AF861655

McGraw Hill Education create™

Course Computer Skills

Course Number **INFT 123**

Bryant and Stratton

McGraw-Hill Education create™

http://create.mheducation.com

ISBN-10: 1259624374 ISBN-13: 9781259624377

Contents

Credits

Microsoft® Office IN PRACTICE

word

CHAPTER 1

WORD

Creating and Editing Documents

CHAPTER OVERVIEW

Microsoft Word (Word) has been and continues to be the leading word processing software in both the personal and business markets. Word improves with each new version and is used for creating and editing personal, business, and educational documents. Word allows you to create letters, memos, reports, flyers, brochures, and mailings without a vast amount of computer knowledge. This chapter covers the basics of creating and editing a Word document.

STUDENT LEARNING OUTCOMES (SLOs)

After completing this chapter, you will be able to:

SLO 1.1 Create, save, and open a Word document (p. W1-3).

SLO 1.2 Customize a document by entering and selecting text, using word wrap, and using *AutoComplete*, *AutoCorrect*, and *AutoFormat* features (p. W1-6).

SLO 1.3 Enhance a document using paragraph breaks, line breaks, spaces, and non-breaking spaces (p. W1-10).

SLO 1.4 Edit a document using cut, copy, paste, the *Clipboard*, and the undo, redo, and repeat features. (p. W1-14).

SLO 1.5 Customize a document using different fonts, font sizes, and attributes (p. W1-17).

SLO 1.6 Enhance a document using text alignment and line and paragraph spacing (p. W1-27).

SLO 1.7 Finalize a document using Word's proofing tools (p. W1-31).

SLO 1.8 Apply custom document properties to a document (p. W1-35).

CASE STUDY

Throughout this book you have the opportunity to put into practice the application features that you are learning. Each chapter begins with a case study that introduces you to the ***Pause & Practice*** *projects in the chapter. These Pause & Practice projects give you a chance to apply and practice key skills. Each chapter contains three to five Pause & Practice projects.*

Placer Hills Real Estate (PHRE) is a real estate company with regional offices throughout central California. In the Pause & Practice projects in this chapter, you create a business document related to the real estate business. PHRE encourages agents to use standard formats for their business documents. This ensures consistency in document appearance while also allowing agents to personalize their correspondence to customers and colleagues.

Pause & Practice 1-1: Create a business letter in block format with mixed punctuation.

Pause & Practice 1-2: Edit the business letter using copy, paste, and *Format Painter*. Modify the font size, color, style, and effects of selected text.

Pause & Practice 1-3: Finalize the business letter by modifying line spacing and paragraph spacing, changing paragraph alignment, translating text, using proofing tools, and adding document properties.

MORE INFO

Appendix D (online resource) contains examples of business documents.

SLO 1.1

Creating, Saving, and Opening Documents

Microsoft Word allows you to create a variety of document types. Your creativity and knowledge of Word allow you to create, edit, and customize high-quality and professional-looking documents.

You can create Word documents from a new blank document, from existing Word templates, or from existing documents. Word allows you to save documents in a variety of formats.

Create a New Document

All new documents are based on the ***Normal template*** (*Normal.dotx*). When you open Word, a blank document is displayed in the Word window. This document has default fonts, font sizes, line and paragraph spacing, and margins, all of which are controlled by the *Normal* template.

HOW TO: Create a New Document

1. Click the **File** tab to open the *Backstage* view (Figure 1-1).
2. Click the **New** button.
3. Select **Blank document**. A new blank document opens in Word.

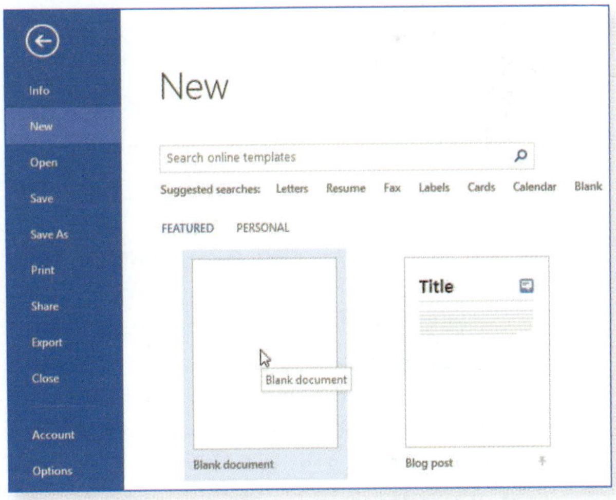

1-1 Open a blank document

ANOTHER WAY

Ctrl+N opens a new blank document.

Save a Document

When you create a blank document, Word automatically assigns a generic file name to this document, such as *Document1*. Save all your new documents using the ***Save As dialog box.***

You can save a Word document in a variety of formats. By default, a Word document is saved as a ***.docx*** file. If you are sharing a document with someone who is using an older version of Word, you might want to save your file as an older version of Word. To change the type of document format, select the format of your choice from the *Save as type* area of the *Save As* dialog box. The following table lists some of the more commonly used available formats.

Save Formats

Type of Document	File Extension	Uses
Word Document	.docx	Standard Word 2013 document
Word Macro-Enabled Document	.docm	Word document with embedded macros
Word 97-2003 Document	.doc	Word document that is compatible with previous versions of Microsoft Word
Word Template	.dotx	Creates a new document based upon a template
Word Macro-Enabled Template	.dotm	Creates a new document based upon a template with embedded macros
Portable Document Format (PDF)	.pdf	PDF files, which are more like pictures of a document, are used to preserve the formatting of a document
Rich Text Format (RTF)	.rtf	RTF files are in a more generic file format and can be read by many different types of word processors while retaining the basic format of the document
Plain Text	.txt	Plain text files contain only text with no special formatting and can be opened with most word processing programs
Open Document Text	.odt	This format is used in the Open Office word processing program

HOW TO: Save a New Document

1. Click the **File** tab to open the *Backstage* view.
2. Click **Save** or **Save As** to display the *Save As* area on the *Backstage* view (Figure 1-2).
3. Select the location where you want to store your document.
   - You can save to your *SkyDrive*, computer, or storage device.

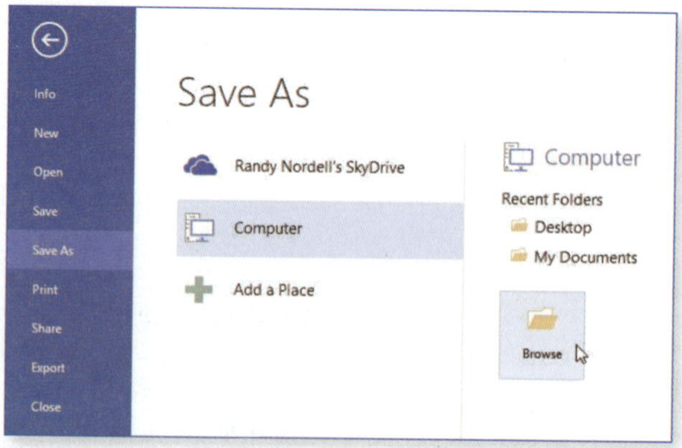

1-2 *Save As* area of the *Backstage* view

4. Select a folder in the *Recent Folders* area or click the **Browse** button to open the *Save As* dialog box (Figure 1-3).
5. Browse to the location on your *SkyDrive*, computer, or USB drive to save the file.
6. Type the file name in the *File name* area.
7. Click the **Save** button.

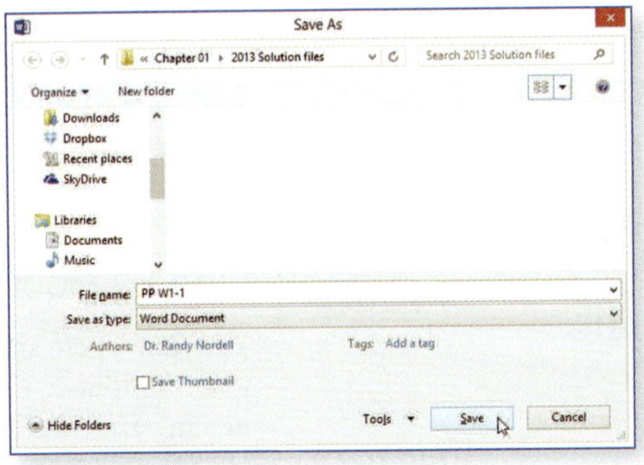

1-3 *Save As* dialog box

ANOTHER WAY

F12 opens the *Save As* dialog box.

After you have saved a document once, you can save the document again by pressing **Ctrl+S** or clicking the **Save** button on the *Quick Access* toolbar. Word saves changes to an existing document without opening the *Save As* dialog box.

Save As a Different File Name

You can save a document as a different name by opening the *Save As* dialog box and giving the document a different file name. When you save as a different file name, the original document is not changed and is still available. Saving as a different file name creates a new version of the original document, but the new document has a different file name.

HOW TO: Save As a Different File Name

1. Click the **File** tab to open the *Backstage* view.
2. Click the **Save As** button to display the *Save As* area.
3. Select a recent folder or click the **Browse** button. The *Save As* dialog box opens (see Figure 1-3).
   - From within Word (not the Backstage view), you can also press **F12** to open the *Save As* dialog box.
4. Browse to the location on your computer or USB drive to save the file.
5. Type the file name in the *File name* area.
6. Click the **Save** button.

MORE INFO

Avoid saving too many different versions of the same document. Rename only when you have a good reason to have multiple versions of a document.

Share and Export Options

Word 2013 provides you with other sharing and export options. From the ***Share*** and ***Export*** area of the *Backstage* view, you have the options of saving a document to the cloud (*SkyDrive*), emailing a document, or saving it as a PDF document. Here are the *Share* and *Export* options, also seen in Figure 1-4.

- Invite People [*Share* area]
- Email [*Share* area]

- Present Online [*Share* area]
- Publish as Blog Post [*Share* area]
- Create PDF/XPS Document [*Export* area]
- Change File Type [*Export* area]

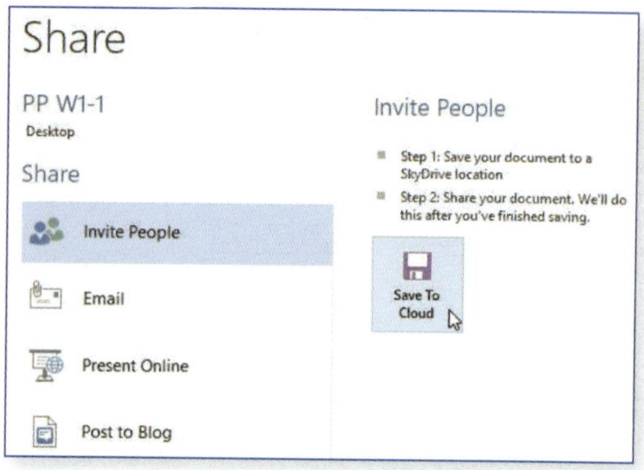

1-4 ***Share*** **area of the** ***Backstage*** **view**

Open a Document

You can open an existing document from your computer, USB drive, SkyDrive drive, or an attachment from an email. One advantage of using Microsoft Word is the program's ability to open different types of file formats and to save documents as different types of files.

HOW TO: Open a Document

1. Click the **File** tab to open the *Backstage* view.
2. Click the **Open** button to display the *Open* area on the *Backstage* view.
3. In the *Places* area, select the location where the document is stored.
   - You can click **Recent Documents** and select a document at the right to open it.
   - You can also open a document from *SkyDrive* or *Computer*.
4. Select a folder or click **Browse** to open the *Open* dialog box (Figure 1-5).
5. Select the file and click the **Open** button.

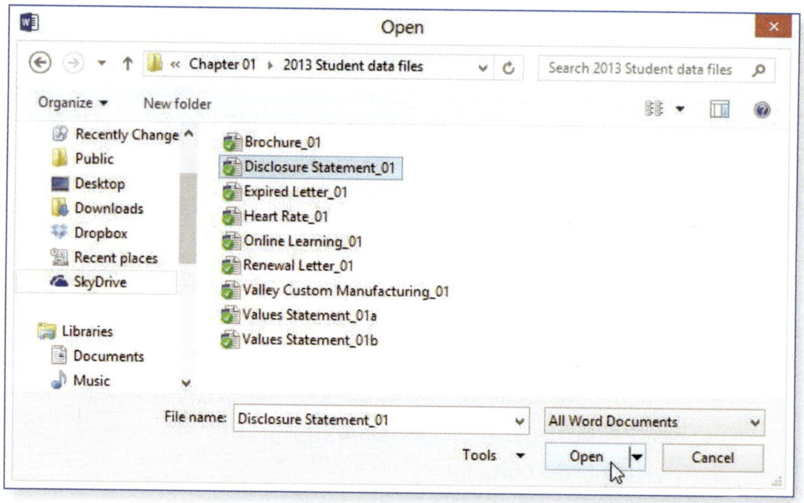

1-5 ***Open*** **dialog box**

> **ANOTHER WAY**
>
> **Ctrl+F12** opens the *Open* dialog box.

SLO 1.2

Entering and Selecting Text

When creating or editing a document, you can type new text, insert text from another document, or copy text from a web page or another document. It is important to understand how to enter text, use word wrap, and select text to create clean and professional-looking documents. Word provides you with options to automatically insert and correct text as well as the ability to control which words are automatically corrected by Word.

Type Text and Word Wrap

Word inserts text at the point in the document where the insertion point is flashing. By default, text is aligned at the left margin and the text wraps to the next line when it reaches the right margin, which is called ***word wrap***.

Show/Hide Formatting Symbols

You can turn on or off the display of formatting symbols. When the ***Show/Hide*** feature is turned on, the formatting symbols are visible in the document. You are able to see paragraph breaks, line breaks, spaces, tabs, and other formatting symbols that help you create clean documents and edit existing documents (Figure 1-6).

Click the **Show/Hide** button in the *Paragraph* group on the *Home* tab to toggle on and off *Show/Hide*. These symbols do not print, but they allow you to see the formatting that is in the document when you view it on your screen.

> **ANOTHER WAY**
>
> **Ctrl+Shift+8** turns on/off *Show/Hide*.

> **MORE INFO**
>
> When editing a document that has inconsistent formatting, begin by turning on **Show/Hide**.

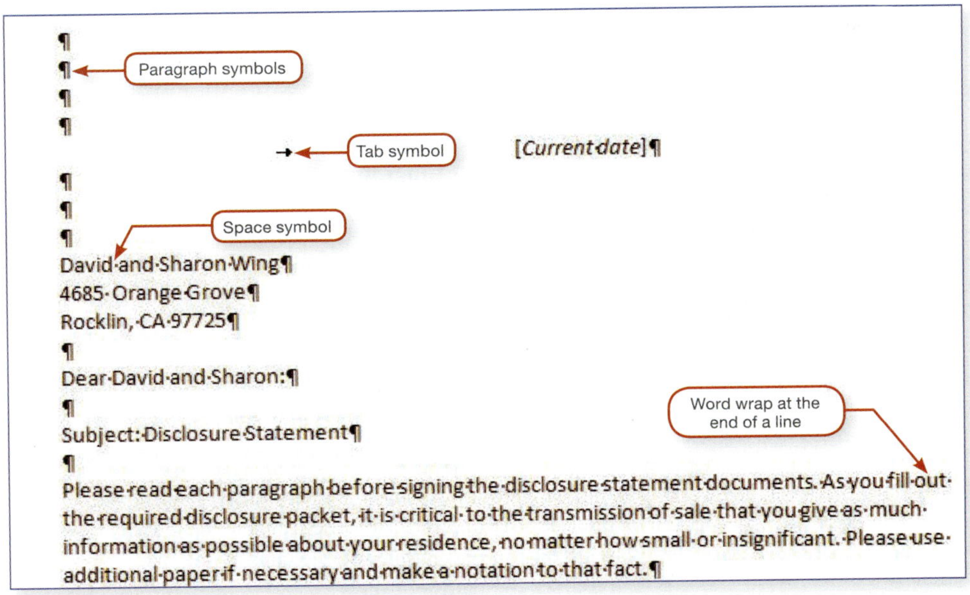

1-6 Document with *Show/Hide* turned on

Select Text

Word allows you select words, lines, sentences, paragraphs, or the entire document. You do this by clicking and dragging the pointer over the desired text, but there are a variety of additional quick methods to select text. The following table lists ways to select text.

> **ANOTHER WAY**
>
> **F8** is the selection function key.
>
> Press once—use the arrow keys to select text.
> Press twice—select word.
> Press three times—select sentence.
> Press four times—select paragraph.
> Press five times—select entire document.
>
> Press **Esc** to turn off **F8** selection.

Selecting Text

Select	Method
Word	Double-click the word.
Line	Click in the *Selection* area, which is to the left of the left margin. Your pointer becomes a right-pointing arrow.
Multiple lines of text	Click in the *Selection* area and drag up or down.
Sentence	Press **Ctrl+Click**. Hold down the **Ctrl** key and click the sentence.
Paragraph	Double-click in the *Selection* area to the left of the paragraph.
Multiple paragraphs	Click in the *Selection* area to the left of the first line of the paragraph and drag down.
Entire document	Press **Ctrl+A** or **Ctrl+Click** in the *Selection* area. You can also click the **Select** button [*Home* tab, *Editing* group] and choose **Select All**.
Non-adjacent text	Select text, press and hold the **Ctrl** key, and select non-adjacent text.

AutoComplete

When you type a day, month, or date, Word uses the ***AutoComplete*** feature to automatically complete typing the day, month, or date for you, which saves you a few key strokes and allows you to be more efficient and accurate when entering dates. As you begin to type the date, Word displays the information in an *AutoComplete* tag (Figure 1-7). Press **Enter** to accept the *AutoComplete* entry. If you do not want this *AutoComplete* entry, keep typing and the *AutoComplete* entry disappears.

1-7 *AutoComplete*

AutoCorrect and AutoFormat

When you're typing, do you ever misspell a word by transposing letters or omitting a letter or adding a letter? Because we all regularly make typing mistakes, the ***AutoCorrect*** feature recognizes and corrects commonly misspelled words.

Word automatically makes the following corrections:

- Eliminates two initial capitals in a word
- Capitalizes the first letter of a sentence
- Capitalizes the first letter of table cells
- Capitalizes the names of days
- Resolves accidental usage of the Caps Lock key

Word's ***AutoFormat*** controls the formatting of items such as numbered and bulleted lists, fractions, ordinal numbers, hyphens and dashes, quotes, indents, and hyperlinks. For example, when you type 3/4 followed by a space, *AutoFormat* automatically changes the format of the fraction to ¾.

AutoCorrect Options

When Word automatically makes a correction or formatting change, you have the option to accept the change, undo the change, stop Word from making the change, or open the *AutoCorrect Options* dialog box. If you keep typing, the change is accepted. Often when Word automatically corrects a word, you don't even recognize a change has been made.

AutoCorrect Smart Tag

If you do not want to accept a change, you can click the ***AutoCorrect Options smart tag*** on the changed word to open the *AutoCorrect Options* menu (Figure 1-8). For example, when you type reference initials at the end of a business letter, Word automatically capitalizes the first letter. You can undo this automatic capitalization by clicking on the *AutoCorrect Options* smart tag and selecting **Undo Automatic Capitalization**.

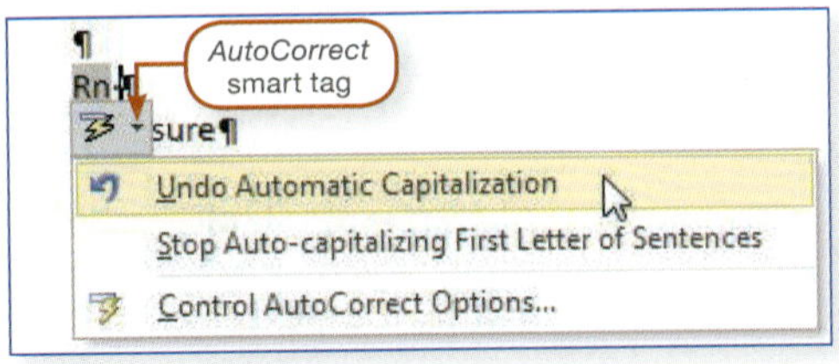

1-8 *AutoCorrect Options*

> **ANOTHER WAY**
>
> **Ctrl+Z** is *undo*. Press **Ctrl+Z** to reverse an automatic correction made by Word.

Add Custom AutoCorrect Entry

The *AutoCorrect* dialog box allows you to customize how Word automatically corrects and formats items in a document. In this dialog box, you can also add custom items to the *AutoCorrect* menu. For example, you can add a custom entry to the *AutoCorrect* menu to type your name every time you type your initials.

HOW TO: Add a Custom AutoCorrect Entry

1. Click the **File** tab to open the *Backstage* view.
2. Choose the **Options** button to open the *Word Options* dialog box.
3. Click the **Proofing** button on the left.
4. Select the **AutoCorrect Options** button. The *AutoCorrect* dialog box opens (Figure 1-9).
5. Type in the text you want to replace in the *Replace* box.
6. Type in the word(s) to replace the original text in the *With* box.
7. Choose **Add** to add this custom *AutoCorrect* entry.
8. Click **OK** to close the *AutoCorrect* dialog box.
9. Click **OK** to close the *Word Options* dialog box.

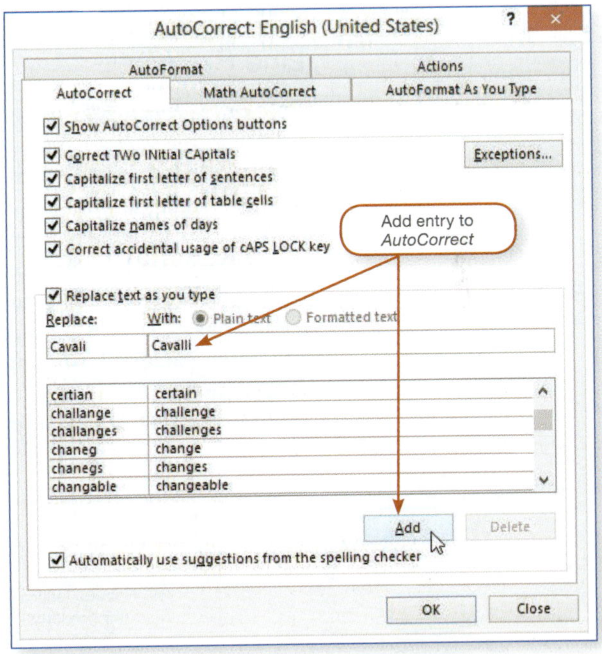

1-9 *AutoCorrect* dialog box

You can delete *AutoCorrect* entries in the *AutoCorrect* dialog box by selecting the entry and pressing **Delete**. You can also add exceptions to *AutoCorrect* by clicking the **Exceptions** button.

SLO 1.3

Using Paragraph Breaks, Line Breaks, and Non-Breaking Spaces

It is important to create attractive and readable documents. Using paragraph and line breaks allows you to break up a document into more readable chunks of information. The different types of breaks can be used for different purposes when you are formatting documents.

Paragraph Breaks

The ***Enter*** key inserts a ***paragraph break*** and is marked by a ***paragraph symbol*** that displays at the end of each paragraph when *Show/Hide* is turned on (Figure 1-10). Use paragraph breaks to control the amount of white space between paragraphs of text within a document.

Many formatting features, such as indents, numbering, bullets, text alignment, line spacing, and paragraph spacing, are applied to an entire paragraph. For example, if your insertion point is within a paragraph and you change the line spacing to double space, double spacing is applied to that paragraph only. It is not applied to the entire document or just the line where the insertion point is located.

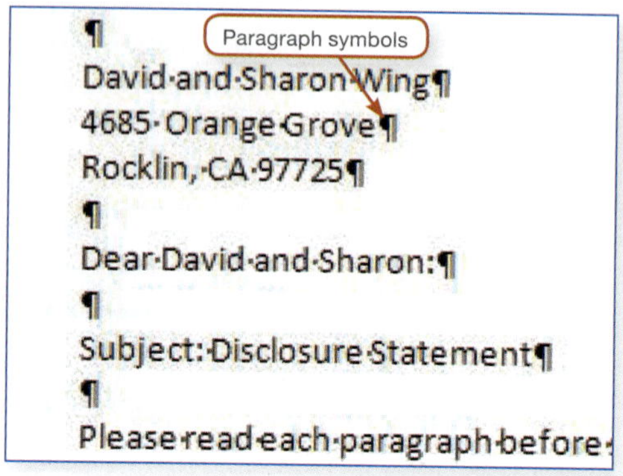

1-10 Paragraph breaks after and between lines

Line Breaks

You can use ***line breaks*** to control breaks between lines or sentences of text. They function similar to the way a paragraph break functions. The distinction between a paragraph break and a line break is that when line breaks are used, the text separated by line breaks is treated as one paragraph.

You can use line breaks within a numbered or bulleted list to allow for multiple lines of text on separate lines and blank lines between the text without creating a new number or bullet (Figure 1-11). You can also use line breaks to control the amount of space between paragraphs when you are using before and after spacing for paragraphs. For more on before and after paragraph spacing, see *SLO 1.6: Changing Text Alignment, Line Spacing, and Paragraph Spacing.*

Press **Shift+Enter** to insert a line break.

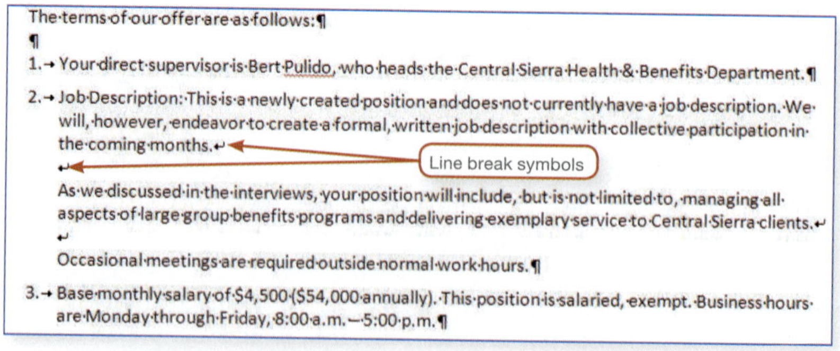

1-11 Line breaks used in a numbered list

Spaces and Non-Breaking Spaces

Spaces are included between words. Use the **spacebar** to insert a space. Add just one space after most punctuation marks, including periods, commas, semicolons, and ending quotation marks. Do not use spaces after a beginning quotation mark, before or after a hyphen in a hyphenated word, or when using a dash.

There might be times when you are typing a document and word wrap breaks up words that you want to keep together. For example, you might want to keep a person's first and last name or a date together on the same line, but you don't want to add a line break or paragraph break at that point in your document. In this case, you can use a ***non-breaking space*** to keep these words together. In Figure 1-12, there is a non-breaking space between 8:00 and a.m., which keeps this information together.

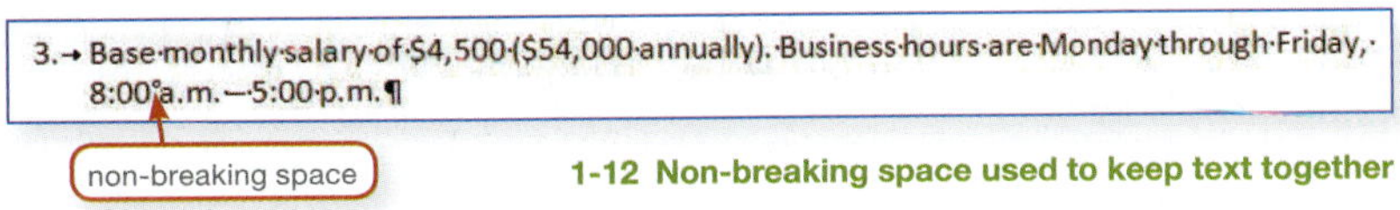

1-12 Non-breaking space used to keep text together

Press **Ctrl+Shift+Spacebar** to insert a non-breaking space between words. Don't insert an additional regular space between words when using a non-breaking space.

PAUSE & PRACTICE: WORD 1-1

In this project, you create a block format business letter for Emma Cavalli, a realtor consultant for Placer Hills Real Estate. In a block format business letter, all lines begin at the left margin. This document uses mixed punctuation, which means there is a colon after the salutation and a comma after the complimentary close (e.g., Best regards,). For more examples of business documents, see *Appendix D* (online resource).

File Needed: None
Completed Project File Name: ***[your initials] PP W1-1.docx***

1. Open a new document.
   a. Press **Ctrl+N** or click the **File** tab, click **New**, and click **Blank Document**.
2. Save the document.
   a. Press **F12** to open the *Save As* dialog box (Figure 1-13). You can also use **Save** or **Save As** in the *Backstage* view.
   b. Browse to the location on your computer or storage device to save the document.
   c. Type [your initials] PP W1-1 in the *File name* area.
   d. Click **Save** to close the dialog box and save the document.

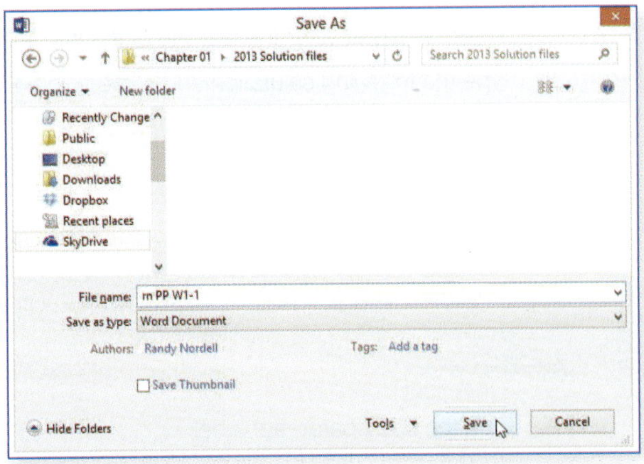

1-13 *Save As* dialog box

3. Create an *AutoCorrect* entry.
   a. Click the **File** tab to open the *Backstage* view and select **Options** to open the *Word Options* dialog box.
   b. Click the **Proofing** button on the left and select **AutoCorrect Options** to open the *AutoCorrect* dialog box (Figure 1-14).
   c. Click the **AutoCorrect** tab.
   d. Type Cavali in the *Replace* area and Cavalli in the *With* area.
   e. Click the **Add** button to add the *AutoCorrect* entry.
   f. Click **OK** to close the *AutoCorrect* dialog box.
   g. Click **OK** to close the *Word Options* dialog box.

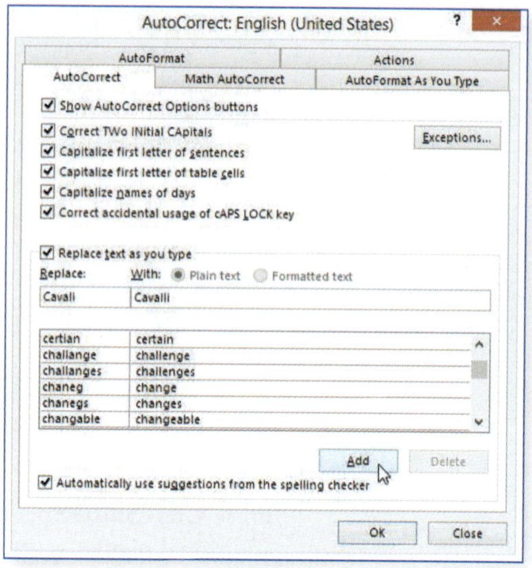

1-14 Add an ***AutoCorrect*** entry

4. Click the **Show/Hide** button [*Home* tab, *Paragraph* group] to turn on the *Show/Hide* feature.
5. Type the current date on the first line of the document. Type the date in month, day, year format (e.g., September 1, 2015).
   a. If the *AutoComplete* tag appears, press **Enter**, and the month is automatically inserted (Figure 1-15).
   b. Continue typing the rest of the date; press **Enter** if the *AutoCorrect* tag displays the current date.

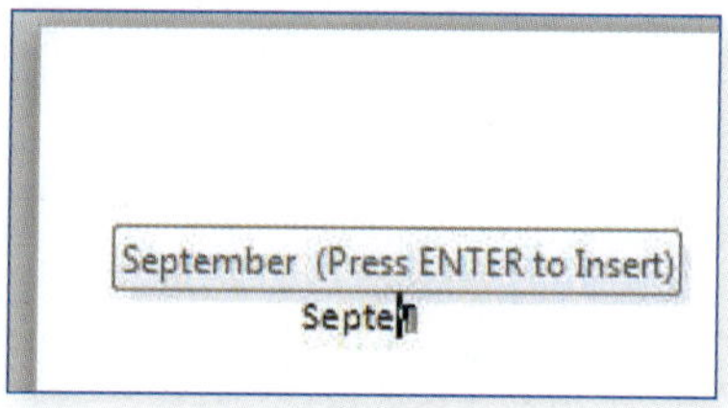

1-15 ***AutoComplete*** tag

6. Press **Enter** two times after typing the date.
7. Type the following information as the inside address of the letter (the recipient of the letter).
   a. Press **Shift+Enter** to insert a line break after the first and second lines to keep the lines together.

      David and Sharon Wing
      4685 Orange Grove Road
      Rocklin, CA 97725

   b. Press **Enter** after the last line of the inside address.
8. Type the following salutation and subject line. Press **Enter** after typing each line.

      Dear Mr. and Mrs. Wing:
      Subject: Disclosure Statement

MORE INFO

In a business letter, use "Dear" followed by a courtesy title (such as Mr., Mrs., Ms., Miss, or Dr.) and the person's last name.

9. Type the body paragraphs below.
   a. Use word wrap for line endings. Do not press Enter at the end of each line.
   b. Press **Enter** at the end of each paragraph.

c. Press **Ctrl+Shift+Spacebar** to insert a non-breaking space between the words "Real" and "Estate" in the second paragraph. Use only a single non-breaking space; do not include a regular space.

Please read each paragraph before signing the disclosure statement documents. As you fill out the required disclosure packet, it is critical to the transmission of sale that you give as much information as possible about your residence, no matter how small or insignificant. Please use additional paper if necessary and make a notation to that fact.

If there is information about the neighborhood or neighbors that you as a buyer would want to know about, be sure to reveal that information. Be sure to address those types of questions on the Real Estate Transfer Disclosure Statement, item #11 on page 2.

10. Type Best regards, as the complimentary close and press **Enter** two times after. Be sure to include the comma after the complimentary close.
11. Type the letter writer's name, title, and company name.
    a. Insert a line break (**Shift+Enter**) at the end of the first two lines.

    Emma Cavalli
    Realtor Consultant
    Placer Hills Real Estate

    b. Press **Enter** after the company name.
12. Type your initials in lower case letters and press **Shift+Enter** to insert a line break.
    a. Word automatically capitalizes the first letter because it is the first word in a new paragraph.
    b. Click the **AutoCorrect** smart tag and select **Undo Automatic Capitalization** (Figure 1-16) or press **Ctrl+Z** to undo automatic capitalization.

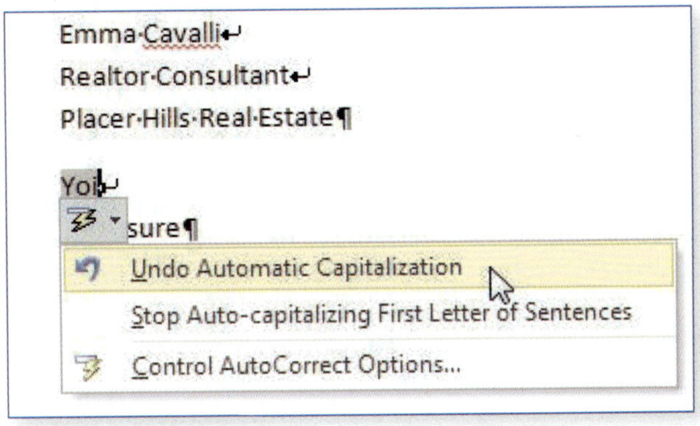

1-16 *AutoCorrect* smart tag

13. On the next line below the reference initials, type Enclosure. An enclosure notation indicates to the reader that something is enclosed with the letter.
14. Press **Ctrl+S** to save the document (Figure 1-17). You can also save the document by clicking on the **Save** button on the *Quick Access* toolbar or in the *Backstage* view.
15. Click the **File** tab and select **Close** (or press **Ctrl+W**) to close the document.

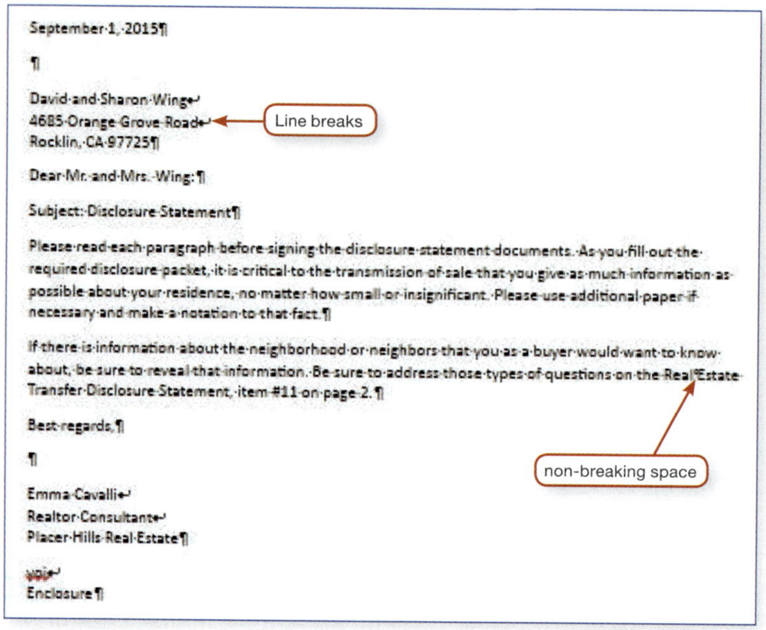
September 1, 2015

David and Sharon Wing
4685 Orange Grove Road
Rocklin, CA 97725

Dear Mr. and Mrs. Wing:

Subject: Disclosure Statement

Please read each paragraph before signing the disclosure statement documents. As you fill out the required disclosure packet, it is critical to the transmission of sale that you give as much information as possible about your residence, no matter how small or insignificant. Please use additional paper if necessary and make a notation to that fact.

If there is information about the neighborhood or neighbors that you as a buyer would want to know about, be sure to reveal that information. Be sure to address those types of questions on the Real Estate Transfer Disclosure Statement, item #11 on page 2.

Best regards,

Emma Cavalli
Realtor Consultant
Placer Hills Real Estate

yoi
Enclosure

1-17 PP W1-1 completed

SLO 1.4

Moving and Copying Text

> **ANOTHER WAY**
> **Ctrl+C** to copy
> **Ctrl+X** to cut
> **Ctrl+V** to paste

Editing is an important phase in document creation. Editing involves not only proofreading and correcting grammar and spelling mistakes but also arranging text within a document, which can include cutting, copying, and pasting. Word makes it easy to move and copy information within a document or between multiple documents.

Move Text

Moving is actually removing text from one location (cutting) and placing it in another location (pasting). There are two methods you can use to move text: ***drag and drop*** or ***cut*** and ***paste.***

HOW TO: Move Text Using Drag and Drop

1. Select the text you want to move.
2. Click and hold the selected text with your pointer.
3. Drag the text to the desired new location and release the pointer (Figure 1-18).

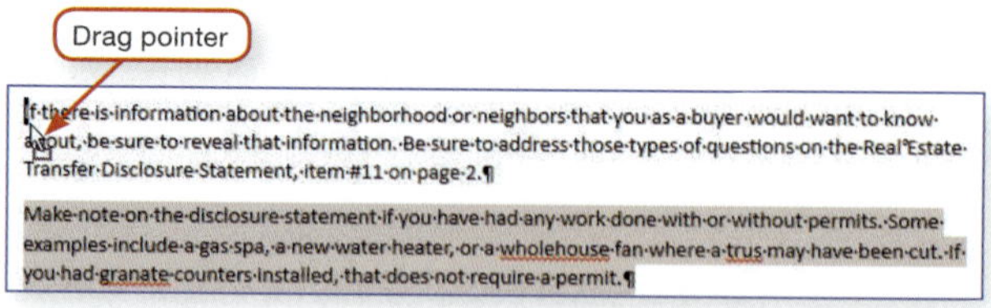
If there is information about the neighborhood or neighbors that you as a buyer would want to know about, be sure to reveal that information. Be sure to address those types of questions on the Real Estate Transfer Disclosure Statement, item #11 on page 2.

Make note on the disclosure statement if you have had any work done with or without permits. Some examples include a gas spa, a new water heater, or a wholehouse fan where a trus may have been cut. If you had granate counters installed, that does not require a permit.

1-18 Move using drag and drop

There are a variety of ways to move text using cut and paste.

- ***Cut and Paste buttons:*** These buttons are in the *Clipboard* group on the *Home* tab.
- ***Shortcut commands:*** Press **Ctrl+X** to cut and **Ctrl+V** to paste.
- ***Context menu:*** Right-click the selected text to display this menu.

HOW TO: Move Text Using Cut and Paste

1. Select the text you want to move.
2. Click the **Cut** button [*Home* tab, *Clipboard* group].
   - You can also press **Ctrl+X** or right-click the selected text and choose **Cut** from the context menu.
3. Place your insertion point in the desired location.
4. Click the **Paste** button [*Home* tab, *Clipboard* group].
   - You can also press **Ctrl+V** or right-click the selected text and click the first **Paste** icon. *Note: See the **Paste Text and Paste Options** section below for the different paste options available.*

Copy Text

An efficient method of inserting text into a document is to copy it from another location, such as a web page or a different document, and paste it into your document. Copying text leaves the text in its original location and places a copy of the text in a new location.

You can ***copy*** text by using the ***drag and drop*** method or the ***Copy and Paste*** buttons. Use the drag and drop method when copying text within the same document. The drag and drop method for copying is similar to the method for moving, except that you hold the **Ctrl** key when dragging the text to be copied to an additional location. A + (plus sign) appears next to your pointer, indicating this text is being copied.

HOW TO: Copy Text Using Drag and Drop

1. Select the text you want to copy.
2. Hold the **Ctrl** key and click and hold the selected text with your pointer.
3. Drag to the desired new location and release the pointer (Figure 1-19).

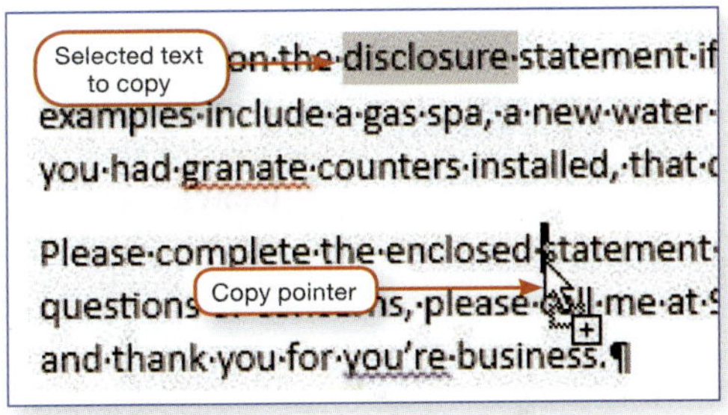

1-19 Copy using drag and drop

Copying text using the following copy and paste method is similar to moving text using the cut and paste method.

- ***Copy and Paste buttons:*** These buttons are in the *Clipboard* group on the *Home* tab.
- ***Shortcut commands:*** Press **Ctrl+C** to copy and **Ctrl+V** to paste.
- ***Context menu:*** Right-click the selected text to display this menu.

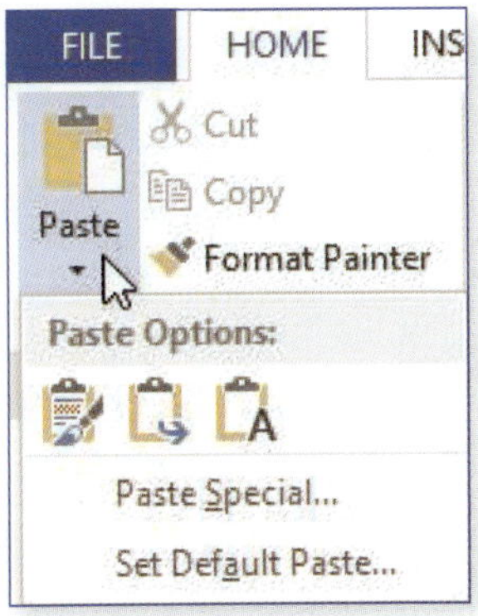

1-20 *Paste* options

Paste Text and Paste Options

You might want to paste text into a document and only want the plain text, or you might want to merge the format from the source document into the new document. Word provides multiple paste options.

You have three primary paste options when you use the *Paste* button in the *Clipboard* group (Figure 1-20) or from the context menu.

- ***Keep Source Formatting***—*retains formatting from source document (the document where the text was copied)*
- ***Merge Formatting***—*merges formatting from source document and current document*
- ***Keep Text Only***—*pastes only unformatted text*

The default paste option is *Keep Source Formatting.* In addition to these paste options, there are other context-specific paste options that are available when you paste information from lists or paste text with a style applied.

> **MORE INFO**
>
> If you're having trouble with the format of pasted text, try pasting the text as plain text and formatting the text *after* you have pasted it into the document.

The Clipboard

When you copy or cut an item from a document, Word stores this information in the ***Clipboard.*** From the *Clipboard,* you can select a previously copied item and paste it into a document. When Word is open, the *Clipboard* stores multiple items copied from Word documents and also items from web pages or other documents. The *Clipboard* stores text, pictures, tables, lists, and graphics.

Open the Clipboard Task Pane

The ***Clipboard task pane*** displays all of the items stored in *Clipboard.* To display the *Clipboard* task pane, click the **launcher** in the bottom right corner of the *Clipboard* group on the *Home* tab (Figure 1-21). The *Clipboard* task pane is displayed on the left side of the Word window.

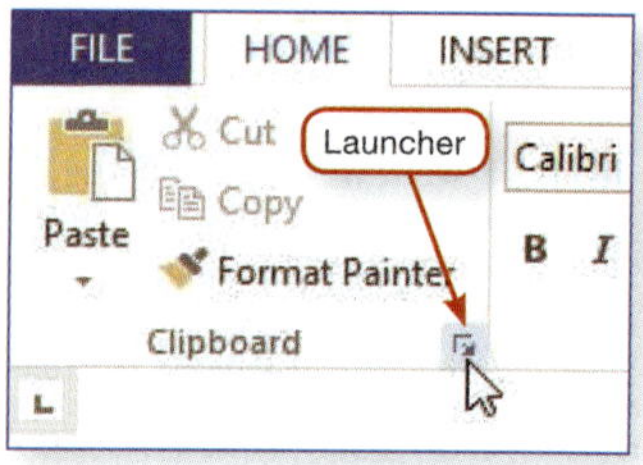

1-21 *Clipboard* launcher

> **MORE INFO**
>
> The ***launcher*** (also referred to as the ***dialog box launcher***) is referred to throughout this text. Click the **launcher** in the bottom right corner of a group to open a dialog box or pane to give you additional options.

Paste from the Clipboard

To paste an item from the *Clipboard* into a document at the insertion point in the document, select the item or click the drop-down arrow to the right of the item and choose **Paste** (Figure 1-22).

Other Clipboard Options

Paste All pastes all of the items in the *Clipboard* at the insertion point in the document. Selecting **Clear All** empties the content of the *Clipboard.* When you exit Word, the contents of the *Clipboard* are removed.

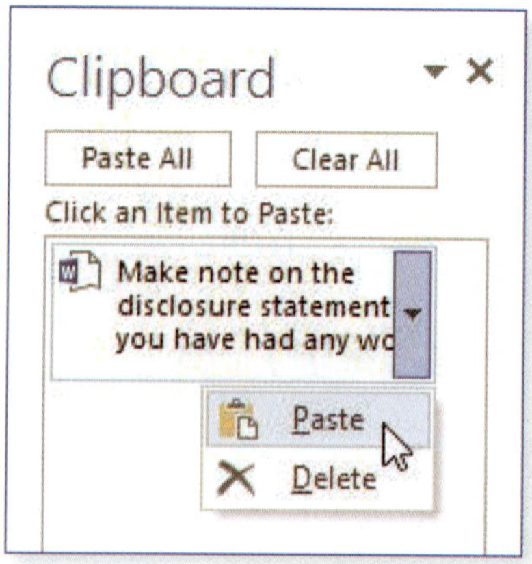

1-22 *Clipboard* task pane

At the bottom of the *Clipboard* task pane, there are a variety of display options. Choose from these by clicking on the **Options** button (Figure 1-23). Click the **X** in the upper right corner of the pane to close it.

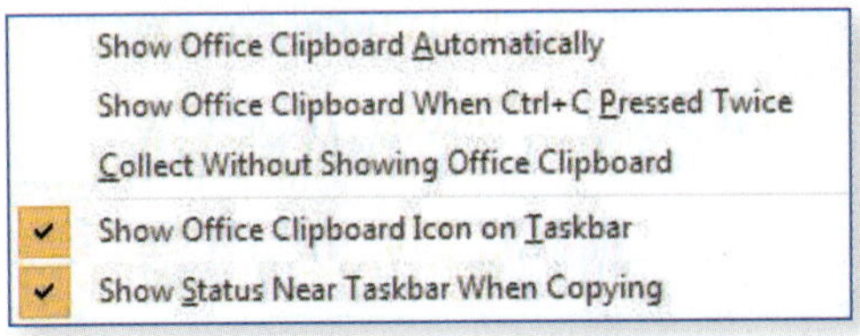

1-23 ***Clipboard*** **options**

Undo, Redo, and Repeat Changes

You can undo, redo, or repeat previous actions. All of these buttons are available on the ***Quick Access toolbar.***

Undo

When you click the ***Undo*** button, the last action you performed is undone. You can undo multiple actions by clicking on the **Undo** drop-down arrow to the right of the button and selecting the items to undo (Figure 1-24).

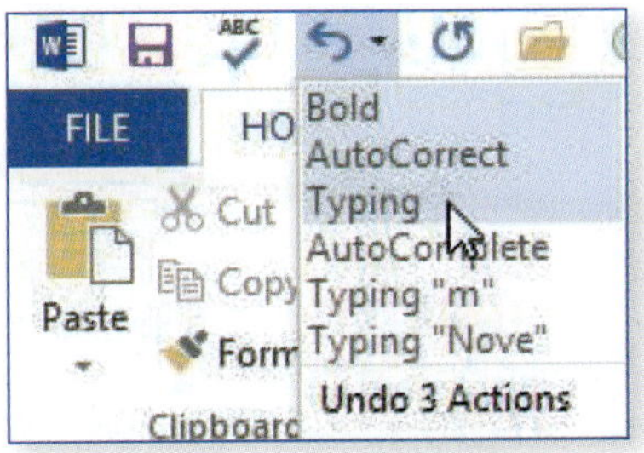

1-24 ***Undo*** **button on the** ***Quick Access*** **toolbar**

Redo and Repeat

The ***Redo*** and ***Repeat*** features are similar to the undo feature. The same button is used for both of these features, and it is context sensitive. Depending on the previous action performed, the button is either *Redo* or *Repeat.*

When you use the *Undo* button, the *Redo* button is activated so you can redo the previous change (Figure 1-25).

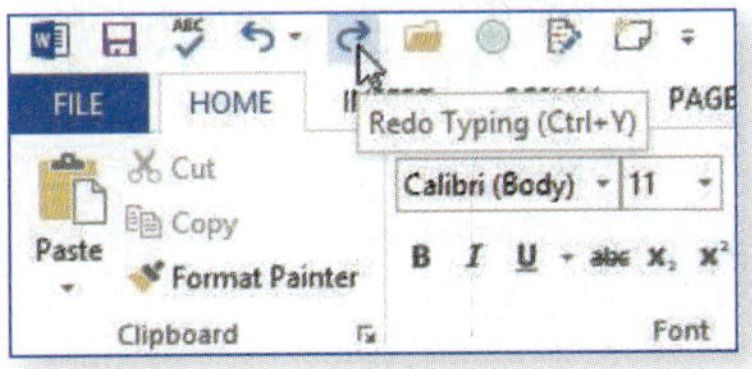

1-25 ***Redo*** **button on the** ***Quick Access*** **toolbar**

When you perform an action or apply formatting in a document, the *Repeat* button is activated so you can repeat the previous action or formatting (Figure 1-26). For example, if you need to copy the date or a name into a document in multiple places, you can use the *Repeat* feature to accomplish this task quickly and accurately.

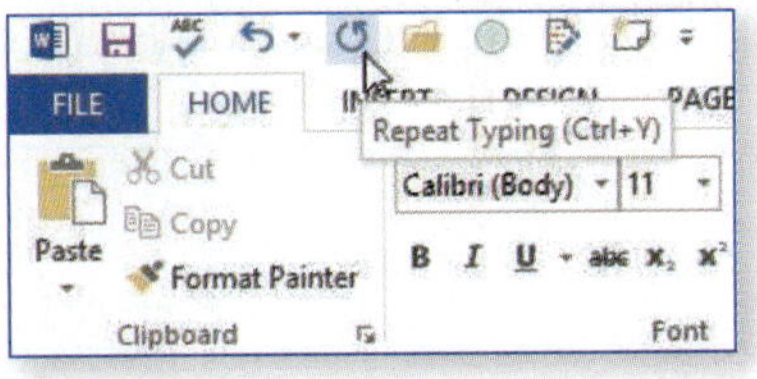

1-26 ***Repeat*** **button on the** ***Quick Access*** **toolbar**

ANOTHER WAY

Ctrl+Z is undo.
Ctrl+Y is redo and repeat.

SLO 1.5

Changing Fonts, Font Sizes, and Attributes

Word has many features that you can use to customize the appearance of the text within a document. You can change the font and size of font; add styles such as bold, italics, and underlining; change the case of the text; add font and text effects; adjust the scale, spacing, and position of text; and change the default font settings. You can use buttons in the *Font* group on the *Home* tab, the *Font* dialog box, and the mini toolbar to apply formatting to text.

Font and Font Size

There are two main categories of fonts: serif and sans serif. ***Serif fonts*** have structural details (flair) at the top and bottom of most of the letters. Some commonly used serif fonts are Cambria, Times New Roman, and Courier New. ***Sans serif fonts*** have no structural details on the letters. Commonly used sans serif fonts are Calibri, Arial, and Century Gothic.

Font size is measured in ***points*** (pt.); the larger the point, the larger the font. Most documents use between 10 and 12 pt. font sizes. Titles and headings generally are larger font sizes.

> **MORE INFO**
>
> The default font and font size in Microsoft Word are *Calibri* and *11 pt.*, respectively.
>
> Font size of 72 pt. is approximately 1" in height.

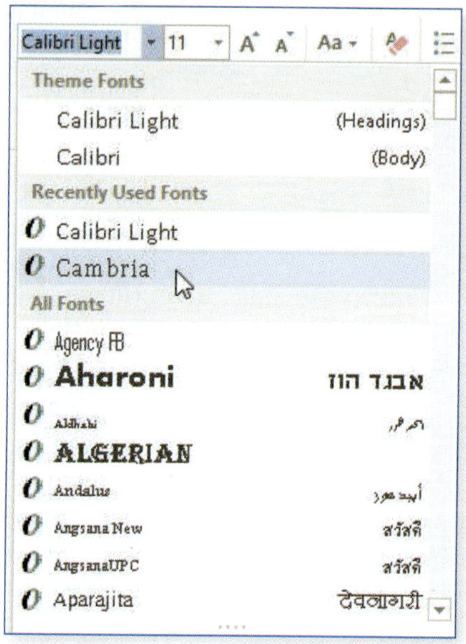

1-27 *Font* drop-down list

HOW TO: Change Font and Font Size

1. Select the text you want to change.
2. Click the **Font** drop-down list to display the list of available fonts (Figure 1-27).
   - The *Font* drop-down list has three sections: *Theme Fonts*, *Recently Used Fonts*, and *All Fonts.*
3. Select the font you want to apply to the selected text.
4. Click the **Font Size** drop-down list to display the list of available font sizes (Figure 1-28).
5. Select a font size to apply to selected text.
   - You can also click in the **Font Size** area and type a size.
   - Use the **Increase Font Size** and **Decrease Font Size** buttons to increase or decrease the size of the font in small increments.

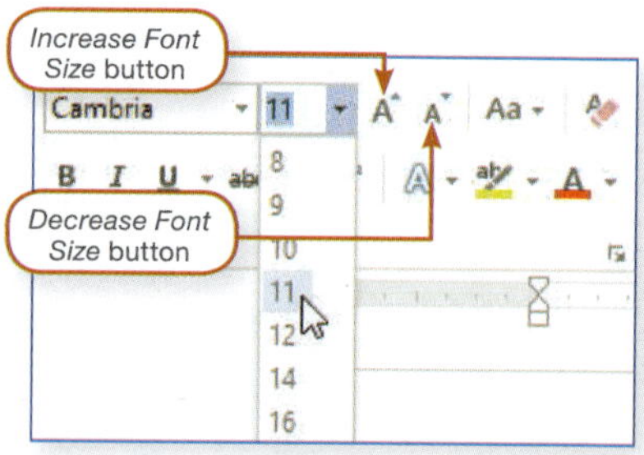

1-28 *Font Size* drop-down list

> **ANOTHER WAY**
>
> **Ctrl+> (Ctrl+Shift+.)** is *Increase Font Size.*
>
> **Ctrl+< (Ctrl+Shift+,)** is *Decrease Font Size.*

When creating a new document, you can choose a font and it applies to the entire document. If you want to change the font of an existing document, you must first select the text before applying the change.

Font Styles

You can add styles such as ***Bold, Italic,*** and ***Underline*** to fonts to improve their appearance or call attention to specific text. The font style buttons for *Bold, Italic,* and *Underline* are available in the *Font* group on the *Home* tab.

Bold, Italic, and Underline

To apply a font style, select the desired text and click the **Bold**, **Italic**, or **Underline** button in the *Font* group on the *Home* tab (Figure 1-29). You can also click one or more of the font style buttons to turn on a style. Type the text and click the font style button(s) again to turn off the style.

The ***mini toolbar*** displays when you select or right-click text (Figure 1-30). You can use the mini toolbar to apply text formatting. Like the content menu, the mini toolbar is context-sensitive and displays different options depending on the selection you right-click.

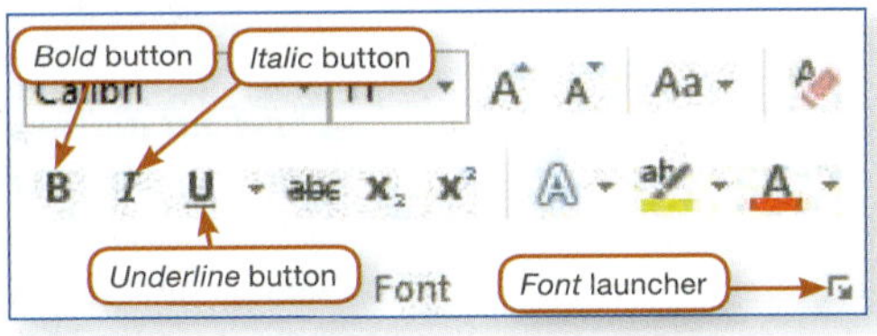

1-29 *Font* group on the *Home* tab

1-30 Select or right-click text to display the mini toolbar

> **ANOTHER WAY**
>
> **Ctrl+B** is *Bold.*
> **Ctrl+I** is *Italic.*
> **Ctrl+U** is *Underline.*

Other Font Style Buttons

There are other styles and effects in the *Font* group on the *Home* tab and on the mini toolbar.

- *Strikethrough*
- *Subscript*
- *Superscript*
- *Text Effects and Typography,* which includes *Outline, Shadow, Reflection, Glow, Number Styles, Ligatures, and Style Sets*
- *Text Highlight Color*
- *Font Color*

Change Case

The ***Change Case*** feature is a quick and easy way to change the case of a single word or group of words. The *Change Case* button is in the *Font* group on the *Home* tab (Figure 1-31).

Your different case options are:

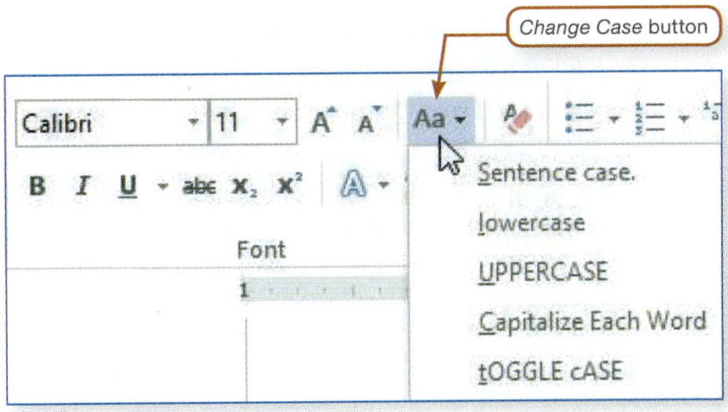

1-31 *Change Case* options

- *Sentence case* (capitalizes the first letter of the sentence)
- *lowercase*
- *UPPERCASE*
- *Capitalize Each Word*
- *tOGGLE cASE* (changes letters that are uppercase to lowercase and lowercase letters to uppercase)

Font Dialog Box

The ***Font dialog box*** combines many of the font style and ***effect options*** in one location for easy access. You can open the *Font* dialog by clicking the **Font** launcher in the bottom right corner of the *Font* group (Figure 1-32).

In addition to the *Font, Font Style,* and *Size* areas on the *Font* tab in this dialog box, there are also areas to change *Font Color, Underline Style, Underline Color,* and *Effects.* The *Preview* area gives you a preview of applied changes, styles, and effects.

The *Advanced* tab lists *Character Spacing* options such as *Scale, Spacing, Position,* and *Kerning.* From this tab, you can also open the *Format Text Effects* dialog box.

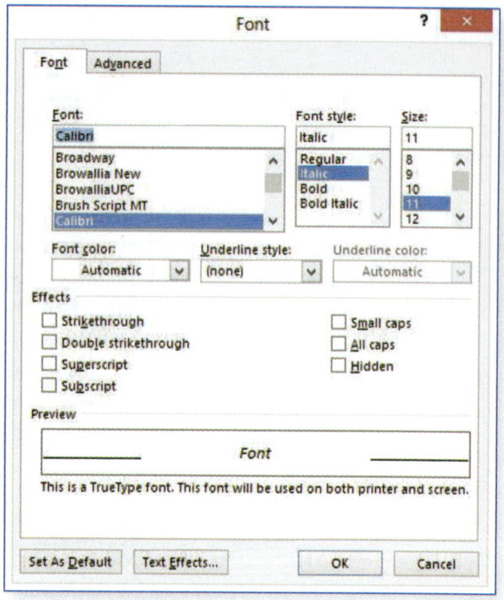

1-32 ***Font* dialog box**

> **ANOTHER WAY**
>
> **Ctrl+D** opens the *Font* dialog box.

Font Color

By default, the font color in a Word document is black. You can change the font color of selected text to add emphasis. The ***Font Color*** drop-down list in the *Font* dialog box displays a list of available font colors.

HOW TO: Change Font Color

1. Select the text you want to be a different color.
2. Click the **Font** launcher [*Home* tab, *Font* group]. The *Font* dialog box opens (Figure 1-33).
3. Click the **Font Color** drop-down arrow to display the list of font colors.
   - The drop-down list of font color options includes *Theme Colors*, *Standard Colors*, and *More Colors.* Theme colors are those colors associated with the theme of the document. For more on themes, see *Section 2.7: Using Styles and Themes.*
4. Choose **OK** to close the *Font* dialog box.

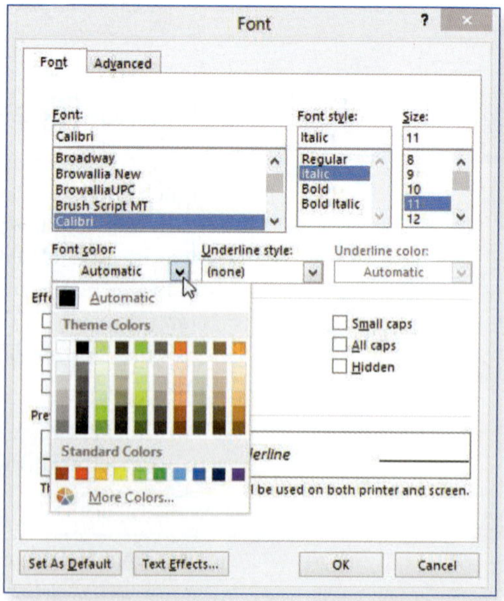

1-33 **Change font color in the *Font* dialog box**

ANOTHER WAY

Change the font color by clicking on the **Font Color** button [*Home* tab, *Font* group].

Underline Style and Color

When you underline selected text, the default underline style is a solid black underline. Word provides a variety of additional underline styles. You can also change the color of the underline.

The ***Underline Style*** and ***Underline Color*** drop-down lists are available in the *Font* dialog box (Figure 1-34). A preview of how the formatted text will appear in your document is displayed in the *Preview* area of the *Font* dialog box.

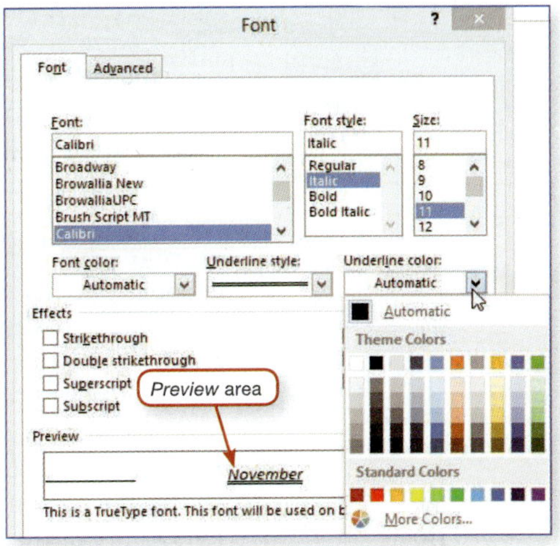

1-34 Change *Underline* style and color

Font Effects

In the *Font* dialog box you can choose a variety of font effects from the ***Effects*** section. Some of these font effects are available in the *Font* group on the *Home* tab. The following table lists the different font styles and effects.

Font Styles and Effects

Style/Effect	Example
Bold	This **word** is in bold.
Italic	This *word* is in italic.
Bold and Italic	This ***word*** is in bold and italic.
Underline	This sentence is underlined.
Double Underline	This word is double underlined.
Underline Words Only	This sentence is words only underlined.
Thick Underline with Color	This word has a thick, colored underline.
Strikethrough	This ~~word~~ has a strikethrough.
Double Strikethrough	~~This sentence has a double strikethrough.~~
Subscript	H_2O uses a subscript number.
Superscript	Footnotes and endnotes use superscript numbers or letters.[1]
Small Caps	MICROSOFT WORD 2013 is in small caps.
All Caps	THIS SENTENCE IS IN ALL CAPS.
Hidden	
Text Highlight Color	This word has a highlight color.
Font Color	This sentence has a font color applied.

> **MORE INFO**
>
> *Hidden* text appears in your on-screen document, but it does not print or display in print preview.

Character Spacing

The ***Character Spacing*** options allow you to add more or less space between letters and words. You can also raise and lower letters and words (Figure 1-35).

The ***Scale*** option allows you to change the spacing of a word or group of words by a percentage. You can choose from preset percentages, or you can type in a custom percentage for scaling.

Spacing has three options: *Normal, Expanded,* and *Condensed.* For *Expanded* and *Condensed,* you can choose the amount of points by which to expand the selected text.

The ***Position*** option raises or lowers text by a selected number of points.

Kerning adjusts the space between letters in a proportional font.

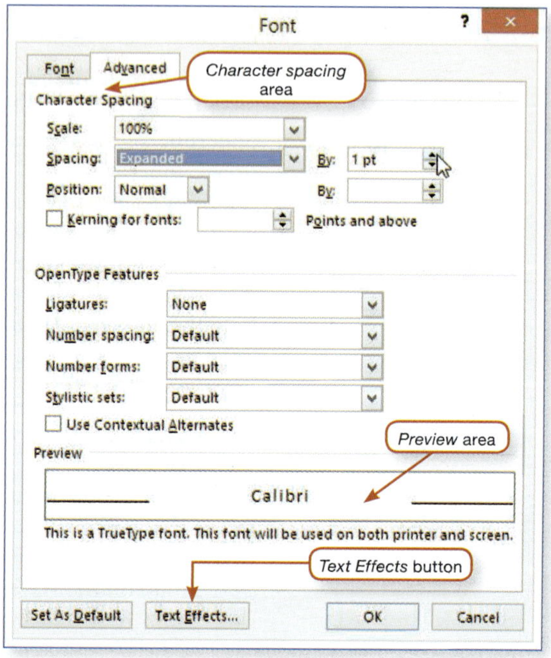

1-35 *Font* dialog box *Advanced* tab

Text Effects

With ***Text Effects,*** you can add special formatting features to selected text, such as *Outline, Shadow, Reflection,* and *Glow* (Figure 1-36).

The *Text Effects* button is located in the *Font* group on the *Home* tab. There are many preset options for each of the different text effects, and there are more custom text effect options available in the *Format Text Effects* dialog box.

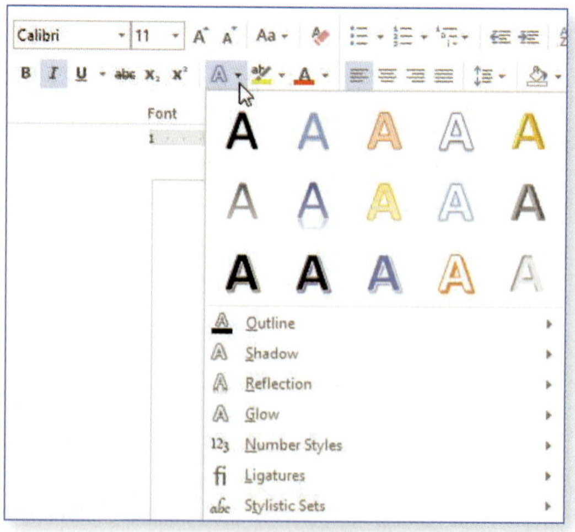

1-36 ***Text Effects*** button in the ***Font*** group

HOW TO: Use the Format Text Effects Dialog Box

1. Select the text you want to format.
2. Click the **Font** launcher [*Home* tab, *Font* group]. The *Font* dialog box opens.
3. Click the **Text Effects** button at the bottom. The *Format Text Effects* dialog box opens (Figure 1-37).
4. Click the **Text Fill & Outline** button to display fill and outline options.
   - Select **Text Fill** or **Text Outline** to expand and display options.
5. Click the **Text Effects** button to display text effect options.
   - Select **Shadow**, **Reflection**, **Glow**, **Soft Edges**, or **3-D Format** to expand and display options.
   - Each of these categories has *Presets* you can choose or you can customize the effect.
6. Select the text effect of your choice on the left.
7. To the right of each option you can choose a preset option from the drop-down list or customize the text effect as desired.
8. Click **OK** to close the *Format Text Effects* dialog box and click **OK** to close the *Font* dialog box.

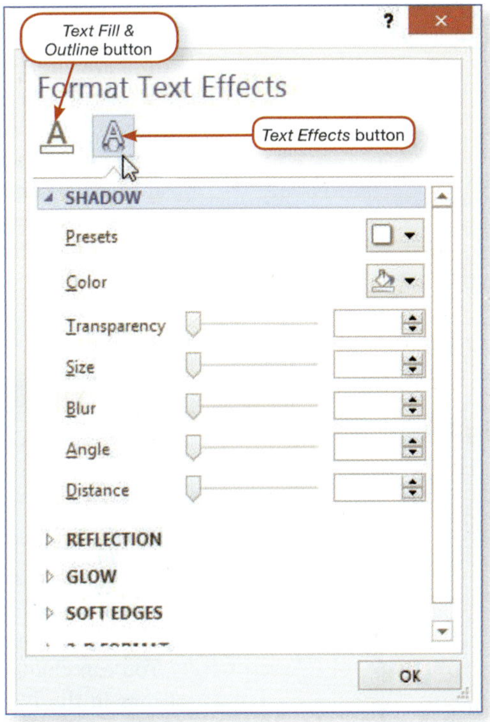

1-37 ***Format Text Effects* dialog box**

Format Painter

The ***Format Painter*** copies font, font size, line spacing, indents, bullets, numbering, styles, and many other features in Word and applies the formatting to a word, phrase, or entire paragraph. This feature saves time in applying formats and keeps your document consistent in format.

HOW TO: Use the Format Painter

1. Select the text that has the formatting you want to copy.
2. Click the **Format Painter** button [*Home* tab, *Clipboard* group (Figure 1-38). The *Format Painter* icon appears as your pointer (Figure 1-39).
3. Click the word or select the paragraph you want to format and Word applies the formatting to the selected text.
   - Double-click the **Format Painter** button to apply formatting to multiple non-adjacent selections.
   - Click the **Format Painter** button again to turn off the *Format Painter.*

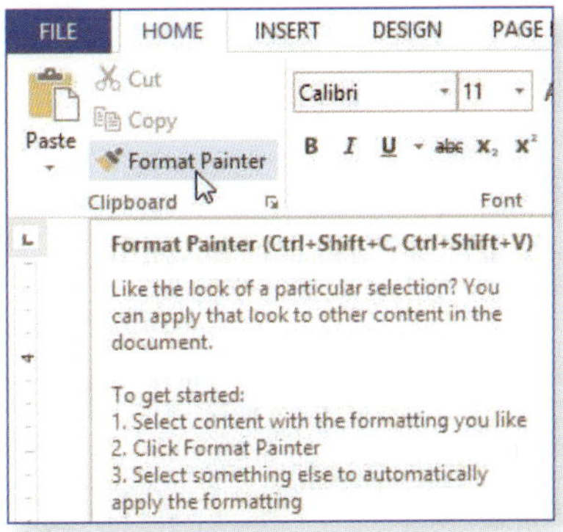

1-38 ***Format Painter* button**

1-39 ***Format Painter* icon**

Clear Formatting

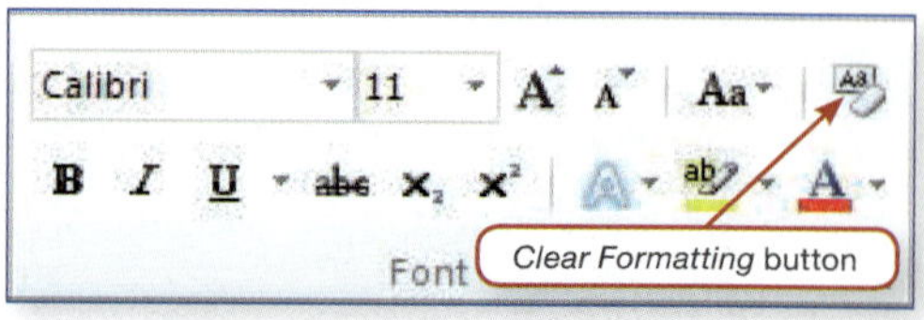

1-40 ***Clear Formatting*** **button in the** ***Font*** **group**

If you have applied multiple formatting features to text and you decide to remove the formatting, you don't have to individually deselect all of the formatting options previously selected. The ***Clear Formatting*** feature allows you to remove all formatting for the selected text and change it back to plain text (Figure 1-40).

> **MORE INFO**
>
> Be careful when using the *Clear Formatting* feature. It not only clears all text formatting but also clears line and paragraph spacing, numbering, bullets, and style formatting.

Change Default Font and Font Size

Recall that the default font in Microsoft Word is *Calibri,* and the default font size is *11 pt.* This ***default*** setting is used on each new blank document you create. Each new document is based on the *Normal.dotx* template. This template stores the default settings for documents and controls document elements such as font, font size, line spacing, paragraph spacing, alignment, and styles.

You can change the default settings on the current document only or change the default settings in the *Normal* template. If you change the default settings for the *Normal* template, each new blank document you create uses this new default font and font size.

HOW TO: Change the Default Font and Font Size

1. Select the text you want to format.
2. Click the **Font** launcher [*Home* tab, *Font* group]. The *Font* dialog box opens (Figure 1-41).
3. Click the **Font** tab if it is not already selected.
4. Select the font and font size to set as the default.
5. Click the **Set As Default** button at the bottom left. A confirmation dialog box opens giving you two options: *This document only?* or *All documents based on the Normal template?* (Figure 1-42).
6. Select an option.
7. Click **OK** to close the dialog box.

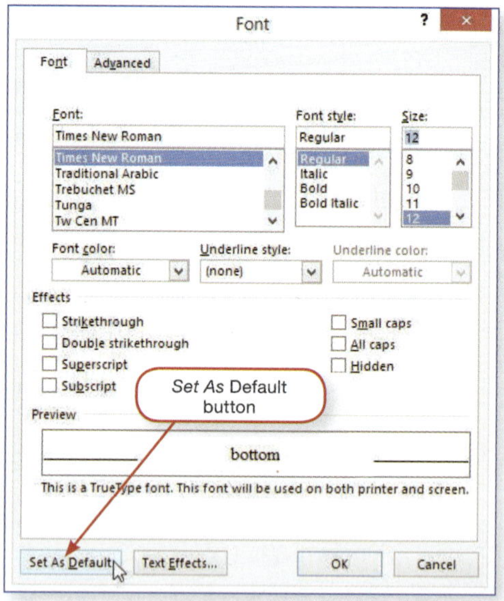

1-41 ***Set As Default*** **button in the** ***Font*** **dialog box**

> **MORE INFO**
>
> Be careful about changing the default settings in the *Normal* template. Do this only when you are sure you want to make this global default settings change.

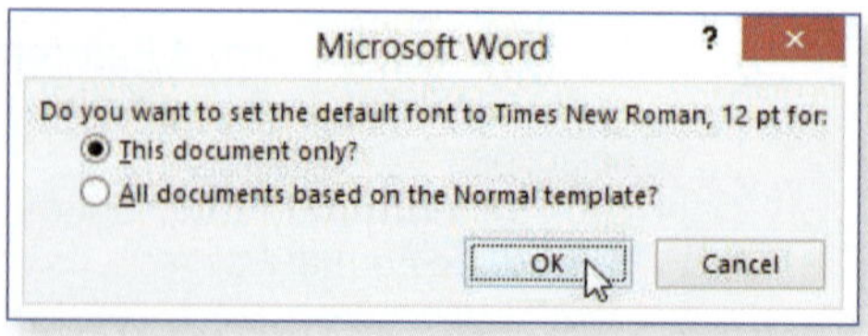

1-42 Change default setting confirmation options

PAUSE & PRACTICE: WORD 1-2

In this Pause & Practice project, you customize the content of your block format letter using cut, copy, paste, and the *Clipboard.* You also enhance your document by changing the font and applying font attributes.

Files Needed: ***[your initials] PP W1-1.docx***, ***DisclosureStatement-01.docx***
Completed Project File Name: ***[your initials] PP W1-2.docx***

1. Open the ***[your initials] PP W1-1*** document.
2. Save this document as ***[your initials] PP W1-2***.
   a. Press **F12** to open the *Save As* dialog box.
   b. Change the file name to [your initials] PP W1-2.
   c. Click **Save** to rename the document and close the *Save As* dialog box.
3. Open the ***DisclosureStatement-01*** document. Ignore any spelling and grammar errors in this document; you will fix these in Pause & Practice 1-3.
4. In the ***DisclosureStatement-01*** document, copy both paragraphs of text to the *Clipboard.*
   a. Press **Ctrl+A** to select the text.
   b. Press **Ctrl+C** or click the **Copy** button [*Home* tab, *Clipboard* group].
   c. Close the document without saving.
5. Paste the contents of the *Clipboard* into the document.
   a. In the ***[your initials] PP W1-2*** document, place your insertion point to the left of "Best regards,".
   b. Click the **Clipboard** launcher [*Home* tab, *Clipboard* group] to display the *Clipboard* pane.
   c. Click the **drop-down arrow** to the right of the copied text in the *Clipboard* (Figure 1-43).
   d. Select **Paste**. The paragraphs of text are pasted in the document at the insertion point.
   e. Close the *Clipboard* by clicking on the **X** in the upper right corner.

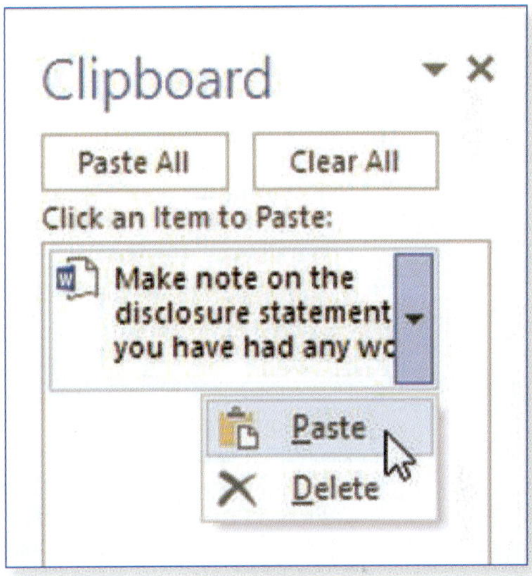

1-43 Paste text from the *Clipboard*

6. Copy the formatting of the first paragraph to the two new paragraphs.
   a. Place your insertion point in the first body paragraph of the letter.
   b. Click the **Format Painter** button [*Home* tab, *Clipboard* group].
   c. Select the last two paragraphs in the body of the letter. Be sure to include the paragraph mark at the end of the last body paragraph (Figure 1-44).

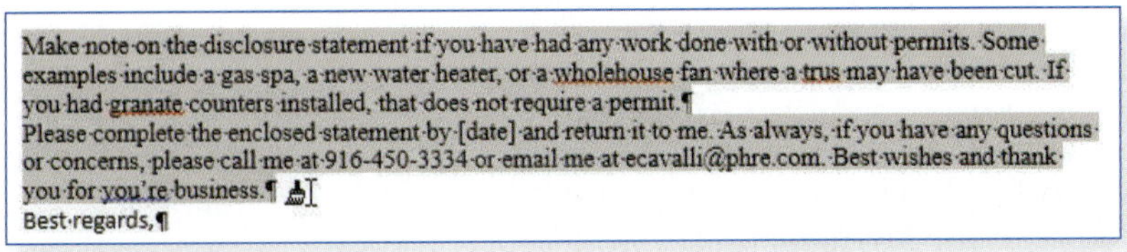

1-44 Apply the *Format Painter* to selected text

7. Copy text using the drag and drop method.
   a. Select the word "**disclosure**" in the first sentence of the third body paragraph.
   b. Hold down the **Ctrl** key and drag and drop the text between the words "enclosed" and "statement" (Figure 1-45).

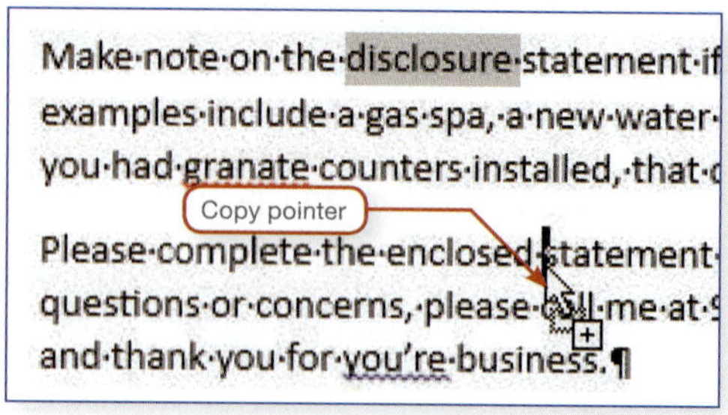

1-45 Copy text using drag and drop

8. Move the third body paragraph ("Make note . . .") so it becomes the second body paragraph.
   a. Select the third paragraph in the body of the letter, including the paragraph mark at the end of the paragraph.
   b. Click the **Cut** button [*Home* tab, *Clipboard* group] or press **Ctrl+X**. The selected paragraph is cut from the document and stored in the *Clipboard.*
   c. Place your insertion point at the beginning of the second body paragraph.
   d. Click the **Paste** button [*Home* tab, *Clipboard* group] or press **Ctrl+V**.

9. Insert and format a date.
   a. Replace the placeholder "[date]" in the last paragraph with the date one week from today.
   b. Use month, day, year format (e.g., September 8, 2015).
   c. Select the date.
   d. On the **Text Highlight Color** drop-down list button [*Home* tab, *Font* group], choose **yellow** text highlight color (Figure 1-46).

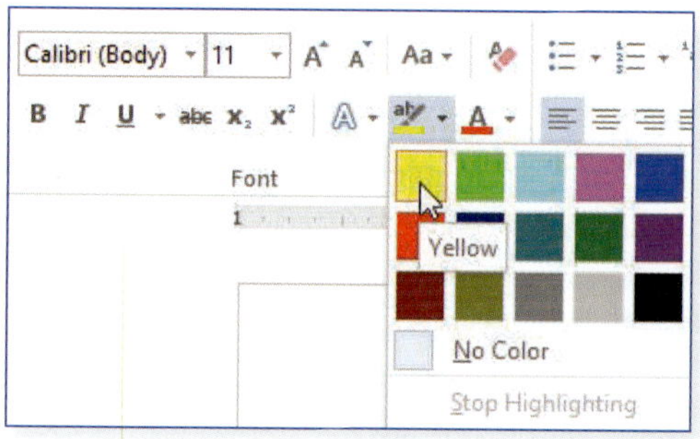

1-46 Apply text highlight color

10. Change the font and font size of the entire document.
    a. Press **Ctrl+A** to select all of the text in the document.
    b. Click the **Font** drop-down list button [*Home* tab, *Font* group] and select **Cambria**.
    c. Click the **Font Size** drop-down list button [*Home* tab, *Font* group] and select **12**.

11. Change the case and spacing of selected text.
    a. Select the word "**Subject**" in the subject line of the document.
    b. Click the **Change Case** button [*Home* tab, *Font* group] and select **UPPERCASE**.
    c. Select the entire subject line.
    d. Click the **Font** launcher [*Home* tab, *Font* group] to open the *Font* dialog box. **Ctrl+D** also opens the *Font* dialog box (Figure 1-47).
    e. Click the **Advanced** tab.
    f. In the *Character Spacing* area, click the **Spacing** drop-down list and select **Expanded**.
    g. In the *By* area to the right of *Spacing*, click the up arrow to change the character spacing to be expanded by **1.5 pt**.
    h. Click **OK** to close the *Font* dialog box.

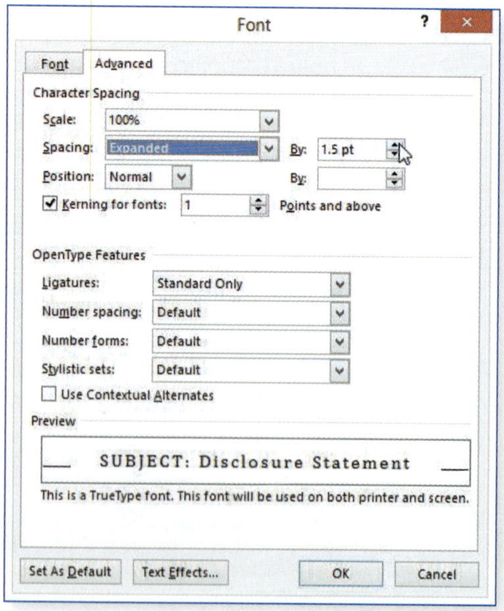

1-47 Change character spacing

12. Apply font styles to selected text.
    a. Select the email address "**ecavalli@phre.com**" in the last body paragraph.
    b. Click the **Font Color** drop-down list button [*Home* tab, *Font* group] and select **Dark Blue** in the *Standard Colors* area.
    c. Click the **Underline** button or press **Ctrl+U** to apply an underline to the selected email address.
    d. Select the writer's name "**Emma Cavalli**" (below "Best regards,") and open the *Font* dialog box.
    e. In the *Effects* area on the *Font* tab, check the **Small caps** box.
    f. Click **OK** to close the *Font* dialog box.
    g. Select the writer's title "**Realtor Consultant**" and click the **Italic** button or press **Ctrl+I**.
    h. Select the company name "**Placer Hills Real Estate**" and click the **Bold** button or press **Ctrl+B**.
13. Save and close the document (Figure 1-48).

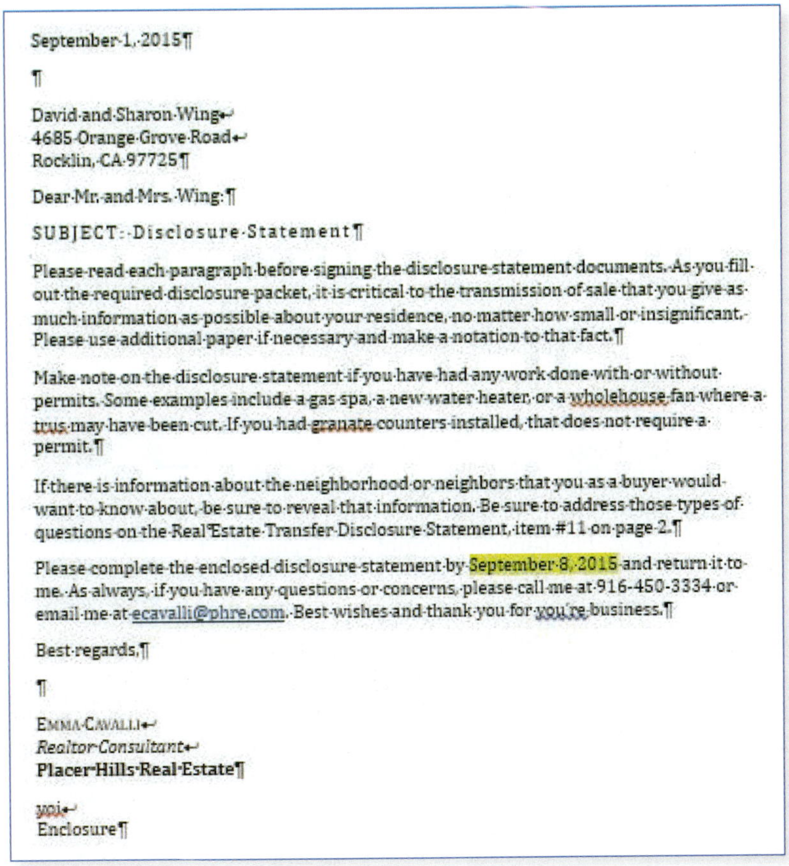

September 1, 2015

David and Sharon Wing
4685 Orange Grove Road
Rocklin, CA 97725

Dear Mr. and Mrs. Wing:

SUBJECT: Disclosure Statement

Please read each paragraph before signing the disclosure statement documents. As you fill out the required disclosure packet, it is critical to the transmission of sale that you give as much information as possible about your residence, no matter how small or insignificant. Please use additional paper if necessary and make a notation to that fact.

Make note on the disclosure statement if you have had any work done with or without permits. Some examples include a gas spa, a new water heater, or a wholehouse fan where a trus may have been cut. If you had granate counters installed, that does not require a permit.

If there is information about the neighborhood or neighbors that you as a buyer would want to know about, be sure to reveal that information. Be sure to address those types of questions on the Real Estate Transfer Disclosure Statement, item #11 on page 2.

Please complete the enclosed disclosure statement by September 8, 2015 and return it to me. As always, if you have any questions or concerns, please call me at 916-450-3334 or email me at ecavalli@phre.com. Best wishes and thank you for you're business.

Best regards,

EMMA CAVALLI
Realtor Consultant
Placer Hills Real Estate

yoi
Enclosure

1-48 PP W1-2 completed

SLO 1.6

Changing Text Alignment, Line Spacing, and Paragraph Spacing

In addition to word wrap, line breaks, and paragraphs breaks, you can use text alignment, line spacing, and paragraph spacing to control the layout and the white space between parts of your document.

Understand Default Settings

Just as there are default settings for font and font size, there are default settings for paragraph alignment, line spacing, and paragraph spacing. These default settings are stored in the *Normal* template on which all new blank documents are based. The following table summarizes these default settings:

Normal Template Default Settings

Setting	Default Setting
Font	Calibri
Font Size	11 pt.
Horizontal Paragraph Alignment	Left
Line Spacing	1.08 lines
Paragraph Spacing—Before	0 pt.
Paragraph Spacing—After	8 pt.

Paragraph Alignment

Paragraph alignment controls how a paragraph is aligned horizontally on the page. A paragraph can be a single word, a group of words, a sentence, or multiple sentences. Paragraphs are separated by paragraph breaks. A group of words using word wrap and line breaks is considered one paragraph.

The four different paragraph alignment options are:

- ***Left*** (default): The paragraph is aligned at the left margin.
- ***Center:*** The paragraph is centered between the left and right margins.
- ***Right:*** The paragraph begins and is aligned at the right margin.
- ***Justify:*** The paragraph is aligned flush with both the left and right margins.

ANOTHER WAY

Ctrl+L is *Align Text Left.*
Ctrl+E is *Center* text.
Ctrl+R is *Align Text Right.*
Ctrl+J is *Justify* text.

Change the alignment of a paragraph by clicking a paragraph alignment button in the *Paragraph* group on the *Home* tab (Figure 1-49). When changing the alignment of a paragraph, the entire paragraph need not be selected; the insertion point only needs to be within the paragraph for the alignment to be applied. Text alignment can also be changed in the *Paragraph* dialog box, which we discuss later.

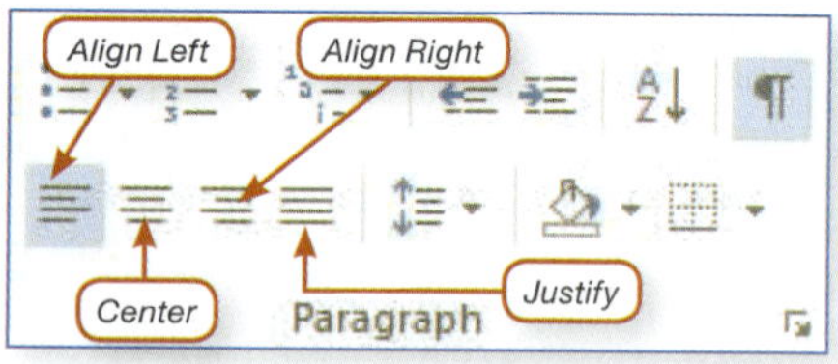

1-49 Paragraph alignment options in the *Paragraph* group

Line Spacing

Line spacing refers to the amount of blank space between lines of text within a paragraph. The default setting in Word is 1.08 lines, which is slightly more than single spaced. Most documents you type are single spaced or 1.08 line spacing, but there are times you may want to use double spacing (2 lines), such as when typing an academic report.

As with paragraph alignment, you can apply line spacing to an individual paragraph, multiple paragraphs, or an entire document.

You can change the line spacing using the **Line and Paragraph Spacing** button in the *Paragraph* group on the *Home* tab (Figure 1-50). You can choose from the preset line spacing options, or you can select **Line Spacing Options** and set custom line spacing in the *Paragraph* dialog box.

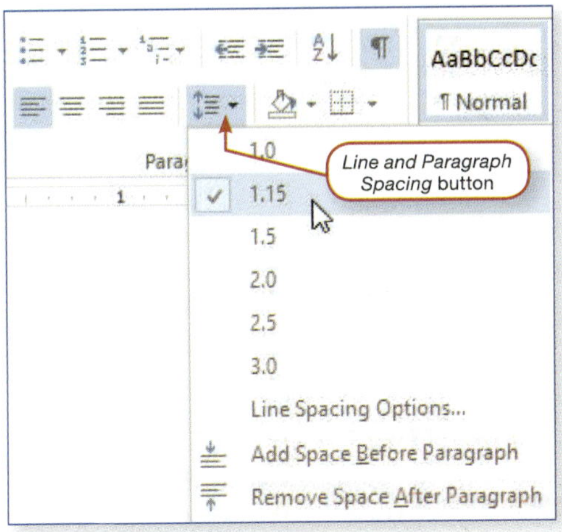

1-50 ***Line and Paragraph Spacing*** **button in the** ***Paragraph*** **group**

ANOTHER WAY

Ctrl+1 is single space (1 line).
Ctrl+5 is 1.5 line spacing.
Ctrl+2 is double space (2 lines).

When you select **Line Spacing Options**, the *Paragraph* dialog box opens. In the box, you see different line spacing options (Figure 1-51).

The *At Least* and *Exactly* options allow you to specify points of spacing, rather than lines of spacing, between lines of text. The *Multiple* option allows you to set a line spacing option that is not a whole number, such as 1.3 or 2.25 line spacing.

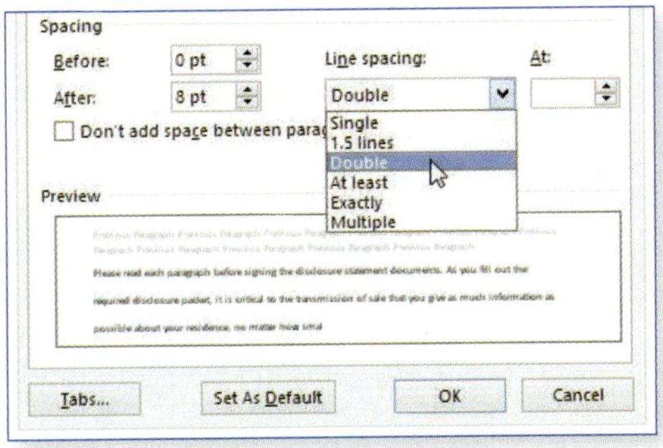

1-51 Line spacing options in the ***Paragraph*** **dialog box**

MORE INFO

If a document has inconsistent line spacing, it looks messy and unprofessional. Select the entire document and set the line spacing to enhance consistency. Consistent line spacing also improves readability.

Paragraph Spacing

While line spacing controls the amount of space between lines of text in a paragraph, ***paragraph spacing*** controls the amount of spacing before and after paragraphs (before and after a paragraph break). For example, you might want the text of a document to be single spaced, but you prefer to have more blank space between paragraphs. You can use paragraph spacing to accomplish this task. You can also do this by inserting multiple paragraph breaks—pressing *Enter* more than once.

Before and *After* paragraph spacing is set in points. The default after paragraph spacing in Word is 8 pt., which is a little less than one blank line.

Change before and after paragraph spacing from the *Paragraph* group on the *Page Layout* tab (Figure 1-52). You can also change before and after paragraph spacing in the *Paragraph* dialog box and from the *Line and Paragraph Spacing* button in the *Paragraph* group on the *Home* tab.

From the *Line and Paragraph Spacing* button in the *Paragraph* group on the *Home* tab, you can **Add/Remove Space Before Paragraph** or **Add/Remove Space After Paragraph** (Figure 1-53). These options are context sensitive, depending on whether there is already *Before* or *After* paragraph spacing.

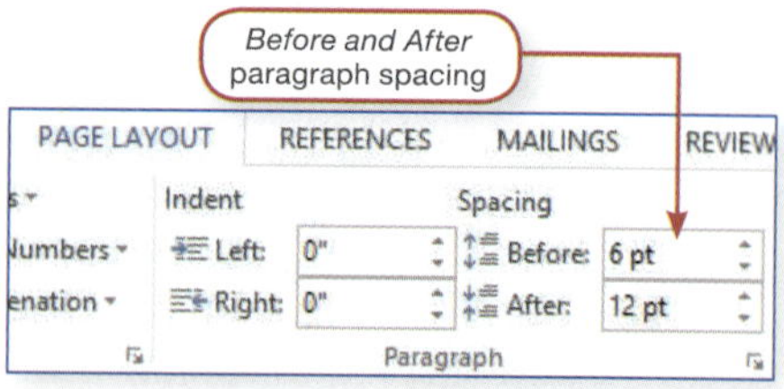

1-52 ***Paragraph* group on the *Page Layout* tab**

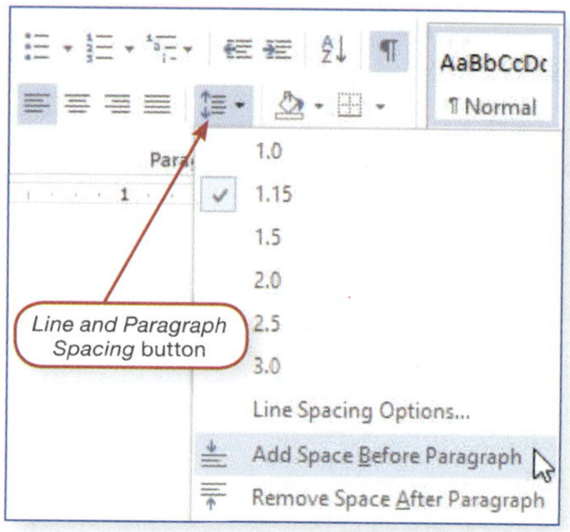

1-53 **Add/Remove paragraph spacing options**

> **MORE INFO**
>
> Use line breaks to keep lines of text together. *Before* and *After* paragraph spacing is not applied to lines of text where line breaks are used.

Paragraph Dialog Box

The ***Paragraph* dialog box** combines many of the alignment and spacing options included in the *Paragraph* groups on the *Home* and *Page Layout* tabs.

HOW TO: Change Alignment and Spacing in the Paragraph Dialog Box

1. Select the text you want to format.
2. Click the **Paragraph** launcher [*Home* or *Page Layout* tab, *Paragraph* group] to open the *Paragraph* dialog box (Figure 1-54).
3. Click the **Alignment** drop-down list in the *General* area and select **Left**, **Centered**, **Right**, or **Justified**.
4. The *Indentation* section of this dialog box lets you control indents. (For more on indents, see Chapter 2.)
5. In the *Spacing* section, you can change paragraph spacing and line spacing.
   - Type the number of points for spacing or use the up and down arrows.
   - The *Don't add space between paragraphs of the same style* check box controls paragraph spacing between paragraphs of the same style, which is primarily used with numbered and bulleted lists and outlines.
6. Click the **Line spacing** drop-down list to select line spacing.
   - You can select **Multiple** and type in a specific line spacing in the *At* area.
7. The *Preview* area displays how your document will look with changes.
8. Click **OK** to close the *Paragraph* dialog box.

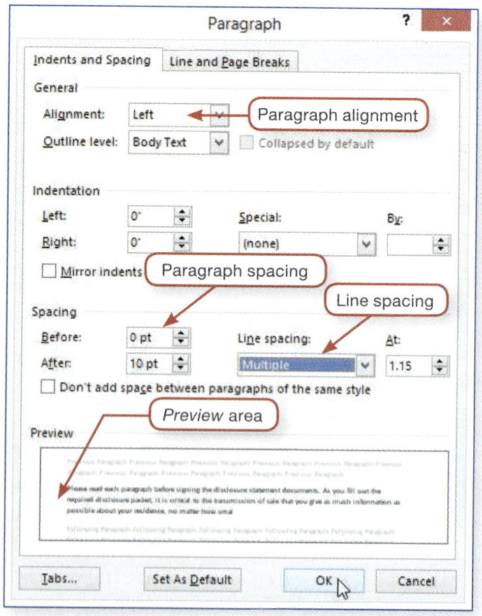

1-54 ***Paragraph* dialog box**

Change Default Line and Paragraph Spacing

You can set default paragraph alignment and spacing settings in the *Paragraph* dialog box. This process is similar to changing the font and font size default settings.

HOW TO: Change the Default Paragraph Alignment and Spacing

1. Click the **Paragraph** launcher [*Home* or *Page Layout* tab, *Paragraph* group] to open the *Paragraph* dialog box.
2. Click the **Indents and Spacing** tab if it is not already selected.
3. Make the desired changes to paragraph and line spacing.
4. Click the **Set As Default** button on the bottom left. Select one of the two options in the confirmation dialog box that opens: *This document only* or *All documents based on the Normal template* (Figure 1-55).
5. Click **OK**.

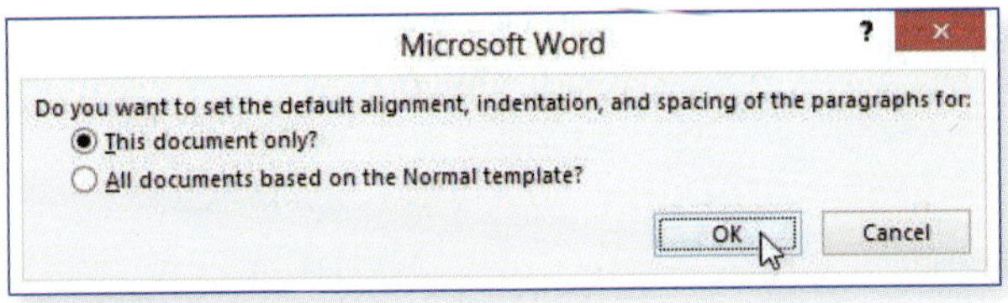

1-55 Change default setting confirmation options

SLO 1.7

Checking Spelling and Grammar and Using the Thesaurus

The words and grammar you use in a document reflect your professionalism and the reputation of your organization. Word provides you with many proofing and editing tools to improve the quality of the documents you produce. The spelling, grammar, thesaurus, and research features help you to produce high-quality and professional-looking documents.

Automatic Spelling and Grammar Notifications

Recall that Word uses *AutoCorrect* to automatically correct many commonly misspelled words. But there are many ***spelling errors*** that Word does not automatically correct. When you are typing a document, Word is constantly checking the words you type against the words in its dictionary. When Word doesn't recognize a word, it marks it with a ***red wavy underline.***

Word also checks the grammar of what you are typing and marks potential word choice or ***grammatical errors*** with a ***blue wavy underline.***

> **MORE INFO**
>
> Just because Word marks a word as a possible spelling or grammatical error, it does not necessarily mean that the word is misspelled. Many proper nouns are not included in the dictionary.

HOW TO: Correct Spelling and Grammatical Errors

1. Right-click a word that has a red or blue wavy underline. A context menu opens (Figure 1-56).
2. This menu provides different editing options.
   - Select the correct word from the list to replace the misspelled word.

- Select **Ignore All** to ignore all instances of this spelling throughout the document. Select **Ignore Once** to ignore a potential grammar error.
- Select **Add to Dictionary** to add the word to the Word dictionary.

3. When you select an option, the context menu closes.
4. Right-click the next item with a wavy red or blue underline to repeat the editing process.

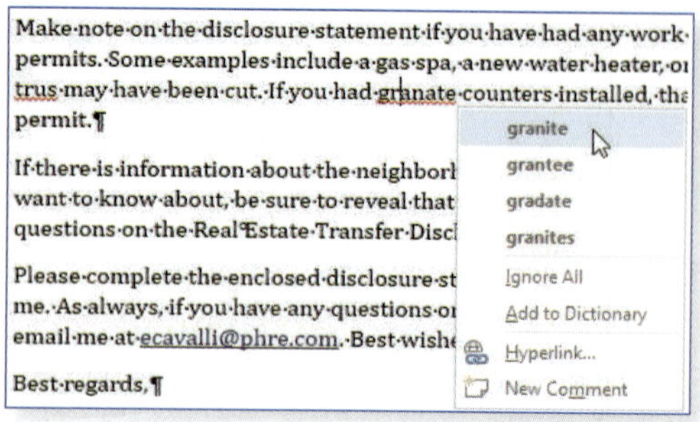

1-56 Correct a spelling error

MORE INFO

Don't rely solely on Word's spelling and grammar checkers to proofread your document. These helpful features cannot replace the proofreading and editing that you should do on every document you produce.

Spelling and Grammar Checking

When finalizing a document, it is important to proofread it one last time and give it one last spelling and grammar check. This is especially true with longer documents. You can use the ***Spelling and Grammar pane*** to check your entire document for potential spelling and grammatical errors.

The *Spelling and Grammar* pane is context-sensitive. The name of the pane (*Spelling* or *Grammar*) and the available options change depending on whether a potential spelling or grammatical error is detected.

HOW TO: Use the Spelling and Grammar Pane

1. Click the **Spelling & Grammar** button [*Review* tab, *Proofing* group] to open the *Spelling* pane (Figure 1-57).
   - The first potential spelling or grammatical error is displayed in the *Spelling* or *Grammar* pane.
2. If the word does not need to be changed, select **Ignore**, **Ignore All**, or **Add**.
   - If you select *Add*, the selected word is added to the dictionary so it is not detected as a potential error in the future.
3. If the word needs to be changed, select the correct word and select **Change** or **Change All**.
   - *Change* changes the word and *Change All* changes all instances of the misspelled word.
   - A definition of the selected word is displayed below the list of word options.
   - If no word options are available, retype the word in the body of the document.
4. When the spell and grammar check is complete, a dialog box opens.
5. Click **OK** to finish.

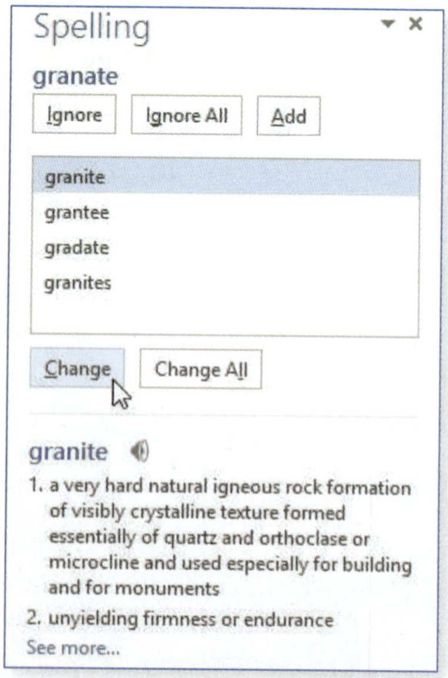

1-57 *Spelling and Grammar* pane

ANOTHER WAY

F7 opens the *Spelling and Grammar* pane.

Customize the Dictionary

When you are spell checking a document, you can easily add a word to the ***Word dictionary.*** When you add a word to the dictionary, Word actually creates a custom dictionary for you. You can manually add or delete words from the custom dictionary.

HOW TO: Add Words to the Custom Dictionary

1. Click the **File** tab to open the *Backstage* view.
2. Click the **Options** button to open the *Word Options* dialog box.
3. Click the **Proofing** button.
4. Click the **Custom Dictionaries** button. The *Custom Dictionaries* dialog box opens (Figure 1-58).
5. Select the dictionary to edit in the *Dictionary List.*
   - The *RoamingCustom.dic* is the default dictionary.
6. Click the **Edit Word List** button. Your custom dictionary dialog box opens (Figure 1-59). The words that have been previously added to your dictionary are displayed in the *Dictionary* area.
7. Click in the **Word(s)** area, type a word to add to your dictionary, and click the **Add** button to add the word to your dictionary.
   - Words can be deleted from the dictionary by clicking the **Delete** button.
8. Click **OK** when finished to close the *RoamingCustom.dic* dialog box.
9. Click **OK** to close the *Custom Dictionaries* dialog box.
10. Click **OK** to close the *Word Options* dialog box.

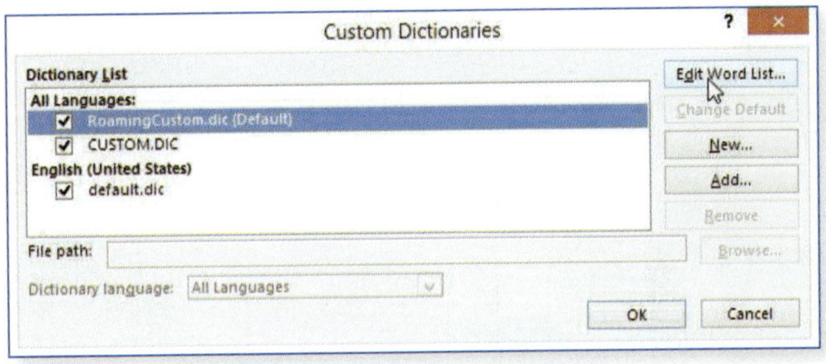

1-58 *Custom Dictionaries* dialog box

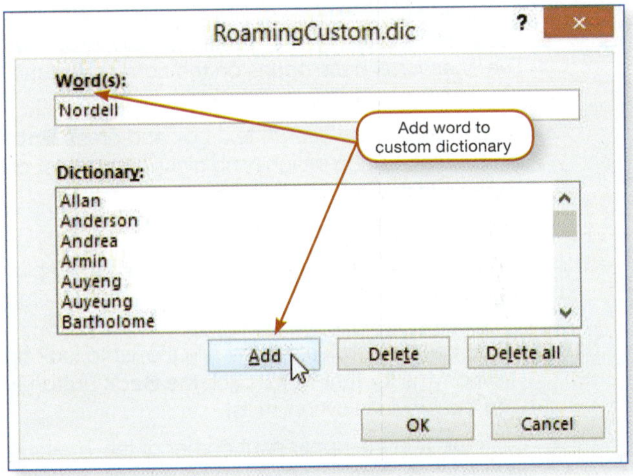

1-59 Add word to custom dictionary

The Thesaurus

Word provides a ***Thesaurus*** that you can use to find ***synonyms*** of words to add variety to your writing. A varied vocabulary makes you appear more educated and professional.

There are two ways to use the *Thesaurus* to find synonyms. The first and quickest way is to select a word in the document and use the context menu (right-click) to replace a selected word with an appropriate synonym.

HOW TO: Find Synonyms Using the Context Menu

1. **Select** the word you want to replace with an appropriate synonym.
2. Right-click the selected word to display the context menu (Figure 1-60).
3. Put your pointer on **Synonyms**. Another context menu appears with a list of synonym choices.
4. Select the synonym you prefer. The selected synonym replaces the selected word in the text and the menus close.

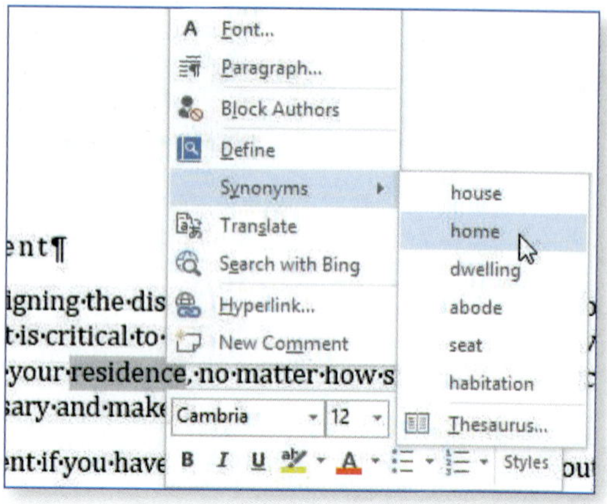

1-60 Use *Thesaurus* to find synonyms

You can also use the *Thesaurus* feature in the *Thesaurus* pane. This method allows you to search for synonyms of any word, not just a selected word in your document.

HOW TO: Use the Thesaurus

1. Click the **Thesaurus** button [*Review* tab, *Proofing* group]. The *Thesaurus* pane opens on the right side of the Word window (Figure 1-61).
2. Type a word in the *Search* text box and press **Enter** or click the **Search** button (magnifying glass icon). A list of synonyms appears in the *Thesaurus* area.
3. Choose from the synonyms listed.
   - Click the **arrow** to the right of the word to display the drop-down list. You have options to *Insert* or *Copy* the synonym.
   - You can also click a synonym in the list to look up synonyms for that word. Click the **Back** button to return to the previous synonym list.
4. Click the **X** in the upper right corner of the *Thesaurus* pane to close this pane.

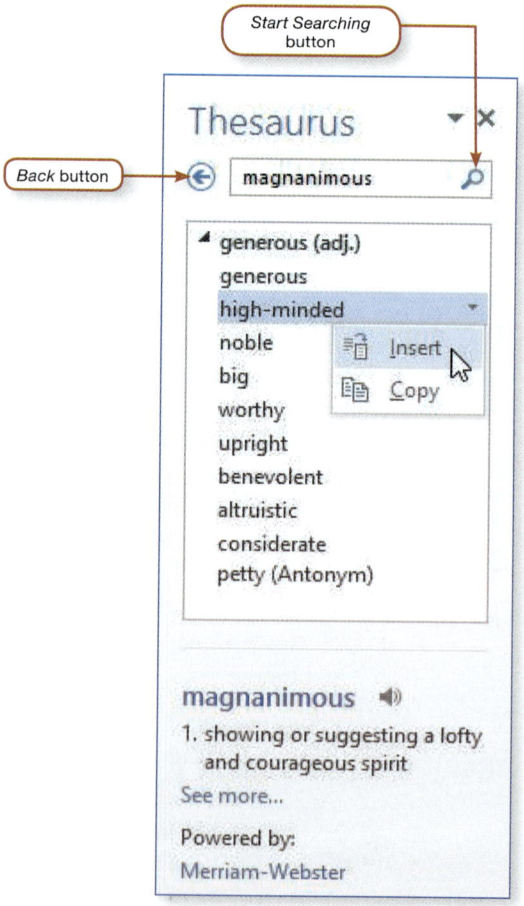

1-61 *Thesaurus* pane

> **ANOTHER WAY**
>
> **Shift+F7** opens the *Thesaurus* pane.

Word Count

Word also provides you with a ***word count*** option. Click the **Word Count** button in the *Proofing* group on the *Review* tab (Figure 1-62) to get the following information: number of pages, words, characters (no spaces), characters (with spaces), paragraphs, and lines (Figure 1-63). You can also choose to have Word count words in text boxes, footnotes, and endnotes, which are not by default included in the word count.

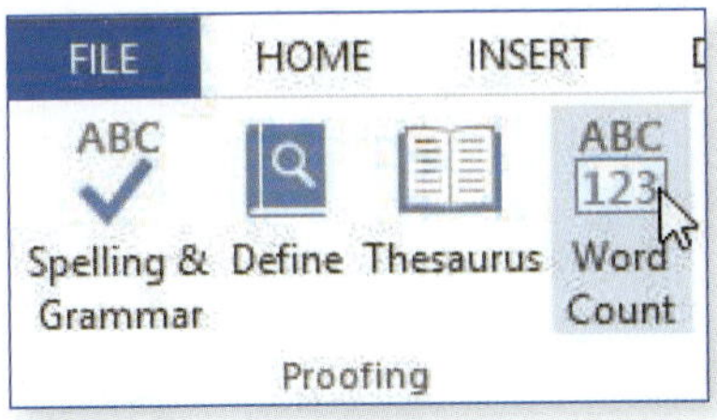

1-62 *Word Count* button

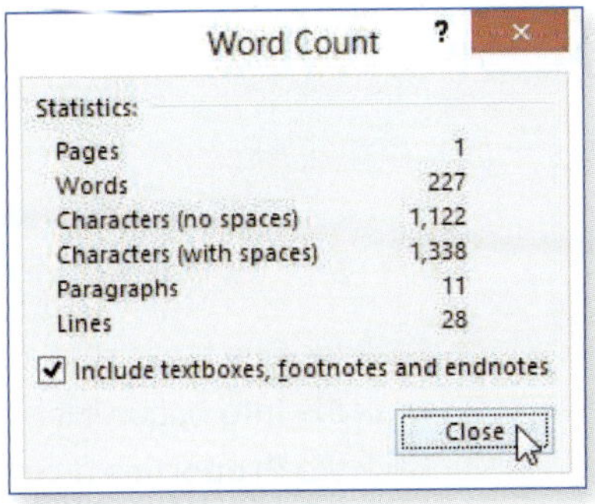

1-63 *Word Count* dialog box

> **ANOTHER WAY**
>
> Click **WORDS** at the bottom left of the *Status* bar to open the *Word Count* dialog box.

SLO 1.8

Customizing Document Properties

Word allows you to include details about a document, which are called ***document properties.*** These details are not visible in the text of the document but are included as hidden information within the document. These include fields such as *Title, Author, Comments, Subject, Company, Created,* and *Last Modified.* Some of the document properties are automatically generated, such as *Words, Total Editing Time,* and *Last Modified,* whereas other document property details can be edited individually.

Document Properties

The document properties can be viewed and edited in the *Info* area on the *Backstage* view. Document properties are saved within the document and can be viewed by others who view or use the document.

HOW TO: Add Document Properties

1. Click the **File** tab to display the *Backstage* view.
2. Click the **Info** button if it is not already selected.
3. The document properties are displayed on the right side of the window (Figure 1-64).
4. Document property field names are listed on the left, and the information in these fields is listed on the right.
5. Click in a field and type information to edit the document property.
   - Some properties cannot be changed. These properties are automatically generated by Word.

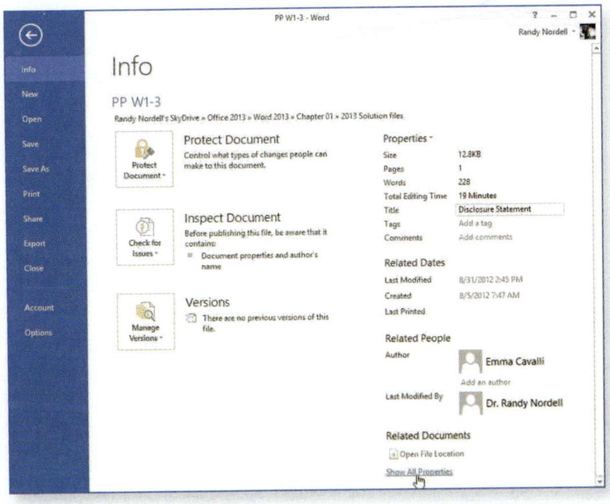

1-64 Document properties on the *Backstage* view

6. Click the **Show All/Fewer Properties** link at the bottom to display more or fewer document property fields.
7. After entering document properties, click the **Back** arrow in the upper left corner of the Backstage view to return to the document.

Document Panel

In addition to viewing and editing the document properties on the *Backstage* view, you can also display the properties in the ***Document panel,*** which appears in the regular Word window above the document and below the tab.

HOW TO: Use the Properties Panel

1. Click the **File** tab to display the *Backstage* view.
2. Click the **Info** button if it is not already selected.
3. Click the **Properties** drop-down list at the top of the *Properties* area (Figure 1-65).
4. Select **Show Document Panel**. The *Backstage* view closes and the *Document* panel is displayed above the document in the Word window (Figure 1-66).
5. Edit or add text in the *Document Properties* fields as desired.
6. Click the **X** in the upper right corner of the *Document* panel (not the Word window) to close the panel.

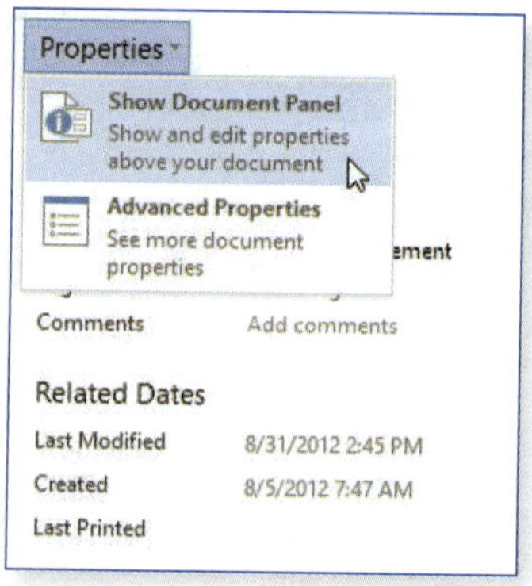

1-65 ***Show Document Panel***

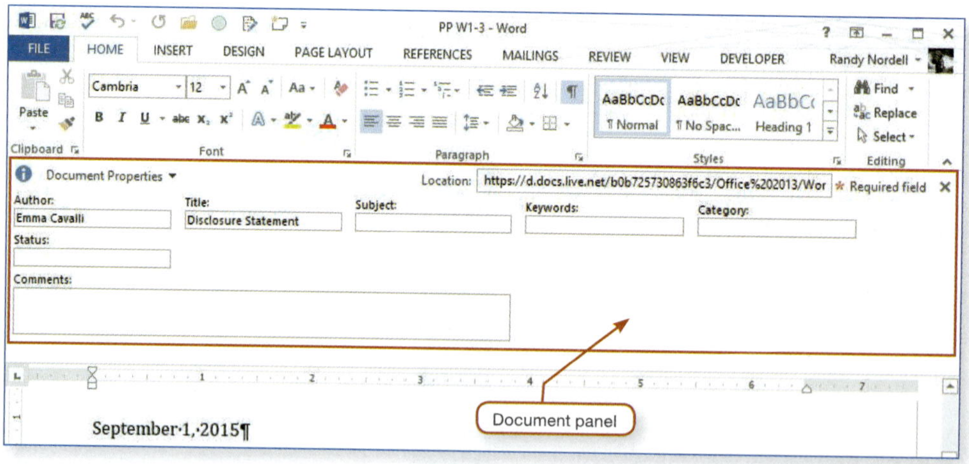

1-66 ***Document* panel**

PAUSE & PRACTICE: WORD 1-3

In the final Pause & Practice project in this chapter, you put the finishing touches on a document. You customize paragraph and line spacing, change paragraph alignment, and use spelling and grammar checkers to produce an error-free document. You also modify the document properties.

File Needed: ***[your initials] PP W1-2.docx***
Completed Project File Name: ***[your initials] PP W1-3.docx***

1. Open the ***[your initials] PP W1-2*** document.
2. Save this document as ***[your initials] PP W1-3***.
   a. Press **F12** to open the *Save As* dialog box.
   b. Change the file name to [your initials] PP W1-3.
   c. Click **Save** to rename the document and close the *Save As* dialog box.
3. Change the line and paragraph spacing on the entire document and set as the default for this document only.
   a. Press **Ctrl+A** to select the entire document.
   b. Click the **Paragraph** launcher [*Home* or *Page Layout* tab, *Paragraph* group] to open the *Paragraph* dialog box (Figure 1-67).
   c. Change the *Line spacing* to **Single**.
   d. Change the *After* spacing to **12 pt**., using the up arrow or typing in the amount of spacing.
   e. Click the **Set As Default** button. A dialog box opens.
   f. Click the **This document only?** radio button and click **OK** to close the dialog box.

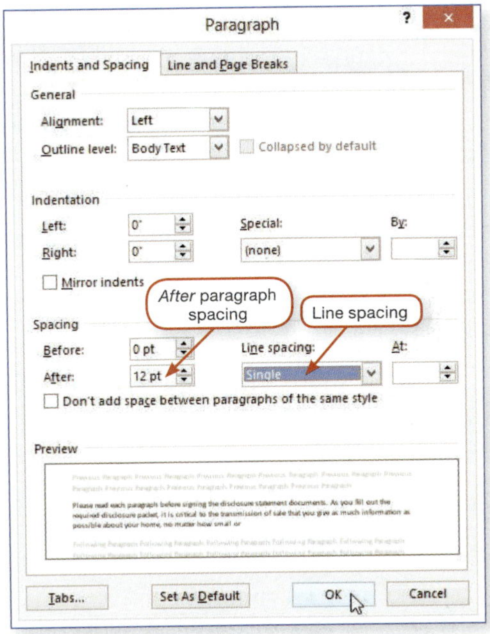

1-67 Change line and paragraph spacing in the *Paragraph* dialog box

> **ANOTHER WAY**
>
> Change line spacing in the *Paragraph* group on the *Home* tab. Change *Before* and *After* paragraph spacing in the *Paragraph* group on the *Page Layout* tab.

4. Add paragraph spacing before the date line of the business letter.
   a. Select or place your insertion point in the first line (date line) of the business letter.
   b. Click the **Page Layout** tab.
   c. Change the *Before* spacing to **72 pt**. Note: 72 pt. is approximately 1", which is commonly used as the spacing before the date line on business letters (Figure 1-68).

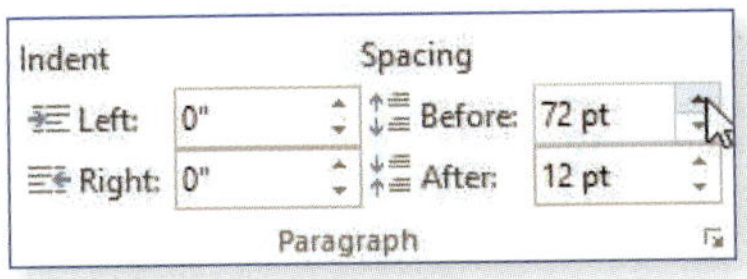

1-68 Change paragraph spacing in the *Paragraph* group

5. Change the paragraph alignment of selected text.
   a. Select or place your insertion point in the subject line of the business letter.
   b. Click the **Center** button [*Home* tab, *Paragraph* group] or press **Ctrl+E**.

6. Use the *Thesaurus* to find synonyms for selected words.
   a. Select the word "**reveal**" in the third body paragraph.
   b. Click the **Thesaurus** button [*Review* tab, *Proofing* group]. The *Thesaurus* pane opens on the right side of the Word window with a list of synonyms for the selected word (Figure 1-69).
   c. Click the **drop-down arrow** to the right of the word "divulge" and choose **Insert**. The word "reveal" is replaced with "divulge."
   d. Click the **X** in the upper right corner of the *Thesaurus* pane to close the pane.
   e. Right-click the word "**residence**" in the first body paragraph. A context menu opens.
   f. Put your pointer on **Synonyms** and a list of synonyms appears.
   g. Select "**home**" from the list of synonyms. The word "residence" is replaced with "home."

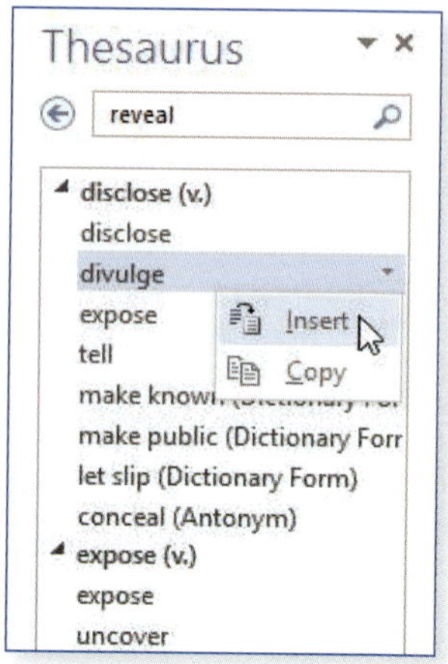

1-69 Insert a synonym from the *Thesaurus* pane

7. Add a word to the custom dictionary.
   a. Click the **File** tab to open the *Backstage* view.
   b. Click the **Options** button to open the *Word Options* dialog box.
   c. Click the **Proofing** button.
   d. Click the **Custom Dictionaries** button in the *When correcting spelling in Microsoft Office programs* area. The *Custom Dictionaries* dialog box opens.
   e. Select **RoamingCustom.dic** in the *Dictionary List.*
   f. Click the **Edit Word List** button. The *RoamingCustom.dic* dialog box opens (Figure 1-70).
   g. Type your last name in the *Word(s)* area and click the **Add** button.
   h. Click **OK** to close the *RoamingCustom.dic* dialog box.
   i. Click **OK** to close the *Custom Dictionaries* dialog box.
   j. Click **OK** to close the *Word Options* dialog box.

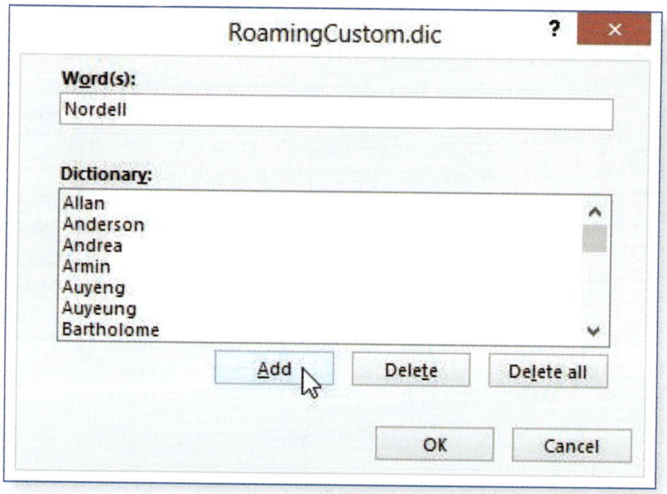

1-70 Add a word to the custom dictionary

8. Spell and grammar check the document.
   a. Right-click the word "**whole house**" in the second paragraph. A context list of words appears (Figure 1-71).
   b. Select "**whole house**." The correctly spelled word replaces the incorrectly spelled word.
   c. Click the **Spelling & Grammar** button [*Review* tab, *Proofing* group] or press **F7** to open the *Spelling* pane on the right (Figure 1-72).
   d. Select "**truss**" and click **Change**.
   e. Continue spell checking the remainder of the document. Change "granate" to "granite" and "you're" to "your."
   f. Click **Add** for "Cavalli."

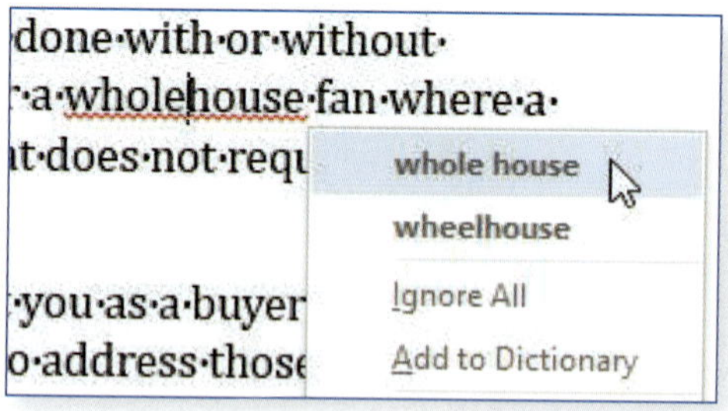

1-71 Correct spelling using the context menu

g. Click **Ignore** for your reference initials (if it is marked as incorrect).
h. Click **Ignore** for the capitalization grammar error (lower case reference initials).
i. Click **OK** to close the dialog box that opens and informs you that the spelling and grammar check is complete. The *Spelling and Grammar* pane closes.

9. Add document properties to your letter.
   a. Click the **File** tab to open the *Backstage* view.
   b. Click the **Info** button on the left if it is not already selected. The document properties are displayed on the right side of the *Backstage* view (Figure 1-73).
   c. Click in the *Title* field and type Disclosure Statement.
   d. In the *Author* area, right-click the existing author and select **Remove Person**.
   e. In the *Author* area, click **Add an author**, type Emma Cavalli, and press **Tab**.
   f. Click the **Show All Properties** link at the bottom. More document properties are displayed.
   g. Click in the *Company* area and type Placer Hills Real Estate.
   h. Click the **Properties** drop-down list at the top of the *Properties* area and choose **Show Document Panel**. The document properties are displayed in the *Document* panel.
   i. Click the **X** in the upper right corner of the *Document* panel to close it.

10. Save and close the document (Figure 1-74).

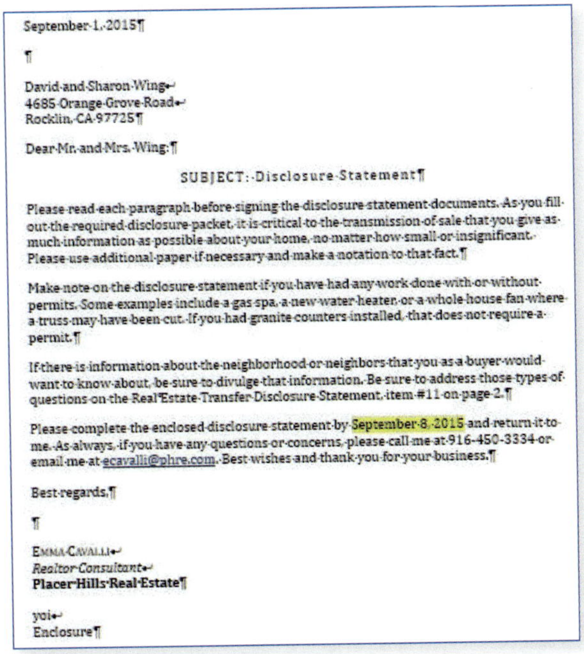
September 1, 2015

David and Sharon Wing
4685 Orange Grove Road
Rocklin, CA 97725

Dear Mr. and Mrs. Wing:

SUBJECT: Disclosure Statement

Please read each paragraph before signing the disclosure statement documents. As you fill out the required disclosure packet, it is critical to the transmission of sale that you give as much information as possible about your home, no matter how small or insignificant. Please use additional paper if necessary and make a notation to that fact.

Make note on the disclosure statement if you have had any work done with or without permits. Some examples include a gas spa, a new water heater, or a whole house fan where a truss may have been cut. If you had granite counters installed, that does not require a permit.

If there is information about the neighborhood or neighbors that you as a buyer would want to know about, be sure to divulge that information. Be sure to address those types of questions on the Real Estate Transfer Disclosure Statement, item #11 on page 2.

Please complete the enclosed disclosure statement by September 8, 2015 and return it to me. As always, if you have any questions or concerns, please call me at 916-450-3334 or email me at ecavalli@phre.com. Best wishes and thank you for your business.

Best regards,

EMMA CAVALLI
Realtor Consultant
Placer Hills Real Estate

yoi
Enclosure

1-74 PP W1-3 completed

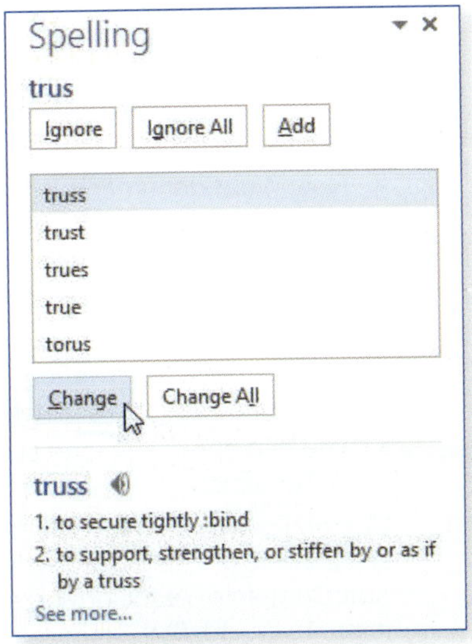

1-72 *Spelling and Grammar* pane

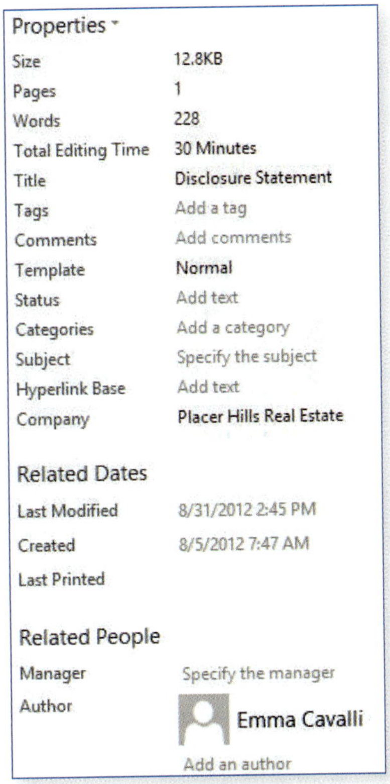

1-73 Document properties on the *Backstage* view

Chapter Summary

1.1 Create, save, and open a Word document (p. W1-3).

- New Word documents are based on the ***Normal template*** (*Normal.dotx*).
- You can save documents with the existing file name or with a different file name.
- A ***Word document*** (***.docx***) is the standard file format. There are a variety of Word file formats in which to save a document.
- You can open, edit, and save existing Word documents.

1.2 Customize a document by entering and selecting text, using word wrap, and using AutoComplete, AutoCorrect, and AutoFormat features (p. W1-6).

- ***Word wrap*** automatically wraps text to the next line as you reach the right margin of the document.
- The ***Show/Hide*** button displays formatting symbols in the document to properly and consistently format documents.
- You can select text in a variety of ways, and you can select individual words, an entire line, multiple lines of text, a sentence, a paragraph, multiple paragraphs, or the entire document.
- ***AutoComplete*** automatically completes a day, month, or date for you.
- ***AutoCorrect*** automatically corrects commonly misspelled words and capitalization errors.
- ***AutoFormat*** automatically controls the formatting of items such as numbered and bulleted lists.
- You can add, delete, and edit *AutoCorrect* entries and customize *AutoCorrect* options in Word.

1.3 Enhance a business document using paragraph breaks, line breaks, spaces, and non-breaking spaces (p. W1-10).

- The ***Enter*** key on the keyboard inserts a ***paragraph break***. The ***paragraph symbol*** is visible when Show/*Hide* is turned on.
- ***Line breaks*** control breaks between lines or sentences to retain paragraph formatting between lines.
- ***Non-breaking spaces*** keep related words together.

1.4 Edit a business document using cut, copy, paste, the Clipboard, and the undo, redo, and repeat features (p. W1-14).

- You can move or copy selected text within a document. There are a variety of methods to ***cut***, ***copy***, and ***paste*** text in a document.
- The ***Clipboard*** stores text that you have cut or copied. You can use the *Clipboard* to paste text into your document.
- You can ***Undo***, ***Redo***, and ***Repeat*** previous actions when working on a document. These features are available on the ***Quick Access*** toolbar.

1.5 Customize a business document using different fonts, font sizes, and attributes (p. W1-17).

- ***Serif*** and ***sans serif*** are the two main categories of ***fonts***.
- Fonts are measured in ***points*** (pt.). Most documents use between 10 and 12 pt. font size.
- You can change fonts and font size for specific text or the entire document.
- ***Bold***, ***italic***, and ***underline*** are font styles that you can apply quickly to text.
- Other font effects include ***strikethrough***, ***subscript***, ***superscript***, ***small caps***, and ***all caps***.
- You can change the case of text in Word.
- The ***Font dialog box*** provides many font, size, style, and ***effect*** options.
- You can modify the ***scale***, ***spacing***, ***position***, and ***kerning*** of selected text.
- The ***Format Painter*** applies formatting from selected text to other text.
- The ***Clear Formatting*** feature removes all formatting applied to selected text.
- You can change the ***default*** font and font size in Word.

1.6 Enhance a document using text alignment and line and paragraph spacing. (p. W1-27).

- ***Paragraph alignment*** describes how text is aligned horizontally between the margins of a document: ***left***, ***center***, ***right***, or ***justified***.
- ***Line spacing*** refers to the amount of blank space between lines of text in a paragraph.
- ***Paragraph spacing*** is the amount of space between paragraphs. Paragraph spacing is measured in points.

- You can modify alignment, line spacing, and paragraph spacing on the *Home* or *Page Layout* tab or in the ***Paragraph dialog box***.
- You can change the default line and paragraph spacing in Word.

1.7 Finalize a document using Word's proofing tools (p. W1-31).

- By default, Word automatically checks documents for ***spelling*** and ***grammatical errors***.
- Word marks potential spelling, incorrect word, or grammatical errors with a colored wavy line under the words. You can correct errors by selecting from options in the context menu.
- You can manually spell and grammar check a document using the *Spelling and Grammar* pane.
- You can customize the ***Word dictionary*** by adding, deleting, or modifying words in the word list.
- The ***Thesaurus*** finds synonyms for words in your document.
- Word also provides you with ***Word Count***.

1.8 Apply custom document properties to a document (p. W1-35).

- *You can add* ***document properties***, such as *Title*, *Author*, *Company*, *Subject*, *Created*, and *Last Modified*, into a document.
- You can add document properties on the *Backstage* view or in the ***Document panel***.

Check for Understanding

In the ***Online Learning Center*** for this text (www.mhhe.com/office2013inpractice), there are a variety of resources that can be used to review the concepts covered in this chapter.

The following Online Learning Resources are available in the Online Learning Center.

- Multiple choice questions
- Short answer questions
- Matching exercises

USING MICROSOFT WORD 2013

Guided Project 1-1

In this project, Jennie Owings at Central Sierra Insurance is writing a business letter to Hartford Specialty regarding the renewal of the insurance policy for Valley Custom Manufacturing. This business letter is typed in block format and uses open punctuation. See *Appendix D* (online reference) for an example of a block format business letter and open and mixed punctuation.
[Student Learning Outcomes 1.1, 1.2, 1.3, 1.4, 1.5, 1.6, 1.7]

File Needed: ***ValleyCustomManufacturing-1.docx***
Completed Project File Name: ***[your initials] Word 1-1.docx***

Skills Covered in This Project

- Use business letter format.
- Change line spacing.
- Change paragraph spacing.
- Use *AutoComplete*.
- Use paragraph breaks for proper spacing between the parts of a business letter.
- Copy and paste using the *Clipboard*.
- Use *Show/Hide*.
- Undo automatic capitalization.
- Change font size.
- Apply font styles.
- Use spelling and grammar checker.
- Add words to dictionary.

1. Open a new Word document and save it as ***[your initials] Word 1-1***.
2. Change the line and paragraph spacing of the document.
   a. Click the **Paragraph** launcher [*Home* or *Page Layout* tab, *Paragraph* group]. (Figure 1-75).
   b. Change the *Line spacing* to **Single**.
   c. Change the *After* paragraph spacing to **0 pt**.
   d. Choose **OK** and close the *Paragraph* dialog box.
3. Type the current date on the first line of the document.
   a. Use month, day, year format (e.g., September 1, 2015).
   b. As you begin typing the date, press **Enter** as *AutoComplete* completes the month and current date.
   c. Press **Enter** four times (quadruple space, QS) after the date.
4. Type the inside address.
   a. Press **Enter** once (single space, SS) at the end of each of the first three lines.

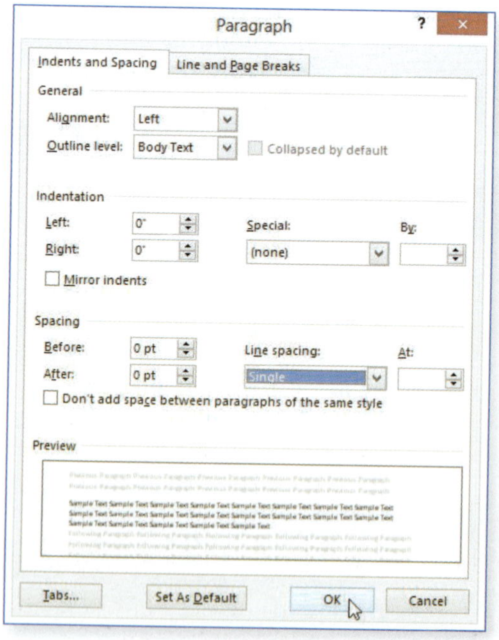

1-75 *Paragraph* dialog box

b. Press **Enter** twice (double space, DS) after the last line of the inside address.

Mrs. Cammie Speckler
Hartford Specialty
4788 Market Street, Suite A205
San Francisco, CA 95644

5. Type Dear Mrs. Speckler as the salutation. No colon is used after the salutation when using open punctuation.
6. Press **Enter** two times.
7. Type RE: Valley Custom Manufacturing as the subject line.
8. Press **Enter** two times.
9. Copy text from another document and paste it into the current document.
   a. Open the ***ValleyCustomManufacturing-01*** document from your student data files.
   b. Press **Ctrl+A** to select the entire document.
   c. Click the **Copy** button [*Home* tab, *Clipboard* group] or press **Ctrl+C**.
   d. Close ***ValleyCustomManufacturing-01*** without saving the document.
   e. In the ***[your initials] Word 1-1*** document, place your insertion point at the end of the document (a DS below the subject line).
   f. Click the **Clipboard** launcher [*Home* tab, *Clipboard* group] to open the *Clipboard* pane (Figure 1-76).

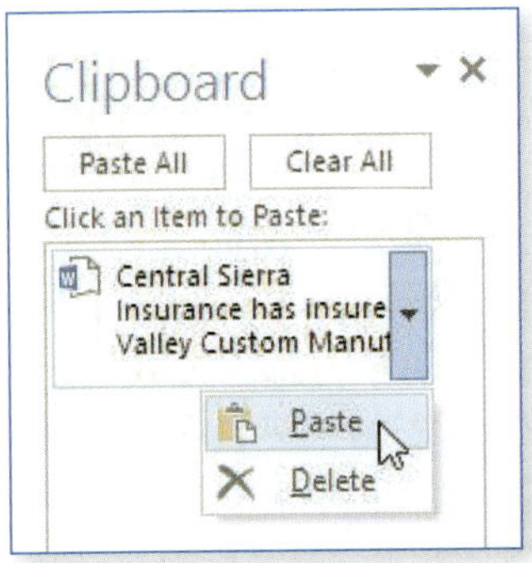

1-76 Paste from the *Clipboard*

   g. Select the **drop-down arrow** to the right of the copied text in the *Clipboard* and click **Paste**. The paragraphs of text are pasted in the body of the document.
   h. Click the **X** in the upper left corner of the *Clipboard* pane to close it.
10. Use the *Format Painter* to format the inserted paragraphs.
   a. Place your insertion point in the first line of the document.
   b. Click the **Format Painter** button [*Home* tab, *Clipboard* group].
   c. Select the body paragraphs of the letter to apply the formatting (Figure 1-77).

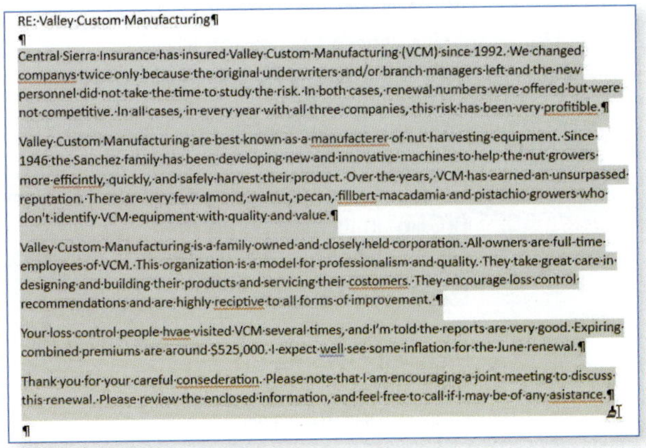

RE:·Valley·Custom·Manufacturing¶
¶
Central·Sierra·Insurance·has·insured·Valley·Custom·Manufacturing·(VCM)·since·1992.·We·changed·companys·twice·only·because·the·original·underwriters·and/or·branch·managers·left·and·the·new·personnel·did·not·take·the·time·to·study·the·risk.·In·both·cases,·renewal·numbers·were·offered·but·were·not·competitive.·In·all·cases,·in·every·year·with·all·three·companies,·this·risk·has·been·very·profitible.¶

Valley·Custom·Manufacturing·are·best·known·as·a·manufacterer·of·nut·harvesting·equipment.·Since·1946·the·Sanchez·family·has·been·developing·new·and·innovative·machines·to·help·the·nut·growers·more·efficintly,·quickly,·and·safely·harvest·their·product.·Over·the·years,·VCM·has·earned·an·unsurpassed·reputation.·There·are·very·few·almond,·walnut,·pecan,·fillbert·macadamia·and·pistachio·growers·who·don't·identify·VCM·equipment·with·quality·and·value.¶

Valley·Custom·Manufacturing·is·a·family·owned·and·closely·held·corporation.·All·owners·are·full-time·employees·of·VCM.·This·organization·is·a·model·for·professionalism·and·quality.·They·take·great·care·in·designing·and·building·their·products·and·servicing·their·costomers.·They·encourage·loss·control·recommendations·and·are·highly·reciptive·to·all·forms·of·improvement.·¶

Your·loss·control·people·hvae·visited·VCM·several·times,·and·I'm·told·the·reports·are·very·good.·Expiring·combined·premiums·are·around·$525,000.·I·expect·well·see·some·inflation·for·the·June·renewal.¶

Thank·you·for·your·careful·consederation.·Please·note·that·I·am·encouraging·a·joint·meeting·to·discuss·this·renewal.·Please·review·the·enclosed·information,·and·feel·free·to·call·if·I·may·be·of·any·asistance.¶
¶

1-77 Use the *Format Painter* to copy formatting

11. Insert a blank line between each of the body paragraphs so there is a double space after each body paragraph (one blank line between paragraphs).
   a. Turn on **Show/Hide** [*Home* tab, *Paragraph* group] if it is not already turned on.
   b. Place your insertion point at the end of the first body paragraph and press **Enter**.
   c. Repeat for each of the body paragraphs.

12. Enter the closing lines of the document.
    a. Place your insertion point on the blank line below the body of the letter, press **Enter**, and type Sincerely. No comma is used after the salutation when using open punctuation.
    b. Press **Enter** four times and type the writer's name, title, and company.

       Jennie Owings, Vice President
       Central Sierra Insurance

    c. Press **Enter** two times and type your reference initials (your first and last initials in lower case letters).
    d. Press **Enter**. *AutoCorrect* automatically capitalizes the first letter of your reference initials.
    e. Click the **AutoCorrect Options** smart tag (Figure 1-78). The *AutoCorrect Options* smart tag appears when you place your pointer below your reference initials.
    f. Click **Undo Automatic Capitalization** to undo the automatic capitalization of your reference initials.
    g. Place your insertion point on the blank line below your reference initials and type Enclosure.

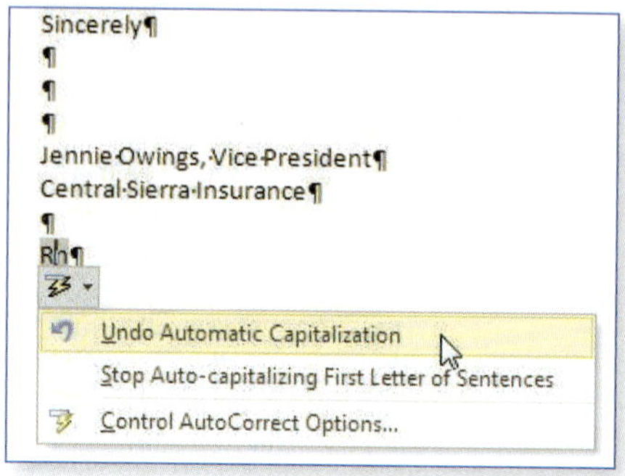

1-78 *AutoCorrect* smart tag

13. Select the entire document (**Ctrl+A**) and change the font size to **10 pt**.
14. Add paragraph spacing before the date line.
    a. Select or place your insertion point in the date line.
    b. Click the **Page Layout** tab.
    c. Change the *Before* spacing to **72 pt**. [*Paragraph* group] (Figure 1-79).

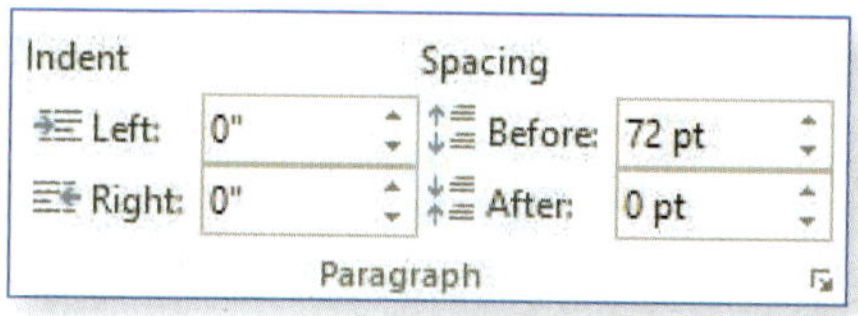

1-79 Change *Before* paragraph spacing on the date line

15. Apply font styles to selected text.
    a. Select the words "**Central Sierra Insurance**" in the first paragraph.
    b. Click the **Underline** button [*Home* tab, *Font* group] or press **Ctrl+U**.
    c. Select the words "**Valley Custom Manufacturing (VCM)**" in the first paragraph.
    d. Click the **Bold** button [*Home* tab, *Font* group] or press **Ctrl+B**.
16. Spell and grammar check the entire document.
    a. Press **Ctrl+Home** to move to the top of the document.
    b. Click the **Review** tab.
    c. Click the **Spelling & Grammar** button [*Proofing* group]. The *Spelling* pane opens (Figure 1-80).
    d. Click **Add** to add "Cammie" and "Speckler" to the dictionary.

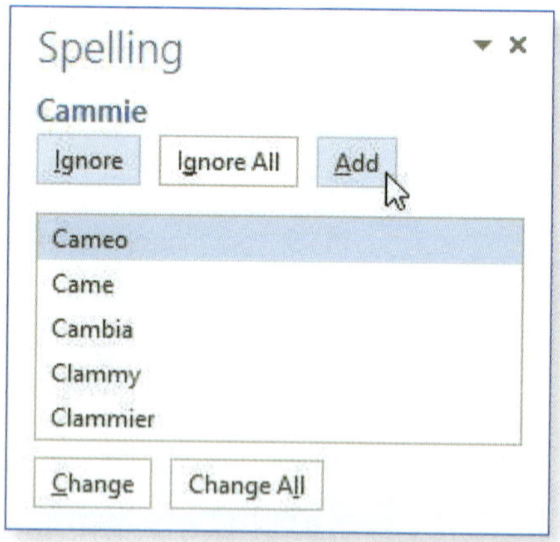

1-80 Add word to the dictionary

e. Change other words as necessary to correct spelling, incorrect word usage, and grammatical errors. If prompted to continue checking the document from the beginning, choose **Yes**.

f. Click **Ignore Once** if your reference initials are marked as a potential spelling or grammatical error.

17. Save and close the document (Figure 1-81).

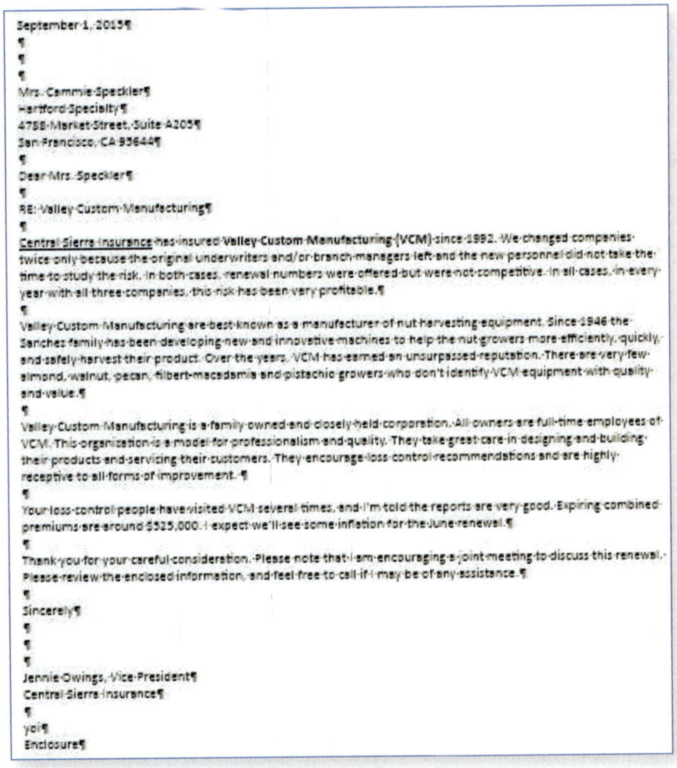

September 1, 2015

Mrs. Cammie Speckler
Hartford Specialty
4788 Market Street, Suite A205
San Francisco, CA 93644

Dear Mrs. Speckler

RE: Valley Custom Manufacturing

Central Sierra Insurance has insured Valley Custom Manufacturing (VCM) since 1992. We changed companies twice only because the original underwriters and/or branch managers left and the new personnel did not take the time to study the risk. In both cases, renewal numbers were offered but were not competitive. In all cases, in every year with all three companies, this risk has been very profitable.

Valley Custom Manufacturing are best known as a manufacturer of nut harvesting equipment. Since 1946 the Sanchez family has been developing new and innovative machines to help the nut growers more efficiently, quickly, and safely harvest their product. Over the years, VCM has earned an unsurpassed reputation. There are very few almond, walnut, pecan, filbert-macadamia and pistachio growers who don't identify VCM equipment with quality and value.

Valley Custom Manufacturing is a family owned and closely held corporation. All owners are full-time employees of VCM. This organization is a model for professionalism and quality. They take great care in designing and building their products and servicing their customers. They encourage loss control recommendations and are highly receptive to all forms of improvement.

Your loss control people have visited VCM several times, and I'm told the reports are very good. Expiring combined premiums are around $325,000. I expect we'll see some inflation for the June renewal.

Thank you for your careful consideration. Please note that I am encouraging a joint meeting to discuss this renewal. Please review the enclosed information, and feel free to call if I may be of any assistance.

Sincerely

Jennie Owings, Vice President
Central Sierra Insurance

yoi
Enclosure

1-81 Word 1-1 completed

Guided Project 1-2

Sierra Pacific Community College District is a multi-campus community college district. In this project, you format an informational handout regarding online learning.
[Student Learning Outcomes 1.1, 1.3, 1.4, 1.5, 1.6, 1.7, 1.8]

File Needed: ***OnlineLearning-01.docx***
Completed Project File Name: ***[your initials] Word 1-2.docx***

Skills Covered in This Project

- Open and edit an existing document.
- Change line spacing.
- Change paragraph spacing.
- Change default paragraph settings in your current document.
- Use *Show/Hide*.
- Change font size and apply color, styles, and effects.
- Cut and paste to move a paragraph.
- Use drag and drop to move a paragraph.
- Apply a shadow text effect.
- Use the *Format Painter*.
- Use spelling and grammar checker.
- Add document properties.

1. Open the ***OnlineLearning-01*** document from your student data files.
2. Save this document as ***[your initials] Word 1-2***.
3. Change the line and paragraph spacing of the entire document, and use these settings as the default for this document.
   a. Press **Ctrl+A** to select the entire document.
   b. Click the **Paragraph** launcher [*Home* or *Page Layout* tab, *Paragraph* group] to open the *Paragraph* dialog box (Figure 1-82).
   c. In the *Line spacing* area, select **Multiple** from the drop-down list.
   d. In the *At* area, type 1.2.
   e. Change the paragraph spacing *After* to **12 pt**.
   f. Click **Set As Default**. A dialog box opens (Figure 1-83).
   g. Select the **This Document Only?** radio button.
   h. Click **OK** to close the *Paragraph* dialog box.
4. Turn on **Show/Hide** [*Home* tab, *Paragraph* group] and **delete** the one extra blank line between each paragraph including the title.
5. Change the font and font size of the entire document.
   a. Select the entire document (**Ctrl+A**).
   b. Change the font to **Cambria** and the size to **11 pt**. [*Home* tab, *Font* group].
6. Change the paragraph spacing, alignment, font size, styles, effects, and color of the title.
   a. Select the title of the document (**Online Learning Information**).
   b. Click the **Page Layout** tab.
   c. Change the *Before* spacing to **36 pt**. and the *After* spacing to **18 pt**. [*Paragraph* group].
   d. Click the **Center** button [*Home* tab, *Paragraph* group].
   e. Click the **launcher** [*Font* group]. The *Font* dialog box opens (Figure 1-84).
   f. Change the *Font* style to **Bold**.

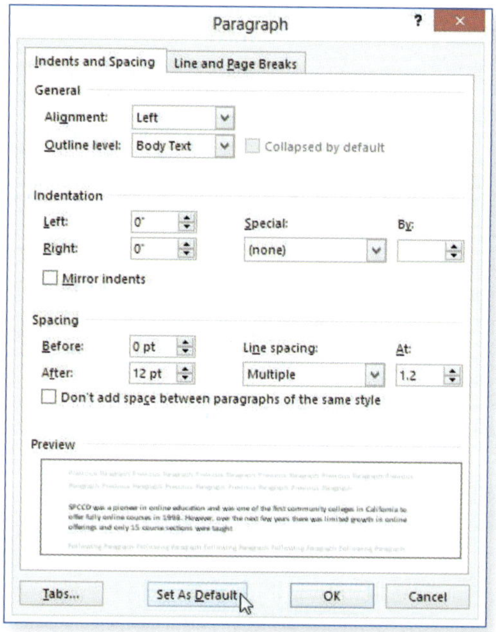

1-82 Change line and *After* paragraph spacing

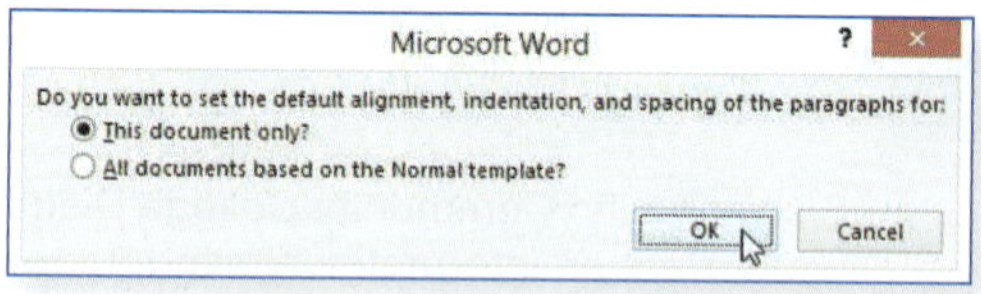

1-83 Set as default for this document only

g. Change the *Size* to **24**.
h. In the *Effects* area, click the **Small caps** check box.
i. On the **Font color** drop-down list [*Font* group], choose **Blue-Gray**, **Text 2** from the *Theme Colors.*
j. Click the **Advanced** tab.
k. Click the **Spacing** drop-down list and select **Expanded**. Change the *By* to **1.2**.
l. Click **OK** to close the *Font* dialog box.

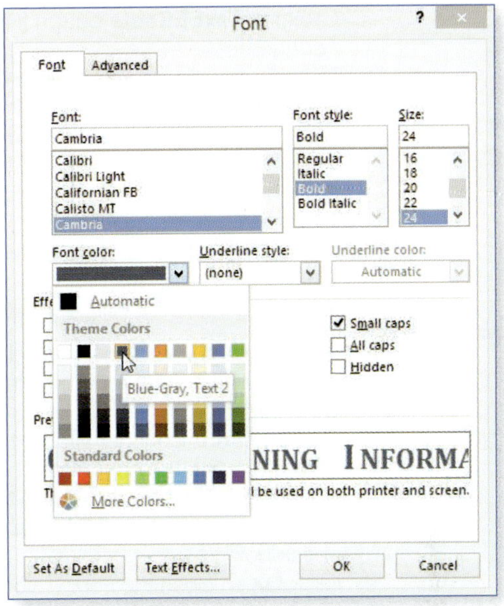

1-84 Change font style, size, effects, and color

7. Move paragraphs in the document and insert a heading.
   a. Select the last paragraph in the document, including the paragraph mark at the end of the document.
   b. Click the **Cut** button [*Home* tab, *Clipboard* group] or press **Ctrl+X**.
   c. Place your insertion point before the second line of the document ("Definition of Online Learning Modalities").
   d. Click the **Paste** button [*Home* tab, *Clipboard* group] or press **Ctrl+V**.
   e. Click at the beginning of the pasted paragraph and type Where are we now with Online Learning?
   f. Press **Enter**.
   g. Select the paragraph that begins "Hybrid Course:", including the paragraph mark at the end of the paragraph.
   h. Move this paragraph using the drag and drop method so it appears before the paragraph that begins with "Television or Tele-Web Course:" (Figure 1-85).

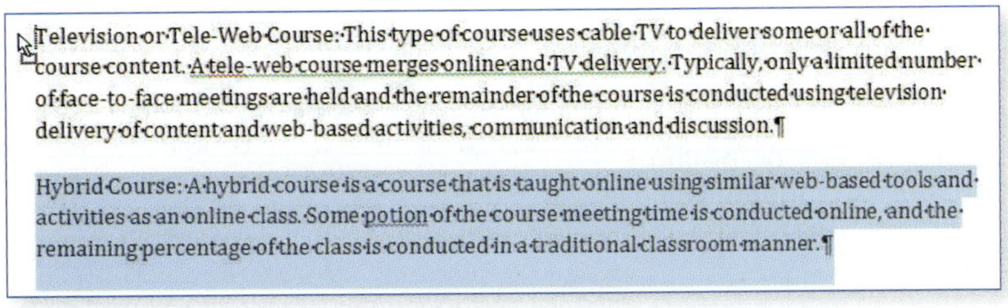

1-85 Move paragraph using drag and drop

8. Format section headings in the document.
   a. Select the first section heading (**"Where are we now with online learning?"**).
   b. Click the **Font** launcher [*Home* tab, *Font* group] to open the *Font* dialog box (Figure 1-86).
   c. Change the font *Size* to **12 pt**.
   d. Change the *Font color* to **Blue-Gray**, **Text 2**.
   e. Change the *Underline style* to **Double Underline**.
   f. Change the *Underline color* to **Blue-Gray**, **Text 2**.
   g. In the *Effects* area, click the **All caps** check box.
   h. Click **OK** to close the *Font* dialog box.

i. Click the **Text Effects** button [*Home* tab, *Font* group].
j. Put your pointer on **Shadow;** a list of shadow options is displayed (Figure 1-87).
k. Select **Offset Diagonal Bottom Right**.
l. With the formatted heading still selected, click the **Format Painter** button [*Home* tab, *Clipboard* group].
m. Select the next heading (**"Definition of Online Learning Modalities"**) to apply formatting.

9. Format paragraph headings in the document.
   a. Select the first paragraph heading ("**Online Course**:"), including the colon.
   b. Click the **Font** launcher [*Home* tab, *Font* group] to open the *Font* dialog box.
   c. Change the *Font color* to **Blue-Gray**, **Text 2**.
   d. In the *Effects* area, click the **Small caps** check box.
   e. Click **OK** to close the *Font* dialog box.
   f. Use the **Format Painter** to copy this format to the other paragraph headings ("Hybrid Course:", "Television or Tele-Web Course:", "Web-Enhanced Course:"). Double-click the **Format Painter** button to apply this formatting to multiple selections. Click the **Format Painter** button again to turn off the *Format Painter.*

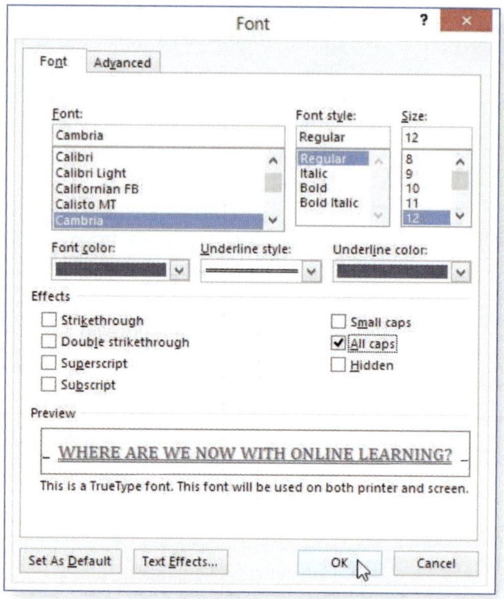

1-86 Format heading using *Font* dialog box

10. Correct spelling and grammar in the document using the context menu.
    a. Right-click the first misspelled word ("**management**") and choose the correct spelling from the list of options.
    b. Repeat this process for "**potion**".
    c. Click **Ignore All** or **Ignore Once** on the other words that are marked as potentially incorrect.

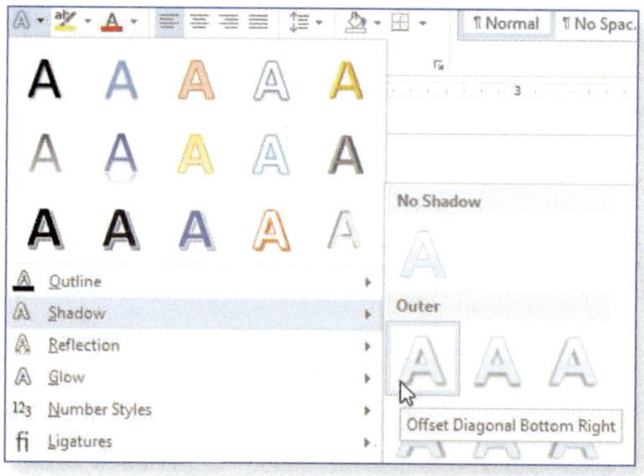

1-87 Apply *Shadow* text effect

11. Select the sentence in parentheses at the end of the document, including the parentheses, and click the **Italic** button [*Home* tab, *Font* group] or press **Ctrl+I**.

12. Add document properties using the *Document* panel.
    a. Click the **File** tab to open the *Backstage* view.
    b. Click the **Info** button if it is not already selected.
    c. Click the **Properties** button on the right and choose **Show Document Panel**. The *Document* panel is displayed above the document.
    d. In the *Author* area, delete the existing author name and type Tanesha Morris.
    e. In the *Title* area, type Online Learning Information.
    f. In the *Subject* area, type Online Learning.
    g. In the *Status* area, type Draft.
    h. Click the **X** in the upper right of the *Document* panel to close it.

13. Save and close the document (Figure 1-88).

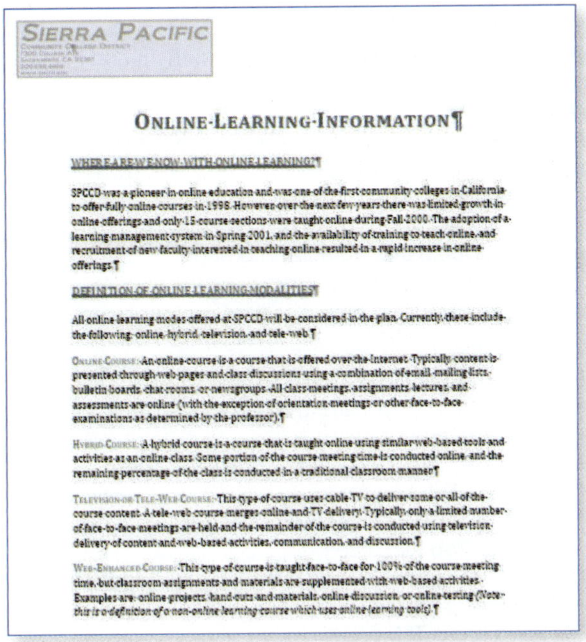

SIERRA PACIFIC

ONLINE LEARNING INFORMATION

WHERE ARE WE NOW WITH ONLINE LEARNING?

SPCCD was a pioneer in online education and was one of the first community colleges in California to offer fully online courses in 1998. However, over the next few years there was limited growth in online offerings and only 15 course sections were taught online during Fall 2000. The adoption of a learning management system in Spring 2001, and the availability of training to teach online, and recruitment of new faculty interested in teaching online resulted in a rapid increase in online offerings.

DEFINITION OF ONLINE LEARNING MODALITIES

All online learning modes offered at SPCCD will be considered in the plan. Currently, these include the following: online, hybrid, television, and tele-web.

ONLINE COURSE: An online course is a course that is offered over the Internet. Typically, content is presented through web pages and class discussions using a combination of email, mailing lists, bulletin boards, chat rooms, or newsgroups. All class meetings, assignments, lectures, and assessments are online (with the exception of orientation meetings or other face-to-face examinations as determined by the professor).

HYBRID COURSE: A hybrid course is a course that is taught online using similar web-based tools and activities as an online class. Some portion of the course meeting time is conducted online, and the remaining percentage of the class is conducted in a traditional classroom manner.

TELEVISION OR TELE-WEB COURSE: This type of course uses cable TV to deliver some or all of the course content. A tele-web course merges online and TV delivery. Typically, only a limited number of face-to-face meetings are held and the remainder of the course is conducted using television delivery of content and web-based activities, communication, and discussion.

WEB-ENHANCED COURSE: This type of course is taught face-to-face for 100% of the course meeting time, but classroom assignments and materials are supplemented with web-based activities. Examples are: online projects, hand-outs and materials, online discussion, or online testing (*Note: this is a definition of a non-online learning course which uses online learning tools*).

1-88 Word 1-2 completed

Guided Project 1-3

In this project, you create a memo about using heart rate to increase the effectiveness of training to send out to American River Cycling Club members.
[Student Learning Outcomes 1.1, 1.2, 1.3, 1.5, 1.6, 1.7, 1.8]

File Needed: ***HeartRate-01.docx***
Completed Project File Name: ***[your initials] Word 1-3.docx***

Skills Covered in This Project

- Open and edit an existing document.
- Change line spacing.
- Change paragraph spacing.
- Use *Show/Hide*.
- Add a memo heading to a document.
- Change paragraph alignment.
- Change font size and apply styles and effects.
- Use the *Format Painter*.
- Add text highlight color.
- Use non-breaking space.
- Use *Thesaurus*.
- Add words to the dictionary.
- Add document properties.

1. Open the ***HeartRate-01*** document from your student data files.
2. Save the document as ***[your initials] Word 1-3***.
3. Change line and paragraph spacing of the entire document and insert a paragraph break between each paragraph.
   a. Press **Ctrl+A** to select the entire document.
   b. Click the **Paragraph** launcher [*Home* or *Page Layout* tab, *Paragraph* group].
   c. In the *Line spacing* area, select **Single** from the drop-down list.
   d. Change the *After* paragraph spacing to **0 pt**.
   e. Click **OK** to close the *Paragraph* dialog box.
   f. Turn on **Show/Hide** [*Home* tab, *Paragraph* group].
   g. Click at the end of each paragraph and press **Enter** once to add a blank line between each of the paragraphs.
4. Add a memo heading to the document.
   a. Place your insertion point at the beginning of the first paragraph and press **Enter**.
   b. Press the **up arrow** key on keyboard to move to the blank line above the first paragraph.
   c. Type TO: and press **Tab** two times.
   d. Type All ARCC Club Members and press **Enter** two times.
   e. Type FROM: and press **Tab** two times.
   f. Type Taylor Mathos, ARCC Coach and press **Enter** two times.
   g. Type DATE: and press **Tab** two times.
   h. Type the current date in month, day, year format (e.g., September 1, 2015) and press **Enter** two times.
   i. Type SUBJECT: and press **Tab** once.
   j. Type Heart Rate Training and press **Enter** two times.
5. Change paragraph alignment and font styles of selected text.
   a. Select the second and third paragraphs in the body of the memo (beginning with "**220 – Your Age. . .**" and ending with "**. . .heart rate is 180.**)"), including the paragraph mark at the end of the third paragraph.
   b. Click the **Center** button [*Home* tab, *Paragraph* group] or press **Ctrl+E**.
   c. Select the paragraph beginning "220 – Your Age . . . " and click the **Bold** button [*Home* tab, *Font* group] or press **Ctrl+B**.
   d. Select the next paragraph and click the **Italic** button [*Home* tab, *Font* group] or press **Ctrl+I**.
   e. Delete the blank line between the second and third paragraphs (Figure 1-89).

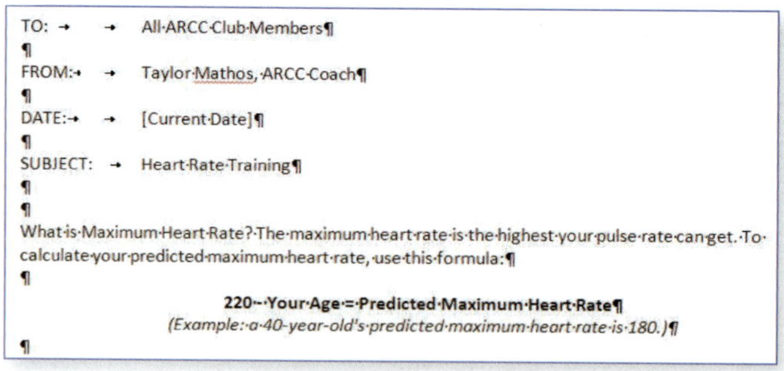
TO: → → All·ARCC·Club·Members¶
¶
FROM:→ → Taylor·Mathos,·ARCC·Coach¶
¶
DATE:→ → [Current·Date]¶
¶
SUBJECT: → Heart·Rate·Training¶
¶
¶
What·is·Maximum·Heart·Rate?·The·maximum·heart·rate·is·the·highest·your·pulse·rate·can·get.·To·calculate·your·predicted·maximum·heart·rate,·use·this·formula:¶
¶
220·–·Your·Age·=·Predicted·Maximum·Heart·Rate¶
(Example:·a·40-year-old's·predicted·maximum·heart·rate·is·180.)¶
¶

1-89 Memo heading added and paragraphs formatted

6. Change the font and style of selected text.
   a. Press **Ctrl+A** to select the entire document.
   b. Click the **Increase Font Size** button [*Home* tab, *Font* group] to increase the font size to 12 pt. (Figure 1-90).
   c. In the first sentence of the first body paragraph, select the words "**Maximum Heart Rate**".

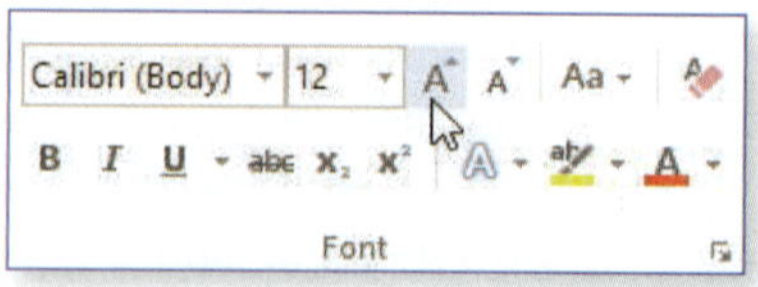

1-90 *Increase Font Size* button

d. Click the **Font** launcher [*Home* tab, *Font* group] to open the *Font* dialog box (Figure 1-91).
e. Change the *Font style* to **Bold**.
f. Change the *Underline style* to **Words only**.
g. Change the *Underline color* to **Green, Accent 6**.
h. In the *Effects* area, select the **Small caps** check box.
i. Click **OK** to close the *Font* dialog box.
j. With the words still selected, click the **Format Painter** button [*Home* tab, *Clipboard* group].
k. Select the words "**Target Heart Rate Zone**" in the first sentence of the fifth paragraph in the body ("You gain the most benefits . . ."). The *Format Painter* applies the formatting to the selected words.
l. Select the last two sentences of the fifth paragraph ("Do not exercise above 85 percent . . .").
m. Click the **Text Highlight Color** drop-down arrow [*Home* tab, *Font* group] (Figure 1-92).
n. Select **Gray-25%** text highlighting.

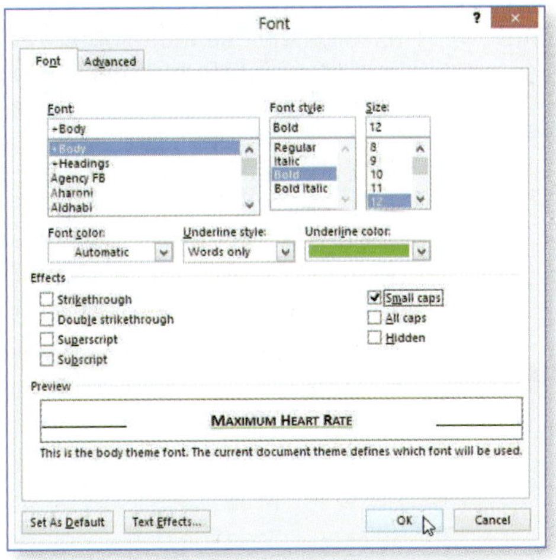

1-91 Change font style and effects

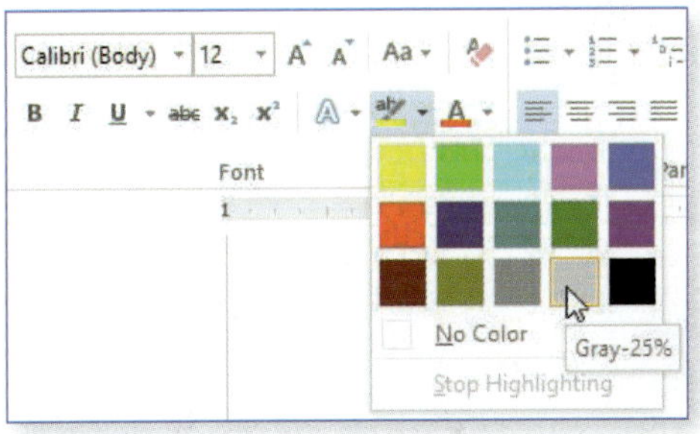

1-92 *Text Highlight Color* button and drop-down list

7. Use a non-breaking space to keep words together.
   a. In the first sentence of the fifth paragraph in the body ("You gain the most benefits . . ."), delete the space between the words "Target" and "Heart."
   b. Place your insertion point between these two words and press **Ctrl+Shift+Spacebar** to insert a non-breaking space. "Target" is wrapped to the next line so the words do not break between lines.

8. Add paragraph spacing before the first line of the document.
   a. Select the first line of the document.
   b. Change the *Before* spacing to **72 pt**. [*Page Layout* tab, *Paragraph* group].

9. Use the thesaurus to find synonyms for selected words.
   a. Right-click the word "**medicines**" in the third sentence of the first body paragraph.
   b. Put your pointer on **Synonyms** to display a list of synonyms (Figure 1-93).
   c. Select **"medications"** as the synonym.
   d. In the last sentence of the fifth paragraph ("You gain the most benefits . . ."), right-click the word "**added**."
   e. Put your pointer on **Synonyms** and select "**additional**."

10. Add reference initials to the document.
   a. Click at the end of the last paragraph and press **Enter** two times.
   b. Type your reference initials in lower case letters.

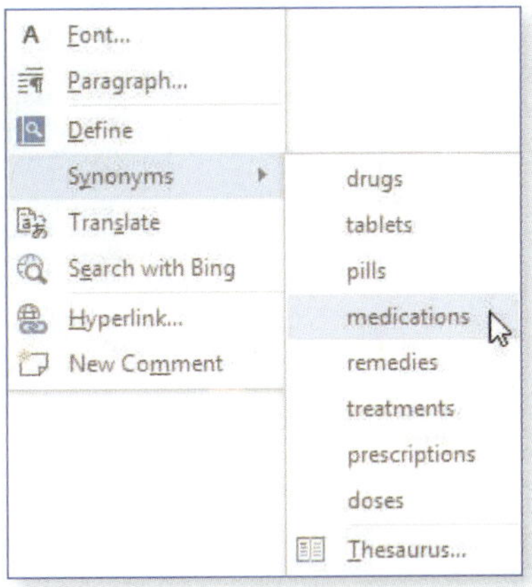

1-93 Select synonym from context menu

11. Add document properties.
    a. Click the **File** tab to open the *Backstage* view.
    b. Click the **Info** button if it is not already selected to display the document properties at the right.
    c. In the *Title* area, type Heart Rate Training.
    d. In the *Author* area, right-click the existing author and select **Remove Person**.
    e. In the *Author* area, type Taylor Mathos.
    f. Click the **Show All Properties** link at the bottom of the document properties.
    g. In the *Company* area, type ARCC.
    h. Click the **Back** arrow in the upper left of the *Backstage* view to the document.
12. Add words to the dictionary.
    a. Right-click the word "**Mathos**" in the second line of the memo heading.
    b. Choose **Add to Dictionary** from the context menu.
    c. If your reference initials are marked as incorrectly spelled (red wavy underline), right-click them and choose **Add to Dictionary**.
13. Save and close the document (Figure 1-94).

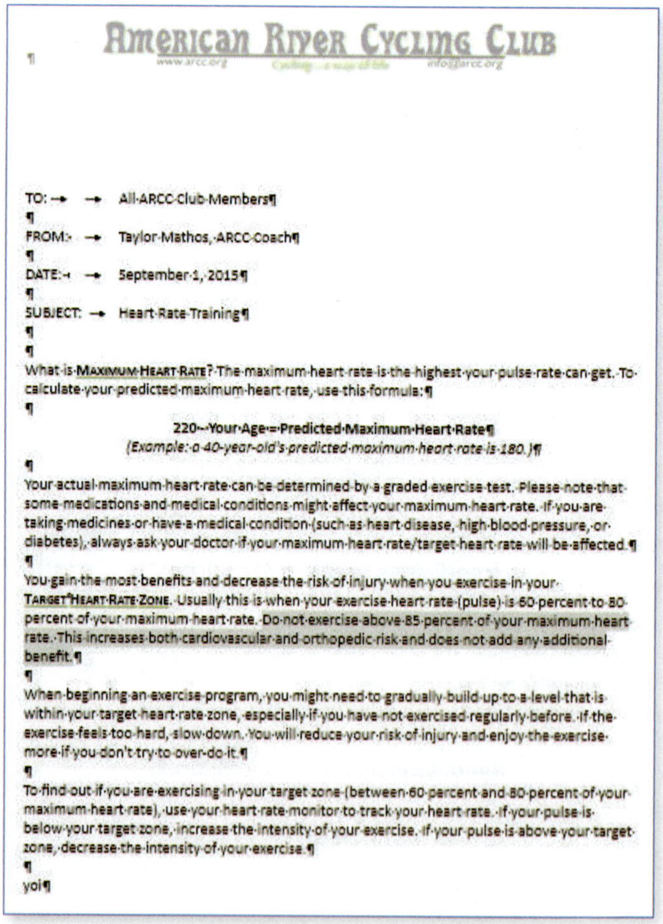

AMERICAN RIVER CYCLING CLUB

TO: All ARCC Club Members

FROM: Taylor Mathos, ARCC Coach

DATE: September 1, 2015

SUBJECT: Heart Rate Training

What is MAXIMUM HEART RATE? The maximum heart rate is the highest your pulse rate can get. To calculate your predicted maximum heart rate, use this formula:

220 – Your Age = Predicted Maximum Heart Rate
(Example: a 40-year-old's predicted maximum heart rate is 180.)

Your actual maximum heart rate can be determined by a graded exercise test. Please note that some medications and medical conditions might affect your maximum heart rate. If you are taking medicines or have a medical condition (such as heart disease, high blood pressure, or diabetes), always ask your doctor if your maximum heart rate/target heart rate will be affected.

You gain the most benefits and decrease the risk of injury when you exercise in your TARGET HEART RATE ZONE. Usually this is when your exercise heart rate (pulse) is 60 percent to 80 percent of your maximum heart rate. Do not exercise above 85 percent of your maximum heart rate. This increases both cardiovascular and orthopedic risk and does not add any additional benefit.

When beginning an exercise program, you might need to gradually build up to a level that is within your target heart rate zone, especially if you have not exercised regularly before. If the exercise feels too hard, slow down. You will reduce your risk of injury and enjoy the exercise more if you don't try to over-do it.

To find out if you are exercising in your target zone (between 60 percent and 80 percent of your maximum heart rate), use your heart rate monitor to track your heart rate. If your pulse is below your target zone, increase the intensity of your exercise. If your pulse is above your target zone, decrease the intensity of your exercise.

yoi

1-94 Word 1-3 completed

Independent Project 1-4

In this project, you format a business letter for Emma Cavalli to send to clients whose current home listings are expiring.
[Student Learning Outcomes 1.1, 1.2, 1.3, 1.4, 1.5, 1.6, 1.7, 1.8]

File Needed: ***ExpiredLetter-01.docx***
Completed Project File Name: ***[your initials] Word 1-4.docx***

Skills Covered in This Project

- Open and edit an existing document.
- Change line spacing.
- Change paragraph alignment and spacing.
- Change font and font size.
- Use *Show/Hide*.
- Format document as a block format business letter with mixed punctuation.
- Use *AutoCorrect*.
- Move text.
- Change font styles and effects.
- Use spelling and grammar checker.
- Add document properties.

1. Open the ***ExpiredLetter-01*** document from your student data files.
2. Save this document as ***[your initials] Word 1-4***.
3. Select the entire document and make the following formatting changes:
   a. Change the before and after paragraph spacing to **0 pt**.
   b. Change the line spacing to **Single**.
   c. Change the paragraph alignment to **Left**.
   d. Change the font and font size to **Calibri** and **11 pt**.
4. Turn on **Show/Hide** and press **Enter** to add an extra space between each paragraph.
5. Add the following information to the top of the business letter:
   a. Press **Ctrl+Home** to move your insertion point to the top of the document.
   b. Type the current date and press **Enter** four times.
   c. Type the following inside address and press **Enter** two times after the last line.

      Mr. Rick Hermann
      9035 Masi Drive
      Fair Oaks, CA 95528

   d. Supply an appropriate salutation and use mixed punctuation.
   e. Press **Enter** two times after the salutation; there should be one blank line between the salutation and the body of the letter.
   f. Add **72 pt**. *Before* paragraph spacing on the date line.
6. Press **Enter** two times after the last paragraph and type in the closing lines.
   a. Type Best regards, and press **Enter** four times.
   b. Type the following closing lines.

      Emma Cavalli
      Realtor Consultant
      Placer Hills Real Estate

   c. Press **Enter** two times after the company name and type your reference initials in lower case letters.

7. Move the third body paragraph so it appears before the second body paragraph. Make sure there is one blank line between each of the body paragraphs.
8. In the second body paragraph ("There was a lot of detail . . ."), move the last two sentences to the beginning of the paragraph. Make sure there is proper spacing between sentences.
9. Select "**Placer Hills Real Estate**" in the first body paragraph and make the company name **Bold**, **Underline**, and **Small caps**.
10. Select the first sentence in the third paragraph ("The service and experience . . .") and make it **Italic**.
11. Apply formatting to the closing lines of the business letter.
    a. Select the writer's name at the bottom and make it **Small caps**.
    b. Select the writer's title and make it **Italic**.
    c. Select the company name below the writer's title and make it **Bold**.
12. Add the following document properties:
    a. *Title*: Expired Letter
    b. *Company*: Placer Hills Real Estate
    c. *Manager*: Kelsey Kroll
    d. *Author*: Emma Cavalli
13. Spell and grammar check the entire document, ignoring proper nouns.
14. Save and close the document (Figure 1-95).

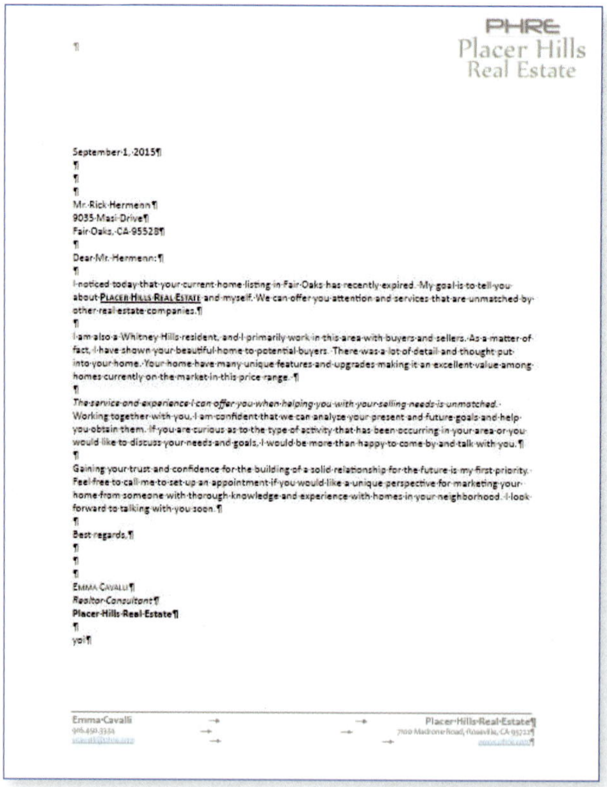
PHRE
Placer Hills
Real Estate

September 1, 2015

Mr. Rick Hermenn
9035 Masi Drive
Fair Oaks, CA 95528

Dear Mr. Hermenn:

I noticed today that your current home listing in Fair Oaks has recently expired. My goal is to tell you about **PLACER HILLS REAL ESTATE** and myself. We can offer you attention and services that are unmatched by other real estate companies.

I am also a Whitney Hills resident, and I primarily work in this area with buyers and sellers. As a matter of fact, I have shown your beautiful home to potential buyers. There was a lot of detail and thought put into your home. Your home have many unique features and upgrades making it an excellent value among homes currently on the market in this price range.

The service and experience I can offer you when helping you with your selling needs is unmatched. Working together with you, I am confident that we can analyze your present and future goals and help you obtain them. If you are curious as to the type of activity that has been occurring in your area or you would like to discuss your needs and goals, I would be more than happy to come by and talk with you.

Gaining your trust and confidence for the building of a solid relationship for the future is my first priority. Feel free to call me to set up an appointment if you would like a unique perspective for marketing your home from someone with thorough knowledge and experience with homes in your neighborhood. I look forward to talking with you soon.

Best regards,

EMMA CAVALLI
Realtor Consultant
Placer Hills Real Estate

yoi

Emma Cavalli — Placer Hills Real Estate

1-95 Word 1-4 completed

Independent Project 1-5

In this project, you combine information from different documents to create a memo for Sierra Pacific Community College District. This memo is a draft of the values statement for the district.
[Student Learning Outcomes 1.1, 1.3, 1.4, 1.5, 1.6, 1.8]

File Needed: ***ValuesStatement-01a.docx***, ***ValuesStatement-01b.docx***
Completed Project File Name: ***[your initials] Word 1-5.docx***

Skills Covered in This Project

- Open and edit an existing document.
- Change line spacing.
- Change paragraph spacing.
- Change font and font size.
- Format document as a memo.
- Use spelling and grammar checker.
- Add words to the dictionary.
- Change font styles and effects.
- Use the *Format Painter*.
- Move text.
- Add document properties.

1. Open the ***ValuesStatement-01a*** document from your student data files.
2. Save this document as ***[your initials] Word 1-5***.
3. Open the ***ValuesStatement-01b*** document from your student data files.
4. Select all of the text in this document and copy to the *Clipboard.*
5. Close the ***ValuesStatement-01b*** document without saving.
6. In the ***[your initials] Word 1-5*** document, press **Enter** at the end of the document and paste the copied text from the *Clipboard.*
7. **Delete** the extra paragraph breaks between the first four paragraphs and at the end of the document.
8. Select the entire document and make the following formatting changes:
   a. Change after paragraph spacing to **12 pt**.
   b. Change the line spacing to **1.15**.
   c. Change the font and font size to **Calibri** and **10 pt**.
9. Press **Enter** at the top of the document and add the memo information above the existing text.
   a. Press **Tab** (once or twice) after the guidewords to line up information at 1".
   b. Press **Enter** once at the end of the first three lines of the memo heading.

   TO: All SPCCD faculty, staff, and managers
   FROM: Lanita Morrow, Chancellor
   DATE: [Current Date]
   SUBJECT: Draft of SPCCD Values Statement
10. Select the first line of the memo heading and change the before paragraph spacing to **24 pt**.
11. Select the last line of the memo heading and change the after paragraph spacing to **18 pt**.
12. Spell and grammar check the entire document.
13. Add the chancellor's first and last names to the dictionary if they are marked as potential spelling errors.

14. Select the first paragraph heading (**“Access”**) in the body of the memo and apply the following style changes:
    a. *Font style*: **Bold**
    b. *Font color*: **Blue-Gray**, **Text 2**
    c. *Underline*: **Double Underline**
    d. *Underline color*: **Blue-Gray**, **Text 2**
    e. *Effects*: **Small caps**
15. Use the *Format Painter* to apply these styles to each of the other paragraph headings in the body of the memo.
16. Use cut and paste or drag and drop to move the body paragraphs so they are ordered alphabetically by paragraph heading. Exclude the first body paragraph. Be sure to include the paragraph symbol at the end of each paragraph when cutting or dragging.
17. Delete any extra blank lines at the end of the document so this document fits on one page.
18. Add the following document properties:
    a. *Title*: SPCCD Values Statement
    b. *Company*: Sierra Pacific Community College District
    c. *Author*: Yoon Soo Park
19. Save and close the document (Figure 1-96).

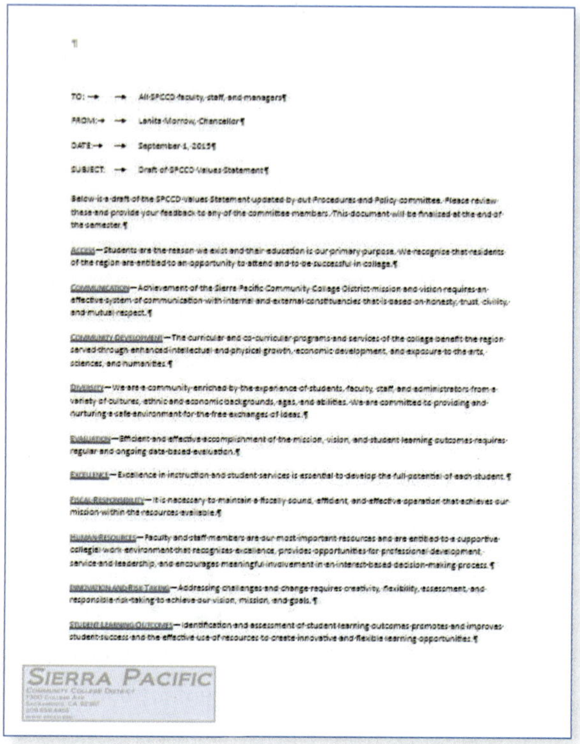
¶

TO: → → All SPCCD faculty, staff, and managers¶

FROM: → → Lanita Morrow, Chancellor¶

DATE: → → September 1, 2015¶

SUBJECT: → Draft of SPCCD Values Statement¶

Below is a draft of the SPCCD Values Statement updated by out Procedures and Policy committee. Please review these and provide your feedback to any of the committee members. This document will be finalized at the end of the semester.¶

ACCESS—Students are the reason we exist and their education is our primary purpose. We recognize that residents of the region are entitled to an opportunity to attend and to be successful in college.¶

COMMUNICATION—Achievement of the Sierra Pacific Community College District mission and vision requires an effective system of communication with internal and external constituencies that is based on honesty, trust, civility, and mutual respect.¶

COMMUNITY DEVELOPMENT—The curricular and co-curricular programs and services of the college benefit the region served through enhanced intellectual and physical growth, economic development, and exposure to the arts, sciences, and humanities.¶

DIVERSITY—We are a community enriched by the experience of students, faculty, staff, and administrators from a variety of cultures, ethnic and economic backgrounds, ages, and abilities. We are committed to providing and nurturing a safe environment for the free exchanges of ideas.¶

EVALUATION—Efficient and effective accomplishment of the mission, vision, and student learning outcomes requires regular and ongoing data-based evaluation.¶

EXCELLENCE—Excellence in instruction and student services is essential to develop the full potential of each student.¶

FISCAL RESPONSIBILITY—It is necessary to maintain a fiscally sound, efficient, and effective operation that achieves our mission within the resources available.¶

HUMAN RESOURCES—Faculty and staff members are our most important resources and are entitled to a supportive collegial work environment that recognizes excellence, provides opportunities for professional development, service and leadership, and encourages meaningful involvement in an interest-based decision-making process.¶

INNOVATION AND RISK TAKING—Addressing challenges and change requires creativity, flexibility, assessment, and responsible risk-taking to achieve our vision, mission, and goals.¶

STUDENT LEARNING OUTCOMES—Identification and assessment of student learning outcomes promotes and improves student success and the effective use of resources to create innovative and flexible learning opportunities.¶

SIERRA PACIFIC
COMMUNITY COLLEGE DISTRICT

1-96 Word 1-5 completed

Independent Project 1-6

In this project, you use formatting features in Word to create a professional and appealing brochure for Emma Cavalli at Placer Hills Real Estate.
[Student Learning Outcomes 1.1, 1.2, 1.3, 1.4, 1.5, 1.6, 1.7, 1.8]

File Needed: ***Brochure-01.docx***
Completed Project File Name: ***[your initials] Word 1-6.docx***

Skills Covered in This Project

- Open and edit an existing document.
- Change font and font size.
- Change paragraph spacing.
- Change line spacing.
- Use line breaks.
- Change paragraph alignment.
- Change font styles and effects.
- Use the *Format Painter*.
- Move text.
- Use the thesaurus to find synonyms.
- Add document properties.

1. Open the ***Brochure-01*** document from your student data files.
2. Save this document as ***[your initials] Word 1-6***.
3. Select the entire document and make the following formatting changes:
   a. Change the font and font size to **Candara** and **10 pt**.
   b. Change thc after-paragraph spacing to **6 pt**.
   c. Change the line spacing to **Single**.
4. On the first five lines of the document ("Emma Cavalli to E-mail . . ."), delete the paragraph symbols at the end of each line and insert a line break (**Shift+Enter**).
5. **Center** the first six lines of the document ("Emma Cavalli to Web . . .").
6. Select the first line of the document and make the following changes:
   a. *Font style*: **Bold**
   b. *Size*: **12 pt**.
   c. *Font color*: **Green**, **Accent 6**, **Darker 50%**
   d. *Underline style*: **Thick Underline**
   e. *Underline color*: **Green**, **Accent 6**, **Darker 50%**
7. Select the second line of the document and make it **Bold**.
8. Select the third line of the document and make it **Italic**.
9. Select the first section heading, "**Personal Statement**," and apply **Bold**, **Underline**, and **Small Caps** formatting. Change the before paragraph spacing to **12 pt**. and the after paragraph spacing to **3 pt**.
10. Use the *Format Painter* to copy this formatting to the other section headings ("Real Estate Experience," "Why I am a Real Estate Agent," "What Clients are Saying," "Professional Credentials," and "Education & Training").
11. In the "Why I am a Real Estate Agent" section, combine the four sentences into one paragraph, deleting paragraph marks and inserting spaces as needed.
12. In the "What Clients are Saying" section, make the following changes:
    a. Select the first quote (don't include the names of the individuals who said the quote), make it **Italic**, and change the after spacing to **0 pt**.
    b. Select the source of the quote ("**-Rod & Luisa Ellisor**, **Rocklin**, **CA**") and right-align this text.
    c. Repeat the above two steps for the second quote in this section.
13. Move the third section heading and the paragraph below it ("Why I am a Real Estate Agent") so it appears before the second section ("Real Estate Experience").
14. Select the lines of text in the "Professional Credentials" section (don't include the heading) and change the after-paragraph spacing to **3 pt**.
15. Use the *Format Painter* to repeat the above formatting to the lines of text (excluding the heading) in the "Education & Training" section.
16. Use the thesaurus to find an appropriate synonym for the following words:
    a. Replace "surpass" (in the "Personal Statement" section) with "**exceed**."
    b. Replace "emotions" (in the "Why I am a Real Estate Agent" section) with "**sentiments**."
17. Add the following document properties:
    a. *Title*: Brochure
    b. *Company*: Placer Hills Real Estate
    c. *Author*: Emma Cavalli

18. Save and close the document (Figure 1-97).

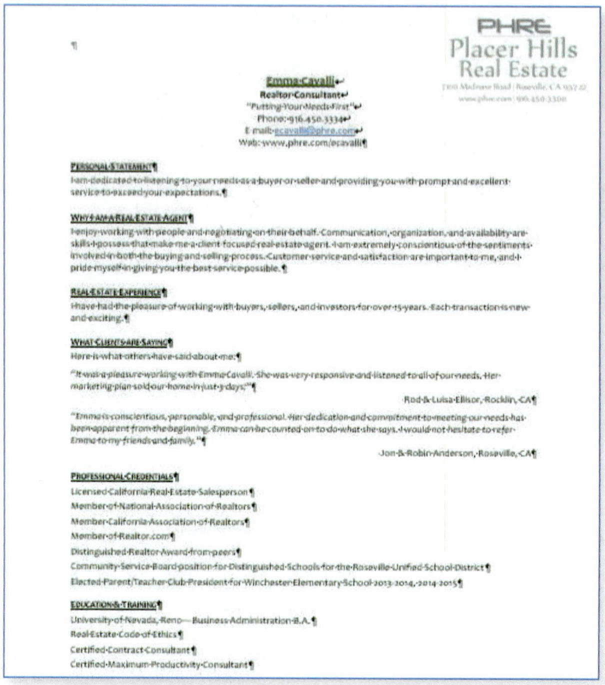

PHRE
Placer Hills Real Estate

Emma Cavalli
Realtor Consultant
"Putting Your Needs First"
Phone: 916.450.3334
E-mail: ecavalli@phre.com
Web: www.phre.com/ecavalli

PERSONAL STATEMENT
I am dedicated to listening to your needs as a buyer or seller and providing you with prompt and excellent service to exceed your expectations.

WHY I AM A REAL ESTATE AGENT
I enjoy working with people and negotiating on their behalf. Communication, organization, and availability are skills I possess that make me a client focused real estate agent. I am extremely conscientious of the sentiments involved in both the buying and selling process. Customer service and satisfaction are important to me, and I pride myself in giving you the best service possible.

REAL ESTATE EXPERIENCE
I have had the pleasure of working with buyers, sellers, and investors for over 15 years. Each transaction is new and exciting.

WHAT CLIENTS ARE SAYING
Here is what others have said about me:

"It was a pleasure working with Emma Cavalli. She was very responsive and listened to all of our needs. Her marketing plan sold our home in just 7 days."

Rod & Luisa Ellisor, Rocklin, CA

"Emma is conscientious, personable, and professional. Her dedication and commitment to meeting our needs has been apparent from the beginning. Emma can be counted on to do what she says. I would not hesitate to refer Emma to my friends and family."

Jon & Robin Anderson, Roseville, CA

PROFESSIONAL CREDENTIALS
Licensed California Real Estate Salesperson
Member of National Association of Realtors
Member California Association of Realtors
Member of Realtor.com
Distinguished Realtor Award from peers
Community Service Board position for Distinguished Schools for the Roseville Unified School District
Elected Parent/Teacher Club President for Winchester Elementary School 2013-2014, 2014-2015

EDUCATION & TRAINING
University of Nevada, Reno—Business Administration B.A.
Real Estate Code of Ethics
Certified Contract Consultant
Certified Maximum Productivity Consultant

1-97 Word 1-6 completed

Improve It Project 1-7

In this project, you create a block format business letter for Margaret Jepson, an insurance agent at Central Sierra Insurance. You fix the formatting and text in this document and add opening and closing lines to create a properly formatted business letter. For more information on creating a correctly formatted block format business letter, see *Appendix D* (online reference).
[Student Learning Outcomes 1.1, 1.2, 1.3, 1.5, 1.6, 1.8]

File Needed: ***RenewalLetter-01.docx***
Completed Project File Name: ***[your initials] Word 1-7.docx***

Skills Covered in This Project

- Open and edit an existing document.
- Change font and font size.
- Change paragraph spacing.
- Change line spacing.
- Use spelling and grammar checker.
- Format a business letter.
- Change paragraph alignment.
- Change font styles and effects.
- Use the *Format Painter.*
- Add document properties.

1. Open the ***RenewalLetter-01*** document from your student data files.
2. Save this document as ***[your initials] Word 1-7***.
3. Use **Single** line spacing and **0 pt**. before- and after-paragraph spacing on the entire document.
4. Use **Calibri** font and **11 pt**. font size.
5. Correct spelling and grammar as needed.
6. Type the current date at the top of the document.
7. Type the inside address.

    Mr. Rick DePonte
    8364 Marshall Street
    Granite Bay, CA 95863

8. Include an appropriate salutation. Use mixed punctuation.
9. Include the insurance policy information in the subject line.

    Policy HO-2887-5546-B

10. At the end of the document, supply an appropriate complimentary close. Use mixed punctuation.
11. Type the information below as the writer's name, title, and company.

    Margaret Jepson, ARM, CIC, CRM
    Insurance Agent
    Central Sierra Insurance

12. Include your reference initials and an enclosure notation at the end of the business letter.
13. **Center** the four lines of renewal premium information in the body of the letter.
14. Apply **Bold** and **Small caps** formatting to the headings for each of these four lines of renewal premium information.
15. Format the "Total Premium" amount as **Bold**, **Italic**, and **Double Underline**.
16. Replace *[Company Name]* with Hartford Specialty.
17. Replace *[First Name]* with the appropriate information.
18. Use **72 pt**. before paragraph spacing on the date line.
19. Add *Title* (Renewal Letter), *Company*, and *Author* document properties to the letter.
20. Proofread and edit the document carefully. Make sure there is proper spacing between each of the parts of the block format business letter. This document fits on one page.
21. Save and close the letter (Figure 1-98).

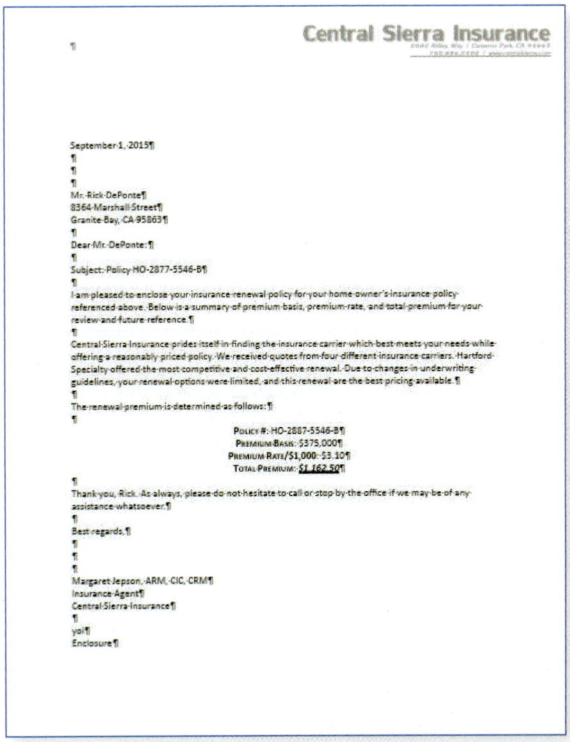

Central Sierra Insurance

September 1, 2015

Mr. Rick DePonte
8364 Marshall Street
Granite Bay, CA 95863

Dear Mr. DePonte:

Subject: Policy HO-2877-5546-B

I am pleased to enclose your insurance renewal policy for your home owner's insurance policy referenced above. Below is a summary of premium basis, premium rate, and total premium for your review and future reference.

Central Sierra Insurance prides itself in finding the insurance carrier which best meets your needs while offering a reasonably priced policy. We received quotes from four different insurance carriers. Hartford Specialty offered the most competitive and cost-effective renewal. Due to changes in underwriting guidelines, your renewal options were limited, and this renewal are the best pricing available.

The renewal premium is determined as follows:

POLICY #: HO-2887-5546-B
PREMIUM BASIS: $375,000
PREMIUM RATE/$1,000: $3.10
TOTAL PREMIUM: ***$1,162.50***

Thank you, Rick. As always, please do not hesitate to call or stop by the office if we may be of any assistance whatsoever.

Best regards,

Margaret Jepson, ARM, CIC, CRM
Insurance Agent
Central Sierra Insurance

yoi
Enclosure

1-98 Word 1-7 completed

Challenge Project 1-8

Create a cover letter for a job application. A cover letter typically accompanies a resume to introduce an applicant to a prospective employer. You can use and modify an existing cover letter, or you can create a new one. It is important to customize each cover letter for each job for which you are applying.

There are many online resources available to help you with both content and format. One of the best online resources for writing is the Online Writing Lab (OWL) from Purdue University (http://owl.english.purdue.edu/owl/). You can search this site for helpful information about cover letters.
[Student Learning Outcomes 1.1, 1.2, 1.3, 1.4, 1.5, 1.6, 1.7, 1.8]

File Needed: None
Completed Project File Name: ***[your initials] Word 1-8.docx***

Open a new document and save this document as ***[your initials] Word 1-8***.

Type this document as a personal business letter in block format. For more information on formatting a personal business letter see *Appendix D* (online reference). Modify your document according to the following guidelines:

- Move sentences and paragraphs as needed to produce a well-organized cover letter.
- Add words to the dictionary as needed.
- Use the thesaurus to find synonyms as needed.
- Include document properties and spell and grammar check the document.

Challenge Project 1-9

Create a list of five places you would like to visit in the next five years. For each of the places you list, compose a short paragraph about that place and why it is interesting to you. Research each of the places you choose on the Internet. Use your own words when composing the paragraphs about each place.
[Student Learning Outcomes 1.1, 1.2, 1.3, 1.4, 1.5, 1.6, 1.7, 1.8]

File Needed: None
Completed Project File Name: ***[your initials] Word 1-9.docx***

Open a new document and save it as ***[your initials] Word 1-9***. Modify your document according to the following guidelines:

- Create and format a title for the document.
- Format each of the headings by modifying the font, style, and attributes.
- Change line and paragraph spacing as needed to create an attractive and readable document.
- Use consistent line and paragraph spacing throughout the document.
- Use the *Format Painter* to keep formatting consistent throughout the document.
- Move the paragraphs so the places are listed in order of your preference.
- Include document properties and spell and grammar check the document.

Challenge Project 1-10

Create a flyer for an upcoming event for an organization to which you belong. Be sure to include all the relevant information for this event and arrange it attractively and professionally on the page. [Student Learning Outcomes 1.1, 1.2, 1.3, 1.5, 1.6, 1.7, 1.8]

File Needed: None
Completed Project File Name: ***[your initials] Word 1-10.docx***

Open a new document and save it as ***[your initials] Word 1-10***. Modify your document according to the following guidelines:

- Create and format a title for the document.
- Format the information by modifying the fonts, styles, and attributes.
- Change line and paragraph spacing as needed to create an attractive and readable document.
- Change the text alignment as desired.
- Use the *Format Painter* to keep formatting consistent throughout the document.
- Include document properties and spell and grammar check the document.

CHAPTER 2

Formatting and Customizing Documents

CHAPTER OVERVIEW

In addition to giving you the ability to create basic business documents, Microsoft Word 2013 provides formatting and editing tools you can use to customize a variety of documents. Formatting features such as custom margins, tab stops, indents, page numbering, headers, footers, breaks, lists, styles, themes, borders, and shading help you to produce readable and attractive professional and personal documents.

STUDENT LEARNING OUTCOMES (SLOs)

After completing this chapter, you will be able to:

SLO 2.1 Format a document by customizing margins, page orientation, paper size, and vertical alignment (p. W2-63).

SLO 2.2 Improve alignment and white-space usage by setting, using, and editing tab stops in a document (p. W2-66).

SLO 2.3 Understand and apply indents to control text alignment (p. W2-71).

SLO 2.4 Enhance document layout by effectively using page numbers, headers, and footers (p. W2-76).

SLO 2.5 Control pagination with page and section breaks (p. W2-83).

SLO 2.6 Present information using customized bulleted and numbered lists (p. W2-85).

SLO 2.7 Increase document consistency and format with styles and themes (p. W2-89).

SLO 2.8 Effectively edit a document using find and replace (p. W2-93).

SLO 2.9 Improve overall document design and format with borders, shading, horizontal lines, and hyperlinks (p. W2-96).

CASE STUDY

Courtyard Medical Plaza has a preschool for its employees' children. The preschool is currently looking for qualified applicants to fill a vacant teacher position.

In the Pause & Practice projects, you are modifying a resume for Richelle Wilkinson. You use features covered in this chapter to create an attractive and informative resume.

Pause & Practice 2-1: Edit the resume to change margins and include tab stops and indents.

Pause & Practice 2-2: Modify the resume to include a header with text and a page number.

Pause & Practice 2-3: Enhance the resume by using bulleted lists, a page break, and a theme.

Pause & Practice 2-4: Finalize the resume by using find and replace, borders, shading, and hyperlinks.

WORD

SLO 2.1

Customizing Margins and Page Layout

You can use margins to create ***white space*** around the edges of a document. White space improves the readability of a document and prevents the document from appearing cluttered. The document type and content influence the margins you choose for the document. You can also customize a document by changing the orientation, page size, or vertical alignment.

Page Layout Settings

When you open a new Word document, the default settings control margins, page orientation, paper size, and vertical alignment. The default settings for a new document are as follows:

Default Page Layout Settings

Page Layout Option	Default Setting
Margins	1" top, bottom, left, and right
Page Orientation	Portrait
Paper Size	8.5"×11" (Letter)
Vertical Alignment	Top

These settings are applied to the entire Word document, and you can easily change all of these settings in Word.

Margin Settings

Margin settings are measured in inches; the default margin settings for a new Word document are 1". Word provides you with a variety of ***preset margins settings.*** You can choose and change margins on the *Page Layout* tab.

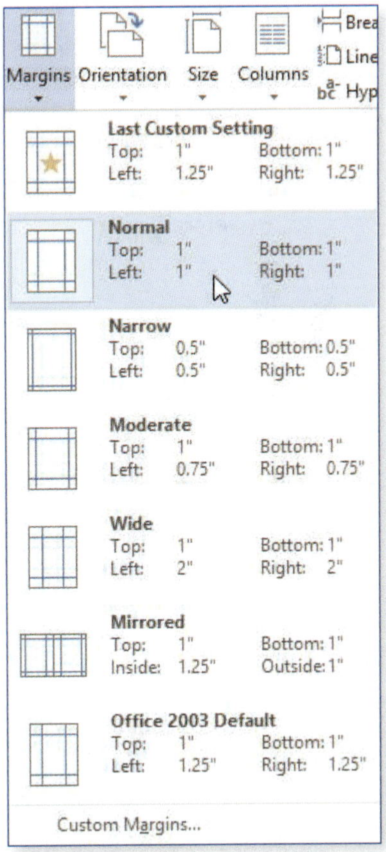

2-1 Preset margin settings drop-down list

HOW TO: Change Margin Settings

1. Click the **Page Layout** tab.
2. Click the **Margins** button [*Page Setup* group]. Preset margin options appear in the *Margins* drop-down list (Figure 2-1).
3. Select the desired margin settings from the drop-down list of options.

The *Margins* drop-down list provides preset margin options. You are not limited to these preset options; you can also create your own custom margin settings.

> **MORE INFO**
>
> At the top of this *Margins* list, the ***Last Custom Setting*** option displays the most recent custom margin settings you have used.

Page Setup Dialog Box

If you want margin settings that are not listed in the preset margin settings in the *Margins* drop-down list, use the ***Page Setup dialog box*** (Figure 2-2) to change one or more of the margin settings and create custom margins.

HOW TO: Set Custom Margins

1. Click the **Page Layout** tab.
2. Click the **Margins** button [*Page Setup* group]. The *Margins* drop-down list opens.
3. Click **Custom Margins**. The *Page Setup* dialog box opens (Figure 2-2).
4. Click the **Margins** tab if it is not already selected.
5. Change the *Top, Bottom, Left,* and *Right* margin settings as desired. You can do this in two different ways.
   - Click in the **Top**, **Bottom**, **Left**, or **Right** margin box, and type in your desired margin setting.
   - Click the **up** or **down arrow** to increase or decrease the margin size. Each click of the *up* or *down arrow* increases or decreases the margins by 0.1".
6. The *Preview* area displays how the margin settings appear when applied to the document.
7. Click **OK** to apply the margin settings.

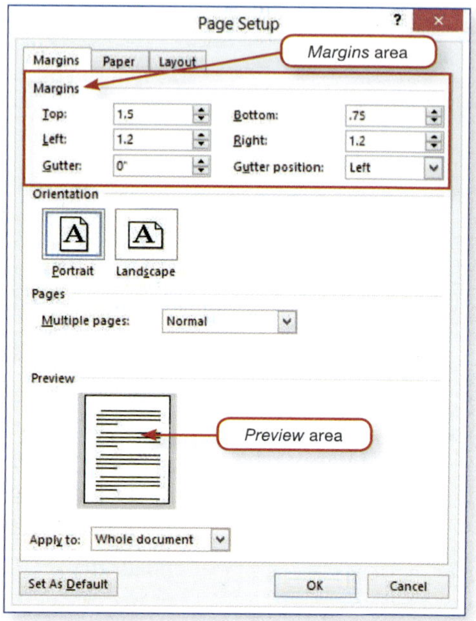

2-2 *Page Setup* dialog box

> **MORE INFO**
>
> Margin settings are applied to the entire document by default. However, you can apply different margin settings to different sections of a document. Sections and section breaks are covered later in this chapter.

Page Orientation

Page orientation refers to the direction of the page. The two different orientation options in Word are ***Portrait*** and ***Landscape.*** Portrait is the tall orientation (8.5"×11") which is the default setting in Word. Landscape is the wide orientation (11"×8.5").

You can change page orientation by clicking the **Orientation** button in the *Page Setup* group on the *Page Layout* tab (Figure 2-3). By default, orientation is applied to the entire document. You can also change page orientation in the *Page Setup* dialog box.

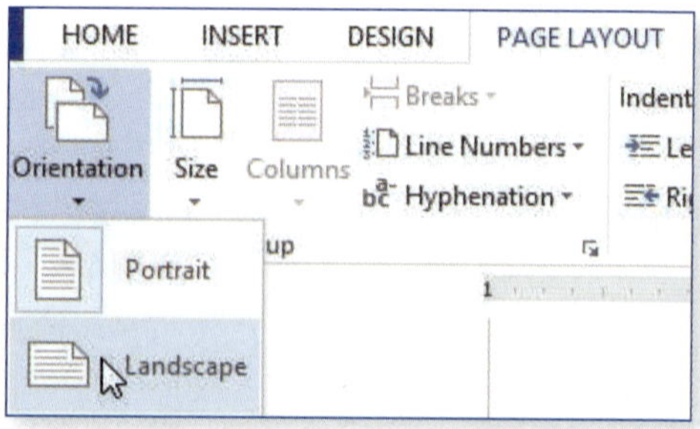

2-3 Page orientation settings

Paper Size

Paper size refers to the actual size of the paper of your final printed document. A new document in Word is letter size, which is 8.5"×11" by default. Word also provides other preset paper size settings, some of which are displayed in Figure 2-4.

You can change paper size by clicking the **Size** button in the *Page Setup* group on the *Page Layout* tab. You can also set a custom paper size in the *Page Setup* dialog box. When a different paper size is set, the margins of the document remain the same. You can change the margins if necessary.

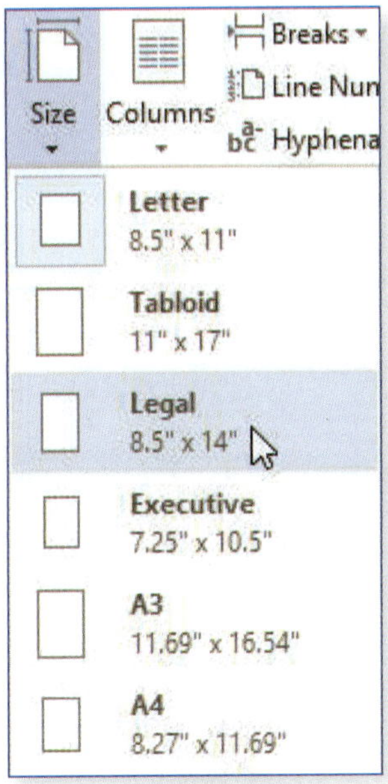

2-4 Paper size preset setting options

Vertical Alignment

If you are creating a flyer or a title page for a report, you might want to balance or center the information vertically on the page. Changing the ***vertical alignment*** of a page, section, or document is a much more effective method than using paragraph breaks (pressing *Enter* multiple times) to align information vertically.

Word gives you four different vertical alignment options.

- ***Top***—The text begins at the top of the document.
- ***Center***—Information is centered vertically between the margins.
- ***Justified***—Space is automatically added between lines to fill up the entire vertical space between the top and bottom margins.
- ***Bottom***—The text begins at the bottom of the document.

HOW TO: Change Vertical Alignment

1. Click the **Page Layout** tab.
2. Click the **Page Setup** launcher [*Page Setup* group]. The *Page Setup* dialog box opens.
3. Click the **Layout** tab.
4. In the *Page* area, click the **Vertical alignment** drop-down list (Figure 2-5).
5. Select the vertical alignment option of your choice.

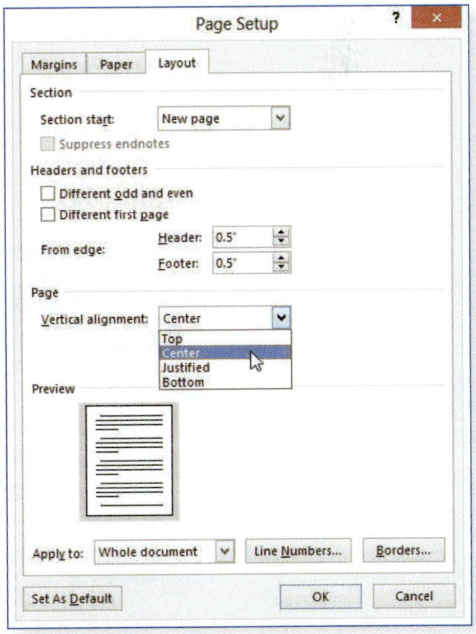

2-5 Change vertical alignment

Use the Ruler

Microsoft Word provides horizontal and vertical rulers that displays both the typing line length and the vertical typing space available in a document. The rulers are broken into 1/8" increments. Half-inch markers are longer vertical lines and inch markers are numerical. The typing area on the rulers is displayed in white, while the margin area is shaded (Figure 2-6).

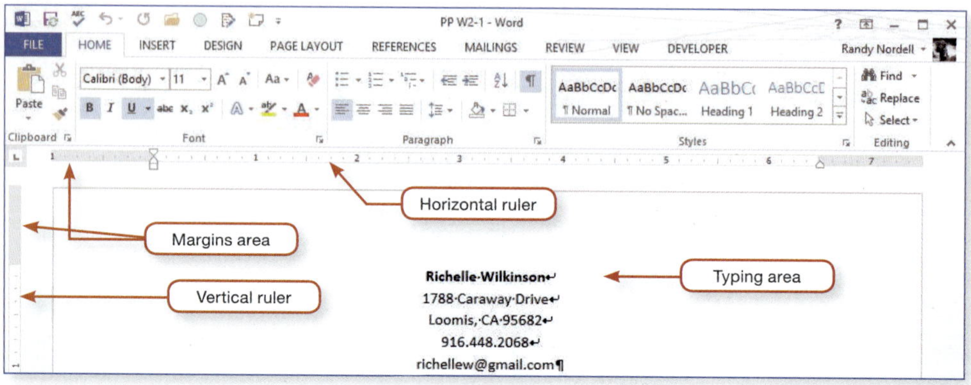

2-6 Horizontal and vertical rulers displayed

To display the rulers, select the **Ruler** check box on the *View* tab in the *Show* group. This check box toggles on and off the display of the rulers.

> **MORE INFO**
>
> The rulers are increasingly important and useful as you begin using tab stops, indents, columns, tables, and section breaks.

SLO 2.2

Setting, Using, and Editing Tab Stops

Tabs are useful tools that you can employ to control the alignment of text. A tab is often used to indent the first line of a paragraph. A ***tab stop*** is where your insertion point stops when you press the *Tab* key. Tabs can also be used, for example, to align text in columns, or to begin the date at the horizontal midpoint on a modified block business letter.

The five different types of tabs stops that you can set and use in your documents are described in the following table.

Types of Tab Stops

Type of Tab Stop	Description	Tab Stop Indicator	Tab Stop in Use
Left	Text is left aligned at the tab stop		Left tab
Center	Text is centered on the tab stop		Center tab
Right	Text is right aligned at the tab stop		Right tab
Decimal	Decimal point is aligned at the tab stop		Decimal tab 620.50 8.375
Bar	A vertical bar (line) is inserted at the tab stop		There is a bar | tab between these words

Set Tabs Stops

Tabs are different from margins because tab stops apply to a paragraph or selected paragraphs rather than an entire document or sections of a document. This is important to keep in mind when setting, using, and editing tab stops.

You can set tab stops before text is typed, or you can set tab stops on existing text. If you open a *new* document and set a left tab stop at 3.25", that tab stop is set on the first line of the document and is set on each subsequent line and paragraph in the document.

On the other hand, if you open an *existing* document and set a tab stop on the first line, the tab stop is only set for that paragraph. When setting a tab stop on existing documents or text, remember to select all the text or paragraphs where you want the tab settings to apply.

There are two ways to set a tab stop in Word.

- *Tabs* dialog box
- Ruler

Use the Tabs Dialog Box to Set Tab Stops

The ***Tabs dialog box*** is an effective and easy method to set single or multiple tab stops. The *Tabs* dialog box is available from the *Paragraph* dialog box, which you can open from the *Paragraph* group on either the *Home* or *Page Layout* tabs.

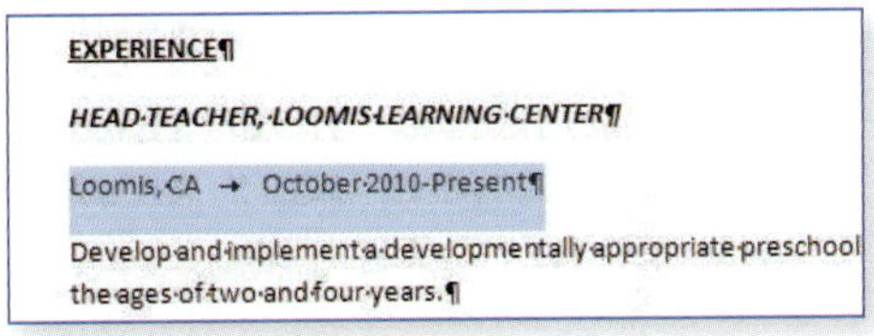

2-7 Select text before setting tab stops

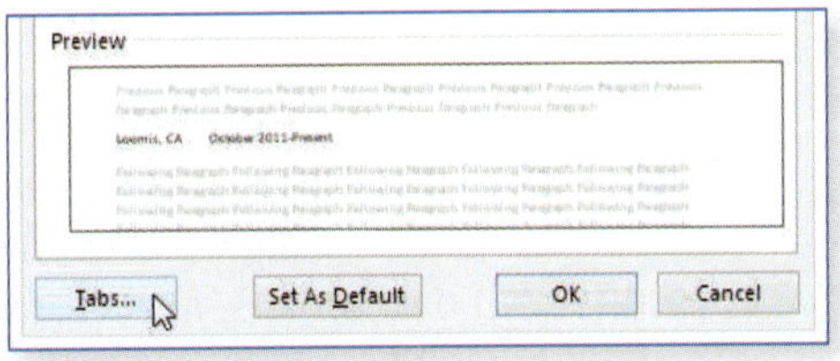

2-8 *Tabs* button in the *Paragraph* dialog box

HOW TO: Set Tab Stops Using the Tabs Dialog Box

1. Select the text where you want to set a tab stop (Figure 2-7).
2. Click the **Home** tab.
3. Click the **Paragraph** launcher to open the *Paragraph* dialog box.
4. Click the **Tabs** button (Figure 2-8). The *Tabs* dialog box opens.
5. Click in the **Tab stop position** area and type the desired tab stop position.
6. In the *Alignment* area, select the type of tab stop radio button you want.
7. Click the **Set** button. The tab stop appears in the list of tab stops below the *Tab stop position* area (Figure 2-9).
8. Click **OK** to close the *Tabs* dialog box.
   - The tab stop is applied to the selected text.
   - The tab stop is visible on the ruler.

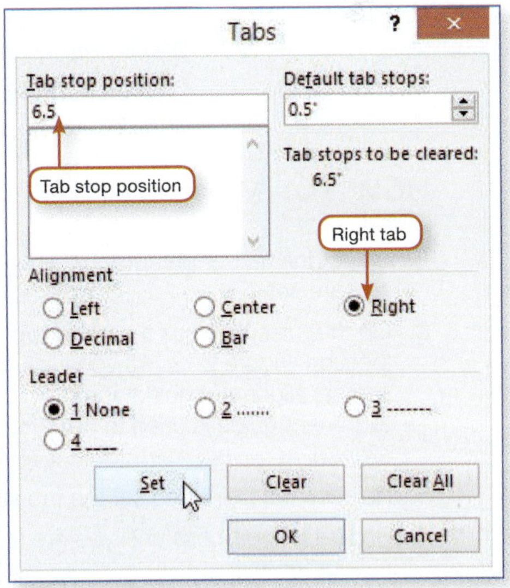

2-9 Set 6.5" right tab stop in the *Tabs* dialog box

MORE INFO

Set and use tab stops to line up and balance columns of text rather than pressing *Tab* multiple times between columns.

Use the Ruler to Set Tab Stops

Using the ruler to set tab stops is a quick way to add them to a document. You can also easily move or remove tab stops using the ruler. Use the ***tab selector*** to select the type of tab stop you want. The tab selector is located at the top of the vertical ruler on the left side of the Word window. When setting tab stops on an existing document, it is very important to select the text or paragraphs where you want the tab stop to apply before setting the tab stop.

HOW TO: Set Tab Stops Using the Ruler

1. Select the text where you want the new tab stop(s) to appear.
2. Click the **tab selector** to select the type of tab stop to apply (Figure 2-10).
3. Click the ruler to set a tab stop.
   - When setting tab stops using the ruler, click the bottom edge of the ruler to set a tab stop (Figure 2-11).

2-10 ***Tab Selector*** **button**

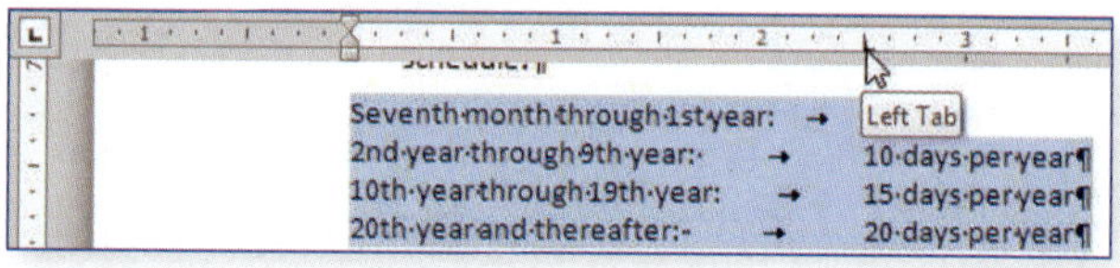

2-11 Set left tab stop at 2.5" on the ruler

> **MORE INFO**
>
> Use the ***Format Painter*** to copy tab stops from one area of your document to other areas.

Edit Tab Stops

Aligning text using tab stops can sometimes be tedious. It can be challenging to get text aligned correctly and balanced between columns. But as you set and use tab stop more regularly, you become more comfortable selecting the correct type of tab stop to use, adjusting the settings of existing tab stops, and removing tab stops. When using multiple columns, adjust tab stops so you have about the same amount of white space between columns.

Move Tab Stops

The easiest way to move tab stops is by using the ruler. When using the ruler to adjust a tab stop, be sure to select the appropriate text before moving a tab stop.

HOW TO: Move Tab Stops

1. Select the text or paragraphs where the tab stops you want to edit are set.
2. On the ruler, left click the **tab stop** and drag it to the new location (Figure 2-12). As you click the tab stop to be moved, a vertical alignment guide appears on your document. This alignment guide is used to help you see where your text is aligned.
3. Release the pointer to set the tab stop in the new location.
4. Repeat this process until you are satisfied with the placement of your tab stops.

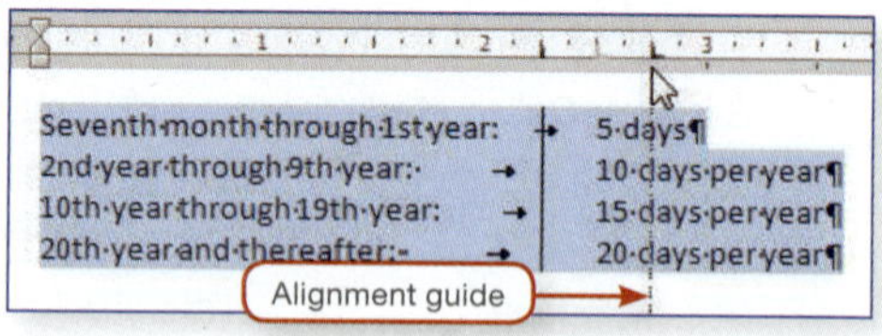

2-12 Move a tab stop using the ruler

> **ANOTHER WAY**
>
> Adjust tab stops in the *Tabs* dialog box by clearing an existing tab stop and setting a new tab stop.

If you hold down the **Alt** key when you are moving a tab stop, a different ruler appears that allows you to place the tab stop at a specific measurement (Figure 2-13).

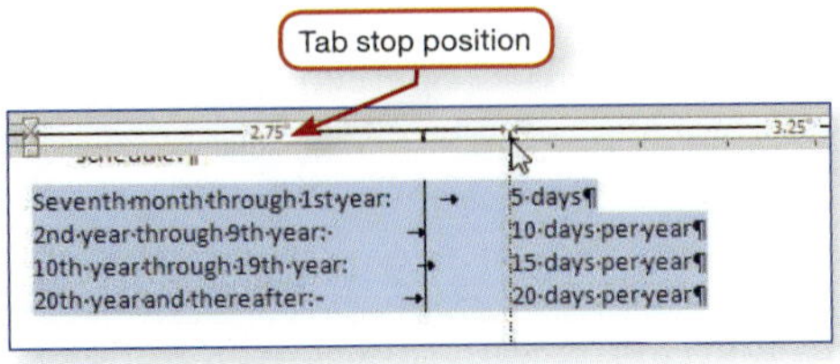

2-13 Use the *Alt* key to adjust a tab stop

Remove Tab Stops

Occasionally, when setting tab stops using the ruler, you unintentionally add unwanted tab stops. Or sometimes you might just want to remove unwanted tab stops to clean up an existing document. It is very important to select the text or paragraphs where the tab stops you want to remove are before performing these actions. Following are three different ways to remove tab stops.

- Drag a tab stop off the ruler.
- Clear a single tab stop in the *Tabs* dialog box.
- Clear all tab stops in the *Tabs* dialog box.

To clear a single tab stop using the ruler, select the text or paragraphs, select the tab stop you want to remove, drag down below the ruler, and release the pointer.

When using the *Tabs* dialog box to remove tab stops, you can clear a single tab stop or clear all existing tab stops on the selected text or paragraphs.

HOW TO: Clear Tab Stops Using the Tabs Dialog Box

1. Select the text or paragraphs that contain the tab stops you want to remove.
2. Click the **Paragraph** launcher [*Home* or *Page Layout* tab] to open the *Paragraph* dialog box.
3. Click the **Tabs** button to open the *Tabs* dialog box.
4. To clear a single tab stop, select the tab stop to be cleared in the list of existing tab stops and click the **Clear** button (Figure 2-14). Repeat on any other tab stops you want to remove.
   - To clear all tab stops, click the **Clear All** button.
5. Click **OK** to close the *Tabs* dialog box.

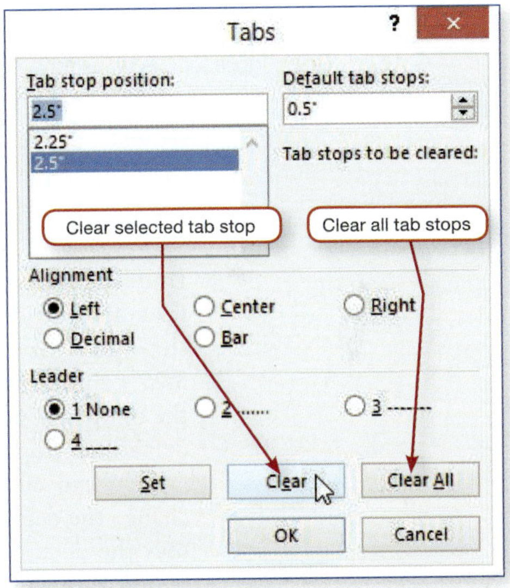

2-14 Clear tab stops in the *Tabs* dialog box

Tab Leaders

You can use ***leaders*** to insert dots or a line between information when using tab stops. The most common type of leader is the dot leader, which is regularly used in a table of contents. In a table of contents, a dot leader is inserted between the text and the right aligned page number. Leaders make it easier for readers to read across a line where there is a gap on the same line. Leaders can also be used to insert a dashed line in the blank space between columns or to create a solid underline when creating a printed form.

Word has three different types of leaders. Examples of each of these are in the following table.

Types of Leaders

Leader	Example of Use
Dot	Chapter 1 4
Dash	Vacation Days ------- 10 days per year
Solid Underline	Name ______________________

You can add leaders to existing or new tab stops, but they can only be added in the *Tabs* dialog box.

HOW TO: Add a Tab Leader

1. Select the text or paragraphs where you want to add a tab leader.
2. Click the **Paragraph** launcher [*Home* or *Page Layout* tab] to open the *Paragraph* dialog box.
3. Click the **Tabs** button to open the *Tabs* dialog box.
4. Select an existing tab stop or type in the *Tab stop position* text box for a new tab stop.
5. In the *Leader* area, select the type of leader to be applied.
6. Click **Set**. Figure 2-15 is an example of a dash leader.
7. Click **OK** to close the *Tabs* dialog box.

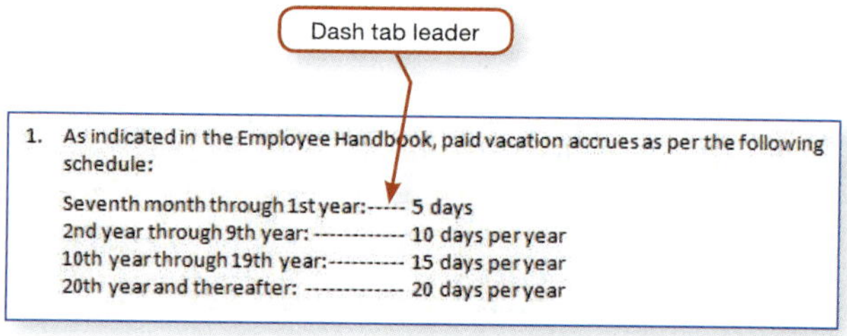

2-15 Tab stop with a dash leader

Change Default Tab Stops

By default, Word has a left tab stop every 0.5". When you set a tab stop in Word, this custom tab stop overrides all preceding default tab stops. The default tab stops after your custom tab stop still remain. For example, if you set a left tab stop at the horizontal midpoint (typically 3.25") and press *Tab* to move to the horizontal midpoint, your insertion point will move to the midpoint, not 0.5". But if you press *Tab* again, your insertion point will stop at the next default tab stop, which would be 3.5".

You can customize the default tab stops. If you change the default tab stop setting, this change affects only the document on which you are working, not all new documents.

HOW TO: Change Default Tab Stops

1. Click the **Paragraph** launcher [*Home* or *Page Layout* tab] to open the *Paragraph* dialog box.
2. Click the **Tabs** button to open the *Tabs* dialog box.
3. In the *Default tab stops* area, use the up or down arrow to change the default tab stops (Figure 2-16).
4. Click **OK** to close the *Tabs* dialog box.

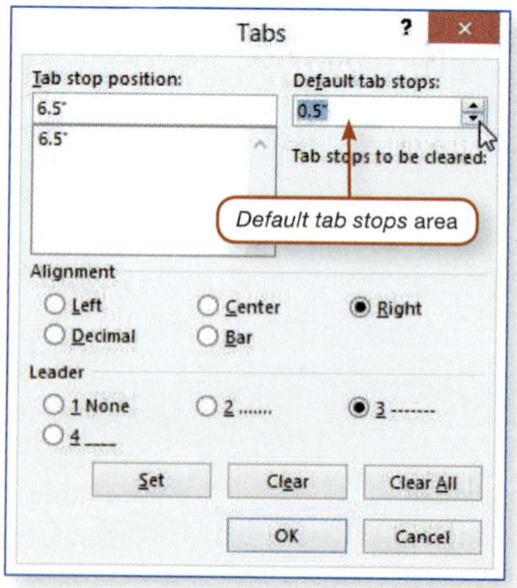

2-16 Change default tab stops

SLO 2.3

Using Indents

Indents are another powerful tool to help you control how text is arranged between the left and right margins. Indents can be thought of as temporary margins. You can use indents to indent the first line of each paragraph, set off a long quote in a report, or indent the carry-over lines when creating bulleted or numbered lists.

The four different types of indents that you can set and use in your document are described in the following table.

Types of Indents

Indent	Example of Use	Ruler Indent Marker
Left Indent	This line has a ***left indent***.	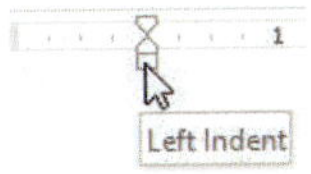
Right Indent	This line has a ***right indent***.	
First Line Indent	This line has a ***first line indent***.	
Hanging Indent	This line has a ***hanging indent***.	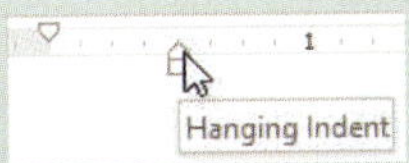

Similar to setting tab stops, it is important to select the text where you want to apply the indent settings before applying the new settings. You can set indents using the ruler, the *Paragraph* group on the *Page Layout* tab, or the *Paragraph* dialog box.

Left and Right Indents

Indents are applied to paragraphs, not just lines of text within a paragraph. When setting an indent, select the text or paragraphs on which to apply the indent. If your insertion point is in a paragraph, the indent you set is applied to that paragraph only.

HOW TO: Set a Left and Right Indent

1. Select the text or paragraph where you want to apply the indent. If it is just one paragraph, place your insertion point in that paragraph.
2. Click the **Page Layout** tab.
3. Change the *Left* and *Right* indent settings [*Paragraph* group]. This change is applied to the selected text (Figure 2-17).

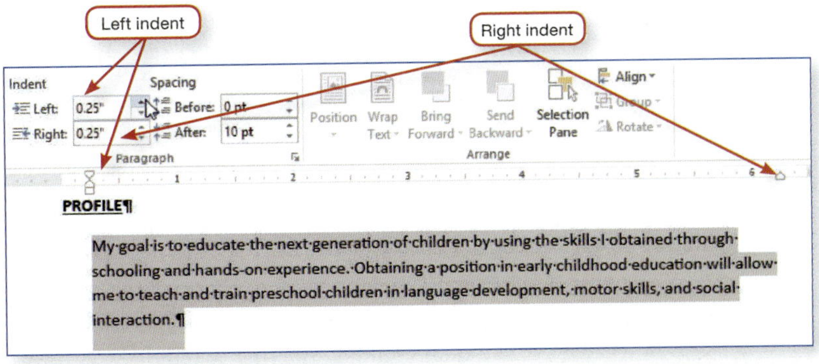

2-17 Change left and right indents

When an indent is set on a paragraph and you press *Enter* at the end of the paragraph, the indent carries over to the next paragraph.

Indents can also be set using the ruler by dragging the indent marker to the desired location after you select the text you want to indent. As you drag the indent marker, an alignment guide appears to display where your text aligns.

HOW TO: Use the Ruler to Set Indents

1. Select the text or paragraph you want to indent. If it is just one paragraph, place your insertion point in that paragraph.
2. Left click the **left indent marker**, drag to the desired location, and release the pointer. The left indent is applied to the text (Figure 2-18).
3. Left click the **right indent marker**, drag to the desired location, and release the pointer. The right indent is applied to the text (Figure 2-19).

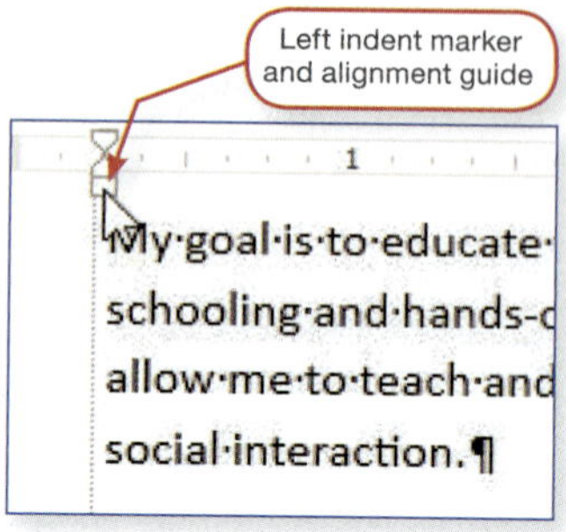

2-18 Change left indent using the ruler

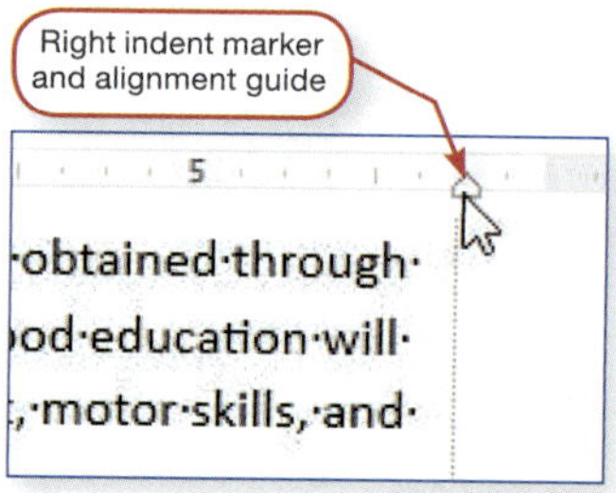

2-19 Change right indent using the ruler

ANOTHER WAY

Set left and right indents using the *Paragraph* dialog box. Click the **Paragraph** launcher to open the *Paragraph* dialog box.

The ***Decrease Indent*** and ***Increase Indent*** buttons in the *Paragraph* group on the *Home* tab increase or decrease the left indent in increments of 0.5" (Figure 2-20). Remove a left indent by clicking at the beginning of the paragraph and pressing **Backspace**.

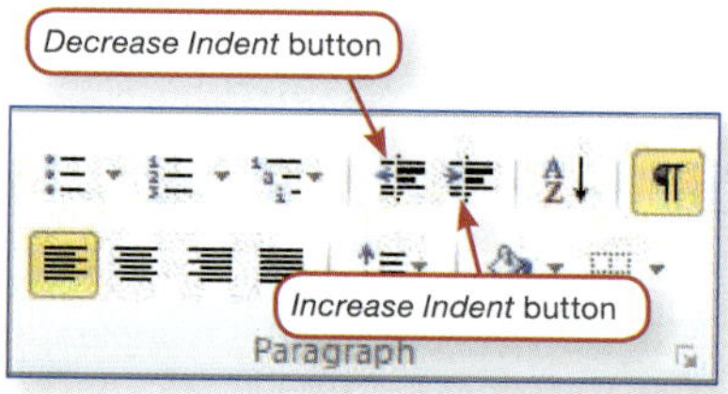

2-20 *Decrease Indent* and *Increase Indent* buttons

First Line and Hanging Indents

You can use ***first line indents*** to indent the first line of a paragraph instead of using a tab. ***Hanging indents*** are typically used with bulleted and numbered lists but can be used effectively to indent text that wraps to a second or more lines.

When using the ruler to set a first line indent, select the text or paragraph you want to indent and drag the first line indent marker to the desired location (Figure 2-21). The alignment guide displays where the first line of each paragraph will align.

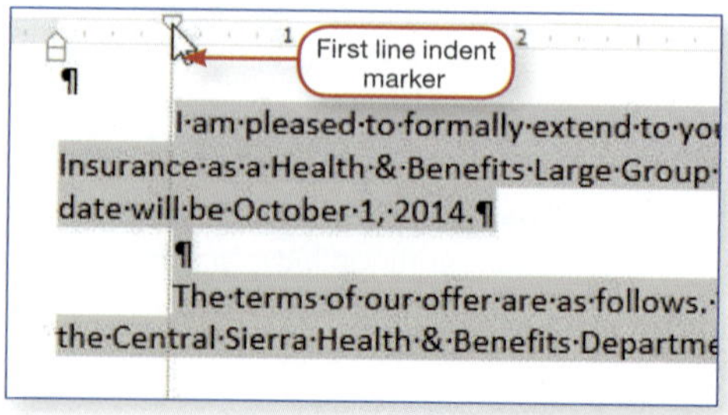

2-21 Set a first line indent using the ruler

To set a hanging indent, select the text or paragraph on which to apply the indent and drag the hanging indent marker to the desired location (Figure 2-22). The alignment guide displays where the carryover lines of the paragraph will align.

You can use the *Paragraph* dialog box to set either a first line or a hanging indent.

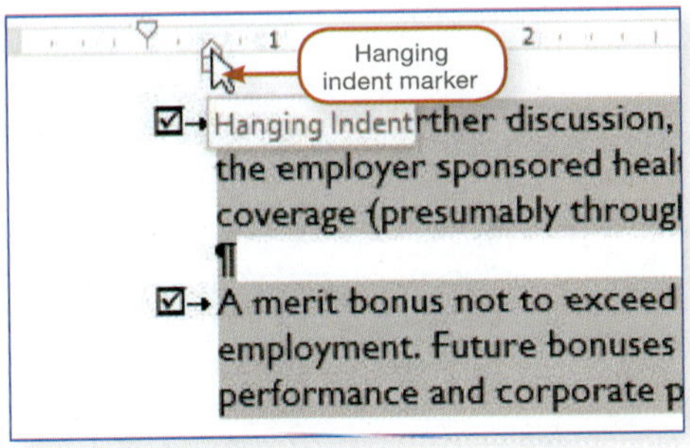

2-22 Set a hanging indent using the ruler

HOW TO: Set a First Line or a Hanging Indent Using the Paragraph Dialog Box

1. Select the text or paragraph you want to indent.
2. Click the **Paragraph** launcher [*Home* or *Page Layout* tab] to open the *Paragraph* dialog box.
3. Click the **Special** drop-down list in the *Indentation* area and choose the type of indent (Figure 2-23).
4. In the *By* area, either type the indent amount or use the up or down buttons to increase or decrease the amount of the indent.
   - The *Preview* area displays how the text will look with the indent applied.
5. Click **OK** to close the *Paragraph* dialog box.

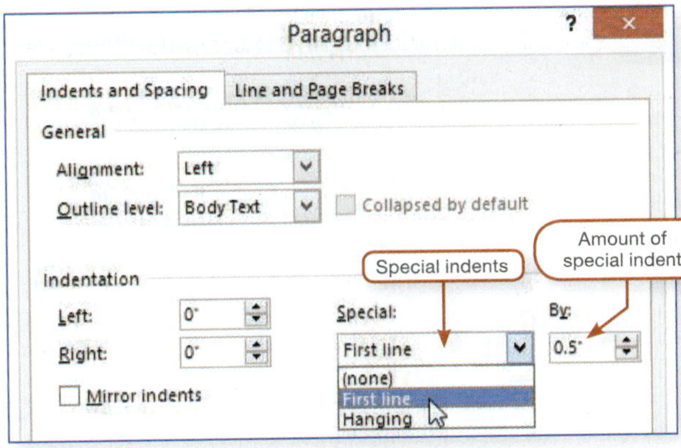

2-23 Set first line or hanging indent using the *Paragraph* dialog box

An ***outdent*** can be used to line up information outside the left or right margins. Outdents are sometimes used to set off section headings so they are slightly to the left of the left margin. You can do this by setting a ***negative value*** (–0.25") in the indents area in the *Paragraph* dialog box or *Paragraph* group on the *Page Layout* tab or by dragging the indent marker outside of the left or right margins.

Remove Indents

Removing indents moves the indent markers back to either the left or right margin, so the margins control the alignment of text rather than the indents. Remember to select the paragraph or paragraphs before removing the indents. You can remove indents using the *Paragraph* dialog box or the *Paragraph* group on the *Page Layout* tab. When using either of these methods, set the indents value to 0" (Figure 2-24).

The ruler can also be used to remove indents. When using this method, select the text or paragraphs on which to remove the indents, and drag the indent marker(s) to the margin.

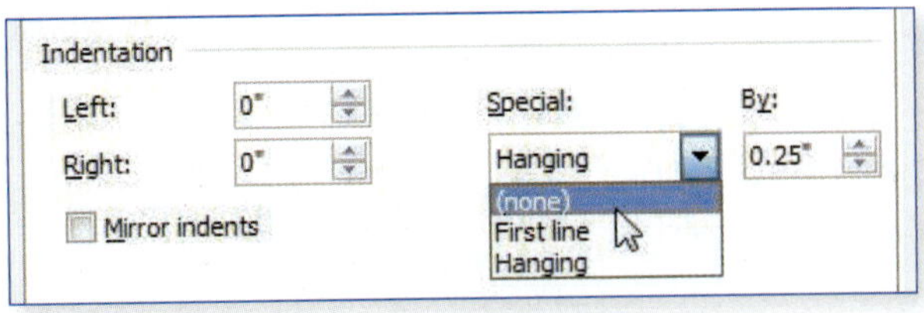

2-24 Remove indents using the *Paragraph* dialog box

PAUSE & PRACTICE: WORD 2-1

In this Pause & Practice project, you format a resume for Richelle Wilkinson. This resume is a two-page document, and you change the margins, set tab stops and leaders, and use indents.

File Needed: ***Resume-02.docx***
Completed Project File Name: ***[your initials] PP W2-1.docx***

1. Open the ***Resume-02*** document in your student data files.
2. Save this document as ***[your initials] PP W2-1.***
3. Change the margins of the resume.
   a. Click the **Page Layout** tab.
   b. Click the **Margins** button [*Page Setup* group]. A drop-down list appears.
   c. Select **Custom Margins** at the bottom of the list. The **Page Setup** dialog box opens.
   d. In the *Margins* area (Figure 2-25), click in the *Top* box, delete the existing margin, and type .75.
   e. Click in the *Bottom* box, delete the existing margin, and type .75.
   f. Click the **down arrow** to the right of the *Left* box to change the left margin to **1"**.
   g. Click the **down arrow** to the right of the *Right* box to change the right margin to **1"**.
   h. Click the **Apply to** drop-down list at the bottom of the dialog box and select **Whole document**.
   i. Click **OK** to apply the new margin settings and close the dialog box.

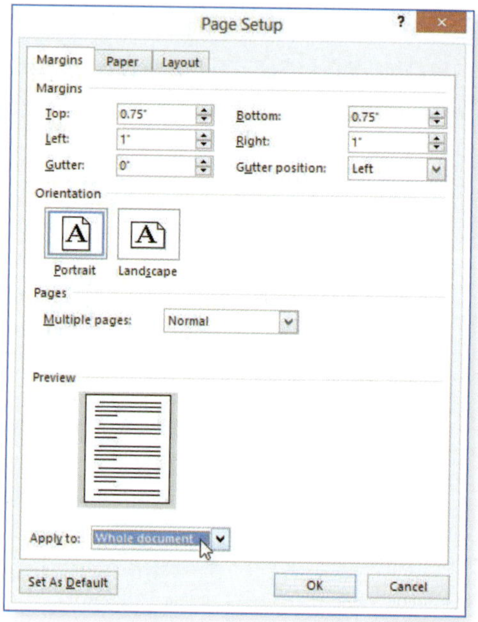

2-25 Change margins in the *Page Setup* dialog box

4. Set a right tab stop with a dash leader.
   a. Select **"Loomis, CA October 2011Present"** below *"Head Teacher, Loomis Learning Center."*
   b. Click the **Paragraph** launcher [*Page Layout* or *Home* tab]. The *Paragraph* dialog box opens.
   c. Click the **Tabs** button in the bottom left of the *Paragraph* dialog box. The *Tabs* dialog box opens (Figure 2-26).
   d. In the *Tab stop position* area, type 6.5.
   e. In the *Alignment* area, click the **Right** radio button.
   f. In the *Leader* area, click the **3** (dash leader) radio button.
   g. Click the **Set** button to set this tab stop and leader.
   h. Click the **OK** button to close the dialog box.
5. Use the *Format Painter* to apply the tab setting to multiple areas of the resume.
   a. Place the insertion point somewhere in the line you just formatted.
   b. Double-click the **Format Painter** button [*Home* tab, *Clipboard* group].

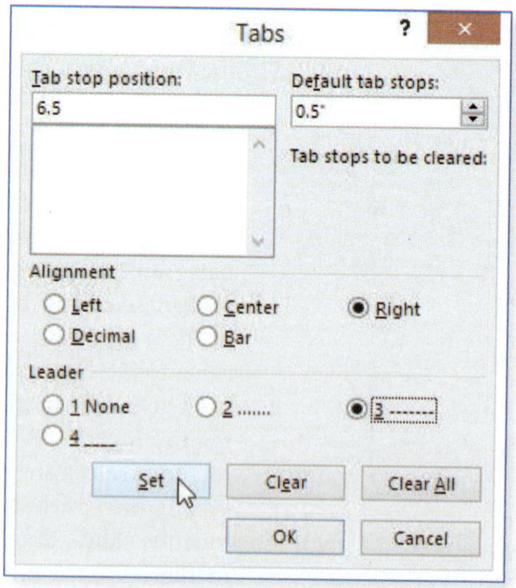

2-26 Set a right tab stop with a dash leader

c. Click each of the city/date lines in the "Experience" and "Education" sections to apply the tab settings to these lines as shown in Figure 2-27.

d. Click the **Format Painter** button to turn it off.

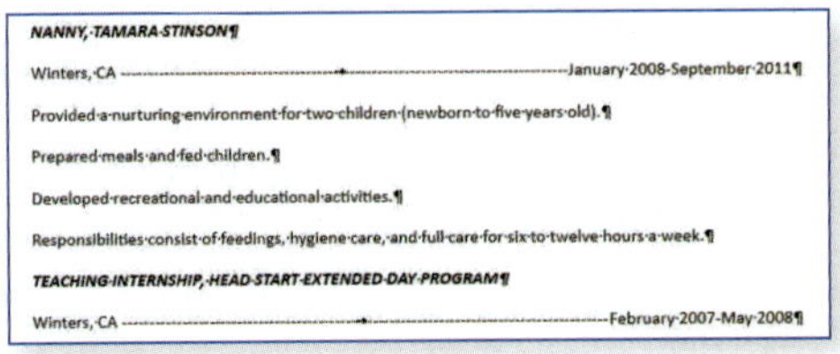

2-27 Use the *Format Painter* to apply tab settings

6. Remove an existing tab stop and set a left tab stop.
   a. On the second page, select the lines of text below the "References" heading.
   b. Click the **Paragraph** launcher [*Page Layout* or *Home* tab] to open the *Paragraph* dialog box.
   c. Click the **Tabs** button in the bottom left of the *Paragraph* dialog box. The *Tabs* dialog box opens (Figure 2-28).
   d. In the *Tab stop position* area, select the existing tab stop and click the **Clear** button to remove the existing tab.
   e. In the *Tab stop position* area, type 3.75.
   f. In the *Alignment* area, click the **Left** radio button.
   g. In the *Leader* area, click the **1 None** radio button.
   h. Click the **Set** button to set this left tab stop.
   i. Click the **OK** button to close the dialog box.

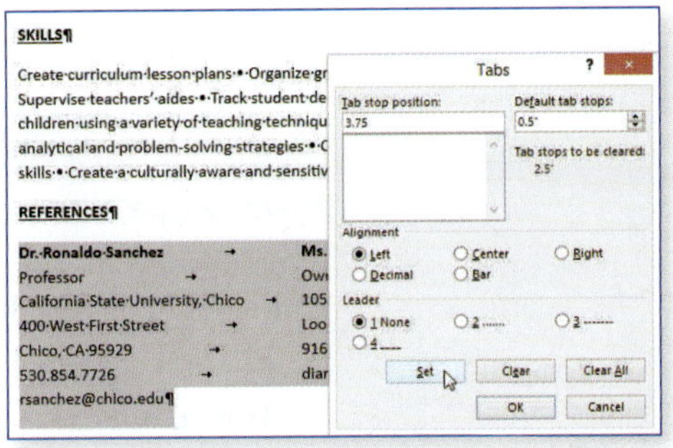

2-28 Set a left tab stop on selected text

7. Apply a left and right indent to selected text.
   a. Place the insertion point in the paragraph below the "Profile" heading on the first page.
   b. Click the **Page Layout** tab.
   c. Click in the **Left** indent area [*Paragraph* group], type .25, and press **Enter**.
   d. Click in the **Right** indent area, type .25, and press **Enter**.

8. Save and close this document (Figure 2-29).

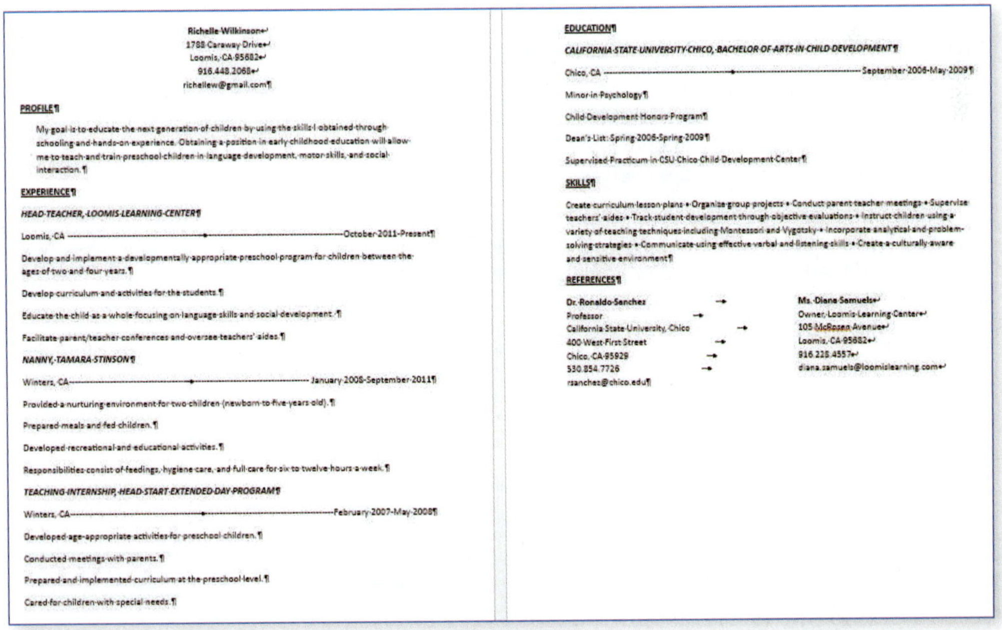

2-29 PP W2-1 completed

SLO 2.4

Inserting Page Numbers, Headers, and Footers

Page numbering, headers, and ***footers*** are regularly used in multiple-page documents. You can set the header and footer information to appear on each page of the document, which means you only have to type the information once, and Word repeats that information on each of the subsequent pages. The header area of a document is above the top margin, and the footer is below the bottom margin.

Page Numbering

When you use Word to insert page numbers, a ***page number field*** is inserted in the header or footer of the document. This page number field automatically displays the current page number. You can control where the page number is placed and the page number format.

Insert Page Number

Word gives you a variety of page number locations, horizontal alignment options, and number format options. The following is a list of the basic page number placement options.

- Top of Page
- Bottom of Page
- Page Margins
- Current Position

Page numbers at the top or bottom of the document can be aligned at the left, center, or right.

HOW TO: Insert a Page Number

1. Click the **Insert** tab.
2. Click the **Page Number** button [*Header & Footer* group]. A drop-down list of options appears (Figure 2-30).
3. Click either **Top of Page** or **Bottom of Page**. Another drop-down list of page number options appears.
   - The top three options in this list are simple page numbers aligned at the left, center, or right.
   - Further down this list there are custom page number options.
4. Click one of the page number options to insert the current page number. The header and footer open with the page number inserted, and the *Headers & Footer Tools Design* tab opens (Figure 2-31).
5. Click the **Close Header and Footer** button [*Close* group].

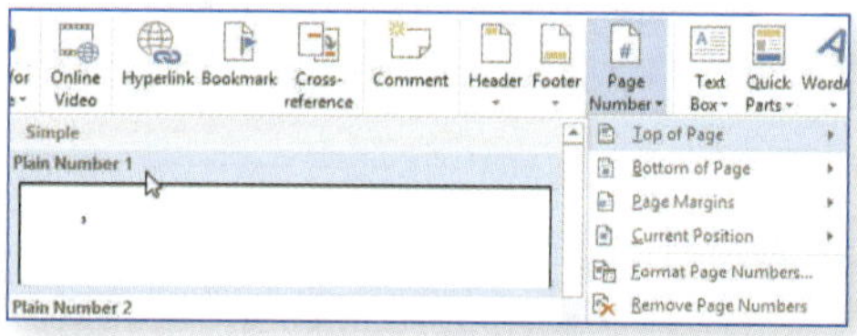

2-30 Insert page number

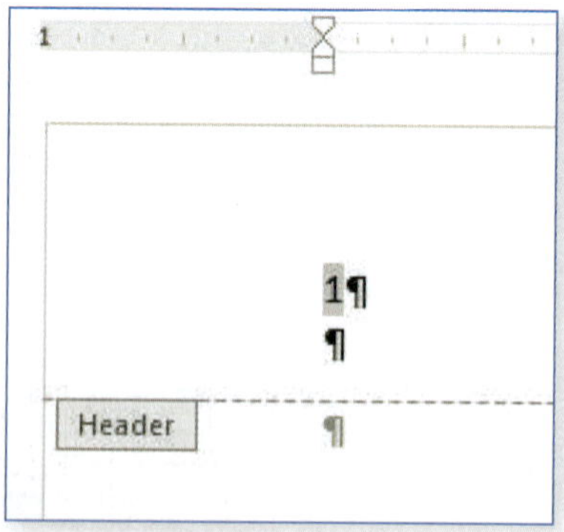

2-31 Page number inserted in the header on the left

ANOTHER WAY

Close the header and footer by **double-clicking** in the body of the document.

When you close the header and footer, the page number appears in gray rather than black like the text of the document. The header and footer are outside the boundaries of the margins. If you want to edit the page number or contents of the header and footer, you have to open the header and footer. There are three ways to do this.

- Double-click in the header or footer area of the document.
- Click the **Insert** tab, click the **Header** or **Footer** button in the *Header & Footer* group, and choose **Edit Header** or **Edit Footer**.
- Right-click the header or footer and select **Edit Header** or **Edit Footer**.

Different First Page

There are times when you might not want the page number and header or footer to print on the first page, but you want it to appear on the second and continuing pages. For example on both multiple-page business letters and reports, the page number is typically not on the first page but is on the second and subsequent pages. Word gives you the option to set a ***different first page***.

HOW TO: Set a Different First Page Header and Footer

1. After inserting a page number in the header or footer, open the header and footer if it is not already open.
2. Click the **Different First Page** check box [*Options* group] (Figure 2-32).
3. Click the **Close Header and Footer** button [*Close* group]. The page number, header, and footer no longer appear on the first page but do appear on the second and continuing pages.

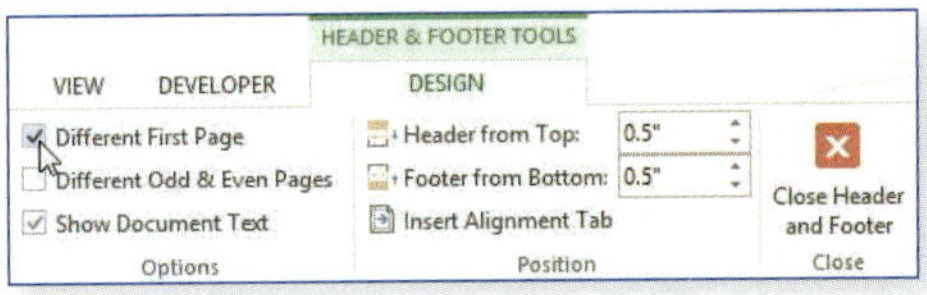

2-32 ***Different First Page*** **option check box**

MORE INFO

When inserting a page number, header, or footer, it is best to insert it on the first page of the document. This becomes increasingly important as you add section breaks to a document.

Page Number Format

When using page numbering, you might want a different type of page number format, numbering to begin with a different page number, or a chapter number before the page number. The *Page Number Format* dialog box provides you with page numbering options (Figure 2-33).

HOW TO: Format Page Numbers

1. After inserting a page number, click the **Page Number** button [*Insert* tab, *Header & Footer* group].
2. From the drop-down list, select **Format Page Numbers**. The *Page Number Format* dialog box opens (Figure 2-33).
3. In the *Number format* area, click the **drop-down list** and select a page number format. There are six preset page numbering options from which to choose.
4. In the *Page numbering* section, you have the option to *Continue from previous section* (default setting) or *Start at* a different page number.
5. Click the **Start at** radio button to set a different starting page number.
6. Type in the starting page number or use the up or down arrow to set the starting page number.
7. Click **OK** to close the *Page Number Format* dialog box.

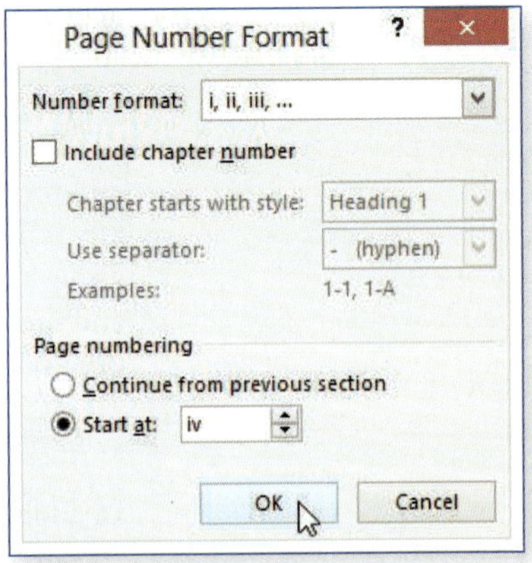

2-33 Page numbering options

Remove Page Number

If you want to remove the page numbering from a document, there are two different ways to do this.

- Open the header and footer and manually delete the page number.
- Select **Remove Page Numbers** from the *Page Numbers* drop-down list (Figure 2-34).

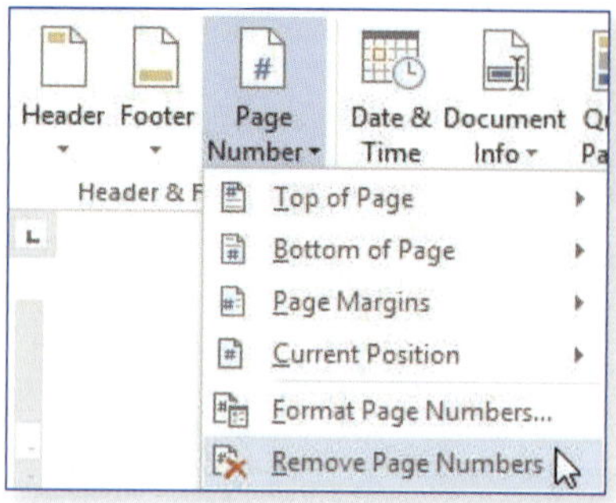

2-34 Remove page numbers

Insert Header and Footer Content

In addition to inserting page numbers into the header or footer of a document, you might want to include the number of pages in the document, date or time, title of the document, or company name. You can enter information manually into the header or footer, or you can have Word insert document property fields.

HOW TO: Manually Enter Information in the Header or Footer

1. Click the **Insert** tab.
2. Click the **Header** button and choose **Edit Header** in the drop-down list, or double-click in the *Header* area of the document (above the top margin). The header of the document opens and the *Header & Footer Tools Design* tab is displayed.
3. In the *Header* area, type in your information (Figure 2-35).
   - You can change the formatting and alignment as desired.
   - You can insert a page number with the header or footer open.
4. Close the header.

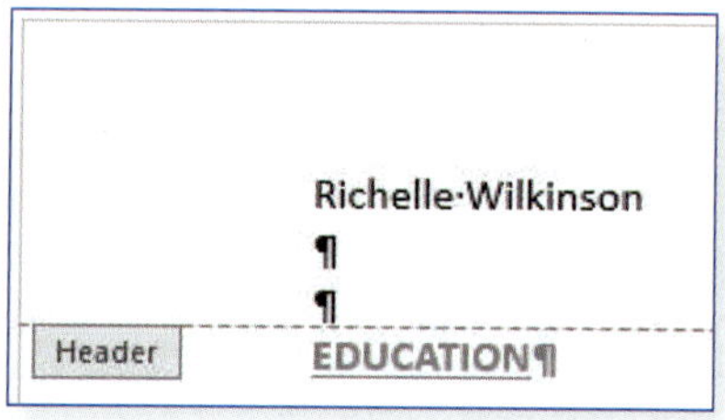

2-35 Manually enter information in the header

MORE INFO

In the header and footer, there is a center tab stop at the horizontal midpoint and a right tab stop at the right margin. You can move these tab stops, remove them, or add additional tab stops.

When you edit a header or footer, both the header and footer open and the *Header & Footer Tools Design* tab is displayed. On this tab, there is a *Navigation* group to help you move between the header and footer and move through the different headers and footers in the document (Figure 2-36).

2-36 *Navigation* group in the *Header & Footer Tools Design* tab

Number of Pages Field

In addition to inserting the current page number in a document, you can add a field code to automatically insert the total number of pages in a document (*NumPages* field).

HOW TO: Insert the Number of Pages Field

1. Open the header or footer. The page number should already be inserted in the document.
2. Click before the page number, type Page, and press **spacebar**.
3. Click after the page number and press **spacebar**, type of, and press **spacebar**.
4. Click the **Quick Parts** button [*Header & Footer Tools Design* tab, *Insert* group] (Figure 2-37).
5. Select **Field** from the drop-down list. The *Field* dialog box opens (Figure 2-38).
6. In the *Field names* area, scroll down and select **NumPages**. The description of the field is displayed in the *Description* area.
7. In the *Format* area, click **1, 2, 3**. This is the format of the page number.
8. Click **OK** to close the *Field* dialog box. The number of pages in the document is inserted (Figure 2-39).
9. Close the header or footer.

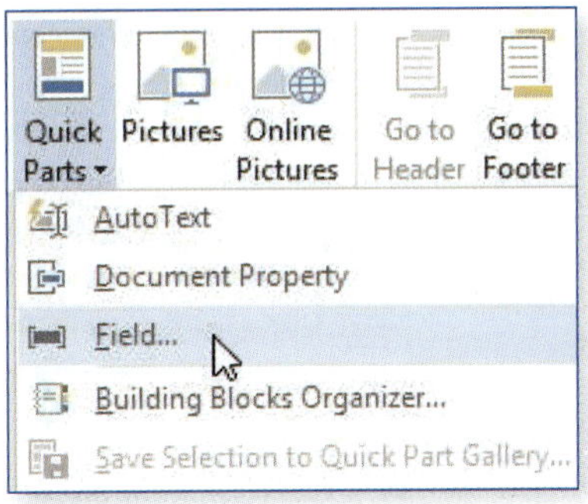

2-37 Insert field code

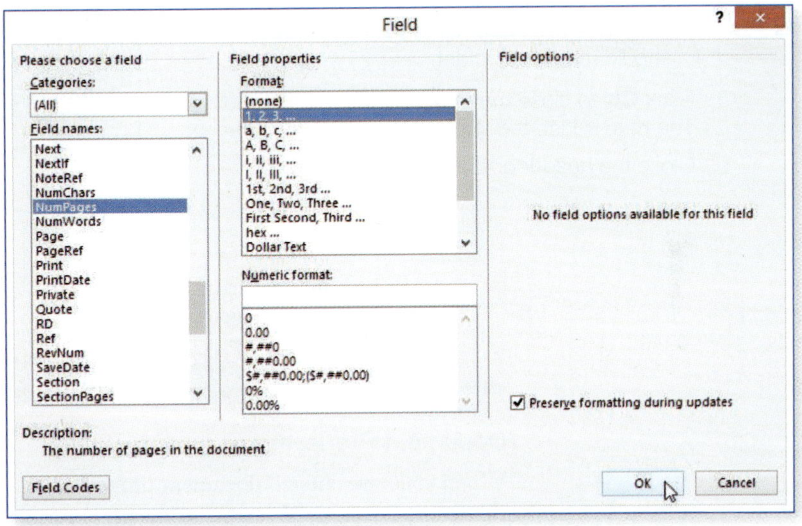

2-38 Insert *NumPages* field from the *Field* dialog box

MORE INFO

When inserting text before or after a page number, be sure to include a space between the word and the page number. Word does not automatically do this for you.

2-39 Page number and number of pages fields inserted into the header

Date and Time

You can type a date or the time in the header or footer of a document, or you can have Word insert this information. The advantages of inserting the date and time are that you have a variety of date and time formats from which to choose, and you can choose to have the date and time update automatically.

HOW TO: Insert the Date and Time

1. Open the header or footer and position the insertion point at the position where you want the date inserted.
2. Click the **Date & Time** button [*Header & Footer Tools Design* tab, *Insert* group]. The *Date and Time* dialog box opens (Figure 2-40).
3. In the *Available formats* area, select the date or time format to use
4. If you want the date to update automatically, check the **Update automatically** check box.
   - Don't use the *Update automatically* on time-sensitive documents where the date should remain constant.
5. Click **OK** to close the *Date and Time* dialog box. The date is inserted into the header.
6. Close the header or footer.

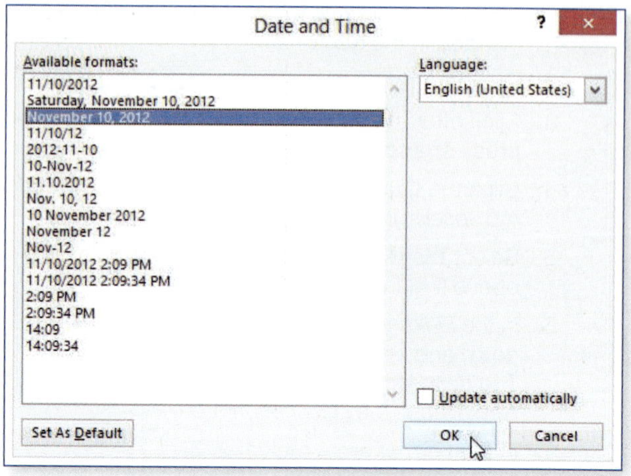

2-40 ***Date and Time* dialog box**

> **MORE INFO**
>
> Inserting a date or time is not limited to headers and footers. You can insert the date or time in the body of a document by clicking **Date & Time** [*Insert* tab, *Text* group].

Document Properties

When you have entered document properties in a Word document, you can automatically insert this information in the header or footer. For example, you might want to include the title of the document, name of the author, or date last modified. One of the advantages of inserting document properties rather than typing this information is that when you update the document properties, these fields are automatically updated in the header or footer and throughout the document.

HOW TO: Insert Document Properties

1. Open the header or footer and place the insertion point at the location where you want the document property inserted.
2. Click the **Document Info** button [*Header & Footer Tools Design* tab, *Insert* group] (Figure 2-41).
3. Select the document property field or click **Document Property** and select the document property field of your choice from the drop-down list. The document property field is inserted in the document.
   - You can also click the **Quick Parts** button [*Header & Footer Tools Design* tab, *Insert* group] and select **Document Property**.
4. Close the header or footer.

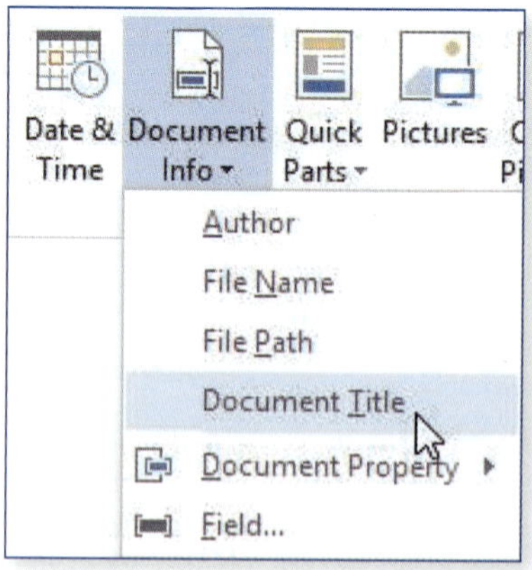

2-41 Insert document property field

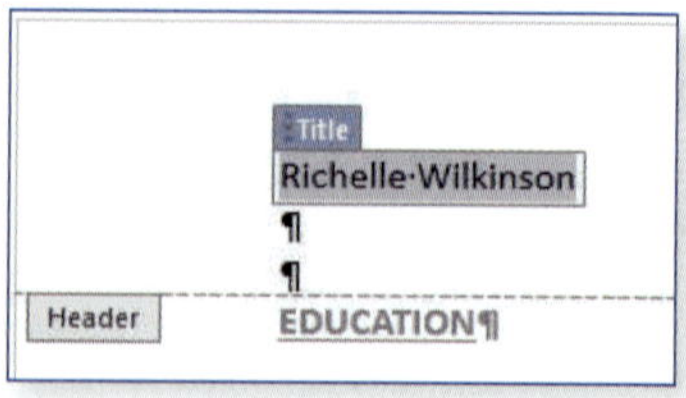

2-42 ***Title* document property field inserted in the header**

> **MORE INFO**
>
> Inserting document properties is not limited to headers and footers. Click the **Quick Parts** button [*Insert* tab, *Text* group] to insert this information in the body of a document.
>
> Press the **right arrow** key to deselect a field code.

Built-In Headers, Footers, and Page Numbers

In addition to inserting basic page numbers, manually adding header or footer content, and inserting date and time, Word provides you with a variety of built-in custom header, footer, and page number format options. Many of the header and footer options include document properties that are automatically inserted and updated.

HOW TO: Insert a Built-In Header

1. Click the **Insert** tab.
2. Click the **Header** button [*Header & Footer* group] and select a built-in header from the choices in the drop-down list. (Figure 2-43) The selected header is inserted into the document.
   - Document property fields are automatically updated with the document information.
   - Some fields, such as *Pick the date,* require you to input or select information.
3. Close the header.

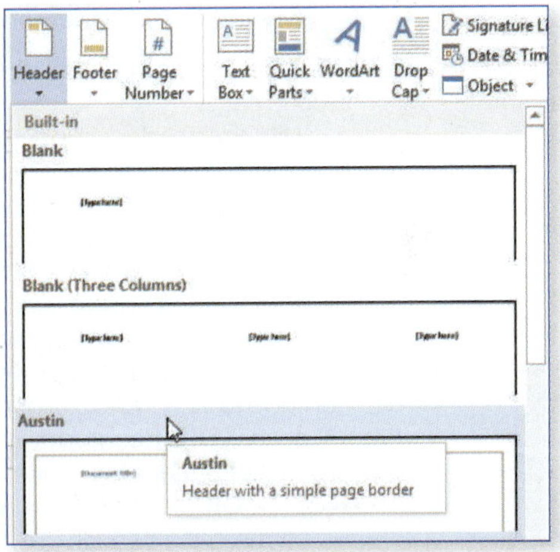

2-43 List of built-in headers

Keep in mind when you are using built-in headers, footers, and page numbers that many of these use tables, graphics, and advanced formatting, which makes editing more challenging without a thorough understanding of this type of content.

PAUSE & PRACTICE: WORD 2-2

In this Pause & Practice project, you modify the resume from *Pause & Practice 2-1*. You add a header that appears only on the second page of this document and insert a document property field, page number, and Word field into the header.

File Needed: ***[your initials] PP W2-1.docx***
Completed Project File Name: ***[your initials] PP W2-2.docx***

1. Open the ***[your initials] PP W2-1*** document created in *Pause & Practice 2-1*.
2. Save this document as ***[your initials] PP W2-2***.

3. Edit the document properties.
   a. Click the **File** tab to open the *Backstage* view.
   b. In the *Info* area, click in the *Title* document property text box and type Richelle Wilkinson.
   c. Click the **Back** arrow to return to the resume.
4. Insert a document property field in the header of the resume.
   a. Place the insertion point at the beginning of the first page.
   b. Click the **Insert** tab.
   c. Click the **Header** button [*Header & Footer* group], and select **Edit Header** from the drop-down list. The header on the first page opens.
   d. Click the **Quick Parts** button [*Header & Footer Tools Design* tab, *Insert* group], select **Document Property**, and select **Title** from the drop-down list.
   e. Press the **right arrow** key once to deselect the document property field you just inserted.
   f. Press **Tab** two times to move to the right margin.
   g. Type Page and **space** once. Leave the header open.
5. Insert a page number and number of pages field to the header and make it display only on the second page.
   a. With the header still open, click the **Page Number** button [*Header & Footer* group].
   b. From the drop-down list, select **Current Position**, and then select **Plain Number**. The page number is inserted.
   c. **Space** once, type of, and **space** once.
   d. Click the **Quick Parts** button [*Header & Footer Tools Design* tab, *Insert* group] and select **Field** from the drop-down list. The *Field* dialog box opens (Figure 2-44).
   e. In the *Field names* area, scroll down and select **NumPages**. This is a field code to insert the total number of pages in the document.
   f. In the *Format* area, select **1, 2, 3**.
   g. Click **OK** to insert the number of pages in the header.
   h. Press **Enter** two times to insert two blank lines after the header.
   i. Check to ensure that there are spaces between each of the words and page numbers.
   j. Check the **Different First Page** check box [*Options* group]. This removes the page number from the first page; the page number is still displayed on the second and subsequent pages (Figure 2-45).

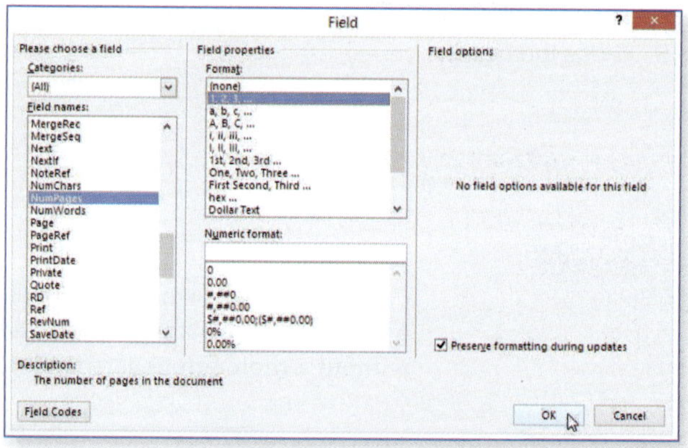

2-44 Insert *NumPages* field

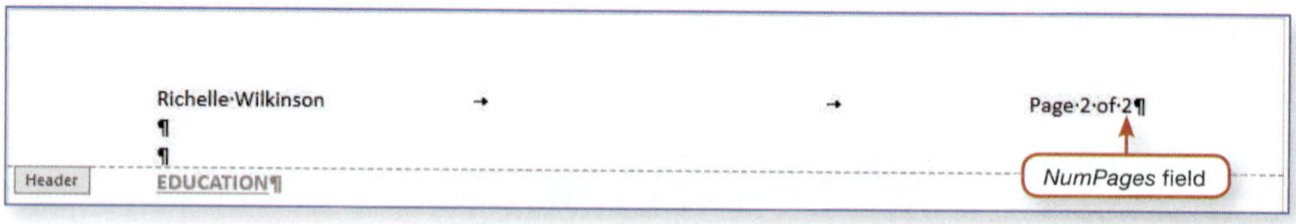

2-45 Header with custom text, page number, and number of pages

   k. Click the **Close Header and Footer** button [*Close* group] to close the header and return to the document.

6. Save and close the document (Figure 2-46).

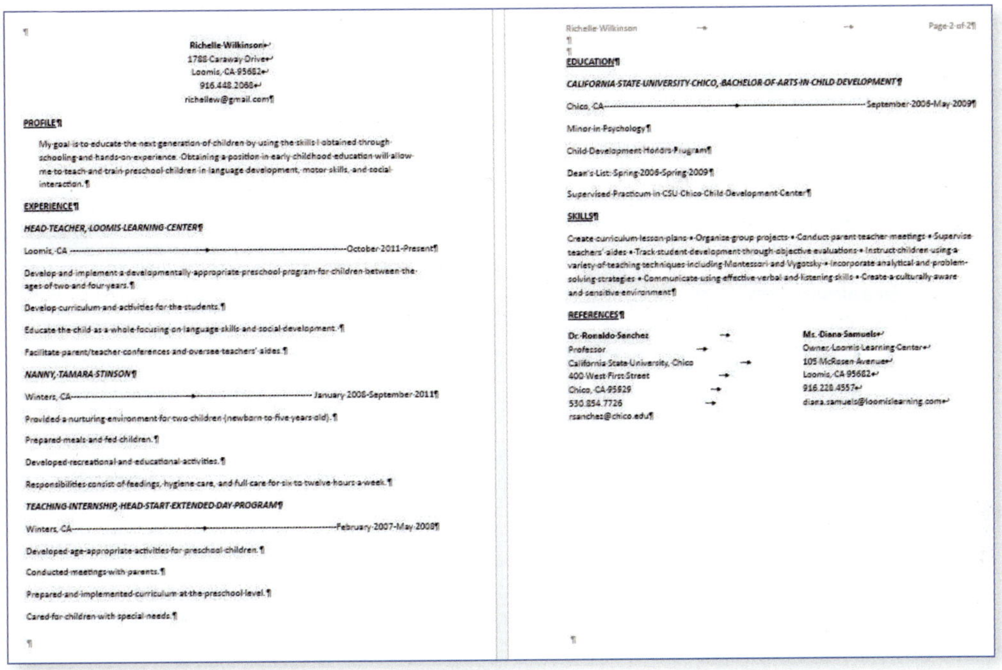

2-46 PP W2-2 completed

SLO 2.5

Using Page and Section Breaks

As you're typing a document and you get to the bottom of the page, Word automatically moves to the top of the next page so you can continue typing; this is referred to as a ***soft page break.*** The document's content and margins determine how much information fits on a page and what information flows to a new page.

There may be times when you want to start a new page before you get to the bottom margin or you might want different margins or page orientation in a different section of your document. When this happens, Word provides options for page and section breaks (Figure 2-47).

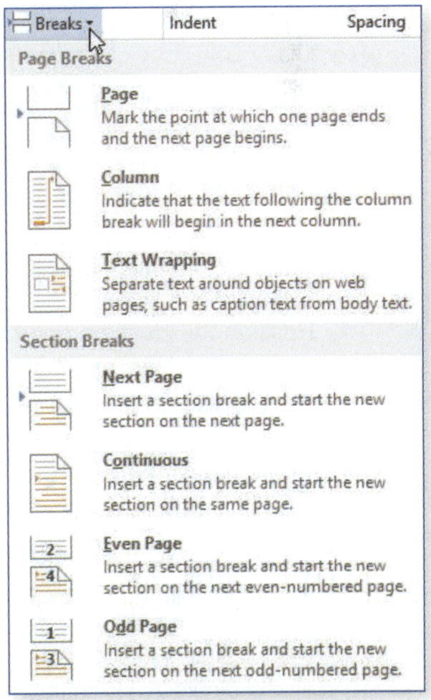

2-47 Page and section breaks

> **MORE INFO**
>
> Turn **Show/Hide** [*Home* tab, *Paragraph* group] on when working with page and section breaks, so you can view the placement of these breaks.

Page Breaks

Page breaks end one page and begin a new page. When you insert page breaks, you, rather than the margins, control where one page ends and a new page begins. There are three different types of page breaks: *Page*, *Column*, and *Text Wrapping*.

HOW TO: Insert a Page Break

1. Position the insertion point at the point in your document where you want to end one page and begin a new page.
2. Click the **Page Layout** tab.
3. Click the **Breaks** button [*Page Setup* group]. A drop-down list appears (Figure 2-48).
4. Select **Page** from the drop-down list. A page break is inserted in the document.
   - Make sure *Show/Hide* [*Home* tab, *Paragraph* group] is turned on.
   - The *Page Break* indicator is visible and displays where the page breaks (Figure 2-49).

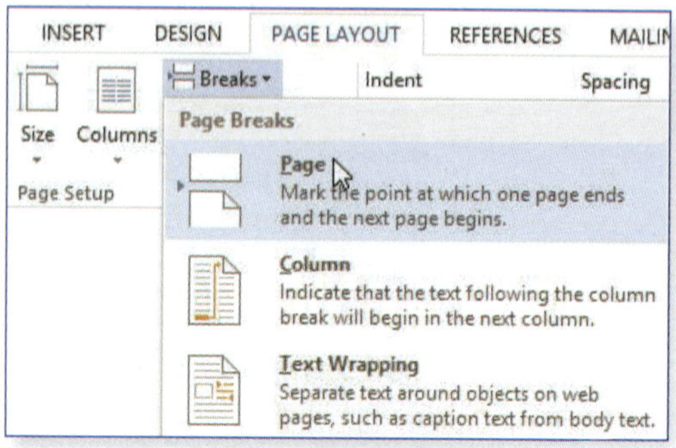

2-48 Insert page break

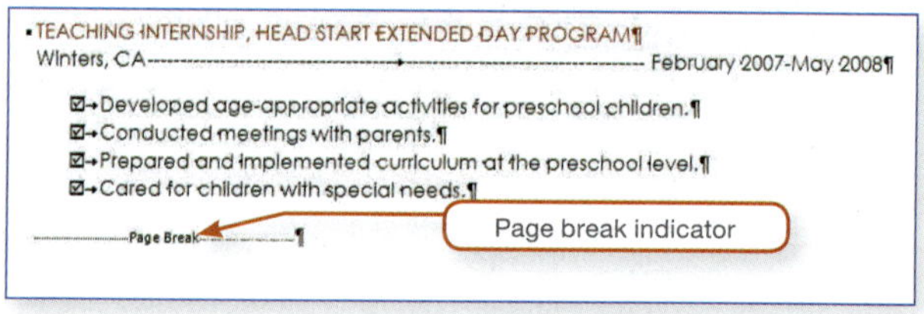

2-49 Page break inserted in a document

> **ANOTHER WAY**
>
> Press **Ctrl+Enter** to insert a page break at the insertion point.

Section Breaks

Section breaks allow you even more formatting control over your document than page breaks. Section breaks can be used to format different headers, footers, and page numbering in different sections of your document. For example, if you want one page in your document to be landscape orientation, you can use a section break to control this. There are four different types of section breaks: *Next Page*, *Continuous*, *Even Page*, and *Odd Page*.

HOW TO: Insert a Next Page Section Break

1. Position the insertion point at the point in your document where you want to end one page and begin a new page.
2. Click the **Page Layout** tab.
3. Click the **Breaks** button [*Page Setup* group]. A drop-down list appears.
4. Select **Next Page** from the drop-down list. A next page section break is inserted in the document.
   - Make sure *Show/Hide* [*Home* tab, *Paragraph* group] is turned on.
   - The *Section Break (Next Page)* indicator is visible and displays where the next page section break occurs (Figure 2-50).

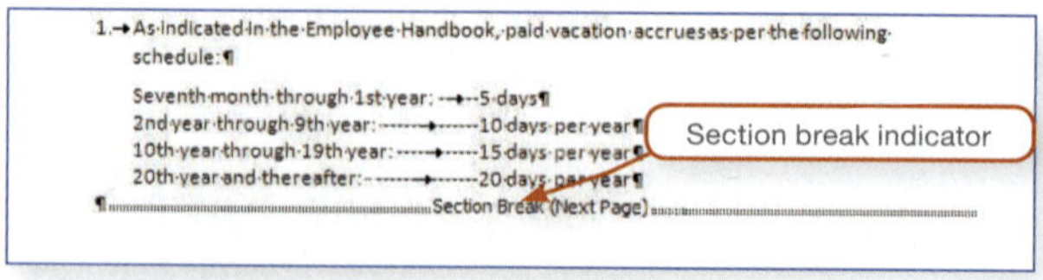

2-50 *Next Page* section break inserted in a document

Edit Page and Section Breaks

When finalizing a document, you might need to change the placement of a page or section break or remove one or more of these from the document. You can move and delete breaks in the same way you move or delete text from a document.

There are two different ways to move a section or page break to a new location. First select the **Page Break** or **Section Break**, and then use one of the move options below.

- Cut and paste
- Drag and drop (Figure 2-51)

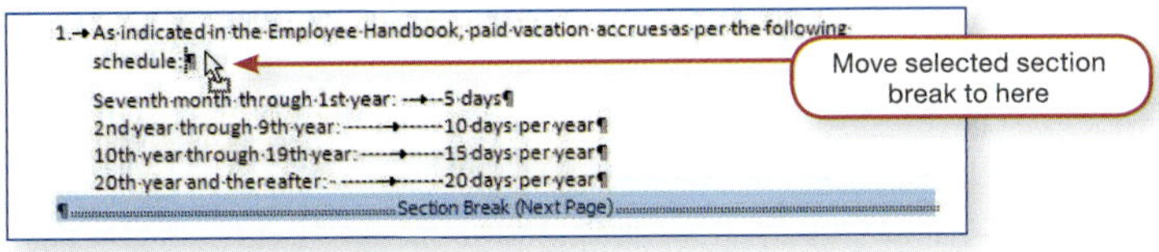

2.51 Move section break using drag and drop

To delete a page or section break, select the break and press **Delete**.

SLO 2.6

Using Bulleted and Numbered Lists

Bulleted and ***numbered lists*** highlight important information. Generally, bulleted lists are used when the order of information is not important, while numbered lists are used for sequential information. Word provides you with automatic bulleted and numbered lists, but you can also customize how your list information is displayed and aligned.

> **MORE INFO**
>
> When using bulleted and numbered lists, do not use a period at the end of lists containing only words or short phrases. If you are using complete sentences in your list, use a period at the end of each sentence.

Create Bulleted Lists

You can create a bulleted list from existing text or you can create a new bulleted list. When you turn on bullets, you choose the type of bullet to use from a library of bullet options.

HOW TO: Create a Bulleted List

1. Select the text to be converted to a bulleted list, or, if you are beginning a new bulleted list, place the insertion point at the location where you want to begin the list.
2. Click the **Home** tab.
3. Click the **Bullets** drop-down arrow [*Paragraph* group] to open the library of bullet options (Figure 2-52).
   - If you click the *Bullets* button, the most recently used bullet will be applied.
4. Select the bullet to be used from the list of options.
5. Type your information after the bullet.
6. Press **Enter** to add another bullet.
7. Click the **Bullet** button to turn off bullets or press **Enter** two times after the last bullet.

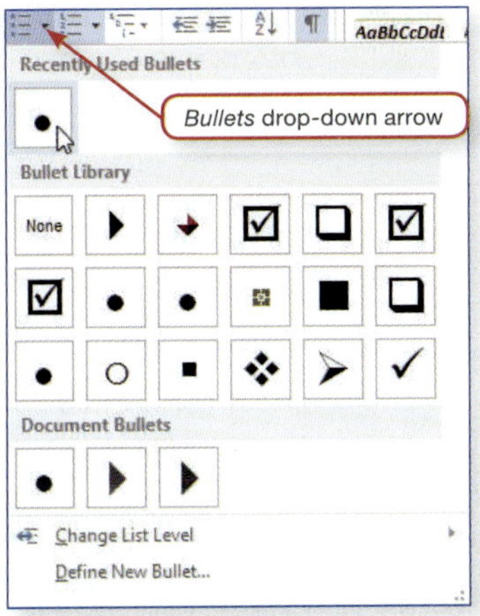

2-52 *Bullets* drop-down list

By default, bulleted lists are formatted using a hanging indent. The first line is indented 0.25" and the hanging indent is set at 0.5". You can adjust the indent using the *Decrease Indent* or *Increase Indent* buttons, ruler, or *Paragraph* dialog box.

You can add new bulleted items in the middle or at the end of the list by pressing **Enter** in front of or at the end of an existing bulleted item. To add a bulleted item before the first item in the list, click at the beginning of the first item and press **Enter**.

> **MORE INFO**
>
> You can use a line break (**Shift+Enter**) at the end of a bulleted sentence to add a blank line between bulleted items.

Customize Bullets

In addition to using the bullets listed in the bullets library, you can select and use a custom bullet. You have the option of using a symbol from one of the font groups or you can use a picture. If you are using a picture, you can select one from the picture library or import a graphic of your own to use as a bullet.

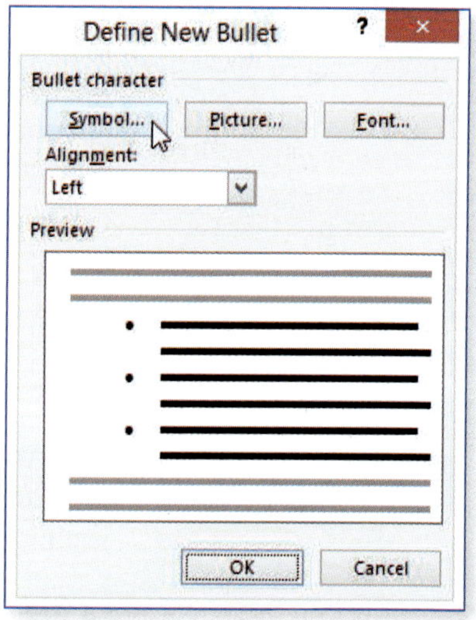

2-53 *Define New Bullet* dialog box

HOW TO: Use Custom Bullets

1. Click the **Bullets** drop-down arrow [*Home* tab, *Paragraph* group] and select **Define New Bullet**. The *Define New Bullet* dialog box opens (Figure 2-53).
2. Click the **Symbol** or **Picture** button to open the *Symbol* or *Picture Bullet* dialog box.
   - If you click the **Symbol** button, the *Symbol* dialog box opens (Figure 2-54). You can select a symbol from any of the font sets (the most common are *Symbol, Wingdings,* and *Webdings*) or from *Recently used symbols*.
   - If you click the **Picture** button, the *Insert Pictures* dialog box opens. You can import your own picture bullet from a file or search Office.com or Bing for a picture to use as a bullet.
3. Select the bullet to use and click **OK** (or **Insert** or **Open** depending on the open dialog box) to close the dialog box.
4. Click **OK** to close the *Define New Bullet* dialog box.

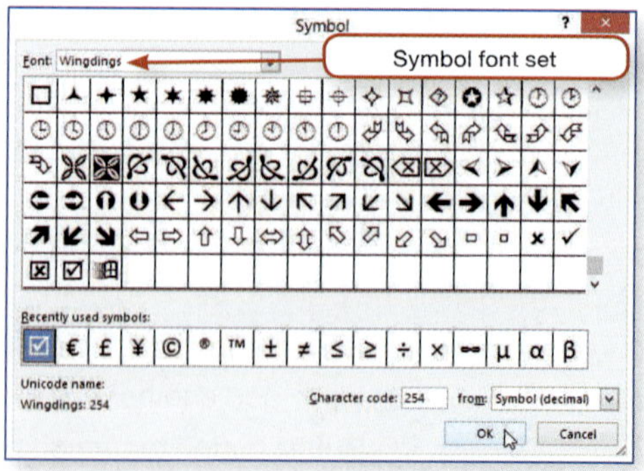

2-54 *Symbol* dialog box

You also have the option of having multiple levels of bullets with a different bullet for each level. Each subsequent level of bullet is indented to distinguish it from the previous level. There are a few ways to increase or decrease the bullet level.

- Click the **Bullets** drop-down arrow [*Home* tab, *Paragraph* group], and select a bullet list level from the **Change List Level** drop-down list (Figure 2-55).
- Select or click at the beginning of a bulleted item, and press **Tab** to increase bullet level.
- Select or click at the beginning of a bulleted item and click the **Increase Indent** button [*Home* tab, *Paragraph* group] to increase bullet level.

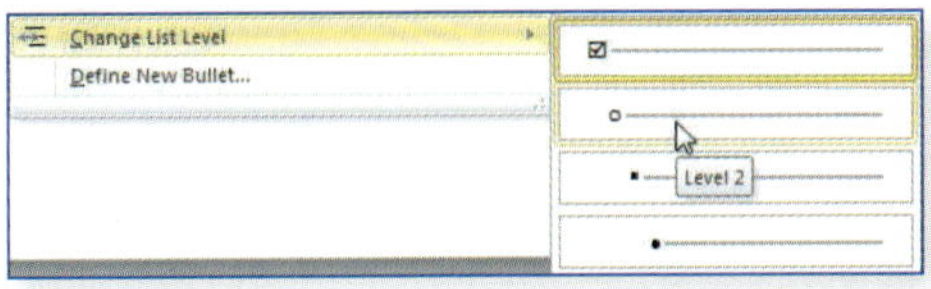

2-55 Change bulleted list level

MORE INFO

Shift+Tab or **Decrease Indent** decreases the bullet level.

Create Numbered Lists

Creating a numbered list is similar to creating a bulleted list. There is a ***Numbering Library*** that contains number format options.

HOW TO: Create a Numbered List

1. Select the text you want to convert to a numbered list, or, if you are beginning a new numbered list, place the insertion point at the location where you want to begin the list.
2. Click the **Home** tab.
3. Click the **Numbering** drop-down arrow [*Paragraph* group] to open the *Numbering Library* of number format options (Figure 2-56).
   - If you click the *Numbering* button, the most recently used number format is applied.
4. Select the number format to be used from the list of options. The number format is applied to selected text.

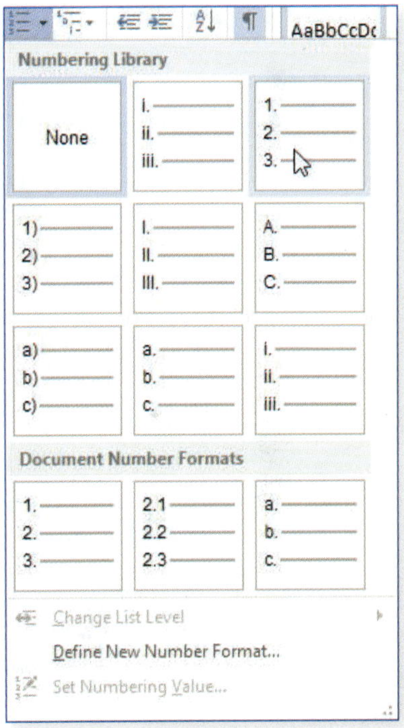

2-56 Number format options

ANOTHER WAY

Both the *Numbering* and *Bullets* drop-down lists are available from the context menu.

Customize Numbering

In addition to being able to select a format from the *Numbering Library*, you also have the options to *Change List Level*, *Define New Number Format*, and *Set Numbering Value*.

The *Change List Level* option in the *Numbering* drop-down list allows you to select the level of the list. The numbering of each subsequent level of the list is dependent upon the number format you select.

You are not limited to the numbering formats available in the *Numbering* drop-down list. The *Define New Number Format* option allows you to customize how the numbered list is displayed.

HOW TO: Define New Number Format

1. Select the text where you want to change the number format, or, if you are beginning a new numbered list, place the insertion point at the location where you want to begin the list.
2. Click the **Numbering** drop-down arrow [*Home* tab, *Paragraph* group], and select **Define New Number Format**. The *Define New Number Format* dialog box opens (Figure 2-57).
3. In the *Number style* area, you can select from a list of number format options. You can also change the font of the numbering.
4. In the *Number format* area, you can customize how the numbers are displayed. Typically, a period follows the numbers, but you can change this to an ending parenthesis, hyphen, other character, or nothing.
5. Numbers are aligned at the left by default, but you can change the number alignment to center or right in the *Alignment* area.
6. The *Preview* area displays how your number format will appear in your document.
7. Click **OK** to apply the number format and close the dialog box.

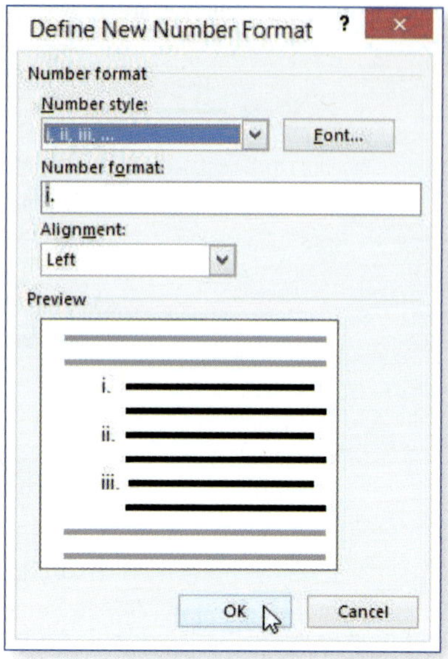

2-57 *Define New Number Format* dialog box

The *Set Numbering Value* option allows you to *Start new list* or *Continue from previous list*. You can also set the number value to begin a new list. The *Set Numbering Value* dialog box can be opened from the *Numbering* drop-down list or from the context menu (Figure 2-58).

When using numbering, the context menu gives you the options to *Adjust List Indents*, *Restart at 1*, *Continue Numbering*, and *Set Numbering Value* (Figure 2-59).

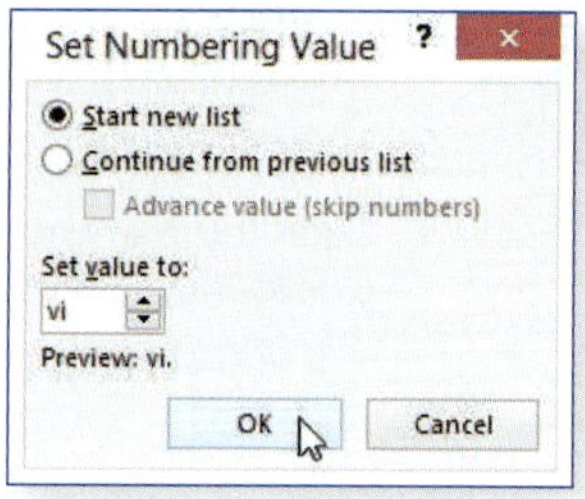

2-58 *Set Numbering Value* dialog box

> **MORE INFO**
>
> Use the *Format Painter* to copy numbered or bulleted list formatting to other areas in a document.

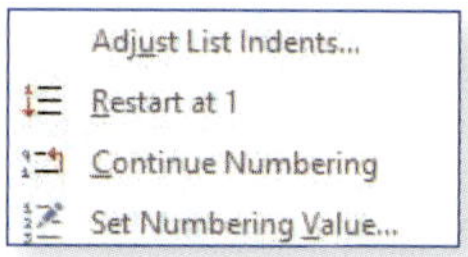

2-59 Context menu numbering options

Multilevel Lists

Multilevel lists allow you to customize a list using a combination of numbers, letters, or bullets. Word provides you with a *List Library* from which to select a multilevel list. You can customize an existing multilevel list or you can define your own.

As you define a new multilevel list, you have the option to make the following customizations on each level of the list.

- Number format including font and starting number
- Number style, which can be a number, letter, Roman numeral, or bullet
- Position of the number and the text that follows

HOW TO: Define a New Multilevel List

1. Select the text or the beginning point on which to apply a multilevel list.
2. Click the **Multilevel List** button [*Home* tab, *Paragraph* group].

3. From the drop-down list, select **Define new Multilevel list**. The *Define new Multilevel list* dialog box opens (Figure 2-60).
4. Click the **More** button at the bottom left of the dialog box to display all formatting options.
5. In the *Click level to modify* area, select the level you want to modify.
6. In the *Number format* area, select the number format, starting number, and number style for the selected level.
7. In the *Position* area, set the number alignment, the position at which the number is aligned, and the position of the text indent (which is a hanging indent).
8. The **Set for All Levels** button opens a dialog box that allows you to set the indents for all levels.
9. Click **OK** to apply the multilevel list settings.

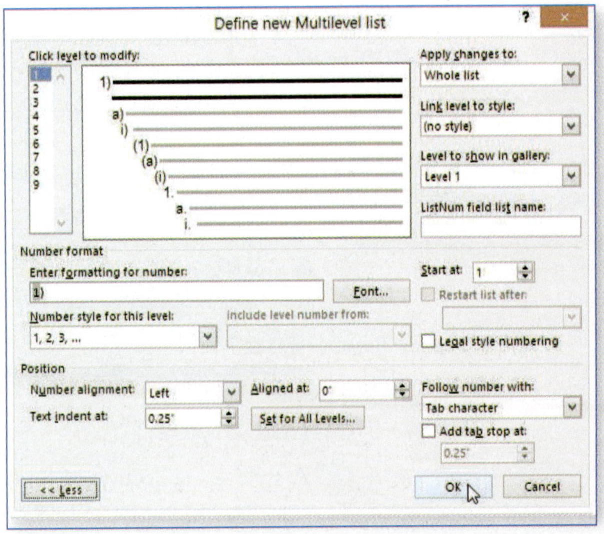

2-60 ***Define New Multilevel List*** **dialog box**

SLO 2.7

Using Styles and Themes

Styles are a collection of preset formatting that you can apply to selected text. You can use styles to apply preset formatting to titles, section headings, paragraph headings, text, lists, and tables. ***Themes*** are a collection of fonts, colors, and effects that you can apply to an entire document. Both styles and themes keep the formatting consistent throughout a single document or multiple documents.

Style Gallery

The ***Style gallery*** in the *Styles* group on the *Home* tab provides you with numerous built-in styles to apply to selected text in a document (Figure 2-61). The *Style* gallery does not display all of the available styles but rather a list of the more commonly used styles.

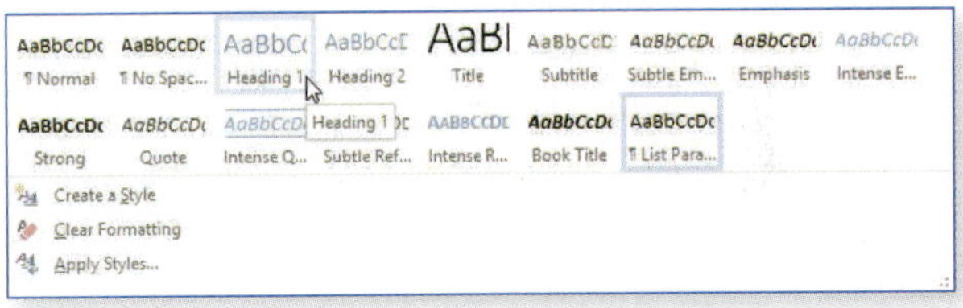

2-61 ***Style*** **gallery**

Apply Built-In Styles

You can quickly preview or apply styles to selected text or paragraphs. To preview a style, put the pointer on a style in the *Style* gallery. A live preview of the style is displayed on the selected text or paragraph. You can apply a style to the text by clicking a style.

HOW TO: Use the Style Gallery

1. Select the text or paragraph where you want to apply the style.
2. From the *Style* gallery [*Home* tab, *Styles* group], select a style to apply to the text.
   - To see the second row of styles available in the *Style* gallery, click the **down arrow** at the right side of the gallery (Figure 2-62).
   - To see all of the styles in the *Style* gallery, click the **More** button.

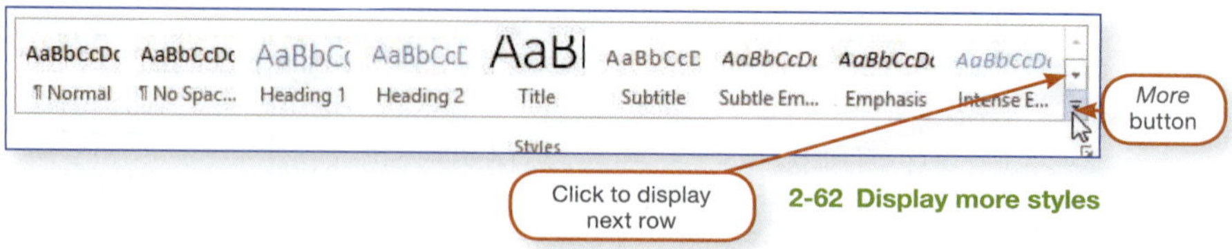

2-62 Display more styles

> **ANOTHER WAY**
>
> Apply a style to selected text by **right-clicking** the text, choosing **Styles** from the mini toolbar, and selecting the desired style to apply.

Edit Styles

A style is a collection of fonts, font sizes, styles, color, effects, indents, line spacing, paragraph spacing, and borders. Once a style has been applied to the text, you can change the formatting of this text. One way to do this is to make changes to font, font size, color, style, effects, etc. to the selected text without actually changing the style. The other option you have is to modify the style. The advantage of modifying a style when you make a change is that the style will be consistent when applied to text in a document. When a style is modified, existing text with that style applied is automatically updated to match the modified style.

There are two ways to modify a style.

- Update style to match selection
- Modify style

HOW TO: Update Style to Match Selection

1. Apply a style to selected text.
2. Make the desired changes to the text where the style was applied.
3. Select the text that you changed.
4. Right-click the style in the *Style* gallery and choose **Update *[name of style]* to Match Selection** (Figure 2-63).

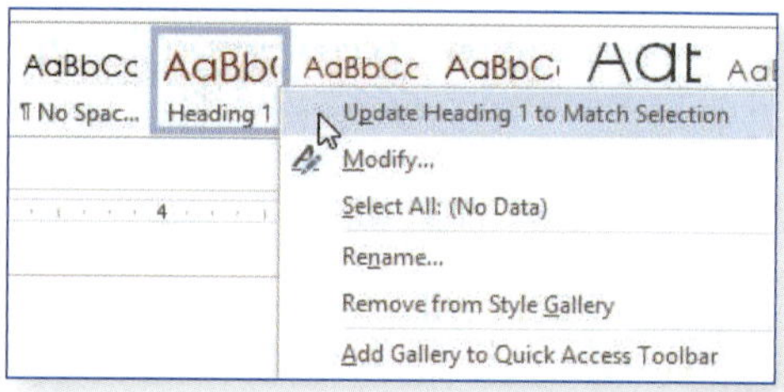

2-63 Update style from the *Style* gallery

You can also modify a style using the *Modify Style* dialog box.

HOW TO: Modify an Existing Style

1. Right-click the style to modify in the *Style* gallery and select **Modify**. The *Modify Style* dialog box opens (Figure 2-64).
2. Make desired changes to the style. You can make basic formatting changes from this dialog box.
   - Click the **Format** button to open other dialog boxes, such as *Font, Paragraph, Tabs, Borders,* etc.
   - Click **OK** to apply changes from another dialog box.
   - The formatting changes are shown and described in the *Preview* area.
3. Click **OK** to apply the style change and close the *Modify Style* dialog box.

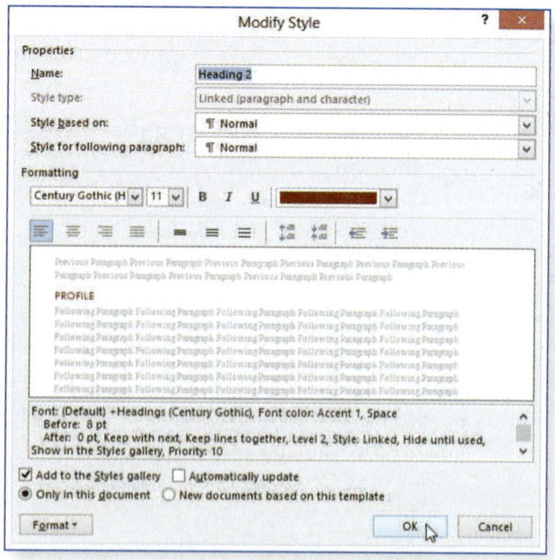

2-64 *Modify Style* dialog box

Apply Themes

A theme is a collection of fonts, colors, and effects. Themes are similar to styles, but instead of applying to just selected text, themes apply to an entire document. All documents have a theme; the default theme for a new document is *Office*. You can change the theme of a document or you can individually change the colors, fonts, or effects set in a document.

HOW TO: Change the Document Theme

1. Click the **Design** tab.
2. Click the **Themes** button [*Document Formatting* group].
3. From the *Themes* gallery, select the theme to be applied (Figure 2-65).
4. You can also click the **Colors**, **Fonts**, or **Effects** buttons to change each of these individually within the existing theme.

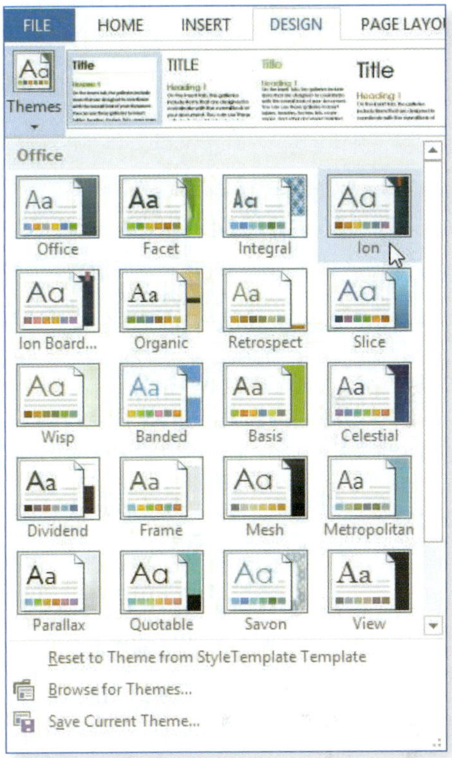

2-65 Change the theme of a document

PAUSE & PRACTICE: WORD 2-3

In this Pause & Practice project, you modify the resume you edited in *Pause & Practice 2-2*. You add a bulleted list, customize the bulleted list, insert a page break, apply and modify styles, and apply a document theme.

File Needed: ***[your initials] PP W2-2.docx***
Completed Project File Name: ***[your initials] PP W2-3.docx***

1. Open the ***[your initials] PP W2-2*** document created in *Pause & Practice 2-2*.
2. Save this document as ***[your initials] PP W2-3***.
3. Convert text to bulleted list and customize the bullet.
   a. Select the four paragraphs of text below the "Experience" heading and the city, state, and date line.
   b. Click the **Bullets** button [*Home* tab, *Paragraph* group]. The selected text is converted to a bulleted list (Figure 2-66).

c. With the bulleted paragraphs still selected, click the **Bullets** drop-down arrow, and select **Define New Bullet**. The *Define New Bullet* dialog box opens.
d. Click the **Symbol** button. The *Symbol* dialog box opens (Figure 2-67).
e. Click the **Font** drop-down list and scroll down to select **Wingdings**.
f. In the list of symbols, scroll down and select the **check box** symbol (*Character code 254*).
g. Click **OK** to close the *Symbol* dialog box.
h. Click **OK** to close the *Define New Bullet* dialog box.

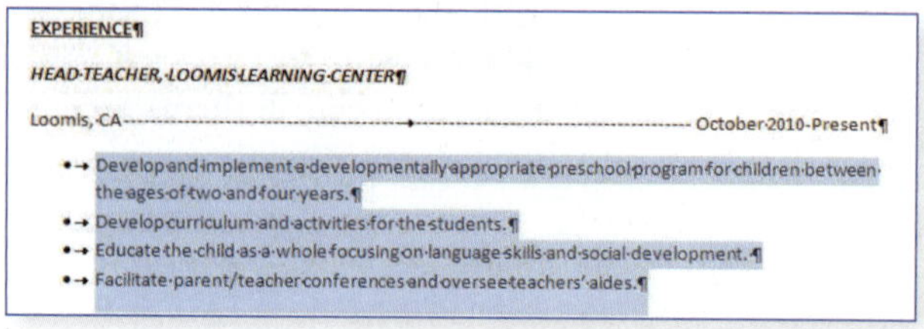

2-66 Apply bullets to selected text

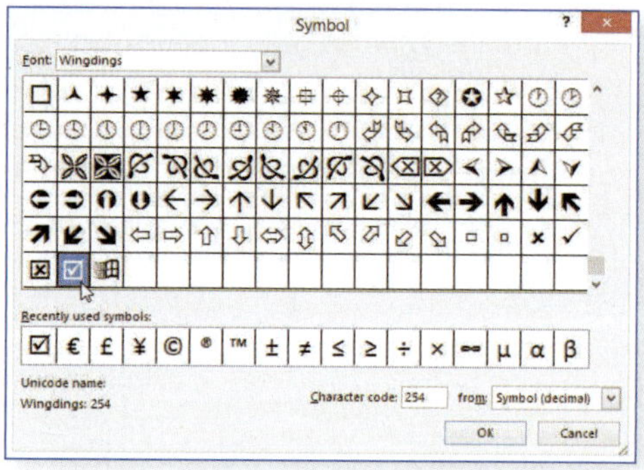

2-67 *Symbol* dialog box

4. Use the *Format Painter* to apply this bullet format to lines of text in the other "Experience" sections and the "Education" section. Don't apply bullet formatting to the city, state, and date lines with the tab stop and leader applied.
5. Insert a page break in the document.
   a. Turn on the **Show/Hide** feature [*Home* tab, *Paragraph* group].
   b. Place the insertion point in front of the "Education" heading.
   c. Click the **Page Layout** tab.
   d. Click the **Breaks** button [*Page Setup* group].
   e. From the drop-down list select **Page** in the *Page Breaks* section. A page break is inserted at the bottom of the first page and the "Education" section is pushed to the next page.

ANOTHER WAY

Ctrl+Enter inserts a page break.

6. Change the theme of the document.
   a. Click the **Design** tab.
   b. Click the **Themes** button [*Document Formatting* group].
   c. Scroll down the list of themes and select **Ion**.
7. Apply styles from the *Style* gallery to text.
   a. On the first page of the letter, select **"Richelle Wilkinson"** and click the **Title** style from the *Style* gallery [*Home* tab].
   b. With this text still selected, change the font size to **20 pt**.
   c. Apply the **Heading 1** style to each of the main headings ("Profile," "Experience," "Education," "Skills," and "References").
   d. Apply the **Heading 2** style to each of the bold and italicized subheadings in the "Experience" and "Education" sections.
8. Modify a style.
   a. Select the **"Profile"** heading.
   b. Change the *Before* paragraph spacing to **16 pt**.

c. Right-click the **Heading 1** style in the *Style* gallery and select **Update Heading 1 to Match Selection** (Figure 2-68). This style change is applied to all text with *Heading 1* style.
d. On the second page, select **"CALIFORNIA STATE UNIVERSITY CHICO, BACHELOR OF ARTS IN CHILD DEVELOPMENT"** and change the font size to **11 pt**.
e. Right-click the **Heading 2** style in the *Style* gallery and select **Update Heading 2 to Match Selection**.

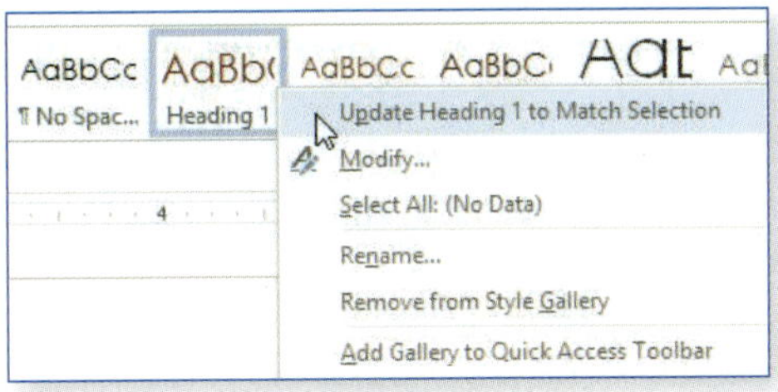

2-68 Update style to match selection

9. Save and close the document (Figure 2-69).

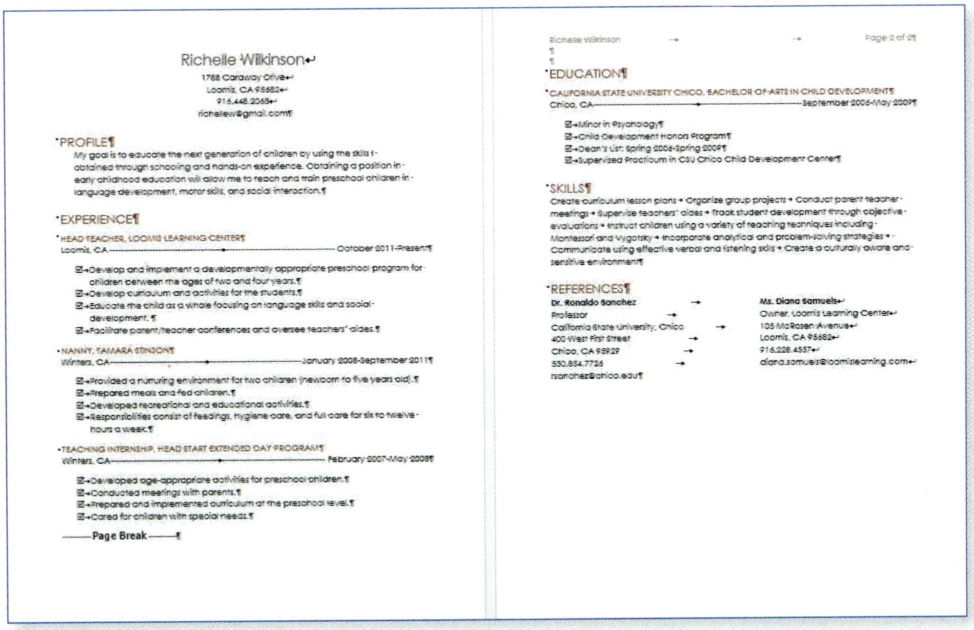

2-69 PP W2-3 completed

SLO 2.8

Using Find and Replace

Find and ***Replace*** are two extremely useful and powerful tools in Word. The *Find* feature allows you to search for and locate words and phrases in a document. The *Replace* feature allows you to search for a word or phrase and replace it with other text. You can also use *Find* and *Replace* to search for a specific type of formatting in a document and replace it with different formatting. These features are particularly useful in longer documents.

Find

You can use the *Navigation* pane in Word to search for text and display all instances of the matching text. Word highlights in yellow each instance of the matching text in the document. You are able to navigate through the document, see each instance, and make edits as desired.

HOW TO: Use Find in the Navigation Pane

1. Click the **Find** button [*Home* tab, *Editing* group]. The *Navigation* pane is displayed at the left side of the Word window.
2. Click in the **Search Document** text box at the top of the *Navigation* pane and type in the text you want to search. The matching results are displayed below the text box and the matching text in the document is highlighted.
3. Click the **Next** or **Previous** search result buttons to move through each matching instance in the document (Figure 2-70). You can also click the matching instances below the *Search Document* text box to go to a specific occurrence of the matching text.

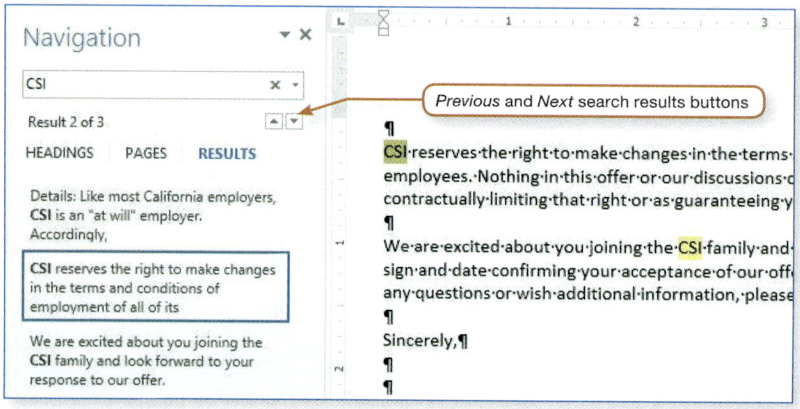

2-70 Use *Find* in the *Navigation* pane

4. Edit the highlighted text in the document if you want to make changes.
5. Click the **X** to the right of the *Search Document* text box to clear the current search.
6. Click the **X** in the upper right of the *Navigation* pane to close the pane.

ANOTHER WAY

Ctrl+F opens the *Find* feature in the *Navigation* pane.

Find and Replace

The ***Find and Replace*** dialog box gives you three different advanced options for searching your document.

- Find
- Replace
- Go To

The *Find* tab of the *Find and Replace* dialog box not only searches for text in your document but also searches for specific formatting (such as font styles, line spacing, or paragraph spacing). For example, you can search for all text that is bold or italic, or that has 6 pt. after paragraph spacing.

Using the *Replace* feature you can search for text, formatting, or a combination of text and formatting and replace the matching text with other text, formatting, or formatted text. This feature is a quick and efficient way to find and replace information in a document.

HOW TO: Use Replace

1. Click the **Replace** button [*Home* tab, *Editing* group] or press **Ctrl+H**. The *Find and Replace* dialog box opens with the *Replace* tab displayed (Figure 2-71).
2. Click in the **Find what** text box and type the text for which you are searching.
3. Click in the **Replace with** text box and type the text you want to replace the found text.
4. Click the **More** button to display advanced find options. The *Less* button hides the advanced find options.
5. Click the **Format** or **Special** button to add formatting options or special characters to either the text for which you are searching or the replacement text.
6. When the first occurrence is found you have the options to *Replace* (this occurrence), *Replace All* (all occurrences), or *Find Next* (skip this occurrence without replacing and move on to the next).
7. Click the **Find Next** button to move to the next occurrence of the matching text and formatting.
8. When you finish finding and replacing text in the document, a dialog box opens informing you that Word has finished searching the document. Click **OK** to close this dialog box.
9. Click the **X** in the upper right corner to close the *Find and Replace* dialog box.

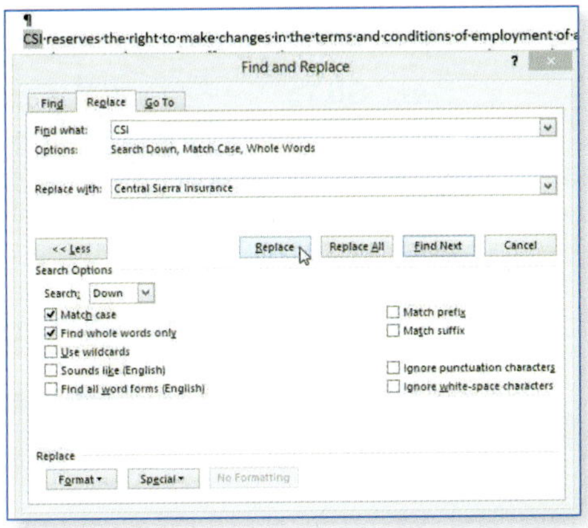

2-71 Replace text

When using *Find* or *Replace*, wildcards can be used to help find information. You can use wildcards before, after, or between words.

- Use the question mark (?) as a wildcard for a single character. For example, ***w???*** finds any words that begins with "w" and contains four letters (e.g., when, with, or wish).
- Use an asterisk (*) as a wildcard for a string of characters. For example, **search*** finds any form of the word "search" (e.g., searches, searching, or searched).

ANOTHER WAY

Ctrl+H opens the *Find and Replace* dialog box.

MORE INFO

It is a good idea to use **Match Case** when replacing acronyms (capital letters) with words so the replaced words will not be all upper case. Also, use **Find whole words only** to refine your search.

Go To

The ***Go To*** feature allows you to go quickly to specific items in your document. This feature is available in the *Find and Replace* dialog box. This feature is different from *Find* in that *Go To* moves you to specific objects in your document such as a page, section, or bookmark.

HOW TO: Use the Go To Feature

1. Click the **Find** drop-down arrow [*Home* tab, *Editing* group].
2. Select **Go To**. The *Find and Replace* dialog box opens with the *Go To* tab displayed (Figure 2-72).
3. In the *Go to what* area, select the item to go to from the list of options. The text box to the right is context sensitive and changes depending on the item chosen.
4. In the text box to the right, type in a page number, section, line, etc.
5. Click the **Go To** button.
6. Click **Close** to close this dialog box.

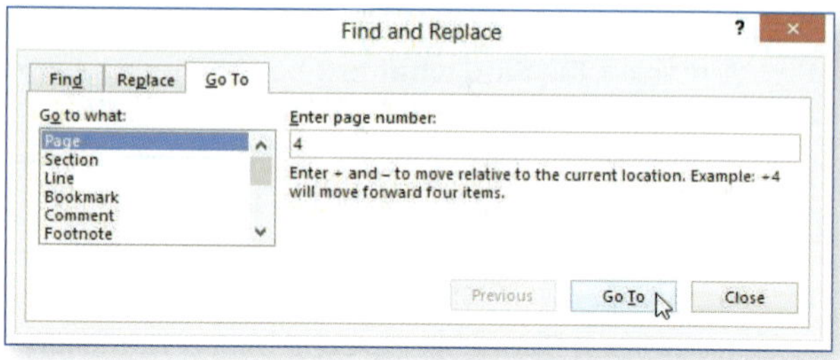

2-72 *Go To* in the *Find and Replace* dialog box

ANOTHER WAY

Ctrl+G or **F5** opens the *Find and Replace* dialog box with the *Go To* tab selected.

SLO 2.9

Using Borders, Shading, and Hyperlinks

Borders and ***shading*** are excellent ways to set off or emphasize important information in a document. In Word, there are many different border and shading options including many preset border options. You also have the option of applying custom borders and shading to selected text or areas of your document.

A ***hyperlink*** functions like a button and can be used to take a reader to a web page, open an existing or new document, open an email message, or take a reader to another location in the current document. You can add a hyperlink to text or a graphic in a document.

Apply Built-In Borders

You can use the built-in border options to quickly apply borders to selected text. Borders are typically applied to paragraphs, but they can also be applied to other selected text. Borders are, by default, applied to the paragraph where your insertion point is unless specific text is selected.

The built-in borders are available from the *Borders* button in the *Paragraph* group on the *Home* tab. Figure 2-73 shows the different types of built-in borders.

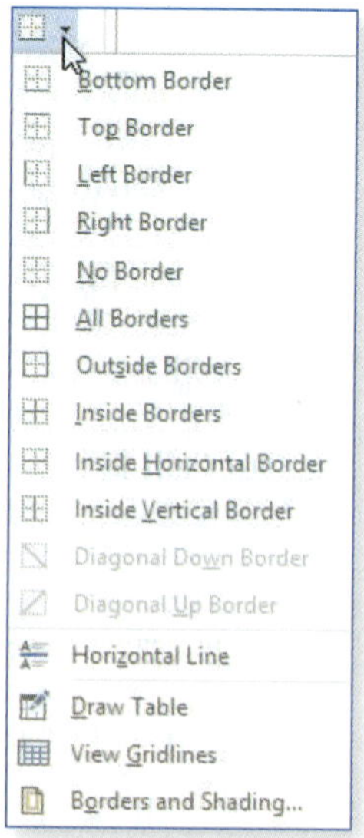

2-73 *Borders* drop-down list

HOW TO: Apply Built-In Borders

1. Select the paragraph or place the insertion point in the paragraph where you want to apply the border.
2. Click the **Home** tab.
3. Click the **Borders** drop-down arrow [*Paragraph* group] (Figure 2-73).
4. Click the border option to apply to the paragraph.

MORE INFO

You can remove borders by selecting the paragraph or text on which the border is applied and clicking the **No Border** option in the *Borders* drop-down list.

Customize Borders

The ***Borders and Shading*** dialog box gives you many more options to customize the type of border you use. Not only can you customize the style, width, and color of border line, but also you can customize where the border is placed in relation to the selected text. The *Borders and Shading* dialog box is available from the *Borders* drop-down list in the *Paragraph* group on the *Home* tab.

HOW TO: Apply Custom Borders

1. Select the paragraph(s) you want to border.
2. Click the **Borders** drop-down arrow [*Home* tab, *Paragraph* group] and choose the **Borders and Shading** option at the bottom of the list. The *Borders and Shading* dialog box opens (Figure 2-74).
3. In the *Setting* area, select the type of border to use. Your options are *None, Box, Shadow, 3-D,* and *Custom.*
4. In the *Style* area, select a style of the line from the list of options.
5. In the *Color* area, select line color.
6. In the *Width* area, select the width of the border line. The width of the line is measured in points.
7. The *Preview* area shows you how the border will appear in your document.
   - You can turn on or off a specific border by either clicking any of the border buttons in the *Preview* area or clicking the border itself.
8. Click the **Options** button to open the *Borders and Shading Options* dialog box (Figure 2-75). This dialog box gives you the option to add in additional space (padding) between the border and the text at the *Top, Bottom, Left,* and *Right*. The spacing is measured in points.
9. Click **OK** to close the *Borders and Shading Options* dialog box.
10. Click **OK** to close the *Borders and Shading* dialog box.

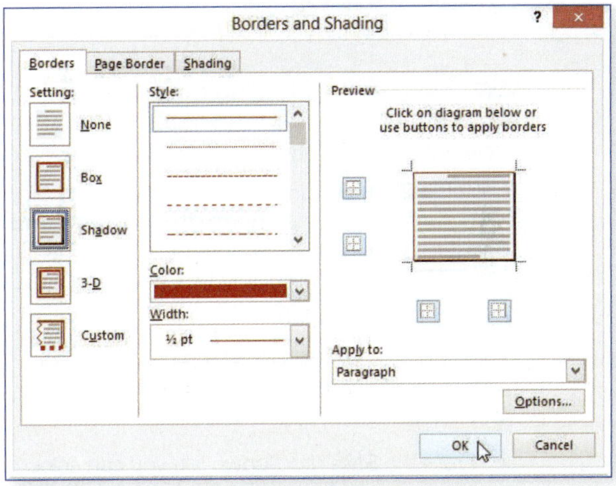

2-74 *Borders and Shading* dialog box

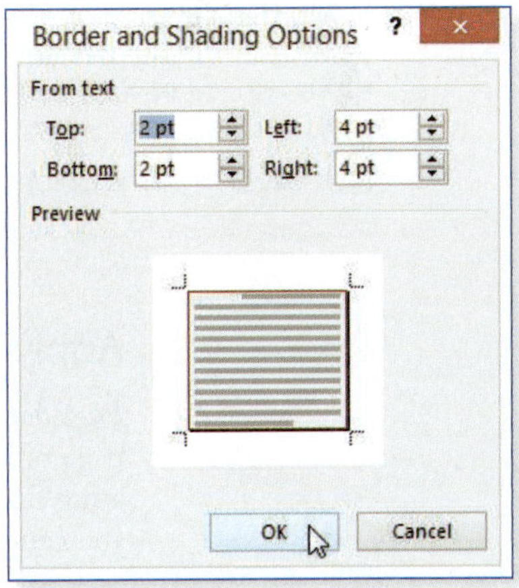

2-75 *Border and Shading Options* dialog box

MORE INFO

When you use the *Borders* button [*Paragraph* group], the last border you choose becomes the function of the *Borders* button. For example, if you last applied a bottom border, you can apply a bottom border again by clicking the **Borders** button.

Apply Shading

2-76 Shading color options from the *Shading* drop-down list

Applying shading to a paragraph or text is very similar to applying borders. The *Shading* option is available from the *Shading* button in the *Paragraph* group on the *Home* tab or in the *Borders and Shading* dialog box on the *Shading* tab.

The shading colors available are dependent upon the theme of the document. In the *Shading* drop-down list, you can select from *Theme Colors* or *Standard Colors* (Figure 2-76). If you want a color that is not available in the menu, you can click *More Colors* to select from a color palette.

HOW TO: Apply Shading from the Borders and Shading Dialog Box

1. Select the paragraph(s) you want to shade.
2. Click the **Borders** drop-down arrow [*Home* tab, *Paragraph* group] and choose the **Borders and Shading** option at the bottom of the list. The *Borders and Shading* dialog box opens (Figure 2-77).
3. Click the **Shading** tab.
4. In the *Fill* area, select a shading color.
5. In the *Patterns* area, you can select a shading *Style* and *Color*.
   - From the *Style* drop-down list, you can select a gradient percent or a fill pattern as the shading style.
   - From the *Color* drop-down list, you can select a fill color for the gradient or pattern you selected.
   - You do not have to use a pattern style or color for shading. Usually just a fill color is sufficient.
6. Click **OK** to close the *Borders and Shading* dialog box.

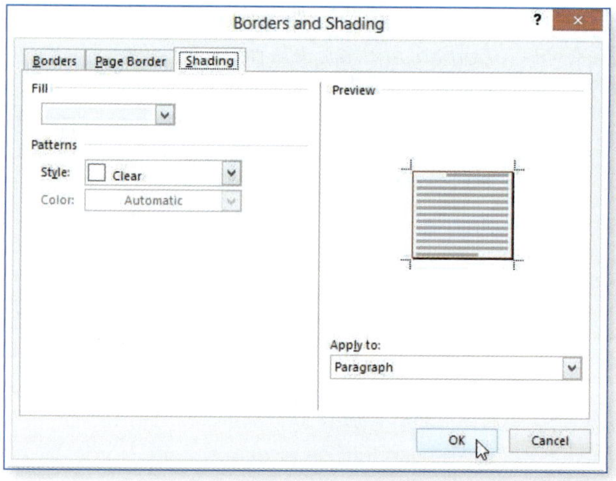

2-77 Shading options in the *Borders and Shading* dialog box

Apply a Page Border

Page borders are different from paragraph or text borders; a page border is around the entire page rather than selected paragraphs or text. Page borders are useful and attractive when creating flyers or handouts. A page border can be a line with varying styles, widths, and colors, or you can use art graphics as a page border.

HOW TO: Apply a Page Border

1. Click the **Design** tab.
2. Click the **Page Borders** button [*Page Background* group]. The *Borders and Shading* dialog box opens with the *Page Border* tab displayed (Figure 2-78).
3. In the *Setting* area, select the type of page border you want to apply.

4. You can select either a page border *Style* or *Art* from the drop-down lists.
5. You can change the *Color* and *Width* as desired.
6. In the *Preview* area, you can customize how the page border appears by turning on or off top, bottom, left, or right borders.
7. In the *Apply to* area, you can select the page(s) where you want to apply the page border. Your options are:
   - *Whole document*
   - *This section*
   - *This section – First page only*
   - *This section – All except first page*
8. Click **OK** to close the *Borders and Shading* dialog box.

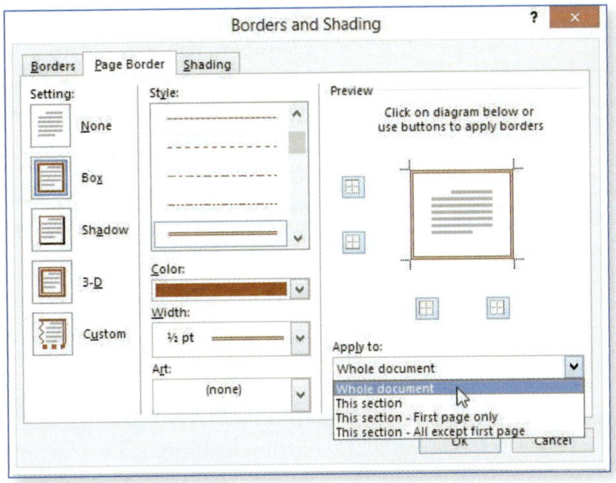

2-78 Apply a page border

MORE INFO

When you apply a page border, the text in the document is not affected because the page border is placed outside the margin boundaries.

Insert a Horizontal Line

In addition to being able to insert top and bottom borders on selected text, you can also insert a ***horizontal line*** to use as a border to separate information on a page. A horizontal line is actually a graphic that is inserted into the document. When you insert a horizontal line, the line is the width of the page. More information about using and customizing graphics is covered in *SLO 4.5: Working with Graphics.*

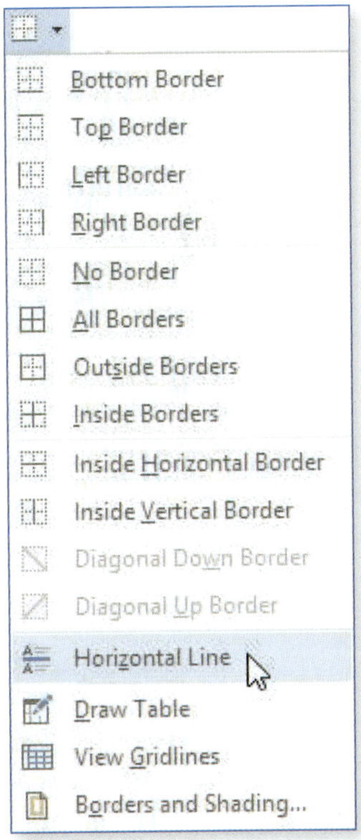

2-79 Insert a horizontal line

HOW TO: Insert a Horizontal Line

1. Place your insertion point in the document where you want a horizontal line.
2. Click the **Borders** drop-down arrow *[Home* tab, *Paragraph* group].
3. Select **Horizontal Line** from the drop-down list (Figure 2-79).
   - The horizontal line is treated as a separate paragraph and has a paragraph mark to the right.

Create a Hyperlink

A hyperlink is an excellent way to direct users to information on a web site, another document, or a location in the same document. You can also create a hyperlink for an email address, which automatically opens a new Outlook email message addressed to the recipient. You can create a hyperlink by selecting the text or figure you want to turn into a hyperlink and then providing the information about the online location where the user will be directed. You can also customize the ScreenTip and the target frame.

> **MORE INFO**
>
> Typically, hyperlinks are underlined and a different color to distinguish them from regular text in a document. In a Word document, **Ctrl+Click** opens a hyperlink.

The ***ScreenTip*** is the text that is displayed when you place your pointer over the hyperlink in the document. The ***target frame*** is the window where the hyperlink document or web site opens. There are many different target frame options from which to choose. Usually it is best to choose **New window** if the link is to a different document or a web page. An email message always opens in a new window.

HOW TO: Create a Hyperlink

1. Select the text or graphic where you want to create a hyperlink.
2. Click the **Insert** tab.
3. Click the **Hyperlink** button [*Links* group]. The *Insert Hyperlink* dialog box opens (*Figure 2-80*).
4. In the *Link to* area, select the type of hyperlink you want to create. Your options are:
    - *Existing File or Web Page*
    - *Place in This Document*
    - *Create New Document*
    - *E-mail Address*
5. The text you selected in the document as the hyperlink is displayed in the *Text to display* area. If you type other text in this text box, it will replace the text you selected in the document.
6. Select the file to link to in the *Look in* area, or type a web address in the *Address* area.
    - If you are linking to a file, you can browse your computer in the *Look in* area to locate and select the file.
    - If you are linking to a place in the document, you are given a list of headings and bookmarks from which to choose.
    - If you are inserting a link to create a new document, you are given options for the new document.
    - If you are linking to an email address, you type in the email address and are given the option to create a subject line for the email.
7. Click the **ScreenTip** button to insert text that will be displayed when the pointer is placed over the hyperlink (Figure 2-81).
8. Type the ScreenTip text.
9. Click **OK** to close the *Set Hyperlink ScreenTip* dialog box.

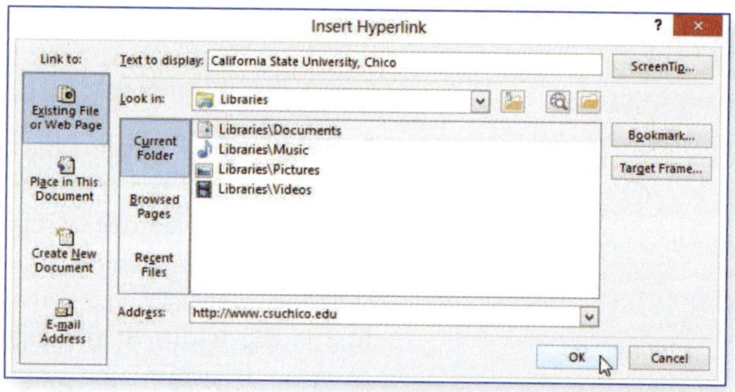

2-80 *Insert Hyperlink* dialog box

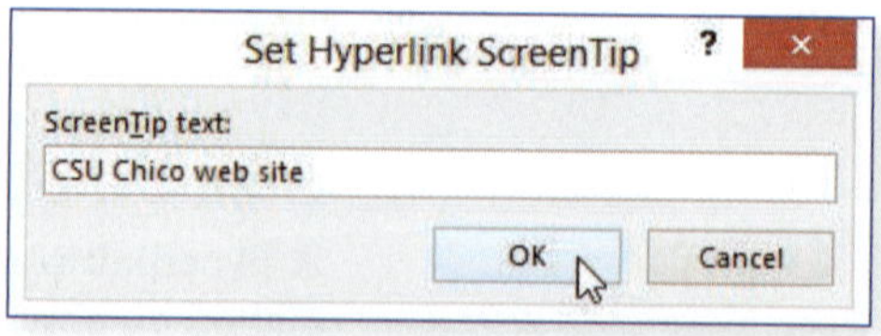

2-81 *Set Hyperlink ScreenTip* dialog box

10. Click the **Target Frame** button to open the *Set Target Frame* dialog box (Figure 2-82)
    - From the drop-down list of options, select where the hyperlink destination will be opened .
    - The *Set as default for all hyperlinks* check box allows you to make your target frame selection the default for all hyperlinks in your document.
11. Click **OK** to close the *Set Target Frame* dialog box.
12. Click **OK** to insert the hyperlink and close the *Insert Hyperlink* dialog box.

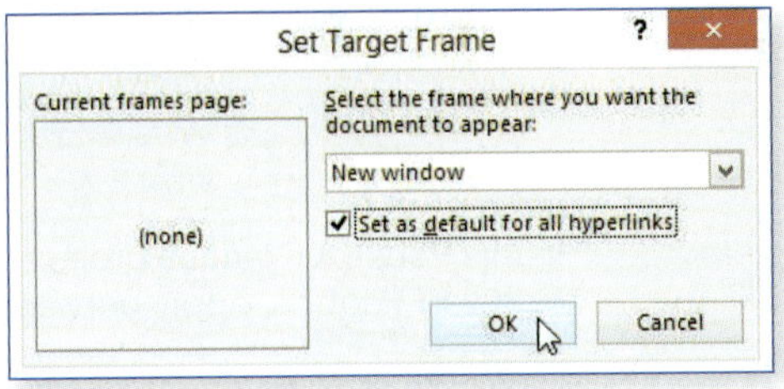

2-82 *Set Target Frame* dialog box

ANOTHER WAY

Ctrl+K opens the *Insert Hyperlink* dialog box.

Edit or Remove a Hyperlink

There might be times when you have incorporated text from a web site or another document that includes hyperlinks to a document, or you might want to edit a hyperlink in an existing document. Word allows you to quickly edit hyperlinks to change hyperlink information, add a ScreenTip, or change the target frame.

HOW TO: Edit a Hyperlink

1. Select or click the hyperlink to be edited.
2. Click the **Hyperlink** button [*Insert* tab, *Links* group]. You can also press **Ctrl+K** or right-click the selected hyperlink and select **Edit Hyperlink**. The *Edit Hyperlink* dialog box opens.
3. Make the desired changes to the hyperlink information or options.
4. Click **OK** to close the *Edit Hyperlink* dialog box.

You can quickly remove a hyperlink from a document without deleting the text in the document. When you remove a hyperlink from existing text, the text is not deleted. Only the hyperlink attached to the text is deleted.

HOW TO: Remove a Hyperlink

1. Select or click the hyperlink to be removed.
2. Click the **Hyperlink** button [*Insert* tab, *Links* group] or press **Ctrl+K** to open the *Edit Hyperlink* dialog box (Figure 2-83).
3. Click the **Remove Link** button.
4. Click **OK** to close the *Edit Hyperlink* button.

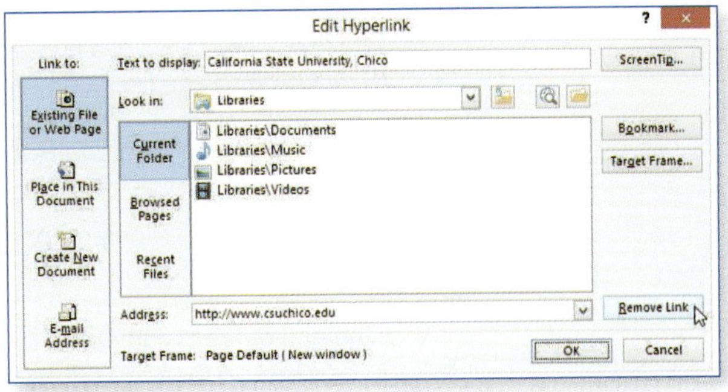

2-83 Remove hyperlink

ANOTHER WAY

Right-click a hyperlink and select **Remove Hyperlink**.

PAUSE & PRACTICE: WORD 2-4

In this Pause & Practice project, you finalize the resume you worked on in *Pause & Practice 2-3*. You use *Find and Replace,* apply borders and shading to selected text, and add hyperlinks to the document.

File Needed: ***[your initials] PP W2-3.docx***
Completed Project File Name: ***[your initials] PP W2-4.docx***

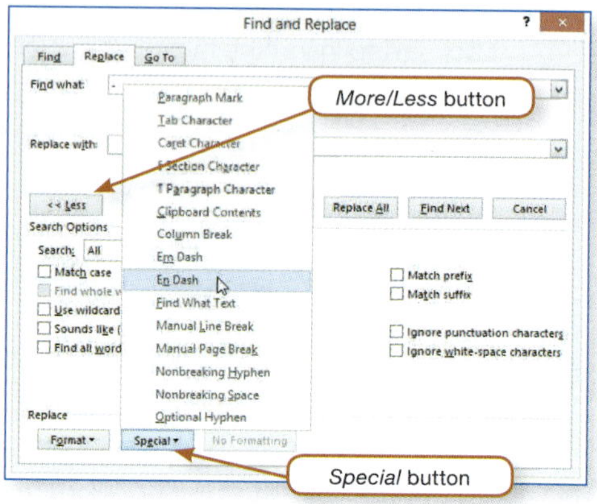

2-84 Use Find and Replace

1. Open the ***[your initials] PP W2-3*** document created in *Pause & Practice 2-3*.
2. Save this document as ***[your initials] PP W2-4.***
3. Use *Find and Replace* to replace the hyphen between dates with an en dash.
   a. Press **Ctrl+Home** to move to the top of the document.
   b. Click the **Replace** button [*Home* tab, *Editing* group] or press **Ctrl+H** to open the *Find and Replace* dialog box (Figure 2-84).
   c. Type - (hyphen) in the *Find what* text box.
   d. Place the insertion point in the *Replace with* text box.
   e. Click the **More** button if the *Search Options* are not already displayed.
   f. Click the **Special** button and select **En Dash**.
   g. Click the **Less** button to make the **Find and Replace** dialog box smaller.
   h. Click the **Find Next** button to locate the first instance of the text for which you are searching.

> **MORE INFO**
>
> Word highlights each found occurrence. If you need to, you can move the *Find and Replace* dialog box to view highlighted text.

   i. Choose **Find Next** to skip the hyphenated word in the first paragraph.
   j. Click the **Replace** button to replace the hyphen between the dates with an en dash.
   k. Choose **Replace** to replace each occurrence of a hyphen between dates; choose **Find Next** to skip and not replace each occurrence of a hyphenated word.
   l. Click **OK** when Word has finished searching the document.
   m. Click **Close** to close the *Find and Replace* dialog box.
4. Add borders and shading to a paragraph.
   a. Select the paragraph after the "Profile" heading on the first page. Be sure to include the paragraph mark at the end of the paragraph.
   b. Click the **Borders** drop-down arrow [*Home* tab, *Paragraph* group] and select **Borders and Shading** to open the *Borders and Shading* dialog box (Figure 2-85).

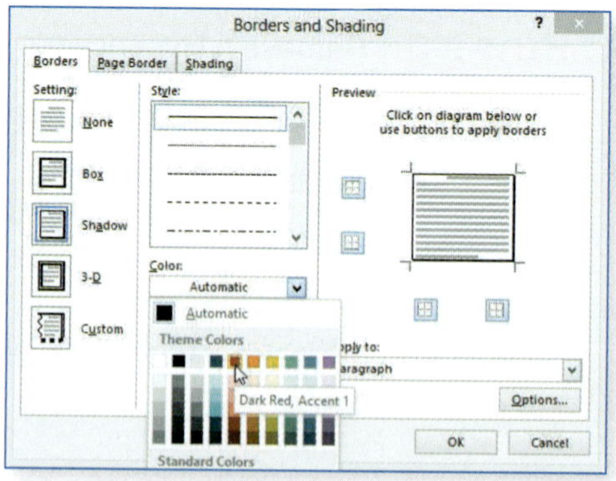

2-85 Select border color in the *Borders and Shading* dialog box

c. Select **Shadow** in the *Setting* area.
d. Select the **solid line** in the *Style* area.
e. Click the **Color** drop-down list and select **Dark Red**, **Accent 1**.
f. Select **½ pt** in the *Width* area.
g. Select **Paragraph** in the *Apply to* area.
h. Click the **Options** button to open the *Borders and Shading Options* dialog box.
i. Change *Top* and *Bottom* to **2 pt**.
j. Click **OK** to close the *Borders and Shading Options* dialog box.
k. Click the **Shading** tab (Figure 2-86).
l. Click the **Fill** drop-down list and choose **White**, **Background 1**, **Darker 5%**.
m. Click **OK** to close the *Borders and Shading* dialog box.

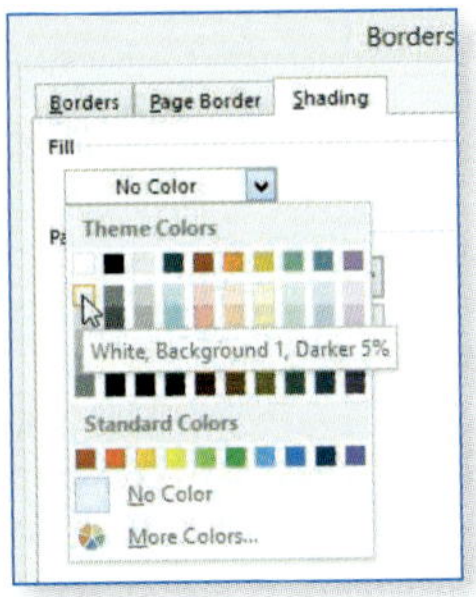

2-86 Apply shading to selected text

5. Add bottom border to the header.
   a. Double-click the header on the second page of the resume to open the second-page header.
   b. Place the insertion point in the first line of the header.
   c. Click the **Borders** drop-down arrow [*Home* tab, *Paragraph* group].
   d. Select **Bottom Border**. A bottom border is applied below the header text.
   e. Click the **Close Header and Footer** button [*Header & Footer Tools Design* tab, *Close* group].
6. Insert a hyperlink to an email address.
   a. Select the email address in the heading information on the first page.
   b. Click the **Hyperlink** button [*Insert* tab, *Links* group] or press **Ctrl+K** to open the *Insert Hyperlink* dialog box (Figure 2-87).
   c. Click the **E-mail Address** button in the *Link to* area.
   d. Type richellew@gmail.com in the *Text to display* area.
   e. Type richellew@gmail.com in the *E-mail address* area. Word automatically inserts "mailto:" before the email address.
   f. Click **OK** to close the *Insert Hyperlink* dialog box.

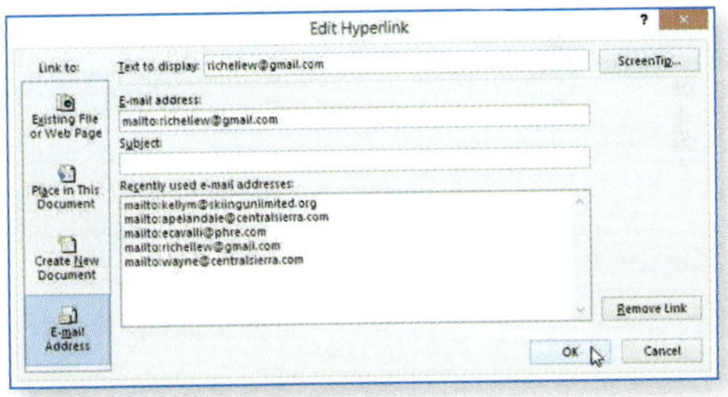

2-87 Insert hyperlink to an email address

7. Insert a hyperlink to a web site.
   a. Select **"California State University, Chico"** in the "References" section on the second page.
   b. Click the **Hyperlink** button or press **Ctrl+K** to open the *Insert Hyperlink* dialog box (Figure 2-88).
   c. Select **Existing File or Web Page** in the *Link to* area. The *Text to display* area has *California State University, Chico* already filled in.
   d. In the *Address* area, type www.csuchico.edu. Word automatically inserts "*http://*" before the web address.
   e. Click the **ScreenTip** button. The *Set Hyperlink ScreenTip* dialog box opens (Figure 2-89).
   f. Type CSU Chico web site in the *ScreenTip text* area.

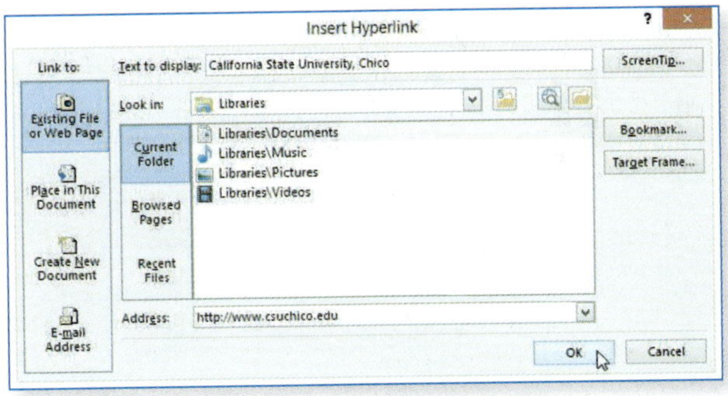

2-88 Insert hyperlink to a web page

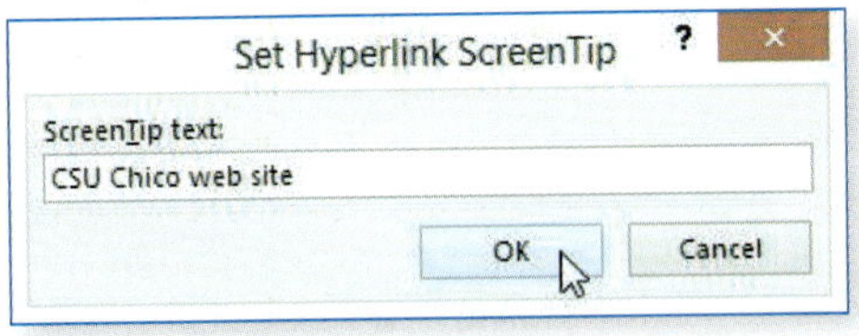

2-89 *Set Hyperlink ScreenTip* dialog box

g. Click **OK** to close the *Set Hyperlink ScreenTip* dialog box.
h. Click the **Target Frame** button in the *Insert Hyperlink* dialog box to open the *Set Target Frame* dialog box (Figure 2-90).
i. Select **New window** from the drop-down list.
j. Check the **Set as default for all hyperlinks** check box.
k. Click **OK** to close the *Set Target Frame* dialog box.
l. Click **OK** to close the *Insert Hyperlink* dialog box.

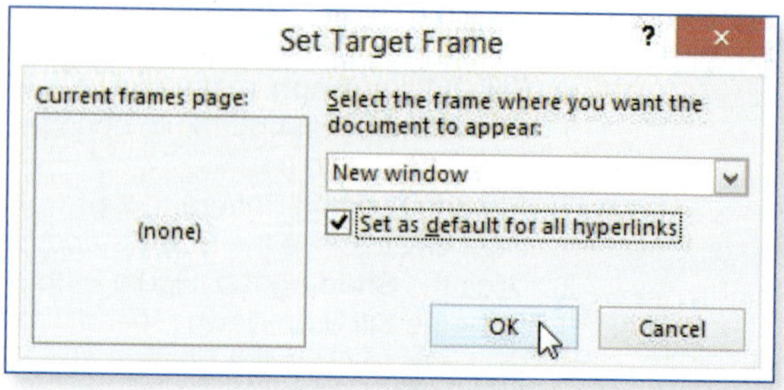

2-90 *Set Target Frame* dialog box

8. Automatically add hyperlinks to email addresses.
   a. Place the insertion point after "rsanchez@chico.edu" in the "References" section on the second page.
   b. Press the **spacebar** once to automatically add a hyperlink to the email address.
   c. Repeat the above steps to automatically add a hyperlink to the "diana.samuels@loomislearning.com" email address.
9. Save and close the document (Figure 2-91).

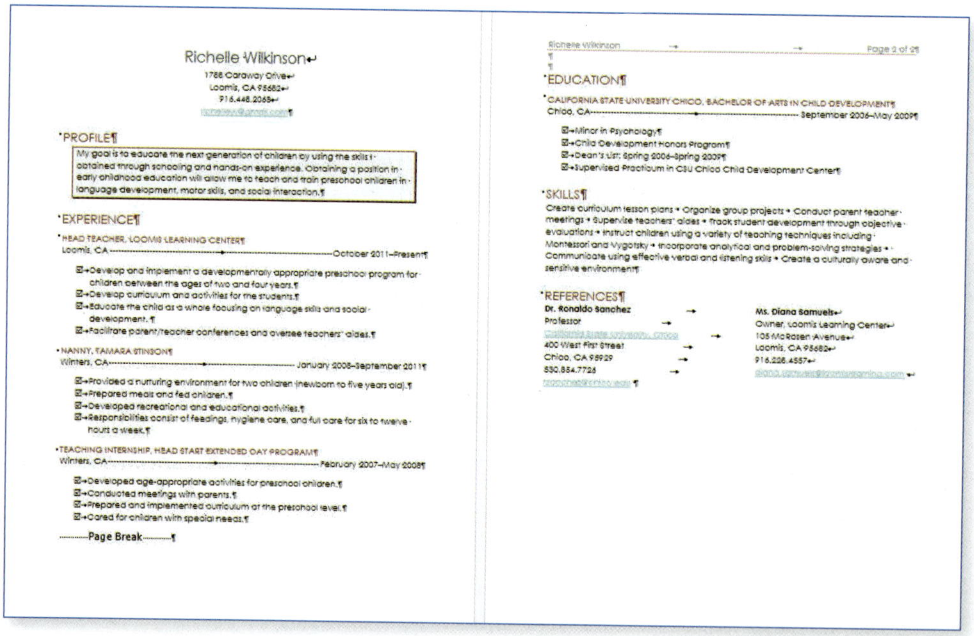

2-91 PP W 2-4 completed

Chapter Summary

2.1 Format a document by customizing margins, page orientation, paper size, and vertical alignment (p. W2-63).

- Adjust the ***margins*** of a document to increase or decrease the ***white space*** surrounding the text. You can adjust the top, bottom, left, and right margins of a document.
- ***Landscape*** and ***portrait*** are the two ***page orientation*** options.
- A standard sheet of paper is 8½"×11". Select other paper sizes or create a custom paper size.
- By default, text is aligned vertically at the top of the document. You can also ***vertically align*** text center, justified, or bottom.
- Use horizontal and vertical ***rulers*** to display the typing area on a document.
- You can change default page settings in the *Page Setup* dialog box.

2.2 Improve alignment and white-space usage by setting, using, and editing tab stops in a document (p. W2-66).

- There are five different types of tab stops: ***left***, ***center***, ***right***, ***decimal***, and ***bar***.
- Set, modify, or remove tab stops using the ruler or the *Tabs* dialog box.
- Leaders can be used with tab stops. There are three different types of leaders: ***dot***, ***dash***, and ***solid underline***.
- In a Word document, default tab stops are set every 0.5". You can change the default tab stops.

2.3 Understand and apply indents to control text alignment (p. W2-71).

- ***Indents*** can function as temporary margins and allow you to arrange paragraphs horizontally between the margins.
- There are four different types of indents: ***left***, ***right***, ***first line***, and ***hanging***.
- You can apply, modify, and remove indents with the ruler, *Page Layout* tab, or *Paragraph* dialog box.

2.4 Enhance document layout by effectively using page numbers, headers, and footers (p. W2-76).

- You can insert a ***page number*** into the header or footer in various locations.
- The ***Different First Page*** option allows you to remove a page number from the first page or have a header and footer.
- ***Headers*** and ***footers*** are areas above and below a document's top and bottom margins.
- You type header and footer content once and it appears on subsequent pages.
- You can customize headers and footers with text, page numbers, the date, and other document property fields.
- You have a variety of built-in header, footer, and page numbering options.

2.5 Control pagination with page and section breaks (p. W2-83).

- *Use* ***page breaks*** to control the ending and beginning of pages in a document.
- *Use* ***section breaks*** to allow for different page setup formatting on different sections of a document.
- There are four different types of section breaks: ***next page***, ***continuous***, ***even page***, and ***odd page***.
- Section breaks are visible in a document when the *Show/Hide* feature is turned on.

2.6 Present information using customized bulleted and numbered lists (p. W2-85).

- *Use* ***bulleted*** and ***numbered lists*** to emphasize important information.
- You can customize lists by using different symbols or pictures as bullets.
- Use numbering to display an ordered list.
- You can customize number format and levels.
- ***Multilevel lists*** allow you to customize a list using a combination of numbers, letters, or bullets.

2.7 Increase document consistency and format with styles and themes (p. W2-89).

- A ***style*** is a collection of preset formatting that you can apply to selected text.
- The ***Style gallery*** is a collection of built-in styles available in a document.
- You can modify existing styles.
- A ***theme*** is a collection of fonts, colors, and effects that you can apply to a document.

2.8 Effectively edit a document using find and replace (p. W2-93).

- The ***Find*** feature in Word allows you to search for specific information in a document.
- The ***Navigation pane*** displays all occurrences of the text for which you are searching.
- The ***Replace*** feature allows you to search for specific information in a document and replace it with other information.
- Both *Find* and *Replace* allow you to search for and replace formatting in a document.
- Use the ***Go To*** feature to go directly to a page, section, line, or other area in your document.

2.9 Improve overall document design and format by using borders, shading, horizontal lines, and hyperlinks (p. W2-96).

- *You can apply* ***borders*** and ***shading*** to text and paragraphs in a document.
- Word provides a variety of built-in border and shading options that you can apply to text, or you can customize borders and shading using the *Borders and Shading* dialog box.
- You can apply ***page borders*** to an individual page or all pages in a document.
- A ***horizontal line*** is a graphic that you can insert into a document.
- A ***hyperlink*** takes readers to a web page, a different document, or a different location in a document.

Check for Understanding

On the ***Online Learning Center*** for this text (www.mhhe.com/office2013inpractice), there are a variety of resources that can be used to review the concepts covered in this chapter.

The following Online Learning Resources are available on the Online Learning Center.

- Multiple choice questions
- Short answer questions
- Matching exercises

USING MICROSOFT WORD 2013

Guided Project 2-1

In this project, you create a form for contractors seeking insurance coverage at Central Sierra Insurance. You use a theme, styles, a multilevel list, tab stops, leaders, indents, borders and shading, a page break, and page numbering.
[Student Learning Outcomes 2.1, 2.2, 2.3, 2.4, 2.5, 2.6, 2.7, 2.9]

File Needed: ***InsuranceQuestionnaire-02.docx***
Completed Project File Name: ***[your initials] Word 2-1.docx***

Skills Covered in This Project

- Modify an existing document.
- Change margins.
- Apply a document theme.
- Change font size, line spacing, and paragraph spacing.
- Apply a style to selected text.
- Modify an existing style.
- Apply borders and shading to selected text.
- Set and use a tab stop with an underline leader.
- Apply and modify a multilevel list.
- Insert a page break.
- Insert a page number in the footer.

1. Open the ***InsuranceQuestionnaire-02*** document from your student data files.
2. Save this document as ***[your initials] Word 2-1***.
3. Change the margins of the document.
   a. Click the **Margins** button [*Page Layout* tab, *Page Setup* group] and select **Custom Margins**. The *Page Setup* dialog box opens.
   b. Change the *Left* and *Right* margins to **0.75"**.
   c. Click **OK** to close the *Page Setup* dialog box.
4. Change the theme and color set of the document.
   a. Click the **Themes** button [*Design* tab, *Document Formatting* group].
   b. Select **Integral** from the drop-down list.
   c. Click the **Colors** button [*Document Formatting* group] (Figure 2-92).
   d. Select **Aspect** from the drop-down list.
5. Change the font size, paragraph spacing, and line spacing on the entire document.
   a. Press **Ctrl+A** to select the entire document.
   b. Change the font size to **11 pt**.
   c. Change the line spacing to **Single** (1.0).
   d. Change the *After* paragraph spacing to **6 pt**.

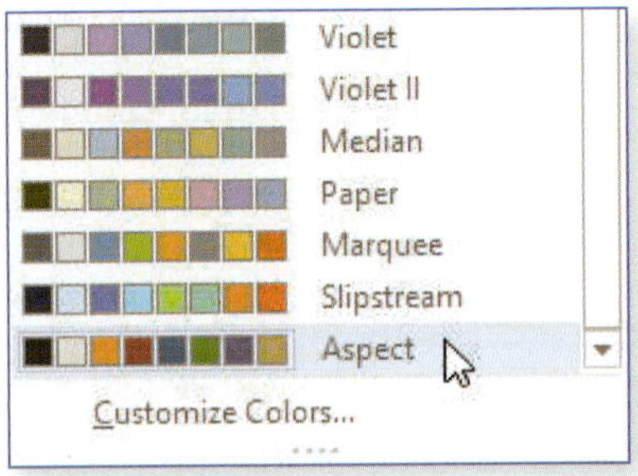

2-92 Select color set

6. Apply styles to selected text.
   a. Place the insertion point in the first line of text ("Contractor's Insurance Questionnaire").
   b. Click the **Title** style [*Home* tab, *Styles* group] in the *Style* gallery.
   c. Select the second line of the document (**"Please carefully . . . "**).
   d. Right-click the selected text and click **Styles** on the mini toolbar. The *Style* gallery list appears.
   e. Select **Book Title** from the *Style* gallery.
   f. With this text still selected, click the **Change Case** button in the *Font* group, and select **UPPERCASE**.
   g. Select **"Applicant's Instructions"** and apply the **Intense Quote** style from the *Style* gallery.
   h. In the next paragraph ("Please answer ALL questions . . ."), apply the **Strong** style to the three words in all caps ("ALL," "NONE," and "NONE").
   i. On the second page of the document, select **"Insurance Application Disclaimer"** and apply the **Intense Quote** style.

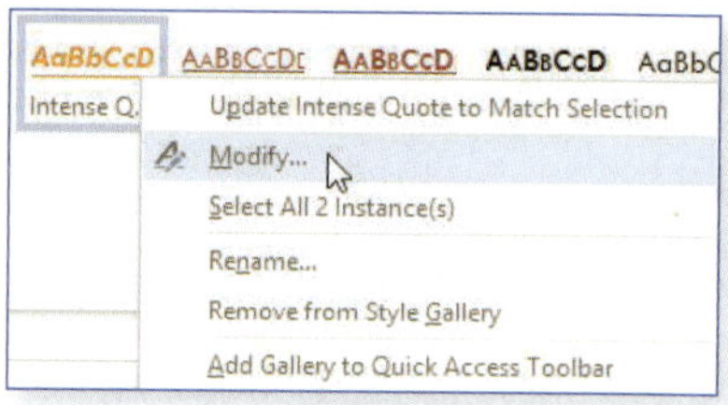

2-93 Modify an existing style

7. Modify an existing style.
   a. Click the **More** button [*Home* tab, *Styles* group] to display the *Style* gallery.
   b. Right-click the **Intense Quote** style in the *Style* gallery and select **Modify** (Figure 2-93). The *Modify Style* dialog box opens.
   c. In the *Formatting* area, change the font size to **12 pt**.
   d. Click the **Format** button on the bottom left and select **Paragraph**. The *Paragraph* dialog box opens.
   e. Change the *Left* and *Right* indent to **0**.
   f. Click **OK** to close the *Paragraph* dialog box.
   g. Click the **Only in this document** radio button to apply the style changes to only this document.
   h. Click **OK** to close the *Modify Style* dialog box. The change should be applied to all text formatted with the *Intense Reference* style on both the first and second pages.

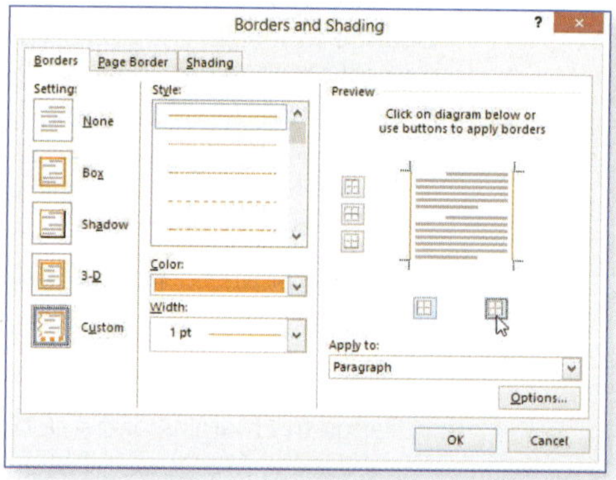

2-94 Border option settings

8. Add borders and shading to selected text.
   a. On the second page, select the three paragraphs below "Insurance Application Disclaimer."
   b. Click the **Borders** drop-down arrow [*Home* tab, *Paragraph* group] and select **Borders and Shading**. The *Borders and Shading* dialog box opens (Figure 2-94).
   c. In the *Setting* area, select **Custom**.
   d. In the *Style* area, select the solid line border.
   e. In the *Color* area, select **Orange**, **Accent 1**.
   f. In the *Width* area, select **1 pt**.
   g. In the *Preview* area, click the **Left** and **Right** border buttons.
   h. In the *Apply to* area, select **Paragraph**.
   i. Click the **Options** button. The *Border and Shading Options* dialog box opens.
   j. Change the *Left* and *Right* settings to **5 pt**. and click **OK** to close the *Border and Shading Options* dialog box.
   k. Click the **Shading** tab (Figure 2-95).
   l. From the *Fill* drop-down list, select **Orange**, **Accent 1**, **Lighter 80%**.
   m. Click **OK** to close the *Borders and Shading* dialog box.

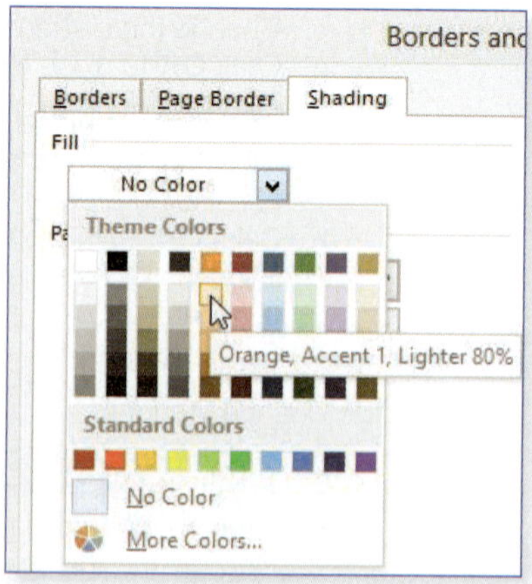

2-95 Select shading fill color

9. Change the paragraph spacing and add a tab stop with an underline leader to selected text.
   a. Select the last three lines of text on the second page.
   b. Click the **Paragraph** launcher [*Home* or *Page Layout* tab].

c. Change the *Before* paragraph spacing to **12 pt**.
d. Click the **Tabs** button to open the *Tabs* dialog box (Figure 2-96).
e. In the *Tab stop position* area, type 7.
f. Click the **Right** radio button in the *Alignment* area.
g. Click the **4** (solid underline) radio button in the *Leader* area.
h. Click the **Set** button to set this tab stop.
i. Click **OK** to close the *Tabs* dialog box.
j. Click at the end of the "Name and Title of the Insured" line and press **Tab**. A solid underline is inserted across the page to the right margin.
k. Repeat the above step (j.) on the next two lines.

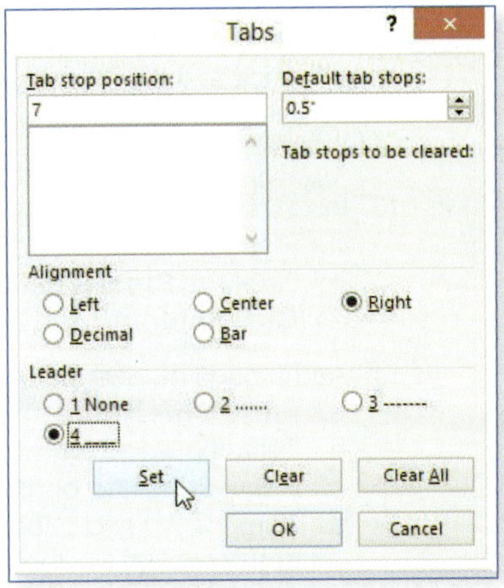

2-96 Set a right tab stop with an underline leader

10. Add a multilevel list to selected text and modify lists settings.
  a. Select the lines of text beginning with "Applicant" on the first page and ending with the last "If yes, please explain:" on the second page.
  b. Click the **Multilevel List** button [*Home* tab, *Paragraph* group] and select the **1), a), i)** option.
  c. With the text still selected, click the **Multilevel List** button and select **Define new Multilevel list**. The *Define new Multilevel list* dialog box opens (Figure 2-97).
  d. Click the **Set for All Levels** button. The *Set for All Levels* dialog box opens.
  e. Set the *Bullet/Number position for first level* to **0"**.
  f. Set the *Text position for first level* to **0.3"**.
  g. Set the *Additional indent for each level* to **0.3"**.
  h. Click **OK** to close the *Set for All Levels* dialog box.
  i. Click **OK** to close the *Define new Multilevel list* dialog box.

11. Increase indent on selected lines.
  a. Click anywhere on the list to deselect it.
  b. Place your insertion point in 13 in the numbered list ("If yes, . . .") and click **Increase Indent** [*Home* tab, *Paragraph* group]. This line is now letter *a)*.
  c. Repeat the above step (b.) on each of the lines in the list that begin with "If yes, . . .". There should be 28 numbered items in the list when you finish this process.

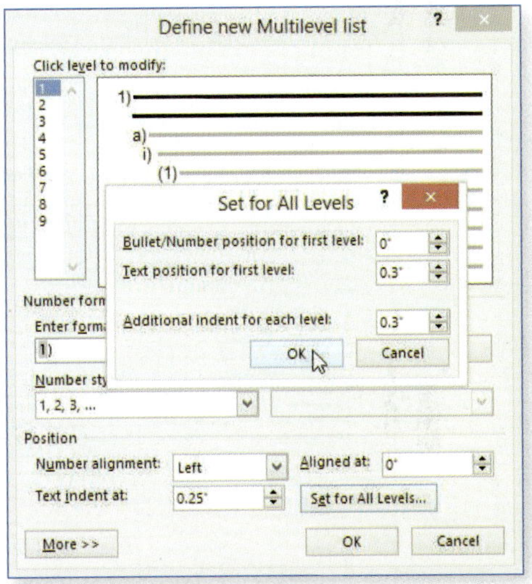

2-97 Change settings for a multilevel list

12. Change paragraph spacing to the multilevel list and add a right tab stop with an underline leader.
  a. Select the entire multilevel list.
  b. Click the **Paragraph** launcher [*Home* or *Page Layout* tab].
  c. Deselect the **Don't add space between paragraphs of the same style** check box (Figure 2-98).
  d. Click the **Tabs** button to open the *Tabs* dialog box.
  e. In the *Tab stop position* area, type 7.
  f. Click the **Right** radio button in the *Alignment* area.
  g. Click the **4** (solid underline) radio button in the *Leader* area.
  h. Click the **Set** button to set this tab stop.

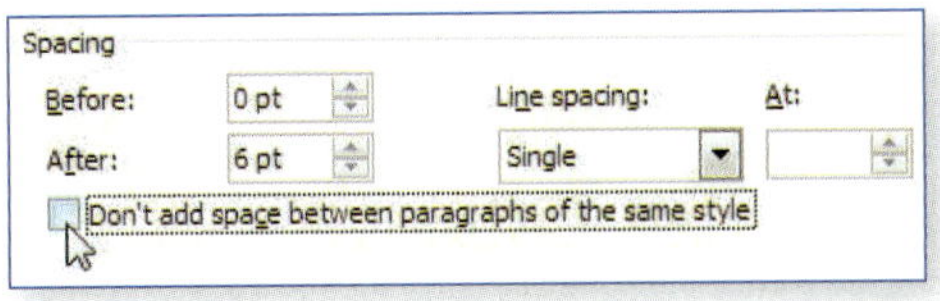

2-98 Add spacing between lines of text with the same style

i. Click **OK** to close the *Tabs* dialog box.
j. Click at the end of the first numbered item ("Applicant:") and press **Tab**. A solid underline will be inserted across the page to the right margin.
k. Repeat the above step (j.) on each of the numbered and lettered paragraphs.

13. Insert a page break in the document.
    a. Place the insertion point before the text in number 22 in the multilevel list.
    b. Click the **Breaks** button [*Page Layout* tab, *Page Setup* group] and select **Page Break**, or press **Ctrl+Enter** to insert a page break.
14. Add a page number in the footer of the document.
    a. Press **Ctrl+Home** to move to the top of the document.
    b. Click the **Page Number** button [*Insert* tab, *Header & Footer* group].
    c. Put your pointer on **Bottom of Page** to display the drop-down list.
    d. Scroll down and choose **Bold Numbers 3** in the *Page X of Y* section. The page number is inserted at the right of the footer.
    e. Click the blank line below the page number in the footer and press **Backspace** to delete the blank line.
    f. Click the **Close Header and Footer** button [*Header & Footer Tools Design* tab, *Close* group].
15. Save and close the document (Figure 2-99).

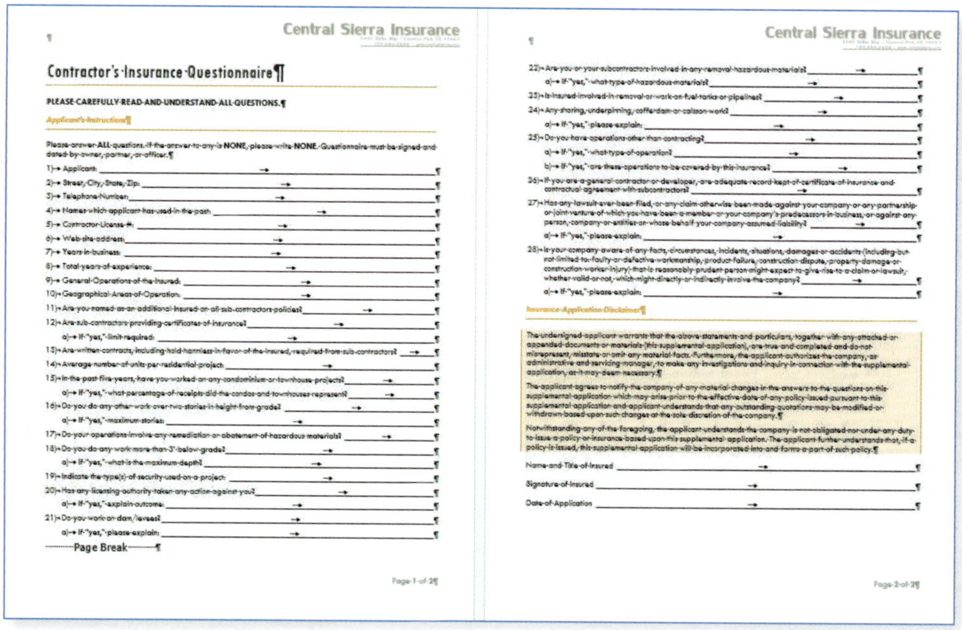
Central Sierra Insurance

Contractor's Insurance Questionnaire

PLEASE CAREFULLY READ AND UNDERSTAND ALL QUESTIONS.

Applicant's Instructions

Please answer ALL questions. If the answer to any is NONE, please write NONE. Questionnaire must be signed and dated by owner, partner, or officer.

1) Applicant:
2) Street, City, State, Zip:
3) Telephone Number:
4) Names which applicant has used in the past:
5) Contractor License #:
6) Web site address:
7) Years in business:
8) Total years of experience:
9) General Operations of the Insured:
10) Geographical Areas of Operation:
11) Are you named as an additional Insured on all sub-contractors policies?
12) Are sub-contractors providing certificates of insurance?
    a) If "yes," limit required:
13) Are written contracts, including hold harmless in favor of the insured, required from sub-contractors?
14) Average number of units per residential project:
15) In the past five years, have you worked on any condominium or townhouse projects?
    a) If "yes," what percentage of receipts did the condos and townhouses represent?
16) Do you do any other work over two stories in height from grade?
    a) If "yes," maximum stories:
17) Do your operations involve any remediation or abatement of hazardous materials?
18) Do you do any work more than 3' below grade?
    a) If "yes," what is the maximum depth?
19) Indicate the type(s) of security used on a project:
20) Has any licensing authority taken any action against you?
    a) If "yes," explain outcome:
21) Do you work on dam/levees?
    a) If "yes," please explain:

Page Break

Page 1 of 2

Central Sierra Insurance

22) Are you or your subcontractors involved in any removal hazardous materials?
    a) If "yes," what type of hazardous materials?
23) Is insured involved in removal or work on fuel tanks or pipelines?
24) Any shoring, underpinning, cofferdam or caisson work?
    a) If "yes," please explain:
25) Do you have operations other than contracting?
    a) If "yes," what type of operation?
    b) If "yes," are these operations to be covered by this insurance?
26) If you are a general contractor or developer, are adequate record kept of certificate of insurance and contractual agreement with subcontractors?
27) Has any lawsuit ever been filed, or any claim otherwise been made against your company or any partnership or joint venture of which you have been a member or your company's predecessors in business, or against any person, company or entities on whose behalf your company assumed liability?
    a) If "yes," please explain:
28) Is your company aware of any facts, circumstances, incidents, situations, damages or accidents (including but not limited to: faulty or defective workmanship, product failure, construction dispute, property damage or construction worker injury) that is reasonably prudent person might expect to give rise to a claim or lawsuit, whether valid or not, which might directly or indirectly involve the company?
    a) If "yes," please explain:

Insurance Application Disclaimer

The undersigned applicant warrants that the above statements and particulars, together with any attached or appended documents or materials (this supplemental application), are true and completed and do not misrepresent, misstate or omit any material facts. Furthermore, the applicant authorizes the company, as administrative and servicing manager, to make any investigations and inquiry in connection with the supplemental application, as it may deem necessary.

The applicant agrees to notify the company of any material changes in the answers to the questions on this supplemental application which may arise prior to the effective date of any policy issued pursuant to this supplemental application and applicant understands that any outstanding quotations may be modified or withdrawn based upon such changes at the sole discretion of the company.

Notwithstanding any of the foregoing, the applicant understands the company is not obligated nor under any duty to issue a policy or insurance based upon this supplemental application. The applicant further understands that, if a policy is issued, this supplemental application will be incorporated into and forms a part of such policy.

Name and Title of Insured
Signature of Insured
Date of Application

Page 2 of 2

2-99 Word 2-1 completed

Guided Project 2-2

In this project, you create a checklist for employees at Placer Hills Real Estate to track the tasks they need to complete when a house enters escrow. You create a bulleted list, modify a bullet in a list, set and modify tab stops, apply and modify styles, and insert document properties in the footer.
[Student Learning Outcomes 2.1, 2.2, 2.3, 2.4, 2.6, 2.7, 2.9]

File Needed: ***SellerEscrowChecklist-02.docx***
Completed Project File Name: ***[your initials] Word 2-2.docx***

Skills Covered in This Project

- Modify an existing document.
- Change margins, line spacing, font, and font size.
- Set a tab stop using the ruler.
- Set a tab stop with leader.
- Apply a style to selected text.
- Modify an existing style.
- Apply and customize a bulleted list.
- Use the *Format Painter.*
- Insert a document property field and date in the footer.
- Apply a border in the footer.

1. Open the ***SellerEscrowChecklist-02*** document from your student data files.
2. Save this document as ***[your initials] Word 2-2***.
3. Change margins, vertical alignment, line spacing, and font and font size, and delete blank lines.
   a. Click the **Margins** button [*Page Layout* tab, *Page Setup* group].
   b. Select **Normal** from the drop-down list.
   c. Click the **Page Setup** launcher to open the *Page Setup* dialog box.
   d. Click the **Layout** tab.
   e. In the *Page* area, change *Vertical alignment* to **Center**.
   f. Click **OK** to close the *Page Setup* dialog box.
   g. Press **Ctrl+A** to select the entire document.
   h. Change the font to **Calibri**.
   i. Change the font size to **12 pt**.
   j. Change the line spacing to **2.0** (Double).
   k. Turn on **Show/Hide** and delete all of the blank lines between the lines of text.
4. Add text to the document.
   a. Click after "Seller" in the second line of the document and press **Tab** once.
   b. Type Property Address.
   c. Click after "Escrow Company" and press **Tab** once.
   d. Type Escrow #.
   e. Click after "Tasks to be Completed" and press **Tab** once.
   f. Type Date Completed.
5. Set tab stops using the ruler to line up information.
   a. Select the second and third lines of text (beginning with "Seller").
   b. Ensure that the **Left Tab** is selected in the tab selector area to the left of the horizontal ruler.
   c. Click the ruler at **3.5"**. If you click the wrong location on the ruler, drag the tab stop to the correct location (Figure 2-100).

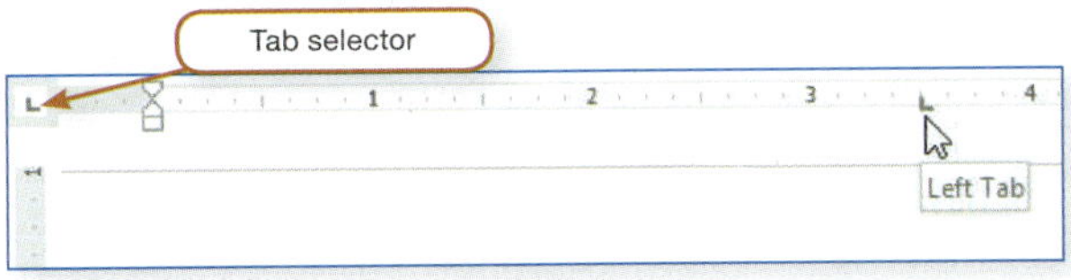

2-100 Set left tab stop using the ruler

   d. Select the fourth line of text (beginning with "Tasks").
   e. Click to the **tab selector** to change to a center tab stop (Figure 2-101).
   f. Click the ruler at **5.5"**.

2-101 Center tab stop

6. Set tab stops and add leaders to create lines for users to fill in information.
   a. Select the second and third lines of text (beginning with "Seller").
   b. Click the **Paragraph** launcher. The *Paragraph* dialog box opens.
   c. Click the **Tabs** button. The *Tabs* dialog box opens.
   d. In the *Tab stop position* area, type 3.
   e. Click the **Right** radio button in the *Alignment* area.
   f. Click the **4** (solid underline) radio button in the *Leader* area.
   g. Click the **Set** button to set this tab stop.
   h. In the *Tab stop position* area, type 6.5.
   i. Click the **Right** radio button in the *Alignment* area.
   j. Click the **4** (solid underline) radio button in the *Leader* area.
   k. Click the **Set** button to set this tab stop.
   l. Click **OK** to close the *Tabs* dialog box.
7. Use tab stops to align text.
   a. Place the insertion point before "Property Address" and press **Tab** once.
   b. Click after "Property Address" and press **Tab** once.
   c. Place the insertion point before "Escrow #" and press **Tab** once.
   d. Click after "Escrow #" and press **Tab** once.
8. Apply styles to selected text and modify a style.
   a. Place the insertion point in the first line of text ("Seller Escrow Checklist").
   b. Select **Title** style in the *Style* gallery [*Home* tab, *Styles* group].
   c. Change the *After* paragraph spacing to **24 pt**. [*Page Layout* tab, *Paragraph* group].
   d. Click the **Center** alignment button to center the title.
   e. Select **"Tasks to be Completed"**.
   f. Apply the **Book Title** style from the *Style* gallery.
   g. Change the font size of the selected text to **14 pt**. and apply a **Double underline**.
   h. Right-click the **Book Title** style in the *Style* gallery and select **Update Book Title to Match Selection**. The *Book Title* style is updated.
   i. Select **"Date Completed"** and apply the **Book Title** style.
9. Create a bulleted list to selected text and apply a custom bullet.
   a. Select the remaining lines of text beginning with "Open Escrow . . .".
   b. Click the **Bullets** drop-down arrow [*Home* tab, *Paragraph* group] and select **Define New Bullet**. The *Define New Bullet* dialog box opens.
   c. Click the **Symbol** button. The *Symbol* dialog box opens (Figure 2-102).
   d. Click the **Font** drop-down arrow and select **Wingdings**.
   e. Scroll down the list and select the **open square** bullet (Character code 113).
   f. Click **OK** to close the *Symbol* dialog box.
   g. Click the **Font** button in the *Define New Bullet* dialog box. The *Font* dialog box opens.
   h. Change the *Size* to **14 pt**.
   i. Click **OK** to close the *Font* dialog box.
   j. Click **OK** to close the *Define New Bullet* dialog box.
   k. With the bulleted list still selected, click the **Decrease Indent** button to align the bullet at the left margin.

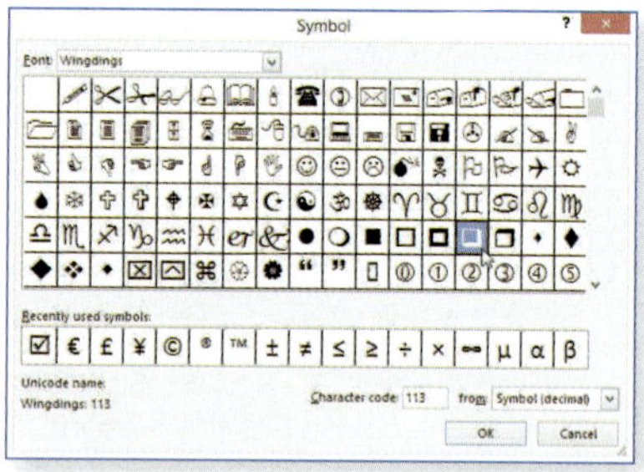

2-102 Select a symbol for a custom bullet

10. Change the hanging indent and add tab stops.
    a. Select the bulleted list.
    b. Click the **Paragraph** launcher to open the *Paragraph* dialog box.
    c. Change the hanging indent to **0.3"**.

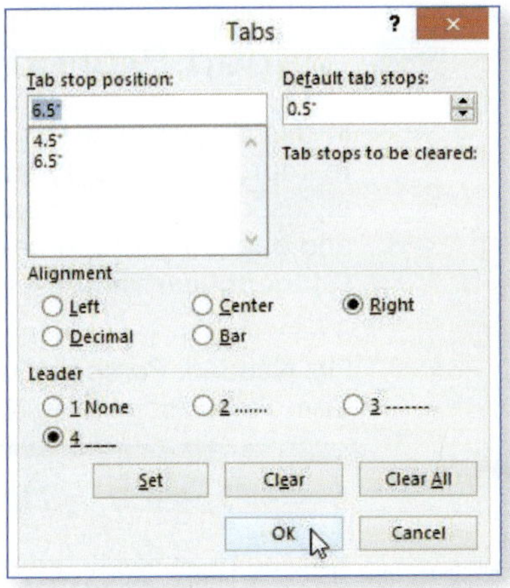

2-103 *Tabs* dialog box

d. Click the **Tabs** button. The *Tabs* dialog box opens (Figure 2-103).
e. In the *Tab stop position* area, type 4.5.
f. Click the **Left** radio button in the *Alignment* area.
g. Click the **1 None** radio button in the *Leader* area.
h. Click the **Set** button to set this tab stop.
i. In the *Tab stop position* area, type 6.5.
j. Click the **Right** radio button in the *Alignment* area.
k. Click the **4** (solid underline) radio button in the *Leader* area.
l. Click the **Set** button to set this tab stop.
m. Click **OK** to close the *Tabs* dialog box.
n. Place the insertion point after "Open Escrow with Escrow Company" and press **Tab** two times. A solid underline is inserted between 4.5" and 6.5".
o. Repeat the step above (n.) on the remaining lines in the bulleted list.

11. Add text to the document.
    a. Press **Enter** after the last line of text in the document.
    b. Click the **Bullets** button [*Home* tab, *Paragraph* group] to turn off the bullet on this line.
    c. Type Fax/Email Clear Pest Report and press **Enter**.
    d. Type Title and press **Enter**.
    e. Type Lender and press **Enter**.
    f. Type Buyer's Agent.

12. Apply a style to selected text and use the *Format Painter*.
    a. Select **"Fax/Email Clear Pest Report"** and apply the **Subtle Reference** style.
    b. Click one of the bulleted items.
    c. Click the **Format Painter** button [*Home* tab, *Clipboard* group] to copy the formatting of this bulleted item.
    d. Select the last three lines of text (beginning with "Title . . ."). The *Format Painter* copies the bullet formatting and tab settings to these lines of text.
    e. Press **Tab** two times after each of these last three lines to insert the tab stops and leaders.

13. Insert a document property field, the date, and a border in the footer of the document.
    a. Click the **Footer** button [*Insert* tab, *Header & Footer* group].
    b. Select **Edit Footer** from the drop-down list. The footer opens.
    c. Click the **Quick Parts** button [*Header & Footer Tools Design* tab, *Insert* group].
    d. Click **Document Property** and select **Company**. The *Company* document property field is inserted.
    e. Press the **right arrow** key once to deselect the *Company* field.
    f. Press **Tab** two times, type Last Updated:, and **space** once. The text aligns at the right side of the footer.
    g. Click the **Date & Time** button [*Header & Footer Tools Design* tab, *Insert* group]. The *Date and Time* dialog box opens.
    h. Select the third option (month, day, year) and click the **Update automatically** check box.
    i. Click **OK** to close the dialog box.
    j. Select all of the text in the footer and change the font to **Calibri** and the font size to **10 pt**.
    k. Click the **Borders** drop-down arrow [*Home* tab, *Paragraph* group] and select **Top Border**.
    l. Click the **Close Header and Footer** button [*Header & Footer Tools Design* tab, *Close* group].

14. Save and close the document (Figure 2-104).

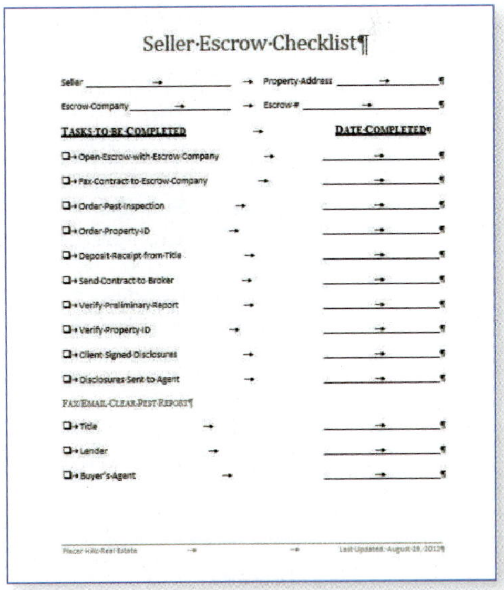

2-104 Word 2-2 completed

Guided Project 2-3

In this project, you edit and format the personal training guide for the American River Cycling Club to improve readability and effectiveness. You use find and replace, apply a document theme, modify styles, customize numbered and bulleted lists, apply borders and shading, and insert headers, footers, and document properties.
[Student Learning Outcomes 2.3, 2.4, 2.6, 2.7, 2.8, 2.9]

File Needed: ***PersonalTrainingProgram-02.docx***
Completed Project File Name: ***[your initials] Word 2-3.docx***

Skills Covered in This Project

- Modify an existing document.
- Apply a document theme.
- Change line spacing and paragraph spacing.
- Apply a style to selected text.
- Modify an existing style.
- Apply borders and shading to selected text.
- Customize a multilevel bulleted list.
- Use *Find* and *Replace*.
- Insert a hyperlink.
- Insert header, footer, page number, and document properties.

1. Open the ***PersonalTrainingProgram-02*** document from your student data files.
2. Save this document as ***[your initials] Word 2-3***.
3. Apply a document theme and change the line and paragraph spacing.
   a. Click the **Themes** button [*Design* tab, *Document Formatting* group].
   b. Select **Slice** from the drop-down list of theme options.
   c. Select the entire document.
   d. Change the line spacing to **1.15**.
   e. Change the after paragraph spacing to **10 pt**.
   f. Turn on **Show/Hide** and delete any blank lines in the document.
4. Apply styles to the title, subtitle, and section headings.
   a. Select the title (first line) of the document.
   b. Apply the **Title** style from the *Style* gallery [*Home* tab, *Styles* group].
   c. Change the font size to **20 pt**., make it **bold**, and **center** it horizontally.
   d. Select the subtitle (second line) of the document.
   e. Apply the **Subtitle** style from the *Style* gallery.
   f. Change the font size to **16 pt**. and **center** horizontally.
   g. Select the first section heading **("General Guidelines")**.
   h. Apply the **Heading 1** style from the *Style* gallery.
   i. Apply the **Heading 1** style to the remaining section headings in the document *("Personal Training Program Guidelines," "More About Long Rides," "Training Intensity and Heart Rate," "Tracking Training Miles versus Hours,"* and *"Using a Training Log")*.
5. Modify styles in the document.
   a. Select the first section heading **("General Guidelines")** including the paragraph mark at the end of the line.
   b. Change the *Before* paragraph spacing to **12 pt**. and the *After* paragraph spacing to **6 pt**.
   c. Click the **Borders** drop-down arrow [*Home* tab, *Paragraph* group] and select **Borders and Shading**. The *Borders and Shading* dialog box opens.

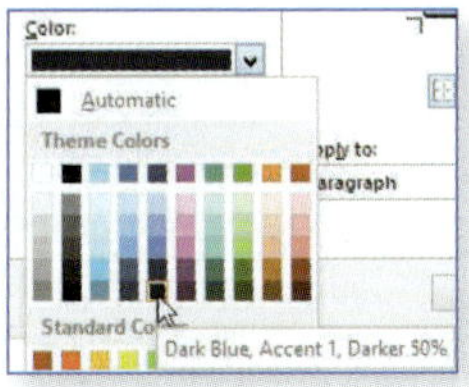

2-105 Select border line color

d. In the *Setting* area, select **Shadow**.
e. In the *Style* area, select the solid line.
f. In the *Color* area, select **Dark Blue**, **Accent 1**, **Darker 50%** (Figure 2-105).
g. In the *Width* area, select **1 pt**.
h. In the *Apply to* area, make sure that **Paragraph** is selected.
i. Click the **Shading** tab and in the *Fill* area, select **Dark Blue**, **Accent 1**, **Lighter 80%**.
j. In the *Apply to* area, make sure that **Paragraph** is selected and click **OK** to close the *Borders and Shading* dialog box.
k. With the heading still selected, right-click the **Heading 1** style in the *Style gallery*.
l. Select **Update Heading 1 to Match Selection**. All of the headings with the *Heading 1* style applied are automatically updated in the document.

6. Customize the bullets and indents for the bulleted list.
   a. Right-click the first bulleted item on the first page and select **Adjust List Indents**. The *Define new Multilevel list* dialog box opens.
   b. Click **1** in the *Click level to modify* area.
   c. In the *Number style for this level* area, select **New Bullet** from the drop-down list (Figure 2-106). The *Symbol* dialog box opens.
   d. In the *Font* area, select **Webdings** from the drop-down list (Figure 2-107).
   e. Click the **right pointing triangle** (Character code 52) and click **OK** to close the *Symbol* dialog box.
   f. Click **2** in the *Click level to modify* area in the *Define new Multilevel list* dialog box.
   g. In the *Number style for this level* area, select **New Bullet** from the drop-down list. The *Symbol* dialog box opens.
   h. In the *Font* area, select **Webdings** from the drop-down list.
   i. Click the **double right pointing triangle** (Character code 56) and click **OK** to close the *Symbol* dialog box.
   j. Click the **Set for All Levels** button in the *Define new Multilevel list* dialog box. The *Set for All Levels* dialog box opens (Figure 2-108).
   k. Change the *Bullet/Number position for first level* to **0.25"**.
   l. Change the *Text position for first level* to **0.5"**.
   m. Change *Additional indent for each level* to **0.25"**.
   n. Click **OK** to close the *Set for All Levels* dialog box.
   o. Click **OK** to close the *Define new Multilevel list* dialog box. All of the first and second level bullets and indents in the entire document are changed.

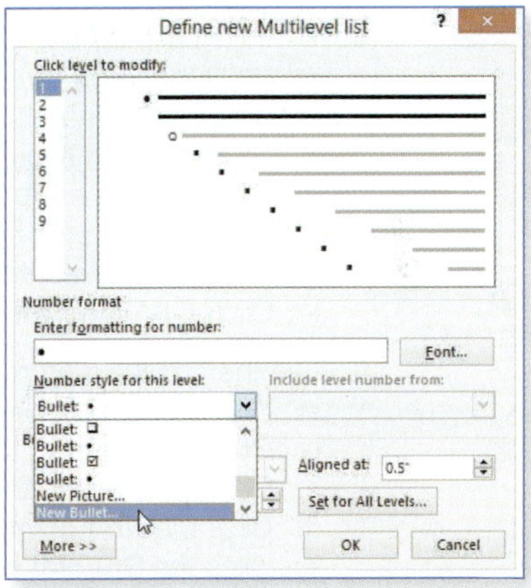

2-106 Customize bulleted list

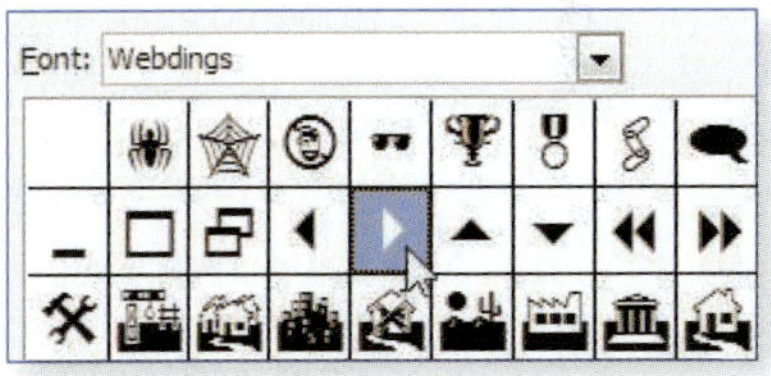

2-107 Select bullet from Webdings font set

7. Use the *Find* feature to find text in the document.
   a. Press **Ctrl+Home** to go to the beginning of the document.
   b. Press **Ctrl+F** to open *Find* in the *Navigation* pane.
   c. Type personal training program in the *Search Document* area. All instances of this text appear below in the *Navigation* pane.
   d. Click after "personal training program" in the first body paragraph on the first page and type (PTP). Make sure there is one space before and after the parentheses.
   e. Select **"PTP"** and make **italic**.
   f. Click the **X** in the upper right of the *Navigation* pane to close this pane.

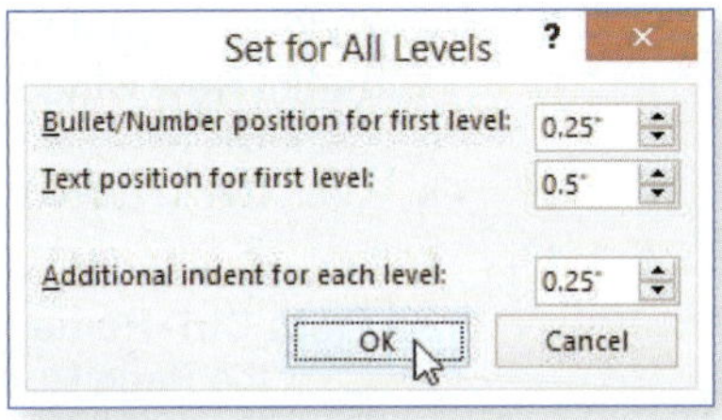

2-108 Set indents for all levels

8. Use the replace feature to find and replace text in the document.
   a. Press **Ctrl+Home** to go to the beginning of the document.
   b. Click the **Replace** button [*Home* tab, *Editing* group]. The *Find and Replace* dialog box opens with the *Replace* tab selected (Figure 2-109).
   c. In the *Find what* area, type personal training program.
   d. In the *Replace with* area, type PTP.
   e. Click the **More** button to display more search options.
   f. Click the **Format** button and select **Font**. The *Replace Font* dialog box opens.
   g. Click **Italic** in the *Font style* area and click **OK** to close the *Replace Font* dialog box.
   h. Click the **Less** button to make the *Find and Replace* dialog box smaller.
   i. Click the **Find Next** button to find the first occurrence of "personal training program" in the document.
   j. Do not replace this text in the title, first body paragraph, or section heading. Replace all other occurrences of "personal training program" with "*PTP*." Click the **Replace** button to replace the highlighted occurrence or click the **Find Next** button to skip and not replace an occurrence.
   k. Click **OK** when you are finished searching the document.

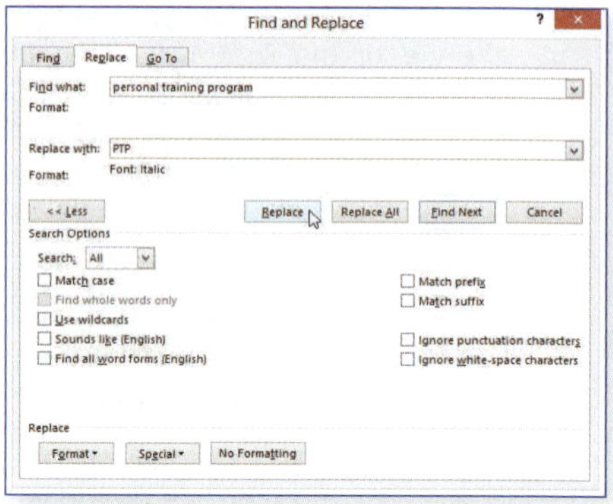

2-109 Replace text with text and formatting

9. Use the replace feature to replace some hyphens with an em dash.
   a. With the *Find and Replace* dialog box still open, delete the text in the *Find what* area and type - (hyphen).
   b. Click the **More** button.
   c. Delete the text in the *Replace with* area.
   d. Click the **No Formatting** button at the bottom of the dialog box to clear the *Replace with* formatting.
   e. Click the **Special** button and select **Em Dash**.
   f. Click the **Less** button.
   g. Click the **Find Next** button to find the first occurrence of the hyphen. Replace the hyphen with an em dash when a hyphen is used to set off part of a sentence; skip (click **Find Next**) when the hyphen is used in a hyphenated word.
   h. Click **OK** when you are finished searching the document (click **No** if a dialog box opens asking if you want to search from the beginning of the document).
   i. Click **Close** to close the *Find and Replace* dialog box.

10. Add a hyperlink to the document.
   a. Select the subtitle of the document **("American River Cycling Club")**.
   b. Click the **Hyperlink** button [*Insert* tab, *Links* group] or press **Ctrl+K**. The *Insert Hyperlink* dialog box opens.
   c. Click the **Existing File or Web Page** button in the *Link to* area.
   d. Type www.arcc.org in the *Address* area.
   e. Click the **Target Frame** button. The *Set Target Frame* dialog box opens.
   f. Select **New window** from the drop-down list.
   g. Click **OK** to close the *Set Target Frame* dialog box.
   h. Click **OK** to close the *Insert Hyperlink* dialog box.

11. Insert header and footer on the second and continuing pages.
   a. Press **Ctrl+Home** to move to the beginning of the document.
   b. Click the **Page Number** button [*Insert* tab, *Header & Footer* group].
   c. Click **Top of Page** and select **Accent Bar 2** from the drop-down list. The header is inserted and remains open with the *Header & Footer Tools Design* tab displayed.
   d. Check the **Different First Page** check box [*Options* group] to remove the header from the first page so it only displays on the second and continuing pages.

12. Insert document property fields in the footer.
    a. With the header still open, click the **Go to Footer** button [*Navigation* group].
    b. Click the **Next** button [*Navigation* group] to move to the footer on the second page.
    c. Click the **Quick Parts** button [*Insert* group] and select **Document Property**.
    d. Select **Company** to insert the company document property field.
    e. Press the **right arrow** key once to deselect the property field.
    f. Press **Tab** two times to move the insertion point to the right margin in the footer.
    g. Click the **Quick Parts** button [*Insert* group] and select **Document Property**.
    h. Select **Title** to insert the title document property field.
    i. Press **Ctrl+A** to select all of the text in the footer.
    j. Make this text **bold** and **italic**.
    k. Click the **Close Header and Footer** button [*Header & Footer Tools Design* tab, *Close* group]. The header and footer information should appear on the second and continuing pages in the document.
13. Save and close the document (Figure 2-110).

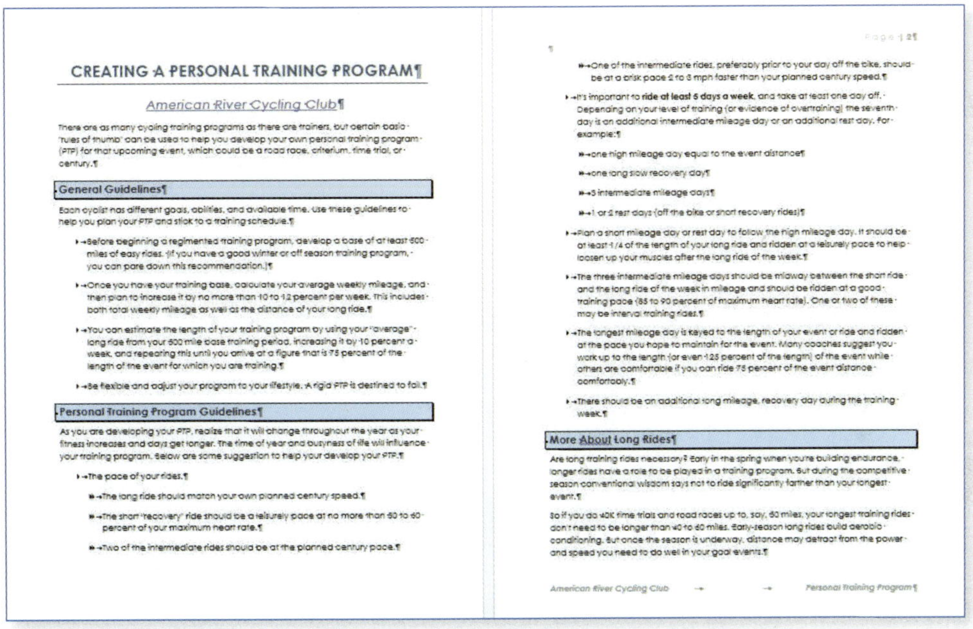

2-110 Word 2-3 completed (pages 1 and 2 of 5)

Independent Project 2-4

In this project, you use styles, indents, lists, tab stops, the replace feature, footers, and document properties to customize the Emergency Procedures document for Sierra Pacific Community College District. [Student Learning Outcomes 2.1, 2.2, 2.3, 2.4, 2.6, 2.7, 2.9]

File Needed: ***EmergencyProcedures-02.docx***
Completed Project File Name: ***[your initials] Word 2-4.docx***

Skills Covered in This Project

- Modify an existing document.
- Apply a document theme.
- Change margins and font size.
- Apply and modify a style.
- Apply borders to selected text.
- Apply and customize a numbered and bulleted list.
- Use the *Format Painter*.
- Set and modify tab stops.
- Use *Replace*.
- Insert a footer with document properties and current date.
- Insert a page border.
- Center text vertically.

1. Open the ***EmergencyProcedures-02*** document from your student data files.
2. Save this document as ***[your initials] Word 2-4***.
3. Format the entire document.
   a. Change the document theme to **Integral** and the color set to **Red**.
   b. Change the top, bottom, left, and right margins to **0.75"**.
   c. Select the entire document and change the font size to **12 pt**.
4. Format the title of the document.
   a. Select the title of the document and apply **Heading 1** style.
   b. Format this text in **all caps**.
   c. Change the font size to **16 pt**.
   d. Change the before paragraph spacing to **0 pt**.
   e. Add a **bottom border** to the title.
5. Select each of the section headings and apply the **Heading 2** style.
6. Modify the **Heading 2** style. Select the first section heading **("Emergency Telephones [Blue Phones]")** and make the following changes.
   a. Change before paragraph spacing to **12 pt**. and after paragraph spacing to **3 pt**.
   b. Apply **small caps** effect and **underline**.
   c. Update **Heading 2** style to match this heading. All of the section headings are updated.
7. Delete all of the blank lines in the document.
8. Select the bulleted list in the first section and change to a numbered list.
9. Apply numbering format, make formatting changes, and use the *Format Painter*.
   a. Apply numbering format to the text in the following sections: "*Assaults, Fights, or Emotional Disturbances*"; "*Power Failure*"; "*Fire*"; "*Earthquake*"; and "*Bomb Threat*."
   b. With the numbered list in the "Bomb Threat" section selected, use the *Paragraph* dialog box to set before and after paragraph spacing to **2 pt**., and deselect the **Don't add space between paragraphs of the same style** check box.
   c. Use the **Format Painter** to copy this numbering format to each of the other numbered lists.
   d. Reset each numbered list so it begins with **1**.
10. Select the text in the "Accident or Medical Emergency" section and apply and customize a bulleted list.
    a. Use a **solid square bullet** (Wingdings, Character code 110).
    b. Set left indent at **0.25"** and hanging indent at **0.25"**.
    c. Set before and after paragraph spacing to **2 pt**.
    d. Deselect the **Don't add space between paragraphs of the same style** check box.
11. Use the *Format Painter* to apply this bulleted list format to the following text in the following sections: "*Tips to Professors and Staff*" and "*Response to Students*."
12. Select the text in the "Emergency Telephone Locations" section and change indent, paragraph spacing, and style.

a. Set a **0.25"** left indent.
b. Set before and after paragraph spacing to **2 pt**.
c. Deselect the **Don't add space between paragraphs of the same style** check box.
d. Apply **Book Title** style to each of the telephone locations. Select only the location, not the text in parentheses or following text.

13. Select the text in the "Emergency Phone Numbers" section, change left indent and paragraph spacing, and set a tab stop with a dot leader.
    a. Set a **0.25"** left indent for this text.
    b. Set before and after paragraph spacing to **2 pt**.
    c. Deselect the **Don't add space between paragraphs of the same style** check box.
    d. Set a **right tab stop** at the right margin and use a **dot leader (2)**.
    e. Press **Tab** before the phone number on each of these lines. The phone numbers align at the right margin with a dot leader between the text and phone number.
14. Apply the **Intense Reference** style to the paragraph headings in the "Accident or Medical Emergency" section ("*Life-Threating Emergencies*" and "*Minor Emergencies*").
15. Use the *Replace* feature to replace all instances of "Phone 911" with "PHONE 911" with **bold** font style.
16. Insert a footer with document property fields and the current date that appears on every page.
    a. Edit the footer and use the ruler to move the center tab stop to **3.5"** and the right tab stop to **7"**.
    b. Insert the **Title** document property field at the left.
    c. Insert the **Company** document property field at center. Use the center tab stop for alignment.
    d. Insert the **current date** (third date format) that is updated automatically at the right. Use the right tab stop for alignment.
    e. Change the font size of all the text in the footer to **10 pt**.
    f. Add a **top border** to the text in the footer.
17. Insert a page border on the entire document. Use **Shadow** setting, **solid line** style, **Dark Red**, **Accent 1** color, and **1 pt**. line width.
18. Center the entire document vertically.
19. Save and close the document (Figure 2-111).

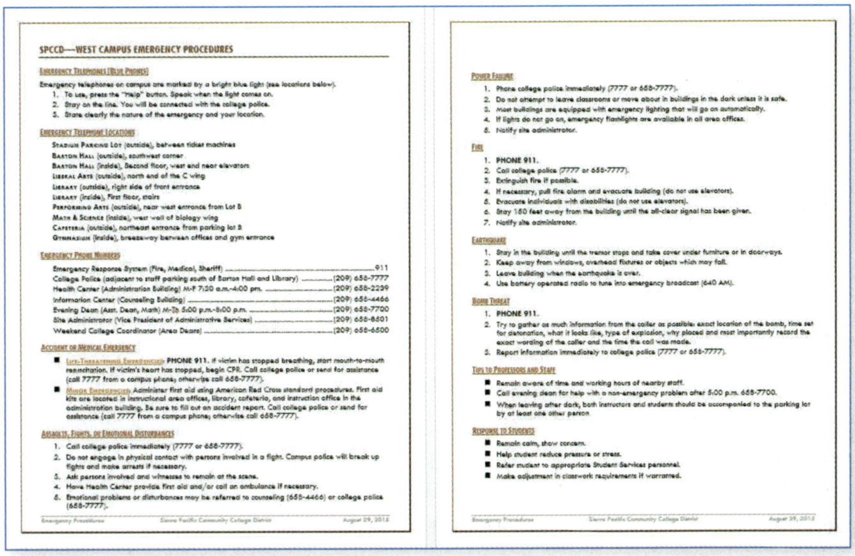

2-111 Word 2-4 completed

Independent Project 2-5

In this project, you format a bank authorization letter for Placer Hills Real Estate. You modify the formatting of an existing document, apply a theme, apply and modify styles, set tab stops, apply borders, and insert and edit hyperlinks.
[Student Learning Outcomes 2.1, 2.2, 2.7, 2.9]

File Needed: ***BankAuthorization-02.docx***
Completed Project File Name: ***[your initials] Word 2-5.docx***

Skills Covered in This Project

- Modify an existing document.
- Apply a document theme.
- Change margins.
- Insert automatically updated date.
- Apply and modify a style.
- Expand font spacing.
- Change paragraph spacing.
- Use the *Format Painter*.
- Set and use tab stops.
- Apply borders and shading to selected text.
- Insert a hyperlink.
- Edit a hyperlink.

1. Open the ***BankAuthorization-02*** document from your student data files.
2. Save this document as ***[your initials] Word 2-5***.
3. Format the document.
   a. Change the document theme to **Whisp**.
   b. Change the margins to **Normal**.
   c. Select the entire document and change the after paragraph spacing to **18 pt**.
4. Insert a blank line after the first line of the document and insert the **current date** (third date format) that is updated automatically.
5. Click at the end of the document, press **Enter**, and type the following information. Use line breaks after the first three lines. (Note: the email address is automatically converted to a hyperlink; you will edit this later).
   Emma Cavalli
   Placer Hills Real Estate
   ecavalli@phre.com
   916-450-3334
6. Select the date line and change the after paragraph spacing to **30 pt**. Use the *Format Painter* to copy this formatting to the "Sincerely," line.
7. Apply the **Title** style to the first line of the document and change the before paragraph spacing to **36 pt**.
8. Select **"Authorization Letter to Lender,"** apply the **Intense Reference** style, and expand the font spacing to **1 pt**. on this text.
9. Select the five lines of text beginning "Bank/Financial Institution" and apply the **Book Title** style. Use the *Format Painter* to copy the style to "Seller/Borrower Signature(s)".

10. Select the five lines of text beginning "Bank/Financial Institution" and set a **right tab stop** at the right margin with a **solid underline leader**. Press **Tab** after each of these lines to insert the solid underline leader to the right margin.
11. Select the paragraph beginning "Please consider . . ." and apply a border and shading to the paragraph.
    a. Use **Shadow** setting, **solid line** style, **Black**, **Text 1**, **Lighter 50%** color, and **1½ pt**. line width.
    b. Change the options so there is **4 pt**. padding from text on the top, bottom, left, and right.
    c. Set the shading fill color to **White**, **Background 1**, **Darker 5%**.
12. Select the **"Seller/Borrower Signature(s)"** line and apply a top border that is **solid line**, **black**, and **2¼ pt**. width.
13. Select **"Placer Hills Real Estate"** in the closing lines and insert a hyperlink.
    a. Type www.phre.com as the web page address.
    b. Set the target frame to **New window** and make this the default for all hyperlinks.
14. Edit the "ecavalli@phre.com" email hyperlink and type Email Emma Cavalli as the ScreenTip.
15. Save and close the document (Figure 2-112).

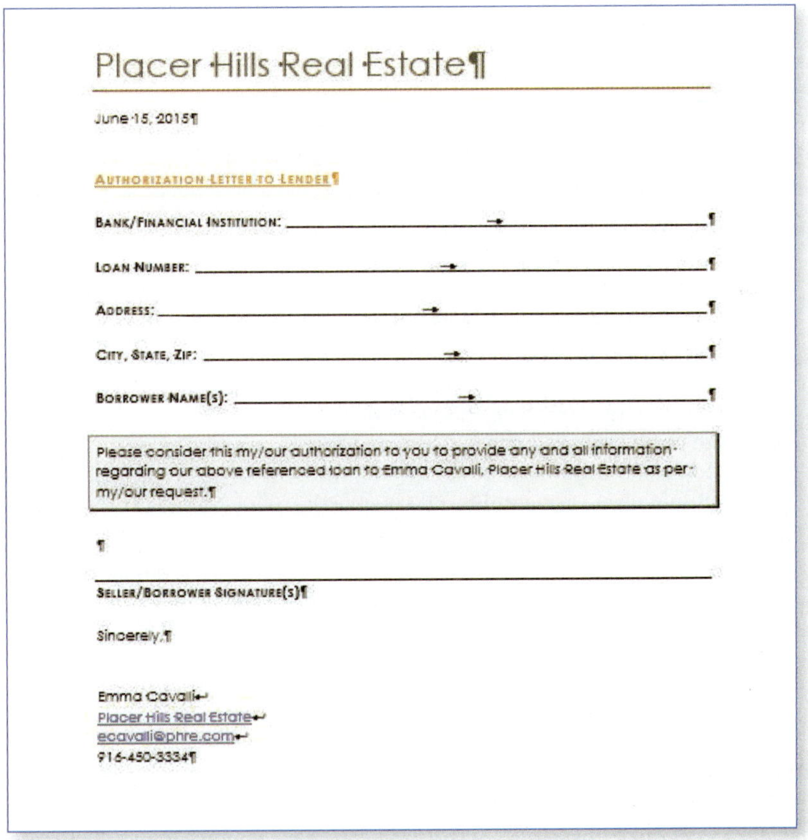

2-112 Word 2-5 completed

Independent Project 2-6

In this project, you edit, format, and customize the conference registration form for Central Sierra Insurance's Agriculture Insurance Conference. You use a continuous section break, *Find and Replace*, tab stops and leaders, styles, bullets, indents, borders, shading, and hyperlinks.
[Student Learning Outcomes 2.1, 2.2, 2.3, 2.4, 2.5, 2.6, 2.7, 2.9]

File Needed: ***ConferenceRegistrationForm-02.docx***
Completed Project File Name: ***[your initials] Word 2-6.docx***

Skills Covered in This Project

- Modify an existing document.
- Change margins, font, font size, line spacing, and paragraph spacing.
- Insert a header.
- Apply a style.
- Use *Find and Replace*.
- Insert a continuous section break.
- Insert a horizontal line.
- Set different margins for different sections.
- Customize a bulleted list and indents.
- Set and use tab stops and leaders.
- Apply borders and shading to selected text.
- Insert hyperlinks.

1. Open the ***ConferenceRegistrationForm-02*** document from your student data files.
2. Save this document as ***[your initials] Word 2-6***.
3. Format the document.
   a. Change the top and bottom margins to **0.5"**.
   b. Select all of the text in the document and change the font size to **10 pt**., line spacing to **1** (SS), and after paragraph spacing to **6 pt**.
4. Apply styles to title and subtitle.
   a. Cut the first line of the document and paste it in the header. Apply **Title** style, align **center**, and change the after paragraph spacing to **6 pt**.
   b. Delete the blank line below the text in the header.
   c. In the body of the document, select the first two lines beginning with "Central Sierra Insurance," apply **Subtitle** style, align **center**, and change the after paragraph spacing to **6 pt**.
5. Use *Find* and *Replace*.
   a. Use *Find* to find all occurrences of "Agriculture Insurance Conference."
   b. Apply **italic** formatting to each occurrence except in the header.
   c. Use *Replace* to find all occurrences of "Oct." and replace with **"May"**.
   d. Use *Replace* to find all occurrences of "Westfield Hotel & Spa" and replace with **"Northgate Resort"** with **bold** and **italic** font style.
6. Click at the end of the second body paragraph ("Please help us to determine . . .") and insert a **continuous** section break.
7. On the blank line below the section break, insert a **horizontal line**.
8. Click in the document below the section break and change the left and right margins to **1.25"** and apply to **This section**.

9. Select the two lines of text below the horizontal line and set a **right tab stop** with a **solid underline leader** at the right margin. Press **Tab** after each of these lines to insert the **solid underline leader** to the right margin.
10. Customize bullets and indents for the different levels.
    a. Use the *Define new Multilevel list* dialog box (in the *Multilevel List* drop-down list).
    b. On the first, second, and third levels, change the bullet to an open square bullet and change the font size of the bullet to **12 pt**.
    c. Set the indents for all levels so that the first level begins at **0"**, the text for the first level begins at **0.25"**, and additional indent for each level is **0.25"**.
    d. Apply this formatting to all of the bulleted lists.
11. Set tab stops with a leader.
    a. Select the **"Flying—Arrival time:"** line and set a **right tab stop** at **3"** with a solid underline leader.
    b. Press **Tab** after this line to insert the leader.
    c. Select the **"I need directions to *Northgate Resort* from:"** line and set a **right tab stop** at **5"** with a **solid underline leader**.
    d. Press **Tab** after this line to insert the leader.
12. Change indents and apply custom borders and shading to selected text.
    a. Select the last two lines of the document, align **center**, and change the left and right indents to **1"**.
    b. With these two lines selected, apply a double border, **¾ pt**., and **Dark Blue**, **Text 2** to the top and bottom border of the selected text.
    c. Apply **Dark Blue**, **Text 2**, **Lighter 80%** shading to the selected text.
13. Insert a hyperlink to an email address at each of the two occurrences of "apelandale@centralsierra.com."
    a. Make sure the *Text to display* area just displays the email address and not "mailto: . . ."
    b. Type Email Asia Pelandale as the ScreenTip for each of these hyperlinks.
14. Save and close the document (Figure 2-113).

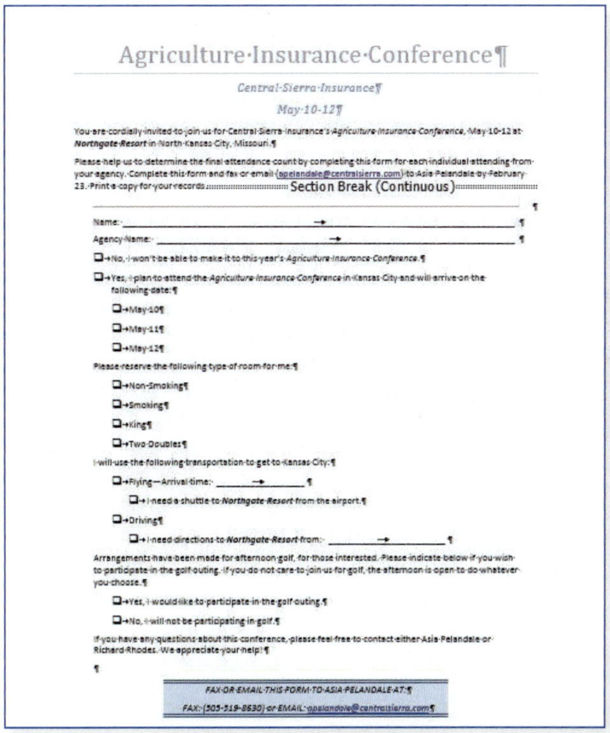

Agriculture·Insurance·Conference¶

Central·Sierra·Insurance¶

May·10-12¶

You·are·cordially·invited·to·join·us·for·Central·Sierra·Insurance's·*Agriculture·Insurance·Conference*,·May·10-12·at·***Northgate·Resort***·in·North·Kansas·City,·Missouri.¶

Please·help·us·to·determine·the·final·attendance·count·by·completing·this·form·for·each·individual·attending·from·your·agency.·Complete·this·form·and·fax·or·email·(apelandale@centralsierra.com)·to·Asia·Pelandale·by·February·23.·Print·a·copy·for·your·records.::::::::::::: Section Break (Continuous) :::::::::::::

¶

Name:· ______→______¶

Agency·Name:· ______→______¶

❑→No,·I·won't·be·able·to·make·it·to·this·year's·*Agriculture·Insurance·Conference*.¶

❑→Yes,·I·plan·to·attend·the·*Agriculture·Insurance·Conference*·in·Kansas·City·and·will·arrive·on·the·following·date:¶

❑→May·10¶

❑→May·11¶

❑→May·12¶

Please·reserve·the·following·type·of·room·for·me:¶

❑→Non-Smoking¶

❑→Smoking¶

❑→King¶

❑→Two·Doubles¶

I·will·use·the·following·transportation·to·get·to·Kansas·City:¶

❑→Flying—Arrival·time:· ______→______¶

❑→I·need·a·shuttle·to·***Northgate·Resort***·from·the·airport.¶

❑→Driving¶

❑→I·need·directions·to·***Northgate·Resort***·from:· ______→______¶

Arrangements·have·been·made·for·afternoon·golf,·for·those·interested.·Please·indicate·below·if·you·wish·to·participate·in·the·golf·outing.·If·you·do·not·care·to·join·us·for·golf,·the·afternoon·is·open·to·do·whatever·you·choose.¶

❑→Yes,·I·would·like·to·participate·in·the·golf·outing.¶

❑→No,·I·will·not·be·participating·in·golf.¶

If·you·have·any·questions·about·this·conference,·please·feel·free·to·contact·either·Asia·Pelandale·or·Richard·Rhodes.·We·appreciate·your·help!¶

¶

FAX·OR·EMAIL·THIS·FORM·TO·ASIA·PELANDALE·AT:¶

FAX:·(505-519-8630)·or·EMAIL:·apelandale@centralsierra.com¶

2-113 Word 2-6 completed

Improve It Project 2-7

In this project, you clean up a document that contains shortcuts for Microsoft Outlook. Courtyard Medical Plaza wants to make this document available to all of its employees. You use tab stops, styles, and many other page layout features that you have learned in this chapter to create a professional and attractive reference document.
[Student Learning Outcomes 2.1, 2.2, 2.4, 2.5, 2.7, 2.9]

File Needed: ***OutlookShortcuts-02.docx***
Completed Project File Name: ***[your initials] Word 2-7.docx***

Skills Covered in This Project

- Modify an existing document.
- Change margins, line spacing, and paragraph spacing.
- Apply and modify a style.
- Apply borders and shading to selected text.
- Set and modify tab stops and leaders.
- Use the *Format Painter.*
- Insert a page break.
- Edit footer content and tab stops.

1. Open the ***OutlookShortcuts-02*** document from your student data files.
2. Save this document as ***[your initials] Word 2-7***.
3. Format the document.
   a. Change the page orientation to **Landscape**.
   b. Change the top margin to **0.5"** and the bottom, left, and right margins to **0.75"**.
   c. Select the entire document and change the line spacing to **1** and the after paragraph spacing to **4 pt**.
4. Modify and apply styles.
   a. Remove the bottom border from the title and change the after paragraph spacing to **0 pt**.
   b. Select **"Global Outlook Commands,"** add a **1 pt.**, **Dark Blue**, **Text 2** top and bottom border, and apply **White**, **Background 1**, **Darker 5%** shading.
   c. Change the before paragraph spacing to **12 pt**. and the after spacing to **0 pt**.
   d. Update **Heading 1** to match selected text.
   e. Apply the **Heading 1** style to each of the remaining headings ("*Mail,*" "*Calendar,*" "*Contacts,*" "*Tasks,*" "*Notes,*" "*Journal,*" and "*Formatting*").
   f. Select the third line of text on the first page ("Activity Shortcut . . .") and change the before paragraph spacing to **6 pt**. and the after spacing to **3 pt**.
   g. Set **left tab stops** on the selected text at **3"**, **5"**, and **8.25"**.
   h. Update **Heading 2** to match selected text.
   i. Apply the **Heading 2** style to the first line of text ("Activity Shortcut . . .") after each section heading.
5. Select the tabbed text below the column headings ("Activity Shortcut . . .") in the first section and set tab stops to match the column headings. Include a dot leader between the text in the first and second columns and between the third and fourth columns.
6. Use the *Format Painter* to apply the tab settings to the text in the other sections.
7. Delete any blank lines and extra tabs.

8. Remove the existing footer and insert a footer with **Courtyard Medical Plaza** at the left, **Outlook Shortcuts** aligned at the center tab stop, and **Page X of Y** aligned at the right tab stop.
   a. You need to adjust the tab stops on the ruler in the footer.
   b. For the page number, use *Page X of Y* format where *X* is the page number and *Y* is the number of pages in the document (Hint: for *Y*, insert *NumPages* field).
   c. Apply a **1 pt.**, **Dark Blue**, **Text 2** top border in the footer.
   d. Set the footer so it does not appear on the first page.
9. Insert page breaks where necessary to keep groupings together. This document fits on four pages.
10. Check the document for consistent formatting. Make any necessary changes.
11. Save and close the document (Figure 2-114).

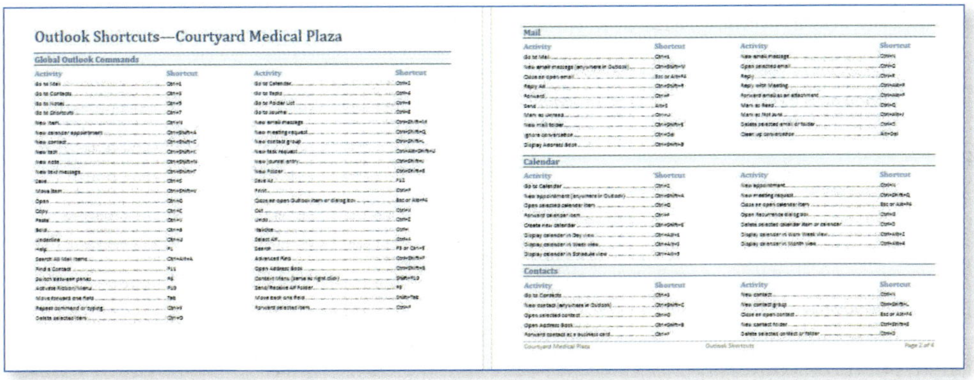

2-114 Word 2-7 completed (pages 1 and 2 of 4)

Challenge Project 2-8

Create an agenda for an upcoming meeting for an organization you are a member of, such as a club, church, volunteer organization, student group, or neighborhood association. Do some online research to find out some of the common components of agendas. Robert's Rules of Order is a good source of information about meetings and guidelines for meeting protocol.
[Student Learning Outcomes 2.1, 2.2, 2.3, 2.6, 2.7, 2.9]

File Needed: None
Completed Project File Name: ***[your initials] Word 2-8.docx***

Create a new document and save it as ***[your initials] Word 2-8***. An agenda can include, but is not limited to, the following items:

- Organization name as the title
- Meeting date, start time, and end time

- Meeting location
- Meeting attendees
- Topic headings
- Topic subheadings—include details for each topic heading
- The time each topic is expected to last

Modify your document according to the following guidelines:

- Apply styles.
- Use a multilevel list for the agenda items and subheadings.
- Customize number or bullet format and indents as needed.
- Use a right tab stop with a leader to line up the amount of time to be spent on each main topic heading.
- Apply borders, shading, and/or a horizontal line to create an attractive agenda.
- Adjust margins as needed.
- Include an appropriate header and/or footer.

Challenge Project 2-9

Update your resume using some of the document formatting features learned in this chapter. Edit your resume so it is consistently formatted, easy to read, and professional looking. Do some online research on resumes to get ideas about formatting and content.
[Student Learning Outcomes 2.1, 2.2, 2.3, 2.4, 2.5, 2.6, 2.7, 2.8, 2.9]

File Needed: None
Completed Project File Name: ***[your initials] Word 2-9.docx***

Open your existing resume or create a new document and save it as ***[your initials] Word 2-9***. Modify your document according to the following guidelines:

- Apply a document theme.
- Apply styles to headings and subheadings to improve consistency in format.
- Adjust margins as needed.
- Use bulleted lists with customized bullets and indents to attractively arrange information.
- Set and use tab stops and indents as necessary to line up information.
- Apply borders, shading, and/or a horizontal line to set off information in your resume.
- Use page or section breaks as needed.
- Use *Find and Replace* as needed.
- Insert hyperlinks for appropriate information (e.g., email address and company names).
- If your resume is more than one page, include a header and/or footer on the second and continuing pages.

Challenge Project 2-10

Format your favorite recipe using some of the formatting features learned in this chapter. You can look up recipes online on the Food Network, Epicurious, Simply Recipes, or other food web sites.
[Student Learning Outcomes 2.1, 2.2, 2.3, 2.6, 2.7, 2.9]

File Needed: None
Completed Project File Name: ***[your initials] Word 2-10.docx***

Create a new document and save it as ***[your initials] Word 2-10***. Your recipe should include, but is not limited to, the following:

- Recipe title
- Descriptive paragraph about the recipe
- Tab stops to arrange quantity and ingredients (and special instructions if needed)
- Numbered, step-by-step instructions
- Recipe source and/or additional information

Modify your document according to the following guidelines:

- Apply a document theme.
- Apply styles.
- Adjust margins as needed.
- Set and use a combination of tab stops (e.g., left, right, center, decimal, bar, and leaders) as necessary to attractively line up information.
- Use a numbered list for instructions.
- Use left, right, first line, and/or hanging indents as necessary.
- Apply borders, shading, page border, and/or a horizontal line to set off information in your recipe.
- Insert hyperlinks to appropriate information (e.g., link to online recipe).

CHAPTER 3

Working with Reports and Multipage Documents

CHAPTER OVERVIEW

Creating a long report with a table of contents, citations, footnotes or endnotes, a reference page, and headers and footers can be a challenging task. Word 2013 has numerous tools that automatically create these components in report or multipage document. Using these tools not only saves you time when you are working on this type of document, but also improves consistency within your documents.

STUDENT LEARNING OUTCOMES (SLOs)

After completing this chapter, you will be able to:

- **SLO 3.1** Insert and edit footnotes and endnotes in a document (p. W3-129).
- **SLO 3.2** Create a bibliography with properly formatted sources and insert citations into a document (p. W3-134).
- **SLO 3.3** Create and edit a table of contents based on headings (p. W3-144).
- **SLO 3.4** Insert a cover page and modify content and content control fields (p. W3-148).
- **SLO 3.5** Integrate bookmarks into a multipage document (p. W3-153).
- **SLO 3.6** Apply and customize headers and footers in a multipage document (p. W3-156).

Case Study

American River Cycling Club (ARCC) is a community cycling club that promotes fitness for the entire region. ARCC members include recreational cyclists who enjoy the exercise and camaraderie and competitive cyclists who compete in road, mountain, and cyclo-cross races throughout the cycling season.

For the Pause & Practice projects, you create a report for club members about how to develop a personal training program. In this report, you incorporate many of the report features covered in the chapter to produce a professional-looking and useful report.

Pause & Practice 3-1: Insert endnotes into the report, convert endnotes to footnotes, add reference sources, insert citations, and create a bibliography page.

Pause & Practice 3-2: Apply styles to headings in the report, create a table of contents based on the headings in the document, modify the table of contents, and insert a cover page.

Pause & Practice 3-3: Insert and view bookmarks, create hyperlinks and cross-references to bookmarks, and customize headers and footers in the report.

WORD

SLO 3.1

Using Footnotes and Endnotes

Footnotes and ***endnotes*** cite reference sources used in a document. You can also use them to include additional notational information that does not cleanly fit within the text of the document. Footnotes appear at the bottom of each page, while endnotes are listed at the end of the document.

As you insert footnotes and endnotes into your document, Word numbers them consecutively. If another footnote or endnote is inserted before or between existing notes, Word automatically reorders notes. You can also customize number format and convert footnotes to endnotes or endnotes to footnotes.

Insert Footnotes

When a footnote is inserted into a document, a ***reference marker,*** which is a number or letter in superscript format (in a smaller font and slightly raised above the typed line), is inserted directly after the word. Word then places the insertion point at the bottom of the page to insert the text of the footnote. A thin top border above the note distinguishes it from the text in the body of the document.

Footnotes are placed in the body of the document at the bottom of the page, not in the footer, and the text on a page with a footnote is adjusted to allow space for the footnote.

HOW TO: Insert a Footnote

1. Position the insertion point directly after the word where the footnote is to be inserted.
2. Click the **References** tab.
3. Click the **Insert Footnote** button [*Footnotes* group] (Figure 3-1).
   A reference marker is inserted in the body of the document (Figure 3-2), and the insertion point is positioned after the corresponding reference marker in the footnote area of the page.

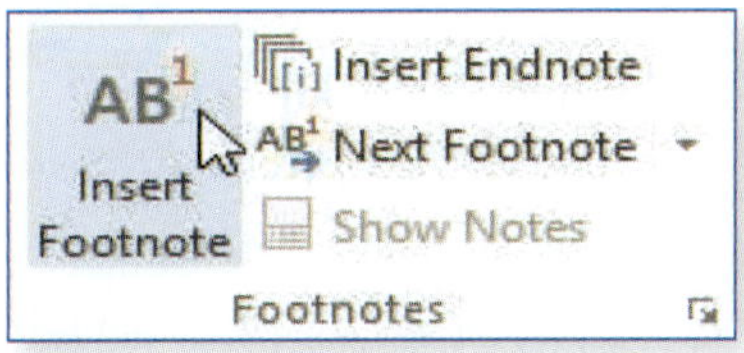

3-1 *Insert Footnote* button

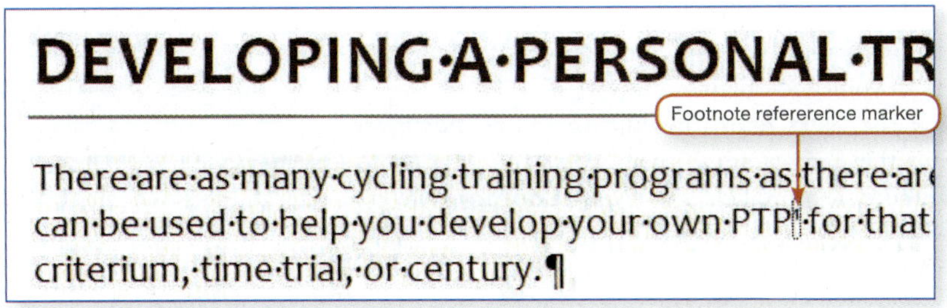

3-2 Footnote reference marker in the body of the document

4. Type the footnote text in the footnote area of the page (Figure 3-3).

3-3 Footnote text at the bottom of the page

Insert Endnotes

Inserting endnotes is similar to inserting footnotes. The main difference is the text for the endnote is placed after the text at the end of the document rather than at the bottom of the page where the note appears.

HOW TO: Insert an Endnote

1. Position the insertion point directly after the word where the endnote is to be inserted.
2. Click the **References** tab.
3. Click the **Insert Endnote** button [*Footnotes* group] (Figure 3-4). The reference marker is inserted in the body of the document and the insertion point is positioned after the corresponding reference marker at the end of the document.
4. Type the endnote text.

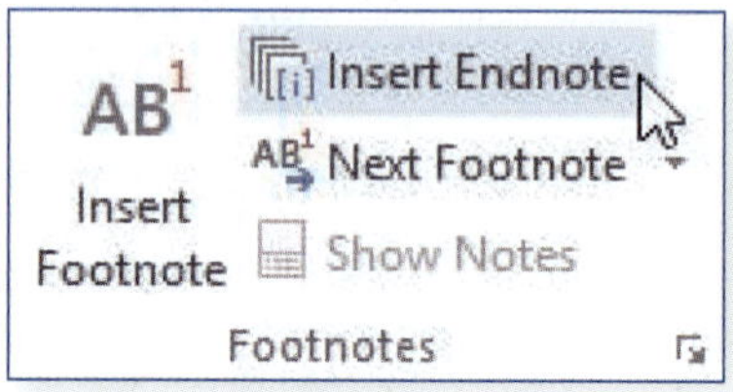

3-4 ***Insert Endnote*** **button**

ANOTHER WAY

Alt+Ctrl+F inserts a footnote.
Alt+Ctrl+D inserts an endnote.

View Footnotes and Endnotes

Once you have footnotes or endnotes in your document, it is easy to see the footnote or endnote text at the bottom of a page or at the end of the document, but you might have a difficult time locating the reference markers in the body of the document. Word provides you with a tool to easily locate footnote reference markers in your document.

Click the **Next Footnote** button in the *Footnotes* group on the *References* tab to move to the next footnote (Figure 3-5). Click the **Next Footnote** drop-down arrow to display a list of options to move to next or previous footnotes or endnotes. Click the **Show Notes** button in the *Footnotes* group to toggle between the note reference markers and the note text.

Word also displays the text of the footnote or endnote when you place your pointer over a reference marker (Figure 3-6).

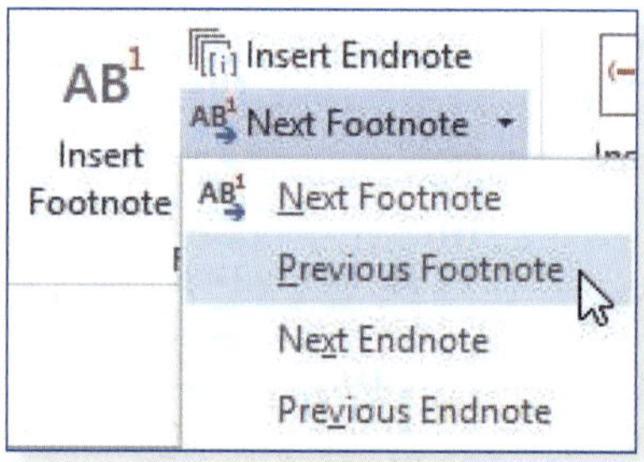

3-5 ***Next Footnote*** **drop-down list**

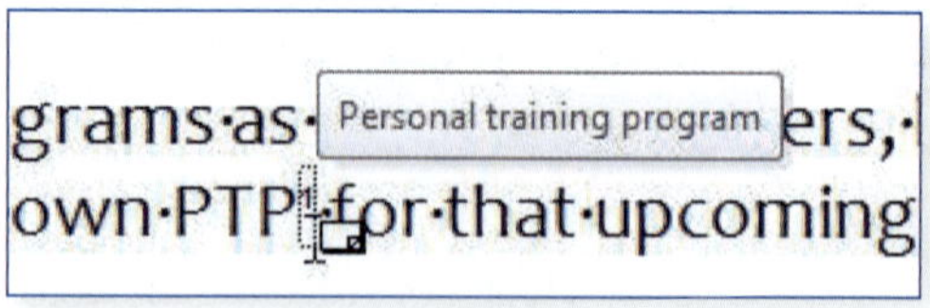

3-6 **Footnote text displayed**

Customize Footnotes and Endnotes

By default, footnotes are numbered consecutively with numbers (e.g., 1, 2, 3) and endnotes are numbered with lowercase Roman numerals (e.g., i, ii, iii). You might decide to use letters or symbols such as an asterisk (*), section mark (§), or number or pound symbol (#) as reference markers. You can customize how notes are numbered and where they are displayed in a document.

HOW TO: Customize Footnotes and Endnotes

1. Select the **References** tab.
2. Click the **Footnotes** launcher [*Footnotes* group] to open the *Footnote and Endnote* dialog box (Figure 3-7).
3. In the *Location* area, select either **Footnotes** or **Endnotes**.
   - In the drop-down list for *Footnotes,* you have the option to position the footnote text at the *Bottom of page* (default) or *Below text*.
   - In the drop-down list for *Endnotes,* you have the option to position the endnote text at the *End of document* (default) or *End of section*.
4. In the *Format* area, you can change any of the following: *Number format, Custom mark, Start at,* or *Numbering.*
5. In the *Apply changes* area, you can apply changes to the *Whole document* or *This section* (if there are sections in your document).
6. Click **Apply** to close the dialog box and apply the changes. Do not press *Insert,* which inserts a footnote or endnote in the document.

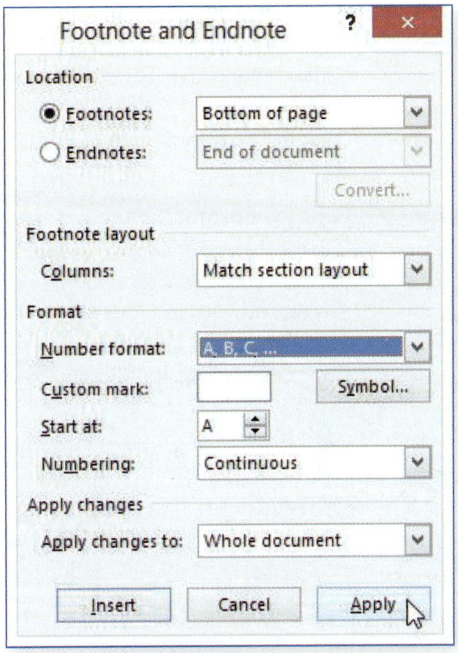

3-7 ***Footnote and Endnote*** **dialog box**

> **MORE INFO**
>
> You can also use the *Footnote and Endnote* dialog box to insert a footnote or endnote.

Modify Footnote and Endnote Format

In addition to customizing placement and note format, you can also change how the text of the footnotes and endnotes appears. You do this the same way you format regular text in the document.

Select the footnote or endnote text and apply any formatting changes such as font, font size, style, line or paragraph spacing, or text effects (Figure 3-8). You can apply changes using the buttons on the *Home* or *Page Layout* tab, the context menu (right-click selected text), the mini toolbar, or keyboard shortcuts.

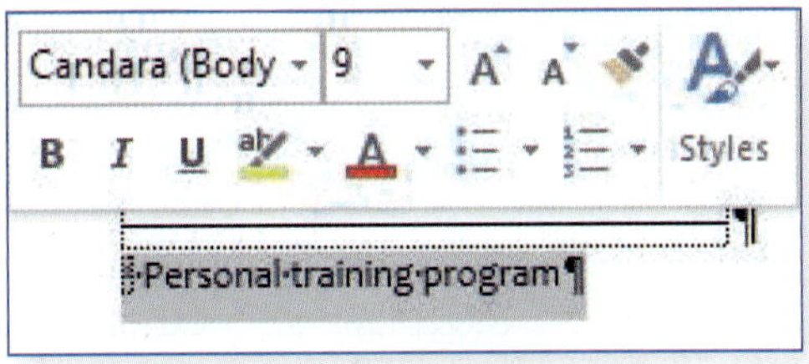

3-8 Apply formatting to footnote text

Modify Footnote and Endnote Styles

The appearance of the footnotes and endnotes in your document is determined by styles. Styles control the font, font size, text styles and effects, and paragraph formatting. When you insert a footnote in your document, Word applies the *Footnote Text* style; this style controls the formatting of all of the footnote text in your document.

You can modify the footnote or endnote style, which automatically updates all of your footnote or endnote text to reflect the changes you made to the style.

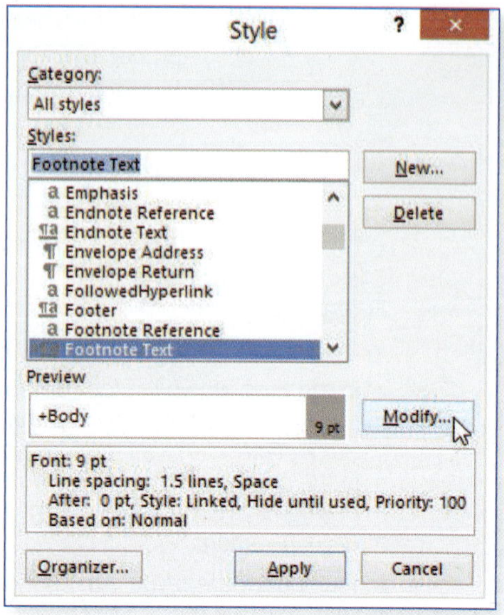

3-9 *Style* dialog box

HOW TO: Modify the Footnote or Endnote Style

1. Right-click the footnote or endnote text and select **Style** from the context menu. The *Style* dialog box opens and the name of the style is displayed in the *Styles* area (Figure 3-9).
2. Click the **Modify** button to open the *Modify Style* dialog box.
3. You can change the basic font formatting in the *Formatting* area.
4. Click the **Format** button to display a list of other formatting options (Figure 3-10).
   - When you select an option, another dialog box opens.
   - Make any desired formatting changes and click **OK** to close the dialog box.
5. Click **OK** to close the *Modify Style* dialog box.

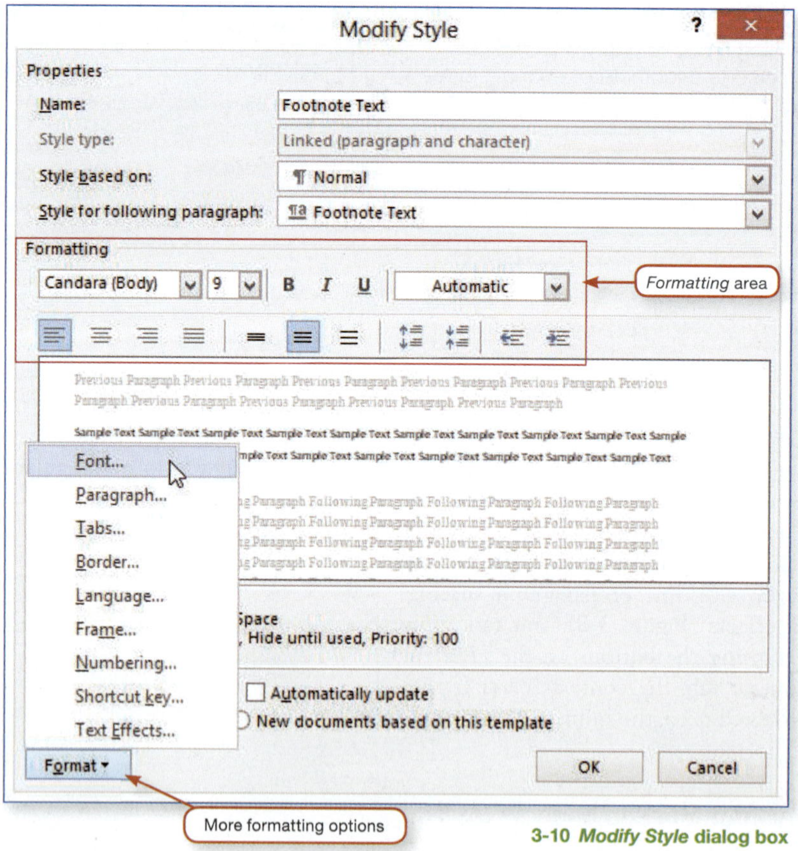

3-10 *Modify Style* dialog box

6. Click **Apply** to apply any changes to the style and close the *Style* dialog box.

Convert Footnotes and Endnotes

There might be times when you want to convert footnotes to endnotes or endnotes to footnotes. Rather than deleting and re-creating them, you can convert notes. When you convert notes, Word automatically renumbers the reference markers and moves the note text to the correct location in the document.

HOW TO: Convert All Notes

1. Click the **Footnotes** launcher [*References* tab, *Footnotes* group] to open the *Footnote and Endnote* dialog box.
2. In the *Location* area, click the **Convert** button. The *Convert Notes* dialog box opens (Figure 3-11).
3. Select from one of the three convert options.
4. Click **OK** to close the *Convert Notes* dialog box.
5. Click **Close** to close the *Footnote and Endnote* dialog box. Do not click *Insert* or Word will insert a footnote or endnote.

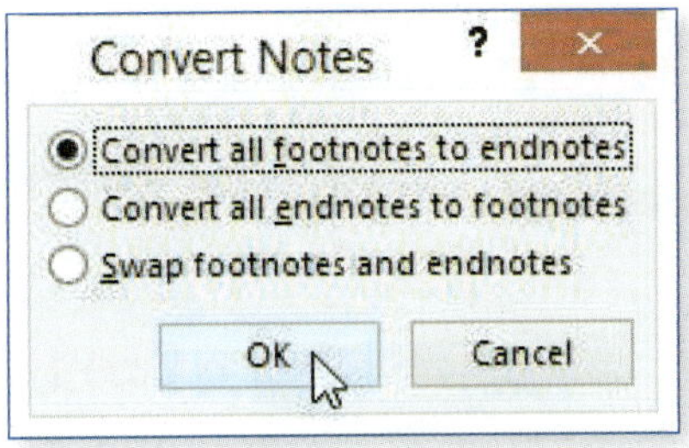

3-11 *Convert Notes* dialog box

> **MORE INFO**
>
> All three of the convert options are active *only* if you have both footnotes and endnotes in your document. Otherwise, only one option is active.

You can convert individual notes using the context menu. Right-click a footnote or endnote (*not* the reference marker in the text of the document) and select **Convert to Endnote** or **Convert to Footnote** (Figure 3-12).

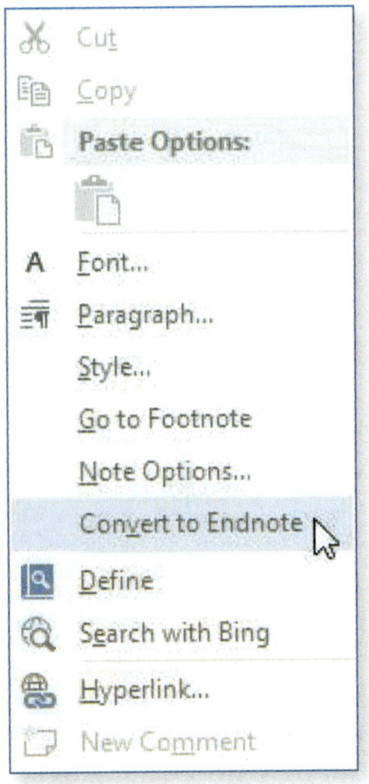

3-12 Convert individual notes

Move Footnotes and Endnotes

You can move footnotes and endnotes in the same way you move text in a document. To move a note, select the **reference marker** in the body of the document (Figure 3-13) and use one of the following methods:

- Drag and drop
- **Ctrl+X** to cut and **Ctrl+V** to paste
- **Cut** and **Paste** buttons [*Home* tab, *Clipboard* group]
- **Cut** and **Paste** options in the context menu

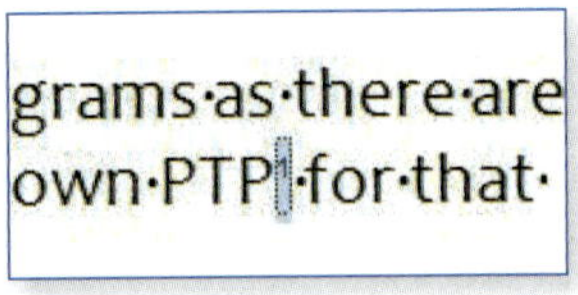

3-13 Select note to move

> **MORE INFO**
>
> When moving a note, select the note carefully to ensure that you are only moving the note and not any spaces or text.

Delete Footnotes and Endnotes

When you delete a note, Word removes the reference marker and the text of the note. Your remaining notes are renumbered and remain in consecutive order.

HOW TO: Delete a Note

1. Select the **reference marker** in the body of the document (*not* the text of the footnote or endnote at the bottom of the page or end of the document).
2. Press **Delete** on the keyboard.
   - Deleting footnote or endnote text in footnote or endnote area will not delete note reference.
3. Check to ensure proper spacing around text where the note was deleted.

SLO 3.2

Creating a Bibliography and Inserting Citations

Typically, the most tedious and time-consuming aspect of writing a research paper is compiling sources, creating a bibliography page, and citing sources in the body of the report. A ***source*** is the complete bibliographic reference for a book, journal article, or web page. A ***citation*** is the abbreviated source information that you place in the body of the report to give credit to the source of the information you use. A ***bibliography*** or ***works cited*** page lists the sources used in the report. Word has tools to create sources, insert citations, and create a bibliography or works cited page at the end of your report.

Report Styles

There are a variety of report styles, and each differs not only in the overall format of the report but also in the format for sources and citations. The most common report styles are the following:

- APA (American Psychological Association)
- Chicago *(The Chicago Manual of Style)*
- MLA (Modern Language Association)
- Turabian

MLA and APA are the two most common report formats. The following table lists some of the general characteristics of each of these two report styles. Within each of these report formats, there can be much variance depending on the preference of your instructor. Always follow the formatting instructions your instructor provides.

Common Report Styles

Report Features	APA	MLA
Font	11 or 12 pt.	11 or 12 pt.
Line Spacing	Academic APA is double spaced and business APA is single spaced.	Double space.
Margins	For an unbound report use 1" for all margins. For a left bound report use 1.5" left margin and 1" top, bottom, and right margins.	Use 1" margins.

Heading Information	Heading information is typically typed on a title page.	Left align at the top of the first page and include author's name, instructor's name, class, and date on separate lines.
Title	The title is either on the title page or centered on the first page of the report.	Centered on the first page of the report.
Header	Include report title and page number on the right.	Include author's last name and page number on the right.
Uses	Typically use in social and behavioral sciences, business, and nursing.	Typically use in humanities.

Bibliography Styles

As you begin compiling your sources for your report, the first thing you need to do is select the ***bibliography style*** of the report. Most likely your instructor will tell you what style to use. You can then select this bibliography style in Word so Word correctly formats sources and citations.

HOW TO: Set the Bibliography Style of the Report

1. Click the **Reference** tab.
2. Click the **Style** drop-down arrow [*Citations & Bibliography* group].
3. Select the style of the report from the drop-down list of report styles (Figure 3-14).

> **MORE INFO**
>
> The report style you select controls the formatting of sources and citations; it does not control the overall formatting of your report. To do that, you must apply the correct formatting to the body of your report.

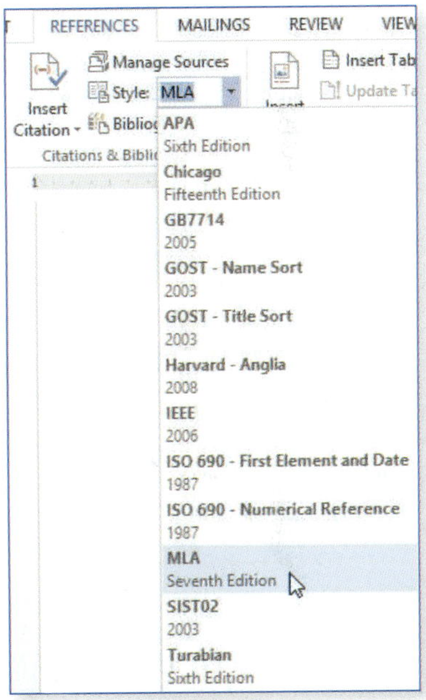

3-14 Select bibliography style

Add a New Source

As you are writing a report, you should be gathering bibliographic information about sources used in your report (e.g., author; title of book, journal, or article; publication date and edition; publisher or online location). You need to add this information to your report in Word. Word inserts a citation in your report at the insertion point and stores this source information. You then can access these stored sources to insert additional citations and create a bibliography page.

HOW TO: Add a New Source

1. Position the insertion point in your document at the point where you want to insert a citation.
2. Click the **Insert Citation** button [*References* tab, *Citations & Bibliography* group].

3. Select **Add New Source**. The *Create Source* dialog box opens (see Figure 3-16).
4. Select the type of source in the *Type of Source* area.
   - The fields for the source change depending on the type of source you choose.
5. Click the **Edit** button to the right of the *Author* area. The *Edit Name* dialog box opens (Figure 3-15).
   - Type the author name in this box so you can specify first, middle, and last names.
   - Add additional authors if your source has more than one author.
   - If the source is an organization or company (e.g., USA Cycling or Velo News), click the **Corporate Author** check box instead of the *Edit* button in the *Create Source* dialog box (see Figure 3-16).
6. Type in the author information and click **OK** when finished (see Figure 3-15).
   - Click the **Add** button to add additional authors.
   - You can also reorder multiple authors by selecting an author in the *Names* area and clicking the **Up** or **Down** button.
7. Type in other source information as needed (Figure 3-16).
   - As you type in other source information, Word automatically creates a *Tag name* for your source.
   - You can edit the *Tag name* if desired.

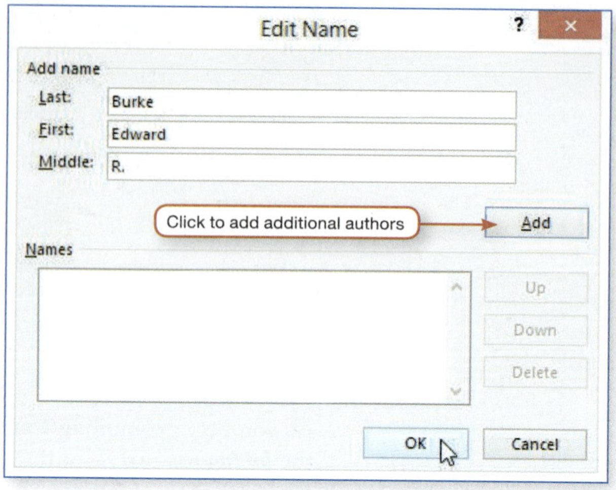

3-15 *Edit Name* dialog box

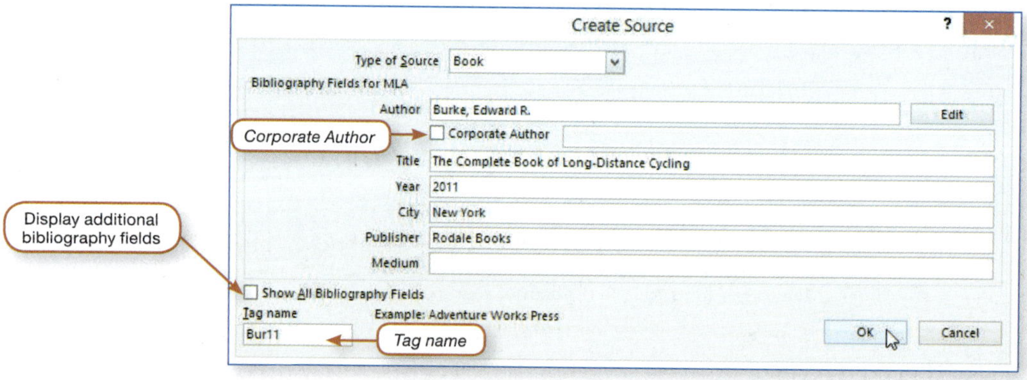

3-16 *Create Source* dialog box

8. Click the **Show All Bibliography Fields** check box to display more fields. For example, you might need to type in the edition of the book.
9. Click **OK** to close the *Create Source* dialog box.
10. The citation is inserted in the document in the report style you selected (Figure 3-17).

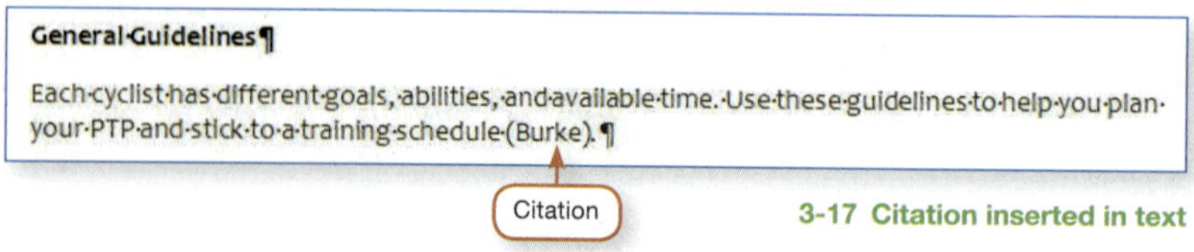

3-17 Citation inserted in text

Insert Citations

Many times you will cite a source more than once in a report. Once you have added a source to your document, you can insert this same citation again in your document without entering source information again. When inserting a citation, you can choose from citations you have previously created.

HOW TO: Insert a Citation

1. Position the insertion point in your document at the point where you want a citation inserted.
2. Click the **Insert Citation** button [*References* tab, *Citations & Bibliography* group].
   - A list of previously used or created sources is displayed in the drop-down list (Figure 3-18).
3. Select from your list of sources.
4. The citation is inserted in the document.
   - When a citation is inserted, Word automatically inserts a space between the citation and the preceding word.

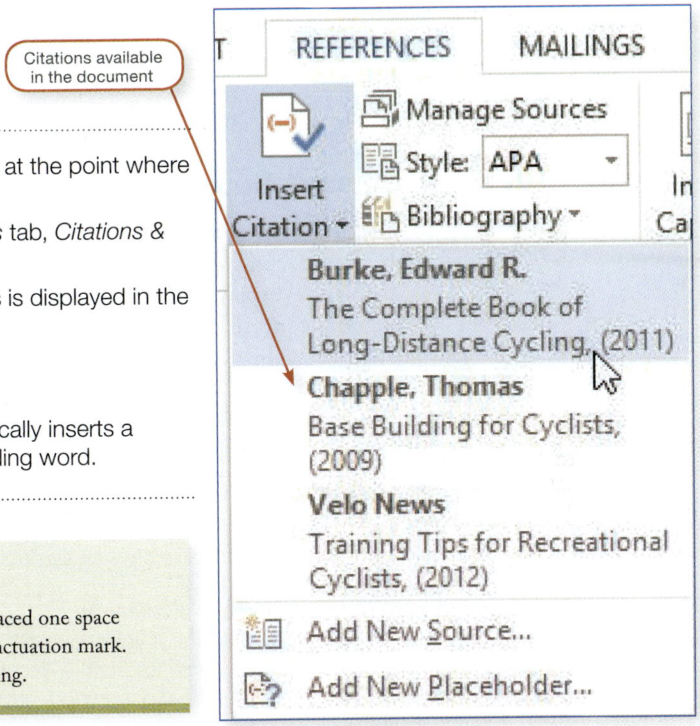

3-18 Insert citation from a previously created source

MORE INFO

When inserting citations, the citation typically is placed one space after the preceding word and directly before the punctuation mark. Always check your document to ensure proper spacing.

Insert a Placeholder

There might be times when you need to insert a citation but do not have all of the bibliographic information to create the source. You can insert a ***placeholder*** in the report to temporarily mark a spot where a citation needs to be completed. Later, you can go back in and add bibliographic source information for any placeholders inserted in the document.

HOW TO: Insert a Placeholder

1. Position the insertion point in your document at the point where you want a placeholder inserted.
2. Click the **Insert Citation** button [*References* tab, *Citations & Bibliography* group].
3. Select **Add New Placeholder**. The *Placeholder Name* dialog box opens (Figure 3-19).

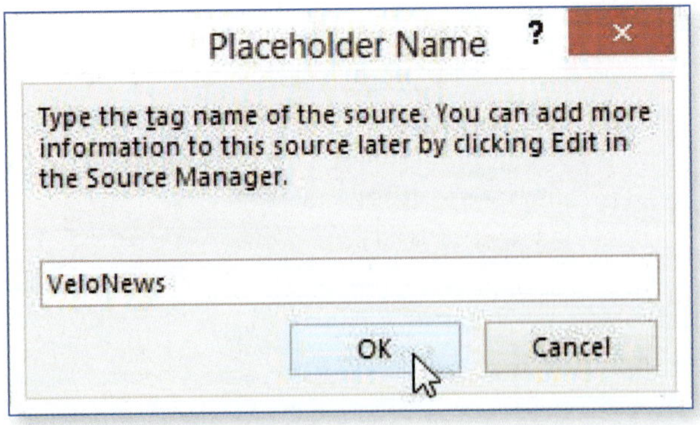

3-19 Insert a placeholder

4. Type in the name of the placeholder.
    - You can't use spaces between words in the placeholder text.
    - Use an underscore or merge words together when naming a placeholder.
5. Click **OK**. The placeholder is inserted into the document and looks similar to a citation (Figure 3-20).

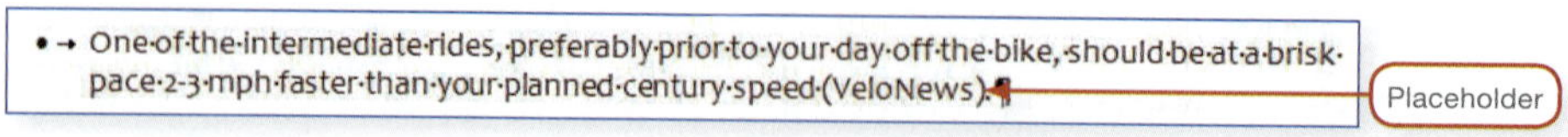

3-20 Placeholder in the body of the document

Manage Sources

The ***Source Manager*** dialog box allows you to create sources, copy sources created and used in other documents, modify sources, and add bibliographic information to placeholders. This dialog box displays which sources are used in your report and the placeholders that need bibliographic information.

HOW TO: Manage Sources

1. Click the **Manage Sources** button [*References* tab, *Citations & Bibliography* group]. The *Source Manager* dialog box opens (Figure 3-21).
    - The *Master List* of sources on the left displays *all* available sources. Some of these may have been created in other Word documents.
    - The *Current List* displays the sources available in your current document.
    - The *Preview* area displays the contents of your source.
    - The sources in the *Current List* that are cited in the document have a check mark next to them.
    - The sources in the *Current List* that are placeholders have a question mark next to them. These placeholders need additional information.

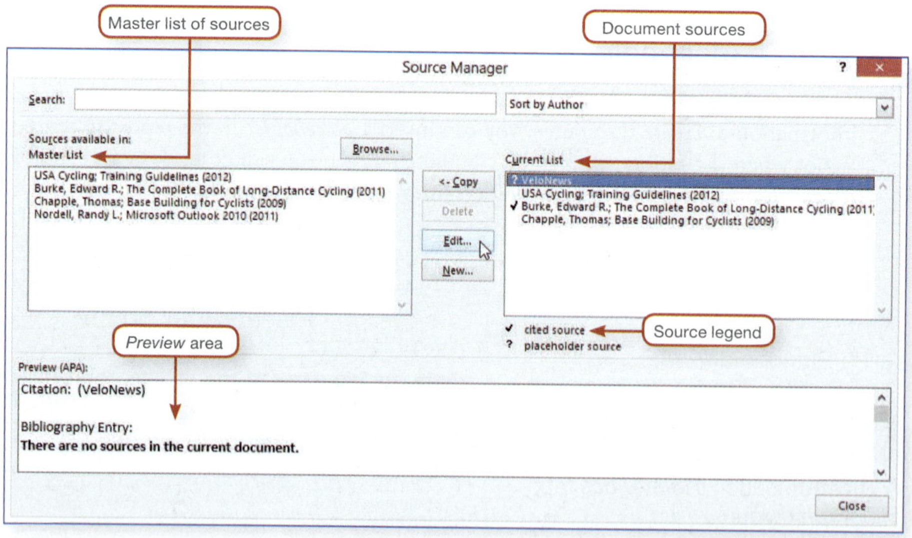

3-21 *Source Manager* dialog box

2. To copy a source from the *Master List* to the *Current List,* select the source and press the **Copy** button. The copied source remains on the *Master List.*

3. To edit a source from either list, select the source and click the **Edit** button. The *Edit Source* dialog box opens.
   - Make changes to the source and press **OK**.
   - Word automatically updates any citations in your document if you make changes to the source.
4. To add bibliographic information to a placeholder, select the placeholder and click the **Edit** button. The *Edit Source* dialog box opens.
   - Add bibliographic information to the placeholder and press **OK**.
   - When bibliographic information is added to a placeholder, it becomes a complete source and the question mark next to it changes to a check.
   - Word automatically replaces the placeholder with a citation in your document when you add bibliographic information to a placeholder.
5. Click the **New** button to create a new source. The *Create Source* dialog box opens.
   - Type in the bibliographic information and press **OK**.
   - This source is now available as a citation to insert in your document.
   - This source is also added to the *Master List*.
6. To delete a source from either list, select the source and click the **Delete** button.
   - You cannot delete a source from the *Current List* if it is cited in the document.
   - If a source is in both lists and you delete it from one list, it is not deleted from the other list.
7. Click **Close** to close the *Source Manager* dialog box and apply any changes made.

Edit Citations and Sources

After citations are inserted into the document, you can edit the citation or source without using the *Source Manager* dialog box. When you click a citation in your document, you see a drop-down list of editing options (Figure 3-22).

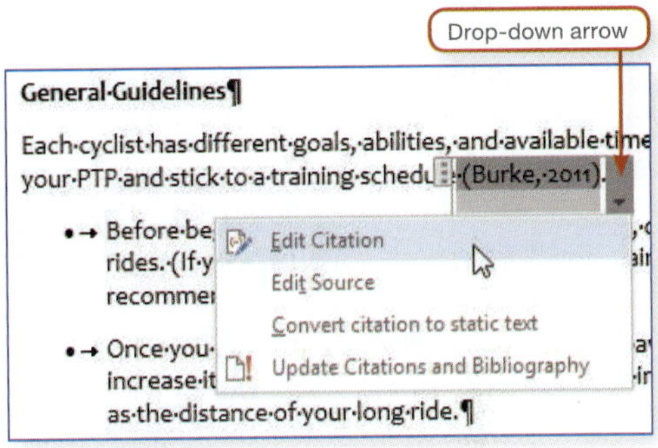

3-22 Edit citation options

- ***Edit Citation:*** Options in the *Edit Citation* dialog box allow you to add a page number to the citation or suppress any currently displayed information.
- ***Edit Source:*** Options in the *Edit Source* dialog box allow you to update source bibliographic information.
- ***Convert citation to static text:*** This option changes the citation from a Word field that is automatically generated and updated to static text that is not updated.
- ***Update Citations and Bibliography:*** This option updates your bibliography page to reflect any changes you have made to citations or sources.

MORE INFO

You can edit placeholders using either the drop-down list or context menu.

You can move or delete a citation or placeholder in the body of the text by clicking the citation or placeholder handle on the left and dragging to a new location (to move) or by pressing **Delete** (to delete) on your keyboard (Figure 3-23).

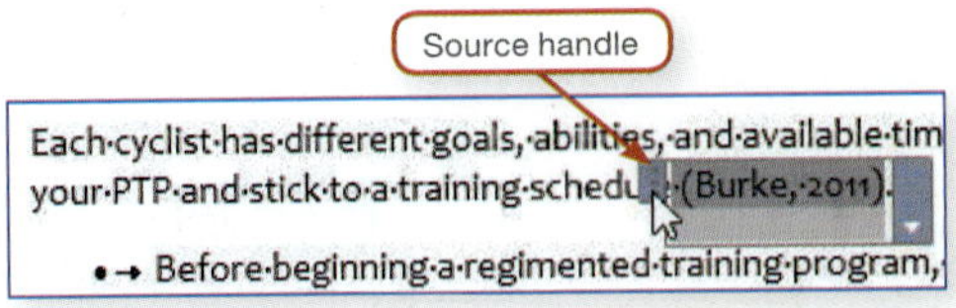

3-23 Select a citation to move or delete

Insert a Bibliography

Once you have created your sources and inserted citations in the body of the report, you are now ready to create a bibliography page. The bibliography page is automatically generated from the sources in your document and is formatted according to the style of report you selected. Word provides you with a few bibliography options.

The *Bibliography, References*, and *Works Cited* built-in options insert a title before the sources. The *Insert Bibliography* option just inserts the sources; you can add a title of your choice. If you are planning on using a table of contents in your report, it is best to use one of the built-in options because Word applies a style for the bibliography title, which allows the bibliography page to automatically be included in the table contents.

HOW TO: Insert a Bibliography

1. Position the insertion point in your document at the point where you want the bibliography to begin.
   - It is usually good to insert a page break (**Ctrl+Enter**) at the end of the document and begin the bibliography on a new page.
2. Click the **Bibliography** button [*References* tab, *Citations & Bibliography* group] to display the list of options (Figure 3-24).
3. Select your bibliography option. The bibliography is inserted in the document.

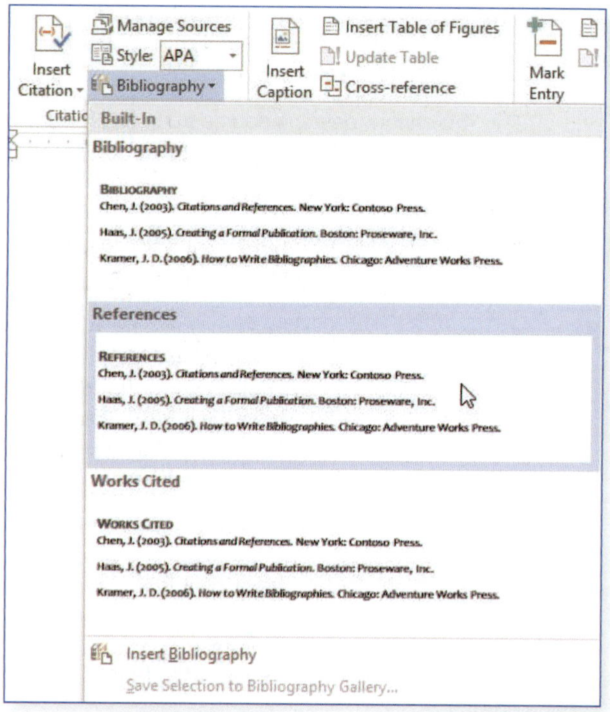

3-24 Insert bibliography

If changes are made to sources after the bibliography page has been inserted, you have to update the bibliography. Click one of the references on the bibliography page to select the entire bibliography and click the **Update Citations and Bibliography** (Figure 3-25).

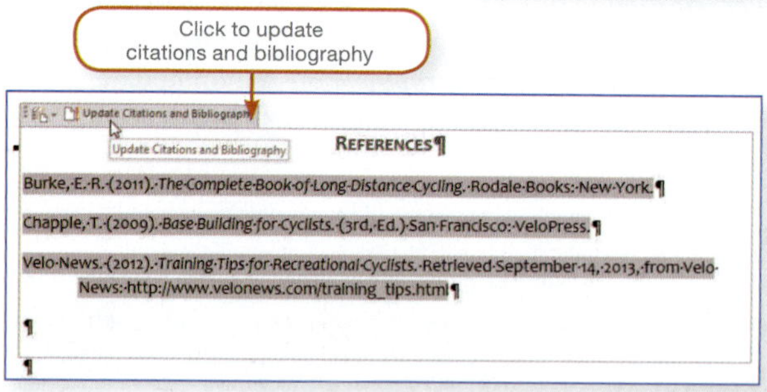

3-25 Bibliography inserted into the document

ANOTHER WAY

Right-click your bibliography and choose **Update Field** or press **F9** to update your bibliography.

PAUSE & PRACTICE: WORD 3-1

For this Pause & Practice project, you modify the *Developing a Personal Training Program* report for American River Cycling Club. You select the report style, add and modify notes, add sources and citations, and insert a bibliography page.

File Needed: ***PersonalTrainingProgram-03.docx***
Completed Project File Name: ***[your initials] PP W3-1.docx***

1. Open the ***PersonalTrainingProgram-03*** document from your student data files.
2. Save this document as ***[your initials] PP W3-1***.
3. Insert endnotes into the report.
   a. Position the insertion point after "PTP" (first page, first paragraph).
   b. Click **Insert Endnote** [*References* tab, *Footnotes* group]. Word moves the insertion point to the endnote area on the last page.
   c. Type Personal training program.
   d. Position the insertion point after the first instance of "Max VO2" (third page, "Training Intensity and Heart Rate" section).

> **MORE INFO**
> Use the *Find* feature in the *Navigation* pane to locate specific words.

   e. Click **Insert Endnote** [*References* tab, *Footnotes* group].
   f. Type The highest rate of oxygen consumption attainable during maximal or exhaustive exercise.
   g. Position the insertion point after "RPM" (third page, "Training Intensity and Heart Rate" section).
   h. Click **Insert Endnote** [*References* tab, *Footnotes* group].
   i. Type Revolutions per minute.
   j. Apply **bold** and **italic** formatting to the words "maximal" and "exhaustive" in the second endnote (Figure 3-26).

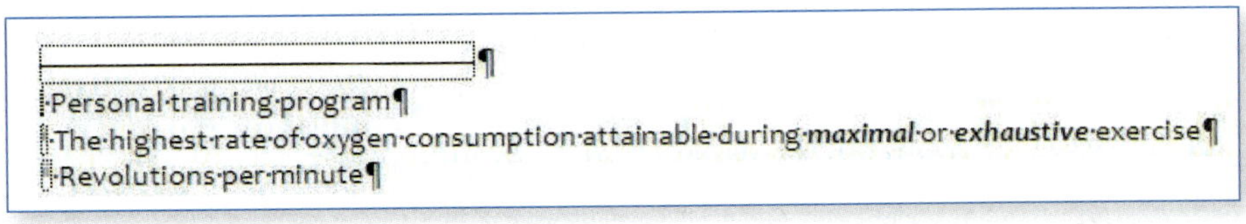

3-26 Endnotes added to report

4. Convert endnotes to footnotes and change numbering.
   a. Click the **Footnotes** launcher [*References* tab, *Footnotes* group]. The *Footnote and Endnote* dialog box opens.
   b. Click the **Convert** button to open the *Convert Notes* dialog box (Figure 3-27).
   c. Select **Convert all endnotes to footnotes** and click **OK**.

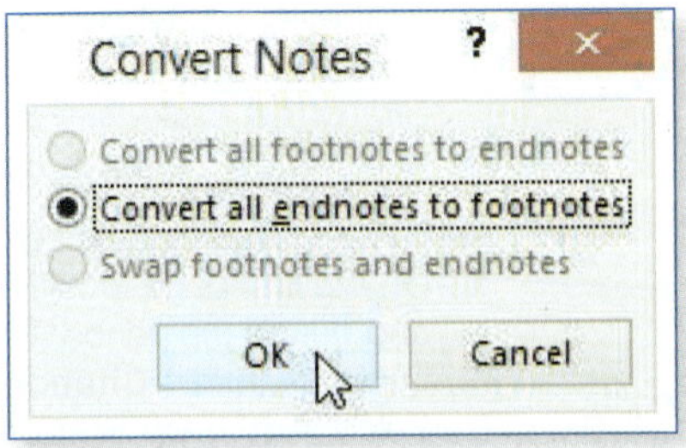

3-27 Convert endnotes to footnotes

d. Click **Close** to the close the *Footnote and Endnote* dialog box.
e. Click the **Footnotes** launcher again to open the *Footnote and Endnote* dialog box.
f. Click the **Footnotes** radio button.
g. Click the **Number format** drop-down arrow and select **a**, **b**, **c . . .** option (Figure 3-28). Don't change any of the other *Format* settings.
h. Choose **Apply** to close the *Footnote and Endnote* dialog box and apply the changes.
i. Check your document to confirm that endnotes have been converted to footnotes and that the number format has been changed.

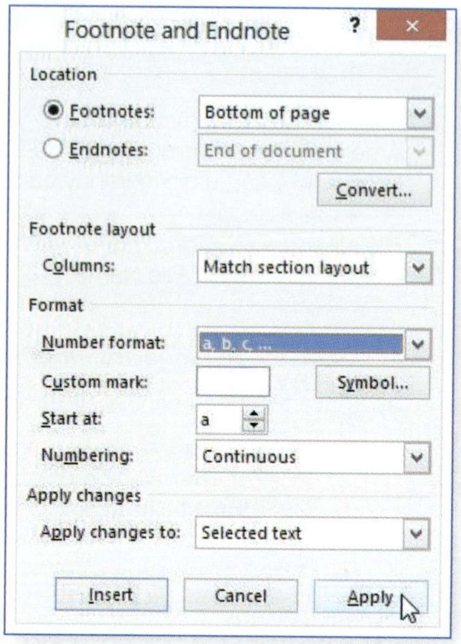

3-28 Change number format of footnotes

5. Change the style of the footnotes.
   a. Right-click the footnote text at the bottom of the first page.
   b. Select **Style** from the context menu. The *Style* dialog box opens.
   c. Click the **Modify** button to open the *Modify Style* dialog box (Figure 3-29).
   d. Change the font size to **9 pt**.
   e. Change line spacing to **1.5**.
   f. Click **OK** to close the *Modify Style* dialog box.
   g. Choose **Apply** to close the *Style* dialog box.

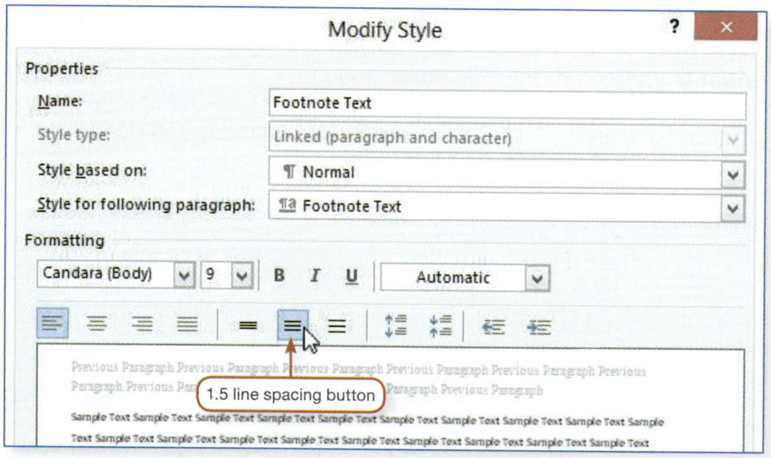

3-29 Modify *Footnote Text* style

6. Select the report style for sources and citations.
   a. Click the **Style** drop-down list [*References* tab, *Citations & Bibliography* group].
   b. Select **MLA Seventh Edition**.
7. Add a new source and insert a citation.
   a. On the first page, position the insertion point after the word "schedule" and before the period (first paragraph, "General Guidelines" section).
   b. Click the **Insert Citation** button [*References* tab, *Citations & Bibliography* group].
   c. Select **Add New Source**. The *Create Source* dialog box opens.
   d. Select **Book** as the type of source.

e. Click the **Edit** button to open the *Edit Name* dialog box.
f. In the *Author* area, type Burke for *Last,* Edward for *First,* and R. for *Middle*.
g. Click **OK** to close the dialog box.
h. Type the following in the *Create Source* dialog box:

Title: The Complete Book of Long-Distance Cycling
Year: 2011
City: New York
Publisher: Rodale Books
Tag name: Burke

i. Click **OK** to add the source, insert the citation, and close the dialog box.

8. Add a placeholder to the report.
   a. On the first page, position the insertion point after the word "speed" and before the period (last bulleted item, "Pace of Rides" section).
   b. Click the **Insert Citation** button [*References* tab, *Citations & Bibliography* group].
   c. Select **Add New Placeholder**. The *Placeholder Name* dialog box opens.
   d. Type VeloNews (no space between words) as the placeholder text.
   e. Press **OK** to insert the placeholder and close the dialog box.

9. Manage sources to add a new source and complete bibliographic information for the placeholder.
   a. Click the **Manage Sources** button [*References* tab, *Citations & Bibliography* group]. The *Source Manager* dialog box opens.
   b. Select **VeloNews** in the *Current List* area and click the **Edit** button.
   c. Type the following:

   Type of Source: **Document from Web Site**
   Corporate Author (check **Corporate Author** check box): Velo News
   Name of Web Page: Training Tips for Recreational Cyclists
   Name of Web Site: Velo News
   Year: 2012
   Year Accessed: 2013 (check **Show All Bibliography Fields** box)
   Month Accessed: September
   Day Accessed: 14
   URL: http://www.velonews.com/training_tips.html

   d. Click **OK** to close the *Edit Source* dialog box. The placeholder is updated as a complete source.
   e. Click the **New** button to create a new source.
   f. Type the following:

   Type of Source: **Book**
   Author: Thomas Chapple
   Title: Base Building for Cyclists
   Year: 2009
   City: San Francisco
   Publisher: VeloPress
   Edition (check **Show All Bibliography Fields** check box): 3rd
   Tag name: Chapple

   g. Click **OK** to close the *Create Source* dialog box.
   h. Click **Close** to close the *Source Manager* dialog box.

10. Insert citations into the report.
    a. On the second page, position the insertion point after "rest day" and before the period (first paragraph, "Number of Rides per Week" section).

b. Click the **Insert Citation** button [*References* tab, *Citations & Bibliography* group] (Figure 3-30).
c. Select the **Chapple**, **Thomas** source. The citation is inserted into the report.
d. Using the **Insert Citation** button, insert the following citations:

Burke, **Edward**, **R.:** after "training week" and before the period (page 2, last bulleted item in the "Duration of Rides" section).
Chapple, **Thomas:** after "maximum heart rate" and before the period (page 3, first paragraph in "Training Intensity and Heart Rate" section).
Velo News: after "overtraining" and before the period (page 3, at the end of "Other Heart Rate Factors" section).

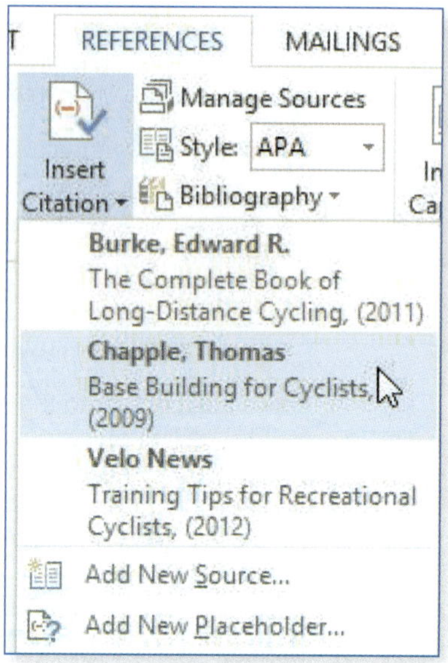

3-30 Insert a citation

11. Insert a bibliography and change report style.
    a. Position the insertion point on the blank line at the end of the document and press **Ctrl+Enter** to insert a page break.
    b. Click the **Bibliography** button [*References* tab, *Citations & Bibliography* group] and select **References** from the drop-down list. The *Reference* page is inserted on the blank page at the end of the document.
    c. **Center** the *References* title and apply **10 pt**. after paragraph spacing.
    d. Click the **Style** drop-down list [*References* tab, *Citations & Bibliography* group].
    e. Select **APA Sixth Edition**.

12. Save and close the document (Figure 3-31).

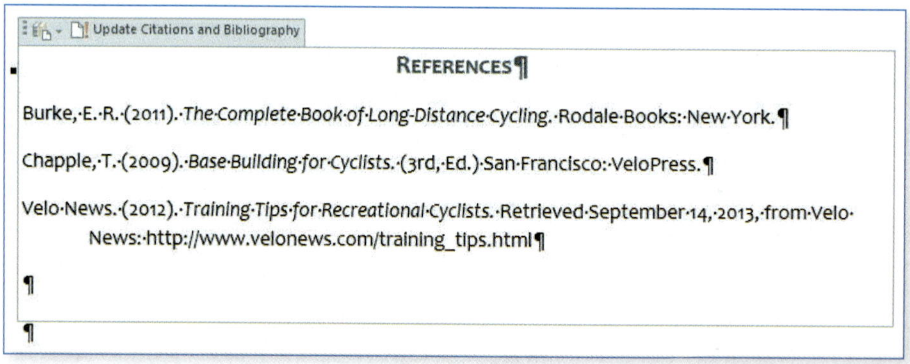

3-31 PP W3-1 References page

SLO 3.3

Inserting a Table of Contents

Most long reports have a ***table of contents*** to provide readers with an overview of the material covered in the report. The table of contents reflects the headings in the report; some tables of contents list only the main headings while others might list second- and third-level headings. Typically, a table of contents lists headings on the left and page numbers on the right with a dot leader separating them.

You can create a table of contents manually by typing in the headings, using a tab with a dot leader, and then typing the page number. But with Word you can automatically generate a table of contents based upon the headings in your report. This saves you time, and, if you generate your table of contents this way, it automatically updates if topics are moved or page numbering changes in the report.

Use Heading Styles for a Table of Contents

Word can automatically generate a table of contents listing the headings in your report if ***heading styles*** are applied to each heading. Styles control the appearance of text by applying a specific font, font size, color, font styles and effects, and spacing to the text on which a style is applied. The document ***theme*** determines the appearance of the styles. Many of the commonly used styles are displayed in the *Styles* gallery.

> **MORE INFO**
>
> Styles and themes were introduced in Chapter 2.

The first step in automatically generating a table of contents in a report is to apply a heading style to each heading in the document. Word provides you with multiple levels of heading styles (e.g., Heading 1, Heading 2, etc.).

HOW TO: Apply Heading Styles

1. Select the heading where you want to apply a style.
2. Click the heading style to apply [*Home* tab, *Styles* group] (Figure 3-32). The style is applied to the heading.
   - Apply *Heading 1* to main headings, *Heading 2* to second level headings, and other heading styles as needed.
   - When you place the insertion point on a style, Word displays a live preview of the style and temporarily applies the style to the selected text.
   - Click the **More** button to expand the *Style* gallery to display more styles.

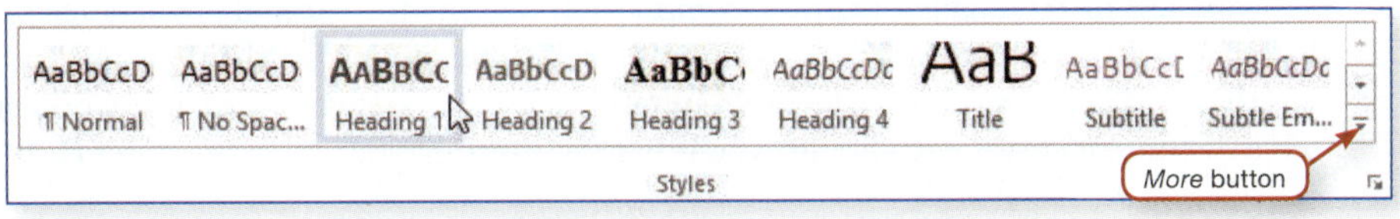

3-32 Document styles displayed in the *Style* gallery

3. Continue to select headings and apply styles. Every heading that you want to have in your table of contents must have a style.
   - When a heading style has been applied to text, there is an *Expand/Collapse* button to the left of the heading (Figure 3-33). Click the **Expand/Collapse** button to expand or collapse the text below the heading.

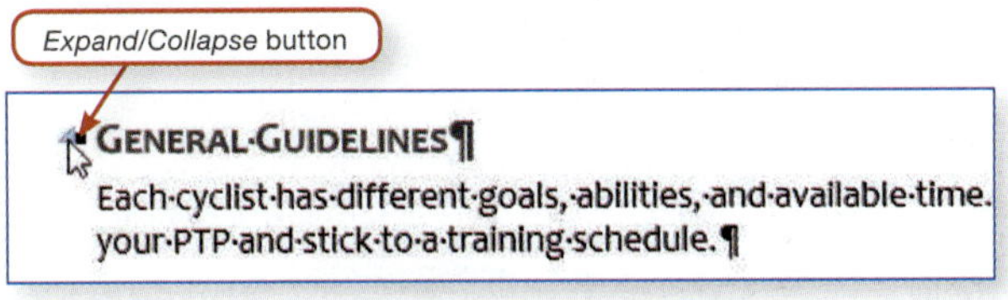

3-33 Expand or collapse text below heading

Insert a Built-In Table of Contents

You can insert a built-in table of contents that includes the headings in your document. Word inserts the table of contents at the point in your report where the insertion point is located. It is a good idea to insert a blank page before the first page of your report for your table of contents.

HOW TO: Insert a Built-In Table of Contents

1. Place the insertion point before the first line of the report and press **Ctrl+Enter** to insert a page break.
2. Position the insertion point at the top of the new first page.
3. Click the **References** tab.
4. Click the **Table of Contents** button [*Table of Contents* group] (Figure 3-34).
5. Select a built-in table of contents to insert. The table of contents is inserted into your report (Figure 3-35).

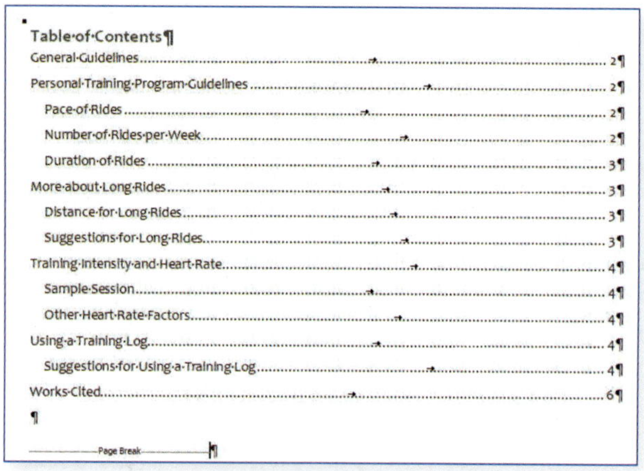

3-35 Table of contents inserted into the report

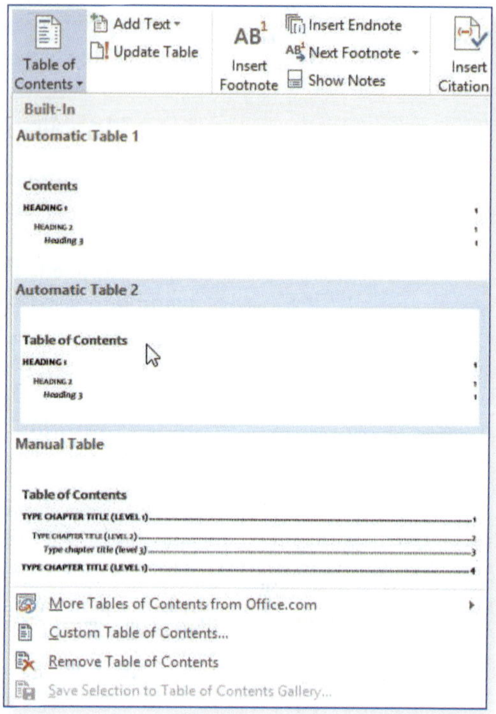

3-34 Insert built-in table of contents

Insert a Custom Table of Contents

You can also insert a table of contents and customize the format and appearance of the table. When you insert a custom table of contents, the "Table of Contents" title is not automatically inserted as it is when you insert a built-in table of contents. If you want a title on your custom table of contents page, you should type it before inserting your table of contents.

> **MORE INFO**
>
> It is usually best to just apply font formatting (not a heading style) to the table of contents title. If a heading style is applied to the table of contents title, the table of contents title is included as an item in the table of contents when it is updated.

HOW TO: Insert a Custom Table of Contents

1. Place the insertion point before the first line of your report and press **Ctrl+Enter** to insert a page break.
2. Position the insertion point at the top of the new first page.
   - If desired, type a title for the table of contents and press **Enter**. Do not apply a heading style to the title.
3. Click the **Table of Contents** button [*References* tab, *Table of Contents* group].

4. Select **Custom Table of Contents**. The *Table of Contents* dialog box opens (Figure 3-36).
   - A preview of the table of contents appears in the *Print Preview* area.
   - Below the *Print Preview* area, you can choose to not display page numbers or not have them aligned on the right and select the type of leader to use with right-aligned page numbers.
5. In the *General* area, select a table of contents format from the **Formats** drop-down list.
6. Select the number of heading levels to display in the *Show levels* area.
7. Click **OK** to insert the table of contents.

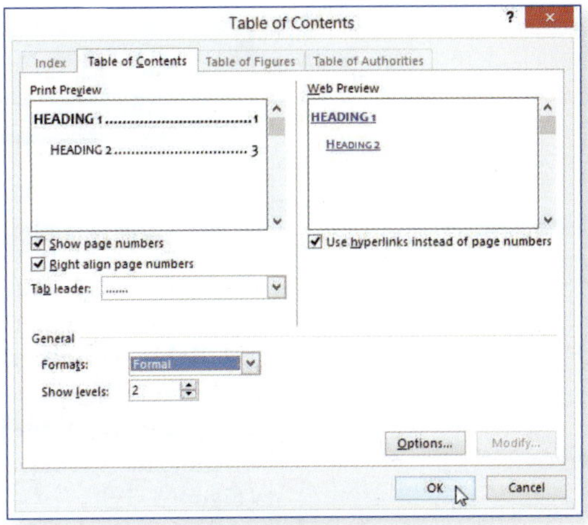

3-36 ***Table of Contents* dialog box**

Modify a Table of Contents

After inserting a table of contents, you might decide that you want a different format or to change the levels of headings that are displayed. When you update a table of contents, you are actually replacing the old table of contents with a new one.

HOW TO: Modify a Table of Contents

1. Click anywhere in the table of contents.
2. Click the **Table of Contents** button [*References* tab, *Table of Contents* group].
3. Select **Custom Table of Contents**. The *Table of Contents* dialog box opens.
4. Make changes to the table of contents.
5. Click **OK**. A dialog box opens, confirming you want to replace the existing table of contents (Figure 3-37).
6. Click **YES** to insert the new table of contents.

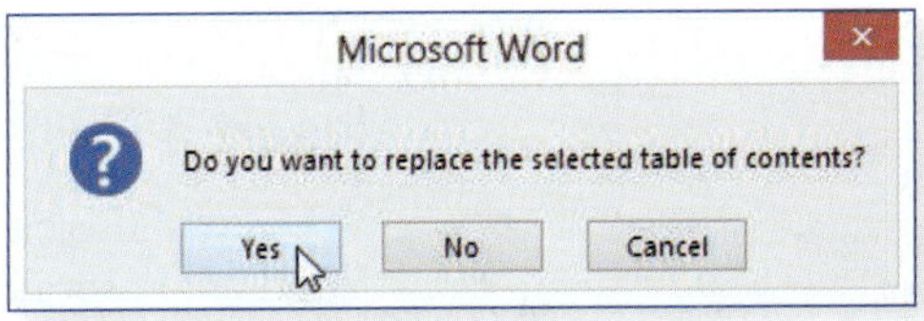

3-37 Replace existing table of contents

Update a Table of Contents

When you make changes to your report such as adding or modifying headings, content, or page breaks, the content and page numbers in the table of contents may no longer be accurate. You need to update the table of contents to reflect these changes. You have the option of updating only page numbers or updating the entire table of contents, which includes both content and page numbers.

HOW TO: Update a Table of Contents

1. Click anywhere in the table of contents.
2. Click the **Update Table** button [*References* tab, *Table of Contents* group]. The *Update Table of Contents* dialog box opens (Figure 3-38).
3. Select either **Update page numbers only** or **Update entire table**.
4. Click **OK** to update the table of contents.

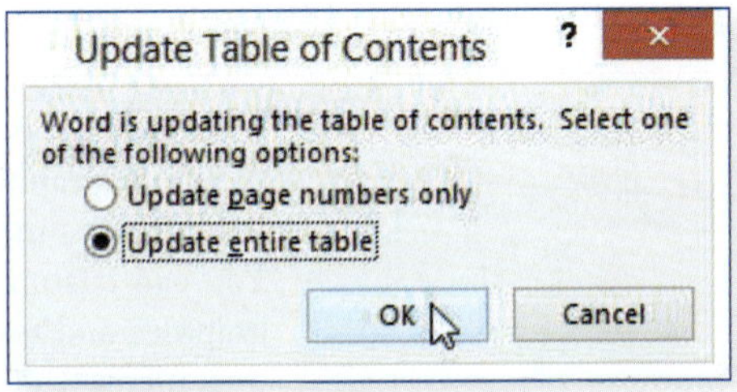

3-38 Update table of contents

> **ANOTHER WAY**
>
> Press **F9** or right-click the table of contents and select **Update Field** to update the table of contents.

Remove a Table of Contents

If you no longer want a table of contents in your report, you can easily remove it. Click the **Table of Contents** button in the *Table of Contents* group on the *References* tab and select **Remove Table of Contents.** The table of contents is removed from your document (Figure 3-39).

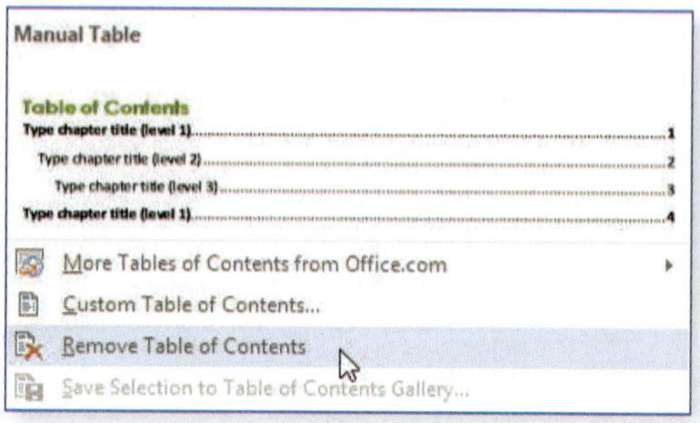

3-39 Remove table of contents

SLO 3.4

Inserting a Cover Page

Some reports have a title page as the cover or introduction. If you're writing a formal report in APA style, there is a specific way you must organize the title page. But if you're presenting a market analysis or product feasibility report at work, you might want a ***cover page*** to introduce the report with professional appeal. Word provides you with a variety of cover page options.

Insert a Built-In Cover Page

When you insert a cover page into a document, Word automatically inserts it at the beginning of the document and inserts a page break to push the existing first page content to the second page.

To insert a cover page, click the **Cover Page** button in the *Pages* group on the *Insert* tab and select one of the built-in cover pages from the drop-down list (Figure 3-40). More custom cover pages are available on Office.com. Select **More Cover Pages from Office.com** to display a list of additional cover pages.

3-40 Insert built-in cover page

Customize Cover Page Content

The built-in cover pages in Word are arrangements of graphics, text boxes, and Word fields. Some of the fields are document property fields and some are ***content control fields,*** fields where you can type custom information. You can customize the content of the fields, delete unwanted Word fields, and modify the graphics and text boxes on the cover page. Cover pages are controlled by the theme of your document, which means the colors and fonts change depending on the theme selected for the document.

Customize Document Property Content

If you have added information to the document properties of your document, Word automatically populates the document properties fields in the cover page. When you type information into a document property field on the cover page, Word adds this information to your document properties.

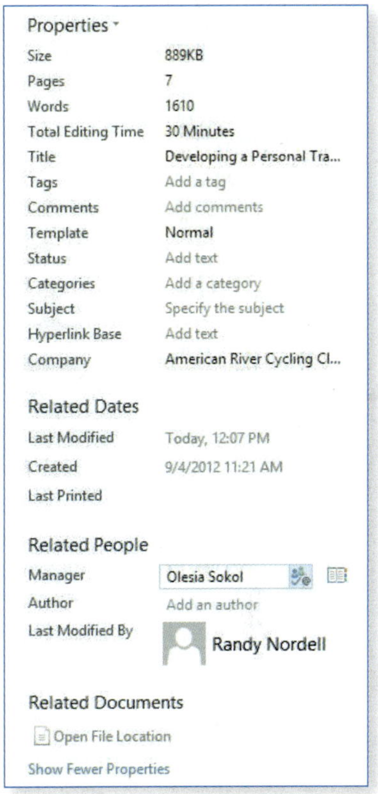

3-41 Document properties on the *Backstage* view

HOW TO: Customize Document Properties

1. Click the **File** tab to open the *Backstage* view and select **Info** to display document properties (Figure 3-41).
2. Click the **Show All Properties** link at the bottom.
   - This link toggles between *Show All Properties* and *Show Fewer Properties*.
3. Add or modify document property content.
   - Some fields, such as *Last Modified* and *Created,* cannot be modified.
   - To remove the *Author,* right-click the author and select **Remove Person**.
4. Click the **Back** arrow to return to the document. Word updates the document property fields on the cover page.

Add or Remove Document Property Fields

You can also add document property fields to the cover page or remove them. When you add a document property field to a cover page, the content of this field is automatically populated with the information from your document properties.

HOW TO: Add Document Property Fields

1. Position the insertion point at the place where you want to insert the document property field.
2. Click the **Insert** tab.
3. Click the **Quick Parts** button [*Text* group] (Figure 3-42).
4. Choose **Document Property**.
5. Select a document property field from the drop-down list. The document property field is inserted into the document.

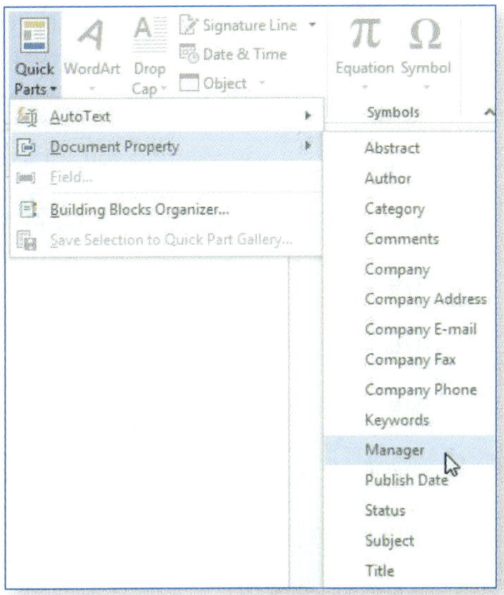

3-42 Insert document property field

> **MORE INFO**
>
> You can insert document property fields anywhere in a document.

To remove a document property field, click the **field handle** and press **Delete** (Figure 3-43). Make sure to check for proper spacing and paragraph breaks when you delete a document property field.

3-43 Delete document property field

Print Document Properties

After customizing document properties, you can print the document properties included in a document. When you print document properties, only a page listing the document properties prints, not the document itself.

HOW TO: Print Document Properties

1. Click the **File** tab to open the *Backstage* view.
2. Click **Print** on the left.
3. Click **Print All Pages** and select **Document Info** from the drop-down list (Figure 3-44).
4. Click the **Print** button to print the document properties.

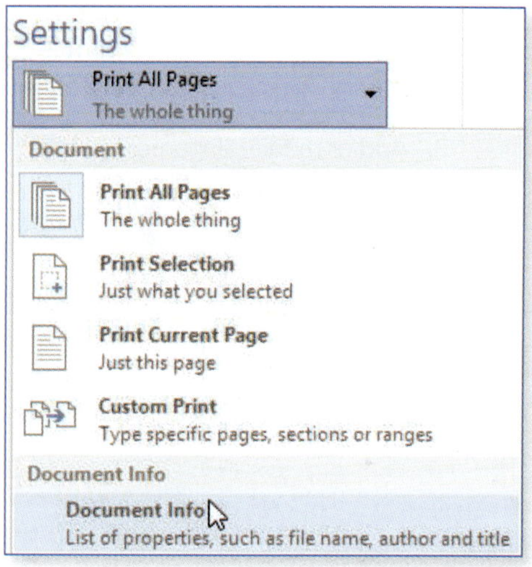

3-44 Print document properties

Customize Content Control Fields

When you insert a cover page into a document, many of the fields are content control fields, which are fields where you type or select custom content (Figure 3-45). You may want to add content to some of these fields and remove others. You can remove Word content control fields the same way you remove a document property field (see Figure 3-43).

To insert custom content into a content control field, click in the field and type the information. You can type whatever information you want into a content control field. For example, you can type a web address into the *Address* field (Figure 3-45).

3-45 Insert text into a content control field

Remove a Cover Page

You might decide that you no longer want a cover page or that you want to insert a different one. Removing a cover page is similar to removing a table of contents. Click the **Cover Page** button and select **Remove Current Cover Page** (Figure 3-46). When you remove a cover page, Word deletes the entire contents of the cover page and removes the page break.

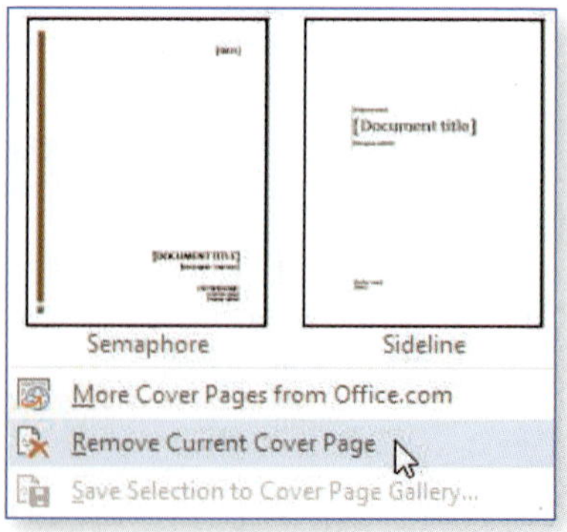

3-46 Remove cover page

PAUSE & PRACTICE: WORD 3-2

For the Pause & Practice project, you continue to modify the *Personal Training Program* report for American River Cycling Club. You apply styles to headings in the report, insert and modify a table of contents, and insert and modify a cover page.

File Needed: ***[your initials] PP W3-1.docx***
Completed Project File Name: ***[your initials] PP W3-2.docx***

1. Open the ***[your initials] PP W3-1*** document created in *Pause & Practice 3-1*.
2. Save this document as ***[your initials] PP W3-2***.
3. Apply styles to the headings in the report.
   a. Select the "**General Guidelines**" heading on the first page.
   b. Click the **Heading 1** style [*Home* tab, *Styles* group] to apply this style to the selected heading (Figure 3-47). If the *Heading 1* style is not visible, click the **More** button to display the entire *Styles* gallery.

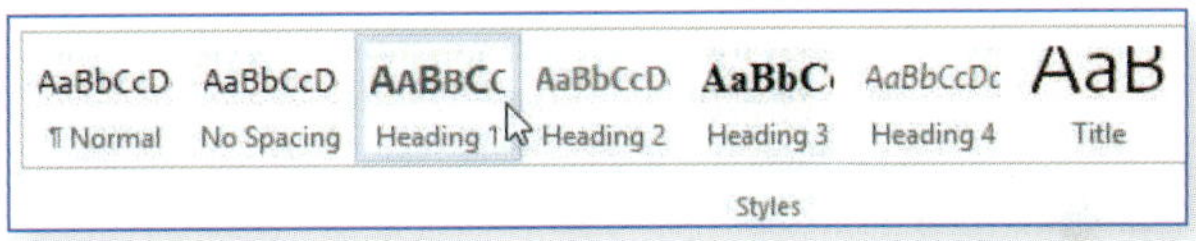

3-47 Apply *Heading 1* style

   c. Apply the **Heading 1** style to the following headings (bolded headings in the document):

      Personal Training Program Guidelines
      More about Long Rides
      Training Intensity and Heart Rate
      Using a Training Log

   d. Apply the **Heading 2** style to the following headings (underlined headings in the document):

      Pace of Rides
      Number of Rides per Week
      Duration of Rides
      Distance for Long Rides
      Suggestions for Long Rides
      Sample Session
      Other Heart Rate Factors
      Suggestions for Using a Training Log

4. Insert a page break and add a table of contents.
   a. Turn on **Show/Hide** [*Home* tab, *Paragraph* group].
   b. Position the insertion point at the beginning of the document before the title ("Developing a Personal Training Program") and press **Ctrl+Enter** to insert a page break.
   c. Position the insertion point before the page break on the new first page.
   d. Click the **Table of Contents** button [*References* tab, *Table of Contents* group] (Figure 3-48).
   e. Select **Automatic Table 2** from the drop-down list. The table of contents is inserted on the first page of the report.

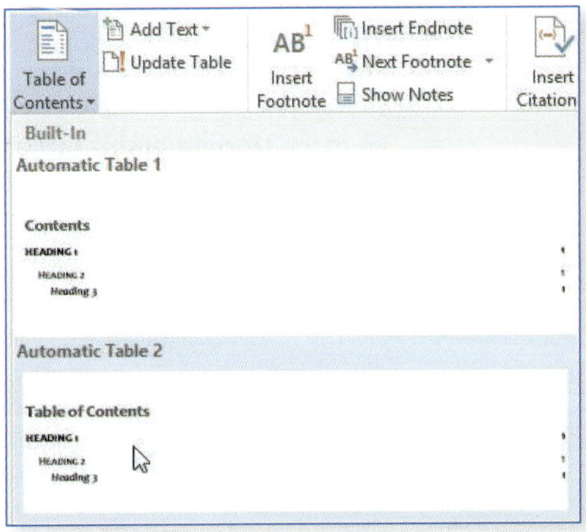

3-48 Insert table of contents

5. Customize the table of contents.
   a. Position the insertion point anywhere in the body of the table of contents.
   b. Click the **Table of Contents** button [*References* tab, *Table of Contents* group].
   c. Select **Custom Table of Contents** to open the *Table of Contents* dialog box (Figure 3-49).
   d. Click the **Formats** drop-down list and select **Formal**.
   e. In the *Show levels* area, set the number of levels at **2**.
   f. Check the **Right align page numbers** check box if it is not already checked.
   g. Select the dot leader option from the *Tab leader* drop-down list if it is not already selected.
   h. Click **OK** to close the dialog box. A dialog box opens, confirming you want to replace the existing table of contents (Figure 3-50).
   i. Click **YES** to replace the existing table of contents.

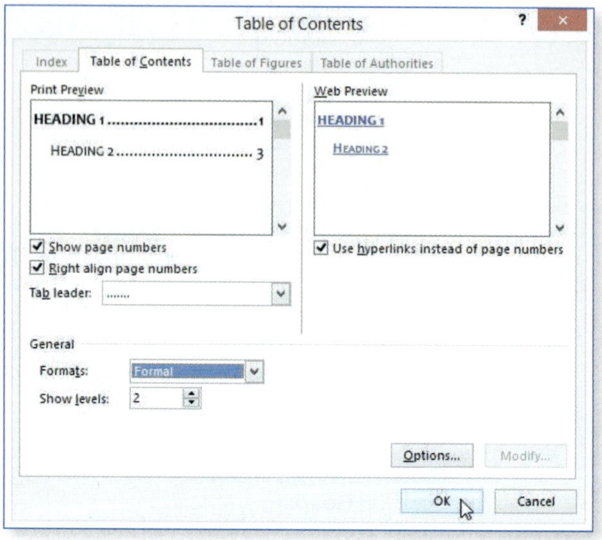

3-49 Customize table of contents

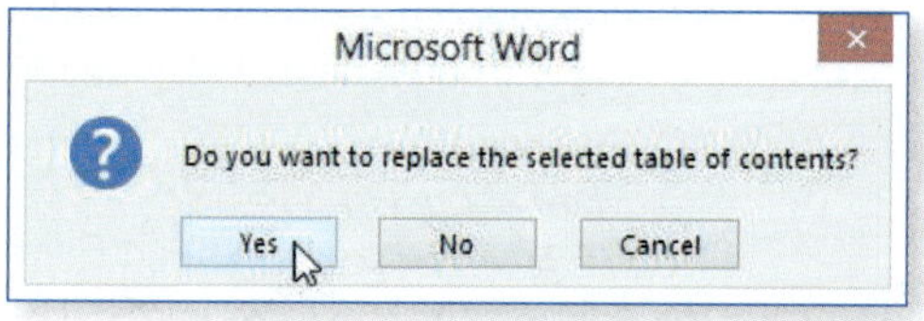

3-50 Replace existing table of contents

6. Insert page breaks and update table of contents.
   a. On the second page, position the insertion point in front of the "Number of Rides per Week" heading and press **Ctrl+Enter** to insert a page break and push this heading to the next page.
   b. Repeat this process on the following headings:

      Suggestions for Long Rides
      Using a Training Log

   c. Press **Ctrl+Home** to move to the beginning of the document.
   d. Click the **Update Table** button [*References* tab, *Table of Contents* group]. The *Update Table of Contents* dialog box opens (Figure 3-51).
   e. Select the **Update entire table** radio button and click **OK**.
   f. If there is a blank line above the table of contents, select it and press **Delete**.

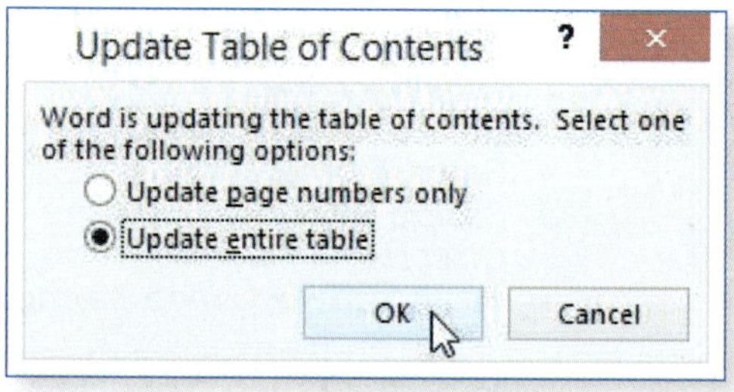

3-51 Update entire table of contents

7. Customize document properties.
   a. Click the **File** tab to open the *Backstage* view and select **Info** to display document properties.
   b. Click the **Show All Properties** link in the document properties area.
   c. Add the following document properties:
      Title: Developing a Personal Training Program
      Company: American River Cycling Club
      Manager: Olesia Sokol
   d. In the *Author* area, right-click the author's name and select **Remove Person**.
   e. Click the **Back** arrow to return to the report.

8. Add a cover page and customize fields.
   a. Click the **Cover Page** button [*Insert* tab, *Pages* group] and select **Semaphore**. The cover page is inserted on a page before the table of contents.
   b. Click the **Date** field drop-down arrow to display the calendar and select the current date.
   c. Click the **Author** document property field, select the field handle, and press **Delete** to delete the field (Figure 3-52). The insertion point is positioned on the blank line where the *Author* field was removed.

3-52 Delete document property field

   d. Click the **Quick Parts** button [*Insert* tab, *Text* group].
   e. Choose **Document Property** and select **Manager** from the drop-down list. The *Manager* document property field is inserted into the cover page.
   f. Click in the **Company Address** field and type: www.arcc.org.
   g. Select and delete the **Subject** field ("[Document Subtitle]").
   h. Click in the **Title** field and apply **bold** format. The bold formatting is applied to the entire title.
9. Save and close the document (Figure 3-53).

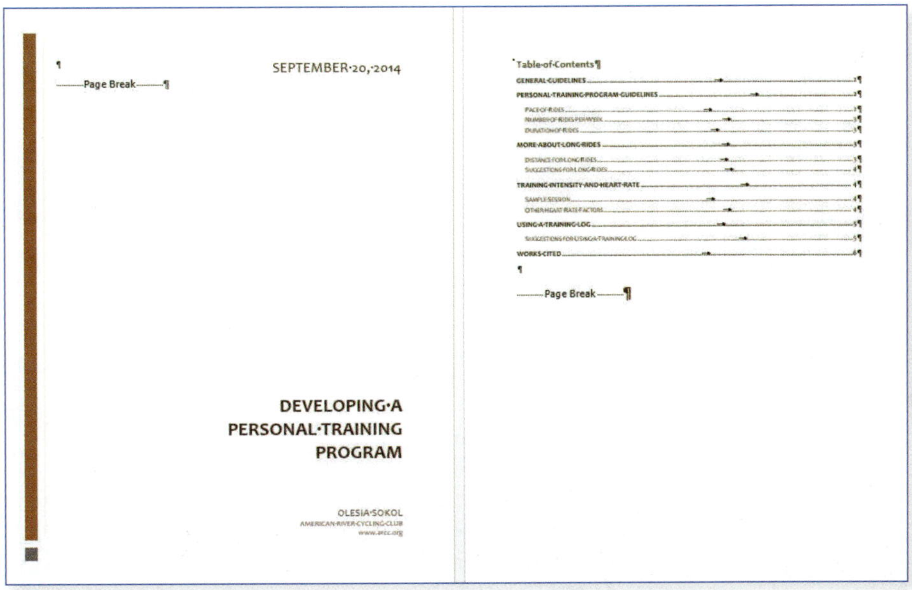

3-53 PP W3-2 cover page and table of contents

SLO 3.5

Using Bookmarks

When working with long documents, you can add a ***bookmark*** for a location or selected text in the document. Once you have inserted a bookmark, you can create a hyperlink to this location, create a cross-reference to this location, or index the bookmark to be included on an index page.

Add a Bookmark

Use bookmarks to mark a specific location, a word, or selected text, including a table.

HOW TO: Add a Bookmark

1. Position the insertion point or select the text you want to bookmark.
2. Click the **Insert** tab.
3. Click the **Bookmark** button [*Links* group] to open the *Bookmark* dialog box (Figure 3-54).
4. Type the name of the bookmark.
   - Bookmark names must be one word.
5. Click **Add** to add the bookmark and close the dialog box.

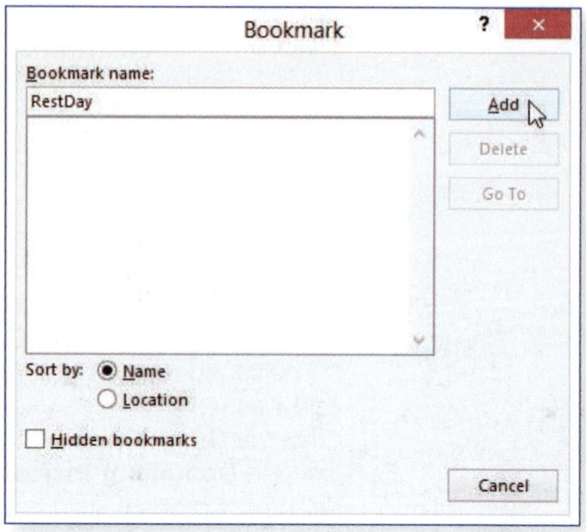

3-54 ***Bookmark* dialog box**

View Bookmarks in a Document

When a bookmark is added, by default it is not visible in your document. But you can make bookmarks visible in Word by changing a setting in the ***Word Options*** dialog box.

HOW TO: Make Bookmarks Visible in Your Document

1. Click the **File** tab to open the *Backstage* view.
2. Click the **Options** button to open the *Word Options* dialog box.
3. Select **Advanced** on the left of the *Word Options* dialog box (Figure 3-55).
4. Check the **Show bookmarks** check box in the *Show document content* area.
5. Click **OK** to close the dialog box.

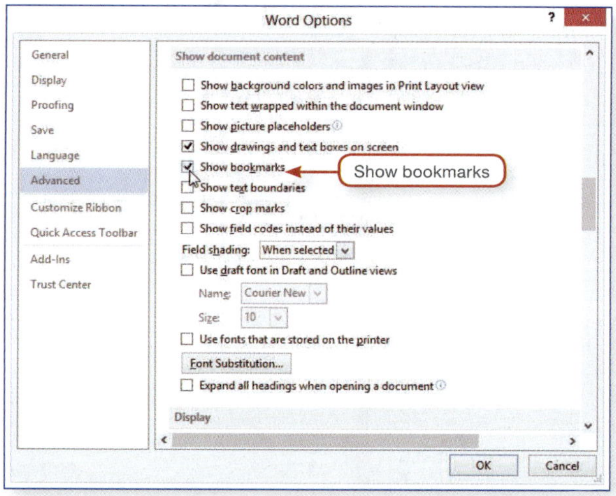

3-55 Display bookmarks in document

When bookmarks are made visible, a bookmark at a specific location is marked with a gray I-beam (Figure 3-56), and a bookmark on selected text is marked with gray brackets (Figure 3-57).

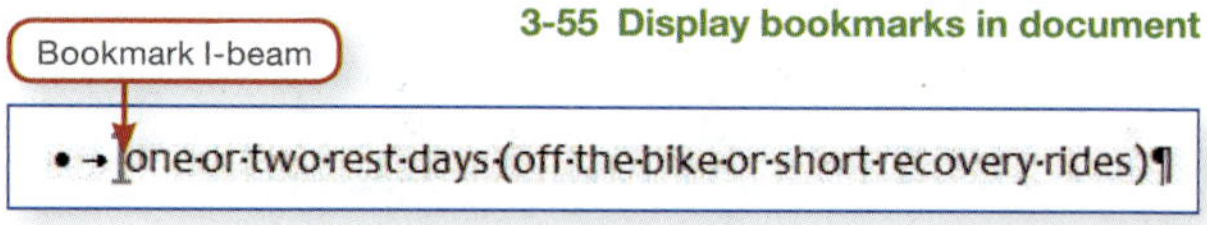

3-56 Bookmark at specific location in the document

Go To a Bookmark

There are a couple of ways to quickly move to a bookmark in your document.

- **Insert Bookmark** button [*Insert* tab, *Links* group]: In the *Bookmark* dialog box, select the bookmark and click **Go To.**
- **Find and Replace** dialog box: Click the **Find** drop-down arrow [*Home* tab, *Editing* group] and select **Go To** (Figure 3-58). Select **Bookmark** in the *Go to what* area, select the bookmark, and click **OK.**

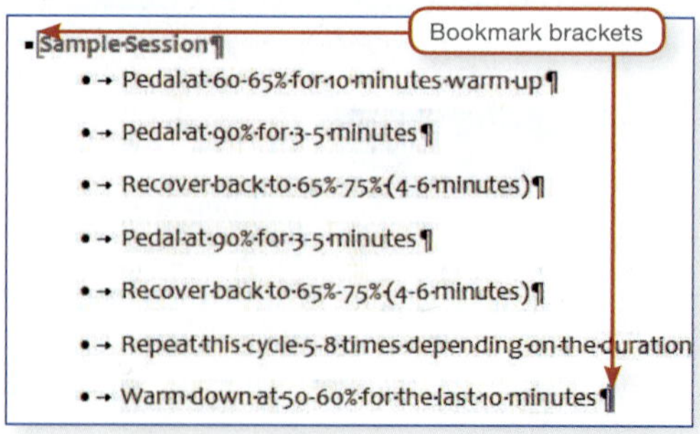

3-57 Bookmark on selected text

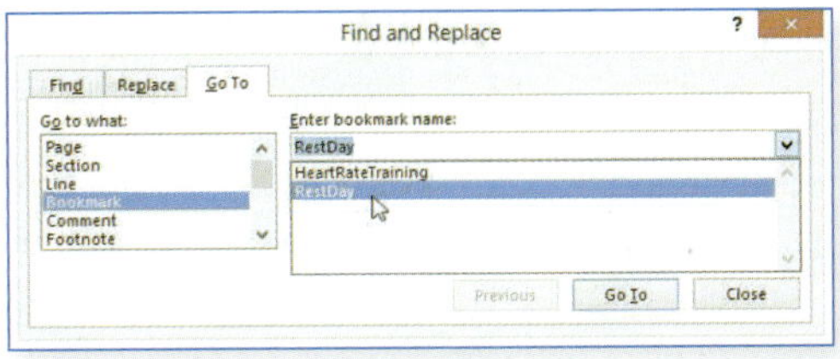

3-58 Go to selected bookmark

> **ANOTHER WAY**
>
> **Ctrl+G** opens the *Go To* tab in the *Find and Replace* dialog box.

Hyperlink to a Bookmark

You can create a ***hyperlink*** in your document that takes the reader to the bookmarked area.

HOW TO: Create a Hyperlink to a Bookmark

1. Select the text on which to create a hyperlink.
2. Click the **Hyperlink** button [*Insert* tab, *Links* group] or press **Ctrl+K**. The *Insert Hyperlink* dialog box opens (Figure 3-59).
3. Choose **Place in This Document** in the *Link to* area.

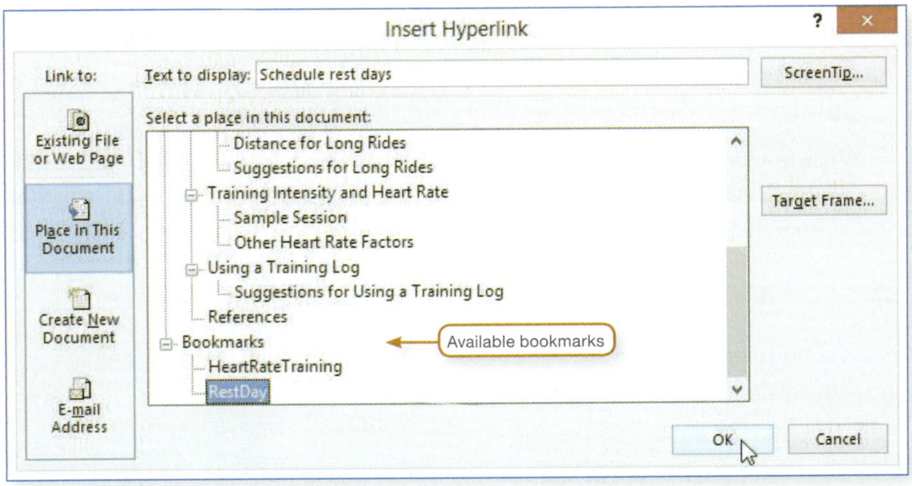

3-59 Insert hyperlink to a bookmark

4. Select from the available bookmarks.
5. Click **OK** to insert the hyperlink and close the dialog box.
   - The selected text is blue and underlined.
   - Press **Ctrl** and click the hyperlink to move to the bookmark.

Cross-Reference a Bookmark

You can also ***cross-reference*** a bookmark. For example, you can insert a page number that references a bookmark at another location in the document (e.g., "Schedule rest days (*see page 3*)"). When a cross-reference page number is linked to a bookmark, the page number is automatically updated if the bookmarked text moves to a different page.

HOW TO: Create a Cross-Reference to a Bookmark

1. Type any preceding text and position the insertion point where you want the cross-reference inserted.
2. Click the **Cross-reference** button [*Insert* tab, *Links* group]. The *Cross-reference* dialog box opens (Figure 3-60).
3. Select **Bookmark** in the *Reference type* area.
   - Check the **Insert as hyperlink** check box if you want the cross-reference to be a hyperlink to the bookmark.
4. In the *Insert reference to* area, select the type of reference from the drop-down list.
   - You can reference a page number, the bookmarked text, or the words "above" or "below."
   - If you choose *Page number,* you can also include the words "above" or "below" after the page number (e.g., "see page 3 above").
5. Select the bookmark in the *For which bookmark* area.
6. Click **Insert** to insert the cross-reference.
7. Click **Close** to close the dialog box.

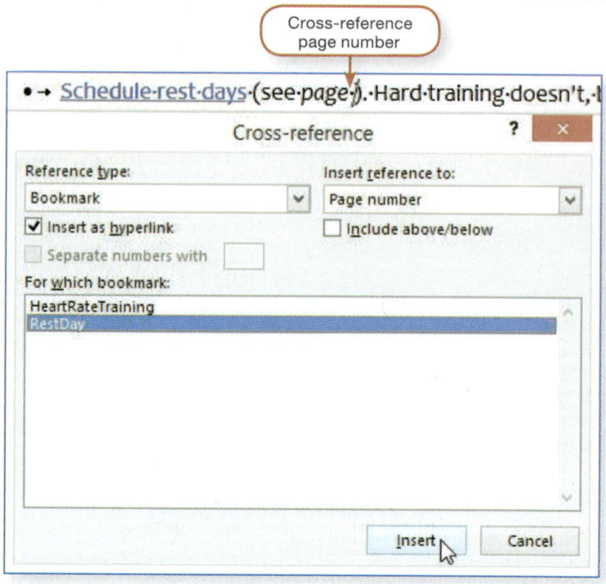

3-60 Insert cross-reference to a bookmark

Delete a Bookmark

When you delete a bookmark from a document, Word does not remove hyperlinks or cross-references associated with this bookmark. You must manually remove a hyperlink or cross-reference to a bookmark.

HOW TO: Delete a Bookmark

1. Click the **Bookmark** button [*Insert* tab, *Links* group]. The *Bookmark* dialog box opens.
2. Select the bookmark to delete.
3. Click **Delete**.
4. Click **Close** to close the *Bookmark* dialog box.

SLO 3.6

Using Advanced Headers and Footers

You can use headers and footers to include page numbers and document information at the top or bottom of each page in a report or multipage document. Headers appear at the top of the page and footers appear at the bottom. You type headers and footers just once and then they are automatically displayed on subsequent pages. Page numbers can automatically be inserted in the header or footer. You can also add custom content such as text, document property fields, the date, or borders.

Page and Section Breaks

For multipage documents, it is a good idea to insert page or section breaks to control page endings or special formatting in different sections. A *Page* break controls where one page ends and another begins. Use a *Next Page* section break when special document layout formatting is applied to a whole page or multiple pages of a document, such as landscape orientation to one page of the document. Use a *Continuous* section break when special formatting is applied to a section of the document, such as two-column format to specific text on one page.

> **MORE INFO**
>
> Don't use a section break to control page endings where a page break will suffice.

HOW TO: Insert a Page or Section Break

1. Place the insertion point in the document at the point where you want the page or section break.
   - If you are inserting a continuous section break, it is best to select the text on which to apply the section break.
   - When you insert a continuous break on selected text, Word inserts a continuous section break before and after the selected text.
2. Click the **Breaks** button [*Page Layout* tab, *Page Setup* group] (Figure 3-61).
3. Select the type of break from the drop-down list.

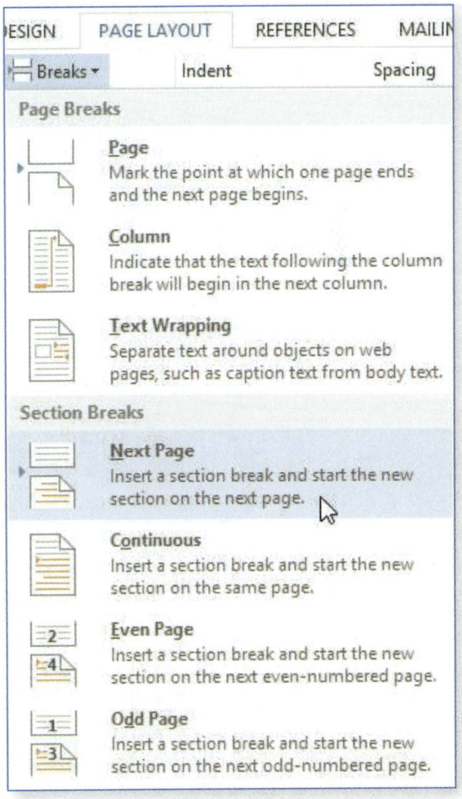

3-61 Insert page or section break

> **ANOTHER WAY**
>
> **Ctrl+Enter** inserts a page break.

When working with page and section breaks, it is best to have the *Show/Hide* feature turned on so you can see where these breaks are located in a document. To delete a page or section break, select the break and press **Delete.**

Built-In Headers, Footers, and Page Numbers

Word provides you with a variety of built-in headers, footers, and page numbering options that you can insert into a document. You can also customize this built-in content. You can insert this content with the header or footer open or while you are in the main document.

HOW TO: Insert a Built-In Header or Footer

1. Click the **Insert** tab.
2. Click the **Header**, **Footer**, or **Page Number** button [*Header & Footer* group].

3. Select the built-in header, footer, or page number from the drop-down list (Figure 3-62). The content is inserted and the header or footer opens.
   - If you're inserting a page number, select the position (*Top of Page, Bottom of Page, Page Margins,* or *Current Position*) to insert the page number.
   - The colors and fonts of the built-in headers, footers, and page numbers are determined by the theme of your document.
   - More built-in headers, footers, and page numbers are displayed when you place your pointer on *More Headers (Footer* or *Page Numbers) from* Office.com.
   - You can insert odd and even headers, footers, and page numbering into a document. We discuss odd and even headers and footers in the next section.

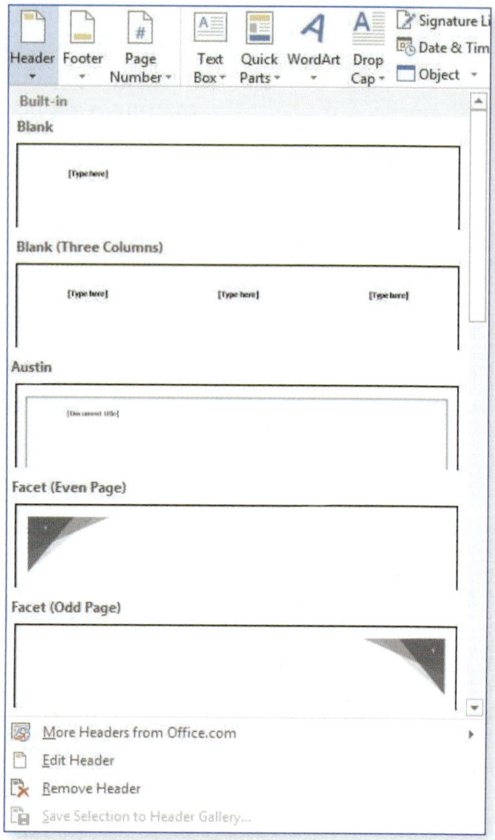

3-62 Insert built-in header

Many of the built-in headers and footers in Word contain document property fields or content control fields. You can enter information in the document property area and these fields are automatically populated. For content control fields such as *Date* or *Year,* you can select or type the content to be displayed in these fields (see Figure 3-62).

Customize Header and Footer Content

You are not limited to built-in content in the header and footer of your document. You can type text or insert content control fields. You can format header and footer text as you would other text in your document; you can apply font formatting and borders, insert graphics, and modify or set tabs for alignment.

You can open a header or footer in the following ways:

- Double-click on the header or footer area of the document.
- Right-click the header or footer area and select **Edit Header** or **Edit Footer.**
- Click the **Header** or **Footer** button [*Insert* tab, *Header & Footer* group] and select **Edit Header** or **Edit Footer.**

HOW TO: Insert Custom Content in the Header or Footer

1. Open the header or footer. See above for different ways to open the header or footer. The *Header & Footer Tools Design* tab open (Figure 3-63).
2. Insert content from the *Header & Footer Tools Design* tab.

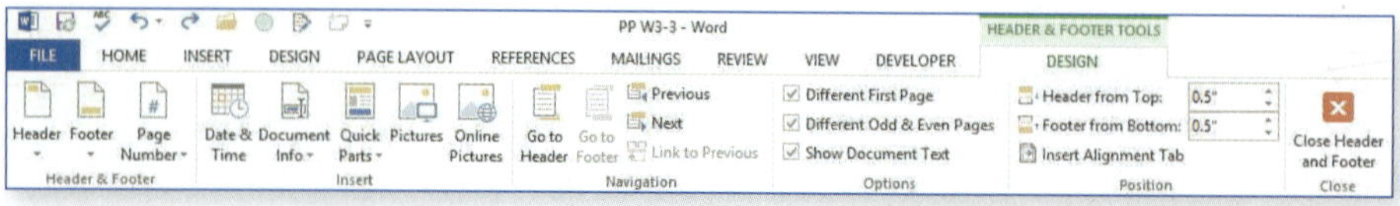

3-63 *Header & Footer Tools Design* tab

3. Type content to display in the header or footer.
4. Align information in the header or footer (Figure 3-64).
   - By default a center tab is set at the midpoint between the left and right margins and a right is set at the right margin.
   - You can insert a tab by clicking the **Insert Alignment Tab** button [*Position* group].
   - You can modify, add, or remove tabs on the ruler or in the *Tabs* dialog box [*Paragraph* dialog box, *Tabs* button].

3-64 Built-in and custom content inserted in the footer

5. You can change the position of the header and footer in the *Position* group.
   - By default, the header and footer are positioned 0.5" from the top and bottom of the page.
   - The settings can also be changed in the *Page Setup* dialog box on the *Layout* tab.
6. Click **Close Header and Footer** to return to the main document.

Different Headers and Footers

It's common on long documents to have different header and footer content on different pages. Word options allow you to have a different first page header and footer as well as different headers and footers on odd and even pages.

Different First Page

On many reports, you don't include a page number or header and footer content on the first page, but this information is included on subsequent pages. When you select the ***Different First Page*** option, Word removes existing content from the header and footer on the first page. You can choose to leave the first page header and footer blank, or you can insert content that is different from the second and subsequent pages headers and footers.

HOW TO: Insert a Different First Page Header and Footer

1. Open the header or footer on the first page of the document.
2. Check the **Different First Page** check box [*Header & Footer Tools Design* tab, *Options* group] (Figure 3-65).
   - When the *Different First Page* check box is checked, the header (or footer) tab displays *First Page Header* (or *First Page Footer*) to distinguish it from other headers and footers in the document, which are labeled *Header* (or *Footer*) (Figure 3-66).
   - The header (or footer) tab label changes when you apply other header and footer formatting such as odd and even pages or have different headers for different sections of your document.
3. Click **Close Header and Footer**.

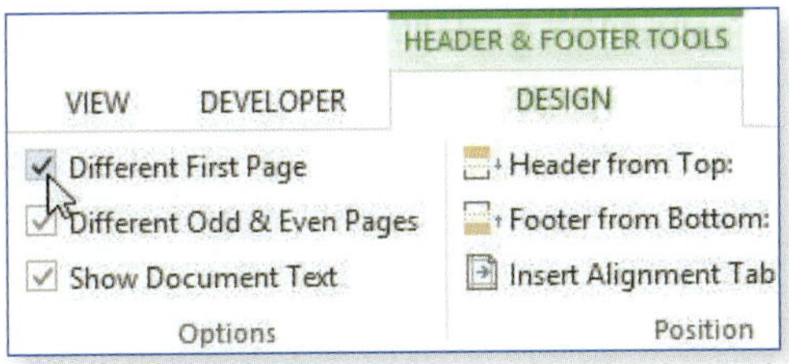

3-65 Set different first page header and footer

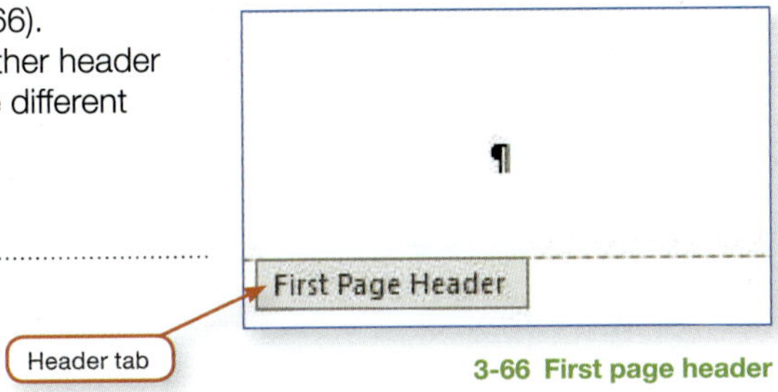

3-66 First page header

Different Odd and Even Pages

Just as you can have different header and footer content on the first page, Word provides you with the option of having ***different odd and even*** header and footer content on a multipage document. For example, you might want the title of the report to appear on all even pages in the footer and the page number and a company name to appear on odd pages.

> **MORE INFO**
>
> It's best to insert header and footer content on the first page of your document and then make any desired header and footer option changes.

HOW TO: Insert Different Odd and Even Headers and Footers

1. Open the header or footer on the first page of the document.
2. Check the **Different Odd & Even Pages** check box [*Header & Footer Tools Design* tab, *Options* group].
   - When the *Different Odd & Even Pages* check box is checked, the header (or footer) tab displays *Odd* (or *Even*) *Page Header* (or *Footer*) to distinguish it from other headers and footers in the document (Figure 3-67).
3. Click **Close Header and Footer**.

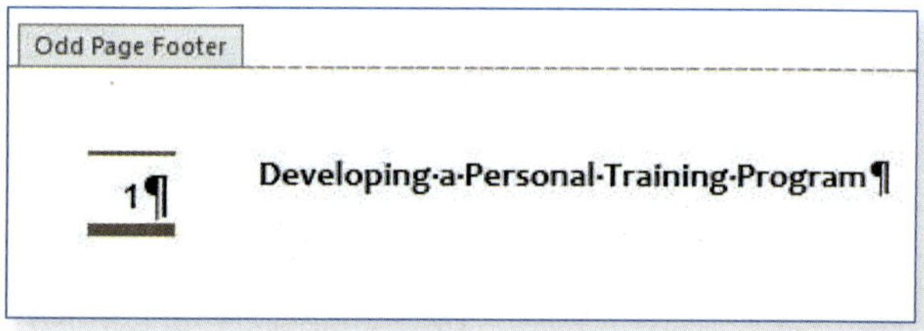

3-67 Odd page footer

Link to Previous

When you have different sections in your document, the headers and footers are by default linked to previous headers and footers. For example, a page number that appears in the footer of the first section of a document will also appear in the same position in the next section footer because it is linked to the previous footer. You can break this link to format header and footer content in one section independently of the header or footer in another section.

HOW TO: Link or Unlink Headers or Footers

1. Open the header or footer to be unlinked from the previous section (Figure 3-68).
   - By default the *Link to Previous* button is on (highlighted).
   - The *Same as Previous* label is displayed on the right of the header or footer.

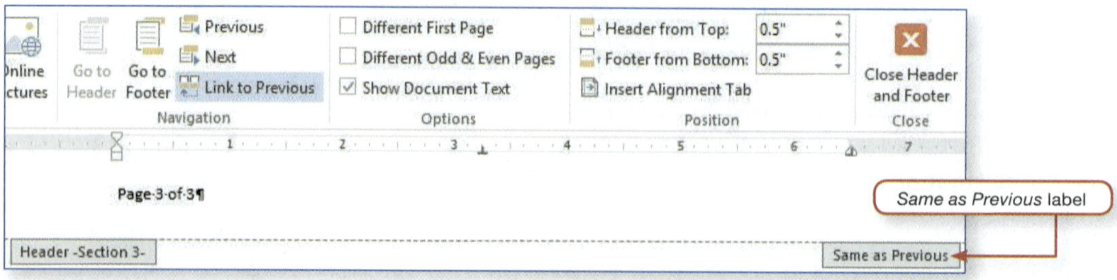

3-68 ***Link to Previous*** **button**

2. Click the **Link to Previous** button [*Header & Footer Tools Design* tab, *Navigation* group] to unlink it from the previous section.
   - The *Same as Previous* label is no longer displayed.
   - The header or footer content is still displayed, but you can now change it without it changing the header or footer content in the previous section.
   - The *Link to Previous* button is no longer highlighted.
3. If you want to link header or footer content to a previous section after it has been unlinked, click the **Link to Previous** button. A dialog box opens asking if you want to link the header or footer to the previous section (Figure 3-69).
4. Click **Yes**.
5. Click **Close Header and Footer**.

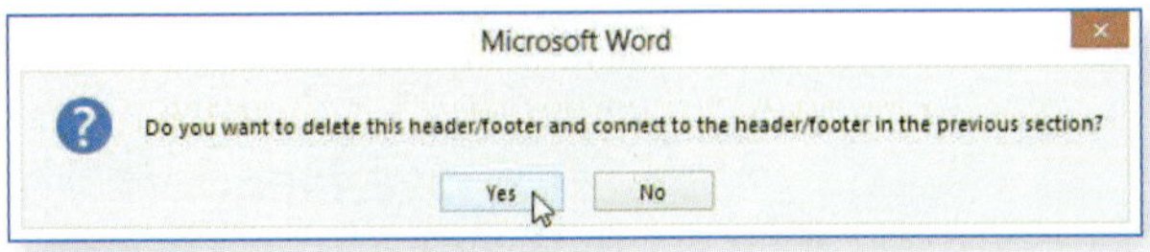

3-69 Link header or footer to previous section

Format Page Numbers

When you number the pages in your document, you can change the page number format and starting page number. For example, on a report you might want to number the front matter pages (title page, table of contents, executive summary) with Roman numerals and number the body pages with regular numbers. If you are using different numbering for different sections of a document, you need to insert a next page section break between sections. This allows you to format the page numbering of each section differently.

HOW TO: Format Page Numbers

1. Select the page number to format in the header or footer.
2. Click the **Page Number** button [*Header & Footer Tools Design* tab, *Header & Footer* group].
3. Select **Format Page Numbers** from the drop-down list. The *Page Number Format* dialog box opens (Figure 3-70).
4. In the *Number format* area, select the number format from the drop-down list.
5. In the *Page numbering* area, select either the **Continue from previous section** or **Start at** radio button.
   - If you select *Continue from previous section,* the numbering continues consecutively from the previous section.
   - If you select *Start at,* you select the starting page number for the section.
6. Click **OK** to close the *Page Number Format* dialog box.

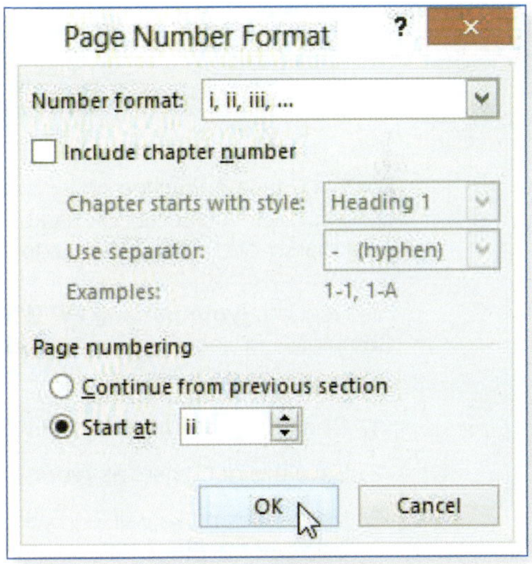

3-70 *Page Number Format* dialog box

When you include a Word cover page in a multipage document, the cover page is *not* considered the first page. Word considers the cover page as "page 0" when inserting page numbers in the header or footer, table of contents, or cross-reference links. For this reason, the page numbering in your document might be different from the page number displayed in the *Status* bar (bottom left of the Word window) of the document.

Navigate between Headers and Footers

When you are in a header or footer of a document, there are a variety of buttons you can use to move from the header to the footer or to the next or previous header or footer. These navigation buttons are in the *Navigation* group on the *Header & Footer Tools Design* tab (Figure 3-71).

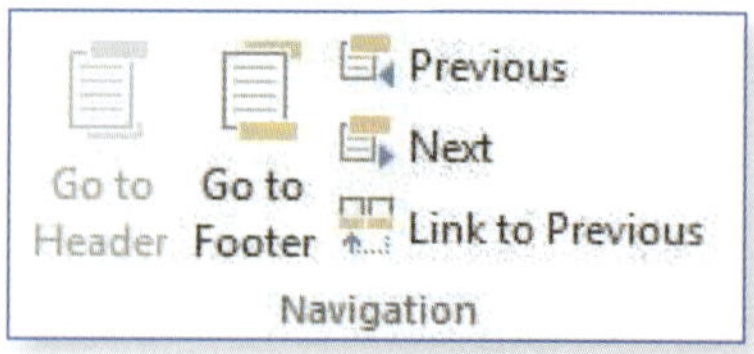

3-71 Header and footer navigation buttons

Remove Headers and Footers

To remove a header or footer from a document, you can open the header or footer and manually delete the content. All linked header or footer content is also removed when you do this. Word can also automatically remove the header or footer from a document.

HOW TO: Remove a Header or Footer

1. Click the **Insert** button.
2. Click the **Header or Footer** button [*Header & Footer* group].
3. Select **Remove Header** or **Remove Footer** from the drop-down list (Figure 3-72). The header or footer content is removed.

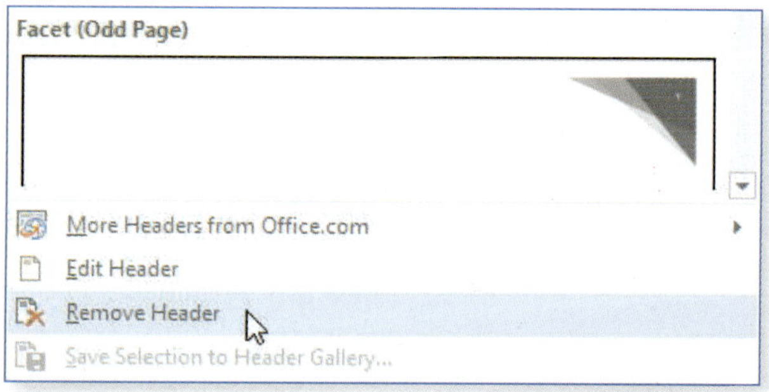

3-72 Remove header

PAUSE & PRACTICE: WORD 3-3

For this Pause & Practice project, you finalize the *Personal Training Program* report for American River Cycling Club. You add bookmarks, create hyperlinks to bookmarks, create cross-reference links to bookmarks, and customize headers and footers.

File Needed: ***[your initials] PP W3-2.docx***
Completed Project File Name: ***[your initials] PP W3-3.docx***

1. Open the ***[your initials] PP W3-2*** document created in *Pause & Practice 3-2*.
2. Save this document as ***[your initials] PP W3-3***.
3. Make bookmarks visible in your document.
   a. Click the **File** tab to open the *Backstage* view.
   b. Select **Options** to open the *Word Options* dialog box (Figure 3-73).
   c. Select **Advanced** on the left.
   d. Check the **Show bookmarks** check box in the *Show document content* area.
   e. Click **OK** to close the dialog box.

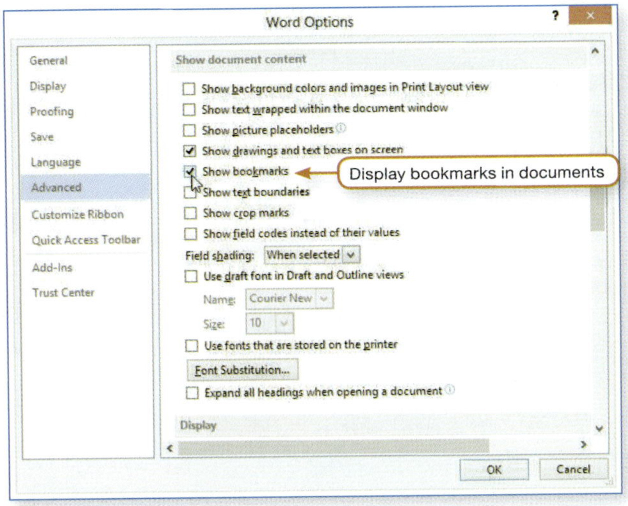

3-73 Display bookmarks in document

4. Insert bookmarks.
   a. Place the insertion point before "one or two rest days" (fourth page, fourth bullet).
   b. Click the **Bookmark** button [*Insert* tab, *Links* group]. The *Bookmark* dialog box opens (Figure 3-74).
   c. Type RestDay and click **Add** to add the bookmark and close the dialog box. An I-beam bookmark is displayed before the text.
   d. On the fifth page, select the text beginning with "**Sample Session**" and ending with the last bulleted item in that section.
   e. Click the **Bookmark** button.
   f. Type HeartRateTraining and click **Add** to add the bookmark and close the dialog box. Bookmark brackets are displayed around the selected text.

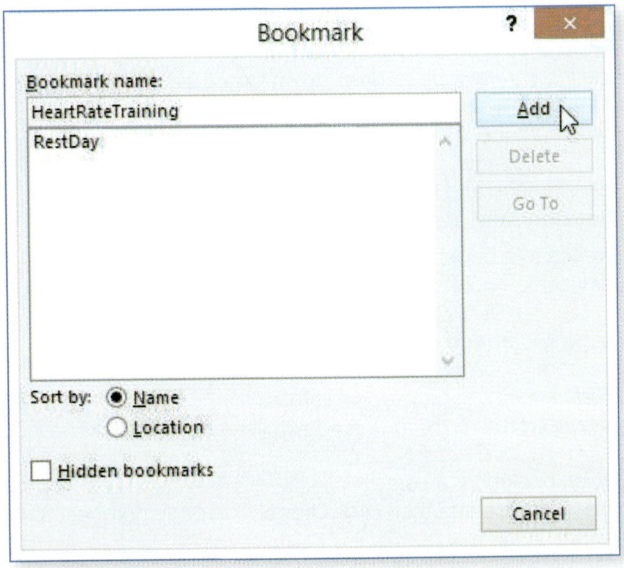

3-74 Insert bookmarks

5. Insert a cross-reference to a bookmark.
   a. On the sixth page, place your insertion point after "Record heart rate levels" (second bulleted item) and before the period.
   b. **Space** once and type (see Sample Session and **space** once.
   c. Click the **Cross-reference** button [*Insert* tab, *Links* group] to open *the Cross-reference* dialog box (Figure 3-75).

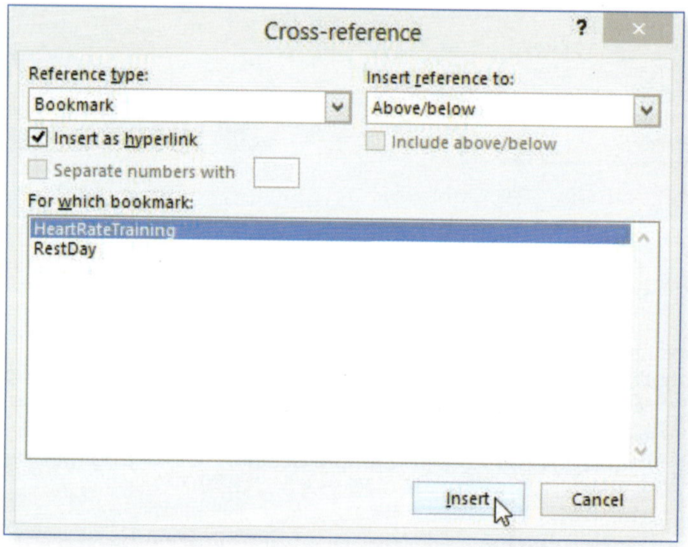

3-75 Insert cross-reference to a bookmark

   d. Select **Bookmark** from the *Reference type* drop-down list.
   e. Select **Above/below** from the *Insert reference to* drop-down list.
   f. Select **HeartRateTraining** in the *For which bookmark* area.
   g. Click **Insert** to insert the cross-reference and then click **Close**. The word "above" is inserted after the text.
   h. Type) after the inserted cross-reference and before the period.
   i. Select the words "**Sample Session**" and apply **italic** formatting.
6. Insert a page number cross-reference to a bookmark.
   a. On the sixth page, place your insertion point after "Schedule rest days" (fifth bulleted item) and before the period.
   b. **Space** once and type (see page and **space** once.
   c. Click the **Cross-reference** button.
   d. Select **Bookmark** from the *Reference type* drop-down list.
   e. Select **Page number** from the *Insert reference to* drop-down list. Do not check the *Include above/below* check box.
   f. Select **RestDay** in the *For which bookmark* area.
   g. Click **Insert** to insert the cross-reference and then click **Close**. The page number "3" is inserted after the text.
   h. Type) after the inserted cross-reference and before the period.
   i. Select the words "**page 3**" and apply **italic** formatting.

7. Insert hyperlinks to bookmarks.
   a. On the sixth page, select "**Record heart rate levels**" (second bulleted item).
   b. Click the **Hyperlink** button [*Insert* tab, *Links* group] to open *the Insert Hyperlink* dialog box (Figure 3-76).

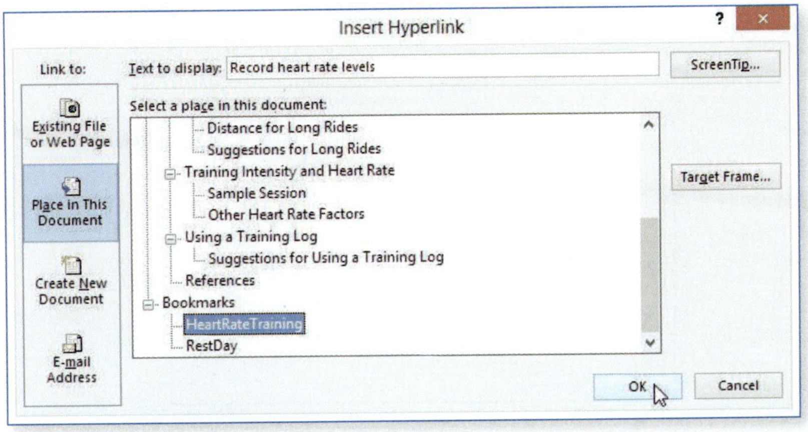

3-76 Insert hyperlink to a bookmark

   c. Select **Place in This Document** in the *Link to* area.
   d. Select **HeartRateTraining** in the *Bookmarks* list.
   e. Click **OK** to insert the hyperlink to the bookmark.
   f. On the sixth page, select "**Schedule rest days**" (fifth bulleted item).
   g. Click the **Hyperlink** button [*Insert* tab, *Links* group] to open *the Insert Hyperlink* dialog box.
   h. Select **Place in This Document** in the *Link to* area.
   i. Select **RestDay** in the *Bookmarks* list.
   j. Click **OK** to insert the hyperlink to the bookmark (Figure 3-77).

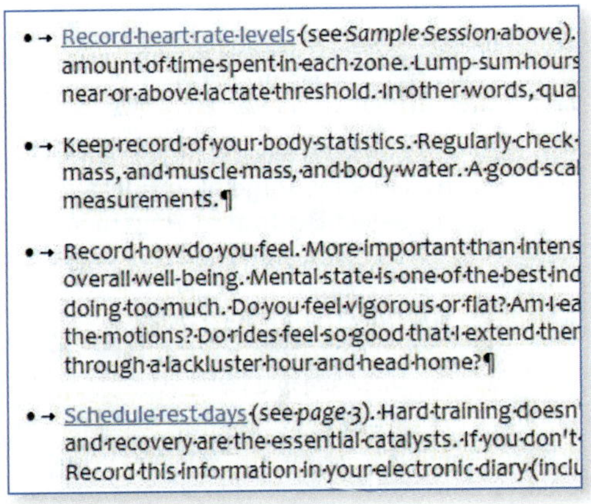

3-77 Cross-references and hyperlinks to bookmarks

8. Insert odd page and even page footers.
   a. Press **Ctrl+Home** to move to the top of the document.
   b. Click the **Footer** button [*Insert* tab, *Header & Footer* group] and select **Edit Footer** to open the footer.
   c. Check the **Different First Page** (if it is not already checked) and the **Different Odd & Even Pages** check boxes [*Header & Footer Tools Design* tab, *Options* group].
   d. Click the **Next** button [*Navigation* group] to move to the footer on the second page (Figure 3-78).

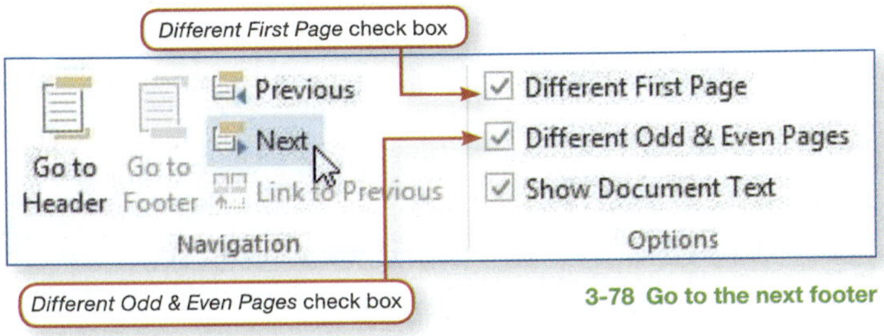

3-78 Go to the next footer

e. Click the **Page Number** button [*Header & Footer* group].
f. Select **Bottom of Page** and select **Two Bars 1** from the drop-down list of built-in page numbers (Figure 3-79). The page number "1" is inserted on the second page.

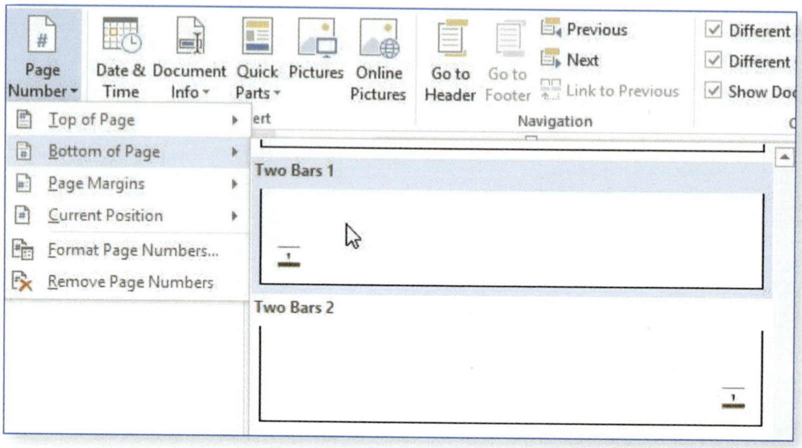

3-79 Select built-in page number

> **MORE INFO**
>
> Word considers the cover page as page 0. The table of contents page is page 1.

g. Click the **Next** button [*Navigation* group] to move to the footer on the next page.
h. Click the **Page Number** button [*Header & Footer* group].
i. Select **Bottom of Page** and select **Two Bars 2** from the drop-down list of built-in page numbers. The page number "2" is inserted on the right. Leave the footer open to add custom content in the next step.

9. Add custom content to the odd and even footers.
   a. The insertion point should be in the even page footer.
   b. Press **Ctrl+R** to align the insertion point on the right.
   c. Click the **Document Info** button [*Header & Footer Tools Design* tab, *Insert* group] (Figure 3-80).
   d. Select **Document Property** and choose **Company** from the drop-down list. The *Company* document property field is inserted with the company name displayed in this field.
   e. Select the **Company** document property field, change the font size to **10 pt.**, and apply **bold** formatting.
   f. Click the **Previous** button [*Header & Footer Tools Design* tab, *Navigation* group] to move to the odd page footer on the previous page. The insertion point should be on the left after the page number "1."

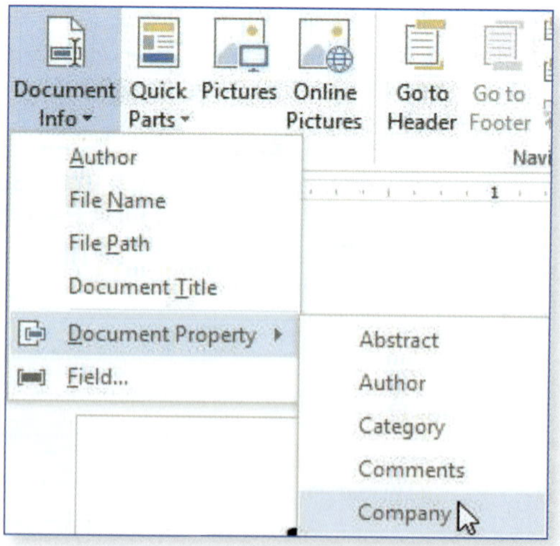

3-80 Insert document property field

g. Click the **Quick Parts** button [*Header & Footer Tools Design* tab, *Insert* group].
h. Select **Document Property** and choose **Title** from the drop-down list. The *Title* document property field is inserted with the document title displayed in this field.
i. Select the **Title** document property field, change the font size to **10 pt.**, and apply **bold** formatting.
j. Click the **Close Header and Footer** button [*Header & Footer Tools Design* tab, *Close* group].

10. Review the document to ensure correct page numbering.
    a. There should be no header or footer on the cover page of the document.
    b. The table of contents page should be numbered "1" in the footer on the left with the title of the report following the page number.
    c. The first body page of the report should be numbered "2" in the footer on the right with the company name preceding the page number.
    d. Each subsequent page should be numbered consecutively with odd and even footers.

11. Save and close the document (Figure 3-81).

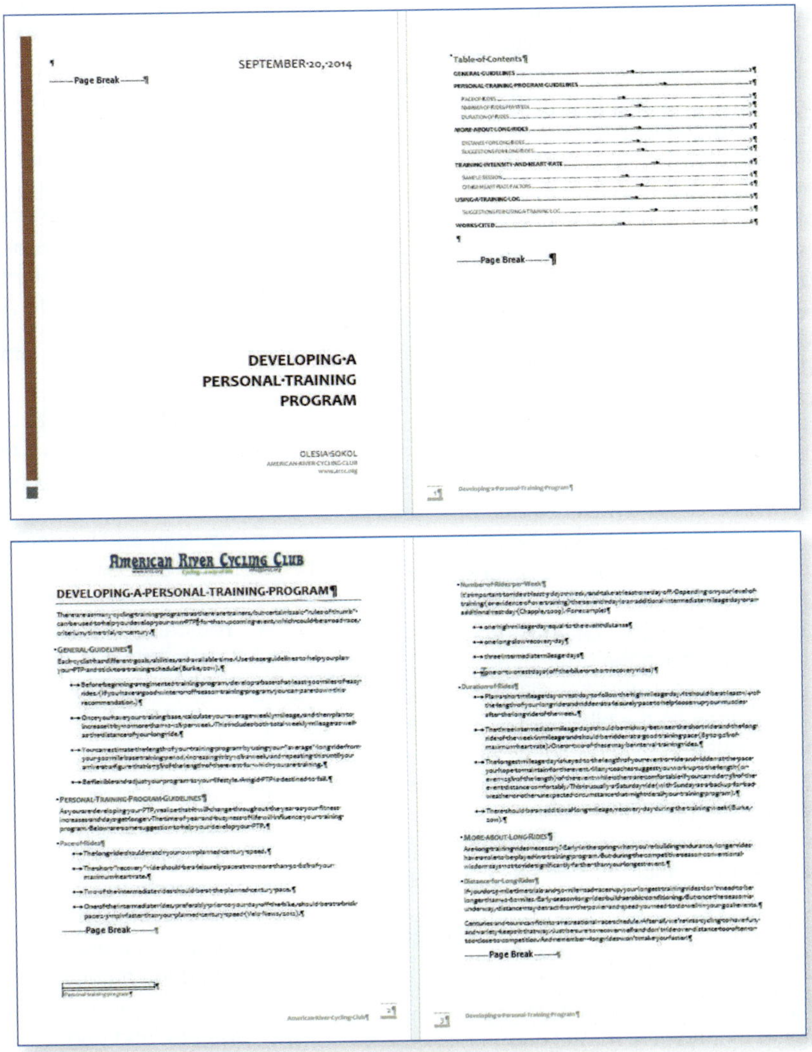

3-81 PP W3-3 completed (first four of seven pages)

Chapter Summary

3.1 Insert and edit footnotes and endnotes in a document (p. W3-129).

- *Use **Footnotes*** and ***endnotes*** to include additional information or reference sources.
- Footnotes appear at the bottom of the page and endnotes appear at the end of the document.
- A ***reference marker*** is a number, letter, or symbol that marks a footnote or endnote in the body of the document.
- Change the location, number format, and starting number for footnotes and endnotes in the ***Footnote and Endnote*** dialog box.
- Word styles control the format of footnotes and endnotes. Change these styles to modify how your footnote and endnote text appears in the document.
- Convert footnotes to endnotes or endnotes to footnotes using the ***Convert Notes*** dialog box.
- Move footnotes and endnotes using the drag and drop method or using cut and paste.
- When you delete a footnote or endnote reference marker, the associated footnote and endnote text is also deleted. Footnotes and endnotes are automatically renumbered if one is deleted or inserted.

3.2 Create a bibliography using proper source format and insert citations in a document (p. W3-134).

- A ***source*** is the complete bibliographic information for a reference (e.g., book, web page, journal article) used in a report.
- A ***citation*** is the abbreviated source information used in the body of a report.
- The ***bibliography style*** controls the format of the sources on the bibliography page and citations in the body of the document.
- Add a ***placeholder*** to temporarily mark a citation in the body of a report.
- Use the ***Source Manager*** dialog box to create and edit sources, edit placeholders, and view available sources.
- Insert a ***bibliography*** or ***works cited*** page to list the sources in your document.

3.3 Create and edit a table of contents based on headings in a document (p. W3-144).

- Word can automatically generate a ***table of contents*** for a document.
- ***Heading styles*** (e.g., Heading 1, Heading 2) determine the content for a table of contents.
- You can use built-in table of contents formats or customize the format of the table of contents.
- Use the ***Table of Contents*** dialog box to customize the format and levels displayed in the table of contents.
- When document heading or pagination is changed, the table of contents can be updated to reflect these changes.

3.4 Insert a cover page and modify content and document fields (p. W3-148).

- There are a variety of built-in ***cover pages*** available to use on your documents.
- A cover page has graphics, colors, text boxes, and Word fields that you can customize. The document theme controls the colors and fonts on the cover page.
- Use ***document property*** and ***content control fields*** to display information on the cover page. This content can be customized or deleted.

3.5 Integrate bookmarks into a multipage document (p. W3-153).

- Use a ***bookmark*** to mark a specific location or selected text in a document.
- In ***Word Options***, you can set bookmarks in your documents.
- You can add a ***hyperlink*** to a bookmark; this takes the user to the bookmark when the hyperlink is clicked.
- You can add a ***cross-reference*** to a bookmark; this provides the page number for the bookmark or a general location in the document.

3.6 Apply custom headers and footers in multipage documents (p. W3-156).

- ***Headers*** and ***footers*** provide information and page numbers in a document. Headers are located at the top and footers are located at the bottom of a document.
- ***Page*** and ***section breaks*** control pagination and page numbering in a document.
- You can insert a variety of built-in headers, footers, and page numbers into a document.
- You can customize content and page numbering in headers and footers.

- ***Different first page*** headers and footers allow you to include different information on the first page of a document.
- *Use* ***odd and even page*** headers and footers to display different information on odd and even pages in a document.
- Change the page number format and starting page number in the ***Page Number Format*** dialog box.

Check for Understanding

In the ***Online Learning Center*** for this text (www.mhhe.com/office2013inpractice), there are a variety of resources that can be used to review the concepts covered in this chapter.

The following Online Learning Resources are available in the Online Learning Center:

- Multiple-choice questions
- Short answer questions
- Matching exercises

USING MICROSOFT WORD 2013

Guided Project 3-1

For this project, you customize the *Online Learning Plan* for Sierra Pacific Community College District. You add a customized cover page, apply styles, create a table of contents, insert and modify footnotes, and insert headers and footers.
[Student Learning Outcomes 3.1, 3.3, 3.4, 3.6]

File Needed: ***OnlineLearningPlan-03.docx***
Completed Project File Name: ***[your initials] Word 3-1.docx***

Skills Covered in This Project

- Customize document properties.
- Insert a cover page and add content.
- Delete and add document property fields.
- Apply font formatting to text.
- Apply styles to selected text.
- Insert page breaks.
- Create a table of contents based on heading styles.
- Insert footnotes.
- Modify footnote number format.
- Insert built-in page numbers in the header.
- Insert document property fields and the date in the footer.
- Modify header and footer text formatting.
- Update a table of contents.

1. Open the ***OnlineLearningPlan-03*** document from your student data files.
2. Save this document as ***[your initials] Word 3-1***.
3. Add document properties.
   a. Click the **File** tab to open the *Backstage* view.
   b. Click **Show All Properties** in the *Properties* area.
   c. Add the following document properties:
      Title: Online Learning Plan
      Company: Sierra Pacific Community College District
      Manager: Hasmik Kumar
   d. Click the **Back** arrow to return to the document.
4. Insert a cover page and modify content control fields.
   a. Press **Ctrl+Home** to move to the top of the document.
   b. Click the **Cover Page** button [*Insert* tab, *Pages* group].
   c. Select the **Austin** built-in cover page from the drop-down list. The cover page is inserted before the first page of the document.
   d. Click the **Subtitle** content control field handle and press **Delete** (Figure 3-82).

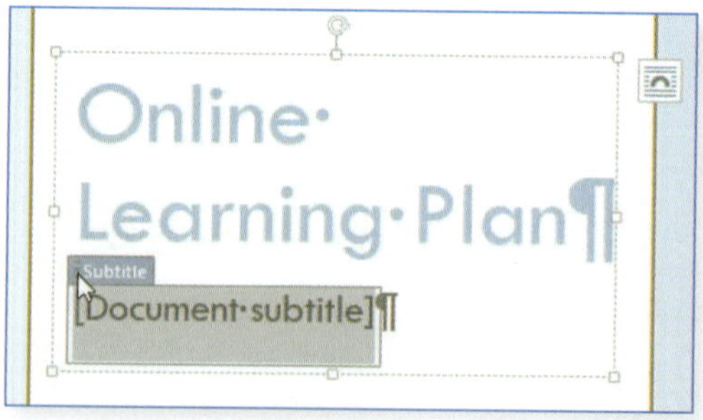

3-82 Delete content control field

e. Delete the blank line after the *Title* field.
f. Select the **Title** field and change the font size to **48 pt**.
g. Click the **Abstract** content control field and type This report was developed by the Online Learning Task Force at Sierra Pacific Community College District to review and update the district's strategic plan for online learning.
h. Select the **Abstract** field, change the text alignment to **left**, and apply **italic** formatting.
i. Click the **Author** content control field handle and press **Delete**.
j. With the insertion point on the blank line where the *Author* field was deleted, click the **Quick Parts** button [*Insert* tab, *Text* group] (Figure 3-83).
k. Select **Document Property** and select **Manager** from the drop-down list.
l. Apply **bold** formatting to the *Manager* document property field.

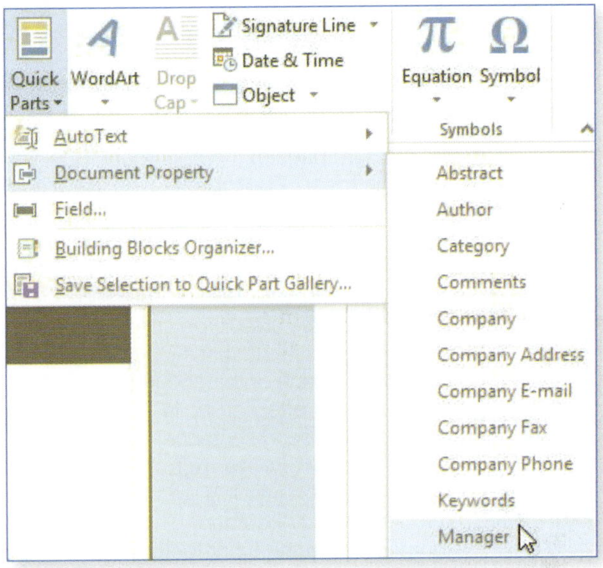

3-83 Insert document property field

5. Apply styles to the document.
   a. Apply the **Heading 1** style to all of the main headings (those in all caps and bold) in the document. Do not include information on the cover page.
   b. Apply the **Heading 2** style to all subheadings (those underlined) in the document.
   c. On the second page of the document, select the title ("**Online Learning Plan**") and apply the **Title** style.
   d. On the second page of the document, select the subtitle ("**Sierra Pacific Community College District**") and apply the **Subtitle** style.
6. Insert a table of contents into the report.
   a. Click in front of the first main heading in the document ("Purpose of this Plan") and insert a page break.
   b. On the second page of the document, click directly after the subtitle and press **Enter**.
   c. With the insertion point on the blank line below the subtitle, click the **Table of Contents** button [*References* tab, *Table of Contents* group] (Figure 3-84).
   d. Select **Automatic Table 2**. The table of contents is inserted below the subtitle.

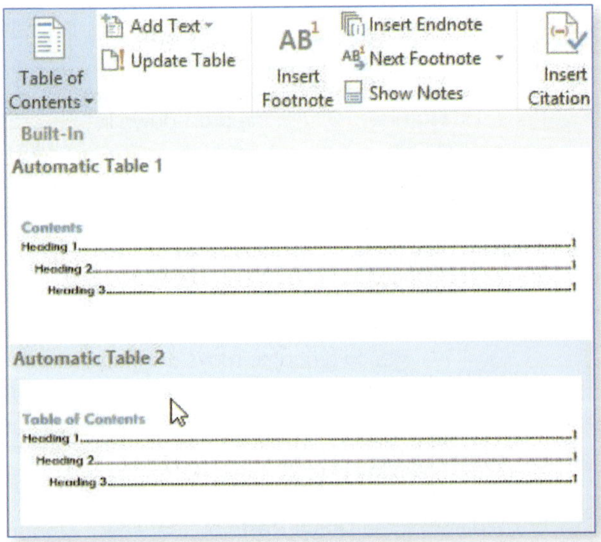

3-84 Insert table of contents

e. Select the words "**Table of Contents**" in the table of contents and apply **Black**, **Text 1** font color.
f. If there is a blank line between the subtitle and "Table of Contents," delete it.

7. Insert footnotes into the document.
   a. On the third page of the document, position the insertion point after "Web-Enhanced course."
   b. Click the **Insert Footnote** button [*References* tab, *Footnotes* group]. A footnote reference marker is inserted after the text and the insertion point is positioned at the bottom of the page in the *Footnotes* area.
   c. In the *Footnotes* area, type Just for clarification, this is a non-OL course that uses OL tools.
   d. On the third page of the document, position the insertion point after "online learning" (first body paragraph, second sentence).
   e. Click the **Insert Footnote** button and in the footnote area type Online learning will be referred to as OL throughout this document. This footnote becomes footnote 1 and the other footnote automatically becomes number 2.

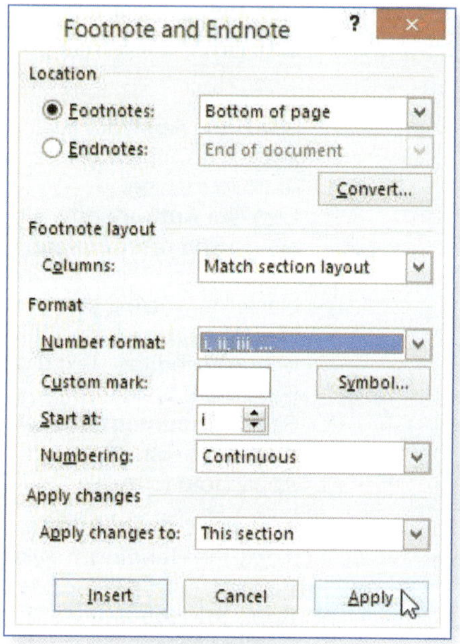

3-85 Modify footnote number format

8. Modify footnote number format.
   a. Click the **Footnotes** launcher to open the *Footnote and Endnote* dialog box (Figure 3-85).
   b. Select **i, ii, iii, . . .** from the *Number format* drop-down list.
   c. Click **Apply** to close the dialog box and apply the number format change.

9. Insert and modify content in the header.
   a. Position the insertion point at the top of the table of contents page.
   b. Click the **Page Number** button [*Insert* tab, *Header & Footer* group].
   c. Select **Top of Page** and select **Bold Numbers 3** from the drop-down list (Figure 3-86).
   d. Delete the blank line below the page number.
   e. Select the text in the header and change the font size to **10 pt**.

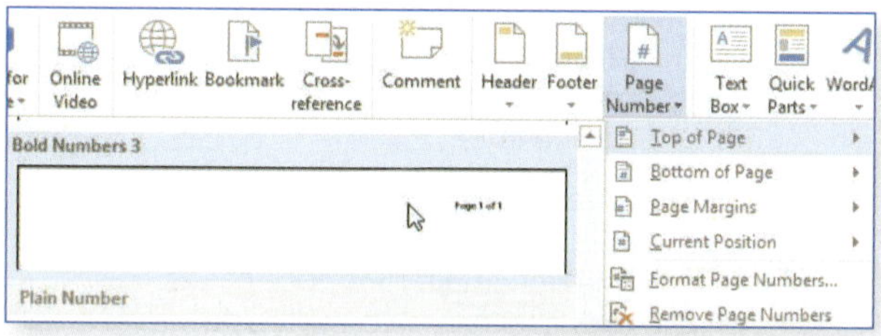

3-86 Insert page number

10. Insert and modify content in the footer.
    a. With the header still open, click the **Go to Footer** button [*Header & Footer Tools Design* tab, *Navigation* group] to move the insertion point to the footer.
    b. Click the **Quick Parts** button [*Header & Footer Tools Design* tab, *Insert* group], select **Document Property**, and select **Title** from the drop-down list to insert the *Title* document property field into the footer.
    c. Press the **right arrow** once to deselect the document property field and press **Tab** to move to the center preset tab.
    d. Click the **Quick Parts** button, select **Document Property**, and select **Company** from the drop-down list.

e. Press the **right arrow** once to deselect the document property field and press **Tab** to move to the right preset tab.

f. Type Last modified: and **space** once.

g. Click the **Date & Time** button [*Header & Footer Tools Design* tab, *Insert* group] to open the *Date and Time* dialog box.

h. Select the first date format (e.g., 1/31/2015) and deselect the **Update automatically** check box.

i. Click **OK** to close the dialog box and insert the date.

j. Select the text in the footer and change the font size to **10 pt**.

k. Click the **Close Header and Footer** button [*Header & Footer Tools Design* tab, *Close* group].

11. Insert a page break.
    a. Position the insertion point before the last subheading ("How are Courses and Programs Selected for Online Learning Delivery?") on the first body page of the report (the page after the table of contents).
    b. Press **Ctrl+Enter** to insert a page break.

12. Update the table of contents.
    a. Click in the table of contents.
    b. Click the **Update Table** button [*References* tab, *Table of Contents* group]. The *Update Table of Contents* dialog box opens (Figure 3-87).
    c. Select the **Update entire table** radio button.
    d. Click **OK** to close the dialog box and update the table.

13. Save and close the document (Figure 3-88).

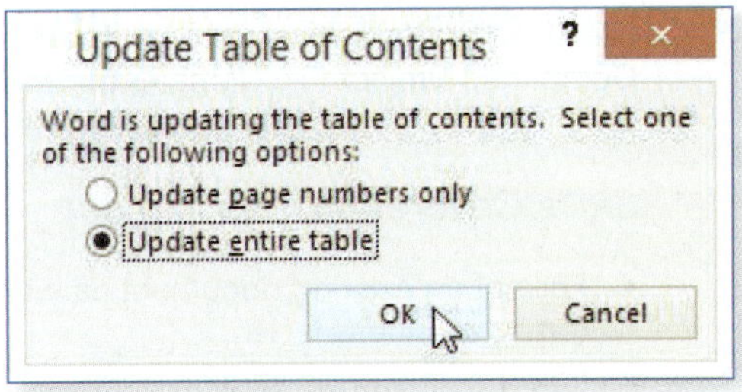

3-87 *Update Table of Contents* dialog box

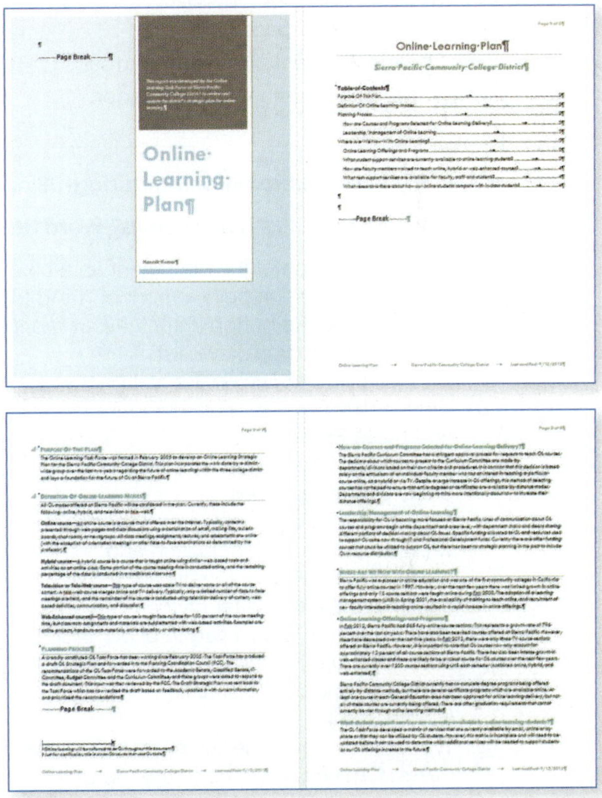

3-88 Word 3-1 completed (first four of six pages)

Guided Project 3-2

For this project, you create a multipage insurance renewal letter that Central Sierra Insurance will send on behalf of Valley Custom Manufacturing. You format this document as a business letter, insert and customize header content, use footnotes and endnotes, and insert a bookmark.
[Student Learning Outcomes 3.1, 3.5, 3.6]

File Needed: ***ValleyCustomManufacturing-03.docx***
Completed Project File Name: ***[your initials] Word 3-2.docx***

Skills Covered in This Project

- Format an existing document as a block format business letter.
- Insert a next page section break.
- Change margins and header location on a section of a document.
- Use a different first page header.
- Insert header content and page number.
- Format the page number in the header.
- Apply bottom border.
- Insert footnotes.
- Convert footnotes to endnotes and change number format.
- Insert a bookmark for selected text.
- Insert a cross-reference to a bookmark.
- Create a hyperlink to a bookmark.
- Insert a page break to control pagination.

1. Open the ***ValleyCustomManufacturing-03*** document from your student data files.
2. Save this document as ***[your initials] Word 3-2***.
3. Format the first page of the document as a block format business letter.
   a. Place your insertion point in front of "LIABILITY" on the first page.
   b. Click the **Breaks** button [*Page Layout* tab, *Page Setup* group] and select **Next Page** section break from the drop-down list.
   c. On the last blank line on the first page, type Sincerely, and press **Enter** four times.
   d. Type Jennie Owings, Vice President and press **Enter** once.
   e. Type Central Sierra Insurance and press **Enter** two times.
   f. Type your initials in lower case letters with no spaces or punctuation and press **Enter**. Word automatically capitalizes the first letter of your initials. Use the **smart tag** to undo automatic capitalization or press **Ctrl+Z** to undo the last action (Figure 3-89).

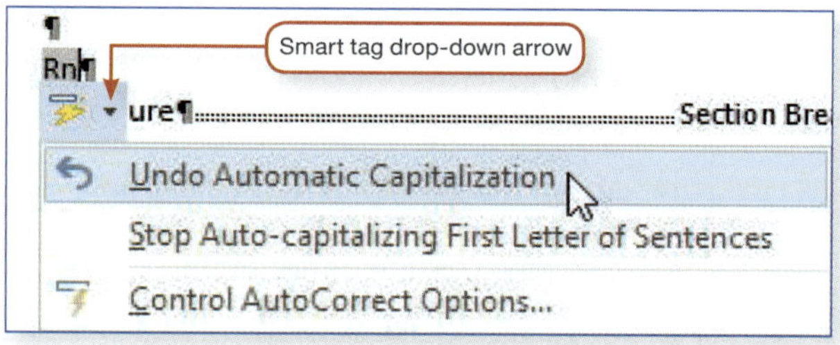

3-89 Use smart tag to undo automatic capitalization

   g. Type Enclosure on the line after your reference initials.
   h. Press **Ctrl+Home** to go to the top of the document and press **Enter** four times.
   i. Place the insertion point on the first blank line at the top and click the **Date & Time** button [*Insert* tab, *Text* group]. The *Date and Time* dialog box opens.
   j. Select the date in proper business letter format (e.g., April 12, 2014) and check the **Update automatically** check box.
   k. Click **OK** to close the dialog box and insert the date.
   l. On the dateline, apply **24 pt**. before paragraph spacing.
4. Modify the margins and header position in the second section of the document.
   a. Place your insertion point in the second section of the document (page 2 or 3).
   b. Click the **Margins** button [*Page Layout* tab, *Page Setup* group] and select **Custom Margins** from the drop-down list. The *Page Setup* dialog box opens.
   c. Change the *Top* margin to **1.5"** and the *Left* and *Right* margins to **1.25"**.

d. Click the **Layout** tab (Figure 3-90).
e. In the *Headers and footers* area, change the *From edge Header* setting to **1"**.
f. In the *Apply to* area, select **This section** from the drop-down list.
g. Click **OK** to close the dialog box and apply the settings.

5. Insert header content on the second and continuing pages.
   a. Press **Ctrl+Home** to move to the top of the document.
   b. Click the **Header** button [*Insert* tab, *Header & Footer* group].
   c. Select **Edit Header** from the drop-down list.
   d. Check the **Different First Page** check box [*Header & Footer Tools Design* tab, *Options* group].
   e. Click the **Next** button [*Header & Footer Tools Design* tab, *Navigation* group] to move to the header in section 2.
   f. Type Valley Custom Manufacturing and press **Enter**.
   g. Click the **Date & Time** button [*Header & Footer Tools Design* tab, *Insert* group]. The *Date and Time* dialog box opens.
   h. Select the date in proper business letter format (e.g., April 12, 2014) and check the **Update automatically** check box.
   i. Click **OK** to close the dialog box and insert the date.

6. Insert page number in the header and format page number.
   a. With the header still open, press **Enter** after the date.
   b. Type Page and **space** once.
   c. Click the **Page Number** button [*Header & Footer Tools Design* tab, *Header & Footer* group].
   d. Select **Current Position** and **Plain Number** from the drop-down list of page number options.
   e. Click the **Page Number** button and select **Format Page Numbers** to open the *Page Number Format* dialog box (Figure 3-91).
   f. In the *Page numbering* area, click the **Start at** radio button and change the page number to **2**.
   g. Click **OK** to close the dialog box.

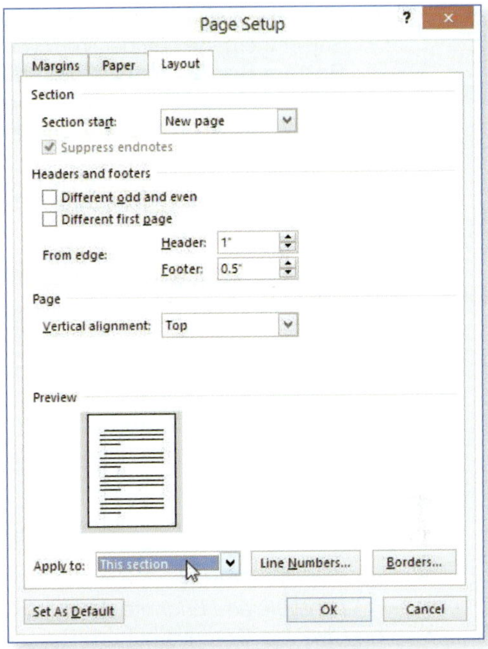

3-90 Change header position in this section of the document

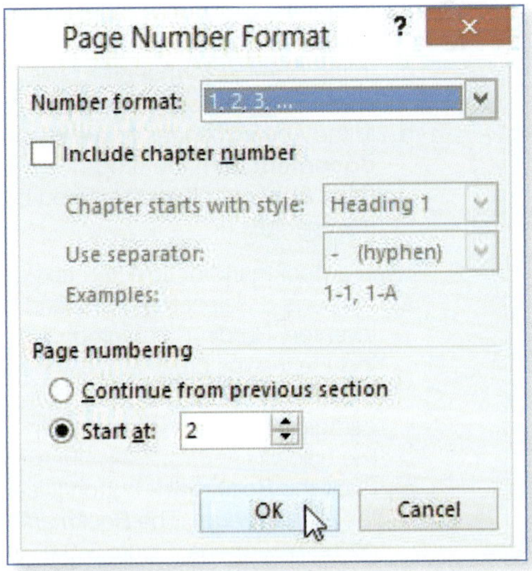

3-91 Format page number

h. Place the insertion point after the page number and press **Enter** two times.
i. Select the page number line, click the **Borders** button [*Home* tab, *Paragraph* group], and select **Bottom Border** from the drop-down list.
j. Click the **Close Header and Footer** button [*Header & Footer Tools Design* tab, *Close* group].

7. Insert footnotes.
   a. Place the insertion point after the period at the end of the last line of text on page 4.
   b. Click the **Insert Footnote** button [*References* tab, *Footnotes* group].
   c. In the footnotes area, type A list of drivers was faxed as a separate attachment.
   d. On the first page, place the insertion point at the end of the fourth body paragraph (after "2013 renewal.").
   e. Click the **Insert Footnote** button.
   f. In the footnotes area, type Inflation is anticipated to be 2 percent.

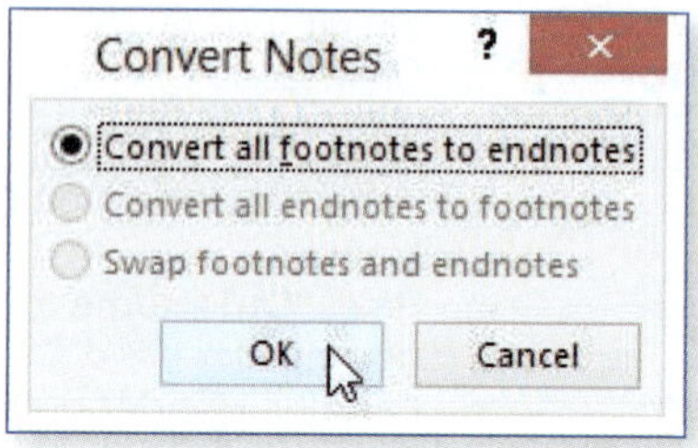

3-92 Convert footnotes to endnotes

8. Convert footnotes to endnotes and change number format.
   a. Click the **Footnotes** launcher to open the *Footnote and Endnote* dialog box.
   b. Click the **Convert** button. The *Convert Notes* dialog box opens (Figure 3-92).
   c. Select the **Convert all footnotes to endnotes** radio button and click **OK** to close the *Convert Notes* dialog box.
   d. Click **Close** to close the *Footnote and Endnote* dialog box.
   e. Click the **Footnotes** launcher to open the *Footnote and Endnote* dialog box (Figure 3-93).
   f. Select the **Endnotes** radio button if it is not selected.
   g. In the *Number format* area, select **a, b, c, . . .** from the drop-down list.
   h. In the *Apply changes to* area, select **Whole document** from the drop-down list.
   i. Click **Apply** to close the dialog box and apply the changes.

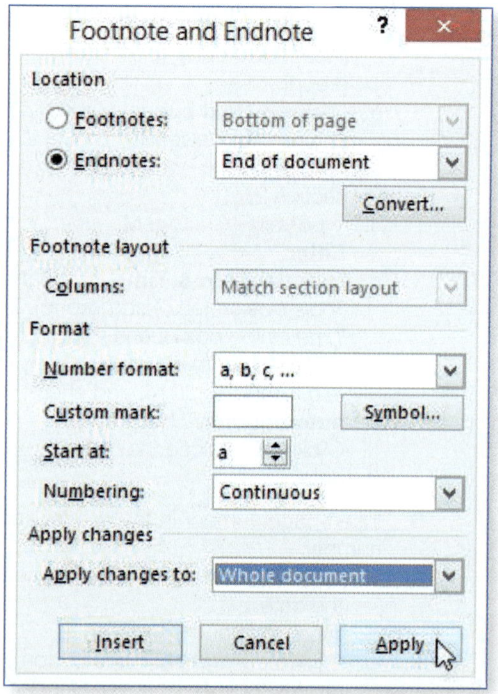

3-93 Change endnote number format

9. Insert a bookmark for selected text.
   a. On page 3, select the "Parts and Inventory Building" paragraph. Include the line break at the end of the paragraph, but do *not* include the paragraph break on the blank line below.
   b. Click the **Bookmark** button [*Insert* tab, *Links* group]. The *Bookmark* dialog box opens (Figure 3-94).

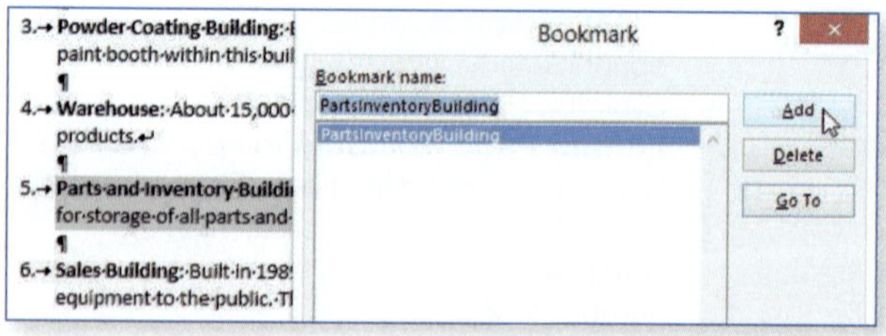

3-94 Insert bookmark on selected text

c. In the *Bookmark name* area, type PartsInventoryBuilding.
d. Click **Add** to close the dialog box and add the bookmark for selected text.

10. Insert a cross-reference link to a bookmark.
    a. On page 2 in the "Farm Equipment Dealers" section, place the insertion point after "2001" and before the period.
    b. **Space** once and type (see #5 on page and **space** once.
    c. Click the **Cross-reference** button [*Insert* tab, *Links* group] to open the *Cross-reference* dialog box (Figure 3-95).
    d. In the *Reference type* area, select **Bookmark**.
    e. In the *Insert reference to* area, select **Page number**.
    f. In the *For which bookmark* area, select **PartsInventoryBuilding**.
    g. Click **Insert** and then click **Close**.
    h. Type) after the inserted cross-reference page number.

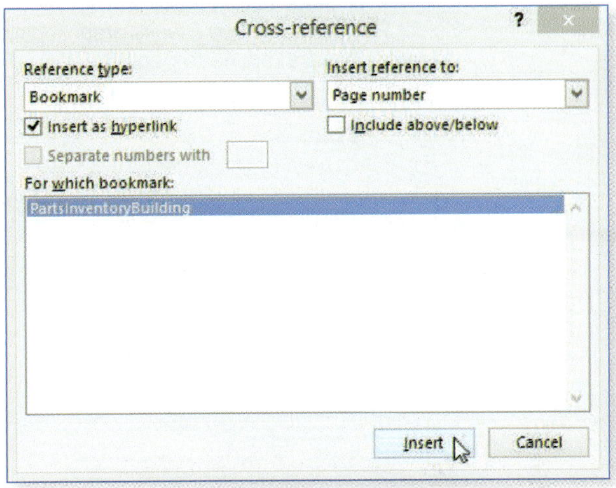

3-95 Insert cross-reference to a bookmark

11. Create a hyperlink to a bookmark.
    a. On page 2 in the "Farm Equipment Dealers" section, select "**new building completed in 2001**."
    b. Click the **Hyperlink** button [*Insert* tab, *Links* group] to open the *Insert Hyperlink* dialog box (Figure 3-96).
    c. In the *Link to* area, select **Place in This Document**.
    d. In the *Select a place in this document* area, select the **PartsInventoryBuilding** bookmark.
    e. Click **OK** to close the dialog box and insert the hyperlink.

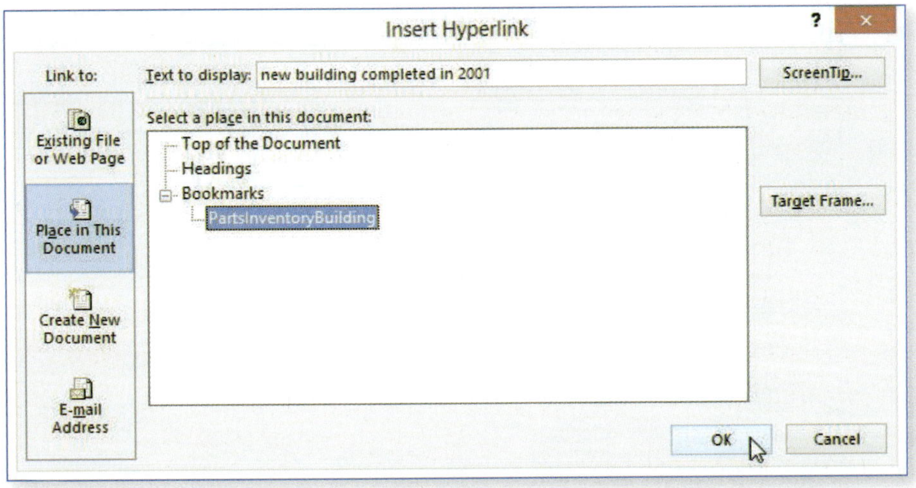

3-96 Insert hyperlink to a bookmark

12. Insert a page break to control pagination.
    a. On page 2, place the insertion point in front of the "PROPERTY" heading.
    b. Click the **Breaks** button [*Page Layout* tab, *Page Setup* group].
    c. Select **Page** in the *Page Breaks* area. A page break is inserted and the "PROPERTY" heading and following text are moved to page 3.
13. Save and close the document (Figure 3-97).

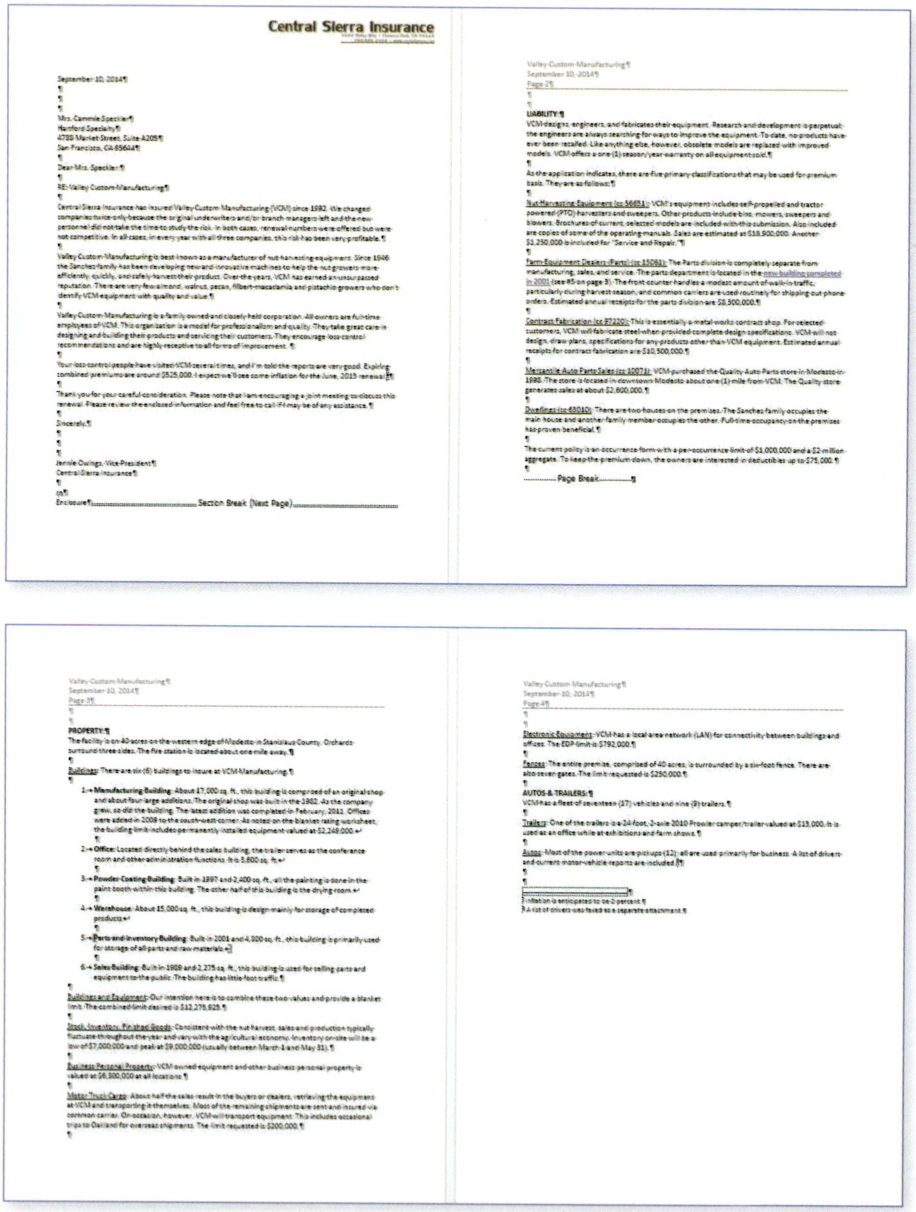

3-97 Word 3-2 completed

Guided Project 3-3

For this project, you customize the *Teen Substance Abuse* report for Courtyard Medical Plaza. You insert citations and a placeholder, manage sources, create a bibliography, and use odd and even page headers and footers.
[Student Learning Outcomes 3.2, 3.3, 3.6]

File Needed: ***TeenSubstanceAbuse-03.docx***
Completed Project File Name: ***[your initials] Word 3-3.docx***

Skills Covered in This Project

- Set bibliography style.
- Insert a placeholder for a citation.
- Create a source and insert a citation.
- Use the *Source Manager* to edit a placeholder and create a new source.
- Insert a bibliography page.
- Use styles to format title and headings.
- Create a table of contents.
- Insert built-in odd and even headers and footers.
- Insert a document property field into a header.
- Update a table of contents.

1. Open the ***TeenSubstanceAbuse-03*** document from your student data files.
2. Save this document as ***[your initials] Word 3-3***.
3. Select the report style and insert placeholders for a citation.
   a. Click the **Style** drop-down list [*References* tab, *Citations & Bibliography* group].
   b. Select **Chicago Fifteenth Edition**.
   c. On the first page in the "What Problems Can Teen Substance Abuse Cause?" section, place the insertion point at the end of the last sentence in the second paragraph and before the period.
   d. Click the **Insert Citation** button [*References* tab, *Citations & Bibliography* group].
   e. Select **Add New Placeholder**. The *Placeholder Name* dialog box opens.
   f. Type Foundation and click **OK**. The placeholder for the citation is inserted into the report.
   g. On the second page in the "Can Teen Substance Use And Abuse Be Prevented?" section, place the insertion point at the end of the last sentence in the first paragraph and before the period.
   h. Click the **Insert Citation** button and select the **Foundation** placeholder from the drop-down list (Figure 3-98).

3-98 Insert placeholder for a citation

4. Insert a citation into the report.
   a. On the first page in the "What Is Teen Substance Abuse?" section, place the insertion point at the end of the last sentence in the second paragraph and before the period.

b. Click the **Insert Citation** button and select **Add New Source**. The *Create Source* dialog box opens (Figure 3-99).

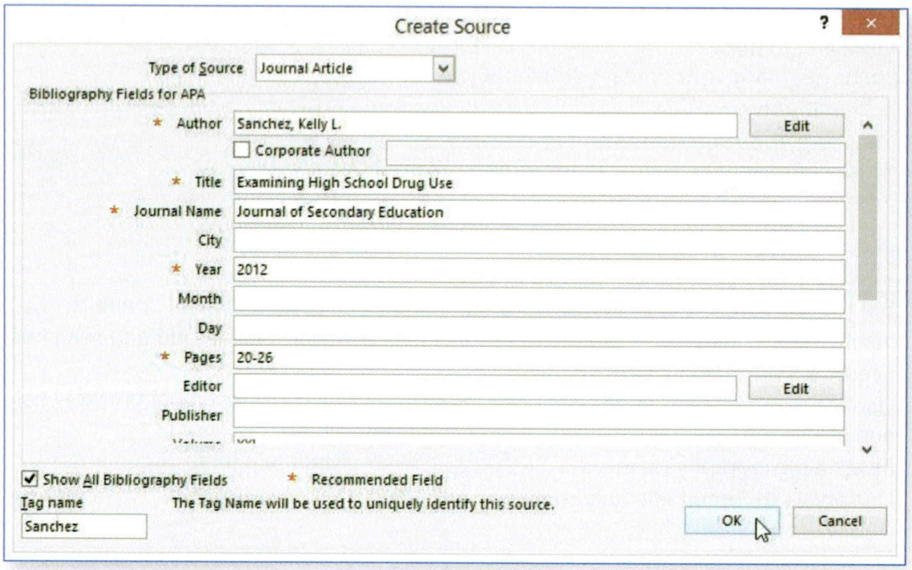

3-99 *Create Source* dialog box

c. Create a new source with the following information:

Type of Source: **Journal Article**
Author: Kelly L. Sanchez
Title: Examining High School Drug Use
Journal Name: Journal of Secondary Education
Year: 2012
Pages: 22-26
Volume: XXI (check the **Show All Bibliography Fields** check box to display these last two fields)
Issue: 2
Tag Name: Sanchez

d. Click **OK** to close the dialog box and insert the citation. The citation is inserted into the report.

5. Use the *Source Manager* to create a new source and provide source information for a placeholder.
   a. Click the **Manage Sources** button [*References* tab, *Citations & Bibliography* group] to open the *Source Manager* dialog box.
   b. In the *Current List* area, select the **Foundation** placeholder and click **Edit**. The *Edit Source* dialog box opens.
   c. Use the following information to edit the placeholder source:

Type of Source: **Web site**
Corporate Author: Foundation for Teen Health
Name of Web Page: Making Good Choices
Year: 2013
Year Accessed: 2013
Month Accessed: June
Day Accessed: 25
URL: http://foundationforteenhealth.org/choices.htm
Tag Name: Foundation

d. Click **OK** to close the dialog box and update the placeholders. The placeholders in the report are updated with the proper citation from the source information.
e. With the *Source Manager* dialog box still open, click the **New** button. The *Create Source* dialog box opens.
f. Create a new source with the following information:

   Type of Source: **Document From Web site**
   Corporate Author: Courtyard Medical Plaza
   Name of Web Page: Teen Mental Health
   Name of Web Site: Courtyard Medical Plaza
   Year: 2013
   Month: March
   Day: 6
   URL: http://cmp.com/Teen_Mental_Health.pdf
   Tag Name: CMP

g. Click **OK** to close the dialog box and click **Close** to close the *Source Manager* dialog box.

6. Insert citations into the report.
   a. On the first page in the "Why Do Teens Abuse Drugs and Alcohol?" section, place the insertion point at the end of the last sentence in the second paragraph and before the period.
   b. Click the **Insert Citation** button and select the **Courtyard Medical Plaza** citation from the drop-down list.
   c. On the second page in the "What You Should Do If You Find Out That Your Teen Is Using?" section, place the insertion point at the end of the last sentence in the second paragraph and before the period.
   d. Click the **Insert Citation** button and select the **Sanchez**, **Kelly L**. citation from the drop-down list.
7. Insert a bibliography page at the end of the document.
   a. Press **Ctrl+End** to move to the end of the document.
   b. Insert a **page break**.
   c. With the insertion point on the blank last page, click the **Bibliography** button [*References* tab, *Citations & Bibliography* group].
   d. Select **Bibliography** to insert a bibliography into the document.
8. Apply styles to the title and section headings and insert a table of contents.
   a. Apply the **Title** style to the title of the report on the first page.
   b. Apply the **Heading 1** style to each of the bold section headings in the report.
   c. Press **Ctrl+Home** to move the insertion point to the beginning of the report.
   d. Click the **Blank Page** button [*Insert* tab, *Pages* group] to insert a blank page before the first page of the report.
   e. Place your insertion point at the top of the new first page, type Teen Substance Abuse, and press **Enter**. The text should be formatted as *Title* style. If it's not, apply the **Title** style.
   f. Click the **Table of Contents** button [*References* tab, *Table of Contents* group] and select **Automatic Table 1** from the drop-down list. The table of contents is inserted below the title.
9. Insert odd and even page headers and customize content.
   a. With the insertion point still on the first page, click the **Header** button [*Insert* tab, *Header & Footer* group] and click **More Headers from Office.com**.
   b. Select **Origin (Odd Page)** from the drop-down list of built-in headers.
   c. In the header, click the **Title** document property handle and press **Delete**.
   d. Click the **Document Info** button, click **Document Property**, and select **Company** from the drop-down list.

e. Select the **Company** document property field and change the after paragraph spacing to **0 pt**. and line spacing to **1** (single).
f. Check the **Different Odd & Even Pages** check box [*Header & Footer Tools Design* tab, *Options* group and click the **Next** button to move to the *Even Page Header*.
g. Click the **Header** button [*Header & Footer Tools Design* tab, *Header & Footer* group].
h. Click **More Headers from Office.com** and select **Origin (Even Page)** from the drop-down list.
i. Delete the **Title** document property field and insert the **Company** document property field.
j. Select the **Company** document property field and change the after paragraph spacing to **0 pt**. and line spacing to **1**.

10. Insert odd and even page footers.
   a. With the header still open, click the **Go to Footer** button [*Header & Footer Tools Design* tab, *Navigation* group] to move to the *Even Page Footer*.
   b. Click the **Page Number** button [*Header & Footer* group], click **Bottom of Page**, and select **Brackets 2**.
   c. Click the **Previous** button [Navigation group] to move to the *Odd Page Footer*.
   d. Click the **Page Number** button [*Header & Footer* group], click **Bottom of Page**, and select **Brackets 2**.
   e. Click the **Close Header and Footer** button [*Close* group].

11. Insert page breaks to control pagination.
   a. On page 2, click before the last section heading and insert a **page break**.
   b. On page 3, click before the last section heading and insert a **page break**.

12. Update the table of contents.
   a. Click the table of contents on the first page.
   b. Click the **Update Table** button at the top of the content control field. The *Update Table of Contents* dialog box opens (Figure 3-100).

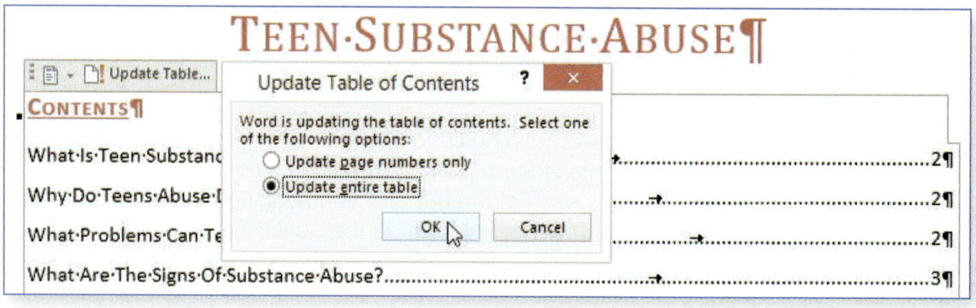

3-100 Update table of contents

   c. Select the **Update entire table** radio button and click **OK**.

13. Save and close the document (Figure 3-101).

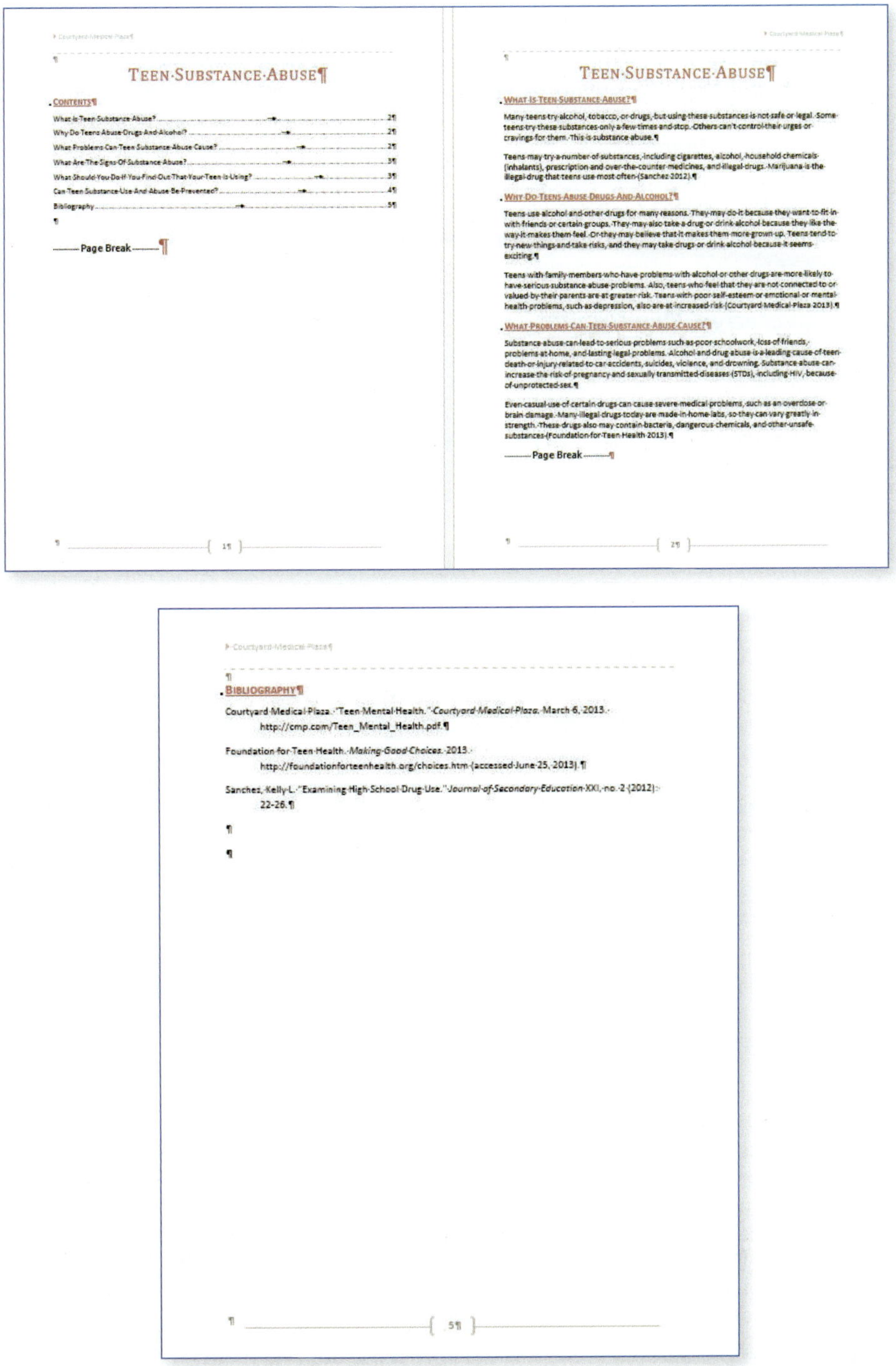

Courtyard Medical Plaza

TEEN SUBSTANCE ABUSE

CONTENTS

Page Break

1

Courtyard Medical Plaza

TEEN SUBSTANCE ABUSE

WHAT IS TEEN SUBSTANCE ABUSE?

Many teens try alcohol, tobacco, or drugs, but using these substances is not safe or legal. Some teens try these substances only a few times and stop. Others can't control their urges or cravings for them. This is substance abuse.

Teens may try a number of substances, including cigarettes, alcohol, household chemicals (inhalants), prescription and over-the-counter medicines, and illegal drugs. Marijuana is the illegal drug that teens use most often (Sanchez 2012).

WHY DO TEENS ABUSE DRUGS AND ALCOHOL?

Teens use alcohol and other drugs for many reasons. They may do it because they want to fit in with friends or certain groups. They may also take a drug or drink alcohol because they like the way it makes them feel. Or they may believe that it makes them more grown up. Teens tend to try new things and take risks, and they may take drugs or drink alcohol because it seems exciting.

Teens with family members who have problems with alcohol or other drugs are more likely to have serious substance abuse problems. Also, teens who feel that they are not connected to or valued by their parents are at greater risk. Teens with poor self-esteem or emotional or mental health problems, such as depression, also are at increased risk (Courtyard Medical Plaza 2013).

WHAT PROBLEMS CAN TEEN SUBSTANCE ABUSE CAUSE?

Substance abuse can lead to serious problems such as poor schoolwork, loss of friends, problems at home, and lasting legal problems. Alcohol and drug abuse is a leading cause of teen death or injury related to car accidents, suicides, violence, and drowning. Substance abuse can increase the risk of pregnancy and sexually transmitted diseases (STDs), including HIV, because of unprotected sex.

Even casual use of certain drugs can cause severe medical problems, such as an overdose or brain damage. Many illegal drugs today are made in home labs, so they can vary greatly in strength. These drugs also may contain bacteria, dangerous chemicals, and other unsafe substances (Foundation for Teen Health 2013).

Page Break

2

Courtyard Medical Plaza

BIBLIOGRAPHY

Courtyard Medical Plaza. "Teen Mental Health." *Courtyard Medical Plaza.* March 6, 2013. http://cmp.com/Teen_Mental_Health.pdf.

Foundation for Teen Health. *Making Good Choices.* 2013. http://foundationforteenhealth.org/choices.htm (accessed June 25, 2013).

Sanchez, Kelly L. "Examining High School Drug Use." *Journal of Secondary Education* XXI, no. 2 (2012): 22-26.

5

3-101 Word 3-3 completed (pages 1, 2, and 5 displayed)

Independent Project 3-4

For this project, you modify the *Tips for Better Heart Rate Monitor Training* document from the American River Cycling Club. You insert and modify endnotes, insert placeholders, create sources, insert a bibliography page, bookmark selected text, and use custom headers and footers.
[Student Learning Outcomes 3.1, 3.2, 3.4, 3.5, 3.6]

File Needed: ***HeartRateMonitorTraining-03.docx***
Completed Project File Name: ***[your initials] Word 3-4.docx***

Skills Covered in This Project

- Insert endnotes.
- Insert a placeholder for a citation.
- Use the *Source Manager* to edit placeholders and create a new source.
- Change the bibliography style.
- Insert a bibliography page.
- Create a bookmark for selected text.
- Create a hyperlink to a bookmark.
- Add document properties.
- Insert and modify a cover page.
- Insert custom headers and footers.
- Insert page breaks.

1. Open the ***HeartRateMonitorTraining-03*** document from your student data files.
2. Save this document as ***[your initials] Word 3-4***.
3. Insert endnotes.
   a. Insert an endnote at the end of the first paragraph on the first page.
   b. In the endnote area, type See the bibliography for related books and articles.
   c. Insert an endnote at the end of the first sentence in the "Analyze Your Heart Rate Data" section.
   d. In the endnote area, type See the ARCC web site (www.arcc.org) for information about specific heart rate monitors.
   e. Insert an endnote at the end of the second sentence of the second paragraph in the "Comparing Heart Rate Values with Others" section.
   f. In the endnote area, type 220-age is a rough estimate of maximum heart rate.
4. Insert placeholders for citations.
   a. Place the insertion point at the end of the last sentence and before the period in the "Know Your Resting Heart Rate" section.
   b. Insert a placeholder named **VeloNews**.
   c. Place the insertion point at the end of the last sentence and before the period in the "Perform a Threshold Test" section.
   d. Insert a placeholder named **Burke**.
   e. Place the insertion point at the end of the last sentence and before the period in the "Analyze Your Heart Rate Data" section.
   f. Insert a placeholder named **Chapple**.
   g. Place the insertion point at the end of the last sentence and before the period in the "A Heart Rate Monitor Is Not Effective for Anaerobic Intervals" section.
   h. Insert the **Chapple** placeholder.
5. Use the *Source Manager* dialog box to provide source information for the three placeholders.
   a. Edit the *VeloNews* placeholder to include the following information:

Type of Source: **Web site**
Corporate Author: Velo News
Name of Web Page: Training Tips for Recreational Cyclists
Year: 2012
Year Accessed: 2013
Month Accessed: May
Day Accessed: 2
URL: http://velonews.com/training_tips.html

b. Edit the *Burke* placeholder to include the following information. When you save the edit, click **No** if a dialog box opens and asks if you want to update the source.

Type of Source: **Book**
Author: Edward R. Burke
Title: The Complete Book of Long-Distance Cycling
Year: 2011
City: New York
Publisher: Rodale Books

c. Edit the *Chapple* placeholder to include the following information. When you save the edit, click **No** if a dialog box opens and asks if you want to update the source.

Type of Source: **Book**
Author: Thomas Chapple
Title: Base Building for Cyclists
Year: 2009
City: San Francisco
Publisher: VeloPress

6. Change the style of the report to **APA Sixth Edition**.
7. Convert all endnotes to footnotes and change the footnote number format to **A**, **B**, **C**.
8. Insert a bibliography at the end of the document.
   a. Insert a page break at the end of the document.
   b. Insert the built-in **References** page on the last page.
   c. **Center** the *References* heading.
9. Insert a bookmark for selected text.
   a. Select the "**Perform a Threshold Test**" heading on the first page and insert a bookmark.
   b. Name the bookmark **LactateThreshold**.
10. Create a hyperlink to a bookmark.
   a. On the first page, select "**maximum heart rate**" in the first paragraph (third sentence).
   b. Insert a hyperlink to the **LactateThreshold** bookmark.
11. Add the following text to the document properties.

   Title: Tips for Better Heart Rate Training
   Company: American River Cycling Club
   Manager: Olesia Sokol

12. Insert a cover page.
   a. Insert the **Ion (Dark)** built-in cover page.
   b. In the *Year* field, select the current date.
   c. Delete the **Subtitle** and **Author** fields.
   d. In the *Company Address* field, type www.arcc.org.
   e. Select the **Title** field, change the font size to **40 pt.**, apply **bold** formatting, and align **center**.

13. Insert a header and footer.
    a. In the header of the second page, type Page, **space** once, and insert a plain page number in the current position.
    b. **Right align** the header information.
    c. In the footer, type American River Cycling Club on the left and www.arcc.org on the right (use tabs to align the text on the right).
    d. Change the font size of the information in the header and footer to **10 pt**.
    e. Apply a **½ pt**. **top** and **bottom black border** to the information in the footer.
    f. No header or footer should appear on the cover page.
14. Insert **page breaks** where necessary to keep headings on the same page with the text that follows.
15. Save and close the document (Figure 3-102).

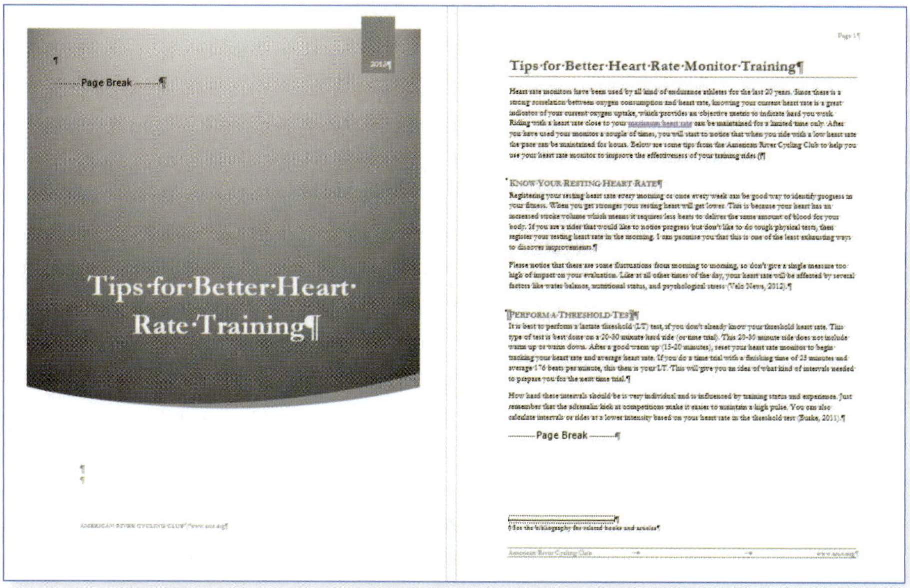

3-102 Word 3-4 completed (cover page and page 1 displayed)

Independent Project 3-5

Sierra Pacific Community College District gives incoming college students a *Student Success Tips* document. For this project, you modify the document to include heading styles, a table of contents, footnotes, and bookmarks.
[Student Learning Outcomes 3.1, 3.3, 3.5, 3.6]

File Needed: ***StudentSuccess-03.docx***
Completed Project File Name: ***[your initials] Word 3-5.docx***

Skills Covered in This Project

- Change margins.
- Apply title and heading styles.
- Insert a bookmark for selected text.
- Create a cross-reference and a hyperlink to a bookmark.
- Insert and modify footnotes.
- Insert a table of contents.
- Use a different first page footer.
- Insert page numbers and a document property field into the footer.
- Modify text format and right indent.
- Insert page breaks.
- Update a table of contents.

---

1. Open the ***StudentSuccess-03*** document from your student data files.
2. Save this document as ***[your initials] Word 3-5***.
3. Change the margins to **1"** top, bottom, left, and right on the entire document.
4. Apply styles to the title and headings.
   a. Apply the **Title** style to the title on the first page.
   b. Apply the **Heading 1** style to all the bold headings
   c. Apply the **Heading 2** style to all the underlined headings.
5. Insert a bookmark for selected text.
   a. Select the "**Procrastination**" heading and all of the text in that section.
   b. Insert a bookmark named **Procrastination** on the selected text.
   c. If bookmarks are not visible in your document, change the *Word Options* settings to make them visible.
6. Create a cross-reference to a bookmark.
   a. Find the word "Procrastination" in the "How to Reduce Test Anxiety" section.
   b. After "Procrastination," create a cross-reference to insert the page number of the *Procrastination* bookmark.
   c. Insert text so the cross-reference reads "(see page x)" where "x" is the inserted page number of the bookmark.
7. Create a hyperlink to a bookmark.
   a. Select the word "**Procrastination**" in the "How to Reduce Test Anxiety" section.
   b. Insert a hyperlink to the **Procrastination** bookmark on the selected text.
   c. Test the hyperlink to make sure it takes the reader to the *Procrastination* bookmark.
8. Insert footnotes and apply text formatting.
   a. Insert a footnote after "Weekly Schedules" in the "Schedule Your Time" section on the first page.
   b. For the footnote text, type Weekly Schedules are available from your counselor or in the college bookstore.
   c. In the "Schedule Your Time" section, insert a footnote at the end of "Be sure to schedule your time for all these in your 119 hours."
   d. For the footnote text, type Be sure to schedule recreational and down time in your 119 hours.
   e. Apply **italic** formatting to the text of the footnotes.
9. Move a footnote and modify footnote number format.
   a. Move the first footnote so it appears after "Weekly Schedule" in the "Track Your Time" section.
   b. Change the footnote number format to **a**, **b**, **c**.
10. Insert a table of contents.
    a. Insert a page break before the first page.
    b. Type Student Success Tips on the first line on the new first page and press **Enter**.

c. Apply the **Title** style to the title on the new first page.
d. On the blank line below the title, insert the **Automatic Table 1** table of contents.

11. Insert a footer on the second and continuing pages.
    a. Edit the footer on the first page of the document (table of contents).
    b. Set the first page footer to be different from the remaining footers.
    c. Go to the footer on the second page.
    d. Insert the **Vertical**, **Right** built-in page number format from the *Page Margins* page numbering options.
    e. In the footer, change the alignment to **right** and insert the **Company** document property field (Figure 3-103).
    f. Change the font size to **10 pt**. and apply **bold** formatting to the document property field.
    g. Change the right indent in the footer to **–.5"**.
    h. Close the footer.

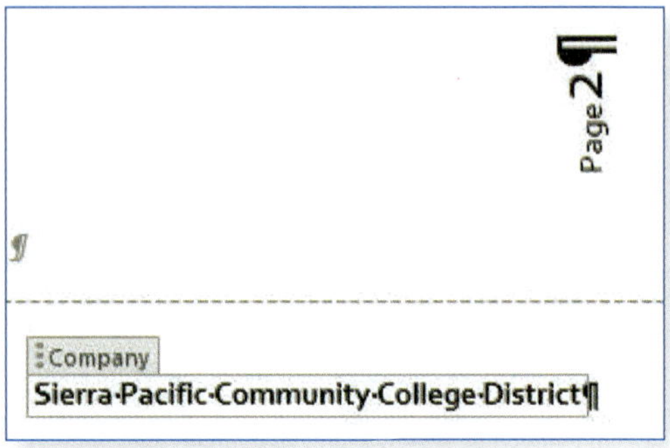

3-103 Footer on second and continuing pages

12. Insert page breaks to keep headings and text together.
13. Update the table of contents.
14. Save and close the document (Figure 3-104).

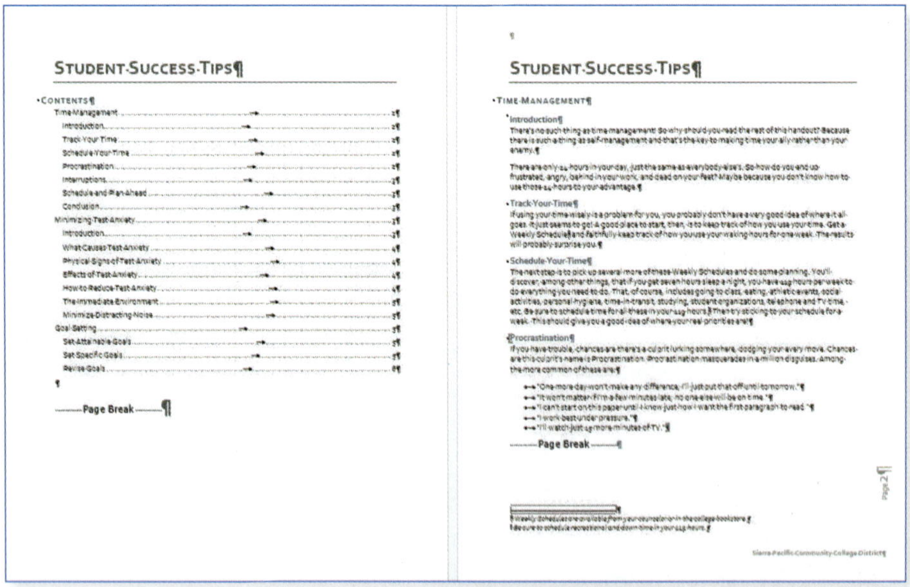

3-104 Word 3-5 completed (first two pages of six)

Independent Project 3-6

Courtyard Medical Plaza works closely with the Skiing Unlimited winter ski program. In this project, you modify the *Skiing Unlimited Training Guide* to include a table of contents, cover page, and odd and even headers.
[Student Learning Outcomes 3.3, 3.5, 3.6]

File Needed: ***SkiingUnlimitedTrainingGuide-03.docx***
Completed Project File Name: ***[your initials] Word 3-6.docx***

Skills Covered in This Project

- Change margins.
- Edit document properties.
- Apply title and heading styles.
- Insert a custom table of contents.
- Insert and customize odd and even headers.
- Insert a document property field into headers.
- Insert a cover page.
- Customize content and insert document property fields.
- Insert page breaks.
- Update a table of contents.

1. Open the ***SkiingUnlimitedTrainingGuide-03*** document from your student data files.
2. Save this document as ***[your initials] Word 3-6***.
3. Change the left and right margins to **1"**.
4. Edit the following document properties.
   Title: Skiing Unlimited Training Guide
   Company: Courtyard Medical Plaza
   Manager: Kallyn Nickols
5. Apply styles to the title and headings.
   a. Apply the **Title** style to the title on the first page.
   b. Apply the **Heading 1** style to all the bold headings.
   c. Apply the **Heading 2** style to all the underlined headings.
   d. Apply the **Heading 3** style to all the italicized headings.
6. Insert a custom table of contents.
   a. Insert a page break before the first page.
   b. Type Table of Contents on the first line on the new first page and press **Enter**.
   c. Apply the **Title** style to the title on the new first page.
   d. On the blank line below the title and before the page break, click the **Table of Contents** button and select **Custom Table of Contents** to insert a custom table of contents.
   e. Select **Fancy** format and show **2** levels of headings.
7. Insert header and footer.
   a. On the first page, insert the **Bold Numbers 3** built-in page number at the top of the page.
   b. Delete the extra **Enter** in the header.
   c. In the footer, insert the **Title** document property field on the left and the **Company** field on the right. Use tabs to align the field on the right.
   d. **Bold** the text in the footer.

8. Insert and modify a cover page.
   a. Insert the **Grid** cover page.
   b. Delete the **Subtitle** field and insert the **Company** document property field.
   c. Change the font size of the *Company* document property field to **20 pt**.
   d. In the *Abstract* field, type On behalf of the Skiing Unlimited winter ski program, Courtyard Medical Plaza has developed this training guide for Skiing Unlimited volunteers.
   e. On the Abstract field, apply **italic** formatting and change the text color to **Black**, **Text 1**.
9. Insert page breaks where necessary to keep headings with the text below.
   a. Insert a page break before the "Visual Impaired (VI)" heading.
   b. Insert other page breaks as necessary to keep headings with the text below.
10. Update the table of contents.
11. Save and close the document (Figure 3-105).

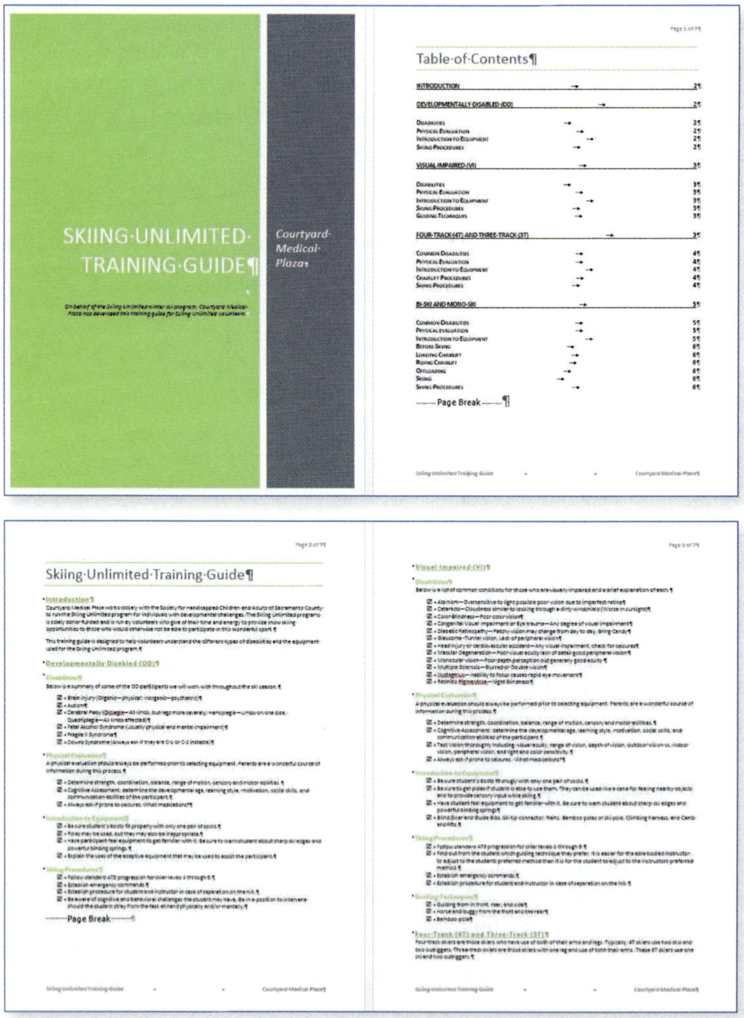

3-105 Word 3-6 completed (first four pages of eight)

Improve It Project 3-7

American River Cycling Club is working with a cycling tour company to set up a trip to cycle through the Tuscany region of Italy. The original document from the cycling tour company needs to be improved. Modify this document to remove some of the existing content and add a cover page, footnotes, bookmarks, and a footer.
[Student Learning Outcomes 3.1, 3.4, 3.5, 3.6]

File Needed: ***ItalyTourItinerary-03.docx***
Completed Project File Name: ***[your initials] Word 3-7.docx***

Skills Covered in This Project

- Change margins.
- Edit document properties.
- Apply a title and heading styles.
- Insert a custom table of contents.
- Insert and customize odd and even headers.
- Insert a document property field into headers.
- Insert a cover page.
- Customize content and insert document property fields.
- Insert and align pictures.
- Insert page breaks.
- Update a table of contents.

1. Open the ***ItalyTourItinerary-03*** document from your student data files.
2. Save this document as ***[your initials] Word 3-7***.
3. Remove existing content.
   a. Remove the existing cover page.
   b. Remove the existing table of contents.
   c. Remove the existing headers and footers on all pages of the itinerary.
   d. Delete the existing bookmark in the document.
4. Change the page orientation to **Landscape**.
5. Apply the **Day** style to each of the day headings in the itinerary.
6. Insert page breaks.
   a. Click in front of "Day 3" and insert a page break.
   b. Repeat this on each of the odd numbered days so only two days appear on each page.
7. Add text and apply style.
   a. Place your insertion point on the blank line after the text in the "Day 2" section.
   b. Press **Enter** and type Notes and Questions at the insertion point.
   c. Apply **Day** style to the text you just typed.
   d. Repeat steps b and c to insert this information at the end of the "Day 4," "Day 6," and "Day 8" sections.

8. Insert a bookmark for selected text.
   a. On the last page, select the text beginning with "**Kilometers to Miles Conversion**" to "**49.6 miles**."
   b. Insert a bookmark named **kmConversion** for the selected text.
9. Insert hyperlinks to a bookmark.
   a. On the first page in the "Day 2" section, select "**Distance: 83 km**" (don't select the paragraph mark) and insert a hyperlink to the **kmConversion** bookmark.
   b. Repeat this on each of the other riding days of the tour. Don't select the footnote after the "Day 3" distance.
   c. Test the hyperlink on page 1. It should take you to the bookmarked text on page 4.
10. Move and delete footnotes.
   a. Move the first footnote (after the distance on "Day 3") to appear after the distance on "Day 2."
   b. Change the footnote text to Day 2 is the longest day of the tour.
   c. Delete the second footnote reference marker after "Day 4." The footnote text is removed when you delete the footnote reference marker.
11. Insert footnotes.
   a. After the "Day 4" distance, insert a footnote and type Day 4 is an optional riding day.
   b. After the "Day 5" distance, insert a footnote and type Day 5 has two routes from which to choose.
   c. After the "Day 6" distance, insert a footnote and type Day 6 has three routes from which to choose. The 68 km route has a couple of substantial climbs.
12. Edit the following document properties.

    Title: Cycling Classic Tuscany: Tour Itinerary
    Company: American River Cycling Club
13. Insert and modify a cover page.
   a. Insert the **Semaphore** cover page.
   b. Select next **June 15** as the date.
   c. Change the font size of the *Title* field to **32 pt.**
   d. Delete the **Subject** (*Document Subtitle*) and **Author** fields.
   e. Change the font size of the *Company* field to **14 pt**.
   f. In the *Address* field, type www.arcc.org.
14. Insert footers on the second and continuing pages.
   a. On the second page of the document, edit the footer.
   b. Change the alignment to **right**, insert the **Company** document property field, deselect the field, and **space** once.
   c. Type | (horizontal line; **Shift+**) and **space** once.
   d. Type Page followed by a **space**.
   e. Insert a plain page number in the current position.
   f. **Bold** all of the text in the footer.

15. Save and close the document (Figure 3-106).

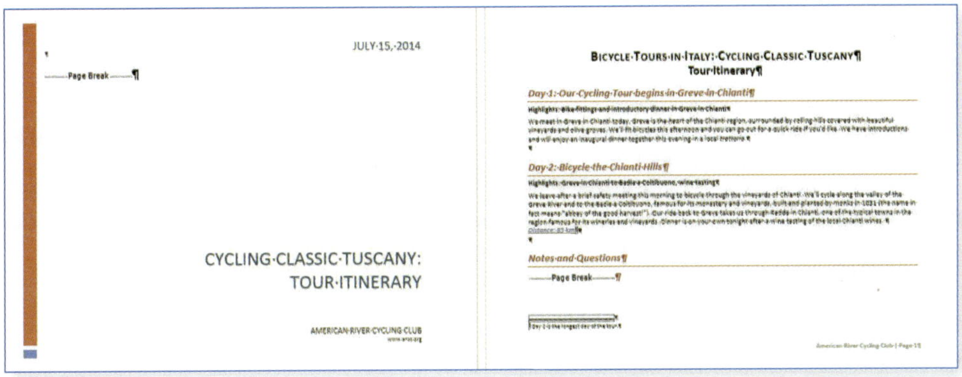

3-106 Word 3-5 completed (first two pages of five)

Challenge Project 3-8

Modify a report you have written for another class to include citations, a bibliography or works cited page, and headers and footers.
[Student Learning Outcomes 3.2, 3.6]

File Needed: None
Completed Project File Name: ***[your initials] Word 3-8.docx***

Open an existing report you have and save it as ***[your initials] Word 3-8***.

Modify your document according to the following guidelines:

- Select the citation style to use for your report (e.g., APA, MLA, Chicago).
- Add citations to the body of your report and create sources.
- Add placeholders for citations in the body of your report.
- Insert a bibliography or works cited page at the end of your report.
- Use the *Source Manager* dialog box to edit placeholders and sources and add new sources, if necessary.
- Insert other citations in the body as necessary.
- Update the bibliography page.
- Insert a header, footer, and page number from the built-in list of options.
- Use different first page headers and footers.
- Insert page breaks to control pagination as necessary.

Challenge Project 3-9

Add footnotes and endnotes, bookmarks, and headers and footers to a multipage document that you have written.
[Student Learning Outcomes 3.1, 3.5, 3.6]

File Needed: None
Completed Project File Name: ***[your initials] Word 3-9.docx***

Open an existing report you have written for another class and save it as ***[your initials] Word 3-9***.

Modify your document according to the following guidelines:

- Add endnotes to the document.
- Convert endnotes to footnotes.
- Change the number format for footnotes.
- Move a footnote to a new location.
- Delete a footnote.
- Add two bookmarks. Insert one at a specific location in your document and another one for selected text.
- Create a hyperlink to a bookmark.
- Create a cross-reference to a bookmark.
- Insert a custom header or footer in your document.
- Add a page number in the header or footer of the document.
- Insert page breaks to control pagination as necessary.

Challenge Project 3-10

Modify a report or multipage document you have written for another class to include a table of contents, a cover page, and headers and footers.
[Student Learning Outcomes 3.3, 3.4, 3.6]

File Needed: None
Completed Project File Name: ***[your initials] Word 3-10.docx***

Open an existing report or multipage document and save it as ***[your initials] Word 3-10***.

Modify your document according to the following guidelines:

- Apply *Heading 1* and *Heading 2* styles to the headings of your document. If the document does not have headings, add two levels of headings to the document.
- Insert a built-in or custom table of contents as the first page of your document.
- Include two levels of headings in the table of contents.
- Customize the title, company, and author document property fields.
- Insert a cover page of your choice.
- Customize the cover page by adding or removing a document property or content control fields.
- Add custom content to content control fields.
- Insert a header, footer, and page number from the built-in list of options.
- Use different first page headers and footers.
- Insert page breaks to control pagination as necessary.
- Update the table of contents.

CHAPTER 4

Using Tables, Columns, and Graphics

WORD

CHAPTER OVERVIEW

Tables, columns, and graphics enhance the appearance and readability of your Word documents. For example, you can use tables to attractively arrange and align information in column and row format. Columns improve readability and provide additional white space in a document. You can also insert and manipulate graphics to add attention-grabbing visual elements to your documents. This chapter introduces you to the Word tools that allow you to add and customize tables, columns, and graphics.

STUDENT LEARNING OUTCOMES (SLOs)

After completing this chapter, you will be able to:

SLO 4.1 Improve the design and readability of a document by using tables to present and arrange information (p. W4-197).

SLO 4.2 Modify a table by changing column and row size, aligning text, using the *Table Properties* dialog box, sorting data, and using *AutoFit* (p. W4-201).

SLO 4.3 Enhance the appearance and function of a table by using the *Table Tools* tabs, applying borders and shading, using table styles, inserting formulas, and converting text into a table (p. W4-207).

SLO 4.4 Modify the layout and design of a document using columns to present information (p. W4-214).

SLO 4.5 Enrich a document by adding and modifying visual elements such as pictures, shapes, *SmartArt*, and *WordArt* (p. W4-218).

Case Study

Placer Hills Real Estate (PHRE) is a real estate company with regional offices throughout central California. In the Pause & Practice projects in this chapter, you modify a brochure for Emma Cavalli, a realtor consultant with PHRE. In the past, Emma distributed brochures that were poorly laid out and designed and that negatively impacted the effectiveness of her message. You modify one of Emma's brochures to include tables, columns, and graphics. Your modifications will improve the overall layout and effectiveness of the document.

Pause & Practice 4-1: Modify an existing brochure to include a table that presents information attractively.

Pause & Practice 4-2: Enhance the table in the brochure by using borders, shading, and table styles.

Pause & Practice 4-3: Improve the readability of the brochure by arranging text in columns.

Pause & Practice 4-4: Add visual elements to the brochure to improve the overall design of the document.

SLO 4.1

Creating and Editing Tables

In Chapter 2 you learned about aligning information into column and row format using tab stops. ***Tables*** are another tool that you can use to organize information into column and row format. In addition to lining up information, tables allow you more formatting options than tabs do for alignment.

> **MORE INFO**
>
> On web pages, most of the information is organized into table and row format even though you might not see table borders or structure.

Tables

You can insert tables almost anywhere in a Word document. A table is made up of individual ***cells***. You enter information in the cells of a table. Cells are grouped into ***columns*** and ***rows***. When using tables, it is important to distinguish between cells, columns, and rows (Figure 4-1).

- ***Cell:*** The area where a column and row intersect
- ***Column:*** A vertical grouping of cells (think of vertical columns that support a building)
- ***Row:*** A horizontal grouping of cells (think of horizontal rows of seating in a stadium or auditorium)

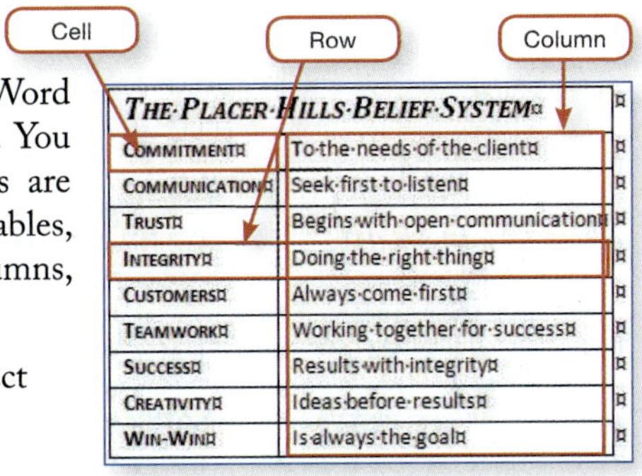

4-1 Table

HOW TO: Insert a Table

1. Place your insertion point in your document where you want to insert a table.
2. Click the **Insert** tab.
3. Click the **Table** button [*Tables* group] to open the drop-down list.
4. Click and drag across the *Insert Table* grid to select the number of columns and rows you want to have in the table (Figure 4-2).
   - As you drag across the grid, the *Insert Table* label changes to display the size of the table (e.g., *3x2 Table*).
5. Select the desired table size to insert into the document. The table is inserted into your document.

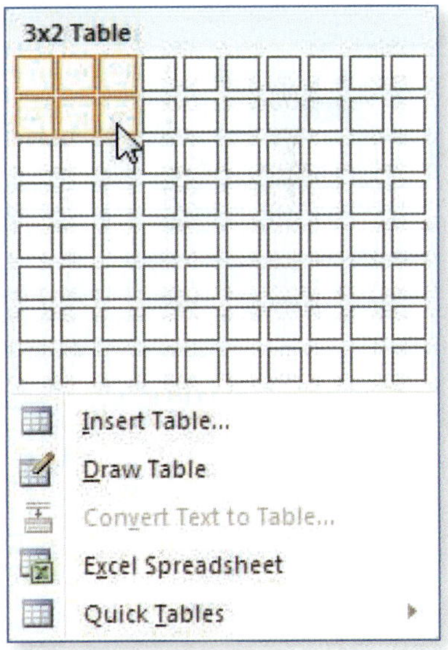

4-2 ***Insert Table*** **drop-down list**

> **MORE INFO**
>
> Word lists table dimensions in column and row format. For example, a three column and two row table is a 3x2 table.

When you insert a table using the *Insert Table* grid, the table size is limited depending on the size and resolution of your computer screen. You can also insert a table using the ***Insert Table*** dialog box.

HOW TO: Insert a Table Using the Insert Table Dialog Box

1. Click the **Insert** tab.
2. Click the **Table** button [*Tables* group] to open the drop-down list.
3. Select **Insert Table.** The *Insert Table* dialog box opens (Figure 4-3).
4. In the *Table size* area, select the desired number of columns and rows.
5. Choose **OK** to insert the table.

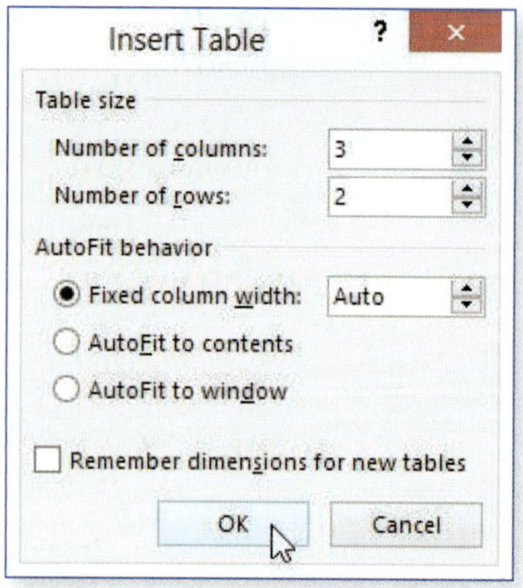

4-3 *Insert Table* dialog box

Navigate within a Table

To move the insertion point within a table, press **Tab** to move forward one cell in the current row. When you get to the end of a row and press *Tab,* the insertion point moves to the first cell in the next row. **Shift+Tab** moves you back one cell at a time. You can also use your pointer and click in a cell to insert the insertion point.

Table Tools Layout Tab

When a table is inserted into a document, the ***Table Tools tabs*** are displayed. There are two *Table Tools* tabs: ***Design*** and ***Layout***. These context-sensitive toolbars are activated whenever the insertion point is in the table or when a region of the table is selected. The *Table Tools Layout* tab lists a variety of formatting options (Figure 4-4). For more on the *Table Tools Design* tab, see *SLO 4.3: Formatting and Editing Tables.*

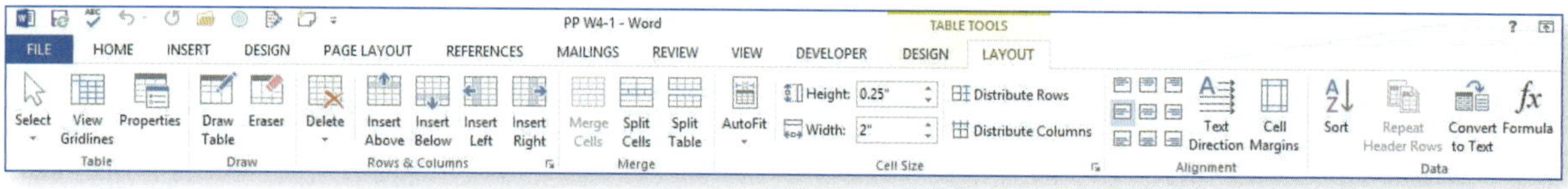

4-4 *Table Tools Layout* tab

Select Table and Text

When you are working with tables, at times you will want to select the entire table, a cell, column, or row, or multiple cells, columns, or rows. Word provides a variety of table selection tools.

- ***Table selector handle:*** This handle appears at the upper left of the table when the pointer is on the table (Figure 4-5). Click the **table selector** to select the entire table.
- ***Row selector:*** The row selector is the right-pointing arrow when your pointer is just to the left of the table row (Figure 4-6). When the pointer becomes the row selector, click to select a single row. To select multiple rows, click and drag up or down.

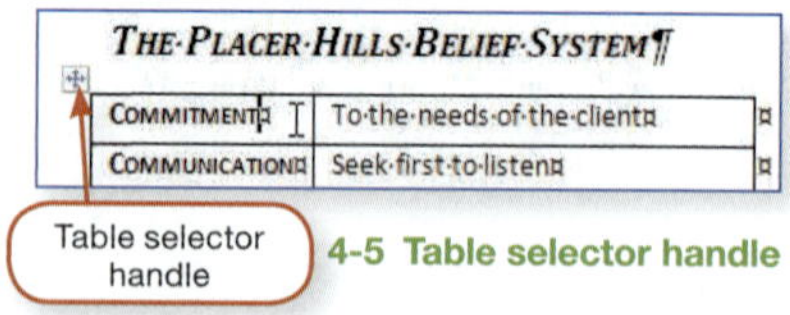

4-5 Table selector handle

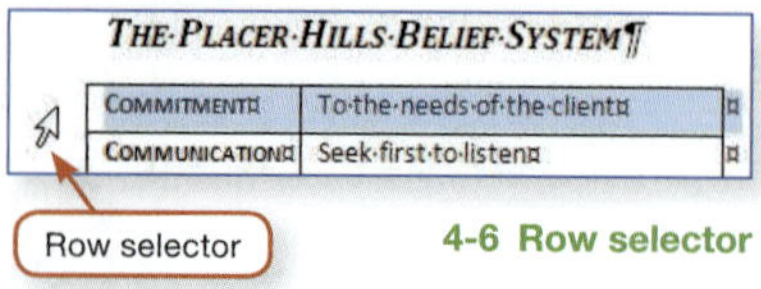

4-6 Row selector

- ***Column selector:*** The column selector is the thick, black down arrow when your pointer is on the top of a column (Figure 4-7). When the pointer becomes the column selector, click to select a single column. To select multiple colums, click and drag left or right.
- ***Cell selector:*** The cell selector is the thick, black right-pointing arrow when your pointer is just inside the left border of a cell (Figure 4-8). When the pointer becomes the cell selector, click to select a single cell. To select multiple cells, click and drag left, right, up, or down. When the cell selector is displayed, double-click to select the entire row.
- ***Select button:*** The select button is on the *Table Tools Layout* tab in the *Table* group. Click the **Select** button to access a drop-down list of table selection options (Figure 4-9).

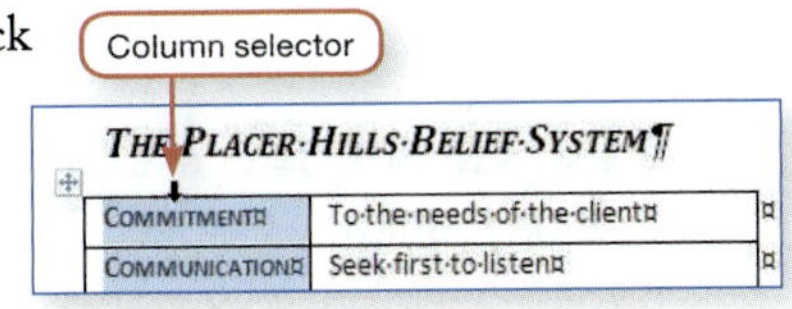

4-7 Column selector

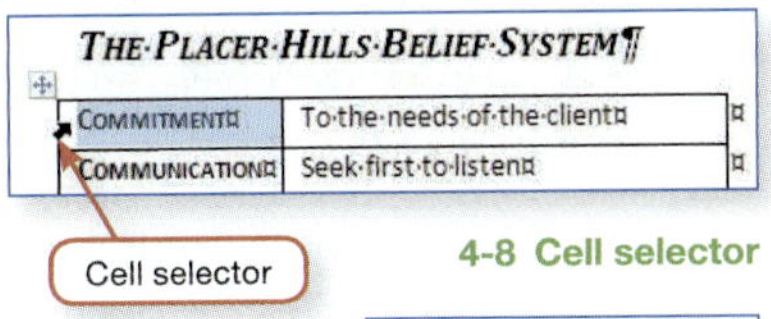

4-8 Cell selector

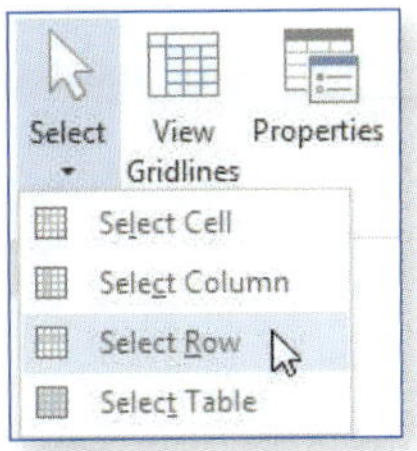

4-9 *Select* drop-down list

Add Rows and Columns

When you insert a table into a document, you are not locked into your original table dimensions; you can always add columns and rows to the table in a variety of ways.

- ***Insert Control:*** Place your pointer on the left outside edge of a row or top outside edge of a column to display the insert row or column control (plus sign). Click the **insert control** to add a row or column (Figure 4-10). Select multiple rows or columns and click the insert control to add the number or rows or columns selected.
- ***Table Tools Layout tab***—In the *Rows & Columns* group, you can insert a row above or below the current row or a column to the left or right of the current column (see Figure 4-4).
- ***Mini toolbar:*** Select a cell, row, column, or table to display the mini toolbar. You can also right-click the table to display the mini toolbar. Click the **Insert** button to display a list of insert options (Figure 4-11).
- ***Insert Cells dialog box:*** Open this dialog box by clicking the **Rows & Columns** launcher on the *Table Tools Layout* tab (Figure 4-12).
- ***Tab:*** When your insertion point is in the last cell in the last row, you can press **Tab** to insert a new row below the last row.

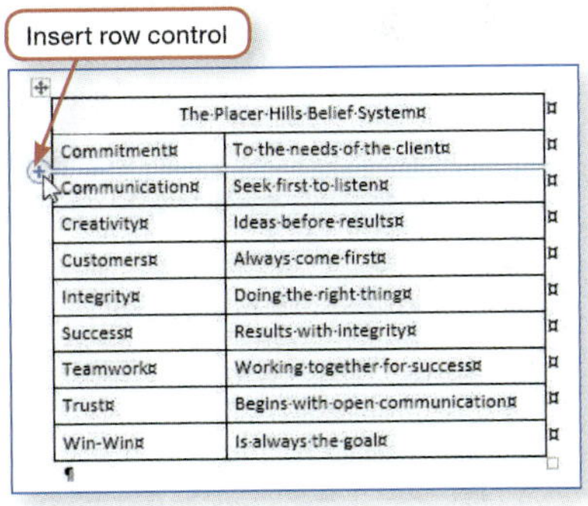

4-10 Insert row control

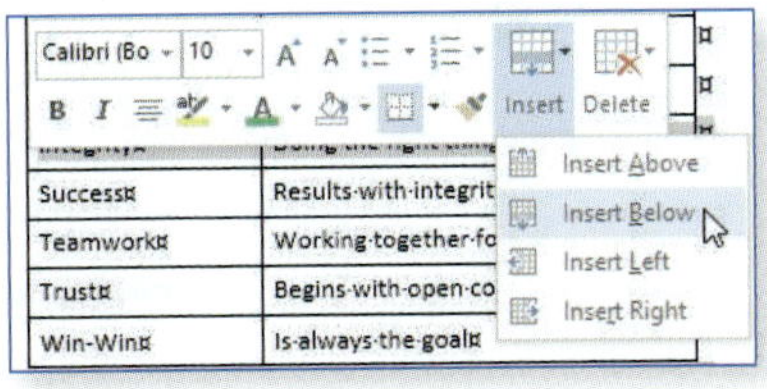

4-11 Use the mini toolbar to insert a row

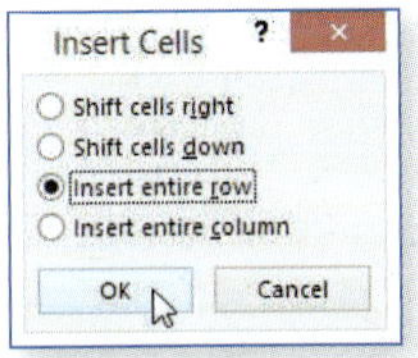

4-12 *Insert Cells* dialog box

> **MORE INFO**
>
> Be careful about *using Shift cells right* from the *Insert Cells* dialog box. This pushes cells to the right creating a new column in that one row, not the entire table.

Merge and Split Cells

Many times when you use tables you want to span information across multiple columns, such as when you are inserting a title or subtitle in a table. You can do this by merging columns, rows, and cells.

HOW TO: Merge Cells

1. Select the cells to be merged.
2. Click the **Table Tools Layout** tab.
3. Click the **Merge Cells** button [*Merge* group] (Figure 4-13).
   The cells are merged into one cell.

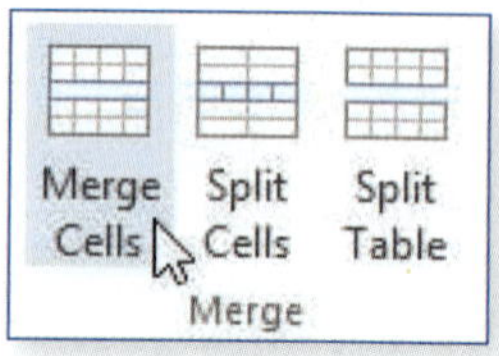

4-13 *Merge Cells* button

Word also allows you to split a cell into multiple cells. You can split cells that have previously been merged or split a single cell into multiple columns and rows. When you are splitting cells, the *Split Cells* dialog box prompts you to specify the number of columns and rows.

HOW TO: Split Cells

1. Select the cell(s) to be split.
2. Click the **Table Tools Layout** tab.
3. Click the **Split Cells** button [*Merge* group]. The *Split Cells* dialog box opens (Figure 4-14).
4. Select the number of columns and rows that you want in the split cell.
   - By default, the *Merge cells before split* check box is selected. When this check box is selected, Word merges the selected cells before splitting them into the desired number of columns and rows.
5. Click **OK** to split the cells.

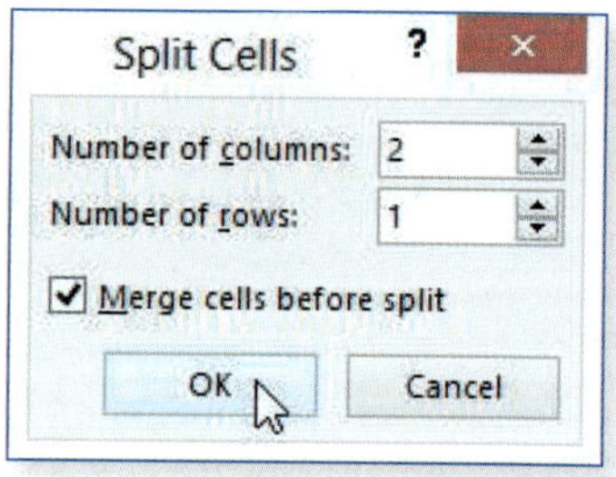

4-14 *Split Cells* dialog box

> **ANOTHER WAY**
>
> Both *Merge Cells* and *Split Cells* are available from the context menu.

Copy or Move Columns and Rows

You can copy or move columns and rows in a table similar to how you copy or move text in a document. Select the column or row to copy or move, and use one of the following methods:

- *Drag and drop:* Drag and drop the column or row in the new location to move it. Hold the **Ctrl** key while dragging and dropping to copy a column or row.
- *Keyboard Shortcuts:* **Ctrl+C** (copy), **Ctrl+X** (cut), and **Ctrl+V** (paste).
- *Context menu:* Right-click on the selected column or row and select **Cut**, **Copy**, or **Paste**.
- *Clipboard group on the Home tab:* Use the **Cut**, **Copy**, and **Paste** buttons in this group.

Remove Columns and Rows

At some point, you will need to remove columns or rows from your table. Removing columns and rows is very similar to inserting columns and rows. Use the *Delete* button in the *Rows & Columns* group on the *Table Tools Layout* tab or the mini toolbar to remove cells, columns, rows, or an entire table. You have the following options (Figure 4-15):

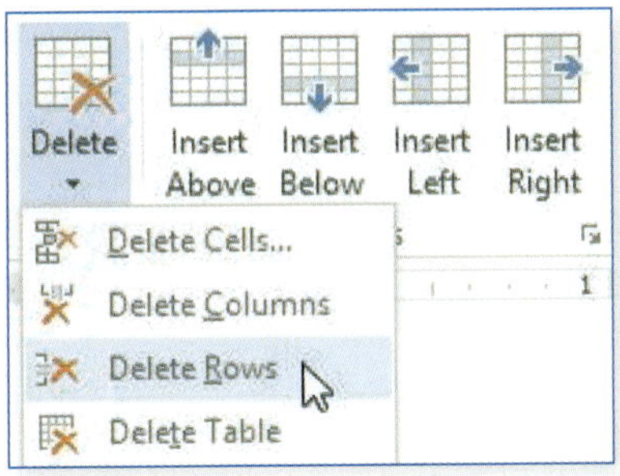

4-15 ***Delete*** **options**

- *Delete Cells . . .*: This will open the *Delete Cells* dialog box.
- *Delete Columns*
- *Delete Rows*
- *Delete Table*

Delete a Table

If you select an entire table and press *Delete* on your keyboard, only the information in the table is deleted; the blank table remains in your document. To delete a table, you select the **Delete Table** option from the *Delete* button on the *Table Tool Layout* tab or mini toolbar (see Figure 4-15).

SLO 4.2

Arranging Text in Tables

You can adjust the width of columns and the height of rows and control how text is aligned within the cells of a table. Word provides you with a variety of table resizing and text alignment options. You also can sort information automatically within a table.

Resize Columns and Rows

Many times you need to adjust columns and rows to better fit the information in the table. When you insert a table into a document, the default size for the table is the width of the document. You can manually adjust the width of columns and height of rows in a couple of ways.

You can manually drag the column or row borders to increase or decrease the size of a column or row. When you put your pointer on the vertical border of a column, the pointer changes to a ***resizing pointer*** (Figure 4-16). You can drag the column border to the left or right to adjust the size of the column. You can use the same method to adjust the height of a row by dragging the top or bottom border of a row up or down.

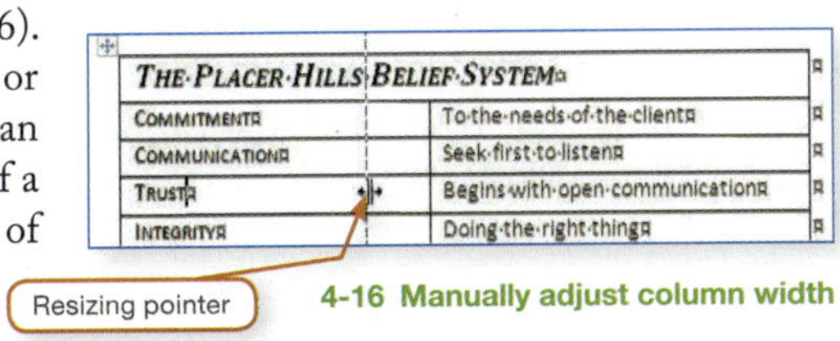

4-16 Manually adjust column width

> **MORE INFO**
>
> When you manually adjust the height of a row, it adjusts the height of the selected row only. Normally, you want to keep the height of rows consistent.

Word also allows you to type in a specific size for columns and rows. It is difficult to adjust column and row sizes of a table with merged cells. It is best to adjust the size of columns and rows before merging cells. If you're adjusting the size of columns or rows after merging cells, be very specific about the cells you select.

HOW TO: Resize Columns and Rows

1. Select the cells, columns, or rows you want to resize.
2. Click the **Table Tools Layout** tab.
3. Change the height or width to the desired size [*Cell Size* group] (Figure 4-17).
   - Manually type in the specific size or use the up or down arrows (spinner box) to resize.

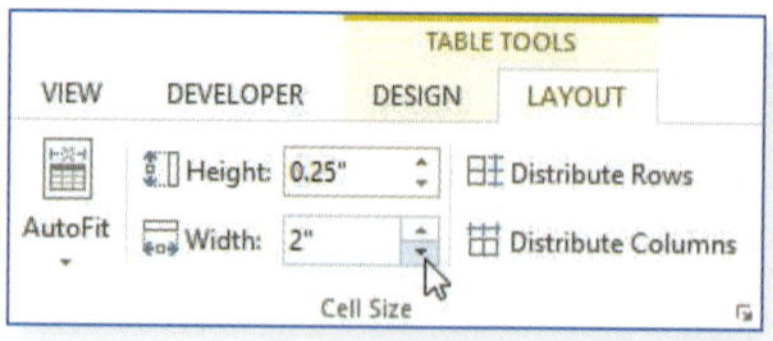

4-17 Set cell *Height* and *Width*

AutoFit Tables

When you insert a table into a document, the table is automatically set to the width of the document (inside the left and right margins). Word has three different ***AutoFit*** options to adjust the column width of the table. The *AutoFit* options are in the *Cell Size* group on the *Table Tools Layout* tab (Figure 4-18).

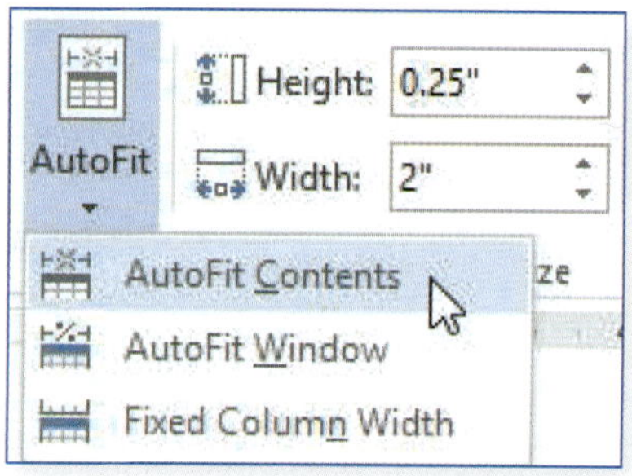

4-18 *AutoFit* options

- ***AutoFit Contents:*** Adjusts column widths to fit the contents of the table.
- ***AutoFit Window:*** Distributes the column widths so the table fits across the width of the page (this is the default setting when you insert a table into a document).
- ***Fixed Column Width:*** Adjusts columns to a fixed column width.

> **MORE INFO**
>
> When you insert a table, the table has the same formatting as the text in the document. If your rows seem too high, it might be because your document contains before or after paragraph spacing that is controlling the height of the rows in your table.

Distribute Rows and Columns

There might be times when you adjust the sizes of columns and rows in a table and the table seems cluttered or uneven afterwards, or you might just want your columns and rows to be the same size as a starting point. Word provides you with features to evenly distribute rows and columns. ***Distribute Rows*** and ***Distribute Columns*** are on the *Table Tools Layout* tab in the *Cell Size* group (Figure 4-19).

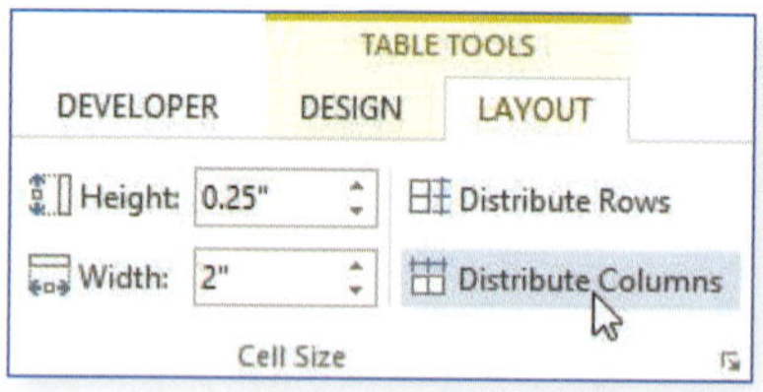

4-19 Distribute rows and columns

- ***Distribute Rows:*** This feature evenly distributes the rows based on the height of the existing table, making all rows a consistent height.
- ***Distribute Columns:*** This feature evenly distributes the columns based on the width of the existing table, making all columns the same width.

> **ANOTHER WAY**
>
> *AutoFit* and *Distribute* options are available from the context menu when a table is selected.

Text Alignment

In Chapter 1, you learned about paragraph alignment and how to left align, right align, center, or justify text. You learned how to change the vertical alignment of a page or section in Chapter 2. Similarly, when using tables, you have both horizontal and vertical alignment options. Text can be aligned vertically and horizontally within a cell and can be aligned independently of other cells. There are nine alignment options within the cell of a table. The following alignment options are in the *Alignment* group on the *Table Tools Layout* tab (Figure 4-20):

- *Align Top Left*
- *Align Top Center*
- *Align Top Right*
- *Align Center Left*
- *Align Center*
- *Align Center Right*
- *Align Bottom Left*
- *Align Bottom Center*
- *Align Bottom Right*

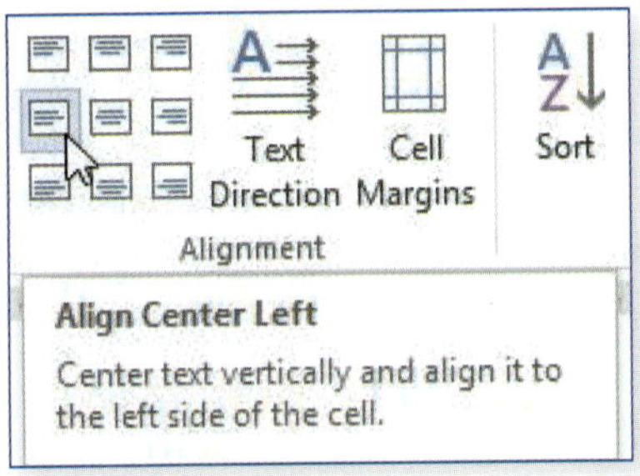

4-20 Text alignment options in a table

> **MORE INFO**
>
> For horizontal alignment, text in the table is usually aligned on the left and numbers are aligned on the right. If you increase row height, it's generally best to vertically center text within a cell.

Cell Margins

In addition to being able to change alignment in cells, you can also adjust ***cell margins***. Just like the margins on a Word document, the cells of a table have top, bottom, left, and right margins. The default cell margins are 0" top and bottom, and 0.08" left and right.

HOW TO: Change Cell Margins

1. To change the cell margins on the entire table, select the entire table. Cell margins can also be changed on individual cells.
2. Click the **Table Tools Layout** tab.
3. Click the **Cell Margins** button [*Alignment* group]. The *Table Options* dialog box opens (Figure 4-21).
4. Make the desired changes to the *Top, Bottom, Left,* and *Right* cell margins.
   - You can also add spacing between cells in the *Default cell spacing* area. This puts padding (space) around the outside of the cells.
   - If you don't want the size of your table to be automatically adjusted, deselect the **Automatically resize to fit contents** check box.
5. Click **OK** to apply the cell margin settings.

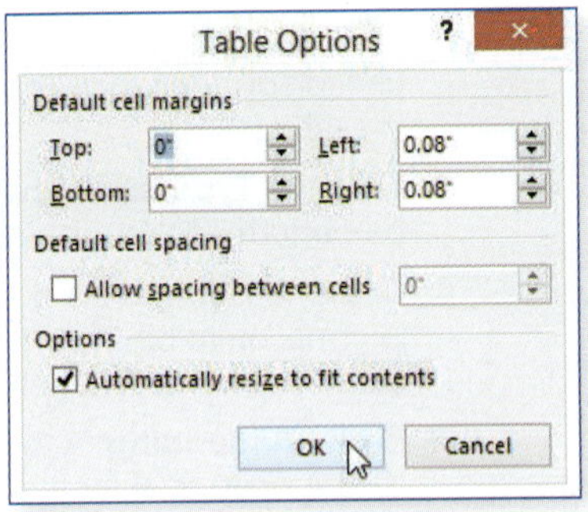

4-21 *Table Options* dialog box

Table Properties Dialog Box

The ***Table Properties*** dialog box consolidates some of table sizing and alignment options in one location. In the dialog box, there are separate tabs for *Table, Row, Column, Cell,* and *Alt Text.* To open the *Table Properties* dialog box, click the **Properties** button in the *Table* group on the *Table Tools Layout* tab (Figure 4-22). You can also open the *Table Properties* dialog box from the context menu.

- *Table* tab: Adjusts the size of the table, alignment, text wrapping, positioning, borders and shading, and cell margins.
- *Row* tab: Adjusts the height of rows and controls how rows break between pages.
- *Column* tab: Adjusts the width of columns.
- *Cell* tab: Adjusts the width of cells, vertical alignment of information in cells, and cell margins.
- *Alt Text* tab: Alternative text (Alt text) is an information tag that is displayed when the pointer is placed on the table. Alt text is also used with screen readers to accommodate those with visual impairments. Alt text is very common with web pages.

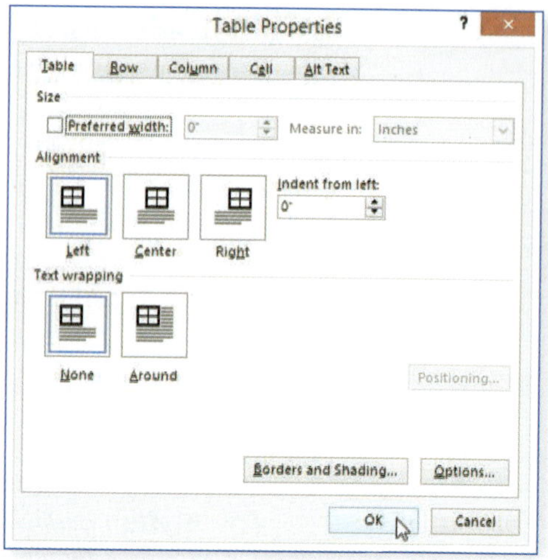

4-22 *Table Properties* dialog box

Sort Data in Tables

A very useful feature in Word is the ability to sort information within a table. You might want to arrange the text in the first column of a table alphabetically or sort numbers in descending order. When you use the ***Sort*** feature on a table, rows of information are rearranged according to how you specify the sort.

HOW TO: Sort Information in a Table

1. Place your insertion point somewhere in the table.
2. Select the **Table Tools Layout** tab.
3. Click the **Sort** button [*Data* group]. The entire table is selected and the *Sort* dialog box opens (Figure 4-23).
4. Click the **Sort by** drop-down list and select the column to use to sort the table. You can sort by any of the columns in the table.
5. Click the **Type** drop-down list and select the type of sort to be performed. You can sort by *Text, Number,* or *Date.*
6. Click the **Using** drop-down list and select the cell information to be used in the sort. *Paragraphs* is the default option and usually this is the only option available.
7. Select **Ascending** (A to Z or 1 to 10) or **Descending** (Z to A or 10 to 1) for the sort order.
8. If desired, you can add a second or third sort on different columns. Use the *Then by* options to add additional sorts.
9. If your table has a header row (title or column headings), click the **Header row** radio button to omit this row from the sort.
10. Click **OK** to perform the sort. Your table is sorted according to your settings.

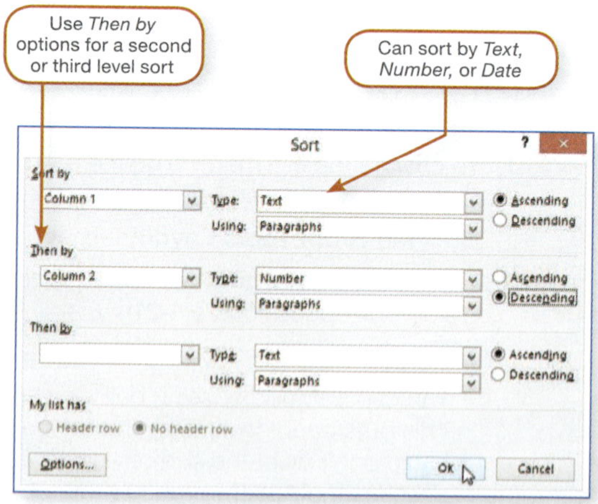

4-23 *Sort* dialog box

MORE INFO

If your table has both a title and column headings, select the rows of the table to be sorted before clicking the *Sort* button so that only the data in the table is sorted.

ANOTHER WAY

Manually sort rows using copy (**Ctrl+C**), cut (**Ctrl+X**), and paste (**Ctrl+V**), or the drag and drop method.

PAUSE & PRACTICE: WORD 4-1

For this Pause & Practice project, you begin modifying Emma Cavalli's brochure. You add a table to the end of this document and then modify the table.

File Needed: ***Brochure-04.docx***
Completed Project File Name: ***[your initials] PP W4-1.docx***

1. Open the ***Brochure-04*** document from your student data files.
2. Save this document as ***[your initials] PP W4-1***.
3. Move to the end of the document and insert a 3x7 table.
   a. Press **Ctrl+End** to move to the end of the document.
   b. Click the **Insert** tab.
   c. Click the **Table** button [*Tables* group] and select a 3x7 table using the table grid. The table is inserted into the document.
4. Type the information in the following table. Press **Tab** to move from one cell to the next cell in the row. Leave the third column blank.

Commitment	To the needs of the client	
Communication	Seek first to listen	
Integrity	Doing the right thing	
Customers	Always come first	
Teamwork	Work together for success	
Success	Results with integrity	
Creativity	Ideas before results	

5. Delete a column and insert rows.
   a. Place the insertion point in any cell in the last column and click the **Delete** button [*Table Tools Layout* tab, *Rows & Columns* group].
   b. Select **Delete Columns**.
   c. Place the insertion point in the second row and click the **Insert Below** button [*Table Tools Layout* tab, *Rows & Columns* group]. A blank row is inserted below the second row.

d. Type the following information in the third row:

Trust	Begins with communication

e. Click in the last cell of the table (bottom right cell) and press **Tab.** A new row is inserted at the bottom of the table.

f. Type the following information in the third row:

Win-Win	Is always the goal

6. *AutoFit* table and adjust column and row size.
   a. Place your insertion point somewhere in the table.
   b. Click the **AutoFit** button [*Table Tools Layout* tab, *Cell Size* group] and select **AutoFit Contents.** The column widths are adjusted to fit the contents of the table.
   c. Place the insertion point in the first column.
   d. Change the *Width* to **1.2"** [*Table Tool Layout* tab, *Cell Size* group]
   e. Place the insertion point in the second column.
   f. Change the *Width* to **2"**.
   g. Use the table selector handle to select the entire table.
   h. Click the **Properties** button [*Table Tool Layout* tab, *Table* group] to open the *Table Properties* dialog box (Figure 4-24).
   i. Click the **Row** tab and check the **Specify height** check box.
   j. Type .25 in the *Specify height* field and select **Exactly** in the *Row height is* drop-down list.
   k. Click **OK** to close the *Tables Properties* dialog box and apply these settings.

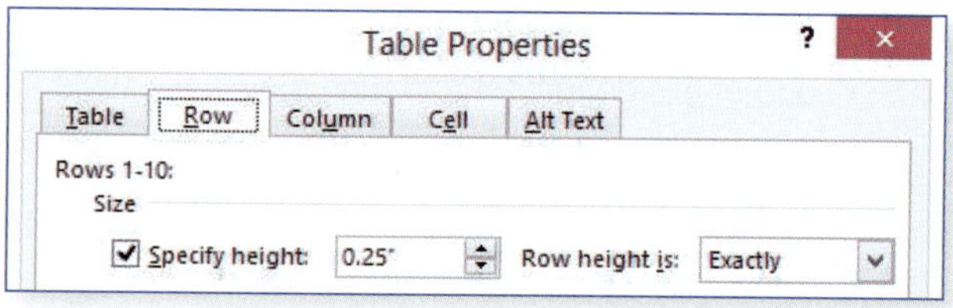

4-24 Change row height on the selected table

7. Insert a row and merge cells.
   a. Click anywhere in the table so the entire table is no longer selected.
   b. Select the first row of the table, select **Insert** on the mini toolbar, and click **Insert Above.** A new row is inserted at the top of the table.
   c. With the first row selected, click the **Merge Cells** button [*Table Tools Layout* tab, *Merge* group]. The cells in the first row are merged into one cell.
   d. Type The Placer Hills Belief System in the merged first row.

8. Sort the table by text in the first column.
   a. Select the **second through tenth (last) rows** of the table.
   b. Click the **Sort** button [*Table Tools Layout* tab, *Data* group]. The *Sort* dialog box opens (Figure 4-25).
   c. Sort by **Column 1** in **Ascending** order. Leave *Type* as **Text** and *Using* as **Paragraphs**.
   d. Click **OK** to perform the sort. The rows below the title are sorted in ascending order.

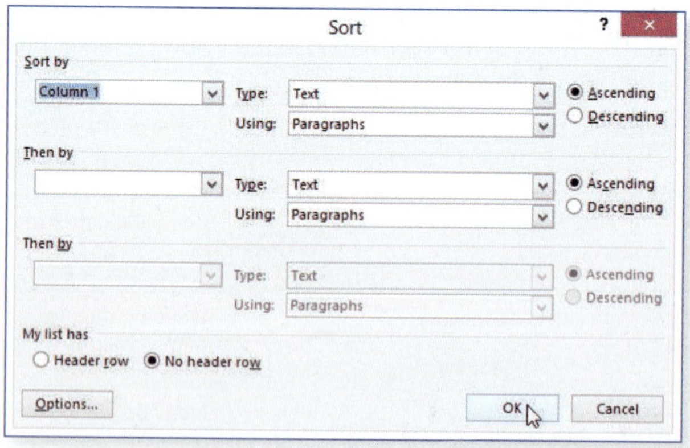

4-25 Sort the table by the first column in ascending order

9. Change cell margins and text alignment.
   a. Select the entire table.
   b. Click the **Cell Margins** button [*Table Tools Layout* tab, *Alignment* group]. The *Table Options* dialog box opens (Figure 4-26).
   c. In the *Left* and *Right* cell margins, type .05.
   d. Select the **Automatically resize to fit contents** check box and press **OK**.
   e. With the table still selected, click the **Align Center Left** button (first button in the second row) [*Table Tools Layout* tab, *Alignment* group].
   f. Click in the first row of the table to deselect the table.
   g. Right-click the first row of the table.
   h. Click the **Center** button on the mini toolbar. The title is centered horizontally.
10. Save and close this document (Figure 4-27).

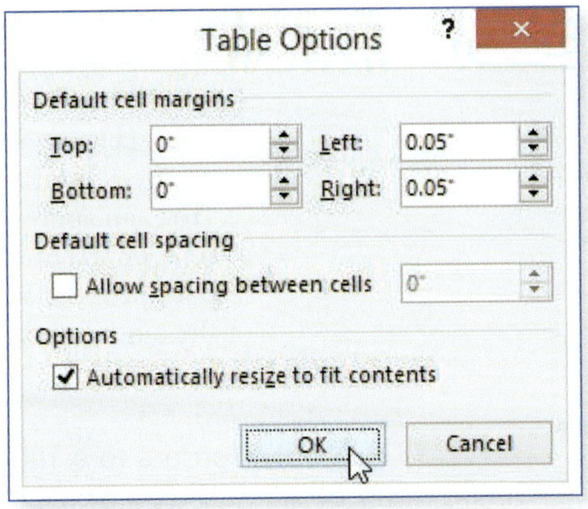

4-26 Change cell margins

The·Placer·Hills·Belief·System¤	
Commitment¤	To·the·needs·of·the·client¤
Communication¤	Seek·first·to·listen¤
Creativity¤	Ideas·before·results¤
Customers¤	Always·come·first¤
Integrity¤	Doing·the·right·thing¤
Success¤	Results·with·integrity¤
Teamwork¤	Work·together·for·success¤
Trust¤	Begins·with·communication¤
Win-Win¤	Is·always·the·goal¤

4-27 PP W4-1 completed (table only displayed)

SLO 4.3

Formatting and Editing Tables

In addition to the ability to adjust the structure of tables, Word provides you with many tools to enhance the overall appearance of tables. For example, you can add custom borders and shading and table styles to tables. You can also add formulas to tables and convert text into tables.

Table Tools Design Tab

Word provides you with two *Table Tools* tabs when you work with tables: *Design* and *Layout*. Both tabs are context-sensitive and are only displayed when the table or portion of the table is selected or when the insertion point is somewhere in the table. The ***Table Tools Design tab*** allows you to apply table styles and options (Figure 4-28). You can also draw tables using the tools on this tab.

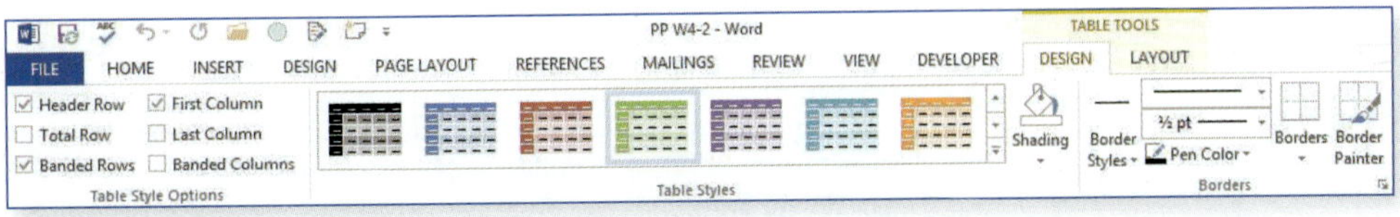

4-28 *Table Tools Design* tab

Table Borders

The *Borders* button is on the *Table Tools Design* tab in the *Borders* group or on the mini toolbar. On the *Borders* drop-down list, there are a variety of border options (Figure 4-29). You can also apply borders using the *Borders and Shading* dialog box.

You can apply borders to an individual cell, a group of cells, or an entire table. When applying borders, it is important to be very specific when selecting the area of the table on which to apply the borders.

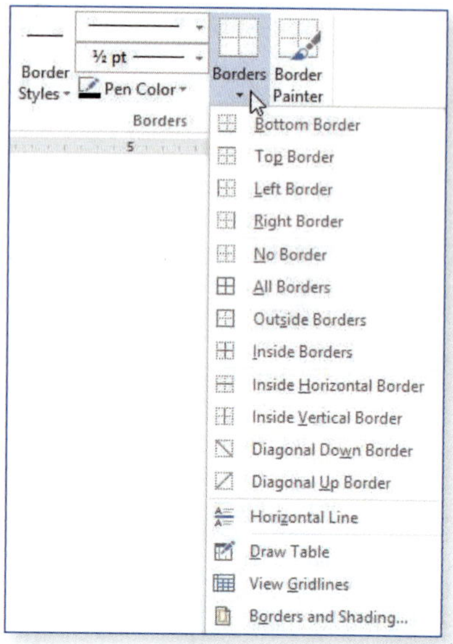

4-29 ***Borders* drop-down list**

HOW TO: Apply Borders to a Table Using the Borders and Shading Dialog Box

1. Select the entire table or the desired area of the table where you want borders.
2. Click the **Borders** button [*Table Tools Design* tab, *Borders* group].
3. Select **Borders and Shading** to open the *Borders and Shading* dialog box (Figure 4-30).
4. In the *Apply to* area, select the portion of the table where you want to apply the border settings.
5. In the *Setting* area, select the border from the list of options.
   - You can remove all borders by selecting **None**.
6. Select the *Style* of the border from the list of options.
7. Choose the color of the border from the *Color* drop-down list.
8. Change the width of the border with the *Width* drop-down list.
9. In the *Preview* area, you can see how your borders will be applied to your table.
   - In the *Preview* area, you can also apply or deselect borders on specific areas of your table.
   - You can click the buttons in the *Preview* area or click the displayed borders to turn borders on or off.
10. Click **OK** to apply the border settings and close the *Borders and Shading* dialog box.

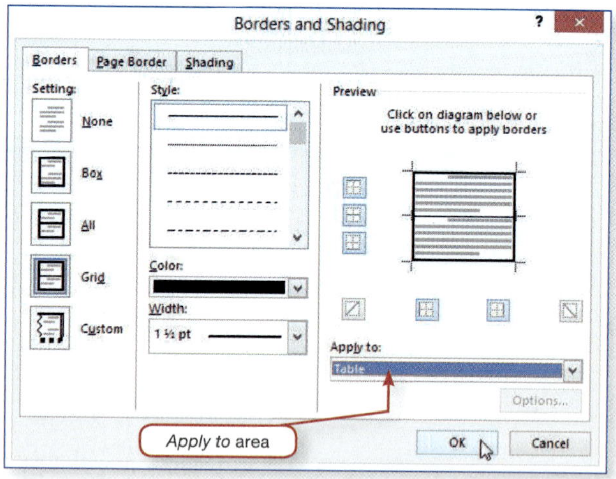

4-30 ***Borders and Shading* dialog box**

> **MORE INFO**
>
> Without borders, it is difficult to see the structure of your table. If you don't have borders, click **View Gridlines** [*Table Tools Layout* tab, *Table* group]. Gridlines are displayed in the document only; they do not print.

Table Shading

Like table borders, you can apply shading to specific cells or to an entire table. In the *Shading* drop-down list in the *Table Styles* group on the *Table Tools Design* tab, you can choose from *Theme Colors* or *Standard Colors* (Figure 4-31). Theme colors change depending on the theme of your document. You can choose a custom color by selecting **More Colors**, which opens the *Colors* dialog box. You can also remove shading by selecting **No Color**.

You can also apply, change, or remove shading with the *Shading* tab in the *Borders and Shading* dialog box.

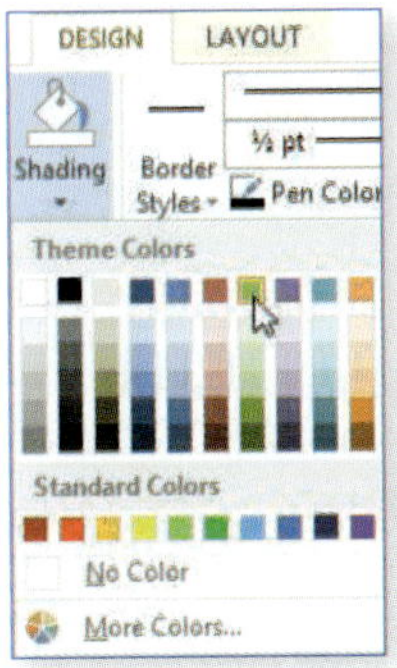

4-31 Table *Shading* options

ANOTHER WAY

Apply borders and shading from the mini toolbar by right-clicking the table or a portion of the table.

Table Styles

Table Styles are built-in styles that you can apply to your tables. These table styles include a variety of borders, shading, alignment, and formatting options. Word provides a wide variety of built-in table styles in the *Table Styles* group on the *Table Tools Design* tab. Click the **More** button on the bottom right to display the *Table Styles* gallery (Figure 4-32).

After you have applied a table style to a table, you can still customize all aspects of the table. You can also remove all formatting of a table by selecting the **Clear** option at the bottom of the *Table Styles* gallery.

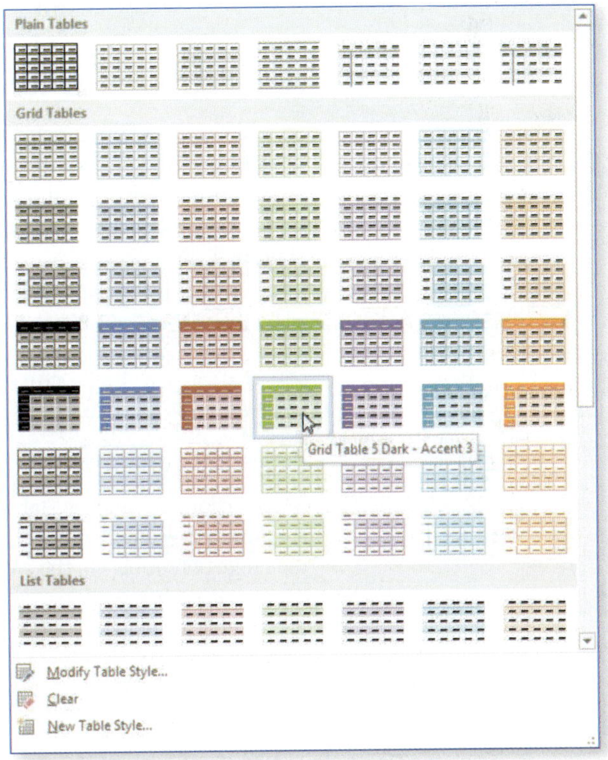

4-32 *Table Styles* gallery

Table Style Options

Word offers a variety of ***Table Style Options*** to customize tables (Figure 4-33). For example, many tables have a header row or column, or a total or last row, where you might want to apply special formatting for emphasis. When any of these options is selected, Word includes special formatting when a table style is applied. Select your table style options before applying a table style.

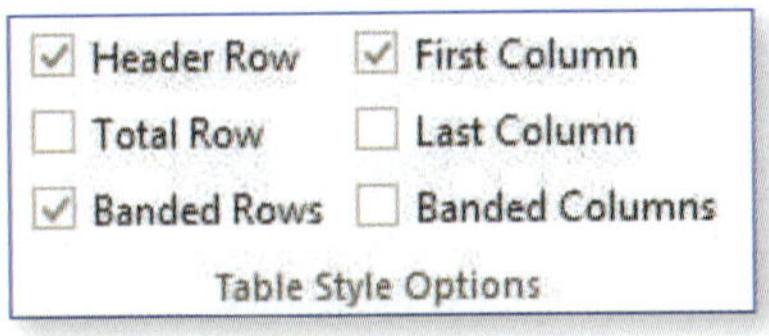

4-33 *Table Style Options* group

> **MORE INFO**
>
> With ***Banded Rows***, every other row is shaded. You can also apply ***Banded Columns*** in the *Table Style Options* group.

HOW TO: Apply a Table Style and Options

1. Select the table on which to apply a table style.
2. Click the **Table Tools Design** tab.
3. Select the options you want to apply to the table [*Table Style Options* group].
   - Consider the content of your table when deciding which table style options to choose.
   - When you select or deselect table style options, the thumbnails of the table styles in the *Table Styles* gallery change to reflect the options you have chosen.
4. Click the **More** button to display the *Table Styles* gallery.
   - You can scroll down in the *Table Styles* gallery to view more table styles.
5. Choose a table style. Word applies the style and options to your table.

Add Formulas to Tables

In addition to making your tables more attractive and easier to read with formatting and style options, you can add ***formulas*** to tables to automatically calculate amounts. For example, you can add a formula in a total row of the table to total the numbers in the rows above (Figure 4-34).

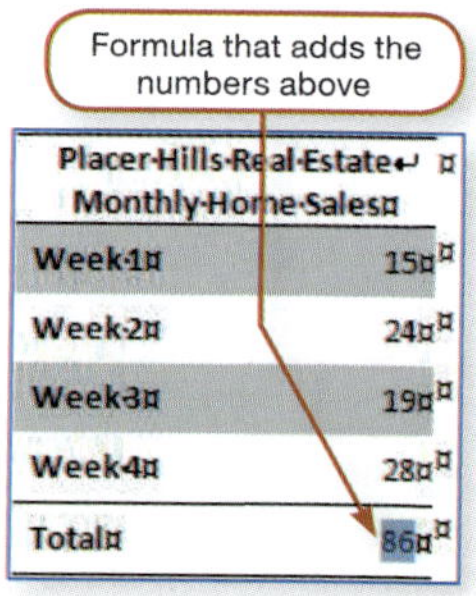

4-34 Formula in a table

> **MORE INFO**
>
> Remember, it's best to align amount figures on the right in a table.

Insert a Formula

Most formulas used in tables in Word are simple formulas that calculate numbers in a column or row. When you insert a formula, Word, by default, inserts the ***SUM*** formula and adds the range of numbers in the column or row. Word also allows you to insert more complex formulas.

HOW TO: Insert a Formula in a Table

1. Place the insertion point in the cell where you want to insert the formula.
2. Click the **Table Tools Layout** tab.
3. Click the **Formula** button [*Data* group]. The *Formula* dialog box opens (Figure 4-35).
4. The formula appears in the *Formula* box.
   - You can select different formula functions from the *Paste function* drop-down list.
5. In the *Number format* area, select number format from the drop-down list.
6. Click **OK** to insert the formula.

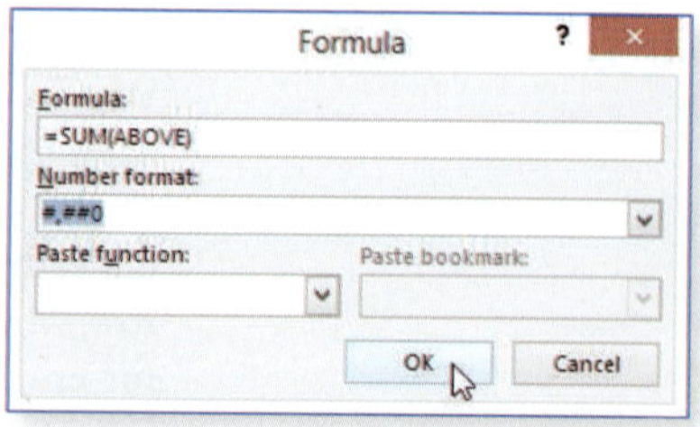

4-35 *Formula* dialog box

Update a Formula

A formula automatically adds values in a table, and you can automatically update it if any of the values change. There are two ways to update a formula:

- Right-click the formula and select **Update Field**.
- Select the formula and press the **F9** function key.

Convert Text into a Table

You will not always be creating a table from scratch. Many times you want to create a table from existing text. For example, you might want to convert information that is arranged into a table using tabs, or you might want to convert a table into text. Word provides you with options to ***convert text to a table*** or ***convert a table to text***.

When converting text into a table, the selected text must be separated by tabs, commas, paragraph breaks, or other characters. Word uses these characters to separate text into individual cells in the table.

HOW TO: Convert Text to a Table

1. Select the text to be converted to a table.
2. Click the **Insert** tab.
3. Click **Tables** [*Tables* group] and select **Convert Text to Table**. The *Convert Text to Table* dialog box opens (Figure 4-36).
4. In the *Table size* area, make desired changes to the number of columns or rows.
   - Word automatically detects the size of the table you need.
   - You might not be able to change one or both of the values, depending on the text you selected.
5. In the *AutoFit behavior* area, select an *AutoFit* option. The default setting is *Fixed column width.*
6. In the *Separate text at* area, select how you want Word to separate columns and rows.
   - Word automatically picks an option based on the text you have selected.
7. Click **OK** to convert the text to a table.

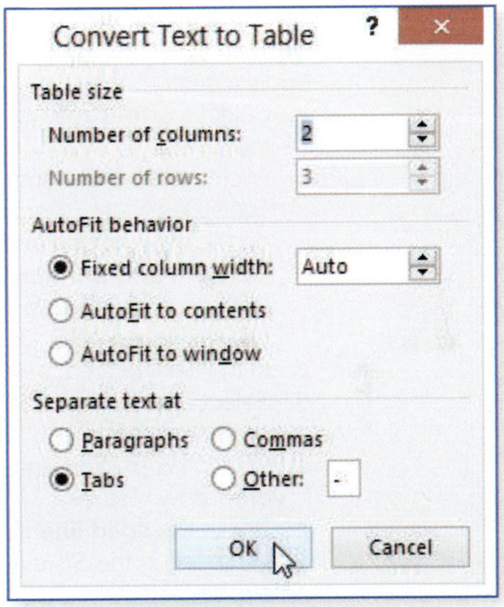

4-36 ***Convert Text to Table*** **dialog box**

MORE INFO

To convert a table to text, click the **Convert to Text** button [*Table Tool Layout* tab, *Data* group] to open the *Convert Table to Text* dialog box.

PAUSE & PRACTICE: WORD 4-2

For this Pause & Practice project, you continue to modify Emma's brochure. You apply a table style and table style options to the table you created in the previous Pause & Practice project. You also convert text to a table and apply borders and shading.

File Needed: ***[your initials] PP W4-1.docx***
Completed Project File Name: ***[your initials] PP W4-2.docx***

1. Open the ***[your initials] PP W4-1*** file you created in *Pause & Practice 4-1.*
2. Save this document as ***[your initials] PP W4-2***.
3. Apply table style options and a table style.
   a. Select the table at the end of the document.
   b. Click the **Table Tools Design** tab.
   c. Select **Header Row**, **Banded Rows**, and **First Column** [*Table Style Options* group] if they are not already selected. The other check boxes should not be selected.
   d. Click the **More** button in the *Table Styles* group to open the *Table Styles* gallery.
   e. Select the **Grid Table 5 Dark – Accent 3** style (Figure 4-37). The style is applied to the table.

4-37 Select table style

4. Apply a custom top and bottom border to the table.
   a. Select the **first row** (title) of the table.
   b. Click the **Borders** button [*Table Tools Design* tab, *Borders* group or on the mini toolbar] and select **Borders and Shading.** The *Borders and Shading* dialog box opens (Figure 4-38).
   c. In the *Setting* area, select **Custom.**
   d. Select **Black**, **Text 1** from the *Color* drop-down list.
   e. Select **1½ pt.** from the *Width* drop-down list.
   f. Select the **solid line** (first line style in the list) in the *Style* area if it is not already selected.
   g. In the *Preview* area, click the **top boundary** of the cell to add a top border.
   h. Click **OK** to close the dialog box and add the border.
   i. Select the **bottom row** of the table.
   j. Open the *Borders and Shading* dialog box and apply the same custom border to the bottom of the selected row (**Black**, **1½ pt.**, **solid line**).
   k. Click **OK** to add the border and close the dialog box.

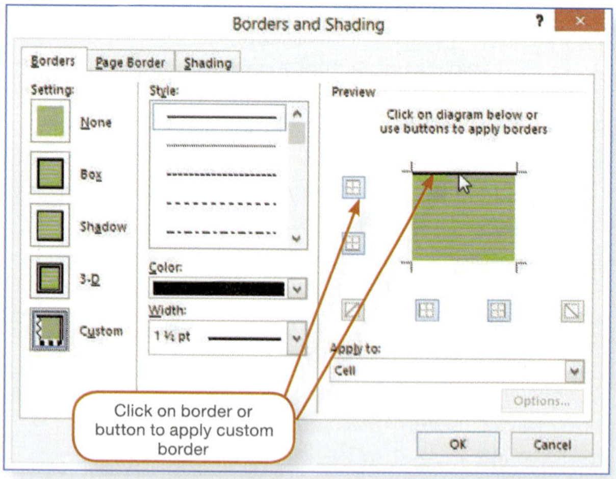

4-38 Apply custom borders

5. Vertically align text in cells.
   a. Select the entire table and click the **Properties** button [*Table Tools Layout* tab, *Table* group] to open the *Table Properties* dialog box.

   b. Click the **Cell** tab and select **Center** in the *Vertical alignment* area.
   c. Click **OK** to close the dialog box.
6. Make formatting changes to the text in the table.
   a. Select the first row.
   b. Open the *Font* dialog box, change *Size* to **12** and *Font color* to **Black**, **Text 1**, and check **All caps** in the *Effects* area.
   c. Click **OK** to close the *Font* dialog box.
   d. Select the first column, not including the title.
   e. Open the *Font* dialog box and check **Small caps** in the *Effects* area.
   f. Click **OK** to close the *Font* dialog box.
7. Convert text to a table.
   a. On the first page, select the three lines of text after "Realtor Consultant" ("Phone" through "www.phre.com/ecavalli"). Be sure to include the paragraph mark at the end of the third line.
   b. Click the **Insert** tab.
   c. Click the **Table** button [*Tables* group] and select **Convert Text to Table**. The *Convert Text to Table* dialog box opens (Figure 4-39).
   d. Change the *AutoFit behavior* to **AutoFit to contents.**
   e. Click **OK** to convert selected text to a table.
8. Remove all borders and add custom borders and shading.
   a. With the table selected, click the **Borders** drop-down arrow [*Table Tools Design* tab, *Borders* group].
   b. Select **No Border** to remove all borders.
   c. With the table still selected, click the **Borders** drop-down arrow and select **Top Border.**
   d. With the table still selected, click the **Borders** drop-down arrow and select **Bottom Border**.
   e. With the table still selected, click the **Shading** drop-down arrow [*Table Tools Design* tab, *Table Styles* group] and select **Olive Green, Accent 3, Lighter 80%** (Figure 4-40).
9. Save and close the document (Figure 4-41).

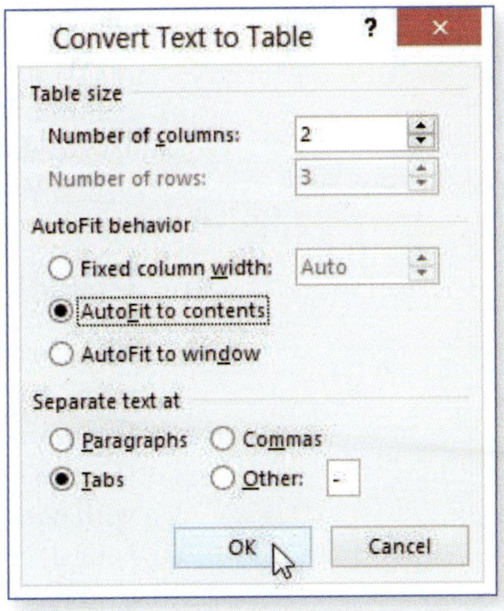

4-39 ***Convert Text to Table* dialog box**

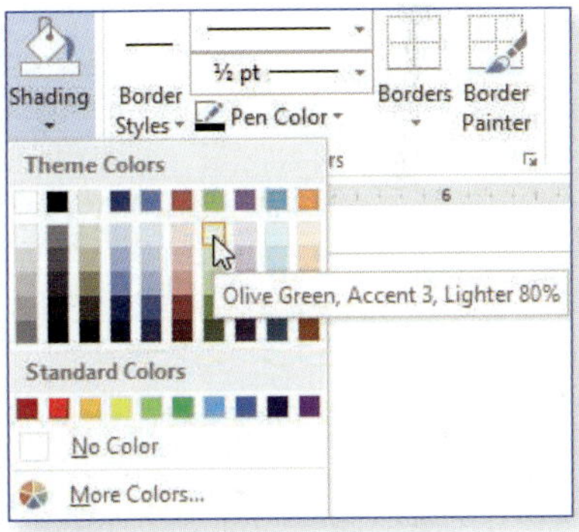

4-40 Select *Shading* color

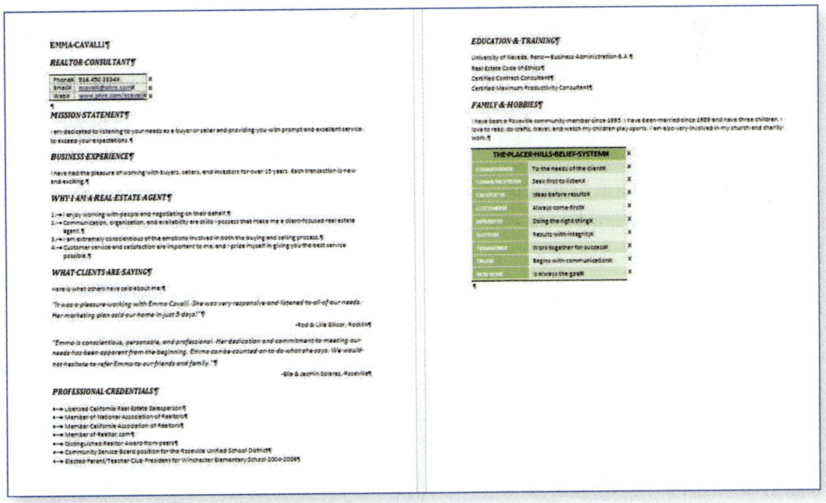

4-41 PP W4-2 completed

SLO 4.4

Using Columns

You can use columns to arrange text and tables into narrower widths and improve the readability, layout, and design of a document. In a normal Word document, text is arranged in a single column. You can apply columns to an entire document or to selected sections of a document. Word has preset column setting options or you can customize column settings to meet your needs. You can use column and section breaks to control column endings and balance columns.

Preset Column Settings

You can apply column settings to a new document or to a document with existing text. To apply preset column settings, click the **Columns** button on the *Page Layout* tab in the *Page Setup* group (Figure 4-42). The *Two* and *Three* column options set columns with equal width, while the *Left* and *Right* column options arrange your document in two columns of unequal width.

When you apply columns to a document, the column settings are applied only to that section of the document. If there are no section breaks, columns are applied to the entire document.

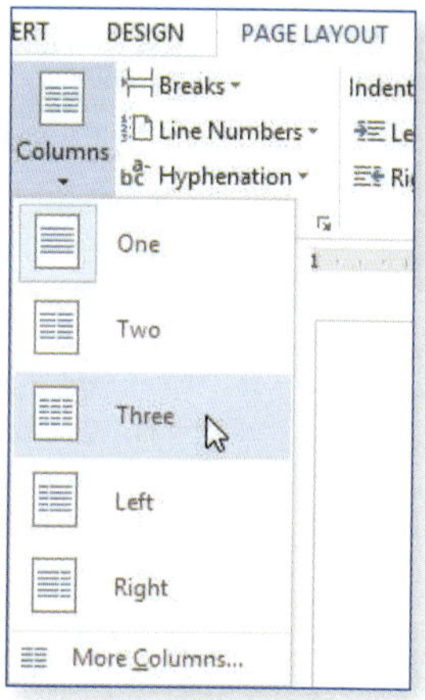

4-42 Preset column options

Customize Columns

Use the ***Columns* dialog box** to apply column settings or customize current column settings. In the *Columns* dialog box you can select the number of columns, adjust the column width and space between columns, insert a line between columns, and select the portion of the document where the column settings will be applied.

HOW TO: Customize Columns Using the Columns Dialog Box

1. Click the **Page Layout** tab.
2. Click the **Columns** button [*Page Setup* group].
3. Select **More Columns**. The *Columns* dialog box opens (Figure 4-43).
4. Select column settings from the *Presets* options or *Number of columns* box.
   - Based on the number of columns you choose, Word automatically sets the column width and spacing.
   - The default spacing between columns is 0.5".
5. In the *Width and spacing* area, adjust the column widths and spacing as desired.
6. To apply unequal column widths, deselect the **Equal column widths** check box.
   - When *Equal column width* is deselected, you can adjust the width and spacing of each column individually.
   - When *Equal column width* is selected, you can adjust the width and spacing to apply to all columns.
7. In the *Apply to* area, select the portion of the document where you want to apply column settings.
   - You can apply column settings to the *Whole document* or from *This point forward.*

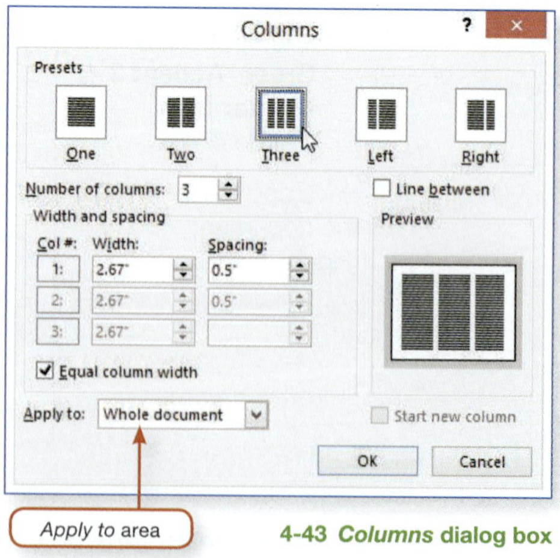

4-43 ***Columns* dialog box**

- When *This point forward* is selected, Word inserts a continuous section break at the insertion point in the document and applies column settings to the text after the continuous section break.
- If you select text, you will be given the option to apply column settings to *Selected text* in the *Apply to* area.

8. Check the **Line between** check box to insert a vertical line between columns.
9. The *Preview* area displays a thumbnail of how your columns will appear.
10. Click **OK** to apply column settings.

Convert Text to Columns

You can apply column settings to the *whole document,* from *this point forward,* or to *selected text.* Depending on the portion of the document where you are applying column settings, Word applies the column settings and inserts any needed section breaks. These options are in the *Columns* dialog box in the *Apply to* area. The following table describes how Word handles each of the options.

Apply to Column Options

Columns Applied to	Actions
Whole Document	Word applies column settings to the entire document. No section breaks are added.
This point forward	Word inserts a continuous section break before the insertion point in the document and applies the column setting beginning at the insertion point, which becomes a new section of the document.
Selected text	When text is selected and column settings are applied, Word inserts a continuous section break before and after the selected text. The column settings apply only to that section.

Use Column Breaks

Column widths control the horizontal text wrapping, while the top and bottom margins or section breaks control where a column ends and wraps to the next column. You can insert ***column breaks*** to end a column and push subsequent text to the next column.

HOW TO: Insert a Column Break

1. Place the insertion point where you want the column to end or the next column to begin.
2. Click the **Page Layout** tab.
3. Click the **Breaks** button [*Page Layout* group].
4. Select **Column** in the *Page Breaks* options (Figure 4-44).
   - You see a column break indicator when *Show/Hide* is turned on (Figure 4-45).

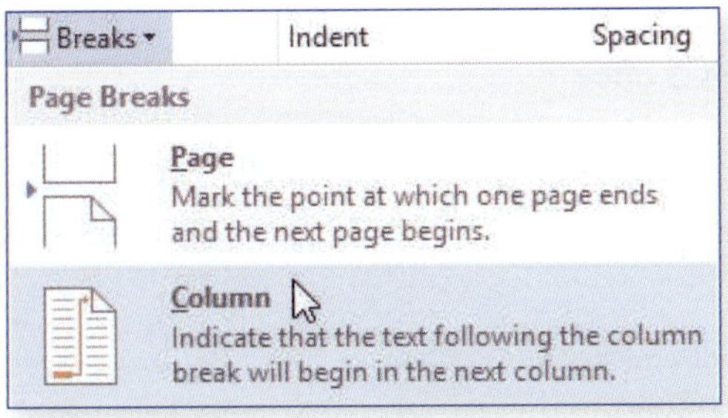

4-44 Insert column break

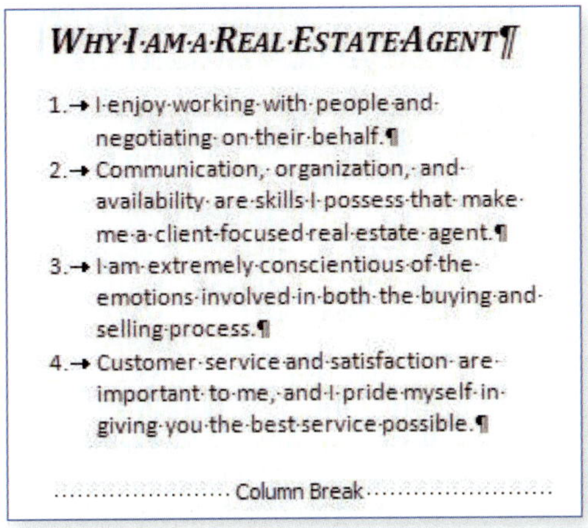

4-45 Column break inserted

ANOTHER WAY

Ctrl+Shift+Enter inserts a column break.

MORE INFO

Always turn on *Show/Hide* (**Ctrl+Shift+8**) when using page, section, or column breaks to help you see these elements in your document.

Balance Columns

Column breaks are one way to balance columns on a page. Another way is to use a ***continuous section break***. To make columns approximately equal in length on a page, insert a continuous section break at the end of the last column on the page. Word automatically adjusts your columns so they are about the same length.

HOW TO: Balance Columns Using a Continuous Section Break

1. Place the insertion point at the end of the last column in your document.
2. Click the **Page Layout** tab.
3. Click the **Breaks** button [*Page Layout* group].
4. Select **Continuous** in the *Section Breaks* options.
   - You see a continuous section break indicator when *Show/Hide* is turned on.

MORE INFO

Balancing columns using a continuous section break works only if there are no other column breaks controlling column endings on that page.

PAUSE & PRACTICE: WORD 4-3

For this Pause & Practice project, you apply columns to Emma's brochure. With the use of columns and column breaks, you attractively arrange the columns and make the document fit on one page.

File Needed: ***[your initials] PP W4-2.docx***
Completed Project File Name: ***[your initials] PP W4-3.docx***

1. Open the ***[your initials] PP W4-2*** file you saved in *Pause & Practice 4-2*.
2. Save this document as ***[your initials] PP W4-3***.
3. Change the page orientation and margins.
   a. Click the **Orientation** button [*Page Layout* tab, *Page Setup* group].
   b. Select **Landscape**.

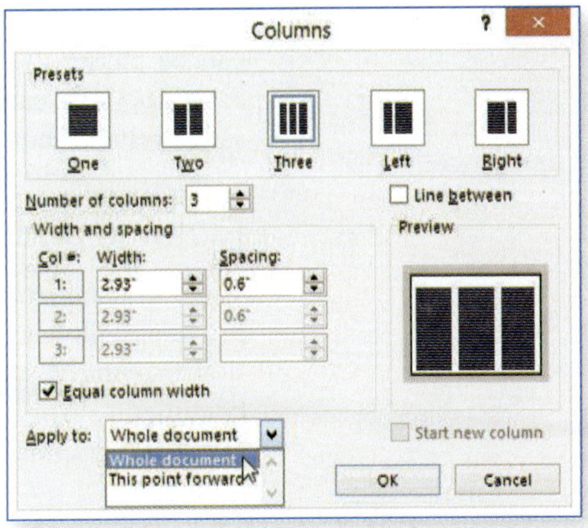

4-46 Customize column settings

   c. Click the **Margins** button and choose *Custom Margins*.
   d. Change the *Top* margin to **1.2"**, and the *Bottom, Left,* and *Right* margins to **0.5"**.
   e. Click **OK** to close the dialog box and apply the margin settings. If a dialog box opens informing you that the margins are outside the printable area, click **Ignore**.

4. Arrange the text in columns.
   a. Move to the top of the document.
   b. Click the **Columns** button [*Page Layout* tab, *Page Setup* group] and choose **Two**. The text is arranged into two columns.

5. Customize column settings using the *Columns* dialog box.
   a. Click the **Columns** button [*Page Layout* tab, *Page Setup* group] and choose **More Columns**. The *Columns* dialog box opens (Figure 4-46).
   b. In the *Presets* area, select **Three**.
   c. In the *Width and spacing* area, change the *Spacing* to **0.6"**.
   d. In the *Apply to* area, select **Whole document**.
   e. Click **OK** to apply custom column settings.

6. Use column breaks to control column endings.
   a. Place the insertion point in front of "What Clients are Saying."
   b. Click the **Breaks** button [*Page Layout* tab, *Page Setup* group].
   c. Select **Column** in the *Page Breaks* options to insert a column break.
   d. Place the insertion point in front of "Education & Training."
   e. Press **Ctrl+Shift+Enter** to insert a column break.

7. Save and close the document (Figure 4-47).

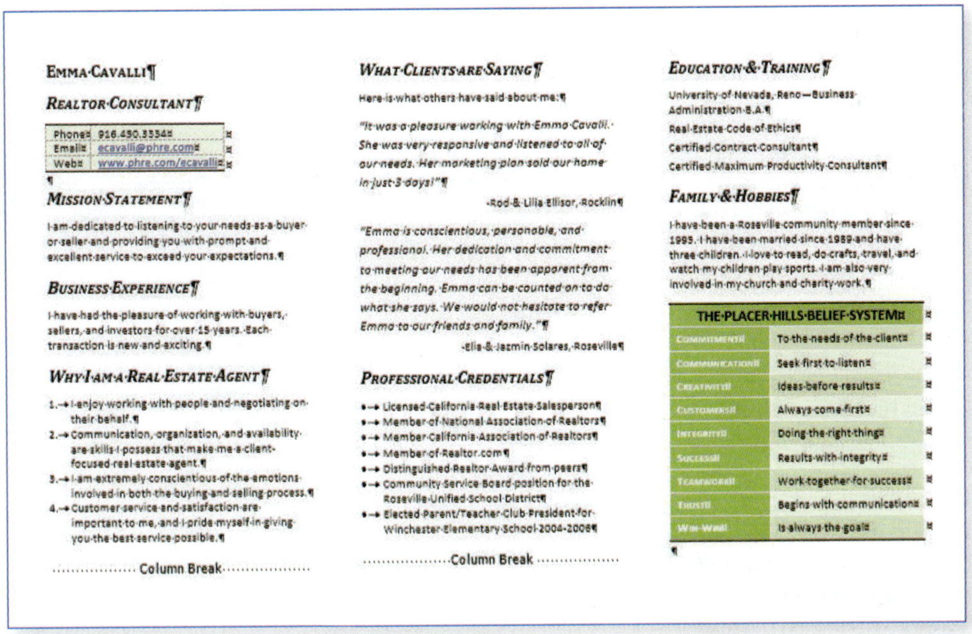
EMMA CAVALLI

REALTOR CONSULTANT

Phone	916.450.3334
Email	ecavalli@phre.com
Web	www.phre.com/ecavalli

MISSION STATEMENT

I am dedicated to listening to your needs as a buyer or seller and providing you with prompt and excellent service to exceed your expectations.

BUSINESS EXPERIENCE

I have had the pleasure of working with buyers, sellers, and investors for over 15 years. Each transaction is new and exciting.

WHY I AM A REAL ESTATE AGENT

1. I enjoy working with people and negotiating on their behalf.
2. Communication, organization, and availability are skills I possess that make me a client-focused real estate agent.
3. I am extremely conscientious of the emotions involved in both the buying and selling process.
4. Customer service and satisfaction are important to me, and I pride myself in giving you the best service possible.

Column Break

WHAT CLIENTS ARE SAYING

Here is what others have said about me:

"It was a pleasure working with Emma Cavalli. She was very responsive and listened to all of our needs. Her marketing plan sold our home in just 3 days!"

-Rod & Lilia Ellisor, Rocklin

"Emma is conscientious, personable, and professional. Her dedication and commitment to meeting our needs has been apparent from the beginning. Emma can be counted on to do what she says. We would not hesitate to refer Emma to our friends and family."

-Elia & Jazmin Solares, Roseville

PROFESSIONAL CREDENTIALS

- Licensed California Real Estate Salesperson
- Member of National Association of Realtors
- Member California Association of Realtors
- Member of Realtor.com
- Distinguished Realtor Award from peers
- Community Service Board position for the Roseville Unified School District
- Elected Parent/Teacher Club President for Winchester Elementary School 2004-2006

Column Break

EDUCATION & TRAINING

University of Nevada, Reno—Business Administration B.A.

Real Estate Code of Ethics

Certified Contract Consultant

Certified Maximum Productivity Consultant

FAMILY & HOBBIES

I have been a Roseville community member since 1995. I have been married since 1989 and have three children. I love to read, do crafts, travel, and watch my children play sports. I am also very involved in my church and charity work.

THE PLACER HILLS BELIEF SYSTEM	
Commitment	To the needs of the client
Communication	Seek first to listen
Creativity	Ideas before results
Customers	Always come first
Integrity	Doing the right thing
Success	Results with integrity
Teamwork	Work together for success
Trust	Begins with communication
Win-Win	Is always the goal

4-47 PP W4-3 completed

SLO 4.5

Working with Graphics

You can use graphics to visually present information and enhance a document. Graphics can be pictures stored on your computer, online pictures or clip art, shapes, *SmartArt,* and *WordArt.* You can insert and customize each of these to meet your specific needs and effectively present information visually.

Pictures and Online Pictures

You can use ***pictures*** and ***clip art*** to enhance your documents with a visual element. Word provides a library of media that includes illustrations, photographs, video, and audio. In addition to using Word's media library, you can also add your own pictures and graphics to Word documents. Word uses the term *picture* generically to refer to any type of visual image that is saved as a graphic file. Below is a table of common types of graphic formats.

Types of Graphics

Format	Full Name	Extension	Details
PNG	Portable Network Graphics	.png	Used with pictures and editing pictures. High-quality resolution.
JPEG	Joint Photographic Experts Group	.jpeg or .jpg	Relatively small file size. Many pictures are saved and distributed in JPEG format.
TIFF	Tagged Image File Format	.tiff	Used with high-quality digital photos and has a larger file size than JPEG or PNG.
GIF	Graphics Interchange Format	.gif	Used with graphics and clip art with fewer colors.
WMF	Windows Metafile	.wmf	Windows format used with many clip art and graphic images.
BMP	Windows Bitmap	.bmp	Proprietary Windows format used with many Microsoft clip art and graphic images.

Insert a Picture

You can use your own picture or a picture from the media library in Word. See the steps below to insert a picture into a document.

HOW TO: Insert a Picture

1. Place the insertion point in the document at the approximate area where you want the picture inserted.
2. Click the **Insert** tab.
3. Click the **Pictures** button [*Illustrations* group]. The *Insert Picture* dialog box opens (Figure 4-48).
4. Browse to the location on your computer and select a picture.
5. Click the **Insert** button to insert the picture and close the *Insert Picture* dialog box.

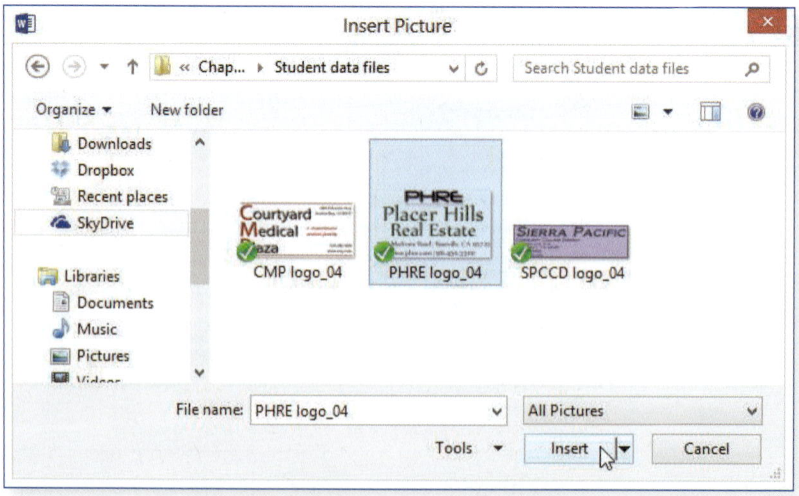

4-48 ***Insert Picture*** **dialog box**

You might find a picture on the Internet and want to use it in a document. You can either save the picture and insert it as explained above or copy the picture and paste it into your document. Press **Ctrl+C** to copy the picture and **Ctrl+V** to paste the picture.

Include pictures obtained from the web only if you have permission from the image owner to avoid copyright infringement. For academic purposes, you may include images if you reference their sources as you would any other research citation.

ANOTHER WAY

Use the context menu (right-click) to both copy the picture and paste it into a document.

Search for an Online Picture

Word provides a variety of clip art and picture choices in its royalty-free media library on Office.com. You can also search for images using ***Bing Image Search***. When using an image from *Bing Image Search,* make sure you have the permission of the image owner to avoid copyright infringement.

HOW TO: Search for and Insert Online Pictures

1. Place the insertion point in the document where you want the picture inserted.
2. Click the **Insert** tab.
3. Click the **Online Pictures** button [*Illustrations* group] to open the *Insert Pictures* dialog box.
4. Click in the *Office.com Clip Art* or *Bing Image Search* text box, type the keywords for the graphic you want to find, and press **Enter**. Thumbnails of the pictures appear in the list below (Figure 4-49).

4-49 Insert graphic from the *Insert Pictures* dialog box

5. Select the picture to insert into your document.
   - Click the **View Larger** button in the bottom right corner of a graphic to view a larger picture.
   - Click the **X** in the upper right corner to close the larger image.
6. Click the **Insert** button to insert the picture into your document.

In the *Insert Pictures* dialog box, you are not limited to inserting clip art only. When you search for a picture, Word provides you with a list of pictures and clip art that match the keywords in your search.

Arrange Graphics within a Document

Once you have inserted an image into a document, you can adjust its size and arrange it in the document. Word provides you with a number of options to resize, align, and wrap text around graphics in your document.

Resize a Graphic

In most cases you will need to resize your graphic to fit properly in your document. You can do this a couple of different ways. You can drag the top, bottom, side, or corner handles to resize the graphic manually, or you can set a specific size for the graphic.

When you select (click) a graphic, ***sizing handles*** appear on each side and in each corner (Figure 4-50). To resize the graphic, click and hold one of the handles and drag in or out to decrease or increase the size of the graphic. Use the corner handles to keep the resized image proportional. If you use the side, top, or bottom handles to resize, the proportions of the image may become distorted. You can also resize the image to a specific size or to a percentage of its original size.

4-50 Resize graphic using the sizing handles

HOW TO: Resize an Image

1. Click the image to select it. The *Picture Tools Format* tab opens.
2. Click the **up** or **down** arrows in the *Height* or *Width* area [*Size* group] to increase or decrease the size (Figure 4-51). Resizing in this manner keeps the graphic proportional.
3. You can also resize the graphic in the *Layout* dialog box.
4. Click the **Size** launcher. The *Layout* dialog box opens with the *Size* tab displayed (Figure 4-52).
5. You can change the size of the graphic to a specific size in the *Height* and *Width* area. You can also scale the graphic to make it a percentage of its original size in the *Scale* area.
   - Keep the *Lock aspect ratio* box selected to prevent the graphic from becoming distorted in size.
   - In the *Original size* area, the original size of the graphic is displayed. You can reset the graphic to its original size by clicking the **Reset** button.
6. Click **OK** to resize the graphic and close the dialog box.

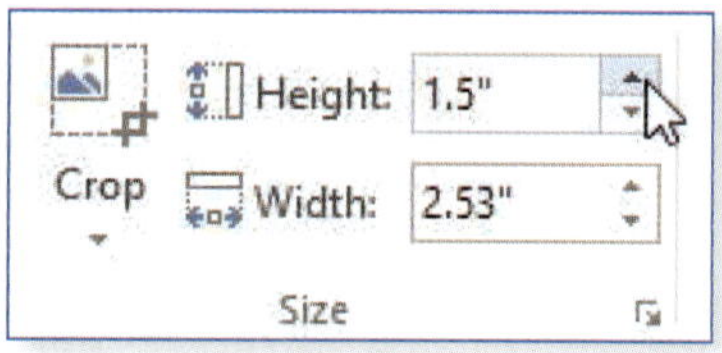

4-51 *Size* group on the *Picture Tools Format* tab

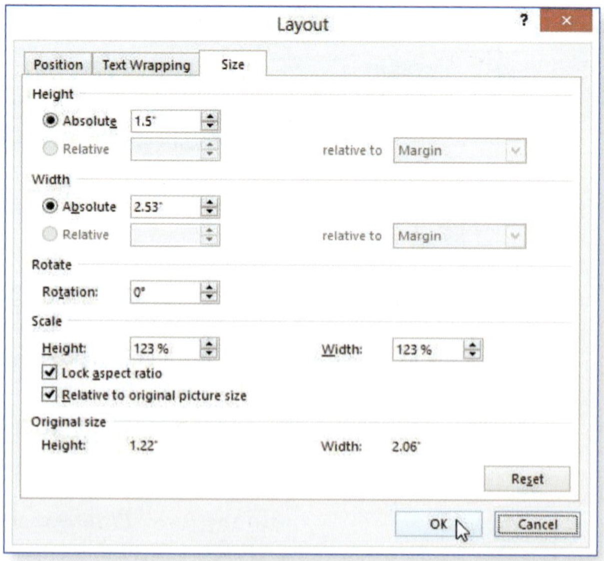

4-52 *Layout* dialog box

ANOTHER WAY

Open the *Layout* dialog box by right-clicking the graphic and selecting **Size and Position**.

Wrap Text around a Graphic

You can select how the text aligns or wraps around your graphic with a variety of ***text wrapping*** options. You can control how the text wraps around the graphic and choose to position the graphic in front of or behind the text.

HOW TO: Wrap Text

1. Click the graphic to select it.
2. Click the **Wrap Text** button [*Picture Tools Format* tab, *Arrange* group] (Figure 4-53).
3. Select a text wrapping option.
   - Select **More Layout Options** to open the *Layout* dialog box with the *Text Wrapping* tab displayed. Options in this dialog box allows you to customize text wrapping.
   - You can also click the **Layout Options** button to the right of a selected graphic and select a text wrapping option.

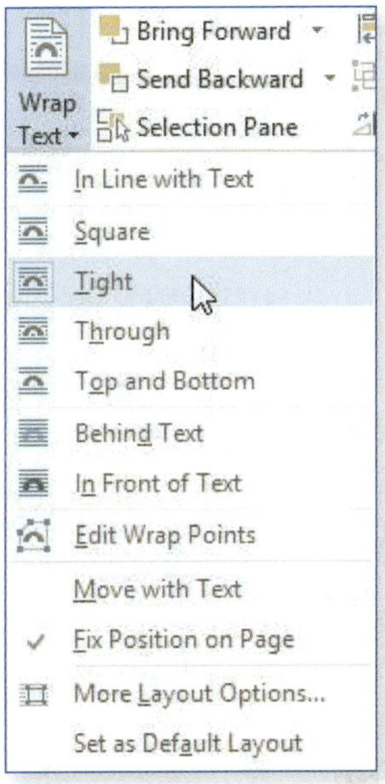

4-53 *Wrap Text* options

In the *Layout* dialog box on the *Text Wrapping* tab, there are additional options to control how text wraps around a graphic (Figure 4-54). In the ***Wrap text*** area, you can choose *Both sides, Left only, Right only,* or *Largest only*. In the ***Distance from text*** area, you can set a specific distance from the graphic to wrap text.

MORE INFO

In Line with Text is the default option when a graphic is inserted into a document.

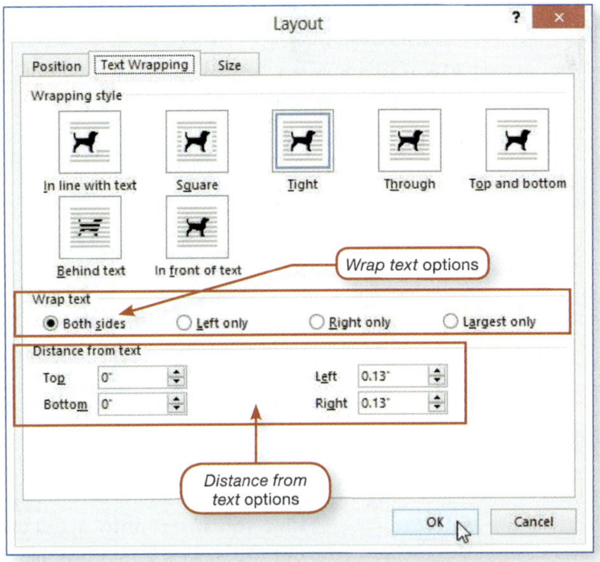

4-54 *Text Wrapping* tab in the *Layout* dialog box

Position a Graphic

In addition to adjusting the size of a graphic and specifying how text wraps around a graphic, you can also determine the position of the graphic in your document. You can align a graphic left, right, or center by selecting the graphic and clicking the **Align** button in the *Arrange* group on the *Picture Tools Format* tab (Figure 4-55).

> **ANOTHER WAY**
>
> The alignment buttons [*Home* tab, *Paragraph* group] also work to horizontally align a graphic, or you can use the following shortcuts:
>
> **Ctrl+L** to align left
> **Ctrl+E** to align center
> **Ctrl+R** to align right

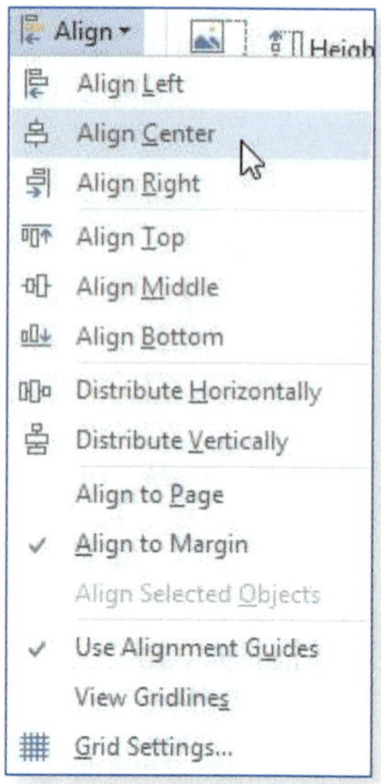

4-55 *Align* options

You can position a graphic in a document in a specific location by dragging the graphic to the desired location. You can also specify the location relative to the margins, page, or column. For example, you can position a graphic 5" from the left margin and 6" from the top margin of the document. The *Position* tab in the *Layout* dialog box offers customization options (see Figure 4-56).

HOW TO: Position a Graphic

1. Select the graphic to be positioned.
2. Click the **Picture Tools Format** tab.
3. Click the **Position** button [*Arrange* group] and select **More Layout Options**. The *Layout* dialog box opens with the *Position* tab selected (Figure 4-56).
4. In this dialog box, you can set both the horizontal and vertical alignment of the graphic.
    - In the *Horizontal* area, you have the following positioning options: *Alignment, Book layout, Absolute position,* and *Relative position.*
    - In the *Vertical* area, you have the following positioning options: *Alignment, Absolute position,* and *Relative position.*
5. Use the radio buttons in these areas to select how the graphic is aligned.
6. Click **OK** to close the dialog box.

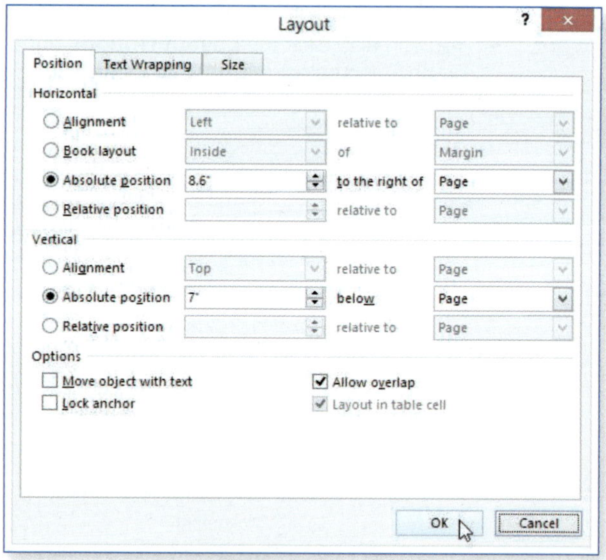

4-56 *Position* tab in the *Layout* dialog box

> **ANOTHER WAY**
>
> Open the *Layout* dialog box by clicking the **Size** launcher [*Picture Tools Format* tab].

Insert a Caption

You might want to add a caption to a picture or chart that you insert into a document. The *Insert Caption* option creates a text box below the graphic where you can enter a caption (Figure 4-57).

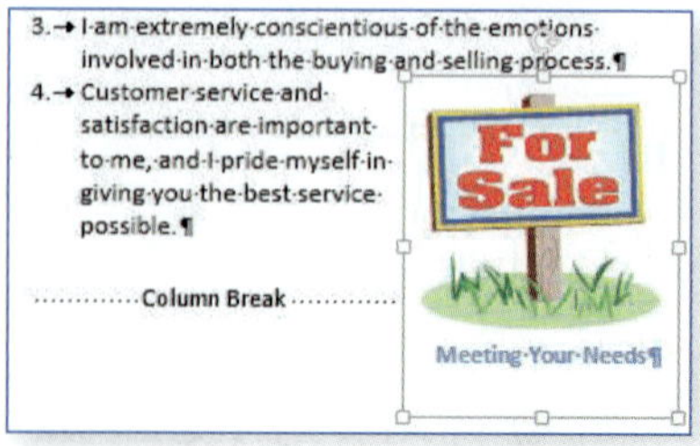

4-57 Graphic with caption below

HOW TO: Insert a Caption

1. Select the graphic that needs a caption.
2. Right-click the graphic and select **Insert Caption** from the context menu. The *Caption* dialog box opens (Figure 4-58).
   - Word automatically creates a caption for the object you have selected.
   - In the *Caption* area, you can add a description after the label, but you cannot delete the label.
   - After a caption is added to a graphic, you can delete the label and number and customize the caption text.
3. In the *Label* area, choose *Equation, Figure,* or *Table.*
   - You can add a custom label by clicking the *New Label* button and typing a custom label.
   - You can remove the label (but not the number) by checking the *Exclude label from caption* option.
4. In the *Position* area, you can choose to place the caption below or above the selected item.
5. Click **OK** to insert the caption.
6. You can edit the caption in the text box after it is added to the graphic (Figure 4-59). You can also customize the size and color of the caption text and adjust the size and positioning of the text box.

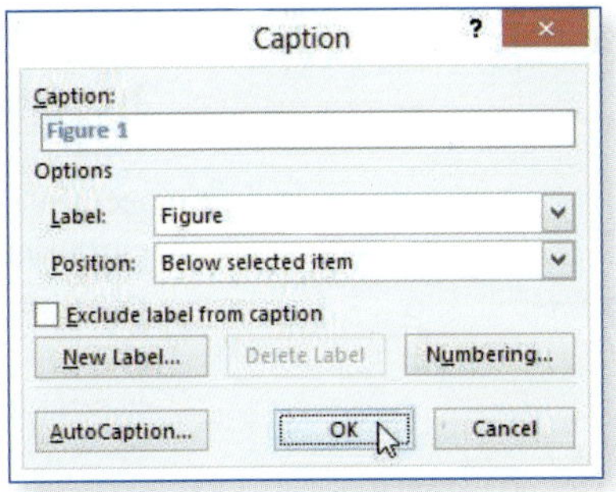

4-58 ***Caption*** **dialog box**

4-59 Caption added to graphic

> **ANOTHER WAY**
>
> Insert a caption by clicking the **Insert Caption** button [*References* tab, *Captions* group].

Group Graphics Objects

When you work with graphics, you may want to ***group*** together related graphics and objects. For example, you might want to group a picture and caption. The advantage of doing this is that the grouped graphics become one object that can be resized and positioned together.

HOW TO: Group and Ungroup Graphics

1. Hold down the **Ctrl** key and click the graphics to be grouped (Figure 4-60).
2. Click the **Group** button [*Picture Tools Format* tab, *Arrange* group].
3. Select **Group**. The selected objects become one grouped object (Figure 4-61).
4. To ungroup grouped items, click the **Group** button in the *Arrange* group on the *Picture Tools Format* tab and select **Ungroup**.

4-60 Multiple objects selected

4-61 Grouped objects

> **ANOTHER WAY**
>
> *Group* and *Ungroup* options are available in the context menu by right-clicking a graphic.

Shapes, SmartArt, and WordArt

In addition to pictures and clip art, you can insert other types of graphic items into your Word documents. For example, Word provides a variety of ***shapes*** that you can insert into your document. ***SmartArt*** and ***WordArt*** can also be added to enhance documents.

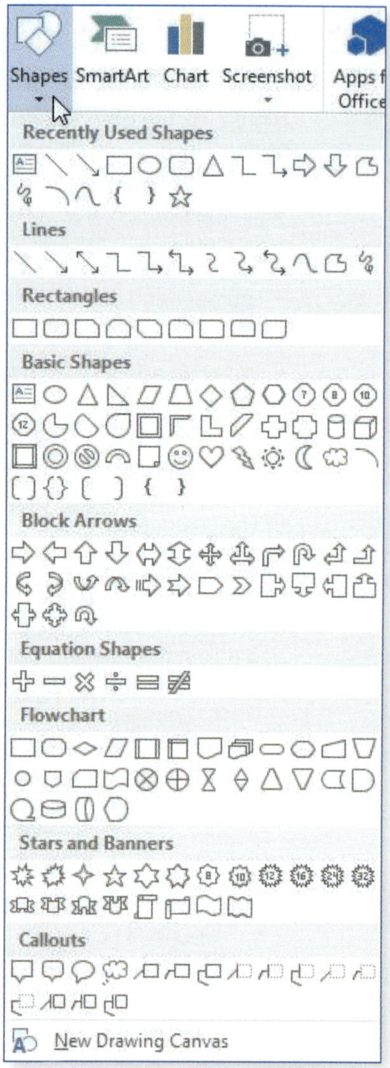

4-62 *Shapes* drop-down list

Insert Shapes

Word's *Shapes* gallery groups shapes into categories (Figure 4-62). When you insert a shape or line into your document, you are actually drawing the object in your document. Once the object is drawn in your document, you can edit the size, position, alignment, and text wrapping of the object.

HOW TO: Insert a Shape

1. Click the **Insert** tab.
2. Click the **Shapes** button [*Illustrations* group] to display the gallery of shape options.
3. Select the shape you want to use. Your pointer becomes a drawing crosshair (large dark plus sign).
4. Click and drag to create the shape (Figure 4-63). When you release the pointer, the shape is inserted into the document.

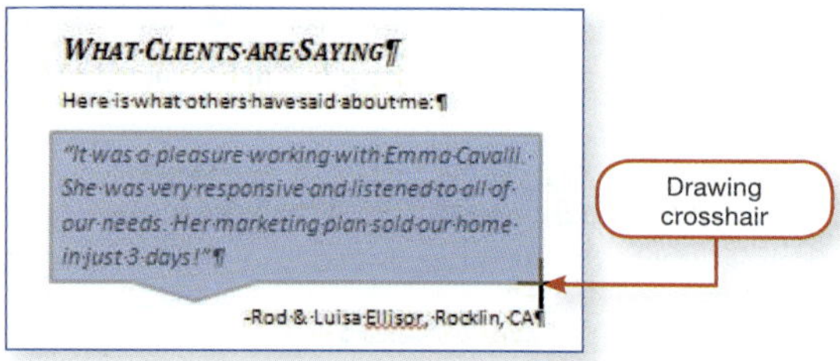

4-63 Draw a shape

- You don't have to be perfectly accurate when you create the shape because you can easily resize the shape after it is inserted.
- You can change the text wrapping on a shape so the shape appears on top of or behind the text, or you can have text wrap around a shape.

MORE INFO

If you want to create a perfect square or circle or to draw a straight line, hold down the **Shift** key while drawing.

Customize Shapes

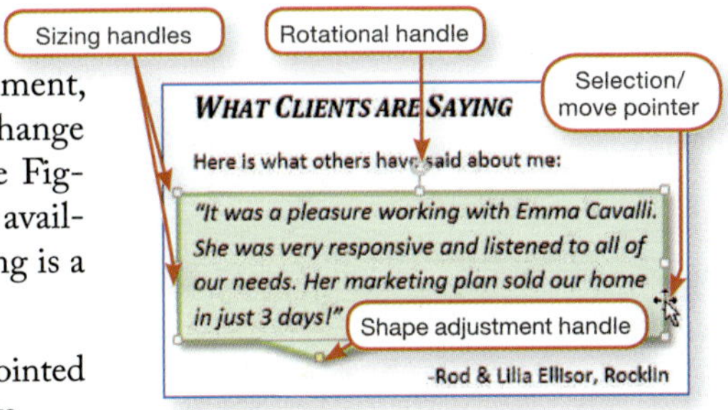

4-64 Shape selected with handles displayed

Once a shape has been inserted into a document, you can move or resize it. Also, you can change the line size, color, and fill of the shapes. See Figure 4-64 and its callouts for examples of the available selection and sizing handles. The following is a list of those options:

- ***Selection/move pointer:*** This pointer (four-pointed arrow) allows you to select and move objects. Select multiple objects by holding down the *Ctrl* key.
- ***Sizing handles:*** There are sizing handles in each corner and on each side of the shape. When you select one of these, the pointer becomes a sizing pointer (two-pointed arrow).
- ***Rotation handle:*** The rotation handle is the circle at the top of the selected shape. Rotate a shape by clicking and dragging this handle to the left or right.
- ***Shape Adjustment handle:*** This handle is the yellow diamond. You can use this handle to change the shape of an object (not all shapes have this handle available). You can also use this handle to change the size or location of a callout, corner roundness, and other shape elements.

You can change the ***Shape Fill***, ***Shape Outline***, and ***Shape Effects*** of a shape. Each of these areas includes many customization options to enhance shapes. When the shape is selected, the *Drawing Tools Format* tab is displayed (Figure 4-65).

4-65 *Drawing Tools Format* tab

Insert SmartArt

SmartArt allows you to graphically present information in your document in a visually attractive way. There are a variety of categories of *SmartArt* and within each category there are numerous options available (Figure 4-66).

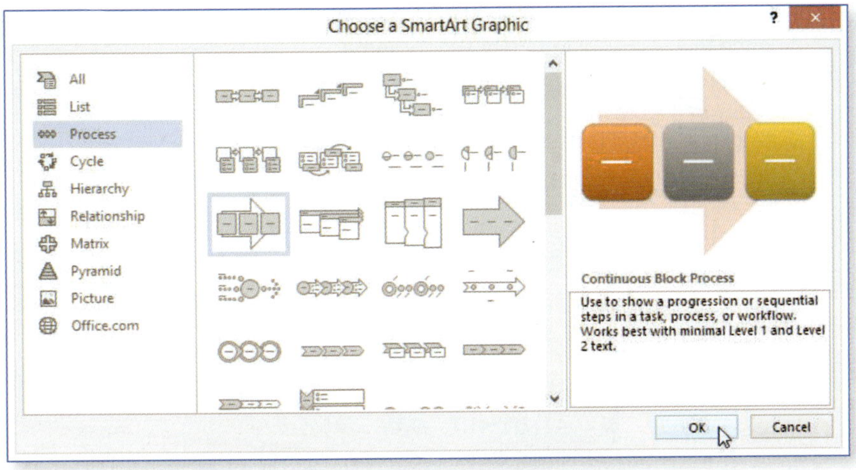

4-66 *Choose a SmartArt Graphic* dialog box

Customize SmartArt

SmartArt graphics are a combination of shapes and text boxes. Once you insert a *SmartArt* graphic into a document, you can use *SmartArt Tools Design* and *Format* tabs to customize the text content and the graphic's structure.

HOW TO: Insert and Customize SmartArt

1. Position your insertion point in your document where you want to insert the *SmartArt.*
2. Click the **Insert** tab.
3. Click the **SmartArt** button [*Illustrations* group]. The *Choose a SmartArt Graphic* dialog box opens (see Figure 4-66).
4. Select a *SmartArt* graphic. A preview and description of the *SmartArt* are displayed on the right of the dialog box.
5. Click **OK** to insert the *SmartArt* into the document.
6. Customize the graphic using the *SmartArt Tools Design* and *Format* tabs.
   - The *SmartArt Tools Design* tab controls the overall design and colors of the *SmartArt* objects.
   - The *SmartArt Tools Format* tab allows you to customize the shape of objects, colors, borders, fill, and effects.

Insert WordArt

WordArt can visually enhance a title of a document or add emphasis to certain text within a document. When you insert *WordArt,* you are actually inserting a text box in the document which can then be manipulated as a graphic. Once you insert *WordArt* in a document, you can resize and move it, and you can change the color, fill, and effects of this object.

HOW TO: Insert WordArt

1. Position your insertion point in your document where you want to insert the *WordArt.*
2. Click the **Insert** tab.
3. Click the **WordArt** button [*Text* group] and select a *WordArt* style from the gallery of options (Figure 4-67). The *WordArt* text box is inserted into your document.
4. Type the text you want to format as *WordArt.*
   - The placeholder text (*Your text here*) is selected when you insert the *WordArt* (Figure 4-68). Type to replace the placeholder text. If the placeholder text is deselected, select it before typing in your text.
5. Click your document away from the text box to deselect the *WordArt* graphic.

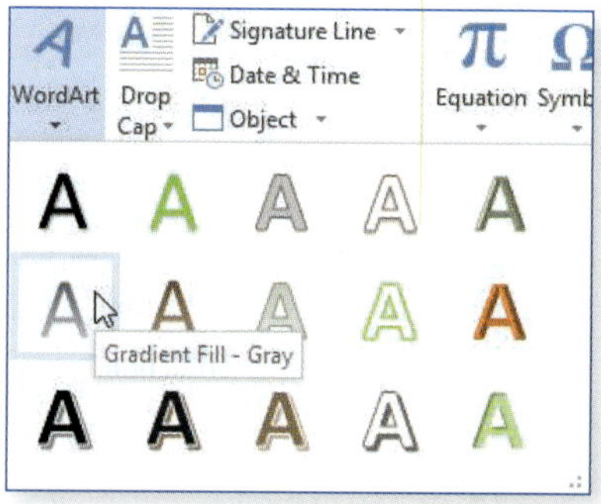

4-67 *WordArt* gallery

4-68 WordArt inserted into a document

ANOTHER WAY

To select text in your document to be converted to *WordArt,* first select the text and then select the *WordArt* format. The selected text is converted to *WordArt* and placed in a text box.

Customize WordArt

Customizing *WordArt* is similar to customizing other graphic objects in Word. When the *WordArt* text box is selected, the *Design Tools Format* tab is displayed (Figure 4-69). From this tab, you can change the style of the *WordArt,* add a border to the text box, and change the fill, outline, and effects of the *WordArt* text.

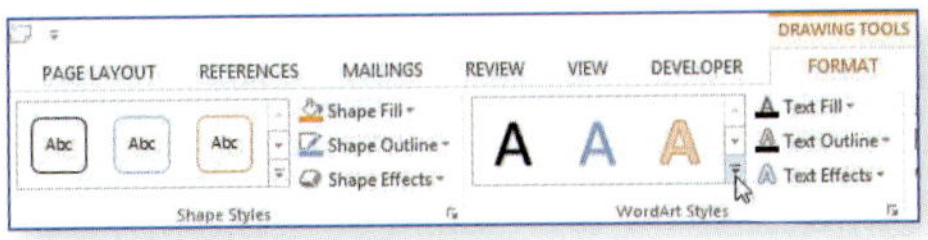

4-69 *Drawing Tools Format* tab

Resize *WordArt* by using the sizing handles on the corners and sides. Rotate the *WordArt* text box with the rotation handle. You can change the position and text wrapping of the *WordArt* in the same way you manipulate other graphics.

Enhance Graphics with Styles

Each of the different types of graphics has a variety of styles, fills, outlines, and effects that you can apply. Context-sensitive tabs appear when you select a graphic object. On each of these context-sensitive tabs, there are a variety of ***styles galleries*** (Figure 4-70).

When applying styles to graphics, Word provides you with a ***live preview***. When you place your pointer on a style from one of the style galleries, Word temporarily applies the style to the selected graphic to preview how it will appear in the document.

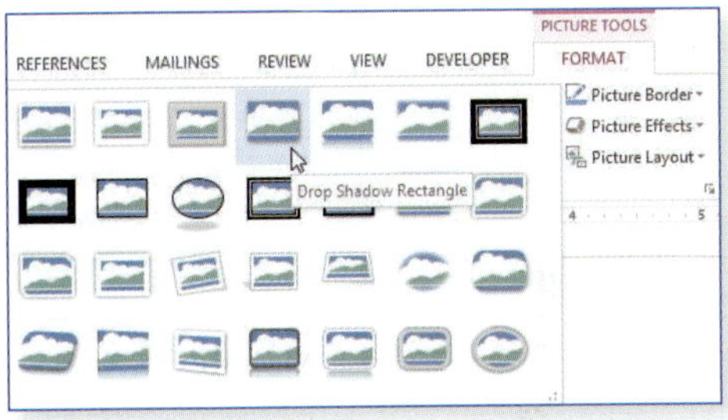

4-70 *Picture Styles* gallery

Insert Symbols and Special Characters

In addition to pictures, Clip Art, *WordArt,* shapes, *SmartArt,* and other types of graphic objects, Word has a variety of symbols and other special characters that you can insert into a document (Figure 4-71). The *Symbols, Wingdings,* and *Webdings* font sets have an assortment of characters and symbols that can be inserted into a document. There are also additional special characters available, such as the em dash, en dash, and copyright and trademark symbols.

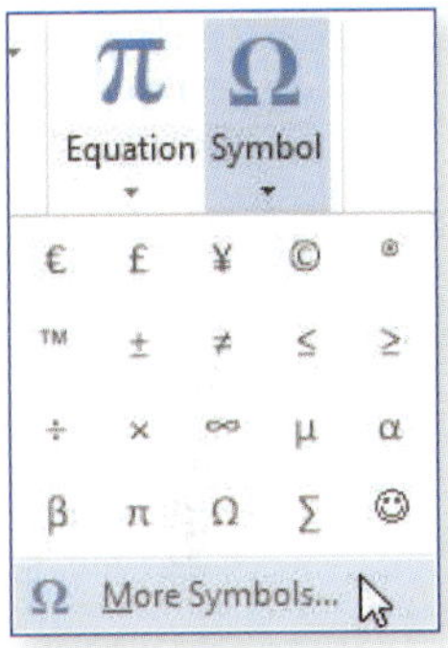

4-71 *Symbol* button on the *Insert* tab

HOW TO: Insert a Symbol

1. Click the **Insert** tab.
2. Click the **Symbol** button [*Symbols* group]. A drop-down list of recently used symbols is displayed.
3. Select **More Symbols** (see Figure 4-71). The *Symbol* dialog box opens (Figure 4-72).
4. Click the **Font** drop-down list on the *Symbols* tab to select the font set.
   - Or click the **Special Character** tab to display the list of available special characters.
5. Click a symbol or special character to insert.
6. Click **Insert** to insert the symbol in the document.
7. Click **Close** to close the dialog box.

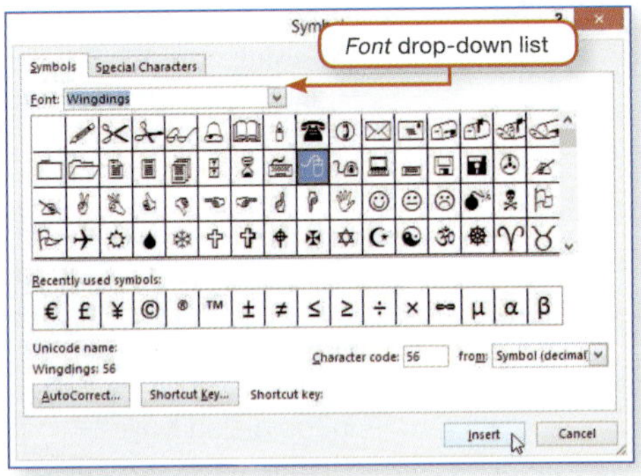

4-72 *Symbol* dialog box

PAUSE & PRACTICE: WORD 4-4

For this Pause & Practice project, you finalize Emma's brochure by inserting a picture, clip art, shapes, and *WordArt.* You format and arrange these graphic objects attractively in the document.

Files Needed: ***[your initials] PP W4-3.docx* and *PHRElogo-04.png***
Completed Project File Name: ***[your initials] PP W4-4.docx***

1. Open the ***[your initials] PP W4-3*** file you saved in *Pause & Practice 4-3.*
2. Save this document as ***[your initials] PP W4-4***.
3. Insert the Placer Hills Real Estate logo at the bottom right corner of the document.
   a. Position the insertion point below the table in the third column.
   b. Click the **Pictures** button [*Insert* tab, *Illustrations* group]. The *Insert Picture* dialog box opens.
   c. Select the ***PHRElogo-04*** file from the student data files and click **Insert.**

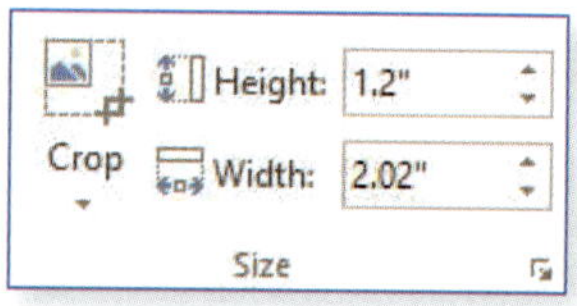

4-73 Adjust the size of a graphic

4. Arrange and format the logo.
   a. With the logo selected, click the **Wrap Text** button [*Picture Tools Format* tab, *Arrange* group] and choose **In Front of Text**.
   b. In the *Height* box [*Size* group] type 1.2 and press **Enter** (Figure 4-73). The width automatically adjusts to keep the graphic proportional.
   c. Click in the middle of the graphic and drag the graphic near the bottom right corner of the document.
   d. Click the **Picture Border** button [*Picture Styles* group] and select **Olive Green**, **Accent 3** (Figure 4-74).
   e. Click the **Picture Border** again, click **Weight**, and select **1½ pt**.
   f. Click the **Position** button [*Arrange* group] and select **More Layout Options.** The *Layout* dialog box opens with the *Position* tab displayed (Figure 4-75).
   g. In the *Horizontal* area, select the **Absolute position** radio button, type 8.6, click the ***to the right of*** drop-down list, and select **Page**.
   h. In the *Vertical* area, select the **Absolute position** radio button, type 7, click the ***below*** drop-down list, and select **Page**.
   i. Click **OK** to close the dialog box.

4-74 Select *Picture Border* color

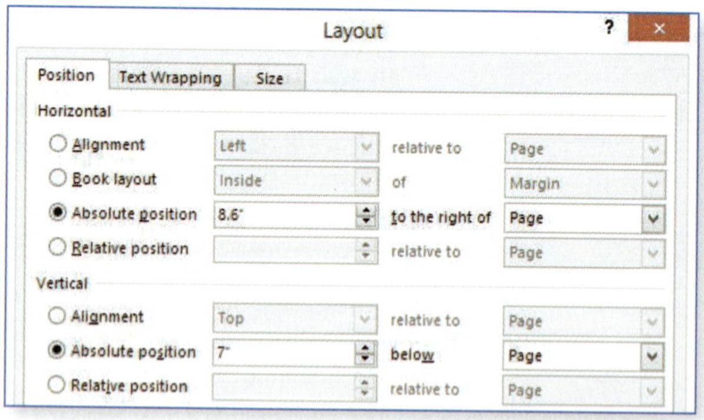

4-75 *Layout* dialog box

5. Add clip art near the bottom of the first column.
   a. Click at the end of the fourth numbered item in the first column.
   b. Click the **Online Pictures** button [*Insert* tab, *Illustrations* group]. The *Insert Pictures* dialog box opens.
   c. Type for sale in the *Office.com Clip Art* text box and press **Enter**. A list of clip art options appears in the dialog box.

d. Select the clip art shown in Figure 4-76 and click **Insert.** The clip art is inserted into the document. Don't be concerned about the clip art at this point. If this clip art is not available, you can insert the ***ForSale-04*** picture from your student data files.

e. With the clip art selected, change the *Height* [*Picture Tools Format* tab, *Size* group] to **1.2"** and press **Enter.**

f. Right-click the clip art, choose **Wrap Text**, and select **Square**.

g. Select the graphic and position it so it is to the right of the fourth numbered item in the first column.

4-76 Insert clip art

6. Insert a caption for the clip art.
   a. Right-click the clip art and choose **Insert Caption.** The *Caption* dialog box opens.
   b. Click **OK** to close the *Caption* dialog box and insert the caption.
   c. In the caption text box, delete the placeholder text and type Meeting Your Needs.
   d. Press **Ctrl+E** or click the **Center** button [*Home* tab, *Paragraph* group] to center the text in the caption.
   e. With the caption still selected, hold down the **Ctrl** key and click the clip art to select it also. Both the clip art and the caption should be selected.
   f. Click the **Group** button [*Picture Format Tools* tab, *Arrange* group] and choose **Group**. The two objects are grouped into one object (Figure 4-77).

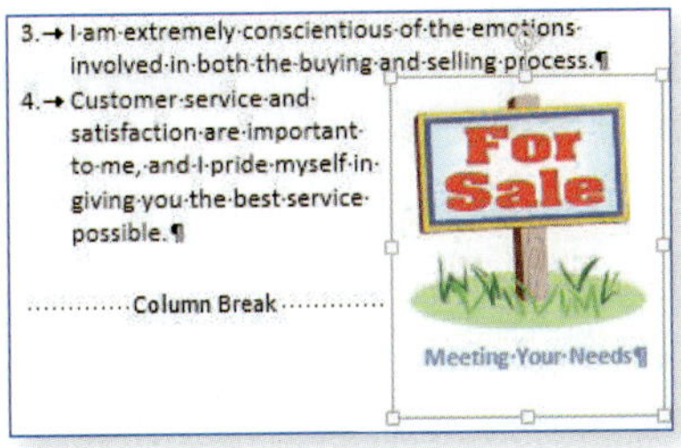

4-77 Clip art and captions grouped

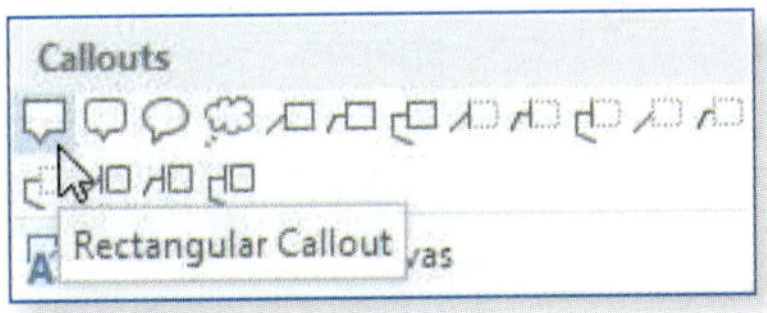

4-78 Select shape

7. Change the paragraph spacing on the two quotes in the second column.
   a. Click in the first quoted paragraph in the second column (beginning with "It was a pleasure . . .").
   b. Change the *After* paragraph spacing to **12 pt**.
   c. Click in the second quoted paragraph in the second column (beginning with "Emma is conscientious . . .").
   d. Change the *After* paragraph spacing to **12 pt**.

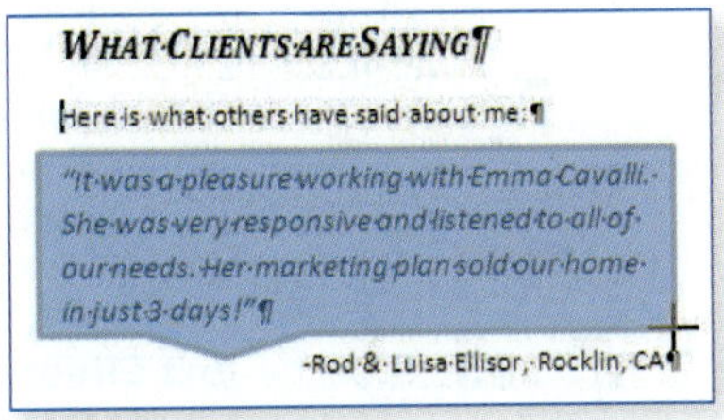

4-79 Draw rectangular shape

8. Add and format a shape to the quoted text.
   a. Click the **Shapes** button [*Insert* tab, *Illustration* group] and select **Rectangular Callout** (Figure 4-78). Your pointer changes to a crosshair (dark plus sign).
   b. On the first quote in the second column, drag from the upper left to the lower right to draw the shape over the quoted text (Figure 4-79).
   c. With the shape still selected, click the **Send Backward** drop-down arrow [*Drawing Tools Format* tab, *Arrange* group] and select **Send Behind Text** (Figure 4-80). The text is displayed over the shape.
   d. Click the **More** button [*Drawing Tools Format* tab, *Shape Styles* group] to display the gallery of shape styles.
   e. Select **Colored Outline – Olive Green**, **Accent 3** (Figure 4-81).
   f. Click the **Shape Fill** button [*Drawing Tools Format* tab, *Shape Styles* group] and select **Olive Green**, **Accent 3**, **Lighter 80%**.

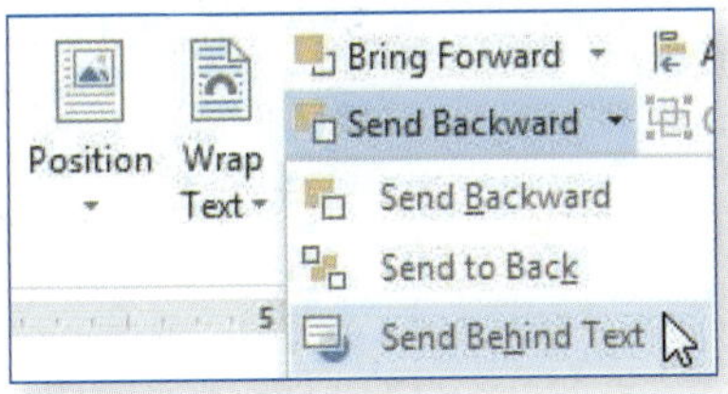

4-80 *Send Behind Text*

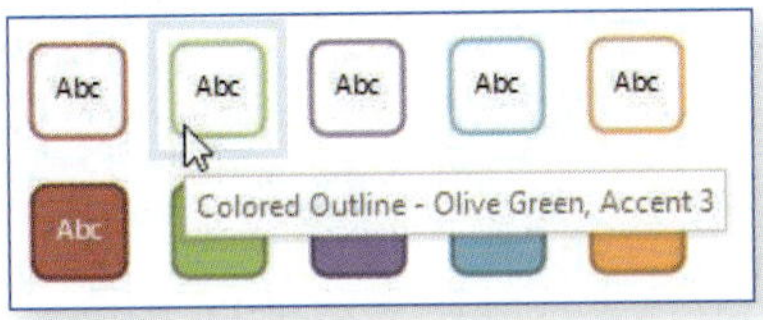

4-81 Apply shape style

g. Click the **Shape Effects** button [*Drawing Tools Format* tab, *Shape Styles* group], select **Shadow**, and choose **Offset Diagonal Bottom Right** (Figure 4-82).
h. With the shape still selected, change the *Shape Height* to **0.9"** and the *Shape Width* to **3"** [*Drawing Tools Format* tab, *Size* group].
i. Drag the shape so it is evenly positioned behind the text. You can also use the keyboard arrow keys to position a selected shape.

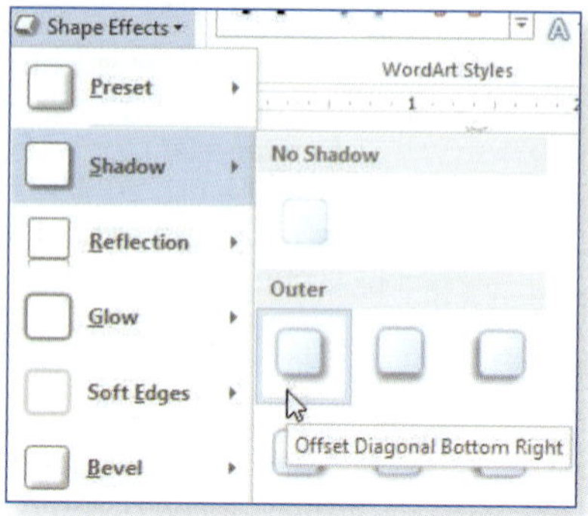

4-82 Select a shape *Shadow* option

9. Replicate and align the callout shape.
   a. With the shape still selected, press **Ctrl+C** to copy it and **Ctrl+V** to paste the copy of the shape into the document.
   b. Drag the new shape over the second quote.
   c. With the second shape still selected, change the *Shape Height* to **1.4"** [*Drawing Tools Format* tab, *Size* group].
   d. Drag the shape so it is evenly positioned behind the text (Figure 4-83).
   e. With the second shape selected, hold down the **Shift** key and click the right edge of the first shape to select both shapes.
   f. Click the **Align** button [*Drawing Tools Format* tab, *Arrange* group] and select **Align Center**.
   g. Make any necessary minor vertical position adjustments by selecting the shape and using the up or down arrow keys.

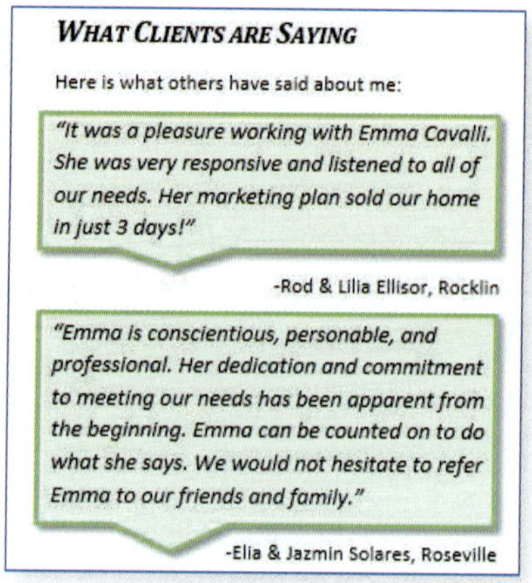

4-83 Shapes positioned behind text

10. Add *WordArt* to the brochure and customize it.
   a. At the top of the first column, select the text **"Emma Cavalli"** (including the paragraph mark).
   b. Click the **WordArt** button [*Insert* tab, *Text* group].
   c. In the *WordArt* gallery, select **Gradient Fill – Gray** (Figure 4-84). The selected text is converted to *WordArt*.
   d. With the *WordArt* selected, change the *Shape Height* to **0.8"** and the *Shape Width* to **3.6"** [*Drawing Tools Format* tab, *Size* group].
   e. Click the **Text Effects** button [*Drawing Tools Format* tab, *WordArt Styles* group], click **Reflection**, and select **Tight Reflection, touching** (Figure 4-85).

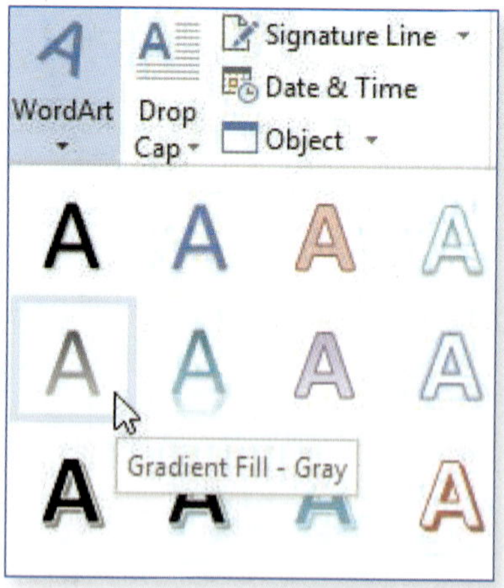

4-84 Select *WordArt* style

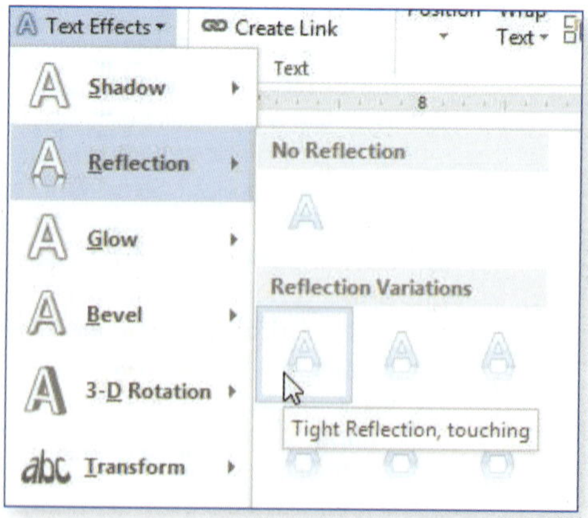

4-85 Apply a *Reflection* text effect

f. Click the **Position** button [*Drawing Tools Format* tab, *Arrange* group] and select **More Layout Options.** The *Layout* dialog box opens.
g. In the *Horizontal* area, change the *Absolute position* to **0.2"** *to the right of* **Page**.
h. In the *Vertical* area, change the *Absolute position* to **0.2"** *below* **Page**.
i. Click **OK** to close the *Layout* dialog box.

11. Save and close the document (Figure 4-86).

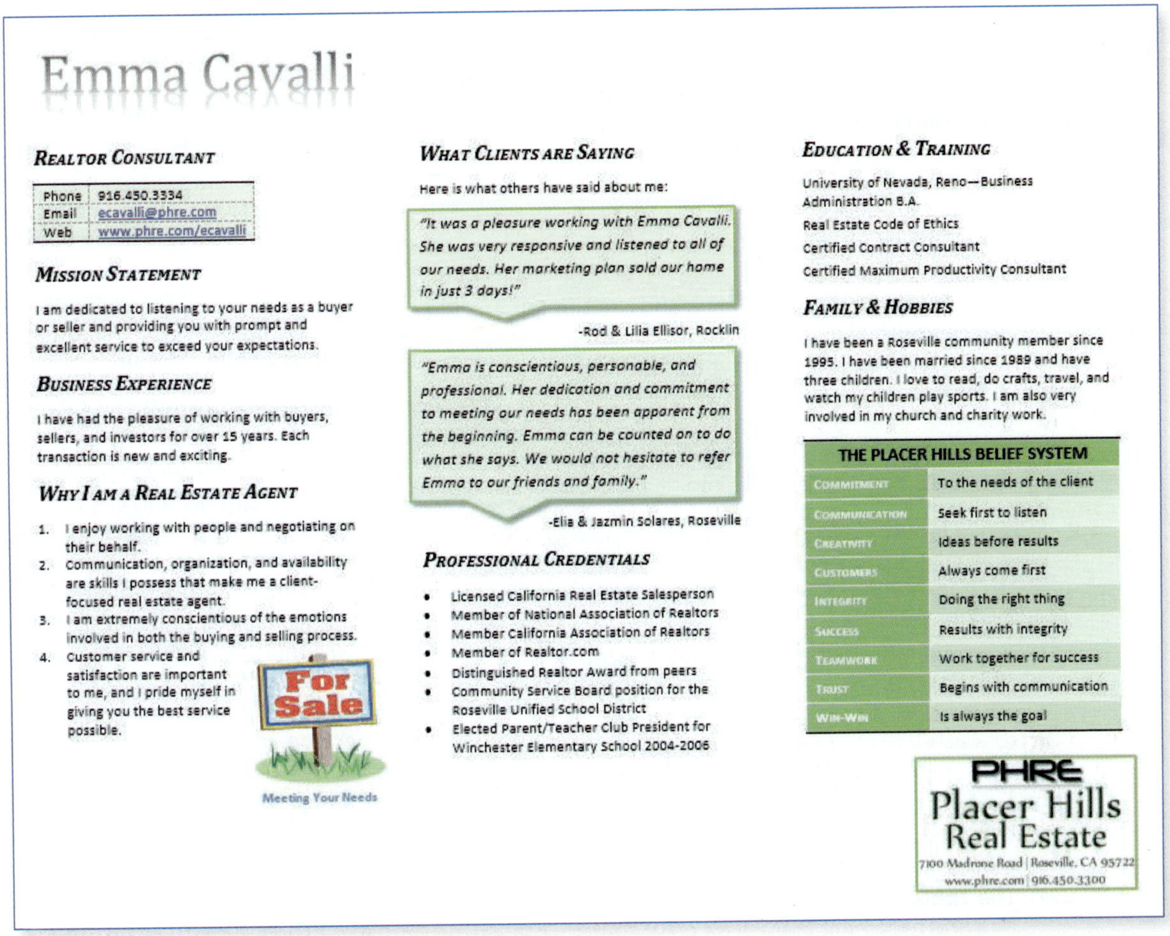

Emma Cavalli

REALTOR CONSULTANT

Phone	916.450.3334
Email	ecavalli@phre.com
Web	www.phre.com/ecavalli

MISSION STATEMENT

I am dedicated to listening to your needs as a buyer or seller and providing you with prompt and excellent service to exceed your expectations.

BUSINESS EXPERIENCE

I have had the pleasure of working with buyers, sellers, and investors for over 15 years. Each transaction is new and exciting.

WHY I AM A REAL ESTATE AGENT

1. I enjoy working with people and negotiating on their behalf.
2. Communication, organization, and availability are skills I possess that make me a client-focused real estate agent.
3. I am extremely conscientious of the emotions involved in both the buying and selling process.
4. Customer service and satisfaction are important to me, and I pride myself in giving you the best service possible.

For Sale

Meeting Your Needs

WHAT CLIENTS ARE SAYING

Here is what others have said about me:

"It was a pleasure working with Emma Cavalli. She was very responsive and listened to all of our needs. Her marketing plan sold our home in just 3 days!"

-Rod & Lilia Ellisor, Rocklin

"Emma is conscientious, personable, and professional. Her dedication and commitment to meeting our needs has been apparent from the beginning. Emma can be counted on to do what she says. We would not hesitate to refer Emma to our friends and family."

-Elia & Jazmin Solares, Roseville

PROFESSIONAL CREDENTIALS

- Licensed California Real Estate Salesperson
- Member of National Association of Realtors
- Member California Association of Realtors
- Member of Realtor.com
- Distinguished Realtor Award from peers
- Community Service Board position for the Roseville Unified School District
- Elected Parent/Teacher Club President for Winchester Elementary School 2004-2006

EDUCATION & TRAINING

University of Nevada, Reno—Business Administration B.A.
Real Estate Code of Ethics
Certified Contract Consultant
Certified Maximum Productivity Consultant

FAMILY & HOBBIES

I have been a Roseville community member since 1995. I have been married since 1989 and have three children. I love to read, do crafts, travel, and watch my children play sports. I am also very involved in my church and charity work.

THE PLACER HILLS BELIEF SYSTEM	
COMMITMENT	To the needs of the client
COMMUNICATION	Seek first to listen
CREATIVITY	Ideas before results
CUSTOMERS	Always come first
INTEGRITY	Doing the right thing
SUCCESS	Results with integrity
TEAMWORK	Work together for success
TRUST	Begins with communication
WIN-WIN	Is always the goal

PHRE
Placer Hills
Real Estate
7100 Madrone Road | Roseville, CA 95722
www.phre.com | 916.450.3300

4-86 PP W4-4 completed

Chapter Summary

4.1 Improve the design and readability of a document by using tables to present and arrange information (p. W4-197).

- ***Tables*** organize information in column and row format. A ***column*** is a vertical grouping of cells, and a ***row*** is a horizontal grouping of cells.
- A ***cell*** is where a column and row intersect.
- Use ***Tab*** to move forward to the next cell and ***Shift+Tab*** to move to the previous cell.
- ***Table Tools Layout*** and ***Table Tools Design*** tabs provide you with many table formatting features.
- You can copy or move columns or rows in a table.
- You can add or delete columns and rows from existing tables.
- When working with tables, you can select individual cells, a range of cells, rows, columns, or an entire table.
- A group of cells can be ***merged*** to create one cell. Cells can also be ***split*** into multiple cells.

4.2 Modify a table by changing the column and row size, aligning text, using the *Table Properties* dialog box, sorting data in tables, and using *AutoFit* (p. W4-201).

- You can resize columns and rows in a table.
- The ***AutoFit*** feature allows you to automatically resize the table to fit the contents or window or change to a fixed width.
- Text in a cell can be ***aligned*** both horizontally and vertically.
- ***Cell margins*** control the amount of spacing around the text within a cell.
- The ***Table Properties*** dialog box provides size and alignment options for cells, rows, columns, or an entire table.
- You can sort table information in ascending or descending order.

4.3 Enhance the appearance and function of a table by using the *Table Tools* tabs, applying borders and shading, using table styles, inserting formulas, and converting text into a table (p. W4-207).

- You can apply ***borders*** and ***shading*** to parts of a table or to the entire table.
- ***Table Styles*** are collections of borders, shading, and formatting that you can apply to a table. Word provides a gallery of table styles.
- You can apply ***Table Style Options*** to a header row, total row, banded rows, first column, or last column.
- ***Formulas*** in a table perform mathematical calculations.
- You can convert existing text into a table in Word.

4.4 Modify the layout and design of a document by using columns to present information (p. W4-214).

- You can arrange text in a document in ***columns***.
- You can choose from preset column settings or you can customize column settings and space between columns using the ***Columns dialog box.***
- ***Column breaks*** control column endings.
- Balance columns with column breaks or a ***continuous section break***.

4.5 Enrich a document by adding and modifying visual elements such as pictures, shapes, *SmartArt,* and *WordArt* (p. W4-218).

- ***Pictures*** and ***clip art*** add visual appeal to a document. Word can insert a variety of graphic file types.
- You can ***resize*** and ***position*** graphics at specific locations in a document.
- ***Text wrapping*** controls how text wraps around graphics.
- The ***Layout dialog box*** has options to change the position, text wrapping, and size of graphic objects.
- You can insert customized ***captions*** for graphics.
- Graphic objects can be ***grouped*** together to create one graphic object, which makes resizing and positioning easier.
- ***Shapes*** can be inserted into a document and resized and customized. You can change fill color, outline color and width, and shape effects.
- ***SmartArt*** graphically presents information in a document.
- ***WordArt*** is special text formatting that you can insert into a document.
- Word provides a variety of formatting options and styles for *SmartArt, WordArt,* and other graphic objects.
- You can insert a variety of ***symbols*** and ***special characters*** into documents. Use the ***Symbols dialog box*** to select different symbols and characters.

Check for Understanding

In the ***Online Learning Center*** for this text (www.mhhe.com/office2013inpractice), there are a variety of resources that can be used to review the concepts covered in this chapter.

The following Online Learning Resources are available in the Online Learning Center:

- Multiple choice questions
- Short answer questions
- Matching exercises

USING MICROSOFT WORD 2013

Guided Project 4-1

For this project, you modify the values statement document for Sierra Pacific Community College District to arrange text in columns, insert the company logo, and use shapes.
[Student Learning Outcomes 4.4, 4.5]

Files Needed: ***ValuesStatement-04.docx* and *SPCCDlogo-04.png***
Completed Project File Name: ***[your initials] Word 4-1.docx***

Skills Covered in This Project

- Modify an existing document.
- Change page orientation.
- Change margins.
- Apply columns to text.
- Modify column settings.
- Insert a column break.
- Insert a picture.
- Change picture color.
- Modify picture size and position.
- Insert a shape.
- Modify shape size and position.
- Modify shape fill and outline.

1. Open the ***ValuesStatement-04*** document from your student data files.
2. Save this document as ***[your initials] Word 4-1.***
3. Change the orientation and change the margins of the document.
   a. Change the orientation of the document to **Landscape**.
   b. Change the top and bottom margins to **0.5"**.
   c. Change the left and right margins to **0.75"**.
4. Apply column formatting to the text in the body of the document.
   a. Place the insertion point in front of the first paragraph heading ("Access").
   b. Click the **Columns** button [*Page Layout* tab, *Page Setup* group] and select **More Columns**. The *Columns* dialog box opens (Figure 4-87).
   c. Select **Three** in the *Presets* area.
   d. In the *Width and spacing* area, change the *Spacing* to **0.4"**.
   e. In the *Apply to* area, select **This point forward** from the drop-down list.
   f. Click **OK** to close the *Columns* dialog box.
5. Insert a column break to balance the columns on the page.
   a. Place the insertion point in front of the "Student Learning Outcomes" paragraph heading.
   b. Click the **Breaks** button [*Page Layout* tab, *Page Setup* group] and select **Column**.

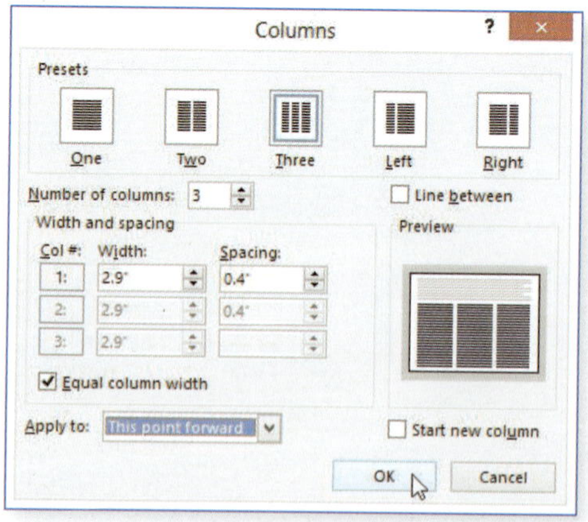

4-87 ***Columns* dialog box**

6. Insert the company logo on the bottom left of the document and resize and position it.
   a. Click at the end of the first column.
   b. Click the **Pictures** button [*Insert* tab, *Illustrations* group].
   c. Select the ***SPCCDlogo-04*** file from the student data files and click **Insert**.
   d. Click the **Wrap Text** button [*Picture Tools Format* tab, *Arrange* group] and select **Behind Text**.
   e. Right-click the logo and choose **Size and Position**. The *Layout* dialog box opens (Figure 4-88).
   f. In the *Scale* area, change the *Height* to **120%** and press **Tab**. The width automatically adjusts to keep the logo proportional.
   g. Click the **Position** tab.
   h. In the *Horizontal* area, change the *Absolute position* to **0.3"** *to the right of* **Page**.
   i. In the *Vertical* area, change the *Absolute position* to **7.2"** *below* **Page**.
   j. Click **OK** to close the *Layout* dialog box.

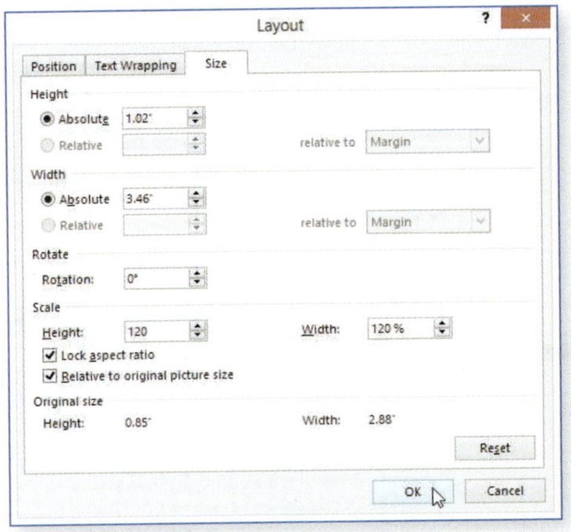

4-88 Resize logo as a percentage of its original size

7. Change the color of the logo.
   a. With the logo selected, click the **Color** button [*Picture Tools Format* tab, *Adjust* group].
   b. Select **Saturation**: **0%** in the *Color Saturation* area (Figure 4-89).

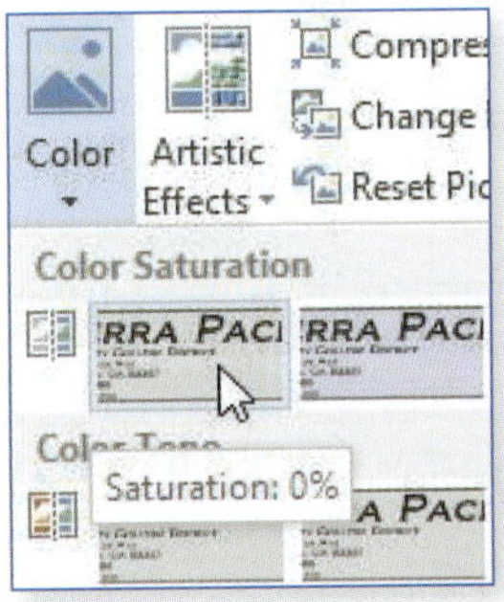

4-89 Change *Color Saturation*

8. Add a shape around the title, and then resize the shape and modify the outline and fill.
   a. Click the **Shapes** button [*Insert* tab, *Illustrations* group].
   b. Select **Snip Single Corner Rectangle** from the *Shapes* gallery. Your pointer becomes a crosshair (dark plus sign) (Figure 4-90).
   c. Click and drag the crosshair over the title and then release the pointer (Figure 4-91).
   d. Click the **Shape Fill** button [*Drawing Tools Format* tab, *Shape Styles* group] and select **White**, **Background 1**, **Darker 15%**.
   e. Click the **Shape Outline** button [*Drawing Tools Format* tab, *Shape Styles* group] and select **White**, **Background 1**, **Darker 50%**.
   f. Click the **Shape Outline** button again, select **Weight**, and select **1½ pt**.
   g. Click the **Send Backward** drop-down arrow [*Drawing Tools Format* tab, *Arrange* group] and select **Send Behind Text** from the drop-down list.
   h. Change the *Shape Height* [*Drawing Tools Format* tab, *Size* group] to **0.4"** and the *Shape Width* to **6.3"**.
   i. Click the **Align** button [*Drawing Tools Format* tab, *Arrange* group] and select **Align Center**.
   j. Use the up and down arrow keys on the keyboard to vertically center the shape behind the title.

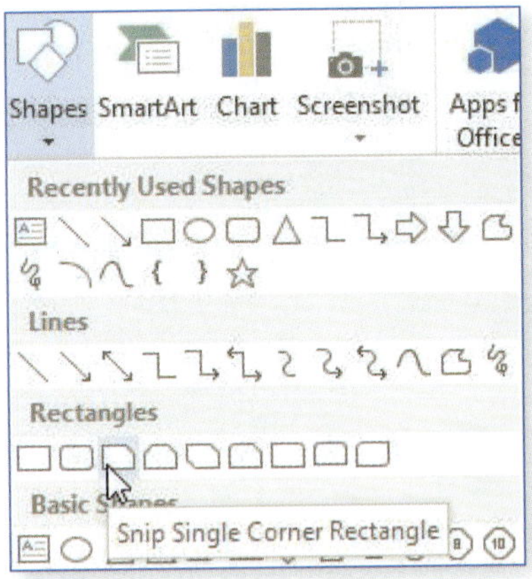

4-90 Select shape

4-91 Draw shape around the title

9. Save and close the document (Figure 4-92).

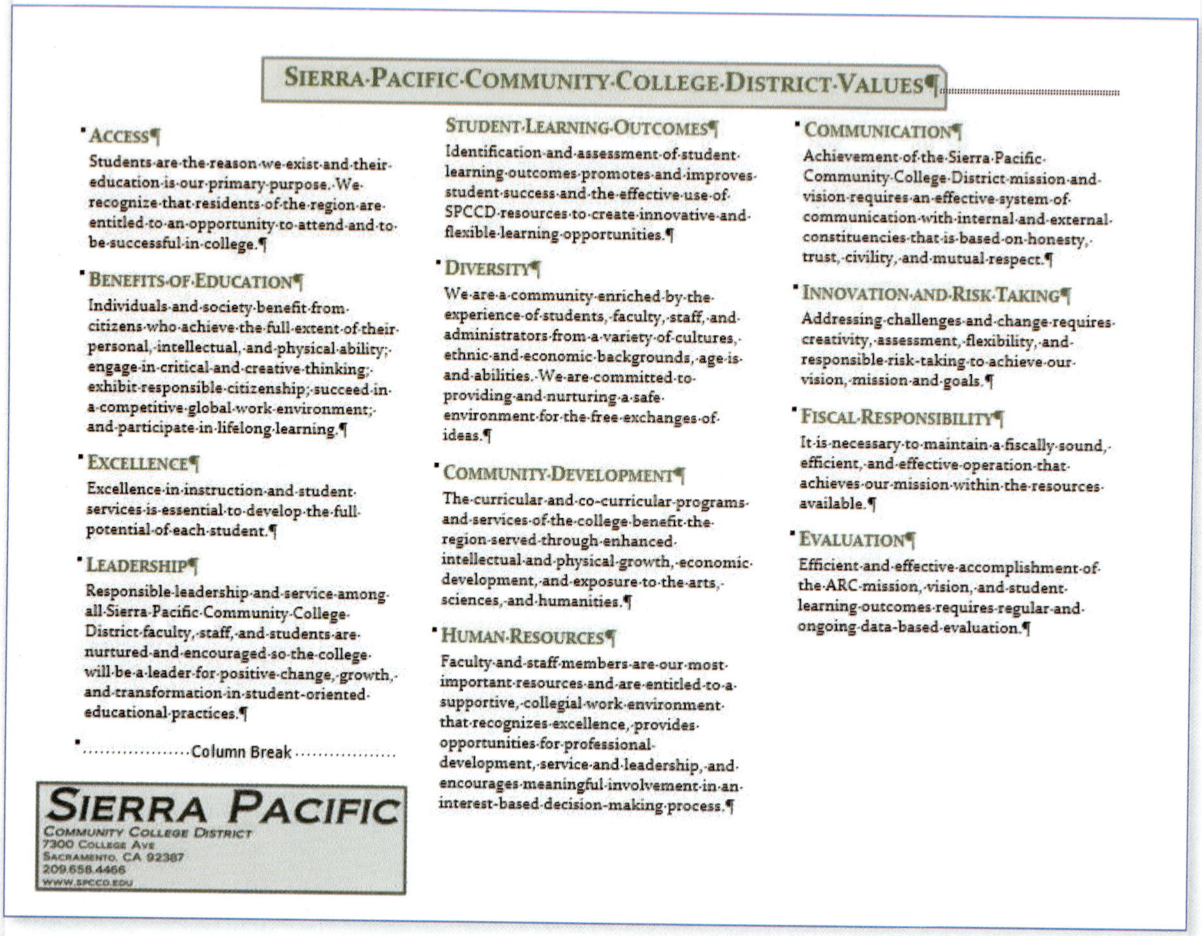

SIERRA·PACIFIC·COMMUNITY·COLLEGE·DISTRICT·VALUES¶

ACCESS¶
Students·are·the·reason·we·exist·and·their·education·is·our·primary·purpose.·We·recognize·that·residents·of·the·region·are·entitled·to·an·opportunity·to·attend·and·to·be·successful·in·college.¶

BENEFITS·OF·EDUCATION¶
Individuals·and·society·benefit·from·citizens·who·achieve·the·full·extent·of·their·personal,·intellectual,·and·physical·ability;·engage·in·critical·and·creative·thinking;·exhibit·responsible·citizenship;·succeed·in·a·competitive·global·work·environment;·and·participate·in·lifelong·learning.¶

EXCELLENCE¶
Excellence·in·instruction·and·student·services·is·essential·to·develop·the·full·potential·of·each·student.¶

LEADERSHIP¶
Responsible·leadership·and·service·among·all·Sierra·Pacific·Community·College·District·faculty,·staff,·and·students·are·nurtured·and·encouraged·so·the·college·will·be·a·leader·for·positive·change,·growth,·and·transformation·in·student-oriented·educational·practices.¶

..................Column Break..................

SIERRA PACIFIC
COMMUNITY COLLEGE DISTRICT
7300 COLLEGE AVE
SACRAMENTO, CA 92387
209.658.4466
WWW.SPCCD.EDU

STUDENT·LEARNING·OUTCOMES¶
Identification·and·assessment·of·student·learning·outcomes·promotes·and·improves·student·success·and·the·effective·use·of·SPCCD·resources·to·create·innovative·and·flexible·learning·opportunities.¶

DIVERSITY¶
We·are·a·community·enriched·by·the·experience·of·students,·faculty,·staff,·and·administrators·from·a·variety·of·cultures,·ethnic·and·economic·backgrounds,·age·is·and·abilities.·We·are·committed·to·providing·and·nurturing·a·safe·environment·for·the·free·exchanges·of·ideas.¶

COMMUNITY·DEVELOPMENT¶
The·curricular·and·co-curricular·programs·and·services·of·the·college·benefit·the·region·served·through·enhanced·intellectual·and·physical·growth,·economic·development,·and·exposure·to·the·arts,·sciences,·and·humanities.¶

HUMAN·RESOURCES¶
Faculty·and·staff·members·are·our·most·important·resources·and·are·entitled·to·a·supportive,·collegial·work·environment·that·recognizes·excellence,·provides·opportunities·for·professional·development,·service·and·leadership,·and·encourages·meaningful·involvement·in·an·interest-based·decision-making·process.¶

COMMUNICATION¶
Achievement·of·the·Sierra·Pacific·Community·College·District·mission·and·vision·requires·an·effective·system·of·communication·with·internal·and·external·constituencies·that·is·based·on·honesty,·trust,·civility,·and·mutual·respect.¶

INNOVATION·AND·RISK·TAKING¶
Addressing·challenges·and·change·requires·creativity,·assessment,·flexibility,·and·responsible·risk-taking·to·achieve·our·vision,·mission·and·goals.¶

FISCAL·RESPONSIBILITY¶
It·is·necessary·to·maintain·a·fiscally·sound,·efficient,·and·effective·operation·that·achieves·our·mission·within·the·resources·available.¶

EVALUATION¶
Efficient·and·effective·accomplishment·of·the·ARC·mission,·vision,·and·student·learning·outcomes·requires·regular·and·ongoing·data-based·evaluation.¶

4-92 Word 4-1 completed

Guided Project 4-2

For this project, you modify a document about maximum and target heart rate for the American River Cycling Club. You arrange text in a table and insert and modify *SmartArt* and clip art.
[Student Learning Outcomes 4.1, 4.2, 4.3, 4.5]

File Needed: ***MaximumHeartRate-04.docx***
Completed Project File Name: ***[your initials] Word 4-2.docx***

Skills Covered in This Project

- Modify an existing document.
- Insert and resize *WordArt.*
- Position and modify *WordArt.*
- Convert text to a table.
- Apply a table style.
- Modify table and text alignment.
- Change cell margins in a table.
- Insert and add text to a *SmartArt* graphic.
- Resize, position, and format *SmartArt.*
- Insert, resize, and position a graphic.
- Insert a caption
- Align and group graphic objects.

---

1. Open the ***MaximumHeartRate-04*** document from your student data files.
2. Save this document as ***[your initials] Word 4-2.***
3. Insert *WordArt* as the title of the document and modify the *WordArt.*
   a. Select the title of the document, **"American River Cycling Club."**
   b. Click the **WordArt** button [*Insert* tab, *Text* group].
   c. Select **Fill – Red, Accent 2, Outline – Accent 2** from the *WordArt* gallery (Figure 4-93).
   d. Change the *Shape Width* [*Drawing Tools Format* tab, *Size* group] to **6.5"**.
   e. Click the **Position** button [*Drawing Tools Format* tab, *Arrange* group] and select **More Layout Options**. The *Layout* dialog box opens (Figure 4-94).
   f. In the *Horizontal* area select **Alignment** and **Centered** *relative to* **Margin**.
   g. In the *Vertical* area select **Absolute position** and enter **0.2"** *below* **Page**.
   h. Click **OK** to close the *Layout* dialog box.
   i. Click the **Text Effects** button [*Drawing Tools Format* tab, *WordArt Styles* group] and select **Reflection**.
   j. Select **Tight Reflection, touching** (Figure 4-95).

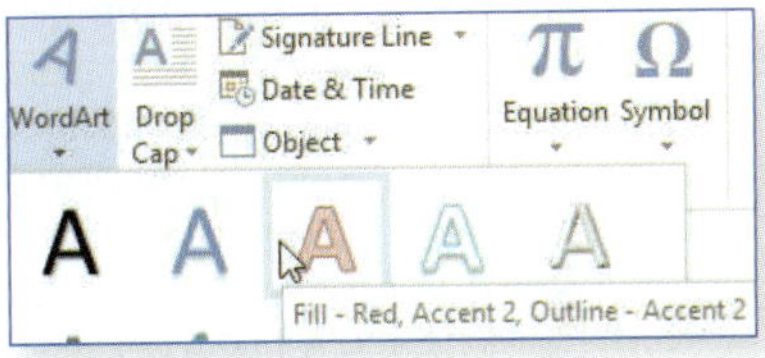

4-93 Insert *WordArt*

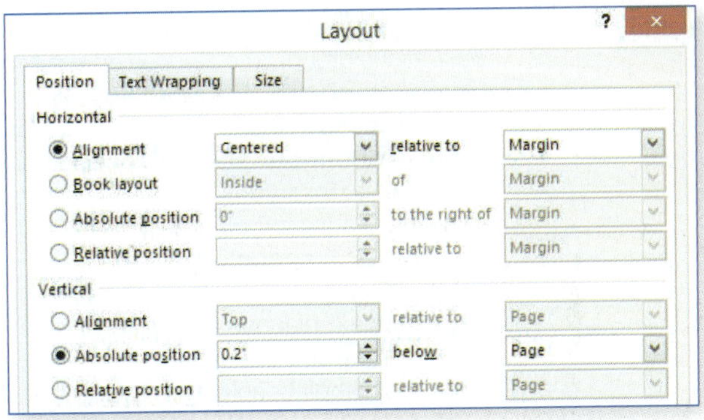

4-94 Adjust position of *WordArt*

4. Convert text into a table and format the table.
   a. Select all of the tabbed text at the bottom of the document.
   b. Click the **Table** button [*Insert* tab, *Tables* group] and select **Convert Text to Table**. The *Convert Text to Table* dialog box opens.
   c. In the *AutoFit behavior* area, click the **AutoFit to contents** radio button.
   d. Click **OK** to close the dialog box.
   e. Click the **Table Tools Design** tab.
   f. Select the **Header Row** and **Banded Rows** check boxes [*Table Style Options* group] and deselect the other check boxes.
   g. In the *Table Styles* group, click the **More** button to display the *Table Styles* gallery.

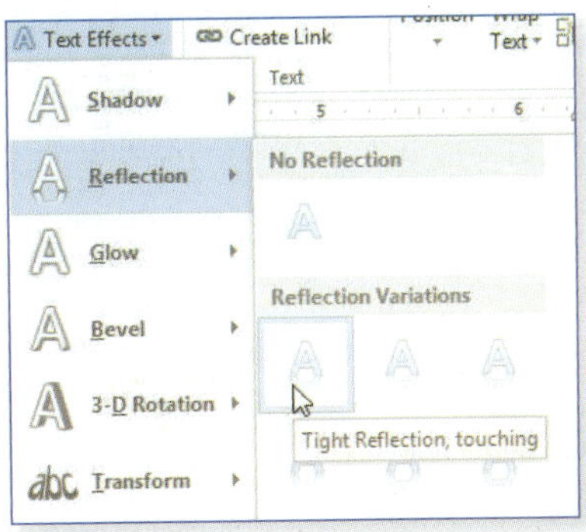

4-95 *Reflection* options

h. Select **Grid Table 4 – Accent 2** (Figure 4-96).
i. In the second column of the first row, place the insertion point before "Zone" and press **Enter**.
j. In the third column of the first row, place the insertion point before "Heart" and press **Enter**.

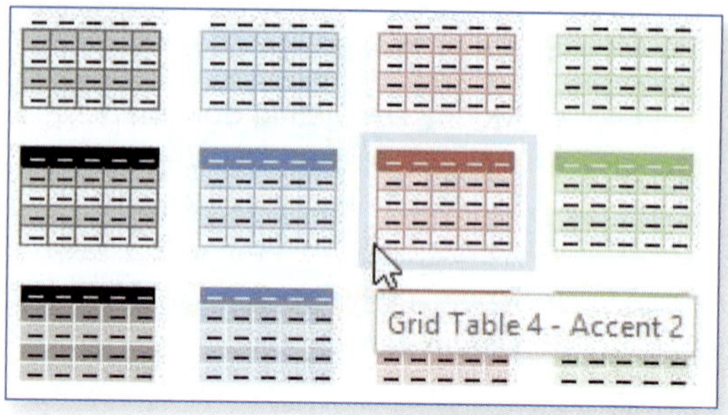

4-96 *Table Styles* gallery

5. Adjust the size and alignment of the table.
   a. Use the table selector handle to select the entire table.
   b. Click the **Align Center** button [*Table Tool Layout* tab, *Alignment* group] (Figure 4-97).
   c. With the table still selected, click the **Properties** button [*Table Tools Layout* tab, *Table* group].
   d. Click the **Table** tab, select **Center** in the *Alignment* area, and click **OK** to close the dialog box.
   e. Click the **Cell Margins** button [*Table Tools Layout* tab, *Alignment* group]. The *Table Options* dialog box opens.
   f. Change the *Top* and *Bottom* cell margins to **0.03"** and the *Left* and *Right* cell margins to **0.1"**.
   g. Click **OK** to close the *Table Options* dialog box.

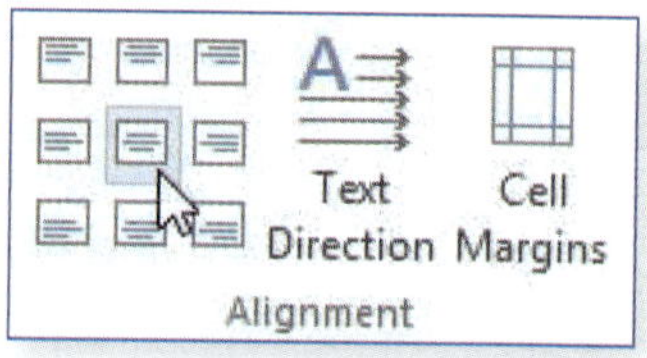

4-97 Text alignment options

6. Insert and modify a *SmartArt* graphic.
   a. Place the insertion point at the end of the "(Example: . . ." line near the top of the document.
   b. Click the **SmartArt** button [*Insert* tab, *Illustrations* group]. The *Choose a SmartArt Graphic* dialog box opens (Figure 4-98).
   c. Click **Process** in the list of *SmartArt* types.
   d. Select **Continuous Block Process** and press **OK** to insert the *SmartArt*.
   e. Click the first placeholder text (*[Text]*) and type 220, **space** once, and type – (hyphen or minus).
   f. Click the next placeholder text and type Your Age, **space** once, and type =.
   g. Click the last placeholder text and type Predicted Maximum Heart Rate.

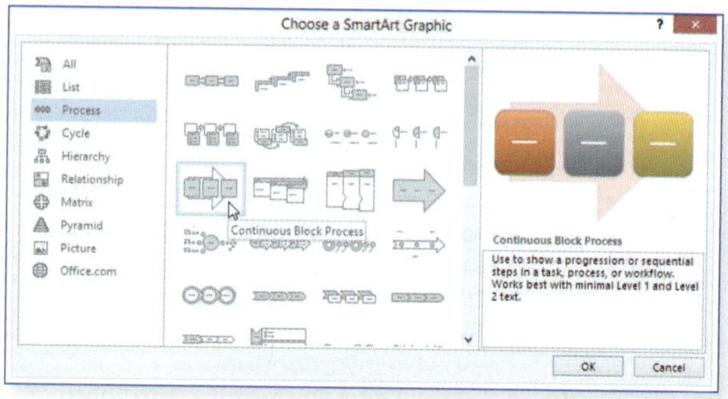

4-98 *Choose a SmartArt Graphic* dialog box

7. Format, resize, and position the *SmartArt*.
   a. Click the outside frame of the *SmartArt* graphic. *Note: make sure the entire* SmartArt *is selected and not an object within the graphic.*
   b. In the *Size* group [*SmartArt Tools Format* tab], change the *Shape Height* to **1.5"** and the *Shape Width* to **2.6"**.
   c. Click the **Wrap Text** button [*SmartArt Tools Format* tab, *Arrange* group] and select **Square**.
   d. Click the **Position** button [*SmartArt Tools Format* tab, *Arrange* group] and select **More Layout Options**. The *Layout* dialog box opens (Figure 4-99).

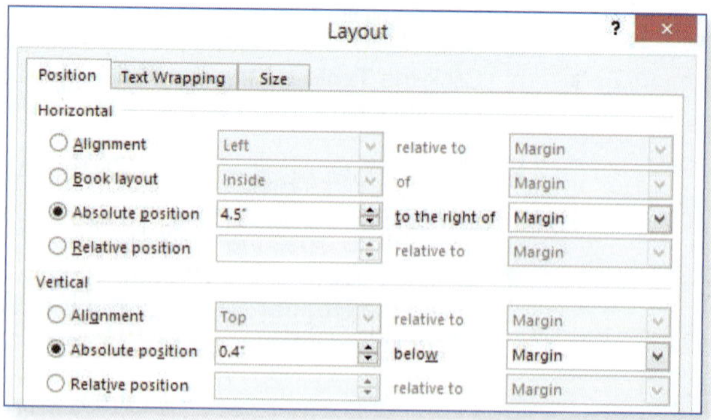

4-99 Adjust *SmartArt* position

e. In the *Horizontal* area select **Absolute position** and enter **4.5"** *to the right of* **Margin**.
f. In the *Vertical* area select **Absolute position** and enter **0.4"** *below* **Margin**.
g. Click **OK** to close the *Layout* dialog box.
h. With the *SmartArt* still selected, select **Intense Effect** as the *SmartArt* style [*SmartArt Tools Design* tab, *SmartArt Styles* group] (Figure 4-100).
i. Click the edge of the first text box to select it, and press **Ctrl+B** to make the text bold. Repeat this on the other two text boxes.
j. Select the last text box and click the **SmartArt Tools Format** tab.
k. Click the **Shape Fill** button and select **Red**, **Accent 2** as the fill color (Figure 4-101).

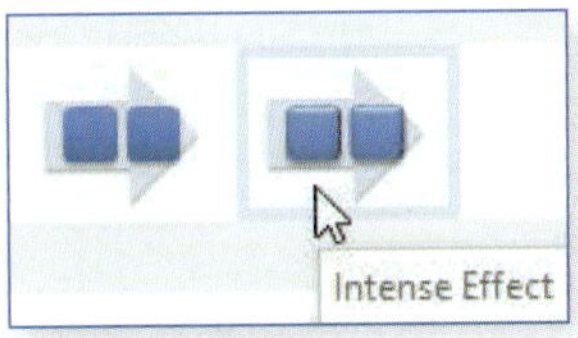

4-100 Apply *SmartArt* style

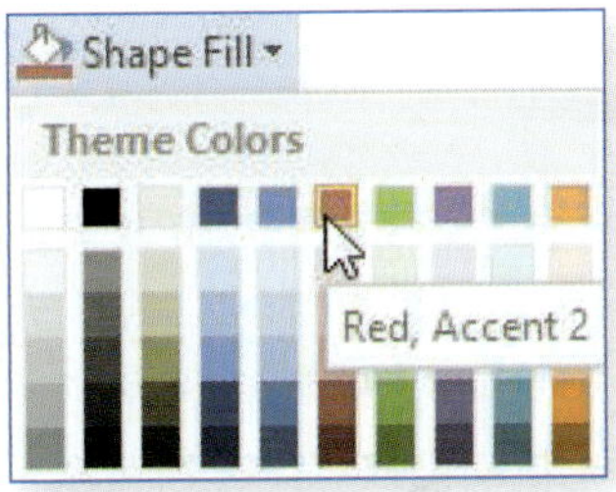

4-101 Change text box fill color

8. Insert clip art and resize and position the graphic.
   a. Place the insertion point at the end of the second paragraph heading ("Target Heart Rate").
   b. Click the **Online Pictures** button [*Insert* tab, *Illustrations* group] to open the *Insert Pictures* dialog box.
   c. Type heart rate in the *Office.com Clip Art* text box and press **Enter**.
   d. Select the **Heart cardiogram illustration** clip art and click **Insert** to insert it into the document (Figure 4-102). If this clip art is not available, insert the ***HeartRate-04*** picture from your student data files.
   e. Change the *Height* [*Picture Tools Format* tab, *Size* group] to **1"** and press **Enter**. The width automatically adjusts.
   f. Click the **Wrap Text** button [*Picture Tools Format* tab, *Arrange* group] and select **Tight**.
   g. Drag the clip art to the right of the heading and first paragraph in the "Target Heart Rate" section and place it approximately 0.5" from the right edge of the document.

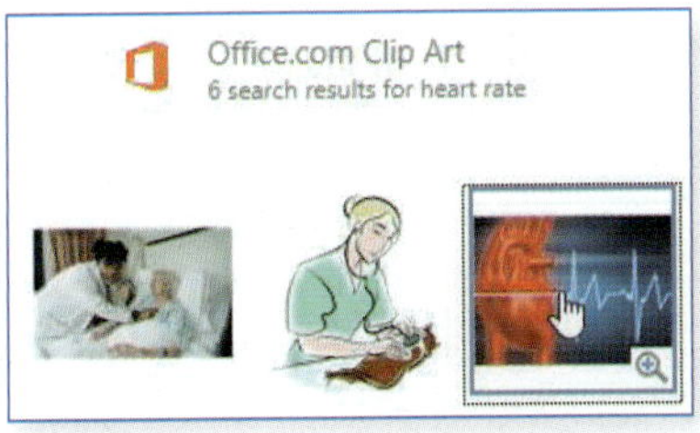

4-102 Insert clip art

9. Format the clip art and insert a caption.
   a. With the clip art selected, click the **More** button in the *Pictures Styles* group [*Picture Tools Format* tab] to display the gallery of styles.
   b. Select the **Bevel Rectangle** picture style (Figure 4-103).
   c. Right-click the clip art and select **Insert Caption** from the context menu. The *Insert Caption* dialog box opens.
   d. Press **Enter** to insert the caption.
   e. Select the caption text, click the **Text Fill** button [*Drawing Tools Format* tab, *WordArt Styles* group], and select **Red**, **Accent 2** as the text color.
   f. With the caption text still selected, type Know your target heart rate to replace the caption placeholder text.
   g. In the *Size* group [*Drawing Tools Format* tab], change the *Height* to **0.2"** and the *Width* to **1.5"**.
   h. Press the **Ctrl** key and click the clip art. Both the caption and text box should be selected.
   i. Click the **Align** button [*Drawing Tools Format* tab, *Arrange* group] and select **Align Center**.
   j. Click the **Group** button [*Arrange* group] and select **Group**. The clip art and caption are grouped into one object.
   k. Drag the grouped clip art and caption so it is approximately 0.5" from the right edge of the document.

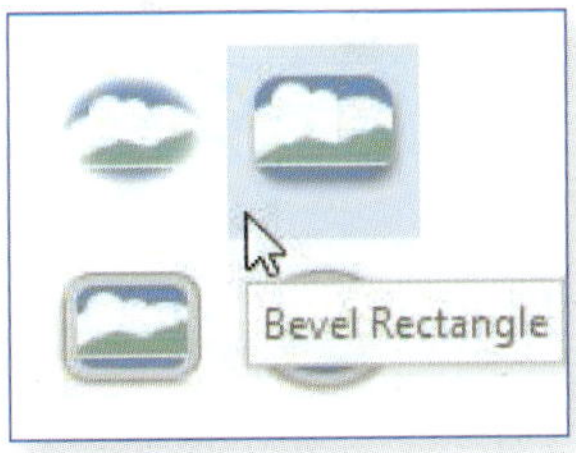

4-103 Apply *Picture Style* to clip art

10. Save and close the document (Figure 4-104).

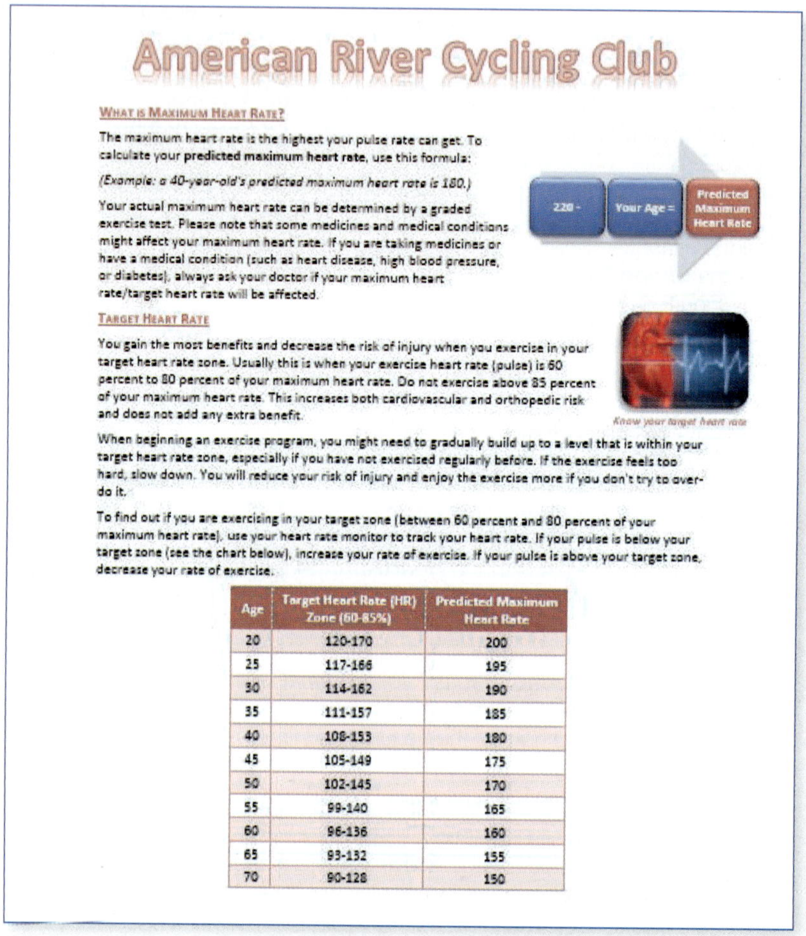

American River Cycling Club

WHAT IS MAXIMUM HEART RATE?

The maximum heart rate is the highest your pulse rate can get. To calculate your **predicted maximum heart rate**, use this formula:

(Example: a 40-year-old's predicted maximum heart rate is 180.)

220 - Your Age = Predicted Maximum Heart Rate

Your actual maximum heart rate can be determined by a graded exercise test. Please note that some medicines and medical conditions might affect your maximum heart rate. If you are taking medicines or have a medical condition (such as heart disease, high blood pressure, or diabetes), always ask your doctor if your maximum heart rate/target heart rate will be affected.

TARGET HEART RATE

You gain the most benefits and decrease the risk of injury when you exercise in your target heart rate zone. Usually this is when your exercise heart rate (pulse) is 60 percent to 80 percent of your maximum heart rate. Do not exercise above 85 percent of your maximum heart rate. This increases both cardiovascular and orthopedic risk and does not add any extra benefit.

Know your target heart rate

When beginning an exercise program, you might need to gradually build up to a level that is within your target heart rate zone, especially if you have not exercised regularly before. If the exercise feels too hard, slow down. You will reduce your risk of injury and enjoy the exercise more if you don't try to over-do it.

To find out if you are exercising in your target zone (between 60 percent and 80 percent of your maximum heart rate), use your heart rate monitor to track your heart rate. If your pulse is below your target zone (see the chart below), increase your rate of exercise. If your pulse is above your target zone, decrease your rate of exercise.

Age	Target Heart Rate (HR) Zone (60-85%)	Predicted Maximum Heart Rate
20	120-170	200
25	117-166	195
30	114-162	190
35	111-157	185
40	108-153	180
45	105-149	175
50	102-145	170
55	99-140	165
60	96-136	160
65	93-132	155
70	90-128	150

4-104 Word 4-2 completed

Guided Project 4-3

For this project, you format a buyer escrow checklist for Placer Hills Real Estate. You convert text to a table, format the table, and insert clip art and a picture.
[Student Learning Outcomes 4.1, 4.2, 4.3, 4.5]

Files Needed: ***BuyerEscrowChecklist-04.docx*** **and** ***PHRElogo-04.png***
Completed Project File Name: ***[your initials] Word 4-3.docx***

Skills Covered in This Project

- Modify an existing document.
- Convert text to a table.
- Add columns to a table.
- Apply bullets and modify alignment.
- Apply table styles and borders.
- Modify row width and column height.
- Center text vertically in a table.
- Insert and position clip art.
- Insert and resize a graphic.
- Use absolute position and text wrapping.
- Insert and resize a picture.
- Apply border and effects to a picture.

---

1. Open the ***BuyerEscrowChecklist-04*** document from your student data files.
2. Save this document as ***[your initials] Word 4-3***.
3. Convert text to a table.
   a. Select the text beginning with **"Task"** through **"Verify Preliminary Report with Lender**."
   b. Click the **Table** button [*Insert* tab, *Tables* group].
   c. Click the **Convert Text to Table** button. The *Convert Text to Table* dialog box opens.
   d. Click **OK** to accept the default settings. The text is converted to a table with 1 column and 14 rows.
4. Add columns and column headings to the table.
   a. With the table selected click the **Table Tools Layout** tab.
   b. Click the **Insert Right** button [*Rows & Columns* group]. A blank column is inserted to the right of the existing column.
   c. Click the **Insert Right** button two more times to insert two more columns. Your table should now have four columns.
   d. Type the following column headings in the first row:
      Column 2: Date Completed
      Column 3: Initials
      Column 4: Notes
   e. **Center** column headings.
5. Add bullets to selected text.
   a. Select all of the text in the first column below "Task."
   b. Apply an **open square bullet** to these items.
   c. Click the **Decrease Indent** button once so the first line indent is at 0" and the hanging indent is at 0.25".
6. Apply table style and apply formatting.
   a. Place your insertion point in the first cell in the first column.
   b. Click the **AutoFit** button [*Table Tools Layout* tab, *Cell Size* group] and select **AutoFit Contents**.
   c. Click the **Table Tools Design** tab.
   d. In the *Table Style Options* group, select **Header Row** and **Banded Rows**. The other options should be unchecked.
   e. Click the **More** button in the *Table Styles* group to open the gallery of table styles.
   f. Select **Grid Table 5 Dark** style (Figure 4-105).
   g. Select the column headings (first row of the table).
   h. **Bold** the column headings.
7. Modify cell size and alignment.
   a. Use the table selector handle to select the entire table, or use the **Select** button [*Table Tools Layout* tab, *Table* group] and click **Select Table**.

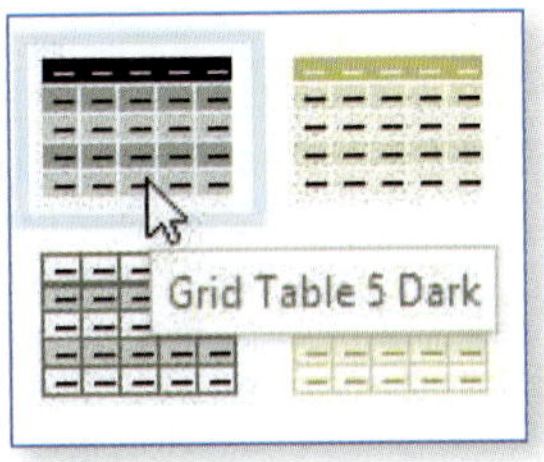

4-105 Apply table style

b. Change the *Height* [*Table Tools Layout* tab, *Cell Size* group] to **0.35"**. The row height changes on the entire table.
c. With the table still selected, click the **Properties** [*Table Tools Layout* tab, *Table* group] button. The *Table Properties* dialog box opens.
d. Click the **Cell** tab and select **Center** in the *Vertical alignment* area.
e. Click **OK** to close the *Table Properties* dialog box
f. Place your insertion point in the fourth column and change the *Width* [*Table Tools Layout* tab, *Cell Size* group] to **1.5"**.

8. Insert clip art and position it in the document.
   a. Place your insertion point at the end of the "Buyer(s):" line after the solid underline tab leader.
   b. Click the **Online Pictures** button [*Insert* tab, *Illustrations* group]. The *Insert Pictures* dialog box opens.
   c. In the *Office.com Clip Art* text box, type check and press **Enter**.
   d. Select the clip art shown in Figure 4-106 and click **Insert**. If this clip art is not available, insert the ***Check-04*** picture from your student data files.
   e. In the *Size* group [*Picture Tools Format* tab], change the *Height* to **1.5"** and press **Enter**. The width automatically adjusts to keep the clip art proportional.
   f. Click the **Wrap Text** button [*Picture Tools Format* tab, *Arrange* group] and select **Tight**.
   g. Click the **Position** button [*Picture Tools Format* tab, *Arrange* group] and select **More Layout Options** to open the *Layout* dialog box (Figure 4-107).
   h. In the *Horizontal* area, change the *Absolute position* to **5.2"** *to the right of* **Margin**.
   i. In the *Vertical* area, change the *Absolute position* to **0.8"** *below* **Margin**.
   j. Click **OK** to close the *Layout* dialog box.

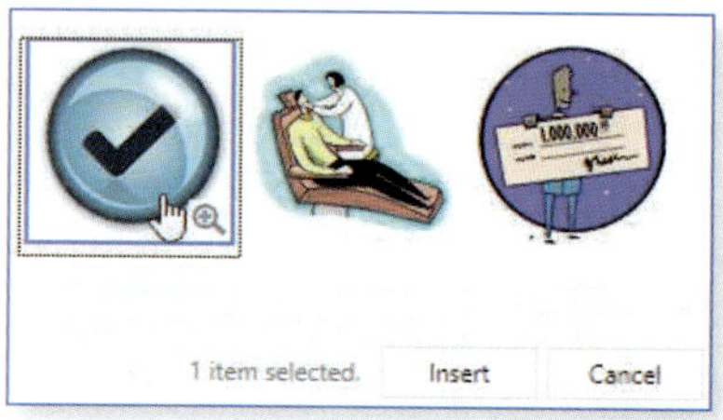

4-106 Insert clip art

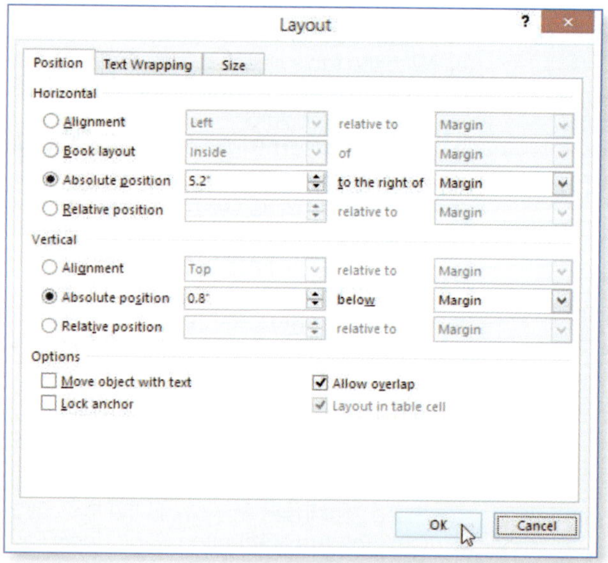

4-107 Position clip art

9. Insert a picture in the upper right of the document.
   a. Place your insertion point at the end of the title.
   b. Click the **Pictures** button [*Insert* tab, *Illustrations* group]. The *Insert Picture* dialog box opens.
   c. Select the ***PHRElogo-04*** file from the student data files and click **Insert**.
   d. Right-click the picture, select **Wrap Text**, and choose **In Front of Text**.
   e. Drag the picture so it is near the upper right corner of the document.
   f. Click the **Picture Border** button [*Picture Tools Format* tab, *Picture Styles* group] and select **Olive Green**, **Accent 2** (Figure 4-108).

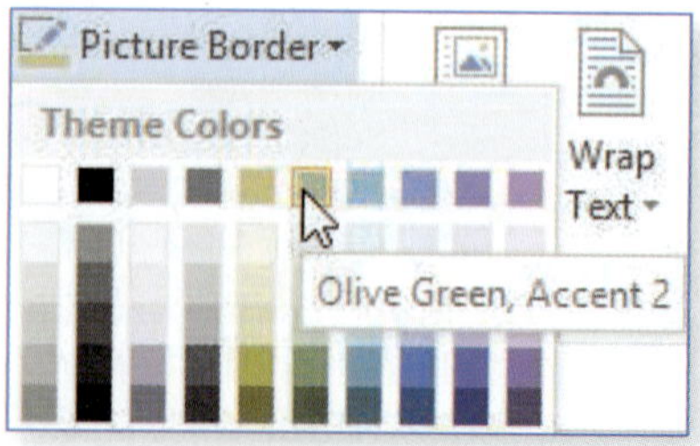

4-108 Apply *Picture Border* color

g. Click the **Picture Border** button, click **Weight**, and select **1½ pt**.
h. Click the **Picture Effects** button [*Picture Tools Format* tab, *Picture Styles* group], select **Shadow**, and select **Offset Bottom** (middle option in first row).

10. Save and close the document (Figure 4-109).

PHRE
Placer Hills
Real Estate

BUYER ESCROW CHECKLIST

Buyer(s): ______________________

Phone/Fax: ______________________

Email: ______________________

Agent: ______________________

Property Address: ______________________

Task	Date Completed	Initials	Notes
❑ Fax Contract to Buyer(s)			
❑ Fax Contract to Lender			
❑ Verify Property ID with Buyer(s)			
❑ Verify Property ID with Lender			
❑ Turn in new sale to PHRE			
❑ Send check to Title Company			
❑ Notified Buyer of EM deposit			
❑ Fax/Email Pest Report to Buyer(s)			
❑ Fax/Email Pest Report to Lender			
❑ Fax/Email *Clear* Pest Report to Buyer(s)			
❑ Fax/Email *Clear* Pest Report to Lender			
❑ Verify Preliminary Report with Buyer(s)			
❑ Verify Preliminary Report with Lender			

Emma Cavalli

Placer Hills Real Estate

4-109 Word 4-3 completed

Independent Project 4-4

For this project, you format a vaccination schedule for Courtyard Medical Plaza by converting text to a table, formatting the table, and inserting a picture.
[Student Learning Outcomes 4.1, 4.2, 4.3, 4.5]

Files Needed: ***VaccinationSchedule-04.docx, CMPLogo-04.png,*** **and** ***Vaccination-04.png***
Completed Project File Name: ***[your initials] Word 4-4.docx***

Skills Covered in This Project

- Modify an existing document.
- Convert text to a table.
- Apply a table style.
- *AutoFit* table and change row height.
- Center text vertically.
- Sort text in a table.
- Insert rows and add information.
- Merge cells.
- Apply custom borders.
- Apply a style to text.
- Insert a picture.
- Adjust size and position.
- Apply picture effect.
- Insert and position clip art.
- Resize clip art.
- Add and format a caption.
- Align and group caption and clip art.

1. Open the ***VaccinationSchedule-04*** document from your student data files.
2. Save this document as ***[your initials] Word 4-4.***
3. Convert the tabbed text in the middle of the document to a table.
4. Select the entire table and make the following changes:
   a. Select **Banded Rows** in the *Table Style Options* group [*Table Tools Design* tab] and deselect all other check boxes.
   b. Apply the **List Table 1 Light – Accent 2** table style.
   c. Change the font size to **10 pt**.
   d. Choose **AutoFit Window**.
   e. Change row height to **0.25"**.
   f. Center all text vertically within each cell *(Hint: Use the* Cell *tab in the* Table Properties *dialog box).*
   g. Sort the table in ascending order by **Name of Vaccine**. Be sure to select **Header row** in the *My list has* area of the *Sort* dialog box.
5. Make the following changes to the table:
   a. Insert a row above the first row.
   b. Merge the three cells in the new first row and type **RECOMMENDED VACCINATION SCHEDULE**.
   c. **Bold** and **center** the first row.
   d. **Bold** and **italicize** the second row.
   e. On the first row, apply a **black**, **1½ pt**. top and bottom border.
   f. On the second row, apply a **black**, **1½ pt**. bottom border.
   g. On the last row, apply a **black**, **1½ pt**. bottom border.
   h. Horizontally center the column headings and the text in the third column.

6. Insert the following information alphabetically into the table. Insert rows where needed.

Meningococcal conjugate (MCV)	At 11-12 years	1
Hepatitis B (HepB)	At birth, 1-2 months, and 6 months	3

7. Modify the title of the document ("Vaccination Schedule").
   a. Apply **Title** style to the title of the document.
   b. Change the *After* paragraph spacing to **8 pt**.
   c. **Center** the title horizontally.
   d. Apply **small caps** and **bold** formatting to the title.
8. Insert the ***CMPLogo-04*** picture in the upper left of the document.
   a. Change text wrapping to **Top and Bottom**.
   b. Change the height of the logo to **1"**. Make sure that the logo remains proportional.
   c. Apply the **Offset Diagonal Bottom Right** shadow picture effect.
   d. Set the horizontal and vertical absolute position at **0.2"** to the right of and below page.

4-110 Insert clip art

9. Insert clip art and add a caption.
   a. Search for vaccination in *Office.com Clip Art.*
   b. Insert the clip art displayed in Figure 4-110. If this clip art is not available, insert the ***Vaccination-04*** picture from your student data files.
   c. Change the text wrapping to **Square**.
   d. Change the height of the clip art to **1.3"**. Make sure the graphic remains proportional.
   e. Position the clip art so it is to the right of the first and second paragraphs.
   f. Add Don't neglect your vaccinations! as the caption.
   g. **Center** the caption text, change the font color to **Red**, **Accent 2**, and turn off italics if it is applied to the text.
   h. Adjust the size of the caption text box as needed.
   i. Select the caption and the clip art and **Align Center**.
   j. **Group** the caption and the clip art.
   k. Position the grouped graphic to the right of the first and second paragraphs approximately 0.5" from the right edge of the document and adjust vertically so it does not interfere with the title alignment or the table.
10. Save and close the document (Figure 4-111).

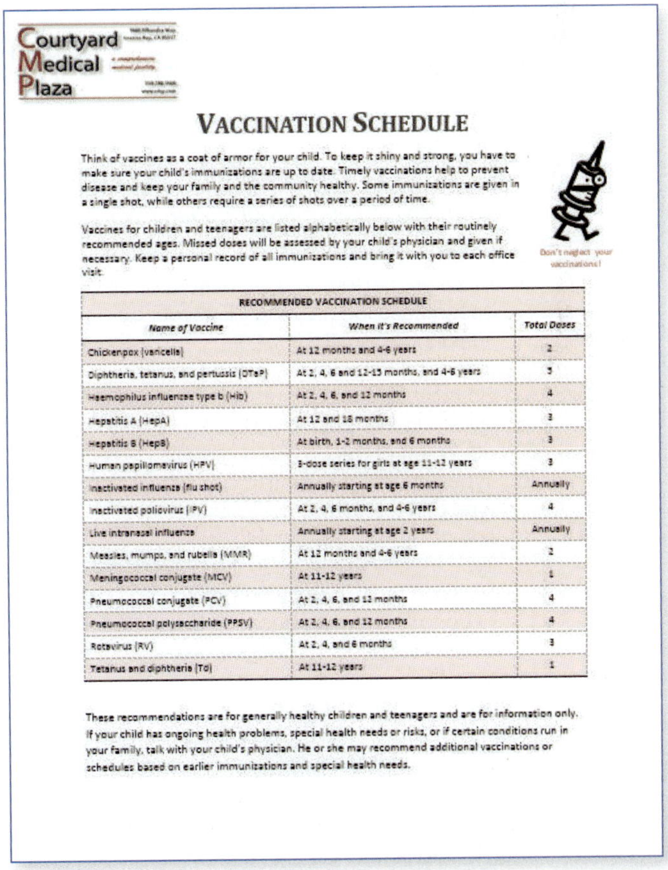

Courtyard Medical Plaza

VACCINATION SCHEDULE

Think of vaccines as a coat of armor for your child. To keep it shiny and strong, you have to make sure your child's immunizations are up to date. Timely vaccinations help to prevent disease and keep your family and the community healthy. Some immunizations are given in a single shot, while others require a series of shots over a period of time.

Vaccines for children and teenagers are listed alphabetically below with their routinely recommended ages. Missed doses will be assessed by your child's physician and given if necessary. Keep a personal record of all immunizations and bring it with you to each office visit.

Don't neglect your vaccinations!

RECOMMENDED VACCINATION SCHEDULE		
Name of Vaccine	*When It's Recommended*	*Total Doses*
Chickenpox (varicella)	At 12 months and 4-6 years	2
Diphtheria, tetanus, and pertussis (DTaP)	At 2, 4, 6 and 12-15 months, and 4-6 years	5
Haemophilus influenzae type b (Hib)	At 2, 4, 6, and 12 months	4
Hepatitis A (HepA)	At 12 and 18 months	3
Hepatitis B (HepB)	At birth, 1-2 months, and 6 months	3
Human papillomavirus (HPV)	3-dose series for girls at age 11-12 years	3
Inactivated influenza (flu shot)	Annually starting at age 6 months	Annually
Inactivated poliovirus (IPV)	At 2, 4, 6 months, and 4-6 years	4
Live intranasal influenza	Annually starting at age 2 years	Annually
Measles, mumps, and rubella (MMR)	At 12 months and 4-6 years	2
Meningococcal conjugate (MCV)	At 11-12 years	1
Pneumococcal conjugate (PCV)	At 2, 4, 6, and 12 months	4
Pneumococcal polysaccharide (PPSV)	At 2, 4, 6, and 12 months	4
Rotavirus (RV)	At 2, 4, and 6 months	3
Tetanus and diphtheria (Td)	At 11-12 years	1

These recommendations are for generally healthy children and teenagers and are for information only. If your child has ongoing health problems, special health needs or risks, or if certain conditions run in your family, talk with your child's physician. He or she may recommend additional vaccinations or schedules based on earlier immunizations and special health needs.

4-111 Word 4-4 completed

Independent Project 4-5

For this project, you create an emergency telephone information sheet for Sierra Pacific Community College District (SPCCD). You add and modify a *SmartArt* graphic, convert text to a table, insert a new table, format the tables, and insert the company logo.
[Student Learning Outcomes 4.1, 4.2, 4.3, 4.5]

Files Needed: ***EmergencyTelephones-04.docx*** **and** ***SPCCDlogo.png***
Completed Project File Name: ***[your initials] Word 4-5.docx***

Skills Covered in This Project

- Modify an existing document.
- Insert a *SmartArt* graphic.
- Add text to a *SmartArt* graphic.
- Resize, change color of, and apply style to *SmartArt.*
- Convert text to a table and *AutoFit.*
- Sort text in a table.
- Insert a row, merge cells, and add information.
- Apply a table style.
- Change cell margins and alignment.
- Apply a style to text.
- Insert a table and type text.
- Insert a picture.
- Adjust picture size and position.
- Insert a symbol and the current date.

1. Open the ***EmergencyTelephones-04*** document from your student data files.
2. Save this document as ***[your initials] Word 4-5.***
3. Insert a *SmartArt* graphic and add text.
   a. Place your insertion point in front of the second section heading ("Emergency Telephone Locations").
   b. Insert the **Vertical Chevron List** *SmartArt* graphic (Figure 4-112).
   c. Type 1 in the graphic text box in the upper left of the *SmartArt* graphic.
   d. Type 2 in the graphic text box below and type 3 in the third graphic text box in the first column of the graphic.
   e. Type the following text in the bulleted text boxes in the second column. You do not need to add bullets because bullets are already included in the *SmartArt.*

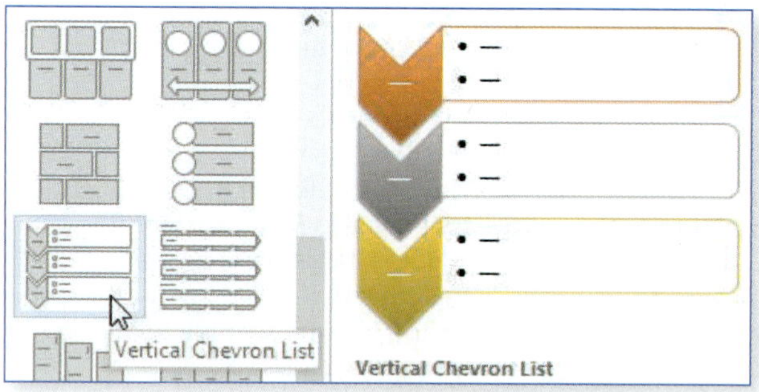

4-112 Insert *SmartArt* graphic

• Press the "Help" button • Speak when the light comes on
• Stay on the line • You will be connected with the college police
• State clearly the nature of the emergency and your location

   f. Delete the extra bullet in the last graphic in the second column.

4. Resize and format the *SmartArt* graphic.
   a. Change the size of the *SmartArt* to **70%** of its original size. Be sure to lock aspect ratio.
   b. Change the text wrapping to **Top and Bottom**.
   c. Change the color of the entire *SmartArt* graphic to **Dark 2 Fill** (Figure 4-113).
   d. Apply the **Intense Effect** *SmartArt* style.

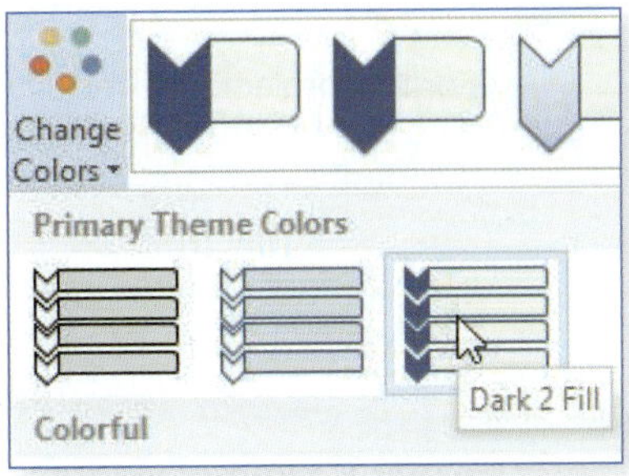

4-113 Change the *SmartArt* colors

5. Convert text to a table.
   a. Select the tabbed text below the second section heading ("Emergency Telephone Locations"). Do not select the paragraph mark below the last row.
   b. Convert this text to a table and **AutoFit to contents**.
6. Sort the table text in ascending order by the first column.
7. Add a title row and insert text.
   a. Add a row above the first row.
   b. Merge the cells in this row.
   c. Type Blue Emergency Telephones in the merged first row.
8. Format the table.
   a. In the *Table Style Options* group, select **Header Row**, **First Column**, and **Banded Rows**.
   b. Apply the **List Table 2 – Accent 4** table style.
   c. Select the entire table and change the top and bottom cell margins to **0.04"** and the left and right cell margins to **0.1"**.
   d. Vertically **center** all text in the table (*Hint: use the* Cell *tab in the* Table Properties *dialog box)*.
   e. Horizontally **center** the text in the first row. This text should be centered vertically and horizontally.
9. Insert, resize, and position the SPCCD logo.
   a. Insert the ***SPCCDlogo_04*** picture at the top of the document.
   b. Change the width to **3"** and keep the size proportional.
   c. Change the text wrapping to **Top and Bottom** and drag the logo above the title.
   d. Set the horizontal and vertical absolute position at **0.3"** to the right of the page and below the page.
10. Modify the footer to include a symbol and the current date.
   a. Open the footer and **space** once at the end of the footer.
   b. Insert a **solid circle** from the *Symbol* font set (Character code 183) and **space** once after it.
   c. Type Revised: and **space** once.
   d. Insert the current date in MM/DD/YY format and set it so that it does not update automatically.
11. Save and close the document (Figure 4-114).

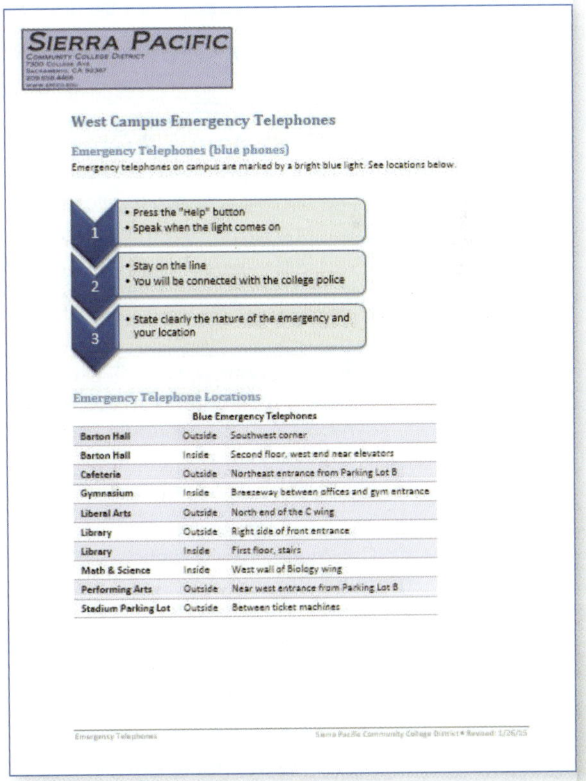
SIERRA PACIFIC

West Campus Emergency Telephones

Emergency Telephones (blue phones)

Emergency telephones on campus are marked by a bright blue light. See locations below.

1
• Press the "Help" button
• Speak when the light comes on

2
• Stay on the line
• You will be connected with the college police

3
• State clearly the nature of the emergency and your location

Emergency Telephone Locations

Blue Emergency Telephones		
Barton Hall	Outside	Southwest corner
Barton Hall	Inside	Second floor, west end near elevators
Cafeteria	Outside	Northeast entrance from Parking Lot B
Gymnasium	Inside	Breezeway between offices and gym entrance
Liberal Arts	Outside	North end of the C wing
Library	Outside	Right side of front entrance
Library	Inside	First floor, stairs
Math & Science	Inside	West wall of Biology wing
Performing Arts	Outside	Near west entrance from Parking Lot B
Stadium Parking Lot	Outside	Between ticket machines

Emergency Telephones   Sierra Pacific Community College District • Revised: 1/26/15

4-114 Word 4-5 completed

Independent Project 4-6

For this project, you modify a memo for Life's Animal Shelter. You edit an existing table, add rows and a column, format the table, insert formulas into the table, and insert and modify *WordArt.* [Student Learning Outcomes 4.1, 4.2, 4.3]

File Needed: ***WeeklyExpenses-04.docx***
Completed Project File Name: ***[your initials] Word 4-6.docx***

Skills Covered in This Project

- Modify an existing document.
- Modify a table row height.
- Change cell alignment.
- Add rows and a column to a table.
- Merge table rows.
- Modify borders and shading of the table.
- Insert formulas into a table.
- Set formula number format.
- Update formulas.
- Format selected text.
- Insert *WordArt.*
- Modify and position *WordArt.*
- Change paragraph spacing.
- Insert a date.

1. Open the ***WeeklyExpenses-04*** document from your student data files.
2. Save this document as ***[your initials] Word 4-6.***
3. Select the entire table and change the font size to **10 pt**.
4. Sort the table in ascending order by the first column excluding the header row.
5. Add rows, a column, and text to the table.
   a. Insert two rows above the first row.
   b. Insert one row below the last row.
   c. Insert one column to the right of the last column.
   d. Merge the cells in the first row.
   e. Merge the cells in the second row.
   f. In the first row, type Life's Animal Shelter.
   g. In the second row, type Weekly Expenses.
   h. If there is a paragraph symbol at the end of the title and subtitle text, delete the paragraph symbols in these two rows.
   i. In the last column in the third row, type Totals.
   j. In the first column in the last row, type Totals.
6. Modify row height and text alignment.
   a. Change the row height on the entire table to **0.3"**.
   b. **Align Center** (vertical and horizontal) the first two rows.
   c. **Align Center Left** the first column below the two merged rows.
   d. **Align Center Right** columns 2-9 below the two merged rows.
7. Modify table borders and shading.
   a. Select the table and remove all borders.
   b. Add a **1½ pt**, **black**, **double line** top border to the first row.
   c. Add a **1½ pt**, **black**, **double line** bottom border to the last row.
   d. Add a **½ pt**, **black**, **single line** top and bottom border to the third row.

e. Add a **½ pt**, **black**, **single line** top border to the last row.
f. Add a **½ pt**, **black**, **single line** right border to the first column. Don't include the first two rows (title and subtitle).
g. Add a **½ pt.**, **black**, **single line** left border to the last column. Don't include the first two rows (title and subtitle).
h. Apply **Orange**, **Accent 6**, **Lighter 60%** shading fill to the first two rows.
i. Apply **Orange**, **Accent 6**, **Lighter 60%** shading fill to the last row.
j. Apply **Orange**, **Accent 6**, **Lighter 60%** shading fill to the last column.

8. Insert formulas into the table.
   a. In the last row of the second column, insert a formula [*Table Tools Layout* tab, *Data* group] to add the figures above. The formula should be **=SUM(ABOVE)**. Use the **$#,##0.00;($#,##0.00)** number format (Figure 4-115).
   b. Insert the same formula and number format in remaining cells in the last row.
   c. In the last column of the fourth row, insert a formula to add the figures to the left. The formula should be **=SUM(LEFT)**. Use the **$#,##0.00;($#,##0.00)** number format.
   d. Insert the same formula and number format in remaining rows in the last column. Make sure to insert the correct formula in each of these cells **=SUM(LEFT)**. Replace "ABOVE" with "LEFT" in the formula, if needed.

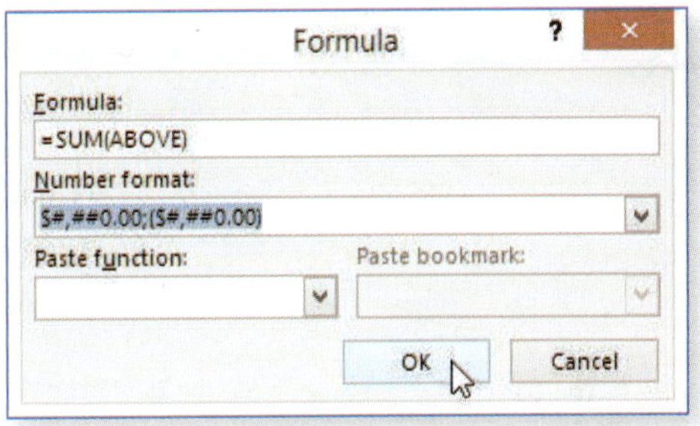

4-115 Insert a formula into the table

9. Change expense data and update formulas.
   a. Change the wages for Wednesday to 592.75.
   b. Select the total amounts in this column and row and press **F9** to update the formulas.
   c. Use **F9** to update the formulas for the wages total and grand total (bottom right cell).
10. Format text in the table.
    a. Apply **bold**, **small caps**, and **12 pt**. font size to the text in the first two rows.
    b. **Bold** and **italicize** text in the third and last rows.
    c. **Bold** and **italicize** text in the last column.
    d. **Italicize** the expense categories in the first column.
    e. Select the table and **AutoFit Contents**.
11. Insert *WordArt* for the company logo.
    a. At the top of the document, insert *WordArt* and use **Fill – Red**, **Accent 2**, **Outline – Accent 2** (Figure 4-116).
    b. Type Life's Animal Shelter as the text for the *WordArt.*

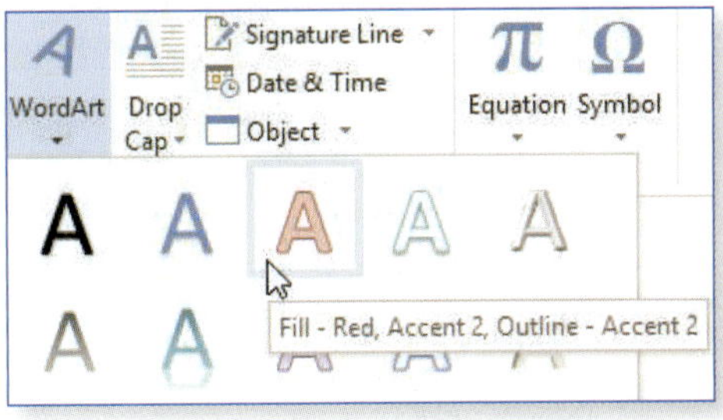

4-116 Insert *WordArt*

12. Modify and position *WordArt.*
    a. Change the text to **small caps** and **40 pt**.
    b. Change the text fill to **Orange**, **Accent 6**.
    c. Change the **Shadow** text effect to **Offset Right**.
    d. Using the *Layout* dialog box, change the horizontal **Alignment** to **Centered** relative to **Margin** and change vertical **Absolute position** to **0.2"** below **Page**.

13. Modify the heading lines of the memo.
    a. Add **36 pt**. before paragraph spacing on the first line ("TO: . . .") of the document.
    b. Insert the current date on the date line in the memo heading to replace the placeholder text and set it to update automatically.
14. Save and close the document (Figure 4-117).

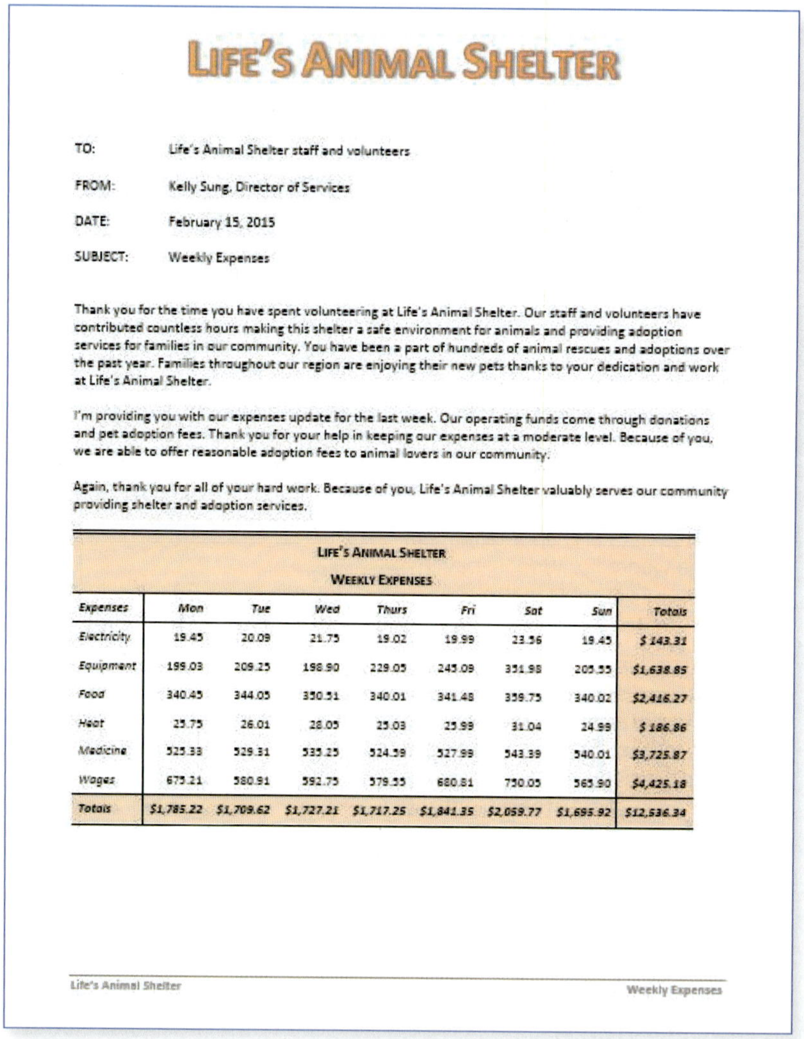

LIFE'S ANIMAL SHELTER

TO: Life's Animal Shelter staff and volunteers

FROM: Kelly Sung, Director of Services

DATE: February 15, 2015

SUBJECT: Weekly Expenses

Thank you for the time you have spent volunteering at Life's Animal Shelter. Our staff and volunteers have contributed countless hours making this shelter a safe environment for animals and providing adoption services for families in our community. You have been a part of hundreds of animal rescues and adoptions over the past year. Families throughout our region are enjoying their new pets thanks to your dedication and work at Life's Animal Shelter.

I'm providing you with our expenses update for the last week. Our operating funds come through donations and pet adoption fees. Thank you for your help in keeping our expenses at a moderate level. Because of you, we are able to offer reasonable adoption fees to animal lovers in our community.

Again, thank you for all of your hard work. Because of you, Life's Animal Shelter valuably serves our community providing shelter and adoption services.

LIFE'S ANIMAL SHELTER WEEKLY EXPENSES								
Expenses	*Mon*	*Tue*	*Wed*	*Thurs*	*Fri*	*Sat*	*Sun*	*Totals*
Electricity	19.45	20.09	21.75	19.02	19.99	23.56	19.45	*$ 143.31*
Equipment	199.03	209.25	198.90	229.05	245.09	351.98	205.55	*$1,638.85*
Food	340.45	344.05	350.51	340.01	341.48	359.75	340.02	*$2,416.27*
Heat	25.75	26.01	28.05	25.03	25.99	31.04	24.99	*$ 186.86*
Medicine	525.33	529.31	535.25	524.59	527.99	543.39	540.01	*$3,725.87*
Wages	675.21	580.91	592.75	579.55	680.81	750.05	565.90	*$4,425.18*
Totals	*$1,785.22*	*$1,709.62*	*$1,727.21*	*$1,717.25*	*$1,841.35*	*$2,059.77*	*$1,695.92*	*$12,536.34*

Life's Animal Shelter Weekly Expenses

4-117 Word 4-6 completed

Improve It Project 4-7

For this project, you edit a document for Courtyard Medical Plaza. You arrange text in columns, position the company logo, and apply formatting to improve the overall layout of the document. [Student Learning Outcomes 4.4, 4.5]

Files Needed: ***StayingActive-04.docx* and *CMPlogo.png***
Completed Project File Name: ***[your initials] Word 4-7.docx***

Skills Covered in This Project

- Modify an existing document.
- Apply style formatting to the title and headings.
- Change font size and alignment.
- Change paragraph spacing.
- Arrange text in columns.
- Change spacing between columns.
- Use a column break to balance columns.
- Insert a picture.
- Update formulas.
- Format selected text.
- Insert *WordArt.*
- Modify and position *WordArt.*
- Change paragraph spacing.
- Insert a date.

1. Open the ***StayingActive-04*** document from your student data files.
2. Save this document as ***[your initials] Word 4-7***.
3. Modify the title of the document.
   a. Apply **Intense Reference** style.
   b. Change to **18 pt**. font size.
   c. Align **center**.
   d. Change paragraph spacing to **36 pt**. before and **12 pt**. after.
4. Modify section headings of the document ("Try Some of the Following Suggestions" and "To Keep Exercise Fun and Interesting").
   a. Apply **Subtle Reference** style.
   b. Change to **14 pt**. font size.
   c. Align **center**.
   d. Change paragraph spacing to **12 pt**. before and **6 pt**. after.
5. Format the last line of the document to make it part of the bulleted list that precedes it and format it consistently with the other bulleted items.
6. Apply column format to the multilevel list following the first section heading.
   a. Arrange the multilevel list in two-column format. Do not include the section heading. If the section break above the list has a number, turn off numbering on this line.
   b. Use **0.75"** space between columns.

7. Apply column format to the bulleted list following the second section heading.
   a. Arrange the bulleted list in two-column format. Do not include the section heading. If the section break above the list has a bullet, turn off bullets on this line.
   b. Use **0.75"** space between columns.
   c. Insert a **column break** before the third bulleted item to balance the columns.
8. Insert the ***CMPlogo-04*** picture at the top of the document.
9. Resize and position the logo.
   a. Change the width to **2.5"** and keep the size proportional.
   b. Change the text wrapping to **In Front of Text**.
   c. Set the horizontal and vertical absolute position at **0.2"** to the right of and below page.
10. Save and close the document (Figure 4-118).

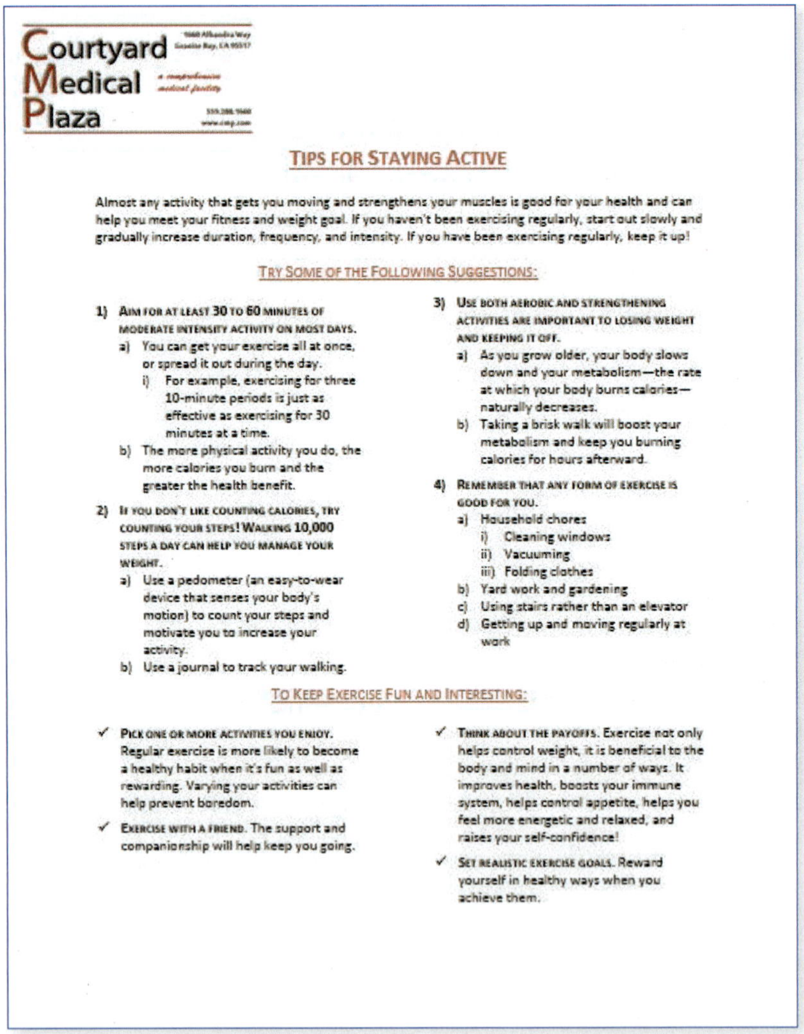
Courtyard Medical Plaza

TIPS FOR STAYING ACTIVE

Almost any activity that gets you moving and strengthens your muscles is good for your health and can help you meet your fitness and weight goal. If you haven't been exercising regularly, start out slowly and gradually increase duration, frequency, and intensity. If you have been exercising regularly, keep it up!

TRY SOME OF THE FOLLOWING SUGGESTIONS:

1) AIM FOR AT LEAST 30 TO 60 MINUTES OF MODERATE INTENSITY ACTIVITY ON MOST DAYS.
   a) You can get your exercise all at once, or spread it out during the day.
      i) For example, exercising for three 10-minute periods is just as effective as exercising for 30 minutes at a time.
   b) The more physical activity you do, the more calories you burn and the greater the health benefit.
2) IF YOU DON'T LIKE COUNTING CALORIES, TRY COUNTING YOUR STEPS! WALKING 10,000 STEPS A DAY CAN HELP YOU MANAGE YOUR WEIGHT.
   a) Use a pedometer (an easy-to-wear device that senses your body's motion) to count your steps and motivate you to increase your activity.
   b) Use a journal to track your walking.
3) USE BOTH AEROBIC AND STRENGTHENING ACTIVITIES ARE IMPORTANT TO LOSING WEIGHT AND KEEPING IT OFF.
   a) As you grow older, your body slows down and your metabolism—the rate at which your body burns calories—naturally decreases.
   b) Taking a brisk walk will boost your metabolism and keep you burning calories for hours afterward.
4) REMEMBER THAT ANY FORM OF EXERCISE IS GOOD FOR YOU.
   a) Household chores
      i) Cleaning windows
      ii) Vacuuming
      iii) Folding clothes
   b) Yard work and gardening
   c) Using stairs rather than an elevator
   d) Getting up and moving regularly at work

TO KEEP EXERCISE FUN AND INTERESTING:

- ✓ PICK ONE OR MORE ACTIVITIES YOU ENJOY. Regular exercise is more likely to become a healthy habit when it's fun as well as rewarding. Varying your activities can help prevent boredom.
- ✓ EXERCISE WITH A FRIEND. The support and companionship will help keep you going.
- ✓ THINK ABOUT THE PAYOFFS. Exercise not only helps control weight, it is beneficial to the body and mind in a number of ways. It improves health, boosts your immune system, helps control appetite, helps you feel more energetic and relaxed, and raises your self-confidence!
- ✓ SET REALISTIC EXERCISE GOALS. Reward yourself in healthy ways when you achieve them.

4-118 Word 4-7 completed

Challenge Project 4-8

It is always good to live within your means. A budget can help you track actual or anticipated spending and compare the amount you spend with your earnings. Using some of the skills you learned in this chapter, for this project you create a weekly or monthly budget.
[Student Learning Outcomes 4.1, 4.2, 4.3, 4.5]

File Needed: None
Completed Project File Name: ***[your initials] Word 4-8.docx***

Create a new document and save it as ***[your initials] Word 4-8.***

A budget can include, but is not limited to, the following elements:

- Document title
- Time frame of the budget
- Expenditure categories
- Days in the week or weeks in the month
- Row and column totals

Modify your document according to the following guidelines:

- Set up your budget in table format.
- Use column headings for days or weeks.
- Use row headings for expense categories.
- Use formulas to total rows and columns.
- Sort table by expenditure amounts.
- Apply table style formatting.
- Adjust shading and borders as needed.
- Adjust column width and row height.
- Modify cell margins.
- Format row and column totals.
- Insert a picture or clip art.
- Format, resize, and position clip art.
- Adjust document margins as needed.
- Include an appropriate header and/or footer.

Challenge Project 4-9

Most newspapers and magazines arrange text in column format to improve readability and overall attractiveness of the document. For this project, you arrange an existing document you have written (such as an essay, blog entry, article for a newspaper, or posting for Craigslist) in column format. [Student Learning Outcomes 4.4, 4.5]

File Needed: None
Completed Project File Name: ***[your initials] Word 4-9.docx***

Create a new document and save it as ***[your initials] Word 4-9.***

A document in column format can include, but is not limited to, the following elements:

- Document title
- Byline
- Section headings
- Graphics

Modify your document according to the following guidelines:

- Set up your article in column format. Don't include the title as part of the columns.
- Change space and/or add a line between columns.
- Use a column or continuous section break to balance the columns.
- Insert a graphic.
- Adjust size, wrapping, and position of the graphic.
- Add a caption to the graphic.
- Adjust margins as needed.
- Include an appropriate header and/or footer.

Challenge Project 4-10

A weekly schedule can help you get organized and manage work, school, family, and personal time more effectively. In this project, you use a table to create a weekly schedule and figure out the time you spend on each activity you engage in each day.
[Student Learning Outcomes 4.1, 4.2, 4.3, 4.5]

File Needed: None
Completed Project File Name: ***[your initials] Word 4-10.docx***

Create a new document and save it as ***[your initials] Word 4-10.***

A weekly schedule can include, but is not limited to, the following elements:

- Document title
- Days of the week
- Time commitment categories
- Row and column totals

Modify your document according to the following guidelines:

- Set up your weekly schedule in table format.
- Use column headings for days of the week.
- Use row headings for time commitment categories.
- Use formulas to total rows and columns.
- Apply table style formatting.
- Adjust shading and borders as needed.
- Adjust column width and row height.
- Adjust cell margins as needed.
- Format row and column totals.
- Insert a picture or clip art.
- Format, resize, and position clip art.
- Adjust document margins as needed.
- Include an appropriate header and/or footer.

Microsoft® Office IN PRACTICE

excel

CHAPTER 1

Creating and Editing Workbooks

CHAPTER OVERVIEW

Microsoft Excel (Excel) is a spreadsheet program you can use to create electronic workbooks to organize numerical data, perform calculations, and create charts. Using Excel, both new and advanced users can create useful and powerful business spreadsheets. This chapter covers the basics of creating and editing an Excel workbook.

STUDENT LEARNING OUTCOMES (SLOs)

After completing this chapter, you will be able to:

SLO 1.1 Create, save, and open an Excel workbook (p. E1-3).

SLO 1.2 Edit a workbook by entering and deleting text and numbers, using the *Fill Handle* to complete a series, and using the cut, copy, and paste features (p. E1-6).

SLO 1.3 Create a basic formula using *AutoSum* (p. E1-16).

SLO 1.4 Format a worksheet using different font attributes, borders, shading, cell styles, themes, and the *Format Painter* (p. E1-19).

SLO 1.5 Resize, insert, delete, and hide and unhide columns and rows in a worksheet (p. E1-26).

SLO 1.6 Insert, delete, edit, format, and rearrange worksheets (p. E1-31).

SLO 1.7 Customize the Excel window by changing views, adjusting zoom level, freezing panes, and splitting a worksheet (p. E1-36).

SLO 1.8 Finalize a workbook by spell checking, adding document properties, applying page setup options, and printing (p. E1-41).

CASE STUDY

Paradise Lakes Resort (PLR) is a vacation company with four resort chains located throughout northern Minnesota. PLR asks employees to use standard formats for spreadsheets to ensure consistency in spreadsheet appearance. In the Pause & Practice projects for Chapter 1, you create business workbooks for the Paradise Lakes Resort.

Pause & Practice 1-1: Create a business workbook.

Pause & Practice 1-2: Create basic formulas using *AutoSum* and format a workbook.

Pause & Practice 1-3: Customize cell contents and edit spreadsheet structure.

Pause & Practice 1-4: Customize the window and finalize the workbook.

EXCEL

SLO 1.1

Creating, Saving, and Opening Workbooks

In Microsoft Excel, the file you create and edit is called a ***workbook***. You can create an Excel workbook from a blank workbook or from an existing, customizable Excel template. Each workbook file contains many ***worksheets***, which are comparable to individual pages in a Word document. A worksheet is also referred to as a ***spreadsheet*** or a ***sheet***, and you can use these terms interchangeably. This book also uses the terms "workbook" and "file" interchangeably. To create a new workbook, first open Excel on your computer.

Create a New Workbook

By default, a workbook includes one worksheet, but a workbook can include multiple worksheets. The worksheet tab is located near the bottom left of the workbook window and is labeled *Sheet1*.

When you first open Excel, the ***Excel Start page*** displays. From the *Start* page, you can create a new blank workbook, open a previously saved workbook, or create a new workbook from an Excel template. Click **Blank workbook** to open a new blank workbook. Alternatively, you can create a new blank workbook from the *New* area on the ***Backstage view***.

> **ANOTHER WAY**
>
> Press **Esc** to leave the Excel *Start* page and open a blank workbook.

HOW TO: Create a New Workbook

1. Click the **File** tab to display the *Backstage* view.
2. Select **New** on the left to display the *New* area on the *Backstage* view (Figure 1-1).
3. Click **Blank workbook** to create a new blank workbook.

> **ANOTHER WAY**
>
> **Ctrl+N** opens a new blank workbook.

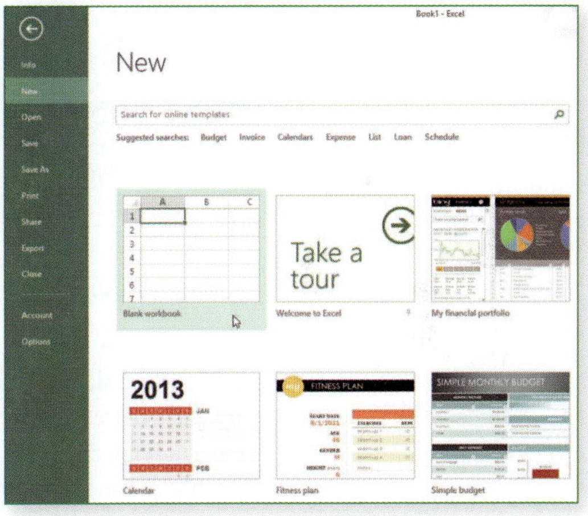

1-1 *Backstage* view for creating new workbooks

Save a Workbook

When you open a blank workbook, Excel automatically assigns a file name to the file, such as *Book1*. The first time you save a new workbook you must type a file name for the workbook into the *Save As* dialog box (see Figure 1-3).

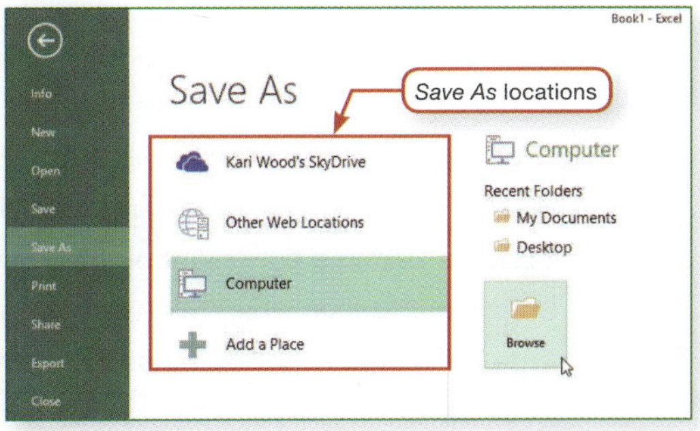

1-2 *Save As* locations

HOW TO: Save a New Workbook

1. Click the **File** tab to display *Backstage* view.
2. Select **Save As** on the left to display the *Save As* area (see Figure 1-2).
   - You can also press **Ctrl+S** to open the *Save As* area on *Backstage* view when saving a workbook that has not yet been saved.
3. Select the location where you want to save your document.
   - You can save the document on your computer, in a *SkyDrive* folder, or on an external storage device.
   - If you click one of the *Recent Folders* options, the *Save As* dialog box opens.
4. Click the **Browse** button to open the *Save As* dialog box (Figure 1-3).
5. Select the location where you want to save the workbook in the left area of the *Save As* dialog box.
6. Type the name of the file in the *File name* area.
7. Click **Save** to close the *Save As* dialog box and save the file.

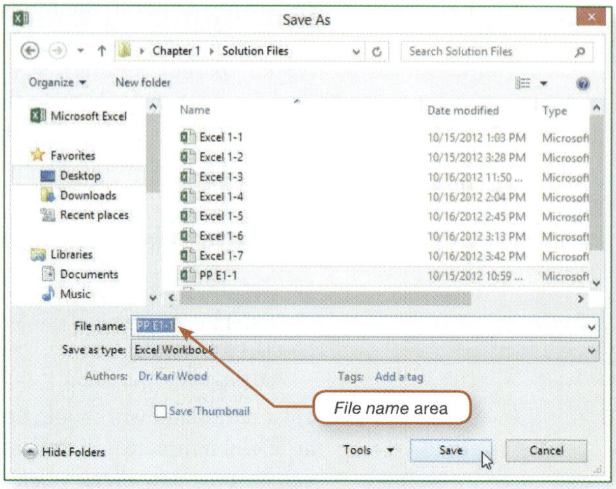

1-3 *Save As* dialog box

> **ANOTHER WAY**
>
> Press **F12** to open the *Save As* dialog box.

Once a workbook has been saved, you can re-save it by pressing **Ctrl+S** or clicking the **Save** button on the ***Quick Access*** toolbar.

Save a Workbook with a Different File Name

You can save a workbook as a different name by opening the *Save As* dialog box and giving the workbook a different file name. This action does not remove the existing workbook but instead creates a copy of the file with a new name. For example, you might want to rename an existing expense report before updating it with current data. Saving a workbook with a different file name is similar to saving a new workbook.

HOW TO: Save As a Different File Name

1. Click the **File** tab to open *Backstage* view.
   - You can also press **F12** from the working area of Excel to open the *Save As* dialog box.
2. Click **Save As** to display the *Save As* area.
3. Select the location to save your document.
4. Click the **Browse** button to open the *Save As* dialog box (see Figure 1-3).
5. Select the location where you want to save the workbook in the left pane of the *Save As* dialog box.
6. Type the name of the file in the *File name* area.
7. Click **Save** to close the *Save As* dialog box and save the file.

Workbook File Formats

You can save an Excel workbook in a variety of formats. For example, you might want to save a workbook in an older Excel format to share with someone who uses an earlier version of Excel, or you may want to save a workbook in portable document format (.pdf) to create a static image of the file.

By default, Excel workbooks are saved as ***.xlsx*** files. To change the type of file format, select the format of your choice from the *Save as type* area of the *Save As* dialog box (Figure 1-4). The following table lists several common formats for saving an Excel workbook.

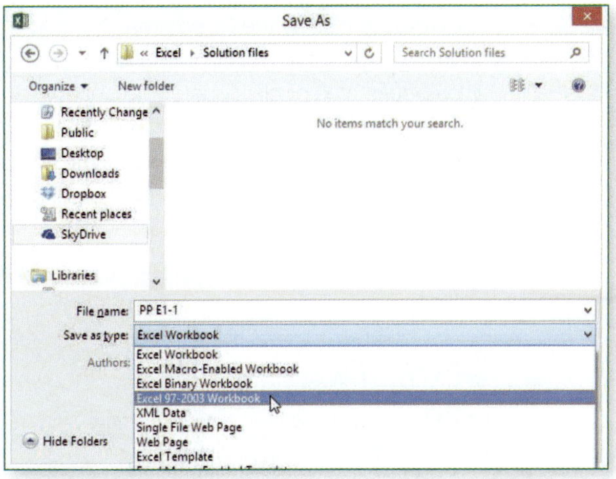

1-4 Workbook file formats

Save Formats

Type of Document	File Extension	Uses of This Format
Excel Macro-Enabled Workbook	.xlsm	Excel workbook with embedded macros
Excel 97-2003 Workbook	.xls	Excel workbook compatible with older versions of Microsoft Excel
Excel Template	.xltx	A new workbook based on a template
Excel Macro-Enabled Template	.xltm	A new workbook based on a template with embedded macros
Portable Document Format (PDF)	.pdf	A static image, similar to a picture, of a workbook; used to preserve the formatting of a file
Plain Text	.txt	Workbook can be opened with most spreadsheet applications and contains text only, with no special formatting.
Comma Separated Values (CSV)	.csv	A common file format that can be opened by most spreadsheet programs and is used to import and export data
Open Document Text	.ods	The spreadsheet software in the Open Office suite
Web Page	.htm, .html	A workbook that is formatted for web sites

Open a Workbook

You can open workbooks from your computer, USB drive, or *SkyDrive*. You can open a previously saved workbook from the *Start* page, *Open* area on the *Backstage* view, or *Open* dialog box.

HOW TO: Open a Workbook

1. Click the **File** tab to open *Backstage* view.
2. Click **Open** to display the *Open* area.
   - Select a workbook to open in the *Recent Workbooks* area or click one of the options in the *Open* area.
3. Select the location where the workbook is stored.
4. Click **Browse** or click a folder to display the *Open* dialog box.
5. Select the workbook and click **Open** (Figure 1-5).

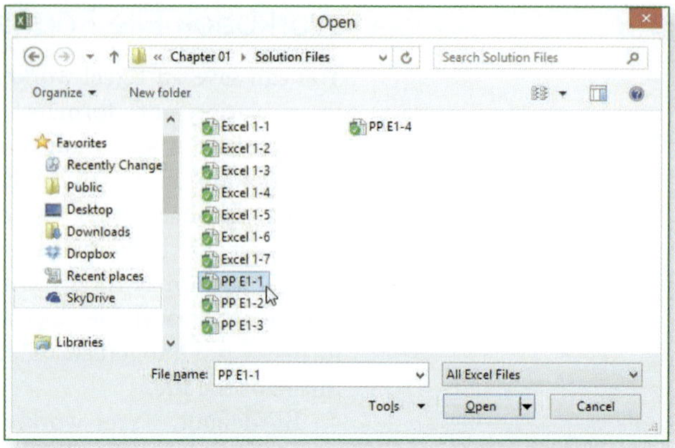

1-5 *Open* dialog box

ANOTHER WAY

Ctrl+O displays the *Open* area on the *Backstage* view.
Ctrl+F12 displays the *Open* dialog box.

SLO 1.2

Working with Text and Numbers

When you create or edit a workbook, you can type data, import data from another file, or copy data from a web page or another source. It is important to enter text and numbers correctly to create professional-looking workbooks. A ***label*** is text in a worksheet that identifies a title and subtitle, row and column headings, and other descriptive information. Labels are not included in calculations. A ***value*** is a number that you type in a cell. Use values for numbers, currency, dates, and percentages. Values are included in calculations. Occasionally you may need to enter a number as a label. To type a number as a label, click the cell, type an apostrophe ('), and type the number value.

A worksheet is arranged in ***columns*** (vertical) and ***rows*** (horizontal). Columns are labeled with letters and rows are labeled with numbers. You type text and numbers in a ***cell***, which is the intersection of a column and a row. Each cell is identified with a ***cell reference*** (or ***cell address***), which is the column letter and row number that represent the location of the cell. Cell A1 is the intersection of column A and row 1.

Before entering data in a worksheet, verify the workbook view settings. Click the **View** tab, and select the **Gridlines**, **Formula Bar**, and **Headings** options in the *Show* group. *Gridlines* display the cell boundaries, and the *Headings* option displays row and column headings. Use the *Formula bar* to insert formulas and to edit data.

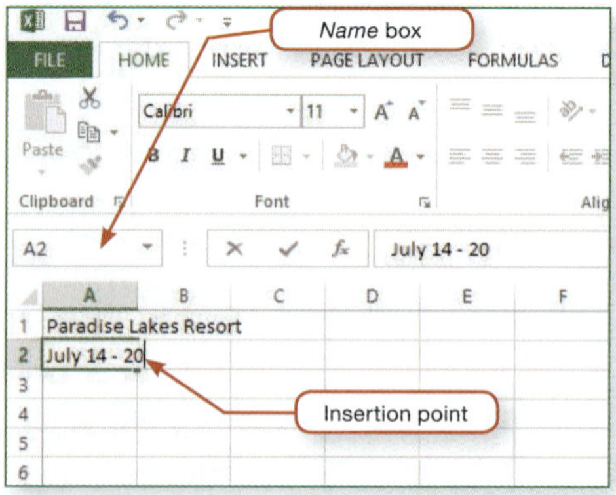

1-6 Entering text

Enter Text and Numbers

To enter data into a spreadsheet, click the cell with your pointer to activate the cell. The ***active cell*** displays a solid border around the cell, and the reference for the active cell appears in the ***Name box*** (Figure 1-6).

HOW TO: Enter Data into a Workbook

1. Select the cell and type the information.
   - The text appears inside the active cell with a blinking insertion point (see Figure 1-6).
2. Press **Enter** to accept the information you typed in the cell and to activate the cell below.
   - Press **Tab** to activate the cell to the right.
   - You can also use the arrow keys on your keyboard to activate a cell.

MORE INFO

When text is longer than the width of the cell, the text displays only if adjacent cells are empty. If the adjacent cells are not empty, the text appears cut off in the cell, but the *Formula bar* displays the entire entry. To display the entire entry, adjust the column width.

Edit Cell Contents

You can edit the content of the cell as you type or after the entry is complete. To edit text as you type (before you press *Enter*), use the **Backspace** key to delete characters to the left of the insertion point. Use arrow keys to move the insertion point, and use the **Delete** key to delete characters to the right of the insertion point. To edit a completed entry (after you press *Enter*), you must activate ***edit mode*** in the cell. To activate edit mode, double-click the cell or press **F2**. Either method displays an insertion point, and "EDIT" displays on the *Status bar.*

ANOTHER WAY

Click the **Enter** button on the *Formula bar* to complete an entry.

HOW TO: Edit Cell Contents (Completed Entry)

1. Activate edit mode by double-clicking the cell (Figure 1-7).
   - Another way to activate edit mode is to press **F2**.
2. Position the insertion point and edit the contents of the cell.
3. Press **Enter**.

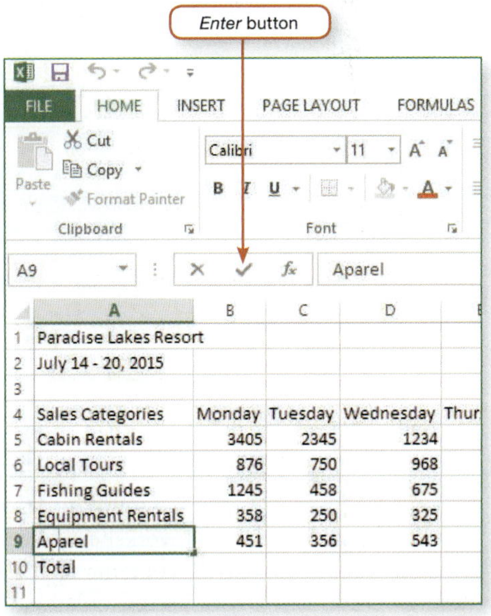

1-7 Activated cell for editing

Replace or Clear Cell Contents

To replace the contents of an existing cell, click to activate the cell, and type the new text. Press **Enter** or click the **Enter** button on the *Formula bar.* To remove the contents of the cell, select the cell and press **Delete** or click the **Clear** button [*Home* tab, *Editing* group]. When you click the *Clear* button, you can choose to *Clear All, Clear Formats,* or *Clear Contents.*

HOW TO: Clear Cell Contents

1. Select the cell or cells.
2. Click the **Clear** button [*Home* tab, *Editing* group].
   - Another way to remove cell contents is to press **Delete**.
3. Choose an option from the drop-down list (Figure 1-8).
   - *Clear All* removes formatting and content.
   - *Clear Formats* only clears formatting.
   - *Clear Contents* deletes content.

1-8 *Clear* options

Align and Indent Cell Contents

Excel recognizes any combination of letters, numbers, spaces, and other characters as text and aligns each entry in the bottom left corner of the cell. When you type only numbers into a cell, Excel recognizes your entry as numeric data (values). Excel aligns numeric entries in the bottom right corner of the cell.

You can change both the vertical and horizontal ***alignment*** of information in a cell. A number of horizontal and vertical alignment and indent options are available in the *Alignment* group on the *Home* tab (Figure 1-9). The vertical alignment options are *Top Align, Middle Align,* and *Bottom Align.* Horizontal alignment options are *Align Left, Center,* and *Align Right.*

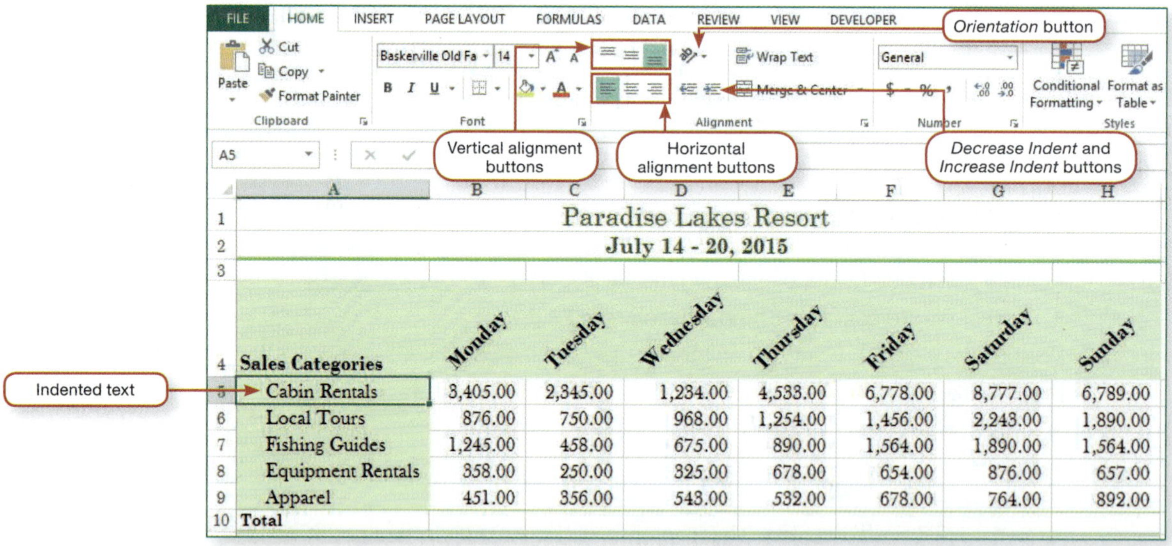

1-9 Alignment and indent options

You can also indent information in a cell. An ***indent*** increases the distance between the cell contents and the left boundary of the cell. It is common practice to indent row headings in a worksheet (see Figure 1-9). Use ***Increase Indent*** [*Home* tab, *Alignment* group] to indent cell contents to the right. Use ***Decrease Indent*** [*Home* tab, *Alignment* group] to remove a previously added indent and move cell contents to the left.

HOW TO: Align and Indent Text

1. Select the cell.
2. Select a horizontal alignment option [*Home* tab, *Alignment* group].
   - *Align Left* aligns text on the left side of the cell.
   - *Center* centers text between the left and right sides of the cell.
   - *Right Align* aligns text on the right side of the cell.
3. Select a vertical alignment option [*Home* tab, *Alignment* group].
   - *Top Align* aligns text at the top of the cell.
   - *Middle Align* aligns text between the top and bottom of the cell.
   - *Bottom Align* aligns text at the bottom of the cell.
4. Select an indent option [*Home* tab, *Alignment* group].
   - *Increase Indent* moves text to the right of the left cell boundary.
   - *Decrease Indent* moves text toward the left cell boundary.

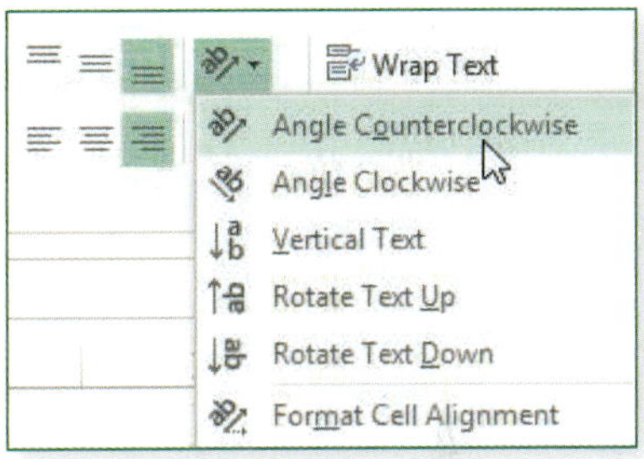

1-10 Text orientation options

By default, text and values are oriented horizontally from left to right, but you can change ***text orientation*** to display text vertically or at an angle. Click the **Orientation** button [*Home* tab, *Alignment* group] to select a text orientation from the drop-down list (Figure 1-10). Select the **Format Cell Alignment** option from the *Orientation* drop-down list to open the *Format Cells* dialog box and adjust the orientation to a specific degree.

> **MORE INFO**
>
> Click the **Alignment** launcher [*Home* tab, *Alignment* group] or press **Ctrl+1** to open the *Format Cells* dialog box, where you can further customize cell contents.

Select Cells

When you format or edit worksheets, the first step is to select a cell, ranges, columns, or rows. A group of cells is a ***range*** (or cell range). In a range of cells, a colon is used to represent "through" while a comma is used to represent "and." For example, (A1:A3) includes the cell A2 while (A1, A3) does not.

Excel uses multiple ***pointers*** to indicate various selecting, copying, and moving options within a worksheet. The following table describes the pointers in Excel.

Pointers

Pointer Icon	Pointer Use
	***Selection pointer*** (block plus sign) selects a cell or ***cell range*** (group of cells); the selection pointer appears when you move your pointer over the center of a cell.
	***Fill pointer*** (crosshair or thin black plus sign) copies cell contents, completes lists, and fills patterns of selected data; it appears when you place your pointer on the *Fill Handle* or black square in the bottom right corner of an active cell or cells.
	***Move pointer*** (white pointer and four-pointed arrow) moves data; it appears when you place your pointer on the border of an active cell or cells.
	***Resize pointer*** (two-pointed arrow) adjusts cell ranges in a formula and adjusts object sizes; it appears when you place your pointer on the selection handle in a range in a formula or on a sizing handle when an object is selected.

There are many different ways to select data in a worksheet (Figure 1-11). The following table lists the various selection methods.

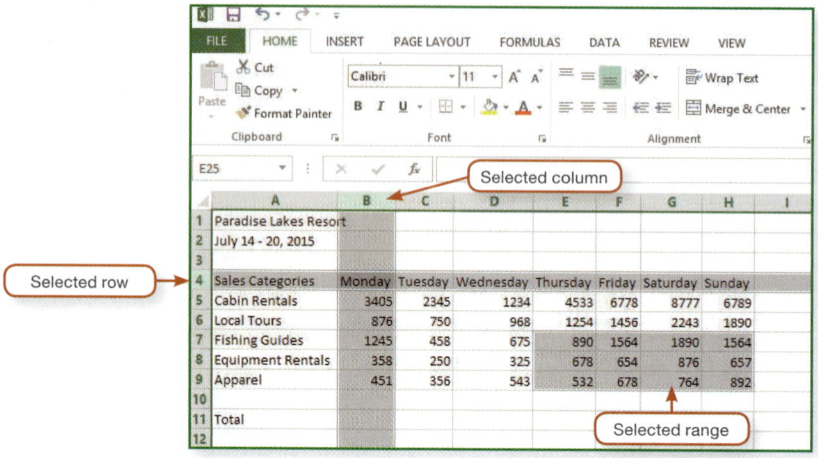

1-11 Selected text

Selection Methods

Name	Instructions
Select an Entire Column or Row	To select an entire column, point to and click a column heading. To select an entire row, point to and click a row heading.
Select the Worksheet	Press **Ctr+A** or click the **Select All** button (above the row 1 heading and to the left of the column A heading) to select the entire sheet. *Select All* button 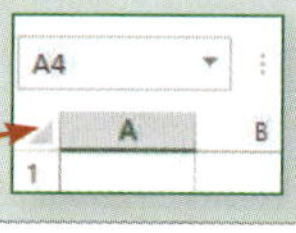
Select Adjacent Cells	To select groups of cells that are *adjacent* (next to each other), click and drag the selection pointer over the range of cells. Alternatively, you can select the first cell in the range, press **Shift**, and select the last cell in the range. You can also use the **arrow keys+Shift** to select adjacent cells.
Select Non-Adjacent Cells	To select groups of cells that are *non-adjacent* (not next to each other), use the selection pointer to select the first cell(s), hold down **Ctrl**, and select the next cell(s).
Use the *Name Box* to Select Cells	Type a cell reference or cell range in the *Name* box and press **Enter** to select cells. Type a colon (:) between cell references to select a range of cells. *Name* box 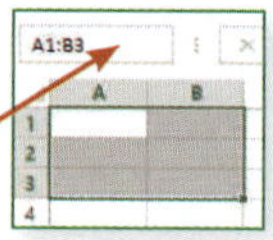

MORE INFO

Selecting a *cell range* prior to entering data is a quick method for data entry in a defined area. Select the cell range, type the first entry, and press **Enter**. Continue typing and pressing **Enter** after each entry. When the last cell in the first column of the range is completed, the active cell automatically moves to the top of the second column.

Fill Handle

When you are typing data that is in a series, such as days of the week or months of the year, you can use the ***Fill Handle*** to complete the list. You can also use this tool to repeat numeric patterns, such as in a numbered list, or to copy cell contents to another location.

HOW TO: Use the Fill Handle to Create a Series

1. Type the first item in the series.
2. Press **Enter** and reselect the cell.
3. Place your pointer on the *Fill Handle* (small black square in the lower right corner of the cell) until a fill pointer (thin black plus sign) appears (Figure 1-12).
4. Click and drag the fill pointer through the last cell in the range. Release the pointer to complete the series.
   - The items in the series appear in the cell range.
   - The *Auto Fill Options* button displays and includes options to change the fill selection (Figure 1-13).

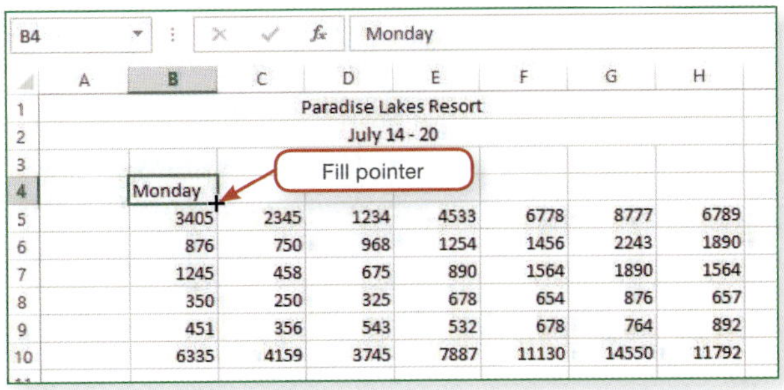

1-12 Use the *Fill Handle* to complete a series

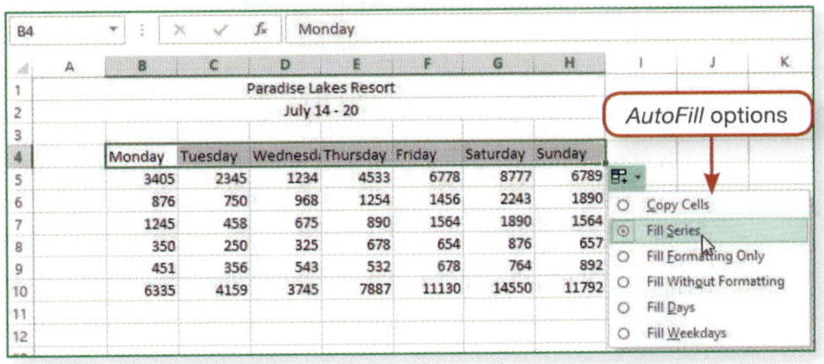

1-13 Completed series

Cut, Copy, and Paste Cell Contents

You can reorganize labels or numeric data quickly using *Cut, Copy,* and *Paste.* Use the *Cut* command to move cells or a cell range. The *Copy* command duplicates cell content from one cell or range to another location. When you cut or copy a cell or a range of cells, it is stored on the Windows *Clipboard.* When you use *Cut, Copy,* and *Paste* commands, the cell you cut or copy from is a ***source cell*** or cells and the cell you paste to is a ***destination cell*** or cells.

ANOTHER WAY

Use **Ctrl+C** to copy.
Use **Ctrl+X** to cut.
Use **Ctrl+V** to paste.

Move or Cut Cell Contents

You can move cell content using drag and drop, keyboard shortcuts, or *Cut* and *Paste* in the *Clipboard* group on the *Home* tab. When you use the drag and drop method, the selected cells are not placed on the clipboard.

HOW TO: Move Cell Contents Using Drag and Drop

1. Select the cell(s) you want to move.
2. Place your pointer on the border of the selection until the move pointer (white pointer and four-pointed arrow) appears.
3. Click and hold the move pointer on the border of the selected cell(s) (Figure 1-14).
4. Drag to the desired new location and release the pointer.

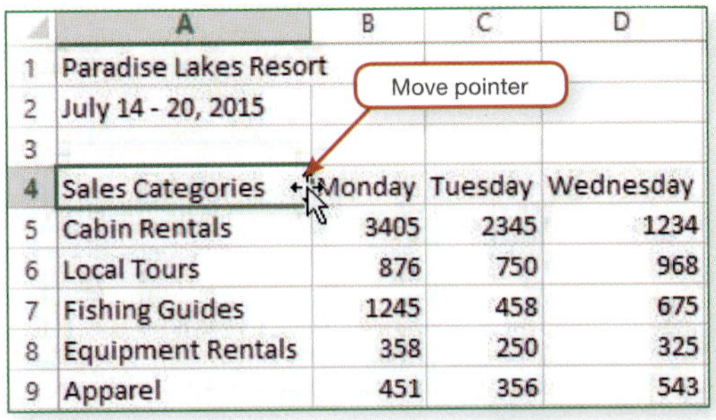

1-14 Move pointer

After you select and cut cells, the cells are placed on the *Clipboard.* To place the contents of the *Clipboard* in the spreadsheet, use the *Paste* command. There are three ways to move text using *Cut* and *Paste.*

- ***Ribbon buttons:*** **Cut** and **Paste** buttons [*Home* tab, *Clipboard* group]
- ***Shortcut commands:*** **Ctrl+X** to cut and **Ctrl+V** to paste
- ***Context menu:*** Right-click a cell or range of cells to display the context menu, and click **Cut**.

HOW TO: Move Cell Contents Using Cut and Paste

1. Select the cell or cell range you want to move.
2. Click **Cut** [*Home* tab, *Clipboard* group]. A moving border appears around the selected source cell or cell range (Figure 1-15).
   - If you choose not to move data, press **Esc** to remove the moving border.
3. Select the destination cell location.
   - Click the cell in the top left of the range where you want to paste.
4. Click **Paste** [*Home* tab, *Clipboard* group].
   - If the destination cell or cell range is not empty, pasted data overwrites existing data. To prevent loss of data, use **Insert Cut Cells** [*Home* tab, *Insert* group].
   - You can paste data that you cut only one time.

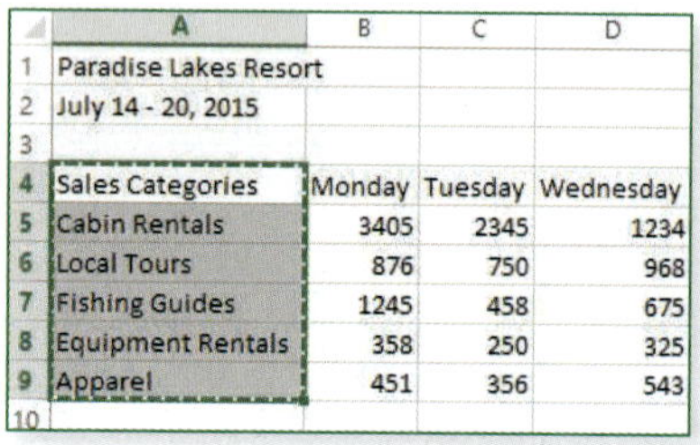

1-15 Moving cell contents using *Cut* and *Paste*

ANOTHER WAY

Press **Ctrl+X** to cut or right-click the cell and select **Cut** from the context menu. Alternatively, you can press **Ctrl+V** to paste or right-click the destination cell and select **Paste** from the context menu.

Office Clipboard

The Office ***Clipboard*** stores cut or copied data from Excel or other Office applications, and the data stored on the *Clipboard* is available to Excel or to other applications such as Word and PowerPoint. The *Clipboard* can hold up to 24 items. Click the **Clipboard** launcher to open the *Clipboard* pane. Each time you cut or copy, the item appears at the top of the *Clipboard* pane. You can paste one item from the *Clipboard* or paste the entire contents of the *Clipboard.*

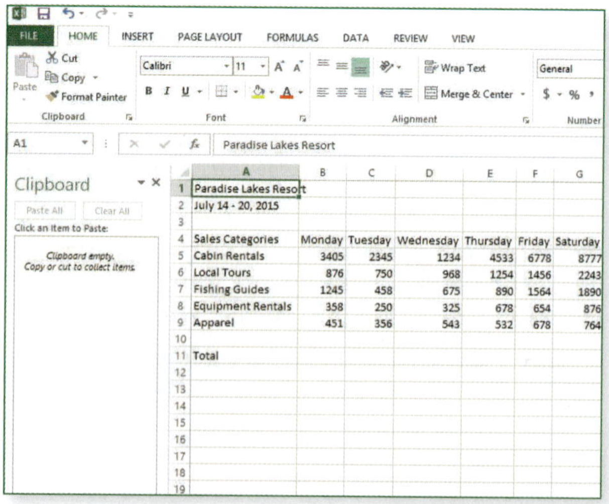

1-16 *Clipboard* pane

HOW TO: Use the Office Clipboard

1. Click the **Home** tab.
2. Click the **Clipboard** launcher to display the *Clipboard* pane (Figure 1-16).
3. Click **Clear All** to empty the *Clipboard.*

4. Cut or copy spreadsheet data to place data on the *Clipboard*. Each item you cut or copy is added to the top of the *Clipboard* pane.
5. Paste items from the *Clipboard* by clicking the item in the task pane. The data is pasted in the active cell.
6. Delete an item from the *Clipboard* by pointing to a *Clipboard* item and clicking the drop-down arrow that appears to the right of the item. Choose **Delete**.
7. Click **Close** to hide the *Clipboard*.

Copy Cell Contents

Copying a cell or a cell range places a duplicate of the selection on the *Clipboard*. The selected data remains in its original location, and a copy of the cell data is pasted in another location. You can copy text using the drag and drop method or *Copy* and *Paste* commands. Data that is copied can be pasted multiple times and in multiple locations.

HOW TO: Copy Using Drag and Drop

1. Select the cell(s) you want to copy.
2. Place your pointer over the border of the selection until the move pointer appears.
3. Press and hold **Ctrl** and click the border of the selected cell(s).
   - A small plus sign appears next to the pointer indicating the move pointer has changed to the copy pointer.
4. Drag the cell or cell range to the desired new location on the worksheet, release the pointer first, and then release **Ctrl** (Figure 1-17).

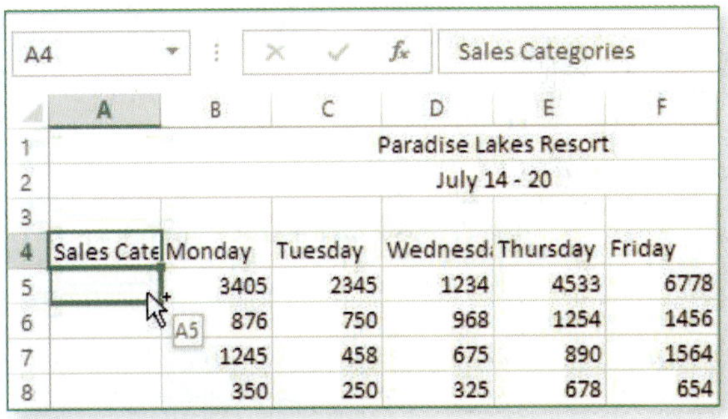

1-17 Copy data using drag and drop

Copying cells using the copy and paste method is similar to moving cells using the cut and paste method. The *Copy* command places the selection on the *Clipboard*, and the *Paste* command places the *Clipboard* contents in the worksheet.

- ***Ribbon buttons:*** **Copy** and **Paste** buttons [*Home* tab, *Clipboard* group]
- ***Shortcut commands:*** **Ctrl+C** to copy and **Ctrl+V** to paste
- ***Context menu:*** Right-click to display the menu, and click **Copy**.

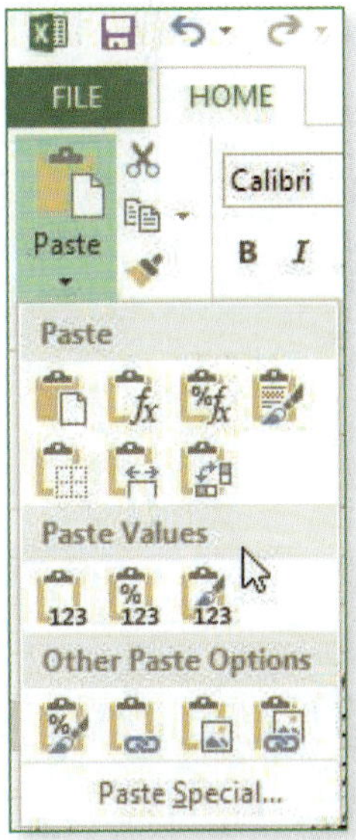

1-18 *Paste Options* gallery

Paste Cell Contents and Paste Options

When you are pasting cell data into a worksheet, you may want to paste plain text or cell formatting or formulas. Excel provides multiple paste options. After copying or cutting cells from your worksheet, click the bottom half of the **Paste** button in the *Clipboard* group on the *Home* tab to display the ***Paste Options gallery*** (Figure 1-18). The following groups are available in the *Paste Options* gallery:

- *Paste*
- *Paste Values*
- *Other Paste Options*

Within these paste groups, there are many context-sensitive paste options. The following table describes each of these paste options.

Paste Options

Group	Paste Icon	Paste Option	Description
Paste		Paste	Copy contents and format of source cell(s); this is the default option.
		Formulas	Copy formulas from the source cell(s) but not contents or formats.
		Formulas & Number Formatting	Copy formulas and format for numbers and formulas of source area but not the contents.
		Keep Source Formatting	Copy contents, format, and styles of source cell.
		No Borders	Copy contents and format of source area but not borders.
		Keep Source Column Widths	Copy contents and format of source cell(s); change destination column widths to source column widths.
		Transpose	Copy the contents and format of the source cell(s), but transpose the rows and columns.
		Merge Conditional Formatting	Context-sensitive: Copy the contents, format, and *Conditional Formatting* rules of the source cell(s) to the destination cell(s).
Paste Values		Values	Copy contents of source cell(s) without formatting or formulas.
		Values & Number Formatting	Copy contents and formatting of source cell(s), but use the format of the destination area for labels.
		Values & Source Formatting	Copy contents and formatting of source cell(s) without formulas.
Other Paste Options		Formatting	Copy format of source cell(s) without the contents.
		Paste Link	Copy contents and format and link cells so that a change to the cells in the source area updates corresponding cells in the destination area.
		Picture	Copy an image of the source cell(s) as a picture.
		Linked Pictures	Copy an image of the source area as a picture so that a change to the cells in the source area updates the picture in the destination area.

MORE INFO

The default paste option is *Keep Source Formatting*. This option applies when you click the top half of the *Paste* button [*Home* tab, *Clipboard* group].

PAUSE & PRACTICE: EXCEL 1-1

Businesses use spreadsheets to display data in a useful and meaningful manner. For this project, you create a business spreadsheet that displays one week's sales for Paradise Lakes Resort.

File Needed: None
Completed Project File Name: ***[your initials] PP E1-1****.xlsx*

1. Create a new workbook.
   a. Click the **File** tab.
   b. Click **New**.
   c. Click **Blank workbook** to open a new workbook.
2. Save the workbook.
   a. Press **F12** to open the *Save As* dialog box.
   b. Select a location to save the workbook (Figure 1-19).
   c. Name the file ***[your initials] PP E1-1*** in the *File name* area.
   d. Click **Save**. The *Save As* dialog box closes.

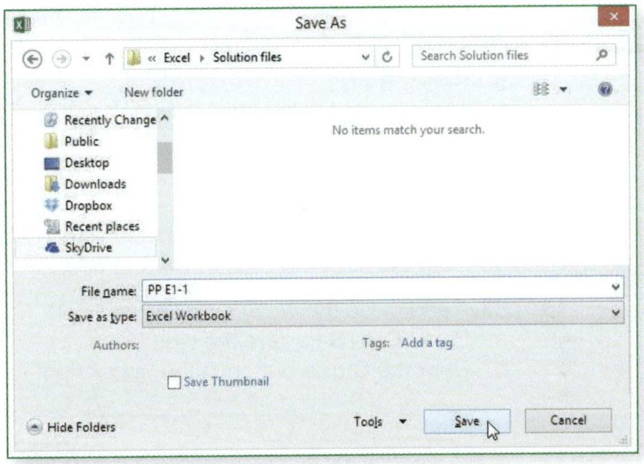

1-19 *Save As* dialog box

3. Enter data.
   a. Click to select cell **A1**, and type Paradise Lakes Resort.
   b. Press **Enter** and type July 14 – 20, 2015.
   c. Press **Enter** again.
   d. Type the remaining data in Figure 1-20. The data in the spreadsheet is displayed so that you can easily read the text for each column and row. You will learn the procedure to increase column width in SLO 1.5. To widen column A, drag the right column heading border to the right.

	A	B	C	D	E	F	G	H
1	Paradise Lakes Resort							
2	July 14 - 20, 2015							
3								
4	Sales Categories	Sunday						
5	Cabin Rentals	6789	3405	2345	1234	4533	6778	8777
6	Local Tours	1890	876	750	968	1254	1456	2243
7	Fishing Guides	1564	1245	458	675	890	1564	1890
8	Equipment Rentals	657	358	250	325	678	654	876
9	Apparel	892	451	356	543	532	678	764
10	Total	11792						

1-20 PP E1-1 data

4. Use the *Fill Handle* to create a series.
   a. Select **B4**.
   b. Place the pointer on the *Fill Handle* (small black square in the lower right corner of the cell) until a fill pointer appears.
   c. Click and drag to cell **H4**.
   d. Release the pointer.

5. Edit worksheet data.
   a. Select **B10**.
   b. Press **Delete** to remove the contents.
   c. Select **F5**.
   d. Type 4583 and press **Enter**.
6. Indent and align text.
   a. Select **A5:A9**.
   b. Click the **Increase Indent** button [*Home* tab, *Alignment* group].
   c. Select **B4:H4**.
   d. Click the **Align Right** button [*Home* tab, *Alignment* group].
7. Move text.
   a. Select **B4:B9**.
   b. Click the **Cut** button [*Home* tab, *Clipboard* group].
   c. Select **I4**.
   d. Click the **Paste** button [*Home* tab, *Clipboard* group].
   e. Select **C4:I9**.
   f. Point to the right border of the selected cell range.
   g. Drag the selected cells to **B4** and release the move pointer.
8. Save and close the workbook (Figure 1-21).
   a. Press **Ctrl+S** to save the workbook.
   b. Click the **Close** button in the upper right corner.

	A	B	C	D	E	F	G	H	I
1	Paradise Lakes Resort								
2	July 14 - 20, 2015								
3									
4	Sales Categories	Monday	Tuesday	Wednesday	Thursday	Friday	Saturday	Sunday	
5	Cabin Rentals	3405	2345	1234	4583	6778	8777	6789	
6	Local Tours	876	750	968	1254	1456	2243	1890	
7	Fishing Guides	1245	458	675	890	1564	1890	1564	
8	Equipment Rentals	358	250	325	678	654	876	657	
9	Apparel	451	356	543	532	678	764	892	
10	Total								
11									

1-21 PP E1-1 completed

SLO 1.3

Using the Sum Function

Sum is a built-in formula that adds the values in a selected range. To insert the *Sum* function, click the cell to make it active. When you click **AutoSum** [*Home* tab, *Editing* group], a formula (=SUM) displays in the cell followed by the suggested range of cells (for example, B5:B9). A moving border surrounds the cells in the range, and the function displays. Press **Enter** to complete the formula or adjust the cell range. The cell displays the result of the sum function, and the *Formula bar* displays the formula. Once a formula has been entered, it is automatically updated if the content of the worksheet is edited.

ANOTHER WAY

The *Function Library* group on the *Formulas* tab includes the *AutoSum* function.

HOW TO: Use the Sum Function

1. Click the cell where you want to display the calculation results.
2. Click the **AutoSum** button [*Home* tab, *Editing* group].
3. Press **Enter** to complete the formula (Figure 1-22).
   - You can double-click **AutoSum** to enter the formula. Click once to see the range and click a second time to complete the entry.

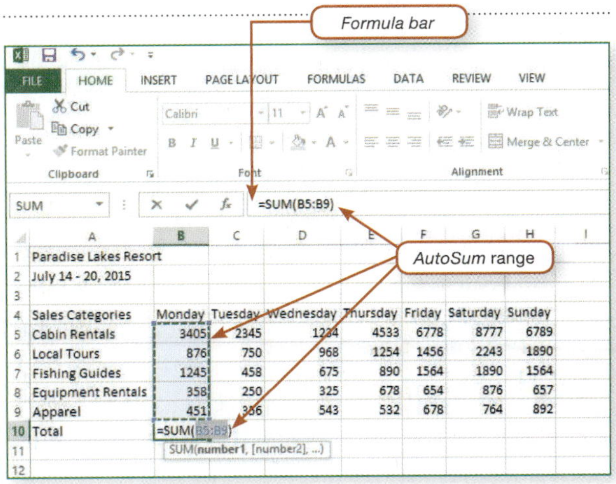

1-22 *AutoSum* function

MORE INFO

To display formulas in the worksheet, click the **Formula** tab, and click **Show Formulas** or press **CTRL+`**.

Copy the Sum Function

The *Fill Handle* is a useful tool to copy functions and formulas, such as *Sum*, into adjacent cells. Notice that in Figure 1-23 each day of the week contains the same number of figures to total. The formula to sum the numbers in the "Tuesday" column is the same as the formula to add the numbers in the "Monday" column except for the cell references. When you drag the *Fill Handle*, Excel automatically adjusts cell references. The formula automatically changes relative to its location on the worksheet.

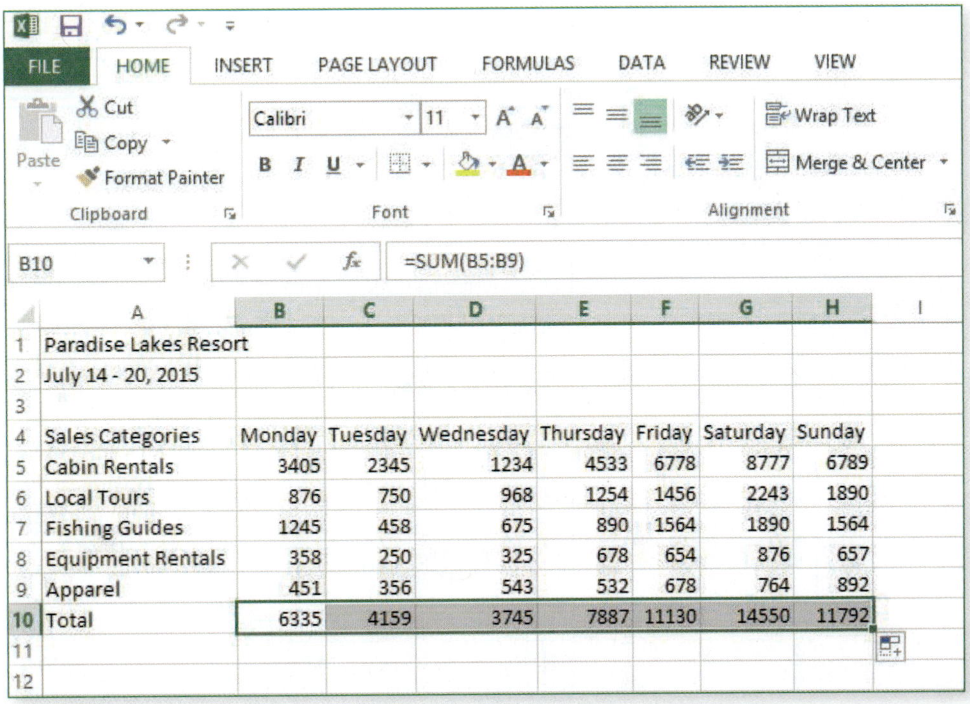

1-23 Using the *Fill Handle* to copy a formula

> **MORE INFO**
>
> Chapter 2 covers many other types of functions and formulas.

HOW TO: Use the Fill Handle to Copy Formulas

1. Click the cell containing the formula.
2. Point to the *Fill Handle* in the lower right corner of the cell.
3. Click and drag the fill pointer to the adjacent cells (see Figure 1-23).

Edit the Formula Cell Range

As you edit worksheet structure and contents, it may be necessary to adjust the cell range in a formula. You can edit the cell range using the *Formula bar* or by dragging the border that surrounds a range of cells. Remember that a cell displays the result of the formula and the ***Formula bar*** displays the formula.

You can also edit a cell reference or the cell range in a formula by dragging the border to reduce or expand the range. When dragging to include more or fewer cells, you will see a two-pointed arrow (resize pointer) when you point to a selection handle on the border.

HOW TO: Edit a Cell Reference Range Using the Formula Bar

1. Select the cell containing the formula.
2. Click the cell range displayed in the *Formula bar*. The range is highlighted, and a border displays around the cell range (Figure 1-24).
3. Edit the cell range.
4. Press **Enter**.

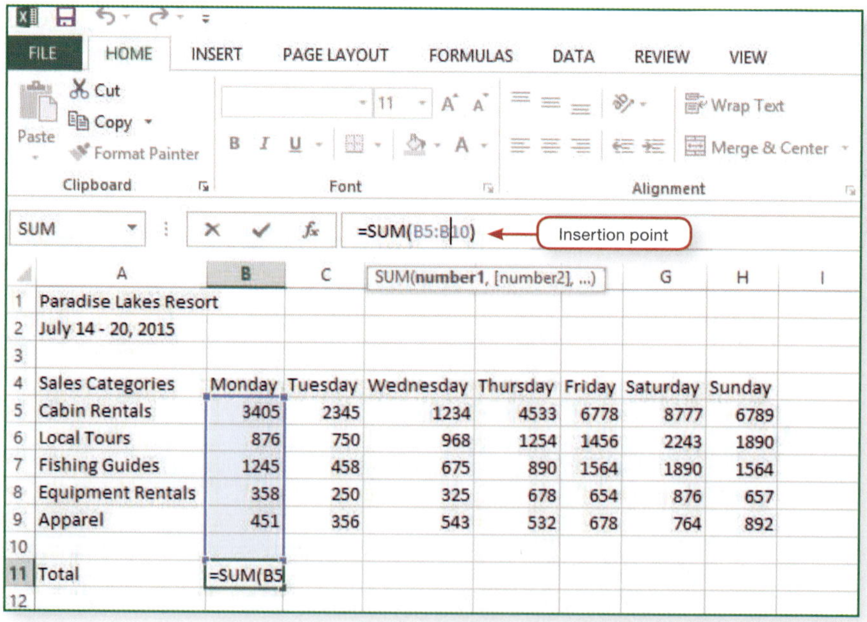

1-24 Editing the cell range in the *Formula bar*

HOW TO: Edit a Formula Cell Range by Dragging

1. Double-click the cell containing the formula.
2. Drag the border handle in the lower right corner to expand or contract the border (Figure 1-25).
3. Press **Enter** to complete the edit.
   - Click the **Enter** button on the *Formula bar* to complete an entry.

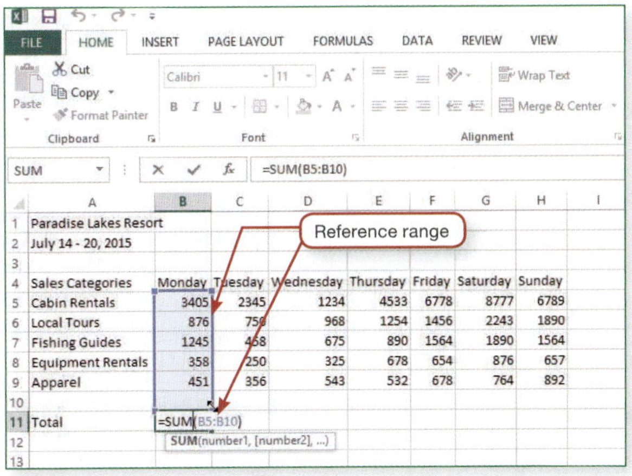

1-25 Edit a cell reference range by dragging

SLO 1.4

Formatting a Worksheet

There are a variety of ways you can change the appearance of your worksheet. You can apply font attributes and add borders, or you can apply a format using ***cell styles***. ***Themes*** provide consistency in format and help you create professional-looking workbooks.

Font Face, Size, Style, and Color

A font is a type design applied to an entire set of characters including the alphabet, numbers, punctuation marks, and other keyboard symbols. *Font size* describes the size of text and is measured in points. There are 72 points in one inch. *Font style* is the weight or angle of text, such as **bold**, underline, or *italic text*. *Font color* refers to the color of the characters. You can change the font attributes in a single cell, a group of cells, a worksheet, or an entire workbook.

The default font attributes for Excel 2013 workbooks are:

- ***Font:*** Calibri
- ***Font Size:*** 11 pt.
- ***Font Color:*** Black, Text 1

MORE INFO

The *Font* drop-down list has two sections: *Theme Fonts* and *All Fonts*.

HOW TO: Customize Font, Style, Font Size, and Font Color

1. Select the cell or range of cells to be formatted and choose an option from the *Font* group [*Home* tab] (Figure 1-26).
2. Click the **Font** drop-down list and select a font.
3. Click the **Font Size** drop-down list and select a font size or type a font size in the *Font Size* area.
   - You can also click the **Increase Font Size** or **Decrease Font Size** buttons to change the font size.
4. Click **Bold**, **Italic**, or **Underline** to apply one or more font styles.
5. Click the **Font Color** drop-down list [*Home* tab, *Font* group] and select a color.
   - Click the **Font Color** button (left of the drop-down arrow) to apply the last font color selected.

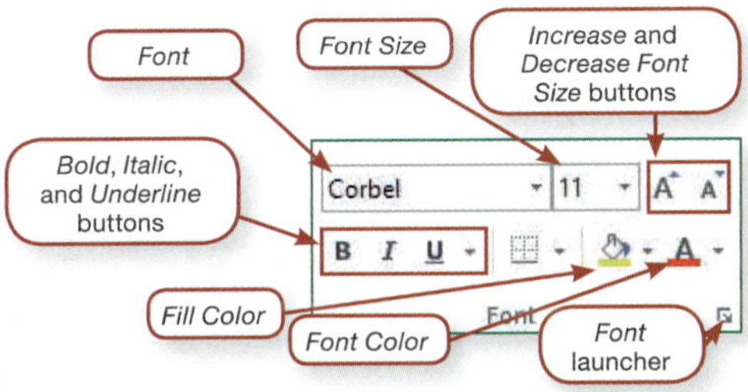

1-26 *Font* group on the *Home* tab

You can also apply font formats using one of the following methods:

- ***Mini toolbar:*** Right-click a cell or range of cells to display the mini toolbar (Figure 1-27).
- ***Format Cells dialog box:*** Click the **Font** launcher in the bottom right corner of the *Font* group on the *Home* tab or press **Ctrl+1** (Figure 1-28).
- ***Context menu:*** Right-click a cell or range of cells and select **Format Cells**.
- Keyboard shortcuts
  Bold: **Ctrl+B**
  Italic: **Ctrl+I**
  Underline: **Ctrl+U**

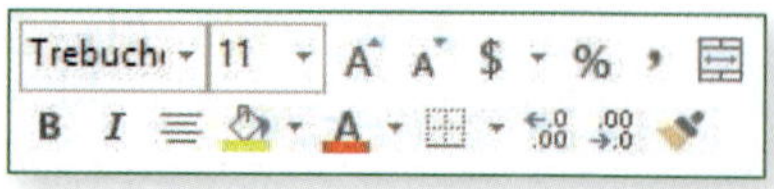

1-27 Mini toolbar

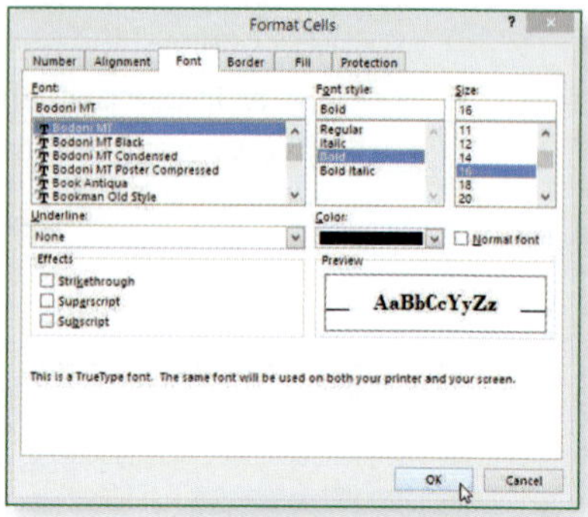

1-28 *Format Cells* dialog box

Format Painter

The ***Format Painter*** option allows you to copy formatting attributes and styles from one cell to another cell or group of cells. This method is a quick and easy way to apply a consistent look to worksheet data.

HOW TO: Use the Format Painter Button

1. Select the cell that contains the formatting you want to copy.
2. Click **Format Painter** [*Home* tab, *Clipboard* group].
3. Select the cell(s) where you want to apply the copied format (Figure 1-29).
   - The *Format Painter* automatically turns off after you apply the copied format one time.
   - To apply formatting to multiple areas, double-click **Format Painter**, apply the copied format to multiple areas, and click **Format Painter** again to turn off the option. You can also press **Esc** to cancel copying format.

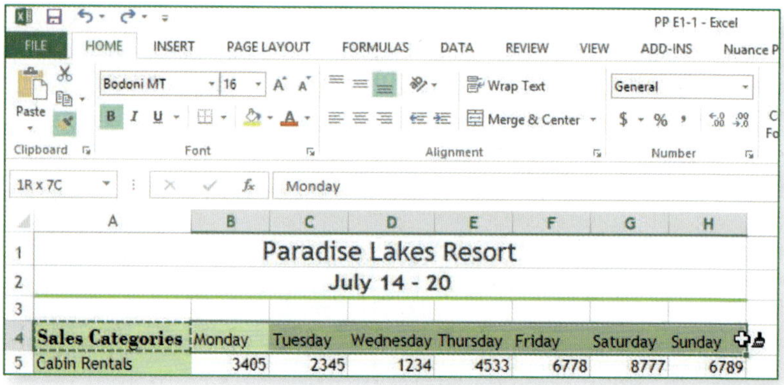

1-29 Copy formats to a range using *Format Painter*

Number Formats

In addition to text formatting, you can apply various number formats to cells so the numbers in your worksheet are clear and easy to understand. Common numeric formats used in worksheets include *Currency, Accounting,* and *Percentage.* You can also specify the number of decimal places a number displays by using the *Increase Decimal* or *Decrease Decimal* button. Open the *Format Cells* dialog box to customize number formatting. For example, the *Currency* format includes options to specify the number of decimal places, apply the $ symbol or no symbol, and control the appearance of negative numbers.

HOW TO: Format Numbers

1. Select the cell range you want to format.
2. Click one of the numeric format buttons [*Home* tab, *Number* group] (Figure 1-30) or click the **Number Format** drop-down list and select an option.
3. Click **Increase Decimal** or **Decrease Decimal** to specify the number of decimal places after the whole number.
   - If pound signs (###) appear in any cell, it means your column is not wide enough to accommodate the entry. Adjusting column width is covered in *SLO 1.5: Editing Columns and Rows*.

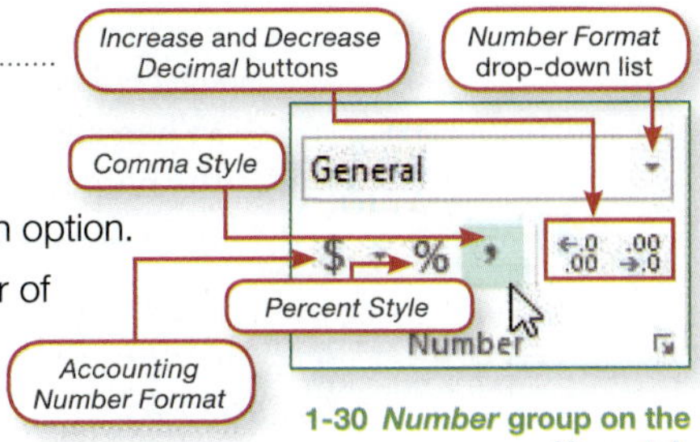

1-30 *Number* group on the *Home* tab

> **MORE INFO**
>
> Click the **Number** launcher [*Home* tab, *Number* group] or press **Ctrl+1** to open the *Format Cells* dialog box where you can further customize a number format.

Borders and Shading

You can apply borders to a worksheet to place lines under headings, to show totals, or to group information. Use shading (or fill) to apply a background color or pattern to cells. You can use the *Ribbon* or *Format Cells* dialog box to apply a border or shading to selected cells.

HOW TO: Add Borders and Shading Using the Ribbon

1. Select the cell or range of cells to be formatted.
2. Click the arrow next to the *Borders* button [*Home* tab, *Font* group] and select a border option from the *Borders* drop-down list (Figure 1-31).
   - The *Borders* button displays the most recently used border style.
   - To remove a cell border, choose the **No Border** option from the *Borders* drop-down list.
3. Click the arrow next to the *Fill Color* button [*Home* tab, *Font* group] and select a background color (Figure 1-32).
   - Click **More Colors** to apply a custom color.
   - Click the **Fill Color** button to apply the most recently selected color.
   - To remove cell shading, click the arrow next to *Fill Color* and then select **No Fill**.

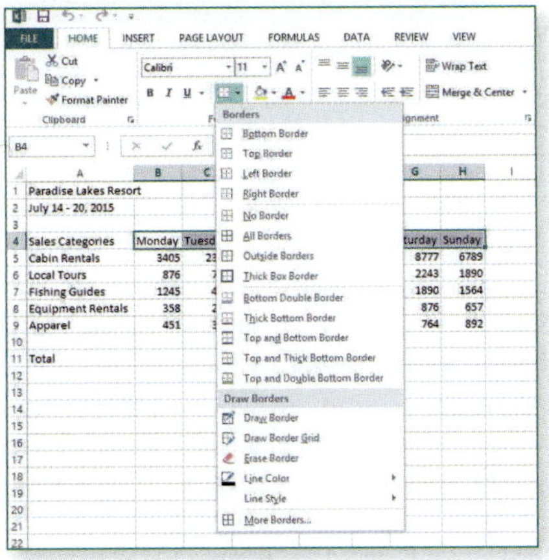

1-31 *Borders* drop-down list

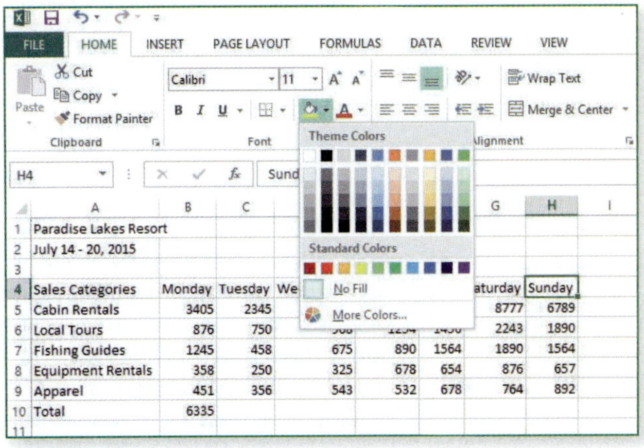

1-32 *Fill Color* palette

The *Format Cells* dialog box includes a tab for defining borders and applying a fill to selected cells. Each tab provides more borders and fill color choices than the *Ribbon* does. When creating a border design, select the border color and border line style before you apply the border to a preset or custom location. When selecting a solid or pattern fill, consider the content of the cell and whether readability will be affected.

HOW TO: Add Borders and Shading Using the Format Cells Dialog Box

1. Select the cell or range of cells to be formatted.
2. Click the **Font** launcher [*Home* tab, *Font* group] or press **Ctrl+1** to display the *Format Cells* dialog box.
3. Click the **Border** tab (Figure 1-33).
4. Select a line style in the *Style* area.
5. Choose a color from the *Color* drop-down list.
6. Click **Outline** in the *Presets* area to apply an outside border.
   - The *Preview* area displays the change.
7. Click **None** to remove the border.
8. Set individual borders by clicking a button in the *Border* area.
9. Click the **Fill** tab (Figure 1-34).
10. Select a color under *Background Color*.
    - To create a pattern with two colors, click a color in the *Pattern Color* box.
    - To create a gradient special effect, click **Fill Effects**, and select color and shading options.
11. Click a pattern style in the *Pattern Style* box.
12. Click **OK** to close the *Format Cells* dialog box.

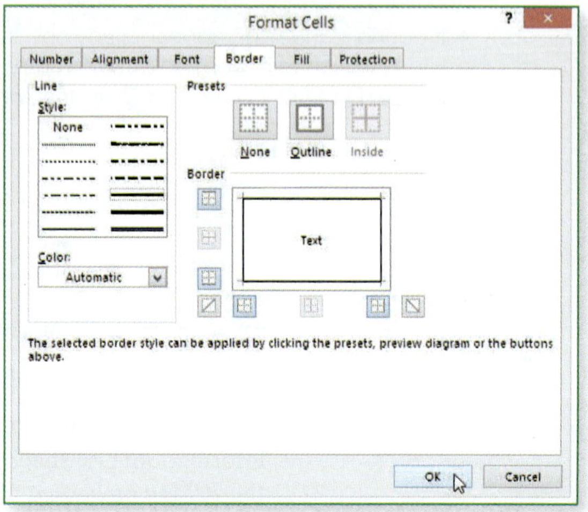

1-33 ***Border* tab in the *Format Cells* dialog box**

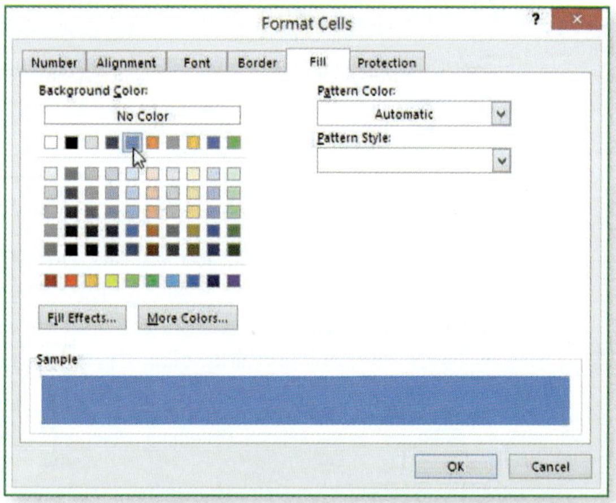

1-34 ***Fill* tab in the *Format Cells* dialog box**

Cell Styles

Cell Styles are a set of predefined formatting you can apply to titles, subtitles, column headings, row totals, and other areas of your worksheet. Styles apply formatting to the text, background, and border of a cell. You can also create your own cell styles to include specific character formatting, numeric formatting, borders, shading, or alignment. If you plan to use a *Cell Style*, apply the cell style before changing individual font attributes because the *Cell Style* overwrites other formats. Your screen may differ from the figures in this section. If you do not see a style gallery, click the **Cell Styles** button.

HOW TO: Apply Cell Styles to a Range of Cells

1. Select the cell or cell range where you want to apply a *Cell Style*.
2. Click the **More** button or the **Cell Styles** button [*Home* tab, *Styles* group] to display the *Cell Styles* gallery (Figure 1-35).
3. Select a style to apply to the selected cell(s) (Figure 1-36).
   - When you position your pointer on a *Cell Style* in the *Cell Styles* gallery, Excel provides a live preview of the style by temporarily applying the style to the selected cell(s).

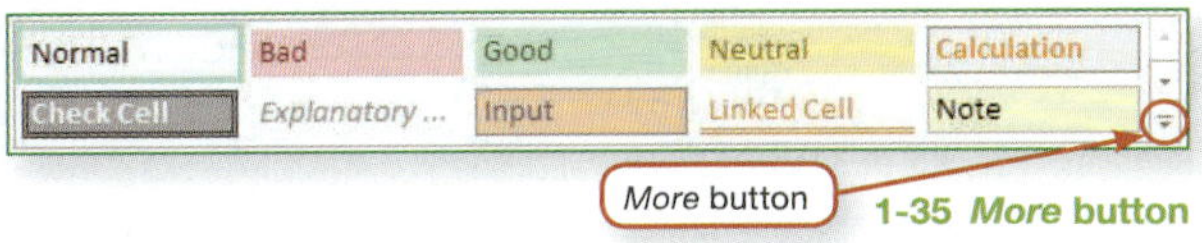

1-35 *More* button

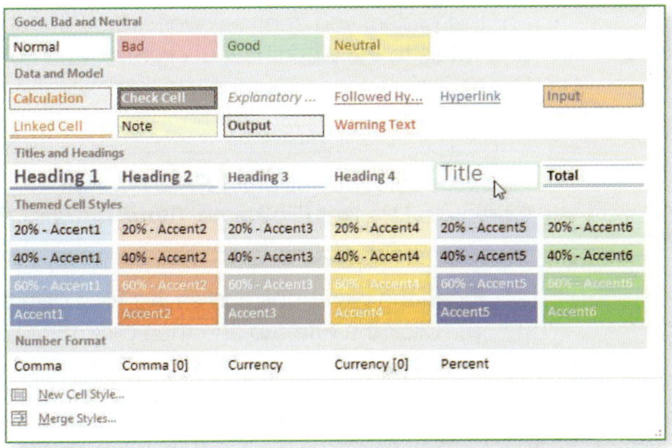

1-36 *Cell Syles* gallery

Workbook Themes

Applying a ***theme*** to a workbook formats a workbook quickly and applies a consistent design to the entire workbook. Themes include three combined elements: colors, fonts, and effects. The *Themes* gallery includes several themes to format a workbook; the default theme is called ***Office***. Themes can be customized, and you can individually change ***theme colors***, ***theme fonts***, or ***theme effects***. Additional themes are available online.

HOW TO: Apply Themes to a Workbook

1. Open the workbook.
2. Click the **Theme** button [*Page Layout* tab, *Themes* group] to display the *Themes* gallery (Figure 1-37).
   - Place your pointer on a theme to temporarily apply a live preview of the theme in your workbook.
3. Select a theme to apply to a workbook.
   - You can individually apply theme colors, theme fonts, or theme effects by clicking the **Colors**, **Fonts**, and **Effects** buttons [*Page Layout* tab, *Themes* group] and selecting from the drop-down lists.

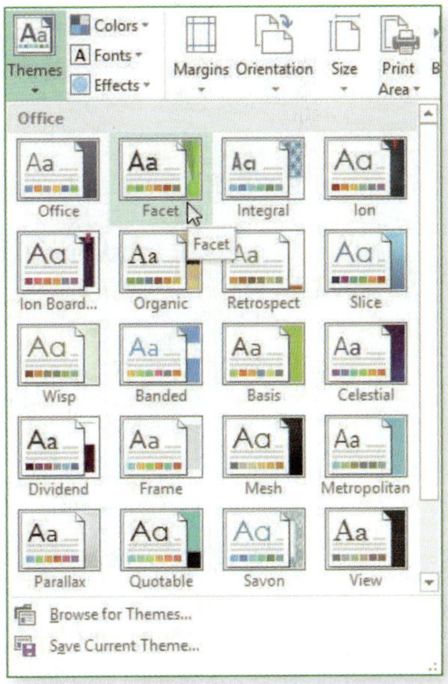

1-37 *Themes* gallery

MORE INFO

Themes change the colors that are available in a workbook. Place your pointer over each button in the *Themes* group on the *Page Layout* tab to view the current theme.

PAUSE & PRACTICE: EXCEL 1-2

For this project you continue working on the spreadsheet you created in *Pause & Practice Excel 1-1*. You add totals to the worksheet using *Sum* and copy formulas using *AutoFill*. You also format the spreadsheet. Formatting changes you apply in this exercise may cause the spreadsheet data to appear crowded or missing. You will adjust column width for the spreadsheet in Student Learning Objective 1.5.

File Needed: ***[your initials] PP E1-1.xlsx***
Completed Project File Name: ***[your initials] PP E1-2.xlsx***

1. Open the workbook and save it as a different name.
   a. Click the **File** tab and then click the **Open** button.
   b. Locate the folder where your files are saved.
   c. Open the workbook ***[your initials] PP E1-1***.
   d. Press **F12** to open the *Save As* dialog box.
   e. Locate the folder where your files are saved.
   f. Save the workbook as ***[your initials] PP E1-2***.
2. Calculate daily totals using *Sum*.
   a. Click cell **B10**.
   b. Click the **AutoSum** button [*Home* tab, *Editing* group].
   c. Press **Enter** to complete the formula.
3. Copy a formula across cells using the *Fill Handle*.
   a. Click cell **B10**.
   b. Point to the *Fill Handle* in the lower right corner of the cell.
   c. Click and drag to cell **H10** (Figure 1-38).

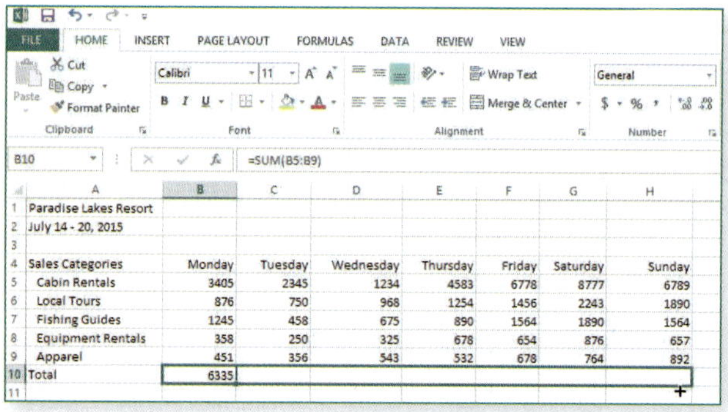

1-38 Copying a formula

4. Calculate sales category totals.
   a. Click cell **J5**.
   b. Double-click the **AutoSum** button [*Home* tab, *Editing* group].
5. Edit the cell reference range to remove the blank cell reference.
   a. Click cell **J5**.
   b. Click the cell range **B5:I5** in the *Formula bar* (Figure 1-39).

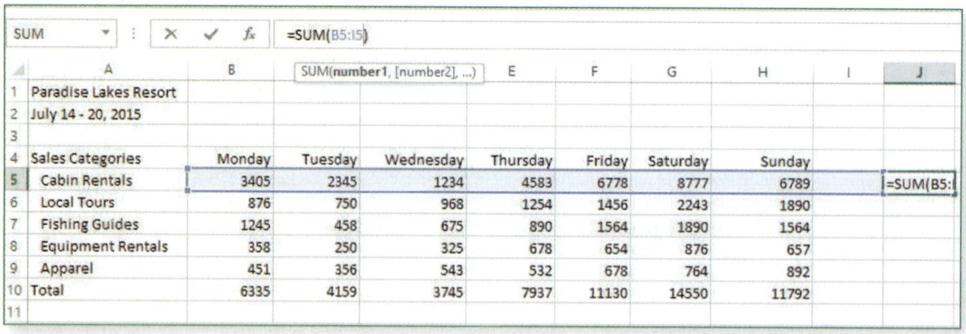

1-39 Edit cell reference in *Formula bar*

c. Change the cell range to **B5:H5**.
d. Press **Enter**.

6. Copy a formula down using the *Fill Handle*.
   a. Select **J5**.
   b. Point to the *Fill Handle* in the lower right corner of the cell.
   c. Click and drag to **J10**.

7. Apply *Cell Styles*.
   a. Select **A1** and then click the **More** button or the **Cell Styles** button [*Home* tab, *Styles* group] to display the *Styles* gallery (Figure 1-40).

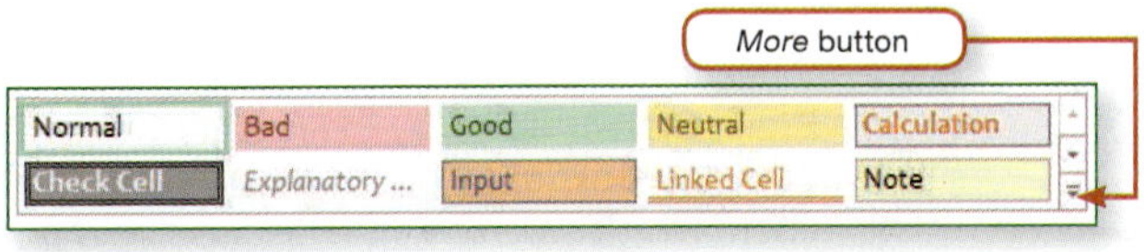

1-40 *More* button

   b. Locate the *Titles and Headings* category and select **Title**.
   c. Select **A2** and click the **More** button or the **Cell Styles** button [*Home* tab, *Styles* group].
   d. Locate the *Titles and Headings* category and select **Heading 2**.
   e. Drag to select **A10:H10** and then click the **More** button [*Home* tab, *Styles* group].
   f. Select **Total** in the *Titles and Headings* category.
   g. Select **A4:A9**, hold down and press **Ctrl**, and then select **B4:H4**.
   h. Click the **More** button [*Home* tab, *Styles* group].
   i. Select **20%**, **Accent 1** in the *Themed Cell Styles* category.

8. Apply themes.
   a. Click the **Themes** button [*Page Layout* tab, *Themes* group], and choose **Facet** from the gallery.
   b. Click the **Theme Fonts** button [*Page Layout* tab, *Themes* group] and select **Candara** from the gallery.

9. Apply font attributes to cell A4.
   a. Select **A4** and click the **Home** tab.
   b. Click the **Font** drop-down list [*Font* group], and select **Bodoni MT** in the *All Fonts* section.
   c. Click the **Font Size** drop-down list and select **16 pt**.
   d. Click the **Bold** button.
   e. Click the **Font Color** button and select **Blue-Grey**, **Text 2**, **Darker 50%** (fourth column, last row). Drag column heading border to widen if needed.

10. Apply font attributes to cells A1:A2.
   a. Select **A1:A2**.
   b. Click the **Font Color** button [*Home* tab, *Font* group].
   c. Select **Green**, **Accent 1**, **Darker 50%** (fifth column, last row in the *Theme Colors* category).

11. Apply font attributes to the cell range A5:H10.
   a. Select **A5:H10**.
   b. Change the font to **Arial Narrow** [*Home* tab, *Font* group, *Font*].
   c. Click the **Font Size** drop-down arrow and choose **12 pt**.

12. Use the *Format Painter* button to apply the formatting in A4 to the cell range B4:H4.
   a. Click **A4**.
   b. Double-click **Format Painter** [*Home* tab, *Clipboard* group] to turn on the option.
   c. Select the range **B4:H4** by clicking and dragging your pointer or select each cell in the range.
   d. Click **Format Painter** [*Home* tab, *Clipboard* group] to turn off the option.

13. Apply numeric formatting and align text.
   a. Select **B5:H9**.
   b. Click **Comma Style** [*Home* tab, *Number* group].
   c. Select **B10:H10**.
   d. Click the **Accounting Number Format** button [*Home* tab, *Number* group].

e. Select **B4:H4**.
f. Click **Align Right** [*Home* tab, *Alignment* group].

14. Delete text.
    a. Select the cell range **J5:J10**.
    b. Press **Delete**.
15. Add a bottom border and an outside border.
    a. Select cells **A1:H10**.
    b. Press **Ctrl+1** to display the *Format Cells* dialog box.
    c. Click the **Border** tab.
    d. Click a thick solid line style (second column, fifth style).
    e. Click the **Color** drop-down list, and select **Black** (Automatic).
    f. Click **Outline** in the *Presets* area.
    g. Click **OK** to close the *Format Cells* dialog box.
    h. Select **A4:H4**.
    i. Click the **Border** button drop-down list [*Home* tab, *Font* group] (Figure 1-41).
    j. Select **Bottom Border**.

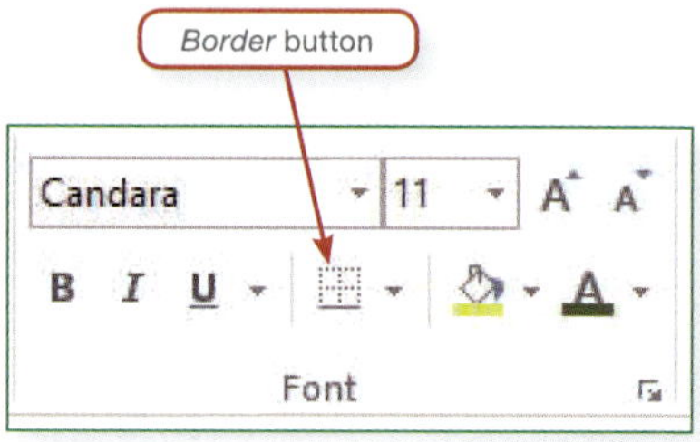

1-41 *Border* button

16. Press **Ctrl+S** to save the workbook (Figure 1-42). You can also save the workbook by clicking the **Save** button on the *Quick Access* toolbar or in *Backstage* view.

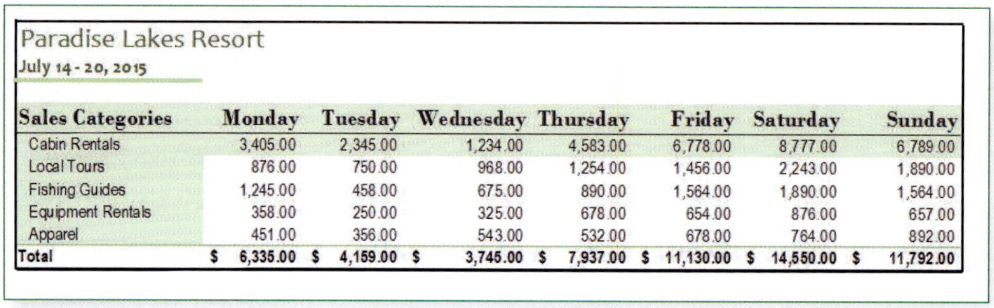

Paradise Lakes Resort
July 14 - 20, 2015

Sales Categories	Monday	Tuesday	Wednesday	Thursday	Friday	Saturday	Sunday
Cabin Rentals	3,405.00	2,345.00	1,234.00	4,583.00	6,778.00	8,777.00	6,789.00
Local Tours	876.00	750.00	968.00	1,254.00	1,456.00	2,243.00	1,890.00
Fishing Guides	1,245.00	458.00	675.00	890.00	1,564.00	1,890.00	1,564.00
Equipment Rentals	358.00	250.00	325.00	678.00	654.00	876.00	657.00
Apparel	451.00	356.00	543.00	532.00	678.00	764.00	892.00
Total	$ 6,335.00	$ 4,159.00	$ 3,745.00	$ 7,937.00	$ 11,130.00	$ 14,550.00	$ 11,792.00

1-42 PP E1-2 completed

17. Click the **File** tab and click **Close**, or press **Ctrl+W** to close the workbook.

SLO 1.5

Editing Columns and Rows

There are many ways to control the display of data within each column and row. Often the default column width and row height settings of Excel do not fit the requirements of the cell contents and require adjustment. You may also want to hide columns or rows containing sensitive data such as employee salaries. This section teaches you how to adjust column width and row height, as well as how to insert, delete, hide, and unhide columns and rows.

MORE INFO

Excel 2013 has 16,384 columns and 1,048,576 rows.

Adjust Column Width and Row Height

The default setting for each column is 8.43 characters. This number represents the number of characters that are viewable within the cell in the default font. You may change this width to any value between 0 and 255 characters. The default height of each row is 15 points. There are several ways to edit column width or row height, including dragging column or row heading borders, displaying the context menu, or selecting options from the *Format* drop-down list [*Home* tab, *Cells* group]. When you adjust column width or row height, the entire column or row changes.

HOW TO: Change Column Width or Row Height

1. Select a cell in the column or row you want to adjust.
   - To apply the same column width or row height to multiple columns or rows, select multiple columns or rows.
2. Click the **Format** button [*Home* tab, *Cells* group] and select **Row Height** or **Column Width** from the drop-down list to open the *Row Height* or *Column Width* dialog box (Figure 1-43).
3. Enter the desired height or width.
4. Click **OK** to close the dialog box.

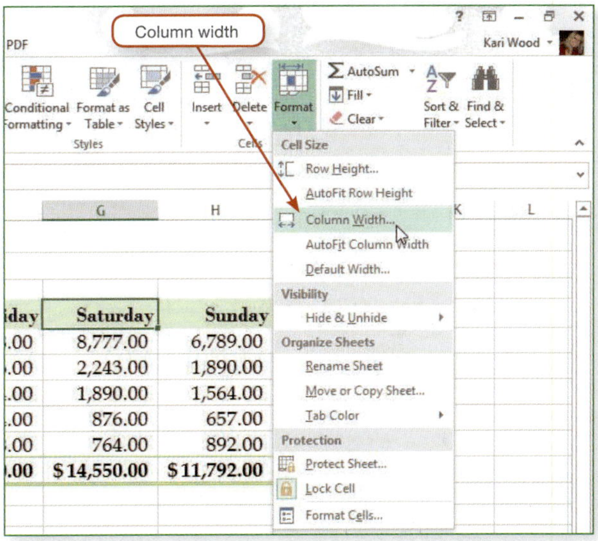

1-43 ***Format* button drop-down list**

ANOTHER WAY

To apply the same column width or row height to multiple columns or rows, select the columns or rows and right-click. Choose **Column Width** or **Row Height** from the context menu. Enter the new measurement and click **OK**.

MORE INFO

You can change the default sheet settings for column width by selecting the sheet tab or tabs, clicking **Format** [*Home* tab, *Cells* group], and selecting **Default Width** in the *Cell Size* category. Enter the new width for the selected sheets.

AutoFit Columns and Rows

The ***AutoFit*** feature resizes column width or row height to accommodate the width or height of the largest entry. You can use the *Format* button in the *Cells* group on the *Home* tab, or the context menu to *AutoFit* columns and rows. Another way to *AutoFit* a column is to double-click the right border of the column heading. When you point to the border, the pointer changes to a *sizing pointer* (Figure 1-44). To *AutoFit* a row, double-click the bottom border of the row heading.

HOW TO: Change Column Width or Row Height Using AutoFit

1. Select the columns or rows to adjust.
2. Click **Format** [*Home* tab, *Cells* group].
3. Click **AutoFit Column Width** or **AutoFit Row Height** (see Figure 1-44).

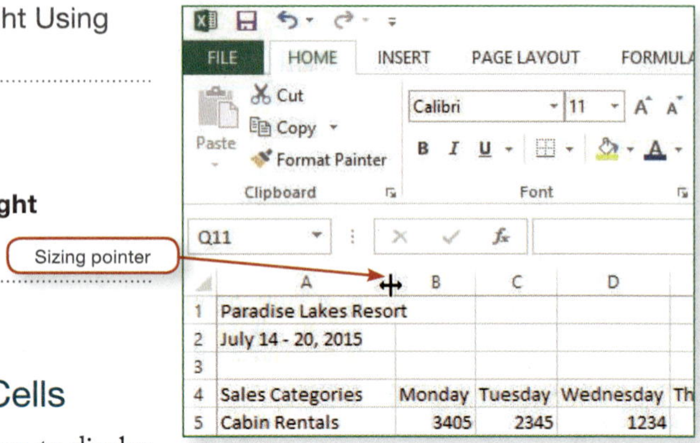

1-44 Double-click a column border to *AutoFit* column contents

Wrap Text and Merge Cells

The ***Wrap Text*** feature enables you to display the contents of a cell on multiple lines. You can format the cell to wrap text automatically, or you can enter a manual line break by pressing **Alt+Enter**. The cell contents wrap to fit the width of the column. If the text is not visible, it may be necessary to adjust the row height.

HOW TO: Wrap Text in a Cell

1. Select the cells to format.
2. Click the **Home** tab.
3. Click the **Wrap Text** button [*Alignment* group] (Figure 1-45).

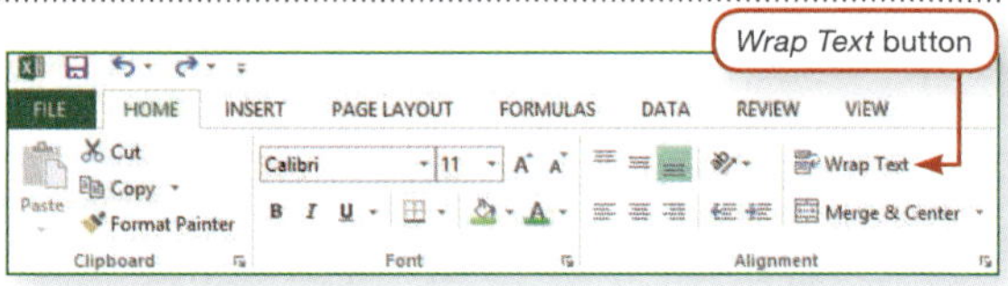

1-45 *Wrap Text* button

ANOTHER WAY

Double-click a cell or press **F2** to activate edit mode in a cell and click to position the insertion point where you want to break the line. Press **Alt+Enter**.

The ***Merge & Center*** command combines two or more cells into one cell and centers the text. This feature is useful for centering worksheet titles over multiple columns. Before you merge cells, be sure the data appears in the upper-left cell. All data included in any other selected cell will be overwritten during the merge process.

HOW TO: Merge and Center

1. Select the cells you want to merge and center.
2. Click the **Home** tab.
3. Click the **Merge & Center** button [*Alignment* group] (Figure 1-46).

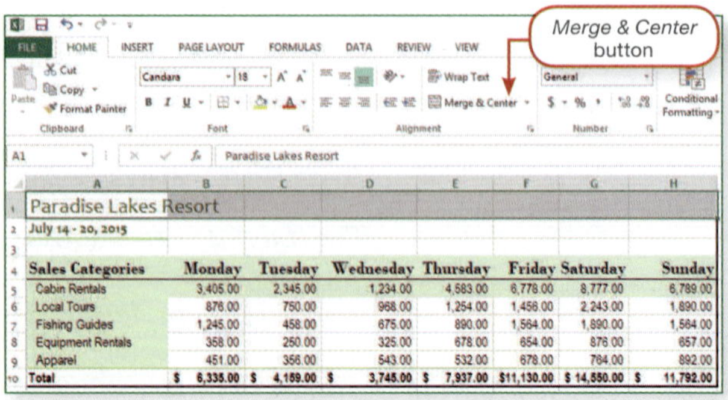

1-46 Select cells to merge and center

To merge cells without centering text, click the arrow next to *Merge & Center,* and choose **Merge Across** or **Merge Cells**. To unmerge cells, click the **Merge & Center** button or click the **Merge & Center** drop-down list and choose **Unmerge Cells**.

> **MORE INFO**
>
> Use the ***Undo*** button on the *Quick Access* toolbar or press **Ctrl+Z** to undo single or multiple actions.

Insert and Delete Columns and Rows

There are times when you need to insert or delete a row or column of information in your spreadsheet. For example, you can insert a row for an additional sales category or you might want to combine Saturday and Sunday sales figures into one column and delete the extra column. When you insert or delete columns and rows, Excel automatically shifts cells to make room for the new cells or fills the gap for deleted cells.

HOW TO: Insert Columns or Rows

1. Select a cell in the column that is to the right of where you want to insert a column, or click the row immediately below the row where you want to insert a new row.
2. Click the bottom half of the **Insert** button [*Home* tab, *Cells* group].
3. Select **Insert Sheet Rows** to add a row (Figure 1-47).
   - The new row appears directly above the originally selected row.

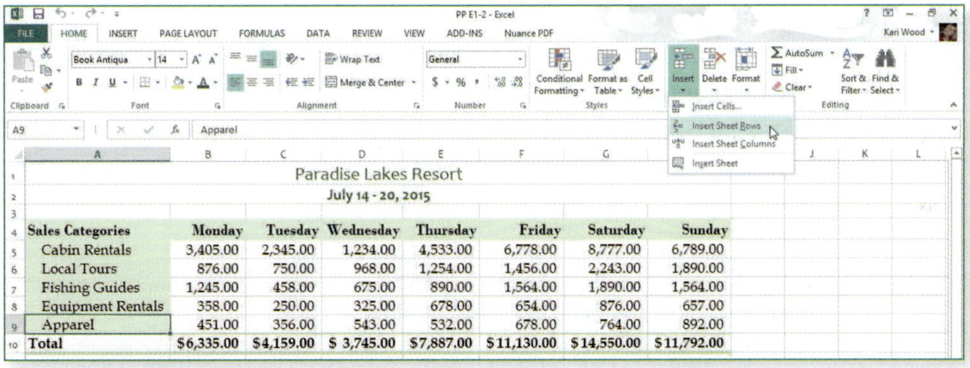

1-47 Insert a row

4. Select **Insert Sheet Columns** to add a column.
   - The new column appears directly to the left of the column you originally selected.
5. Select an individual cell and click the top half of the *Insert* button to insert a single cell rather than an entire row.
6. Select an entire column or row and click the top half of the *Insert* button to insert a column or row. To insert multiple columns or rows, select the number of columns or rows you want to insert.

> **ANOTHER WAY**
>
> To insert a column or row, select a column heading or row heading, right-click, and select **Insert** from the context menu. An alternative is to select column(s) or row(s), and press **Ctrl+plus sign** (+) on the numeric keypad.

When you delete a column or row, the contents in the cells of that column or row are deleted. Remaining columns and rows shift to the left or up after a deletion.

HOW TO: Delete Columns or Rows

1. Select a cell in the column or row you want to delete.
2. Click the bottom half of the **Delete** button [*Home* tab, *Cells* group].
3. Select **Delete Sheet Rows** to remove a row (Figure 1-48).
   - All the remaining rows below the deleted row shift up.

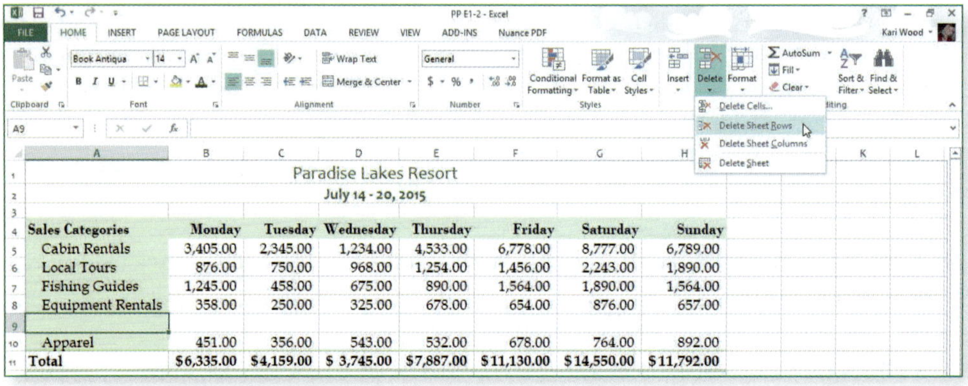

1-48 Delete a row

4. Select **Delete Sheet Columns** to remove a column.
   - All remaining columns to the right of the deleted column shift to the left.
5. Select an individual cell and click the top half of the *Delete* button to delete a cell rather than an entire row.
6. Select an entire column or row and click the top half of the *Delete* button to delete the column or row.

> **MORE INFO**
>
> Delete or insert single cells by choosing **Insert Cells** from the *Insert* drop-down list or **Delete Cells** from the *Delete* drop-down list [*Home* tab, *Cells* group].

Hide and Unhide Columns and Rows

If there is sensitive data in a worksheet, you may want to hide it before sharing the worksheet with others. Hiding a column or row does not delete the information in the worksheet nor does it affect the results of calculations. After hiding a column or row, you can unhide it so it again displays in the worksheet.

HOW TO: Hide and Unhide Columns or Rows

1. Select the column or row (or a cell in the column or row) you want to hide.
   - The hide feature applies to an entire column or row, not individual cells.
   - You can select multiple columns or rows to hide.
2. Click the **Format** button [*Home* tab, *Cells* group] and select **Hide & Unhide** in the *Visibility* category.

3. Select **Hide Columns** or **Hide Rows**.
   - When a column or row is hidden, there is a small gap between the letters in column headings or numbers in row headings indicating that the column or row is hidden.
   - Column or row headings are not lettered or numbered consecutively when a column or row is hidden.
4. To unhide a column or row, select the columns to the left and right of the hidden column or select the rows above and below the hidden row.
5. Click the **Format** button and select **Hide & Unhide** in the *Visibility* category (Figure 1-49).

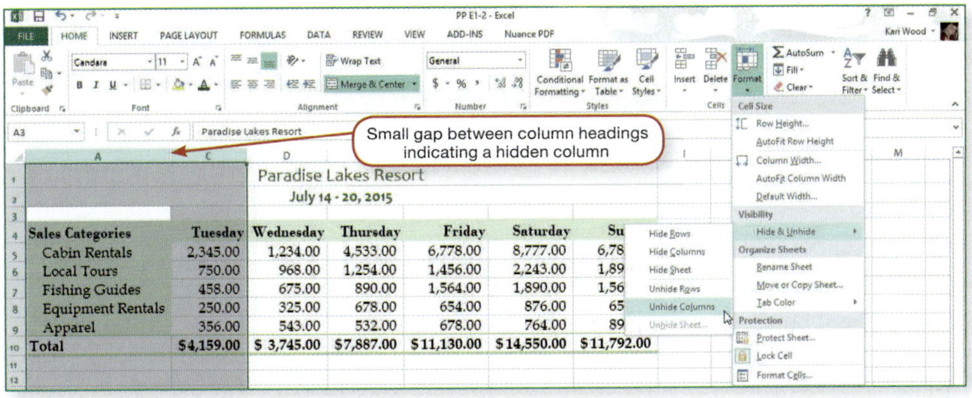

1-49 Unhide a column

6. Select **Unhide Columns** or **Unhide Rows** to display the hidden column or row.

ANOTHER WAY

Ctrl+9 hides selected rows.
Ctrl+Shift+(unhides hidden rows from a selection.
Ctrl+0 hides selected columns.

MORE INFO

To hide or unhide multiple columns or rows, select the columns or rows, right-click one of the selected columns or rows, and choose **Hide** or **Unhide** from the context menu.

SLO 1.6

Customizing Worksheets

An Excel workbook consists of one or more worksheets (or sheets), and each worksheet has a ***worksheet tab*** near the bottom left of the Excel window that displays the name of the worksheet.

The number of worksheets you can insert in a workbook is limited only by the amount of memory available on your computer. By default each workbook contains one sheet. Excel provides options to insert additional sheets, delete unwanted sheets, rename sheets, and change the tab color of sheets. Also, you may want to hide sheets if sensitive data should not be available to others. In this section, you learn to format, name, insert, delete, copy, rearrange, hide, and unhide worksheet tabs.

Insert and Delete Worksheets

There are times when you need to insert a worksheet to store additional information in your workbook. When there is more than one worksheet in a workbook, you select a worksheet by clicking the worksheet tab. There are multiple ways to both insert and delete worksheets. Inserted worksheets are automatically named.

> **MORE INFO**
>
> Press **Ctrl+Page Down** to move to the next worksheet. Press **Ctrl+Page Up** to move to the previous worksheet.

HOW TO: Insert and Delete Worksheets

1-50 ***New Sheet*** **button**

1. Select a cell in the current worksheet.
2. To insert a worksheet, use one of the following methods:
   - Click the **New Sheet** button (plus sign) to the right of the existing worksheet tabs (Figure 1-50).
   - Click the bottom half of the **Insert** button [*Home* tab, *Cells* group] and select **Insert Sheet** (Figure 1-51).
   - Right-click a worksheet tab and select **Insert** from the context menu to open the *Insert* dialog box. Select **Worksheet** and click **OK**.
3. To delete a worksheet from a workbook, click the bottom half of the **Delete** button [*Home* tab, *Cells* group] and select **Delete Sheet** to remove the active worksheet.
   - Alternatively, you can right-click the worksheet tab and select **Delete** from the context menu.

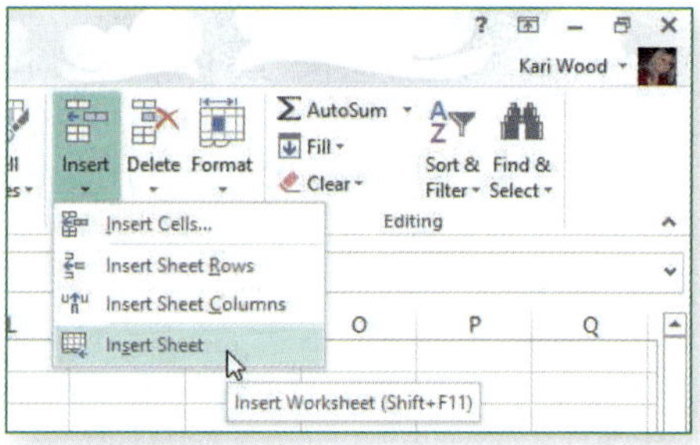

1-51 ***Insert*** **button: Adding a new worksheet**

> **ANOTHER WAY**
>
> Press **Shift+F11** to insert a new worksheet.

> **MORE INFO**
>
> To delete or insert multiple worksheets, click the worksheet tabs while pressing **Ctrl**, right-click one of the selected worksheet tabs, and choose **Delete** or **Insert** from the context menu.

Rename Worksheets and Change Tab Color

The default names for the sheets within a workbook are *Sheet1, Sheet2,* and so on. After adding worksheets to a workbook, you might want to ***rename*** each worksheet with a more meaningful name. The size of the sheet tab adjusts to fit the name. You can also apply a ***tab color*** to further distinguish each worksheet. There is no default color for worksheet tabs.

HOW TO: Rename a Worksheet and Apply a Tab Color

1. Right-click the worksheet tab and choose **Rename** from the context menu (Figure 1-52).
2. Type the new name on the worksheet tab and press **Enter**.
   - You can also click the **Format** button [*Home* tab, *Cells* group] and select **Rename Sheet**.
3. Right-click the worksheet tab, choose **Tab Color** from the context menu, and select a color to apply to the background of the worksheet tab.
   - When a worksheet tab is active (selected), it displays as a light version of the tab color, and when a worksheet is not active, it displays the tab color (Figure 1-53).
   - You can also apply a tab color to the active worksheet by clicking the **Format** button, selecting **Tab Color**, and then choosing a color.

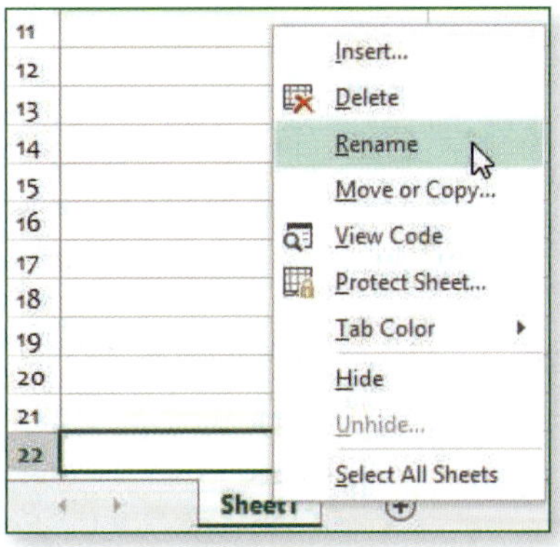

1-52 Rename a worksheet

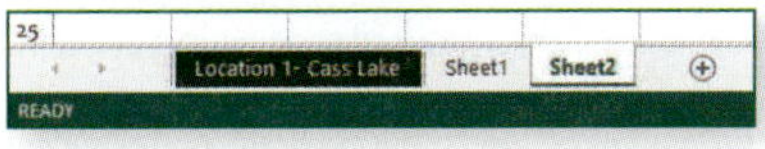

1-53 Tab color applied to a worksheet

MORE INFO

To color multiple sheet tabs in a workbook the same color at the same time, select the sheet tabs you want to apply the color to, right-click one of the selected sheet tabs, and choose **Tab Color** from the context menu.

ANOTHER WAY

Rename a sheet tab by double-clicking the sheet tab name, typing the new name, and pressing **Enter**.

Move and Copy Worksheets

You can use the move feature to change the order of worksheets within a workbook or to move worksheets to a different workbook. The copy feature saves time by eliminating the need to reenter data. If you need to move or copy a worksheet a short distance, use the drag and drop method. Otherwise, use move, copy, and paste.

HOW TO: Move Worksheets

1. Right-click the worksheet tab you want to move.
2. Select **Move or Copy** from the context menu (Figure 1-54). The *Move or Copy* dialog box opens (Figure 1-55).
   - Alernatively, you can click the **Format** button [*Home* tab, *Cells* group] and select **Move or Copy Sheet**.
   - To move or copy the selected worksheet into a workbook other than the current one, select a different workbook from the *To book* drop-down list.
   - If you are moving a worksheet between workbooks, the destination workbook must be open prior to opening the *Move* or *Copy* dialog box.
3. Locate the *Before sheet* area, and select the worksheet that the active sheet will precede when it is moved.
4. Deselect the **Create a copy** check box if it is checked.
5. Click **OK** to close the dialog box.

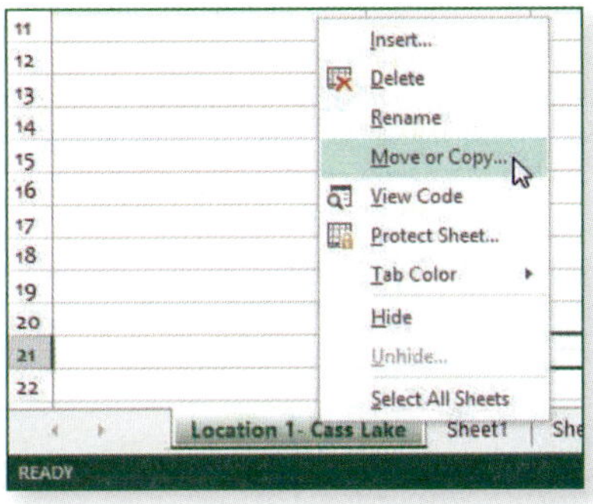

1-54 Move or copy a worksheet

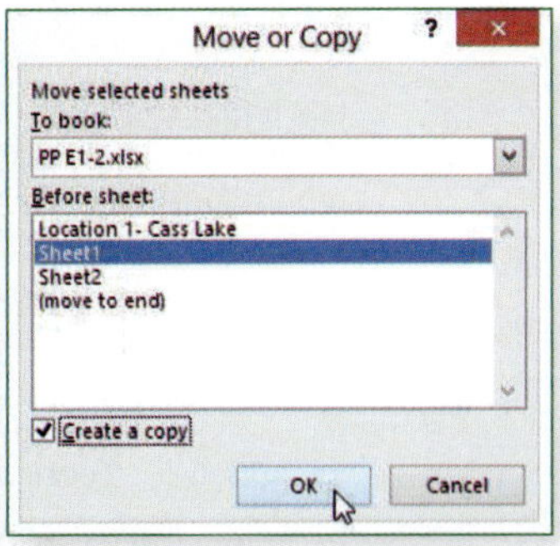

1-55 *Move or Copy* dialog box

When you move or copy worksheets, you can select multiple sheets to move or copy. Selecting multiple worksheets creates a group, and the title bar displays "[Group]" after the workbook name. To select multiple sheets, select a sheet tab, press **Shift**, and click another sheet tab. Once you have moved or copied the grouped worksheets, "[Group]" disappears from the title bar. To ungroup the sheets (prior to moving or copying), right-click a grouped tab, and choose **Ungroup**.

HOW TO: Copy Worksheets

1. Right-click the worksheet tab you want to copy and select **Move or Copy** from the context menu (see Figure 1-54). The *Move or Copy* dialog box opens (see Figure 1-55).
   - You can also click the **Format** button [*Home* tab, *Cells* group] and select **Move or Copy Sheet**.
   - To copy the selected worksheet into a workbook other than the current one, select a destination workbook from the *To book* drop-down list.
   - If you are copying a worksheet between workbooks, the destination workbook must be open prior to opening the *Move or Copy* dialog box.
2. Select the worksheet that the active sheet will precede when it is copied in the *Before sheet* area.
3. Check the **Create a copy** box in the bottom left corner of the dialog box.
4. Click **OK** to close the dialog box.
   - The copied sheet has the same name as the original worksheet with a (2) after it, as shown in Figure 1-56.

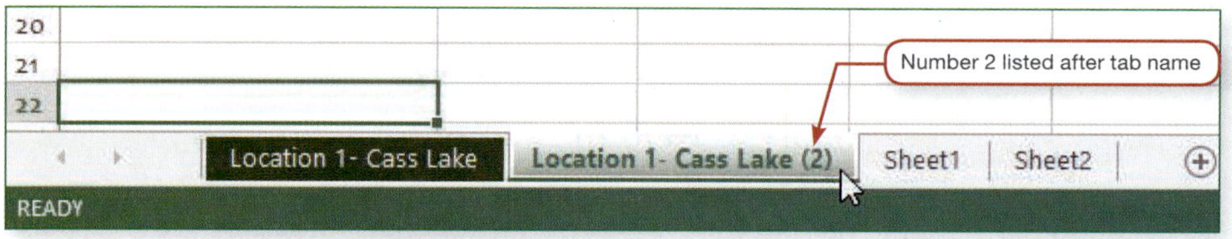

1-56 New worksheet copy

ANOTHER WAY

To move a worksheet, click the worksheet tab and drag to the left or right. To copy a worksheet, press and hold **Ctrl** while you drag the worksheet tab to the left or right.

PAUSE & PRACTICE: EXCEL 1-3

For this project, you open your previous Pause & Practice file (***[your initials] PP E1-2***) to adjust the column and row widths; insert a row for a new sales category; delete unwanted sheets; and copy, rename, and format a spreadsheet for another location of Paradise Lakes Resorts.

File Needed: ***[your initials] PP E1-2.xlsx***
Completed Project File Name: ***[your initials] PP E1-3.xlsx***

1. Open the ***[your initials] PP E1-2*** workbook.
2. Save the file as ***[your initials] PP E1-3***.

3. Change the width of columns B through H.
   a. Click and drag column headings **B** through **H** to select the columns.
   b. Click the **Format** button [*Home* tab, *Cells* group].
   c. Select **Column Width** from the menu.
   d. Enter 20.0 characters as the new width.
   e. Click **OK**.
4. Apply new row heights to rows 4 and 10.
   a. Click row heading **4**, hold down **Ctrl**, and click row heading **10**.
   b. Right-click row heading **4**.
   c. Choose **Row Height** from the context menu.
   d. Enter 24.0 as the new height.
   e. Click **OK**.
5. Insert a new row and row label above row 9.
   a. Right-click row heading **9**.
   b. Choose **Insert** from the context menu to add a new row.
   c. The new row appears directly above the originally selected row.
   d. Select cell **A9** and type Food & Beverages.
   e. Press **Enter**.
6. Hide the newly inserted row 9.
   a. Click cell **A9**.
   b. Click the **Format** button [*Home* tab, *Cells* group].
   c. Select **Hide & Unhide** in the *Visibility* category.
   d. Select **Hide Rows**.
7. Merge and center the worksheet title and date.
   a. Select **A1:H1**.
   b. Click the **Merge & Center** button [*Home* tab, *Alignment* group].
   c. Select **A2:H2** and merge and center the cells.
8. Rename *Sheet1* and color the sheet tab.
   a. Double-click the **Sheet1** tab.
   b. Type the following new name for the sheet: Location 1- Cass Lake.
   c. Press **Enter**.
   d. Click the **Format** button [*Home* tab, *Cells* group].
   e. Select **Tab Color** in the *Organize Sheets* category.
   f. Select **Green Accent 1**, **Darker 50%** (last color in the fifth *Theme Color* column).
9. Insert a new sheet.
   a. Click the bottom half of the **Insert** button [*Home* tab, *Cells* group] and select **Insert Sheet**. The sheet appears to the left of the *Location 1- Cass Lake* sheet.
   b. Click the **New Sheet** button to insert another sheet.
10. Delete the extra blank sheets.
    a. Click the **Sheet2** tab, press and hold **Shift**, and click the **Sheet3** tab. Release **Shift** (both worksheet tabs are selected).
    b. Click the **Delete** button drop-down list [*Home* tab, *Cells* group].
    c. Select **Delete Sheet** to remove the selected worksheets.
11. Create a copy of the worksheet *Location 1- Cass Lake* and rename the new worksheet tab.
    a. Right-click the **Location 1- Cass Lake** tab.
    b. Choose **Move or Copy** from the context menu.
    c. The *Move or Copy* dialog box displays.
    d. Choose **(move to end)** in the *Before Sheet* box.
    e. Check the **Create a copy** box in the bottom left corner of the window.

f. Click **OK**. The new sheet is automatically named *Location 1- Cass Lake (2)*.
g. Double-click the new worksheet tab **Location 1- Cass Lake (2)**, and type the new sheet name: Location 2- Breezy Point.
h. Press **Enter**.
i. Color the tab **Orange**, **Accent 4**, **Darker 50%** (last color in the eighth *Theme Color* column).

12. Press **Ctrl+S** to save the workbook.
13. Click the **File** tab and click **Close** to close the workbook (Figure 1-57).

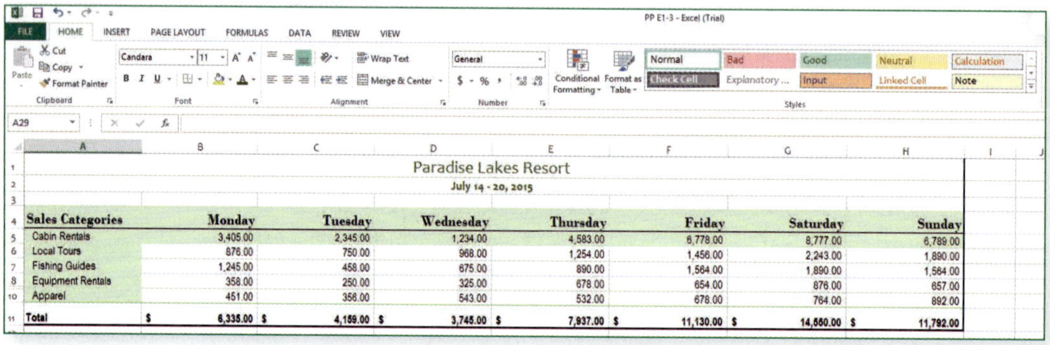

1-57 PP E1-3 completed worksheet with hidden row

SLO 1.7

Customizing the Window

In this section you explore several ways to customize the Excel window including changing workbook views, zooming options, freezing panes, splitting a worksheet into panes, and switching windows.

Workbook Views

Excel has three main views: ***Normal***, ***Page Layout***, and ***Page Break Preview***. A fourth view, ***Full Screen*** view, displays a spreadsheet without screen elements so you can see more of the sheet. Each view in Excel has a specific purpose.

- *Normal* view is the default view. Use *Normal* view to create and modify spreadsheets.
- Use *Page Layout* view to apply headers and footers and to view the layout of the spreadsheet prior to distribution.
- Use *Page Break Preview* to adjust page breaks within your workbook using the drag and drop technique.
- Use *Full Screen* view to display worksheet data without the *Ribbon* and other screen elements.

The *Normal* view, *Page Layout* view, and *Page Break Preview* buttons are on the right side of the *Status bar*. You can also change views using *Normal, Page Layout,* and *Page Break Preview* buttons located on the *View* tab in the *Workbook Views* group (Figure 1-58).

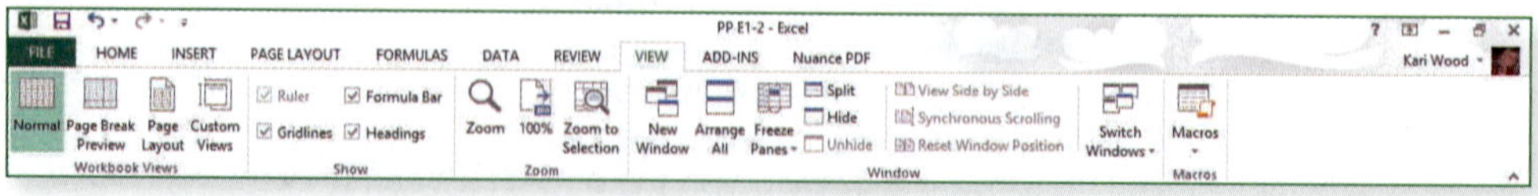

1-58 ***View*** **tab**

HOW TO: Switch Workbook Views Using the Ribbon

1. Open a workbook. The *Normal* view displays by default.
2. Click the **View** tab.
3. Click the **Page Layout** button [*View* tab, *Workbook Views* group].
   - This view displays spreadsheet headers, footers, and page breaks (Figure 1-59).
4. Click **Page Break Preview** [*View* tab, *Workbook Views* group] to view page breaks.
   - Click and drag the dark blue page break lines to adjust page breaks (Figure 1-60).
5. Click **Normal** [*View* tab, *Workbook Views* group] to return to the default view.
6. Click **Ribbon Display Options** in the upper right corner of the Excel window and select **Auto-Hide Ribbon** to display *Full Screen* view (Figure 1-61).
   - *Full Screen* view increases the spreadsheet view by hiding the *Ribbon* and the *Status bar*.
   - The *Ribbon Display Options* menu includes three options: *Auto-Hide Ribbon*, *Show Tabs*, or *Show Tabs and Commands* (Figure 1-62). The entire *Ribbon* disappears from view when you select *Auto-Hide Ribbon*. *Show Tabs* displays *Ribbon* tabs only. Click a tab to display *Ribbon* commands. The *Show Tabs and Commands* option displays the *Ribbon* tabs and commands.

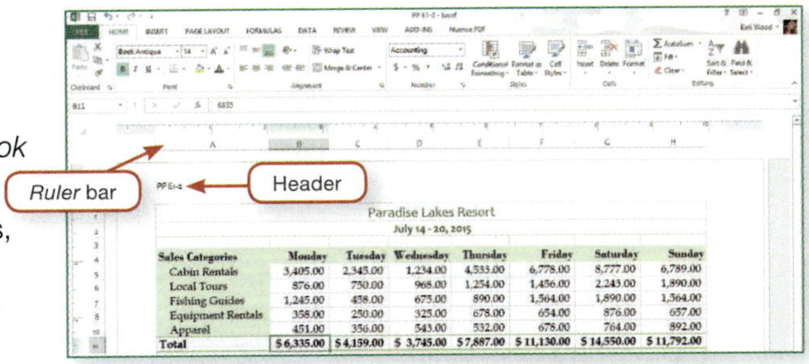

1-59 *Page Layout view*

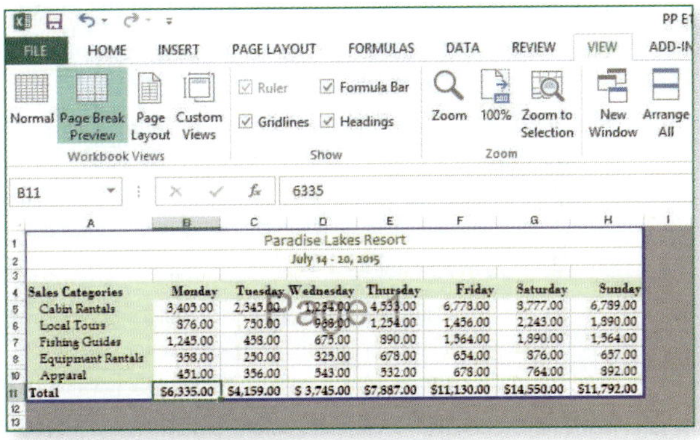

1-60 *Page Break Preview*

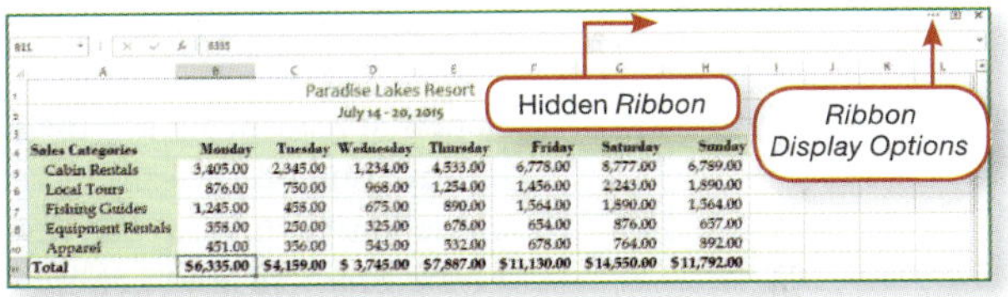

1-61 *Full Screen view*

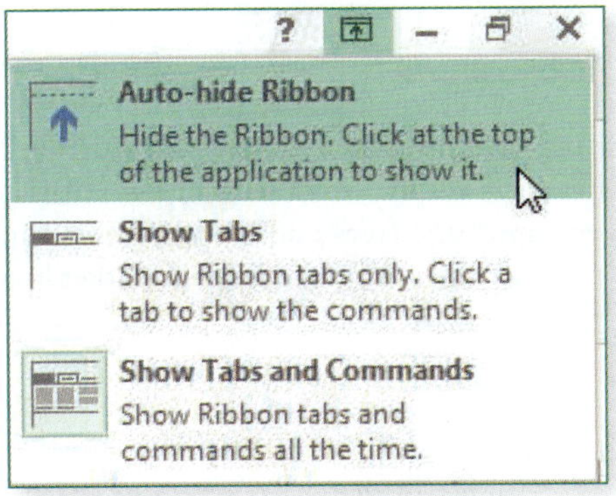

1-62 *Ribbon Display Options*

7. Click **Ribbon Display Options** and choose **Show Tabs and Commands** to display the *Ribbon* and tab commands.

ANOTHER WAY

Use the *Status bar* buttons in the bottom right corner of the window to switch views.

Zoom Options

You can change a window's zoom level to see more of its content (zoom out) or to read the content more easily (zoom in). Zoom controls increase or decrease the magnification of the spreadsheet contents. You can increase or decrease the zoom level using *Zoom* in the *Zoom* group on the *View* tab (Figure 1-63) or the zoom controls on the *Status bar.*

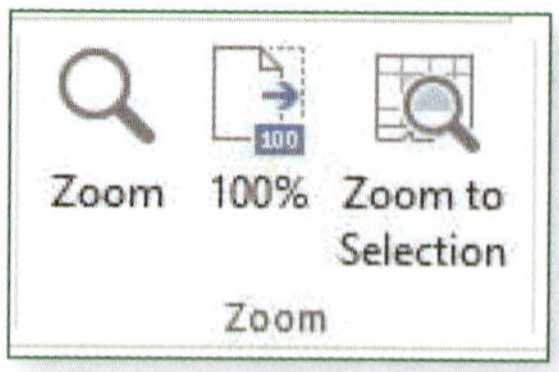

1-63 ***View* tab, *Zoom* options**

HOW TO: Increase Zoom Using the Ribbon

1. Click the **Zoom** button [*View* tab, *Zoom* group].
   - The *Zoom* dialog box opens.
2. Click to select the radio button next to the desired *Magnification.*
   - Select **Fit selection** for a range of cells to fill the entire screen.
   - Choose **Custom** to enter an exact magnification (Figure 1-64).
3. Click **OK** to see the change in magnification in your workbook.

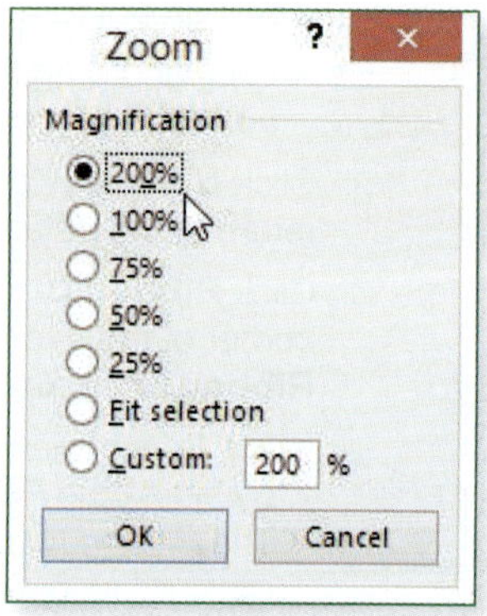

1-64 ***Zoom* dialog box**

> **ANOTHER WAY**
>
> Other useful buttons are located in the *Zoom* group on the *View* tab: ***100%*** and ***Zoom to Selection.*** The *100%* option returns the magnification to the default. The *Zoom to Selection* option fills the entire screen with the range of cells selected in the worksheet.

Freeze Panes

When spreadsheets are magnified or contain multiple pages, it is difficult to see all of the information on the same screen. You can use scroll bars to move to those sections that are not immediately in view, but this process is tedious if you have to scroll repeatedly. You can also *Freeze Panes* so that column and row headings display whether you are at the top, bottom, left, or right of the spreadsheet. When you apply the freeze option, the Excel window is split into one or more panes, and displays multiple areas of a spreadsheet. A darker border displays when a row or column is frozen.

HOW TO: Freeze Panes Using the Ribbon

1. Select a cell in the worksheet that is located below the rows and to the right of the columns you want to freeze.
2. Click the **Freeze Panes** button [*View* tab, *Window* group].
   - Choose **Freeze Panes** to keep rows and columns visible.
   - Select **Freeze Top Row** to keep the top row visible.
   - Choose **Freeze First Column** to keep the first column visible.
3. Select **Freeze Panes** (Figure 1-65).
   - All rows above the active cell are frozen, and all columns to the left of the active cell are frozen.

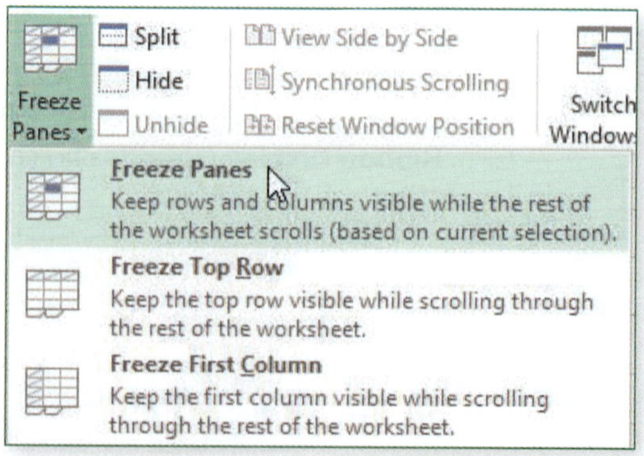

1-65 ***Freeze Panes* button**

4. Use the right horizontal scrolling arrow to view other columns of information.
   - Notice the row headings do not move (Figure 1-66).
5. Use the down vertical scrolling arrow to view the last row of data.
   - Notice the column headings remain constant.
6. Click the **Freeze Panes** button [*View* tab, *Window* group].
   - A new option, *Unfreeze Panes*, displays.
7. Select **Unfreeze Panes** to return the workbook to its original viewing state.

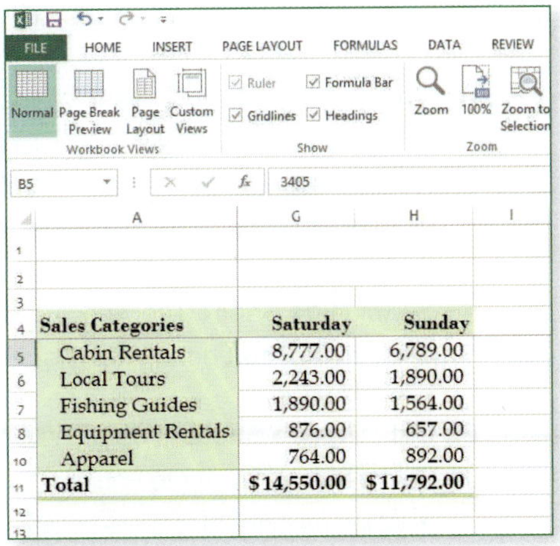

1-66 ***Freeze Panes*** **view results**

Split a Worksheet into Panes

You can use the split feature to show different parts of the same spreadsheet in separate panes. The split feature can divide a worksheet into two or four scrollable windows (panes) that you can view simultaneously. You can scroll and edit each window independently and size the panes by dragging the *Splitter bar.*

HOW TO: Split a Worksheet into Panes

1. Select the row, column, or cell where you want to split a worksheet into panes.
   - Click a cell to split a worksheet into four panes.
   - Click the first cell in the row or column to split a worksheet into two panes.
2. Click the **Split** button [*View* tab, *Window* group].
3. Adjust the size of the panes by pointing to the *Splitter bar* and dragging to reposition the splitter bar (Figure 1-67).
4. Click the **Splitter** button [*View* tab, *Window* group] to remove the splitter bar.

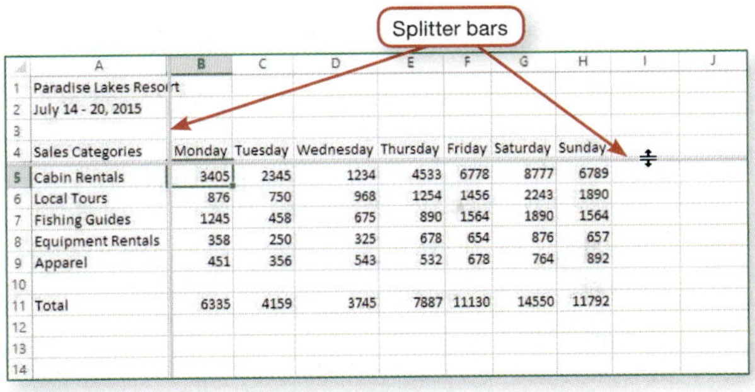

1-67 Split worksheet

> ### ANOTHER WAY
> Remove a window split by double-clicking the *Splitter bar.*

Hide or Unhide Worksheets

When worksheets contain confidential information, you can hide the sheets without affecting the worksheet data or calculations in the sheet. Hidden worksheets do not appear in a printout. You can hide a worksheet using the *Ribbon* or by right-clicking a sheet tab. You cannot hide a sheet if there is only one sheet in the workbook.

HOW TO: Hide and Unhide Worksheets

1. Click the sheet tab you want to hide.
   - You can use the **Ctrl** key to select multiple sheets to hide.
2. Click the **Home** tab.
3. Click the **Format** button [*Cells* group] and choose **Hide & Unhide** in the *Visibility* group.
4. Select **Hide Sheet**. The worksheet tab does not display.
5. Click the **Format** button [*Cells* group] and choose **Hide & Unhide** in the *Visibility* group.
6. Click **Unhide Sheet** to open the *Unhide* dialog box (Figure 1-68).
7. Select the worksheet to unhide.
   - When multiple sheets are hidden, you must unhide each sheet individually.
8. Click **OK**.

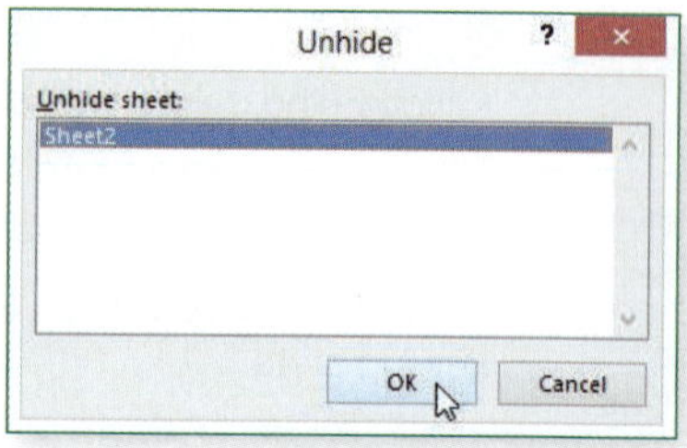

1-68 *Unhide* dialog box

ANOTHER WAY

To hide the worksheet, right-click the worksheet you want to hide and choose **Hide** from the context menu. To unhide the worksheet, right click a worksheet tab and choose **Unhide**. Select the worksheet to unhide.

You can hide an open workbook window by clicking the **View** tab and clicking the **Hide** button. To unhide a workbook, click the **View** tab and click the **Unhide** button.

Switch Windows Option

The ***Switch Windows*** feature is useful for viewing or editing multiple open workbooks.

HOW TO: Switch Windows Using the Ribbon

1. Verify that you have more than one workbook open.
2. Click the **Switch Windows** button [*View* tab, *Window* group].
   - A list of open workbooks displays.
3. Select the workbook you want to view.
   - You can view workbooks side-by-side by selecting **View Side by Side** [*View* tab, *Window* group] (Figure 1-69).
   - The *Synchronous Scrolling* option is available when viewing two workbooks side by side. *Synchronous Scrolling* scrolls both files in the same direction at the same time. It is useful for editing different versions of similar spreadsheets or sharing information between two different workbooks.
4. Click **Maximize** to restore a workbook to full size.

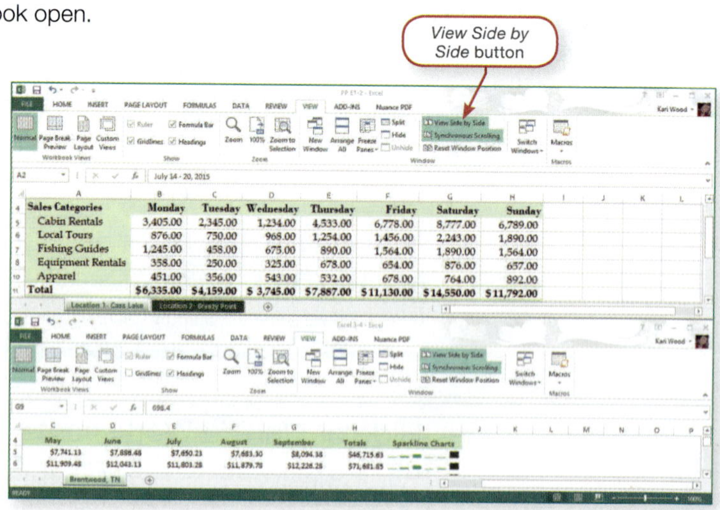

1-69 *View Side by Side*

View Multiple Worksheets at the Same Time

You can view multiple worksheets at the same time. Use the *New Window* feature to open a second window and to view different parts of the same worksheet. Use the *Arrange All* feature to position open windows. Click **Maximize** to restore a workbook to full size.

HOW TO: View Multiple Worksheets at the Same Time

1. Verify that you have more than one workbook open.
2. Click **Arrange All** [*View* tab, *Window* group] to open the *Arrange Windows* dialog box (Figure 1-70).
3. Choose an option to display more than one workbook: *Tiled*, *Horizontal*, *Vertical*, or *Cascade*.
4. Click **OK**.
5. Click **Maximize** to restore a workbook to full size.
6. Click the **View** tab, and click **New Window**.
   - A second window of the worksheet displays. Notice the change in the title bar. Each window displays a number after the name of the workbook.
7. Click **Arrange All** [*View* tab, *Window* group].
8. Choose **Vertical** in the *Arrange Windows* dialog box.
9. Select the **Windows of active workbook** check box.
10. Click **OK**.
11. Scroll the windows to display cells to edit.
12. **Close** the windows.

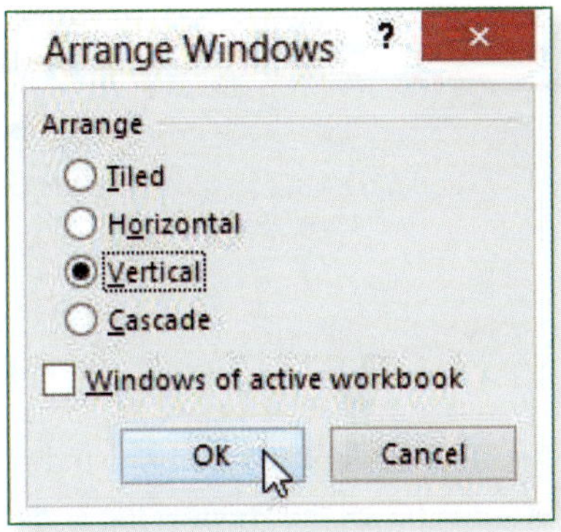

1-70 *Arrange Windows* dialog box

SLO 1.8

Finalizing a Workbook

After customizing your workbook content, structure, and format, Excel provides you with features to finalize your workbook. It's important to spell check a workbook for accuracy before printing or sending to others. You can also add document properties and a header and footer to your worksheet for document identification. If you are working with a large worksheet, you can customize page breaks and how your worksheet prints.

Check Spelling

The ***Spelling*** feature scans a worksheet and locates words that do not match entries in its main dictionary. You can add entries to the main dictionary such as proper names or technical terms. Duplicated words are also identified when you check spelling. You can check an entire worksheet or a selected range of cells. If you are not at the beginning of your worksheet, Excel starts spell checking at the active cell and checks to the end of the worksheet. When it reaches the end of the worksheet, a dialog box displays and asks if you want to continue checking at the beginning of the sheet. The *Spelling* dialog box displays several options when Excel finds an error. The following table describes each option.

Spelling Dialog Box Options

Option	Action
Ignore Once	Skips the word
Ignore All	Skips all occurrences of the word in the spreadsheet
Add to Dictionary	Adds the word to the default dictionary file. You can also create a custom dictionary.
Change	Changes the word to the entry you choose in the *Suggestions* box
Change All	Same as *Change*, but changes the word throughout the worksheet
Delete	Appears for duplicated words. Click to delete one occurrence of the word.
AutoCorrect	Adds the word to the list of corrections Excel makes automatically
Options	Changes the spelling options in Excel
Undo Last	Changes back to the most recent correction made
Cancel	Discontinues the checking operation

HOW TO: Spell Check a Worksheet

1. Press **Ctrl+Home** to move to the beginning of the worksheet.
2. Click the **Review** tab and click the **Spelling** button [*Proofing* group] (Figure 1-71).
3. Use the buttons on the right to change or ignore each identified error.
   - If a recommendation that is acceptable does not appear in the *Suggestions* box, edit the *Not in Dictionary* text box and click **Change**.

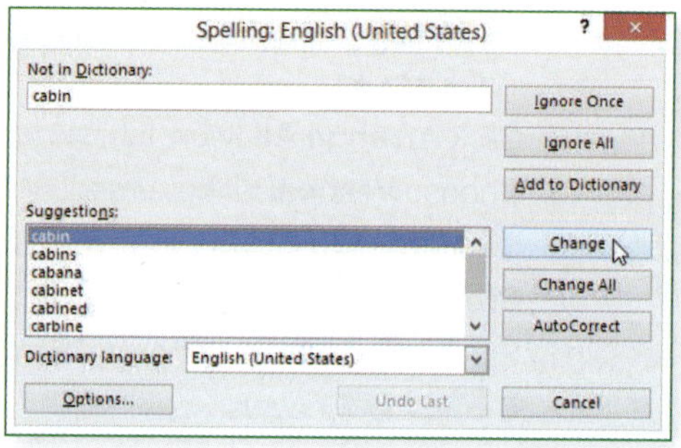

1-71 *Spelling* dialog box

Document Properties

Document Properties are details that you can add to any Office file. Document properties are also called ***metadata***, and you can use them to organize or to gather basic information about workbooks. Several properties are created automatically by Excel including *Creation* date, *Modified* date, *Accessed* date, and file *Size*. You can edit other document properties, such as *Title, Author, Comments, Subject,* and *Company*. You can view or edit document properties using *Backstage* view, displaying the *Document Panel*, or opening the *Property* dialog box.

HOW TO: Add Document Properties

1. Click the **File** tab to display *Backstage* view.
2. Click **Info** if it is not already selected (Figure 1-72).
   - Document property field names are listed on the left and the property fields are listed on the right.
3. Click a field property and type or edit the entry.
4. Click the **Show All/Show Fewer Properties** link at the bottom to display more or fewer document property fields.

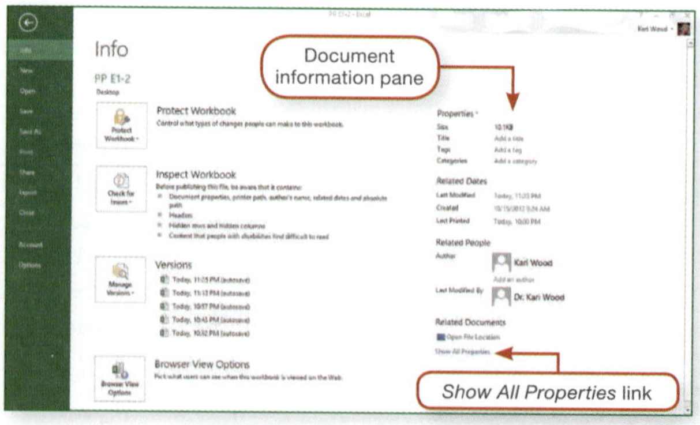

1-72 Workbook properties

Document Panel

You can view and edit document properties using the *Document* panel in *Normal, Page Layout,* or *Page Break Preview* views. The panel appears above the *Formula bar* and below the *Ribbon* (Figure 1-73). To display the *Document* panel, use the *Backstage* view. Close the *Document* panel by clicking the *Document* panel close button.

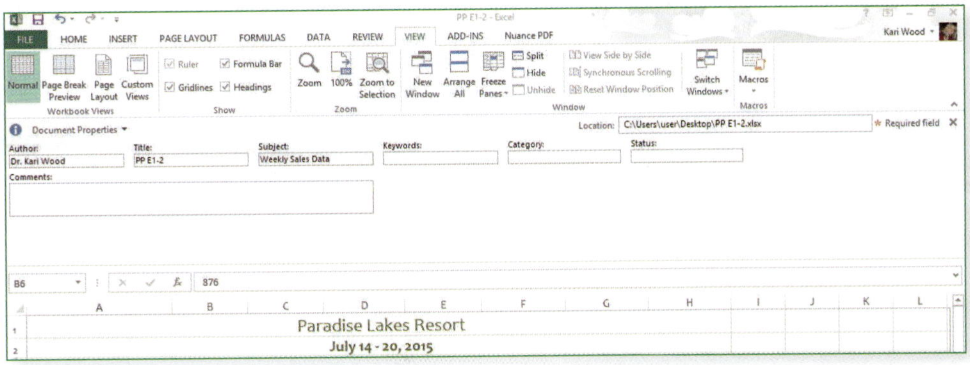

1-73 *Document Properties* panel

HOW TO: Display the Document Properties Panel

1. Click **File** to display *Backstage* view.
2. Click **Info** if it is not already selected.
3. Click the **Properties** drop-down list at the top of the *Properties* pane (Figure 1-74).
4. Select **Show Document Panel**.
   - The *Backstage* view closes and the *Document* panel displays above the *Formula bar* in the Excel window.
5. Edit or add text in the *Document Properties* fields.
6. Click **X** in the upper right corner of the *Document* panel to close the panel.

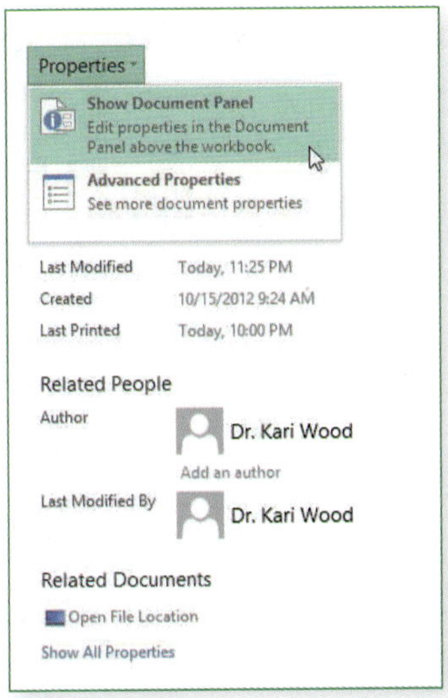

1-74 *Show Document Panel*

Advanced Properties

The ***Advanced Properties*** option displays the *Properties* dialog box. You can open the *Properties* dialog box using the *Backstage* view or the *Document* panel (Figure 1-75).

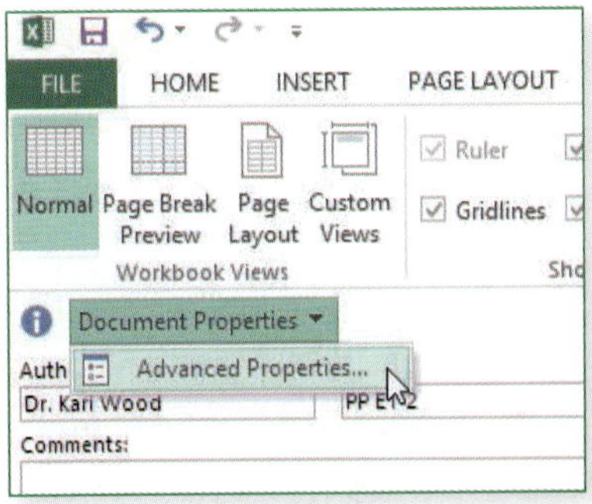

1-75 *Advanced Properties*

HOW TO: Open the Properties Dialog Box

1. Display the *Backstage* view and click **Info**.
2. Click the **Properties** button to display the drop-down list (see Figure 1-74).
3. Select **Advanced Properties**. The *Properties* dialog box opens (Figure 1-76).
   - The *General*, *Statistics*, and *Contents* tabs provide document properties that are automatically created by Excel.
   - The *Summary* and *Custom* tabs allow you to edit fields.
   - Use the *Custom* tab to add custom document property fields to your workbook.

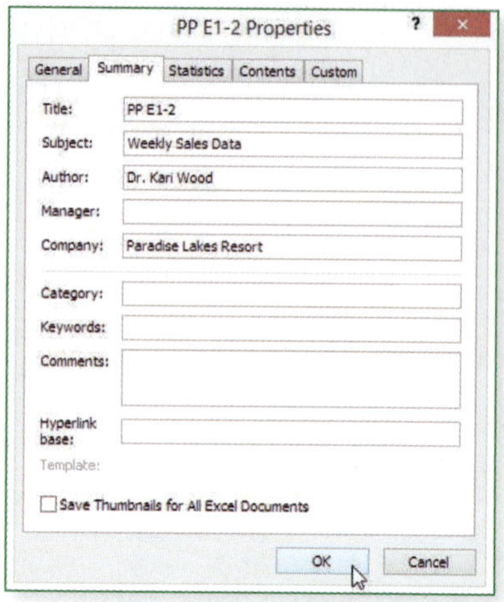

1-76 ***Properties*** **dialog box**

Page Layout

The *Page Layout* tab includes options that allow you to control the appearance of your worksheet such as margins, page orientation, and paper size (Figure 1-77). You can also use the *Page Setup* dialog box to customize worksheet settings (Figure 1-78). To view page layout changes, you can preview or print the worksheet.

Open the *Page Setup* dialog box to change multiple page setup options at one time. Click the **Page Setup, Scale to Fit,** or **Sheet Options** launcher on the *Page Layout* tab to open the *Page Setup* dialog box (see Figure 1-78). The following table describes each of the tabs in the *Page Setup* dialog box.

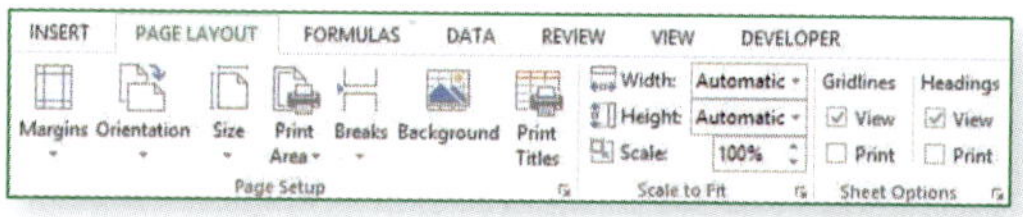

1-77 Customize page setup and print options

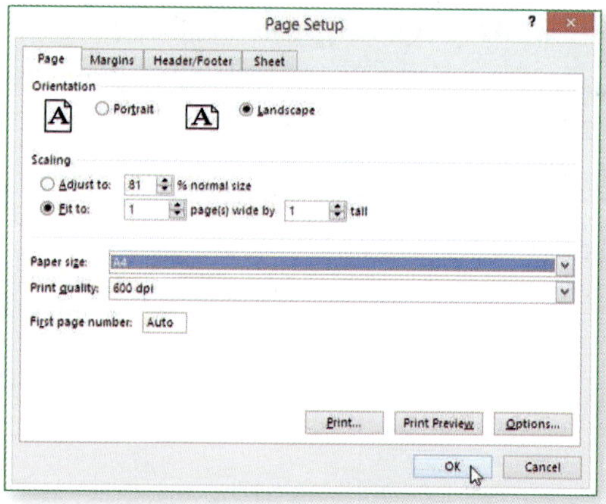

1-78 ***Page*** **tab in the** ***Page Setup*** **dialog box**

Page Setup Dialog Box Options

Tab	Tab Options
Page	Set the *Orientation* to *Portrait* or *Landscape*. *Scaling* adjusts the size of the printed worksheet as a percentage of the normal size, or you can use *Fit to* area to scale the worksheet to print on a specific number of pages. Use the *Paper size* drop-down list to select a paper size (see Figure 1-78).
Margins	Set the *Top*, *Bottom*, *Left*, and *Right* margins of the worksheet. You can also set the margins for the header and footer text in the worksheet. In the *Center on page* area, check the *Horizontally* and/or *Vertically* boxes to center the data in the worksheet on a printed page (see Figure 1-79).
Header/Footer	Add and customize headers and footers in the worksheet.
Sheet	Set the *Print area* by selecting a specified range of cells. In the *Print titles* area, you can designate certain rows or columns to repeat each time spreadsheet data spans more than one page. You can also specify printing options such as printing titles, gridlines, and row and column headings.

ANOTHER WAY

Open the *Page Setup* dialog box by clicking the **Page Setup** link in the *Print* area on *Backstage* view.

Margins, Page Orientation, and Paper Size

The default settings for page layout for an Excel spreadsheet include the following:

- Top and bottom margins: 0.75
- Left and right margins: 0.7
- Header and footer margins: 0.3
- Portrait orientation
- Letter size paper

You can modify each of these settings for individual worksheets or multiple worksheets. To format multiple worksheets, select the worksheet tabs. Use **Shift** to select adjacent sheets. Use **Ctrl** to select non-adjacent sheets. Right-click a sheet tab and choose **Select All Sheets** to format an entire workbook. When changing margin settings, the top and bottom margin settings must be greater than the header and footer values or the worksheet data prints over the header and footer text.

HOW TO: Customize Margins, Page Orientation, and Paper Size

1. Click the **Margins** button [*Page Layout* tab, *Page Setup* group] and select a preset option from the drop-down list.
   - Select **Custom Margins** from the *Margins* drop-down list to open the *Page Setup* dialog box to enter a precise measurement (Figure 1-79).
   - Select the **Horizontally** and/or **Vertically** check boxes in the *Center on Page* area to center your worksheet [*Page Setup* dialog box, *Margins* tab]. *Horizontally* centers data between the left and right margins. *Vertically* centers data between the top and bottom margins.
2. Click the **Orientation** button [*Page Layout* tab, *Page Setup* group] and select **Portrait** or **Landscape** from the drop-down list.
   - When you select *Portrait*, the page is taller than it is wide; if you select *Landscape*, the page is wider than it is tall.
   - Use the *Page* tab in the *Page Setup* dialog box to change the page orientation.
   - You can also change orientation when you are ready to print. Select an option from the *Page Orientation* drop-down list in the *Print* area on the *Backstage* view.
3. Click the **Size** button [*Page Layout* tab, *Page Setup* group] and select a paper size from the drop-down list.
   - The default paper size is 8 ½"×11", which is called *Letter*.
   - Click **More Paper Sizes** to open the *Page Setup* dialog box.

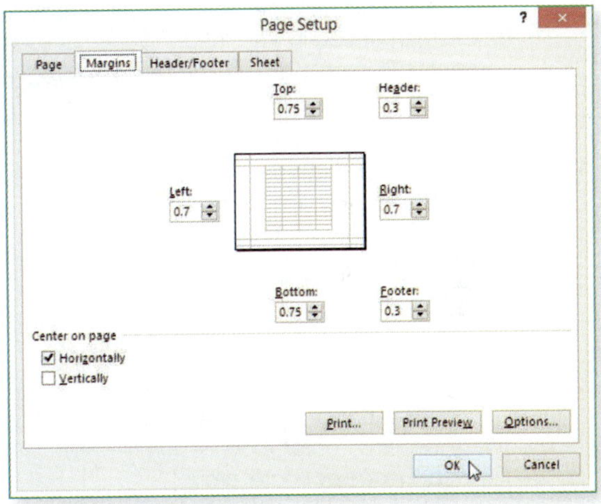

1-79 *Margins* tab in the *Page Setup* dialog box

ANOTHER WAY

You can change the margins using the *Ruler* in *Page Layout* view. Click the **View** tab and click the **Page Layout** button. Select the **Ruler** option if necessary. Point to a margin boundary and drag to change margin settings.

Headers and Footers

Headers appear at the top of the worksheet in the *Header* area, while ***footers*** appear in the *Footer* area at the bottom of the worksheet. Each header and footer area has a left, middle, and right section where you can insert a page number, file name, date, or other information in text boxes.

Note that headers and footers appear on the worksheets only when you choose to add them. They do not appear on every sheet automatically. To add headers and footers to multiple worksheets at one time, select the worksheet tabs and open the *Page Setup* dialog box. Headers and footers do not display in *Normal* view. To view header and footer text, switch to *Print Layout* view or *Print Preview.*

HOW TO: Insert a Header and Footer Using the Ribbon

1. Select the worksheet.
2. Click the **Insert** tab.
3. Click the **Header & Footer** button [*Text* group].
   - The worksheet view changes to *Page Layout* view.
   - The header displays three text boxes. Information entered in the left text box is left aligned, text in the middle text box is centered, and text in the right text box is right aligned.
4. Click a text box in the header area.
   - Clicking a header or footer text box displays the *Header & Footer Tools Design* tab.
5. Click the **Design** tab to activate it (Figure 1-80).
6. Click an option in the *Header & Footer Elements* group [*Header & Footer Tools Design* tab].
   - A field is inserted with an ampersand (&) followed by the code enclosed in brackets.
   - If the header or footer contains text, you can edit or delete the contents.
   - To insert a pre-defined header or footer such as the page number or worksheet name, click the **Header** or **Footer** button [*Header & Footer Tools Design* tab, *Header & Footer* group].
7. Click **Go To Footer** [*Header & Footer Tools Design* tab, *Navigation* group].
8. Click one of the text boxes in the footer area.

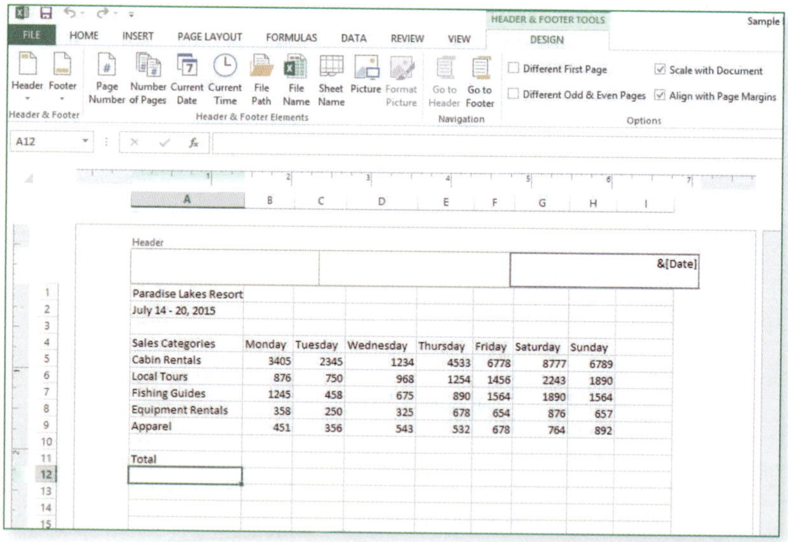

1-80 *Header area in Page Layout view*

9. Type text or click an element [*Header & Footer Elements* group].
   - If the text you type includes an ampersand (&), type two ampersands (&&) to distinguish text from the header or footer code. For example, you type "Research && Development" to display "Research & Development".
10. Scroll to the top of the worksheet and then click any cell to close the header and footer area.
    - The header and footer text displays in *Page Layout* view.
11. Switch to **Normal** view.
    - The header and footer are not visible in *Normal* view.

You can insert headers and footers using the *Page Setup* dialog box. One advantage of using the *Page Setup* dialog box to insert headers or footers is that this option allows you to add headers or footers to multiple sheets. The *Page Setup* dialog box includes preset header and footer fields located in the *Custom Header* or *Custom Footer* drop-down lists on the *Header/Footer* tab.

HOW TO: Insert Headers or Footers Using the Page Setup Dialog Box

1. Click the worksheet tab (or tabs if applying the header or footer to multiple sheets).
   - To select two or more adjacent worksheets, use **Shift**.
   - To select two or more nonadjacent sheets, use **Ctrl**.
   - To select all worksheets in the workbook, right-click a tab and click **Select All Sheets**.
2. Click the **Page Layout** tab and then click the **Page Setup** launcher [*Page Setup* group].
   - The *Page Setup* dialog box displays.
3. Select the **Header/Footer** tab.
4. Click the drop-down arrow for the *Header* or *Footer* text box to see a list of predefined headers or footers (Figure 1-81).
   - Scroll to see additional options.
5. Choose **(none)** to create a new header or footer.
6. Click the **Custom Header** or **Custom Footer** button to open the *Header* or *Footer* dialog box (Figure 1-82).
7. Type text in the *Left* section, *Center* section, or *Right* section, or click a button to insert a field code.
   - Each button has a *ScreenTip* to identify the button (Figure 1-83).
8. Click **OK** to close the *Header or Footer* dialog box.
   - The information appears in the *Header or Footer* text box.
9. Click **OK** to close the *Page Setup* dialog box.

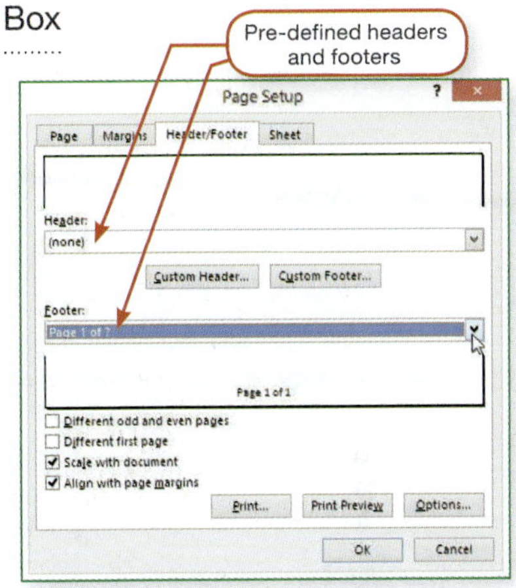

1-81 ***Header/Footer* tab in the *Page Setup* dialog box**

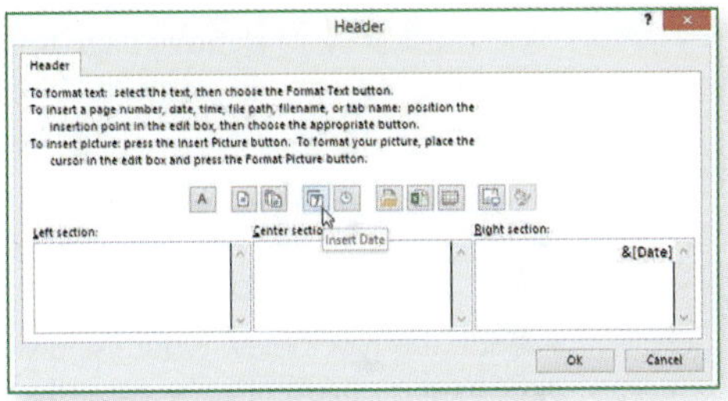

1-82 ***Header* dialog box**

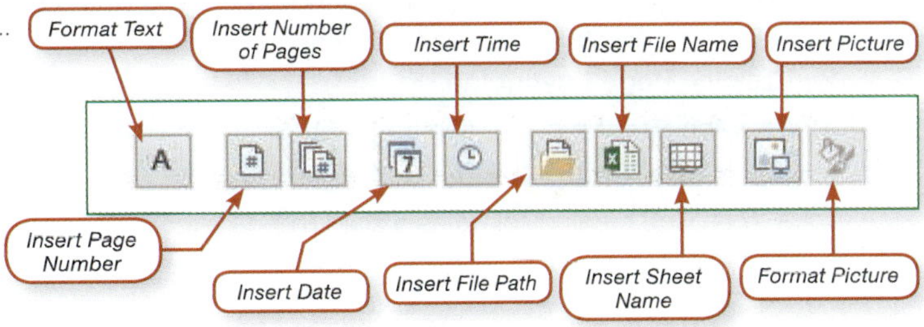

1-83 Buttons to insert header and footer content

Figure 1-83 displays the buttons available in the *Header* and *Footer* dialog boxes. When you click the *Format Text, Insert Picture,* or *Format Picture* button, another dialog box opens that provides you with additional options.

There are two ways to remove a header or footer. One method uses the *Page Setup* dialog box and the other uses the *Text* group on the *Insert* tab. Remember to use the *Page Setup* dialog box method to remove headers and footers from multiple sheets.

HOW TO: Remove Headers and Footers

1. Select the worksheet.
2. Click the **Page Layout** tab and click the **Page Setup** launcher.
3. Click the **Header/Footer** tab.
4. Click the **Header** or **Footer** drop-down list and select **(none)** (Figure 1-84).
5. Click **OK** to close the *Page Setup* dialog box.

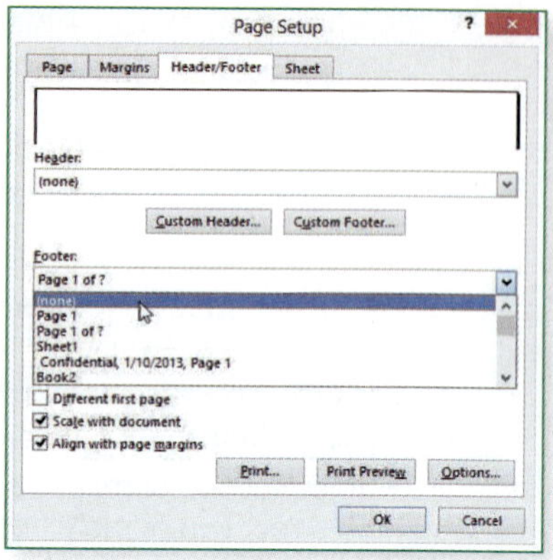

1-84 *Footer* drop-down list

ANOTHER WAY

To remove a header or footer, click the **Insert** tab and click **Header & Footer** [*Text* group]. Click the left, right, or center area, select the header or footer text, and press **Delete** or **Backspace**.

Page Breaks

When you complete a workbook you can preview the content before printing or distributing the workbook electronically. If the worksheet data is larger than one page, page breaks are inserted automatically. Paper size, margins, and scale options control the position of automatic page breaks. You can manually insert page breaks to change the number of rows or columns printed on the page. Use *Page Break Preview* to insert page breaks, move page breaks, or remove page breaks. Manual page breaks display as a solid line. Automatic page breaks display as a dotted or dashed line.

HOW TO: Insert a Page Break

1. Select the location to insert a page break.
   - Click the row below where you want to insert a horizontal page break.
   - Click the column to the right of where you want to insert a vertical page break.
   - Click the cell below and to the right of where you want to insert a horizontal and vertical page break.
2. Click the **Page Layout** tab.
3. Click the **Breaks** button (Figure 1-85).
4. Select **Insert Page Break**.
   - The page break displays as a solid line.

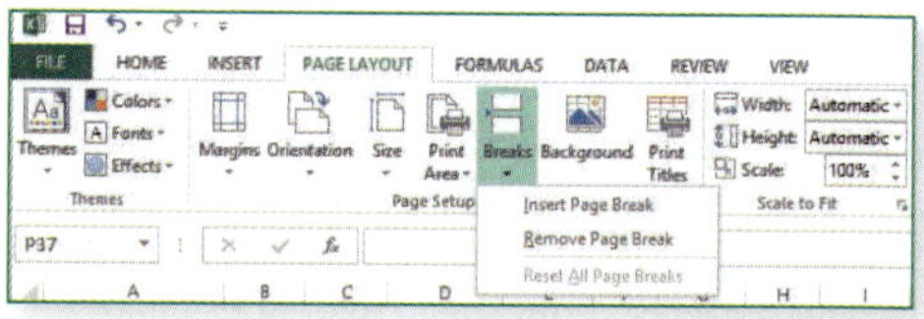

1-85 *Breaks* options

ANOTHER WAY

To insert a page break, right-click a row or column and choose **Insert Page Break** from the context menu.

Preview and Move a Page Break

In *Normal* view, you can use the *Breaks* command to insert, remove, and reset page breaks. You cannot drag page breaks to another location in *Normal* view. Use *Page Break Preview* to move a page break. Moving an automatic page break changes it to a manual page break.

HOW TO: Preview and Move a Page Break

1. Click the **View** tab.
2. Click the **Page Break Preview** button (Figure 1-86).
3. Drag the page break (solid line) to a new location.
   - The pointer changes to a resize pointer (two-pointed arrow) while dragging the page break.
4. Return to *Normal* view [*View* tab, *Workbook Views* group].

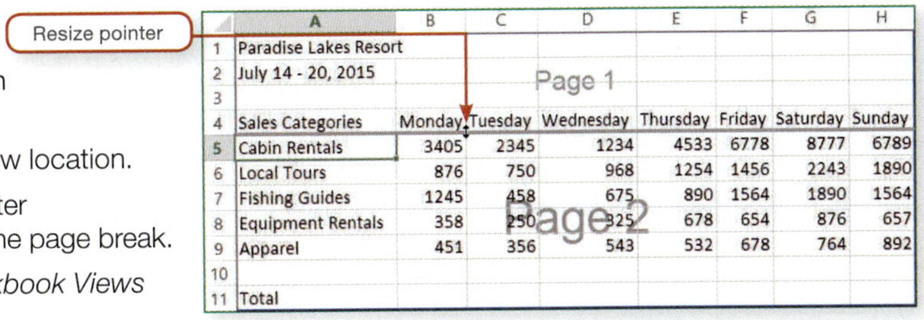

1-86 *Page Break Preview*

Remove a Manual Page Break

To remove a manual page break, use *Page Break Preview*. You cannot delete an automatic page break. You can, however, reposition an automatic page break by inserting or deleting columns and rows, changing page orientation, or adjusting column width and row height.

HOW TO: Remove a Manual Page Break

1. Switch to **Page Break Preview** [*View* tab, *Workbook Views* group].
2. Select the column or row next to the page break to be removed.
   - To delete a vertical page break, select the column to the right of the page break.
   - To delete a horizontal page break, select the row below the page break.
3. Click **Breaks** [*Page Layout* tab, *Page Setup* group] (Figure 1-87).
4. Click **Remove Page Break**.
   - To remove all manual page breaks, click **Reset All Page Breaks**.

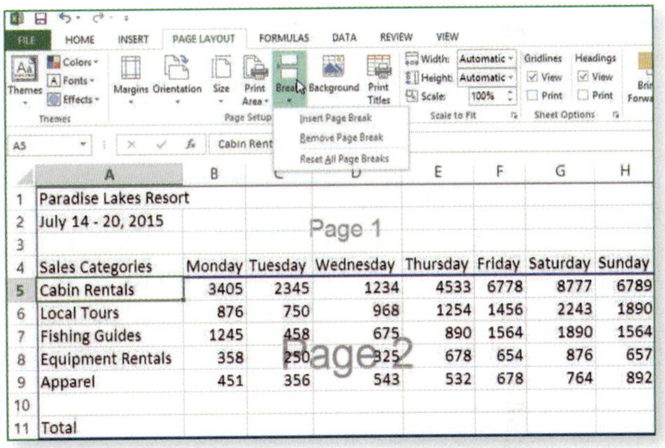

1-87 Remove page break

Customize Worksheet Printing

You can print an entire workbook, a single worksheet, or a section of a worksheet. You can also control the appearance of the printout by displaying gridlines, printing column letters and row numbers, or including titles that repeat on each page.

HOW TO: Print Titles, Gridlines, Column Letters, and Row Numbers

1. Click the **Page Layout** tab and locate the *Sheet Options* group (Figure 1-88).

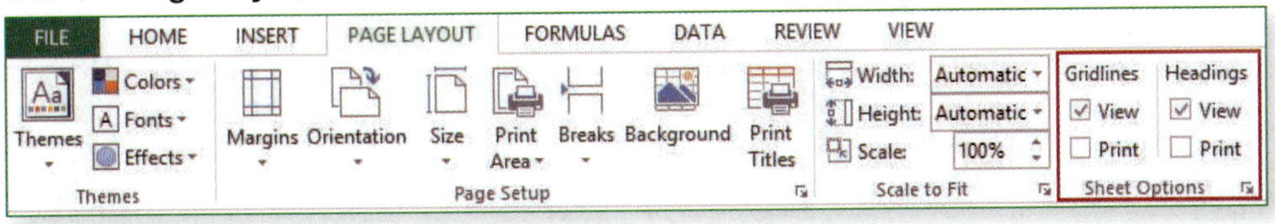

1-88 *Sheet Options*

2. Select the **Print** checkbox under *Gridlines*.
3. Select the **Print** checkbox under *Headings*.
   - Both *Gridlines* and *Row and column headings* are available in the *Print* area on the *Sheet* tab in the *Page Setup* dialog box.
4. Click the **Print Titles** button [*Page Layout* tab, *Page Setup* group] to open the *Page Setup* dialog box.
5. Click the **Rows to repeat at top** text box (Figure 1-89).
6. Drag to select the row or rows to repeat.
   - You can also type the reference of the row(s) that contains the column labels. For example, type $1:$1 to repeat the first row. Type $1:$2 to repeat the first two rows.
7. Click the **Columns to repeat at left** text box.
8. Click column **A** to select the column.
   - A second method is to type the reference of the column that contains the row labels. Type $A:$A to repeat the first column.
9. Click **OK**.

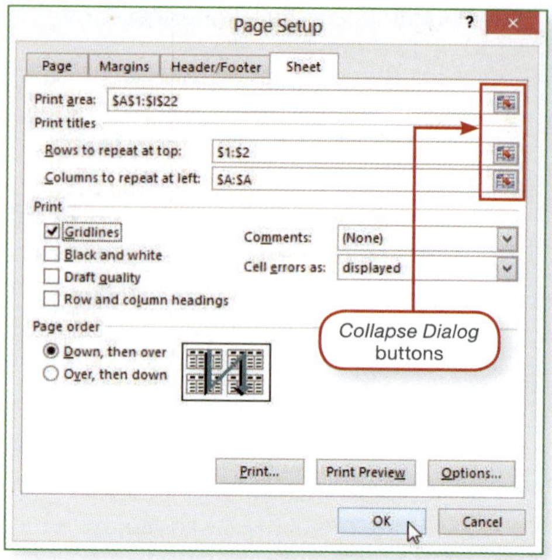

1-89 ***Sheet* tab in the *Page Setup* dialog box**

ANOTHER WAY

Click the **Collapse Dialog** button on the right side of *Rows to repeat at top* or *Columns to repeat at left* and select the rows or columns to repeat. Click the **Collapse Dialog** button again to expand the *Page Setup* dialog box.

Scale to Fit

The ***Scale to Fit*** feature expands or reduces a worksheet to fit on a specific number of pages or a specific paper size. You can adjust the worksheet as a percentage of the normal size or change the height or width values.

HOW TO: Scale to Fit

1. Click the **Page Layout** tab.
2. Select a scaling option [*Scale to Fit* group] (Figure 1-90).
   - Click the **Width** drop-down list and select the number of pages.
   - Click the **Height** drop-down list and select the number of pages.
   - Click the **Scale** up and down arrows to scale the worksheet a percentage of the normal size (100%).
   - You can also click the **Scale to Fit** launcher to display the *Page* tab in the *Page Setup* dialog box where you can make adjustments in the *Scaling* area (Figure 1-91).

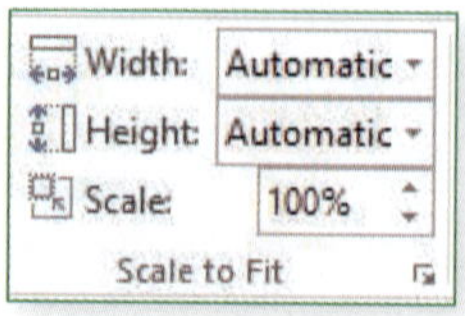

1-90 ***Scale to Fit* options**

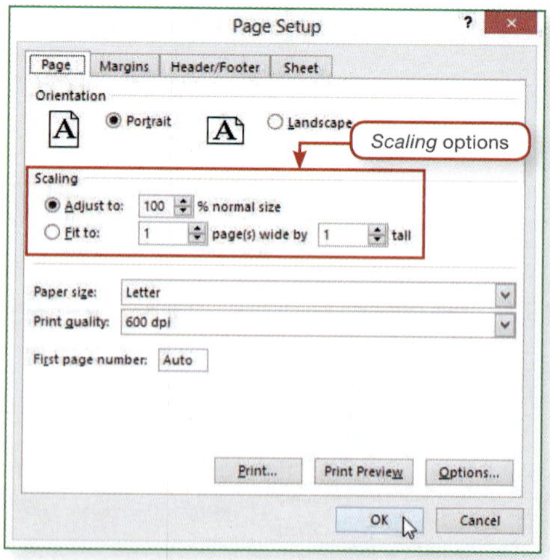

1-91 ***Scaling* options in the *Page Setup* dialog box**

Print Area

The ***print area*** is the section of the worksheet that prints. A print area consists of a single cell or a range of cells. You can add cells to a print area and you can clear the print area in order to print an entire worksheet.

HOW TO: Set and Clear Print Area

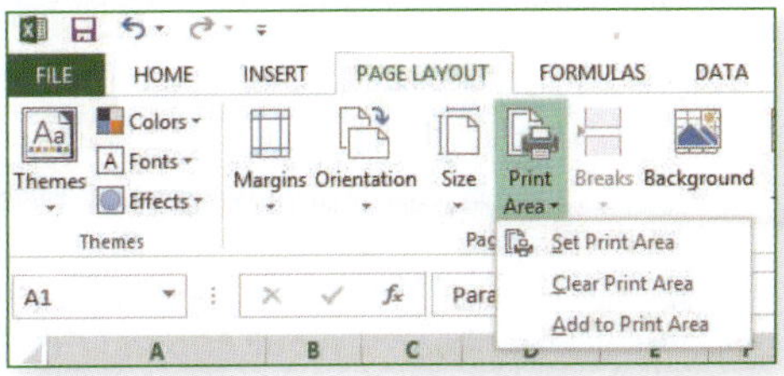

1-92 ***Print Area*** **options**

1. Select the cells to print.
   - Use **Ctrl** and drag to select multiple print areas.
2. Click the **Page Layout** tab.
3. Click the **Print Area** button [*Page Setup* group] (Figure 1-92).
4. Select **Set Print Area**.
   - Change the view to *Page Break Preview* to see the print area.
   - A print area is saved when the workbook is saved.
5. To enlarge the print area, select adjacent cells, click the **Print Area** button [*Page Layout* tab, *Page Setup* group], and then select **Add to Print Area**.
   - Switch to *Page Break Preview* to view the print area.
6. To clear the print area, click the **Print Area** button [*Page Layout* tab, *Page Setup* group] and select **Clear Print Area**.

ANOTHER WAY

You can print part of a worksheet using the *Page Setup* dialog box. Display the **Page Setup** dialog box and select the **Sheet** tab. Type the cell range to print in the *Print area* text box. Click **OK**.

Print a Worksheet or Workbook

Once you complete a worksheet, you can preview the worksheet to verify layout and formatting changes. There are two ways to preview a worksheet. One way is to click the **File** tab and then click **Print**. The other way is to open the *Page Setup* dialog box and click **Print Preview**.

HOW TO: Preview and Print a Worksheet

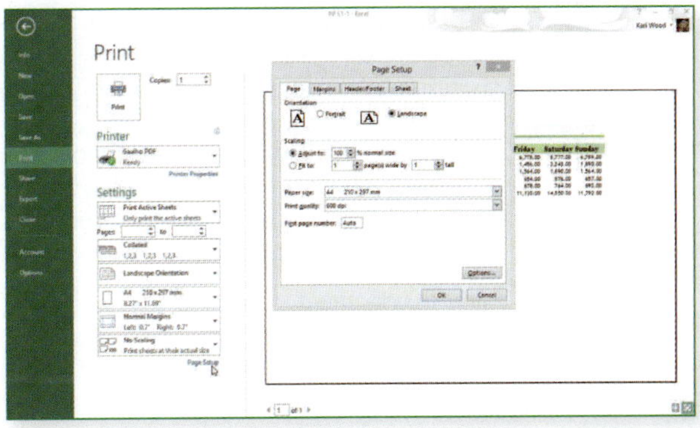

1-93 ***Backstage* view: *Page Setup* dialog box**

1. Click the **File** tab.
2. Click **Print** (Figure 1-93). A preview of your worksheet appears on the right.
   - If the workbook is more than one page, use the **Next Page** and **Previous Page** arrows to review each page.
   - Click **Show Margins** to manually adjust the header and page margins.
   - Click **Zoom to Page** to adjust the zoom level.
3. In the *Copies* area, set the number of copies to print.
4. Select an option to print the active sheet, print the entire workbook, or print a selection.
5. Specify the pages to print.
6. Verify orientation, paper size, and margin settings.
7. Click the **Page Setup** link to display the *Page Setup* dialog box and adjust settings.
8. Click **Print**.

ANOTHER WAY

Ctrl+P opens the *Print* area.

PAUSE & PRACTICE: EXCEL 1-4

For this project, you open your previous Pause & Practice file (***[your initials] PP E1-3.xlsx***) and change the display and view options, hide and unhide rows and worksheets, add document properties, and apply page setup formatting to finalize your Paradise Lakes Resorts workbook.

File Needed: ***[your initials] PP E1-3.xlsx***
Completed Project File Name: ***[your initials] PP E1-4.xlsx***

1. Open the ***[your initials] PP E1-3*** workbook.
2. Save the workbook as ***[your initials] PP E1-4***.
3. Select the **Location 1 – Cass Lake worksheet**.
4. Unhide row 9 from the previous Pause & Practice (the "Food & Beverage" row).
   a. Drag to select row headings **8** and **10**.
   b. Right-click one of the selected row headings.
   c. Choose **Unhide** from the context menu. Row 9 appears between rows 8 and 10.
5. Enter the following "Food & Beverage" data in row 9 for the cell range **B9:H9**.

	B	C	D	E	F	G	H
9	254.00	209.00	198.00	402.00	519.00	677.00	399.00

6. Increase the zoom to 150%.
   a. Click the **Zoom** button [*View* tab, *Zoom* group].
   b. The *Zoom* dialog box opens.
   c. Select the **Custom** radio button and enter 150 for the magnification.
   d. Click **OK** to see the change in magnification in your workbook.
7. Use *Freeze Panes* in the worksheet.
   a. Select **B5** in the worksheet.
   b. Click the **Freeze Panes** button [*View* tab, *Window* group].
   c. Choose the **Freeze Panes** option.
   d. Use the right horizontal scrolling arrow to view the last two columns of information (Figure 1-94).
8. Hide a worksheet.
   a. Click the **View** tab and click the **100%** zoom button [*Zoom* group].
   b. Click the **Freeze Panes** button and select **Unfreeze Panes**.
   c. Right-click the **Location 2** worksheet tab.
   d. Select **Hide**.

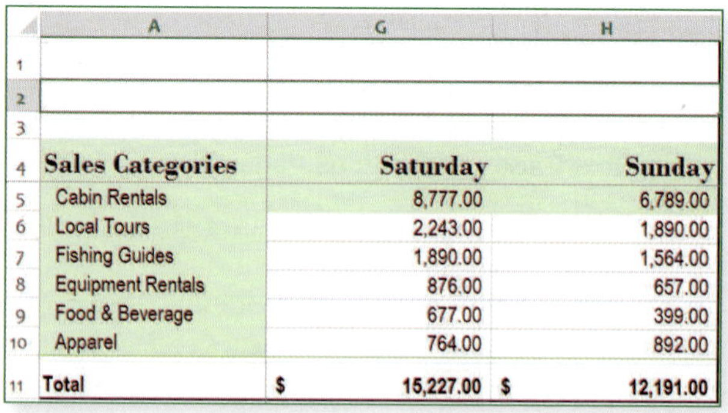

1-94 ***Freeze Panes* view**

9. Check the spelling of the worksheet.
   a. Click the **Spelling** button [*Review* tab, *Proofing* group].
   b. Correct any misspelled words in the worksheet.
10. Add document properties using the *Document Properties* panel.
    a. Click the **File** tab to display *Backstage* view.
    b. Click **Info** if it is not already selected.
    c. Click the **Properties** drop-down list at the top of the *Properties* pane and select **Show Document Panel**. The *Backstage* view closes and the *Document* Panel displays above the *Formula bar* in the Excel window.
    d. Add text in the following *Document Properties* fields (Figure 1-95):

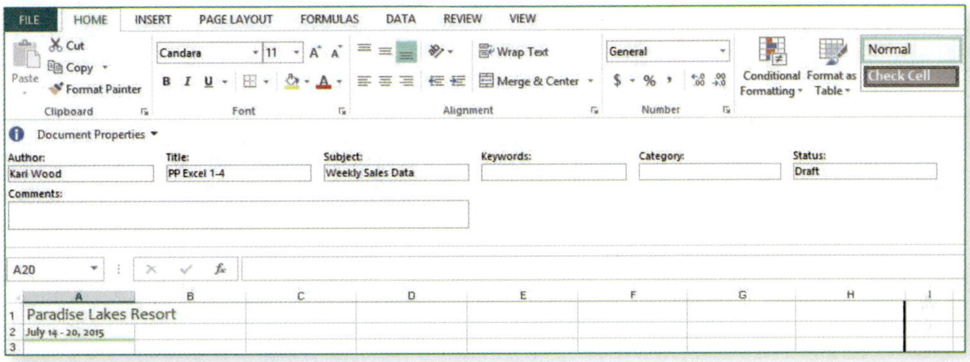

1-95 *Document* Panel

Title: PP Excel 1-4
Subject: Weekly Sales Data
Status: Draft

    f. Click the **X** in the upper right corner of the *Document* Panel to close the panel.
11. Change page setup options.
    a. Click the **Page Layout** tab.
    b. Click the **Orientation** button and select **Landscape**.
    c. Click the **Page Setup** launcher to display the *Page Setup* dialog box and select the **Margins** tab.
    d. Click the **Horizontally** check box in the *Center on page* area.
    e. Click **OK** to close the *Page Setup* dialog box.
12. Add a header and footer.
    a. Click the **Page Layout** tab.
    b. Open the *Page Setup* dialog box by clicking the **Page Setup** launcher.
    c. Click the **Header/Footer** tab.
    d. Click the **Header** drop-down list and select ***[your initials] PP E1-4***. The name of the file displays in the header.
    e. Click the **Footer** drop-down list and select **Page 1** to insert a page number in the footer.
    f. Click **OK** to close the *Page Setup* dialog box.
13. Select the print area and preview the worksheet.
    a. Select the cell range **A1:H11**.
    b. Select the **Page Layout** tab.
    c. Click the **Print Area** button and select **Set Print Area**.
    d. Deselect the text.
    e. Click the **File** tab and select **Print**. The workbook *Print Preview* displays.

14. Save and close the workbook (Figure 1-96).

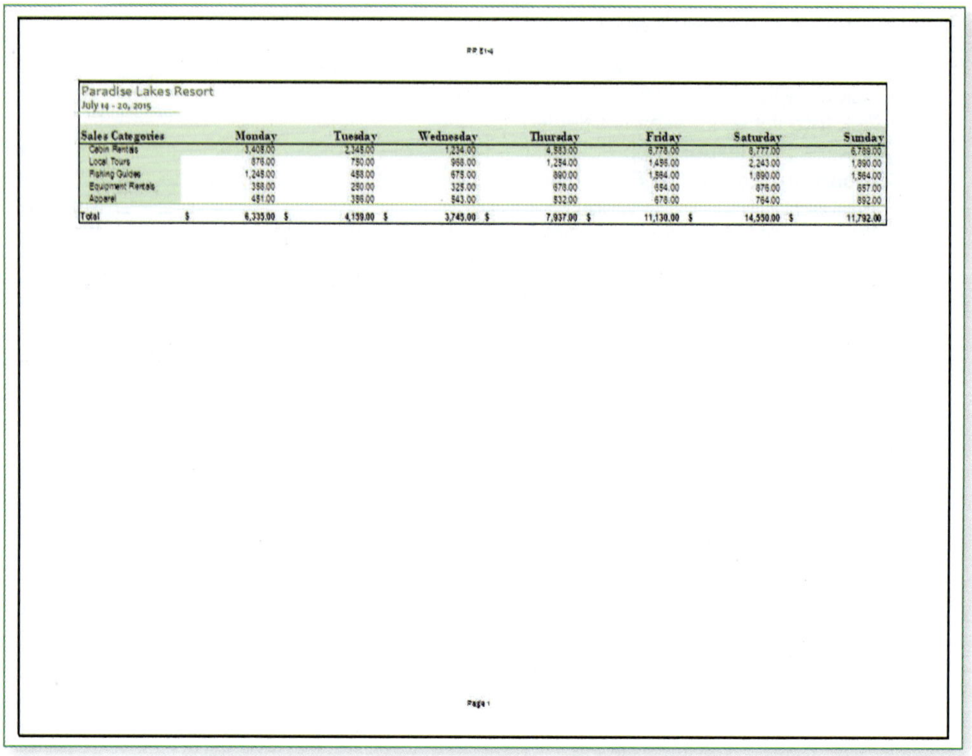

PP E1-4

Paradise Lakes Resort
July 14 - 20, 2015

Sales Categories	Monday	Tuesday	Wednesday	Thursday	Friday	Saturday	Sunday
Cabin Rentals	3,408.00	2,345.00	1,234.00	4,583.00	6,778.00	8,777.00	6,789.00
Local Tours	876.00	750.00	968.00	1,254.00	1,496.00	2,243.00	1,890.00
Fishing Guides	1,248.00	458.00	675.00	890.00	1,564.00	1,890.00	1,564.00
Equipment Rentals	358.00	250.00	325.00	678.00	654.00	876.00	657.00
Apparel	451.00	396.00	543.00	532.00	678.00	764.00	892.00
Total	$ 6,335.00	$ 4,159.00	$ 3,745.00	$ 7,937.00	$ 11,130.00	$ 14,550.00	$ 11,792.00

Page 1

1-96 PP E1-4 completed

Chapter Summary

1.1 Create, save, and open an Excel workbook (p. E1-3).

- When you create a blank workbook, Excel automatically assigns a file name to the file, such as *Book1*.
- You can save an Excel workbook in a variety of formats. By default, Excel workbooks are saved as ***.xlsx*** files.
- From the ***Share*** and ***Export*** areas of *Backstage* view, you have the option of saving in different online locations and saving a workbook as a PDF document.
- You can open workbooks from your computer, external storage device, or *SkyDrive*.

1.2 Edit a workbook by entering and deleting text, using the *Fill Handle* to complete a series, and using the cut, copy, and paste features (p. E1-6).

- When creating or editing a workbook, you can type data, import data from another file, or copy data from a web page or another source.
- Excel uses multiple pointers to indicate various selection, copying, resizing and moving options within a worksheet.
- Excel recognizes any combination of letters, numbers, spaces, and other characters as text and aligns each entry to the bottom left corner of the cell. Numeric entries align at the bottom right corner of the cell.
- Vertical alignment options include *Top Align, Middle Align,* and *Bottom Align*. Horizontal alignment options include *Align Left, Center,* and *Align Right*.
- Use the ***Fill Handle*** to complete lists, repeat numeric patterns, or copy cell contents to another location.
- Cut, copy, and paste data using the ***drag and drop*** method; ***Cut***, ***Copy***, and ***Paste*** buttons on the *Home* tab; the context menu; or shortcut keys on the keyboard.

1.3 Create a basic formula using *AutoSum* (p. E1-16).

- ***AutoSum*** is a button that automates the *Sum* function and other popular functions. *Sum* is used for adding values in a range.
- To adjust the cell range in a formula, use the *Formula bar* or drag the cell range border to reduce or expand the range.

1.4 Format a worksheet using different font attributes, borders, shading, cell styles, themes, and the *Format Painter* (p. E1-19).

- The default format for worksheet entries is 11 pt. Calibri.
- Customize font attributes using the *Font* group on the *Ribbon* or opening the *Format Cells* dialog box. You can change the ***Font Face***, ***Font Size***, ***Font Style***, and ***Font Type*** in a single cell, a group of cells, a worksheet, or an entire workbook.
- Add borders, shading, and number formatting to a worksheet to improve readability and to add emphasis.
- The ***Format Painter*** option allows you to copy formatting attributes and styles from one cell to another.
- Use ***Cell Styles*** to format a worksheet attractively using predefined settings such as alignment, color, borders, and fill color.
- Apply ***themes*** to a workbook for consistency in color, font, and effects.

1.5 Resize, insert, delete, and hide and unhide columns and rows in a worksheet (p. E1-26).

- Control the display of data by adjusting column width or row height.
- Two methods you can use to insert or delete columns and rows are the context menu and the ***Insert*** or ***Delete*** button.
- Display multiple lines in a cell using ***Wrap Text*** or use ***Merge & Center*** to combine two or more cells.
- You can hide sensitive data in a column or incomplete information in a row using the context menu or the *Format* button.

1.6 Insert, delete, edit, format, and rearrange worksheets (p. E1-31).

- The number of worksheets contained in a workbook is limited only by the amount of your computer memory.
- The default names for the sheets within a workbook are *Sheet1, Sheet2,* and so on.
- The two methods you can use to insert or delete worksheets are the context menu and the ***Insert*** or ***Delete*** buttons.
- The context menu and the *Format* button include options to ***Move*** and ***Copy*** worksheets.

1.7 Customize the Excel window by changing views, adjusting zoom level, freezing panes, and splitting a worksheet (p. E1-36).

- Excel has three main views: ***Normal***, ***Page Layout***, and ***Page Break Preview***.
- Display options such as ***Zoom***, ***Freeze Panes***, ***Gridlines***, and ***Headings*** can help make larger spreadsheets easier to view.
- You can ***Hide*** and ***Unhide*** sheets if they include sensitive data.

1.8 Finalize a workbook by spell checking, adding document properties, applying page setup options, and printing (p. E1-41).

- Check spelling using the *Review* tab.
- Various ***Document Properties*** are created automatically. These include *Creation* date, *Modified* date, *Accessed* date, and file *Size*. You can add properties such as *Title*, *Author*, *Comments*, *Subject*, and *Company*.
- The *Document Information Panel* on the right side of *Backstage* view displays details that are available for update or change.
- The ***Advanced Properties*** option in the *Document Information* panel displays the *Properties* dialog box.
- Use *Page Setup* options to customize page layout settings and print preview to review worksheets.

Check for Understanding

In the ***Online Learning Center*** for this text (www.mhhe.com/office2013inpractice), there are a variety of resources that can be used to review the concepts covered in this chapter.

The following Online Learning Resources are available on the Online Learning Center:

- Multiple choice questions
- Short answer questions
- Matching exercises

USING MICROSOFT EXCEL 2013

Guided Project 1-1

Abdul Kohl has just been hired at Life's Animal Shelter and asked to track the organization's weekly expenses on a spreadsheet.
[Student Learning Outcomes 1.1, 1.2, 1.3, 1.4, 1.5, 1.6, 1.8]

File Needed: None
Completed Project File Name: ***[your initials] Excel 1-1.xlsx***

Skills Covered in This Project

- Create and save a workbook.
- Enter text and numbers.
- Change font size and attributes.
- Create a formula using *AutoSum*.
- Use the *Fill Handle*.
- Apply *Cell Styles*.
- Apply a theme.
- Apply page layout options.
- Insert a row and adjust column width and row height.
- Rename and apply color to sheet tabs.
- Merge and center titles.
- Apply number formatting.
- Insert and delete sheets.
- Use spell check.

1. Open a new workbook.
   a. Click the **File** tab to open the *Backstage* view.
   b. Click **New** and then click **Blank workbook** to open a new blank workbook.
2. Save the workbook as ***[your initials] Excel 1-1***.
   a. Press **F12** to open the *Save As* dialog box.
   b. Rename the file ***[your initials] Excel 1-1*** in the *File name* area.
   c. Select the folder or **Browse** to the location on your *SkyDrive*, computer, or storage device to save the workbook.
   d. Click **Save**.
3. Enter the data.
   a. Select **A1**, type Life's Animal Shelter, and then press **Enter**. Type September 1 – 7, 2015 and press **Enter**.
   b. Type the remaining data in Figure 1-97.

	A	B	C	D	E	F	G	H
1	Life's Animal Shelter							
2	September 1 - 7, 2015							
3								
4	Expense Categories	Monday						
5	Food	340.45	344.05	350.51	340.01	341.18	359.75	340.02
6	Medicine	525.33	529.31	535.25	524.59	527.99	543.39	540.01
7	Wages	675.21	580.91	575.88	579.55	680.81	750.05	565.9
8	Heat	25.75	26.01	28.05	25.03	25.99	31.04	24.99
9	Electricity	19.45	20.09	21.75	19.02	19.99	23.56	19.45
10	Total							

1-97 Excel 1-1 data

4. Use the *Fill Handle* to copy a series.
   a. Select **B4**.
   b. Place the pointer on the *Fill Handle* (small black square in the lower right corner of the cell) until the fill pointer (thin black plus sign) appears.
   c. Click and drag the fill pointer to **H4**.

5. Apply *Merge & Center* to the title and subtitle of your worksheet.
   a. Select **A1:H1** and click the **Merge & Center** button [*Home* tab, *Alignment* group].
   b. Select **A2:H2** and click the **Merge & Center** button [*Home* tab, *Alignment* group].
6. Apply *Cell Styles*.
   a. Select **A1** and click the **More** button [*Home* tab, *Styles* group].
   b. Select **Title** in the *Titles and Headings* category.
   c. Select **A2** and click the **More** button [*Home* tab, *Styles* group].
   d. Select **Heading 2** in the *Titles and Headings* category.
   e. Select **A4:A9**, hold down **Ctrl**, and select **B4:H4**.
   f. Click the **More** button [*Home* tab, *Styles* group].
   g. Select **60%**, **Accent 1** in the *Themed Cell Styles* category.
   h. Select **A10:H10** and click the **More** button [*Home* tab, *Styles* group].
   i. Select **Total** in the *Titles and Headings* category.
7. Apply font attributes.
   a. Select **A4:A9**, hold down **Ctrl**, and then select **B4:H4**.
   b. Click the **Bold** button [*Home* tab, *Font* group].
   c. Select **A5:A9**, hold down **Ctrl**, and then select **B4:H4**.
   d. Click the **Increase Indent** button [*Home* tab, *Alignment* group] three times.
   e. Click the **Font size** drop-down list [*Home* tab, *Font* group] and select **12 pt**.
8. Increase column width.
   a. Select **A4:H10**.
   b. Click the **Format** button [*Home* tab, *Cells* group].
   c. Select **AutoFit Column Width**. Deselect the cells.
9. Apply themes to the worksheet.
   a. Click the **Themes** button [*Page Layout* tab, *Themes* group] and choose **Integral** from the gallery (Figure 1-98).
   b. Click the **Theme Fonts** button [*Page Layout* tab, *Themes* group] and select **Franklin Gothic** from the gallery.
10. Apply font attributes to the labels in the spreadsheet.
    a. Select **A4**.
    b. Click the **Font** drop-down list [*Home* tab, *Font* group] and select **Arial**.
    c. Click the **Font Size** drop-down list and select **14**.
11. Use *AutoSum* to calculate a total and copy the formula using the *Fill Handle*.
    a. Select **B10**.
    b. Click **AutoSum** [*Home* tab, *Editing* group] and press **Enter**.
    c. Select **B10** and place the pointer on the *Fill Handle* (small black square in the lower right corner of the cell) until the fill pointer (thin black plus sign) appears.
    d. Click and drag the fill pointer to cell **H10**.
12. Apply number formatting to the numeric data.
    a. Select **B5:H10**.
    b. Click the **Accounting Number Format** button [*Home* tab, *Number* group].
13. Adjust column width.
    a. Select **A4:H10**.
    b. Click the **Format** button [*Home* tab, *Cells* group].
    c. Select **AutoFit Column Width**.

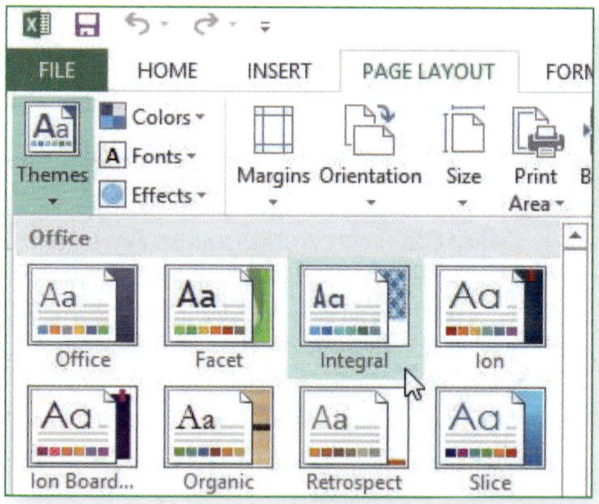

1-98 *Integral* theme button

14. Press **Ctrl+S** to save the workbook.
15. Change column width on a range of columns.
    a. Click and drag to select the column headings **B:H**.
    b. Click the **Format** button [*Home* tab, *Cells* group].
    c. Select **Column Width** from the menu.
    d. Enter 15.0 characters as the new width.
    e. Click **OK**.
16. Apply new row heights.
    a. Click row heading **4**, hold down **Ctrl**, and click row heading **10**.
    b. Right-click row heading **4**.
    c. Choose **Row Height** from the context menu.
    d. Enter 21.0 as the new height.
    e. Click **OK**.
17. Insert a new row and row heading.
    a. Right-click row heading **9**.
    b. Choose **Insert** from the context menu to add a new row. The new row appears directly above the originally selected row.
    c. Select cell **A9** and type: Cages & Equipment.
18. Increase the width of column A to **29.00**.
19. Enter the following information into the cell range **B9:H9**.

	B	C	D	E	F	G	H
9	199.03	209.25	198.90	229.05	245.09	351.98	205.55

20. Rename and color sheet tab.
    a. Double-click the **Sheet1** tab.
    b. Type the following name: Park Rapids, MN Location.
    c. Press **Enter**.
    d. Click the **Format** button [*Home* tab, *Cells* group].
    e. Select **Tab Color** in the *Organize Sheets* category to add a fill color to the background of the sheet tab.
    f. Select **Blue Accent 2, Darker 50%** (last color in the sixth *Theme Color* column) (Figure 1-99).

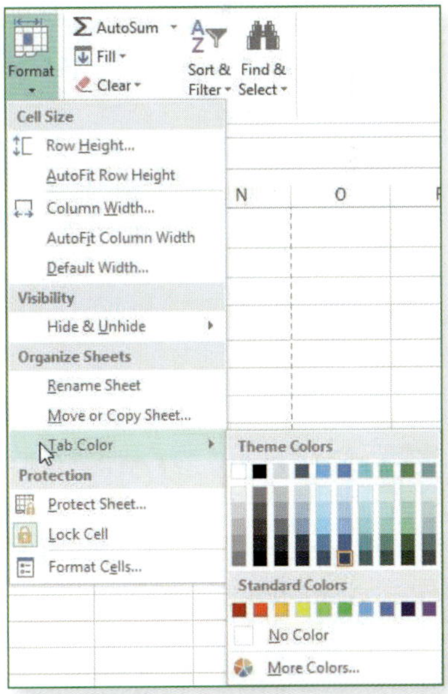

1-99 Worksheet *Tab Color* options

21. Insert a new sheet.
    a. Click the **Insert** button drop-down arrow [*Home* tab, *Cells* group] and select **Insert Sheet**. The new sheet named **Sheet2** appears to the left of the *Park Rapids* worksheet tab.
    b. Add another sheet to the workbook by clicking the **New Sheet** button.
22. Delete *Sheet2* and *Sheet3*.
    a. Click the **Sheet2** tab, press and hold **Shift**, click the **Sheet3** tab, and release **Shift**.
    b. Click the **Delete** button drop-down arrow [*Home* tab, *Cells* group] and select **Delete Sheet**.
23. Press **Ctrl+S** to save the workbook.

24. Change *Page Setup* options.
    a. Click the **Page Layout** tab and click the **Page Setup** launcher.
    b. Select the **Page** tab in the *Page Setup* dialog box.
    c. Click the **Landscape** radio button under *Orientation*.
    d. Click the **Fit to:** radio button under *Scaling* and enter 1 page wide by 1 tall.
    e. Click the **Header/Footer** tab.
    f. Click the **Header:** drop-down list and select ***[your initials] Excel 1-1*** from the list.
    g. Click the **Margins** tab.
    h. Click the **Horizontally** check box under *Center on page*.
    i. Click **OK**.
25. Spell check the worksheet.
    a. Press **Ctrl+Home** to go to cell **A1**.
    b. Click the **Spelling** button [*Review* tab, *Proofing* group].
    c. Correct any misspelled words.
26. Click the **File** tab and select **Print** to preview the workbook.
27. Save and close the workbook (Figure 1-100).

Excel 1-1

	A	B	C	D	E	F	G	H
1	Life's Animal Shelter							
2	September 1-7, 2015							
3								
4	Expense Categories	Monday	Tuesday	Wednesday	Thursday	Friday	Saturday	Sunday
5	Food	$ 340.45	$ 344.05	$ 350.51	$ 340.01	$ 341.18	$ 359.75	$ 340.02
6	Medicine	$ 525.33	$ 529.31	$ 535.25	$ 524.59	$ 527.99	$ 543.39	$ 540.01
7	Wages	$ 675.21	$ 580.91	$ 575.88	$ 579.55	$ 680.81	$ 750.05	$ 565.90
8	Heat	$ 25.75	$ 26.01	$ 28.05	$ 25.03	$ 25.99	$ 31.04	$ 24.99
9	Cages & Equipment	$ 199.03	$ 209.25	$ 198.90	$ 229.05	$ 245.09	$ 351.98	$ 205.55
10	Electricity	$ 19.45	$ 20.09	$ 21.75	$ 19.02	$ 19.99	$ 23.56	$ 19.45
11	**Total**	**$ 1,785.22**	**$ 1,709.62**	**$ 1,710.34**	**$ 1,717.25**	**$ 1,841.05**	**$ 2,059.77**	**$ 1,695.92**

1-100 Excel 1-1 completed

Guided Project 1-2

For this project, you edit and format a spreadsheet for a sales representative for Eller Software Services. The spreadsheet contains clients' personal information and a listing of their product purchases. **[Student Learning Outcomes 1.1, 1.2, 1.3, 1.4, 1.5, 1.6, 1.7, 1.8]**

File Needed: ***EllerSoftwareServices-1.xlsx***
Completed Project File Name: ***[your initials] Excel 1-2.xlsx***

Skills Covered in This Project

- Open and save a workbook.
- Enter and format text and numbers.
- Copy text using the *Fill Handle*.
- Create a formula using *AutoSum*.
- Apply a theme and *Cell Styles*.
- Merge and center titles and subtitles.
- Change orientation.
- Apply font attributes.
- Apply numeric formatting.
- Apply date formatting.
- Apply a border.
- Change zoom level.
- Hide and insert a row and adjust column width.
- Rename and apply color to sheet tabs.
- Use spell check.
- Apply page layout options.

1. Open a workbook.
   a. Click the **File** tab and click **Open**.
   b. Locate the folder where your files are saved.
   c. Open the workbook ***EllerSoftwareServices-1.xlsx***.
2. Rename the workbook ***[your initials] Excel 1-2***.
   a. Press **F12** to open the *Save As* dialog box.
   b. Locate the folder where your files are located.
   c. Rename the file ***[your initials] Excel 1-2*** in the *File name* area.
   d. Click **Save**.
3. Apply a theme to the worksheet.
   a. Click the **Themes** button [*Page Layout* tab, *Themes* group].
   b. Choose **Retrospect** from the *Office* gallery.
4. Enter and format data.
   a. Select **E5**, type **MN**, and press **Enter**.
   b. Select **E5** and point to the *Fill Handle*.
   c. Click and drag the fill pointer to **E13**.
   d. Select **C5:C13**.
   e. Press **Ctrl+1** to open the *Format Cells* dialog box.
   f. Click the **Number** tab and click **Special** under *Category*.
   g. Select **Phone Number** and click **OK** to close the *Format Cells* dialog box.
5. Use *AutoSum* to calculate the total of gross sales and adjust the reference range.
   a. Type Total in **A15**.
   b. Select cell **I15**.
   c. Click **AutoSum** [*Home* tab, *Editing* group] and press **Enter**.
   d. Select **I15** and click the cell reference range in the *Formula bar*.
   e. Edit the cell range to **I13** and press **Enter**.
6. Apply *Merge & Center* to the title and subtitle of the worksheet.
   a. Select **A1:I1** and click the **Merge & Center** button [*Home* tab, *Alignment* group].
   b. Select **A2:I2** and click the **Merge & Center** button.
7. Apply *Cell Styles*.
   a. Select **A1** and click the **More** button [*Home* tab, *Styles* group].
   b. Select **Title** in the *Titles and Headings* category.
   c. Select **A2** and click the **More** button and select **Heading 2** in the *Titles and Headings* category.

d. Select **A4:A15**, hold down **Ctrl**, and then select **B4:I4**.
e. Click the **More** button and select **40%- Accent 1** in the *Themed Cell Styles* category.
f. Select **I15**, click the **More** button, and then select **Total** in the *Titles and Headings* category.

8. Apply diagonal rotation to text.
   a. Select **A4:I4**.
   b. Click the **Orientation** button [*Home* tab, *Alignment* group].
   c. Select **Angle Counterclockwise**.

9. Apply font attributes.
   a. Select the cell range **A4:A15**, hold down **Ctrl**, and click and drag to select **B4:I4**.
   b. Click the **Font size** drop-down list [*Home* tab, *Font* group] and select **12**.
   c. Click the **Font type** drop-down list [*Home* tab, *Font* group] and select **Verdana**.
   d. Click the **Bold** button [*Home* tab, *Font* group].
   e. Select the non-adjacent cell ranges **C5:C13** and **E5:F13**.
   f. Click **Center** [*Home* tab, *Alignment* group].
   g. Select **A1:A2** and click the **Increase Font Size** button [*Home* tab, *Font* group] two times.

10. Apply numeric formatting to your spreadsheet.
    a. Select **I5:I15**.
    b. Click **Comma Style** [*Home* tab, *Number* group].
    c. Select **I5**, press **Ctrl**, and select **I15**.
    d. Press **Ctrl+1** to open the *Format Cells* dialog box.
    e. Select the **Number** tab, if necessary, and select the **Accounting** category.
    f. Change the **Symbol** drop-down list to **$**.
    g. Click **OK** to close the *Format Cells* dialog box.

11. Apply date formatting to your spreadsheet.
    a. Select **H5:H13**.
    b. Click the **Short Date** format from the *Number Format* drop-down list [*Home* tab, *Number* group].

12. Increase the width of your columns.
    a. Select **A4:I15**.
    b. Click the **Format** button [*Home* tab, *Cells* group].
    c. Select **AutoFit Column Width**.

13. Press **Ctrl+S** to save the workbook.

14. Edit a cell.
    a. Double-click cell **G9** to activate edit mode.
    b. Delete the word **Software** from the cell contents and press **Enter**.

15. Change the width of a column.
    a. Click the column **G** heading to select the column.
    b. Click the **Format** button [*Home* tab, *Cells* group] and select **Column Width** from the menu.
    c. Enter 31.0 characters as the new width.
    d. Click **OK**.

16. Hide an existing row and insert a new row and row heading.
    a. Right-click row heading **10**.
    b. Choose **Hide** from the context menu.
    c. Right-click row heading **11**.
    d. Choose **Insert** from the context menu to add a new row. The new row appears directly above the originally selected row.
    e. Select cell **A11** and type Hilary Marschke.

f. Enter the following information into the cell range **B11:I11**. (Figure 1-101).

B11: 245 West Third Avenue
C11: 3203555443
D11: Saint Cloud
E11: MN
F11: 56301
G11: Training
H11: 11/15/2015
I11: 750.00

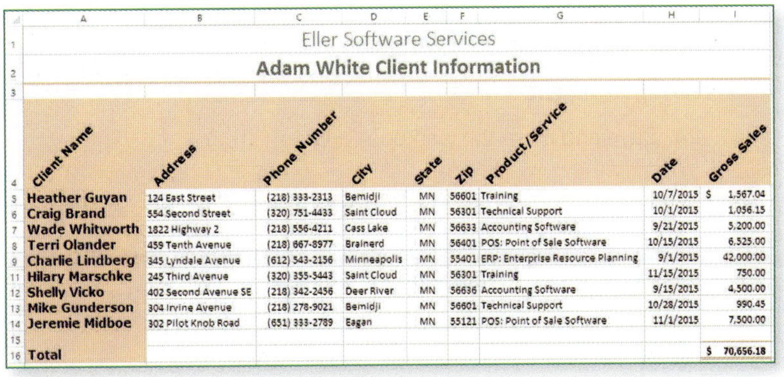

1-101 Adjusted column width

17. Rename and color a sheet tab.
   a. Double-click the **Sheet1** tab.
   b. Type the following name: MN Clients.
   c. Press **Enter**.
   d. Right-click the **MN Clients** tab.
   e. Point to **Tab Color** to add a fill color to the background of the sheet tab.
   f. Select **Orange Accent 1**, **Darker 50%** (last color in the fifth *Theme Color* column) (Figure 1-102).

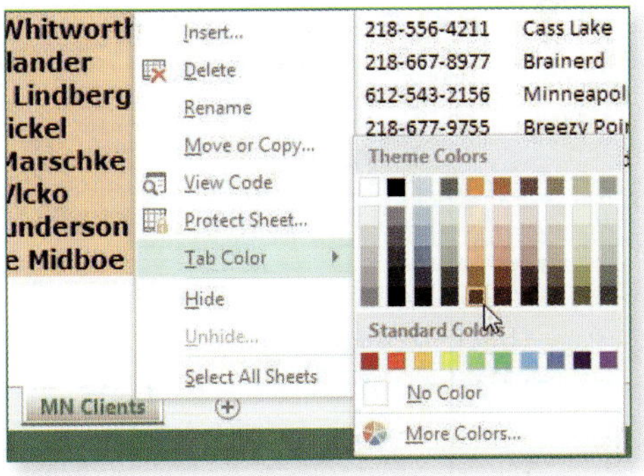

1-102 Worksheet *Tab Color* options

18. Save the workbook.

19. Apply a bottom border.
   a. Select **A4:I4**.
   b. Press **Ctrl+1** to open the **Format Cells** dialog box.
   c. Click the **Border** tab.
   d. Select the fifth line style in the second column and select **Orange**, **Accent 1**, **Darker 50%** for the line color (last color in the fifth column).
   e. Select the bottom border button in the **Border** area (third button under the *Border* heading).
   f. Click **OK**.

20. Change the zoom level.
   a. Click the **View** tab.
   b. Click **Zoom**.
   c. Select the **75%** ***Magnification*** level.
   d. Click **OK**.

21. Select the **Spelling** button [*Review* tab, *Proofing* group] and correct any misspellings in the worksheet.

22. Preview the worksheet.
   a. Select **Print** from the *File* tab.
   b. Review the workbook layout and format, and then return to the worksheet.
   c. Use the **Zoom** slider in the *Status bar* to return to *100%* magnification.

23. Change *Page Setup* options.
   a. Display the *Page Layout* tab and click the **Page Setup** launcher [*Page Setup* group].
   b. Select the **Page** tab and click the **Landscape** radio button under *Orientation*.
   c. Click the **Fit to:** radio button under *Scaling*, enter 1 page wide by 1 tall.

d. Select the *Margins* tab and click the **Horizontally** check box under *Center on page*.
e. Select the **Header/Footer** tab.
f. Click the **Footer:** drop-down button and select **MN Clients** to print the sheet name in the footer.
g. Click **OK**.

24. Save and close the workbook (Figure 1-103).

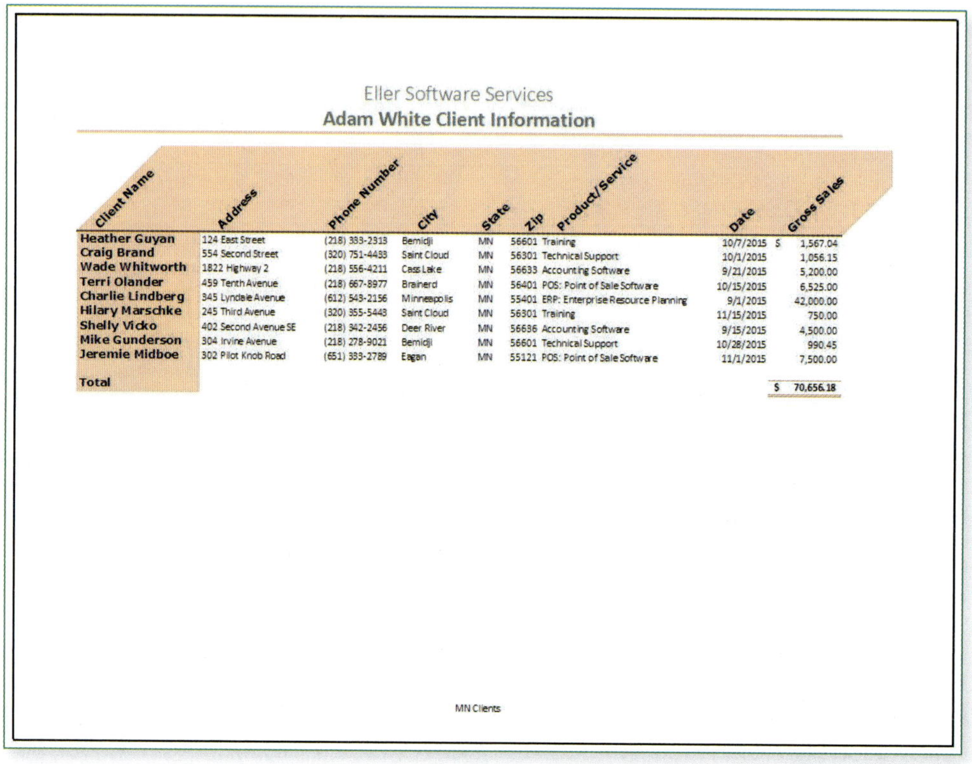
Eller Software Services

Adam White Client Information

Client Name	Address	Phone Number	City	State	Zip	Product/Service	Date	Gross Sales
Heather Guyan	124 East Street	(218) 333-2313	Bemidji	MN	56601	Training	10/7/2015	$ 1,567.04
Craig Brand	554 Second Street	(320) 751-4433	Saint Cloud	MN	56301	Technical Support	10/1/2015	1,056.15
Wade Whitworth	1822 Highway 2	(218) 556-4211	Cass Lake	MN	56633	Accounting Software	9/21/2015	5,200.00
Terri Olander	459 Tenth Avenue	(218) 667-8977	Brainerd	MN	56401	POS: Point of Sale Software	10/15/2015	6,525.00
Charlie Lindberg	345 Lyndale Avenue	(612) 543-2156	Minneapolis	MN	55401	ERP: Enterprise Resource Planning	9/1/2015	42,000.00
Hilary Marschke	245 Third Avenue	(320) 355-5443	Saint Cloud	MN	56301	Training	11/15/2015	750.00
Shelly Vicko	402 Second Avenue SE	(218) 342-2456	Deer River	MN	56636	Accounting Software	9/15/2015	4,500.00
Mike Gunderson	304 Irvine Avenue	(218) 278-9021	Bemidji	MN	56601	Technical Support	10/28/2015	990.45
Jeremie Midboe	302 Pilot Knob Road	(651) 333-2789	Eagan	MN	55121	POS: Point of Sale Software	11/1/2015	7,500.00
Total								$ 70,656.18

MN Clients

1-103 Excel 1-2 completed

Guided Project 1-3

For this project, you create an Excel spreadsheet that consists of the product inventory information for Wear-Ever Shoes.

[Student Learning Outcomes 1.1, 1.2, 1.3, 1.4, 1.5, 1.6, 1.7, 1.8]

File Needed: ***WearEverShoes-1.xlsx***
Completed Project File Name: ***[your initials] Excel 1-3.xlsx***

Skills Covered in This Project

- Open and save a workbook.
- Enter and format text and numbers.
- Use the *Fill Handle* to copy a formula.
- Apply a theme and *Cell Styles*.
- Merge and center title and subtitle.
- Apply numeric formatting.
- Adjust column width and row height.
- Insert a column.
- Use *Page Layout* view to insert a footer.
- Move cell contents.
- Check spelling.
- Rename sheet tabs and apply color to sheet tabs.
- Apply page layout options.

1. Open and rename the workbook file.
   a. Press **Ctrl+O** to display the *Open* area.
   b. Locate the folder where your files are located.
   c. Open the workbook file ***WearEverShoes-1.xlsx***.
   d. Press **F12** and locate the folder where your files are saved.
   e. Save the workbook as ***[your initials] Excel 1-3***.
2. Click the **Themes** button [*Page Layout* tab, *Themes* group] and choose **Ion** from the gallery.
3. Increase column width.
   a. Select **A4:I12**.
   b. Click the **Format** button [*Home* tab, *Cells* group].
   c. Select **AutoFit Column Width**.
4. Apply *Cell Styles*.
   a. Select **A1**, click the **More** button [*Home* tab, *Styles* group], and select **Title** in the *Titles and Headings* category.
   b. Select **A3**, click the **More** button, and select **Heading 2** in the *Titles and Headings* category.
   c. Select **A4:A12**, press **Ctrl**, and select **B4:I4**.
   d. Click the **More** button and select **40%- Accent 1** in the *Themed Cell Styles* category.
   e. Select **B5:I12**.
   f. Click the **More** button and select **20%- Accent 2** in the *Themed Cell Styles* category.
5. Apply *Merge & Center* to the title and subtitle of your worksheet.
   a. Select **A1:I1** and click **Merge & Center** [*Home* tab, *Alignment* group].
   b. Select **A3:I3** and click **Merge & Center**.
6. Apply formatting.
   a. Select the cell range **A4:A12**, press **Ctrl**, and select **B4:I4**.
   b. Click the **Font size** drop-down list [*Home* tab, *Font* group] and select **12 pt**.
   c. Click the **Font type** drop-down list [*Home* tab, *Font* group] and select **Trebuchet MS**.
   d. Select **A4:I4** and click the **Center** button [*Home* tab, *Alignment* group].
   e. Select **I5:I12** and click the **Center** button [*Home* tab, *Alignment* group].
   f. Select **E5:E12** and click the **Increase Indent** button [*Home* tab, *Alignment* group].
7. Use the *Fill Handle* to copy a formula.
   a. Click **H5**.
   b. Point to the *Fill Handle* in the lower right corner and drag the fill pointer to **H12**.
8. Apply numeric formatting and adjust column width.
   a. Select **F5:H12**.
   b. Click **Comma Style** [*Home* tab, *Number* group].

c. Select **A4:I12**.
d. Click the **Format** button [*Home* tab, *Cells* group] and select **AutoFit Column Width**.

9. Save your workbook (Figure 1-104).

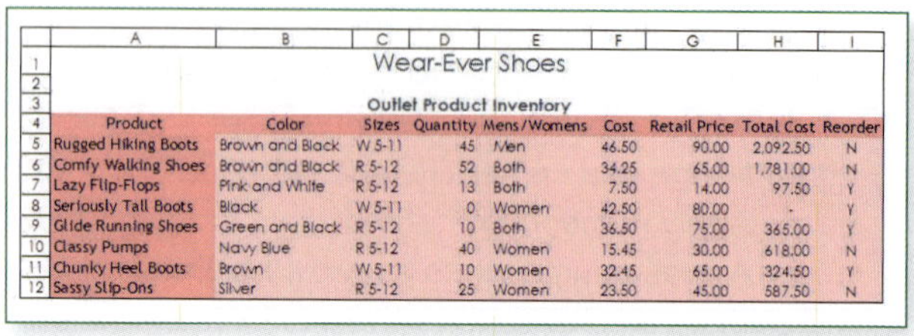

	A	B	C	D	E	F	G	H	I
1	Wear-Ever Shoes								
2									
3	Outlet Product Inventory								
4	Product	Color	Sizes	Quantity	Mens/Womens	Cost	Retail Price	Total Cost	Reorder
5	Rugged Hiking Boots	Brown and Black	W 5-11	45	Men	46.50	90.00	2,092.50	N
6	Comfy Walking Shoes	Brown and Black	R 5-12	52	Both	34.25	65.00	1,781.00	N
7	Lazy Flip-Flops	Pink and White	R 5-12	13	Both	7.50	14.00	97.50	Y
8	Seriously Tall Boots	Black	W 5-11	0	Women	42.50	80.00	-	Y
9	Glide Running Shoes	Green and Black	R 5-12	10	Both	36.50	75.00	365.00	Y
10	Classy Pumps	Navy Blue	R 5-12	40	Women	15.45	30.00	618.00	N
11	Chunky Heel Boots	Brown	W 5-11	10	Women	32.45	65.00	324.50	Y
12	Sassy Slip-Ons	Silver	R 5-12	25	Women	23.50	45.00	587.50	N

1-104 Formatted worksheet

10. Edit a cell.
    a. Double-click cell **B7** to activate edit mode.
    b. Edit the cell's contents so it appears as Pink.
11. Change the width of a column.
    a. Click column heading **A** to select the column.
    b. Click the **Format** button [*Home* tab, *Cells* group] and select **Column Width**.
    c. Enter 24.0 as the new width and click **OK**.
12. Apply a new row height.
    a. Right-click row heading **4**.
    b. Choose **Row Height** from the context menu.
    c. Enter 21.0 as the new height and click **OK**.
13. Insert a new column and type a column heading and data in the new column.
    a. Right-click column heading **D**.
    b. Choose **Insert** from the context menu to add a new column.
    c. Select cell **D4** and type: Discontinue.
    d. Increase the width of the new column if needed to automatically fit the contents of the column.
    e. Enter the following information into the cell range **D5:D12**:

	D
5	No
6	No
7	No
8	No
9	No
10	Yes
11	No
12	Yes

14. Rename and color the sheet tab.
    a. Double-click the **Sheet1** tab.
    b. Type the following name: Northern Warehouse and press **Enter**.
    c. Click the **Format** button [*Home* tab, *Cells* group].
    d. Select **Tab Color** in the *Organize Sheets* category to add a fill color to the background of the sheet tab.
    e. Select **Dark Red, Accent 1, Darker 50%** (last color in the fifth *Theme Color* column).
15. Click the **Save** button on the *Quick Access* toolbar to save the workbook changes.
16. Move cell contents and adjust column width.
    a. Select the cell range **D4:D12**.
    b. Click the **Cut** button [*Home* tab, *Clipboard* group].

c. Click cell **K4** and click the **Paste** button [*Home* tab, *Clipboard* group].
d. Select **E4:K12**.
e. Place the pointer on the right border of the selected cell range, drag the cell range to **D4**, and release the pointer.
f. Select **B4:J12**, click the **Format** button [*Home* tab, *Cells* group], and select **AutoFit Column Width**.

17. Click the **Spelling** button [*Review* tab, *Proofing* group] and correct any misspellings in the worksheet.

18. Use *Page Layout* view to insert a footer.
    a. Click the **Insert** tab and click **Header & Footer**.
    b. Click the **Header & Footer Tools Design** tab.
    c. Click **Go to Footer** [*Header & Footer Tools Design* tab, *Navigation* group].
    d. Click in the middle section of the footer area and select **File Name** in the *Header & Footer Elements* group. Click in the worksheet to see the file name.
    e. Switch to *Normal* view.

19. Change the *Page Setup* options.
    a. Click the **Page Layout** tab and click the **Page Setup** launcher.
    b. Select the **Page** tab from the *Page Setup* dialog box and click the **Landscape** radio button under *Orientation*.
    c. Click the **Fit to:** radio button and enter 1 page wide by 1 tall.
    d. Click **OK**.

20. Save and close the workbook (Figure 1-105).

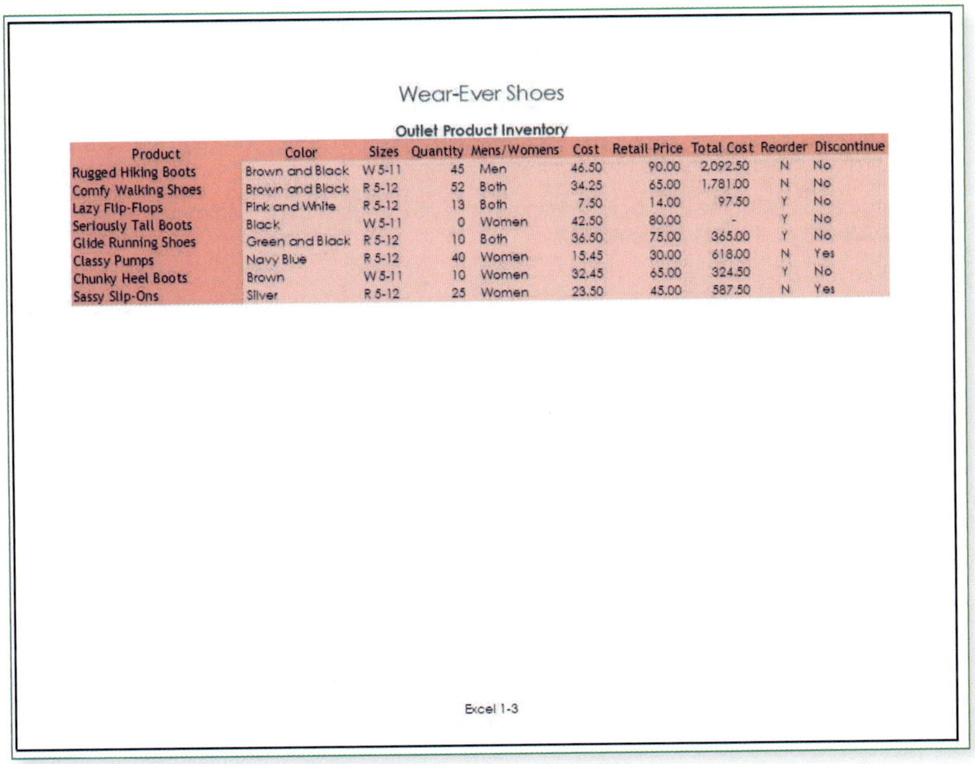

Wear-Ever Shoes

Outlet Product Inventory

Product	Color	Sizes	Quantity	Mens/Womens	Cost	Retail Price	Total Cost	Reorder	Discontinue
Rugged Hiking Boots	Brown and Black	W 5-11	45	Men	46.50	90.00	2,092.50	N	No
Comfy Walking Shoes	Brown and Black	R 5-12	52	Both	34.25	65.00	1,781.00	N	No
Lazy Flip-Flops	Pink and White	R 5-12	13	Both	7.50	14.00	97.50	Y	No
Seriously Tall Boots	Black	W 5-11	0	Women	42.50	80.00	-	Y	No
Glide Running Shoes	Green and Black	R 5-12	10	Both	36.50	75.00	365.00	Y	No
Classy Pumps	Navy Blue	R 5-12	40	Women	15.45	30.00	618.00	N	Yes
Chunky Heel Boots	Brown	W 5-11	10	Women	32.45	65.00	324.50	Y	No
Sassy Slip-Ons	Silver	R 5-12	25	Women	23.50	45.00	587.50	N	Yes

Excel 1-3

1-105 Excel 1-3 completed

Independent Project 1-4

You have just been hired as an administrative assistant at Blue Lake Sport Company. Your supervisor has asked you to convert her daily sales report into a spreadsheet that she can distribute at the department meeting.
[Student Learning Outcomes 1.1, 1.2, 1.3, 1.4, 1.5, 1.6, 1.7, 1.8]

File Needed: ***BlueLakeSports-1.xlsx***
Completed Project File Name: ***[your initials] Excel 1-4.xlsx***

Skills Covered in This Project

- Open and save a workbook.
- Enter and format text and numbers.
- Merge and center title and date.
- Use *AutoSum*.
- Create a formula and use the *Fill Handle*.
- Apply a theme and apply *Cell Styles*.
- Use *Page Layout* view to insert a header and footer.
- Apply page layout options.
- Adjust column width and row height.
- Rename and apply color to sheet tabs.

1. Open the workbook file ***BlueLakeSport-1.xlsx***.
2. Save the presentation as ***[your initials] Excel 1-4***.
3. Apply the **Slice** theme to the worksheet.
4. Edit worksheet data.
   a. Edit the title in **A1** so that the word "Sports" contains an apostrophe and appears as follows: Sport's.
   b. Edit the value in cell **B6** to 5102.
5. Merge and center the title in cell **A1** across the cell range **A1:H1**, and merge and center the date in cell **A2** across the cell range **A2:H2**.
6. Delete row **8**.
7. Use the *Fill Handle* to complete a series.
   a. Select **B4**.
   b. Use *Fill Handle* to add headings for columns **C:H**.
8. Apply *Cell Styles* to the labels in the spreadsheet.
   a. Apply the **Title Style** to **A1**.
   b. Apply the **Heading 1** style to the subtitle in **A2**.
   c. Apply the **20%- Accent 1** themed cell style to **B4:H4** and **A4:A8**.
   d. Apply the **20%- Accent 3** themed cell style to **B5:H8**.
   e. Select **A3:H3**, and apply the **Heading 1** style.
9. Format cell contents.
   a. Increase the font size of **A4:H8** to **12 pt**.
   b. Select **A5:A7** and click the **Increase Indent** button.
   c. Apply the **Comma** format to cells **B5:H8**.
10. Use *AutoSum* and the *Fill Handle* to calculate daily totals.
    a. Use *AutoSum* to create a *Sum* formula for **B8**.
    b. Use the *Fill Handle* to copy the formula in **B8** to cells **C8:H8**.

11. Apply additional formatting to the spreadsheet.
    a. Apply the **Total** cell style to cells **A8:H8**.
    b. Increase the font size to **12 pt.** in cells **B8:H8**.
    c. **Bold** all non-numeric entries in **A4:H8**.
    d. **Center** the days of the week.
    e. Select **B5:H7** and apply the *Comma Style* format.
    f. Select **B8:H8** and select **Accounting** from the *Number Format* drop-down list.
12. Adjust column width and row height.
    a. Change the width in column **A** to 22.0.
    b. Change the row height for rows **1:8** to 22.0.
13. Rename and color a sheet tab.
    a. Rename *Sheet1* Week 1 of May.
    b. Color the sheet tab **Dark Blue Accent 1**, **Darker 50%** (last color in the fifth *Theme Color* column).
14. Spell check the worksheet.
15. Apply page layout options.
    a. Change the page orientation to **Landscape**.
    b. Fit the spreadsheet to 1 page wide by 1 tall.
    c. Center the worksheet horizontally on the page.
16. Add a header and footer.
    a. Click the **Insert** tab and click **Header & Footer**.
    b. Click the left header section and add the **Sheet Name** field.
    c. Click **Go to Footer**, click the middle section, and add the **Page Number** field.
    d. Click a cell in the worksheet and switch to *Normal* view.
17. Preview the workbook.
18. Save and close the workbook (Figure 1-106).

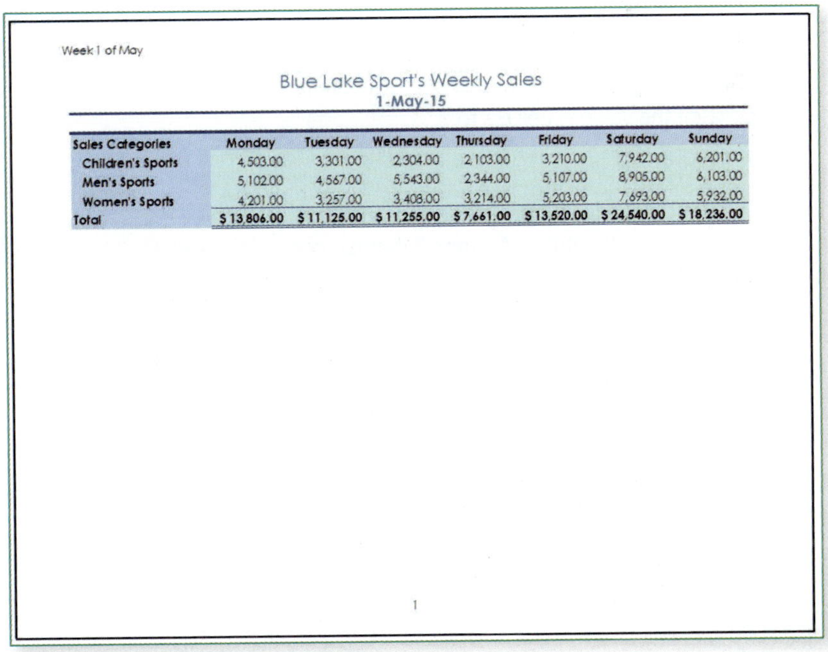
Week 1 of May

Blue Lake Sport's Weekly Sales
1-May-15

Sales Categories	Monday	Tuesday	Wednesday	Thursday	Friday	Saturday	Sunday
Children's Sports	4,503.00	3,301.00	2,304.00	2,103.00	3,210.00	7,942.00	6,201.00
Men's Sports	5,102.00	4,567.00	5,543.00	2,344.00	5,107.00	8,905.00	6,103.00
Women's Sports	4,201.00	3,257.00	3,408.00	3,214.00	5,203.00	7,693.00	5,932.00
Total	$ 13,806.00	$ 11,125.00	$ 11,255.00	$ 7,661.00	$ 13,520.00	$ 24,540.00	$ 18,236.00

1

1-106 Excel 1-4 completed

Independent Project 1-5

Clemenson Imaging is a privately owned organization that employs certified staff to perform mobile medical imaging at many hospitals statewide. You have been hired as the scheduling dispatch coordinator. It is your job to schedule all the mobile technicians at various hospital locations every day. Your supervisor has requested that you convert your schedule to an Excel spreadsheet.
[Student Learning Outcomes 1.1, 1.2, 1.3, 1.4, 1.5, 1.6, 1.7]

File Needed: ***ClemsonImaging-1.xlsx***
Completed Project File Name: ***[your initials] Excel 1-5.xlsx***

Skills Covered in This Project

- Open and save a workbook.
- Enter and format text and numbers.
- Merge and center title and subtitle.
- Spell check.
- Add a border.
- Apply a theme and *Cell Styles*.
- Create a formula using *AutoSum*.
- Adjust column width and row height.
- Rename and apply color to sheet tabs.
- Apply *Freeze Panes*.
- Apply page layout options.

1. Open ***ClemensonImaging-1.xlsx*** and save it as ***[your initials] Excel 1-5***.
2. Apply the **Ion Boardroom** theme to the worksheet.
3. Edit the title in **A1** so that "LLC" appears after the word "Imaging" and appears as Clemenson Imaging LLC.
4. Merge and center the title in cell **A1** across the cell range **A1:H1** and the subtitle in cell **A2** across the cell range **A2:H2**.
5. Edit the value in cell **E7** to 3.
6. Apply *Cell Styles*.
   a. Apply the **Title** style to **A1**.
   b. Apply the **Heading 1** style to the subtitle in **A2**.
   c. Apply the **40%- Accent 2** themed cell style to **A4:H4**.
7. Apply format changes.
   a. Increase the font size of **A4:H11** to **12 pt**.
   b. Increase the indent of cells **A5:A11**.
8. Add the title Total in cell **A13** and calculate the total number of patients in **E13** using *AutoSum*. Edit the formula cell range to **E11**.
9. Apply additional formatting to the spreadsheet.
   a. Apply the **Total Cell** style to **A13:H13**.
   b. Increase the font size to **12 pt.** in cells **A13:H13**.
   c. Select **A13** and **Decrease Indent**.
   d. **Bold** and center the data in **E5:E13** and **H5:H11**.
   e. Apply **bold** format to cells **A4:H4**.

10. Adjust column widths and row heights.
    a. Change the width in column **A** to 20.0.
    b. *AutoFit* the remaining columns (**B:H**).
    c. Change the row height for rows **4** and **13** to 21.00.
    d. Delete row **12**.
11. Apply **Freeze Panes** to cell **A5**.
    a. Click the **View** tab.
    b. Select **A5**.
    c. Click **Freeze Panes** and select **Freeze Panes**.
12. Rename *Sheet1* as 12-1-2015 and color the sheet tab **Plum Accent 1, Darker 50%**.
13. Select **A4:H4** and apply a thick bottom border using the **Plum, Accent 1, Darker 50%** color.
14. Spell check the worksheet.
15. Apply page layout options.
    a. Change the orientation to **Landscape** and fit the spreadsheet to one page.
    b. Center the worksheet horizontally on the page.
    c. Add the automatic footer **12-1-2015** to the worksheet using the *Footer* drop-down list.
16. Preview the spreadsheet.
17. Save and close the workbook (Figure 1-107).

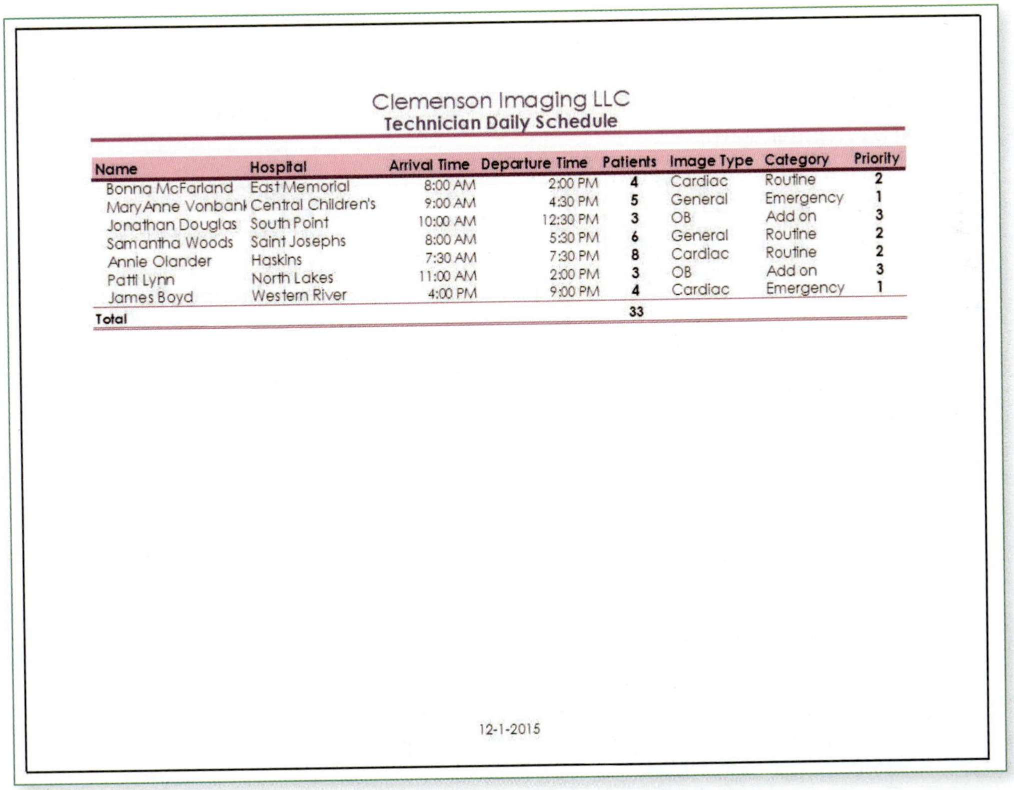

Clemenson Imaging LLC
Technician Daily Schedule

Name	Hospital	Arrival Time	Departure Time	Patients	Image Type	Category	Priority
Bonna McFarland	East Memorial	8:00 AM	2:00 PM	4	Cardiac	Routine	2
Mary Anne Vonbank	Central Children's	9:00 AM	4:30 PM	5	General	Emergency	1
Jonathan Douglas	South Point	10:00 AM	12:30 PM	3	OB	Add on	3
Samantha Woods	Saint Josephs	8:00 AM	5:30 PM	6	General	Routine	2
Annie Olander	Haskins	7:30 AM	7:30 PM	8	Cardiac	Routine	2
Patti Lynn	North Lakes	11:00 AM	2:00 PM	3	OB	Add on	3
James Boyd	Western River	4:00 PM	9:00 PM	4	Cardiac	Emergency	1
Total				**33**			

12-1-2015

1-107 Excel 1-5 completed

Independent Project 1-6

You have been hired as the accounts receivable clerk for a privately owned accounting company called Livingood Income Tax & Accounting. It is your job to track all the payments from clients every day. Your supervisor has requested that you convert your payment table to an Excel spreadsheet. **[Student Learning Outcomes 1.1, 1.2, 1.3, 1.4, 1.5, 1.6, 1.7, 1.8]**

File Needed: None
Completed Project File Name: ***[your initials] Excel 1-6.xlsx***

Skills Covered in This Project

- Create and save a workbook.
- Enter text and numbers.
- Change font size and attributes.
- Use *AutoSum*.
- Adjust column width and row height.
- Spell check.
- Apply *Freeze Panes*.
- Change zoom level.
- Apply a theme and *Cell Styles*.
- Apply page layout options.
- Hide a row.
- Rename and apply color to sheet tabs.

1. Start a new workbook and save it as ***[your initials] Excel 1-6***.
2. Apply the **Organic** theme to the worksheet. Change the theme font to **Gill Sans MT**.
3. Select **A1** and type Livingood Income Tax and Accounting, press **Enter**, type Payment Schedule, and press **Enter** again.
4. Type in the remaining worksheet data from Figure 1-108.
5. Edit the title in **A1** to replace the word "and" with the symbol &.
6. Edit the value in cell **B5** to 451.25. Change "Over Due" in cell **F4** to Overdue.
7. Apply the **Title** style to **A1**.
8. Apply formatting to cell ranges.
   a. Increase the font size of **A4:G11** to **12 pt**.
   b. Select cells **B5:B11** and display the *Format Cells* dialog box. Select the **Accounting** format and change the *Symbol* to **None**.

	A	B	C	D	E	F	G
1	Livingood Income Tax and Accounting						
2	Payment Schedule						
3							
4	Invoice	Amount	Due Date	Paid	Payment Type	Over Due	Contact
5	4567	450.5	42278	Yes	Check 2005	No	No
6	3421	465.78	42248	No	Due	Yes	Letter
7	2456	250.25	42217	No	Due	Yes	Phone
8	4569	585.65	42278	Yes	Discover	No	No
9	4572	1245.89	42278	No	Due	No	No
10	1428	1245.67	42186	No	Due	Yes	Collections
11	2576	345.08	42217	Yes	Check 2345	No	No

1-108 Excel 1-6 data

9. Add the title Total in cell **A13** and calculate the total for **B13** using *AutoSum*. Adjust the cell range reference in the *Formula bar*.
10. Apply additional formatting.
    a. Apply the **Total** cell style to cells **A13:G13**.
    b. Select **A13:G13** and increase the font size to **12 pt**.
    c. **Bold** the entries in **A4:G4**.
    d. **Center** the data in **A4:G4, A5:A13, D5:D13**, and **F5:F13**.

e. Select **A4:G4** and open the *Format Cells* dialog box. Add a thick **Green, Accent 1, Darker 50%** bottom border and a **Green, Accent 1, Lighter 80%** fill color using the second color in the fifth column.
f. Select the cells in rows **6**, **8**, and **10** and apply the same fill color.
g. Use the **Border** button and apply a bottom border to cells **A2:G2**.

11. Adjust column width and row height.
    a. Change the width of columns **A:G** to 14.0.
    b. Change the row height for rows **4** and **13** to 19.50.
12. Hide row **12**.
13. Rename *Sheet1* 10-27-2015 and color the sheet tab **Green, Accent 1** (first color in the fifth *Theme Color* column).
14. Spell check the worksheet.
15. Apply *Freeze Panes* to **B5**.
16. Increase the magnification of the view to **125%**.
17. Apply page layout options.
    a. Change the orientation to **Landscape** and scale the page to fit on one page.
    b. Center the worksheet horizontally on the page.
    c. Click the **Custom Header** button and add the **Insert Sheet Name** field in the *Left Header* section. Click the **Format Text** button and apply the font color **Green, Accent 1, Darker 50%** to the header field.
    d. Add the page number to the right section of the footer.
    e. Select print preview in the *Page Setup* dialog box to view your settings.
18. Save and close the workbook (Figure 1-109).

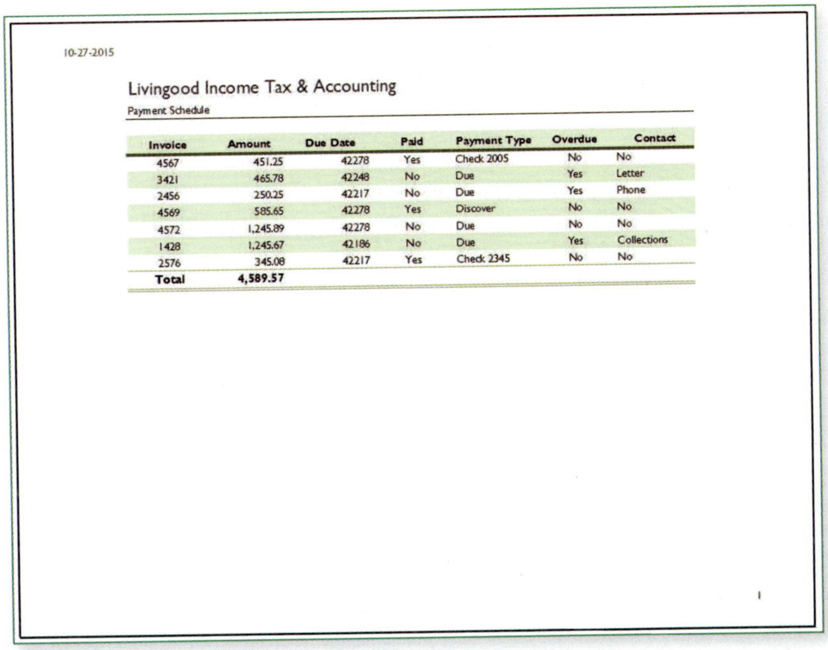
10-27-2015

Livingood Income Tax & Accounting

Payment Schedule

Invoice	Amount	Due Date	Paid	Payment Type	Overdue	Contact
4567	451.25	42278	Yes	Check 2005	No	No
3421	465.78	42248	No	Due	Yes	Letter
2456	250.25	42217	No	Due	Yes	Phone
4569	585.65	42278	Yes	Discover	No	No
4572	1,245.89	42278	No	Due	No	No
1428	1,245.67	42186	No	Due	Yes	Collections
2576	345.08	42217	Yes	Check 2345	No	No
Total	4,589.57					

1

1-109 Excel 1-6 completed

Improve It Project 1-7

For this project, you create a flight schedule for the manager of Boyd Air. You edit and format the data in a spreadsheet and add page layout formatting.
[Student Learning Outcomes 1.1, 1.2, 1.3, 1.4, 1.5, 1.6, 1.7, 1.8]

File Needed: ***BoydAirFlightSchedule-1.xlsx***
Completed Project File Name: ***[your initials] Excel 1-7.xlsx***

Skills Covered in This Project

- Open and save a workbook.
- Enter and format text and numbers.
- Merge and center title and subtitle.
- Format and delete rows and columns.
- Spell check.
- Use *AutoSum* to create a formula.
- Apply a theme and apply *Cell Styles*.
- Apply page layout options.
- Adjust column width and row height.
- Rename and apply color to sheet tabs.
- Freeze panes and change the zoom level.

1. Open the workbook ***BoydAirFlightSchedule-01.xlsx***.
2. Rename the workbook ***[your initials] Excel 1-7***.
3. Type Boyd Air in **A1** and type Flight Schedule in **A2**.
4. Merge and center the title in cell **A1** and the subtitle in cell **A2**.
5. Apply *Cell Styles* to the labels in the spreadsheet.
   a. Apply the **Title** style to **A1**.
   b. Apply the **Heading 1** style to the subtitle in **A2**.
   c. Apply the **Accent 1** cell style to **A4:F4**.
   d. Apply the **20%-Accent 1** cell style to **A5:F13**.
6. Apply formatting.
   a. Increase the font size of **A4:F4** to **14 pt**.
   b. Apply the **Total** cell style to cells **A13:F13**.
   c. **Bold** the entries in **A4:F4**.
   d. Select **A4**, **C4**, and **D4**, and click **Wrap Text** [*Home* tab, *Alignment* group].
7. Apply row and column formatting.
   a. Change the row height for row **4** to 38.00.
   b. Change the row height for row **13** to 21.00.
   c. Right align the text in **C4** and **D4**.
8. Delete row **12**.
9. Use *AutoSum* to calculate the total number of passengers.
10. Color the sheet tab **Dark Blue**, **Accent 1**, **Darker 50%** (last color in the fifth *Theme Color* column).
11. Edit the sheet tab name by deleting **Monday**.
12. *AutoFit* columns **A:F**.
13. Spell check the worksheet.

14. Apply *Freeze Panes* to **B5**.
15. Increase the magnification of the sheet to **150%**.
16. Apply page layout options.
    a. Change the orientation to **Landscape** and fit the spreadsheet to one page.
    b. Center the worksheet horizontally on the page.
    c. Add the **Insert File Name** field in the *Left Header* section and apply the font color **Dark Blue, Accent 1**.
17. Preview your settings.
18. Save and close the workbook (Figure 1-110).

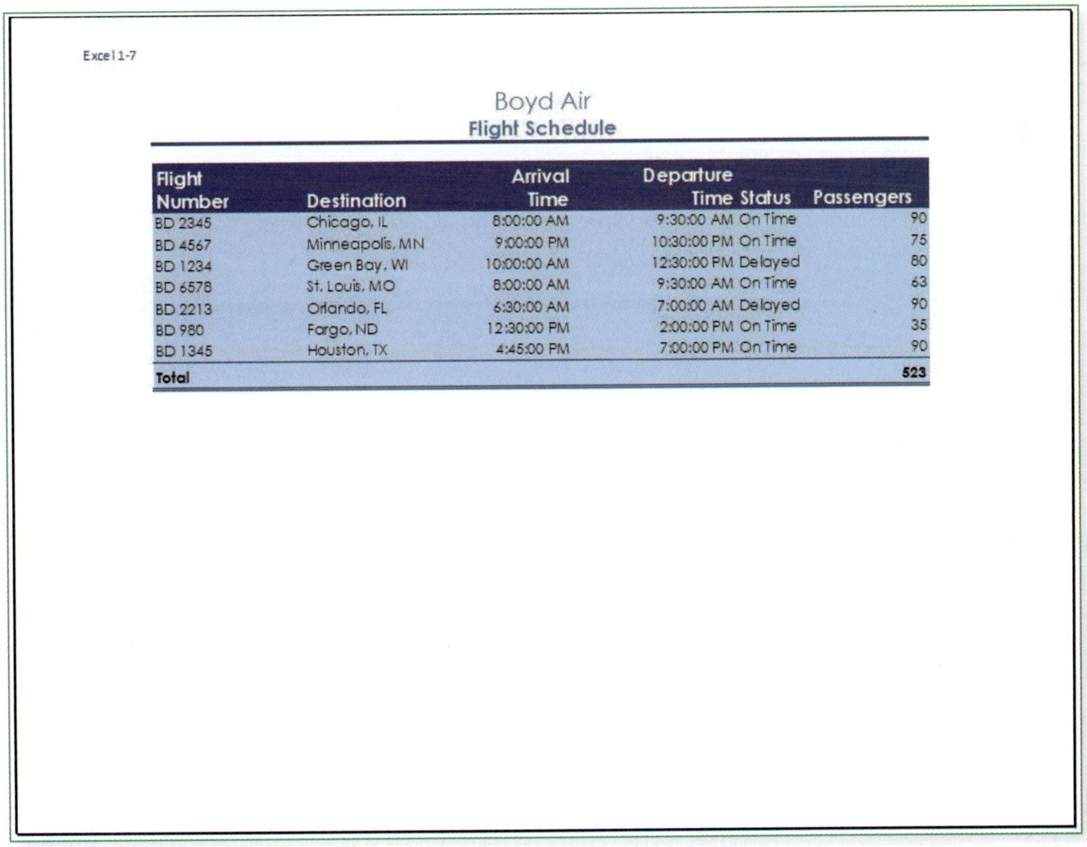

Excel 1-7

Boyd Air
Flight Schedule

Flight Number	Destination	Arrival Time	Departure Time	Status	Passengers
BD 2345	Chicago, IL	8:00:00 AM	9:30:00 AM	On Time	90
BD 4567	Minneapolis, MN	9:00:00 PM	10:30:00 PM	On Time	75
BD 1234	Green Bay, WI	10:00:00 AM	12:30:00 PM	Delayed	80
BD 6578	St. Louis, MO	8:00:00 AM	9:30:00 AM	On Time	63
BD 2213	Orlando, FL	6:30:00 AM	7:00:00 AM	Delayed	90
BD 980	Fargo, ND	12:30:00 PM	2:00:00 PM	On Time	35
BD 1345	Houston, TX	4:45:00 PM	7:00:00 PM	On Time	90
Total					523

1-110 Excel 1-7 completed

Challenge Project 1-8

For this project, you create a spreadsheet that lists sales for a gourmet chocolate store. The sales report lists data for popular holidays within a calendar year.
[Student Learning Outcomes 1.1, 1.2, 1.3, 1.4, 1.5, 1.6, 1.7, 1.8]

File Needed: None
Completed Project File Name: ***[your initials] Excel 1-8.xlsx***

Create a new workbook and save it as ***[your initials] Excel 1-8***. Name the gourmet chocolate store and list five types of chocolate as row headings. For column headings, list four popular holidays for chocolate sales. Modify your workbook according to the following guidelines:

- Type sales data for each holiday.
- Include a date in the worksheet title area.
- Incorporate a theme, *Cell Styles,* and formatting.
- Use *AutoSum* to calculate totals.
- Insert header and footer text.
- Include document properties and spell check the workbook.

Challenge Project 1-9

For this project, you create a spreadsheet for a photography club. The photography club rents retail space for selling used photography equipment. The equipment available in the store includes camera bodies, lenses, tripods, and books. Each month a master list is created which includes the type of equipment for sale and current prices.
[Student Learning Outcomes 1.1, 1.2, 1.3, 1.4, 1.5, 1.6, 1.7, 1.8]

File Needed: None
Completed Project File Name: ***[your initials] Excel 1-9.xlsx***

Create a new workbook and save it as ***[your initials] Excel 1-9***. Modify your workbook according to the following guidelines:

- Name the photography club for the main title and create a subtitle to reflect the purpose of the spreadsheet.
- Create rows and columns of data for listing the photography equipment, price, and quantity available.
- Include other information that would be helpful to potential customers.
- Use *AutoSum* to calculate the value of the inventory.
- Incorporate a theme, *Cell Styles,* and other formatting to create a professional-looking spreadsheet.
- Include document properties and spell check the workbook.

Challenge Project 1-10

For this project, you create a spreadsheet that lists your monthly financial responsibilities. This spreadsheet is a valuable tool for money management.
[Student Learning Outcomes 1.1, 1.2, 1.3, 1.4, 1.5, 1.6, 1.7, 1.8]

File Needed: None
Completed Project File Name: ***[your initials] Excel 1-10.xlsx***

Enter data for a monthly budget. Create a new workbook and save it as ***[your initials] Excel 1-10***. Modify your workbook according to the following guidelines:

- Use blank rows to divide your worksheet into groups. For example, include a section for income and another section for expenses. You can create additional groups for expenses that occur monthly, quarterly, or annually.
- Insert worksheets for each month and name each sheet.
- Incorporate themes, *Cell Styles*, and formatting. (Remember that you can select multiple sheet tabs and apply Page Setup formatting to each sheet in a single step.)
- Use *AutoSum* to calculate total income and expenses.
- Include document properties and spell check the workbook.

CHAPTER 2

Working with Formulas and Functions

CHAPTER OVERVIEW

Excel is a powerful tool for creating mathematical computations. You can use Excel to create a simple addition formula or a formula that includes complex calculations. When creating formulas, you can take advantage of Excel's error correcting techniques to ensure accuracy in your worksheets. This chapter introduces the basics of using formulas and functions in an Excel worksheet.

STUDENT LEARNING OUTCOMES (SLOs)

After completing this chapter, you will be able to:

SLO 2.1 Create and edit basic formulas (p. E2-79).

SLO 2.2 Use range names and relative, absolute, and mixed cell references in a formula (p. E2-83).

SLO 2.3 Apply mathematical order of operations when using parentheses, exponents, multiplication, division, addition, and subtraction (p. E2-88).

SLO 2.4 Use *AutoSum* and other common functions such as *AVERAGE, COUNT, MAX, MIN, TODAY,* and *NOW* (p. E2-93).

SLO 2.5 Apply financial, logical, and lookup functions such as *PMT, IF, VLOOKUP,* and *HLOOKUP* (p. E2-99).

SLO 2.6 Apply math and trigonometry functions such as *SUMIF, SUMPRODUCT,* and *ROUND* (p. E2-106).

CASE STUDY

In the Pause & Practice projects in this chapter, you create business workbooks related to a northern Minnesota resort business, Paradise Lakes Resort (PLR), which was introduced in Chapter 1. PLR is asking all managers to incorporate formulas into their monthly sales workbooks to determine future costs and net income projections. PLR is also considering several investment options and is using various formulas to examine and evaluate these opportunities.

Pause & Practice 2-1: Modify a workbook to include basic formulas.

Pause & Practice 2-2: Insert common functions into a workbook.

Pause & Practice 2-3: Apply financial, logical, lookup, math and trigonometry functions in a workbook.

EXCEL

SLO 2.1

Creating and Editing Basic Formulas

One reason why Excel is one of the most popular business software applications is because it gives users the ability to incorporate formulas into a workbook. A ***formula*** evaluates values and returns a result. Basic formula creation can involve adding weekly expenses, multiplying inventory by unit price to determine inventory value, or subtracting expenses from income. The formulas in Excel workbooks automatically update when cell values change.

Formula Syntax

The term ***syntax*** refers to the required parts of a formula and the rules controlling the order of the parts. As discussed in Chapter 1, the intersection of a column and row is a cell. Each cell has a ***cell reference*** (or cell address), which is the specific location of a cell within a worksheet. When you create formulas, you use cell references to identify cells rather than an actual number. For example, the formula to add the values in cells B5 and B6 is =**B5+B6**.

The equals sign [=] is always the first character you type when creating a formula. The equals sign alerts Excel that you are entering a formula and not text. The second component of the formula is the first cell reference (B5 in the example =**B5+B6**). The third component is the mathematical operator, which signifies the type of calculation. (In the example =**B5+B6**, the plus sign is the operator.) The final part of the sample formula is the last cell reference (B6 in the example =**B5+B6**).

Enter a Formula Using the Keyboard

There are two ways to enter cell references into a formula. You can type the formula manually using the keyboard or use the select method. Both methods require identifying the location of the formula, typing the equals sign, and then entering (by typing or selecting) the first cell reference, an arithmetic operator (+, -, *, or /), and the next cell reference. Formulas are not case sensitive, and Excel automatically changes cell references to uppercase. In both methods, you press **Enter** to complete the entry or click the **Enter** button (the check mark) on the *Formula bar*. To cancel a formula before it is complete, press **Esc**. Do not navigate using an arrow key while you are entering a formula. The cell you navigate to may accidentally be included in the formula.

HOW TO: Enter a Formula in a Cell Using the Keyboard

1. Click the cell where you want to create the formula (Figure 2-1).
2. Type = (equals sign) to begin the formula.
3. Type the first cell reference.
4. Enter the mathematical operator (+, -, *, or /).
5. Type the second cell reference.
   - Once a cell reference is entered using the keyboard, Excel color codes each cell reference.
6. Press **Enter**.
   - The result of the formula appears in the cell where the formula is located (Figure 2-2).
   - The *Formula bar* displays the formula.
   - You can use the **Enter** button (the check mark) on the *Formula bar* instead of pressing **Enter** on the keyboard (Figure 2-3). This button is only active when a cell is in ***edit mode*** (the insertion point is present within a cell).

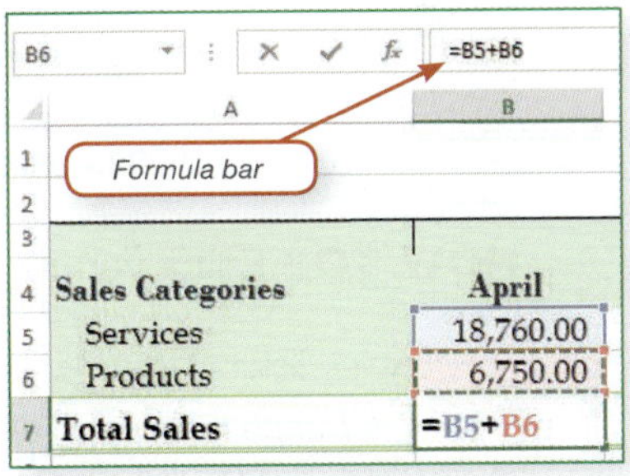

2-1 Formula syntax

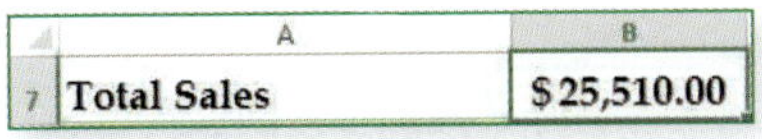

2-2 Formula result

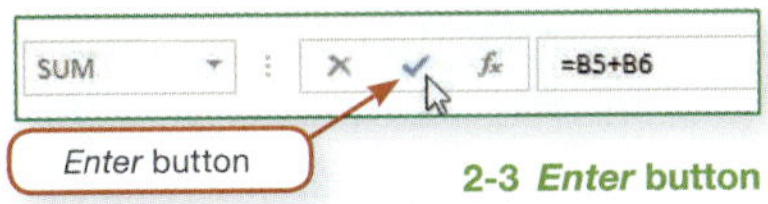

2-3 *Enter* button

> **MORE INFO**
>
> Use the numeric keypad or the symbol keys to insert math operators.

Enter a Formula Using the Select Method

A popular and accurate technique of creating formulas is the ***select method***. When creating a formula, you can select a cell with your pointer instead of manually typing the cell reference, which prevents typographical errors. When you click a cell or select a cell range, Excel automatically enters the cell addresses into the formula.

HOW TO: Enter a Formula in a Cell Using Selection

1. Click the cell where you want to create the formula (Figure 2-4).
2. Type = (equals sign).
3. Using your pointer, click the first cell you want to include in the formula.
4. Enter a mathematical operator.
5. Move the pointer to the next cell reference and select the cell.
6. Click the **Enter** button on the *Formula bar* to finalize the formula.
   - If you select a cell by mistake, press **Backspace**.
   - The result of the calculation appears in the cell where the formula is located.
   - Select the cell where the formula is located to display the formula in the *Formula bar*.

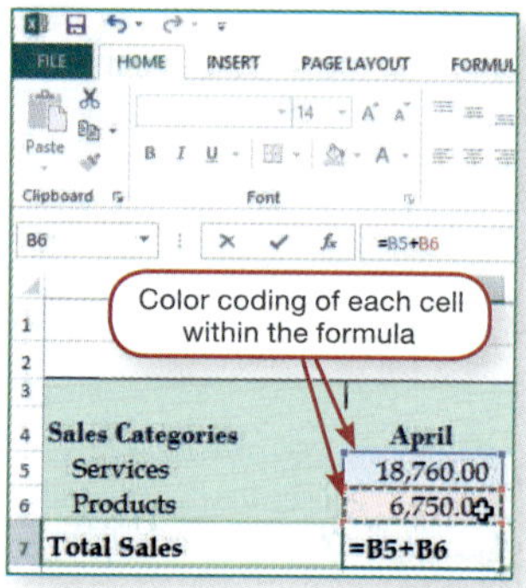

2-4 Formula syntax

Edit a Formula

There will be times when you make an error when creating a formula. You can edit a formula by double-clicking the cell where the formula is located and using edit mode to correct the formula. Another way to edit a formula is to use time-saving, color-coded editing options such as the ***Range Finder*** and ***Formula Auditing*** tools.

Range Finder

The *Range Finder* is a color-coded editing tool that applies different colors to each cell or cell range included within a formula. To activate the *Range Finder*, double-click the cell that contains the formula you want to edit or select the cell that contains the formula and click the *Formula bar*. The color-coded cells automatically appear and indicate each cell location within the formula.

HOW TO: Edit a Formula in a Cell Using the Range Finder

1. Double-click the formula you want to edit.
   - The *Range Finder* activates and the cell references appear color-coded.
   - The cell formula appears in the *Formula bar*.
2. Edit the formula.
   - Insert or delete text.
   - Drag a range finder border to move the frame to include the correct cells (Figure 2-5).
   - Drag a corner of the border to include additional cells or to reduce the number of cells.
3. Press **Enter** or click the **Enter** button on the *Formula bar* once your edit is complete.

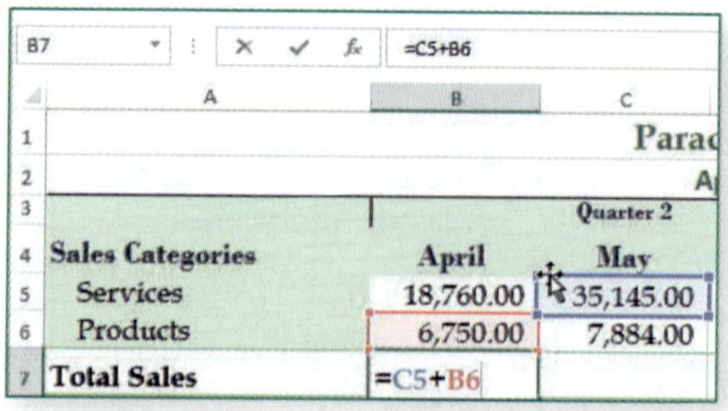

2-5 Formula in edit mode using *Range Finder*

> **ANOTHER WAY**
>
> Activate the *Range Finder* by clicking the cell that contains the formula and clicking the *Formula bar* or pressing **F2**.

Formula Auditing

Formula Auditing refers to a group of editing options on the *Formulas* tab that you can use to review and correct errors in formulas. ***Trace Precedents*** and ***Trace Dependents*** are auditing tools that include a color-coded editing system. When you use these tools, different colors are applied to each cell or cell range and display arrows point to the cells and cell ranges included within a formula. *Trace Precedents* displays all cells referenced in a formula. *Trace Dependents* indicates which formulas reference a particular cell.

Evaluate Formula

Evaluate Formula is an additional auditing tool that is typically used for more complex formulas. Complex formulas may contain a syntax error. A syntax error occurs when a formula contains a typographical error, unnecessary or missing punctuation, incorrect order of arguments, or an incorrect cell reference. If your formula includes a syntax error, Excel displays an error message or returns an error code as the formula result. The *Evaluate Formula* tool reviews each part of a formula in sequence to determine where the error is.

To apply *Formula Auditing* options, display the *Formulas* tab, and choose an option in the *Formula Auditing* group (Figure 2-6). The following table describes the auditing options.

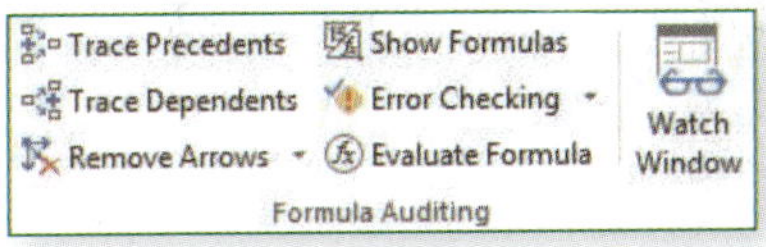

2-6 *Formula Auditing* options

Formula Auditing Tools

Button	Description
Trace Precedents	Displays arrows that point to the cells referenced in the selected formula
Trace Dependents	Displays arrows that point to the cells that contain a formula
Remove Arrows	Removes arrows for *Trace Precedents* or *Trace Dependents*
Show Formulas	Displays formulas instead of results
Error Checking	Checks for common errors
Evaluate Formula	Steps through each part of a formula
Watch Window	Adds cells to the *Watch Window*. Values are watched as the worksheet is updated.

HOW TO: Use Auditing Tools

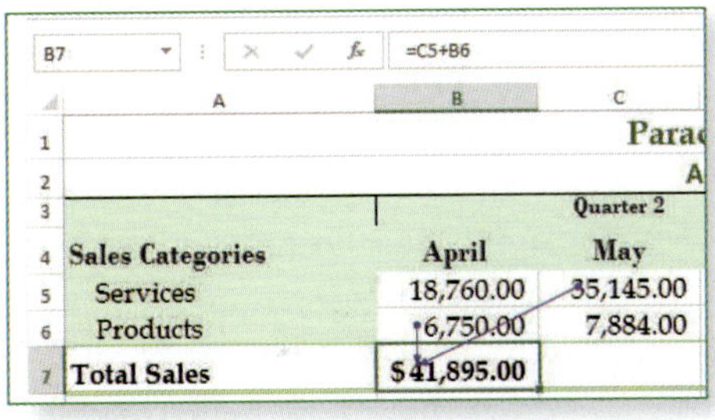

2-7 *Trace Precedents* arrows

1. Select the cell you want to edit (Figure 2-7).
2. Click the **Show Formulas** button [*Formulas* tab, *Formula Auditing* group].
   - The formula displays instead of the formula result. You may need to *AutoFit* the width of your columns to view the formula.
   - Press **Ctrl+`** to switch between formula and results views.
3. Select a cell containing a formula.

4. Click the **Trace Precedents** button [*Formulas* tab, *Formula Auditing* group].
   - Arrows display indicating which cells in your workbook are included in the current cell's formula (see Figure 2-7).
   - Blue arrows indicate cells with no errors.
   - Red arrows indicate cells that cause errors.
   - Black arrows point from the selected cell to a worksheet icon.
5. Click **Remove Arrows** [*Formulas* tab, *Formula Auditing* group] to remove the *Trace Precedents* arrows.
6. Click a cell that is included in a formula (not the formula cell).
7. Click **Trace Dependents**.
   - An arrow displays leading from the selected cell to the formula cell.
8. Click **Remove Arrows** to remove the *Trace Dependents* arrows.
   - Click the **Remove Arrows** drop-down list to specify the type of arrow to remove.
9. Click **Show Formulas** to display formula results.

> **MORE INFO**
>
> The *Error Checking* and *Evaluate Formulas* tools are helpful if a syntax error occurs. If the error occurs because you selected the incorrect cell, it may be more useful to use *Trace Precedents.*

> **MORE INFO**
>
> To print the formula view of a spreadsheet, click the **Show Formulas** button [*Formulas* tab, *Formula Auditing* group] prior to printing the worksheet.

Message Window

There are times when a typographical error may be the cause of your syntax error. After you complete a formula containing an error, a Microsoft Excel message window may display (Figure 2-8). The window indicates an error was found, and a corrected formula appears in the box. Click **Yes** to accept the correction or **No** to edit the formula manually.

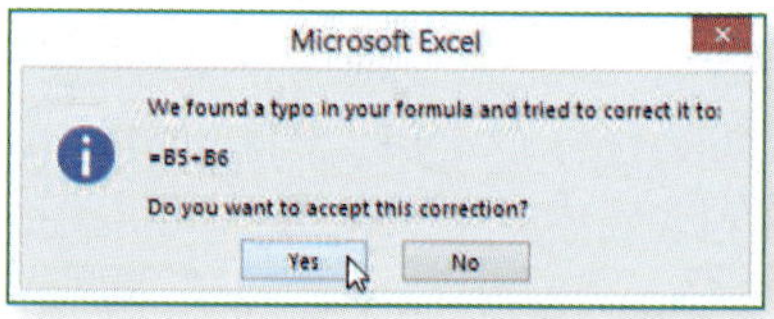

2-8 Microsoft Excel message window

Trace Error

A green triangle in the top left corner of a cell indicates that the formula in the cell may contain an error. When you select a cell with the green triangle, the *Trace Error* button displays. You can point to the button to see a ScreenTip identifying the error. Click the drop-down arrow to view a list of options to ignore or repair the error.

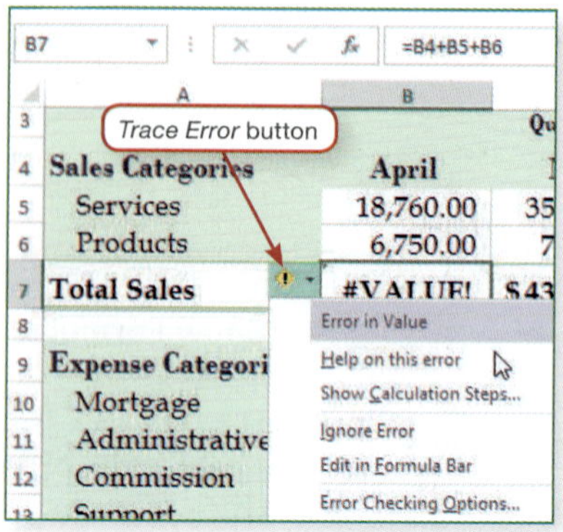

2-9 *Trace Error* options

HOW TO: Correct a Formula in a Cell Using the Trace Error Button

1. Click a cell with an incorrect formula (Figure 2-9).
   - The green triangle appears in the top left corner of the cell.
2. Move the pointer over the *Trace Error* button that appears to the left of the selected cell.
   - The *Trace Error* button looks like a yellow diamond with an exclamation mark (!).

3. Click the **Trace Error** drop-down arrow.
4. Select an option from the *Trace Error* button list.
   - Select the **Ignore Error** option if the formula is correct.

Circular Reference

A ***circular reference*** occurs when a formula includes the cell address of the formula. For example, if the cell containing the formula is B7, and the syntax of the formula is **=B5+B7**, then you would have a circular reference because B7 is included in the calculation. When a circular reference occurs, a Microsoft Excel message appears (Figure 2-10). You can either click **OK** to accept the result or click **Help**.

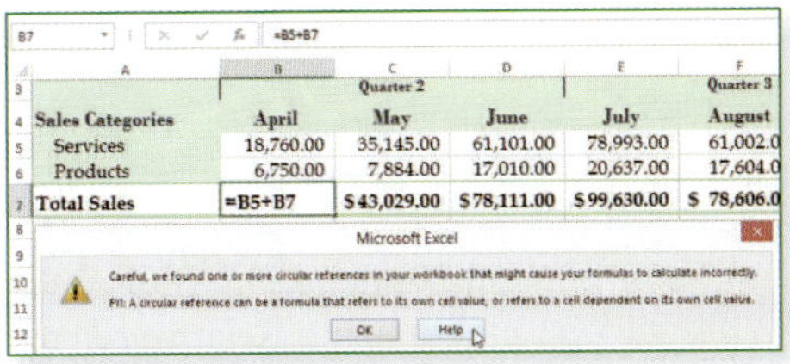

2-10 Circular reference and Microsoft Excel message window

SLO 2.2

Working with Cell References

There are three types of cell references you can use in a formula. The type of cell references included in a formula determines the result of a formula when it is copied. The three types of cell references are ***relative***, ***absolute***, and ***mixed***.

- ***Relative cell references*** identify the location of a cell. When you are creating formulas, the default cell reference is *relative*. Column and row references automatically change when you copy a formula that contains a relative cell address. The cell address **B2** is an example of a relative cell reference.
- ***Absolute cell reference*** is the fixed location of a cell referenced in a formula or dialog box. Absolute cell addresses include a **$** (dollar sign) around both the column and row references. Cells that contain absolute references do not change when copied. The cell address **$B$2** is an absolute cell reference. You can quickly insert dollar signs around a cell reference in the *Formula bar* by pressing **F4**.
- ***Mixed cell references*** contain one relative reference (either the row number or column letter) and one absolute reference (the remaining row number or column letter). The cell address **$B2** refers to an absolute column address ($B) and a relative row address (2).
- ***3D cell references*** indicate cells in multiple workbooks or worksheets. To create a 3D cell reference, you include the name of the workbook (if referring to a different workbook), the name of the worksheet, and the cell reference. An example of a 3D cell reference is **='[2016 Sales.xlsx]Sheet2'!B2**. Square brackets surround the workbook name ([2016 Sales]), and an exclamation point follows the sheet name (Sheet2!). If the name of the worksheet or workbook contains non-alphabetic characters, you need to enclose the name in single quotes. Excel automatically places absolute value symbols ($) around each cell reference if you select the cell from a different workbook or worksheet rather than type the reference.

The following table lists examples of cell reference types:

Cell Reference Examples

Cell Reference	Reference Type	Description
B2	*Relative*	The cell address changes when copied.
$B$2	*Absolute*	The cell address does not change when copied.

continued

Cell Reference Examples

Cell Reference	Reference Type	Description
$B2	*Mixed*	The column portion of the cell address is absolute; the row component changes when copied.
B$2	*Mixed*	The row portion of the cell address is absolute; the column component changes when copied.
Sheet2!B2	*3D Relative*	The cell address is located on a different worksheet and changes when copied.

Copy a Formula with a Relative Cell Reference

Relative cell references within a formula adjust automatically when you copy them. For example, if you create a formula that totals the sales for the month of January, you can copy that formula to calculate the totals for February and March. The cell references change automatically.

You can use the following methods to copy formulas:

- *Fill Handle*
- *Copy* and *Paste* buttons in the *Clipboard* group on the *Home* tab
- Shortcut commands **Ctrl+C** to copy and **Ctrl+V** to paste
- *Context-sensitive menu;* right-click to display the menu
- *Control* key combined with drag and drop

HOW TO: Copy a Formula with Relative Cell References

1. Select the cell that contains the formula you want to copy (Figure 2-11).
2. Click and drag the *Fill Handle* to the destination cell or range of cells.
3. Release the *Fill Handle.*
   - The formula in the destination cell adjusts to the corresponding relative cell references.
   - Click the **Show Formulas** and **Trace Precedents** buttons [*Formulas* tab, *Formula Auditing* group] to see how the formula's cell reference changes from the source cell to the destination cell during the copy process (Figure 2-12).

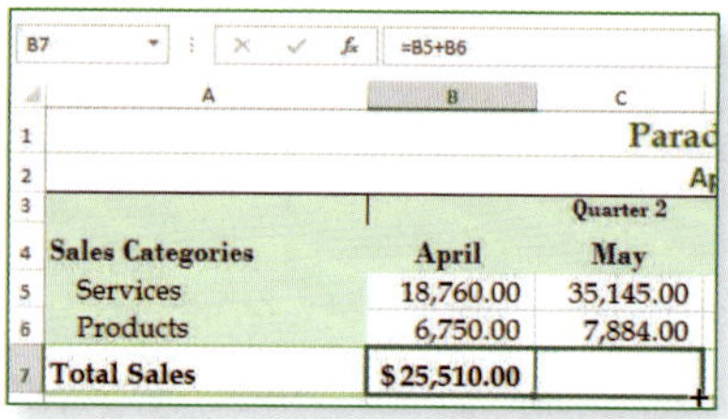

2-11 Using the *Fill Handle* to copy

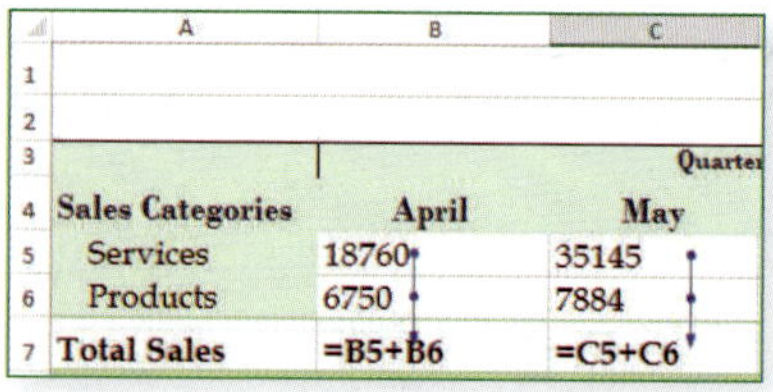

2-12 *Trace Precedence* arrows

After you drag the *Fill Handle* over a range, the ***AutoFill Options*** button displays. The drop-down list includes three options to control the fill data. Choose to *Copy Cells, Fill Formatting Only,* or *Fill Without Formatting.*

Copy a Formula with an Absolute Cell Reference

An absolute reference in a cell refers to a specific location, and it does not change when you copy or fill the formula. To change a relative cell reference to an absolute cell reference, type a **$** in front of the column letter and the row number of the cell address or select the cell address and press **F4** to insert the dollar signs quickly.

HOW TO: Copy a Formula with an Absolute Cell Reference

1. Select the cell that contains the formula you want to copy.
2. Click the *Formula bar* and click the cell reference you want to be absolute.
3. Press **F4** to change the cell address to an absolute cell reference.
4. Press **Enter** and re-select the cell to copy the formula.
5. Click and drag the *Fill Handle* to the destination cell.
6. Release the *Fill Handle.*
   - The absolute cell reference remains constant when the formula is copied to the destination cell.
   - Figure 2-13 displays *Trace Precedents* for the formulas with the correct formula syntax.

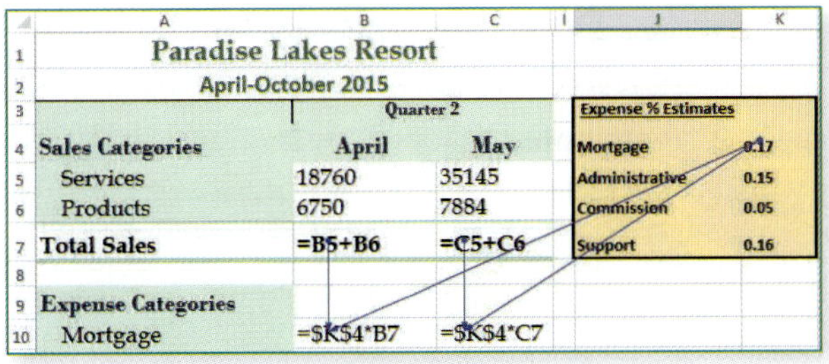

2-13 *Trace Precedence* arrows illustrate cell references

MORE INFO

F4 is a four-way toggle key in the *Formula bar.* Press **F4** to toggle from absolute reference to mixed references to relative reference.

Range Names

You can use ***range names*** to navigate a worksheet or to identify a cell or group of cells (recall from Chapter 1 that a group of cells is called a ***range***). Range names describe the cell or purpose of a group of cells and make it easier to interpret a formula. For example, instead of referring to cell K4 in the formula **=K4*B7**, you can name cell K4 "Mortgage", and use the range name in the formula. The example formula would change to **=Mortgage*B7**.

When you name a cell or range, the name becomes an absolute reference. The first character of a name must be a letter, an underscore (_), or a backslash (\). Range names cannot contain spaces, special characters (#, $, &), or cell references. To signify a space between words, use the underscore (_) (e.g., "Mortgage_Payment" or "MortgagePayment"). You can create a range name using the *Name* box on the *Formula bar,* the *Create from selection* button [*Formulas* tab, *Defined Names* group], or the *New Name* dialog box (Figure 2-14).

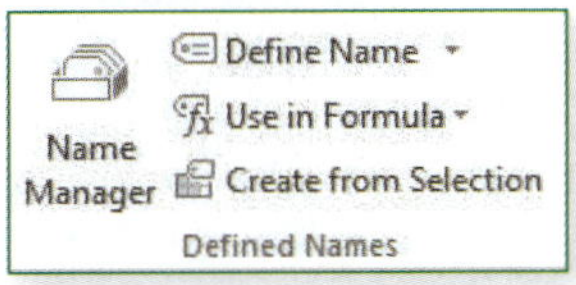

2-14 *Defined Names* group on the *Formulas* tab

To create range names using the *Name* box, select the cell or group of cells, and type the name of the range in the *Name* box.

HOW TO: Name a Cell and Use the Range Name in a Formula

1. Select the cell(s) you want to name.
2. Click the **Name** box beside the *Formula bar.*
3. Type a range name (e.g., "Tax_Rate") and press **Enter** (Figure 2-15).
4. Select the cell where you want the formula to appear and press = to begin the formula.
5. Type the beginning letters of the range name.
   - A list of names appears matching the letters typed.

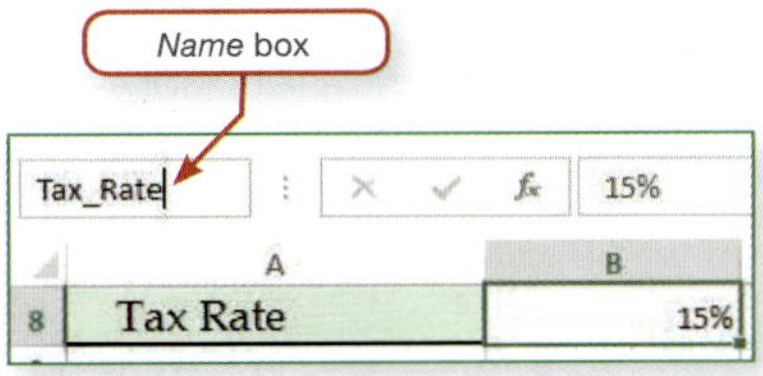

2-15 Tax_Rate range name

6. Double-click the range name from the list.
   - The drop-down list is known as *Formula AutoComplete*.
7. Type a mathematical operator.
8. Select the next cell reference or cell range (Figure 2-16).
9. Press **Enter**.

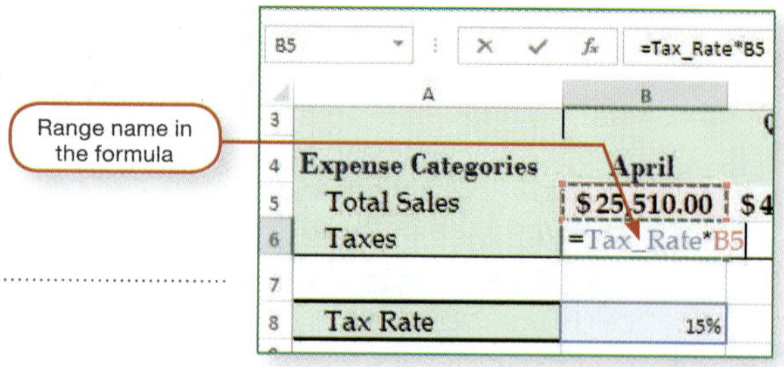

2-16 Formula with range name

MORE INFO

Manage range names by clicking the **Name Manager** button [*Formulas* tab, *Defined Names* group]. The *Name Manager* dialog box provides options for creating, editing, and deleting range names.

ANOTHER WAY

To insert a range name, press **F3** to display the *Paste Name* dialog box. Select a name and click **OK**.

A second method to name a range is to convert existing row and column labels to names. If a range in your worksheets contains column and or row headings, you can use these headings to name multiple cells simultaneously.

HOW TO: Name Multiple Cells Simultaneously Using the Ribbon

1. Select the range and include the row or column labels (Figure 2-17).
   - The cells and their labels must be adjacent to each other.
   - A range can consist of one cell, a range of cells, a formula, or a constant.
2. Click the **Create from Selection** button [*Formulas* tab, *Defined Names* group] to open the *Create Names from Selection* dialog box (see Figure 2-17).
3. Select the check box that best describes the label location in relation to the selected cells.
4. Click **OK**.
   - To view a list of range names, click the **Name** box arrow on the *Formula bar* (Figure 2-18).
   - The formula syntax shows the range name in place of the cell address (Figure 2-19).

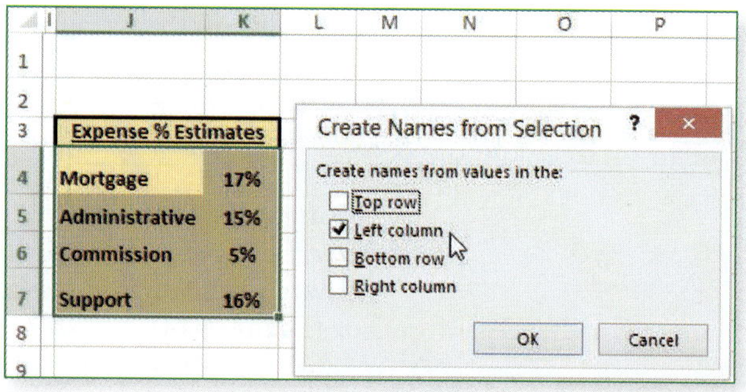

2-17 *Create Names from Selection* dialog box

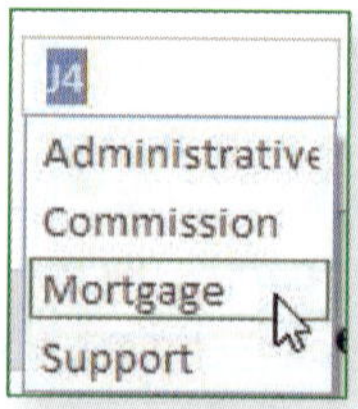

2-18 *Name* box

2-19 Formula with range name

If you have already created formulas and are naming cells after copying formulas, select **Apply names** from the *Define Name* drop-down arrow [*Formulas* tab, *Defined Names* group] to open the *Apply Names* dialog box (Figure 2-20). Click **OK** to apply all newly created range names to existing formulas.

A third method to define range names is to use the *New Name* dialog box. The New Name dialog box includes an option to specify a range name for the entire workbook or an individual worksheet. After range names have been added to a worksheet, use the *Paste Name* dialog box to create a two-column list in a blank area of a worksheet to display defined names and their locations.

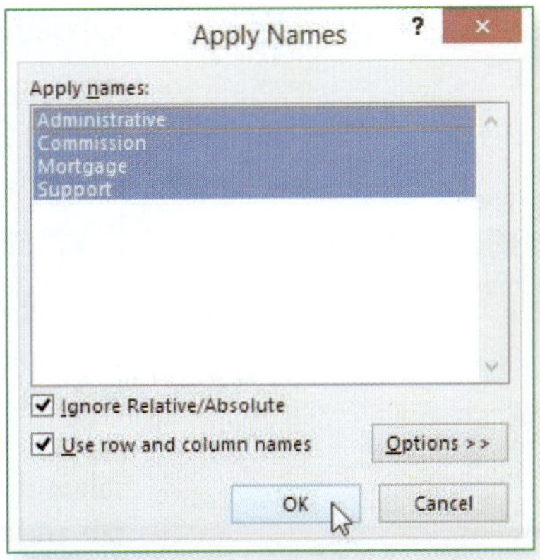

2-20 ***Apply Names* dialog box**

HOW TO: Use the New Name Dialog Box and the Paste Names Dialog Box

1. Select the cell range.
2. Click the **Define Name** button [*Formulas* tab, *Defined Names* group] to open the *New Name* dialog box (Figure 2-21).
3. Type the range name in the **Name** box.
4. Click the **Scope** drop-down arrow to select *Workbook* or *Worksheet.*
5. Click **OK**.
6. Click a cell in a blank area of the worksheet or a cell on a new sheet.
7. Click the **Use in Formula** button [*Formulas* tab, *Defined Names* group].
8. Select **Paste Names** to open the *Paste Name* dialog box.
9. Click **Paste List** to display the range names and their locations in the worksheet.

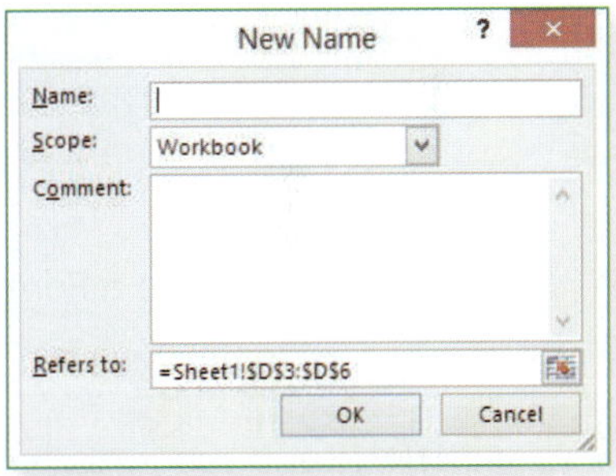

2-21 ***New Name* dialog box**

Copy a Formula with a Mixed Cell Reference

Mixed cell references are a combination of relative and absolute cell references within a single cell address. For example, you can copy a formula in a cell to another location and keep the column reference of the cell addresses constant but allow the row reference to be relative. The same rules that apply to mixed cell references apply to absolute cell references. Place a dollar sign before the part of the cell address that you want to remain absolute prior to copying.

HOW TO: Copy a Formula with a Mixed Cell Reference

1. Select the cell that contains the formula you want to copy.
2. Click the *Formula bar* and type a dollar sign next to the column letter or row number that you want to remain absolute (Figure 2-22).
3. Press **Enter**.
4. Select the cell you want to copy.
5. Click and drag the *Fill Handle* to the destination cell.
6. Release the *Fill Handle.*

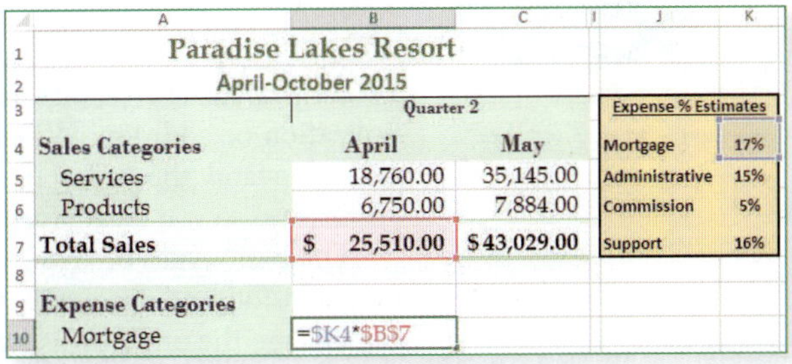

2-22 Formula with mixed cell reference

Create a Formula with a 3D Reference

Sometimes data for your formula may be located in different worksheets. For example, sales for 2015 may be saved in a different worksheet than sales for 2016. To reference cells in both sheets within a formula, you can use *3D* references. The process of using cells in other workbooks is known as ***linking workbooks***.

A formula containing a *3D* cell reference follows the same rules and requirements of non-*3D* cell references with one exception. Because a *3D* cell reference is not physically located in the same sheet as the cell containing the formula, one extra step is required when using *3D* cell references. You must click the sheet tab that contains the cell you want to use in your formula before you select the cell. To select a cell in another sheet within a different workbook, select the open workbook from the *Excel* button on the *Taskbar* and then select the worksheet tab and cell within the tab.

Sample 3D References

Active Cell	Formula	Explanation
Sheet 1 – Cell B4	=Sheet2!B2+Sheet2!B3	Adds cells B2 and B3 on sheet 2.
Sheet 1 – Cell B4	=A4+February!D5+ '[Sales.xslx]10-27-2015'!$B$10+ '[Sales.xslx]10-27-2015'!$C$12	Adds cell A4 in current sheet, D5 on the February sheet in the current workbook, and cells B10 and C12 from the 10-27-2015 worksheet in the Sales workbook.

HOW TO: Create a Formula with a 3D Relative Cell Reference

1. Click the cell where you want to create the formula.
2. Type =.
3. Select the sheet tab of the first cell in the formula.
   - If copying a cell reference from another workbook, open that workbook before creating the formula.
4. Select the cell address of the first cell of the formula.
5. Type the mathematical operator.
6. Select the sheet tab of the next cell in the formula.
7. Select the cell address of the next cell in the calculation (Figure 2-23).
8. Press **Enter** or click the **Enter** button (check mark) on the *Formula bar.*
   - You can copy a *3D* formula using the *Fill Handle*.

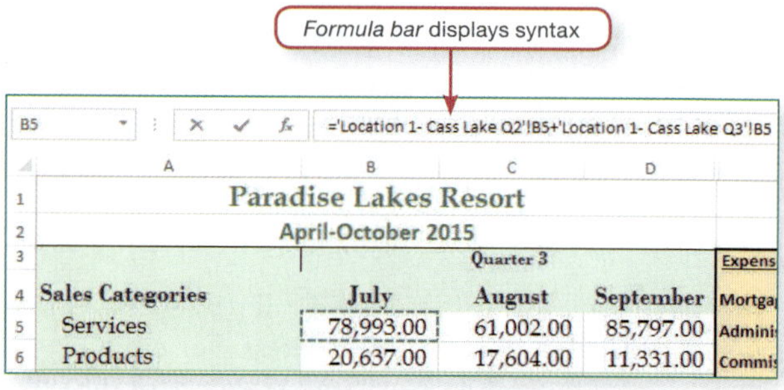

2-23 3D cell reference

Applying Mathematical Order of Operations

SLO 2.3

When you create formulas, arithmetic operators specify the type of calculation such as multiplication or addition. When more than one operator appears in a formula, it is important to understand the order in which Excel performs each operation (***mathematical order of operations***) so you create formulas that correctly calculate results.

The basic types of arithmetic operators in formulas are: addition, subtraction, multiplication, division, and exponentiation. Excel executes these operations in a specified order, but you can change the order by using parentheses.

You can use the following acronym to help remember the order: **P**lease **E**xcuse **M**y **D**ear **A**unt **S**ally. The first letter of each word in the acronym signifies an operator. The order of the words indicates which operator has precedence over another. In the event that two operators have the same level of precedence, Excel calculates the operations of the formula from left to right.

The following table describes the specific rules Excel follows in formulas with multiple operators.

Mathematical Order of Precedence in Formulas

Character	Operator Name	Order of Precedence	Acronym
()	*Parentheses*	First	Please
^	*Exponent*	Second	Excuse
*	*Multiplication*	Third	My
/	*Division*	Third	Dear
+	*Addition*	Fourth	Aunt
-	*Subtraction*	Fourth	Sally

Addition and Subtraction

Since addition and subtraction are on the same precedence level, Excel calculates from left to right if they are both included in a formula.

For example, consider the mathematical expression: **2+5-3**.
The addition operation (2+5) is completed first.
The result (7) is used in the subtraction operation (7-3).
The result is 4.

HOW TO: Use Addition and Subtraction in a Formula

1. Click the cell where you want to create the formula (Figure 2-24).
2. Type =.
3. Enter the cell address or select the first cell reference of the formula.
4. Type +.
5. Enter or select the next cell address of the calculation.
6. Type –.
7. Enter or select the last cell address of the formula.
8. Press **Enter**.
   - The result of the calculation appears in the cell containing the formula.
   - Use the *Formula bar* to view the syntax of the formula.

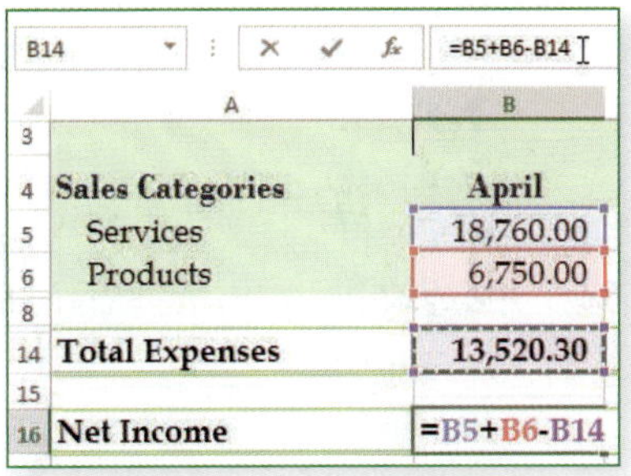

2-24 Formula with multiple operators

Multiplication and Division

Like subtraction and addition, multiplication and division are on the same precedence level. Excel calculates from left to right if multiplication and division appear in the same formula. If the syntax of the formula also includes addition or subtraction, the multiplying or dividing operators are computed before the addition or subtraction operators.

For example, consider the mathematical expression: **2+5*3**.
The multiplication operation (5*3) occurs first.
The result (15) is used in the addition operation (15+2).
The result is 17.

Conversely, consider the mathematical expression: **2*5+3**.
The multiplication operation (2*5) occurs first.
The result (10) is used in the addition operation (10+3).
The result is 13.

HOW TO: Use Multiplication and Addition in a Formula

1. Click the cell where you want to create the formula (Figure 2-25).
2. Type =.
3. Enter or select the first cell address of the formula.
4. Type +.
5. Enter or select the next cell address.
6. Type *.
7. Enter or select the last cell address of the formula.
8. Press **Enter**.

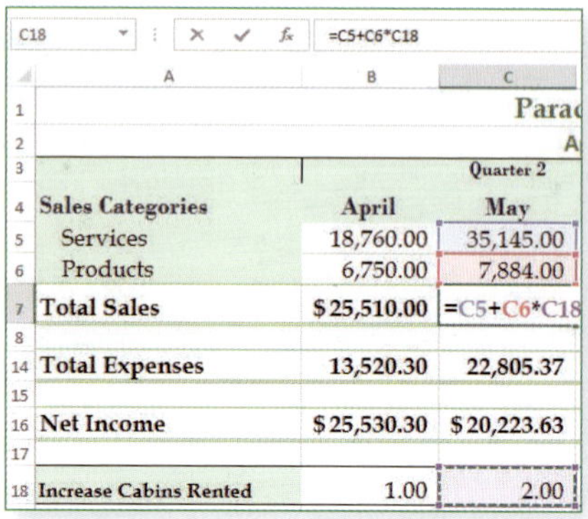

2-25 Addition and multiplication formula

Parentheses and Exponents

Excel calculates operations within parentheses before any other operation is performed. Within parentheses, Excel uses the order of operations to perform calculations.

For example, in the mathematical expression **4+(2+5)*3**.
The operation (2+5) in parentheses occurs first.
The result (7) is used in the multiplication operation (7*3).
The result (21) is used in the addition operation (21+4).
The result is 25.

HOW TO: Use Parentheses, Multiplication, Addition, and Subtraction in a Formula

1. Click the cell where you want to create the formula (Figure 2-26).
2. Type =.
3. Type ((open parenthesis).
4. Enter or select the first cell address of the formula.
5. Type +.
6. Select the next cell address and then type) (close parenthesis).
7. Type *.
8. Select the next cell address.
9. Type –.
10. Select the last cell address.
11. Press **Enter**.

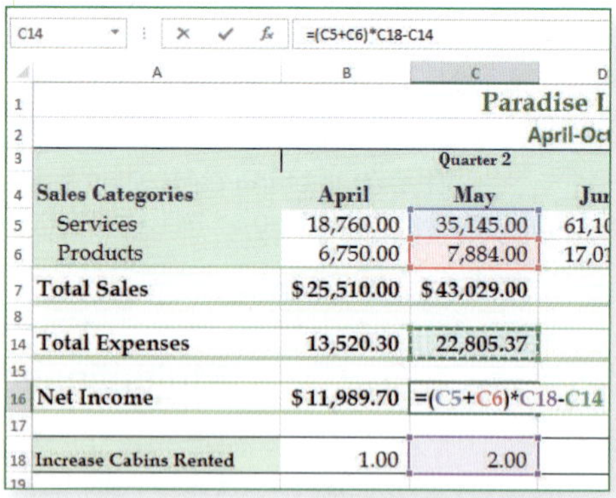

2-26 Multiple operators

Exponents raise a number to a power. Use the caret symbol (^) when writing a formula that includes an exponent. The formula **3^3** raises 3 to the power of 3 and produces the result of 27.

PAUSE & PRACTICE: EXCEL 2-1

You can use the formulas in Excel to convey calculations in a time-saving and meaningful fashion. In this project, you add formulas to a business spreadsheet that displays two quarters of sales and expenses for Paradise Lakes Resort.

File Needed: ***PLRSalesandExpenses-02.xlsx***
Completed Project File Name: ***[your initials] PP E2-1.xlsx***

1. Open the ***PLRSalesandExpenses-02.xlsx*** workbook and save the workbook as ***[your initials] PP E2-1***. (If you see a yellow bar at the top of the workbook entitled "Protected View," click **Enable Editing.**)
2. Enter an addition formula.
   a. Click cell **B7**.
   b. Type =.
   c. Select **B5**, the cell address of the first cell of the formula.
   d. Type +.
   e. Select **B6**, the next cell address of the formula.
   f. Press **Enter** or click the **Enter** button on the *Formula bar.* The syntax of the formula should read =B5+B6.
3. Copy the addition formula.
   a. Select cell **B7**.
   b. Place your pointer in the lower right corner of **B7**, click and drag the *Fill Handle* through the cell range **C7:G7**, and release the *Fill Handle* (Figure 2-27).

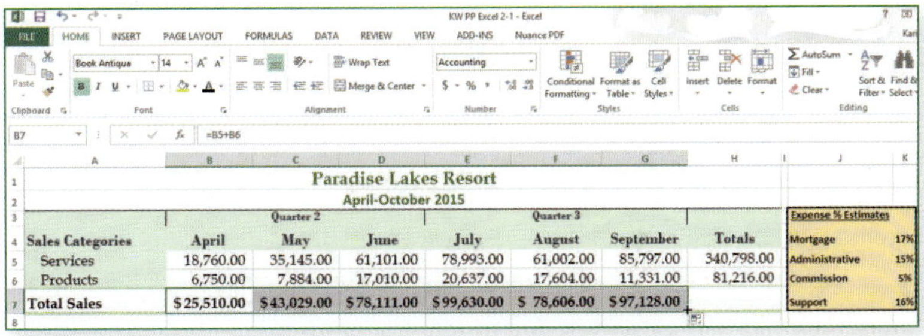

2-27 Using the *Fill Handle* to copy a formula

4. Create and copy the mortgage expense formula using absolute cell references.
   a. Select cell **B10**.
   b. Type the following formula to determine mortgage expenses: =K4*B7.
   c. Click to the left of the **K** column reference letter in the *Formula bar* and type $.
   d. Click to the left of the **4** row reference number and type $. You can also use **F4** to add the dollar signs in the cell reference (Figure 2-28). The formula should read: =$K$4*B7.

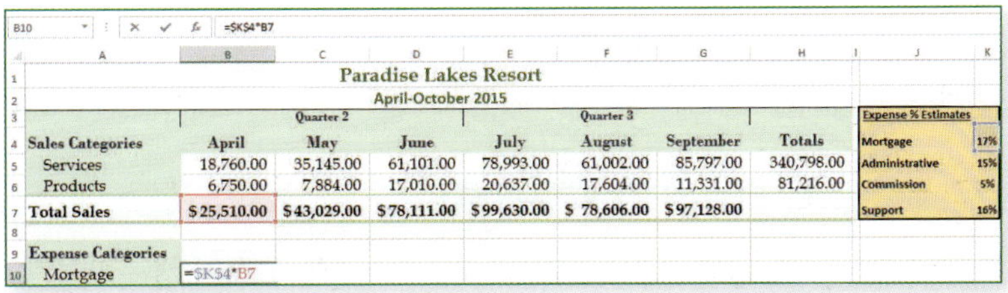

2-28 Mortgage expense formula

e. Press **Enter**.
f. Click and drag the *Fill Handle* on cell **B10** through the cell range **C10:G10**.

5. Create and copy expense formulas using multiplication and absolute cell references.
   a. Enter the formulas listed in the table at right.
   b. Select cells **B11:B14**.
   c. Use the *Fill Handle* of cell **B14** to copy the formulas to **C11:G14**.

B11	=$K$5*B7
B12	=$K$6*B7
B13	=$K$7*B7
B14	=B10+B11+B12+B13

6. Create and copy a net income formula with a *3D* reference, multiple operators, and apply the mathematical order of precedence.
   a. Click cell **B16** and type =(B5+.
   b. Select cell **B6** and type).
   c. Type -, select cell **B14**, and type -.
   d. Click the **Cass Lake Tax** sheet tab.
   e. Select **B5** on the *Cass Lake Tax* tab.
   f. Press **Enter**.
   g. Review the formula syntax. It should be =(B5+B6)-B14-'Cass Lake Tax'!B5.
   h. Select cell **B16** and place your pointer over the *Fill Handle* of cell **B16**.
   i. Use the *Fill Handle* to copy the formula to **C16:G16**.
   j. Release the pointer.
7. Use auditing tools to review the formula in cell B16.
   a. Select cell **B16**.
   b. Click **Show Formulas** and **Trace Precedents** [*Formulas* tab, *Formula Auditing* group]. The black arrow indicates a cell reference on another worksheet.
   c. Click **Remove Arrows** [*Formulas* tab, *Formula Auditing* group].
   d. Click **Show Formulas** [*Formulas* tab, *Formula Auditing* group] to return to *Normal* view.
8. Copy and paste an existing formula without the formatting.
   a. Select cell **H6** and use the *Fill Handle* to copy the formula to **H7:H16**.
   b. Click the **AutoFill Options** arrow button and select **Fill Without Formatting** to prevent overwriting existing cell formats.
   c. Delete unnecessary formulas in cells **H8, H9**, and **H15**.
9. Save and close the workbook (Figure 2-29).

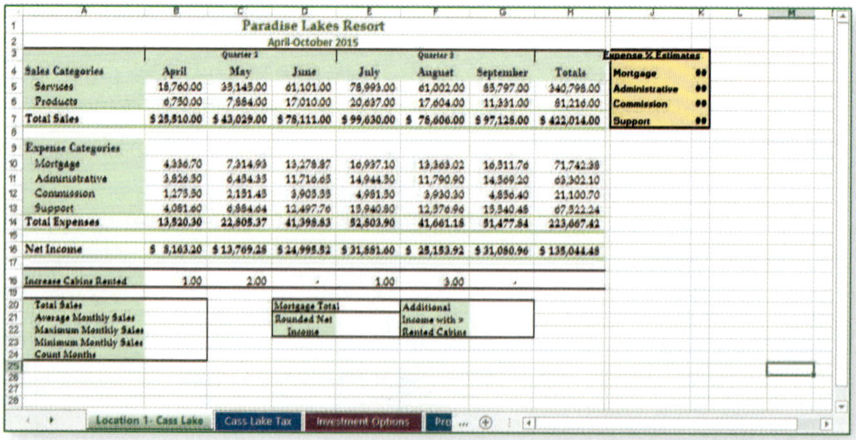

2-29 PP E2-1 completed

SLO 2.4

Working with Common Functions

Functions are pre-defined formulas and each function has a specific syntax pattern. Functions start with an equals sign (=) followed by the function name, an opening parenthesis, the arguments for the function separated by commas, and a closing parenthesis. ***Arguments*** are the pieces of information within parentheses that determine what value a function returns. For example, in the function =SUM(B2:B6), SUM is the function name and the cell range B2:B6 is the argument.

When you type a formula, ***Formula AutoComplete*** and ***Function Screen Tips*** appear to help you create and edit formulas. After you type an = and beginning letters of the function, *Formula AutoComplete* displays a list of functions and range names. Use the down arrow to move through the list or continue typing the function name. Press *Tab* or double-click the function name to insert it. A ScreenTip appears after you type the function name and an opening parenthesis. The ScreenTip includes the required syntax and arguments for the function. Click the ScreenTip function name to display the *Help* topic for the function.

In addition to the *AutoSum* function, which was introduced in Chapter 1 (see *SLO 1.3: Using the Sum Function*), there are other common functions that you can use to calculate values in a spreadsheet. Many times you may need to find an average or a minimum or maximum value in a range of numbers or you may want to count the numbers in a given range within a group of cells.

> **MORE INFO**
>
> Functions and formulas are similar but not exactly the same. All functions are also considered formulas, =SUM(B2:B6), but not all formulas are functions since they do not contain a function name, =B2+B3-B6.

AUTOSUM Function

As discussed in Chapter 1, the *AutoSum* button automates the insertion of the *SUM* function. Recall that when you use *AutoSum,* instead of typing a formula to add cell contents that separates each cell reference with a plus sign, you use the *SUM* function to add the cells. You can use *AutoSum* to insert the *SUM* function by clicking the *AutoSum* button in the *Function Library* group on the *Formulas* tab. In this chapter, we discuss the *AutoSum* function in more detail and explain how you can use the *AutoSum* drop-down list to insert other functions including *Average, Count Numbers, Max,* and *Min.*

HOW TO: Enter the SUM Function with AutoSum

1. Click the cell where you want to enter the function.
2. Click the **AutoSum** arrow [*Formulas* tab, *Function Library* group] (Figure 2-30).
   - When you click the upper half of **AutoSum**, the *SUM* function is inserted. Click the bottom half of **AutoSum** (the arrow) to display a list of functions.
3. Select **Sum** from the list.
   - The equals sign, function name, parentheses, and assumed cell range are entered automatically.
4. Select the cell range you wish to total if the range that Excel entered automatically is not correct.
   - The cell range appears between the parentheses in the function syntax (Figure 2-31).
5. Press **Enter**.

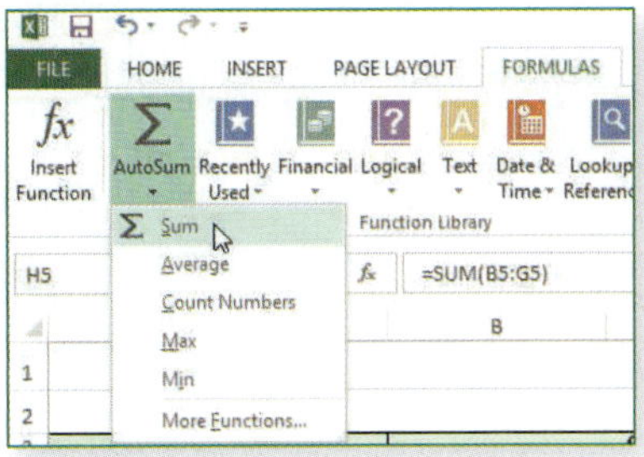

2-30 *AutoSum* function list

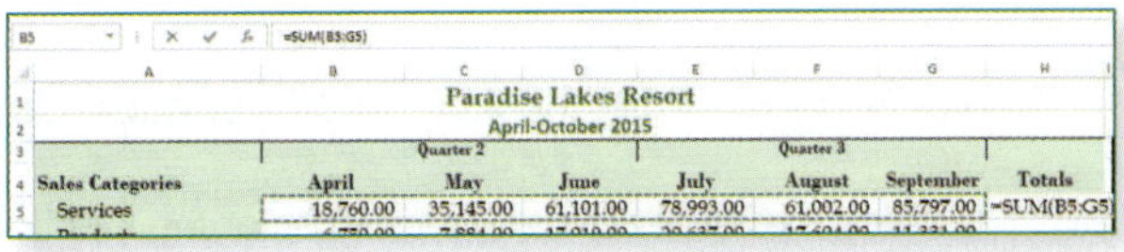

2-31 Selection of correct range

If you are entering multiple *AutoSum* functions in a worksheet, you can do this in one step rather than individually entering each *AutoSum* function.

HOW TO: Enter Multiple SUM Functions Simultaneously with AutoSum

1. Select the cells where you want to enter the functions (Figure 2-32).

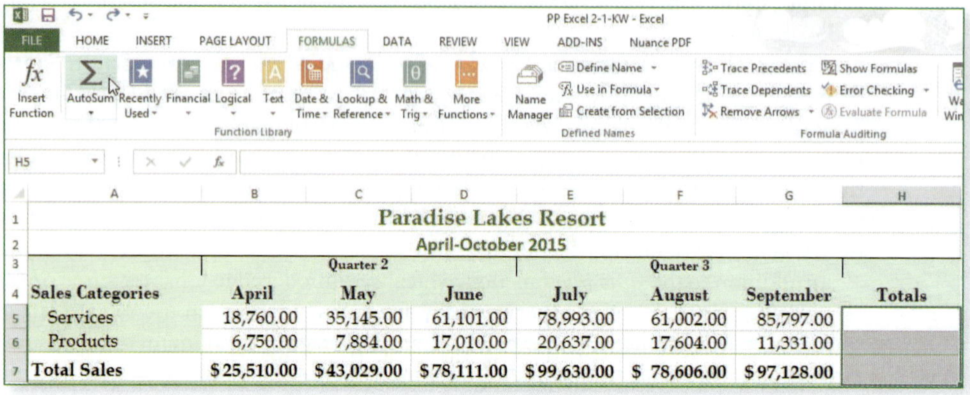

2-32 Selected cell range for simultaneous SUM function

2. Click the **AutoSum** arrow [*Formulas* tab, *Function Library group*].
3. Select **Sum** from the list.
   - It is not necessary to press **Enter**.
   - The results appear in the cells containing the formulas.

ANOTHER WAY

AutoSum is also located on the *Home* tab in the *Editing* group.
Press **Alt+=** for the *SUM* function.

MORE INFO

The *AutoSum* button is also called the ***Sigma*** button.

AVERAGE Function

The ***AVERAGE*** function calculates an average by adding cell values together and dividing the total of the values by the number of values. The *AVERAGE* function performs the calculation quickly and eliminates the need to key cell addresses and mathematical operators manually. You can apply the *AVERAGE* function by using the *AutoSum* button in the *Function Library* group on the *Formulas* tab.

HOW TO: Enter the AVERAGE Function Using the AutoSum Button

1. Click the cell where you want to enter the function.
2. Click the **AutoSum** arrow [*Formulas* tab, *Function Library* group].

3. Select **Average**.
   - The equals sign, function name, parentheses, and assumed cell range appear in the cell (Figure 2-33).

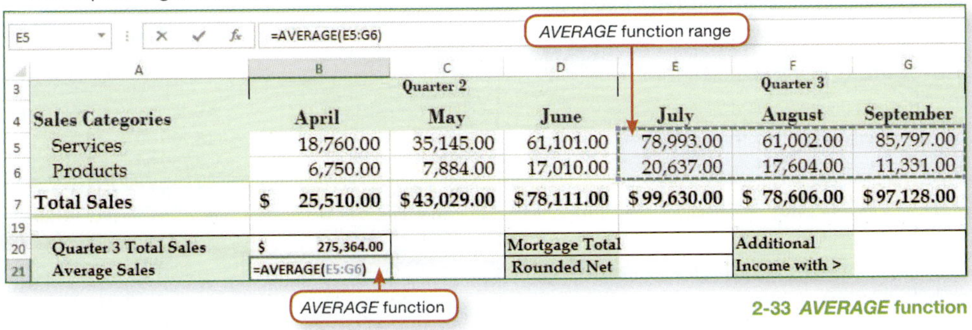

2-33 *AVERAGE* function

4. Select a cell range if the range Excel automatically highlights is not correct.
   - The cell range appears between the parentheses in the function syntax.
5. Press **Enter** or click the **Enter** button on the *Formula bar.*

COUNT Functions

Although you can manually count each number in a group of cells or each cell that contains descriptive labels, *COUNT* functions provide a more error-free method to accomplish this task. To add a *COUNT* function to the worksheet, use the *AutoSum* arrow in the *Function Library* group on the *Formulas* tab (Figure 2-34).

There are several *COUNT* functions. For example, you could use a *COUNTIF* function to insert a function that calculates all cells in a range that contain the product description label "Services." The following table lists several *COUNT* functions.

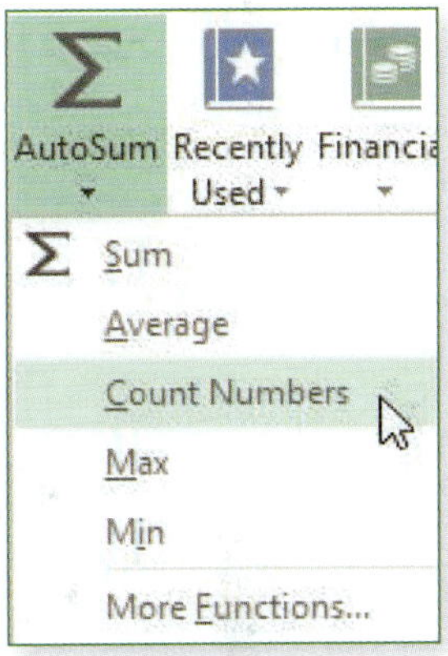

2-34 *AutoSum* function list

Common Count Functions

Count Functions	Description	Example Syntax
COUNT	Counts the number of cells in a range that contain numbers	=COUNT(A1:A15)
COUNTA	Counts the number of cells in a range that contain any data type, text, or numbers	=COUNTA(A1:A15)
COUNTBLANK	Counts the number of blank cells in a range	=COUNTBLANK(A1:A15)
COUNTIF	Counts the number of cells in a range based on specified criteria	=COUNTIF(A1:A15, "Services")
DCOUNT	Counts the amount of numbers in a database range that meet specified criteria	=DCOUNT(database, field, criteria)
DCOUNTA	Counts the amount of text entries in a database range that meet specified criteria	=DCOUNTA(database, field, criteria)

HOW TO: Enter the COUNT Function Using the AutoSum Button

1. Click the cell where you want to enter the function (Figure 2-35).
2. Click the **AutoSum** arrow [*Formulas* tab, *Function Library group*].
3. Select **Count Numbers** from the list to choose the *COUNT* function (see Figure 2-35).
   - The *COUNT* function counts the number of cells in a range that contain numbers.
4. Select a cell range if the range that Excel automatically highlights is not correct.
5. Press **Enter**.

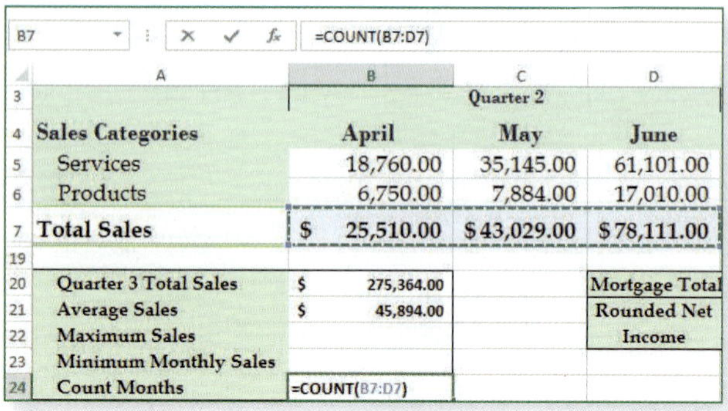

2-35 ***COUNT*** **function**

> **MORE INFO**
>
> You can use a "?" to take the place of one character in the *COUNT* function criteria. For example, the criteria "**Sal?**" finds results of 4-letter words beginning with *Sal* such as **Sale** or **Salt**. You can use an "*" to represent multiple characters in criteria. For example, the criteria "**Sal***" finds results such as **Salmon** or **Salt**.

MAX and MIN Functions

The *MAX* function finds the largest value in a cell range, and the *MIN* function finds the smallest value in a cell range. To apply the *MAX and MIN* functions use the *AutoSum* arrow in the *Function Library* group on the *Formulas* tab.

HOW TO: Enter the MAX or MIN Function Using the AutoSum Button

1. Click the cell where you want to enter the function.
2. Click the **AutoSum** arrow [*Formulas* tab, *Function Library group*].
3. Select the **MAX** or **MIN** function from the list (Figure 2-36).
4. Select a cell range if the range that Excel highlights is not correct.
5. Press **Enter**.

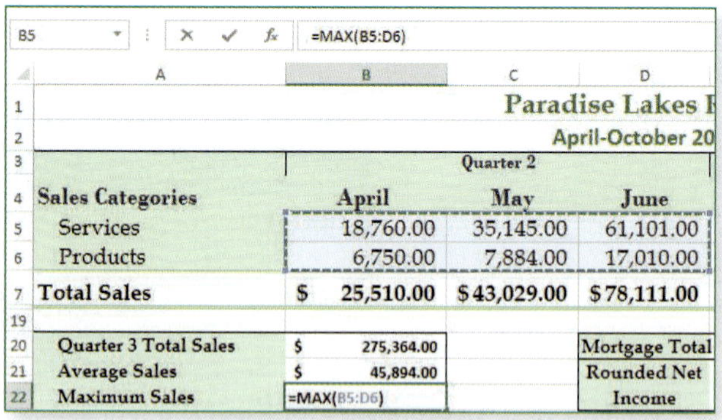

2-36 ***MAX*** **function**

AutoCalculate

AutoCalculate allows you to view totals, averages, or other statistical information without creating a formula. The *AutoCalculate* area is located on the *Status bar.* Right-click the *Status bar* to select *AutoCalculate* options. The *Average, Count,* and *Sum* options are selected by default. *AutoCalculate* results do not display in the spreadsheet.

HOW TO: Use AutoCalculate for a Range of Cells

1. Select the appropriate cell range.
2. Right-click the **Status bar** to display the *Customize Status Bar* menu (Figure 2-37).
3. Select the desired functions from the shortcut menu.
   - If a function has a checkmark to the left, it is already active.
4. View the *Status bar* to see the results of selected functions (Figure 2-38).

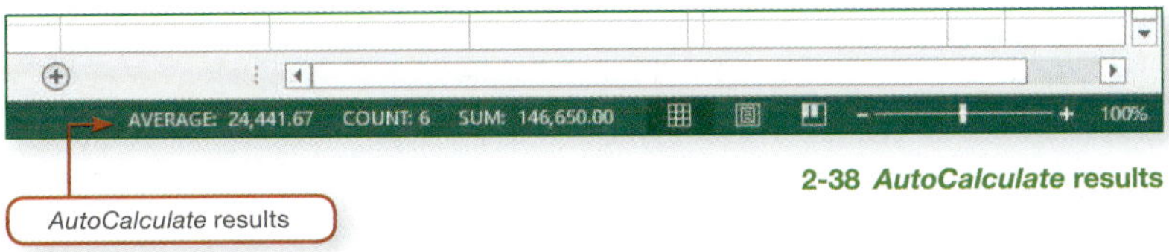

2-38 *AutoCalculate* results

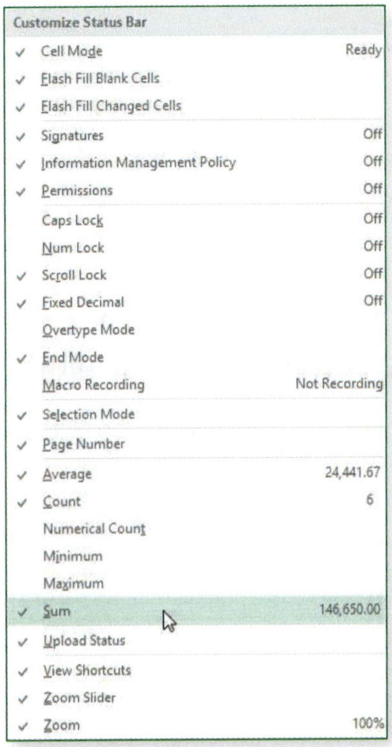

2-37 *Customize Status Bar* menu

TODAY and NOW Functions

Excel has 24 date and time functions. *TODAY* and *NOW* are useful functions that are often included in spreadsheets to track the current date of reports. These functions reflect your computer's date and time stamp.

The *TODAY* function uses the syntax =TODAY() to automatically insert the current date. The TODAY() function does not have any arguments. The TODAY() function updates each time the spreadsheet is opened.

The *NOW* function uses the syntax =NOW() and is similar to the *TODAY* function. However, the *NOW* function includes the current time with the date. Like the *TODAY* function, the *NOW* function is updated each time the spreadsheet opens. Several formats are available for the date and time data. For example, if you prefer to view the date as 12/21/2015, you can choose the ***Short Date*** format from the *Number Format* drop-down list located in the *Number* group on the *Home* tab.

The *Function Library* group on the *Formulas* tab includes a ***Date & Time*** button. Click the **Date & Time** arrow to view the list of date and time functions.

PAUSE & PRACTICE: EXCEL 2-2

For this project, you open your previous Pause & Practice file and insert the *SUM, AVERAGE, COUNT, MIN*, and *MAX* functions to the Paradise Lakes Resort net income spreadsheet.

File Needed: ***[your initials] PP E2-1.xlsx***
Completed Project File Name: ***[your initials] PP E2-2.xlsx***

1. Open the workbook ***[your initials] PP E2-1*** and save the workbook as ***[your initials] PP E2-2***.

2. Enter the *SUM* function using *AutoSum.*
   a. Click cell **B20**.
   b. Click the **AutoSum** arrow button [*Formulas* tab, *Function Library* group].
   c. Select **Sum**.
   d. Select the cell range **B7:G7**. Verify that the formula syntax is =SUM(B7:G7) (Figure 2-39).
   e. Press **Enter**.

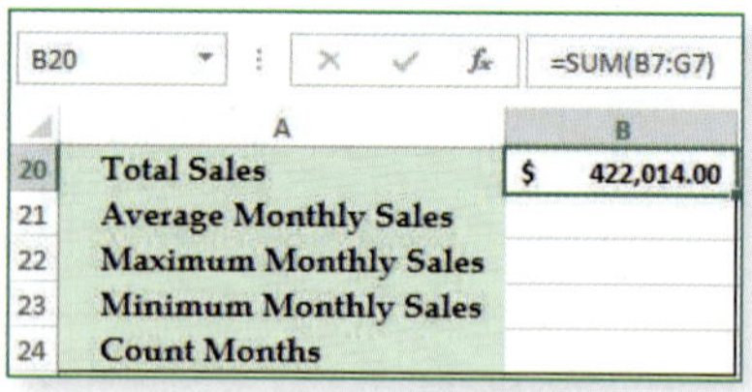

2-39 ***SUM*** **function**

3. Enter the *AVERAGE* function using *AutoSum.*
   a. Click cell **B21**.
   b. Click the **AutoSum** arrow button [*Formulas* tab, *Function Library group*].
   c. Select **Average**.
   d. Select the cell range **B7:G7**.
   e. Verify that the formula syntax is =AVERAGE(B7:G7).
   f. Press **Enter**.
4. Enter a *COUNT* function using *AutoSum.*
   a. Click cell **B24**.
   b. Click the **AutoSum** arrow button [*Formulas* tab, *Function Library* group].
   c. Select **Count Numbers**.
   d. Select the cell range **B7:G7**.
   e. Verify that the formula syntax is =COUNT(B7:G7).
   f. Press **Enter**. The formula's result should be 6.00 (Figure 2-40).

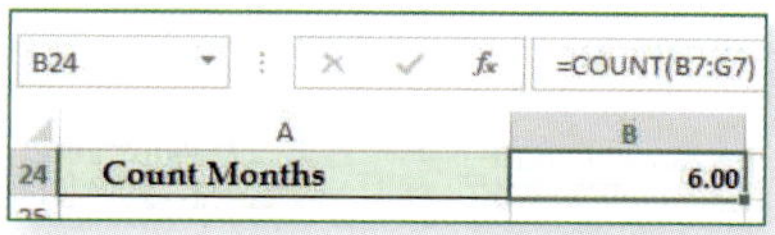

2-40 ***COUNT*** **function**

5. Enter the *MAX* function using *AutoSum.*
   a. Click cell **B22**.
   b. Click the **AutoSum** arrow [*Formulas* tab, *Function Library group*].
   c. Select **Max**.
   d. Select the cell range **B7:G7**.
   e. Verify that the formula syntax is =MAX(B7:G7).
   f. Press **Enter**.
6. Use auditing tools to review the formula in B22.
   a. Select **B22**.
   b. Click **Show Formulas** and **Trace Precedents** [*Formulas* tab, *Formula Auditing* group].
   c. Review the position of the arrows.
   d. Click **Remove Arrows** [*Formulas* tab, *Formula Auditing* group].
   e. Click **Show Formulas** [*Formulas* tab, *Formula Auditing* group] to return to *Normal* view.
7. Add absolute cell references to an existing formula.
   a. Select **B22**.
   b. Click the **Formula bar** and select the cell range **B7:G7** but not the parentheses.
   c. Press **F4** to add absolute references.
   d. Press **Enter**.
   e. Verify the formula syntax =MAX($B$7:$G$7).
8. Copy an existing formula and edit the function name.
   a. Select **B22** and use the *Fill Handle* to copy the formula to **B23**.
   b. Select cell **B23**.
   c. Click the **Formula bar** and replace the function name *MAX* with MIN.
   d. Press **Enter**.

9. Save and close the workbook (Figure 2-41).

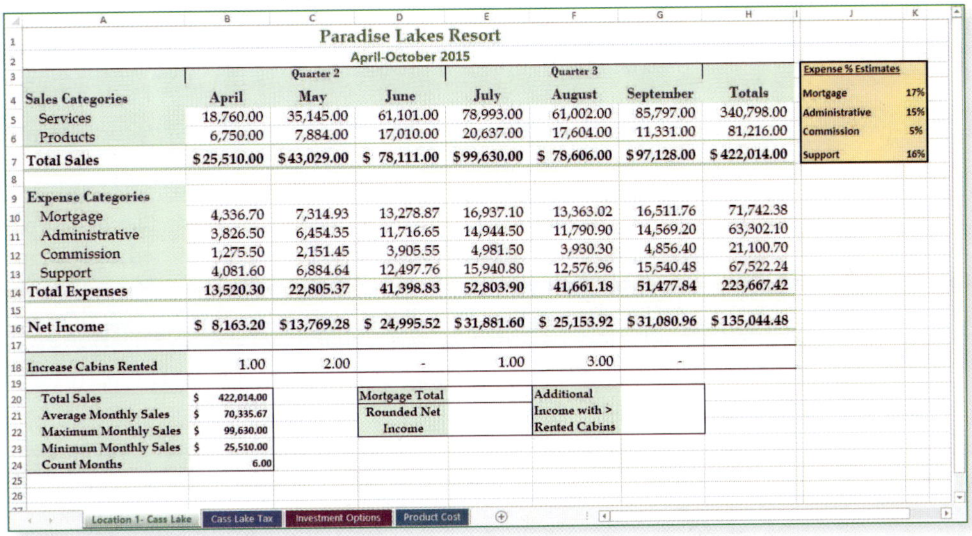

Paradise Lakes Resort							
April-October 2015							
	Quarter 2			Quarter 3			
Sales Categories	**April**	**May**	**June**	**July**	**August**	**September**	**Totals**
Services	18,760.00	35,145.00	61,101.00	78,993.00	61,002.00	85,797.00	340,798.00
Products	6,750.00	7,884.00	17,010.00	20,637.00	17,604.00	11,331.00	81,216.00
Total Sales	**$ 25,510.00**	**$ 43,029.00**	**$ 78,111.00**	**$ 99,630.00**	**$ 78,606.00**	**$ 97,128.00**	**$ 422,014.00**
Expense Categories							
Mortgage	4,336.70	7,314.93	13,278.87	16,937.10	13,363.02	16,511.76	71,742.38
Administrative	3,826.50	6,454.35	11,716.65	14,944.50	11,790.90	14,569.20	63,302.10
Commission	1,275.50	2,151.45	3,905.55	4,981.50	3,930.30	4,856.40	21,100.70
Support	4,081.60	6,884.64	12,497.76	15,940.80	12,576.96	15,540.48	67,522.24
Total Expenses	**13,520.30**	**22,805.37**	**41,398.83**	**52,803.90**	**41,661.18**	**51,477.84**	**223,667.42**
Net Income	**$ 8,163.20**	**$ 13,769.28**	**$ 24,995.52**	**$ 31,881.60**	**$ 25,153.92**	**$ 31,080.96**	**$ 135,044.48**
Increase Cabins Rented	1.00	2.00	-	1.00	3.00	-	

Expense % Estimates	
Mortgage	17%
Administrative	15%
Commission	5%
Support	16%

Total Sales	$ 422,014.00
Average Monthly Sales	$ 70,335.67
Maximum Monthly Sales	$ 99,630.00
Minimum Monthly Sales	$ 25,510.00
Count Months	6.00

Mortgage Total		Additional Income with > Rented Cabins	
Rounded Net Income			

2-41 PP E2-2 completed

SLO 2.5

Working with Financial, Logical, and LOOKUP Functions

Excel's financial, logical, and lookup functions contain many advanced options. The *Insert Function* button automates hundreds of functions that are available in Excel. This section of the chapter focuses on using the *Insert Function* button to insert *PMT, IF, VLOOKUP,* and *HLOOKUP* functions.

The search feature within the ***Insert Function dialog box*** helps to quickly locate the function you need and tells you which arguments to include. Once the function is selected, you can complete most of the ***arguments*** (components or parts of the function) of the function by using point and click. This method can be very useful when you are not sure how to create the formula syntax or what the required arguments for a formula are. You can access the *Insert Function* button in the *Function Library* group on the *Formulas* tab (Figure 2-42) or click the f_x button located on the *Formula bar.*

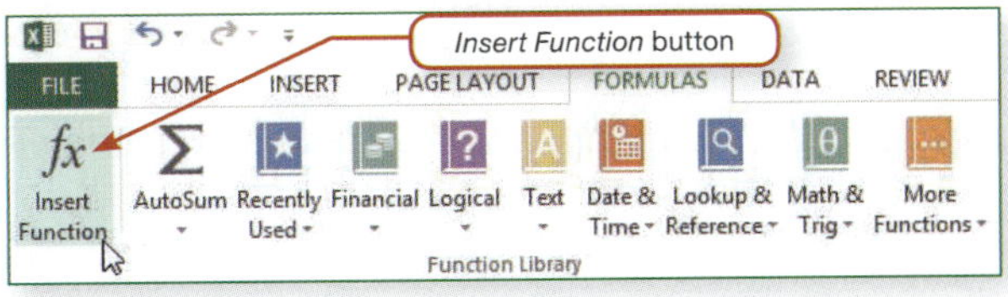

2-42 *Function Library* group

> **ANOTHER WAY**
>
> **Shift+F3** opens the *Insert Function* dialog box.

PMT Function

The *PMT* function calculates loan payment amounts. The *PMT* function assumes the borrower makes regular payments and the loan has a constant interest rate. The *PMT* function includes the principal (amount of money borrowed) and the interest rate when calculating the payment amount. It does not include other fees such as insurance costs or taxes.

The *PMT* function has five arguments, and the formula syntax for the function is:

=PMT(rate, nper, pv, [fv], [type])

- The ***rate*** argument is the interest rate per period for the loan; this argument is required.
- The ***nper*** argument is the total number of periods for repayment of the loan; this argument is required.
- The ***pv*** argument is the present value or the principal; this argument is required.
- The ***fv*** argument is the future value after you make the last payment; this argument is optional. If the fv argument is omitted, it is assumed the future value of the loan is zero.
- The ***type*** argument indicates when payments are due; this argument is optional. A zero or omitted argument indicates payments are due at the end of the period; this is the default setting. If the type argument is 1, payments are due at the beginning of the period.

Refer to Figure 2-43 to understand the following *PMT* function example:

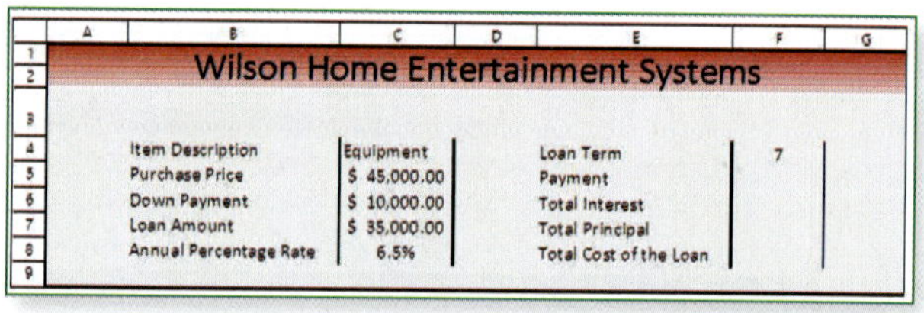

2-43 *PMT* function sample worksheet

The PMT function **=PMT(C8/12,F4*12,C7)**

- **C8/12** is the ***rate*** argument and indicates an annual rate of 6.5% and that the borrower is making monthly payments (period is equal to one month), in other words 6.5% divided by 12.
- **F4*12** is the ***nper*** argument and indicates that the loan term is 7 years (cell F7) and there are 12 payments per year. (The total number of periods is 7 years times 12 periods per year.)
- **C7** is the ***pv*** argument (amount of the loan or the present value).

The result of this *PMT* function is ($519.73). The payment result is a negative number, which is indicated by the red color and the parentheses; the borrower is paying this amount and not receiving it.

HOW TO: Enter the PMT Function with the Insert Function Button

1. Click the cell where you want to enter the function.
2. Click the **Insert Function** (**f_x**) button to the left of the *Formula bar* to open the *Insert Function* dialog box (Figure 2-44).
3. Click the **Search for a function** box, type Payment, and click **Go**.
4. Select **PMT** from the function list and click **OK**. The *Function Arguments* dialog box opens (Figure 2-45).
5. Click the **Rate** argument text box and click the cell that contains the interest per period for the loan.
   - If the cell contains an APR (annual percentage rate), it must be converted to interest per period. Divide the interest rate by the number of payments that will be made in a year. For example, if the borrower is paying monthly, divide by 12; if the borrower is paying quarterly, divide by 4.

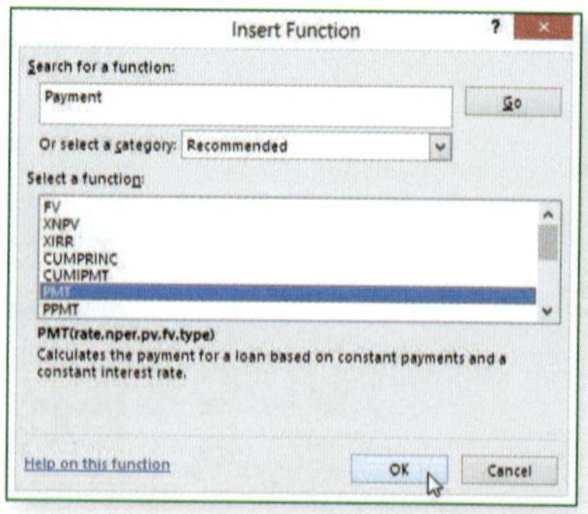

2-44 *Insert Function* dialog box

6. Click the **Nper** argument text box and click the cell that contains the term of the loan. The cell must contain the total number of periods for repayment of the loan.
    - If the loan term is in years and payments are monthly, the total number of periods is the number of years * 12.
    - If the loan term is in years and payments are quarterly, then the total number of periods is the number of years * 4.
7. Click the **Pv** argument text box and click the cell that contains the amount of the loan.
    - You can omit the last two arguments because there will be a zero balance after the last payment is made, and payments will be made at the end of each period.
8. Click **OK** to close the dialog box and insert the function.

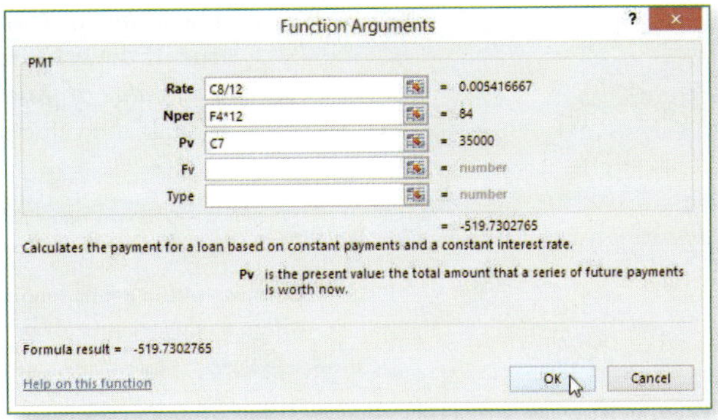

2-45 *PMT Function Arguments* dialog box

ANOTHER WAY

Use the **Financial** button [*Formulas* tab, *Function Library* group] to locate financial functions described in this section.

MORE INFO

To create an amortization schedule, you can use the ***Loan Amortization Schedule*** template in the *Templates* category from the *New* button [*File* tab]. Select the **Loan Amortization Schedule** from the *Business Schedules* subfolder located in the *Schedules* folder.

IF Function

The ***IF*** function evaluates a specified condition and returns one value if the condition is true and another value if the condition is false. For example, if you work for an organization that determines bonuses on the amount of sales revenue generated, you could use the *IF* function to determine if a sales goal was met and if a bonus should be paid and then calculate the amount of the bonus.

To evaluate the condition, you can use comparison operators. The table at the right lists comparison operators:

Comparison Operators

Operator	Description
=	Equal to
<>	Not equal to
>	Greater than
>=	Greater than or equal to
<	Less than
<=	Less than or equal to

The *IF* function has three arguments and the formula syntax for the function is:

=IF (logical_test, value_if_true, value_if_false)

- **The *logical_test*** argument is the value or expression to be evaluated as true or false; this argument is required. You can use any comparison operator in the logical test.

- The ***value_if_true*** argument is the value returned if the logical test argument is true. If the value returned is text, enclose the text in quotes.
- The ***value_if_false*** argument is the value returned if the logical test argument is false. If the value returned is text, enclose the text in quotes.

> **MORE INFO**
>
> Commas within a function indicate the start of a new argument, so it is a good idea to omit commas within a value argument. For example, type "5000," not "5,000," in a value argument.

Refer to Figure 2-46 to understand the following examples of using an *IF* function. The formula shown here determines if an item should be reordered:

	A	B	C	D	E	F
1	Product Catalog					
2						
3	Product #	Description	Qty on Hand	Unit Cost	Unit Price	Reorder?
4	101	T-Shirt	120	$ 4.00	$ 11.00	
5	102	Shorts	45	$ 2.50	$ 6.88	
6	103	Coffee Mug	25	$ 1.25	$ 3.44	
7	104	Pants	36	$ 7.25	$ 19.94	
8	105	Beach Towel	22	$ 3.50	$ 9.63	

2-46 *IF* function sample worksheet

=IF(C4<=100,"Yes","No")

- C4<=100 is the ***logical_test*** argument and determines whether *Qty on Hand* is less than or equal to 100.
- "Yes" is the ***value_if_true*** argument. "Yes" is the value returned if the quantity on hand is less than or equal to 100. A "Yes" response indicates that the quantity on hand is below the minimal amount required on hand and should be reordered. The logical test argument is true if this value is returned.
- "No" is the ***value_if_false*** argument. "No" is the value returned if the quantity on hand is greater than 100. A "No" response indicates that it is not necessary to reorder. The logical test argument is false if this value is returned.
- The value returned for this *IF* function is "No."

The following formula is based again on information in Figure 2-46 and determines how many items to order:

=IF(C5<50,50-C5,0)

- C5<50 is the ***logical_test*** argument.
- 50-C5 is the ***value_if_true*** argument. The result of 50-C5 is the value returned if the quantity on hand is less than 50. The amount to order is calculated. The logical test argument is true if this value is returned.
- 0 is the ***value_if_false*** argument. 0 is the value returned if the quantity on hand is greater than or equal to 50. Reordering is not necessary. The logical test argument is false if this value is returned.
- The value returned for this *IF* function is 5.

You can insert the *IF* function by typing the formula, using the *Insert Function* button on the *Formula bar*, or using the *Insert Function* button on the *Formulas* tab.

HOW TO: Enter the IF Function

1. Click the cell where you want to enter the function.
2. Click the **Insert Function** button [*Formulas* tab, *Function Library group*] to open the *Insert Function* dialog box.

3. Type IF in the **Search for a function** box and click **Go**.
4. Select **IF** from the function list and click **OK**. The *Function Arguments* dialog box opens (Figure 2-47).
5. Click the **Logical_test** argument text box, and select the cell that will be compared.
6. Type the comparison operator or operators.
7. Click the cell that contains the comparison amount or type the value.
   - Include absolute cell references if you plan to copy the formula to another location and are referencing a cell that must remain constant.
8. Click the **Value_if_true** argument text box and click the cell that contains the true value, type the true value, or type the argument text surrounded with quotation marks.
9. Click the **Value_if_false** argument text box and click the cell that contains the false value, type the false value, or type the argument text surrounded with quotation marks.
10. Click **OK** to close the dialog box and insert the function.

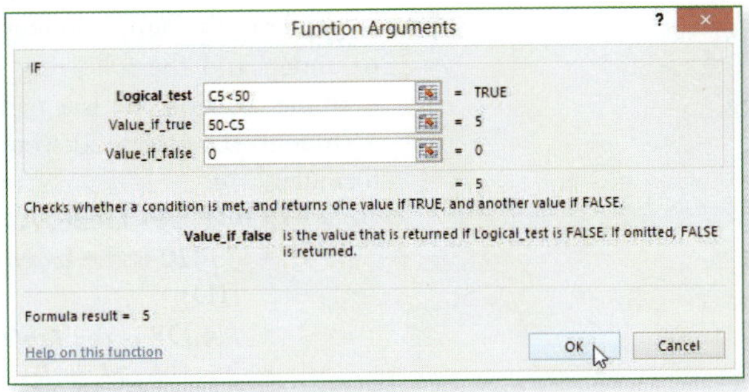

2-47 ***IF Function Arguments*** **dialog box**

> **MORE INFO**
>
> You can create nested *IF* functions that allow for more than one logical test.

LOOKUP Functions

LOOKUP functions retrieve a value from a range or table of cells located in another area of the worksheet or workbook. The two main types of *LOOKUP* functions are ***VLOOKUP*** (vertical lookup) and ***HLOOKUP*** (horizontal lookup). The *VLOOKUP* function finds a value in the first column of a range of cells and returns a value from any cell on the same row of the range. In order for the *VLOOKUP* function to work properly, the first column must be sorted in ascending order and each cell must contain a unique value.

The *VLOOKUP* function has four arguments and the formula syntax for the function is:

=VLOOKUP (lookup_value, table_array, col_index_num, [range_lookup])

- The ***lookup_value*** argument is required and Excel searches for this value in the first column of the cell range or table. If the cells in the first column contain text, you must enclose the text in quotes when creating the formula. When searching for the lookup value in the first column of the range, Excel finds the largest value less than or equal to the value in the first column of the range.
- The ***table_array*** argument is the range used for looking up data; this argument is required. You can enter a cell range or a range name. The data in the first column must be in ascending order.
- The ***col_index_num*** argument is the column number of the cell range or table (counting from the left); this argument is required.
- The ***[range lookup]*** argument is a logical value (True or False) that is used to find the nearest value (True) or an exact match (False); this argument is optional. The default value is "True."

Refer to the sample lookup table in Figure 2-48 to understand the following *VLOOKUP* function example. To find the last name of a student with a student ID of 33420, you enter the following formula:

=VLOOKUP(33420, A4:D8, 2)

- **33420** is the ***lookup_value*** argument (ID).
- **A4:D8** is the ***table_array*** argument (cell range).
- **2** is the ***col_index_num*** argument (the second column in the table which lists the last names of the students).
- The result of this *VLOOKUP* function is "Rosch."

	A	B	C	D
1	**Student Data Table**			
2				
3	**ID**	**Last Name**	**First Name**	**Degree**
4	11123	Boney	John	Business
5	22234	Eisenhauer	DeAnn	Education
6	33420	Rosch	Ariel	Psychology
7	42002	Bowman	Larry	Education
8	56009	Kranz	Sandra	Accounting

2-48 Lookup table

To find the degree of a student with an identification number of 33420, key the following formula:

=VLOOKUP(33420,A4:D8,4)

The result of this *VLOOKUP* function is "Psychology."

Apply the *VLOOKUP* and *HLOOKUP* functions by using the *Insert Function* button on the *Formula bar* or on the *Formulas* tab or by typing the function name into a cell.

HOW TO: Enter the VLOOKUP Function

1. Click the cell where you want to enter the function.
2. Click the **Insert Function** button [*Formulas* tab, *Function Library* group] to open the *Insert Function* dialog box (Figure 2-49).
3. Type VLOOKUP in the **Search for a function** text box and click **Go**.
4. Select **VLOOKUP** from the function list and click **OK** to open the *Function Arguments* dialog box (Figure 2-50).
5. Click the **Lookup_value** text box.
6. Click a cell in the first column of the cell range or table.
7. Click the **Table_array** argument text box and select the appropriate cell range.
   - When you drag to select, the *Function Arguments* dialog box collapses. The dialog box expands after the range is selected.
   - Apply absolute cell reference symbols to this range if you plan to copy the formula to another location.
8. Click the **Col_index_num** argument text box, and type the column number (count from the left).
   - Do not include the *Range_lookup* argument; it will default to *TRUE* and find the closest match instead of an exact match.
9. Click **OK** to close the *Functions Arguments* dialog box.

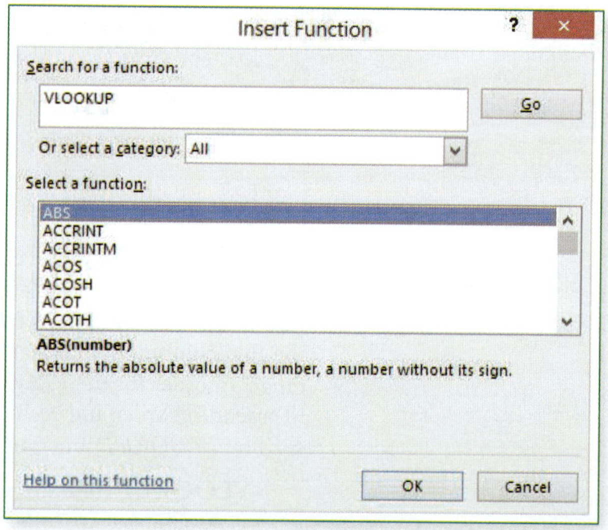

2-49 *Insert Function* dialog box

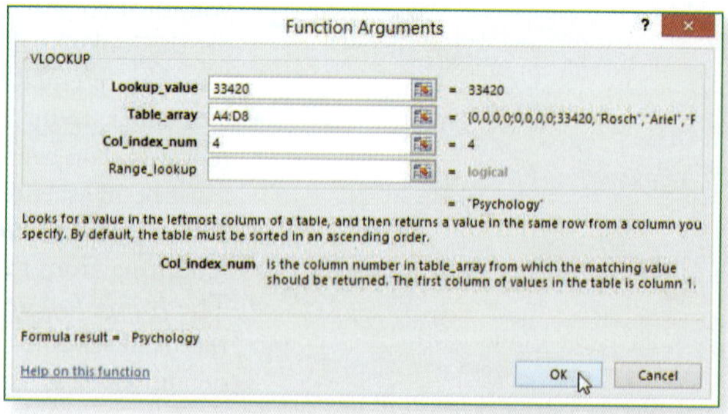

2-50 *VLOOKUP Function Arguments* dialog box

MORE INFO

Make sure you type the column number and not the column letter for the third argument in the *VLOOKUP* function.

The ***HLOOKUP*** function is very similar to *VLOOKUP*. You can use *HLOOKUP* to find a value in the first row of a table or cell range and return a value from any cell in the same column of the range. Each entry in the first row must be a unique value.

The *HLOOKUP* function has four arguments, and the formula syntax for the function is:

=HLOOKUP (lookup_value, table_array, col_index_num, [range_lookup])

- The ***lookup_value*** argument is required and is the value Excel searches for in the first row of the cell range or table. If the cells in the first row contain text, you must enclose the text in quotes when creating the formula. When searching for the lookup value in the first row of the range, Excel finds the largest value less than or equal to the value in the first column of the range.
- The ***table_array*** argument is the range used for looking up data; this argument is required. You can enter a cell range or a range name. The data in the first row must be in ascending order from left to right if looking for an exact match.
- The **row_*index_num*** argument is the row number of the cell range or table (counting from the top); this argument is required.
- The ***[range lookup]*** argument is a logical value (True or False) that is used to find the nearest value (True) or an exact match (False); this argument is optional. The default value is "True."

Refer to the sample lookup table in Figure 2-51 to understand the following example:

=HLOOKUP("Last Name", A3:D8, 5)

- **Last Name** is the ***lookup_value*** argument found in the top row.
- **A3:D8** is the ***table_array*** argument (cell range).
- **5** is the ***row_index_num*** argument (the fifth row from the top of the cell range).
- The result of this *HLOOKUP* function is "Bowman".

	A	B	C	D
1	Student Data Table			
2				
3	ID	Last Name	First Name	Degree
4	11123	Boney	John	Business
5	22234	Esienhauer	DeAnn	Education
6	33420	Rosch	Aariel	Psychology
7	42002	Bowman	Larry	Education
8	56009	Dranz	Sandra	Accounting

2-51 Lookup table

HOW TO: Enter the HLOOKUP Function

1. Click the cell where you want to enter the function.
2. Click the **Insert Function** button [*Formulas* tab, *Function Library* group] to open the *Insert Function* dialog box.
3. Type HLOOKUP in the **Search for a function** box and click **Go**.
4. Select **HLOOKUP** and click **OK** to open the *Function Arguments* dialog box (Figure 2-52).

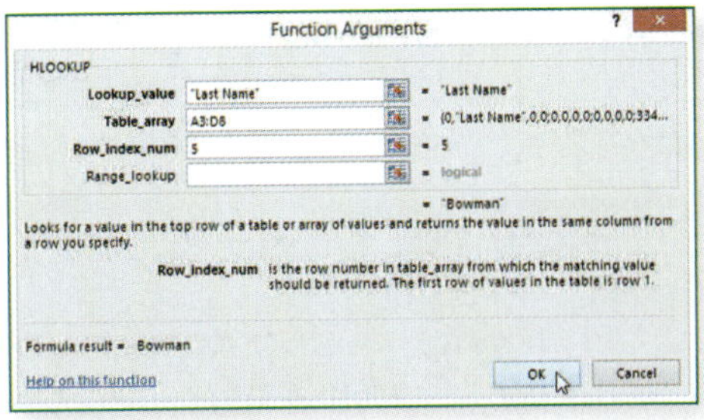

2-52 *HLOOKUP Function Arguments* dialog box

5. Click the **Lookup_value** argument text box and click a cell in the top row of the cell range or table.
6. Click the **Table_array** argument text box and select the cell range.
   - Be sure to apply absolute cell reference symbols to this range if you plan to copy the formula to another location.
7. Click the **Row_index_num** argument text box and type the row number (count from the top row).
   - Do not include the *Range_lookup* argument; it will default to *TRUE* and find the closest match instead of an exact match.
8. Click **OK** to close the dialog box and insert the function.

SLO 2.6

Working with Math and Trigonometry Functions

Excel includes many pre-defined math and trigonometry functions. In this section you learn to insert *SUMIF, SUMPRODUCT,* and *ROUND* functions in a spreadsheet.

SUMIF Function

The *SUMIF* function combines the *SUM* function with the logical criteria component of the *IF* function. The *SUMIF* includes cells in a calculation only if they meet a certain condition. For example, you may only want to add together cells that have values larger than 20.

The *SUMIF* function has three arguments and the formula syntax for the function is:

=SUMIF (range, criteria, [sum_range])

- The ***range*** argument is the range of cells to be added; this argument is required.
- The ***criteria*** argument defines which cells will be added (which condition must be met); this
  argument is required. Text criteria or logical or mathematical symbols must be enclosed in quotation marks (" ").
- The ***[sum_range]*** argument is optional. It is used to add cells that are not included in the range argument.

Refer to Figure 2-53 for an example that adds values in a range if the "*Unit Price*" value is greater than 25.

=SUMIF(E4:E6,">25",F4:F6).

- E4:E6 is the ***range*** argument (unit price).
- >25 is the ***criteria*** argument (unit price greater than 25).
- F4:F6 is the ***sum_range*** argument and adds the line total amounts.
- The result of this *SUMIF* function is $147.26.

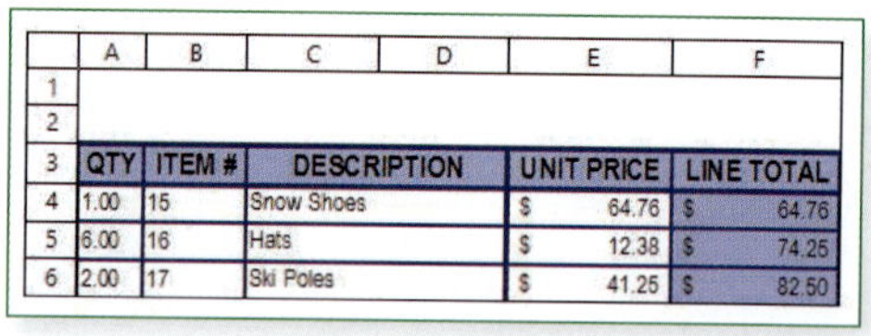

	A	B	C	D	E	F
1						
2						
3	QTY	ITEM #	DESCRIPTION		UNIT PRICE	LINE TOTAL
4	1.00	15	Snow Shoes		$ 64.76	$ 64.76
5	6.00	16	Hats		$ 12.38	$ 74.25
6	2.00	17	Ski Poles		$ 41.25	$ 82.50

2-53 *SUMIF* function sample worksheet

HOW TO: Enter the SUMIF Function

1. Click the cell where you want to enter the function.
2. Click the **Math & Trig** button [*Formulas* tab, *Function Library* group] (Figure 2-54).
3. Scroll and select the **SUMIF** function. The *Function Arguments* dialog box opens (Figure 2-55).

4. Click the **Range** argument text box if necessary.
5. Drag to select the cell range.
6. Click the **Criteria** argument text box and type the condition.
   - Enclose the argument in quotes.
7. Click the **Sum_range** argument text box and select a range.
   - The *sum_range* identifies the actual range of cells to add. If the text box is blank, the cells in the range argument are added.
8. Click **OK**.

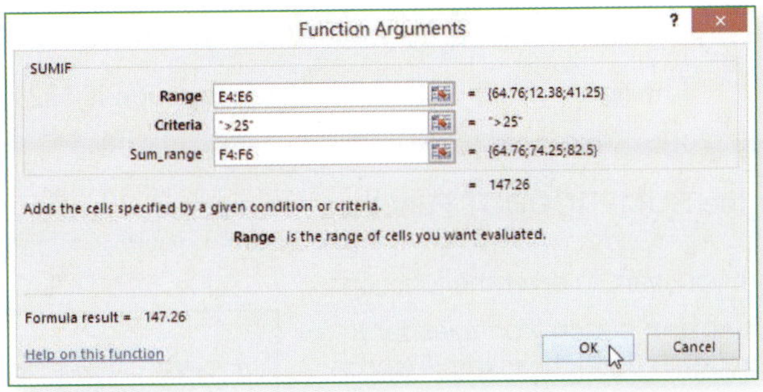

2-55 ***SUMIF Function Arguments*** **dialog box**

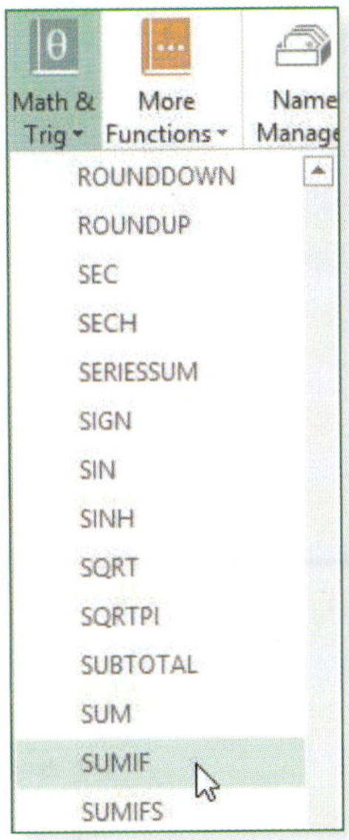

2-54 ***Math & Trig*** **functions**

> **ANOTHER WAY**
>
> Use ***wild cards*** (such as the asterisk [*]) in conjunction with criteria to sum all cells that meet corresponding criteria. For example, to sum all cells that have an associated criteria cell that begins with the letter A, type (**"A*"**) as the criteria.

SUMPRODUCT Function

The *SUMPRODUCT* function combines the *Sum* and *Product* mathematical operations. This function multiplies and then adds a series of arrays. An ***array*** is a range of cells in a row or column, such as A1:A4. An example of two arrays with the same dimension is A1:A5 and C1:C5. Two arrays with different dimensions are A1:A5 and C1:G1. The *SUMPRODUCT* is the sum of the products of several arrays. All arrays in a *SUMPRODUCT* function must have the same number of rows and columns.

The SUMPRODUCT function has the following arguments and the formula syntax is:

=**SUMPRODUCT (array1, array2, [array_n], ...)**

- The ***array1*** argument is the argument that contains cells to multiply with the corresponding cells in the next array, and then those products are added together; this argument is required.
- The ***array2*** argument must have the same number of cells and the same dimension as array1; this argument is required.

Refer to Figure 2-56 to understand the following example. The *SUMPRODUCT* function is:

=SUMPRODUCT (A4:A6,D4:D6)

	A	B	C	D	E
1					
2					
3	QTY	Item #	Description	Unit Price	Line Total
4	1	15	Snow Shoes	64.76	64.76
5	6	16	Hats	12.38	74.28
6	2	17	Ski Poles	41.25	82.50

2-56 ***SUMPRODUCT*** **function sample worksheet**

The function multiplies each specified cell in column A (quantity) times the specified cell in column D (unit price) and then adds the products.

QTY		Unit Price		Line Total
A4	*	D4	=	64.76
A5	*	D5	=	74.28
A6	*	D6	=	82.50
				221.54

The result of this *SUMPRODUCT* function is $221.54.

HOW TO: Enter the SUMPRODUCT Function

1. Click the cell where you want to enter the function.
2. Click the **Insert Function** button [*Formulas* tab, *Function Library* group] to open the *Insert Function* dialog box.
3. Type SUMPRODUCT in the **Search for a function** box and click **Go**.
4. Select **SUMPRODUCT** and click **OK** to open the *Function Arguments* dialog box (Figure 2-57).
5. Click the **Array1** argument text box and select a cell range.
6. Click the **Array2** argument text box and select a cell range.
   - Each selected array must contain the same number of cells and have the same dimensions.
7. Click **OK** to insert the function and close the dialog box.

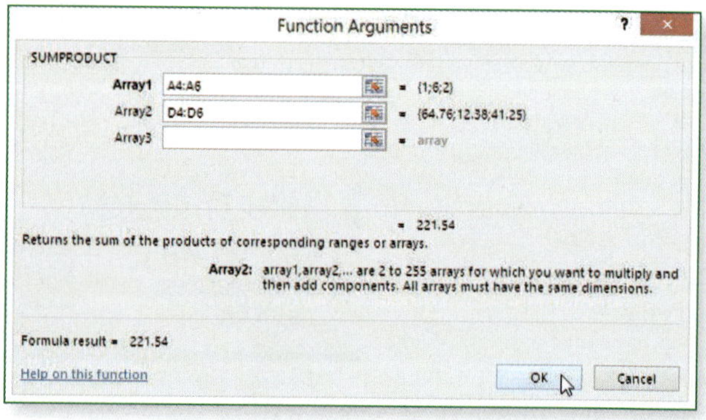

2-57 *SUMPRODUCT Function Arguments* dialog box

> **MORE INFO**
>
> Excel treats any empty cell in an array as if it has a value of 0.

ROUND Function

The *ROUND* function rounds a number to a specified number of decimal places. The *ROUND* function has two arguments and the formula syntax is:

=ROUND(number, num_digits)

- The ***number*** argument represents the number to round; this argument is required.
- The ***num_digits*** argument specifies the number of decimal places to round the number argument; this argument is required. If the *num_digits* argument is greater than zero, the number argument is rounded to the specified number of decimal places. If *num_digits* argument is zero, the number is rounded to the nearest whole number. If the *num_digits* argument is less than zero, the number is rounded to the left of the decimal point.

You can use the *ROUND* function to round the results of another formula. For example, if cell A1 contains the number 25.346, and you want to round the number to 1 decimal place, type the formula:

=ROUND(A1,1).

The result of this ROUND function is 25.3.

HOW TO: Enter the ROUND Function

1. Click the cell where you want to create the formula.
2. Click the **Insert Function** button [*Formulas* tab, *Function Library* group] to open the *Insert Function* dialog box.
3. Type ROUND in the **Search for a function** box and click **Go**.
4. Select the **ROUND** function and click **OK** to open the *Function Arguments* dialog box (Figure 2-58).
5. Click the **Number** argument text box and select a cell.
6. Click the **Num_digits** argument text box and type the number of digits you want to round the specified number.
7. Click **OK** to insert the function and close the dialog box.

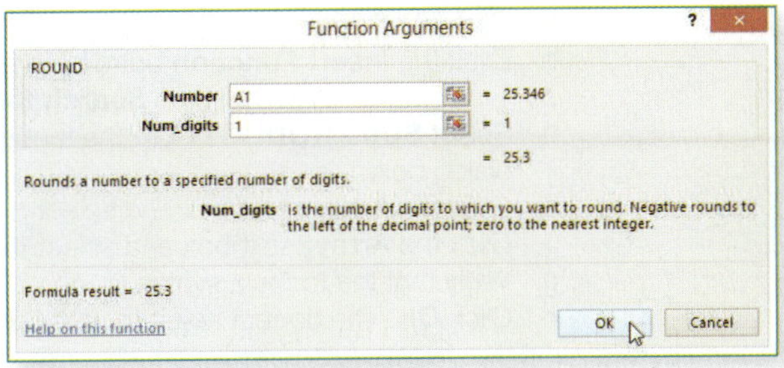

2-58 ***ROUND Function Arguments*** **dialog box**

MORE INFO

Excel also has a *ROUNDDOWN* function that always rounds a number down. The *ROUNDUP* function always rounds a number up.

PAUSE & PRACTICE: EXCEL 2-3

For this project, you open the previous Pause & Practice file and add the following kinds of functions: math and trigonometry, financial, logical, lookup, and date and time. These functions provide important financial information on sales and future investment opportunities to finalize the Paradise Lakes Resort workbook.

File Needed: ***[your initials] PP E2-2.xlsx***
Completed Project File Name: ***[your initials] PP E2-3.xlsx***

1. Open the ***[your initials] PP E2-2*** workbook, and save the workbook as ***[your initials] PP E2-3***.
2. Enter the *SUMIF* function to determine the total mortgage.
   a. Click cell **E20**.
   b. Click the **Insert Function** button [*Formulas* tab, *Function Library* group] to open the *Insert Function* dialog box.
   c. Type SUMIF in the **Search for a function** box and click **Go**.

d. Select **SUMIF** from the function list and click **OK** to open the *Function Arguments* dialog box.
e. Click the **Range** argument text box and select the cell range A10:A13.
f. Click the **Criteria** argument text box and type "Mortgage".
g. Click the **Sum_range** argument and type H10:H13.
h. Verify that the formula syntax is =SUMIF(A10:A13,"Mortgage",H10:H13).
i. Click **OK**. The correct result for cell E20 is $71,742.38.

3. Enter a *SUMPRODUCT* function to determine additional income for extra rented cabins.
   a. Click cell **G20**.
   b. Click the **Insert Function** button [*Formulas* tab, *Function Library* group].
   c. Type SUMPRODUCT in the **Search for a function** box and click **Go**.
   d. Select **SUMPRODUCT** from the function list and click **OK** to open the *Function Arguments* dialog box.
   e. Click the **Array1** text box and select B16:H16.
   f. Click the **Array2** text box and select the cell range B18:H18.
   g. Verify that the formula syntax is =SUMPRODUCT(B16:H16,B18:H18).
   h. Click **OK**. The correct result for cell G20 is $143,045.12.

4. Enter a *ROUND* function to round the net income in the spreadsheet.
   a. Click cell **E21** and use the **Insert Function** button to insert the *ROUND* function.
   b. In the *Function Arguments* dialog box, type H16 in the *Number* argument text box.
   c. Type 1 in the *Num_digits* argument text box.
   d. Verify that the formula syntax is =ROUND(H16,1).
   e. Press **Enter**.
      The correct result for cell E21 is $135,044.50 (Figure 2-59).

	D	E	F	G
20	Mortgage Total	$ 71,742.38	Additional	
21	Rounded Net	$ 135,044.50	Income with >	$ 143,045.12
22	Income		Rented Cabins	

2-59 *ROUND* function results

5. Enter a *PMT* function to determine payments if the organization were to purchase additional cabins.
   a. Click the **Investment Options** sheet tab.
   b. Click cell **B7** and use the **Insert Function** button to insert the *PMT* function.
   c. In the *Function Arguments* dialog box, click the **Rate** argument text box and click cell **B6**. Be sure to divide B6 by 12 (**B6/12**); the organization will be making monthly payments.
   d. Click the **Nper** argument text box and then click cell **B5**. Be sure to multiply B5 times 12 (**B5*12**); the organization will be making monthly payments.
   e. Click the **Pv** argument text box and then click cell **B4**.
   f. Omit the last two arguments because we want a zero balance after the last payment is made and payments will be made at the end of each period.
   g. Click **OK**.
   h. Verify that the formula syntax is =PMT(B6/12,B5*12,B4).
   i. Press **Enter**. The correct result for cell B7 is ($2,415.70) (a negative value).

6. Enter an *IF* function to determine if the organization should take out the loan for the investment. Compare the monthly payment to the lowest monthly sales total from the *Location 1- Cass Lake* sheet tab. If the monthly payment is lower, choose to make the investment.
   a. Click cell **B13** and use the **Insert Function** button to insert the *IF* function (Figure 2-60).

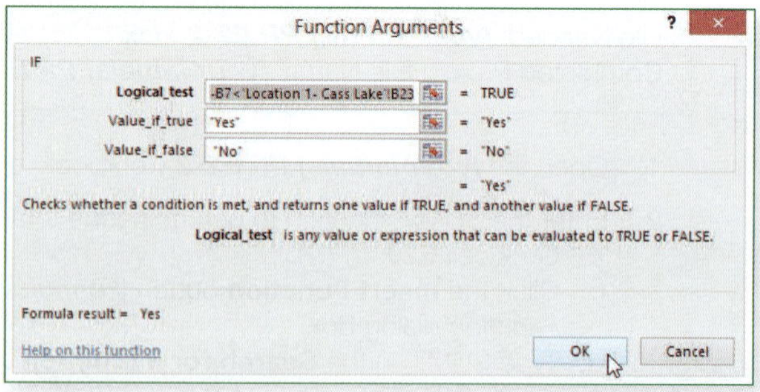

2-60 *IF Function Arguments* dialog box

b. In the *Function Arguments* dialog box, click the **Logical_test** argument box and then type -B7<, click the **Location 1- Cass Lake** sheet, and select **B23**.
c. Verify that the the **Logical_test** argument is -B7<'Location 1- Cass Lake'!B23.
d. Click the **Value_if_true** argument text box and type "Yes".
e. Click the **Value_if_false** argument text box and type "No".
f. Click **OK**. The result of the calculation appears in the cell containing the formula.
g. Verify that the formula syntax is =IF(-B7<'Location 1- Cass Lake'!B23,"Yes", "No").
h. Press **Enter**. The correct result for cell B13 is "Yes" (Figure 2-61).

2-61 *PMT* function result

7. Enter a *VLOOKUP* function to determine the cost of various products.
   a. Select the **Product Cost** sheet tab.
   b. Click cell **B4** and use the **Insert Function** button to insert the *VLOOKUP* function (Figure 2-62).
   c. In the *Function Arguments* dialog box, click the **Lookup_value** argument text box and click **A4**.
   d. Click the **Table_array** argument box and select the cell range **E4:G8**, and then apply absolute cell reference symbols by pressing **F4**.
   e. Click the **Col_index_num** argument text box and type the column number 3.
   f. Omit the **Range_lookup** argument; it will default to *TRUE* and find the closest match.
   g. Click **OK**. The result of the calculation appears in B4.
   h. Verify that the formula syntax is =VLOOKUP(A4,$E$4:$G$8,3).
   i. Press **Enter**. The correct result in B4 is $25.50.
   j. Copy the formula in **B4** to **B5:B6**. Apply **Accounting** formatting to **B4:B6**. Apply any borders needed to **A2:B6**.

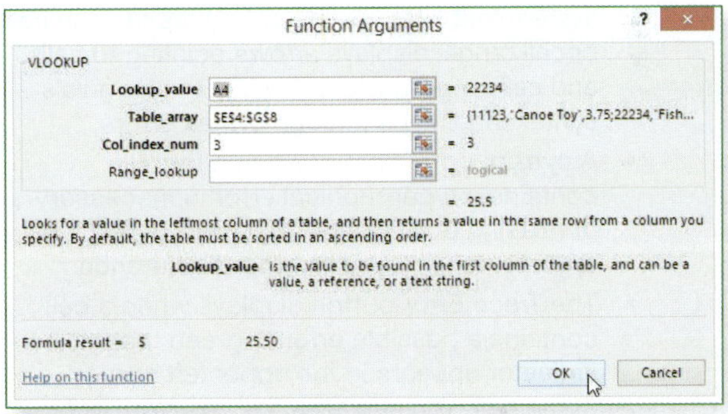

2-62 *VLOOKUP Function Arguments* dialog box

8. Save and close the workbook (Figure 2-63).

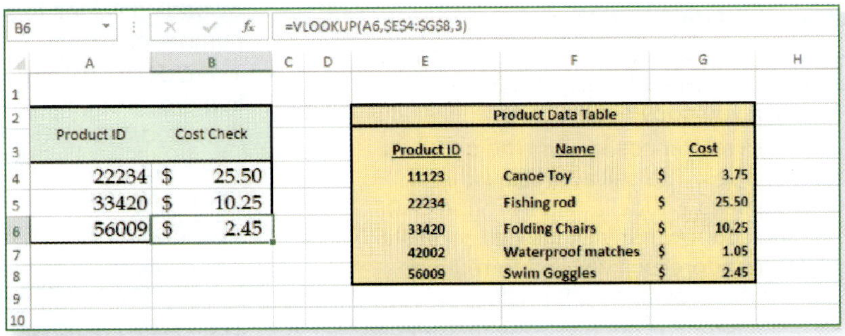

2-63 *VLOOKUP* function results after copying and formatting

Chapter Summary

2.1 Create and edit basic formulas (p. E2-79).

- The ***syntax*** of a formula refers to the required parts of the formula and the rules controlling the sequence of the parts.
- A popular and accurate technique for entering cells in formulas is the ***select*** method.
- Formulas calculate and update automatically when values in the worksheet change.
- Double-clicking a cell or pressing **F2** activates edit mode and allows you to modify a formula.
- The ***Range Finder*** is a color-coded editing tool that applies different colors to each cell or cell range within the formula syntax.
- ***Formula Auditing*** is a color-coded editing system that applies different colors to each cell or cell range, displays arrows pointing to cells and cell ranges included within the formula's syntax, and steps through syntax errors.
- A ***syntax error*** occurs when a formula contains a typographical error, unnecessary or missing punctuation, incorrect order of arguments, or an incorrect cell reference.
- The *Trace Error* button displays when a cell contains a possible error. A green triangle indicator appears in the upper left corner of the cell. You can click the down arrow to display a list of options to repair or ignore the error.
- A ***circular reference*** occurs when a formula includes the cell address of the formula.

2.2 Use range names and relative, absolute, and mixed cell references in a formula (p. E2-83).

- There are three basic types of cell references: ***relative***, ***absolute***, and ***mixed***.
- Relative cell references identify the location of a cell. Relative cell addresses within a formula adjust when you copy a formula.
- Absolute cell references identify the constant location of a cell. The cell address within a formula contains a $ (dollar sign) around both the column and row parts of the cell address. Absolute cell addresses within a formula *do not* adjust when you copy a formula.
- Mixed cell references contain one relative cell address component (either the row number or column letter) and one absolute cell address component.
- ***3D*** cell references identify cells in worksheets other than where the formula resides. Using a *3D* cell reference in another workbook is called ***linking workbooks***.
- You can apply a ***range name*** to a cell or groups of cells to describe the purpose of the group of cells and make it easier to interpret a formula. A range name is an absolute cell reference.
- The *Fill Handle* is a tool that allows you to copy formulas, lists, and numeric patterns.

2.3 Apply mathematical order of operations when using parentheses, exponents, multiplication, division, addition, and subtraction (p. E2-88).

- Excel follows a specified set of rules when it calculates a formula that has more than one operation.
- If the syntax of the formula includes parentheses, exponents, multiplication or division, and addition or subtraction, the operation within the parentheses is performed first, exponent operation is second, multiplying or dividing operators are computed third, and addition and subtraction are completed last.
- Use the following acronym to help remember the order of operations: **P**lease **E**xcuse **M**y **D**ear **A**unt **S**ally.

2.4 Use *AutoSum* and other common functions such as *AVERAGE, COUNT, MAX, MIN, TODAY*, and *NOW* (p. E2-93).

- Use the ***AutoSum*** button to insert frequently used functions.
- The ***AVERAGE*** function calculates an average by adding values together and dividing by the number of values.
- The ***COUNT*** function counts each number in a group of cells or each cell that contains specified descriptive labels.
- The ***MAX*** and ***MIN*** functions find the largest or the smallest value in a cell range.
- ***AutoCalculate*** allows you to view totals, averages, or other statistical information on the *Status bar* without creating any formulas.
- The ***TODAY*** function returns the current date each time a workbook is opened.
- The ***NOW*** function returns the current date and time each time a workbook is opened.

2.5 Apply financial, logical, and lookup functions such as *PMT, IF, VLOOKUP,* and *HLOOKUP* (p. E2-99).

- ***Functions*** are pre-defined formulas that include function names and arguments.
- The ***Insert Function*** dialog box automates the functions available in Excel.
- You can use the point and click method to complete most of the ***arguments*** (or components) of a function.
- The ***PMT*** function calculates payments for a loan if regular payments are made and the interest rate is constant.
- ***IF*** functions evaluate a specified condition and return one value if the condition is true and another value if the condition is false.
- ***LOOKUP*** functions retrieve a value from a range or table of cells located in another area of the worksheet.
- Two main types of *LOOKUP* functions are ***VLOOKUP*** (vertical lookup) and ***HLOOKUP*** (horizontal lookup).

2.6 Apply math and trigonometry functions such as *SUMIF, SUMPRODUCT,* and *ROUND* (p. E2-106).

- The ***SUMIF*** function combines the *SUM* function with the *IF* function. The *SUMIF* function includes cells in a calculation if they meet a certain condition.
- The ***SUMPRODUCT*** function combines the *SUM* and *PRODUCT* mathematical operations. The function multiplies and then adds together a series of ***arrays***.
- The ***ROUND*** function rounds a value to a specified number of decimal places.

Check for Understanding

In the ***Online Learning Center*** for this text (www.mhhe.com/office2013inpractice), there are a variety of resources that can be used to review the concepts covered in this chapter.

The following Online Learning Resources are available in the Online Learning Center:

- Multiple choice questions
- Short answer questions
- Matching exercises

USING MICROSOFT EXCEL 2013

Guided Project 2-1

Courtyard Medical Plaza (CMP) is a full-service medical office complex providing customers with a variety of medical services. CMP has doctor offices, a pharmacy, x-ray and lab services, insurance and billing support, specialty physicians, optometry and dental offices, and a restaurant for clients.

Larry Bowman is the manager for the restaurant division. He has been asked to forecast the net monthly income of the restaurant and display it on a spreadsheet. The owner has also asked to see some investment options for a new restaurant listed on the spreadsheet.
[Student Learning Outcomes 2.1, 2.2, 2.3, 2.4, 2.5, 2.6]

File Needed: ***CMPRestaurantIncome-02.xlsx***
Completed Project File Name: ***[your initials] Excel 2-1.xlsx***

Skills Covered in This Project

- Create and copy formulas.
- Apply mathematical order of operations.
- Use relative, absolute, and mixed cell references.
- Use *AutoSum.*
- Apply *AVERAGE, MAX,* and *MIN* functions.
- Apply the *PMT* function.
- Apply the *SUMPRODUCT* function
- Apply the *TODAY* function.
- Use formula auditing tools.

1. Open the ***CMPRestaurantIncome-02.xlsx*** workbook and save the workbook as ***[your initials] Excel 2-1***.
2. Enter an addition formula on the *Restaurant* sheet tab to add the food and beverages sales.
   a. Click cell **B7**.
   b. Type = (equals sign).
   c. Select the first cell of the formula (**B5**), press the + (plus sign), and then select the next cell address (**B6**).
   d. Click the **Enter** button (check mark) on the *Formula bar*.
   e. Verify that the formula syntax is =B5+B6. The result of the formula is $4,251.68.
3. Copy the *Total Sales* formula from Week 1 through Week 4.
   a. Select cell **B7**.
   b. Click and drag the *Fill Handle* to cells **C7:E7**.
4. Create an addition formula to total the food monthly sales, and use the *Fill Handle* to copy the formula without formatting.
   a. Click cell **F5**.
   b. Type =.
   c. Select **B5**, press +, select **C5**, press +, select **D5**, press +, and select **E5**.
   d. Press **Enter**.
   e. Verify that the syntax of the formula is =B5+C5+D5+E5. The result of the formula is $22,333.17.
   f. Select cell **F5**.
   g. Click and drag the *Fill Handle* to cells **F6:F7**.

h. Select the **AutoFill Options** button drop-down arrow and select **Fill Without Formatting** to ensure borders are not overwritten.
i. Release the pointer. The totals for F6 and F7 are $7,546.84 and $29,880.01, respectively.

5. Create a formula to calculate the rent expense (estimated to be 17% of total sales). Apply absolute cell references and copy the rent expense formula.
   a. Select **B10** (Figure 2-64).

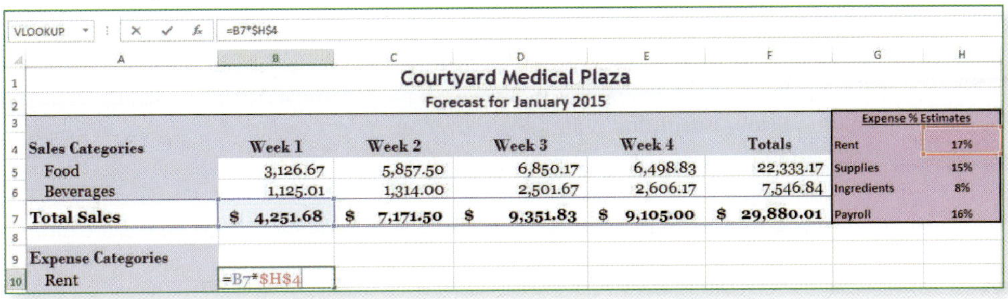

2-64 Rent expense formula with an absolute reference

   b. Type the following formula =B7*H4.
   c. Click the *Formula bar* to the left of the column letter **H** and then press **F4** to apply absolute cell references.
   d. Press **Enter**. Verify that the formula syntax is =B7*$H$4.
   e. Select **B10** and click and drag the fill pointer to cells **C10:F10**.

6. Name a cell to make it an absolute reference.
   a. Click **H7**.
   b. Click the **Name** box.
   c. Type Payroll in the *Name* box and press **Enter**.

7. Create and copy expense formulas for "Supplies", "Ingredients", and "Payroll". Use multiplication to calculate the expense and absolute cell references for the estimated percent of total sales.
   a. Enter the formulas in the table in the corresponding cells as shown in the following table.

B11	=B7*$H$5
B12	=B7*$H$6
B13	=B7*Payroll

   b. Select cells **B11:B13**.
   c. Place your pointer over the *Fill Handle* of cell range **B11:B13**.
   d. Click and drag the fill pointer through cells **C11:F13**.

8. Create an addition formula to total the expenses for week 1 and copy the formula.
   a. Click **B14**.
   b. Type = (equals sign).
   c. Select **B10** and type +.
   d. Select **B11** and type +.
   e. Select **B12** and type +.
   f. Select **B13**.
   g. Press **Enter**.
   h. Verify that the syntax of the formula is =B10+B11+B12+B13. The result of the formula is $2,380.94.
   i. Select **B14** and click and drag the *Fill Handle* to cells **C14:F14**.

9. Create and copy a formula with multiple operators.
   a. Click **B16**.
   b. Type =(B5+B6)-B14.
   c. Press **Enter**. Verify the formula syntax is =(B5+B6)-B14.
   d. Select **B16** and click and drag the *Fill Handle* to cells **C16:F16**.
10. Use auditing tools to review a formula.
    a. Select cell **B16**.
    b. Click the **Show Formulas** button and the **Trace Precedents** button [*Formulas* tab, *Formula Auditing* group]. A blue dot appears in each cell referenced in the formula.
    c. Click the **Remove Arrows** button [*Formulas* tab, *Formula Auditing* group].
    d. Click the **Show Formulas** button [*Formulas* tab, *Formula Auditing* group] to return to results view.
11. Enter a *SUM* function to calculate monthly sales.
    a. Click cell **B20**.
    b. Click the **AutoSum** button drop-down arrow [*Formulas* tab, *Function Library* group] and select **SUM** from the drop-down list.
    c. Select the cell range **B7:E7**. Verify the formula syntax is =SUM(B7:E7).
    d. Press **Enter**. The formula result is $29,880.01.
12. Calculate average weekly sales by entering an *AVERAGE* function using the *AutoSum* button.
    a. Click cell **B21**.
    b. Click the **AutoSum** button drop-down arrow [*Formulas* tab, *Function Library* group] and select **Average** from the drop-down list.
    c. Select the cell range **B7:E7**.
    d. Press **Enter**. Verify the formula syntax =AVERAGE(B7:E7). The formula's result should be $7,470.00.
13. Calculate maximum weekly sales by entering a *MAX* function using the *AutoSum* button.
    a. Click cell **B22**.
    b. Click the **AutoSum** button drop-down arrow [*Formulas* tab, *Function Library* group] and select **Max** from the drop-down list.
    c. Select cell range **B7:E7**.
    d. Press **Enter**. Verify the formula syntax =MAX(B7:E7). The formula result is $9,351.83.
14. Use auditing tools to review a formula.
    a. Select cell **B22**.
    b. Click the **Show Formulas** button and the **Trace Precedents** button [*Formulas tab, Formula Auditing* group].
    c. Click the **Remove Arrows** button [*Formulas* tab, *Formula Auditing* group].
    d. Click the **Show Formulas** button [*Formulas* tab, *Formula Auditing* group] to return to results view.
15. Edit the maximum weekly sales formula to add absolute cell references.
    a. Select cell **B22**.
    b. Click the *Formula bar* and select the cell range **B7:E7**. Do not include the parentheses in your selection.
    c. Press **F4** key to add absolute reference symbols.
    d. Press **Enter**. The formula syntax should be =MAX($B$7:$G$7).
16. Copy an existing formula and edit the function name.
    a. Select cell **B22** and click and drag the *Fill Handle* to **B23**.
    b. Choose the **AutoFill Options** button and select **Fill Without Formatting** to ensure your borders are not overwritten.

c. Select cell **B23**.
d. Click the *Formula bar*, delete the function name **MAX**, and type MIN.
e. Press **Enter**. Verify the syntax of the formula is =MIN($B$7:$G$7). The formula result is $4,251.68.

17. Enter the *SUMIF* function to determine the rent total.
   a. Click cell **E20**.
   b. Click the **Insert Function** button [*Formulas* tab, *Function Library group*] to open the *Insert Function* dialog box.
   c. Type SUMIF in the **Search for a function** box and click **Go**.
   d. Select **SUMIF** from the function list and click **OK** to open the *Function Arguments* dialog box.
   e. Click the **Range** argument text box and select the cell range A10:A13.
   f. Click the **Criteria** argument text box and type "Rent".
   g. Click the **Sum_range** argument and type F10:F13.
   h. Verify that the formula syntax is =SUMIF(A10:A13,"Rent",F10:F13).
   i. Click **OK**. The correct result for cell E20 is $5,079.60.

18. Enter a *SUMPRODUCT* function to determine additional income for extra meal and beverage sales.
   a. Click cell **E24**.
   b. Click the **Insert Function** button [*Formulas* tab, *Function Library* group] to open the *Insert Function* dialog box.
   c. Type SUMPRODUCT in the **Search for a function** box and click **Go**.
   d. Select **SUMPRODUCT** and click **OK** to open the *Function Arguments* dialog box.
   e. Click the **Array1** argument text box and select the cell range **E22:F22**.
   f. Click the **Array2** argument text box and select the cell range **E23:F23**.
   g. Verify that the formula syntax is =SUMPRODUCT(E22:F22,E23:F23).
   h. Click **OK**. The correct result in E24 is $33.25. See Figure 2-65 for the complete *Restaurant* tab results.

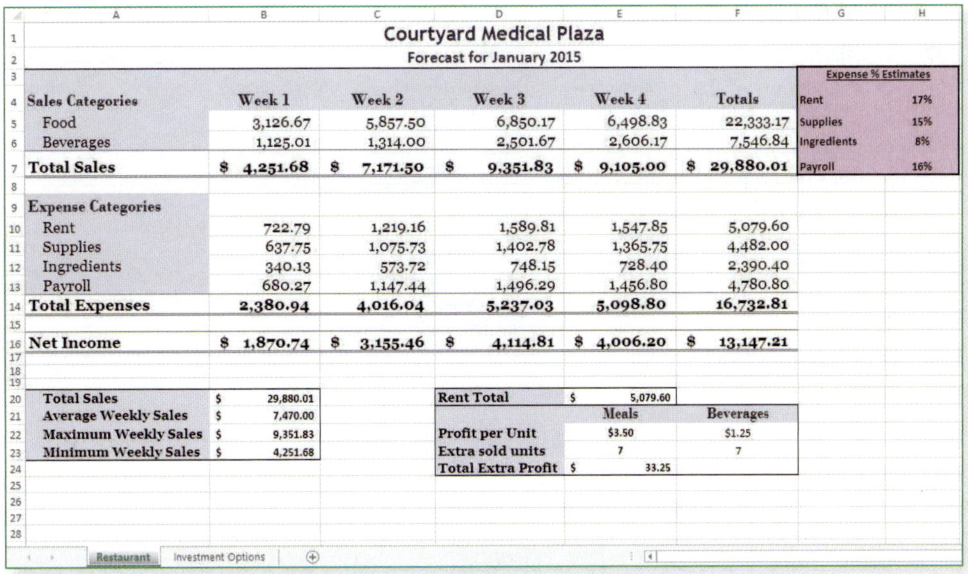

2-65 Excel 2-1 *Restaurant* tab results

19. Enter a *PMT* function on the *Investment Options* sheet tab to calculate the payment amount if the organization purchased another restaurant.
    a. Click the *Investment Options* sheet tab and select cell **B7**.
    b. Click the **Insert Function** button [*Formulas* tab, *Function Library* group].
    c. Type Payment in the **Search for a function** box and click **Go**.
    d. Select **PMT** and click **OK** to open the *Function Arguments* dialog box.
    e. Click the **Rate** argument text box, click cell **B6** (the interest rate), and type /12 (B6/12) since the organization will be making monthly payments.
    f. Click the **Nper** argument text box, click cell **B5**, and type *12 (B5*12) since the organization will be making monthly payments.
    g. Click the **Pv** argument text box and click cell **B4**, which is the amount of the loan.
    h. Omit the last two arguments because a zero balance is desired after the last payment is made and payments will be made at the end of each period.
    i. Click **OK**. The formula syntax should be =PMT(B6/12,B5*12,B4).
    j. Press **Enter**. The correct result is ($2,952.52).
20. Enter the **TODAY** function to update the worksheet date every time you open the file.
    a. Click cell **G3**.
    b. Type =TODAY() and press **Enter**. The current date appears in cell G3.
21. Save and close the workbook (Figure 2-66).

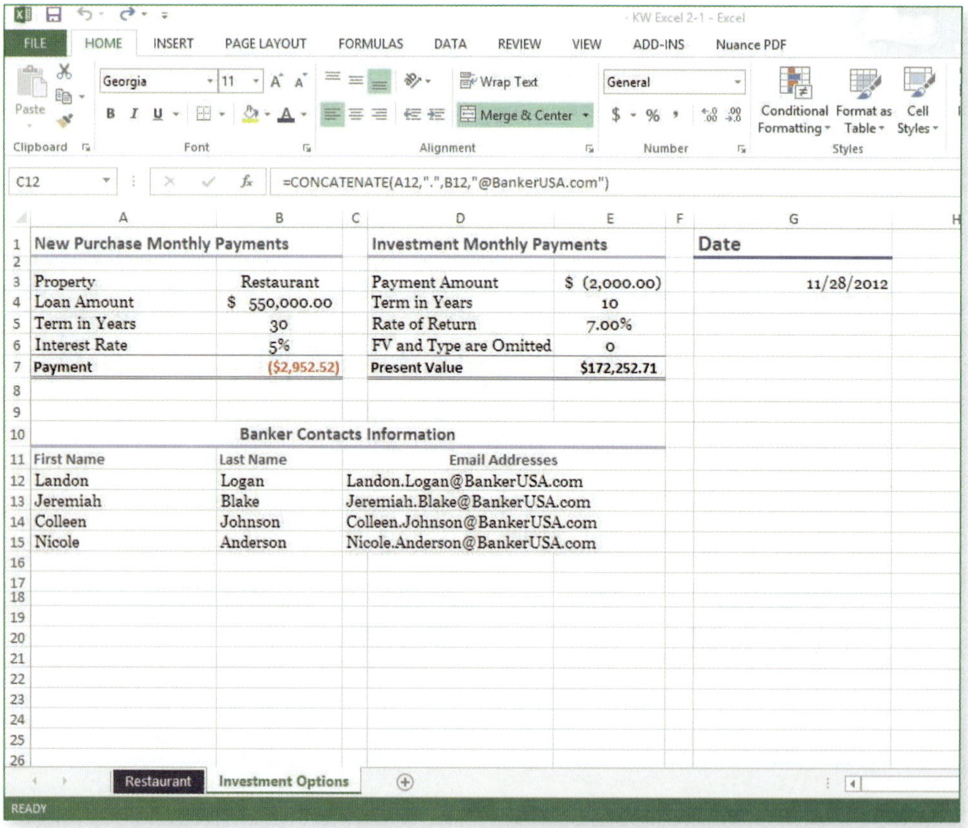

2-66 Excel 2-1 *Investment Options* tab results

Guided Project 2-2

Hamilton Civic Center (HCC) is a nonprofit community fitness center with an indoor pool, sauna, indoor track, project room, racquetball courts, meeting rooms, and a gift shop. HCC provides training and sponsors athletic and social events for adults and children. Tara Strachan is HCC's administrator for the gift shop. She has been asked to create an invoice template that links to the gift shop's product inventory spreadsheet.
[Student Learning Outcomes 2.1, 2.2, 2.3, 2.4, 2.5, 2.6]

File Needed: ***HCCInvoice-02.xlsx***
Completed Project File Name: ***[your initials] Excel 2-2.xlsx***

Skills Covered in This Project

- Create and copy basic formulas.
- Apply mathematical order of operations.
- Use relative, absolute, and mixed cell references.
- Apply the *VLOOKUP* function.
- Apply the *IF* function.
- Apply the *SUMIF* function.
- Apply the *TODAY* function.

1. Open the ***HCCInvoice-02.xlsx*** workbook from your student data files and save the workbook as ***[your initials] Excel 2-2.***
2. Enter a *VLOOKUP* function with *3D* references on the *Invoice* sheet tab.
   a. Click cell **C15** on the *Invoice* sheet tab.
   b. Click the **Insert Function** button [*Formulas* tab, *Function Library* group] to open the *Insert Function* dialog box.
   c. Type VLOOKUP in the **Search for a function** box and click **Go**.
   d. Select the **VLOOKUP** function from the list and click **OK** to open the *Function Arguments* dialog box (Figure 2-67).
   e. Click the **Lookup_value** argument text box and click cell **B15** (Item #).
   f. Click the **Table_array** argument text box and click the **Gift Shop Products** sheet tab.
   g. Select the cell range **A4:F18**.
   h. Press **F4** to apply absolute cell reference symbols to the A4:F18 range.
   i. Click the **Col_index_num** argument box and type 2, the column number.
   j. Omit the **Range_lookup** argument; if you include a *Range_lookup* argument, it will default to *TRUE* and find the closest match instead of the exact match you want to find.
   k. Click **OK**. The formula syntax should be =VLOOKUP(B15,'Gift Shop Products'!$A$4:$F$18,2). The result is "Shorts" and displays in C15 on the *Invoice* tab.

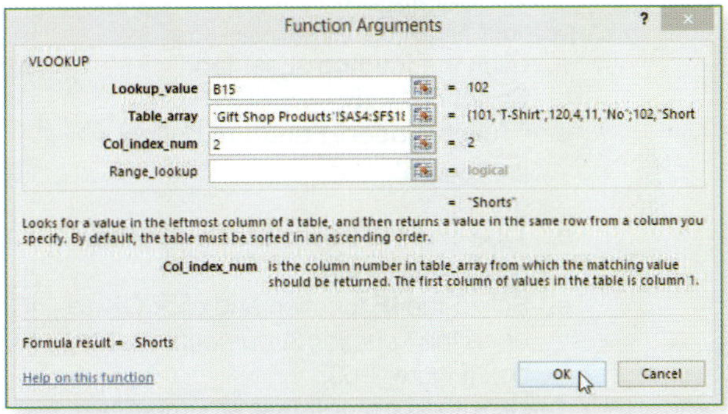

2-67 ***VLOOKUP Function Arguments* dialog box**

3. Copy the *VLOOKUP* formula.
   a. Select cell **C15**.
   b. Place your pointer over the *Fill Handle*.
   c. Click and drag the fill pointer through cells **C16:C17**.

4. Enter another *VLOOKUP* function with *3D* references on the *Invoice* sheet tab to insert unit price.
   a. Click cell **F15** on the *Invoice* sheet tab.
   b. Click the **Recently Used** button [*Formulas* tab, *Function Library* group].
   c. Select **VLOOKUP** to open the *Function Arguments* dialog box (Figure 2-68).
   d. Click the **Lookup_value** argument text box and click cell **B15**.
   e. Click the **Table_array** argument text box and click the *Gift Shop Products* sheet tab.
   f. Select the cell range **A4:F18** and press **F4** to apply absolute cell reference symbols to the range.
   g. Type 5 in the *Col_index_num* argument text box.
   h. Click **OK**. Verify that the formula syntax is =VLOOKUP(B15,'Gift Shop Products'!$A$4:$F$18,5). The result of the calculation is $6.88 and appears in cell F15 on the *Invoice* tab.

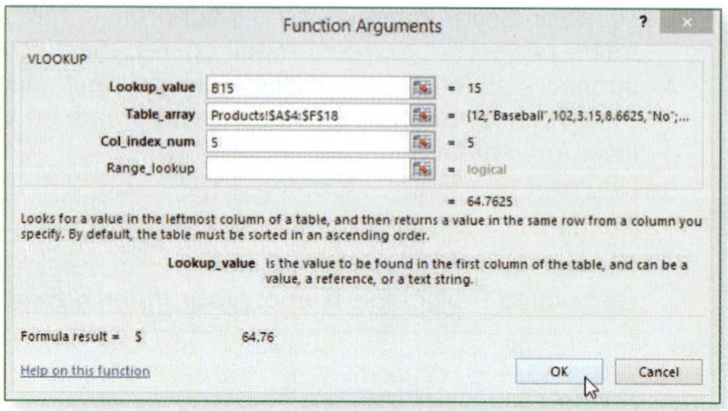

2-68 ***VLOOKUP Function Arguments* dialog box**

5. Copy the *VLOOKUP* formula.
   a. Select cell **F15**.
   b. Drag the *Fill Handle* through cells **F16:F17**.

6. Create an *IF* function to determine if the product is backordered.
   a. Click the **Invoice** sheet tab.
   b. Select cell **E15**.
   c. Click the **Insert Function** button [*Formulas* tab, *Function Library* group].
   d. Type IF in the **Search for a function** box and click **Go**.
   e. Select the **IF** function and click **OK** to open the *Function Arguments* dialog box (Figure 2-69).
   f. Click the **Logical_test** argument text box and click cell **A15**.
   g. Type <=.
   h. Click the **Gift Shop Products** sheet and select **C5**. The argument syntax is A15<='Gift Shop Products'!C5.
   i. Type "No" in the *Value_if_true* argument box.
   j. Type "Yes" in the *Value_if_false* argument box.
   k. Click **OK**. Verify that the formula syntax is =IF(A15<='Gift Shop Products'!C5,"No", "Yes"). The result of the calculation is "No" and displays in E15.
   l. Press **Enter**.
   m. Copy the formula in **E15** to **E16:E17**.

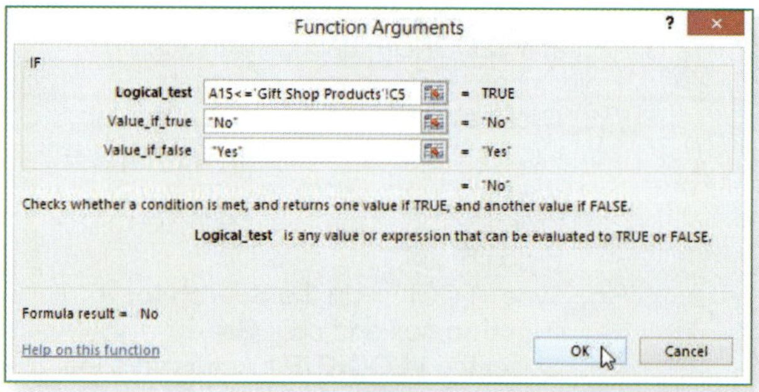

2-69 ***IF Function Arguments* dialog box**

7. Create a multiplication formula to calculate the sales total for shorts and use the *Fill Handle* to copy the formula.
   a. Click cell **G15**.
   b. Type =.

c. Select **A15**, type * (multiplication sign), and select **F15**.
d. Press **Enter**. Verify that the formula syntax is =A15*F15. The result should be $13.75.
e. Select cell **G15**.
f. Drag the *Fill Handle* through cells **G16:G17**. The totals for G16 and G17 should be $10.31 and $39.88.
g. Apply the **Accounting** numeric formatting to cells **F15:G17** if needed.

8. Create a *SUMIF* formula to total the line items that are not backordered.
   a. Click cell **G31** and insert the **SUMIF** function.
   b. Type E15:E17 in the *Range* argument box.
   c. Type "No" in the *Criteria* argument box.
   d. Click the **Sum_range** argument text box and select **G15:G17**.
   e. Click **OK**. Verify that the formula syntax is =SUMIF(E15:E17,"No",G15:G17). The result in G31 should be $63.94.
   f. Apply the **Accounting** formatting to **G31** if needed.
9. Create a formula with multiple operators and apply the mathematical order of precedence.
   a. Click cell **G33**.
   b. Type =G31+(G31*G32) and press **Enter**. Verify that the formula syntax is =G31+(G31*G32). The result in G33 should be $68.09.
   c. Apply the **Accounting** formatting to **G33** if needed.
10. Use auditing tools to review a formula.
    a. Select cell **G31**.
    b. Click the **Show Formulas** button and the **Trace Precedents** button [*Formulas* tab, *Formula Auditing* group].
    c. Review the formulas.
    d. Click the **Remove Arrows** button [*Formulas* tab, *Formula Auditing* group].
    e. Click the **Show Formulas** button [*Formulas* tab, *Formula Auditing* group] to return to results view.
11. Insert a date that will update every time you open the file.
    a. Click cell **E5**.
    b. Type =TODAY() and press **Enter**.
    c. Format the date to **Short Date**.
12. Save and close the workbook (Figure 2-70).

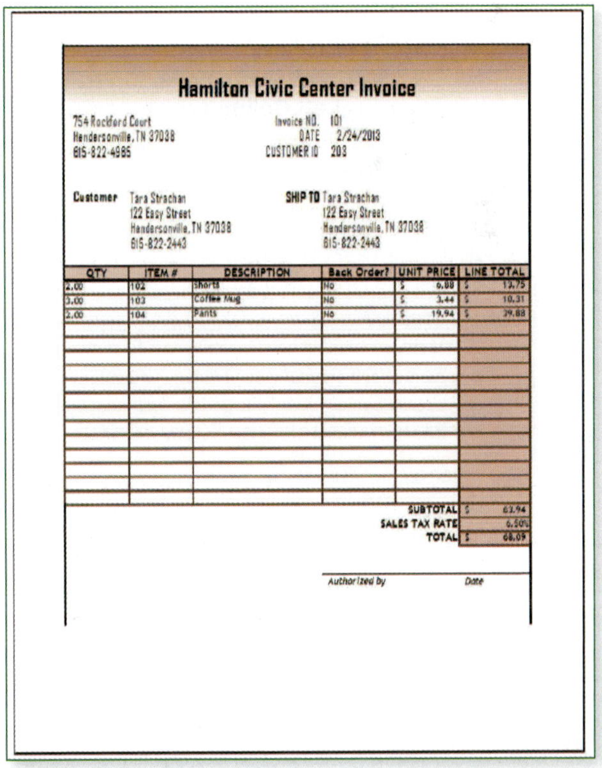

Hamilton Civic Center Invoice

754 Rockford Court
Hendersonville, TN 37038
615-822-4985

Invoice NO. 101
DATE 2/24/2013
CUSTOMER ID 203

Customer Tara Strachan
122 Easy Street
Hendersonville, TN 37038
615-822-2443

SHIP TO Tara Strachan
122 Easy Street
Hendersonville, TN 37038
615-822-2443

QTY	ITEM #	DESCRIPTION	Back Order?	UNIT PRICE	LINE TOTAL
2.00	102	Shorts	No	$ 6.88	$ 13.75
3.00	103	Coffee Mug	No	$ 3.44	$ 10.31
2.00	104	Pants	No	$ 19.94	$ 39.88
				SUBTOTAL	$ 63.94
				SALES TAX RATE	6.50%
				TOTAL	$ 68.09

Authorized by Date

2-70 Excel 2-2 completed

Guided Project 2-3

Sierra Pacific Community College District (SPCCD) is a community college district composed of four individual community colleges. Ashlyn Varriano is the SPCCD administrator for the smallest of the four community colleges. She has been asked to explore an investment option and create an amortization schedule.

[Student Learning Outcomes 2.1, 2.2, 2.3, 2.5]

File Needed: ***SPCCDInvestments-02.xlsx***
Completed Project File Name: ***[your initials] Excel 2-3.xlsx***

Skills Covered in This Project

- Create and copy formulas.
- Apply mathematical order of operations.
- Use relative, absolute, and mixed cell references.
- Name cells and use the name range in a formula.
- Apply *PMT* function.

1. Open the ***SPCCDInvestments-02.xlsx*** workbook, and save the workbook as ***[your initials] Excel 2-3***.
2. Apply range names.
   a. Select **C4:D8**.
   b. Click the **Create from Selection** button [*Formulas* tab, *Defined Names* group].
   c. Select the **Left Column** check box in the *Create Names from Selection* window. Deselect **Top row**.
   d. Click **OK**.
   e. Click the **Name** box drop-down arrow on the *Formula bar* to see a list of the new range names.
   f. Select **F4:G8**.
   g. Repeat steps 2b–d.
3. Enter the loan amount formula.
   a. Click **D7**.
   b. Type =.
   c. Select **D5** (*Purchase_Price*), press -, and select **D6** (*Down_Payment*).
   d. Press **Enter**. Verify that the formula syntax is =Purchase_Price – Down_Payment. The result of the formula should be $250,000.00.
4. Enter a *PMT* function.
   a. Click **G5**.
   b. Click the **Insert Function** button [*Formulas* tab, *Function Library* group] and insert the **PMT** function.
   c. Click the **Rate** argument box, click **D8** (named *Annual_Percentage_Rate*), and type /12 after D8 to divide it by 12 (*Annual_Percentage_Rate* /12) for monthly payments.
   d. Click the **Nper** argument box, click **G4** (*Term_of_the_Loan_in_Years*), and type *12 after G4 to multiply it by 12 (*Term_of_the_Loan_in_Years* *12) for monthly payments.
   e. Click **D7** (*Loan_Amount*) for the *Pv* argument.
   f. Click **OK**. Verify that the formula syntax is =PMT(Annual_Percentage_Rate/12,Term_of_the_Loan_in_Years*12,Loan_Amount). The correct result in G5 should be ($2,590.96).
   g. Edit the formula to create a positive number for the amortization schedule by typing a – (minus sign) in front of *Loan_Amount*. Verify that the formula syntax is =PMT(Annual_Percentage_Rate/12,Term_of_the_Loan_in_Years*12,-Loan_Amount).

5. Create a total interest formula.
    a. Click **G6** (*Total_Interest*).
    b. Type =.
    c. Select **G5** (*Payment*), type *, select **G4** (Term_of_the_Loan_in_Years), type *, type 12, type –, and select **D7** (*Loan_Amount*).
    d. Press **Enter**. Verify that the formula syntax is =Payment*Term_of_the_Loan_in_Years*12-Loan_Amount. The result of the formula should be $60,915.23.
6. Create the total principal formula.
    a. Click **G7** (*Total_Principal*).
    b. Type =.
    c. Select **G5** (*Payment*), type *, select **G4** (Term_of_the_Loan_in_Years), type *, type 12, type –, and select **G6** (*Total_Interest*).
    d. Press **Enter**. Verify that the formula syntax is =Payment*Term_of_the_Loan_in_Years*12-Total_Interest. The formula result should be $250,000.00.
7. Create an addition formula to calculate the cost of the loan.
    a. Click **G8** (*Total_Cost_of_the_Loan*).
    b. Type =.
    c. Select **G6**, type +, and select **G7**.
    d. Press **Enter**. Verify that the formula syntax is =Total_Principal+Total_Interest. The result of the formula should be $310,915.23 (Figure 2-71).

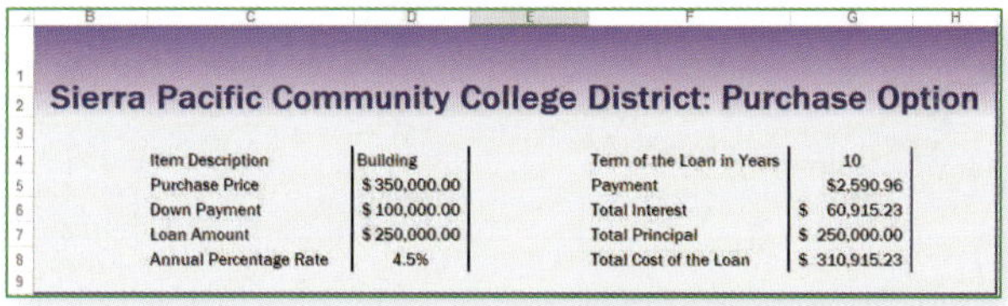

2-71 Formula results

8. Create and copy formulas for the amortization schedule.
    a. Create the formulas listed in the table at right.
    b. Select **C13** and double-click the *Fill Handle* to copy the contents through **C14:C131**.
    c. Select the range **D12:G12**, and double-click the *Fill Handle* to copy the contents through **D13:G131**. (The values in the columns will not be correct until the formulas in all columns have been copied.)
9. Save and close the workbook (Figure 2-72).

C12	=Total_Cost_of_the_Loan
C13	=G12
D12	=C12*(Annual_Percentage_Rate/12)
E12	=Payment-D12
F12	=D12+E12
G12	=C12-F12

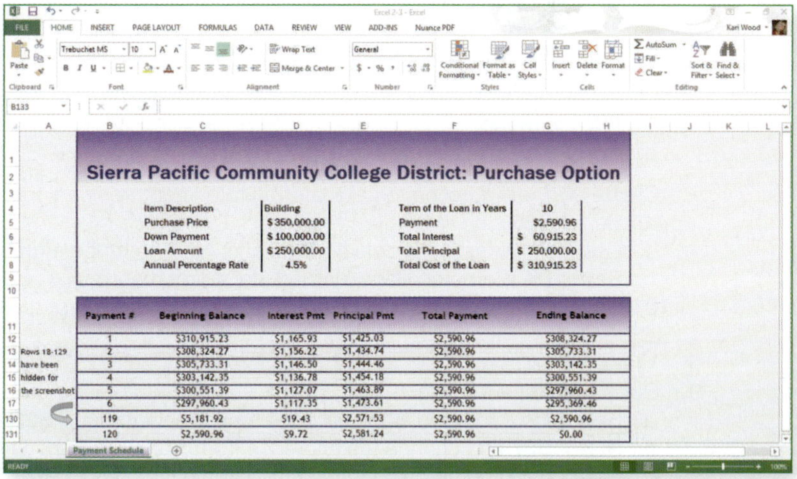

2-72 Excel 2-3 completed

Independent Project 2-4

Central Sierra Insurance (CSI) is a multi-office insurance company that handles all lines of commercial and personal insurance policies. CEO Eliana Lingle is planning to pay a bonus to employees calculated on each employee's base monthly salary. For this project, you create a spreadsheet for Ms. Lingle to summarize the bonus payments.
[Student Learning Outcomes 2.1, 2.2, 2.3, 2.4, 2.5, 2.6]

File Needed: ***CentralSierra-02.xlsx***
Completed Project File Name: ***[your initials] Excel 2-4.xlsx***

Skills Covered in This Project

- Create and copy formulas.
- Apply mathematical order of operations.
- Use relative, absolute, and mixed cell references.
- Use *AutoSum.*
- Apply the *VLOOKUP* function.
- Apply the *SUMIF* function.

1. Open the ***CentralSierra-02.xlsx*** workbook and save the workbook as ***[your initials] Excel 2-4***.
2. Create a *VLOOKUP* function to calculate the bonus amount for each employee.
   a. Click the **Employees** sheet tab, and select **I4**.
   b. Type a formula to reference the *Base Monthly Salary* amount as the *lookup_value*.
   c. Click the **Bonus** sheet tab for the *table_array* argument.
   d. Use the second column of the table for the *col_index_num*.
   e. Verify that the formula syntax is =VLOOKUP(H4,Bonus!A4:B8,2).
3. Select the formula in **I4** and apply absolute values to the cell references.
4. Copy the formula in **I4** to **I5:I13**.
5. Type a formula in **J4** to calculate the total monthly salary.
   a. Use parentheses in the formula to calculate the amount of the bonus and then add the bonus to the *Base Monthly Salary*.
   b. Copy the formula in **J4** to **J5:J13**.
6. Select **J15** and use *AutoSum* to calculate a total for the *Total Monthly Salary* column.
   a. Edit the range.
   b. Apply the **Total** cell style to **J15**.
7. Create a *SUMIF* function to calculate the total monthly salary for each office.
   a. Select **B26**.
   b. Use the information in column **D** (Branch) for the range argument.
   c. Select **D4** (Cameron Park) for the criteria argument.
   d. Use the information in column **J** (Total Monthly Salary) for the sum_range argument.
8. Edit the formula in **B26** to include absolute cell references in all cell ranges.
9. Copy and edit a formula.
   a. Select the formula in **B26** and copy the formula through **B28**.
   b. Select **B27** and change the reference from Cameron Park (**D4**) to Folsom (**D8**).
   c. Select **B28** and change the reference from Cameron Park (**D4**) to Granite Bay (**D7**).

10. Select cell **B29** and create a formula to add the salary amounts for each branch.
11. Format the data in column **I** using the **Percent Style** button.
12. Format the salary amounts in columns **H** and **J** and the "Branch Totals" section to the **Accounting** style with no symbol.
13. Select the data from **A3:J30** and change the font to **Gill Sans MT** and the font size to **11 pt**.
14. Select **E26** and type Highest Salary.
15. Type Lowest Salary in **E27** and Average Salary in **E28**.
16. Select **F26** and type =ma. When you see *MAX*, double-click to insert the function. Drag to select **J4:J13**. Press **Enter** to complete the formula.
17. Select **F27** and use the **MIN** function to calculate the lowest salary.
18. Select **F28** and use the **AVERAGE** function to calculate the average salary.
19. Select **E25** and type Salary Summary.
20. Merge and center "Salary Summary" in cells **E25** and **F25**.
21. Format the "Salary Summary" section to match the "Branch Totals" section.
    a. Apply a fill color.
    b. Apply **All Borders** from the *Borders* button drop-down list.
22. Format the two total amounts (**B29** and **J15**) to include a dollar sign.
23. Adjust column widths if necessary.
24. Save and close the workbook (Figure 2-73).

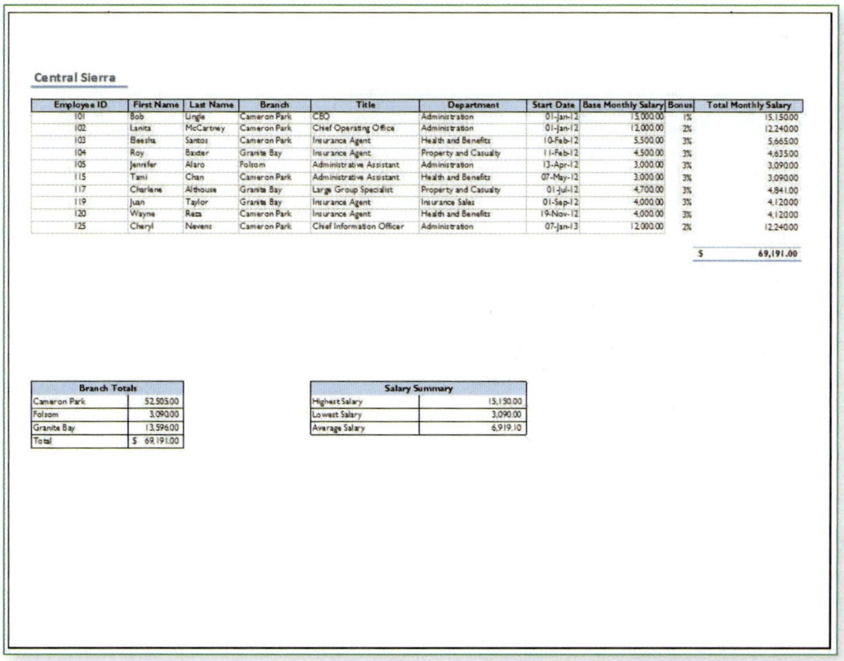

Central Sierra

Employee ID	First Name	Last Name	Branch	Title	Department	Start Date	Base Monthly Salary	Bonus	Total Monthly Salary
101	Bob	Lingle	Cameron Park	CEO	Administration	01-Jan-12	15,000.00	1%	15,150.00
102	Lanita	McCartney	Cameron Park	Chief Operating Office	Administration	01-Jan-12	12,000.00	2%	12,240.00
103	Beesha	Santos	Cameron Park	Insurance Agent	Health and Benefits	10-Feb-12	5,500.00	3%	5,665.00
104	Roy	Baxter	Granite Bay	Insurance Agent	Property and Casualty	11-Feb-12	4,500.00	3%	4,635.00
105	Jennifer	Alaro	Folsom	Administrative Assistant	Administration	13-Apr-12	3,000.00	3%	3,090.00
115	Tami	Chan	Cameron Park	Administrative Assistant	Health and Benefits	07-May-12	3,000.00	3%	3,090.00
117	Charlene	Althouse	Granite Bay	Large Group Specialist	Property and Casualty	01-Jul-12	4,700.00	3%	4,841.00
119	Juan	Taylor	Granite Bay	Insurance Agent	Insurance Sales	01-Sep-12	4,000.00	3%	4,120.00
120	Wayne	Reza	Cameron Park	Insurance Agent	Health and Benefits	19-Nov-12	4,000.00	3%	4,120.00
125	Cheryl	Nevens	Cameron Park	Chief Information Officer	Administration	07-Jan-13	12,000.00	2%	12,240.00
									$ 69,191.00

Branch Totals	
Cameron Park	52,505.00
Folsom	3,090.00
Granite Bay	13,596.00
Total	$ 69,191.00

Salary Summary	
Highest Salary	15,150.00
Lowest Salary	3,090.00
Average Salary	6,919.10

2-73 Excel 2-4 completed

Independent Project 2-5

When San Diego Sailing received its end-of-year financial reports, its financial officers decided to evaluate the rental rates schedule for boats. You have been asked to create a spreadsheet to compare three different proposed rate changes that the group is considering implementing in the new year and to update information on the boat fleet.
[Student Learning Outcomes 2.1, 2.2, 2.3, 2.5]

File Needed: ***SanDiego-02.xlsx***
Completed Project File Name: ***[your initials] Excel 2-5.xlsx***

Skills Covered in This Project

- Create and copy formulas.
- Apply mathematical order of operations.
- Use relative, absolute, and mixed cell references.
- Apply the *IF* function.
- Name cells and use the name range in a formula.
- Apply the *TODAY* function.

1. Open the ***SanDiego-02.xlsx*** workbook and save the workbook as ***[your initials] Excel 2-5***.
2. Select **H4** and create an *IF* function formula to determine which boats include a stove with the galley. Boats must be able to seat 8 or more people to have a stove in the galley.
   a. Use "Yes" for the *value_if_true* argument.
   b. Use "No" for the *value_if_false* argument.
3. Insert a worksheet and name the sheet Data.
4. Type the following information in the new worksheet:

	A	B
Row 3	Projected Increases	
Row 4	5% Increase	105%
Row 5	10% Increase	110%
Row 6	15% Increase	115%

5. Format the table text on the *Data* sheet.
   a. **Merge and Center** the text in **A3** over **A3:B3** and apply **bold** format.
   b. Apply **Accent 1** cell style to **A3**.
   c. Select **A3:B6** and apply the **All Borders** format.
6. Select **A4:B6** and assign range names using the **Create from Selection** button on the *Formulas* tab.
7. Select **J4** on the *Fleet* worksheet, and create a formula to calculate a 5% increase for the data in the "4 Hr. Rate" column using the range name assigned on the *Data* sheet.
   a. Type =.
   b. Select **F4** and type *.
   c. Press **F3** to open the *Paste Name* dialog box.
   d. Select **_5_Increase** and click **OK**.
   e. Press **Enter**.

8. Create formulas for **K4:O4** and copy the formulas to row 18.
9. Select the amounts in columns F, G, and J:O and apply **Currency** format with no symbol.
10. Select **A1** and type San Diego Sailing.
11. Format **A1** using the **Title** cell style and apply **bold** format. Adjust the column width.
12. Insert a row above the current row 2. Clear the formatting of the new row 2.
13. Insert the **TODAY()** function in **A2**. Format the date as **11 pt. bold** and align left.
14. Change the date format to display the month as a word followed by the day and year.
15. Apply the **All Borders** format to rows **4** through **19**.
16. Click the **Insert** tab and click the **Header & Footer** button.
    a. Switch to the *Footer* area.
    b. Click the right text box and type Page followed by a space.
    c. Click the **Page Number** button on the *Header & Footer Tools Design* tab.
    d. Click the worksheet and return to *Normal* view.
17. Paste range names in a worksheet.
    a. Click the **Data** sheet tab and select cell **A15**.
    b. Click the **Use in Formula** button [*Formulas* tab, *Defined Names* group].
    c. Click **Paste Names**.
    d. Click the **Paste List button** in the *Paste Name* dialog box.
    e. Click **OK**.
18. Save and close the workbook (Figure 2-74).

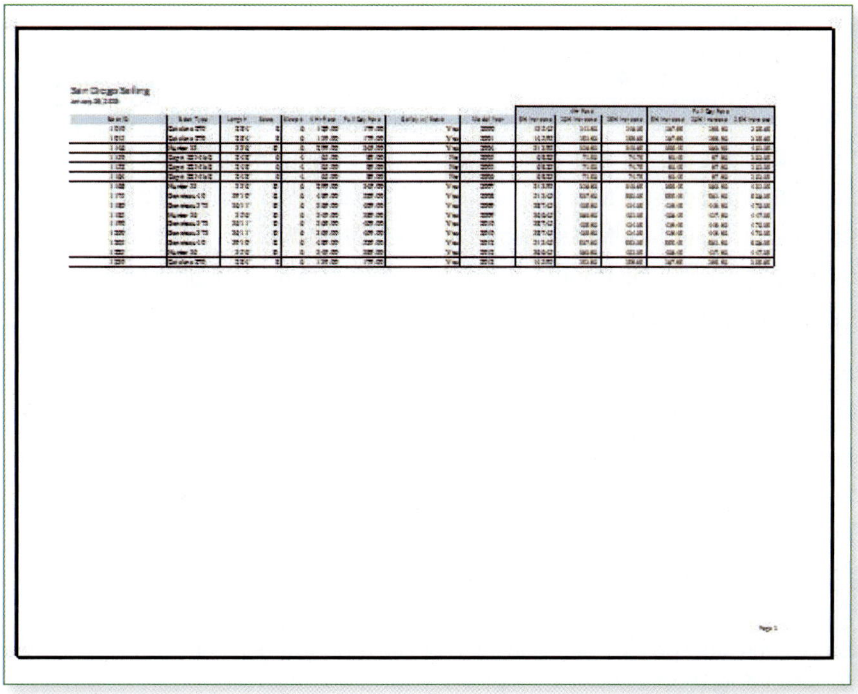

2-74 Excel 2-5 completed

Independent Project 2-6

Placer Hills Real Estate is a real estate company with regional offices throughout central California. In this project, you create a spreadsheet for the real estate company to provide summary information to its agents.
[Student Learning Outcomes 2.1, 2.2, 2.3, 2,4, 2.5]

File Needed: ***PlacerHills-02.xlsx***
Completed Project File Name: ***[your initials] Excel 2-6.xlsx***

Skills Covered in This Project

- Create and copy formulas.
- Apply mathematical order of operations.
- Use relative, absolute, and mixed cell references.
- Apply the AVERAGE, MAX, MIN, and COUNT functions.
- Apply the *VLOOKUP* function.

1. Open the ***PlacerHills-02.xlsx*** workbook and save the workbook as ***[your initials] Excel 2-6.***
2. Type Placer Hills in cell **A1**, and apply the **Heading 1** style. Copy the contents of cell **A1** to the *Agent* worksheet cell **A1**.
3. Use the "SoldPrice" column data and the "ListPrice" column data on the *Listing* worksheet to calculate the percentage of list price.
   a. Select **O4**.
   b. Press = and click **N4**.
   c. Press / and click **C4**.
4. Copy the formula in **O4** to cells **O5:O12** and apply the **Percent Style** format to cells **O4:O12**.
5. Select **B20** and use the **Average** function to calculate the *Average List Price*.
6. Select **B21** and use the **Max** function to calculate the *Maximum List Price*.
7. Select **B22** and use the **Min** function to calculate the *Minimum List Price*.
8. Select **B23** and use the **Count** function to calculate the *Number of Listings*.
9. Calculate the number of brick homes by combining two functions.
   a. Select **B25**.
   b. Type =COUNTIF(
   c. Select **K4:K12**.
   d. Type ,"=Brick").
   e. Apply absolute cell references to the selected cell range.
   f. Press **Enter**.
10. Create individual formulas for **B26, B27, B29, B30, B31,** and **B32**, or copy the formula in **B25** and edit the formula.
11. Use the *VLOOKUP* function to insert the agent's last name in cells **E21:E26**.
    a. Use the agent number for the *lookup_value* argument.
    b. Use the table on the *Agent* sheet for the *table_array* argument.
    c. Use the *Last Name* column for the *col_index_num* argument.

d. Add absolute cell reference to the table_array argument.
e. Copy the formula in **B21** to **B22:B27**.

12. Select **D20:E26** and apply the **All Borders** format.
13. Format **D20:E20** with the **Accent 5** cell style and **bold** format.
14. Select **A3:O12** and apply the **All Borders** format.
15. Save and close the workbook (Figure 2-75).

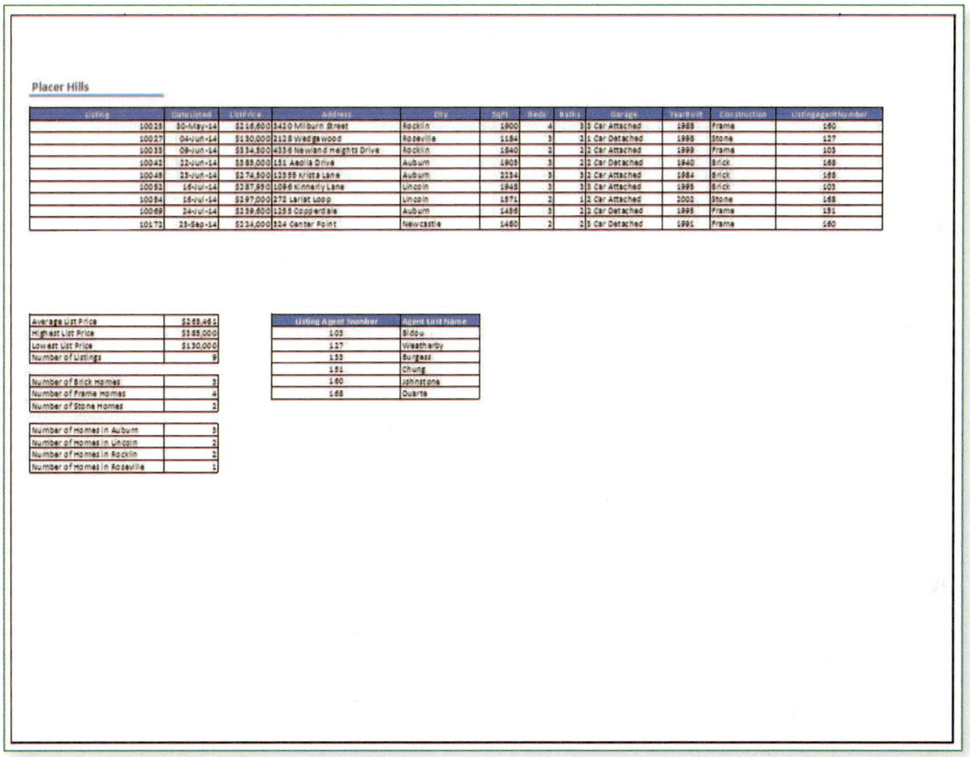

Placer Hills

Listing	Date Listed	List Price	Address	City	SqFt	Beds	Baths	Garage	Year Built	Construction	ListingAgentNumber
10025	30-May-14	$216,600	3410 Milburn Street	Rocklin	1900	4	3	3 Car Attached	1988	Frame	160
10027	04-Jun-14	$130,000	2128 Wedgewood	Roseville	1184	3	2	1 Car Detached	1998	Stone	127
10033	09-Jun-14	$334,500	4336 Newland Heights Drive	Rocklin	1840	2	2	2 Car Attached	1999	Frame	103
10042	22-Jun-14	$385,000	131 Aeolia Drive	Auburn	1905	3	2	2 Car Detached	1940	Brick	168
10045	23-Jun-14	$274,500	12355 Krista Lane	Auburn	2234	3	3	2 Car Attached	1984	Brick	168
10052	16-Jul-14	$287,950	1096 Kinnerly Lane	Lincoln	1948	3	3	3 Car Attached	1995	Brick	103
10054	16-Jul-14	$297,000	272 Lariat Loop	Lincoln	1571	2	1	2 Car Attached	2002	Stone	168
10069	24-Jul-14	$239,600	1255 Copperdale	Auburn	1456	3	2	2 Car Detached	1995	Frame	151
10172	23-Sep-14	$234,000	324 Center Point	Newcastle	1460	2	2	3 Car Detached	1991	Frame	160

Average List Price	$268,461
Highest List Price	$385,000
Lowest List Price	$130,000
Number of Listings	9

Number of Brick Homes	3
Number of Frame Homes	4
Number of Stone Homes	2

Number of Homes in Auburn	3
Number of Homes in Lincoln	2
Number of Homes in Rocklin	2
Number of Homes in Roseville	1

Listing Agent Number	Agent Last Name
103	Bidou
127	Weatherby
133	Burgess
151	Chung
160	Johnstone
168	Duarte

2-75 Excel 2-6 completed

Improve It Project 2-7

Mary's Rentals serves the rental equipment needs of contractors and the general public. In this exercise you create formulas and format a spreadsheet for the rental company.
[Student Learning Outcomes 2.1, 2.2, 2.3, 2.4, 2.5, 2.6]

File Needed: ***MarysRentals-02.xlsx***
Completed Project File Name: ***[your initials] Excel 2-7.xlsx***

Skills Covered in This Project

- Create and copy formulas.
- Apply mathematical order of operations.
- Use relative, absolute, and mixed cell references.
- Edit formulas.
- Name cells and use range names in formulas.
- Apply the *SUM* function.
- Apply the *SUMPRODUCT* function.

1. Open the ***MarysRentals-02.xlsx*** workbook and save the workbook as ***[your initials] Excel 2-7***.
2. Select **B20** and use the *SUMPRODUCT* function to create a formula to calculate income from daily rentals.
    a. Use **C5:C12** for the *array1* argument.
    b. Use **D5:D12** for the *array2* argument.
3. Create formulas for **B21** and **B22** using *SUMPRODUCT.*
4. Select **B23** and use **Sum** to calculate total rental income for the month of March.
5. Select **C5:C12** and name the range Daily.
6. Select **E5:E12** and name the range Weekly.
7. Select **G5:G12** and name the range Monthly.
8. Select **B26** and use the *Sum* function and the *Daily* range name to calculate the number of daily rentals.
    a. Type =Su to display a list of functions beginning with "SU."
    b. Double-click **SUM**.
    c. Type da to display a list of functions and range names.
    d. Double-click **Daily**.
    e. Press **Enter**.
9. Create formulas for **B27** and **B28** using *Sum* and range names.
10. Select **B29** and create a formula to add the **Daily**, **Weekly**, and **Monthly** range names together.
11. Change the theme to **Slice**.
12. Format **A1** and **A2**.
    a. **Merge & Center** the text in **A1** over **A1:H1**, and merge and center the text in **A2** over **A2:H2**.
    b. Edit **A2** to Month of March.
    c. Apply **Accent 1** cell style to **A1**.
    d. Apply **bold** formatting to **A1** and **A2**.
    e. Change the font size of **A1** to **18 pt**.
13. Format the column headings (**A4:H4**) with cell style **20% Accent 1**.
14. AutoFit column width and row height.
15. Format the numbers in columns **D, F**, and **H** using **Accounting** style with no symbol. Apply the **Accounting** style with no symbol format to cells **B20:B22**.
16. Apply **All Borders** to **A4:H12, A20:B23**, and **A26:B29**.
17. Change the orientation to **landscape**.
18. Save and close the workbook (Figure 2-76).

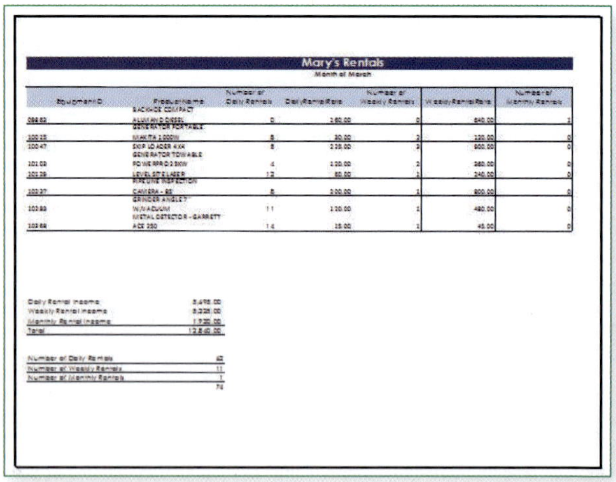

2-76 Excel 2-7 completed

Challenge Project 2-8

In this project, you create a spreadsheet to compare three purchase options you may be considering. Plan the spreadsheet layout so that a comparison of the three options is easy to read and understand. [Student Learning Outcomes 2.1, 2.2, 2.3, 2.5]

File Needed: None
Completed Project File Name: ***[your initials] Excel 2-8.xlsx***

Create and save a workbook as ***[your initials] Excel 2-8***. Enter data in a spreadsheet that will be useful in planning a major purchase such as a car or home. Modify your workbook according to the following guidelines:

- Include headings to identify the cells. Headings may include "Description," "Loan Amount," "Term of the Loan," "Interest Rate," and "Payment." Assign range names to easily identify cell references in formulas.
- Create a *PMT* formula.
- Create a payment schedule with formulas.
- Add two sheets to your workbook. Create a second spreadsheet using the original parameters except change the interest rate. Calculate the amount of payment. Create a third spreadsheet using the original parameters except change the term of the loan. Calculate the amount of the payment.
- Add another sheet to the workbook to create a side-by-side comparison of the three loan scenarios.
- Include a date formula that automatically updates when you open the spreadsheet.
- Incorporate *Themes, Cell Styles*, and formatting.
- Include document properties and spell check your workbook.

Challenge Project 2-9

In this project, you create a spreadsheet to calculate your monthly expenditures and monthly income for one year. You also calculate the percentage of total expenses each of your individual expenses represents. [Student Learning Outcomes 2.1, 2.2, 2.3, 2.4]

File Needed: None
Completed Project File Name: ***[your initials] Excel 2-9.xlsx***

Create and save a blank workbook as ***[your initials] Excel 2-9***. Plan the layout of the workbook to include one sheet for expenses and one sheet for income. You may want to plan a third sheet to compare expenses with income. Modify your workbook according to the following guidelines:

- On the income sheet, list all your sources of income including full-time and part-time employment. Arrange the data so that each column heading is a month of the year.
- On the expense sheet, place the months across the sheet and the expenses in the first column.
- Create a row of cells that lists the total expenses for each month. Consider grouping expenses by month, quarter, or year. Include subtotals for each section.
- Add a formula to calculate the percentage of your total expenses each expense represents. Use an absolute cell reference in the formula.
- Use formulas to calculate your net income, average income, and maximum income.
- Add a sheet to compare projected income and projected expenses for one month to actual income and actual expenses for one month.
- Incorporate *Themes, Cell Styles*, and formatting.
- Include document properties and spell check the workbook.

Challenge Project 2-10

In this project, you create a form for a store that sells and ships merchandise. You include a lookup table to calculate shipping costs and calculate the total cost of buying an item.
[Student Learning Outcomes 2.1, 2.2, 2.3, 2.4, 2.5, 2.6]

File Needed: None
Completed Project File Name: ***[your initials] Excel 2-10**.xlsx*

Create and save a blank workbook as ***[your initials] Excel 2-10***. Modify your workbook according to the following guidelines:

- At the top of the spreadsheet, create a section to include the name of the store, address, telephone number, web site, and store hours.
- Include bill-to and ship-to sections. Arrange and format the data.
- Include a section below the bill-to and ship-to sections to include purchasing information such as "Item Number," "Quantity," "Item Description," "Price Subtotal," "Sales Tax," "Shipping," and "Total Cost."
- Name the worksheet tab and insert a second worksheet. Name the second sheet "Shipping Charges."
- On sheet 2 ("Shipping Charges"), create a *VLOOKUP* table for shipping charges. Use a price range to calculate charges. For example, for orders up to $50, the shipping cost is $6.95; for orders of $50.01 to $100.00, the shipping cost is $8.95; etc.
- Add borders and shading as well as cell styles and a theme to format the spreadsheets attractively.
- Use 6% as the sales tax rate.
- Add range names if appropriate.
- Add formulas to calculate the cost of buying an item including tax and shipping charges.
- Test the worksheet formulas.
- Include document properties and spell check the workbook.

CHAPTER 3

Creating and Editing Charts

CHAPTER OVERVIEW

In addition to building formulas and functions in a worksheet, you can use Excel to graph or chart worksheet data. After selecting the correct data in a worksheet, you can quickly create a professional-looking chart with a few clicks of the mouse. This chapter introduces you to the basics of creating, editing, and formatting Excel charts.

STUDENT LEARNING OUTCOMES (SLOs)

After completing this chapter, you will be able to:

SLO 3.1 Create, size, and position an Excel chart object and create a chart sheet (p. E3-134).

SLO 3.2 Design a chart using *Quick Layouts* and chart styles (p. E3-137).

SLO 3.3 Switch row and column data, add or remove chart elements, change chart type, and edit source data (p. E3-141).

SLO 3.4 Format chart elements with shape styles, fill, outlines, and special effects (p. E3-148).

SLO 3.5 Use images, shapes, and *WordArt* in a chart (p. E3-152).

SLO 3.6 Create a pie chart and a combination chart (p. E3-157).

SLO 3.7 Insert and format sparklines in a worksheet (p. E3-161).

CASE STUDY

In the Pause & Practice projects in this chapter, you use Excel workbooks for the northern Minnesota resort business Paradise Lakes Resort (PLR). PLR has asked its managers to develop various charts for monthly sales data to better monitor the resort's business and to help formulate goals for next year.

Pause & Practice 3-1: Create and style charts in a workbook.

Pause & Practice 3-2: Edit and format charts in a workbook.

Pause & Practice 3-3: Create a combination chart and insert sparklines in a workbook.

EXCEL

SLO 3.1

Creating a Chart Object and a Chart Sheet

An Excel ***chart*** is a visual representation of numeric data in a worksheet. A chart helps you to easily identify trends, make comparisons, and recognize patterns in the numbers. Charts are dynamic and linked to the data, so if the numbers in your worksheet change, the chart is automatically redrawn.

There are different kinds of charts, and Excel can recommend the best chart type based on your selected data range or you can choose a chart type on your own. You can display a chart in the worksheet with the data or you can place a chart on its own sheet.

Create a Chart Object

A ***chart object*** is a selectable object surrounded by a square border that contains many customizable chart elements like data labels or a chart title. The chart elements are displayed as selectable components within the chart object. You can size and position a chart object on a worksheet.

Source data are the cells that contain values and labels to be graphed in the chart. In Figure 3-1, the source data includes the categories names, the month names, and four values for each of three months. Each of these values is a ***data point***, a cell containing a value. Each group of data points or values is a ***data series***. In this example, Figure 3-1 sets up three data series for a clustered bar chart (the four items under each month). Each data series has a name (i.e., *April*, *May*, and *June*).

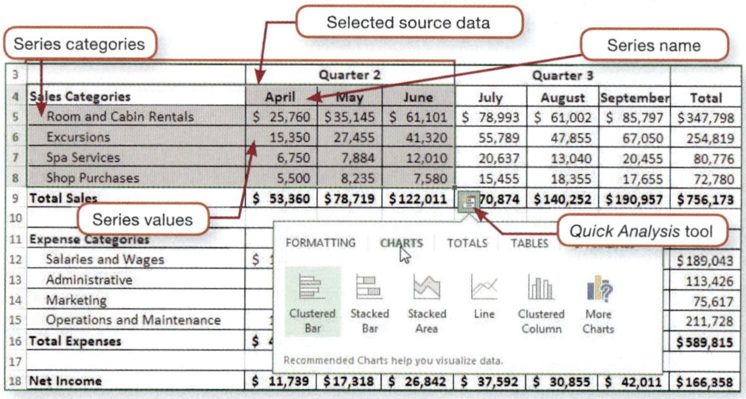

3-1 Source data and *Quick Analysis* suggestions

The text label that describes each data series is a ***category label***. In Figure 3.1, the categories are the sales categories in column A (i.e., *Room and Cabin Rentals*, *Excursions*, *Spa Services*, and *Shop Purchases*).

> **MORE INFO**
>
> You can create a default chart object by selecting the appropriate data and pressing **Alt+F1**.

When you select source data that is adjacent (all the cells are next to each other), the ***Quick Analysis*** button appears at the lower right corner of the selection. The *Quick Analysis* tool lists tabs with the commands you are most likely to choose for your selected data, including *Charts*. After you click the *Charts* command, Excel displays recommended chart types. As you point to each chart type, you see a preview of the chart. This preview helps you to determine if you have selected the correct range. Click your preferred chart type to create a new chart object in the worksheet. The chart object is placed in the sheet next to the source data.

HOW TO: Create a Chart Object

1. Select the cell range that includes the data series and category labels you want to display in chart format.
2. Click the **Quick Analysis** button and select **Charts**.
3. Point at the preferred chart type and click to insert a chart (Figure 3-2).

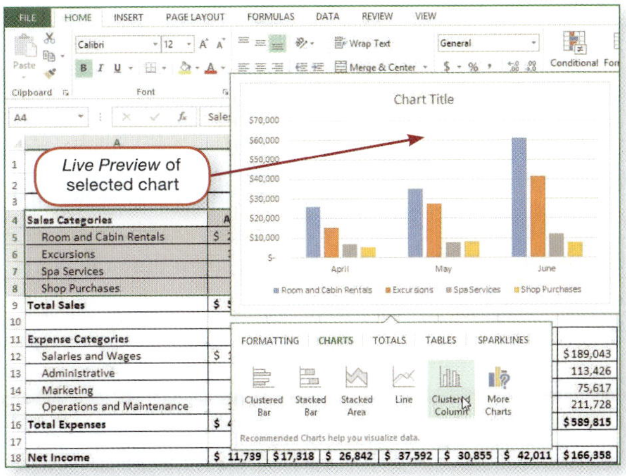

3-2 Chart object previewed

MORE INFO

When the source data range is non-adjacent, the *Quick Analysis* tool does not display.

Excel Chart Types

Excel has many chart types that you can use to graph your data. Most chart types have several subtypes or variations. Excel recommends chart types based on your selected data, or you can choose the type of chart you want to use. The most common chart types are column or bar, line, and pie. Excel can also build powerful scientific and statistical charts when needed. The following table describes Excel chart types.

Excel Chart Types

Chart Type	Description	Category (Labels)	Values (Numbers)
Column	Illustrates data changes over a period of time or shows comparisons among items	Horizontal axis	Vertical axis
Bar	Displays comparisons among individual items or values at a specific period of time	Vertical axis	Horizontal axis
Pie	Uses one data series to display each value as a percentage of the whole		One data series shown by slice size
Line	Displays trends in data over time, emphasizing rate of change	Horizontal axis	Vertical axis
Area	Displays the magnitude of change over time and shows the rate of change	Horizontal axis	Vertical axis
XY (Scatter) or Bubble	Displays relationships among numeric values in two or more data series; these charts do not have a category	Horizontal axis (value 1-x)	Vertical axis (value 2-y)
Stock	Displays three series of data to show fluctuations in stock prices from high to low to close	Horizontal axis	Vertical axis
Surface	Displays optimum combinations of two sets of data on a surface	Horizontal axis (value 1-x)	Horizontal axis (value 1-x)
Radar	Displays the frequency of multiple data series relative to a center point. There is an axis for each category	NA	NA
Combo Chart	Uses two types of charts to graph values that are widely different	Either	Either

Size and Position a Chart Object

A chart object can be selected, sized, and positioned. When you select a chart object or it is active, it is surrounded by eight selection handles. A **selection handle** is a small round or rectangular shape on each corner and in the middle of each side. When you point at a selection handle, the pointer changes to a two-pointed arrow that you drag to make the chart smaller or larger. Drag a corner handle to size both height and width of the chart proportionally.

To move a chart object, point at the chart background to display a four-pointed move pointer. Then drag the chart to the desired location.

> **MORE INFO**
>
> When a chart object is selected, the *Chart Tools* tabs are visible in the *Ribbon* and three *Quick Chart Tools* are available at the top right corner of the object.

HOW TO: Move and Size a Chart Object

1. Select the chart object (Figure 3-3).
2. Place your pointer on the outside border of the chart to display a move pointer.
3. Drag the chart object to a new location and release.
4. Place your pointer on a selection handle to display a resize pointer.
5. Drag the pointer to resize the chart.

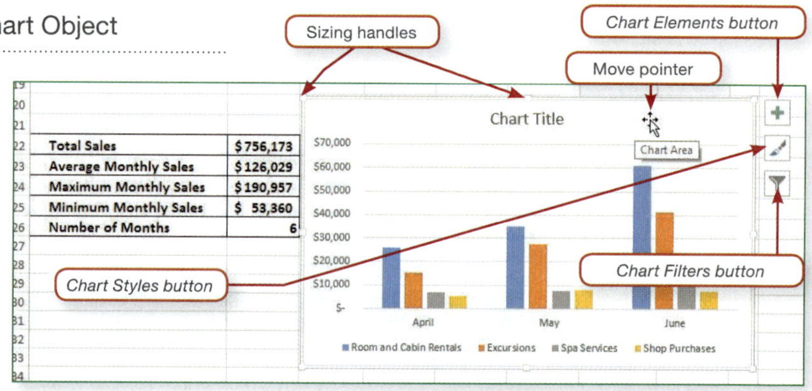

3-3 Selected chart object and move pointer

Creating a Chart Sheet

A ***chart sheet*** is an Excel chart that is displayed on its own sheet in the workbook. The chart sheet does not include rows, columns, and cells like a regular worksheet, but the chart is linked to its data on another worksheet.

When you create a chart from the *Quick Analysis* tool or from the *Insert* tab in the *Ribbon*, Excel creates a chart object. You can move any chart object that you have already created to its own sheet using the *Chart Tools Design* tab. When you do that, Excel moves the chart to a new sheet named *Chart1, Chart2,* and so on. You can type a new name for the chart sheet in the *Move Chart* dialog box. You can also create a new chart sheet from a new chart object.

From the *Charts* group on the *Insert* tab, you can click the **Recommended Charts** button or the specific chart type button to create the chart object.

HOW TO: Create a Chart Sheet

1. Select the cell range that includes the data series and category labels you want to display in chart format.
   - If the cell range is non-adjacent, hold down the **Ctrl** key to select each range (Figure 3-4).
2. Click the **Recommended Charts** button [*Insert* tab, *Charts* group].

3. Click the preferred chart type.
4. Click **OK**.
5. Click the **Move Chart** button [*Chart Tools Design* tab, *Location* group].
6. Click the **New sheet** radio button (Figure 3-5).
7. Type the name of the new sheet tab.
8. Click **OK**.

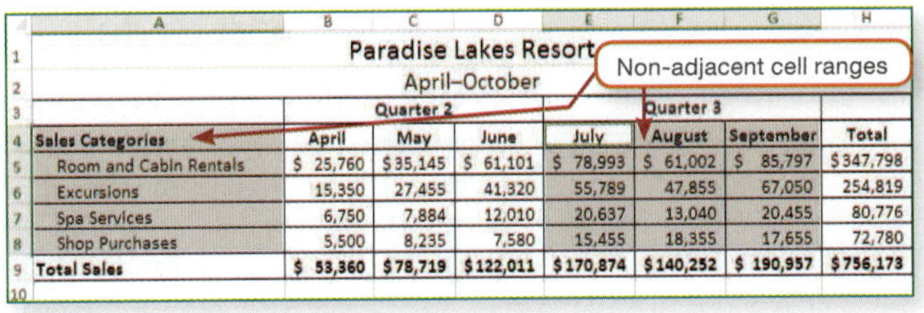

	A	B	C	D	E	F	G	H
1		Paradise Lakes Resort						
2		April–October						
3		Quarter 2			Quarter 3			
4	Sales Categories	April	May	June	July	August	September	Total
5	Room and Cabin Rentals	$ 25,760	$35,145	$ 61,101	$ 78,993	$ 61,002	$ 85,797	$347,798
6	Excursions	15,350	27,455	41,320	55,789	47,855	67,050	254,819
7	Spa Services	6,750	7,884	12,010	20,637	13,040	20,455	80,776
8	Shop Purchases	5,500	8,235	7,580	15,455	18,355	17,655	72,780
9	Total Sales	$ 53,360	$78,719	$122,011	$170,874	$140,252	$ 190,957	$756,173

3-4 Source data ranges that are not next to each other

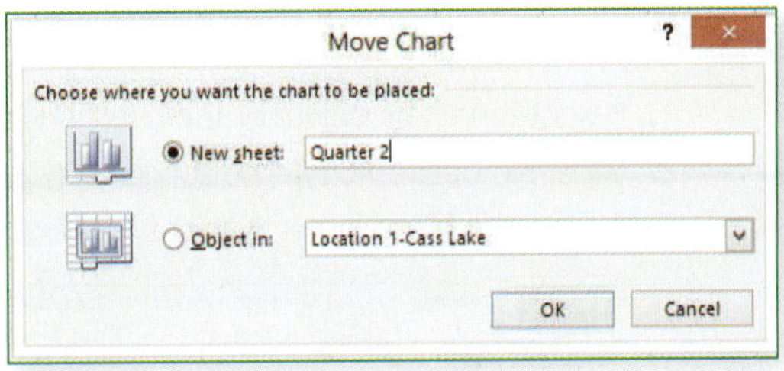

3-5 *Move Chart* dialog box

ANOTHER WAY

To move a chart object to its own sheet, right-click the chart object and choose **Move Chart**.

MORE INFO

You can create a default chart sheet for selected data by pressing **F11**.

SLO 3.2

Designing a Chart with Quick Layouts and Styles

Excel has many tools to help you develop consistent and appealing designs for your charts. From the *Chart Tools Design* tab, you can apply different chart layouts or choose from predefined styles. These choices affect the appearance of the entire chart.

Apply a Quick Layout

A **chart layout** is the complete set of elements that is displayed in the chart. These include parts of a chart such as the main title, axis titles, legend, and others. The *Quick Layout* command allows you to choose from 10 predefined layouts. After selecting a *Quick Layout,* you can add or remove individual chart elements, too.

To apply a *Quick Layout* use the ***Quick Layout*** button in the *Chart Layouts* group on the *Chart Tools Design* tab. As you point to each layout option, *Live Preview* redraws your chart so that you can decide if the layout is right for your needs.

HOW TO: Apply a Quick Layout to a Chart

1. Click the chart object or the chart sheet.
2. Click the **Quick Layout** button [*Chart Tools Design* tab, *Chart Layouts* group].
3. Point to a layout to preview its effect.
4. Click the preferred **Layout** (Figure 3-6).

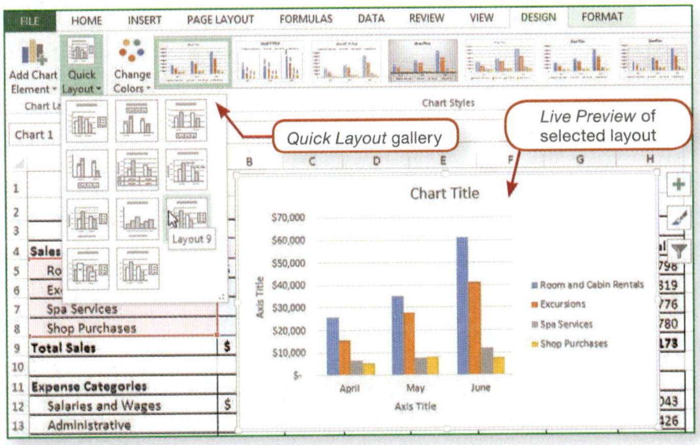

3-6 *Quick Layout* gallery

Apply a Chart Style

A **chart style** is a preset combination of colors and effects for a chart, its background, and its elements. The chart styles that are available for a chart are based on the current workbook theme. If you change the workbook theme, the chart style colors are updated, and your chart will reflect the new color palette. You can find chart styles in the *Chart Styles* group on the *Chart Tools Design* tab. Like a chart layout, you can preview the effects of a chart style as you point to each style in the gallery.

HOW TO: Apply a Chart Style

1. Select the chart object or the chart sheet.
2. Click the desired **Style** button [*Chart Tools Design* tab, *Chart Styles* group].
   - Click the **More** button [*Chart Tools Design* tab, *Chart Styles* group] to display the entire *Chart Styles* gallery (Figure 3-7).

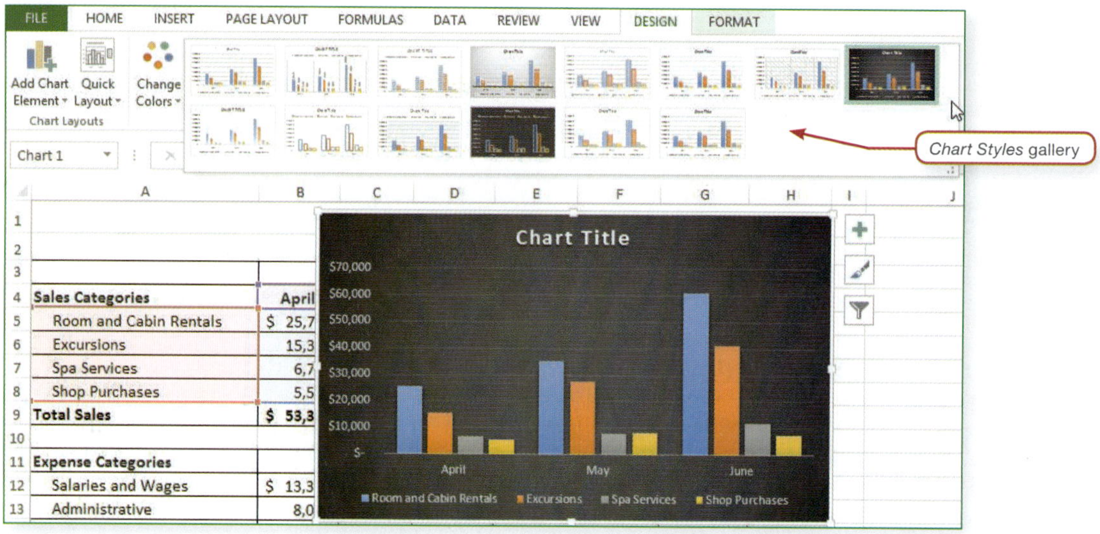

3-7 ***Chart Styles*** **gallery and preview of selected style**

> **MORE INFO**
>
> Chart styles may affect the current chart layout.

Print a Chart

You can print chart objects with the worksheet data or individually. When you want to print a worksheet with the chart object, you need to size and position the chart so that it fits on the page or scale the sheet to fit the complete worksheet contents. You can choose whether the data and chart should print in portrait or landscape orientation and you can insert headers or footers as well in a worksheet.

> **MORE INFO**
>
> Use the *Page Setup* dialog box or the *Insert* tab to insert a header or footer on a chart sheet.

You can print a chart sheet with a regular *Print* command. By default, a chart sheet prints in landscape orientation.

To print a chart object with its source data, click any cell in the worksheet. Then use the *Print* command from the *File* tab in the *Backstage* view and make your usual print choices. If you prefer to print a chart object on its own sheet, select the object first and then choose print.

HOW TO: Print a Chart with its Source Data

1. Click any cell in the worksheet.
   - To print a chart sheet, click the sheet tab.
2. Click the **File** tab to open the *Backstage* view (Figure 3-8).
3. Select **Print** at the left and set print options if necessary.
4. Click **Print**.

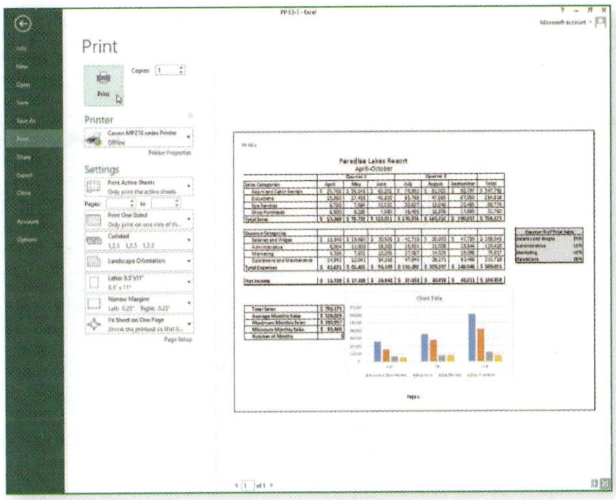

3-8 *Backstage* view, print options

PAUSE & PRACTICE: EXCEL 3-1

Charts illustrate worksheet data and make it clearer and easy to understand. For this project you insert a clustered column chart object in a worksheet that tracks sales and expenses for Paradise Lakes Resort. You also insert a clustered bar chart sheet to highlight second quarter results.

File Needed: ***ParadiseLakes-03.xlsx***
Completed Project File Name: ***[your initials] PP E3-1.xlsx***

1. Open the ***ParadiseLakes-03*** workbook.
2. Save this document as ***[your initials] PP E3-1***.
3. Create a chart object.
   a. Select the cell range **A4:D8** for your chart.
   b. Click the **Quick Analysis** button and choose the **Charts** tab.
   c. Click **Clustered Column**.
4. Position and size the chart object.
   a. Click the chart object if it is not selected.
   b. Point at the chart area to display a move pointer.
   c. Drag the chart object so that its top left corner is at cell **C20**.

d. Point at the lower right selection handle to display a resize pointer.

e. Drag the pointer to reach cell **H35** as shown in Figure 3-9.

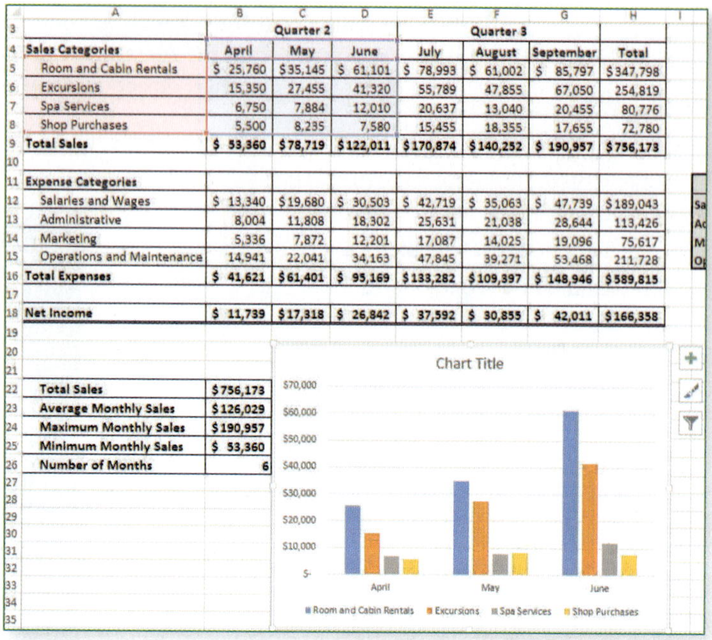

3-9 Chart object sized and positioned

5. Apply a *Quick Layout*.
   a. Click the chart object if necessary.
   b. Click the **Quick Layout** button [*Chart Tools Design* tab, *Chart Layouts* group].
   c. Click **Layout 7**.
6. Create a chart sheet.
   a. Select the cell range **A4:A8**.
   b. Hold down **Ctrl** and select the cell range **E4:G8**.
   c. Click the **Recommended Charts** button [*Insert* tab, *Charts* group].
   d. Select **Clustered Bar**.
   e. Click **OK**.
   f. Click the **Move Chart** button [*Chart Tools Design* tab, *Location* group].
   g. Click the **New sheet** radio button.
   h. Type Quarter 3 as the new sheet name.
   i. Click **OK**.
7. Choose a chart style.
   a. Click the **Chart Styles** More button [*Chart Tools Design* tab, *Chart Styles* group] to display the gallery.
   b. Click **Style 10** (Figure 3-10).

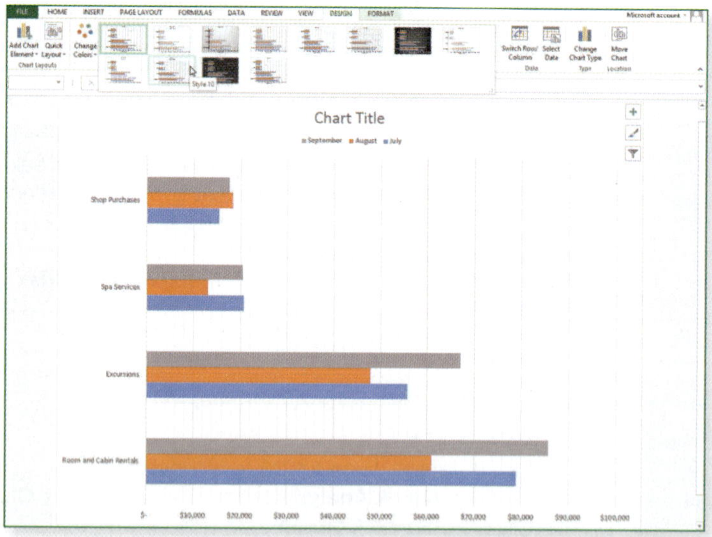

3-10 Chart sheet with new style

8. Preview the charts.
   a. Select the **Quarter 3** sheet if necessary.
   b. Click the **File** tab to open the *Backstage* view.
   c. Click **Print** at the left to preview the chart sheet (see Figure 3-11).
   d. Click the **Back** button to return to the worksheet.
   e. Select the **Location 1 Cass Lake** sheet.
   f. Click cell **A1**.
   g. Click the **File** tab to open the *Backstage* view.
   h. Click **Print** to preview the worksheet and chart object.
   i. Click the **Back** button to return to the worksheet.

9. Save and close the workbook (Figure 3-11).

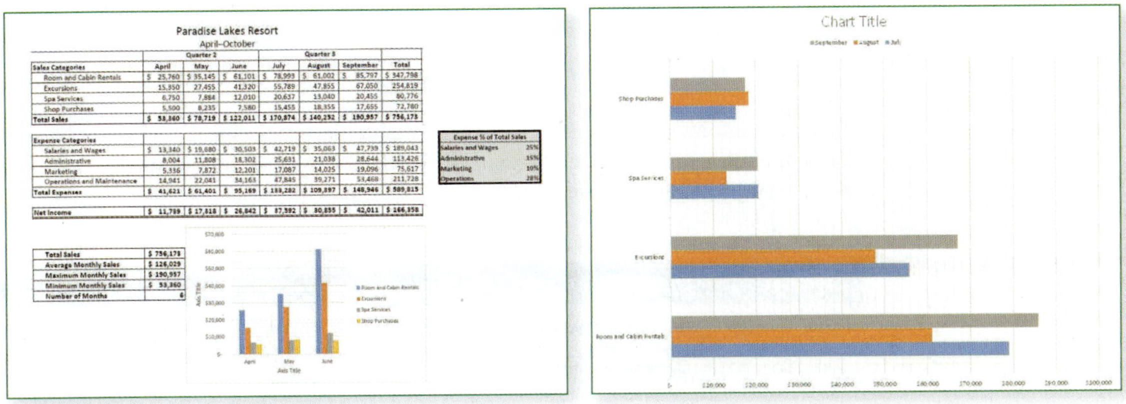

3-11 PP E3-1 completed chart object and chart sheet

SLO 3.3

Editing a Chart

You can edit a chart in many ways. For example, you will want to edit the contents of the placeholder text boxes that are inserted in your chart if you use a *Quick Layout*, or you might insert a legend to explain colors used for a data series. You can also add data labels that indicate the actual values on the chart, or you might decide to switch row and column data.

Switch Row and Column Data

When you choose a recommended chart, Excel plots the data series based on the number of rows and columns selected in the worksheet and the chart type. If you prefer, however, you can choose which data series is plotted on the X-axis and which is plotted on the Y-axis. In a column chart, by default, the X-axis is along the bottom of the chart; the y-axis is along the left.

HOW TO: Switch Row and Column Data

1. Click the chart object or chart sheet tab.
2. Click the **Switch Row/Column** button [*Chart Tools Design* tab, *Data* group] (Figure 3-12).
   - Click the **Switch Row/Column** button [*Chart Tools Design* tab, *Data* group] to toggle how the columns and rows are plotted.

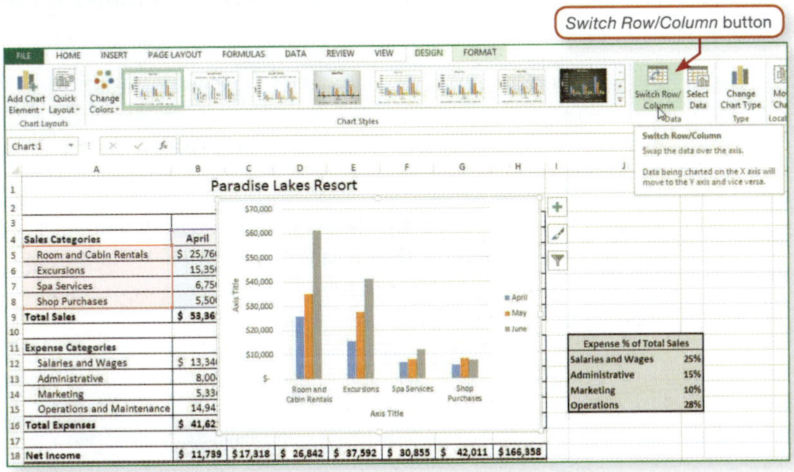

3-12 Column and row data switched

> **ANOTHER WAY**
>
> Click the **Chart Filters** button in the top right corner of a selected chart and click **Select Data** at the bottom of the pane to switch the row and column data.

Add and Remove Chart Elements

A **chart element** is a separate, clickable, editable part of a chart. The chart layout and style that you choose affect which elements are initially displayed in a chart. You can add, remove, and format individual elements in a chart. The following table describes the chart elements.

Excel Chart Elements

Element	Description
Axis	Horizontal or vertical boundary that identifies what is plotted (the plural of axis is axes)
Axis title	Optional title for the categories or values
Chart area	Background for the chart; can be filled with a color, gradient, or pattern
Chart floor	Base or bottom for a 3-D chart
Chart title	Optional title or name for the chart
Chart wall	Vertical background or wall for a 3-D chart
Data label	Optional element that displays values with the marker for each data series
Data marker	Element that represents individual values. The marker is a bar, a column, a slice, or a point on a line
Data point	A single value or piece of data from a data series
Data series	Group of related values that are in the same column or row and translate into the columns, lines, pie slices, and other markers
Gridline	Horizontal or vertical line that extends across the plot area to help in identifying values
Horizontal (category) axis	Describes what is shown in the chart and is created from row or column headings. In a bar chart, the category axis is the vertical axis; the category axis is the horizontal axis in a column chart
Legend	Element that explains the symbols, textures, or colors used to differentiate data series
Plot area	Rectangular area bounded by the horizontal and vertical axes
Tick mark	Small line or marker on an axis to guide in reading values
Trendline	Displays averages in your data and can be used to forecast data by plotting future approximate averages
Vertical (value) axis	Shows the numbers on the chart. In a bar chart, the vertical axis is along the bottom; in a column chart, the vertical axis is along the side

You can show or remove chart elements by clicking the **Chart Elements** button to the right of the chart. When you click the button, the *Chart Elements* pane opens. In this pane, click the corresponding box to show or remove the element. To hide the pane, click the *Chart Elements* button again.

> **ANOTHER WAY**
>
> Click the **Add Chart Elements** button [*Chart Tools Design* tab, *Chart Layouts* group] to add or remove a chart element.

When you point at a chart element, a ScreenTip describes the element. You can click the element to select it and make it active. When a chart element is active, it is surrounded by selection handles, as shown in Figure 3-13. The name of an active element also appears in the *Chart Elements* box on the *Chart Tools Format* tab.

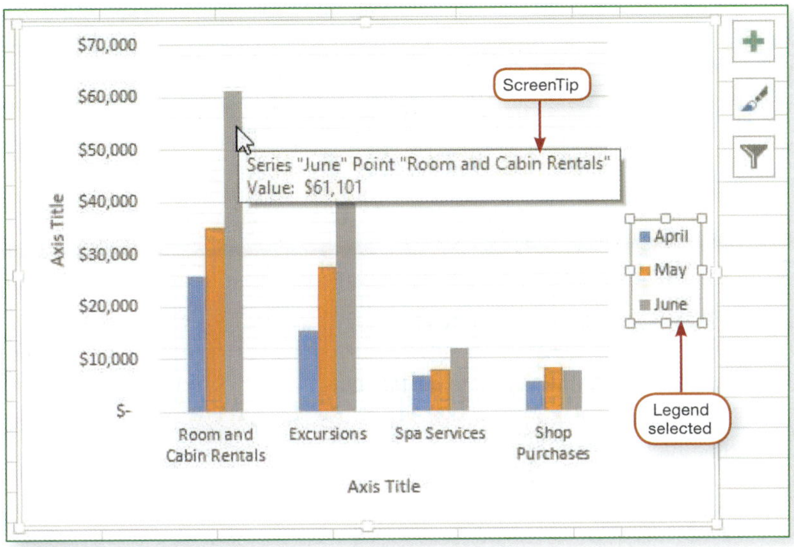

3-13 Selected legend and ScreenTip for a data series

Chart and Axes Titles

Some chart layouts include a placeholder or text box for a main chart title and axes titles. When a placeholder is shown, you need to edit the sample text to fit your data. When the layout does not include a placeholder title, you can add a placeholder or text box and then edit the text.

You can position a main chart title above the chart or within the chart area. Once you have created a text box, you can select it and move it anywhere on the chart. You can use an axis title to clarify what is represented by the categories or the values. However, keep in mind that many times an axis title is not required because the chart itself represents the data well.

HOW TO: Add a Chart Title

1. Click the chart object or chart sheet.
2. Click the **Chart Elements** button to the right of the chart.
3. Click to place a check mark next to **Chart Title** (Figure 3-14).
4. Click the menu arrow to choose a position for the title.
5. Type the title and press **Enter**.
   - To edit the chart title, triple-click the *Chart Title* placeholder, type the title, and click the chart background to deselect the element.

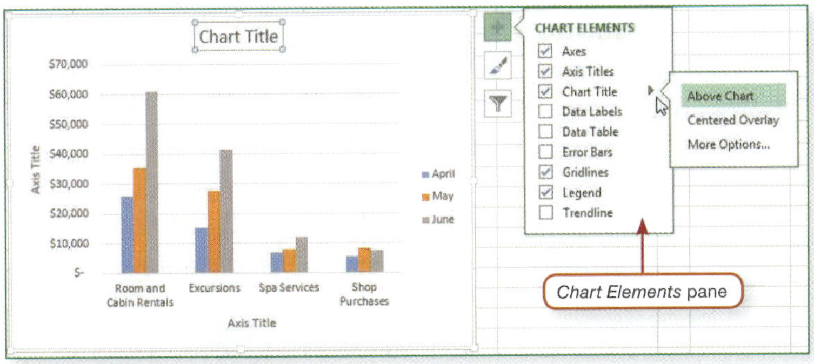

3-14 Chart title element added to chart object

In addition to adding and removing elements, you can edit placeholder text that is automatically placed in your chart when you select a chart layout or style. Select the element and type the new title. As you type a title, it appears in the *Formula bar*. It is placed in the chart when you press **Enter**.

If you select the placeholder element, you can triple-click the text to select all of it and display the mini toolbar. You can type new data and use the commands on the mini toolbar to reformat it. After you type the new text, click the chart background to deselect the element and complete your edit. If you press **Enter** while typing in a text box, you insert a second line for the title.

> **MORE INFO**
>
> Double-clicking a chart element opens its *Format* pane.

HOW TO: Edit Placeholder Text

1. Click the placeholder text box to display the selection handles.
2. Point at the label and triple-click to select all the text (Figure 3-15).
3. Type the new title.
4. Click the chart background to accept the edit.

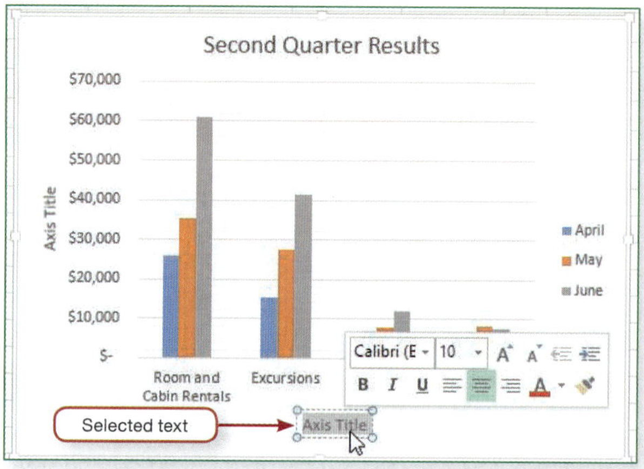

3-15 Placeholder text to be edited

You can delete chart elements when they are not necessary. For example, in a chart that illustrates dollar sales such as the one in Figure 3-15, the values on the vertical (y-axis) represent the amount of the sales. In a case like this, the vertical axis title is probably not necessary. To delete a chart element, click it to select it and press **Delete**. The chart may resize when certain elements are deleted.

Data Labels

Data labels display the value of a column, bar, pie slice, or other marker. Because the value axis uses a scale, it cannot show exact numbers, but a data label can.

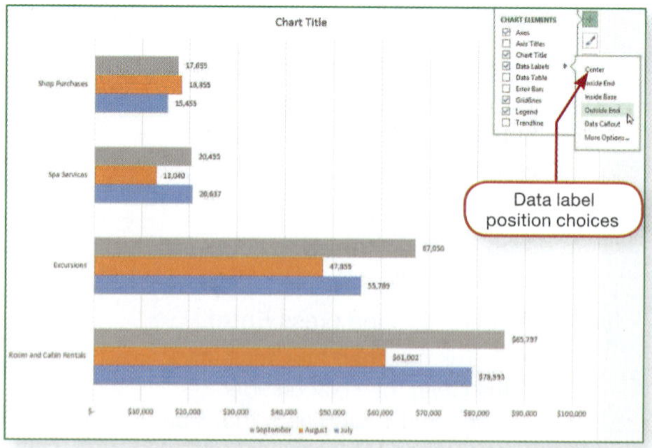

3-16 Data labels shown outside bar markers

HOW TO: Add Data Labels

1. Select the chart object or chart sheet.
2. Click the **Chart Elements** button to the right of the chart.
3. Click to place a check mark for **Data Labels**.
4. Click the menu arrow to choose a position for the labels (Figure 3-16).

> **ANOTHER WAY**
>
> Display data labels by clicking the **Add Chart Element** [*Chart Tools Design* tab, *Chart Layouts* group].

Data Table

A ***data table*** displays a table of the values of each data series based on your selected source data cells. You can add a data table to the bottom of your chart with or without legend markers (e.g., a mini legend to the left of the data table). By default, Excel does not include data tables with charts. To add a data table below your chart, use the ***Data Table*** button on the *Chart Tools Design* tab in the *Chart Layouts* group (Figure 3-17).

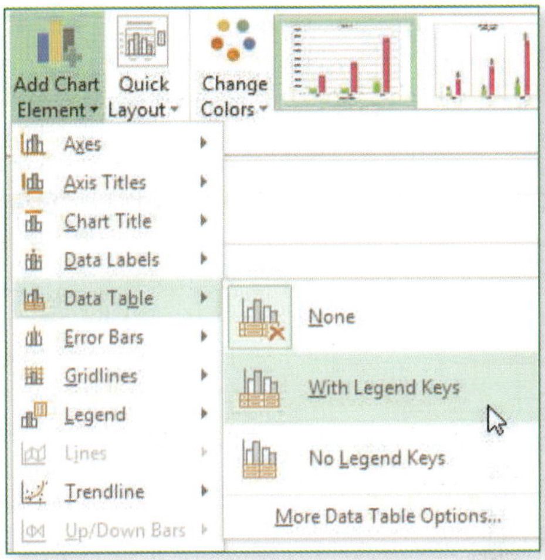

3-17 ***Data Table* options**

Trendlines

After adding chart elements, you may want to see any trends that occur. It is also useful to display trends in data to help predict future values. For example, a manager may need to forecast the next quarter's sales based on historical numbers. A ***trendline*** is a chart element that demonstrates averages in your data and that can be used to forecast data by plotting future approximate averages.

HOW TO: Add a Trendline to a Chart

1. Click the chart if it is not already selected.
2. Click the **Chart Elements** customization button in the top right corner of the chart.
3. Place your pointer over the *Trendline* check box until the arrow button appears and then click the **Trendline** arrow button.
4. Select the type of trendline you want to apply (Figure 3-18) to open the *Add Trendline* dialog box (Figure 3-19).
5. Select the data series you want to apply the *Trendline* to.
6. Click **OK** (Figure 3-20).

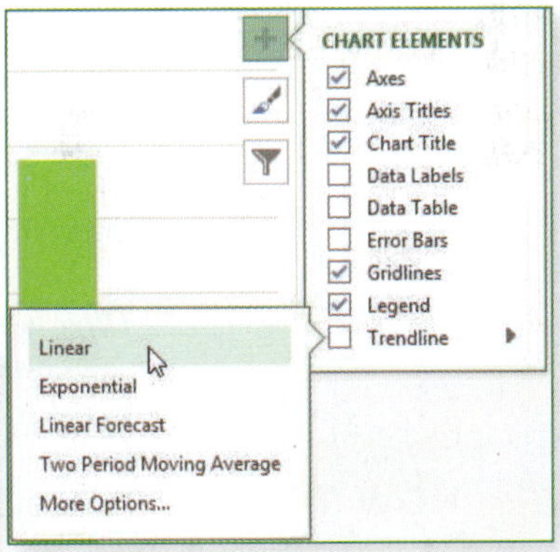

3-18 ***Trendline* options**

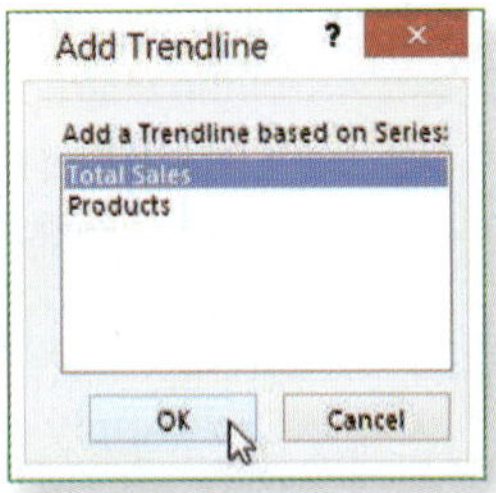

3-19 ***Add Trendline* dialog box**

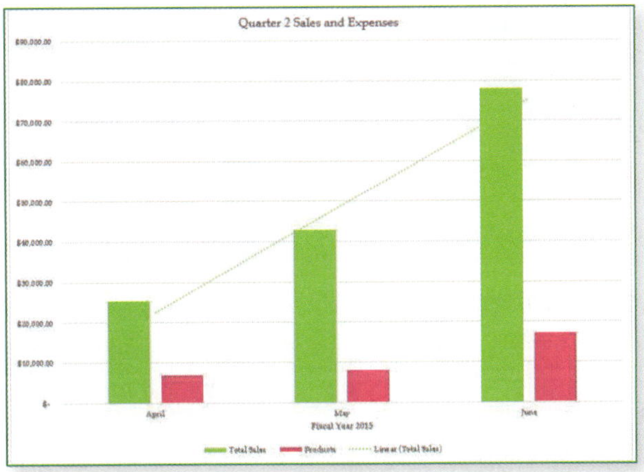

3-20 **2-D clustered column chart with "Total Sales" linear trendline**

Change the Chart Type

It is possible to change the chart type. For example, you may decide to change some bar charts into column charts for consistency in a report to make it easier for your audience to quickly compare one chart to the next, or you might decide to use 3-D pie charts instead of 2-D.

> **MORE INFO**
>
> Excel 3-D charts add the perception of depth to a chart.

HOW TO: Change the Chart Type

1. Click the chart object or chart sheet.
2. Click the **Change Chart Type** button [*Chart Tools Design* tab, *Type* group].
3. Click the *Recommended Charts* tab.
4. Scroll the chart types in the left pane and click a tile to see a larger preview in the right pane.
5. Choose the preferred chart type and click **OK** (Figure 3-21).

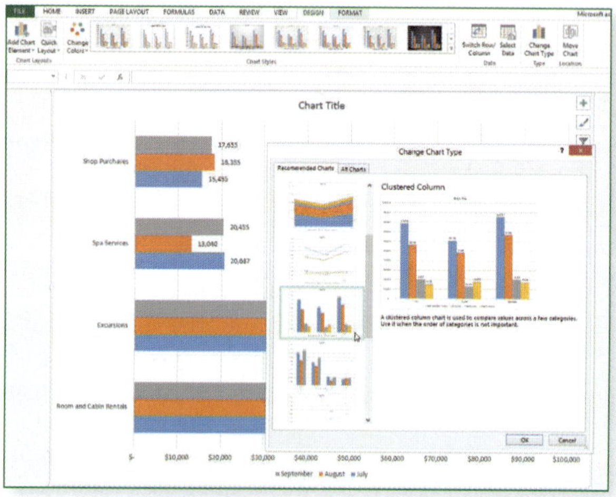

3-21 ***Change Chart Type*** **options for selected chart sheet**

Filter the Source Data

Once a chart is created, you can refine which data is displayed in the chart without changing the original source data range. This allows you to switch between several scenarios for your data without changing the underlying cell range.

You can accomplish this by applying a filter to either the values, the categories, or both. A ***filter*** is criteria that specifies which data is shown and which is hidden. Filters do not alter the source data range so you can return to the initial chart at any time.

HOW TO: Filter Source Data

1. Select the chart object or chart sheet.
2. Click the **Chart Filters** button in the top right corner of the chart.
   - The *Chart Filters* button is the bottom button and resembles a funnel-type filter.
3. Click to remove the check mark for the series or category you want to hide.
4. Click **Apply** (Figure 3-22).
5. Click the **Chart Filters** button to close the pane.

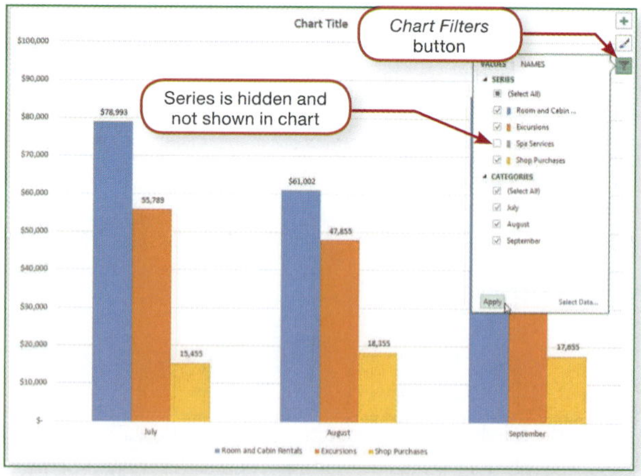

3-22 ***Chart Filters*** **pane**

> **ANOTHER WAY**
>
> Apply and remove filters from the *Select Data Source* dialog box [*Chart Tools Design* tab, *Data* group].

Edit a Chart Data Source

In addition to filtering chart data, you can edit the existing chart data source or add a data series to a chart. In a column chart, adding a data series adds another column. To add a data series to a chart object, drag the sizing pointer in the lower right corner of the data range to expand or reduce the data range, as shown in Figure 3-23. Reducing the data range deletes the data series from the chart. To add a data series to a chart sheet, you use the *Select Data Source* dialog box.

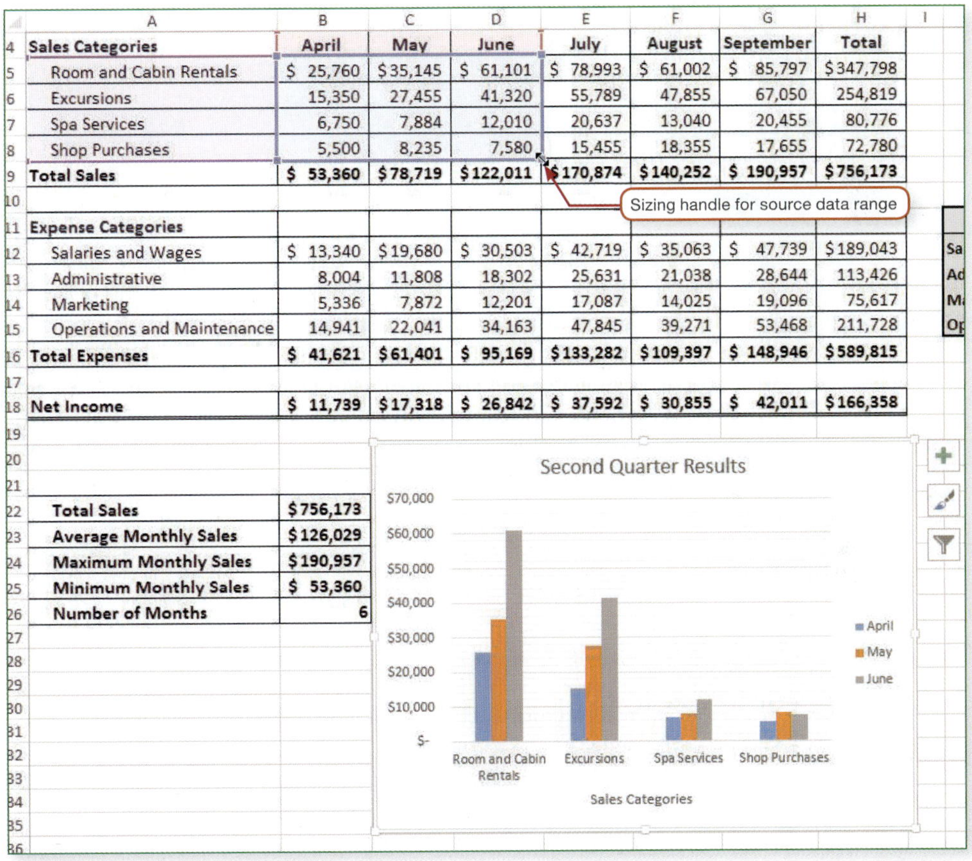

	A	B	C	D	E	F	G	H
4	Sales Categories	April	May	June	July	August	September	Total
5	Room and Cabin Rentals	$ 25,760	$35,145	$ 61,101	$ 78,993	$ 61,002	$ 85,797	$347,798
6	Excursions	15,350	27,455	41,320	55,789	47,855	67,050	254,819
7	Spa Services	6,750	7,884	12,010	20,637	13,040	20,455	80,776
8	Shop Purchases	5,500	8,235	7,580	15,455	18,355	17,655	72,780
9	Total Sales	$ 53,360	$78,719	$122,011	$170,874	$140,252	$ 190,957	$756,173
10								
11	Expense Categories							
12	Salaries and Wages	$ 13,340	$19,680	$ 30,503	$ 42,719	$ 35,063	$ 47,739	$189,043
13	Administrative	8,004	11,808	18,302	25,631	21,038	28,644	113,426
14	Marketing	5,336	7,872	12,201	17,087	14,025	19,096	75,617
15	Operations and Maintenance	14,941	22,041	34,163	47,845	39,271	53,468	211,728
16	Total Expenses	$ 41,621	$61,401	$ 95,169	$133,282	$109,397	$ 148,946	$589,815
17								
18	Net Income	$ 11,739	$17,318	$ 26,842	$ 37,592	$ 30,855	$ 42,011	$166,358
22	Total Sales	$756,173						
23	Average Monthly Sales	$126,029						
24	Maximum Monthly Sales	$190,957						
25	Minimum Monthly Sales	$ 53,360						
26	Number of Months	6						

3-23 Chart object selected, sizing handle visible

While a chart filter does not change the source data range, editing the data source or adding a data series does change the source data range in the worksheet.

HOW TO: Add a Data Series in a Chart Sheet

1. Click the chart sheet.
2. Click the **Select Data** button [*Chart Tools Design* tab, *Data* group] to open the *Select Data Source* dialog box.
   - When the source data range is adjacent, you can click the **Collapse** button at the right of the *Chart data range* text box and drag to select a new range. Then click the **Expand** button and click **OK**.

3. Edit the cell references in the *Chart data range* text box to identify the new range (Figure 3-24).
4. Click **OK**.

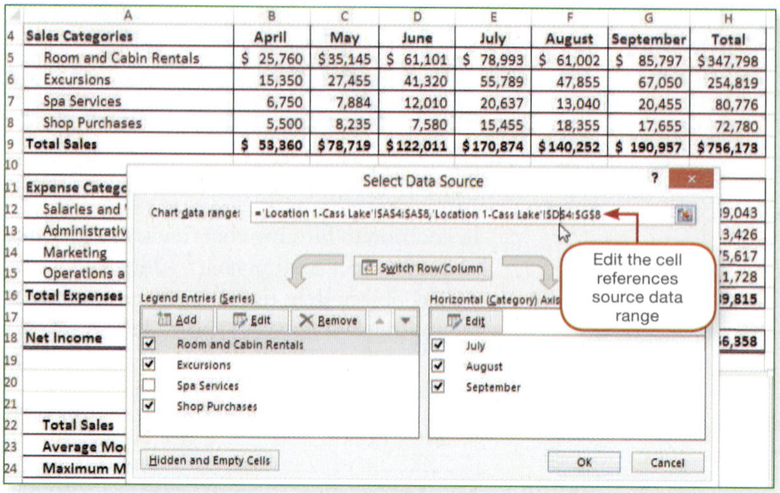

3-24 *Select Data Source* dialog box for a chart sheet

ANOTHER WAY

You can open the *Select Data Source* dialog box by clicking **Select Data** in the *Chart Filters* pane.

MORE INFO

You can apply or remove filters from the *Select Data Source* dialog box.

SLO 3.4

Formatting Chart Elements

In *SLO 3.2* and *SLO 3.3* you saw how you can quickly change the overall appearance and layout of a chart using *Quick Layouts* and *Chart Styles* and by adding or deleting chart elements. These commands are the first stages of designing a chart, but you will usually want to add your own format choices too.

Being able to personalize your charts is important. For example, your employer may have specific design requirements, or you may want to use colors and shapes from your organization or school in a chart. In either case, there are a variety of ways to enhance your charts to increase their readability.

MORE INFO

Making your own format choices enables you to distinguish your charts from those of other Excel users.

You can format each element in a chart. Some chart elements consist of a group of related elements. A data series, for example, is the group of values for a particular item. Within each data series, there are several data points. You can format the entire data series or an individual data point.

When you select an individual chart element, certain options on the *Chart Tools Design* tab apply to only that element. For example, when the chart area (background) is selected, you can change its fill or border color.

Apply a Shape Style

A ***Shape Style*** is a predesigned set of borders, fill colors, and effects for a chart element. ***Shape fill*** is the background color for the element. ***Shape outline*** is the border around an element. ***Shape effects*** include shadows, glows, bevels, or soft edges.

You choose a shape style from the gallery. As soon as you click the style, it is applied to the selected element and you see the results. There is a *Live Preview* for chart elements, and you can click the **Undo** button to remove the style if you change your mind after selecting it.

HOW TO: Apply a Shape Style

1. Click the chart element to select it.
   - Select a chart element by name by clicking the **Chart Elements** drop-down arrow [*Chart Tools Format* tab, *Current Selection* group] and choosing the element.
   - If the *Format* pane for the chart element opens, close it.
2. Click the **More** button [*Chart Tools Format* tab, *Shape Styles* group] to open the *Shape Styles* gallery (Figure 3-25).
3. Click the selected style.

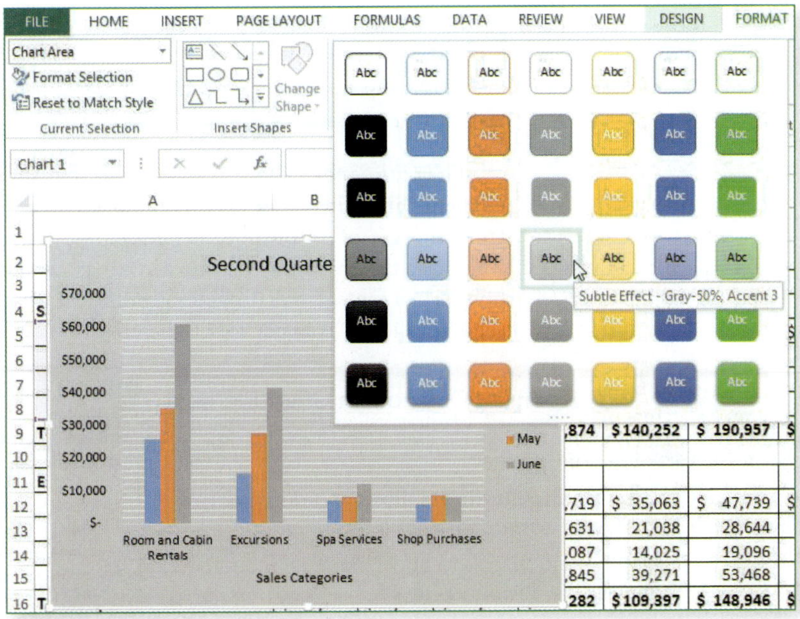

3-25 ***Shape Style*** **gallery for the chart area**

Apply Shape Fill, Outline, and Effects

Once you select a chart element, you can apply fill color, set outline width and color, or special effects. These three format options are available in the *Shape Styles* group on the *Chart Tools Format* tab. If a *Shape Style* has already been applied to the object, individual choices override the style.

When you set a fill color, you choose from the workbook theme colors shown in the gallery. In addition to theme colors, the standard colors are also available, or you can build a custom color. After you choose a color, you can refine it to use a ***gradient***, a variegated blend of the color.

Live Preview is available for shape fill so you can preview the results of your choice before committing to it. To preview, just point at a color tile in the gallery. When you find the color you want, click the color tile.

The *Shape Fill, Shape Outline,* and *Shape Effects* buttons apply the choice you made most recently when you click the icon. To make a choice from a gallery, click the drop-down arrow for the option.

HOW TO: Apply Gradient Fill to a Chart Element

1. Click the chart element.
2. Click the **Shape Fill** button drop-down arrow [*Chart Tools Format* tab, *Shape Styles* group].
   - Click the button icon to apply the most recently used color.
3. Select the desired color.
4. Click the **Shape Fill** drop-down arrow again.
5. Choose **Gradient** (Figure 3-26) to open the gallery.
6. Click the preferred gradient.

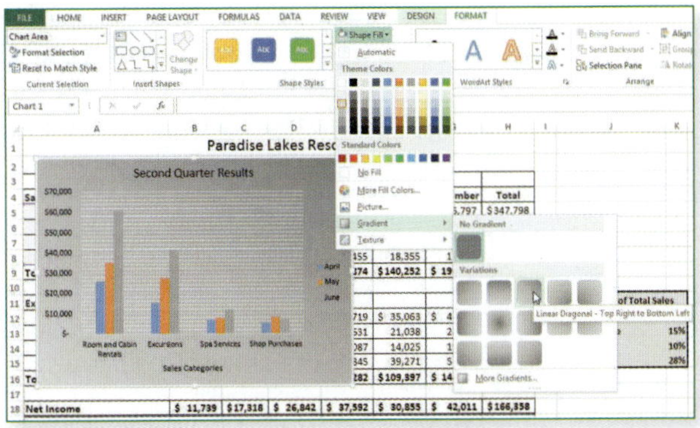

3-26 ***Shape Fill*** **gallery and** ***Gradient*** **gallery**

ANOTHER WAY

You can apply some formats, such as fill or font color, from the *Home* tab for a selected chart element.

The outline for a shape is the border that surrounds or encircles the element. Not all chart elements are suited to an outline, but elements such as the chart or plot area often benefit from the use of an outline. When you add an outline to a chart element, you can select a weight or thickness for the line as well as a color. The thickness of an outline is measured in points, like fonts. Excel provides a gallery of weights to help you visualize the width. After you set an outline, it is easier to see the effect if you deselect the chart object.

HOW TO: Apply an Outline to a Chart Element

1. Click the chart element.
2. Click the **Shape Outline** button drop-down arrow [*Chart Tools Format* tab, *Shape Styles* group].
   - Click the button icon to apply the most recently used outline color and weight.
3. Click the desired color for the outline.
4. Click the **Shape Outline** drop-down arrow again.
5. Click **Weight**.
6. Choose a point size (Figure 3-27).

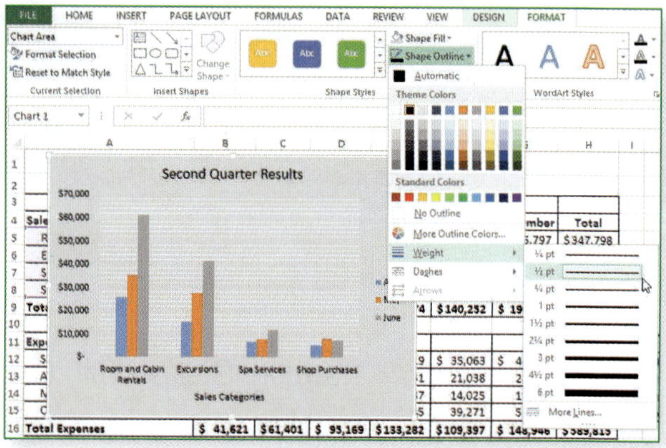

3-27 *Outline color* and *Weight* galleries

MORE INFO

To remove shape fill or outline, select the object and click the button corresponding to the effect that you want to change. Then choose **No Fill** or **No Outline**.

You can also apply special effects to a chart element. Popular effects include bevels and shadows, which give the element a realistic, three-dimensional look. These types of effects are best used on larger elements, such as the chart area, because they can overwhelm smaller elements.

HOW TO: Apply an Effect to a Chart Element

1. Click the chart element.
2. Click the **Shape Effects** button [*Chart Tools Format* tab, *Shape Styles* group].
3. Click the desired effect group for the object (Figure 3-28).
4. Choose the effect.

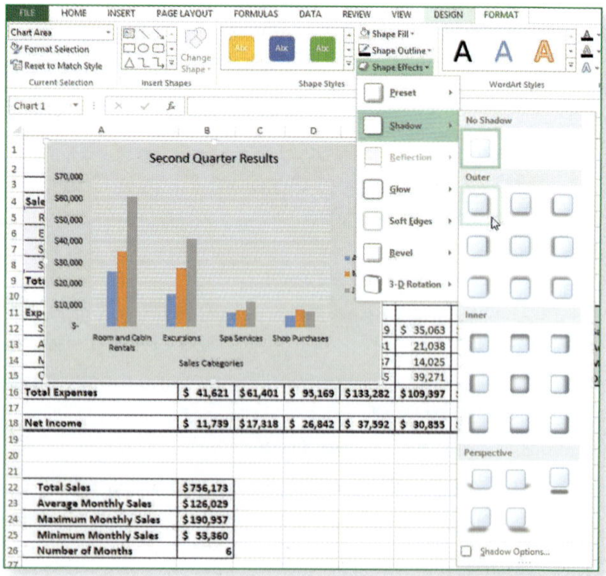

3-28 *Shape Effects* gallery for a chart object

To remove an effect, select the element and click the **Shape Effects** button drop-down arrow. Choose the type of effect and click the first option such as **No Shadow** or **No Bevel**.

The Format Task Pane

You can apply many format choices quickly from the *Chart Tools Format* tab. There are, however, several options for chart elements that are not available on the tab. Every chart element has a *Format* task pane that consolidates shape, fill, and color options and provides custom commands for the element (Figure 3-29).

To open the *Format* pane for a chart element, double-click the element or right-click it and choose *Format [Element Name]* from the menu. The *Format* pane opens to the right of the workbook window and automatically changes to reflect the selected element. For example, if you display the task pane for a data series and then select the chart title, the pane changes to the *Chart Title Format* pane.

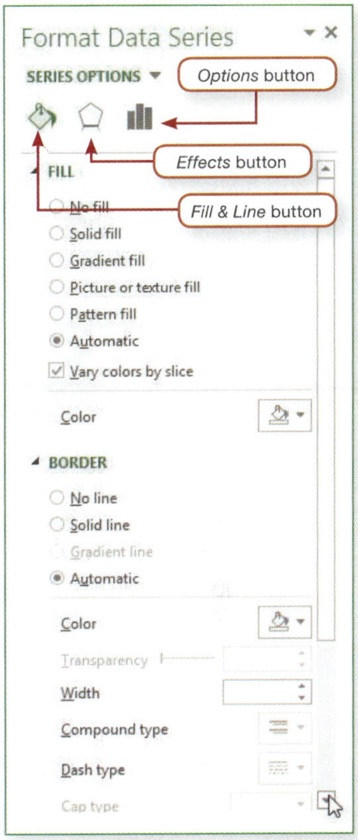

3-29 ***Format Data Series*** **pane**

> **ANOTHER WAY**
>
> Open a *Format* task pane by clicking the **Format Selection** button [*Chart Tools Format* tab, *Selection* group].

> **MORE INFO**
>
> Expand or collapse a command group in the *Format* task pane by clicking the small triangle to the left of the group name.

Most *Format* task panes have three buttons at the top: *Fill & Line, Effects,* and *Options*. When you click a button, the pane displays the relevant commands. *Fill & Line* and *Effects* are similar for all chart elements. The *Options* panes are specific to the element.

HOW TO: Use the Format Task Pane to Change Shape Fill

1. Double-click the chart element.
   - Verify the name of the task pane. If the wrong task pane opens, click the element again.
   - You can also select an element from the **Chart Elements** button drop-down arrow [*Chart Tools Format* tab, *Current Selection* group].
2. Click the **Fill & Line** button in the *Format* task pane.
3. Click **Fill** to expand the group.
4. Click the **Fill Color** button to open the gallery.
5. Click the desired color (Figure 3-30).

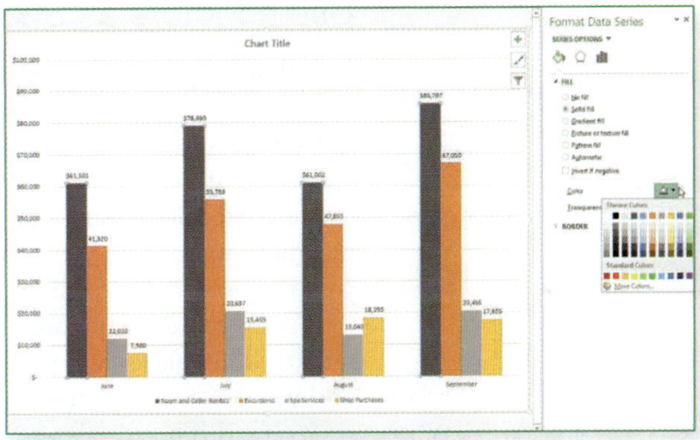

3-30 ***Fill & Line*** **command in the *Format* task pane**

There is an *Effects* command group in many *Format* task panes with the same options as the *Ribbon*. You can set shadows, bevels, glows, and more, depending on the selected element. Use these commands sparingly in most charts. Overuse of these commands can make the chart look too busy and overdesigned.

An *Options* group in a *Format* task pane is the command set that enables you to accomplish tasks that are specific to the type of element you select. For a data series in a column chart, for example, these commands determine whether numbers are shown on the right or left of the chart (secondary or primary axis), or you can choose to have the columns overlap. A pie chart, on the other hand, has series options that allow you to rotate the pie and explode the slices.

HOW TO: Use the Format Task Pane to Set Data Label Options

1. Double-click a data label element.
   - Right-click the element and choose **Format *[Element Name]***.
   - If you have difficulty selecting the desired element, click the *Options* triangle next to the group name and choose the element from the drop-down list.
2. Click the **Label Options** button in the *Format* task pane.
3. Click **Label Options** or **Number** to expand the group.
4. Enter your format preferences in the task pane (Figure 3-31).

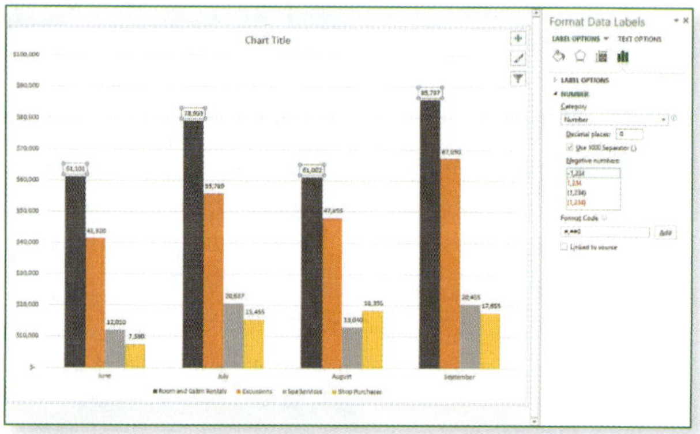

3-31 ***Format Data Labels*** **pane**

SLO 3.5

Using Images, Shapes, and WordArt in a Chart

A chart includes several selectable elements as part of its basic layout. You can add images, shapes, or *WordArt* in a chart to further personalize it. For example, a chart that illustrates the number of fish caught in a tournament could use a small image of a fish as fill for a data series rather than a fill color, or you might add a shape as a callout to a particular data point on a chart, such as a star to highlight the best sales record. You can also replace a chart title box with *WordArt* for a distinctive look.

Pictures, shapes, or *WordArt* are chart elements that you can size, position, and format.

Use a Picture as Shape Fill

In a chart, you can fill bars, columns, or pie slices with a picture that helps illustrate the data. To clarify, you might use a small stick-figure in a chart that graphs numbers of customers. You can use images that are filed on your computer or external storage device. You can search for and insert an online image, or you can copy an image from another application.

The size and design of an image are important. You cannot edit all images in Excel, so you may have to experiment with pictures to learn what works well in your charts. For example, you may not be able to change the color of a picture, or it may have a transparent background.

When you use a picture as a fill, you can use the ***Stretch*** option to stretch it across the data marker. This places a single copy of the image and stretches it to fill the shape. The ***Stack*** options resizes the picture to fit the width of the marker and repeats it to signify the values represented. There is also a ***Stack and Scale*** setting for more detailed sizing and placement of the picture.

> **MORE INFO**
>
> When you first click the *Picture or texture fill* option in the *Format* task pane, it may display the most recently used image in the selected element.

HOW TO: Use a Picture as Fill

1. Select the data series and open its *Format* task pane.
2. Click the **Fill & Line** button in the *Format* task pane.
3. Click **Fill** to expand the group.
4. Click the **Picture or texture fill** button to open the gallery.
5. Click **Online** to search for an image or click **File** to choose a stored image.
6. Find and select the image you want to use as fill.
7. Click **Stack** to scale and repeat the image (Figure 3-32).

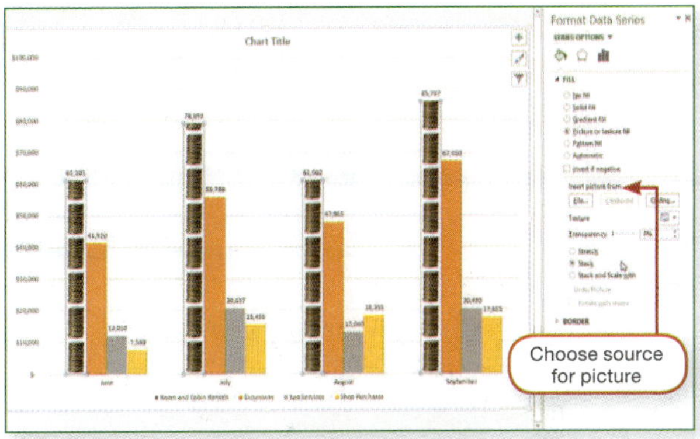

3-32 Online image used as fill for data series

> **MORE INFO**
>
> You can insert an image as a separate design element on a chart from the *Insert* tab. Edit it from the *Picture Format* tab.

Insert Shapes

Shapes such as arrows, circles, or callouts can be used to highlight important parts of a chart. For example, you can insert an arrow shape to emphasize the highest sales month or add a banner with text to congratulate the sales team.

The shapes that are available for use on a chart are the same shapes available in other Office applications. The *Shapes* gallery opens when you click the **More** button from the *Insert Shapes* group on the *Chart Tools Format* tab.

Once you place a shape in a chart, you can select it and format it from the *Picture Tools Format* tab.

HOW TO: Insert a Shape in a Chart

1. Select the chart object or chart sheet.
2. Click the **More** button [*Chart Tools Format* tab, *Insert Shapes* group].
3. Select the shape.
4. Click and drag to draw the shape on the chart (Figure 3-33).
5. Format the shape as needed.
6. Add text to the shape by right-clicking and selecting **Edit Text** from the context-sensitive menu.

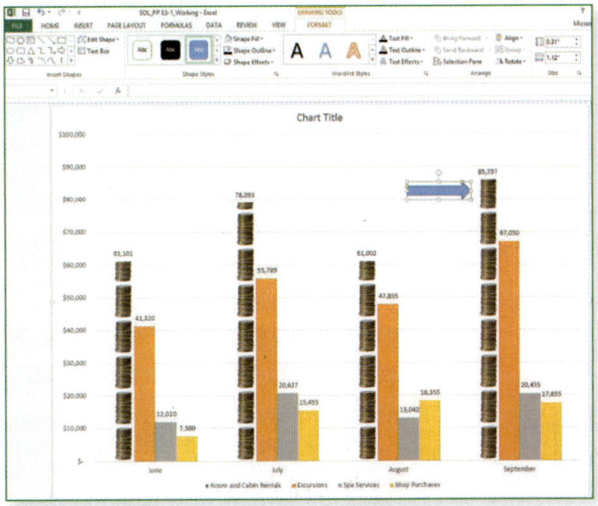

3-33 Shape inserted in chart

> **ANOTHER WAY**
>
> Insert a shape in a chart from the **Shapes** button on the *Insert* tab [*Illustrations* group].

Use WordArt in a Chart

WordArt is a text box with preset font style, fill, and text effects. You might use *WordArt* in a chart in place of a regular chart title. You can apply a *WordArt* style to an existing chart title, or if a chart has no title, you can insert a *Text Box* shape and format it with a *WordArt* style.

> **ANOTHER WAY**
>
> Insert a *WordArt* text box in a chart from the **Insert WordArt** button [*Insert* tab, *Text* group].

HOW TO: Use WordArt in a Chart

1. Select the chart title or other chart element.
2. Click the **More** button to display *WordArt Styles* [*Chart Tools Format* tab, *WordArt Styles* group].
3. Click the preferred style (Figure 3-34).

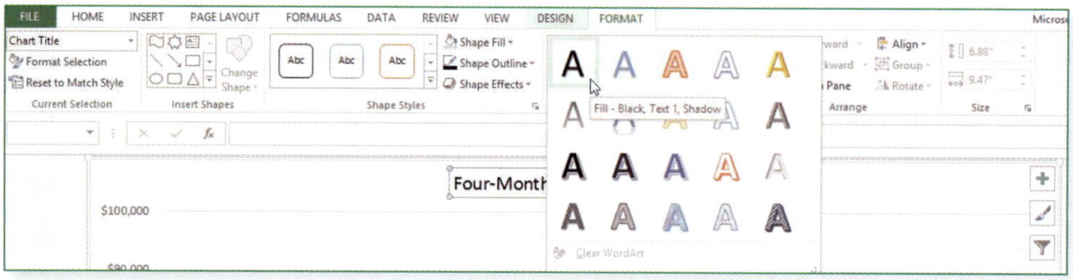

3-34 *WordArt Style* gallery for selected chart title

PAUSE & PRACTICE: EXCEL 3-2

For this project, you open your first Pause & Practice file to edit and format the Paradise Lakes Resort charts. You switch row and column data and add and delete several chart elements. You also change the chart type so that the two charts in the workbook are consistent. Finally, you format the charts for easier reading.

File Needed: ***[your initials] PP E3-1.xlsx***
Completed Project File Name: ***[your initials] PP E3-2.xlsx***

1. Open the ***[your initials] PP E3-1*** workbook.
2. Save the workbook as ***[your initials] PP E3-2***.
3. Switch the row and column data in the chart object.
   a. Click the **Location 1-Cass Lake** worksheet tab.
   b. Click the chart object.
   c. Click the **Switch/Row Column** button [*Chart Tools Design* tab, *Data* group].

4. Add and remove chart elements.
   a. Click the **Location 1-Cass Lake** worksheet tab and select the chart object if it is not already selected.
   b. Click the **Chart Elements** button to the right of the chart.
   c. Add a title by clicking the **Chart Title** check box.
   d. Click the **Chart Title** menu arrow and choose **Above Chart**.
   e. Point at the placeholder text and triple-click.
   f. Type Second Quarter Activity.
   g. Click the chart to deselect the title.
   h. Click the horizontal axis title placeholder.
   i. Press **Delete**.
   j. Delete the vertical axis title placeholder.
   k. Double-click the legend element at the right of the chart area to open its *Format* task pane.
   l. Click the **Legend Options** button if necessary (Figure 3-35).
   m. Click the **Bottom** radio button to reposition the legend.
   n. Close the *Format Legend* task pane.

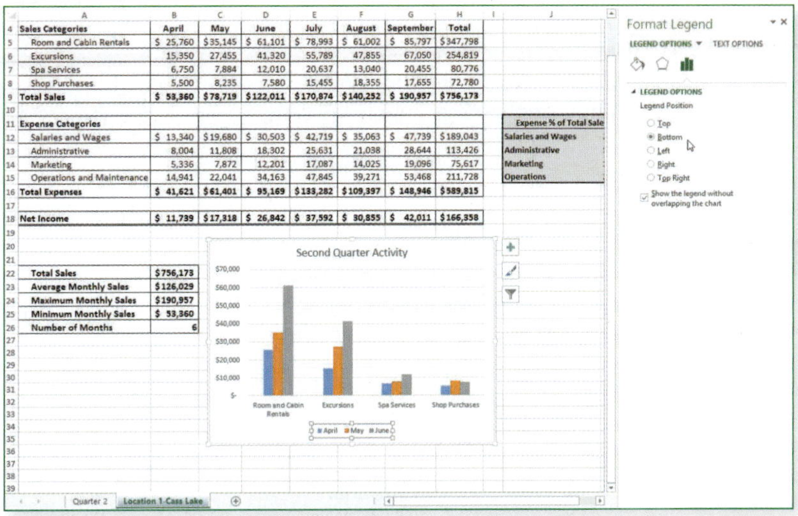

3-35 Chart in worksheet with elements added and removed

5. Change the chart type.
   a. Click the **Quarter 3** tab.
   b. Click the **Change Chart Type** button [*Chart Tools Design* tab, *Type* group] to open the *Change Chart Type* dialog box.
   c. Click the **Recommended Charts** tab.
   d. Find and select the first **Clustered Column** in the pane on the left.
   e. Click **OK**.

6. Filter the source data.
   a. Click the **Chart Filters** button in the top right corner of the chart.
   b. Click the **Excursions** check box to remove the check mark.
   c. Click **Apply**.
   d. Click the **Chart Filters** button to close the pane.

7. Apply shape styles and outlines to chart elements.
   a. Click the **Location 1-Cass Lake** tab.
   b. Click the chart object.
   c. Click the **Chart Elements** drop-down arrow [*Chart Tools Format* tab, *Current Selection* group].
   d. Choose **Plot Area** to select the plot area of the chart.
   e. Click the **More** button [*Chart Tools Format* tab, *Shape Styles* group].
   f. Click **Subtle Effect – Gold, Accent 4**.

g. Click the **Shape Outline** button drop-down arrow [*Chart Tools Format* tab, *Shape Styles* group].
h. Choose **Black, Text 1** in the top row of the *Theme Colors.*
i. Click the **Chart Elements** drop-down arrow [*Chart Tools Format* tab, *Current Selection* group].
j. Choose **Vertical (Value) Axis Major Gridlines** to select the major gridlines in the plot area.
k. Click the icon for the **Shape Outline** button [*Chart Tools Format* tab, *Shape Styles* group] to apply the last-used color (**Black, Text 1**).
l. Select the **Vertical (Value) Axis Minor Gridlines** and apply the same black outline color.
m. Click the chart area to see the change (Figure 3-36).
n. Click the **Chart Elements** drop-down arrow [*Chart Tools Format* tab, *Current Selection* group] and choose **Chart Area**.
o. Apply **Black, Text 1** for the outline.

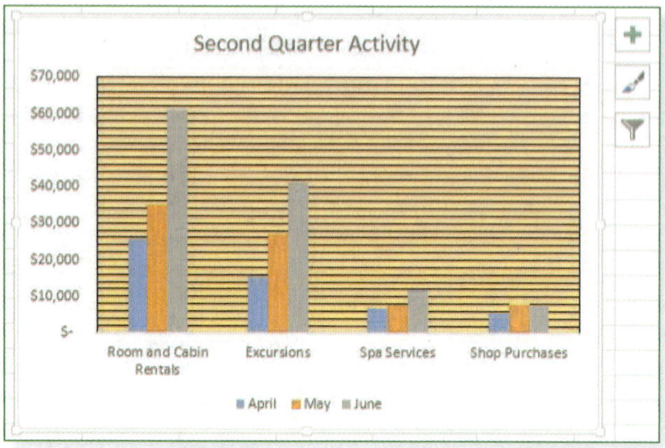

3-36 Plot area formatted

8. Use a picture as fill.
   a. Click the **Quarter 3** tab.
   b. Double-click one of the "Room and Cabin Rentals" columns to open the *Format Data Series* task pane.
   c. Click the **Fill & Line** button.
   d. Click **Fill** to expand the command group.
   e. Click the **Picture or texture fill** button to open the gallery.
   f. Click **Online**, type cabins in the *Office.com Clip Art* text box, and press **Enter** (Figure 3-37).
   g. Choose an image and insert it.
   h. Click **Stack** in the *Format Data Series* task pane.
   i. Close the task pane.

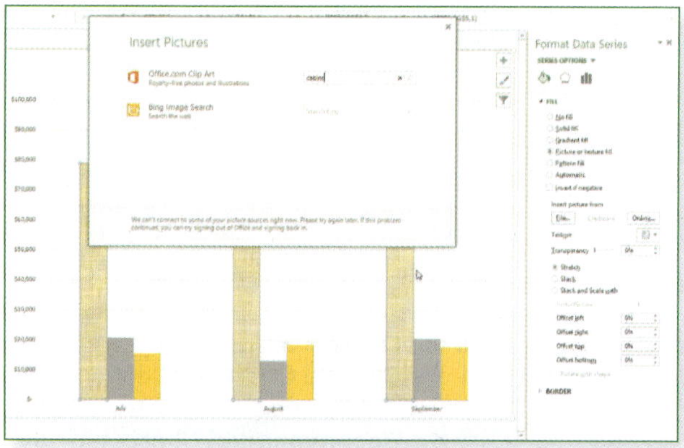

3-37 Online search for a picture to use as fill

9. Use *WordArt* in a chart.
   a. Triple-click the **Chart Title** placeholder to select the text.
   b. Type Third Quarter Activity.
   c. Click the chart area to deselect the title.
   d. Triple-click the title text again.
   e. From the mini toolbar, change the font size to **24 pt**.
   f. Click the chart area to deselect the title.
   g. Select the chart title to display the selection handles.
   h. Click the **More** button [*Chart Tools Format* tab, *WordArt Style* group].
   i. Choose **Fill – Black, Text 1, Shadow**.

10. Move the legend.
    a. Double-click the legend element below the chart title to open its *Format* task pane.
    b. Click the **Legend Options** button if necessary.
    c. Choose **Bottom** to reposition the legend.
11. Save and close the workbook (Figure 3-38).

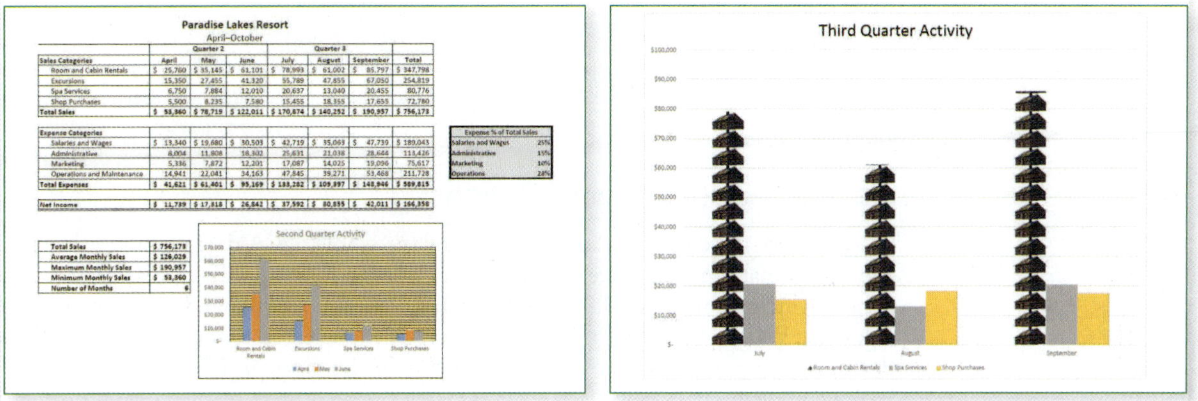

3-38 PP E3-2 completed worksheet and chart sheet

SLO 3.6

Creating and Editing a Pie Chart and a Combination Chart

When you use the *Quick Analysis* or *Recommended Charts* button, Excel chooses chart types that are suited to the data you have selected. As you develop your Excel skills and build more charts, you can choose your chart types directly from the *Charts* group on the *Insert* tab. With this method, when you click the specific chart type button, you see a small gallery with the available subtypes of the chart. As you point at each option, *Live Preview* previews the chart.

Charts created from a chart type button on the *Insert* tab are created as chart objects in the worksheet. Like any chart objects, you can move them to their own sheets.

Create a 3-D Pie Chart

A ***pie chart*** graphs one data series, one set of numbers. For most pie charts, you want to limit the number of categories to six or seven. A pie chart with many slices is difficult to interpret and often does not illustrate the relationship among the values. A pie chart illustrates how each number relates to the whole. In fact, you can set a value for the data series to show a percentage in the data label.

On the *Insert Pie or Doughnut Chart* button on the *Insert* tab, you can choose from a gallery of 2-D or 3-D pie types as well as a doughnut shape (see Figure 3-39). A doughnut chart is a pie chart with a hollow center. There are also two options for a pie chart with a bar or another pie chart.

HOW TO: Create a 3-D Pie Chart

1. Select the cell ranges that include the data series and the category labels.
2. Click the **Insert Pie or Doughnut Chart** button [*Insert* tab, *Charts* group] (Figure 3-39).
3. Choose **3-D Pie**.
   - Click the **Move Chart** button [*Chart Tools Design* tab, *Location* group] to move a pie chart to its own sheet.

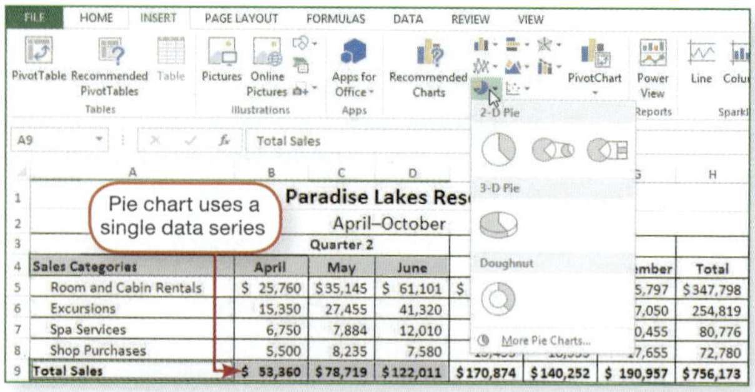

3-39 Selected data series and categories for a pie chart

Pie Chart Elements and Options

In a pie chart, the data series is represented by the whole pie. A data point is a slice of the pie. You can format the data series as a whole and you can format individual slices. It is important to note which element you have selected when you give a command. Remember the *Format* task pane. When you use it, it shows the name of the selected element. You can also view the element's name in the *Chart Elements* text box in the *Current Selection* group on the *Chart Tools Format* tab.

A pie chart can display a legend and a title. It does not, however, have axes and does not use axes titles. Data labels are often used instead of a legend for a pie chart because they show the same information. The chart area, as usual, is the background for the chart.

Pie charts do have *Quick Layouts* and *Quick Styles*. You can also set shape fill, color, and effects for the elements or objects, use a picture as fill, add an image, or insert *WordArt*.

Specialized commands for a pie chart are the angle of the first slice and the percent of explosion. The angle of the first slice allows you to rotate the pie. The first slice starts at the top of the chart at 0° (zero degrees). As you increase that value, the slice arcs to the right. *Live Preview* displays the results.

Exploding a pie slice emphasizes that slice because it moves the slice away from the rest of the pie. You set explosion as a percentage.

HOW TO: Rotate a Pie Chart and Explode a Slice

1. Double-click the pie chart to open the *Format Data Series* task pane.
   - You can also right-click the pie chart and choose **Format Data Series** to open the task pane.
2. Click the **Series Options** button to open the command group (Figure 3-40).
   - If the wrong *Format* task pane opens, click the arrow with **Series Options** and choose **Series 1**.
3. Set the angle for the first slice by dragging the slider control to the degree setting (see Figure 3-40).
   - You can also type the desired value in the text box or use the up or down spinner arrows to set a degree value.
4. Click the data point (slice) you want to explode.
   - Verify that the *Format Data Point* task pane is open.

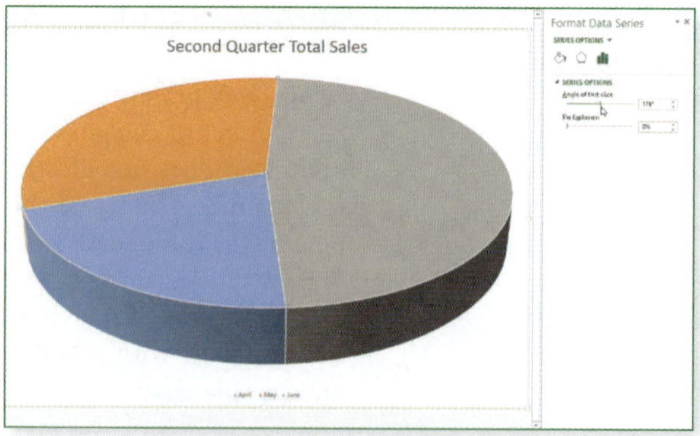

3-40 Angle of first slice adjusted

5. Set the percentage for the amount of explosion by dragging the slider control to the percent setting (Figure 3-41).
   - You can also type the new value in the text box or use the up or down spinner arrows to set a percent value.

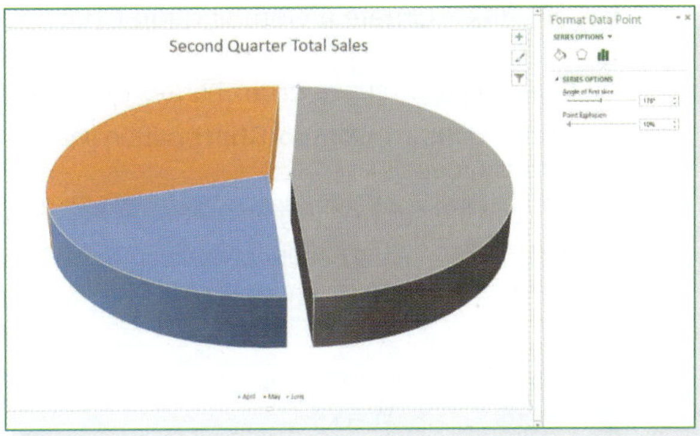

3-41 Exploded pie slice

> **MORE INFO**
>
> You can explode all the slices in a pie chart by selecting the data series, not a data point.

Create a Combination Chart

A combination chart includes two chart types such as a line chart and a column chart. Paradise Lakes Resort can use a combination chart, for example, to compare revenue from cabin and room rentals to the operations and maintenance expense. These two values reflect different types of numbers, so showing one series as a line and the other as a column focuses the revenue/expense comparison (Figure 3-42).

	A	B	C	D	E
1	Paradise Lakes Resort				
2	April–October				
3		Quarter 2			
4	**Sales Categories**	**April**	**May**	**June**	**July**
5	Room and Cabin Rentals	$ 25,760	$35,145	$ 61,101	$ 78,993
6	Excursions	15,350	27,455	41,320	55,789
7	Spa Services	6,750	7,884	12,010	20,637
8	Shop Purchases	5,500	8,235	7,580	15,455
9	**Total Sales**	**$ 53,360**	**$78,719**	**$122,011**	**$170,874**
10					
11	**Expense Categories**				
12	Salaries and Wages	$ 13,340	$19,680	$ 30,503	$ 42,719
13	Administrative	8,004	11,808	18,302	25,631
14	Marketing	5,336	7,872	12,201	17,087
15	Operations and Maintenance	14,941	22,041	34,163	47,845
16	**Total Expenses**	**$ 41,621**	**$61,401**	**$ 95,169**	**$133,282**

3-42 Source data for a combo chart

The most common combination of chart types is line and column, but you can also use a line and area combination. Excel offers an option to create a custom combination, but it is best to use this only after you have experience charting your data.

> **MORE INFO**
>
> Some chart types cannot be combined. If you try to do so, Excel opens a message box to inform you.

In a combination chart, you can display two sets of values with two vertical axes. The axis on the left is the primary axis; the one on the right is secondary. This option is best when the values are very different such as when comparing the number of rooms booked to dollars earned.

You can create a combination chart from the *Charts* group on the *Insert* tab as well as from the *Recommended Charts* button in the same group.

HOW TO: Create a Combination Chart

1. Select the cell ranges to be charted.
2. Click the **Insert Combo Chart** button [*Insert* tab, *Charts* group].
3. Choose the subtype (Figure 3-43).
   - You can move a combination chart to its own sheet if desired.

ANOTHER WAY

Create a combination chart for selected data from the **Recommended Charts** button [*Insert* tab, *Charts* group] by clicking the *All Charts* tab.

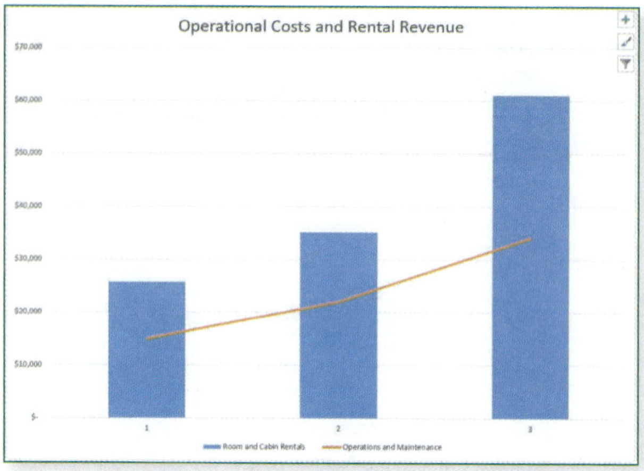

3-43 Line-Column combination chart

Combination Chart Elements and Options

A combination chart can have several data series, each shown in its own chart type. Keep this type of chart relatively simple, however, because its purpose is to compare unlike items.

A combination chart has most of the same elements as a regular column or line chart. You can apply chart styles and layouts, as well as shape fill, outline, effects, pictures, shapes, and *WordArt*, to a combination chart.

You can display or hide the secondary axis for a combination chart in the *Change Chart Type* dialog box. When you use a secondary axis, Excel builds the number scale based on the data. You can edit which data uses a line or a column from this dialog box as well (Figure 3-44).

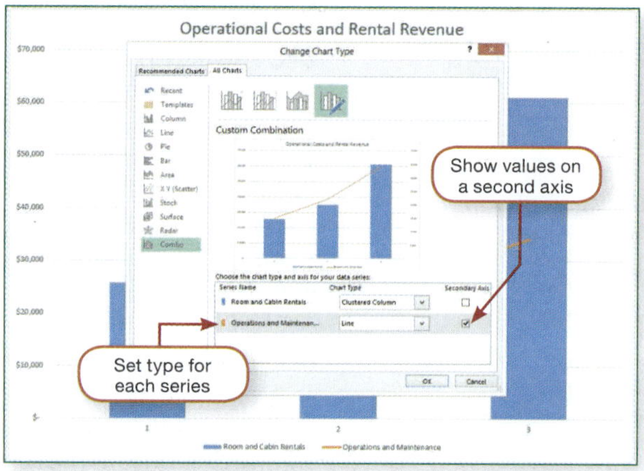

3-44 *Change Chart Type* dialog box for a combo chart

HOW TO: Display a Secondary Axis on a Combination Chart

1. Select the chart object.
2. Click the **Change Chart Type** button [*Chart Tools Design* tab, *Type* group].
3. Choose the chart type for each series if desired.
4. Click to place or remove a check mark for a secondary axis.
5. Click **OK** (Figure 3-45).

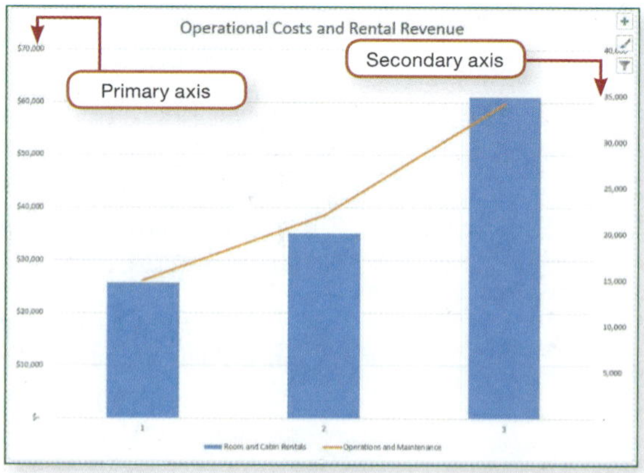

3-45 Secondary axis for a combo chart

SLO 3.7

Inserting Sparklines in a Worksheet

Sparklines are miniature charts displayed in a cell or cell range next to your data. They can be used to illustrate trends and patterns without adding a separate chart object or sheet.

Sparklines are created from a selected data range like a chart. You can place them in a location range, usually next to the worksheet data (Figure 3-46).

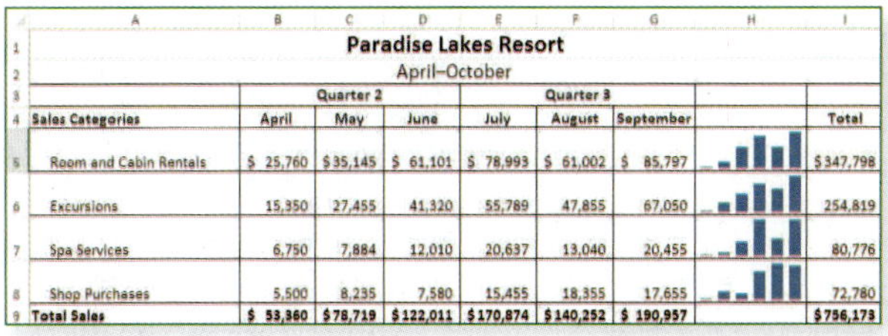

3-46 Column sparklines in a worksheet

There are three sparkline types: ***Line***, ***Column***, and ***Win/Loss***. The *Sparklines* command is located on the *Insert* tab for the worksheet. After you insert sparklines, they act like other objects in a worksheet. The ***Sparkline Tools Design*** tab opens when you click the sparkline object.

To insert sparklines, you may need to insert a column at the appropriate location in your data, or, if it is empty, you may be able to use the right-most column. Depending on the type of sparkline, you may also want to increase the row height or column width to better present the sparklines.

Insert Sparklines

To insert sparklines in a worksheet, decide where you want to place them and insert a column if necessary. Select the data range that includes the values to be illustrated. This range cannot include the range where the sparklines display.

The *Sparklines* group is on the *Insert* tab and in the *Type* group on the *Sparkline Tools Design* tab.

HOW TO: Insert Column Sparklines in a Worksheet

1. Select the cell range to be used for sparklines.
   - When you select the data range first, it is displayed in the *Data Range* box within the *Create Sparklines* dialog box.
2. Click the **Column Sparkline** button [*Insert* tab, *Sparklines* group].
3. Click in the **Location Range** box.
4. Click and drag in the worksheet to select the cell range for the sparklines (Figure 3-47).
5. Click **OK**.

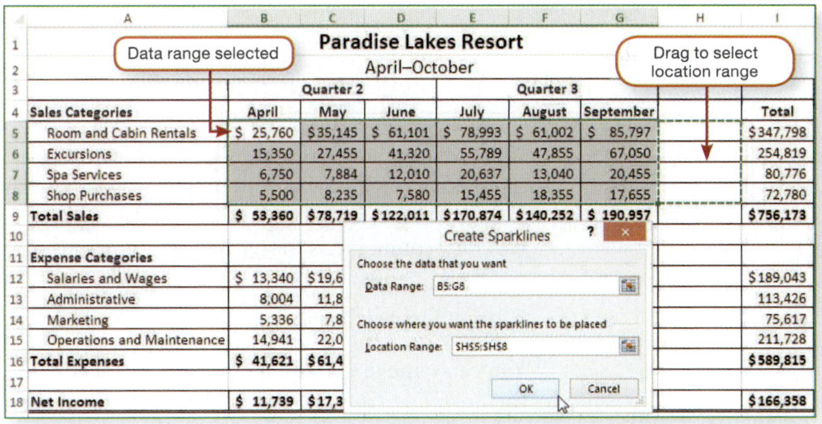

3-47 *Create Sparklines* dialog box

ANOTHER WAY

Click the **Column Sparkline** button [*Insert* tab, *Sparklines* group] and select the *Data Range* and *Location Range* from the dialog box to insert sparklines.

Sparkline Design Tools

When sparklines are selected in a worksheet, the *Sparkline Tools Design* tab opens. This context-sensitive tab includes several choices for changing the appearance of your sparklines. There is a *Shape Style* option that changes the color of the sparkline group. You can also change the color with the *Sparkline Color* command. The *Marker Color* command enables you to choose a different color for identified values in the sparklines. A ***marker*** for a sparkline is the data point value. You can highlight a specific value or the high, low, first, or last value as well as negative values.

Other choices on the *Sparkline Tools Design* tab are in the *Type* and *Show* groups. For example, you can change a column sparkline to a line sparkline. The *Show* commands set the color of the identified values in the data range.

HOW TO: Format Sparklines

1. Click the sparkline group in the worksheet.
2. Click the *Sparkline Line Tools Design* tab if necessary.
3. Click the **High Point** check box in the *Show* group (Figure 3-48).
   - A default color is applied to the highest value in the sparklines for each row.
4. Click the **Marker Color** button [*Sparkline Tools Design* tab, *Style* group].
5. Choose **High Point** and select a color from the gallery.

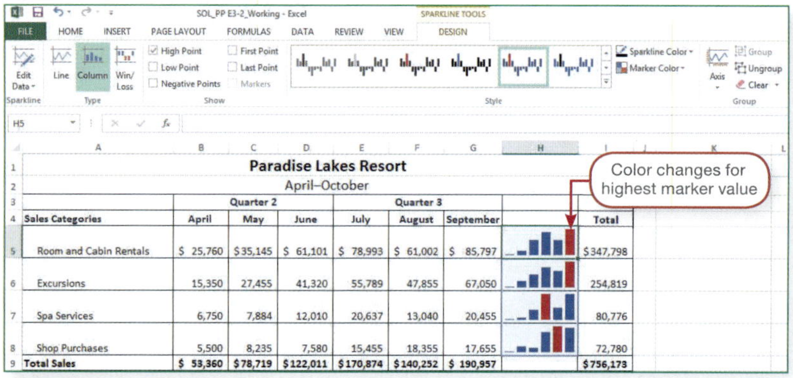

3-48 ***High Point*** **marker selected for sparklines**

6. Click the **Sparkline Color** button [*Sparkline Tools Design* tab, *Style* group].
7. Choose a color for the sparkline group that is different from the color you chose for the *High Point.*

Sparklines are inserted as a group in the location range. When you click any cell in the range with sparklines, the group is selected. Sparklines can be ungrouped if you need to make format choices for one sparkline cell or if you want to delete one sparkline in a range. The *Ungroup* command is in the *Group* group on the *Sparkline Tools Design* tab.

Clear Sparklines

You can remove sparklines from a worksheet with the *Clear* command in the *Group* group on the *Sparkline Tools Design* tab. After sparklines are cleared from a worksheet, you may need to delete the column where they were located or reset row heights and column widths.

HOW TO: Clear Sparklines

1. Select any cell in the sparklines range.
2. Click the **Clear Selected Sparklines** button [*Sparkline Tools Design* tab, *Group* group].
3. Choose **Clear Selected Sparklines Group**.

PAUSE & PRACTICE: EXCEL 3-3

For this project, you continue to build Paradise Lakes' sales report by inserting a pie chart that shows the proportion of each sales category in the organization's total sales. You also insert a combination chart sheet to compare rentals and maintenance expense. Finally, you insert sparklines in the worksheet.

File Needed: ***[your initials] PP E3-2.xlsx***
Completed Project File Name: ***[your initials] PP E3-3.xlsx***

1. Open the ***[your initials] PP E3-2*** workbook.
2. Save the workbook as ***[your initials] PP E3-3***.
3. Create a pie chart for total sales revenue.
   a. Select the **Location 1 – Cass Lake** tab.
   b. Select cells **A5:A8** as the category.
   c. Hold down **Ctrl** and select cells **H5:H8** as the data series.
   d. Click the **Insert Pie or Doughnut Chart** button [*Insert* tab, *Charts* group].
   e. Choose **3-D Pie** (Figure 3-49).
   f. Click the **Move Chart** button [*Chart Tools Design* tab, *Location* group].
   g. Click the **New sheet** button and type Pie Chart as the sheet name.
   h. Click **OK**.

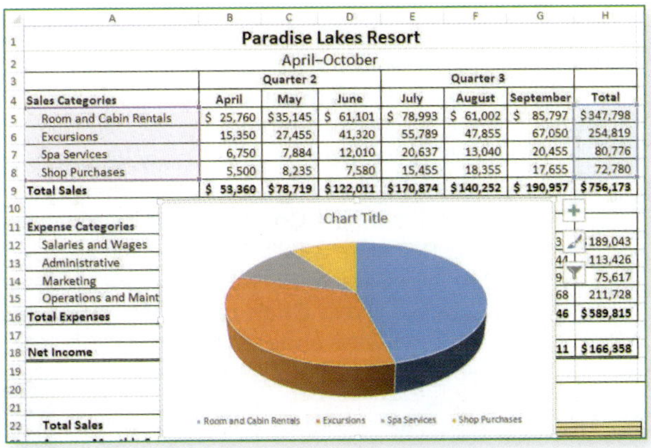

3-49 Pie chart object inserted

4. Format a pie chart.
   a. Select the **Pie Chart** tab.
   b. Click the **Chart Title** placeholder to select it and then triple-click the **Chart Title** placeholder text.
   c. Type Second and Third Quarters and press **Enter**.
   d. Type Sources of Revenue on the second line.
   e. Drag to select the first line of the title.
   f. From the mini toolbar, change the font size to **24 pt**.
   g. Drag to select the second line of the title.
   h. From the mini toolbar, change the font size to **18 pt**. (Figure 3-50).
   i. Click the chart area to deselect the title.
   j. Double-click the pie to open the *Format Data Series* task pane.
   k. Click the **Series Options** button in the *Format Data Series* task pane.
   l. Click the **Room and Cabin Rentals** slice to change to the *Format Data Point* task pane.

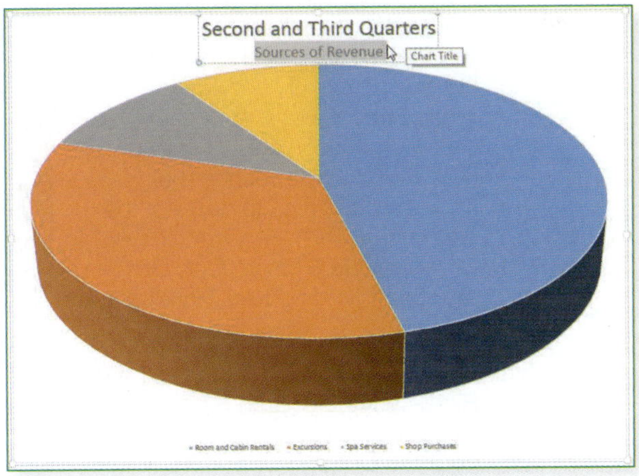

3-50 Chart titles typed and sized

m. Set the pie explosion percentage at **10%**.
n. Close the task pane.
o. Select the legend at the bottom of the chart to display selection handles.
p. Click the *Home* tab and change the font size to **12 pt**.
q. Point at the legend border (its edge) to display a move pointer.
r. Drag the legend object slightly closer to the chart (Figure 3-51).
s. Click the chart area to deselect the legend.

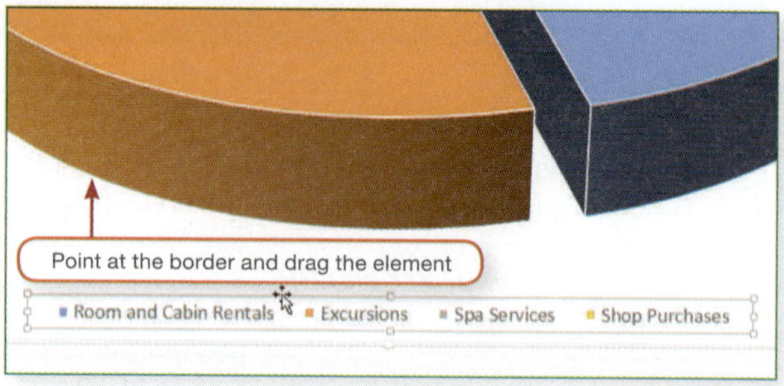

3-51 Selected legend and move pointer

5. Create a combination chart for total sales revenue and room and cabin rentals.
   a. Select the **Location 1 – Cass Lake** tab.
   b. Select cells **A4:G5** as one data series and category.
   c. Hold down **Ctrl** and select cells **A9:G9** as another data series and category.
   d. Click the **Insert Combo Chart** button [*Insert* tab, *Charts* group] (Figure 3-52).
   e. Choose **Clustered Column – Line on Secondary Axis**.
   f. Click the **Move Chart** button [*Chart Tools Design* tab, *Location* group].
   g. Click the **New sheet** button and type Combo Chart as the sheet name.
   h. Click **OK**.

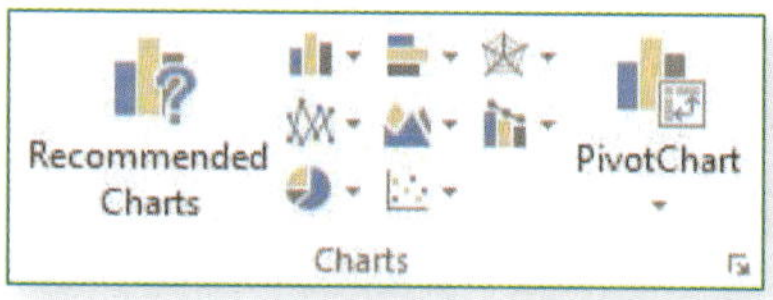

3-52 ***Insert Combo Chart* button**

6. Format a combination chart.
   a. Select the **Combo Chart** tab.
   b. Click to select the **Chart Title** placeholder and then triple-click the **Chart Title** placeholder text.
   c. Type Second and Third Quarters and press **Enter**.
   d. Type Comparison of Rentals and Total Sales on the second line.
   e. Click the chart area to deselect the chart title.
   f. Choose **Style 6** [*Chart Tools Design* tab, *Chart Styles* group] (Figure 3-53).

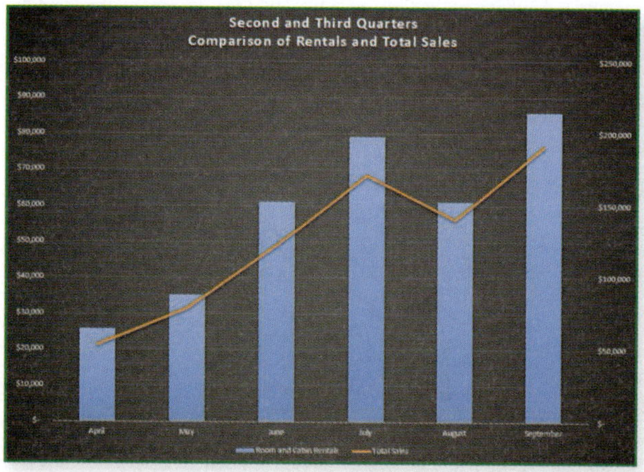

3-53 Combo chart with Style 6

7. Insert sparklines in a worksheet.
   a. Select the **Location 1 – Cass Lake** tab.
   b. Right-click the column **H** heading and choose **Insert** to insert a new column.
   c. Select the cell range **B5:G8** as the data to be charted with sparklines.
   d. Click the **Column Sparkline** button [*Insert* tab, *Sparklines* group].
   e. Click in the **Location Range** box.
   f. Click and drag to select cells **H5:H8**.
   g. Click **OK**.

8. Format sparklines.
    a. Click any cell in the sparkline group.
    b. Click the **Sparkline Color** button [*Sparkline Tools Design* tab, *Style* group] and select **Green, Accent 6, Darker 25%**.
    c. While the sparkline group is selected, click the **Format** button [*Home* tab, *Cells* group] and change the **Row Height** to **30 (40 pixels)**.
    d. Set column **H** to a width of **16.00 (117 pixels)**.
    e. Click **OK**.
9. Save and close the workbook (Figure 3-54).

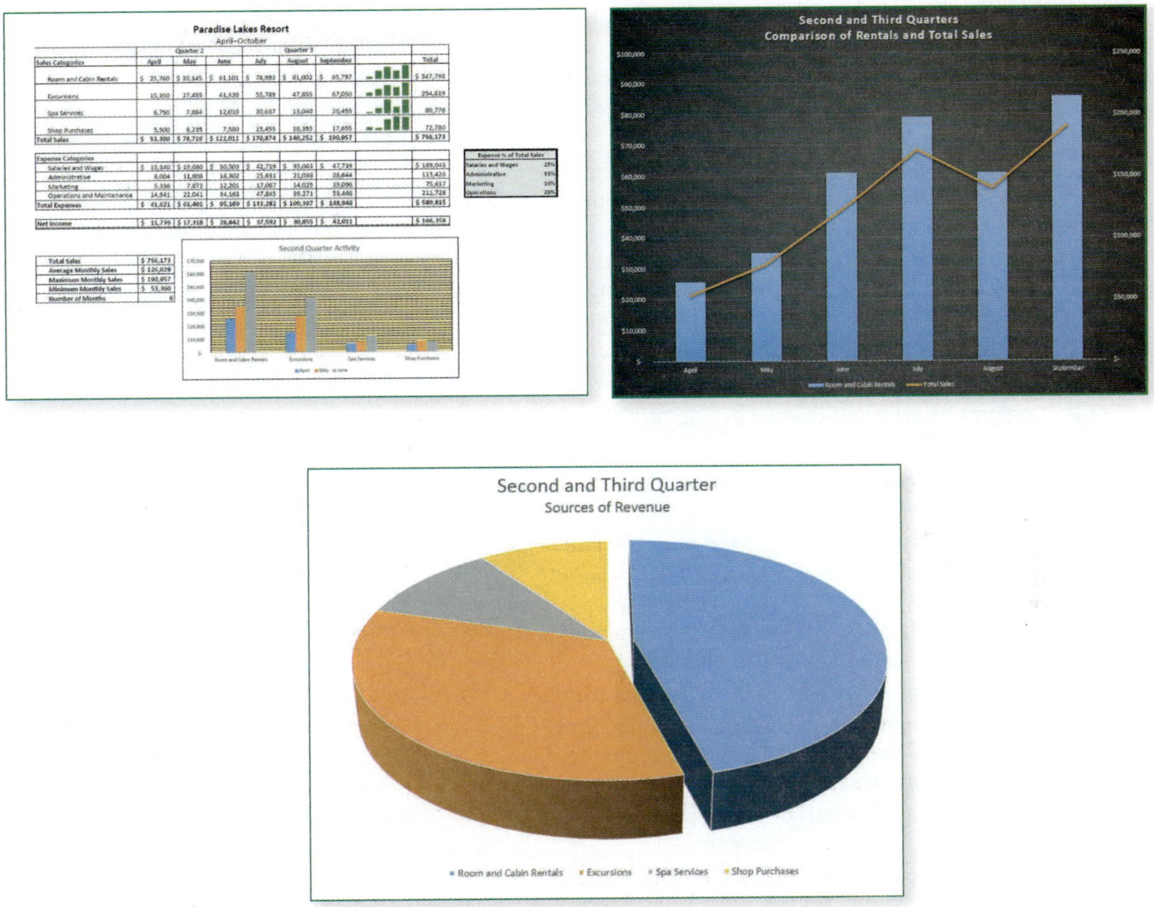

3-54 PP E3-3 completed worksheet and chart sheets

Chapter Summary

3.1 Create, size, and position an Excel chart object and create a chart sheet (p. E3-134).

- A ***chart object*** is a selectable object surrounded by a square border that contains many customizable chart elements like data labels or a chart title.
- Commonly used chart types are ***Column***, ***Line***, ***Pie***, and ***Bar***, but Excel can also create sophisticated statistical, financial, and scientific charts.
- The cells used to build a chart are its ***source data***.
- You can size and position the chart object in a worksheet.
- A ***chart sheet*** is an Excel chart that is displayed on its own sheet tab in the workbook but is still linked to the source data.
- You can move a chart object to its own sheet by clicking the ***Move Chart*** button in the *Location* group on the *Chart Tools Design* tab.
- You can name a chart sheet tab to indicate the purpose or type of its chart.

3.2 Design a chart using *Quick Layouts* and chart styles (p. E3-137).

- A ***chart layout*** is a preset group of elements in a chart.
- You can apply a *Quick Layout* from the ***Quick Layout*** button [*Chart Tools Design* tab, *Chart Layouts* group].
- A ***Chart Style*** is a predefined combination of colors and effects for chart elements.
- Chart styles are based on the workbook theme.
- Apply a chart style by selecting a style from the gallery in the *Chart Styles* group on the *Chart Tools Design* tab.
- You can print a chart object with its worksheet data using the *Backstage* view.
- Print options for charts are the same as for a worksheet.
- A chart sheet prints on its own sheet in landscape orientation.

3.3 Switch row and column data, add or remove chart elements, change the chart type, and edit source data (p. E3-141).

- Excel plots source data based on the number of rows and columns selected; this determines what is shown on the horizontal or vertical axis.
- You can switch the row and column data when appropriate.
- A ***chart element*** is a selectable component that is part of the chart.
- Chart elements include chart and axes titles, data labels, legends, gridlines, and trendlines.
- You can change some chart types into another type. Use the ***Change Chart Type*** button on the *Chart Tools Design* tab.
- You can filter chart data to show or hide values or categories without changing the source data.
- Source data for a chart can be edited to add or delete a data series.

3.4 Format chart elements with shape styles, fill, outlines, and special effects (p. E3-148).

- Select a chart element with the pointer to format it or use the ***Current Selection*** group on the *Chart Tools Format* tab.
- A ***Shape Style*** is a predesigned combination of fill, borders, and effects.
- You can apply ***Shape Fill***, ***Shape Outline,*** and ***Shape Effects*** separately from the *Chart Tools Format* tab.
- A chart element has its own *Format* task pane that includes fill, outline, and effects commands as well as specific options for the element.

3.5 Use images, shapes, and *WordArt* in a chart (p. E3-152).

- You can use a picture as fill for a shape.
- Select appropriately sized and designed images from your own or online sources.
- Insert shapes into a chart from the *Insert Shapes* group on the *Chart Tools Format* tab.
- You can apply ***WordArt*** to a chart title for special effect.
- Use the *Text Box* or *WordArt* buttons in the *Text* group on the *Insert* tab to add extra labels.

3.6 Create a pie chart and a combination chart (p. E3-157).

- A ***pie chart*** has one data series; it shows each data point as a part of the whole.
- Pie charts have many of the same elements as other charts, but they do not have axes.

- A ***combination chart*** uses two chart types to highlight differences in data or values.
- You can format a combination chart to show a secondary axis on the right side of the chart when values are widely different.

3.7 Insert and format sparklines in a worksheet (p. E3-161).

- A ***sparkline*** is a miniature chart in a cell or range of cells in the worksheet.
- Three sparkline types are available: ***Line, Column***, and ***Win/Loss***.
- Add sparklines to a worksheet from the *Sparklines* group on the *Insert* tab.
- Sparklines are grouped and can be formatted from the *Sparkline Tools Design* tab.
- Formatting options for sparklines include changing the color and identifying markers such as high and low values.
- Delete sparklines from a worksheet with the ***Clear Selected Sparklines*** button on the *Sparkline Tools Design* tab.

Check for Understanding

On the ***Online Learning Center*** for this text (www.mhhe.com/office2013inpractice), there are a variety of resources that can be used to review the concepts covered in this chapter.

The following Online Learning Resources are available on the Online Learning Center:

- Multiple choice questions
- Short answer questions
- Matching exercises

USING MICROSOFT EXCEL 2013

Guided Project 3-1

Life's Animal Shelter (LAS) is an animal care and adoption agency that accepts all unwanted or stray domestic animals. For this project, you create several expense charts and insert sparklines to help the agency track its expenses for the first six months of the year.
[Student Learning Outcomes 3.1, 3.2, 3.3, 3.4, 3.5, 3.6, 3.7]

File Needed: ***LASExpenses-03.xlsx***
Completed Project File Name: ***[your initials] Excel 3-1.xlsx***

Skills Covered in This Project

- Create a chart object.
- Create a chart sheet.
- Apply *Quick Layouts* and chart styles.
- Add and format chart elements.
- Change chart type.
- Filter the data series.
- Insert a shape in a chart.
- Create and format a combination chart.
- Insert and format sparklines in a sheet.

---

1. Open the ***LASExpenses-03*** workbook from your student data files folder.
2. Save the workbook as ***[your initials] Excel 3-1***.
3. Create a pie chart object.
   a. Select cells **A4:A10**. Hold down **Ctrl** and select cells **I4:I10**.
   b. Click the **Insert Pie or Doughnut Chart** button [*Insert* tab, *Charts* group].
   c. Select the **2D-Pie** chart subtype.
4. Apply a chart style.
   a. Select the chart object.
   b. Click the **More** button [*Chart Tools Design* tab, *Chart Styles* group] and select **Style 12**.
5. Edit and format chart elements.
   a. Click the chart title.
   b. Place the insertion point in front of "Totals" in the title.
   c. Type Year-to-Date Expense and press the **spacebar** once.
   d. Click the chart area to deselect the title.
   e. Select the legend element.
   f. Click the **Font Size** arrow [*Home* tab, *Font* group] and change the size to **12 pt**. (Figure 3-55).
   g. Select the chart area.

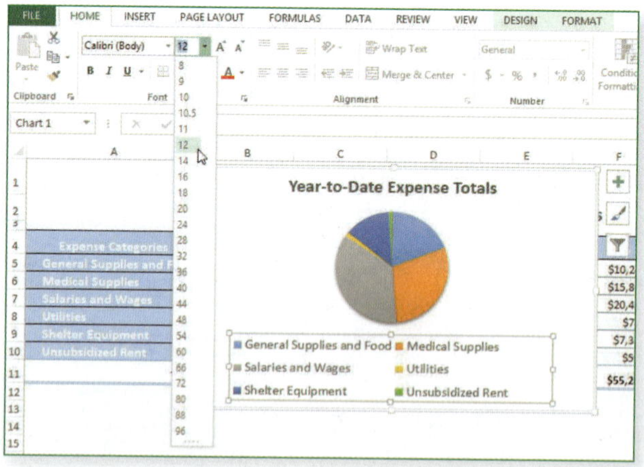

3-55 Legend selected for font size change

h. Click the **Shape Outline** button drop-down arrow [*Chart Tools Format* tab, *Shape Styles* group].
i. Choose **Black, Text 1** as the color.
j. Click the **Shape Outline** drop-down arrow again.
k. Choose **Weight** and **1 pt**.

6. Create a chart sheet.
   a. Click the pie chart object to select it.
   b. Click the **Move Chart** button [*Chart Tools Design* tab, *Location* group].
   c. Click the **New sheet** button.
   d. Type Pie Chart in the text box.
   e. Click **OK**.

7. Create a bar chart object.
   a. Click the **Half-Year Expenses** sheet tab.
   b. Select cells **A4:G10** as the source data range.
   c. Click the **Quick Analysis** button and select **Charts**.
   d. Select **Clustered Bar**.
   e. Point at the chart area to display a move pointer.
   f. Drag the chart object so its top left corner is at cell **B13**.
   g. Point at the bottom right selection handle to display a resize pointer.
   h. Drag the pointer to reach cell **G30** (Figure 3-56).

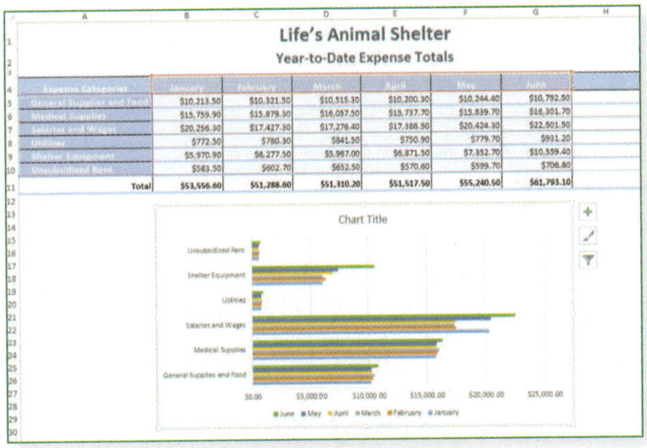

3-56 Bar chart object sized and positioned

8. Change the chart type.
   a. Click the chart object.
   b. Click the **Change Chart Type** button [*Chart Tools Design* tab, *Type* group].
   c. Click the **Recommended Charts** tab.
   d. Choose **Clustered Column** in the left pane.
   e. Click **OK**.

9. Filter the source data.
   a. Click the chart object.
   b. Click the **Chart Filters** button at the top right corner of the chart.
   c. Click to remove the check marks for **January**, **February**, and **March**.
   d. Click **Apply** in the *Chart Filters* pane (Figure 3-57).
   e. Click the **Chart Filters** button to close the pane.

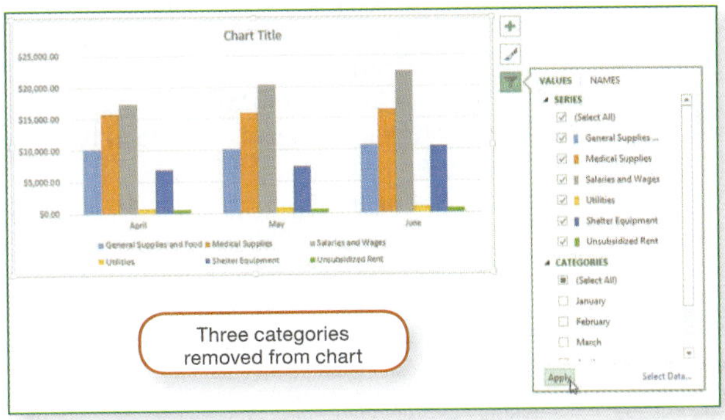

3-57 Chart filter applied

10. Edit and format chart elements.
   a. Click the chart title placeholder.
   b. Point at the text and triple-click or drag to select all the text.
   c. Type Second Quarter Expenses.
   d. Click the chart area to deselect the title.

e. Click to select the legend element.
f. Click the **Font Size** arrow [*Home* tab, *Font* group] and change the size to **8 pt**.
g. Click to select the chart area.
h. Click the **Shape Outline** button drop-down arrow [*Chart Tools Format* tab, *Shape Styles* group].
i. Choose **Black**, **Text 1** as the color.
j. Click the **Shape Outline** drop-down arrow again.
k. Choose **Weight** and **1 pt**.

11. Create a combination chart sheet.
    a. Select cells **A8:G8**. Hold down **Ctrl** and select cells **A11:G11**.
    b. Click the **Insert Combo Chart** button [*Insert* tab, *Charts* group].
    c. Select the **Clustered Column-Line** chart subtype.
    d. Click the combo chart object to select it.
    e. Click the **Move Chart** button [*Chart Tools Design* tab, *Location* group].
    f. Click the **New sheet** button.
    g. Type Combo Chart.
    h. Click **OK**.
    i. Click the **Change Chart Type** button [*Chart Tools Design* tab, *Type* group].
    j. Click the **Secondary Axis** check box for the line chart (Figure 3-58).
    k. Click **OK**.

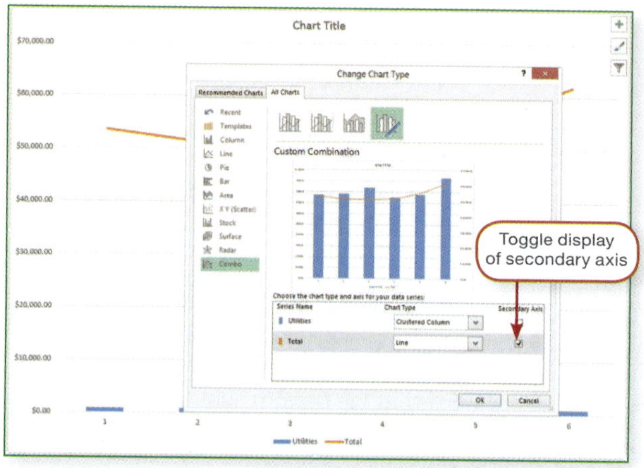

3-58 Combo chart and a secondary axis

12. Edit and format chart elements.
    a. Click the chart title placeholder.
    b. Point at the text and triple-click or drag to select all the text.
    c. Type Utilities Expense and Total Expenses.
    d. Click the chart area to deselect the title.
    e. Apply a **1 pt**. **black** outline to the chart area.

13. Insert sparklines in worksheet.
    a. Click the **Half-Year Expenses** sheet tab.
    b. Select cells **B5:G10** as the data range.
    c. Click the **Column Sparkline** button [*Insert* tab, *Sparklines* group].
    d. Click in the **Location Range** box.
    e. Click and drag to select cells **H5:H10**.
    f. Click **OK**.
    g. Click the **Format** button [*Home* tab, *Cells* group] and set the **Row Height** to **35**.
    h. Click the **Sparkline Color** button [*Sparkline Tools Design* tab, *Style* group] and select **White**, **Background 1**, **Darker 50%**.

14. Insert a shape in a chart.
    a. Click the **More** button [*Chart Tools Format* tab, *Insert Shapes* group].
    b. Select the text box shape.
    c. Draw a text box like the one shown in Figure 3-59.

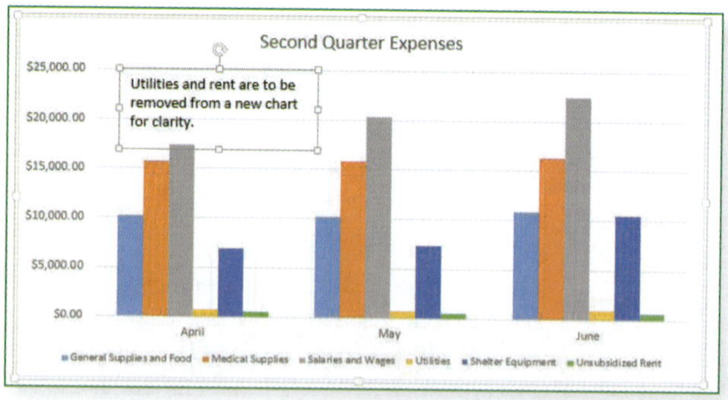

3-59 Text box shape inserted in chart

d. Type Utilities and rent are to be removed from a new chart for clarity.
e. Drag a selection handle to size the text box shape if necessary.
f. Point at an edge of the shape to display a four-pointed arrow and position it if needed.

15. Save and close the workbook (Figure 3-60).

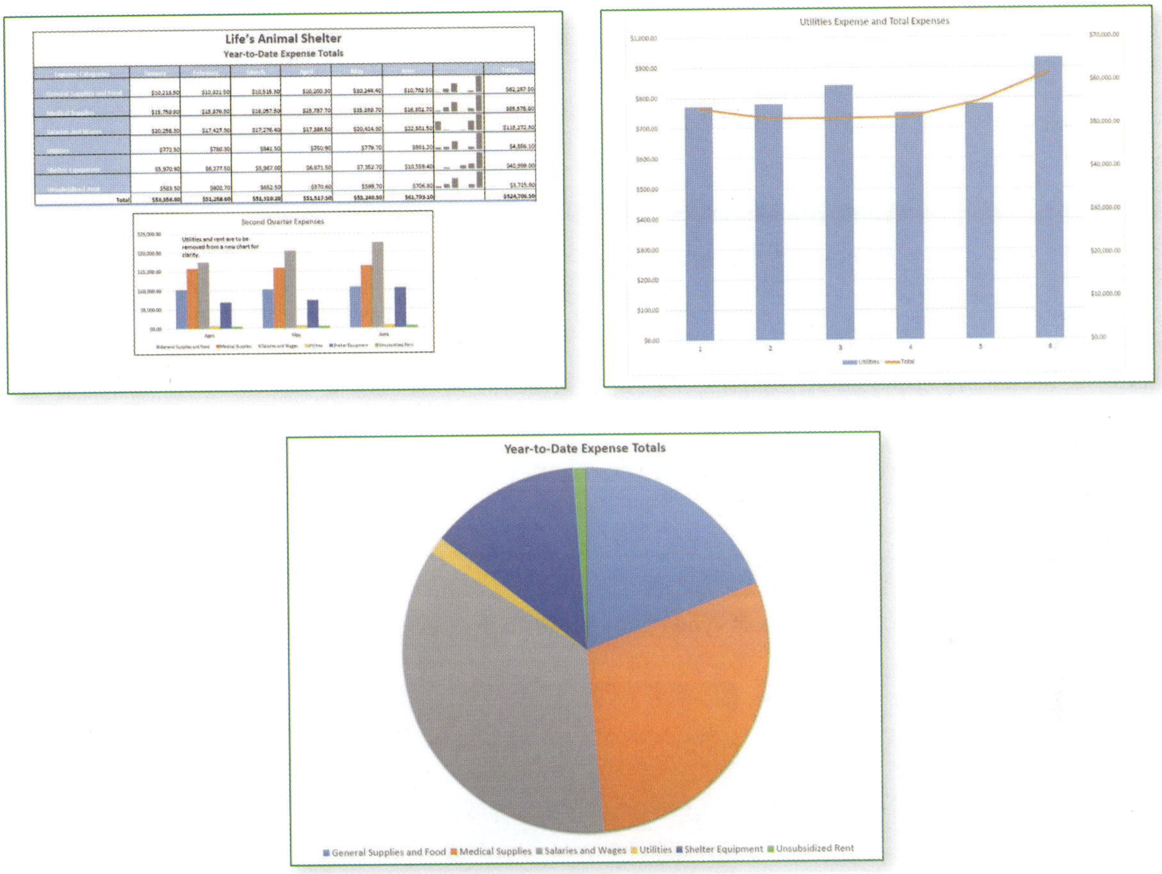

3-60 Excel 3-1 completed charts and worksheet

Guided Project 3-2

Wear-Ever Shoes is an shoe outlet with several locations. In a worksheet that tracks sales of popular items for the past six months, you create a bar chart to compare the number of pairs sold by style. You also create a combination chart to compare the number of pairs sold and the unit cost for each style.
[Student Learning Outcomes 3.1, 3.2, 3.3, 3.4, 3.5, 3.6]

File Needed: ***WearEverSales-03.xlsx***
Completed Project File Name: ***[your initials] Excel 3-2.xlsx***

Skills Covered in This Project

- Create a chart sheet.
- Change the chart type.
- Apply a chart style.
- Add and format chart elements.
- Use a picture as fill.
- Create and format a combination chart.
- Use *WordArt* in a chart.

1. Open the ***WearEverSales-03*** workbook from your student data files folder.
2. Save the workbook as ***[your initials] Excel 3-2***.
3. Create a column chart sheet.
   a. Select cells **A5:B16**.
   b. Click the **Quick Analysis** button and choose **Charts**.
   c. Select **Clustered Column**.
   d. Click the chart object to select it.
   e. Click the **Move Chart** button [*Chart Tools Design* tab, *Location* group].
   f. Click the **New sheet** button.
   g. Type Sales Chart.
   h. Click **OK**.
4. Change the chart type.
   a. Click the **Sales Chart** sheet tab if necessary.
   b. Click the **Change Chart Type** button [*Chart Tools Design* tab, *Type* group].
   c. Click the **Recommended Charts** tab.
   d. Choose **Clustered Bar** in the left pane.
   e. Click **OK**.
5. Apply a chart style.
   a. Select the chart sheet if necessary.
   b. Click the **Chart Styles** button in the top right corner of the chart.
   c. Select **Style 7** (Figure 3-61).
   d. Click the **Chart Styles** button to close the pane.
6. Use a picture as fill for a data point.
   a. Select the chart sheet if necessary.

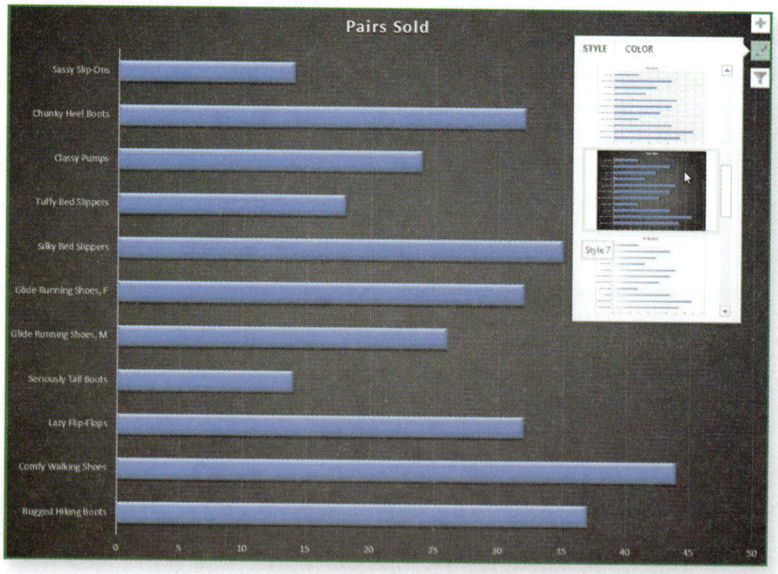

3-61 *Chart Styles* button and pane

b. Double-click any one of the bars to select the data series and open the *Format Data Series* task pane.
c. Point and click at the "Classy Pumps" bar to select it and display the *Format Data Point* task pane.
d. Click the **Fill & Line** button in the task pane.
e. Click **Fill** to expand the command group.
f. Click the **Picture or texture fill** button.
g. Click **Online** to open the *Insert Pictures* dialog box.
h. Type heels in the *Office.com Clip Art* search box and press **Enter** (Figure 3-62).
i. Select the image and click **Insert**.
j. Click **Stack** in the task pane.
k. Close the task pane and click the chart area.

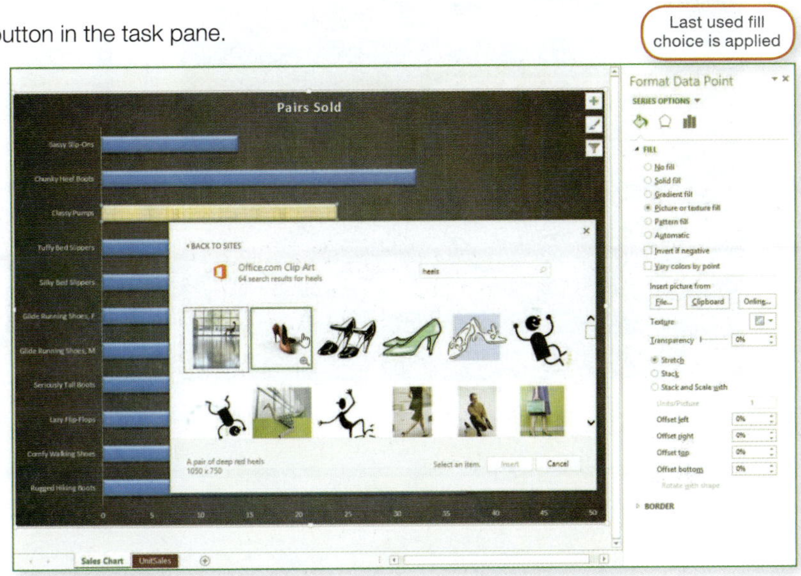

3-62 Online image search for fill in a data point

7. Create a combination chart sheet.
   a. Click the **Unit Sales** sheet tab.
   b. Select cells **A5:A16**. Hold down **Ctrl** and select cells **E5:F16**.
   c. Click the **Insert Combo Chart** button [*Insert* tab, *Charts* group].
   d. Select the **Clustered Column-Line on Secondary Axis** chart subtype.
   e. Select the combo chart object.
   f. Click the **Move Chart** button [*Chart Tools Design* tab, *Location* group].
   g. Click the **New sheet** button.
   h. Type Cost vs. Selling Price.
   i. Click **OK**.

8. Edit chart elements.
   a. Click the chart title placeholder.
   b. Select all the text in the placeholder.
   c. Type Cost and Selling Price Comparison.
   d. Select all the text in the chart title again.
   e. From the mini toolbar, change the font size to **20 pt**.
   f. Select the chart area.
   g. Apply a **1 pt**. **black** outline.

9. Use *WordArt* in a chart.
   a. Click the chart title.
   b. Click the **More** button [*Chart Tools Format* tab, *WordArt Style* group].
   c. Choose **Fill–Blue**, **Accent 1**, **Shadow**.
   d. Click the chart area to deselect the title.

10. Save and close the workbook (Figure 3-63).

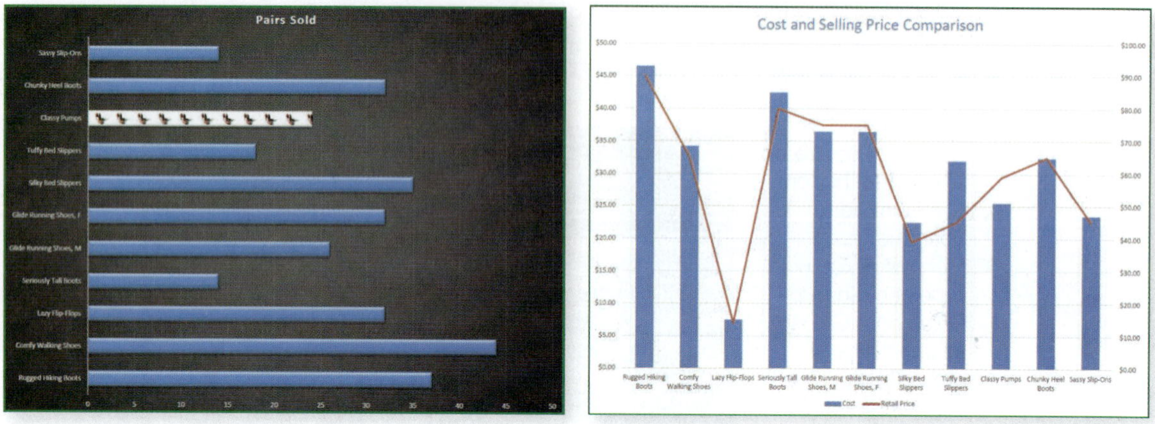

3-63 Excel 3-2 completed chart sheets

Guided Project 3-3

Blue Lake Sports has locations in several major cities and tracks sales by department in each store. For this project, you create a pie chart that shows each store's share of golf-related sales for the first quarter. You also create a line chart to illustrate week-to-week sales for specific departments in one of the stores and insert sparklines in the data.
[Student Learning Outcomes 3.1, 3.2, 3.3, 3.4, 3.6, 3.7]

File Needed: ***BlueLakeSports-03.xlsx***
Completed Project File Name: ***[your initials] Excel 3-3.xlsx***

Skills Covered in This Project

- Create, size, and position a pie chart object.
- Apply a chart style.
- Change chart type.
- Add and format chart elements in a pie chart.
- Create a line chart sheet.
- Apply a chart layout.
- Add and format chart elements in a line chart.
- Insert and format sparklines in a sheet.

1. Open the ***BlueLakeSports-03*** workbook from your student data files folder.
2. Save the workbook as ***[your initials] Excel 3-3***.
3. Select the **Revenue by Department** tab.

4. Create a pie chart object.
    a. Select cells **A4:F4**, hold down **Ctrl**, and select cells **A13:F13**.
    b. Click the **Recommended Charts** button [*Insert* tab, *Charts* group].
    c. Choose **Pie** and click **OK**.
5. Apply a chart style.
    a. Select the chart object.
    b. Click the **More** button [*Chart Tools Design* tab, *Chart Styles* group].
    c. Select **Style 12**.
6. Size and position a chart object.
    a. Point at the chart area to display the move pointer.
    b. Drag the chart object so its top left corner is at cell **A21**.
    c. Point at the bottom right selection handle to display the resize pointer.
    d. Drag the pointer to cell **G36**.
7. Change the chart type.
    a. Click the pie chart object.
    b. Click the **Change Chart Type** button [*Chart Tools Design* tab, *Type* group].
    c. Click the **All Charts** tab.
    d. Choose **Pie** in the left pane.
    e. Choose **3-D Pie** and click **OK**.
8. Format pie chart elements.
    a. Double-click the pie to open the *Format Data Series* task pane.
    b. Click the **Atlanta** slice to update the pane to the *Format Data Point* task pane.
    c. Click the **Series Options** button in the *Format Data Series* task pane.
    d. Set the pie explosion percentage at **10%**.
    e. Close the task pane and click the chart area to deselect the **Atlanta** slice.
9. Add and format chart elements in a pie chart.
    a. Select the chart object if necessary.
    b. Click the **Chart Elements** button at the top right corner of the chart.
    c. Click the **Data Labels** check box (Figure 3-64).
    d. Display the submenu for **Data Labels** and choose **More Options**.
    e. In the *Format Data Point* task pane, click the **Label Options** button if necessary.

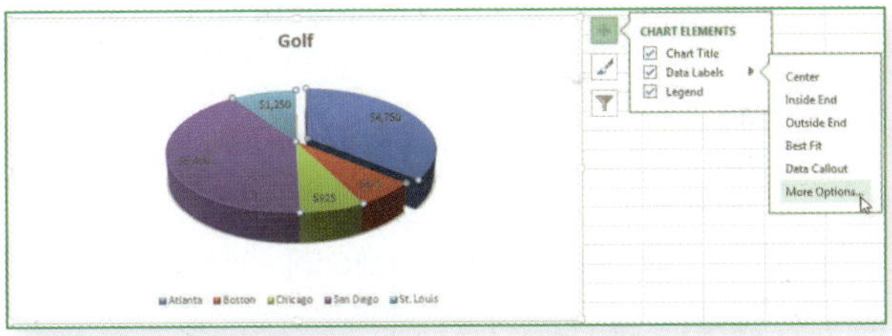

3-64 Data labels added to chart

    f. Click **Label Options** to expand the menu and click **Percentage** check box to show the percentage for each slice.
    g. Click to clear the **Value** check box and close the task pane.
    h. While the data labels are selected, press **Ctrl+B** to apply bold to the labels.
    i. While the data labels are selected, change the font size to **12 pt**. [*Home* tab, *Font* group].
    j. Click a worksheet cell to deselect the data labels and click the chart object to select it.
    k. Click the **Shape Outline** button drop-down arrow [*Chart Tools Format* tab, *Shape Styles* group] and choose **Purple**, **Accent 4**, **Darker 50%** as the color.
    l. Click the **Shape Outline** drop-down arrow again and choose **Weight** and **1 pt**.
10. Create a line chart sheet.
    a. Select the **Atlanta Revenue by Week** tab.
    b. Select cells **A4:E7**.

c. Click the **Quick Analysis** button and choose **Charts**.
d. Select **Line**.
e. Click the **Move Chart** button [*Chart Tools Design* tab, *Location* group].
f. Click the **New sheet** button.
g. Type Promo Depts.
h. Click **OK**.

11. Apply a chart layout.
    a. Select the chart sheet if necessary.
    b. Click the **Quick Layout** button [*Chart Tools Design* tab, *Chart Layouts* group].
    c. Select **Layout 5** to add a data table to the chart sheet (Figure 3-65).

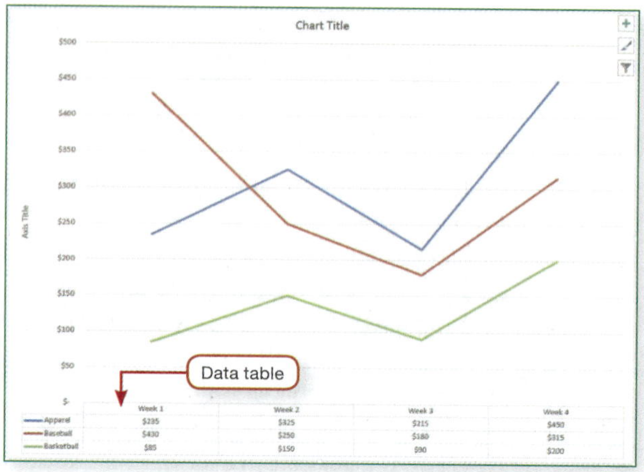

3-65 Data table added by chart layout

12. Change the chart type.
    a. Right-click the **Promo Depts** chart and select **Change Chart Type**.
    b. On the **All Charts** tab, choose **Line with Markers** in the **Line** category.
    c. Click **OK**.

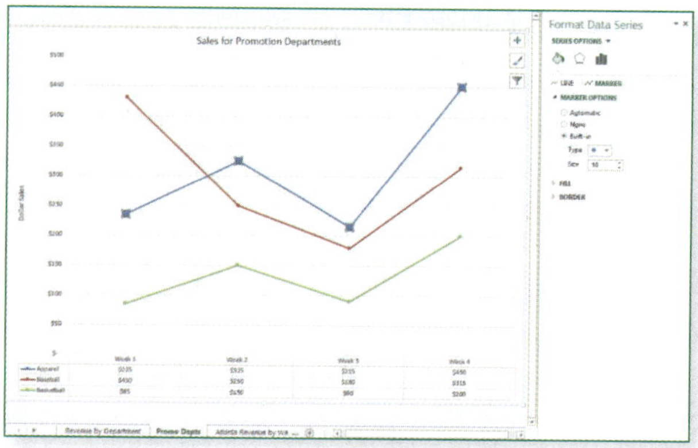

3-66 Marker options for the data series

13. Edit chart elements in a line chart.
    a. Click the chart title placeholder.
    b. Type Sales for Promotion Departments and press **Enter**.
    c. Click the vertical axis title placeholder.
    d. Type Dollar Sales and press **Enter**.
    e. Click the **Chart Elements** drop-down arrow [*Chart Tools Format* tab, *Current Selection* group].
    f. Choose **Series "Apparel"** to select the line in the chart.
    g. Click the **Format Selection** button [*Chart Tools Format* tab, *Current Selection* group].
    h. Click the **Fill & Line** button in the *Format Data Series* task pane.
    i. Click **Marker** and then click **Marker Options** to expand the group (Figure 3-66).
    j. Click **Built-in** and set a size of **10 pt**.
    k. Click the **Series Options** triangle and choose **Series "Baseball"** to select that data series (Figure 3-67).
    l. Make the same marker changes for the baseball series.
    m. Select the basketball series and make the same marker changes.
    n. Close the task pane and select the chart area.

14. Insert sparklines in worksheet.
    a. Click the **Atlanta Revenue by Week** sheet tab.
    b. Right-click the **column F** heading and choose **Insert** to insert a new column.
    c. Select cells **B5:E18** as the data range.

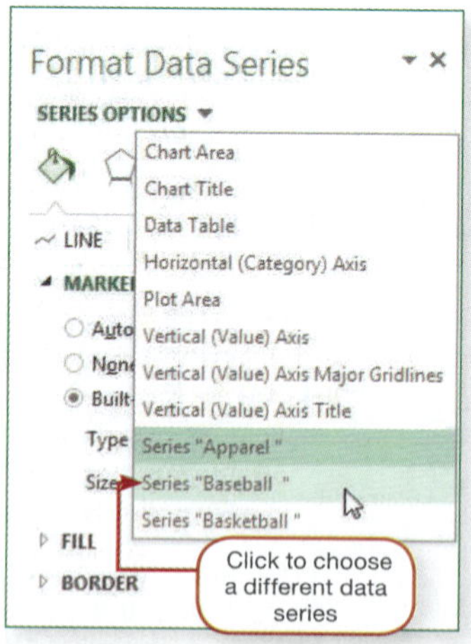

3-67 New data series selected

d. Click the **Line Sparkline** button [*Insert* tab, *Sparklines* group].
e. Click in the **Location Range** box.
f. Click and drag to select cells **F5:F18**.
g. Click **OK**.

15. Format sparklines in worksheet.
    a. Click the **Format** button [*Home* tab, *Cells* group] and set the **Row Height** to **24**.
    b. Click the **Format** button [*Home* tab, *Cells* group] and set the **Column Width** to **35**.
    c. Click to place a check mark for **Markers** in the *Show* group in the *Sparkline Tools Design* tab.
    d. Click the **Sparkline Color** button [*Sparkline Tools Design* tab, *Style* group].
    e. Choose **Black, Text 1** for the line color.
16. Change the page orientation to landscape.
17. Save and close the workbook (Figure 3-68).

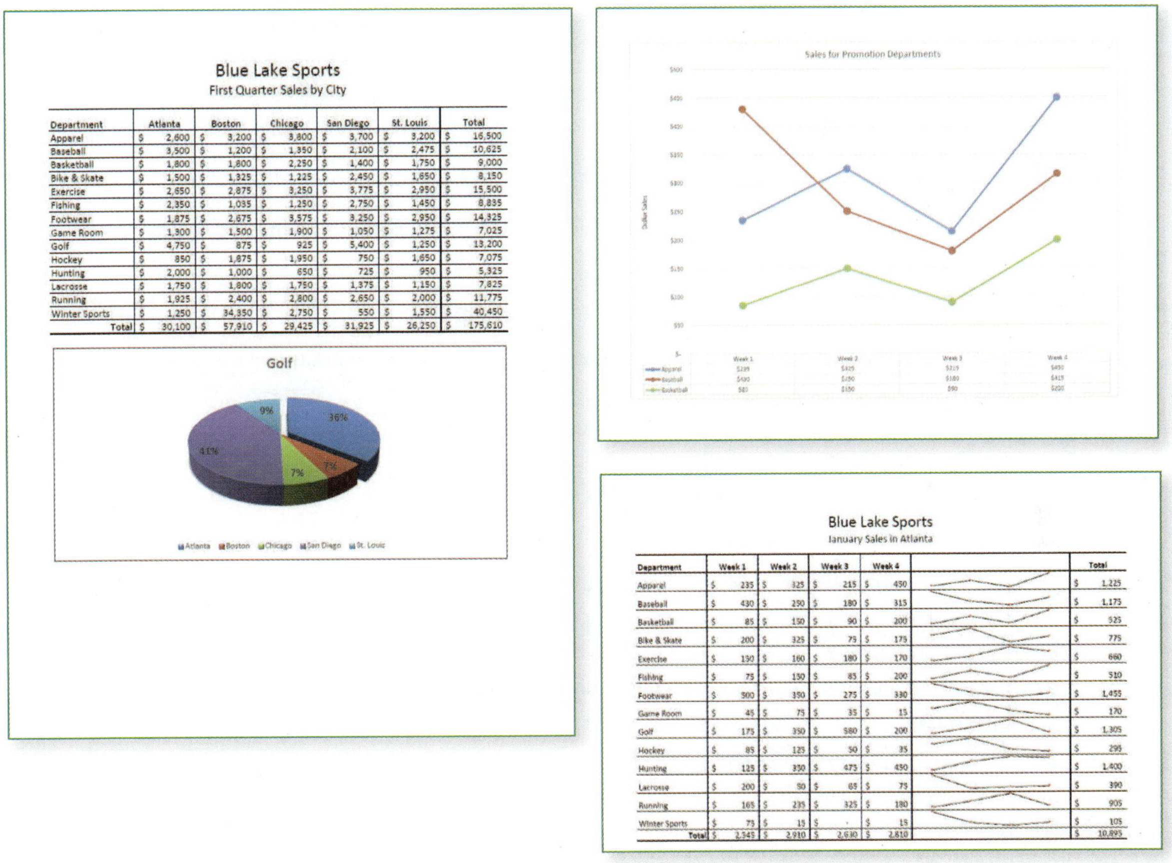

Department	Atlanta	Boston	Chicago	San Diego	St. Louis	Total
Apparel	$ 2,600	$ 3,200	$ 3,800	$ 3,700	$ 3,200	$ 16,500
Baseball	$ 3,500	$ 1,200	$ 1,350	$ 2,100	$ 2,475	$ 10,625
Basketball	$ 1,800	$ 1,800	$ 2,250	$ 1,400	$ 1,750	$ 9,000
Bike & Skate	$ 1,500	$ 1,325	$ 1,225	$ 2,450	$ 1,650	$ 8,150
Exercise	$ 2,650	$ 2,875	$ 3,250	$ 3,775	$ 2,950	$ 15,500
Fishing	$ 2,350	$ 1,035	$ 1,250	$ 2,750	$ 1,450	$ 8,835
Footwear	$ 1,875	$ 2,675	$ 3,575	$ 3,250	$ 2,950	$ 14,325
Game Room	$ 1,300	$ 1,500	$ 1,900	$ 1,050	$ 1,275	$ 7,025
Golf	$ 4,750	$ 875	$ 925	$ 5,400	$ 1,250	$ 13,200
Hockey	$ 850	$ 1,875	$ 1,950	$ 750	$ 1,650	$ 7,075
Hunting	$ 2,000	$ 1,000	$ 650	$ 725	$ 950	$ 5,325
Lacrosse	$ 1,750	$ 1,800	$ 1,750	$ 1,375	$ 1,150	$ 7,825
Running	$ 1,925	$ 2,400	$ 2,800	$ 2,650	$ 2,000	$ 11,775
Winter Sports	$ 1,250	$ 34,350	$ 2,750	$ 550	$ 1,550	$ 40,450
Total	$ 30,100	$ 57,910	$ 29,425	$ 31,925	$ 26,250	$ 175,610

Department	Week 1	Week 2	Week 3	Week 4		Total
Apparel	$ 235	$ 325	$ 215	$ 450		$ 1,225
Baseball	$ 430	$ 250	$ 180	$ 315		$ 1,175
Basketball	$ 85	$ 150	$ 90	$ 200		$ 525
Bike & Skate	$ 200	$ 325	$ 75	$ 175		$ 775
Exercise	$ 150	$ 160	$ 180	$ 170		$ 660
Fishing	$ 75	$ 150	$ 85	$ 200		$ 510
Footwear	$ 500	$ 350	$ 275	$ 330		$ 1,455
Game Room	$ 45	$ 75	$ 35	$ 15		$ 170
Golf	$ 175	$ 350	$ 580	$ 200		$ 1,305
Hockey	$ 85	$ 125	$ 50	$ 35		$ 295
Hunting	$ 125	$ 350	$ 475	$ 450		$ 1,400
Lacrosse	$ 200	$ 50	$ 65	$ 75		$ 390
Running	$ 165	$ 235	$ 325	$ 180		$ 905
Winter Sports	$ 75	$ 15	$ -	$ 15		$ 105
Total	$ 2,545	$ 2,910	$ 2,630	$ 2,810		$ 10,895

3-68 Excel 3-3 completed worksheet and charts

Independent Project 3-4

For this project, you create a column chart to illustrate April–September revenue for Classic Gardens and Landscapes. You also create a pie chart sheet to graph the proportion that each category contributes to total revenue.
[Student Learning Outcomes 3.1, 3.2, 3.3, 3.4, 3.5, 3.6]

File Needed: ***ClassicGardensRevenue-03**.xlsx*
Completed Project File Name: ***[your initials] Excel 3-4**.xlsx*

Skills Covered in This Project

- Create a chart object.
- Size and position a chart object.
- Edit and format chart elements.
- Edit the source data for a chart.
- Use the *SUM* function in a worksheet.
- Create a pie chart sheet.
- Use texture as fill.
- Add and format data labels in a chart.

1. Open the ***ClassicGardensRevenue-03*** workbook from your student data files folder.
2. Save the workbook as ***[your initials] Excel 3-4***.
3. Create a *Clustered Column* chart object for cells **A4:G9**.
4. Move the chart object so that its top left corner is at cell **A12**. Size the bottom of the chart to reach cell **H30**.
5. Edit the chart title to display CGL Major Sales Revenue on one line and Second and Third Quarters on the second line.
6. Set the first line of the chart title to a font size of **20 pt**. Set the second title line to a size of **14 pt**.
7. Apply chart **Style 14** to the chart.
8. Apply a ½ **point Black**, **Text 1** outline to the chart.
9. Remove the *Design Consulting* data series from the chart using the resizing pointer.
10. Enter *SUM* functions for the total column **H5:H9** and total row **B10:H10**.
11. Create a **3-D Pie** chart sheet named Revenue Breakdown for cells **A4:A9** and **H4:H9**.
12. Edit the chart title to display Revenue by Category. Set the font size to **32**.
13. Apply the **Oak** texture fill to the *Tree and Shrubbery* slice.
14. Add a data label in the center of each slice.
    a. Choose the **Accounting** format and set **0** decimal places (Figure 3-69).
    b. While the data labels are selected, set the font size to **14 pt**. and make them **bold** [*Home* tab, *Font* group].

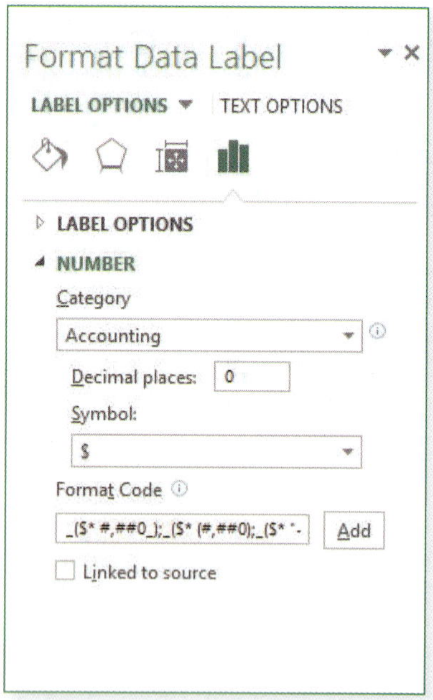

3-69 Data label options

15. Save and close the workbook (Figure 3-70).

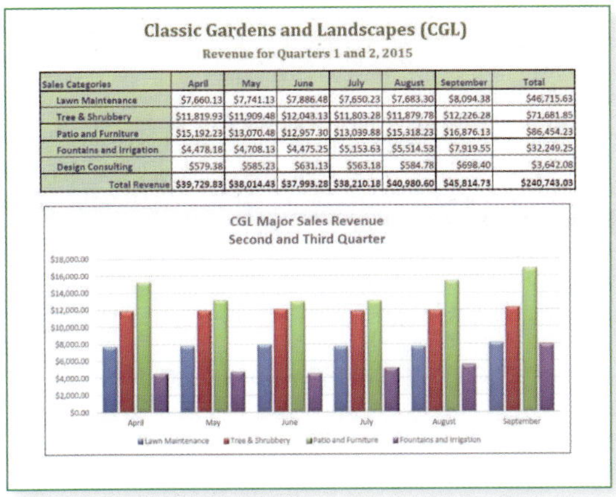
Classic Gardens and Landscapes (CGL)

Revenue for Quarters 1 and 2, 2015

Sales Categories	April	May	June	July	August	September	Total
Lawn Maintenance	$7,660.13	$7,741.13	$7,886.48	$7,650.23	$7,683.30	$8,094.38	$46,715.63
Tree & Shrubbery	$11,819.93	$11,909.48	$12,043.13	$11,803.28	$11,879.78	$12,226.28	$71,681.85
Patio and Furniture	$15,192.23	$13,070.48	$12,957.30	$13,039.88	$15,318.23	$16,876.13	$86,454.23
Fountains and Irrigation	$4,478.18	$4,708.13	$4,475.25	$5,153.63	$5,514.53	$7,919.55	$32,249.25
Design Consulting	$579.38	$585.23	$631.13	$563.18	$584.78	$698.40	$3,642.08
Total Revenue	$39,729.83	$38,014.43	$37,993.28	$38,210.18	$40,980.60	$45,814.73	$240,743.03

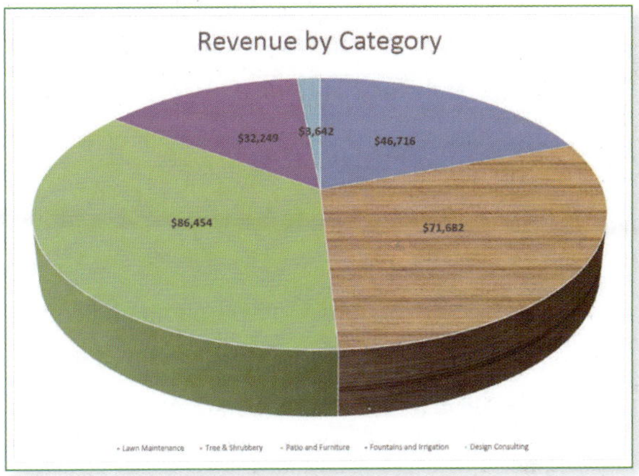

3-70 Excel 3-4 completed chart sheets

Independent Project 3-5

For this project, you create a stacked bar chart to illustrate projected tuition and fee amounts for Sierra Pacific Community College District (SPCCD). You also create a pie chart to show total projected revenue for the time period and add sparklines to the worksheet.
[Student Learning Outcomes 3.1, 3.2, 3.3, 3.4, 3.6, 3.7]

File Needed: ***SierraPacificCC-03.xlsx***
Completed Project File Name: ***[your initials] Excel 3-5.xlsx***

Skills Covered in This Project

- Create a chart object.
- Size and position a chart object.
- Apply a chart style.
- Switch row and column data.
- Edit chart source data.
- Create a pie chart sheet.
- Edit and format chart elements.
- Insert and format sparklines in a sheet.

1. Open the ***SierraPacificCC-03*** workbook from your student data files folder.
2. Save the workbook as ***[your initials] Excel 3-5***.
3. Select cells **A3:E7** and create a stacked bar chart object.
4. Size and position the chart below the worksheet data in cells **A10:G28**.
5. Apply **Chart Style 6**.

6. Edit the chart title to display Tuition Revenue Projection.
7. Apply a dark blue **½ pt**. outline to the chart object.
8. Switch the row and column data for the chart.
9. Edit the source data to remove the fees values from the chart.
10. Create a 3-D pie chart sheet for cells **A4:A7** and cells **G4:G7**. Move the chart to a new sheet named Total Revenue.
11. Apply **Chart Style 3** and a black **½ pt**. outline.
12. Edit the chart title to Projected Revenue Sources.
13. Move the legend to the bottom and change its font size to **12 pt**.
14. Create column sparklines for cells **B4:E7** in the worksheet so that they appear in cells **F4:F7**.
15. Save and close the workbook (Figure 3-71).

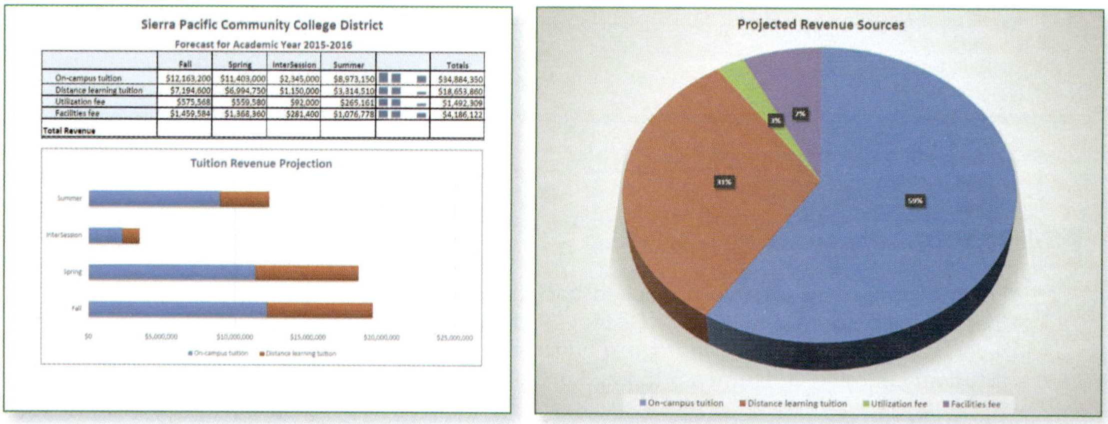

3-71 Excel 3-5 completed worksheet and chart

Independent Project 3-6

Courtyard Medical Plaza (CMP) is a full-service medical office complex providing customers with a variety of medical services in one location. For this project you create charts to illustrate data about the number of procedures performed at CMP as well as how patients come to the facility.
[Student Learning Outcomes 3.1, 3.2, 3.3, 3.4, 3.5]

File Needed: ***CourtyardMedical-03.xlsx***
Completed Project File Name: ***[your initials] Excel 3-6.xlsx***

Skills Covered in This Project

- *AutoFill* month names.
- Use the *SUM* function.
- Create a column chart sheet.
- Add and edit chart elements.
- Add and format a trendline in a chart.
- Insert a text box shape in a chart.
- Display gridlines in a chart.
- Use gradient fill for a chart object.

1. Open the ***CourtyardMedical-03*** workbook from your student data files folder.
2. Save the workbook as ***[your initials] Excel 3-6***.
3. On the **Patient Count** worksheet, select cell **C5** and use the *Fill Handle* to complete the month names.
4. Complete the totals in **N6:N10** and **B10:M10** using the *SUM* function.
   a. Select all the values and apply **Comma Style** with no decimal places.
   b. *AutoFit* columns **B:N**.
5. Create a clustered column chart sheet named Immed Care for cells **A5:M5** and cells **A7:M7**.
6. Edit the chart title to display Immediate Care Patient Count.
7. Click the **Chart Elements** button and add a linear trendline to the chart.
8. Format the trendline.
   a. In the *Forecast* group, set the **Forward** value to **12**.
   b. Choose **Olive Green, Accent 3** for the line color.
   c. Set the **Width** of the trendline to **4 pt**.
9. Insert a text box in the chart. Draw a text box between the 300 and 400 gridlines and type The number of patients who come in for Immediate Care services will continue to grow. (Figure 3-72).

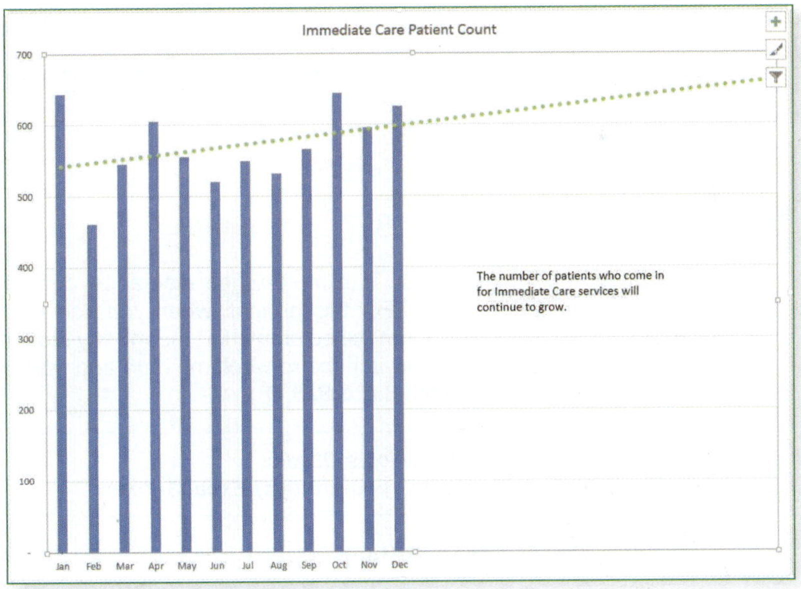

3-72 Text box shape in a chart

10. On the **Procedures Count** worksheet, select cells **A5:D16** and create a clustered column chart object. Move the chart to a new sheet named Procedures Chart.
11. Edit the chart title to display Number of Procedures on the first line and Three-Year Period on the second line.

12. Add **Primary Major Vertical** gridlines.
13. Format the plot area.
    a. Apply the fill **Tan**, **Background 2**, **Darker 10%**.
    b. Apply the **Gradient** shape fill. Choose **Linear Down**.
14. Save and close the workbook (Figure 3-73).

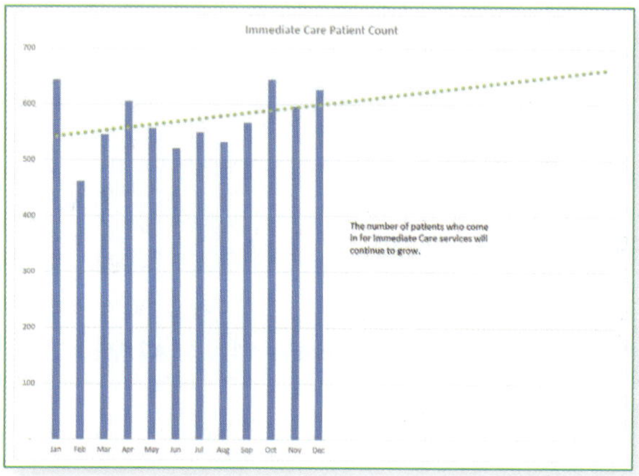

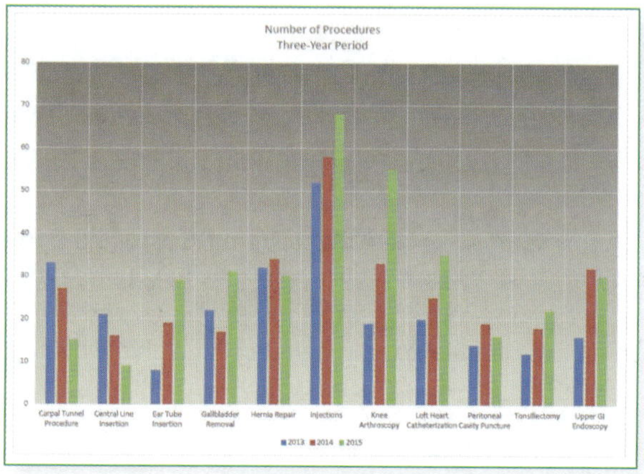

3-73 Excel 3-6 completed chart sheets

Improve It Project 3-7

Central Sierra Insurance (CSI) is a multi-office insurance company that handles commercial and personal insurance products. For this project, when you add missing data to a worksheet, the pie chart automatically updates, but the column chart incorrectly plots row and column data and does not update. To address this, you switch the row/column data and then edit the source data range. **[Student Learning Outcomes 3.2, 3.3, 3.4]**

File Needed: ***CentralSierraPolicies-03.xlsx***
Completed Project File Name: ***[your initials] Excel 3-7.xlsx***

Skills Covered in This Project

- Insert a row within a chart source range.
- Switch row and column data.
- Apply a new color scheme to a chart and to a data series.
- Edit source data.
- Add and format elements in a 3-D chart.
- Use gradient fill for a chart object.
- Change chart type.
- Apply a chart style.
- Format chart elements.

1. Open the ***CentralSierraPolicies-03*** workbook from your student data files folder.
2. Save the workbook as ***[your initials] Excel 3-7***.
3. Insert a new row at row 8.
4. In cell **A8,** type Motorcycle. In cells **B8:D8**, type these values: 15, 82, and 24.
5. Switch the row and column data for the column chart.
6. Edit the source data for the column chart to show cells **A5:D10**.
7. Change the chart color scheme to **Color 11** in the **Monochromatic** list.
8. Format chart elements.
   a. Apply the **Olive Green**, **Accent 3**, **Lighter 80%** shape fill to the **Side Wall** of the chart.
   b. Apply the **Linear Down** gradient for the shape fill.
   c. Apply the same fill and gradient to the **Walls** element.
   d. Apply the **Olive Green**, **Accent 3**, **Lighter 60%** with no gradient to the **Floor** element.
9. Change the pie chart to a **3-D Pie** and apply **Chart Style 3**.
10. Select the **Chart Area** of the pie chart and apply **Color 11** color scheme, **Olive Green**, **Accent 3**, **Lighter 80%** shape fill, and **Linear Down** gradient fill.
11. Apply a ½ **pt**. **Olive Green**, **Accent 3**, **Darker 25%** outline to both chart objects.
12. Select the pie (**Series AJP**) and change the color to **Color 11** in the **Monochromatic** list.
13. Save and close the workbook (Figure 3-74).

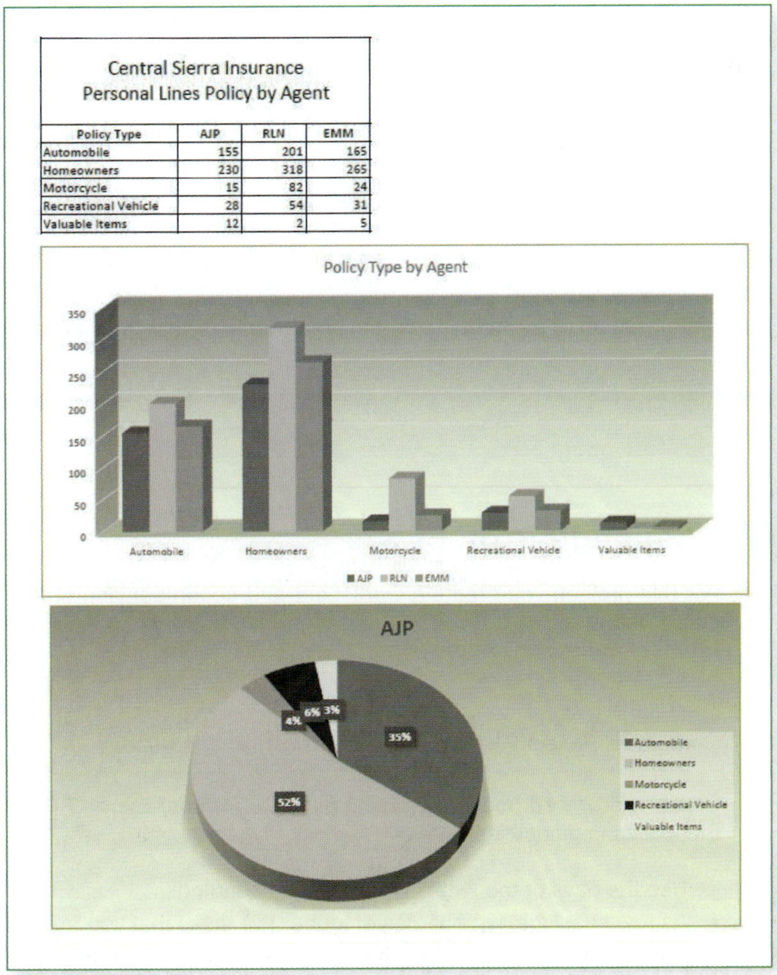

3-74 Excel 3-7 completed worksheet with charts

Challenge Project 3-8

For this project, you create a worksheet that outlines costs for trips to three of your favorite cities. From the data, you will create column or bar charts to compare the costs of the visits to each city.
[Student Learning Outcomes 3.1, 3.2, 3.3, 3.4, 3.5, 3.6]

File Needed: None
Completed Project File Name: ***[your initials] Excel 3-8.xlsx***

Create a new workbook and save it as ***[your initials] Excel 3-8***. Modify your workbook according to the following guidelines:

- As column headings, type the names of three cities that you would like to visit.
- As row headings, type five or six major expense categories for a trip. These might be labels such as “Air, Train, or Bus”, “Hotel”, “Entertainment”, and similar expenses.
- Enter estimated costs for a five-day trip for each city using your own research about the city. Format your data as needed.
- Type a main and secondary title for your data.
- Create a column or bar chart sheet that compares the trips.
- Change the layout or apply a chart style.
- Use a picture as fill for one of the data series.
- Edit the chart title placeholder to display an appropriate title. Change the font size of the title to balance the chart.
- Format chart elements to create an attractive, easy-to-understand chart of your data.

Challenge Project 3-9

For this project, you create a worksheet and accompanying charts to track your daily usage of your smart phone.
[Student Learning Outcomes 3.1, 3.2, 3.3, 3.4, 3.5, 3.6]

File Needed: None
Completed Project File Name: ***[your initials] Excel 3-9.xlsx***

Create a new workbook and save it as ***[your initials] Excel 3-9***. Modify your workbook according to the following guidelines:

- Use the days of the week as the column headings.
- As row headings, type names of four or five tasks that you might do each day with your smart phone. You might use labels such as “Send text”, “Receive phone call”, “Use GPS”, or similar tasks.
- Enter a value for the number of times you perform each task on each day.

- Type a main title for your data in row 1. Format your data.
- Create a column chart object that compares the number of times you did each task on Monday.
- Size and position the chart object below the worksheet data.
- Change the layout or apply a chart style.
- Edit the chart title placeholder to display an appropriate title.
- Format chart elements to create an attractive, easy-to-understand chart of your data.
- For the task with the greatest Monday value, create another column chart that displays the daily numbers for that one task.
- Size and position this chart object below the first chart.
- Format the second chart to complement the first chart.

Challenge Project 3-10

For this project, you create a worksheet and line chart that compares the temperature in your city or town at 12 noon for the past 10 days. You also insert a single sparkline in the data.
[Student Learning Outcomes 3.1, 3.2, 3.3, 3.4, 3.5, 3.6, 3.7]

File Needed: None
Completed Project File Name: ***[your initials] Excel 3-10.xlsx***

Create a new workbook and save it as ***[your initials] Excel 3-10***. Modify your workbook according to the following guidelines:

- In a worksheet, enter the dates for the last 10 days and enter a temperature in degrees for each date at 12 noon. Use a weather reference or your recollection of the day.
- Type a main title for your data (insert a row if necessary). Format your data.
- Create a line chart sheet that illustrates the daily temperature for 10 days.
- Change the layout or apply a chart style.
- Edit and format the chart elements as needed.
- In the worksheet, select the range of values and insert a line sparkline in the column to the right, in one cell, next to the first value.
- Format the sparkline and adjust the row height or column width to better display the sparkline.

CHAPTER 4

Importing, Creating Tables, Sorting and Filtering, and Using Conditional Formatting

CHAPTER OVERVIEW

Sharing data among software programs is essential in professional and personal work. Excel can both import data from several sources and export data in a number of formats. Because shared data is typically in the form of a list or table, Excel features a ***Table*** style with enhanced commands to help you manage list-type data. This chapter teaches you how to import data, create and format Excel tables, and protect your worksheets in an Excel workbook.

STUDENT LEARNING OUTCOMES (SLOs)

After completing this chapter, you will be able to:

SLO 4.1 Import data into Excel from a text file, database file, or a web site and use *Flash Fill* and data connections (p. E4-187).

SLO 4.2 Create and format an Excel table and a *PivotTable* and export data for use in other programs (p. E4-194).

SLO 4.3 Sort data by text, number, color, or icon (p. E4-205).

SLO 4.4 Apply an *AutoFilter* or an *Advanced Filter* to data (p. E4-209).

SLO 4.5 Use the *Subtotal* command and create groups and outlines (p. E4-212).

SLO 4.6 Apply and manage *Conditional Formatting* using cell rules, *Color Scales*, *Icon Sets*, and *Data Bars* (p. E4-218).

SLO 4.7 Use *Goal Seek* and protect a worksheet (p. E4-222).

CASE STUDY

For the Pause & Practice projects in this chapter, you create Excel workbooks for the northern Minnesota company, Paradise Lakes Resort (PLR), introduced in Chapters 1–3. In preparation for its annual department meetings, PLR is asking managers to import and sort data from external sources, format lists as tables and PivotTables, *and subtotal data for analysis.*

Pause & Practice 4-1: Import data for a workbook from text files and use *Flash Fill*.

Pause & Practice 4-2: Format an Excel list as a table, remove duplicate records, and create a *PivotTable*.

Pause & Practice 4-3: Sort and filter data in an Excel workbook and apply subtotals.

Pause & Practice 4-4: Use *Goal Seek*, apply conditional formatting, and protect a worksheet.

EXCEL

SLO 4.1

Importing Data

Data is available in many formats. A key Excel skill is knowing how to access and convert data for use in your Excel worksheets. ***Importing*** data refers to the task of obtaining data from another software program, another file format, or an Internet location. In many situations importing data saves time and increases accuracy. For example, at a retail business, you might import a supplier's catalog into a worksheet to help employees prepare routine orders. Or you might import calendar data from co-workers to build a daily schedule in a worksheet. Many companies buy customer or client lists and import the data from those lists into Excel to build prospect lists.

External data is data in a worksheet that originated in another program or format. You can import or copy external data into Excel from the ***source***. The source can be a text file, a database, or a web location. If you import external data using the *Get External Data* group, you establish live connections that update the data in your worksheet if a change is made to the original data. If you simply copy data into a worksheet, you do not maintain a connection to the source. Data connections are discussed later in this section.

For most uses, it is best to import data in list format. List format features data organized in rows and columns with analogous information in the same column in each row.

Text Files

A ***text file*** is a document that includes basic data, no formatting, and commas or other characters to separate the data into columns and rows. Text files include *.txt* (text) documents such as those created in NotePad or WordPad. Another widely used format is *.csv* (comma separated values); you might see this type of file when you download a bank statement. Most software can save a *.prn* (printer) file, which is a simple text file that can be printed.

Text files separate data into columns, often called ***fields,*** in one of two ways. In one type of text file, a character, such as a comma or a tab, separates the fields. When a text file uses a special character, it is referred to as a ***delimited*** file (e.g., tab-delimited file). The ***delimiter*** in the file is the character used to separate the data.

The other text file type identifies fields or columns by a ***fixed width.*** Each field is a specified width, followed by a space. For example, if the first name field occupies 25 spaces and an individual's name is "Tom," it is imported as 3 characters followed by 22 empty spaces.

When you click the *From Text* button in the *Get External Data* group on the *Data* tab (Figure 4-1), the ***Text Import Wizard*** guides you through the data importing steps. The wizard usually is able to determine if the file you are working with is delimited or fixed width.

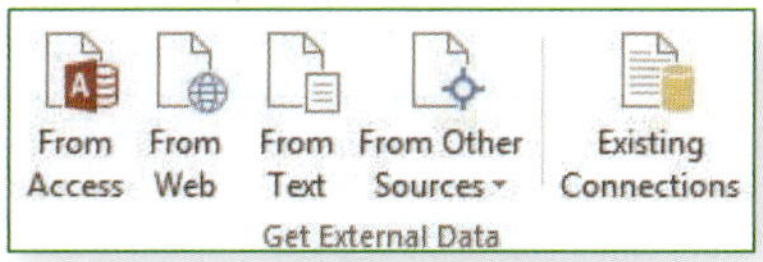

4-1 *Get External Data* group

> **MORE INFO**
>
> Many legacy or mainframe computer systems use fixed width files for data.

HOW TO: Import a Delimited Text File into a Worksheet

1. Select the cell where you want the imported data to start.
2. Click the **From Text** button [*Data* tab, *Get External Data* group].
3. Select the name of the text file in the *Import Text File* dialog box and click **Import** (Figure 4-2).
4. In the *Text Import Wizard – Step 1 of 3* window, click the **Delimited** radio button if necessary and click **Next** (Figure 4-3).

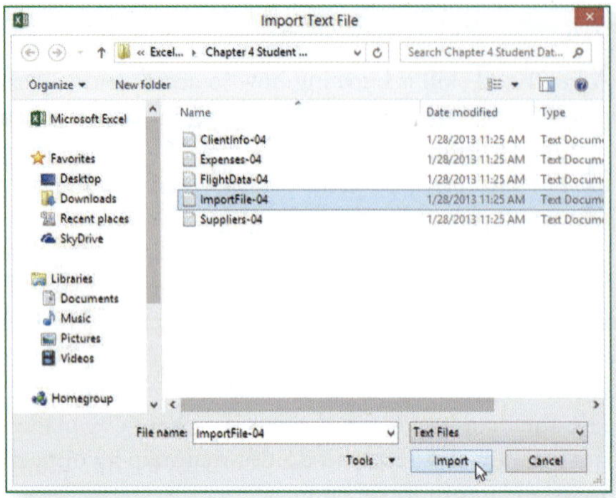

4-2 *Import Text File* dialog box

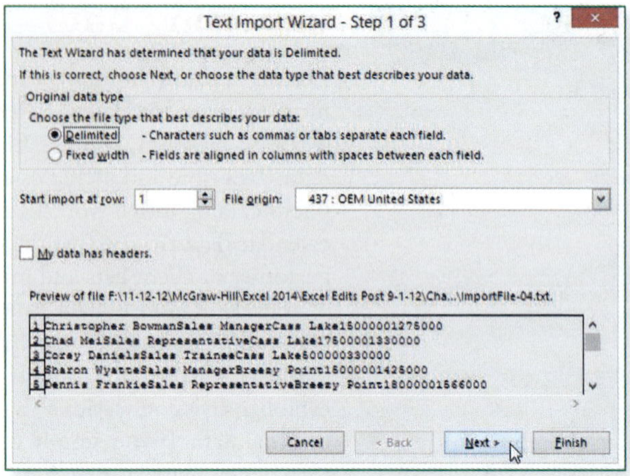

4-3 *Text Import Wizard – Step 1*

5. In the *Text Import Wizard – Step 2 of 3* window, check the **Tab** box if necessary and click **Next** (see Figure 4-4).
   - Look at the *Data preview* to determine if the correct delimiter is selected. You can try any of the listed delimiters or type a custom character.
6. Click **Finish** (Figure 4-5).
   - Select a column in the *Data preview* area and set its format in the *Column data format* group.
   - You can also format the data after it is imported.
7. Click **OK** in the *Import Data* dialog box (Figure 4-6).
   - Click **Properties** to open the *External Data Range Properties* dialog box. You can set options for imported data such as a *Refresh data* time or *Preserve cell formatting*. Click **OK** to close this dialog box.

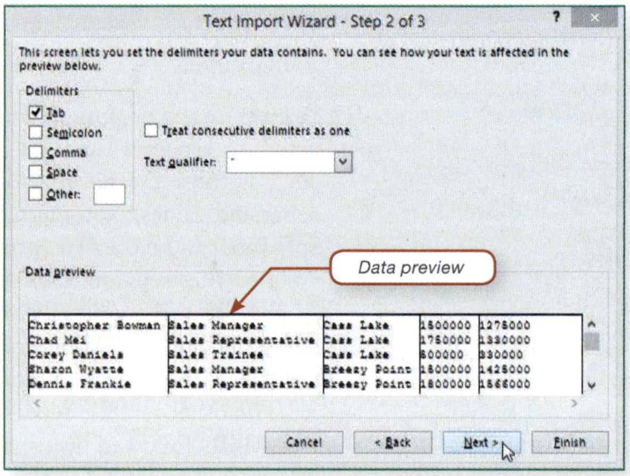

4-4 *Text Import Wizard – Step 2*

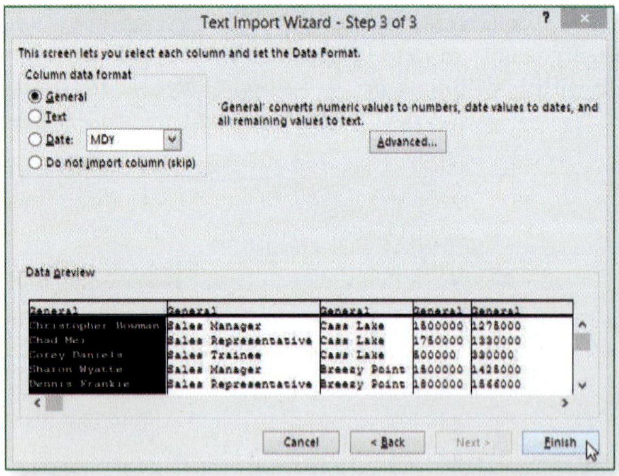

4-5 *Text Import Wizard – Step 3*

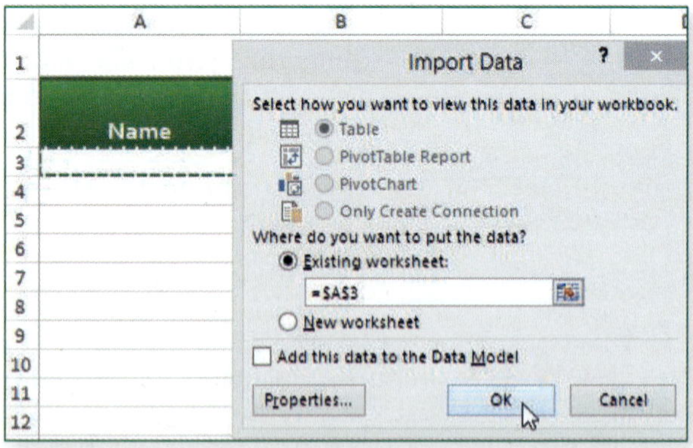

4-6 *Import Data* dialog box

You cannot directly import text from a Word document into Excel. However, you can copy and paste data from Word into an Excel worksheet. When you paste the data in Excel, you can retain the formatting used in the Word document, or you can choose the current format in the worksheet.

HOW TO: Copy Data from a Word Document

1. Select the cell in the worksheet where you want the imported data to start.
2. Open the Word document and select the table or list you want to import to Excel.
3. Click the **Copy** button [*Home* tab, *Clipboard* group].
4. Switch to the Excel worksheet.
5. Click the **Paste** button [*Home* tab, *Clipboard* group] or press **Ctrl+V**.
   - To retain the formatting from the Word document, click the arrow with the **Paste** drop-down button to choose the option to *Match Destination Formatting*.

ANOTHER WAY

Save a Word document as a Text file (*.txt*) and import the text file into Excel.

MORE INFO

To split data in a single column into separate columns, insert as many blank columns to the right as needed for the split data. Select the column to be split and click the **Text to Columns** button [*Data* tab, *Data Tools* group]. Complete the *Convert Text to Columns Wizard* to split the column.

Access Database Files

A ***database*** is a collection of related tables, queries, forms, and reports. ***Microsoft Access*** is a relational database management system that is part of the Office suite of products. Most companies, service organizations, schools, and other enterprises keep great amounts of data in databases, so it is quite common to import data from a database for use in Excel. For example, Access cannot illustrate data in a chart. If there is chartable sales data in a database table, you can import the relevant data from Access into Excel and build the chart.

You can import a table or a query from an Access database into an Excel worksheet. To do this, you import the data as an Excel table and then you convert a table into a normal data range (this topic is covered later in this chapter).

Access database files have an *.accdb* extension. When a database includes many tables and queries, the *Select Table* dialog box opens so that you can choose the table or query you want to import.

MORE INFO

If a database has a single table or query, it is automatically imported into Excel; the *Select Table* dialog box does not open.

HOW TO: Import an Access Table into a Worksheet

1. Select the worksheet cell where you want the imported data to start.
   - Because all Access tables or queries have column or field headings, you do not need column headings in the worksheet.
2. Click the **From Access** button [*Data* tab, *Get External Data* group].
3. Select the database name in the *Select Data Source* dialog box.
4. Click **Open** (Figure 4-7).
5. Select the name of the table or query you want to import in the *Select Table* dialog box (Figure 4-8).
6. Click **OK**.
7. In the *Import Data* dialog box, select **Table** and **Existing worksheet**.
   - You can choose a new worksheet for the imported data. If you do this, the data is imported starting at cell A1.
   - Click **Properties** to change options such as refresh timing.
8. Click **OK**.
   - An Excel table displays *AutoFilter* buttons with each column heading for sorting and filtering (Figure 4-9). Filters are covered in *SLO 4.4: Filtering Data*.

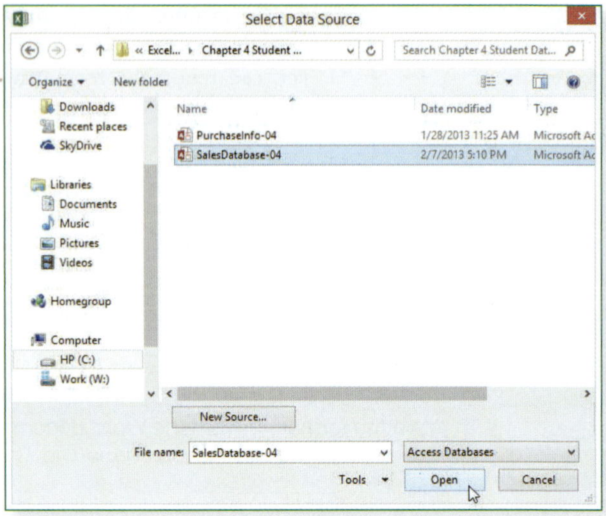

4-7 *Select Data Source* dialog box

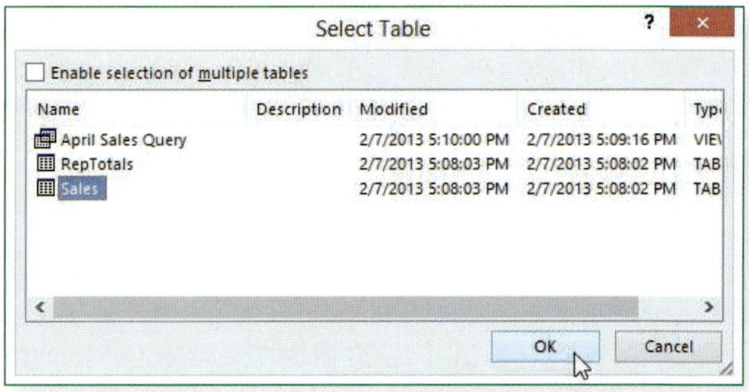

4-8 *Select Table* dialog box

MORE INFO

You can import tables and queries from relational databases such as SQL Server with the **From Other Sources** button [*Data* tab, *Get External Data* group].

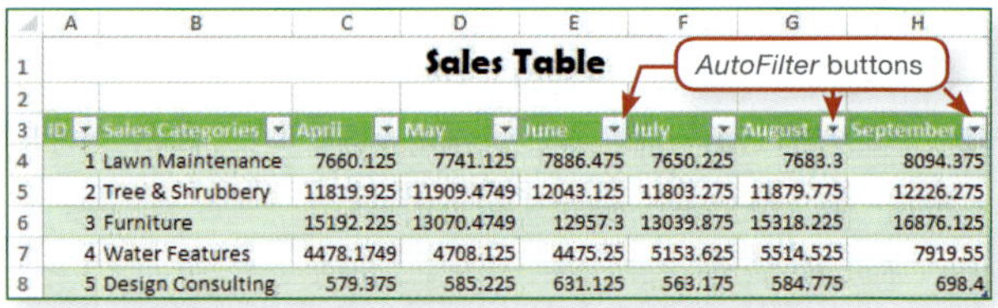

ID	Sales Categories	April	May	June	July	August	September
1	Lawn Maintenance	7660.125	7741.125	7886.475	7650.225	7683.3	8094.375
2	Tree & Shrubbery	11819.925	11909.4749	12043.125	11803.275	11879.775	12226.275
3	Furniture	15192.225	13070.4749	12957.3	13039.875	15318.225	16876.125
4	Water Features	4478.1749	4708.125	4475.25	5153.625	5514.525	7919.55
5	Design Consulting	579.375	585.225	631.125	563.175	584.775	698.4

4-9 Imported Access table

Web Site Data

Many web sites include table-formatted data that you can import into a worksheet. For example, a company like Paradise Lakes Resort might import data from a web site about vacation spending so that company officers can project future rentals and purchases. Or they might import data from a weather site to build a chart about average temperatures and rainfall to plan marketing campaigns.

Web pages include a wealth of data, images, and sometimes even video. When you use the *From Web* command, data that you can import into Excel as a list or table is indicated on a web page with a small black arrow in a yellow box. This identifier enables you to easily locate which data you can import and format in columns and rows. When you click a yellow box with an arrow, the related table is selected, and the arrow changes to a green box with a check mark. The data is ready for importing.

> **MORE INFO**
> Most data that you import from another source needs to be formatted in Excel to match your other worksheet data.

Data that you import from a web page establishes a connection to the site that you can refresh whenever necessary.

HOW TO: Import Web Data into a Worksheet

1. Select the worksheet cell where you want the imported data to start.
   - Depending on how data is formatted on the web page, you may not need to insert column headings after importing.
2. Click the **From Web** button [*Data* tab, *Get External Data* group].
3. In the *New Web Query* dialog box, browse to locate the web site and data you want to import (Figure 4-10).
4. Click the **Click to select this table** arrow (yellow box with black arrow) next to the data you want to import.
   - Click the **Options** button to set options such as *Formatting* (Figure 4-11) and click **OK**.
5. Click the **Import** button in the *New Web Query* dialog box.
   - Click the **Properties** button to edit options such as *Refresh Control* or *Data Formatting and layout*. Click **OK** to save changes.
6. Click **OK** in the *Import Data* dialog box.
   - A message on screen may inform you that Excel is obtaining the data. When the import is complete, the data is displayed in the worksheet and looks similar to the example shown in Figure 4-12.

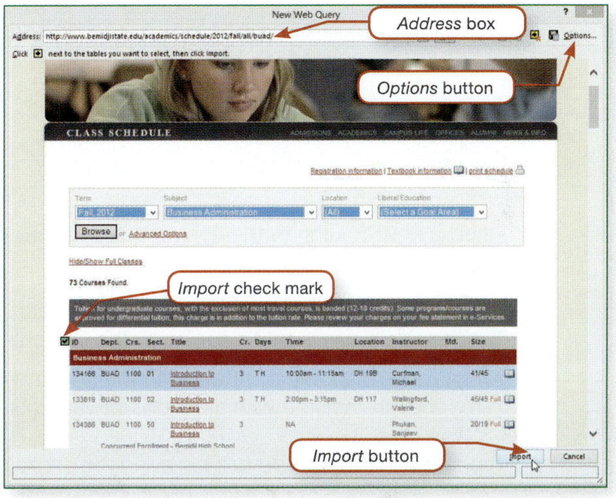

4-10 ***New Web Query*** **window**

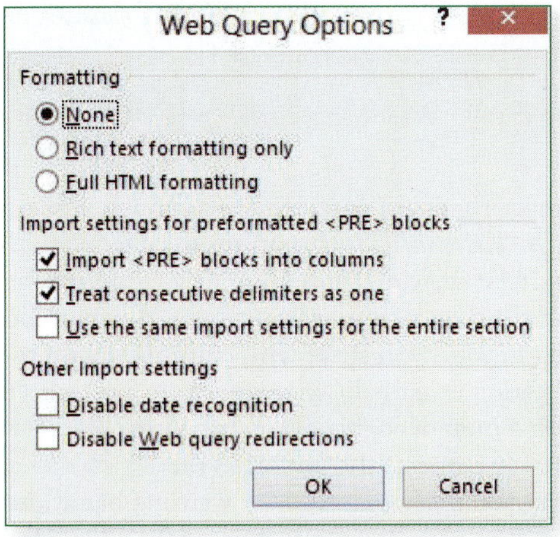

4-11 ***Web Query Options*** **dialog box**

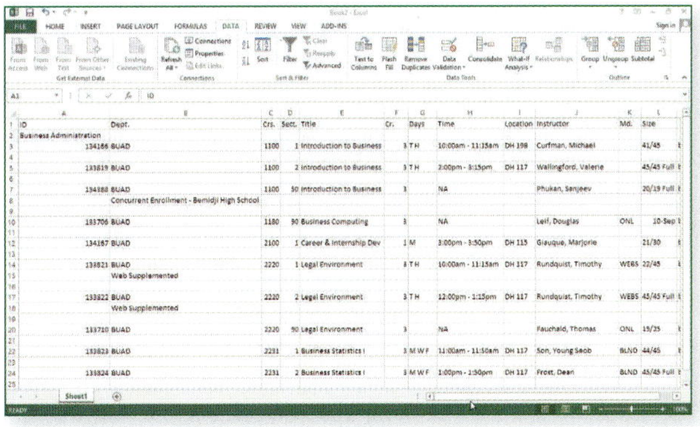

4-12 Data imported from a web site

> **ANOTHER WAY**
>
> You can copy and paste from a web page into an Excel worksheet. However, there is no connection to the web site when you do this.

Flash Fill

Flash Fill is a new command in Excel 2013 that recognizes a pattern and duplicates it for matching cells. For example, imagine that in data that you import from a text file or a web site, individuals' first and last names are together in a single column. You want the first and last names to be in separate columns in your Excel document so in a new column in the first row, you type the first name of the first individual. When you enter the first name of the second person in the second row, *Flash Fill* completes the remaining cells in the column. The **Flash Fill Options** button appears after you press **Enter** so that you can undo the fill if necessary or accept all the suggestions.

HOW TO: Flash Fill Data in a Worksheet

1. Insert a new column to the right of the data you want to use in the *Flash Fill* column.
2. Click in the first cell in the new column for data.
3. Type the data you want to appear in the first cell in the column.
   - Figure 4-13 shows a pattern with the first and last name from the "Name" column with a period between names, followed by "@go.com."
4. Type data in the second cell following the same pattern.
   - If the *Flash Fill* suggestion list does not appear after the second item, type the third item.
5. Press **Enter** to complete the *Flash Fill.*
   - If the *Flash Fill* suggestion list does not appear, click the **Flash Fill** button [*Data* tab, *Data Tools* group] with the insertion point still in the column.

	A	B	C
1	Sales Table		
2	Name		Title
3	Christopher Bowman	christopher.bowman@	Sales Manager
4	Chad Mei	chad.mei@go.com	Sales Representative
5	Corey Daniels	corey.daniels@go.com	
6	Sharon Wyatte	sharon.wyatte@go.co	Sales Manager
7	Dennis Frankie	dennis.frankie@go.co	Sales Representative
8	BJ Francine	bj.francine@go.com	Sales Representative
9	Kendal Shaedon	kendal.shaedon@go.c	Sales Representative
10	Ella Jamison	ella.jamison@go.com	Sales Manager
11	Alec Mikayla	alec.mikayla@go.com	Sales Representative
12	Natasha Ari	natasha.ari@go.com	Sales Trainee
13	Nikolai Jalowiec	nikolai.jalowiec@go.c	Sales Manager
14	Tammy Christine	tammy.christine@go.	Sales Representative
15	Josie Daddiline	josie.daddiline@go.c	Sales Representative
16	Christopher Bowman	christopher.bowman@	Sales Manager

4-13 *Flash Fill* suggestion list

Data Connections

A ***connection*** is an identifier for data that originated outside the workbook. For any data that you import using a command in the *Get External Data* group on the *Data* tab, Excel establishes a connection that you can update, refresh, name, or remove. If you import the data from a text file or a database, you can refresh the data by importing it again. If you import the data as a web query, you can replace the data in your worksheet with current data on the web site.

A data connection to an Internet location is named *Connection.* You can access the properties for any connection and label it with a more recognizable name. A data connection to the file you import is named with the same file name as the imported file.

Depending upon your Excel options, you may see a security warning bar at the top of the worksheet when you open a workbook that has data connections. Click **Enable Editing** to work with the data.

HOW TO: Manage Data Connections

1. Click the **Connections** button [*Data* tab, *Connections* group] to open the *Workbook Connections* dialog box.
2. Select the name of the connection in the top pane (Figure 4-14).
3. Click **Refresh** to update the imported data.
   - The *Import Text File* dialog box opens if you have selected a connection for an imported text file.
4. Click the link **Click here to see where the selected connections are used** to identify where the data is located in the workbook.
5. Click **Properties** to open the *Connections Properties* dialog box.
   - You can set how the data is refreshed, change the connection name, or add a description.
6. Click **Close** to save changes.

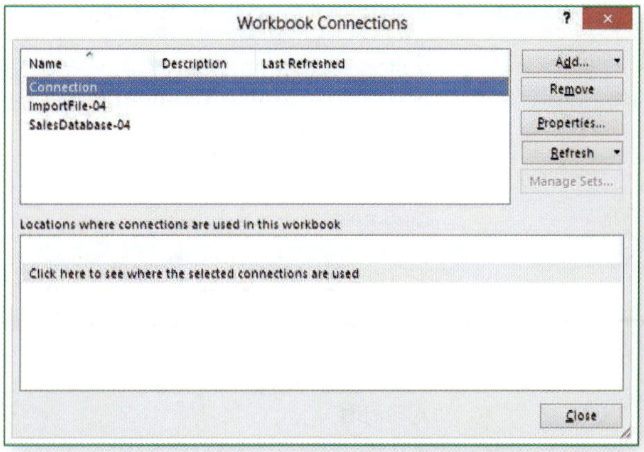

4-14 ***Workbook Connections*** **dialog box**

PAUSE & PRACTICE: EXCEL 4-1

For this project, you import data from a text file into an Excel worksheet, copy data from a Word document into the same worksheet, and use *Flash Fill* to build a worksheet for Paradise Lakes Resort.

Files Needed: ***Sales-04.xlsx***, ***ImportFile-04.txt***, and ***ImportWord-04.docx***
Completed Project File Name: ***[your initials] PP E4-1.xlsx***

1. Open the ***Sales-04*** workbook from the student data files folder. Click the **Enable Editing** button.
2. Save the workbook as ***[your initials] PP E4-1***.
3. Import data from a text file.
   a. Select cell **A3**.
   b. Click the **From Text** button [*Data* tab, *Get External Data* group].
   c. Select the ***ImportFile-04.txt*** file in the *Import Text File* dialog box.
   d. Click **Import**.
   e. Select the **Delimited** button in the *Text Import Wizard – Step 1 of 3* dialog box.
   f. Click **Next**.
   g. Place a check mark for **Tab** in the *Text Import Wizard – Step 2 of 3* dialog box.
   h. Click **Next**.
   i. Click **Finish** in the last dialog box.
   j. Click **OK** in the *Import Data* dialog box.
4. Copy data from a Word document.
   a. Select cell **A17**.
   b. Open Microsoft Word and open the ***ImportWord-04*** Word document. Click the **Enable Editing** button.
   c. Select all the data and click the **Copy** button [*Home* tab, *Clipboard* group].

d. Switch to the Excel window.
e. Click the arrow with the **Paste** button [*Home* tab, *Clipboard* group] and choose **Match Destination Formatting** (Figure 4-15).
f. Select cells **D3:E26** and apply the **Currency** number format with zero decimals.
g. Adjust the widths of columns **C:E** to 15.00.

5. Create an email address column using *Flash Fill*.
   a. Insert a new column between columns **A** and **B**.
   b. Type Email Address in cell **B2**.
   c. Increase the width of the "Email Address" column to 37.00.
   d. Type Christopher.Bowman@somewhere.com in **B3** and press **Enter**.
   e. Type Chad.Mei@somewhere.com in **B4** and press **Enter** to complete the *Flash Fill* (Figure 4-16).
   f. If the *Flash Fill* suggestion list does not appear, click the **Flash Fill** button [*Data* tab, *Data Tools* group].
6. Save and close the workbook. Close the Word document.

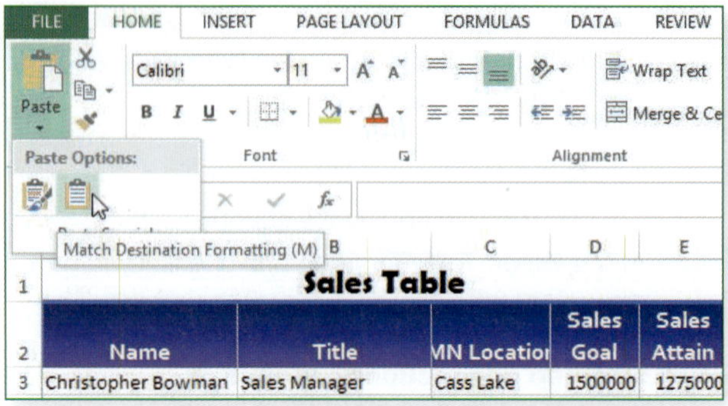

4-15 *Paste Options* for copied data

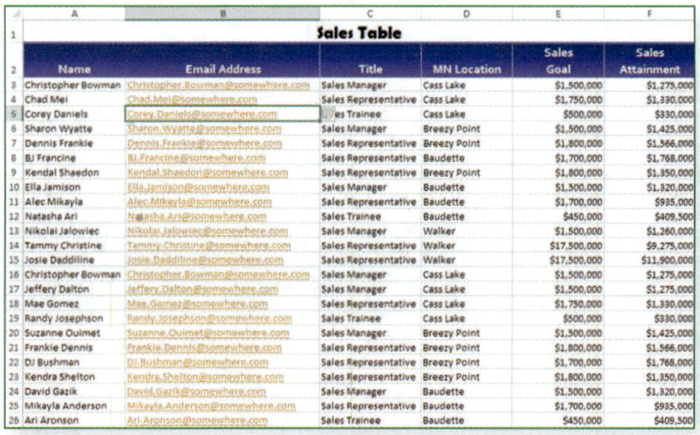

	A	B	C	D	E	F
1	Sales Table					
2	Name	Email Address	Title	MN Location	Sales Goal	Sales Attainment
3	Christopher Bowman	Christopher.Bowman@somewhere.com	Sales Manager	Cass Lake	$1,500,000	$1,275,000
4	Chad Mei	Chad.Mei@somewhere.com	Sales Representative	Cass Lake	$1,750,000	$1,330,000
5	Corey Daniels	Corey.Daniels@somewhere.com	es Trainee	Cass Lake	$500,000	$330,000
6	Sharon Wyatte	Sharon.Wyatte@somewhere.com	Sales Manager	Breezy Point	$1,500,000	$1,425,000
7	Dennis Frankie	Dennis.Frankie@somewhere.com	Sales Representative	Breezy Point	$1,800,000	$1,566,000
8	BJ Francine	BJ.Francine@somewhere.com	Sales Representative	Baudette	$1,700,000	$1,768,000
9	Kendal Shaedon	Kendal.Shaedon@somewhere.com	Sales Representative	Breezy Point	$1,800,000	$1,350,000
10	Ella Jamison	Ella.Jamison@somewhere.com	Sales Manager	Baudette	$1,300,000	$1,320,000
11	Alec Mikayla	Alec.Mikayla@somewhere.com	Sales Representative	Baudette	$1,700,000	$935,000
12	Natasha Ari	Natasha.Ari@somewhere.com	Sales Trainee	Baudette	$450,000	$409,500
13	Nikolai Jalowiec	Nikolai.Jalowiec@somewhere.com	Sales Manager	Walker	$1,500,000	$1,260,000
14	Tammy Christine	Tammy.Christine@somewhere.com	Sales Representative	Walker	$17,500,000	$9,275,000
15	Josie Daddiline	Josie.Daddiline@somewhere.com	Sales Representative	Walker	$17,500,000	$11,900,000
16	Christopher Bowman	Christopher.Bowman@somewhere.com	Sales Manager	Cass Lake	$1,500,000	$1,275,000
17	Jeffery Dalton	Jeffery.Dalton@somewhere.com	Sales Manager	Cass Lake	$1,500,000	$1,275,000
18	Mae Gomez	Mae.Gomez@somewhere.com	Sales Representative	Cass Lake	$1,750,000	$1,330,000
19	Randy Josephson	Randy.Josephson@somewhere.com	Sales Trainee	Cass Lake	$500,000	$330,000
20	Suzanne Ouimet	Suzanne.Ouimet@somewhere.com	Sales Manager	Breezy Point	$1,500,000	$1,425,000
21	Frankie Dennis	Frankie.Dennis@somewhere.com	Sales Representative	Breezy Point	$1,800,000	$1,566,000
22	DJ Bushman	DJ.Bushman@somewhere.com	Sales Representative	Breezy Point	$1,700,000	$1,768,000
23	Kendra Shelton	Kendra.Shelton@somewhere.com	Sales Representative	Breezy Point	$1,800,000	$1,350,000
24	David Gazik	David.Gazik@somewhere.com	Sales Manager	Baudette	$1,500,000	$1,320,000
25	Mikayla Anderson	Mikayla.Anderson@somewhere.com	Sales Representative	Baudette	$1,700,000	$935,000
26	Ari Aronson	Ari.Aronson@somewhere.com	Sales Trainee	Baudette	$450,000	$409,500

4-16 PP E4-1 completed worksheet

SLO 4.2

Creating Excel Tables

An Excel ***table*** is a list of related pieces of information that is formatted with a title row followed by rows of data. When your data is in table format, Excel commands allow you to organize, sort, filter, and calculate the data easily and quickly, much like a database.

The ***header row*** is the first row of the table with descriptive titles or labels. Each row of data is a ***record*** and each column is a ***field***. The label in the header row is sometimes referred to as the ***field name***. When you format your Excel data as a table, follow these guidelines to make your tables easier to use and navigate:

- Type descriptive labels in the first row and begin each label with a letter, not a number.
- Give each header a unique label; do not repeat any of the descriptive labels.
- Keep the same type of data within each column (e.g., text or values).
- Do not leave blank cells within the data.

Create an Excel Table

When data is arranged as a list and conforms to the guidelines just described, it is a straightforward format command to create an Excel table. Select the data you want to include in the table and click the **Format as Table** button in the *Styles* group on the *Home* tab. There is also a **Table** button in the *Tables* group on the *Insert* tab.

After your data is formatted as a table, each label in the header row displays an ***AutoFilter*** button. Recall from Chapter 3 that a ***filter*** specifies which data is shown and which is hidden. In other words, a filter is a criterion or a specification that data must meet to be shown. The *AutoFilter* buttons allow you to quickly hide or display rows of data. For example, you might want to display only those persons from a particular location or only those who reached a certain level of sales. In *SLO 4.4: Filtering Data,* you learn how to create and customize filters.

MORE INFO

The *AutoFilter* buttons do not print.

The *Table Tools Design* tab appears when any cell is selected within a table.

HOW TO: Create an Excel Table

1. Select the cells that you want to include in a table, including the header row.
2. Click the **Format as Table** button [*Home* tab, *Styles* group].
3. Choose a **Table Style** from the *Style* gallery (Figure 4-17).
4. Verify the cell range in the *Format As Table* dialog box.
   - If the cell range for the table is incorrect, drag to reselect the correct cell range in the worksheet.
5. Verify that there is a check in the **My table has headers** box in the *Format As Table* dialog box.
   - If there is no header row in the cell range you select originally, Excel inserts a row above the data and names the columns *Column1*, *Column2*, and so on. You can edit these names.
6. Click **OK** to create the table (Figure 4-18).
   - When the selected range includes imported data, you will see a message box asking to remove the connection. Click **Yes** to create the table.

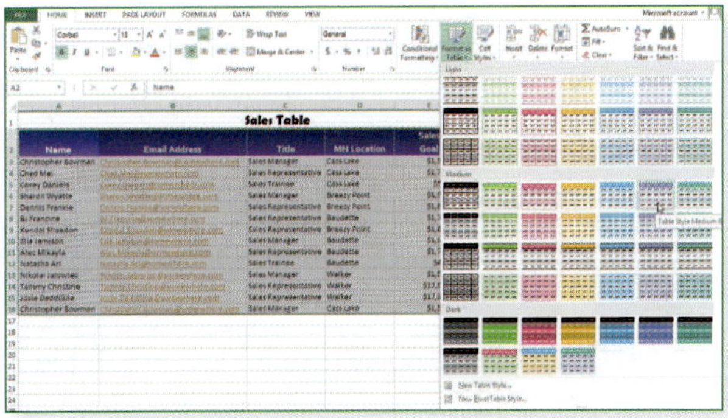

4-17 *Table Style* gallery

Sales Table

Name	Email Address	Title	MN Location	Sales Goal	Sales Attainment
Christopher Bowman	Christopher.Bowman@somewhere.com	Sales Manager	Cass Lake	$1,500,000	$1,275,000
Chad Mei	Chad.Mei@somewhere.com	Sales Representative	Cass Lake	$1,750,000	$1,330,000
Corey Daniels	Corey.Daniels@somewhere.com	Sales Trainee	Cass Lake	$500,000	$330,000
Sharon Wyatte	Sharon.Wyatte@somewhere.com	Sales Manager	Breezy Point	$1,500,000	$1,425,000
Dennis Frankie	Dennis.Frankie@somewhere.com	Sales Representative	Breezy Point	$1,800,000	$1,566,000
BJ Francine	BJ.Francine@somewhere.com	Sales Representative	Baudette	$1,700,000	$1,768,000
Kendal Shaedon	Kendal.Shaedon@somewhere.com	Sales Representative	Breezy Point	$1,800,000	$1,350,000
Ella Jamison	Ella.Jamison@somewhere.com	Sales Manager	Baudette	$1,500,000	$1,320,000
Alec Mikayla	Alec.Mikayla@somewhere.com	Sales Representative	Baudette	$1,700,000	$935,000
Natasha Ari	Natasha.Ari@somewhere.com	Sales Trainee	Baudette	$450,000	$409,500
Nikolai Jalowiec	Nikolai.Jalowiec@somewhere.com	Sales Manager	Walker	$1,500,000	$1,260,000
Tammy Christine	Tammy.Christine@somewhere.com	Sales Representative	Walker	$17,500,000	$9,275,000
Josie Daddiline	Josie.Daddiline@somewhere.com	Sales Representative	Walker	$17,500,000	$11,900,000
Christopher Bowman	Christopher.Bowman@somewhere.com	Sales Manager	Cass Lake	$1,500,000	$1,275,000

4-18 Formatted Excel table

ANOTHER WAY

Select the header and data rows and click the **Quick Analysis** tool. Choose **Tables** and click the **Table** button to format the data in a default table style.

MORE INFO

If you type a new label in the header row to the right of the last column, Excel makes the new label part of the table.

Table Styles

A ***table style*** is a predesigned set of built-in format options such as borders, fill colors, and effects for a table. A table style includes a color scheme and may display alternating fill for the rows, vertical borders, and more. You select a style when you create a table, but you can apply a different style to a table once it exists to change the look of your data. Predefined table styles are classified as *Light*, *Medium*, and *Dark*.

HOW TO: Apply a Style to an Existing Table

1. Click any cell within the table to display the *Table Tools Design* tab.
2. Click the **More** button [*Table Tools Design* tab, *Table Styles* group] to open the *Table Styles* gallery.
3. Point at a style to see a *Live Preview* of its effect on the table.
4. Click to select and apply a style.

Table Style Options

The *Table Style Options* group on the *Table Tools Design* tab includes commands for showing or hiding various parts of the table. You can hide the header row or display a total row. You can choose banded columns or rows, which alternates shading on the rows or columns. You can also hide the *AutoFilter* buttons, if you like.

If you choose to show a total row, you can choose the calculation that is displayed in the row.

HOW TO: Display a Total Row in a Table

1. Click any cell within the table.
2. Click to check the **Total Row** box [*Table Tools Design* tab, *Table Style Options* group].
   - The total row displays after the last row in the table (Figure 4-19).

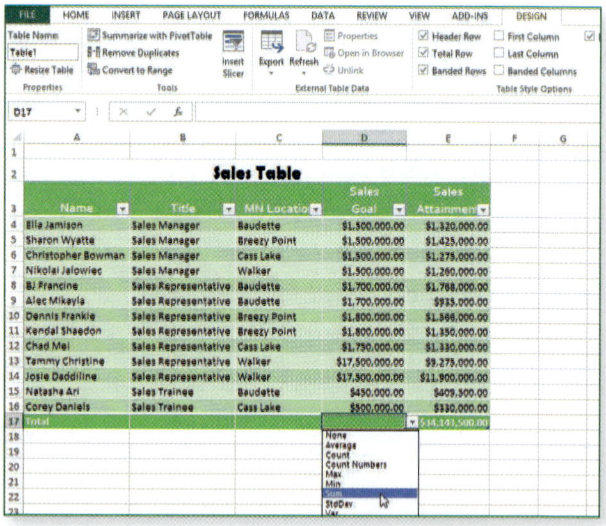

4-19 Table with total row

Save a New Table Style

You may have a preference for a particular table style, or your organization may have specific requirements. You can create and name custom table styles so that you can apply preferred format choices to tables you create with one click.

In the *New Table Style* dialog box, select an individual part of a table and specify how it should be formatted. For example, you can set the first column feature a different font color or bold italic font.

When you create your own table style, it is listed in a *Custom* group at the top of the *Table Styles* gallery.

HOW TO: Save a New Table Style

1. Click any cell within a table.
2. Click the **Table Styles** More button [*Table Tools Design* tab, *Table Styles* group].
3. Click the **New Table Style** button (Figure 4-20).
4. Type a style name in the *Name* box.
5. Select a *Table Element* and click **Format** to open the *Format Cells* dialog box.
   - Make format selections on the *Font*, *Border*, or *Fill* tabs in the dialog box and click **OK**.
6. Check or uncheck the set as default box to indicate if the new style should be the default for the current document.
7. Click **OK**.

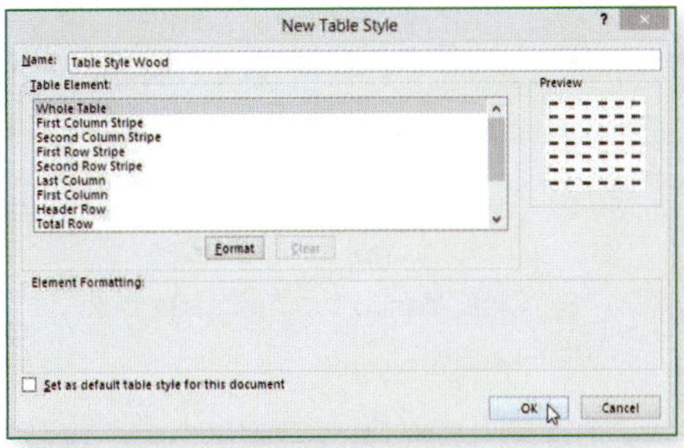

4-20 ***New Table Style*** **dialog box**

The Table Tools Group

The ***Tools*** group on the *Table Tools Design* tab has four commands: *Summarize with PivotTable, Remove Duplicates, Convert to Range,* and *Insert Slicer* (Figure 4-21). *PivotTables* are covered later in this section. First, the other three commands are introduced.

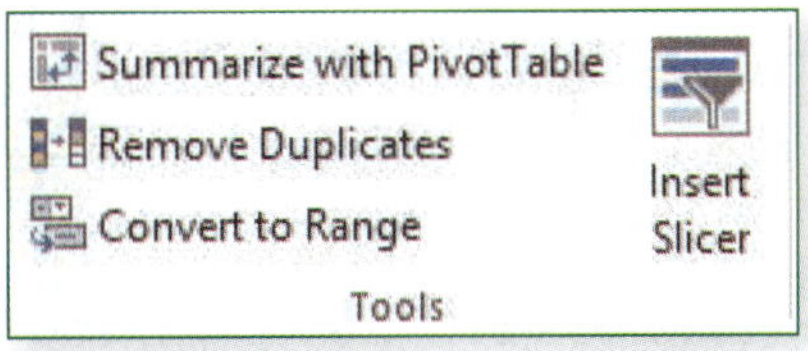

4-21 ***Tools*** **group**

A ***duplicate row*** is a row in a table that has exactly the same information in one or more columns. The *Remove Duplicates* command scans a table to locate and delete any rows with repeated data in the specified columns. In the *Remove Duplicates* dialog box, you specify which columns might have duplicate data.

HOW TO: Remove Duplicates

1. Click any cell within the table.
2. Click the **Remove Duplicates** button [*Table Tools Design* tab, *Tools* group] (Figure 4-22).
3. Place a check mark next to each column that you suspect may have duplicate data.
   - If you check all the columns, those rows containing the same data in every column are considered a duplicate and removed.
4. Click **OK**.
   - A message box indicates how many duplicate values were found and removed as well as how many unique values are still in the table (Figure 4-23).
   - This command does not preview which rows are deleted.
5. Click **OK** in the message box.

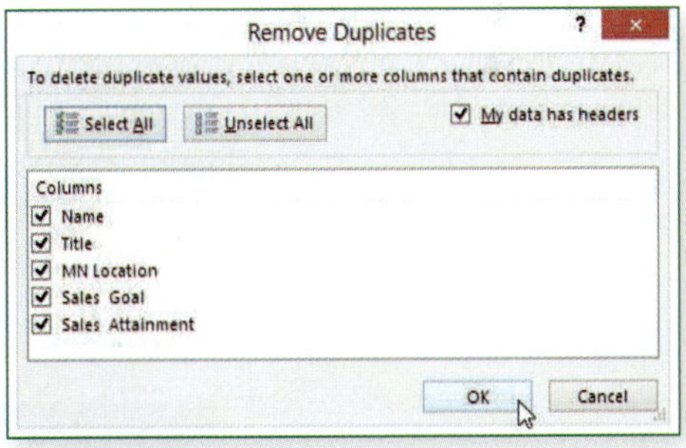

4-22 ***Remove Duplicates*** **dialog box**

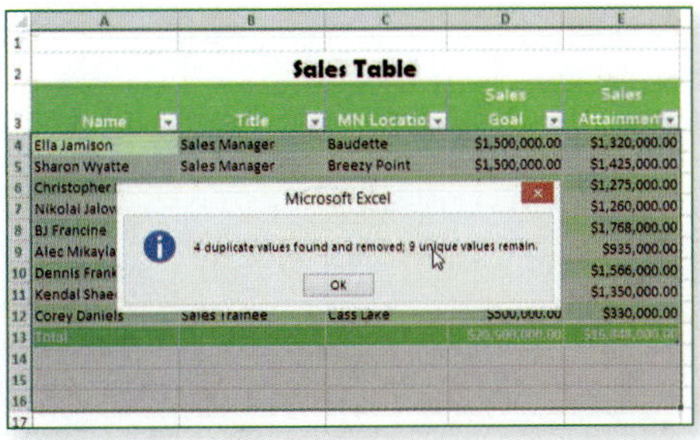

4-23 ***Duplicates Found*** **message box**

In the *Tools* group, you can use the *Convert to Range* command to convert a table to a normal data in the worksheet. This removes all table formatting and the *AutoFilter* buttons.

HOW TO: Convert a Table to Range

1. Click any cell within the table.
2. Click the **Convert to Range** button [*Table Tools Design* tab, *Tools* group] (Figure 4-24).
3. Click **Yes** in the message box.

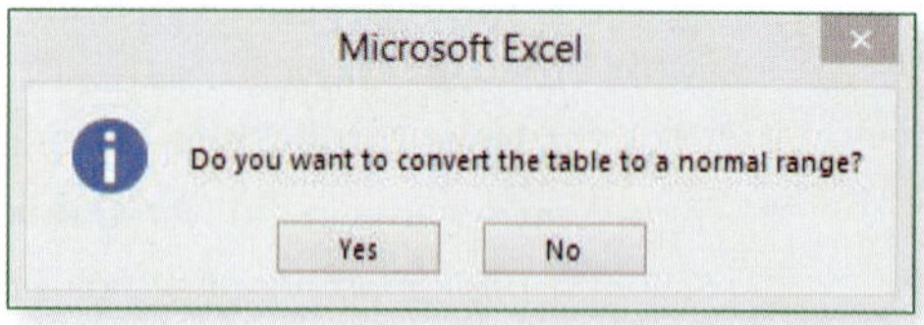

4-24 *Convert to Normal Range* dialog box

MORE INFO

You can show *AutoFilter* buttons in a normal data range by clicking the *Filter* button on the *Data* tab.

The *Insert Slicer* command opens a window where you can filter data to analyze smaller pieces of the whole. This command is also available for *PivotTables,* which are discussed later in this section.

Table Name and Structured References

By default, when you first create an Excel table, it is initially named *TableN* where *N* is a number. You can give an Excel table a more descriptive name using the *Table Tools Design* tab in the *Properties* group.

In an Excel table, each column is assigned a specific name based on the label in its header row. This name is known as a ***structured reference***. There is a structured reference for every column, and structured references are each preceded by the @ symbol. There are also several automatic structured references in a table. They include: #All, #Data, #Headers, #This Row, and #Totals.

You view these structured references when you build a formula by pointing to them (Figure 4-25). You can also refer to them elsewhere in the worksheet when creating a formula.

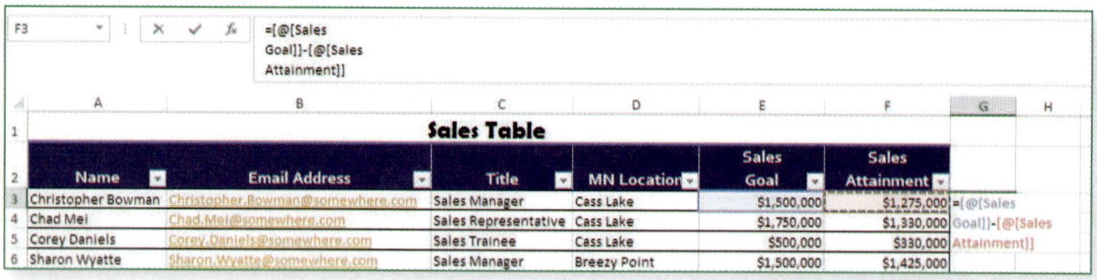

4-25 Structured references in a table

MORE INFO

To force your table formulas to use regular cell referencing in place of table headings, select **Options** from the *File* tab. Select **Formulas** on the left, navigate to the *Working with formulas* category, and remove the check next to *Use table names in formulas.*

PivotTables

A ***PivotTable*** is a summary report based on a list-type range of data in a worksheet. The list of data in a *PivotTable* is dynamic and contains movable field buttons and filter options; you can move and manipulate different components of a *PivotTable* for different analysis options.

In other words, a *PivotTable* is a separate worksheet in which you can sort, filter, and calculate large amounts of data. *PivotTables* are interactive, because you can rearrange parts of the report for analysis by clicking or dragging. Rearranging data is *pivoting* the data; pivoting allows you to look at data from a different perspective. A ***PivotChart*** can be built from a *PivotTable* and has similar features. It contains charted data that is dynamic (updates in real time) and contains the same movable field buttons and filter options that a *PivotTable* does. The *PivotChart* button is on the *PivotTable Tools Analyze* tab.

MORE INFO

If you create a *PivotChart* directly from list data in a worksheet, an underlying *PivotTable* is also automatically created.

PivotTables are sophisticated analysis tools. They enable you to "drill-down" into your data and assess various types of results or changes. For example, in a table or list with thousands of records, you can arrange a *PivotTable* to quickly show average sales by state, by city, or by other criteria, and, just as quickly, return to the entire list.

A *PivotTable* is based on a range of data, like a table, with a header row, although the data does not have to be formatted as an Excel table (Figure 4-26). Data for a *PivotTable* should follow the same guidelines as those recommended for an Excel table in the beginning of this section. A *PivotTable* is placed on its own sheet in the workbook.

The *Tables* group on the *Insert* tab includes the *PivotTable* button as well as the *Recommended PivotTables* button. When you are first learning about *PivotTables*, use the **Recommended PivotTables** button until you gain experience building these reports.

After you create a *PivotTable*, the *PivotTable Tools Analyze* and *Design* tabs are available for additional format choices and data commands.

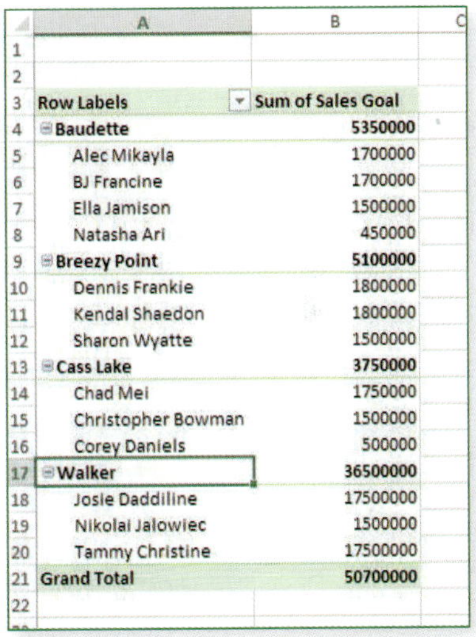

	A	B
1		
2		
3	Row Labels	Sum of Sales Goal
4	Baudette	5350000
5	Alec Mikayla	1700000
6	BJ Francine	1700000
7	Ella Jamison	1500000
8	Natasha Ari	450000
9	Breezy Point	5100000
10	Dennis Frankie	1800000
11	Kendal Shaedon	1800000
12	Sharon Wyatte	1500000
13	Cass Lake	3750000
14	Chad Mei	1750000
15	Christopher Bowman	1500000
16	Corey Daniels	500000
17	Walker	36500000
18	Josie Daddiline	17500000
19	Nikolai Jalowiec	1500000
20	Tammy Christine	17500000
21	Grand Total	50700000
22		

4-26 An Excel *PivotTable*

MORE INFO

You must refresh a *PivotTable* after changes are made to the underlying worksheet data.

HOW TO: Create a PivotTable

1. Click anywhere within the data range.
   - The data range must have a header row.
   - You can select the entire range.

2. Click the **Recommended PivotTables** button [*Insert* tab, *Tables* group] (Figure 4-27).
    - A data range in the worksheet is assumed.
    - Click *Change Source Data* if the assumed range is incorrect.
    - You can create a blank *PivotTable* from this dialog box.
3. Click a preview tile and review the description of the proposed *PivotTable.*
4. Select the preferred *PivotTable* and click **OK**.

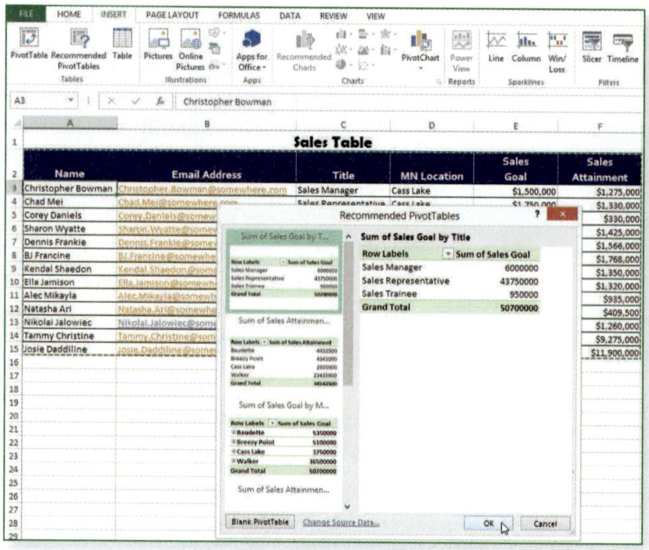

4-27 ***Recommended PivotTables* for a data range**

A *PivotTable* is created on a new sheet in the workbook and the *PivotTable Fields* pane opens at the right. From this pane, you can choose fields to be added to the report and hide or display other fields. You can drag field names into different areas in the pane to regroup how the data is organized.

> **MORE INFO**
>
> Delete the *PivotTable* layout by clicking the **Clear** button [*PivotTable Tools Analyze* tab, *Actions* group]. You can build a new *PivotTable* from the same data.

In the *PivotTable* report itself, each column label includes a filter arrow so that you can hide or display selected rows. Similarly, row labels may include collapse/expand buttons to hide or show data for that part of the report. In addition, you can add a report filter by dragging a field name into the *Filter* part of the *PivotTable Fields* pane.

It takes time and practice to create a useful *PivotTable* and to understand all its features. It is a good idea to experiment as you build *PivotTables* to develop skill in placing fields, and sorting and filtering data.

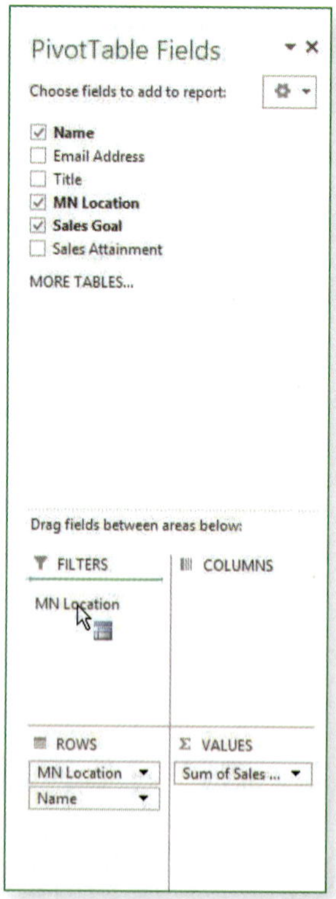

4-28 ***PivotTable Fields* pane**

HOW TO: Add a PivotTable Report Filter and Pivot Fields

1. Click anywhere in the *PivotTable.*
2. Drag the field name into the *Filter* area and release the field (Figure 4-28).
    - Drag the field name from the *Choose fields to add to report* area or from another area in the *PivotTable Fields* pane.
    - The field is added with a filter button in row 1 of the *PivotTable.*

3. Point and drag a field name from the *Choose fields to add to report* area into the *Values* area in the *PivotTable Fields* pane and release the field.
   - A new column is added to the report (Figure 4-29).
   - The calculation used for the *Values* fields is *Sum*. Change it by clicking in the column and selecting the **Field Settings** button [*PivotTable Tools Analyze* tab, *Active Field* group].

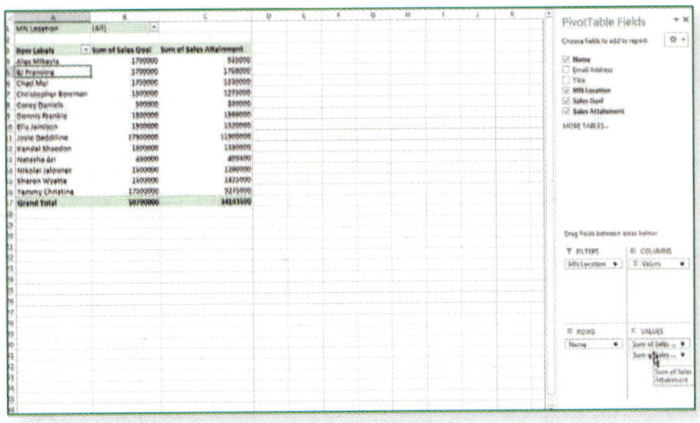

4-29 *PivotTable* results

Export Data

You have seen how you can import data from various sources for use in Excel. Similarly, you can export or save Excel data in a format that is usable in other programs and applications. For example, you can save an Excel table as a text file for use in any program that can read a text file. Since most software applications can read a text file, this is a common way to transfer or share data.

When you save worksheet data as a text file, Excel renames the sheet with the same file name that you type for the text file. You can save only one worksheet in a text file. If a workbook has multiple sheets, a message box will alert you that only the current sheet will be saved.

HOW TO: Save an Excel Table as a Text File

1. Save the workbook file you want to export.
2. Click the worksheet tab with the table or list you want to save and export.
3. Open the *Backstage* view and click **Export**.
4. Click the **Change File Type** button.
5. Select **Text (Tab delimited)** as the file type (Figure 4-30).
6. Click **Save As**.
7. Navigate to the location where you want the exported material to be saved and type the file name.
8. Click **Save**.

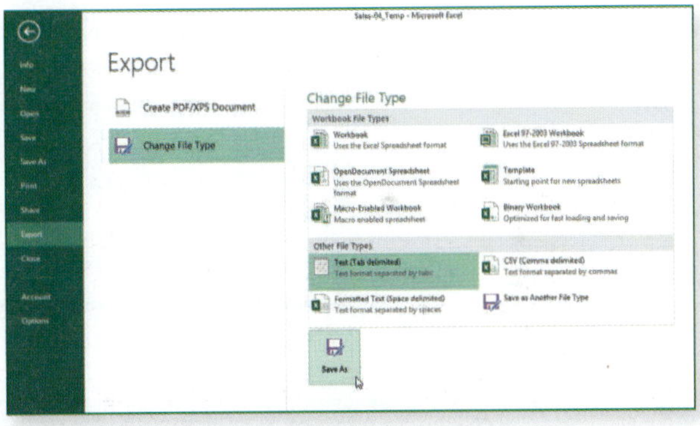

4-30 *Backstage* view to export data

A ***SharePoint web server*** is a server that runs *Microsoft SharePoint Services,* a network product that allows for collaboration and simultaneous work by groups of people via the Internet. You can export table data to a custom list on the server and make your data available for others with the *Export Table to SharePoint List Wizard.* A list on a SharePoint server stores and displays content that users can edit online. To work with the SharePoint server, you must have an Internet connection and permission from the network administrator.

HOW TO: Export an Excel Table to a SharePoint List

1. Click any cell within the table you wish to export.
2. Click the **Export** button [*Table Tools Design* tab, *External Table Data* group].
3. Select the *Export Table to SharePoint List* option.

4. Type the web address of the SharePoint site in the *Address* box (Figure 4-31).
   - Check the **Create a read-only connection to the new SharePoint list** box if you do not want others to edit the data.
   - Two columns are added to the table with a read-only connection. An *Item Type* column indicates whether a row represents a SharePoint list item or a folder. A *Path* column displays the folder path for a list item (mylist/foldername).
5. Type the *List* name and *Description* in the *Export Table to SharePoint List* dialog box.
   - A list name is required and is displayed at the top of the list page.
6. Click **Next**.
7. Click **Finish** if the columns and data types are correct.
8. Click **OK**.
   - Click the **Unlink** button [*Table Tools Design* tab, *External Table Data* group] to disconnect the Excel table from the SharePoint server.

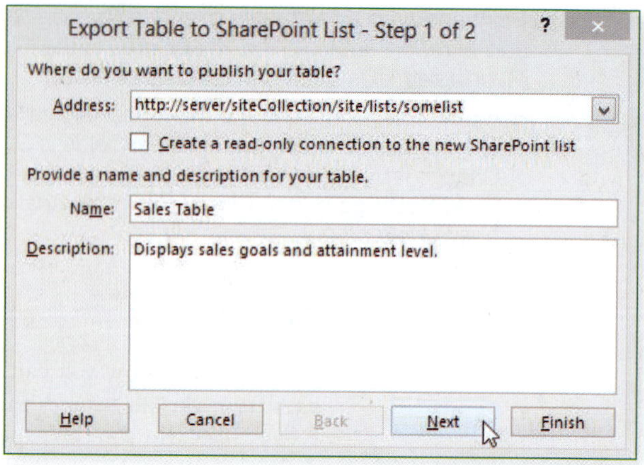

4-31 ***Export Table to SharePoint List* wizard**

MORE INFO

You can access and use SharePoint data in an Excel worksheet, or unlink the data to keep your own copy of the data separate.

ANOTHER WAY

View your SharePoint list by clicking the **Open in Browser** button [*Table Tools Design* tab, *External Table Data* group].

PAUSE & PRACTICE: EXCEL 4-2

For this project, you format data as an Excel table, add a total row, and remove duplicate records. Then you create a *PivotTable* for Paradise Lakes Resort using the Excel table as its source. Because the workbook has data connections, you will need to enable editing to work with it.

File Needed: ***[your initials] PP E4-1.xlsx***
Completed Project File Name: ***[your initials] PP E4-2.xlsx***

1. Open the ***[your initials] PP E4-1*** workbook. Click **Enable Editing**.
2. Save the workbook as ***[your initials] PP E4-2***.
3. Delete column **B**.

4. Select cells **A2:E2** and clear the formats.
5. Rename the sheet tab Sales Quota Data.
6. Format the data as an Excel table.
   a. Select cells **A2:E26**.
   b. Click the **Format as Table** button [*Home* tab, *Styles* group].
   c. Select **Table Style Medium 27** from the *Style* gallery.
   d. Verify that there is a check mark for **My table has headers** in the *Format As Table* dialog box.
   e. Click **OK**.
   f. Click **Yes** in the message box about external connections (Figure 4-32).
7. Add a total row to a table.
   a. Click a cell within the table.
   b. Click to place a check mark for **Total Row** [*Table Tools Design* tab, *Table Style Options* group].
   c. Click cell **D27** and choose **SUM** from the drop-down list.
8. Remove duplicate rows in a table.
   a. Click a cell within the table.
   b. Click the **Remove Duplicates** button [*Table Tools Design* tab, *Tools* group].
   c. Click **Unselect All** to remove all the check marks.
   d. Click **Name** to place a check mark (Figure 4-33). If you know that duplicate data is in a specific column, you can speed up the search by choosing only that column.
   e. Click **OK** in the *Remove Duplicates* dialog box.
   f. Click **OK** in the message box.

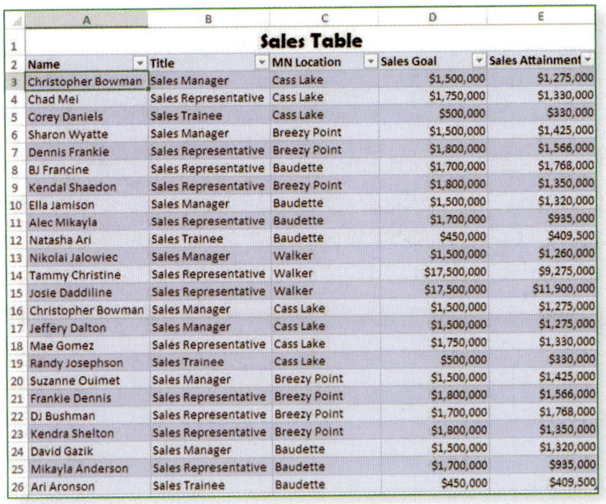

	A	B	C	D	E
1	Sales Table				
2	Name	Title	MN Location	Sales Goal	Sales Attainment
3	Christopher Bowman	Sales Manager	Cass Lake	$1,500,000	$1,275,000
4	Chad Mei	Sales Representative	Cass Lake	$1,750,000	$1,330,000
5	Corey Daniels	Sales Trainee	Cass Lake	$500,000	$330,000
6	Sharon Wyatte	Sales Manager	Breezy Point	$1,500,000	$1,425,000
7	Dennis Frankie	Sales Representative	Breezy Point	$1,800,000	$1,566,000
8	BJ Francine	Sales Representative	Baudette	$1,700,000	$1,768,000
9	Kendal Shaedon	Sales Representative	Breezy Point	$1,800,000	$1,350,000
10	Ella Jamison	Sales Manager	Baudette	$1,500,000	$1,320,000
11	Alec Mikayla	Sales Representative	Baudette	$1,700,000	$935,000
12	Natasha Ari	Sales Trainee	Baudette	$450,000	$409,500
13	Nikolai Jalowiec	Sales Manager	Walker	$1,500,000	$1,260,000
14	Tammy Christine	Sales Representative	Walker	$17,500,000	$9,275,000
15	Josie Daddiline	Sales Representative	Walker	$17,500,000	$11,900,000
16	Christopher Bowman	Sales Manager	Cass Lake	$1,500,000	$1,275,000
17	Jeffery Dalton	Sales Manager	Cass Lake	$1,500,000	$1,275,000
18	Mae Gomez	Sales Representative	Cass Lake	$1,750,000	$1,330,000
19	Randy Josephson	Sales Trainee	Cass Lake	$500,000	$330,000
20	Suzanne Ouimet	Sales Manager	Breezy Point	$1,500,000	$1,425,000
21	Frankie Dennis	Sales Representative	Breezy Point	$1,800,000	$1,566,000
22	DJ Bushman	Sales Representative	Breezy Point	$1,700,000	$1,768,000
23	Kendra Shelton	Sales Representative	Breezy Point	$1,800,000	$1,350,000
24	David Gazik	Sales Manager	Baudette	$1,500,000	$1,320,000
25	Mikayla Anderson	Sales Representative	Baudette	$1,700,000	$935,000
26	Ari Aronson	Sales Trainee	Baudette	$450,000	$409,500

4-32 Excel data formatted as a table

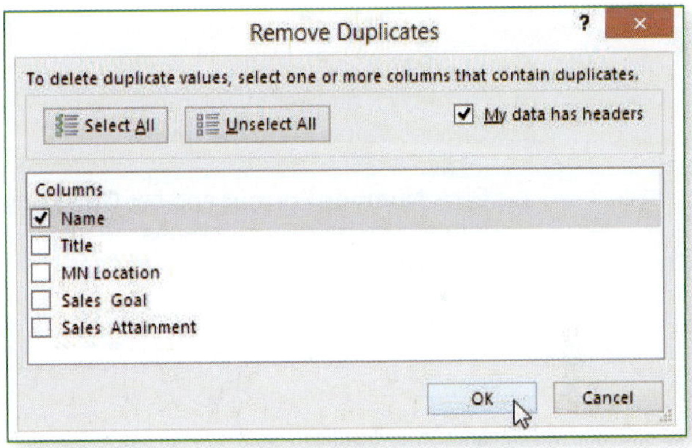

4-33 Duplicate record search in a single field

9. Create a *PivotTable*.
   a. Click cell **A3**.
   b. Click the **Recommended PivotTables** button [*Insert* tab, *Tables* group].
   c. Locate and click the **Sum of Sales Goal by MN Location (+)** preview tile.
   d. Click **OK**.
   e. Name the worksheet tab PivotTable.
10. Add a report filter in a *PivotTable*.
    a. Click a cell in the *PivotTable* to open the *PivotTable Fields* pane.
    b. Drag the **MN Location** field from the *Rows* group to the *Filters* group in the *PivotTable Fields* pane.
    c. Click the filter arrow in cell **B1** and click to place a check mark for **Select Multiple Items**.
    d. Click to remove the check marks for **Baudette** and **Breezy Point** (Figure 4-34).
    e. Click **OK**.

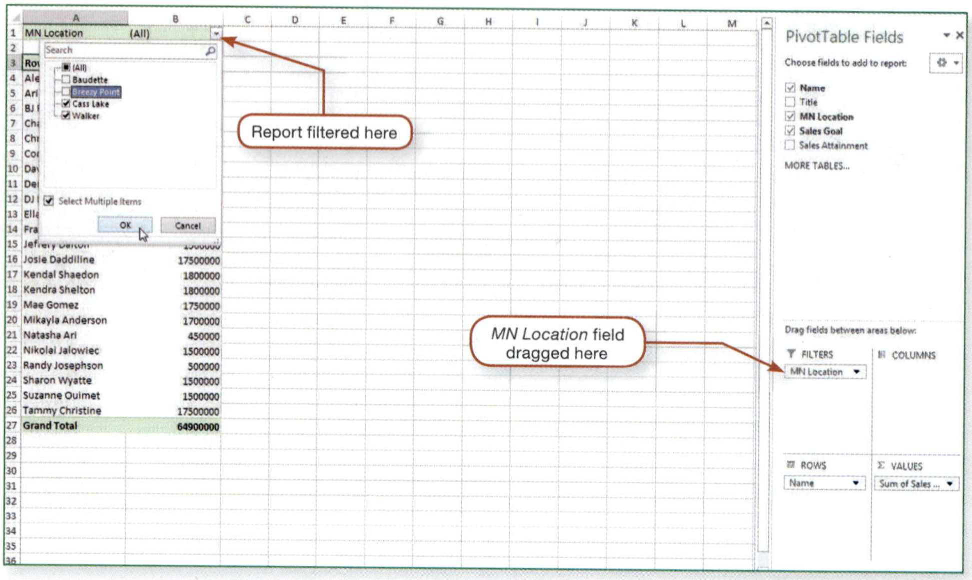

4-34 Report filter settings

11. Format data in a *PivotTable*.
    a. Right-click any cell in column B.
    b. Choose **Value Field Settings** (Figure 4-35).
    c. Click **Number Format** and set **Currency** format with no decimal places.
    d. Click **OK** to close each dialog box.
12. Save and close the workbook (Figure 4-36).

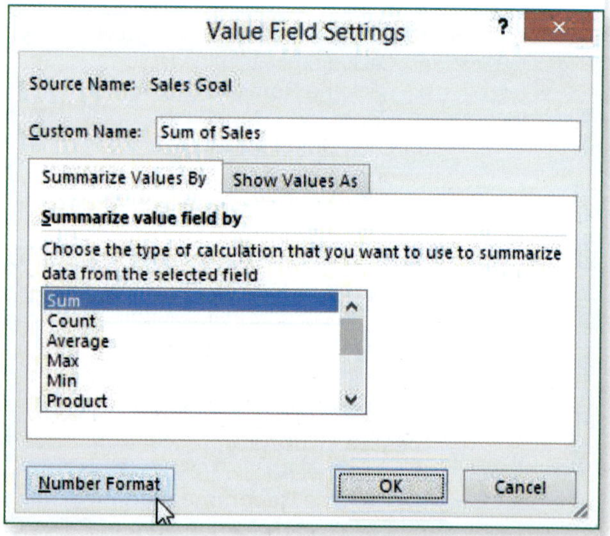

4-35 *Value Field Settings* dialog box

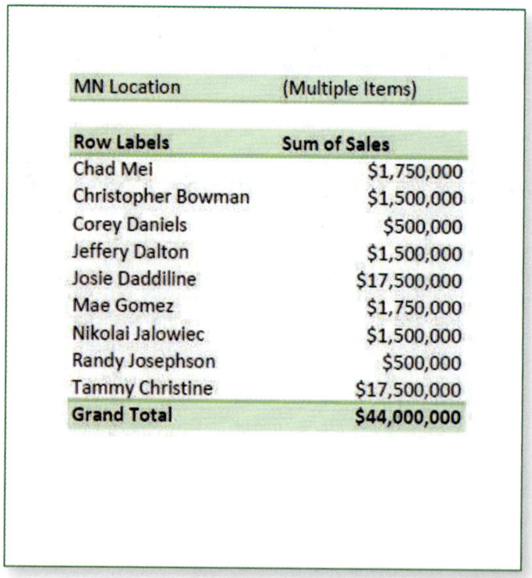

MN Location	(Multiple Items)
Row Labels	**Sum of Sales**
Chad Mei	$1,750,000
Christopher Bowman	$1,500,000
Corey Daniels	$500,000
Jeffery Dalton	$1,500,000
Josie Daddiline	$17,500,000
Mae Gomez	$1,750,000
Nikolai Jalowiec	$1,500,000
Randy Josephson	$500,000
Tammy Christine	$17,500,000
Grand Total	**$44,000,000**

4-36 PP E4-2 completed *PivotTable*

SLO 4.3

Sorting Data

Sorting is the process of arranging rows of data in an identified order. For Paradise Lakes Resort, for example, you may want to arrange the sales table by location to compare the sites. Or you may want to order the rows from best sales attainment to lowest.

You can sort data in ascending or descending order. ***Ascending*** order sorts data alphabetically from A to Z or numerically from smallest to largest value. In a ***descending*** sort, data are arranged alphabetically Z to A or numerically from largest to smallest value.

Sort Options

You can sort all Excel data that is organized in rows and columns. You can sort by one column or by multiple columns. In addition to normal text or number sorting, you can sort data by cell fill color, font color, or cell icons (from *Conditional Formatting,* covered later in this chapter in *SLO 4.6: Applying Conditional Formatting*).

The ***Sort & Filter*** button on the *Home* tab in the *Editing* group lists the *A to Z* sort, the *Z to A* sort, and the *Custom Sort* (multiple columns) commands. The same commands are available in the *Sort & Filter* group on the *Data* tab.

Sort Text Data

In a cell range that has a header row followed by rows of data, you can click any cell in the column you want to sort and click the appropriate button.

HOW TO: Sort Text Data by a Single Column

1. Select a cell in the column that contains the data you want to sort.
2. Click the **A to Z** button [*Data* tab, *Sort & Filter* group].
   - The records are arranged in alphabetical order based on the first character in the cell.
   - If the first character in a row is a value or special character, that record is sorted at the top.
   - Click the **Undo** button [*Home* tab, *Clipboard* group] to undo a sort.
3. Click the **Z to A** button [*Data* tab, *Sort & Filter* group].
   - The records are arranged in reverse alphabetical order based on the first character in the cell (Figure 4-37).
   - If the first character in a row is a value or special character, that record is sorted at the bottom.

	A	B	C	D	E
1	Sales Table				
2	Name	Title	MN Location	Sales Goal	Sales Attainment
3	Tammy Christine	Sales Representative	Walker	$17,500,000.00	$9,275,000.00
4	Sharon Wyatte	Sales Manager	Breezy Point	$1,500,000.00	$1,425,000.00
5	Nikolai Jalowiec	Sales Manager	Walker	$1,500,000.00	$1,260,000.00
6	Natasha Ari	Sales Trainee	Baudette	$450,000.00	$409,500.00
7	Kendal Shaedon	Sales Representative	Breezy Point	$1,800,000.00	$1,350,000.00
8	Josie Daddiline	Sales Representative	Walker	$17,500,000.00	$11,900,000.00
9	Ella Jamison	Sales Manager	Baudette	$1,500,000.00	$1,320,000.00
10	Dennis Frankie	Sales Representative	Breezy Point	$1,800,000.00	$1,566,000.00
11	Corey Daniels	Sales Trainee	Cass Lake	$500,000.00	$330,000.00
12	Christopher Bowman	Sales Manager	Cass Lake	$1,500,000.00	$1,275,000.00
13	Chad Mei	Sales Representative	Cass Lake	$1,750,000.00	$1,330,000.00
14	BJ Francine	Sales Representative	Baudette	$1,700,000.00	$1,768,000.00
15	Alec Mikayla	Sales Representative	Baudette	$1,700,000.00	$935,000.00

4-37 "Name" column sorted Z to A

MORE INFO

When you sort a cell range using the **A to Z** or **Z to A** buttons, complete rows of data are rearranged, not just the cells in the selected column.

To sort text data in more than one column or field, use the *Sort* dialog box. This dialog box opens when you click the **Sort** button [*Data* tab, *Sort & Filter* group] or when you choose **Custom Sort** from the **Sort & Filter** button options [*Home* tab, *Editing* group]. A common multiple column sort involves data that includes cities and states. You can first sort by state so that Alabama is before Arizona, and then within that sort, you can further sort by city. Another example of a common multiple column sort involves persons' names. When first and last names are listed in separate columns, you can sort by last name and then first name. If a list includes 15 people named "Smith," you can further sort them by first name.

The data in Figure 4-38 is sorted with a multiple sort.

	A	B	C	D	E
1	**Sales Table**				
2	Name	Title	MN Location	Sales Goal	Sales Attainment
3	Ella Jamison	Sales Manager	Baudette	$1,500,000.00	$1,320,000.00
4	Sharon Wyatte	Sales Manager	Breezy Point	$1,500,000.00	$1,425,000.00
5	Christopher Bowman	Sales Manager	Cass Lake	$1,500,000.00	$1,275,000.00
6	Nikolai Jalowiec	Sales Manager	Walker	$1,500,000.00	$1,260,000.00
7	BJ Francine	Sales Representative	Baudette	$1,700,000.00	$1,768,000.00
8	Alec Mikayla	Sales Representative	Baudette	$1,700,000.00	$935,000.00
9	Kendal Shaedon	Sales Representative	Breezy Point	$1,800,000.00	$1,350,000.00
10	Dennis Frankie	Sales Representative	Breezy Point	$1,800,000.00	$1,566,000.00
11	Chad Mei	Sales Representative	Cass Lake	$1,750,000.00	$1,330,000.00
12	Tammy Christine	Sales Representative	Walker	$17,500,000.00	$9,275,000.00
13	Josie Daddiline	Sales Representative	Walker	$17,500,000.00	$11,900,000.00
14	Natasha Ari	Sales Trainee	Baudette	$450,000.00	$409,500.00
15	Corey Daniels	Sales Trainee	Cass Lake	$500,000.00	$330,000.00

4-38 Data sorted first by "Title" and then by "MN Location"

HOW TO: Sort Text Data by Multiple Columns

1. Select a cell in the range of cells that you want to sort.
2. Click the **Sort** button [*Data* tab, *Sort & Filter* group].
3. Check the **My data has headers** box if your data has a header row.
4. Click the **Sort by** arrow and select the column heading for the first sort (Figure 4-39).
   - The *Sort On* option specifies *Values*, *Cell Color*, *Font Color*, or *Cell Icon*. Use *Values* for sorting text or numbers.
5. Click the **Order** arrow and choose a sort option.
6. Click **Add Level** to add a second sort column.
7. Click the **Then by** arrow and select the second column heading.
8. Click the **Order** arrow and choose a sort option.
   - Click the **Options** button in the *Sort* dialog box to specify case-sensitive sorting.
9. Click **OK**.

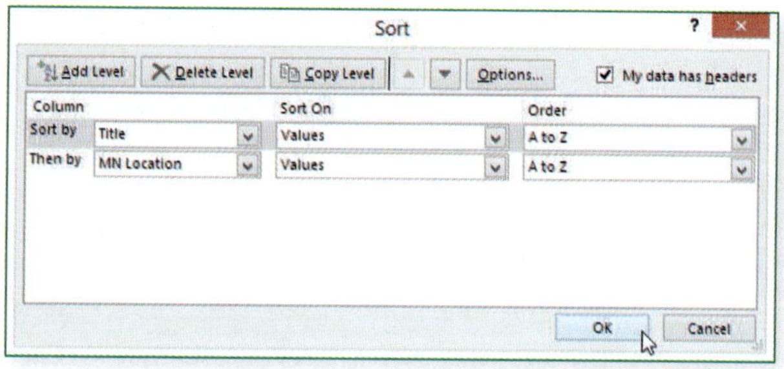

4-39 *Sort* dialog box

Sort Data with Values

To sort data that contains values, take the same steps you took to sort text data. A value sort can be smallest to largest or largest to smallest.

Dates are treated as values. When dates are sorted smallest to largest, the earliest dates are listed first. To show the most recent date at the top of a sort, sort largest to smallest.

HOW TO: Sort Values by a Single Column

1. Select a cell in the column you want to sort.
2. Click the **A to Z** button [*Data* tab, *Sort & Filter* group].
   - If some of the beginning characters are values and some are text, rows that begin with a value are sorted first.
3. Click the **Z to A** button [*Data* tab, *Sort & Filter* group].

MORE INFO

A warning message may appear when you select a cell range for sorting. The warning asks if you would prefer to select the whole data set; you can ignore the warning and sort only the selected data.

In a multiple column sort, you can use both a value column and a text column if necessary. The same *Sort* dialog box is used, and the *Sort On* option is *Values* for both fields. The data in Figure 4-40 is sorted first by the "MN Location" column, a text sort, and then by the "Sales Attainment" column, a value sort.

	A	B	C	D	E
1	Sales Table				
2	Name	Title	MN Location	Sales Goal	Sales Attainment
3	Natasha Ari	Sales Trainee	Baudette	$450,000.00	$409,500.00
4	Alec Mikayla	Sales Representative	Baudette	$1,700,000.00	$935,000.00
5	Ella Jamison	Sales Manager	Baudette	$1,500,000.00	$1,320,000.00
6	BJ Francine	Sales Representative	Baudette	$1,700,000.00	$1,768,000.00
7	Kendal Shaedon	Sales Representative	Breezy Point	$1,800,000.00	$1,350,000.00
8	Sharon Wyatte	Sales Manager	Breezy Point	$1,500,000.00	$1,425,000.00
9	Dennis Frankie	Sales Representative	Breezy Point	$1,800,000.00	$1,566,000.00
10	Corey Daniels	Sales Trainee	Cass Lake	$500,000.00	$330,000.00
11	Christopher Bowman	Sales Manager	Cass Lake	$1,500,000.00	$1,275,000.00
12	Chad Mei	Sales Representative	Cass Lake	$1,750,000.00	$1,330,000.00
13	Nikolai Jalowiec	Sales Manager	Walker	$1,500,000.00	$1,260,000.00
14	Tammy Christine	Sales Representative	Walker	$17,500,000.00	$9,275,000.00
15	Josie Daddiline	Sales Representative	Walker	$17,500,000.00	$11,900,000.00

4-40 Sorted data by "MN Location" and then by "Sales Attainment"

HOW TO: Sort Values and Text in Multiple Columns

1. Select a cell in the range you want to sort.
2. Click the **Sort** button [*Data* tab, *Sort & Filter* group].
3. Check the **My data has headers** box if your data has headers.
4. Click the **Sort by** arrow and select the column heading for the first sort.
5. Click the **Order** arrow and choose a sort option.
6. Click **Add Level** to add another column sort.
7. Click the **Then by** arrow and select the second column heading.
8. Click the **Order** arrow and choose a sort option.
9. Add more levels if necessary.
10. Click **OK**.

ANOTHER WAY

To sort data in a column, right-click a cell in the column to be sorted, choose **Sort**, and then choose the type of sort.

Sort by Font or Cell Color

In addition to basic sorting by the value or text content of data, you can sort data based on the font color or the cell fill color. For example, you might use color-coding in a large worksheet to identify cities, months, or individuals. You can use *Conditional Formatting* (discussed in detail later in this chapter in *SLO 4.6: Applying Conditional Formatting*) to apply fill or font color to cells. If font or fill color is used to classify data, you can group items with a sort command. In Figure 4-41 the cells with yellow fill are grouped at the top of the "Sales Attainment" column.

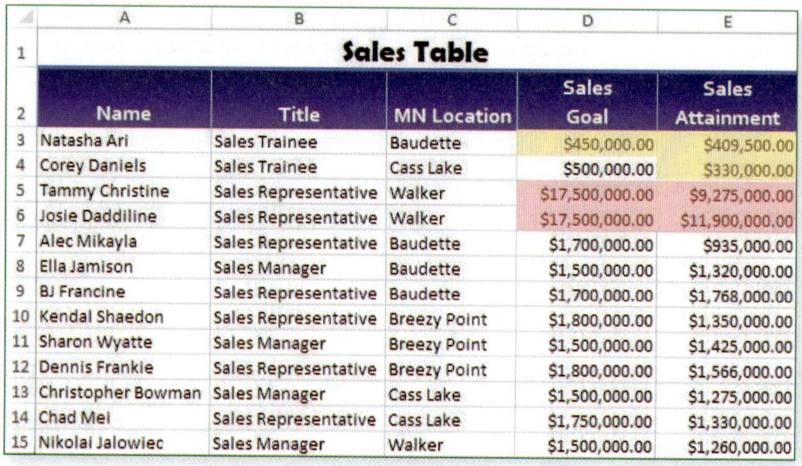

	A	B	C	D	E
1	**Sales Table**				
2	Name	Title	MN Location	Sales Goal	Sales Attainment
3	Natasha Ari	Sales Trainee	Baudette	$450,000.00	$409,500.00
4	Corey Daniels	Sales Trainee	Cass Lake	$500,000.00	$330,000.00
5	Tammy Christine	Sales Representative	Walker	$17,500,000.00	$9,275,000.00
6	Josie Daddiline	Sales Representative	Walker	$17,500,000.00	$11,900,000.00
7	Alec Mikayla	Sales Representative	Baudette	$1,700,000.00	$935,000.00
8	Ella Jamison	Sales Manager	Baudette	$1,500,000.00	$1,320,000.00
9	BJ Francine	Sales Representative	Baudette	$1,700,000.00	$1,768,000.00
10	Kendal Shaedon	Sales Representative	Breezy Point	$1,800,000.00	$1,350,000.00
11	Sharon Wyatte	Sales Manager	Breezy Point	$1,500,000.00	$1,425,000.00
12	Dennis Frankie	Sales Representative	Breezy Point	$1,800,000.00	$1,566,000.00
13	Christopher Bowman	Sales Manager	Cass Lake	$1,500,000.00	$1,275,000.00
14	Chad Mei	Sales Representative	Cass Lake	$1,750,000.00	$1,330,000.00
15	Nikolai Jalowiec	Sales Manager	Walker	$1,500,000.00	$1,260,000.00

4-41 Yellow fill sorted on top in "Sales Attainment" column

When you sort by color, there are two choices about the *Order* in the *Sort* dialog box. You set which color is to be first. Then you specify whether that color should sort to the top or the bottom. If you have three colors, you can indicate where each color should fall in the sort order.

HOW TO: Sort Data by Font or Cell Color

1. Select a cell in the column you want to sort.
2. Click the **Sort** button [*Data* tab, *Sort & Filter* group].
3. Check the **My data has headers** box if your data has headers.
4. Click the **Sort by** arrow and select the column heading for the first sort.
5. Click the **Sort On** arrow and choose **Cell Color** or **Font Color**.
6. Click the first **Order** arrow (on the left) and choose the first color (Figure 4-42).
7. Click the second **Order** arrow (on the right) and choose **On Top** or **On Bottom**.
8. Click the **Add Level** to add another column sort option as desired.
9. Click the **Then by** arrow and select the second column heading.
   - Add as many sort levels as there are colors to be sorted.
   - Choose the color and the sort position for each color.
10. Click **OK**.

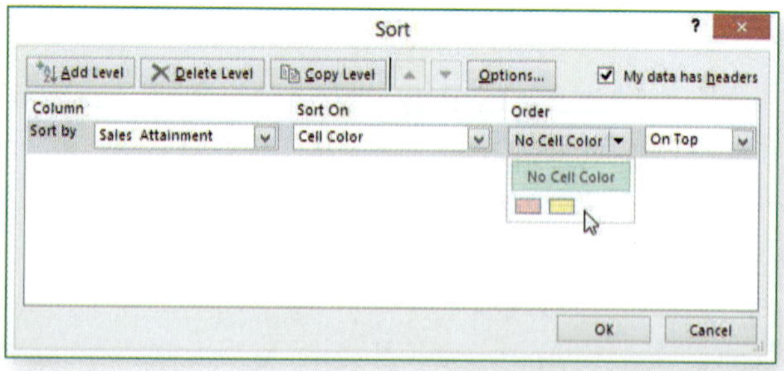

4-42 Cell color options in the *Sort* dialog box

Sort by Cell Icon

A cell icon is a small image that you can place in a cell with a *Conditional Formatting* command (see *SLO 4.6: Applying Conditional Formatting* in this chapter). You can apply icons in sets of three, four, or five, and you can sort by icon. The sorted data in Figure 4-43 has a two-set icon, sorted with the green icons on the top.

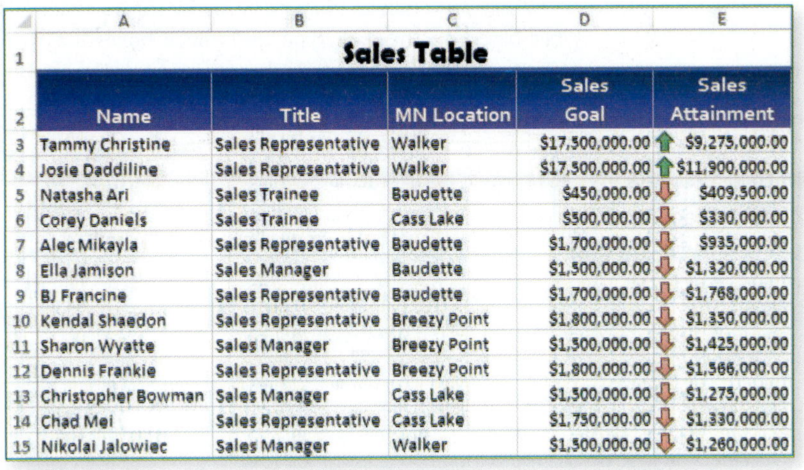

	A	B	C	D	E
1	Sales Table				
2	Name	Title	MN Location	Sales Goal	Sales Attainment
3	Tammy Christine	Sales Representative	Walker	$17,500,000.00	$9,275,000.00
4	Josie Daddiline	Sales Representative	Walker	$17,500,000.00	$11,900,000.00
5	Natasha Ari	Sales Trainee	Baudette	$450,000.00	$409,500.00
6	Corey Daniels	Sales Trainee	Cass Lake	$500,000.00	$330,000.00
7	Alec Mikayla	Sales Representative	Baudette	$1,700,000.00	$935,000.00
8	Ella Jamison	Sales Manager	Baudette	$1,500,000.00	$1,320,000.00
9	BJ Francine	Sales Representative	Baudette	$1,700,000.00	$1,768,000.00
10	Kendal Shaedon	Sales Representative	Breezy Point	$1,800,000.00	$1,350,000.00
11	Sharon Wyatte	Sales Manager	Breezy Point	$1,500,000.00	$1,425,000.00
12	Dennis Frankie	Sales Representative	Breezy Point	$1,800,000.00	$1,566,000.00
13	Christopher Bowman	Sales Manager	Cass Lake	$1,500,000.00	$1,275,000.00
14	Chad Mei	Sales Representative	Cass Lake	$1,750,000.00	$1,330,000.00
15	Nikolai Jalowiec	Sales Manager	Walker	$1,500,000.00	$1,260,000.00

4-43 Data sorted by the cell icon in "Sales Attainment" column

HOW TO: Sort Data by Cell Icon

1. Select a cell with an icon in the column you want to sort.
2. Click the **Sort** button [*Data* tab, *Sort & Filter* group].
3. Check the **My data has headers** box if your data has headers.
4. Click the **Sort by** arrow and select the column heading for the first sort.
5. Click the **Sort On** arrow and choose **Cell Icon**.
6. Click the first **Order** arrow and select the first icon.
7. Click the second **Order** arrow (on the right) and choose **On Top** or **On Bottom** (Figure 4-44).
8. Click the **Add Level** button to add another sort option.
9. Click the **Then by** arrow and select the second column heading.
   - Add as many levels as there are icons.
   - Choose the sort order for each icon.
10. Click **OK**.

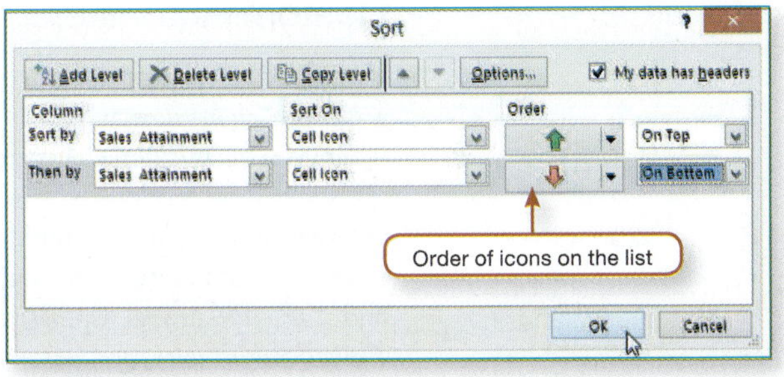

4-44 *Sort* dialog box

SLO 4.4

Filtering Data

When you work with large lists or tables, it is not practical to display thousands of rows of data on screen at once. It is easier to work with data if you filter the data to show the rows for the current month, the selected individual, or a specific product. Recall that a filter specifies which data is shown and which is hidden based on a specified criteria. When you filter data, information that doesn't meet the specified requirements is temporarily hidden.

The AutoFilter Command

Recall from earlier in the chapter that the *AutoFilter* button allows you to quickly hide or display rows of data. In list-type data or an Excel table, the ***AutoFilter*** command displays a filter arrow for each label in the header row. A table automatically shows *AutoFilter* arrows, but you need to activate them for a normal data range.

When you click an *AutoFilter* arrow for a header label, a pane displays sort options, filter types based on the data type, and check boxes for every piece of data. You can select check boxes to mark which records should be displayed or you can build a filter.

HOW TO: Use AutoFilters

1. Select a cell in the cell range to be filtered.
2. Click the **Filter** button [*Data* tab, *Sort & Filter* group].
3. Click the **AutoFilter** button so the column is filtered.
4. Click **(Select All)** to remove all check marks.
5. Check each record you want displayed (Figure 4-45).
6. Click **OK**.
   - Records that meet the criteria are visible with row headings in blue.
   - Records that do not meet the criteria and their row numbers are hidden.
   - A filter symbol appears with the column *AutoFilter* button (Figure 4-46).

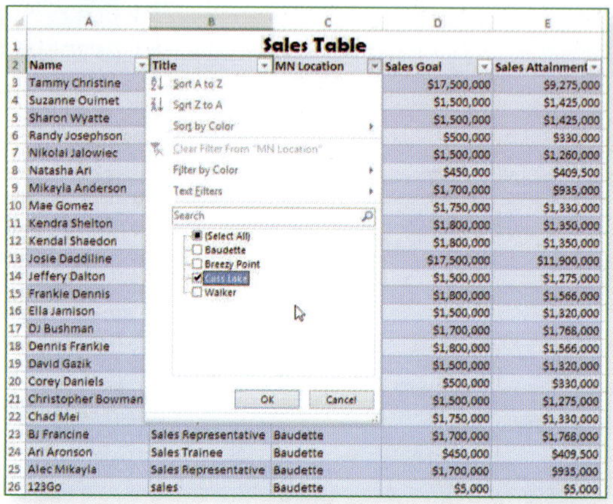

4-45 *AutoFilter* for "MN Location"

Custom AutoFilter

From the *AutoFilter* button, you can build a custom *AutoFilter*, which is a dialog box where you build criteria. A custom *AutoFilter* gives you more options to specify how rows are displayed. You can build criteria to select ranges of data using relational operators *AND*, and *OR*. Relational operators are words like *Equals*, *Begins with*, or *Contains* (Figure 4-47).

The available filters depend on the type of data in the column. For example, if the column is text, *Text Filters* are available. There are also *Number Filters* and *Date Filters*.

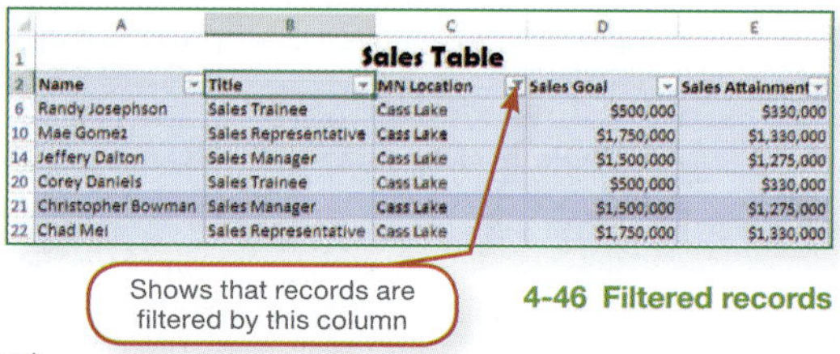

4-46 Filtered records

> **ANOTHER WAY**
>
> To turn off an *AutoFilter*, click the **Filter** button [*Data* tab, *Sort & Filter* group].

To remove any filter and return to the complete list, click the **Clear** button in the *Sort & Filter* group on the *Data* tab. Alternatively, you can click the *AutoFilter* button for the column and choose **Clear Filter From (ColumnName)**.

4-47 Text filters for a custom *AutoFilter*

HOW TO: Create a Custom Text AutoFilter

1. Select a cell in the cell range you want to filter.
2. Click the **Filter** button [*Data* tab, *Sort & Filter* group].
3. Click the **AutoFilter** button for the column you want to filter.
4. Select **Text Filters** and choose an operator.
5. Type the desired criteria in the *Custom AutoFilter* dialog box.
   - In Figure 4-48, the letter *B* is entered in the text box to filter for location names that contain the letter *B*.
6. Click **OK** in the *Custom AutoFilter* dialog box.
   - Rows that do not contain the letter *B* are hidden in Figure 4-49.

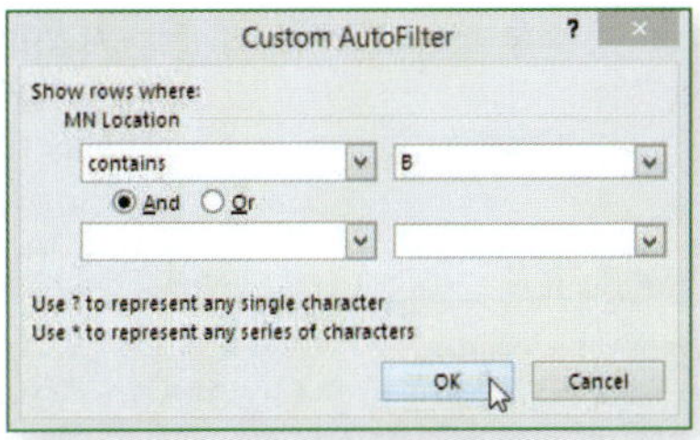

4-48 ***Custom AutoFilter*** **dialog box**

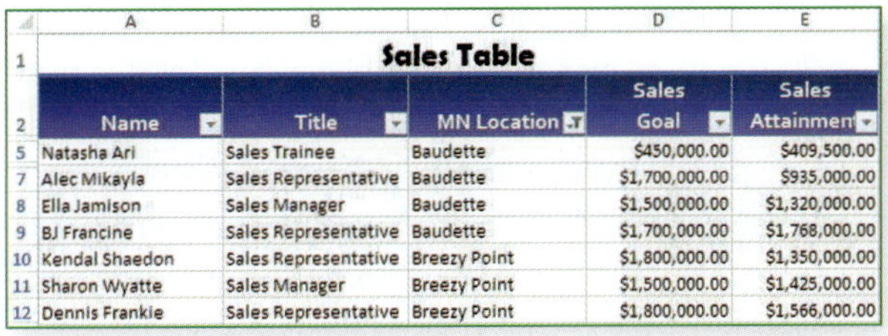

Sales Table

	Name	Title	MN Location	Sales Goal	Sales Attainment
5	Natasha Ari	Sales Trainee	Baudette	$450,000.00	$409,500.00
7	Alec Mikayla	Sales Representative	Baudette	$1,700,000.00	$935,000.00
8	Ella Jamison	Sales Manager	Baudette	$1,500,000.00	$1,320,000.00
9	BJ Francine	Sales Representative	Baudette	$1,700,000.00	$1,768,000.00
10	Kendal Shaedon	Sales Representative	Breezy Point	$1,800,000.00	$1,350,000.00
11	Sharon Wyatte	Sales Manager	Breezy Point	$1,500,000.00	$1,425,000.00
12	Dennis Frankie	Sales Representative	Breezy Point	$1,800,000.00	$1,566,000.00

4-49 ***AutoFilter*** **results for "MN Location" data containing the letter B**

Advanced Filter

An *Advanced Filter* is similar to a query in a database. When you use an *Advanced Filter*, you build a criteria range separate from the actual data and type the criteria within that range. You can filter the data in the worksheet range or you can output data to another location on the sheet. Being able to output filter results allows you to create separate reports that include only filtered rows. An *Advanced Filter* requires more set-up work but allows you to apply more complex filters. You can even use a formula in your criteria.

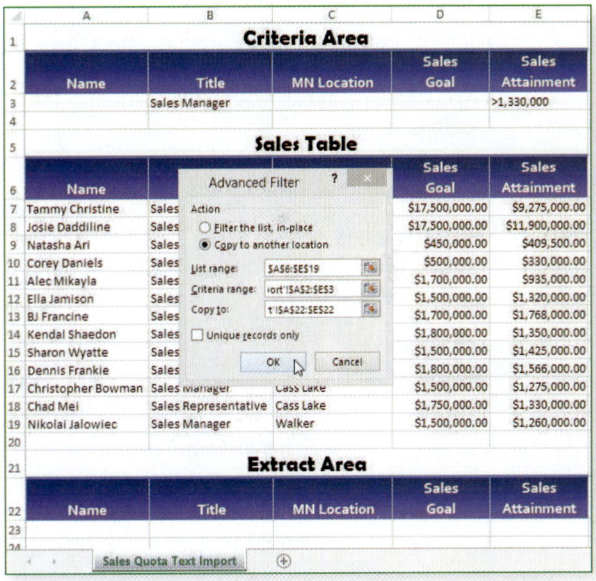

4-50 ***Advanced Filter*** **set-up and dialog box**

To use an *Advanced Filter*, you need to create a ***criteria range***. The criteria range must be at least two rows. The first row must use column names from the worksheet data but you need not use all of them. You type the actual criteria in the second row. You can create a criteria range in empty rows anywhere on the worksheet or on another sheet. In Figure 4-50, the criteria range is A2:E3.

You can use multiple rows after the header row in the criteria range to set *AND* or *OR* conditions. If you enter criteria on the same row, they are treated as *AND* conditions. This means both criteria must be met for the record to be displayed. In Figure 4-50, "Sales Manager" in cell B3 and ">1,330,000" in cell E3 are the criteria. This is an *AND* condition because both criteria are on the same row. For an *OR* condition, use a second (or third) row in the criteria range. An *OR* filter displays the record if any one of the requirements is met.

If you want to output filtered results to another location, you also create an ***extract range***. You only need to specify one row for this range, and it should include the same column headings as the data. The filter results are copied to the area below these headings and take up as many rows as necessary. In Figure 4-50, the extract range is A22:E22. Filter results appear below the extract area header.

HOW TO: Create an Advanced Filter

1. Select the header row and copy the labels to a *Criteria* area on the same worksheet or to another sheet in the same workbook.
   - If you plan to use only one or two fields in the criteria, you only need to copy those labels to the criteria range.
   - If you place the criteria range above the data, leave at least one blank row between it and the data.
2. Select the header row and copy the labels to an *Extract* area in the same worksheet.
   - The output or extract area must be on the same sheet as the data you want to filter.
   - Leave enough blank rows below the labels for the filtered results.
3. Enter the criteria in the criteria range.
4. Click the **Advanced** button [*Data* tab, *Sort & Filter* group] to open the *Advanced Filter* dialog box (see Figure 4-50).
5. Select the **Copy to another location** button to display results in the extract area.
6. In the *List range* text box, verify or select the range (including the header row).
7. In the *Criteria range* text box, select the criteria cell range in the worksheet with its header row.
   - If the criteria range is on another sheet, click the worksheet tab and then select the range.
   - You can type in cell references to identify the criteria range.
8. In the *Copy to* text box, select the extract range in the worksheet.
9. Click **OK** (Figure 4-51).

	A	B	C	D	E
21			Extract Area		
22	Name	Title	MN Location	Sales Goal	Sales Attainment
23	Sharon Wyatte	Sales Manager	Breezy Point	$1,500,000.00	$1,425,000.00
24					

4-51 ***Advanced Filter*** **results for "Sales Managers" with a "Sales Attainment" greater than $1,330,000**

SLO 4.5

Using the Subtotal Command and Creating Outlines and Groups

The ***Subtotal*** command automatically inserts summary rows for data that are arranged in related groups. To obtain the summary amounts, you can use functions such as *SUM, AVERAGE, MAX,* or *MIN.* Although you can insert summary rows and formulas on your own, that would be a daunting task if you had 10,000 records sorted into 200 groups. For example, you would have to insert 200 rows in the correct location for each group and then copy the formula to each of those rows. The *Subtotal* command does this automatically.

Use the Subtotal Command with SUM

The *Subtotal* command is available for a normal range of cells. The command is not available when the range is formatted as an Excel table, because a table has its own total and sorting commands. If your data is formatted as a table, you must first convert it to a normal cell range before you can display subtotals.

For the *Subtotal* command to work properly, you must sort the rows by the main field (column) to be totaled. To display sales totals by city location, for example, sort the data by the city name. The *Subtotal* command groups the rows by this field.

The *Subtotal* command formats the list data as an ***outline***. An **outline** is a summary that groups records so that they can be displayed or hidden from view. The *Subtotal* button is located in the *Outline* group on the *Data* tab.

HOW TO: Display Subtotals

1. Sort the data in the first column where you want to show subtotals.
   - Convert the data to a normal range if needed.
2. Select the cell range including the header row.
3. Click the **Subtotals** button [*Data* tab, *Outline* group].
4. Click the **At each change in** arrow and choose the column heading for the subtotals.
   - This is the same column you used to sort the data.
5. Click the **Use function** arrow and choose the function.
6. In the **Add subtotal to** list, check each field that should display a subtotal.
   - You can include a subtotal for other columns (fields).
7. Choose command options such as **Replace current subtotals** and **Summary below data** (Figure 4-52) as desired.
   - You can run the *Subtotal* command numerous times with different functions to analyze data by replacing any existing subtotals.
   - You can allow a group to split across pages.
   - The "Summary" row can be placed above the data if you prefer.
   - You can remove subtotals from this dialog box.
8. Click **OK** (Figure 4-53).
   - A subtotal row appears below each group.
   - A grand total appears after the last row of data.
   - Outline buttons appear to the left of the column and row headings.
   - The outline is expanded, showing all details.

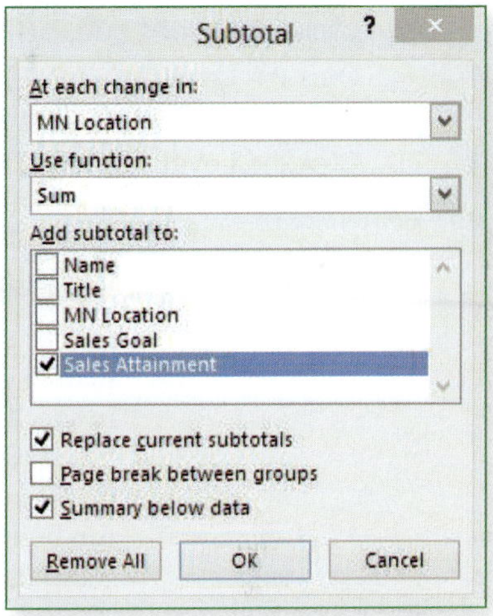

4-52 *Subtotal* dialog box

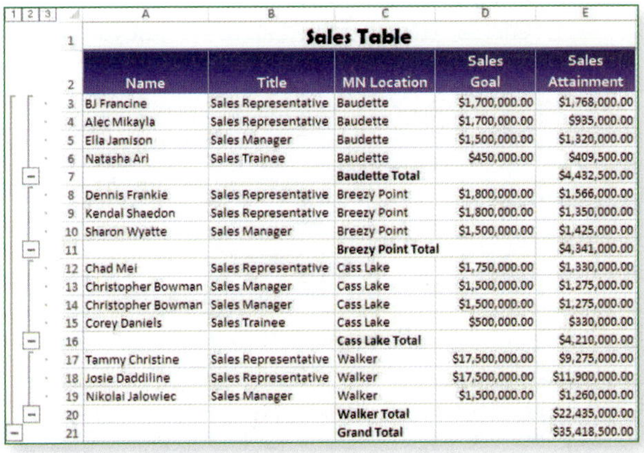

	A	B	C	D	E
1	Sales Table				
2	Name	Title	MN Location	Sales Goal	Sales Attainment
3	BJ Francine	Sales Representative	Baudette	$1,700,000.00	$1,768,000.00
4	Alec Mikayla	Sales Representative	Baudette	$1,700,000.00	$935,000.00
5	Ella Jamison	Sales Manager	Baudette	$1,500,000.00	$1,320,000.00
6	Natasha Ari	Sales Trainee	Baudette	$450,000.00	$409,500.00
7			**Baudette Total**		$4,432,500.00
8	Dennis Frankie	Sales Representative	Breezy Point	$1,800,000.00	$1,566,000.00
9	Kendal Shaedon	Sales Representative	Breezy Point	$1,800,000.00	$1,350,000.00
10	Sharon Wyatte	Sales Manager	Breezy Point	$1,500,000.00	$1,425,000.00
11			**Breezy Point Total**		$4,341,000.00
12	Chad Mei	Sales Representative	Cass Lake	$1,750,000.00	$1,330,000.00
13	Christopher Bowman	Sales Manager	Cass Lake	$1,500,000.00	$1,275,000.00
14	Christopher Bowman	Sales Manager	Cass Lake	$1,500,000.00	$1,275,000.00
15	Corey Daniels	Sales Trainee	Cass Lake	$500,000.00	$330,000.00
16			**Cass Lake Total**		$4,210,000.00
17	Tammy Christine	Sales Representative	Walker	$17,500,000.00	$9,275,000.00
18	Josie Daddiline	Sales Representative	Walker	$17,500,000.00	$11,900,000.00
19	Nikolai Jalowiec	Sales Manager	Walker	$1,500,000.00	$1,260,000.00
20			**Walker Total**		$22,435,000.00
21			**Grand Total**		$35,418,500.00

4-53 Sales Attainment subtotals for each location

> **MORE INFO**
>
> If you apply a filter to data with subtotals, you can hide the subtotal rows.

Outline Buttons

An ***outline*** groups and summarizes data. A worksheet can have only one outline; the outline can include all of the data on the sheet or a portion of it. Outlines have levels, indicated by the numbered buttons to the left of the column headings. Each of the *Outline Level* buttons shows increasing level of detail. The worksheet in Figure 4-53 has three levels. An outline can have up to eight levels.

Each level has an *Expand/Collapse* button. This button is a toggle and shows a minus sign (-) or a plus sign (+). When an individual group is collapsed, you do not see details for that group, only the subtotal.

HOW TO: Use Outline Buttons

1. Click a collapse button (-) to hide details for a row.
2. Click an expand button (+) to display details for a row.
3. Click the **Level 1** button (1) to reveal the grand total.
4. Click the **Level 2** button (2) to see the second outline level details (Figure 4-54).
5. Click the **Level 3** button (3) to display all details.

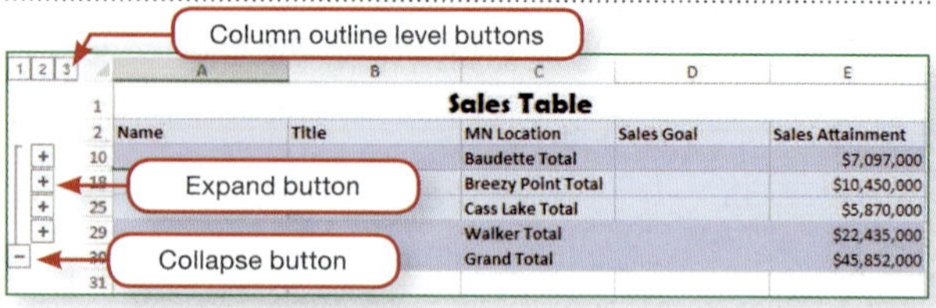

4-54 Level 2 outline results

Create an Auto Outline

If your data is consistently formatted, you can create an automatic outline. Consistently formatted data is grouped with related formulas in the same location. The formulas can be either in specific rows or columns, because an outline can use either. An ***Auto Outline*** inserts groups based on where the formulas are located in your data.

The data in Figure 4-55 is grouped and there is a *SUM* formula after each group. Excel can build an *Auto Outline* group from this type of data. If your data is not properly formatted, Excel displays a message that an *Auto Outline* cannot be created.

HOW TO: Apply an Auto Outline

1. Click a cell within the data range that you want to automatically outline.
2. Click the **Group** button arrow [*Data* tab, *Outline* group] and select **Auto Outline** (Figure 4-56).
   - Expand or collapse the outline to show or hide details.

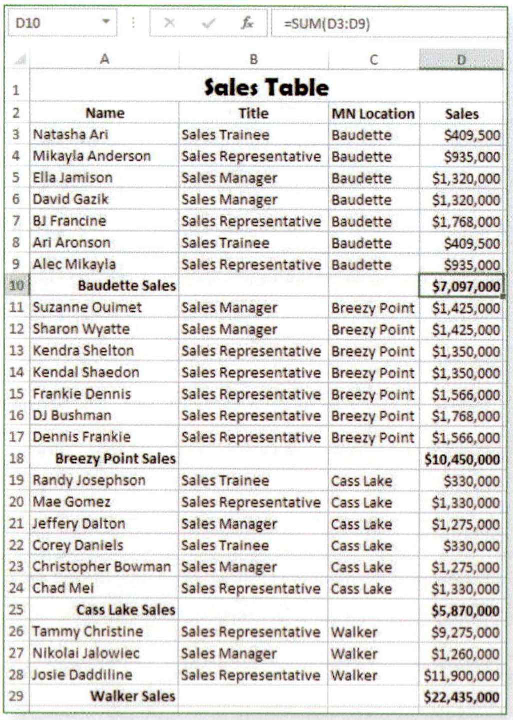

4-55 Data sorted by city with formulas after each city

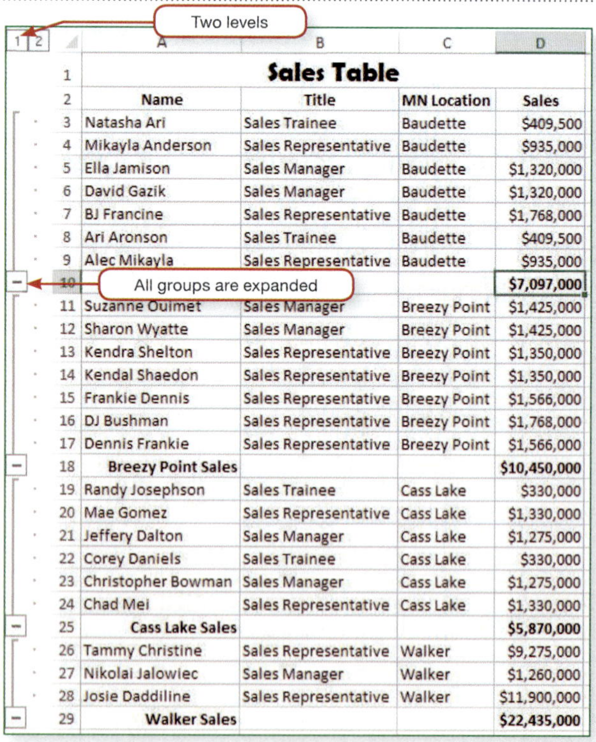

4-56 *AutoOutline* with two levels

> **MORE INFO**
>
> To clear an *Auto Outline,* click the **Ungroup** button arrow [*Data* Tab, *Outline* group] and select **Clear Outline**.

Define Groups

In addition to outlining data, you can create a group, by rows or columns, for data that does not have totals or formulas. To create a group, your data must be sorted or arranged so that you can select a range of cells to indicate the group, and you can insert a summary row either above or below the group (or a summary column to the left or right of the group). You can use these blank rows to enter subtitles for the data before or after grouping.

When you work with large numbers of records in a worksheet, you can use groups to hide data that is not needed at the moment. You can concentrate only on those groups that require editing or other work.

The data in Figure 4-57 is sorted by the "Title" column, so that groups can be created for each title. Note that a blank row has been inserted after each group.

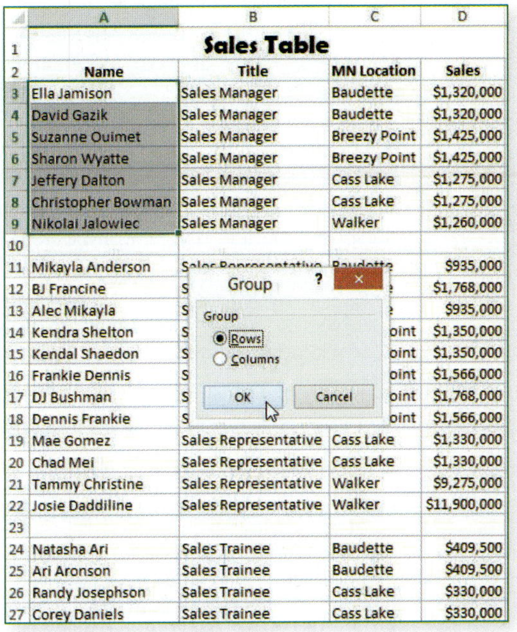

	A	B	C	D
1		Sales Table		
2	Name	Title	MN Location	Sales
3	Ella Jamison	Sales Manager	Baudette	$1,320,000
4	David Gazik	Sales Manager	Baudette	$1,320,000
5	Suzanne Ouimet	Sales Manager	Breezy Point	$1,425,000
6	Sharon Wyatte	Sales Manager	Breezy Point	$1,425,000
7	Jeffery Dalton	Sales Manager	Cass Lake	$1,275,000
8	Christopher Bowman	Sales Manager	Cass Lake	$1,275,000
9	Nikolai Jalowiec	Sales Manager	Walker	$1,260,000
10				
11	Mikayla Anderson			$935,000
12	BJ Francine	S		$1,768,000
13	Alec Mikayla	S		$935,000
14	Kendra Shelton	S	oint	$1,350,000
15	Kendal Shaedon	S	oint	$1,350,000
16	Frankie Dennis	S	oint	$1,566,000
17	DJ Bushman	S	oint	$1,768,000
18	Dennis Frankie	S	oint	$1,566,000
19	Mae Gomez	Sales Representative	Cass Lake	$1,330,000
20	Chad Mei	Sales Representative	Cass Lake	$1,330,000
21	Tammy Christine	Sales Representative	Walker	$9,275,000
22	Josie Daddiline	Sales Representative	Walker	$11,900,000
23				
24	Natasha Ari	Sales Trainee	Baudette	$409,500
25	Ari Aronson	Sales Trainee	Baudette	$409,500
26	Randy Josephson	Sales Trainee	Cass Lake	$330,000
27	Corey Daniels	Sales Trainee	Cass Lake	$330,000

4-57 Data sorted by Title; blank rows inserted after each title

HOW TO: Define a Group

1. Sort the data (or arrange columns) based on the preferred grouping.
2. Insert a blank row at the end of each sort group (or at the start of each group).
   - Include a blank row above the first group if you want to display a subtitle row for each group.
   - For column data, the summary column is usually to the right of the group.
3. Select a range of cells that includes each row (or column) of your first group.
   - Do not include the blank row or column.
   - You can select the entire range in the row or column.
4. Click the **Group** button [*Data* tab, *Outline* group].
5. Choose **Rows** or **Columns** (see Figure 4-57).
   - For example, you can create column groups for data that show 12 months in the header row to group them by quarters.
6. Click **OK**.
7. Repeat steps 1-6 for each group (Figure 4-58).

	A	B	C	D
1		Sales Table		
2	Name	Title	MN Location	Sales
3	Ella Jamison	Sales Manager	Baudette	$1,320,000
4	David Gazik	Sales Manager	Baudette	$1,320,000
5	Suzanne Ouimet	Sales Manager	Breezy Point	$1,425,000
6	Sharon Wyatte	Sales Manager	Breezy Point	$1,425,000
7	Jeffery Dalton	Sales Manager	Cass Lake	$1,275,000
8	Christopher Bowman	Sales Manager	Cass Lake	$1,275,000
9	Nikolai Jalowiec	Sales Manager	Walker	$1,260,000
10				
11	Mikayla Anderson	Sales Representative	Baudette	$935,000
12	BJ Francine	Sales Representative	Baudette	$1,768,000
13	Alec Mikayla	Sales Representative	Baudette	$935,000
14	Kendra Shelton	Sales Representative	Breezy Point	$1,350,000
15	Kendal Shaedon	Sales Representative	Breezy Point	$1,350,000
16	Frankie Dennis	Sales Representative	Breezy Point	$1,566,000
17	DJ Bushman	Sales Representative	Breezy Point	$1,768,000
18	Dennis Frankie	Sales Representative	Breezy Point	$1,566,000
19	Mae Gomez	Sales Representative	Cass Lake	$1,330,000
20	Chad Mei	Sales Representative	Cass Lake	$1,330,000
21	Tammy Christine	Sales Representative	Walker	$9,275,000
22	Josie Daddiline	Sales Representative	Walker	$11,900,000
23				
24	Natasha Ari	Sales Trainee	Baudette	$409,500
25	Ari Aronson	Sales Trainee	Baudette	$409,500
26	Randy Josephson	Sales Trainee	Cass Lake	$330,000
27	Corey Daniels	Sales Trainee	Cass Lake	$330,000
28				

4-58 Defined groups

> **MORE INFO**
>
> To remove groups, click the **Ungroup** button [*Data* Tab, *Outline* group] and select **Clear Outline**.

PAUSE & PRACTICE: EXCEL 4-3

For this project, you sort and filter data for Paradise Lakes Resort. You sort data according to location and sales values and use a *Number Filter* to display the best sales. You also build an advanced filter and include subtotals in your workbook. Because the workbook has data connections, you must enable editing.

File Needed: ***[your initials] PP E4-2.xlsx***
Completed Project File Name: ***[your initials] PP E4-3.xlsx***

1. Open the ***[your initials] PP E4-2*** workbook. Click **Enable Editing**.
2. Save the workbook as ***[your initials] PP E4-3***.
3. Click the **Sales Quota Data** sheet tab.
4. Convert a table to a normal data range.
   a. Click any cell in the table.
   b. Click to remove the check mark for **Total Row** [*Table Tools Design* tab, *Table Style options* group].
   c. Click the **Convert to Range** button [*Table Tools Design* tab, *Tools* group].
   d. Click **Yes**.
   e. Select cells **A2:E25** and apply **No Fill** [*Home* tab, *Font* group].
5. Sort data in a worksheet.
   a. Click any cell in the data range.
   b. Click the **Sort** button [*Data* tab, *Sort & Filter* group].
   c. Click the **My data has headers** check box if necessary.
   d. Click the **Sort by** arrow and select **MN Location**.
   e. Choose **Values** for *Sort On* and **A to Z** for *Order*.
   f. Click the **Add Level** button.
   g. Click the **Then by** arrow and select **Sales Goal**.
   h. Choose **Values** for *Sort On* and **Largest to Smallest** for *Order* (Figure 4-59).
   i. Click **OK**. The data is sorted alphabetically first by "MN Location" and then by "Sales Goal" numbers in descending order.

4-59 Multiple column sort with text and numeric data

6. Use a *Number AutoFilter*.
   a. Click any cell in the data range.
   b. Click the **Filter** button [*Data* tab, *Sort & Filter* group]. *AutoFilter* buttons appear with each label in the header row.
   c. Click the **AutoFilter** button for "Sales Attainment".
   d. Point at **Number Filters** and select **Greater Than Or Equal To**.
   e. In the **is greater than or equal to** text box, enter 1700000.
   f. Click **OK** (Figure 4-60).

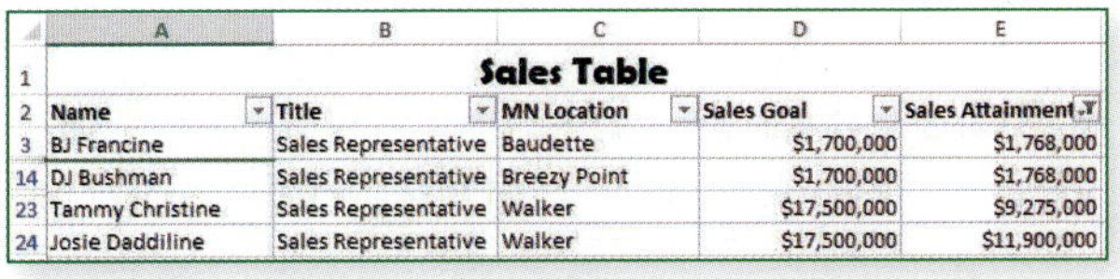

4-60 *AutoFilter* results for Sales Attainment data greater than or equal to $1,700,000

7. Make a copy of the **Sales Quota Data** sheet to the right of the original. *Hint: Right-click the worksheet tab*.
8. Name the copied worksheet Advanced Filter.
9. Click the **Clear** button [*Data* tab, *Sort & Filter* group] to remove the filter.
10. Click the **Filter** button [*Data* tab, *Sort & Filter* group] to remove the *AutoFilter* buttons.
11. Create a criteria range and an extract range.
    a. Insert four rows above row 1.
    b. Select cells **A6:E6**. Copy and paste them in cells **A2:E2** and then in cells **A32:E32**.
    c. Type Criteria Area in cell **A1** and Extract Area in cell **A31**.
    d. Select **A5**, double-click the **Format Painter** button, and apply the formats to cells **A1** and **A31**. Click the **Format Painter** to turn it off.
    e. In cell **B3**, type Sales Trainee.
    f. In cell **E3**, type <400000.
12. Run an *Advanced Filter*.
    a. Click in **A7**.
    b. Click the **Advanced** button [*Data* tab, *Sort & Filter* group].
    c. Select the **Copy to another location** radio button.
    d. Verify that the correct data range is shown in the **List range** text box. If the data range is not correct, select cells **A6:E29**.
    e. Click in the **Criteria range** text box and select cells **A2:E3**.
    f. Click in the **Copy to** text box and select cells **A32:E32** (Figure 4-61).
    g. Click **OK**. Two records that meet the criteria, Corey Daniels and Randy Josephson, are displayed in rows 33:34.

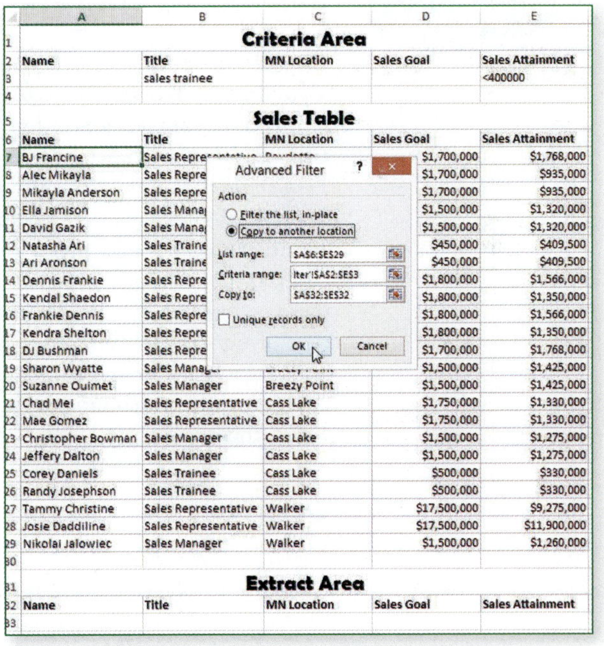

4-61 Criteria and extract ranges; *Advanced Filter* dialog box

13. Make a copy of the *Sales Quota Data* sheet to the right of the *Advanced Filter* sheet.
14. Name the copied worksheet Subtotals.
15. Click the **Clear** button [*Data* tab, *Sort & Filter* group] to remove the filter.

16. Click the **Filter** button [*Data* tab, *Sort & Filter* group] to remove the *AutoFilter* buttons.
17. Show subtotals in a list.
    a. Click a cell in the **Title** column and click the **Sort A to Z** button [*Data* tab, *Sort & Filter* group].
    b. Click the **Subtotal** button [*Data* tab, *Outline* group].
    c. Click the **At each change in** arrow and choose **Title**.
    d. Click the **Use function** arrow and choose **Average**.
    e. In the **Add subtotal to list** box, click to place check marks for **Sales Goal** and **Sales Attainment**.
    f. Click **OK** (Figure 4-62).
18. Save and close the workbook.

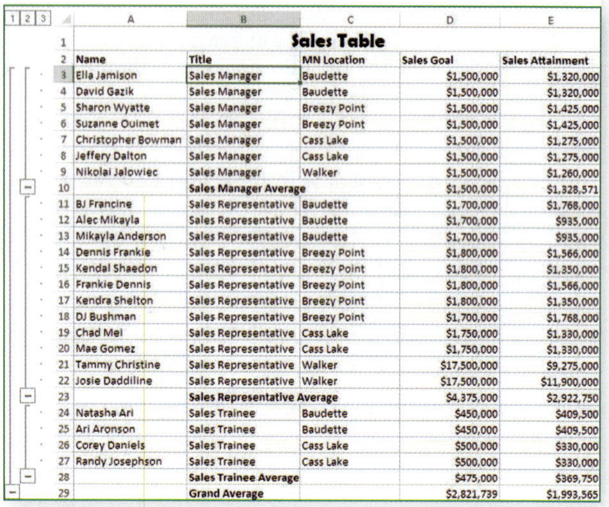

	A	B	C	D	E
1		Sales Table			
2	Name	Title	MN Location	Sales Goal	Sales Attainment
3	Ella Jamison	Sales Manager	Baudette	$1,500,000	$1,320,000
4	David Gazik	Sales Manager	Baudette	$1,500,000	$1,320,000
5	Sharon Wyatte	Sales Manager	Breezy Point	$1,500,000	$1,425,000
6	Suzanne Ouimet	Sales Manager	Breezy Point	$1,500,000	$1,425,000
7	Christopher Bowman	Sales Manager	Cass Lake	$1,500,000	$1,275,000
8	Jeffery Dalton	Sales Manager	Cass Lake	$1,500,000	$1,275,000
9	Nikolai Jalowiec	Sales Manager	Walker	$1,500,000	$1,260,000
10		Sales Manager Average		$1,500,000	$1,328,571
11	BJ Francine	Sales Representative	Baudette	$1,700,000	$1,768,000
12	Alec Mikayla	Sales Representative	Baudette	$1,700,000	$935,000
13	Mikayla Anderson	Sales Representative	Baudette	$1,700,000	$935,000
14	Dennis Frankie	Sales Representative	Breezy Point	$1,800,000	$1,566,000
15	Kendal Shaedon	Sales Representative	Breezy Point	$1,800,000	$1,350,000
16	Frankie Dennis	Sales Representative	Breezy Point	$1,800,000	$1,566,000
17	Kendra Shelton	Sales Representative	Breezy Point	$1,800,000	$1,350,000
18	DJ Bushman	Sales Representative	Breezy Point	$1,700,000	$1,768,000
19	Chad Mei	Sales Representative	Cass Lake	$1,750,000	$1,330,000
20	Mae Gomez	Sales Representative	Cass Lake	$1,750,000	$1,330,000
21	Tammy Christine	Sales Representative	Walker	$17,500,000	$9,275,000
22	Josie Daddiline	Sales Representative	Walker	$17,500,000	$11,900,000
23		Sales Representative Average		$4,375,000	$2,922,750
24	Natasha Ari	Sales Trainee	Baudette	$450,000	$409,500
25	Ari Aronson	Sales Trainee	Baudette	$450,000	$409,500
26	Corey Daniels	Sales Trainee	Cass Lake	$500,000	$330,000
27	Randy Josephson	Sales Trainee	Cass Lake	$500,000	$330,000
28		Sales Trainee Average		$475,000	$369,750
29		Grand Average		$2,821,739	$1,993,565

4-62 Completed PP E4-3 worksheet with subtotals

SLO 4.6

Applying Conditional Formatting

Conditional Formatting commands apply specified formats to cells only when the cells meet some criteria. You can use *Conditional Formatting* to highlight information in a worksheet by setting different fill colors or font styles for selected cells. For example, a sales manager might use *Conditional Formatting* to display sales amounts that are below a certain level in a bold red font.

Conditional Formatting is dynamic; the formatting adapts if the data changes. In our sales example, if sales values are updated and a particular person or department that was below the specified level has now met a goal, the bold red formatting is removed.

Basic *Conditional Formatting* commands are *Highlight Cells Rules* and *Top/Bottom Rules*. For these commands, you set the rule or criteria in a dialog box and choose the format. Another type of *Conditional Formatting* is ***data visualization***, in which specified data is indicated with a fill color, a horizontal bar, or an icon within the cell. *Data visualization* commands include *Data Bars, Color Scales,* and *Icon Sets.*

Cells Rules

Highlight Cells Rules uses relational or comparison operators to determine if the value or label in a cell should be formatted. *Highlight Cells Rules* includes common operators such as *Equal to* and *Greater Than.* You can also create your own rule using other operators or a formula.

You can access all of the conditional formatting options from the *Conditional Formatting* button in the *Styles* group on the *Home* tab (Figure 4-63). You can also choose a recommended conditional formatting style from the *Quick Analysis* tool options.

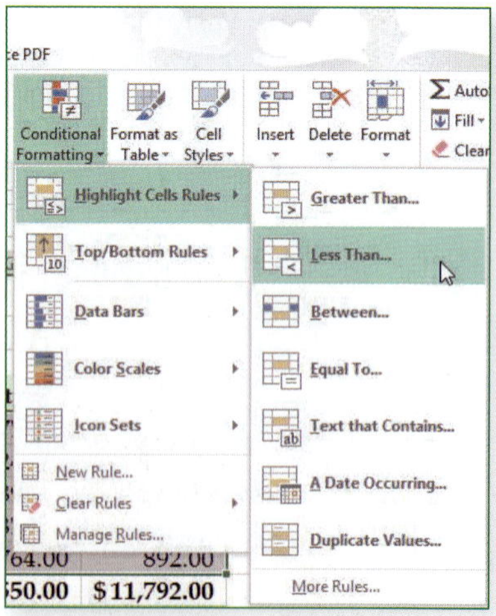

4-63 *Highlight Cells Rules* menu

HOW TO: Create a "Less Than" Highlight Cells Rule

1. Select the cell range to be formatted.
2. Click the **Conditional Formatting** button [*Home* tab, *Styles* group].
3. Click **Highlight Cells Rules** and select **Less Than**.
4. In the *Format cells that are LESS THAN* box, type a value. If the number in a cell is below this value, the cell will be conditionally formatted.
   - You can click a cell in the worksheet to enter a value.
5. Click the arrow in the *with* entry box and choose a preset option (Figure 4-64).
   - Alternatively, you can choose *Custom Format* to open the *Format Cells* dialog box and build a custom format.
6. Click **OK**.

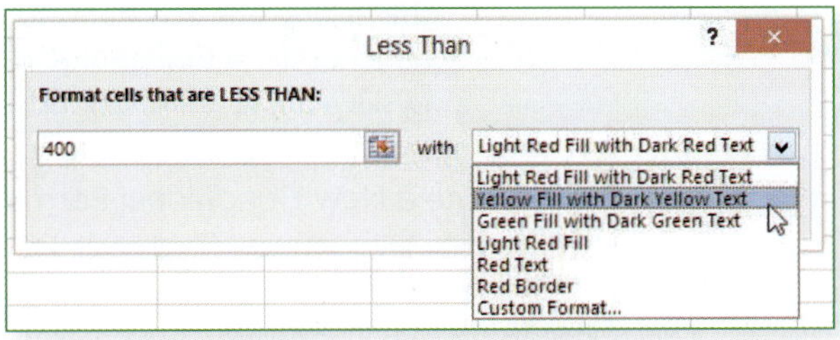

4-64 *Less Than* dialog box

Top/Bottom Rules use a ranking to format the highest (top) or lowest (bottom) items or a specified percentage of a list. You can also set a rule to format values that are above or below average (Figure 4-65). You are not limited to the percentages or numbers shown in the menu.

When you select a range of values, the *Quick Analysis* tool appears in the bottom right corner of the range. The *Totals* group typically provides likely conditional format choices. When you make your choice this way, the same dialog box opens so that you can build the format.

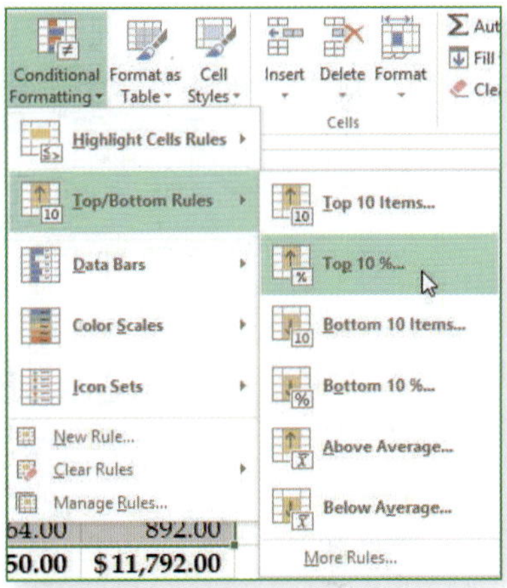

4-65 *Top/Bottom Rules*

HOW TO: Create a Top 10% Rule

1. Select the cell range you want to format.
2. Click the **Quick Analysis** button.
3. Click **Formatting** and choose **Top 10%** (Figure 4-66).
4. Click the arrow for the *with* box and choose **Custom Format**.
5. Click the appropriate tab to set a fill color, a font, or a border.
6. Click **OK** to close the *Format Cells* dialog box.
7. Click **OK** to close the *Top 10%* dialog box.

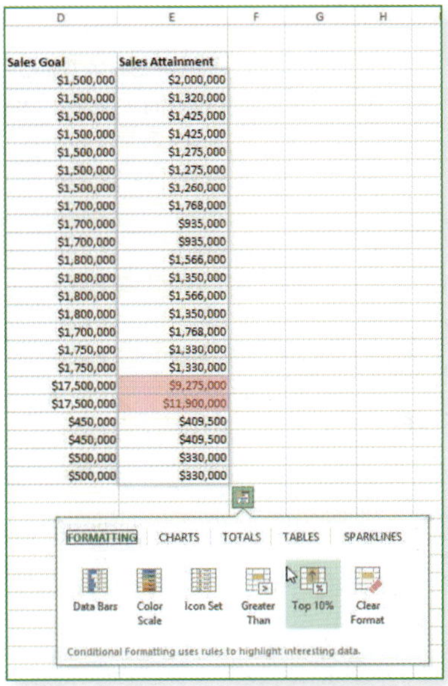

4-66 *Quick Analysis* options for conditional formatting

If you cannot find a *Highlight Cells* or *Top/Bottom* rule that fits your needs, create your own rule using operators, criteria, and formats in the *New Formatting Rule* dialog box. Options in this dialog box allow you to create a rule based on a formula as well. You can, for example, build a rule to format only cells that display a particular percentage of a specified value, such as sales that are 108% of the sales goal.

HOW TO: Create a New Conditional Formatting Rule

1. Select the cell range to be formatted.
2. Click the **Conditional Formatting** button [*Home* tab, *Styles* group].
3. Click **New Rule** to open the *New Formatting Rule* dialog box (Figure 4-67).
4. Select a rule type from the *Select a Rule Type* list.
5. In the *Edit the Rule Description* area, make choices to build the new rule.
   - The options that are available depend on the type of rule.
   - Click **Format** (when available) to set the format in the *Format Cells* dialog box.
   - Click **OK** to close the *Format Cells* dialog box.
6. Click **OK** to close the *New Formatting Rule* dialog box.

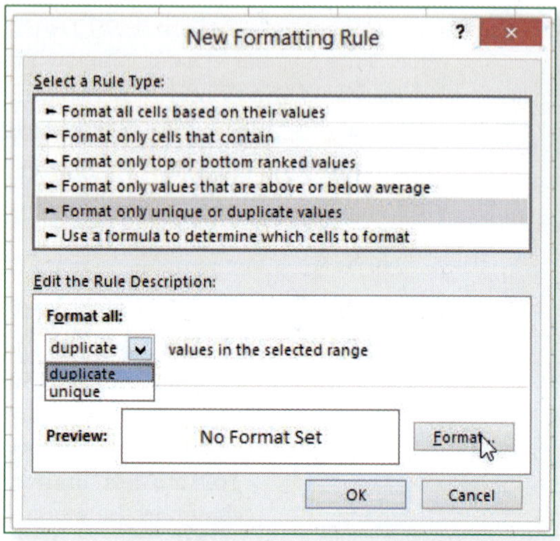

4-67 *New Formatting Rule* dialog box

Data Bars, Color Scales, and Icon Sets

Excel's data visualization *Conditional Formatting* commands format cells with icons, cell shading, or shaded bars to distinguish the values. They generally highlight the low, middle, or top values or compare the values to each other.

You can access the *Conditional Formatting* button in the *Styles* group on the *Home* tab, or the *Quick Analysis* tool. When you use the *Quick Analysis* tool, a default data bar (or other format) is applied. You can edit it by choosing a different color or style from the *Conditional Formatting* button menu.

HOW TO: Format Data with Data Bars

1. Select the cell range you want to format.
2. Click the **Quick Analysis** button.
3. Click **Formatting** and choose **Data Bars** (Figure 4-68).
   - A default data bar style and color are applied.
   - The length of the data bars compares the value in each cell to the other values in the selected cell range.
   - *Color Scales* use a variation of two or three colors to indicate low, middle, and high values.
   - *Icon Sets* inserts icons that represent the upper, middle, or lower values of the cell range.

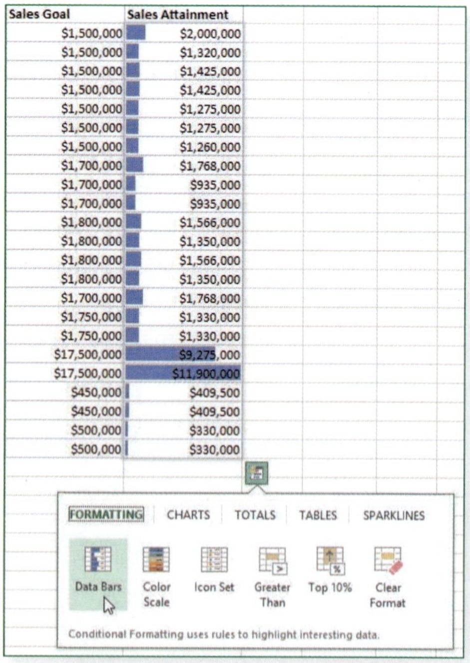

4-68 *Conditional Formatting: Data Bars*

Manage Conditional Formatting Rules

To edit, delete, or review any *Conditional Formatting* rule, use the ***Manage Rules*** command. You can update the range to be formatted, edit the actual format, or change the rule.

In the *Conditional Formatting Rules Manager* dialog box, you can choose to display all the rules in the worksheet or rules from other sheets in the workbook. If you choose a cell range before you give the command, the rule for the *Current Selection* is shown (Figure 4-69).

When you click **Edit Rule**, the *Edit Formatting Rule* dialog box opens. This dialog box is very similar to the *New Formatting Rule* dialog box, and you make your changes in the same way.

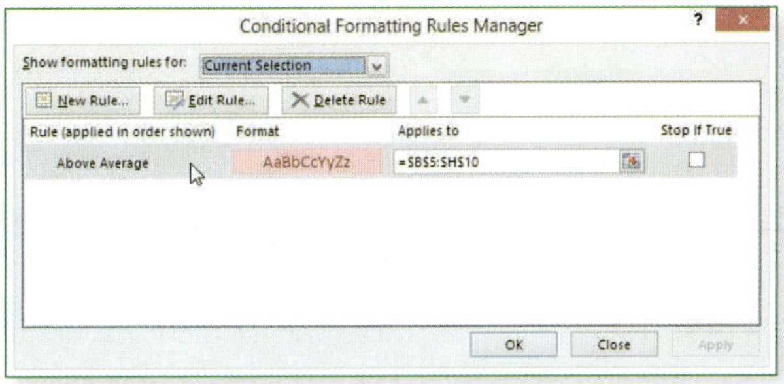

4-69 *Conditional Formatting Rules Manager* dialog box

HOW TO: Manage Conditional Formatting Rules

1. Click the **Conditional Formatting** button [*Home* tab, *Styles* group].
2. Choose **Manage Rules**.
3. In the *Show formatting rules for* list, make a choice.
   - If you selected a cell range, the option is *Current Selection*.
   - Choose **This Worksheet** if you did not select a range or want to see all rules in the worksheet.
4. Select the rule to edit.
5. Click **Edit Rule**.
6. In the *Select a Rule Type* list, choose another type if needed.
7. In the *Edit the Rule Description* area, make choices to change the rule.
   - The choices depend on the rule type (Figure 4-70).
   - Click **Format** when it is an option and make changes in the *Format Cells* dialog box.
8. Click **OK** to close the *Edit Formatting Rule* dialog box.
9. Click **OK** to close the *Conditional Formatting Rules Manager* dialog box and apply the change.

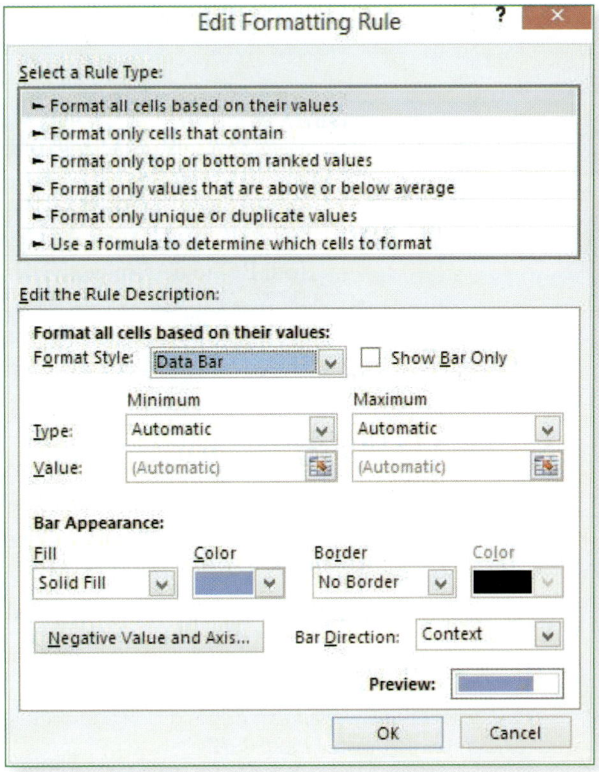

4-70 *Edit Formatting Rule* dialog box for data bars

Clear Conditional Formatting Rules

You can clear rules from a selected cell range or from an entire sheet. Access the ***Clear Rules*** option by clicking the *Conditional Formatting* button in the *Styles* group on the *Home* tab. For a selected range, you can click the **Quick Analysis** button and choose **Clear Format**.

HOW TO: Clear All Rules

1. Click the **Conditional Formatting** button [*Home* tab, *Styles* group].
2. Choose **Clear Rules**.
3. Click **Clear Rules from Entire Sheet** (Figure 4-71).

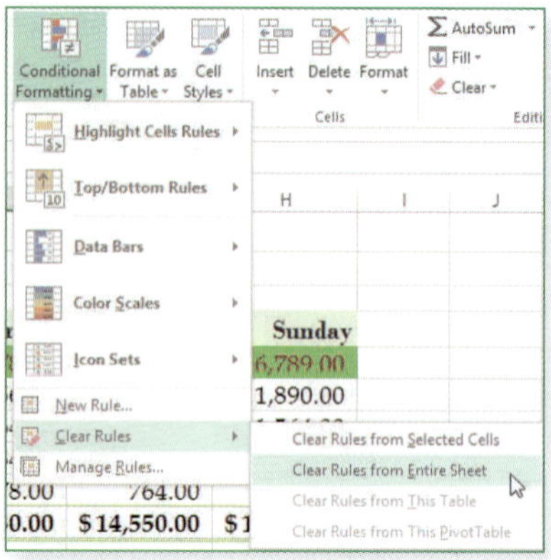

4-71 *Clear Rules* options

SLO 4.7

Using Goal Seek and Worksheet Protection

Goal Seek is one type of what-if analysis. It allows you to test values in a cell to "backsolve" a formula. ***Backsolving*** means knowing the desired results and determining the value needed to reach those results. For example, if you can afford to pay $500 per month for a new car, you can use *Goal Seek* to determine how much you can borrow and end up with a $500 per month car payment.

Worksheet protection allows you to set which cells can be edited in a worksheet. When you share work with others, worksheet protection can safeguard your work from accidental changes by others.

Use Goal Seek

Goal Seek solves a formula for one cell (one argument) in the formula. In the *Goal Seek* dialog box, you enter the cell reference for the formula in the *Set cell* text box. You type a target or goal number in the *To value* text box. For example, in Figure 4-72, an organization is solving the *PMT* function so that it results in a payment of $2,200. *Goal Seek* adjusts the interest rate (cell B6) to determine the desired payment.

You can access *Goal Seek* from the *What-if Analysis* button in the *Data Tools* group on the *Data* tab. The solution appears in the *Goal Seek Status* dialog box. You can click **OK** to accept the solution or keep the original value by clicking **Cancel**.

HOW TO: Use Goal Seek

1. Click the cell with the formula to be solved.
2. Click the **What-if Analysis** button [*Data* tab, *Data Tools* group].
3. Choose **Goal Seek**.
4. Verify the formula cell address in the *Set cell* text box.
5. Click in the *To value* text box and type in your desired formula result.
6. Click in the *By changing cell* text box and click the cell that can be adjusted (Figure 4-72).
   - In Figure 4-72, the interest rate is chosen as the value that can be adjusted.
   - *Goal Seek* can change only one cell.
   - You can key the cell reference instead of selecting the cell.
7. Click **OK**.
   - The solution is shown in the *Goal Seek Status* dialog box (Figure 4-73).
   - The solution is displayed in the cell in the worksheet.

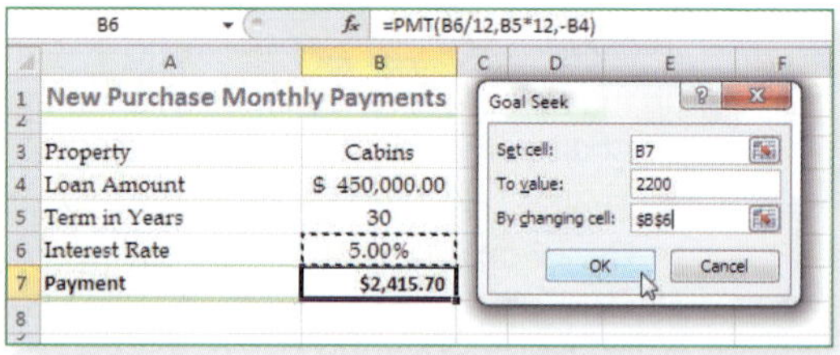

4-72 *Goal Seek* dialog box

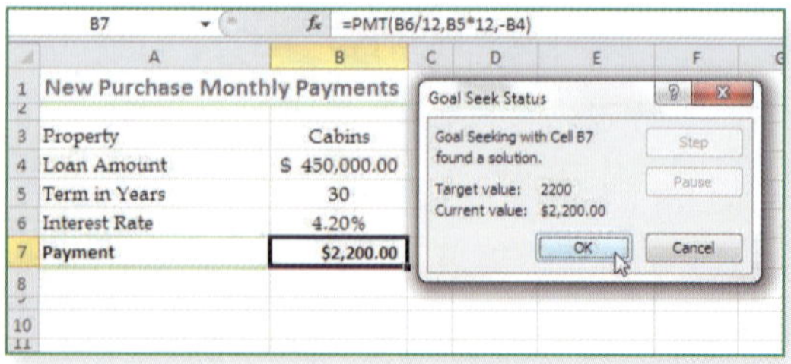

4-73 *Goak Seek Status* dialog box

8. Click **OK** to accept the solution.
   - You can press **Enter** to accept the solution.
   - Choose **Cancel** to ignore the solution.

Worksheet Protection

Worksheet protection is a good way to prohibit changes to your work. It employs the *Locked* cell property. This property is active for all cells in a worksheet by default. However, it has no effect until you set worksheet protection. If you set worksheet protection, no editing is possible in the sheet. When you protect a worksheet, you need to select the cells that can still be edited and disable the *Locked* property. Typically, you do this before protecting the sheet.

Unlock Worksheet Cells

When you protect a sheet, you or others may still want to edit some cells in the worksheet. In an inventory worksheet, for example, you need to update item counts, but you don't need to change the product name or code. In a protected inventory worksheet, you can unlock the item-count cells so that their values can be changed while the other values and codes cannot be edited.

The *Locked* property is on the *Protection* tab in the *Format Cells* dialog box. Open the dialog box from the *Format* button on the *Home* tab [*Cells* group] or by pressing **Ctrl+1**. Alternatively, you can toggle the *Locked* property on and off from the *Format* button menu. When a cell is locked, the command in the menu shows an outline; when a cell is unlocked, there is no outline (Figure 4-74).

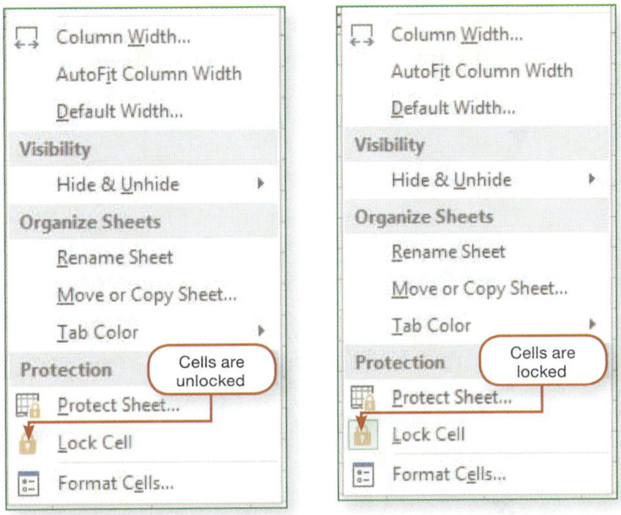

4-74 ***Locked*** **property off and on**

HOW TO: Unlock Cells for Editing

1. Select the cell(s) that you still want to be able to edit.
2. Right-click a selected cell.
3. Choose **Format Cells**.
4. Click the **Protection** tab.
5. Click the **Locked** check box to remove the check mark (Figure 4-75).
6. Click **OK**.

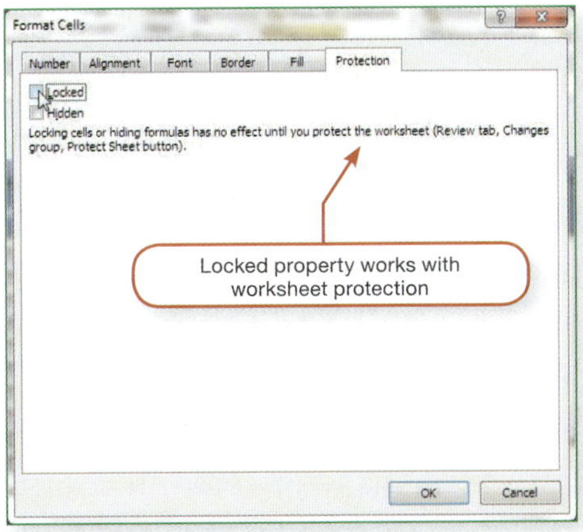

4-75 ***Format Cells*** **dialog box;** ***Protection*** **tab**

> **MORE INFO**
>
> Many users leave the *Locked* property on for formula cells in a protected sheet so that they are not accidentally changed or deleted.

Protect a Worksheet

The *Protect Worksheet* command includes a list of editing options that you can allow for locked cells. For example, you can allow users to select cells, but they will not be able to edit them. Or you can give users permission to format cells or to insert or delete rows or columns.

As you set worksheet protection, you can also set a password. Once this added security is enforced, all users must enter the password before they can edit anything in the worksheet. Once the password is entered, the protection is removed.

The *Protect Sheet* button is in the *Changes* group on the *Review* tab. This button is a toggle; when a worksheet is protected, it becomes the *Unprotect Sheet* button. You can also protect a worksheet from the *Format* button [*Home* tab, *Cells* group] (see Figure 4-74).

HOW TO: Protect a Worksheet

1. Unlock the cells that you want to still be able to edit.
2. Click the **Protect Sheet** button [*Review* tab, *Changes* group].
3. Check the commands that should still be available after protection is set.
4. Type a password if desired.
   - You see a placeholder as you type a password (Figure 4-76).
   - A second message box requires that you rekey the password.
   - Passwords are case sensitive.
5. Click **OK**.

> **MORE INFO**
>
> Keep track of passwords. You cannot recover a lost or forgotten password without the use of a password recovery program.

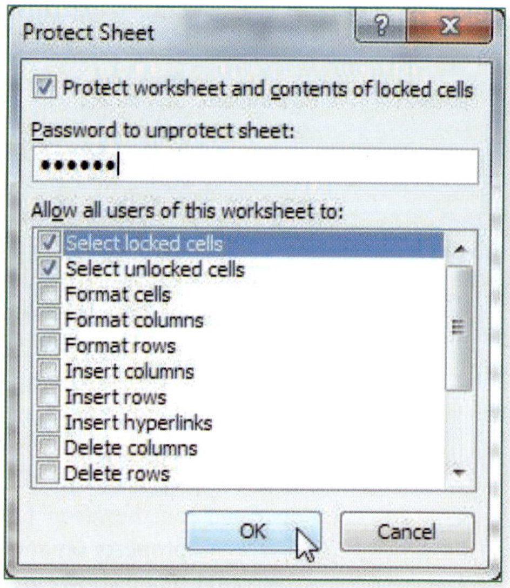

4-76 *Protect Sheet* dialog box

Unprotect a Worksheet

If you try to edit a cell in a protected sheet, a message box tells you that the sheet is protected (Figure 4-77). When a worksheet is protected, it cannot be edited until the protection is removed. If there is no password, you just need to click the **Unprotect Sheet** button.

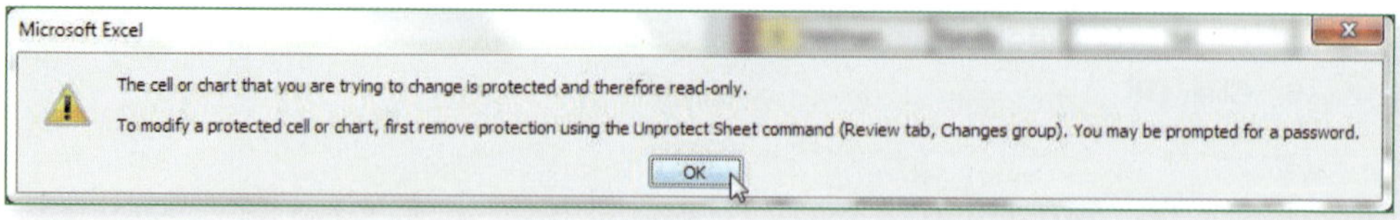

4-77 Message window for a protected sheet

When a password has been set, you need to enter the password to remove the protection.

The *Unprotect Sheet* button is in the *Changes* group on the *Review* tab. If a password has been used, a message box for entering the password appears (Figure 4-78).

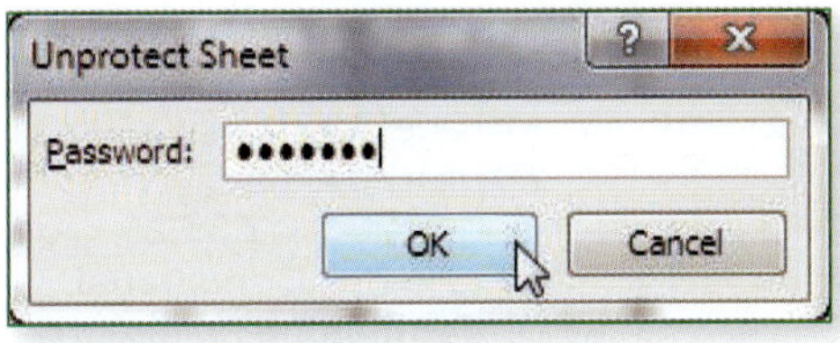

4-78 *Unprotect Sheet* dialog box

HOW TO: Unprotect a Worksheet

1. Click the **Unprotect Sheet** button [*Review* tab, *Changes* group].
2. Type the password if necessary and click **OK**.

PAUSE & PRACTICE: EXCEL 4-4

For this project, you set conditional formatting using data bars in Paradise Lakes Resort's workbook. You use *Goal Seek* to calculate a possible sales amount for one of the representatives so that average sales can reach a particular goal. Finally, you protect the worksheet but allow editing to the attainment figures.

File Needed: ***[your initials] PP E 4-3.xlsx***
Completed Project File Name: ***[your initials] PP E4-4.xlsx***

1. Open the ***[your initials] PP E4-3*** workbook. Enable editing.
2. Save the workbook as ***[your initials] PP E4-4***.
3. Click the **Sales Quota Data** sheet tab.
4. Click the **Filter** button [*Data* tab, *Sort & Filter* group] to remove the filter.
5. Apply *Conditional Formatting* using *Highlight Cells Rules*.
   a. Select cells **D3:D25**.
   b. Click the **Quick Analysis** button and choose **Formatting**.
   c. Choose **Greater Than**.
   d. Type 2000000.
   e. Select **Green Fill with Dark Green Text** from the *with* drop-down list.
   f. Click **OK**.
   g. Select cells **B3:B25**.
   h. Click the **Quick Analysis** button and choose **Formatting**.
   i. Choose **Text Contains**.
   j. Type sales trainee.
   k. Select **Light Red Fill with Dark Red Text**.
   l. Click **OK**.
6. Apply *Conditional Formatting* using *Data Bars*.
   a. Select cells **E3:E25**.
   b. Click the **Quick Analysis** button and choose **Formatting**.
   c. Choose **Data Bars**.

7. Manage *Conditional Formatting* rules.
   a. Select cells **E3:E25**.
   b. Click the **Conditional Formatting** button [*Home* tab, *Styles* group].
   c. Choose **Manage Rules**.
   d. Click **Edit Rule**.
   e. Click the **Fill** arrow and choose **Gradient Fill** (Figure 4-79).
   f. Click the **Color** arrow; choose **Gold**, **Accent 3**.
   g. Click **OK** to close the *Edit Formatting Rule* dialog box.
   h. Click **OK** to close the *Conditional Formatting Rules Manager*.

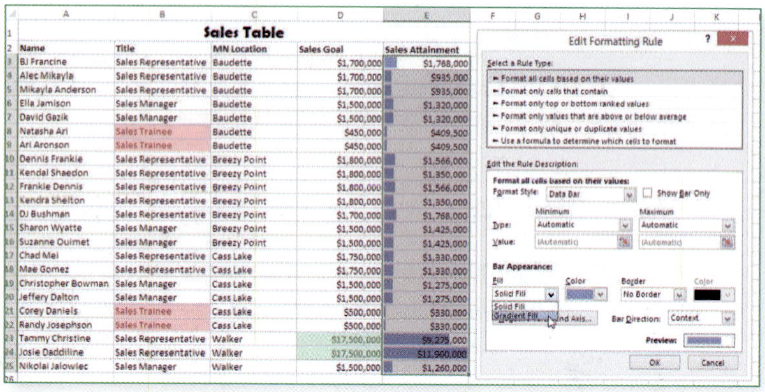

4-79 Edited rule for data bars

8. Click the **Subtotals** sheet tab.
9. Use Goal Seek.
   a. Click cell **E10**.
   b. Click the **What-if Analysis** button [*Data* tab, *Data Tools* group].
   c. Select **Goal Seek**.
   d. Type 1500000 in the *To value* box.
   e. Click in the *By changing cell* box and click cell **E5**. This finds a value for Sharon Wyatte's sales that would result in average sales of $1,500,000.
   f. Click **OK** to run *Goal Seek* (Figure 4-80). Sharon's new sales would have to reach $2,625,000.
   g. Click **OK** to accept the solution.

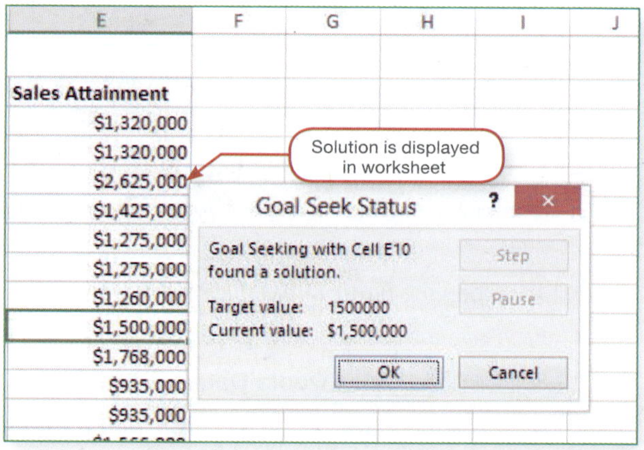

4-80 ***Goal Seek*** **solution**

10. Click the **Sales Quota Data** sheet tab.
11. Protect a worksheet with a password.
    a. Select cells **E3:E25**.
    b. Right-click a selected cell.
    c. Choose **Format Cells** from the menu.
    d. Click the **Protection** tab.
    e. Click to remove the check mark for **Locked**.
    f. Click **OK**.
    g. Click the **Protect Sheet** button [*Review* tab, *Changes* group].
    h. Show check marks for **Select locked cells** and **Select unlocked cells**.
    i. Type the password 123 and click **OK**.
    j. Retype the password and click **OK**.
12. Save and close the workbook (Figure 4-81).

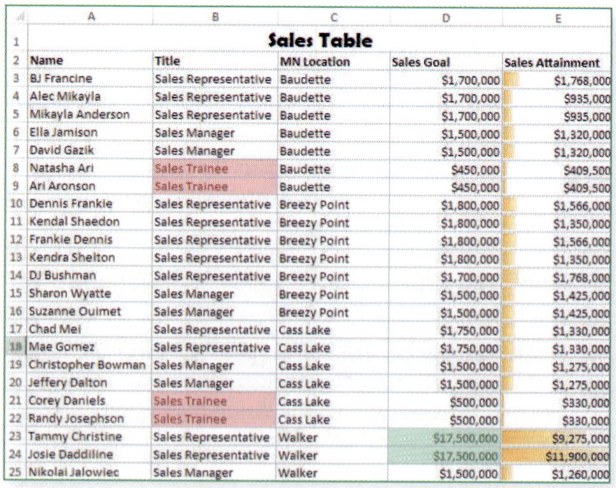

Sales Table

Name	Title	MN Location	Sales Goal	Sales Attainment
BJ Francine	Sales Representative	Baudette	$1,700,000	$1,768,000
Alec Mikayla	Sales Representative	Baudette	$1,700,000	$935,000
Mikayla Anderson	Sales Representative	Baudette	$1,700,000	$935,000
Ella Jamison	Sales Manager	Baudette	$1,500,000	$1,320,000
David Gazik	Sales Manager	Baudette	$1,500,000	$1,320,000
Natasha Ari	Sales Trainee	Baudette	$450,000	$409,500
Ari Aronson	Sales Trainee	Baudette	$450,000	$409,500
Dennis Frankie	Sales Representative	Breezy Point	$1,800,000	$1,566,000
Kendal Shaedon	Sales Representative	Breezy Point	$1,800,000	$1,350,000
Frankie Dennis	Sales Representative	Breezy Point	$1,800,000	$1,566,000
Kendra Shelton	Sales Representative	Breezy Point	$1,800,000	$1,350,000
DJ Bushman	Sales Representative	Breezy Point	$1,700,000	$1,768,000
Sharon Wyatte	Sales Manager	Breezy Point	$1,500,000	$1,425,000
Suzanne Oulmet	Sales Manager	Breezy Point	$1,500,000	$1,425,000
Chad Mei	Sales Representative	Cass Lake	$1,750,000	$1,330,000
Mae Gomez	Sales Representative	Cass Lake	$1,750,000	$1,330,000
Christopher Bowman	Sales Manager	Cass Lake	$1,500,000	$1,275,000
Jeffery Dalton	Sales Manager	Cass Lake	$1,500,000	$1,275,000
Corey Daniels	Sales Trainee	Cass Lake	$500,000	$330,000
Randy Josephson	Sales Trainee	Cass Lake	$500,000	$330,000
Tammy Christine	Sales Representative	Walker	$17,500,000	$9,275,000
Josie Daddiline	Sales Representative	Walker	$17,500,000	$11,900,000
Nikolai Jalowiec	Sales Manager	Walker	$1,500,000	$1,260,000

4-81 Completed PP E4-4 worksheet

Chapter Summary

4.1 Import data into Excel from a text file, database file, or web site and use *Flash Fill* and data connections (p. E4-187).

- You can ***import*** text files in Excel including *.txt* (text) documents, *.csv* (comma separated values) files, and *.prn* (printer) files.
- The *From Text* button is in the *Get External Data* group on the *Data* tab.
- The ***Text Import Wizard*** guides you through the steps of importing the data.
- You can import data from a Word document and tables and queries in a Microsoft Access database into a worksheet.
- You can import table-formatted data on a web site into a worksheet using the *From Web* button on the *Data* tab.
- Imported data establishes a data connection in the workbook.
- The ***Flash Fill*** command copies your typing actions from nearby cells.

4.2 Create and format an Excel table and a *PivotTable*, and export data for use in other programs (p. E4-194).

- There are several methods for sorting, filtering, and calculating rows of data in Excel ***tables***.
- Data that is set up like a list with a header row and the same type of data in each column can be formatted as a table.
- Create a table by clicking the **Format as Table** button in the *Styles* group on the *Home* tab or by clicking the **Quick Analysis** tool and choosing **Tables**.
- An ***AutoFilter*** button accompanies each label in the header row of an Excel table.
- When any cell in a table is selected, the *Table Tools Design* tab is available.
- Apply a table style by clicking the **More** button in the *Table Styles* group on the *Table Tools Design* tab.
- Save a customized table style with the *New Table Style* button in the *Table Styles* gallery in the *Table Styles* group on the *Table Tools Design* tab.
- ***Table Tools*** include commands to remove duplicate rows and to convert a table to a normal cell range. The *Tools* group is on the *Table Tools Design* tab.
- An Excel table is named and uses structured references (names) for each column and other predefined parts.
- A ***PivotTable*** is a summary report based on a cell range in the worksheet.
- For a selected cell range, use the *Recommended PivotTables* button on the *Insert* tab in the *Tables* group.
- In a *PivotTable*, fields can be repositioned to display different views of the data.
- Use the *PivotTable Fields* pane to reposition fields in a *PivotTable* report.
- Use the ***Export*** command in the *Backstage* view to save data in a different format.

4.3 Sort data by text, number, color, or icon (p. E4-205).

- List-type data can be sorted alphabetically or by value by one or more columns.
- Sorts can be in ***ascending*** order (A to Z) or ***descending*** (Z to A).
- Values can be sorted from smallest to largest (A to Z) or largest to smallest (Z to A).
- To sort a single column, use the *Sort A to Z* or *Sort Z to A* button in the *Sort & Filter* group on the *Data* tab.
- To sort by multiple columns, open the *Sort* dialog box by clicking the **Sort** button on the *Data* tab.
- In the *Sort* dialog box, you can choose to sort by font color, cell color, or cell icon when this type of formatting is used in the data.

4.4 Apply an *AutoFilter* or an *Advanced Filter* to data (p. E4-209).

- The ***AutoFilter*** command displays an *AutoFilter* button arrow in each column heading.
- Click the **AutoFilter** button to select which records are shown or hidden.
- You can build a custom *AutoFilter* using operators such as *Equals*. There are different operators for text, number, and date filters.
- An ***Advanced Filter*** provides sophisticated filter options such as using a formula in the filter definition.
- An *Advanced Filter* requires a criteria range in the same workbook to define the criteria.
- An *Advanced Filter* can show the filtered results separate from the actual data.
- The *Advanced* button is in the *Sort & Filter* group on the *Data* tab.

4.5 Use the *Subtotal* command and create groups and outlines (p. E4-212).

- The ***Subtotal*** command inserts summary rows using a function such as *SUM*, *AVERAGE*, *MAX*, or *MIN* in a normal cell range.
- The *Subtotal* command requires that the data be sorted by at least one column.
- The *Subtotal* command formats the results as an ***outline***. An outline groups records so that they can be displayed or hidden.
- The *Subtotal* button is in the *Outline* group on the *Data* tab.
- The ***Auto Outline*** command creates groups based on formulas that are located in a consistent pattern in the data.
- The *Auto Outline* command is available from the *Group* button in the *Outline* group on the *Data* tab.
- You can manually define groups by sorting the data and using the *Group* button in the *Outline* group on the *Data* tab.

4.6 Apply and manage *Conditional Formatting* using cell rules, *Color Scales*, *Icon Sets*, and *Data Bars* (p. E4-218).

- ***Conditional Formatting*** formats only cells that meet specified criteria.
- Cells rules formatting uses relational or comparison operators such as *Greater Than* or *Equals*.
- In the rule dialog box, you define the rule and choose the format.
- You can create your own conditional formatting rule as well as edit existing rules with the ***Manage Rules*** command.
- Conditional formatting commands include *Icon Sets*, *Color Scales*, and *Data Bars*.
- An icon, color, or data bar represents a value in relation to other values in the range.
- You can ***Clear Rules*** from a selected cell range or from an entire sheet.

4.7 Use *Goal Seek* and protect a worksheet (p. E4-222).

- ***Goal Seek*** is a command that finds a solution for one of the arguments in a formula.
- In a *Goal Seek* command, you set the desired result for the formula to a value and find out how to arrive at that result by changing one cell.
- The *Goal Seek* command is part of the ***What-If Analysis*** button options on the *Data* tab.
- Worksheet protection is a first step in prohibiting unwanted changes to your work.
- The *Protect Sheet* button is in the *Changes* group in the *Review* tab; it is the *Unprotect Sheet* button when the worksheet is protected.
- To allow cell editing in a protected worksheet, you must disable or remove the *Locked* property for the cells you want to be able to edit.
- The *Locked* property is toggled off and on in the *Format Cells* dialog box on the *Protection* tab.
- Worksheet protection can be set with or without a password.
- Worksheet protection must be removed or turned off before the worksheet can be edited.

Check for Understanding

On the ***Online Learning Center*** for this text (www.mhhe.com/office2013inpractice), there are a variety of resources that can be used to review the concepts covered in this chapter.

The following Online Learning Resources are available on the Online Learning Center:

- Multiple choice questions
- Short answer questions
- Matching exercises

USING MICROSOFT EXCEL 2013

Guided Project 4-1

For this project you import supplier data in a text file into the inventory worksheet for Wear-Ever Shoes. You use *Flash Fill* to enter product codes and sort the data by supplier and code. You use *AutoFilter* for several tasks, use the *Subtotal* command, and work with *Goal Seek*. Finally, you protect one of the sheets in the workbook.
[Student Learning Outcomes 4.1, 4.3, 4.4, 4.5, 4.7]

Files Needed: ***WearEverInventory-04.xlsx*** and ***Suppliers-04.txt***
Completed Project File Name: ***[your initials] Excel 4-1.xlsx***

Skills Covered in This Project

- Import a text file.
- Use *Flash Fill*.
- Sort data.
- Use an *AutoFilter*.
- Create and copy a formula.
- Insert columns.
- Use the *Subtotal* command.
- Use *Goal Seek*.
- Copy and move a worksheet.
- Protect a worksheet without a password.

1. Open the ***WearEverInventory-04*** workbook from your student data files folder. Click the **Enable Editing** button.
2. Save the workbook as ***[your initials] Excel 4-1***.
3. Import a text file.
   a. Select cell **J4**.
   b. Click the **From Text** button [*Data* tab, *Get External Data* group].
   c. Find and select the ***Suppliers-04.txt*** file in the *Import Text File* window.
   d. Click **Import**.
   e. Select the **Delimited** button in the first *Wizard* window. Excel recognizes that this file separates the data into columns with a tab character.
   f. Click **Next**.
   g. Click to place a check mark for **Tab** if necessary.
   h. Click **Next**.
   i. Click **Finish**.
   j. Click **OK**.
   k. Use the **Format Painter** button to copy formatting from **I4** to **J4:K4**.
   l. *AutoFit* columns **J:K**.
4. Use *Flash Fill* to insert a product code.
   a. Insert a column between columns **B** and **C**.
   b. Type Code in cell **C4**.
   c. Type RHB in cell **C5**.
   d. Type r and press **Enter** in cell **C6**.

e. Type r and press **Enter** in cell **C7**. *AutoFill* completes the entries based on what is already in the column. The *Flash Fill* suggestion list does not appear because you did not type a second item to identify the pattern.

f. Click the **Fill** button [*Home* tab, *Editing* group].

g. Choose **Flash Fill**.

h. *AutoFit* column **C**.

5. Sort data in multiple columns.

   a. Click any cell in cells **A5:L40**.

   b. Click the **Sort** button [*Data* tab, *Sort & Filter* group].

   c. Click the **My data has headers** check box if necessary.

   d. Click the **Sort by** arrow and choose **Supplier**.

   e. Check that **Sort On** is **Values** and **Order** is **A to Z**.

   f. Click **Add Level**.

   g. Click the **Then by** arrow and choose **Code**.

   h. Check that **Sort On** is **Values** and **Order** is **A to Z**.

   i. Click **OK** (Figure 4-82).

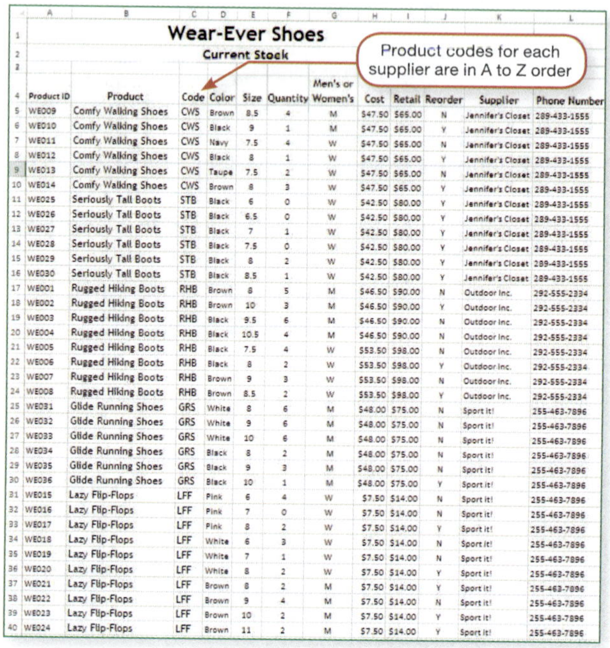

Wear-Ever Shoes

Current Stock

	A	B	C	D	E	F	G	H	I	J	K	L
4	Product ID	Product	Code	Color	Size	Quantity	Men's or Women's	Cost	Retail	Reorder	Supplier	Phone Number
5	WE009	Comfy Walking Shoes	CWS	Brown	8.5	4	M	$47.50	$65.00	N	Jennifer's Closet	289-433-1555
6	WE010	Comfy Walking Shoes	CWS	Black	9	1	M	$47.50	$65.00	Y	Jennifer's Closet	289-433-1555
7	WE011	Comfy Walking Shoes	CWS	Navy	7.5	4	W	$47.50	$65.00	N	Jennifer's Closet	289-433-1555
8	WE012	Comfy Walking Shoes	CWS	Black	8	1	W	$47.50	$65.00	Y	Jennifer's Closet	289-433-1555
9	WE013	Comfy Walking Shoes	CWS	Taupe	7.5	2	W	$47.50	$65.00	N	Jennifer's Closet	289-433-1555
10	WE014	Comfy Walking Shoes	CWS	Brown	8	3	W	$47.50	$65.00	Y	Jennifer's Closet	289-433-1555
11	WE025	Seriously Tall Boots	STB	Black	6	0	W	$42.50	$80.00	Y	Jennifer's Closet	289-433-1555
12	WE026	Seriously Tall Boots	STB	Black	6.5	0	W	$42.50	$80.00	Y	Jennifer's Closet	289-433-1555
13	WE027	Seriously Tall Boots	STB	Black	7	1	W	$42.50	$80.00	Y	Jennifer's Closet	289-433-1555
14	WE028	Seriously Tall Boots	STB	Black	7.5	0	W	$42.50	$80.00	Y	Jennifer's Closet	289-433-1555
15	WE029	Seriously Tall Boots	STB	Black	8	2	W	$42.50	$80.00	Y	Jennifer's Closet	289-433-1555
16	WE030	Seriously Tall Boots	STB	Black	8.5	1	W	$42.50	$80.00	Y	Jennifer's Closet	289-433-1555
17	WE001	Rugged Hiking Boots	RHB	Brown	8	5	M	$46.50	$90.00	N	Outdoor Inc.	292-555-2334
18	WE002	Rugged Hiking Boots	RHB	Brown	10	3	M	$46.50	$90.00	Y	Outdoor Inc.	292-555-2334
19	WE003	Rugged Hiking Boots	RHB	Black	9.5	6	M	$46.50	$90.00	N	Outdoor Inc.	292-555-2334
20	WE004	Rugged Hiking Boots	RHB	Black	10.5	4	M	$46.50	$90.00	N	Outdoor Inc.	292-555-2334
21	WE005	Rugged Hiking Boots	RHB	Black	7.5	4	W	$53.50	$98.00	N	Outdoor Inc.	292-555-2334
22	WE006	Rugged Hiking Boots	RHB	Black	8	2	W	$53.50	$98.00	Y	Outdoor Inc.	292-555-2334
23	WE007	Rugged Hiking Boots	RHB	Brown	9	3	W	$53.50	$98.00	N	Outdoor Inc.	292-555-2334
24	WE008	Rugged Hiking Boots	RHB	Brown	8.5	2	W	$53.50	$98.00	Y	Outdoor Inc.	292-555-2334
25	WE031	Glide Running Shoes	GRS	White	8	6	M	$48.00	$75.00	N	Sport it!	255-463-7896
26	WE032	Glide Running Shoes	GRS	White	9	6	M	$48.00	$75.00	N	Sport it!	255-463-7896
27	WE033	Glide Running Shoes	GRS	White	10	6	M	$48.00	$75.00	N	Sport it!	255-463-7896
28	WE034	Glide Running Shoes	GRS	Black	8	2	M	$48.00	$75.00	N	Sport it!	255-463-7896
29	WE035	Glide Running Shoes	GRS	Black	9	3	M	$48.00	$75.00	N	Sport it!	255-463-7896
30	WE036	Glide Running Shoes	GRS	Black	10	1	M	$48.00	$75.00	Y	Sport it!	255-463-7896
31	WE015	Lazy Flip-Flops	LFF	Pink	6	4	W	$7.50	$14.00	N	Sport it!	255-463-7896
32	WE016	Lazy Flip-Flops	LFF	Pink	7	0	W	$7.50	$14.00	N	Sport it!	255-463-7896
33	WE017	Lazy Flip-Flops	LFF	Pink	8	2	W	$7.50	$14.00	Y	Sport it!	255-463-7896
34	WE018	Lazy Flip-Flops	LFF	White	6	3	W	$7.50	$14.00	N	Sport it!	255-463-7896
35	WE019	Lazy Flip-Flops	LFF	White	7	1	W	$7.50	$14.00	N	Sport it!	255-463-7896
36	WE020	Lazy Flip-Flops	LFF	White	8	2	W	$7.50	$14.00	Y	Sport it!	255-463-7896
37	WE021	Lazy Flip-Flops	LFF	Brown	8	2	M	$7.50	$14.00	Y	Sport it!	255-463-7896
38	WE022	Lazy Flip-Flops	LFF	Brown	9	4	M	$7.50	$14.00	N	Sport it!	255-463-7896
39	WE023	Lazy Flip-Flops	LFF	Brown	10	2	M	$7.50	$14.00	Y	Sport it!	255-463-7896
40	WE024	Lazy Flip-Flops	LFF	Brown	11	2	M	$7.50	$14.00	Y	Sport it!	255-463-7896

4-82 Data sorted by "Supplier" and "Code"

6. Use an *AutoFilter*.

   a. Click any cell in cells **A5:L40**.

   b. Click the **Filter** button [*Data* tab, *Sort & Filter* group].

   c. Click the **AutoFilter** button for **Supplier** column.

   d. Click **(Select All)** to remove all the check marks.

   e. Click **Jennifer's Closet** to place a check mark for only that supplier.

   f. Click **OK**. The data is filtered to show only records from one supplier.

7. Copy the *Northern Warehouse* worksheet.

   a. Name the copied sheet Subtotals.

   b. Move the *Subtotals* sheet to the right of the *Northern Warehouse* sheet.

8. Use the *Subtotal* command.

   a. Click cell **K5** in the *Subtotals* sheet.

   b. Click the **Filter** button [*Data* tab, *Sort & Filter* group] to remove the filter.

   c. Click the **Subtotal** button [*Data* tab, *Outline* group].

   d. Click the **At each change in** arrow and choose **Supplier**.

   e. Click the **Use function** arrow and choose **Count**.

   f. Check the **Supplier** box in the *Add subtotal to* area and remove check marks for all other fields (Figure 4-83).

   g. Click **OK**. A subtotal row is inserted at the bottom of each group and shows how many products are available from each supplier.

   h. Format the label in cell **J17** as **right-aligned**.

   i. **Right-align** the remaining subtotal labels in column **J** (Figure 4-84).

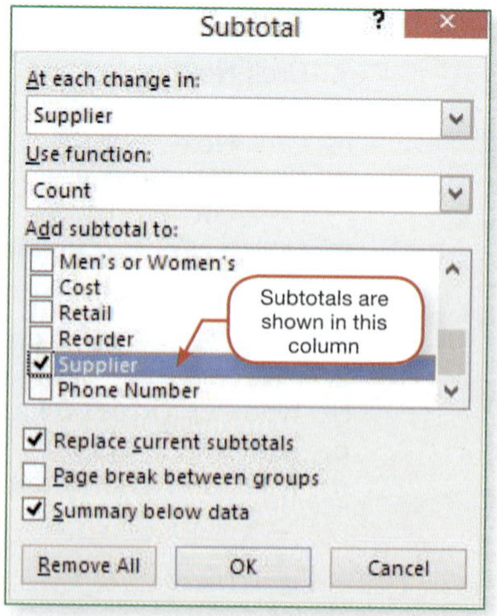

4-83 *Subtotal* dialog box to count the number of products by supplier

9. Copy the **Subtotals** sheet, name it Goal Seek, and move it to the right of the *Subtotals* sheet.
10. Prepare a *Goal Seek* worksheet.
    a. Click cell **K5** in the **Goal Seek** sheet.
    b. Click the **Subtotals** button [*Data* tab, *Outline* group].
    c. Click **Remove All** in the *Subtotal* dialog box.
    d. Insert a column between columns **I** and **J**. Type Margin in cell **J4**. Increase the width of column **J** to **7.43**.
    e. Type the profit margin formula in cell **J5** =(I5-H5)/H5 and press **Enter**. The profit margin subtracts the unit cost from the retail price and divides those results by the cost.
    f. Since the result is a percentage, format the results in cell **J5** as **Percent Style** with no decimals.
    g. Copy the formula in cell **J5** to cells **J6:J40**.
    h. Click the **Filter** button [*Data* tab, *Sort & Filter* group].
    i. Click the **AutoFilter** button for the **Margin** column.
    j. Click **(Select All)** to remove all the check marks.
    k. Click **37%** to place a check mark for that profit margin.
    l. Click **OK**. The data is filtered to show only the rows with the lowest profit margin.

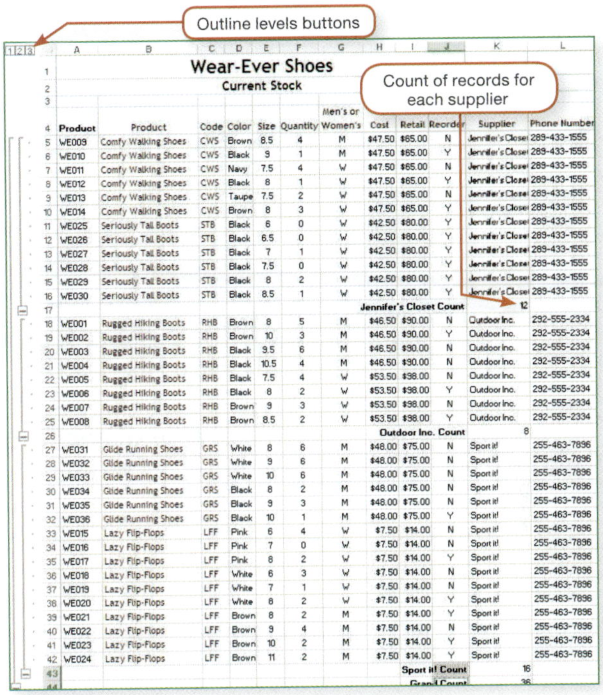

4-84 Subtotals inserted for each group

11. Use *Goal Seek*.
    a. Type New Retail Price to Reach 55% Margin in cell **N6** and make it **bold**.
    b. Click cell **J5**.
    c. Click the **What-If Analysis** button [*Data* tab, *Data Tools* group] and choose **Goal Seek**.
    d. In the *To value* box, type 55%.
    e. In the *By changing cell* box, click cell **I5** (Figure 4-85).
    f. Click **OK** to view the solution in cell **I5**.
    g. Make a note of the results and click **Cancel**.
    h. Click cell **O7** and type $73.63.

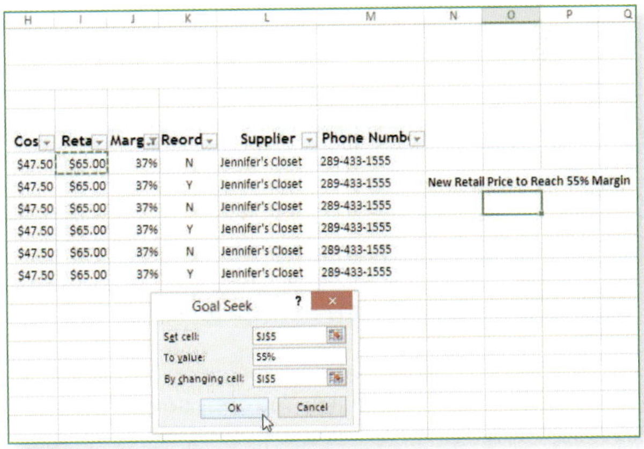

4-85 *Goal Seek* to find new retail price

12. Protect a worksheet without a password.
    a. Click the **Subtotals** sheet tab.
    b. Click the **Protect Sheet** button [*Review* tab, *Changes* group].
    c. Verify that there are check marks for **Select locked cells** and **Select unlocked cells**.
    d. Click **OK**.

13. Save and close the workbook (Figure 4-86).

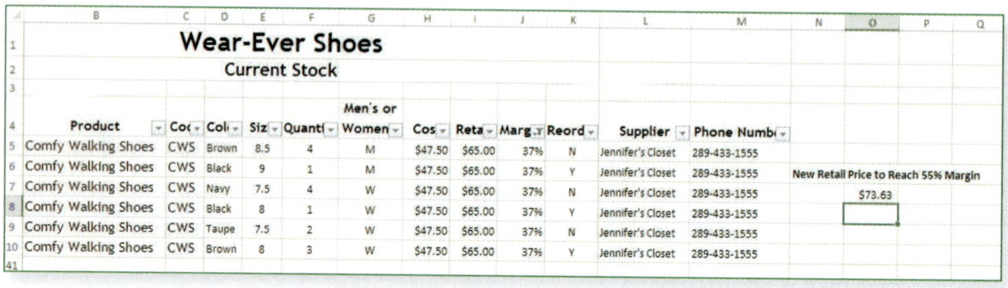

Wear-Ever Shoes												
Current Stock												
Product	Coc	Col	Siz	Quanti	Men's or Women	Cos	Reta	Marg	Reord	Supplier	Phone Numb	
Comfy Walking Shoes	CWS	Brown	8.5	4	M	$47.50	$65.00	37%	N	Jennifer's Closet	289-433-1555	
Comfy Walking Shoes	CWS	Black	9	1	M	$47.50	$65.00	37%	Y	Jennifer's Closet	289-433-1555	New Retail Price to Reach 55% Margin
Comfy Walking Shoes	CWS	Navy	7.5	4	W	$47.50	$65.00	37%	N	Jennifer's Closet	289-433-1555	$73.63
Comfy Walking Shoes	CWS	Black	8	1	W	$47.50	$65.00	37%	Y	Jennifer's Closet	289-433-1555	
Comfy Walking Shoes	CWS	Taupe	7.5	2	W	$47.50	$65.00	37%	N	Jennifer's Closet	289-433-1555	
Comfy Walking Shoes	CWS	Brown	8	3	W	$47.50	$65.00	37%	Y	Jennifer's Closet	289-433-1555	

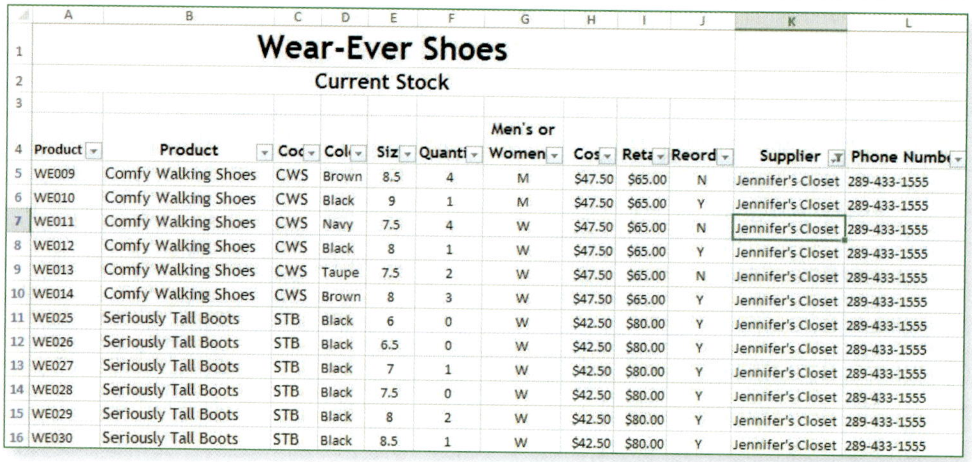

Wear-Ever Shoes											
Current Stock											
Product	Product	Coc	Col	Siz	Quanti	Men's or Women	Cos	Reta	Reord	Supplier	Phone Numb
WE009	Comfy Walking Shoes	CWS	Brown	8.5	4	M	$47.50	$65.00	N	Jennifer's Closet	289-433-1555
WE010	Comfy Walking Shoes	CWS	Black	9	1	M	$47.50	$65.00	Y	Jennifer's Closet	289-433-1555
WE011	Comfy Walking Shoes	CWS	Navy	7.5	4	W	$47.50	$65.00	N	Jennifer's Closet	289-433-1555
WE012	Comfy Walking Shoes	CWS	Black	8	1	W	$47.50	$65.00	Y	Jennifer's Closet	289-433-1555
WE013	Comfy Walking Shoes	CWS	Taupe	7.5	2	W	$47.50	$65.00	N	Jennifer's Closet	289-433-1555
WE014	Comfy Walking Shoes	CWS	Brown	8	3	W	$47.50	$65.00	Y	Jennifer's Closet	289-433-1555
WE025	Seriously Tall Boots	STB	Black	6	0	W	$42.50	$80.00	Y	Jennifer's Closet	289-433-1555
WE026	Seriously Tall Boots	STB	Black	6.5	0	W	$42.50	$80.00	Y	Jennifer's Closet	289-433-1555
WE027	Seriously Tall Boots	STB	Black	7	1	W	$42.50	$80.00	Y	Jennifer's Closet	289-433-1555
WE028	Seriously Tall Boots	STB	Black	7.5	0	W	$42.50	$80.00	Y	Jennifer's Closet	289-433-1555
WE029	Seriously Tall Boots	STB	Black	8	2	W	$42.50	$80.00	Y	Jennifer's Closet	289-433-1555
WE030	Seriously Tall Boots	STB	Black	8.5	1	W	$42.50	$80.00	Y	Jennifer's Closet	289-433-1555

4-86 Excel 4-1 completed worksheets

Guided Project 4-2

Classic Gardens and Landscapes is building a workbook with data about sales revenue and recent promotion campaigns. You copy some data from Word and import other data from an Access database. You also use *Conditional Formatting* and create tables.
[Student Learning Outcomes 4.1, 4.2, 4.4, 4.5, 4.6]

Files Needed: ***ClassicGardensRevenue-04.xlsx***, ***SalesDatabase-04.accdb***, and ***ClassicGardensWord-04.docx***
Completed Project File Name: ***[your initials] Excel 4-2.xlsx***

Skills Covered in This Project

- Copy data from Word.
- Apply *Conditional Formatting* using an icon set.
- Import a table from a database file.
- Apply a table style.
- Insert a total row in a table.
- Use the *SUM* function.
- Insert a column.
- Copy a formula.
- Create an *Auto Outline*.
- Create a *PivotTable*.
- Set a report filter in a *PivotTable*.
- Move fields in a *PivotTable*.

1. Open the ***ClassicGardensRevenue-04*** workbook from your student data files folder. Click the **Enable Editing** button.
2. Save the workbook as ***[your initials] Excel 4-2***.
3. Click the **Quarterly** sheet tab.
4. Insert six columns between columns **G** and **H**.
5. Copy data from Word.
   a. Open the Word document ***ClassicGardensWord-04*** from your student data files folder. Click the **Enable Editing** button.
   b. Select all the data in Word and copy it.
   c. Return to the Excel workbook.
   d. Click cell **H4**.
   e. Click the **Paste** button arrow [*Home* tab, *Clipboard* group] and choose **Match Destination Formatting**.
   f. Select cells **N5:N10** and click the *AutoSum* button [*Home* tab, *Editing* group].
   g. Select cells **B10:M10** and sum the columns.
6. Apply *Conditional Formatting*.
   a. Select cells **J5:J9**.
   b. Click the **Quick Analysis** button.
   c. Click **Formatting**.
   d. Choose **Icon Set** (Figure 4-87). The cells display an icon to represent the upper, middle, or lower values of the range.

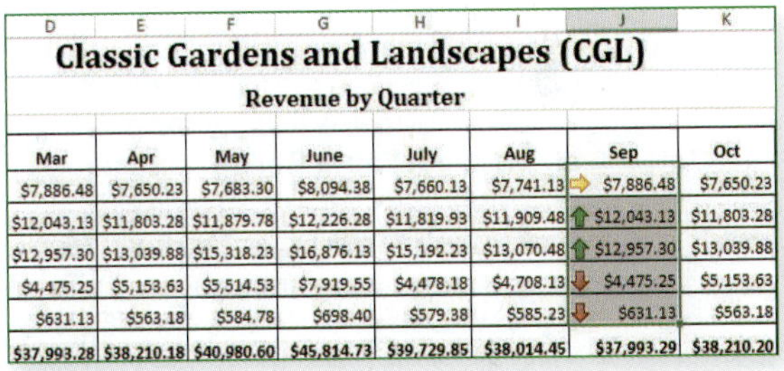

D	E	F	G	H	I	J	K
Classic Gardens and Landscapes (CGL)							
Revenue by Quarter							
Mar	Apr	May	June	July	Aug	Sep	Oct
$7,886.48	$7,650.23	$7,683.30	$8,094.38	$7,660.13	$7,741.13	$7,886.48	$7,650.23
$12,043.13	$11,803.28	$11,879.78	$12,226.28	$11,819.93	$11,909.48	$12,043.13	$11,803.28
$12,957.30	$13,039.88	$15,318.23	$16,876.13	$15,192.23	$13,070.48	$12,957.30	$13,039.88
$4,475.25	$5,153.63	$5,514.53	$7,919.55	$4,478.18	$4,708.13	$4,475.25	$5,153.63
$631.13	$563.18	$584.78	$698.40	$579.38	$585.23	$631.13	$563.18
$37,993.28	$38,210.18	$40,980.60	$45,814.73	$39,729.85	$38,014.45	$37,993.29	$38,210.20

4-87 Icon set conditional formatting

7. *AutoFit* the columns and make sure all data is visible.
8. Click the **AutoOutline** sheet tab.
9. Enter *SUM* functions.
   a. Enter the *SUM* function in cells **E5:E18**, **I5:I18**, **M5:M18**, and **Q5:Q18**.
   b. Enter the *SUM* function in cells **R5:R18** to add the four quarter totals.
   c. Enter the *SUM* function in cells **B19:R19**.
   d. Do the same to show sums for the remaining sections on the sheet. You can hold down the **Ctrl** key, select multiple nonadjacent ranges, and click the **AutoSum** button.

10. In cell **B35**, type the formula =B19+B26+B34 and press **Enter**.
11. Copy the formula in cell **B35** to cells **C35:R35**. *Autofit* the columns.
12. Create an *Auto Outline*.
    a. Click cell **B5**.
    b. Click the **Group** button arrow [*Data* tab, *Outline* group] and choose **Auto Outline** (Figure 4-88). The *Auto Outline* command uses the column and row formulas to group the data.
    c. Click the **Level 2** column outline button (above the column headings). Only the quarter totals are displayed (Figure 4-89).

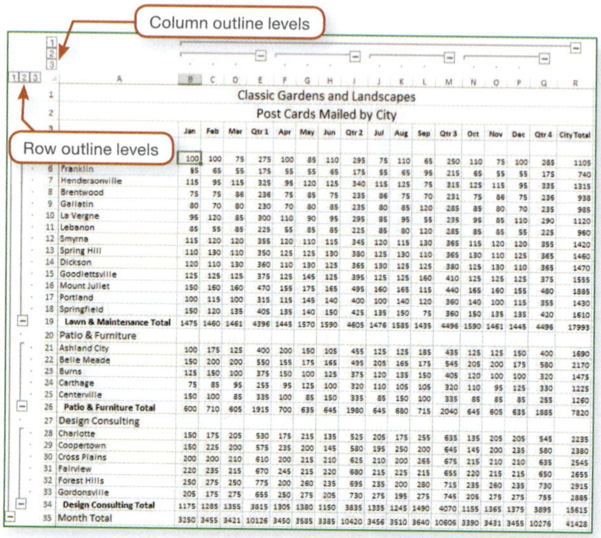

4-88 AutoOutline with three row levels and three column levels

13. Import a table from an Access database.
    a. Click the **Table** sheet tab.
    b. Click cell **A4**.
    c. Click the **From Access** button [*Data* tab, *Get External Data* group].
    d. Select ***SalesDatabase-04.accdb*** in the *Select Data Source* window.
    e. Click **Open**.
    f. Click **tblMailings** in the *Select Table* dialog box.
    g. Click **OK**.
    h. Select **Table** and **Existing worksheet** if necessary.
    i. Click **OK**.
14. Apply a table style and show a total row.
    a. Click any cell within the table.
    b. Click the **Table Styles** More button [*Table Tools Design* tab, *Table Styles* group].
    c. Choose **Table Style Medium 15**.
    d. Click to place a check mark for **Total Row** [*Table Tools Design* tab, *Table Style Options* group].
    e. Click each cell in the range **C30:M30** and choose **SUM**.
15. Merge and center the title across **A1:N1**, and the subtitle across **A2:N2**. Set the font size of the labels to **18 pt.** (Figure 4-90).
16. Click the **PivotTable** sheet tab.
17. Create a *PivotTable*.
    a. Select cells **A3:D28**.
    b. Click the **PivotTable** button [*Insert* tab, *Tables* group]. Depending on how data is arranged, Excel cannot always recommend *PivotTable* layouts. Select the correct cell range if you did not do so before clicking the **PivotTable** button.

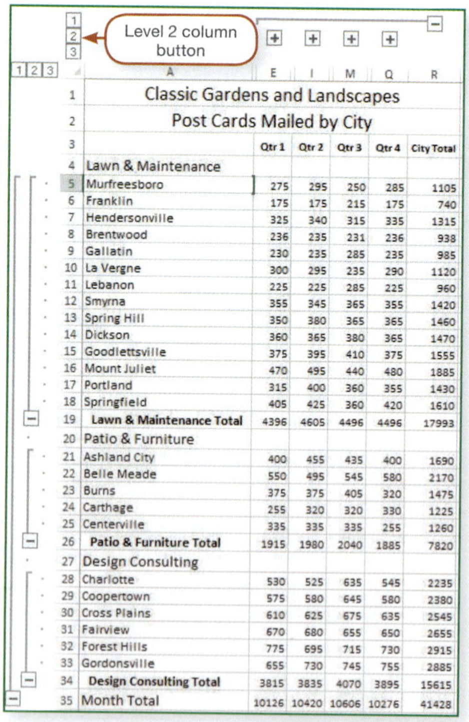

	A	E	I	M	Q	R
1	Classic Gardens and Landscapes					
2	Post Cards Mailed by City					
3		Qtr 1	Qtr 2	Qtr 3	Qtr 4	City Total
4	Lawn & Maintenance					
5	Murfreesboro	275	295	250	285	1105
6	Franklin	175	175	215	175	740
7	Hendersonville	325	340	315	335	1315
8	Brentwood	236	235	231	236	938
9	Gallatin	230	235	285	235	985
10	La Vergne	300	295	235	290	1120
11	Lebanon	225	225	285	225	960
12	Smyrna	355	345	365	355	1420
13	Spring Hill	350	380	365	365	1460
14	Dickson	360	365	380	365	1470
15	Goodlettsville	375	395	410	375	1555
16	Mount Juliet	470	495	440	480	1885
17	Portland	315	400	360	355	1430
18	Springfield	405	425	360	420	1610
19	Lawn & Maintenance Total	4396	4605	4496	4496	17993
20	Patio & Furniture					
21	Ashland City	400	455	435	400	1690
22	Belle Meade	550	495	545	580	2170
23	Burns	375	375	405	320	1475
24	Carthage	255	320	320	330	1225
25	Centerville	335	335	335	255	1260
26	Patio & Furniture Total	1915	1980	2040	1885	7820
27	Design Consulting					
28	Charlotte	530	525	635	545	2235
29	Coopertown	575	580	645	580	2380
30	Cross Plains	610	625	675	635	2545
31	Fairview	670	680	655	650	2655
32	Forest Hills	775	695	715	730	2915
33	Gordonsville	655	730	745	755	2885
34	Design Consulting Total	3815	3835	4070	3895	15615
35	Month Total	10126	10420	10606	10276	41428

4-89 Outline collapsed at Level 2 column group

c. Select **New Worksheet** if necessary.
d. Click **OK**.
e. In the *Choose fields to add to report* area in the *PivotTable Fields* pane, click to place a check for **City**, **# Mailed**, and **# Responses**. These fields are shown in the report layout and in the *Row* and *Values* areas in the pane. The *Columns* area in the pane indicates that the numbers in the columns are summed or totaled in the *Grand Total* row (Figure 4-91).
f. Drag the **Department** field from the *Choose fields to add to report* area to the *Filters* area in the *PivotTable Fields* pane.
g. Click the filter arrow for the **Department** field in cell **B1**.
h. Click to place a check mark for **Select Multiple Items**.
i. Click to remove the check mark for **All**.
j. Click to place a check mark for **Landscape Design** and click **OK**.
k. Format cells **A1:B1** as bold.
l. Close the *PivotTable Fields* pane (Figure 4-92).

18. Save and close the workbook.

Classic Gardens and Landscapes
Post Card Mailings by City

ID	City	Jan	Feb	Mar	Apr	May	Jun	Jul	Aug	Sep	Oct	Nov	Dec
1	Murfreesboro	100	100	75	100	85	110	75	110	65	110	75	100
2	Franklin	55	65	55	55	55	65	55	65	95	65	55	55
3	Hendersonville	115	95	115	95	120	125	115	125	75	125	115	95
4	Brentwood	75	75	86	75	85	75	86	75	70	75	86	75
5	Gallatin	80	70	80	70	80	85	80	85	120	85	80	70
6	La Vergne	95	120	85	110	90	95	85	95	55	95	85	110
7	Lebanon	85	55	85	55	85	85	85	80	120	85	85	55
8	Smyrna	115	120	120	120	110	115	120	115	130	115	120	120
9	Spring Hill	110	130	110	125	125	130	125	130	110	130	110	125
10	Dickson	120	110	130	110	130	125	130	125	125	125	130	110
11	Goodlettsville	125	125	125	125	145	125	125	125	160	125	125	125
12	Mount Juliet	150	160	160	155	175	165	160	165	115	165	160	155
13	Portland	100	115	100	115	145	140	100	140	120	140	100	115
14	Springfield	150	120	135	135	140	150	135	150	75	150	135	135
15	Ashland City	100	175	125	200	150	105	125	125	185	125	125	150
16	Belle Meade	150	200	200	155	175	165	205	165	175	205	200	175
17	Burns	125	150	100	150	100	125	120	135	150	120	100	100
18	Carthage	75	85	95	95	125	100	110	105	105	110	95	125
19	Centerville	150	100	85	100	85	150	85	150	100	85	85	85
20	Charlotte	150	175	205	175	215	135	205	175	255	135	205	205
21	Coopertown	150	225	200	235	200	145	195	250	200	145	200	235
22	Cross Plains	200	200	210	200	215	210	210	200	265	215	210	210
23	Fairview	220	235	215	245	215	220	215	225	215	220	215	215
24	Forest Hills	250	275	250	200	260	235	235	200	280	235	260	235
25	Gordonsville	205	175	275	250	275	205	275	195	275	205	275	275
Total		3250	3455	3421	3450	3585	3385	3456	3510	3640	3390	3431	3455

4-90 Imported data formatted as a table

Row Labels	Sum of # Mailed	Sum of # Responses
Ashland City	1690	473
Belle Meade	2170	602
Brentwood	938	125
Burns	1475	413
Carthage	1225	343
Centerville	1260	353
Charlotte	2235	618
Coopertown	2380	668
Cross Plains	2545	712
Dickson	1470	322
Fairview	2655	743
Forest Hills	2915	815
Franklin	740	207
Gallatin	985	325
Goodlettsville	1555	435
Gordonsville	2885	807
Hendersonville	1315	368
La Vergne	1120	314
Lebanon	960	175
Mount Juliet	1885	527
Murfreesboro	1105	309
Portland	1430	389
Smyrna	1420	300
Spring Hill	1460	460
Springfield	1610	450
Grand Total	**41428**	**11253**

PivotTable Fields
Choose fields to add to report:
City
Department
Mailed
Responses
MORE TABLES...
Drag fields between areas below:
FILTERS
COLUMNS
Σ Values
ROWS
City
Σ VALUES
Sum of # Mail...
Sum of # Res...

4-91 *PivotTable* layout

Department	Landscape Design	
Row Labels	**Sum of # Mailed**	**Sum of # Responses**
Centerville	1260	353
Charlotte	2235	618
Forest Hills	2915	815
Gallatin	985	325
La Vergne	1120	314
Portland	1430	389
Springfield	1610	450
Grand Total	**11555**	**3264**

Report Filter button

4-92 *PivotTable* with report filter

Guided Project 4-3

Clemenson Imaging wants to analyze expense reports from field representatives as well as its patient data and image data. To complete the necessary worksheets, you import a comma-separated text file (*.csv*), use the *Subtotal* command, and run *Goal Seek*. You also format data as a table and build an advanced filter. Finally, you display data in a *PivotTable*.
[Student Learning Outcomes 4.1, 4.2, 4.3, 4.4, 4.5, 4.6, 4.7]

Files Needed: ***ClemensonForecasts-04.xlsx*** and ***ClemensonExpenseData-04.csv***
Completed Project File Name: ***[your initials] Excel 4-3.xlsx***

Skills Covered in This Project

- Create an Excel table.
- Apply a table style.
- Create an *Advanced Filter*.
- Apply *Conditional Formatting*.
- Copy, move, and name a worksheet.
- Insert a row and set column widths.
- Import a comma-separated values text file.
- Sort data.
- Use the *Subtotal* command.
- Expand and collapse groups in an outline.
- Use *Goal Seek*.
- Create a *PivotTable*.
- Create a *PivotChart*.
- Unlock cells.
- Protect a worksheet with a password.

1. Open the ***ClemensonForecasts-04*** workbook from your student data files folder. Click the **Enable Editing** button.
2. Save the workbook as ***[your initials] Excel 4-3***.
3. Copy the **Past&Projected** sheet and name the copied sheet Adv Filter. Move the **Adv Filter** sheet to the right of the *Past&Projected* sheet.
4. Create and format an Excel table.
   a. Select cells **A4:E60** on the *Adv Filter* sheet.
   b. Click the **Quick Analysis** tool and choose **Tables**.
   c. Click **Table**.
5. Apply a table style.
   a. Click a cell within the table.
   b. Click the **More** button [*Table Tools Design* tab, *Table Styles* group].
   c. Select **Table Style Medium 15**.
6. Create a criteria range for an *Advanced Filter*.
   a. Select cells **A4:E4** and copy and paste them to cell **G4**.
   b. Type Criteria Range in cell **G3** and set the font to **Cambria 16 pt**.
   c. Adjust column **K** width to show the complete label.
   d. Type Extract Range in cell **G8** and set the same font and size.
   e. Copy the labels from cells **G4:K4** to cell **G9**.
7. Create an *Advanced Filter*.
   a. In cell **G5**, type >12/31/16.
   b. In cell **H5**, type mri.

c. In cell **H6**, type ct scan. These criteria will find records dated 2017 or later for MRIs ***and*** records for CT scans from any year (Figure 4-93).

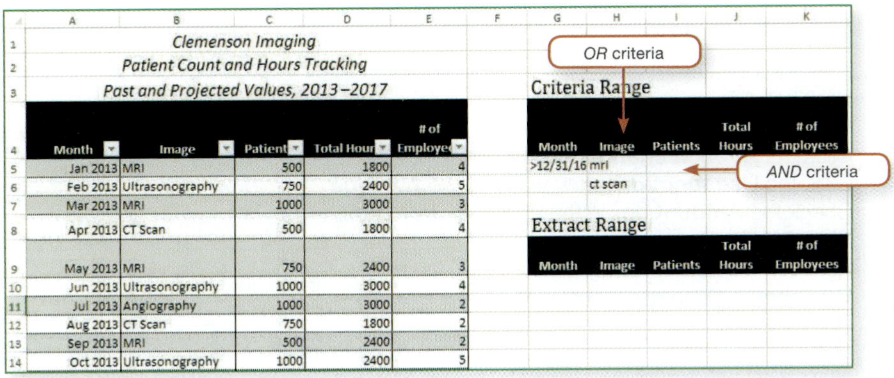

4-93 Criteria range and extract range

d. Click a cell in the table.
e. Click the **Advanced** button [*Data* tab, *Sort & Filter* group].
f. Select the **Copy to another location** radio button.
g. Verify that the **List range** is cells **A4:E60**. If the range is incorrect, click and drag to select the range. The list range includes the header row.
h. Click in the **Criteria range** box and select cells **G4:K6**.
i. Click in the **Copy to** box and select cells **G9:K9**.
j. Click **OK** (Figure 4-94). The CT scan records are from all years; the MRI records are only those from 2017 and later.

Extract Range

Month	Image	Patients	Total Hours	# of Employees
Apr 2013	CT Scan	500	1800	4
Aug 2013	CT Scan	750	1800	2
Dec 2013	CT Scan	500	2400	3
Apr 2014	CT Scan	750	1800	2
Aug 2014	CT Scan	1000	1800	4
Dec 2014	CT Scan	750	2400	4
Apr 2015	CT Scan	1000	1800	5
Aug 2015	CT Scan	500	2400	3
Dec 2015	CT Scan	500	2400	2
Apr 2016	CT Scan	500	2400	3
Aug 2016	CT Scan	750	2400	3
Dec 2016	CT Scan	500	1800	4
Jan 2017	MRI	1000	1800	3
Apr 2017	CT Scan	750	2400	2
May 2017	MRI	750	3000	4
Aug 2017	CT Scan	500	2400	3

4-94 *Advanced Filter* results

8. Apply *Conditional Formatting*.
a. Select cells **I10:I25**.
b. Click the **Conditional Formatting** button [*Home* tab, *Styles* group].
c. Choose **Highlight Cells Rules** and **Greater Than**.
d. Type 751 and choose **Green Fill with Dark Green Text**.
e. Click **OK**.

9. Import a comma-separated values text file.
a. Click the **Expense Info** sheet tab.
b. Select cell **A3**.
c. Click the **From Text** button [*Data* tab, *Get External Data* group].
d. Find and select the ***ClemensonExpenseData-04.csv*** file in the *Import Text File* window.
e. Click **Import**.
f. Select the **Delimited** button in the first *Wizard* window. Excel recognizes that this file separates the data into columns with a comma.
g. Click **Next**.
h. Click to remove the check mark for **Tab** and click to place a check mark for **Comma**.
i. Click **Finish** and click **OK**.
j. Insert two rows at row **3**.
k. Type Representative in cell **A4**, Date in cell **B4**, and Amount in cell **C4**.
l. *AutoFit* column **C**.

10. Sort data.
    a. Click cell **A5**.
    b. Click the **Sort & Filter** button [*Home* tab, *Editing* group].
    c. Choose **Sort A to Z**.
11. Use the *Subtotal* command.
    a. Click cell **A5**.
    b. Click the **Subtotal** button [*Data* tab, *Outline* group].
    c. Click the **At each change in** arrow and choose **Representative**.
    d. Click the **Use function** arrow and choose **Average**.
    e. Check the **Amount** box in the *Add subtotal to* area.
    f. Click **OK**.
    g. Format the values in column **C** as **Currency** with no decimal places.
12. Use *Goal Seek*.
    a. Type Target March Expense in cell **E4**.
    b. Click cell **C8**.
    c. Click the **What-If Analysis** button [*Data* tab, *Data Tools* group] and choose **Goal Seek**.
    d. In the *To value* box, type 600. This value sets a lower expense for Mary Jo.
    e. In the *By changing cell* box, click cell **C7**.
    f. Click **OK**.
    g. Note the target expense and click **Cancel**.
    h. Type $600 in cell **F5**.

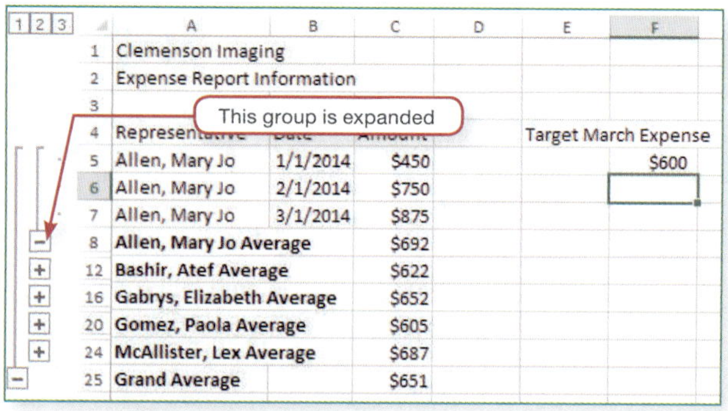

4-95 Expanded and collapsed groups after the Subtotal Command

13. Collapse outline groups.
    a. Click the collapse symbol (-) for row **12**.
    b. Click the collapse symbol (-) for each of these rows: **16**, **20**, and **24** (Figure 4-95).
14. Create a *PivotTable*.
    a. Click the **Past&Projected** sheet tab.
    b. Select cells **A4:E60**. You must select the range to display the *Quick Analysis* tool.
    c. Click the **Quick Analysis** tool and choose **Tables**.
    d. Point at several *PivotTable* options to see the *Live Preview*.
    e. Choose the option that shows a sum of each field (Figure 4-96).
    f. Rename the sheet PivotTable.

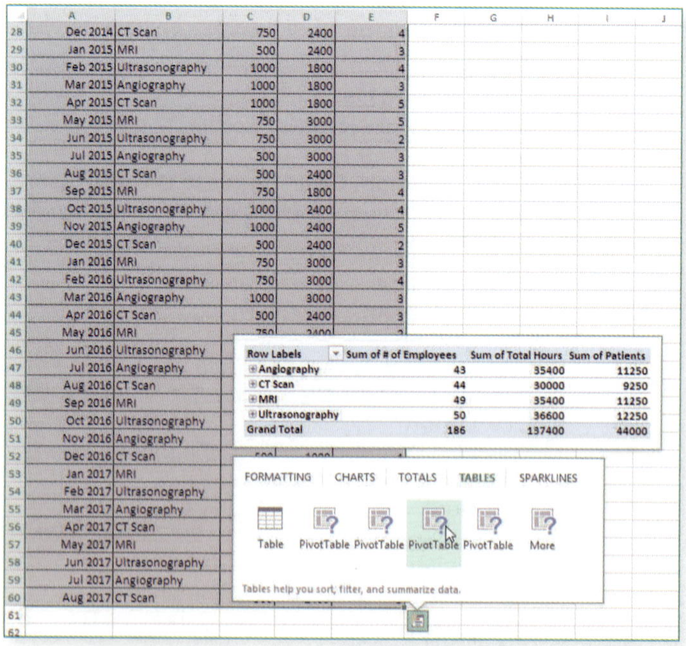

4-96 Suggested *PivotTable* choices from the *Quick Analysis* tool

15. Add a *PivotChart* to the *PivotTable* worksheet.
    a. Click a cell within the *PivotTable*.
    b. Click the **PivotChart** button [*PivotTable Tool Analyze* tab, *Tools* group].
    c. Click **Line** in the type list, and choose **Line with Markers** *PivotChart*.
    d. Click **OK**.
    e. Position the chart to the right of the *PivotTable*.
    f. In the *PivotChart Fields* pane, click to remove the check mark for **# of Employees** (Figure 4-97). The *PivotTable* and *PivotChart* are linked so that field is removed from the table and the chart. The task pane toggles between the *PivotTable* and *PivotChart* fields panes based on which element is active.

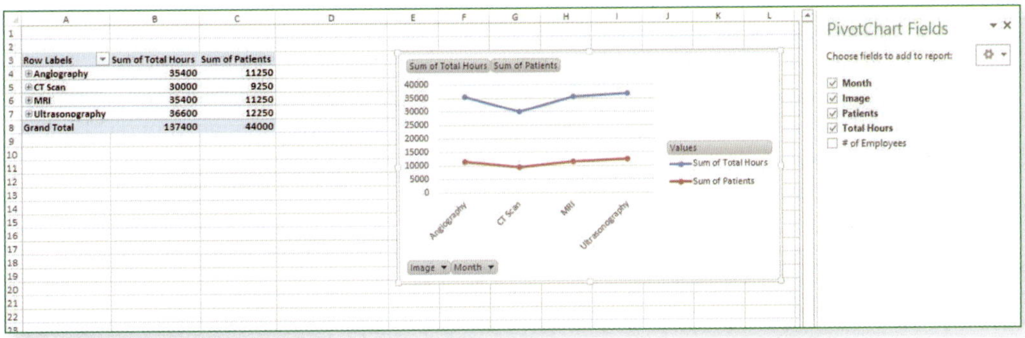

4-97 *PivotChart* and its *PivotTable*

16. Remove the *Locked* property.
    a. Click the **Past&Projected** sheet tab.
    b. Select cells **C5:E60** and right-click any cell in the range.
    c. Select **Format Cells** from the menu.
    d. Click the **Protection** tab.
    e. Clear the check mark for **Locked**.
    f. Click **OK**.

17. Protect a worksheet with a password.
    a. Click the **Protect Sheet** button [*Review* tab, *Changes* group].
    b. Click to place check marks for **Select locked cells** and **Select unlocked cells** if necessary.
    c. Type the password: 321.
    d. Click **OK**.
    e. Retype the password: 321.
    f. Click **OK**. The cells for which the *Locked* property was disabled can be edited.

18. Save and close the workbook.

Independent Project 4-4

Eller Software Services has received updated client information with sales numbers. You import the data into the worksheet, sort and filter it, and apply conditional formatting. You also format the data as an Excel table and create a *PivotTable*.
[Student Learning Outcomes 4.1, 4.2, 4.3, 4.4, 4.5, 4.6, 4.7]

Files Needed: ***EllerSales-04.xlsx*** and ***ClientInfo-04.txt***
Completed Project File Name: ***[your initials] Excel 4-4.xlsx***

Skills Covered in This Project

- Import a text file.
- Sort data.
- Use an *AutoFilter*.
- Filter data by cell color.
- Copy, name, and move a worksheet.
- Use the *Subtotal* command.
- Apply *Conditional Formatting*.
- Clear filters and conditional formatting.
- Create an Excel table.
- Create a *PivotTable*.
- Protect a worksheet with a password.

1. Open the ***EllerSales-04*** workbook from your student data files folder.
2. Save the workbook as ***[your initials] Excel 4-4***.
3. Import the ***ClientInfo-04.txt*** file in cell **A4**. The text file is tab-delimited.
4. Unhide row **10**. Fix the phone number in cell C12.
5. Set *Conditional Formatting* to show cells **I5:I13** with **Yellow Fill with Dark Yellow Text** for values that are less than **1500**.
6. Sort the data first by **Product/Service** in **A to Z** order and next by **Client Name** in **A to Z** order (Figure 4-98).

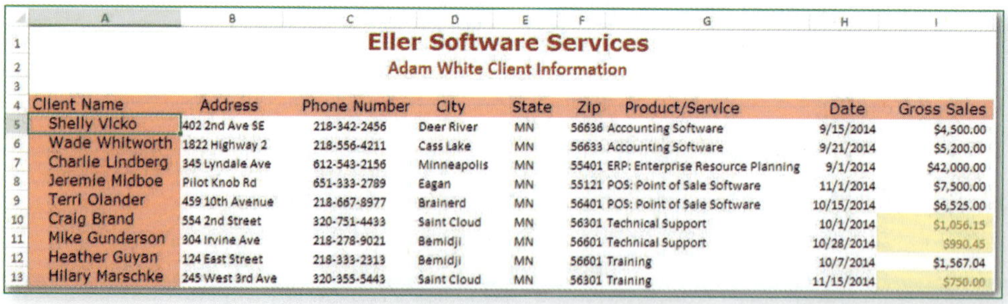

Eller Software Services
Adam White Client Information

Client Name	Address	Phone Number	City	State	Zip	Product/Service	Date	Gross Sales
Shelly Vicko	402 2nd Ave SE	218-342-2456	Deer River	MN	56636	Accounting Software	9/15/2014	$4,500.00
Wade Whitworth	1822 Highway 2	218-556-4211	Cass Lake	MN	56633	Accounting Software	9/21/2014	$5,200.00
Charlie Lindberg	345 Lyndale Ave	612-543-2156	Minneapolis	MN	55401	ERP: Enterprise Resource Planning	9/1/2014	$42,000.00
Jeremie Midboe	Pilot Knob Rd	651-333-2789	Eagan	MN	55121	POS: Point of Sale Software	11/1/2014	$7,500.00
Terri Olander	459 10th Avenue	218-667-8977	Brainerd	MN	56401	POS: Point of Sale Software	10/15/2014	$6,525.00
Craig Brand	554 2nd Street	320-751-4433	Saint Cloud	MN	56301	Technical Support	10/1/2014	$1,056.15
Mike Gunderson	304 Irvine Ave	218-278-9021	Bemidji	MN	56601	Technical Support	10/28/2014	$990.45
Heather Guyan	124 East Street	218-333-2313	Bemidji	MN	56601	Training	10/7/2014	$1,567.04
Hilary Marschke	245 West 3rd Ave	320-355-5443	Saint Cloud	MN	56301	Training	11/15/2014	$750.00

4-98 Rows sorted by "Product/Service" and then by "Client Name"

7. Display the *AutoFilter* buttons and filter the **Gross Sales** data by color to show only those cells with yellow fill.
8. Copy the **MN Clients** sheet, name the copied sheet Subtotals, and move it to the right of the *MN Clients* sheet.
9. Clear the filter and the conditional formatting on the **Subtotals** sheet.

10. Sort by **City** in **A to Z** order if necesssary.

11. Use the *Subtotal* command to show a **SUM** function in the **Gross Sales** column at each change in **City** (Figure 4-99).

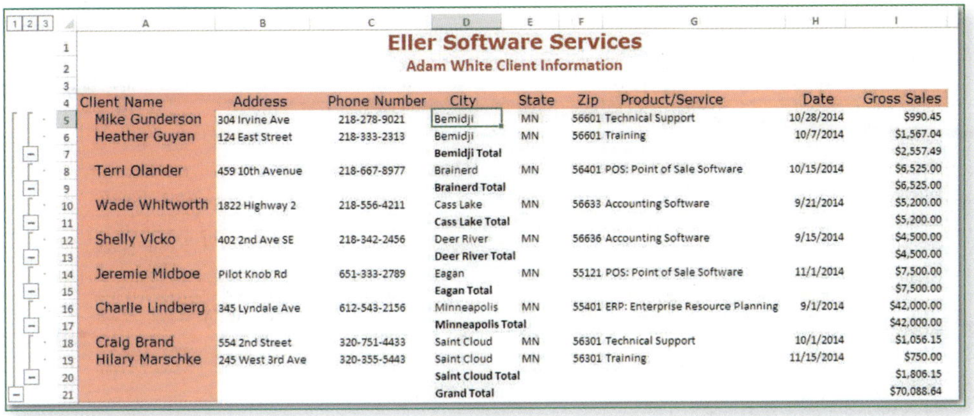

Eller Software Services

Adam White Client Information

Client Name	Address	Phone Number	City	State	Zip	Product/Service	Date	Gross Sales
Mike Gunderson	304 Irvine Ave	218-278-9021	Bemidji	MN	56601	Technical Support	10/28/2014	$990.45
Heather Guyan	124 East Street	218-333-2313	Bemidji	MN	56601	Training	10/7/2014	$1,567.04
			Bemidji Total					$2,557.49
Terri Olander	459 10th Avenue	218-667-8977	Brainerd	MN	56401	POS: Point of Sale Software	10/15/2014	$6,525.00
			Brainerd Total					$6,525.00
Wade Whitworth	1822 Highway 2	218-556-4211	Cass Lake	MN	56633	Accounting Software	9/21/2014	$5,200.00
			Cass Lake Total					$5,200.00
Shelly Vicko	402 2nd Ave SE	218-342-2456	Deer River	MN	56636	Accounting Software	9/15/2014	$4,500.00
			Deer River Total					$4,500.00
Jeremie Midboe	Pilot Knob Rd	651-333-2789	Eagan	MN	55121	POS: Point of Sale Software	11/1/2014	$7,500.00
			Eagan Total					$7,500.00
Charlie Lindberg	345 Lyndale Ave	612-543-2156	Minneapolis	MN	55401	ERP: Enterprise Resource Planning	9/1/2014	$42,000.00
			Minneapolis Total					$42,000.00
Craig Brand	554 2nd Street	320-751-4433	Saint Cloud	MN	56301	Technical Support	10/1/2014	$1,056.15
Hilary Marschke	245 West 3rd Ave	320-355-5443	Saint Cloud	MN	56301	Training	11/15/2014	$750.00
			Saint Cloud Total					$1,806.15
			Grand Total					$70,088.64

4-99 Subtotal results for gross sales at each change in city

12. Copy the **Subtotals** worksheet, name the copied sheet Table Data, and move it to the right of the *Subtotals* sheet.

13. Remove all subtotals on the **Table Data** sheet.

14. Format cells **A4:I13** as an Excel table with **Table Style Medium 9**. The external connection is from the imported data; click **Yes** in the message box.

15. Display a **Total Row** in the table (Figure 4-100).

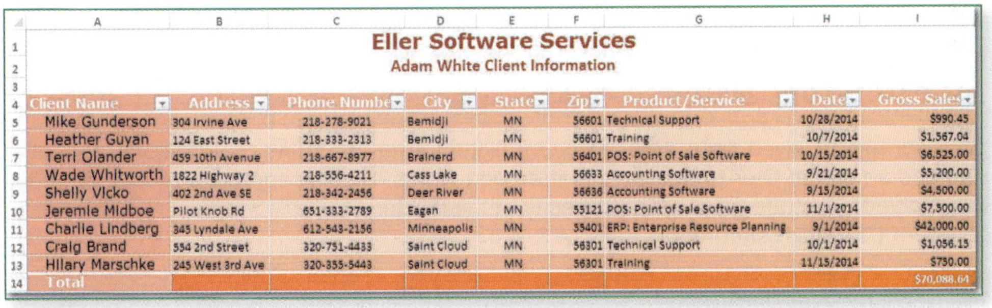

Eller Software Services

Adam White Client Information

Client Name	Address	Phone Number	City	State	Zip	Product/Service	Date	Gross Sales
Mike Gunderson	304 Irvine Ave	218-278-9021	Bemidji	MN	56601	Technical Support	10/28/2014	$990.45
Heather Guyan	124 East Street	218-333-2313	Bemidji	MN	56601	Training	10/7/2014	$1,567.04
Terri Olander	459 10th Avenue	218-667-8977	Brainerd	MN	56401	POS: Point of Sale Software	10/15/2014	$6,525.00
Wade Whitworth	1822 Highway 2	218-556-4211	Cass Lake	MN	56633	Accounting Software	9/21/2014	$5,200.00
Shelly Vicko	402 2nd Ave SE	218-342-2456	Deer River	MN	56636	Accounting Software	9/15/2014	$4,500.00
Jeremie Midboe	Pilot Knob Rd	651-333-2789	Eagan	MN	55121	POS: Point of Sale Software	11/1/2014	$7,500.00
Charlie Lindberg	345 Lyndale Ave	612-543-2156	Minneapolis	MN	55401	ERP: Enterprise Resource Planning	9/1/2014	$42,000.00
Craig Brand	554 2nd Street	320-751-4433	Saint Cloud	MN	56301	Technical Support	10/1/2014	$1,056.15
Hilary Marschke	245 West 3rd Ave	320-355-5443	Saint Cloud	MN	56301	Training	11/15/2014	$750.00
Total								$70,088.64

4-100 Table with total row

16. Create a *PivotTable* based on cells **A4:I13** in the **Table Data** sheet on its own sheet named PivotTable.

17. Arrange the fields in the *PivotTable* like this: **City** (*FILTERS* area), **Product/Service** (*ROWS* area), and **Gross Sales** (*VALUES* area).

18. Filter the report to display only the data for **Bemidji** and **Brainerd**.

19. Apply **Currency** style to **B4:B7**.

20. Insert a **Clustered Column PivotChart** on the *PivotTable* sheet.

21. Delete the legend from the *PivotChart* and insert the following chart title: Bemidji & Brainerd Gross Sales (Figure 4-101).

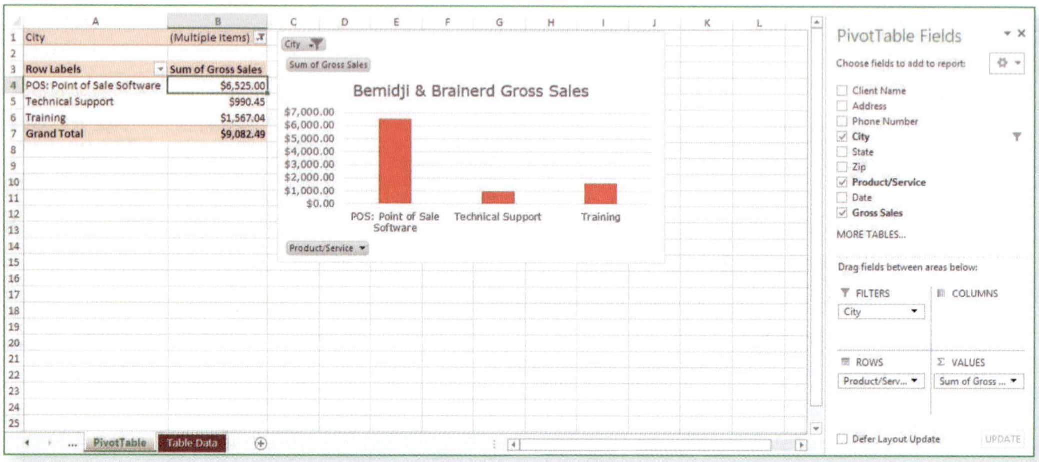

4-101 *PivotTable* with *PivotChart* results

22. Protect the **Table Data** sheet with the password **PasswordC**.

23. Save and close the workbook.

Independent Project 4-5

Boyd Air has received flight data for recent flights. After importing the data, you format it as a table and use a number filter to display the afternoon flights. Display subtotals by city of origin and use a *PivotTable* to illustrate the average capacity of the flights.
[Student Learning Outcomes 4.1, 4.2, 4.3, 4.4, 4.5]

File Needed: ***FlightData-04.txt***
Completed Project File Name: ***[your initials] Excel 4-5.xlsx***

Skills Covered in This Project

- Import a text file.
- Create an Excel table.
- Filter data.
- Convert a table to a normal range.
- Sort data.
- Use the *Subtotal* command.
- Copy, name, and move a worksheet.
- Create a *PivotTable*.
- Create a *PivotChart*.

1. Open a new workbook and save it as ***[your initials] Excel 4-5***.
2. Import the ***FlightData-04.txt*** text file starting at cell **A3**. The text file is tab-delimited.
3. Click a cell within the data range and format the range as an Excel table using **Table Style Medium 21**.
4. Use the **AutoFilter** button and **Number Filters** to filter the table to display only those flights with a Departure Time after 12 PM (Figure 4-102).
5. Type Boyd Air in cell **A1**. Type Flight Statistics in cell **A2**. Set the font size to **20 pt.** for both labels.
6. Center the labels in cells **A1:A2** across the table data.

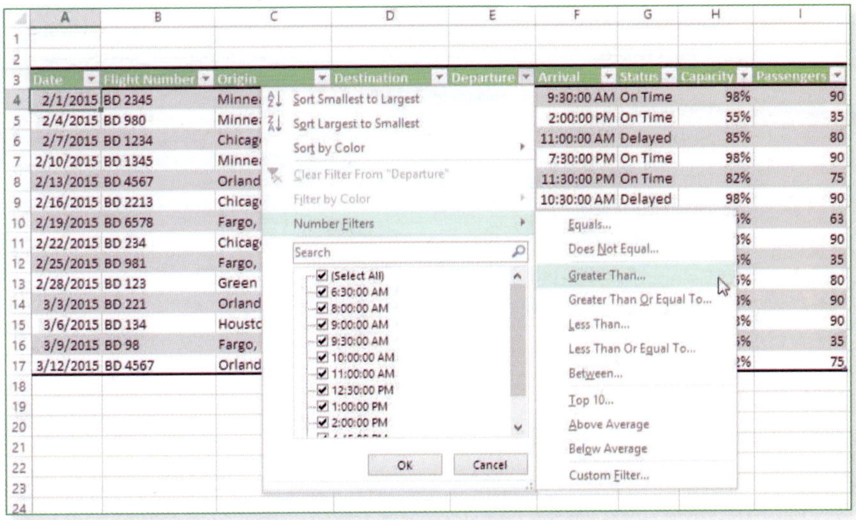

4-102 Number filter for departure time field

7. Name the worksheet Afternoon Flights.
8. Copy the **Afternoon Flights** worksheet, name the copy Subtotals, and move the **Subtotals** sheet to the right of the *Afternoon Flights* sheet.
9. On the **Subtotals** sheet, clear the filter.
10. On the **Subtotals** sheet, sort the data by **Origin** in **A to Z** order.
11. Convert the table on the **Subtotals** sheet to a normal range.
12. Select cells **A3:I17** and use the **Subtotal** command to display a sum for the **Passengers** field at each change in **Origin** (Figure 4-103). You must select the cells for the *Subtotal* command, because the main labels are not separated from the data range by a blank row.

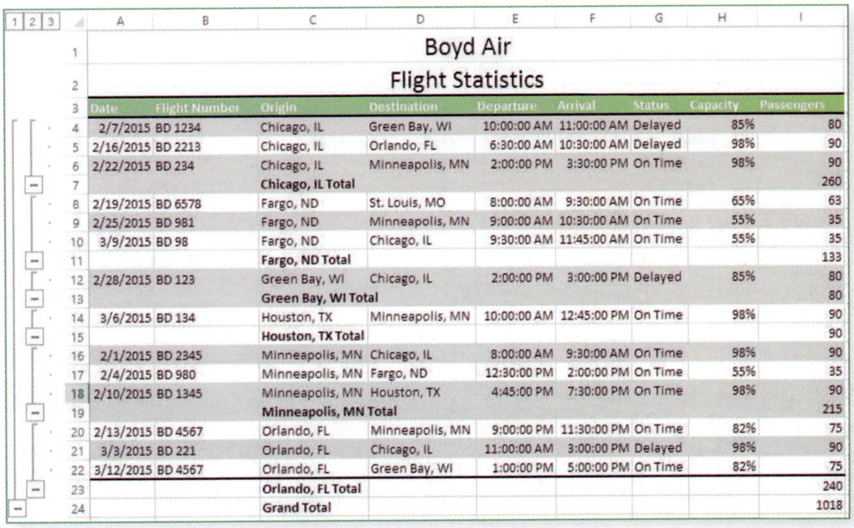

4-103 Subtotals for Passenger field at each change in Origin field

13. Copy the **Afternoon Flights** worksheet, name the copy PivotTable Source, and move the **PivotTable Source** sheet to the right of the *Subtotals* sheet.
14. On the **PivotTable Source** sheet, clear the filter.
15. Select cells **A3:I17** and use the **Quick Analysis** tool to create a *PivotTable* to display average of capacity by origin (Figure 4-104).

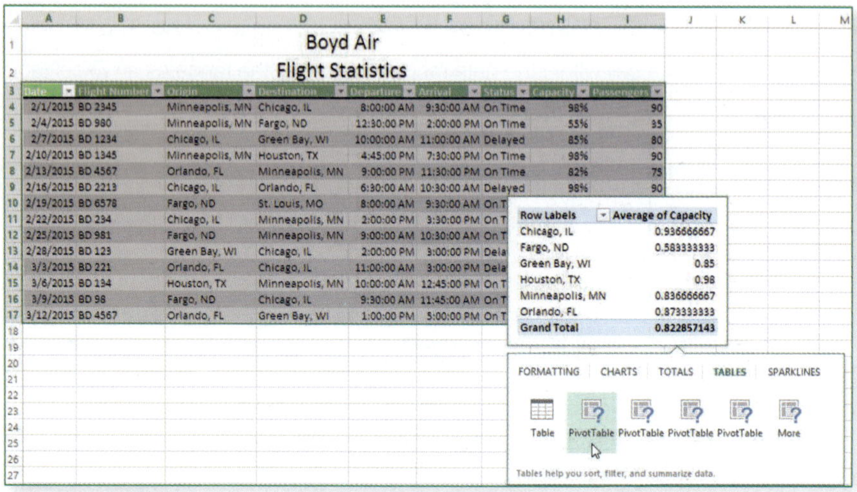

4-104 *PivotTable* suggestions from the *Quick Analysis* tool

16. Click cell **B3** in the *PivotTable*. On the *PivotTable Tools Analyze* tab, click **Field Settings** and set a **Number Format** of **Percentage** with 2 decimal places.
17. In the *PivotTable Fields* pane, place a check mark to add the **Passengers** field to the *PivotTable VALUES* area showing a sum.
18. Add a **3-D Pie PivotChart** to the sheet and position the chart to the right of the *PivotTable*.
19. Rename the worksheet PivotTable&Chart and close the task pane (Figure 4-105).
20. Save and close the workbook.

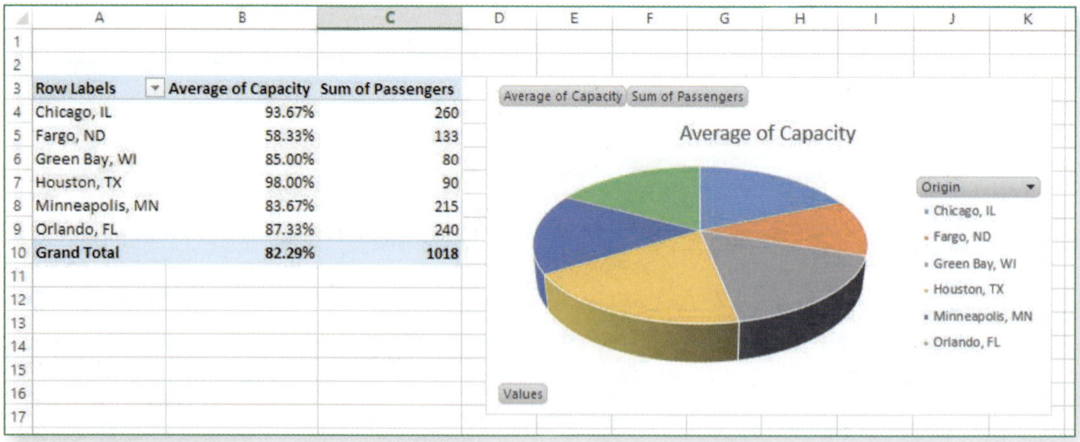

Row Labels	Average of Capacity	Sum of Passengers
Chicago, IL	93.67%	260
Fargo, ND	58.33%	133
Green Bay, WI	85.00%	80
Houston, TX	98.00%	90
Minneapolis, MN	83.67%	215
Orlando, FL	87.33%	240
Grand Total	82.29%	1018

4-105 Excel 4-5 completed *PivotTable* and *PivotChart*

Independent Project 4-6

Life's Animal Shelter maintains its supplier list in a worksheet. You need to copy this data to a Word document for use by a coworker. You also need to define groups so that you can display and hide rows by supplier name.
[Student Learning Outcomes 4.1, 4.3, 4.5, 4.6, 4.7]

File Needed: ***LASSuppliers-04.xlsx***
Completed Project File Name: ***[your initials] Excel 4-6.xlsx***

Skills Covered in This Project

- Copy Excel data to Word.
- Sort data.
- Use *Flash Fill*.
- Insert and delete a column.
- Define a group.
- Collapse a group.
- Apply conditional formatting.
- Protect a worksheet.

1. Open the ***LASSuppliers-04*** workbook from your student data files folder.
2. Save the workbook as ***[your initials] Excel 4-6***.
3. Select cells **A4:D18** and copy them to the *Clipboard*.
4. Open Word and create a new document. Save the document as ***[your initials] Excel 4-6***. Note that because Word and Excel use different file name extensions, you can use the same file name.
5. Paste the data into Word.
6. Save and close the Word document (Figure 4-106).
7. Return to the worksheet and press **Esc** to remove the selection marquee if necessary.
8. In cell **E5**, type (651) 555-6788. In cell **E6**, start to type the number that is in cell **D6** and press **Enter** when the *Flash Fill* suggestion appears.
9. Type Phone in cell **E4**.
10. Delete column **D**.

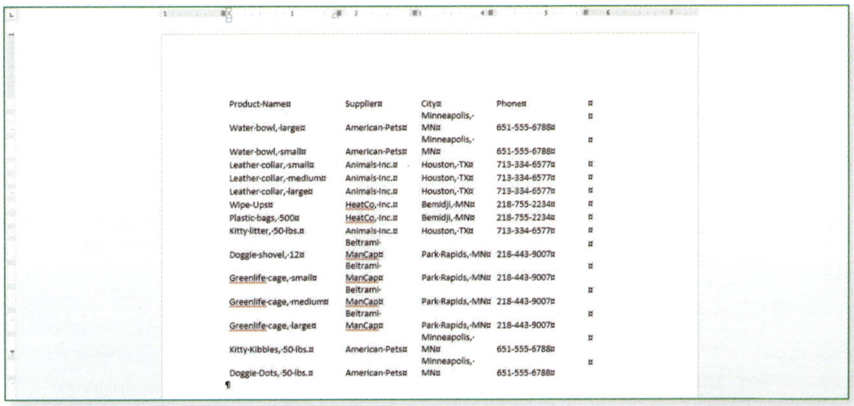

Product Name	Supplier	City	Phone
Water bowl, large	American Pets	Minneapolis, MN	651-555-6788
Water bowl, small	American Pets	Minneapolis, MN	651-555-6788
Leather collar, small	Animals Inc.	Houston, TX	713-334-6577
Leather collar, medium	Animals Inc.	Houston, TX	713-334-6577
Leather collar, large	Animals Inc.	Houston, TX	713-334-6577
Wipe-Ups	HeatCo, Inc.	Bemidji, MN	218-755-2234
Plastic bags, 500	HeatCo, Inc.	Bemidji, MN	218-755-2234
Kitty litter, 50 lbs.	Animals Inc.	Houston, TX	713-334-6577
Doggie shovel, 12	Beltrami ManCap	Park Rapids, MN	218-443-9007
Greenlife cage, small	Beltrami ManCap	Park Rapids, MN	218-443-9007
Greenlife cage, medium	Beltrami ManCap	Park Rapids, MN	218-443-9007
Greenlife cage, large	Beltrami ManCap	Park Rapids, MN	218-443-9007
Kitty Kibbles, 50 lbs.	American Pets	Minneapolis, MN	651-555-6788
Doggie Dots, 50 lbs.	American Pets	Minneapolis, MN	651-555-6788

4-106 Excel data copied to Word

11. Unmerge cell **A1** and then **Merge & Center** it across cells **A1:D1**. Repeat for cell **A2** (Figure 4-107).

12. Copy the worksheet, name the copy Groups and move the copy to the right of the *LAS Suppliers* sheet.

13. On the *Groups* sheet, select and format the labels in row **4** as **bold** and **centered**. You need to distinguish the labels in the header row from the other rows.

14. Select cells **A5:D18** and open the *Sort* dialog box. Sort by **Supplier** in **A to Z** order and then by **Product Name** in **A to Z** order.

15. Insert a blank row at row **5** and type Minneapolis in cell **A5**. Left-align the label.

16. Insert a row at row **10** and type Houston in cell **A10**. **Bold** the label.

17. Repeat step 16 for Park Rapids and Bemidji.

18. Select cells **A6:A9**. Group this data by **Rows**. Do not include the city label in the group.

	A	B	C	D
1	**Life's Animal Shelter**			
2	Supplier List			
3				
4	Product Name	Supplier	City	Phone
5	Water bowl, large	American Pets	Minneapolis, MN	(651) 555-6788
6	Water bowl, small	American Pets	Minneapolis, MN	(651) 555-6788
7	Leather collar, small	Animals Inc.	Houston, TX	(713) 334-6577
8	Leather collar, medium	Animals Inc.	Houston, TX	(713) 334-6577
9	Leather collar, large	Animals Inc.	Houston, TX	(713) 334-6577
10	Wipe-Ups	HeatCo, Inc.	Bemidji, MN	(218) 755-2234
11	Plastic bags, 500	HeatCo, Inc.	Bemidji, MN	(218) 755-2234
12	Kitty litter, 50 lbs.	Animals Inc.	Houston, TX	(713) 334-6577
13	Doggie shovel, 12	Beltrami ManCap	Park Rapids, MN	(218) 443-9007
14	Greenlife cage, small	Beltrami ManCap	Park Rapids, MN	(218) 443-9007
15	Greenlife cage, medium	Beltrami ManCap	Park Rapids, MN	(218) 443-9007
16	Greenlife cage, large	Beltrami ManCap	Park Rapids, MN	(218) 443-9007
17	Kitty Kibbles, 50 lbs.	American Pets	Minneapolis, MN	(651) 555-6788
18	Doggie Dots, 50 lbs.	American Pets	Minneapolis, MN	(651) 555-6788

4-107 Phone numbers completed with *Flash Fill*; title recentered

	A	B	C	D
1	**Life's Animal Shelter**			
2	Supplier List			
3				
4	**Product Name**	**Supplier**	**City**	**Phone**
5	**Minneapolis**			
6	Doggie Dots, 50 lbs.	American Pets	Minneapolis, MN	(651) 555-6788
7	Kitty Kibbles, 50 lbs.	American Pets	Minneapolis, MN	(651) 555-6788
8	Water bowl, large	American Pets	Minneapolis, MN	(651) 555-6788
9	Water bowl, small	American Pets	Minneapolis, MN	(651) 555-6788
10	**Houston**			
11	Kitty litter, 50 lbs.	Animals Inc.	Houston, TX	(713) 334-6577
12	Leather collar, large	Animals Inc.	Houston, TX	(713) 334-6577
13	Leather collar, medium	Animals Inc.	Houston, TX	(713) 334-6577
14	Leather collar, small	Animals Inc.	Houston, TX	(713) 334-6577
15	**Park Rapids**			
20	**Bemidji**			
21	Plastic bags, 500	HeatCo, Inc.	Bemidji, MN	(218) 755-2234
22	Wipe-Ups	HeatCo, Inc.	Bemidji, MN	(218) 755-2234
23				

Group can be expanded

4-108 Data manually defined in groups; Park Rapids group collapsed

19. Repeat the command to group the selected data for each supplier.

20. Collapse the *Park Rapids* group (Figure 4-108).

21. Click the **LAS Suppliers** sheet tab.
22. Apply conditional formatting to show the *American Pets* supplier name with **Green Fill with Dark Green Text** (Figure 4-109).
23. Do not remove the *Locked* property for any cells, but protect the *LAS Suppliers* sheet without a password.
24. Save and close the workbook.

	A	B	C	D
1	**Life's Animal Shelter**			
2	**Supplier List**			
3				
4	Product Name	Supplier	City	Phone
5	Water bowl, large	American Pets	Minneapolis, MN	(651) 555-6788
6	Water bowl, small	American Pets	Minneapolis, MN	(651) 555-6788
7	Leather collar, small	Animals Inc.	Houston, TX	(713) 334-6577
8	Leather collar, medium	Animals Inc.	Houston, TX	(713) 334-6577
9	Leather collar, large	Animals Inc.	Houston, TX	(713) 334-6577
10	Wipe-Ups	HeatCo, Inc.	Bemidji, MN	(218) 755-2234
11	Plastic bags, 500	HeatCo, Inc.	Bemidji, MN	(218) 755-2234
12	Kitty litter, 50 lbs.	Animals Inc.	Houston, TX	(713) 334-6577
13	Doggie shovel, 12	Beltrami ManCap	Park Rapids, MN	(218) 443-9007
14	Greenlife cage, small	Beltrami ManCap	Park Rapids, MN	(218) 443-9007
15	Greenlife cage, medium	Beltrami ManCap	Park Rapids, MN	(218) 443-9007
16	Greenlife cage, large	Beltrami ManCap	Park Rapids, MN	(218) 443-9007
17	Kitty Kibbles, 50 lbs.	American Pets	Minneapolis, MN	(651) 555-6788
18	Doggie Dots, 50 lbs.	American Pets	Minneapolis, MN	(651) 555-6788

4-109 Excel 4-6 completed worksheet

Improve It Project 4-7

Eller Software Services has created a software release workbook, but the sheets contain several errors. For this project, you edit the workbook and correct sorting, filtering, and *PivotTable* problems. [Student Learning Outcomes 4.2, 4.3, 4.4, 4.5]

File Needed: ***SoftwareRelease-04***
Completed Project File Name: ***[your initials] Excel 4-7.xlsx***

Skills Covered in This Project

- Sort data.
- Remove subtotals.
- Use the *Subtotal* command.
- Edit fields in a *PivotTable*.
- Create a *PivotChart*.
- Edit chart elements.

1. Open the ***SoftwareRelease-04*** workbook from your student data files folder.
2. Save the workbook as ***[your initials] Excel 4-7***.
3. On **Phase 1 Release Dates** sheet, click the **Name Box** arrow and select **Data** to select cells **A5:F19** by its range name. Sort the data by **Platform** in **A to Z** order and then by **Release Date** in **Oldest to Newest** order.

4. On the *Subtotals* sheet, remove the subtotals. Sort the data by **Platform** in **A to Z** order.
5. Use the **Subtotal** command to count the number of projects by platform, showing the count in the **Software Project** column.
6. On the *PivotTable* sheet, click to place check marks for **Software Project**, **Price**, and **Release Date** in the *Choose fields to add to report* area. Remove other check marks.
7. Drag the **Release Date** field into the *Filters* area in the *PivotTable Fields* task pane.
8. Use the **Report** filter to show only the projects that will be released in 2015.
9. Place the **Software Project** field in the *Values* area in the *PivotTable Fields* task pane. This field is in both the *Row* and the *Values* areas.
10. Add a **3-D Pie PivotChart** to the *PivotTable* worksheet. Place the chart to the right of the *PivotTable*.
11. Change the chart title to: Revenue by Project.
12. Click the **Field Buttons** button on the *PivotChart Tools Analyze* tab to hide the pivot buttons in the chart.
13. Close the task pane.
14. Save and close the workbook (Figure 4-110).

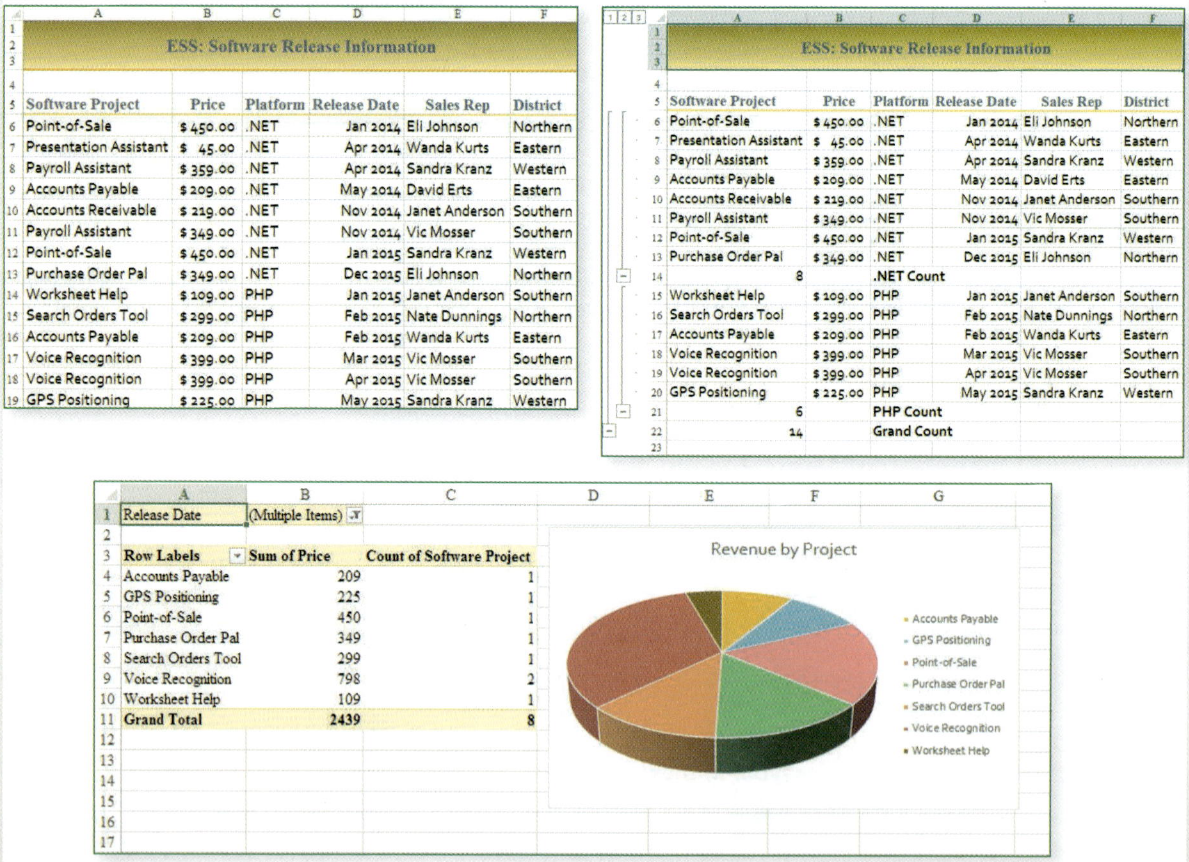

ESS: Software Release Information

Software Project	Price	Platform	Release Date	Sales Rep	District
Point-of-Sale	$ 450.00	.NET	Jan 2014	Eli Johnson	Northern
Presentation Assistant	$ 45.00	.NET	Apr 2014	Wanda Kurts	Eastern
Payroll Assistant	$ 359.00	.NET	Apr 2014	Sandra Kranz	Western
Accounts Payable	$ 209.00	.NET	May 2014	David Erts	Eastern
Accounts Receivable	$ 219.00	.NET	Nov 2014	Janet Anderson	Southern
Payroll Assistant	$ 349.00	.NET	Nov 2014	Vic Mosser	Southern
Point-of-Sale	$ 450.00	.NET	Jan 2015	Sandra Kranz	Western
Purchase Order Pal	$ 349.00	.NET	Dec 2015	Eli Johnson	Northern
Worksheet Help	$ 109.00	PHP	Jan 2015	Janet Anderson	Southern
Search Orders Tool	$ 299.00	PHP	Feb 2015	Nate Dunnings	Northern
Accounts Payable	$ 209.00	PHP	Feb 2015	Wanda Kurts	Eastern
Voice Recognition	$ 399.00	PHP	Mar 2015	Vic Mosser	Southern
Voice Recognition	$ 399.00	PHP	Apr 2015	Vic Mosser	Southern
GPS Positioning	$ 225.00	PHP	May 2015	Sandra Kranz	Western

ESS: Software Release Information

Software Project	Price	Platform	Release Date	Sales Rep	District
Point-of-Sale	$ 450.00	.NET	Jan 2014	Eli Johnson	Northern
Presentation Assistant	$ 45.00	.NET	Apr 2014	Wanda Kurts	Eastern
Payroll Assistant	$ 359.00	.NET	Apr 2014	Sandra Kranz	Western
Accounts Payable	$ 209.00	.NET	May 2014	David Erts	Eastern
Accounts Receivable	$ 219.00	.NET	Nov 2014	Janet Anderson	Southern
Payroll Assistant	$ 349.00	.NET	Nov 2014	Vic Mosser	Southern
Point-of-Sale	$ 450.00	.NET	Jan 2015	Sandra Kranz	Western
Purchase Order Pal	$ 349.00	.NET	Dec 2015	Eli Johnson	Northern
8		.NET Count			
Worksheet Help	$ 109.00	PHP	Jan 2015	Janet Anderson	Southern
Search Orders Tool	$ 299.00	PHP	Feb 2015	Nate Dunnings	Northern
Accounts Payable	$ 209.00	PHP	Feb 2015	Wanda Kurts	Eastern
Voice Recognition	$ 399.00	PHP	Mar 2015	Vic Mosser	Southern
Voice Recognition	$ 399.00	PHP	Apr 2015	Vic Mosser	Southern
GPS Positioning	$ 225.00	PHP	May 2015	Sandra Kranz	Western
6		PHP Count			
14		Grand Count			

Release Date (Multiple Items)

Row Labels	Sum of Price	Count of Software Project
Accounts Payable	209	1
GPS Positioning	225	1
Point-of-Sale	450	1
Purchase Order Pal	349	1
Search Orders Tool	299	1
Voice Recognition	798	2
Worksheet Help	109	1
Grand Total	2439	8

4-110 Excel 4-7 completed worksheets

Challenge Project 4-8

For this project, you import your debit or checkbook account records into an Excel workbook. You format the data as a table and sort and filter the data. Finally, you protect your data with a password.
[Student Learning Outcomes 4.1, 4.2, 4.3, 4.6, 4.7]

File Needed: None
Completed Project File Name: ***[your initials] Excel 4-8.xlsx***

Create a new workbook and save it as ***[your initials] Excel 4-8***. Modify your workbook according to the following guidelines:

- Import several months of your account activity from your bank's web site into the worksheet.
- If each month is a separate file on the web site, import each month separately so that the data follows one another in the sheet.
- If column headings are not included in the imported data, add headings such "Date", "Transaction", and "Balance" where appropriate.
- Format the data as an Excel table or change the style if you imported it as a table. If you have multiple tables, select all the rows and convert the tables to a normal range. Then format the entire range as a single table.
- If the records are sorted in ascending order by date, reverse the sort order.
- Review your data and apply conditional formatting to a transaction name that appears more than once or to a transaction type that you want to highlight.
- Filter the data by the color used in your conditional formatting command.
- Password protect the sheet without unlocking any cells.

Challenge Project 4-9

For this project, you build a worksheet that will allow you to analyze costs of a decorating or remodeling project in your home or apartment.
[Student Learning Outcomes 4.6, 4.7]

File Needed: None
Completed Project File Name: ***[your initials] Excel 4-9.xlsx***

Create a new workbook and save it as ***[your initials] Excel 4-9***. Modify your workbook according to the following guidelines:

- Type labels for at least five tasks in a decorating or remodeling project, such as "Purchase paint", "Consult with contractor", etc.
- Type an estimated cost for each task and use a *SUM* formula to show an estimated total.

- Determine a slightly lower total cost than your original estimate and use *Goal Seek* to adjust one of the tasks so that you can reach this preferred lower cost.
- Review your data and apply conditional formatting to display the two most expensive tasks in a different color.
- Add a main title to your worksheet and use different font sizes and borders to effectively display your information.

Challenge Project 4-10

For this project, you create a worksheet that lists names, birth dates, and hair color for 12 people. You format the list as a table and build a *PivotTable*.
[Student Learning Outcomes 4.2, 4.3, 4.4, 4.5]

File Needed: None
Completed Project File Name: ***[your initials] Excel 4-10.xlsx***

Create a new workbook and save it as ***[your initials] Excel 4-10***. Modify your workbook according to the following guidelines:

- Type your first name, your last name, your birthdate, and your hair color in four columns in a row.
- Type the same information for 11 more people, using real or fictitious data. Use birthdates that are the same year as yours as well as two other years, so that your data has only three birth years. Use only three hair colors for all your people, such as brown, blond, and red.
- Format the data as a table and apply a table style.
- Sort the date by birthdate with the youngest people listed first. Then filter the data to show only those records from the first year listed in the data.
- Make a copy of the table sheet and convert the table to normal range. Use the *Subtotal* command to count the number of persons with each hair color.
- Copy the table again for use as a *PivotTable* source. Create a *PivotTable* that displays something of interest about your list.

Microsoft® Office
IN PRACTICE
powerpoint

CHAPTER 1

POWERPOINT

Creating and Editing Presentations

CHAPTER OVERVIEW

Microsoft PowerPoint is the leading presentation software. Whether you need to create a quick display or a very polished presentation with dazzling graphics, creative animation effects, and video, PowerPoint has all the tools you need. You can use PowerPoint for slide shows with computer projection equipment in meeting rooms, for self-running presentations viewed by individuals, or for presentations shown on the web. This chapter covers the basics of starting and editing a PowerPoint presentation.

STUDENT LEARNING OUTCOMES (SLOs)

After completing this chapter, you will be able to:

SLO 1.1 Create, open, and save a presentation (p. P1-3).

SLO 1.2 Develop presentation content by adding slides, choosing layouts, moving and resizing placeholders, editing text, and reusing slides from another presentation (p. P1-14).

SLO 1.3 Rearrange presentation content by moving, copying and pasting, duplicating, and deleting slides (p. P1-22).

SLO 1.4 Use the *Slide Master* to change theme colors and fonts (p. P1-26).

SLO 1.5 Use headers and footers to add identifying information (p. P1-29).

SLO 1.6 Insert, resize, and align a picture from a file (p. P1-33).

SLO 1.7 Apply and modify transition effects to add visual interest (p. P1-35).

SLO 1.8 Preview a presentation and print slides, handouts, and outlines (p. P1-37).

SLO 1.9 Change presentation properties (p. P1-39).

CASE STUDY

Hamilton Civic Center (HCC) is a nonprofit community fitness center with an indoor pool, sauna, indoor track, exercise room, racquetball courts, and meeting rooms. HCC partners with the local hospital to bring doctors and nurses in to provide classes on a variety of health and wellness issues for adults. It also works with local schools to support their academic programs and sponsors events for children, including a summer day care program.

For the Pause & Practice projects in this chapter, you create and modify a presentation about training for an upcoming marathon that is being promoted to members by the Civic Center.

Pause & Practice 1-1: Create a presentation and develop text content.

Pause & Practice 1-2: Impose consistency to a presentation's design.

Pause & Practice 1-3: Add interest with pictures and apply transitions. Print supplements.

SLO 1.1

Creating, Opening, and Saving Presentations

In this section, you explore how to start and view a PowerPoint presentation and to save a presentation in different formats. It is important to save a presentation before closing it so you can access it again if necessary. If you close the presentation before saving it, your content is lost.

Create a Presentation

When PowerPoint first opens, you are presented with several ways to start a new presentation or open an existing presentation. Clickable images called ***thumbnails*** have a name below each one. If you prefer to work on text content only, click the **Blank Presentation** thumbnail to go directly to your first slide so you can begin developing content.

Other thumbnails represent built-in ***Themes*** that provide a unified look for all the slides in a presentation. One theme has a plain, dark background while most of them have a background design. When you click a theme, a dialog box opens where you can choose from different color combinations called ***Variants.*** Then you start developing content.

The following examples demonstrate ways to start a presentation.

HOW TO: Create a Presentation When First Opening PowerPoint

1. Open PowerPoint and you will automatically see the *Backstage* view (Figure 1-1).
2. Click the **Blank Presentation** theme to go directly to your first slide.

Or

3. Click a **Theme** to open a dialog box (Figure 1-2).
4. Click the arrow buttons below the slide to see h ow colors are applied to different layouts.

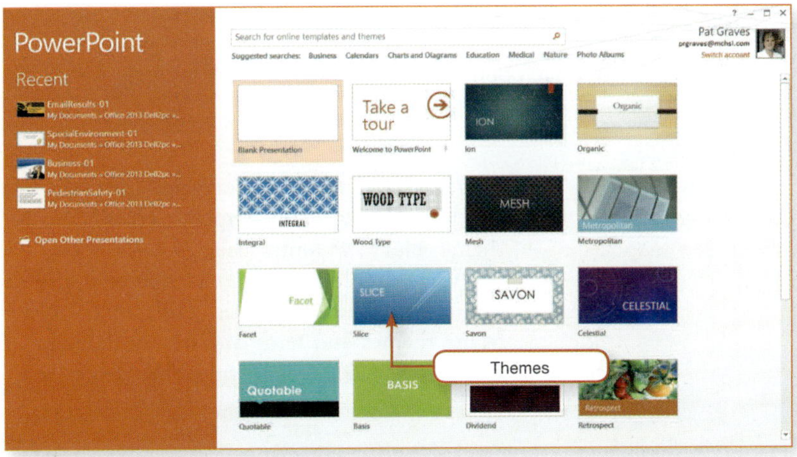

1-1 PowerPoint *Backstage* view

5. Select one of four *Variants* that provide different color combinations.
6. Click **Create**.

1-2 Theme *Variants*

When you create a new presentation, the PowerPoint title bar displays the generic name *Presentation1*. When you create additional new presentations, PowerPoint names them *Presentation2, Presentation3,* and so on, until you save the presentations and the new names appear in the title bar.

> **MORE INFO**
>
> When your content is complete, save your presentation (discussed on pages P1-10–P1-13) and then close it. Click the **File** tab, and then click **Close**. To close PowerPoint, click the **Close** button in the upper right corner of the title bar.

HOW TO: Create a New Presentation when PowerPoint is Open

1. Click the **File** tab to open the *Backstage* view.
2. Click the **New** button.
3. Select a *Theme* and *Variant*.
4. Click **Create**.

Or

5. Press **Ctrl+N** to open a new blank presentation.

Themes simplify the process of creating professional-looking presentations. They provide consistent background graphics, colors, and font settings. For more on selecting different theme colors and fonts, see *SLO 1.4: Working with Themes.*

A ***template*** contains the characteristics of a theme and usually provides sample content you can edit for your own slides or delete if you want only the background a template provides. Many themes and templates are available at Office.com and the online collection is ever-growing. You can save downloaded themes and templates so they are available for future use.

> **MORE INFO**
>
> Your computer must be connected to the Internet to download themes and templates.

HOW TO: Create a New Presentation from Online Templates and Themes

1. Click the **File** tab to open the *Backstage* view.
2. Click the **New** button. In the search box, type a keyword and click the **Start searching** button (Figure 1-3). Available templates and themes appear.
   - Filter your results by typing the word or before another search word and searching again.

Or

3. Click one of the *Suggested searches* for general topics, and available templates and themes will appear.
   - Filter your results by clicking one of the terms in the *Category* list on the right (Figure 1-4).
   - Filter your results by typing the word or before another search word and searching again.
4. Click a template thumbnail to open a dialog box to review other slides in addition to the title slide. Some templates include a description.
5. Click **Create**.
6. The presentation opens; it may contain sample content that you need to delete before adding your content.

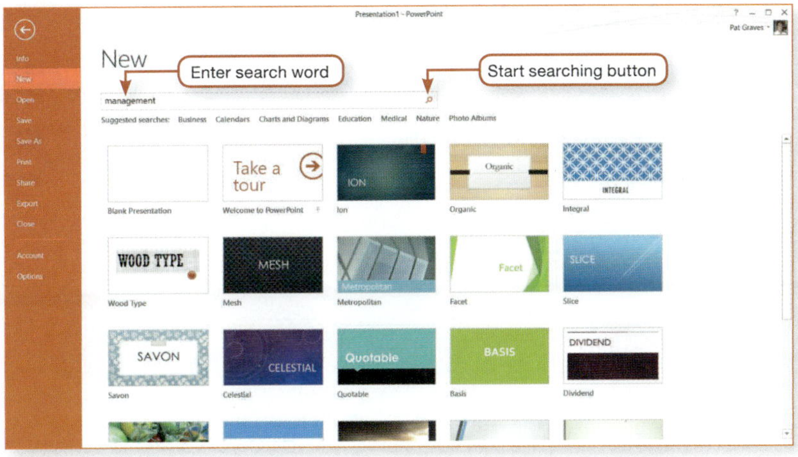

1-3 Search for online themes and templates

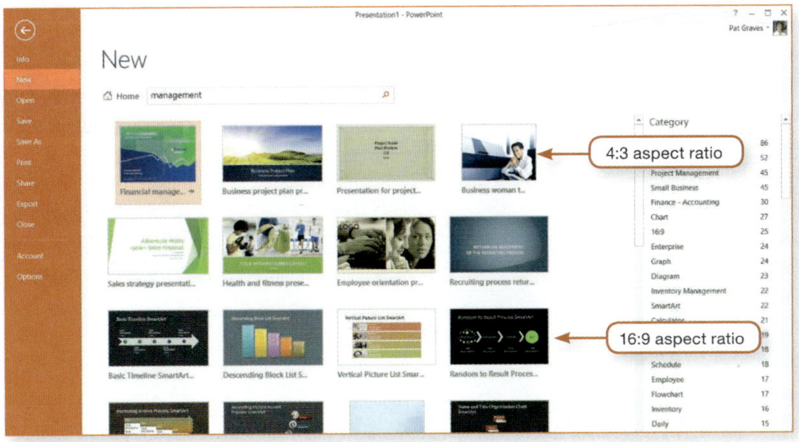

1-4 Search results for online themes and templates

You can use an existing presentation to start a new presentation. To do this, open a presentation file from a source such as your computer, USB drive, local network, cloud space such as SkyDrive, or an email attachment.

HOW TO: Open a Recent Presentation

1. With PowerPoint open, click the **File** tab to open the *Backstage* view.
2. Click the **Open** button.

3. Select **Recent Presentations** below the *Open* title.
4. Click a presentation on the right (Figure 1-5) to open it.

Or

5. Select your **SkyDrive**, then click **Browse** to locate the file (Figure 1-6).

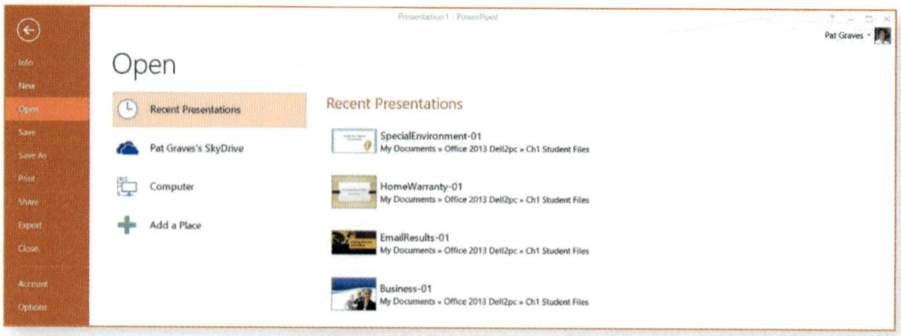

1-5 Open a recent presentation

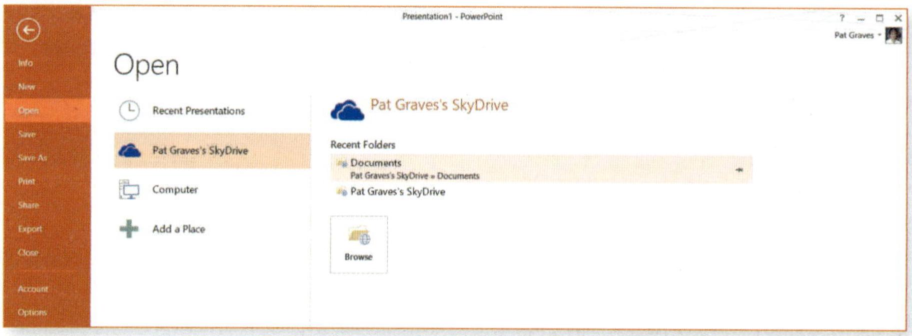

1-6 Open a presentation saved on your *SkyDrive*

MORE INFO

For instructions to set up a SkyDrive account, refer to *SLO 1.1 Using Windows 8 and Office 2013 in Office Chapter 1, Windows 8 and Office 2013 Overview.*

Or

6. Select **Computer** and then click **Browse** to locate the file on your computer or other place such as a USB drive or local network (Figure 1-7).
7. Select the file and click **Open**.

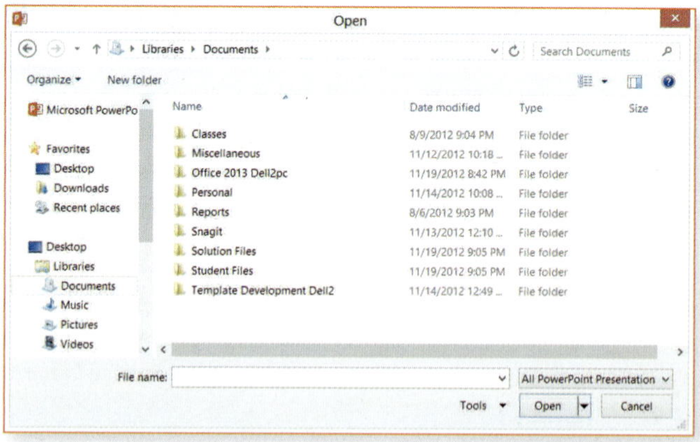

1-7 *Open* dialog box

ANOTHER WAY

Ctrl+O opens the *Backstage* view where you can open a presentation.

Views

PowerPoint provides different views to help you create slides, organize them, and display them in a slide show. When you start a new presentation, it opens in ***Normal*** view. The *Ribbon* is displayed across the top of the window and has nine tabs with commands organized in groups (Figure 1-8). Additional tabs, such as the *Drawing Tools Format* tab, open depending on what you are doing. Some tabs contain commands similar to those in Word, whereas other tabs display features that are unique to PowerPoint.

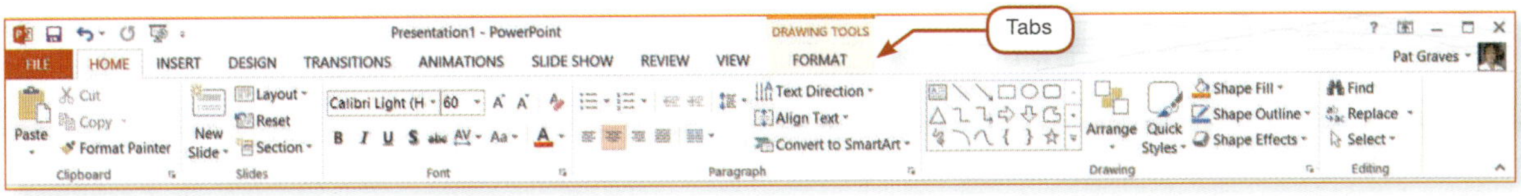

1-8 PowerPoint *Ribbon* with *Home* tab displayed

The area below the *Ribbon* is divided into two panes that display slide thumbnails on the left and a large area for working on individual slides. You can change views using commands on the *View* tab [*View* tab, *Presentation Views* group] (Figure 1-9) or the *View* buttons on the *Status bar* at the bottom of the window.

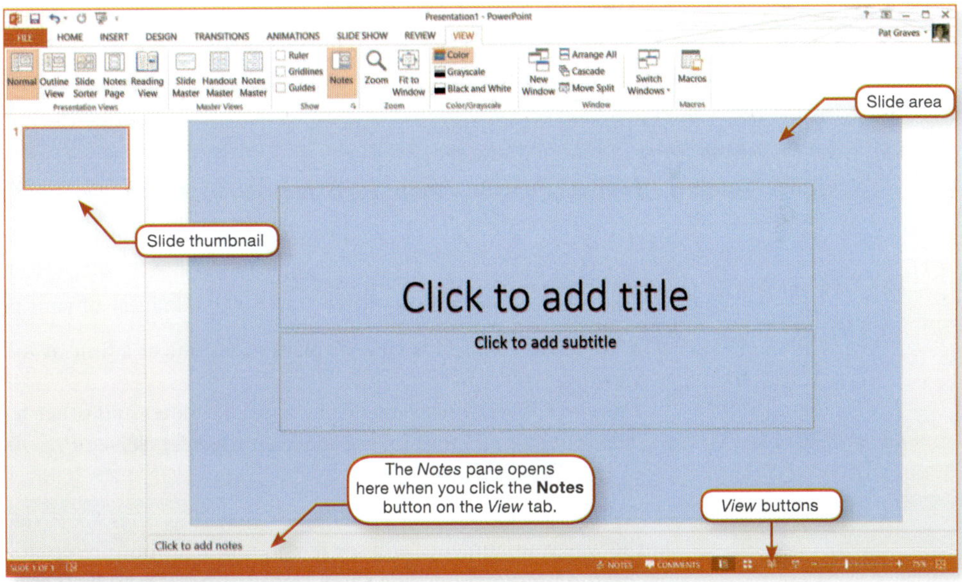

1-9 *Normal* view with *View* tab and *Notes* pane displayed

The five *Presentation Views* with commands on the *View* tab include the following:

- ***Normal:*** This is the default view where you enter the content of the slides and move between slides as you develop them. Click the *Normal* button or the *Notes* button to open a *Notes* pane below the slide to add speaker notes for individual slides.
- ***Outline View:*** This view expands the pane at the left of your slide area to show slide titles and bulleted text. Slide thumbnails are not displayed.

- ***Slide Sorter:*** This view displays slides as thumbnails so it is easy to reorganize slides and apply transition effects to control how the slides advance.
- ***Notes Page:*** This view displays each slide on a page with space below the slide where you can type speaker notes. You can also use the *Notes* pane below each slide to type speaker notes.
- ***Reading View:*** This view displays the slide show at full-screen or another window size controlled by the viewer. Navigation controls are in the *Status bar* at the bottom of the window.
- ***Slide Master, Handout Master, and Notes Master:*** These views are used to make changes that affect the whole presentation.

View Buttons are located on the *Status bar* to provide easy access regardless of which tab is currently open (Figure 1-10).

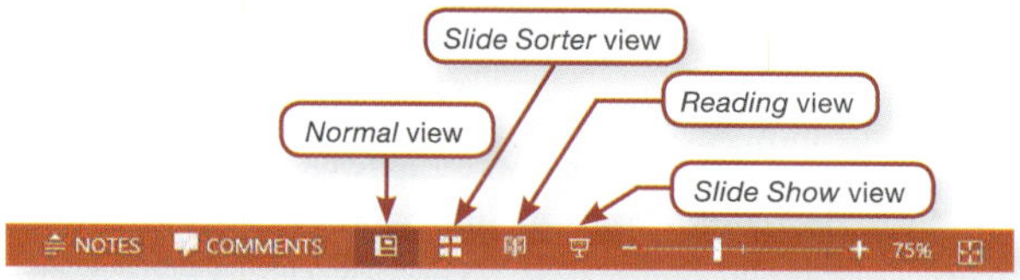

1-10 *View* buttons

HOW TO: Change Views

1. Click the **View** tab. Note that *Normal* is selected in the *Presentation Views* group.
2. Click the **Outline** button on the *View* tab.
3. Click the **Slide Sorter** button on the *View* tab or *Status bar.*
4. Click the **Notes Page** button on the *View* tab.
5. Click the **Reading View** button on the *View* tab or *Status bar.* To return to *Normal* view, click the **Normal** button on the *Status bar.*

Two more views are very important for the delivery of your presentation.

- ***Slide Show view:*** This view displays slides one at a time at full-screen size for audience viewing.
- ***Presenter View:*** This view displays speaker notes and other features that are helpful for delivering a presentation. For more on this feature, see *Presenter View* in *SLO 3.5: Controlling Display Options.*

While developing your presentation, test it in *Slide Show* view so you can see the content in the way your audience will see it, and rehearse your presentation before using it.

Start a presentation slide show from the beginning by pressing **F5**; start with the current slide by clicking the **Slide Show** button on the *Status bar.* You may also use buttons on the *Slide Show* tab (Figure 1-11).

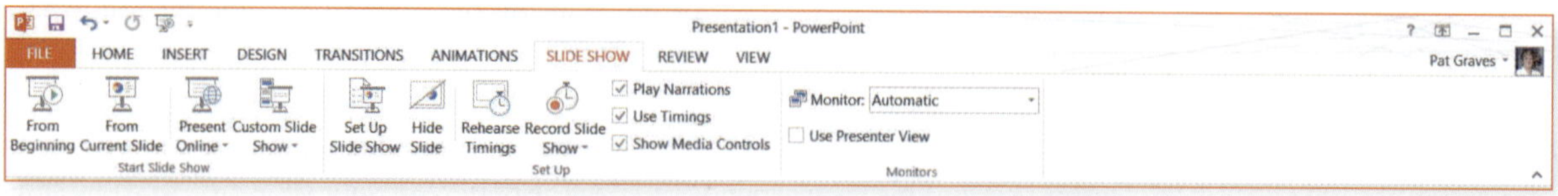

1-11 *Slide Show* tab

HOW TO: Start a Presentation from the Slide Show Tab

1. Click the **Slide Show** tab.
2. Click the **From Beginning** button [*Start Slide Show* group] to display slides from the beginning, regardless of which slide is the current slide.
3. Click the **From Current Slide** button to display slides starting with the current slide.
4. To move through the slides, click the screen or press one of several keys on the keyboard: **spacebar**, **arrow keys**, **Enter**, **Page Down**, or **N**.

Adjust Pane Sizes in Normal View

You can adjust the pane size to help you better focus on one aspect of your presentation. For example, you can make slide thumbnails larger or increase the area for notes. In each case, the slide becomes a little smaller.

HOW TO: Adjust Pane Sizes

1. Point to the border line separating the slide thumbnails and the slide area until your pointer turns into a sizing pointer with two arrows (Figure 1-12).
2. Click and drag the pane border to the right to make the thumbnails larger and to the left to make the thumbnails smaller.
3. If the *Notes* pane is not open, click the **Notes** button [*View* tab, *Show* group].
4. With the sizing pointer, click and drag the pane border line between the *Slide* area and the *Notes* pane up to make the *Notes* pane larger or down to make it smaller.
5. With the sizing pointer, click and drag the *Notes* pane border line down to the bottom of the window or click the **Notes** button to remove this area.

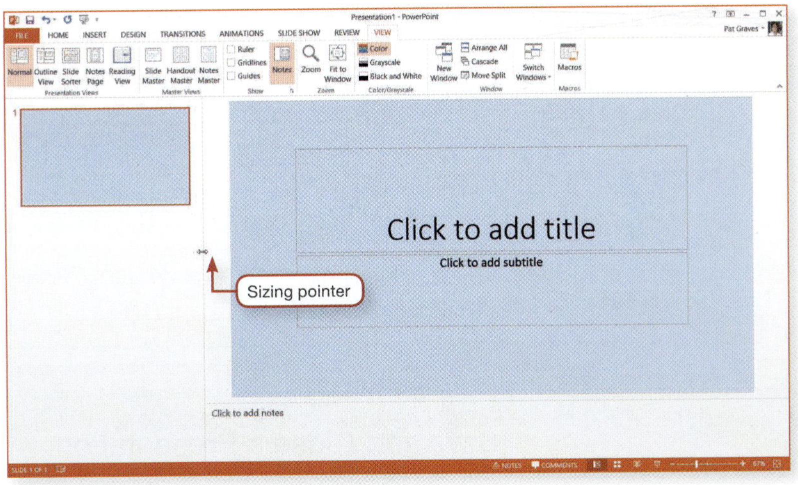

1-12 Slide thumbnail and *Notes* pane size is increased

Use Zoom

Use ***Zoom*** to increase the size of the slide on which you are working when you need to see detail. You can set a specific magnification level by using the *Zoom* dialog box or adjust the magnification by using the *Zoom* slider. You can use *Zoom* on the *Slide Sorter* view also.

HOW TO: Use the Zoom Dialog Box

1. Click the **Zoom** button [*View* tab, *Zoom* group].
2. Select a preset zoom percentage or enter a percentage number such as 200% (Figure 1-13).
3. Click **OK**. The slide size is increased and you can see only a portion of the slide
4. Click the **Fit slide to window** button [*View* tab, *Zoom* group] to return to the default setting so the entire slide is displayed.

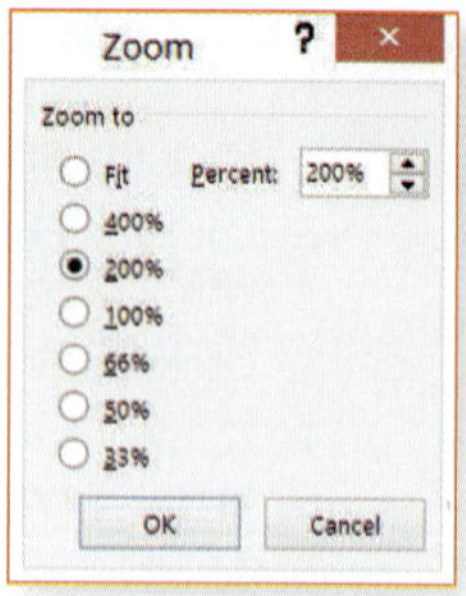

1-13 *Zoom* dialog box

The *Zoom* controls are located on the right side of the *Status bar* and the current slide size percentage is shown. At 100%, the slider is in the center. Drag the slider or click the **Zoom** buttons to adjust the slide size.

HOW TO: Use the Zoom Controls

1. Click the **Zoom Out** button several times to decrease the view to 50% (Figure 1-14).
2. Drag the *Zoom* slider to the center.
3. Click the **Zoom In** button several times to increase the view to 150%.
4. Click the left or right of the *Zoom* slider to increase or decrease the percentage.
5. Click the **Fit slide to current window** button to return to the default setting.
6. Click the percentage to open the *Zoom* dialog box. Select a percentage and click **OK** to close the dialog box.

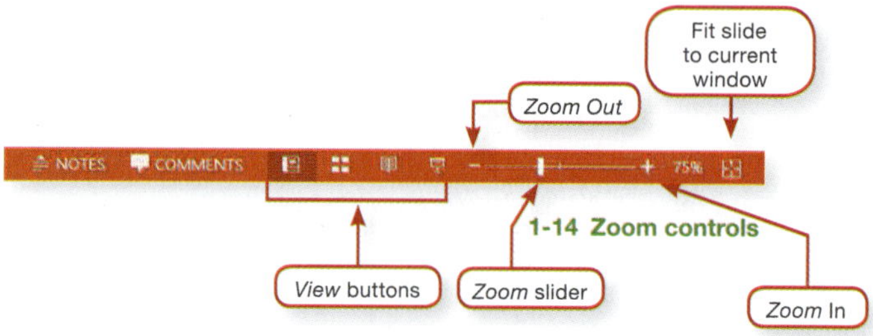

1-14 Zoom controls

Save and Close a Presentation

PowerPoint gives each new presentation a generic name, so you should name each presentation the first time you save it.

HOW TO: Save a Presentation

1. Click the **File** tab to open the *Backstage* view.
2. Click **Save** or **Save As** to display the *Save As* area (Figure 1-15).
3. Select the place where you want to save your presentation. You can save to your SkyDrive, computer, or other place such as a different web location.
4. Select a folder in the *Current Folder* or *Recent Folders* area or click the **Browse** button to open the *Save As* dialog box (Figure 1-16).

5. Browse to the folder on your computer or other place to save the file.
6. Type the file name in the *File name* area.
7. Click the **Save** button.

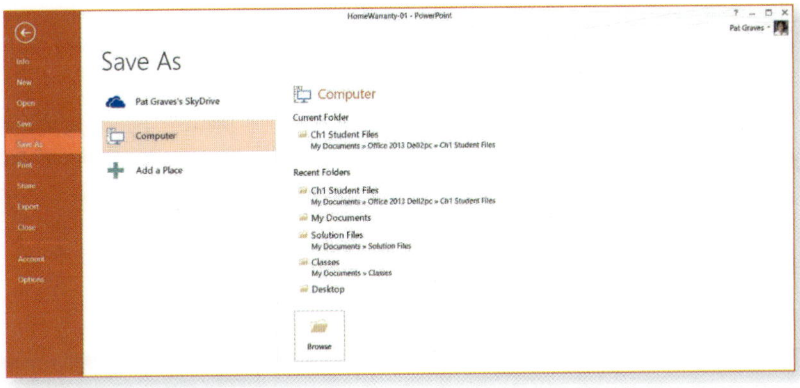

1-15 *Save As* area on the *Backstage* view

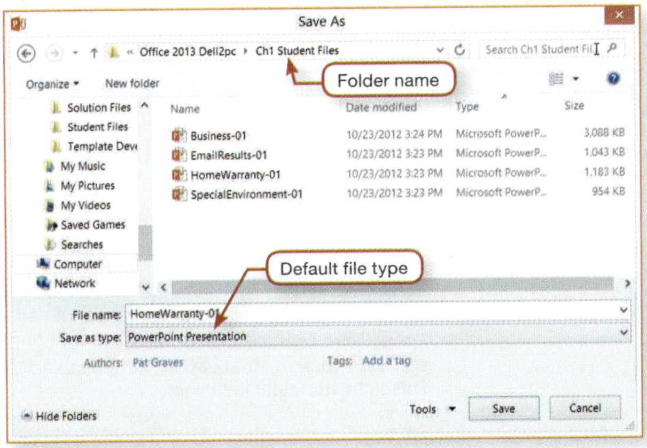

1-16 *Save As* dialog box

When saving for the first time, you can also click the **Save** button on the *Quick Access* toolbar, or press **Ctrl+S**, to open the *Save As* area on the *Backstage* view. As you make revisions to your presentation, simply clicking the **Save** button on the *Quick Access* toolbar will resave it with the same name in the same location.

If you want to create a second version of that file, then click the **File** tab and the **Save As** button to resave it with a different name in the same or different location. The original presentation is not affected by any changes you make to the second presentation.

ANOTHER WAY

Press **F12** to open the *Save As* dialog box.

You can save PowerPoint presentations in a variety of formats. By default, PowerPoint 2013 presentations are saved with the *.pptx* file extension. To change the type of presentation format, select the format of your choice from the *Save as type* area in the *Save As* dialog box (Figure 1-17).

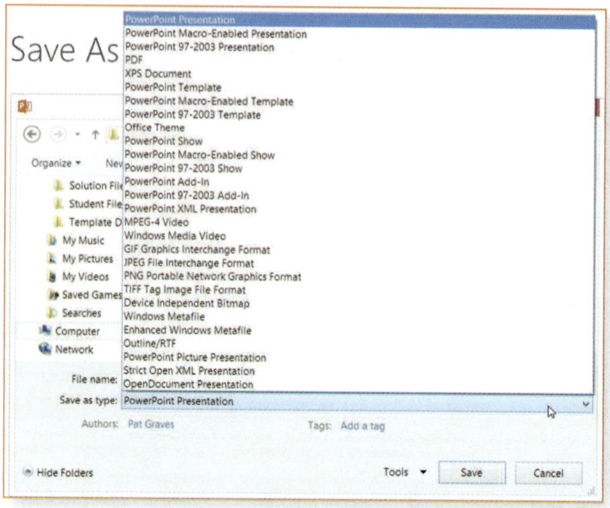

1-17 ***Save As* file types**

The following table lists some of the available formats that are most commonly used for PowerPoint.

Save Formats

Type of Presentation	File Extension	Uses of this Format
PowerPoint Presentation	.pptx	PowerPoint presentation compatible with 2007–2013 software versions that use an XML-enabled file format. This is the default file format.
PowerPoint 97-2003 Presentation	.ppt	PowerPoint presentation compatible with 1997–2003 software versions. Current software features are not supported.
PDF (Portable Document Format)	.pdf	Similar to pictures of slides, with each slide shown as a separate page. The file size may be smaller than the original presentation, so this format often works well for presentations distributed electronically.
PowerPoint Template	.potx	PowerPoint template that can be used to format future presentations.
Windows Media Video or MPEG-4 Video	.wmv or .mp4	PowerPoint presentation saved as a video that will play on many media players. Three resolution sizes are available, and all create large file sizes.
Outline/RTF	.rtf	A presentation text-only outline with a small file size for easy sharing.
PowerPoint Picture Presentation	.pptx	PowerPoint presentation that converts each slide into an image. It helps to reduce file size or create images for inclusion in other documents.
Open Document Presentation	.odp	PowerPoint presentation that can be opened in applications that use the *Open Document Presentation* format, such as Google.Docs or Open Office.org.

MORE INFO

Other file formats are used to save individual slides or images on slides. These graphic file formats include .jpg, .png, .tif, .bmp, .wmf, or .emf. These formats are explained on page P1-34.

When you are finished with a presentation, save your final version and then close the presentation. Click the **File** tab, and then click **Close**. To close PowerPoint, click the **Close** button in the upper right corner of the title bar.

Share and Export Options

From the *Backstage* view you have options for ***sharing*** (Figure 1-18) or ***exporting*** (Figure 1-19) your presentation using different file formats. Although these options take advantage of the distribution capabilities of Microsoft Office, not all classroom computer lab configurations permit access to shared online sites or network locations.

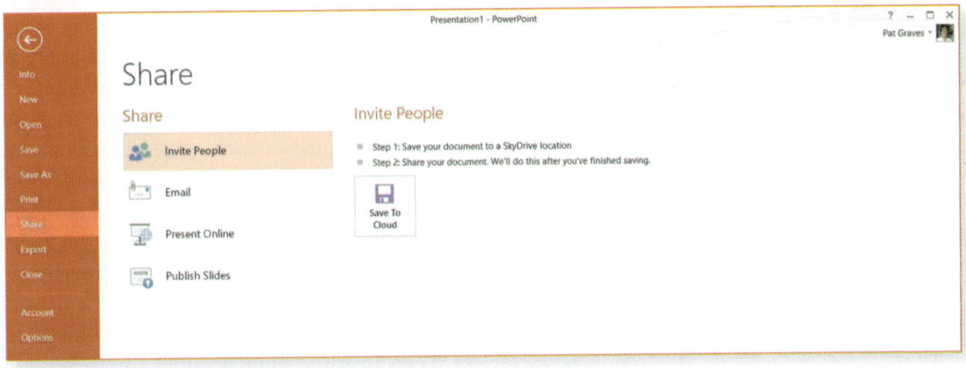

1-18 *Share* options

Share

- ***Invite People:*** Saves your presentation to a *SkyDrive* location so you can share it with people.
- ***Email:*** Sends your presentation as an attachment in the file type you choose.
- ***Present Online:*** Requires a Microsoft account so people can link to your slide show through a web browser.
- ***Publish Slides:*** Sends presentation files to a shared library or SharePoint site.

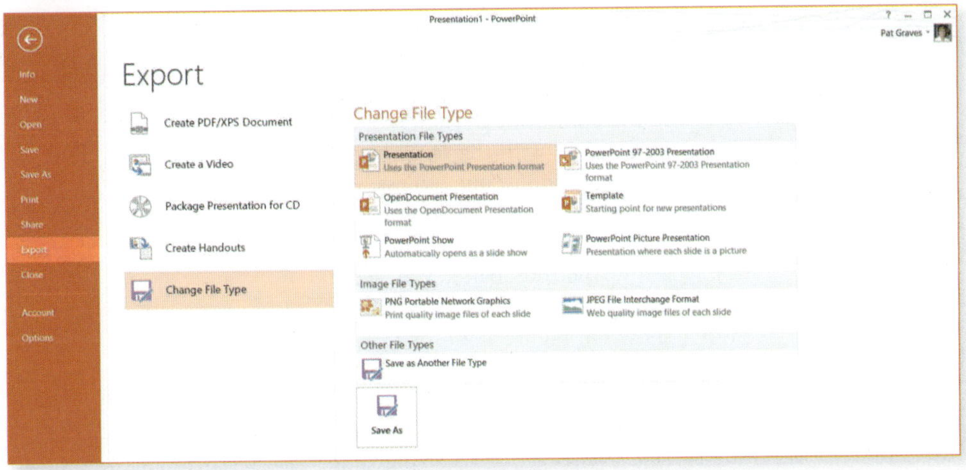

1-19 *Export* options

Export

- ***Create PDF/XPS Document:*** Preserves formatting and reduces file size for easier distribution.
- ***Create a Video:*** Saves your presentation as a video.
- ***Package Presentation for CD:*** Saves your presentation and all linked or embedded files.
- ***Create Handouts:*** Transfers slides and notes to a Word document that you can re-format.
- ***Change File Type:*** Saves your presentation or individual slides in different file formats.

SLO 1.2

Adding and Editing Presentation Text

As you begin developing presentation content, you will enter most text and objects such as pictures, tables, and charts using ***placeholders*** on slides in *Normal* view. By default, these placeholders have no fill color or border, but you may choose to emphasize them by adding color. You can resize placeholders as needed to fit text content. Usually, slide titles and subtitles contain a single line of text; body placeholders contain bulleted text.

When PowerPoint first opens or when you start a blank presentation, the first slide has a ***Title Slide*** layout with two placeholders: a presentation title and a subtitle. You can add text directly into these placeholders or you can type slide titles and bulleted text in *Outline* view. The font, font size, and alignment are preset, but you can change them as you develop your presentation.

As you write text, keep in mind that it should be brief, straight to the point, and easy to read.

Add Slides and Choose Layouts

After a title slide, PowerPoint automatically inserts a ***Title and Content*** layout when you click the **New Slide** button. This layout is the one used for developing most slides; it has a placeholder for the slide title and a placeholder for inserting bulleted text or graphic elements. From that point forward, each time you click the top of the **New Slide** button, you add a new slide with the same layout as the previous one unless you use the **Title Slide** layout again. If you click the **New Slide** list arrow (bottom half), you see a gallery of layouts such as the ones shown in Figure 1-20 for a blank presentation.

Layouts control the position of placeholders on a slide and provide a starting point for your slide designs. You can change layouts or

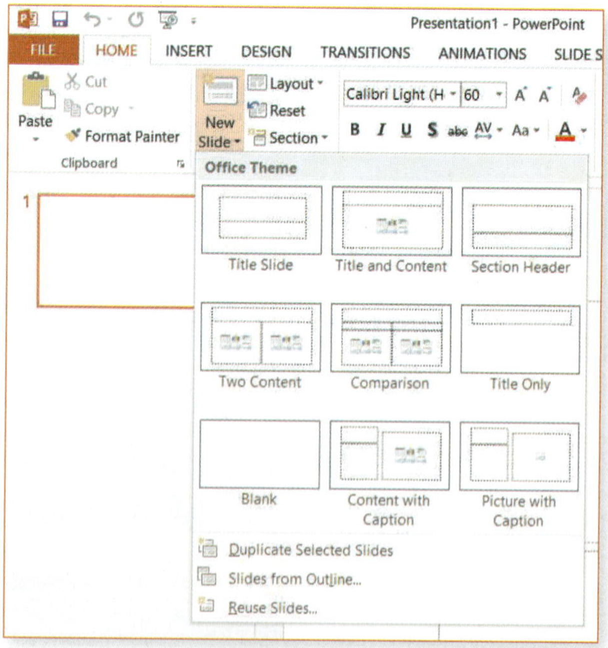

1-20 Slide layouts

customize each slide for the content you are developing. The available layouts vary based on the current theme. The most common layouts are described in the following table.

Slide Layouts

Layout Name	Layout Description
Title Slide	This layout is used for a presentation's opening slide. It contains a title and subtitle placeholder.
Title and Content	This slide layout makes up the body of a presentation. It contains a placeholder for the slide title and a larger placeholder for many different kinds of content.
Section Header	Similar to a title slide layout, it has a title and subtitle placeholder. Depending on the theme being used, it usually has a different appearance from the title slide. Slides with this layout can divide a lengthy presentation or introduce different topics or speakers.
Two Content	This layout has a slide title placeholder and two smaller content placeholders to display either two brief lists or a list and a graphic object, such as a picture or chart.
Comparison	This layout is similar to the *Two Content* layout, but it works better for comparing two lists because it provides a heading area above each content placeholder.
Title Only	Only one placeholder is provided for the title (usually at the top) of the slide.
Blank	This layout has no placeholders.
Content with Caption	This layout is similar to the *Two Content* layout, but one area is designated for the content, such as a table or chart, while the other area is meant for descriptive text.
Picture with Caption	This layout has a large area for a picture and another area for descriptive text.

HOW TO: Choose and Change Slide Layouts

1. Click the **New Slides** button [*Home* tab, *Slides* group] to insert a slide with the default layout after the current slide.
2. Click the **New Slides** list arrow [*Home* tab, *Slides* group], and select the layout you want from the *Office Theme Layout* gallery.
3. To change the layout of a selected slide, click **Layout** [*Home* tab, *Slides* group].
4. From the *Office Theme Layout* gallery, select the layout you want. Repeat this process to try another layout.
5. Click the **Undo** button to remove the layout change.

Enter Text in Placeholders

1-21 Edit text in a selected placeholder

When you first see placeholders on slides, they appear as boxes with a thin border. When you click inside the placeholder, it becomes active with a blinking insertion point where you can type or edit text (Figure 1-21). Click the border to select the placeholder (Figure 1-22). In both cases, sizing handles that are small white squares appear on the corners and sides. A rotation handle that is a circular arrow appears at the top.

Keep the wording of titles concise so the text does not become too small. Depending on the font that is used, title text for individual slides is usually 36–44 points. When using the *Title Slide* layout, the title text is usually 54–72 points.

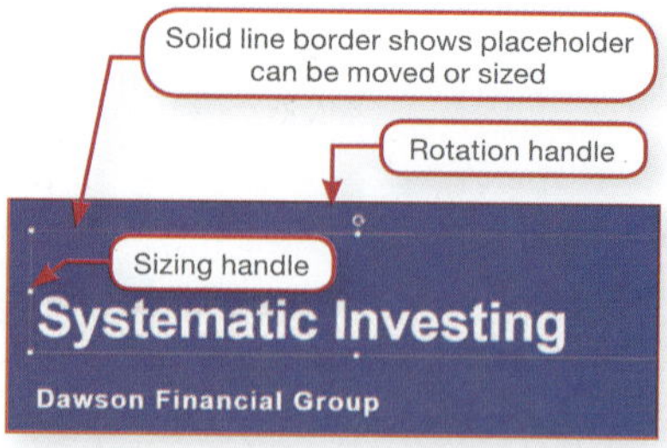

1-22 Selected placeholder to move or resize

In body placeholders, a bullet automatically appears when you type text and press **Enter**. Bullets help mark the beginning point, so people recognize items as separate. You can also add subpoints that are indented below a bulleted item. Be sure your list is very concise, usually no more than six items, and the text size is 20–28 points. Larger font sizes are very important if you are presenting in a large room so your audience can read slide text from a distance. However, if you are preparing a presentation to be viewed on a computer or online, you can use smaller font sizes.

Bulleted lists are appropriate when items require no particular order. If you need to show items in order, use a numbered list instead.

HOW TO: Work with Lists

1. In the body placeholder, click after the first bullet and type the text.
2. Press **Enter** to type another bulleted item in the same position (the list level).
3. To indent a bulleted item to the right (Figure 1-23), press **Tab** or click the **Increase List Level** button [*Home* tab, *Paragraph* group] (Figure 1-24).
4. If you need to enter several text slides, click the **Outline View** button [*View* tab, *Presentation Views* group] to display all slide titles and bulleted text on the left of the window.
5. Use *Outline View* to move a bulleted item to the left to create a slide title.
   a. Position your insertion point before the text to move left (Figure 1-25).
   b. Press **Shift+Tab** or click the **Decrease List Level** button [*Home* tab, *Paragraph* group].
   c. Change text capitalization as needed for a title (Figure 1-26).
6. To switch to a numbered list, click the **Numbering** button [*Home* tab, *Paragraph* group].

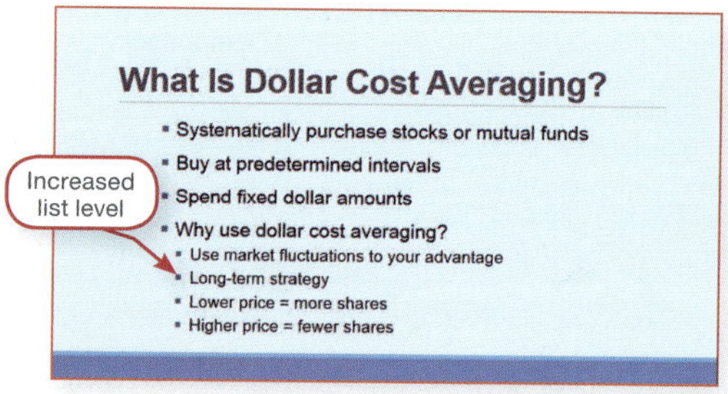

1-23 Bulleted list slide

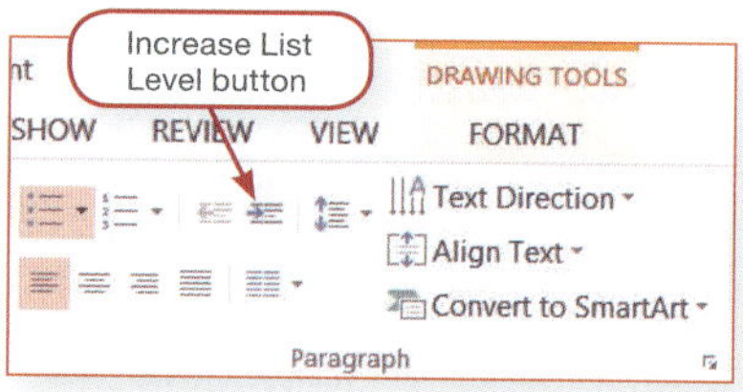

1-24 Paragraph group on the *Home* tab

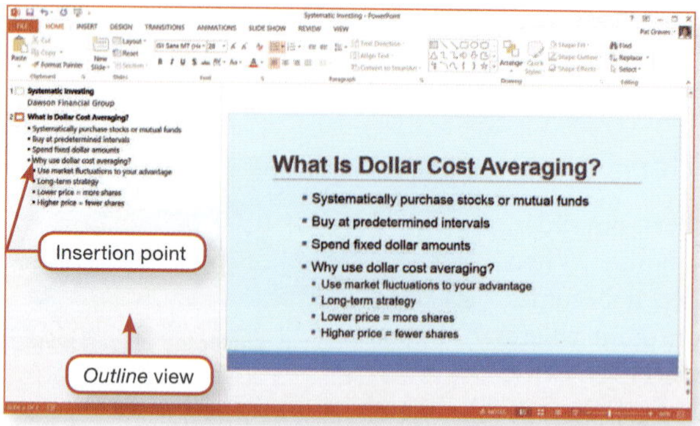

1-25 Slide with bulleted text before list level changes

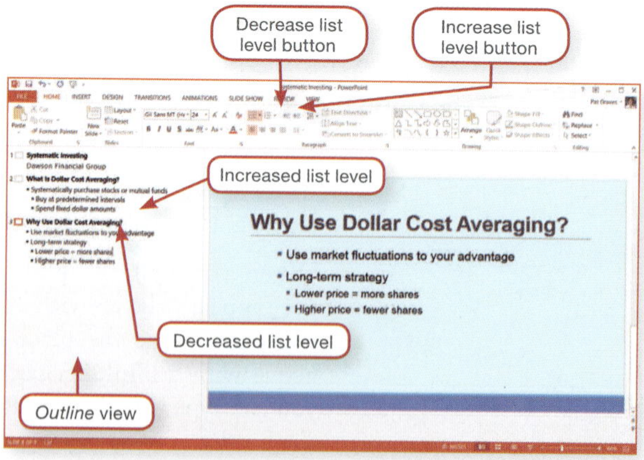

1-26 New slide created by decreasing the list level

> **MORE INFO**
> To move from the title to the body placeholder, press **Ctrl+Enter**. If you are in the last placeholder, press **Ctrl+Enter** to create a new slide.

Move, Align, and Resize Placeholders

To move a placeholder, point to the border so your pointer changes to a move arrow (with four points) and then drag the placeholder to its new position.

Align text within placeholders using the buttons on the *Home* tab in the *Paragraph* group.

- ***Horizontal alignment:*** **Left**, **Center**, **Right**, or **Justified** (rarely used on slides) buttons
- ***Vertical alignment:*** **Top**, **Middle**, or **Bottom** buttons

Align placeholders with one another or with the slide by clicking the **Align** button in the *Arrange* group on the *Drawing Tools Format* tab (Figure 1-27). Select from the following alignment options from the drop-down list:

- ***Horizontal alignment:*** **Left**, **Center**, **Right**
- ***Vertical alignment:*** **Top**, **Middle**, **Bottom**

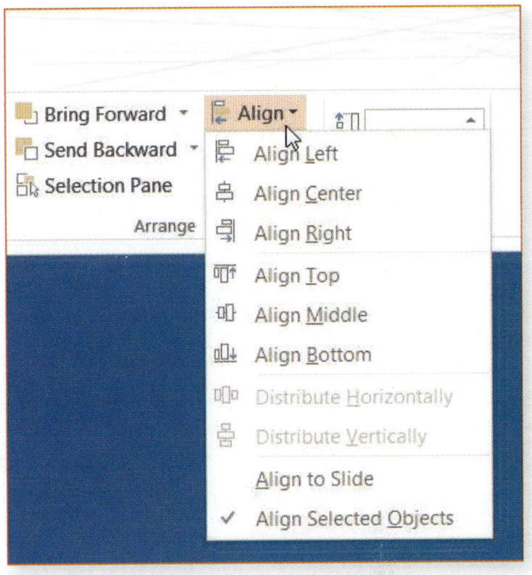

1-27 Alignment options

To increase or decrease placeholder size, point to one of the corner or side ***sizing*** handles (Figure 1-28) until your pointer changes to a two-pointed arrow (Figure 1-29). Drag to resize. The corner sizing handles move diagonally to change both the horizontal and vertical dimensions at the same time.

1-28 Sizing handles on a placeholder

You can control the way placeholders and other objects are resized by pressing one of three keys as you drag:

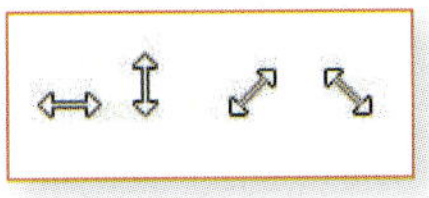
1-29 Sizing pointers

- ***Ctrl:*** The placeholder size changes from a fixed center point.
- ***Shift:*** The height and width proportions are maintained as the size changes.
- ***Ctrl+Shift:*** The placeholder resizes from the center and remains in proportion.

Another way to precisely resize a placeholder is to enter the exact dimensions on the *Drawing Tools Format* tab.

All of these techniques for moving, aligning, and resizing also apply to pictures and other objects. If you make a change to a slide layout that you do not like, click the **Reset** button in the *Slides* group on the *Home* tab.

Edit Text

As you are writing text, you can cut, copy, or paste text. All of your font commands, such as bold, italic, underline, font, and font size are available in the *Font* group on the *Home* tab. Also, these text formatting options are available on the mini toolbar (Figure 1-30), which appears when text is selected. You can undo or redo actions using commands on the *Quick Access* toolbar.

1-30 Mini toolbar

Notice that your pointer changes when you are working with text. When you see a blinking insertion point, PowerPoint is waiting for you to type text. When you point to text, your pointer changes to a text selection tool so you can click and drag to select text.

ANOTHER WAY

Ctrl+X Cut
Ctrl+C Copy
Ctrl+V Paste
Ctrl+Z Undo
Ctrl+Y Redo

HOW TO: Delete Text

1. Press **Delete** to remove text to the right of the insertion point.
2. Press **Backspace** to remove text to the left of the insertion point.
3. Select text and press **Delete** to remove several words at one time.

Click outside a text placeholder to deselect it. Handles no longer appear.

Change Text Case

Text case refers to how text is capitalized. Sometimes text appears in a placeholder in uppercase (all capital) letters. Be careful when using uppercase letters, because text may not be as easy to read as text with initial caps (the first letter only is capitalized). People are more experienced at reading lowercase text and, therefore, can generally read that text faster. Also, uppercase words in email are thought to represent shouting, and this negative connotation might carry over to your presentation if you overuse capital letters. Use uppercase letters when you really want to emphasize selected words or brief phrases.

HOW TO: Change Case

1. Select the text to be changed.
2. Click the **Change Case** button [*Home* tab, *Font* group].
3. Choose from the options **Sentence case**, **lowercase**, **UPPERCASE**, **Capitalize Each Word**, or **tOGGLE cASE** (Figure 1-31).

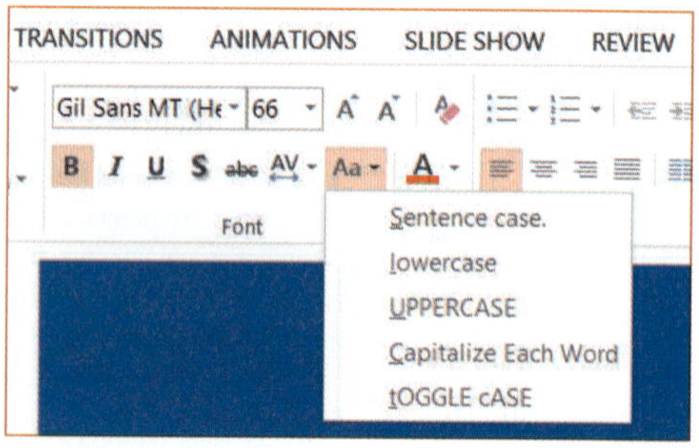

1-31 *Change Case* options

Change List Bullet Symbols

If a bullet that automatically appears seems inappropriate or if its color blends too much with the slide background, you can change the bullet symbol.

HOW TO: Change Bullet Symbols

1. Select the text where you want to change the bullet.
2. Click the **Bullets** button list arrow [*Home* tab, *Paragraph* group] and then select **Bullets and Numbering** to open the *Bullets and Numbering* dialog box.
3. Select one of the pre-defined bullets (Figure 1-32).
4. In the *Size* box, enter a different number to increase or decrease the bullet size.
5. Click the **Color** button to select a different bullet color.
6. Click the **Customize** button to open the *Symbol* dialog box (Figure 1-33), where you can select from many symbols displayed in several fonts.
7. After you select a symbol, click **OK** to add that symbol to the *Bullets and Numbering* dialog box.
8. Select the bullet and click **OK** to change the bullets on selected text.

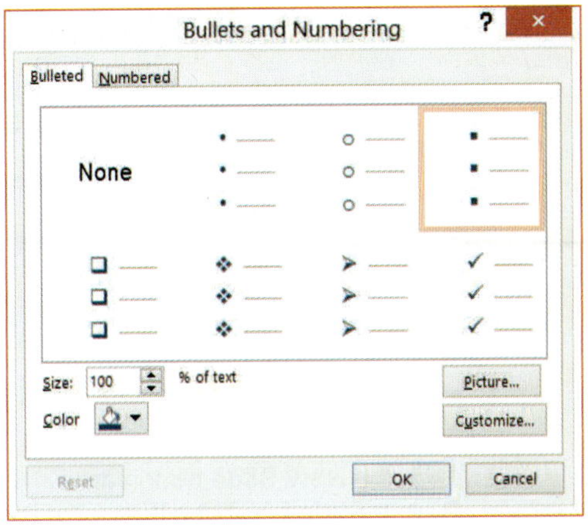

1-32 ***Bullets and Numbering*** **dialog box**

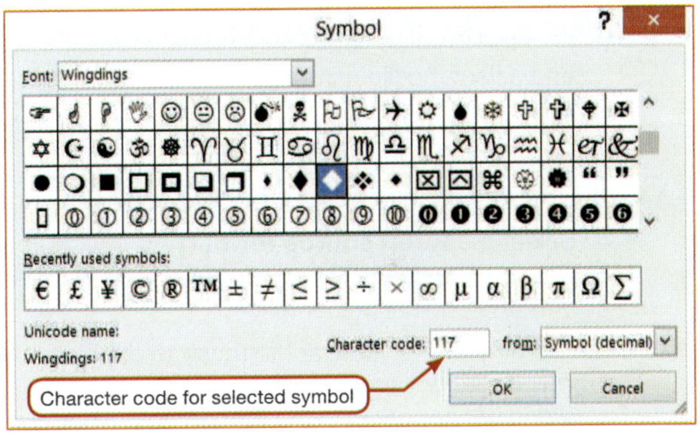

1-33 ***Symbol*** **dialog box**

The three ***Wingdings*** fonts have most of the available character bullets from the *Symbols* dialog box. You can also select picture bullets that are more decorative from the *Bullets and Numbering* dialog box.

The Format Painter

To copy formatting changes from text, shapes, or pictures and apply these changes to another selection, use the ***Format Painter***. You can apply the changes on the same slide or on different slides.

HOW TO: Use the Format Painter

1. Select the text or other object with the format that you want to copy.
2. Click **Format Painter** [*Home* tab, *Clipboard* group] (Figure 1-34).

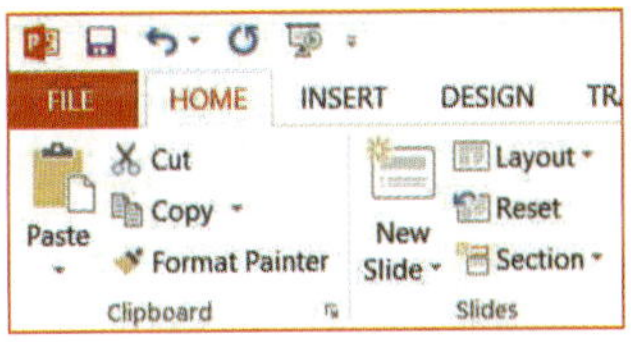

1-34 ***Format Painter*** **button on the** ***Home*** **tab**

3. Your pointer changes to a paintbrush.
4. Select the text or other object and click to apply the formatting.
5. If you want to apply the change to multiple selections, double-click the **Format Painter** button. Press **Esc** to stop formatting.

Reuse Slides from Another Presentation

You can add slides from another presentation without opening it as long as you can access the location where it is stored.

HOW TO: Reuse Slides

1. In the thumbnail area, click between two slides where you want the new slide inserted.
2. Click the **New Slide** button arrow [*Home* tab, *Slides* group] and select **Reuse Slides** from the bottom of the *Office Theme Layout* gallery.
3. In the *Reuse Slides* pane that automatically opens, click **Browse** and then click **Browse File** (Figure 1-35).
4. Find the location where your existing presentation file is saved and select the file name.
5. Click **Open**. The slides in this second presentation appear in the *Reuse Slides* pane (Figure 1-36).
6. Point to each of the slide thumbnails so you can read the slide titles.
7. Select the **Keep source formatting** checkbox at the bottom of the *Reuse Slides* pane if you want the inserted slides to retain their design from the original presentation.
8. Click the slides you want to reuse to duplicate them in your current presentation. By default, the reused slides will appear with the formatting of your current presentation.
9. Click the **Close** button at the top of the *Reuse Slides* pane.

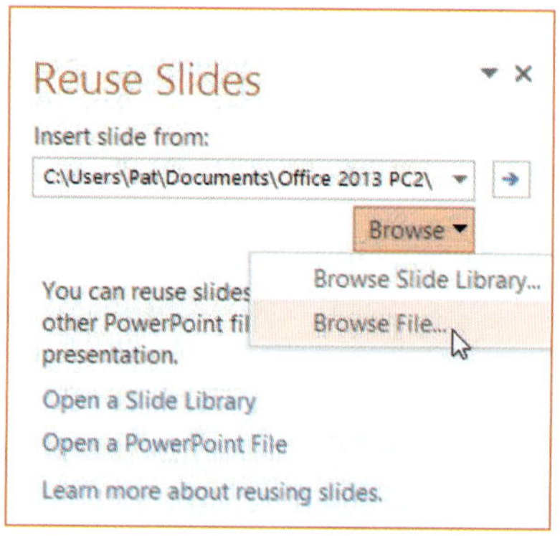

1-35 ***Reuse Slides*** **task pane**

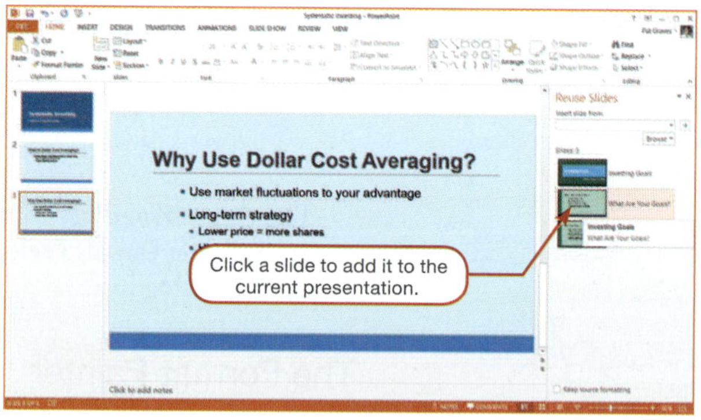

1-36 Reuse slides

MORE INFO

When task panes open, they are docked on the right side of the PowerPoint window. If you have a wide computer screen and you are using PowerPoint in a window size that does not fill the screen, you can drag a task pane away from the window so your slide size becomes larger. Double-click the task pane to dock it on the right of the window again.

Check Spelling and Word Usage

PowerPoint's *AutoCorrect* feature fixes many simple errors as you are typing. You can customize *AutoCorrect* options. Even when using *AutoCorrect*, you still need to check for errors when your presentation is complete. If your audience sees mistakes when viewing your slide show, your credibility is undermined. After using PowerPoint's spelling feature, carefully read the content to find any words that may have been missed, such as names or words that might not be in the spelling dictionary.

HOW TO: Check Spelling

1. From any slide in your presentation, click the **Spelling** button [*Review* tab, *Proofing* group] (Figure 1-37).
2. From the *Spelling* pane that opens on the right (Figure 1-38), consider each word that is identified and whether or not the suggested spelling is correct.
3. Click the **Audio** button on the *Spelling* pane to hear the word pronounced.
4. Click the **Change** button to insert a suggested spelling; click the **Ignore** button if you want to skip the suggestion.
5. When the spell check is complete, click **OK**.
6. Click the **Close** button at the top of the *Spelling* pane.

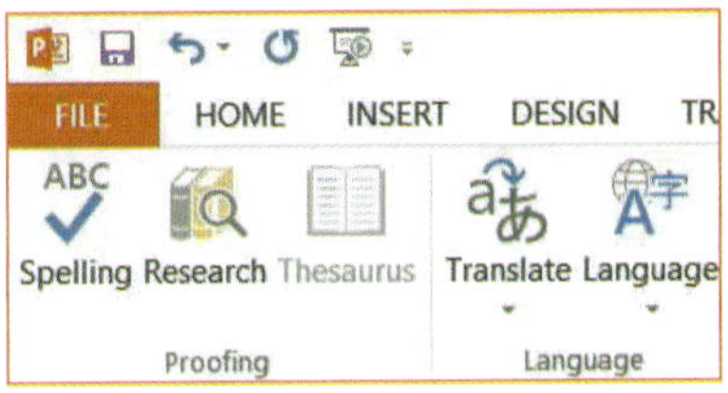

1-37 *Spelling* button on the *Review* tab

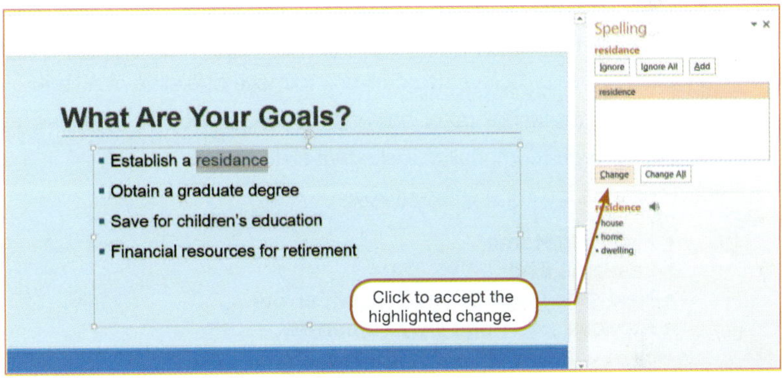

1-38 *Spelling* pane

If you want to replace an awkward word or one that is used too frequently, use PowerPoint's ***Thesaurus*** to find a more appropriate word.

HOW TO: Use the Thesaurus

1. Click in the word you want to change.
2. Click the **Thesaurus** button [*Review* tab, *Proofing* group]. Your word is selected and the *Thesaurus* pane opens (Figure 1-39).
3. Your selected word appears in the search box, and words with similar meanings appear below it.
4. Click a word from this list to see more options; click the **Back** arrow to return to the original list.
5. On a highlighted word in the list, click the **Down** arrow and choose **Insert** to replace the selected word.
6. Click the **Close** button at the top of the *Thesaurus* pane.

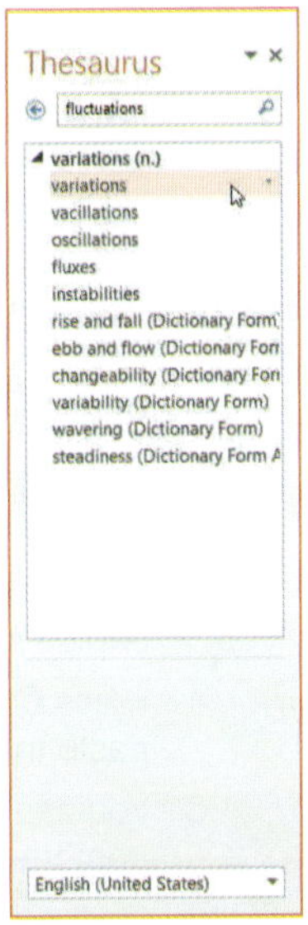

1-39 *Thesaurus* word choices

SLO 1.3

Rearranging Slides

When developing a presentation, you might need to move between slides as ideas occur to you or when you have new information to add. You can rearrange slides at any time. However, always carefully examine your sequence when all slides are complete. The final order must be logical to you and to your audience.

Move between Slides

In *Normal* view, you can move between slides by clicking the **Next** and **Previous** buttons, clicking scroll arrows, or dragging the scroll box on the right of the window. You can also click thumbnails or use keyboard shortcuts.

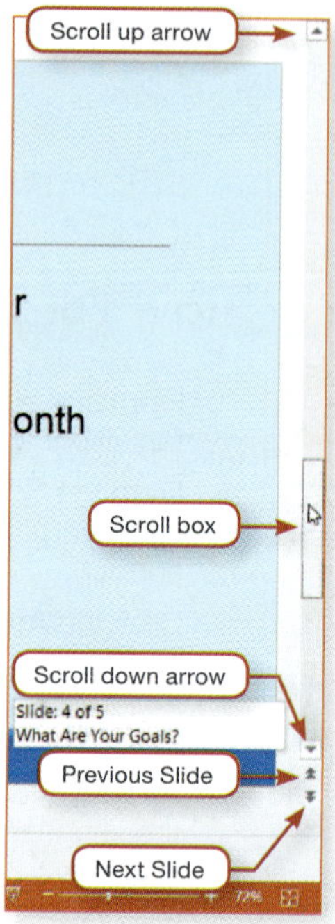

1-40 Move between slides

HOW TO: Move between Slides

1. Click the **Next** button or the **scroll down arrow** to go to the next slide (Figure 1-40).
2. Click the **Previous** button or **scroll up arrow** to go to the previous slide.
3. Click above or below the scroll box to move one slide at a time.
4. Drag the *Scroll* box up or down to move to a specific slide, using the slide indicator.
5. Click a slide thumbnail to make that slide active.
6. Press the following shortcut keys:
   - First slide **Home**
   - Last slide **End**
   - Next slide **Page Down** or **down arrow**
   - Previous slide **Page Up** or **up arrow**

Copy, Paste, and Duplicate Slides

To reuse a slide's content or format, copy the thumbnail. The original slide remains in its position. Paste the copied slide where you need it and edit the text.

HOW TO: Copy and Paste Slides

1. Select the thumbnail of the slide to be copied (Figure 1-41).
2. Press **Ctrl+C** or click the **Copy** button [*Home* tab, *Clipboard* group] to copy the slide.
3. Move the insertion point to the place between slides where you want the copied slide to appear.
4. Press **Ctrl+V** or click the **Paste** button [*Home* tab, *Clipboard* group] to paste the slide.
5. You can also right-click a slide thumbnail and then select **Copy** or **Paste** from the shortcut menu.
6. On the new slide, edit the text with new content.

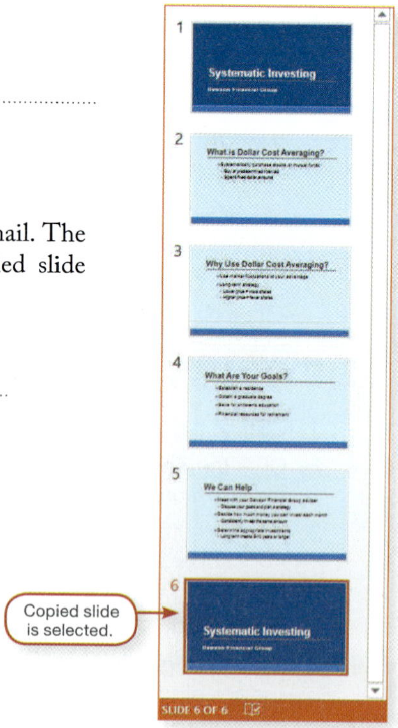

1-41 Copy and paste a selected slide

Duplicating slides is similar to *Copy* and *Paste,* except it requires only one step to make the second slide.

HOW TO: Duplicate Slides

1. Select the thumbnail of the slide to be duplicated.
2. Press **Ctrl+D** to duplicate the slide. The second slide is placed immediately after the original slide.
3. You can also right-click a slide thumbnail and select **Duplicate Slide** from the shortcut menu.

Select Multiple Slides

If you need to make the same changes to more than one slide, you can select more than one slide thumbnail.

HOW TO: Select Multiple Slides

1. To select multiple slides in order, select the first slide and then press **Shift** while you click the last slide (Figure 1-42).
2. To select multiple nonadjacent slides (not in order), select the first slide and then press **Ctrl** while you click each of the slides you need to select (Figure 1-43).

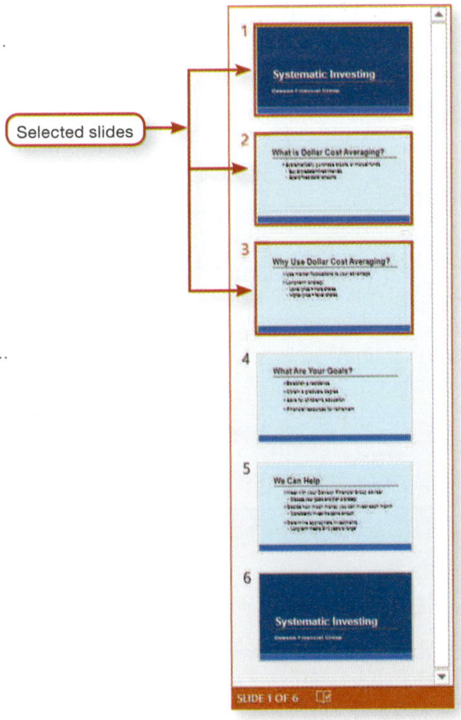

1-42 Adjacent slides selected

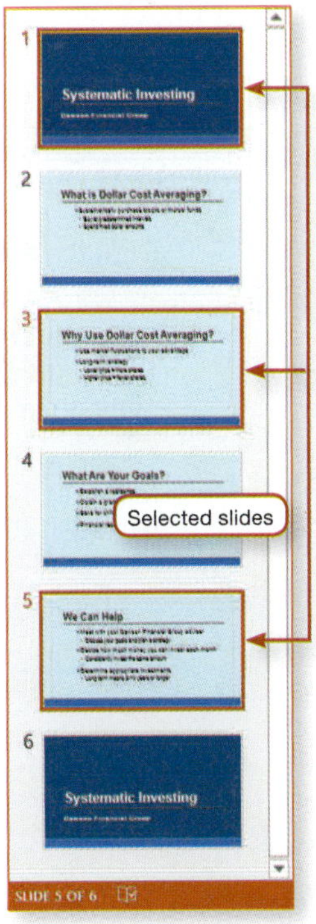

1-43 Nonadjacent slides selected

Rearrange Slide Order

You can rearrange slides at any time while developing a presentation. You can drag slide thumbnails up or down. On the *Outline* view, you can drag the slide icons. You can also cut slides and paste them into a different position. However, when your presentation has more slides than can be seen in the thumbnail pane, it is best to rearrange slides using *Slide Sorter* view (Figure 1-44).

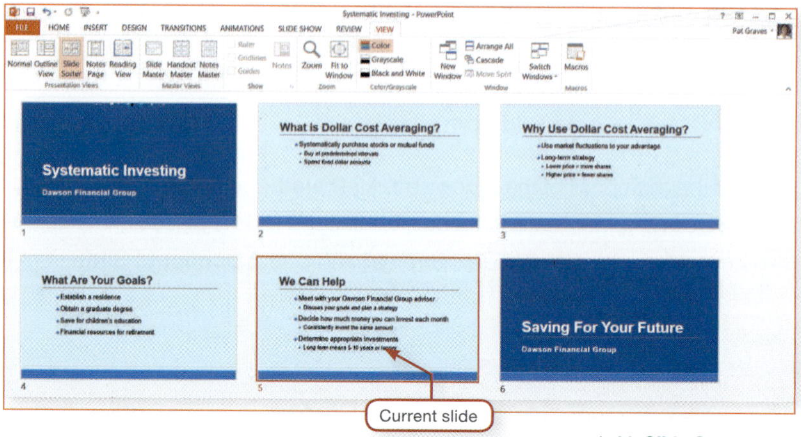

1-44 ***Slide Sorter*** **view**

The *Slide Sorter* view enables you to see your presentation as a whole. The thumbnails are arranged from left to right in rows. By default, they are shown at a 100% size. Click the **Zoom In** button to increase the slide thumbnail size if you need to see the slide content better; click the **Zoom Out** button to decrease the slide thumbnail size and see more slides at one time.

HOW TO: Rearrange Slides in Slide Sorter View

1. Click the **Slide Sorter** button on the *Status bar.*
2. Click the **Zoom In** or **Zoom Out** buttons to adjust the size of the thumbnails.
3. Click and drag the slide thumbnails into their new positions (Figure 1-45).

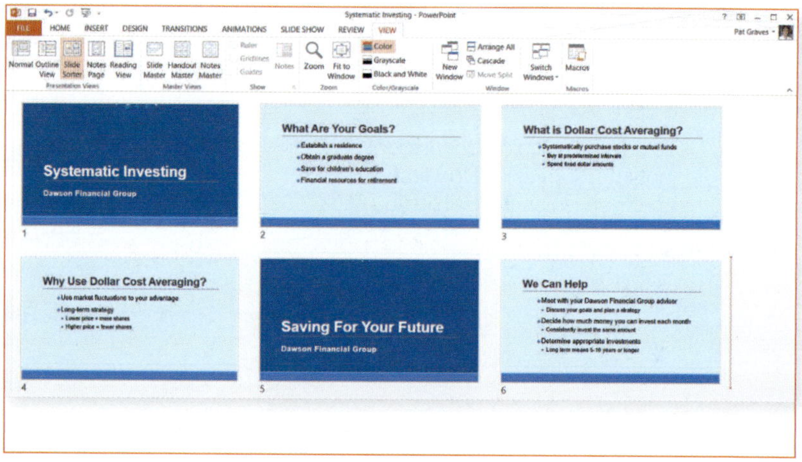

1-45 Slides rearranged

Delete Slides

Remove slides by deleting slide thumbnails in *Normal* view and *Slide Sorter* view or by deleting the slide icon in *Outline* view. You can also use the **Cut** button on the *Home* tab in the *Clipboard* group. This method is helpful because if you change your mind about the deletion later, you can paste the deleted slides back into the presentation from the *Clipboard.*

HOW TO: Delete Slides

1. Right-click the slide thumbnail (or the *Slide* icon in *Outline* view) and click **Delete Slide** from the shortcut menu.
2. Select the slide thumbnail (or the *Slide* icon in *Outline* view) and press **Delete**.
3. Select the slide thumbnail (or the *Slide* icon in *Outline* view) and click **Cut** [*Home* tab, *Clipboard* group].

PAUSE & PRACTICE: POWERPOINT 1-1

In this project, you develop the text for a presentation about upcoming marathon events. At the Hamilton Civic Center, this presentation promotes event preparation for participants. You start with a blank presentation, add slides, reuse slides from another presentation, and make format changes.

File Needed: ***MarathonInfo-01.pptx***
Completed Project File Name: ***[your initials] PP P1-1.pptx***

1. Start a new presentation. Press **Ctrl+N**, or click the **File** tab, click **New**, and then click **Blank Presentation**.
2. Name and save the presentation.
   a. Press **F12** to open the *Save As* dialog box.
   b. Browse to the location where you want to save your files.
   c. Type [your initials PP P1-1] in the *File name* area (Figure 1-46).
   d. Be sure that the *Save as type* says "PowerPoint Presentation."
   e. Click **Save**. The *Save As* dialog box closes.

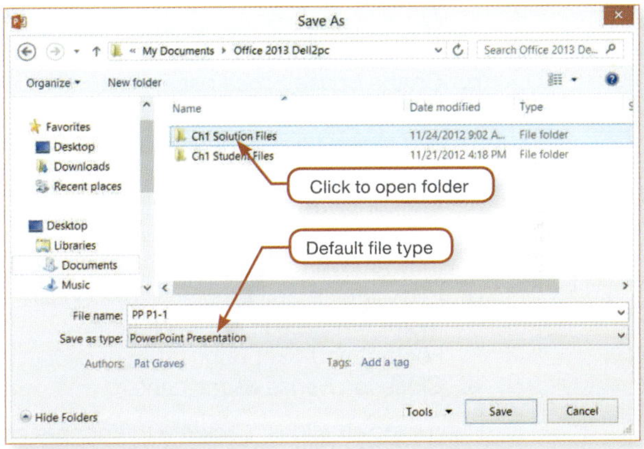

1-46 *Save As* dialog box

3. On slide 1, type the following text in the placeholders:

Title	Take the Right Steps
Subtitle	Train for a Marathon

4. Click the **New Slide** button [*Home* tab, *Slides* group] twice to add two new slides that automatically have the *Title and Content* layout. Type the following text in slides 2 and 3:

Slide 2 Title	What Is Your Goal?
Bulleted items	Run the second half faster
	Beat a time you've run before
	Or
	Finish the marathon
Slide 3 Title	Start Early to Be Ready
Bulleted items	Begin 5–16 weeks in advance
	Get a physical check up
	Prepare gear for running
	Join a training group
	Enjoy camaraderie
	Be accountable
	Run 3-4 times a week

5. Change slide 3 to a *Two Context* layout and adjust the text.
   a. Select slide 3 and click the **Layout** button [*Home* tab, *Slides* group]. Next, select the **Two Content** layout.
   b. Select the last four bulleted items on the left placeholder and press **Ctrl+X** to cut them.

c. Click in the right placeholder and press **Ctrl+V** to paste them.
d. If an extra bullet appears after the last text, delete it by pressing the Backspace key.
e. Select the middle two bulleted items on the right placeholder and press **Tab** or click the **Increase List Level** button [*Home* tab, *Paragraph* group] to format them as sub-points under the first-level item (Figure 1-47).

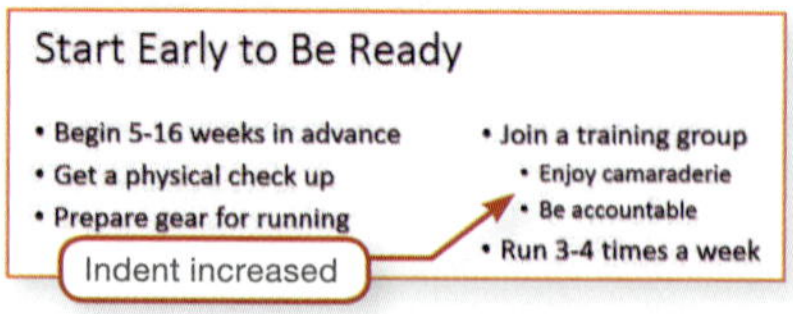

1-47 *Two Content* layout

6. Insert three slides from another presentation after slide 3.
   a. Click the **New Slide** list arrow and select **Reuse Slides**.
   b. On the *Reuse Slides* pane, click **Browse;** then select **Browse file** and locate your student files.
   c. Select the presentation ***MarathonInfo-01*** and click **Open**. (This presentation has spelling errors that you will fix later.)
   d. Click three slides (Figure 1-48) to insert them: "Practice Runs," "Eat Energy Foods," and "Get Running Apparel."
   e. Close the *Reuse Slides* pane.

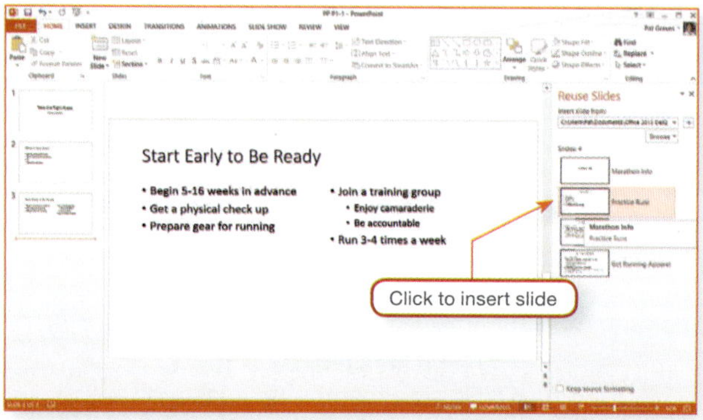

1-48 Reuse slides

7. Rearrange six slides. Click the thumbnails and drag them up or down so the six slides are in this order: "Take the Right Steps," "What is Your Goal?," "Start Early to Be Ready," "Get Running Apparel," "Eat Energy Foods," and "Practice Runs."
8. Insert a new slide.
   a. With slide 6 selected, click the **New Slide** list arrow and select the **Title Only** layout.
   b. In the title placeholder, type Look It UP! (Figure 1-49).
   c. Select the title text and change the font size to **72 pts**.
   d. Select this slide thumbnail and press **Ctrl+D** to duplicate it to create slide 8.

1-49 Placeholder text resized

9. Edit and duplicate slide 8.
   a. On slide 8, edit the title text and type Mark It DOWN!
   b. Select this slide thumbnail and press **Ctrl+D** to duplicate it to create slide 9.
10. On slide 9, edit the title text and type See You THERE!
11. Click the **Spelling** button [*Review* tab, *Proofing* group] and correct each of the spelling errors.
12. Save the presentation. You will continue to work on this presentation for *Pause & Practice PowerPoint 1-2* and *PowerPoint 1-3*.

SLO 1.4

Working with Themes

You can use the same themes for presentations, documents, and worksheets created in all Microsoft Office applications to create a cohesive look. In PowerPoint, the ***Slide Master*** stores information about slide backgrounds, layouts, and fonts for each theme. Changing the *Slide Master* can help you work more efficiently because the entire presentation is affected. In this section, you change theme colors and fonts. In Chapter 3 you create unique backgrounds.

When you start a new presentation and search online, you may find themes or templates that contain artwork or pictures that fit your topic perfectly. The file names you see below each thumbnail do not distinguish between themes and templates. Many of the presentations that appear in a search will have the PowerPoint default file extension (.pptx). Those saved as template files will have a different file extension (.potx). Depending on how your software is set up, you may not see these file extensions when you open files.

You can search through general categories or enter a specific search word to get more targeted results. Themes and templates are provided by Microsoft and other companies.

Your searches will provide results that include the following:

- ***Theme:*** A slide show with only background graphics and text treatments but no content. Different layouts control where slide objects are positioned. You can control design elements with the *Slide Master* to create custom designs.
- ***Template:*** A slide show with the characteristics of a theme but also with sample content on several slides. You can edit the content or remove individual slides you do not need to create your presentation. You can control design elements with the *Slide Master* to create custom designs.
- ***Template, title slide only:*** While the thumbnail may show a title slide, that slide might be the only content in the presentation. Other slides may be blank or have no related graphic background. The *Slide Master* has not been used.
- ***Template, individual slide only:*** Some thumbnails show only a single diagram or chart that can be revised for a new presentation. Usually, the *Slide Master* has not been used.
- ***Different slide sizes:*** Two slide sizes will appear. The thumbnails that have an almost square appearance are shown in a 4:3 aspect ratio, the ratio of width to height, which has been the standard for many years. The thumbnails in a wide-screen size are shown in a 16:9 aspect ratio, which is the newer size that reflects the shape of current computer screens.

People who see a lot of presentations become very familiar with the designs that appear in common software. So seeing a presentation with a contemporary looking design that truly fits the topic is refreshing. Caring enough to match your theme to your topic speaks volumes to people about your preparedness and competence. Consider carefully what you select so the design is suitable for your topic and for how your presentation will be used.

HOW TO: Apply a Theme to an Existing Presentation

1. Click the **Design** tab.
2. Click the **More** list arrow in the *Themes* gallery to see additional themes.
3. Point to a thumbnail to see a live preview of that theme on the current slide (Figure 1-50).
4. Click the thumbnail to apply the theme.

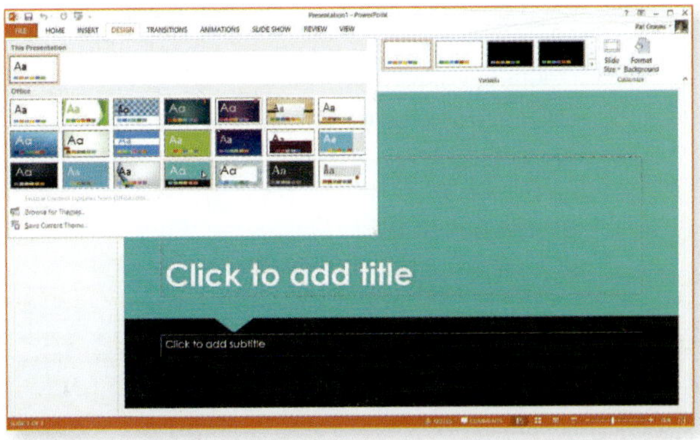

1-50 *Themes* gallery

ANOTHER WAY

To apply two themes in one presentation, apply your first theme to all slides then select the slides that should be different. Right-click another theme and select **Apply to Selected Slides**. Be careful when using this option so that your content does not seem disjointed.

Use the Slide Master to Change Theme Colors

When you choose theme colors for your slide show, consider colors that are appropriate for your topic. Also consider where you will present. Because of room lighting, colors for a slide show projected on a large-screen are not as clear or vibrant as what you see on the computer screen directly in front of you. These differences can influence your color choices. Be sure your text is easy to read with a high contrast between the text and background colors (dark on light or light on dark).

Every presentation, even a blank one, begins with a set of colors that have been chosen to work well together. With each built-in theme, PowerPoint provides ***Variants*** on the *Design* tab that show different theme colors. Many more theme colors are available from the *Design* tab and from the *Slide Master* tab. Generally, the *Design* tab is best to use when you want to change only theme colors or theme fonts. You will use this technique in Chapter 3 when you customize theme colors and theme fonts.

It is best to use the *Slide Master* tab to change theme colors or theme fonts when you want to make additional changes to customize slide layouts or background graphics such as to add a company logo to all slides in a presentation.

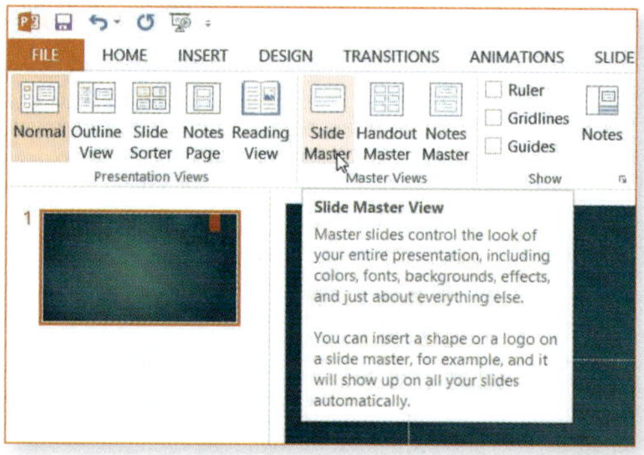

1-51 ***Slide Master*** **button on the** ***View*** **tab**

HOW TO: Change Theme Colors

1. Click the **View** tab.
2. Click the **Slide Master** button [*Master Views* group] (Figure 1-51).
3. Click the **Colors** button [*Slide Master* tab, *Background* group] (Figure 1-52).
4. A list of theme colors appears and you see a live preview of those colors as you point to each one. The blank, Office theme will show a live preview only if the background colors have been changed.
5. Click a theme color name to apply it.
6. Select one or more Slide Master layouts on the left and click the **Background Styles** button [*Slide Master* tab, *Background* group] to change the background to light or dark variations.
7. Click the **Close Master View** button [*Slide Master* tab, *Close* group].

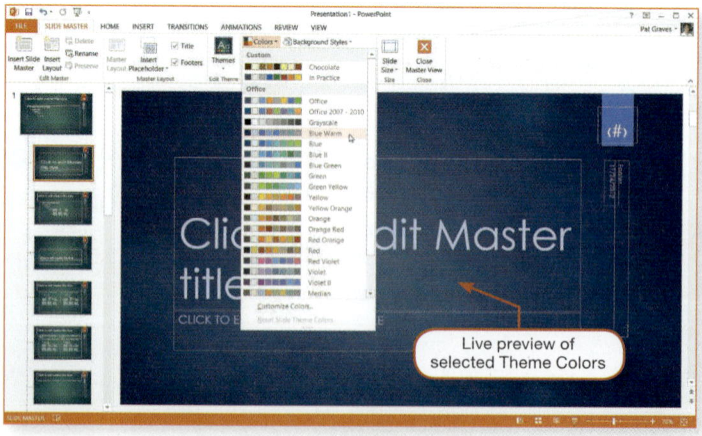

1-52 ***Slide Master*** **tab and** ***Theme Colors***

The first two colors shown represent the background and text colors; the remaining six show accent colors. For more on customizing theme colors, see *SLO 3.1: Creating Custom Theme and Background Colors.*

Not all of the themes you find online permit color changes in the same way. It depends on how the background design was created originally.

Use the Slide Master to Change Theme Fonts

Select your fonts carefully. Some seem very traditional and serious; others appear more playful and flamboyant. Use fonts that are appropriate for your presentation topic.

Consider how legible the font is with the background color you are using. In some fonts, the letters appear very thin and are not easy to read unless you make the text bold. Also consider the issues related to where you present. The lighting and room size affect how readable the text is on a large screen and you must use large font sizes. If you design a presentation to be displayed for a single person on your notebook or tablet computer, you can use smaller font sizes.

Every presentation, even a blank one, begins with a pair of ***Theme Fonts***. The heading font is used for slide titles and the body font is used for all other text. Sometimes the same font is used for both. You can view or change *Theme Fonts* from the *Design* tab or from the *Slide Master* tab.

HOW TO: Change Theme Fonts

1. Click the **View** tab.
2. Click the **Slide Master** button [*Master Views* group].
3. Click the **Fonts** button [*Slide Master* tab, *Background* group] (Figure 1-53).
4. A list of Theme Fonts appears and you see a live preview of Theme Fonts applied to placeholder text as you point to each pair.
5. Click a Theme Font pair to apply it.
6. Click the **Close Master View** button [*Slide Master* tab, *Close* group].

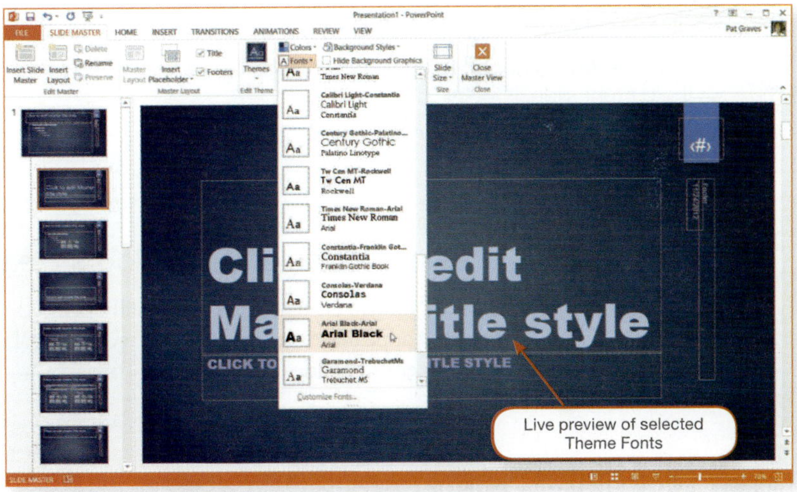

1-53 ***Slide Master*** **tab and** ***Theme Fonts***

SLO 1.5 Inserting Headers and Footers

If you want to include identifying information on all slides of a presentation, use the ***Header & Footer*** command on the *Insert* tab (Figure 1-54). Footers are displayed on every slide with placeholders for the date and time, slide number, and footer text. These placeholders often appear across the bottom of the slide, but depending on the theme, they may appear in different places. You can choose to show footers on all slides or only on selected slides.

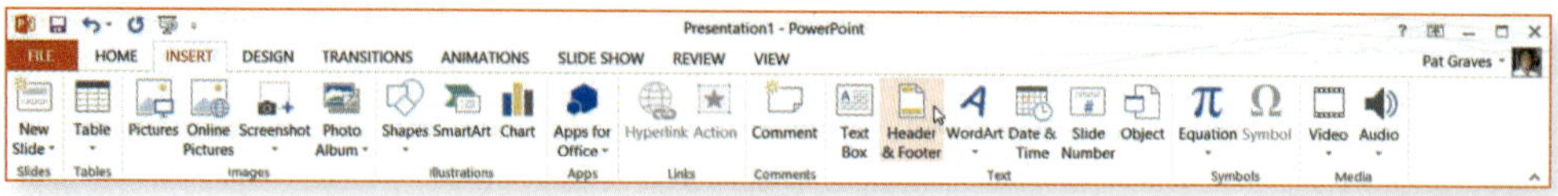

1-54 *Insert* tab

Create a Slide Footer

When you enter information using the *Header and Footer* dialog box, placeholders appear on the slides. You can move these placeholders if you wish.

HOW TO: Create a Slide Footer

1. Click the **Insert** tab.
2. Click the **Header & Footer** button [*Text* group].
3. In the *Header and Footer* dialog box, click the **Slide** tab (Figure 1-55).
4. Click the check boxes to select the following:
   a. **Date and time:** Choose between **Update automatically** to show the current date or **Fixed** to enter a specific date.
   b. **Slide number:** Each slide is numbered.
   c. **Footer:** Type text you want to appear on each slide.
5. Check the box for **Don't show on title slide** if you do not want footer information to appear on any slide created with the *Title Slide* layout.
6. Click the **Apply** button to apply the settings only to the current slide.
7. Click the **Apply to All** button to apply the settings to all slides.

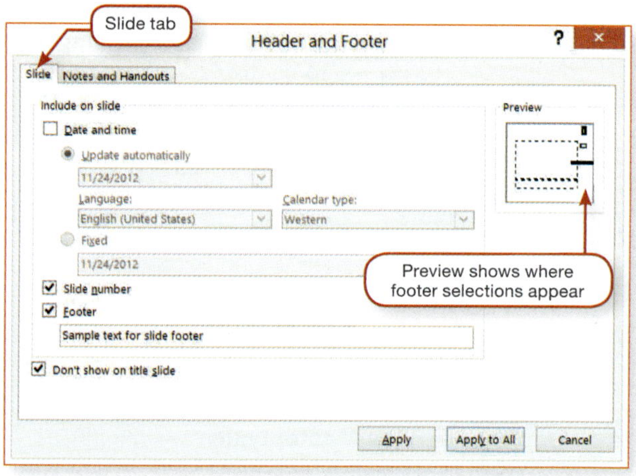

1-55 *Slide* tab on the *Header and Footer* dialog box

Create a Notes and Handouts Header

Because notes and handouts are usually printed documents, they can include header information that appears at the top of each page. Control all settings for notes and handouts in the same way you control slide footers.

HOW TO: Create a Notes and Handouts Header

1. Click the **Insert** tab.
2. Click the **Header & Footer** button [*Text* group].
3. In the *Header and Footer* dialog box, click the **Notes and Handouts** tab (Figure 1-56).
4. Click the check boxes to select the following:
   a. **Date and time:** Choose between **Update automatically** to show the current date or **Fixed** to enter a specific date.
   b. **Page number:** Each page is numbered.

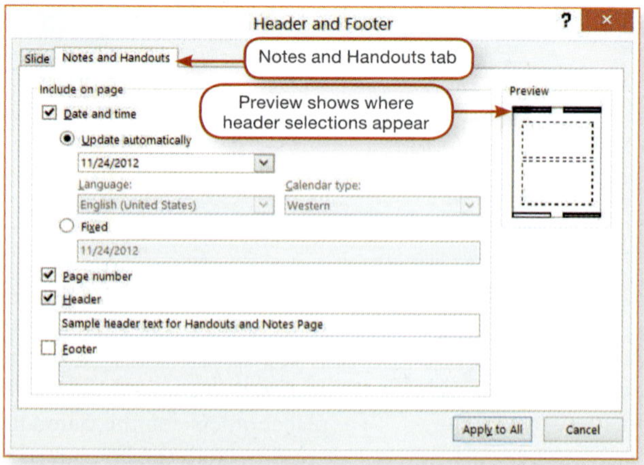

1-56 *Notes and Handouts* tab in the *Header and Footer* dialog box

c. **Header:** Type text you want to appear on each page.
d. **Footer:** Type text you want to appear on each page.

5. Click the **Apply to All** button to apply your settings to all pages.

If you leave items blank in the *Header and Footer* dialog box, empty placeholders show on your slide, but no information appears in *Slide Show* view.

PAUSE & PRACTICE: POWERPOINT 1-2

For this project, you continue working on the presentation you created in *Pause & Practice: PowerPoint 1-1*. You apply a theme then change theme colors and fonts to revise two individual slides. Finally, you add a footer to your slides and add page numbering to the notes and handout pages.

File Needed: ***[your initials] PP P1-1.pptx***
Completed Project File Name: ***[your initials] PP P1-2.pptx***

1. Open and rename the presentation file.
   a. Click the **File** tab; then click the **Open** button.
   b. Locate the folder where your files are saved.
   c. Open the presentation file **[your initials] PP P1-1**.
   d. Click the **File** tab; then click **Save As** or press **F12**.
   e. Locate the folder where your files are saved.
   f. Save the presentation as **[your initials] PP P1-2**.
2. Apply a theme.
   a. Click the **Design** tab.
   b. Click the **More** button [*Themes* group] to open the *Themes* gallery (Figure 1-57).
   c. Click the **Facet** theme so it is applied to all slides.

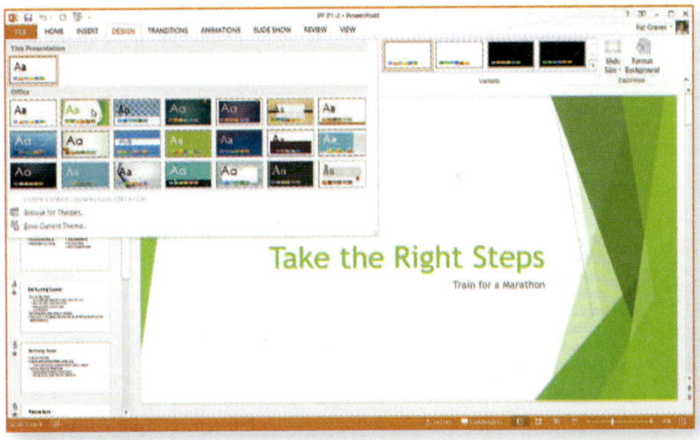

1-57 *Themes* gallery

3. Change the background style.
   a. Click the **View** tab.
   b. Click the **Slide Master** button.
   c. Scroll to the top of the slide master layouts and select the first layout (Facet Slide Master) so your color change is applied to all slides.
   d. Click the **Colors** button [*Slide Master* tab, *Background* group].
   e. Scroll down the list and select the **Aspect** theme.
   f. Click the **Background Styles** button [*Slide Master* tab, *Background* group].
   g. Select **Style 4**, which applies a solid black background (Figure 1-58).

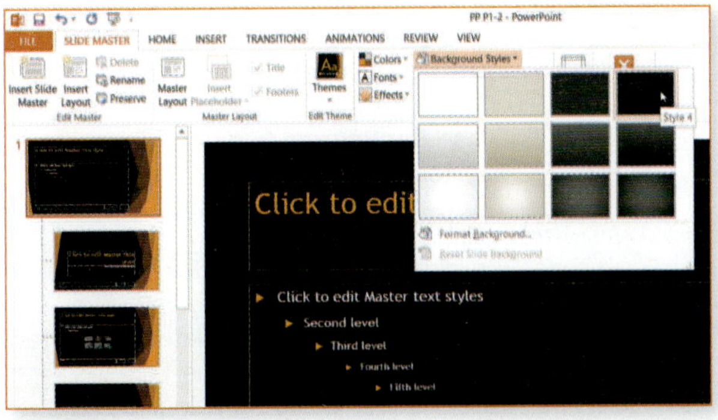

1-58 *Background Styles*

4. Change the fonts.
    a. Click the **Fonts** button [*Slide Master* tab, *Background* group].
    b. Scroll down the list and click the **TrebuchetMS** font pair (Figure 1-59).
    c. Click the **Close Master View** button [*Slide Master* tab].
5. On slide 1, modify the title and subtitle text.
    a. Select all of the title text and make these changes:
        - Apply **bold**, change to **left alignment**, and increase the font size to **60 pts**. [*Home* tab, *Font* group].
        - Click the **Arrange** button [*Home* tab, *Drawing* group], **Align**, and select **Align Top**.
        - Select the word **Right**. Click the **Change Case** button [*Home* tab, *Font* group] and select **UPPERCASE**.
        - Resize the placeholder on the right by dragging the horizontal sizing handle so the text fits on one line.
    b. Select the subtitle and make these changes:
        - Apply **bold**, change to **left alignment**, and increase the font size to **36 pts**. [*Home* tab, *Font* group].
        - Position the subtitle below the title.
6. On slide 2, change the bullet.
    a. Select the bulleted text and click the **Bullets** list arrow [*Home* tab, *Font* group].
    b. Select **Bullets and Numbering**.
    c. Change the *Size* to **100%** of text.
    d. Click the **Color** button and select **Red**, **Accent 2** (Figure 1-60).
    e. Click the **Customize** button to open the *Symbol* dialog box. Change the font (if necessary) to **Wingdings** (Figure 1-61)
    f. Scroll down and select the **solid square** (Character code 110) and click **OK**.
    g. Click **OK** again to close the *Bullets and Numbering* dialog box.
    h. Click to put your insertion point before the word "Or" on the third bulleted item.
    i. Press **Backspace** to remove the bullet from this item only. Make this text bold.
7. Add a slide footer.
    a. On slide 2, click the **Header & Footer** button [*Insert* tab, *Text* group] (Figure 1-62).
    b. On the *Slide* tab, select **Slide number** and **Footer**.
    c. In the *Footer* text box, type Take the Right Steps, Train for a Marathon.
    d. Select **Don't show on title slide**.

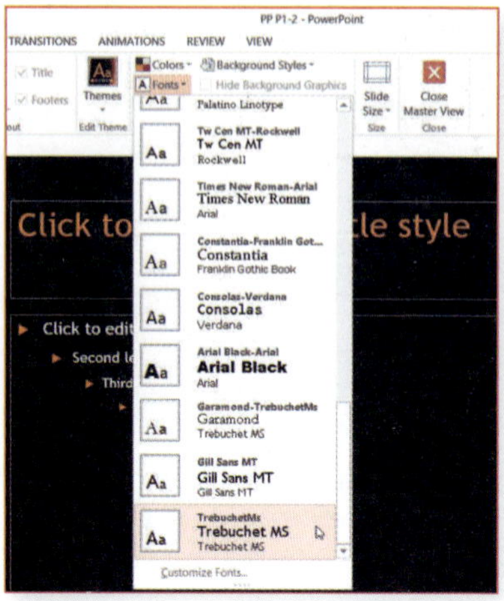

1-59 *Theme* font change

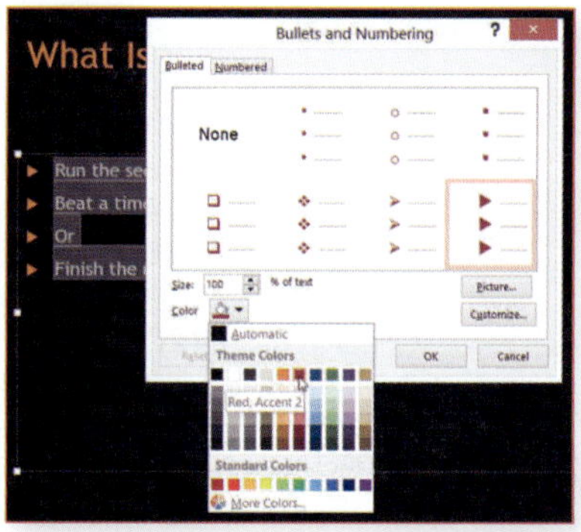

1-60 Change bullet size and color

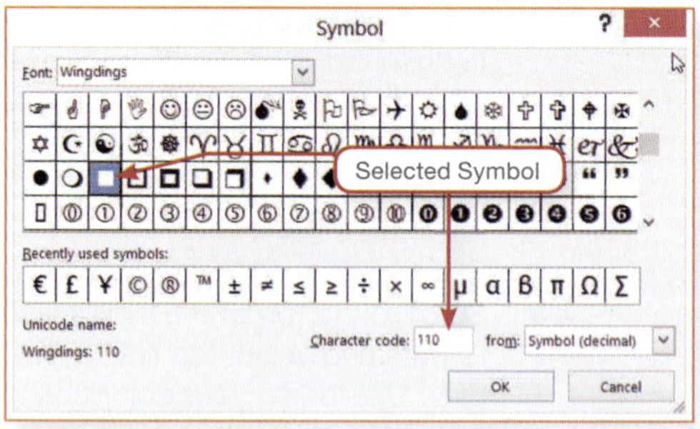

1-61 *Symbol* dialog box

e. Click the **Apply** button. The dialog box closes and the footer appears only on this slide.
f. Select the footer text and the page number. Increase the font size to **18 pts**.

8. Add page numbers for a handout.
   a. On slide 2, click the **Header & Footer** button [*Insert* tab, *Text* group].
   b. Click the **Notes and Handouts** tab.
   c. Select **Page number**.
   d. Click the **Apply to All** button and the dialog box closes.
9. Save the presentation.

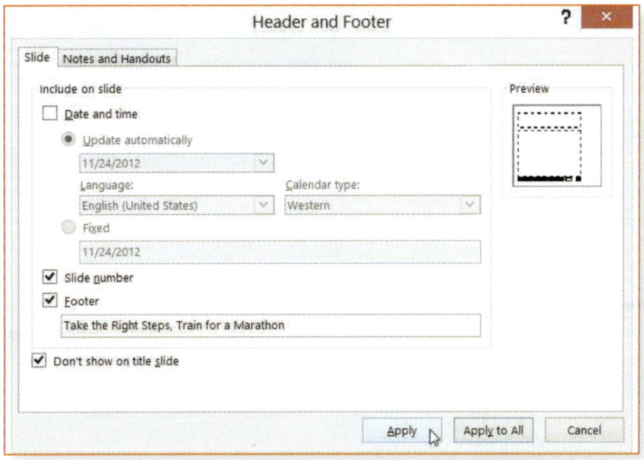

1-62 ***Header and Footer*** **dialog box with changes**

SLO 1.6 Working with a Picture from a File

There is an old adage, "A picture is worth a thousand words." That saying is still true today, because pictures bring a sense of realism to a presentation. Select pictures appropriate for your topic. Include pictures obtained from web sites only if you have the permission of the image owner to avoid copyright infringement. For academic purposes, you may include images if you reference their sources as you would any other research citation.

Insert a Picture

PowerPoint supports different graphic file types, so you can insert almost any digital image from a camera, or one created by scanning a document, into a slide show. To insert a picture, click the **Picture** button in the *Images* group on the *Insert* tab. Be aware that pictures can increase the file size of your presentation dramatically.

HOW TO: Insert a Picture

1. Click the **Insert** tab.
2. Click the **Pictures** button.
3. Select the drive and folder where your picture is saved.
4. Select the file you want to insert (Figure 1-63).
5. Click **Insert**.

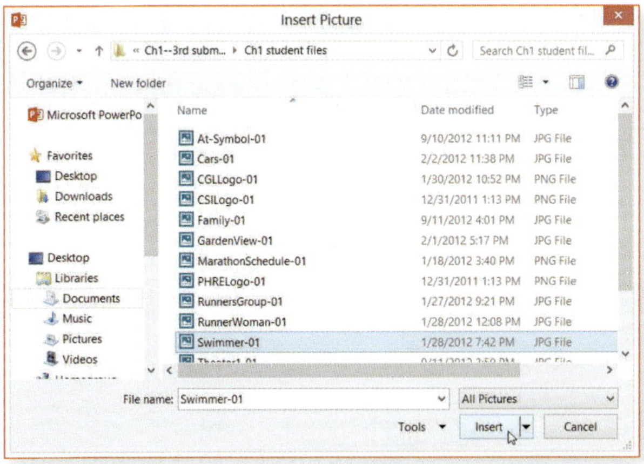

1-63 ***Insert Picture*** **dialog box**

ANOTHER WAY

Once you have located your picture file, insert the picture by double clicking the file name.

Graphic File Formats

Picture File Type	Extension	Uses of This Format
JPEG (Joint Photographic Experts Group)	.jpg	Designed for photographic images. Handles gradual color blending and complex graphics well. Produces a smaller file size than most other formats because of compression.
PNG (Portable Network Graphics)	.png	Handles photographic images and complex graphics well. Originally designed for web applications, this format works well for presentations also. Supports transparency so areas removed from the image appear blank on the slide.
GIF (Graphics Interchange Format)	.gif	Suited for line art and simple drawings, but not optimal for photographs because it only supports 256 colors. Used for simple animated graphics. Does not handle gradual color blending well. Supports transparency.
Windows Metafile and Enhanced Windows Metafile	.wmf and .emf	Used for many Windows illustrations available through searches using the Clip Art task pane.
Device Independent Bitmap	.bmp	Images usually display well in their original size, but if you increase size, the image will be distorted.
TIFF (Tagged Image File Format)	.tiff	Designed for print publications. Produces high-quality images with large file sizes. Supports transparency.

Resize a Picture

You can make a picture smaller and still retain its clarity, but some pictures cannot be made larger without becoming blurred or distorted.

To resize a picture, point to one of the corner or side sizing handles and drag it. The corner sizing handles move diagonally to change both horizontal and vertical dimensions at the same time.

You can precisely resize a picture by entering the exact dimensions on the *Picture Tools Format* tab that appears when a picture is selected. When changing the size of pictures, maintain the correct ratio between height and width to avoid distorting the image. The selected picture of the swimmer in Figure 1-64 is shown in the original size on the left. The pictures on the right were resized horizontally to be too wide and too narrow.

If you change the size incorrectly, restore the picture's original dimensions by clicking the **Reset Picture** button in the *Adjust* group on the *Picture Tools Format* tab (Figure 1-65).

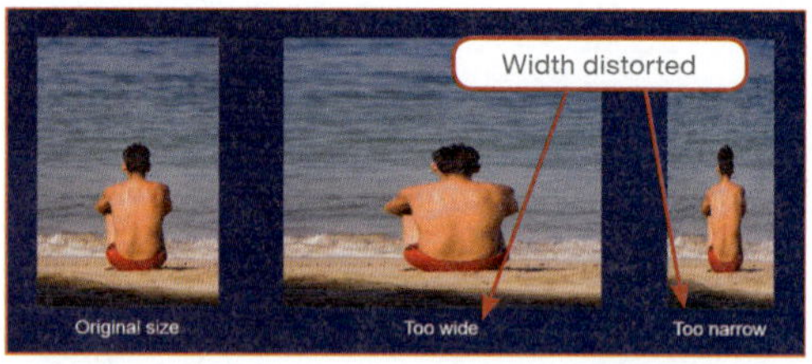

1-64 Resizing examples

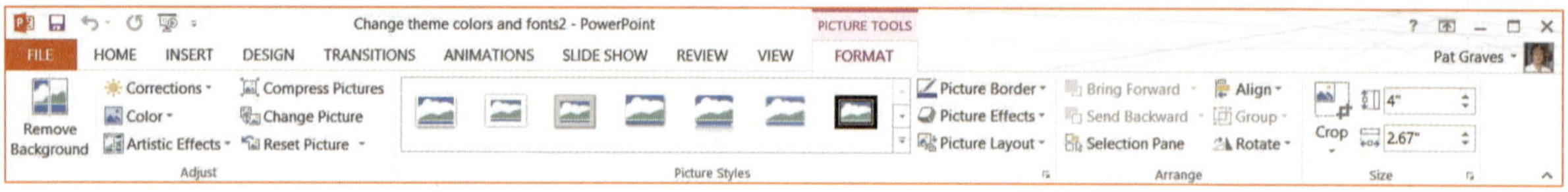

1-65 *Picture Tools Format* tab

Align a Picture

As you place pictures and other graphic objects on slides, consider how they are aligned on the slide and how they align with other objects on the slide. Everything on the slide should align in some way. You can align pictures and other objects with each other or on the slide by clicking the *Align* button in the *Arrange* group on the *Picture Tools Format* tab and selecting the alignment from the drop-down list (Figure 1-66).

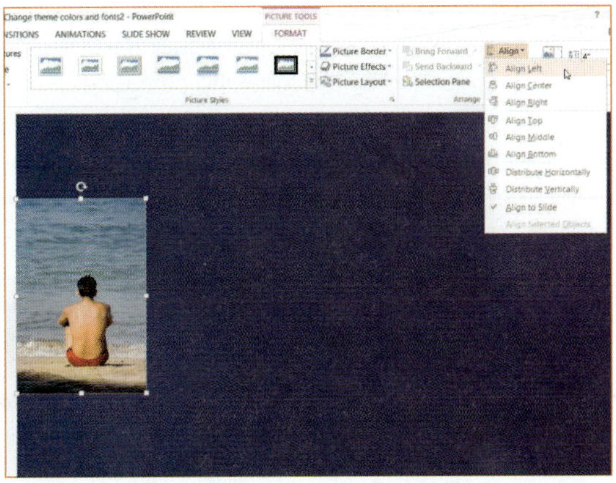

1-66 Left align on the slide

- ***Horizontal alignment:*** *Left, Center,* or *Right*
- ***Vertical alignment:*** *Top, Middle,* or *Bottom*

SLO 1.7

Applying Transitions

A ***transition*** is the visual effect of movement that occurs when one slide changes into another slide. Each transition effect in PowerPoint provides a different type of movement. You can find these in the *Transition to This Slide* gallery on the *Transitions* tab (Figure 1-67).

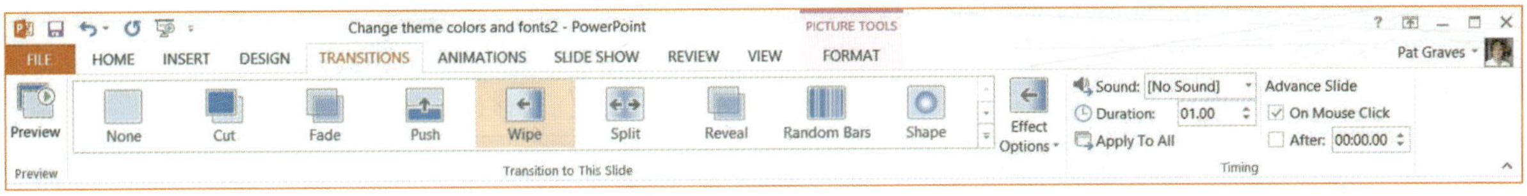

1-67 *Transitions* tab

Each slide can have only one transition. You can set transitions for one slide at a time in *Normal* view or apply the same transition to all slides. If you want to use different transitions, select thumbnails in *Normal* view or *Slide Sorter* view. Once a transition has been applied, an icon symbolizing movement appears with the slide thumbnails.

Although it is possible to apply different transitions on every slide in a presentation, it is neither practical nor advisable. People are very accustomed to PowerPoint use today and know that slides are going to change in some way. Random movements using many different transitions do not entertain an audience and may be distracting or even annoying. Control movement skillfully to reinforce your message. Some people prefer to use a "quiet" transition for most of a presentation (sort of like turning pages in a book or an e-reader). They apply a more "energetic" transition to key slides to grab attention or signal the beginning of a new topic. Use the *Slide Sorter* view to see more slides at once and decide which slides might benefit from a different movement.

In the *Timing* group, the **Advance Slide** options control whether slides advance **On Mouse Click** (the default) or after a specific number of seconds that you choose. Sound can also be associated with a transition.

HOW TO: Apply Transitions

1. Select the slide thumbnail where you want a transition to appear.
2. Click the **Transitions** tab.

3. Click the **More** button [*Transition to This Slide* group] to see additional transitions (Figure 1-68) organized by the following categories:
   a. *Subtle*
   b. *Exciting*
   c. *Dynamic Content*
4. Apply one transition to all slides in the presentation.
   a. Select a transition effect for the current slide.
   b. Be sure **On Mouse Click** is checked.
   c. Click the **Apply to All** button [*Timing* group]
5. Apply more than one transition.
   a. Click the **Slide Sorter** button on the *Status bar*.
   b. Press **Ctrl** as you click to select two or more slides that should have a different transition.
   c. Click a different transition effect and a live preview shows on the selected slides.
   d. Be sure **On Mouse Click** is checked (Figure 1-69).
6. Click the **Normal View** button on the *Status bar*.
   a. Select the first slide and click **Preview** [*Transitions* tab, *Preview* group] to test the movement.
   b. Click the **Next Slide** button and click **Preview** again for each slide.
7. Click the **Slide Show** tab.
   a. Click the **From Beginning** button to view the slide show from the first slide.
   b. Click to advance from slide to slide.

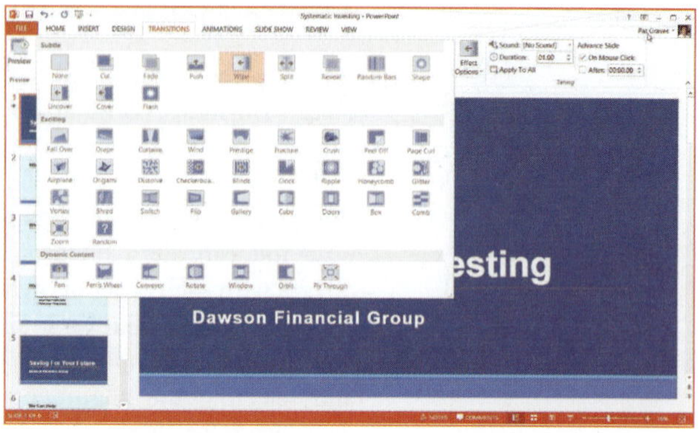

1-68 *Transitions* gallery

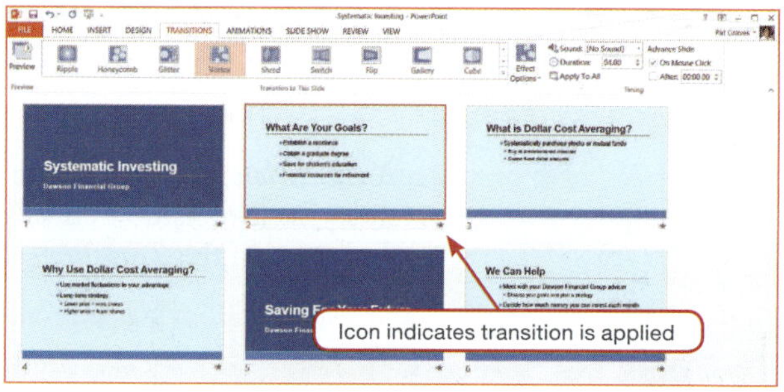

1-69 Change transitions on selected slides in *Slide Sorter* view

Duration, shown in seconds, controls how fast the slides change. Duration seconds vary based on the selected transition effect. Movement might be barely visible if the duration is fast; a slower duration of five or more seconds can make the movement much more noticeable. Enter a different number to change the duration and experiment to see what works best for your content.

Select Effect Options

Effect Options control the direction of transition movement and options vary based on the transition. Each transition can have only one effect option.

HOW TO: Select Effect Options

1. In *Slide Sorter* view, select the slide (or slides) with the same transition.
2. Click the **Transitions** tab.
3. Click the **Effect Options** button to see a drop-down list showing directional movements (Figure 1-70).
4. Select an option to apply it.
5. Repeat this process if you have more than one transition.

6. Click **Preview** to test the movement in *Normal View.*
7. Click the **Slide Show** tab.
8. Click the **From Beginning** button to view the slide show from the first slide.
9. Click to advance from slide to slide.

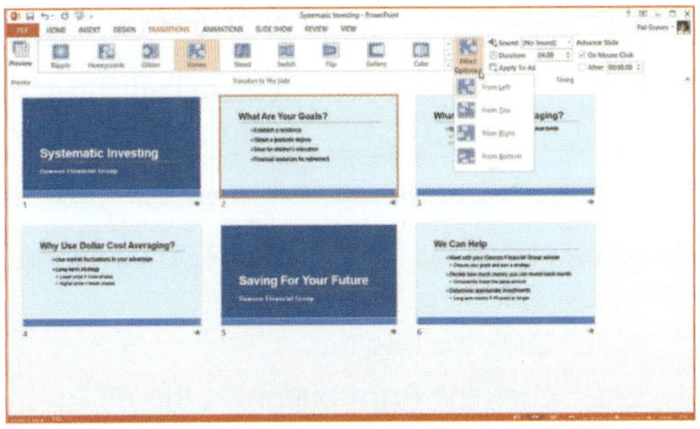

1-70 ***Transition Effect*** **options**

SLO 1.8

Exploring Print Options

You may want to proofread your presentation content on paper or review the slides with a colleague. Or you may want to prepare audience handouts or your own printed materials to use while you are giving the presentation. PowerPoint 2013 provides convenient ways to preview and print presentation slides, handouts, notes pages, or outlines.

Preview a Presentation

Before printing, check your slides to ensure everything looks as you intended. The *Backstage* view [*File* tab, *Print* button] displays each slide or handout page in your presentation as it will look when printed. Use the navigation controls at the bottom of the window to go through the slides or pages one at a time. You can also press **Page Up** or **Page Down**, or you can use the scroll bar on the right. Adjust slide sizes using the *Zoom* controls on the lower right.

The look of your slides in *Backstage* view is influenced by the selected printer. If you are using a color printer, the preview image is shown in color; if it prints in black and white, the preview image will be shown in ***grayscale*** (shades of black). In a work setting, you may have a small desktop printer for printing rough draft copies with black print and a network printer for printing more expensive, high-quality color pages. If you design slides in color and plan to print slides or handouts in grayscale, preview your slides to make sure that all text is readable. You may need to adjust some colors to get good results.

In *Backstage* view, select a printer from the available list of local and network printers. Print ***Settings*** are shown as buttons with the current setting displayed. Click the list arrow for a list of the following options:

- ***Which Slides to Print:*** Choose among *Print All Slides, Print Selection, Print Current Slide,* or *Custom Range* using slide numbers entered in the *Slides* box (e.g., slides 1-3 or slides 1-3, 5, 8).
- ***What to Print:*** Choose *Full Page Slides, Notes Pages, Outline,* or *Handouts.* You can print handouts with three to nine slides on a page using a horizontal or vertical arrangement on the page. You can also specify *Frame Slides, Scale to Fit Paper* (makes slides larger), or *High Quality.*
- ***Print Side:*** Choose between *Print One Side* or *Print Both Sides.* However, not all printers can print on both sides.
- ***Print Order:*** Choose between *Collated* and *Uncollated.* Usually slides print in order, but you may want to print multiple copies page by page.
- ***Orientation:*** Choose between *Landscape* and *Portrait.* By default, slides print in landscape orientation; notes and handouts print in portrait orientation. This option is not available if you are printing full-size slides.
- ***Color Range:*** Choose among *Color, Grayscale,* or *Pure Black and White.*

Below the print *Settings* in *Backstage* view, you can click the **Edit Header & Footer** link to open the *Header and Footer* dialog box and then enter or revise information.

Print a Slide

The default print settings print each slide on letter-size paper. Adjust settings as needed to print the current or selected slides.

HOW TO: Print a Slide in Grayscale

1. Click the **File** tab.
2. Click the **Print** button on the left.
3. For *Settings*, choose the options you need, such as the following:
   a. Which Slides to Print: **Print Current Slide**.
   b. What to Print: **Full Page Slides**.
   c. Print Order: **Collated**.
   d. Color Range: **Grayscale** (Figure 1-71).
4. Enter the number of copies, if you need more than one.
5. Click the **Print** button at the top.

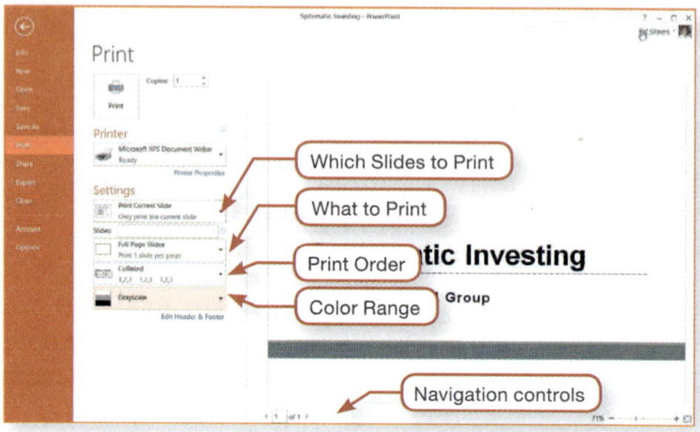

1-71 Print settings for a full-size slide

Print a Handout

Handouts print one to nine slides on a page. You can use these pages as audience handouts or for your own reference during a presentation. Selecting *Scale to Fit Paper* makes the slides larger. *Framing* shows the shape of slides, which is helpful when printing slides with a white background on white paper. Depending on the number of slides, changing the page orientation to landscape can make slides larger.

When preparing handouts for an audience, consider which slides will be important for the audience to have. If not all slides are necessary, you can specify which slides to include and perhaps reduce the number of pages required for printing.

HOW TO: Print a Handout for Selected Slides in Color

1. Click the **File** tab.
2. Click the **Print** button on the left.
3. Select a color printer.
4. For *Settings*, choose the options you need, such as the following:
   a. Which Slides to Print: Enter the specific slides needed (such as **1**, **3–4**, **6**) in the *Slides* box to print a *Custom Range*.
   b. What to Print: **6 Slides Horizontal**, **Collated**, and **Portrait Orientation**.
   c. Color Range: **Color** (Figure 1-72).
5. Enter the number of copies, if you need more than one.
6. Click the **Print** button at the top.

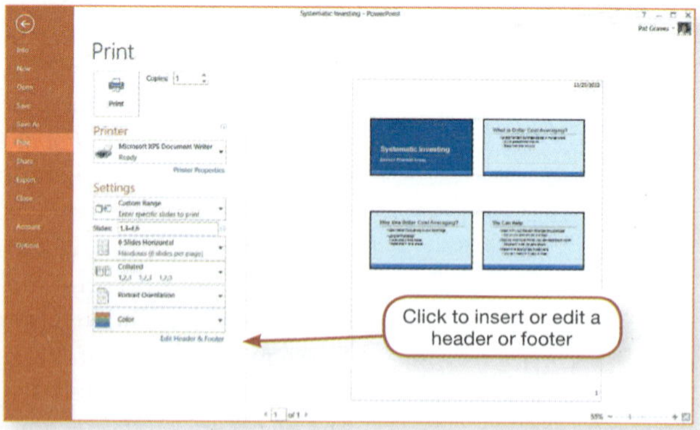

1-72 Print settings for a handout

Print an Outline

If a presentation consists of mostly slides with bulleted lists, printing an outline is a very concise way to display the content. Only the text is shown.

HOW TO: Print an Outline in Pure Black and White

1. Click the **File** tab.
2. Click the **Print** button on the left.
3. For *Settings*, choose the options you need, such as the following:
   a. Which Slides to Print: **Print All Slides**.
   b. What to Print: **Outline**.
   c. What Side: **Print One Sided**.
   d. Print Order: **Collated**.
   e. Orientation: **Portrait Orientation**.
   f. Color Range: **Pure Black and White** (Figure 1-73).
4. Enter the number of copies, if you need more than one.
5. Click the **Print** button at the top.

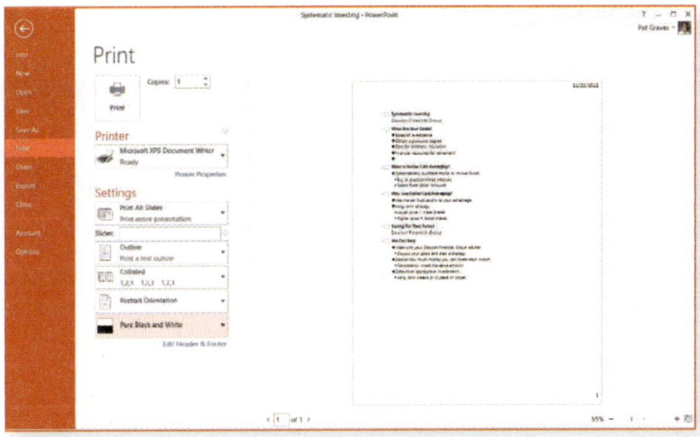

1-73 Print settings for an outline

SLO 1.9

Applying Properties

PowerPoint automatically records information in your presentation file, such as the file size, creation date, and number of slides. These ***document properties***, also called ***metadata***, can help you manage and track files. Click the **File** tab and click the **Info** button to see these properties on the right side of the *Backstage* view. You can edit some of these properties, such as title and author, in this view.

HOW TO: Change Properties Using Backstage View

1. Click the **File** tab.
2. Click the **Info** button.
3. Document properties are listed on the right. Point to the fields to see which ones you can edit (Figure 1-74).
4. Click **Show All Properties** to access additional information.
5. Click in a **field** and type information to edit the document property.

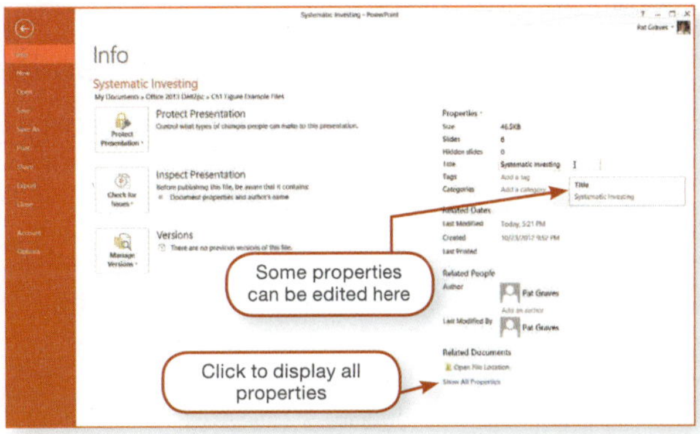

1-74 Document properties on *Backstage* view

Change Document Panel Information

You can change additional properties, such as subject, keywords, or category, using the *Document Properties* panel that appears in the PowerPoint window between the *Ribbon* and the slide area.

HOW TO: Change Properties Using the Document Panel

1. Click the **File** tab.
2. Click the **Info** button.
3. Click the **Properties** list arrow at the top of the *Properties* area.
4. Select **Show Document Panel** (Figure 1-75). The *Backstage* closes, and the *Document Properties Panel* displays (Figure 1-76).
5. Click in the fields and type appropriate information.
6. Click the *Document Properties* **Close** button at the top right of the panel to close the panel.

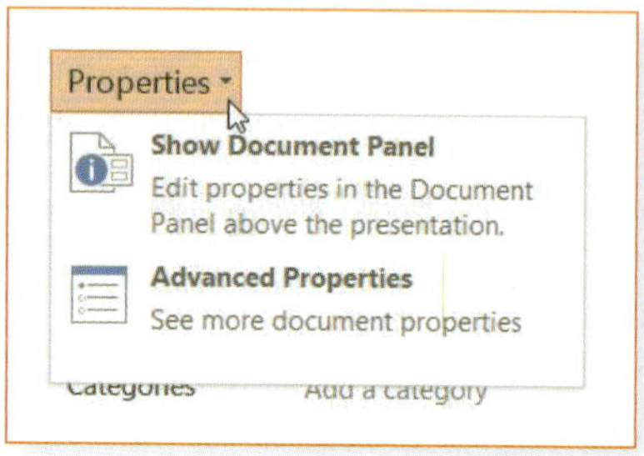

1-75 *Properties* options

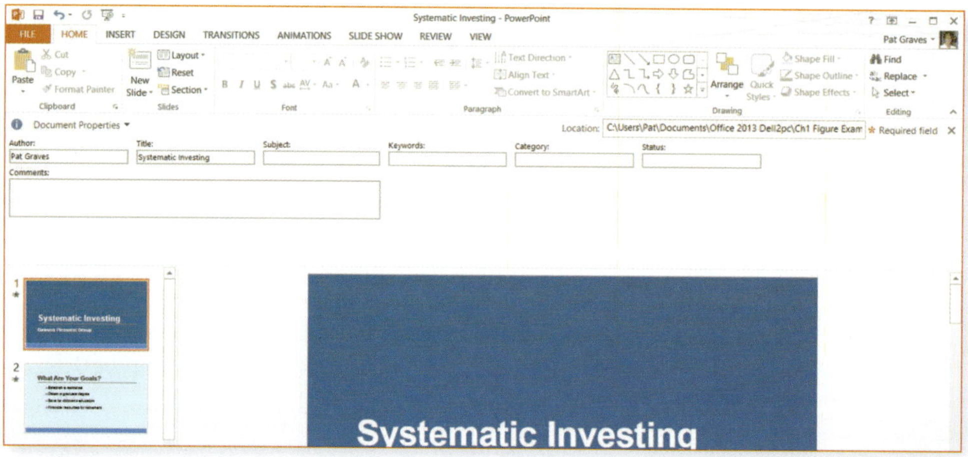

1-76 *Document Properties* Panel

Review Advanced Properties

The *Properties* dialog box displays properties organized in the following five tabs: *General, Summary, Statistics, Contents,* and *Custom.*

HOW TO: Change Properties Using the Properties Dialog Box

1. Click the **File** tab.
2. Click the **Info** button.
3. Click the **Properties** list arrow at the top of the *Properties* area.

4. Select **Advanced Properties**. The *Properties* dialog box is displayed (Figure 1-77).
5. Tabs display properties automatically generated by PowerPoint.
6. Click the **Summary** and **Custom** tabs to add or edit information.
7. Click **OK** to close the *Properties* dialog box.

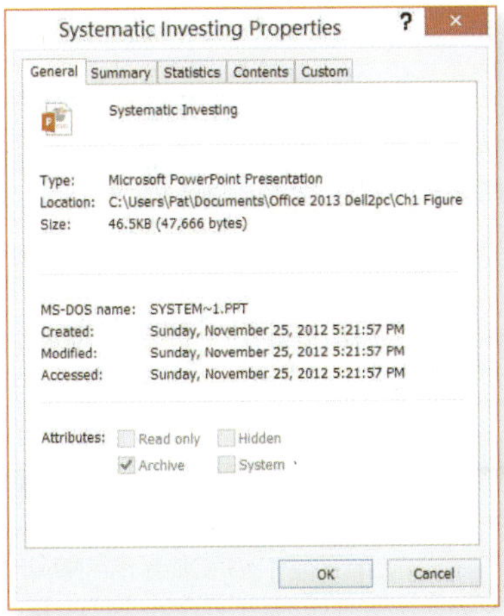

1-77 *Properties* dialog box

ANOTHER WAY

Open the *Advanced Properties* dialog box from the *Document* Panel by clicking **Document Properties** and selecting **Advanced Properties.**

PAUSE & PRACTICE: POWERPOINT 1-3

For this final Pause & Practice project, you finish the presentation about training for a marathon. You insert, resize, and align several pictures, apply transitions, change the presentation properties, and print a handout.

Files Needed: ***[your initials] PP P1-2.pptx MarathonInfo-01.pptx***, ***RunnersGroup-01.jpg***, ***RunnerWoman-01.jpg***, and ***MarathonSchedule-01.png***
Completed Project File Name: ***[your initials] PP P1-3.pptx***

1. Open and rename the ***[your initials] PP P1-2*** presentation.
   a. Click the **File** tab and click the **Open** button.
   b. Locate your saved files.
   c. Open the ***[your initials] PP P1-2*** presentation.
   d. Click the **File** tab; then click **Save As**.
   e. Browse to the location on your computer or storage device to save the presentation.
   f. Save this presentation as ***[your initials] PP P1-3***.
2. On slide 1, insert, resize, and align a picture on the slide.
   a. Click the **Insert** tab; then click the **Pictures** button.
   b. Locate the folder where your student files are saved.
   c. Select ***RunnersGroup-01.jpg*** and click **Insert** (or double click the file name) to insert the picture (Figure 1-78). (The .jpg file name extension may not show in your file list.)
   d. Resize the picture using the horizontal sizing arrows so it is **8.5"** wide. Because the picture is already blurred to reflect the speed of running, it looks fine when you stretch the picture.
   e. With the picture selected, click the **Align** button [*Picture Tools Format* tab, *Arrange* group].
      - Select **Align Bottom** (Figure 1-79).
      - Repeat to select **Align Right**.

1-78 Picture of runners inserted

1-79 Picture resized and aligned

3. On slide 6, repeat the process to insert a picture and align it.
   a. Click the **Insert** tab and click the **Pictures** button.
   b. Locate the folder where your files are saved.
   c. Select ***RunnerWoman-01.jpg*** and click **Insert** (or double click the file name) to insert the picture.
   d. No resizing is required for this picture.
   e. With the picture selected, click the **Align** button [*Picture Tools Format* tab, *Arrange* group] and select **Align Right** (Figure 1-80).

1-80 Picture aligned

4. With slide 6 selected, add a new slide and insert a picture of a table.
   a. Click the **New Slide** list arrow [*Home* tab, *Slides* group].
   b. Select the **Title Only** layout.
   c. Type the title Upcoming Marathons.
   d. Click the **Insert** tab; then click the **Pictures** button.
   e. Locate the folder where your files are saved.
   f. Select ***MarathonSchedule-01.jpg*** and click **Insert** (or double click the file name) to insert the picture.
   g. Move the table so it is approximately centered in the black area (Figure 1-81).

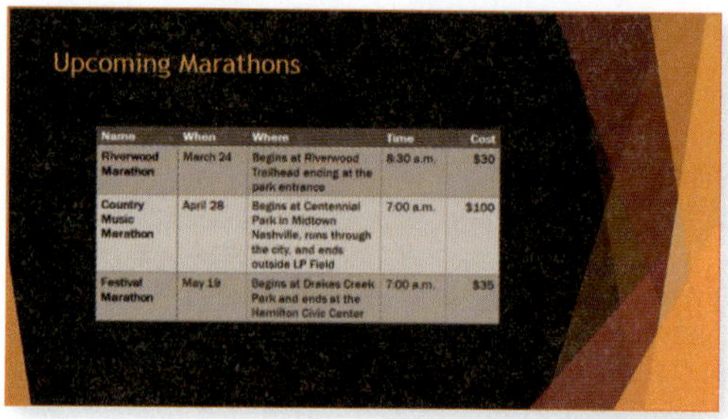

Name	When	Where	Time	Cost
Riverwood Marathon	March 24	Begins at Riverwood Trailhead ending at the park entrance	8:30 a.m.	$30
Country Music Marathon	April 28	Begins at Centennial Park in Midtown Nashville, runs through the city, and ends outside LP Field	7:00 a.m.	$100
Festival Marathon	May 19	Begins at Drakes Creek Park and ends at the Hamilton Civic Center	7:00 a.m.	$35

1-81 Picture of table inserted and positioned

5. On slides 8, 9, and 10, only the large title text appears. Resize the placeholders horizontally on the right side so the text fits in the placeholder without extra horizontal space or word wrapping.
6. On slide 10, change the font color for the word "THERE!" to **Tan**, **Text 2**.
7. On slides 8, 9, and 10, adjust where the text aligns. Repeat this process for each slide.
   a. Select the title text placeholder and click the **Align** button [*Drawing Tools Format* tab, *Arrange* group].
   b. Click **Align** and select the following alignment:

      Slide 8: **Align Left**, **Align Top** (Figure 1-82)
      Slide 9: **Align Center**, **Align Bottom**
      Slide 10: **Align Right**, **Align Middle**

1-82 Title placeholder aligned top and left

8. Apply one transition to all slides and a different transition to selected slides.
   a. Click the **Slide Sorter** button [*Status bar*].
   b. Press **Ctrl+A** to select all slides.
   c. Click the **Transitions** tab.
   d. Click the **Wipe** transition from the gallery.
   e. Click **Effect Options** [*Transition* tab, *Transition to This Slide* group].
   f. Select **From Left** (Figure 1-83).
   g. Click off a slide to remove the selections.

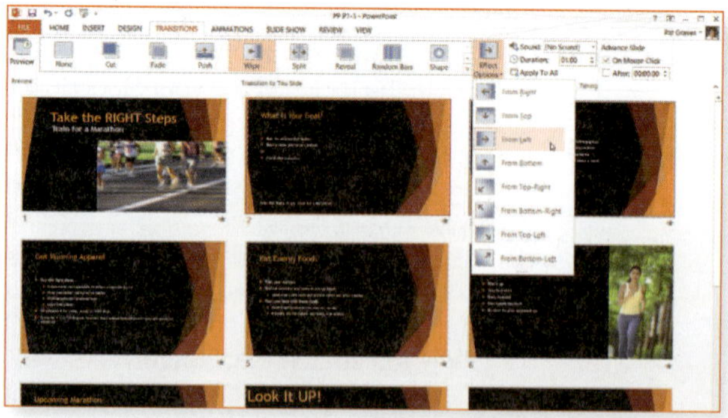

1-83 *Transition Effect* options

h. Select each of the following slides and apply transitions and effect options from the *Transition* tab to emphasize the content with different movements:

Slide 1: **Zoom**, **In**
Slide 7: **Doors**, **Vertical**
Slide 8: **Pan**, **From Bottom**
Slide 9: **Pan**, **From Top**
Slide 10: **Pan**, **From Left**

i. Press **Ctrl+A** to select all slides.
j. Click **Preview** [*Transitions* tab] to see the movements in *Slide Sorter* view.
k. Click the **Slide Show** button [*Status bar*] and click to advance each slide so you can see the movements in *Slide Show* view.

9. Now change some of the presentation properties.
   a. Click the **File** tab, then the **Info** button.
   b. Under *Properties*, change the *Title* to Train for a Marathon.
   c. Click the **Properties** button, then click **Show Document** Panel (Figure 1-84). Type the following information in the respective fields:

Author:	Your Name *(unless it already appears)*
Title:	Train for a Marathon *(already entered)*
Subject:	Athletic Event Promotion
Comments:	This presentation will be shown at the Civic Center to explain how to get ready for upcoming marathon events.

   d. Click the **Close** button to close the *Document Properties* panel.

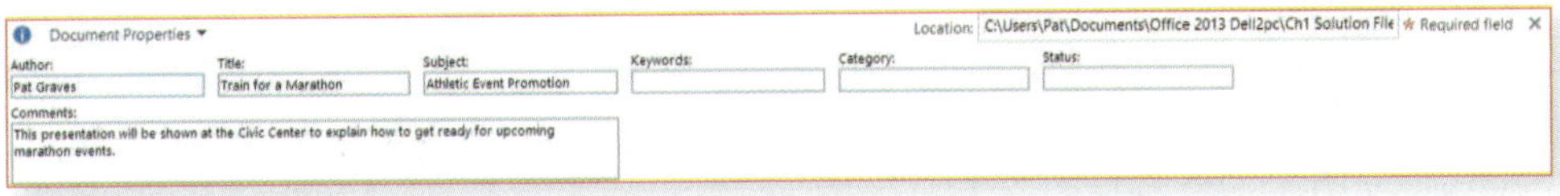

1-84 ***Document Properties*** Panel

10. Print slides as a handout.
   a. Click the **File** tab, then the **Print** button on the left.
   b. Select the appropriate printer.
   c. Change the following *Settings* by clicking the **list arrow** for each option (repeat as necessary to make more than one change) (Figure 1-85):

      Which Slides to Print: **Print All Slides**
      What to Print: **Handouts**, **6 Slides Horizontal**, **Frame Slides**, **Scale to Fit Paper**
      Print Order: **Collated**
      Orientation: **Portrait**
      Color Range: **Grayscale** (or **color** if you prefer)

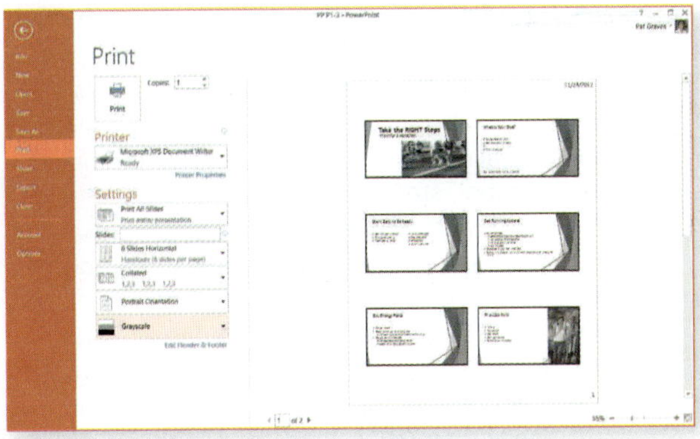

1-85 ***Print* settings**

   d. Preview the handout by clicking the navigation buttons so you can see both pages.
   e. Click the **Print** button at the top of the *Backstage* view.

11. Press **Ctrl+S** to save the presentation (or click the **Save** button on the *File* tab or the *Quick Access* toolbar).

Chapter Summary

1.1 Create, open, and save a presentation (p. P1-3).

- You can start creating a presentation with a blank presentation, a ***theme***, an existing presentation, or a ***template***.
- Different ***views*** in PowerPoint enable you to look at your content in different ways.
- The ***Zoom*** feature allows you to adjust the size of the slide on which you are working.
- The standard file format for presentation files has an extension of ***.pptx***.
- In ***Backstage*** view, PowerPoint provides a variety of save and send options. For example, you can save a presentation as a ***PDF*** file or email a presentation file as an attachment.
- Additional themes and templates are available at Office.com.

1.2 Develop presentation content by adding slides, choosing layouts, moving and resizing placeholders, editing text, and reusing slides from another presentation (p. P1-14).

- Use ***placeholders*** for presentation text and objects such as pictures, tables, and charts. You can resize, reposition, and align text placeholders on slides.
- The ***New Slide*** button displays a gallery of slide layouts with placeholders arranged for different content.
- You can make font changes using commands on the *Home* tab or the mini toolbar.
- ***Change Case*** changes the way words are capitalized.
- In bulleted lists, you can change the bullet symbol, size, and color.
- Use the ***Format Painter*** to copy formatting from one object and apply it to another object.
- The ***Reuse Slides*** feature enables you to insert slides from another presentation.
- Although potential spelling errors are automatically marked, you also can use the ***Spelling*** dialog box to check for errors.
- Use the ***Thesaurus*** to find synonyms for words in your presentation.

1.3 Rearrange presentation content by moving, copying and pasting, duplicating, and deleting slides (p. P1-22).

- You can move selected slides using a variety of methods to rearrange their sequence.
- ***Copy***, ***paste***, ***duplicate***, and ***delete*** slides using the ***Slides*** tab or ***Slide Sorter*** view.

1.4 Modify a theme to change slide size and use the Slide Master to change theme colors and fonts (p. P1-26).

- Presentation ***themes*** provide a cohesive look through the consistent use of backgrounds, designs, colors, and font treatments.
- Consider the topic and tone of your presentation when choosing theme colors and fonts.

1.5 Use headers and footers to add identifying information (p. P1-29)

- ***Footers*** usually appear at the bottom of slides but can appear in other locations. They are applied to all slides or to individual slides.
- Both ***headers*** and ***footers*** are used for notes pages and handouts. They are applied to all pages.

1.6 Insert, resize, and align a picture from a file (p. P1-33).

- PowerPoint supports different ***graphic file types***; you can insert almost any digital image into slide shows.
- Use ***sizing handles*** or enter exact dimensions to increase or decrease a picture's size.
- Avoid distortion when resizing pictures by maintaining accurate height and width ratios.
- You can ***align*** pictures with one another or with the slide.

1.7 Apply and modify transition effects to add visual interest (p. P1-35).

- A ***transition*** is the visual effect that appears when one slide changes into another slide.
- The ***Effect Options*** command enables you to control the direction of transition movement.
- You can apply transitions to one slide or to all slides in a presentation.

1.8 Preview a presentation and print slides, handouts, and outlines (p. P1-37).

- *Backstage* view allows you to examine each slide in your presentation before printing.
- The printer you select influences how slides appear in *Backstage* view.
- ***Grayscale*** shows shades of black.
- ***Print settings*** control which slides to print, what to print, and the print order, orientation, and color range.

1.9 Change properties (p. P1-39).

- Document properties are automatically recorded in your presentation file.
- You can add properties such as subject, keywords, or category to help manage and track files.
- Edit document properties in *Backstage* view under *Info* or by opening either the *Document Properties* panel or the *Advanced Properties* dialog box.

Check for Understanding

In the ***Online Learning Center*** for this book (www.mhhe.com/office2013inpractice), there are a variety of resources that can be used to review the concepts covered in this chapter.

The following Online Learning Resources are available in the Online Learning Center:

- Multiple choice questions
- Short answer questions
- Matching exercises

USING MICROSOFT POWERPOINT 2013

Guided Project 1-1

Jason Andrews is a sales associate for Classic Gardens and Landscaping (CGL) and frequently talks to customers when they visit the CGL showroom. For this project, you prepare a presentation he can use when introducing customers to CGL services.
[Student Learning Outcomes 1.1, 1.2, 1.3, 1.4, 1.5, 1.6]

Files Needed: ***GardenView-01.jpg*** and ***CGLLogo-01.png***
Completed Project File Name: ***[your initials] PowerPoint 1-1.pptx***

Skills Covered in This Project

- Create a new presentation using a theme.
- Change theme colors.
- Change theme fonts.
- Add slides.
- Change font size.
- Rearrange slides.
- Use the Format Painter.
- Insert a footer.
- Check spelling.
- Adjust placeholder position.
- Insert a picture.
- Save a presentation.

1. Create a new presentation using a theme.
   a. Click the **File** tab, then click **New**.
   b. Double-click the **Ion** theme (Figure 1-86).
2. Save the presentation as ***[your initials] PowerPoint 1-1***.
3. Change the theme colors.
   a. Click the **Slide Master** button [*View* tab, *Master Views* group].
   b. Select the first layout on the left, **Ion Slide Master**, so your color changes are applied to all slides.
   c. Click the **Colors** button [*Slide Master* tab, *Background* group].
   d. Scroll down the list and click the **Paper** theme.
   e. Click the **Background Styles** button [*Slide Master* tab, *Background* group] and select **Style 3** (Figure 1-87).
4. Change the theme fonts.
   a. Click the **Theme Fonts** button [*Slide Master* tab, *Background* group].
   b. Scroll down the list and click the **Candara** font group.
   c. Click the **Close Master View** button [*Slide Master* tab].

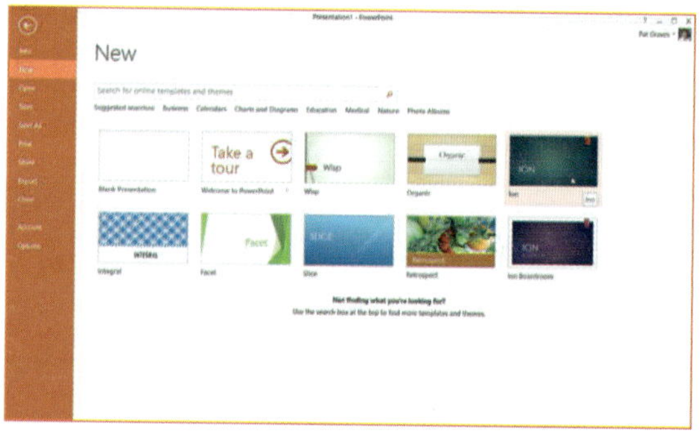

1-86 Ion theme selected

1-87 Background Style 3

5. Type the following text in the placeholders on slide 1:

Title	Creating Beautiful Outdoor Spaces
Subtitle	Jason Andrews, Sales Associate

6. Apply **bold** and a **shadow** [*Home* tab, *Font* group] to both the title and subtitle. Change the title font size to **66 pts**. and the subtitle font size to **28 pts**. [*Home* tab, *Font* group].

7. Add slides.
   a. Click the **New Slide** button [*Home* tab, *Slides* group] to add a new slide that automatically has the **Title and Content** layout. Type the following text for slide 2:

   Slide 2 Title — Our Services
   Bulleted items — Garden center
   Tree nursery
   Gift shop
   Delivery and installation
   Patios and irrigation systems

   b. Repeat this process to create three new slides with the following text:

   Slide 3 Title — Available Products
   Bulleted items — Shrubs, perennials, annuals
   Soils and mulches
   Garden décor including fountains
   Shade trees and evergreen screening trees
   Flowering or ornamental trees
   Trees and plants for Christmas

   Slide 4 Title — Why Sustainable Design?
   Bulleted items — Energy efficiency increased
   Water efficiency increased
   Dependency on chemicals decreased
   Vigor assured through native and hardy plants

   Slide 5 Title — We Make It Easy
   Bulleted items (indent as shown) — We can do the entire project or we can assist
   - You can do as much, or as little, as you like

   We will provide:
   - Landscape design planning or just advice
   - Soil testing
   - Low-cost delivery
   - Fountain set up

   c. Click the **New Slide** list arrow [*Home* tab, *Slides* group] and click the **Title Slide** layout. Type this text in the placeholders:

Title	Call for a Consultation
Subtitle	615-792-8833

8. Move the slide 5 thumbnail before slide 4.

9. Apply bold and use the *Format Painter*.
   a. On slide 2, select the title text and apply **bold**.
   b. Double-click the **Format Painter** button [*Home* tab, *Clipboard* group] so you can apply this change more than one time.

c. Press **Page Down** and click the title text on slide 3 to apply the same change.
d. Repeat for slides 4 and 5.
e. Click the **Format Painter** button or press **Esc** to stop applying formatting.

10. Increase the font size on other slides.
    a. On slide 2, select the bulleted text placeholder and click the **Increase Font Size** button [*Home* tab, *Font* group] to increase the font size to **24 pts**.
    b. Repeat for slides 3-5. On slide 4, the font size for level 2 bulleted text changes to **20 pts**.
    c. On slide 6, increase the font size for the phone number to **32 pts**.

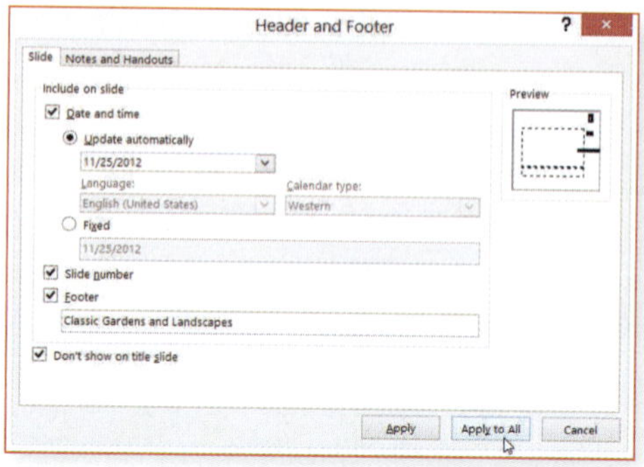

1-88 *Header and Footer* dialog box

11. Create a footer with the company name in the footer text.
    a. Click the **Header & Footer** button [*Insert* tab, *Text* group].
    b. On the *Slide* tab, select **Date and time** with **Update automatically**, **Slide number**, and **Footer** (Figure 1-88).
    c. In the *Footer* text box, type Classic Gardens and Landscapes.
    d. Select **Don't show on title slide**.
    e. Click the **Apply to All** button.

1-89 Completed title slide

12. Click the **Spelling** button [*Review* tab, *Proofing* group] and correct any spelling errors you find.

13. Make the title slide look more distinctive by adjusting the placeholders and inserting the company logo and a picture.
    a. On slide 1, select the subtitle and click the **Change Case** button; then select **Capitalize Each Word**.
    b. Click the **Insert** tab; then click the **Pictures** button.
    c. Locate the folder where your files are saved.
    d. Select ***GardenView-01.jpg*** and click **Insert** to insert the picture.
    e. Align the picture, title, and subtitle as shown in Figure 1-89.
    f. Follow the same procedure to insert the logo, which is a picture file named ***CGLLogo-01.png***.

14. Resize the logo width to **5.5"** [*Picture Tools Format* tab, *Size* group] and the height will automatically adjust. Position the logo as shown in Figure 1-89.

15. Save and close the presentation (Figure 1-90).

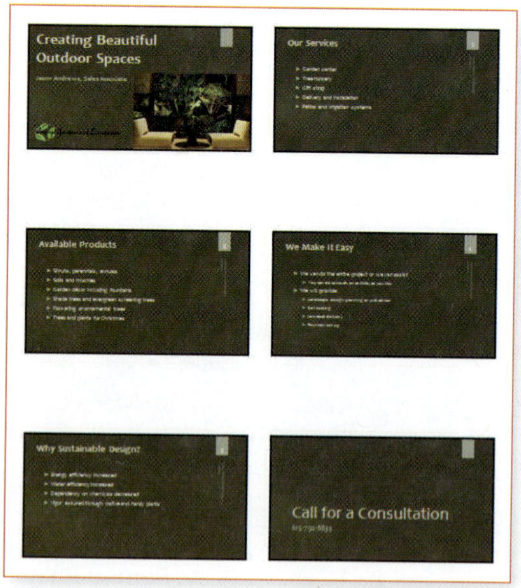

1-90 PowerPoint 1-1 completed

Guided Project 1-2

Solution Seekers, Inc., a management consulting firm, is preparing a series of brief presentations to be used in a training program for new hires. For this project, you develop a presentation about how to get better results when writing email messages.
[Student Learning Outcomes 1.1, 1.2, 1.3, 1.6, 1.7, 1.8, 1.9]

Files Needed: ***EmailResults-01.pptx***, ***EmailContent-01.pptx***, and ***AtSymbol-01.jpg***
Completed Project File Name: ***[your initials] PowerPoint 1-2.pptx***

Skills Covered in This Project

- Open a presentation.
- Change bullets.
- Reuse slides from another presentation.
- Rearrange slides.
- Check spelling.
- Adjust placeholder position.
- Insert a picture.
- Apply transitions.
- Preview a presentation.
- Change presentation properties.
- Print a handout.
- Save a presentation.

1. Open and rename a presentation.
   a. Open the ***EmailResults-01*** presentation from your student files.
   b. Press **F12** to open the *Save As* dialog box and save this presentation as ***[your initials] PowerPoint 1-2***.
2. On slide 2, change the bullets to emphasize them more.
   a. Select the bulleted text.
   b. Click the **Bullets** list arrow [*Home* tab, *Paragraph* group].
   c. Select **Bullets and Numbering**.
   d. Click the **Color** button and select **Brown**, **Text 2** (Figure 1-91).
   e. Change the size to **80%** of text.
   f. Click the **Customize** button and change the font (if necessary) to **Wingdings 2** (Figure 1-92).
   g. Select the bold **X** (Character code 211) and click **OK** to close the *Symbol* dialog box.
   h. Click **OK** again to close the *Bullets and Numbering* dialog box.
3. Reuse slides from another presentation.
   a. Click the **New Slide** list arrow and select **Reuse Slides**.
   b. On the *Reuse Slides* pane, click **Browse**; then select **Browse file** and locate your student files.
   c. Select the presentation ***EmailContent-01*** and click **Open**. (This presentation has spelling errors that you will fix later.)

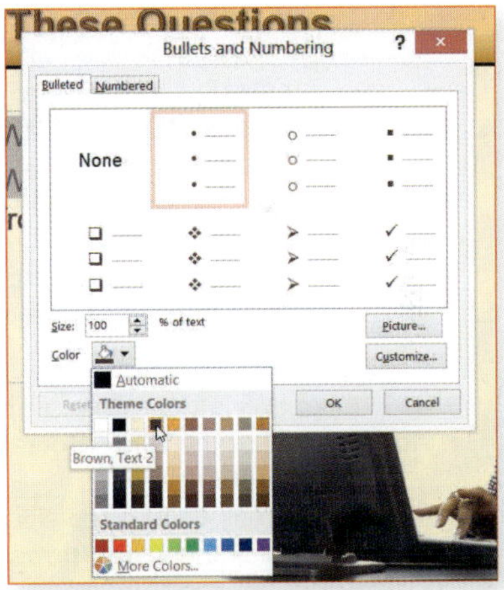

1-91 Change bullet color

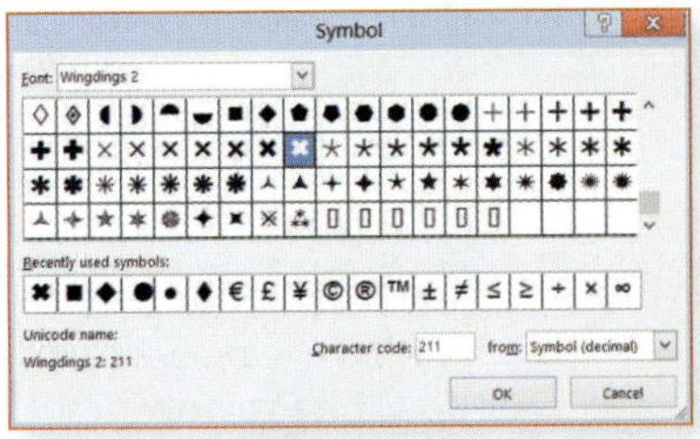

1-92 Change bullet symbol

d. On the *Reuse* Slides pane (Figure 1-93), click all four slides to insert them.
e. Close the *Reuse Slides* pane.

4. On the *Slides* tab, rearrange the six slides in this order: "Getting Results with Email," "Ask These Questions, Why?," "Write a Meaningful Subject Line," Organize It!," and "Keep It Short."
5. Click the **Spelling** button [*Review* tab, *Proofing* group] and correct each of the spelling errors.
6. Use the *Format Painter* to change bullets.
   a. On slide 2, select the body placeholder with the bulleted text.
   b. Double-click the **Format Painter** button [*Home* tab, *Clipboard* group] so you can apply what you have copied more than one time.
   c. Press **Page Down** and click the list on slide 3 to apply the change for the first-level bullets.
   d. Repeat for slides 4 and 5.
   e. Press **Esc** to end formatting.

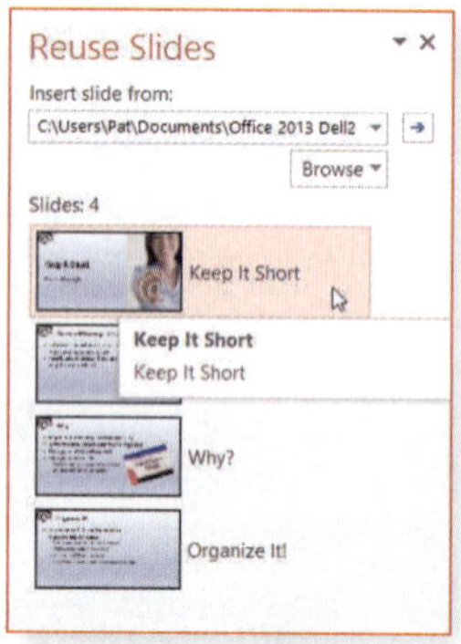

1-93 *Reuse Slides* pane

7. On slide 3, move the picture down so it does not overlap the listed text.
8. On slide 6, use a different picture and adjust text position.
   a. Delete the picture on the right.
   b. Click the **Insert** tab; then click the **Pictures** button.
   c. Locate the folder where your student files are saved.
   d. Select ***AtSymbol-01.jpg*** and click **Insert** to insert the picture.
   e. Adjust the size of the title and subtitle placeholders to fit the text; then position them both on the gold shape.
   f. Align the picture, title, and subtitle as shown in Figure 1-94.

1-94 Completed ending slide

9. Apply one transition to all slides.
   a. Click the **Slide Sorter** button [*Status bar*].
   b. Press **Ctrl+A** to select all slides.
   c. Click the **Transitions** tab.
   d. Click the **Switch** transition from the gallery.
10. Change the movement direction.
   a. With all slides selected, click **Effect Options** [*Transition* tab, *Transition to This Slide* group] (Figure 1-95).
   b. Select **Left**.

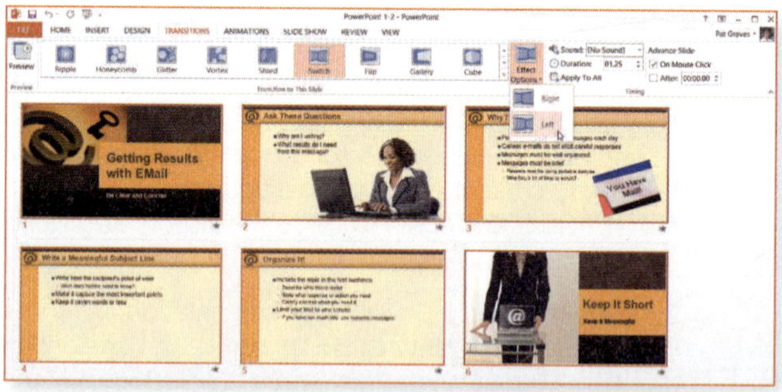

1-95 *Effect Options*

11. Preview the presentation.
   a. Click **Preview** [*Transitions* tab] to examine the movements in *Slide Sorter* view.
   b. Click off a slide to remove the selections.
   c. Click the **Slide Show** button [*Status bar*] and advance through the slides to see the movements in *Slide Show* view.

12. Change some of the presentation properties.
    a. Click the **File** tab, then the **Info** button.
    b. Click the **Properties** button; then click **Show Document Panel**. Type this information in the respective fields.

       Author: Your Name *(unless it already appears)*
       Title: Getting Results with Email *(already entered)*
       Subject: Writing
       Comments: This presentation is for the new hire seminar.

    c. Click the **Close** button to close the *Document Properties* panel.
13. Print slides as a handout.
    a. Click the **File** tab, then the **Print** button on the left.
    b. Select the appropriate printer.
    c. Change the following *Settings* by clicking the button list arrow for each option:

       Which Slides to Print: **Print All Slides**
       What to Print: **Handouts**, **6 Slides Horizontal**, **Frame Slides**, **Scale to Fit Paper**
       Print Order: **Collated**
       Orientation: **Portrait**
       Color Range: **Grayscale** (or **Color** if you prefer)

    d. Click the **Print** button at the top of the *Backstage* view.
14. Save and close the presentation (Figure 1-96).

1-96 PowerPoint 1-2 completed

Guided Project 1-3

At Placer Hills Real Estate, realtors are always thinking of ways to help sellers make their homes more marketable and help buyers find the right home. For this project, you prepare a presentation for realtors to use when they speak with individual clients to explain how sellers can provide an added-value benefit by offering a home warranty.
[Student Learning Outcomes 1.1, 1.2, 1.5, 1.6, 1.7, 1.9]

Files Needed: ***PHRELogo-01.png*** and ***HomeWarranty-01.pptx***
Completed Project File Name: ***[your initials] PowerPoint 1-3.pptx***

Skills Covered in This Project

- Create a new presentation using an online template.
- Change font size.
- Adjust picture position.
- Insert a picture.
- Reuse slides from another presentation.
- Check spelling.
- Insert a footer.
- Apply transitions.
- Change presentation properties.
- Save a presentation.

1. Create a new presentation using an online template.
   a. Click the **File** tab; then click **New**.
   b. In the search box, type the search term real estate and click the **Start Searching** button or press **Enter**.
   c. Select the **For sale design template** (Figure 1-97) and click **Create** to download it. Although it is called a template, it contains only background graphics and no content that you need to remove. This template uses the 4:3 aspect ratio. (If you are unable to download the file, it is available as the presentation ***ForSale-01.pptx*** in your student files.)

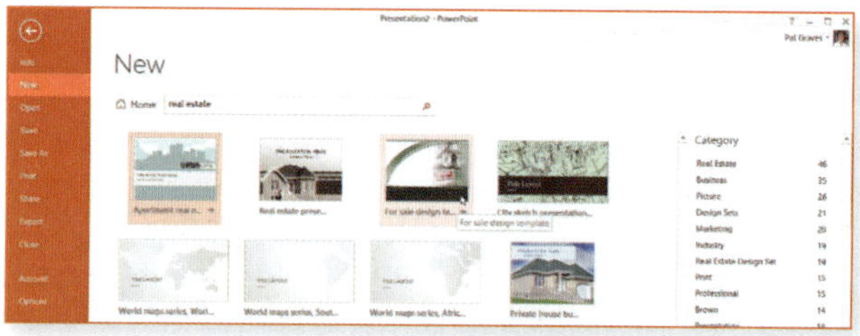

1-97 Online real estate themes and templates

2. Save the presentation as ***[your initials] PowerPoint 1-3***.
3. Type the following text in the placeholders on slide 1:

Title	Gremlin-Proof Sales
Subtitle	Angie O'Connor Sales Associate

4. Increase the font size of the title to **60 pts**. and move the placeholder down slightly.
5. Insert the PHRE company logo.
   a. Click the **Picture** button [*Insert* tab, *Images* group] and locate your student files.
   b. Select ***PHRELogo-01.png*** and click **Insert** (or double-click the file name) to insert the picture.
   c. Position this logo in the upper left as shown in Figure 1-98.

1-98 Completed title slide

6. Reuse slides from another presentation.
   a. Click the **New Slide** list arrow and select **Reuse Slides**.
   b. On the *Reuse Slides* pane, click **Browse**. Select **Browse file** and locate your student files.
   c. Select the presentation ***HomeWarranty-01*** and click **Open**.
   d. On the *Reuse Slides* pane (Figure 1-99), click slides 2–6 to insert them.
   e. Close the *Reuse Slides* pane.
7. Click the **Spelling** button [*Review* tab, *Proofing* group] and correct any spelling errors.

8. On slide 6, resize the picture on the top to stretch it to the top of the slide.
9. Add a footer to all slides except the title slide.
   a. Click the **Header & Footer** button [*Insert* tab, *Text* group].
   b. On the *Slide* tab, select *Slide number* and *Footer*.
   c. In the *Footer* text box, type Placer Hills Real Estate.
   d. Select *Don't show on title slide*.
   e. Click the **Apply to All** button.
10. Apply one transition to all slides.
   a. Click the **Slide Sorter** button [*Status bar*].
   b. Press **Ctrl+A** to select all slides.
   c. Click the **Transitions** tab.
   d. Click the **More** button to open the gallery; then click the **Box** effect.
   e. Click **Effect Options** [*Transitions* tab, *Transition to This Slide* group].
   f. Select **From Bottom** (Figure 1-100).
   g. Click **Preview** [*Transitions* tab] to see the movements in *Slide Sorter* view.
   h. Click the **Slide Show** button [*Status bar*] and advance through the slides to see the movements in *Slide Show* view.
   i. Double-click slide 1 to return to *Normal* view.

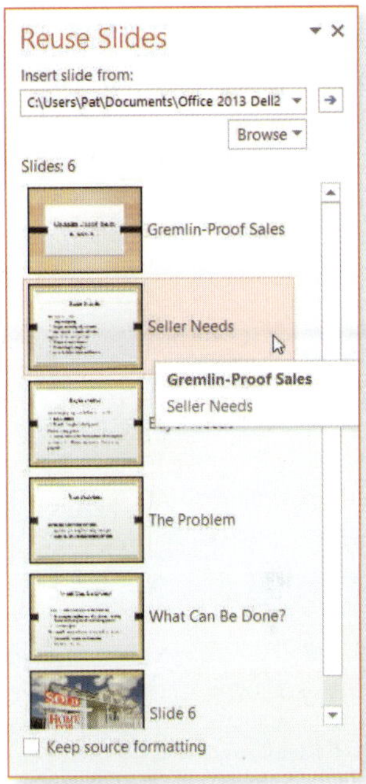

1-99 *Reuse Slides* pane

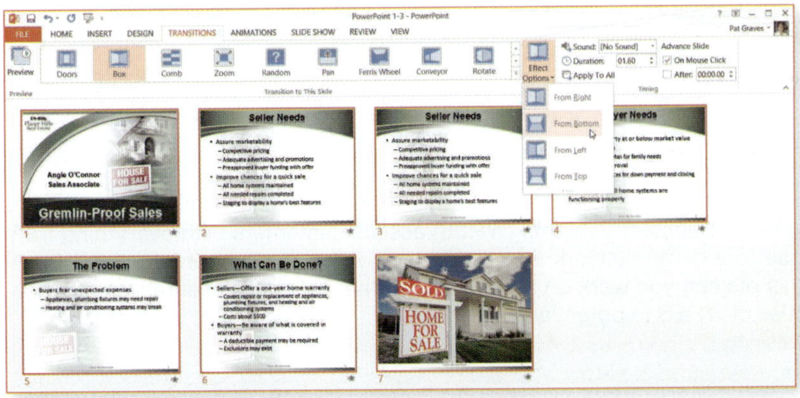

1-100 Transition Effect Options

11. Change some of the presentation properties.
   a. Click the **File** tab; then click the **Info** button.
   b. Click the **Properties** button; then click **Show Document Panel**. Type the following information in the respective fields:

Author	Angie O'Connor
Title	Gremlin-Proof Sales
Subject	Sales Strategies
Comments	Seller can offer a home warranty to encourage buyer purchase.

   c. Click the **Close** button to close the *Document Properties Panel*.

12. Save and close the presentation (Figure 1-101).

1-101 PowerPoint 1-3 completed

Independent Project 1-4

Wilson Home Entertainment Systems (WHES) assists customers with everything from a single television purchase to a home network installation to the design and construction of an elaborate home theater. In this project, you work on a presentation that sales representatives can use to demonstrate the capabilities of WHES to potential customers.
[Student Learning Outcomes 1.1, 1.2, 1.4, 1.6, 1.7, 1.9]

Files Needed: ***SpecialEnvironment-01.pptx***, ***WHESLogo-01.png***, ***Family-01.jpg***, and ***Theater1-01.jpg***
Completed Project File Name: ***[your initials] PowerPoint 1-4.pptx***

Skills Covered in This Project

- Open a presentation.
- Add slides.
- Apply a theme.
- Change theme colors.
- Insert a picture.
- Adjust placeholders.
- Check spelling.
- Apply transitions.
- Change presentation properties.
- Save a presentation.

1. Open the presentation ***SpecialEnvironment-01***.
2. Save the presentation as ***[your initials] PowerPoint 1-4***.
3. After slide 1, insert two new slides. Type the following text for slides 2 and 3:

Slide 2 Title	Our Residential Services
Bulleted items	Design Sales Installation Maintenance
Slide 3 Title	Sales
Bulleted items	Authorized dealer for the highest-quality home theater technology in the industry Televisions Video Projectors Blu-Ray Players Audio Systems

4. Apply a theme and change theme colors.
   a. Select the **Integral** theme and the third **Variant** (Figure 1-102).
   b. Click the **View** tab then the **Slide Master** button.
   c. Scroll to the top of the layouts and select the first layout, *Integral Slide Master Layout* on the left so your color changes are applied to all slides.
   d. Click the **Colors** button.
   e. Scroll down the list and click the **Orange Red** theme colors.
   f. Click the **Close Master View** button.

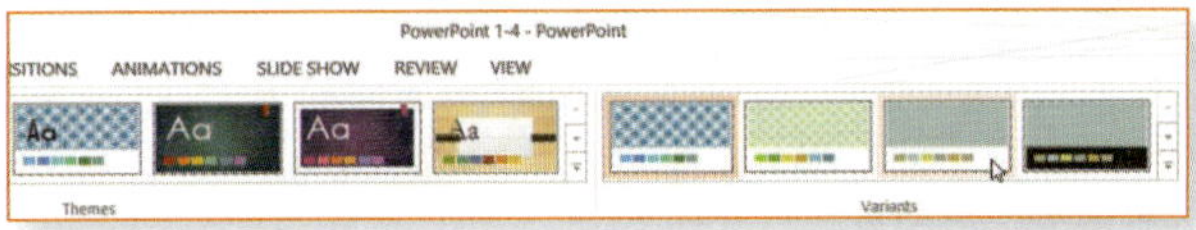

1-102 Change Variant

5. On slide 1, insert different pictures.
   a. Delete the popcorn picture.
   b. Delete the subtitle placeholder.
   c. From your student files, insert ***Family-01.jpg*** and ***WHESLogo-01.png***.
   d. Increase the family picture size (height **5"** and width **7.52"**) and align it on the top right (Figure 1-103).
   e. Align the logo on the bottom right.
   f. Move the title placeholder up and resize it so it fits in the red area on the left and word wraps as shown. Make the text **bold**, change the font color to **White**, increase the font size to **66 pts.**, and apply a **shadow**.

1-103 Completed title slide

6. Click the **Spelling** button and correct any spelling errors you find.
7. On slide 2, increase the text size and insert a picture.
   a. Select the bulleted text placeholder and change the font size to **40 pts**.
   b. From your student files, insert ***Theater1-01.jpg*** and increase the picture size (height **5"** and width **7.52"**) and align it on the bottom right.

8. On slide 6, increase the picture size (height **2.18"** and width **9"**) and center it horizontally in the space below the text.
9. Apply one transition to all slides.
   a. In *Slide Sorter* view, select all the slides and apply the **Cube** transition.
   b. Apply the **From Right** effect option.
   c. Double-click slide 1 to return to *Normal* view.
10. Insert the following presentation properties using the **Document Properties Panel:**

    Author Liam Martin
    Title Create Your Special Environment
    Subject Residential Services

11. Save and close the presentation (Figure 1-104).

1-104 PowerPoint 1-4 completed

Independent Project 1-5

The Advising Offices in the Sierra Pacific Community College (SPCC) District work to assist students throughout the completion of their academic programs. Because SPCC has a large population of students who are retraining themselves for different types of employment, job-related information is especially important. For this project, you prepare a presentation about writing resumes.
[Student Learning Outcomes 1.1, 1.2, 1.3, 1.4, 1.7, 1.8]

File Needed: ***ResumeUpdates-01.pptx***
Completed Project File Name: ***[your initials] PowerPoint 1-5.pptx***

Skills Covered in This Project

- Open a presentation using an online template.
- Add slides.
- Reuse slides from another presentation.
- Rearrange slides.
- Change theme colors.
- Change bullets.
- Adjust placeholders.
- Check spelling.
- Apply transitions.
- Print a handout.
- Save a presentation.

1. Create a new presentation from an online template.
   a. Click the **File** tab; then click **New**.
   b. In the search box, type business woman design template and press **Enter**.
   c. Select the **Business woman design template** (Figure 1-105) and click **Create** to download it. This template uses the 4:3 aspect ratio. (If you are unable to download the file, it is available as the presentation ***Business-01.pptx*** in your student files.)
2. Save the presentation as ***[your initials] PowerPoint 1-5***.

1-105 Online business woman themes and templates

3. On slide 1, type the following text:

Title	Resume Updates
Subtitle	Your First Impression

4. After slide 1, insert two new slides. Type the following text for slides 2 and 3:

Slide 2 Title: Accomplishments, Not Duties
Bulleted items:
- Include only the most impressive details about your career
- Quantify your day-to-day tasks
  - How many times?
  - What was the result?
  - How much money was saved?

Slide 3 Title: Proofread
Bulleted items:
- Employers take spelling and grammar errors as signs of carelessness
- Ask a trusted friend or colleague to look at your resume

5. Reuse slides from another presentation.
   a. Click the **New Slide** list arrow and select **Reuse Slides**.
   b. On the *Reuse Slides* pane, click **Browse** and select **Browse file**. Locate the student file ***ResumeUpdates-01*** and click **Open**.
   c. On the *Reuse Slides* pane, click all three slides to insert them.
   d. Close the *Reuse Slides* pane.
6. Move the slide 3 (*Proofread*) thumbnail to the end of the presentation.
7. Change theme colors.
   a. Click the **View** tab; then the **Slide Master** button.
   b. Select the first *Master Layout* on the left so your color changes are applied to all slides.
   c. Click the **Colors** button and select the **Blue II** theme colors (Figure 1-106).
   d. Click the **Close Master View** button.

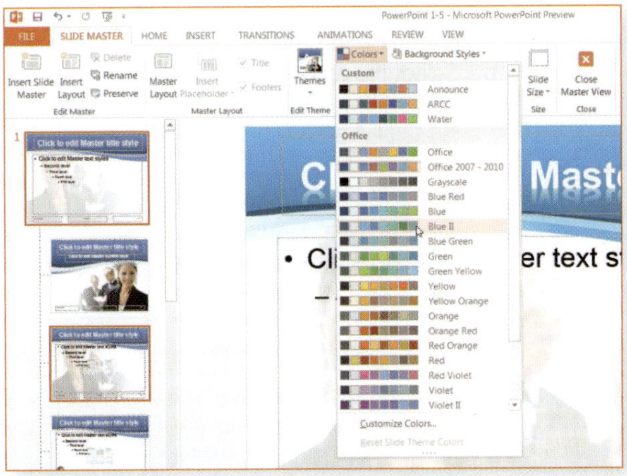

1-106 Change theme colors

8. On slide 2, change the bullets to emphasize them more.
   a. Select the level 1 bulleted text.
   b. Click the **Bullets** list arrow and select **Bullets and Numbering**.
   c. Click the **Color** button and select **Dark Teal**, **Text 2**.
   d. Change the size to **80%** of text if necessary.
   e. Click the **Customize** button and change the font to **Wingdings 2** (Figure 1-107).
   f. Select the large diamond (Character code 191) and click **OK** to close the *Symbol* dialog box.
   g. Click **OK** again to close the *Bullets and Numbering* dialog box.
9. On slide 2, resize the top of the bulleted text placeholder by dragging it down so the text does not overlap the decorative blue title area. Repeat for all other slides.
10. Use **Format Painter** to change the level 1 bullets on all other slides.
11. On slide 1, change the title and subtitle placeholders to **Left alignment**; then align both placeholders on the left (but not to the slide) (Figure 1-108).
12. Click the **Spelling** button and correct any spelling errors you find.
13. Apply one transition to all slides.
    a. Click the **Transitions** tab and apply the **Reveal** transition.
    b. Apply the **Through Black from Right** effect option.
    c. Click **Apply To All**.
14. Print slides as an outline (Figure 1-109).
    a. Click the **File** tab; then click the **Print** button on the left.
    b. Select the appropriate printer.
    c. Change the following *Settings* by clicking the list arrow for each option as necessary:

       Which Slides to Print: **Print All Slides**
       What to Print: **Outline**
       Print Side: **Print One Sided**
       Print Order: **Collated**
       Orientation: **Portrait**
       Color Range: **Grayscale**

    d. Click the **Print** button at the top of the *Backstage* view.

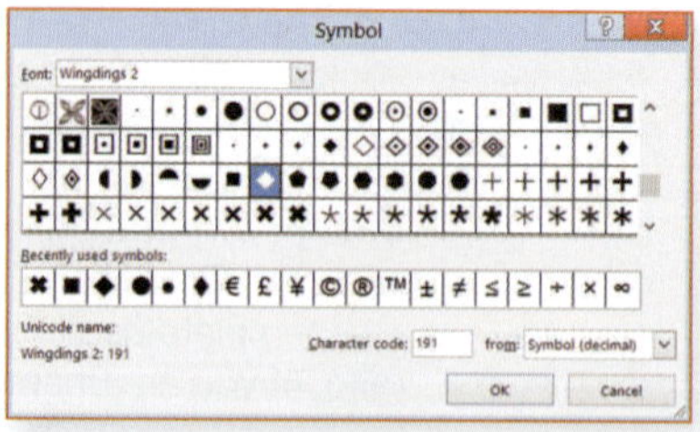

1-107 Change bullet symbol

1-108 Completed title slide

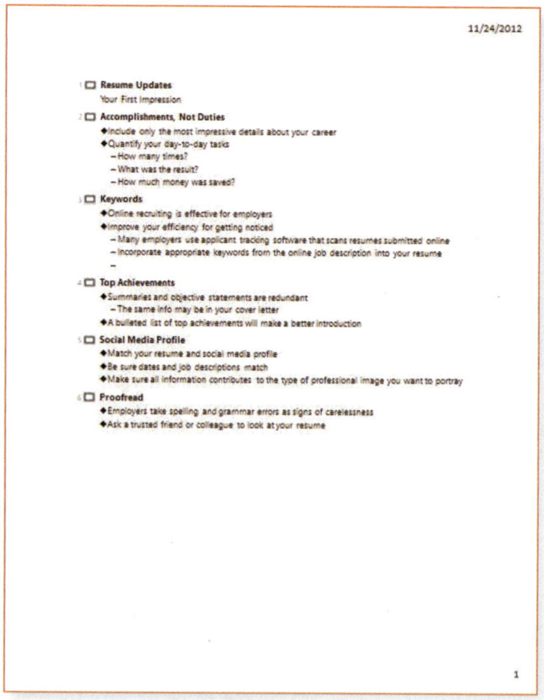

11/24/2012

1 Resume Updates
Your First Impression
2 Accomplishments, Not Duties
◆Include only the most impressive details about your career
◆Quantify your day-to-day tasks
– How many times?
– What was the result?
– How much money was saved?
3 Keywords
◆Online recruiting is effective for employers
◆Improve your efficiency for getting noticed
– Many employers use applicant tracking software that scans resumes submitted online
– Incorporate appropriate keywords from the online job description into your resume
–
4 Top Achievements
◆Summaries and objective statements are redundant
– The same info may be in your cover letter
◆A bulleted list of top achievements will make a better introduction
5 Social Media Profile
◆Match your resume and social media profile
◆Be sure dates and job descriptions match
◆Make sure all information contributes to the type of professional image you want to portray
6 Proofread
◆Employers take spelling and grammar errors as signs of carelessness
◆Ask a trusted friend or colleague to look at your resume

1

1-109 Outline

15. Save and close the presentation (Figure 1-110).

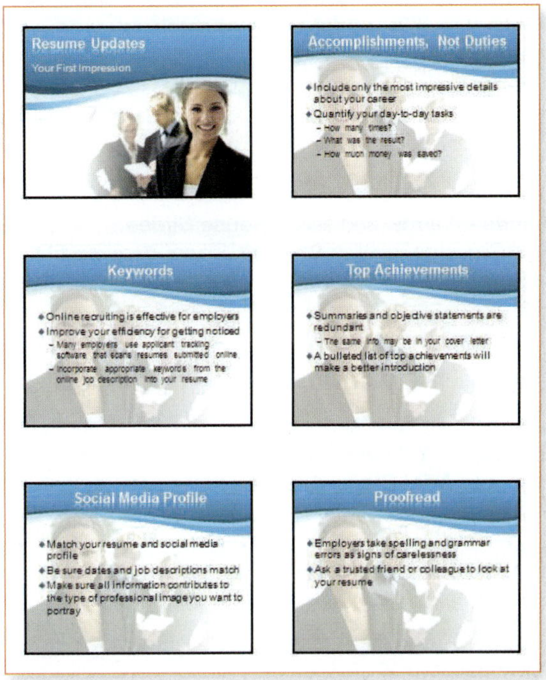

1-110 PowerPoint 1-5 completed

Independent Project 1-6

At the Hendersonville Civic Center, workshops are given for the community to address fitness, health, and wellness issues. For this project, you develop a presentation for an upcoming series about helping families become more active.
[Student Learning Outcomes 1.1, 1.2, 1.3, 1.4, 1.5, 1.6, 1.7, 1.9]

Files Needed: ***PedestrianSafety-01.pptx***, ***Walk1-01.jpg***, and ***Walk2-01.jpg***
Completed Project File Name: ***[your initials] PowerPoint 1-6.pptx***

Skills Covered in This Project

- Create a new presentation using a theme.
- Change case.
- Reuse slides from another presentation.
- Check spelling.
- Change theme colors.
- Change theme fonts.
- Rearrange slides.
- Insert a picture.
- Adjust placeholders.
- Insert a footer.
- Apply transitions.
- Change presentation properties.
- Save a presentation.

1. Create a new presentation and select the **Retrospect** theme and **Green** variant.
2. Save the presentation as ***[your initials] PowerPoint 1-6***.
3. On slide 1, type the following text:

   Title Pedestrian Safety Matters
   Subtitle Keeping That New Year's Resolution To Be More Active

4. Select the subtitle text and change the case to **Capitalize Each Word**.
5. Click the **New Slide** list arrow and select **Reuse Slides**.
   a. On the *Reuse Slides* pane, click **Browse**. Select **Browse file** and locate your student file ***PedestrianSafety-01***. Click **Open**.
   b. On the *Reuse Slides* pane, click all slides to insert them.
   c. Close the *Reuse Slides* pane.
6. Click the **Spelling** button [*Review* tab, *Proofing* group] and correct any spelling errors.
7. Click **View**, then **Slide Master**, and change theme colors and fonts.
   a. Change the colors to **Yellow Orange** and the background style to **Style 6**.
   b. Change the font to **Arial Black-Arial** (the font pairs are not listed in alphabetical order).
   c. Click **Close Master View**.
8. Adjust slide order to match the sequence shown in Figure 1-111.

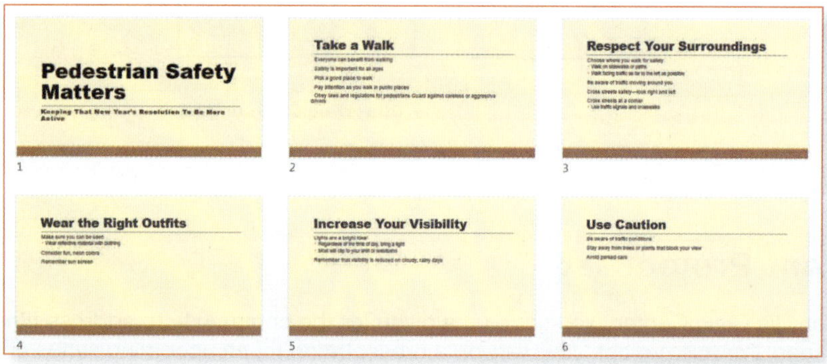

1-111 Slide order

9. On slide 1, insert a picture and resize the placeholders.
   a. From your student files, insert the picture ***Walk1-01.jpg***.
   b. Change the picture height to **7.5"** and align it to the slide on the top right.
   c. Adjust the size of the title and subtitle placeholders so the text wraps as shown in Figure 1-112.
10. On slide 2, put your insertion point in front of the word "Guard" and press **Enter**.

1-112 Completed title slide

11. Add a footer to all slides except the title slide.
    a. Click the **Header and Footer** button.
    b. On the *Slide* tab, select *Slide number* and *Footer*.
    c. In the *Footer* text box, type Pedestrian Safety Matters.
    d. Select **Don't show on title slide**.
    e. Click the **Apply to All** button.
12. On slide 6, insert a picture and resize the placeholder.
    a. From your student files, insert the picture ***Walk2-01.jpg***.
    b. Change the picture height to **7.5"** and align it to the slide on the top right.
13. Apply one transition to all slides.
    a. In *Slide Sorter* view, select all the slides.
    b. Select the **Push** transition and apply the **From Right** effect option.
14. Preview the transitions in *Slide Show* view.
15. Change these presentation properties using the *Document Properties* panel.

Author	Anna Lorenzo
Title	Pedestrian Safety Matters
Subject	Active Lifestyle

16. Click the **Close** button to close the *Document Properties* panel.
17. Save and close the presentation (Figure 1-113).

1-113 PowerPoint 1-6 completed

Improve It Project 1-7

For this project, you revise a presentation for Margaret Jepson, insurance agent at Central Sierra Insurance. You apply a design theme, adjust its appearance, and add other information to the slide show, including a picture.
[Student Learning Outcomes 1.1, 1.2, 1.3, 1.4, 1.5, 1.6, 1.7, 1.8, 1.9]

Files Needed: ***TotaledCar-01.pptx***, ***Cars-01.jpg***, and ***CSILogo-01.png***
Completed Project File Name: ***[your initials] PowerPoint 1-7.pptx***

Skills Covered in This Project

- Open a presentation.
- Change theme colors.
- Check spelling.
- Insert a picture.
- Adjust placeholders.
- Insert a footer.
- Apply transitions.
- Change presentation properties.
- Print a handout.
- Save a presentation.

1. Open the presentation ***TotaledCar-01***.
2. Save the presentation as ***[your initials] PowerPoint 1-7***.
3. Use the *Slide Master* to change the theme colors and fonts.
   a. Theme colors: **Yellow**
   b. Theme background style: **Style 6**
   c. Theme font: **Gil Sans MT**
4. Check spelling and correct any spelling errors.
5. On slide 1, make text changes and insert a picture and logo (Figure 1-114).
   a. Change the title font size to **66 pts**., make the text fit on two lines, and position the placeholder on the right of the slide beside the picture.
   b. Delete the subtitle placeholder.
   c. Insert ***Cars-01*** and align it on the left of the slide.
   d. Insert ***CSILogo-01***, change the width to **5"**, and position it below the title text on the lower right of the slide.

1-114 Completed title slide

6. On slide 5, make the following changes:
   a. Change the slide layout to **Title Only**.
   b. Change the font size to **54 pts**. and apply right alignment.
   c. Align the placeholder on the middle right of the slide.
7. Add header and footer text and slide numbering to all slides except the title slide.

   Slide footer text: The Totaled Car
   Handout header text: Central Sierra Insurance

8. Apply the **Reveal** transition to all slides with the **Through Black from Right** effect option.

9. Change the effect option on slide 5 to **Through Black from Left**.
10. Preview the transitions.
11. Change these presentation properties using the **Document Properties Panel**.

    Author: Margaret Jepson
    Title: Totaled Car? What Next?
    Subject: Accident Insurance

12. Print a handout with 6 slides on a page, horizontal, framed, and sized to fit paper.
13. Save and close the presentation (Figure 1-115).

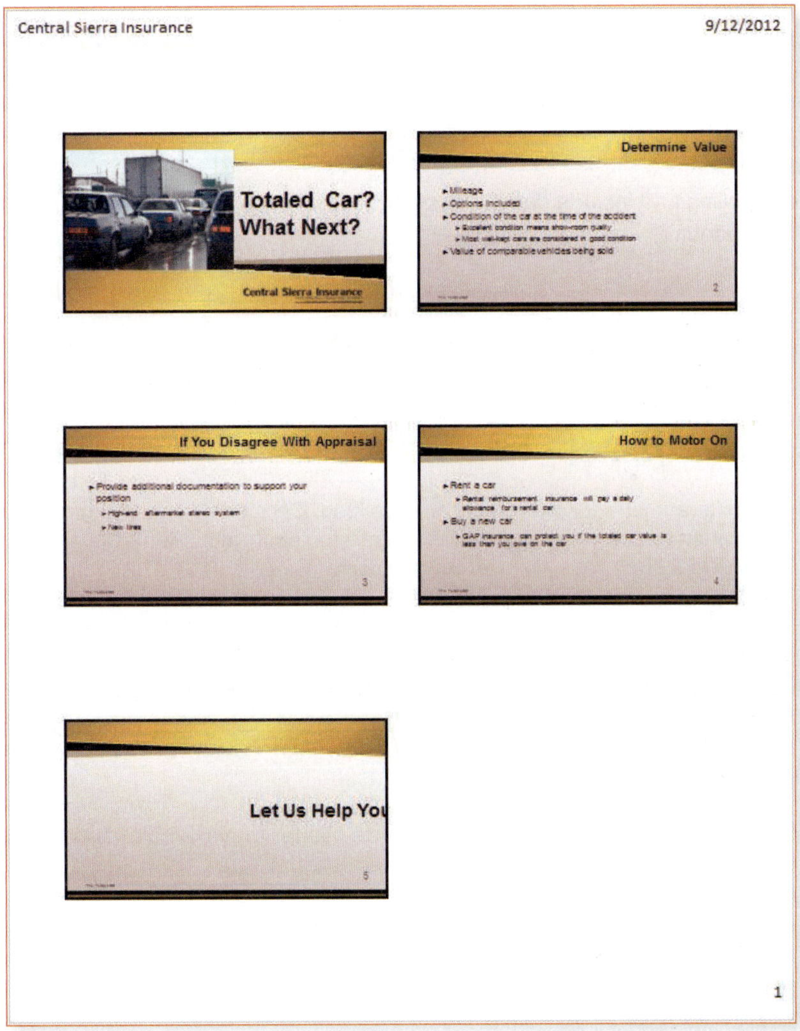

1-115 PowerPoint 1-7 completed

Challenge Project 1-8

For this project, tell the story of your favorite vacation. Create six slides that introduce the topic and describe your main points with bulleted lists. Insert photographs to illustrate locations and resize them to fit with related text.
[Student Learning Outcomes 1.1, 1.2, 1.4, 1.5, 1.6, 1.7, 1.8, 1.9]

File Needed: None
Completed Project File Name: ***[your initials] PowerPoint 1-8.pptx***

Create a new presentation and save it as ***[your initials] PowerPoint 1-8***. Modify your presentation according to the following guidelines:

- Select an appropriate theme from Office.com for your topic.
- Use different slide layouts for variety.
- Insert three or more pictures.
- Add a footer.
- Apply transitions.
- Check spelling and include document properties.
- Print a handout.

Challenge Project 1-9

Think about different jobs for which you are qualified. On the Internet, research four different jobs and identify several characteristics and requirements for each job. Many online resources provide job-related information, such as www.careerbuilder.com.
[Student Learning Outcomes 1.1, 1.2, 1.3, 1.4, 1.5, 1.6, 1.7, 1.8, 1.9]

File Needed: None
Completed Project File Name: ***[your initials] PowerPoint 1-9.pptx***

Create a new presentation and save it as ***[your initials] PowerPoint 1-9***. Modify your presentation according to the following guidelines:

- Select an appropriate theme and use the Slide Master to make color and font changes as needed for your topic.
- Create a distinctive title slide.
- Write bulleted lists describing the characteristics and requirements of each different job with no more than seven lines of text on each slide.
- Apply transitions.
- Check spelling and include document properties.
- Print handouts with six slides on a page.

Challenge Project 1-10

For this project, develop a presentation about how a presenter can manage nervous tendencies when presenting in front of an audience. Include information from your own experiences and refer to online resources, such as www.presentationmagazine.com.
[Student Learning Outcomes 1.1, 1.2, 1.3, 1.4, 1.5, 1.6, 1.7, 1.8, 1.9]

File Needed: None
Completed Project File Name: ***[your initials] PowerPoint 1-10.pptx***

Create a new presentation and save it as ***[your initials] PowerPoint 1-10***. Modify your presentation according to the following guidelines:

- Select an appropriate theme and use the Slide Master to make color and font changes as needed for your topic.
- Create a distinctive title slide.
- Write bulleted lists describing typical causes of nervousness and suggest ways to control nervousness when presenting.
- Insert pictures to illustrate concepts.
- Apply transitions.
- Check spelling and include document properties.
- Print an outline of the presentation.

CHAPTER 2

POWERPOINT

Illustrating with Pictures and Information Graphics

CHAPTER OVERVIEW

In our world today, we are surrounded by information graphics. We see them in television programming, web sites, and published material of all kinds. We interpret signage that helps us get from place to place and readily recognize many iconic images that help us with everyday tasks. These graphics communicate visually and can be more effective than long passages of text.

PowerPoint gives you the ability to create information graphics—to visually display information in ways that help an audience quickly grasp the concepts you are presenting. You can choose from many options, such as adding shapes or color for emphasis, pictures to illustrate, diagrams to show processes, and charts to show data relationships.

STUDENT LEARNING OUTCOMES (SLOs)

After completing this chapter, you will be able to:

- **SLO 2.1** Work with shapes, select theme colors and standard colors, and apply styles (p. P2-67).
- **SLO 2.2** Create interesting and eye-catching text with *WordArt* styles and text effects (p. P2-75).
- **SLO 2.3** Search for pictures and illustrations, modify picture appearance, and compress picture file size (p. P2-78).
- **SLO 2.4** Organize information in a grid format using tables and customize the arrangement of columns and rows (p. P2-85).
- **SLO 2.5** Emphasize portions of a table by applying styles, colors, and effects (p. P2-90).
- **SLO 2.6** Show processes and relationships with *SmartArt* graphics (p. P2-94).
- **SLO 2.7** Improve the appearance of *SmartArt* graphics by applying styles, colors, and effects (p. P2-97).
- **SLO 2.8** Create charts that show relationships between data values and emphasize data in different ways (p. P2-101).
- **SLO 2.9** Enhance a chart by applying preset styles or manually customizing individual chart elements (p. P2-105).

CASE STUDY

Classic Gardens and Landscapes (CGL) is a landscape design company that creates beautiful and low-maintenance landscapes for outdoor living spaces. Frank and Sandra Hunter recently bought a home with minimal landscaping from a builder. They contacted Gerod Sunderland, a landscape designer for CGL, to discuss improvements.

Gerod visited the property and designed plans with several options for trees, shrubs, and plants. You have been asked to prepare a presentation illustrating his key points for his meeting with the Hunters.

Pause & Practice 2-1: Add visual interest with picture enhancements and creative text designs.

Pause & Practice 2-2: Prepare a table.

Pause & Practice 2-3: Create an organization chart and convert text to a *SmartArt* graphic.

Pause & Practice 2-4: Create column and pie charts with an enhanced appearance.

SLO 2.1

Working with Shapes, Colors, and Styles

Shapes can emphasize key points. For example, an arrow can point to an object, or a line can connect two related objects. You can draw a variety of shapes using PowerPoint's ***Shapes*** gallery; each shape has both an outline and fill color. The ***Quick Style***, ***Color***, and ***Effects*** galleries make it easy to customize shapes and the other objects you use to illustrate your slides.

Shapes and Text Boxes

To insert a shape, select the shape you want from the *Shapes* gallery [*Insert* tab, *Illustrations* group] and use the following features to draw and adjust your shape:

- ***Crosshair:*** A large plus sign used to draw the shape
- ***Sizing handles:*** Squares on the corners and sides of the shapes used to change shape size
- ***Rotation handle:*** Circular arrow on the top used to make shapes angle
- ***Adjustment handle:*** Squares used to change curves or points

You can add text to shapes and format the text as you do text in a placeholder or in a text box. However, the text in shapes or in text boxes does not appear in *Outline* view.

The *Shapes* gallery (Figure 2-1) is on the *Home* tab, the *Insert* tab, and the *Drawing Tools Format* tab. Shapes are grouped in the following categories:

- *Recently Used Shapes*
- *Lines*
- *Rectangles*
- *Basic Shapes*
- *Block Arrows*
- *Equation Shapes*
- *Flowchart*
- *Stars and Banners*
- *Callouts*
- *Action Buttons*

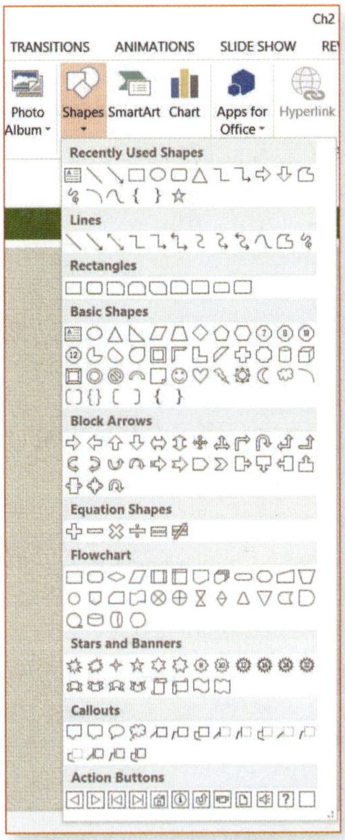

2-1 ***Shapes*** **gallery**

HOW TO: Insert a Shape

1. Click the **Insert** tab.
2. Click the **Shapes** button [*Illustrations* group] to display the *Shapes* gallery.
3. Select the shape you want and your pointer becomes a crosshair (Figure 2-2).
4. Click and drag to draw the shape in the approximate size you need (Figure 2-3). The shape appears with sizing handles and a rotation handle. It may have adjustment handles.
5. Press the **Shift** key while you drag to make oval shapes round, make rectangles square, and make lines straight.
6. Add text if needed.
7. Resize the shape if necessary and move it to the appropriate position on the slide.

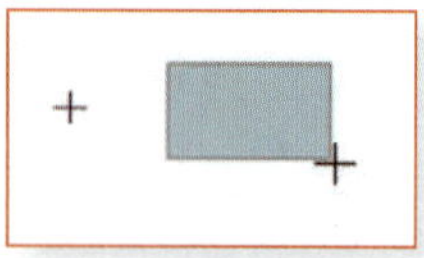

2-2 Crosshair and crosshair drawing a shape

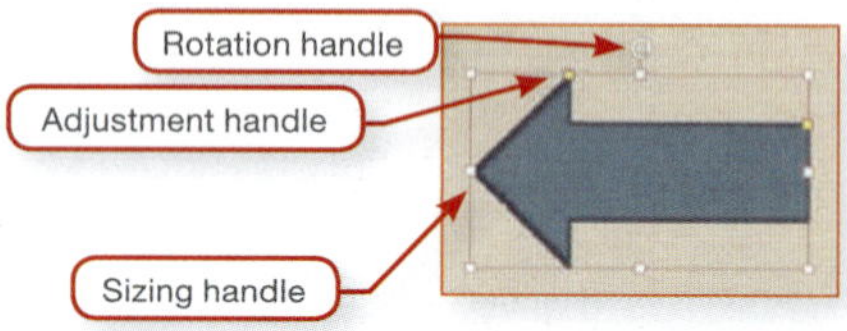

2-3 Shape with handles

When you need more than one of the same shape, you can efficiently draw them using ***Lock Drawing Mode***.

HOW TO: Insert Multiple Shapes

1. Click the **Insert** tab.
2. Click the **Shapes** button [*Illustrations* group] to display the *Shapes* gallery.
3. Right-click the shape you want, and click **Lock Drawing Mode** (Figure 2-4).
4. Draw the first shape. Repeat to draw more of the same shape.
5. When you are finished, press **Esc** to turn off **Lock Drawing Mode**.

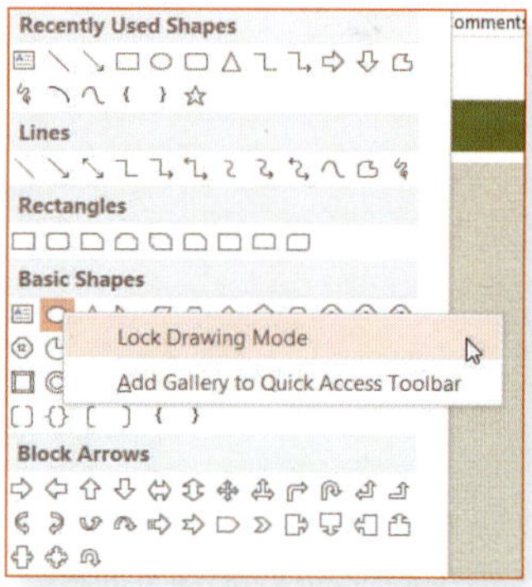

2-4 *Lock Drawing Mode*

When you select an existing shape, the *Drawing Tools Format* tab opens and the *Shapes* gallery is displayed on the left. If the existing shape does not fit your purpose, you can easily change the shape.

HOW TO: Change a Shape to Another Shape

1. Select the shape to be changed.
2. Click the **Edit Shape** arrow [*Drawing Tools Format* tab, *Insert Shapes* group] (Figure 2-5).
3. Select **Change Shape** and click a different shape from the *Shapes* gallery.
4. Click **Undo** to return to your original shape.
5. Click a blank area of the slide to deselect the shape.

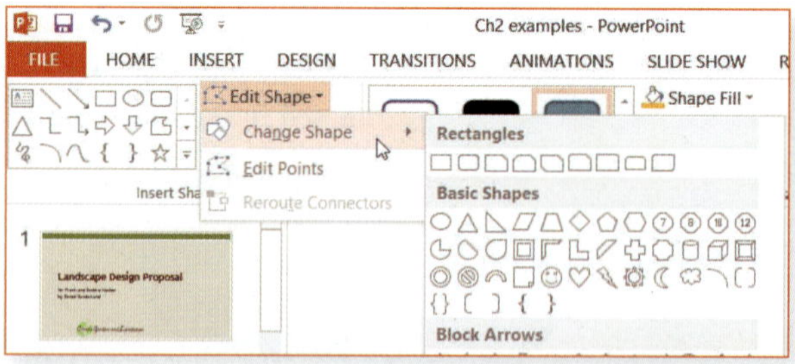

2-5 Change Shape

Using ***text boxes***, you can add text anywhere on a slide without using placeholders. For example, you can add notations to identify slide objects or insert brief phrases you want to emphasize. Text boxes can be sized and moved around like any other shape.

HOW TO: Insert a Text Box

1. Click the **Insert** tab.
2. Click the **Text Box** button and your pointer changes to an insertion point. Create a text box using one of the following methods:
   - Begin typing at the insertion point and the text box grows to fit the text you type in it. The *Home* tab opens.
   - Click to change the pointer to a crosshair and draw a text box (Figure 2-6) in the approximate width you need. The *Home* tab opens. The text box height adjusts as you type text.
3. Resize if necessary by dragging sizing handles or entering height and width sizes [*Drawing Tools Format* tab, *Size* group] (Figure 2-7).
4. Click and drag the text box to move it to an appropriate position on the slide.

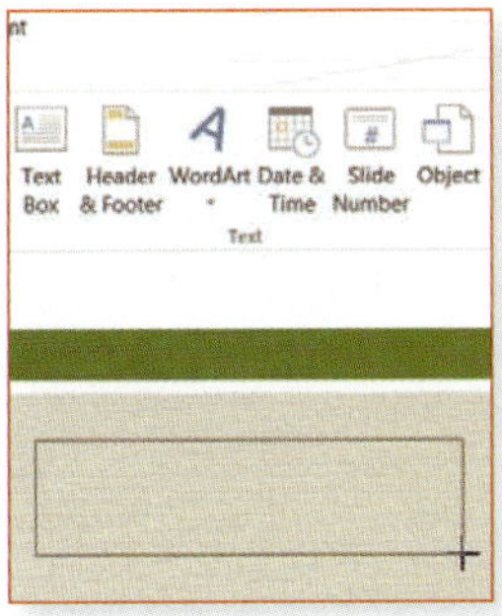

2-6 Draw a text box

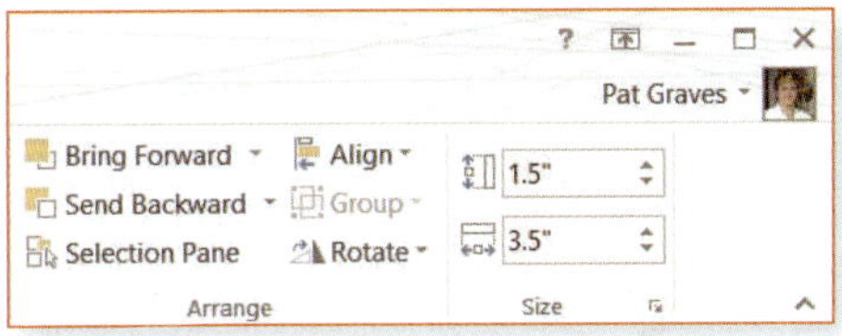

2-7 Size measurements

Style Galleries

Different *Style* galleries provide collections of preset effects for shapes, pictures, or other objects. You can customize all effects using the related button such as ***Shape Effects***, ***Picture Effects***, or ***Text Effects*** to access drop-down galleries. You can choose from *Shadow*, *Reflection*, *Glow*, *Soft Edges*, *Bevel*, or *3D Rotation*. These options are described in the following table. The *Transform* effect is only available for ***Text Effects***. You can also apply one or more effects without first using styles from a gallery.

Style Effect Options

Effect	Options
Shadow	***Shadow*** effects appear in three groupings. An ***Outer*** shadow shows behind an object from different directions. An ***Inner*** shadow makes part of the object looked raised. A ***Perspective*** shadow makes an object "float" with the shadow below.
Reflection	A ***Reflection*** shows a mirror image below an object, like a reflection on a shiny surface or on water. You can control how close the reflection is to the object.
Glow	***Glow*** provides a colored area around an object that fades into the background color on your slide. It is not available for text. Glow colors by default are based on the current theme colors but you can use other colors. The size of the *Glow* is measured in points.
Soft Edges	Some objects, such as pictures or text boxes, have a straight edge on all sides. ***Soft Edges*** creates a feathered edge that gradually blends into the background color. The size of the blending area is measured in points from the edge of the object inward. The larger the point size, the less you see of the object.
Bevel	***Bevel*** effects add light and dark areas to create a dimensional appearance. Objects or text can look raised or inset.
3D Rotation	***3D Rotation*** effects include ***Parallel***, ***Perspective***, and ***Oblique*** options that create an illusion of depth by rotating an object from front to back.
Transform	***Transform*** is a *Text Effect* used to change the shape of words. It is not available for shapes.

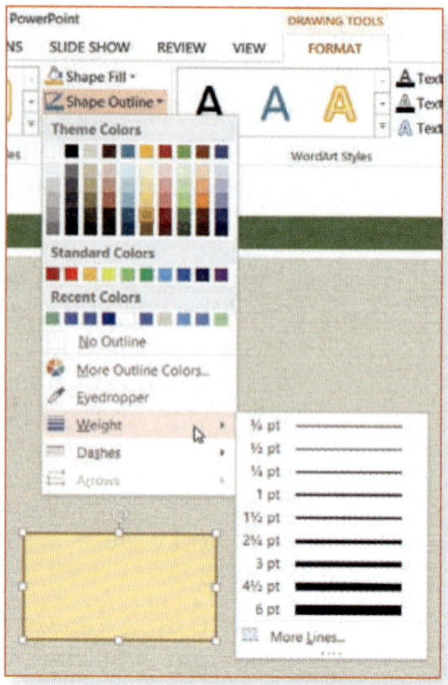

2-8 *Shape Outline Weight*

The width of your PowerPoint window affects how galleries are displayed on the various tabs where they appear. If you have a narrow PowerPoint window, you need to click a quick style button to open a gallery. If your window is wide, part of a gallery is displayed and you click the **More** button to open the complete gallery.

Adjust Outline Weight and Style

You can emphasize an outline by making it wider with a contrasting color; you can deemphasize an outline by making it thinner. You can choose to show no outline or match its color to the shape to make the outline disappear. Select a shape and click the **Shape Outline** button [*Drawing Tools Format* tab, *Shape Styles* group]. Choose one of the following options to see drop-down lists of options (Figure 2-8):

- ***Weight:*** Displays line thickness measured in points
- ***Dashes:*** Displays lines made with various combinations of dots and dashes (Figure 2-9)
- ***Arrows:*** Displays arrowheads or other shapes for both ends of a line.

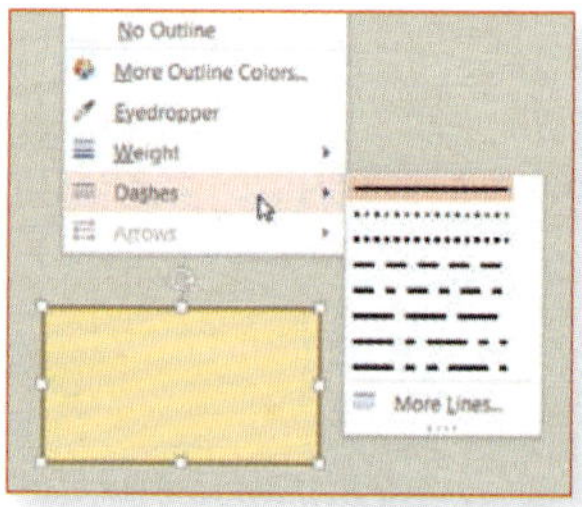

2-9 *Shape Outline Dashes*

At the bottom of each drop-down list, select **More Lines** to open the *Format Shape* pane (Figure 2-10) where you can customize the following *Line* options:

- ***Color:*** Provides color choices
- ***Transparency:*** Adjusts transparency percentages
- ***Width:*** Controls the thickness of lines measured in points
- ***Compound type:*** Provides outlines with two or more lines in different thicknesses
- ***Dash type:*** Displays lines made with various combinations of dots and dashes
- ***Cap type:*** Controls the look (*Square, Round,* or *Flat*) of the ends of lines; it is usually applied to single lines or arrows
- ***Join type:*** Controls the look (*Round, Bevel, Miter*) for the connection point where two lines meet (for example, at the corner of a rectangle or square)
- ***Begin and End Arrow type:*** Controls the shape for both ends of an arrow
- ***Begin and End Arrow size:*** Controls the size of the shape at both ends of an arrow

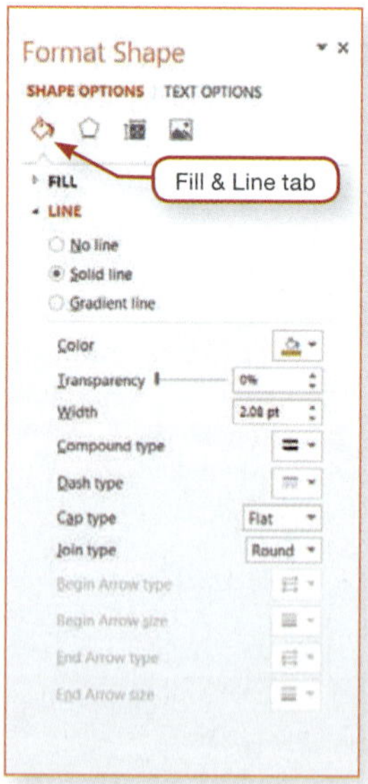

2-10 *Format Shape* pane

The *Format Shape* pane is a convenient place to change many options. Figure 2-10 shows the *Fill & Line* tab with *Line* options displayed because a line was selected when the pane opened. Different options appear if you have a shape selected or if you choose a *Gradient* line. Above *Line* you can select *Fill* to change shape colors. You can click the arrow in front of these options to expand or collapse each list.

Additional tabs include *Effects, Size & Properties,* and *Picture* with related options on each tab. Click the buttons at the top of the pane to select different tabs.

> **ANOTHER WAY**
>
> Right-click a shape and then select **Format Shape** from the shortcut menu to open the *Format Shape* pane.

Themes and Standard Colors

As you learned in Chapter 1, each PowerPoint *Theme* starts with a set of *Theme Colors* that provide background and accent colors. When you apply *Theme Colors* for shapes and text, these colors automatically change when you select a different set of *Theme Colors.*

Consider all of the colors used throughout your presentation when you make color choices because some colors seem more appropriate than others. This section explains how colors are arranged in PowerPoint and describes different ways to "mix" custom colors. The same techniques for choosing colors apply to color fills or outline colors.

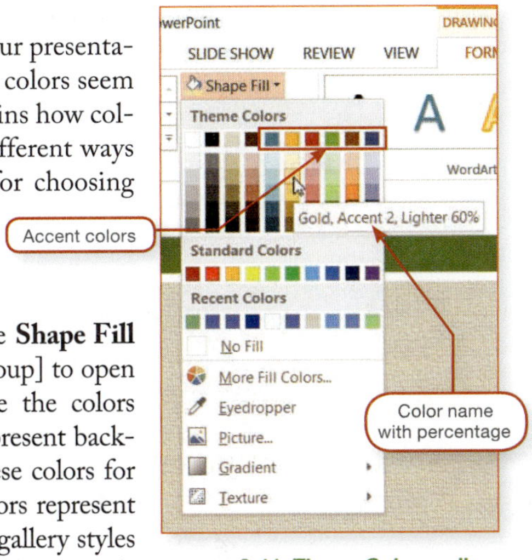

2-11 ***Theme Colors* gallery**

Change Solid and Gradient Fill Colors

To change the color of a selected shape, click the **Shape Fill** button [*Drawing Tools Format* tab, *Shape Styles* group] to open the ***Theme Colors*** gallery (Figure 2-11). Notice the colors arranged in the first row. The first four colors represent background and text colors; however, you can use these colors for other slide objects as well. The remaining six colors represent accent colors. These colors appear when viewing gallery styles and some effects. Beneath each color on the first row is a column of lighter and darker shades (shown as percentages) of that color. When you point to any color, a ScreenTip shows its name.

Below the *Theme Colors* is a single row of ***Standard Colors*** arranged in the order of a rainbow. When standard colors are used, they remain in effect even if *Theme Colors* change.

Gradient colors blend two or more colors together. Using the *Format Shape* pane, you can select from preset colors or customize your own gradient color by changing the colors and how they blend.

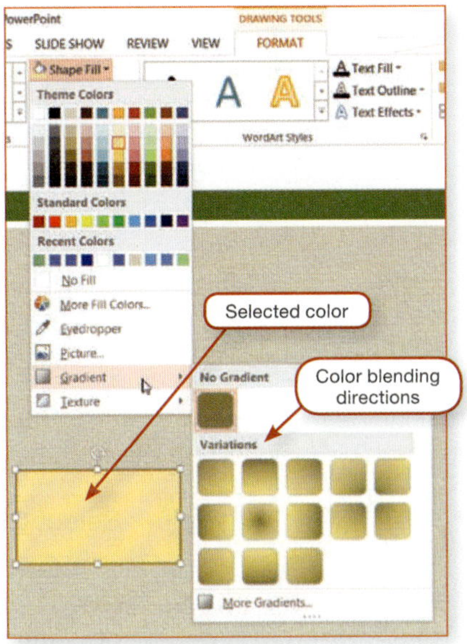

2-12 Gradient color variations for the selected color

HOW TO: Change Gradient Colors Using the Format Shape Pane

1. Select a slide object and click the **Shape Fill** button [*Drawing Tools Format* tab, *Shape Styles* group].
2. Select **Gradient** to select from a gallery of light and dark variations of the current fill color that blend the colors in different directions (Figure 2-12).

3. Click **More Gradients** at the bottom of the gallery to open the *Format Shape* pane to customize the colors.
4. Under *Fill* options, select **Gradient fill** and make selections from the following:
   - *Preset gradients:* Theme color variations (Figure 2-13)
   - *Type: Linear, Radial, Rectangular,* or *Path*
   - *Direction:* Options change based on the selected *Type.*
   - *Angle:* The percentage changes with each *Type* and *Direction.*
   - *Gradient stops:* Shapes on the gradient bar slider that you can move to control where colors change (Figure 2-14)
5. Each *Gradient stop* can be changed in the following ways to control color blending:
   - *Delete a stop:* Click the **Remove Gradient Stop** button or drag the stop off the slider.
   - *Add a stop:* Click the **Add Gradient Stop** button and click on the slider where you want it to appear.
   - *Color:* Select the stop; then change the color.
   - *Position:* Enter a different percentage or drag the stop on the slider to change its position.
   - *Transparency:* Click the arrows to change the percentage. When *Transparency* is 0%, the color is opaque (solid); as the percentage increases, the color becomes increasingly transparent and more of the background color shows through.
   - *Brightness:* Click the arrows to change the percentage. As the percentage decreases from 100%, the color softens.
6. Check **Rotate with shape** to maintain the color settings when a shape or text is rotated so it angles on the slide.
7. Under *Line* options, *select* **No line** or **Solid line** to control whether or not an outline shows around a shape or text.
8. Click **Close** and the new color is applied.

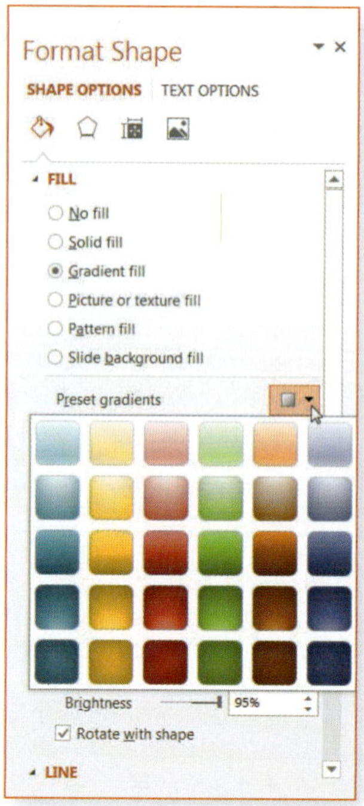

2-13 Preset gradients based on theme colors

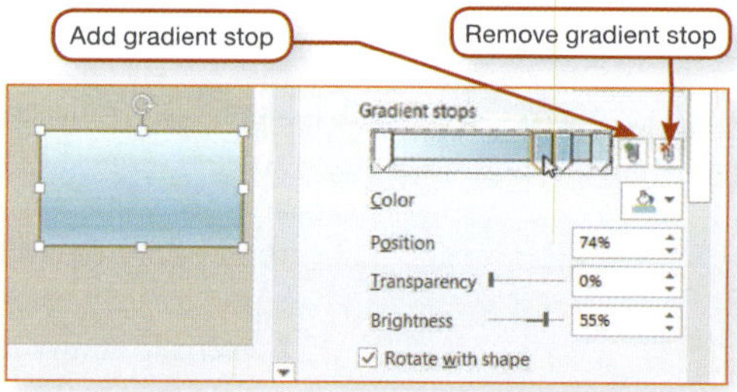

2-14 Gradient stops

MORE INFO

To apply gradient colors to *WordArt,* click the **Text Fill** button [*Drawing Tools Format* tab, *WordArt Styles* group] and select **Gradient** or select **Text Options**, then **Gradient fill** on the *Format Shape* pane.

Select Custom Colors

The *Colors* dialog box provides many solid color options on two tabs so you can either pick from displayed colors or mix a custom color. The new color appears on the lower right so you can compare it to the original color. Custom colors are not affected by any changes made to theme colors.

HOW TO: Use the Standard Tab to Select a Color

1. Select a shape and click the **Shape Fill** button [*Home* tab or *Drawing Tools Format* tab, *Shape Styles* group].
2. Click **More Fill Colors** to open the *Colors* dialog box.
3. On the *Standard* tab (Figure 2-15), colors are arranged in a honeycomb shape with colors blending from white to black below.
4. Click a color to apply it and notice the *New* color that appears on the right above the *Current* color.
5. Adjust the *Transparency* as needed.
6. Click **OK** to apply the new color.

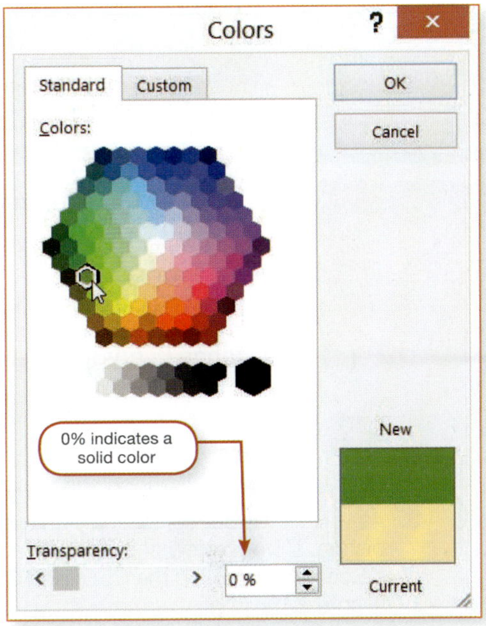

2-15 *Standard* tab on *Colors* dialog box

When you need more precision in selecting a color, use the *Custom* tab on the *Colors* dialog box. Colors are arranged like a rainbow and you drag a crosshair to select a different color. You drag the crosshair up or down to change the color intensity and then move a slider to adjust how light or dark the color appears. ***Color model*** information is shown on the *Custom* tab also. The ***RGB*** model is typically used for computer displays and colors are formed by blending values of the three numbers for *Red, Green,* and *Blue.* Highly saturated colors at the top have higher number values (255 maximum). You can use these numbers to match colors in different shapes and in different presentations.

HOW TO: Use the Custom Tab to Mix a Color

1. Select a shape and click the **Shape Fill** button [*Home* tab or *Drawing Tools Format* tab, *Shape Styles* group].
2. Click **More Fill Colors** to open the *Colors* dialog box.
3. On the *Custom* tab (Figure 2-16), a crosshair is positioned for the *Current* color.
   - Drag the crosshair to select a different color.
   - When the crosshair is at the top, colors are highly ***saturated*** (intense and vibrant).
   - As you move the crosshair down, colors become less saturated (duller and less intense).
4. Use the slider on the right to adjust the amount of white and black in the color to raise and lower the ***luminosity*** (lightness).
5. The current color and the new color appear in the lower right.
6. Adjust the *Transparency* as needed.
7. Click **OK** to apply the new color.

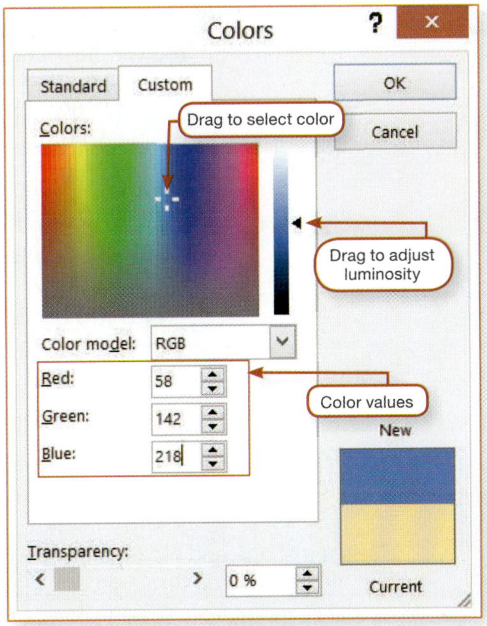

2-16 *Custom* tab on *Colors* dialog box

MORE INFO

Use the *Custom* tab if you need to match a specific color such as one of the colors in a business or college logo.

Use the Eyedropper for Color Matching

You can match the exact color of an object in PowerPoint with the ***Eyedropper*** and apply it to a shape.

HOW TO: Use the Eyedropper

1. Have an object, such as a picture, and the shape to be changed on the same slide. Select the shape.
2. Click the **Shape Fill** button and select **Eyedropper**.
3. As you move your pointer (now an eyedropper) around the picture, a live preview of each color appears. Pause to see a ScreenTip showing the *RGB* (Red Green Blue) values (Figure 2-17).
4. Click to select the color.

Or

5. Press **Esc** to cancel the eyedropper without selecting a color.

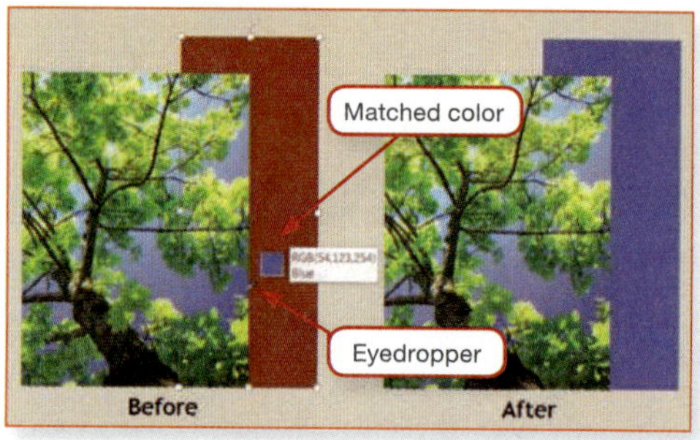

2-17 ***Eyedropper*** **live preview and** ***RGB*** **colors**

To match a color anywhere on your computer screen, left-click and hold as you drag the eyedropper pointer to other areas of the screen outside of PowerPoint.

Apply Picture, Texture, or Pattern Fills

You can fill *WordArt* and other shapes with more than colors. The following options are available from the *Shape Fill* drop-down list or from the *Format Shape* pane.

- *Texture:* Applies an image such as woven fabric or wood
- *Pattern:* Applies a mixture of two colors in various dotted or crosshatch designs
- *Picture:* Fills the *WordArt* or shape with a picture from a file or from the *Office.com Clip Art* collection

2-18 ***Texture*** **fills**

HOW TO: Apply Texture and Pattern Fills

1. Select a shape and click the **Shape Fill** button [*Drawing Tools Format* tab, *Shape Styles* group].
   - Select **Texture** to open the gallery (Figure 2-18).
   - Click a texture to apply it.

2. Select a shape and right-click. Click **Format Shape** from the callout menu to open the *Format Shape* pane.
   - Select **Pattern fill** (Figure 2-19).
   - Click a pattern to apply it.
   - Change *Foreground* and *Background* colors as needed.

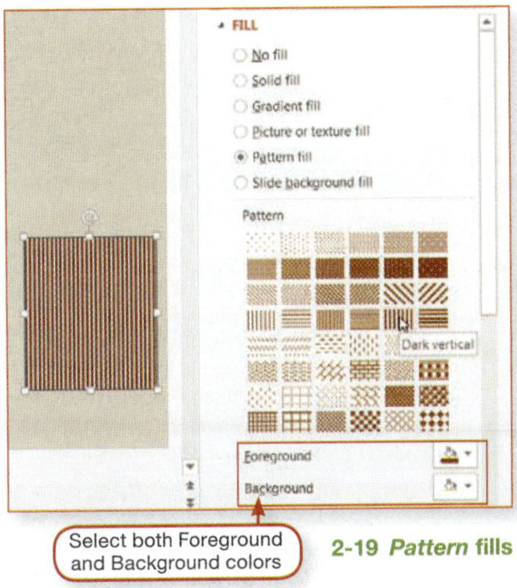

2-19 *Pattern* fills

You can also use the *Format Background* pane to insert textures and adjust how they are positioned. Inserting pictures from the *Office.com Clip Art* collection is covered in *SLO 2.3 Working with Pictures.*

SLO 2.2

Adding Text Effects and WordArt

You can apply interesting ***text effects*** for many purposes. For example, you can make slide titles more attractive and easier to read, or you can provide a bold focal point on a slide. One way is to start by inserting ***WordArt***.

HOW TO: Apply Text Effects with WordArt

1. Click the **WordArt** button [*Insert* tab, *Text* group] to choose a style from the *WordArt Quick Styles* gallery (Figure 2-20).
2. The gallery has preset text effects showing a variety of solid, gradient, and pattern fill colors.
3. Click to select a *WordArt* style.
4. A text box is inserted on your slide with sample text that you edit to create a *WordArt* object (Figure 2-21).
5. Use the *Font* group [*Home* tab] to make the following changes:
   - Select a different font or attribute such as bold or italic.
   - Change the font size by entering a point size or using the **Increase Font Size** and **Decrease Font Size** buttons.
   - Click the **Character Spacing** button to make letters fit more closely or to spread letters apart.

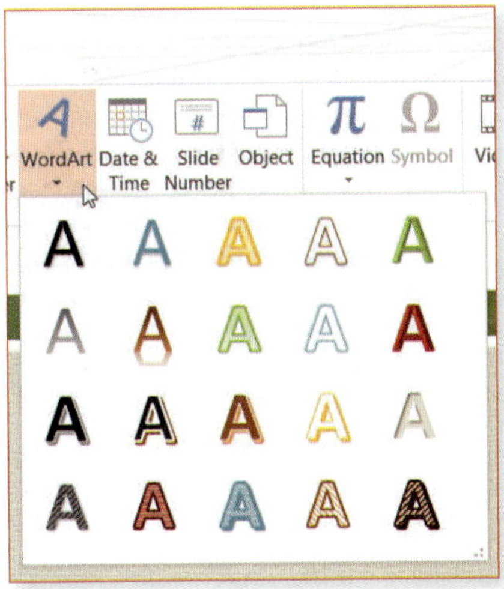

2-20 *WordArt Quick Styles* gallery

2-21 *WordArt* as it first appears

> **MORE INFO**
>
> When using text in a large size, tight character spacing conserves space yet keeps the text easy to read.

You can also start with text in a placeholder or text box and then apply text effects. With either method, you use commands on the *WordArt Styles* group [*Drawing Tools Format* tab] (Figure 2-22) to customize your text. These commands—*Text Fill, Text Outline, and Text Effects*—are similar to the *Shape* commands.

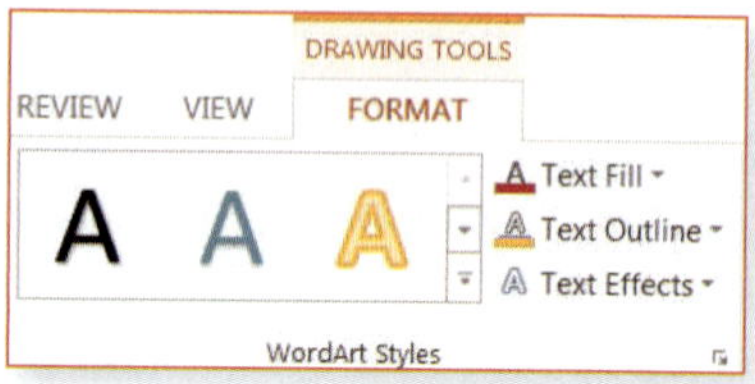

2-22 *WordArt Styles* group

HOW TO: Apply Text Effects to Existing Text

1. Select a *WordArt* object or text in a placeholder or text box.
2. Click the **More** button [*Drawing Tools Format* tab, *WordArt Styles* group] to open the *Quick Styles* gallery (Figure 2-23).
3. Point to a style to see a live preview applied to your text.
4. Click a style to apply it.
5. Use the *WordArt Styles* group [*Drawing Tools Format* tab] to make the following changes:
   - Click the **Text Fill** button to select **Theme** or other color options.
   - Click the **Text Outline** button to select **Theme** or other color options as well as line weight and style.
   - Apply different *Text Effects* (*Shadow, Reflection, Glow, Bevel, 3D Rotation,* or *Transform*).
6. With the WordArt object selected, right-click and then click **Format Shape** to open the *Format Shape* pane. Select **Shape Options** or **Text Options** and make adjustments as needed.

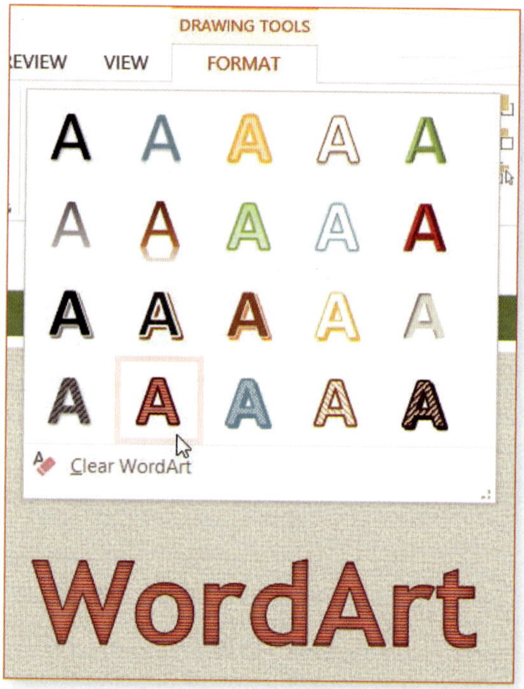

2-23 *WordArt* with style changed

> **MORE INFO**
>
> If the *WordArt Quick Styles* gallery is not open on your *Drawing Tools Format* tab, click the **Quick Styles** button.

Changing the text outline color and increasing line weight emphasizes the outline just as it does on shapes. Different line styles can create interesting effects. Using pictures or patterns as fill colors can add a creative touch when text is shown in a large size. A variety of different color and effects are shown in Figure 2-24.

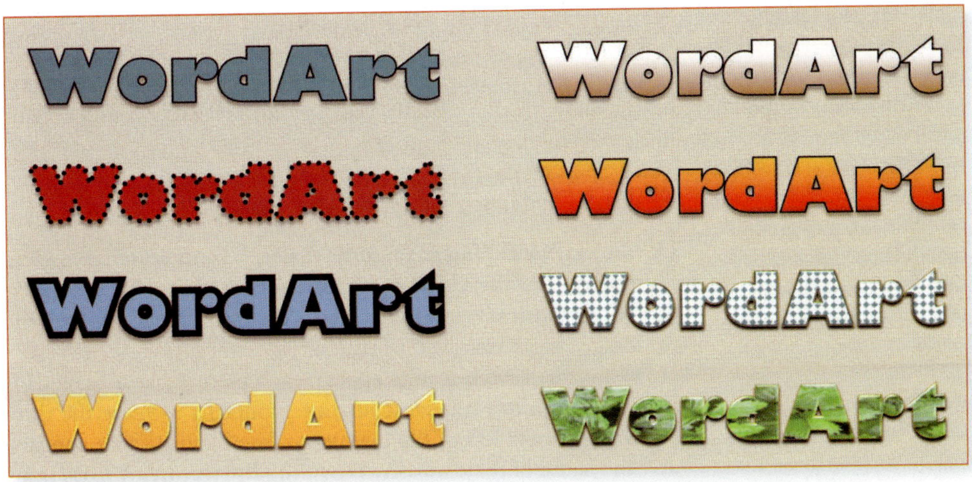

2-24 Sample fill and line effects

ANOTHER WAY

Select the text in a *WordArt* object and right-click. Click **Format Text Effects** from the shortcut menu to open the *Format Shape* pane with *Text Options* listed.

Transform effects are unique to text and make a word or phrase warp to fit different shapes or follow a path. For example, text can angle, flow in a circle, and arc up or down. As you point to different *Transform* effects, a live preview shows how your text will look in that shape. Once a *Transform* effect has been applied, text size is not limited to the font size because you can drag the *WordArt* sizing handles. Some *Transform* effects also provide one or more pink adjustment handles that control the slant of letters or the curve of text.

HOW TO: Apply a Transform Effect

1. Select a *WordArt* object.
2. Click the **Text Effects** button [*Format* tab, *WordArt Styles* group].
3. From the drop-down list, select **Transform** (Figure 2-25).
4. On the *Transform* gallery, point to an effect to see a live preview applied to your text.
5. Click an effect to apply it.
6. Adjust as needed using sizing and adjustment handles.

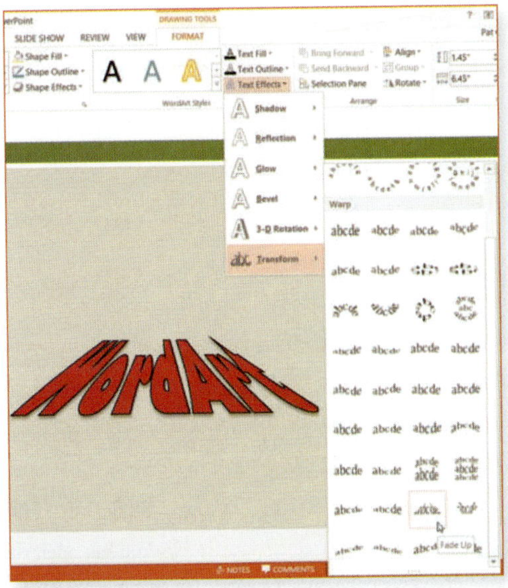

2-25 *Transform Fade Up* effect

SLO 2.3

Working with Pictures

In Chapter 1, you learned how to insert pictures from files, change their size, and align them on the slide. In this section, you use PowerPoint's search capabilities to find images to help illustrate presentation concepts.

Online Pictures and Illustrations

Use PowerPoint's ***Insert Pictures*** dialog box to search for pictures (digital photographs or illustrations) in the *Office.com Clip Art* collection. You can search the web using *Bing Image Search* but pictures you find may have licensing restrictions or require fees. You can also browse for images you have saved in your *SkyDrive* location.

When the search results appear, each picture has a ScreenTip identifying its name and a magnifying button you can click to temporarily increase the thumbnail size.

On the lower left of the dialog box, the picture name appears with its dimension in pixels and the name of the company providing the picture. A ***pixel*** is an abbreviated term for *picture element,* a single unit of information about color.

HOW TO: Search for and Insert a Picture or Illustration

1. On a slide, click the **Online Pictures** button [*Insert* tab, *Images* group] (Figure 2-26) to open the *Insert Pictures* dialog box.
2. In the *Search* box, type the search word (Figure 2-27).
3. Click the **Search** button (or press **Enter**) to activate the search.
4. Thumbnails of all the pictures that match your search word appear (Figure 2-28).
5. Click to select the picture you want.
6. Press **Ctrl** while you click to select more than one picture.
7. Click the **Insert** button. The picture will download and the *Insert Pictures* dialog box will close.

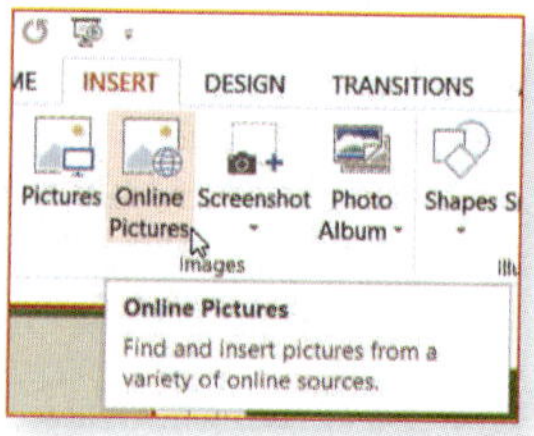

2-26 *Online Pictures* button

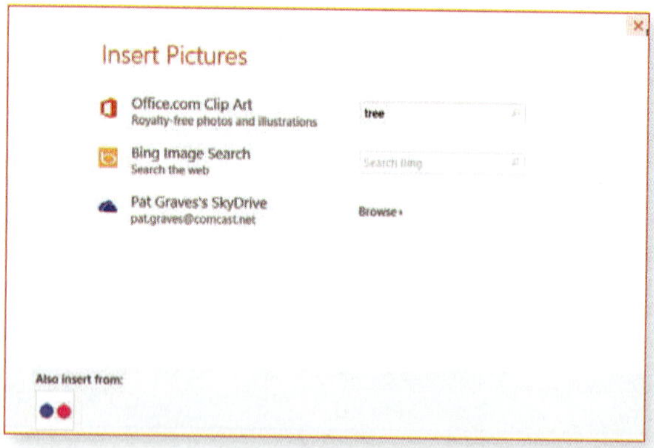

2-27 *Insert Pictures* dialog box

2-28 Pictures from search

MORE INFO

You can open the *Insert Pictures* dialog box when creating a new slide by clicking the **Online Pictures** button on the content placeholder.

> **MORE INFO**
>
> Be careful to select images that are appropriate for your topic. Some cartoon-like illustrations look amateurish and may not be appropriate for academic or business situations.

Apply Picture Quick Styles

When you have selected a picture, the *Picture Tools Format* tab becomes available. Different quick styles allow you to frame pictures, give them a 3D appearance, add a reflection, or apply other treatments. You can customize each of these options using the *Picture Effects* drop-down galleries.

When you use multiple pictures in a presentation, try to maintain consistency and use the same or a similar style for each of them. If you use different styles, be sure you have a reason for making them look different so the effects do not appear random.

HOW TO: Apply a Picture Style

1. Select a picture and click the **Picture Tools Format** tab.
2. Click the **More** button on the gallery [*Picture Styles* group] to see the pre-defined effects (Figure 2-29).
3. Drag your pointer over the styles to see a live preview applied to your picture. A ScreenTip showing the style name appears.
4. Click a style to apply it to your picture.
5. To change to a different style, simply select a different one.

2-29 Picture style applied

Picture Effects are similar to *Shape Effects*. Each different effect has many options you can adjust.

HOW TO: Apply or Modify Picture Effects

1. Select a picture and click the **Picture Effects** button [*Picture Tools Format* tab, *Picture Styles* group].
2. As you point to each effect, a drop-down gallery (Figure 2-30) provides many variations. Select **Options** at the bottom of each *Effects* drop-down gallery and make the needed changes to fine-tune a specific effect.
3. You can also right-click the picture and select **Format Picture** from the short-cut menu to open the *Format Picture* pane where you can make changes.
4. To remove a picture style, select the picture and click the **Reset Picture** button [*Picture Tools Format* tab, *Adjust* group].

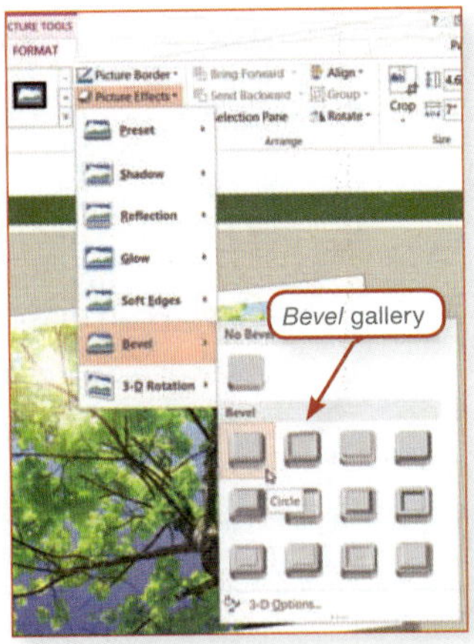

2-30 *Picture Effects*

Crop a Picture

You can ***crop*** (trim) unwanted areas of a selected picture by dragging black ***cropping handles*** on the corners and sides of the picture that appear when **Crop** is selected. When you point to these handles, your pointer changes to a shape that resembles the handle. Be careful when dragging to be sure you are moving a cropping handle and not a sizing handle.

HOW TO: Crop a Picture

1. Select a picture and click the **Crop** button [*Picture Tools Format* tab, *Size* group].
2. Drag one or more cropping handles toward the center of the picture; the area to be removed from the edges is grayed out (Figure 2-31).
3. When you are satisfied, click the **Crop** button again to accept this change.

2-31 Cropped area of a picture

Always check your pictures to be sure they have a strong focal point. Excess detail clutters a picture and does not help your viewers quickly grasp what you want them to see.

Change Picture Colors

Pictures are digital photographs usually made up of many colors to achieve the realism that they portray. If an image is faded or if you want a muted image for a background area so text is easy to read, PowerPoint's *Color* feature allows you to apply different color options.

HOW TO: Change Picture Colors

1. Select a picture you want to change.
2. Click the **Color** button [*Picture Tools Format* tab, *Adjust* group].
3. A gallery appears showing different color options (Figure 2-32). The current option within each group is highlighted.
4. Click an option to apply it.
5. Click **Picture Color Options** to open the *Format Picture* pane with the **Picture Color** options listed where you can make your selections.
6. Options include the following:
   - ***Color Saturation:*** Colors are more muted as you move from the center to the left as saturation becomes lower; colors are more intense as you move from the center to the right as saturation increases.

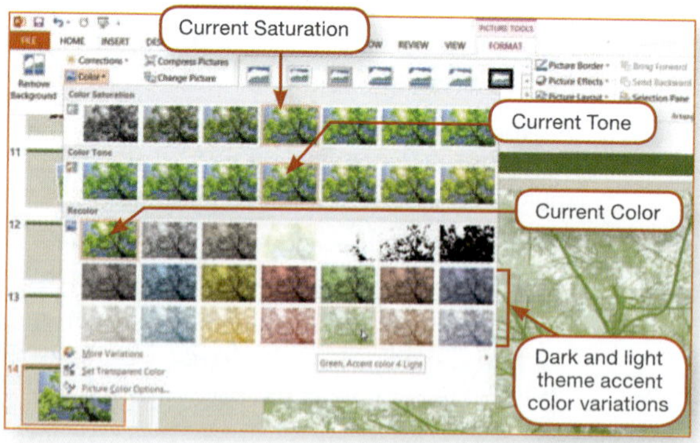

2-32 *Color* gallery

- ***Color Tone:*** Colors on the left have cool tones and lower temperature values; colors on the right have warm tones and higher values.
- ***Recolor:*** Options on the first row include *Grayscale, Sepia, Washout,* and percentages of *Black and White.* The second and third rows display dark and light monotone variations of accent colors.

Set a Transparent Color

An image with a white background works well on a slide with a white background (or on a typical Word document) because you see just the image. However, a white background can detract from an image if you place it on a slide background with a contrasting color.

Use the ***Set Transparent Color*** feature to remove a single-color background. Because this feature removes only one color, it does not work well for pictures that have a lot of detail and many colors.

HOW TO: Set a Transparent Color

1. Select a picture.
2. Click the **Color** button [*Picture Tools Format* tab, *Adjust* group].
3. Click **Set Transparent Color** and your pointer changes to a pen tool.
4. Point to the area of the picture you want to remove, and click.
5. All of the pixels with that color value disappear, revealing what is behind the picture (Figure 2-33).

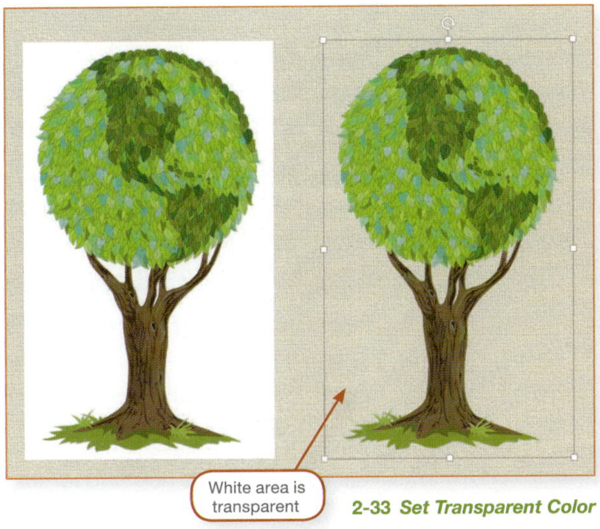

2-33 ***Set Transparent Color***

Compress Pictures

Pictures can greatly increase your presentation file size. You can ***compress*** single pictures or all pictures at one time to reduce the picture resolution depending on the quality you need. For print you generally need a higher resolution, and for on-screen viewing a lower resolution is usually fine. Resolution options are expressed in *pixels per inch (ppi)—Print (220 ppi), Screen (150 ppi),* and *E-mail (96 ppi).* The ppi measurement for viewing on screen is very different from the *dots per inch* (*dpi*) print measurement for printing on paper. An inexpensive printer can produce 1,200 or more *dpi*, which produces crisp, clear letterforms that are easy to read on paper.

Deleting cropped areas of pictures removes unused information and, therefore, reduces file size. Compression only affects how the pictures display in the presentation file and not the original picture files.

HOW TO: Compress Picture File Size

1. Select a picture.
2. Click the **Compress Picture** button [*Picture Tools Format* tab, *Adjust* group].
3. On the *Compress Pictures* dialog box (Figure 2-34), deselect **Apply only to this picture** if you want the compression to apply to all pictures in the presentation.
4. If you have cropped pictures, select **Delete cropped areas of pictures**.
5. Select the appropriate *Target output.*
6. Click **OK** to close the dialog box.

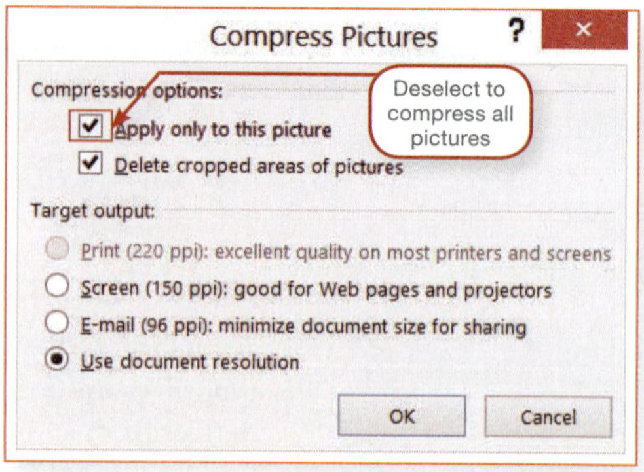

2-34 ***Compress Pictures*** **dialog box**

PAUSE & PRACTICE: POWERPOINT 2-1

When Gerod Sunderland shares his landscaping proposal with homeowners, he provides detailed printed information and uses a presentation to illustrate concepts. In this project, you add pictures and other objects to his presentation and apply a variety of styles and colors to enhance the content.

File Needed: ***LandscapingProposal-02.pptx***
Completed Project File Name: ***[your initials] PP P2-1.pptx***

1. Open the presentation ***LandscapingProposal-02.***
2. Save the presentation as ***[your initials] PP P2-1.***
3. Add a rectangle.
   a. On slide 1, click the **Shapes** button [*Insert* tab, *Illustrations* group].
   b. Select the rectangle shape.
   c. Click and drag to draw a rectangle across the slide.
   d. Change the rectangle height to **.4"** and width to **13.33"** [*Drawing Tools Format* tab, *Size* group].
   e. Click the **Shape Fill** button [*Drawing Tools Format* tab, *Shape Styles* group] and select **Brown, Accent 5**, **Darker 25%**.
   f. Click the **Shape Outline** button and select **No Outline**.
   g. Position the rectangle below the white line as shown in Figure 2-35.

2-35 Change ***Shape Fill*** **color**

4. Add text effects.
   a. On slide 1, select the title and click the **Text Effects** button [*Drawing Tools Format* tab, *Word Art Styles* group].
   b. Select **Bevel** and then **Circle**.
   c. Repeat to select **Shadow** and then **Offset Diagonal Bottom Right** (Figure 2-36).

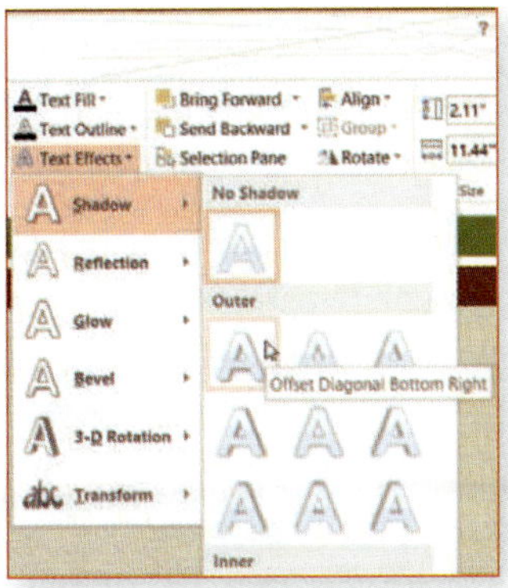

2-36 Apply *Text Effects*

5. Add a frame shape.
   a. On slide 3, click the **Shape** button [*Insert* tab, *Illustrations* group] and select the **Frame** shape under the *Basic Shapes* heading.
   b. Click and drag to draw a frame.
   c. In the frame shape type Allow three days.
   d. Change the font size to **24 pts**.
   e. Adjust the frame size with a height of **1"** and width of **3.3"** [*Drawing Tools Format* tab, *Size* group].

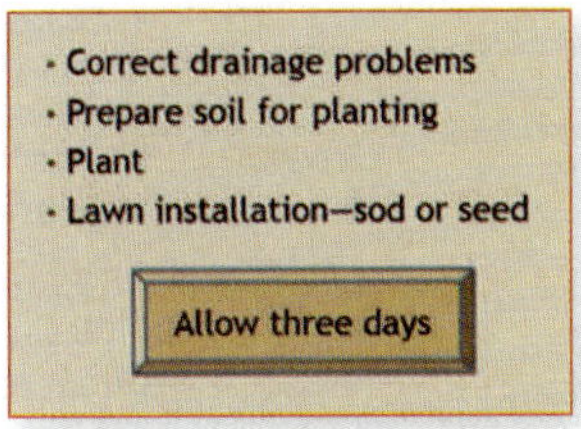

2-37 Text box positioned below list

6. Change to a different shape and color.
   a. Click the **Edit Shape** button arrow [*Drawing Tools Format* tab, *Insert Shapes* group] and select **Change Shape**.
   b. Click the **Bevel** shape under the *Basic Shapes* heading.
   c. Change the *Shape Fill* to **Tan**, **Background 2**, **Darker 25%**.
   d. Position this shape below the bulleted text (Figure 2-37).

7. On slide 8, add *WordArt* text.
   a. Click the **WordArt** button [*Insert* tab, *Text* group].
   b. Select the style **Gradient fill - Green, Accent 4, Outline - Accent 4.**
   c. In the *WordArt* text box type Thank you for your business!
   d. Move the *WordArt* object so it is at the top of the picture (Figure 2-38).
   e. Change the *Character Spacing* [*Home* tab, *Font* group] to **Tight**.

2-38 *WordArt* with gradient

8. Change the *WordArt* gradient fill and outline colors.
   a. Click the **Text Fill** button [*Drawing Tools Format* tab, *WordArt Styles* group] and select **Gradient**.
   b. Click **More Gradients** to open the *Format Shape* pane.
   c. Select the second gradient stop (at Position **4%**) and click the **Remove gradient stop** button.
   d. Select the left gradient stop (at Position **0%**) and change the color to **Green**, **Accent 4**, **Lighter 40%**.
   e. Select the right gradient stop and change the color to **Green**, **Accent 4**, **Darker 50%** (Figure 2-39).
   f. Close the *Format Shape* pane.
   g. Click the **Text Outline** button and change the outline color to **Black**, **Text 1**.

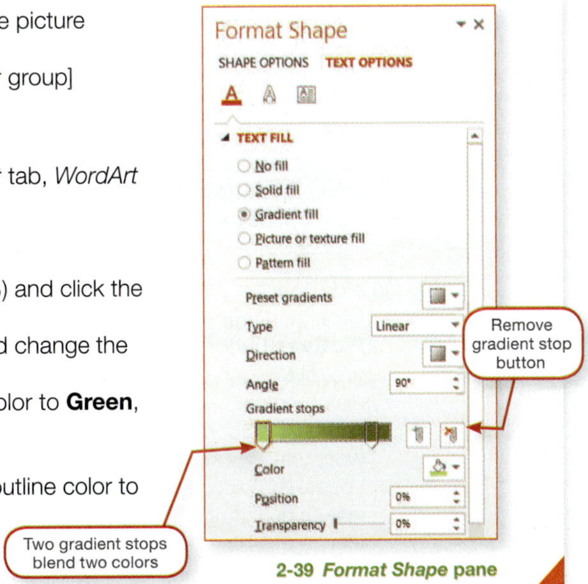

2-39 *Format Shape* pane

9. Apply a *Transform* effect to the *WordArt*.
   a. Click the **Text Effects** button [*Format* tab, *WordArt Styles* group]. From the drop-down list, select **Transform**.
   b. On the *Transform* gallery, click the **Deflate Bottom** effect (Figure 2-40).
   c. Resize the *WordArt* to fit across the top of the picture (Figure 2-41).
10. Apply effects and use the *Format Painter*.
   a. On slide 2, select the left list heading placeholder.
   b. Change the text to **bold**.
   c. Click the **Shape Fill** button [*Drawing Tools Format* tab, *Shape Styles* group] and select **Texture**.
   d. Click the **Parchment** option.
   e. Click the **Format Painter** button [*Home* tab, *Clipboard* group]. Click the list heading placeholder on the right to apply the same changes.
11. On slide 3, search for and insert a picture.
   a. Click the **Online Pictures** button [*Insert* tab, *Images* group] to open the *Insert Pictures* dialog box.
   b. In the *Office.com* search box, type the word soil.
   c. Click **Search** (or press **Enter**) to activate the search.
   d. Locate the picture shown in Figure 2-42.
   e. Click **Insert**.
12. On slide 3, resize and crop the picture.
   a. Resize the picture to a height of **6"** and the width automatically adjusts to **4.01"** [*Picture Tools Format* tab, *Size* group].
   b. Click the **Crop** button [*Picture Tools Format* tab, *Size* group] and crop a little space from all four edges to focus more on the plant.
   c. Click the **Crop** button again to accept the crop.
   d. Click the **More** button [*Picture Tools Format* tab, *Picture Styles* group] and select the **Rotated, White** picture style.
   e. Position the picture on the right (Figure 2-43).
13. On slide 1, insert a picture.
   a. Click the **Online Pictures** button [*Insert* tab, *Images* group] to open the *Insert Pictures* dialog box.
   b. In the *Office.com* search box, type the word leaf.
   c. Locate the picture of a red maple leaf on a white background (Figure 2-44).

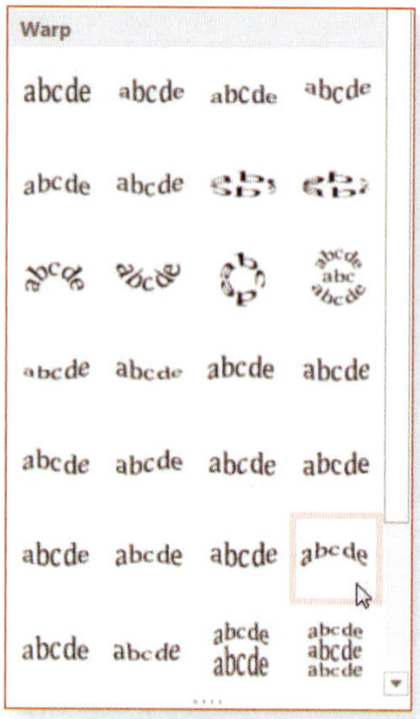

2-40 *WordArt Transform* gallery

2-41 *Deflate Bottom Transform* effect applied and adjusted

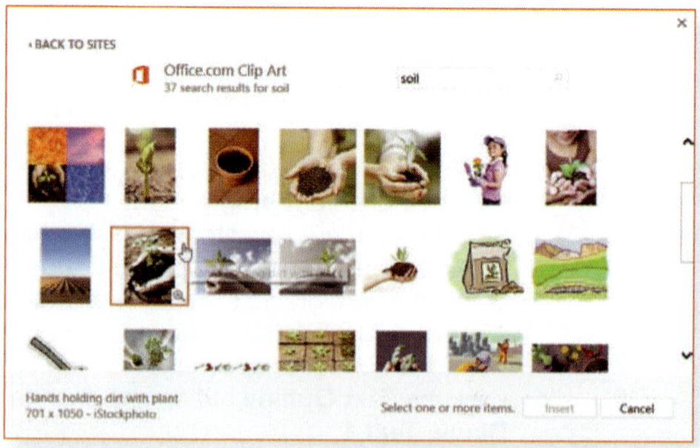

2-42 *Online Pictures* search results

d. Select the thumbnail and click **Insert**.
e. On the *Picture Tools Format* tab, change the leaf height to **5"** and the width automatically adjusts.
f. With the leaf selected, click **Color** [*Picture Tools Format* tab, *Adjust* group].
g. Select **Set Transparent Color** and your pointer changes to a pen tool.
h. Click the white area around the leaf so it becomes transparent.
i. Position the leaf on the right (Figure 2-44).

14. Compress a picture file size.
    a. Select the leaf and click **Compress Pictures** [*Picture Tools Format* tab, *Adjust* group].
    b. Deselect **Apply only to this picture**.
    c. For the *Target output,* select **Use document resolution**.
    d. Click **OK**.
15. Save and close your presentation.

2-43 Completed slide 3

2-44 Completed slide 1

SLO 2.4

Creating a Table

Tables show data in an organized and easy-to-read way because information is arranged in ***columns*** (vertical) and ***rows*** (horizontal). The intersection of a column and row is a ***cell***. ***Border*** lines and ***shading*** show the table structure. Working with PowerPoint tables is much like working with tables in Word.

Once you create a table, you can change its size as well as column width and row height. Use table formatting to emphasize the contents in different ways and help your audience interpret the data. If you plan to project your slides on a large screen, be sure your table information is concise so you can use a minimum font size of 20 points. If a table requires a lot of detailed information, then prepare the table as a full-page handout with body text at an 11–12 point size. You can prepare a PowerPoint slide to reference the handout as you explain the table, or perhaps show on a slide only a portion of the table.

Insert and Draw Methods

You can create a table using the **Table** button [*Insert* tab, *Tables* group]. As you drag over the columns and rows to select them, the table dimensions (such as *3×4 Table*) are shown at the top of the drop-down list. The first number represents columns and the second number represents rows. By default, columns and rows appear on the slide with even sizing, but you can adjust column width and row height as you add information.

HOW TO: Insert a Table and Select Columns and Rows

1. Display the slide where you want the table.
2. Click the **Insert** tab.
3. Click the **Table** button [*Tables* group] to open the drop-down list (Figure 2-45).
4. Drag across and down to select the number of columns and rows you need.
5. Click to insert the table.

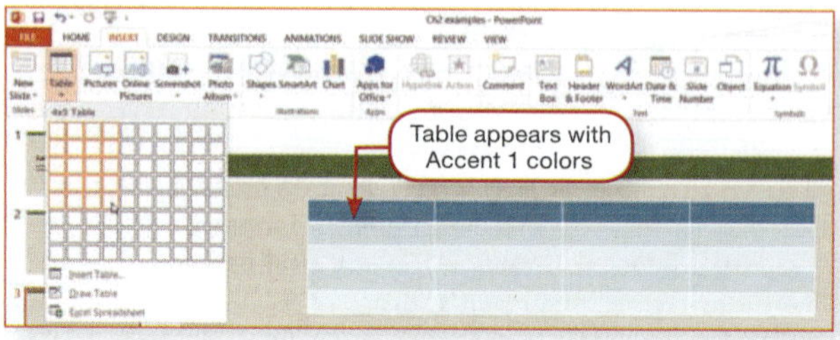

2-45 Table cells selected

By using the **Insert Table** command [*Insert* tab, *Tables* group], you can create a table by entering a specific the number of columns and rows.

HOW TO: Insert a Table and Enter the Number of Columns and Rows

1. Display the slide where you want to insert the table.
2. Click the **Insert** tab.
3. Click the **Table** button [*Tables* group] to open the drop-down list.
4. Click **Insert Table** and the *Insert Table* dialog box opens (Figure 2-46).
5. Specify the number of columns and rows you need.
6. Click **OK** to close the *Insert Table* dialog box and insert the table.

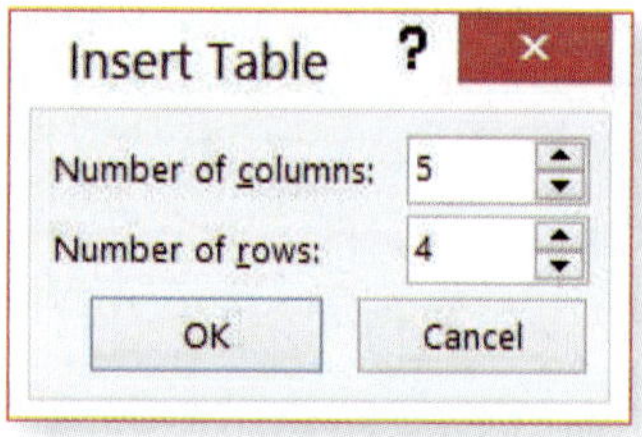

2-46 *Insert Table* dialog box

ANOTHER WAY

When you add a new slide, click the **Table** icon in the empty content placeholder and enter the number of columns and rows to create a table. The table width will be slightly wider than when you click the **Insert** button to create a table.

The final way to create a table is by drawing the table area and dividing it into columns and rows.

HOW TO: Draw a Table

1. Display the slide where you want the table.
2. Click the **Insert** tab.
3. Click the **Table** button [*Tables* group] to open the drop-down list.

4. Click **Draw Table** and your pointer changes to a pen tool.
5. Drag to create the table size you want.
6. Click the **Draw Table** button [*Table Tools Design* tab, *Draw Borders* group] to activate the pen tool again, and drag the pen within the table to insert horizontal and vertical lines that divide the table into rows and columns (Figure 2-47).
7. Press **Esc** to turn off the pen tool.

2-47 *Draw Table*

Regardless of the method you use to create a table, the *Table Tools Design* tab (Figure 2-48) and *Table Tools Layout* tab (Figure 2-49) are available when the table is active.

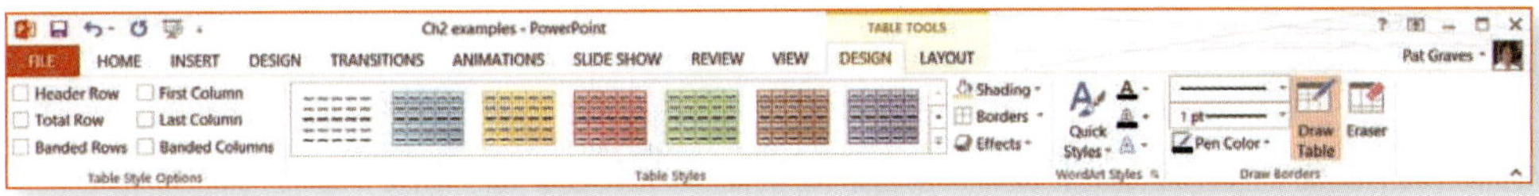

2-48 *Table Tools Design* tab

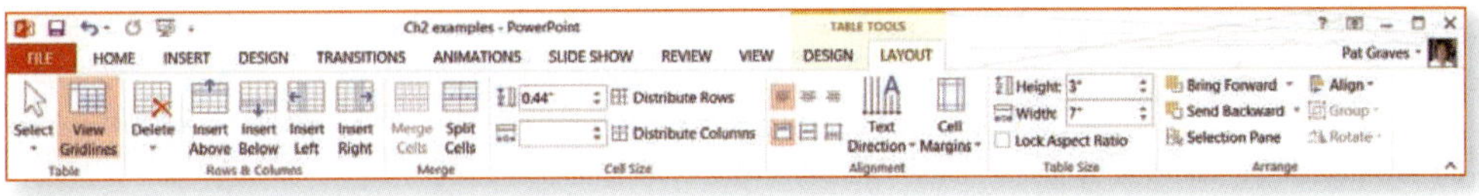

2-49 *Table Tools Layout* tab

Move and Select

Your insertion point indicates where you are within a table to add text. To move from cell to cell, use one of the following methods:

- Press **Tab** to move to the next cell on the right (or the first cell in the next row).
- Press **Shift+Tab** to move to the next cell on the left.
- Click a cell to move the insertion point to that cell.
- Use arrow keys to move in different directions from the current cell.

Where you point within a table influences whether you select individual cells, columns, rows, or the entire table. Your pointer changes to a selection pointer (a black arrow that points in different directions based on what you are selecting).

HOW TO: Select Cells, Columns, Rows, and the Table

1. To select a cell, point inside the left border and click when your pointer turns into a black arrow.
2. To select a column, use one of the following methods:
   - Point above its top border and click when your pointer turns into a downward-pointing black arrow (Figure 2-50).
   - Move your insertion point to any cell in the column. Click the **Select** button [*Table Tools Layout* tab, *Table* group] and click **Select Column**.

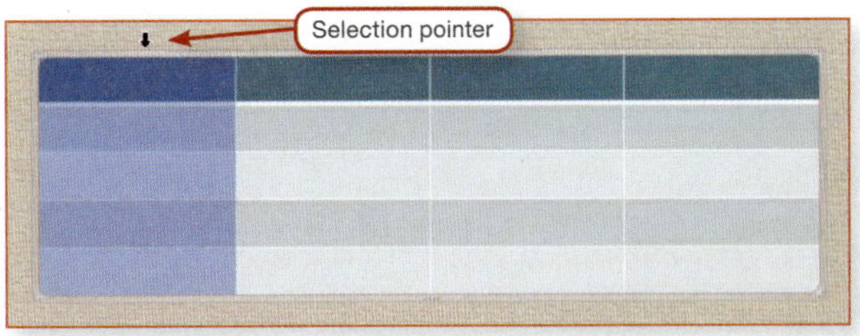

2-50 Select table column

3. To select a row, use one of the following methods:
   - Point outside the table to the left of a row and click when your pointer turns into a right-pointing black arrow (Figure 2-51).
   - Move your insertion point to **any cell** in the row. Click the **Select** button [*Table Tools Layout* tab, *Table* group] and click **Select Row**.

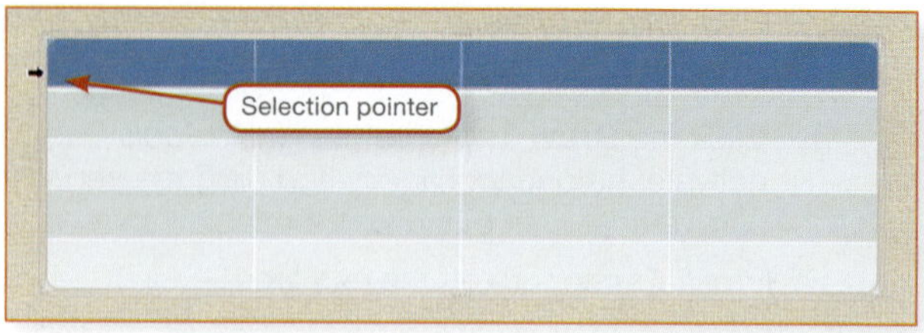

2-51 Select table row

4. To select multiple cells, columns, or rows, use one of the following methods:
   - Drag across adjacent cells.
   - Press **Shift** as you click additional adjacent cells.
5. To select an entire table, use one of the following methods:
   - Drag across all cells in the table.
   - Move your insertion point to any cell in the table. Click the **Select** button [*Table Tools Layout* tab, *Table* group] and click **Select Table**.

Insert and Delete Rows and Columns

After you begin entering table content, you may need to add rows or columns. You can change a table's structure in several ways:

- Insert rows above or below the current row.
- Insert columns to the left or right of the current column.
- Delete rows and columns.

HOW TO: Insert and Delete Rows and Columns

1. Click inside the table.
2. Click the **Table Tools Layout** tab.
3. Insert a row or column.
   - Click in a table cell next to where you want to add a column or row.
   - Click the **Insert Above** or **Insert Below** buttons [*Rows & Columns* group] to add rows.
   - Click the **Insert Left** or **Insert Right** buttons [*Rows & Columns* group] to add columns.
4. Delete a row or column.
   - Click in a table cell where you want to delete a column or row.
   - Click the **Delete** button and select **Delete Columns** or **Delete Rows** [*Rows & Columns* group] (Figure 2-52).

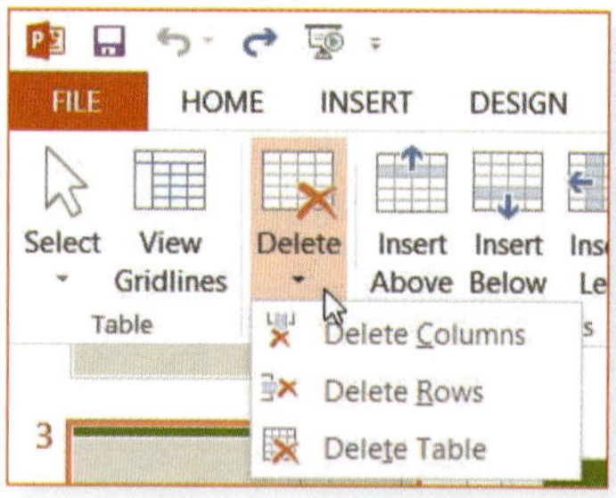

2-52 ***Delete*** **button**

ANOTHER WAY

Right-click a row or column and insert or delete rows and columns by selecting the appropriate option from the mini toolbar.

Merge and Split Cells

You can ***merge*** (combine) two or more cells in a row or column. For example, you can combine all the cells in the top row of a table so a title spans all columns (see Figure 2-53). You can ***split*** (divide) any single cell into two or more cells.

HOW TO: Merge and Split Cells

1. Select the cells to be merged.
   - Click the *Table Tools Layout* tab.
   - Click the **Merge Cells** button [*Merge* group] to combine those cells into one cell.
2. Select the cell (or cells) to be split.
   - Click the *Table Tools Layout* tab.
   - Click the **Split Cells** button [*Merge* group] to open the *Split Cells* dialog box and enter the number of columns and rows that you need.
   - Click **OK** to close the dialog box.

> **ANOTHER WAY**
>
> Click the **Eraser** button [*Table Tools Design* tab, *Draw Borders* group] and your pointer turns into an eraser. Click a border within the table to remove it and merge cells.

Adjust Sizing

You often need to resize tables to fit information appropriately. Column widths will vary based on content, but row height should usually be consistent.

HOW TO: Resize a Table, Cells, Columns, and Rows

1. Resize a table.
   - Enter sizes in the *Height* and *Width* boxes [*Table Tools Layout* tab, *Table Size* group].
   - Click and drag table sizing handles as you would to resize a shape.
2. Resize a cell, column, or row.
   - Point to a cell, column, or row inside a border. When your pointer changes to a splitter (Figure 2-53), click and drag to make the cell, column, or row larger or smaller.
   - Select the cell, column, or row you want to change; then enter the size you want in the *Height* and *Width* boxes [*Table Tools Layout* tab, *Cell Size* group].
3. To resize a column to fit the text within it, point to a border and double-click when your pointer changes to a splitter.
4. To evenly distribute column width or row height,
   - Select the columns or rows to be changed.
   - Click the **Distribute Rows** or **Distribute Columns** buttons [*Table Tools Layout* tab, *Cell Size* group].

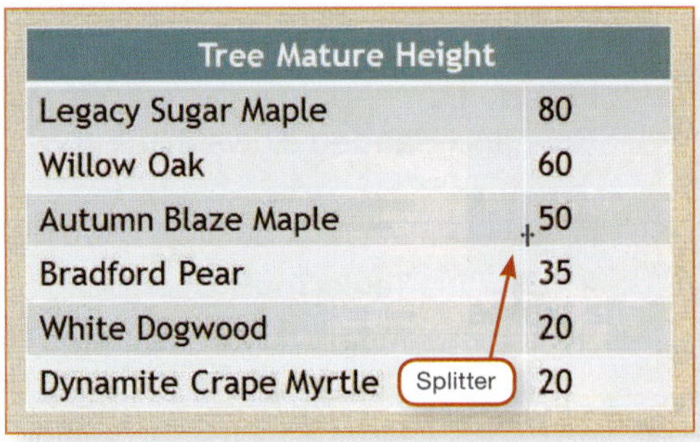

Tree Mature Height	
Legacy Sugar Maple	80
Willow Oak	60
Autumn Blaze Maple	50
Bradford Pear	35
White Dogwood	20
Dynamite Crape Myrtle	20

2-53 Change column width

> **MORE INFO**
>
> To maintain column width proportions, press **Shift** as you drag table sizing handles or select **Lock Aspect Ratio** before entering *Height* or *Width* sizes.

SLO 2.5

Enhancing a Table

You can format text in a table as you can any other text such as changing alignment and applying *WordArt Quick Styles.* You can also change cell margins and text direction. The following are table formatting options:

- Apply a *Table Style.*
- Customize the style by changing effect options.
- Add shading, borders, and other effects to cells, columns, or rows.

Table Style Options and Effects

On the *Table Tools Design* tab, ***Table Styles*** provide a gallery of built-in options for a table's design. The first style on each row of options is shown in black and white while the other six styles are in theme accent colors. Table styles are arranged in the following categories:

- *Best Match for Document*
- *Light*
- *Medium*
- *Dark*

Each table style is influenced by the features checked for ***Table Style Options*** [*Table Tools Design* tab]. Fill colors that emphasize table cells vary depending on which of the following options you select:

- ***Header Row*** or ***Total Row:*** The first or last row has a darker color and has bold text in a contrasting color.
- ***First Column*** or ***Last Column:*** The first or last column has a darker color and has bold text in a contrasting color.
- ***Banded Rows*** or ***Banded Columns:*** The rows or columns have alternating colors. *Banded Rows* makes reading across the table easier. *Banded Columns* emphasizes the separate columns.

HOW TO: Apply a Table Style with Header Row and Banded Rows

1. Click anywhere in the table you want to change.
2. Click the **Table Tools Design** tab.
3. Check **Header Row** and **Banded Rows** [*Table Style Options* group].
4. Click the **More** list arrow in the *Table Styles* group to see the complete gallery. The current style is highlighted.
5. Point to a style to see a live preview (Figure 2-54). ScreenTips identify each style name.
6. Click a style to apply it.

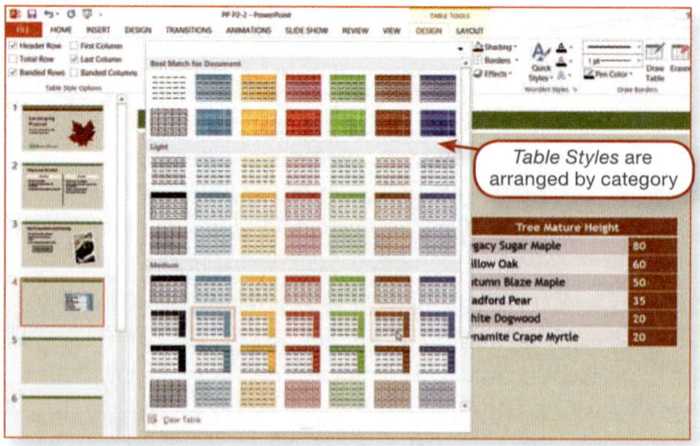

2-54 ***Table Styles***

If you want to clear table formatting, click the **More** button [*Table Tools Design* tab, *Table Styles* group] and click **Clear Table**. To emphasize the table or cells within the table, such as a heading row, you can apply effects.

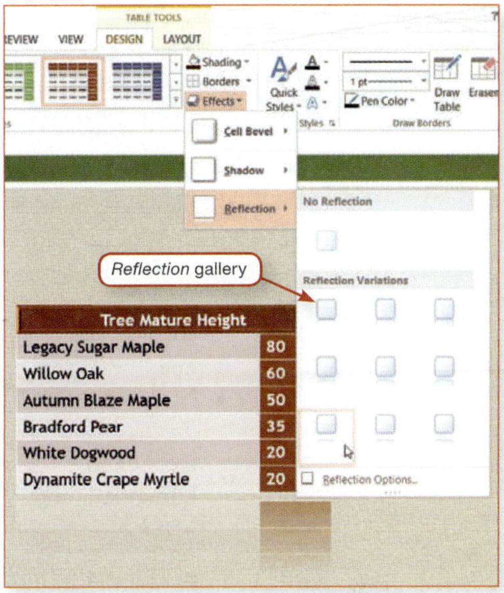

2-55 *Reflection Effects*

HOW TO: Apply Table Effects

1. Select the table, or the cells, to be changed.
2. Click the **Effects** button [*Table Tools Design* tab, *Table Styles* group (Figure 2-55).
3. Click one of the following effects and select a specific option:
   - **Cell Bevel**
   - **Shadow**
   - **Reflection**

Shading and Border Colors

After you apply a built-in table style, you can change colors to emphasize your content or better match other aspects of your presentation. Select the cells you want to change and use the **Shading** button [*Table Tools Design* tab, *Table Styles* group] to select a different color (Figure 2-56). The icon for this button is the same as a **Shape Fill** button.

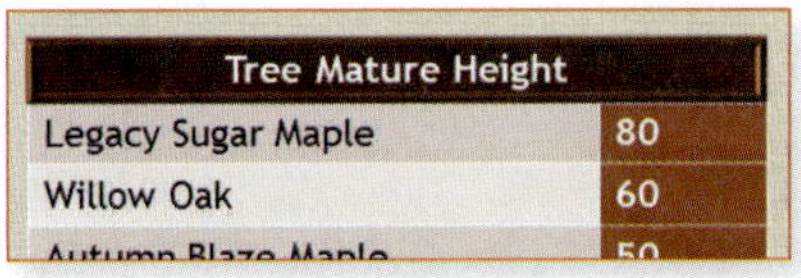

2-56 Row shading emphasizes text

Border lines separate cells and outline the edge of the table. Some table styles do not show border lines. To add lines, use the **Borders** button [*Table Tools Design* tab, *Table Styles* group] and each available option shows where the border line will be applied when that option is selected (Figure 2-57). Make sure to select the appropriate area before you apply the border change. If you want to make the border lines thicker, increase the **Pen Weight** [*Table Tools Design* tab, *Draw Borders* group] before you apply the border change. You can remove borders from selected cells by clicking the **Borders** button and selecting **No Border**.

Also, you can apply, change, and remove borders using the ***Pen*** tools [*Table Tools Design* tab, *Draw Borders* group].

- ***Pen Color:*** Change line color.
- ***Pen Style:*** Choose a different line style.
- ***Pen Weight:*** Change line thickness.
- ***Draw Table:*** Draw table area as well as column and row border lines.
- ***Eraser:*** Remove border lines.

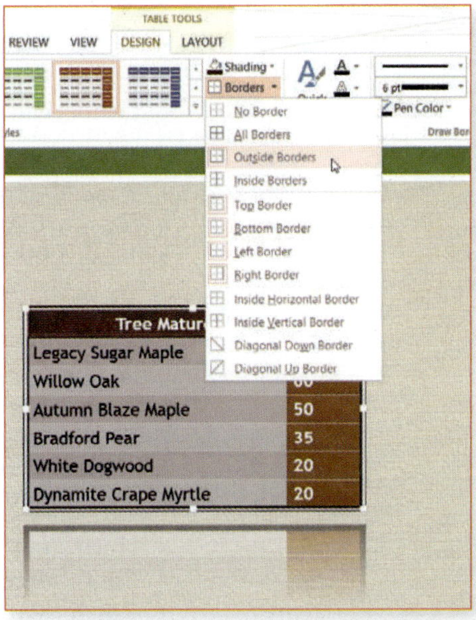

2-57 Border color and weight changed

It may take a little practice to use the pen to change table lines and not start a new table. The *Eraser* removes each line you click.

Cell Alignment

Within cells, text is aligned on the left by default, which is appropriate for words and phrases. However, numbers should usually be right-aligned to make it easy for your audience to interpret values.

If cells have a single line of text, center the text vertically in the cells. If some cells contain more text than other cells, top alignment generally works best because it imposes consistency. Bottom alignment works well for column headings when they have more than one line of text.

Click the **Align** buttons [*Table Tools Layout* tab, *Alignment* group] and choose from the following horizontal and vertical alignment options:

- ***Horizontal alignment:*** *Align Text Left, Center, Align Text Right*
- ***Vertical alignment:*** *Align Top, Center Vertically, Align Bottom*

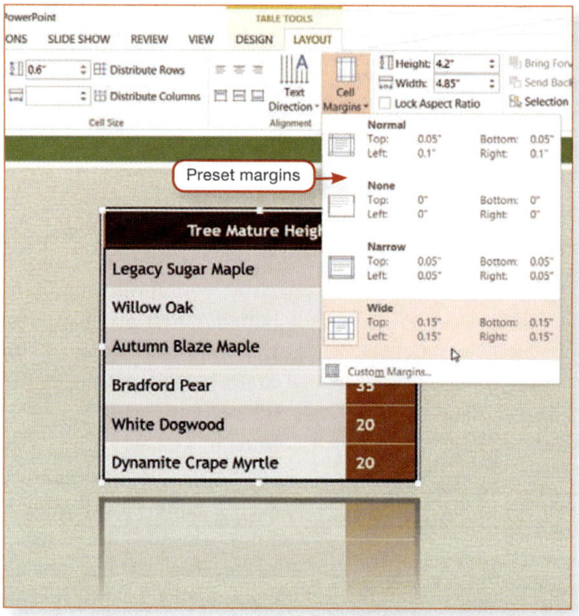

2-58 *Cell Margins* increased

Cell Margins and Text Direction

Some space is needed between the border lines that define a cell and the text that goes in the cell. The default ***Internal Margin*** spacing is *Normal*. You can change the spacing by clicking the **Cell Margins** button [*Table Tools Layout* tab, *Alignment* group] and choose from one of the following options (Figure 2-58):

- *Normal:* **.05"** top/bottom, **.1"** left/right
- *None:* **0"** all sides
- *Narrow:* **0.05"** all sides
- *Wide:* **0.15"** all sides

Click **Custom Margins** to open the *Cell Text Layout* dialog box to enter other measurements.

If text becomes too long to fit in a cell, you can change from the default horizontal direction. Be careful when using this option because your text may not be as easy to read. Click **Text Direction** and choose one of the following four options (Figure 2-59):

- **Horizontal**
- **Rotate all text 90°**
- **Rotate all text 270°**
- **Stacked**

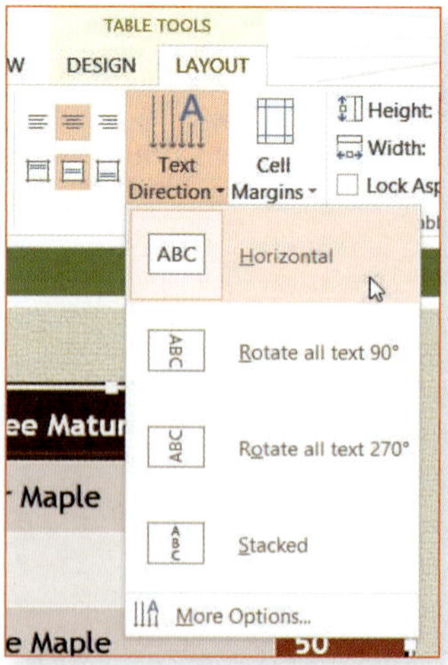

2-59 *Text Direction* options

PAUSE & PRACTICE: POWERPOINT 2-2

For this project you create a table of costs, insert a row of data, and format the table to blend with other colors used in the landscaping presentation. You also add a text box to show an alternative cost.

File Needed: ***[your initials] PP P2-1.pptx***
Completed Project File Name: ***[your initials] PP P2-2.pptx***

1. Open the presentation ***[your initials] PP P2-1*** and save it as ***[your initials] PP P2-2***.
2. Create a table.
   a. On slide 4, click the **Table** button on the content placeholder.
   b. On the *Insert Table* dialog box, enter 4 columns and 5 rows. Click **OK** to close the dialog box.
   c. Type the following table text. It will first appear as shown in Figure 2-60.

Item	Quantity	Cost Each	Totals
Trees—shade	3	500	1,500
Trees—ornamental	3	150	450
Perennials	30	12	360
Hydroseeding sq. ft.	8,000	.10	800

Item	Quantity	Cost Each	Totals
Trees—shade	3	500	1,500
Trees—ornamental	3	150	450
Perennials	30	12	360
Hydroseeding sq. ft.	8,000	.10	800

2-60 Table as it first appears

   d. Select all table **cells** and change the font size to **20 pts**.
3. Adjust table sizing and alignment.
   a. Make each column the appropriate size for its content by pointing to each line separating the columns, including the right side of the table, and double-clicking when your pointer changes to a splitter.
   b. Select the "Quantity," "Cost Each," and "Totals" columns and click the **Align Right** button [*Table Tools Layout* tab, *Alignment* group].
4. Insert rows and add text.
   a. Click in the "Perennials" cell and click the **Insert Above** button [*Table Tools Layout* tab, *Rows & Columns* group].
   b. Add the following row text:

      Shrubs 10 40 400

   c. Click in the "Hydroseeding" cell and click the **Insert Below** button [*Table Tools Layout* tab, *Rows & Columns* group].
   d. On this new row, select the last three cells and click the **Merge Cells** button [*Table Tools Layout* tab, *Merge* group].
   e. Add the following row text:

      Total 3,510

5. Select styles, options, and shading.
   a. Click the **More** button [*Tables Tools Design* tab, *Table Styles* group] and select the **Medium Style 3**, **Accent 4** style.
   b. Select **Header Row**, **Total Row**, and **Banded Rows** [*Tables Tools Design* tab, *Table Style Options* group].

c. Select each of the rows with gray shading and click the **Shading** button [*Table Tools Design* tab, *Table Styles* group]; then select **Green**, **Accent 4**, **Lighter 80%**.
d. Select the last row and click the **Shading** button and select **Green**, **Accent 4**, **Lighter 60%**.
e. Select the first row and click the **Effects** button [*Table Tools Design* tab, *Table Styles* group], click **Cell Bevel**, and select **Circle** (Figure 2-61).

Item	Quantity	Cost Each	Totals
Trees–shade	3	500	1,500
Trees–ornamental	3	150	450
Shrubs	10	40	400
Perennials	30	12	360
Hydroseeding sq. ft.	8,000	.10	800
Total			3,510

2-61 Style, row shading, and *Bevel* effect applied

6. Add borders and a shadow effect.
   a. Select the first column.
   b. Click the **Pen Color** button [*Table Tools Design* tab, *Draw Borders* group] and select **Black**.
   c. Click the **Pen Weight** button [*Table Tools Design* tab, *Draw Borders* group] and select **1 pt**.
   d. Click the **Border** button [*Table Tools Design* tab, *Table Styles* group] and select **Left Border**.
   e. Select the last column.
   f. Click the **Border** button and select **Right Border**.
   g. Select the table and click the **Effects** button [*Table Tools Design* tab, *Table Styles* group]. Click **Shadow** and select **Offset Diagonal Bottom Right**.
7. Move the table so it is centered on the slide.
8. Insert a text box.
   a. Click the **Text Box** button [*Insert* tab, *Text* group] and click the slide to start a text box. Type the following text:
      Sod cost for 8,000 sq. ft. @ .60 = $4,800
   b. Change the font size to **20 pts** [*Home* tab, *Font* group].
   c. Click the **Shape Fill** button [*Home* tab, *Drawing* group] and select **Green**, **Accent 4**, **Lighter 60%**.
   d. Resize the text box as necessary so the text fits on one line. Move it to the lower right of the slide (Figure 2-62).

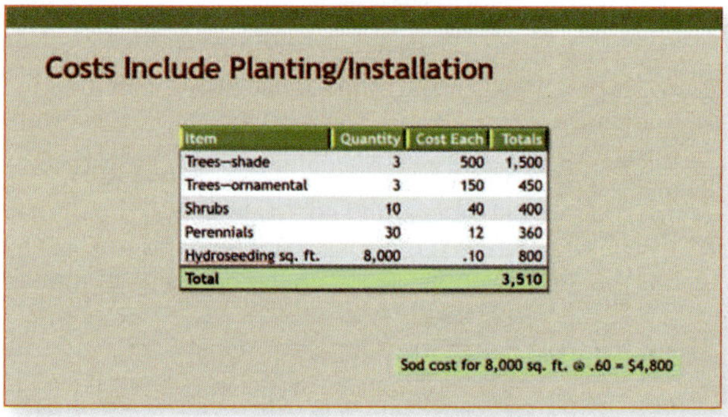

2-62 Completed table

9. Save and close your presentation.

SLO 2.6

Creating a SmartArt Graphic

To clearly illustrate concepts such as processes, cycles, or relationships, you can create a diagram using ***SmartArt graphics*** to help your audience see connections or sequences. This is a very important communication strategy; the shapes of the diagram are concisely labeled for each concept and the shapes you use can help people recognize relationships. For example, you can show subtopics radiating from a central topic or sequential steps in a work flow.

The *SmartArt Tools Design* tab (Figure 2-63) provides options for the overall design and styles of the *SmartArt* graphics. You can add shapes and rearrange the order of shapes.

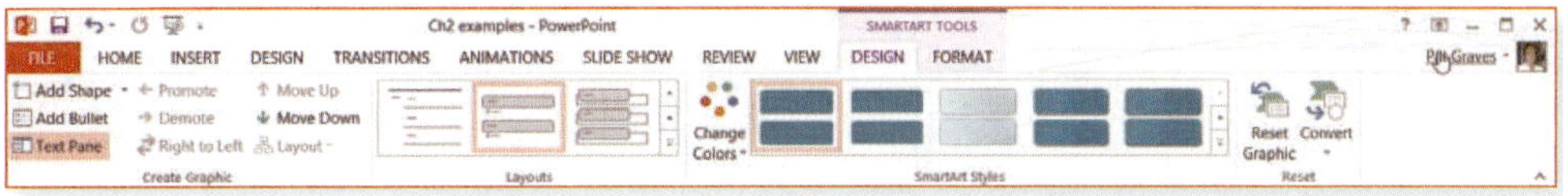

2-63 *SmartArt Tools Design* tab

The *SmartArt Tools Format* tab (Figure 2-73) provides options to customize shape and text styles, fill colors, outline colors, and effects.

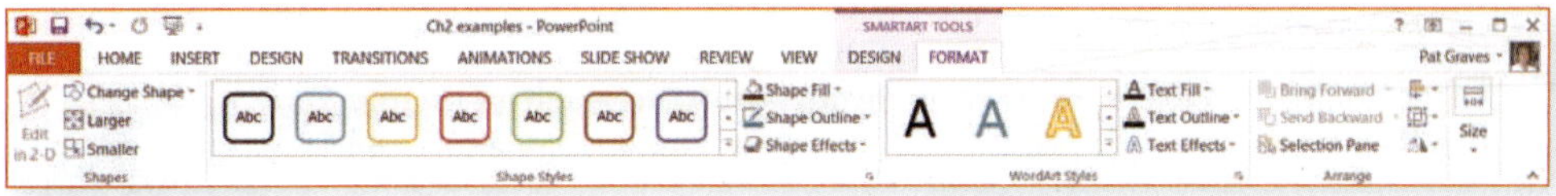

2-64 *SmartArt Tools Format* tab

SmartArt Layouts

SmartArt layouts (diagrams) are organized by type in the *Choose a SmartArt Graphic* dialog box; each type is described in the following table. When you select a layout, PowerPoint provides more information about using that specific layout.

SmartArt Graphic Types and Purposes

Type	Purpose
List	Illustrates non-sequential or grouped information
Process	Illustrates sequential steps in a process or workflow
Cycle	Illustrates a continuing sequence or concepts related to a central idea
Hierarchy	Illustrates a decision tree or top-to-bottom relationship such as an organizational chart
Relationship	Illustrates concepts that are connected such as contrasting, opposing, or converging
Matrix	Illustrates the relationship of four parts to the whole
Pyramid	Illustrates proportional or interconnected relationships
Picture	Shows pictures as integral parts of many different diagrams
Office.com	Shows diagrams from layouts on Office.com

HOW TO: Create a SmartArt Graphic

1. Display the slide where you want to insert the *SmartArt* graphic.
2. Click the **Insert** tab.
3. Click the **SmartArt** button [*Illustrations* group] to open the *Choose a SmartArt Graphic* dialog box.
4. Select a type from the list on the left (Figure 2-65).
5. Click a layout in the gallery to select it.
6. Click **OK** to close the dialog box. The *SmartArt* graphic appears on the slide with sample text.

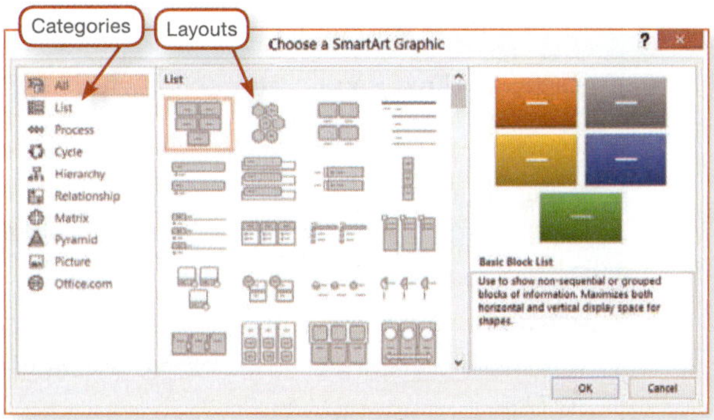

2-65 *Choose a SmartArt Graphic* dialog box

> **ANOTHER WAY**
>
> To insert a *SmartArt* graphic on a new slide, click the **Insert SmartArt Graphic** button on the content placeholder to open the *Choose a SmartArt Graphic* dialog box.

When you insert a *SmartArt* graphic using the **SmartArt** button on the *Insert* tab, the initial size of the *SmartArt* frame may be different than if you inserted the *SmartArt* graphic using the content placeholder on a new slide with a Title and Content layout. You may need to resize the frame for your content and to fit appropriately on your slide.

If the layout you choose has picture placeholders on the shapes, such as the *Continuous Picture List* layout shown in Figure 2-66, click each picture icon to open the *Insert Pictures* dialog box. Locate the picture you want to insert and click **Insert**. The picture is sized automatically and shaped to fit the current picture placeholder.

2-66 *SmartArt Continuous Picture List* layout

Add Text

Keep text very concise because space is limited for each shape within the *SmartArt* frame. *List* layouts often work well if you have both Level 1 and Level 2 information (shown as indented text in a bulleted list).

Use the Text Pane

You can enter text using the ***Text Pane*** [*SmartArt Tools Design* tab, *Create Graphic* group] just as you would a bulleted list. As you enter text in the *Text Pane,* it also appears in the *SmartArt* shapes. Text becomes smaller in the shapes as you enter more text. You can resize or move the *Text Pane.*

Typically, only a few words appear in each shape. After the first bulleted text is entered (Level 1 text), press **Enter** to add a second bullet. If the layout you are using has enough space, press **Tab** to indent for Level 2 text. Notice in Figure 2-67 that Level 1 text is in a shape and Level 2 text is in a bulleted list below the shape.

HOW TO: Type SmartArt Text Using the Text Pane

1. Open the *Text Pane,* if necessary, by using one of the following methods:
   - Click the **Text Pane** button [*SmartArt Tools Design* tab, *Create Graphic* group].
   - Click the **Text Pane** control on the left side of the *SmartArt* frame.
2. Type text after the first bullet to add Level 1 text.
3. Press **Enter** to add a new item. Another shape appears in your diagram, and shape sizes automatically adjust.
4. Press **Tab** to indent for Level 2 text (Figure 2-67).
5. Use arrow keys to move through the listed items.
6. To remove a shape, delete the related bulleted text in the *Text Pane.*

2-67 *SmartArt Text Pane*

Enter Text in SmartArt Shapes

You can type text directly into each *SmartArt* shape.

HOW TO: Type Text in SmartArt Shapes

1. Close the *Text Pane* by clicking the **Close** button in the top-right corner of the pane.
2. Click each *SmartArt* shape to select it and type your text. A dashed border appears as you type or edit your text.
   - Pressing **Tab** does not move your insertion point between shapes.
   - You cannot drag text into a *SmartArt* shape, but you can paste copied text.
3. Press **Delete** to remove a selected shape.
4. Click outside the *SmartArt* frame, or press **Esc**, when you are finished (Figure 2-68).

2-68 Completed picture *SmartArt* graphic

Convert Text to a SmartArt Graphic

You can change bulleted text to a *SmartArt* graphic.

HOW TO: Convert Text to a SmartArt Graphic

1. Select the bulleted text placeholder or the text within the placeholder that you want to convert to a *SmartArt* graphic.
2. Click the **Home** tab.
3. Click the **Convert to SmartArt Graphic** button [*Paragraph* group] (Figure 2-69). The gallery displays layouts that are designed to show listed information.
4. Select the layout you want and click **OK** to close the dialog box and insert the *SmartArt* graphic.

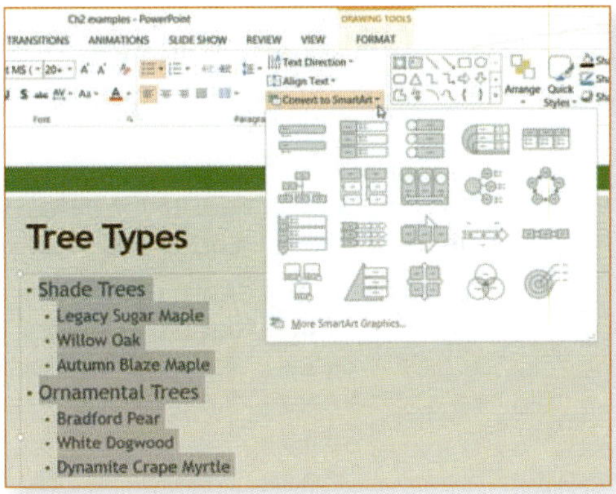

2-69 Convert to *SmartArt* graphic

SLO 2.7

Enhancing a SmartArt Graphic

When you create a *SmartArt* graphic, by default it appears using the first accent color in the current color theme. You can customize many style options and colors using the *SmartArt Tools Design* tab as well as rearrange shape order, add shapes, or change layouts.

SmartArt Styles

The ***SmartArt Styles*** gallery provides different effects for emphasizing the diagram shapes. In the ***3-D*** category, the layouts have a dimensional effect. When choosing these layouts, be sure that your diagram is not distorted or difficult to interpret.

HOW TO: Apply SmartArt Styles

1. Select the *SmartArt* graphic.
2. Click the **SmartArt Tools Design** tab.
3. Click the **More** button [*SmartArt Styles* group] to open the *SmartArt Styles* gallery (Figure 2-70).
4. Point to a style to see a live preview.
5. Click a style to apply it.

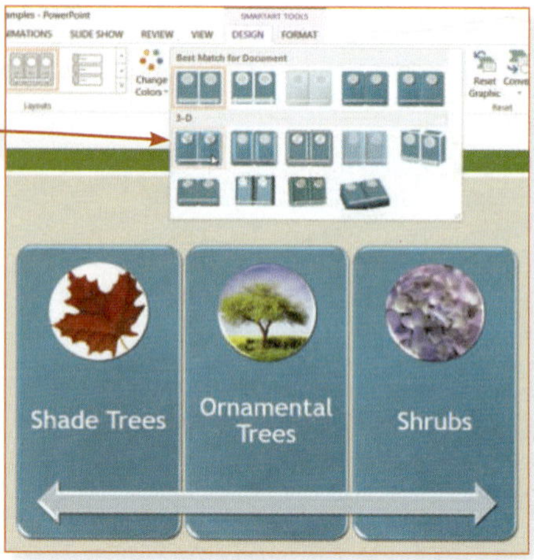

2-70 ***SmartArt* graphic styles**

Change Colors

How color is applied can help to differentiate between the various parts of a *SmartArt* graphic. The ***Change Colors*** gallery provides a quick way to change all the colors at the same time. Color options are arranged in categories; some show variations of the same color while others have different colors.

Individual shape colors within a *SmartArt* graphic can be changed as you would any other shape.

HOW TO: Change SmartArt Colors

1. Select the *SmartArt* graphic.
2. To change colors for the entire diagram, click the **Change Colors** button [*SmartArt Tools Design* tab, *SmartArt Styles* group] and select a gallery option (Figure 2-71) to apply it.
3. To change the color of a selected shape within a diagram, click the **Shape Fill** button or the **Shape Outline** button [*SmartArt Tools Format* tab, *Shape Styles* group] and choose an appropriate color.

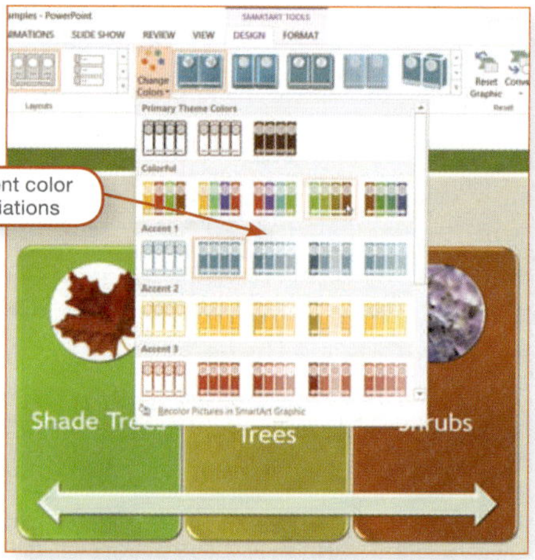

2-71 ***SmartArt* graphic *Change Colors* options**

Change Layouts

You may find that the *SmartArt* layout you have chosen does not fit your particular process or the relationship you are trying to show. Or you might need a layout that would better fit two levels of information.

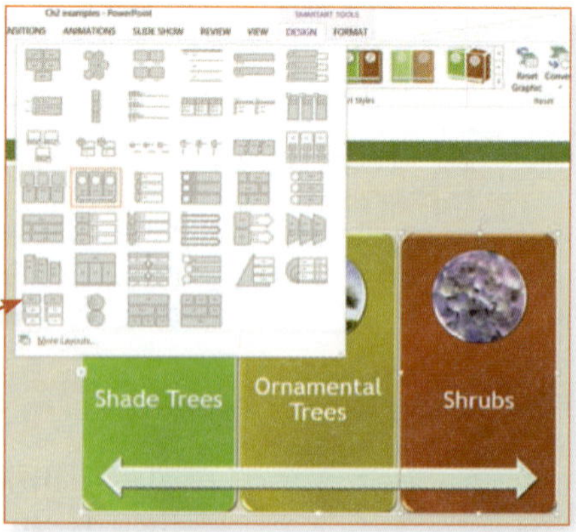

2-72 ***SmartArt* layouts**

HOW TO: Change Layouts

1. Select the *SmartArt* graphic.
2. On the *SmartArt Tools Design* tab, click the **More** button [*Layouts* group] to open the *Layouts* gallery (Figure 2-72).

3. Point to a layout to see a live preview of the current layout.
4. Click **More Layouts** to open the *Choose a SmartArt Graphic* dialog box.
5. Select an appropriate type from the list on the left.
6. Double-click a **layout** to apply it, or select the layout and then click **OK**.

Add Shapes

The ***Add Shape*** button on the *SmartArt Tools Design* tab inserts shapes in relation to the selected shape. The available options include the following:

- *Add Shape After*
- *Add Shape Before*
- *Add Shape Above*
- *Add Shape Below*
- *Add Assistant*

Being able to control where a new shape appears is important. For example, you can add shapes to an organization chart as new employees are hired. Adding a shape before or after a selected shape could show a new managerial position at the same level. Adding a shape above a selected shape could show a director position above a managerial position. Adding a shape below a selected shape could show a subordinate position reporting to a manager. An Assistant shape is only available for organization charts.

HOW TO: Add Shapes

1. Select the shape closest to where you want to add a shape.
2. Click the **SmartArt Design Tools** tab.
3. Click the **Add Shape** button list arrow [*Create Graphic* group] (Figure 2-73) and select the position where you want to add the new shape.

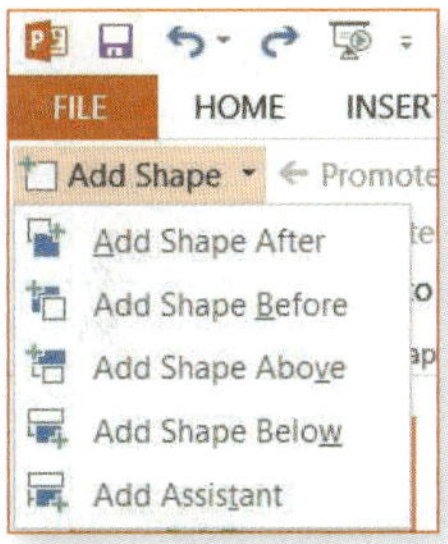

2-73 *Add Shape* options

To change the flow of a diagram, click the **Right to Left** button [*SmartArt Tools Design* tab, *Create Graphic* group].

PAUSE & PRACTICE: POWERPOINT 2-3

For this project you create an organization chart showing the CGL employees who will be managing various aspects of the landscaping for Frank and Sandra Hunter. You also convert one of the existing lists to a *SmartArt* graphic and rearrange slide objects for an interesting appearance. The *SmartArt* styles applied blend with other colors in the presentation.

File Needed: ***[your initials] PP P2-2.pptx***
Completed Project File Name: ***[your initials] PP P2-3.pptx***

1. Open the presentation ***[your initials] PP P2-2*** and save it as ***[your initials] PP P2-3***.
2. Create a new slide.
   a. On slide 1, click the **New Slide** button list arrow and select the **Title and Content** layout.
   b. Type the slide title Your CGL Team.
   c. Click the **Insert a SmartArt Graphic** button on the content placeholder to open the *Choose a SmartArt Graphic* dialog box.
   d. Select the *Hierarchy* type from the list on the left.
   e. Click the **Organization Chart** layout and click **OK** to close the dialog box and insert the *SmartArt* graphic.
3. Add the text displayed in Figure 2-74 to the shapes. Press **Enter** after each name and let the job titles word wrap as needed.
4. Make changes to the organization chart using the *SmartArt Tools Design* tab.
   a. Change the flow by clicking the **Right to Left** button [*Create Graphic* group].
   b. Click the **More** button [*SmartArt Styles* group] and select the **Inset** effect (Figure 2-75).
   c. Click the **Change Colors** button [*SmartArt Styles* group] and select **Gradient Loop, Accent 4** (Figure 2-76).
5. Change bulleted text to *SmartArt.*
   a. On slide 4, select the bulleted text and click the **Convert to SmartArt** button [*Home* tab, *Paragraph* group].
   b. Click the **Vertical Bullet List**. The *SmartArt* list fills the slide and is too large since other objects are already on the slide (Figure 2-77).
6. Make changes to the *SmartArt* graphic so it fits on the slide with the other objects.
   a. Select all shapes and change the font to **24 pts**.
   b. Select the *SmartArt* frame and resize it to better fit the text as shown (Figure 2-78).
   c. Change the style to **Inset** [*SmartArt Tools Design* tab, *SmartArt Styles* group].

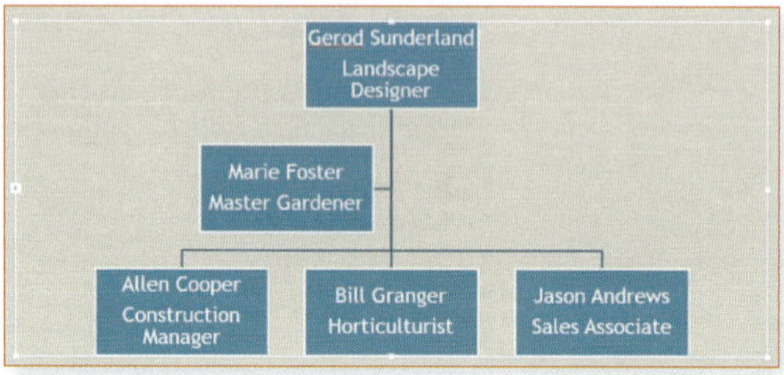

2-74 Organization chart

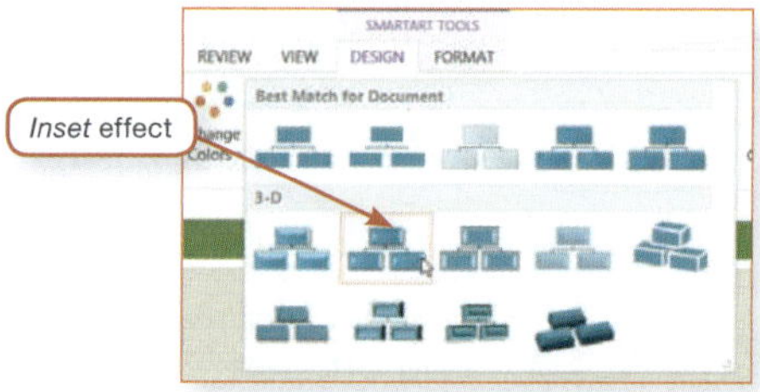

2-75 *SmartArt* graphic styles

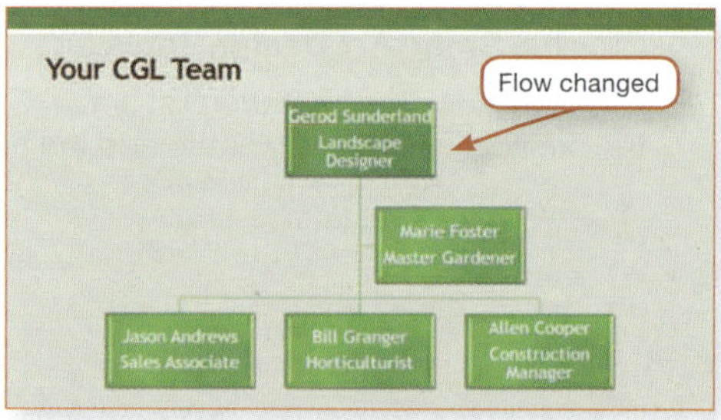

2-76 Completed organization chart

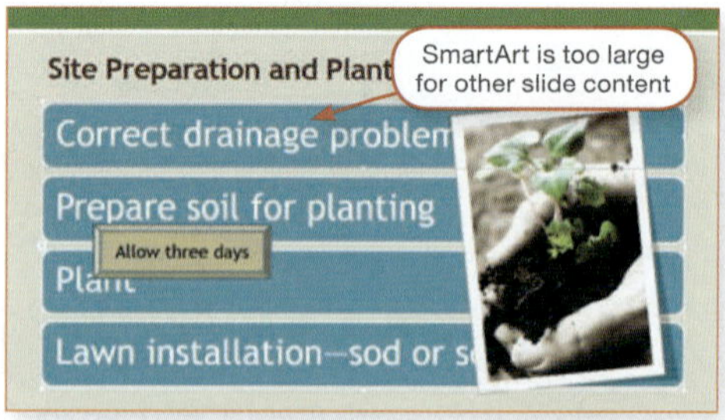

2-77 *SmartArt* graphic shapes as they originally appear

2-78 Resize the *SmartArt* graphic

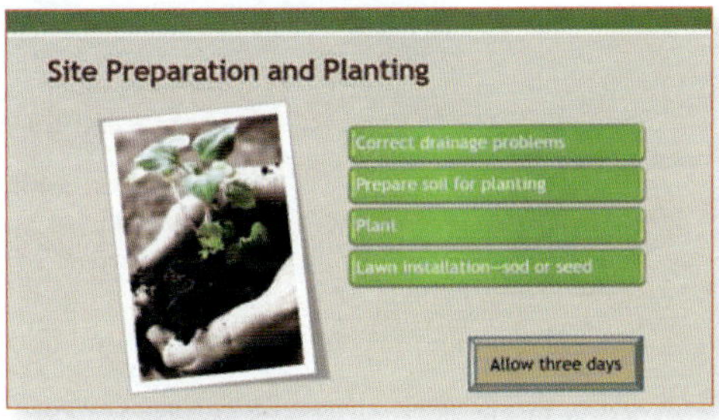

2-79 Completed slide

d. Click the **Change Colors** button [*SmartArt Tools Design* tab, *SmartArt Styles* group] and select **Colored Fill - Accent 4**.

e. Rearrange slide objects as displayed in Figure 2-79. Be careful to point to the *SmartArt* frame when moving it so the whole diagram moves and not just an individual shape within the frame.

7. Save and close your presentation.

SLO 2.8

Creating a Chart

Charts help viewers interpret data and make comparisons. If you have lots of data, then create your chart in Excel and copy it to a PowerPoint slide. However, for most situations, PowerPoint's *Chart* feature will provide all the options you need.

To insert a chart in PowerPoint 2013, click the **Insert Chart** button on a new slide content placeholder or click the **Insert** tab and then click the **Chart** button [*Illustrations* group] to add a chart to an existing slide. You can choose a chart type to control how data is represented such as with columns, bars, lines, or pie slices. The following table lists chart types and describes their purposes.

Chart Types and Purposes

Type	Purpose
Column	Shows a comparison of values or data changes over time. Categories are shown on the horizontal axis and values are shown on the vertical axis. Columns may be clustered to show a range of values or groupings. Columns in a category may be stacked to emphasize the total category value rather than the subsections that make up the category.
Line	Shows data changes over time; works well to show trends with data plotted at even intervals. Categories are shown on the horizontal axis and values are shown on the vertical axis.
Pie	Shows the values in a data series in proportional sizes that make up a whole pie. Values cannot be negative or zero values. Percentages or actual values can be displayed near or on pie slices. This category also includes *Doughnut* charts that also show parts of a whole but can contain more than one data series as rings.
Bar	Similar to column charts except bars are horizontal; works well for comparison of values.
Area	Shows data changes over time; emphasizes the total value of a trend.
X Y (Scatter)	Shows the relationships between several data series using values on both the X and Y axes; works well to emphasize where data sets have similar values. This category also includes *Bubble* charts.
Stock	Shows fluctuation of stock prices with high, low, and close values displayed over time.

(continued)

Chart Types and Purposes *(continued)*

Type	Purpose
Surface	Shows the differences between two sets of data. Instead of values, the color bands represent the same range of values as in a topographic map showing land elevations.
Radar	Shows the combined values of several data series with values relative to a center point.
Combo	Combines two charts such as a column chart with a line chart displayed over it.

MORE INFO

Use *Help* to search for "chart types" to see examples and get tips on how to arrange data in a worksheet.

The *Chart Tools Design* tab (Figure 2-80) and the *Chart Tools Format* tab (Figure 2-81) are available when a chart is active.

2-80 *Chart Tools Design* tab

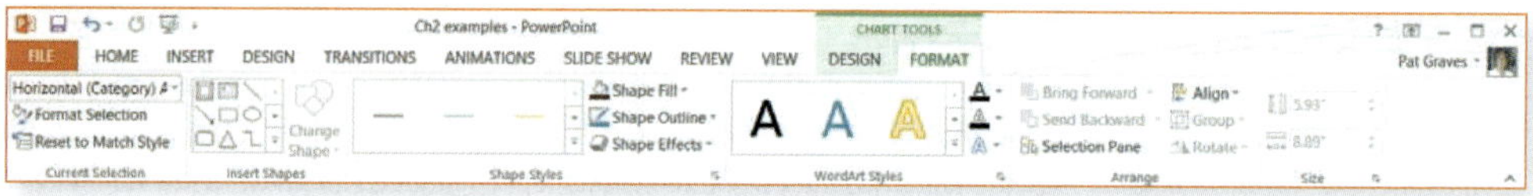

2-81 *Chart Tools Format* tab

When you insert a chart in PowerPoint, a ***spreadsheet*** opens with sample data in rows and columns. A group of data values from each column is a ***data series;*** a group of data values from each row is a ***category***. You can edit the sample data by entering your own information or you could copy and paste data from Excel, Word, or Access. If you need to revise the data in Excel, click the **Excel** button in the spreadsheet title bar.

Because the spreadsheet and PowerPoint chart are linked, the changes you make to the spreadsheet are automatically reflected in the chart.

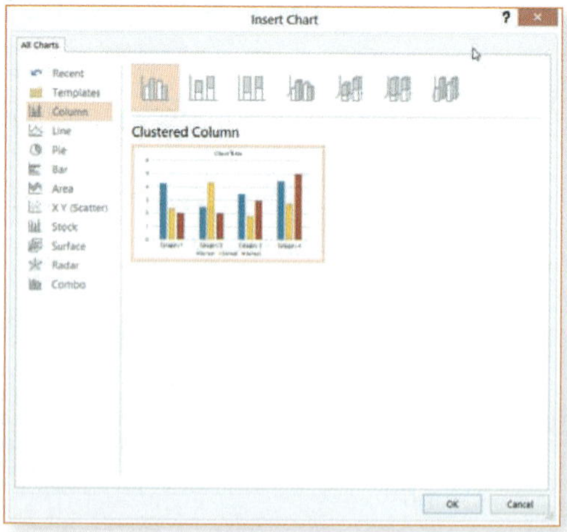

2-82 *Insert Chart* dialog box

HOW TO: Insert a Chart

1. Click the **Insert** tab; then click the **Chart** button [*Illustrations* group]. You can also click the **Insert Chart** button on a new slide content placeholder.
2. In the *Insert Chart* dialog box (Figure 2-82), chart categories are listed in the left pane and a variety of chart layouts for each category appear in the right pane. A ScreenTip identifies chart names.

3. Click a layout to select a chart.
4. Click **OK** to close the dialog box.
5. A spreadsheet automatically opens showing sample data that you edit (Figure 2-83).

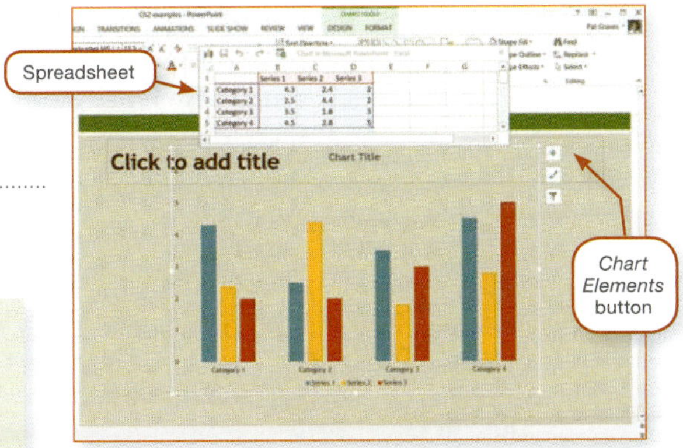

2-83 Spreadsheet linked to a chart

> **MORE INFO**
>
> The chart frame that appears on your slide when it is inserted using the *Insert* tab may be sized differently than when you insert a chart on a new slide from the *Title and Content* placeholder. Resize the chart frames as needed.

The chart frame displays ***chart elements***, the objects that make up the chart. Chart elements vary based on the type of chart used. You can see which chart elements are shown by clicking the **Chart Elements** button, the top button on the right of the chart frame. You can add or remove elements by changing selections from the list. Other chart elements appear in the list box in the *Current Selection* group on the *Chart Tools Format* tab and in the *Format* pane when you are working on the chart. The following table defines chart elements.

Chart Elements and Definitions

Element	Definition
Y-Axis (Vertical)	Also called the *Value Axis;* displayed vertically with numbers usually arranged on the left of a chart
X-Axis (Horizontal)	Also called the *Category Axis;* displayed horizontally with word or number labels across the bottom of the chart
Axis Titles	Both the Y-Axis and the X-Axis can include titles
Chart Area	The background area where the entire chart is displayed in a frame
Chart Title	A chart may include a title
Data Labels	Used to identify series and category names; may include values
Data Markers	The graphical representation of values shown as columns, bars, slices, or data points
Data Table	The data that creates the chart shown in table format below the chart
Error Bars	Used to show margins of error or standard deviation amounts
Gridlines	Lines that appear behind a chart to help the viewer judge values
Legend	The key that identifies the data series by color
Plot Area	The rectangle between the vertical and horizontal axes that is behind the data markers
Tick Marks	Used to identify the categories, values, or series on each axis
Trendline	Shows averages on 2-D charts that are not stacked and can extend beyond actual data to predict future values

Enter Data and Edit

After you replace the spreadsheet sample data with your data, you can close the spreadsheet. If you need to revise the data as you work on the chart in PowerPoint, you can open the spreadsheet again.

HOW TO: Edit Data in the Spreadsheet

1. Select the chart you want to modify.
2. Click the top of the **Edit Data** button [*Chart Tools Design* tab, *Data* group] (Figure 2-84) to open the spreadsheet. (If you need to modify the data in Excel, click the **Edit Data** button list arrow and choose **Edit Data in Excel 2013**.)
3. Resize the spreadsheet window, if necessary, to display all of your data.
4. Replace cell contents (Figure 2-85) by clicking in the **cell** and typing your data.
5. To move around in the spreadsheet,
   - Press **Enter** to move the insertion point down one row.
   - Press **Tab** to move the insertion point to the next cell on the right.
   - Press **Shift+Tab** to move to the next cell on the left.
   - Press arrow keys to move in any direction.
6. Click the spreadsheet **Close** button to return to PowerPoint.

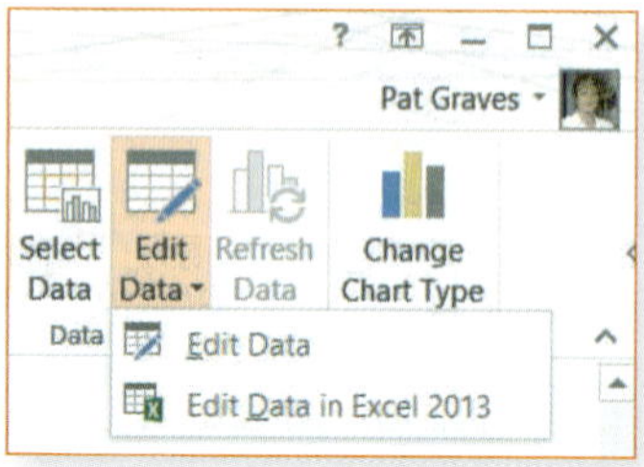

2-84 *Edit Data* button

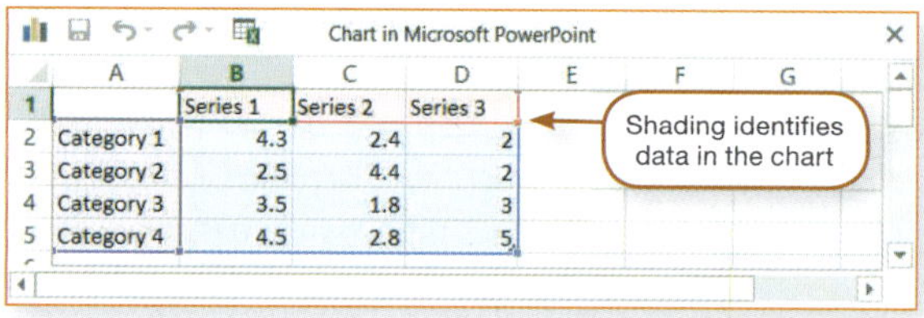

2-85 Default spreadsheet data

MORE INFO

Remove the sample data on the spreadsheet by clicking the **Select All** button (above the row 1 heading and to the left of the column A heading) and pressing your keyboard **Delete**.

Rows and columns on the spreadsheet may need adjustments.

- If a cell displays number signs (#) rather than the data you entered, the cell is not wide enough to display cell contents. You need to make the column wider.
- Be sure the shading correctly identifies the category, series, and data cells. If necessary, drag the sizing handles to adjust.
- If you need to add new columns or rows, edit the spreadsheet in Excel.

HOW TO: Modify the Spreadsheet

1. Select the chart you want to modify.
2. Click the top of the **Edit Data** button [*Chart Tools Design* tab, *Data* group].
3. Adjust column width. Position your pointer on the vertical line to the right of the column heading (Figure 2-86); then use one of these methods:
   - Drag to the correct width.
   - Double-click and the column automatically expands to fit the widest data entered in that column.

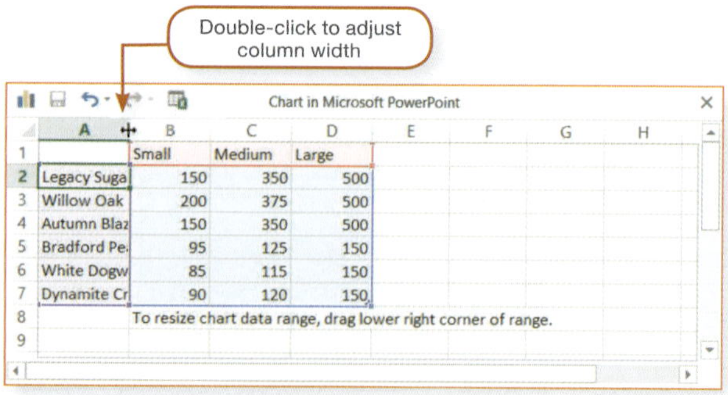

2-86 Adjust column width

- Right-click and select **Column Width**, then width number on the *Column Width* dialog box. Click **OK** to close the dialog box.

4. To add columns and rows, click the **Edit Data** button list arrow [*Chart Tools Design* tab, *Data* group] and choose **Edit Data in Excel 2013**.
   - Click in the column to the right of where you want to add a column.
   - Click in the row below where you want to add a row.
   - Click the **Insert Cells** button [*Home* tab, *Cells* group] and select the option you need to insert cells, columns, or rows.
5. If necessary, resize the shaded areas on the spreadsheet so the data is accurately represented on your chart.

In PowerPoint, switch the data series by clicking the **Switch Row/Column** button [*Chart Tools Design* tab, *Data* group].

Change Chart Type

Click the **Change Chart Type** button [*Chart Tools Design* tab, *Type* group] to open the *Change Chart Type* gallery where you can choose from the many different layouts. For example, Figure 2-87 shows data in a line chart and Figure 2-88 shows the same data in a clustered column chart.

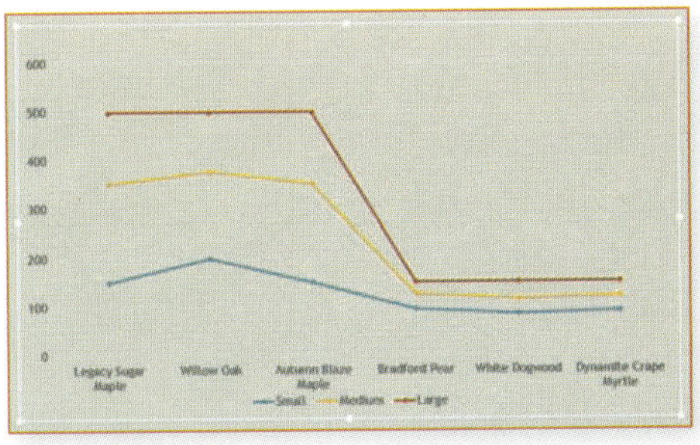

2-87 Line Chart

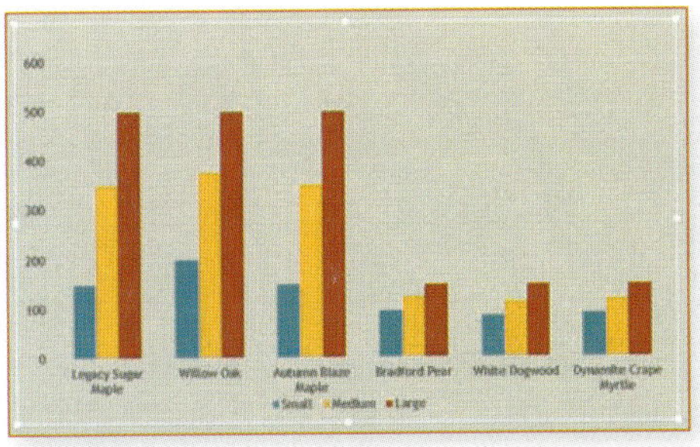

2-88 Clustered column chart

> **MORE INFO**
>
> If your PowerPoint window is narrow, you may need to click the **Quick Styles** button [*Chart Tools Design* tab] to open the *Chart Styles* gallery.

SLO 2.9

Enhancing a Chart

You can change the look of a chart by applying preset styles or manually customizing individual chart elements.

Chart Styles

The ***Chart Styles*** gallery [*Chart Tools Design* tab] provides preset effects for chart elements including the chart background. Click the **More** button to see styles arranged by number. Click a style to apply it (Figure 2-89).

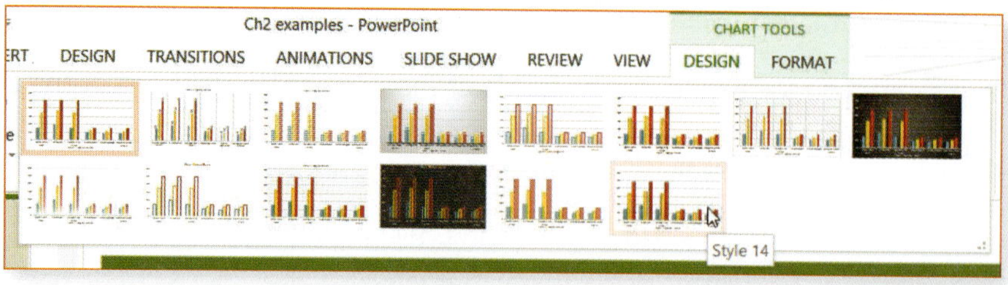

2-89 *Chart Styles* gallery

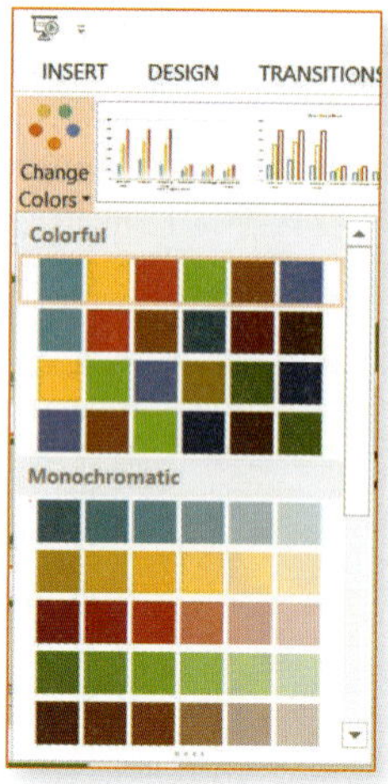

2-90 *Chart Colors* gallery

Click the **Change Colors** button [*Chart Tools Design* tab] to select ***Colorful*** or ***Monochromatic*** (shades of one color) combinations based on theme colors (Figure 2-90). The colors you choose then show in all the available chart styles. Be careful when selecting colors so the chart shapes (columns, bars, lines, or pie slices) are easy to distinguish for value comparisons. The colors also need to coordinate with your overall presentation (Figure 2-91).

If possible, avoid arranging red and green colors together. People who have difficulty recognizing different colors are most likely to have problems with red and green because they can look beige or gray.

ANOTHER WAY

You can also access *Chart Styles* and *Chart Colors* using the **Chart Styles** button on the right of each chart.

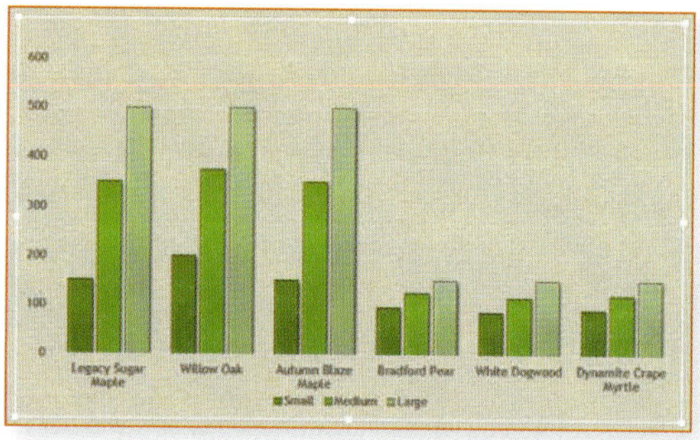

2-91 Chart style applied

Format Chart Elements

You can select chart elements (objects) and apply formatting in several ways.

HOW TO: Format a Chart Element

1. Use one of these methods to select a chart element and open the appropriate *Format* pane:
   - Select an element directly on the slide then double-click or right-click to open the appropriate *Format* pane for that element.
   - Click the **Chart Elements** button on the right of the chart, select a particular element, then click **More Options** to open the appropriate *Format* pane.
   - Use the *Chart Elements* list box [*Chart Tools Format* tab, *Current Selection* group] to select the element you need to change and then click **Format Selection** to open the *Format* pane for that element.

2. Use one or more of these commands on the *Chart Tools Format tab:*
   - Click the **More** button [*Shape Styles* group] and select a style.
   - Click the **Shape Fill**, **Shape Outline**, or **Shape Effects** buttons [*Shape Styles* group] and choose appropriate colors and effects (Figure 2-92).
   - When text is selected, click the **WordArt Quick Styles** button and select from the gallery of effects. You can also click the **Text Fill**, **Text Outline**, or **Text Effects** buttons [*WordArt Styles* group] and choose appropriate colors and effects.

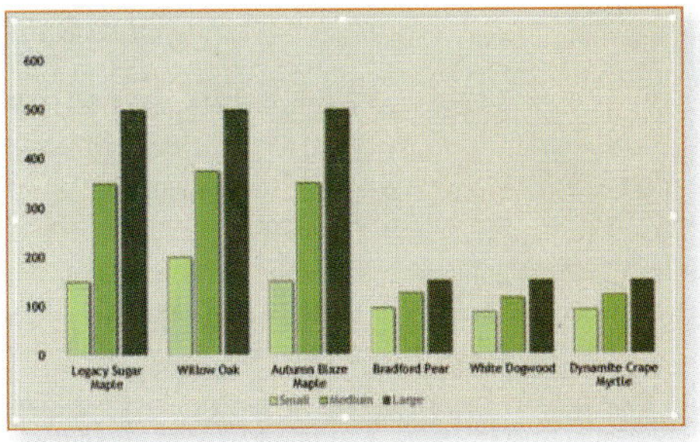

2-92 Colors changed on data series

To change the chart area size, point to any handle (the white squares on the chart frame) and resize by dragging. You can resize chart elements, but be careful not to distort size relationships.

HOW TO: Change the Chart Background

1. Select the chart.
2. Click the **Chart Tools Format** tab.
3. Click an element in the *Chart Elements* list box [*Current Selection* group].
4. Click the **Format Selection** button and the appropriate pane opens with options specific to each different element. Some options are available for 3-D charts only.
5. Chart background elements will vary based on the chart type. They may include:
   - *Chart Area*
   - *Plot Area*
   - *Back Wall*
   - *Side Wall*
   - *Walls*
   - *Floor*

You can fill elements of a chart with pictures. While a chart area picture might provide an interesting background, be careful when using pictures to avoid making the chart cluttered or the text difficult to read. The goal is always to create a chart that is easy to interpret.

In Figure 2-93, the plot area has a gradient fill with the darkest color at the bottom which helps to emphasize the height of the columns. In Figure 2-94, the chart type is a *3-D Column Chart*. The column heights (especially for the shorter columns) are not as easy to compare in this chart as they are in Figure 2-93.

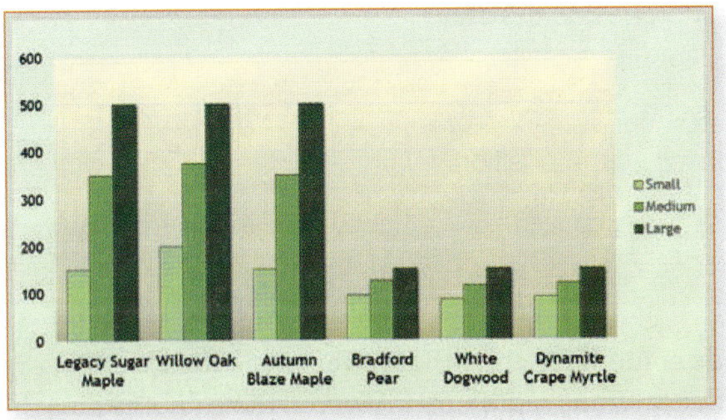

2-93 Chart plot area with gradient fill

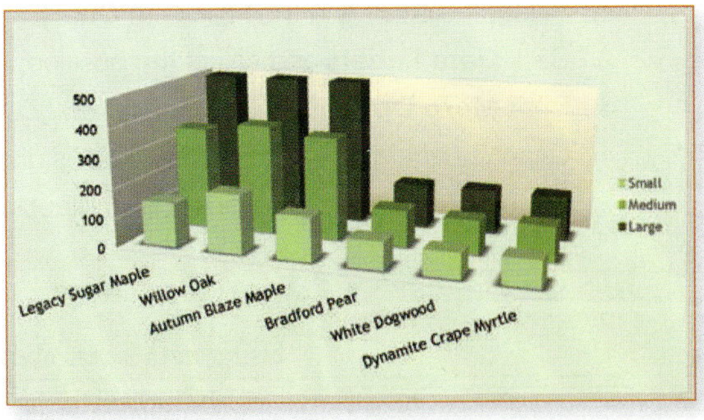

2-94 Chart with *3-D Rotation*

Legends and Labels

The ***legend*** identifies each data series by color. It is usually displayed on the right, but you can move it to other positions, display it horizontally above or below the plot area, or remove it.

HOW TO: Change Legend Position and Colors

1. To change the selected legend's position, use one of the following methods:
   - Click the **Chart Tools Format** tab, select **Legend** in the *Current Selection* list box, and click **Format Selection** to open the *Format Legend* pane.
   - Right-click the legend and choose **Format Legend** to open the *Format Legend* pane and select a different position. Deselect **Show the legend without overlapping the chart** if you want the legend to appear over the plot area that can be resized if necessary (Figure 2-95).
   - Click the **Chart Elements** button beside the chart, select the **Legend** list arrow, and then select the appropriate position.
   - Select the legend and drag it to another position within the chart area.

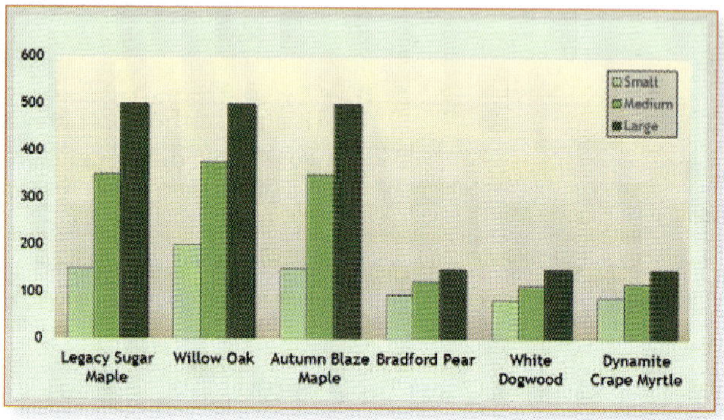

2-95 Legend moved

2. To change the selected legend's fill and outline colors, use one of the following methods:
   - Click the **Chart Tools Format** tab, click the **Shape Fill** or **Shape Outline** buttons, and select different colors.
   - Right-click the legend and choose **Format Legend** to open the *Format Legend* pane. Click the **Fill & Line** tab and then select appropriate fill and border colors. Click **Close**.
3. To remove a selected legend, use one of the following methods:
   - Click the **Chart Elements** button beside the chart and deselect the **Legend**.
   - Press **Delete**.

Labels appear in different places based on the chart style. Use the *Format Data Labels* pane to customize labels.

HOW TO: Change Chart Labels

1. Select the chart and then click the **Chart Element** button beside the chart.
2. Click **Data Labels** and select the position.
3. Click **More Options** to open the *Format Data Labels* pane.
4. Change *Label Options* to control what is displayed as well as the position.
5. Change *Text Options* to control fill and outline colors.

Using data labels above or inside columns enables the viewer to see the exact data value as well as the size relationships that the columns represent. However, the columns must be wide enough to display the numbers without overlapping. If they are too narrow (Figure 2-96), using a data table for this purpose will be more effective (Figure 2-97).

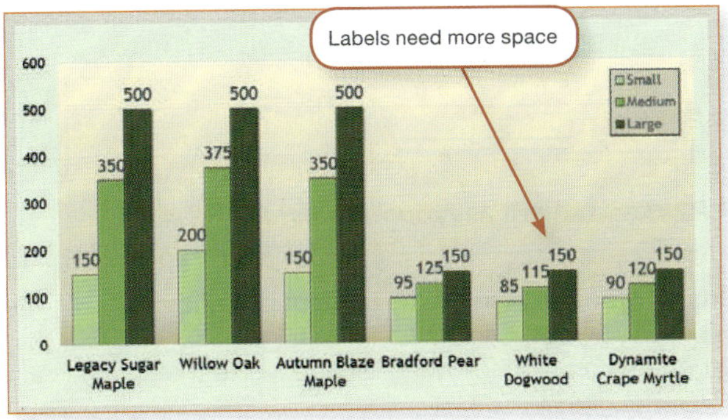

2-96 Data labels

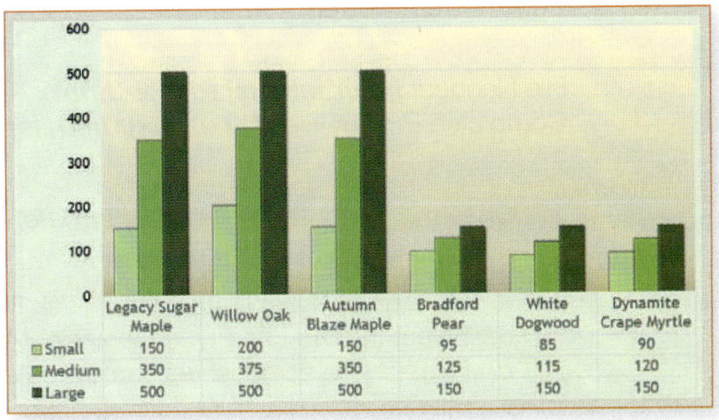

2-97 Data table

Separate a Pie Slice

You can separate pie chart slices (called ***exploding***) by dragging the pie slices away from the center. However, when all slices are separated, no single slice is emphasized. To emphasize just one slice, it is best to first design a pie chart as you want it to look and then pull that slice away from the pie. Consider, also, how your colors are applied so the most noticeable or brightest color is used for the slice that you want to emphasize (Figure 2-98).

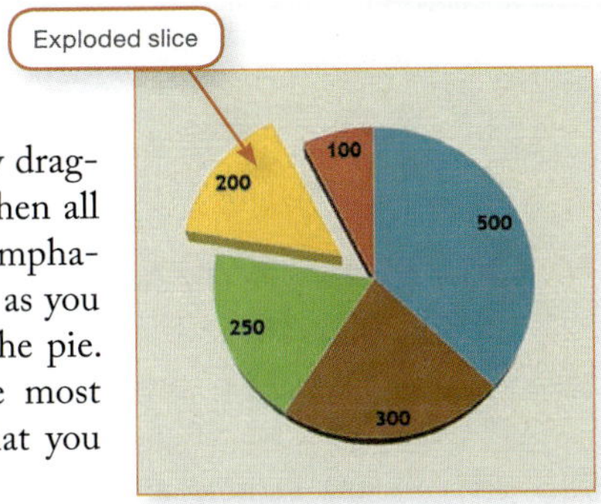

2-98 3-D pie chart with exploded slice

HOW TO: Explode a Pie Slice

1. Click a pie to select the pie object.
2. Click again to select just one pie slice. Check the handles to be sure you have selected the correct slice and not a label on the slice.
3. Drag slightly away from the center of the pie so the slice is emphasized.

As you drag a pie slice away from the center, the remainder of the pie becomes smaller. You may need to make the whole pie larger by resizing the plot area. Removing the legend creates more space for the pie, too. Pie charts are easier to interpret when short labels are shown directly on or beside slices instead of in a legend.

PAUSE & PRACTICE: POWERPOINT 2-4

For this project you create a pie and two clustered column charts showing the cost distribution for CGL landscaping, cost comparisons for tree sizes, and the height of mature trees being considered for the new landscape.

File Needed: ***[your initials] PP P2-3.pptx***
Completed Project File Name: ***[your initials] PP 2-4.pptx***

1. Open the presentation file ***[your initials] PP P2-3*** and save it as ***[your initials] PP P2-4.***
2. Create a 3-D pie chart.
   a. On slide 6, "Cost Distribution," click the **Insert Chart** button on the content placeholder.
   b. Select the **Pie** chart type then select the **3-D Pie** layout. Click **OK.**
   c. Replace the spreadsheet sample data with the data in the following list and resize the columns as needed:

	Cost
Trees—Shade	1,500
Trees—Ornamental	450
Shrubs	400
Perennials	360
Hydroseeding sq. ft.	800

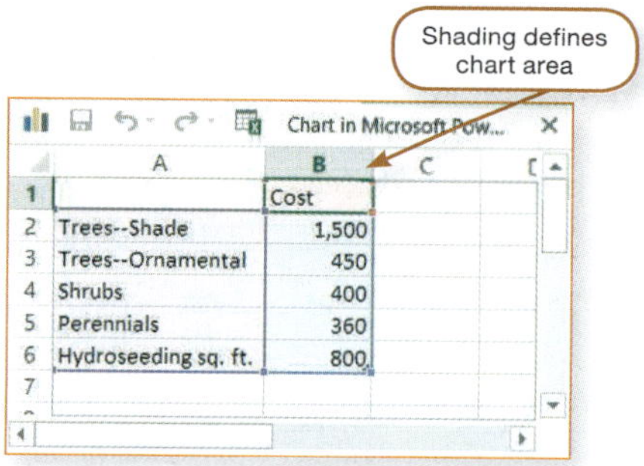

2-99 Spreadsheet linked to a chart

3. Be sure all chart data is selected. Resize the spreadsheet so you can proof all entries (Figure 2-99).
4. Close the spreadsheet.
5. Make changes to the chart.
   a. In the chart area, delete the *Cost* chart title because it duplicates the slide title.
   b. Click **Style 3** [*Chart Tools Design* tab, *Chart Styles* group].
   c. Select **Chart Area** [*Chart Tools Format* tab, *Current Selection* group] and click the **Shape Fill** button [*Chart Tools Format* tab, *Shape Styles* group]; then select **No fill**.
   d. Select the **Series "Cost" Data Labels** [*Chart Tools Format* tab, *Current Selection* group] and increase the font size to **20 pts**. [*Home* tab].
   e. Select the **Legend** and increase the font size to **20 pts**. [*Home* tab].
   f. Move the legend to the upper right of the **Chart Area.**
   g. Select the **Plot Area** and increase the size of the plot area to make the pie larger (Figure 2-100).
   h. Select the single slice for "Trees—Ornamental" and explode that slice by dragging it down slightly.

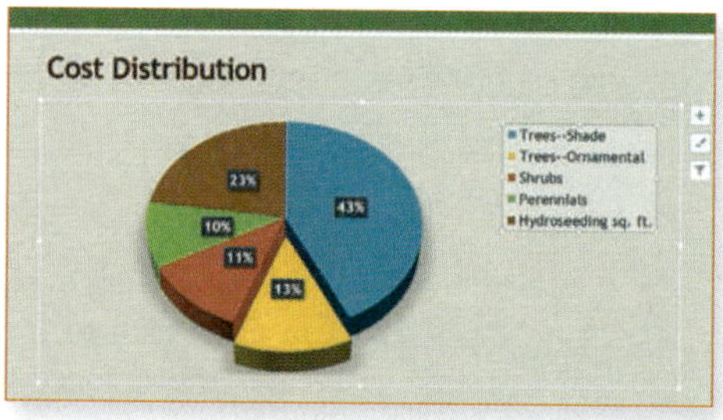

2-100 Slice exploded and legend repositioned

6. Create a clustered column chart.
   a. On slide 7, "Tree Size Cost Comparisons," click the **Insert Chart** button on the content placeholder.
   b. Click the **Clustered Column** layout and click **OK**.
   c. Replace the spreadsheet data with the following data:

	Small	Medium	Large
Legacy Sugar Maple	150	350	500
Willow Oak	200	375	500
Autumn Blaze Maple	150	350	500
Bradford Pear	95	125	150
White Dogwood	85	115	150
Dynamite Crape Myrtle	90	120	150

d. Close the spreadsheet. If you need to check the data, click the **Edit Data** button [*Chart Tools Design* tab, *Data* group].
e. Change the chart style to **Style 8** [*Chart Tools Design* tab, *Chart Styles* group] which has a dark fill for the chart area.

7. Click the **Chart Elements** button on the right side of the chart (Figure 2-101). Select the following: **Axes, Axis Titles, Data Table, Gridlines,** and **Legend**. The **Data Table** automatically appears below the columns.
   a. Make adjustments to the following chart elements:

      Axis Titles: Edit the *Primary Vertical (Y-axis)* rotated text by typing Tree Cost. Delete the *Primary Horizontal (X-axis) title* text below the data table.

      Legend: Select the **Legend** and click **Format Selection** [*Chart Tools Format* tab, *Current Selection* group] to open the *Format Legend* pane. Deselect *Show the legend without overlapping the chart* and select the **Right** *Legend Position.* Move the legend to the right of the plot area.

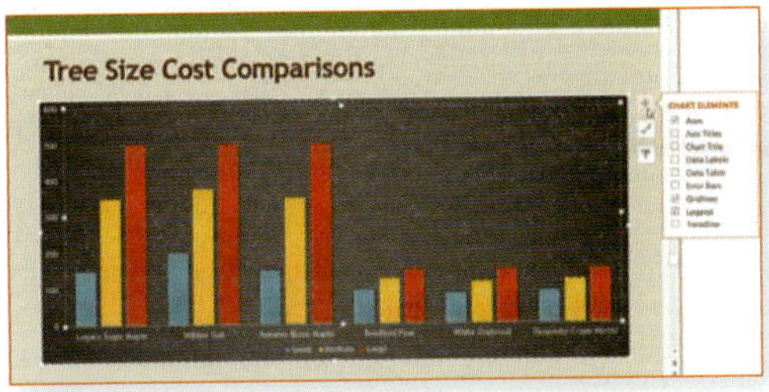

2-101 Clustered column chart with data table, axis title, and legend

   b. Select each of the following chart elements and click **Shape Fill** [*Chart Tools Format* tab, *Shape Styles* group] to change the colors:

      Chart Area: **Tan, Background 2, Darker 10%**
      Plot Area: **Tan, Background 2**
      Legend: **Tan, Background 2, Darker 10%**
      Large Series: **Green, Accent 4, Darker 50%**
      Medium Series: **Green, Accent 4**
      Small Series: **Green, Accent 4, Lighter 40%**

   c. Make all text **black**. Increase the font size on the axis title and legend to **20 pts**. Increase the table text and axis number to **18 pts**. The completed slide is shown in Figure 2-102.

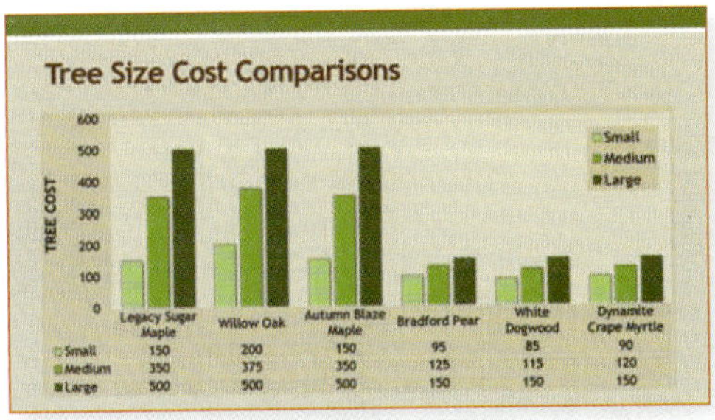

2-102 Column fill colors changed

8. Create another clustered column chart.
   a. On slide 8, "Growth Potential" click **Chart** [*Insert* tab, *Illustrations* group] because this slide does not have a content placeholder.
   b. Click the **Clustered Column** layout and click **OK** to close the dialog box.
   c. Replace the spreadsheet data with the following data:

	Height
Legacy Sugar Maple	80
Willow Oak	60
Autumn Blaze Maple	50
Bradford Pear	95
White Dogwood	20
Dynamite Crape Myrtle	20

   d. This data is in one data series, so delete the extra columns in the spreadsheet. Be sure you delete the entire spreadsheet columns so the PowerPoint chart columns can expand in the available space (Figure 2-102). An empty column in the spreadsheet creates too much blank space between columns in the PowerPoint chart.
   e. Select spreadsheet **Column C** and **Column D** headings and the entire columns are selected.

f. Right-click, then click **Delete**, and the columns appear blank.
g. Check to be sure the data is correctly selected and adjust borders if necessary.
h. Close the spreadsheet.
i. The chart area is smaller than in the previous chart because you inserted the chart directly on the slide rather than inserting it through a content placeholder that is in a larger size.

9. Make changes to the chart.
    a. Increase the chart area to a width of **10"** and height of **5.5"** [*Chart Tools Format* tab, *Size* group] and position it evenly on the slide (Figure 2-103).
    b. Delete the chart title and the legend.
    c. Click the **More** button [*Chart Tools Design* tab, *Chart Styles* group] and change the chart style to **Style 14**.
    d. Select the columns and change the color to **Green**, **Accent 4**.
    e. Make the text **black** and increase the font size.
        - *Vertical (Value) Axis:* **bold** and **20 pts**.
        - *Horizontal (Category) Axis:* **bold** and **18 pts**.

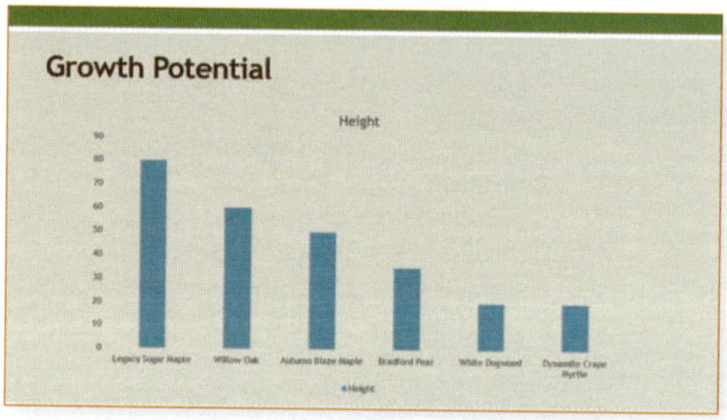

2-103 Column chart as it first appears

10. Select the *Chart Area* and apply a picture fill.
    a. Click the **Shape Fill** button [*Chart Tools Format* tab, *Shape Styles* group] and select **Picture** to open the *Insert Pictures* dialog box.
    b. In the *Office.com* search box, enter the search word tree and click **Search**.
    c. On the *Insert Pictures* dialog box, scroll down the gallery to locate the picture of "Trees with the leaves changing color for autumn" (Figure 2-104) and click **Insert**.
    d. If the *Format Chart Area* pane is not open, double-click the picture. Change the *Transparency* percentage to **60%**.
    e. Close the *Format Chart Area* pane.

2-104 Chart resized, colors changed, and picture fill

11. Click the **Transitions** tab, apply the **Wipe** transition to all slides, and change the *Effect Options* to **From Left**.

12. Save and close your presentation.

Chapter Summary

2.1 Work with shapes, select theme colors and standard colors, and apply styles (p. P2-67).

- Change shape size by entering exact height and width sizes or by dragging sizing handles.
- Use ***Lock Drawing Mode*** to draw the same shape multiple times.
- Use ***text boxes*** to position text anywhere on a slide.
- PowerPoint's various ***Styles*** galleries provide collections of preset effects for shapes, pictures, or other objects.
- When you apply ***Theme Colors*** to shapes, the colors change when a different theme is applied.
- ***Standard*** colors do not change when a different theme is applied.
- Highly ***saturated*** colors are intense and vibrant; colors that are not saturated are muddy and dull.
- ***Luminosity*** is a measure of lightness that is adjusted by the amount of white or black in the color.
- Computer screens use the ***RGB*** color model that displays colors by blending values for *red, green,* and *blue.*
- The ***Eyedropper*** is used to match any color on your computer screen.

2.2 Create interesting and eye-catching text effects with *WordArt* (p. P2-75).

- The ***WordArt Styles*** gallery shows a collection of preset ***Text Effects***.
- The ***Transform*** effect makes text warp into different shapes or follow a path.
- You can fill *WordArt* with solid or gradient colors, textures, patterns, or pictures.
- ***Line Weight*** is the line thickness measured in points.
- ***Dashes*** show lines with a combination of dots and dashes.
- Use the ***Line Style*** option on the ***Format Shape*** dialog box to customize line styles.

2.3 Search for pictures and illustrations, modify picture appearance, and compress picture file size (p. P2-78).

- Use the ***Insert Pictures*** dialog box to search for online pictures and illustrations.
- The ***Picture Styles*** gallery shows a collection of preset ***Picture Effects***.
- To remove a picture style, click the ***Reset Picture*** button.
- ***Cropping*** trims unwanted areas of a selected picture.
- Increase ***Color Saturation*** to make picture colors more vibrant; decrease color saturation to make picture colors more muted.
- ***Color Tone*** changes a picture's cool or warm tones.
- Select ***Color*** and then ***Recolor*** to change a picture's color to a monotone color.
- The ***Set Transparent Color*** feature can make one color in a picture transparent. This feature works well to remove white backgrounds.
- ***Compressing*** pictures reduces the file size of your presentation.

2.4 Organize information in a grid format using tables and customize the arrangement of columns and rows (p. P2-85).

- You can insert and delete table ***columns*** and ***rows***.
- Table ***cells*** can be ***merged*** or ***split*** to create multiple cells.
- ***Column width*** usually varies based on content; ***row height*** is usually a consistent size.

2.5 Emphasize portions of a table by applying styles, colors, and effects (p. P2-90).

- You can apply ***WordArt Styles*** to table text.
- ***Table Styles*** provide options for a table's design using theme accent colors.
- ***Table Style Options*** control how columns and rows are emphasized to feature areas of the table.
- ***Border lines*** or ***shading*** can separate cells.
- Horizontal cell alignment options include ***Align Text Left***, ***Center***, or ***Align Text Right***; vertical cell alignment options include ***Align Top***, ***Center Vertically***, or ***Align Bottom***.

2.6 Show processes and relationships with *SmartArt* graphics (p. P2-94).

- Use ***SmartArt graphics*** to create diagrams that illustrate concepts such as processes, cycles, or relationships.
- ***SmartArt layouts*** are organized by categories.
- Each layout includes information about how you can use it or the meaning it conveys.

- Type text directly in each *SmartArt* shape or type in the *Text Pane*.
- Change bulleted text to a *SmartArt* graphic by clicking the **Convert to SmartArt Graphic** button.

2.7 Improve the appearance of *SmartArt* graphics by applying styles, colors, and effects (p. P2-97).

- ***SmartArt Styles*** provide a gallery of effect options.
- The ***Change Colors*** button provides a gallery of color options arranged in categories.
- The ***Add Shapes*** button inserts shapes in relation to the selected shape.
- You can format or individually resize shapes within a *SmartArt* graphic.

2.8 Create charts that show relationships between data values and emphasize data in different ways (p. P2-101).

- Charts in PowerPoint are linked to spreadsheets in Excel; therefore, changes made to data in the worksheet automatically appear in the chart that represents the data.
- A group of data values is a ***data series***.
- ***Chart Layouts*** are arranged in categories including ***Column***, ***Line***, ***Pie***, ***Bar***, and ***Area***.
- The ***Chart Area*** displays the entire chart including all ***Chart Elements***.
- The ***Plot Area*** provides a background for ***Data Markers***, the columns, bars, or slices that represent data.

2.9 Enhance a chart by applying preset styles or manually customizing individual chart elements (p. P2-105).

- ***Chart Styles*** provide a gallery of preset effects for chart elements.
- The ***legend*** is a key that identifies each data series by color.
- The ***Change Colors*** button provides a gallery of colorful or monochromatic colors for chart elements.
- You can customize chart elements individually to enhance their appearance.
- To emphasize a pie slice, you can **explode** it by separating the slice from the rest of the pie chart.

Check for Understanding

In the ***Online Learning Center*** for this text (www.mhhe.com/office2013inpractice), there are a variety of resources that can be used to review the concepts covered in this chapter.

The following Online Learning Resources are available in the Online Learning Center:

- Multiple choice questions
- Short answer questions
- Matching exercises

USING MICROSOFT POWERPOINT 2013

Guided Project 2-1

Guest satisfaction has always been important to the success of Paradise Lakes Resort (PLR) in Minnesota. The general manager plans to use feedback from social media to identify problems and to guide improvements at the resort. In this project you illustrate a presentation the general manager will use to explain these concepts to employees at BLR.
[Student Learning Outcomes 2.1, 2.2, 2.3, 2.6, 2.7]

File Needed: ***SocialMedia-02.pptx***
Completed Project File Name: ***[your initials] PowerPoint 2-1.pptx***

Skills Covered in This Project

- Insert an online picture.
- Apply a picture style.
- Adjust size dimensions.
- Apply text effects.
- Insert a text box.
- Create a *SmartArt* graphic.
- Apply a *SmartArt* style and effects.

1. Open the presentation ***SocialMedia-02***. This design theme shows slide titles at the bottom of all slides except the title slide.
2. Save the presentation as ***[your initials] PowerPoint 2-1***.
3. On slide 1, search online for a picture.
   a. Click the **Insert** tab.
   b. Click the **Online Pictures** button to open the *Insert Pictures* dialog box.
   c. In the *Office.com* search box, type the word lake and click **Search**.
   d. Locate the picture showing two chairs on a deck facing the lake (Figure 2-105) and click **Insert**.
   e. Apply the **Metal Oval** picture style [*Picture Tools Format* tab, *Picture Styles* group].
   f. Resize the picture width to **6"** and the height automatically adjusts.
   g. Position the picture on the lower left.

2-105 Title slide

4. On slide 1, adjust the title text to complement the wood decking shown in the picture.
   a. Increase the font size to **60 pts**.
   b. Adjust the placeholder so it fits the text and move it up slightly.
   c. Click the **Text Fill** button [*Drawing Tools Format* tab, *WordArt Styles* group], select **Texture**, and select **Medium Wood**.

d. Click the **Text Effects** button, select **Shadow**, and select **Shadow Options**. The *Format Shape* pane opens.
e. Change the following settings:
Transparency: **20%**
Blur: **5 pt**.
Angle: **50°**
Distance: **3 pt**.
f. Close the *Format Shape* pane.

5. On slide 1, make the subtitle **bold** and increase the font size to **32 pts**. Adjust the placeholder size so it fits the text and move it down.
6. After slide 2, insert a new slide with a *Title and Content* layout.
7. On slide 3, add text and a shape.
   a. Type the slide title Why Social Media?
   b. Type the following bulleted text:

      Revenue
      Market Share
      Guest Satisfaction
      Guest Loyalty

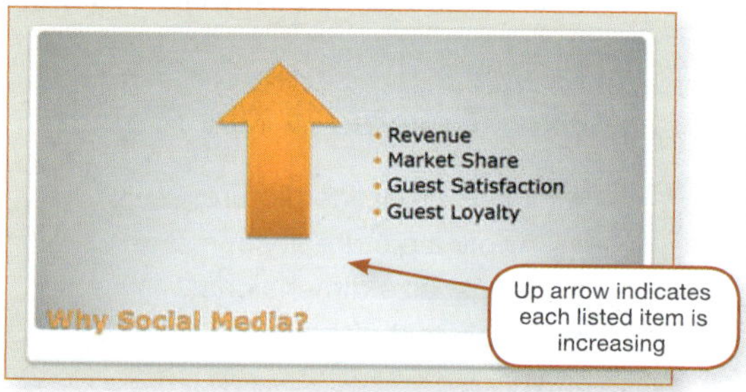

2-106 Slide 3 with a shape

   c. Resize the bulleted list placeholder so it fits the text and move the text to the right (Figure 2-106).
   d. To show that each item in the list is increasing, click the **Shape** button [*Insert* tab, *Illustrations* group] and select the *Up Arrow* shape.
   e. Draw an arrow (height **3.5"** and width **2.5"**); then position the arrow to the left of the text.
   f. With the arrow selected, click the **More** button [*Drawing Tools Format* tab, *Shape Styles* group] and apply the **Intense Effect**, **Orange**, **Accent 1**.
8. After slide 4, insert a new slide with a *Blank* layout.
9. On slide 5, create a *SmartArt* graphic using a cycle layout and insert an additional shape.
   a. Click the **Insert** tab.
   b. Click the **SmartArt** button and select the **Cycle** type.
   c. Select the **Continuous Cycle** layout and click **OK**.
   d. Add the following text to each shape starting with the top shape and continuing in a clockwise direction around the circle:

      More Rentals
      Rentals
      Social Media Comments
      Improvements
      Better Social Media Comments

   e. With the Better Social Media Comments shape selected, click the **Add Shape** list arrow [*SmartArt Tools Design* tab, *Create Graphic* group] and select **Add Shape After**.
   f. In the new shape, type Higher Ratings.
   g. Click the **Intense Effect** style [*SmartArt Tools Design* tab, *SmartArt Styles* group].

h. Select all the shapes, change the font size to **20 pts.**, and apply **bold**.
i. With all the shapes selected, resize the shapes horizontally so the word "Improvements" fits on one line (Figure 2-107).

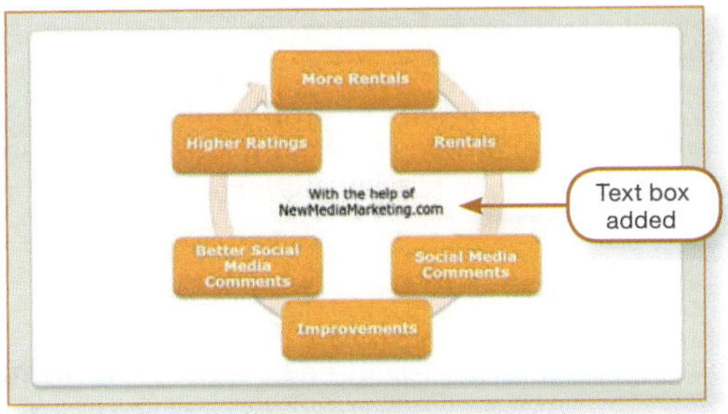

2-107 Slide 4 with *SmartArt graphic* and effects added

10. Insert a text box.
    a. Click the **Text Box** button [*Insert* tab, *Text* group] and click inside the cycle diagram.
    b. Type the following text on two lines:

       With the help of NewMediaMarketing.com

    c. Change the font size to **20 pts**. and center the text.
    d. Adjust the text box size, if necessary.
11. Click the **Reveal** button [*Transitions* tab, *Transition to This Slide* group] and then click **Apply To All**.
12. Save and close the presentation (Figure 2-108).

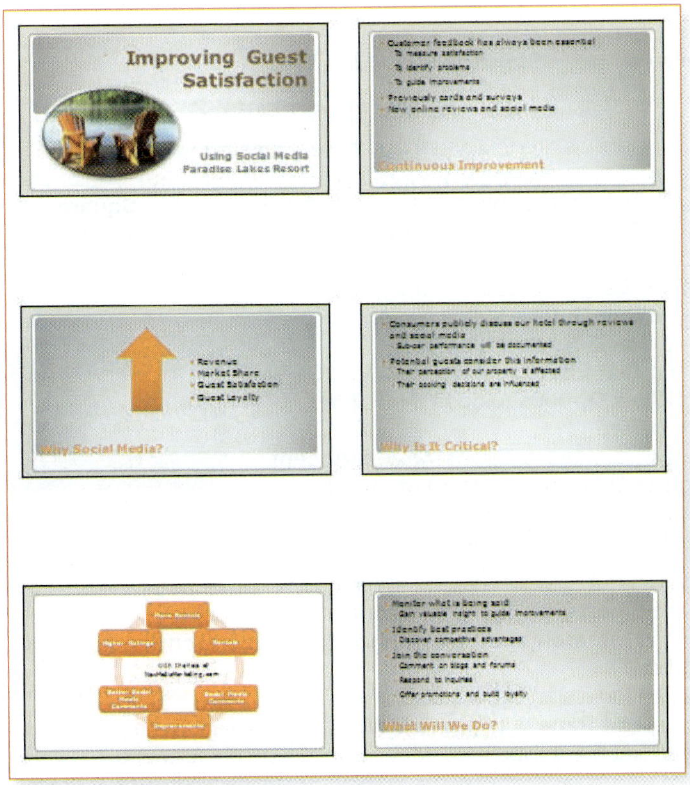

2-108 PowerPoint 2-1 completed

Guided Project 2-2

In this project, you prepare a presentation with key points essential to maintain a healthy lifestyle and show examples of weight loss calorie requirements for men and women at different ages. The doctors at Courtyard Medical Plaza will use this presentation to encourage clients to be more active. [Student Learning Outcomes 2.1, 2.2, 2.3, 2.4, 2.5, 2.6, 2.7]

File Needed: ***StayingActive-02.pptx***
Completed Project File Name: ***[your initials] PowerPoint 2-2.pptx***

Skills Covered in This Project

- Apply text effects.
- Create a *SmartArt* graphic.
- Apply a *SmartArt* style and effects.
- Insert an online picture.
- Crop a picture.
- Apply a picture style.
- Adjust size dimensions.
- Insert a text box.
- Insert and format a table.

1. Open the presentation ***StayingActive-02***.
2. Save the presentation as ***[your initials] PowerPoint 2-2***.
3. On slide 1, select the title text and make these changes using the *Drawing Tools Format* tab, *WordArt Styles* group.
   a. Click the **Text Effects** button, click **Transform**, and select **Square**. Text fills the title placeholder.
   b. Click the **Text Fill** button, select **Texture**, and click **More Textures** to open the *Format Shape* pane.
   c. Select **Pattern fill** and change the *Background Color* to **Teal**, **Accent 6**.
   d. Select the **Large checker board** pattern.
   e. Click the **Text Outline** button and change the color to **Black**, **Background 1**.
   f. Click the **Text Effects** button and select **Glow**. Select **Glow Options** to open the *Format Shape* pane.
   g. For *Glow,* change the *Color* to **Green**, **Accent 1**, **Lighter 60%**; the *Size* to **10 pt**.; and the *Transparency* to **20%** (Figure 2-109).
   h. Close the *Format Shape* pane.

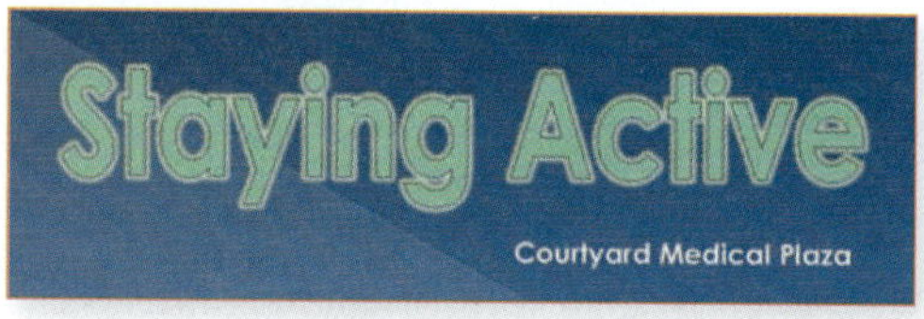

2-109 *Text Effects* for presentation title

4. On slide 2, insert a *SmartArt* graphic and modify the style using the *SmartArt Tools Design* tab.
   a. Click the **SmartArt** button on the content placeholder.
   b. Select the **Hierarchy** type and the **Horizontal Hierarchy** layout. Click **OK** to close the dialog box.
   c. Delete the three shapes on the right.
   d. Click the **Text Pane** button on the left of the SmartArt frame.
   e. After the first bullet, type Keep Moving; then type the following items after the indented bullets:

      Moderate Intensity Activity
      Count Steps (Press **Enter** to add another bullet.)
      Combine Aerobic and Strengthening

   f. Close the *Text Pane.*

g. Apply the *Subtle Effect* style [*SmartArt Styles* group].
h. Click the **Change Colors** button and select **Colorful Range, Accent Colors 5 to 6** (Figure 2-110).

2-110 *SmartArt graphic* with effects added

5. On slide 3, search for a picture and apply a picture style.
   a. Click the **Online Pictures** button [*Insert* tab, *Images* group] to open *the Insert Pictures* dialog box.
   b. Search for a picture using *Office.com* and the search word **gardening**.
   c. Select the picture "Women smiling while gardening" and click **Insert**.
   d. Resize the picture (height **4.5"** and width will automatically change to the same size since this picture is square).
   e. Move the picture to the right of the slide.
   f. Apply the *Rotated White* picture style [*Picture Tools Format* tab, *Picture Styles* group].
6. On slide 5, repeat the process in step 5 to search for a picture using the search word walk.
   a. Select the picture "Family of four walking on the beach" and click **Insert**.
   b. Click the **Crop** button [*Picture Tools Format* tab, *Size* group] and crop the picture on the top and left to focus only on the family. Click **Crop** again to accept your change.
   c. Apply the same style to match the previous picture.
   d. Resize the picture (height **5"** and width will automatically change).
   e. Move the picture to the right of the slide.
7. After slide 6, insert a new slide with a *Title and Content* layout.
8. On slide 7, add text.
   a. Type the title text **Calorie Examples**.
   b. Insert a text box with the text **Gaining 5 pounds a year** and position it below the slide title. Apply **bold** and change the font size to **20 pts**.
9. On slide 7, insert a table, add text, and modify formatting.
   a. Click the **Table** button on the content placeholder and enter **6** columns and **5** rows on the *Insert Table* dialog box. Click **OK** to close the dialog box.
   b. Type the text shown in Figure 2-111 using a font size of **20 pts**.

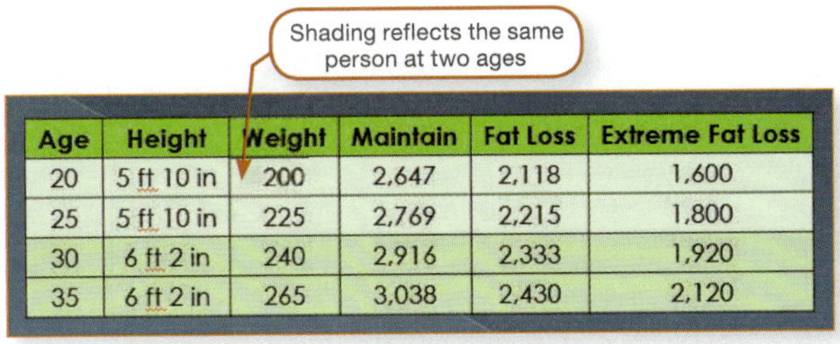

Age	Height	Weight	Maintain	Fat Loss	Extreme Fat Loss
20	5 ft 10 in	200	2,647	2,118	1,600
25	5 ft 10 in	225	2,769	2,215	1,800
30	6 ft 2 in	240	2,916	2,333	1,920
35	6 ft 2 in	265	3,038	2,430	2,120

2-111 Table with formatting changes

   c. Resize the last column so the heading text fits on one line.
   d. Make the column width fit each column by double-clicking the border line between columns.
   e. Select all cells and change to **Center** alignment [*Table Tools Layout* tab, *Alignment* group].
   f. Change the *Pen Color* to **Black** and the *Pen Weight* to **1 pt**. [*Table Tools Design* tab, *Draw Borders* group].
   g. Click the **Borders** button, and select **All Borders** [*Table Tools Design* tab, *Table Styles* group].
   h. Select the top table row and change the *Text Fill* to **Black** [*Table Tools Design* tab, *WordArt Styles* group].
   i. Select the second and third rows and change the *Shading* to **Green, Accent 1, Lighter 80%** [*Table Tools Design* tab, *Table Styles* group].
   j. Select the fourth and fifth rows and change the *Shading* to **Green, Accent 1, Lighter 60%**.
   k. Move the table up slightly and center it on the slide.

10. On slide 7, duplicate the table and edit the text in the second table.
    a. Select the table and press **Ctrl+D** to duplicate it. Position the second table centered near the bottom of the slide.
    b. Edit the table content (Figure 2-112).

Age	Height	Weight	Maintain	Fat Loss	Extreme Fat Loss
20	5 ft 7 in	150	2,041	1,633	1,225
25	5 ft 7 in	175	2,163	1,730	1,400
30	5 ft 9 in	180	2,204	1,763	1,440
35	5 ft 9 in	205	2,325	1,860	1,640

2-112 Table with formatting changes

11. On slide 7, insert and format a shape to label table contents.
    a. Click the **Shapes** button [*Insert* tab, *Illustrations* group] and select the **Oval**. Draw an oval shape and adjust its size (height **0.9"** and width **2"**) [*Drawing Tools Format* tab, *Size* group].
    b. Type the word Female with **black** text and **bold**.
    c. Click the **Shape Outline** button [*Drawing Tools Format* tab, *Shape Styles* group] and change the outline color to **Teal**, **Accent 6**.
    d. Click the **Edit Shape** button [*Drawing Tools Format* tab, *Insert Shapes* group] and select **Change Shape**. Select **Explosion 1**.
    e. Position this shape at the left corner of the bottom table (Figure 2-113).

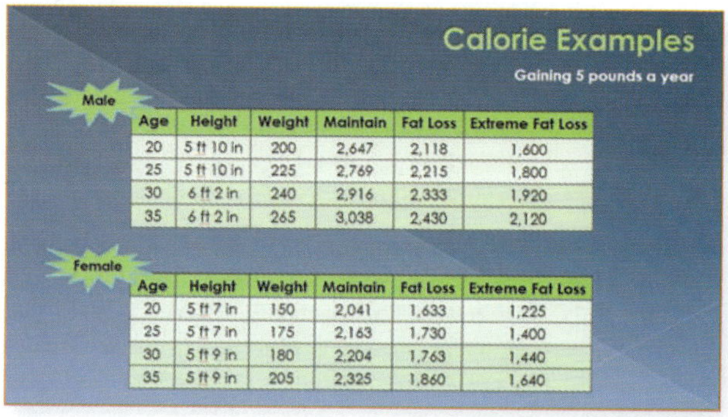

Age	Height	Weight	Maintain	Fat Loss	Extreme Fat Loss
20	5 ft 10 in	200	2,647	2,118	1,600
25	5 ft 10 in	225	2,769	2,215	1,800
30	6 ft 2 in	240	2,916	2,333	1,920
35	6 ft 2 in	265	3,038	2,430	2,120

Age	Height	Weight	Maintain	Fat Loss	Extreme Fat Loss
20	5 ft 7 in	150	2,041	1,633	1,225
25	5 ft 7 in	175	2,163	1,730	1,400
30	5 ft 9 in	180	2,204	1,763	1,440
35	5 ft 9 in	205	2,325	1,860	1,640

2-113 Slide 7 completed tables

12. Select the shape and press **Ctrl+D** to duplicate it.
    a. Position the second shape at the left corner of the top table.
    b. Change the text to Male.

13. After slide 7, insert a new slide with a *Title and Content* layout.

14. On slide 8, insert a table and add text.
    a. Type the title Make It Fun.
    b. Click the **Table** button on the content placeholder. Enter 2 columns and 8 rows and click **OK**.
    c. Type the following text:

Exercise Benefits	Motivation
Control weight	Enjoy the activities
Improve health	Keep it a priority
Boost immune system	Vary activities
Control appetite	Share with a friend
Feel more energetic	Enjoy companionship
Be more relaxed	Set realistic goals
Raise self-confidence	Reward yourself

15. On slide 8, make the following changes to the table:
    a. Select the table. If necessary, change the *Pen Color* to **Black** and the *Pen Weight* to **1 pt**. Click **All Borders**.
    b. Change the font size for all text to **20 pts**.
    c. Change the heading row text to **black**.

d. Select all cells and click the **Center Vertically** button [*Table Tools Layout* tab, *Alignment* group].
e. Change the table size (height **4.5"** and width **9"**) and center it horizontally on the slide.

16. Apply the **Cube** transition to all slides.
17. Save and close the presentation (Figure 2-114).

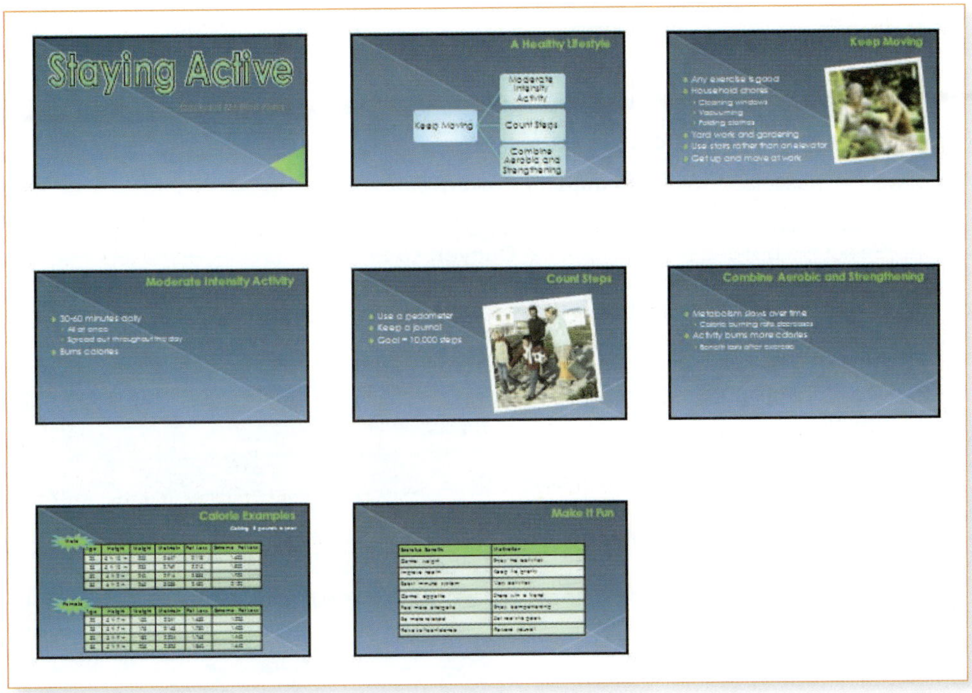

2-114 PowerPoint 2-2 completed

Guided Project 2-3

Solution Seekers, Inc., has been asked to develop a presentation for a meeting of personnel managers about salary trends for information technology workers. In the current economy, some jobs are paying less than they were a few years ago. For this project, you prepare tables and charts showing average salaries and salary changes for selected jobs.
[Student Learning Outcomes 2.1, 2.2, 2.3, 2.5, 2.6, 2.7, 2.8]

File Needed: ***InfoTechSalaries-02.pptx***
Completed Project File Name: ***[your initials] PowerPoint 2-3.pptx***

Skills Covered in This Project

- Convert text to a *SmartArt* graphic.
- Apply a *SmartArt* style and effects.
- Create a pie chart.
- Format a table.
- Create a column chart.
- Apply chart styles.
- Format chart elements.
- Insert *WordArt* and apply effects.
- Apply a picture style.
- Insert and align text boxes.

1. Open the presentation ***InfoTechSalaries-02***
2. Save the presentation as ***[your initials] PowerPoint 2-3.***
3. On slide 2, convert the bulleted text to a *SmartArt* graphic and modify the style and colors.
   a. Select the bulleted text and click the **Convert to SmartArt** button [*Home* tab, *Paragraph* group].
   b. Select **More SmartArt Graphics** to open the *Choose a SmartArt Graphic* dialog box.
   c. Select the **Relationship** type and the **Counterbalance Arrows** layout. Click **OK** to close the dialog box.
   d. Apply the **Cartoon** style [*SmartArt Tools Design* tab, *SmartArt Styles* group].
   e. Select the down arrow shape pointing to "Fewer Layoffs" and click the **Shape Fill** button list arrow [*SmartArt Tools Format* tab, *Shape Styles* group].
   f. Select **Gradient** and under *Dark Variations,* click **Linear Down** to emphasize the downward movement.
   g. Select the up arrow and repeat step f to apply a **Linear Up** gradient (Figure 2-115).

2-115 Slide 2 *SmartArt graphic* with color changes

4. After slide 2, insert a new slide with a *Title and Content* layout.
5. On slide 3, create a pie chart and modify it.
   a. Type the slide title **Employee Salary Satisfaction**.
   b. Click the **Chart** button in the content placeholder.
   c. Click the **Pie** chart type; then select the **3-D Pie**. Click **OK** to close the dialog box.
   d. Replace the spreadsheet data with the data shown in Figure 2-116. Close the spreadsheet.
   e. Drag the chart title to the top left of the chart area. Increase the font size to **24 pts**. [*Home* tab, *Font* group].
   f. Click the **Chart Elements** button on the right side of the slide and select **Legend**. Click **Right**.
   g. Increase the font size to **20 pts**. and drag the legend to the bottom right of the chart area.

Chart in Microsoft P

	A	B
1		Satisfaction %
2	Very Satisfied	13
3	Somewhat Satisfied	36
4	Undecided	16
5	Somewhat Dissatisfied	24
6	Very Dissatisfied	11
7		

2-116 Spreadsheet linked to a chart

h. Click the **Chart Elements** button again and select **Data Labels**. Click **Inside End**.

i. Click the **Chart Elements** list box arrow and select **Series "Satisfaction%" Data Labels** [*Chart Tools Format* tab, *Current Selection* group]. Increase the font size to **24 pts**. and apply **bold** (Figure 2-117).

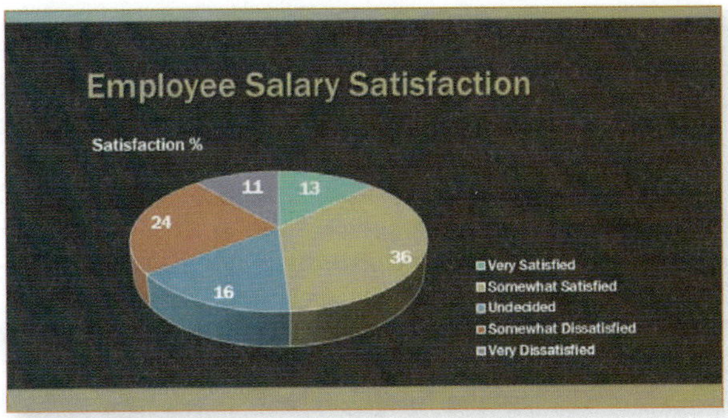

2-117 Slide 3 completed pie chart

6. On slide 4, modify table formatting.
   a. Select the table. Increase the font size to **20 pts**.
   b. Select **Header Row** and **Banded Rows** [*Table Tools Design* tab, *Table Style Options* group].
   c. Apply the **Themed Style 1, Accent 2** style [*Table Tools Design* tab, *Table Styles* group].
   d. Increase the table height to **4"** and click the **Center Vertically** button [*Table Tools Layout* tab].
   e. Select columns 2–4 and change to **Right** alignment.

7. After slide 4, insert a new slide with a *Title and Content* layout.

8. On slide 5, create a column chart and modify it.
   a. Type the title **Salary Change, Selected Jobs**.
   b. Click the **Chart** button on the content placeholder.
   c. Select the **3-D Clustered Column** and click **OK**.
   d. Replace the spreadsheet data with the data shown in Figure 2-118. Select **Column D**, right-click, and select **Delete**. By removing the blank column, the chart displays correctly with no blank space. Close the spreadsheet.

	A	B	C
1		2013	2014
2	Project Manager	101,256	104,897
3	Applications Developer	86,783	90,250
4	Security Analyst	79,498	82,663
5	Network Manager	61,245	62,871
6	Technical Support	53,387	52,296
7	Help Desk	41,854	41,532
8			

2-118 Spreadsheet linked to a chart

   e. Delete the chart title.
   f. Click the **Chart Elements** button on the right side of the chart, select **Legend**, and then click **More Options** to open the *Format Legend* pane. Select **Top Right** and deselect **Show the legend without overlapping the chart**.
   g. Click the **Shape Fill** button [*Table Tools Format* tab, *Shape Styles* group] and change the legend color to **Brown, Accent 2, Darker 50%**.
   h. Click the chart frame to select the **Chart Area** and change the **Shape Fill** color to **Teal, Accent 1, Darker 50%**.
   i. Select the **Legend** and increase the font size to **18 pts**. Repeat to increase the **Vertical (Value) Axis** font size to **18 pts**.
   j. Select the **Horizontal (Category) Axis** and increase the font size to **20 pts**. (Figure 2-119).
   k. On slide 6, apply the *Moderate Frame, Black* picture style [*Picture Tools Format* tab, *Picture Styles* group].

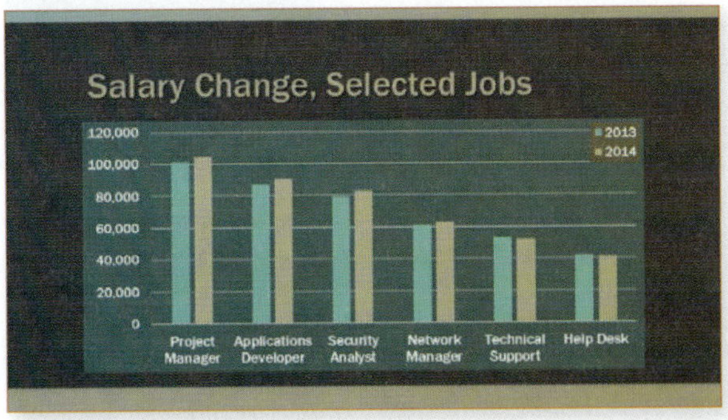

2-119 Slide 5 completed clustered column chart

9. On slide 6, insert *WordArt* text.
   a. Click the **WordArt** button [*Insert* tab, *Text* group] and select the **Fill - White, Text 1, Outline - Background 1, Hard Shadow - Background 1** style (Figure 2-120).
   b. Type the text **Employees Are Valuable** and move this text above the picture.
   c. Click the **Text Effects** button [*Drawing Tools Format* tab, *WordArt Styles* group], select **Shadow**, and click **Offset Diagonal Bottom Right**.
   d. Click the **Text Outline** button [*Drawing Tools Format* tab, *WordArt Styles* group] and select **Black, Background 2**.
   e. Deselect the *WordArt* text.

2-120 Slide 6 picture style, text effects, and text boxes

10. On slide 6, insert text boxes.
    a. Click the **Text Box** button [*Insert* tab, *Text* group] and type the first salary of **$74,270**. Change the font color to **black**, increase the font size to **20 pts.**, and apply **bold**.
    b. Position this salary below the first person on the left of the picture.
    c. With the salary text box selected, press **Ctrl+D** and position the duplicated text box below the second person. Repeat for the remaining figures.
    d. Edit the text boxes to change the salaries to **$62,844**, **$54,340**, and **$48,982**.
    e. Select all of the salary text boxes and click the **Arrange** button [*Drawing Tools Format* tab, *Drawing* group]. Select **Align** and **Align Bottom** (Figure 2-120).

11. Apply the **Blinds** transition to all slides; then apply the **Zoom** transition to slide 6.

12. Save and close the presentation (Figure 2-121).

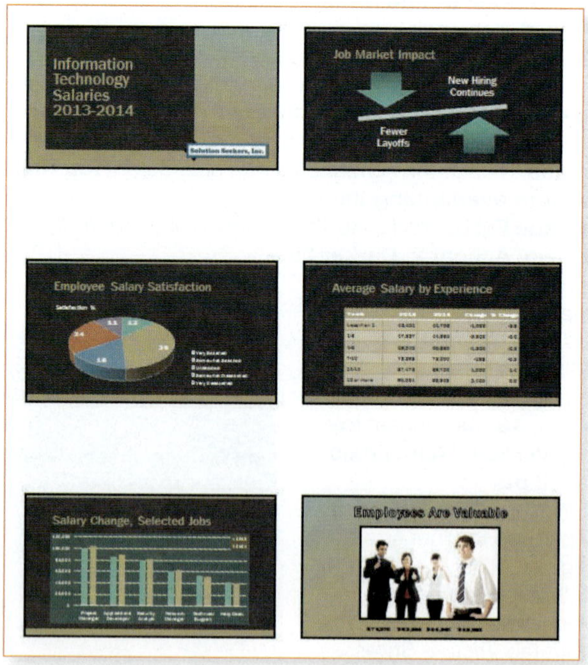

2-121 PowerPoint 2-3 completed

Independent Project 2-4

At Pool & Spa Oasis, sales associates must educate new spa owners about keeping spa water safe with proper maintenance. For this project, you prepare a presentation that emphasizes the routine to follow, explains pH level numbers, and lists available products that are typically used to balance water. [Student Learning Outcomes 2.1, 2.2, 2.3, 2.4, 2.5, 2.6, 2.7]

Files Needed: ***Balancing-02.pptx***
Completed Project File Name: ***[your initials] PowerPoint 2-4.pptx***

Skills Covered in This Project

- Insert *WordArt* and apply effects.
- Adjust size dimensions.
- Insert an online picture.
- Apply a picture style.
- Create a *SmartArt* graphic.
- Apply a *SmartArt* style and effects.
- Insert and format a table.
- Insert a text box.
- Change solid and gradient colors.

1. Open the presentation ***Balancing-02***.
2. Save the presentation as ***[your initials] PowerPoint 2-4***.
3. On slide 1, change the title text arrangement.
   a. Delete the title text "Balancing Act," but leave the word "The" as shown.
   b. Insert *WordArt* with the style **Fill – White**, **Outline – Accent 1**, **Glow – Accent 1**.
   c. Type Balancing Act.
   d. Click **Text Effects**, select **Shadow**, and **Offset Right**. Click **Shadow Options** to open the *Format Shape* pane and change the *Transparency* setting to **30%**.
   e. Change the *Character Spacing* to **Tight**.
   f. Apply the *Transform* text effect of **Cascade Up**.
   g. Increase the *WordArt* size to height **3"** and width **9"** and position as shown in Figure 2-122.
   h. Close the *Format Shape* pane.

2-122 Slide 1 with *WordArt*

4. On slide 2, the bulleted list placeholder has a fill color so it cannot be resized without distorting the slide. Adjust text spacing and insert a picture.
   a. On the last bulleted item, place your insertion point in front of the word "such" and press **Shift+Enter**.
   b. Search on *Office.com* using the search word swim and insert the picture "Young woman in swimming pool."
   c. Resize the picture (height **5.5"** and the width will automatically change to **3.71"**).
   d. Apply the **Bevel Rectangle** picture style.
   e. Position the picture as shown in Figure 2-123.

2-123 Slide 2 with inserted picture and picture style

5. On slide 4, insert a *SmartArt* graphic, add text, and change formatting.
   a. Insert a *SmartArt* graphic from the *Process* category with the **Continuous Block Process layout**.
   b. In the three shapes, type Test Water, Add Necessary Products, and Enjoy!
   c. Resize the *SmartArt* graphic (height **5"** and width **9.5"**).
   d. Apply the **Polished** SmartArt style.
   e. Select the arrow and apply **Gradient** colors. Select **More Gradient** to open the *Format Shape* pane. Select a **Linear** type and **Linear Right** direction and three gradient stops.

      First stop: Position **0%**, **Light Turquoise, Background 2**, **Darker 50%**
      Second stop: Position **40%**, **Light Turquoise, Background 2**, **Darker 10%**
      Third stop: Position **100%**, **Light Turquoise, Background 2**
   f. Close the *Format Shape* pane.
   g. Apply **bold** to all *SmartArt* text (Figure 2-124).

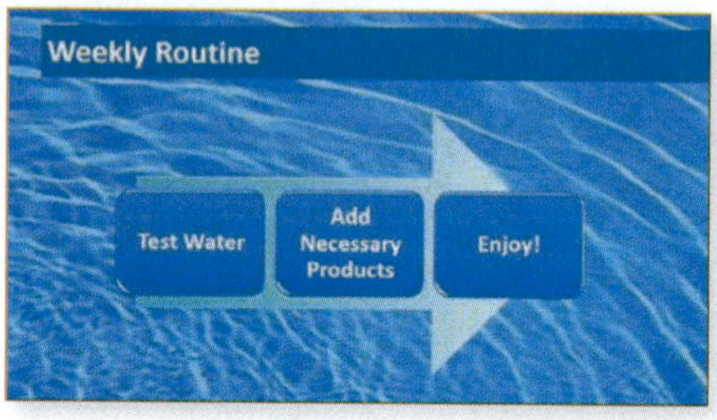

2-124 Slide 4 *SmartArt graphic* with style and color changes

6. On slide 5, insert a table, add text, and change formatting.
   a. Insert a table with 3 columns and 4 rows.
   b. Select **Header Row** and **Banded Rows**.
   c. Type the following text:

Level	Numbers	Results
High	8.0	Scale, Alkaline
Good	7.2 – 7.6	Ideal pH Range
Low	6.0	Corrosion, Acidic

   d. Change the font size to **20 pts**. for all table text.
   e. Apply the **Themed Style 1, Accent 1** table style.
   f. Select each column and adjust the cell width as follows: left column is **1.5"**, middle column is **2.75"**, and right column is **2.75"**.
   g. Change the alignment on the middle column to **Center**.
   h. Center the table on the slide.
7. On slide 5, insert a text box below the table.
   a. Type Drain and replace spa water every 60-90 days.
   b. Change the font size to **20 pts**.
   c. Change the shape fill to **Turquoise, Accent 3, Lighter 40%.**
   d. Resize the text box, if necessary, to fit the text and position it below the table aligned with the right of the table.
8. Copy the table on slide 5.
9. On slide 6, paste the table and make revisions.
   a. Delete the middle column and make the table **9"** wide.
   b. Delete the table text and add three rows.
   c. Type the following text:

Products	Purpose
Sanitizer	Type needed depends on sanitizer system
Test Strips	Measures chemical levels
Shock Treatment	Breaks down organic or unfiltered material
Total Alkalinity	Increases or decreases to balance pH levels
Calcium Increaser	Balances dissolved calcium
Stain and Scale Prevention	Removes metallic impurities

d. Adjust the column width as needed to avoid word wrapping.
e. Center the table on the slide.

10. Apply the **Ripple** transition with the **From Top-Left** effect option to all slides.
11. Save and close the presentation (Figure 2-125).

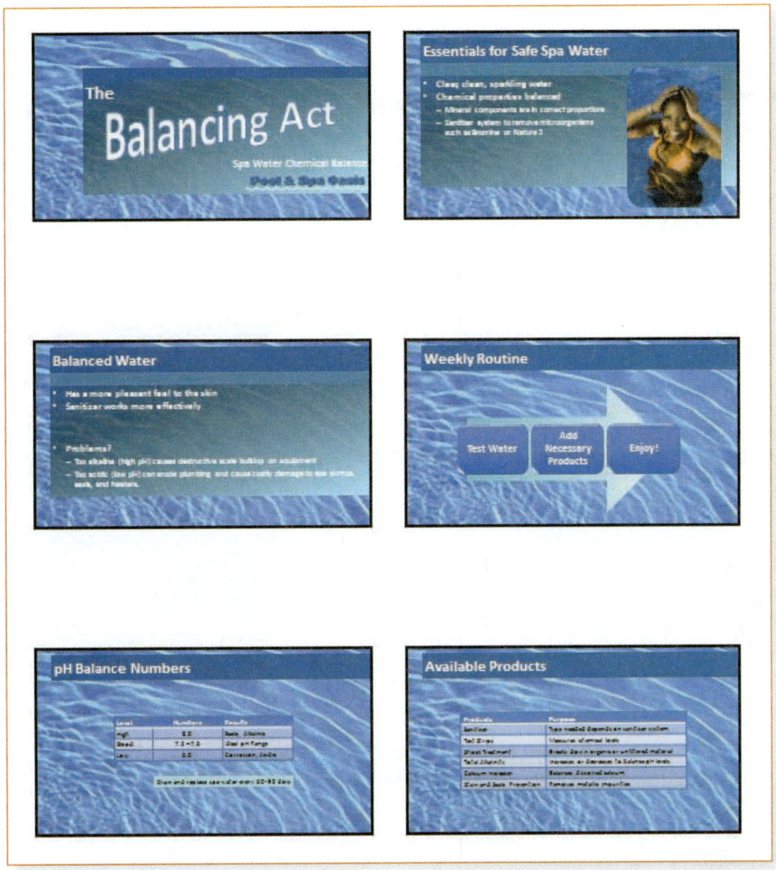

2-125 PowerPoint 2-4 completed

Independent Project 2-5

Prospective home buyers need to understand mortgage requirements and how to prepare to apply for a mortgage. Angie O'Connor at Placer Hills Real Estate frequently discusses these issues with clients, so she wants to use a presentation on her notebook computer to help guide her discussions with clients. For this project, you develop the presentation.
[Student Learning Outcomes 2.1, 2.3, 2.4, 2.5, 2.6, 2.7, 2.8]

File Needed: ***PreparetoBuy-02.pptx***
Completed Project File Name: ***[your initials] PowerPoint 2-5.pptx***

Skills Covered in This Project

- Insert an online picture.
- Crop a picture.
- Apply a picture style.
- Adjust size dimensions.
- Insert a chart and edit data.
- Apply chart styles.
- Format chart elements.
- Insert text boxes.
- Insert and format a table.
- Convert text to a *SmartArt* graphic.
- Apply a *SmartArt* style and effects.

1. Open the presentation ***PreparetoBuy-02*** that has a Standard size (4:3 aspect ratio). The slide size is 10" x 7.5" compared to the slide size of 13.333" x 7.5" for the Widescreen (16:9 aspect ratio).
2. Save the presentation as ***[your initials] PowerPoint 2-5.***
3. On slide 1, search at *Office.com* for the picture shown in Figure 2-126 using the search word home.
   a. Insert the picture and crop it slightly on the left to remove part of the sky.
   b. Resize the picture so it is **3"** wide and the height remains in proportion.
   c. Apply the **Moderate Frame, Black** picture style.
   d. Align the picture on the right side of the slide. The black frame portion extends beyond the slide on the right.

2-126 Slide 1 with inserted picture and picture style

4. On slide 4, insert a chart showing how fixed mortgage rates have changed over time.
   a. Click the **Line** chart type; then select the **Line with Markers** chart layout. Click **OK**.
   b. Replace the spreadsheet data with the data shown in Figure 2-127.
      - Increase the selection area to include *row 10* to avoid error messages.
      - Delete *Column D* so the corresponding chart area is correct with no blank space.
      - Close the spreadsheet.

	A	B	C	
1		Rate	Points	Co
2	1974	9.19	1.2	
3	1979	11.2	1.6	
4	1984	13.88	2.5	
5	1989	10.32	2.1	
6	1994	8.38	1.8	
7	1999	7.44	1	
8	2004	5.84	0.7	
9	2009	5.04	0.7	
10	2014	3.95	0.8	
11				

2-127 Spreadsheet linked to a chart

5. The chart now shows accurate information, but it is difficult to distinguish the data series lines from the gridlines in the background. The data markers that reflect the value of each number can barely be seen (Figure 2-128). The following changes will make the chart easier to interpret.
6. Delete the chart title.
7. Change the chart area *Shape Fill* to **Blue-Gray, Accent 5, Darker 25%**.

8. Select the "Rate" series line, right-click, and select **Format Data Series** to open the *Format Data Series* pane (Figure 2-129).
   a. Click the **Fill & Line** tab at the top of the pane. Select *Line* options and make one change:
      - *Width:* **3 pt**.
   b. Select *Marker* options and make changes so the marker on the selected series line is more noticeable. Click the option name to access the choices for each option.
      - *Marker Options:* **Built-in**, *Type* **Square**, *Size* **15** (Figure 2-130)
      - *Fill:* **Solid fill**, **Color Dark Red**, **Accent 1**, **Lighter 40%**

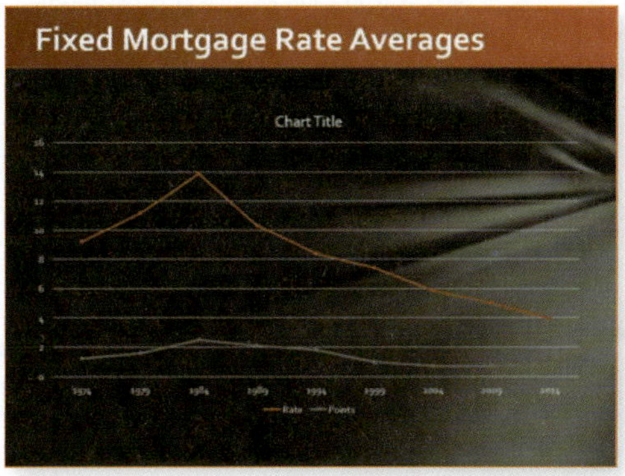

2-128 Line chart as it first appears

9. Select the "Points" series line and make the following similar changes:
   a. For *Line* options, make two changes:
      - *Line Color:* **Solid line**, **Brown**, **Accent 3**
      - *Line Style:* **Width**, **3 pt**
   b. Click the **Marker** button and make two changes:
      - *Marker Options:* **Built-in** *Type* **Diamond**, *Size* **20**
      - *Marker Fill:* **Solid fill**. **Brown**, **Accent 3**, **Lighter 40%**

2-129 Format Data Series pane

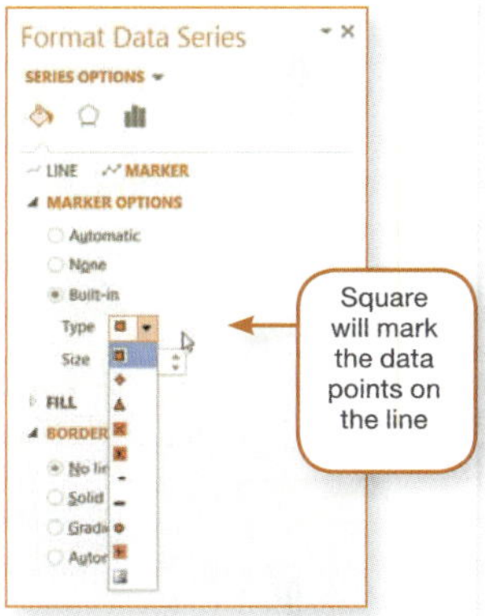

2-130 *Format Data Series* pane with *Marker* options

10. Close the *Format Data Series* pane.
11. Increase the font size to **16 pts**. and make the text **bold** for the *Horizontal (Category) axis* and the *Vertical (Value) axis*.
12. Move the chart area up slightly to make room for a source notation at the bottom of the slide.
    a. Insert a text box and type the following:

       Information based on Freddie Mac survey data
       http://www.freddiemac.com/pmms

    b. Position the text box as displayed in Figure 2-131.

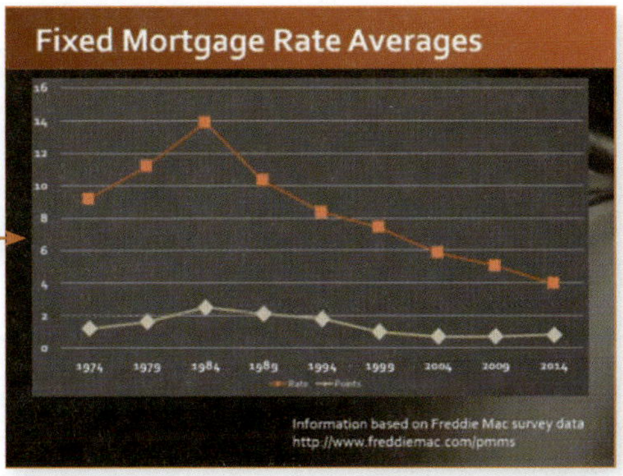

2-131 Slide 4 completed line chart

13. On slide 5, insert a table with 5 columns and 3 rows. Make the following changes:
    a. Type the text shown in Figure 2-132.
    b. Select columns 2–4 and change to **Center** alignment.
    c. In the first row, change to **Bottom** alignment and change the row *Shading* to **Dark Red**, **Accent 1**.
    d. Align the table in the horizontal and vertical center on the slide.

14. Insert a text box above the table.
    a. Type $250,000.
    b. Change the font to **40 pts**. and **bold**.
15. Insert a text box below the table.
    a. Type the following text on three lines:

       Lender rates are influenced by credit scores.
       Plan for a 20% down payment to avoid cost of points.
       Add taxes and insurance premiums.

    b. Position the text boxes as shown in Figure 2-132.
16. On slide 6, convert the list to a *SmartArt* graphic.
    a. Select the bulleted text and convert it to the **Vertical Curved List** *SmartArt* layout.
    b. Resize the *SmartArt* frame on the right so it fits the longest line of text.
17. Make the following changes to the *SmartArt* graphic:
    a. Change the colors to **Colorful Range, Accent 4 to 5**.
    b. Apply the **Moderate Effect SmartArt** style.
    c. Select all of the white circles and change the *Shape Fill* to **Dark Red, Accent 1** and apply the *Bevel* effect of **Cool Slant**.
    d. Center the *SmartArt* graphic on the slide (Figure 2-133).
18. Apply the **Shape** transition with the **Out** effect option to all slides.
19. Save and close the presentation (Figure 2-134).

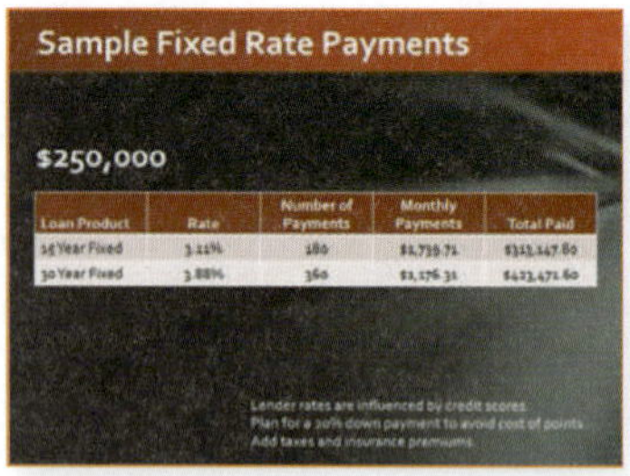

2-132 Slide 5 table with text boxes added

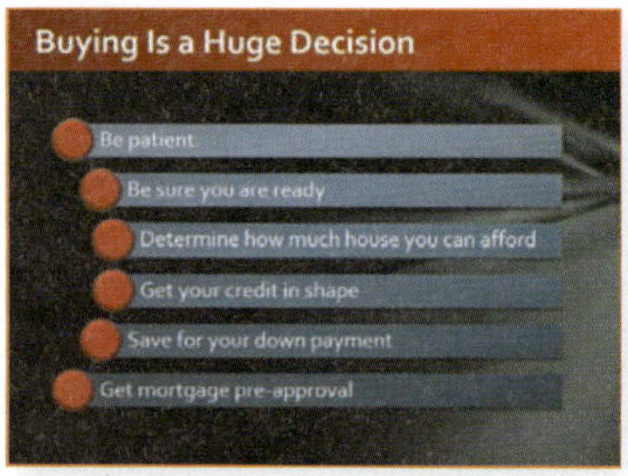

2-133 Slide 6 SmartArt graphic with style and effects changed

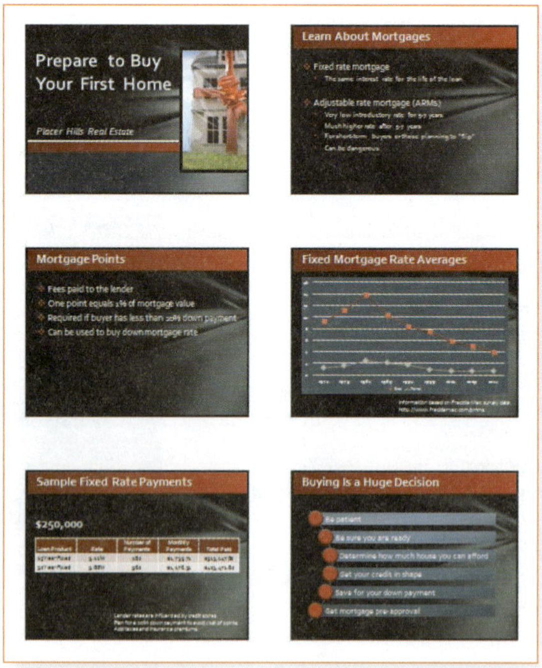

2-134 PowerPoint 2-5 completed

Independent Project 2-6

Kathy Sung, Director of Services at Life's Animal Shelter (LAS), will talk to a luncheon group of businesspeople to explain the important work of LAS and to solicit financial support. For this project you develop the presentation she will use to explain the needs of LAS and describe ways people can contribute through donations or by volunteering their time.
[Student Learning Outcomes 2.1, 2.2, 2.3, 2.4, 2.5, 2.6, 2.7]

Files Needed: ***YouCanHelp-02.pptx, CountryStroll-02.jpg, DayCare-02.jpg, Food-02.jpg, Groom-02.jpg,* and *RoyalTreatment-02.jpg***
Completed Project File Name: ***[your initials] PowerPoint 2-6.pptx***

Skills Covered in This Project

- Insert an online picture.
- Apply text effects.
- Apply a picture style.
- Set transparent color.
- Recolor a picture.
- Adjust size dimensions.
- Insert a text box.
- Insert and format a table.
- Convert text to a *SmartArt* graphic.
- Create a *SmartArt* graphic with pictures.
- Apply a *SmartArt* style and effects.

1. Open the presentation ***YouCanHelp-02***.
2. Save the presentation as ***[your initials] PowerPoint 2-6***.
3. On slide 1, change the title text fill to **Dark Red**, **Accent 1**, **Darker 25%**. Apply the *Bevel* text effect of **Angle**.
4. Change the font size to **80 pts**. and resize the placeholder on the right so one word is on each line.
5. Use the *Insert Pictures* dialog box to search for three pictures from Office.com and insert them on slides. Type the search word dog.
   a. On slide 1, add the picture of a German Shepherd dog with a white background.
   b. On slide 2, add the picture of three boys with a dog on grass.
   c. On slide 3, add the picture of a Golden Retriever dog with a white background.
6. On slide 1, adjust the picture.
   a. Increase the picture size (height **5.9"** and width **4.7"**).
   b. Use *Set Transparent Color* to remove the white area in the picture.
   c. Position the dog picture as shown in Figure 2-135.
7. On slide 2, adjust the picture.
   a. Decrease the picture size (height **5.84"** and width **8"**).
   b. Apply the *Moderate Frame, Black* picture style.
   c. Center the picture horizontally and position it near the top of the slide.

2-135 Slide 1 with picture added, white background removed

8. Insert a text box below the picture and type the following text on two lines:

   Our operating funds come through
   donations and pet adoption fees.

   a. Change the text to **White** and font size to **20 pts**.
   b. Change the *Shape Outline* to **White** and the *Weight* to **3 pts**.
   c. Change the *Shape Fill* to **Black**.
   d. Center the text box horizontally below the picture (Figure 2-136).

2-136 Slide 2 with picture and text box

9. On slide 3, adjust the picture.
   a. Use *Set Transparent Color* to remove the white area in the picture.
   b. Increase the picture size (height **5.23"** and width **6"**).
   c. Position the picture as shown in Figure 2-137.

2-137 Slide 3 with picture added, white background removed

10. Select the slide 2 thumbnail and press **Ctrl+C** to copy it.
    a. Put your insertion point after slide 3 and press **Ctrl+V** to paste the copied slide.

11. Make changes to the new slide 4.
    a. In the text box, replace the text with the words **We Need Your Help!**
    b. Resize the text box to fit the text and center it horizontally under the picture.
    c. Select the picture and click the **Color** button.
    d. In the *Recolor* group click the **Orange**, **Accent color 2**, **Dark** option (Figure 2-138).

2-138 Slide 4 with picture recolored

12. On slide 5, convert the list to a *Vertical Bullet List SmartArt* graphic.
    a. Increase the *SmartArt* frame height to **4.7"** so the text size increases.
    b. Reduce the width to **9"**).
    c. Center the *SmartArt* horizontally.
    d. Apply the **Cartoon** *SmartArt* style as displayed in Figure 2-139.

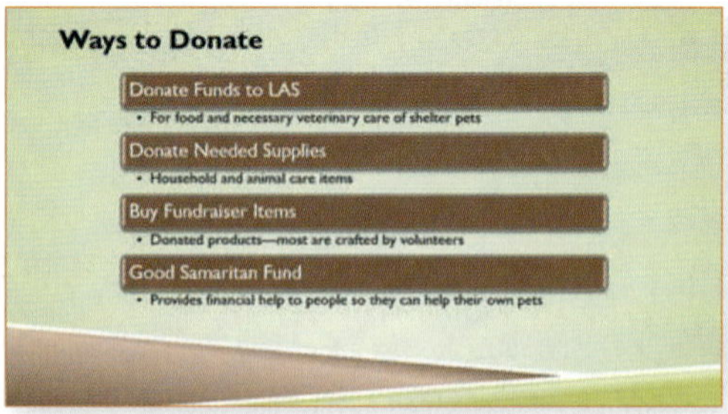

2-139 Slide 5 *SmartArt* graphic converted from bulleted text

13. On slide 6, convert the list to a **Picture Lineup** *SmartArt* graphic. Click the **Picture** icon on each shape to open the *Insert Pictures* dialog box. Browse to locate your student files and insert the following pictures going from left to right (Figure 2-140):

1	***DayCare-02***
2	***CountryStroll-02***
3	***RoyalTreatment-02***
4	***Food-02***
5	***Groom-02***

    Each picture is automatically resized to fit the SmartArt shape where it is inserted.

14. After slide 6, insert a new slide with a *Title and Content* layout.
    a. Type the title Items We Need
    b. Insert a table with 3 columns and 5 rows.
    c. Type the table text shown in Figure 2-141.
    d. Increase the font size to **20 pts**.
    e. Adjust column width so each column fits the longest line of text.
    f. Center the table on the slide.
15. Apply the *Gallery* transition to all slides.
16. Save and close the presentation (Figure 2-142).

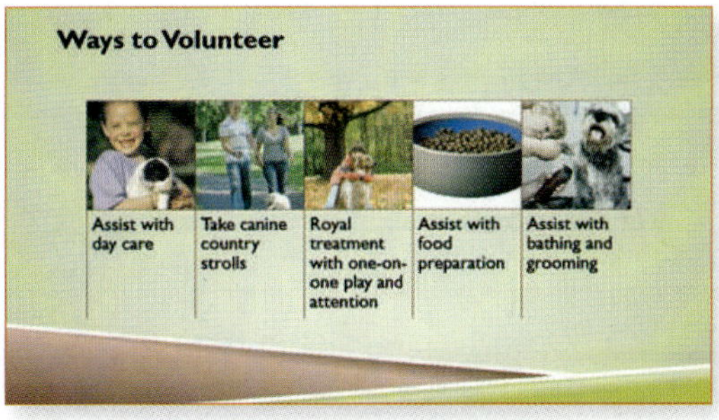

2-140 Slide 6 *SmartArt* graphic picture layout

Cleaning	Paper Products and Bedding	Dog and Cat Play
Bleach	Paper Towels	Dog and Cat Treats
Pine Sol	Paper Plates	Chewies
Mop Heads	Plastic Containers with Lids	Collars
Towels	Blankets	Leashes

2-141 Table text

2-142 PowerPoint 2-6 completed

Improve It Project 2-7

The Hamilton Civic Center needs a presentation to explain benefits of yoga and encourage members to join yoga classes. In this project you revise a presentation to give it a cohesive look and illustrate it with pictures, a *SmartArt* graphic, and a table. You apply various styles and effects for a contemporary appearance. [Student Learning Outcomes 2.2, 2.3, 2.4, 2.5, 2.6, 2.7]

File Needed: ***Yoga-02.pptx***
Completed Project File Name: ***[your initials] PowerPoint 2-7.pptx***

Skills Covered in This Project

- Apply text effects.
- Insert an online picture.
- Apply a picture style.
- Reposition slide objects.
- Convert text to a *SmartArt* graphic.
- Apply a *SmartArt* style and effects.
- Format a table.
- Compress pictures.

1. Open the presentation ***Yoga-02*** that has a Standard size (4:3 aspect ratio). The slide size is 10" x 7.5" compared to the slide size of 13.333" x 7.5" for the Widescreen (16:9 aspect ratio).
2. Save the presentation as ***[your initials] PowerPoint 2-7***.
3. Make the title slide more dynamic.
   a. Search online at Office.com and insert a yoga picture.
   b. Apply a **Bevel Rectangle** picture style.
   c. Select the title placeholder; then click **Text Effects** from the *WordArt Styles* group. Select **Transform** and then select **Wave 1**.

2-143 Title slide

4. Recolor the logo.
   a. Select the logo and then click **Color**. Select the *Recolor* option **Blue, Accent color 5 Light** to replace the black with a color that will better match theme colors.
   b. Use *Set Transparent Color* to remove the white so your background color shows.
   c. Make the logo width **2.5"** and the height will automatically adjust.
5. Size and position title slide objects as shown in Figure 2-143.
6. On slide 3, change the listed text to a *SmartArt* graphic.
   a. Click the **Convert to SmartArt** button and select the **Vertical Block List**.
   b. Apply the **White Outline** *SmartArt* style.
   c. Click **Change Colors** and apply the **Colorful Range – Accent Colors 4 to 5** (Figure 2-144).

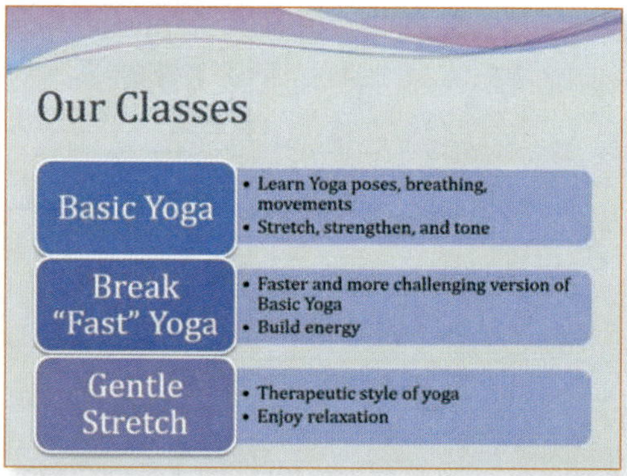

2-144 *SmartArt*

7. On slides 4 and 5, search online at *Office.com* for appropriate yoga pictures and insert them.
   a. Resize and position the pictures appropriately.
   b. With a picture selected, click **Compress Pictures**. Use document resolution, delete cropped areas of pictures, and apply compression to all pictures.
8. On slide 6, modify the table.
   a. Increase the font size to **20 pts**.
   b. Apply the **Medium Style 2 – Accent 4** table style.
   c. Select the title row, click **Cell Bevel,** and apply the **Riblet** effect.
   d. Add a **1 pt** border to all cells using the **Blue, Accent 4, Darker 50%** pen color (Figure 2-145).

9. Apply the **Dissolve** transition to all slides.
10. Save and close your presentation (Figure 2-146).

Classes	Days	Hours
Basic Yoga	Mon/Wed	4:15 – 5:15 p.m.
Break "Fast" Yoga	Tues/Thurs	7:00 – 8:10 a.m.
Gentle Stretch	Fri	10:00 – 11:30 a.m.

2-145 Slide 6 table

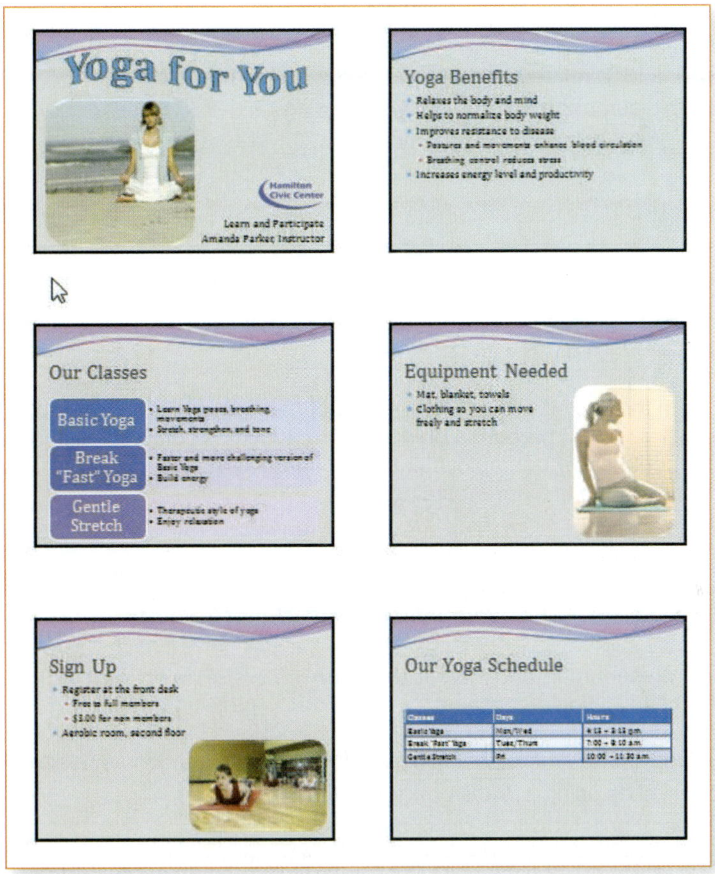

2-146 PowerPoint 2-7 completed

Challenge Project 2-8

For this project, do some online comparison shopping for items you would be likely to buy such as clothing, household products, or automotive supplies. Prepare slides describing the products and apply text effects to the slide titles. Prepare a chart that shows costs either for the same product at several stores or similar products at the same store.
[Student Learning Outcomes 2.1, 2.2, 2.3, 2.4, 2.5, 2.6, 2.7, 2.8]

File Needed: None
Completed Project File Name: ***[your initials] PowerPoint 2-8.pptx***

Create a new presentation and save it as ***[your initials] PowerPoint 2-8***. Modify your presentation according to the following guidelines:

- Select an appropriate theme and make color and font changes as needed for your topic.
- Prepare a title slide and product description slides.
- Search online for a related image and insert it on the title slide.
- Create a table summarizing some of your findings.
- Create two charts to compare specific items.

Challenge Project 2-9

Using data from the United States Department of Labor published online by the Bureau of Labor Statistics (http://www.bls.gov) prepare a presentation explaining some current trends in the labor force. For example, you could show unemployment rate comparisons from different regions or wage estimates for various occupations in different states.
Student Learning Outcomes 2.1, 2.2, 2.3, 2.4, 2.5, 2.6, 2.7, 2.8]

File Needed: None
Completed Project File Name: ***[your initials] PowerPoint 2-9.pptx***

Create a new presentation and save it as ***[your initials] PowerPoint 2-9***. Modify your presentation according to the following guidelines:

- Select an appropriate theme and make color and font changes as needed for your topic.
- Create a title slide using a *Transform* text effect.
- Include several bulleted slides describing current trends.
- Search for appropriate pictures, resize as needed, and apply a picture style to each one.
- Prepare a table showing salaries for several jobs in different locations or for data changing over time.
- Prepare a chart comparing employment statistics from your state or region.

Challenge Project 2-10

Using information from one of your favorite coffee or soft drink manufacturers, such as the information you can find at www.thecoca-colacompany.com or www.pepsico.com, prepare a presentation comparing different products. You could show the diversity of the product line or list promotional products with pricing. From financial information provided on the sites, you could feature total revenue, total profits, or other interesting performance data in your presentation.
[Student Learning Outcomes 2.1, 2.2, 2.3, 2.4, 2.5, 2.6, 2.7, 2.8]

File Needed: None
Completed Project File Name: ***[your initials] PowerPoint 2-10.pptx***

Create a new presentation and save it as ***[your initials] PowerPoint 2-10***. Modify your presentation according to the following guidelines:

- Select an appropriate theme and make color and font changes as needed for your topic.
- Create a distinctive title slide using *WordArt*.
- Search online for appropriate pictures and insert three or more.
- Adjust picture sizes and apply picture styles.
- Prepare slides listing key factors contributing to the company's growth.
- Prepare a *SmartArt* graphic illustrating a specific process or relationship from historical or operational information.
- Create a chart showing comparisons for data such as net revenue or operating profit.

CHAPTER 3

Preparing for Delivery and Using a Slide Presentation

POWERPOINT

CHAPTER OVERVIEW

In this chapter you learn more methods to help you work with PowerPoint more efficiently and effectively. This chapter teaches you how to create new theme colors customized for your topic, apply animation so selected slide objects appear just at the right time in your presentation, and link to a video from a web site. You also explore PowerPoint's rehearsal features to help you perfect your delivery timing and techniques, project your presentation more effectively, and prepare a presentation to be self-running. Finally, you learn how to save a presentation so it can be distributed on a CD.

STUDENT LEARNING OUTCOMES (SLOs)

After completing this chapter, you will be able to:

SLO 3.1 Create custom theme and background colors (p. P3-139).

SLO 3.2 Apply animation to add interest and reinforce content (p. P3-147).

SLO 3.3 Link to an online video (p. P3-149).

SLO 3.4 Use rehearsal techniques to prepare for presentation delivery (p. P3-156).

SLO 3.5 Control display options for different screen sizes (p. P3-159).

SLO 3.6 Present effectively and professionally using projection equipment (p. P3-164).

SLO 3.7 Use annotation pens to highlight information and save presentation markings (p. P3-167).

SLO 3.8 Prepare a self-running presentation that loops (p. P3-170).

SLO 3.9 Use the *Package Presentation for CD* feature to prepare a slide show for display on other computers (p. P3-171).

CASE STUDY

Specialists at Solution Seekers, Inc., frequently present to both large and small groups as they work with clients to improve business performance. Davon Washington is creating a series of seminars for new hires to help them be more productive and professional. For this project, you work with Davon to finish the presentation he has developed about presentation planning.

Pause & Practice 3-1: Create custom theme and background colors. Add interest with animation and video.

Pause & Practice 3-2: Rehearse a presentation and prepare for a widescreen display.

Pause & Practice 3-3: Practice slide show delivery features.

Pause & Practice 3-4: Prepare a self-running presentation and package a presentation to a folder.

SLO 3.1

Creating Custom Theme and Backgrounds Colors

Themes create a unified appearance for your presentation. When you use themes effectively, the information you present on a topic is seen by your viewers as one "package" and not a collection of random slides. You may need to match specific colors in a company logo or a school's colors, so in this section you will prepare custom theme colors that create a unique palette and help you work more efficiently. Then you will explore different ways to apply pattern, gradient, and picture fills and consider some issues to keep in mind when applying these fills to slide backgrounds.

Custom Theme Colors

3-1 *Theme Colors* gallery

As you worked with shapes, colors, and styles in previous chapters, you saw how theme colors are arranged across the top of the *Theme Colors* gallery. Recall that various percentages of each color appear below the top row colors (Figure 3-1). This section takes a closer look at where PowerPoint automatically applies theme colors to various graphics you create.

Four sample slides are shown in Figure 3-2. These samples feature the *Facet* theme and the *Blue* color theme. The background for these slides is white (Background 1) with decorative shapes in Background 2, Text 2, and Accent 1 colors.

- ***Slide 1:*** The photograph has a border color of Text 2.
- ***Slide 2:*** The first row of circles shows background and text colors. The second row of circles shows Accent colors 1–6.
- ***Slide 3:*** The bullets and the *SmartArt* shapes are shown in the Accent 1 color.
- ***Slide 4:*** Accent 2 color variations are applied to the table; the chart shows Accent colors 1–6 based on the order data is entered on the spreadsheet.

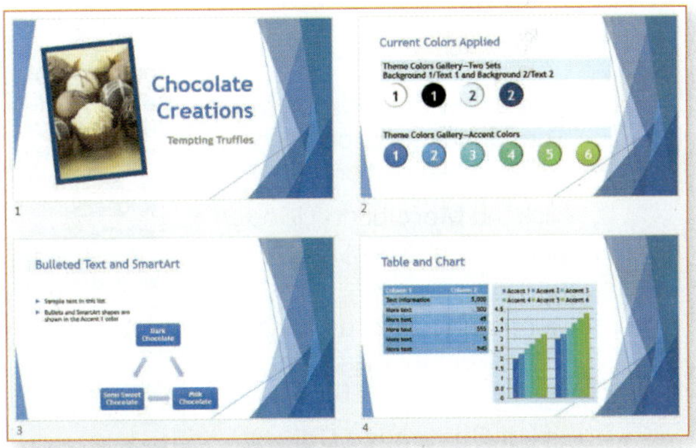

3-2 Sample slides showing graphics with the *Facet* theme

Accent colors (Figure 3-3) appear from left to right in both the *Shape Styles* gallery and the *Table Styles* gallery (Figures 3-4 and 3-5). Other galleries show options in a similar way.

You can boost productivity by creating custom theme colors because the colors you choose are available to you in the galleries as you develop your slide show. When you save custom theme colors, the colors are also available to use again in another presentation. Keep the following guidelines in mind when you create custom theme colors:

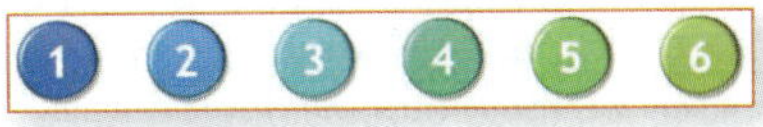

3-3 *Blue* theme accent colors

- Select your background color first and then select other colors that work well on the background.

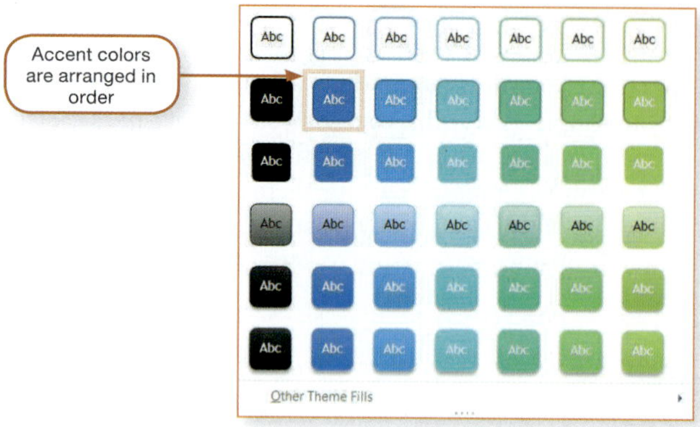

3-4 ***Shapes Styles*** **gallery**

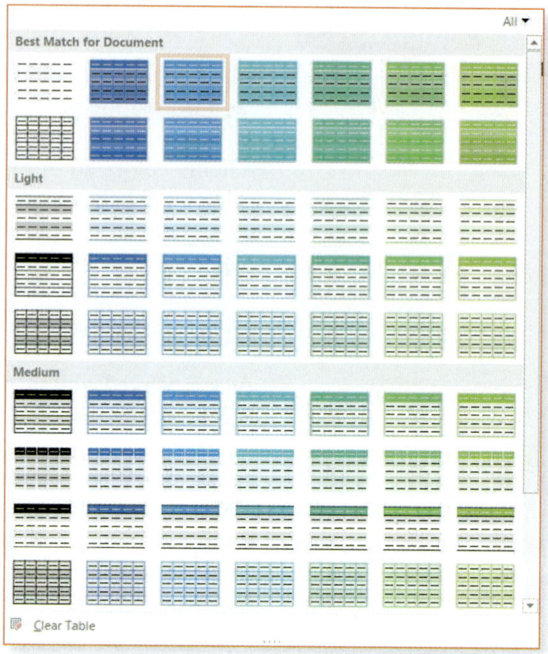

3-5 ***Table Styles*** **gallery**

- Pick a text color that has a high contrast with your background color so words are easy to read.
- The Accent 1 theme color appears first when you draw shapes and is the first choice in galleries for table and *SmartArt* effects.

The following example illustrates how to change theme colors from the *Design* tab to a new set of colors that is more appropriate for a presentation about chocolate.

HOW TO: Create New Theme Colors

1. Start a new presentation using a design theme or open an existing presentation.
2. Click the **More** button [*Design* tab, *Variants* group].
3. Select **Colors** to open the list of built-in theme colors. The current theme colors are selected (Figure 3-6).
4. Select **Customize Colors** to open the *Create New Theme Colors* dialog box (Figure 3-7). For this example, the *Text/Background – Dark 1* (black) color does not change.
5. Change each color as needed to create your custom theme. This example has a brown and

3-6 ***Theme Colors*** **gallery**

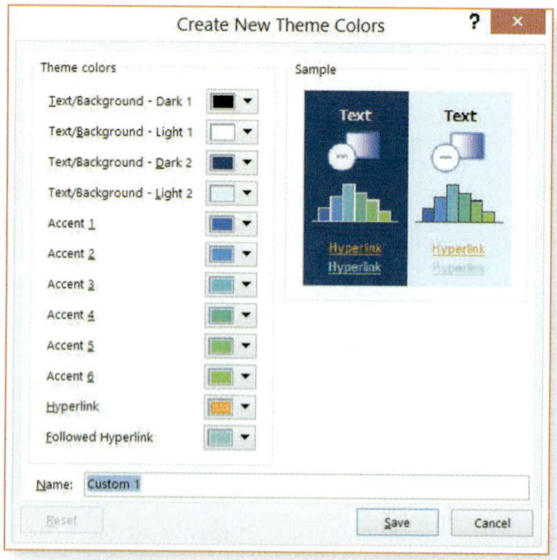

3-7 ***Create New Theme Colors*** **dialog box showing** ***Blue*** **theme colors**

yellow color palette that works for a presentation about chocolate (Figure 3-8).

- Click the **list arrow** on a color button to open the *Theme Colors* gallery.
- Click **More Colors** to open the *Colors* dialog box.
- Click the *Standard* or *Custom* tab, choose a color, and click **OK**.
- Repeat for each of the colors you want to change.

6. Name the new custom theme.
7. Click the **Save** button. The new custom theme is automatically applied and the name will appear in the *Custom* section of your list of available theme colors so you can use it again.

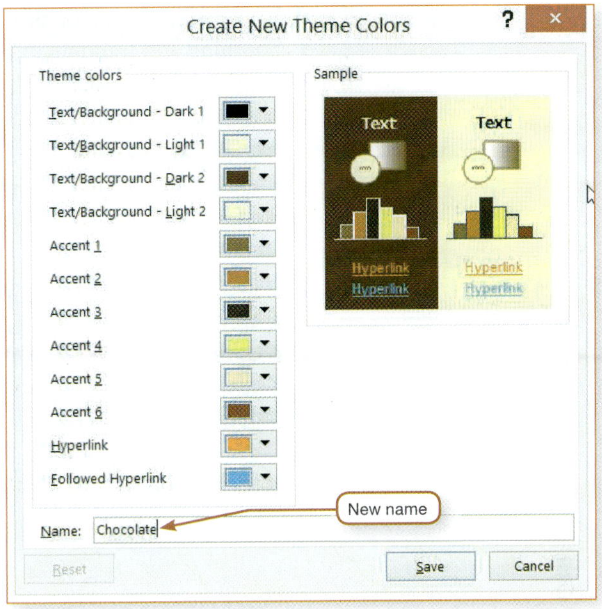

3-8 ***Create New Theme Colors*** **dialog box showing custom colors**

ANOTHER WAY

Use the *Design* tab when you need to customize colors and fonts. When you also need to change background graphics or insert pictures such as a company logo, use the *Slide Master* tab to make all changes.

Figure 3.9 shows sample slides with the new colors. Controlling color this way is much more efficient than using an existing theme and having to select a custom color each time you create various illustrations. If any slide text, such as a slide title, retains the original colors, click the **Reset** button [*Home* tab, *Slides* group] to update the colors.

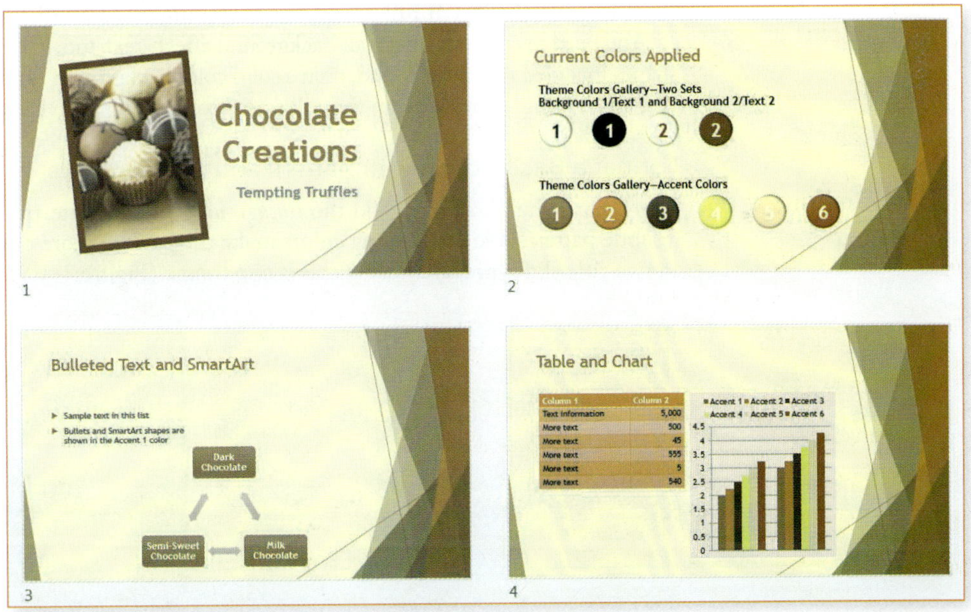

3-9 Chocolate theme colors applied to sample slides

Color combinations influence the tone of your presentation. Your options are endless, but you may want to consider a few of the following tonal effects:

- Varied and vibrant, or similar with subtle differences
- Soothing and tranquil, or lively and energetic
- Youthful or mature
- Historic or high tech

When you think about colors for your topic, consider your audience and be respectful of cultural differences. People tend to assign meaning to colors based on their cultural background and life experiences. A few examples of colors that have symbolic meaning include the following:

- ***White:*** Purity and cleanliness in the American culture, death in some other cultures
- ***Red:*** Health (red blood) in the medical field, loss (negative values) in the financial field
- ***Green:*** Sickness (infection) in the medical field, wealth (money) in the financial field

MORE INFO

To examine this concept further, look online for information about color meaning, symbolism, or the psychology of color.

Custom Background Colors

The *Format Background* pane has options similar to those you have used on the *Format Shape* pane (*See SLO 2.1: Working with Shapes, Colors, and Styles*). When you change background colors, text colors do not change. Also, the position of placeholders or the graphic shapes that are included on some design themes do not change.

When you choose colors and creative effects for backgrounds, remember that your color choices will fill the entire slide area behind everything else you design on a slide. These changes are visible throughout the presentation if you apply them to all slides, so you should examine your changes at full screen size to be sure you are satisfied with the results.

You need to consider how your background affects text, too. If a theme or template has graphic shapes included in a background, then a solid color background fill is a good choice. Select a color that has a strong contrast from the color used for text (light on dark or dark on light).

Format a Background with Pattern and Gradient Fills

Two colors (the *Foreground* and the *Background*) create pattern fills. Two similar colors make a subtle pattern; two contrasting colors make the pattern more obvious. Notice the differences in two title slides prepared using the *Whisp* theme (Figure 3-10).

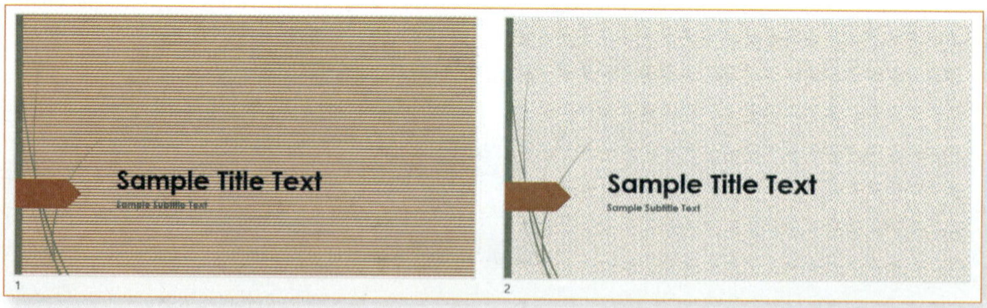

3-10 *Whisp* theme title slide with two background patterns

- ***Slide 1 (Left):*** Contrasting colors in a bold pattern make the title text difficult to read.
- ***Slide 2 (Right):*** The same colors with a subtle pattern improve the appearance.

HOW TO: Add a Background Pattern Fill

1. Point to the slide background and right-click to open the shortcut menu.
2. Click **Format Background** to open the *Format Background* pane.
3. Select the **Pattern fill** option.
4. Choose an appropriate *Foreground Color* and *Background Color.*
5. Choose one of the patterns.
6. By default, this change is applied to the current slide only. Click **Apply to All** to apply this change to the entire presentation.
7. If you want to restore the background's original design, click **Reset Background**.
8. Close the *Format Background* pane.

ANOTHER WAY

To open the *Format Background* pane, click the **Format Background** button on the *Design* tab or click the **Background Styles** list arrow [*Slide Master* tab, *Background* group] and then click **Format Background**.

You can use preset gradient colors based on theme colors or select custom colors. You first choose the type of gradient such as *Linear, Radial, Rectangular, Path,* or *Shade from title.* Then you choose the direction of color change. Based on these choices, gradient stops appear on the color bar. Move, delete, or add gradient stops to control how the colors blend. The color change is more gradual with more distance between the stops. Compare the title slides of the *Whisp* design theme shown in Figures 3-11 and 3-12. These two slides started with the same preset gradient fill of *Bottom Spotlight – Accent 4* with a type of *Linear*. The settings were changed differently.

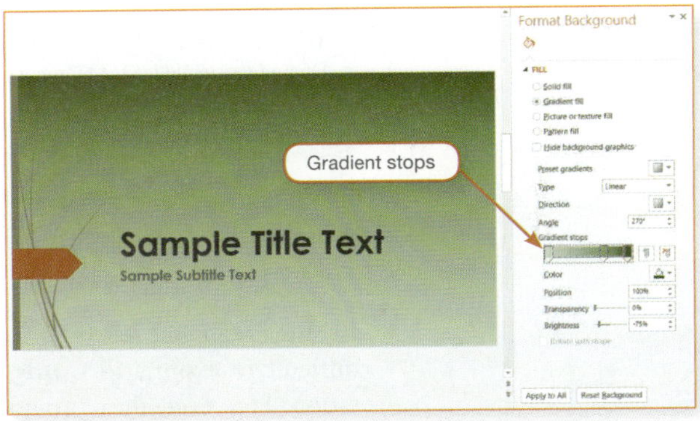

3-11 ***Whisp*** **theme title slide with a custom background gradient fill**

Figure 3-11

- *Linear Up* direction
- Three gradient stops are used

Figure 3-12

- *Linear Diagonal – Top Left to Bottom Right* direction
- The three gradient stops on the left of the color bar are close together for a defined color change; the three right stops are spread apart for a more gradual color change.

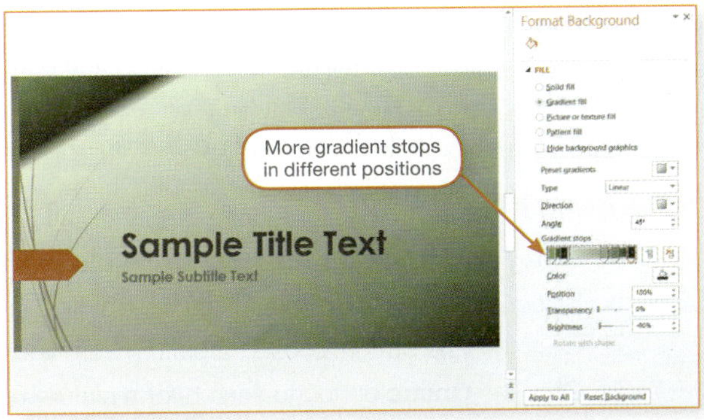

3-12 ***Whisp*** **theme title slide with a custom background gradient fill showing different gradient stops**

HOW TO: Add a Background Gradient Fill

1. Point to the slide background and right-click to open the shortcut menu.
2. Click **Format Background** to open the *Format Background* pane.
3. Select the **Gradient fill** option.
4. Click the **Preset gradients** list arrow and select a color style.
5. Click the **Type** list arrow and choose one of the options: *Linear, Radial, Rectangular, Path*, or *Shade from title.*
6. Click the **Direction** list arrow and choose a direction for color blending if one is available.
7. The **Angle** degree is available only for the *Linear* type and it automatically adjusts based on the direction you choose. You can type a different number or click the spin box to change the number in 10 degree increments.
8. Add or remove gradient stops.
   - To add gradient stops, click the **Add gradient stop** button.
   - To remove gradient stops, click the **Remove gradient stop** button or drag the gradient stop off the color bar.
9. Change colors by selecting a gradient stop and clicking the **Color** button. Choose a different color.
10. To change color blending, select the gradient stop and drag it to a different position on the color bar. If you want to change the order, drag the stops to rearrange them. For precise adjustments, change percentages for each stop position.
11. Adjust *Brightness* and *Transparency* as needed.
12. By default, this change is applied to the current slide only. Click **Apply to All** to apply this background to every slide in your presentation.
13. Close the *Format Background* pane.

ANOTHER WAY

You can access various *Background Styles* [*Design* tab, *Variants* group or *Slide Master* tab, *Background* group] that show light and dark color combinations based on theme colors.

Format a Background with Picture and Texture Fills

Pictures help you tell your story, communicate without words, and convey emotions that are difficult to express in words. Pictures can provide a dramatic background for your presentation. However, they provide some special challenges when text is displayed over pictures because of the many colors that are used in pictures. Textures have similar issues if they use many colors or show a lot of detail. Pictures in a small size can be used as textures to fill a slide with many small pictures. The examples in this section will show you several ways to combine background pictures and text.

HOW TO: Add a Background Picture Fill

1. Point to the slide background and right-click to open the shortcut menu.
2. Click **Format Background** to open the *Format Background* pane.
3. Select the **Picture or texture fill** option.
4. Click the **File** button to insert a picture from your collection.
5. Click the **Online** button to search for a picture using the *Insert Picture* dialog box.
   - Type your search word and click the **Search** button or press **Enter**.
   - Select the picture you want to use and click **Insert**.

6. To soften the picture colors so text and other objects on the slide are easy to see, use one of the following methods:
   - On the *Format Background* pane, increase the *Transparency* percentage. This setting mutes the colors but the original colors are still evident.
   - Click **Picture** at the top of the *Format Background* pane; then click **Picture Color**. Click **Presets** to choose from different saturation levels or click **Recolor** to choose from dark and light accent colors for a monotone effect. If you decide not to change colors, click the **Reset** button to restore the picture to its original state.
7. By default, this change is applied to the current slide only. Click **Apply to All** to apply this background to every slide in your presentation.
8. To restore the background to its original state, click the **Reset Background** button.
9. Close the *Format Background* pane.

MORE INFO

You can change a slide background at any time while you are working on a presentation.

The following figures show some options you can explore using the *Format Background* pane to soften background pictures or use placeholder fill colors to make text over pictures or textures easy to read. In these examples, a single flower that is almost a square image (Figure 3–13) is used in different ways. In Figures 3-13–3-17, the first slide illustrates a problem while the other two slides show possible solutions.

3-13 A flower used in backgrounds

Notice the following characteristics for the slides shown in Figure 3-14:

- ***Slide 1 (Left):*** Because this picture is almost square (522 × 529 pixels) when it is stretched to fit the width of a widescreen display (height 7.5" and width 13.333"), part of the flower is cut off at the top and bottom. This is not necessarily a problem, just something that happens if you use a square picture. The title text, however, is not easy to read over the dark colors of the flower. This is a problem as your slide text should be legible no matter what designs you use.
- ***Slide 2 (Center):*** The title placeholder is the same width as the slide. A dark red fill is applied and the white text has a shadow so now the text is easy to read.
- ***Slide 3 (Right):*** The title placeholder treatment is the same as slide 2. The picture was recolored using the preset *Black and White: 25%* color. This creates a more abstract image.

3-14 A large square picture used as a background fill with color changes

Notice the following characteristics for the three slides shown in Figure 3-15:

- ***Slide 4 (Left):*** The actual size of this large flower does not fill the slide, so now the complete flower is displayed. The *Tile picture as texture* option was selected with *Alignment* changed to *Center.* ***Tiling*** causes the picture to be repeated to fill the slide area so parts of the flower are shown around the center flower. Like slide 1 in Figure 3-14, the text is difficult to read.
- ***Slide 5 (Center):*** The title placeholder resembles slide 2 in Figure 3-14, but this time the fill color transparency is 30%. More of the flower shows through, yet the text is still easy to read.
- ***Slide 6 (Right):*** The picture was recolored with preset *Gray – 25%, Background color 2 Light*. Black text is used with no shadow. (This was done because black text with a black shadow makes the text look blurred.)

3-15 A large square picture used as a tiled background fill with color changes

If you tile a picture or texture that is small, many images fill the screen for an effect like wallpaper. If these images still seem too large, you can adjust the *Tiling Options* and reduce the *Scale* percentage to display each image in a smaller size. *Offset* points control how much the tiled images are indented from the left (*Offset X*) and top (*Offset Y*).

Notice the following characteristics for the three slides shown in Figure 3-16:

- ***Slide 7 (Left):*** The *Tile picture as texture* option was selected so many of these small flower images (200×203 pixels) fill the screen. For an appropriate fit on the slide, *Alignment* was changed to *Top left;* then *Offset* and *Scale* were adjusted. Like slide 4 in Figure 3-15, the text is difficult to read.
- ***Slide 8 (Center):*** The flower picture was recolored with preset *Grayscale.* The title placeholder colors were changed to a black fill with red text. The placeholder size was increased, too, for greater emphasis.
- ***Slide 9 (Right):*** The repeating picture for this slide is a small rectangle (40 by 77 pixels) with a bevel effect to make it look like a real tile. The title text is left aligned and the placeholder is filled with a gold color. A rectangle was added on the right so the date would be easy to read and to help create an asymmetrical focal point with the single large flower. This flower has a transparent background rather than white as in the previous examples.

3-16 Small pictures tiled for a background fill with color changes

Textures available on the *Format Background* pane are small images, so it is generally best to tile them because the effect is more pleasing. When stretched to fill a slide, the textures will appear blurred. Notice the following characteristics for the slides shown in Figure 3-17:

- ***Slide 10 (Left):*** The *Paper bag* texture was applied and it is blurred.
- ***Slide 11 (Center):*** The same texture was tiled so multiple small images repeat and no other change was made.
- ***Slide 12 (Right):*** The same texture was tiled and the *Mirror type* changed to *Both* so this creates an interesting pattern with horizontal and vertical mirror images.

3-17 The same texture used as a background fill with different settings

SLO 3.2

Applying Animation

Animation is the movement of objects on a slide. Animation can make your presentation more dynamic and keep your audience focused on concepts.

You can observe creative animation techniques by noticing how objects and text move in movies or in television commercials. As you decide what effects to use, try to select movements that enhance your content and support your message. Animation can be overdone when it is not used skillfully. Be sure you are applying animation for the right reasons and not just for entertainment value. Use animation sparingly because too much can be distracting.

When planning movement, also consider the transitions (the movement between slides). When a presentation is supporting a speaker, you want to keep the transitions calmer and apply animation effects to draw attention to information on selected slides only.

Add Entrance, Exit, and Emphasis Effects

Animation effects are arranged in three categories that are shown in different colors on the gallery (Figure 3-18):

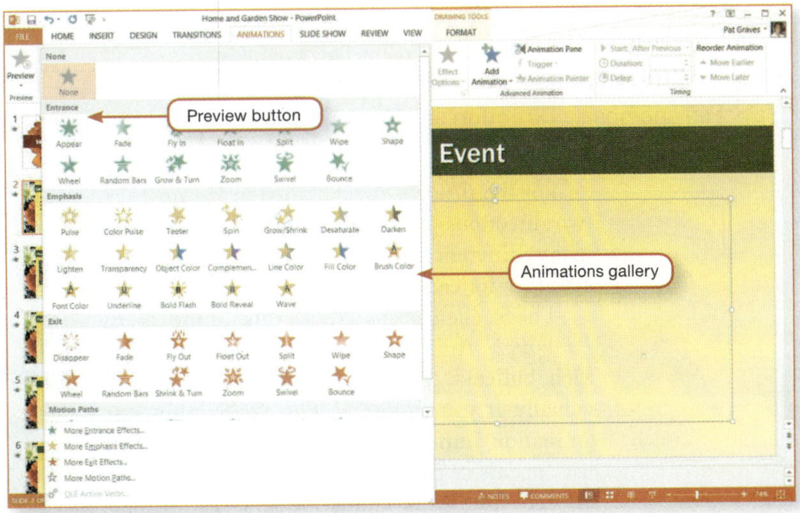

3-18 *Animations* gallery

- ***Entrance:*** A movement that occurs when an object appears on the slide (green)
- ***Emphasis:*** A movement that calls attention to an object that remains on the slide (yellow)
- ***Exit:*** A movement that occurs when an object leaves the slide (red)

Note that some effects are for text only. When animating objects, those effects are gray in the gallery and are not available.

HOW TO: Apply an Animation Effect

1. Select the text or object to be animated.
2. Click the **Animations** tab.
3. Click the **More** button on the *Animations* gallery to see all available effects.
   Or
   If the *Animations* gallery is not open because your PowerPoint window is narrow, click the **Add Animation** button [*Advanced Animation* group] to open the gallery.
4. Click an effect to apply it. A number appears on the slide, showing that the object is animated.
5. Click the **Preview** button to test the animation.
6. Repeat to animate additional objects as desired. Each animated object is numbered in sequence to show animation order.
7. To remove an animation, click the animation number and press **Delete**.

> **MORE INFO**
>
> Animation numbers are displayed only when the *Animations* tab is open.

Effect Options, Timing, and Duration

Each different animation effect has options that control the direction of movement.

HOW TO: Change Effect Options

1. Select the animated object.
2. Click the **Effect Options** button [*Animations* tab, *Animation* group].
3. Select an appropriate **Direction** and **Sequence** if it is available.

For the *Float In* effect shown in Figure 3-19, two directions are available. Other effects have many different options. You select only one direction for each animation.

The sequence shown in this figure is *By Paragraph*. Animation numbers display before each bulleted text item so they appear individually. If you choose *As One Object*, only one animation number displays and the complete list appears at the same time. If you choose *All at Once*, the same animation number displays for each text item and the complete list appears at the same time.

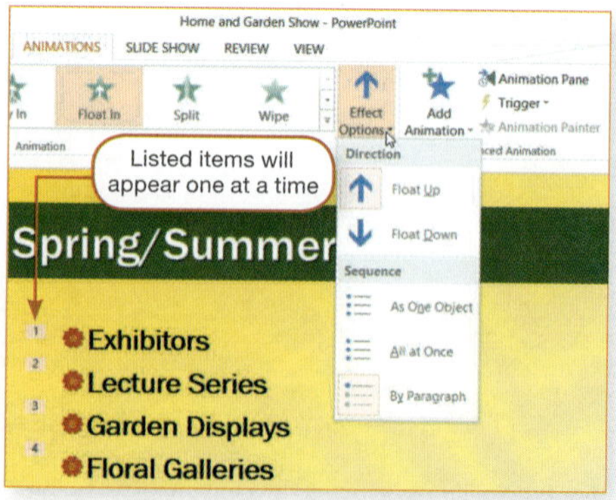

3-19 Animation and effect options applied

Some people are critical of animating text because viewers cannot read text until it stops moving. If you are going to spend significant time discussing each item in a list, adding each item as you start talking about it makes sense. However, animating a list has no value if you are only making brief statements or discussing the complete list in general terms.

You can adjust animation ***timing*** using the following commands on the *Animations* tab in the *Timing* group:

- ***Start:*** This controls when animation begins. With *On Click* the speaker controls the timing; *With Previous* or *After Previous* makes animation occur automatically.
- ***Duration:*** By default, the time to complete each animation ranges from .50 to 2.00 seconds depending on the movement. Increasing the duration seconds extends the time an object is moving so the movement appears slower.
- ***Delay:*** The default is no delay, but you can enter seconds in the spin box to make the animation begin after a specified time.
- ***Reorder Animation:*** When multiple objects are animated, click *Move Earlier* or *Move Later* to adjust the sequence of animation.

HOW TO: Adjust Animation Timing and Duration

1. Select the animated object.
2. Click the **Start** list box arrow [*Animations* tab, *Timing* group] and select from *On Click*, *With Previous*, or *After Previous* (Figure 3-20).
3. Increase or decrease **Duration** by editing the time or clicking the spin box arrows.
4. Enter seconds or click the **Delay** spin box to specify the time (in seconds) before the animation starts.
5. Click the **Preview** button to test the animation.
6. Reorder animation if necessary using the *Move Earlier* and *Move Later* buttons.

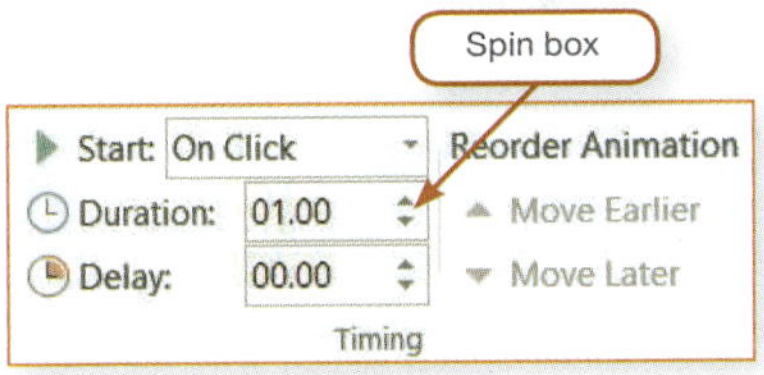

3-20 *Animations* tab, *Timing* group

When you animate several objects, check the animation numbers to be sure the objects will appear in the order you want (Figure 3-21).

3-21 Numbers indicate animation order

If your presentation is designed to support you as a speaker, coordinate the animation timing with your speaking. This technique usually works best in small segments only because precise timing is almost impossible to predict when you are presenting in real time to an audience. If you are designing a self-running presentation for a trade show exhibit, for example, your animation can be much more dramatic and extensive because the slide show is not dependent on a speaker's pace.

SLO 3.3

Linking to an Online Video

Many videos are available online, but not all of them can be played within PowerPoint. When you search for a video using the *Insert Video* dialog box, the videos found from YouTube are most likely to play within PowerPoint as long as you have Internet access. You click **Insert** to put the video on your slide, but the actual video is not saved in your presentation.

An image of the video will appear and the necessary information to link to it is saved in your presentation.

When you search for videos, you may find a compelling interview or demonstration that will enliven your presentation, but be sure the video fits your topic and adds value.

HOW TO: Link a Presentation to an Online Video

1. Be sure your computer has Internet access. Select the PowerPoint slide where you want to show the video.
2. Click the **Insert** tab.
3. Click the **Video** button list arrow [*Media* group] and select **Online Video** (Figure 3-22) to open the *Insert Video* dialog box (Figure 3-23). The search options that appear depend on how your software is installed.
4. Type a search word in one of the search boxes, *Bing Video Search* or *YouTube* if it is available, and click the **Search** button.
5. Available video clips (brief video segments) appear with ScreenTips that identify names.
   - The video name, source, and number of minutes appear in the lower left corner of the dialog box (Figure 3-24). You may want to use this information in a source notation.
6. Click **Insert** and the video will appear on your slide. Below the video, add the appropriate source information as needed.

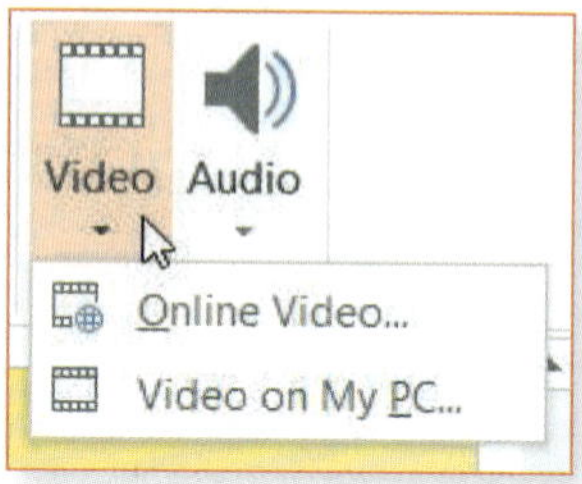

3-22 *Video* button on the *Insert* tab

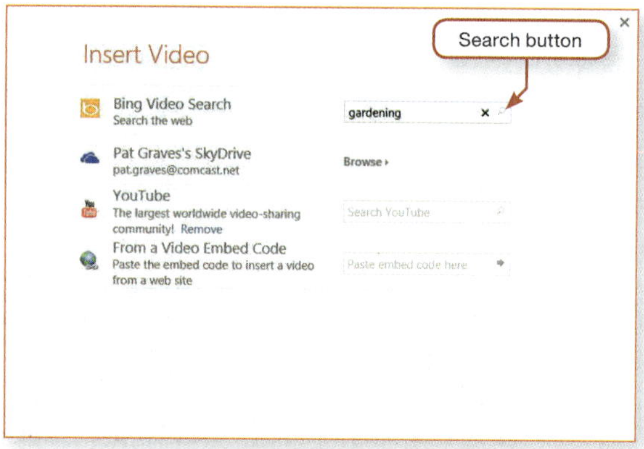

3-23 *Insert Video* dialog box showing search options

3-24 *Insert Video* dialog box showing search results

MORE INFO

A linked video will not play in a presentation that you send by email.

Play the Online Video

To play an online video in PowerPoint, the computer used to display your presentation must have Internet access.

The clarity you see in playback depends on the resolution of the original video and how it was compressed for online distribution. Resolution is expressed in pixel width and height. With more pixels, image clarity and detail improve.

As with all computer technology, video capabilities continue to improve and many videos can be played at full-screen size from their online source. However, video sharing sites often provide video in the standard definition size (640×480 pixels) or even smaller. Be careful when increasing the video size on your slide to avoid degrading image quality. Test how the video plays before you use it in your presentation.

HOW TO: Play an Online Video

1. In *Normal* view, select the video object.
2. If you wish, increase the size of the video by using one of these methods:
   - Drag handles.
   - Enter specific **Height** and **Width** measurements [*Video Tools Format* tab, *Size* group].
   - Click the *Size* launcher to open the *Format Video* pane (Figure 3-25). Click the *Size & Properties* option at the top of the pane. Adjust size by changing **Height** and **Width** measurements or changing the **Scale Height** and **Scale Width** measurements.
3. On the *Format Video* pane, check **Lock aspect ratio** and **Relative to original picture size** to maintain dimensions as your resize.
4. Check **Best scale for slide show** to select a different resolution.
5. Reposition the video as needed.
6. Notice the clarity of the video as you test it in the next steps. If the image is degraded, click the **Reset** button on the *Format Video* pane. You can also click the **Reset Design list arrow** [*Video Tools Format* tab, *Adjust* group] and click **Reset Design & Size** to restore the video to its original dimensions.

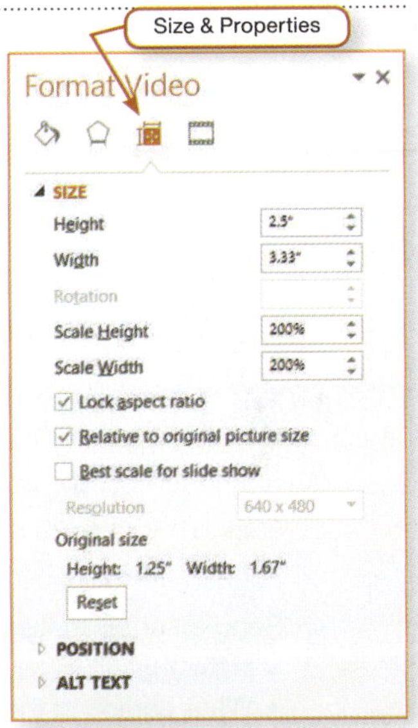

3-25 *Format Video* pane

7. To play the video in *Normal* view:
   - Click the **Play** button [*Video Tools Playback* tab, *Preview* group] to activate the video.
   - If the video can play within PowerPoint, a timeline will appear below the video with playback controls you can use to pause, mute, and access other options (Figure 3-26).
   - Click the **Play** button on the video to play it.
8. To play the video in *Slide Show* view:
   - Click the **Slide Show** button [*Status* bar] to start your slide show on the current slide.
   - Click the **Play** button on the video.
   - The same timeline described in step 7 appears at the bottom of the video as it plays.
   - Press **Esc** to stop the slide show and return to *Normal* view.

3-26 Video playing in *Normal* view

9. To make the video start automatically in *Slide Show* view:
   - Click the **Start** list box arrow [*Video Tools Playback* tab, *Video Options* group] and select **Automatically**.
   - If the video can be played at full screen size, select **Play Full Screen** [*Video Tools Playback* tab, *Video Options* group].
   - Click the **Slide Show** tab and the **From Beginning** button [*Start Slide Show* group]. Advance to the slide with the video to test that it begins playing automatically.
10. Move your pointer so it does not appear on the video while it is playing.
11. When the video is complete, advance to the next slide.

> **MORE INFO**
>
> If you find an online video that you want to use in PowerPoint, you may be able to link to it without searching for it in PowerPoint. You can copy the video's embed codes (the host web address, name of the video, and playback size information) that are included with a video in a sharing section on the host page. Then open the *Insert Video* dialog box and paste the embed codes. Information to link to the video is saved in your presentation, so Internet access is required to play the video.

Obtain Permission

Linking to a video for classroom purposes falls under the guidelines of ***fair use*** for education, and crediting the source may be sufficient. However, business use is different. Just like television programming or movies in a theater, videos are copyrighted by the creator. You need permission before you link to, display, or distribute video that is copyrighted. Obtaining permission is time consuming and can be expensive. If the creator does not give you permission, you must find another video and start the process again.

HOW TO: Obtain Permission to Use an Online Video

1. From the web site where the video is posted, identify the user name of the creator.
2. Click a link to go to more profile information or, in some cases, another web site.
3. Look for terms of use and find contact information.
4. Send an email message explaining the following:
   - How you want to use the video
   - What portion of the video you will use
   - When you will use the video
   - How you will show credits on the slide where the video is displayed such as in Figure 3-26
   - Your contact information for the creator's response

With the dynamic nature of the web, a video you find may be available for only a limited time. You may need to request a high resolution copy of the video, and the creator may charge you for this service.

> **MORE INFO**
>
> The ***Copyright Act of 1976*** is the primary basis of copyright law in the United States. It specifies fair use that permits limited use for such purposes as research, teaching, and scholarship. The ***Digital Millennium Copyright Act of 1998*** addresses issues of online copyright infringement.

PAUSE & PRACTICE: POWERPOINT 3-1

Davon Washington has almost finished the slide show for his seminar on presentation planning. In this project you create custom theme colors that better match the Solution Seekers, Inc., logo, modify a background style, animate several slide objects, and link to a video on a web site. You will later change the slide size from standard to widescreen.

File Needed: ***PresentationPlanning-03.pptx***
Completed Project File Name: ***[your initials] PP P3-1.pptx***

1. Open the presentation ***PresentationPlanning-03***.
2. Save the presentation as ***[your initials] PP P3-1***.
3. Create new theme colors.
   a. Click the **More** button [*Design* tab, *Variants* group].
   b. Select **Colors** and click **Customize Colors** to open the *Create New Theme Colors* dialog box (Figure 3-27).
   c. Change four colors. For each change, click the **color list arrow** and select **More Colors**. Click the **Custom** tab and enter the numbers for *Red*, *Green*, and *Blue* from the following table.

	Text/Background – Light 2	Accent 1	Accent 2	Accent 3
Red	234	3	102	181
Green	214	110	0	139
Blue	184	131	51	128

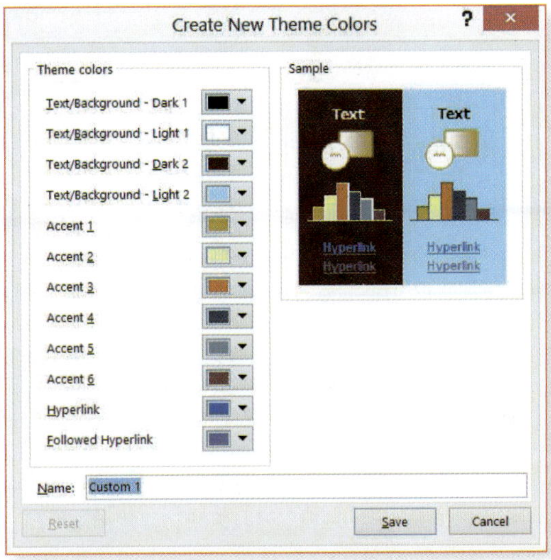

3-27 Original theme colors

   d. Name the new custom theme Planning (Figure 3-28).
   e. Click the **Save** button. The new custom theme is saved in the *Custom* section of your list of available theme colors.
4. On slide 1, apply a gradient fill.
   a. Point to the slide background and right-click.
   b. Select **Format Background** to open the *Format Background* pane.
   c. Select the **Gradient fill** option.
   d. Click the **Type** list arrow and choose **Linear**.
   e. Click the **Direction** list arrow and **Linear Diagonal – Top Right to Bottom Left**.
   f. The *Angle* percentage automatically adjusts to 135°.
   g. If necessary, click the **Add gradient stop** button so you have four gradient stops.

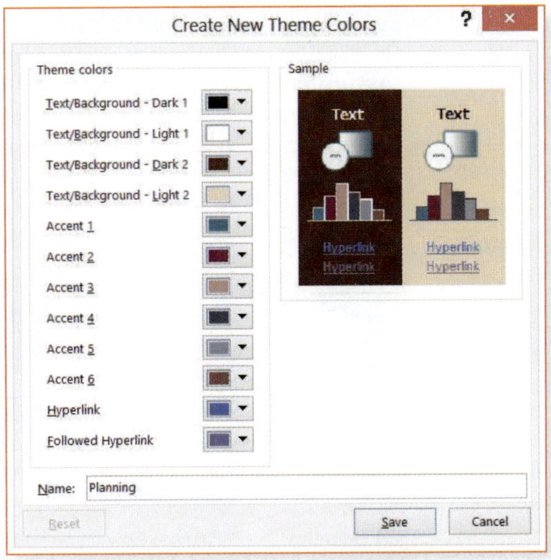

3-28 *Planning* theme colors

h. Click each gradient stop from left to right (Figure 3-29) and adjust the *Color*, *Position*, *Brightness*, and *Transparency* to the values shown in the following table:

Gradient Stops	Stop 1	Stop 2	Stop 3	Stop 4
Color	Dark Teal, Accent 1	Dark Teal, Accent 1, Lighter 60%	Tan, Text 2	Tan, Text 2, Darker 50%
Position	0%	30%	70%	100%
Transparency	0%	50%	0%	0%
Brightness	0%	0%	0%	−50%

i. The title slide gradient fill is shown in Figure 3-30.

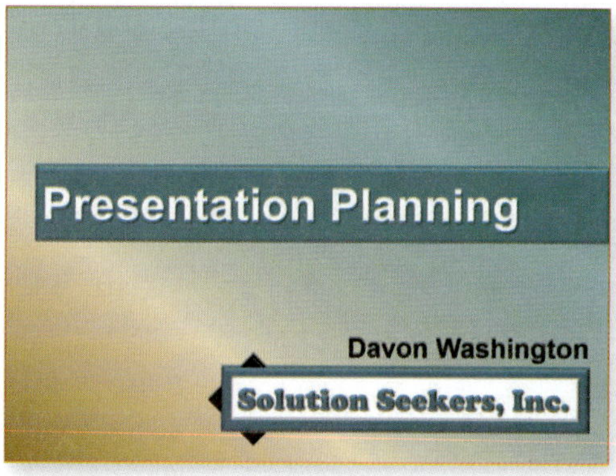

3-30 Title slide with new design

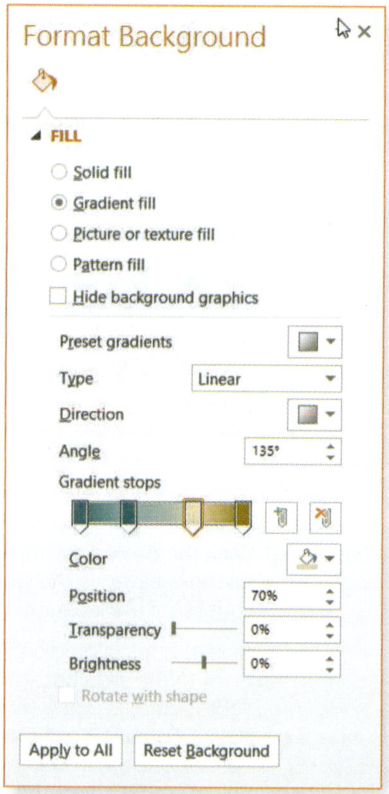

3-29 Gradient stops adjusted

5. On slide 14, create a *Picture fill* background.
   a. On the *Format Background* pane, select **Picture or texture fill** and click the **Online** button to open the *Insert Pictures* dialog box.
   b. In the *Office.com Clip Art* search box, type audience and click **Search**.
   c. Select the picture "Instructor speaking to a group of students" (Figure 3-31) and click **Insert**.

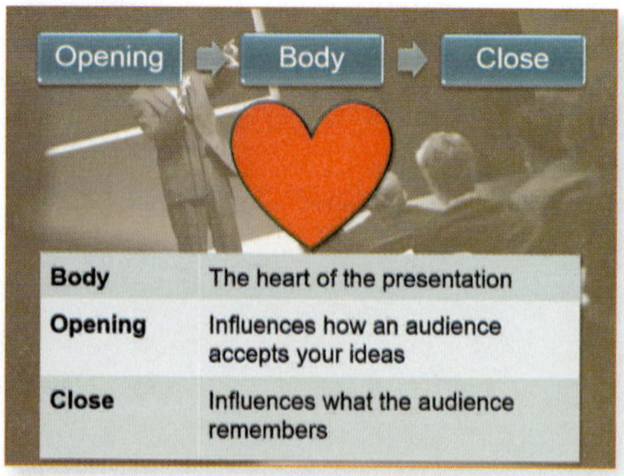

3-31 Background picture fill

d. Click the **Picture** button at the top of the *Format Background* pane and then select **Picture Color**.
e. Click the **Recolor** list arrow, and choose **Brown**, **Accent color 3 Light**.
f. Close the *Format Background* pane.

6. On slide 4, select the text box "Possible body sequence" and change the *Shape Fill* color to **Tan**, **Background 2**, **Darker 50%** and the *Shape Outline* color to **Dark Teal**, **Accent 1** (Figure 3-32).
7. On slide 13, change the *Text fill* color for the text at the top of the slide to **Brown**, **Text 2**, **Lighter 50%**.

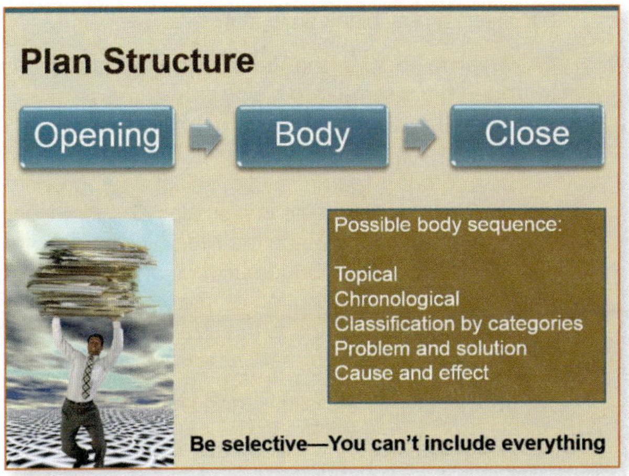

3-32 *SmartArt* resized and text box colors changed

8. Apply a transition.
   a. Click the **Transitions** tab and apply the **Wipe** transition.
   b. Click the **Effect Options** button and select **From Left**.
   c. Click **Apply to All** [*Timing* group].
9. Apply animation.
   a. Click the **Animations** tab and repeat steps b–g for each object in the following table.
   b. Select the **text or object** to be animated.
   c. Click the **More** button on the *Animation* gallery or click the **Add Animation** button [*Advanced Animation* group] if the gallery is not open.
   d. Click an **effect** to apply it.
   e. Click the **Effect Options** button and select the listed **Direction** and **Sequence** or **Amount**.
   f. Adjust settings for *Start*, *Duration*, and *Delay*.
   g. Click the **Preview** button or **Slide Show** button to test the animation.

Slide	Object	Animation Effect	Effect Options	Start	Duration	Delay
4	Possible body sequence text box	*Fade* (Entrance)	*As One Object*	*On Click*	*02.00*	None
5	First impression text	*Wave* (Emphasis)	*By Paragraph*	*After Previous*	*00.50*	None
7	Quoted text	*Bounce* (Entrance)	*As One Object*	*After Previous*	*02.00*	*01:00*
8	Road picture	*Grow & Turn* (Entrance)	None	*With Previous*	*02.00*	*01:00*
13	Prepare text	*Float In* (Entrance)	*Float Up*	*After Previous*	*01.00*	None
13	Slide show text	*Float In* (Entrance)	*Float Up, By Paragraph*	*After Previous*	*01.00*	*01:00*
14	Heart	*Spin* (Emphasis)	*Clockwise, Two Spins*	*With Previous*	*02.00*	None

10. Insert a new blank slide after slide 14.
11. On slide 15, click the **Video** button list arrow [*Insert* tab, *Media* group] and select **Online Video** to open the *Insert Video* dialog box.
    a. In the *Bing Video Search* box (or the *YouTube Search* box if it is available), type the search words presentation skills and click **Search**.
    b. From the search results, select an appropriate video from *YouTube* and click **Insert**.
    c. The video appears in a small size. Increase the size so the width is approximately **5"** wide.
    d. Center the video on the slide.
    e. Click the **Play** button [*Video Tools Playback* tab, *Preview* group] to activate the video.
    f. Click the **Play** button on the video to test it.
    g. If necessary, reduce the size of the video for a clear image.
    h. Add source information below the video.
12. Test all of your transitions and animations in your presentation.
13. Save and close the presentation.

SLO 3.4

Using Rehearsal Techniques

Everyone, no matter how experienced, can benefit from rehearsing a presentation. Practicing your delivery ensures that each slide's information supports what you are saying. Practice builds confidence, too.

Speaker Notes

Speaker notes help you remember what you need to say in your presentation, but they should never include text that would tempt you to read to your audience. Notes should be your personal reminders, such as items to emphasize or terminology to define. Notes should not be a script for everything you are going to say. For example, you could include statistics you want to mention, a quote you want to say but not show on a slide, a list of upcoming events, or additional resources for your audience. Even if you don't use the speaker notes you prepare, having them available while you present can be comforting and help to reduce nervousness.

As you think about what to include in your notes, plan for smooth and logical transitions between the various topics of your presentation. You can compose your notes using the *Notes* pane in *Normal* view or you can change to *Notes Page* view.

HOW TO: Use the Notes Pane in Normal View

1. In *Normal* view, the *Notes* pane is below the slide.
2. If the *Notes* pane is not showing, click the **Notes** button [*View* tab, *Show* group].
3. You can expand the *Notes* pane by dragging the border up (Figure 3-33).
4. If you drag the border too low and the *Notes* pane disappears, click the **Notes** button or the **Normal** button to restore it.

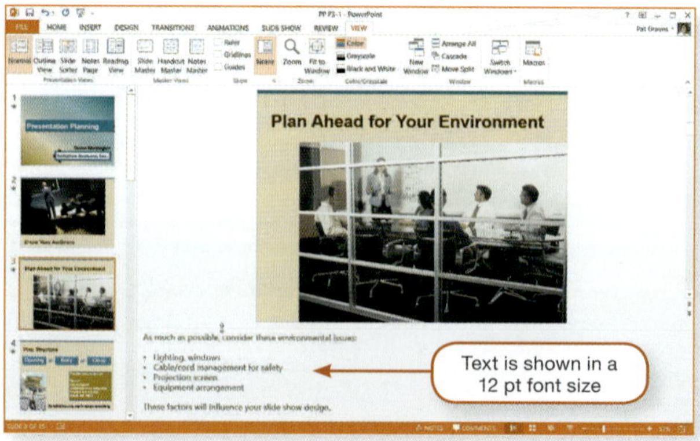

3-33 Increased *Notes* pane size

The *Notes Page* view provides much more space to type text than you have when using the *Notes* pane in *Normal* view.

HOW TO: Use Notes Page View

1. Click the **Notes Page** button [*View* tab, *Presentation Views* group] to show a slide as it will print.
2. Type your text in the text box below the slide to add notes (Figure 3-34).

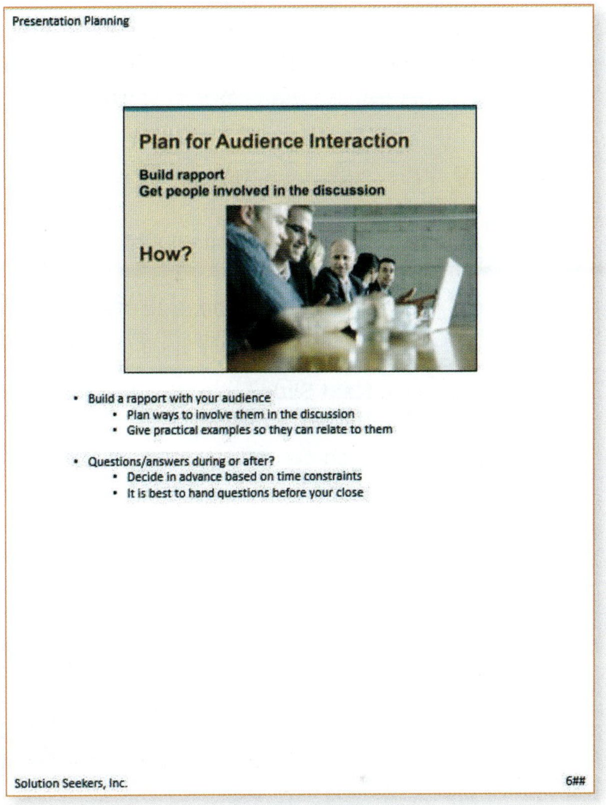

3-34 ***Notes Page*** **view with slide and text**

You may want to increase the font size before you print the pages because large text is easier for you to see on a lectern or podium while you are speaking. You will need your notes to be visible even if overhead lighting is dimmed so slide colors display better on the projection screen.

> **ANOTHER WAY**
>
> Some people find that printed handouts with a few handwritten reminders work well for speaker notes.

HOW TO: Print Notes Pages

1. Click the **File** tab and click **Print**.
2. For *Print Layout*, choose **Notes Pages** and check **Scale to Fit Paper** to make the slide images larger (Figure 3-35).
3. Omit the **Frame Slide** option for *Notes Pages*. A single-line border around the entire page is unnecessary.
4. Click the **Print** button.

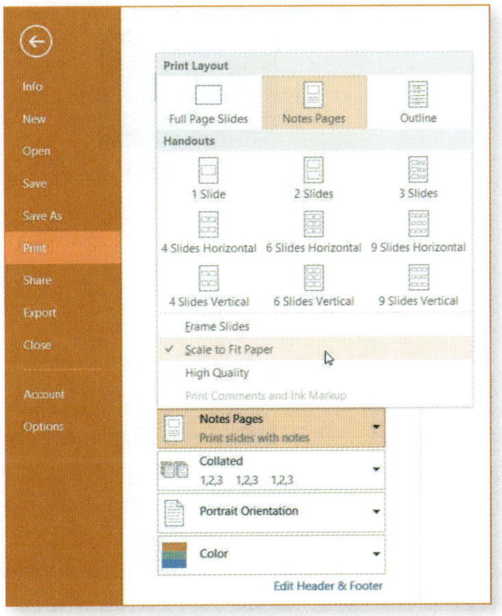

3-35 Print settings for *Notes Pages*

Rehearse Timings

PowerPoint's ***Rehearse Timings*** feature makes it easy to judge the pace of your presentation. When you use this feature to rehearse, the time you spend on each slide is recorded as you move through the presentation. The timings that you save from rehearsing appear below each slide in *Slide Sorter* view. This view enables you to see the "big picture" aspect of your presentation. You can compare the time spent on each slide and make decisions to spend less time on some slides and more time on other slides where the content takes longer to explain. You can save the timings to automate the presentation and make it self-running. If you are presenting to an audience, remove the timings so you can control when the slides advance.

HOW TO: Rehearse Timings

1. Click the **Rehearse Timings** button [*Slide Show* tab, *Set Up* group] and your slide show will start.
   - A *Recording* dialog box appears in the upper left corner (Figure 3-36). It shows the time each slide is displayed and the total elapsed time.
   - Click the **Next Slide** button (or press the **spacebar**) to advance.
   - Click the **Pause** or **Repeat** buttons as needed.
2. When you reach the end of your presentation, a message will ask if you want to save your timings.
3. Click **Yes** and the timings, in seconds, will display below each slide in *Slide Sorter* view (Figure 3-37). (The seconds shown in this example are brief because they were recorded when testing the presentation. The times would be much longer in an actual presentation.)

3-36 Current slide time and total elapsed time

3-37 Slide timings appear below each slide thumbnail

In rehearsal, go through your presentation and practice what you will say while each slide is displayed. Use printed notes pages while you are practicing. If possible, stand to replicate more closely the experience you will have when speaking to your audience. Sometimes knowing how and where to stand in relation to the keyboard and monitor you are using takes a little practice. Your body posture is important. Good posture makes you appear confident and it positively affects how your voice projects. If possible, rehearse with the equipment you will use to deliver the presentation.

Set Timings Manually

You can enter all timings manually, but it is quicker to rehearse your presentation, save the timings, and adjust the time as needed for individual slides.

HOW TO: Modify Timings

1. Click the **Transitions** tab and be sure the **After** option is selected [*Transitions* tab, *Timing* group] and second numbers are showing (Figure 3-38).
2. For each slide, change the number of seconds as needed to increase or decrease the amount of time the slide is displayed.
3. If you want the slides to advance automatically, deselect the **On Mouse Click** option.
4. To remove the timings, click the **Record Slide Show** button list arrow [*Slide Show* tab, *Set Up* group], select **Clear**, and then select **Clear Timing on Current Slide** or **Clear Timings on All Slides** (Figure 3-39).

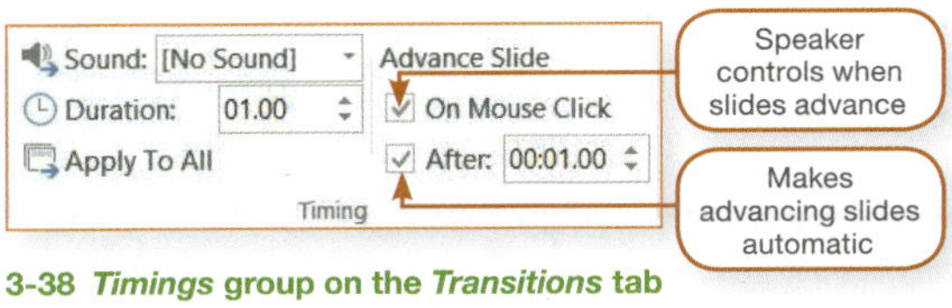

3-38 *Timings* group on the *Transitions* tab

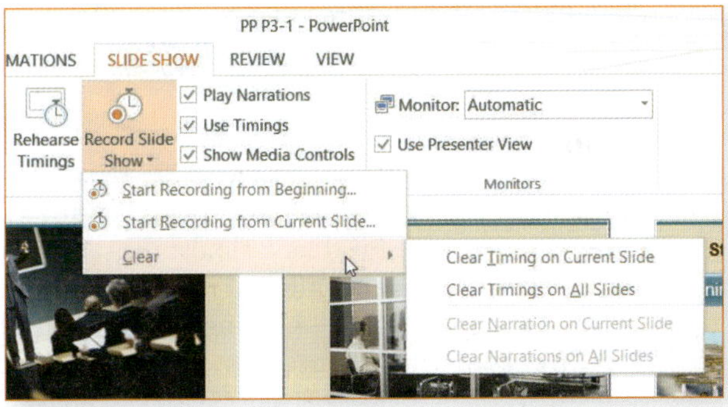

3-39 *Clear Timings* options

Prepare for Mishaps

Be sure you have backup copies of your presentation in case you experience equipment failure and you need to switch to a different computer. In a worst-case situation, where both your computer and projector have malfunctioned, you can present using your handouts to support what you say. All experienced presenters encounter such problems at some time during their careers.

SLO 3.5

Controlling Display Options

As you learned in Chapter 1, themes and templates that you obtain online are available in different sizes called ***Standard*** and ***Widescreen***. The default sizing for PowerPoint 2013 is *Widescreen* but for previous versions of PowerPoint it was *Standard*. Therefore, you may encounter files that require updating to fit your current screen size, or you may need to adjust the size of your presentation to fit an older projection screen in a room where you will give your presentation.

Adjust Slide Size

Today widescreen computers (like television screens) use a 16:9 or 16:10 aspect ratio (the ratio of width to height). A slide show designed in the 16:9 aspect ratio takes advantage of this wide horizontal space because it fills the screen. A slide show designed in the 4:3 aspect ratio (more square) and displayed on a widescreen will be positioned in the center of the screen with black areas on both sides. Both of these slide sizes are available on the *Design* tab in the *Customize* group and you can change from one to the other by clicking the **Slide Size** button and choosing **Standard (4:3)** or **Widescreen (16:9)**. Two other sizes are available on the *Slide Size* dialog box and you can create a custom size if necessary. These sizes are listed in the following table and illustrated as blue and green thumbnails in Figure 3-40:

Slide Sizes

Aspect Ratios	Width in Inches	Height in Inches
Standard 4:3	10	7.5
16:9	10	5.625
16:10	10	6.25
Widescreen 16:9	13.333	7.5

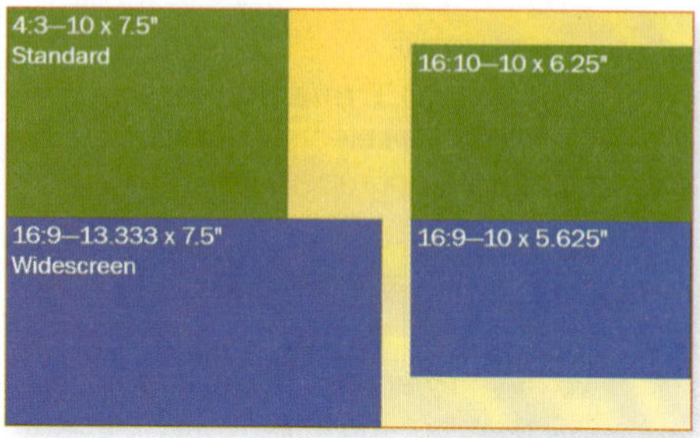

3-40 Screen sizes

The two wide sizes available in the *Slide Size* dialog box look smaller in Figure 3-40 because their width is 10", the same as the Standard 4:3 width. On your computer screen they will look almost the same as the *Widescreen* size, but ruler measurements and object sizes will be different because of the difference in width and height.

Changing between slide show sizes is a simple process, but necessary adjustments after the change can be time consuming. You need to consider how the change affects the text and graphics on your slide. Both *Standard* and *Widescreen* sizes have the same vertical measurement, so the width is what changes and adjustments are usually needed to make slide objects fit appropriately.

If you change from 4:3 to one of the other sizes (16:9 or 16:10), the vertical size is reduced, which compresses the slide vertically. Pictures or text in placeholders may not fit appropriately.

Be aware of these height and width differences when changing slide sizes. If you think you may need to change back to your original size, save the original presentation as a separate file before you begin making changes for the new size. By doing this, you can avoid all the resizing changes that would be necessary to return to the original size.

HOW TO: Change the Aspect Ratio

1. Click the **Design** tab.
2. Click the **Slide Size** button [*Customize* group]; then click either **Standard (4:3)** or **Widescreen (16:9)**.
3. Click **Custom Slide Size** to open the *Slide Size* dialog box. Sizes for printing and four sizes for on-screen viewing are available. You can choose from the following:
   - ***On-screen Show (4:3):*** 10×7.5" (Standard)
   - ***On-screen Show (16:9):*** 10×5.625"
   - ***On-screen Show (16:10):*** 10×6.25"
   - ***Widescreen (16:9):*** 13.333×7.5"
4. Click **OK** (Figure 3-41).

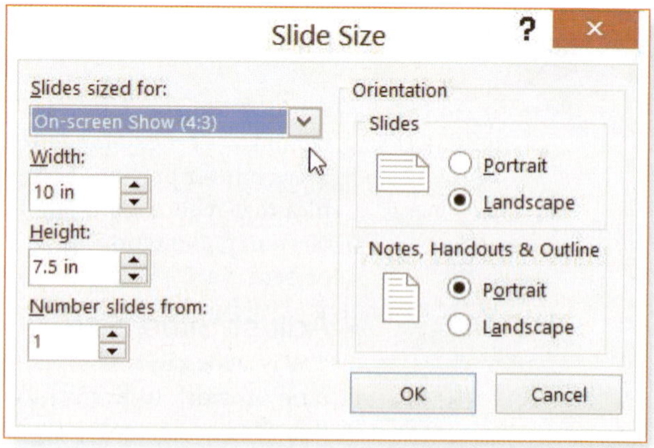

3-41 ***Slide Size*** **dialog box**

Presenter View

Presenter View allows you to display your presentation on the screens of two monitors or a monitor and a projector. PowerPoint can automatically detect when two monitors are connected and will recognize one monitor as your main monitor for *Presenter View* and extend the display to the second monitor for your full-screen slide show. Using *Presenter View* is helpful because while you are speaking you can:

- View the current slide and see the next slide in your presentation.
- Click thumbnails to display slides out of sequence.
- Have speaker notes available on the monitor for easy reading instead of needing printed notes.
- Make the screen that's visible to your audience black yet still have speaker notes available to you.
- Magnify sections of a slide.
- Use convenient navigation and pen tools.

Your monitor shows your view of the presentation and includes the displayed slide, the navigation tools, the next slide, and an area for notes. When you are using a second monitor (or projector), only the slide is displayed on that monitor for your audience. You can click the **Display Settings** button to swap between the monitors used for *Presenter View* and your full-size slide show.

If you do not have two monitors connected to your computer, you can still use *Presenter View* by pressing **Alt+F5**.

HOW TO: Use Presenter View

1. Click the **Slide Show** tab.
2. Select **Use Presenter View** [*Monitors* group] (Figure 3-42).
   - If you are using two monitors, confirm that the monitor you want your audience to see the slide show on appears in the *Show Presentation On* list box. Click the **From Beginning** button to start your slide show.
   - If you are using one monitor, press **Alt+F5**.

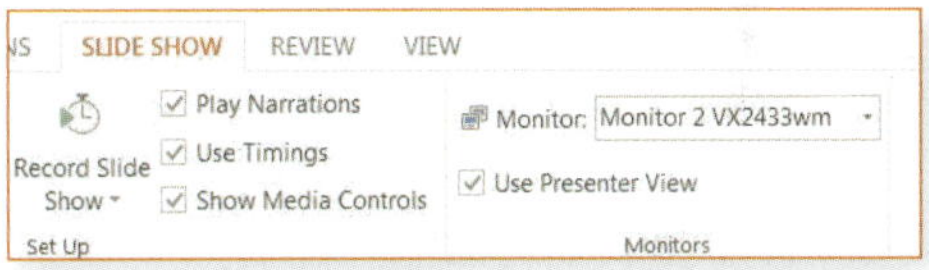

3-42 ***Use Presenter View* option on the *Slide Show* tab**

3. Review your slide show using *Presenter View* (Figure 3-43).
   - Click the **Advance to the next slide** button in the navigation area to move through your slides.
   - Click the **See all slides** button to see slide thumbnails. Click a thumbnail to display a different slide out of sequence.
   - Click the **Zoom into the slide** button, then drag the selection area over an object or text you want to magnify, and then click. That portion of the screen is displayed for your audience. Click the same button again (now **Zoom out**) to return to normal screen size.
   - Notice the slide show time displayed above the slide.
   - Press **Esc** to exit the slide show.

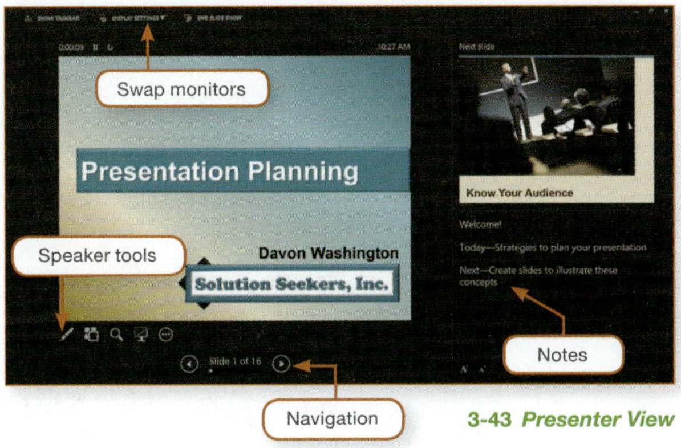

3-43 ***Presenter View***

PAUSE & PRACTICE: POWERPOINT 3-2

For this project, you add speaker notes, print notes pages, and rehearse a presentation. You will save the presentation in its original standard size and then resave it in the widescreen size. For the widescreen version, you will adjust object positioning as needed and then use *Presenter View* to display your slide show.

File Needed: ***[your initials] PP P3-1.pptx***
Completed Project File Name: ***[your initials] PP P3-2a.pptx*** and ***[your initials] PP P3-2b pptx***.

1. Open the presentation ***[your initials] PP P3-1***.
2. Save the presentation as ***[your initials] PP P3-2a***.
3. Create a visual transition between topics. Insert a new slide with the *Section Header* layout after slides 3, 9, and 15. On each of these new slides, delete the subtitle placeholder and type the title text as follows:
   a. Slide 4 title: Presentation Structure (Figure 3-44).
   b. Slide 10 title: Presentation Practice.
   c. Slide 16 title: Summary.

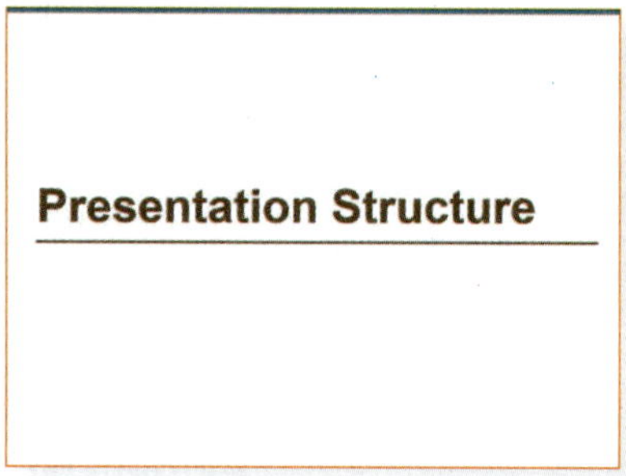

3-44 *Section Header* slide layout

4. Prepare speaker notes for two slides that do not have notes.
   a. On slide 11, click the **Notes Page** button [*View* tab, *Presentation Views* group].
   b. Add the following text with blank space for easy reading (Figure 3-45):
      - Print slide with discussion points below
        - Make notes brief (like cue cards)
        - Keep text large so it is easy to read
      - Can be a "safety net" (builds confidence)
      - Use to rehearse a presentation
      - Do not read during a presentation
   c. On slide 12, add the following text:
      - Experience is the best teacher
      - Identify strengths and develop them
      - Identify weaknesses and work to overcome them
      - Reduce tendency to be nervous
   d. Click the **Normal** button [*View* tab, *Presentation Views* group].

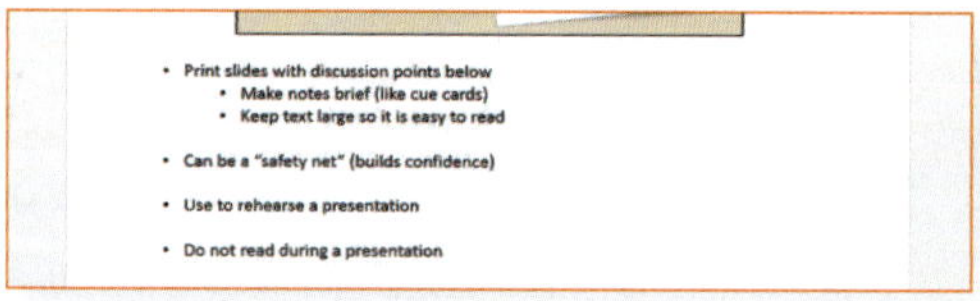

3-45 *Notes Page* view with text

5. Print notes pages for slides 11 and 12.
   a. Click the **File** tab and click **Print**.
   b. Select the appropriate printer and make sure that you are printing just one copy.
   c. For *Slides*, type 11–12 to print a Custom Range.
   d. For *Print Layout*, choose **Notes Pages** and select **Scale to Fit Paper** (Figure 3-46).
   e. Click the **Print** button.

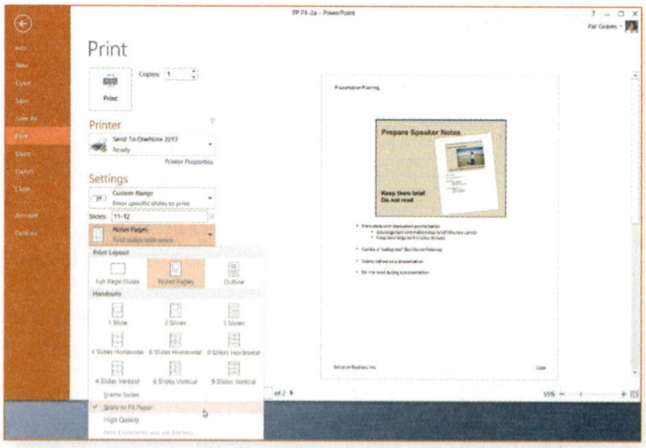

3-46 Print settings for *Notes Pages*

6. Rehearse your presentation and save timings.
   a. Click the **Slide Show** tab.
   b. Click the **Rehearse Timings** button [*Set Up* group].
   c. Using the *Recording* dialog box, click the **Next Slide** button to advance each slide after approximately 3–5 seconds (for the purpose of practicing this feature).
   d. At the end of your presentation, click **Yes** to save your timings.
   e. Click the **Slide Sorter** button [*Status bar*] to see the timings displayed below each slide.
7. Beginning with slide 1, change how slides advance and modify presentation timings.
   a. Click the **Transitions** tab.
   b. Deselect **On Mouse Click** [*Transitions* tab, *Timing* group].
   c. Change the *After* timing to **3** seconds (shown as 00:03:00).
   d. Click the **Apply To All** button.
   e. Change the *After* timing on the *Section Header* slides (slides 4, 10, and 16) to **1** second (shown as 00:01) (Figure 3-47).

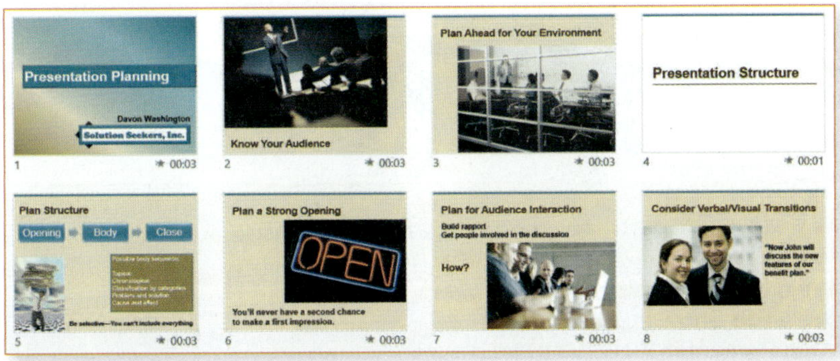

3-47 Rehearsal timings modified

8. Save the presentation to preserve the standard size (4:3 aspect ratio, 10×7.5") on the ***[your initials] PP P3-2a*** file.
9. Save the presentation again as ***[your initials] PP P3-2b*** to create a separate file for a widescreen size (16:9 aspect ratio, 13.333×7.5").
10. Click the **Slide Size** button [*Design* tab, *Customize* group] and select **Widescreen (16:9)**.
11. Slide objects are not aligned as they were in the standard size (Figure 3-48). Slide title text remains in the same position, but space has been added to both sides of the slide to stretch slides from 10" wide to 13.333" wide.

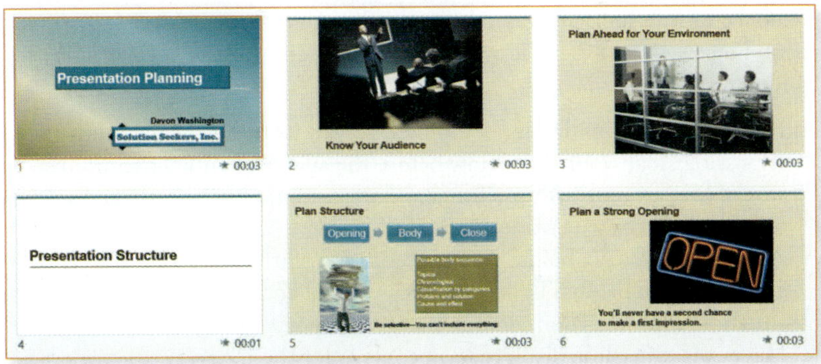

3-48 Slide object alignment changed with widescreen size

12. On some slides, the new object position is acceptable. Double-click Slide 1 to return to *Normal* view. Change the following slides as described (Figure 3-49):
    a. ***Slide 1:*** Increase the size of the title placeholder by dragging the right sizing handle to the edge of the slide (*Width* **11.2"**). Move the logo and name to the right.
    b. ***Slide 2:*** Left align the picture. Move the text to the left about **.5"** from the edge of the slide.
    c. ***Slide 3:*** Right-align the picture.
    d. ***Slide 9:*** Right-align the picture and the text below it. Move the slide title down.
    e. ***Slide 12:*** Right-align the picture. Resize the title placeholder so it fits the text and move the title down so it is closer to the picture.

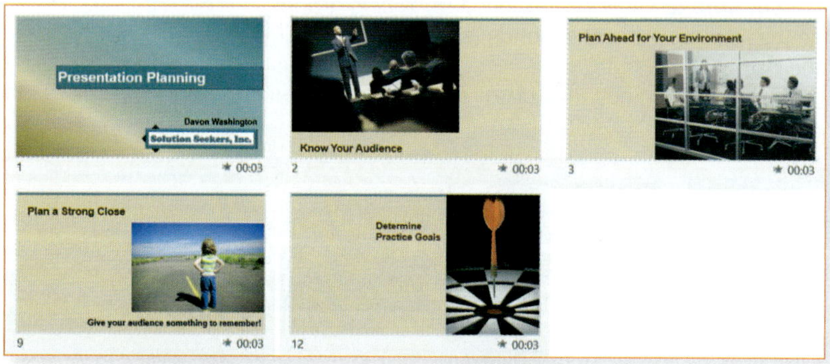

3-49 Alignment adjusted on selected slides

13. Review your presentation using *Presenter View*.
    a. Click the **Slide Show** tab.
    b. Click **Use Presenter View** [*Monitors* group].
    c. Review your slides.
        - If you have two monitors, click the **From Beginning** button [*Start Slide Show* group].
        - If you have one monitor, press **Alt+F5**.
14. Save and close the presentation.

SLO 3.6

Presenting Using Projection Equipment

When facing the front of a presentation room, the ideal location for a speaker is to the left of the projection screen. People are conditioned to read from left to right, so it is natural for the audience to first look at you and then at the projection screen. Many situations are less than ideal, however, so be flexible when you cannot control the speaker area. Keep the following guidelines in mind:

- Become familiar with your equipment so you won't feel awkward using it.
- If possible, load your slide show before the audience enters the room so you are not seen scrambling around with preliminary preparations. Arrive early and test your presentation to be sure all content works correctly.
- Allow time to relax before your presentation starts. Almost everyone feels nervous before a presentation begins. This reaction is normal and just shows you are respectful of the situation. Harness your nervous energy in a positive way.
- Have your title slide displayed as people enter the room.
- If possible, greet people to make them feel welcome. Let people know that you are glad to have the opportunity to share with them.

Position Equipment

3-50 Poor electrical connections

Using a computer while you speak creates some challenges. You may have a tablet computer to control your slide show, but it must work with your projector. If you are using a desktop or notebook computer, you must see the computer screen when facing the audience and be able to access the computer to advance slides. In some presentation rooms, you may need to place your computer on a table. A podium (or lectern) may be available to hold your computer and/or printed notes pages. Be careful, however, that the podium does not create a barrier between you and the audience. Move away from it when you can.

Even if your computer has a wireless Internet connection and is running on battery power, you may need to manage power cords for other equipment. Connections may not be convenient. (Figure 3-50). Be sure to keep cables and cords away from the area where you and audience members will be walking or tape cords to the floor.

Navigate in a Slide Show

You have advanced through a slide show by pressing the spacebar or clicking on a slide. You can use other methods to advance, to go to specific slides, or to end a slide show.

During a slide show, navigation buttons are on the lower left of each slide. They are barely noticeable unless you point to that area. Use buttons (Figure 3-51) to move between slides or to bring up a shortcut menu of presentation options.

3-51 Slide show navigation buttons

Control Slide Display

The audience needs to focus on you, the speaker. Slides support your message, but you may not want a slide displayed all the time. Also, going from a blank screen to your next slide can seem more dramatic.

Blank Slides

If you know in advance that you need to discuss something unrelated to your slides, then plan ahead and place one or more slides with a black background in specific places in your slide show.

During a presentation, you can blank the screen by pressing **B** to display an empty black screen or **W** to display an empty white screen. Be careful about using the white option, however, because an all-white screen can create glare that will be unpleasant for your audience.

Hide and Reveal Slides

Hiding a slide is helpful when you have information that is not essential to your presentation but you want to have that slide available if you need it depending on time and audience interest. For example, you could hide slides containing information such as:

- References
- Additional pictures
- Additional details about a topic
- Optional charts, diagrams, or tables

To hide the current slide, click the **Hide Slide** button [*Slide Show* tab, *Set Up* group] (Figure 3-52). You can hide multiple slides by selecting thumbnails on the *Slides* pane or in *Slide Sorter* view. In *Normal* and *Slide Show* views, the slide thumbnail for a hidden slide appears grayed out with a diagonal line through the slide number.

During a slide show, you can display a hidden slide by typing the slide number and pressing **Enter**.

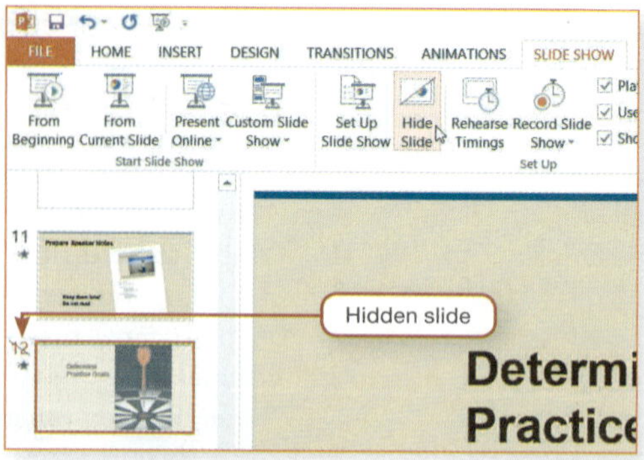

3-52 ***Hide Slide*** **button and hidden slide 12**

> **MORE INFO**
>
> You can print hidden slides. Click the **File** tab and then select **Print.** Click the **Print All Slides** option and select **Print Hidden Slides.**

Use Keyboard Shortcuts

Keyboard shortcuts are convenient if you have easy access to your keyboard while speaking.

Slide Show Navigation Shortcuts

Press	Action
N, spacebar, right arrow, down arrow, **Enter**, or **Page Down**	Advance to the next slide.
P, **Backspace**, left arrow, up arrow, or **Page Up**	Go to the previous slide.
Slide number, then **Enter**	Go to a particular slide.
Ctrl+S	Open *All slides* dialog box, select slide, and click **Go To**.
B or period	Blanks the screen to black.
W or comma	Blanks the screen to white.
S	Stop or restart an automatic show.
plus sign	Zoom in.
minus sign	Zoom out.
H or slide number, **Enter**	Go to a hidden slide.

The presentation shortcut menu is available during a slide show by right-clicking when you point anywhere on a slide.

Remote Control and Laser Pointer

A ***remote control*** enables you to move away from your computer as you are presenting. If you do this, you can interact with your audience more naturally because you don't need to stay close to your computer to control how slides advance. Remote control devices come in many styles from small clickers to clickers that resemble pens with USB storage. When presenting, be sure you have extra batteries available for the remote control.

Some remote controls have a built-in ***laser pointer***, or you can purchase a separate pointing device. A laser pointer shows a small dot (usually red) on the slide where you point. PowerPoint's laser pointer feature resembles this dot. To use this feature, press **Ctrl** while you are pointing on the screen and your pointer changes to a dot that can be red, green, or blue.

HOW TO: Change Laser Pointer Color

1. Click the **Set Up Slide Show** button [*Slide Show* tab, *Set Up* group] to open the *Set Up Show* dialog box (Figure 3-53).

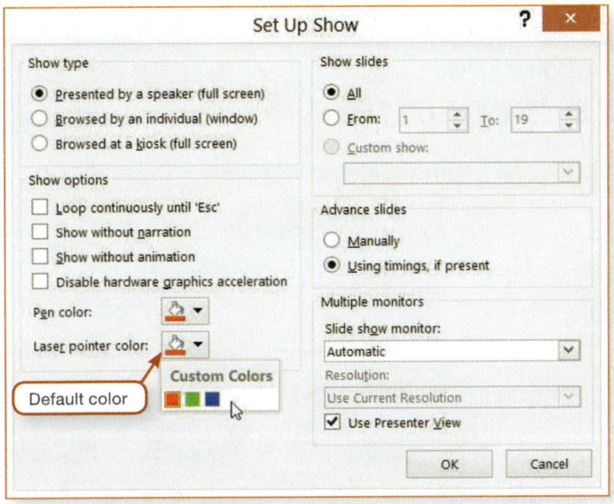

3-53 Changing laser pointer color

2. Click the **Laser pointer color** list box arrow and select **green or blue**.
3. Click **OK**.

A dot on the screen directs audience attention to a particular location. Be sure you show the dot long enough for your audience to find it and keep the dot steady. Do not bounce it around on the screen with random movements because this distracts viewers. A very small pointer movement on your computer screen makes a large movement on a projection screen.

SLO 3.7

Using Annotation Pens

During a presentation, you can call attention to information by writing or drawing on slides. These markings are called ***ink annotations***. While controlling the pointer to write with a hand-held mouse is a little awkward, you can record audience feedback and make simple drawings on slides. When you reach the end of your presentation, you can save ink annotations. All markings, even if you draw a rectangle, are saved as lines and not as shapes.

Select Pen Style and Ink Color

To write or draw on a slide, use the ***Pen***. To add a color overlay on text, use the ***Highlighter*** just as you would mark text to highlight information on paper. When you change ***Ink Color***, be sure the color you select contrasts with the slide background so it is easy to see.

HOW TO: Use the Pen and Highlighter

1. Start a slide show and go to the slide you want to annotate.
2. Select the *Pen* or *Highlighter* using one of the following methods:
   - Click the **Pen** button in the navigation area (Figure 3-54) to open the shortcut menu. Select an option as desired.

Or

   - Right-click anywhere on the slide to open the shortcut menu and select **Pointer Options**. Select an option as desired (Figure 3-55).
3. Begin writing or drawing on one or more slides.
4. To remove markings, select the **Eraser** options from the shortcut menu. Click markings to delete each continuous pen stroke (Figure 3-56).
5. To change annotation color, select the **Ink Color** option from the shortcut menu and then select a different color.
6. At the end of a presentation, click **Keep** to save ink annotations. The markings are saved as lines that you can edit.

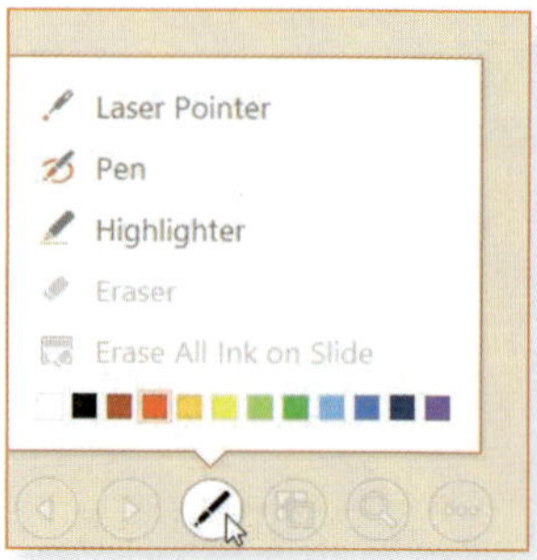

3-54 Navigation area

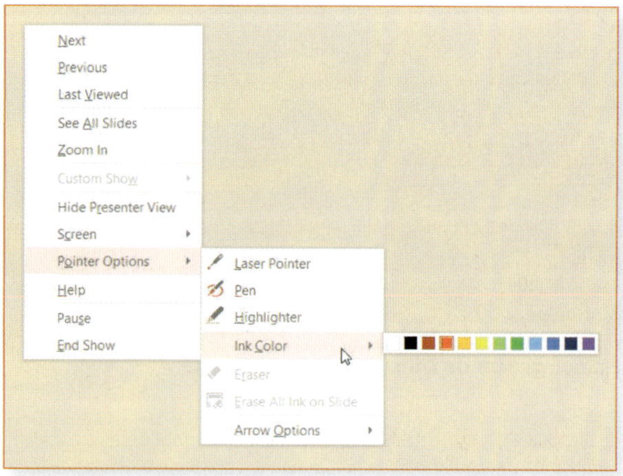

3-55 Shortcut menu

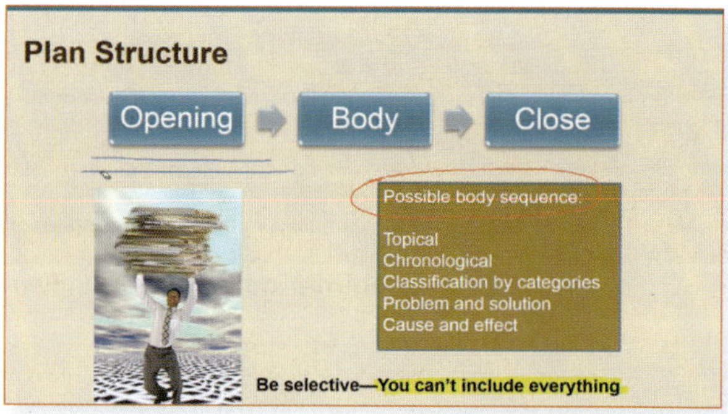

3-56 Ink annotations and the *Eraser* tool

Pen tools are available in *Presenter View,* also. You can control many of these options during a slide show using keyboard shortcuts summarized in the following table:

Ink Markup Shortcuts

Press	Action
Ctrl+P	Changes the pointer to a pen.
Ctrl+A	Changes the pointer to an arrow.
Ctrl+E	Changes the pointer to an eraser.
Ctrl+M	Shows or hides ink markup.
E	Erases markings on the screen.

PAUSE & PRACTICE: POWERPOINT 3-3

For this project, you use PowerPoint features to present more effectively. You hide and reveal slides, blank slides, practice with the laser pointer, change pen colors, use the pen and highlighter, and save annotations.

File Needed: ***[your initials] PP P3-2b.pptx***
Completed Project File Name: ***[your initials] PP P3-3.pptx***

1. Open the presentation ***[your initials] PP P3-2b***.
2. Save the presentation as ***[your initials] PP P3-3***.
3. Click the **Transitions** tab and change the slide transitions.
   a. Select **On Mouse Click** and deselect **After** [*Timing* group].
   b. Click **Apply To All** [*Timing* group].
4. Select slide 4 and click the **Hide Slide** button [*Slide Show* tab, *Set Up* group].
   a. Start a slide show from slide 3 to confirm that you automatically advance directly from slide 3 to slide 5.
   b. On slide 6, type 4 and press **Enter** to show the hidden slide.
5. In *Slide Show* view, practice blanking slides.
   a. Press **B** to blank a slide to black. Press **B** to return to the slide.
   b. Press **W** to blank a slide to white. Press **W** to return to the slide.
   c. Press **Esc** to exit *Slide Show* view.
6. Change the laser pointer color.
   a. Click the **Set Up Slide Show** button [*Slide Show* tab, *Set Up Slide Show* group] to open the *Set Up Show* dialog box.
   b. Click the **Laser Pointer** list box arrow and select **blue**.
   c. Click **OK**.
   d. In *Slide Show* view, press **Ctrl** while you move your pointer to practice using the laser pointer.
7. Use the pen and highlighter.
   a. In *Slide Show* view, go to slide 7.
   b. Right-click to open the shortcut menu, select **Pointer Options**, and then select **Ink Color**. Select the standard color **Blue**.
   c. Use the **Pen** to draw a rectangle around the word "How" (Figure 3-57).
   d. Right-click to open the shortcut menu, select **Pointer Options**, and then select **Ink Color**. Select **Yellow**.
   e. Right-click to open the shortcut menu, select **Highlighter**, and then highlight the word "involved."
   f. Type 13 and press **Enter** to go to slide 13. Use the **Highlighter** to highlight the words "Get help" and "feedback."
   g. Type 17 and press **Enter** to go to slide 17. Use the **Highlighter** to highlight the words "heart," "how an audience," "accepts," "what the audience," and "remembers."
   h. Right-click to open the shortcut menu, select **Pointer Options**, and then select **Eraser**. Click to remove the highlights from the words "how an audience" and "what the audience."
   i. Advance to the end of the presentation and click **Keep** to save your annotations.
8. Save and close your presentation.

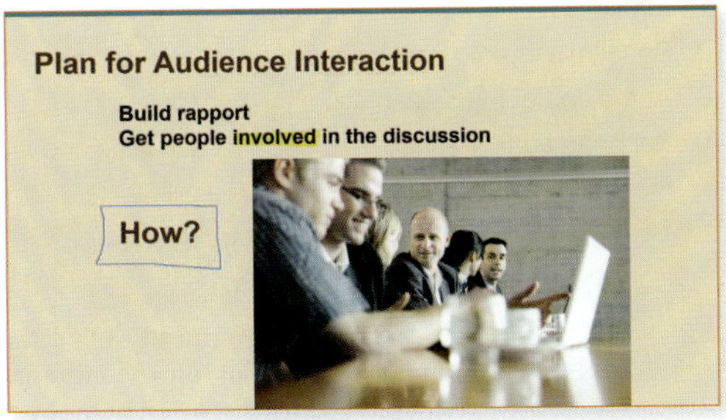

3-57 Pen color changed

SLO 3.8

Preparing a Self-Running Presentation

A self-running slide show, also referred to as a ***kiosk presentation***, can be set up to run continuously without someone being present to advance the slides of the presentation. This type of presentation works well for trade shows or open house events where people walk up to a computer screen and watch the slide show. For example, self-running presentations can be used for marketing products to customers or to educate patients in medical office waiting rooms. You can record narration to accompany the slides. You can also set up the slide show to ***loop*** so it will automatically repeat and cycle continuously from beginning to end.

Record a Slide Show with Narration

To record voice narration for your presentation, your computer must have a microphone and sound card. Like rehearsal, you can use this feature to practice what you will say during a presentation and evaluate your vocal qualities. You can also make a narrated slide show available as a complete presentation to distribute on CDs or DVDs or to post online for viewers.

Prepare carefully to decide what you will say as each slide is displayed. Use notes pages or other resources as references.

HOW TO: Record Narration

1. Click the **Slide Show** tab.
2. Click the **Record Slide Show** button list arrow [*Set Up* group] and then select **Start Recording from Beginning** or **Start Recording from Current Slide** to open the *Record Slide Show* dialog box.
3. Select **Slide and animation timings**.
4. Select **Narrations and laser pointer**. (This option is available only if your computer has a microphone.)
5. Click **Start Recording** (Figure 3-58).
6. A *Recording* box appears in the top left corner of the screen. You can advance, pause, or resume recording in the same way you do when you rehearse a presentation (see *Section 3.4: Using Rehearsal Techniques*).
7. Speak clearly into your microphone as each slide is displayed.
8. At the end of the presentation, the narration and slide timings will automatically be saved.
9. Separate audio files are recorded on each slide and an audio icon appears in the lower right. Review your slide show and listen to your narration.
10. Save your presentation.

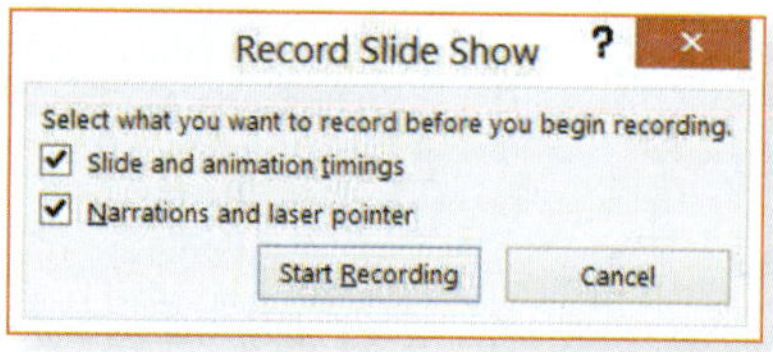

3-58 ***Record Slide Show* dialog box**

Press **Esc** if you need to end the slide show before reaching the last slide. You can clear timing or narration on the current slide or all slides. When you play back a narration, the recording is synchronized with the presentation.

HOW TO: Clear Timings or Narration

1. Click the **Slide Show** tab.
2. Click the **Record Slide Show** button list arrow [*Set Up* group] and then select **Clear**.
3. Select from these options:

Clear Timing on Current Slide | *Clear Timings on All Slides*

Clear Narration on Current Slide | *Clear Narrations on All Slides*

If you need to display the slide show without narration, click the **Set Up Show** button [*Slide Show* tab, *Set Up* group]. Select **Show without narration** and click **OK**.

Set Up a Kiosk Presentation with Looping

Depending on how you plan to use it, a kiosk presentation may need different design guidelines than a slide show that is shown by a presenter. While other presentations provide minimal text because the slides support the speaker's message, a kiosk presentation may contain more information because it is a stand-alone product. If your kiosk presentation is displayed in a public place with a lot of distractions, then splashy graphics can be used to grab attention. On the other hand, if your kiosk presentation is for educational purposes in a quiet setting such as a doctor's office, the slides might be designed more like pages in a book with smaller text and more detailed information.

HOW TO: Set Up a Kiosk Presentation

1. Click the **Slide Show** tab.
2. Click the **Set Up Slide Show** button [*Set Up* group] to open the *Set Up Show* dialog box (Figure 3-59).
3. Choose the following settings:
   - For *Show type,* select **Browsed at a kiosk (full screen)**.
   - For *Show options*, **Loop continuously until 'Esc'** is automatically selected and grayed out because you chose a kiosk.
   - For *Show slides*, select **All** or enter the first and last slide numbers you want to display.
   - For *Advance slides*, **Use timings**, **if present** is automatically selected for a kiosk.
   - If you are using more than one monitor, select the appropriate monitor for the slide show.
   - For *Resolution*, select **Use Current Resolution** or the highest resolution possible for your equipment.
   - For a kiosk presentation, **Use Presenter View** is not available.
4. Click **OK**.
5. Save the presentation with these changes.

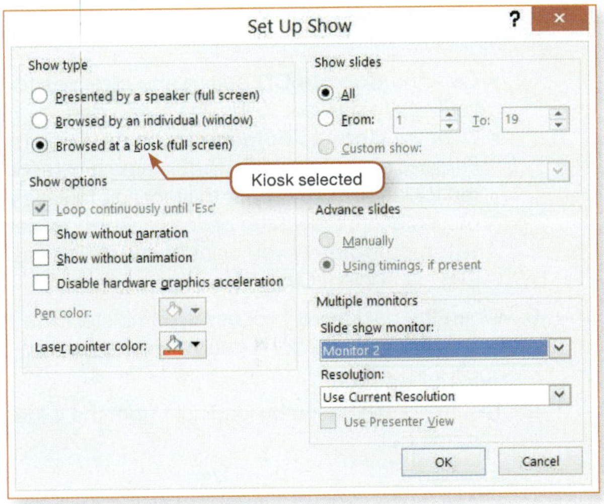

3-59 *Set Up Show* dialog box

SLO 3.9

Packaging a Presentation to a CD or Folder

The ***Package Presentation for CD*** feature allows you to easily transport one or more presentations for use on another computer. You can copy your presentation file and any linked files to a blank CD (CD-R, recordable or CD-RW, rewritable) or to a folder on your computer, network location, or removable drive.

HOW TO: Save a Presentation to a CD or Folder

1. Insert a CD in your CD/DVD drive if you are saving to that location.
2. Click the **File** tab and select **Export**.

3. Select **Package Presentation for CD**. Click the **Package for CD** button to open the *Package for CD* dialog box.
4. Type a name for the CD (Figure 3-60).
5. Click the **Options** button to open the *Options* dialog box (Figure 3-61) and choose from the following options:
   - ***Linked Files:*** Preserves links and copies any external files such as audio or video files.
   - ***Embedded TrueType fonts:*** Assures that the fonts used in your presentation are available on the playback computer.
   - ***Password:*** Enhances security for opening or modifying a presentation.
   - ***Inspect:*** Checks for inappropriate or private information.
6. Click **OK**.
7. To save the presentation use one of the following methods:
   - Click the **Copy to CD** button and click **Yes** to verify that you want to include linked files.
   - Click the **Copy to Folder** to open the *Copy to Folder* dialog box (Figure 3-62). Type a name for the folder and browse for the location to save the presentation. Select the option to **Open folder when complete** if you want to see all the files that are copied. Click **OK**.
8. When the packaging process is complete, click **No** to indicate that you don't need to make another copy. Click **Close**.
9. Test the presentation by loading it from the folder or from the CD.

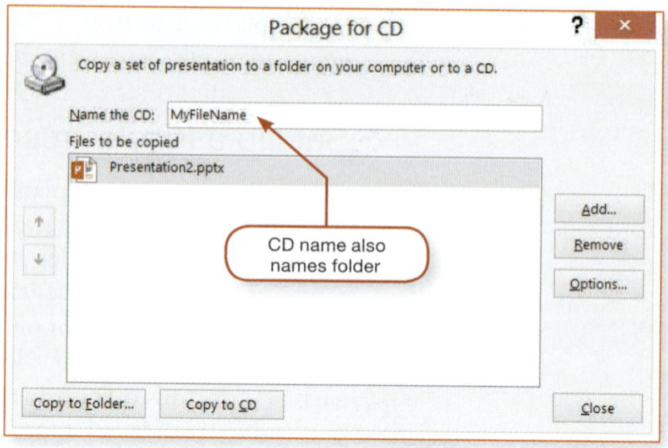

3-60 ***Package for CD*** **dialog box**

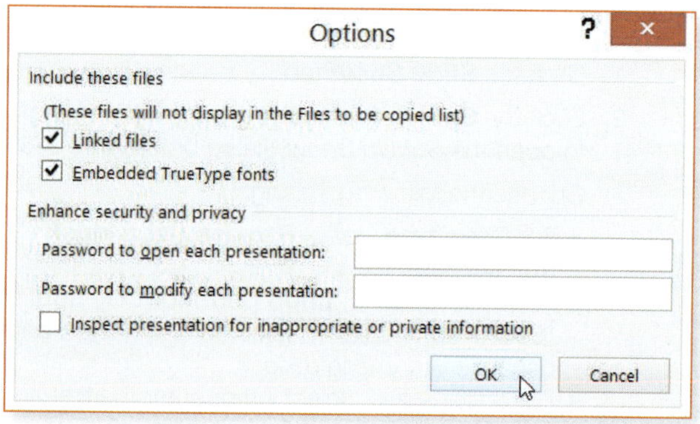

3-61 ***Options*** **dialog box**

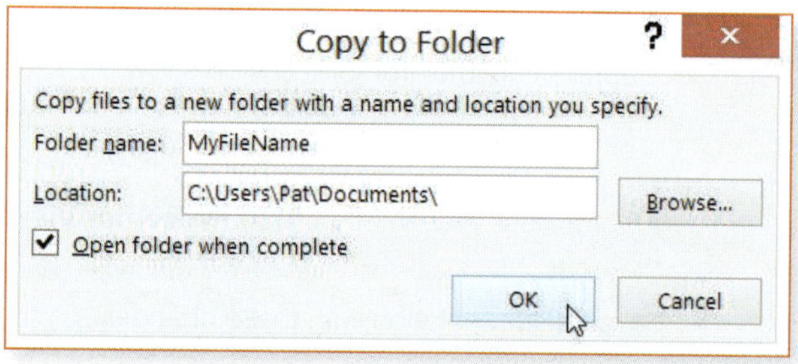

3-62 ***Copy to Folder*** **dialog box**

MORE INFO

If file size requirements exceed the storage capacity of a CD, you can convert your slide show to a video and then use DVD burning software to save the files to a DVD. PowerPoint does not support direct burning to DVDs.

PAUSE & PRACTICE: POWERPOINT 3-4

This project consists of two parts. You record a presentation with audio in Part A if you have a microphone connected to your computer. In Part B, you prepare a kiosk presentation, set it up to loop so it is self-running, and then use the *Package Presentation for CD* feature to save it to a folder.

File Needed: ***[your initials] PP P3-2b.pptx***
Completed Project File Name: ***[your initials] PP P3-4b.pptx***

Part A (Microphone Required)

1. Open the presentation ***[your initials] PP P3-2b***.
2. Save the presentation as ***[your initials] PP P3-4a*** and change to *Slide Sorter* view.
3. For the purpose of this project, you need only slides 1–5. Delete all other slides in the presentation.
4. Remove the timings.
   a. Click the **Record Slide Show** button list arrow [*Slide Show* tab, *Set Up* group] and select **Clear**.
   b. Select **Clear Timings on All Slides** (Figure 3-63).

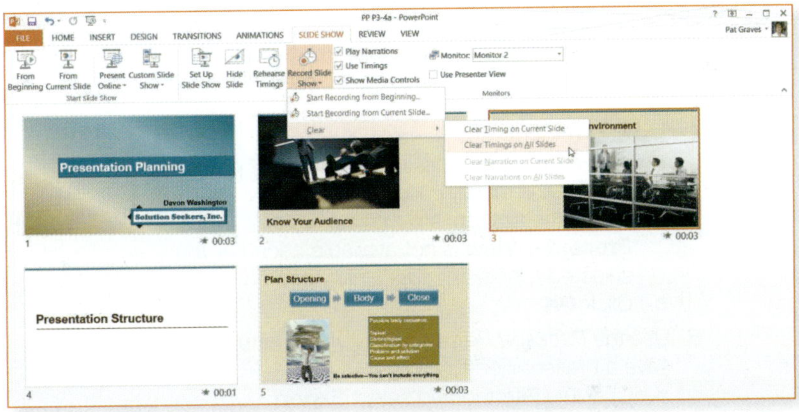

3-63 Clear timings on all slides

5. Click the **Notes Page** button and add notes to two slides.
   a. For slide 2, add four items after the first line of text:
      - What is their background?
      - What is their educational level?
      - How familiar are they with your topic?
      - Are they likely to be accepting of your ideas or resistant?
   b. For slide 3, add two items to the bulleted text:
      - Overall cleanliness and organization of the room
      - Temperature level for comfort
   c. Print the notes pages.
6. Using the notes pages as a reference, click the **Record Slide Show** button list arrow [*Slide Show* tab, *Set Up* group] and select **Start Recording from Beginning**.
   a. Select **Slide and animation timings** and **Narrations and laser pointer** (Figure 3-64).
   b. Click **Start Recording**.
   c. Speak clearly into your microphone as you go through the slide show.
   d. At the end of the presentation, click **Yes** to save your timings and narration.

3-64 *Record Slide Show* dialog box

7. Review the presentation and listen to the narration.
8. Save and close the presentation.

Part B

1. Open the presentation ***[your initials] PP P3-2b***.
2. Save the presentation as ***[your initials] PP P3-4b***.
3. For the purpose of this project, apply timing so slides change rapidly.
   a. Confirm that **On Mouse Click** [*Transitions* tab, *Timing* group] is not selected.
   b. Change the *After* seconds to **00:02:00**.
   c. Click **Apply to All** (Figure 3-65).

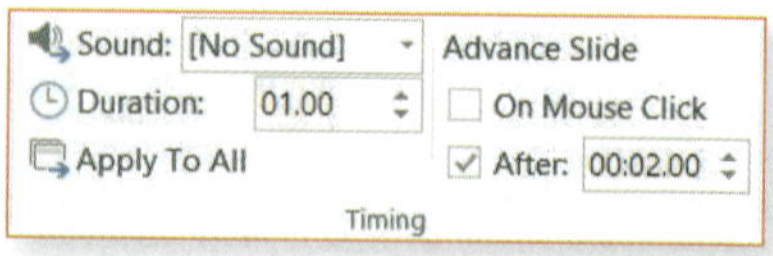

3-65 *Timing* group on the *Transitions* tab

4. Click the **Set Up Slide Show** button [*Slide Show* tab, *Set Up* group] to open the *Set Up Show* dialog box.
   a. Select the following settings (Figure 3-66):
      - For *Show type*, select **Browsed at a kiosk (full screen)**.
      - For *Show options*, **Loop continuously until 'Esc'** is automatically checked for a kiosk.
      - For *Show slides*, select **All**.
      - For *Advance slides*, **Use timings**, **if present** is automatically checked for a kiosk.
   b. Select the appropriate monitor. **Use Presenter View** is not available because you selected a kiosk.
   c. Click **OK**.

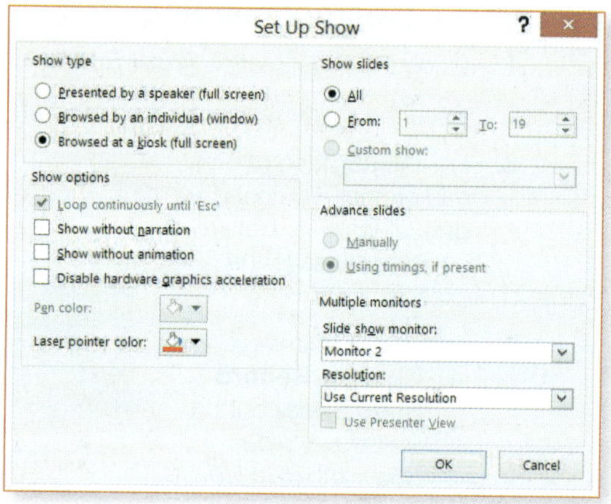

3-66 *Set Up Show* dialog box

5. Use the *Package Presentation for CD* feature to save a presentation to a folder.
   a. Click the **File** tab and select **Export**.
   b. Click **Package Presentation for CD** and click the **Package for CD** button to open the *Package for CD* dialog box.
   c. Type Planning for the name of the CD.
6. Click the **Options** button to open the *Options* dialog box and select the following:
   - Choose **Linked Files** to preserve links and copy any external files such as audio or video files.
   - Choose **Embedded TrueType fonts** to assure that the fonts you use in your presentation are available on the playback computer.
7. Click **OK** and the dialog box closes.
8. Click the **Copy to Folder** button to open the *Copy to Folder* dialog box. The name you typed for the CD automatically appears.
   a. Click **Browse** to open the *Choose Location* dialog box and find the place where you want to save the presentation. Click **Select** and the dialog box closes.
   b. Select the option to **Open folder when complete**.
   c. Click **OK** and the dialog box closes.
   d. If you receive a message about including linked files, click **Yes**.
9. A *File Explorer* window opens showing the files in the open *Planning* folder.
10. Close the *Package for CD* dialog box.
11. Close your original ***[your initials] PP P3-4b*** presentation.
12. Test the saved presentation by loading it from the *Planning* folder. Double-click the ***[your initials] PP P3-4b*** file name.
13. Close the presentation and folder.

Chapter Summary

3.1 Create custom theme colors and background styles (p. P3-139).

- Design themes create a unified appearance for your presentation.
- The Accent 1 theme color is the color that appears, by default, each time you draw a shape.
- Create custom theme colors by selecting different colors for background, text, and accent colors. Select the background color first and then select other colors that work well on that background.
- Modify backgrounds using the *Format Background* dialog box to apply a custom pattern, gradient, or picture fill.
- Carefully control how text is placed over background pictures and other fills so text is easy to read.

3.2 Apply animation to add interest and reinforce content (p. P3-147).

- Animation adds movement to slide objects and text.
- Animation is applied through ***Entrance***, ***Exit***, and ***Emphasis*** effects.
- If more than one animation is used, each animation is numbered in sequence.
- ***Effect Options*** control the direction and sequence of movement.
- Animation can start ***On Click***, ***With Previous***, or ***After Previous***.
- ***Duration*** is the time that it takes to complete an animation.

3.3 Link to an online video (p. P3-149).

- Search for an online video using the *Insert Video* dialog box.
- You need Internet access and a video must currently be available online if you want to link to it during a PowerPoint presentation.
- Some video can be played at full screen size.
- Playback controls appear at the bottom of the video.

3.4 Use rehearsal techniques to prepare for presentation delivery (p. P3-156).

- Type speaker notes using the *Notes* pane or *Notes Page* view.
- Print speaker notes for reference during a presentation.
- Use ***Rehearse Timings*** to practice and judge the pace of your presentation.
- You can manually adjust timings to increase or decrease the time a slide is displayed.
- Prepare backup copies of your presentation and your notes.

3.5 Control display options for different screen sizes (p. P3-159).

- The shape of your slides varies based on the aspect ratio (the ratio of width to height) you use.
- PowerPoint's default aspect ratio is *Widescreen 16:9;* the *Standard 4:3* is available.
- *Presenter View* displays the current slide, next slide, notes, and navigation controls on one monitor, while the slide show displays on a second monitor or projection screen.
- *Presenter View* can be used with one monitor.

3.6 Present effectively and professionally using projection equipment (p. P3-164).

- Use the slide show toolbar, shortcut menu, or keyboard shortcuts to navigate to different slides in a presentation.
- To blank a slide to black, press **B**; to blank a slide to white, press **W**.
- When you ***Hide*** a slide, it is still in the presentation but will not display during a slide show unless you go to that specific slide.
- Use ***remote controls*** to advance slides so you can move away from your computer.
- Use PowerPoint's ***laser pointer*** to place a dot on the slide during a slide show.

3.7 Use annotation pens to highlight information and save presentation markings (p. P3-167).

- Use the ***Pen*** or ***Highlighter*** to mark or draw on a slide during a slide show.
- Use the ***Eraser*** to remove markings during a slide show.
- These markings, called ***ink annotations***, can be saved at the end of the presentation.

3.8 Prepare a self-running presentation that loops (p. P3-170).

- If your computer has a microphone, you can include narration in a presentation.
- A self-running presentation, a ***kiosk presentation***, is set to automatically loop so it runs continuously.
- Use the ***Set Up Show*** dialog box to set up a kiosk presentation.
- The ***Package Presentation for CD*** feature saves linked files to a CD or other location.
- To assure that the fonts you used to create your presentation are available on the computer you will use to display your presentation, select ***Embedding TrueType Fonts***.

3.9 Use the *Package Presentation for CD* feature to prepare a slide show for display on other computers (p. P3-171).

Check for Understanding

In the ***Online Learning Center*** for this text (www.mhhe.com/office2013inpractice), there are a variety of resources that can be used to review the concepts covered in this chapter.

The following Online Learning Resources are available in the Online Learning Center:

- Multiple choice questions
- Short answer questions
- Matching exercises

USING MICROSOFT POWERPOINT 2013

Guided Project 3-1

One of the community colleges in the Sierra Pacific Community College District has finished construction of a new building for its business program. A dedication ceremony and open house is planned. In this project, you finalize the presentation for this special program and prepare a kiosk presentation to be displayed on monitors throughout the building while people tour after the opening ceremony. You save the standard slide size version in Part A and then change to a widescreen version in Part B.
[Student Learning Outcomes 3.1, 3.2, 3.4, 3.5, 3.6, 3.8]

File Needed: ***Dedication-03.pptx***
Completed Project File Names: ***[your initials] PowerPoint 3-1a.pptx*** and ***[your initials] PowerPoint 3-1b.pptx***

Skills Covered in This Project

- Apply a background picture fill.
- Apply animation and effect options.
- Create and print notes pages.
- Rehearse a presentation and save timings.
- Change to a widescreen slide size.
- Use *Presenter View.*
- Use slide show navigation tools, use keyboard shortcuts, and insert blank slides.
- Prepare a kiosk presentation.

Part A

1. Open the presentation ***Dedication-03*** that has a standard size (4:3 aspect ratio, 10 x 7.5").
2. Save the presentation as ***[your initials] PowerPoint 3-1a***.
3. Apply a background picture fill with a softened effect to all slides.
   a. Right-click to open the shortcut menu. Click **Format Background** to open the *Format Background* pane.
   b. Select the **Picture or texture fill** option.
   c. Click the **Online** button to open the *Insert Pictures* dialog box.
   d. In the *Office.com Clip Art* search box, type the word building and click the **Search** button (or press **Enter**).
   e. Select the picture, "Office building with reflection" shown in Figure 3-67 and click **Insert**.
   f. Click the **Picture** button at the top of the pane and then click **Picture Color**. Click the **Recolor** list arrow and select **Blue**, **Accent color 2, Dark**.
   g. Click **Apply to All** so this slide is used as the background for all slides.

3-67 ***Insert Picture*** **dialog box with search results**

4. On slides 1 and 2, restore the background picture to its original color. On the *Format Background* pane under *Picture Color*, click the **Reset** button for each slide.
5. On slide 2, delete the subtitle placeholder and move the title down slightly (Figure 3-68).

3-68 Slide title moved down

6. On slide 6, change the background color to black.
   a. On the *Format Background* pane, click **Fill** at the top of the pane if it is not selected. Select the **Solid fill** option.
   b. Click the **Color** list arrow and select **Black**, **Background 1**.
   c. Close the *Format Background* pane.
7. Select slide 2 and press **Ctrl+D** to duplicate. Move the new slide to the end of the presentation so it becomes slide 9. Change the slide 9 title text to Take a Tour.
8. Apply a transition to all slides.
   a. Click the **Transitions** tab and apply the **Shape** transition.
   b. Click the **Effect Options** button and select **Diamond**.
   c. Click **Apply to All** [*Timing* group] (Figure 3-69).

3-69 *Transition Effect Options*

9. Apply animation on four slides and change effect options as shown in the following table.
   a. Select the text or object to be animated.
   b. Click the **More** button on the *Animation* gallery. If the *Animation* gallery is not displayed, click the **Add Animation** button [*Animations* tab, *Advanced Animation* group].
   c. Click an effect to apply it.
   d. Click the **Effects Options** button [*Animations* group] to apply *Direction*, *Sequence*, or *Amount* settings.
   e. Adjust settings for *Start* and *Duration*.
   f. Click the **Preview** button or **Slide Show** button to test the animation.

Slide	Object	Animation Effect	Effect Options	Start	Duration
1	Text box for agenda	*Wipe* (Entrance)	*From Bottom, By Paragraph*	*On Click*	*00.50*
3	Picture	*Shape* (Entrance)	*Out, Diamond*	*After Previous*	*02:00*
7	Text box for space design	*Zoom* (Entrance)	*Object center, As One Object*	*On Click*	*00:50*
7	Text box for wireless access	*Zoom* (Entrance)	*Object center, As One Object*	*On Click*	*00:50*
8	Text box for donors	*Wipe* (Entrance)	*From Bottom, All At Once*	*After Previous*	*00:50*

10. Prepare speaker notes on two slides.
    a. Click the **Notes Page** button [*View* tab, *Presentation Views* group].
    b. Click the **Zoom** button and increase the *Percent* to **150%** so you can more easily see the text. Click **OK**.
    c. Add the following text with a blank line between each item on two notes pages (Figure 3-70):

    Slide 1: Welcome the audience.
    Review today's agenda—go through animation.

    Slide 9: The tours will now begin and last until 4 p.m.
    Student leaders are available outside this auditorium to guide small groups.
    Or tour on your own.

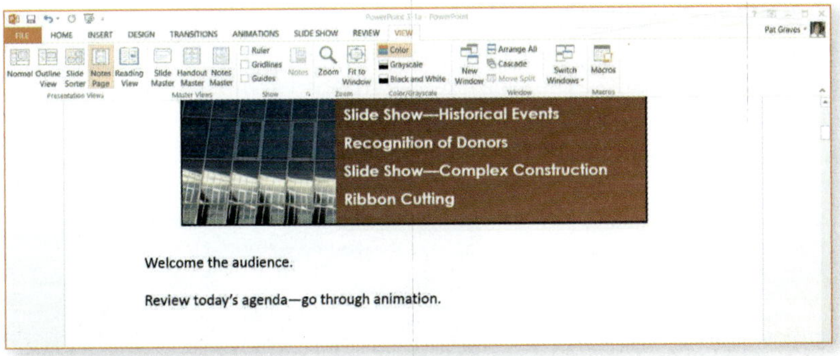

3-70 ***Notes Page*** **view showing speaker notes**

    d. Click the **Normal** button to return to *Normal* view.

11. Print notes pages for slides 4 and 5.
    a. Click the **File** tab and click **Print**.
    b. Select the appropriate printer and make sure that you are printing just one copy.
    c. For *Slides*, type 4–5 to print a *Custom Range*.
    d. For *Print Layout*, choose **Notes Pages** and check **Scale to Fit Paper** (Figure 3-71).
    e. Click the **Print** button.

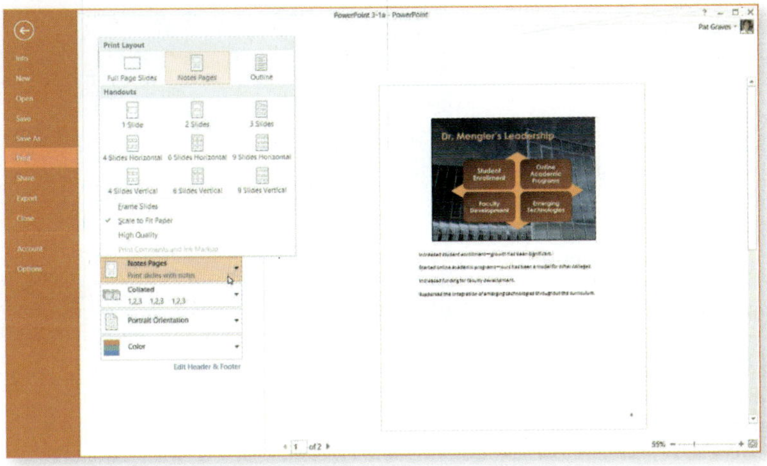

3-71 Print view of notes page

12. Rehearse and save timings.
    a. Click the **Rehearse Timings** button [*Slide Show* tab, *Set Up* group].
    b. Using the *Recording* dialog box, click the **Next Slide** button to advance each slide after approximately 3–5 seconds.
    c. At the end of your presentation, click **Yes** to save your timings. The timings are displayed below each slide in *Slide Show* view.
13. Save the presentation to preserve the current standard (4:3) slide size.

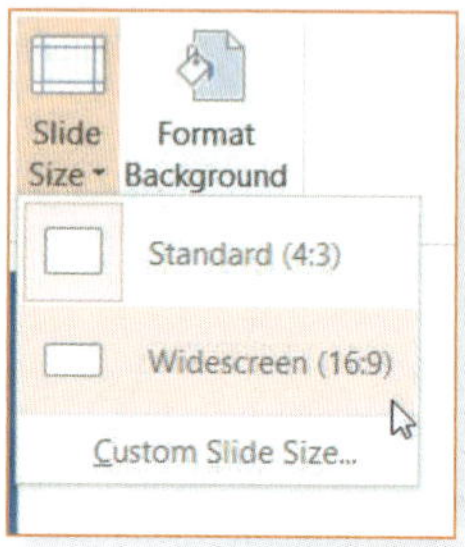

3-72 *Slide Size*

Part B

14. Resave the presentation as ***[your initials] PowerPoint 3-1b***.
15. Deselect the **After** timings [*Transitions* tab, *Timing* group] and click **Apply To All**.
16. Click the **Slide Size** button [*Design* tab, *Customize* group] and click **Widescreen (16:9)** (Figure 3-72). The slide size has changed from 10" to 13.333" wide.
17. Reposition objects on the following slides to fit the widescreen size:
    a. ***Slide 1:*** Right-align the text box.
    b. ***Slide 2:*** Move the slide title to the left to match other slide titles.
    c. ***Slide 7:*** Right-align both text boxes (Figure 3-73).
    d. ***Slide 8:*** Move the text at the top of the slide to the left. Right-align the text box.
    e. ***Slide 9:*** Move the slide title to the left to match other slide titles.

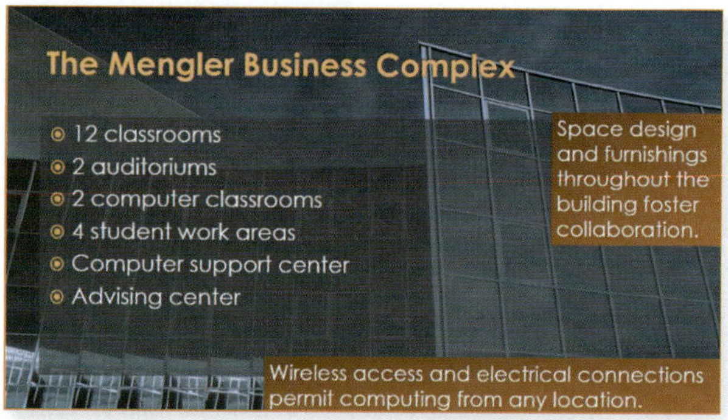

3-73 Text boxes right-aligned

18. Use *Presenter View* to review your presentation.
    a. Click the **Slide Show** tab.
    b. Click **Use Presenter View** [*Monitors* group].
    c. Start your presentation.
       - If you have two monitors, click the **From Beginning** button [*Start Slide Show* group].
       - If you have one monitor, press **Alt+F5**.
    d. Click the **Presenter View** right arrow button to advance slides as you review them.
    e. Click the **Zoom into the slide** button to magnify a section of the slide. Click **Zoom Out** to return to the normal slide size (Figure 3-74).
    f. Click the **See all slides** button to view thumbnails of all slides. Click to display different slides.
    g. Press **Esc** to exit *Presenter View*.

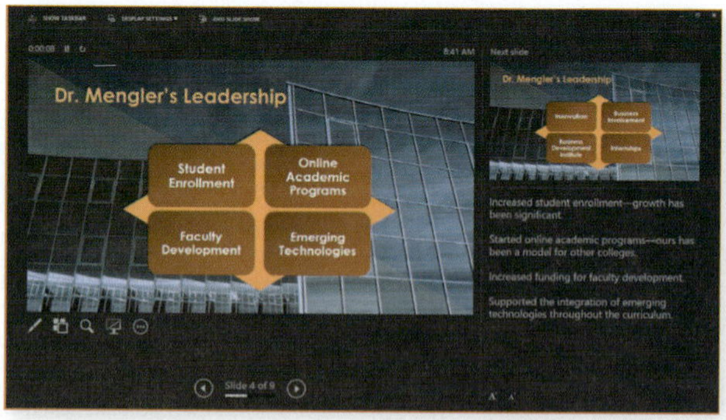

3-74 *Presenter View*

19. In *Slide Show* view, practice use of navigation tools, keyboard shortcuts, and blanking slides.
    a. Click the **right arrow** button in the slide navigation area to advance slides.
    b. Click the **Menu** button in the slide navigation area to open the shortcut menu and go to a specific slide.
    c. Right-click to open the shortcut menu and go to a specific slide.
    d. Press **N** to advance to the next slide; press **P** to go to the previous slide.
    e. Type 6 and press **Enter** to go to slide 6.
    f. Press **B** to blank a slide; press **B** to view the screen again.
20. Prepare a kiosk presentation with looping.
    a. Select the **After** timing [*Transitions* tab, *Timing* group] and click **Apply To All** so timings will be available for the kiosk presentation.
    b. On slides 1 and 7, select each animated object and change **Start** [*Animations* tab, *Timing* group] to **After Previous**.
    c. Click the **Set Up Slide Show** button [*Slide Show* tab, *Set Up* group] to open the *Set Up Show* dialog box.
    d. Select the following settings:
        - *For Show type*, select **Browsed at a kiosk (full screen)**.
        - *For Show options*, **Loop continuously until 'Esc'** is automatically selected for a kiosk.
        - *For Show slides*, select **All**.
        - *For Advance slides*, **Use timings**, **if present** is automatically selected for a kiosk.
    e. Select the appropriate monitor.
    f. Click **OK**.
21. Test the presentation to make sure slide transitions and animations work correctly.
22. Save and close the presentation (Figure 3-75).

3-75 PowerPoint 3-1 completed

Guided Project 3-2

For the second training session for new hires on presenting effectively, Davon Washington, Management Consultant at Solution Seekers, Inc., is preparing guidelines for designing slides and developing content in a visual way. For this project, you finish the presentation that Davon has prepared and save it on a CD so participants can refer to it after the session.
[Student Learning Outcomes 3.1, 3.2, 3.3, 3.4, 3.7, 3.9]

Files Needed: ***SlideShowDevelopment-03.pptx***, ***Background-03.jpg***, and ***Applause-03.jpg***
Completed Project File Names: ***[your initials] PowerPoint 3-2.pptx*** and folder ***Develop Slides***

Skills Covered in This Project

- Apply a background picture fill.
- Create custom theme colors.
- Apply animation and effect options.
- Link to an online video.
- Create and print notes pages.
- Add ink annotations.
- Use the *Package Presentation for CD* feature.

1. Open the presentation ***SlideShowDevelopment-03***.
2. Save the presentation as ***[your initials] PowerPoint 3-2***.
3. Apply a background picture fill to all slides.
   a. Right-click and select **Format Background** to open the *Format Background* pane.
   b. Select the **Picture or texture fill** option.
   c. Click the **File** button to open the *Insert Pictures* dialog box.
   d. Locate the student file ***Background-03*** and click **Insert** (Figure 3-76).
   e. Click **Apply to All** so this picture is the background for all slides.

3-76 Title slide with new background picture fill

4. On slide 12, repeat step 3 to apply a different background picture, ***Applause-03***, for this slide only.
   a. Change the *Offset left* to **–9%** and the *Offset top* to **–5%** for better picture positioning. (*Offset right* is 0% and *Offset bottom* is –9%.)
   b. Close the *Format Background* pane.
5. Prepare a new custom color theme to blend with the background picture.
   a. Click the **More** button [*Design* tab, *Variants* group].
   b. Select **Colors** and click **Customize Colors** to open the *Create New Theme Colors* dialog box.
   c. Change five accent colors.
      - For each change, click the color list arrow and select **More Colors** to open the *Colors* dialog box.
      - Click the **Custom** tab and enter the numbers for *Red*, *Green*, and *Blue* shown in the following table.

	Accent 1	Accent 2	Accent 3	Accent 4	Accent 5
Red	255	157	255	38	95
Green	247	175	217	203	30
Blue	220	210	82	236	60

d. Name the new custom theme Development (Figure 3-77).
e. Click the **Save** button.

6. Adjust text and object colors on the following selected slides:
   a. ***Slide 3:*** Change the black text on the *SmartArt* shapes to white.
   b. ***Slide 4 and 5:*** Click **Reset** [*Home* tab, *Slides* group] so the list bullet updates for the new *Accent 1* color.
   c. ***Slide 7 and 11:*** Change the *SmartArt* graphic color. Click the **Change Colors** button [*SmartArt Tools Design* tab, *SmartArt Styles* group] and select the **Colored Fill – Plum, Accent 5** style (Figure 3-78).
   d. ***Slide 12:*** Change the text box *Shape Fill* to **Plum, Accent 5**.

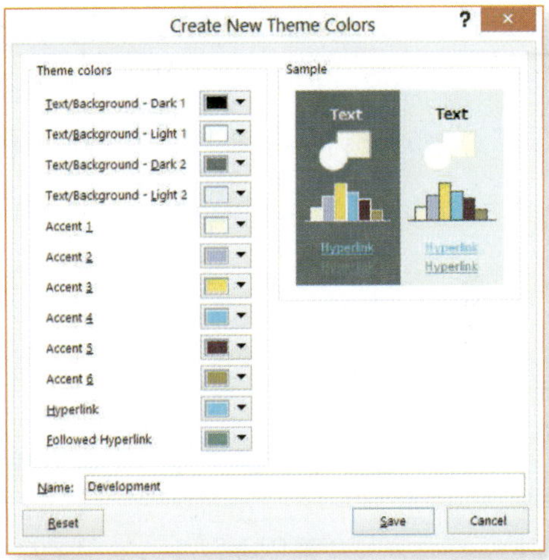

3-77 New theme colors

7. Apply a transition to all slides.
   a. Click the **Transitions** tab and apply the **Reveal** transition.
   b. Click the **Effect Options** button and the select **Smoothly from Right**.
   c. Change the *Duration* to **02:00** [*Timing* group].
   d. Click **Apply to All**.

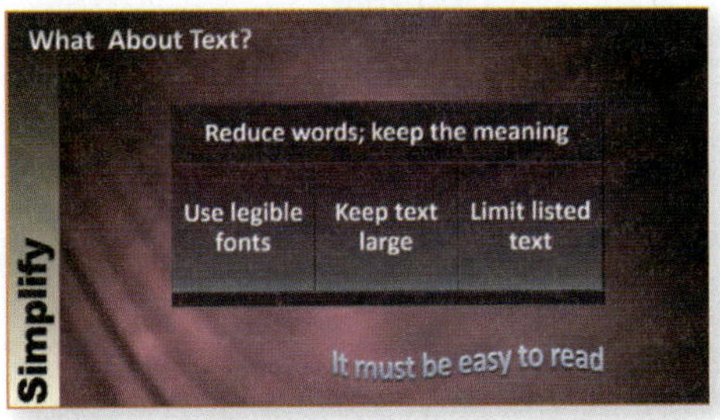

3-78 *SmartArt* recolored

8. Apply animation on four slides and change effect options as shown in the following table.
   a. Select the text or object to be animated.
   b. Click the **Animations** tab and click the **More** button on the *Animation* gallery. (Click the **Add Animation** button [*Advanced Animation* group] if the gallery is not open.)
   c. Click an effect to apply it.
   d. Click the **Effects Options** button to apply *Direction*, *Sequence*, or *Amount* settings.
   e. Adjust settings for *Start and Duration* as needed to match the table.
   f. Click the **Preview** button or **Slide Show** button to test the animation.

Slide	Object	Animation Effect	Effect Options	Start	Duration
2	Ducks	*Fly In* (Entrance)	*From Left*	*On Click*	*02.00*
2	Slide Show Development text box	*Bounce* (Entrance)	None	*After Previous*	*02.00*
4 and 5	Up text box	*Float In* (Entrance)	*Float Up*	*After Previous*	*01.00*

(Continued)

Slide	Object	Animation Effect	Effect Options	Start	Duration
4 and 5	Down text box	*Float In* (Entrance)	*Float Down*	*After Previous*	*01.00*
6	Color wheel	*Spin* (Emphasis)	*Clockwise, Two Spins*	*After Previous*	*03.00*
12	Text box	*Wheel* (Entrance)	*2 Spokes, As One Object*	*After Previous*	*02.00*

9. After slide 11, insert a new blank slide.
10. On the new slide 12, find and insert an online video.
    a. Click the **Insert** tab.
    b. Click the **Video** button list arrow [*Media* group] and select **Online Video** to open the *Insert Video* dialog box.
    c. Use the search words presentation slide design and select an appropriate video. Click **Insert**.
    d. Increase the size of the video (*Width* **6.5"**) if the quality remains acceptable.
    e. Below the video, add the appropriate source information.
    f. Play the video in *Slide Show* view, by clicking the **Start** button on the video.
    g. Press **Esc** to exit *Slide Show* view.
11. Beginning on slide 1, click the **Notes Page** button [*View* tab, *Presentation Views* group] and advance through all slides and read the speaker notes to review tips for slide design.
12. Print notes pages for slides 7 and 11.
    a. Click the **File** tab and click **Print**.
    b. Select the appropriate printer and make sure that you are printing just one copy.
    c. For *Slides,* type 7, 11 to choose a *Custom Range*.
    d. For *Print Layout*, choose **Notes Pages** and check **Scale to Fit Paper** (Figure 3-79).
    e. Click the **Print** button.

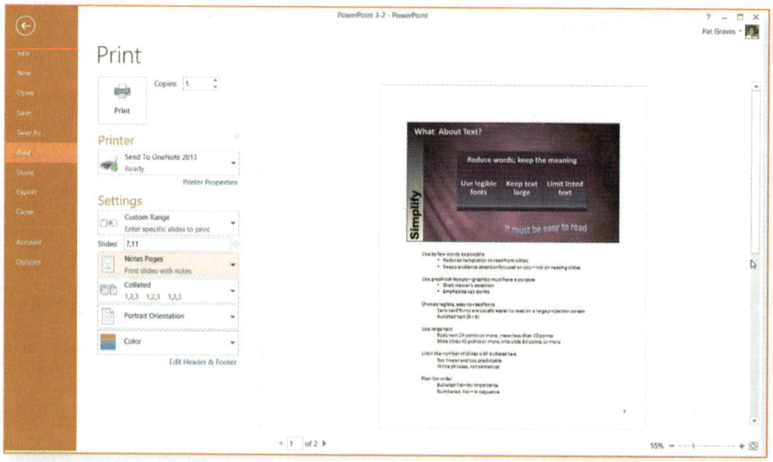

3-79 Print *Notes Pages*

13. Add ink annotations on slides 4, 5, and 7.
    a. In *Slide Show* view, go to slide 4.
    b. Right-click to open the shortcut menu and select **Pointer Options** and **Highlighter**. Highlight the word "organization."
    c. On slide 5, repeat step 14b and highlight the words "creative thinking."
    d. On slide 7, right-click to open the shortcut menu. Select **Pointer Options** and **Pen**. Circle the words "Reduce words" and "keep the meaning."
    e. Advance to the end of the presentation and click **Keep** to save your ink annotations.

14. Save the presentation (Figure 3-80).
15. Use the *Package Presentation for CD* feature to save the presentation to a folder.
    a. Click the **File** tab and select **Export**.
    b. Click **Package Presentation for CD** and click the **Package for CD** button to open the *Package for CD* dialog box.
    c. Type Develop Slides to name the CD.
    d. Click the **Options** button to open the *Options* dialog box and select **Linked Files** and **Embedded TrueType fonts**.
    e. Click **OK**.
    f. Click the **Copy to Folder** button to open the *Copy to Folder* dialog box. The folder name appears and is the same name you typed for the CD. Deselect the **Open folder when complete** option (Figure 3-81).
    g. Browse for the location to save the presentation and click the **Select** button.
    h. Click **OK** to close the *Copy to Folder* dialog box.
    i. A message appears asking if you want to include linked files. Click **Yes**.
    j. Another message appears telling you that ink annotations will not be included. Click **Continue**.
    k. Close the *Package for CD* dialog box.
    l. Close the presentation.

3-80 PowerPoint 3-2 completed

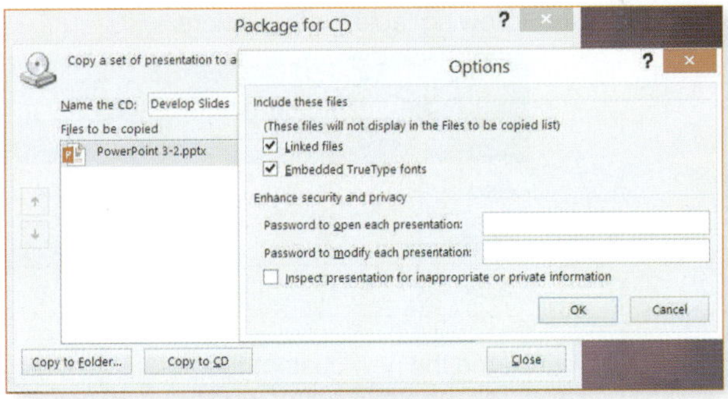

3-81 *Package for CD* and *Copy to Folder* dialog boxes

16. Test the presentation.
    a. Open the folder where you "packaged" the presentation. Notice that additional files have been saved in this folder.
    b. Double-click the file name in the folder to open the presentation. If you receive a security warning, click the **Enable** button. Test the presentation and then close it.
    c. To show the presentation from a different computer, the online video link will be broken. You will need to delete the existing video and insert the video again from the presentation computer.

Guided Project 3-3

At an upcoming meeting of the American River Cycling Club, Eric Salinas is giving a presentation about the importance of knowing your target heart rate and exercising with your heart rate at an appropriate target level. For this project, you finalize the presentation.
[Student Learning Outcomes 3.1, 3.3, 3.4, 3.5, 3.8]

Files Needed: ***HeartRateARCC-03.pptx*** and ***RiderAir.jpg***
Completed Project File Name: ***[your initials] PowerPoint 3-3.pptx***

Skills Covered in This Project

- Create custom theme colors.
- Apply a background picture fill.
- Link to a video on a web site.
- Use *Presenter View*.
- Create and print notes pages.
- Record a presentation with narration.
- Prepare a kiosk presentation.

1. Open the presentation ***HeartRateARCC-03***.
2. Save the presentation as ***[your initials] PowerPoint 3-3***.
3. Prepare a new custom color theme to blend with the heart picture on slide 3.
   a. Click the **More** button [*Design* tab, *Variants* group].
   b. Select **Colors** and click **Customize Colors** to open the *Create New Theme Colors* dialog box.
   c. For each change, click the **Color** list arrow and select **More Colors** to open the *Colors* dialog box. Click the **Custom** tab and enter the numbers for *Red*, *Green*, and *Blue* shown in the following table for four colors.

	Text/ Background – Dark 2	Accent 1	Accent 2	Accent 3
Red	24	36	204	227
Green	66	99	0	108
Blue	77	116	0	9

   d. Name the new custom theme ARCC (Figure 3-82).
   e. Click the **Save** button and the new colors will automatically be applied to all slides.
4. Format the title slide by adding a background picture fill.
   a. Right-click and select **Format Background** to open the *Format Background* pane.
   b. Select the **Picture or texture fill** option.
   c. Click the **File** button to open the *Insert Pictures* dialog box.
   d. Locate the student file ***RiderAir-03*** and click **Insert**.

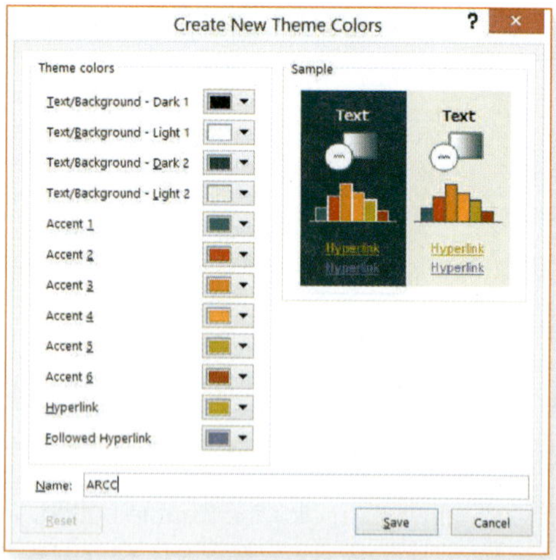

3-82 New ARCC color theme

e. Click **Picture** at the top of the pane and select **Picture Color**. Click the **Recolor** list arrow and select **Black and White**, **25%** (Figure 3-83).
f. Close the *Format Background* pane.

5. On the title slide, increase the subtitle font size to **36 pt.** and resize the placeholder so one word fits on each line.

3-83 Completed title slide

6. On slide 5, find and insert an online video.
   a. Click the **Insert** tab.
   b. Click the **Video** button list arrow [*Media* group] and select **Online Video** to open the *Insert Video* dialog box.
   c. Use the search words Col de la Madone and select an appropriate video. Click **Insert**.
   d. Position the video to the left of the picture and increase the video size (*Width* **5.5"**) if the quality remains acceptable.
   e. Below the video, add the appropriate source information.
   f. Play the video in *Slide Show* view by clicking the **Start** button in the middle of the video.

7. Apply a transition. Choose the **Cube** [*Transitions* tab, *Transition to This Slide* group] with the **From Right** effect options. Click **Apply To All**.

8. Use *Presenter View* to review your presentation.
   a. Click the **Slide Show** tab.
   b. Click **Use Presenter View** [*Monitors* group].
   c. Start your presentation.
      - If you have two monitors, click the **From Beginning** button [*Start Slide Show* group].
      - If you have one monitor, press **Alt+F5**.
   d. Click the **Presenter View** right arrow button to advance slides as you review them.
   e. If the notes text seems too small, click the **Make the text larger** button to adjust the text size in the *Notes* pane and then scroll to read the text (Figure 3-84).
   f. Press **Esc** to end the slide show.

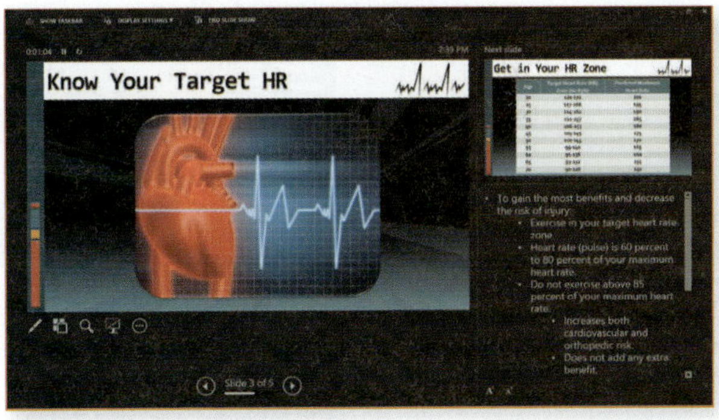

3-84 *Presenter View*

9. Print notes pages for slides 3 and 4.
   a. Click the **File** tab. Click **Print**.
   b. Select the appropriate printer and make sure that you are printing just one copy.
   c. For *Slides,* type 3–4 to choose a *Custom Range.*
   d. For *Print Layout,* choose **Notes Pages** and select **Scale to Fit Paper**.
   e. Click the **Print** button.

10. Record a slide show with narration.
    a. Click the **Record Slide Show** button [*Slide Show* tab, *Set Up* group] and select **Start Recording from Beginning** to open the *Record Slide Show* dialog box.

b. Select both options and click **Start Recording** (Figure 3-85). The *Recording* dialog box appears.
c. Speak clearly into your microphone as each slide is displayed.
d. Click the **Next Slide** navigation button to advance each slide.

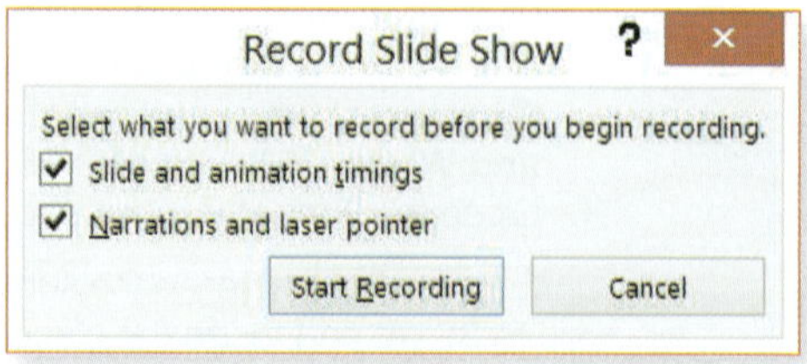

3-85 *Record Slide Show* dialog box

11. Prepare a kiosk presentation with looping.
    a. Click the **Set Up Slide Show** button [*Slide Show* tab] to open the *Set Up Show* dialog box.
    b. Select the *Show type* **Browsed at a kiosk (full screen)**.
    c. For *Show slides* select **All**.
    d. Select the appropriate monitor.
    e. Click **OK**.
12. Save and close your presentation (Figure 3-86).

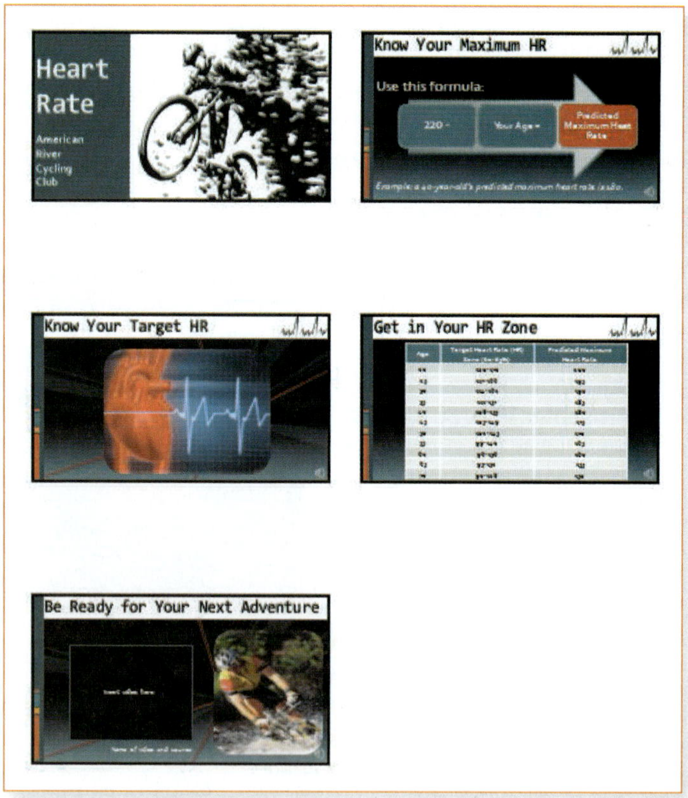

3-86 PowerPoint 3-3 completed

Independent Project 3-4

The sales representatives at Wilson Home Entertainment Systems review acceptable viewing distances when talking with clients who are in the early stages of planning a home theater or media room. They discuss options for televisions or projection systems for the spaces being planned. For this project, you complete a presentation to prepare clients for an in-home consultation.
[Student Learning Outcomes 3.1, 3.2, 3.4, 3.6, 3.7, 3.8]

File Needed: ***ScreenSizes-03.pptx***, ***TVCabinet-03.jpg***, and ***Projector-03.jpg***
Completed Project File Name: ***[your initials] PowerPoint 3-4.pptx***

Skills Covered in This Project

- Apply a background picture fill.
- Apply animation and effect options.
- Create and print notes pages.
- Rehearse a presentation and save timings.
- Use slide show navigation tools, keyboard shortcuts, and blank slides.
- Hide and reveal slides.
- Use the laser pointer feature.
- Use annotation pens.
- Prepare a kiosk presentation.

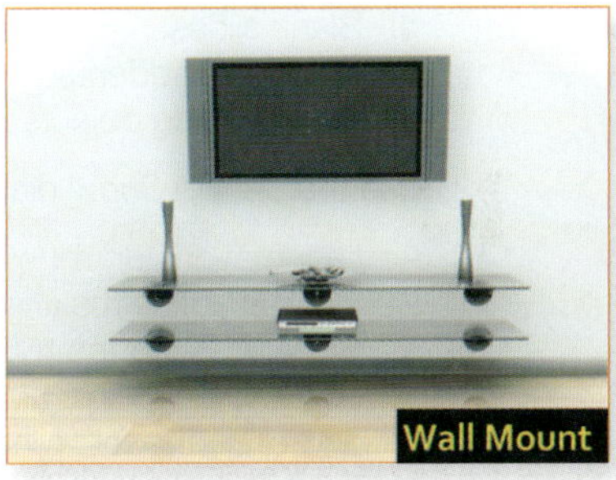

3-87 Background picture fill

1. Open the presentation ***ScreenSizes-03***.
2. Save the presentation in its current standard slide size as ***[your initials] PowerPoint 3-4***.
3. Using the *Format Background* pane, change the background fill on three slides to a picture fill.
   a. ***Slide 5:*** Insert **TVCabinet-03** from your student files.
   b. ***Slide 6:*** Search *Online* using the *Insert Pictures* dialog box and the search word television. Locate a picture of a wall-mounted flat screen television (Figure 3-87).
   c. ***Slide 7:*** Insert **Projector-03** from your student files.
   d. Close the *Format Background* pane.
4. Apply the **Vortex** transition with the **From Bottom** effect option. Change the *Duration* to **3.00**. Apply these settings to all slides (Figure 3-88).
5. Apply animation on four slides and change effect options as shown in the following table:

Slide	Object	Animation Effect	Effect Options	Start	Duration
2	Question mark	*Spin* (Emphasis)	*Clockwise, Two Spins*	*After Previous*	*02.00*
5, 6, 7	Text box	*Fly In* (Entrance)	*From Top-Left, As One Object*	*After Previous*	*00.50*

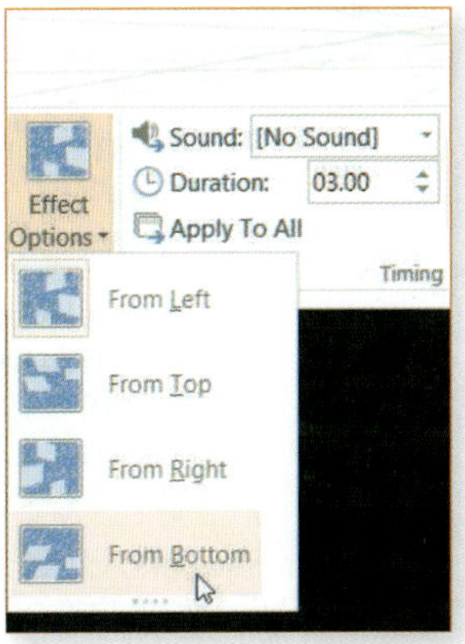

3-88 *Vortex* transition

6. Prepare speaker notes on the following three slides. Insert blank space between each item.
   a. ***Slide 5:*** Provides storage for related equipment and media.
      Select appropriate height for viewing.
      Some cabinets have a lift to hide TV when not in use.
   b. ***Slide 6:*** Creates an uncluttered, contemporary look.
      Where will you keep related equipment?
   c. ***Slide 7:*** Most equipment is concealed in some way.
      Projector
      Receiver
         Sound system
         DVD player
      Remote controls operate equipment.
      Wires and cables are in the walls.
7. Print notes pages for slides 5, 6, and 7 (Figure 3-89).
8. Rehearse the presentation and save timings.
9. Modify the timings to advance each slide after approximately 3–5 seconds.
10. Hide slide 4.
11. In *Slide Show* view, practice the following slide show features:
    a. Use the navigation area buttons.
    b. Right-click and use the shortcut menu.
    c. Use keyboard shortcuts.
    d. Blank slides.
    e. Go to the hidden slide 4.
    f. Point to slide objects with the laser pointer.

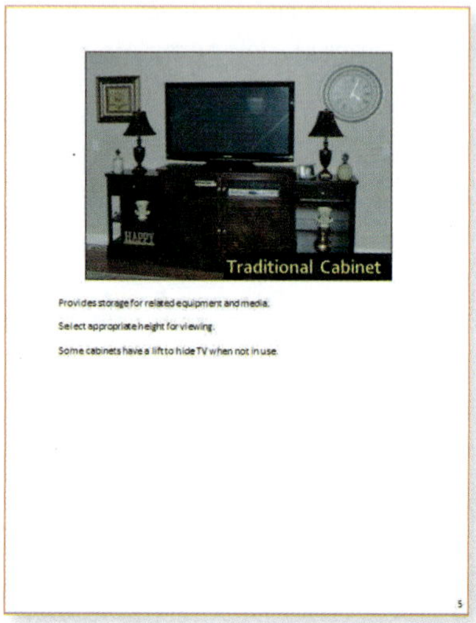

3-89 Notes page

12. Use the *Set Up Show* dialog box to change *Advance Slides* to **Manually**. Click **OK**.
13. Add annotations on slides 3 and 4 using the **Pen** with **Red** ink and keep annotations. Use *Presenter View* and practice making annotations on the presenter slide.
    a. ***Slide 3:*** Circle the "55-60" and "100" screen sizes.
    b. ***Slide 4:*** Go to this hidden slide and circle the following phrases in the bulleted items: "level with the middle," "reduce color clarity," and "visibility at all seats."
    c. Keep ink annotations.
14. Use the *Set Up Show* dialog box to prepare a kiosk presentation with looping.
    a. For *Advance Slides*, select **Use timings, if present**.
    b. Select **Browsed at a kiosk (full screen)** and show **All** slides.
    c. Select the appropriate monitor.
    d. Click **OK**.
15. Save and close the presentation (Figure 3-90).

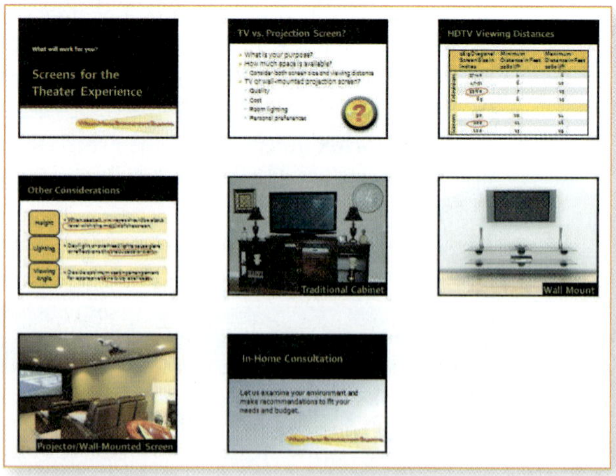

3-90 PowerPoint 3-4 completed

Independent Project 3-5

For the third training session for new hires on presenting effectively, Davon Washington, Management Consultant at Solution Seekers, Inc., is preparing guidelines for delivering a presentation with projection equipment. For this project, you finish the presentation that Davon has prepared.
[Student Learning Outcomes 3.1, 3.2, 3.4, 3.5, 3.7, 3.8]

File Needed: ***PresentationDelivery-03.pptx***
Completed Project File Name: ***[your initials] PowerPoint 3-5.pptx***

Skills Covered in This Project

- Apply a background picture fill.
- Apply animation and effect options.
- Create and print notes pages.
- Hide and reveal slides.
- Rehearse a presentation and save timings.
- Use *Presenter View.*
- Use ink annotation pens.
- Record a presentation with narration.

1. Open the presentation ***PresentationDelivery-03***.
2. Save the presentation as ***[your initials] PowerPoint 3-5***.
3. On slide 3, make the following changes:
   a. From the *Block Arrows* category in the *Shapes* gallery, select the **right arrow** and draw an arrow (*Height* **1.7"** and *Width* **4"**). The **Shape Fill** color is **Dark Red**, **Accent 1**.
   b. Apply the *Shape Effect of* **Shadow**, **Offset Bottom**.
   c. Adjust the arrow position as shown in Figure 3-91.
   d. Delete the "Answer" text box.
4. Apply the **Fade** transition with the **Smoothly** effect option. Change the *Duration* to **01.00**. Apply these settings to all slides.

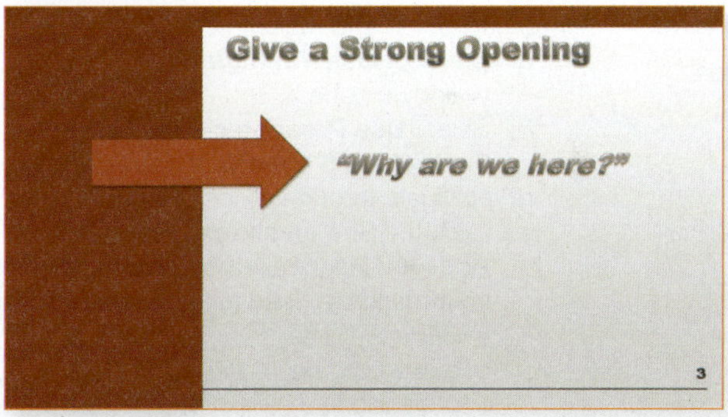

3-91 Shape added

5. Apply animation on five slides and change effect options as shown in the following table.

Slide	Object	Animation Effect	Effect Options	Start	Duration
2	Text, You get only one . . .	*Bounce* (Entrance)	*As One Object*	*After Previous*	02.00
5	Butterfly image	*Grow & Turn* (Entrance)	None	*After Previous*	02.00
7	Graphic	*Wipe* (Entrance)	*From Left*	*After Previous*	02.50
11	Text, Make it memorable	*Bounce* (Entrance)	*As One Object*	*After Previous*	02.00
12	Success shape	*Grow/Shrink* (Emphasis)	*Both, Larger*	*After Previous*	02.50

6. Prepare speaker notes on two slides. Apply bullets and indent the bulleted text (Figure 3-92).
   a. ***Slide 2:*** Never underestimate the importance of a first impression
      If possible, welcome people as they arrive for your presentation
   b. ***Slide 9:*** Be careful with how you use humor
      - Use humor only if it is appropriate
      - Avoid jokes—you could unintentionally offend someone

      Humor works best when it fits the presentation and seems natural
      - Break the ice
      - Be yourself; be real
      - Make your audience feel comfortable

      Choose stories or examples from your own experience
7. Print notes pages for slides 5, 6, and 7.
8. Hide slide 8.
9. Review the presentation to check transitions and animations.
   a. On the *Transitions* tab, deselect **On Mouse Click**.
   b. Change *After* to **00:03:00** seconds.
   c. Click **Apply To All**.
   d. Start your slide show from the beginning and review all slide movements.

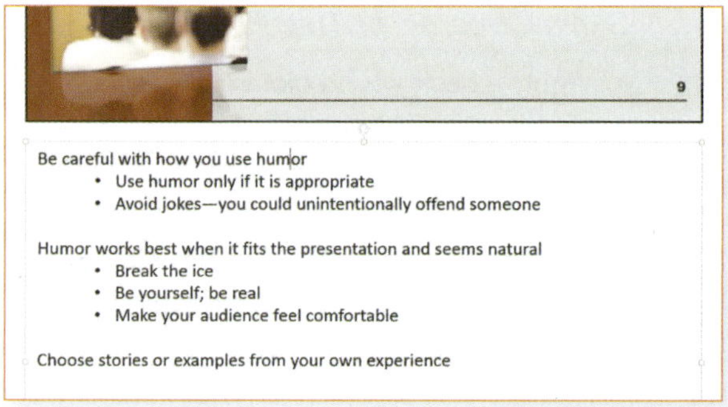

3-92 Notes with bullets and indents

10. Use *Presenter View* to review your presentation and make ink annotations.
    a. Deselect **Use Timings** [*Slide Show* tab, *Set Up* group] so you can advance through the slides at your own pace.
    b. Select **Use Presenter View**.
    c. Press **Alt+F5** to begin the presentation.
    d. Navigate through slides using the *Presenter View* arrow buttons.
    e. Click the **See all slides** button and click thumbnails to move to different slides.
    f. Add annotations on the following slides using the **Pen** with **Blue** ink. If you are not satisfied with your markings, then use the **Eraser** and try again.
       - ***Slide 2:*** Circle the words "Be professional."
       - ***Slide 4:*** Draw a rectangle around the words "Eye Contact" and "Smile" (Figure 3-93).
       - ***Slide 7:*** Circle the words "Avoid monotone."
       - ***Slide 10:*** Circle "End on time."
    g. At the end of the presentation, click **Keep** to save annotations.

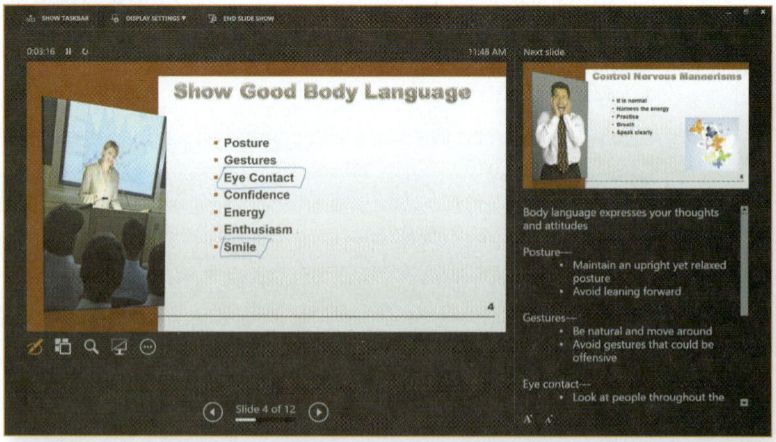

3-93 *Presenter View* showing ink annotations

11. If you have a microphone on your computer, record a slide show with narration.
    a. Print notes pages for additional slides where you need reminders of what to discuss.
    b. On the *Slide Show* tab, click **Record Slide Show** and select both **Slide and animation timings** and **Narrations and laser pointer**.
    c. Begin on the first slide and speak clearly into your microphone as each slide is displayed.
    d. Save and close your presentation (Figure 3-94).

3-94 PowerPoint 3-5 completed

Independent Project 3-6

At the Hamilton Civic Center (HCC), classes are offered for a variety of fitness activities. For this project, you complete a presentation to promote the water aerobics classes at several community events. It will also be used as a self-running presentation at the HCC front desk.
[Student Learning Outcomes 3.1, 3.2, 3.3, 3.4, 3.5, 3.6, 3.8]

File Needed: ***WaterAerobics-03.pptx***
Completed Project File Names: ***[your initials] PowerPoint 3-6a.pptx*** and ***[your initials] PowerPoint 3-6b.pptx***

Skills Covered in This Project

- Create custom theme colors.
- Modify background fill colors.
- Change object colors on selected slides.
- Apply animation and effect options.
- Change to a widescreen slide size.
- Hide and reveal a slide.
- Use slide show navigation tools, keyboard shortcuts, and blank slides.
- Link to an online video.
- Prepare a kiosk presentation.

1. Open the presentation ***WaterAerobics-03***.
2. Save the presentation as ***[your initials] PowerPoint 3-6a***.
3. Use the *Create New Theme Colors* dialog box to create a custom theme. Change four colors according to the *Red*, *Green*, and *Blue* numbers shown in the following table. Name the custom theme Water and save it (Figure 3-95).

	Text/ Background - Dark 2	Accent 1	Accent 3	Accent 5
Red	7	53	16	255
Green	55	151	89	51
Blue	99	241	100	153

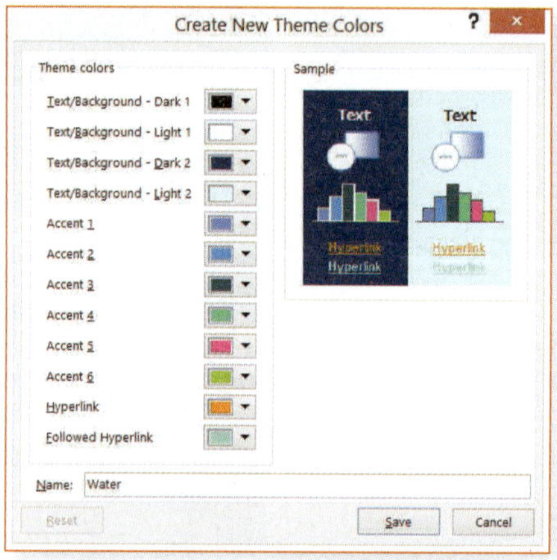

3-95 *Water* theme colors

4. Change the background colors.
   a. Click the **More** button [*Design* tab, *Variants* group] and select **Background Styles**. Click **Style 2** so a light blue is applied to all slides in the presentation.
   b. On slides 1 and 8, use the *Format Background* pane to change the **Solid Fill** to **Dark Blue**, **Text 2**.
   c. On slides 1 and 8, change the color for the text at the bottom of these slides to **White**, **Background 1** (Figure 3-96).

3-96 Title slide in standard slide size

5. Change the color for the following two objects to **Pink**, **Accent 5:**
   a. ***Slide 3:*** *Text Fill for* "Fun"
   b. ***Slide 4:*** *Shape Fill* for the table heading row
6. Type the following speaker notes on slide 4 (Figure 3-97):

   Swimming classes, scuba classes, and the local swim team practice sessions are scheduled at other times.
   Check with the front desk for unscheduled time when the pool is open.
   Each class is 6 weeks long.

7. Apply the **Ripple** transition with the **From Top-Left** effect option. Apply this transition to all slides.

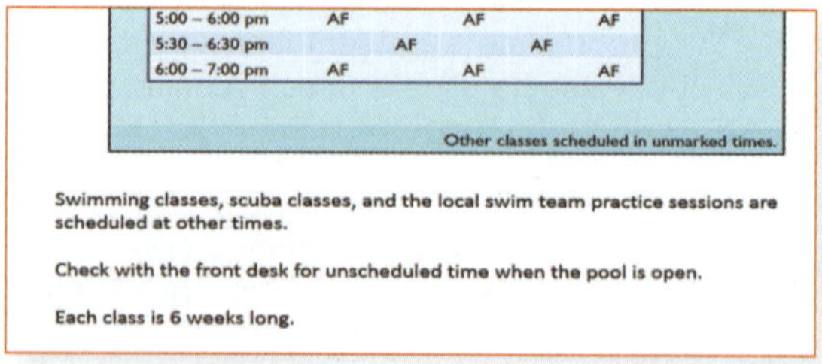

3-97 Notes page

8. Apply animation on four slides and change effect options as shown in the following table:

Slide	Object	Animation Effect	Effect Options	Start	Duration
2	Bulleted list	*Fly In* (Entrance)	*From Bottom-Right, By Paragraph*	*After Previous*	*01.00*
3	Bulleted list	*Fly In* (Entrance)	*From Bottom, As One Object*	*After Previous*	*01.00*
3	*WordArt* "Fun"	*Bounce* (Entrance)	*As One Object*	*After Previous*	*02.50*
5	Text box	*Wipe* (Entrance)	*From Left, As One Object*	*After Previous*	*02.00*

9. Save the presentation to preserve the file in the **Standard 4:3** slide size.
10. Resave the presentation as ***[your initials] PowerPoint 3-6b***.
11. Click the **Design** tab and change *Slide Size* to **Widescreen 16:9**.
    a. Make the following adjustments so objects better fit the wider screen size:
        - *Slide 1:* Increase the picture size (*Height* **4"** and *Width* **6"**). Move the picture and text as shown in Figure 3-98.
        - ***Slide 4:*** Resize the text box on the right so the text fits on four lines (Figure 3-99). Align it to the slide on the right.
        - ***Slide 4:*** Right-align the text box at the bottom of the slide and then extend the left end of the box to fit across the bottom of the slide.
        - ***Slide 5:*** Repeat the same alignment and size increase process for the text box at the bottom of the slide.

3-98 Title slide in widescreen slide size

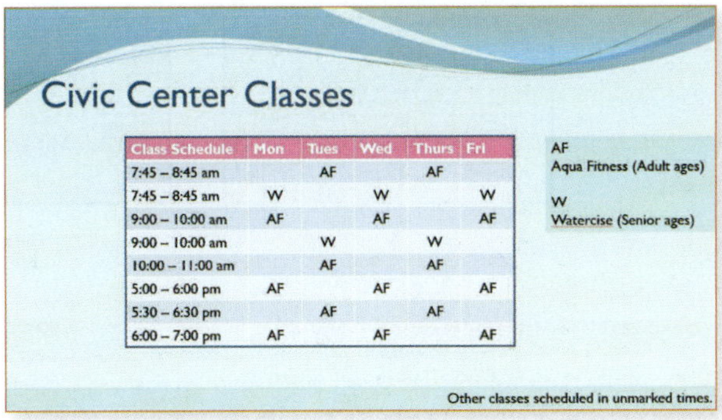

3-99 Text boxes adjusted

12. Hide slide 5.
13. Use *Slide Show* view to practice the following features:
    a. Use the navigation buttons.
    b. Right-click and use the shortcut menu.
    c. Use keyboard shortcuts.
    d. Blank slides.
    e. Go to the hidden slide 5.
    f. Point to slide objects with the laser pointer.
14. After slide 4, insert a new slide with the *Title Only* layout. Type the title Learn Online.

15. On slide 5, use the *Insert Video* dialog box to find and insert an online video.
    a. Use the search words water aerobics exercises and select an appropriate video. For referencing purposes, write down the name of the video and online source from the lower left of the dialog box. Click **Insert**.
    b. Increase the video size if the quality remains acceptable.
    c. Below the video, add the name of the video and online source.
    d. Test the video in *Slide Show* view to be sure it plays correctly.
16. Rehearse the presentation and save timings.
    a. Modify the timings to advance each slide after approximately 3–5 seconds.
17. Set up a kiosk presentation so it automatically loops.
    a. Show all slides and use timings.
18. Test the presentation and make any needed timing adjustments.
19. Save and close the presentation (Figure 3-100).

3-100 PowerPoint 3-6 completed

Improve It Project 3-7

Delivering news that employees may perceive as bad news is a difficult task. Improve this text-only presentation about presenting news to employees. Use existing slide text to create notes pages. Create custom theme colors. To communicate the message in a more visual way, add *SmartArt* graphics, brief text, and appropriate pictures. The figures in this section provide slide examples; your slides may differ slightly from these examples.
[Student Learning Outcomes 3.1, 3.2, 3.4, 3.8]

File Needed: ***Announcement-03.pptx***
Completed Project File Names: ***[your initials] PowerPoint 3-7.pptx***

Skills Covered in This Project

- Create custom theme colors.
- Modify slide content using pictures. *SmartArt,* and text boxes.
- Create and print notes pages.
- Apply appropriate transitions.
- Rehearse a presentation and save timings.
- Prepare a kiosk presentation.

1. Open the presentation ***Announcement-03***.
2. Save the presentation as ***[your initials] PowerPoint 3-7***.
3. Create custom theme colors. Change five colors and save the custom theme with the name Announce.

	Text/Background - Dark 2	Text/Background - Light 2	Accent 1	Accent 2	Accent 3
Red	38	255	255	124	204
Green	19	230	153	26	236
Blue	0	193	0	26	255

4. On slide 1, make the text more distinctive.
   a. Apply bold to the slide placeholders.
   b. Increase the title text **66 pts**. and "Big" to **96 pts**. Change the font color to **Orange**, **Accent 1**, **Lighter 40%**.
   c. Increase the subtitle text to **32 pts**. and "You" to **48 pts**. (Figure 3-101).

3-101 Revised title slide

5. On slide 2, use the existing bulleted text to create a notes page.
   a. Click the **Notes** button so you can see the *Notes* pane in *Normal* view. Increase the size of the *Notes* pane so you can see it while you are working on each slide.
   b. Copy the existing bulleted text and paste it in the *Notes* pane. Arrange this text neatly (Figure 3-102).

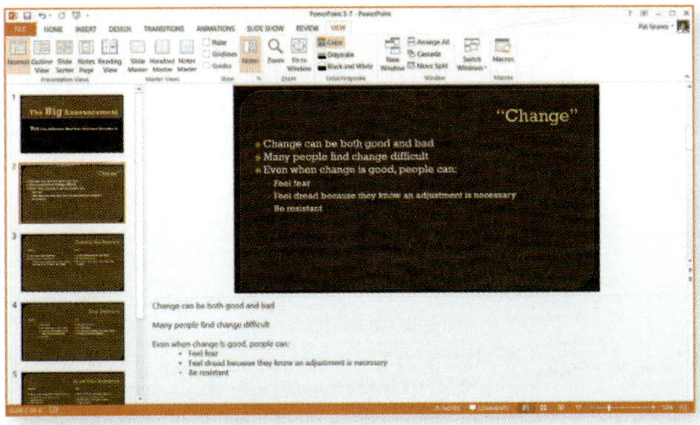

3-102 *Notes* pane expanded

6. On slide 2, show that "change" can be perceived as both good and bad (Figure 3-103).
   a. Replace the bulleted text with three short items: Fear, Dread, Be resistant. Resize the body placeholder and move it to the lower right.

b. Use the search word anxiety to find a similar picture and insert it. Apply the **Rounded Corner Diagonal**, **White** picture style and change the **Picture Border** to **Black**, **Background 2**.
c. Insert a *SmartArt* **Opposing Arrows** layout from the *Relationship* category. Type the text Good and Bad. Apply the **Inset** *SmartArt Style.*
d. Resize chart objects and position them as shown in Figure 3-103.

3-103 Slide 2 revised

7. Prepare the remaining notes pages on slides 3-6:
   a. Cut the existing bulleted text and paste this text on notes pages for each slide. Also include the words "Do" and "Don't."
   b. On each slide, delete the title and heading placeholders.
8. On slide 3, using a picture, emphasize what you should and should not do to control rumors (Figure 3-104).
   a. Insert a text box and type Don't create false expectations. Change the font size to **24 pts**. and emphasize the word "Don't" by increasing the font size to **32 pts**. and changing the color to **Orange**, **Accent 1**. Change the shape fill color to **Black**, **Background 2** (this is a very dark brown).
   b. Duplicate this text box and change the text to Do explain things in a positive way.
   c. Use the search word excitement to find a similar picture and insert it. To match the picture on slide 1, apply the **Rounded Corner Diagonal**, **White** picture style and change the **Picture Border** to **Black**, **Background 2**.

3-104 Slide 3 revised

9. On slide 4, using a picture, emphasize what you should and should not do in your delivery of bad news (Figure 3-105).
   a. Copy the "Don't" and "Do" text boxes from slide 3 and paste them on slide 4. Change the slide 4 text boxes to: Don't be insincere or "slick" and Do be confident and caring.
   b. Use the search word relax to find a similar picture and insert it. Apply the same picture style.
   c. Resize the picture and position objects as shown.

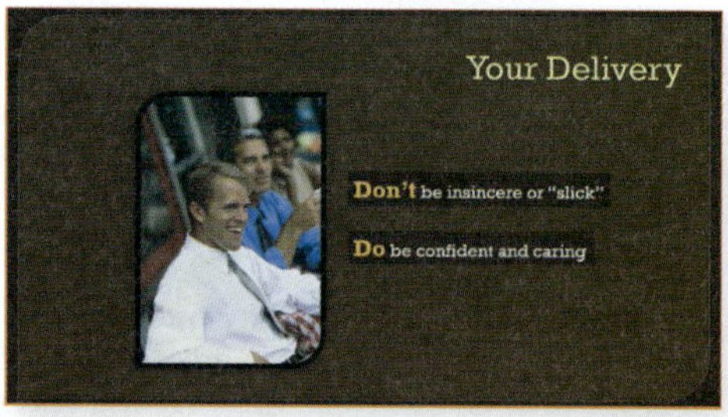

3-105 Slide 4 revised

10. On slide 5, using a picture, emphasize what you should and should not do to reflect your understanding of your audience (Figure 3-106).
   a. Copy the "Don't" and "Do" text boxes from slide 4 and paste them on slide 5. Change the slide 5 text boxes to: Don't be condescending and Do show your understanding.
   b. Use the search word meeting to find a similar picture and insert it. Apply the same picture style.
   c. Resize the picture and position objects as shown.

3-106 Slide 5 revised

11. On slide 6, using a picture, provide a strong summary statement (Figure 3-107).
    a. Insert a text box and type this text: Treat people as you would like to be treated.
    b. Make the text bold, increase the font size to **32 pts**., and change the shape fill to **Black, Background 2**.
    c. Use the search word meeting to find a similar picture and insert it. Apply the same picture style.
    d. Resize the picture and position objects as shown.

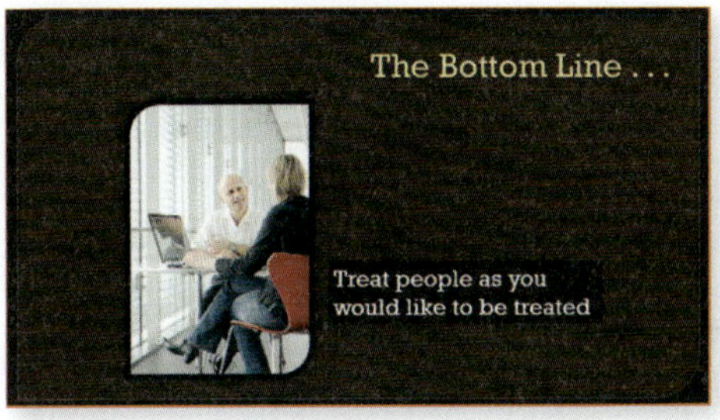

3-107 Slide 6 revised

12. Apply the **Gallery** transition to all slides.
13. Print notes pages for slides 2-5.
14. Rehearse the presentation and save timings.
15. Modify the timings and change the *After* seconds to **00:03:00**.
16. Set up the slide show for a kiosk presentation.
17. Save and close the presentation (Figure 3-108).

3-108 PowerPoint 3-7 completed

Challenge Project 3-8

For this project, explain the benefits of tablet computing and factors to consider when purchasing a tablet. Using sources such as www.pcmag.com, list some of the top-rated products and their prices. Describe common features, applications, and accessories.
[Student Learning Outcomes 3.1, 3.2, 3.3, 3.4, 3.5, 3.9]

File Needed: None
Completed Project File Name: ***[your initials] PowerPoint 3-8.pptx***

Create a new presentation and save it as ***[your initials] PowerPoint 3-8***. Modify your presentation according to the following guidelines:

- Select an appropriate theme and create custom theme colors for a high-tech appearance.
- Change to a widescreen format.
- Include pictures from www.pcmag.com or other sources and credit the source below each picture.
- Animate approximately three objects for emphasis and apply appropriate effects.
- Rehearse the presentation and save timings.
- Link to an online video.
- Prepare a slide listing your references and include it as the last slide in your presentation.
- Use *Package Presentation for CD* to save the presentation to a folder.

Challenge Project 3-9

Prepare a presentation to promote a student or civic organization. Use pictures and very brief text to convey the aim and purpose of the organization. Consider using an organization chart to illustrate the officer or committee structure. Apply styles and text treatments consistently.
[Student Learning Outcomes 3.1, 3.2, 3.3, 3.4, 3.6, 3.9]

File Needed: None
Completed Project File Name: ***[your initials] PowerPoint 3-9.pptx***

Create a new presentation and save it as ***[your initials] PowerPoint 3-9***. Modify your presentation according to the following guidelines:

- Select an appropriate theme and then create custom theme colors for your topic.
- Modify backgrounds by applying a gradient fill to all slides and a picture fill to one slide.
- Design slides with a variety of illustration techniques and minimal text.
- Add transitions and animations with appropriate effects.
- Create and print notes pages.
- Include an online video if one is available and credit your source.
- Prepare a slide listing your references and include it as the last slide in your presentation.
- Rehearse the presentation and use a variety of navigation techniques.
- Use *Package Presentation for CD* to save your presentation to a folder.

Challenge Project 3-10

Create a presentation about living green. Focus on ways to conserve water and other resources. Use web sites such as www.mygreenside.org and others. Prepare a slide listing your references and include it as the last slide in your presentation.
[Student Learning Outcomes 3.1, 3.2, 3.3, 3.4, 3.6, 3.8]

File Needed: None
Completed Project File Name: ***[your initials] PowerPoint 3-10.pptx***

Create a new presentation and save it as ***[your initials] PowerPoint 3-10***. Modify your presentation according to the following guidelines:

- Create custom theme colors that fit the "green" topic.
- Modify backgrounds and use at least one picture fill.
- Design slides with a variety of illustration techniques and minimal text.
- Add transitions and animations with appropriate effects.
- Create and print notes pages.
- Include an online video about "green" living and credit your source.
- Hide slides and blank slides.
- Rehearse the presentation, save timings during the rehearsal and then modify timings.
- Prepare a kiosk presentation.

CHAPTER 1

Outlook Overview and Email Basics

OUTLOOK

CHAPTER OVERVIEW

Microsoft Outlook (usually referred to as ***Outlook***) is the most widely used email and personal management software today. It is used in both business and personal environments. Outlook 2013 is part of the Microsoft Office 2013 suite of application software. This book covers the different aspects of Outlook and how this software is used to help manage your electronic communication, schedule your appointments and meetings, organize your personal and business contacts, and arrange your list of to-do items.

This first half of this book (Chapters 1–5) introduces you to all the main features of Outlook; the more advanced and special features of Outlook are presented in the second half of the book (Chapters 6-10). After going through the first half of the book, you will be very proficient in using all the main features in Outlook. The remaining chapters will take you more in depth into each of these areas and introduce you to some of the more advanced aspects of Outlook. After going through this book and practicing what you are learning, you will become the Outlook expert in your workplace, family, and neighborhood. Hopefully, that's a good thing!

Today, most people equate Microsoft Outlook with email, and these two terms have become almost synonymous in their use. Email is an integral part of Outlook, but it is much more than just email, as you will discover as you continue through this text. Most people use email on a daily basis, and Outlook is widely used in both the business and home environment to manage email accounts. It is important to remember that Outlook is not email but rather a computer software program that handles email accounts. Just as your mail carrier is not the mail itself but rather the person who delivers your mail to your home mailbox, Outlook delivers email received through your existing email account(s). You must have an email account to use Outlook to send and receive email.

Outlook allows you to create and send email, reply to received email, forward email to other recipients, save and manage email, and flag and categorize email. Email is also useful as a method of sending pictures and other types of computer files to others. Most individuals cannot imagine their daily work and personal business without the use of email.

STUDENT LEARNING OUTCOMES (SLOs)

After completing this chapter, you will be able to:

- **SLO 1.1** Identify the basic components of Microsoft Outlook 2013 (p. O1-2).
- **SLO 1.2** Navigate throughout the Outlook environment and identify the different panes in the Outlook window (p. O1-6).
- **SLO 1.3** Distinguish between Outlook being used as a stand-alone program and in a Microsoft Exchange environment (p. O1-13).
- **SLO 1.4** Distinguish between the different types of email accounts and set up an email account in Outlook (p. O1-14).
- **SLO 1.5** Use Outlook to create, send, and receive email (p. O1-17).
- **SLO 1.6** Use attachments in email (p. O1-28).
- **SLO 1.7** Differentiate email arrangements and icons (p. O1-32).
- **SLO 1.8** Explain the importance and process of cleaning up an *Inbox* (p. O1-35).

CASE STUDY

Central Sierra Insurance (CSI) is a multi-office insurance company that handles all lines of commercial and personal insurance policies. As a thriving and growing insurance agency, Central Sierra is regularly hiring qualified personnel to enhance their sales and support staff. CSI encourages its employees to be active in community organizations and events.

Pause & Practice 1-1: You set up an email account using Microsoft Outlook. You will need an email account that is provided by your school or a free email service such as Gmail.com or Outlook.com.

Pause & Practice 1-2: You send an email message to your instructor and use the *Cc* function to send a copy to yourself. You also read the message, reply to it, and print it for your records.

Pause & Practice 1-3: You reply to a message with an email attachment. You also forward the message to your instructor as an attachment and delete a message.

SLO 1.1

Working with Outlook

When most people think of or hear about Microsoft Outlook, their first thought is email. One of the main features in Outlook is handling email, but Outlook is so much more! It is personal management software that contains the following features:

- *Email*
- *Calendar*
- *Contacts*
- *Tasks*
- *Notes*
- *Journal*

Microsoft Outlook 2013 combines the email, calendar, contacts, tasks, notes, and journal features into one piece of personal management software (Figure 1-1). Each of these different features in Outlook operates as an independent piece of a personal information

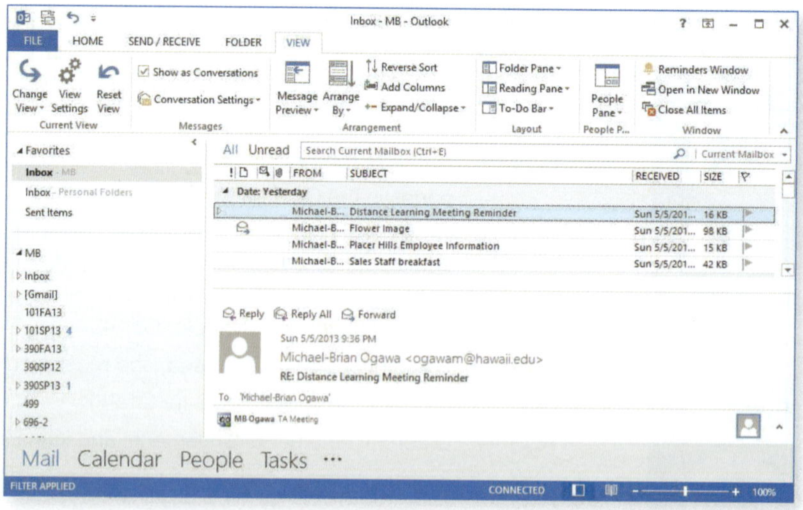

1-1 Outlook interface

management system; yet these different tasks integrate seamlessly together in Outlook. In addition, Outlook can be used in conjunction with Microsoft Word, Excel, Access, and other Microsoft products.

Email

Email is the commonly used term for ***electronic mail*** (Figure 1-2) Outlook gives users the capability of creating, sending, and receiving email. It can manage a single email account or multiple email accounts. In Outlook, email is activated by clicking on the *Mail* button.

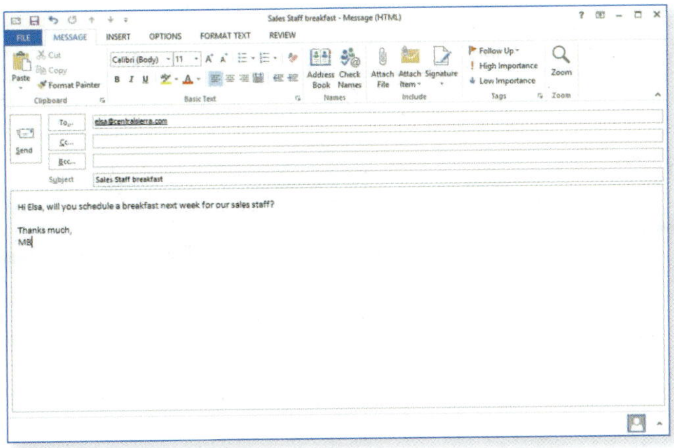

1-2 Email message

> **MORE INFO**
>
> Chapter 2 goes into more detail and covers the special email features available in Outlook. Chapter 6 discusses the use of rules for handling both incoming and outgoing email, and Chapter 7 provides the reader with information about setting up the different types of email accounts.

Calendar

Most individuals organize their daily, weekly, and monthly schedule with some type of calendar. This might be a daily planner you keep with you or a calendar that hangs on your wall at work or at home. ***Outlook Calendar*** (Figure 1-3) is an electronic calendar that makes it easy to create appointments or events, edit these items, replicate calendar items, set electronic reminders, create meeting requests, and share calendar items with other Outlook users or other devices. Additional information and details can be stored in a calendar item.

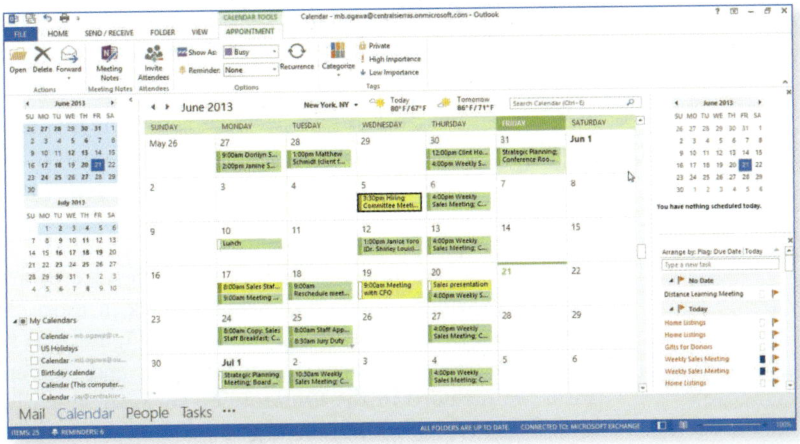

1-3 Outlook Calendar

Another advantage of an Outlook calendar is that users can synchronize their work and home calendars. As the popularity of multifunction (smart) cell phones increases, the potential to have your Outlook calendar synchronized between your work, home, and cell phone is not only a reality but also commonplace for working professionals.

> **MORE INFO**
>
> Outlook Calendar will be covered in Chapters 4 and 9 of this text.
>
> Outlook Contacts will be thoroughly covered in Chapters 3 and 8.

Contacts

Outlook also provides an area to keep names, email addresses, phone numbers, and other information about business contacts, coworkers, friends, and family. Similar to the way the Outlook calendar replaces the old paper calendar, ***Outlook Contacts*** (Figure 1-4) allows users to electronically store personal information. It functions as a database, which is a collection of information. One of the many benefits of Outlook Contacts is that it can be used without having any knowledge of the organizational structure or database.

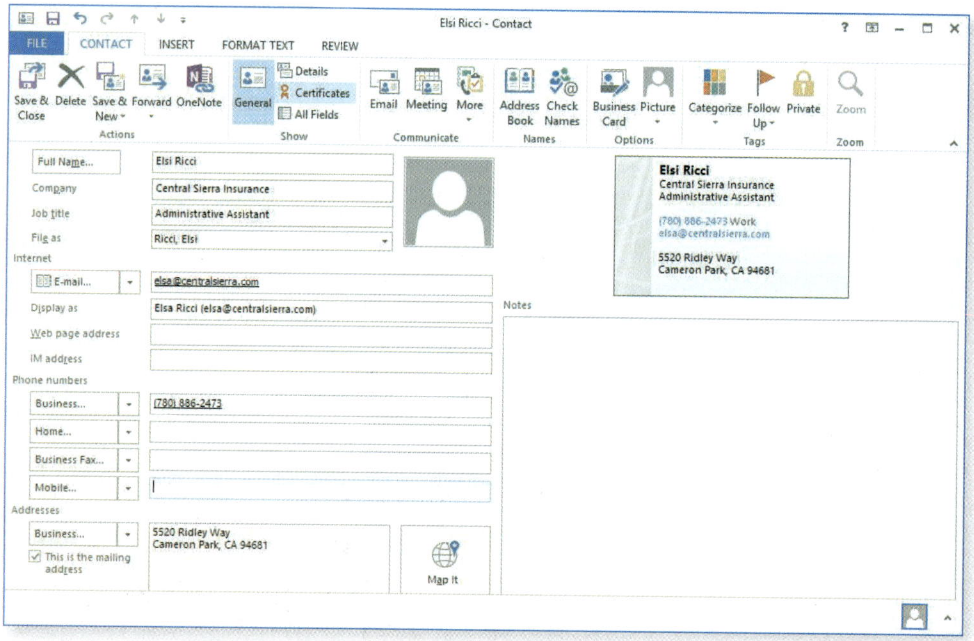

1-4 Outlook contact

Contacts are used to save personal and company information in Outlook and also when populating a recipient list in an email, meeting request, or tasks request.

Tasks

Are you a list person? Do you constantly have a list of things to get done today or this week? Outlook provides a method of keeping track of those things that need to be accomplished with the use of Outlook Tasks. The ***Tasks*** (Figure 1-5) function is very similar to a notepad that you use to write down your to-do items and then cross them off as they are completed. Tasks are included in the Outlook ***To-Do List***, which lists both tasks and emails that have been flagged for some action.

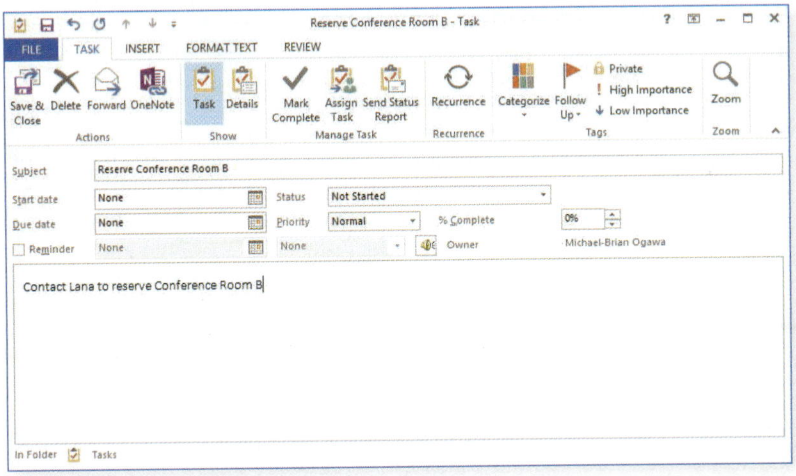

1-5 Outlook task

Some of the advantages of using Outlook Tasks are listed here:

- Tasks are electronic and can be shared between computers and cell phones.
- Many details, which are not typically written down on a piece of paper, can be added to a task.
- Reminders can be set to alert you to an upcoming due date and time for a task.
- A task can be assigned to another Outlook user.

> **MORE INFO**
>
> Outlook tasks and to-do items will be covered in Chapter 5.

Notes

Outlook Notes (Figure 1-6) are used to keep track of information that does not necessarily or neatly fall into the category of a calendar item, contact, or task. Do you ever end the day with a pocket full of scraps of paper with pieces of information written on them? Do you have sticky notes stuck to your computer monitor or refrigerator? Outlook Notes functions like electronic sticky notes—actually they look just like them. Notes are an excellent way of storing information such as a user name and password to log into a web site, gift ideas for family and friends, or a list of books you'd like to read.

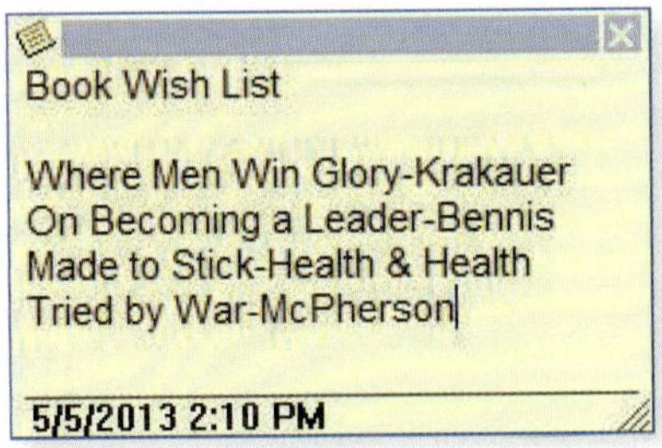

1-6 Outlook note

> **MORE INFO**
>
> Outlook Notes will be covered in Chapter 10.

Journal

Outlook Journal (Figure 1-7) is a way to keep track of the amount of time spent working on a particular document or project. The journal is primarily used in the business environment and enables you to associate specific Microsoft Office documents to a journal entry.

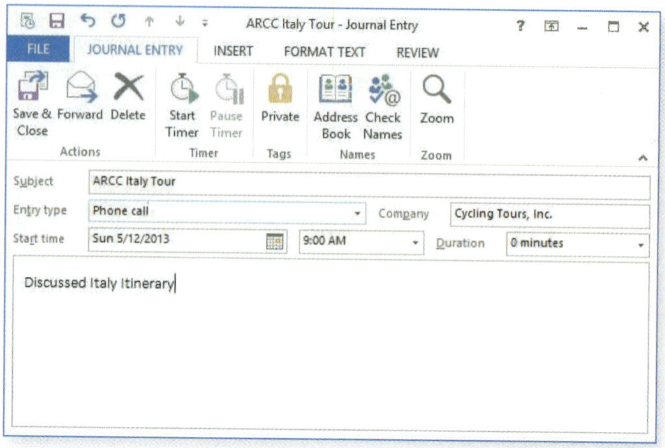

1-7 Outlook journal

MORE INFO

Chapter 10 will teach you how to use the Outlook Journal and provide you with ideas of how this feature might be used in the business setting.

SLO 1.2

Navigating Outlook

The Outlook working environment (Figure 1-8) has a much different look and feel than that of Microsoft Word, Excel, PowerPoint, and Access. The Outlook user interface is divided into multiple sections, called ***panes***. When working with different items in Outlook, you select them by clicking on each item. Selected items are typically highlighted in blue.

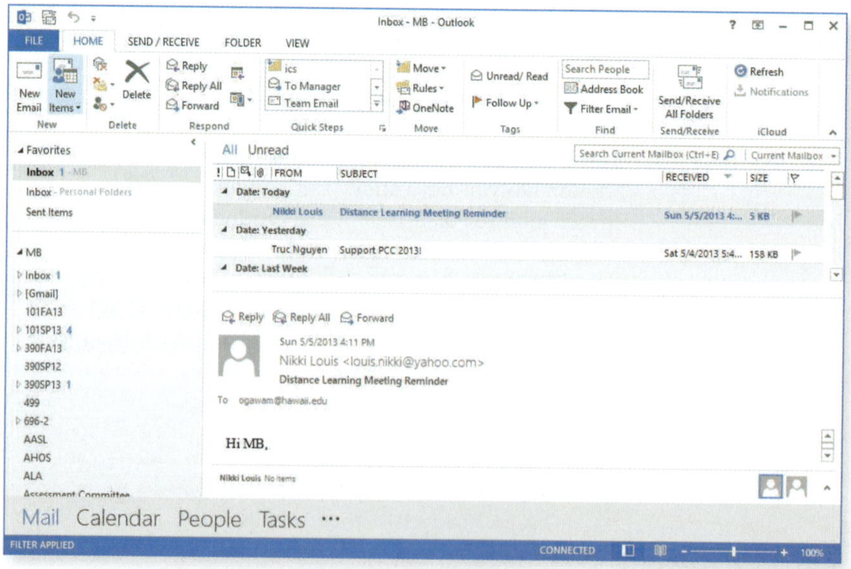

1-8 Outlook environment

As you work through this book and use Outlook, you will become familiar with the Outlook user interface and the different panes available. Outlook has provided much consistency throughout this program to allow you to quickly become comfortable navigating through its working environment.

Outlook Today

Outlook Today (Figure 1-9) is an introductory screen that will provide you with information about your Inbox and other email folders, current calendar items, and upcoming tasks. *Outlook Today* is displayed in the ***Folder pane*** and is the default view when you open Outlook each time. *Outlook Today* can be customized to meet your personal needs.

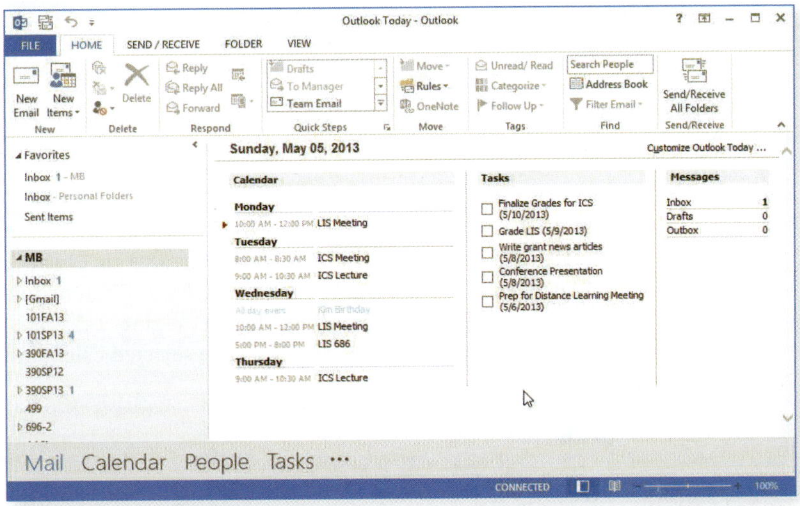

1-9 Outlook Today

> **MORE INFO**
>
> Chapter 5 will provide more information about customizing Outlook Today.

Outlook Panes

The Outlook program window is divided into four main panes: *Navigation* pane, *Folder* pane (Figure 1-10), *Reading* pane, and the new *People* pane.

Use the ***Navigation pane*** to help you navigate through the different features available in Outlook. It is located on the left side of the Outlook window, and the buttons at the bottom of the *Navigation* pane allow you to choose which task you want to work on in Outlook. The main functions in Outlook—***Mail***, ***Calendar***, ***People***, and ***Tasks***—are represented by text at the bottom of the *Navigation* pane, while the less commonly used features in Outlook—***Shortcuts***, ***Notes***, ***Folder List***, and ***Journal***—are represented by smaller icons which are visible when you click the . . . (more) button.

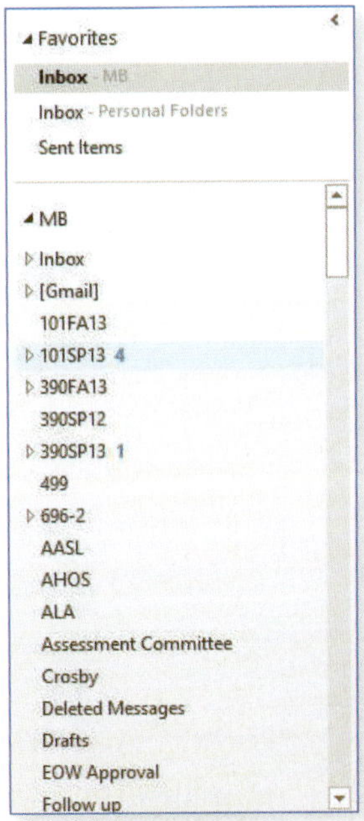

1-10 Navigation pane

ANOTHER WAY

Mail: **Ctrl+1**
Calendar: **Ctrl+2**
Contacts: **Ctrl+3**
Tasks: **Ctrl+4**
Notes: **Ctrl+5**
Folder List: **Ctrl+6**
Shortcuts: **Ctrl+7**
Journal: **Ctrl+8**

The look of the *Navigation* pane changes depending on the feature chosen, but the large and small navigation buttons at the bottom of the *Navigation* pane remain consistent. The navigation buttons can be customized to better meet your needs. This will be covered in Chapter 5. The width of the *Navigation* pane can be adjusted using the steps outlined in the following *How To* section.

HOW TO: Adjust the Width of the Navigation Pane

1. Click and hold the right border of the *Navigation* pane.
2. Drag the border to the left or right as desired.

The ***Folder pane*** is the main working area in Outlook and displays the contents of the folder selected in the *Navigation* pane. As a different folder is selected, the contents of the *Folder* pane change. The screenshot in Figure 1-11 is an example of the *Calendar* being selected in the *Navigation* pane, and the selected calendar is displayed in the *Folder* pane.

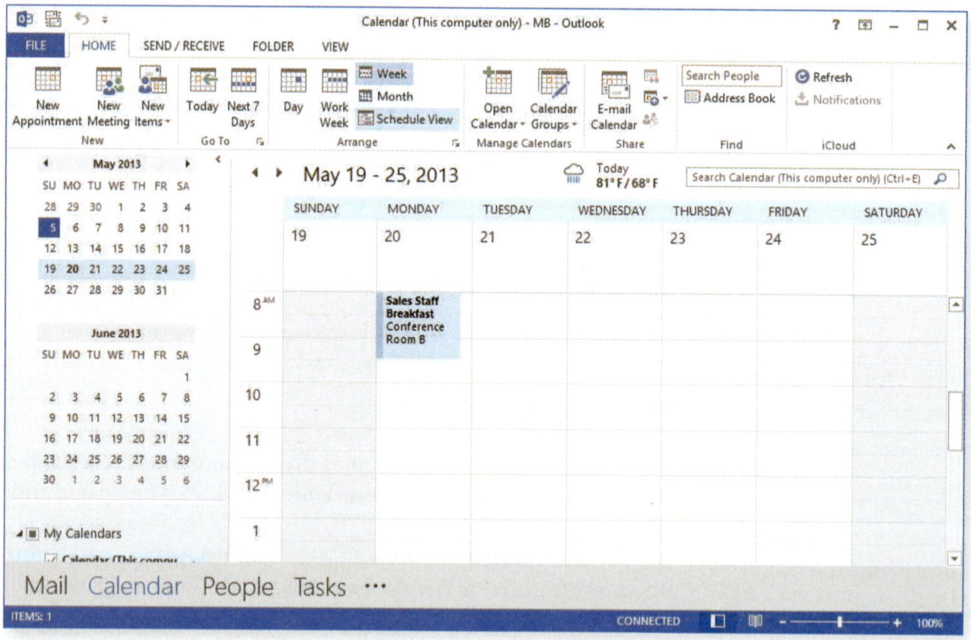

1-11 Calendar displayed in the Folder pane

The ***Reading pane*** (Figure 1-12) is an optional pane that is available in most of the different main functions in Outlook, although it is primarily used with the *Mail* feature. The *Reading* pane displays the contents of the item selected in the *Folder* pane. The *Reading* pane can be set to appear below or to the right of the *Folder* pane, or it can be turned off. The *Reading* pane will vary depending on the task (e.g., Mail, Calendar, or Contacts) selected in the *Navigation* pane.

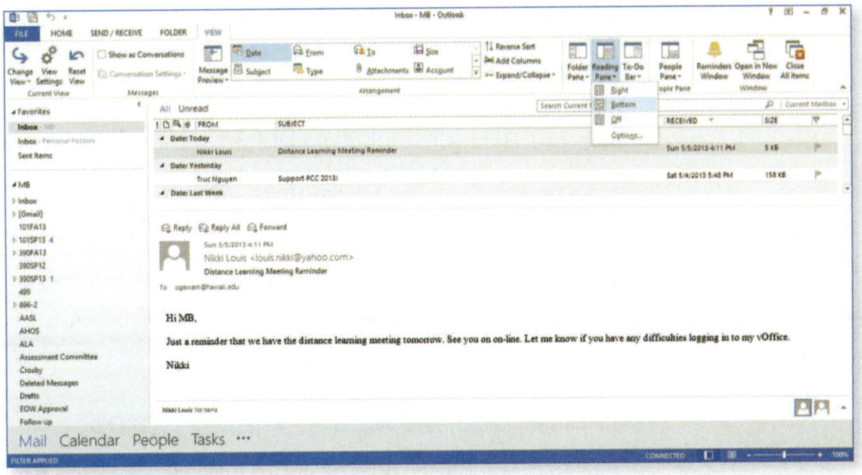

1-12 Reading pane

HOW TO: Change the Location of the Reading Pane

1. Click the **Mail** button in the *Navigation* pane.
2. Click the **View** tab.
3. In the *Layout* group, click the **Reading Pane** button.
4. Choose the desired location: *Right*, *Bottom*, or *Off* (see Figure 1-12).

The *Reading* pane can also be resized in the same manner as the *Navigation* pane. The boundary can be moved to the desired height or width by clicking and holding on the top edge (when the *Reading* pane is displayed at the bottom) or the left edge (when the *Reading* pane is displayed at the right).

The ***People pane*** (Figure 1-13) is connected with the new ***Outlook Social Connector***. The *People* pane provides a collection of information associated with the sender including communication history, meeting requests, attachments, and other social networks. The Outlook

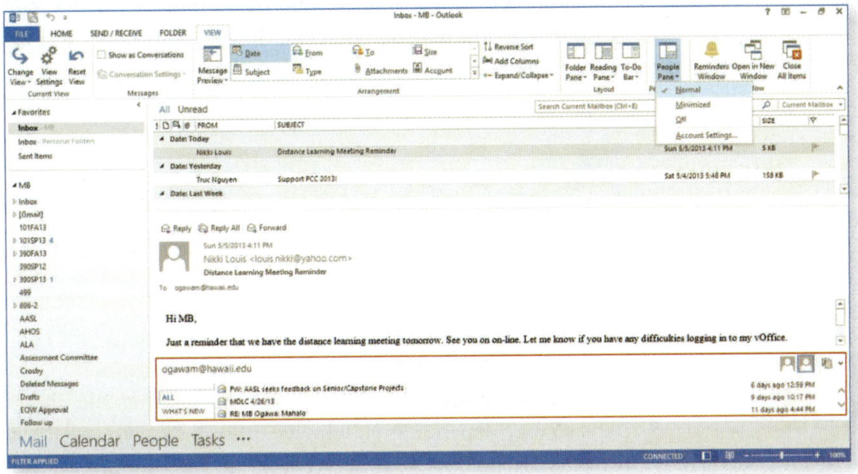

1-13 People pane

Social Connector and *People* pane also integrate with SharePoint. The *People* pane can be expanded or collapsed by clicking on the small arrow in the upper right corner of the pane.

The *People* pane is not only available in the main interface of Outlook but also on email messages, meetings, contacts, and task requests. The *People* pane helps to consolidate all activities associated with an individual into one area. The links in the *People* pane can be used to open an associated Outlook item.

MORE INFO

The *People* pane and *Outlook Social Connector* will be covered in Chapters 2 and 3.

The Ribbon, Tabs, and Dialog Boxes

The main working environment in Outlook 2013 has a ***Ribbon*** (Figure 1-14), which includes a variety of ***tabs***. The *Ribbon* appears at the top of the Outlook window and at the top of any open Outlook item (e.g., email, calendar item, contact, or task). Each tab has a variety of groups, and groups contain a variety of buttons, drop-down lists, and galleries.

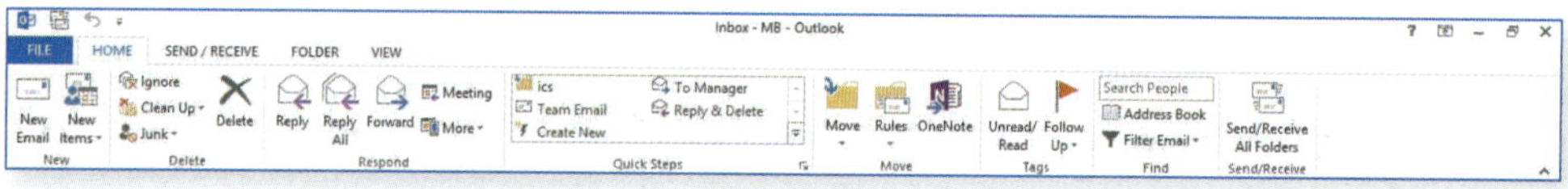

1-14 Outlook Ribbon

ANOTHER WAY

The *Ribbon* can be minimized by pressing **Ctrl+F1** or by clicking on the small up arrow in the upper right corner of the Outlook window. You can restore the *Ribbon* by pressing **Ctrl+F1** or by clicking the small up arrow in the upper right corner of the Outlook window and selecting **Show Tabs and Commands**.

When you move your pointer over a button on the *Ribbon*, ***ScreenTips*** (Figure 1-15) will appear that will tell you what that button represents and provide a shortcut key combination, if available.

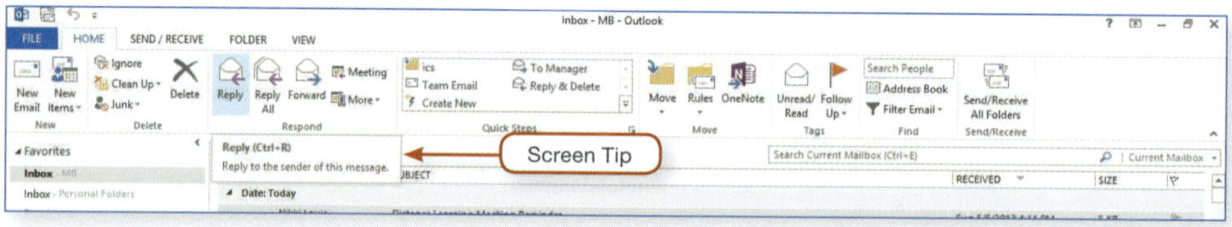

1-15 Screen Tip

Tabs are ***context sensitive***, which means that the choices of tabs and the content of the tabs change depending on which Outlook item you select. Each tab has different user features available that are divided into ***groups***. The size of the buttons in each group will vary depending on the size of the open window.

Some of the groups on each tab have a ***launcher*** button at the bottom right corner of the group. When the expand button is clicked, the ***dialog box*** (Figure 1-16) for that particular group opens. The opened dialog box contains additional options for the selected group.

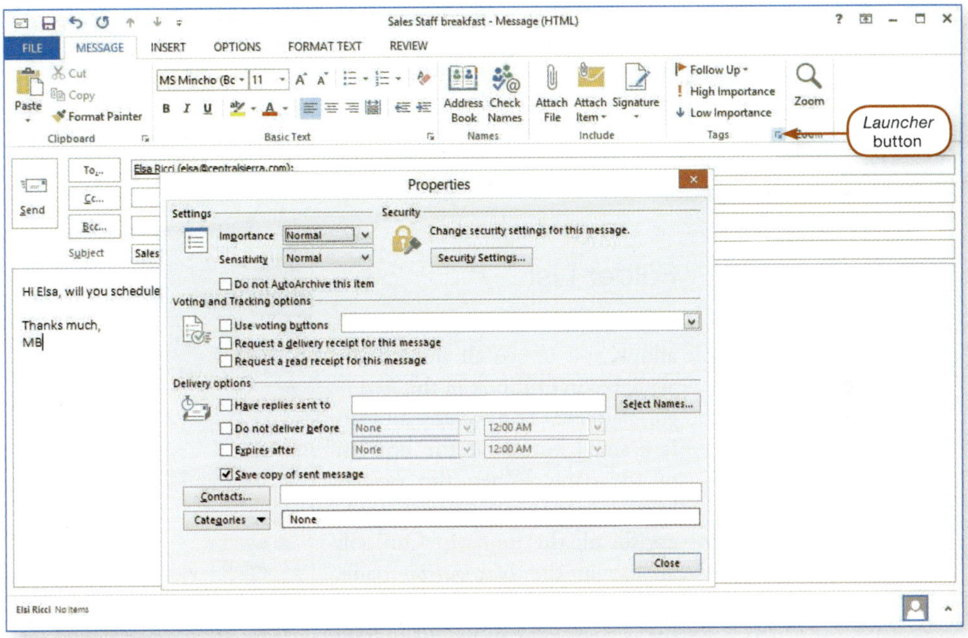

1-16 Dialog box

> **MORE INFO**
>
> The name of the dialog box is not always the same as the name of the group that was expanded. Some dialog boxes contain features that are distributed between a few groups.

> **MORE INFO**
>
> Many of the dialog boxes that you will use in Outlook 2013 are the same as or very similar to the dialog boxes used in previous versions of Outlook.

Views

Each of the different main tasks in Outlook (Mail, Calendar, Contacts, Tasks, Notes, and Journal) has numerous different preset views from which to choose, as well as the option to customize each view or create your own personal view. The selected view will control how the folder selected in the *Navigation* pane will be displayed in the *Folder* pane.

HOW TO: Change to a Different View

1. Click the **View** tab.
2. Click the **Change View** button [*Current View* group] (Figure 1-17).

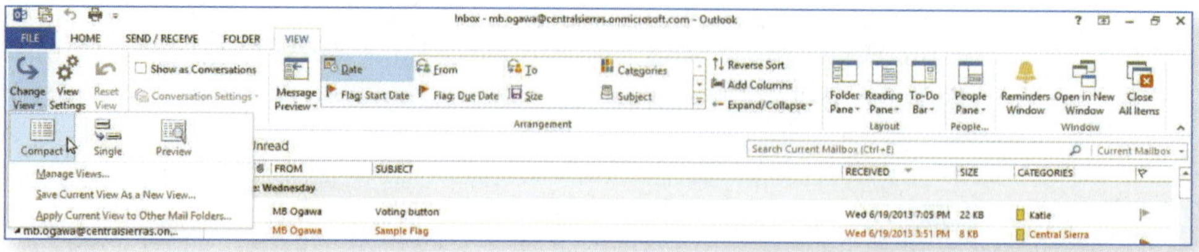

1-17 Change View button

3. Select the view you want. Notice the different views available; the different views are context sensitive.

Folder List

The ***Folder list*** (Figure 1-18) allows you to see all the folders available in Outlook in the *Navigation* pane. The *Folders* button is a small button at the bottom of the pane. When the *Folders* button is selected, all the folders for all the items in Outlook appear in the *Navigation* pane. The benefit of viewing the *Folder* list is that you can see all folders available in the folder hierarchy in which they reside, rather than viewing just one set of folders at a time. This view can be used to move folders up or down a level or can be used to drag specific items into a folder.

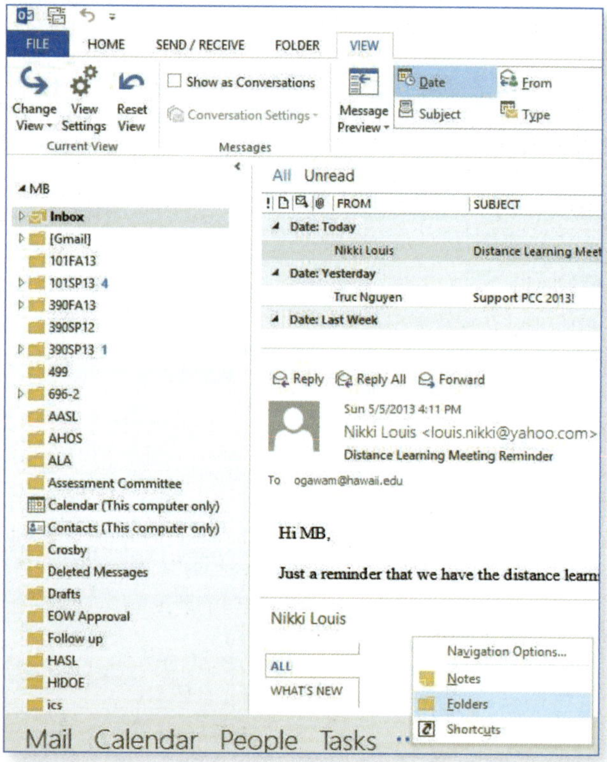

1-18 Folder list

ANOTHER WAY

Ctrl+6 displays the *Folder* list in the *Navigation* pane.

MORE INFO

The *Folder* list will be covered more thoroughly in Chapter 6 when we start using multiple folders for email, contacts, and tasks.

Outlook Help

Outlook Help (Figure 1-19) is an online search engine that is available throughout Outlook and will provide you with specific information about topics on which you might have a question or need additional information. The *Microsoft Outlook Help* button is located in the upper right corner of any open Outlook window.

When the *Outlook Help* button is clicked, the *Outlook Help* dialog box opens. You will be given the choice of either typing in keywords related to your search or choosing from a list of common Outlook topics.

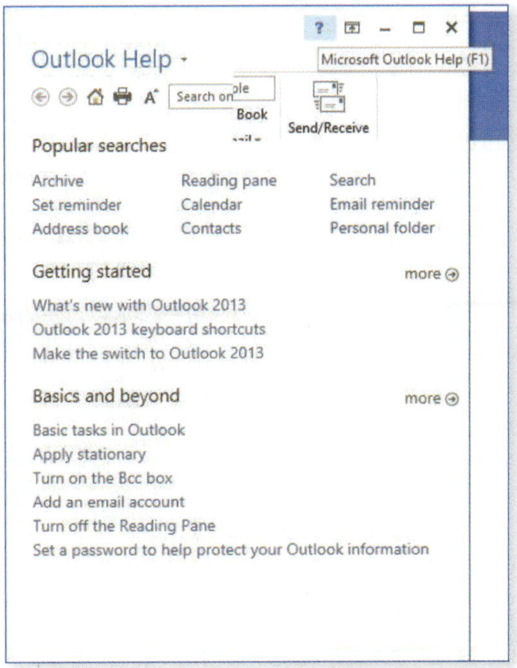

1-19 Help function

> **ANOTHER WAY**
>
> The **F1** function key on your computer keyboard opens the *Outlook Help* dialog box.

SLO 1.3

Understanding Outlook Environments

Microsoft Outlook can be used as either a ***stand-alone program*** or in conjunction with a ***Microsoft Exchange Server*** (also referred to as an Exchange server or Exchange). Many individuals use Outlook on their home computer, and this is what is meant by a stand-alone program. Outlook is still part of the Microsoft Office 2013 suite of software and is still capable of performing all the main functions of this personal management software.

Outlook as a Stand-Alone Program

When using Outlook in the home or personal environment, Outlook connects directly with your ***Internet Service Provider*** (***ISP***) and manages your email through the accounts you set up. Outlook can handle a single email account or multiple email accounts. Some of the more advanced and specialty features in Outlook are only available when Outlook is used in conjunction with Exchange.

> **MORE INFO**
>
> Chapter 1 will show you how to set up an email account in Outlook. Managing multiple email accounts will be covered in Chapter 7.

Outlook in an Exchange Environment

In the business environment, Microsoft Outlook is typically connected to a ***Microsoft Exchange Server***. Exchange on a business network handles all the incoming and outgoing mail. Each individual user of Exchange is actually a client of this Exchange network, and the network administrator sets up an account for each individual user. In addition to handling email, Exchange also stores all the data associated with calendars, contacts, tasks, notes, and journals.

Outlook in an Exchange environment has the same user interface as in a stand-alone environment, but Outlook with an Exchange server does allow you more functionality. Some of the enhanced features an Exchange server will enable you to perform include:

- Using voting buttons and tracking responses
- Sending meeting requests and tracking responses
- Recalling messages
- Sharing your calendar, contacts, tasks, and email with others
- Using *MailTips*
- Using a common global contact list

MORE INFO

As you progress through this book, you will be informed when Outlook performs functions differently when using Outlook as a stand-alone program or with Exchange. Also, Appendix D provides a summary of Outlook features unique to an Exchange environment.

SLO 1.4

Adding an Email Account in Outlook

Multiple email accounts can be set up in Outlook. In previous versions of Outlook, only one Exchange account could be connected, but Outlook 2013 gives you the ability to set up multiple Exchange accounts. There are four different types of email accounts that can be set up in Outlook, and Outlook provides you with an ***Auto Account Setup Wizard*** to walk you through the process of adding an email account to Outlook.

Types of Email Accounts

Microsoft Exchange accounts are used primarily in medium- to large-business settings. These email accounts are set up through the company network or email administrator. An Exchange account has an individual mailbox assigned to each user and resides on an Exchange file server. Outlook connects to the Exchange server to retrieve your email. Exchange accounts use Messaging Application Programming Interface (MAPI) and provide enhanced functionality when used with Outlook. Recalling messages, tracking voting responses, and sharing Outlook with others on your Exchange system are features that are associated with Exchange accounts and Outlook.

POP3 accounts are Internet email accounts that are associated with your Internet service provider (ISP). If you have an ISP such as Comcast or AT&T, you will have an email account (or multiple email accounts) through your provider. This POP3 account can be set up in Outlook to send and receive email. When using Outlook with this type of account, your email messages are downloaded to Outlook.

IMAP accounts are also Internet accounts but are not always associated with an ISP. IMAP accounts create folders on a server to store and organize messages for retrieval by other computers and give you the options to read message headers only and to select which messages to download. These types of accounts are becoming increasingly popular as personal email accounts. Gmail is an example of an IMAP email account.

HTTP accounts use the hypertext transfer protocol used on the web to create, view, send, and receive messages. This type of account is not automatically supported by Outlook but can be configured by installing an add-in. Windows Live Mail is an HTTP account that can be configured to work with Outlook by using the MSN Connector for Outlook.

Add an Email Account

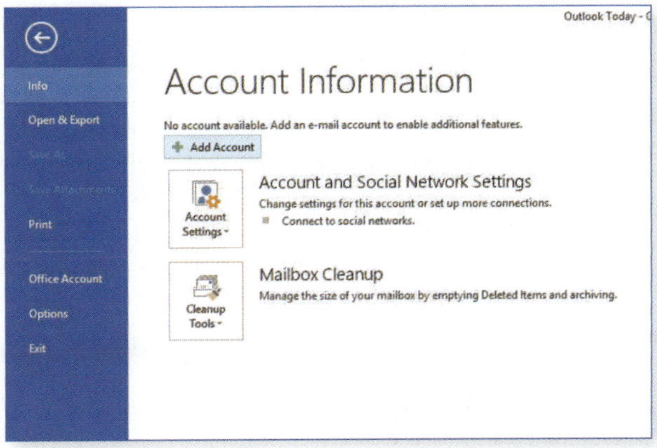

1-20 Account set up

To create, send, and receive email, Outlook must be set up to recognize your email account. In the past, it has been a challenge to get all the specific information needed to set up an email account, but beginning with Outlook 2007, an ***Auto Account Setup*** (Figure 1-20) feature was added to automatically detect the incoming and outgoing server.

To set up your account, you will need to supply your email address and password to access the account. This will give Outlook the location of your Exchange or Internet mailbox, and your password provides access to the account. An account only needs to be set up once, and it will be stored in Outlook for future use.

> **MORE INFO**
>
> The first time you open Outlook, you will be prompted to set up an account. The *Add New Account* dialog box automatically opens for you.
>
> Outlook will automatically detect the type of email account being configured.

HOW TO: Set Up an Email Account

1. Click the **File** tab. The *Backstage* view opens.
2. Click the **Add Account** button. The *Add Account* dialog box opens (Figure 1-21).

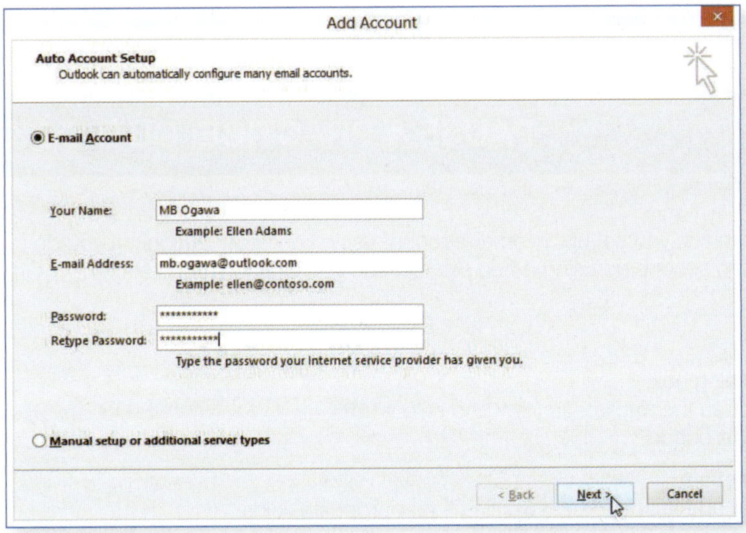

1-21 Add account dialog box

3. Enter the following account settings in the text boxes:
   - *Your Name* (as you want it to appear in email)
   - *E-mail Address*

- *Password*
- *Retype Password*

4. Click **Next**.
5. Outlook will automatically detect your email account and validate it with your password. Three green check marks display when your account has been configured properly (Figure 1-22).
6. Click **Finish** and you're ready to use Outlook.

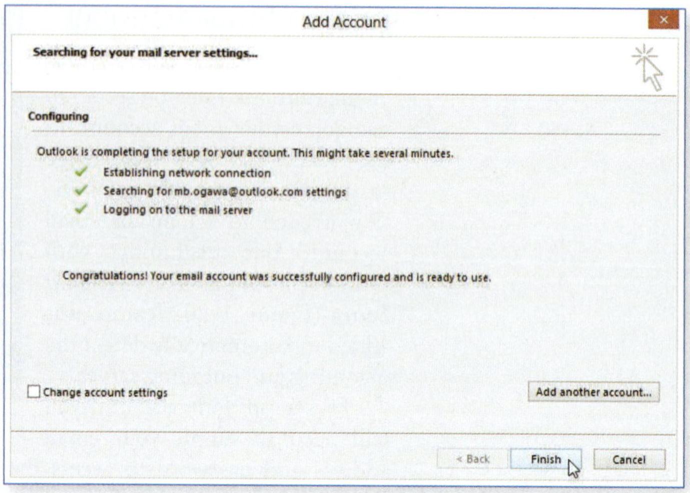

1-22 Successful configuration of an account

MORE INFO

Chapter 7 will provide additional information on setting up multiple email accounts.

ANOTHER WAY

An email account can be added to Outlook when Outlook is closed by clicking on **Mail** and then on **Email Accounts** in your computer's *Control Panel.*

PAUSE & PRACTICE: OUTLOOK 1-1

For this Pause and Practice project, you set up an email account using Microsoft Outlook. If you do not have an email account, you can set one up using a free service, such as Outlook (outlook.com) or Gmail (gmail.com).

1. Launch Outlook 2013.
2. Open the *Add Account* dialog box.
   a. Click the **File** tab to open the *Backstage* view and select **Info**.
   b. Click the **Add Account** button.
3. Input your account information.
   a. Type your name, email address, and password in the appropriate fields.
   b. Click **Next**.
   c. If you are using a school email account, you may need to contact your system administrator for the manual setup information.

SLO 1.5

Creating, Sending, and Receiving Email

Creating and sending an email message is very similar to sending a letter—just much easier and quicker! You select recipients, type the subject of the message, type the message, and send—no stamp or going to the post office.

> **ANOTHER WAY**
>
> **Ctrl+N** opens a new email message when you are in Outlook *Mail*.

Create New Email

To create a new email message, make sure the *Mail* button (Figure 1-23) is selected in the *Navigation* pane and then click the **New Email** button in the *New* group on the *Home* tab. Outlook opens a new email message (Figure 1-24).

> **MORE INFO**
>
> When you click the **New** button or press **Ctrl+N**, Outlook creates a new item of the task selected in Outlook. For example, if you select *Calendar* in the *Navigation* pane and click **New**, you get a new calendar appointment.

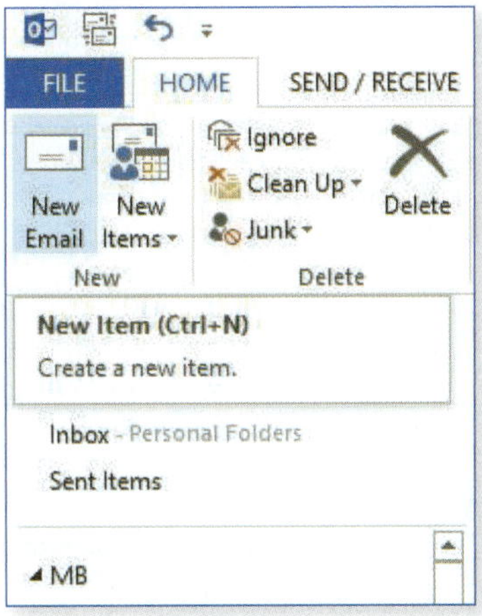

1-23 New mail button

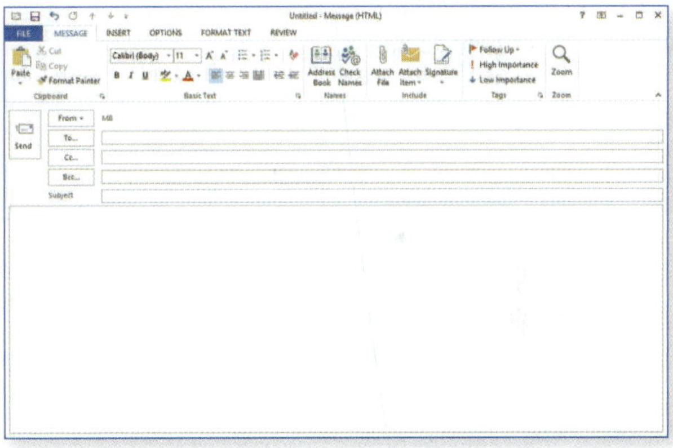

1-24 New email message

Select Recipients

An email message can be sent to one recipient or multiple recipients. You can type the email address into the *To* field or click the **To** button and select from your *Contact* list. If you are typing in the email addresses, separate each email address with a semicolon (;).

When you click the *To* button (Figure 1-25), Outlook opens your *Contacts*. A single recipient can be chosen or multiple recipients can be selected.

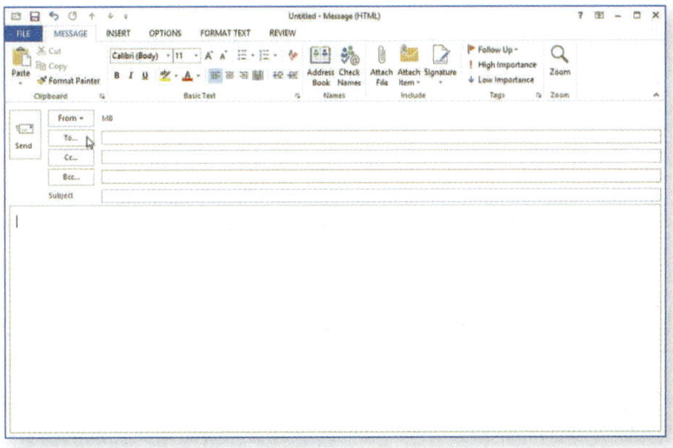

1-25 Select the **To** button

HOW TO: Select Recipients

1. Click the **Mail** button in the *Navigation* pane.
2. Click the **New Email** button to open a new email message.
3. Click the **To** button on the new email message. The *Select Names* dialog box opens.
   - You can also type in an email address in the *To* field.
4. Select recipient(s) (Figure 1-26).

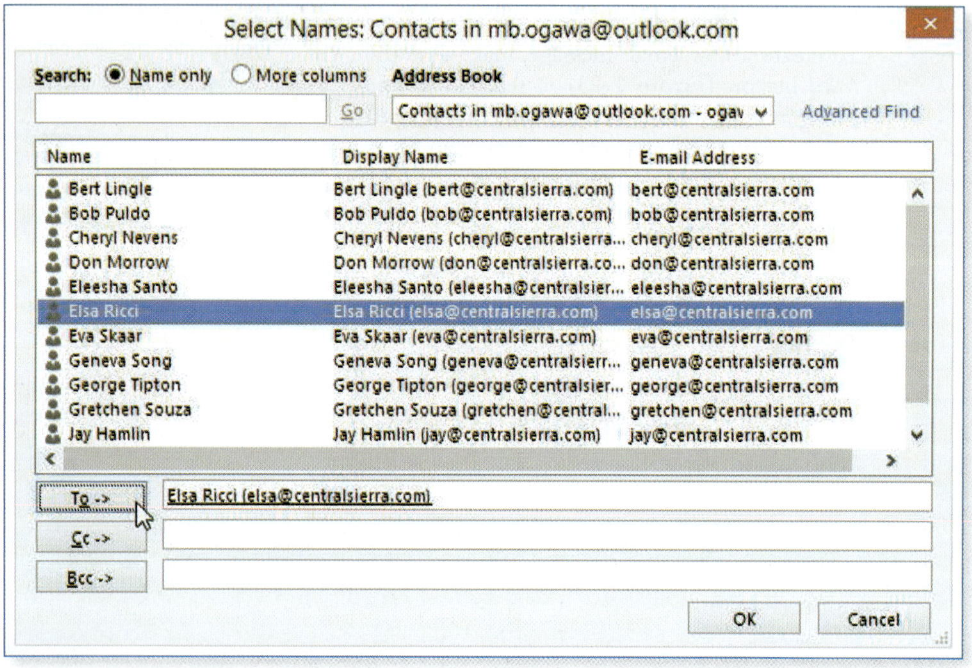

1-26 Select recipients from contacts list

5. Click the **To** button below the names.
6. Click **OK** to close the *Select Names* dialog box.

ANOTHER WAY

When selecting multiple recipients from the contact list, holding down the **Ctrl** key while clicking allows you to select nonadjacent entries. Using the **Shift** key allows you to select a range of recipients. Click the first item in the range, hold down the **Shift** key, and select the last item in the range. These shortcuts are common throughout many of the Microsoft Office applications.

Cc and Bcc

There are two other options that are available when selecting recipients for your email message: ***Carbon Copy*** (*Cc*) and ***Blind carbon copy*** (*Bcc*) (Figure 1-27). *Cc* is used when someone is not the main recipient of the message, but they need to be kept informed of the contents of the message or ongoing email discussion.

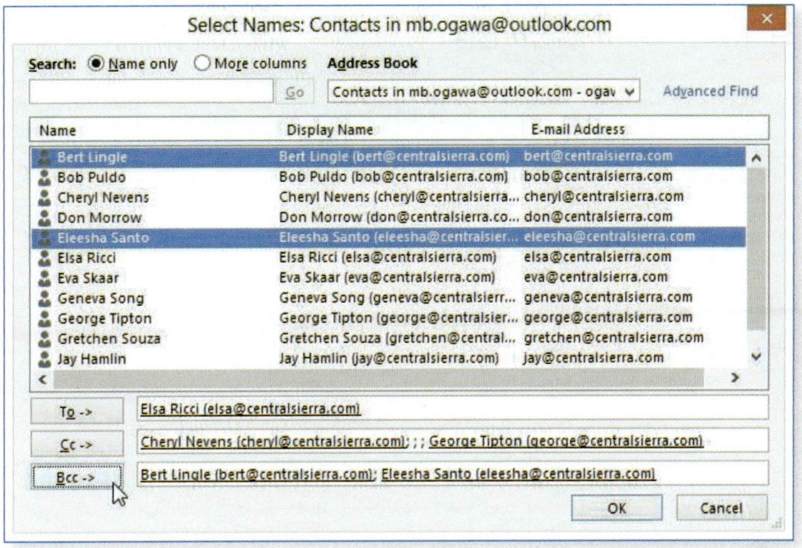

1-27 Select recipients in the Cc and Bcc fields

Bcc is used when you do not want those receiving the email message to see other recipients' email addresses or names (Figure 1-28). When a recipient receives an email, he or she will be able to see other recipients' names and email addresses in both the *To* and *Cc* fields, but the *Bcc* field is hidden.

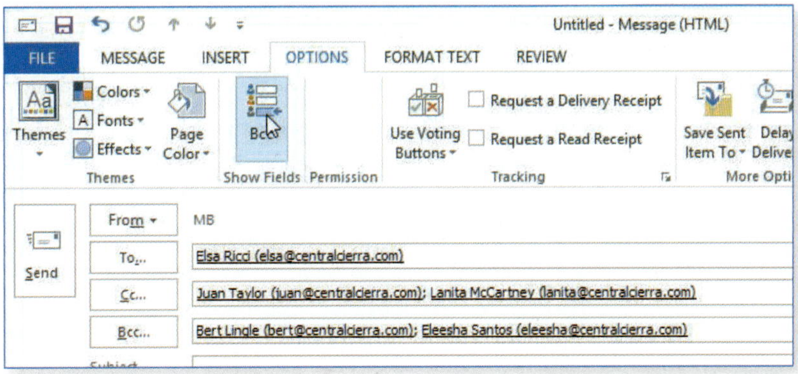

1-28 Select the Bcc option

MORE INFO

Be careful about sharing email addresses with those outside of your organization. *Bcc* is a great feature to provide confidentiality in email by hiding others' email addresses. To send an email, there must be at least one recipient in one of the recipient fields.

The *Cc* button appears on a new message and can be used like the *To* button to select recipients. By default, the *Bcc* button or field is not available when you open a new email message. You can click either the *To* or *Cc* button to open the *Select Names* dialog box. Once this dialog box is open, the *Bcc* field is available.

ANOTHER WAY

In a new email message, click the **Options** tab and then click the **Bcc** button in the *Show Fields* group. *Bcc* recipients can now be selected by clicking on the **Bcc** button (Figure 1-29).

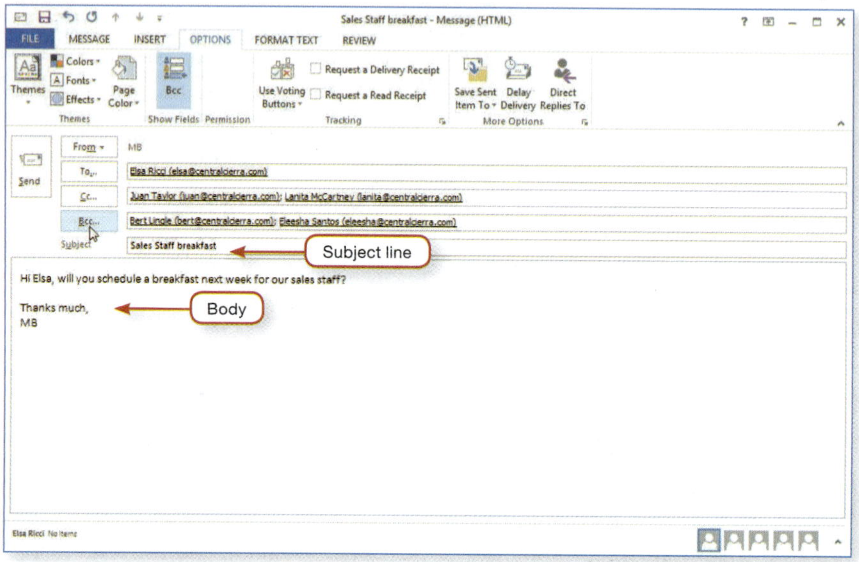

1-29 Select the Bcc button

Subject Line and Body

The ***Subject line*** alerts recipients to the subject of the email, and the ***body*** contains the contents of the email (Figure 1-29). When a new email message is created, the email is untitled (top center), but once a subject is typed in, it becomes the message title.

MORE INFO

Use a subject line on every email, and keep it short and descriptive. Your subject line might determine whether or not your message gets read.

Format Text

Outlook provides users with many of the same formatting features that are available in Microsoft Word. These text formatting features can be used in the body of the email message. Many of the commonly used formatting features are available on the *Message* tab in the *Basic Text* group (Figure 1-30). This *Basic Text* group can be expanded (by clicking the small box in the bottom right corner of the group) to open the *Font* dialog box.

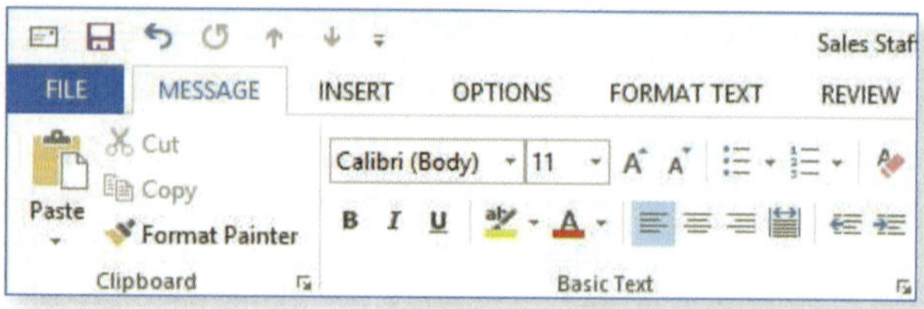

1-30 Formatting options

More formatting options are available by clicking on the *Format Text* tab, which opens this tab for additional formatting features (Figure 1-31).

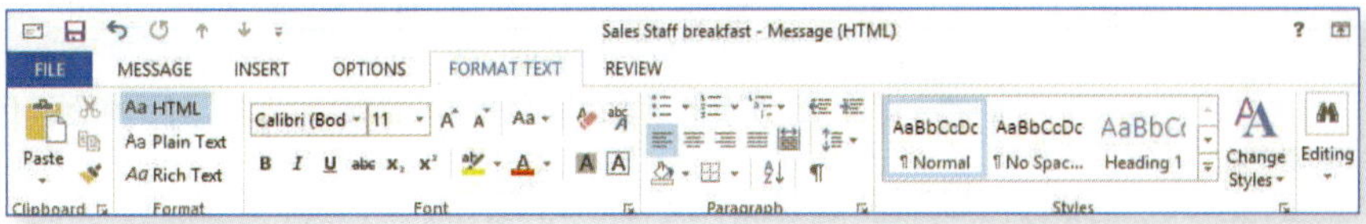

1-31 Additional formatting options

> **MORE INFO**
>
> Don't overuse text formatting in the body of an email message. Depending on the type of email account the recipient has, some of the text formatting might not be visible to the recipient.

Send an Email

Once you select your recipients and type in the subject and body of the email, you are ready to send the email message. Click the **Send** button to the left of the *To* and *Cc* buttons and your email message will be sent. A copy of it will be automatically saved in the ***Sent Items*** folder in your *Folder* list.

HOW TO: Send an Email Message

1. Click the **New Email** button [*Home* tab, *New* group]. A new email message opens in a new window.
2. Click the **To** button and select the names or email addresses from the *Select Names* dialog box. You can also add recipients to the *Cc* and *Bcc* fields.
3. Click **OK**. The email addresses will appear in the *To*, *Cc*, and/or *Bcc* fields.
4. Type a brief subject in the *Subject* field.
5. Type a brief message in the body of the message. Remember to always include your name in the body of the email.
6. Click **Send** (Figure 1-32).

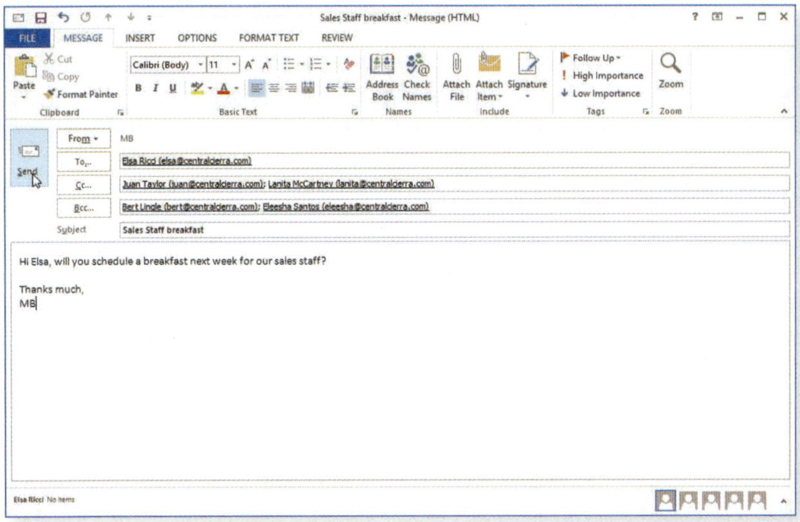

1-32 Sample email message

> **MORE INFO**
>
> Be careful about the information you include in an email message. An email can easily be forwarded to others, which can have ethical and confidentiality implications.

Save an Email Draft

If you are working on an email and do not have time to finish it or would like to look it over later before sending it, you can save and close the message and it will be available for later use. When you save a message in Outlook, it is kept in the ***Drafts*** folder in the *Folder* list.

To save an unfinished message, click the **Save** button on the ***Quick Access*** toolbar or press **Ctrl+S**. Microsoft Office Outlook automatically saves all unfinished messages for you. By default, unfinished messages are saved to your *Drafts* folder every three minutes (Figure 1-33). You can, however, change this time interval or location.

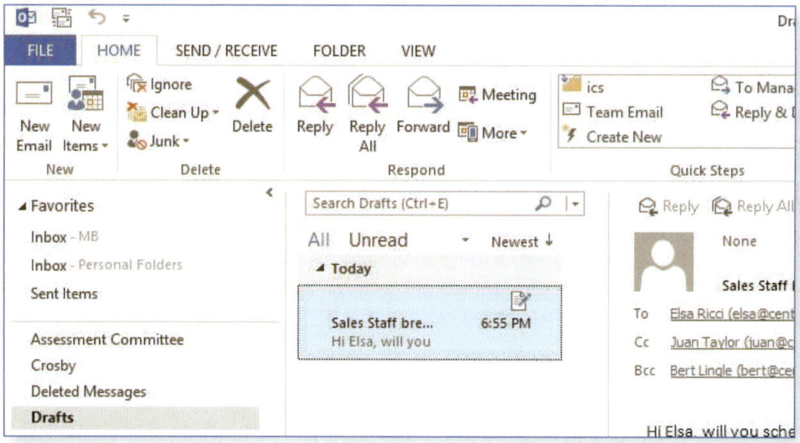

1-33 Saved draft message

> **MORE INFO**
>
> Changing the default time interval for saving drafts will be covered in Chapter 7.

Open an Email

When you open an email, it opens into a new window. To open an email in your Inbox, double-click the message; the message opens in a new window. Outlook provides users with a *Reading* pane, which allows the message to be read without opening it in a new window. To view the message in the *Reading* pane, click once on the message in the *Folder* pane and the contents of the message will be displayed in the *Reading* pane (either to the right or at the bottom).

> **ANOTHER WAY**
>
> **Ctrl+O** opens a selected email from the *Folder* or *Reading* pane in a new window.

> **MORE INFO**
>
> Throughout this text when you are asked to open an email, use a new window; do not just view it in the *Reading* pane. Double-click an email in the *Folder* pane to open it.

Reply, Reply All, and Forward

When responding to an email, you have three main options: *Reply*, *Reply All*, and *Forward*. ***Reply*** allows you to send a message to the original sender (Figure 1-34). ***Reply All*** will let you send a response to the sender and the other email recipients (those in the *To* and *Cc* lines). ***Forward*** will enable you to forward the email message you received to recipients of your choice.

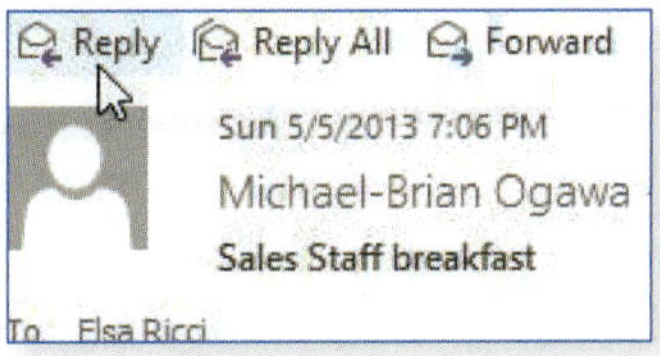

1-34 Reply to a message

Unlike previous versions, Outlook 2013 creates replies and forwarded messages within the Outlook window. If you prefer to write replies in a new window, click the **Pop Out** button in the reply message.

Both *Reply* and *Reply All* will keep the same body and subject line. The body text will be moved down to make room for your message, and the subject will be preceded by "RE:" to indicate this email is a reply. Either the original sender (*Reply*) or the sender and other recipients (*Reply All*) will automatically be in the *To* or *Cc* lines. The difference when using *Forward* is the *To* field will be empty and the subject will include "FW:" in front of the subject (Figure 1-35).

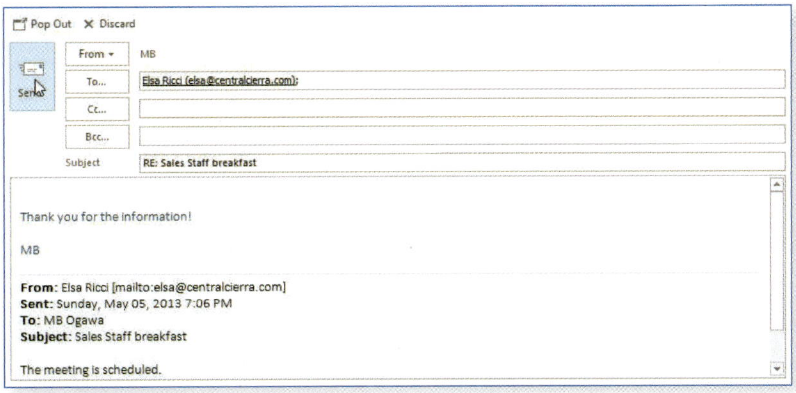

1-35 Sample reply message

To use any of the response options, open the email and choose either *Reply*, *Reply All*, or *Forward*.

> **ANOTHER WAY**
>
> *Reply:* **Ctrl+R**
> *Reply All:* **Ctrl+Shift+R**
> *Forward:* **Ctrl+F**

> **MORE INFO**
>
> When viewing a message in the *Folder* or *Reading* pane, the *Reply*, *Reply All*, and *Forward* buttons are located in the *Respond* group on the *Home* tab. Clicking on any of these buttons opens the message.

> **MORE INFO**
>
> Use *Reply All* sparingly and only when it is absolutely necessary, Don't unnecessarily clutter up others' email Inboxes.

Save an Email in a Windows Folder

When an email message is sent, the original message remains in your Inbox and a copy of the response is automatically saved in the *Sent Items* folder. There might be times when you want to save an important or sensitive email message outside of Outlook. You can save email messages to a different folder on your computer.

HOW TO: Save an Email in a Windows Folder

1. Either click the message to be saved in the *Folder* pane or open the message in a new window.
2. Click the **File** tab. The *Backstage* view opens.
3. Click the **Save As** button to open the *Save As* dialog box (Figure 1-36).
4. Browse to the desired location to save the file.
   - By default, the *File name* will be the subject line of the email. You can change this as desired.
5. Click the **Save** button.

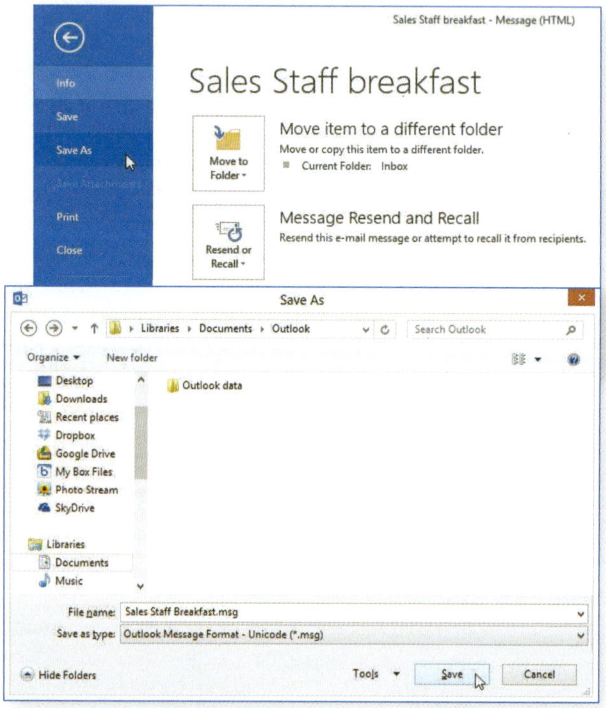

1-36 Save a message

> **ANOTHER WAY**
>
> **F12** opens the *Save As* dialog box.

Print an Email

If you are on your way to a meeting and need some information from an email in your Inbox, you might want to print the email to take with you. Also, you might want to print the contents of one of your Inbox folders. The *Print* option in Outlook allows you to print either an individual email in ***Memo Style*** or the contents of a folder in ***Table Style***.

HOW TO: Print an Email

1. Select the email or folder to be printed.
2. Click the **File** tab to open the *Backstage* view.

3. Click the **Print** button (Figure 1-37).
4. Select the type of printout you would like in the *Print What* area.
5. Click the **Print** button.

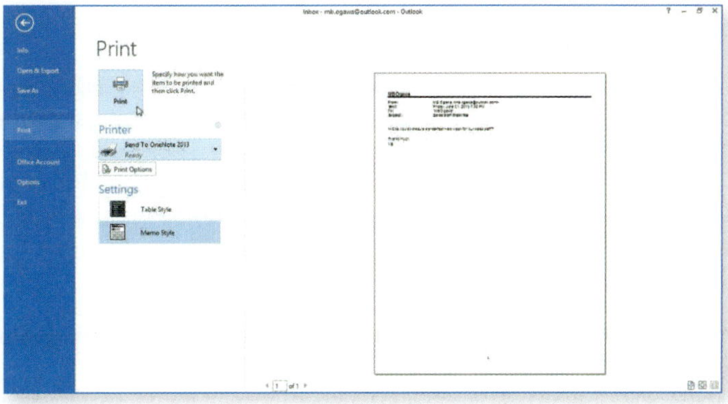

1-37 Print a message

ANOTHER WAY

Ctrl+P opens the *Print* area on the *Backstage* view.

Recall an Email Message

Have you ever sent a message and realized, after you pressed the *Send* button, that you omitted information, included incorrect information, or forgot to include an attachment? Outlook provides us imperfect users with a ***Recall*** feature (Figure 1-38) that allows you to recall a message and gives the option of replacing it with a new message.

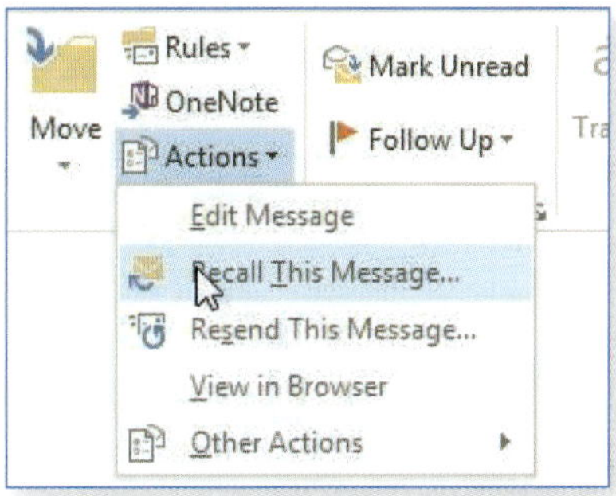

1-38 Recall This Message

HOW TO: Recall an Email Message

1. Locate and open the message to be recalled in your *Sent Items* folder.
2. Click the **Actions** button [*Message* tab, *Move* group].
3. Choose **Recall This Message**. The *Recall This Message* dialog box opens (Figure 1-39).
4. You are given the option to *Delete unread copies of this message* or *Delete unread copies and replace with a new message*. Outlook will also track this action to let you know if the recall was successful.
5. Select one of the options and click **OK**.
   - If you are just deleting unread copies, Outlook performs the recall.
   - If you are replacing the email message with a new one, the original message opens so you can modify it. Press **Send** after editing the message to perform the recall and replace the original message with the new one.

1-39 Recall This Message dialog box

This Outlook feature will only work when used in conjunction with an Exchange server. Assuming the original message has not been read, the original message is deleted and the recipient is informed that you, the sender, deleted the message from his or her mailbox. If you are replacing the original message with a new one, the original message will be deleted when the *Recall* message is opened. The recall will fail if the recipient opens the original message before it is deleted or opened before the recall message. If you have selected the *Tell me if recall succeeds or fails for each recipient* check box, you will receive an email notification in your Inbox informing you of the recall status.

MORE INFO

If you are recalling a message that was sent to a large number of recipients, you will not want to select the **Tell me if recall succeeds or fails for each recipient** check box. If you do select it, your Inbox will be filled with recall success/failure notifications.

Resend an Email Message

Resending a message is useful if you want to resend a previously sent message. If someone did not receive your original message or if you want to send the same message to new recipients, you can resend a previously sent message rather than creating and sending a new message. The process to resend a message is similar to recalling a message.

HOW TO: Resend an Email Message

1. Locate and open the message to be resent in your *Sent Items* folder.
2. Click the **Actions** button [*Message* tab, *Move* group].
3. Choose **Resend This Message** (Figure 1-40).
4. Select recipients to receive the message.
5. Click **OK**.

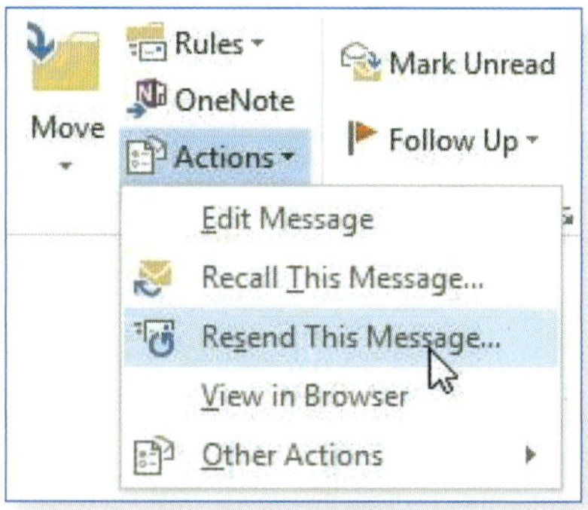

1-40 Resend This Message

ANOTHER WAY

You can also recall or resend an email message by opening the message and clicking on the **File** tab where both the recall and resend options are available on the *Backstage*.

PAUSE & PRACTICE: OUTLOOK 1-2

For this Pause and Practice project, you send an email message to your instructor and use the *Cc* function to send a copy to yourself. You also read the message, reply to it, and print it for your records.

1. Click the **Mail** button in the *Navigation pane*.
2. Create a new email message by clicking the **New Email** button [*Home* tab, *New* group].
3. Enter the following information in the email message fields:

   To: [your instructor's email address]

   CC: [your email address]

   Subject: Central Sierra Information Request

   Body: Hi Don, could you please email me the latest employee information sheet when you have a chance?

   Thank you,

   [your name]
4. Click the **Send** button to send the message.
5. View the message you sent in your Sent Items folder using the *Reading* pane.
   a. Select the message.
   b. Select the *Right* or *Bottom Reading* pane based on your preference [*View* tab, *Layout* group, *Reading Pane* button].
6. Reply to the message.
   a. Click the **Reply** button [*Message* tab, *Respond* group].
   b. Click in the body section of the message and type the following:

   I will look it up and send it to you as soon as I retrieve it.

   [your name]

   c. Click the **Send** button.
7. Print the reply message.
   a. Select the reply message in your Inbox.
   b. Click the **Print** button [*File* tab, *Backstage* view].
8. Print the reply message.
   a. Select the reply message in *Sent Items* folder.
   b. Click the **Print** button [*File* tab, *Backstage* view].
9. Submit the printed copy to your instructor (Figure 1-41).

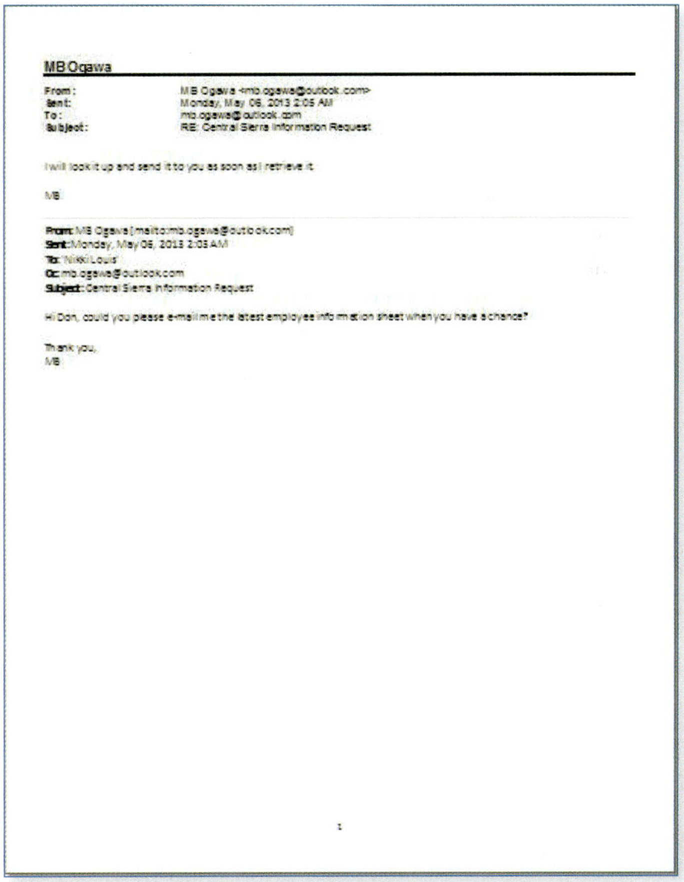
MB Ogawa

From: MB Ogawa <mb.ogawa@outlook.com>
Sent: Monday, May 06, 2013 2:05 AM
To: mb.ogawa@outlook.com
Subject: RE: Central Sierra Information Request

I will look it up and send it to you as soon as I retrieve it.

MB

From: MB Ogawa [mailto:mb.ogawa@outlook.com]
Sent: Monday, May 06, 2013 2:03 AM
To: 'Nikki Louis'
Cc: mb.ogawa@outlook.com
Subject: Central Sierra Information Request

Hi Don, could you please e-mail me the latest employee information sheet when you have a chance?

Thank you,
MB

1-41 Completed Pause & Practice 1-2

SLO 1.6

Handling Attachments

One of the many benefits of email is that a file or multiple files can easily be attached to and sent with an email. Pictures, Word documents, and many other types of files can be attached to an email.

Attach a File

You can attach a file to an email message by clicking on the **Attach File** button (Figure 1-42) on the *Message* tab in the *Include* group.

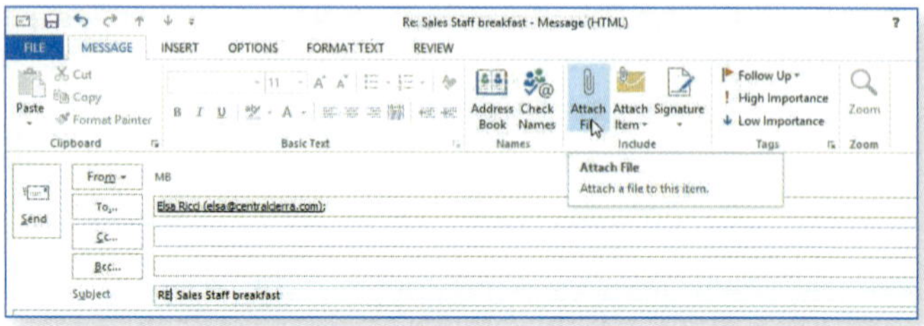

1-42 Attach File button

There are some types of files and objects that cannot be attached to email. Microsoft Access database files and entire folders cannot be attached to an email message. One way to get around this limitation is to ***compress*** or ***zip*** the files or folders and then attach the compressed (zipped) file.

I have sent numerous email messages asking my recipients to refer to an attachment. However, I did not always remember to attach the referenced document to my message. New in 2013, is the ***Attachment Reminder*** feature. If you forgot to attach a file and reference an attachment in your email message, Outlook will warn you. An *Attachment Reminder* will pop up and allow you to select *Don't Send* or *Send Anyway*. This ensures you attach files to email messages. Selecting *Don't Send* will return you to your message, while selecting *Send Anyway* will send your message as is (Figure 1-43).

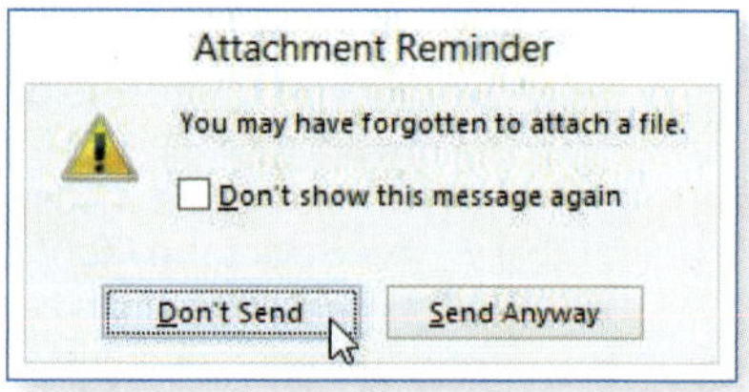

1-43 Attachment Reminder

HOW TO: Attach a File

1. When creating, replying to, or forwarding an email, click the **Attach File** button [*Message* tab, *Include* group].
2. Browse through the files on your computer (Figure 1-44).
3. Select the files. The **Ctrl** and **Shift** keys can be used to select multiple files.
4. Click **Insert**. The attached files will appear below the subject line (Figure 1-45).

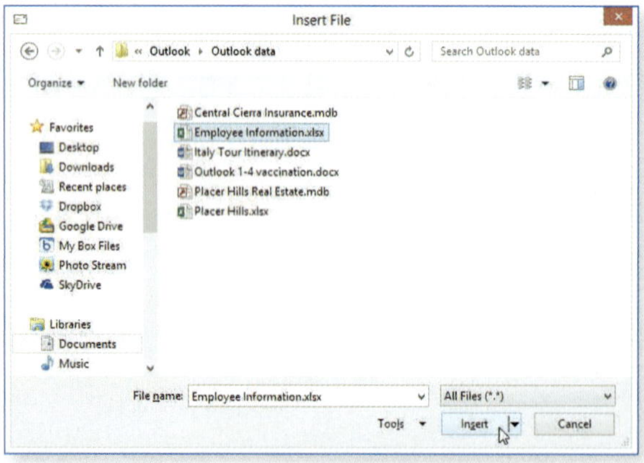

1-44 Insert File dialog box

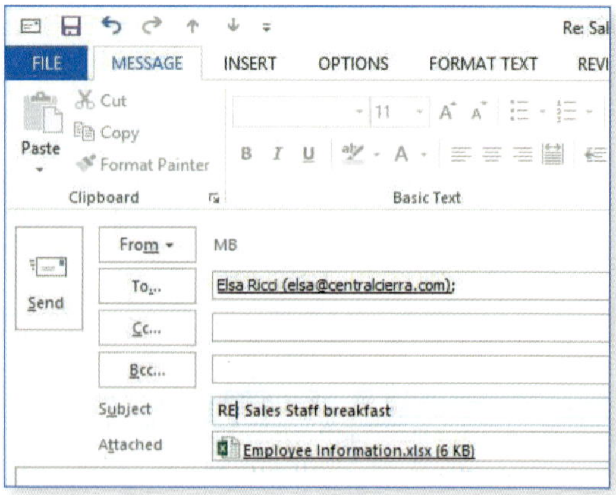

1-45 Attached file

> **MORE INFO**
>
> If you are attaching more than three or four files, consider grouping them in one compressed (zipped) folder and attach that folder to the message.
>
> To compress or zip multiple files into one folder, select the files and then right-click **Send To, Compressed (zipped) Folder**. The compressed folder will have a zipper on it to distinguish it from other folders.

Preview an Attachment

Outlook allows you to preview most types of attachments without opening them. When you click the attachment as shown in Figure 1-45, the attachment will be displayed in the body of the message (Figure 1-46). You can return to the email message by clicking on the **Show Message** button in the *Message* group on the *Attachments* tab.

1-46 Preview an attachment

> **MORE INFO**
>
> When an attachment is being previewed, the area above the attachment displays the file name and the size of the attachment.

Open and Save Attachments

Usually when an attachment is received via email, you will want to open and/or save the attachment. It will be located below the subject line in the email.

Outlook 2013 has made attachment handling much easier with the new ***Attachments*** tab. This tab is automatically displayed when the attachment is selected in an email message. Using the *Attachments* tab, you can open, save, print, copy, or remove the attachment.

> **MORE INFO**
>
> Attachments are usually associated with specific software. For example, if you receive a compressed Excel worksheet, you need Excel on your computer to be able to open the file.

HOW TO: Open an Attachment

1. With an email message open or in the *Reading* pane, click the attachment to display the *Attachments* tab on the *Ribbon*.
   - When you select the attachment, Outlook usually displays a preview of the attachment in the body of the message.
   - Not all file types will display a preview in the body of the message.
2. Click the **Open** button in the *Actions* group to open the attachment. It opens in a new window (Figure 1-47).

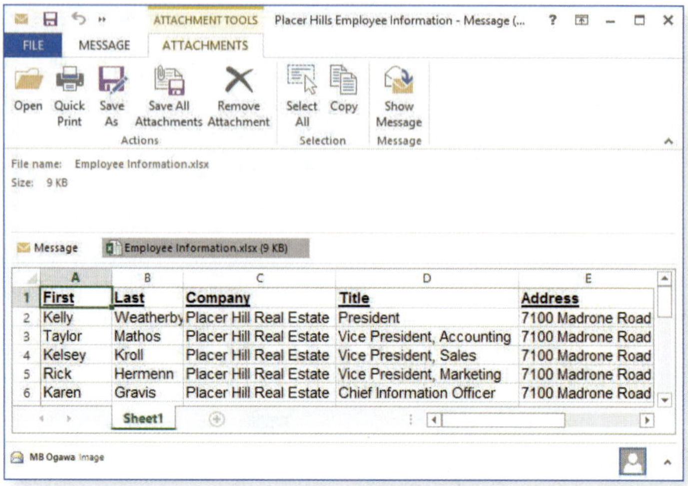

1-47 Opened attachment

MORE INFO

It is important to have virus protection software installed and kept up to date on your computer. Attachments and links in email messages are some of the main ways viruses are spread between computers. Virus protection software could be the best $40–$50 per year you spend.

ANOTHER WAY

An attachment can also be opened by double-clicking on the attachment or by right-clicking the attachment and choosing **Open**.

If an attachment is opened, it can be saved the same way you save any other open document. Typically, you can save an open document by pressing **Ctrl+S** or clicking on the *Save* icon located on the tab or *Quick Access* toolbar. Be sure to specify the location where you want the document saved.

ANOTHER WAY

Ctrl+S is the shortcut for save on most software.

An attachment can also be saved without opening it from the email.

HOW TO: Save an Attachment

1. Click the attachment to be saved. The *Attachments* tab opens.
2. Click the **Save As** button in the *Actions* group. The *Save As* dialog box opens.
3. Choose the desired location to save the file and specify a file name.
4. Click **Save**.

> **MORE INFO**
>
> If an email has multiple attachments, Outlook 2013 has a *Save All Attachments* button. Pressing it will allow you to save multiple attachments all at once rather than saving each one individually.

Forward an Email as an Attachment

When you forward an email with an attachment, the attachment is automatically included in the email to be forwarded. There might be times where you want to forward an entire email as an attachment rather than forwarding only the contents of the email.

HOW TO: Forward an Email as an Attachment

1. Open the message to be forwarded.
2. On the *Message* tab, click the **More** button in the *Respond* group.
3. Select **Forward as Attachment** (Figure 1-48). A new email opens with the selected email as an attachment. The subject line will be the same as the original message with *FW:* in from indicating that the message is being forwarded (Figure 1-49).

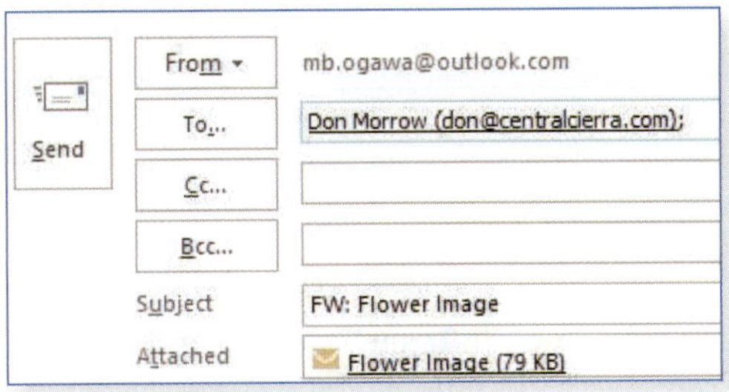

1-49 Forward as Attachment message

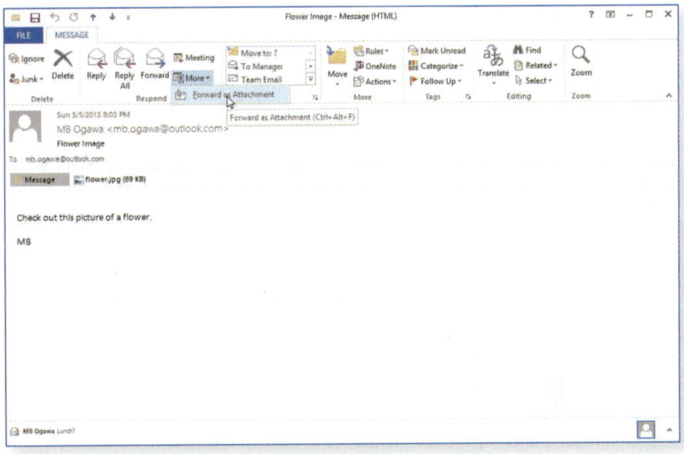

1-48 Forward as Attachment button

4. Select recipients and add any necessary information in the body of the message.
5. Press **Send**.

> **ANOTHER WAY**
>
> Press **Ctrl+Alt+F** to forward an open email or one selected in the *Folder* pane.

Attach Other Outlook Items

Other Outlook items such as contacts, tasks, calendar items, and Outlook business cards can be attached to an email and sent. These items can be sent either as an attachment or as text in the body of the email.

HOW TO: Attach Other Outlook Items

1. Open a **New** email message.
2. Click the **Insert** tab.

3. Click the *Attach Item* button (Figure 1-50) [*Message* tab, *Include* group] or the *Outlook Item* button [*Insert* tab, *Include* group]. The *Insert Item* dialog box opens.
4. Choose the type of item to be attached (*Business Card*, *Calendar*, or *Outlook Item*).
5. Select the items to be attached. Use the **Ctrl** key to select nonadjacent items or the **Shift** key to select a range of items.
6. Choose whether to insert the items as *Text only* or as an *Attachment* (Figure 1-51).
7. Click **OK**. The Outlook item will be attached to the email message.

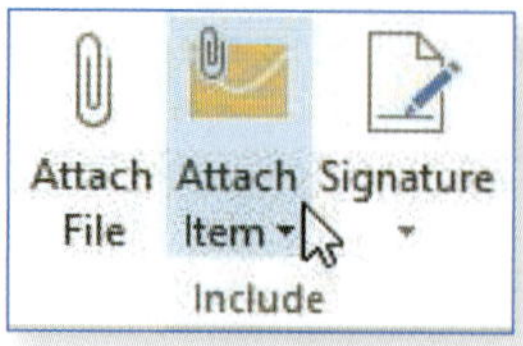

1-50 Attach Item button

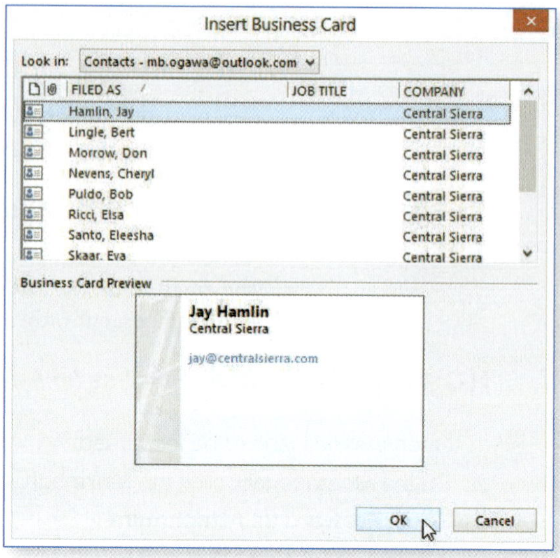

1-51 Insert an Outlook item as an attachment

MORE INFO

The *Attach Item* button is available in the *Include* group on *Message* tab, and the *Outlook Item* button is available in the *Include* group on the *Insert* tab. Both of these buttons open the *Insert Items* dialog box.

SLO 1.7

Understanding Arrangement and Icons

As mentioned in *SLO 1.2: Navigating Outlook*, the working environment in Outlook is broken into panes. There are typically four panes open in Outlook: ***Navigation***, ***Folder***, ***Reading***, *and* ***People***. There is also the ***To-Do bar*** that can be open or collapsed.

In the *Folder* pane, you can arrange emails in numerous different ways to meet your needs and preferences. Outlook also provides users with many ***icons*** to help easily and quickly identify different aspects of an email displayed in the *Folder* pane. The icons on each email in the *Folder* pane can tell you if a message has been read, if it has been replied to or forwarded, if there is an attachment, if it is marked ***important***, if it is ***flagged*** for action, or if it is assigned to a ***category***.

MORE INFO

Message options will be covered in Chapter 2, which will describe how to use the different features associated with some of the Inbox icons. Chapter 5 will cover how to customize the user interface.

Email Arrangement

Arrangement controls the order in which email messages are displayed in the *Folder* pane. Typically email messages are arranged or sorted with the most recently received email at the top of the list (i.e., arranged by date and time in descending order). The *View* tab provides you with different *View* and *Arrangement* options. Outlook 2013 has upgraded the arrangement options to make it easier to quickly change the arrangement of emails.

Conversation arrangement (Figure 1-52) groups all emails related to a particular email conversation (by subject), which is intended to greatly reduce the number of redundant emails displayed

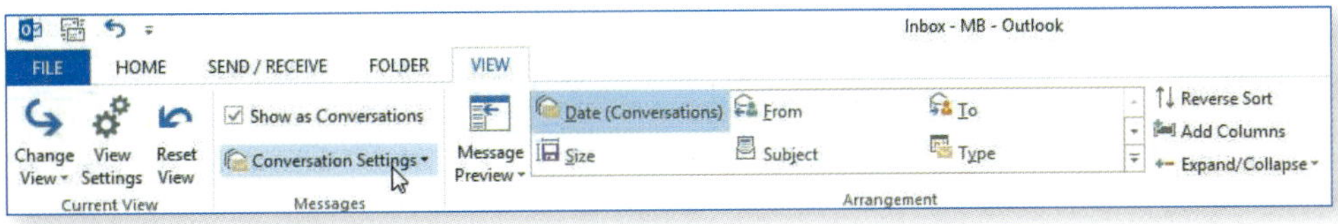

1-52 Conversation Settings button

in the *Folder* list (Figure 1-53). The *Conversation* arrangement groups these emails together to take up less space in your list of emails and gives you the ability to expand the conversation and see all related messages, including those in the *Sent Items* folder.

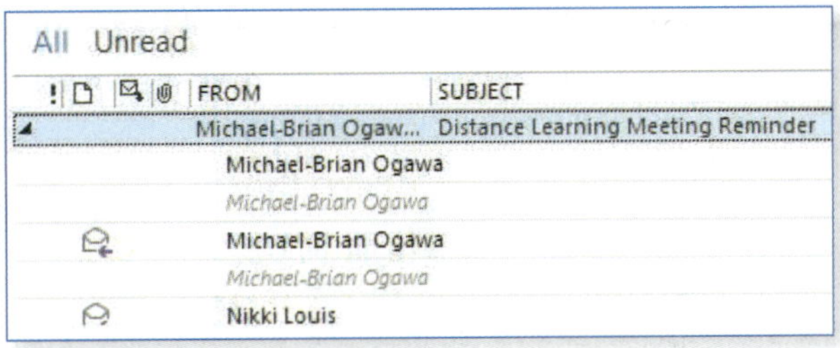

1-53 Conversation arrangement

When there are multiple emails within a conversation, clicking on the small triangle to the left of an email will expand the conversation. The conversation can be collapsed by clicking on the small triangle to the left of the conversation subject in the *Folder* pane.

There are many other preset arrangement options available in Outlook. These can be selected from the *Arrangement* group on the *View* tab.

> **MORE INFO**
>
> When you click the small triangle next to a conversation, the message will be expanded to show the related messages in the current folder. When you click the triangle again, the conversation expands to include related messages in other folders.

Unread/Read Email

When the Inbox (or any other folder) is selected in your *Navigation* pane, the contents of that folder are displayed in the *Folder* pane. The icon to the left of the email shows whether or not the email has been read. When an email has not been read, the email is bold. Once the email has been opened and read, the email will no longer be bold (Figure 1-54).

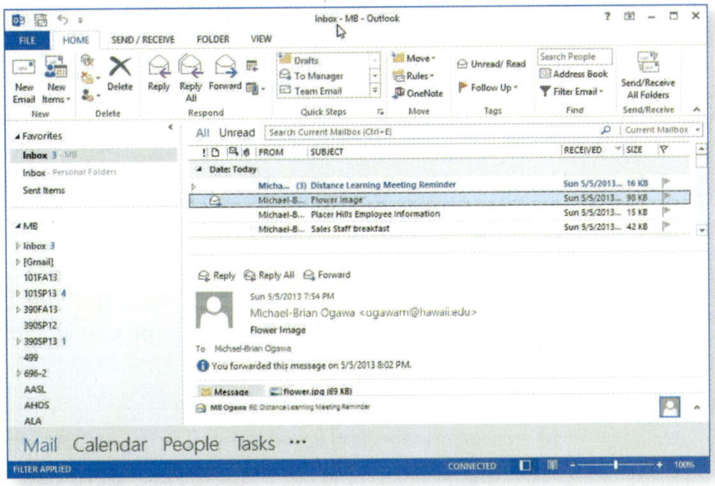

1-54 Read and unread messages

Mark as Unread/Read Email

When an email is opened, Outlook marks it as read. There are times when you might want to mark a message as unread to draw attention to it in the folder or *Folder* pane. Outlook gives you the option of marking an email as ***read*** or ***unread***.

HOW TO: Mark as Unread/Read

1. Select the email in the *Folder* pane to be marked as read or unread.
2. In the *Tags* group on the *Home* tab, click the **Unread/Read** button (Figure 1-55).

1-55 Unread/Read button

ANOTHER WAY

Right-click the email and choose *Mark as Read* or *Mark as Unread*.

MORE INFO

The entire contents of a folder can be marked as read by either right-clicking on the folder and choosing **Mark All as Read** or by clicking on the **Mark All as Read** button in the *Clean Up* group on the *Folder* tab.

Replied to and Forwarded

By scanning your email in the *Folder* pane, you can easily see the response action previously taken on each email. Messages that have been replied to have an envelope icon with an arrow pointing to the left, and those that have been forwarded have an envelope icon with an arrow pointing to the right (Figure 1-56).

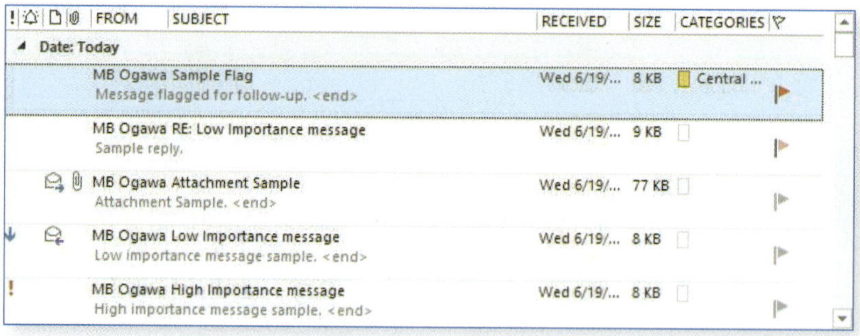

1-56 Sample Inbox

Attachment

Outlook uses a ***paper clip*** icon to indicate that an email has an attachment (Figure 1-56).

Flag

When a message is flagged for follow up or has a flag for recipients, the ***flag*** icon is used. This flag will appear in different shades of red depending on the action of the flag (e.g. *Today*, *Tomorrow*, *This Week*) (Figure 1-56).

Importance

There are three levels of importance that can be set for each email: ***high***, ***low***, and ***normal***. High importance is indicated by a red exclamation point, low importance uses a blue arrow pointed down, and normal importance uses no special icon (Figure 1-56). (Normal importance is the default on all new email messages.)

Category

Categories are used to group Inbox items. Colors are used to distinguish categories, and the category names can be customized to meet your individual needs. Categories are not limited to email messages; they can also be advantageous for grouping contacts, tasks, and calendar items (Figure 1-56).

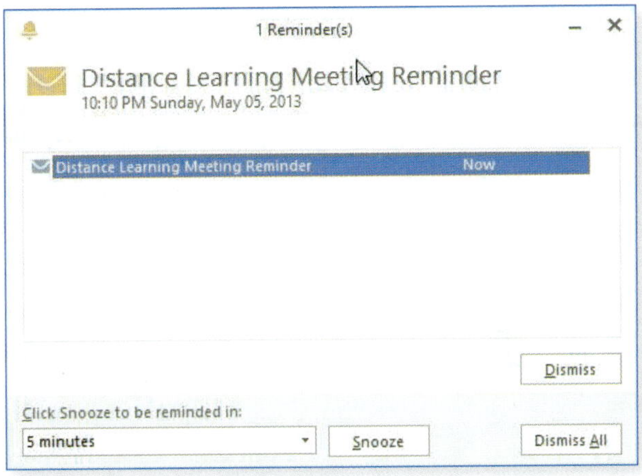

1-57 Reminders window

Reminder

When an email is received that includes a reminder, it is marked with a ***small bell*** icon. An electronic reminder opens on your computer on the reminder day and time (Figure 1-57). You have the options of opening the email, dismissing the reminder, or snoozing the reminder.

SLO 1.8

Cleaning Up Your Inbox

It is important to manage your Inbox effectively. When you receive mail (postal mail) at home or work, you read it and then determine what action needs to be taken. Bills need to be paid, some information needs to be filed and saved, junk mail is discarded, and other mail is thrown away after you've responded to it. Your email Inbox is very similar. Throughout this text, you will learn about many different tools to help you effectively manage your Inbox. For now, it is important to learn how to delete an email you no longer need.

Delete an Email

Select the emails to be deleted, and then either click the *Delete* button (Figure 1-58) in the *Delete* group on the *Home* tab or press the *Delete* key (not *Backspace*) on your computer keyboard. When an email is deleted, it is not gone forever. It has been moved from your *Inbox* (or the folder it is in) to your *Deleted Items* folder.

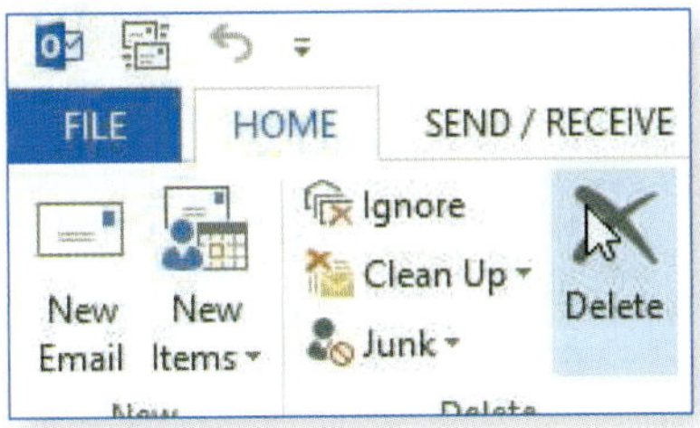

1-58 Delete button

ANOTHER WAY

Outlook items can also be deleted by right-clicking on the item and choosing **Delete**, or select an email message in the *Folder* pane and press **Ctrl+D**.

Deleted Items Folder

Deleted Items is a folder (Figure 1-59) in your list of *Mail* folders. Deleted email, contacts, tasks, calendar items, and other Outlook items are stored in this folder when they are deleted from another location. By default, Outlook does not delete the items in the *Deleted Items* folder, but this is not a good location to store items you might need.

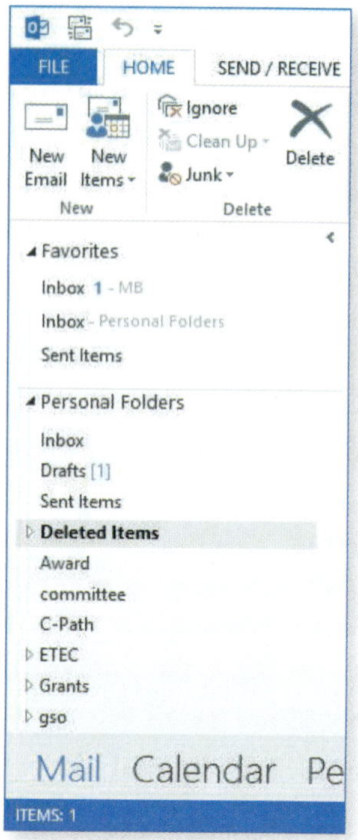

1-59 Deleted Items folder

Clean Up and Ignore

By default, Outlook now arranges emails displayed in the *Folder* pane by conversation. This helps to both group related items together and reduce the clutter and redundant emails in your Inbox. Two new features added to further manage conversations in Outlook are ***Clean Up*** and ***Ignore***. *Clean Up* will remove redundant messages in an email conversation. *Clean Up* can also be used on an entire folder and subfolders (Figure 1-60). *Ignore* will delete all emails related to a specific conversation and delete any new received email that is related to that conversation.

Both *Clean Up* and *Ignore* are handy features to help manage the volume of emails you receive. By default when you *Clean Up* or *Ignore* a conversation, the deleted emails are moved to the *Deleted Items* folder.

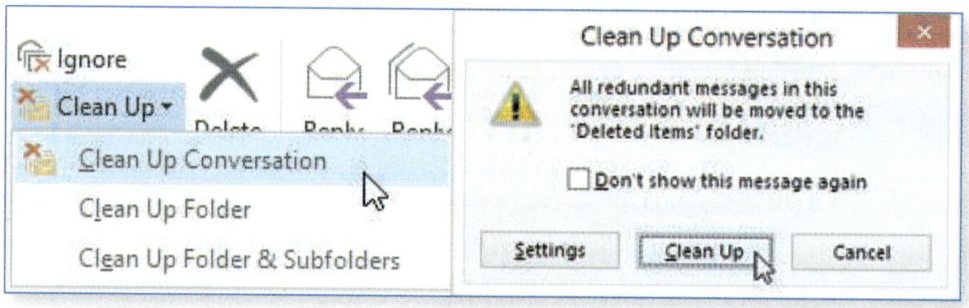

1-60 Clean Up Conversation button and dialog box

Empty Deleted Items

It is a good idea to regularly empty your *Deleted Items* folder. The items in this folder can be manually deleted.

HOW TO: Empty Deleted Items

1. Click the **Deleted Items** folder in the *Navigation* pane.
2. Click the **Folder** tab.
3. Click the **Empty Folder** button (Figure 1-61) in the *Clean Up* group. A dialog box opens confirming that you want to empty the *Deleted Items* folder.
4. Choose **Yes** to delete items in the *Deleted Items* folder.

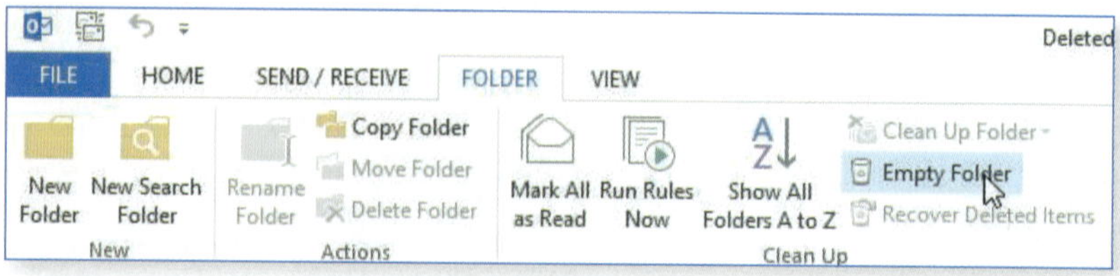

1-61 Empty Folder button

> **ANOTHER WAY**
>
> Right-click the **Deleted Items** folder and choose **Empty Folder**.

It is a good idea to have Outlook automatically empty the *Deleted Items* folder each time you exit Outlook. The default settings in Outlook can easily be changed to do this.

HOW TO: Change the Default Setting to Automatically Empty Deleted Items Each Time You Exit Outlook

1. Click the **File** tab to open the *Backstage*.
2. Click the **Options** button on the left. The *Outlook Options* dialog box opens.
3. Click the **Advanced** button on the left.
4. Select the **Empty Deleted Items folder when exiting Outlook** check box (Figure 1-62).
5. Click **OK** to close the *Outlook Options* dialog box.

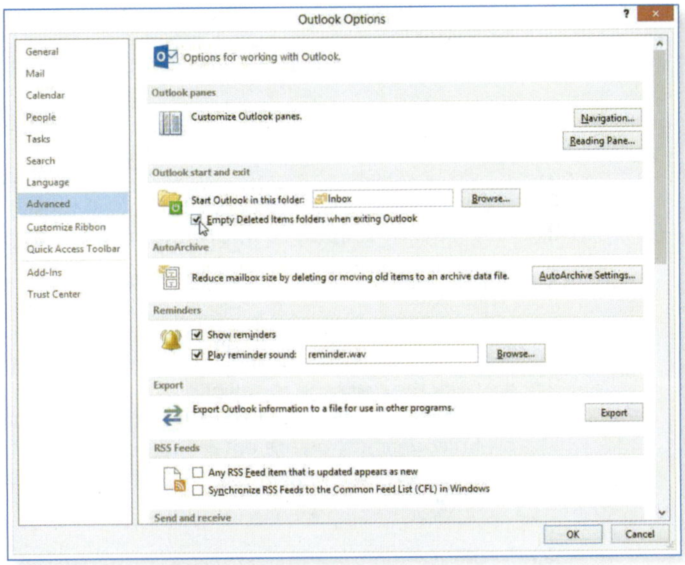

1-62 Empty Deleted Items folder when exiting Outlook option

> **MORE INFO**
>
> The *Outlook Options* dialog box will be referred to throughout this text. This area will allow you to customize the settings in Outlook. *Outlook Options* and other Outlook features are located on the *Backstage* view, which is accessed by clicking on the **File** tab. *Outlook Options* will be covered in Chapter 7.

Even when Outlook items have been deleted and the *Deleted Items* folder has been emptied, Outlook still provides you with the ability to recover deleted items if you are using an Exchange server. The ***Recover Deleted Items*** button (Figure 1-63) in the *Clean Up* group on the *Folder* tab will allow you to select previously deleted items to recover. These recovered items will be placed in your *Deleted items* folder.

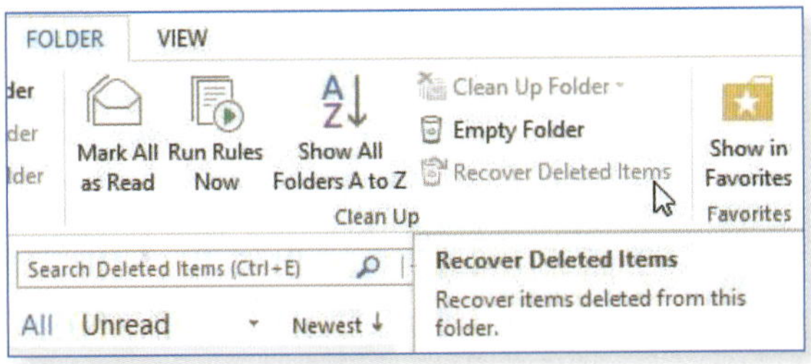

1-63 Recover Deleted Items button

PAUSE & PRACTICE: OUTLOOK 1-3

For this Pause and Practice project, you reply to a message with an email attachment. You also forward the message to your instructor as an attachment and delete a message.

File Needed: ***Employee Information.xlsx***
Completed Project File Name: None

1. Reply to the message with the subject ***Central Sierra Information Request***.
   a. Select the message in your Inbox.
   b. Click the **Reply** button in the message.
2. Add the following text to the body of the message:

   I just found the employee data sheet and attached it to this message.
   [your name]

3. Attach the file ***Employee Information.xlsx*** to the message.
4. Click the **Send** button to send the message.
5. The message will appear in your inbox.
6. Select the message and forward it to your instructor as an attachment.
   a. Click the message to select it.
   b. Click the **Forward as Attachment** option [*Home* tab, *Respond* group, *More* button].
   c. Enter your instructor's email address in the *To* field.
   d. Enter the following text in the body of the message:

   Attached is the requested verification email for the employee data.
   [your name]

   e. Click the **Send** button.
7. Delete the initial reply message that indicated that you would send the message as soon as you retrieved it.
   a. Select the initial reply message in your Inbox.
   b. Click the **Delete** button [*Home* tab, *Delete* group].
8. Empty the *Deleted Items* folder.
   a. Click the **Deleted Items** folder.
   b. Click the **Empty Folder** button [*Folder* tab, *Clean Up* group].
   c. Click **Yes** to confirm the deletion of messages in the *Deleted Items* folder (Figure 1-64).

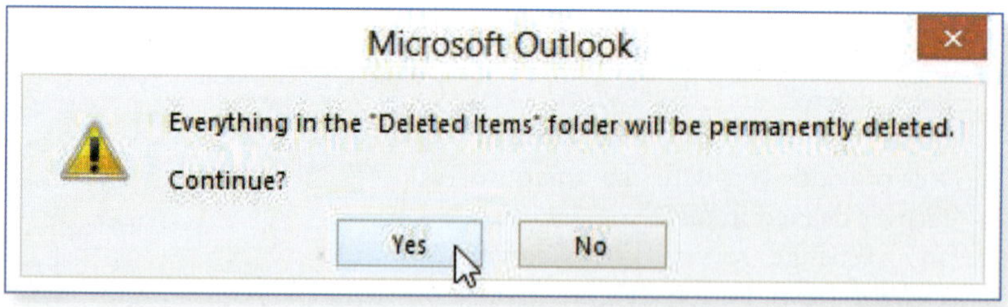

1-64 Confirmation for deleting items

Chapter Summary

1.1 Identify the basic components of Microsoft Outlook 2013 (p. O1-2).

- Outlook includes six major features: *Email*, *Calendar*, *Contacts*, *Tasks*, *Notes*, and *Journal*.
- ***Email:*** Gives users the capability of creating, sending, and receiving email. It can manage a single email account or multiple email accounts.
- ***Calendar:*** An electronic calendar that makes it easy to create appointments or events, edit these items, replicate calendar items, set electronic reminders, create meeting requests, and share calendar items with other Outlook users or other devices.
- ***Contacts:*** An area to keep names, email, phone numbers, and other information about business contacts, coworkers, friends, and family.
- ***Tasks:*** An electronic notepad that you use to write down your to-do items and then cross them off as they are completed.
- ***Notes:*** Electronic sticky notes that are an excellent way of storing information such as a user name and password to log into a web site, gift ideas for family and friends, or a list of books you'd like to read.
- ***Journal:*** Primarily used in the business environment and enables you to keep track of time spent on a project or document.

1.2 Navigate throughout the Outlook environment and identify the different panes in the Outlook window (p. O1-6).

- ***Outlook Today*** is the welcome screen for Outlook which provides you with information about your mailbox, calendar items, and task list.
- The ***Navigation*** pane allows you to quickly switch between different features in Outlook.
- The ***Reading*** pane allows you to quickly read messages or see details in tasks. This can be shown on the bottom or right of the window.
- The ***Ribbon*** appears at the top of the Outlook window and includes a variety of ***tabs***. Each tab has a variety of ***groups;*** groups contain buttons, drop-down lists, and galleries.
- You can choose from a variety of preset views to personalize your experience.
- The ***Folder list*** allows you to see all of the folders in the *Navigation* pane.
- The ***Outlook Help*** button allows you to quickly search for topics on which you might have a question or need additional information.

1.3 Distinguish between Outlook being used as a stand-alone program and in a Microsoft Exchange environment (p. O1-13).

- Outlook as a standalone program connects directly to your Internet Service Provider and can manage multiple email accounts.
- Outlook is typically connected to an ***Exchange Server*** in business environments and has the following features:
  - Using voting buttons and tracking responses
  - Sending meeting requests and tracking responses
  - Recalling messages
  - Sharing your calendar, contacts, tasks, and email with others
  - Using MailTips
  - Using a common global contact list

1.4 Distinguish between the different types of email accounts and set up an email account in Outlook (p. O1-14).

- ***Microsoft Exchange*** accounts are used primarily in medium- to large-business settings. These email accounts are set up through the company network or email administrator. An Exchange account has an individual mailbox assigned to each user and resides on an Exchange file server.
- ***POP3*** accounts are Internet email accounts that are associated with your Internet service provider (ISP). When using this type of account, Outlook downloads the messages.
- ***IMAP*** accounts are also Internet accounts but are not always associated with an ISP. IMAP accounts create folders on a server to store and organize messages for retrieval by other computers and give you the option to read message headers only and select which messages to download.
- ***HTTP*** accounts use the hypertext transfer protocol used on the web to create, view, send, and receive messages. This type of account

is not automatically supported by Outlook but can be configured by installing an add-in.

- You can set up an email account by clicking the **Add Account** button [*File* tab].

1.5 Use Outlook to create, send, and receive email (p. O1-17).

- You select recipients, type the subject of the message, type the message, and send email messages.
- The ***To*** field indicates who a message is addressed to, while the ***Cc*** field is used to send a carbon copy of a message to another person. The ***Bcc*** field is used to send a blind carbon copy of a message to a recipient. *Bcc* is used when you do not want those receiving the email message to see other recipients' email address or names.
- Messages that are sent are automatically copied to the ***Sent Items*** folder.
- If you are not ready to send an email message, you can save it as a draft to the ***Drafts*** folder.
- When you read an email message, you can ***Reply***, ***Reply All***, or ***Forward*** a message.
- You can save email messages as *.msg* files to a location on your computer.

1.6 Use attachments in email (p. O1-28).

- You can attach files from your computer to email messages.
- You cannot attach a Microsoft Access file or a folder to an email message.
- Most common attachments, such as images, can be previewed by clicking on them within a message.
- Attachments can be saved to your computer.
- Email messages can be forwarded to recipients as attachments.
- You can attach Outlook items, such as business cards, to email messages.

1.7 Differentiate email arrangements and icons (p. O1-32).

- Email messages can be grouped in ***Conversations***, which groups all emails related to a particular email conversation. This ensures your email is less cluttered, as only the newest message in a conversation is shown.
- ***Unread*** messages are bolded, while ***read*** messages are not. Outlook allows you to mark messages that are read as unread or unread as read. Marking messages as unread ensures they maintain the bold appearance and are easy to pick out.
- A ***paper clip*** icon is used to indicate that a message has an attachment.
- ***Flags*** are used to indicate that follow-up on a message is needed.
- You can set the importance of an email messages as high, normal, or low to indicate the priority one should place on the message.
- You can add reminders to email messages that require an action.
- Categories can be used to group emails by similar subjects.

1.8 Explain the importance and process of cleaning up an Inbox (p. O1-35).

- When you delete an email message, it is sent to the ***Deleted Items*** folder, as opposed to being deleted from your account.
- Emptying your ***Deleted Items*** folder will delete any messages that were moved to that location.
- ***Clean Up*** removes redundant messages in an email conversation. *Clean Up* can also be used on an entire folder and subfolders.
- ***Ignore*** deletes all emails related to a specific conversation and delete any new received email that is related to that conversation.

Check for Understanding

In the ***Online Learning Center*** for this text (www.mhhe.com/office2013inpractice), there are a variety of resources that can be used to review the concepts covered in this chapter.

The following Online Learning Resources are available in the Online Learning Center:

- Multiple choice questions
- Short answer questions
- Matching exercises

USING MICROSOFT OUTLOOK 2013

Guided Project 1-1

For this project, you request a meeting with Jay Hamlin of Central Sierra Insurance to discuss ways of attracting new customers. You send an email message to request a meeting and include a *Cc* to yourself so that you can keep this message at the top of your message list.
[Student Learning Outcomes 1.1, 1.2, 1.5, 1.7]

Skills Covered in This Project

- Create a new message.
- Select *To* recipient.
- Select *Cc* recipient.
- Add a subject to a message.
- Add a body to a message.
- Mark a message as low importance.
- Flag a message for follow up.
- Send a message.

1. Create a new email message to Jay Hamlin.
   a. Click the **New Email** button [*Home* tab, *New* group].
   b. In the *To* field, type your instructor's email address.
   c. In the *Cc* field, type your email address.
   d. In the *Subject* field, type Attracting New Customers Meeting Request
2. In the body of the message, type the following text:

   Hi Jay, I was wondering if you are available to meet next week to discuss our strategies to attract new customers. I am available on Monday from 2:00 P.M. to 3:00 P.M. or Tuesday from 3:00 P.M. to 4:00 P.M. Please let me know if either of these days work for your schedule. If not, please send me alternative times that you are available.

   Thanks,
   [your name]
3. Mark the message as *Low Importance* and flag the message for follow up.
   a. Click the **Low Importance** button [*Message* tab, *Tags* group].
   b. Click the **Follow Up** button [*Message* tab, *Tags* group] and select **Tomorrow**.
4. Click the **Send** button to send the message (Figure 1-65).

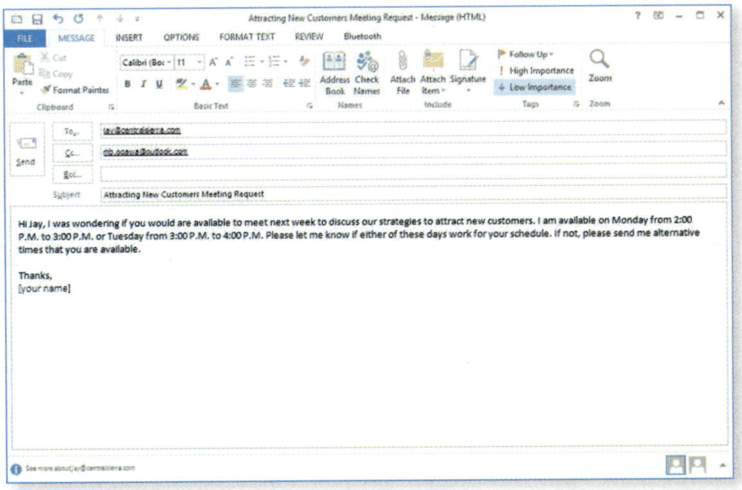

1-65 Completed Guided Project 1-1

Guided Project 1-2

For this project, you follow up with Jay, as he was unable to respond to your first message. You forward your original message to him and ask if he is available to meet.
[Student Learning Outcomes 1.1, 1.2, 1.5, 1.7]

Skills Covered in This Project

- Identify an unread message.
- Open a message.
- Identify a message as low importance.
- Forward a message.
- Select *To* recipient.
- Add a *Bcc* to a message.
- Select *Bcc* recipient.
- Modify the body of a message.
- Remove *Low Importance* tag.
- Mark a message as high importance.
- Send a message.

1. Open the message sent in Guided Practice 1-1.
   a. Click the **Mail** button to confirm you are in your Inbox.
   b. Click the message with the subject ***Attracting New Customers Meeting Request***.
   c. The Information bar states, "The message was sent with Low importance."
2. Forward the message to Jay Hamlin and modify the body of the message.
   a. Click the **Forward** button [*Home* tab, *Respond* group].
   b. In the *To* field, type jay@centralsierra.com.
   c. Click the **Bcc** button [*Message* tab, *Show Fields* group] to ensure the *Bcc* field is available.
   d. In the *Bcc* field, type your email address.
   e. In the body of the message, type:

      Hi Jay, I just wanted to follow up with you regarding our meeting to attract new customers. Are you available next week to meet? Please let me know at your earliest convenience.

      Thank you,
      [your name]

   f. Click the **High Importance** button [*Message* tab, *Tags* group].
3. Click the **Send** button to send the message (Figure 1-66).

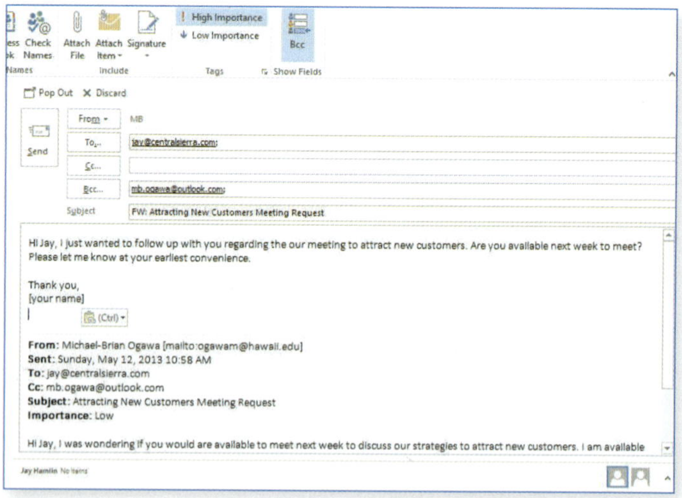

1-66 Completed Guided Project 1-2

Guided Project 1-3

For this project, you reply to the message as Jay Hamlin. You save a draft of your message, save a copy of your message as a *.msg* file, and print a copy of the message.
[Student Learning Outcomes 1.1, 1.2, 1.5, 1.7]

File Needed: None
Completed Project File Name: ***[your initials] Outlook 1-3.msg***

Skills Covered in This Project

- Open a message.
- Identify a message as high importance.
- Reply to a message.
- Select a *Cc* recipient.
- Edit the body of a message.
- Save a message as a file .
- Send a message.
- Create a new message.
- Add an attachment to a message.

1. Open the message sent in Guided Practice 1-2.
   a. Click the **Mail** button to confirm you are in your Inbox.
   b. Click the message with the subject ***FW: Attracting New Customers Meeting Request***.
   c. The Information bar states, "The message was sent with High importance."
2. Forward the message to Jay Hamlin and modify the body of the message.
   a. Click the **Reply** button [*Home* tab, *Respond* group].
   b. Ensure the *To* field has your email address.
   c. In the *Cc* field, type your instructor's email address.
   d. In the body of the message, type:

      Hi [your name], Thanks for checking in with me regarding the meeting about new customers. I accidentally missed your first message. I am available to meet on Tuesday at 2:00 P.M.

      Elsa, could you please schedule the conference room for us next week Tuesday from 2:00 P.M. to 3:00 P.M.

      Jay
3. Save the message to your computer.
   a. Click **Save As** [*File* tab].
   b. Locate the driver and folder where the file is to be stored.
   c. Change the file name to be ***[your initials] Outlook 1-3*** in the *File Name* area.
   d. Click the **Save** button.
4. Click the **Send** button to send the message.
5. Create a new email message to your instructor.
   a. Click the **New Email** button [*Home* tab, *New* group].
   b. In the *To* field, type your instructor's email address.
   c. In the *Cc* field, type your email address.
   d. In the *Subject* field, type [your initials] Outlook 1-3.

6. In the body of the message, type the following text:

   Hi [instructor's name]. Attached are my three guided practice assignments from Outlook Chapter 1.

   Thanks,
   [your name]

7. Attach the message you saved to your computer to the email message.
   a. Click the **Attach File** button.
   b. Locate the message you saved in step 3.
   c. Select the message and click the **Insert** button (Figure 1-67).

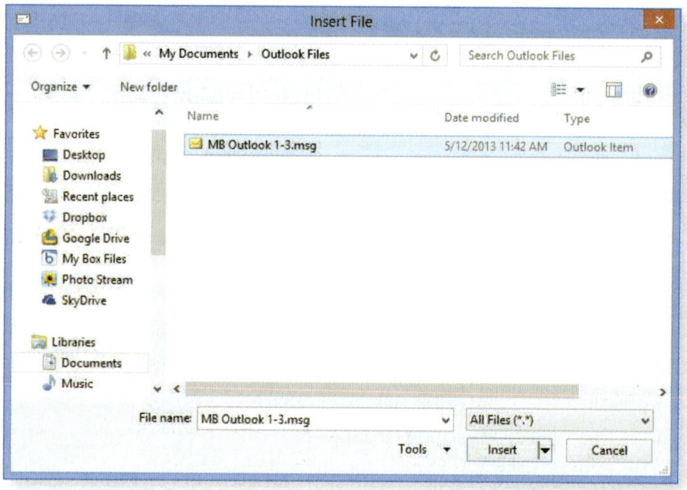

1-67 Attach a saved message

8. Click the **Send** button to send the message (Figure 1-68).

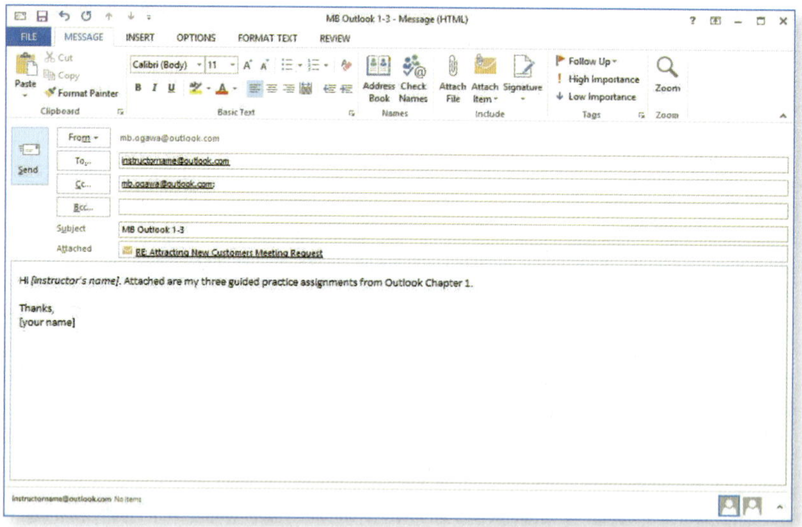

1-68 Completed Guided Project 1-3

Independent Project 1-4

You received a request from Mr. and Mrs. Dodge, over the phone, requesting a vaccination schedule for their newborn child. For this project, you send them an email message with a vaccination schedule. [Student Learning Outcomes 1.1, 1.2, 1.5, 1.6, 1.7]

File Needed: ***Outlook 1-4 vaccination.docx***
Completed Project File Name: None

Skills Covered in This Project

- Create a new message.
- Select a *To* recipient.
- Select a *Cc* recipient.
- Add a subject.
- Add a message.
- Add an attachment to a message.
- Send a message.

1. Create a new email message to the Dodge family using the following information:
   a. In the *To* field, type your partner's email address.
   b. In the *Cc* field, type your email address.
2. In the *Subject* field, type Requested vaccination information for your newborn.
3. Type a short message to the Dodge family indicating that you attached the requested vaccination schedule.
4. Attach the file ***Outlook 1-4 vaccination.docx*** to the message.
5. Send the message (Figure 1-69).

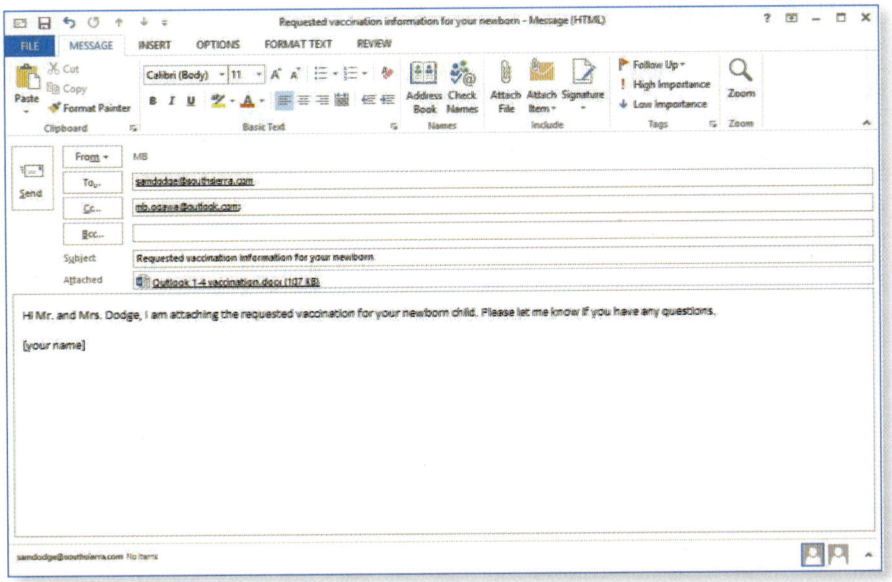

1-69 Completed Independent Project 1-4

Independent Project 1-5

You received a request from Dr. Lee at Courtyard Medical Plaza to verify the message to the Dodge family was sent. For this project, you send him the message that you sent and print a copy for the patient's records.
[Student Learning Outcomes 1.1, 1.2, 1.5, 1.6, 1.7, 1.8]

Skills Covered in This Project

- Open a message.
- Print a message.
- Forward a message as an attachment.
- Select a *To* recipient.
- Select a *Bcc* recipient.
- Add a message.
- Send a message.

1. Locate and open the message sent in Independent Project 1-4 with the subject ***Requested vaccination information for your newborn***. The message has a paper clip icon next to it to indicate that it has an attachment.
2. Print the message in a memo format (Figure 1-70).
3. Forward the message as an attachment to the following recipients:
   a. In the *To* field, type your partner's email address.
   b. In the *Cc* field, type your email address.
4. Edit the body of the message to indicate to Dr. Lee that the attached message was sent to the Dodge family.
5. Send the message (Figure 1-71).

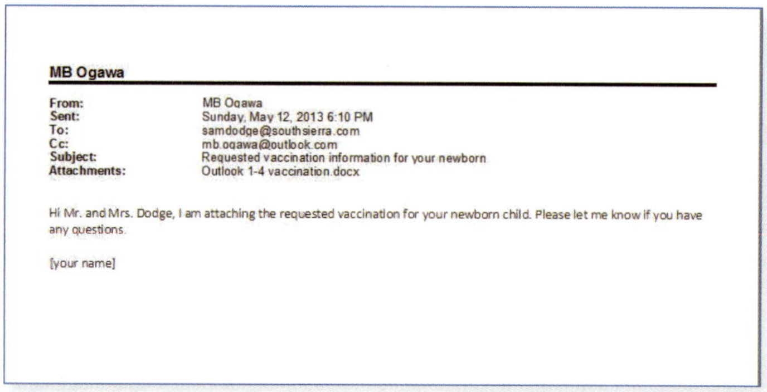

MB Ogawa

From: MB Ogawa
Sent: Sunday, May 12, 2013 6:10 PM
To: samdodge@southsierra.com
Cc: mb.ogawa@outlook.com
Subject: Requested vaccination information for your newborn
Attachments: Outlook 1-4 vaccination.docx

Hi Mr. and Mrs. Dodge, I am attaching the requested vaccination for your newborn child. Please let me know if you have any questions.

[your name]

1-70 Printed message in memo format

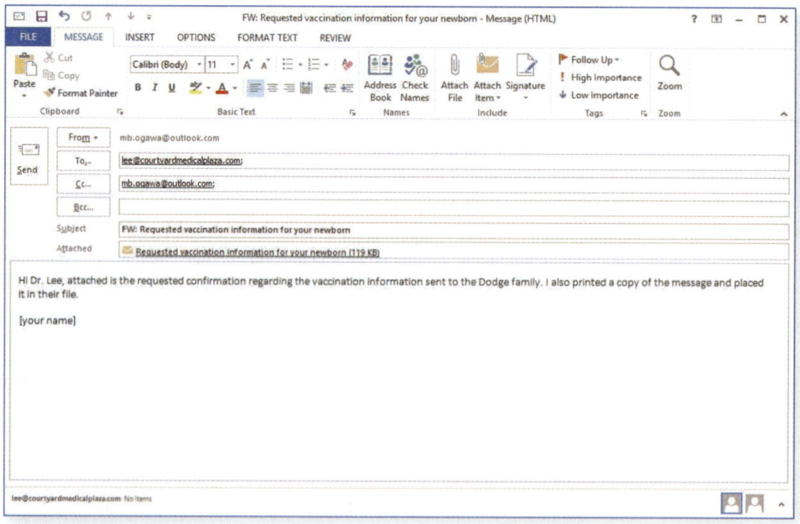

1-71 Completed Independent Project 1-5

Independent Project 1-6

You noticed that your Inbox is becoming cluttered because you included yourself as a *Cc* or *Bcc* on all of your previous messages to the Dodge family and Dr. Lee. For this project, you forward the messages as an attachment to yourself and your instructor to keep it as one message. Next, you clean your Inbox by deleting all previous messages regarding the Dodge family and Dr. Lee.
[Student Learning Outcomes 1.1, 1.2, 1.5, 1.6, 1.7, 1.8]

Skills Covered in This Project

- Open a message.
- Forward a message as an attachment.
- Select a *To* recipient.
- Select a *Cc* recipient.
- Edit the subject.
- Edit the message.
- Send a message.
- Delete messages.

1. Locate and open the message sent in Independent Project 1-5 with the subject ***FW: Requested vaccination information for your newborn***. The message has a paper clip icon next to it to indicate that it has an attachment.
2. Forward the message as an attachment to the following recipients:
   a. In the *To* field, type your email address.
   b. In the *Bcc* field, type your instructor's email address.
3. Edit the subject of the message to indicate that the message contains all of the Dodge family messages.
4. Edit the body of the message to indicate that the message is a summary of all messages related to the Dodge family.
5. Send the message (Figure 1-72).
6. Locate the following messages sent regarding the Dodge family:

   Requested vaccination information for your newborn
   FW: Requested vaccination information for your newborn

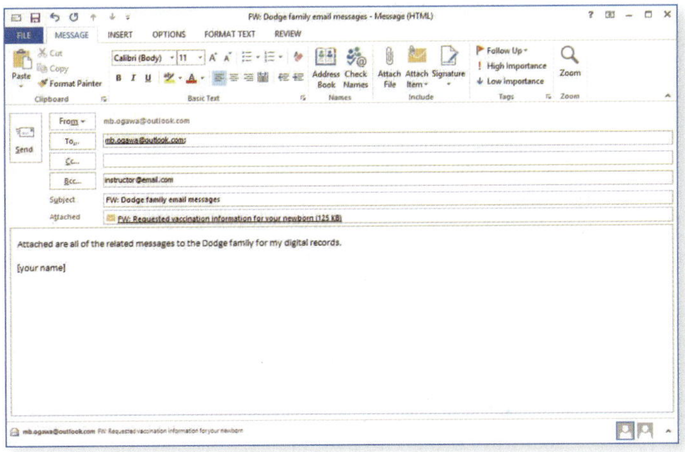

1-72 Message sent for Independent Project 1-6

7. Delete the two messages listed in step 6 (Figure 1-73).

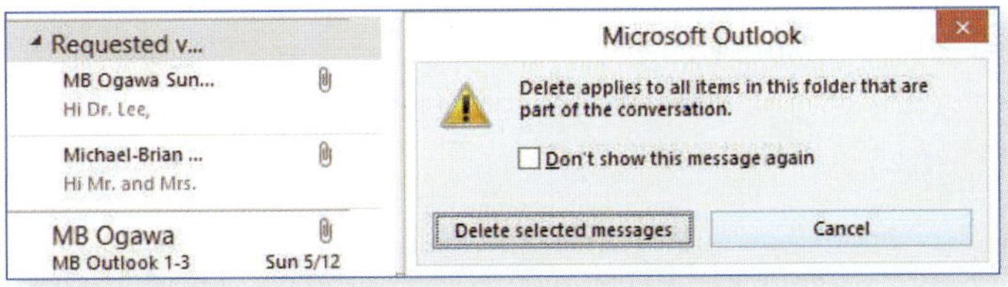

1-73 Deleting messages for Independent Project 1-6

Challenge Project 1-7

Search for an image online that is representative of you. Compose a message to your instructor with the image as an attachment that explains briefly why and how the image represents you.

Note: Use images that are legal under copyright. You may need to use a search engine, such as http://search.creativecommons.org/ to find licensed content.
[Student Learning Outcomes 1.1, 1.2, 1.5, 1.6, 1.8]

- Send the message to your instructor.
- Add your email address to the *Cc* field.
- The subject of the message should be ***Challenge 1-7: Visually Representing [your name]***.
- Include the image as an attachment.
- Explain how the image represents you in three to five sentences.
- Add a citation for the image at the bottom of your message.

Challenge Project 1-8

Compose a message that includes a list of five activities you would like to try in the next five years. For each of the activities you list, compose a short paragraph about that activity and why you find it interesting. Research on the Internet each of the activities you chose. Use your own words when composing the paragraphs about each activity.
[Student Learning Outcomes 1.1, 1.2, 1.5, 1.8]

- Send the message to your instructor.
- Add your email address to the *Cc* field.
- The subject of the message should be ***Challenge 1-8: [your name]'s Activities***.
- Use formatting to differentiate the activity names from their description and explanation for wanting to participate in each.

Challenge Project 1-9

Search for a job online that you would like to have. Compose an application letter to the employer highlighting a few reasons why you would be good for the position. The application letter should be short and concise. Attach your resume to the email message.
[Student Learning Outcomes 1.1, 1.2, 1.5, 1.6, 1.8]

- Send the message to your instructor.
- Add your email address to the *Cc* field.
- The subject of the message should be ***Challenge 1-9: [your name]'s application for [job name]***.
- Include your resume as an attachment.
- Address the body of the email message to your instructor.
- Include a few reasons why you would be good for the position in the body of the message.

CHAPTER 2

Email Special Features

CHAPTER OVERVIEW

One of the benefits of using Outlook to handle your email accounts is the vast array of features available to customize your messages and the Outlook environment. As your understanding of Outlook increases, you will want to customize your email messages and change some of the default settings in Outlook to more fully meet your needs and preferences.

This chapter will prepare you to customize your email by using some of the different email options available in Outlook. These include marking an email as important, using delivery and read receipts, delaying the delivery of an email, flagging an email for recipients, and many more. You will also learn how to use voting buttons and change the look of your email by using stationery, themes, and signatures. After completing Chapter 1 and this chapter, you will be able to customize Outlook and use email options to meet your personal and professional needs.

STUDENT LEARNING OUTCOMES (SLOs)

After completing this chapter, you will be able to:

SLO 2.1 Differentiate between the types of email formats (p. O2-51).

SLO 2.2 Customize your email using the different types of email options available in Outlook (p. O2-52).

SLO 2.3 Use categories to organize email messages into different groups (p. O2-61).

SLO 2.4 Add *Follow Up* flags to email messages to add reminders to messages (p. O2-64).

SLO 2.5 Use email voting buttons to get responses from recipients and to automatically track responses (p. O2-69).

SLO 2.6 Customize your emails by using signatures, themes, and desktop alerts (p. O2-73).

CASE STUDY

For the Pause & Practice projects, you are working with a partner on a business project. You decided to use email to identify meeting dates and locations. You send and reply to email messages with a partner and use Outlook's email special features to make your tasks easier.

Pause & Practice 2-1: You send a plain text formatted message to a peer to request information about your peer's availability to meet about a business project.

Pause & Practice 2-2: You organize your email messages using categories. You also create a custom follow up flag for your message.

Pause & Practice 2-3: You use voting buttons to determine a good location for your lunch meeting.

Pause & Practice 2-4: You create a signature and insert it in an email message to your partner. You also forward the stream of messages to your instructor.

OUTLOOK

SLO 2.1

Understanding Email Format

Not all email accounts operate on the same mail format. Outlook provides flexibility in the type of email messages that are available for different situations. The message format you choose determines the types of formatting features you can use such as fonts, formatted text, colors, styles, bullets, numbering, line spacing, and indents. It is important to note that just because you can and do use some of these advanced formatting features in the body of your email does not mean that the recipient of your email will be able to see them.

There are three different types of mail formats available in Outlook: plain text, Rich Text Format, and Hypertext Markup Language.

Plain Text

All email applications support plain text mail format because it does not include most text formatting features. ***Plain text*** format does not support bold, italic, or any of the other advanced text formatting features. Pictures cannot be displayed in the body of the message when using plain text format; although, pictures can still be attached to the message and sent.

Hypertext Markup Language

Hypertext Markup Language (HTML) message format is the default format in Outlook. HTML format lets you format the body of your email message similar to a Microsoft Word document. HTML is the most commonly used message format and will allow your recipients to receive a message in the same format as you sent it, unless the recipient's email application supports only plain text formatting.

Outlook Rich Text Format

Rich Text Format (RTF) is unique to Outlook users and is supported in an Exchange environment. This format allows users to use the different formatting features available in Outlook. When using RTF, Outlook automatically converts these messages to Hypertext Markup Language (HTML) by default when you send them to an Internet recipient, so that the message formatting is maintained and attachments are received. It is probably best to use HTML format if you are sending messages outside of an Exchange environment.

Set Default and Change Message Format

As mentioned previously, HTML message format is the default setting in Outlook. The default message format can be changed, and the message format for an individual email can also be changed.

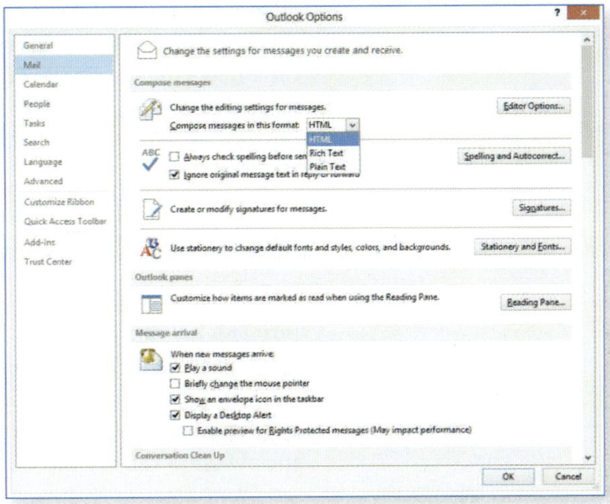

2-1 Outlook Options dialog box

HOW TO: Set Default Message Format

1. Click the **File** tab. The *Backstage* window opens.
2. Click the **Options** button on the left. The *Outlook Options* dialog box opens (Figure 2-1).

3. Click the **Mail** button. The mail options will be displayed.
4. Select the default message desired in the *Compose messages* area.
5. Click **OK** to close the *Outlook Options* dialog box.

If you change the default message setting, then all new emails will have the new default message format.

If you are sending a message to recipients whose email application supports only plain text format, you can change the setting on an individual email rather than changing the default setting.

HOW TO: Change Message Format

1. Open a new email message.
2. Click the **Format Text** tab.
3. In the *Format* group, choose the desired message format (Figure 2-2).

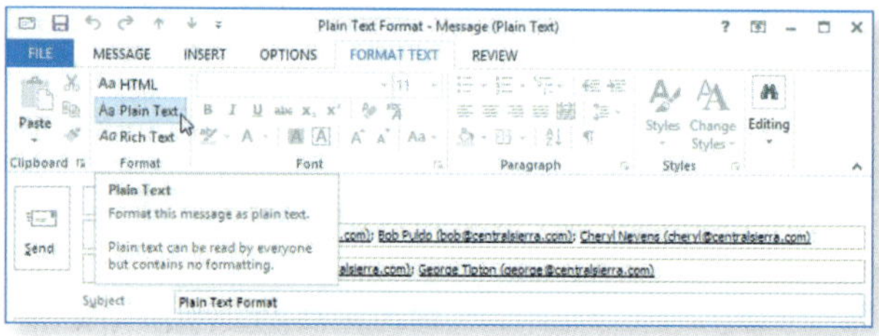

2-2 Select message format

SLO 2.2 Using Message Options

Outlook provides users with a wide variety of message options to enhance an individual email message. The most common message options are available on the *Message* tab. At the bottom right corner of some of the groups is an ***expand*** button (Figure 2-3). Clicking on the expand button opens a dialog box that includes additional options related to the group. Not all groups have an expand button.

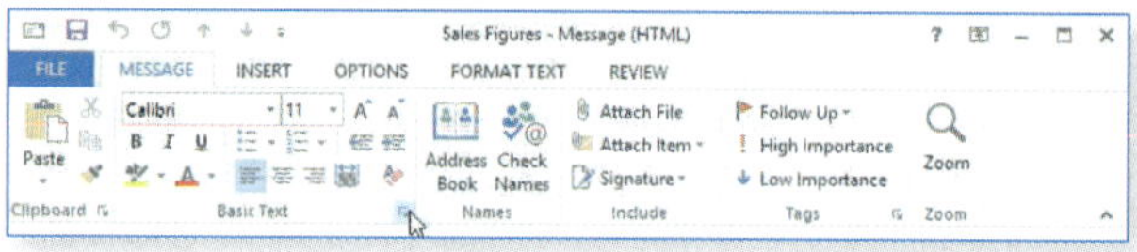

2-3 Expand button

The ***Options tab*** (Figure 2-4) on a new email message provides users an entire tab with many, but not all, of the email message options available.

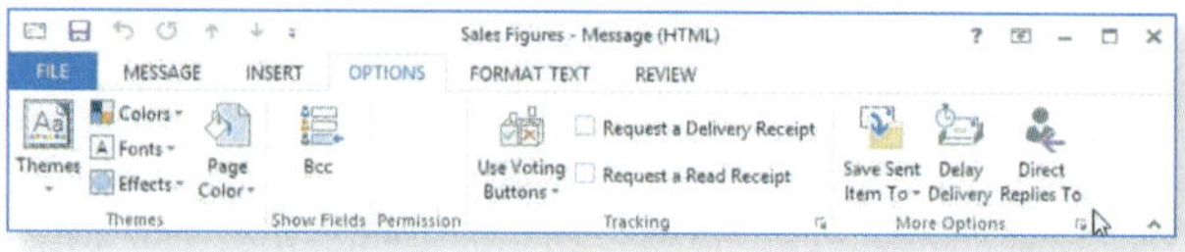

2-4 Options tab

Properties Dialog Box

There is also a ***Properties*** dialog box (Figure 2-5), which can be opened by clicking the **expand** button in the bottom right corner of either the *Tags* group on the *Message* tab or the *Tracking* or *More Options* groups on the *Options* tab.

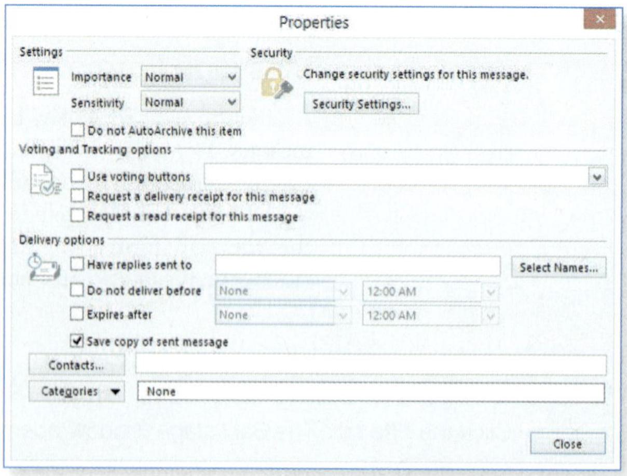

2-5 Properties dialog box

> **MORE INFO**
>
> In all the Microsoft Office products, the ***launcher*** button in the bottom right corner of a group on a tab can be used to open a dialog box.

Importance

Outlook offers you the option of marking an email at one of three levels of importance: ***normal***, ***high***, and ***low***. Normal importance is the default setting for all new email messages.

An email message can be marked as ***High Importance*** to notify your recipients that it is important (Figure 2-6). The **High Importance** button is the red exclamation point in the *Tags* group on the *Message* tab. A message can be marked as ***Low Importance*** by clicking on the **Low Importance** (blue down arrow) button.

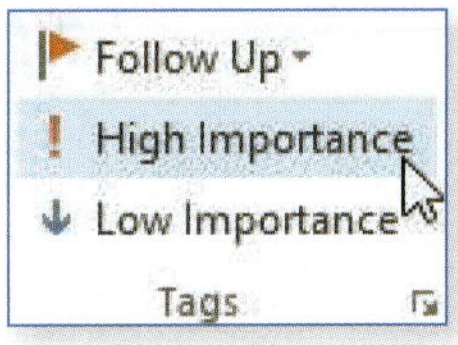

2-6 High Importance tag

> **ANOTHER WAY**
>
> Importance can also be selected from the *Properties* dialog box.

When recipients receive an email marked as *High Importance* or *Low Importance*, the email will be marked with the corresponding Inbox icon (Figure 2-7), which alerts them to the importance of the email.

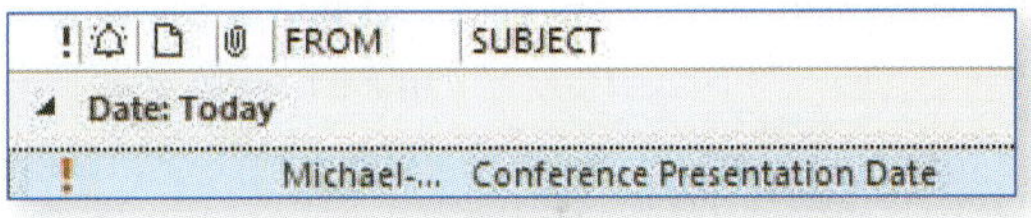

2-7 Message with high importance

> **MORE INFO**
>
> If email is of low importance, marking it as such encourages readers to ignore it. How about not sending it and reducing email clutter?

Sensitivity

If an email is of a sensitive nature, it can be marked as such to alert recipients. Outlook offers several sensitivity options: ***normal*** (default setting), ***personal***, ***private***, and ***confidential***. Sensitivity can only be selected from within the *Properties* dialog box; it is not available on any of the new message tabs.

When a recipient receives an email that has been marked as sensitive, there will be a notification in the ***InfoBar*** (above the *From* line on an open email message). If the message was marked as *Confidential*, the message will read, "Please treat this as Confidential" (Figure 2-8).

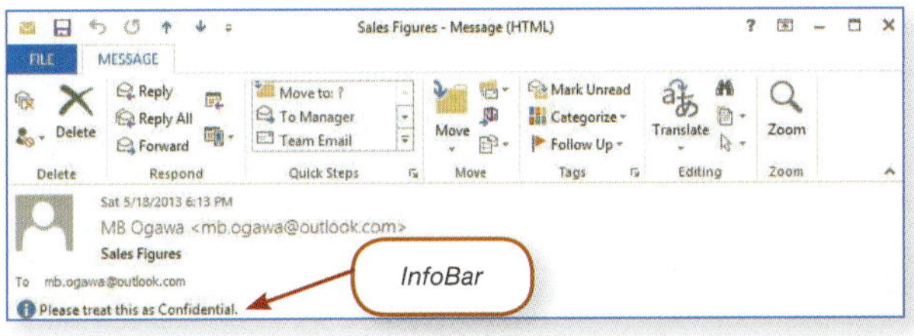

2-8 Confidential message

> **MORE INFO**
>
> The sensitivity marking is only a notification and does not ensure that recipients will treat the information as you have requested.

Security

The ***security settings*** (Figure 2-9) in the *Properties* dialog box provides users with the options of encrypting a message and attachment and including a digital signature. Digital signatures and encryption are available in the *Security Properties* dialog box (Figure 2-10). A ***digital signature*** is a way of authenticating your email to assure recipients you are who you say you are. The process of ***encrypting*** a message and attachment scrambles both the message itself and the attached file, which adds a layer of security. The sender uses a ***public key*** to encrypt a message, and the recipient of an encrypted message must have a ***private key*** to view the contents of the message and attachment.

2-9 Security Settings button

> **MORE INFO**
>
> In the *Properties* dialog box, there is a *Do not AutoArchive this item* check box. Archiving will be covered in Chapter 10.
>
> Digital signatures and encrypting will be covered in Chapter 10.

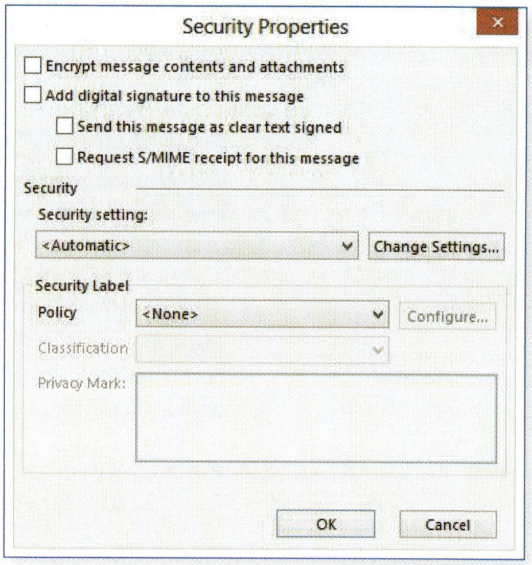

2-10 Security Properties dialog box

Delivery and Read Receipts

Have you ever sent out an email and wondered if the recipients had received or read the email? When using Outlook in conjunction with Exchange, ***delivery*** and ***read receipts*** can be used to provide you, the sender, with an electronic receipt that an email has been delivered to or opened by its intended recipients. When a delivery or read receipt has been requested (Figure 2-11), the sender will receive an email confirmation that the email has been delivered and/or opened by each recipient.

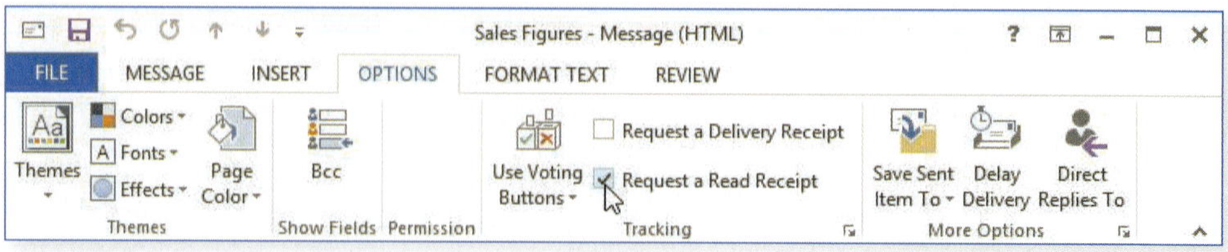

2-11 Request a Read Receipt

When a recipient receives a message that has a delivery receipt, Outlook automatically generates a receipt that is sent to the sender. If an email has a read receipt request, the recipient receives a notification that a read receipt has been requested (Figure 2-12). The recipient is given the option of sending or declining to send a read receipt.

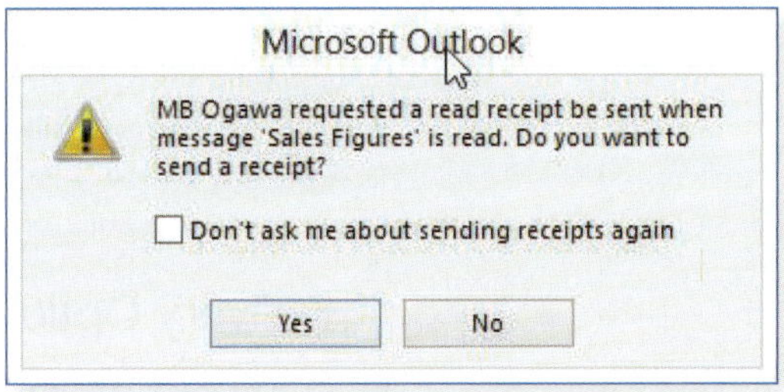

2-12 Read Receipt reply query

> **MORE INFO**
>
> When a sender requests a read receipt, it is good email etiquette to send a receipt, even though Outlook provides you with an option to not send a receipt.

Requesting a delivery or read receipt can be done from the *Tracking* group on the *Options* tab or from the *Properties* dialog box (Figure 2-13).

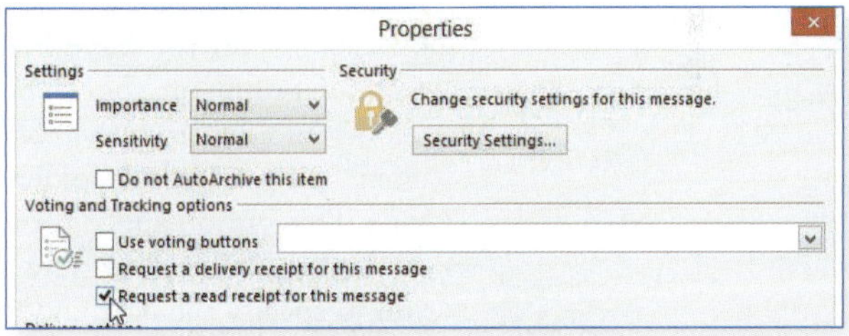

2-13 Request a read receipt for a message in the properties

> **MORE INFO**
>
> Don't solely rely on these receipts because read and delivery receipts work only with Microsoft Exchange. This means that you will not receive these notifications from users not using Exchange. Also, just because a recipient opens an email does not necessarily ensure that he or she will read the email.

Outlook uses ***tracking*** to record this information. Tracking is unique to Exchange and provides the sender with a summary of the receipts received. Once a delivery or read receipt has been received, a *Tracking* button will be available on the original email (usually in the *Sent Items* folder).

HOW TO: View Tracking Results

1. Click the **Sent Items** folder in the *Navigation* pane.
2. Open the sent email that had a delivery or read receipt.
3. Click the **Tracking** button in the *Show* group to view a summary of receipts. The tracking will be displayed in the body of the email (Figure 2-14).
4. Click the **Message** button in the *Show* group to return to the text of the message.

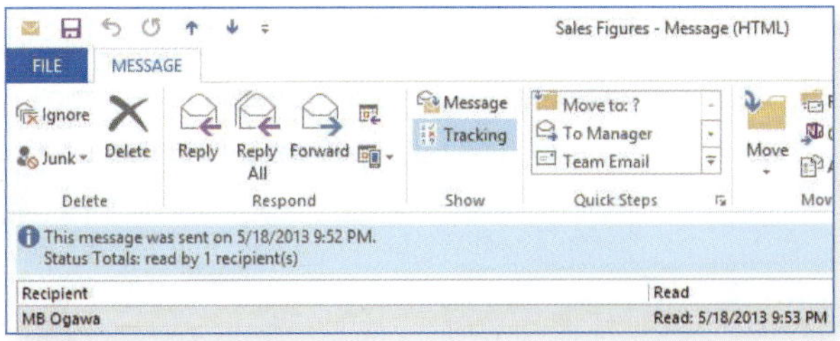

2-14 Tracking a message

> **MORE INFO**
>
> Depending on the size of the email window (or Outlook window) that is open, the buttons and groups might appear differently on the tabs.

Delivery Options

Suppose you are leaving town tomorrow but need to send out an email on Friday, and, since you'll be gone, you want to have replies sent to a coworker in your office. Outlook provides users with customized delivery options. The delivery options include having replies sent to other users, delaying delivery, setting an expiration date and time, and saving the sent email in a different location.

Sent email messages are by default saved in the *Sent Items* folder. This location can be changed for an individual email by clicking on the **Save Sent Item To** button in the *More Options* group on the *Options* tab (Figure 2-15). You can choose a folder from the *Folder* list as the location to save this email, use the default folder, or choose to not save the message. This option applies only to the current message.

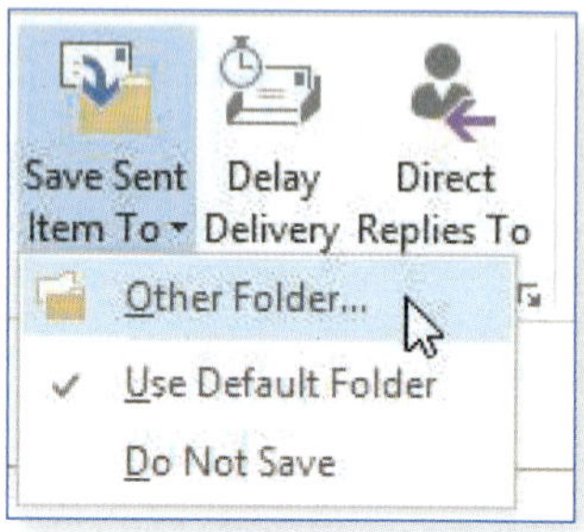

2-15 Save Sent Item To button

Delay Delivery (Figure 2-16) is an option that allows you to specify the date and time when an email is to be sent. When this feature is used, an email can be created and sent, and it will stay in your *Outbox* folder until the scheduled delivery date and time. When you click the **Delay Delivery** button, the *Properties* dialog box opens.

2-16 Delay Delivery button

HOW TO: Set the Delay Delivery Option

1. In a new email message, click the **Options** tab.
2. Click the **Delay Delivery** button. The *Properties* dialog box opens (Figure 2-17).

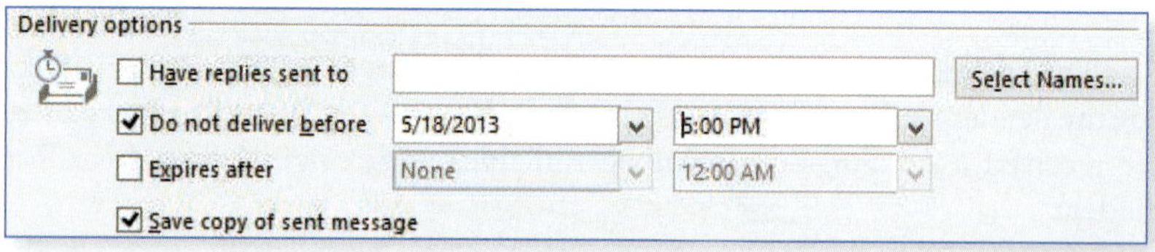

2-17 Delivery options

3. Select the **Do not deliver before** check box.
4. Set the day and time the email is to be delivered.
5. Click **Close** to close the *Properties* dialog box.
6. Click **Send**. The message will be stored in your *Outbox* folder until the specified time to be delivered.

> **MORE INFO**
>
> A rule can also be created to delay the delivery of all emails you send. Rules will be covered in Chapter 6.

There are times when it is beneficial to have other users receive a reply to an email. When the ***Direct Replies To*** option is selected (Figure 2-18), you can select individuals from your contacts to receive replies from an email you've sent.

2-18 Direct Replies To button

HOW TO: Use the Direct Replies To Feature

1. In a new email message, click the **Options** tab.
2. Click the **Direct Replies To** button. The *Properties* dialog box opens.
3. Click the **Select Names** button (Figure 2-19). The *Have Replies Sent To* dialog box opens.

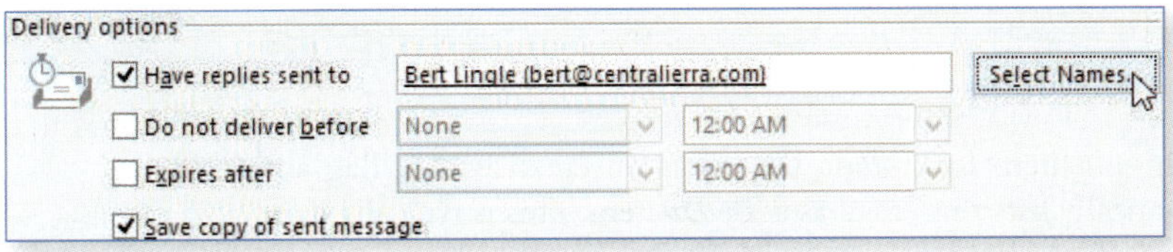

2-19 Direct Replies

4. Select recipients from the contact list and press **OK** to close the *Have Replies Sent To* dialog box.
5. Click **Close** to close the *Properties* dialog box.

ANOTHER WAY

The *Delay Delivery* and *Direct Replies To* options can be directly accessed from the *Properties* dialog box.

Some emails are time sensitive and are no longer relevant to the recipient after a certain time. The ***Expires after*** feature lets you set a time for when an email is to expire. When an email has expired, it still remains visible and can be opened from the recipient's Inbox, but it is marked with a strikethrough (Figure 2-20).

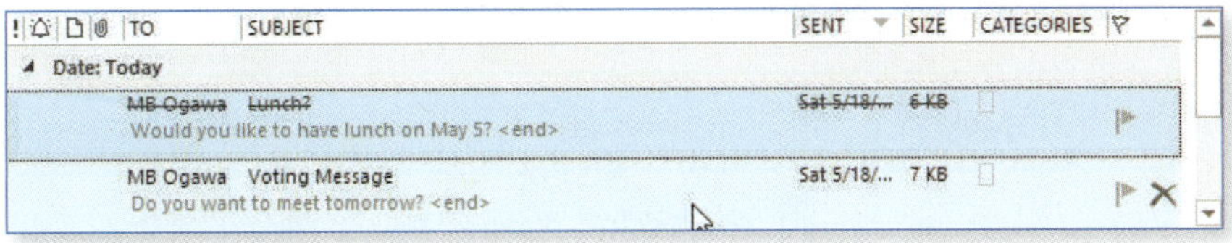

2-20 Expired message

HOW TO: Set an Expiration Day and Time

1. In a new message, click the **expand** button at the bottom right of the *Tags* group on the *Message* tab (Figure 2-21). The *Properties* dialog box opens.

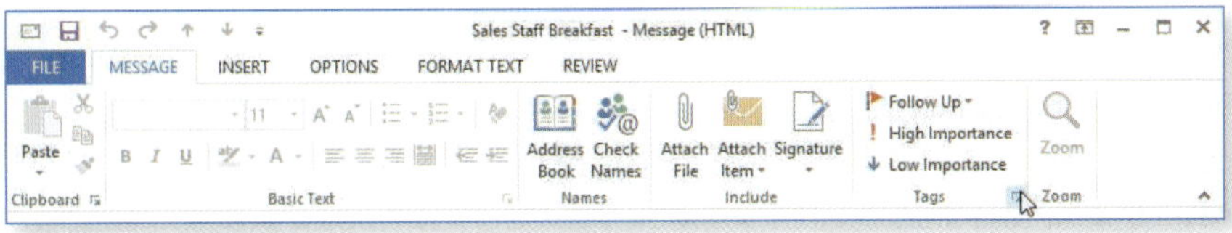

2-21 Expand button

2. Check **Expires after**.
3. Set the date and time the email is to expire (Figure 2-22).
4. Click **Close** to close the *Properties* dialog box.

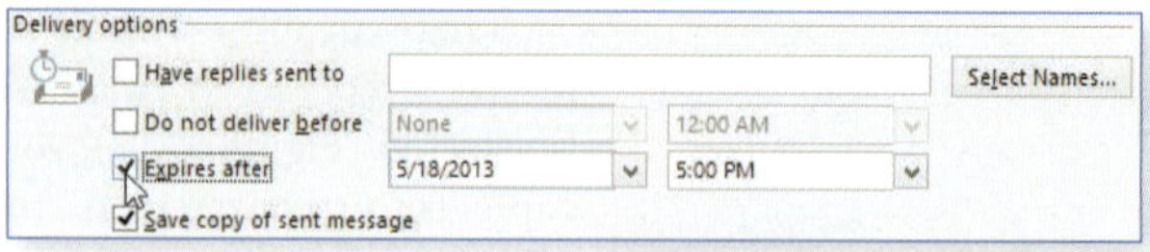

2-22 Set expire date and time

> **MORE INFO**
>
> When a message has expired, the recipient can still reply to the message.

Follow Up Flag

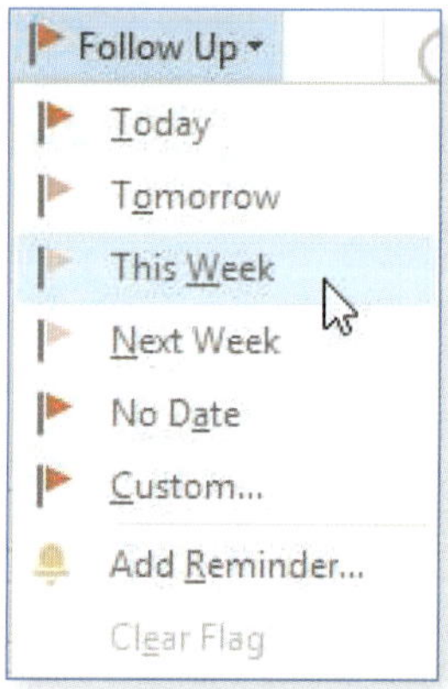

2-23 Flag a message for follow up

Flagging an item for ***Follow Up*** marks an email with a flag and automatically lists this email as a ***To-Do*** item. This is typically done on an email you have received in your Inbox and serves as a reminder that you have to follow up with some action on this email.

An email can be marked for follow up by clicking on the **Follow Up** button in the *Tags* group on the *Message* tab and choosing a flag (Figure 2-23). Email messages marked with a flag will display a flag icon in the *Folder* pane.

Flag for Recipients

A ***Custom flag*** (Figure 2-24) can be used to create a ***Flag for Recipients***. *Flag for Recipients* attaches a flag and message to an email and gives you the option of including a reminder date and time. Outlook provides preset ***Flag to*** messages from which to choose, or you can create your own custom message. If a reminder is set (optional), recipients will receive an Outlook reminder that will open on their computer screen at the designated date and time.

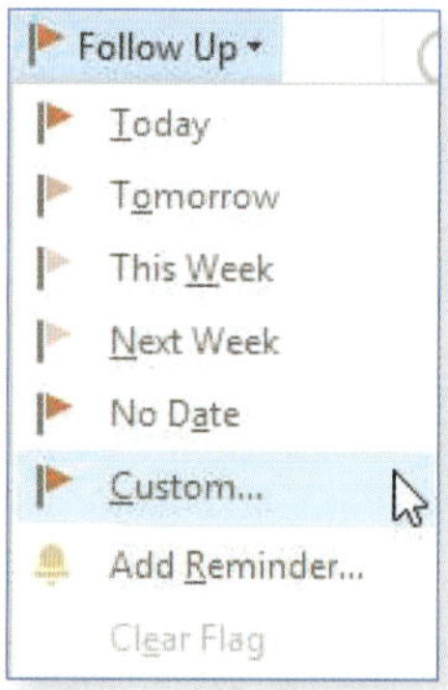

2-24 Flag a message for custom follow up

> **MORE INFO**
>
> The specific follow up options (e.g., *Today*, *This Week*, *Custom*) are only available when using an exchange server. If you are not using an exchange server, you can still add a flag to messages.

HOW TO: Flag an Email for the Recipient

1. In a new email, click the **Follow Up** button in the *Tags* group.
2. Select **Custom**. The *Custom* dialog box opens (Figure 2-25).
3. Deselect the **Flag for Me** check box.
4. Select the **Flag for Recipients** check box.
5. Select a **Flag to** message, or type in your own custom message.

6. If you want the recipients to receive a reminder message, select the **Reminder** check box and set a date and time.
7. Click **OK** to close the *Custom* dialog box.

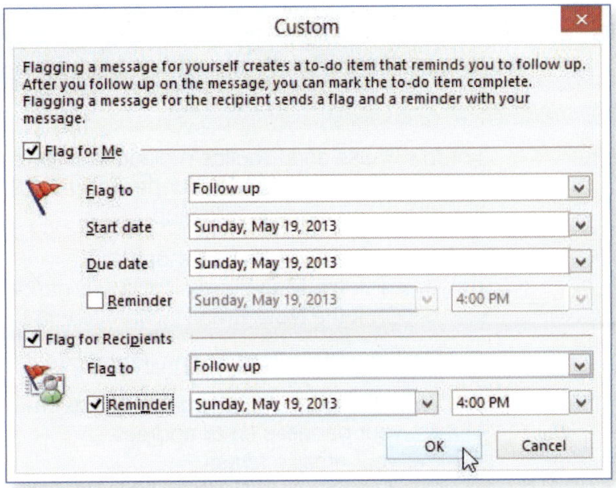

2-25 Custom dialog box

When an email has a *Flag for Recipients*, there will be a notification in the *InfoBar* (above the *From* line on an open email message) visible to both the sender and receiver of the message (Figure 2-26).

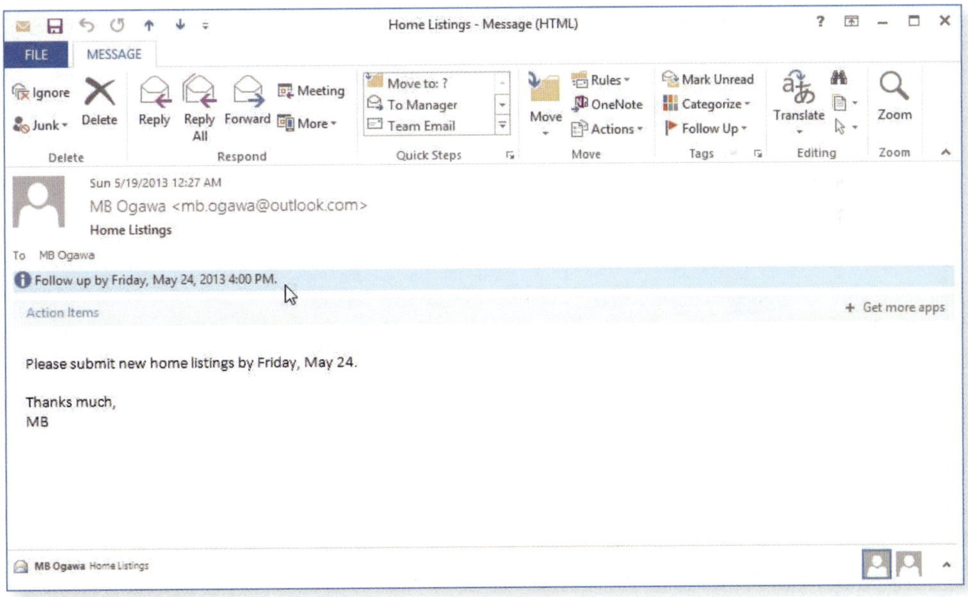

2-26 Follow-up message

Permission

The ***Permission*** option in the *Permission* group on the *Options* tab helps to ensure that sensitive information is not forwarded, printed, or copied. For the permission feature to function properly, your company must enable the ***Information Rights Management (IRM)***. If IRM is not enabled for your company, you will not see any options in the *Permission* group.

If the IRM is enabled, the permission can be set to ***Do Not Forward*** or a custom configuration. When the *Do Not Forward* permission is selected, recipients will receive a notification in the *InfoBar* informing them of the restrictions.

PAUSE & PRACTICE: OUTLOOK 2-1

For this Pause and Practice project, you send a plain text formatted message to a peer. The message will request information about your peer's availability to meet about a business project. The message is very important and requires follow up.

1. Create a new email message.
   a. Click the **Mail** button in the *Navigation pane*.
   b. Click the **New Email** button [*Home* tab, *New* group].
2. Click the **Plain Text** button [*Format Text* tab, *Format* group].
3. Enter the following information in the email message fields.
   To: your partner's email address
   Cc: your email address.
   Subject: Business Project Meeting
   Body: Hi [partner name], are you available to meet next week Monday for our business project?

   Thank you,
   [your name]
4. Click the **High Importance** button [*Message* tab, *Tags* group].
5. Click the **Send** button.
6. Open the message your partner sent to you with the subject *Business Project Meeting*.
7. Reply to the email with following message in the body:

   Monday sounds great! Let's meet for lunch.
   [your name]
8. Click the **Request a Read Receipt** option [*Options* tab, *Tracking* group].
9. Click the **Send** button (Figure 2-27).

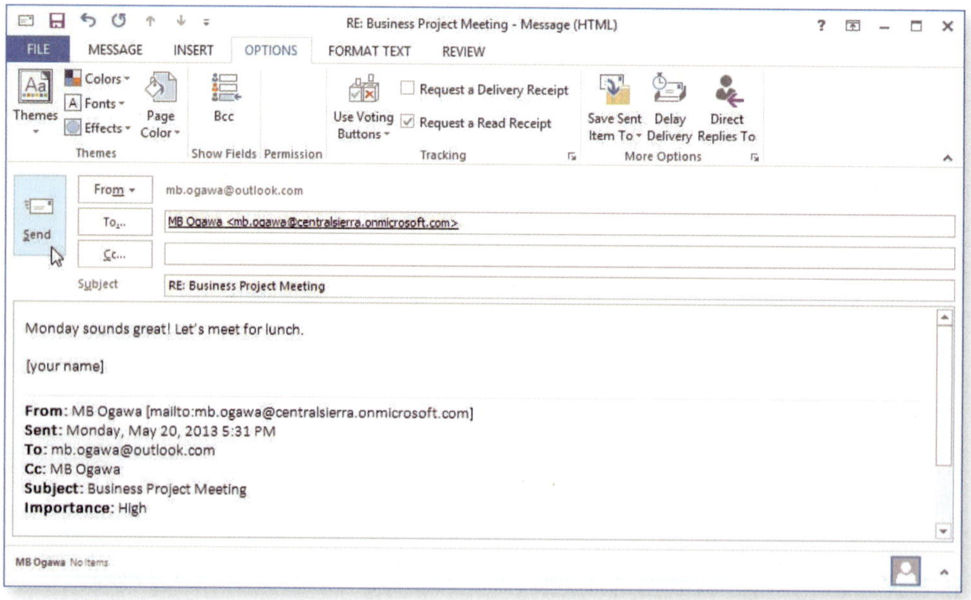

2-27 Completed Pause & Practice 2-1

SLO 2.3

Using Categories

There might be times when you want to group together related emails, tasks, calendar items, or contacts, but you do not want to create a separate folder in which to store these related items. For example, you might want to group all your cycling buddies' contacts together so they are easy to find or group together tasks and emails related to the upcoming fundraiser at work.

The ***Category*** feature can be used to mark Outlook items as part of a particular group. One of the useful and unique aspects of categories is that they are global; they can be used throughout Outlook (emails, calendars, contacts, tasks, notes, and journals) to mark different types of Outlook items. Whereas folders are useful for grouping specific items together, they only store one type of Outlook item. Categories are yet another method provided by Outlook to help you organize information. Each of the different areas of Outlook lets you view these Outlook items by category.

> **MORE INFO**
> Categories were introduced in Chapter 1.

Customize a Category

Outlook is set up with default categories for your use. These categories are really not all that useful until you customize them to meet your individual needs. Each category has a color, and the default name is the name of the color.

Categories can be used extensively in Outlook both for work and personal use. An instructor can set up categories for each of his or her courses so these categories can be used to mark emails from students, students' contact records, and calendar items and tasks associated with each course. At home, you could have a different category for each member of the family, and one for vacation, church, school, birthdays, anniversaries, and others. When almost all calendar items are marked with a category, it is very easy to visually distinguish by color the category of the event or appointment on the calendar.

The default categories in Outlook are labeled by color. ***Customizing*** a category is very easy; pick the color of category and rename it. One of the handy features of categories is that you can ***rename*** or ***create*** a category anywhere in Outlook and it will be available throughout Outlook. Let's start customizing categories.

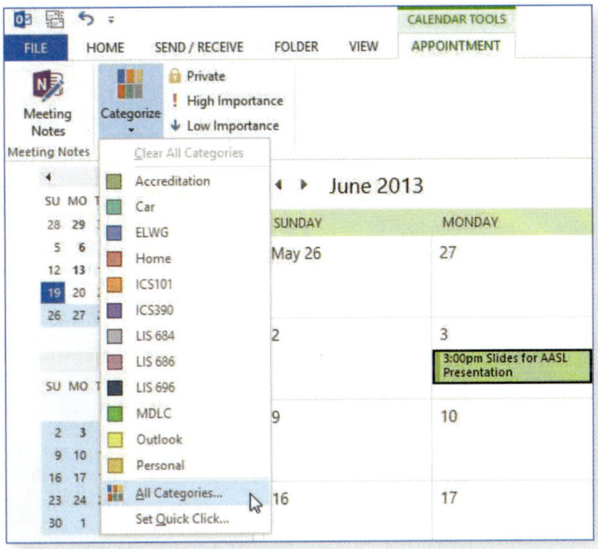

2-28 All categories

HOW TO: Customize Categories

1. Click the **Calendar** button in the *Navigation* pane.
2. Click **Month** view.
3. Click any appointment or event on your calendar. The *Appointment* tab will be displayed.
4. Click the **Categorize** button in the *Tags* group and choose **All Categories** (Figure 2-28), or right-click the calendar item and choose **Categorize** and then **All Categories**. The *Color Categories* dialog box opens (Figure 2-29).

5. Click the color of the category to be renamed.
6. Click the **Rename** button.
7. On the left, type the new name of the category and press **Enter** (you can also click another category).
8. Continue to rename categories as desired.
9. Press **OK** when finished. Your categories are now set up and ready to use.

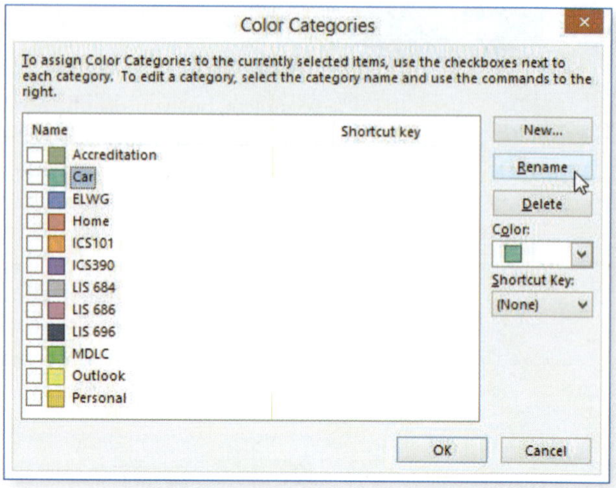

2-29 Rename a category

> **MORE INFO**
>
> The *Color Categories* dialog box can be accessed throughout Outlook. Simply click an email, calendar item, contact, or task and follow the preceding steps.

> **MORE INFO**
>
> When using multiple calendars, you will need to open an appointment to apply a category.

New categories can also be created following a similar process and can be done throughout Outlook. Once your categories are renamed or created, you can assign a category to any Outlook item. You can select or open the item to be categorized. For example, click the **Calendar** button on the *Navigation pane* and select an appointment to be categorized, then click the **Categorize** button in the *Tags* group, and select the category.

HOW TO: Create a New Category

1. Click the **Mail** button in the *Navigation* pane.
2. Select any email in your Inbox.
3. Click the **Categorize** button in the *Tags* group on the *Home* tab and choose **All Categories**, or right-click the mail item and choose **Categorize** and then **All Categories**. The *Color Categories* dialog box opens.
4. Click the **New** button. The *Add New Category* dialog box opens (Figure 2-30).
5. Type the name of the category in the *Name* text box.
6. Click the **Color** drop-down arrow and select a color.
   - You can also add a shortcut key to the category by clicking on the **Shortcut Key** drop-down arrow and selecting an option from the drop-down list.
   - You can apply a category that has a shortcut key assigned by selecting an Outlook item and pressing the shortcut key (e.g., **Ctrl+2**)
7. Click **OK**. The new category is added to your list of categories.

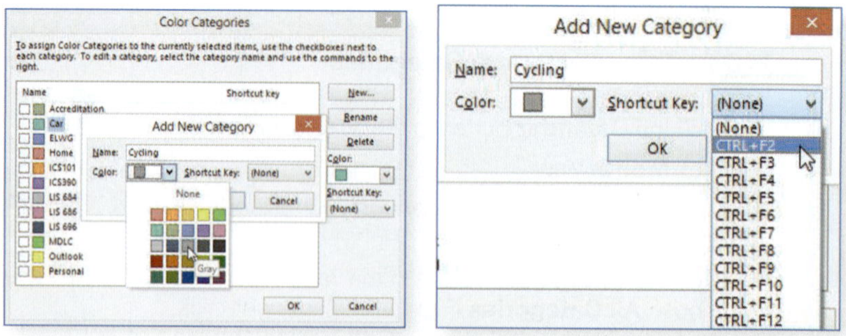

2-30 New category color and shortcut key

Assign a Category

Once your categories are renamed or created, you can assign a category to any Outlook item. You can select or open the item to be categorized, click the **Categorize** button on the tab, and then select the category. You can also right-click the item in the *Folder* pane, choose **Categorize**, and then select the category.

A category can be removed from an Outlook item by following this same process and selecting **Clear All Categories**.

> **MORE INFO**
>
> Outlook items can be assigned to more than one category. When viewing items by category, an item that is assigned to multiple categories will appear in both or multiple category sections; although, it is still only one Outlook item.

View by Categories

When categories have been assigned to Outlook items, you will usually be able to see the color and category when viewing the items in the *Folder* pane (Figure 2-31).

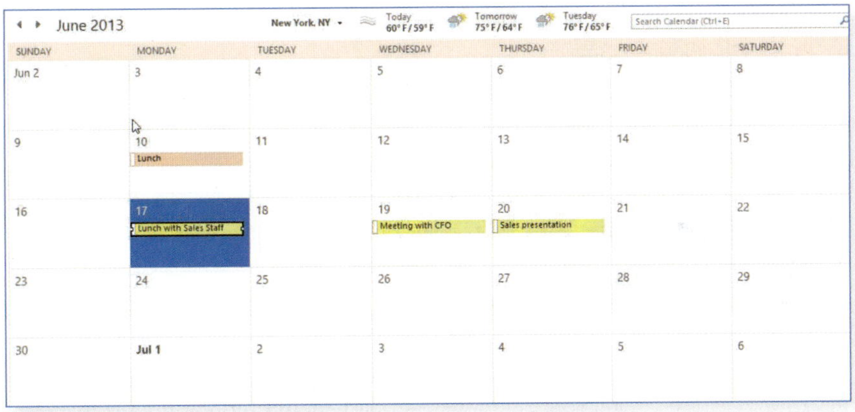

2-31 Outlook calendar folder pane

Within most of the areas in Outlook, you have the option of viewing items by category. This is a filter that can be accessed in the *Advanced View Settings* button in *Current View* group on the *View* tab (Figure 2-32). The *Advanced View Settings: Calendar* dialog box opens. Select the **Filter . . .** (more) button to open the *Filter* dialog box and select the *More Choices* tab. Click the **Categories . . .** (more) button to select the categories that you would like to be visible (Figure 2-33).

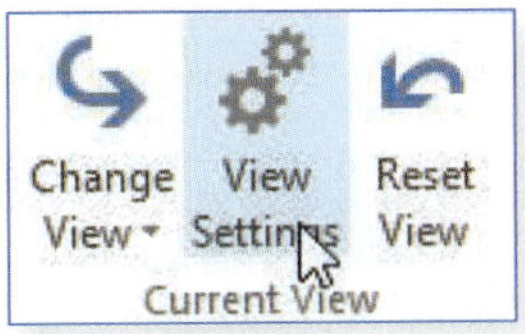

2-32 View Settings button

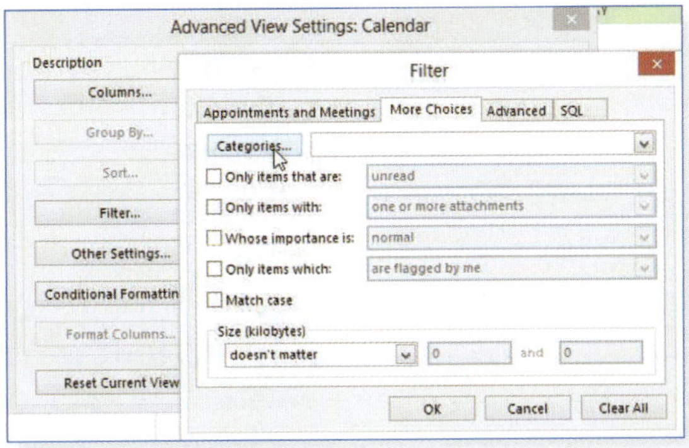

2-33 Categories filter

MORE INFO

In areas of Outlook where items are viewed in list view in the *Folder* pane, you can sort by categories by clicking on the **Categories** column heading.

Set a Quick Click Category

If there is one category you use regularly, this category can be set as the ***Quick Click*** category. By setting a *Quick Click* category, an Outlook item can be quickly added to this category by clicking on the *Categories* field in the *Folder* pane. The *Quick Click* category effectively becomes the default category rather than having to choose a category from the list.

HOW TO: Set a Quick Click Category

1. Click an Outlook item in the *Folder* pane.
2. Click **Categorize** in the *Tags* group and choose **Set Quick Click**. You can also right-click the item in the *Folder* pane, choose **Categorize**, and then **Set Quick Click**. The *Set Quick Click* dialog box opens.
3. Choose the **category** to be used as the *Quick Click* category.
4. Press **OK** (Figure 2-34).

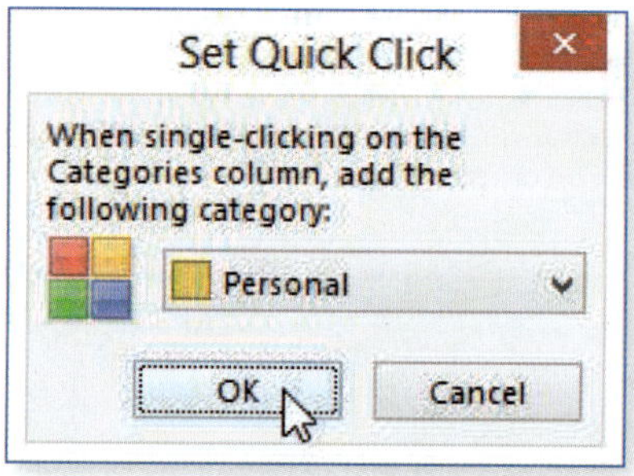

2-34 Set Quick Click dialog box

SLO 2.4

Using Follow Up Flags

Most of you have a stack of to-do items in your office or a pile of papers and bills by your computer at home. At some point you intend to take some kind of action on each of these items. Outlook provides you with *Follow Up* flags (Figure 2-35) to give these items further attention. When an Outlook item is marked with a *Follow Up* flag, it becomes a *To-Do* item.

There are numerous flags available for you to mark items depending on their priority. The types of *Follow Up* flags available in Outlook are:

- *Today*
- *Tomorrow*
- *This Week*
- *Next Week*
- *No Date*
- *Custom*

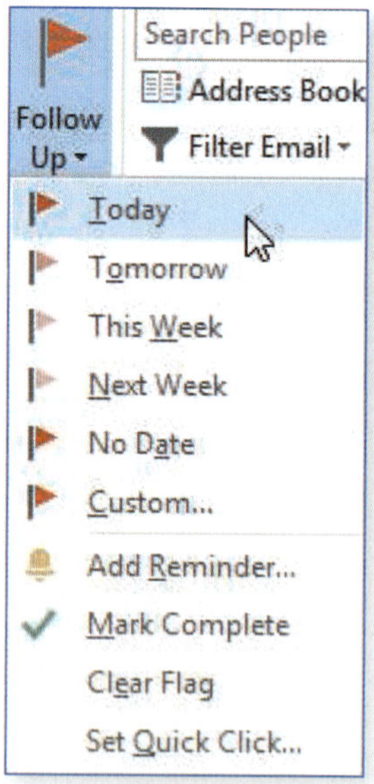

2-35 Follow Up flag

ANOTHER WAY

You can also mark an Outlook item with a *Follow Up* flag by right-clicking on the item, choosing **Follow Up**, and then clicking on the desired **Follow Up flag**.

MORE INFO

Follow Up flags become a darker shade of red as the marked item approaches its due date. Outlook items marked with a *No Date Follow Up* flag are displayed as dark red, which is the same color as a *Today Follow Up* flag. An Outlook item turns red when it is past its due date.

Apply Follow Up Flag

Follow Up flags can be used on email messages and contacts. Tasks are automatically marked with a *Follow Up* flag based on the due date of the task, but these flags can also be changed.

HOW TO: Apply a Follow Up Flag

1. Open the Outlook item (e.g., email, contact, or task).
2. Click the **Follow Up** button in the *Tags* group (Figure 2-36).

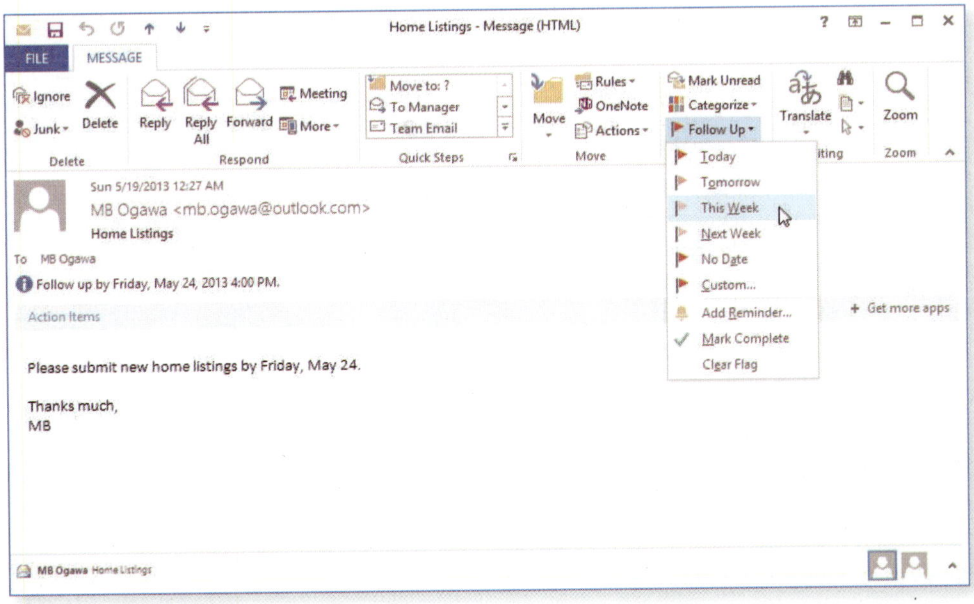

2-36 Apply a This Week Follow Up flag

3. Select the desired **Follow Up flag**. Details of the follow-up status are included in the *InfoBar* of the Outlook item.
4. Close the Outlook item. This marked item is now included in the list of *To-Do* items.

Create a Custom Follow Up Flag

A reminder and/or custom *Follow Up* flag can be added to an Outlook item. If a reminder is set, an electronic reminder will open on your computer screen providing you with details about the marked item.

A custom *Follow Up* flag can be set to give more specific follow-up details on an Outlook item. These include a custom message, start date, due date, and reminder. Outlook provides a few default messages for custom flags, or you can type in your own custom flag message.

HOW TO: Create a Custom Follow Up Flag

1. Open an Outlook item (e.g., email, contact, or task).
2. Click the **Follow Up** button in the *Tags* group.
3. Select *Custom* or *Add Reminder*. The *Custom* dialog box opens (Figure 2-37).
4. Enter the desired details in the *Custom* dialog box.
5. Click **OK** to close the dialog box. Details of the follow-up status are included in the *InfoBar* of the Outlook item.

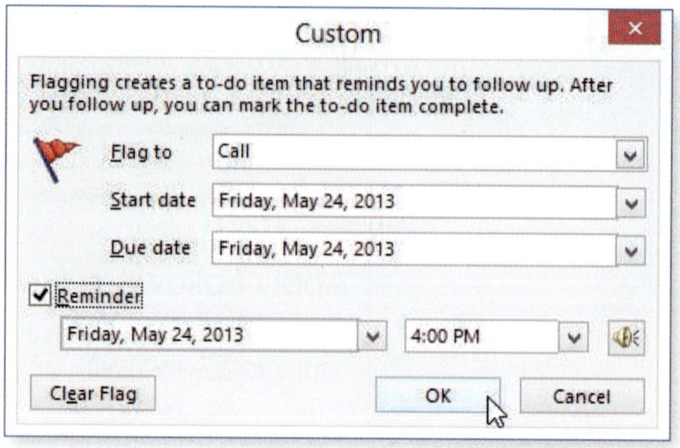

2-37 Custom Follow Up flag

MORE INFO

If you are using a smart phone to synch to Outlook, these reminders will appear on your phone as the item comes due.

Set a Quick Click Follow Up Flag

On the right side of the list of your email messages in the *Folder* pane is a column for *Follow Up* flags. A flag can be added by clicking on this area of the email message without having to select a specific flag.

The ***Quick Click*** flag can be customized to flag the Outlook item with the flag you use most regularly.

HOW TO: Set a Quick Click Follow Up Flag

1. Click the **Follow Up** button in the *Tags* group.
2. Choose **Set Quick Click**. The *Set Quick Click* dialog box opens (Figure 2-38).
3. Choose the desired **Follow Up flag** for *Quick Click* from the list of flag options.
4. Press **OK**.

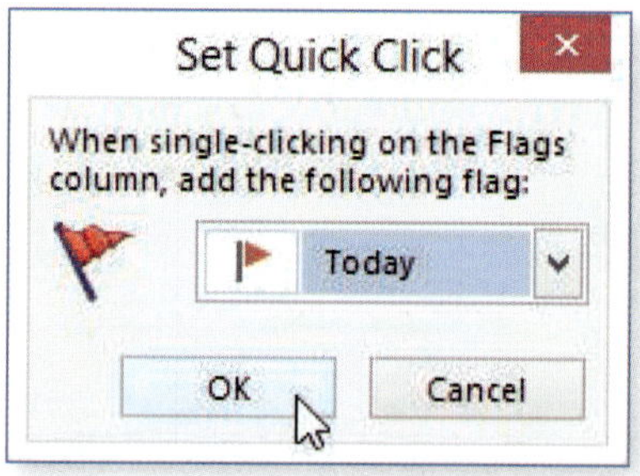

2-38 Quick Click Follow Up flag

To apply the *Quick Click* flag to a selected item, simply click the **Follow Up flag** area of the Outlook item and the *Quick Click* flag will be set on that item.

View To-Do Items

Outlook items marked with a *Follow Up* flag will remain in their location in Outlook (e.g., Inbox, Contacts, or Tasks), but they are also consolidated in the To-Do List (Figure 2-39). As mentioned previously, To-Do items are all Outlook items marked with a *Follow Up* flag and can include email, tasks, and contacts. The To-Do items are also listed in the *To-Do bar*.

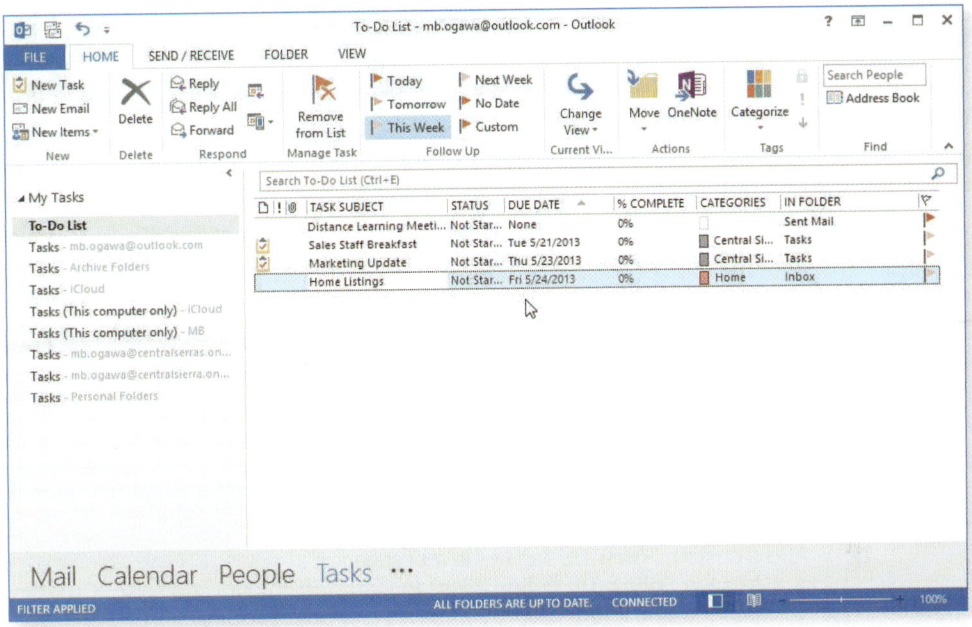

2-39 To-Do List

> **MORE INFO**
>
> In addition to the To-Do List and the *To-Do bar*, rules and search folders can be used to group items that have been flagged for follow up.
>
> Rules and search folders are covered in chapter 6.

Mark a Flagged Item as Complete

When an Outlook item that has been marked with a *Follow Up* flag has been completed, you can use ***Mark Complete*** to indicate the item has been completed and the flag will be replaced with a check mark. Or, if the To-Do List is displayed, the item will be crossed out indicating that it has been marked as complete.

The following list explains the numerous ways in Outlook to use *Mark Complete* for an item that has been flagged:

- Click the **flag** icon and the *Mark Complete* check will replace the flag.
- Right-click the item, choose **Follow Up**, and click **Mark Complete**.
- In the To-Do List, click the **Complete** check box to mark an item as completed.
- Open the item, click the **Follow Up** button in the *Tags* group, and choose **Mark Complete**.

> **MORE INFO**
>
> You can remove a flag (different than marking it as completed) by selecting the Outlook item, opening the **Follow Up** menu, and choosing **Clear Flag**.

PAUSE & PRACTICE: OUTLOOK 2-2

For this Pause and Practice project, you organize your email messages using categories. You also create a custom *Follow Up* flag for your message and mark an item as complete.

1. Select the email message you received in *Pause and Practice Outlook 2-1*. The subject is ***Re: Business Project Meeting***.
2. Create a new category.
   a. Click the **Categorize** button [*Message* tab, *Tags* group] and select **All Categories . . .**
   b. Click the **New** button.
   c. Type the category name Business Project.
   d. Change the color to red (first row, first column).
   e. Click the **OK** button.
3. With the message selected, click the **Categorize** button [*Message* tab, *Tags* group] and select the **Business Project** category.
4. Add a custom *Follow Up* flag to the message.
   a. Click the **Follow Up** button [*Message* tab, *Tags* group] and select **Custom. . .**
   b. Click the **Start date** drop-down arrow and select **Today**.
   c. Click the **Due date** drop-down arrow and select tomorrow's date.
   d. Click the **Reminder** option.
   e. Click the **OK** button.
5. Click the **Reply** button [*Message* tab, *Respond* group].
6. Reply to the message with following message in the body:

   Sure, are there any foods you like to eat?

   [your name]
7. Click the **Send** button.
8. Open the message your partner sent to you and reply with the following message:

   I like to eat Italian and Japanese cuisine. How about you?
9. Change the subject to My lunch preferences.
10. Click the **Send** button.
11. After receiving the message from your partner, mark the initial reply message as complete.
    a. Locate and click on the first reply from your partner (you categorized it in the beginning of this project).
    b. Click the **Follow Up** button [*Message* tab, *Tags* group] and select **Mark Complete**.
12. If you are not using an exchange server, click the **Tasks** button on the *Navigation pane*.
    a. Click the **To-Do List** under *My Tasks*.
    b. Double-click the email in your *To-Do List*.
    c. Click the **Follow Up** button in the *Tags* group, and choose **Mark Complete**.

13. See Figure 2-40 for the completed Pause & Practice 2-2 project.

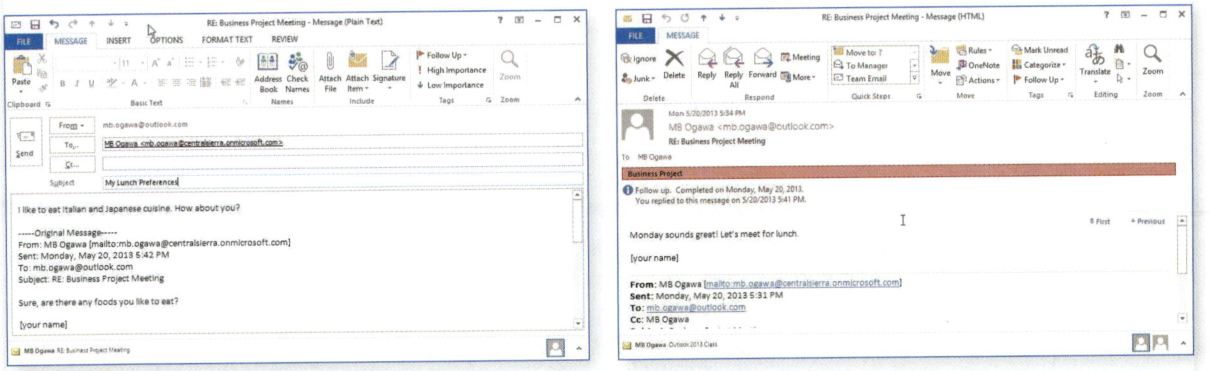

2-40 Completed Pause & Practice 2-2

SLO 2.5

Using Voting Buttons

Voting buttons are a useful way of gathering responses to a question sent via email. The advantage of using voting buttons, rather than having respondents reply to an emailed question, is that you can specify the response choices and Outlook will automatically track and tally the voting responses received. The tracking feature also lets you, the sender of the message, see who has and hasn't voted. You can also export the voting results to Excel.

MORE INFO

Voting buttons and tracking responses will only work in an Exchange environment.

Preset Voting Buttons

A question can be typed into the body of an email or in the subject line. The *Use Voting Buttons* feature is located on the *Options* tab of a new message. Outlook provides you with preset voting buttons. The preset voting buttons are *Approve;Reject*, *Yes;No*, and *Yes;No;Maybe*.

HOW TO: Use Preset Voting Buttons

1. In a new email message, click the **Options** tab.
2. Click the **Use Voting Buttons** button.
3. Choose from one of the three preset options (Figure 2-41).
4. Type and send the email.

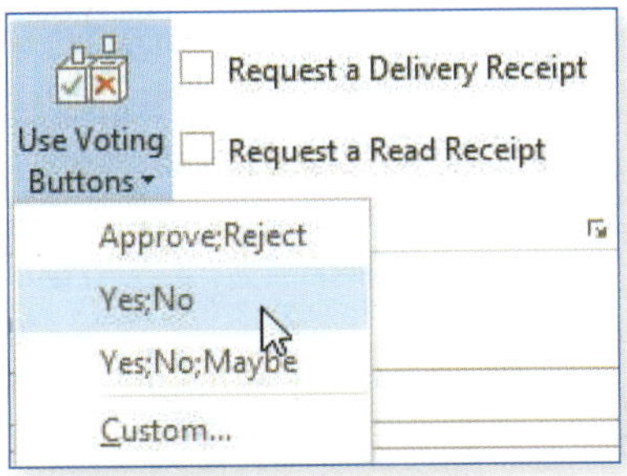

2-41 Preset voting options

> **MORE INFO**
>
> When voting buttons are used, you will see a message in the *InfoBar* stating, "You have added voting buttons to this message."

Custom Voting Buttons

What if you wanted to use the voting buttons to determine your coworkers' preferences for lunch on Friday? The preset buttons would not be effective in this case. Outlook provides you the option of creating custom voting buttons (Figure 2-42). Custom voting buttons could be used to find the day of the week that works best for a team meeting or the choice of restaurant for a Friday lunch. As the sender of the message and question, you can create your own custom voting buttons in the *Properties* dialog box by typing each voting option separated by a semicolon.

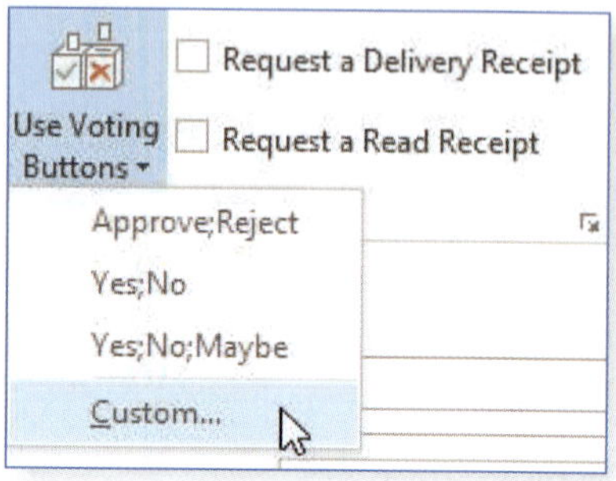

2-42 Custom voting options

HOW TO: Create Custom Voting Buttons

1. In a new email message, click the **Options** tab.
2. Click the **Use Voting Buttons** button.
3. Choose **Custom**. The *Properties* dialog box opens.
4. Select the **Use voting buttons** check box.
5. Select and delete the preset voting buttons (*Accept;Reject*).
6. Type in your voting choices. Separate each choice with a semicolon (Figure 2-43).
7. Click **Close** to close the *Properties* dialog box. The *InfoBar* will inform you that you are using voting buttons on this message.
8. Type and send the email.

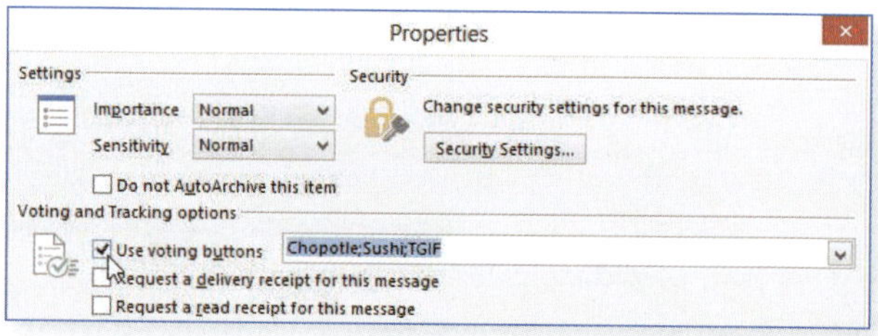

2-43 Custom voting buttons

Respond Using Voting Buttons

When a recipient receives an email with voting buttons, there is a *Vote* button to the left of the *Reply* button in the *Respond* group. Also, there is a message in the *InfoBar* alerting the recipient to vote by using the *Vote* button.

When the *Vote* button is clicked, the voting choices appear in a list below the button. The recipient can make his or her selection from the list of choices.

After the selection is made, the recipient can choose one of the following two options: *Send the response now* or *Edit the response before sending*. If *Send the response now* is selected, Outlook automatically replies to the email and includes the recipient's voting selection.

If *Edit the response before sending* is selected, a reply email opens allowing the recipient to include an email response in addition to his or her voting selection. After typing a response in the body, the recipient must send the response.

HOW TO: Reply Using Voting Buttons

1. Open the email message that has voting buttons.
2. Click the **Vote** button and make a selection (Figure 2-44).
3. Choose *either Send the response now* or *Edit the response before sending*.

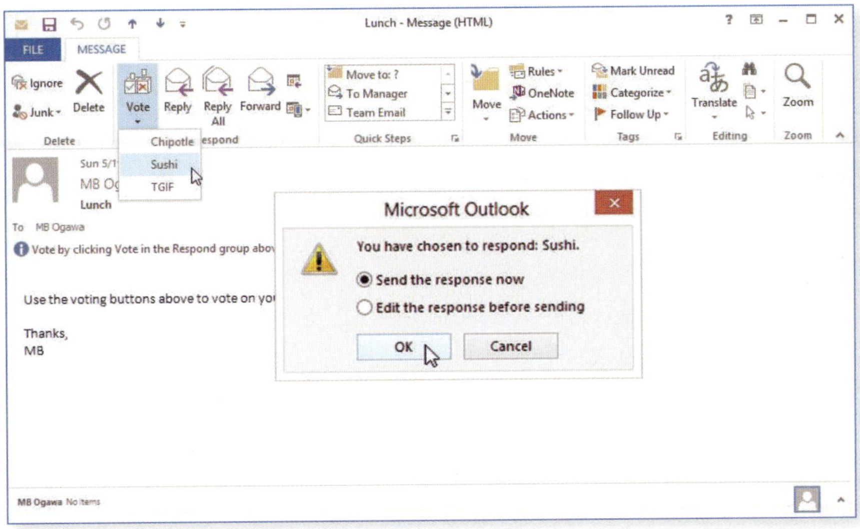

2-44 Voting response

- If you choose *Send the response now*, click **OK** and you are finished and your voting selection has been sent.
- If you chose *Edit the response before sending* and click **OK**, a reply email will automatically open.
- Type any additional information you would like to include in the body of the email.
- Click **Send**.

4. Close the original email.

Track Voting Responses

When recipients respond to an email with voting buttons, the sender of the message will receive the responses. The responses received will include the recipient's voting selection in front of the original subject (Figure 2-45). Also, Outlook uses tracking to record the responses received.

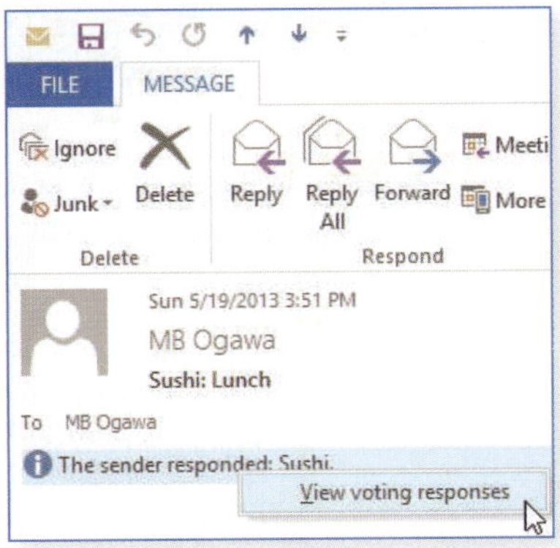

2-45 View voting responses option

HOW TO: Track Voting Responses

1. Open a voting response you received. The voting response is displayed in both the subject line and the *InfoBar*.
2. Click the **InfoBar**, and then click **View voting responses**. The original email message opens. A summary of the voting responses will be displayed in the *InfoBar*, and the individual voting response will be displayed in the body of the message.
3. After you are finished, close both of the open email messages.

ANOTHER WAY

Voting responses can also be viewed by opening the original message from your *Sent Items* folder. Any sent message that has tracking will be marked with a tracking icon rather than a message icon (Figure 2-46).

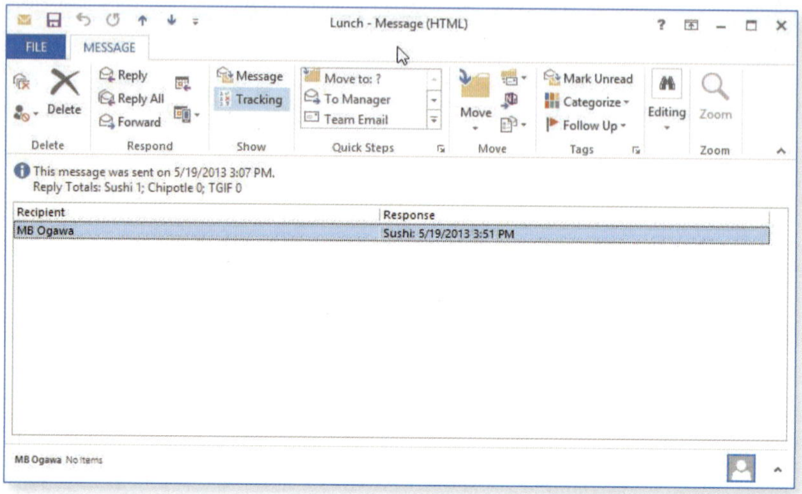

2-46 Voting responses

MORE INFO

Results of the voting can be copied and pasted into Excel.

PAUSE & PRACTICE: OUTLOOK 2-3

For this Pause and Practice project, you use voting buttons to determine a good location for your lunch meeting.

1. Open the message with the subject ***My lunch preferences***.
2. Reply to the message using voting options to determine your partner's top choice.
   a. Click the **Reply** button [*Message* tab, *Respond* group].
   b. Click the **Use Voting Buttons** button [*Options* tab, *Tracking* group] and select **Custom**.
   c. Ensure the **Use voting buttons** option is checked. Delete the text in the text field and type French Cuisine; Italian Cuisine; Japanese Cuisine.
   d. Click the **Close** button.
   e. Add the following text to the body of the message:

      Use the voting options above to select your preference. I do not have a preference, so I would like you to choose.

      [your name]

   f. Click the **Send** button.

3. Open your partner's message to you and select *Italian Cuisine*.
   a. Click the **Vote** button [*Message* tab, *Response* group] and select **Italian Cuisine**.
   b. Click the **Send Response Now** radio button and click **OK**.
4. Check your Inbox for the latest message with the voting response (Figure 2-47).

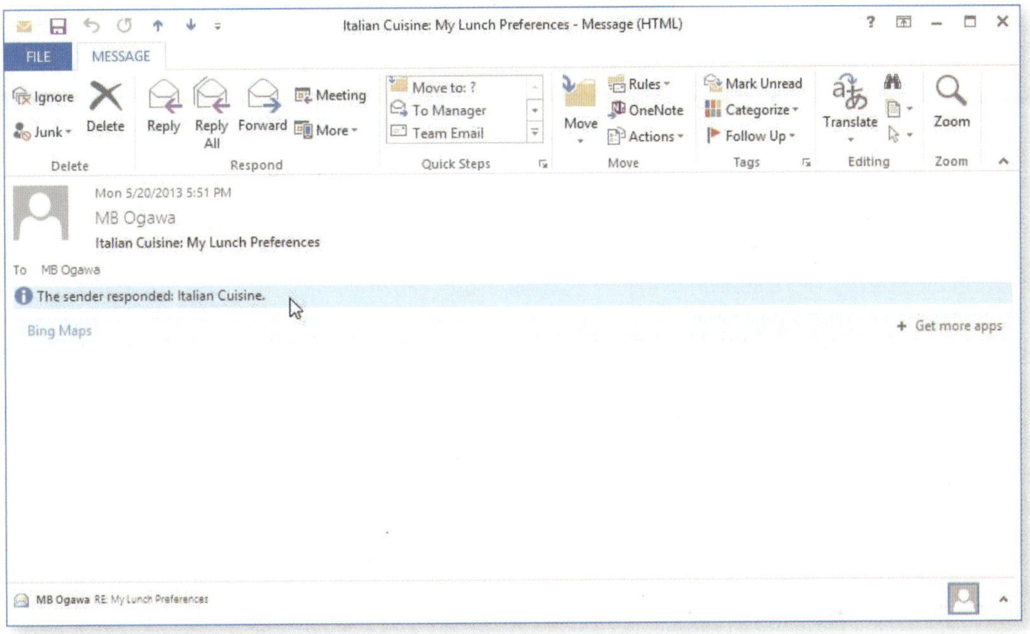

2-47 Completed Pause & Practice 2-3

SLO 2.6

Customizing Your Email

Have you ever received an email where the body of the message had nice fonts, colors, and background graphics? Most likely, the sender did not spend a huge amount of time customizing the design of the email specifically for you.

As covered in Chapter 1, users have a lot control over how to format the body of an email message. But Outlook also provides users with many features to customize the look of emails by using ***signatures***, ***stationery***, and ***themes***. The default settings can be changed so that each new email created will have a consistent and customized look.

Create a Signature

A ***signature*** is a saved group of information that can be inserted into the body of an email. Typically, a signature can include the sender's name, title, company, address, and contact information. Signatures can also include logos and graphics. Signatures save time by storing this information so you don't have to type all of it each time you create an email. Signatures can be manually or automatically inserted at the bottom of each new email you create. You can create and save multiple signatures.

HOW TO: Create a Signature

1. Click the **File** tab to open the *Backstage* window.
2. Click **Options** on the left. The *Outlook Options* dialog box opens (Figure 2-48).
3. Click the **Mail** button on the left.
4. Click **Signatures**. The *Signatures and Stationery* dialog box opens.
5. Click **New**. The *New Signature* dialog box opens (Figure 2-49).
6. Type the name for your signature and press **OK** to close the *New Signature* dialog box.
7. In the *Edit signature* section of the dialog box, type your signature information. You can use different fonts, sizes, styles, colors, and alignments to customize your signature.
8. When you are satisfied with your signature, press **Save** (Figure 2-50).
9. Click **OK** to close the *Signatures and Stationery* dialog box.
10. Click **OK** to close the *Outlook Options* dialog box.

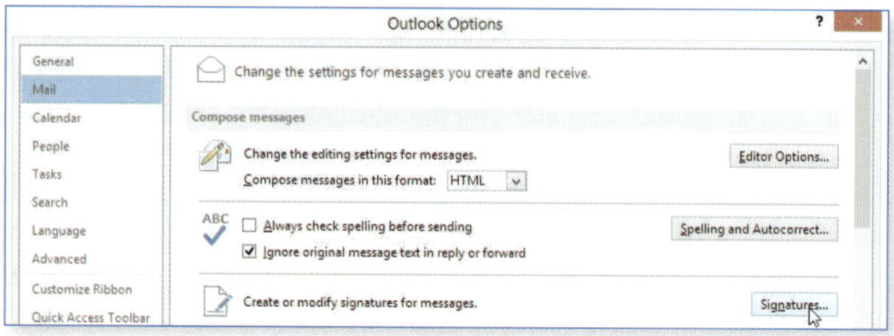

2-48 Outlook Options dialog box

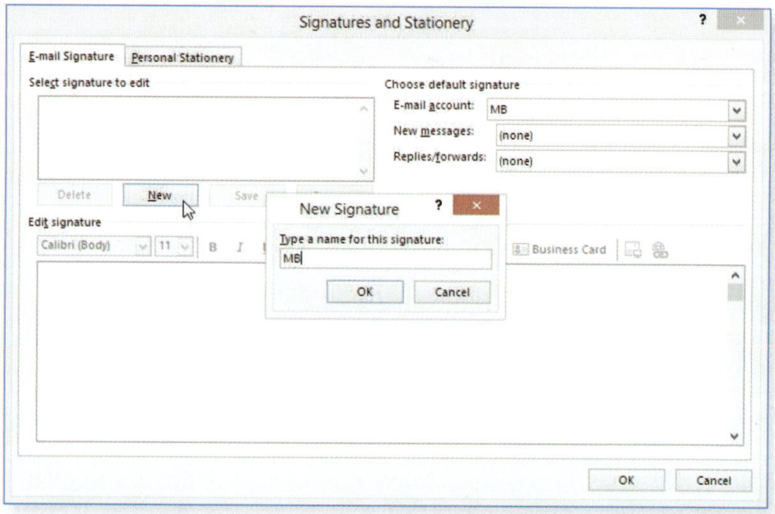

2-49 Signatures and Stationery dialog box

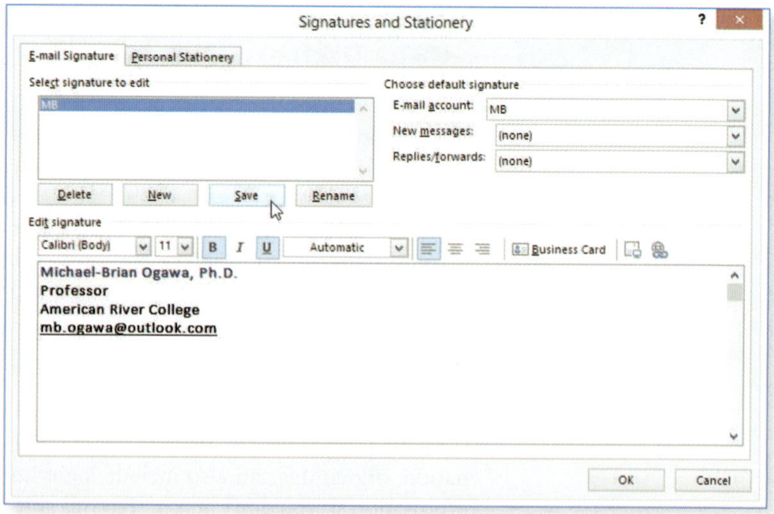

2-50 Sample signature

ANOTHER WAY

The *Signatures and Stationery* dialog box can be opened from a new email message, replies, or forwards by clicking on the **Signature** button on the *Message* tab and selecting **Signatures**.

MORE INFO

Signatures are not limited to names and contact information. Any information that is commonly inserted into the body of an email can be saved as a signature including paragraphs of text. You can create and save multiple signatures.

Signatures are stored on your computer, not on the Exchange server.

Set a Default Signature

The default settings on signatures can be changed to automatically insert your signature on all new emails, on all replies and forwards, or on all new emails, replies, and forwards. Or, the default settings can be set to *(none)*.

HOW TO: Set a Default Signature

1. With a new email open, click the **Signatures** button and choose **Signatures**. The *Signatures and Stationery* dialog box opens. (This dialog box can also be opened from the *Backstage* window by choosing **Options**, **Mail**, and then **Signatures**.)
2. In the *Choose default signature* area, set your desired signature defaults (Figure 2-51).
3. Click **OK** to close the *Signatures and Stationery* dialog box.

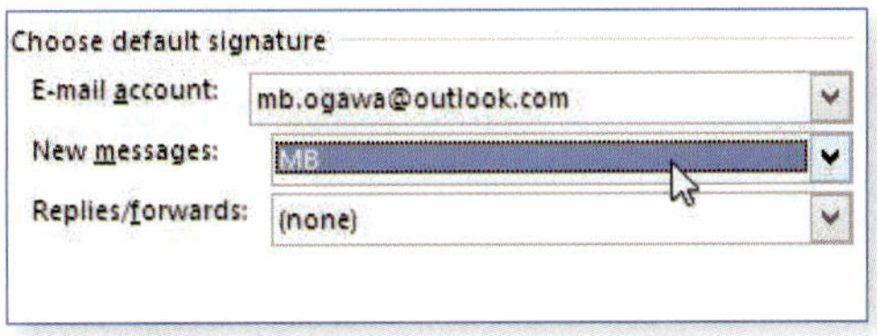

2-51 Default signature

MORE INFO

Be careful to not use your signature as the default on all emails as it might appear pretentious. When sending emails or replying to coworkers, friends, or family, a signature is usually not necessary.

MORE INFO

If you have multiple email accounts in Outlook, you can set up different default signatures for each account.

Manually Insert a Signature

Once your signature is saved, it can be inserted into any new message you create, or it can be inserted into any email that you reply to or forward. The *Signature* button will be available in the *Include* group on both the *Message* and *Insert* tabs on any new, replied to, or forwarded email. Be aware that the signature button icon might appear differently depending on the size of the email window.

HOW TO: Manually Insert a Signature

1. In a new, replied to, or forwarded email, click the **Signature** button in the *Include* group on either the *Message* or *Insert* tab (Figure 2-52).
2. Choose the signature to be inserted into the body of the email.
3. The signature is inserted into the body of the email with a couple of blank lines left above it for the email text.

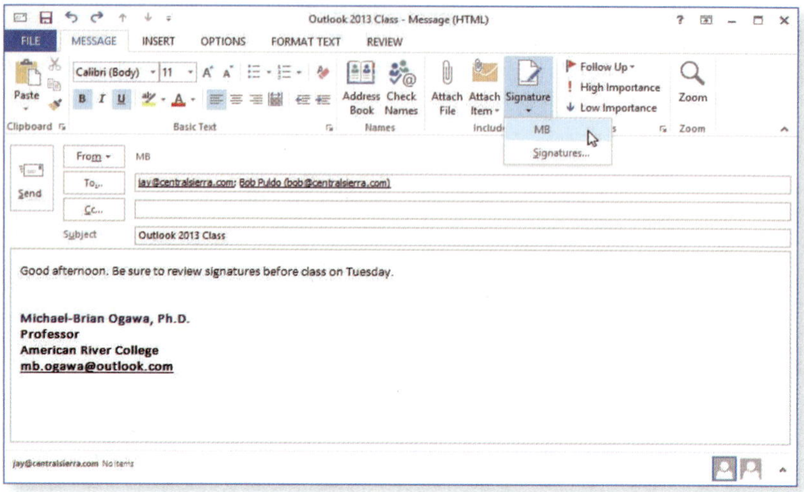

2-52 Signature selection

> **MORE INFO**
>
> Only one signature can be inserted in the body of an email. If you insert a second signature, it will replace the first one.

Themes

Themes are a set of fonts, colors, backgrounds, and fill effects in the body of an email. All emails include a theme. The default setting is the ***Office Theme***, which includes a white background with dark and subtle colors. A theme can be selected and customized for each email you create.

The *Themes* group is on the *Options* tab of an email message (Figure 2-53). You can change the theme, color set, font set, effects, and page color to customize the look of your email. ***Page color*** is the background of the body of an email and is not limited to solid colors; you can change the page color to include a ***gradient***, ***texture***, ***pattern***, or ***picture***.

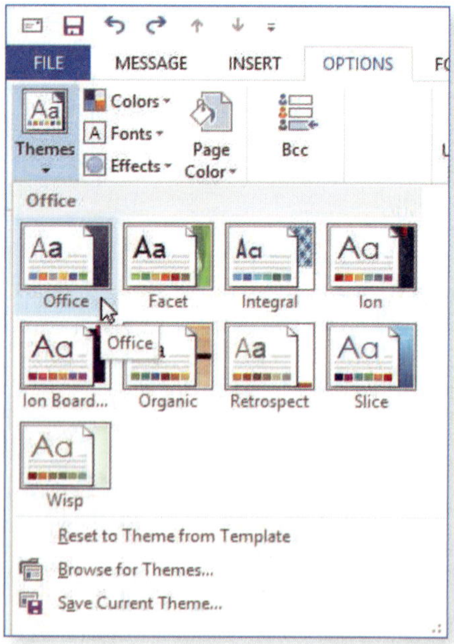

2-53 Themes

> **MORE INFO**
>
> Be careful about making your email message look too fancy and colorful. If you're using email in a business setting, you want your email to look professional. Using a picture as a background will also increase the file size of your email. Sometimes less is more!

Set the Default Theme and Font

To add consistency to your email documents, you might want to change the default settings to control the look of all emails you create. The default settings can be changed to include a theme, consisting of fonts, colors, and background graphics, on all new emails. If you are not using a theme, you can change the default settings on the font, size, style, and color used on all new emails, replies and forwards.

HOW TO: Set the Default Theme and Font

1. Click the **File** tab to open the *Backstage* window.
2. Click the **Options** button on the left. The *Outlook Options* dialog box opens.
3. Click the **Mail** button.
4. Click the **Stationery and Fonts** button. The *Signatures and Stationery* dialog box opens.
5. Click the **Personal Stationery** tab if it is not already displayed (Figure 2-54).

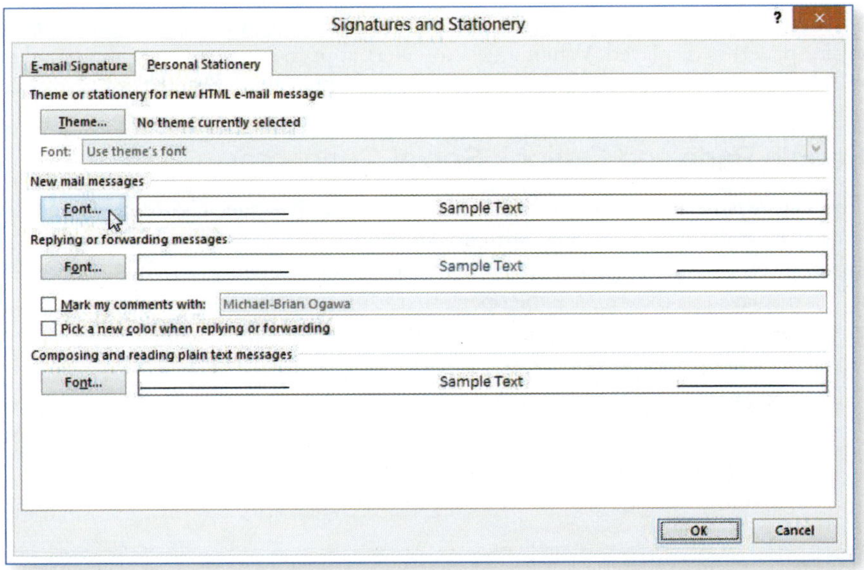

2-54 Personal stationery

6. Set your default preferences for **Theme**, **New mail messages**, and/or **Replying or forwarding messages**.
   - Click the **Font** button under *New mail messages* to modify fonts for new email messages.
   - Click the **Font** button under *Replying or forwarding messages* to modify fonts for replies or forwarded messages.
7. Click **OK** to close the *Signatures and Stationery* dialog box.
8. Click **OK** to close the *Outlook Options* dialog box.

MORE INFO

When a default theme is selected, you have the following choices: *Use the theme's font, Use my font when replying and forwarding messages*, or *Always use my fonts.*

Desktop Alerts

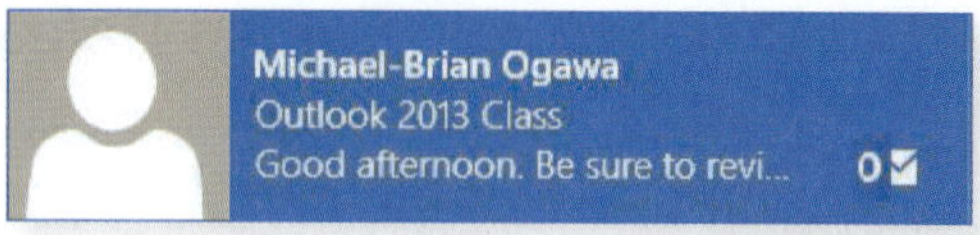

2-55 Desktop alert

A ***desktop alert*** is a notification you receive when a new email arrives in your Inbox (Figure 2-55). The desktop alert appears in a corner of your computer screen and remains there for a few seconds. By default, desktop alerts are turned on. They will also appear when you receive a Meeting Request or Task Request.

> **MORE INFO**
>
> Desktop alerts only appear for items received in your Inbox. A rule can be created to have desktop alerts appear when an email is received in other folders. Rules will be covered in Chapter 6.
>
> A desktop alert will not appear if you are running a PowerPoint presentation.

The desktop alert notifies you of the name of the sender, the subject, and a portion of the body of the message. Outlook allows you to perform some actions on an email when a desktop alert is displayed. When a desktop alert appears, you can open the email message by clicking on the desktop alert. You can also flag or delete the message from the desktop alert.

People Pane and Outlook Social Connector

The ***People pane*** appears at the bottom of each email message (Figure 2-56) and consolidates other Outlook items associated with an individual. The *People* pane will display email messages, meetings, task requests, attachments, and social network activity as links. Clicking on a link displayed in the *People* pane opens that Outlook item. The *People* pane can also be collapsed or expanded by clicking on the small arrow in the upper right corner of the pane.

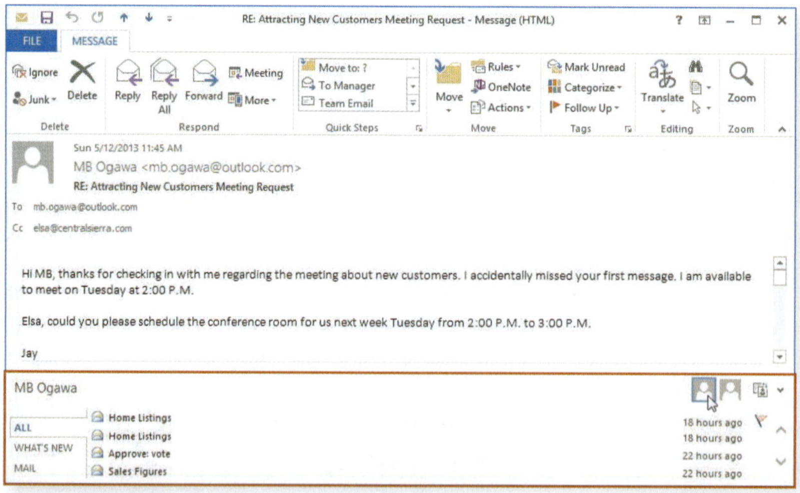

2-56 People pane

If there are multiple recipients of an email, the *People* pane can display items related to each of them. Clicking on one of the picture icons in the top right corner of the *People* pane will allow you to switch between individuals to be displayed in the *People* pane.

The ***Outlook Social Connector (OSC)*** works in conjunction with the *People* pane and can be used to keep track of the social network activity of your personal and business contacts. If your organization is using SharePoint 2013, the OSC can connect with SharePoint to display the activity of your contacts. The OSC can also be used to connect with other social networking sites. To connect to these sites, you will have to download and install an add-in from these sites.

> **MORE INFO**
>
> The *People* pane and Outlook Social Connector will also be discussed in Chapter 3.

PAUSE & PRACTICE: OUTLOOK 2-4

For this Pause and Practice project, you create a signature and insert it in an email message to your peer. You also forward the stream of messages to your instructor.

1. Create a new signature.
   a. Click the **File** tab to open the *Backstage* view and select **Options**. The *Outlook Options* dialog box opens.
   b. Select the **Mail** option.
   c. Click the **Signatures. . .** button. The *Signatures and Stationery* dialog box opens.
   d. Click the **New** button.
   e. Type School Signature and click **OK**.
   f. In the *Edit signature* text area, type:

      [Your Name]
      Student, [Institution Name]
      [your email address]

   g. Select your name and click **Bold** and **Italicize**.
   h. Select the second and third lines of your signature and click **Bold**.
   i. Click the **Save** button.
   j. Click the **OK** button.
   k. Click the **OK** button in the *Outlook Options* dialog box to close it.
2. Select the message from your partner indicating his or her choice, *Italian Cuisine*.
3. Click the **Reply** button to reply to the message including the following information in the email message fields.

   Cc: Your email address
   Body: Thanks, [partner name]. Let's meet at the Italian restaurant on campus for the business project meeting on Monday at noon. See you there!

4. At the end of the body, press the **Enter** key twice.
5. Click the **Signature** button [*Message* tab, *Include* group] and select school signature.
6. Click the **Send** button.
7. Locate and open the message in your Inbox that you sent to your partner and Cc'd to yourself.
8. Click the **Forward** button and enter the following information in the email message fields:
   To: your instructor's email address
   Cc: your email address
   Subject: ***FW: Chapter 2 Pause and Practice***
   Body: Hi [instructor name], this is the Pause and Practice assignments for chapter 2 for class.

9. At the end of the body, press the **Enter** key twice.
10. Click the **Signature** button [*Message* tab, *Include* group] and select school signature.
11. Click the **Send** button (Figure 2-57).

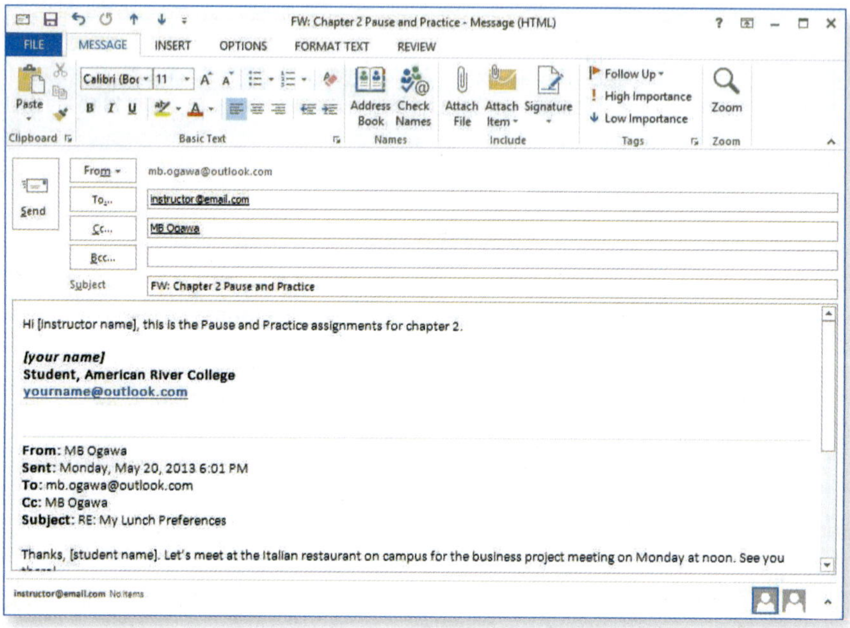

2-57 Completed Pause & Practice 2-4

Chapter Summary

2.1 Differentiate between the types of email formats (p. O2-51).

- There are three types of email formats: Plain text, Hypertext Markup Language, and Rich Text Format.
- **Plain text** format is supported by all email clients. However, it does not support styles such as bold, italic, or underline.
- **Hypertext Markup Language (HTML)** is the default format in Outlook and is most commonly used today. HTML format lets you format the body of your email message similar to a Microsoft Word document.
- **Rich Text Format (RTF)** is unique to Outlook users and is supported in an Exchange environment. This format allows users to use the different formatting features available in Outlook.
- It is probably best to use HTML format if you are sending messages outside of an Exchange environment.

2.2 Customize your email using the different types of email options available in Outlook (p. O2-52).

- There are three levels of importance that can be placed on messages: ***high***, ***normal***, and ***low***. The default level of importance is normal.
- Messages can be marked with different levels of sensitivity. They are ***Normal*** (default setting), ***Personal***, ***Private***, and ***Confidential***.
- Outlook allows you to apply security settings, such as ***digital signatures*** and ***encryption*** on messages.
- You can request ***delivery*** and and/or ***read receipts*** when sending messages.
- By using delivery options, you can change where sent items are saved and delay the delivery of messages.
- You can specify who message replies are directed to.
- You can set messages to expire after a specific date.
- Flags for recipients can be used as reminders.
- You can set permissions on messages to prevent others from forwarding messages (requires IRM to be set up by your administrator).

2.3 Use categories to organize email messages into different groups (p. O2-61).

- ***Categories*** can be used to organize email messages.
- You can create categories based on your needs.
- You can view items within a specific category using the view settings.

2.4 Add *Follow Up* flags to email messages to add reminders to messages (p. O2-64).

- ***Follow Up flags*** can be used as reminders.
- *Follow Up* flags create To-Do items.

2.5 Use email voting buttons to get responses from recipients and to automatically track responses (p. O2-69).

- ***Voting buttons*** allow you to quickly gather replies from other users.
- Voting buttons have the following presets: *Approve;Reject*, *Yes;No*, and *Yes;No;Maybe*.
- You can customize the voting buttons to include any choices.
- Voting buttons allow you to automatically track replies, as opposed to manually counting.

2.6 Customize your emails by using signatures, themes, and desktop alerts (p. O2-73).

- ***Signatures*** allow you to quickly add a group of information to your emails.
- You can create multiple signatures to choose from.
- Signatures can be automatically added to your messages, or you can manually add them.
- ***Themes*** can be used to quickly improve the aesthetics of your messages.
- ***Desktop alerts*** appear in the upper right corner of the screen and give you an overview of a message received, meeting request, or task request.
- The ***People pane*** consolidates multiple Outlook items that are associated with an individual.

Check for Understanding

In the ***Online Learning Center*** for this text (www.mhhe.com/office2013inpractice), there are a variety of resources that can be used to review the concepts covered in this chapter.

The following Online Learning Resources are available in the Online Learning Center:

- Multiple choice questions
- Short answer questions
- Matching exercises

USING MICROSOFT OUTLOOK 2013

Guided Project 2-1

For this project, you work as a Real Estate Agent for Placer Hills Real Estate (PHRE). You recently spoke on the phone with a client who is looking to purchase their first home. You follow up with her using email. [Student Learning Outcomes 2.1, 2.2, 2.6]

Skills Covered in This Project

- Select message format.
- Apply a theme.
- Create a signature.
- Add a signature to a message.

1. Create a new email message to Katie Binstead.
   a. Click the **New Email** button [*Home* tab, *New* group].
   b. In the *To* field, type your instructor's email address.
   c. In the *Cc* field, type your email address.
   d. In the *Subject* field, type Home of your dreams follow-up.
2. Click the **Rich Text** button [*Format Text* tab, *Format* group].
3. Click the **Themes** button [*Options* tab, *Themes* group] and select **Organic**.
4. Create a new signature.
   a. Click the **File** tab and select **Options**.
   b. Click the **Mail** button on the left.
   c. Click **Signatures**. The *Signatures and Stationery* dialog box opens.
   d. Click **New**. The *New Signature* dialog box opens.
   e. Type [your name] PHRE for your signature and press **OK** to close the *New Signature* dialog box.
   f. Click **OK** to close the *Outlook Options* dialog box.
5. Edit the signature.
   a. Click the **File** tab and select **Options**.
   b. Click the **Mail** button on the left.
   c. Click **Signatures**. The *Signatures and Stationery* dialog box opens.
   d. In the *Edit signature* section of the dialog box, type the following information:

      [your name], Real Estate Agent
      Placer Hills Real Estate

   e. Click the **Save** button.
   f. Click OK to close the Signatures and Stationary dialog box.
6. In the body of the message, type the following text:

   Hi Katie, It was great speaking with you about your ideas for a new home for your family. It is definitely an exciting endeavor. I am looking forward to helping you find the home of your family's dreams.

   Thanks,
7. Press the **Enter** key after the "Thanks" line.

8. Click the **Signature** button [*Message* tab, *Include* group] and select **[your name] PHRE** to insert your signature.
9. Click the **Send** button to send the message (Figure 2-58).

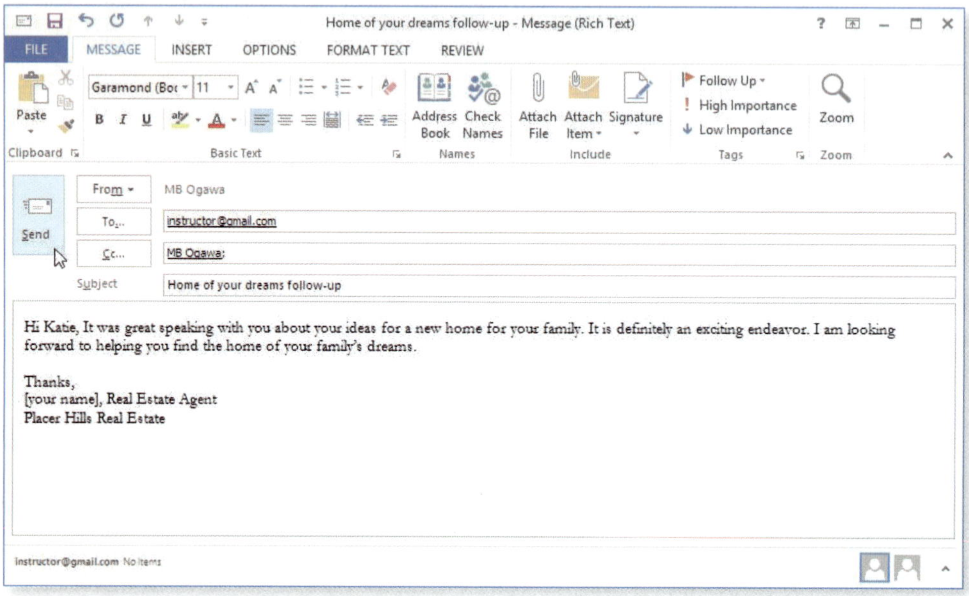

2-58 Completed Guided Project 2-1

Guided Project 2-2

For this project, you follow up with Katie regarding her family's dream home. To help you search for possible options, you ask her to decide on the number of bedrooms her family wants. Since Katie's family is serious about purchasing a home, you create a category for her email messages.
[Student Learning Outcomes 2.1, 2.2, 2.3, 2.5, 2.6]

Skills Covered in This Project

- Create a category.
- Set a Quick Click category.
- Select a message format.
- Apply a theme.
- Add a signature to a message.
- Add custom voting buttons to a message.

1. Open the email message you sent in *Guided Project 2-1*.
2. Create a new category called "Katie" (Figure 2-59).

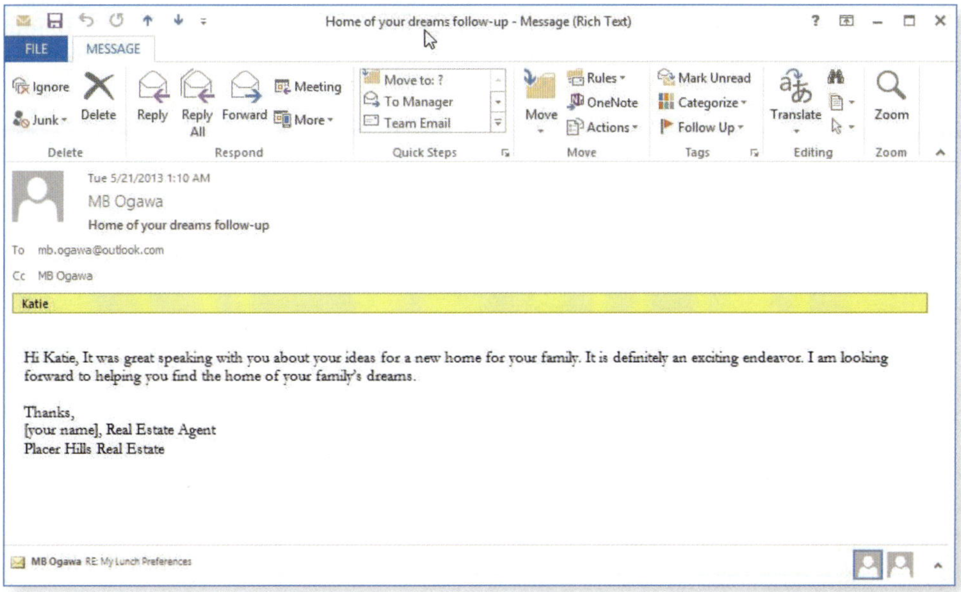

2-59 Katie category

a. Click the **Categorize** button [*Message* tab, *Tags* group] and select **All Categories**.
b. Click the **New** button and type Katie in the *Name* text field.
c. Click the drop-down arrow next to color and select **yellow**.
d. Click the **OK** button to close the *Add New Category* dialog box.
e. Ensure the **Katie** check box is selected and click **OK**.

3. Set the *Katie* category as a *Quick Click*.
   a. Click the **Categorize** button and select **Set Quick Click**.
   b. Click the drop-down arrow and select **Katie**.
   c. Click **OK**.
4. Create a new email message to Katie.
   a. Click the **New Email** button [*Home* tab, *New* group].
   b. In the *To* field, type your instructor's email address.
   c. In the *Cc* field, type your email address.
   d. In the *Subject* field, type Number of bedrooms for property.
5. Click the **Rich Text** button [*Format Text* tab, *Format* group].
6. Click the **Themes** button [*Options* tab, *Themes* group] and select **Organic**.
7. In the body of the message, type the following text:

   Hi Katie, To help me find as many homes as possible for us to check out, could you please use the voting button above to select the number of bedrooms your dream home should have?

   Thanks,
8. Press the **Enter** key after the "Thanks" line.

9. Click the **Signature** button [*Message* tab, *Include* group] and select **[your name] PHRE** to insert your signature.
10. Add voting buttons for two bedrooms, three bedrooms, or four bedrooms to the message.
    a. Click the **Use Voting Buttons** button [*Options* tab, *Tracking* group] and select **Custom**.
    b. Ensure the *Use voting buttons* option is checked and replace the text *Approve;Reject* with 2 bedrooms;3 bedrooms;4 bedrooms.
    c. Click **Close**.
11. Click the **Send** button to send the message (Figure 2-60).

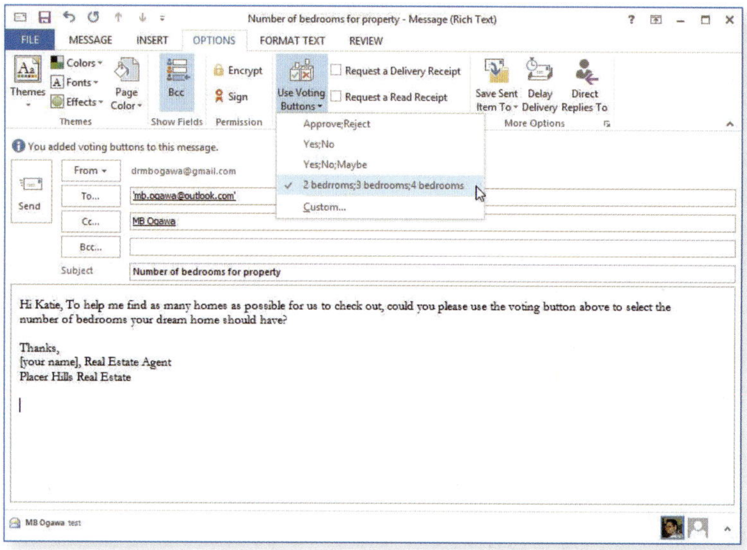

2-60 Completed Guided Project 2-2

Guided Project 2-3

For this project, you send one final message to Katie to confirm a full day of house tours next week on Thursday.
[Student Learning Outcomes 2.1, 2.2, 2.3, 2.4, 2.5, 2.6]

Skills Covered in This Project

- Apply a category to a message.
- Select a message format.
- Apply a theme.
- Add a signature to a message.
- Add preset voting buttons to a message.
- Add a custom Follow Up flag.

1. Open the email message you sent in Guided Project 2-2.
2. Click the **Categorize** button [*Message* tab, *Tags* group] and select **Katie**.
3. Create a new email message to Katie.
   a. Click the **New Email** button [*Home* tab, *New* group].
   b. In the *To* field, type your instructor's email address.
   c. In the *Cc* field, type your email address.
   d. In the *Subject* field, type Property Tour.
4. Click the **Rich Text** button [*Format Text* tab, *Format* group].
5. Click the **Themes** button [*Options* tab, *Themes* group] and select **Organic**.
6. In the body of the message, type the following text:

   Hi Katie, I would like to confirm that you are available next week Thursday for the property tour? I found 6 homes that could be a good fit for your family. Please use the voting button above to approve or reject this date.

   Thanks,

7. Press the **Enter** key after the "Thanks" line.
8. Click the **Signature** button [*Message* tab, *Include* group] and select **[your name] PHRE** to insert your signature.
9. Click the **Use Voting Buttons** button [*Options* tab, *Tracking* group] and select **Approve;Reject**.
10. Add a *Follow Up* flag to the message with a reminder to call Katie tomorrow if you do not receive a response.
    a. Click the **Follow Up** button [*Message* tab, *Tags* group] and select **Custom**.
    b. Click the drop-down arrow next to the due date and select tomorrow's date.
    c. Click the **Reminder** check box.
    d. Click the **OK** button.
11. Click the **Send** button to send the message (Figure 2-61).

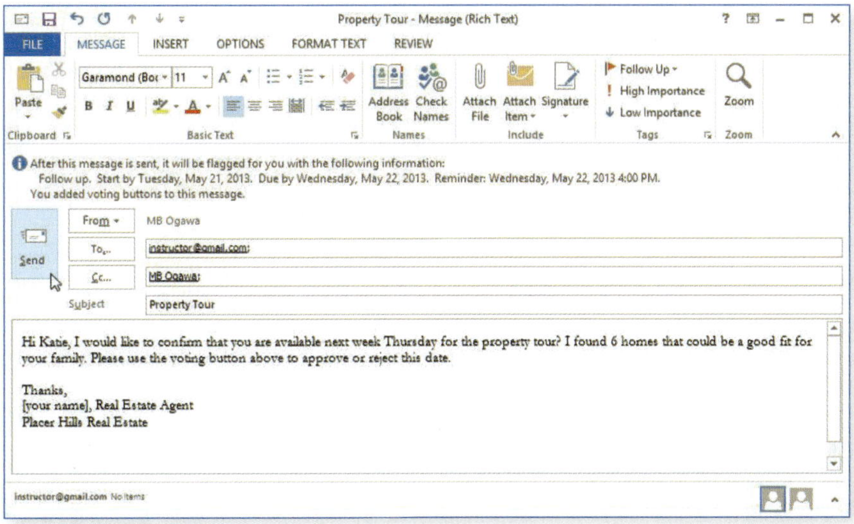

2-61 Completed Guided Project 2-3

Independent Project 2-4

For this project, you are an organizer for the American River Cycling Club (ARCC). You decide to develop a training cycle for the upcoming season. Therefore, you email your members and ask them to vote on a variety of cycling activities to determine priorities for each.
[Student Learning Outcomes 2.1, 2.2, 2.4, 2.5, 2.6]

Skills Covered in This Project

- Select a message format.
- Apply a theme.
- Create a signature.
- Add a signature.
- Add a custom voting button.
- Add a custom voting button.
- Add a *Follow Up* flag

1. Create a new message to the ARCC.
   a. In the *To* field, type your instructor's email address.
   b. In the *Cc* field, type your email address.
2. Type ARCC Training Poll in the subject line.
3. Change the message format to **Rich Text Format**.
4. Apply the **Integral** theme to the message.
5. In the body of the message, type the following text:

   Hi everyone. As we prepare for the upcoming training season, I would like to know which type of training you prefer. If you would like to recommend another type of training, please send me a message containing the type of training. Based on the results of the poll, I will set up a training schedule to accommodate our needs as best as possible.

   Thanks,
6. Create a signature named ***[your name] ARCC***. The signature should have the following format:

   [your name]

   Organizer, ARCC
7. Add the ***[your name] ARCC*** signature to the message after the "Thanks" line.
8. Add a custom voting button with the following options: **Road;Mountain; Cyclocross**.
9. Add a **Follow Up flag** with a reminder for you in one week.
10. Click the **Send** button to send the message (Figure 2-62).

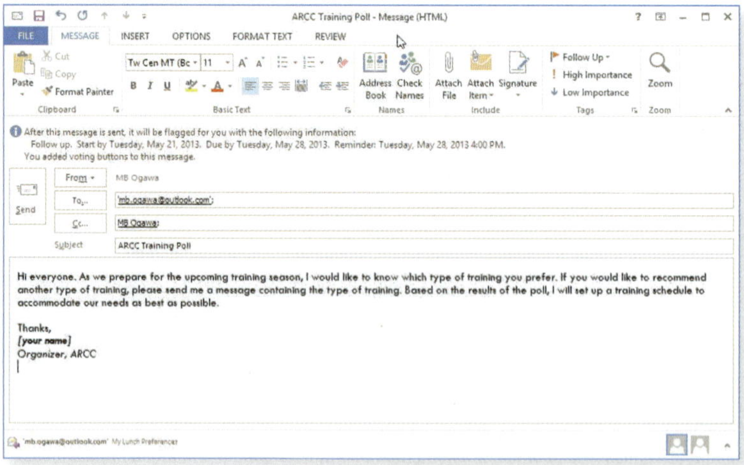

2-62 Completed Independent Project 2-4

Independent Project 2-5

For this project, you categorize the message sent in Independent Project 2-4. You also share the results of the poll from with the ARCC members.
[Student Learning Outcomes 2.1, 2.2, 2.3, 2.4, 2.6]

Skills Covered in This Project

- Create a category.
- Apply a category to a message.
- Select a message format.
- Apply a theme.
- Add a signature.
- Set the message priority.
- Add a *Follow Up* flag.

---

1. Create a new category called **Cycle Training** using red as the category color and apply it to the message you sent in Independent Project 2-4.
2. Create a new message to the ARCC.
   a. In the To field, type your instructor's email address.
   b. In the Cc field, type your email address.
3. Add the subject Results: ARCC Training Poll.
4. Change the message format to **Rich Text Format**.
5. Apply the **Integral** theme to the message.
6. In the body of the message, type the following text:

   Hi everyone. Based on the poll, we have the following results.
   50% Mountain
   25% Road
   25% Cyclocross

   Therefore, we will distribute our training in this manner. A few members also sent me other ideas for training sessions, which I will do my best to incorporate. Please check your email for our schedule.

   Thanks,

7. Add the ***[your name] ARCC*** signature to the message after the "Thanks" line.
8. Set the message priority to **low**.
9. Add a **Follow Up flag** with a reminder in three days and a due date in one week.
10. Click the **Send** button to send the message (Figure 2-63).

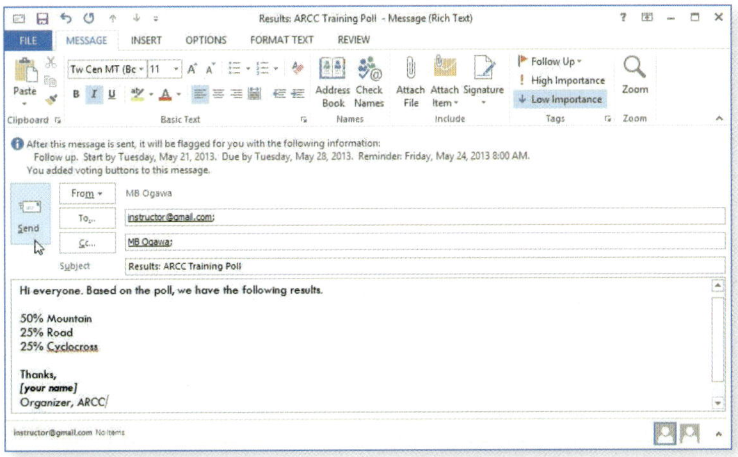

2-63 Completed Independent Project 2-5

Independent Project 2-6

For this project, you familiarize yourself with the basic components of Outlook.
[Student Learning Outcomes 2.1, 2.2, 2.3, 2.4, 2.6]

Skills Covered in This Project

- Apply a category to a message.
- Select a message format.
- Apply a theme.
- Add a preset voting button.
- Add a signature.
- Add a *Follow Up* flag with a reminder.

1. Apply the **Cycle Training** category to the message you sent in Independent Project 2-5.
2. Create a new message to the ARCC.
   a. In the *To* field, type your instructor's email address.
   b. In the *Cc* field, type your email address.
3. Add the subject Training Schedule.
4. Change the message format to **Rich Text Format**.
5. Apply the **Integral** theme to the message.
6. In the body of the message, type the following text:

   Hi everyone. Listed below is our training schedule for the upcoming quarter.

   Monday: Mountain
   Tuesday: Road
   Wednesday: Off
   Thursday: Cyclocross
   Friday: Mountain

   Please use the voting button above to approve or reject the schedule. If you reject, please indicate why in the message.

   Thanks,
7. Add an **Approve;Reject** voting button to the message.
8. Add the ***[your name] ARCC*** signature to the message after the "Thanks" line.
9. Add a **Follow Up flag** with a reminder for you in one week.
10. Click the **Send** button to send the message (Figure 2-64).

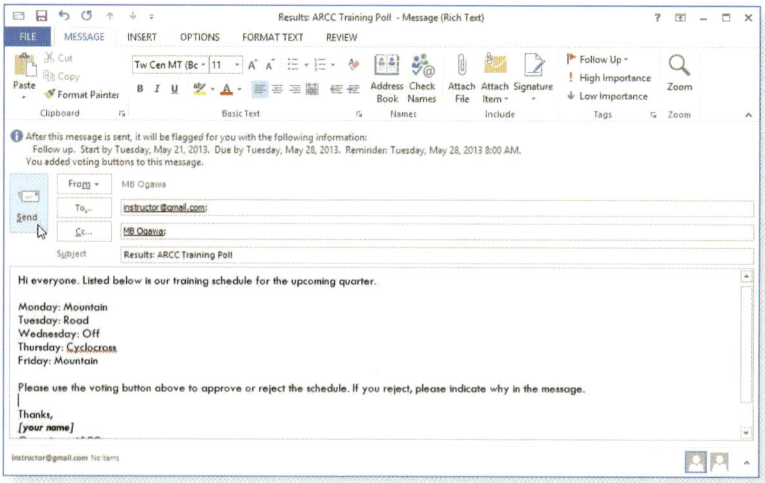

2-64 Completed Independent Project 2-6

Challenge Project 2-7

Compose a message to your instructor to request a meeting regarding your upcoming term paper. This message is of high importance to you. Be sure to use voting options to allow your instructor to quickly select a meeting day.
[Student Learning Outcomes 2.1, 2.2, 2.4, 2.6]

- Send the message to your instructor.
- Add your email address to the *Cc* field.
- The subject of the message should be *Challenge 2-7: Term Paper for ENG 100 Meeting Request*.
- Change the message format to *Rich Text Format*.
- Use voting buttons and the five days of the week to request a day to meet with your instructor.
- Add a *Follow Up* flag to the message and set a reminder for yourself for a week from today.
- Add your signature to the email message.

Challenge Project 2-8

Search for a degree program online that you may be interested in. Develop a set of questions for an academic advisor about the program and how it can suit your educational and lifelong goals. Compose a message to inquire about the program. The application letter should be short and concise.
[Student Learning Outcomes 2.1, 2.2, 2.3, 2.4, 2.6]

- Send the message to your instructor.
- Add your email address to the *Cc* field.
- The subject of the message should be *Challenge 2-8: Potential student inquiry about [educational program]*.
- Change the message format to *HTML Format*.
- Request a delivery receipt.
- Create a category named *School* using a color that you did not assign to a category yet and apply it to the message when you receive it in your Inbox.
- Add a *Follow Up* flag to the message and set a reminder for yourself for a week from today.
- Apply a theme to your email message. The theme should have a professional appearance.
- Print the message and submit it to your instructor.

Challenge Project 2-9

Search online for a job that you would like to have in the future (you may use the position you found in Challenge Project 1-9). Identify a task for your job that requires you to send an email message to coworkers that includes voting options. Compose a message to several coworkers based on the task you identified.
[Student Learning Outcomes 2.1, 2.2, 2.3, 2.4, 2.5, 2.6]

- Send the message to your instructor.
- Add your email address to the *Cc* field.
- The subject of the message should be *Challenge 2-9: Coworkers Inquiry*.
- Change the message format to *Rich Text Format*.
- Add a *Follow Up* flag to the message and set a reminder for yourself for a week from today.
- Categorize your copy of the message using an appropriate category.
- Use voting buttons to automatically track responses based on your inquiry.
- Create and use a signature for your job.
- Apply a theme that is appropriate to the content of the email message.

CHAPTER 3

OUTLOOK

Contacts

CHAPTER OVERVIEW

Before there were various electronic means to store contact information, a physical paper address book was where we kept information about family, friends, neighbors, and business acquaintances. Typically included were names, addresses, and phone numbers; you might have also included birthdays and anniversaries. Microsoft Outlook provides users with a place to electronically store information for emailing, calling, faxing, or sending letters to individuals.

The Outlook ***Contacts*** feature gives you the same benefits of a paper address book, but it also has some unique advantages. In addition to standard personal information, contacts can include company information, a picture, and additional notes. Contacts are stored electronically and integrate seamlessly with other Microsoft Office products so you can create envelopes, labels, and letters. Contacts can easily be shared with other Outlook users. Additionally, Outlook Contacts can be synched with cells phones and other electronic devices.

STUDENT LEARNING OUTCOMES (SLOs)

After completing this chapter, you will be able to:

- SLO 3.1 Differentiate between the *Contacts* folder and the *Global Address List* (p. O3-94).
- SLO 3.2 Create a contact record from different sources (p. O3-95).
- SLO 3.3 Enhance contact records by editing contact information and fields (p. O3-102).
- SLO 3.4 Use and modify the different contact views (p. O3-107).
- SLO 3.5 Create a contact group and produce email from a contact or contact group (p. O3-110).

CASE STUDY

For the Pause & Practice projects, you work with partners in class to create contacts and a contact group to help make communication between you and your classmates more efficient. You also add pictures to contacts to help you match names to faces.

Pause & Practice 3-1: You create a contact with your personal information. You also send it to a partner and create a contact from a business card attached to an email.

Pause & Practice 3-2: You modify your contact to include your picture and a mailing address. You also add a secondary email address.

Pause & Practice 3-3: You create a contact group, update contact information, and send the contact group to your instructor.

SLO 3.1

Understanding Contacts

A ***contact*** is a set of related information about an individual or organization. This could be as simple as a name and email address with the option of storing additional useful information. Outlook Contacts functions similarly to a database, but you do not need to have a thorough understanding of databases to effectively take advantage of the benefits of Outlook Contacts. Since the *Contacts* folder is similar to a database, it is important to understand some basic database terminology.

Database Lingo

An Outlook contact is commonly referred to as a ***record*** or ***contact record***. A record is a group of related information about an individual or organization. Each individual piece of information in a record is called a ***field***. For example, *Full Name, Company, Job Title,* and *Email address* are all fields in a contact record. A group of related records is called a ***file***. In Outlook, a group of related records can be saved in a *Contact* folder. Folders can be created in Contacts to store a group of related contact records.

Contacts versus Global Address List

If you are using Outlook in a home environment (as a stand-alone program rather than on an Exchange server), your contacts will, by default, be saved in the *Contacts* folder (Figure 3-1). You can choose email recipients from your Contacts (Figure 3-2), and you can also create, edit, and delete records in this list of contacts. When you click the *To* button on a new email, your ***Contacts address book*** opens. This address book lists the names and email addresses of those in your Contacts.

If you are using Outlook in an Exchange environment, in addition to your Contacts address book, you will also have a ***Global Address List***. This address book contains the contacts for all the individuals in your organization. Your Exchange server administrator will maintain the *Global Address List*. You cannot add contacts to this folder, but you can save contacts from the *Global Address List* to your *Contacts* folder.

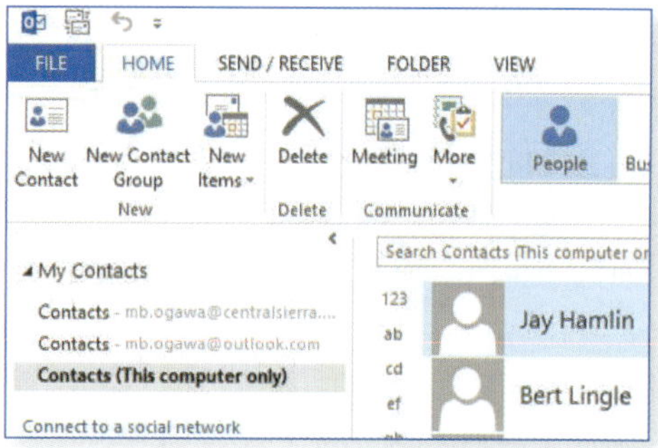

3-1 *Contacts* folder

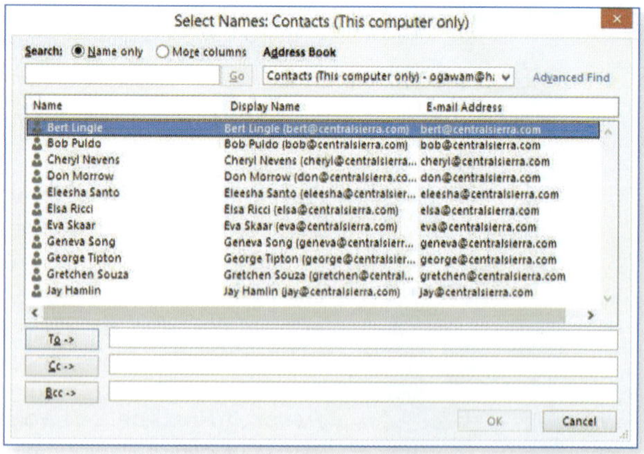

3-2 Choose email recipients from your contacts

> **MORE INFO**
>
> See Chapter 1 for the differences between Outlook as a stand-alone program and Outlook using an Exchange server.

SLO 3.2

Creating Contacts

As with most Microsoft products, there are numerous methods of accomplishing the same task. Adding contact records to your *Contacts* folder can be accomplished in a number of ways. You can create a new contact from scratch, from the same company as an existing contact, from an email you received, from an electronic business card you received, or from the *Global Address List*.

Create a New Contact

To create a new contact, make sure you have selected the **People** button in the *Navigation* pane. When you click the **New Contact** button on the *Home* tab, a new contact record opens. This new contact will be a blank record, and you will be able to add the contact information desired.

HOW TO: Create a New Contact

1. Click the **People** button in the *Navigation* pane.
2. Click the **New Contact** button on the *Home* tab. A new contact record opens (Figure 3-3).

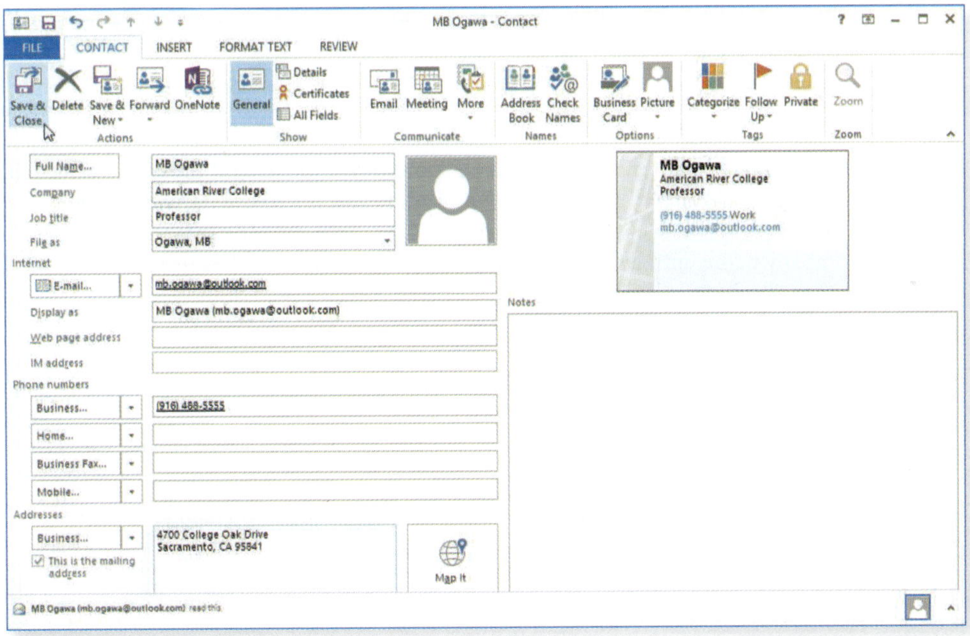

3-3 *New Contact* dialog box

3. Fill in the desired contact information.
4. Click the **Save & Close** button in the *Actions* group on the *Contact* tab when finished. The contact will be saved in your *Contacts* folder.

ANOTHER WAY

Ctrl+N opens a new contact record when you are in Outlook Contacts.
Ctrl+Shift+C opens a new contact record anywhere in Outlook.
Ctrl+S or the *Save* button on the *Quick Access* toolbar saves an open contact.

You can click the **Save & New** button in the *Actions* group on the *Contact* tab (Figure 3-4) to save the current contact in the *Contacts* folder and open a new blank contact.

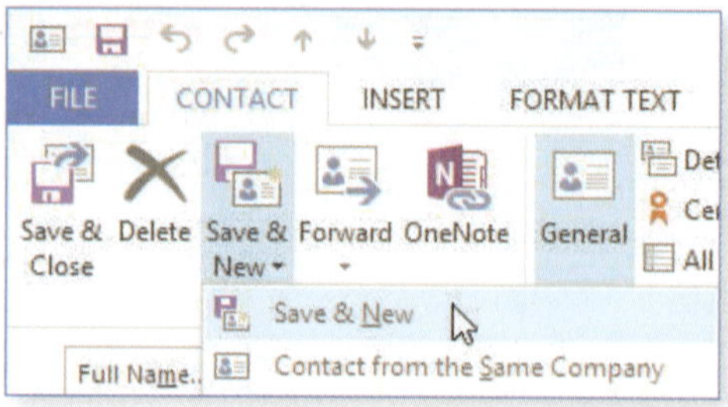

3-4 ***Save & New* contact option**

Create a New Contact from Same Company

There are times when you are adding contacts from the same company and don't want to have to retype some of the common information such as company name, web page address, and business address. When you are creating a new contact from the same company as an existing contact, you can utilize Outlook's ***Contact from Same Company*** feature (Figure 3-5) which preserves existing company information on a new contact record while providing blank fields for the new contact's personal information.

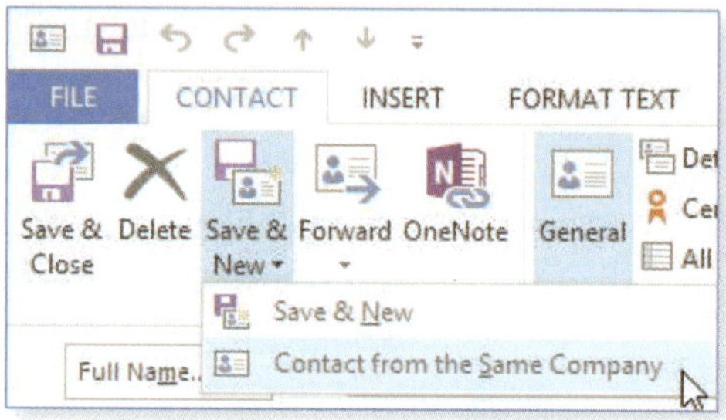

3-5 ***Save & New Contact from the Same Company* option**

When the *Contact from Same Company* option is selected, a new contact record opens that contains company information in some of the fields and provides blank fields for *Full Name, Job title, Email,* and other fields that are specific to the individual being added to your Contacts. The name of the contact (in the *Title bar* at the top center of the contact) will be the company name until an individual's name is typed in the *Full Name* field.

HOW TO: Create a New Contact from the Same Company

1. With an existing contact record open, click the drop-down arrow on the **Save & New** button in the *Actions* group on the *Contact* tab.
2. Click the **Contact from the Same Company** button. A new contact record opens with blank fields for the individual's information (Figure 3-6).
3. Fill in the desired information.
4. Click **Save & Close** when done.

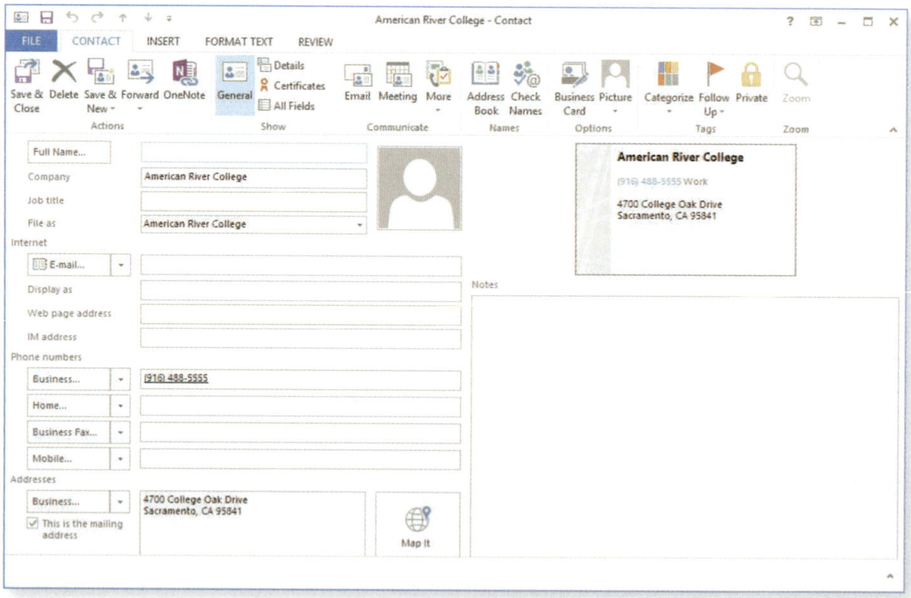

3-6 ***New Contact from the Same Company***

MORE INFO

Entering contact record information can be a time-consuming process if you have numerous contacts to add. Chapter 8 will cover how to import contact records from other files such as a comma separated values (CSV) file.

Create a Contact from a Received Email

Think of the number of times you have received an email and would have liked to add the sender to your contacts; in Outlook there is a very easy way to do this. The most common and efficient method of adding a contact to your *Contacts* folder is from an email that you receive. When you receive an email from someone that is not currently in your *Contacts* folder, you can easily add this new record without having to manually type in all the information.

HOW TO: Create a Contact from a Received Email

1. Put your pointer over the sender's name in an open email or an email in the *Reading* pane. A communications window will appear.
2. Click the **Open Contact Card** button (Figure 3-7) and then click **Add** (Figure 3-8). A new contact record opens.

3-7 *Open Contact Card*

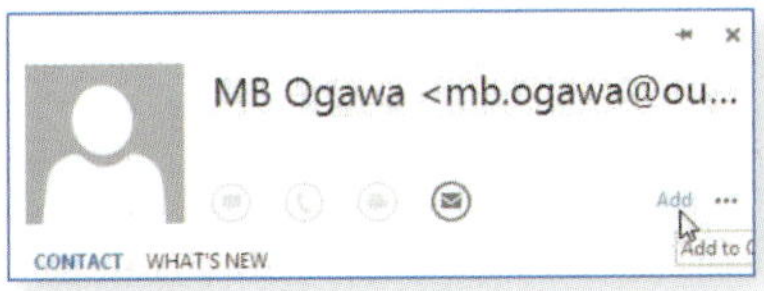

3-8 Add a contact button

3. The *Full Name, Email,* and *Display as* fields are already filled in with the new contact's information. You can edit existing information or add any additional information (Figure 3-9).
4. Click **Save** when done.

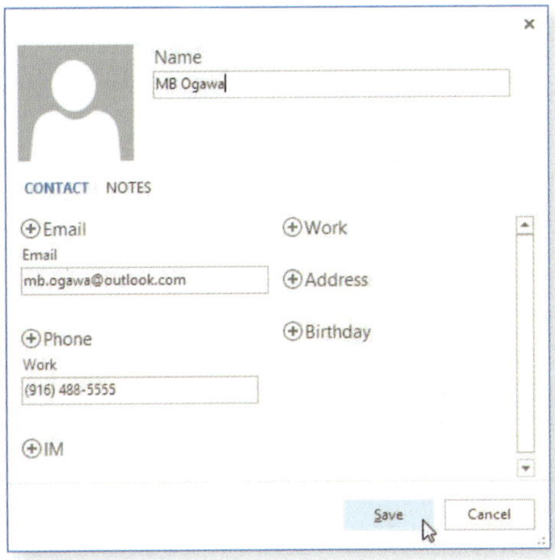

3-9 New contact from email

ANOTHER WAY

With an email open, you can right-click the sender's name and choose **Add to Outlook Contacts.**

Create a Contact from an Electronic Business Card

One of the advantages of using Outlook is being able to send and receive contact records between Outlook users. A very effective and easy method of adding contacts to your *Contacts* folder is by having another Outlook user send you a contact as a business card.

HOW TO: Create a Contact from an Electronic Business Card

1. In an open email or an email in the *Reading* pane, click the attached electronic business card (in the attachment area). The *Attachments* tab opens and the attachment will be displayed in the body of the email (Figure 3-10).

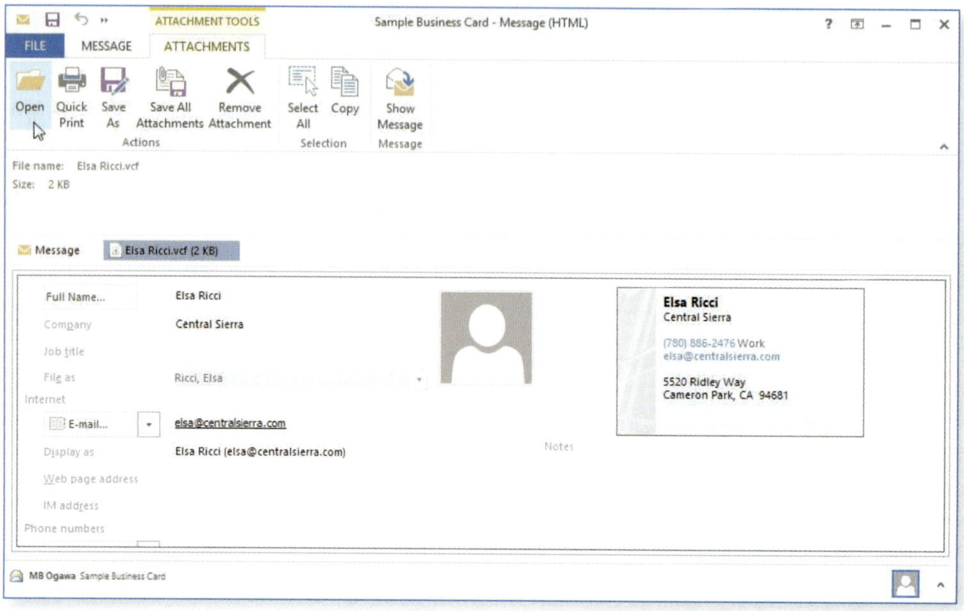

3-10 Business card in the attachments tab

2. Click the **Open** button in the *Actions* group. The contact record opens (Figure 3-11).

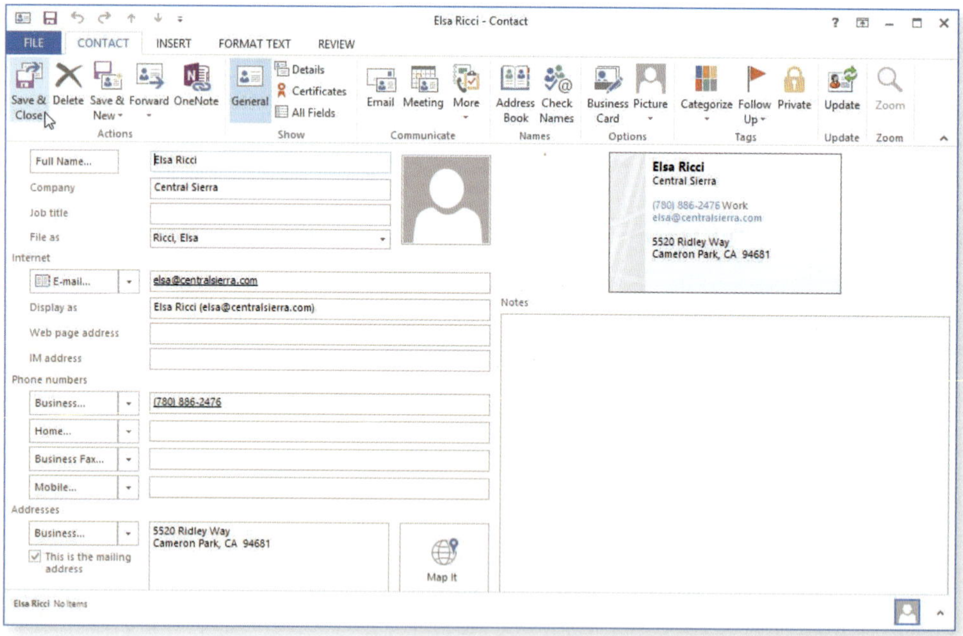

3-11 Business card opened as a contact

3. Make any necessary changes, and then click **Save & Close**.

> **ANOTHER WAY**
>
> You can also drag and drop the attached electronic business card to the *People* button on the *Navigation* pane. This opens the contact record and lets you edit it before saving it to the *Contacts* folder.

> **MORE INFO**
>
> Contact groups will be discussed later in this chapter.

Add a Contact from the Global Address List

If you are using Outlook in a business environment with an Exchange server, most likely you will have a *Global Address List* populated with contacts from within your organization. This global list is created and maintained by the network administrator who is responsible for maintaining the Exchange server.

The *Global Address List* contains the contact records for all employees in the organization and usually contains ***contact groups***. You can add a contact or contact group from the *Global Address List* to your *Contacts* folder.

HOW TO: Add a Contact from the Global Address List

1. In the *Contacts* folder, click the **Address Book** button in the *Find* group on the *Home* tab. The *Address Book* dialog box opens.
2. Click the down arrow on the right side of the *Address Book* drop-down menu (Figure 3-12).
3. Choose **Global Address List**. The list of contacts and contact groups will be displayed.
4. Right-click the contact you want to add to your *Contacts* folder and click **Add to Contacts** (Figure 3-13). The contact record opens in a new window.
5. Click **Save & Close** to save it to your *Contacts* folder.

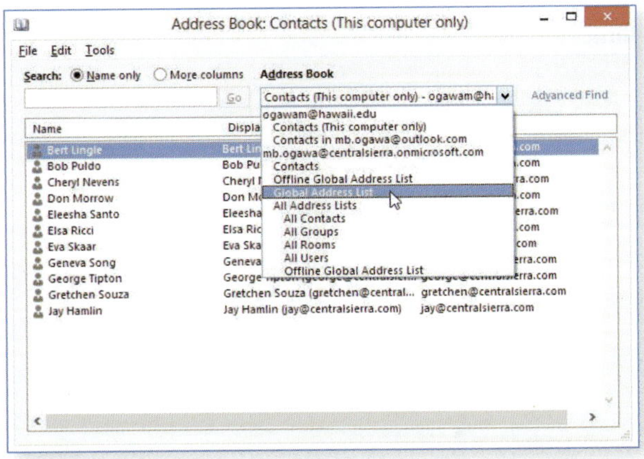

3-12 ***Global Address List*** **option**

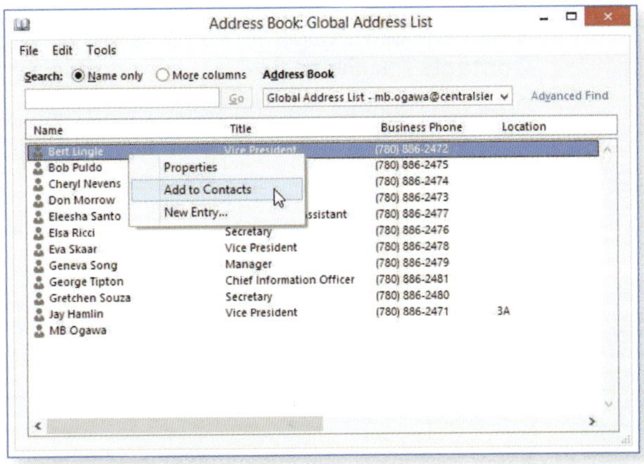

3-13 Add *Global Address* contact to personal contacts

ANOTHER WAY

With the *Address Book* open and the *Global Address List* selected, click the contact you want to add, click the **File** menu, and then click **Add to Contacts.** You can also double-click the contact to open the contact record and then click **Add to Contacts.**

ANOTHER WAY

Ctrl+Shift+B opens the Outlook Address Book.

MORE INFO

You do not have to put a contact in your *Contacts* folder to have access to it. Outlook does allow you to populate a recipient list in an email message from the *Global Address List,* but it is more efficient to keep the contacts you regularly use in your *Contacts* folder.

Duplicate Contacts

If you try to add a contact to your *Contacts* folder and it has the same name as an existing contact, Outlook adds a duplicate entry. Outlook allows you to link contacts together into a single entry, which merges the information in each of the records.

HOW TO: Manage Duplicate Contacts

1. Select one of the duplicate contacts and click the **Link Contacts** link (Figure 3-14).
2. Select the contact that you would like to link to and click **OK** (Figure 3-15). You may need to search for the duplicate contact if you do not see it.

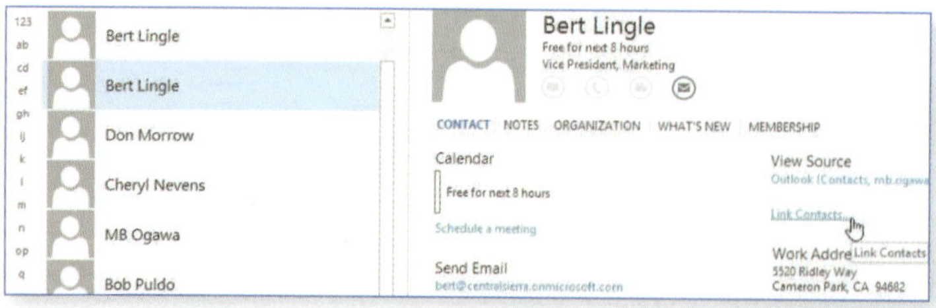

3-14 Link contacts

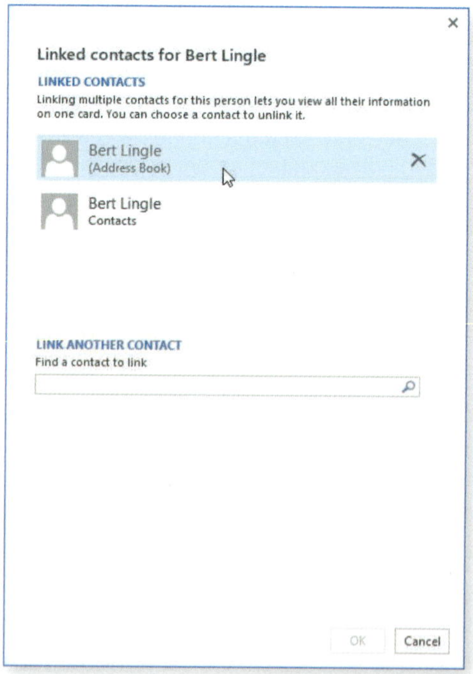

3-15 Select contacts to link

MORE INFO

You should check that the contacts merged correctly and quickly fix errors before you forget to make the appropriate changes.

PAUSE & PRACTICE: OUTLOOK 3-1

For this Pause and Practice project, you create a contact with your personal information. You also send it to a partner and create a contact from a business card attached to an email.

1. Click the **People** button in the *Navigation* pane.
2. Create a contact for yourself.
   a. Click the **New Contact** button [*Home* tab, *New* group].
   b. Enter your full name, company (school name), job title (student), and email address in the appropriate fields.
   c. Click the **Save & Close** button [*Contact* tab, *Actions* group].
3. Create a contact for your instructor.
   a. Click the **New Contact** button [*Home* tab, *New* group].
   b. Enter your instructor's full name, company (school name), job title (Professor), and email address in the appropriate fields.
   c. Click the **Save & Close** button [*Contact* tab, *Actions* group].
4. Forward your contact to a partner.
   a. Select your contact.
   b. Click the **As a Business Card** option [*Home* tab, *Share* group, *Forward Contact* button].
   c. Type your partner's email address in the *To* field.
   d. Click the **Send** button.
5. Save your partner's business card to your contacts (Figure 3-16).

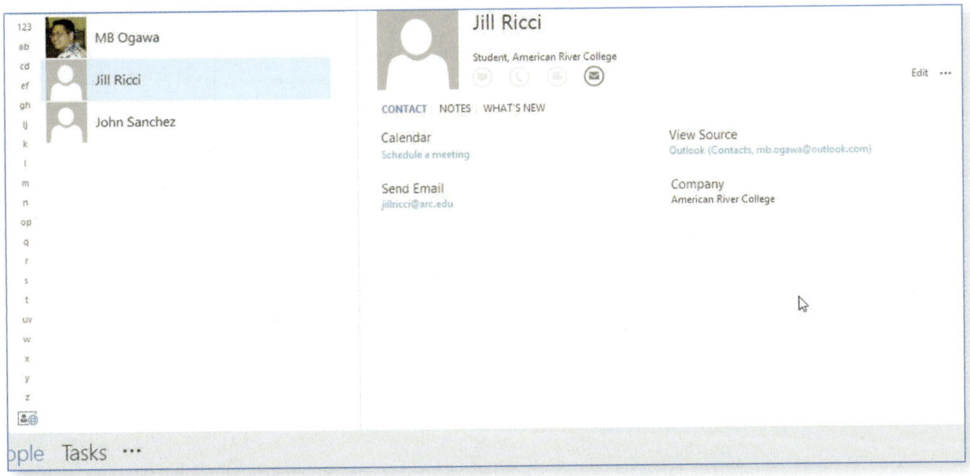

3-16 Completed Pause & Practice 3-1

   a. Open the email message that your partner sent with his or her business card.
   b. Double-click the attached business card to open it.
   c. Click the **Save & Close** button [*Contact* tab, *Actions* group].

SLO 3.3

Editing a Contact Record

Outlook provides you with many fields in a contact record to store information. Not all the information in a contact record has to be completed to save a record. In addition to providing fields to store standard information, Outlook will allow you to change the names of the fields, add multiple email addresses, include a picture, and open a map to the contact's address.

> **MORE INFO**
>
> When creating or editing a contact record, be sure to include the first and last name and begin each name with a capital letter.

Change a Field Name

You can customize many of the fields of a contact record to better meet your needs. Any field with a drop-down menu to the right of the field name is a field name that can be changed. You can select the field name from the choices available. For example, if you would like the mobile (cell) phone number to be listed as the primary phone number, you can change the field from *Mobile* to *Primary*.

HOW TO: Change a Field Name in a Contact Record

1. Change the view to *Business Card* view [*Home* tab, *Current View* group, *Business Card* button].
2. Open the contact record where you want to change a field name.
3. On the field name you would like to change, click the drop-down arrow to the right of the field name (Figure 3-17).
   - A list of available field names opens.
   - Those with a check mark are already being used.
4. Click the desired **field name** to change the field name.

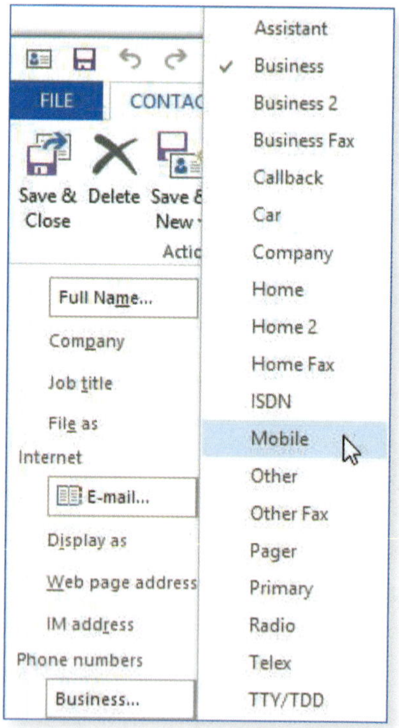

3-17 Change field name

Add an Address

In addition to storing a contact's address, Outlook contact record addresses can be used to generate mailing lists, envelopes, and/or labels. The address field lets you type the address directly into the text box, or an address field dialog box can be opened and the address can be typed into the dialog box. Each contact record can store up to three different addresses. You have the options of business, home, or other addresses.

> **MORE INFO**
>
> If Outlook does not recognize the format in which you type an address, a *Check Address* dialog box opens (Figure 3-18). This will allow you to edit the address.
>
> If you type an email address in a format that Outlook doesn't recognize, a *Check Names* dialog box opens.

> **ANOTHER WAY**
>
> Any of the field names that are displayed as a button can be clicked on and a dialog box will appear. The information for that field can be typed directly into the dialog box.
>
> Click the **Email** button on a contact record; the *Select Names* dialog box opens and allows you to choose an email address from your *Global Address List.*

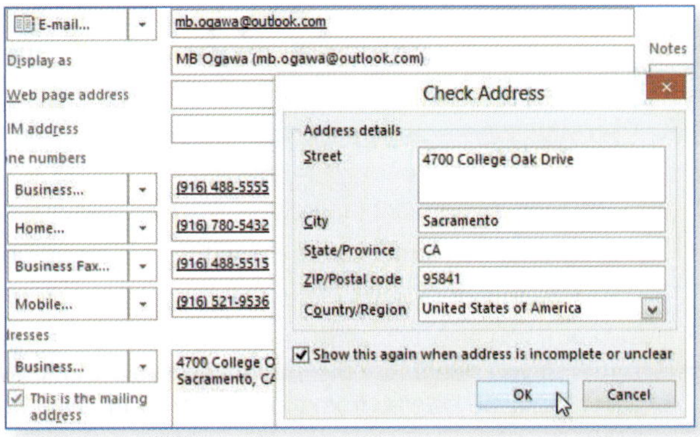

3-18 *Check Address* dialog box

Add Multiple Email Addresses

Do you have more than one email account? Outlook will let you store up to three email addresses per contact record. Each email address is added to the Outlook Address Book. The main email address is labeled ***Email***, and the additional email address fields are labeled ***Email 2*** and ***Email 3*** (Figure 3-19).

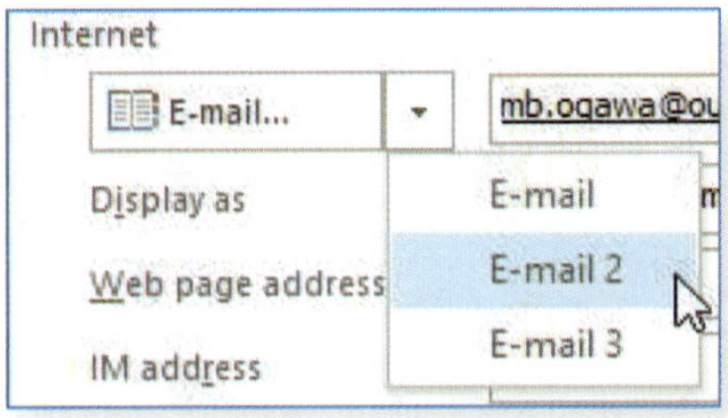

3-19 Add multiple email addresses

Insert a Picture

To further customize a contact record, you can add a contact's picture. Figure 3-20 is the default image before you customize it. The picture will appear on the contact record when it is open. Also, if you have a picture saved in a contact record and you receive an email from that contact, his or her picture will appear on the email message.

3-20 Default contact picture

HOW TO: Insert a Picture in a Contact Record

1. With a contact record open, click the **picture icon**. The *Add Contact Picture* dialog box opens.
2. Find and select the picture you want on the contact record.
3. Click **OK** to close the dialog box.
4. Click **Save & Close** to close the contact record (Figure 3-21).

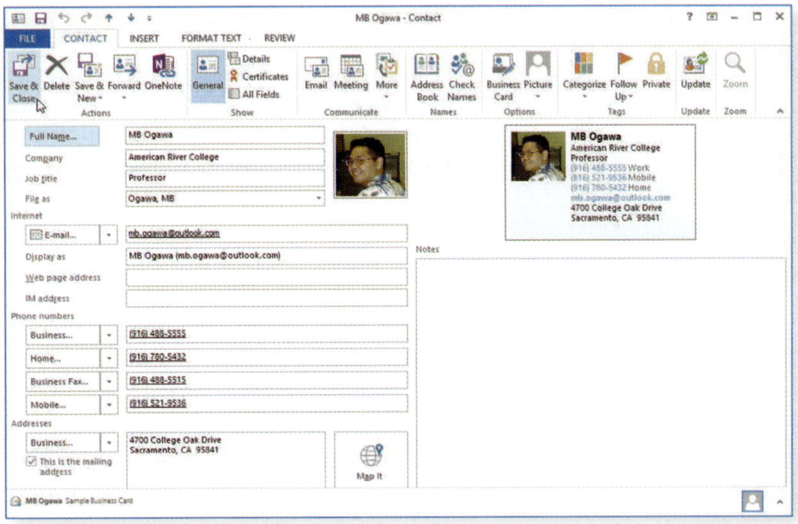

3-21 Contact with a picture

If you decide that you do not want the picture on the contact record or that you would like a different picture, you can easily change or delete it.

HOW TO: Change or Remove a Picture

1. Open the contact record.
2. Click the **Picture** button in the *Options* group on the *Contacts* tab.
3. Click either *Change Picture* or *Remove Picture.*
   - If you select *Change Picture,* the *Add Contact Picture* dialog box opens and you can select a new picture.
   - If you select *Remove Picture* (Figure 3-22), the picture will be removed from the contact record. The picture will only be deleted from the contact record, not from your computer.

3-22 *Remove Picture* option

ANOTHER WAY

You can right-click the picture on the contact record and choose either *Change Picture* or *Remove Picture.*

MORE INFO

If you use your cell phone to sync with Outlook (not all cell phones will do this), you will have the option to sync your Outlook Contacts. If you receive a phone call from a recipient whose contact record has a picture, the picture will be displayed on the cell phone screen during the incoming call.

Use the Map It Feature

How many times have you used the Internet to get a map or driving directions to a location? You had to go to the web site and type in the address to find the desired information. Microsoft Outlook provides users with a ***map*** feature (Figure 3-23) that will link an address from a contact record to an interactive Internet map. So, rather than you having to go to a different web site and type in an address, Outlook opens Bing Maps from an address in a contact record with the click of a button (Figure 3-24).

3-23 *Map It* button

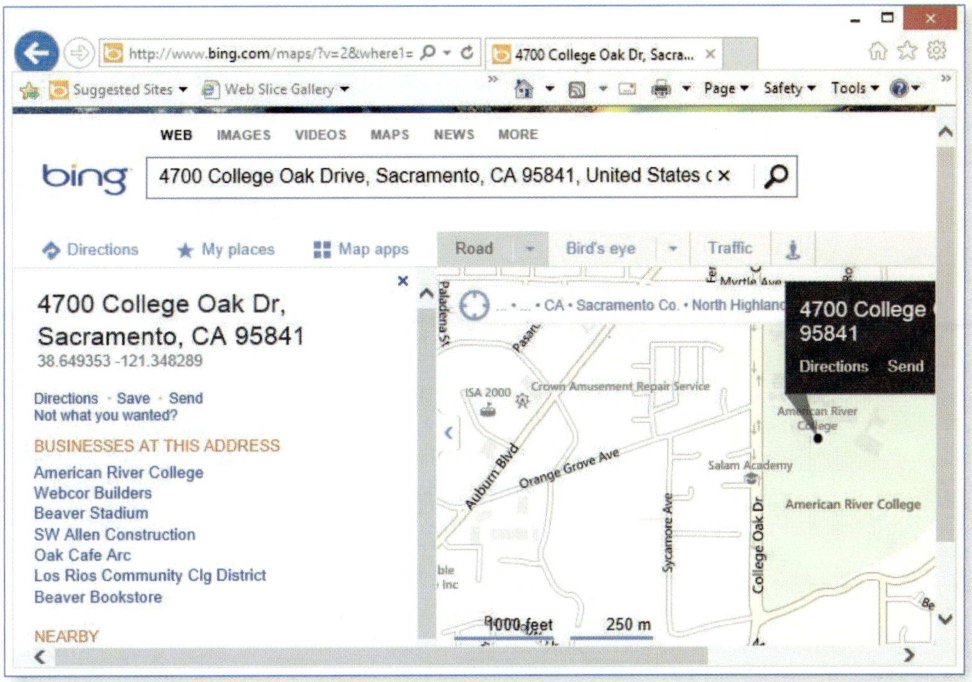

3-24 Bing map

HOW TO: Use the Map It Feature

1. Open an existing contact record that has an address.
2. Click the **Map It** button next to the address in the contact.
3. An Internet window opens with the contact record address mapped.

ANOTHER WAY

Click the **More** button in the *Communicate* group on the *Contact* tab and choose **Map.**

People Pane

The ***People pane***, which is available in the main Outlook interface and on email messages, is also available on contact records (Figure 3-25). This feature provides you with a list of related Outlook activity associated with a contact.

This pane is located at the bottom of the contact record and displays related Outlook items. Clicking on one of the links displayed in the *People pane* opens the selected Outlook item or social networking activity. You can choose how to display or group this information in the *People pane*. Also, the *People pane* can be collapsed or expanded by clicking the small arrow in the upper right corner of the pane.

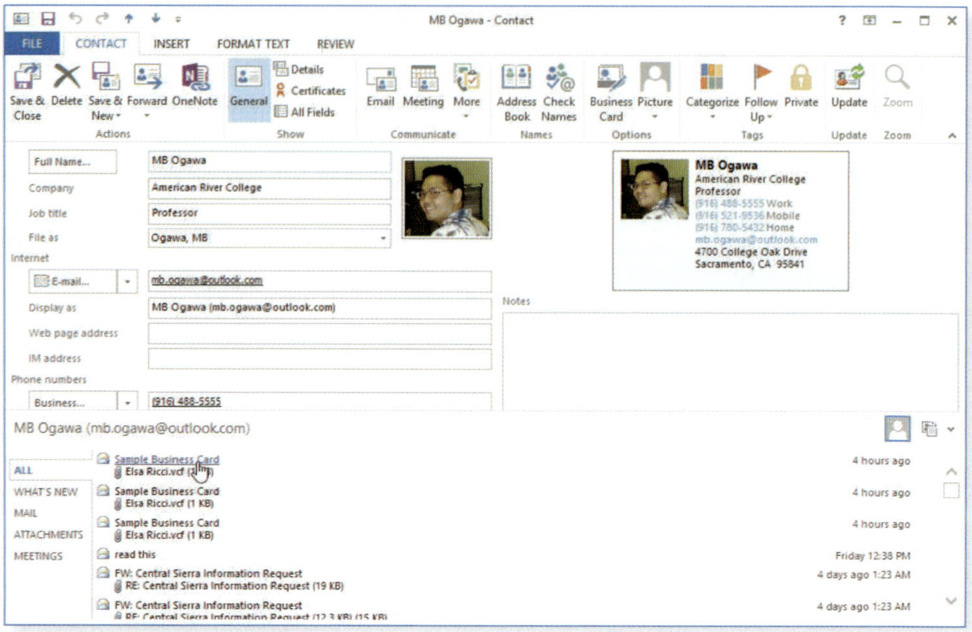

3-25 *People* pane in a contact record

Outlook Social Connector

In addition to consolidating Outlook information related to a contact in the *People* pane, the ***Outlook Social Connector (OSC)*** will also allow you to connect to your social networks such as Facebook, LinkedIn, and MySpace. By using the OSC to connect to your social networks in Outlook, you can view the posts and activity of those in your contacts with whom you are connected on social networks.

By default, Outlook allows you to connect to popular social networks such as Facebook and LinkedIn without a plugin. However, you must install the plugin for other social networking sites, which are available from each provider and provide Outlook with your log in information for the site. This process will vary from site to site.

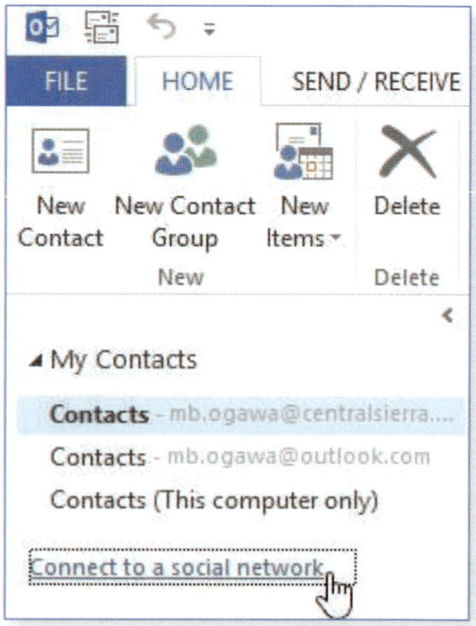

3-26 *Connect to a social network* link

HOW TO: Connect Outlook to Social Network Accounts

1. Install the plugin from the social networking web site if you are using one other than Facebook, LinkedIn, or a Sharepoint server.
2. Once the plugin is installed, you will be prompted to provide your user name and password.
3. Click the **Connect to social network** link in the *Contacts* folder list (Figure 3-26). The *Social Network Accounts* dialog box opens.
4. Enter your user name and password.

5. Click **Connect** to connect Outlook to your social networking site (Figure 3-27).
6. Click **Finish**.
7. Outlook is now connected to your social networking site, and you will receive a confirmation dialog box. Click **Close** to close this dialog box.

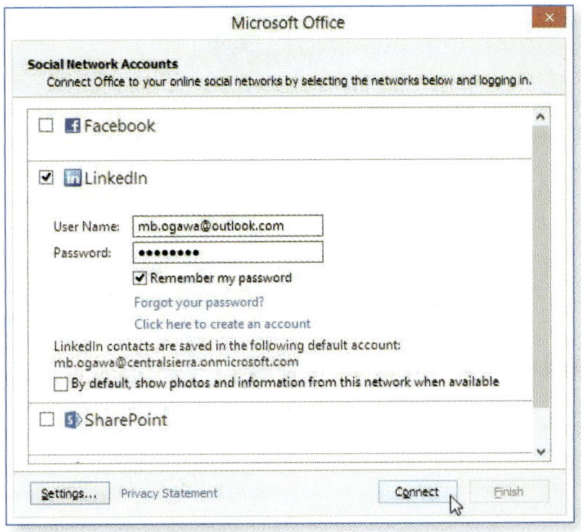

3-27 Enter user name and password for the social network

MORE INFO

This process might be slightly different depending on the social networking site you are setting up in Outlook.

When you open a contact record for a person you are connected with on a social networking site, that contact's activity will be displayed in the *People* pane of the contact record.

Delete a Contact

To delete an existing contact, simply select the contact and press **Delete**. When a contact record is deleted, it is moved to the *Deleted Items* folder where it will stay until it is permanently deleted. If you delete a contact by mistake, you can use the *Undo* button to restore the contact, or you can open the *Deleted Items* folder and drag the contact back to the *Contacts* folder (drag and drop the deleted contact on the *People* button).

ANOTHER WAY

Ctrl+D will delete a selected Outlook item.

You can also select the contact and click the **Delete** button on the *Contact* tab or right-click the contact and choose **Delete.**

MORE INFO

You can select a range of contacts by selecting the first contact in a range, holding down the **Shift** key, and selecting the last item in the range. You can also select nonadjacent contact records by holding down the **Ctrl** key and selecting the contacts.

SLO 3.4

Changing and Modifying Views in Contacts

Outlook provides you with preset views in which to display your contacts. These different views display different contact information and varying amounts of information about each contact. The view can be changed by clicking on one of the views in the *Current View* group on the *Home* tab (Figure 3-28).

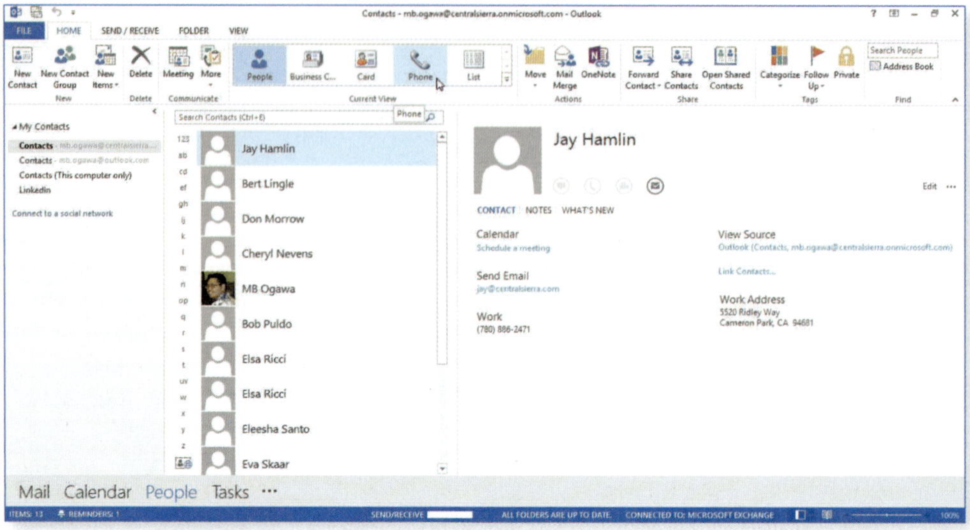

3-28 Contact views

Contact Views

By default there are five different preset contact views. There are mixed, list, and card views.

- People (*People Card* view)
- Business Card (*Card* view)
- Card (*Card* view)
- Phone (*List* view)
- List (*List* view)

You can change views by selecting a view in the *Current View* group on the *Home* tab. Click the **More** button to display all available views in the *Current View* gallery.

ANOTHER WAY

Click the **View** tab, click **Change View**, and select the view you want.

In the *Arrangement* group on the *View* tab, you are given different options to arrange and sort your contacts. The three preset arrangements are: *Categories, Company,* and *Location.*

Sort Contacts

When viewing contacts in a *List* view, the easiest way to sort or arrange records is to click the column heading. The column by which the records are sorted will be shaded, and the sorting order will be indicated by a small triangle pointing up (ascending order) or down (descending order) (Figure 3-29).

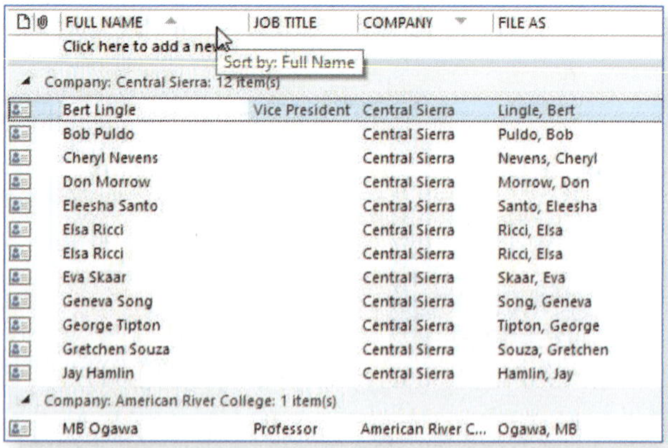

3-29 Sort contacts in a *List* view

Modify a View

As the number of contacts you have stored in Outlook increases, you may want to utilize methods provided by Outlook to help you quickly find a contact. By default, contacts are sorted by last name, but you can group contact records by company or sort them by full name.

In addition, each of the existing contact views can be modified to assist you with finding a contact. You can customize the fields displayed, sort criteria, fonts, font sizes, and styles.

Click the **View Setting** button on the *View* tab to customize the current view.

HOW TO: Modify View Settings

1. Click the **People** button in the *Navigation* pane.
2. Select the desired contacts view in the *Current View* group on the *Contacts* tab.
3. Click the **View** tab.
4. Click the **View Settings** button. The *Advanced View Settings* dialog box for the current view opens (Figure 3-30).
5. Make any desired changes. Each of the buttons on the left opens an additional dialog box.
6. Click **OK** to close the *Advanced View Settings* dialog box.

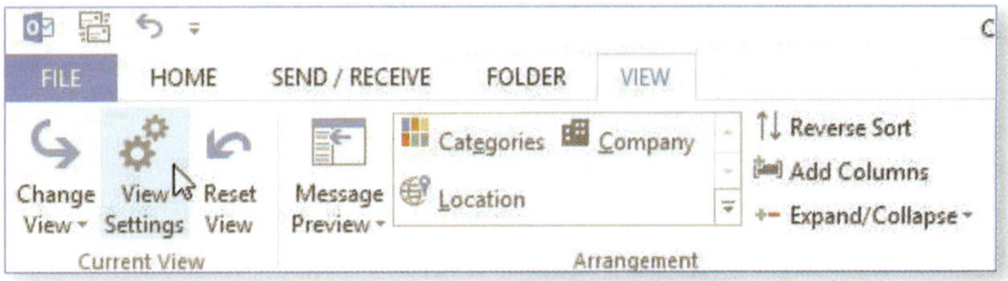

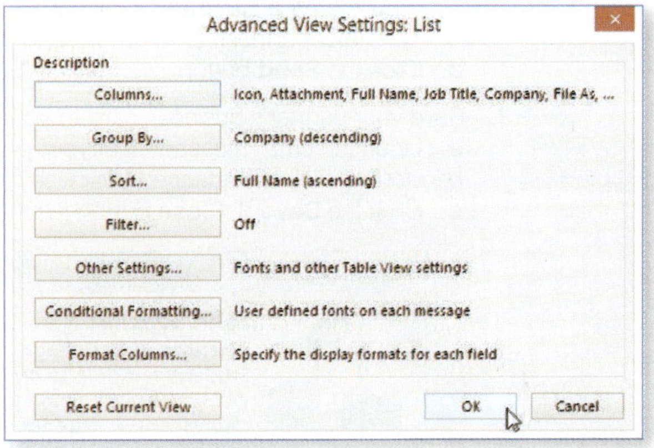

3-30 *Advanced View Settings: List* dialog box

MORE INFO

Feel free to experiment with different views in the *Contacts* folder, because you can easily reset views to their original settings by clicking on the *Reset View* button on the *View* tab or the *Reset Current View* button in the *Advanced View Settings* dialog box.

PAUSE & PRACTICE: OUTLOOK 3-2

For this Pause and Practice project, you modify your contact to include your picture and a mailing address. You also add a secondary email address.

File Needed: A picture of yourself (if you do not have a picture, general picture files are available ***johnsanchez.jpg*** and ***jillricci.jpg***).
Completed Project File Name: None

1. Edit your contact.
   a. Select the **People** button in the *Navigation* pane.
   b. Click **Business Card** view [*Home* tab, *Current View* group].
   c. Double-click your contact.
   d. Select the **Add Picture** option [*Contact* tab, *Options* group, *Picture* button].
   e. Locate your picture and click **OK**. If you do not have a picture, you can use one of the provided images (***johnsanchez.jpg*** or ***jillricci.jpg***) and change it to your image later.
   f. Click the **E-mail** drop-down arrow and select **E-mail 2**.
   g. Type a secondary e-mail address if you have one.
   h. Click the **Business** drop-down arrow under the *Address* section and select **Other**. Click the **This is a mailing address** check box.
   i. Type your school's address.
   j. Click the **Save & Close** button.
2. Forward your updated contact as a business card to a different partner from *Pause & Practice Outlook 3-1*.
   a. Select your contact.
   b. Click the **As a Business Card** option [*Home* tab, *Share* group, *Forward Contact* button].
   c. Type your partner's email address in the *To* field.
   d. Click the **Send** button.
3. Save your partner's business card to your contacts (Figure 3-31).
   a. Open the email message that your partner sent with his or her business card.
   b. Double-click the attached business card to open it.
   c. Click the **Save & Close** button [*Contact* tab, *Actions* group].

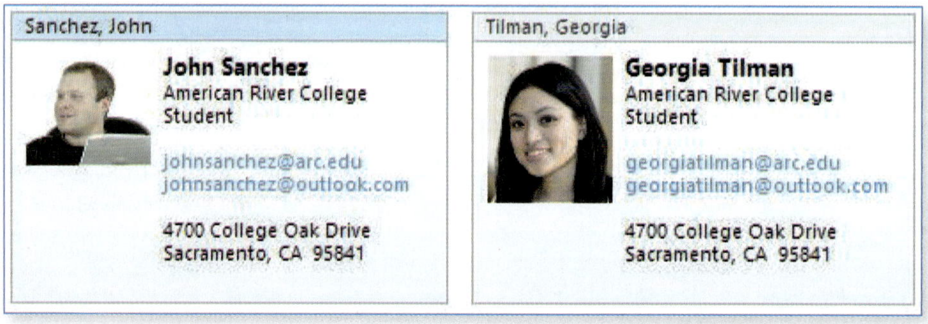

3-31 Completed Pause & Practice 3-2

SLO 3.5

Using Contacts and Contact Groups

One of the most beneficial aspects of the *Contacts* folder is the ability to use this stored information to send emails. An email can be sent to one or more contacts in your *Contacts* folder or the *Global Address List*. You also have the ability to create ***contact groups***, which are saved groups of contacts, and send email to the entire contact group.

Send an Email to a Contact

You can send an email to contacts that are stored in your *Contacts* folder in a couple different ways. When you have an email message open, you can click the *To* button and select the contacts from the *Select Names* dialog box. You can also choose contacts from different address books by selecting from the list in the *Address Book* drop-down menu.

HOW TO: Send an Email to a Contact

1. Click the **To** button on an email message (new, reply, or forward). The *Select Names* dialog box opens.
2. Use the *Address Book* drop-down list to select an address book.
3. Select the desired contacts (Figure 3-32).
   - Use **Ctrl** to select non-adjacent contacts.
   - Use **Shift** to select a range of adjacent contacts.
4. Click the **To** button (you can also put contacts in the *Cc* or *Bcc* fields).
5. Click **OK**. Your email recipient list (*To* field) is populated with these contacts.

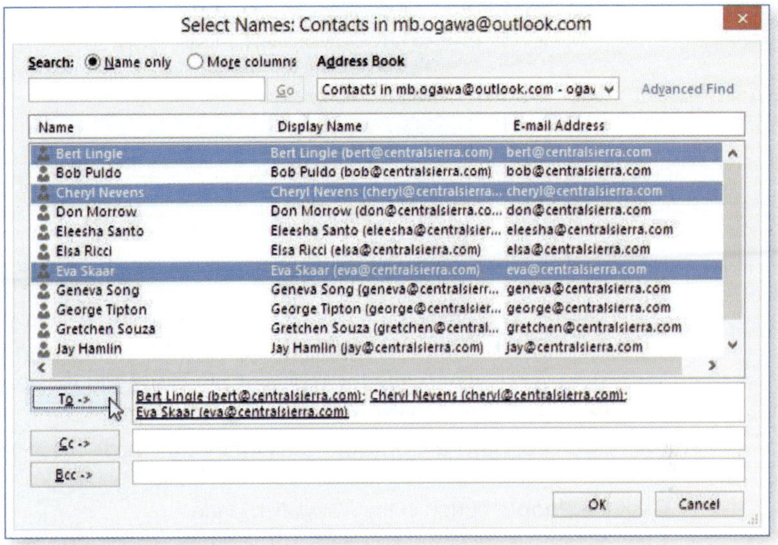

3-32 Select multiple contacts to email

Another way to send a message to a contact is from the contacts in the *Folder* pane. When the *People* button is selected in the *Navigation* pane, your contacts appear in the *Folder* pane. You can create a new email to send to one or more contacts.

HOW TO: Create an Email to a Selected Contact

1. Click the **People** button in the *Navigation* pane.
2. Select the desired contacts.
3. Click the **Email** button in the *Communicate* group on the *Home* tab (Figure 3-33). A new email message opens with the selected contacts in the *To* field.

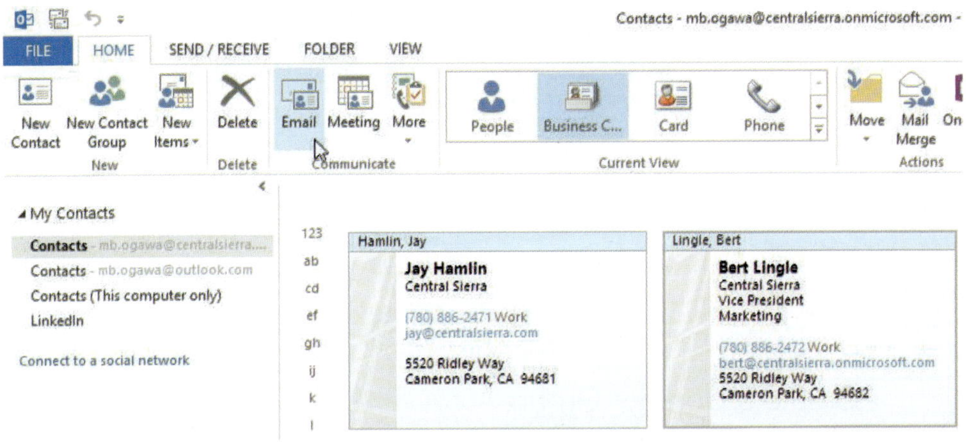

3-33 Create new email message to selected contacts

ANOTHER WAY

With a record selected in the *People* view, click the **Email** button in the contact (Figure 3-34).

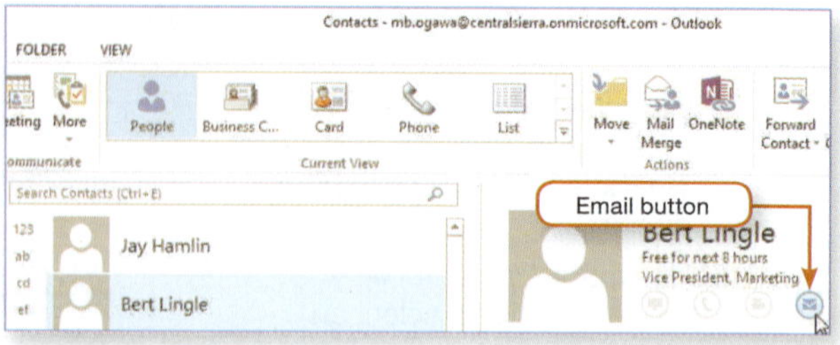

3-34 Create new email message to a contact from the *People* view

Forward a Contact as a Business Card

There are times when you will want to send your contact record or another contact record to others via email. You can send this information as an electronic business card attached to an email, and the recipient can easily add the contact record to their *Contacts* folder.

HOW TO: Forward a Contact as a Business Card

1. Click the **People** button in the *Navigation* pane.
2. Select the contacts to be forwarded in the *Folder* pane.
3. Click the **Forward Contact** button in the *Share* group on the *Home* tab.
4. Choose **As a Business Card** (Figure 3-35). A new email opens with the business card attached, and a graphic of the business card will appear in the body of the email (Figure 3-36). This graphic can be deleted.
5. Populate the recipient list and click **Send**.

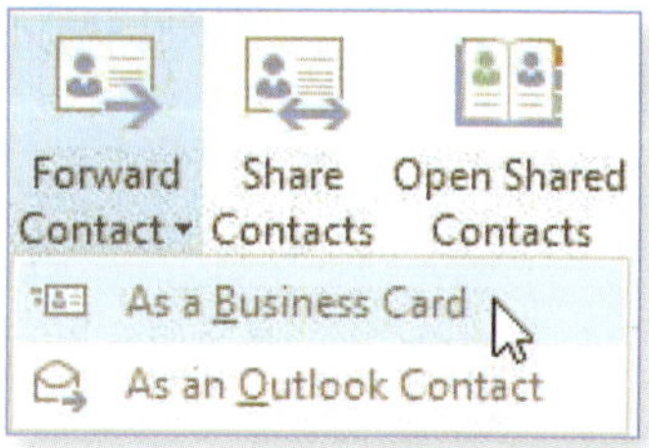

3-35 *Forward Contact As a Business Card*

ANOTHER WAY

With the contact record open, click the **Forward** button in the *Actions* group on the *Contact* tab.

MORE INFO

Contact records can be forwarded as a business card (Internet format), in Outlook format, or as a text message. Business card format is a more generic format that can be used with other email software programs.

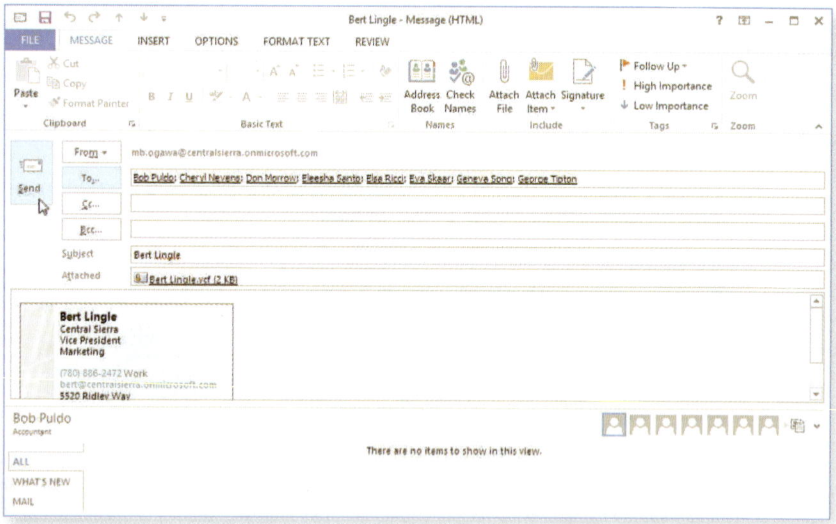

3-36 Attached business card

Create a Contact Group

Contact groups (also known as distribution lists) are commonly used when regularly sending emails to a group of contacts. A contact group is a saved group of contact records. It can include just a few contacts or numerous contacts.

Contact groups are useful to quickly send email to a department, team, or committee. Also, they help to ensure that all members of a group are included in an email and no one is inadvertently left off the recipient list.

Contact groups are named and stored in your *Contacts* folder (or other *Contacts* folder). Most *Global Address Lists* include numerous contact groups that have been created by the Exchange administrator.

HOW TO: Create a Contact Group

1. Click the **People** button in the *Navigation* pane.
2. Click the **New Contact Group** button in the *New* group on the *Home* tab (Figure 3-37). A new *Contact Group* window opens.
3. Type a name for the contact group.
4. Click **Add Members** from the *Member* group and choose **From Outlook Contacts** (Figure 3-38). The *Select Members* dialog box opens.

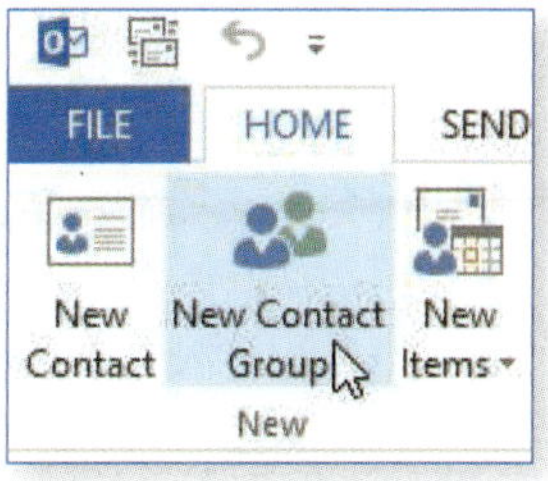

3-37 *New Contact* Group button

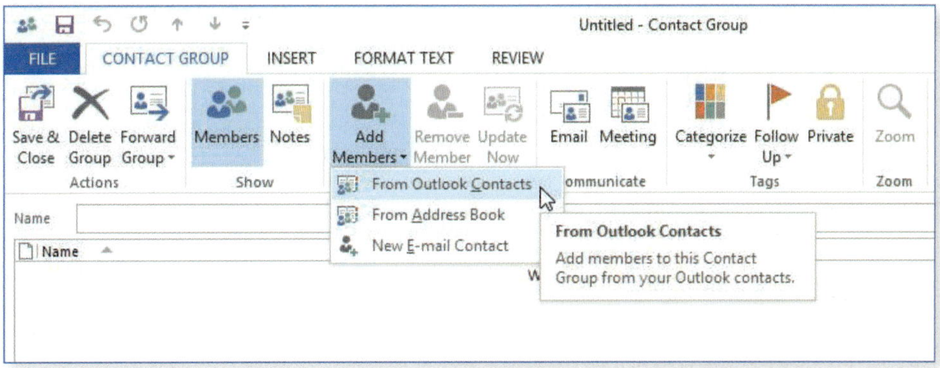

3-38 Select members from *Outlook Contacts* button

5. Select the contacts to be included (Figure 3-39).
6. Click **Members**.
7. Click **OK** to close the *Select Members* dialog box. The contact group is populated with these members.
8. Click **Save & Close** to save the contact group (Figure 3-40).

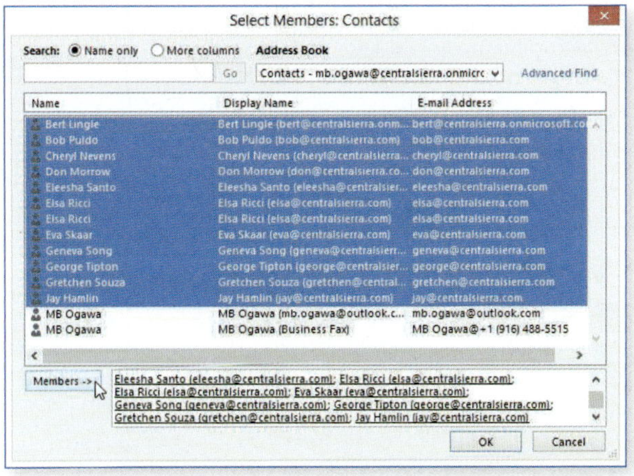

3-39 Select members from Outlook Contacts

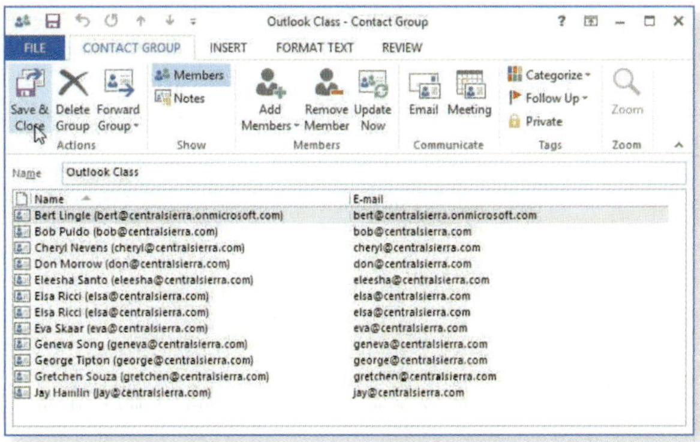

3-40 Contact group members

> **ANOTHER WAY**
>
> **Ctrl+Shift+L** opens a new contact group.

> **MORE INFO**
>
> Members for a contact group can be selected from Outlook Contacts, the Outlook Address Book, or a new email contact.

Send an Email to a Contact Group

A contact group can be used in the same way a contact record is used. On a new email, reply, or forward, you can select a contact group as the recipient by clicking on the *To* button and choosing the contact group from the *Select Names* dialog box. The email message will be sent to all those who are members of the contact group.

You can also create a new message to a contact group directly from your *Contacts* folder.

HOW TO: Send an Email to a Contact Group

1. Click the **People** button in the *Navigation* pane.
2. Select the desired contact group in the *Folder* pane.
3. Click the **Email** button in the *Communicate* group on the *Home* tab (Figure 3-41). A new email opens with the contact group as the recipient.
4. Add a subject and any desired information in the body (Figure 3-42).
5. Click **Send**.

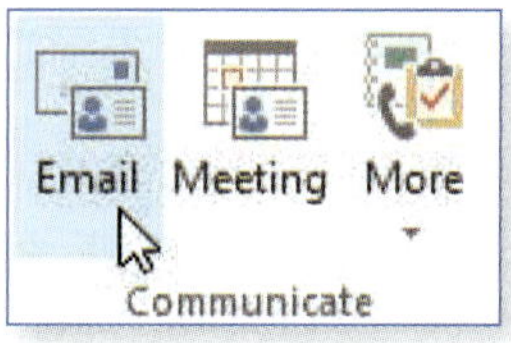

3-41 *Email* button when a contact group is selected

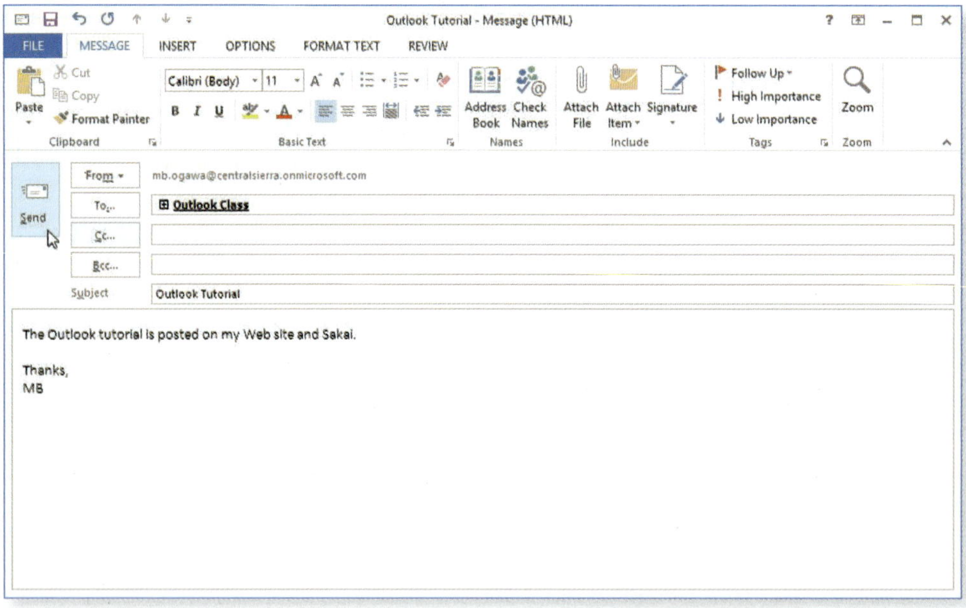

3-42 Email message to a contact group

ANOTHER WAY

With a contact group selected in the *People* view, click the **Email** button in the contact.

MORE INFO

As with *Reply All,* only use contact groups when it is important that all members of the contact group receive the email. You don't want to flood others' Inboxes with unnecessary email.

MORE INFO

The **Email** button is not available in the *Communicate* group when in *People* view, as it is located within each contact.

Modify a Contact Group

You can modify a contact group by opening the contact group and ***selecting members***, ***removing members***, ***adding new members***, or ***updating contact information***.

Once a contact group is created, there are times when you might want to either add members or remove members from this list.

HOW TO: Add Members to a Contact Group

1. Click the **People** button in the *Navigation* pane.
2. Open the contact group to be modified.
3. Click the **Add Members** button in the *Members* group and choose **From Outlook Contacts** (Figure 3-43). The *Select Names* dialog box opens.

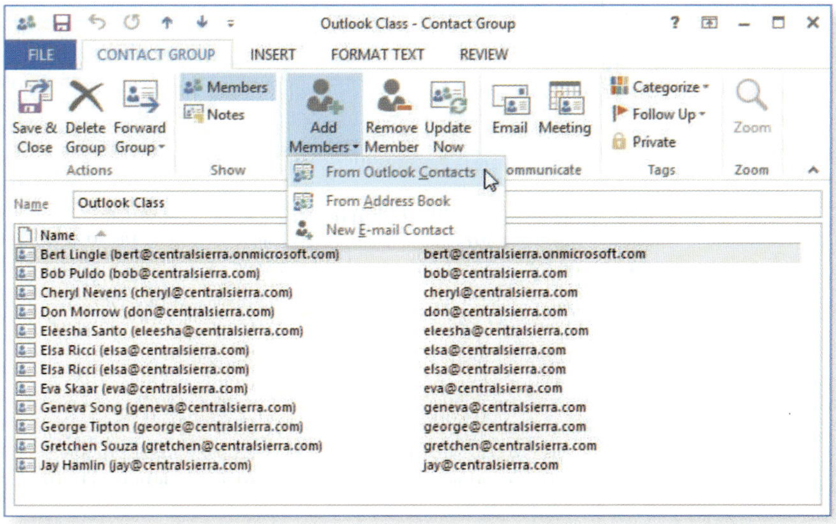

3-43 Add additional members to a contact group

4. Select the contacts to add to your contact group from your *Contacts* folder or the *Global Address List.*

5. Click the **Members** button (Figure 3-44).
6. Click **OK**. The *Select Members* dialog box will close and the new members are now included in your contact group.
7. Click **Save & Close** to save the updated contact group.

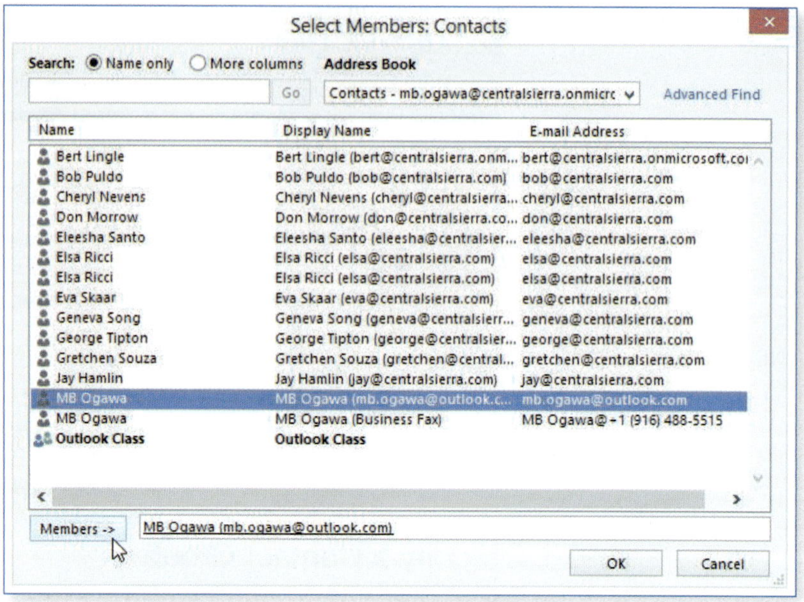

3-44 Select members to add to a contact group

Members can also be easily removed from your contact group.

HOW TO: Remove Members from a Contact Group

1. Click the **People** button in the *Navigation* pane.
2. Open the contact group to be modified.
3. In the body of the contact group, select the members to be removed.
4. Click the **Remove Member** button in the *Members* group (Figure 3-45).
5. Click **Save & Close** to save the updated contact group.

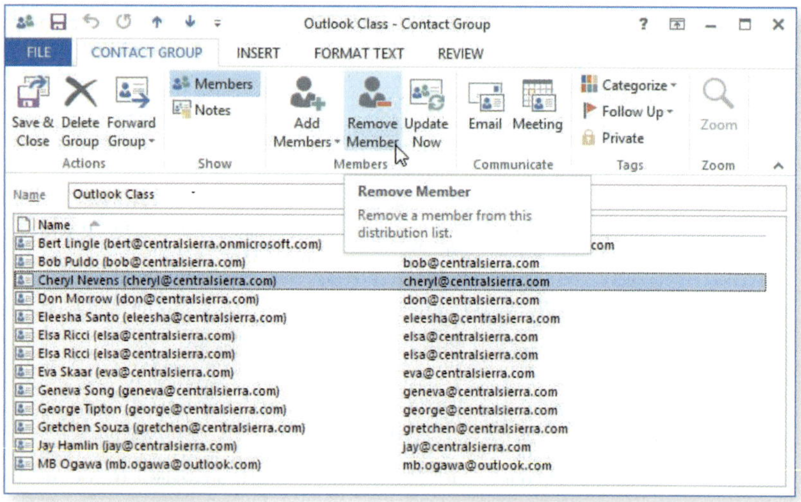

3-45 Remove a member from a contact group

MORE INFO

When removing members from a contact group, *do not* click the *Delete Group* button in the *Actions* group. This will delete the entire contact group rather than the members selected to be removed.

The ***New Email Contact*** option is used to add a member to the contact group who is not currently in your *Contacts* folder.

HOW TO: Add a New Email Contact to a Contact Group

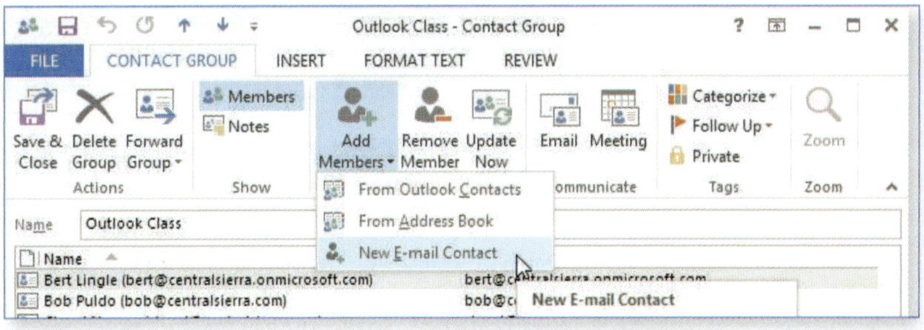

1. Click the **People** button in the *Navigation* pane.
2. Open the contact group to be modified.
3. Click the **Add Members** button in the *Members* group and choose **New Email Contact**. The *Add New Member* dialog box opens.
4. Type in the contact's information. Select the **Add to Contacts** check box, and Outlook will add this contact to your *Contacts* folder.
5. Click **OK** to add the new member to the contact group and to close the *Add New Member* dialog box (Figure 3-46).
6. Click **Save & Close** to save the updated contact group.

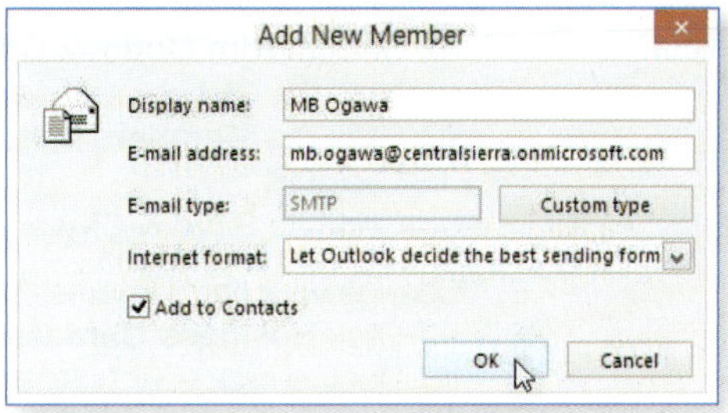

3-46 Add a new contact group member that is not in your contacts list

Update a Contact Group

There will be times when you make changes to a contact in your *Contacts* folder. If this contact is included in a contact group, the changes will not automatically be updated in the contact group. Open the contact group you want to update and click the **Update Now** button in the *Members* group on the *Contact Group* tab to update the members in your contact group to match their contact information in your *Contacts* folder (Figure 3-47).

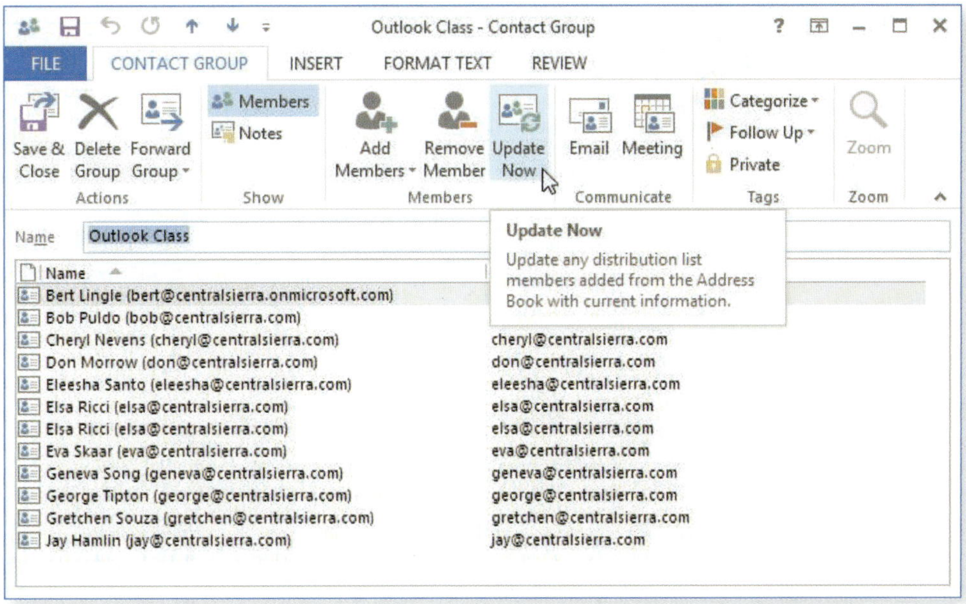

3-47 Update contact group when you modify contact records

PAUSE & PRACTICE: OUTLOOK 3-3

For this Pause and Practice project, you create a contact group, update contact information, and send the contact group to your instructor.

1. Create an Outlook contact group including your two partners from *Pause & Practice Outlook 3-1 and 3-2.*
   a. Click the **New Contact Group** button [*Home* tab, *New* group].
   b. Type Outlook Class Group in the *Name* field.
   c. Select **From Outlook Contacts** [*Contact Group* tab, *Members* group, *Add Members* button].
   d. Hold the **Ctrl** key and select the contact information for your two partners and yourself.
   e. Click the **Members** button.
   f. Click **OK**.
   g. Click the **Save & Close** button [*Contact Group* tab, *Actions* group].
2. Change your email address to your personal email address.
   a. Click **Business Card** view [*Home* tab, *Current View* group].
   b. Double-click your business card.
   c. Change your email address to your personal email address.
   d. Click the **Save & Close** button.
3. Update the addresses in the *Outlook Class Group.*
   a. Double-click the business card for *Outlook Class Group.*
   b. Click the **Update Now** button.
   c. Click the **Save & Close** button.
4. Send an email to your instructor with the *Outlook Class Group* contact as an attachment (Figure 3-48).

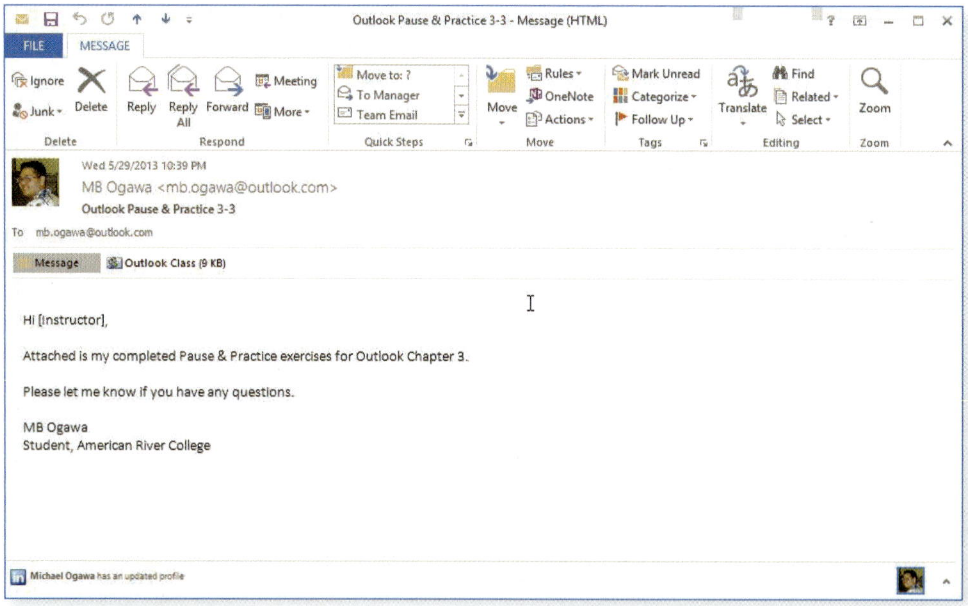

3-48 Completed Pause & Practice 3-3

   a. Select the *Outlook Class Group* contact.
   b. Click the *As an Outlook Contact* option [*Home* tab, *Share* group, *Forward Contact* button].

c. Click the **To** button to open your contacts.
d. Select your instructor and click the **To** button.
e. Click **OK**.
f. Add your email address in the *Cc* field.
g. Change the subject to Outlook Pause & Practice 3-3.
h. Type a short message to your instructor indicating that you attached the completed Pause & Practice exercises.
i. Click the **Send** button.

Chapter Summary

3.1 Differentiate between the *Contacts* folder and the *Global Address List* (p. O3-94).

- An Outlook contact is referred to as a ***record*** or ***contact record***.
- A ***record*** includes a group of related information about a person such as name, phone number, email address, address, company, and job title.
- Each individual piece of information such as an email address or a phone number is called a ***field***.
- Each record is saved to your ***Contacts folder***.
- When using Outlook in an Exchange environment, you will have a ***Global Address List,*** which includes all the members of your organization.

3.2 Create a contact record from different sources (p. O3-95).

- You can create a new contact form using the default template by clicking the *New Contact* button.
- When creating multiple contacts from the same organization, you can use the *Contact from the same Company* option on the *Save & New* button to create a new contact with many of the same fields.
- You can create a contact based on an email you receive.
- A business card can be used to create a contact.
- Contacts in the *Global Address List* (Exchange environments only) can be saved to your personal contacts list.
- You can remove duplicate accounts by linking them.

3.3 Enhance contact records by editing contact information and fields (p. O3-102).

- Field names for specific records can be modified within a record.
- Each record can contain multiple addresses such as business and home.
- Outlook helps you format addresses when it does not recognize the format.
- Each record can contain multiple email addresses.
- You can add pictures to records, which will show up when you receive an email from the contact.
- Outlook can connect to social networks such as LinkedIn and Facebook through the Outlook Social Connector.
- You can receive updates from social networks in the *People* pane.

3.4 Use and modify the different contact views (p. O3-107).

- There are five contact views: *People, Business Card, Card, Phone,* and *List.*
- The ***People*** view includes all of the contacts' information as ***People Cards***. Actions, such as sending an email message, are listed within the People Card.
- The ***Business Card*** view displays each contact as a business card.
- The ***Card*** view displays information as cards and is more condensed than the *Business Card* view.
- The ***Phone*** view displays contacts as a list based on phone number.
- The ***List*** view displays contacts as a list and includes different company groups.
- You can sort your contacts in list view by clicking the column header (field name).
- The *Advanced View Settings: List* dialog box can be used to customize the sorting of contacts.

3.5 Create a contact group and produce email from a contact or contact group (p. O3-110).

- You can create a contact group, which contains multiple contacts, to send email messages to members.
- When you click the *To* button in a new email message, you can select a contact or contact group instead of manually typing in email addresses.
- When selecting multiple email addresses, you can hold the **Ctrl** key to select non-adjacent contacts and the **Shift** key to select adjacent contacts.
- When selecting a contact or contact group in card or list view, you can click the **Email** button in the *Communicate* group to create new message.

- The *People Card* view includes the email button within the People Card.
- You can forward contacts to others as business cards.
- You can add or remove members from a contact group at any time.
- When you update contact fields, you need to update a contact group to ensure it has the most up-to-date fields.

Check for Understanding

In the ***Online Learning Center*** for this text (www.mhhe.com/office2013inpractice), there are a variety of resources that can be used to review the concepts covered in this chapter.
The following Online Learning Resources are available in the Online Learning Center:

- Multiple choice questions
- Short answer questions
- Matching exercises

USING MICROSOFT OUTLOOK 2013

Guided Project 3-1

In this project, you work as an insurance agent for Central Sierra Insurance (CSI). As a new member to the team, you begin setting up your Outlook contacts to make it easy to contact your associates. You will need to work with two partners for this guided project.
[Student Learning Outcomes 3.1, 3.2, 3.5]

Skills Covered in This Project

- Create a new contact.
- Add information in fields.
- Create contacts from the same company.
- Select contacts within the *To* and *Cc* fields of an email.
- Email contacts as a business card.

---

1. Click the **People** button in the *Navigation* pane.
2. Create a contact for your manager (either one of your partners, but be sure each person creates a unique contact).
   a. Click the **New Contact** button [*Home* tab, *New* group].
   b. Partner with another student and enter his or her full name, company (Central Sierra), job title (Manager), business phone number, and email address in the appropriate fields.
   c. Click the **Contact from the Same Company** option [*Contact* tab, *Actions* group, *Save & New* button].
   d. Create another contact for your other partner. Include his or her full name, company (Central Sierra), job title (Insurance Agent), business phone number, and email address in the appropriate fields.
   e. Click **Save & Close**. Click **Save & Close** for both contacts.
3. Create a new message to your instructor.
   a. Click the **Mail** button in the *Navigation* pane.
   b. Click **New Mail** [*Home* tab, *New* group].
   c. In the *To* field, enter your instructor's email ddress.
   d. In the *Cc* field, enter your email address.
   e. In the *Subject* field, type Outlook Guided Project 3-1
   f. In the message area, type:
      Dear [instructor name],
      Attached is my Outlook Guided Project 3-1.
      Thank you,
      [your name]
   g. Click the **Business Card** option [*Message* tab, *Include* group, *Attach Item*] and select **Other Business Cards**.
   h. Select the two cards you created and click **OK**.
   i. Your email message should look similar to figure 3-49.
   j. Click the **Send** button.

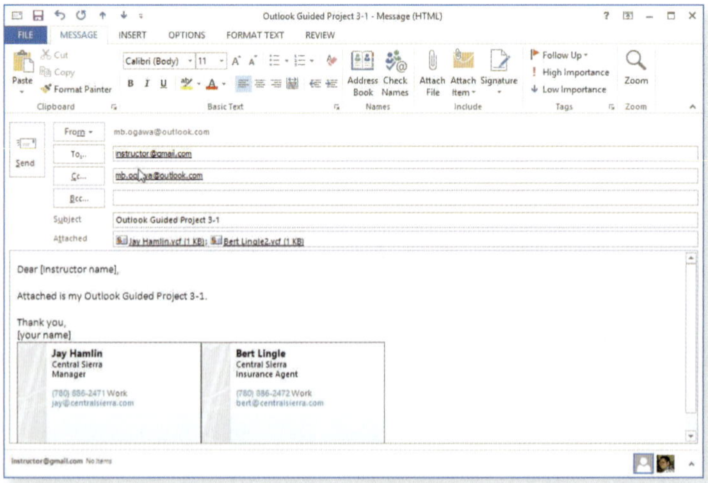

3-49 Completed Guided Project 3-1

Guided Project 3-2

For this project, you edit your contacts to add additional information. You also add a picture to each of the contacts so that you can easily match your coworkers' faces and names when receiving email. [Student Learning Outcomes 3.1, 3.3, 3.4, 3.5]

Files Needed: ***johnsanchez*.jpg and *jillricci.jpg***
Completed Project File Name: None

Skills Covered in This Project

- Edit contacts.
- Include an address in contacts.
- Include a photo in contacts.
- Select contacts within the *To* and *Cc* fields of an email.
- Email contacts as a business card.

1. Edit the two contacts you created in Guided Project 3-1 to include their addresses and pictures.
   a. Click the **Business Card** button [*Home* tab, *Current View* group].
   b. Double-click the first record that you created (your partner that is a manager).
   c. Type the following information in the *Business Address* field:

      5520 Ridley Way
      Cameron Park, CA 94681

   d. Select the **Add Picture** option [*Contact* tab, *Options* group, *Picture* button].
   e. Locate your partner's picture and click **OK**. If you do not have a picture, you can use one of the provided images (***johnsanchez*.jpg** or ***jillricci.jpg***) and change it to his or her image later.
   f. Click the **Save & Close** button.
   g. Double-click the second record that you created (your partner who is an insurance agent).
   h. Type the following information in the *Business Address* field:

      5520 Ridley Way
      Cameron Park, CA 94681

   i. Select the **Add Picture** option [*Contact* tab, *Options* group, *Picture* button].
   j. Locate your partner's picture and click **OK**. If you do not have a picture, you can use one of the provided images (***johnsanchez.jpg*** or ***jillricci.jpg***) and change it to his or her image later.
   k. Click the **Save & Close** button.
2. Create a new message to your instructor (Figure 3-50).

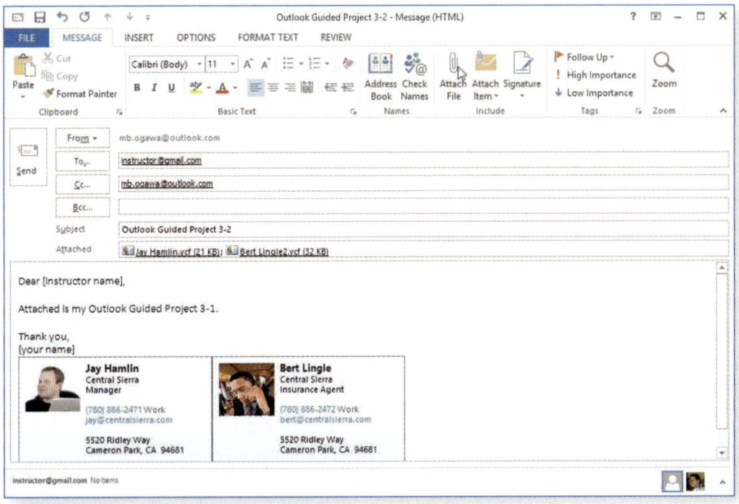

3-50 Completed Guided Project 3-2

a. Click the **Mail** button in the *Navigation* pane.
b. Click **New Mail** [*Home* tab, *New* group].
c. In the *To* field, enter your instructor's email address.
d. In the *Cc* field, enter your email address.
e. In the *Subject* field, enter Outlook Guided Project 3-2.
f. In the message area, type:

Dear [instructor name],
Attached is my Outlook Guided Project 3-2.
Thank you,
[your name]

g. Click the **Business Card** option [*Message* tab, *Include* group, *Attach Item*] and select **Other Business Cards**.
h. Select the two cards you crated and click **OK**.
i. Click the **Send** button.

Guided Project 3-3

For this project, you create a contact group for your coworker and manager. You also include yourself in the contact group.
[Student Learning Outcomes 3.1, 3.5]

Skills Covered in This Project

- Create a contact group.
- Select contacts within the *To* and *Cc* fields of an email.
- Email a contact group as an Outlook item.

1. Create an Outlook contact group using your two coworkers from Guided Project 3-2.
   a. Click the **New Contact Group** button [*Home* tab, *New* group].
   b. Type Central Sierra Team in the *Name* field.
   c. Select **From Outlook Contacts** [*Contact Group* tab, *Members* group, *Add Members* button].
   d. Hold the **Ctrl** key and select the contact information for your two partners and yourself.
   e. Click the **Members** button.
   f. Click **OK**.
   g. Click the **Save & Close** button [*Contact Group* tab, *Actions* group].
2. Send an email to your instructor with the *Central Sierra Team* contact as an attachment (Figure 3-51).
   a. Select the **Central Sierra Team** contact.
   b. Click the **As an Outlook Contact** option [*Home* tab, *Share* group, *Forward Contact* button].
   c. Click the **To** button to open your contacts.
   d. Select your instructor and click the **To** button.
   e. Click **OK**.

f. Add your email address in the *Cc* field.
g. Change the subject to Outlook Guided Project 3-3.
h. In the message area, type:
   Dear [instructor name],
   Attached is my Outlook Guided Project 3-3.
   Thank you,
   [your name]
i. Click the **Send** button.

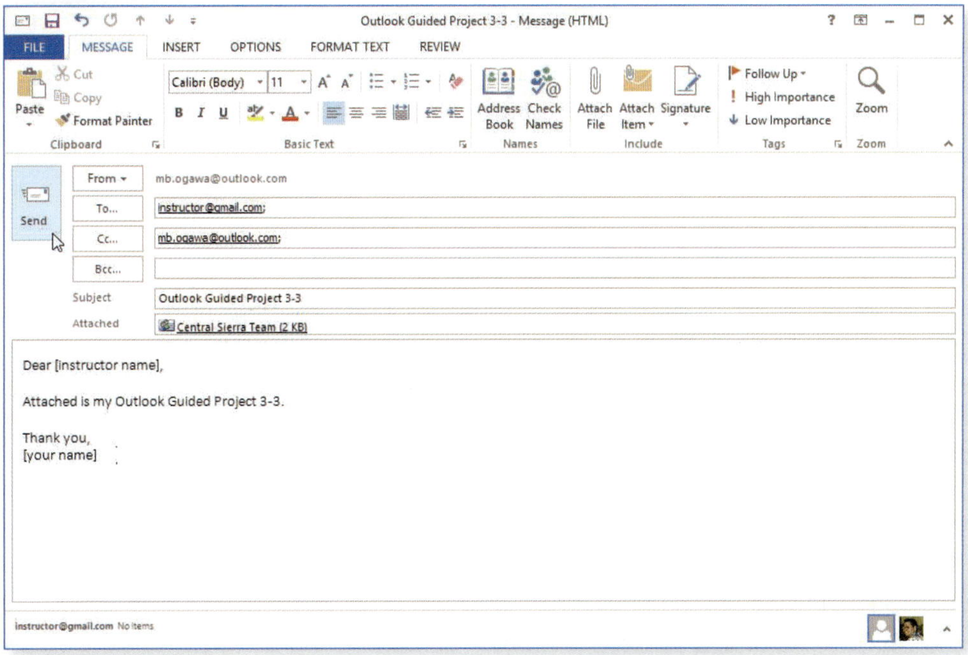

3-51 Completed Guided Project 3-3

Independent Project 3-4

For this project, you work as an academic advisor for Sierra Pacific Community College District (SPCCD), a community college district made up of four individual community colleges. Due to the decentralized nature of the multiple campuses, you realize that it is important that you keep in touch with advisors on the other campuses and you add them to your contacts.
[Student Learning Outcomes 3.1, 3.2, 3.5]

Skills Covered in This Project

- Create contacts.
- Create contacts using the same company.
- Adding information to fields.
- Select contacts within the *To* and *Cc* fields of an email.
- Email contacts as a business card.

1. Create contacts for the following individuals:

Full name	Company	Job title	E-mail	Business Phone
Joy Holland	Sierra Pacific Community College District (North)	Academic Advisor	joy@spccd.edu	209-658-0011
Megan Sharp	Sierra Pacific Community College District (South)	Academic Advisor	megan@spccd.edu	209-658-0891
Jim Hennessey	Sierra Pacific Community College District (East)	Academic Advisor	jim@spccd.edu	209-658-7189
Morgan Santos	Sierra Pacific Community College District (West)	Academic Advisor	morgan@spccd.edu	209-658-5561

2. Send an email to your instructor including the four business cards as attachments.
   a. Include your email address in the *Cc* field.
   b. Type Outlook Independent Project 3-4 in the *Subject* field.
   c. Include a short message indicating that the completed Independent Project is attached to the message (Figure 3-52).

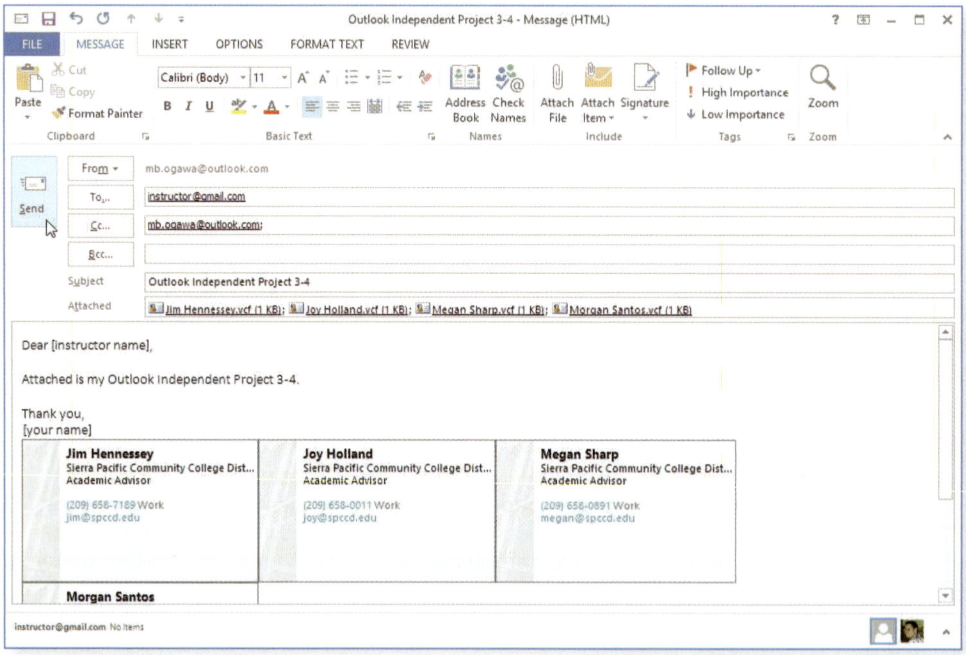

3-52 Completed Independent Project 3-4

Independent Project 3-5

For this project, you familiarize yourself with the basic components of Outlook.
[Student Learning Outcomes 3.1, 3.3, 3.4, 3.5]

Files Needed: ***jim.jpg, joy.jpg, megan.jpg,*** **and** ***morgan.jpg***
Completed Project File Name: None

Skills Covered in This Project

- Edit contacts.
- Include an address in contacts.
- Include a photo in contacts.
- Add a second email address to contacts.
- Add a mobile phone number to contacts.
- Select contacts within the *To* and *Cc* fields of an email.
- Email contacts as a business card.

1. Edit the four contacts you created in Independent Project 3-4 to include the following:

Full name	Photo	Address	E-mail 2	Mobile Phone
Joy Holland	joy.jpg	7300 College Avenue Student Services, 3F Sacramento, CA 92387	joy@outlook.com	818-298-3987
Megan Sharp	megan.jpg	7300 College Avenue Helmsley Hall, 319 Sacramento, CA 92387	megan@outlook.com	818-459-0091
Jim Hennessey	jim.jpg	7300 College Avenue Hamilton Hall, 210A Sacramento, CA 92387	jim@outlook.com	818-928-9916
Morgan Santos	morgan.jpg	7300 College Avenue POST Bld, 312 Sacramento, CA 92387	morgan@outlook.com	818-298-7620

2. Send an email to your instructor including the four business cards as attachments (Figure 3-53).
   a. Include your email address in the *Cc* field.
   b. Type Outlook Independent Project 3-5 in the *Subject* field.
   c. Include a short message indicating that the completed Independent Project is attached to the message.

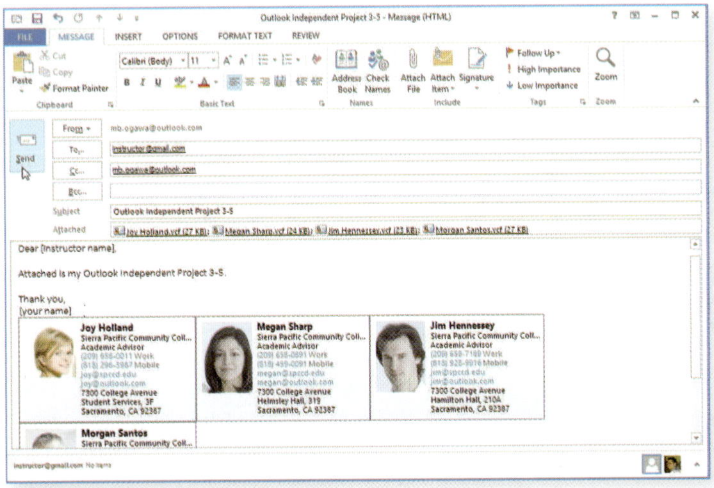

3-53 Completed Independent Project 3-5

Independent Project 3-6

In this project, you continue to familiarize yourself with the basic components of Outlook. [Student Learning Outcomes 3.1, 3.2, 3.3, 3.4, 3.5]

Skills Covered in This Project

- Create a contact group.
- Add a new contact group member.
- Edit a contact.
- Select contacts within the *To* and *Cc* fields of an email.
- Email a contact group as an Outlook item.

1. Create a new contact group with the four advisors called Sierra Pacific Advising Team. Only add their ***spccd.edu*** email addresses.
2. Add a new member to the contact group with the following information:
   Full Name: John Hays
   E-mail: john@spccd.edu
3. Edit John's contact information to include the following:
   Company: Sierra Pacific Community College District (System)
   Job title: Dean
   E-mail 2: jay@outlook.com
   Business phone: 209-981-2975
   Mobile phone: 818-212-0459
   Photo: ***hays.jpg***
   Address:
   7300 College Avenue
   College Hill, 208
   Sacramento, CA 92387
4. Send an email to your instructor including the contact group and Dean Hay's business card as attachments.
   a. Include your email address in the *Cc* field.
   b. Type Outlook Independent Project 3-6 in the *Subject* field.
   c. Include a short message indicating that the completed Independent Project is attached to the message (Figure 3-54).

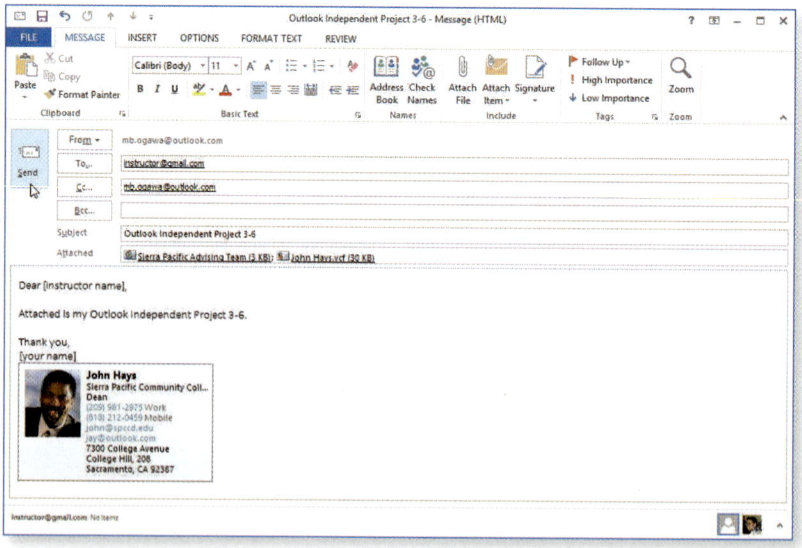

3-54 Completed Independent Project 3-6

Challenge Project 3-7

Develop a contact group for your family and friends to use to send out group updates. Include as much information as possible. If you are concerned about privacy, you can create information for fields that are sensitive.
[Student Learning Outcomes 3.1, 3.2, 3.3, 3.5]

- Create at least five new contacts for friends and family members.
- Use as many fields as possible.
- At minimum, each record should have the full name, email address, phone number, and mailing address completed.
- Include a picture for each contact.
- Create a contact group for the members.
- Use a descriptive name for the group.
- Email the contact group to your instructor as an email attachment.
- Change the subject of your message to ***Outlook Challenge Project 3-7***.
- Include a short message indicating why the contact group name is appropriate.

Challenge Project 3-8

Describe an upcoming event in an email message to an organization in which you're a member. Develop contacts and a contact group list for the organization and email it as a file to your instructor.
[Student Learning Outcomes 3.1, 3.2, 3.3, 3.5]

- Create at least five new contacts for your organization.
- Use as many fields as possible. You can create fictitious information for fields that are sensitive.
- At minimum, each record should have the full name and email address of each member.
- Create a contact group for the members.
- Use a descriptive name for the group.
- Write an email message to the organization describing an upcoming event.
- You can use options, such as themes, to improve the aesthetics of the message.
- Save the message as a draft.
- Save the draft as a file.
- Email the contact group to your instructor as an email attachment.
- Include the draft email message as an attachment.
- Change the subject of your message to ***Outlook Challenge Project 3-8***.

Challenge Project 3-9

Create a contact group including at least five classmates who are in your study sessions. Incorporate as much information in each record as possible since you may need to get in touch with group members via a variety of means. Write a message to the contact group requesting a study session and use voting buttons to select a specific date.
[Student Learning Outcomes 3.1, 3.2, 3.3, 3.5]

- Create at least five new contacts for your study group.
- Use as many fields as possible.
- At minimum, each record should have a full name, two email addresses, a mobile phone number, and an address.
- Apply a category to each of the contacts and the contact group.
- Create a contact group for the members.
- Use a descriptive name for the group.
- Write an email message to the group requesting a study session on a specific date.
- Use voting buttons to have your group vote on a date.
- Save the message as a draft.
- Save the draft as a file.
- Email the contact group to your instructor as an email attachment.
- Include the draft email message as an attachment.
- Change the subject of your message to ***Outlook Challenge Project 3-9***.

CHAPTER 4

OUTLOOK

Calendar

CHAPTER OVERVIEW

If you use a daily planner or a calendar that hangs on your wall or refrigerator and think you would be lost without it, wait until you start using an Outlook calendar and learn about the many advantages it has over a paper calendar. One of the many advantages to using Microsoft Outlook is that it integrates different Outlook tasks. As personal management software, Outlook not only handles your emails (and multiple email accounts) and contacts but also provides an electronic calendar to be used in conjunction with your email.

In this chapter, you'll learn about many of the features of ***Outlook Calendar*** and how it integrates with both email and contacts. In future chapters, you will see how calendar items can be used with Tasks, Categories, and the *To-Do bar.* As you progress though this text and continue to utilize Outlook in your daily life for both business and personal use, you will find that Outlook Calendar not only surpasses your expectations but it is an invaluable organizational tool.

STUDENT LEARNING OUTCOMES (SLOs)

After completing this chapter, you will be able to:

- **SLO 4.1** Identify the different types of calendar items (p. O4-132).
- **SLO 4.2** Distinguish between different calendar views (p. O4-134).
- **SLO 4.3** Create and edit calendar items (p. O4-138).
- **SLO 4.4** Create and use meeting requests (p. O4-144).

CASE STUDY

For the Pause & Practice projects, you begin building your personal calendar by adding a meeting with your instructor and your friend's birthday. You use the features of Outlook to create, modify, and request meetings with others.

Pause & Practice 4-1: For this Pause & Practice project, you create calendar items for an upcoming meeting with your instructor regarding an assignment. You also create a recurring event for your friend's birthday with a reminder set a week in advance to ensure you have time to purchase a gift.

Pause & Practice 4-2: You follow up with the two calendar items you created in *Pause & Practice 4-1.* You had an emergency at home, so you decide to send a meeting request to your instructor to apologize for not being able to make the meeting and reschedule. You also send a meeting request to have lunch with your friend Lynne to give her the gift you purchased.

SLO 4.1

Understanding Calendar Items

Most people who use a calendar to help organize their lives can only imagine having a calendar hanging on their wall or refrigerator instead of keeping all of their appointments on an electronic calendar. But most people who have converted to Outlook Calendar cannot imagine going back to a paper calendar.

An Outlook calendar has many advantages over a paper calendar.

- An Outlook calendar can be viewed in monthly, weekly, daily, or other formats, unlike a paper calendar that has a fixed view.
- Reminders can be set to alert you on your computer or phone about upcoming appointments or events.
- Calendar items can easily be moved, copied, deleted, or set to recur at specific intervals.
- Categories can be used to group calendar items and color them for visual recognition.
- Additional information and details can be included in the body, and items such as contacts and Word documents can be attached to a calendar item.
- Calendar items can be set to recur on a specific interval (daily, weekly, monthly, or yearly).
- Meeting requests can be used to create a meeting on your calendar, invite others to the meeting, and track responses of those attending the meeting.
- Calendars can be synchronized with many cell phones and tablets that have a calendar feature.

There are three main types of calendar items: ***appointments***, ***events***, and ***meeting requests***. Each of these different items has a distinct purpose and use, but all of these items are created in a similar fashion, and you can use the same new calendar item to create each of these different calendar items. For example, an appointment can easily be changed to an event by changing the duration of the calendar item. This consistency makes it easy to learn how to use Outlook Calendar.

Appointments

An ***appointment*** (Figure 4-1) is a calendar item that has a duration of less than 24 hours, such as a sales meeting, your child's water polo game, or a date with your significant other. This is the most common type of calendar item and can be used for storing all types of appointments or for scheduling blocks of time that are less than a day in length.

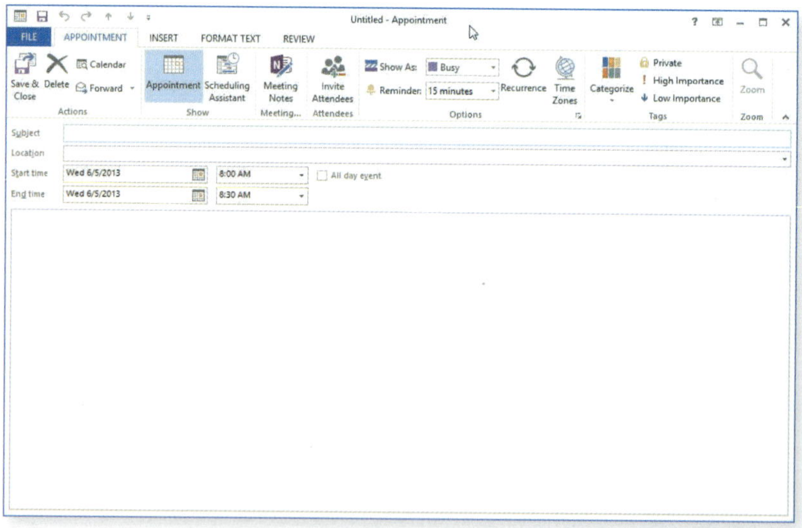

4-1 New appointment

Events

Events (Figure 4-2) are those calendar items that last for 24 hours or more, like vacations, conferences, birthdays, or long holidays.

When a new appointment is open, it can easily be converted to an event by clicking on the **All day event** check box to the right of the *Start time* and *End time.* Conversely, an event can be converted to an appointment by deselecting the **All day event** check box and setting the specific time of the appointment.

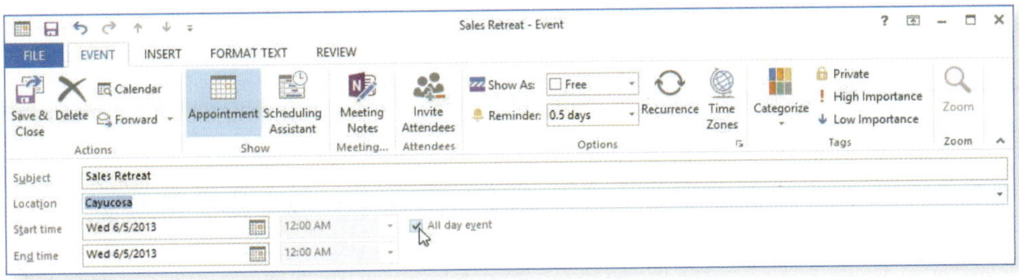

4-2 Event

Meeting Requests

A ***meeting request*** (Figure 4-3) is used to create a calendar item and invite others to this meeting. It looks similar to both an appointment and an event, but the meeting request includes a *To* line used to invite attendees and a *Send* button. A meeting request looks like a combination of a calendar item and a new email and can be either an appointment or event. If you are

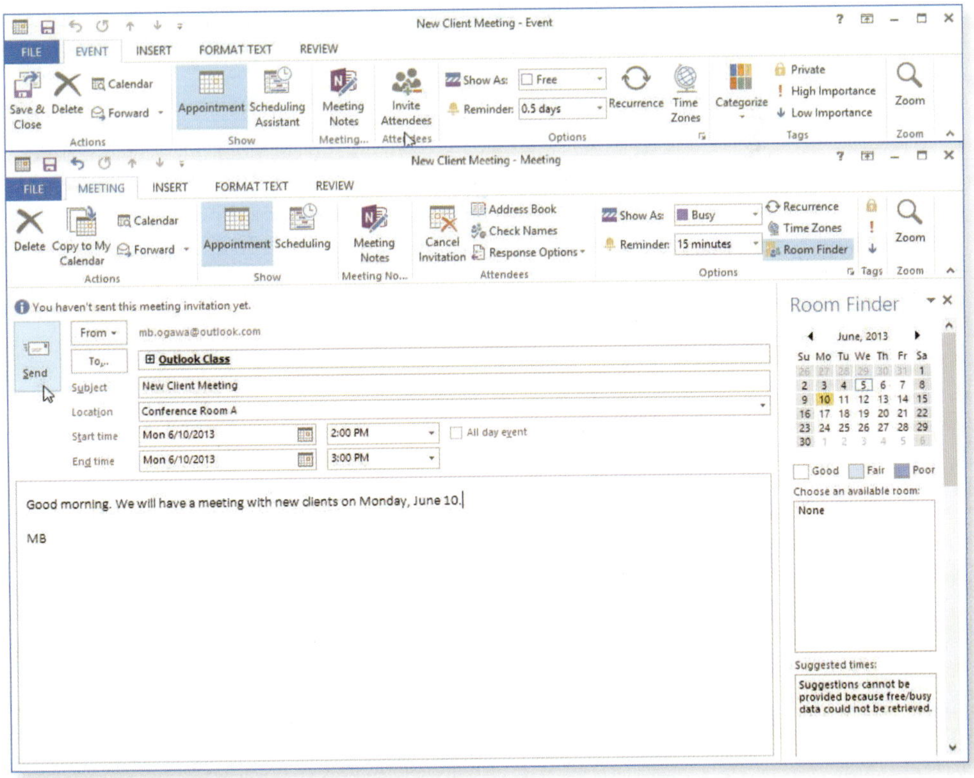

4-3 Meeting request

using an Exchange server, you can select from available rooms if your administrator enabled this feature.

An appointment or event can easily be converted to a meeting request by clicking on the **Invite Attendees** button in the *Attendees* group on the *Appointment* or *Events* tab (the tab name will vary depending on whether the calendar item is an appointment or event).

SLO 4.2

Navigating the Calendar Views

As mentioned previously, one of the advantages of using an Outlook calendar is being able to view the calendar in different formats. There are four main calendar views: ***Day***, ***Week***, ***Month***, and ***Schedule***. There are other views available that list calendar items according to specific criteria. You have to experiment with the different views to find the view or views that work best for you. My preference is the *Month* view.

When **Calendar** is selected in the *Navigation* pane, it is displayed in the *Folder* pane. The way the calendar is displayed in the *Folder* pane is dependent upon the calendar view you have selected. The buttons for *Day*, *Week*, *Month*, and *Schedule* view are in the *Arrange* group on the *Home* tab. Also displayed in the *Navigation* pane are the ***date navigator*** (a thumbnail of a monthly calendar) and the different calendars available (you can have multiple calendars).

MORE INFO

Tasks and To-Do items will be covered in Chapter 5.

ANOTHER WAY

Ctrl+Alt+1 will display the calendar in *Day* view.

Day View

Day view (Figure 4-4) displays the calendar one day at a time with the calendar broken into half-hour segments. Events are displayed at the top of the daily calendar, while appointments appear on the calendar at their scheduled times.

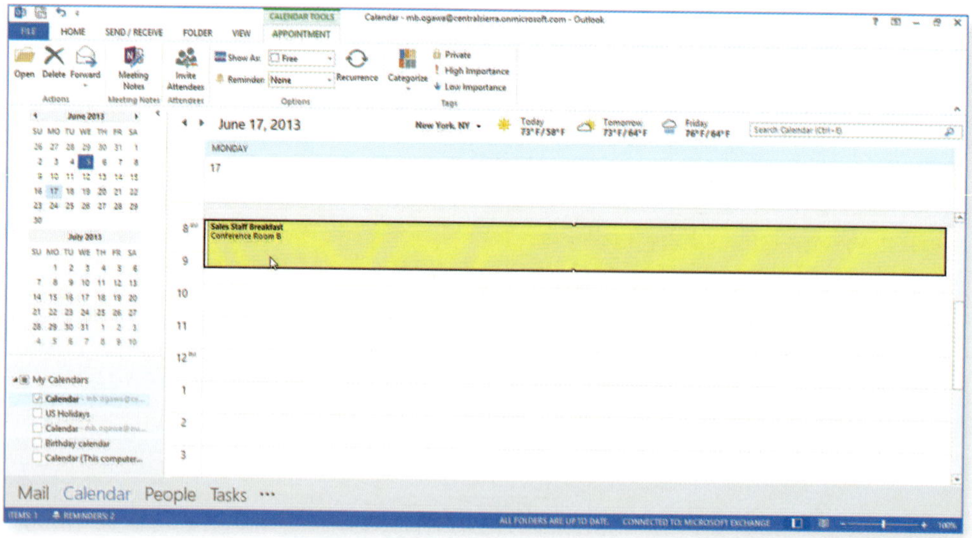

4-4 ***Day* view**

The date is listed at the top of the calendar, and you can move backward or forward one day at a time on the calendar by clicking on the left or right arrow to the left of the date. You can move to a specific date on the calendar by clicking on the date in the thumbnail calendar provided at the top of the *Navigation* pane.

Week View

Week view (Figure 4-5) has two different display options: ***Work Week*** or ***Week.*** *Work Week* view displays a Monday through Friday workweek, while *Week* view displays a Sunday through Saturday week.

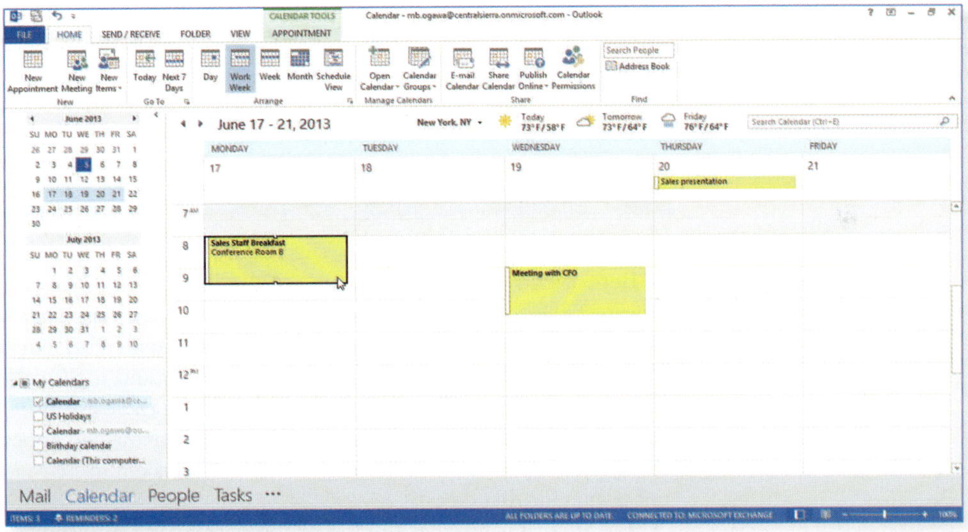

4-5 *Work Week* view

As with *Day* view, *Week* view displays events at the top of the calendar and appointments appear at their set times. The *Daily Task List* is located at the bottom of the *Folder* pane and can either be minimized or turned off.

The date is displayed at the top of the calendar in the *Folder* pane showing the date range for the week. The left and right arrows to the left of the date will move you backward or forward one week at a time.

MORE INFO

Changing work week options, calendar color, and other advanced calendar topics will be covered in Chapter 9.

ANOTHER WAY

Ctrl+Alt+2 displays the calendar in *Work Week* view.
Ctrl+Alt+3 displays the calendar in *Week* view.

Month View

Month view (Figure 4-6) displays an entire month of the calendar. You are given three different options regarding the amount of detail to display on the calendar for each calendar item (*Show Low Detail, Show Medium Detail,* and *Show High Detail*).

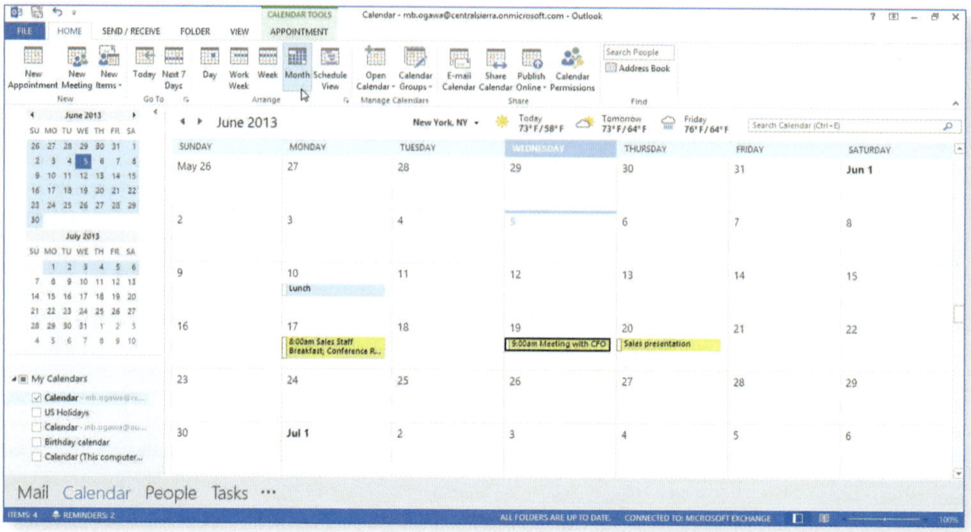

4-6 ***Month*** **view**

Both events and appointments are displayed on the dates on which they occur. Events appear at the top of the date cell, and appointments appear below the events. You can see more detail about any of the items on the calendar by moving your pointer over the item. Depending on the size of your computer monitor and the Outlook window, *Month* view will display three or four calendar items on each day. If there are more events or appointments on a certain date than will fit on the calendar, a small arrow will appear at the bottom right corner of the date. If you click on this arrow, you will be taken to *Day* view to see more appointments and events for that day.

The month is listed at the top of the *Folder* pane, and the left and right arrows to the left of the month will move you backward or forward one month at a time.

ANOTHER WAY

Ctrl+Alt+4 displays the calendar in *Month* view.

MORE INFO

The *Today* button in the *Go To* group on the *Home* tab will always take you to the current day. Also, you can move to a specific day by clicking on the date navigator in the *Navigation* pane.

Schedule View

Schedule view (Figure 4-7) displays your calendar in timeline view in the *Folder* pane. The timeline is displayed horizontally rather than vertically (*Day* and *Week* views). In *Schedule* view you can type a new appointment directly on the calendar, double-click a time slot to open a new appointment, or click the *New Appointment* button on the *Home* tab.

ANOTHER WAY

Ctrl+Alt+5 displays the calendar in *Schedule* view.

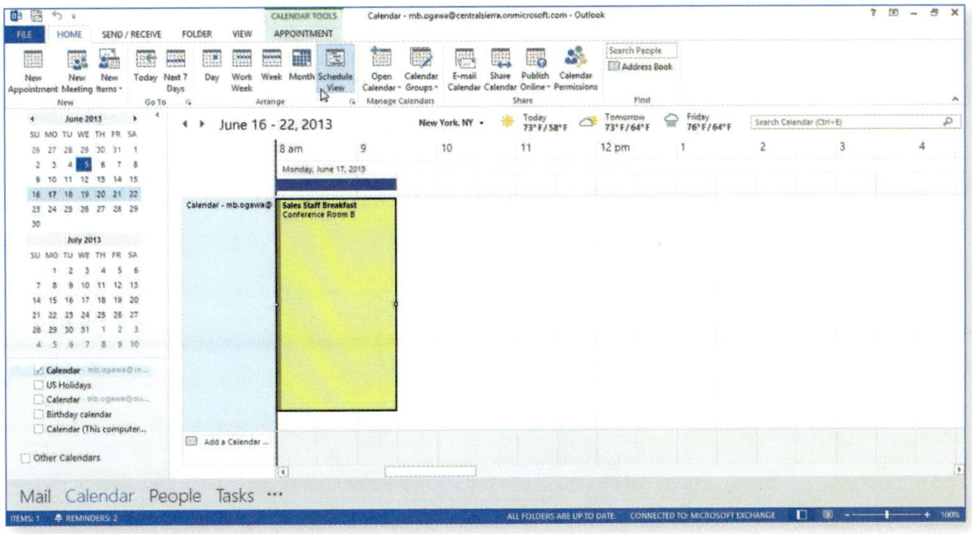

4-7 *Schedule* view

One of the distinct advantages of using the *Schedule* view is the ability to view multiple calendars in the *Folder* pane. When using Outlook in an Exchange environment, it is common to share your calendar with others in your organization. When others have shared their calendars with you, you can select one or more of these shared calendars to be displayed in *Schedule* view, which will help facilitate scheduling meetings, appointments, and events.

> **MORE INFO**
>
> Sharing and opening shared calendars will be covered in Chapter 9.
> Multiple calendars can also be displayed when using *Day, Week, Work Week,* or *Month* views.

Other Views

In addition to the four main calendar views, Outlook also has other preset views available. These different views show calendar items in a list rather than *Day, Week,* or *Month* view. The different preset views are:

- *Calendar* (*Calendar* view)
- *Preview* (*Calendar* view)
- *List* (*List* view)
- *Active* (*List* view)

To access these other views, click **Change View** (Figure 4-8) on the *View* tab and choose the view you want. You can return to *Calendar* view by following the same steps and choosing **Calendar**.

> **MORE INFO**
>
> Any of these views can be customized to better meet your needs. Customizing views will be covered in Chapter 5 and 9.

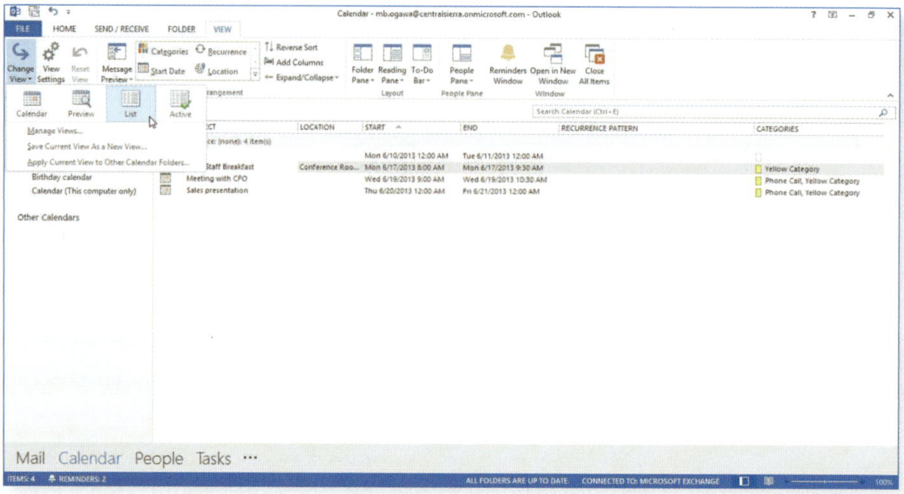

4-8 Additional views

SLO 4.3

Creating and Editing Calendar Items

Creating a calendar item varies depending on the calendar view. In all the calendar views, you can type an appointment directly on the calendar. In *Day* and *Week* views, you can adjust the duration of an appointment by clicking and dragging on the top or bottom edge of the appointment.

Usually the best way to create a calendar item is to open a new calendar item. This will give you more fields to enter detailed information about the appointment or event.

> **ANOTHER WAY**
>
> **Ctrl+N** gives you a new calendar item when you are in your calendar. This shortcut works for all the Outlook tasks. For example, if you're in Contacts and press **Ctrl+N**, you'll get a new contact record. This shortcut works in Mail, Calendar, Contacts, Tasks, Notes, and Journal.

Create an Appointment

When you are in your calendar (it doesn't matter which view), create a new appointment by clicking on the *New Appointment* button on the *Home* tab. The new appointment opens and the date will be the date you were on in the calendar. The date and time can easily be changed.

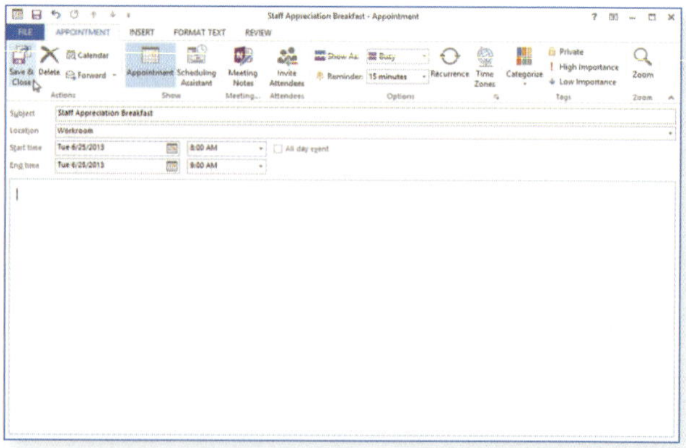

4-9 New appointment

HOW TO: Create an Appointment

1. In your calendar, click the **New Appointment** button on the *Home* tab. A new appointment opens (Figure 4-9).

2. Fill in the *Subject* and *Location* of the appointment. After you enter a subject, the subject appears in the *Title bar* at the top of the open calendar item.
3. Set the *Start time* and *End time* dates and times for this appointment.
4. Enter additional information about this appointment in the body of the new appointment.
5. Click **Save & Close**. The appointment appears on your calendar.

ANOTHER WAY

Ctrl+Shift+A opens a new calendar appointment anywhere in Outlook.

Create an Event

Creating a new event will vary depending on the calendar view. When you are in *Day* or *Week* view, create a new event by double-clicking on the event area at the top of the calendar in the *Folder* pane. In *Month* view, create a new event by double-clicking on the date of the event (or the first day of the event).

An appointment can always be converted to an event by clicking the **All day event** check box to the right of the date and time.

HOW TO: Create an Event

1. Click the **New Appointment** button on the *Home* tab or press **Ctrl+N**. A new appointment opens.
2. Fill in the *Subject* and *Location* of the event.
3. Click the **All day event** check box.
   - The calendar item changes from an appointment to an event (Figure 4-10).
   - In the *Title bar* after the subject, the type of calendar item displays (e.g., *Appointment, Event,* or *Meeting*).
4. Set the *Start time* and *End time* dates for this event.
5. Enter additional information about this event in the body of the new appointment.
6. Click **Save & Close**. The event will appear on your calendar.

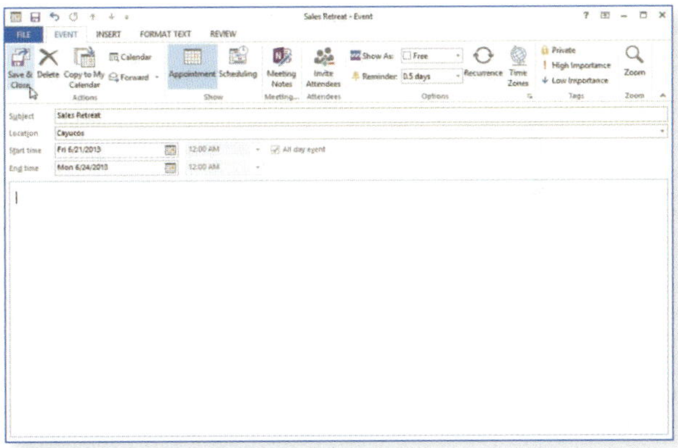

4-10 Event

Reminders

A ***reminder*** can be set on all calendar items. This reminder opens on your computer screen to remind you of an upcoming appointment, event, or meeting.

The default reminder time for an appointment is 15 minutes before the appointment, and an event is 18 hours before the event. You can easily change the reminder time by clicking on the *Reminder* drop-down menu (Figure 4-11) in the *Options* group on the *Appointment* or *Event* tab. You can also choose to set a specific sound for the reminder. The reminder can also be set to *None.*

When the reminder for an appointment or event comes due, it is displayed on your computer screen (Figure 4-12). The reminder displays the subject of the calendar item, the start date and time, and the location. You are given the options of *Dismiss All, Open Item, Dismiss,* and *Snooze.* If you choose *Snooze,* you can choose to be reminded again in a certain amount of time by clicking on the **Snooze** drop-down menu.

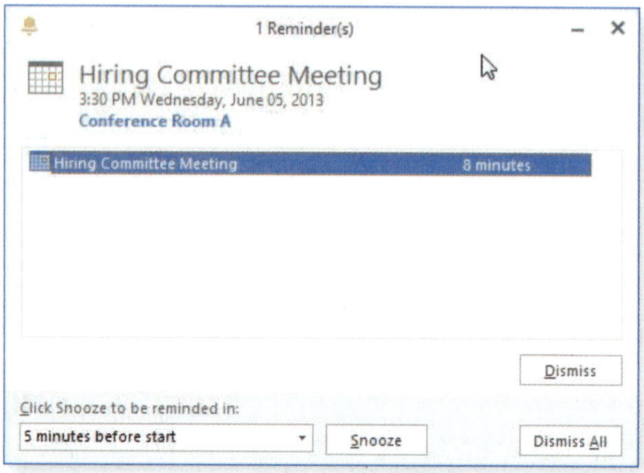

4-12 Reminder window

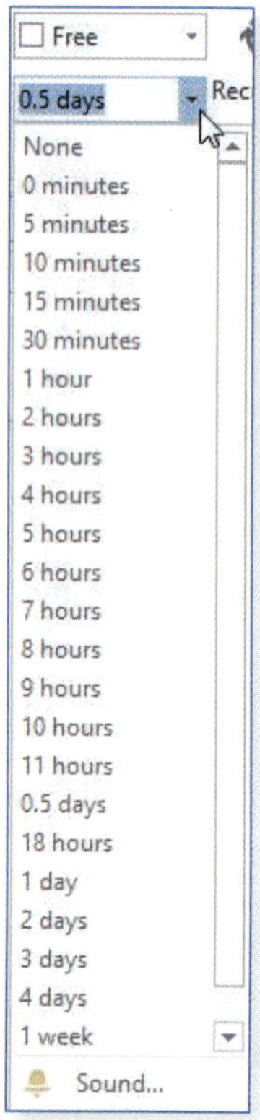

4-11 Reminder drop-down menu

Move and Copy Calendar Items

One of the distinct advantages of using an Outlook calendar is the ability to easily move and replicate calendar items. Many times an appointment is rescheduled, and, when using an Outlook calendar, you can move the item to a new date or time.

To ***move*** a calendar item, you can open the item from the calendar and change the date and/or time of the item. When you save and close the item, it will be moved to its new date and time on the calendar. If an appointment has been moved to another day and has the same time, you can simply drag and drop the calendar item to the new date on the calendar.

Suppose you have jury duty three days in a row and you don't want to create three separate calendar appointments. To ***copy*** an existing appointment to another date, you can select the appointment on the calendar, hold down the **Ctrl** key, and drag and drop the appointment on the new date. As you are dragging the calendar item, you will see a small plus sign by the pointer to indicate that you are copying a calendar item rather than moving it (Figure 4-13). The appointment will be copied to the new date.

4-13 Copy appointment using **Ctrl** + drag and drop

ANOTHER WAY

Ctrl+C copies a selected calendar item.
Ctrl+X cuts a selected calendar item.
Ctrl+V pastes a copied or cut calendar item to a new location.

Recurring Appointments and Events

When a calendar item has a recurring pattern, it is better to set up the item as a ***recurring appointment*** or ***event*** rather than just copying the item to another location. A recurring appointment or event is typically used for appointments or events that occur on a regular basis such as weekly sales meetings, monthly lunch socials, birthdays, or anniversaries.

A calendar item can be set to recur daily, weekly, monthly, or yearly. The recurring calendar item can be set to end after a certain number of occurrences, end on a certain date, or have no end date.

HOW TO: Create a Recurring Appointment or Event

1. Create a new calendar appointment.
2. Fill in the *Subject, Location, Start time, End time,* and any other needed details in the body.
3. Click the **Recurrence** button in the *Options* group (Figure 4-14). The *Appointment Recurrence* dialog box opens (Figure 4-15).
4. Confirm the correct start and end times in the *Appointment time* section.
5. Set the desired *Recurrence pattern.*
6. Select the *Range of recurrence* for *Start* and *End.*
7. Click **OK** to close the dialog box.
8. Click **Save & Close** to close the recurring appointment.

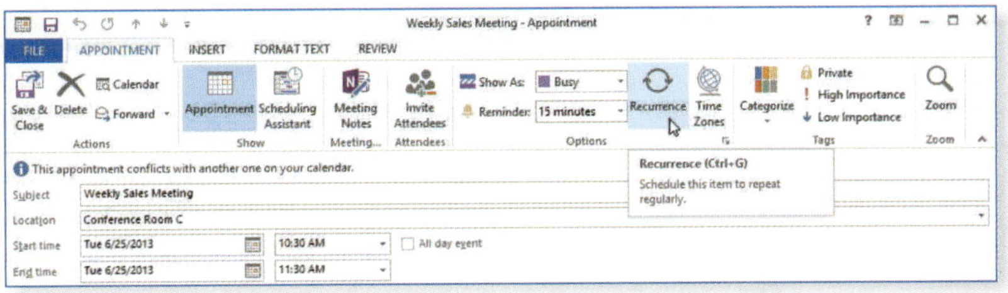

4-14 ***Recurrence* button**

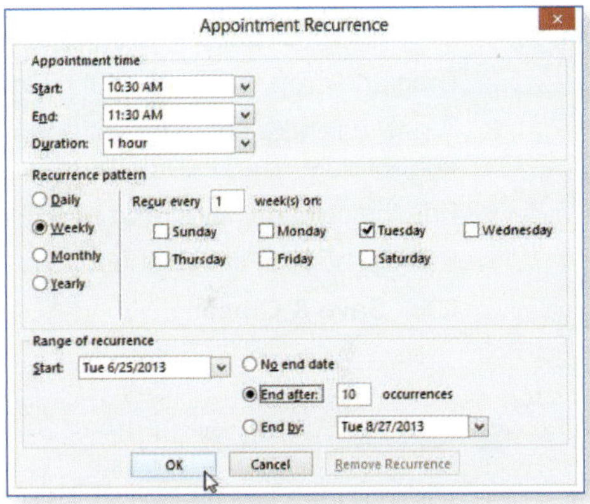

4-15 ***Appointment Recurrence* dialog box**

> **ANOTHER WAY**
>
> When a calendar item is open, **Ctrl+G** opens the *Appointment Recurrence* dialog box.

Recurring items can be edited. When you open a recurring item, Outlook will give you two options. ***Open this occurrence*** will allow you to edit that specific calendar item without changing all the recurring items or the recurrence pattern. ***Open the series*** will allow you to edit the entire series of recurring calendar items (Figure 4-16).

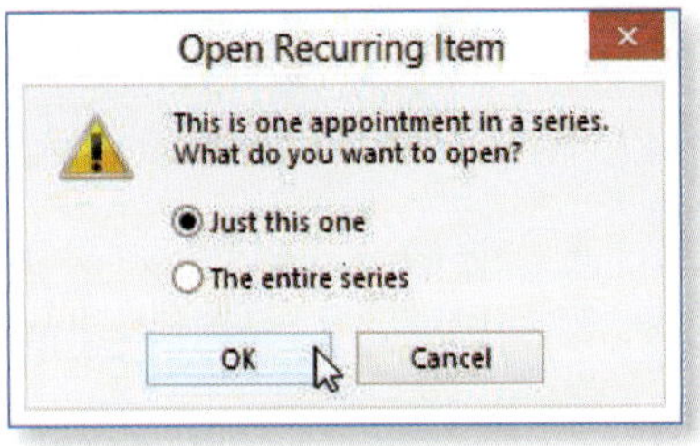

4-16 ***Open Recurring Item* dialog box**

Delete a Calendar Item

You can delete calendar items by selecting the items to be removed from the calendar and either pressing the *Delete* key on your keyboard, clicking on the *Delete* button on the *Appointment* tab, or right-clicking on the calendar item and selecting *Delete.*

When deleting a recurring item, you are given the options to either *Delete Occurrence* or *Delete Series.*

Deleted calendar items are stored in the *Deleted Items* folder and remain there until this folder is permanently emptied. If you delete a calendar item by mistake, you can open the *Deleted Items* folder and drag the calendar item from the *Deleted Items* folder to the *Calendar* button in the *Navigation* pane. The calendar item will be restored to its correct location on the calendar.

ANOTHER WAY

Ctrl+D deletes a selected calendar item.

Create a Calendar Item from an Email

There may be times when you receive an email and would like to create a calendar item based on the information in that email. Rather than retyping all the information in the email, you can easily convert it to a calendar item.

HOW TO: Create a Calendar Item from an Email

1. Click the email to be converted to a calendar item (do not open the email).
2. Drag and drop the email on the *Calendar* button in the *Navigation* pane.
3. A new calendar appointment opens. The subject will be the same as the email subject, and the date will be the current date. The body of the new calendar item will contain the information from the body of the email.
4. Edit the calendar item *Start* and *End* dates and times.
5. Edit the body of the calendar item.
6. Click **Save & Close**.

ANOTHER WAY

Select or open an email, click the **Move** button in the *Move* group, and choose **Other Folder.** Select the **Calendar** in the *Move Item to* dialog box and click **OK.** A new calendar appointment opens. When you save and close the appointment, the original email message will be moved to your *Deleted Items* folder.

PAUSE & PRACTICE: OUTLOOK 4-1

In this Pause & Practice project, you create calendar items for an upcoming meeting with your instructor regarding an assignment. You also create a recurring event for your friend's birthday with a reminder set a week in advance to ensure you have time to purchase a gift.

1. Create a new appointment.
   a. Click the **Calendar** button in the *Navigation* pane.
   b. Click the **New Appointment** button [*Home* tab, *New* group].
   c. Enter the following information for the new appointment:
      Subject: Meeting for ENG 100 Paper
      Location: Hamilton Hall 303A
      Start time: Next week Monday's date, 9:00 AM

End time: Next week Monday's day, 10:00 AM
Body: Email copy of paper to the instructor by Friday.

d. Click the *Reminder* drop-down arrow [*Appointment* tab, *Options* group].
e. Select **3 days**.
f. Click the **Save & Close** button.

2. Create a new appointment.
   a. Click the **New Appointment** button [*Home* tab, *New* group].
   b. Enter the following information for the new appointment:
      Subject: Lynne's Birthday
      Location: None
      Start time: July 17 of the current year
      End time: July 17 of the current year
      Click the checkbox for **All day event**.
      Body: Buy Lynne a present. She like sports and tech gadgets.
   c. Click the *Reminder* drop-down arrow [*Appointment* tab, *Options* group].
   d. Select **1 week**.
   e. Click the **Recurrence** button [*Event* tab, *Options* group].
   f. Click the **Yearly** radio button under *Recurrence pattern* and click **OK**.
   g. Click the **Save & Close** button.
      - The two appointments created are displayed in Figure 4-17.

3. Email the two calendar items to your instructor as Outlook items.
   a. Click the **Mail** button in the *Navigation* pane.
   b. Click the **New Email** button [*Home* tab, *New* group].
   c. Enter the following information in your message:
      To: instructor's email address
      Cc: your email address
      Subject: Pause & Practice 4-1
      Body:
      Hi [instructor name],
      Attached are my calendar items for the Pause & Practice 4-1 exercise.
      Sincerely,
      [student name]
   d. Click the **Attach Item** button [*Message* tab, *Include* group] and select **Outlook Item**.
   e. Select the **Calendar** option and locate the two calendar items you created.
   f. Hold the **Ctrl** key and select the two calendar items and click **OK**.
   g. Click **Send**.

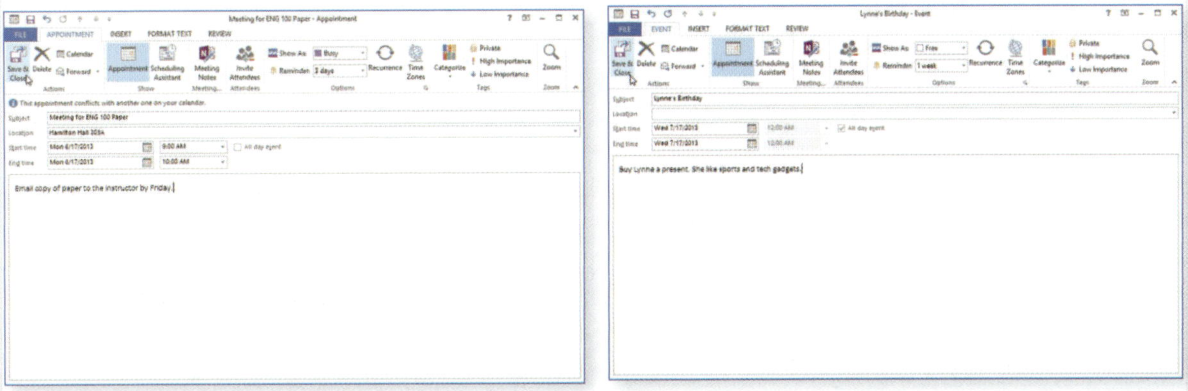

4-17 Completed Pause & Practice 4-1

SLO 4.4

Creating and Using Meeting Requests

Suppose you are organizing a meeting within your company and you want to keep track of those who will be attending and those who are not able to make it to the meeting. Outlook provides you with a calendar feature that not only creates a calendar appointment but also sends this appointment to others via email and tracks whether or not they will be attending the meeting.

Meeting requests are used to invite others to a meeting. It can be either an appointment or event. The advantage of using a meeting request over an email to invite attendees to a meeting is that the recipients receive a meeting invitation and are given the options of *Accept, Tentative, Decline,* or *Propose New Time.* When the recipient accepts the meeting request, the meeting is automatically added to the recipient's Outlook calendar and a response is sent to the sender of the meeting request. The meeting request will automatically keep track of attendees' responses.

> **MORE INFO**
>
> Tracking responses for meeting requests only works when used in an Exchange environment.

Create and Send a Meeting Request

Create a meeting request by clicking on the **New Meeting** button on the *Home* tab or by selecting or opening an existing calendar item and clicking on the **Invite Attendees** button in the *Attendees* group (Figure 4-18).

4-18 *Invite Attendees* button

> **MORE INFO**
>
> When sending a meeting request, provide a brief message and your name in the body.

HOW TO: Create and Send a Meeting Request

1. Create a new meeting request by clicking on the **New Meeting** button in the *New* group on the *Home* tab. An existing appointment or event can be converted to a meeting by clicking on the **Invite Attendees** button in the *Attendees* group.
2. Click the **To** button to invite attendees. The *Select Attendees and Resources* dialog box opens (Figure 4-19).
3. Select attendees from your contacts. Attendees can be either *Required* or *Optional* to attend the meeting.
4. Click **OK** to close the dialog box.

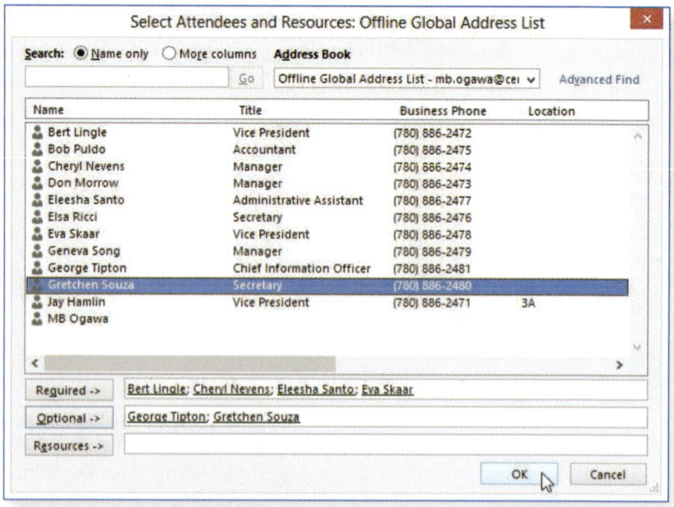

4-19 Select attendees

5. Fill in the *Subject, Location, Start* and *End* times (date and time), and any additional information needed in the body (Figure 4-20).
6. Click **Send** to send the meeting request.

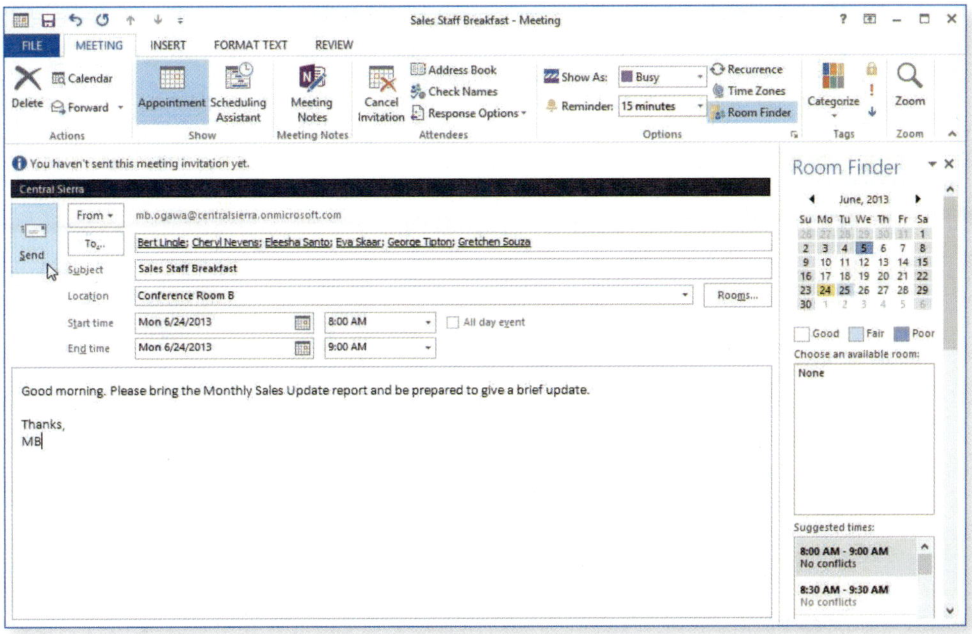

4-20 Filled meeting request

> **MORE INFO**
>
> When you open a new meeting request, it will always be an appointment. The meeting request can be changed to an event by clicking on the **All day event** check box.

> **ANOTHER WAY**
>
> **Ctrl+Shift+Q** opens a new meeting request.

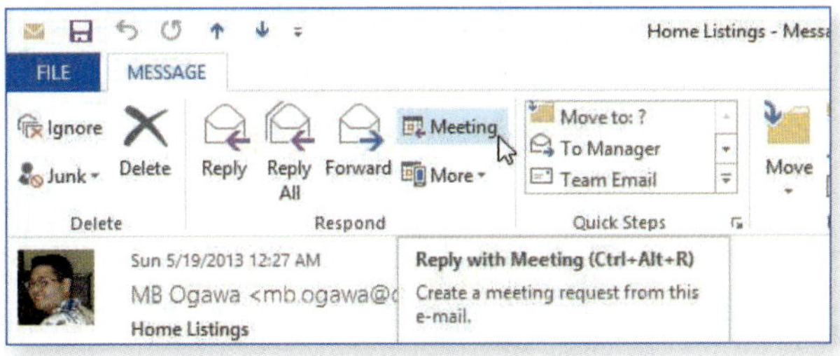

4-21 Create a meeting request from an email message

A meeting can also be created directly from a received email. When you receive an email and need to create a meeting based upon the information in that email, you do not have to go to your calendar to create a new meeting. Create a new meeting from this email by clicking the **Reply with Meeting** button (**Meeting** button) in the *Respond* group on the *Message* tab (Figure 4-21). The contents of the email message are included in the body of the new meeting. You can add attendees and make any other necessary changes before sending the meeting request.

> **ANOTHER WAY**
>
> **Ctrl+Alt+R** creates a new meeting from an existing email message.

> **MORE INFO**
>
> When creating a meeting from an email message, it is a good idea to clean up the body of the meeting to enhance the appearance of this calendar item.

Respond to a Meeting Request

When you receive a meeting request, it will come to your Inbox like other emails you receive. The Inbox icon for a meeting request will look different than an email icon.

When you open the meeting request, it will look similar to an email, but in the *Respond* group you are given four additional options: *Accept, Tentative, Decline,* or *Propose New Time.* When one of these responses is selected, a dialog box is opened and you are given the following options: *Edit the Response Before Sending, Send the Response Now,* or *Do Not Send a Response.*

If you choose *Accept, Tentative,* or *Propose New Time,* the meeting request is removed from your Inbox and added to your calendar and a response email is sent to the meeting organizer. If you choose *Decline,* the meeting request is moved from your Inbox to the *Deleted Items* folder and a response is sent to the meeting organizer.

Calendar Preview inserts a snapshot of your calendar in the body of the meeting request so you can view existing calendar items on the day of the new meeting request. Double-clicking on the calendar preview will take you to your calendar.

HOW TO: Respond to a Meeting Request

1. Open the meeting request from your Inbox.
2. Click one of the response buttons in the *Respond* group: *Accept, Decline,* or *Tentative.*
3. Choose *Edit the Response Before Sending* or *Send the Response Now* (Figure 4-22).
   - If you choose *Edit the Response Before Sending,* the email opens and you are able to enter a response in the body of the email before sending.
   - If you choose *Send the Response Now,* the response is automatically sent to the meeting organizer.
4. Click **OK** to close the dialog box.
5. Click **Send** if necessary.
   - If you chose *Accept* or *Tentative,* the response is sent and the meeting request is removed from your Inbox and placed on your calendar.

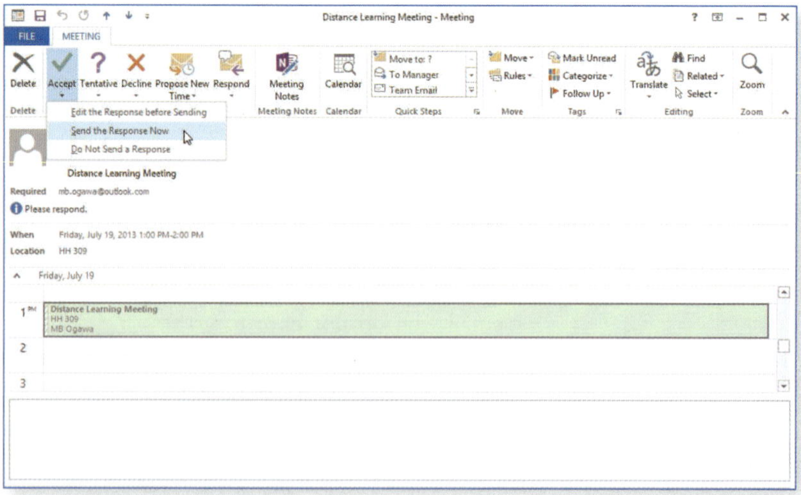

4-22 Respond to a meeting request

> **MORE INFO**
>
> It is probably best not to use the *Don't Send a Response* option. If you use this option, the meeting organizer will not know whether or not you'll be attending the meeting.

Propose a New Time to a Meeting Request

If you can't make a requested meeting at a particular date and time, you have the option of proposing a new time. When you click *Propose New Time* in the *Respond* group, you are given two options: *Tentative and Propose New Time* and *Decline and Propose New Time* (Figure 4-23). The *Propose New Time* dialog box opens. You can propose a new time by either dragging the meeting to a new time slot on the date and time timeline or enter a new date and time in the *Meeting start time* and *Meeting end time* boxes.

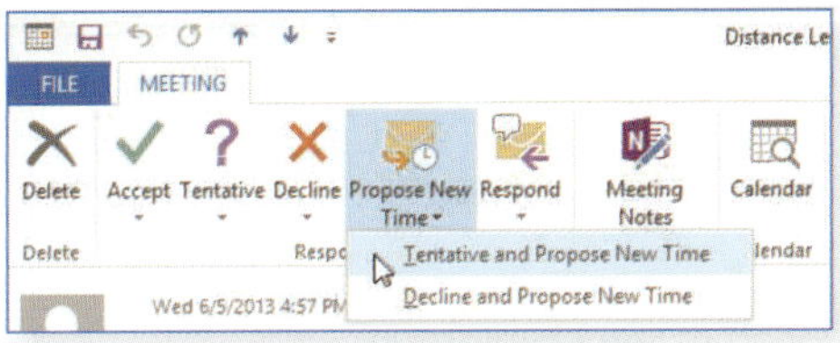

4-23 Propose a new meeting time

HOW TO: Propose a New Time for a Meeting

1. Open the meeting request from your Inbox.
2. Click the **Propose New Time** button and choose either *Tentative and Propose New Time* or *Decline and Propose New Time.* The *Propose New Time* dialog box opens (Figure 4-24).
3. Make changes to the date and/or time.
4. Click **Propose Time**. A *New Time Proposed* meeting request response opens. Notice the proposed changes below the subject line (Figure 4-25).
5. Type a brief message in the body.
6. Click **Send**. The response is sent, and the meeting request is removed from your Inbox and placed on your calendar.

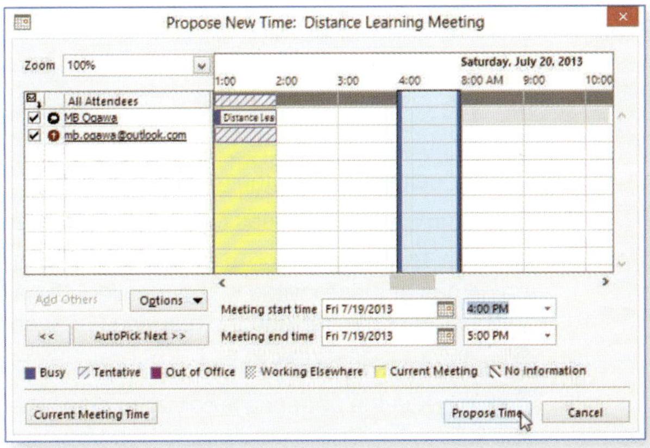

4-24 *Propose New Time* dialog box

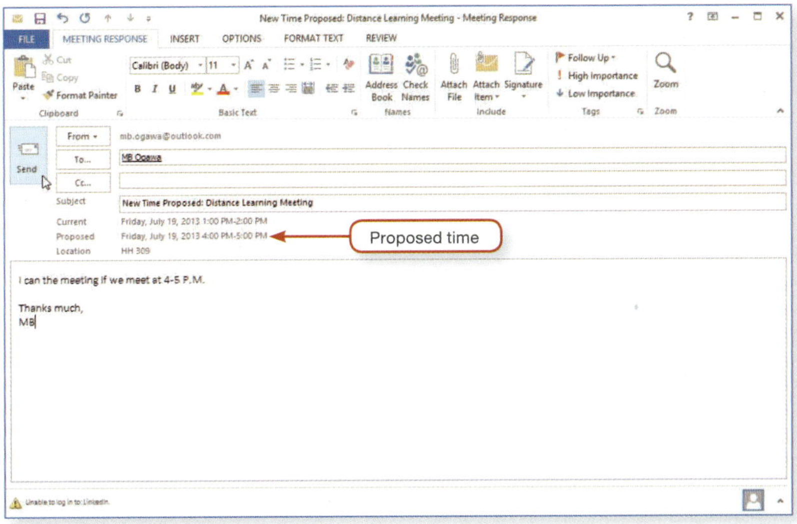

4-25 Proposed meeting time changes

MORE INFO

Outlook can automatically pick a new meeting time that fits on both your schedule and the other attendees' schedules. Using the Scheduling Assistant will be covered in Chapter 9.

Track Meeting Request Respondents

When you organize a meeting and send out a meeting request, you will receive meeting request responses in your Inbox (Figure 4-26). The responses will tell you the attendance status for each individual.

Outlook will track the responses of those individuals who have responded to your meeting request. When you open, from the calendar, the meeting request you created, Outlook displays a summary of responses in the *Info bar* above the *To* button. Also, you can obtain more detailed tracking information by clicking on the **Tracking** button in the *Show* group on the *Meeting* tab.

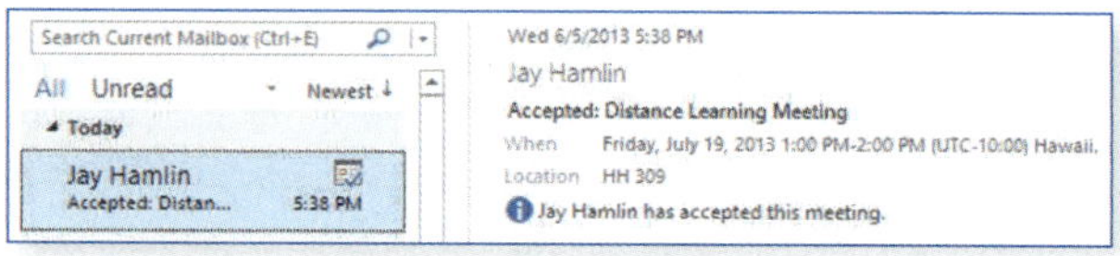

4-26 Meeting request acceptance in the Inbox

HOW TO: Track Meeting Request Respondents

1. On your calendar, open the meeting request you created (Figure 4-27).
2. The summary of responses received is displayed in the *Info bar.*
3. Click the **Tracking** button in the *Show* group on the *Meeting* tab. The body of the meeting request displays the names of those invited to the meeting, the attendance status (*Meeting Organizer, Required Attendance,* or *Optional Attendance*), and the response of each individual.
4. Click the **Appointment** button in the *Show* group to close the tracking and return to the meeting request.
5. Click the **X** in the upper right corner to close the meeting request.

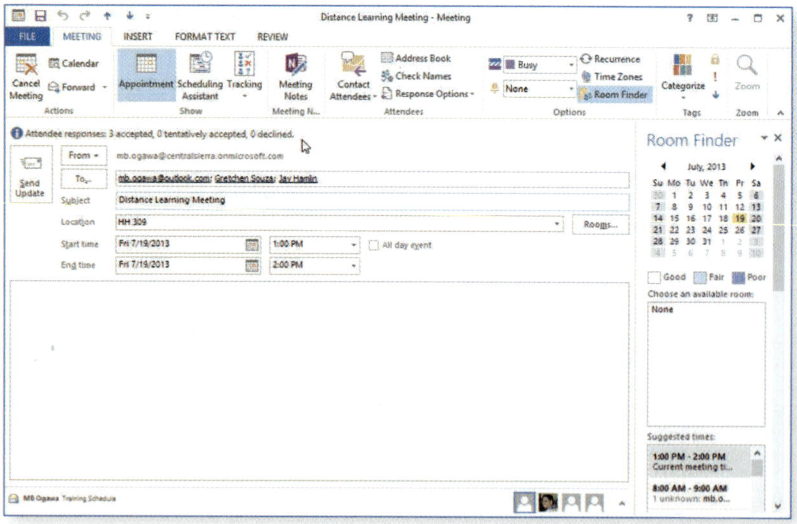

4-27 Open calendar item with meeting responses

ANOTHER WAY

When you open any of the meeting request responses you received in your Inbox, a summary of responses will be displayed above the body of the message.

MORE INFO

When viewing the tracking of a meeting request, you can copy the tracking status to the clipboard and paste it into Excel (Figure 4-28).

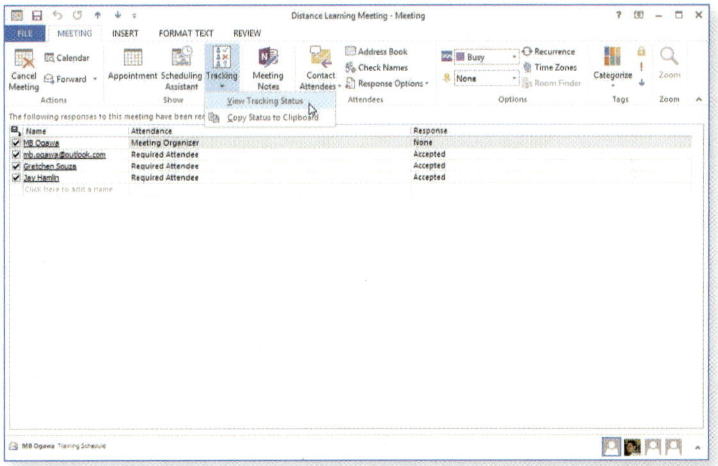

4-28 Tracking status

Change and Update a Meeting Request

It is not uncommon for a meeting to have to be rescheduled to a different day, time, or location. Also, you might need to invite additional attendees to a previously scheduled meeting. The meeting organizer can make changes to the meeting and add attendees. When this is done, a ***meeting update*** must be sent to attendees. Attendees will again be given the option of accepting or declining the changes to the meeting.

HOW TO: Change and Update a Meeting Request

1. On your calendar, open the meeting request you created.
2. Make changes to the meeting date and time or location if necessary (Figure 4-29).
3. The **Contact Attendees** button in the *Attendees* group on the *Meeting* tab provides you with the options to add or remove attendees, send a new email message, or send a reply message.
4. After making any necessary changes, click **Send Update**. Changes will be saved to the meeting on your calendar.

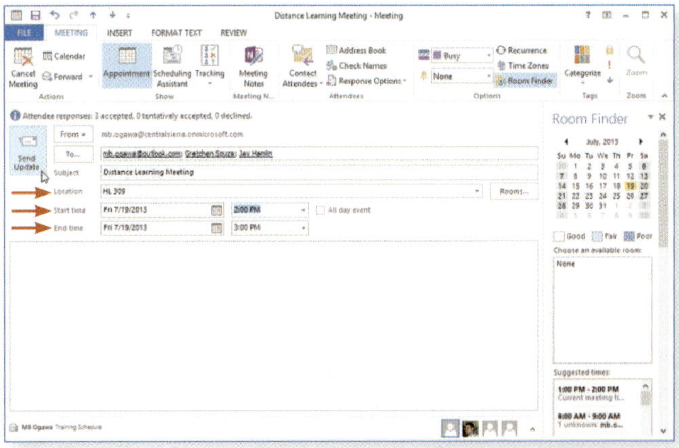

4-29 Updated meeting location and time

MORE INFO

If new attendees are added to or deleted from an existing meeting, you will be given the options of *Send updates to only added or deleted attendees* or *Send update to all attendees.*

Cancel a Scheduled Meeting

Only the meeting organizer can cancel a meeting. When a meeting is canceled, all the attendees will receive a meeting cancellation email. The meeting will be removed from your calendar, and the attendees will have the option of removing the meeting from their calendars.

MORE INFO

When you are the meeting organizer (creator), Outlook will not allow you to delete that meeting without sending a meeting cancellation email.

HOW TO: Cancel a Meeting

1. On your calendar, open the meeting request you created.
2. Click the **Cancel Meeting** button in the *Actions* group (Figure 4-30). The *Send Update* button becomes a *Send Cancellation* button, and there is a message in the *Info bar.*
3. Click the **Send Cancellation** button. The meeting request will be removed from your calendar, and all those invited to the meeting will receive an email notifying them of the meeting cancellation.

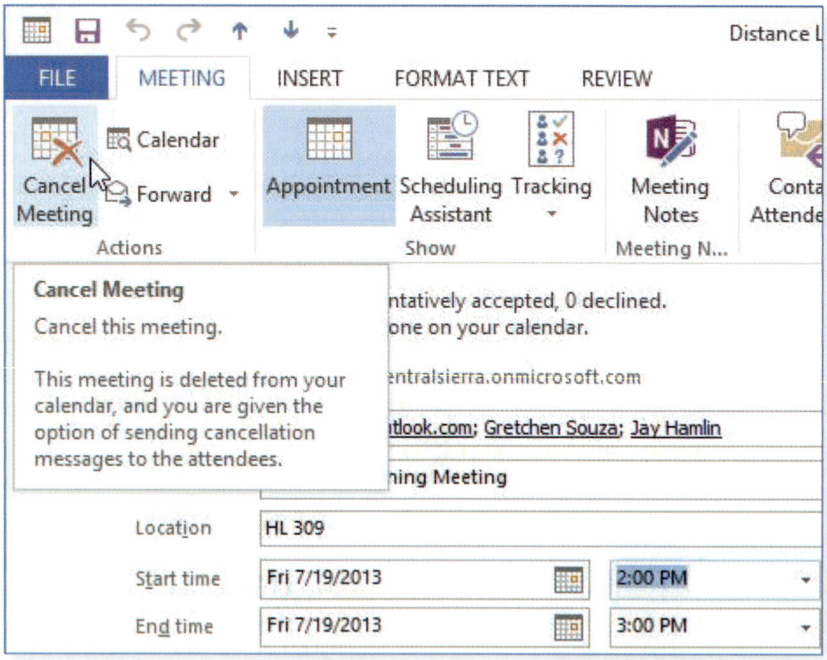

4-30 *Cancel Meeting* button

PAUSE & PRACTICE: OUTLOOK 4-2

For this Pause & Practice project, you follow up with the two calendar items you created in *Pause & Practice 4-1.* You had an emergency at home, so you decide to send a meeting request to your instructor to apologize for not being able to make the meeting and to reschedule. You also send a meeting request to have lunch with your friend Lynne to give her the gift you purchased.

1. Click the **Calendar** button in the *Navigation* pane.
2. Create and send a meeting request to your instructor regarding the ENG 100 paper.
   a. Click the **New Meeting** button [*Home* tab, *New* group].
   b. Enter the following information for the new meeting request:
   To: Instructor's email address
   Subject: Reschedule meeting for ENG 100 paper
   Location: Hamilton Hall 303A
   Start time: One day after your initial meeting, 9:00 AM
   End time: One day after your initial meeting, 10:00 AM
   Body:
   Hi [instructor name],
   My apologies; an emergency came up at home and I need to reschedule our meeting. Are you available on Tuesday at the same time? Please use the meeting request response so that it can automatically be added to our calendars.
   Thanks much,
   [your name]
   c. Click the **Send** button.
3. Create and send a meeting request to Lynne regarding her birthday.
   a. Click the **New Meeting** button [*Home* tab, *New* group].
   b. Enter the following information for the new meeting request:
   To: A partner's email address
   Subject: Birthday Lunch
   Location: ARC Student Center Cafe
   Start time: July 17 of the current year at noon
   End time: July 17 of the current year at 1:00 PM
   Body:
   Hi Lynne,
   Are you available for lunch on your birthday? My treat; let's eat at the ARC Student Center Cafe. Use the meeting request response so that it can automatically be added to our calendars.
   [your name]
   c. Click the **Send** button.
4. Open the meeting request to Lynne that you received from your partner.
5. Propose a new meeting time.
   a. Click the **Propose New Time** button [*Meeting* tab, *Respond* group] and select **Tentative and Propose New Time**.
   b. Select **2:00 PM** as the meeting start time and **3:00 PM** as the meeting end time.
   c. Click the **Propose Time** button.
   d. In the body, type:
   Hi [partner name],
   Sorry, I have lunch plans with my mother. How about coffee at the ARC Student Center Café at 2:00 PM?
   Lynne
   e. Click the **Send** button.

6. Locate the message from your partner and open it.
7. Forward the message proposed time message from your partner to your instructor.
   a. Click the **Forward** button [*Meeting Request* tab, *Respond* group].
   b. Enter the following information in the message:
      To: Instructor's email address
      Cc: Your email address
      Subject: Outlook Pause & Practice 4-2
      Body: A short message indicating that you submitted your Pause & Practice project
   c. Click the **Send** button (Figure 4-31).

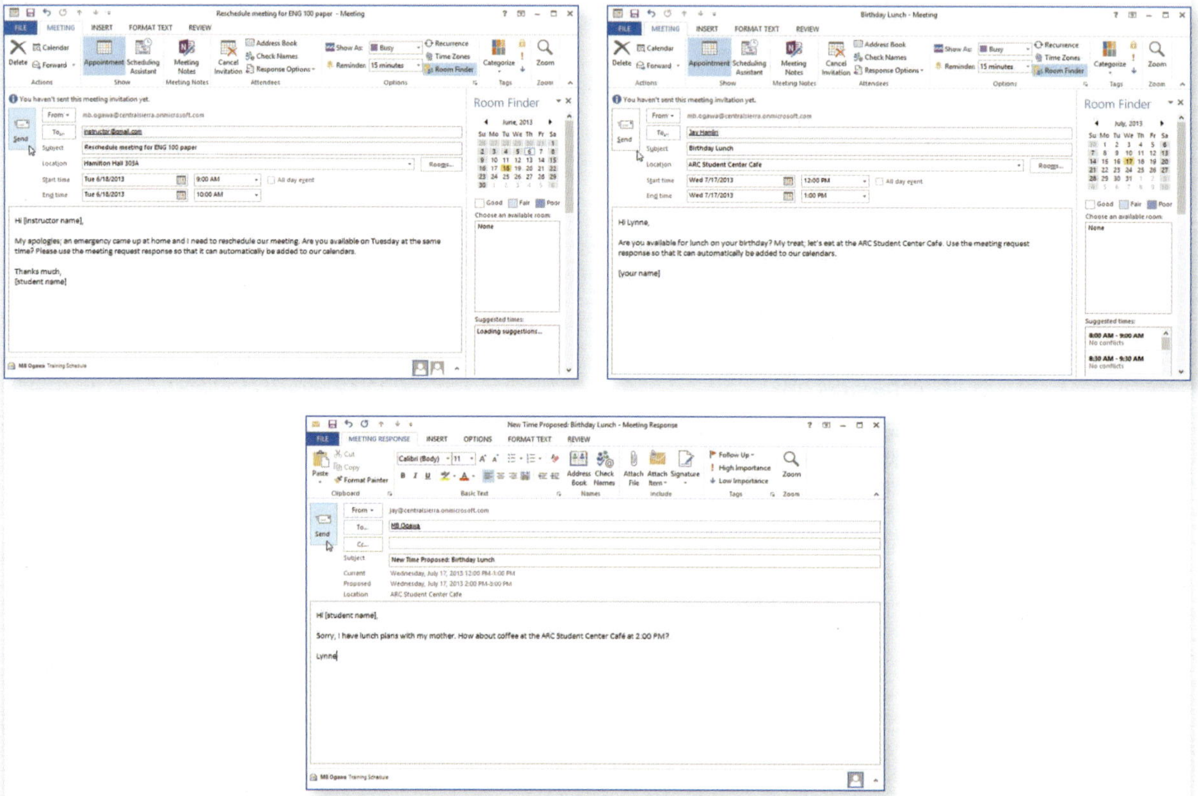

4-31 Completed Pause & Practice 4-2

Chapter Summary

4.1 Identify the different types of calendar items (p. O4-132).

- Unlike paper calendars, an Outlook calendar can be viewed by day, week, month, or other formats.
- You can receive reminders for appointments or events on your computer or mobile device.
- Categories can be used to group certain calendar items together.
- Calendar items can recur at regular intervals.
- Meeting requests can be used to invite others and track their responses.
- Calendars can be synchronized with phones and other mobile devices.
- There are three main types of calendar items: ***appointments, events,*** and ***meeting requests.***
- An ***appointment*** is a calendar item that has a duration of less than 24 hours.
- ***Events*** are those calendar items that last for 24 hours or more.
- A ***meeting request*** is used to create a calendar item and invite others to this meeting.

4.2 Distinguish between different calendar views (p. O4-134).

- Calendars can be displayed in ***Day, Week, Month,*** or ***Schedule*** views.
- ***Day view*** displays the calendar one day at a time with the calendar broken into half-hour segments.
- ***Week view*** displays the calendar as a ***Work Week*** or ***Week*** and breaks the calendar into half-hour segments. The work week is Monday through Friday, while the week is Sunday through Saturday.
- ***Month view*** displays an entire month of the calendar.
- ***Schedule view*** displays your calendar horizontally in timeline view in the *Folder* pane.

4.3 Create and edit calendar items (p. O4-138).

- Appointments and events can include a *Subject, Location, Start time, End time,* and additional information in the body.
- Appointments can be converted to events by clicking the **All day event** check box.
- You can add reminders to appointments and events to alert you prior to their start times.
- Calendar items can be moved or copied.
- Recurring appointments or events can be used for items that occur on a regular schedule such as a weekly meeting or a birthday.
- You can drag and drop an email message to the *Calendar* button to create a new calendar item from an email message.

4.4 Create and use meeting requests (p. O4-144).

- ***Meeting requests*** are used to invite others to a meeting (appointment or event).
- Recipients of meeting requests can respond in the following ways: ***Accept, Tentative, Decline,*** or ***Propose New Time.***
- You can reply to an email message with a meeting request.
- Selecting *Accept, Tentative,* and *Propose New Time* places the meeting time in your calendar.
- Outlook tracks your invitees' responses to your meeting request.
- You can update meeting requests and automatically send an updated message to all recipients.
- Canceling a meeting will delete it from your calendar.
- When you receive a meeting cancellation, the meeting will be marked as canceled in your calendar. You can manually delete the meeting from your calendar since it is not automatically removed with the cancellation.

Check for Understanding

In the ***Online Learning Center*** for this text (www.mhhe.com/office2013inpractice), there are a variety of resources that can be used to review the concepts covered in this chapter.

The following Online Learning Resources are available in the Online Learning Center:

- Multiple choice questions
- Short answer questions
- Matching exercises

USING MICROSOFT OUTLOOK 2013

Guided Project 4-1

For this project, you are an administrative assistant at Courtyard Medical Plaza. You manage calendars for several doctors and make appointments on the phone throughout the day. You use Outlook's calendar feature to keep the appointments organized. Today, you received two appointment requests from patients and record them in the calendar.
[Student Learning Outcomes 4.1, 4.2, 4.3]

Skills Covered in This Project

- Create a new appointment.
- Select start and end times.
- Edit the body of an appointment.
- Set a reminder.

1. Create a new appointment.
   a. Click the **Calendar** button in the *Navigation* pane.
   b. Select the next day on the calendar.
   c. Click the **New Appointment** button [*Home* tab, *New* group].
   d. Enter the following information for the new appointment:
      Subject: Jim Heely (Dr. Greg Lam)
      Location: Exam Room 1
      Start time: Tomorrow at 8:00 AM
      End time: Tomorrow at 9:00 AM
      Body: Sore throat, cough, fever, nausea
   e. Click the *Reminder* drop-down menu [*Appointment* tab, *Options* group].
   f. Select **5 minutes**.
   g. Click the **Save & Close** button.
2. Create a new appointment.
   a. Click the **New Appointment** button [*Home* tab, *New* group].
   b. Enter the following information for the new appointment:
      Subject: Janice Yoro (Dr. Shirley Louis)
      Location: Exam Room 3
      Start time: Next week Tuesday at 1:00 PM
      End time: Next week Tuesday at 2:00 PM
      Body: Annual check up
   c. Click the *Reminder* drop-down menu [*Appointment* tab, *Options* group].
   d. Select **5 minutes**.
   e. Click the **Save & Close** button.
3. Email the two calendar items to your instructor as Outlook items.
   a. Click the **Mail** button in the *Navigation* pane.
   b. Click the **New Email** button [*Home* tab, *New* group].
   c. Enter the following information in your message:
      To: instructor's email address
      Cc: your email address
      Subject: Outlook Guided Project 4-1

Body:
Hi [instructor name],
Attached are my calendar items for the Guided Project 4-1 exercise.
Sincerely,
[your name]

d. Click the **Attach Item** button [*Message* tab, *Include* group] and select **Outlook Item**.
e. Select the **Calendar** option and locate the two calendar items you created.
f. Hold the **Ctrl** key and select the two calendar items and click **OK**.
g. Click **Send** (Figure 4-32).

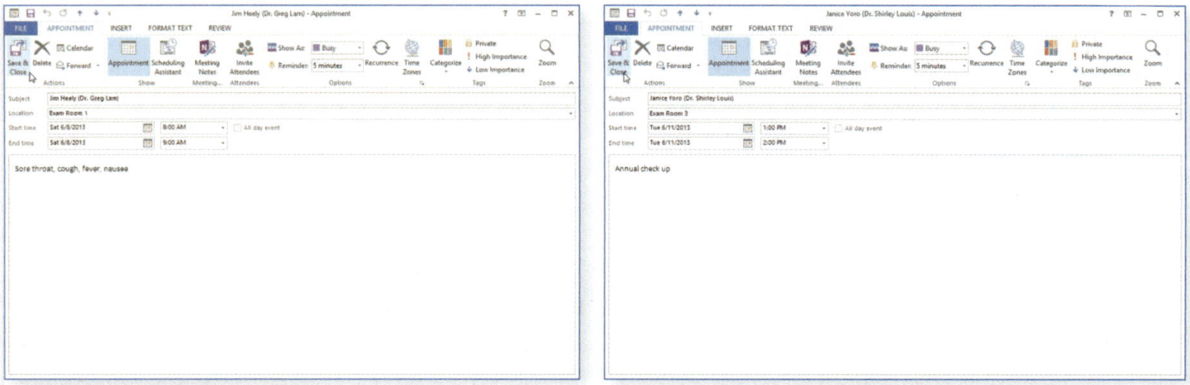

4-32 Completed Guided Project 4-1

Guided Project 4-2

For this project, you send meeting requests to two doctors to ensure they know when they are seeing the patients. Drs. Lam and Louis also indicated that they wanted to set up weekly meetings, so you create a recurring calendar item for the weekly meeting and send the request to both of them.
[Student Learning Outcomes 4.1, 4.2, 4.3, 4.4]

Skills Covered in This Project

- Create a new appointment.
- Select start and end times.
- Edit the body of an appointment.
- Set a reminder.
- Set recurrence.
- Send a meeting request.

1. Send a meeting request to Dr. Lam for the upcoming appointment.
   a. Open the appointment with the subject *Jim Heely (Dr. Greg Lam).*
   b. Click the **Invite Attendees** button [*Appointment* tab, *Attendees* group].
   c. Type a partner's email address in the *To* field.
   d. Click the **Send** button.

2. Send a meeting request to Dr. Louis for the upcoming appointment.
   a. Open the appointment with the subject *Janice Yoro (Dr. Shirley Louis).*
   b. Click the **Invite Attendees** button [*Appointment* tab, *Attendees* group].
   c. Type a partner's email address in the *To* field.
   d. Click the **Send** button.

3. Create a new appointment.
   a. Click the **Calendar** button in the *Navigation* pane.
   b. Click the **New Appointment** button [*Home* tab, *New* group].
   c. Enter the following information for the new appointment:
      Subject: Weekly Doctors' Meeting
      Location: Conference Room
      Start time: Mondays at 3:00 PM
      End time: Mondays at 4:00 AM
      Body: See agenda sent by administrative assistant.
   d. Click the *Reminder* drop-down menu [*Appointment* tab, *Options* group].
   e. Select **30 minutes**.
   f. Click the **Invite Attendees** button [*Appointment* tab, *Attendees* group].
   g. Type a partner's email address in the *To* field.
   h. Click the **Save & Close** button.
   i Figure 4-33 includes each of the appointments created.

4. Email the three meeting requests and to your instructor as Outlook items.
   a. Click the **Mail** button in the *Navigation* pane.
   b. Click the **New Email** button [*Home* tab, *New* group].
   c. Enter the following information in your message:
      To: Instructor's email address
      Cc: Your email address
      Subject: Outlook Guided Project 4-2
      Body:
      Hi [instructor name],
      Attached are my meeting requests for the Guided Project 4-2 exercise.
      Sincerely,
      [your name]
   d. Click the **Attach Item** button [*Message* tab, *Include* group] and select **Outlook Item**.
   e. Select the **Sent Items** option and locate the three meeting requests you sent.
   f. Hold the **Ctrl** key and select the three sent mail items and click **OK**.
   g. Click the **Send** button (Figure 4-33).

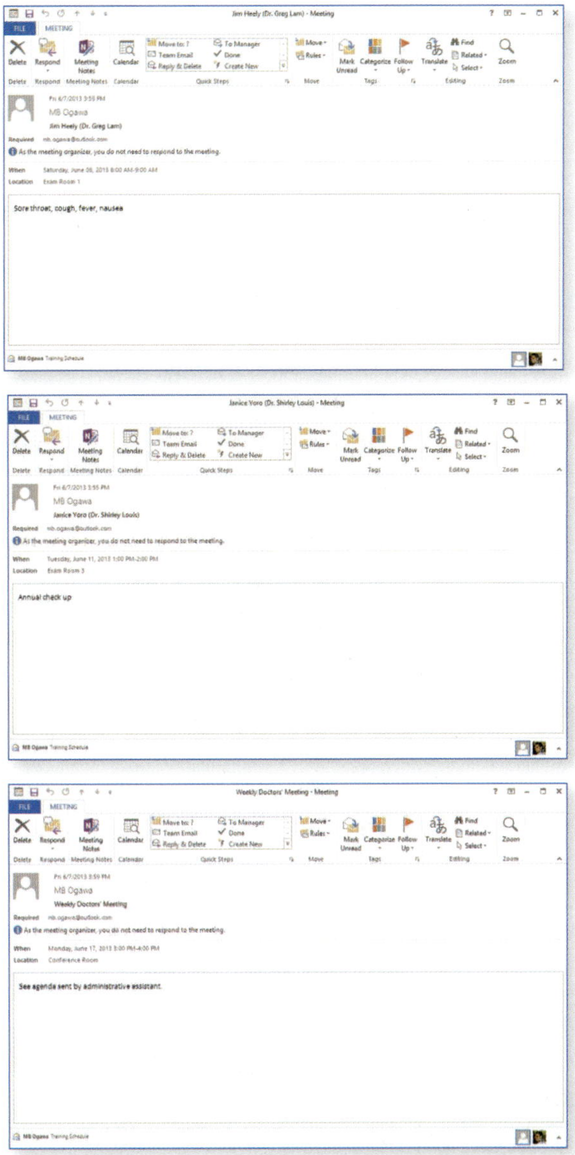

4-33 Completed Guided Project 4-2

Guided Project 4-3

For this project, you must cancel an appointment for Jim, who stated that he was feeling well enough not to come in. You must also reschedule Janice's annual appointment for the next day, as she just found out that she is in charge of snacks for her son's baseball game.
[Student Learning Outcomes 4.1, 4.2, 4.3, 4.4]

Skills Covered in This Project

- Cancel a meeting request.
- Respond to a meeting request.
- Update a meeting request.
- Accept a meeting request.
- Track meeting request responses.

---

1. Cancel Jim Heely's appointment and send the cancellation to Dr. Lam
   a. Open the appointment with the subject *Jim Heely (Dr. Greg Lam).*
   b. Click the **Cancel Meeting** button [*Meeting* tab, *Actions* group].
   c. Click the **Send Cancellation** button.
2. Update Janice Yoro's appointment date.
   a. Open the appointment with the subject *Janice Yoro (Dr. Shirley Louis).*
   b. In the start and end time fields, change the day to Wednesday (keep the same time).
   c. Click the **Send Update** button.
3. Accept the *Weekly Doctors'* meeting request you received.
   a. Open the email with the subject *Weekly Doctors' Meeting.*
   b. Click the **Accept** button [*Meeting* tab, *Respond* group] and select **Send the Response Now**.
4. Click your initial message to ensure you received a response from your partner.
5. Email the three meeting requests to your instructor as Outlook items.
   a. Click the **Mail** button in the *Navigation* pane.
   b. Click the **New Email** button [*Home* tab, *New* group].
   c. Enter the following information in your message:
      To: instructor's email address
      Cc: your email address
      Subject: Outlook Guided Project 4-3
      Body:
      Hi [instructor name],
      Attached are my meeting requests for the Guided Project 4-3 exercise.
      Sincerely,
      [your name]
   d. Click the **Attach Item** button [*Message* tab, *Include* group] and select **Outlook Item**.
   e. Select the **Sent Items** option and locate the meeting cancellation, updated time, and acceptance you sent.
   f. Hold the **Ctrl** key and select the three sent mail items and click **OK**.
   g. Click the **Send** button (Figure 4-34).

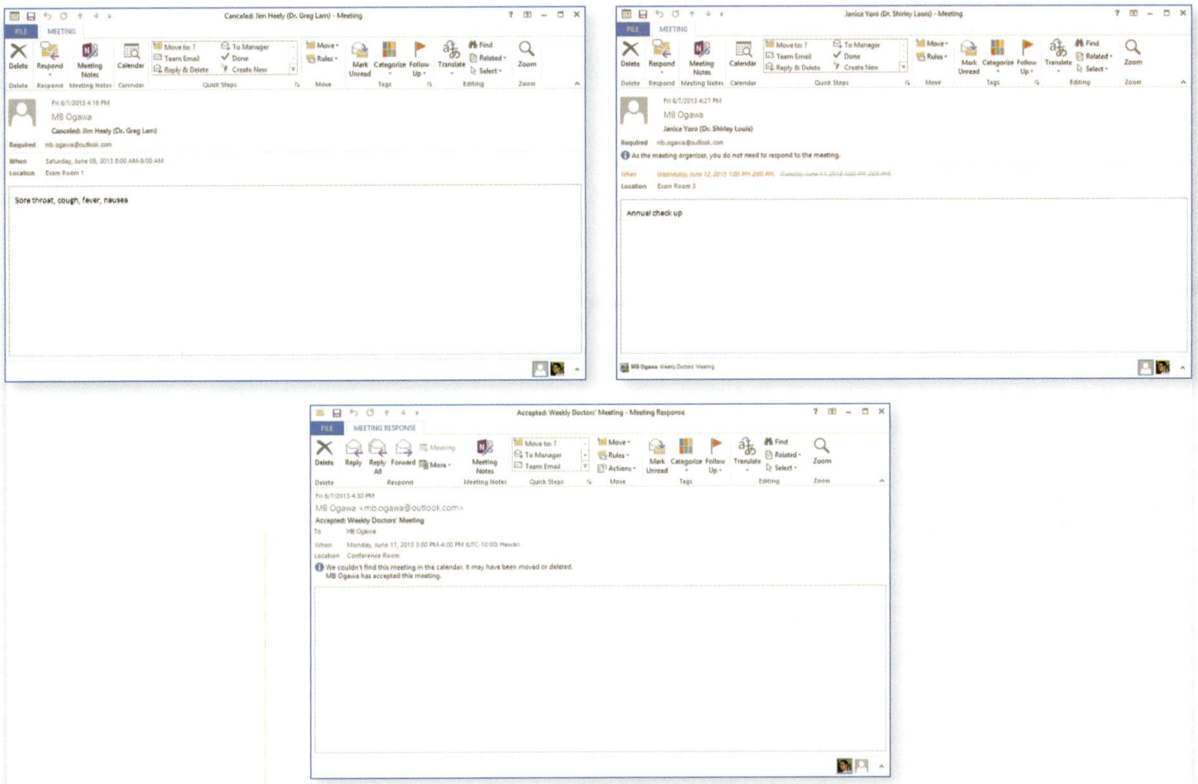

4-34 Completed Guided Project 4-3

Independent Project 4-4

For this project, you work as an insurance agent for Central Sierra Insurance (CSI). As an agent, you make and receive many calls to and from clients to set up meetings in person. You also collaborate with a team of insurance agents. You use Outlook's calendar to help you better organize your schedule. [Student Learning Outcomes 4.1, 4.2, 4.3]

Skills Covered in This Project

- Create a new appointment.
- Create a new event.
- Select start and end times.
- Edit the body of an appointment.
- Set a reminder.

1. Create the following appointments:

Subject	Location	Start time	End time	Body	Reminder
Strategic Planning	Conference Room A	Next week Friday, All day event	Next week Friday, All day event	Prepare slides	1 Day

(Continued)

Subject	Location	Start time	End time	Body	Reminder
Dorilyn Sharuma (New Client)	3A	Next week Monday, 9:00 AM	Next week Monday, 11:00 AM	New customer packet.	15 Minutes
Matthew Schmidt (client for 5 years)	3A	Next week Tuesday, 1:00 PM	Next week Tuesday, 1:30 PM	Client just got married. New insurance options.	30 Minutes
Janine Shephard (client for 3 years)	3A	Next week Monday, 2:00 PM	Next week Monday, 3:00 PM	Review current policy to see where she can lower payments.	30 Minute
Clint Howard (Manager)	Mario's Italian Restaurant	Next week Thursday, 12:00 PM	Next week Thursday, 1:30 PM	Lunch meeting about current clients.	2 Hours

2. Email the five calendar items you created to your instructor as email attachments.
   a. Include your email address in the *Cc* field.
   b. Add a short message indicating that the five Outlook calendar items are attached in the message.
   c. Change the subject of your message to ***Outlook Independent Project 4-4*** (Figure 4-35).

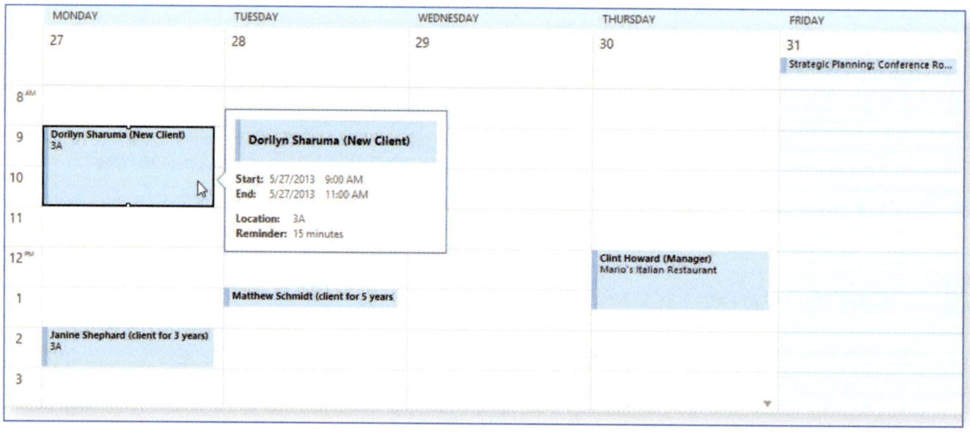

4-35 Completed Independent Project 4-4

Independent Project 4-5

For this project, you categorize all of the calendar items for CSI. You also send out meeting requests to others to ensure everyone is on the same page. You request that your colleague take one of your appointments, as you forgot that you had a doctor's appointment when you decided to meet with Janine because you did not centralize all of your personal and work appointments on one calendar. [Student Learning Outcomes 4.1, 4.2, 4.4]

Skills Covered in This Project

- Create a category.
- Apply categories to calendar items.
- Send meeting requests.
- Modify messages for meeting requests.

1. Create a new category called Central Sierra Insurance.
2. Apply the category to the five appointments you created in Independent Project 4-4.
3. Send the strategic planning event to a partner as a meeting request.
4. Send the *Clint Howard (Manager)* appointment as a meeting request to a partner.
5. Send the *Janine Shephard* meeting to a partner and request that he or she take the meeting for you. You forgot that you had a doctor's appointment at that time. Be sure to include a message indicating why you would like your colleague to meet with your client.
6. Email your instructor with your five calendar items and three meeting requests as attachments.
   a. Include your email address in the *Cc* field.
   b. Add a short message indicating that the five Outlook calendar items are attached in the message.
   c. Change the subject of your message to ***Outlook Independent Project 4-5*** (Figure 4-36).

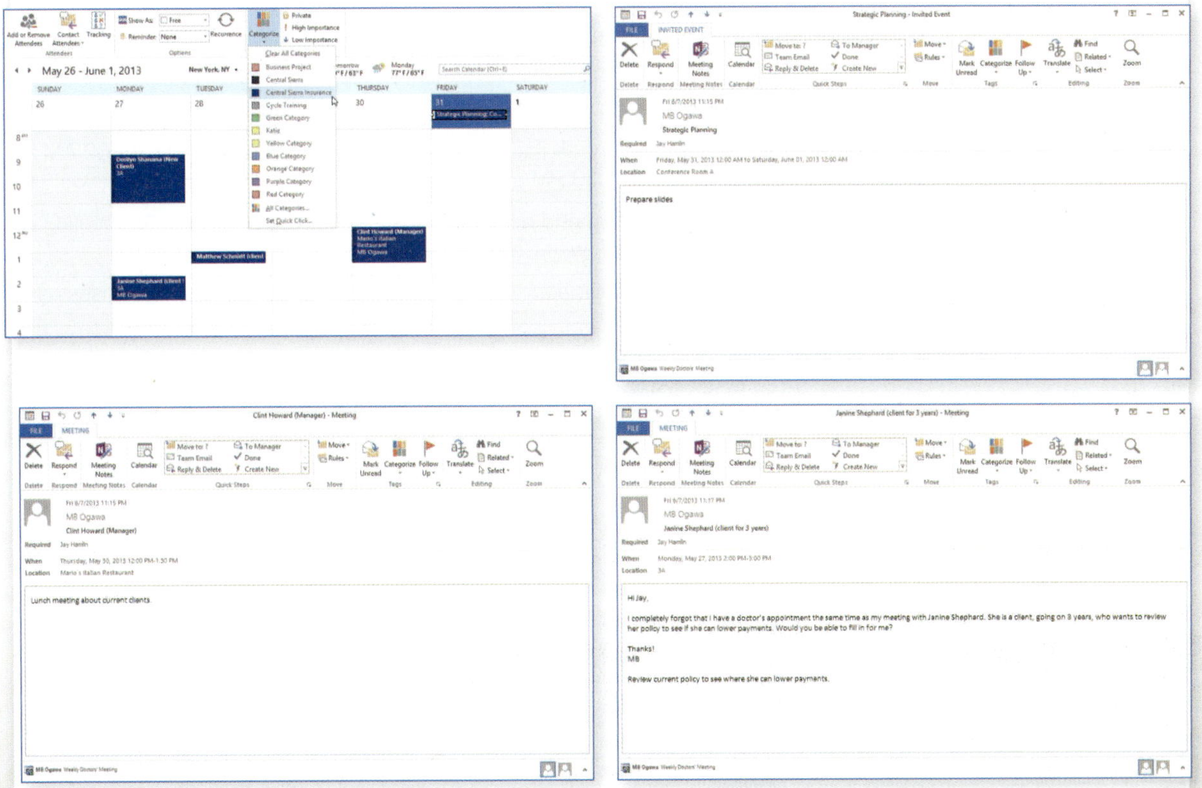

4-36 Completed Independent Project 4-5

Independent Project 4-6

For this project, you add your weekly sales meeting to your calendar. You also respond to the meeting requests you received.
[Student Learning Outcomes 4.1, 4.2, 4.3, 4.4]

Skills Covered in This Project

- Create a new appointment.
- Select start and end times.
- Edit the body of an appointment.
- Set a reminder.
- Set recurrence.
- Apply categories to calendar items.
- Respond to a meeting request.
- Update a meeting request.
- Accept a meeting request.
- Track meeting request responses.

1. Create a new appointment with the following information:
   Subject: Weekly Sales Meeting
   Location: Conference Room B
   Start time: Next week Thursday, 4:00 PM
   End time: Next week Thursday, 5:00 PM
   Reminder: 15 minutes
   Recurrence: Weekly with no end date
   Category: Central Sierra Insurance
2. Open the strategic planning event meeting request from your partner and accept it.
3. Open the *Clint Howard* meeting request and tentatively accept and propose a new time 11:30 AM to 1:00 PM. Indicate that you (Clint) have a 1:30 PM appointment.
4. Open the *Janine Shephard* meeting request and decline it. Indicate that you have another meeting at that time and that the sender should check with Chelsea.
5. Email your instructor with the *Weekly Sales Meeting* calendar item and three meeting responses as attachments.
   a. Include your email address in the *Cc* field.
   b. Add a short message indicating that the five Outlook calendar items are attached in the message.
   c. Change the subject of your message to ***Outlook Independent Project 4-6*** (Figure 4-37).

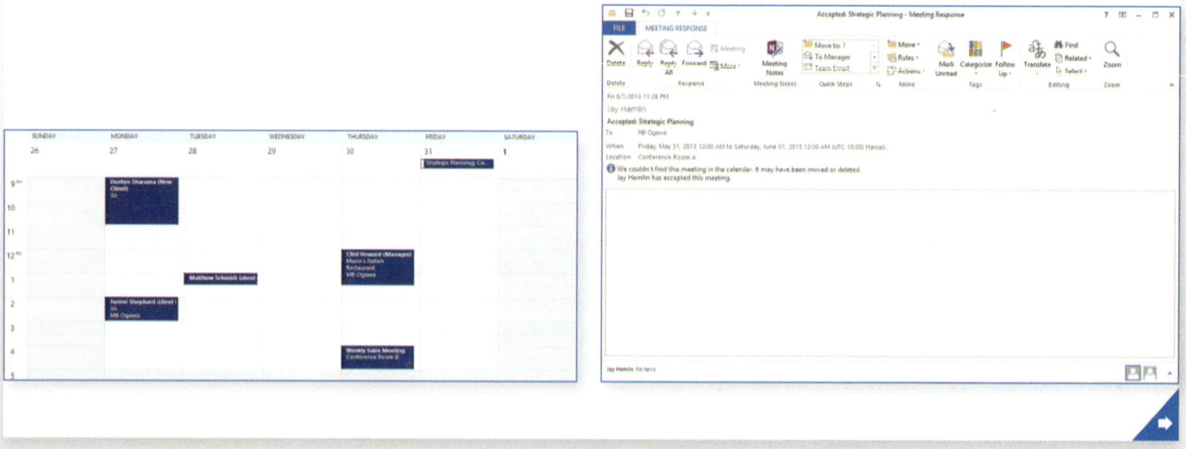

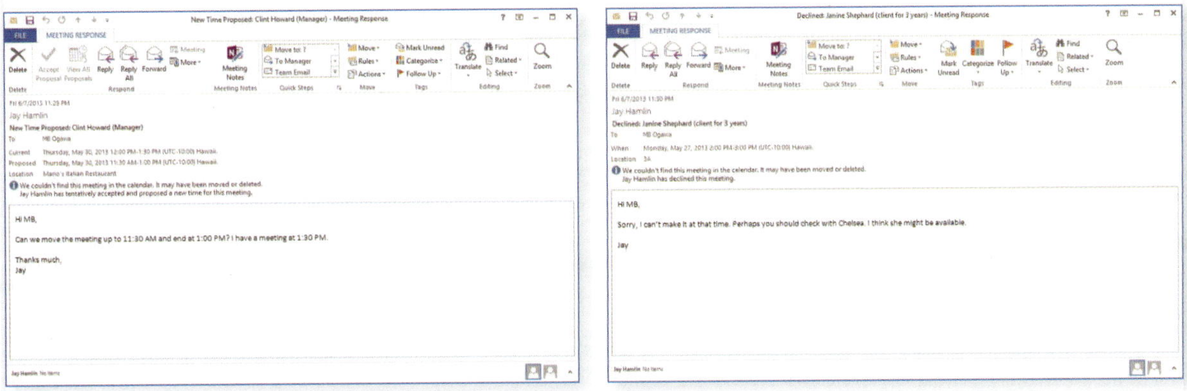

4-37 Completed Independent Project 4-6

Challenge Project 4-7

Create a calendar for yourself based on your current school, work, and personal schedules for the semester. Be sure to include items such as classes, work, appointments, and events such as birthdays or anniversaries.
[Student Learning Outcomes 4.1, 4.2, 4.3]

- Include your class schedule for the semester.
- Include your work schedule if applicable.
- Include events such as birthdays or anniversaries.
- Use *Recurrence* when applicable.
- Email the calendar to your instructor as an email attachment. Specify the dates to include within the current semester.
- Change the subject of your message to ***Outlook Challenge Project 4-7.***

Challenge Project 4-8

Modify the calendar you created in Challenge 4-7 by adding categories and sending out meeting requests. Create at least three categories (school, work, personal). You can add additional categories, such as clubs if it fits your schedule. Send out at least three meeting requests to a partner in class.
[Student Learning Outcomes 4.1, 4.2, 4.3, 4.4]

- Create at least three categories for your calendar and apply them to each item.
- Set up at least three meetings with a partner in class and send the meeting requests.
- Email the calendar to your instructor as an email attachment. Specify the dates to include within the current semester.

- Attach each of the meeting requests to your email message (attach each meeting request message as an Outlook item).
- Change the subject of your message to ***Outlook Challenge Project 4-8.***

Challenge Project 4-9

Modify the calendar you created in Challenge Project 4-8 by responding to meeting requests. For the three meeting requests you received, accept one, decline one, and propose a new time for the third one. [Student Learning Outcomes 4.1, 4.2, 4.4]

- Respond to the three meeting requests you received in Challenge Project 4-8.
- Accept one request, decline a request, and propose a new time for the final request.
- Attach each of the meeting request responses to your email message (attach each meeting request message as an Outlook item).
- Change the subject of your message to ***Outlook Challenge Project 4-9.***

CHAPTER 7

OUTLOOK

Multiple Email Accounts, Advanced Email Options, RSS Feeds, and Search

CHAPTER OVERVIEW

As you begin to use and rely on Outlook to manage your emails and contacts and organize your calendar and tasks, you want to have the ability to customize Outlook to best meet your individual and professional needs. Outlook provides you with the opportunity to have ***multiple email accounts*** set up and manage these accounts through the use of rules and folders. Also, there are many "under the hood" default settings for email that can be used to tailor how Outlook works for you.

In addition to managing multiple email accounts, Outlook can manage your ***RSS feeds.*** RSS is an acronym for "really simple syndication." Essentially, RSS feeds are a way of keeping track of the headlines on your favorite web sites, and Outlook can manage your RSS feeds in a similar way to how it manages your email accounts.

STUDENT LEARNING OUTCOMES (SLOs)

After completing this chapter, you will be able to:

- **SLO 7.1** Connect and use multiple email accounts in Outlook (p. O7-249).
- **SLO 7.2** Manage multiple email accounts (p. O7-251).
- **SLO 7.3** Customize advanced email options (p. O7-256).
- **SLO 7.4** Integrate RSS feeds into Outlook (p. O7-265).
- **SLO 7.5** Utilize search features to find email and other Outlook items (p. O7-270).

CASE STUDY

For the Pause & Practice projects, you become more proficient with using Outlook with multiple accounts, RSS feeds, and searching for email and other Outlook items that you have difficulty finding. You add accounts to Outlook to ensure you can work with both personal and school- or work-related email messages within the Outlook environment. You also add RSS feeds to enable you to receive news that is important to you and to share it with others. Lastly, you learn to search for information quickly and effectively.

Pause & Practice 7-1: You add an email account to Outlook. If you do not have a secondary email account, you can sign up for a free account at gmail.com or outlook.com. After adding the account, you will change the default account and send a message by selecting the account that is not set as default.

Pause & Practice 7-2: You subscribe to CNN RSS news feeds (available at http://www.cnn.com/services/rss/). You subscribe to an RSS feed, rename the feed folder, and share the feed with your instructor.

Pause & Practice 7-3: You search for the previous Pause & Practice email messages that you sent to your instructor because you did not receive a grade for the *Pause & Practice 7-2* assignment. After you find the message, you forward it to your instructor.

SLO 7.1

Setting Up Additional Email Accounts

If you're like most people, you have multiple email accounts: one through your work (an Exchange account) and one through your ISP (Internet service provider) at your home. You might also have a free email account such as Gmail, Outlook.com, or Yahoo Mail.

Outlook gives you the ability to set up multiple email accounts, including multiple Exchange accounts, and to send and receive emails through these accounts. Using Outlook to handle multiple email accounts saves you time because it consolidates your email accounts in one place so that you don't need to go to multiple web sites to check your different email accounts.

MORE INFO

Not all free email accounts can be set up through Outlook. Some types of accounts work seamlessly with Outlook, such as Gmail or Outlook.com. Yahoo Mail accounts will only work with Outlook if you have the Yahoo Plus account, which charges an annual fee.

Auto Account Setup

You don't have to know much about your email account to set it up in Outlook. Outlook 2013 has simplified the process of adding an email account. It determines the type of account (Exchange, Exchange ActiveSync, POP, IMAP, or HTTP) and validates the account settings.

The two pieces of information you will need are your ***user name*** or ***email account*** and your ***password***. Outlook will automatically detect your email account settings and set up your account in Outlook.

MORE INFO

The different types of email accounts were covered in Chapter 1.

MORE INFO

For some online email accounts, you must enable POP on the online account for your email to be delivered to Outlook. This is typically done by logging into your account on the Internet and editing the settings to enable POP. This will vary from account to account.

HOW TO: Add an Email Account to Outlook

1. Click the **File** tab. The *Backstage* opens.
2. Click **Add Account** (Figure 7-1). The *Add Account* dialog box opens (Figure 7-2).
3. Click the **Email Account** radio button.
4. Fill in the following fields: **Your Name, Email Address, Password,** and **Retype Password.** The password is associated with the email account.

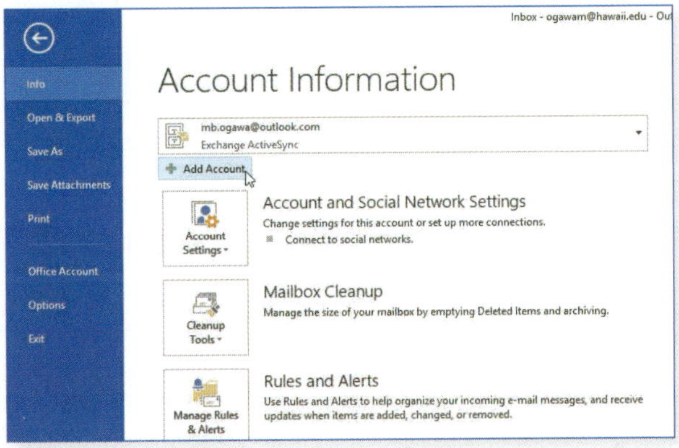

7-1 ***Add Account*** **button**

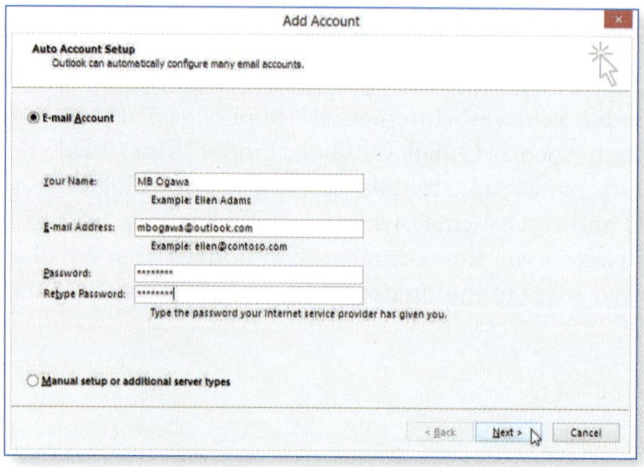

7-2 *Add Account* dialog box

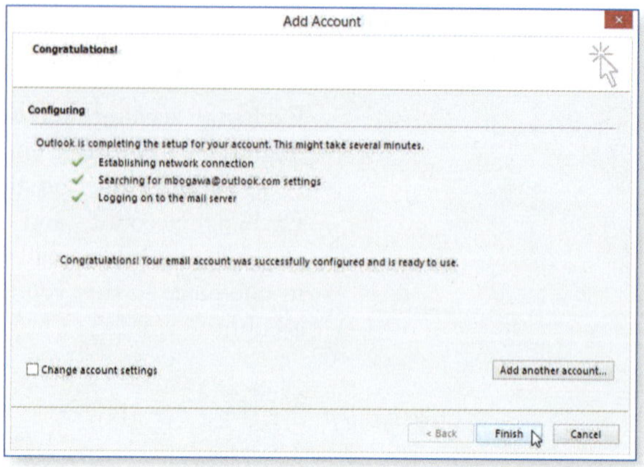

7-3 Auto account setup completion

5. Click **Next.** Outlook will automatically configure and test the account settings. If the account was set up properly, you will see three green check marks and a "*Congratulations!*" message (Figure 7-3).
6. Click **Finish.** The *Account Settings* dialog box appears. Notice your new email account is now included in your list of email accounts.
7. Click **Close.**

MORE INFO

It is not a good idea to set up all your personal email accounts on your work computer because most employers do not want you to be distracted by personal emails while at work.

7-4 Account folders

If you are using Outlook in an Exchange, Exchange ActiveSync, or IMAP environment you will have folders for each of your accounts. Your email account through Exchange, Exchange ActiveSync, and IMAP will be handled in your username@address.com folders (Figure 7.4), and your personal email accounts will, by default, be handled in your *Personal Folders*.

MORE INFO

You will also have another set of folders called *Archive Folders*, which will be covered in Chapter 10.

Troubleshoot Email Problems

There might be times when Outlook is not able to automatically detect the account settings for an email account that you are trying to set up. Outlook will try a couple of different options to configure your account.

If this process does not work, you can manually configure your account settings. You might have to go to the email account web site to find specific setup information to configure your account.

HOW TO: Troubleshoot Email Connection Problems

1. If you receive a *Problem Connecting to Server* message, click **Next** to have Outlook try to configure your account using an unencrypted connection (Figure 7-5).
2. If this next step is unsuccessful, check the **Change account settings** box and click **Next.** A new dialog box opens allowing you to choose the type of account.
3. Select the type of email account to be set up, and click **Next.**
4. Confirm that your account information is correct, and click the **Test Account Settings** button (Figure 7-6). A *Test Account Settings* dialog box opens.
5. When this process is complete, click **Close** to close the *Test Account Settings* dialog box.
6. Click **Next** on the open dialog box. A *Congratulations* dialog box opens.
7. Click **Finish** to close the dialog box.

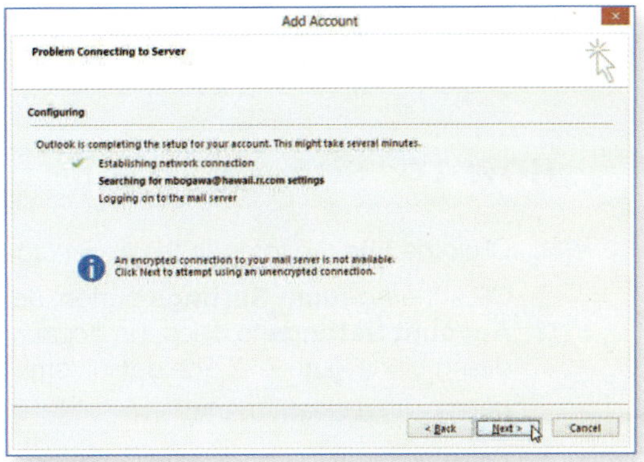

7-5 Unencrypted connection

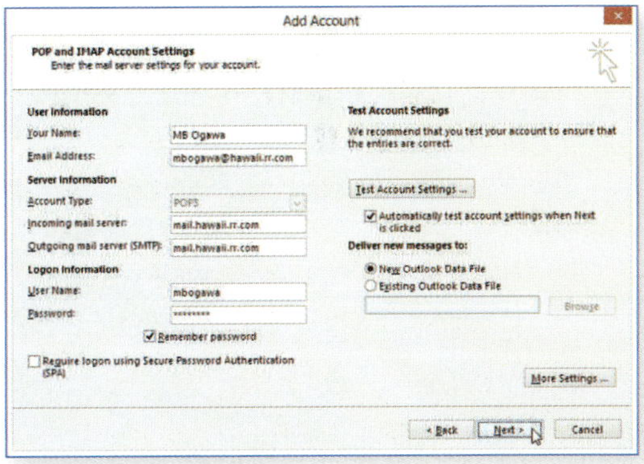

7-6 Account settings

There might also be times when an existing email account in Outlook will stop sending or receiving for no apparent reason. If this email account was previously working and none of the account settings have been changed, you might try using the ***Repair*** feature provided in Outlook. This automated feature in the *Account Settings* dialog box will walk you through a couple of steps and try to automatically repair an existing email account.

> **MORE INFO**
>
> A setting change on the email server end might cause an existing email account in Outlook to stop functioning properly. The *Repair* feature might be able to automatically adjust the account settings to restore this account.

SLO 7.2

Managing Multiple Email Accounts

One of the issues with having multiple email accounts in Outlook is keeping them separate in your mail folders. Managing multiple email accounts can become confusing if emails are all being delivered to the same Inbox. Another issue is choosing the account through which you create and send new emails and respond to or forward emails. Having multiple email accounts somewhat complicates this process, but being deliberate about setting your default email account and having emails delivered to different folders can help you to effectively manage multiple email accounts.

Set the Default Account

The default email account is the account that will, by default, be used to send any new email that is created and sent. This should be the account used most often in Outlook. This will be the first email account you set up in Outlook unless you specify a different account. It is easy to change your default email account.

HOW TO: Set an Account as Default

1. Click the **File** tab to open the *Backstage.*
2. Click the **Account Settings** button, and choose **Account Settings** to open the *Account Settings* dialog box (Figure 7-7). The default email account is noted with a check mark.
3. Click the email account you want as your default account.
4. Click the **Set as Default** button. This account will be moved to the top of the list and will be the default email account.

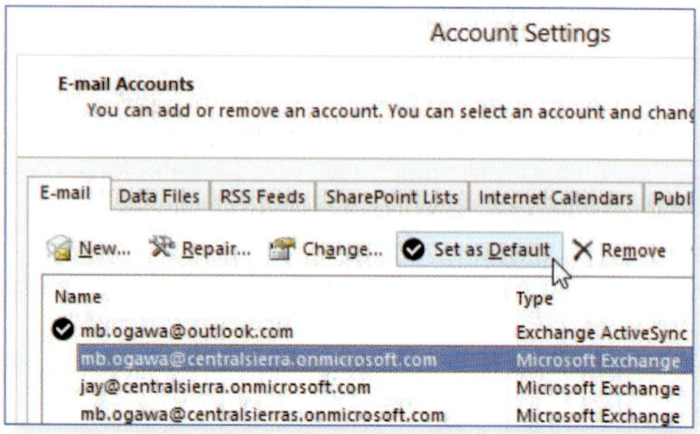

7-7 Set default account

> **MORE INFO**
>
> When you create a new email, the account being used will be displayed to the right of the *From* button. The email will be sent through the default account unless you choose a different account.

> **MORE INFO**
>
> It is probably best to reply to an email using the same account through which the email was received.

Send Email through a Different Account

As mentioned earlier, when you create and send a new email, it will be sent through your default email account. But if you are replying to or forwarding an email, it will be sent through the account through which it was delivered. For example, if you received an email through your Gmail account (assuming this is not your default account), and you reply to or forward this email, it will be sent through your Gmail account unless you choose a different account through which to send this email.

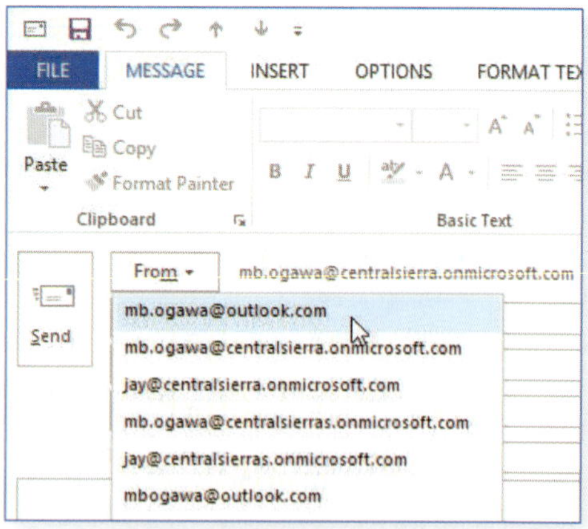

7-8 Set an account to send email

When you have multiple email accounts set up in Outlook, you can decide through which account the email will be sent. This can be done on new emails, replies, or forwards. A ***From*** button will appear to the right of the *Send* button on all your emails when you have multiple accounts set up in Outlook. You can select the account from which to send an email using the *From* button (Figure 7-8).

HOW TO: Send Email through Another Account

1. Open an existing email.
2. Click the *Reply* or *Forward* button. To the right of the *From* button, the account that will be used to send the email is displayed.
3. Click the **From** button and choose a different account. Notice the account displayed to the right.
4. Click **Send** to send the email through the chosen account.

Change the Email Delivery Folder

On personal email accounts that use POP, you can change the folder to which your email is delivered. You do not have this option with an Exchange account. When managing multiple email accounts, it is probably best to have different accounts delivered to different folders. If your default account is being delivered to your Inbox, you might want to create a *Gmail* folder and have your Gmail always delivered to this folder. You can change the default delivery folder for an email account in the *Account Settings* dialog box.

HOW TO: Change the Email Delivery Folder

1. Click the **File** tab to open the *Backstage* view.
2. Click the **Account Settings** button and choose **Account Settings** to open *Account Settings* dialog box.
3. Click one of your accounts that is not the default account. Notice the *delivery folder* to the right of the *Change Folder* button.
4. Click the **Change Folder** button (Figure 7-9). The *New Email Delivery Location* dialog box opens.
5. Select the new delivery folder (Figure 7-10). A new folder can also be created by clicking the **New Folder** button. Click **OK** to close the *New Email Delivery Location* dialog box.
6. Click **Close** to close the *Account Settings* dialog box. All emails from the chosen account will now be delivered to the folder you chose.

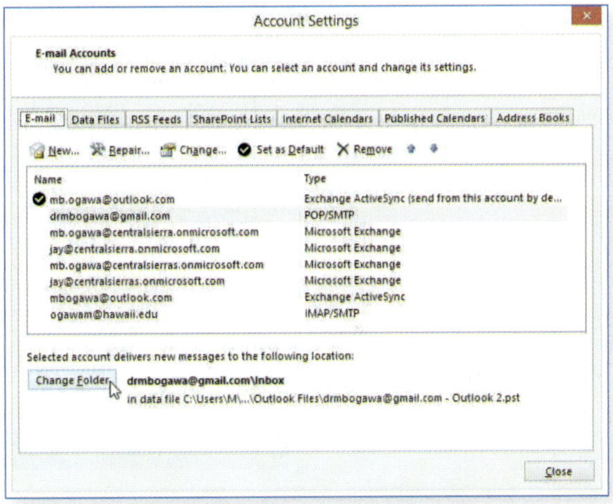

7-9 ***Change Folder* button**

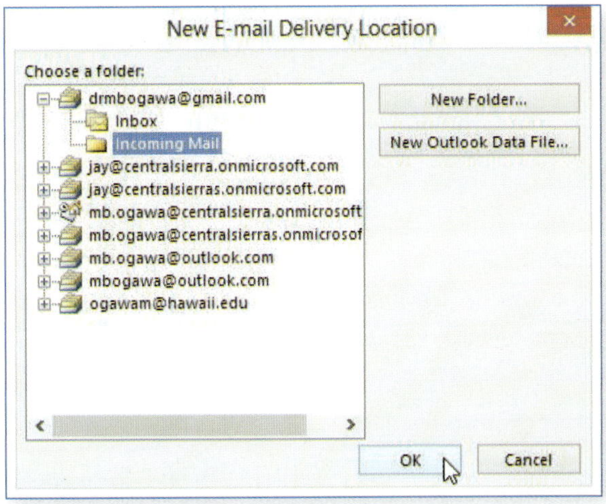

7-10 Select incoming mail folder

MORE INFO

Changing the delivery folder is not available for IMAP email accounts. Rules can be used to deliver email received through these accounts to a different folder.

Create Folders and Use Rules

Rules can also be used to deliver emails from specific accounts to a different folder. The ***condition*** would be looking for emails received through a specified account (for example, a Gmail or Outlook.com account), and the ***action*** would be to move it to a specified folder. This rule would do the same thing as changing the default delivery folder, but it could easily be turned off or on.

> **MORE INFO**
>
> Rules were covered in Chapter 6.

Outlook Web Access

One of the advantages of using email is the ability to access it from any computer that has Internet access. If you have an email account through your Internet service provider (ISP) or a free email account such as Gmail or Yahoo Mail, you can log on to the Internet and access your email account through their web sites. You need to know your user name and password to have access to your online email account.

If you are using Outlook in an Exchange environment, most companies have their Exchange server connected to ***Outlook Web Access*** (***OWA***). OWA allows you to access your Exchange account through the Internet. You need to know the URL (web location) of your company's OWA and log on with your username and password. OWA provides you not only with email access, but also access to your calendar, contacts, tasks, and notes (Figure 7-11).

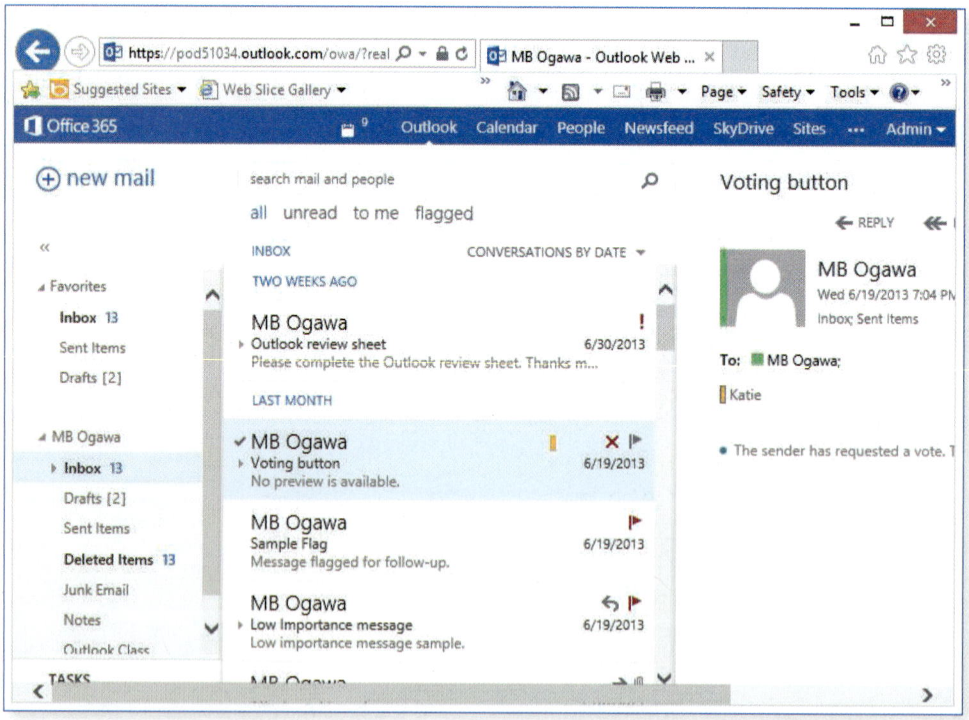

7-11 Outlook Web Access

OWA will be displayed differently depending on the Internet browser you're using (for example, Microsoft Internet Explorer, Google Chrome, or Mozilla Firefox). OWA will look different than Outlook on your computer, but you will still have most of the functionality of your Outlook account.

Outlook for Windows RT

Windows RT, an operating system for Windows tablets will be receiving an update, Windows 8.1, which will include Outlook. Therefore, you will be able to use all of the information you learned in this text while using Microsoft Windows RT based tablet computers.

PAUSE & PRACTICE: OUTLOOK 7-1

For this Pause & Practice project, you add an email account to Outlook. If you do not have a secondary email account, you can sign up for a free account at gmail.com or outlook.com. After adding the account, you will change the default account and send a message by selecting the account that is not set as default.

1. Add a new account to Outlook.
   a. Click the **File** tab. The *Backstage* opens.
   b. Click **Add Account.** The *Add New Account* dialog box opens.
   c. Click the **Email Account** radio button.
   d. Fill in the following fields: **Your Name, Email Address, Password,** and **Retype Password.**
   e. Click **Next.** Outlook will automatically configure and test the account settings. If the account was set up properly, you will see three green check marks and a "*Congratulations!*" message.
   f. Click **Finish.** The *Account Settings* dialog box appears. Notice your new email account is now included in your list of email accounts.
   g. Click **Close.**
2. Change the default email account.
   a. Click the **File** tab to open the *Backstage.*
   b. Click the **Account Settings** button, and choose **Account Settings** to open the *Account Settings* dialog box.
   c. Select the email account you added to Outlook in the first step.
   d. Click the **Set as Default** button.
   e. Click the **Close** button.
3. Send a message by selecting an account (Figure 7-12).
   a. Click the **Mail** button in the *Navigation* pane.
   b. Click the **New Email** button.
   c. Click the **From** button and select the email address that is not the default.
   d. Enter the following information in the new message:
      To: [instructor's email address]
      Cc: [your email address]
      Subject: Outlook Pause & Practice 7-1
      Message: Hi [instructor's name], I added a new address to my Outlook installation. For consistency, I want to be sure you are receiving messages from my school account.
      Thanks,
      [your name]
   e. Click the **Send** button.

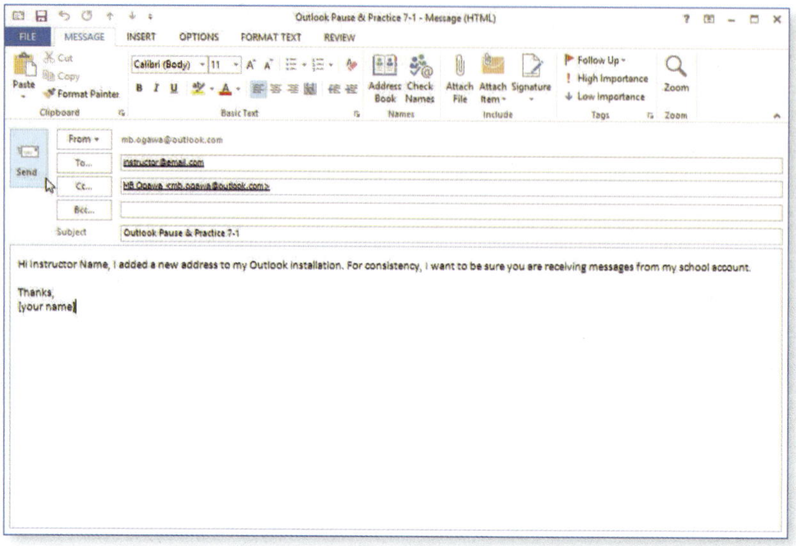

7-12 Completed Pause & Practice 7-1

SLO 7.3

Customizing Email Options

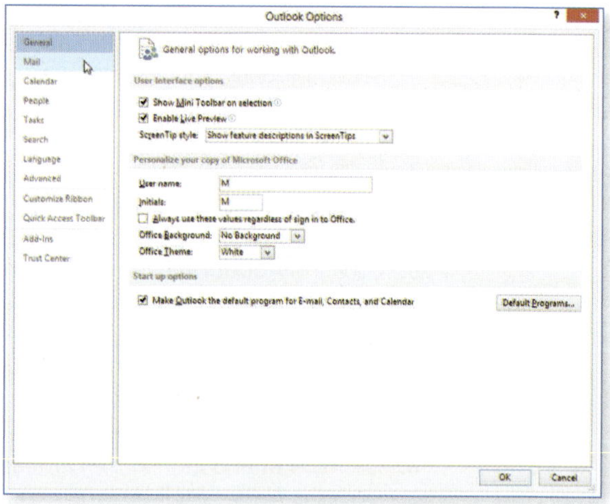

7-13 *Outlook Options* dialog box

After you have been using Outlook for a while and have become familiar with the main tasks, you might want to change some of the default settings to customize Outlook. Within Outlook there are many customization options available, and you are able to modify many of the default settings throughout Outlook. The ***Outlook Options*** dialog box within Outlook (Figure 7-13) provides you with one location to change most of the default settings for email, calendar, contacts, tasks, notes, and other global Outlook settings. The *Outlook Options* dialog box can be accessed by clicking the *File* tab to open the *Backstage* and choosing **Options.**

MORE INFO

The email customization options covered in this section are global or default settings. These differ from message options, which allow you to customize individual email messages. Message options were covered in Chapter 2.

Email Options

The ***Mail Options*** dialog box can be accessed by clicking the *Mail* button in the *Outlook Options* dialog box. In the *Mail Options* dialog box, the different customization options are separated into different sections. Many of these different sections have one or more additional dialog boxes that can be opened for more email options. Clicking the button to the right of the section opens the dialog box for more specific email options.

The following sections are available in *Mail* options:

- *Compose messages*
- *Outlook panes*
- *Message arrival*
- *Conversation Clean Up*
- *Replies and forwards*
- *Save messages*
- *Send messages*
- *MailTips*
- *Tracking*
- *Message format*
- *Other*

Compose Messages

The ***Compose messages*** section allows you to customize the format of email messages, spell checking, AutoCorrect, signatures, stationery, and themes. The button to the left of each of these areas opens a dialog box with many additional features that you are able to customize.

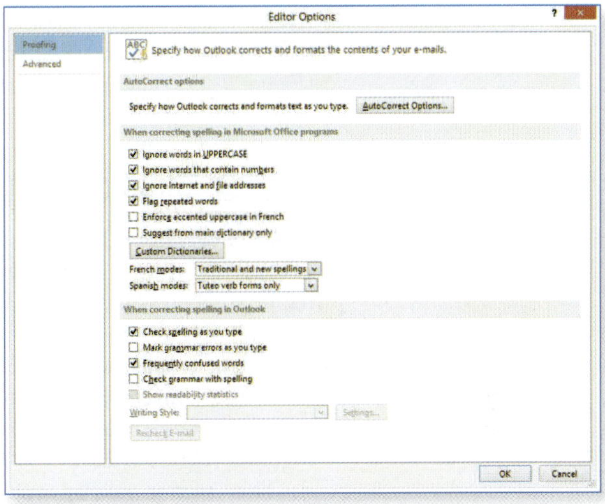

7-14 *Editor Options* dialog box

The *Editor Options* and *Spelling and AutoCorrect* buttons open the *Editor Options* dialog box (Figure 7-14). In this dialog box you are given many options on the *Proofing* and *Advanced* areas.

The *Signatures* and *Stationery and Themes* buttons open the *Signatures and Stationery* dialog box. In this dialog box, you can create and edit signatures, and on the *Personal Stationery* tab you can customize the theme and fonts for emails.

> **MORE INFO**
>
> *Signatures* and *Stationery* were covered in Chapter 2.

Outlook Panes

The ***Outlook panes*** section allows you to control how messages displayed in the *Reading* pane interact with the *Folder* pane. Messages can be set to be marked as read when they are displayed in the *Reading* pane or marked as read when the selection in the *Folder* pane changes (Figure 7-15). Also, the spacebar can be set up and used to move through the text of a message and move to the next message in the *Folder* pane. This is a handy feature to quickly preview and move through messages in the *Reading* pane.

Message Arrival

The ***Message arrival*** section (Figure 7-16) of *Mail Options* controls what happens in Outlook when a message arrives in your Inbox. By default when a new email message arrives, a sound is played, the pointer briefly changes, an envelope is displayed in the notification area, and a desktop alert is displayed. A ***Desktop Alert*** is a message that briefly displays the sender's name, subject line, and part of the body of the message in a corner of your screen when a new email message is received in your Inbox (Figure 7-17). The email message can be opened by clicking the alert.

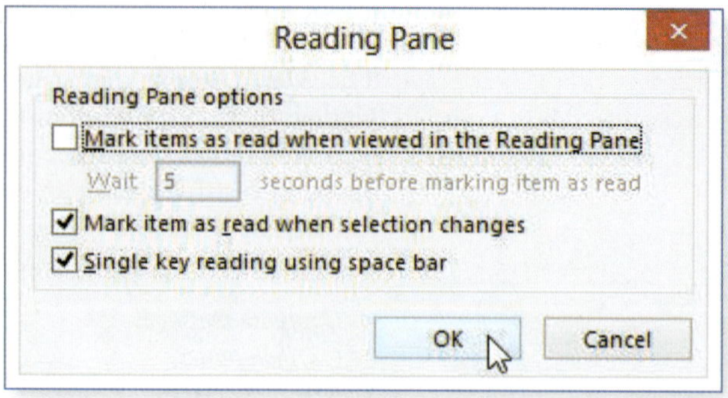

7-15 *Reading Pane* dialog box

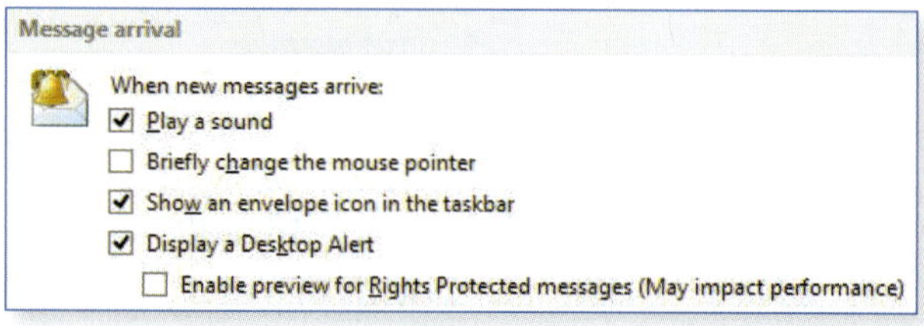

7-16 *Message arrival* options

7-17 Desktop alert

Conversation Clean Up

The ***Conversation Clean Up*** section allows you to control what happens when you use the *Clean Up* feature in Outlook to remove redundant emails in a conversation. The conversation arrangement groups related emails together (Figure 7-18).

This section allows you to determine where cleaned-up messages will be moved (the default is in the *Deleted Items* folder) and the type of messages that Outlook will remove when using the *Clean Up* feature.

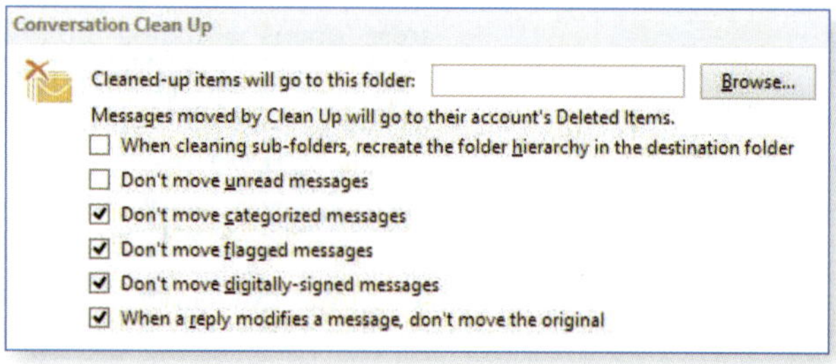

7-18 *Conversation Clean Up* options

> **MORE INFO**
>
> It is good email etiquette to include the original message in the body when replying to or forwarding an email message. By doing this, you provide context for your response.

Replies and Forwards

Outlook allows you to tailor how your email message appears when you receive, or send a reply to, or forward a message (Figure 7-19). By default when you reply to or forward a message, the original message is included below your response in the body of the message.

When ***replying*** to a message, you have the following options as a default setting (Figure 7-20):

- *Do not include the original message*
- *Attach original message* (this option attaches the original message as an attachment and removes it from the body of the response)
- Include original message text (this is the default setting in Outlook)
- *Include and indent the original message text*
- *Prefix each line of the original message* (the default prefix is >)

When ***forwarding*** a message, you have the following options as a default setting (Figure 7-21):

- *Attach original message* (this option attaches the original message as an attachment and removes it from the body of the response)
- *Include original message text* (this is the default setting in Outlook)
- *Include and indent the original message text*
- *Prefix each line of the original message* (the default prefix is >)

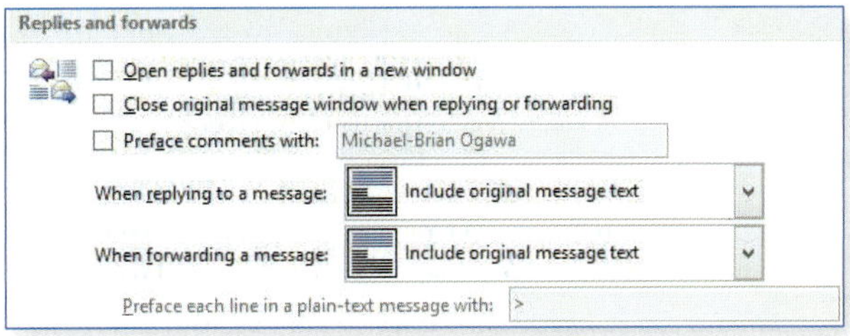

7-19 ***Replies and forwards*** **options**

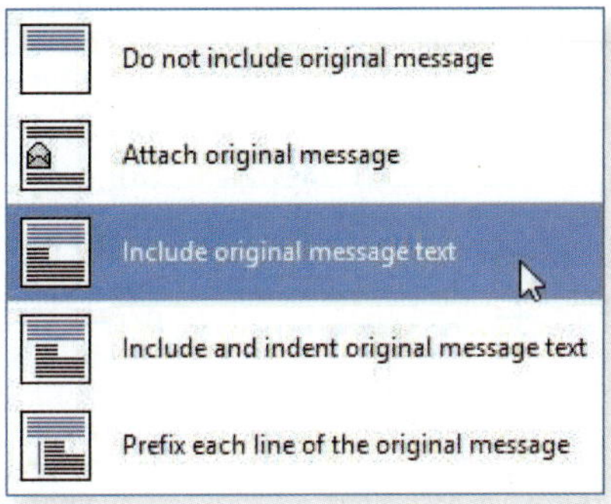

7-20 ***Reply*** **options**

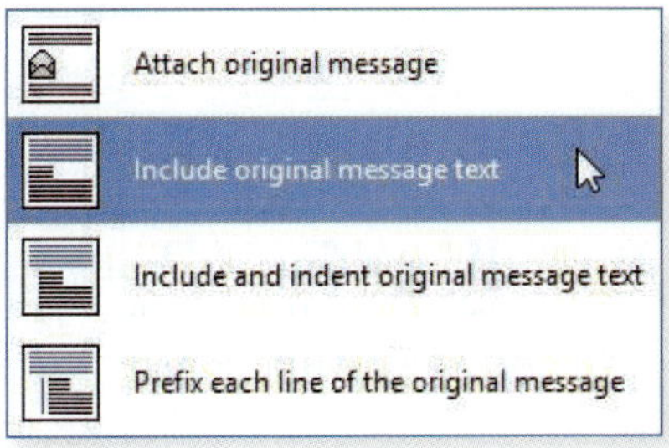

7-21 ***Forward*** **options**

Save Messages

Open messages that are either new, a reply, or a forward are by default saved every three minutes in the ***Drafts*** folder. The time duration and the folder can be customized. Also, by default new messages, replies, and forwards are saved in the *Sent Items* folder (Figure 7-22).

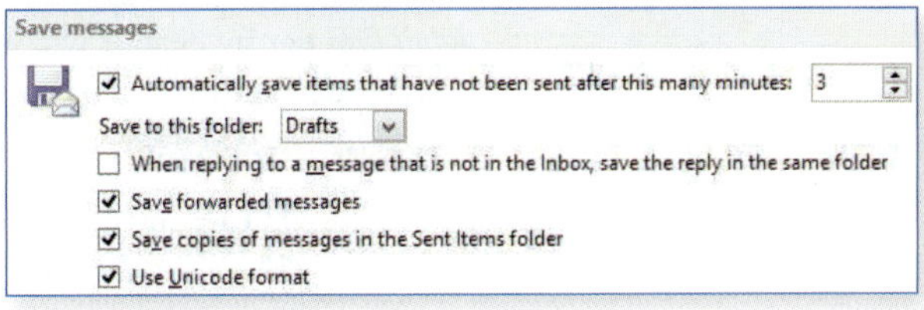

7-22 ***Save messages*** **options**

Send Messages

When a new message is created, the default setting for ***importance*** and ***sensitivity*** is *Normal*, which means there are no special tags or notifications on the message. In the ***Send messages*** section (Figure 7-23), you can customize these default settings as well as set a default expiration.

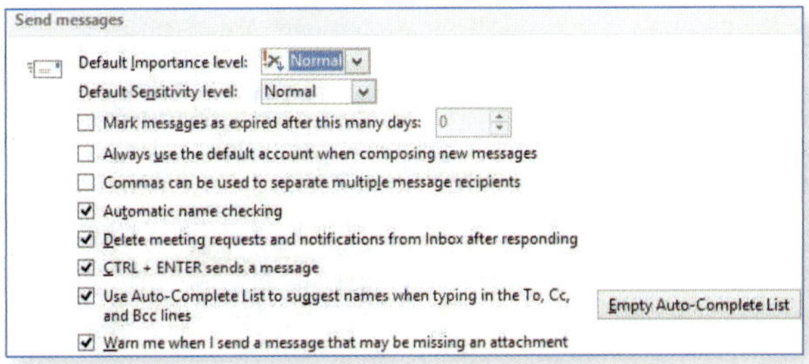

7-23 ***Send messages*** **options**

Typically, a semicolon is used to separate recipients' email addresses in the *To* line of a message, but a comma can also be used to separate recipients. The ***Auto-Complete List*** is used to suggest recently used names when typing names in the *To, Cc,* and *Bcc* lines of an email. This list can be cleared by clicking the **Empty Auto-Complete List** button. By default, Outlook warns you if it you try to send a message that is missing an attachment. This feature can be turned off by unchecking its option.

> **MORE INFO**
>
> It is not a good idea to have all emails marked with *High Importance,* a sensitivity tag, or an expiration date and time. Use these tags only as necessary so they do not lose their effectiveness on recipients.

MailTips

MailTips are used to inform you about when you are sending an email to a large number of recipients, to a recipient who is out of the office, to recipients whose mailbox is full, or to an invalid email address, and about many other email situations. *MailTips* provide you with real-time information about the status of an email message to be sent. The *MailTips* information bar appears in the *Info bar* area of a message.

The *MailTips Options* dialog box (Figure 7-24) allows you to customize the settings for how *MailTips* will appear. The *MailTips* bar by default will only be displayed when one or more of the *MailTips* apply. You can change the setting so that the *MailTips* bar will appear on all email messages.

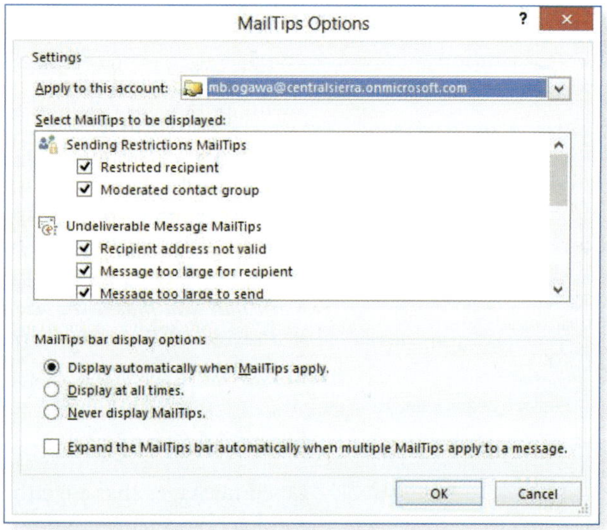

7-24 *MailTips Options* dialog box

> **MORE INFO**
>
> *MailTips* are functional only when using Outlook 2013 in conjunction with an Exchange Server.

> **MORE INFO**
>
> The *MailTips* section does not appear if *MailTips* are not available on your Exchange Server.

Tracking Options

If you are using Outlook in an Exchange environment, Outlook automatically tracks responses when using voting buttons and meeting requests. Outlook will also track receipts received when a read receipt or delivery receipt has been used on an email. The ***Tracking options*** (Figure 7-25) allows you to determine how Outlook tracks and responds to these items.

You can customize how voting buttons and meeting request responses are processed when they arrive in your Inbox. Also, you can change the default settings for read and delivery receipts for outgoing emails and how Outlook should handle read receipts on emails you receive.

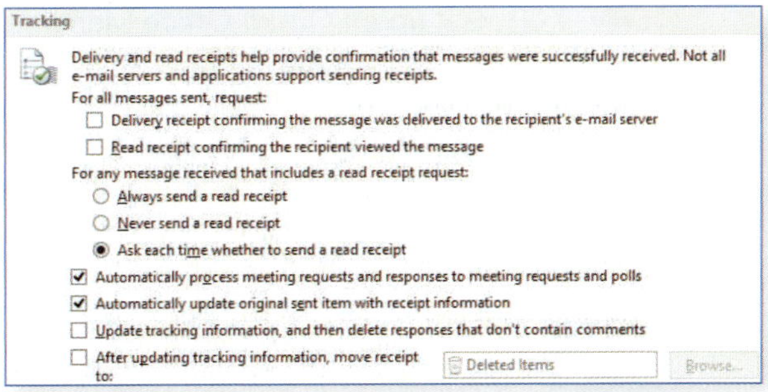

7-25 *Tracking* options

MORE INFO

Use read and delivery receipts sparingly. It can become very annoying to recipients to receive a read receipt on all emails they receive from you.

Also, if you receive an email that is requesting a read receipt, it is courteous to allow Outlook to send a read receipt.

MORE INFO

Delivery receipts, read receipts, and voting buttons were covered in Chapter 2. Meeting requests were covered in Chapter 4.

Message Format and Other

The last two sections of the *Mail Options* dialog box (Figure 7-26) include some behind-the-scenes options for formatting your email messages. Outlook allows you to customize some of these not so common email formatting options. It is probably best to leave the default settings in these areas unless you have specific reasons to change them.

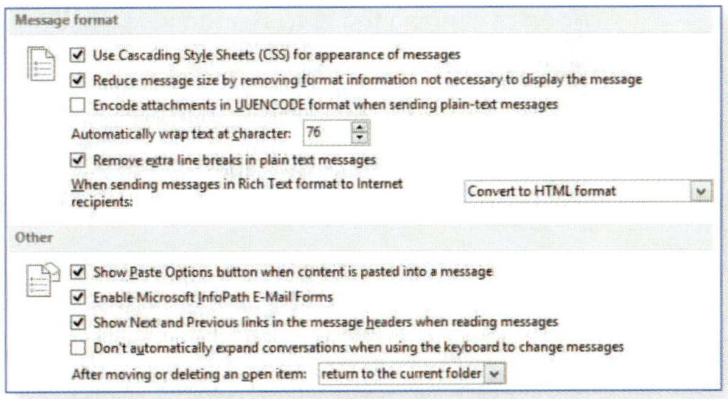

7-26 *Message format* and *Other* options

Out of Office Assistant

Most of us have instances when we are away from the office or home when we are not able to respond to emails for an extended time. You might be on vacation or a business trip and don't want to totally ignore those who send you an email. The ***Out of Office Assistant*** is available if you are using an Exchange account and provides you the option of creating an automated response to reply to all emails you receive while you are not able to answer email.

You can set a specific date range for the *Out of Office Assistant.* If you don't specify a date range, the *Out of Office Assistant* will remain on until you turn it off. A message can be created to automatically respond to all those from whom you receive an email. These automated responses can be sent to those within your organization (those connected to your Exchange server), those outside of your organization, or both.

HOW TO: Set up an Out of Office Message

1. Click on the **File** tab to open the *Backstage.*
2. Click on the **Automatic Replies (Out of Office)** button (Figure 7-27). The *Out of Office Assistant* dialog box opens (Figure 7-28).
3. Click on the **Send Out of Office auto-replies.**

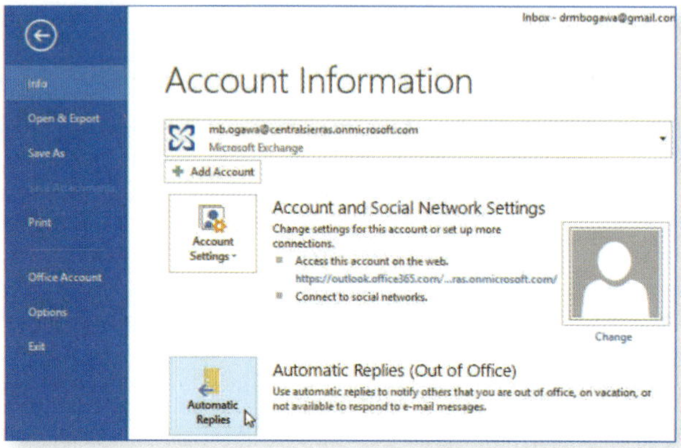

7-27 *Automatic Replies* button

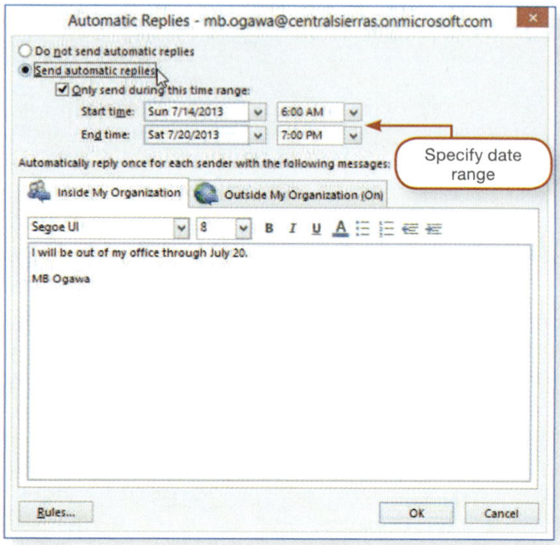

7-28 Set up automatic replies

4. You can set a specific date range if you choose.
5. Compose a brief message in the body.
6. If you want an automated response sent to those outside of your organization, click on the **Outside My Organization** tab and type a brief message. You will have the option of sending the auto-response to *My Contacts only* or *Anyone outside my organization.*
7. Click **OK.** The *Out of Office Assistant* is now activated.

Junk Email Options

If you are like most email users, you receive quite a few junk email messages each day. Antivirus software continues to improve and can identify and move potential junk email messages to a different folder. Online email providers like Gmail, Yahoo Mail, and Outlook.com continue to enhance their efforts to identify spammers (those who send junk mail) and remove junk mail before it is delivered to your Inbox.

But even with these efforts, there are still junk mail messages that make it to your Inbox. Email messages that are identified by Outlook as junk mail are moved to the ***Junk E-mail*** folder in your folder list.

Also, there are times when messages that should make it to your Inbox are identified as junk mail and moved to the *Junk E-mail* folder.

Outlook allows you to customize your junk email settings, add safe senders, add safe recipients, and block senders or domain names.

The ***Junk E-mail Options*** dialog box allows you to control the level of junk email protection in Outlook.

HOW TO: Open Junk E-mail Options

1. Click the **Junk** button in the *Delete* group on the *Home* tab. A menu opens with the junk email options available.
2. Select **Junk E-mail Options.** The *Junk E-mail Options* dialog box opens (Figure 7-29).

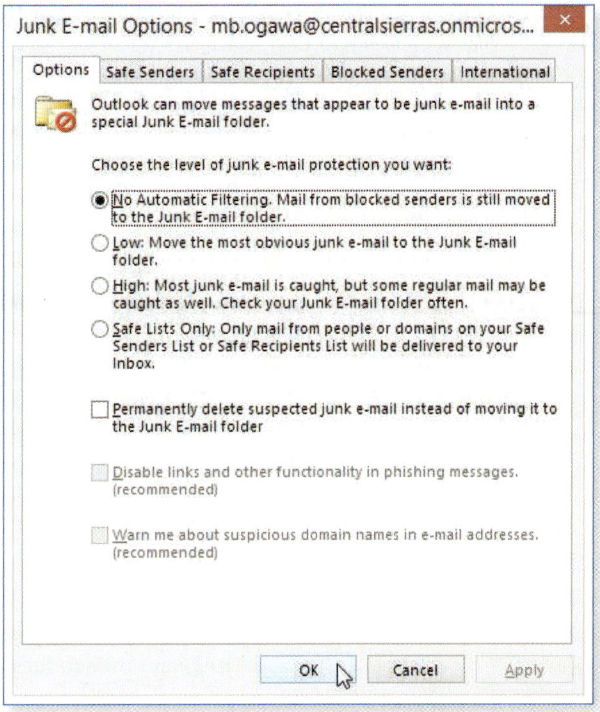

7-29 *Junk E-mail Options* dialog box

ANOTHER WAY

The *Junk E-mail Options* dialog box can also be opened by opening an email and clicking the **Junk** button in the *Delete* group on the *Message* tab.

MORE INFO

The *Junk E-mail Filter* will only function properly on an Exchange account when you are using *Cached Exchange Mode.*

Safe and Blocked Senders and Recipients

Within the *Junk E-mail Options* dialog box, you are given the following options to control junk mail messages.

- ***Safe Senders:*** Senders' email addresses or domains (e.g., @mcgraw-hill.com) can be added to this list to ensure that emails received from these senders or domains are not treated as junk mail.
- ***Safe Recipients:*** Recipients' email addresses or domains can be added to this list to ensure that emails sent to these recipients or domains are not treated as junk mail.
- ***Blocked Senders:*** Senders' email addresses or senders' domains can be added to this list to ensure that emails received from these senders or domains will be treated as junk mail and moved to the *Junk E-mail* folder in your folder list.
- ***International:*** Outlook also allows you to block email messages received in different languages or from different country domains.

Email addresses or domain names can be manually added into these lists (with the exception of international ones) by selecting one of these lists in the *Junk E-mail Options* dialog box by clicking the **Add** button and typing in the email address or domain name.

An email message received in your Inbox can also be added to the *Safe Senders, Safe Recipients,* or *Blocked Senders* list.

HOW TO: Add Senders or Groups to Block or Never Block Lists

1. Open the email to be added to one of these lists.
2. Click the **Junk** button in the *Delete* group.

3. Select *Block Sender, Never Block Sender, Never Block Sender's Domain,* or *Never Block this Group or Mailing List.*
   - If *Block Sender* is selected, the message will be moved to the *Junk E-mail* folder and the sender's email address is added to the *Blocked Senders* list. Outlook will always move email messages received from this sender to the *Junk E-mail* folder.
   - If *Never Block Sender, Never Block Sender's Domain,* or *Never Block this Group or Mailing List* is selected, the sender's email and/or domain name is added to the *Safe Senders* list.

Within the *Junk E-mail Options* dialog box, each of these lists can be edited. You can add or remove email addresses or domains from any of the lists, or you can edit entries included in the lists.

MORE INFO

Email addresses that you have saved in your *Contacts* folder are, by default, treated as safe senders.

Retrieving Email That Is Marked as Junk

If an email is delivered to your *Junk E-mail* folder and it is not a junk email, it can be marked as ***Not Junk,*** and the sender's email address will be added to the *Safe Senders* list.

HOW TO: Open the Junk E-mail Options Dialog Box

1. Select or open an email in the *Junk E-mail* folder.
2. In the *Delete* group, click the **Junk** button and select **Not Junk.** The *Mark as Not Junk* dialog box opens, and you are given the option to always trust email from this sender.
3. Click **OK.** The email will be moved to the *Inbox* folder, and the sender's email address will be added to the *Safe Senders* list.

ANOTHER WAY

Ctrl+Alt+J marks an email message as *Not Junk.*

ANOTHER WAY

You can also drag an email message from the *Junk E-mail* folder to your *Inbox* or another folder in your folder list.

MORE INFO

It is important to check your *Junk E-mail* folder regularly to ensure that important emails that should be delivered to your Inbox do not get overlooked.

SLO 7.4

Using RSS Feeds

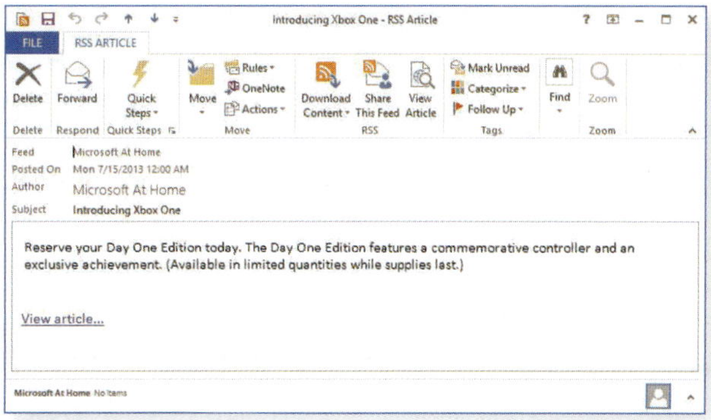

7-30 RSS article

Most of you have watched the news on one of the cable television news shows and have seen the scrolling banner of news headlines at the bottom of the screen. This news feed is similar to an ***RSS*** (really simple syndication) ***feed*** from a web site. RSS feeds are headlines of new articles or information on web sites (Figure 7-30). RSS feeds are useful in that when you subscribe to an RSS feed you are automatically sent the new articles from this web site to your RSS feed reader. So, rather than having to visit each of your favorite news, sports, recipe, and entertainment web sites to search for new information, this new information is automatically sent to you as an RSS feed.

Outlook can manage your RSS feeds like it does your email accounts. When a new item is available on a web site, it is delivered to an RSS feed folder. You will receive RSS feeds like an email. These feeds will come with a subject line and a brief summary of the article. There is also usually a link to take you to the web site to read the full article if you're interested.

Subscribe to an RSS Feed

Outlook provides you with an *RSS Feeds* folder to store the RSS feeds to which you subscribe. Outlook also provides you with a menu of RSS feeds from which to easily subscribe. You must first enable the RSS feeds in the *Outlook Options* dialog box. Once enabled, when you click the *RSS Feeds* folder in the *Navigation* pane, the ***Outlook Syndicated Content (RSS) Directory*** appears in the *Folder* pane. You can click any of these links to subscribe to an RSS feed and automatically add a new folder to your *RSS Feeds* folder.

HOW TO: Subscribe to an RSS Feed

1. Click the **File** button on the *Ribbon* and select **Options.**
2. Click the **Mail** button in the *Navigation* pane.
3. Click the **Advanced** option.
4. Click the **Synchronize RSS Feeds to Common Feed List (CFL) in Windows** check box (Figure 7-31) and click **OK.**
5. Click the **RSS Feeds** folder in the *Mail Folders* list in the *Navigation* pane.
6. Click the **RSS Feeds folder** drop-down arrow to view the available RSS feeds (Figure 7-32).

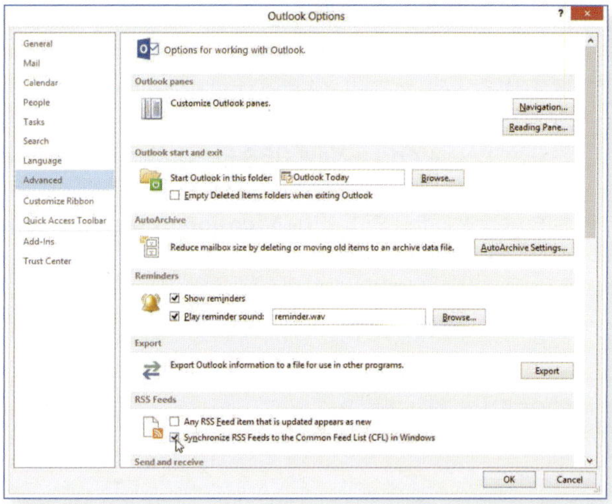

7-31 Subscribe to CFL list

7. Click on any of the feeds to view them.
8. You can click any of the RSS feed articles to open and read any of the interesting articles.

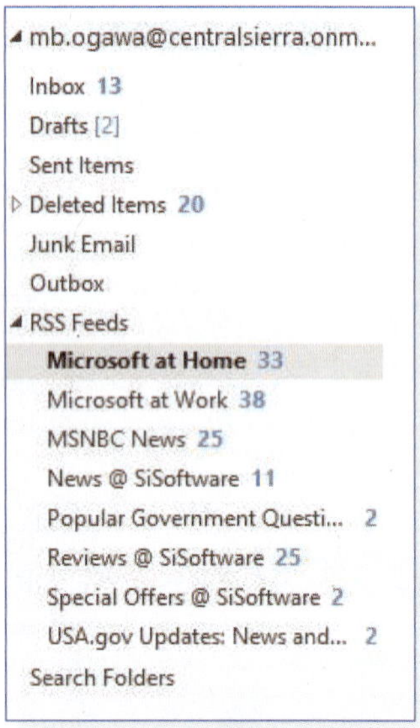

7-32 *RSS Feeds* folder

MORE INFO

The RSS Syndicated Directory might not appear in your Outlook. You can find these Office blogs at www.blogs.office.com.

Although Outlook provides you with many RSS feeds in its RSS Directory, you are not limited to subscribing to only these feeds. Many commercial web sites provide you with RSS links that can be subscribed to in Outlook. Many web sites will also have the RSS feed icon or link to help you to subscribe to the RSS feed link (Figure 7-33).

To subscribe to an RSS feed from a web site, you have to copy the web address (URL) of the RSS feed and paste it into the *New RSS Feed* dialog box.

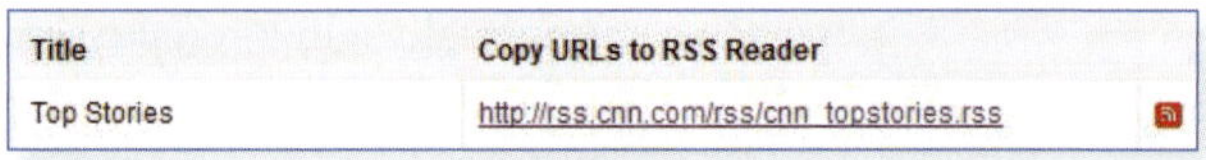

7-33 RSS feed for CNN Top Stories

HOW TO: Subscribe to an RSS Feed from a Web Site

1. Go to the web page of your choice, and locate the RSS feed icon or link. It may take some searching to find the RSS feed icon or link, and not all web sites will have RSS feeds available.
2. Select the RSS URL.
3. Right-click the selected URL and choose **Copy** (Figure 7-34).
4. Go back to Outlook and right-click the **RSS Feeds** folder in the *Navigation* pane.
5. Choose **Add a New RSS Feed.** The *New RSS Feed* dialog box opens.
6. Click in the **Enter the location of the RSS feed you want to add to Outlook** box.
7. Press **Ctrl** + **V** to paste the URL (Figure 7-35).
8. Click **Add.** A dialog box opens asking you *Add this RSS Feed to Outlook?*
9. Click **Yes** (Figure 7-36). The RSS feed is subscribed to, and a new RSS feed folder is added to your *RSS Feeds* folder.

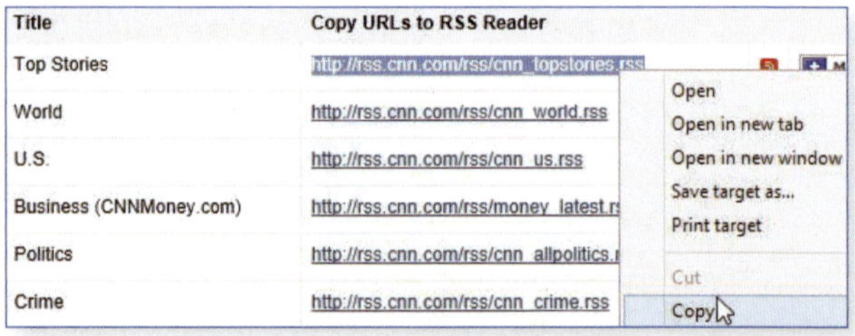

7-34 Copy the RSS address

7-35 *New RSS Feed* dialog box

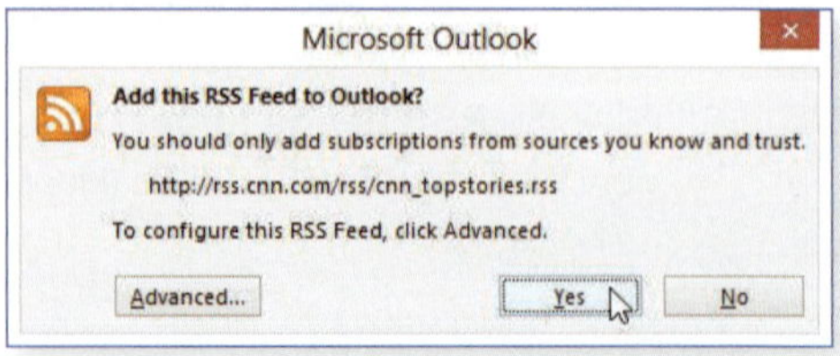

7-36 *Add this RSS Feed* confirmation

MORE INFO

The RSS icon or URL will vary from site to site. If you copy and paste an incorrect URL, Outlook will let you know that it is not a valid RSS feed. You will need to go back to the web page and find the correct RSS feed link or URL.

ANOTHER WAY

To copy a URL, press **Ctrl+C.** To paste a URL, press **Ctrl+V.**

MORE INFO

Be careful when subscribing to many RSS feeds as the volume of RSS feed emails can become overwhelming. You might get 10 to 30 emails a day per RSS feed to which you are subscribed.

Manage RSS Feeds

Inside the *RSS Feeds* folder you will have a separate subfolder for each subscribed to RSS feed. The subfolders contain the RSS feed emails.

Outlook manages RSS feeds in the *Account Settings* dialog box. By opening the *Account Settings* dialog box and clicking the *RSS Feeds* tab, you can see the RSS feeds to which you are subscribed (Figure 7-37). You can rename a feed, change the delivery location, and change how information in the feed is downloaded.

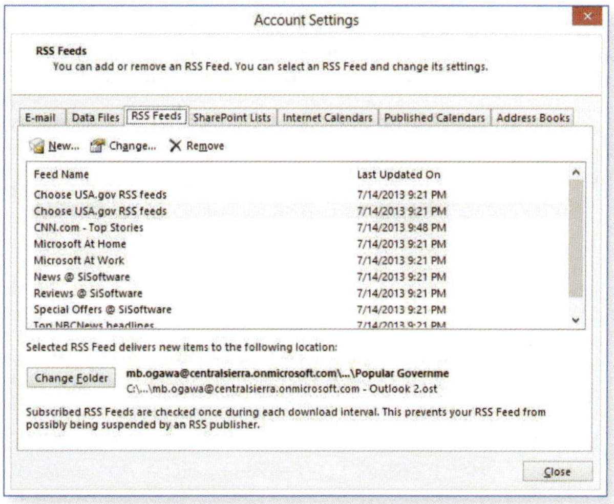

7-37 *RSS Feeds* in account settings

ANOTHER WAY

Right-click the *RSS feed* folder to be renamed, choose **Rename Folder,** type the new name, and press **Enter.**

You can also rename the RSS feed folder in the *Navigation* pane.

HOW TO: Rename RSS Feed Folders

1. In the *Navigation* pane, click the RSS feed folder to be renamed.
2. Click the **Folder** tab at the top of the window.

3. Click the **Rename Folder** button in the *Actions* group (Figure 7-38).
4. Type the new name for the RSS feed folder.
5. Press **Enter.** The folder will be renamed.

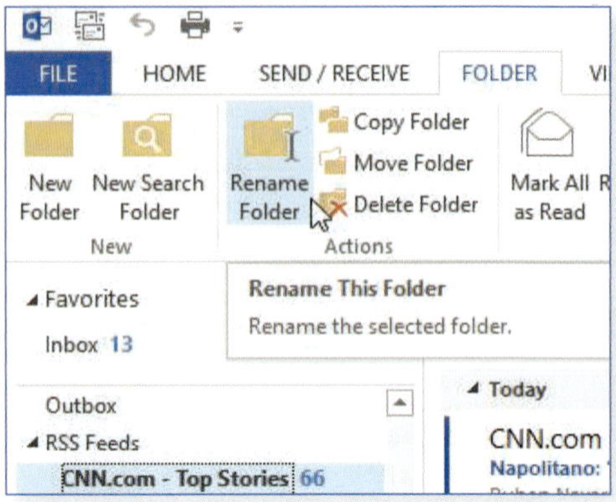

7-38 Rename an RSS feed folder

Share an RSS Feed

RSS feeds can easily be shared with other Outlook users. You might want to send them the URL of the RSS feed and have them add this link as a new RSS feed, but Outlook has provided a much easier way to share an RSS feed.

HOW TO: Share an RSS Feed

1. Click one of the RSS feed folders in the *Navigation* pane. All the RSS feed emails will be displayed in the *Folder* pane.
2. In the *Folder* pane, open one of the RSS feed emails.
3. Click the **Share This Feed** button (Figure 7-39) in the *RSS* group on the *RSS Article* tab. A new email opens (Figure 7-40).
4. Click the **To** button to select recipients and then press **Send.** This RSS feed email will be sent to recipients, and they will be given the option to add this RSS feed to their Outlook.

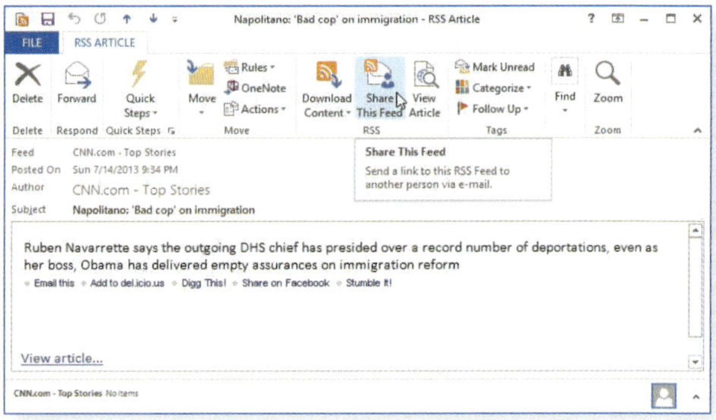

7-39 Share This Feed button

ANOTHER WAY

With an RSS feed email selected in the *Folder* pane, click the **Share This Feed** button in the *RSS* group on the *Home* tab.

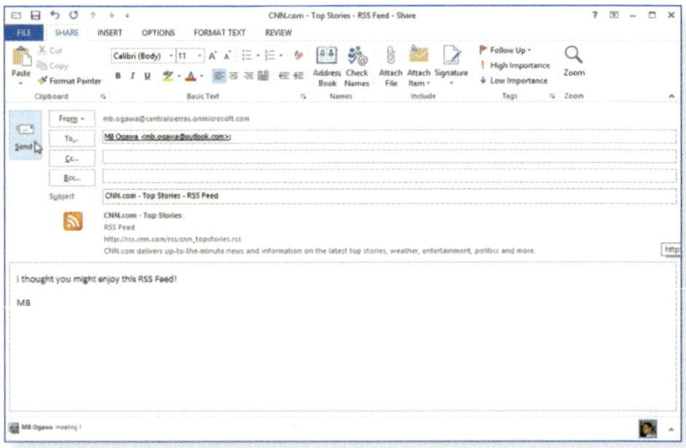

7-40 RSS share email message

When this feed is shared with other Outlook users, they will receive an email in their *Inbox.* They can subscribe to this RSS feed by opening the email and clicking the **Add this RSS Feed** button in the upper left corner of the email (Figure 7-41).

Unsubscribe from an RSS Feed

There are a couple of different ways to unsubscribe from an RSS feed. If you want to unsubscribe from an RSS feed and remove the RSS feed folder and all the RSS feed emails, you can right-click the RSS feed folder and choose **Delete Folder.** A dialog box opens asking if you want to delete the folder and all its contents.

ANOTHER WAY

Ctrl+D deletes the selected folder.

7-41 Add a shared RSS feed

You can also unsubscribe from an RSS feed using the *RSS Feeds* tab in the *Account Settings* dialog box.

HOW TO: Unsubscribe from an RSS Feed

1. In the *Account Settings* dialog box, click the **RSS Feeds** tab.
2. Select the RSS feed to be removed and click the **Remove** button.
3. Click **Yes** on the confirmation dialog box (Figure 7-42).
4. Click **Close** to close the *Account Settings* dialog box.

MORE INFO

When unsubscribing from an RSS feed from the *Account Settings* dialog box, the RSS feed subscription is removed but the RSS feed folder and previously received RSS feed emails are not deleted.

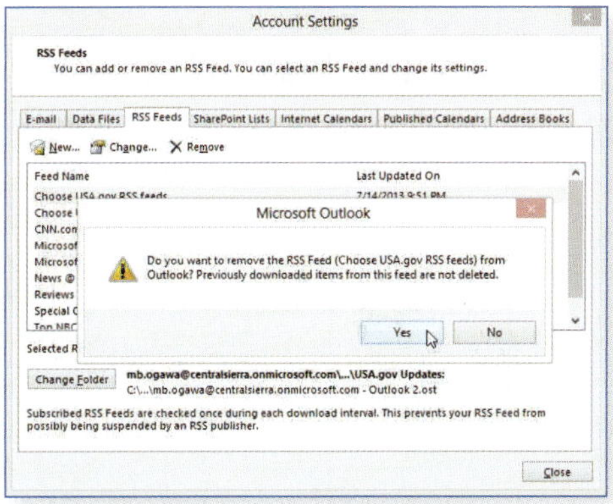

7-42 Remove an RSS feed

PAUSE & PRACTICE: OUTLOOK 7-2

For this Pause & Practice project, you subscribe to CNN RSS news feeds (available at http://www.cnn.com/services/rss/). You subscribe to an RSS feed, rename the feed folder, and share the feed with your instructor.

1. Add the CNN Business feed to your RSS Feeds.
   a. Open a browser and go to the following URL: http://www.cnn.com/services/rss/.
   b. Select the **Technology RSS URL.**
   c. Right-click the selected URL and choose **Copy.**
   d. Go back to Outlook and click the **Mail** button in the *Navigation* pane.
   e. Right-click the **RSS Feeds** folder in the *Folder* pane.
   f. Choose **Add a New RSS Feed.** The *New RSS Feed* dialog box opens.
   g. Click in the **Enter the location of the RSS feed you want to add to Outlook** box.

h. Press **Ctrl** + **V** to paste the URL.
i. Click **Add.** A dialog box opens asking you *Add this RSS Feed to Outlook?*
j. Click **Yes.**

2. Rename the RSS feed you added in the first step to **CNN Tech.**
   a. Right-click the RSS feed you added in the first step and select **Rename Folder.**
   b. Type CNN Tech and press **Enter.**
3. Share the feed with your instructor (Figure 7-43).
   a. Click the **CNN Tech** feed.
   b. Open the first message.
   c. Click the **Share This Feed** button [*RSS Article* tab, *RSS* group]. A new email opens.
   d. Type your instructor's email address in the *To* field.
   e. Type your email address in the *Cc* field.
   f. Modify to subject to include **Outlook Pause & Practice 7-2** before the RSS feed title.
   g. Add the message: Hi [instructor's name], I thought you would be interested in the CNN Tech feed!
   Thank you,
   [your name]
   h. Click the **Send** button.

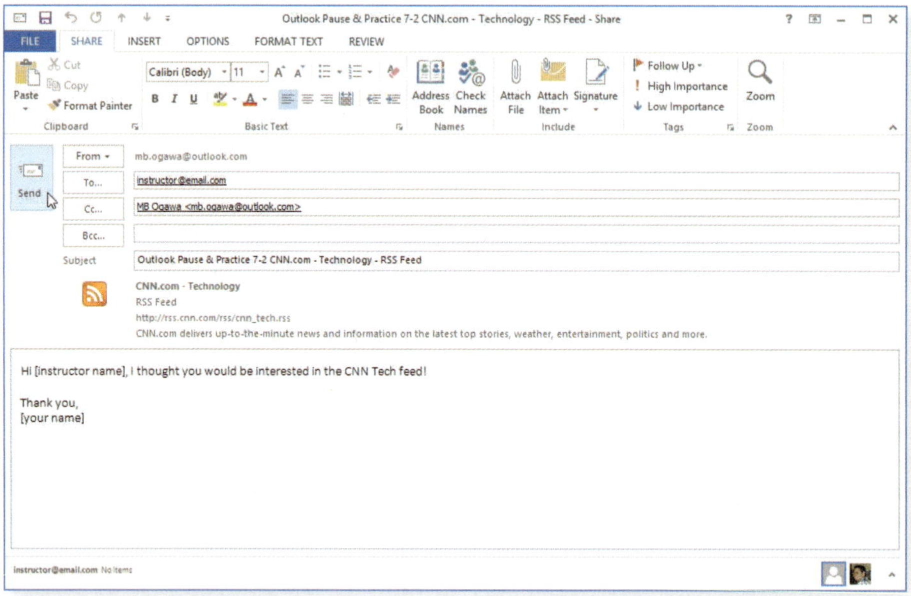

7-43 Completed Pause & Practice 7-2

SLO 7.5

Searching for Outlook Items

Have you ever tried to find an email item that you sent or received months ago? You might have searched through many different folders looking for a specific email. You might not even remember who sent you the email, the subject of the email, or to whom the email was sent. Even if you don't remember all the specifics about the item for which you are looking, you can use the *Instant Search* feature to find Outlook items.

Instant Search

The ***Instant Search*** feature in Outlook provides you with a tool to quickly search for Outlook items in a specific folder or all folders. It indexes all Outlook items in your folders and searches for items that match the specific criteria for which you are looking. For example, you can search all your mailbox folders for emails from your professor, for all emails with the word "Outlook" in the subject or body, or all contacts who work for McGraw-Hill. Outlook will display in the *Folder* pane all items that match your criteria.

MORE INFO

If you are using Windows Vista, 7, or 8, Outlook *Instant Search* is automatically turned on. If you are using a previous version of Windows, you will have to turn on or enable *Instant Search.*

ANOTHER WAY

Ctrl+E activates *Instant Search* on the selected folder. **Ctrl+Alt+A** activates *Instant Search* on *All Mail* Items.

When you click in the *Search* box at the top of the *Folder* pane, the *Search* tab is displayed in Outlook. On the *Search* tab in the *Scope* group, you can select the folders or areas of Outlook to be searched. The *Refine* group will provide you with options to help locate the information for which you are looking. The *Options* group provides you with a list of recent searches and other advanced search tools.

HOW TO: Search for Email Messages

1. Click the **Mail** button in the *Navigation* pane.
2. Click the folder to be searched.
3. Click in the **Search** box at the top of the *Folder* pane (Figure 7-44).
4. Type in the words in the fields to be searched. Outlook will display matching emails in the *Folder* pane.
5. Additional criteria can be selected from the *Refine* group.
6. The *Scope* group will allow you to specify where Outlook performs the search.
7. Click the **Close Search** button (**X**) to the right of the search field to clear the search and close the *Search* area and tab. You can also click one of your mailbox folders to close *Instant Search.*

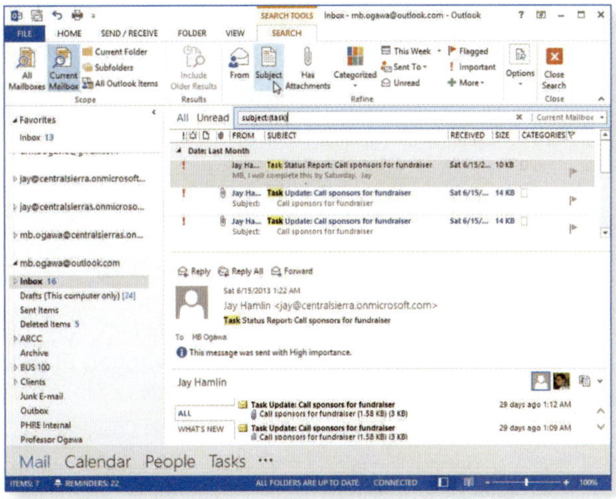

7-44 Search for email messages

When you use *Instant Search,* Outlook will display the matching items in the *Folder* pane, highlight the matching criteria, and list the folder in which the item is located. You can open any of these items from the search results by double-clicking it in the *Folder* pane.

Search Options

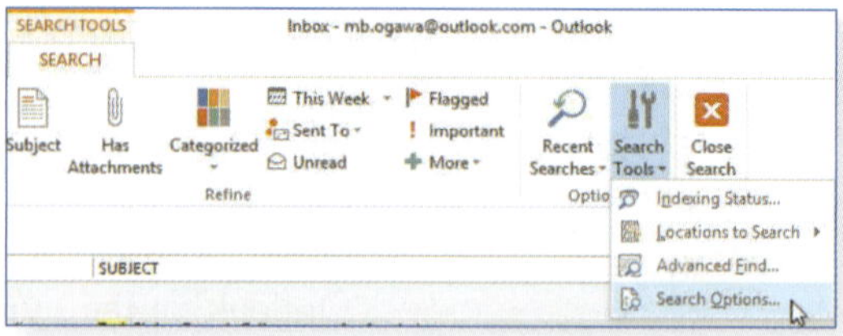

7-45 *Search Options*

You can change the ***search options*** *for Instant Search* to customize which folders are indexed, how the results are displayed, whether or not the *Deleted Items* folder is included in the search, and the default folders to be searched.

You can open the *Search Options* dialog box by clicking the **Search Tools** button in the *Options* group on the *Search* tab and selecting **Search Options** (Figure 7-45). The *Search Options* are displayed in Figure 7-46.

> **ANOTHER WAY**
>
> The *Search Options* dialog box can be opened from the Outlook *Backstage*. Click the **File** tab, choose **Options,** and click **Search.**

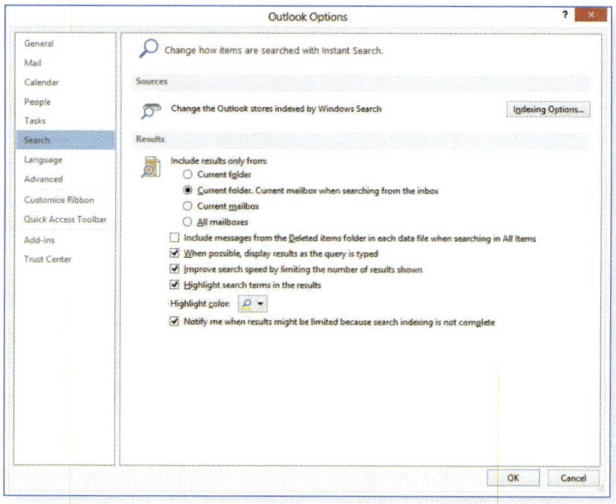

7-46 Search options in *Outlook Options*

Advanced Find

When you use *Instant Search* in Mail, Outlook only searches for email items. However, Outlook also provides you with ***Advanced Find*** to search for any type of Outlook item. *Advanced Find* displays Outlook items that match your criteria in the *Advanced Find* dialog box.

HOW TO: Perform an Advanced Search

1. Click in the **Search** box at the top of the *Folder* pane.
2. Click the **Search Tools** button in the *Options* group on the *Search* tab, and select **Advanced Find** to open the *Advanced Find* dialog box.
3. Select the type of item to find in the *Look* area.
4. Select the location to search in the *In* area. Click the **Browse** button to select the folder to search.
5. Type in the search criteria.
   - You can click the *From* or *Sent To* buttons to select contacts.
   - You can also click either the **More Choices** or *Advanced* tabs for more search options.

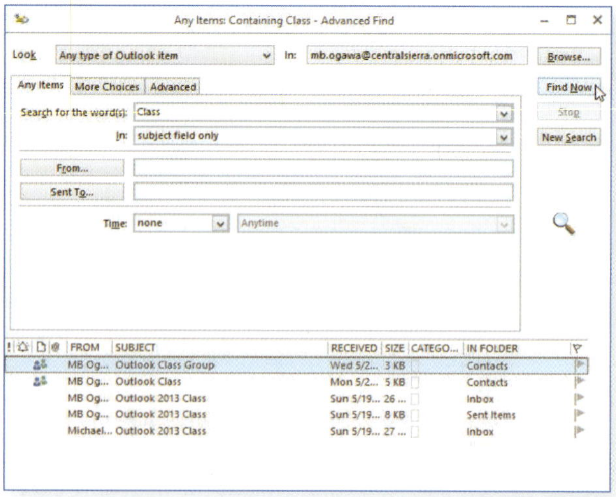

7-47 Search for any Outlook item

6. Click the **Find Now** button to search for items that match your criteria (Figure 7-47). The matching items will be displayed at the bottom of the dialog box.
7. Click **New Search** to clear the current search, or click the **X** in the upper right corner to close the *Advanced Find* dialog box.

ANOTHER WAY

Ctrl + Shift + F opens the *Advanced Find* dialog box.

PAUSE & PRACTICE: OUTLOOK 7-3

For this Pause & Practice project, you search for the email messages from *Pause & Practice 7-2* that you sent to your instructor, because you did not receive a grade for the *Pause & Practice 7-2* assignment. After you find the message, you forward it to your instructor.

1. Click the **Mail** button in the *Navigation* pane.
2. Click the **Sent Items** folder.
3. Click in the **Search** box at the top of the *Folder* pane.
4. Click the **Current Mailbox** button [*Search* tab, *Scope* group].
5. Click the **Subject** button [*Search* tab, *Refine* group].
6. Type Pause Practice 7 as the keywords (Figure 7-48).
7. Locate and open the email message for ***Outlook Pause & Practice 7-2.***
8. Forward the message to your instructor.
   a. Open the email message for *Outlook Pause & Practice 7-2*.
   b. Click the **Forward** button [*Share* tab, *Respond* group].
   c. Type your instructor's email address in the *To* field.
   d. Type your email address in the *Cc* field.
   e. Modify the subject to include *Outlook Pause & Practice 7-3* before the RSS feed title.
   f. Add the following message: Hi [instructor's name], I am resending my Pause & Practice 7-2 assignment for you to check.
   Thank you,
   [student name]

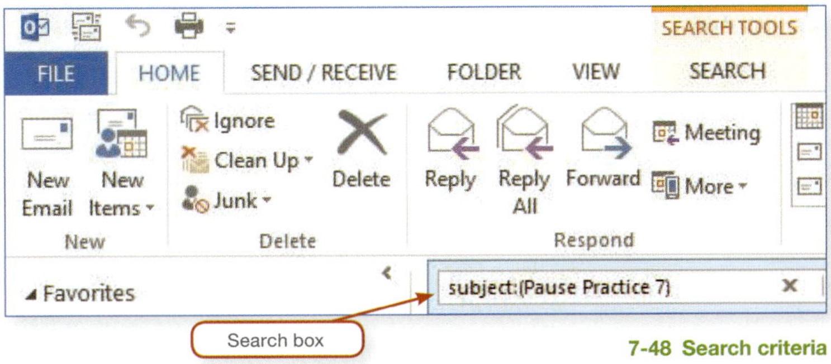

7-48 Search criteria

g. Click the **Send** button (Figure 7-49).

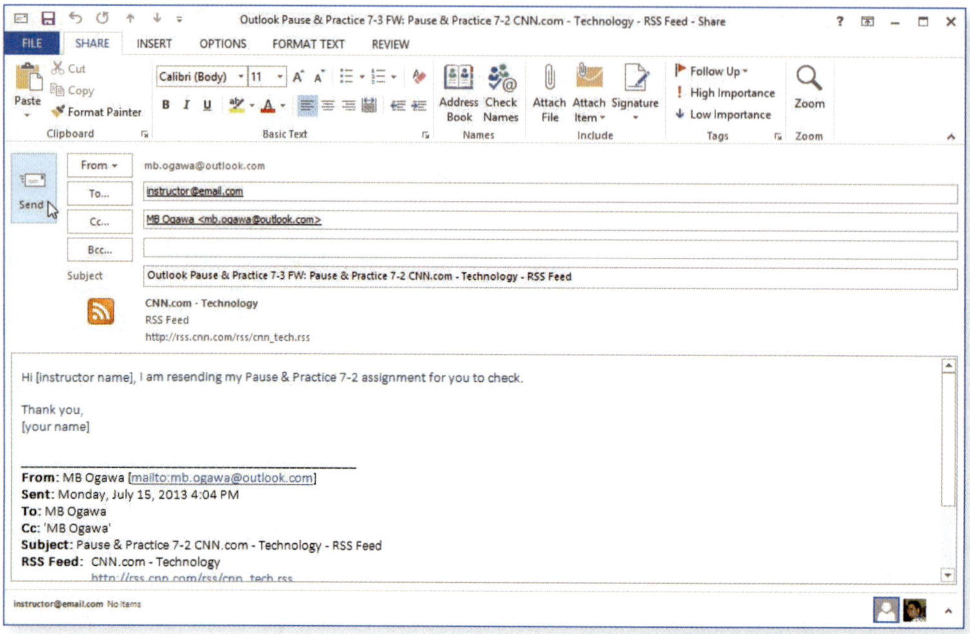

7-49 Completed Pause & Practice 7-3.

Chapter Summary

7.1 Connect and use multiple email accounts in Outlook (p. 249).

- You can manage multiple email accounts in Outlook.
- The ***Auto Account Setup*** automatically detects and validates account settings using your email account and password.
- You can troubleshoot your account by checking encryption and manually setting up your account if the *Auto Account Setup* is unable to detect the correct settings.
- The ***Repair*** feature can help to fix accounts that stop working.

7.2 Manage multiple email accounts (p. 251).

- The default email account is used to send any new email.
- You can change the default email account to fit your preference.
- When you create a new message, you can select which account you would like to send the message from, if multiple accounts are set up.
- If you have multiple POP email accounts, you can change the default folder that receives messages.
- Rules can be used to specify delivery folders for email messages.
- When using an Exchange account, you can use ***Outlook Web Access (OWA)*** to manage your email, tasks, calendar, and contacts from a web browser.
- Windows RT, the Windows based operating system for tablet computers, will have a version of Outlook.

7.3 Customize advanced email options (p. 256).

- Many different options for email can be customized in the *Outlook Options* dialog box.
- The ***Compose messages*** section allows you to customize the format of email messages, spell checking, autocorrect, signatures, stationery, and themes.
- The ***Outlook panes*** section allows you to control how messages displayed in the *Reading* pane interact with the *Folder* pane.
- The ***Message arrival*** section of *Mail Options* controls what happens in Outlook when a message arrives in your Inbox.
- The ***Conversation Clean Up*** section allows you to select options when you use the *Clean Up* feature in Outlook to remove redundant emails in a conversation.
- The ***Replies and forwards*** section allows you to tailor how your email message appears when you receive , send a reply to, or forward a message.
- The ***Send messages*** section allows you to modify how messages are sent.
- The ***MailTips*** section allows you to modify which *MailTips* are shown. *MailTips* are applicable to Exchange environments.
- The ***Tracking Options*** section allows you to determine how Outlook tracks and responds to voting buttons, task assignments, and meeting requests..
- The ***Message Format*** and ***Other*** sections include behind-the-scenes options for formatting your email messages.
- The ***Out of Office Assistant*** helps you to create an automated reply message to people within and outside of your company. The *Out of Office Assistant* is applicable to Exchange environments.
- Outlook detects ***Junk*** email and places it in the ***Junk E-mail*** folder.
- Junk email options allow you to designate ***Safe Senders, Safe Recipients, Blocked Senders,*** and ***International*** messages.

7.4 Integrate RSS feeds into Outlook (p. 265).

- Outlook allows you to receive RSS messages in your mailbox.
- Outlook includes default RSS feeds (Common Feed List).
- You can add RSS feeds that you find on the Internet.
- RSS feeds can be managed from the *Account Settings* dialog box.
- RSS feeds can be shared via email.
- RSS feeds shared via email can be added to your account quickly.
- When unsubscribing from an RSS feed from the *Account Settings* dialog box, all feed messages received are not deleted. They must be deleted manually.

7.5 Utilize search features to find email and other Outlook items (p. 270).

- ***Instant Search*** allows you to quickly find Outlook items because it indexes them.
- The ***Search*** box at the top of the screen can be used to quickly enter search criteria.
- The *Scope* of the search defines where you want to search for items, such as a specific folder.
- The *Refine* group in the *Search* tab allows you to set specific fields for your search (e.g., *From, Subject* or *Has Attachments*).
- ***Search options*** can be customized to determine which folders are indexed, how the results are displayed, whether or not the *Deleted Items* folder is included in the search, and the default folders to be searched.
- ***Advanced Find*** allows you to search for any type of Outlook item, as opposed to solely email messages.

Check for Understanding

In the ***Online Learning Center*** for this text (www.mhhe.com/office2013inpractice), there are a variety of resources that can be used to review the concepts covered in this chapter.

The following Online Learning Resources are available in the Online Learning Center:

- Multiple choice questions
- Short answer questions
- Matching exercises

USING MICROSOFT OUTLOOK 2013

Guided Project 7-1

For this project, you are an academic advisor for Sierra Pacific Community College District (SPCCD). You started using your personal laptop for work because there are many tasks that you need to complete out of the office. Therefore, you have both your personal and work email accounts in Outlook. You decide to change your default email from your personal to work email, as you tend to send messages from your work account.
[Student Learning Outcomes 7.1, 7.2]

Skills Covered in This Project

- Set up an email account.
- Change the default email account.
- Select an account when creating a new message.

---

1. Add a new account to Outlook. (If you completed *Pause & Practice 7-1,* skip this step).
   a. Click the **File** tab. The *Backstage* opens.
   b. Click **Add Account.** The *Add New Account* dialog box opens.
   c. Click the **Email Account** radio button.
   d. Fill in the following fields: **Your Name, Email Address, Password,** and **Retype Password.**
2. Change the default email account to be your work account.
   a. Click the **File** tab to open the *Backstage.*
   b. Click the **Account Settings** button, and choose **Account Settings** to open the *Account Settings* dialog box.
   c. Select your school account (the first one you used to initially set up Outlook in Chapter 1).
   d. Click the **Set as Default** button.
   e. Click the **Close** button.
3. Send a message ensuring the correct **From** address is selected.
   a. Click the **Mail** button in the *Navigation* pane.
   b. Click the **New Email** button.
   c. Click the **From** button and ensure your school account is selected.
   d. Enter the following information in the new message:
      To: [your instructor's email address]
      Cc: [your email address]
      Subject: Outlook Guided Project 7-1
      Message: Hi [instructor's name], I just added my work and personal accounts to my laptop. I wanted to be sure I am sending messages from the correct account. Could you please let me know if this message is coming from my work address?
      Thanks,
      [your name]

e. Click the **Send** button (Figure 7-50).

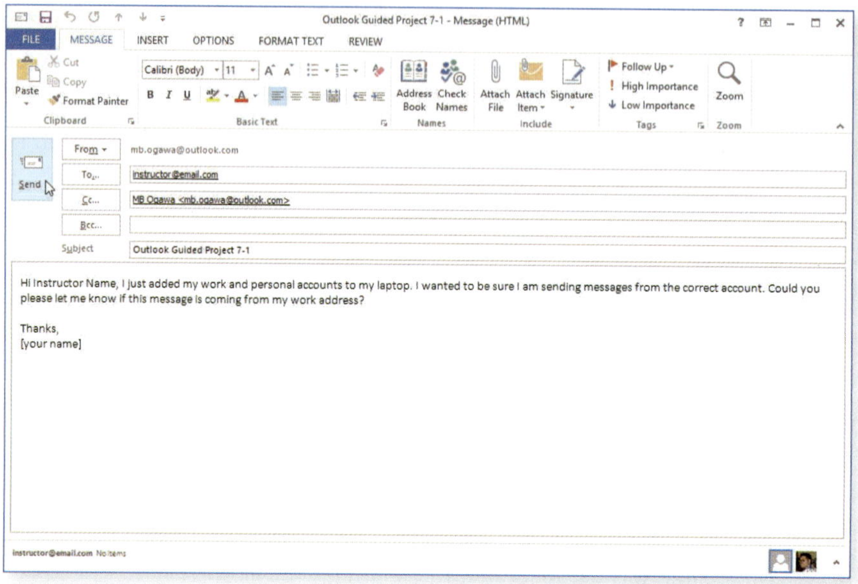

7-50 Completed Guided Project 7-1

Guided Project 7-2

For this project, you want to use Outlook as a central location for information. Therefore, you decide to stay up to date with higher education student services information by subscribing to RSS feeds from the Chronicle of Higher Education (the full RSS feed list is available at http://chronicle.com/sitemap). After reading a few articles, you determine which feed you wanted to keep and which feed you wanted to delete. You decide to share one of the RSS feeds with a colleague.
[Student Learning Outcome 7.4]

Skills Covered in This Project

- Add an RSS feed.
- Rename an RSS feed folder.
- Delete an RSS feed.
- Share an RSS feed.

1. Add the ***Chronicle of Higher Education Leadership & Governance*** RSS feed.
   a. Click the **Mail** button in the *Folder* pane.
   b. Right-click the **RSS Feeds** folder in the *Navigation* pane.
   c. Choose **Add a New RSS Feed.** The *New RSS Feed* dialog box opens.
   d. Click in the **Enter the location of the RSS feed you want to add to Outlook** box.
   e. Type http://chronicle.com/section/Leadership-Governance/18/rss.
   f. Click **Add.** A dialog box opens asking you *Add this RSS Feed to Outlook?*
   g. Click **Yes.**

2. Add the ***Chronicle of Higher Education Students*** RSS feed.
   a. Click the **Mail** button in the *Navigation* pane.
   b. Right-click the **RSS Feeds** folder in the *Navigation* pane.
   c. Choose **Add a New RSS Feed.** The *New RSS Feed* dialog box opens.
   d. Click in the **Enter the location of the RSS feed you want to add to Outlook** box.
   e. Type http://chronicle.com/section/Students/19/rss/.
   f. Click **Add.** A dialog box opens asking you *Add this RSS Feed to Outlook?*
   g. Click **Yes.**
3. Rename the ***Chronicle of Higher Education Students*** RSS feed.
   a. Right-click the ***Chronicle of Higher Education Students*** RSS feed and select **Rename Folder.**
   b. Type Chronicle-Students and press **Enter.**
4. Delete the ***Chronicle of Higher Education Leadership & Governance*** RSS feed.
   a. Right-click the ***Chronicle of Higher Education Leadership & Governance*** RSS feed and select **Delete Folder.**
   b. Click **Yes.**
5. Share the ***Chronicle-Students*** feed with your instructor.
   a. Click the ***Chronicle-Students*** feed.
   b. Open the first message.
   c. Click the **Share This Feed** button [*RSS Article* tab, *RSS* group]. A new email opens.
   d. Type your instructor's email address in the *To* field.
   e. Type your email address in the *Cc* field.
   f. Modify the subject to include ***Outlook Guided Project 7-2*** before the RSS feed title.
   g. Add the following message: Hi [instructor's name], Wow, I just found this RSS feed with a lot of great student information. Feel free to add it to your Outlook if you like the information. Let me know if you find any other great feeds, as I enjoy getting this information delivered to me in Outlook.
      Thank you,
      [your name]
   h. Click the **Send** button (Figure 7-51).

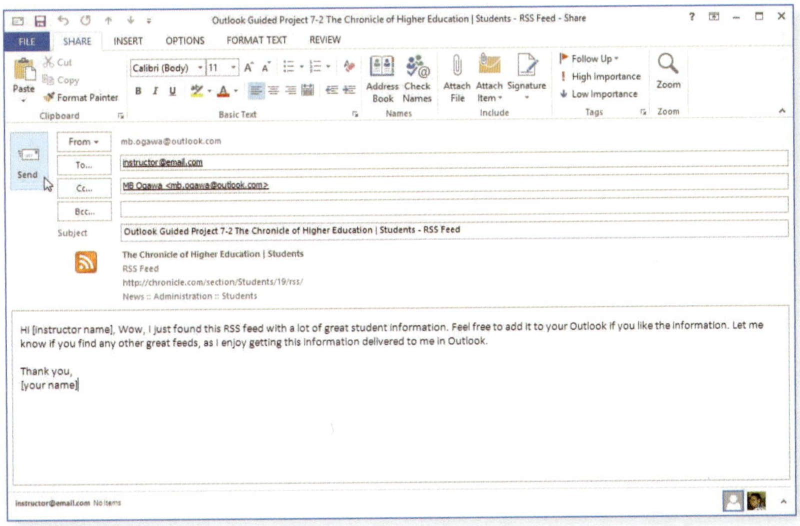

7-51 Completed Guided Project 7-2

Guided Project 7-3

You spoke with your colleague about the RSS feed that you shared. He said that he never received it. You were shocked, so for this project, you search for it and resend it when you get to a WiFi hotspot. [Student Learning Outcome 7.5]

Skills Covered in This Project

- Search using *Instant Search.*
- Use *Scope* to narrow search.
- Use *Refine* to narrow search.

1. Click the **Mail** button in the *Navigation* pane.
2. Click the **Sent Items** folder.
3. Click in the **Search** box at the top of the *Folder* pane.
4. Click the **Current Folder** button [*Search* tab, *Scope* group].
5. Type RSS Feed as the keywords (Figure 7-52).

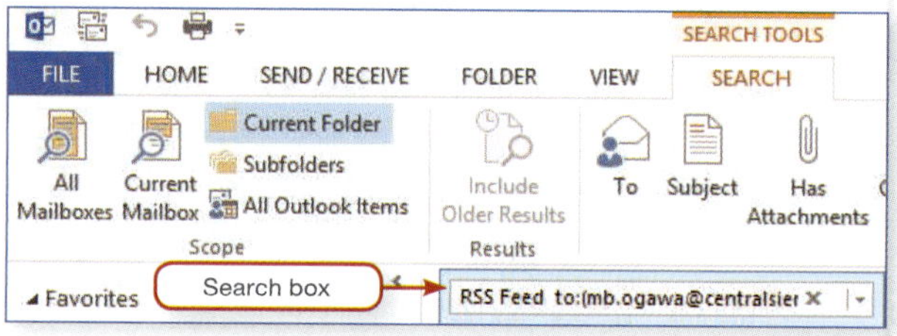

7-52 ***Guided Project 7-3*** **search criteria**

6. Click the **Sent To** button [*Search* tab, *Refine* group] and select **Sent to Another Recipient.**
7. Type your instructor's email address as the keywords.
8. Locate and open the email message for ***Outlook Guided Project 7-2.***
9. Forward the message to your instructor.
   a. Open the email message for ***Outlook Guided Project 7-2.***
   b. Click the **Forward** button [*Share* tab, *Respond* group].
   c. Type your instructor's email address in the *To* field.
   d. Type your email address in the *Cc* field.
   e. Modify the subject to include ***Outlook Guided Project 7-3*** before the RSS feed title.
   f. Add the following message: Hi [instructor's name]. Here is the RSS feed we discussed today. Let me know if you receive it. The news really is awesome!
      Thank you,
      [your name]
   g. Click the **Send** button (Figure 7-53).

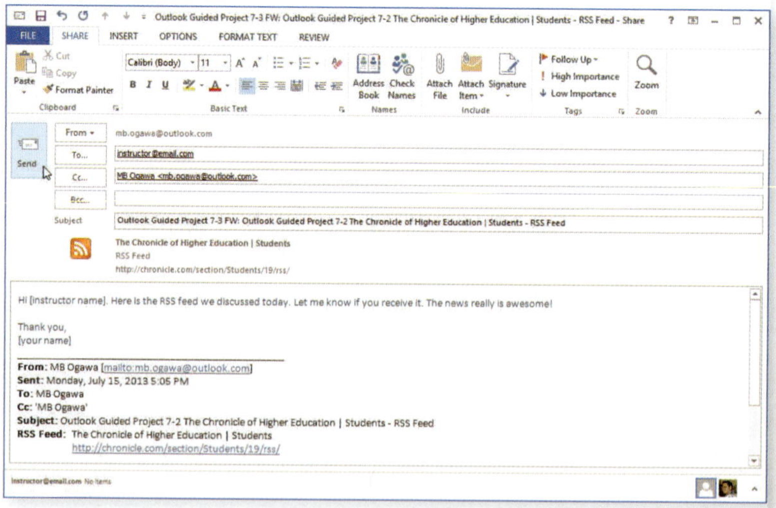

7-53 Completed Guided Project 7-3

Independent Project 7-4

For this project, you are at doctor who works at Courtyard Medical Plaza (CMP). You recently joined the American Medical Association (AMA) using your professional email account. This account is different from your practice account, which you use specifically for email related to your medical practice. Since you use Outlook, you ensure both email accounts are available to make your work more efficient. [Student Learning Outcomes 7.1, 7.2]

Skills Covered in This Project

- Set up an email account.
- Change the default email account.
- Select an account when creating a new message.

1. Add a new account to Outlook. (If you completed *Pause & Practice 7-1* or *Guided Project 7-1,* skip this step).
2. Change the default email account to be your work account (school account).
3. Use the information below to send a message to your patient list indicating that you will be out of town at a conference for the next week (Figure 7-54).

   To: [instructor's email address]
   Cc: [your email address]
   Subject: Outlook Independent Project 7-4
   Message: Hi everyone, I just wanted to let you know that I will be out of town at a conference for the next week. For immediate emergencies, contact my assistant, Jane. She can set up appointments with my colleague, Dr. Goron.
   [your name]

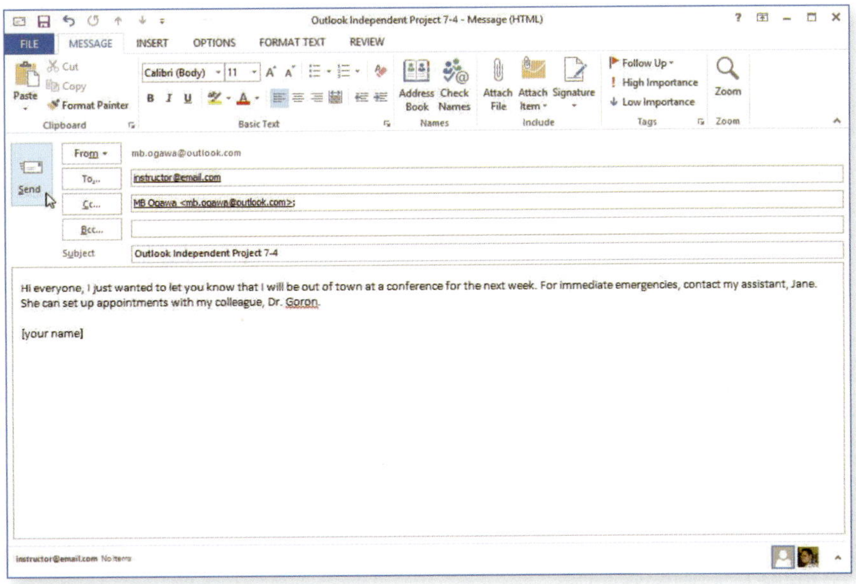

7-54 Completed Independent Project 7-4

Independent Project 7-5

You noticed that more of your patients are discussing stress and nutrition with you. Therefore, for this project, you subscribe to RSS feeds on those subject areas to help you keep abreast of trends. [Student Learning Outcome 7.4]

Skills Covered in This Project

- Add an RSS feed.
- Rename an RSS feed folder.
- Delete an RSS feed.
- Share an RSS feed.

1. Open a browser and navigate to http://www.mayoclinic.com/health/rss/rss.
2. Locate the RSS feeds for ***Stress, Nutrition-wise,*** and ***All MayoClinic.com Topics.***
3. Add all three RSS feeds to your *RSS Feeds* folder.
4. Rename the ***Blog - Stress*** RSS feed ***Stress Information.***
5. Rename the ***Blog – Nutrition-wise*** RSS feed ***Nutrition Information.***
6. Delete the ***All Mayo*** Clinic.com ***Topics*** RSS feed.
7. Share the ***Stress Information*** and ***Nutrition Information*** feeds with your instructor. They will be sent as two messages.
   a. Add the text ***Outlook Independent Project 7-5*** in the subject line before the default subject.
   b. Add your email address to the *Cc* field.
   c. Add a short message to your instructor indicating that you are submitting your completed Independent Project (Figure 7-55).

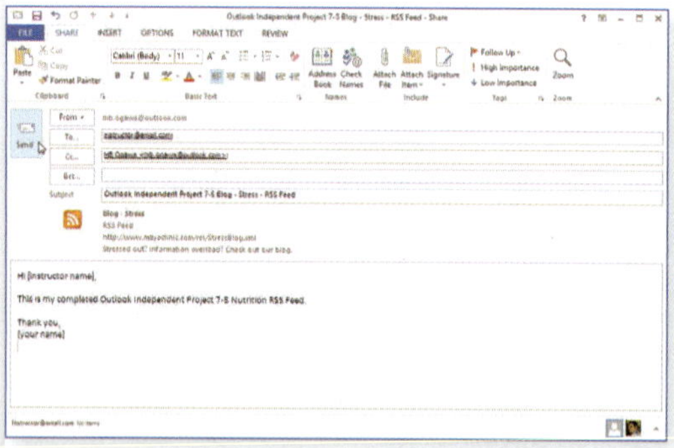

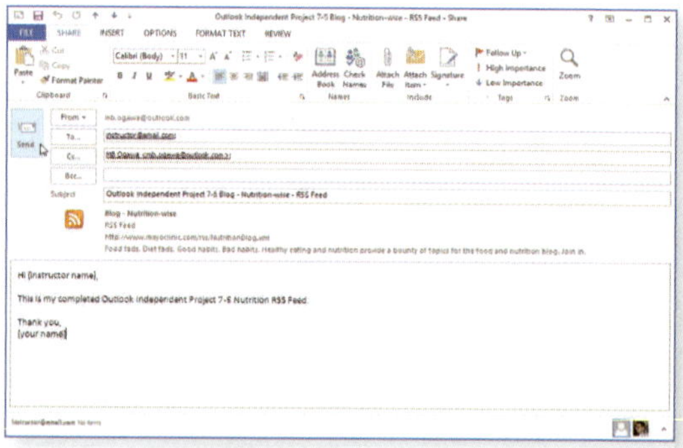

7-55 Completed Independent Project 7-5

Independent Project 7-6

Your patient list email list is not up-to-date. Therefore, some patients may not know that you are away at a conference. For this project, you search for the email you initially sent to your patient list and forward it to the rest of the patients.
[Student Learning Outcome 7.5]

Skills Covered in This Project

- Search using *Instant Search.*
- Use *Scope* to narrow search.
- Use *Refine* to narrow search.
- Use *Advanced Find.*

1. Search for the message you sent in Independent Project 7-4 using *Instant Search* or *Advanced Find.*
2. After locating the message, forward it to your instructor (Figure 7-56).
   a. Be sure to add your address in the *Cc* field.
   b. Add ***Outlook Independent Project 7-6*** in the subject line.
   c. Add a short message to your instructor with the following information:
      Message: Hi everyone. I am not sure if you received this message, so I am forwarding it to you to ensure you are aware that I will be away.
      Thanks,
      [your name]
      Below the message to your patients, include the following search information. Only include the features you utilized:
      Keywords: [keywords for search]
      Scope criteria: [criteria and reason for using it]
      Refine criteria: [criteria and reason for using it]
      Advanced Find criteria: [criteria and reason for using it]

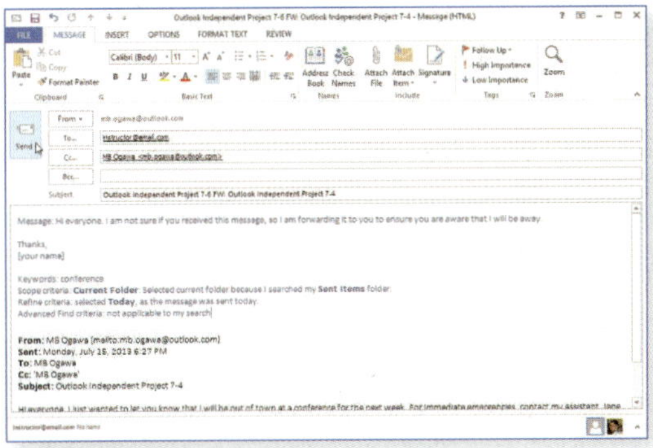

Figure 7-56 Completed Independent Project 7-6

Challenge Project 7-7

Most people have more than one email account. Working with multiple accounts and personalizing Outlook to meet your needs is definitely a challenge. For this project, you identify the different email accounts that you have. Determine if you will need additional accounts for different purposes, such as work, school, and personal. Send an email message to your instructor indicating which one would be set as default and why. Also indicate if and when you would use the Web access counterpart, such as Outlook web access. Lastly, you configure Outlook to better meet your needs and email your instructor which customizations you made to your installation and why. You should customize at least three advanced email options. [Student Learning Outcomes 7.1, 7.2, 7.3]

- Identify the different email accounts that you have.
- Determine if you need additional accounts.
- Determine which account should be the default.
- Determine when the web mail counterpart, such as Outlook Web access would be useful.
- Email your instructor using the following message format:
  Account 1: [purpose for the account]
  Default: [indicate if it is the default account or not and why]
  Web access: [indicate when the Web access counterpart would be useful]
  Account 2: [purpose for the account]
  Default: [indicate if it is the default account or not and why]
  Web access: [indicate when the Web access counterpart would be useful]
  Account 3: [purpose for the account]

Default: [indicate if it is the default account or not and why]
Web access: [indicate when the Web access counterpart would be useful]
Outlook Personalization: [list of features modified]
Feature 1: [indicate modification and reason]
Feature 2: [indicate modification and reason]
Feature 3: [indicate modification and reason]

- Change the subject of your message to Outlook Challenge Project 7-7.

Challenge Project 7-8

Based on your interests, search the web to find at least two RSS feeds that interest you. Add the RSS feeds to your *RSS Feeds* folder and share them with your instructor.
[Student Learning Outcome 7.4]

- Search the web for at least two RSS feeds that interest you.
- Add the feeds to your *RSS Feeds* folder.
- Rename the feeds if you prefer a descriptive title.
- Share the feeds with your instructor (there will be two separate messages).
- Use the following email message format:
  Feed Name: [reason you chose this feed]
  Change the subject of your first message to ***Outlook Challenge Project 7-8 Feed 1.***
- Change the subject of your second message to ***Outlook Challenge Project 7-8 Feed 2.***

Challenge Project 7-9

Identify one email message and one Outlook item that you created in the past year. Email your message and Outlook item as attachments to your instructor. Include your search criteria to find the message and Outlook item and why you would use the criteria for it.
[Student Learning Outcome 7.5]

- Identify an email message and Outlook item you created in the last year.
- Determine search criteria to find the message and Outlook item.
- You should include keywords in your search.
- For the email message, use one scope and one refine search criteria.
- For the Outlook item, use at least two criteria in addition to keywords.
- Include reasons for your search criteria.
- Email your instructor using the following message format:
  Email message: [Outlook attachment name]
  Keywords: [keywords for search]
  Scope criteria: [criteria and reason for using it]
  Refine criteria: [criteria and reason for using it]
  Outlook item: [Outlook attachment name]
  Keywords: [keywords for search]
  Criteria 1: [criteria and reason for using it]
  Criteria 2: [criteria and reason for using it]
- Change the subject of your message to ***Outlook Challenge Project 7-9.***

CHAPTER 6

Folders, Rules, Quick Steps, and Search Folders

OUTLOOK

CHAPTER OVERVIEW

After completing the first half of this book, you now have a good understanding of the main components of Outlook—Email, Contacts, Calendar, and Tasks. Building on this essential foundation, we will delve into the numerous ways you can customize Outlook to best meet your needs. Outlook provides you with a range of features to help organize, categorize, and prioritize items within Outlook. Using *folders, Quick Steps, rules,* and *search folders* will help you to become a more efficient and effective Outlook user.

STUDENT LEARNING OUTCOMES (SLOs)

After completing this chapter, you will be able to:

SLO 6.1 Create, arrange, and modify Outlook folders (p. O6-210).

SLO 6.2 Create, apply, and change Outlook rules (p. O6-214).

SLO 6.3 Customize and use *Quick Steps* (p. O6-224).

SLO 6.4 Utilize search folders to find email messages (p. O6-229).

CASE STUDY

For the Pause & Practice projects, you prepare for a group project and class by using folders, rules, Quick Steps, and search folders to help you more effectively and efficiently manage your email.

Pause & Practice 6-1: You create folders to help you keep your email messages organized. You begin by creating folders for your class, instructor, group project partners, and best friend. You delete the folder for your best friend, as she always sends you text messages, as opposed to email messages.

Pause & Practice 6-2: You create two rules. The first rule is to move email from a specific instructor to the folder you created in the first Pause & Practice. The second rule moves all of your email messages from both of your group members into the folder you created in the first Pause & Practice.

Pause & Practice 6-3: You create two *Quick Steps* to help you be more efficient when working with email. For the first *Quick Step,* your instructor indicated that he or she wants you to email with a specific subject line. Rather than ensuring you type the right subject line for each message, you create a *Quick Step* for those messages. For the second *Quick Step,* you create tasks out of email messages for your group project to ensure you can view your work to complete in your tasks instead of searching through many email messages.

Pause & Practice 6-4: You utilize search folders to help you find information quickly. You create a search folder for email messages from your partners with attachments to allow you to easily locate files you are working with. You also want to use a search folder to quickly locate email messages from your instructor with the word *due* to quickly find messages with due dates or changes to due dates.

SLO 6.1

Using Folders

Most of you have some sort of filing system in your home. You might have a filing cabinet with separate folders for bills, insurance, tax papers, investments, and so forth. Can you imagine having just one drawer in your filing cabinet and throwing everything in that drawer? What a mess it would be and how hard it would be to find a specific item.

When using your computer, you create folders to store various files. You might create and use different folders in the *Documents* folder to store tax information files, Grand Canyon road trip files, or recipes, for example. These Windows folders are generic folders in that they can store various types of files: Word, Excel, .pdf, pictures, and others.

In Outlook, folders can be used to help organize and group your emails, contacts, calendar, tasks, notes, and journals. In contrast to the generic type of folders used in Windows, Outlook folders are specific to the type of Outlook items they store. For example, a *Mail* folder is used to store email and a *Task* folder is used to store tasks.

Create a Folder

Creating folders in Outlook is actually very simple. The most important aspect to remember is that each Outlook folder is created to store a specific type of Outlook item. When the ***Create New Folder*** dialog box is opened, it is important to confirm the type of folder you are creating and the location of the file.

In Outlook the following types of folders can be created:

- *Calendar Items*
- *Contact Items*
- *InfoPath Form Items*
- *Journal Items*
- *Mail and Post Items*
- *Note Items*
- *Task Items*

Follow these steps to create a new *Mail* folder. The steps are the same for creating any type of Outlook folder.

HOW TO: Create a Folder

1. Click the **Mail** button in the *Navigation* pane.
2. Click the **Folder** tab.
3. Click the **New Folder** button in the *New* group (Figure 6-1). The *Create New Folder* dialog box opens (Figure 6-2).
4. Type the name of the new folder to be created.
5. In the *Folder contains* menu, confirm that the folder type is ***Mail and Post Items.***

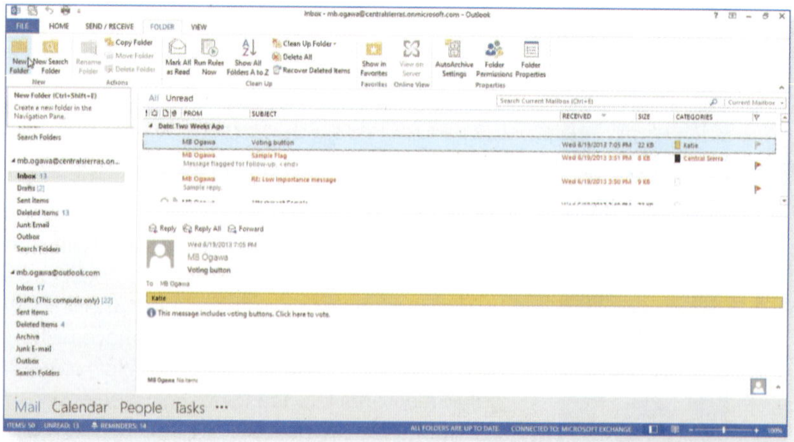

6-1 ***New Folder*** **button**

6. In the *Select where to place the folder* section, specify the location in which to save the new folder.
7. Click **OK.**

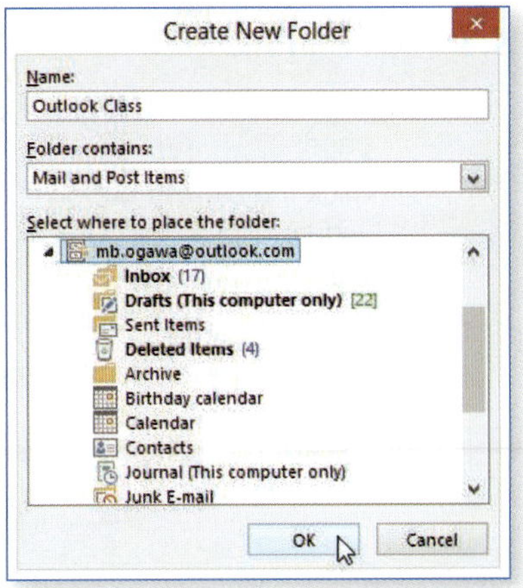

6-2 ***Create New Folder*** **dialog box**

> **ANOTHER WAY**
>
> You can create a new folder by right-clicking the folder inside which you would like to create a new folder and then selecting **New Folder.**

> **ANOTHER WAY**
>
> **Ctrl+Shift+E** opens the *Create New Folder* dialog box throughout Outlook.

Move a Folder

There might be times when you add a new folder in the wrong location or you might just want to move a folder from one location to another. The easiest way to move a folder to a new location is to click the folder in the *Navigation* pane and drag and drop it on the new location. The folder and all its contents will be moved to the new location.

Another way to move a folder is to use the ***Move*** feature.

HOW TO: Move a Folder

1. In the *Navigation* pane, select the folder to be moved.
2. Click the **Folder** tab.
3. Click the **Move Folder** button in the *Actions* group (Figure 6-3). The *Move Folder* dialog box opens (Figure 6-4).
4. In the *Move the selected folder to the folder* section, click the desired location to move the folder.
5. Click **OK.** The folder and all its contents will be moved to the new location.

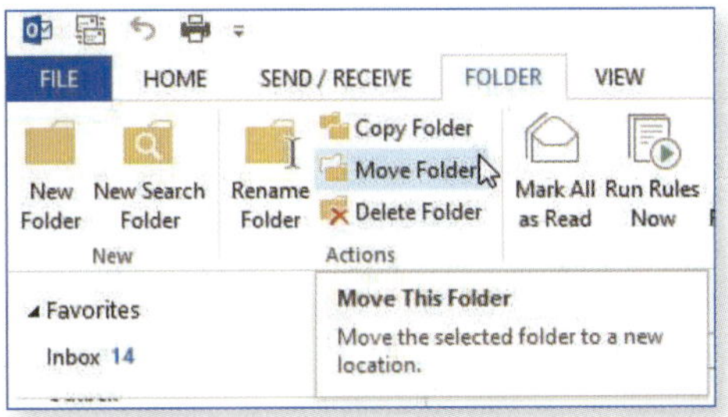

6-3 ***Move Folder*** **button**

> **ANOTHER WAY**
>
> You can right-click the folder to be moved and choose **Move Folder,** or you can simply drag and drop the folder to a new location in the *Navigation* pane.

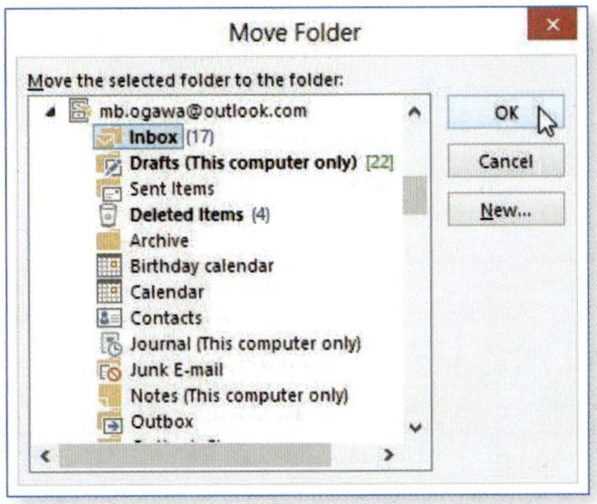

6-4 ***Move Folder*** **dialog box**

Delete a Folder

Folders are sometimes created to store information temporarily. Folders can be deleted when they are no longer needed. When you delete a folder, all the items in the folder are deleted as well. The deleted folder is stored in the *Deleted Items* folder.

HOW TO: Delete a Folder

1. To delete a folder, select the folder to be deleted in the *Navigation* pane.
2. Click the **Delete** button in the *Actions* group on the *Folder* tab (Figure 6-5).
   - A warning dialog box opens asking you if you are sure you want to delete the folder and its contents.
3. Click **Yes** to delete the folder and all its contents.

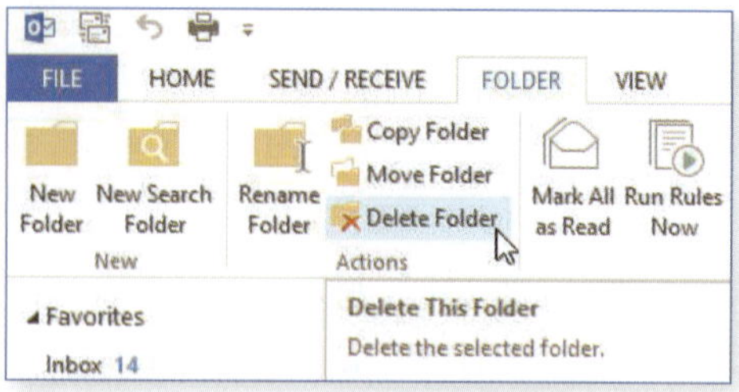

6-5 ***Delete Folder*** **button**

> **ANOTHER WAY**
>
> Right-click the folder to be deleted and choose **Delete Folder.**

> **ANOTHER WAY**
>
> **Ctrl+D** deletes the selected item. This shortcut will delete a folder or other selected Outlook items.

Use the Folders List

When you are in the Mail, Calendar, Contacts, Tasks, Notes, or Journal areas, only those folders associated with that part of Outlook are displayed in the *Navigation* pane. The ***Folders list*** (Figure 6-6) is a useful view to display all your Outlook folders in the *Navigation* pane.

The *Folders* list view can be used to view your folder structure in Outlook. This is also a good view to use when you are moving folders from one location to another.

> **MORE INFO**
>
> In all the areas of Outlook except Mail and the *Folders* list, your folders are not displayed in hierarchical structure. In other words in these other areas, it is hard to know whether or not a folder is located inside of another folder.

The *Folders* list can be displayed in the *Navigation* pane by clicking the *Folders* button at the bottom of the *Navigation* pane.

> **ANOTHER WAY**
>
> **Ctrl+6** displays the *Folders* list in the *Navigation* pane.

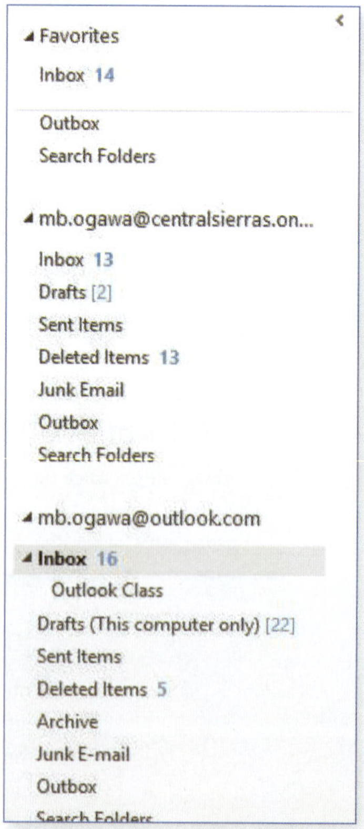

6-6 ***Folders*** **list**

PAUSE & PRACTICE: OUTLOOK 6-1

For this Pause and Practice project, you create folders to help you keep your email messages organized. You begin by creating folders for your class, instructor, group project partners, and best friend. You delete the folder for your best friend, as she always sends you text messages, as opposed to email messages.

1. Create a folder for your class.
   a. Click the **Mail** button in the *Navigation* pane.
   b. Click the **Folder** tab.
   c. Click the **New Folder** button in the *New* group. The *Create New Folder* dialog box opens.
   d. Type BUS 100 in the *Name* text area.
   e. In the *Folder contains* menu, confirm that the folder type is **Mail and Post Items.**
   f. In the *Select where to place the folder* section, specify your main email account folder.
   g. Click **OK.**
2. Create a folder for your instructor.
   a. Click the **Mail** button in the *Navigation* pane.
   b. Click the **Folder** tab.
   c. Click the **New Folder** button in the *New* group. The *Create New Folder* dialog box opens.
   d. Type your instructor's name in the *Name* text area.
   e. In the *Folder contains* menu, confirm that the folder type is **Mail and Post Items.**
   f. In the *Select where to place the folder* section, specify your main email account folder.
   g. Click **OK.**
3. Create a folder for your group project.
   a. Click the **Mail** button in the *Navigation* pane.
   b. Click the **Folder** tab.
   c. Click the **New Folder** button in the *New* group. The *Create New Folder* dialog box opens.
   d. Type Group Project in the *Name* text area.
   e. In the *Folder contains* menu, confirm that the folder type is **Mail and Post Items.**
   f. In the *Select where to place the folder* section, specify your main email account folder.
   g. Click **OK.**
4. Create a folder for your best friend.
   a. Click the **Mail** button in the *Navigation* pane.
   b. Click the **Folder** tab.
   c. Click the **New Folder** button in the *New* group. The *Create New Folder* dialog box opens.
   d. Type Nicole in the *Name* text area.
   e. In the *Folder contains* menu, confirm that the folder type is **Mail and Post Items.**
   f. In the *Select where to place the folder* section, specify your main email account folder.
   g. Click **OK.**
5. Move the *[instructor name]* and *Group Project* folders into the *[class name]* folder.
   a. In the *Navigation* pane, select *[instructor name]* folder.
   b. Click the **Folder** tab.
   c. Click the **Move Folder** button in the *Actions* group. The *Move Folder* dialog box opens.
   d. In the *Move the selected folder to the folder* section, click the **BUS 100** folder.
   e. Click **OK.**
6. Move the *Group Project* folder into the *BUS 100* folder.
   a. In the *Navigation* pane, select **Group Project folder.**
   b. Click the **Folder** tab.
   c. Click the **Move Folder** button in the *Actions* group. The *Move Folder* dialog box opens.

d. In the *Move the selected folder to the folder* section, click the *[class name]* folder.
e. Click **OK.**

7. Delete the *Nicole* folder.
   a. Select the **Nicole folder** in the *Navigation* pane.
   b. Click the **Delete** button in the *Actions* group on the *Folder* tab.
   c. A warning dialog box opens asking you if you are sure you want to delete the folder and its contents. Click **Yes** to delete the folder and all its contents.
8. Figure 6-7 is a sample of your folder list at the end of Pause & Practice 6-1.

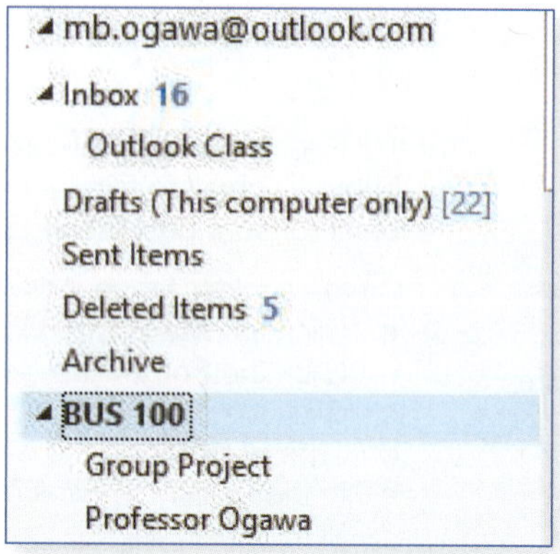

6-7 Completed Pause & Practice 6-1

SLO 6.2

Creating and Using Rules

You might receive an enormous amount of emails everyday. You may receive many email messages from each of your instructors for your courses, or from family members keeping in touch with email instead of social networking sites. If all these emails ended up in your Inbox, it would be hard to distinguish which email message was for a specific course you are enrolled in; or you might miss an important message from a family member. You can create folders and set up rules to automatically move email messages from instructors to an appropriate course folder. This will help you to keep your messages organized without the work of moving them.

Rules might be one of the most useful features in Outlook. It can be used to check incoming or outgoing emails and apply some type of action. If you have ever used the *IF* function in Microsoft Excel, rules operate similar to this if/then logical principle. Most rules have two basic parts: a ***condition*** and an ***action.*** There is also an ***exception*** that can be added to the rule.

- ***Condition:*** The condition is what Outlook is looking for when an email is received or sent. This could be an email that includes a specific word or words in the subject or body, sent from a specific person, received through a specific email account, or marked as high importance.
- ***Action:*** The action is what is done with the email when the condition is met. This could include moving the email to another folder, marking the email as high importance, categorizing the email with a specific category, deleting the email, or forwarding the email to someone else.
- ***Exception:*** An exception can be used to nullify an action. For example, a rule can be set up to look for the word "BUS 310" in the subject line and move it to the *BUS 310* folder, except if it comes from the *Dean of the CSIT* area. Exceptions are not commonly used in rules.

Quick Steps are similar to rules, but do not include a condition. So rather than automatically applying an action to an email when it meets a condition, *Quick Steps* can be applied to email on an individual basis. For example, a *Quick Step* can be used to create a meeting request from a received email message.

Create a Quick Rule

A rule can be created quickly based on an email in your Inbox. These quick rules can be used for many of the common rules used in Outlook. These rules have a limited number of options for the condition and action and do not include options for exceptions.

If an email arrives in your Inbox with the subject "Outlook," and you know that there is going to be an email discussion with others based on this topic, a rule can quickly be created to move all emails with the word "Outlook" to an *Outlook* folder to keep all these related messages together.

HOW TO: Create a Rule Based on an Email in Your Inbox

1. In your *Inbox,* open the email for which you would like to create a new rule.
2. Click the **Rules** button in the *Move* group on the *Message* tab.
3. Choose **Create Rule** (Figure 6-8). The *Create Rule* dialog box opens. The three conditions are at the top and the three actions are at the bottom of this dialog box (Figure 6-9).

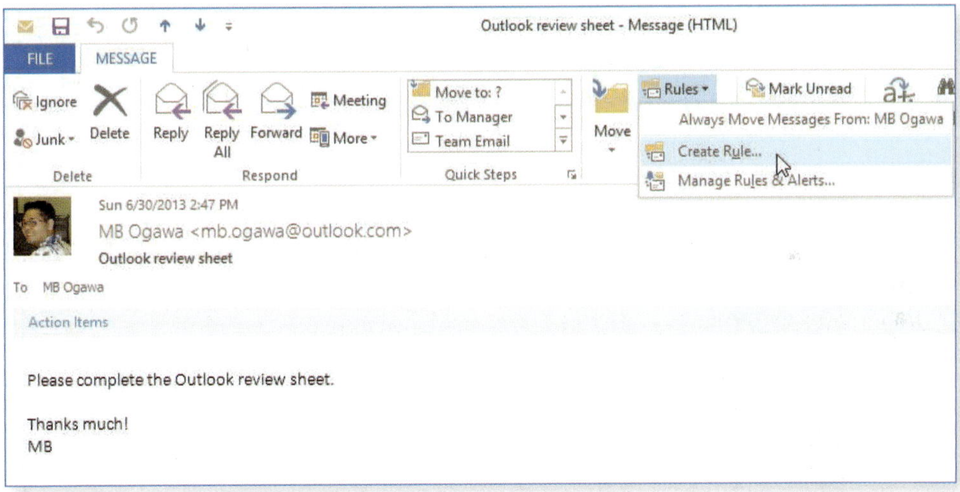

6-8 *Create Rule*

4. In the conditions area (the top half of the dialog box), select the **Subject contains** check box and make sure the word in the subject is correct. If not, correct it.
5. In the actions area (the bottom half of the dialog box), select the **Move the item to folder** check box and click the **Select Folder** button.
6. Select the desired folder from the folder list and press **OK** (Figure 6-10). The *Create Rule* dialog box will still be open. Confirm that the correct folder was selected (Figure 6-10). If not, click the **Select Folder** button and select the correct folder.

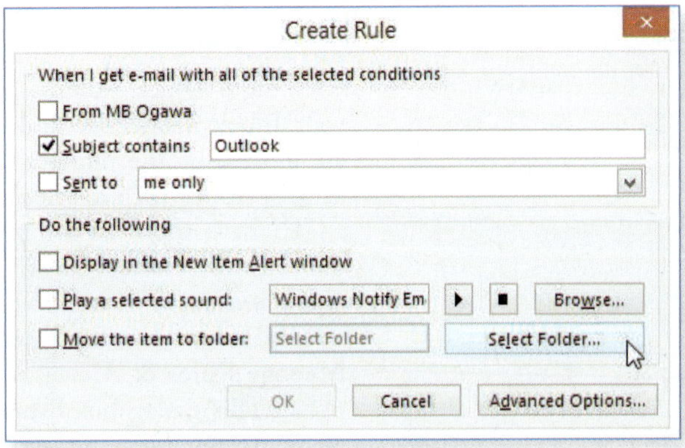

6-9 *Create Rule* dialog box

7. Click **OK.** A *Success* dialog box opens (Figure 6-11).
8. Select the **Run this rule now on messages already in the current folder** check box.
9. Click **OK.**
10. All the emails in your Inbox with a subject that matches the condition will be moved to the specified folder.

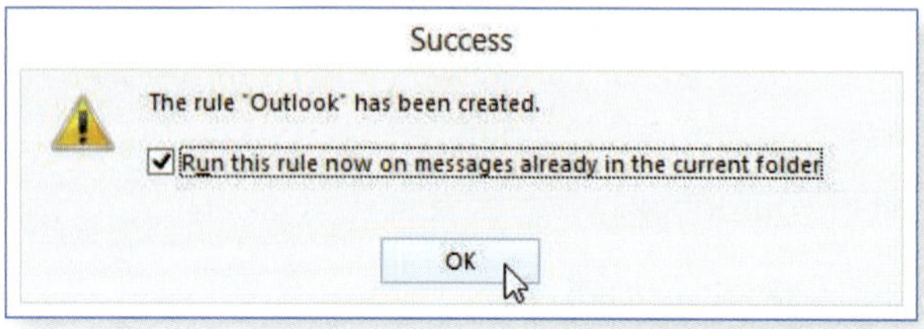

6-11 *Success* dialog box

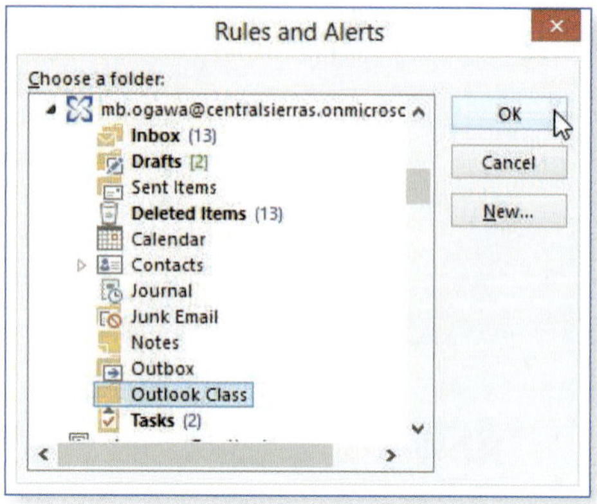

6-10 Select a folder for the rule

MORE INFO

If you forget to create a folder before creating a rule, you can create a new folder in the *Rules and Alerts* dialog box by clicking the **New** button.

MORE INFO

When creating a rule that looks for a word in the subject, Outlook looks for *exactly* what you type. Common errors include misspellings and a space after the word. The word you type is not case sensitive.

ANOTHER WAY

When an email is selected in your *Folder* pane, a Quick Rule can be created by clicking the *Rules* button in the *Move* group or by right-clicking the message and choosing **Rules** and then **Create Rule.**

Create an Advanced Rule

Creating a Quick Rule based on an email in your Inbox is effective and efficient, but you are limited by the number of conditions and actions from which to select.

To have more customization options for the rules you create, you will need to open the ***Rules and Alerts*** dialog box (click the **Home** tab, **Rules** button in the *Move* group, and select **Manage Rules & Alerts** as shown in Figure 6-12). This dialog box lists the rules existing on your computer and allows you to create, modify, delete, and order the existing rules.

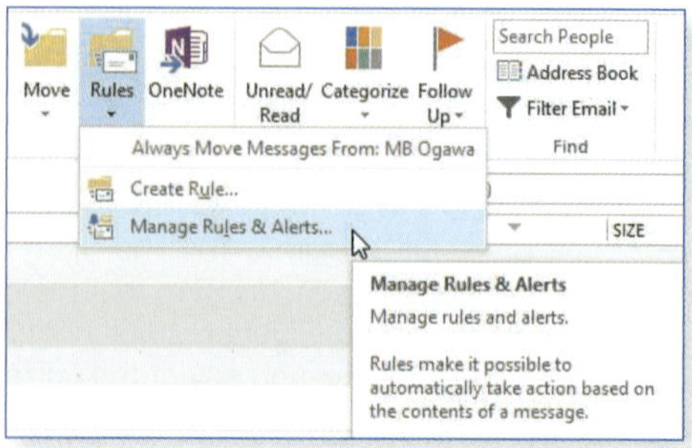

6-12 *Manage Rules & Alerts*

When you click the *New Rule* button (Figure 6-13), the *Rules Wizard* dialog box opens. The *Rules Wizard* will step you through the creation of your rule. There will be five steps in the *Rules Wizard* dialog box to create your new rule.

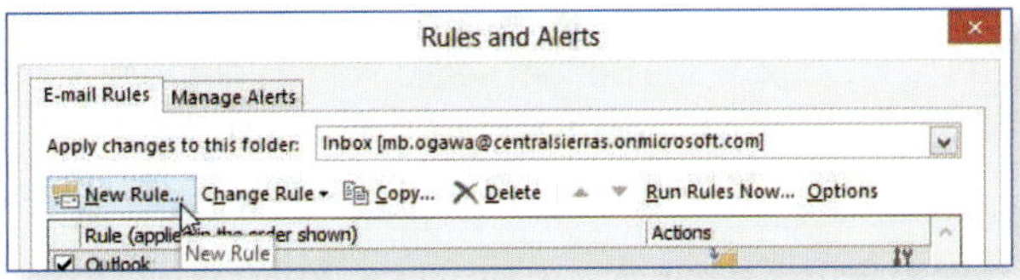

6-13 Create a new rule

- *Step 1:* Choose to use a rule template or create a blank rule. This step will also determine whether this rule is to be applied to incoming or outgoing emails.
- *Step 2:* Select the condition of the rule.
- *Step 3:* Set the action Outlook is to perform if the *condition* is met.
- *Step 4:* Specify any exceptions to the rule.
- *Step 5:* Name and run the rule.

There are rule templates created for the most common types of rules used. When one of these is selected, you will be taken to the next step to specify the condition. You can also choose to start creating a rule from a blank rule.

HOW TO: Create a New Rule

1. Click the **Mail** button in the *Navigation* pane.
2. Create a new folder in your *Inbox.*
3. Click the **Rules** button in the *Move* group on the *Home* tab, and choose **Manage Rules & Alerts.** The *Rules and Alerts* dialog box opens.
4. Click the **New Rule** button. The *Rules Wizard* dialog box opens.
5. Select **Apply rule on messages I receive** in the *Start from a blank rule* section (Figure 6-14).
6. Click **Next.** You will be taken to the next step to select a condition for the rule.

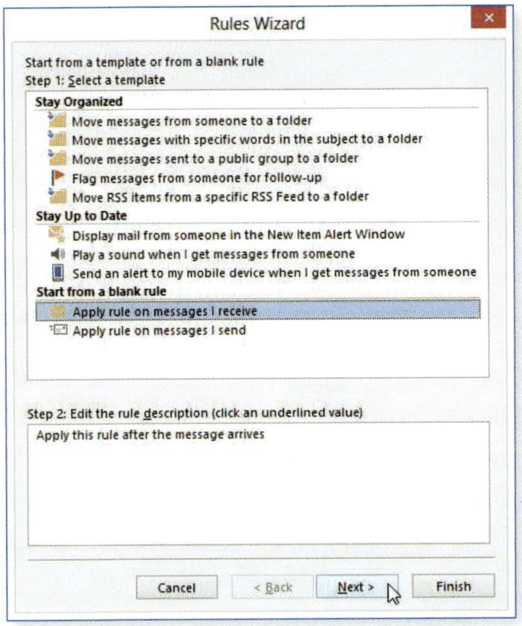

6-14 Create a new blank rule

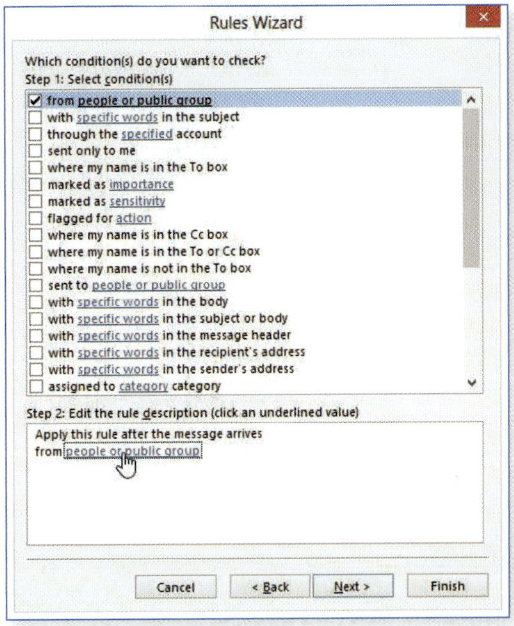

6-15 Click the people or public group link

7. Select the **from people or public group** check box. In the bottom section of this dialog box, the condition is displayed.
8. Click the **people or public group** link in the bottom section (Figure 6-15). The *Rule Address* dialog box opens.
9. Select the name of the individual for the condition of the rule (Figure 6-16).
10. Click **From** and **OK.**
    - The *Rule Address* dialog box will close, and you will be taken back to the *Rules Wizard* dialog box.
    - Notice the person's name appears in the bottom section as the condition for which Outlook is looking.
11. Click **Next.** You will be taken to the *action* step in the *Rules Wizard* dialog box.

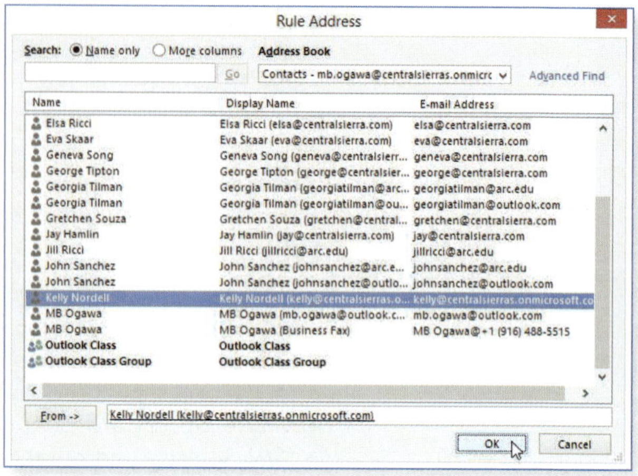

6-16 Select addresses

12. Select the **move it to the specified folder** check box (Figure 6-17).
13. In the bottom section, click the **specified** folder link. The *Rules and Alerts* dialog box opens.
14. Click the desired folder and press **OK** (Figure 6-18). You will be taken back to the *Rules Wizard* dialog box. Always read the rule in the bottom section to make sure the condition and action are correct.
15. Click **Next.** You will be taken to the *exceptions* step.
16. Click **Next.** There will be no exceptions to this rule. The *Finish rule setup* step appears.
17. Customize the name of the rule in the *Step 1* area.
18. Select the **Run this rule now on messages already in "Inbox"** check box (Figure 6-19).

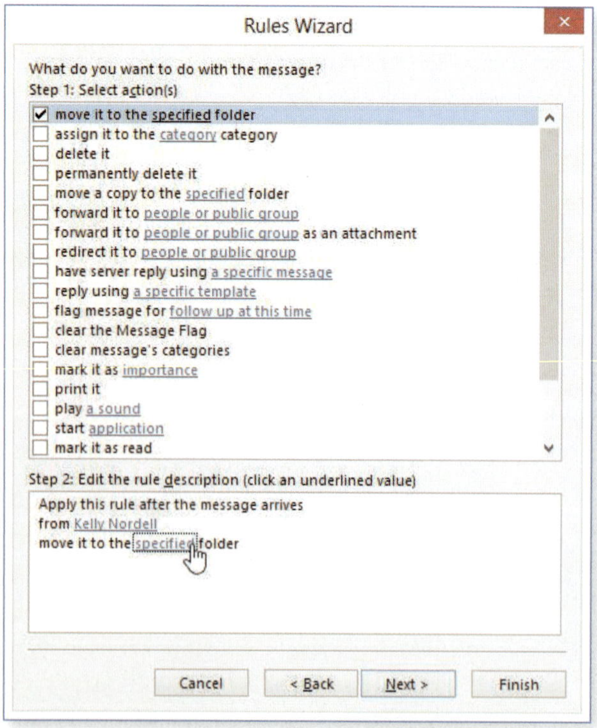

6-17 Select an action

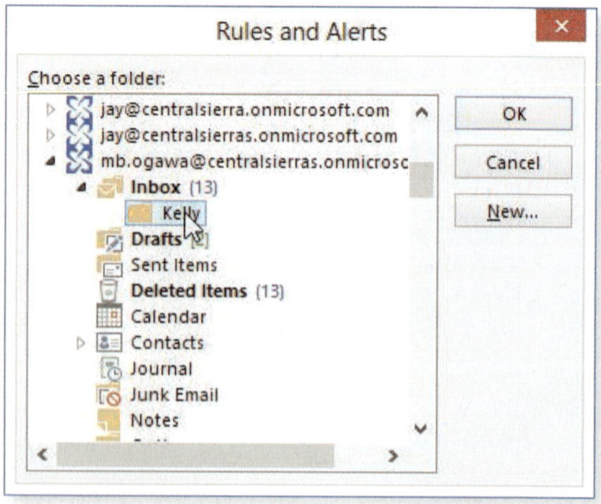

6-18 Select a location

19. Confirm that the **Turn on this rule** box is selected.
20. In the bottom section, read the rule one last time to confirm that the condition and action are correct.
21. Click **Finish.**
    - The rule will check the condition on all the emails in your Inbox.
    - If the condition is met, Outlook will move all emails matching the condition to the folder you created (see Figure 6-19).

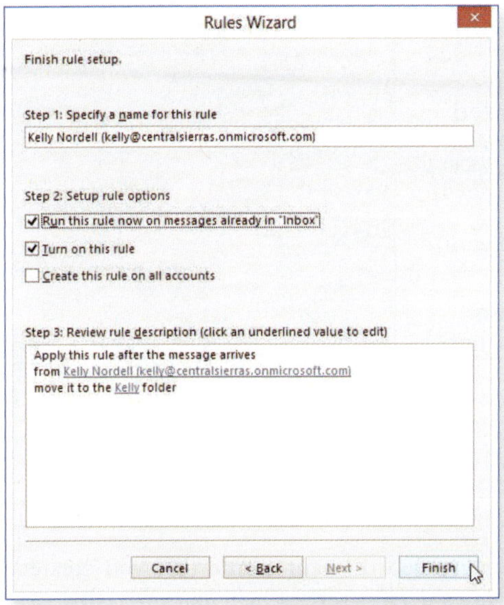

6-19 Setup rule options

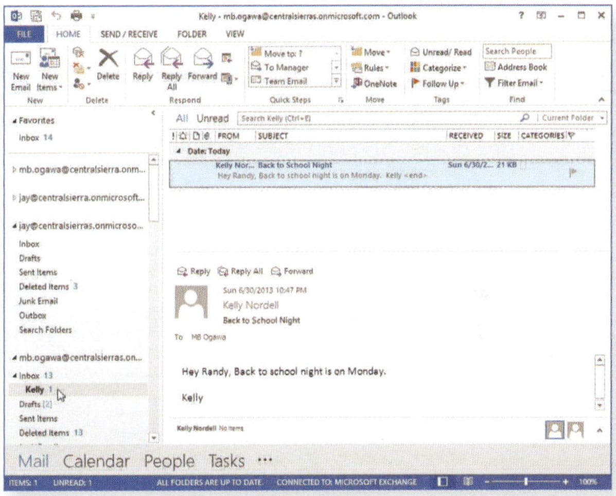

6-20 Email message automatically moved

22. You will be taken back to the *Rules and Alerts* dialog box. Notice the new rule is in the list of rules.
23. Click **Apply** and then **OK.** See how the email from Kelly was automatically moved into the *Kelly* folder (Figure 6-20).

Creating rules might seem like a daunting process, but once you have gone through the steps of creating a rule and understand the logical ***condition, action, exception*** sequence, you'll realize that creating rules is actually very simple. And not only are rules easy to create and use, but they are also very effective in helping you to organize and customize your Inbox, which will ultimately make you a more proficient and productive Outlook user.

> **MORE INFO**
>
> It is best to keep rules simple: one condition and one action (and an exception if necessary). The more conditions and actions you have in one rule, the greater the chance of either diluting the effectiveness of the rule or causing the rule to not function as intended.

> **MORE INFO**
>
> When using Outlook in a stand-alone environment, your rules are stored on your computer. If you are using Outlook in an Exchange environment, your rules are stored on the Exchange server. This means that most rules will run wherever you access Outlook, including Outlook Web Access. Some rules are client-only rules, which means they will only run on the computer on which they were created.

Modify a Rule

Once a rule is created, it is very easy to modify the condition, action, or exception. Rules can also be modified to run on different folders within your mailbox.

HOW TO: Modify a Rule

1. Open the *Rules and Alerts* dialog box.
2. Select the rule to be modified, click the **Change Rule** button, and choose **Edit Rule Settings** (Figure 6-21). The *Rules Wizard* dialog box opens. You can also double-click the rule to open the *Rules Wizard* dialog box.
3. You can change the condition, action, exception, name, or folder on which the rule is to run.
4. If you modify a rule, be sure to select the **Run this rule now on messages already in "Inbox"** check box and click **Finish** to apply the changes and run the rule.

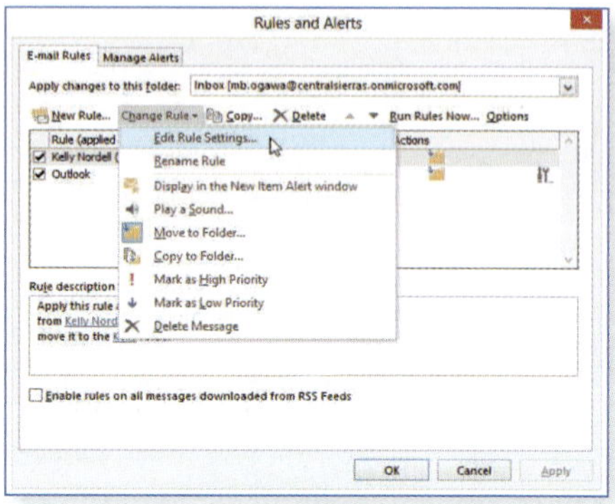

6-21 ***Edit Rule Settings***

Delete or Turn On/Off a Rule

There will be times when you will no longer need or want a rule that you created previously. A rule can easily be deleted by selecting the rule in the *Rules and Alerts* dialog box and either pressing the *Delete* button or right-clicking the rule and choosing *Delete*.

Sometimes you might want to turn off a rule but not delete it because you might use it again sometime in the future. Rules can easily be turned off so that no action will be performed.

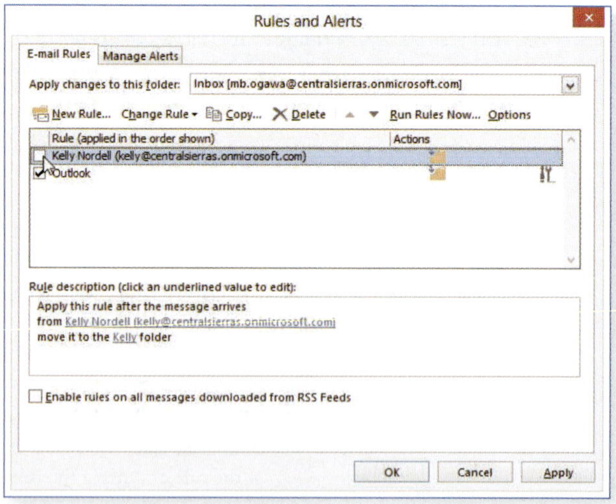

6-22 Turn a rule off

HOW TO: Turn off a Rule

1. Open the *Rules and Alerts* dialog box.
2. Deselect the check box to the left of the rule to turn it off (Figure 6-22).
3. Click **Apply** and then **OK.** The rule is now turned off.

A rule can be turned back on by checking the box to the left of the rule in the *Rules and Alerts* dialog box. It is easy to view which rules are on or off by looking at your list of rules in the *Rules and Alerts* dialog box. A check in the check box indicates that a rule is turned on, and no check in the check box indicates that a rule is turned off.

MORE INFO

Outlook has a default rule (*Clear categories on mail*) that has been created for you. This rule clears any categories on incoming messages. It is important to keep this rule because you do not want others' categories conflicting with your categories.

Run a Rule

When a rule that was turned off is turned back on, it is important to run this rule on messages currently in the Inbox. Outlook provides you with a feature to run specific rules without having to step through the *Rules Wizard.*

You will be given the options of selecting the rules to be run, the folder on which to run each rule, and what type of messages on which to apply each rule (*All Messages, Unread Messages,* or *Read Messages*). A ***Rule Description*** is provided in the middle of this dialog box for the selected rule.

HOW TO: Run a Rule

1. Click the **Rules** button [*Home* tab, *Move* group] and select **Manage Rules & Alerts.**
2. Select the *Rule* you want to run and click the **Run Rules Now** button. The *Run Rules Now* dialog box opens (Figure 6-23).
3. Check the rule to run. The *Rule Description* area will display the condition and action (and exception if applicable) of this rule.
4. Specify the folder on which the rule is to run.
5. Specify the types of messages on which to apply the rule.
6. Click **Run Now.**
7. Click **Close** to close the *Run Rules Now* dialog box.

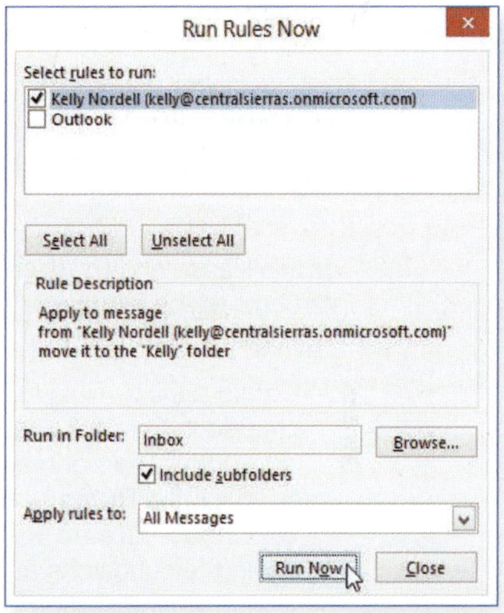

6-23 *Run Rules Now* dialog box

ANOTHER WAY

The *Run Rules Now* dialog box can also be accessed from the *Rules and Alerts* dialog box.

Rearrange Rules

As you begin using rules, you will find more and more uses for them. It will not be long before you have a long list of rules running in Outlook. The rules in Outlook are ***hierarchical,*** which means that those at the top of the list are run before those at the bottom. It is important to order rules properly to prioritize the order in which the rules are run and minimize the potential for conflict. For example, if you have a rule to mark an email as important if it comes from a particular person and a rule to move all emails with attachments to an *Attachments* folder, you might have a conflict if you receive an email from that particular person and it has an attachment. If the attachment rule is above the mark as important rule, the email message will be moved to the *Attachments* folder but not marked as important.

You will need to determine which action is the most important and make sure that rule is above the other rules in the *Rules and Alerts* dialog box. There are up and down buttons in the dialog box that can be used to move rules up or down in the rule hierarchy.

HOW TO: Reorder Rules

1. Open the *Rules and Alerts* dialog box.
2. Select the rule to be moved up or down in priority.
3. Click the *Move Up* or *Move Down* button (Figure 6-24).
4. Click **Apply** and **OK.**

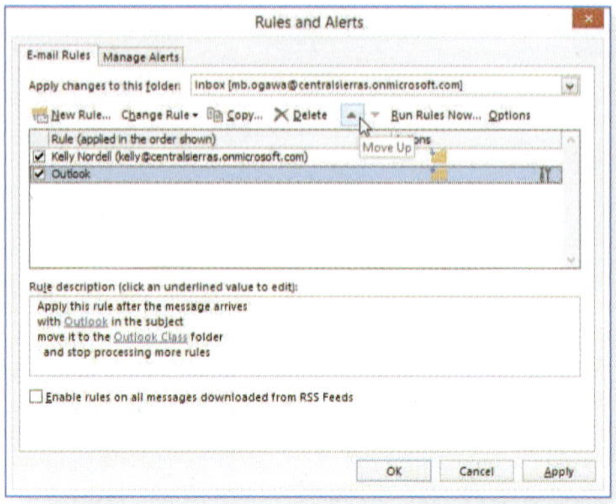

6-24 Move rules up or down

PAUSE & PRACTICE: OUTLOOK 6-2

For this Pause and Practice project, you create two rules. The first rule is to move email from a specific instructor to the folder you created in *Pause & Practice 6-1.* The second rule moves all of your email messages from both of your group members into the folder you created in *Pause & Practice 6-1.*

1. Create a Quick Rule to move email messages from your instructor into the *[instructor name]* folder you created in *Pause & Practice 6-1* (Figure 6-25).
   a. Locate and open a message from your instructor.
   b. Click the **Rules** button in the *Move* group on the *Message* tab.
   c. Choose **Create Rule.** The *Create Rule* dialog box opens.
   d. In the conditions area (the top half of the dialog box), check **From [instructor name]** (the name will vary based on your instructor's name).
   e. In the actions area (the bottom half of the dialog box), check **Move the item to folder** and click the **Select Folder** button.
   f. Select the **[instructor name]** folder from the folder list and press **OK.** The *Create Rule* dialog box will still be open.
   g. Click **OK.**
   h. Select the **Run this rule now on messages already in "Inbox"** check box.
   i. Click **OK.**
2. Create an advanced rule to move emails from your two partners into the *Group Project* folder (Figure 6-25).
   a. Click the **Mail** button in the *Navigation* pane.
   b. Click the **Rules** button in the *Move* group on the *Home* tab and choose **Manage Rules & Alerts.** The *Rules and Alerts* dialog box opens.
   c. Click the **New Rule** button. The *Rules Wizard* dialog box opens.
   d. Select **Apply rule on messages I receive** in the *Start from a blank rule* section.
   e. Click **Next.** You will be taken to the next step to select a condition for the rule.
   f. Check the **from people or public group** box. In the bottom section of this dialog box, the condition is displayed.

g. Click the **people or public group** link in the bottom section. The *Rule Address* dialog box opens.
h. Select the names of your group members if they are in your contacts list or type their email addresses with a semi colon (;) between their email addresses.
i. Click **From** and **OK.**
j. Click **Next.** You will be taken to the *action* step in the *Rules Wizard* dialog box.
k. Check the **move it to the specified folder** box.
l. In the bottom section, click the **specified** folder link. The *Rules and Alerts* dialog box opens.

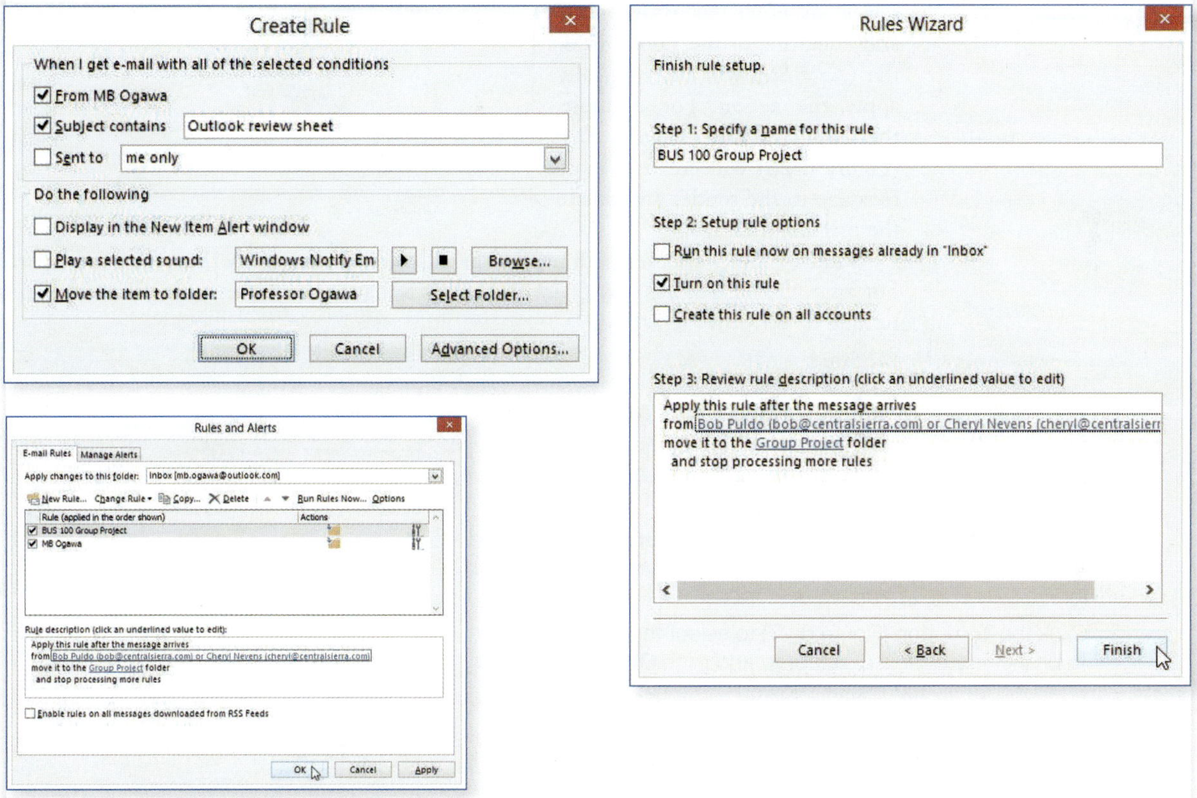

6-25 Completed Pause & Practice 6-2

m. Click the **Group Project** folder and press **OK.** You will be taken back to the *Rules Wizard* dialog box.
n. Click **Next.** You will be taken to the *exceptions* step.
o. Click **Next.** There will be no exceptions to this rule. The *Finish rule setup* step appears.
p. Type Class Name Group Project in the *Step 1* area.
q. Confirm that the **Turn on this rule** box is selected.
r. In the bottom section, read the rule one last time to confirm that the condition and action are correct.
s. Click **Finish.**
t. Click **Apply** and then **OK.**

SLO 6.3

Using Quick Steps

Quick Steps are powerful tools in Outlook. Similar to a rule, a *Quick Step* performs an action on a selected email. The main difference between a *Quick Step* and a rule is that *Quick Steps* are not based on a condition, but rather they are applied to the emails you select.

Modify an Existing Quick Step

Outlook has some preset *Quick Steps* created for you. When you select an email in your Inbox and click one of the *Quick Steps,* the *Quick Step* will automatically apply the action. For example, the *Reply & Delete Quick Step* (Figure 6-26) will create a reply message to the sender and delete the original message.

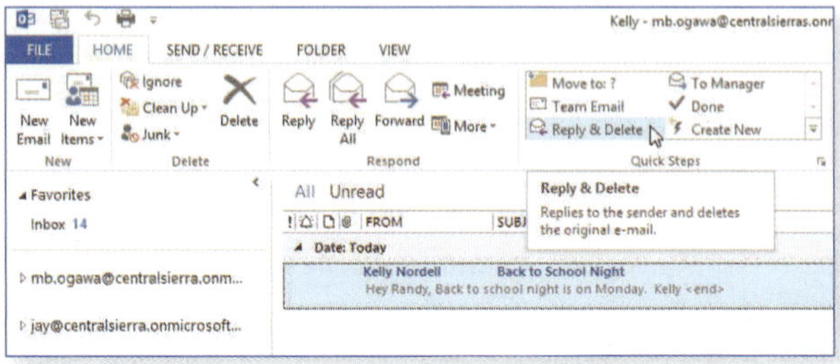

6-26 ***Reply & Delete Quick Step***

Some of the *Quick Steps* will need to be customized to specify the action to be performed. For example, the *Team Email Quick Step* needs to have the recipients on your team selected to be able to perform the action.

HOW TO: Modify an Existing Quick Step

1. Select the email in the *Folder* pane or open an email on which to apply the *Quick Step.*
2. In the *Quick Steps* group, click the **Quick Step** to be applied (*Team Email* used in this example). The *Customize Quick Step* (or *First Time Setup*) dialog box opens.
3. Click the **To** button (Figure 6-27) to select the team members to be included in this *Quick Step* and click **OK.** You can also enter the email addresses followed by semicolon.
4. Change the **Name** of the *Quick Step* as desired.
5. Clicking the **Options** button opens the *Edit [Quick Step's name]* dialog box (Figure 6-28). You can add additional actions to this *Quick Step* in this dialog box.
6. Click the **Show Options** link to display more options available for this action. The **Hide Options** link will hide these available options.
7. Click **Save** to close this dialog box and return to the *Customize Quick Step* dialog box.
8. Click **Save** to save this *Quick Step* and apply it to the selected message.

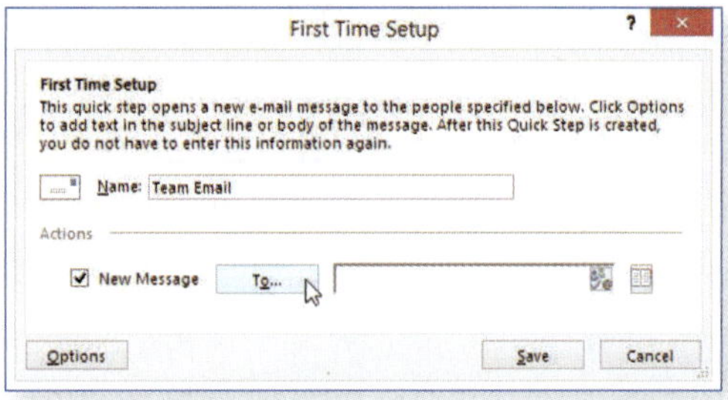

6-27 ***First Time Setup* dialog box**

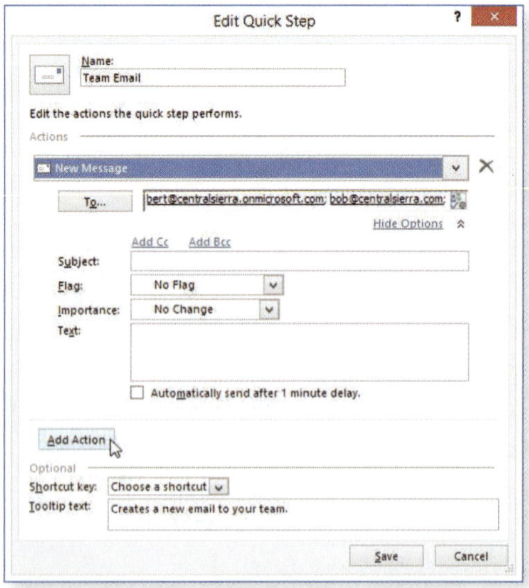

6-28 ***Edit Quick Step* dialog box**

ANOTHER WAY

A *Quick Step* can be applied to an email message by right-clicking the message in the *Folder* pane, choosing **Quick Steps,** and selecting the *Quick Step* to apply.

Create a New Quick Step

As you begin using *Quick Steps,* you will find the need to create your own custom *Quick Steps.* These new custom *Quick Steps* will appear in the *Quick Steps* group on the *Home* and *Message* tabs. *Quick Steps* are not limited to one action but can include multiple actions to be performed on a selected email message. For example, you can create a *Quick Step* to mark an email as high importance, mark it as read, and move it to a folder.

HOW TO: Create a New Quick Step

1. Click the **Create New** *Quick Step* button [*Home* tab, *Quick Steps* group] (Figure 6-29). The *Edit Quick Step* dialog box opens (Figure 6-30). You can also click the **New Quick Step** option and select **Custom** from the expand button.
2. Give the *Quick Step* a **Name.**
3. Click the pull-down arrow to display a list of actions that can be performed. *Note: The list of actions includes more than are displayed in the figure below.*
4. Select the action to be performed (see Figure 6-30). If additional criteria are available, the *Show Options* link will appear below the action.
5. Click the **Add Action** button to add another action (Figure 6-31). An action can be deleted by clicking the **X** (delete) button to the right of the action (see Figure 6-31).

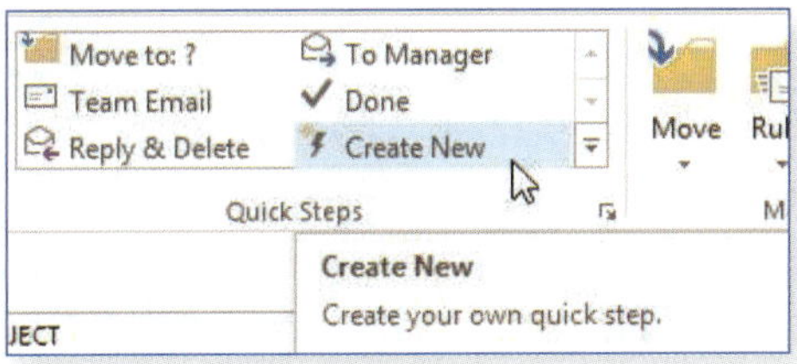

6-29 *Create New Quick Step* button

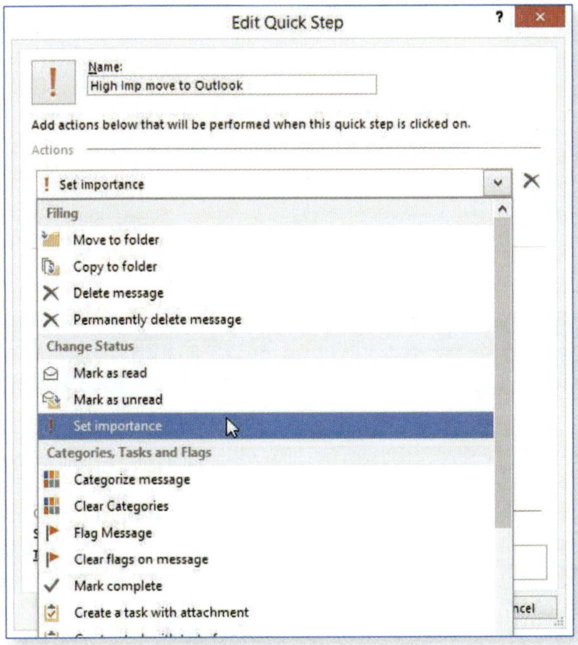

6-30 *Edit Quick Step* dialog box

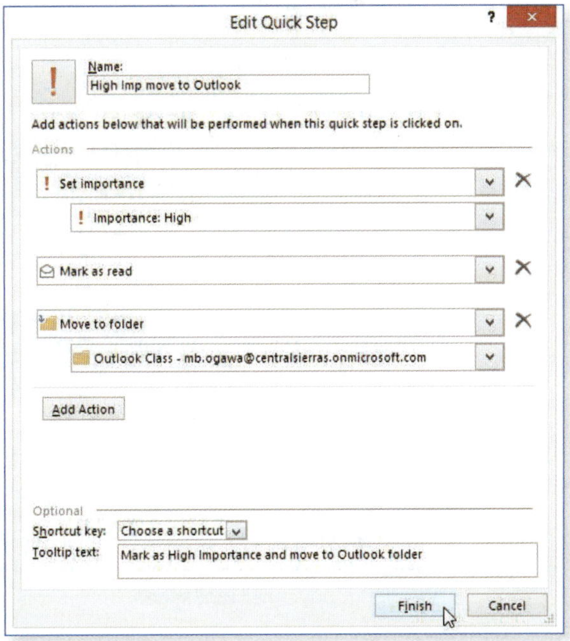

6-31 Completed *Quick Step*

6. In the *Tooltip text* area, type a description for this *Quick Step* (see Figure 6-31). This *Tooltip* will appear when your pointer is placed over the *Quick Step.*
7. When all the actions have been added, click the **Finish** button to create the new *Quick Step* (see Figure 6-31). The new *Quick Step* will be included in the list of *Quick Steps.*

Manage Quick Steps

Like rules, *Quick Steps* can easily be managed. You can open the *Manage Quick Steps* dialog box by clicking the **Manage Quick Steps** option [*Home* tab, *Quick Steps* group, drop-down arrow]. The *Manage Quick Steps* dialog box allows you to create new *Quick Steps* and modify, duplicate, or delete existing ones. You can change the display order of *Quick Steps,* and as you begin to have a lot of them you can create groups in which to organize *Quick Steps* (Figure 6-32).

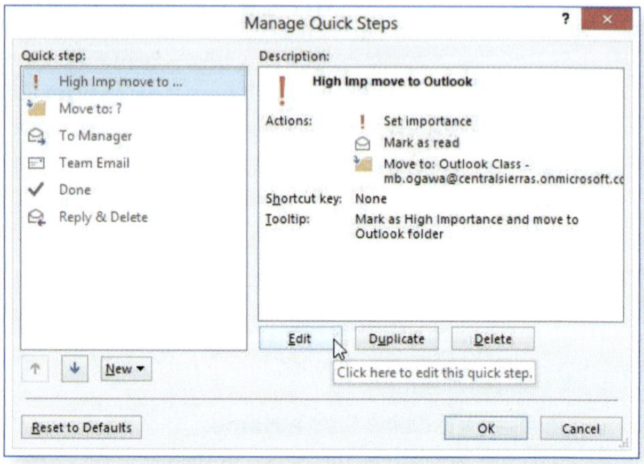

6-32 *Manage Quick Steps* dialog box

ANOTHER WAY

A shortcut can be added to a *Quick Step* by selecting a shortcut keystroke combination when creating or editing a *Quick Step.*

MORE INFO

The *Restore Defaults* button in the *Manage Quick Steps* dialog box will restore the *Quick Steps* to their original settings.

PAUSE & PRACTICE: OUTLOOK 6-3

For this Pause and Practice project, you create two *Quick Steps* to help you be more efficient when working with email. For the first *Quick Step,* your instructor indicated that he or she wants you to email with a specific subject line. Rather than checking that you typed the right subject line for each message, you create a *Quick Step* for those messages. For the second *Quick Step,* you create tasks out of email messages for your group project to ensure you can view your work to complete in your tasks instead of searching through many email messages.

1. Create a *Quick Step* to email your instructor with the subject *[class name]* (Figure 6-33).
   a. Click the **Create New** *Quick Step* button [*Home* tab, *Quick Steps* group]. The *Edit Quick Step* dialog box opens.
   b. In the *Name* text area type Email [instructor name].
   c. Click the pull-down arrow to display a list of actions that can be performed.
   d. Select **New Message.**
   e. Click the **Show Options** link below the action.
   f. Click the **To** button. Select your instructor's email address and click the **To** button followed by **OK.** If your instructor's email address is not in your Contacts, type it into the *To* field in the *Edit Quick Step* dialog box.
   g. In the *Subject* field, type class name].
   h. In the *Tooltip text* area, type Email to instructor for [class name]**.**
   i. Click the **Finish** button to create the new *Quick Step.*

2. Create a *Quick Step* to create a task with an attachment (Figure 6-33).
   a. Click the **Create New** *Quick Step* button [*Home* tab, *Quick Steps* group]. The *Edit Quick Step* dialog box opens.
   b. In the *Name* text area type Group Project Task.
   c. Click the pull-down arrow to display a list of actions that can be performed.
   d. Select **Create a task with attachment.**
   e. Click the **Add Action** button to add another action.
   f. Click the pull-down arrow to display a list of actions that can be performed.
   g. Select **Delete message.**
   h. In the *Tooltip text* area, type Create task and delete message.
   i. Click the **Finish** button to create the new *Quick Step.*

3. Send an email message to one of your partners to request the draft of the executive summary.
   a. Click the **Mail** button in the *Navigation* pane.'
   b. Click the **New Email** button [*Home* tab, *New* group].
   c. Enter the following information in your message:
      To: partner's email address
      Subject: Executive Summary Request
      Body: Hi [partner name],
      Please email me a draft of the executive summary when you finish it.
      Sincerely,
      [your name]
   d. Click **Send.**

4. Create a task from the message (Figure 6-33).
   a. Locate the email your partner sent. It is in the *Group Project* folder.
   b. Click the **Group Project Task** *Quick Step* [*Home* tab, *Quick Steps* group].
   c. Click the **Save & Close** button.

5. Email the task to your instructor as an Outlook item.
   a. Click the **Mail** button in the Navigation pane.
   b. Click the **New Email** button [*Home* tab, *New* group].
   c. Enter the following information in your message:
      To: [instructor's email address]
      Cc: [your email address]
      Subject: Outlook Pause & Practice 6-3
      *Body:*Hi [instructor name],
      Attached is the Outlook item for the Pause & Practice 6-3 exercise.Sincerely,[your name]
   d. Click the **Attach Item** button [*Message* tab, *Include* group] and select **Outlook Item.**
   e. Select the **Tasks** option and locate the task you created.

f. Click **OK.**
g. Click **Send.**

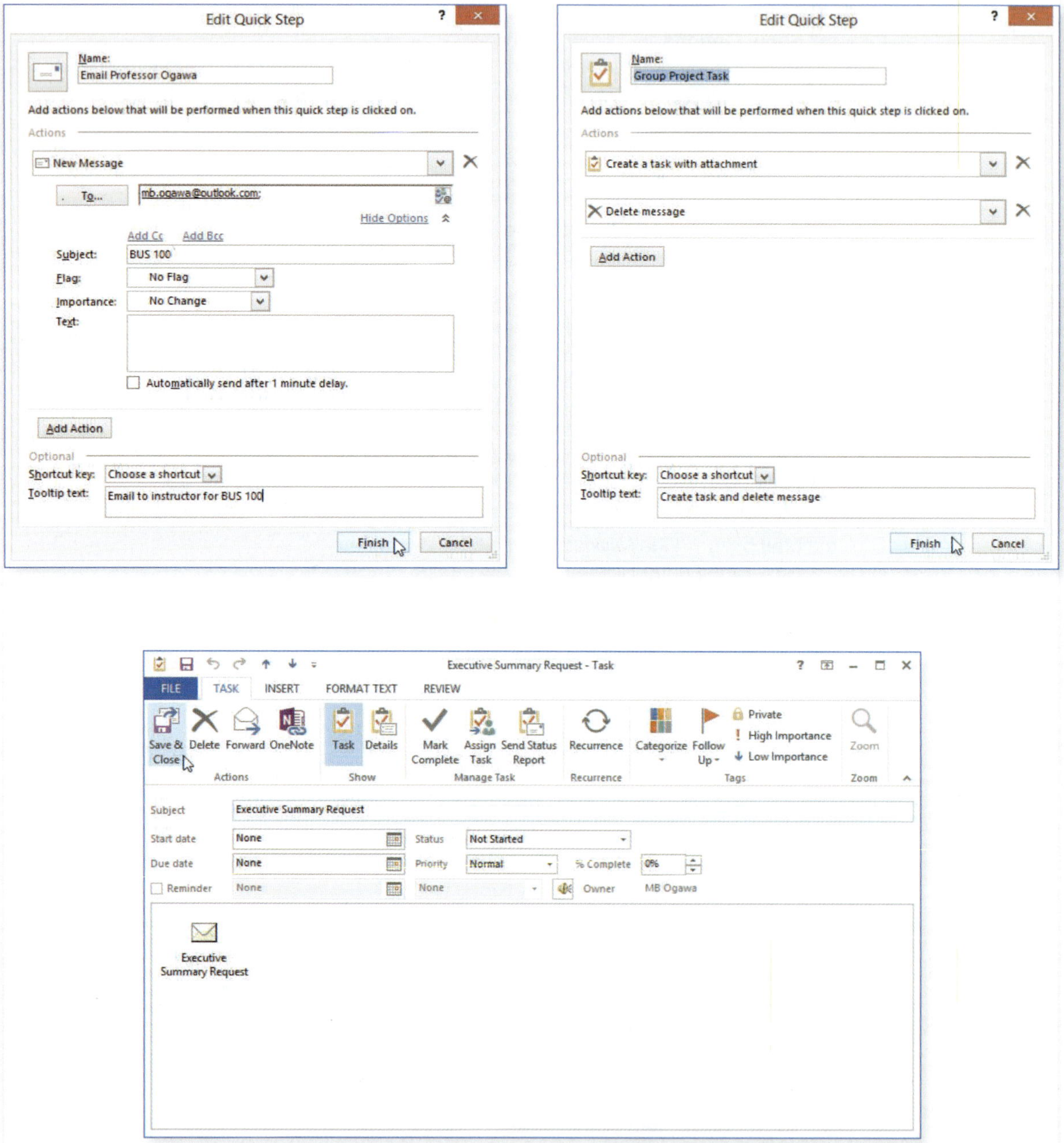

6-33 Completed Pause & Practice 6-3

SLO 6.4

Using Search Folders

Search folders are somewhat related to rules in that they look for a specific condition or criterion in email messages and, if the condition is met, the message will be displayed in the search folder. Search folders differ from rules in that the message is not physically moved to a different location.

Search folders are virtual folders; they don't actually contain any messages, but rather they display email items that are located in other folders that meet a certain condition. For example, you can create a search folder for ***Unread Mail.*** Any email message in your mailbox that is unread will be displayed in the *Folder* pane when you click the **Unread Mail** search folder in the *Navigation* pane (Figure 6-34).

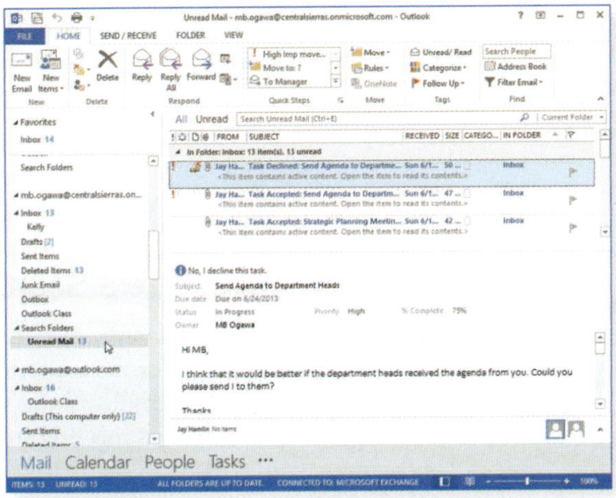

6-34 ***Unread Mail*** **search folder**

MORE INFO

Searching for specific Outlook items will be covered in Chapter 7.

Create a New Search Folder

Suppose you wanted to create a search folder that looks for all the emails from your professor, but you do not want to create a rule to physically move these messages to a separate folder. A search folder can be created to find and display all the messages from your professor.

Search folders are very easy to create, customize, and delete.

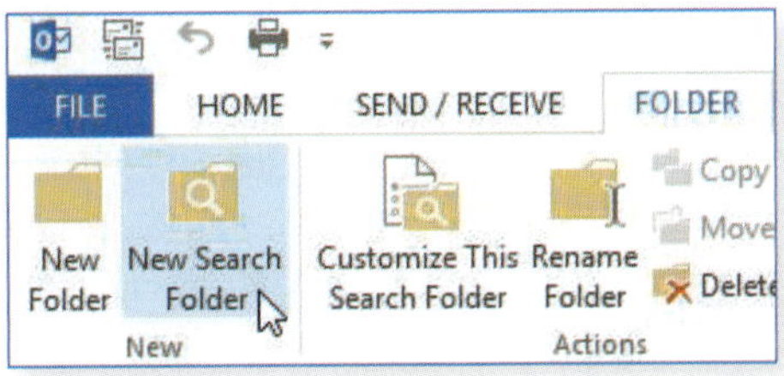

6-35 ***New Search Folder*** **button**

HOW TO: Create a New Search Folder

1. Click the **Mail** button in the *Navigation* pane.
2. Click the **Folder** tab and then the **New Search Folder** button in the *New* group (Figure 6-35). The *New Search Folder* dialog box opens.
3. Select **Mail from specific people** as the condition (Figure 6-36).
4. Click **Choose** to select a contact. The *Select Names* dialog box opens.
5. Select the name of the contact for the condition of the search folder.
6. Click the **From** button to add the contact or double-click the contact.
7. Click **OK** to close the *Select Names* dialog box.
8. Click **OK** to close the *New Search Folder* dialog box. The new search folder will appear in your list of search folders in the *Navigation* pane (Figure 6-37).

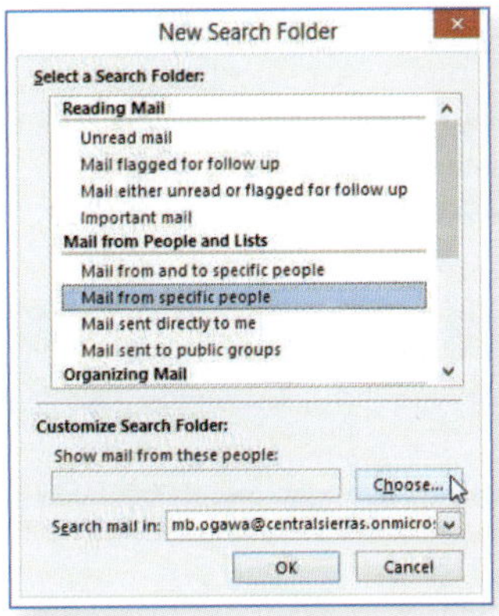

6-36 ***New Search Folder*** **dialog box**

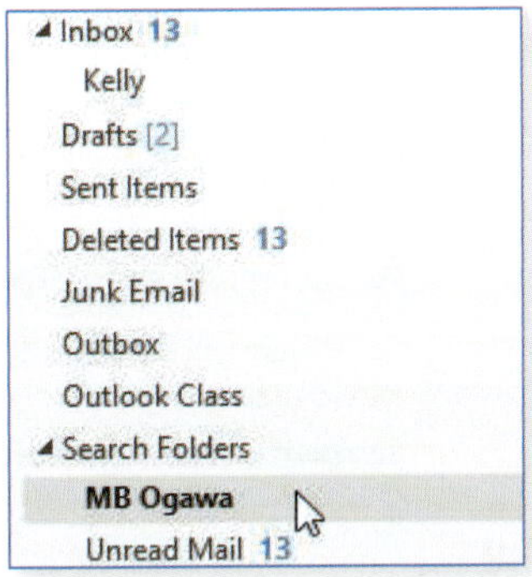

6-37 **Search folder**

ANOTHER WAY

A new search folder can also be created by pressing **Ctrl+Shift+P.**

When creating a new search folder, there are many different criteria options available from which to choose. You can also choose the **Create a custom Search Folder** option at the bottom of the *New Search Folder* dialog box for more customization options.

Customize a Search Folder

You can customize search folders by changing the name of the folder, the criteria for the search, and/or the mailbox folders to be included in the search. When you create a new search folder, by default, all the mailbox folders (or personal folders) are included in the search for mail messages meeting the criterion.

HOW TO: Customize a Search Folder

1. Click the **Mail** button in the *Navigation* pane.
2. Select the search folder to be customized.
3. Click the **Folder** tab and then the **Customize This Search Folder** button in the *Actions* group (Figure 6-38). The *Customize* dialog box opens (Figure 6-39).
4. You can change the name of the search folder, select the criteria, or indicate which folders to include in the *Mail from these folders will be included in the Search Folder* selection box.
5. Click the **Browse** button to change the folders to be included in the search. The *Select Folder(s)* dialog box opens.
6. Select the folders to be included in the search for this search folder. Notice the *Search subfolders* option at the bottom of the dialog box (Figure 6-40).
7. Click **OK** to close the *Select Folder(s)* dialog box.
8. Click **OK** to close the *Customize* dialog box.

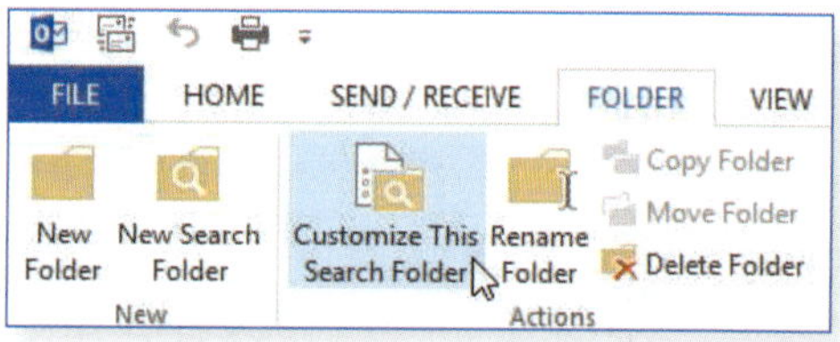

6-38 *Customize This Search Folder* button

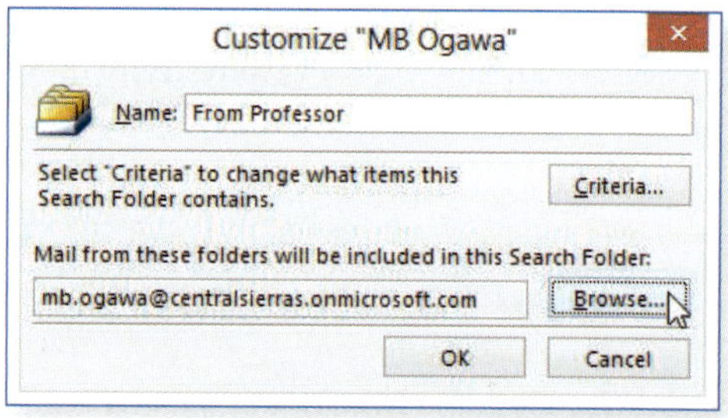

6-39 *Customize Search Folder* dialog box

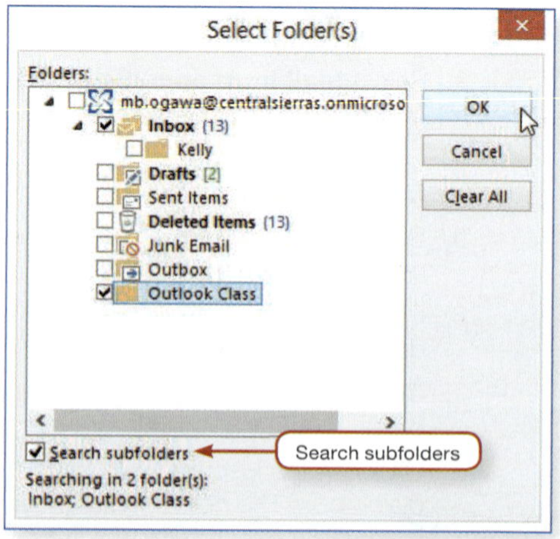

6-40 *Select Folder(s)* dialog box

MORE INFO

There is also a *Rename Folder* button in the *Actions* group on the *Folder* tab, which can be used to rename a search folder.

ANOTHER WAY

Right-click the search folder and choose **Customize This Search Folder.**

Search folders can also be customized to show either the total number of items in the folder or the number of unread items in the folder.

HOW TO: Customize How the Number of Items in the Folder Is Displayed

1. Click one of the search folders.
2. Click the **Folder** tab.
3. Click the **Folder Properties** button in the *Properties* group. The *[Folder's Name] Properties* dialog box opens (Figure 6-41).
4. Click either *Show number of unread items* or *Show total number of items.*
5. Click **Apply** and then **OK.**

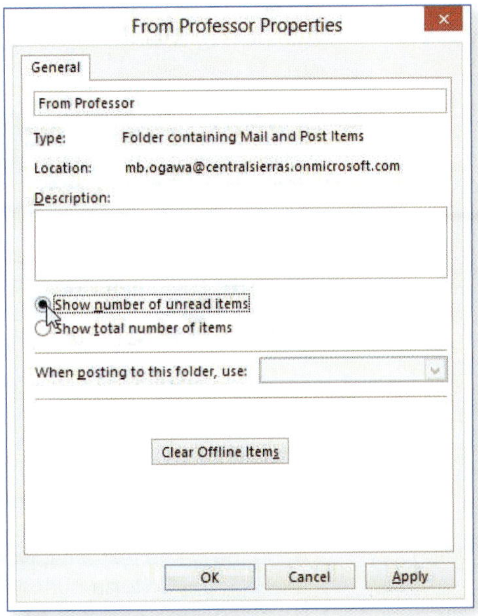

6-41 Search folder properties

ANOTHER WAY

Right-click the search folder and choose **Properties.**

MORE INFO

When a new search folder is created, the default setting is *Show number of unread items.* The number of unread items is displayed in blue parentheses. When *Show total* number of items is selected, the total number of items are displayed in green brackets.

Delete a Search Folder

Because search folders are virtual folders, they don't physically contain any email messages. When a search folder is deleted, none of the messages that were displayed in the search folder are deleted.

To delete a search folder, click the search folder in the *Navigation* pane and click the **Delete** button in the *Actions* group on the *Folder* tab or press **Delete** on your keyboard. You can also right-click the search folder and choose **Delete Folder.** When deleting a search folder, a dialog box opens asking if you want to delete the search folder and informing you that the items contained in the search folder will not be deleted (Figure 6-42). Press **Yes** to delete the search folder.

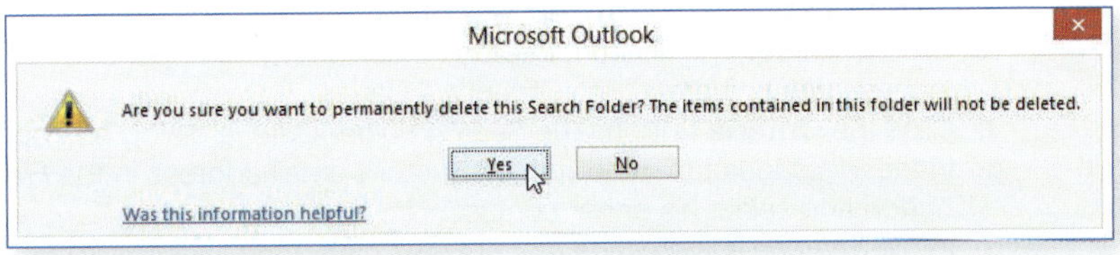

6-42 Delete search folder confirmation

ANOTHER WAY

Ctrl+D deletes a selected search folder throughout Outlook.

MORE INFO

Even though deleting a search folder will not delete the items contained in the search folder, email messages displayed in a search folder can be deleted by selecting the messages in the *Folder* pane and pressing **Delete.**

PAUSE & PRACTICE: OUTLOOK 6-4

For this Pause and Practice project, you utilize search folders to help you find information quickly. You create a search folder for email messages from your partners with attachments to allow you to easily locate files you are working with. You also want to use a search folder to quickly locate email messages from your instructor that contain the word *due* to quickly find messages with due dates or changes to due dates.

1. Create a new search folder to find messages from your partners with attachments.
   a. Click the **Mail** button in the *Navigation* pane.
   b. Click the **Folder** tab and then the **New Search Folder** button in the *New* group. The *New Search Folder* dialog box opens.
   c. Select **Create a custom Search Folder.**
   d. Click **Choose.** The *Custom Search Folder* dialog box opens.
   e. In the *Name* text area, type Group Project Attachments.
   f. Click the **Criteria** button. The *Search Folder Criteria* dialog box opens.
   g. In the *Messages* tab, type your partners' email addresses in the *From* text area or click the **From** button and select their contacts.
   h. Click the **More Choices** tab.
   i. Click the **Only items with** check box and ensure the option is set to **one or more attachments.**
   j. Click **OK** to close the *Search Folder Criteria* dialog box.
   k. Click **OK** to close the *Custom Search Folder* dialog box.
   l. Click **OK** to close the *New Search* Folder dialog box.
   m. The new search folder will appear in your list of search folders in the *Navigation* pane.
2. Customize the *Group Project Attachments* search folder to show the total number of items.
   a. Right-click the *Group Project Attachments* search folder and select **Properties.**
   b. Click the **Show total number of items** radio button.
   c. Click **OK.**
3. Create a new search folder to find messages from your instructor that contain the word *due* in the subject or body of the message.
   a. Click the **Mail** button in the *Navigation* pane.
   b. Click the **Folder** tab and then the **New Search Folder** button in the *New* group. The *New Search Folder* dialog box opens.
   c. Select **Create a custom Search Folder.**
   d. Click **Choose.** The *Custom Search Folder* dialog box opens.
   e. In the *Name* text area, type Class Due Dates.
   f. Click the **Criteria** button. The *Search Folder Criteria* dialog box opens.
   g. In the *Messages* tab, type your instructor's email address in the *From* text area or click the **From** button and select his or her contact.
   h. In the *Search for word(s)* text area type Due.
   i. Click the **In** drop-down arrow and select **subject field and message body.**
   j. Click **OK** to close the *New Search* Folder dialog box.
   k. The new search folder will appear in your list of search folders in the *Navigation* pane.

4. See Figure 6-43 for completed Pause & Practice 6-4.

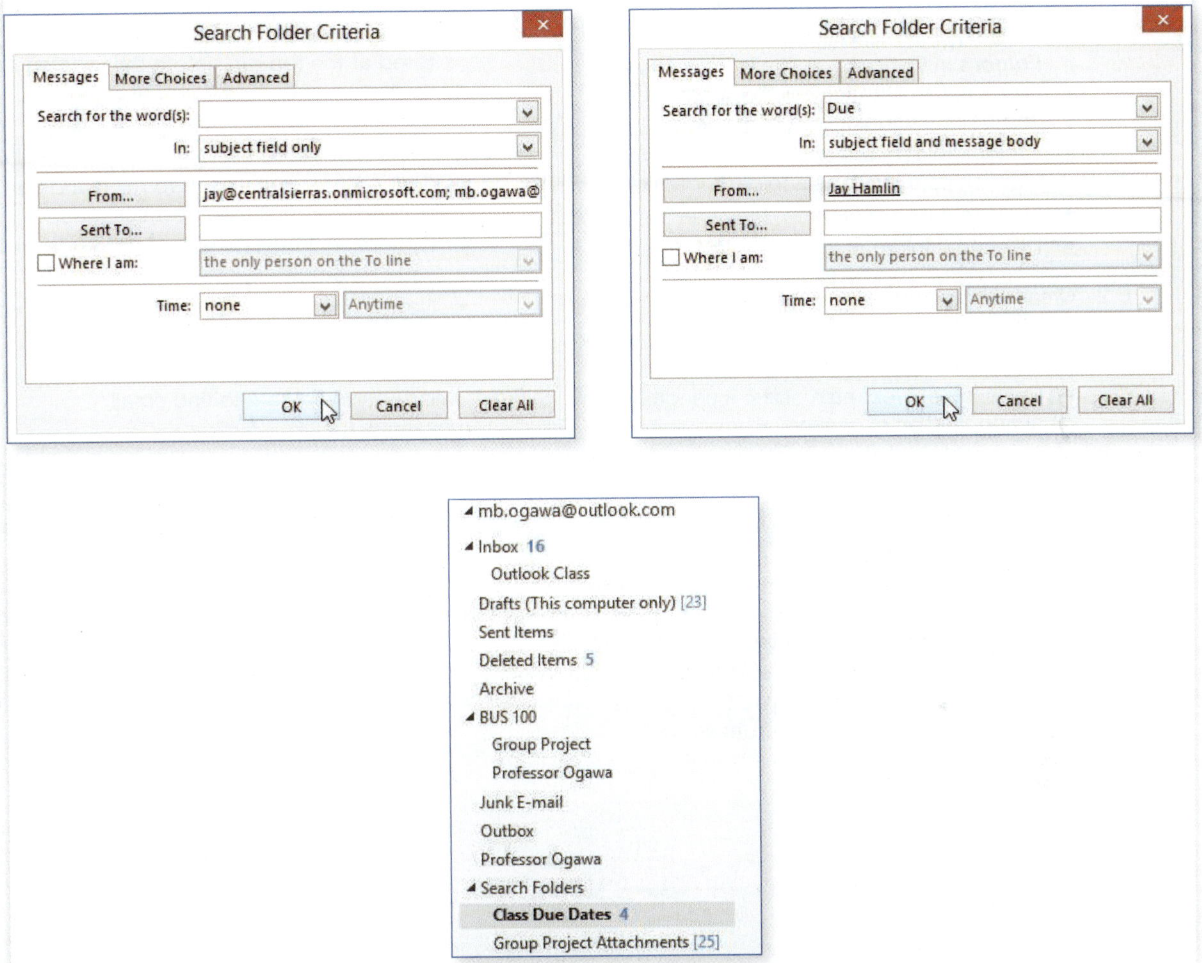

6-43 Completed Pause & Practice 6-4

Chapter Summary

6.1 Create, arrange, and modify Outlook folders (p. O6-210).

- ***Folders*** in Outlook are similar to a physical filing cabinet with folders to organize email and other Outlook items.
- Outlook folders are specific to each type of Outlook item, such as a folder for tasks.
- Once folders are created, they can be moved.
- Deleting a folder also deletes its contents.

6.2 Create, apply, and change Outlook rules (p. O6-214).

- ***Rules*** check incoming or outgoing emails and apply some type of action.
- Rules have three main parts: a condition, an action, and an exception.
- ***A condition*** checks if an email message meets a specific criteria.
- ***An action*** is what is done with the email when the condition is met.
- ***An exception*** nullifies an action if a specific criteria is met.
- A Quick Rule can be created from an email message.
- The *Rules Wizard* guides you through the process of creating a rule from scratch.
- Rules can be edited after they are created.
- Rules run ***hierarchically;*** therefore rules listed at the top run before those listed at the bottom.

6.3 Customize and use *Quick Steps* (p. O6-224).

- ***Quick Steps*** are similar to rules and can be applied to specific email messages.
- Outlook includes default *Quick Steps,* which you can edit.
- New *Quick Steps* can be created for common tasks.

6.4 Utilize search folders to find email messages (p. O6-229).

- ***Search folders*** use virtual folders to display messages that meet specific criteria.
- You can create search folders for a variety of criteria including displaying only *Unread* messages.
- Search folders can display either the number of items in the virtual folder or the number of unread items.
- Deleting a search folder does not delete its contents because it is a virtual folder.

Check for Understanding

In the ***Online Learning Center*** for this text (www.mhhe.com/office2013inpractice), there are a variety of resources that can be used to review the concepts covered in this chapter.

The following Online Learning Resources are available in the Online Learning Center:

- Multiple choice questions
- Short answer questions
- Matching exercises

USING MICROSOFT OUTLOOK 2013

Guided Project 6-1

For this project, you are a real estate agent for Placer Hills Real Estate (PHRE). You just started working with two new clients, Nina Hu and Jim Cross, who are both looking for new homes. You use folders and rules to keep your messages specific to your client and your company email organized.
[Student Learning Outcomes 6.1, 6.2]

Skills Covered in This Project

- Create folders.
- Move folders.
- Delete a folder.
- Create a Quick Rule.
- Create an advanced rule.
- Run a rule.

1. Create a folder for clients.
   a. Click the **Mail** button in the *Navigation* pane.
   b. Click the **Folder** tab.
   c. Click the **New Folder** button in the *New* group. The *Create New Folder* dialog box opens.
   d. Type Clients in the *Name* text area.
   e. In the *Folder contains* menu, confirm that the folder type is **Mail and Post Items.**
   f. In the *Select where to place the folder* section, specify your main email account folder.
   g. Click **OK.**
2. Create a folder for Nina.
   a. Click the **Mail** button in the *Navigation* pane.
   b. Click the **Folder** tab.
   c. Click the **New Folder** button in the *New* group. The *Create New Folder* dialog box opens.
   d. Type Nina Hu in the *Name* text area.
   e. In the *Folder contains* menu, confirm that the folder type is **Mail and Post Items.**
   f. In the *Select where to place the folder* section, specify your main email account folder.
   g. Click **OK.**
3. Create a folder for PHRE Internal Messages.
   a. Click the **Mail** button in the *Navigation* pane.
   b. Click the **Folder** tab.
   c. Click the **New Folder** button in the *New* group. The *Create New Folder* dialog box opens.
   d. Type PHRE Internal in the *Name* text area.
   e. In the *Folder contains* menu, confirm that the folder type is **Mail and Post Items.**
   f. In the *Select where to place the folder* section, specify your main email account folder.
   g. Click **OK.**
4. Create a folder for Jim Cross.
   a. Click the **Mail** button in the *Navigation* pane.
   b. Click the **Folder** tab.
   c. Click the **New Folder** button in the *New* group. The *Create New Folder* dialog box opens.
   d. Type Jim Cross in the *Name* text area.
   e. In the *Folder contains* menu, confirm that the folder type is **Mail and Post Items.**

f. In the *Select where to place the folder* section, specify your main email account folder.
g. Click **OK.**

5. Move the *Nina Hu* folder into the *Clients* folder.
   a. In the *Navigation* pane, select the *Nina Hu* folder.
   b. Click the **Folder** tab.
   c. Click the **Move Folder** button in the *Actions* group. The *Move Folder* dialog box opens.
   d. In the *Move the selected folder to the folder* section, click the *Clients* folder.
   e. Click **OK.**
6. Delete the *Jim Cross* folder since he decided move to another state and will not need your services.
   a. Select the *Jim Cross* folder in the *Navigation* pane.
   b. Click the **Delete** button in the *Actions* group on the *Folder* tab.
   c. A warning dialog box opens asking you if you are sure you want to delete the folder and its contents. Click **Yes** to delete the folder and all its contents.
7. Send an email message to a partner as Nina Hu.
   a. Click the **Mail** button in the *Navigation* pane.
   b. Click the **New Email** button [*Home* tab, *New* group].
   c. Enter the following information in your message:
      To: partner's email address
      Subject: Pre-approval from bank
      Body: Hi [partner's name]
      I just received my pre-approval letter from the bank. I am approved for a purchase up to $375,000 ($75,000 down payment and $300,000 loan).
      Sincerely,
      Nina
   d. Click **Send.**
8. Create a Quick Rule to move email messages from Nina into the *Nina Hu* folder.
   a. Locate and open a message from Nina.
   b. Click the **Rules** button in the *Move* group on the *Message* tab.
   c. Choose **Create Rule.** The *Create Rule* dialog box opens.
   d. In the conditions area (the top half of the dialog box), check **From Nina Hu** (the name may vary based on who sent you the message).
   e. In the actions area (the bottom half of the dialog box), check **Move the item to folder** and click the **Select Folder** button.
   f. Select the **Nina Hu** folder from the folder list and press **OK.** The *Create Rule* dialog box will still be open.
   g. Click **OK.**
   h. Select the **Run this rule now on messages already in "Inbox"** check box.
   i. Click **OK.**
9. Create an advanced rule to move emails from your manager with attachments into the *PHRE Internal* folder.
   a. Click the **Mail** button in the *Navigation* pane.
   b. Click the **Rules** button in the *Move* group on the *Home* tab and choose **Manage Rules & Alerts.** The *Rules and Alerts* dialog box opens.
   c. Click the **New Rule** button. The *Rules Wizard* dialog box opens.
   d. Select **Apply rule on messages I receive** in the *Start from a blank rule* section.
   e. Click **Next.** You will be taken to the next step to select a condition for the rule.
   f. Select the **with specific words in the recipient's address** check box. In the bottom section of this dialog box, the condition is displayed.

g. Click the **specific words** link in the bottom section. The *Search Text* dialog box opens.
h. Type phre.com in the top text area and click **Add.**
i. Click the **OK** button.
j. Click **Next.** You will be taken to the *action* step in the *Rules Wizard* dialog box.
k. Select the **move it to the specified folder** check box.
l. In the bottom section, click the **specified** folder link. The *Rules and Alerts* dialog box opens.
m. Click the **PHRE Internal** folder and press **OK.** You will be taken back to the *Rules Wizard* dialog box.
n. Click **Next.** You will be taken to the *exceptions* step.
o. Click **Next.** There will be no exceptions to this rule. The *Finish rule setup* step appears.
p. Type PHRE Internal in the *Step 1* area.
q. Confirm that the **Turn on this rule** box is selected.
r. In the bottom section, read the rule one last time to confirm that the condition and action are correct.
s. Click **Finish.**
t. Click **Apply** and then **OK** (Figure 6-44).

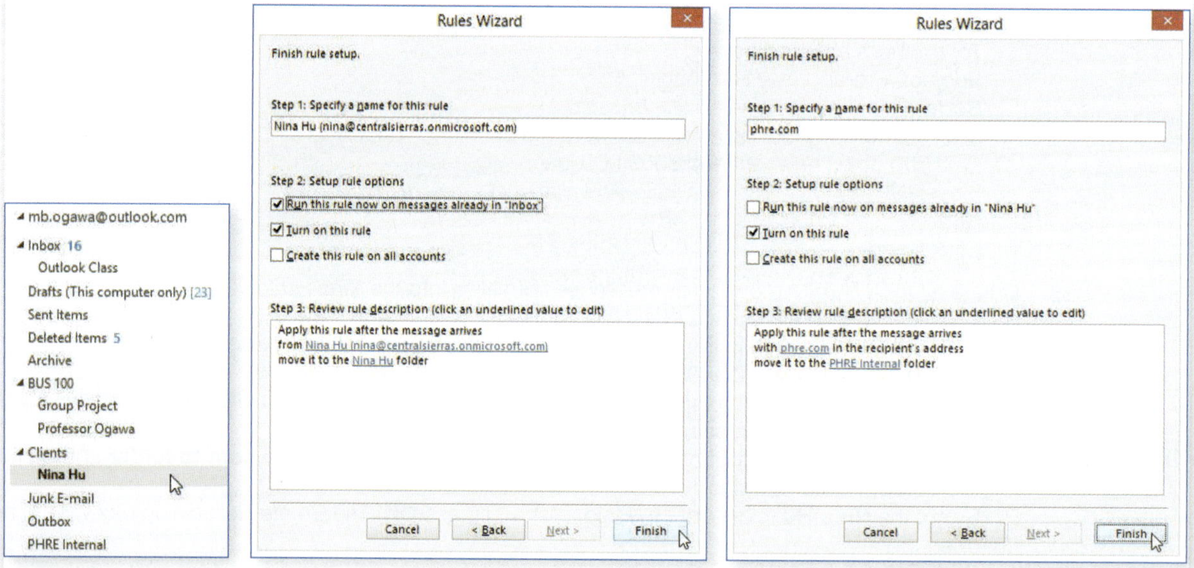

6-44 Completed Guided Project 6-1

Guided Project 6-2

As a real estate agent for PHRE, there are several emails that you send quite often, so you create *Quick Steps* to make your work more efficient. You create a *Quick Step* to forward messages to your manager when you need approval and create an appointment when you meet with your clients.
[Student Learning Outcome 6.3]

Skills Covered in This Project

- Create a *Quick Step.*
- Use the *Forward* feature.
- Use options within actions.
- Add *Tooltips* to *Quick Step.*
- Create an advanced *Quick Step.*
- Create appointments with a *Quick Step.*

1. Create a *Quick Step* to email your instructor with the subject *class name.*
   a. Click the **Create New** *Quick Step* button [*Home* tab, *Quick Steps* group]. The *Edit Quick Step* dialog box opens.
   b. In the *Name* text area type Manager Approval.
   c. Click the pull-down arrow to display a list of actions that can be performed.
   d. Select **Forward.**
   e. Click the **Show Options** link below the action.
   f. Click the **To** button. Select your partner's email address and click the **To** button or type it in the *To* text area. If your partner's email address is not in your Contacts, type it into the *To* field in the *Edit Quick Step* dialog box.
   g. In the *Subject* field, type FW: Contract Approval.
   h. In the *Tooltip text* area, type Email to manager for approval.
   i. Click the **Finish** button to create the new *Quick Step.*

2. Create a *Quick Step* to create a task with an attachment.
   a. Click the **Create New** *Quick Step* button [*Home* tab, *Quick Steps* group]. The *Edit Quick Step* dialog box opens.
   b. In the *Name* text area type Client Meeting.
   c. Click the pull-down arrow to display a list of actions that can be performed.
   d. Select **Create an appointment with attachment.**
   e. In the *Tooltip text* area, type Set up client meetings.
   f. Click the **Finish** button to create the new *Quick Step.*

3. Send an email message to your partners to request a meeting about possible locations.
   a. Click the **Mail** button in the *Navigation* pane.
   b. Click the **New Email** button [*Home* tab, *New* group].
   c. Enter the following information in your message:
      To: partner's email address
      Subject: Possible locations?
      Body: Hi [partner name],
      Can we meet next week Monday at 10:00 AM to discuss possible locations for my new home?
      Thanks,
      [your name]
   d. Click **Send.**

4. Create a task from the message.
   a. Locate the email your partner sent. It is in the ***Group Project*** folder.
   b. Click the **Client Meeting** *Quick Step* [*Home* tab, *Quick Steps* group].
   c. Change the start time to be next week **Monday at 10:00 AM.**
   d. Change the end time to be next week **Monday at 11:00 AM.**
   e. Click the **Save & Close** button.

5. Email the task to your instructor as an Outlook item.
   a. Click the **Mail** button in the *Navigation* pane.
   b. Click the **New Email** button [*Home* tab, *New* group].

c. Enter the following information in your message:
To: [instructor's email address]
Cc: [your email address]
Subject: Outlook Guided Project 6-2
Body: Hi [instructor name],
Attached is the Outlook item for the Guided Project 6-2 exercise.
Sincerely,
[student name]

d. Click the **Attach Item** button [*Message* tab, *Include* group] and select **Outlook Item.**

e. Select the **Calendar** option and locate the appointment you created.

f. Click **OK.**

g. Click **Send** (Figure 6-45).

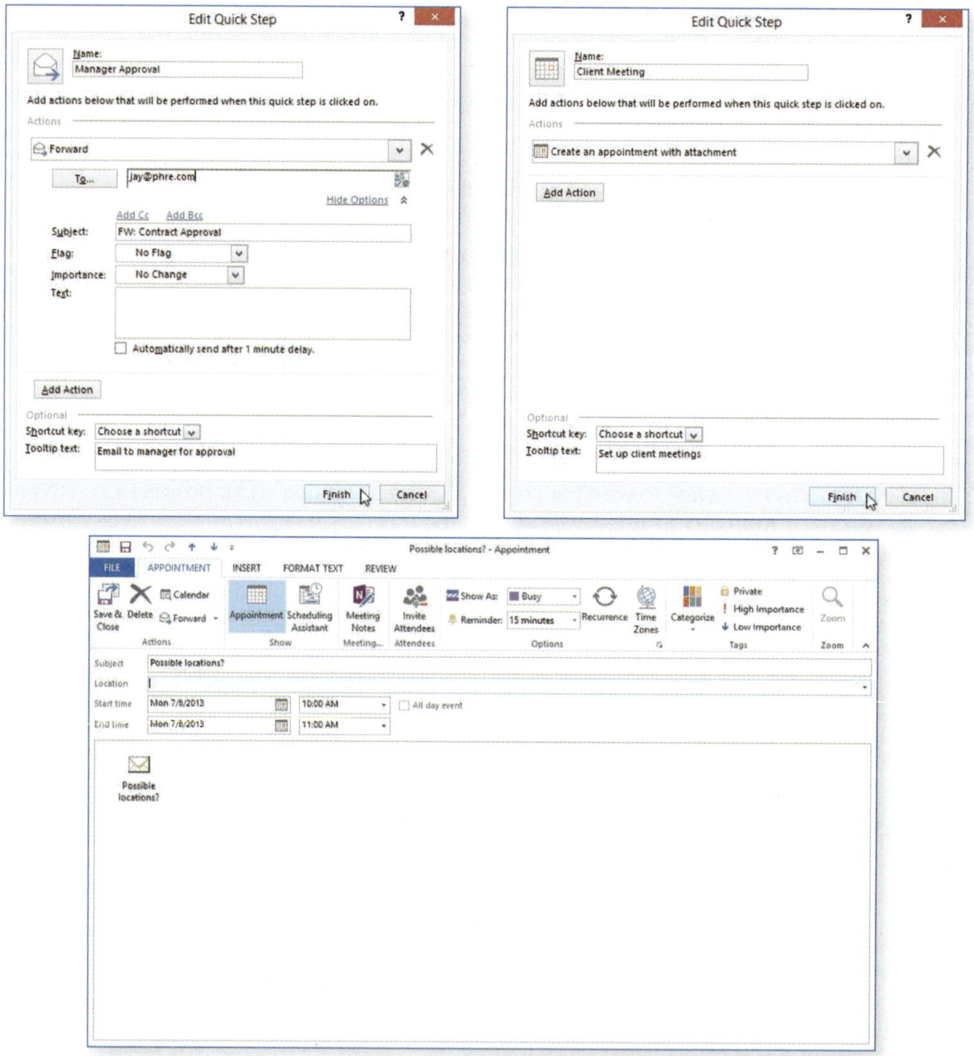

6-45 Completed Guided Project 6-2

Guided Project 6-3

While working with your coworkers and a variety of clients, you identified a handful of email messages that you constantly search for. Therefore, you develop search folders to find messages that deal with executed contracts and messages from your manager with attachments.
[Student Learning Outcome 6.4]

Skills Covered in This Project

- Create a search folder.
- Search for specific words in search folders.
- Search for specific senders in search folders.
- Search for messages with attachments in search folders.
- Use multiple criteria for a search folder.
- Modify the messages shown in search folders.
- Rename search folders.
- Modify a search folder.

1. Create a new search folder to find messages regarding executed contracts.
   a. Click the **Mail** button in the *Navigation* pane.
   b. Click the **Folder** tab and then on the **New Search Folder** button in the *New* group. The *New Search Folder* dialog box opens.
   c. Select **Mail with specific words.**
   d. Click **Choose.** The Search Text dialog box opens.
   e. In the first text area, type execute and click **Add.**
   f. In the first text area, type executed and click **Add.**
   g. In the first text area, type contract and click **Add.**
   h. In the first text area, type contracts and click **Add.**
   i. Click **OK** to close the *New Search* Folder dialog box.
   j. The new search folder will appear in your list of search folders in the *Navigation* pane.
2. Modify the search folder to be named *Executed Contracts* and show the total number of items in the search folder.
   a. Right-click the **Group Project Attachments** search folder and select **Properties.**
   b. Replace the text in the first text area with Executed Contracts.
   c. Click the **Show total number of items** radio button.
   d. Click **OK.**
3. Create a new search folder to find messages from your manager with attachments.
   a. Click the **Mail** button in the *Navigation* pane.
   b. Click the **Folder** tab and then on the **New Search Folder** button in the *New* group. The *New Search Folder* dialog box opens.
   c. Select **Create a custom Search Folder.**
   d. Click **Choose.** The *Custom Search Folder* dialog box opens.
   e. In the *Name* text area, type Manager Attachments.
   f. Click the **Criteria** button. The *Search Folder Criteria* dialog box opens.
   g. In the *Messages* tab, type your partners' email addresses into the *From* text area or click the **From** button and select their contacts.
   h. Click the *More Choices* tab.
   i. Click the **Only items with** check box and ensure the option is set to **one or more attachments.**
   j. Click **OK** to close the *Search Folder Criteria* dialog box.
   k. Click **OK** to close the *Custom Search Folder* dialog box.

l. Click **OK** to close the *New Search* Folder dialog box.
m. The new search folder will appear in your list of search folders in the *Navigation* pane (Figure 6-46).

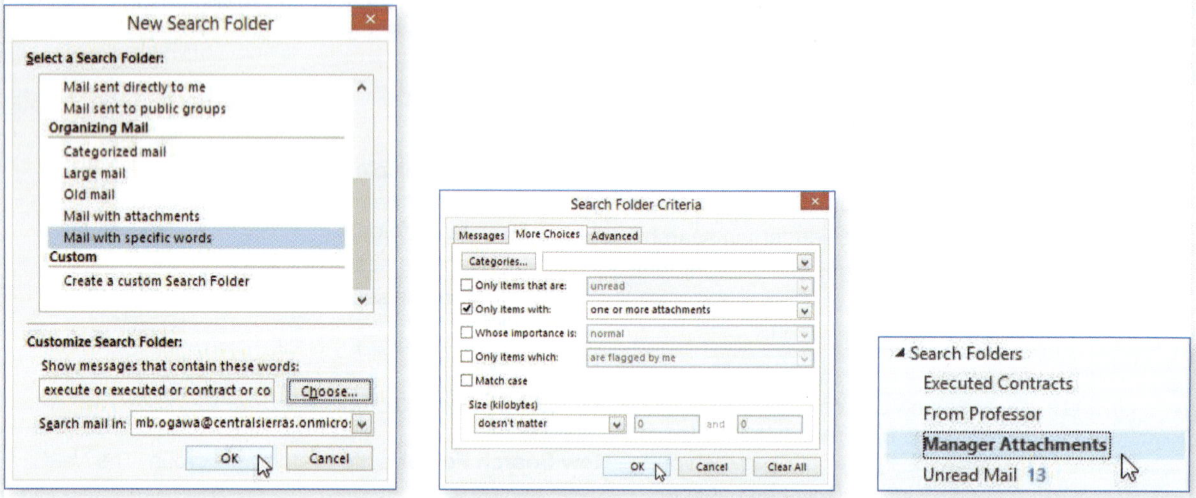

6-46 Completed Guided Project 6-3

Independent Project 6-4

For this project, you are coordinating the Cycling Evolution Event (CEE) for the American River Cycling Club (ARCC). This year, you take registrations via email. Therefore, you create folders and rules to automatically organize registration information for you. You also want to keep email messages you send to the ARCC with updates in a specific folder to ensure you can quickly find the information. [Student Learning Outcomes 6.1, 6.2]

Skills Covered in This Project

- Create folders.
- Move folders.
- Create a Quick Rule.
- Create an advanced rule.
- Run a rule.

1. Create a folders to organize ARCC email.
   a. Create a folder named *ARCC.*
   b. Create a folder named *Registrations.*
   c. Create a folder named *Member updates.*
   d. Move the *Registrations* and *Member updates* folders into the *ARCC* folder.

2. Create a rule to organize registration email messages using the following criteria:
   Condition: Messages received with the term ***Registration*** in the subject.
   Action: Moved into the ***Registrations*** folder.
   Exception: Unless there is a question mark (?) in the message.
3. Create a rule to organize membership updates messages you send based on the following criteria:
   Condition: Messages sent with the term ***Membership update*** in the subject.
   Action: Copy to the *Member updates* folder (Figure 6-47).

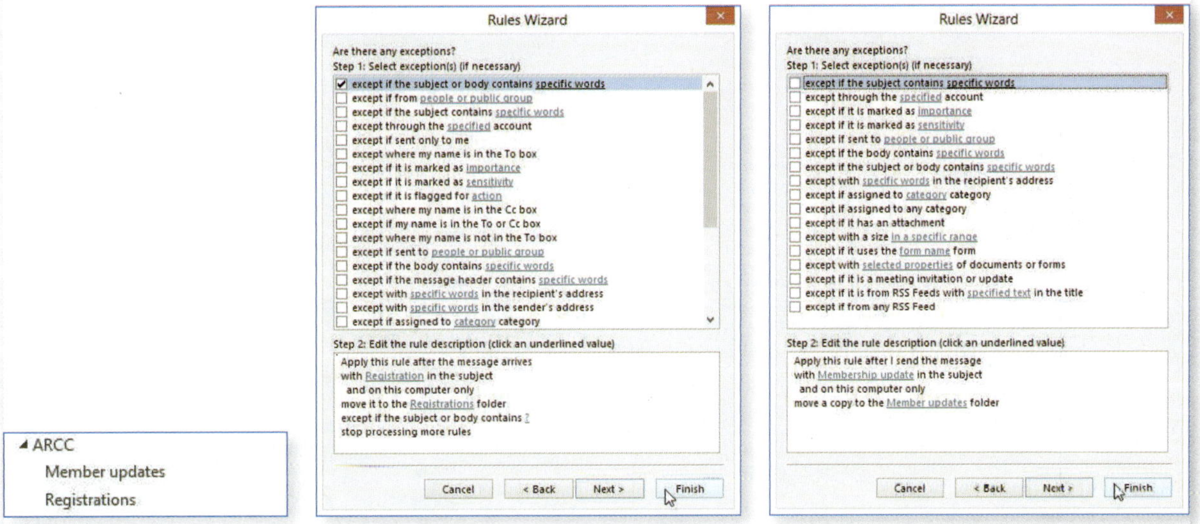

6-47 Completed Independent Project 6-4

Independent Project 6-5

After working on the registration last year, you remember that many of the ARCC members ask similar questions regarding the route. To make your work more efficient, you create a *Quick Step* to reply with the route information. You also create a *Quick Step* to quickly create messages to ARCC members. [Student Learning Outcome 6.3]

Skills Covered in This Project

- Create a *Quick Step.*
- Use the reply feature.
- Use new mail feature.
- Use options within actions.
- Add *Tooltips* to a *Quick Step.*
- Create an advanced *Quick Step.*
- Create appointments with a *Quick Step.*

1. Create a ***Quick Step*** to reply to ARCC members with the following information:
   Name: Route Reply
   Action: Reply
   Options text: Please see the following URL for the most updated route information: http://www.arcc.org/ceeroute/.
   Tooltip text: Reply with up-to-date route information.
2. Create a ***Quick Step*** to send email messages to ARCC members with the following information
   Name: Membership update email
   Action: New Message
   To*:* members@arcc.org
   Subject: Membership update
   Tooltip text: Write membership update messages. (Figure 6-48).

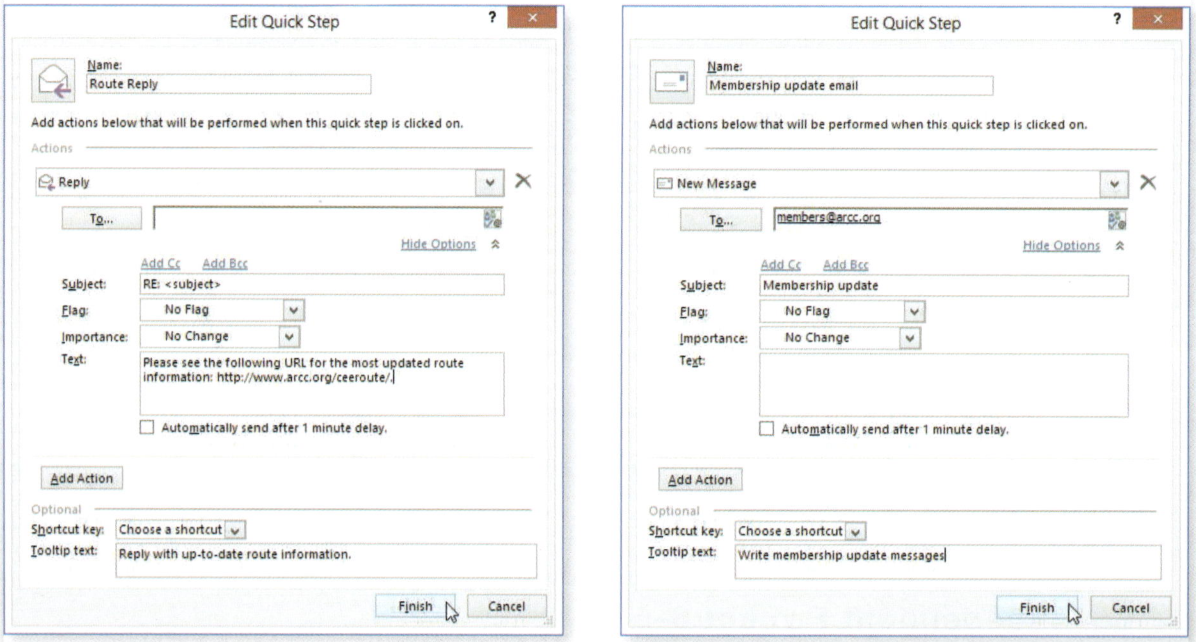

6-48 Independent Project 6-5 completed

Independent Project 6-6

As the CEE coordinator, you recall members asking about receipts for their payments. Since you started giving digital receipts via email, you create a search folder to quickly find receipts to send to participants who accidentally lost the initial message. You also remember participants asking about

their T-shirt size to ensure they receive the correct shirt when they finish the event. Therefore, you create a new search folder to find T-shirt sizes for all participants, which allows you to search within the search folder for a particular member's registration.
[Student Learning Outcome 6.4]

Skills Covered in This Project

- Create a search folder.
- Search for specific words in search folders.
- Search for specific senders.
- Search for messages with attachments in search folders.
- Use multiple criteria for a search folder.
- Modify the messages shown in search folders.
- Rename search folders.
- Modify a search folder.

1. Create a new search folder to find messages regarding receipt messages using the following criteria:
   Search folder name: Receipts
   From: [your email address]
   Search for the term ***Receipt*** in the subject field only.
   Search for items with attachments.
   Show the total number of items for the search folder.
2. Create a new search folder to find T-shirt sizes using the following criteria:
   Search folder name: Shirt size
   To: [your email address]
   Search for the term ***size*** in the subject field and message body.
   All messages received in the last month.
   Show the total number of items for the search folder (Figure 6-49).

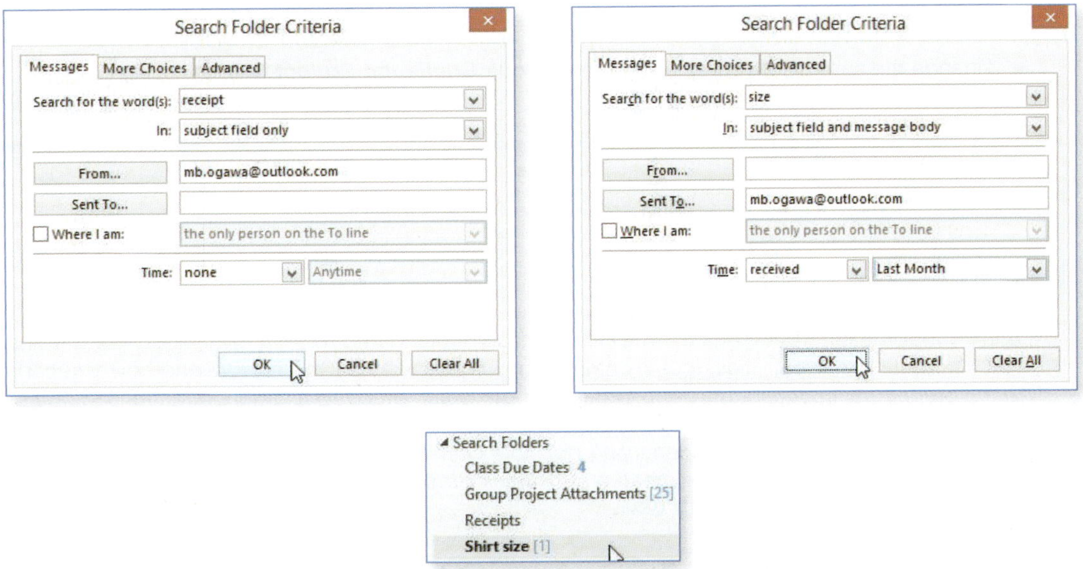

6-49 Completed Independent Project 6-6

Challenge Project 6-7

Consider the different types of email you send and receive for school, work, home, and other extra-curricular activities. Identify at least two types of email you receive or send and how you can apply rules to help keep you organized. For example, you can apply rules to emails received from specific people, words in the subject line, or flagged for action. After identifying the types of email you receive, create folders and rules to apply. Email a description of the folders created and rules applied to your instructor.
[Student Learning Outcomes 6.1, 6.2]

- Create at least two rules.
- Create folders for rules when applicable.
- Ensure you have a reason to justify each rule.
- Explain why the rule performs better than a *Quick Step* or search folder.
- Email your instructor using the following message format:
  Rule 1: [reason you are creating a rule for the type of message including why it performs better than *Quick Steps* and search folders]
  Condition: [description of condition]
  Action: [description of action]
  Exception: [description of exceptions]
  Folder 1: [name and description of folder]

  Rule 2: [reason you are creating a rule for the type of message including why it performs better than *Quick Steps* and search folders]
  Condition: [description of condition]
  Action: [description of action]
  Exception: [description of exceptions]
  Folder 2: [name and description of folder]
- Change the subject of your message to ***Outlook Challenge Project 6-7.***

Challenge Project 6-8

Think about the different types of email messages you send and receive for school, work, home, and other extracurricular activities. Identify at least two types of email you receive and how you can *apply Quick Steps* to help you be efficient. You can apply *Quick Steps* to a variety of actions such as filing, changing status, creating categories, tasks and flags, responding, creating new appointments, and managing conversations. After identifying possible *Quick Steps,* create folders for those that need it. Email a description of the folders created and *Quick Steps* developed to your instructor.
[Student Learning Outcomes 6.1, 6.3]

- Create at least two *Quick Steps.*
- Create folders for *Quick Steps* when applicable.

- Ensure you have a reason to justify each *Quick Step.*
- Use at least two actions for each *Quick Step.*
- Explain why the *Quick Step* performs better than a rule or search folder.
- Email your instructor using the following message format:
  Quick Step 1: [reason you are created a *Quick Step* for the type of message including why it fits better than rules and search folders]
  Action: [description of action]
  Action: [description of action]
  Folder 1: [name and description of folder]
  Quick Step 2: [reason you are created a *Quick Step* for the type of message including why it performs better than rules and search folders]
  Action: [description of action]
  Action: [description of action]
  Folder 2: [name and description of folder]
- Change the subject of your message to be ***Outlook Challenge Project 6-8.***

Challenge Project 6-9

You probably receive many email messages throughout the day for school, work, family, and extracurricular activities. Identify at least two types of emails you send and receive and how you can apply search folders to help you find important messages. After identifying the types of email you send and receive, create search folders for those messages. Email a description of the search folders created to your instructor.
[Student Learning Outcome 6.4]

- Create at least two Search Folders.
- Ensure you have a reason to justify each Search Folder .
- Identify criteria for the Search Folder.
- One of the search folders should contain more than one criteria.
- Email your instructor using the following message format:
  Search Folder 1: [reason you created the search folder including why it fits better than rules and *Quick Steps*]
  Criteria: [description of criteria]
  Search Folder 2: [reason you created the search folder including why it fits better than rules and *Quick Steps*]
  Criteria: [description of criteria]
  Criteria: [description of criteria]
- Change the subject of your message to be ***Outlook Challenge Project 6-9.***

Windows 7 Overview

Software is the set of instructions that directs the computer to process information. These instructions also are called *programs.* Without software, the computer cannot work. A commonly used analogy is that the computer hardware is the engine, while the software is the fuel that allows the engine to operate. Without software, the hardware would be useless. There are two types of software: system software and application software.

System Software

System software consists of four kinds of programs designed to handle the physical complexities of how computer hardware works.

- The bootstrap loader is a program that is stored permanently in the computer's electronic circuitry. When you turn on your computer, the bootstrap loader obtains the operating system from your hard disk (or floppy disk) and loads it into memory. This is commonly called booting the system.
- The diagnostic routines are also programs stored in the computer's electronic circuitry. They start up when you turn on the machine. They test the primary storage, the central processing unit (CPU), and other parts of the system. Their purpose is to make sure the computer is running properly. On some computers, the screen may say "Testing RAM" (a form of computer memory) while these routines are running.
- The basic input-output system consists of service programs stored in primary storage. These programs enable the computer to interpret keyboard characters and transmit characters to the monitor or a storage device, such as a disk.
- The operating system provides the interface between the user and the computer and oversees the processing of the application programs and all input and output of the system. Without the operating system, you could not use the application software programs provided with this book. The operating system controls computer system resources and coordinates the flow of data to and from the microprocessor and to and from input and output devices such as the keyboard and the monitor.

The operating system is usually provided by the computer manufacturer. The various types of computers require different types of operating systems in order to operate. Some of the most popular are Mac OS, Windows, and Unix.

Application Software

Application software is designed for specific uses, or "applications," such as word processing, graphics, or spreadsheet analysis. Application software can be custom written but is usually purchased ready-made.

Normally, to use an application program, you load the program into the computer's memory; execute (run) the program; and then create, edit, or update a file. When you finish, you need to save the work you have done on a disk. If you do not save your work and you turn off the computer, it is erased from memory and everything you have done will be lost.

The operating system acts as a communications link between the hardware and the application program. It is responsible for loading the application software into memory and then starting the program. It also retrieves data files and saves them to disk when directed. When you finish using the application software, you are returned to the operating system.

Microsoft Windows

The most widely used operating system for personal computers is Microsoft Windows. Windows 7 is the newest version of the Windows operating system. Like earlier versions, it has a graphical user interface (GUI, pronounced "gooey"). This kind of interface displays graphical objects called *icons,* which represent the items you use. The icons, when selected, activate the item.

All programs that use the Windows operating system have a common user interface that makes it easy to learn and use different programs that run under Windows. A common user interface means that programs have common features such as the same menu commands. For example, you will find the command to open a file is the same in all Windows applications.

The Windows operating system gets its name from its use of rectangular boxes, called *windows,* that are used to display information and other programs. Multiple windows can be open at the same time, making it easy to move from one task to another. This is how people work. More than likely, you have several projects you are working on during the day and need to be able to switch easily from one to the other.

Case Study for Windows Tutorials

As a recent college graduate, you have accepted a job as advertising coordinator for Adventure Travel Tours, a specialty travel company that organizes active adventure vacations. The company is headquartered in Los Angeles and has locations in other major cities throughout the country. You are responsible for coordination of the advertising program for all locations. Your duties include the creation of brochures, flyers, form letters, news releases, advertisements, and a monthly newsletter, all of which promote Adventure Travel Tour's programs.

The company has recently upgraded to the Windows 7 operating system and you have decided that this is a good time to both learn how the new operating system works and organize the files on your computer. You will begin by using many of the basic Windows features such as using Help, moving and sizing windows, and printing. Then you will learn how to organize the files on your computer and how to use several different application programs that are included with Windows 7. Finally, you will learn about customizing your desktop.

Before You Begin

TO THE STUDENT

The following assumptions have been made:

- Your computer uses the Windows 7 operating system.
- If available, the Aero user interface is on.
- You have a user account established.
- You have Internet access.
- The data files needed to complete the labs are provided by your instructor.

NOTE Data files are also available for download from the O'Leary Series Web site. See Appendix A to learn how to access and download these files.

TO THE INSTRUCTOR

It is assumed that the following Windows 7 settings are in effect. They include the following:

- The Windows 7 Theme is used with the Windows 7 Aurora desktop background.
- Windows and buttons are in the Windows 7 style.
- The following Taskbar settings are on:
    - Lock the taskbar
    - Keep the taskbar on top of other windows
    - Group similar taskbar buttons
    - Show Quick Launch
    - Show window previews (thumbnails)
- Notification area hides inactive icons.
- All System icons are displayed in the Notification area.
- All default Start menu options are on.
- The following Folder options are on:
    - Show preview and filters
    - Open each folder in the same window
    - Use double-click to open an item (single-click to select)
    - All default folder view settings are on except Remember each folder's view settings, which is off to maintain the original default folder settings each time a folder is opened.
    - All default Search options are on
- The default Computer folder window view is Tiles.
- The default Document folder window view is Details.
- The Navigation pane and Details pane are displayed.
- WordPad is associated with .RTF file types.
- If available, the Aero interface is on.

NOTE If the computers in your labs are unable to support the Aero feature, margin notes in the text explain the minor differences that students will encounter with this feature off.

- The Sidebar is displayed.

All figures in the manual reflect the use of a standard VGA display monitor set at 1024 by 768. If another monitor setting is used, there may be more or fewer lines of information displayed in the windows than in the figures.

The data files for students to use to complete the Windows 7 labs are located on the computer's local hard drive in the Student Data Files\Windows 7 sub-folder. If your school uses a different location or folder name, you need to provide alternative instructions for your students.

Additionally, it is assumed that students have user accounts established and Internet access is available.

Instructional Conventions

Hands-on instructions you are to perform appear as a sequence of numbered steps. Within each step, a series of bullets identifies the specific actions that must be performed. Step numbering begins over within each topic heading throughout the lab.

COMMANDS

Commands that are initiated using a command button and the mouse appear following the word "Click." The icon (and the icon name if the icon does not include text) is displayed following "Click." If there is another way to perform the same action, it appears in an Another Method margin note. When the action is first introduced, it will appear as separate steps as shown in Example A. As you become more familiar with the application, commands will appear as shown in Example B.

Example A

1

- **Click Start.**
- **Click** Documents.

Example B

1

- **Choose Start/Documents.**

FILE NAMES AND INFORMATION TO TYPE

Plain green text identifies file names you need to select or enter. Information you are asked to type appears in blue and bold. (See Example C.)

Example C

1

- **Open the file** wn01_Safari Tips.
- **Type Packing List.**

Windows 7 Basic Skills Lab 1

Objectives

After completing this lab, you will know how to:

1. Start Windows 7.
2. Use a mouse.
3. Use the Start menu.
4. Size, move, arrange, and close windows.
5. Scroll a window.
6. Use Help and Support.
7. Print a Help topic.
8. Use dialog boxes.
9. Use folder windows and libraries.
10. Change folder layouts and views.
11. Navigate and sort files and folders.
12. View and organize pictures.
13. Shut down Windows 7.

CASE STUDY

Adventure Travel Tours

As a recent college graduate, you have accepted a job as advertising coordinator for Adventure Travel Tours, a specialty travel company that organizes active adventure vacations. The company is headquartered in Los Angeles and has locations in other major cities throughout the country. You are responsible for coordinating the advertising program for all locations. Your duties include the creation of brochures, flyers, form letters, news releases, advertisements, and a monthly newsletter, all of which promote Adventure Travel Tour's programs.

The company has recently upgraded to the Windows 7 operating system and you have decided that this is a good time to both learn how the new operating system works and organize the files on your computer. You will begin by using many of the basic Windows features that are needed to use a personal computer. These features include how to use a mouse, menus, dialog boxes, the Start menu, and the Help and Support system and how to work with windows, folders, libraries, and files.

Learning to use these features is the foundation upon which your computer skills will continue to grow as you apply and expand your knowledge. This is because the features and concepts that are presented are common to all programs that use the Windows operating system.

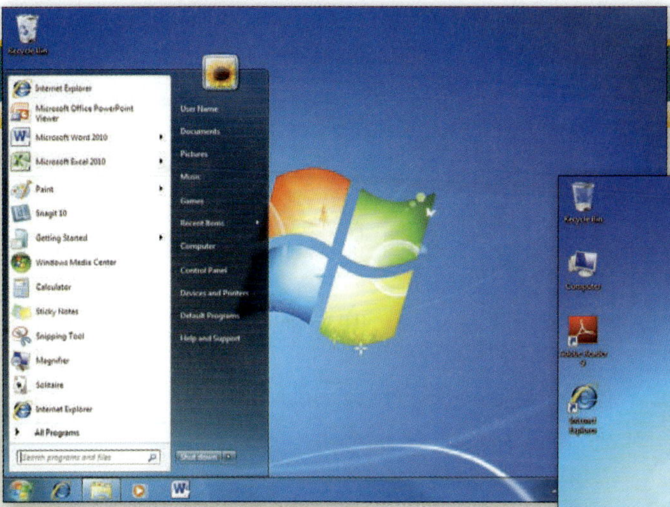

The Start menu provides quick access to features, programs, and files on your computer.

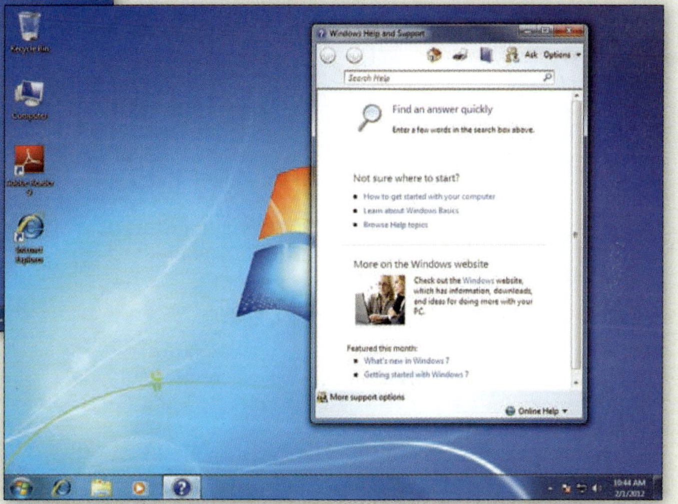

The Help and Support Center provides answers to your questions about Windows 7.

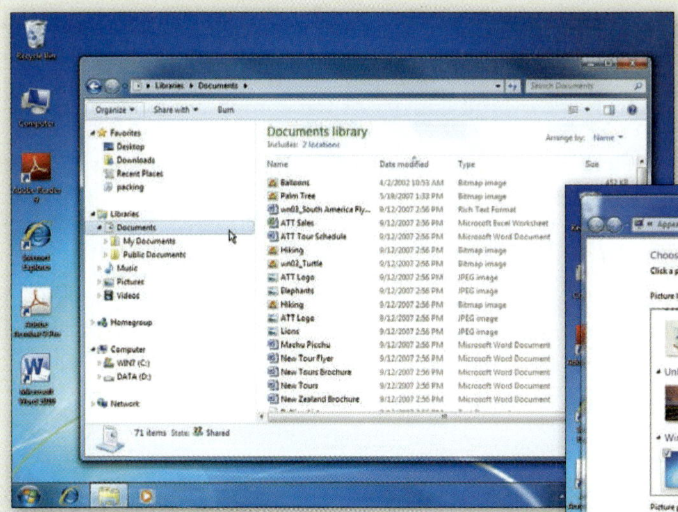

Folder windows display the contents of libraries and folders on your computer.

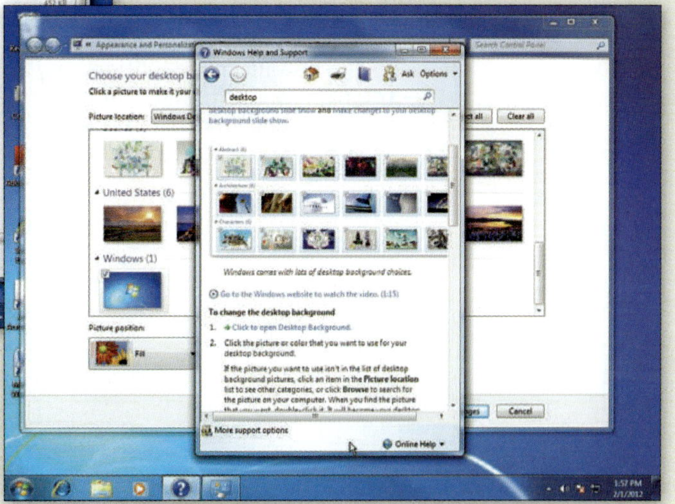

Multiple open windows can be displayed in different arrangements on the desktop.

Concept Overview

The following concepts will be introduced in this lab:

1 **Operating System** An operating system is a collection of programs that helps the computer manage its resources and acts as the interface between the user and the computer.

2 **Desktop** The desktop is the opening screen for Windows 7 and is the place where you begin your work using the computer.

3 **Menu** A menu is one of many methods used to tell a program what you want it to do. When opened, a menu displays a list of commands.

4 **Window** A window is a rectangular section of the screen that is used to display information and other programs.

5 **Dialog Box** A dialog box is a window that is displayed whenever the program requires additional information from you in order to complete a task.

6 **Folders and Libraries** Folders and libraries are used to manage and organize the files on your computer.

Starting Windows 7

Additional Information

Refer to the Overview for a discussion of software.

The primary purpose of a computer is to run **application software**, such as a word processing program, designed to help you accomplish a task. However, in order to run application software, all computers must first load an operating system that controls the overall activity of the computer. (See Concept 1: Operating System)

The operating system you will learn about is Microsoft Windows 7, the newest version of the Windows operating systems. Windows 7 has a Starter edition, Home Basic and Home Premium editions, a Professional edition, an Enterprise edition, and an Ultimate edition. The Starter, Home, Professional, and Ultimate editions are designed for individual computers and small noncorporate networks. The Enterprise edition is used for large corporate networks with more than 25 computers.

Concept 1 Operating System

The **operating system** is the software that helps the computer manage its resources and acts as the interface between the user and the computer. Like all software, the operating system software consists of a collection of programs. **Programs** are a sequence of instructions that direct the computer to perform different tasks and are stored as files on the computer. A **file** is the named unit of storage in your computer that enables the computer to distinguish between one set of information and another.

The three main functions of an operating system are to manage resources, provide a user interface, and run application software.

Function	Description
Manage resources	Coordinates the different parts of the computer system so that all parts work together. This includes coordinating the flow of data to and from the system unit and to and from input and output devices like the keyboard and the display screen. This controls computer system resources and includes providing the means to manage and store information on the computer.
User interface	Provides the means for users to interact with the computer.
Running application software	Loads programs designed for specific uses such as word processing, graphics, and spreadsheet analysis.

Windows employs a **graphical user interface (GUI)** that uses pictures to represent familiar objects. The hardware required to interact with the computer includes a monitor, mouse, and keyboard. Using your mouse or keyboard, you respond to messages displayed on the monitor. The messages that appear are provided by the software. The Windows operating system and most of the applications that can be used with this operating system all use the same or similar interface features. This common user interface makes it easier and faster to learn other applications.

The Windows 7 Professional, Enterprise, Home Premium, and Ultimate editions also include Windows **Aero,** a feature that displays transparent glass designs with subtle window animations and new window colors. To use this feature, certain minimum hardware requirements must be met. The Windows Aero feature is shown in these labs.

NOTE If you are not able to use the Aero feature, your screens will look slightly different and some features may operate differently. These differences are minor and will be addressed in Additional Information margin notes.

TURNING ON THE COMPUTER

Additional Information

On older computer models, you may need to flip the power switch located on the back or the right side of your computer.

The first thing you need to do is to turn on the computer. When you turn it on, system and hardware checks are performed and the Windows 7 operating system program is loaded into main memory automatically. This process is called a **cold start**. The power button on most desktop computer models is located on the front or top edge of the system unit.

When your computer is on, you may hear the fan running and, on most machines, lights are lit on the front. The monitor, however, may be dark or may be displaying a moving picture called a **screen saver**. When a computer has not been used in a while, it goes to "sleep" to conserve energy. You may simply need to "wake up" the system by pressing any key on the keyboard. If the monitor is off, you need to turn it on and adjust the color and brightness. The button to turn it on and the dials to adjust it are generally located on the front of the monitor.

If your computer is on:

1

- **If necessary, press any key or click the mouse button to "wake up" the computer.**
- **If necessary, turn your monitor on and adjust the contrast and brightness.**

If your computer is off:

1

- **Turn on the power.**
- **If necessary, turn your monitor on and adjust the contrast and brightness.**

Your screen should be similar to Figure 1.1

Additional Information

The picture associated with the user account is assigned at random when the account is created; however, it can be changed to another of your choice.

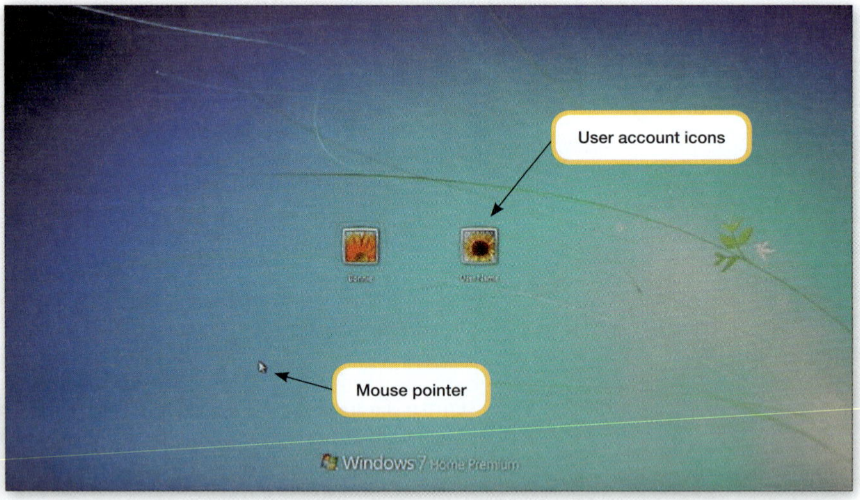

Figure 1.1

Additional Information

Use a "strong" password, one that is hard to break. It should be a minimum of seven characters, contain a symbol character in the second through sixth position, and be different from prior passwords. Do not use your name or a common word or name.

The Windows Welcome screen appears and displays user icons for each user account on the system. At home and in business, multiple users on a single computer are common. As a security measure, separate **user accounts** for each user can be created to control access to information stored on the computer. Each user account requires a user name. In addition, a password may be required. The user account can be set up to limit the user's access to the computer and to restrict use of that user's documents and programs by others. Finally, because people like to work in different ways, each user account automatically stores the user's personal settings and preferences that are activated when the user logs on.

Additional Information

In a network environment, the network administrator creates user accounts and passwords and defines the level of access available on each account.

To gain access to the computer, you need to log on by selecting a user account and entering a password, if needed.

INTERACTING WITH YOUR COMPUTER

To interact with the computer, you use the mouse and keyboard. The **mouse** is used primarily for highlighting text and selecting items on the screen; the keyboard is used primarily for entering information. The symbol on your screen is the **mouse pointer** and is controlled by the mouse that is attached to your computer. Most commonly, the mouse is a handheld device that you move across the surface of your desk. There are two common types of mice: a **wheeled mouse**, which uses a rubber-coated ball, and an **optical mouse**, which uses a light-emitting diode (LED). For the wheeled mouse, the rubber-coated ball on the bottom of the mouse moves as you move the mouse. For the optical mouse, the LED at the bottom of the mouse bounces light off the surface beneath it to calculate coordinates. The movement of the ball or LED is translated into signals that tell the computer how to move the onscreen pointer. These signals are transmitted through a cable that connects the mouse to the computer or through a wireless connection. The direction the ball or LED moves controls the direction the pointer moves on the screen.

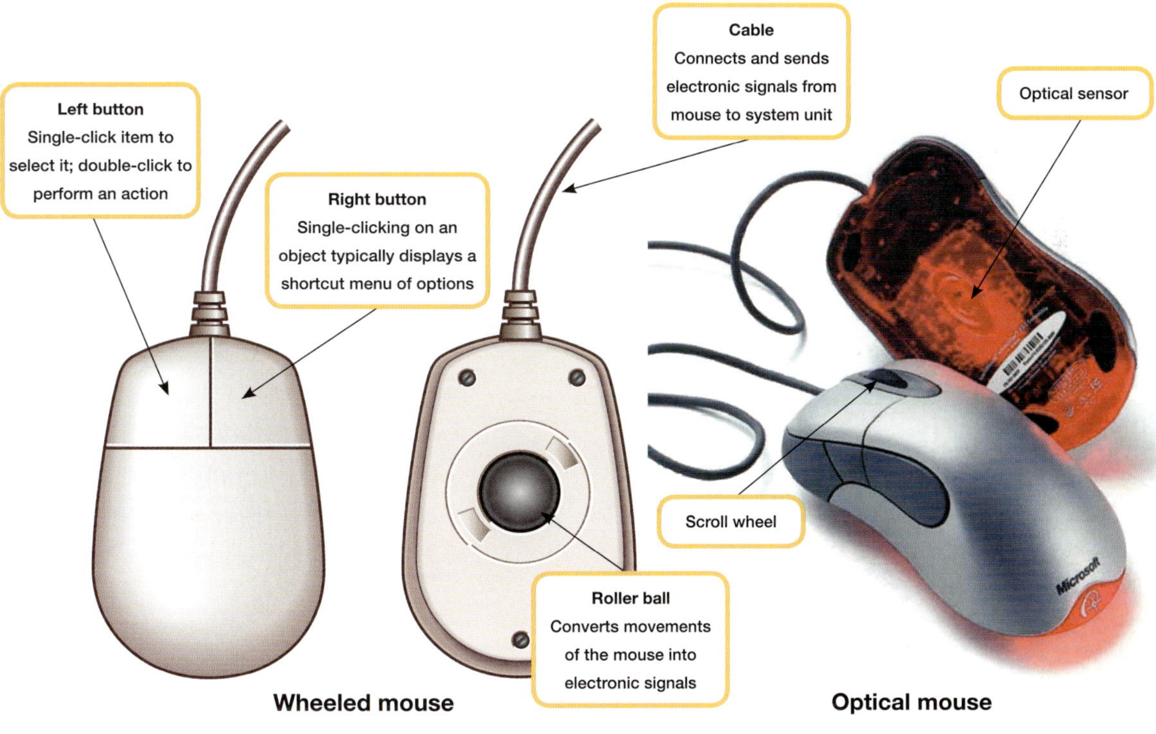

Some computers use a trackball, a stick, or a touch pad to move the mouse pointer. The direction that you move the ball or stick with your fingertips or drag your finger on the pad is the direction the mouse pointer moves on the screen.

The mouse pointer changes shape on the screen depending on what it is pointing to. Some of the most common shapes are shown in the table below.

Pointer Shape	Meaning
	Normal select
	Link or button select
	Move the cursor
	Area is not available
	Busy
	Horizontal/vertical resize
	Diagonal resize

Additional Information

When three buttons are available, the middle button can be programmed as the double-click button.

On top of the mouse are two or three buttons that are used to choose items on the screen. If your system has a stick, ball, or touch pad, the buttons are located adjacent to the device. The buttons are used to **point**, **click**, **double-click**, and **drag**. These mouse actions are described in the table below. Some mice include a wheel button located between the two buttons. The wheel is used differently by different applications but is commonly used to quickly move through information displayed on the screen.

Additional Information

When you pair Windows 7 with a touchscreen PC, you can use your fingertips instead of a mouse to interact with the computer. Icons are fingertip-friendly, and touch-ready!

Action	Description
Point	Move the mouse so the mouse pointer is positioned on the item you want to use.
Click	Press and release the left mouse button.
Right-click	Press and release the right mouse button.
Double-click	Quickly press and release the left mouse button twice.
Drag	Move the mouse while holding down the left or right mouse button.

You will log on to the computer by selecting your user account.

1

- **Move the mouse in all directions (up, down, left, and right) and note the movement of the mouse pointer.**
- **Click on your user account icon.**

Your screen should be similar to Figure 1.2

Figure 1.2

Additional Information

Your instructor will provide the necessary user name and password information.

Clicking on your user account icon displays only your account icon and a password text box in the window. A **text box** is a box in which you type information using the keyboard. A blinking vertical line called the **cursor** or **insertion point** appears in the text box indicating it is ready to accept your entry. The password will appear as a series of dots as you type to maintain the privacy of the password.

2

- **Type your password and click → or press ←Enter to complete the entry.**

Having Trouble?

If the insertion point is not displayed, activate the text box by clicking in it, using the left button on your mouse.

Additional Information

If you enter an Incorrect password, click OK in response to the advisory message, and reenter it correctly.

Your screen should be similar to Figure 1.3

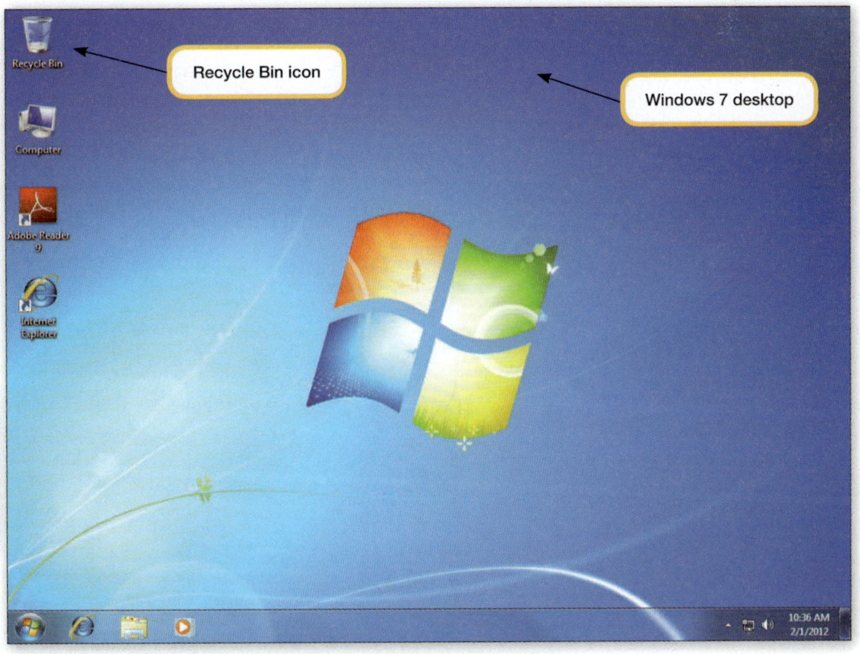

Figure 1.3

Windows 7 loads the personal settings associated with the user account and the Windows desktop is displayed. Your screen may be slightly different, depending upon how your school has set up the computers.

Concept 2 Desktop

The **desktop** is the opening screen for Windows 7 and is the place where you begin your work using the computer. It is called a desktop because it provides quick access to the tools you need to complete your work using the computer. The desktop is made up of many items called **objects**. Each object consists of settings and attributes called **properties** that are unique to the object and that affect what the object looks like, what the object can do, or what you can do to the object. Just about all the objects on the desktop have properties associated with them. For example, the small pictures, called **icons**, on the desktop are each made of properties that control what the icon does. The desktop itself is an object that has properties. The properties can be viewed and changed if necessary to suit your needs. For example, you can change the color of the desktop background.

Like your own desk at home or work, you can add and remove objects from the desktop, rearrange them, or get rid of them by throwing them into the "trash." You also can open some objects, much like a drawer in your desk, to access other tools or materials you have stored in it. You can then place these items on the desktop or take items off the desktop and place them in the "drawer." Just like your own desk, your most frequently used items should be on the desktop so you can quickly access them to begin work. Those items that you use less frequently should be put away for easy access as needed, just as you might put papers in a drawer or on a nearby shelf.

EXPLORING THE DESKTOP

Initially, the Windows 7 desktop displays one icon for the Recycle Bin (trash), where deleted items are stored until they are permanently removed. Because the desktop can be customized to suit individual needs, your desktop may have been modified from the default Windows 7 layout. For example, your desktop may display many additional icons in different locations. Several common icons that may already appear on the desktop are described in the following table.

The desktop also may display Windows **desktop gadgets**, which are fun, popular mini-programs you may use to customize your desktop. A clock or the local weather are examples.

Additional Information

This feature is explained in Appendix B: Customizing the Desktop.

Icon	Description
	Opens the Documents location where documents you create using an application program are stored
	Starts the Internet Explorer program
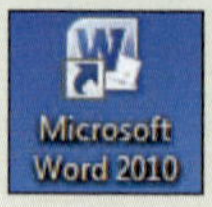	Starts the Microsoft Word 2010 program

1

- **Point to the Recycle Bin icon.**

Your screen should be similar to Figure 1.4

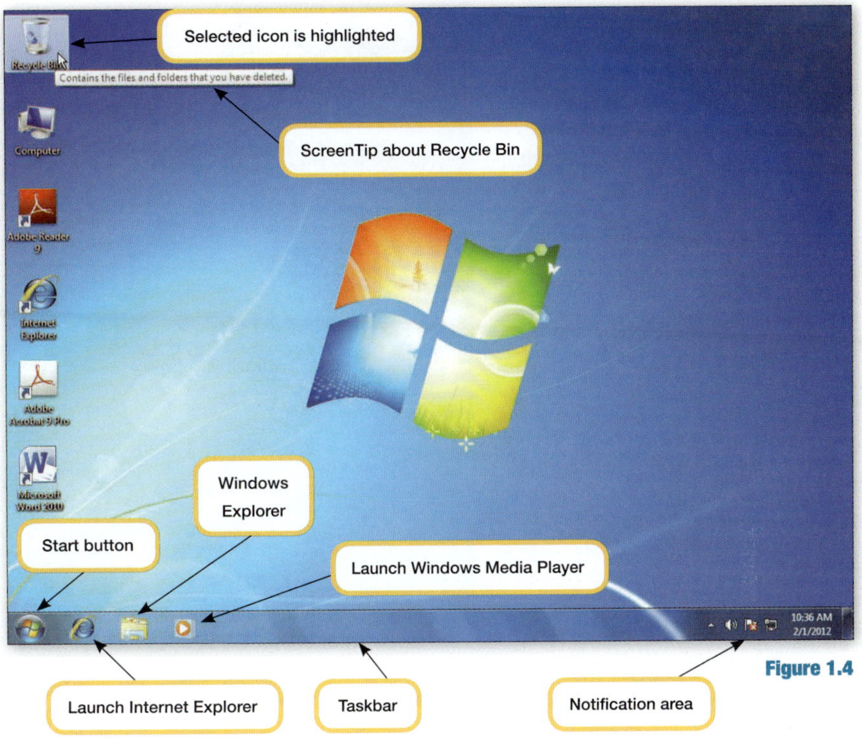

Figure 1.4

Additional Information

The icons in the notification area may be hidden if they have not been used recently. Clicking ▲ displays the icons.

Having Trouble?

If your taskbar is not visible, it may be set to hide automatically when not in use. To redisplay it, point to the area of the screen (the bottom by default) where the taskbar is located.

Having Trouble?

Your taskbar may display different icons than shown in Figure 1.4.

Additional Information

See Appendix B: Customizing the Desktop to learn how to pin items to the taskbar.

When you point to an icon on the desktop, it appears highlighted and displays a **ScreenTip** containing a brief description of the item. You will find that ScreenTips are used throughout Windows programs to quickly provide information about the object you are pointing to. The ScreenTip disappears after a short period of time.

At the bottom of the desktop screen is the **taskbar**. The Start button on the left end of the taskbar is used to start a program, open a document, get help, find information, and change system settings. The center of the taskbar in Figure 1.4 is currently blank. It will display **taskbar buttons** representing programs and files that are currently active, making switching between tasks easy. The right end of the taskbar is the Notification area. It displays the clock icon showing the time as maintained by your computer. To the left of the clock are several icons that indicate those tools that are automatically started when you turn on your computer and are running in the background, such as a speaker if your system includes audio hardware. This area also temporarily displays icons while a tool is in use, such as a printer when printing is in progress.

In addition, the taskbar may display program icons just to the right of the Start button. These items have been attached or **pinned** to the taskbar because they are frequently used programs. Initially, these include a **button** to start the Microsoft Internet Explorer Web browser program that is included with the Windows 7 operating system and a very handy Windows Explorer button that you will learn about shortly. Because you may customize which items are pinned to the taskbar, different icons may be displayed, such as Windows Media Player.

2

- Point to the notification icons and any buttons on the taskbar to view their ScreenTips.
- Point to Start.

Your screen should be similar to Figure 1.5

Figure 1.5

The Start button is one of the most important features in Windows 7, as it is the starting point for most features on your computer.

Using Windows 7

To use your computer, you need to start application programs and access documents you have created. As you learn about Windows 7, you will find there are many ways to perform the same task.

USING THE START MENU

Using the Start button is one of the best places to learn how to use Windows 7. It provides quick and easy access to most features you will use frequently.

1 Click Start.

Another Method

You also can open the Start menu by pressing [Windows] or Ctrl + Esc on your keyboard.

Your screen should be similar to Figure 1.6

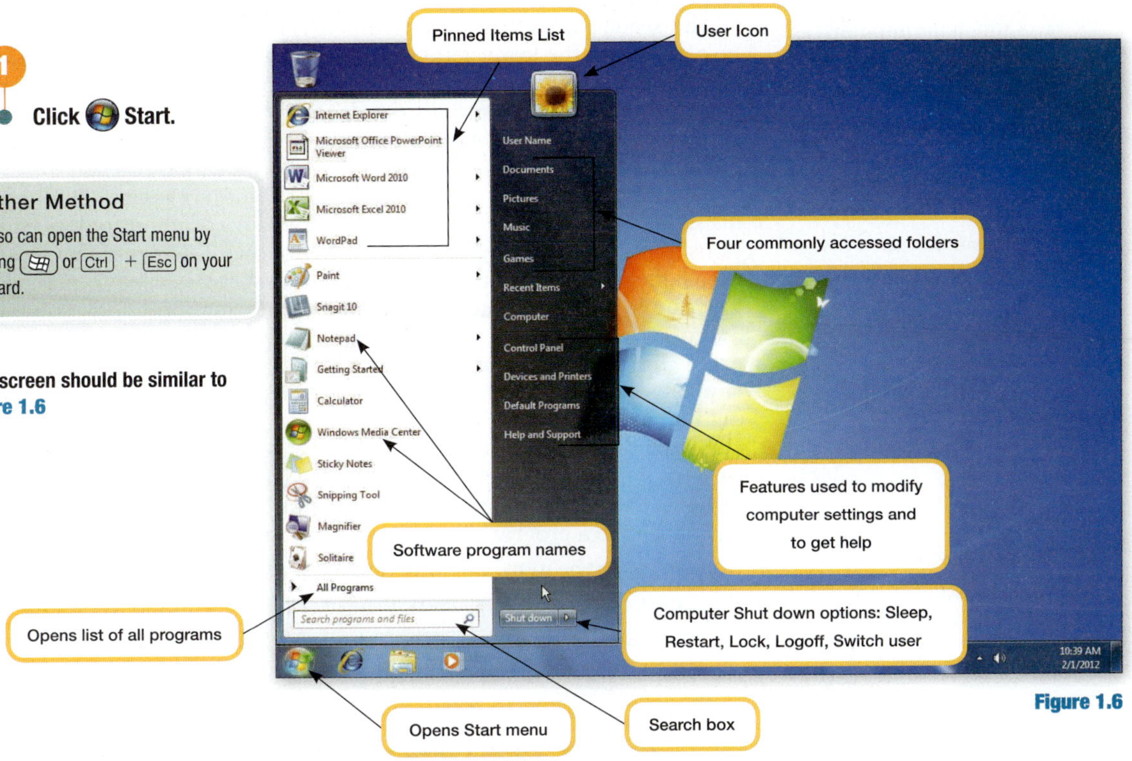

Figure 1.6

The Start menu is displayed and is one of many menus you will see in Windows 7.

Concept 3 Menu

A **menu** is a list of items from which you select an option to tell a program what you want it to do. A colored highlight bar, called the **selection cursor**, appears over the selected item. If the selected item displays a ▸, a **submenu** of additional items automatically appears. This is commonly called a **cascading menu**. Then, to choose an item, you click on it. When the item is chosen, the associated action is performed.

The Start menu consists of items that are used to start programs, access files and documents, adjust computer settings, get help, search for items on your computer, and more. It is divided into three basic areas.

The first area is the left **pane** of the Start menu. It displays a short list of names of application software programs on your computer. The program icons to the left of each name are graphic representations of the feature. The All Programs button at the bottom of the list displays a complete list of all programs on your computer, in alphabetical order, followed by folders, from which you can select.

The upper section of this pane is the **pinned items list** where the names of programs that are always available are listed. The pinned items list can be customized to display program icons for programs you use frequently. The lower section displays the names of frequently used programs. You can customize this list to display from 0 to 30 programs. Programs you have not recently used are removed from the list and replaced with the more recently used programs.

> **Additional Information**
>
> You will learn more about the search feature in Lab 2.

> **Additional Information**
>
> You will learn about folders shortly.

The second area of the Start menu is the [Search programs and files] Search box located in the lower left corner. It is used to search for programs, folders, and files on your computer by typing in words or phrases called **search terms**. When a file, folder, or program is located that contains the search term, the result appears in a list above the search box. Clicking on any search result opens the item.

The third area is on the right pane of the Start menu. The upper section displays your user icon and the names of four common folders, storage locations for items, that are provided with Windows 7. The middle section displays the Games and Computer icons. The Games icon is used to manage and play games and the Computer icon displays information about your disk drives and other hardware on your computer. The icons in the lower section provide access to features that are used to modify computer settings and get program support. Because the Start menu can be customized, yours may display different items.

Below the right pane is the [Shut down ▶] button. Clicking the button will turn off the computer; clicking the arrow will display a submenu of shut-down options: Switch user, Log off, Lock, Restart, and Sleep.

> **Another Method**
>
> You also can move the selection cursor using the four directional arrow keys (←↑→↓) and then press ←Enter to choose a selected item.

Pointing to a program name in the Start menu selects it by moving the selection cursor to the item. Clicking on an item that displays a program icon would then start the program. Clicking the [▶ All Programs] displays a long list of programs in alphabetical order followed by a list of folders. Clicking on an item that displays a (folder) displays a list of additional program or folder items.

2

- **Point to any item in the Start menu to select it.**
- **Click [▶ All Programs].**
- **Click [Accessories] to open the item.**

> **Having Trouble?**
>
> If the Accessories folder is not in view, use your down arrow ↓ directional key on the keyboard until you can see the Accessories folder.

- **Point to [Paint].**

Your screen should be similar to Figure 1.7

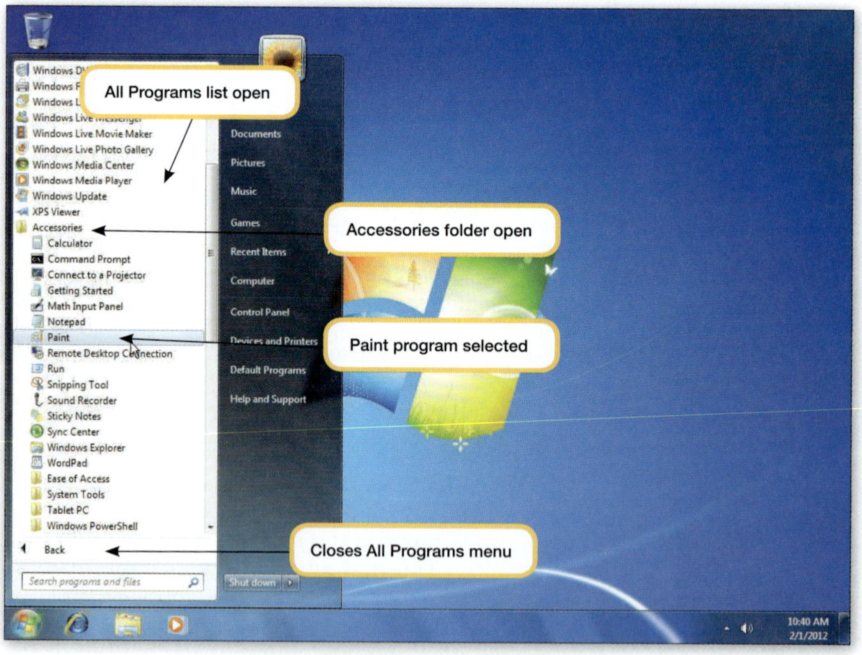

Figure 1.7

Because the Accessories item is a folder, it displays another list of additional programs and folders when selected.

3

- **Click Back to display the original Start menu list.**

Another Method

You may also press Esc to return to the original Start menu.

- **Point to Getting Started in the left pane to display a submenu of items.**

Your screen should be similar to Figure 1.8

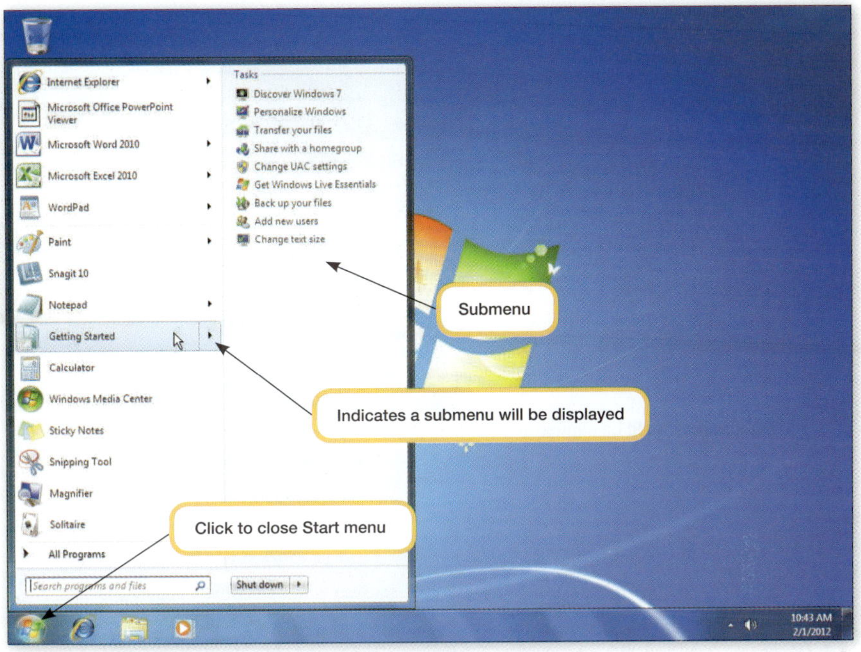

Figure 1.8

4

- **Click outside the Start menu box on a blank area of the desktop to close the menu.**

Another Method

You also can click Start again or press ⊞ or Esc to close the Start menu.

Developing the skill for moving the mouse and correctly positioning the pointer takes some time. If you accidentally find yourself in the wrong location or in a command that you did not intend to select, cancel the selected menu as you did above and try again.

STARTING WINDOWS HELP AND SUPPORT

Next, you will use the Start menu to open Windows 7 Help and Support, a bulit-in help system that is used to access information about using Windows 7. As you are learning to use a program, you will find that using the program's Help feature is an invaluable source of information about commands and procedures.

Clicking most icons in the Start menu starts a program or accesses the item or feature immediately.

1

- **Open the Start menu again.**
- **Click Help and Support in the right pane to choose this item.**

Another Method

Once an item is selected (highlighted), you also can press ←Enter to choose it.

Your screen should be similar to Figure 1.9

Additional Information

Some features have keyboard shortcuts that you can use in place of selecting the command from the menu. The keyboard shortcut to start Windows Help and Support is ⊞ + F1.

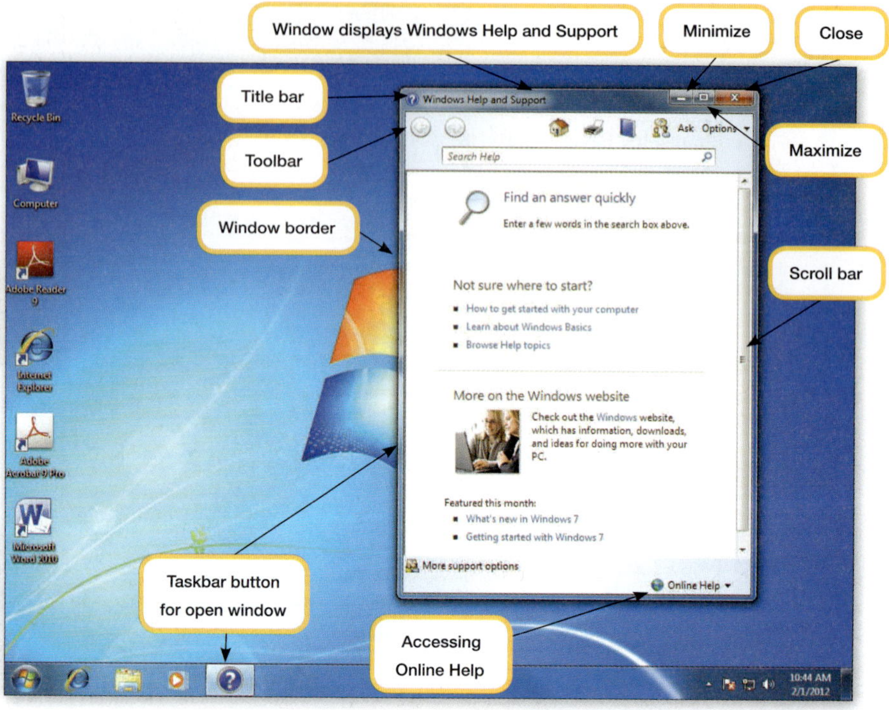

Figure 1.9

You have opened the Windows Help and Support program and the Start menu is closed. If you are connected to the Internet, the Microsoft Windows Online Web site is accessed and Help information from this site is displayed in the window. If you are not connected, the offline Help information that is provided with the application and stored on your computer is located and displayed. Generally, the listing of topics is similar but fewer in number.

Having Trouble?

Do not be concerned if your window is a different size or location. You will learn to use the Windows Help and Support window shortly.

Working with Windows

The Windows Help and Support program displays in a window on the desktop. The taskbar displays a taskbar button consisting of a single, unlabeled icon for the open window.

Concept 4 Window

A **window** is a box or frame that appears on the desktop and is used to display information and other programs. Each program you open is displayed in its own window. Multiple programs, each in its own window, can be open at the same time. This makes it easy to switch from one project to another as you work. The use of windows to display programs and other information is how the Windows operating system got its name.

Most windows have a **title bar** located at the top of the window that displays the program's name, in this case Windows Help and Support. The upper-right corner of a window displays three buttons that are used to control the window. Below the title bar you often will see a menu bar or a toolbar containing commands that are used to work with the program. The **menu bar** generally displays menu titles that when clicked on will display a list of commands or a submenu of additional choices. **Toolbars** contain buttons that provide shortcuts for starting programs or using common features and commands. The content of the window is displayed in the large space below the toolbar.

SIZING AND MOVING WINDOWS

Sometimes the location and size of a window when it opens are not convenient for what you want to do. To make the desktop more workable, you can move and resize windows.

The size of a window can be adjusted to just about any size you want. Using the buttons in the title bar (described in the table below), you can quickly **minimize** a window to its smallest size, **maximize** a window to its largest size, **restore** a window to its previous size, or close a window entirely.

Button	Description
Minimize	Reduces a window to its smallest size by taking it off the desktop. This leaves the program running and simply removes it from the desktop.
Maximize	Enlarges a window to the full screen.
Restore	Returns a window to its previous size after a window has been maximized.
Close	Used to exit the application running in the window and to close the window.

In addition, a window can be custom sized by pointing to the window border and dragging the border in the direction you want to size it. Dragging inward decreases the size and dragging outward increases the size. To change the height of a window, drag the top or bottom window border. To change the width of a window, drag the side window border. Dragging a corner changes the height and width simultaneously. While changing the size of a window, the mouse pointer will change its shape and become ↕ a double-headed arrow.

A window can be moved anywhere on the desktop. Moving a window simply displays the window at another location on the desktop. It does not change the size of the window. To move a window, click on the title bar and drag the window to the new location on the desktop.

You will try out these features by sizing and moving the Windows Help and Support window on your desktop. Your Windows Help and Support window may be a different size than shown in Figure 1.9. This is because Windows remembers and stores in your personal settings the size of a window when you last used it and displays it the same size as it last appeared.

First, you will maximize the window.

1

- **Click Maximize in the Windows Help and Support window title bar.**

Additional Information

A ScreenTip appears that displays the button name when you point to a button.

Your screen should be similar to Figure 1.10

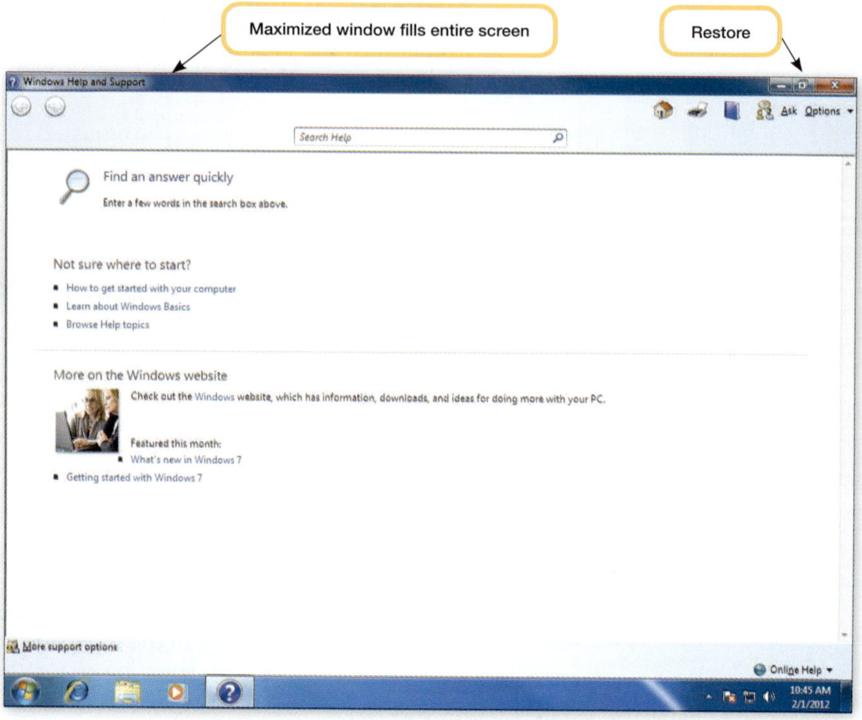

Figure 1.10

The Windows Help and Support window now appears the full size of the screen and occupies the entire desktop. Maximizing a window is helpful when you want to be able to view the maximum amount of content possible in the window. When a window is maximized, the Maximize button changes to Restore. This button is used to return a window to its previous size.

2

Click Restore.

Another Method

You also can double-click the window title bar to maximize or restore a window.

Your screen should be similar to Figure 1.11

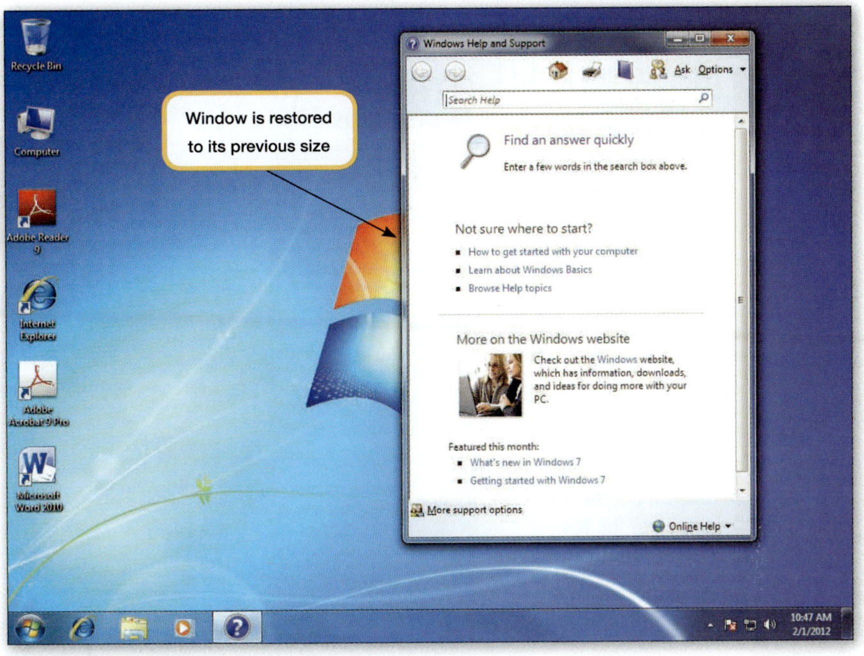

Figure 1.11

Additional Information

You cannot size a window that is maximized.

Having Trouble?

Reminder: To drag, point to an item and hold down the left mouse button while moving the mouse.

The Windows Help and Support window is now the same size as it was before it was maximized.

Next, you will custom size and shape the window by adjusting the window borders. When you point to a window border, the mouse pointer changes to a two-headed arrow. The directions in which the arrowheads point indicate the directions in which you can drag the border. First, you will adjust the height and width of the window.

3

- **Point to a side border of the Windows Help and Support window and, when the pointer changes to ↔, drag the mouse inward and outward to adjust the width of the window.**
- **Point to a top or bottom window border and when the pointer changes to ↕, drag the mouse inward and outward to adjust the height of the window.**
- **Size the window using the borders until the window size is similar to that shown in Figure 1.12.**

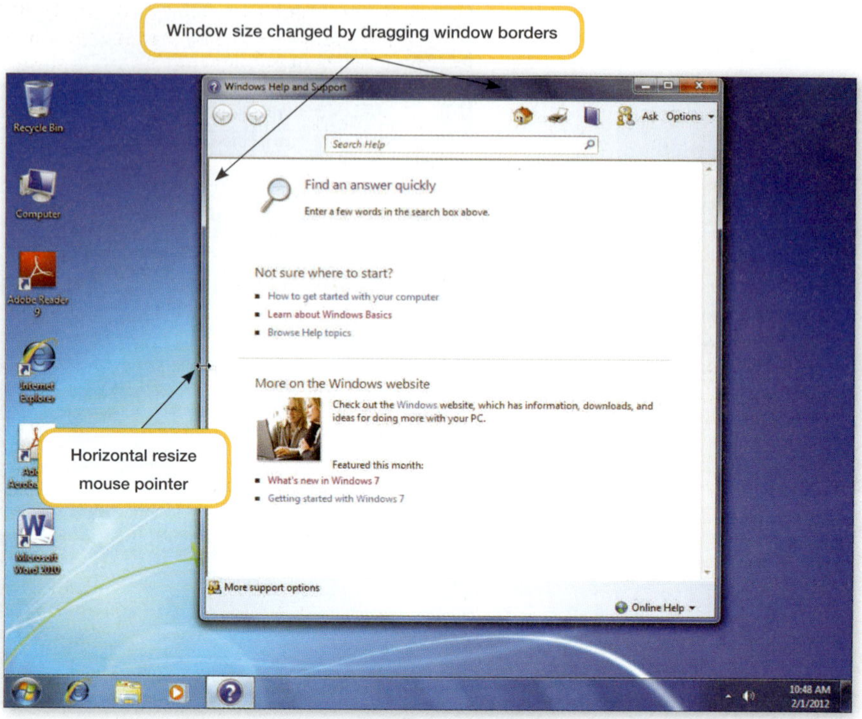

Figure 1.12

Your screen should be similar to Figure 1.12

Generally, it is faster to size a window by dragging the window corner, because this adjusts both the height and width simultaneously. When you point to a window corner, the pointer changes to ⤡.

4

- **Point to a corner of the window and when the pointer changes to ⤡, drag the mouse inward and outward to adjust both the height and width of the window simultaneously.**
- **Size the Windows Help and Support window until the window size is similar to that shown in Figure 1.13.**

Your screen should be similar to Figure 1.13

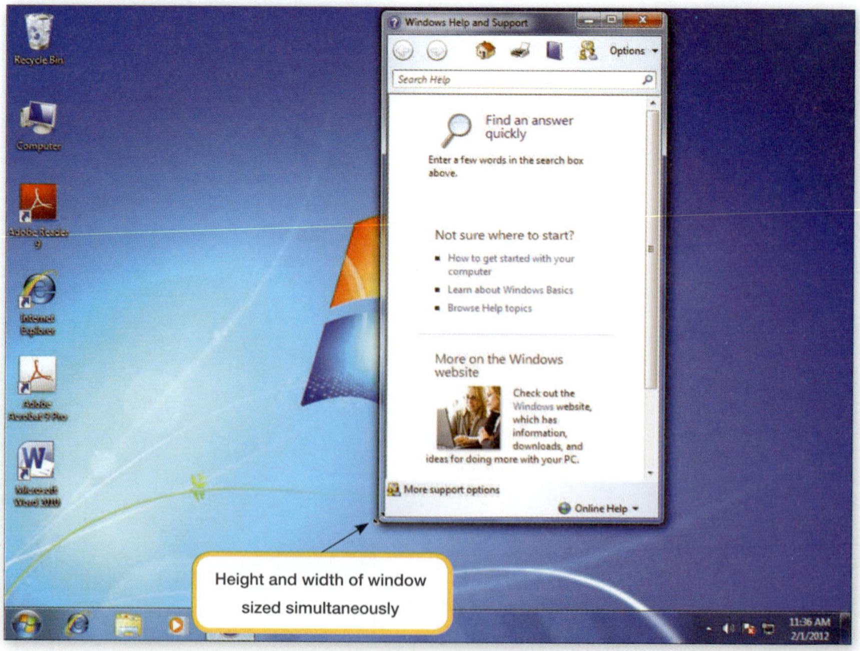

Figure 1.13

Notice as the window is sized that information in the window is reformatted as much as possible to display in the new window space. Once a window has been custom sized, the only way to return it to the original size is by resizing the window again.

You also can move a window to another location on the desktop by dragging the window title bar.

5

- **Point to the Windows Help and Support window title bar and drag the window to the lower-left corner of the desktop.**

Your screen should be similar to Figure 1.14

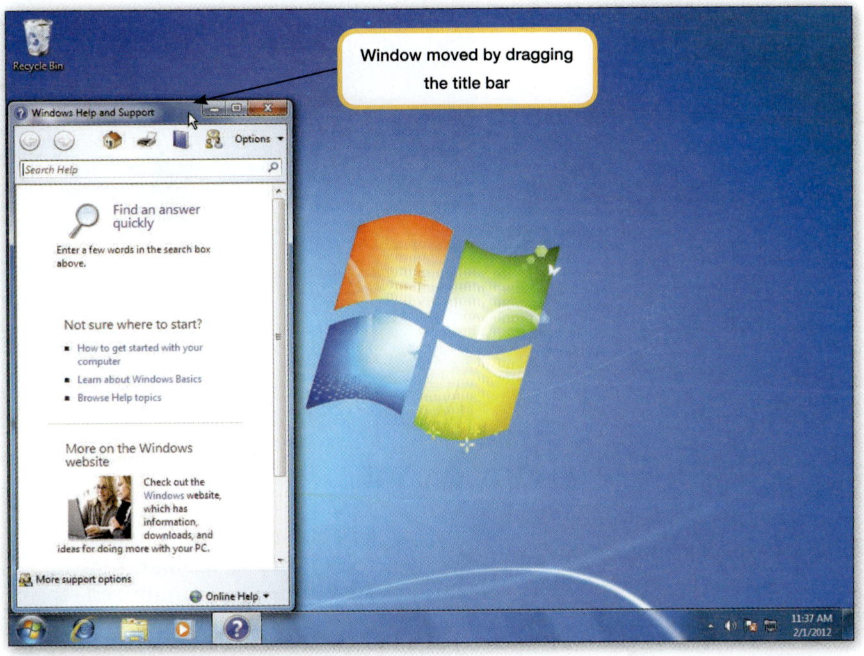

Figure 1.14

Moving a window allows you to see information under it on the desktop or in other open windows while still being able to view the information in the window.

Often you will want to keep a window open for future reference, but you do not want it to occupy space on the desktop. To do this, you can minimize the window.

6

- Click Minimize in the Windows Help and Support window title bar.

Your screen should be similar to Figure 1.15

Figure 1.15

Additional Information

If Aero is not the user interface, the names of the open windows are displayed in a list.

The window is no longer displayed on the desktop. The Windows Help and Support button in the taskbar, however, is still displayed. This indicates the window is still open but minimized. To redisplay the window, simply click on its taskbar button. When you point to a taskbar button, thumbnail previews of any open files associated with the program appear. A **thumbnail** is a miniature window that displays a representation of the window content. This feature is called **Aero Peek**.

7

- Point to to see the preview or list.
- Click .

The Windows Help and Support window is redisplayed on the desktop in the size and location it last appeared.

SCROLLING A WINDOW

As you resized the window, you were able to see more of the window contents as the window was enlarged and less as it was made smaller. When there is more information in the window than space, a **scroll bar** is displayed. It is used with a mouse to bring additional lines of information into view in a space. Scroll bars can run vertically along the right side or horizontally along the bottom. The vertical scroll bar is used to move vertically and the horizontal scroll bar to move horizontally in the space. The scroll bar consists of **scroll arrows** and a **scroll box**. Clicking the arrows moves the information in the direction of the arrows, allowing new information to be displayed in the space.

Additional Information

If there is no scroll box in the scroll bar, this indicates the entire topic is visible in the window.

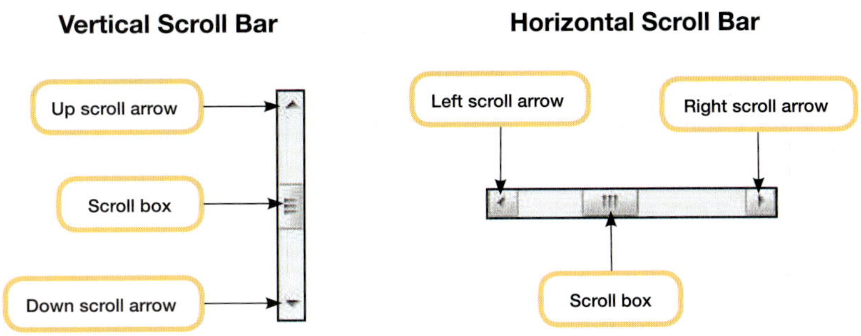

1

- Move the Windows Help and Support window to the center of the desktop.
- Reduce the size of the window similar to that shown in Figure 1.16.
- Click three times to bring more information into view in the window.

Your screen should be similar to Figure 1.16

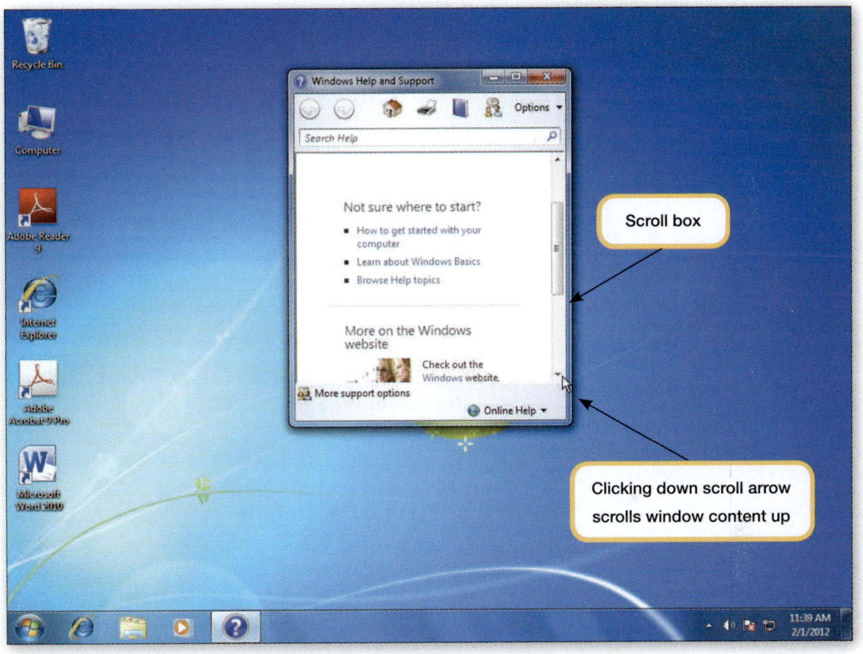

Figure 1.16

The information in the window has moved up line by line, allowing new information to be displayed in the space. Did you notice the movement of the scroll box as you scrolled the pane? It moved down along the scroll bar to show your relative position within the area of available information. In many scroll bars, the size of the scroll box also indicates the relative amount of information available. For example, a small box indicates that only a small amount of the total available information is displayed, whereas a large box indicates that almost all or a large portion of the total amount of available information is displayed.

To move larger distances quickly, you can click above or below the scroll box to move the information in the window up or down a window-full at a time. Additionally, you can drag the scroll box to move to a general location within the window. Finally, by holding down the scroll arrows, you can scroll the window quickly line by line.

2

- **Drag the scroll box to the top of the scroll bar.**
- **Click on the scroll bar below the scroll box.**
- **Point to and hold down the left mouse button for a few seconds to continuously scroll to the top of the window.**

Your screen should be similar to Figure 1.17

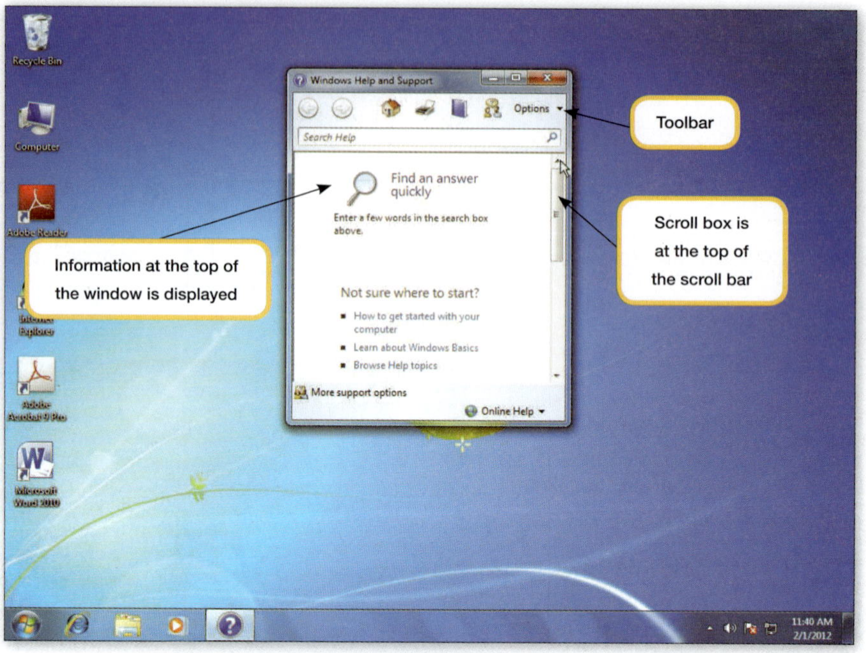

Figure 1.17

The scroll box is at the top of the scroll bar when the information at the top of the window is displayed.

Using Help and Support

The toolbar displayed below the title bar contains buttons that help you use and navigate within Windows Help and Support. The toolbar buttons are described in the following table.

Button	Description
	Displays previous page of information
	Displays next page of information after is used.
	Displays the opening (Home) page of the Help and Support Center.
	Prints the current page of information displayed in the Help and Support window.
	Provides a table of contents list of topics from which you can select to access subtopics.
Ask	Provides links to customer support and additional resources for getting help.
Options	Displays options to modify Help and Support settings.

The main window area displays a list of Help topics you can select.

1

- **Point to Learn about Windows Basics.**

Your screen should be similar to Figure 1.18

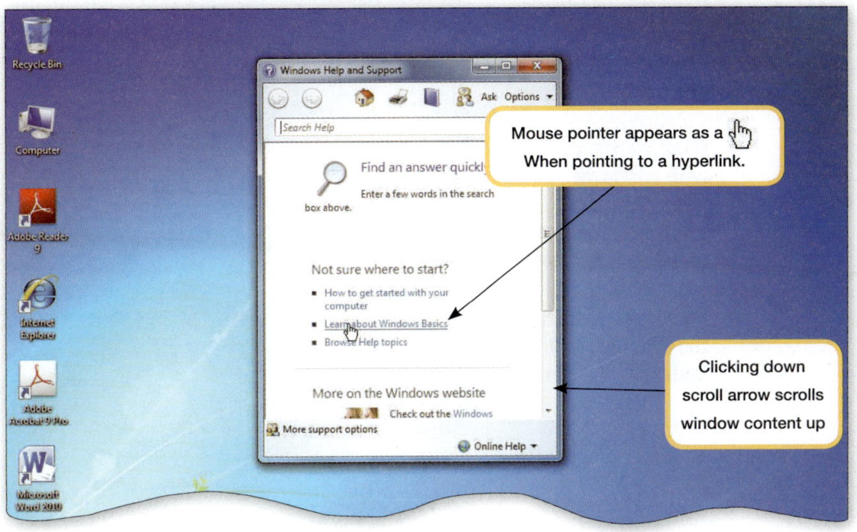

Figure 1.18

Additional Information

The Windows Help system uses Hypertext Markup Language (HTML), a simple programming language that is used to create hyperlinks and format and display information.

Notice that the topic you are pointing to appears in blue text and underlined and that the mouse pointer appears as a . This indicates the item is a hyperlink. **Hyperlinks** typically provide a connection to information at another location. Clicking on a hyperlink jumps to that location and displays the information.

2

- **Click Learn about Windows Basics.**

Your screen should be similar to Figure 1.19

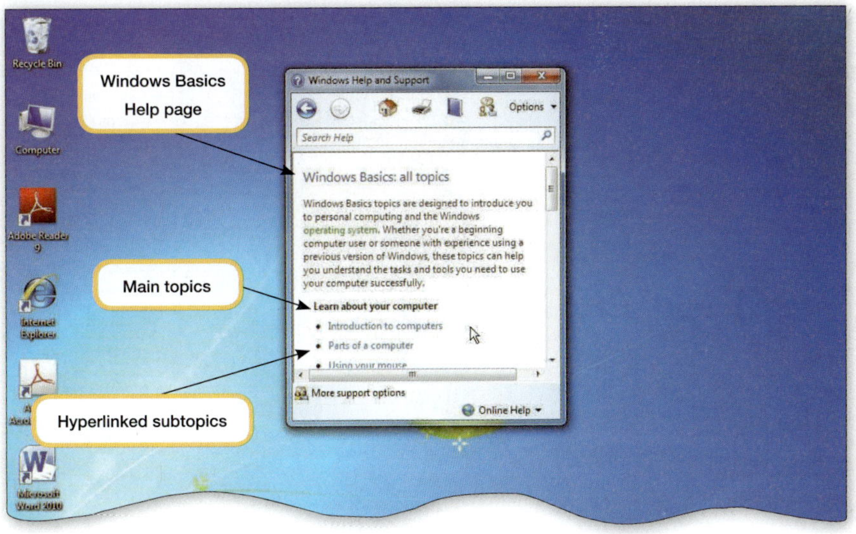

Figure 1.19

The Help and Support window now displays the Windows Basics Help page and a list of main topics and hyperlinked subtopics. A **page** is a unit of information contained in Windows Help. The window also displays a scroll bar because there is more information than can be currently displayed in the window. Clicking on a subtopic will display information about the selected subtopic.

3

- **Scroll the window to see all of the available topics and subtopics.**
- **Click Working with windows in the Desktop fundamentals main topic.**
- **If necessary increase the window size to better see the content.**

Your screen should be similar to Figure 1.20

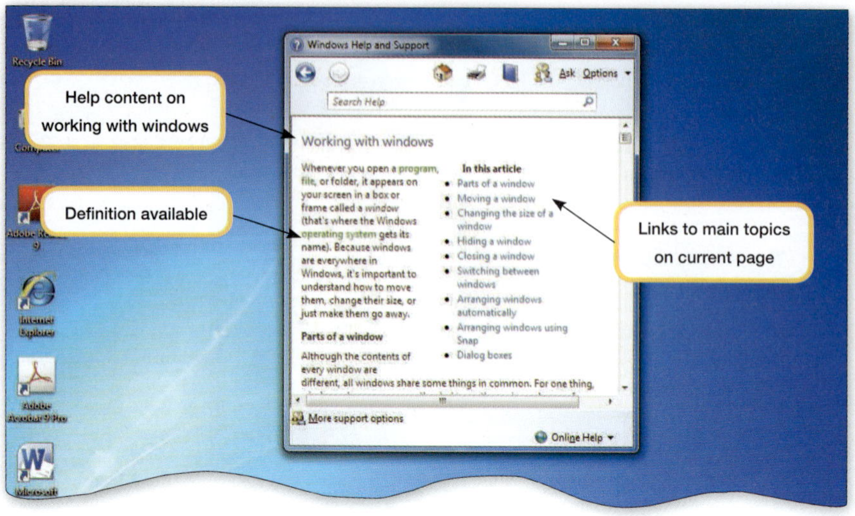

Figure 1.20

The window now displays a page of content about working with windows. The page also displays a list of links to the major topics of the article to help you quickly jump to the selected topic.

Additionally, whenever you see a green word in a Help topic, you can click on it to see a definition of the term.

4

- **Click on the green words "operating system."**

Additional Information

Pointing to a defined term displays the ScreenTip, View Definition.

Your screen should be similar to Figure 1.21

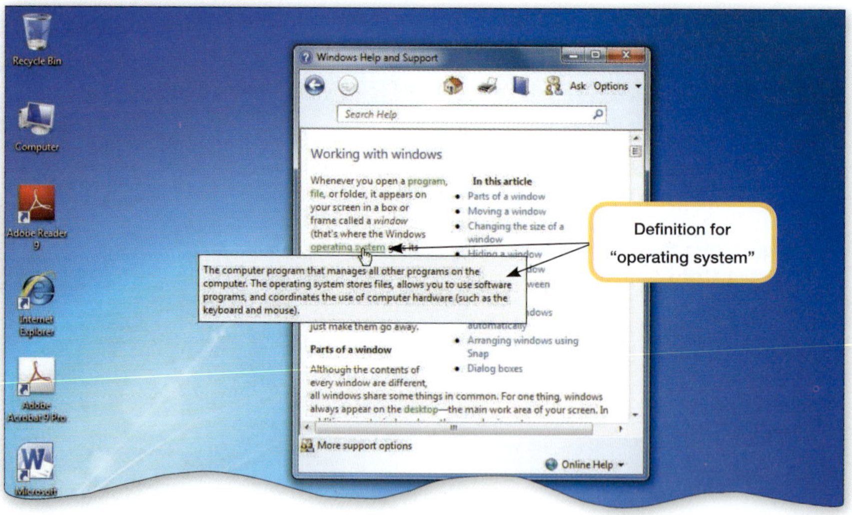

Figure 1.21

A pop-up box containing a definition of an operating system is displayed. Because there is a lot of information about this topic, the scroll box is small, indicating that a small amount of the total available information is displayed in the window. You will increase the size of the Help window to view more information and then quickly jump to a main topic in the current article using a link in the In this article list.

5

- **Click outside the definition box to clear it.**
- **Increase the size of the Help window similar to that shown in Figure 1.22.**
- **Click the Switching between windows topic link.**

Your screen should be similar to Figure 1.22

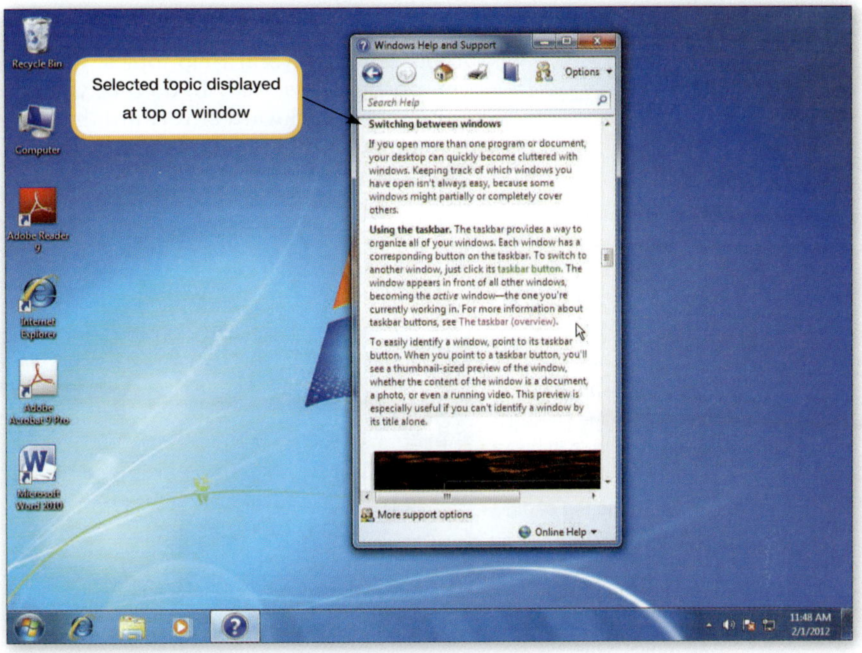

Figure 1.22

Using the topic link, you have quickly jumped to the selected topic in the article and displays it at the top of the window. If you see a purple hyperlink, this means the topic was recently viewed.

6

- **Click The taskbar (overview).**
- **Increase the size of the window as in Figure 1.23.**

Your screen should be similar to Figure 1.23

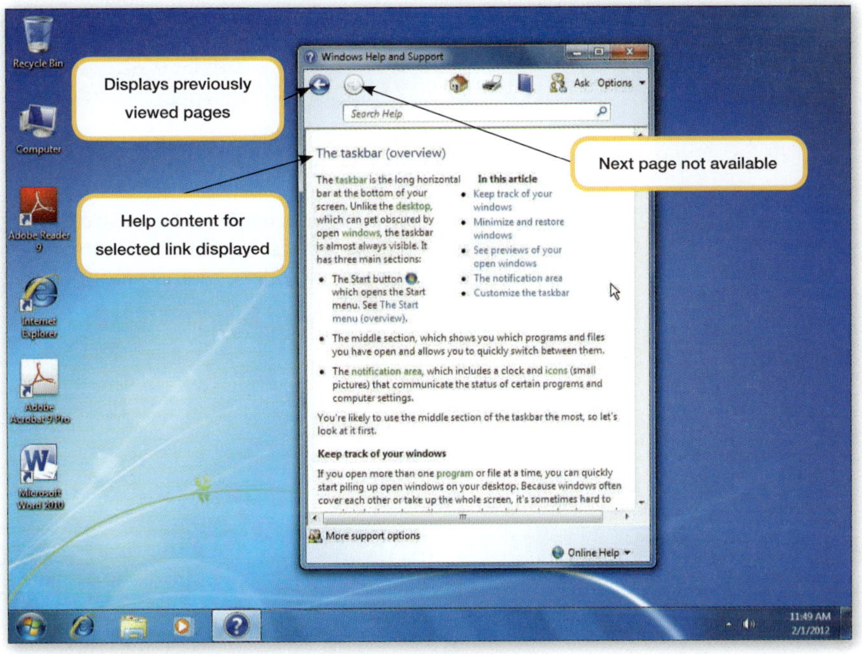

Figure 1.23

A new page of information about this topic is displayed in the Help window.

NAVIGATING HELP AND SUPPORT

After viewing several Help topics, you may want to quickly return to a topic you previously viewed. To do this, you use the and buttons on the toolbar to move backward or forward through viewed topics. Notice the button is dimmed. A dimmed button indicates it is not available until another action has been performed. In this case, it is not available until after the button has been used.

Using will display the last-viewed Help topics in the order in which you displayed them.

1

- **Click to display the previously viewed page.**
- **Scroll to the top of the window.**
- **Click to display the Windows Basics: all topics page.**
- **Click to redisplay the Working with windows page.**

Your screen should be similar to Figure 1.24

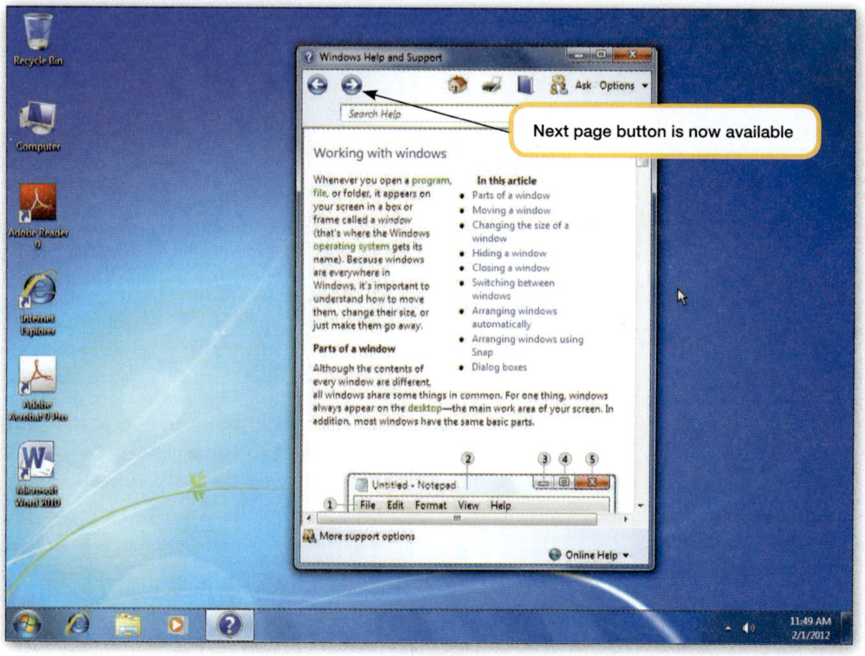

Figure 1.24

You have moved back and forward through several pages of previously displayed Help topics. You also can return quickly to the Windows Help and Support opening window of information, called the **home page**, using the Home button.

2

- **Click Home on the toolbar.**

Your screen should be similar to Figure 1.25

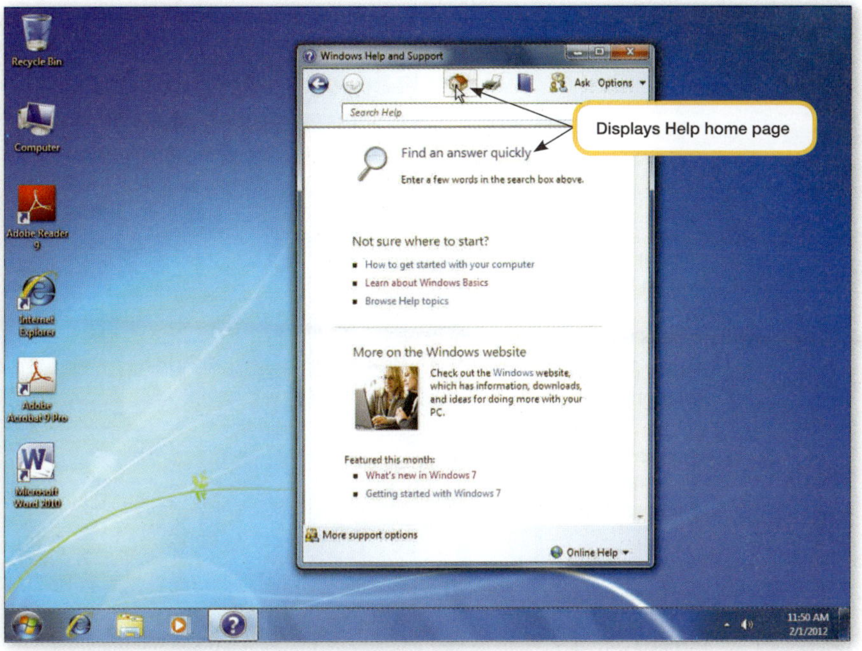

Figure 1.25

USING THE BROWSE HELP FEATURE

Another way to locate information is to use the Browse Help feature. This feature displays a table of contents list of topics that you can use to locate Help topics by subject.

1

- **Click Browse Help on the toolbar.**

Your screen should be similar to Figure 1.26

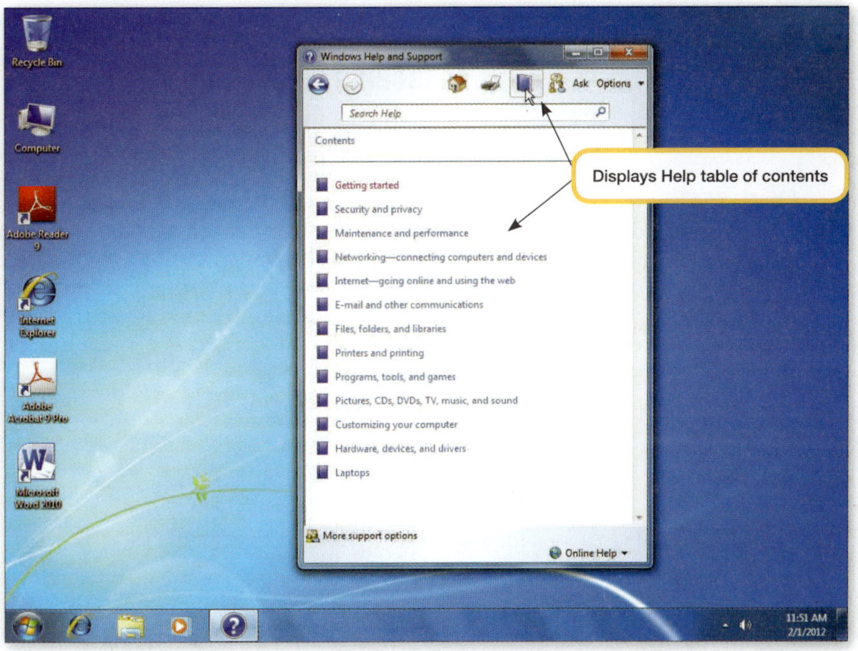

Figure 1.26

The page displays a complete list of subject headings. By clicking on one of the headings, you access a list of Help topics or other subject headings that pertain to the main heading. Topics preceded with display additional topics and those preceded with a display the page of information on that feature.

2

- **Click the topic Getting Started.**
- **Choose Windows Basics (under Categories).**
- **Choose Desktop Fundamentals in Windows.**
- **Choose Working with windows.**

Your screen should be similar to Figure 1.27

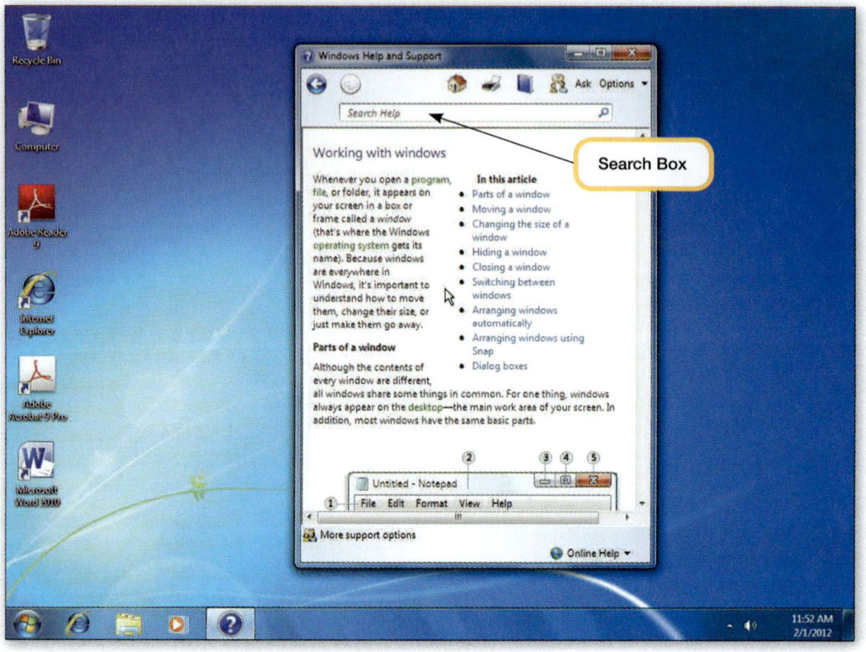

Figure 1.27

You have navigated through the table of contents to again display the Help information on working with windows that you viewed earlier.

SEARCHING HELP

Another way to locate Help information on a specific topic is by typing a word or phrase about the topic you want help on in the Search box. This feature is particularly helpful when you have a good idea of what you are looking for. The Search box is located below the toolbar of the Windows Help and Support window. The Search box is a text box in which you type information. For best search results, type a word or two in the text box that you think are most descriptive of the content you want to find. The more specific the search text, the greater the likelihood of finding the information you want. You do not need to be concerned about capitalization, as the case does not affect the results.

Additional Information

The mouse pointer appears as an I-beam when pointing to a text box. It is used to position the cursor by clicking on the location where you want the cursor to be placed.

1

- **Click in the Search text box.**
- **Type desktop.**
- **Click [Search icon] Search Help.**

Additional Information

You also can press ←Enter to start the search.

Your screen should be similar to Figure 1.28

Additional Information

Because online Help updates frequently, the information displayed in the Help window may be slightly different than shown here.

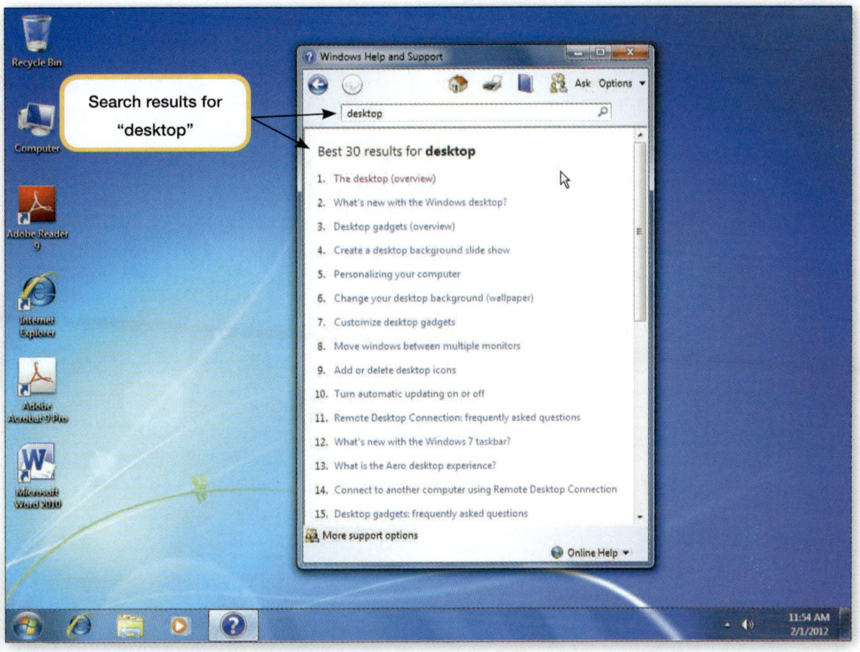

Figure 1.28

Additional Information

By default, the number of results displayed in each page is 30. A link to more results is located at the bottom of the list.

After a few seconds, the search is complete and Windows Help and Support displays a numbered list of located topics. Clicking one of the numbered topics opens a page that displays information about the selected topic.

Many of the topics in the list do not appear to include the information you want. To change the search to more accurately locate the information you want, you could change the search term or add additional descriptive words to it. When searching on multiple words, the results include any topics that include either word, thereby expanding the search. To narrow the search, you can enter a phrase, enclosed in quotes. You will search on "desktop wallpaper" to refine the search to locate only topics that include that phrase, not the individual words.

When a text box already contains an entry, you can select or highlight the entry and then type the new entry. To select text, drag the mouse pointer from one end of the entry to the other. Double-clicking on a word in the text box highlights the entire word. The highlighted text is replaced by the new text you type. Alternatively, you can change the existing entry by adding or deleting characters and words. Use ←Backspace to remove characters to the left of the cursor and Delete to remove characters to the right.

2

- Click at the beginning of the entry in the search box and type **"**.
- Click at the end of the entry, press space, and type **wallpaper"**.
- Press ←Enter.

Your screen should be similar to **Figure 1.29**

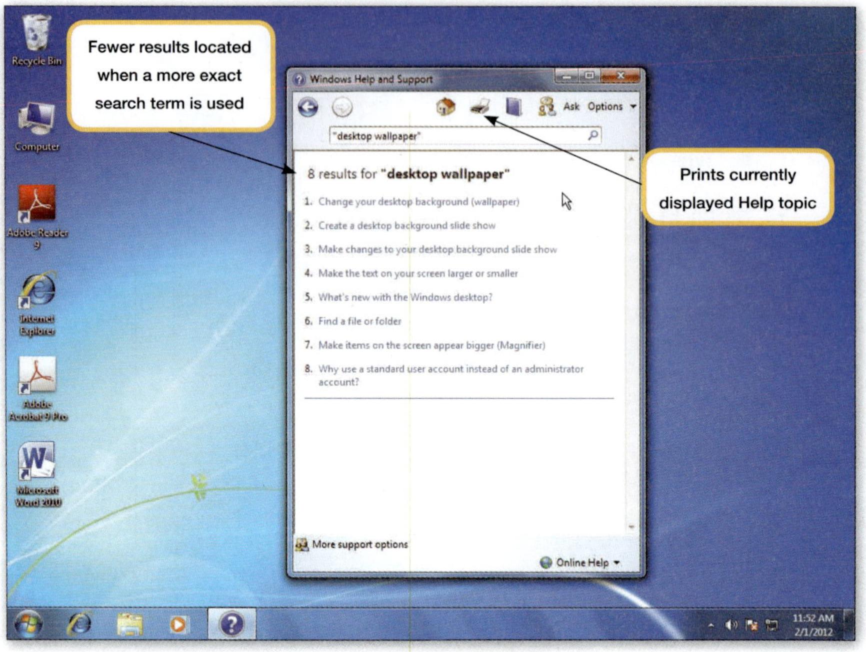

Figure 1.29

Now the search located fewer results. They are, however, more directly related to what you want to find.

PRINTING A HELP TOPIC AND USING DIALOG BOXES

Before leaving Windows Help and Support, you decide you want to view and print a copy of the The Desktop (overview) help topic.

1

- Click .
- Choose The desktop (overview).
- Click Print in the toolbar.

Your screen should be similar to **Figure 1.30**

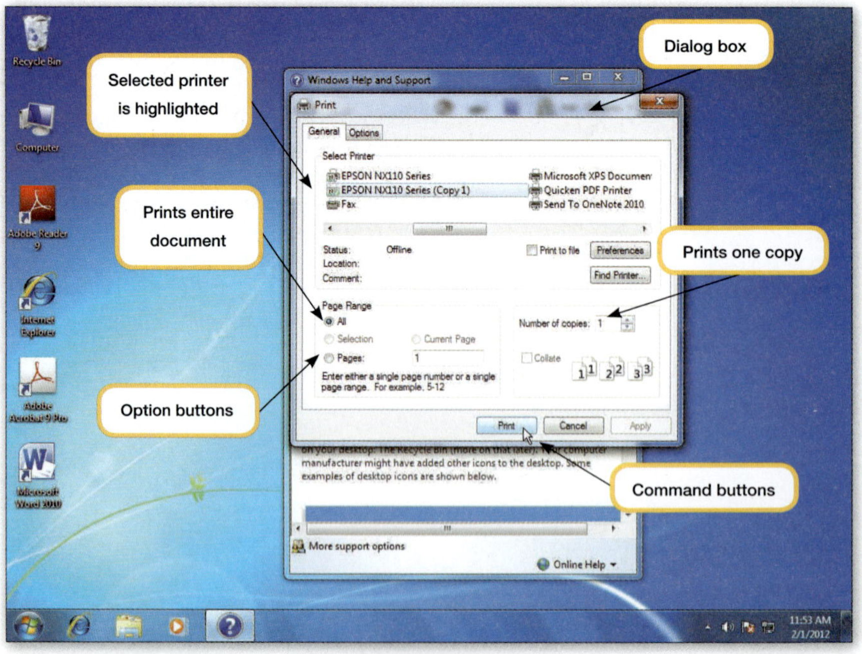

Figure 1.30

A dialog box is displayed in which you need to specify the print settings.

Concept 5 Dialog Box

A **dialog box** is a window that is displayed whenever the program requires additional information to complete a task. All dialog boxes have a title bar at the top, which displays a name identifying the contents of the dialog box, and a X button that is used to close the box. Inside the dialog box are command buttons and areas to select or specify the needed information. Unlike a window, a dialog box cannot be sized. It can be moved, however, just like a window.

The features shown in the table below may be found in dialog boxes; however, not all features are found in every dialog box. Some features such as text boxes and scroll bars also are found in windows and menus. Others are found only in dialog boxes.

Feature	Use
Text box	An area where you type in the requested information.
Drop-down list box	A text box that displays the currently selected item and a ▾ button. Clicking the ▾ button displays a drop-down list of options from which you can select, or you can type the information in the text box.
Option button	Used to select from a group of options. The selected option displays a blue dot in the option button. Only one option can be selected from a list of option buttons.
Check box	Used to select from a group of options. The selected option displays a checkmark. More than one option can be selected from a list of check box options.
List box	A box displaying a list of options from which you can select.
Command button	Instructs Windows to carry out the instructions on the button. The two most common command buttons are OK and Cancel. Others you will see are Save, Print, and Apply.

Additional Information

Dialog boxes always have one command button that is the default button. This button appears with a dark border line. It also can be selected by simply pressing ←Enter.

From the Print dialog box, you need to specify the printer you will be using and the print settings. The printer that is currently selected is highlighted in the Select Printer section of the dialog box.

The Page Range area of the Print dialog box lets you specify how much of the topic you want printed. The range options are described in the following table:

Option	Action
All	Prints entire document.
Selection	Prints portion of text you selected (by highlighting).
Current page	Prints selected page (the page the insertion point is on) of a multiple-page document.
Pages	Prints pages you specify by typing page numbers in the text box.

In Help, the default range setting, All, will print the entire displayed Help topic. In the Copies section, the default setting of one copy of the topic is acceptable.

2

- **If you need to change the selected printer to another printer, click on the appropriate printer (your instructor will tell you which printer to select) to select it.**
- **Click Print.**

The dialog box is closed and your printer should be printing out the Help topic.

USING THE OPTIONS MENU

The Options menu, shown below, includes many features that access and modify Help features. These include menu equivalents for printing a Help topic and browsing Help. Additionally, using this menu you can change the size of the text in the Help window, locate specific words in a page, and turn on or off Windows Online Help. You will take a quick look at these three features next.

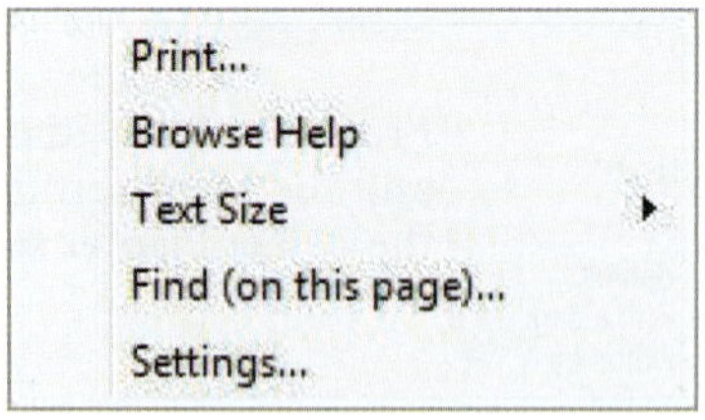

1

- **Click Options and select Text Size.**
- **Choose Largest.**

Your screen should be similar to Figure 1.31

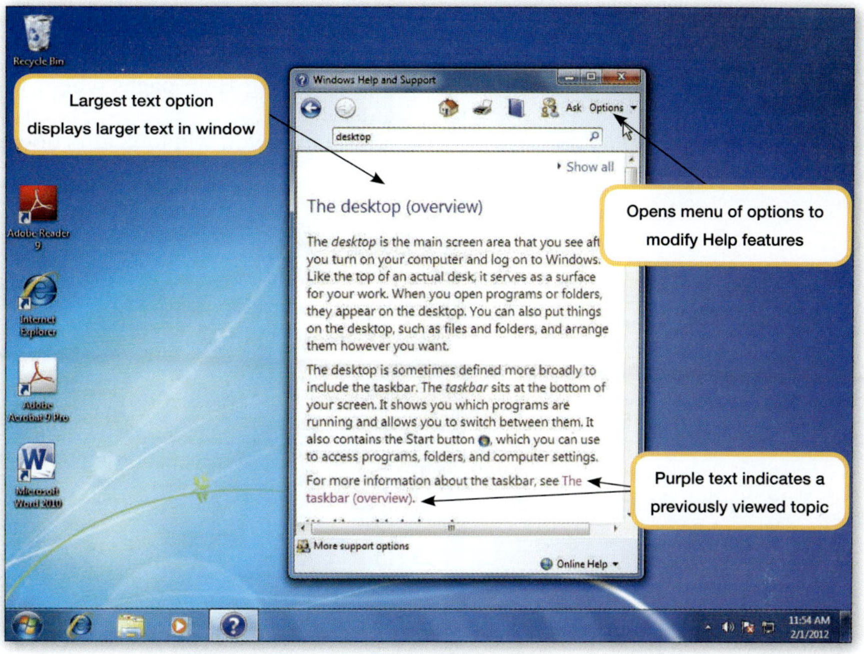

Figure 1.31

The text is much larger and therefore easier to see. However, less information can be displayed in a window. Next, you will use the Find feature to quickly find every occurrence of the word "desktop" in the current help topic. As you type the text to find, the matching text on the page is highlighted in yellow.

2

- **Click Options and choose Find (on this page).**
- **Type desktop in the Find text box.**
- **Click Next 4 times.**

Your screen should be similar to Figure 1.32

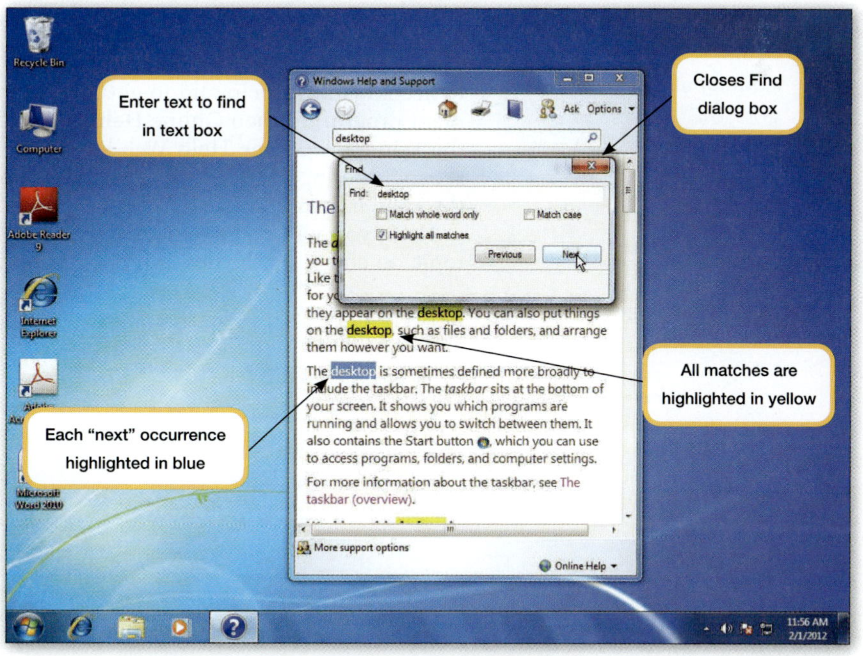

Figure 1.32

Each time you clicked Next, the next occurrence of the word in the Help page was located and the highlighting changed to blue. This feature is particularly helpful in long Help pages where you are looking for information on a specific item.

The last feature you will look at is how to turn Online Help on and off.

3

- **Click X to close the Find box.**
- **Click Options and choose Settings.**

Your screen should be similar to Figure 1.33

Another Method

You also can click Online Help or Offline Help at the bottom of the Help window to turn on/off Online Help and access the Settings menu.

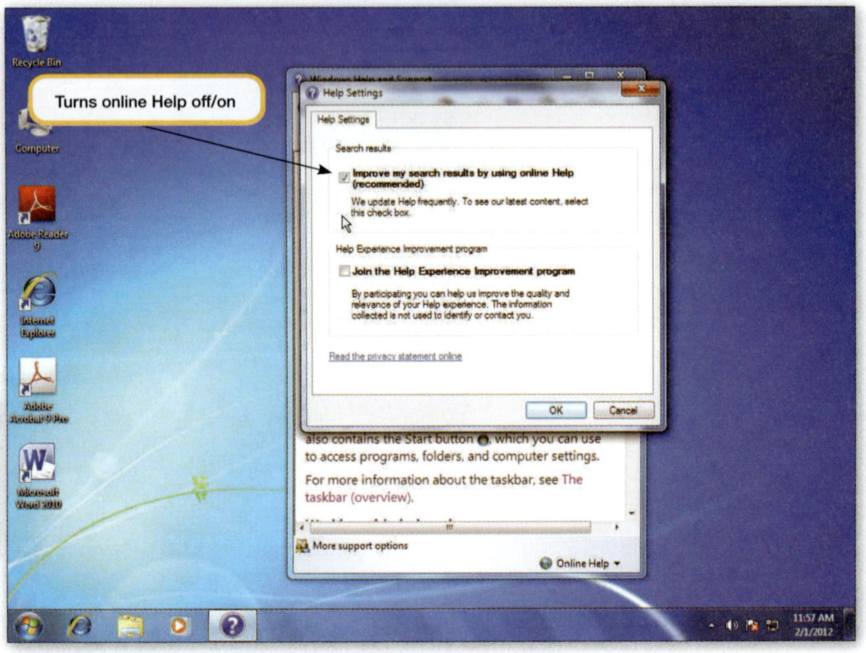

Figure 1.33

Additional Information

When you use Online Help, you also can mark a topic as a Favorite so that it is easy to find again at a later time by selecting the topic from the Favorites list.

The Help Settings dialog box contains options for connecting to the Internet to access Online Help and to get involved with the Help Experience improvement program. When Online Help is on, the option displays a checkmark and the Windows Online Help Web site is accessed whenever you use Help. The second option, when selected, includes you in a program to rate the quality of the Help information.

Next, you will restore the text size to Medium and then take a look at the topic on changing the desktop background.

4

- **Click** [Cancel] **to close the Help Settings dialog box without making any changes.**
- **Click** [Options] **, select Text Size, and choose Medium.**
- **Click** [back arrow] **twice and choose Change your desktop background.**
- **Scroll the window to see the first step.**

Your screen should be similar to Figure 1.34

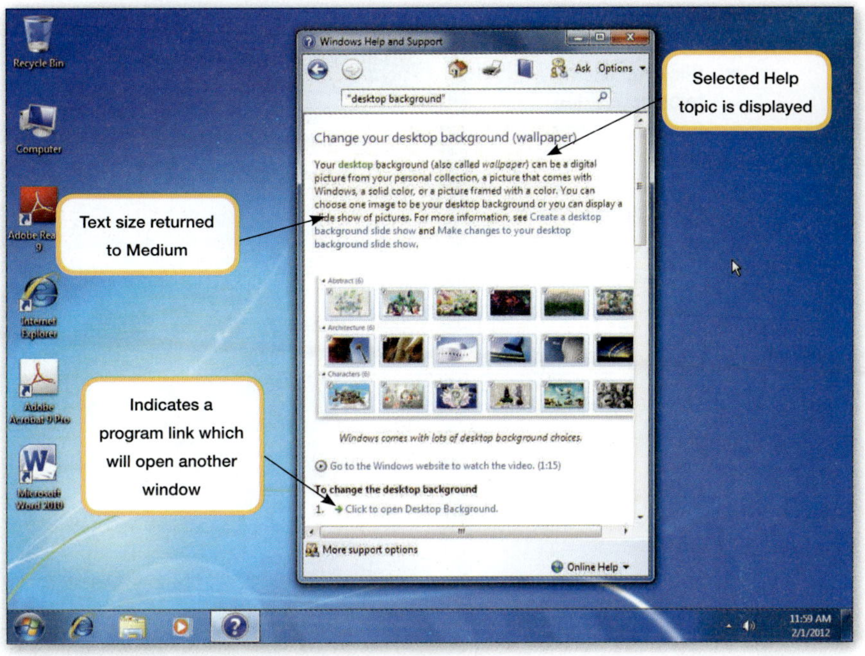

Figure 1.34

The text size of the Help window is restored to the original setting and the selected topic is displayed.

Working with Multiple Windows

It is very common when using your computer that you will have more than one application running at the same time. Each program is displayed in its own window. The capability to run multiple programs at the same time is called **multitasking**. This makes using your computer more like you would actually work, allowing you to switch easily between tasks without having to put one away before beginning the other.

OPENING A SECOND WINDOW

Notice the ➔ preceding the link in the first numbered step. This indicates that clicking this link will open the associated item, such as a program, that is stored on your computer. In this case, it will open the Desktop Background window.

Additional Information

More typically, the Desktop Background window is opened by choosing it from the Control Panel, which is found in the Start menu.

1

- **Click the Click to open Desktop Background link.**

Your screen should be similar to Figure 1.35

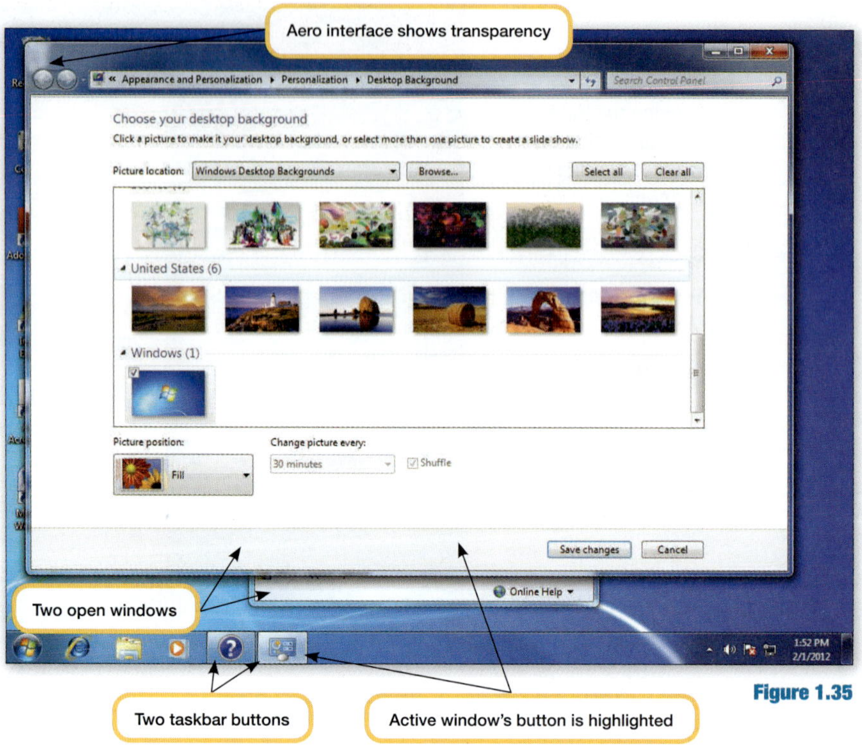

Figure 1.35

A second window opens on the desktop and the taskbar displays a button for this open window. If you are using the Aero desktop effect, parts of the windows are transparent and display underlying items. There are now two programs running at the same time: Windows Help and Support and Desktop Background.

As more windows are opened, their buttons will appear on the taskbar. If you are using Windows Aero and if multiple windows are open within one program, the taskbar button will appear layered.

The Desktop Background window is the **active window**, the window that is currently in use. You can tell it is the active window because the taskbar button appears highlighted, whereas the inactive window button is darker in color. Multiple windows can be open on the desktop at once, but only one window is active at a time.

When a new window is opened, it appears in the size in which it was last used and in any location on the desktop. The newly open window is automatically the active window and appears on top of other open windows on the desktop. To see a window that is below another window and make it the active window, you can click anywhere on the window if it is visible. You can use Peek to preview the contents of the open windows and switch to the one you want by clicking on the thumbnail. If only one window is open in a program, simply click on the taskbar button to switch to it and make it the active window.

Additional Information

If you are not using Aero and you have multiple windows open under a single program, the window title will appear in a list when you point to the program's taskbar button. Clicking on the window title will make it the active window.

2

- **Size the Desktop Background window as in Figure 1.36.**
- **Click [?] on the taskbar to make the Help window active.**

Another Method

You can also press Alt + Tab to switch to the previous window or to cycle through all open windows and the desktop by holding down Alt and repeatedly pressing Tab. When you release Alt, the selected window is active.

Your screen should be similar to Figure 1.36

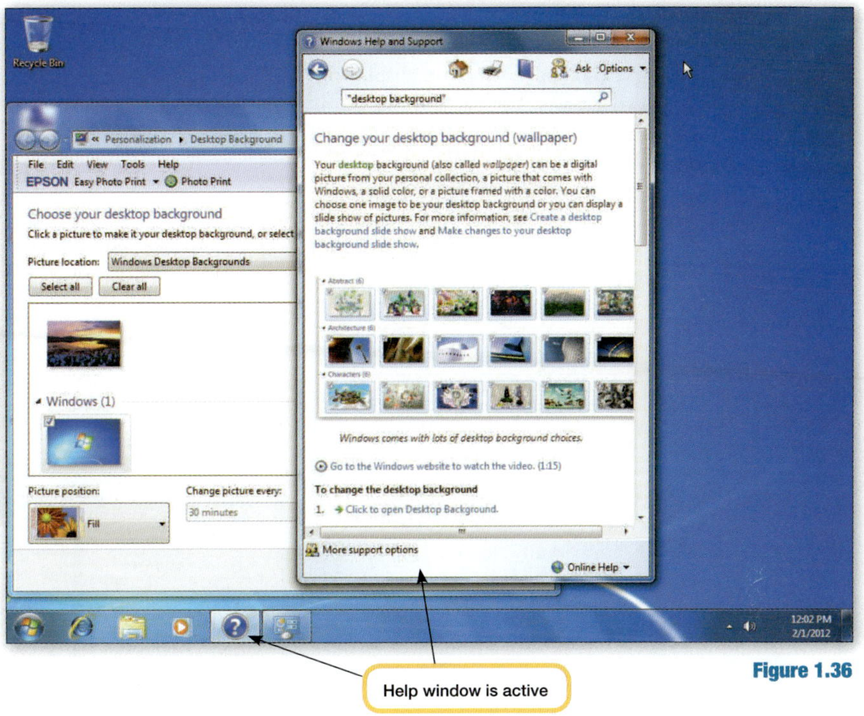

Figure 1.36

Now the Help and Support window is on top of the Desktop Background window and the taskbar button is highlighted.

ARRANGING WINDOWS

When working with multiple open windows, it is often convenient to use Windows 7's standard window-arranging features. There are three ways to arrange windows on the desktop: **cascade**, side by side, and stacked, as described in the following table.

Feature	Description	
Cascade	Layers open windows, displaying the active window fully and only the title bars of all other open windows behind it.	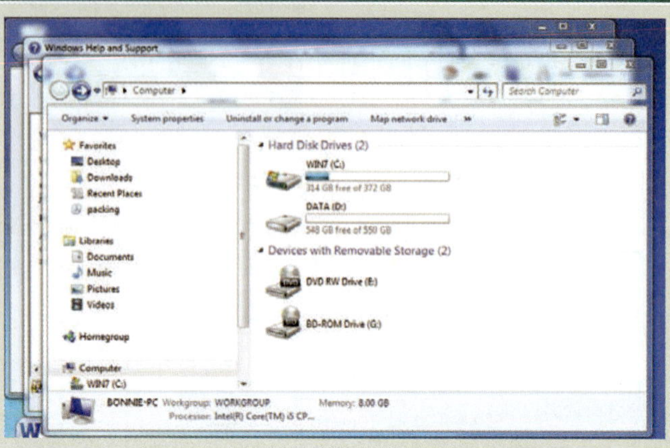
Side by side	Resizes each open window and arranges the windows horizontally side by side.	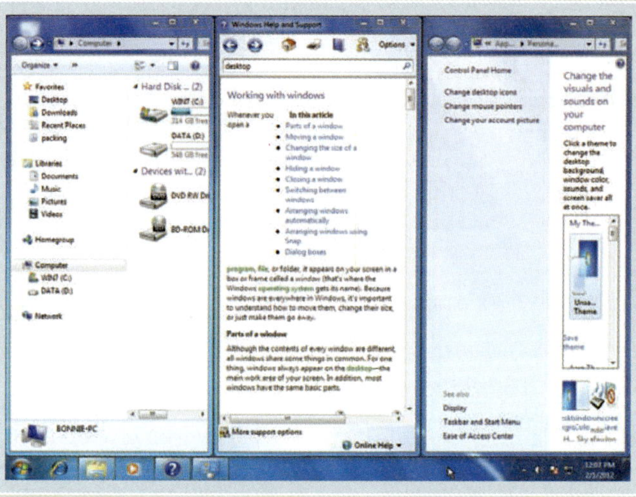
Stacked	Resizes each open window and arranges the windows vertically stacked.	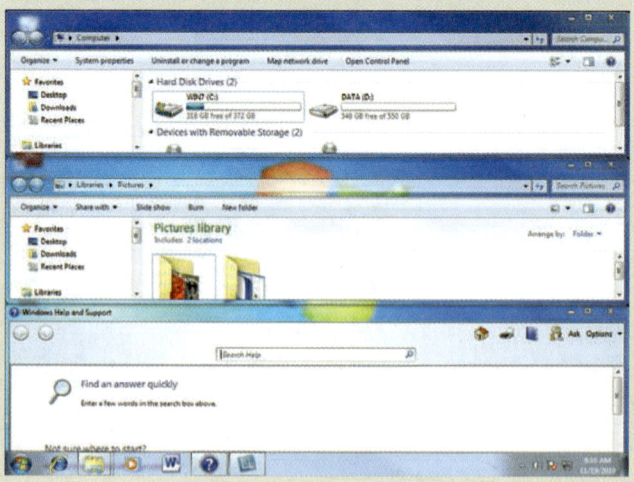

> **Additional Information**
>
> When using the Aero interface, you also can press Ctrl + ⊞ + Tab to activate a special feature called Flip 3D. All open windows are arranged in a three-dimensional stack that you can quickly flip through by pressing Tab.

Cascading windows is useful if you want to work primarily in one window, but you want to see the titles of other open windows. Tiling is most useful when you want to work in several applications simultaneously because it allows you to quickly see the contents of all open windows and move between them. However, the greater the number of open windows, the smaller is the space available to display the **tiled** window contents.

To access the commands to change window arrangements, you need to open the taskbar shortcut menu. A **shortcut menu** is a menu that appears when you right-click on an item or on the desktop. The options in the shortcut menu reflect the most frequently used commands for the item you clicked on. If there are additional menu items for the object, you can hold down ⇧Shift while right-clicking the object to display every available command for that object in the shortcut menu.

You will open the taskbar shortcut menu to cascade the two open windows.

1

- **Right-click an empty area on the taskbar.**

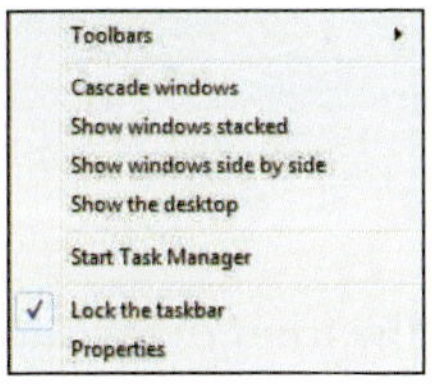

- **Choose Cascade windows.**

Your screen should be similar to Figure 1.37

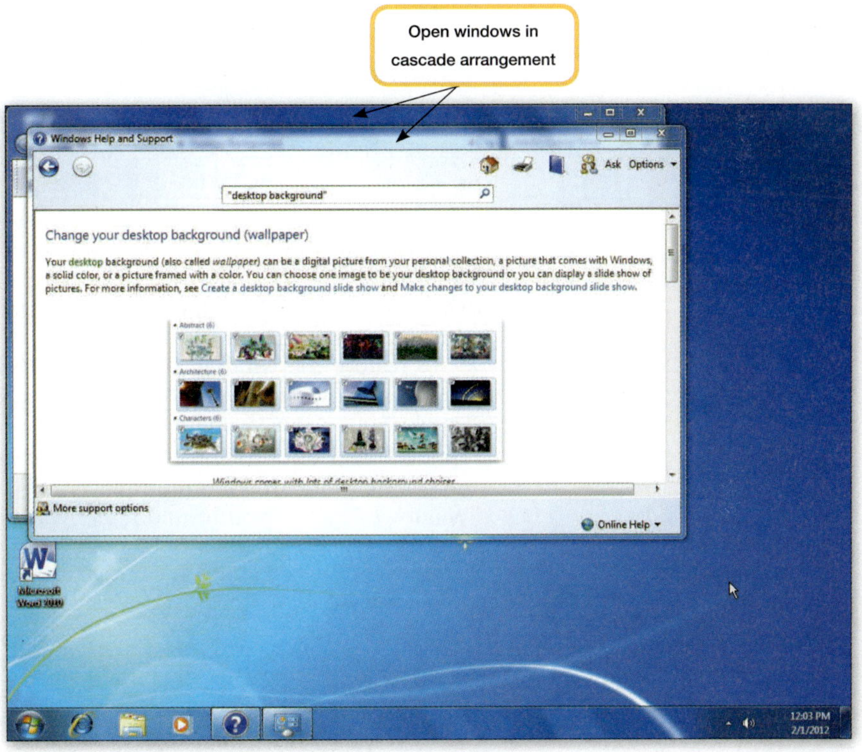

Figure 1.37

> **Additional Information**
>
> Windows that are minimized are not arranged.

The windows are resized and they overlap with the title bars visible. Again, you can click on any visible part of the window or on the window's taskbar button to make it active.

2

Make the Desktop Background window active.

Your screen should be similar to Figure 1.38

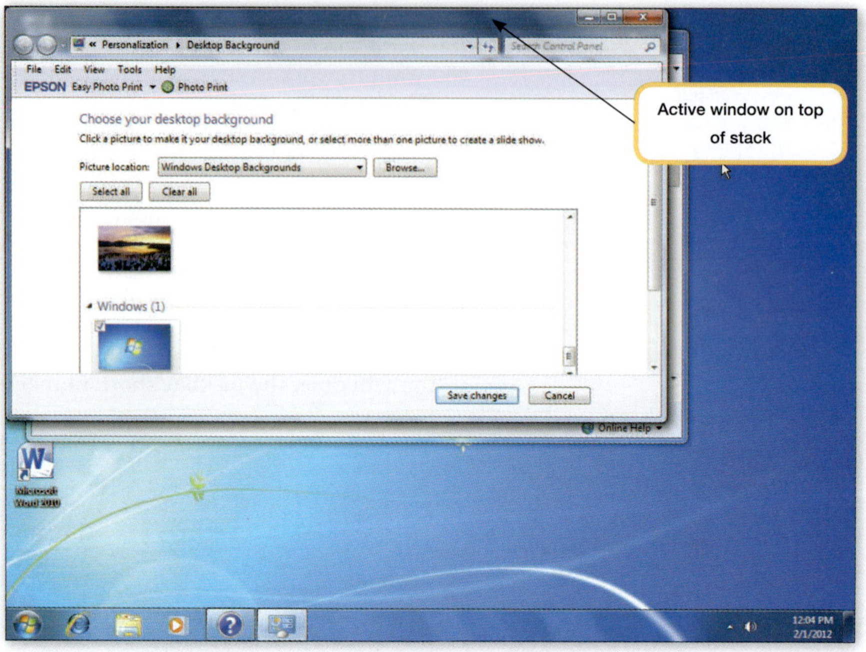

Figure 1.38

The Desktop Background window is pulled to the front of the stack and covers the other cascaded window.

To restore the window size and arrangement as it was prior to cascading the windows, you can use the **Undo** feature. The Undo feature allows you to reverse your last action or command. This feature is available in most software application programs and commonly appears as a toolbar button. In some programs, you can undo multiple actions, up to a certain limit. Others, as in Windows 7, allow you to undo only your last action. You will find that some actions you perform cannot be undone. If the Undo command is unavailable, it appears dimmed and you cannot cancel your last action.

3

- **Display the taskbar shortcut menu.**

Additional Information

The Undo option appears in the taskbar shortcut menu only after windows have been arranged.

- **Choose Undo Cascade.**
- **Make the Windows Help and Support window active again.**

Your screen should be similar to Figure 1.39

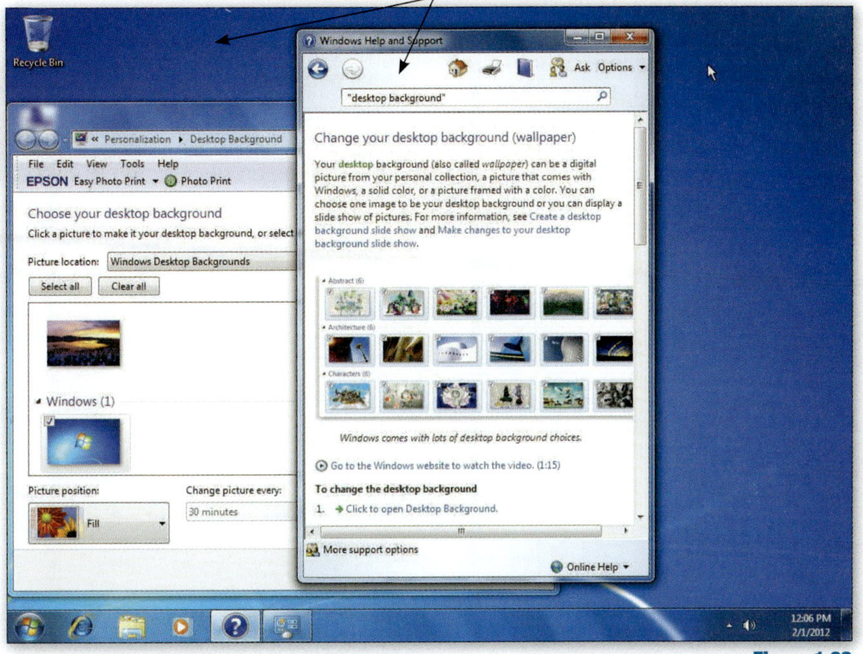

Figure 1.39

The windows are arranged and sized again as they were before using the Cascade command. If you do not undo the arrangement before switching to another arrangement, the windows remain in the size and position set by the second arrangement and cannot be returned to their original size without custom sizing and moving the windows. Next, you will arrange the windows on the desktop without overlapping.

4 **Choose Show windows side by side from the taskbar shortcut menu.**

Your screen should be similar to Figure 1.40

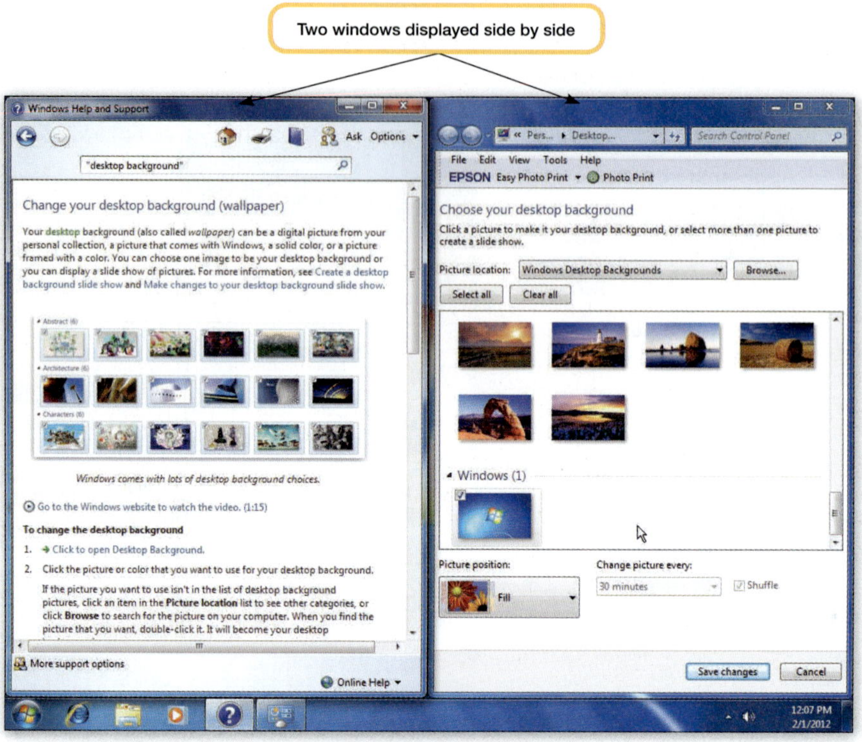

Figure 1.40

The two windows are horizontally arranged side by side on the desktop, each taking up one-half of the horizontal space. Next, you will change the window arrangement to stacked.

5 **Choose Show windows stacked from the taskbar shortcut menu.**

Your screen should be similar to Figure 1.41

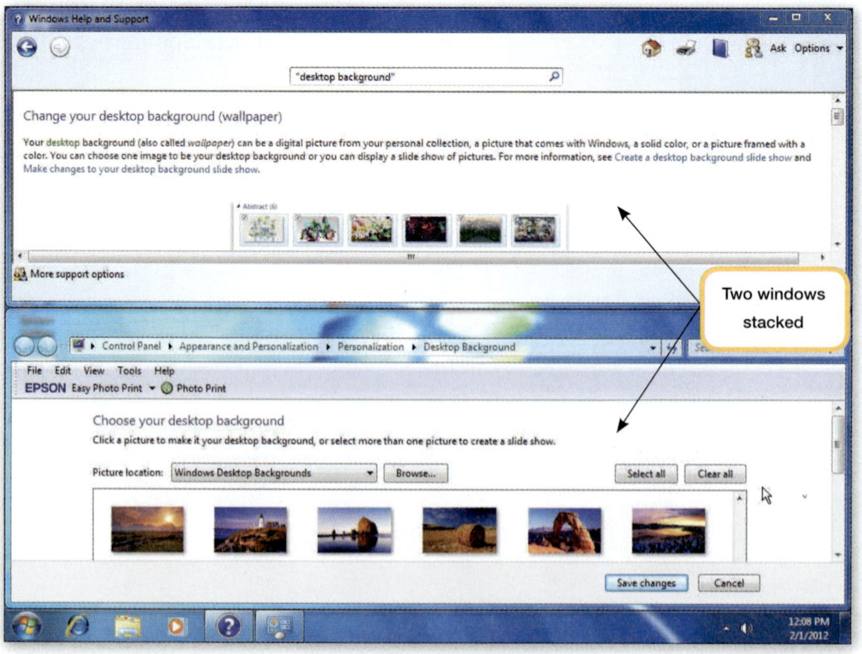

Figure 1.41

Now the two windows are vertically stacked on the desktop, each taking up one-half of the vertical space.

MINIMIZING ALL OPEN WINDOWS

Sometimes you may want to minimize all open windows at once so that you can quickly see the entire desktop. You can do this using Show Desktop on the right end of the taskbar.

1

- **Undo the stacked window arrangement.**
- **Click Show desktop.**

Another Method

You also could choose Show the desktop from the taskbar shortcut menu or use the keyboard shortcut (⊞) + M.

Your screen should be similar to Figure 1.42

Figure 1.42

Additional Information

If using Aero, pointing to the Show Desktop button temporarily fades all open windows from view to reveal the desktop. Then to make the windows reappear, simply move the pointer away from the Show desktop button.

All open windows have been minimized and the desktop window is displayed. This is much quicker than minimizing each window individually. If a dialog box were open, it would be minimized also. However, it would not appear as a taskbar button. Next, you will quickly restore all open windows to the desktop.

2

- **Click Show desktop.**

Another Method

You could also choose Show open windows from the taskbar shortcut menu. You can also use +D to minimize and redisplay all open windows.

- **Resize and position the two windows similar to that shown in Figure 1.43.**

Your screen should be similar to Figure 1.43

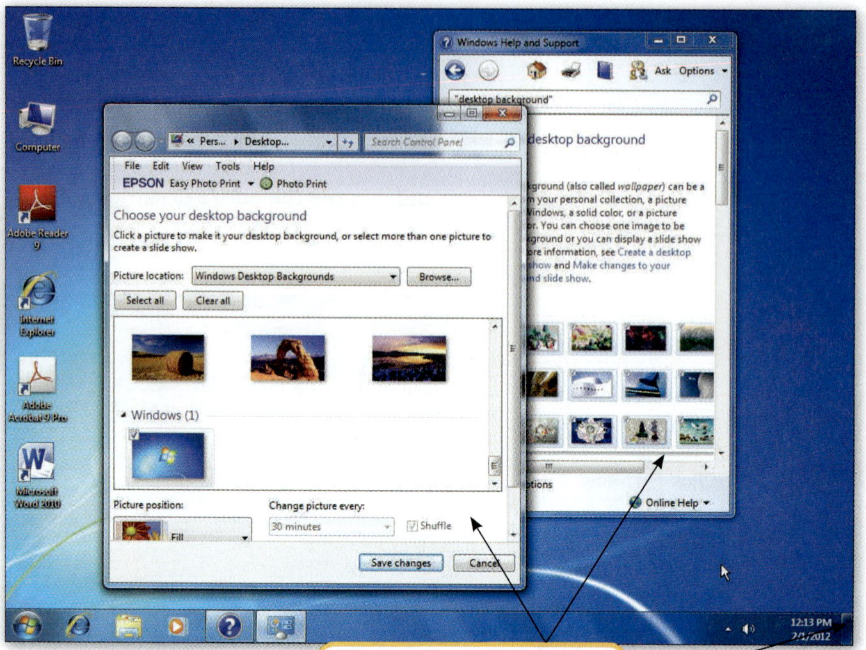

Show desktop restores all open windows after they were minimized

Figure 1.43

Only the windows and dialog boxes that were open on the desktop at the time they were minimized are restored. Because you did not Undo the side-by-side window arrangement before changing to the stacked arrangement, you had to individually resize and position the windows to restore them to how they were prior to using the automatic window arrangement feature.

USING SHAKE AND SNAP

Another way to work with multiple open windows is to use Shake and Snap. **Shake** is used to quickly minimize every open window on your desktop except the one you want to work with by shaking or quickly dragging the title bar of the window back and forth quickly. This can save you time from having to minimize windows on your desktop one by one. To restore the minimized windows to the desktop, shake your open window again.

You can use **Snap** to quickly maximize a window, expand a window vertically, or arrange windows side by side. Dragging the window to the top of the screen maximizes the window. Vertically sizing the window by dragging the top or bottom border of the window expands the window to fill the vertical window space without expanding the window width. This is particularly helpful for reading longer documents.

You will next use Shake to hide the Help window. Then you will use Snap to maximize the window and then to vertically expand the window.

1

- **Drag the title bar of the Desktop window back and forth quickly to shake the window.**

Another Method

Press + Home to minimize all open windows except the active window. Press + Home to restore the minimized windows.

- **Drag the Desktop window to the top of the screen and when the outline of the window expands to fill the entire desktop, release the mouse button.**
- **Drag the window away from the top edge of the screen to restore its size.**
- **Point to the top edge of the window and when the mouse pointer appears as ↕ drag the edge of the window to the top of the screen.**

Your screen should be similar to Figure 1.44

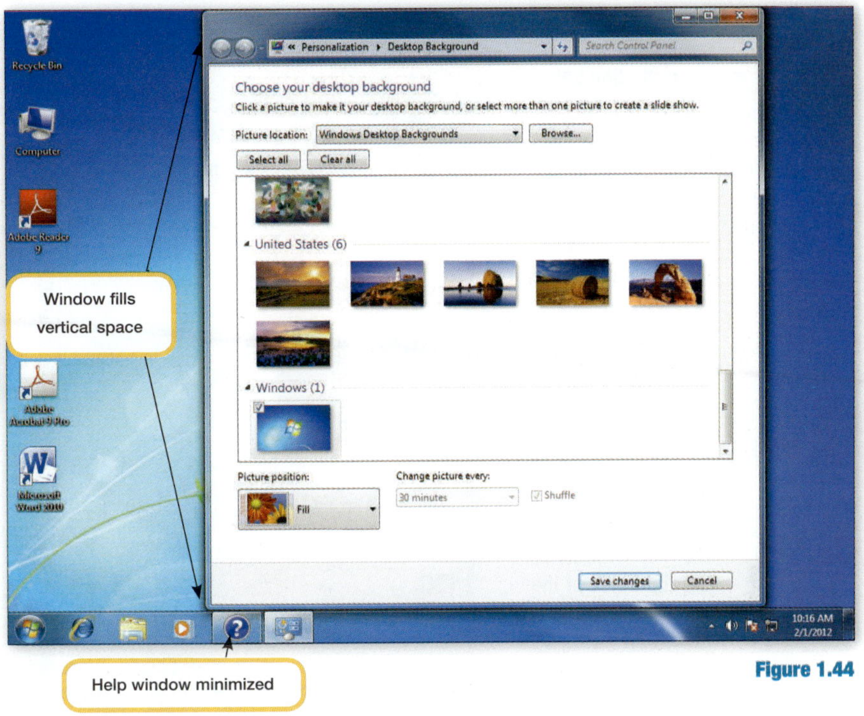

Figure 1.44

When you shook the Desktop window, the Help window was minimized. Dragging the active window to the top of the screen maximized the window and dragging it away from the top of the screen restored the window to its size prior to maximizing. Then, expanding the window vertically to the top of the screen button caused the window to fill the vertical size. The width of the window did not change.

Next, you will return the window to its original size, redisplay the Help window and then you will use Snap to display windows side by side. This is helpful if you need to compare two documents, or when moving files from one location to another. Simply drag the title bar of a window to the left or right side of the screen until you see an outline of the expanded window to half the screen, and release.

2

- **Drag the title bar away from the top edge of the screen to restore the size of the Desktop window.**
- **Shake the window to redisplay the Help window.**
- **Drag the title bar of the Desktop window to the left side of the screen to expand it to half the screen.**
- **Drag the title bar of the Help window to the right side of the screen to expand the other half.**

Figure 1.45

Another Method

Press [Windows key] + the [←] or [→] to snap the active window to the side of the screen.

Your screen should be similar to Figure 1.45

The two open windows are now side by side, each taking up half the screen. To return the windows to their original sizes, drag their title bars away from the top of the screen.

3

- **Restore both windows to their original sizes.**

CLOSING A WINDOW

Now that you are finished using Windows Help and Support, you will exit the program. The [X] button in the title bar is used to close a window and exit a program.

1

- **Click [X] in the Desktop Background window.**
- **Close the Help window.**

Another Method

The keyboard shortcut to close the active window is Alt + F4.

Your screen should be similar to Figure 1.46

Additional Information

If a window is minimized, you can quickly close the program without restoring the window first by clicking [X] in the taskbar buttons thumbnail preview or by choosing Close window from the taskbar button's shortcut menu.

Figure 1.46

Both windows are closed and the taskbar buttons are removed, indicating the programs are no longer active.

Using Folder Windows and Libraries

The next feature in Windows 7 that you will look at is how to view and access the contents of your hard disk, network locations, or removable media such as CD and DVD disks and removable memory—the areas of your computer that can be used to store files. **Files,** as you know, store program instructions or data. **Program files** contain the software instructions that you use to run the program. The information you create while using an application program is stored in document or **data files**. For example, if you write a letter to a friend using a word processing application program, the contents of the letter are stored as a document file. In addition, to organize the file contents, folders and libraries are used.

Concept 6 Folders and Libraries

Folders and libraries are used to manage and organize the files on your computer. A **folder** is a named area on a disk that is used to store related files. Folders are used to organize the information stored on a disk. This is similar to how you store related information in separate folders in a file drawer. Folders also can store other folders. A folder inside another folder is called a **subfolder** (or **secondary folder**) and is used to further refine the organization of your files. Because folders create categories for related items, it makes it easier to locate files.

The folders included on the Windows 7 Start menu—Documents, Pictures, and Music are provided by default to help you organize your document files, image and picture files, and audio files. In addition, there are several Windows folders that provide links to specialized tasks. Among these specialized folders are Computer and Control Panel, to name two. In addition, Windows includes your personal folder, the folder that is labeled with the user name. The personal folder is a folder that contains your most frequently used folders and files making it a quick and convenient method to access those folders.

A **library** is a collection of files and folders whose contents are assembled from a variety of sources that may include your computer, an external hard drive, or even someone else's computer. Unlike folders, libraries do not actually store these items. Instead, libraries monitor specified folders and display their contents to let you access and arrange them in different ways. Because libraries monitor a variety of locations, you can save time by not having to check multiple folders in different locations to find an item. Windows includes four default libraries: Documents, Music, Pictures, and Videos. You can also create new libraries or modify existing libraries.

Additional Information

Refer to Appendix A for more information on working with libraries.

EXPLORING THE COMPUTER WINDOW

To look at the contents of your computer, you will start by displaying the Computer folder window.

1

- **Open the Start menu and choose**  **.**

- **Size and position the Computer window similar to that shown in Figure 1.47.**

Your screen should be similar to Figure 1.47

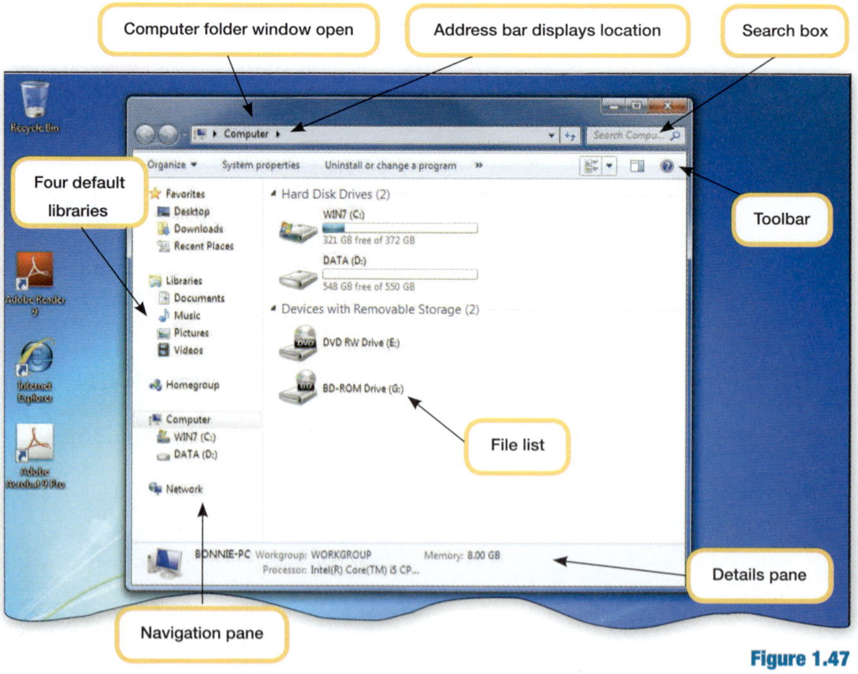

Figure 1.47

Having Trouble?

Don't be concerned if your view of the contents pane is a little different than Figure 1.47; you will learn about changing views a little later.

The Computer window includes an **Address bar** at the top of the window that displays the location you are currently viewing, in this case, the Computer folder. The **location** is any disk drive, folder, or other place in which you can store files and folders. The location consists of a series of links separated by arrows ▸. As you view other locations, the Address bar displays the current location. To the right of the Address bar is a Search text box where you can enter text to locate files in the current location.

Additional Information

Menu buttons display ▾ to the right of the button name.

Below the Address bar is a toolbar that contains both menu and task-specific buttons. The buttons it displays depend on the type of folder you are viewing; however, all folder windows include the Organize ▾ and Views menu buttons and a Help task button. Clicking on a menu button displays a drop-down menu of commands from which you can select. Clicking on a task button immediately opens the related task feature. These buttons, as well as several of the task-specific buttons, are described in the table below.

Button	Use
Organize ▾	Used to perform basic file tasks such as renaming, moving, copying, and deleting. It contains commands for controlling the layout options and the configuration of the folder window.
Views	Controls the display of the folder by allowing you to view Details, Tiles, or Large Icons.
System properties	Shows information about your computer such as the manufacturer and the processor speed
Back	Back arrow will show the previous pane of information.
Forward	Use the forward arrow to show the next pane of information (only if available).
Help	Opens Windows Help and Support and displays help information about the current window.
Uninstall or change a program	Uninstalls (removes) or changes the installation of a program on your computer.
Map network drive	Creates a shortcut to a shared folder or computer on a network.
Open	Used to open a selected file folder or document. When opening a specific document, the pictured icon will show the icon for the associated program (Word, or Notepad, etc.).
Share with ▾	Used to share a selected file folder or document with other people on a network.
Burn	Used to burn the selected file folder or document to disk.
Slide show	Used to display all or selected pictures and videos as a slide show. This option is not always available.
Play all	Used to play all or the selected music files in the selected folder. This option is not always available.

The main window space of the Computer window displays the file list. The **file list** displays icons representing the folders and files at the selected location and is always displayed. Since the Computer folder is the current folder, the locations where files can be stored, including the hard-disk drive, network drives, removable storage devices, and any folders in the Computer folder, are displayed.

The window also can display up to three panes, described in the following table. The panes can be turned on or off. Initially, the Computer window area displays the Navigation and Details panes. If your Computer window displays a different window configuration, this is because Windows remembers the layout settings for each window and displays the window as it last appeared.

Additional Information

If the window is not wide enough, the Navigation pane may not be displayed.

Pane	Description
Details pane	Displays details about a selected file such as the file size and the last modified date.
Preview pane	Displays a preview of the contents of the selected file.
Navigation pane	Displays a list of Favorite links (shortcuts to folders you frequently use), libraries, saved searches, and an expandable list of folders. Use to move to locations that contain the files you want to see.

Because no items are selected in the file list area, the Details pane displays general information about your computer, including the processor and memory information.

CHANGING THE WINDOW LAYOUT

Now that you understand the parts of the folder window, you will use several of the features to change its appearance. First you will use the Layout command on the Organize menu to hide and display different folder window elements.

1

- **Click Organize to display the drop-down menu.**
- **Point to the Layout command to display the submenu.**

Your screen should be similar to Figure 1.48

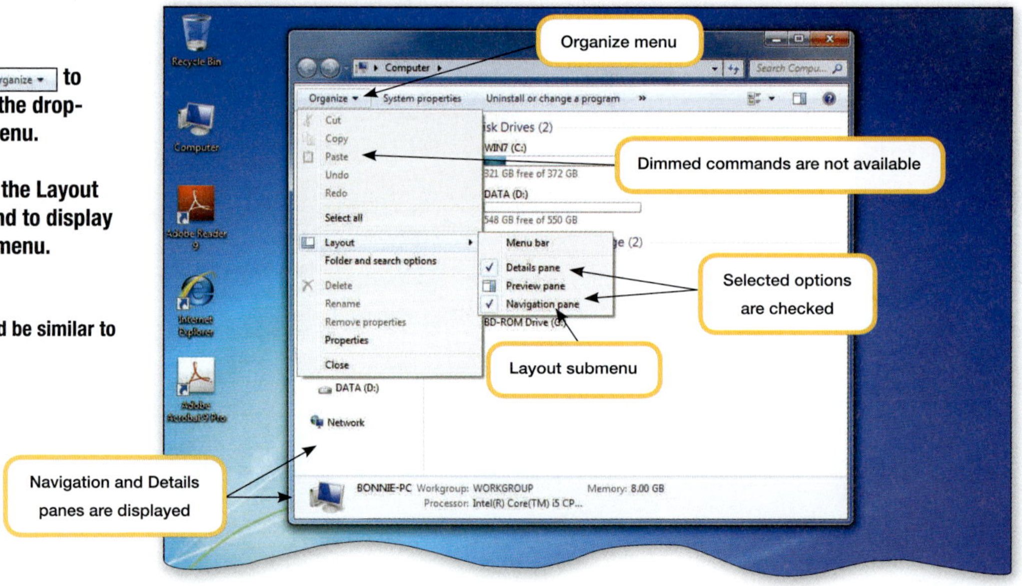

Figure 1.48

Additional Information

The file list area of the window is always displayed and cannot be turned on or off.

The drop-down list of commands contains similar features to the Start menu such as the ▸ to indicate that a submenu will be displayed and operates in a similar fashion to the Start menu. In addition, commands that appear dimmed are not available for selection until certain other conditions are met. Options that are already selected (on) display a checkmark.

The Layout submenu includes a command to display a menu bar as well as the three folder window panes. The two panes that are displayed in your Computer window are checked. You will turn off and then on the Details pane.

2

- **Click on Details pane to choose it.**

Your screen should be similar to Figure 1.49

Having Trouble?

After making a menu choice, the Organize menu is closed. If you need to make another selection, open the menu again.

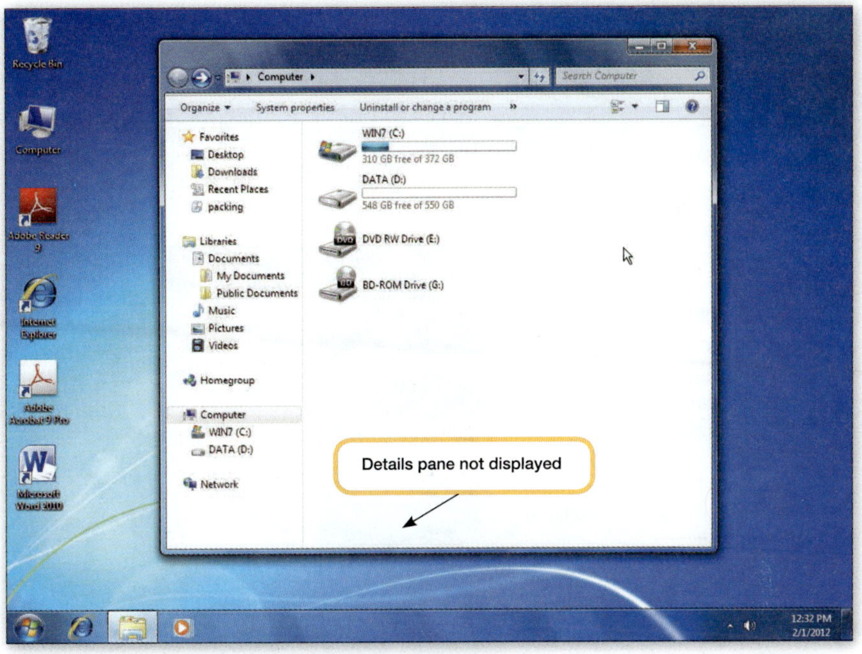

Figure 1.49

The menu closes and the Details pane is no longer displayed. Next, you will change the layout to display the Details pane again.

3

- **Click** Organize **and select Layout.**
- **Choose Details pane to redisplay this pane.**

> **Additional Information**
> Many computers have their hard disk drive space divided into several local hard disk drives.

NAVIGATING THE FOLDER WINDOW

The Computer folder provides an overall view of the organization of the drives on your computer. Next you will view the files and folders on the hard disk drive of your computer. On most computers, the local hard disk drive is the C drive.

1

- **Click** (or the appropriate hard disk drive for your system) to select it.

Your screen should be similar to Figure 1.50

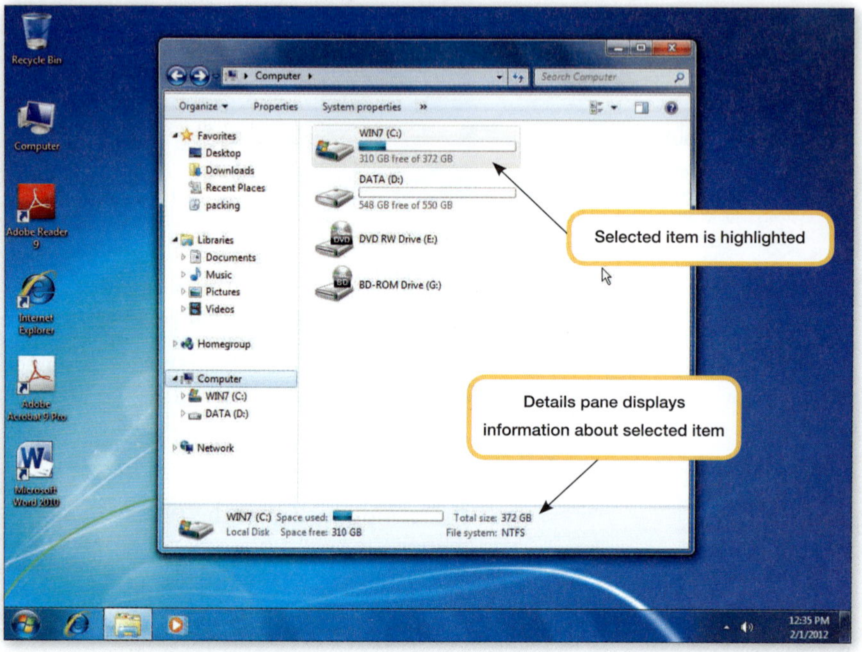

Figure 1.50

> **Additional Information**
> Refer to Concept 2: Desktop to review objects and properties.

> **Additional Information**
> Other features will be used to navigate as you continue to explore Windows 7.

The local hard drive icon you selected is highlighted and the Details pane displays some basic information about the properties of the selected object. In this case, it tells you information about the total size of the disk and the amount of free or available disk space. **Disk size** is the total **capacity** or amount of data the disk is capable of holding.

To actually see the contents of the C drive, you need to change to that location. There are several methods that can be used to navigate in a folder window. You can use the Address bar and either type or click a new location. From the file list, you can double-click on any displayed folder icon to make it the current location. Finally, you can use the features in the Navigation pane. You will use several of these methods now to demonstrate these features.

2

Double click .

Your screen should be similar to Figure 1.51

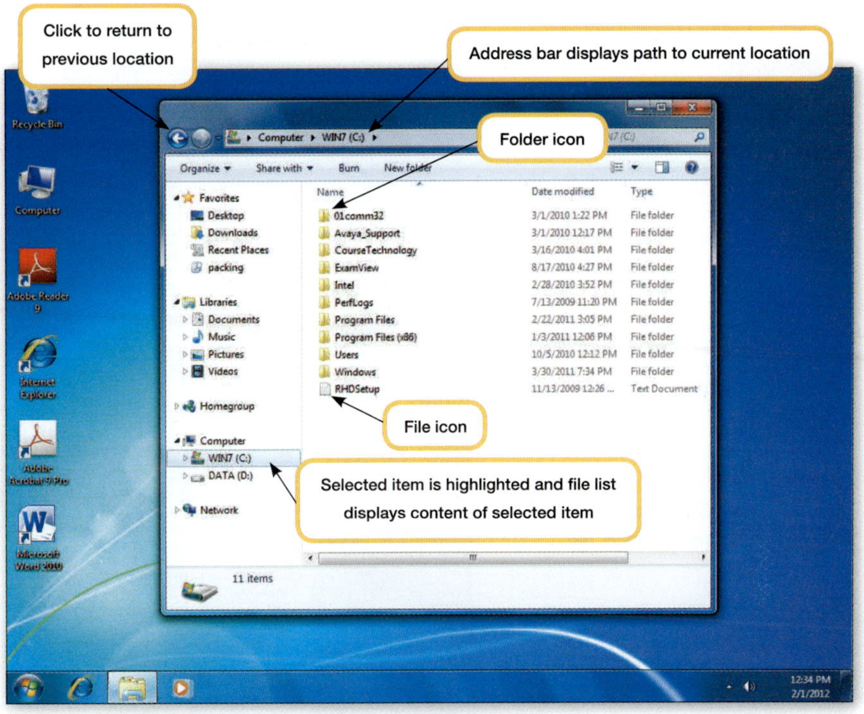

Figure 1.51

Additional Information

The Address bar also is called the "breadcrumb" bar, a nickname that refers to a navigation path that lists all the places you have visited or the route you have taken. This term comes from the fairy tale "Hansel and Gretel," where Hansel leaves a trail of breadcrumbs to help them find their way out of the forest.

Having Trouble?

Do not be concerned if the icons on your screen appear different than in Figure 1.51. You will learn about changing the icon view shortly.

Now the Address bar displays the **path** or route followed by the operating system to the selected location. The first item in the Address bar identifies the starting point of the path—in this case, the name of the Computer folder. This is followed by the subfolder names, each separated by a ▸. To get to this location, you could have typed the path information in the Address bar. However, you must know the exact folder names and type the entry correctly.

The folders and files on your C drive are displayed in the file list. The information and appearance of these items may be different than shown in Figure 1.51. Again, this is because the last-used view is displayed when the folder is displayed. The files and folders are identified by names that are descriptive of the contents of the file or folder. The folder names are listed first and appear in alphabetical order. They are preceded with folder icons. The individual files are listed following the folders, again in alphabetical order. They also are preceded with icons that represent different types of files.

Notice the items in the toolbar have changed to reflect more accurately tasks that you may want to use with the items in the current folder. Also the Details pane tells you the number of items in the current location.

The Navigation Pane still shows the five default groups: Favorites, Libraries, Homegroup, Computer, and Network (described in the following table). Using these groups makes it easier to locate folders and files you will need to work with.

Group	Description
Favorites	By default, shows Desktop, Downloads, and Recent Places. Favorites can be customized.
Libraries	Libraries allow easy access to categories of files. They do not store your folders or files, but rather point to folders on your hard drive or other external drives attached to your computer, so you can easily locate related groups of files no matter where they are stored.
Homegroup	A Homegroup makes it easy to share pictures, music, documents, videos, and printers with other people on your home network.
Computer	Shows drives and external devices on your computer.
Network	Provides access to shared devices if your computer is part of a network.

Next, you will use the Address bar to quickly return to the Computer folder. Then you will use the Navigation pane to display the contents of the Documents library.

3

- **Click on Computer in the Address bar.**

Another Method

You also could click the Back to return to the Computer folder.

- **Click Documents in the Libraries section of the Navigation pane.**
- **Click ▷ to the left of Documents in the Navigation pane to display folder locations included in this library.**

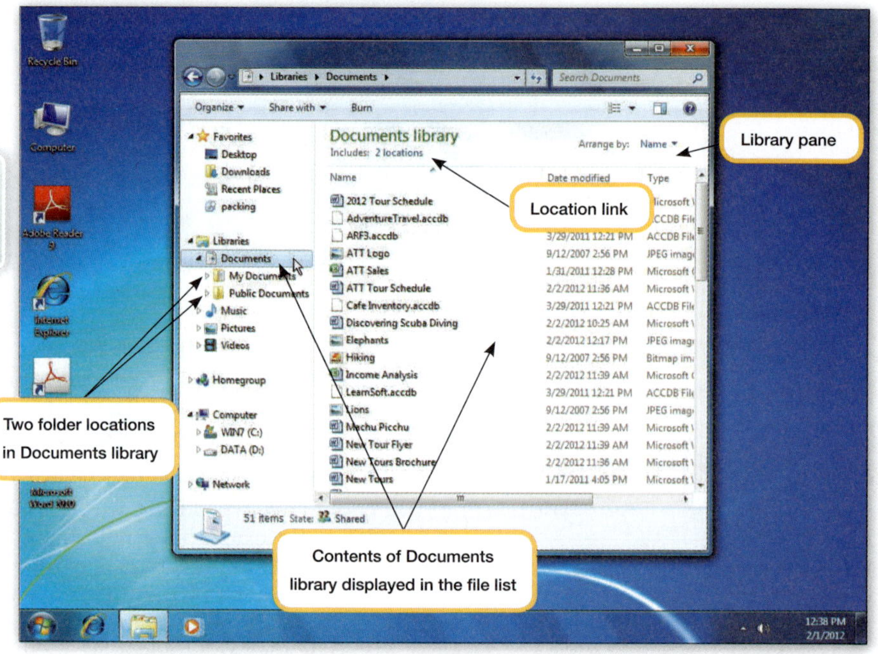

Figure 1.52

Your screen should be similar to Figure 1.52

Additional Information

Because libraries can be customized, your Documents library may include additional folder locations.

Additional Information

You also can point to the locations link in the Library pane to display a ScreenTip showing the library locations.

The selected location is highlighted in the Navigation pane and the two folders included in the Documents library are displayed below it. The file list displays the folders and files gathered by the Documents library from the specified folder locations (your screen will display different folders and files than in Figure 1.52). The Address bar reflects the new location. Notice the first item in the Address bar is the main group (Libraries) name, followed by the location, Documents, within the Libraries group. If you want to see only the contents of a specific folder included in a library in the file list, you can click on the folder name in the Navigation pane. Additionally, because you are viewing a library, the Library pane is displayed above the file list.

You will hide the Documents library folders again and return to the Computer folder.

4

- Click [◢] next to Documents to hide the location folders.
- Click Computer in the Navigation pane to return to the Computer folder.

Your screen should be similar to Figure 1.53

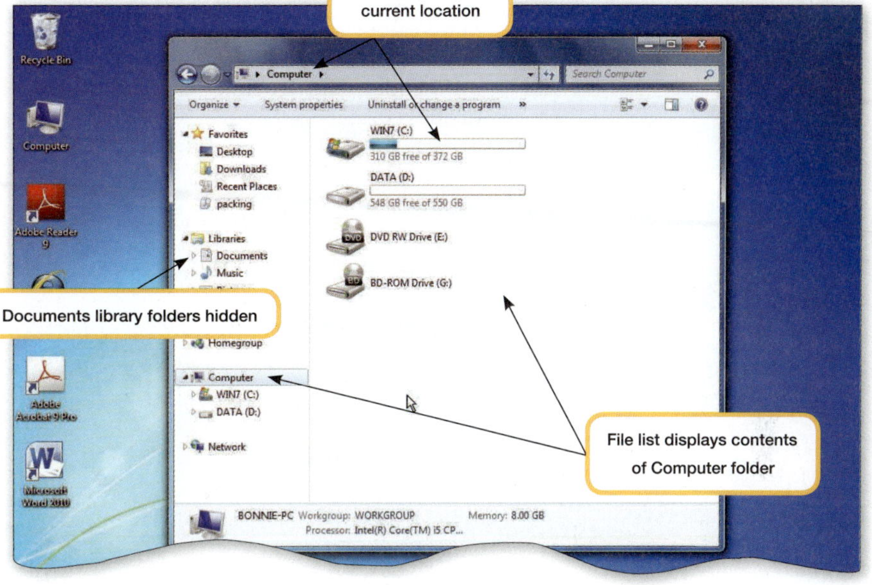

Figure 1.53

The file list again displays the icons for the storage locations on your computer.

CHANGING FOLDER VIEWS

Additional Information

Each supplied folder in Windows 7 has a default folder view. Tiles view (shown in Figure 1.53) is the default view for the Computer window.

Next, you will change how the folder and file icons are displayed in the file list. Icons in a folder window can be viewed or displayed in eight different ways. These views change the icon size, the display order, and the amount of information about the files and folders. Depending upon what you are doing, one view may be more helpful than another. That is why, as you navigate to different locations, different views are displayed. The views are described in the following table.

View	Description
Extra Large Icons	Displays extra large icons across rows with the name below.
Large Icons	Displays large icons across rows with the name below.
Medium Icons	Displays medium icons across rows with the name below.
Small Icons	Displays small icons across rows with the name to the right.
List	Displays very small icons down a multiple-column list with the name to the right.
Details	Displays small icons in a single column list with details about each item in separate columns to the right.
Tiles	Displays medium icons across rows with the name, type, and size to the right.
Content	Displays a smaller version of the icon and file or folder name on the left, and the date modified and the size to the right.

The Views button in the toolbar contains the commands to change the icon display. This button is a split button that consists of two separate parts. Each time you click the folder view switches to one of these five views: Tiles, Large Icons, List, Details, and Content. Clicking the ▾ part of the Views button displays a drop-down menu of all the view choices on a slider-bar. Dragging the slider-bar pointer selects the view that will be displayed.

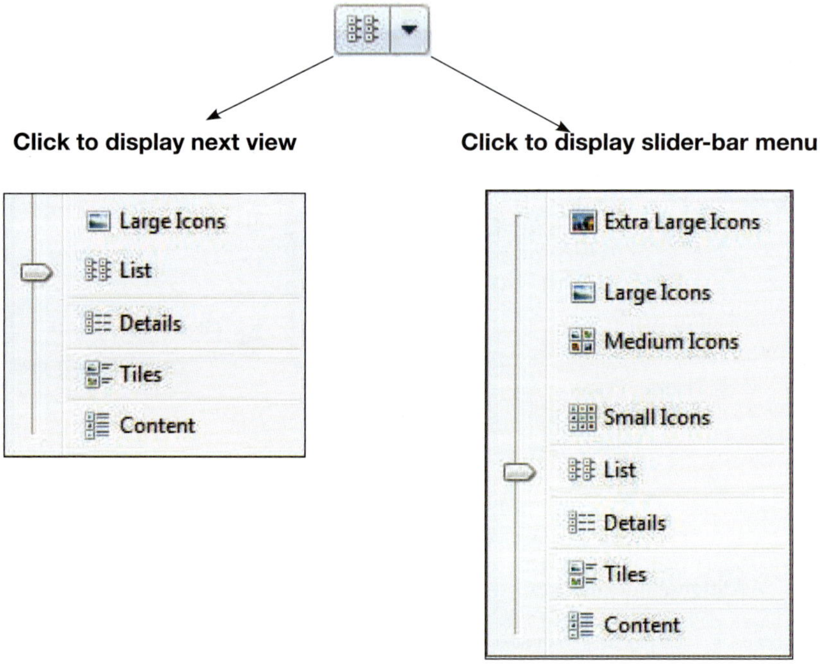

Additional Information

The default view for the Documents library is Details view.

You will first change your location to the Documents library again so you can see folders and files rather than storage locations. Then you will change the view.

1

- **Change the location to the Documents library.**
- **Click ▾ to open the Views drop-down menu.**

Additional Information

The slider-bar pointer next to an option indicates it is selected.

- **Drag the slider-bar pointer to select each of the view options to see the change in the window.**

Additional Information

As you drag the slider between Extra Large Icons and Small Icons, you can fine-tune the icon size to any point between the settings.

- **Point to the Tiles option and release the mouse pointer.**
- **If necessary, increase the width of the window to see multiple columns.**

Another Method

You also can click on the view to immediately choose it.

Your screen should be similar to Figure 1.54

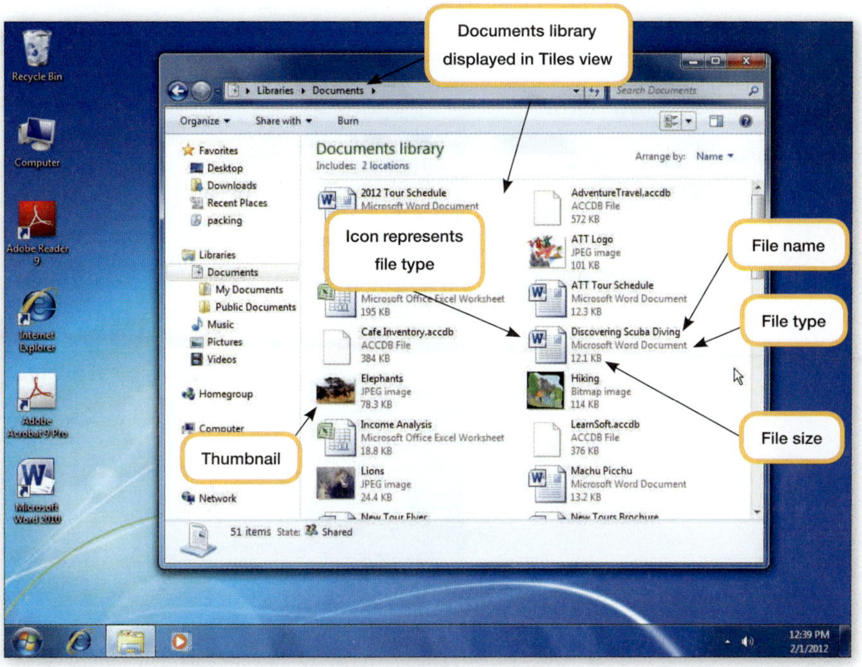

Figure 1.54

Tiles view displays medium icons in a multiple-column list with the file name and type information displayed to the right of the icon. The number of columns will be determined by the size of the window. The icons that represent picture files are thumbnail images of actual content. The other icons represent different types of files: program files, associated files, or another type of file (generally an unassociated document file). An **associated file** is a file that has a specific application program attached to it that will open when the file is opened. The following table describes several common file icons.

Icon	Type of File
	Plain text document
	Rich Text document
	Microsoft Word document
	Microsoft Excel document

Next, you will change to List view. Another way to change the view is to simply click on the view you want to use from the slider-bar menu.

2

- **Open the Views drop-down menu.**
- **Click on List to choose it.**

Your screen should be similar to Figure 1.55

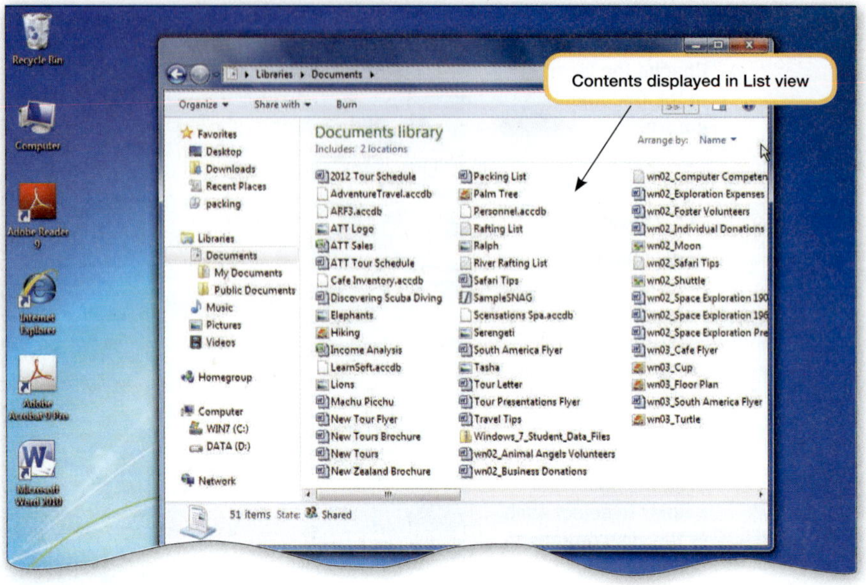

Figure 1.55

This view displays very small icons with the file name to the right arranged alphabetically down a column rather than across the rows. Notice that the picture file icons are no longer thumbnails that represent content. They are simply icons that represent a file type. Using this view, you can see many more items in the window at one time.

The next view setting you will use, Details, displays the file details such as total file size, type, and the date and time of creation/modification in columns.

3

- **Click Views until Details view is displayed as in Figure 1.56.**
- **If necessary, scroll the window to see the file icons.**
- **Click on a file icon to select it.**

Your screen should be similar to Figure 1.56

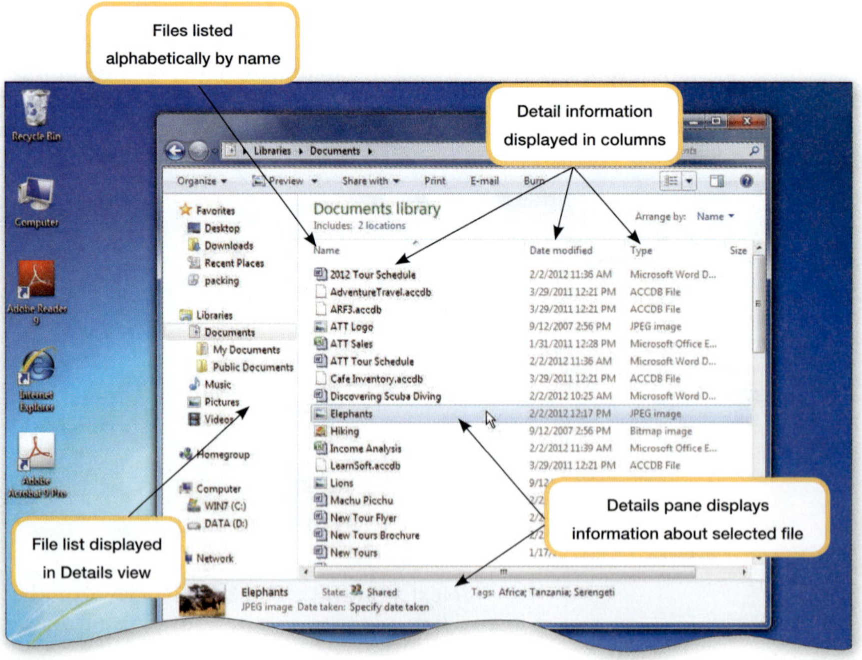

Figure 1.56

Additional Information

The columns to display can be changed by right-clicking on one of the column headings and selecting the desired options.

Additional Information

You can drag the column header divider lines to increase or decrease the size of the columns. You can drag the column header to move the column.

Again, very small folder and file icons appear in a single column down the window with additional file information displayed in columns to the right. The columns are labeled with column headings. The columns display the file or folder name, the date and time the file was last modified, the file type, and the file size. Depending on the type of folder you are viewing, the columns that are displayed in Details view vary. The other file and folder details that can be displayed include the date created, the author, the rating, and the number of pages, to name a few.

This additional information takes up a lot of space in the window. Also, because the items appear in a single column, if there were many files, you would need to vertically scroll the window to locate a file or folder that is not visible. Additionally, most of the same information is displayed in the Details pane when an object is selected. However, this view is useful if you want to compare details between objects.

Now, you will switch to Large Icons view.

4

- **Click Views until Large Icons view is displayed as in Figure 1.57.**
- **Point to a file icon to see the ScreenTip.**

Your screen should be similar to Figure 1.57

Figure 1.57

Additional Information

You also can choose a single picture to identify a folder. The picture does not have to be stored in the folder.

Each icon appears as a large icon with the folder or file name below it. The objects are arranged across rows in alphabetical order. Graphic file icons display a thumbnail of actual content.

Finally, you will look at Content view and display the Preview pane. Although graphic file icons display an actual representation of their contents, most text files do not. Using the Preview pane will display a small portion of the file contents without opening the program it was created in to help you confirm that the file is the file you want to use. You will use the preview pane to display a portion of the contents of a text file.

5

- **Change the view to Content view as displayed in Figure 1.58.**
- **Select a text file.**
- **Click Show Preview Pane.**
- **Maximize the window.**

Your screen should be similar to Figure 1.58

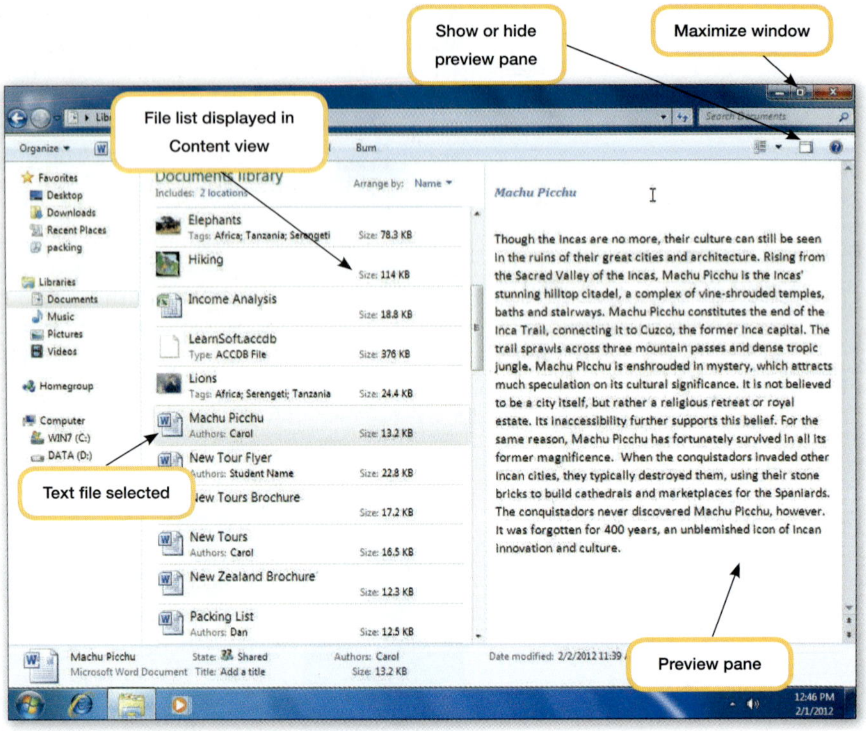

Figure 1.58

> **Additional Information**
>
> The size of the Preview pane can be adjusted by dragging the left border.

Content view displays a smaller version of the icons with the file or folder name on the left and the date modified (if appropriate) and the size to the right. The Preview pane displays a small sample of the information in the beginning of the file.

SORTING FILES AND FOLDERS

> **Additional Information**
>
> You can use the Arrange by drop-down menu to change the arrangement of items in the library or to quickly clear all changes and restore the default folder view settings.

Regardless of the view you are using, folders initially appear first as a group, followed by files. Typically, folders and files are displayed in ascending alphabetical order by name. Sometimes, however, this order is not convenient. For example, you may be unable to remember the name of the file, but you can remember the approximate date you last modified it.

In Details view, the folder and file information is displayed in columns below each heading. The most common headings include Name, Date modified, Type, Size, and Author. Clicking a heading sorts the files and folders by the selected column header. Clicking it again switches the display order between ascending and descending order. To see how this works, you will arrange the files by date modified rather than name. You will do this in Details view so that you can actually see the dates.

1

- **Click Hide Preview Pane.**
- **Click Restore Down to restore the window to its original size.**
- **Change to Details view.**
- **Click on the Date Modified column heading to sort by date.**
- **Click on the Date Modified column heading again to change the order from descending to ascending date order.**

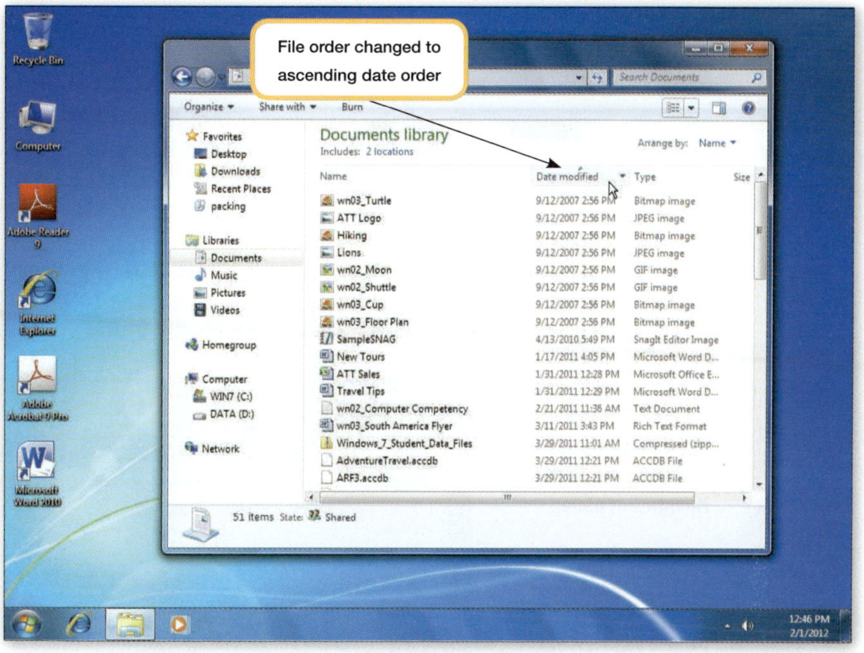

Figure 1.59

Your screen should be similar to Figure 1.59

Additional Information

Ascending sort order is the default order for all file list headings.

Looking at the Date Modified column of information, you can see that the folders are arranged in ascending order by date followed by the files in the same order. The heading by which they are sorted appears highlighted and displays ▲ to indicate ascending order or ▼ for decending order.

You will return the folder display to Tiles view, sorted by name.

2

- **Click on the Name heading.**
- **Switch to Tiles view.**

Your screen should be similar to Figure 1.60

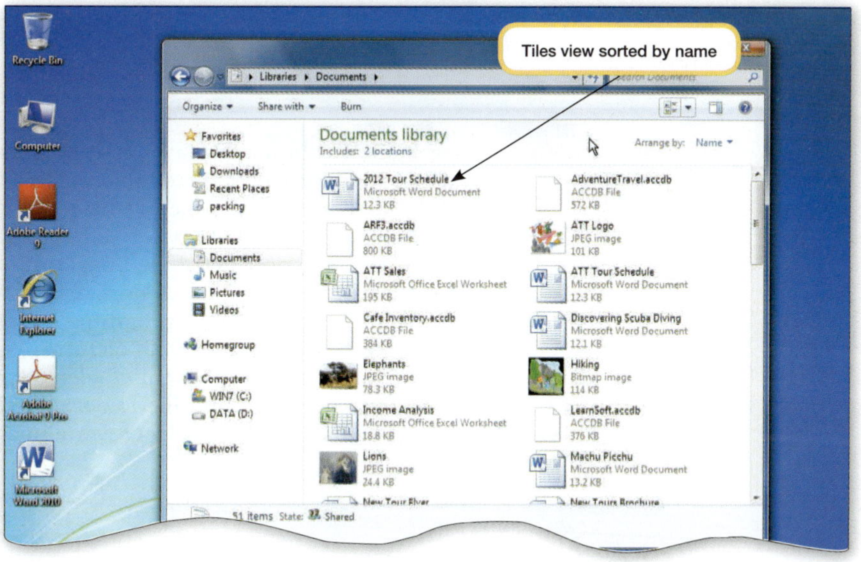

Figure 1.60

The folders and files are again displayed in Tiles view sorted by name.

Viewing and Organizing Pictures

Due to the popularity of digital cameras and the importance of the computer in storing and viewing digital images, Windows includes many features designed just for working with digital images and video. These include features for viewing and organizing images as well as editing, sharing, and printing.

USING THE PICTURES FOLDER

Next you want to look at several pictures that are stored in the Sample Pictures folder. To quickly go to this location, you will display the Pictures library.

1

- **Click Pictures in the Libraries group of the Navigation pane.**
- **If necessary, change to Large Icons view.**
- **Adjust the size of the window as in Figure 1.61.**

Additional Information

You also can get to the Pictures folder by choosing Pictures from the Start Menu.

Your screen should be similar to Figure 1.61

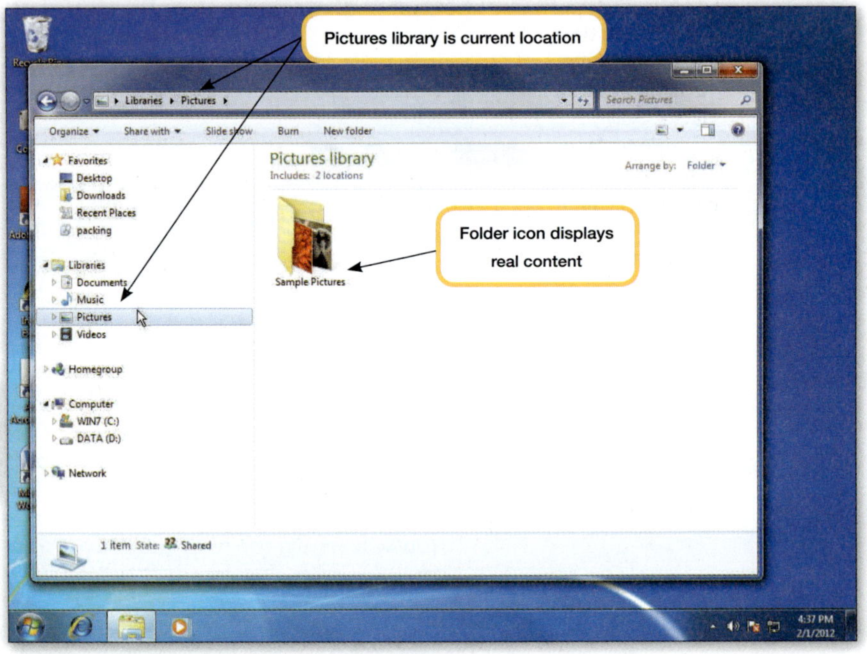

Figure 1.61

The Pictures library displays pictures from two locations by default: the My Pictures and Public Pictures folders. The My Pictures folder is a special folder that is set up to display picture files and video. For example, it displays files by default as thumbnail images in large icon view so you can see not only the file names but a preview of the images. It is also the default location to import pictures from your digital camera or other media device and for many photo editing and graphic design programs.

To help you get started with pictures, Windows includes a Sample Pictures folder. Notice the icon for this folder displays two pictures from this folder. This helps you verify that the folder contains the items you want to use. You will open this folder and select several images.

2

- **If necessary, scroll the window to locate the Sample Pictures folder.**
- **Double-click** .
- **Select the Chrysanthemum icon.**

Your screen should be similar to Figure 1.62

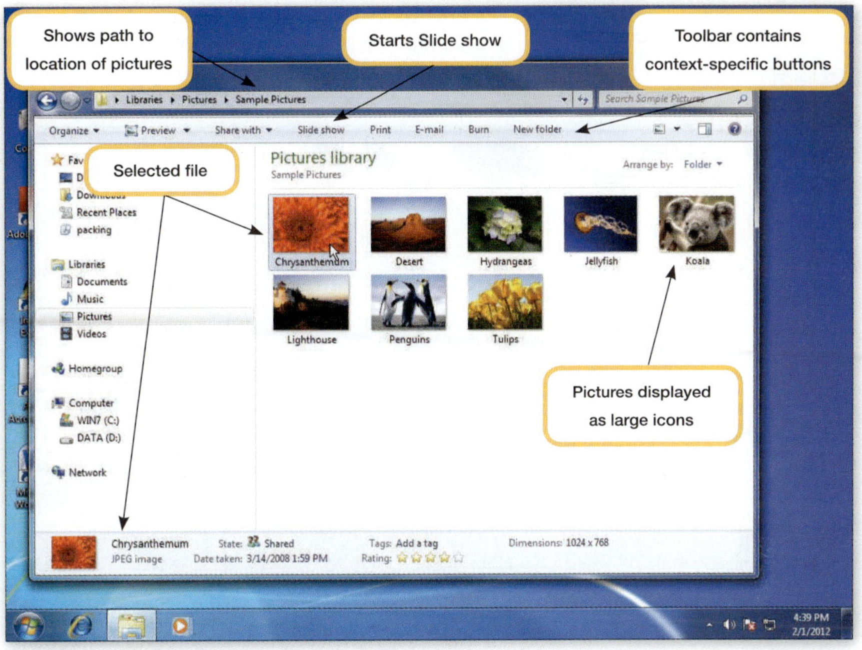

Figure 1.62

The Sample Pictures folder contains eight picture files. Notice that the toolbar now displays a number of context-specific buttons for working with images, such as Slide show and Burn. You will use Slide show to view the pictures full screen and navigate through them easily with the click of the mouse.

3

- **Click** Slide show.

Your screen should be similar to Figure 1.63

The Slide show begins with the first picture, and displays all pictures full-screen.

Figure 1.63

Additional Information

You also can use the ← and → buttons on the keyboard to navigate through the slide show.

The slide show of the images begins automatically. It is timed to display an image for a set period. If you want to advance more quickly through the images, simply click the mouse. You also can display a shortcut menu of options that can be used to modify how the slide show runs.

4

- **Right-click on an image to display the shortcut menu.**

Your screen should be similar to Figure 1.64

Figure 1.64

Now, by selecting a menu option, you can change the slide show speed, temporarily pause the display, go to the next or previous image, or even change the order of the images displayed by shuffling them.

5

- **Press Esc to clear the shortcut menu.**
- **Press Esc to exit the slide show.**

USING WINDOWS PHOTO VIEWER

Next, you will look at Windows Photo Viewer, a program supplied with Windows 7 that makes it easy to view, organize, edit, share, and print digital pictures. Double-clicking on a file icon in any folder opens the file in the associated program, in this case Windows Photo Viewer. You also can easily access other photo editing and viewing programs from Windows Photo Viewer that provide more advanced photo editing capabilities.

1

- **Double-click the Jellyfish icon.**

Your screen should be similar to Figure 1.65

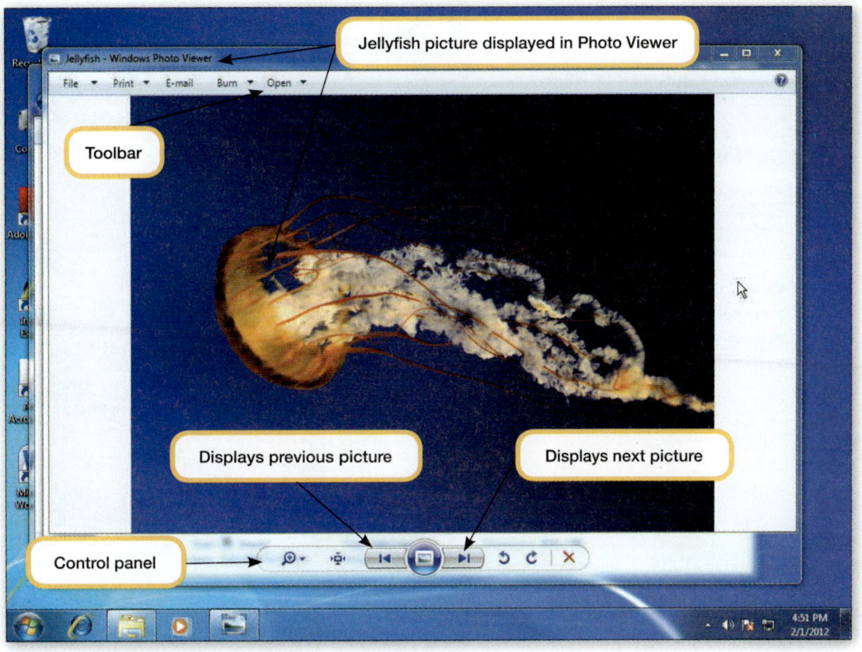

Figure 1.65

The Windows Photo Viewer program is started and the Jellyfish photo is displayed in the window. Above the photo is a toolbar similar to the toolbar in the Pictures folder. Below the picture is a control panel that allows you to change the display size and orientation, rotate the photo, launch the slide show feature, or delete the photo. The control panel also has navigation buttons for moving forward or backward through images in the folder.

2

- **Click [Next button] Next.**

Another Method

You also can press ← to move to the previous image or → to move to the next image.

Your screen should be similar to Figure 1.66

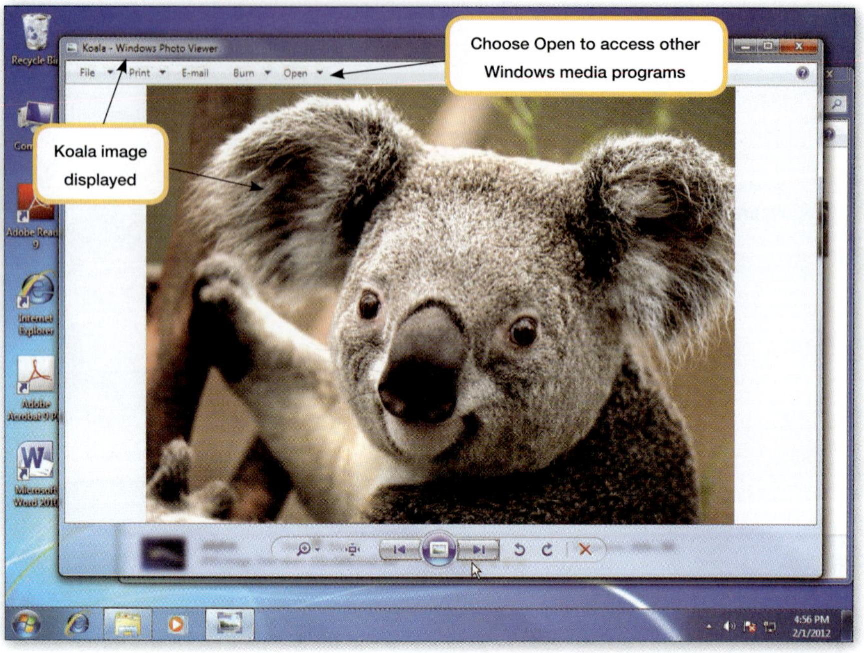

Figure 1.66

The Koala image is displayed. To access more advanced media programs in Windows 7, choose Open from the Photo Viewer toolbar. You will open Windows Live Photo Gallery now.

3

- **Click [Open] on the toolbar.**
- **Choose Windows Live Photo Gallery.**

Your screen should be similar to Figure 1.67

Additional Information

You may start Windows Live Photo Gallery by choosing the program name from the All Programs list in the Start menu.

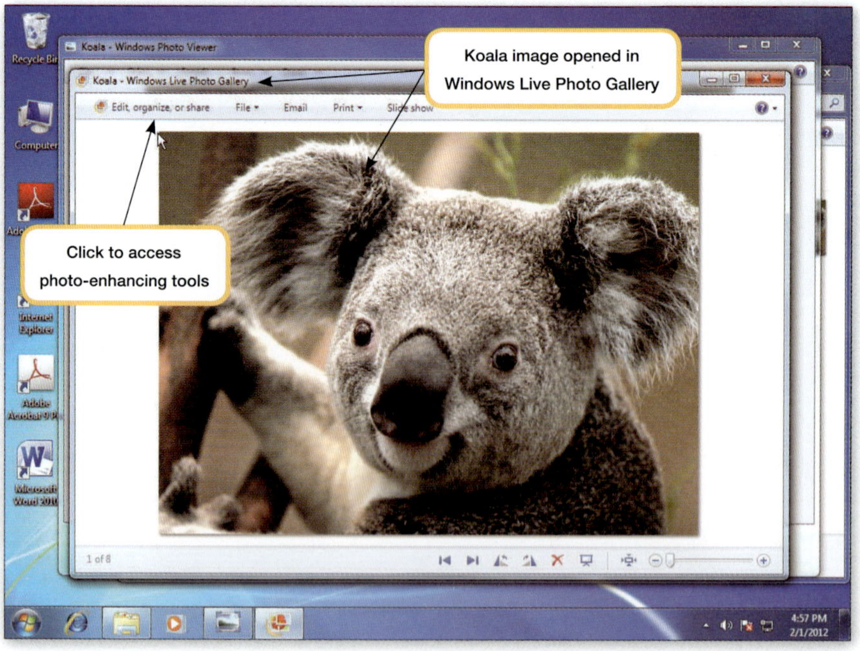

Figure 1.67

Windows Live Photo Gallery includes many additional features for viewing images such as zooming, for color enhancement, and for fixing images such as removing red eye. You will now take a look at some of these tools.

4

- **Click** [Edit, organize, or share].
- **Click the Edit tab to access the photo enhancement features.**

Your screen should be similar to Figure 1.68

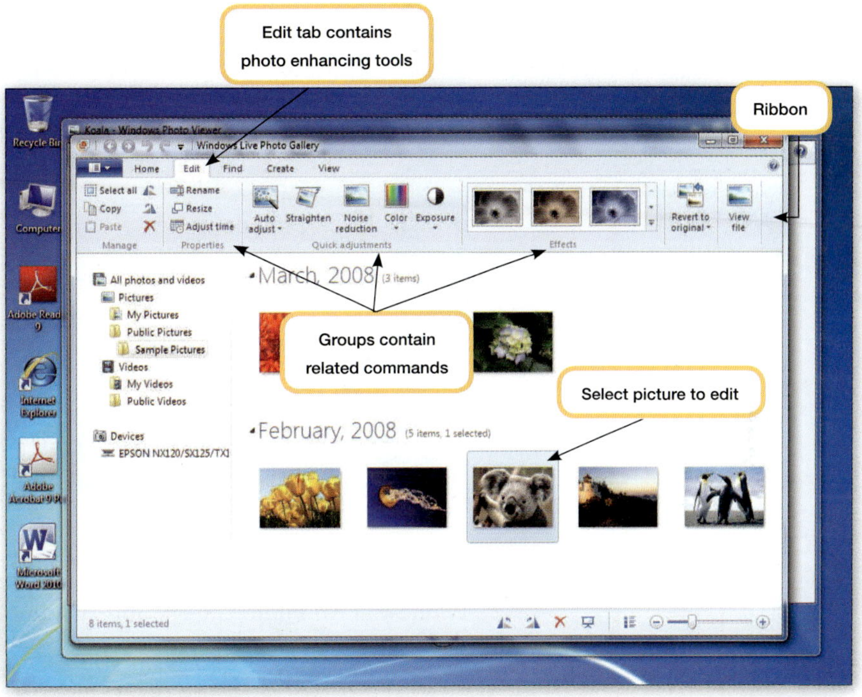

Figure 1.68

Additional Information

A file can have multiple tags consisting of a word or phrase.

Additional Information

The Microsoft Office 2007 and 2010 applications use the Ribbon user interface.

Instead of a toolbar, this application displays a **Ribbon** that consists of tabs, groups and commands. Tabs are used to divide the Ribbon into major activity areas. Each tab is then organized into groups that contain related commands. To edit a specific picture, you would click on the picture to select it and use the features in the Edit tab. For even more editing features, you can double-click on the picture to access even more advanced editing tools.

You will now close the Windows Live Photo Gallery window and the Windows Photo Viewer window to return to the Sample pictures folder in the Pictures library.

5

- **Click Close to close Windows Live Photo Gallery.**
- **Click to close Windows Photo Viewer.**

Your screen should be similar to Figure 1.69

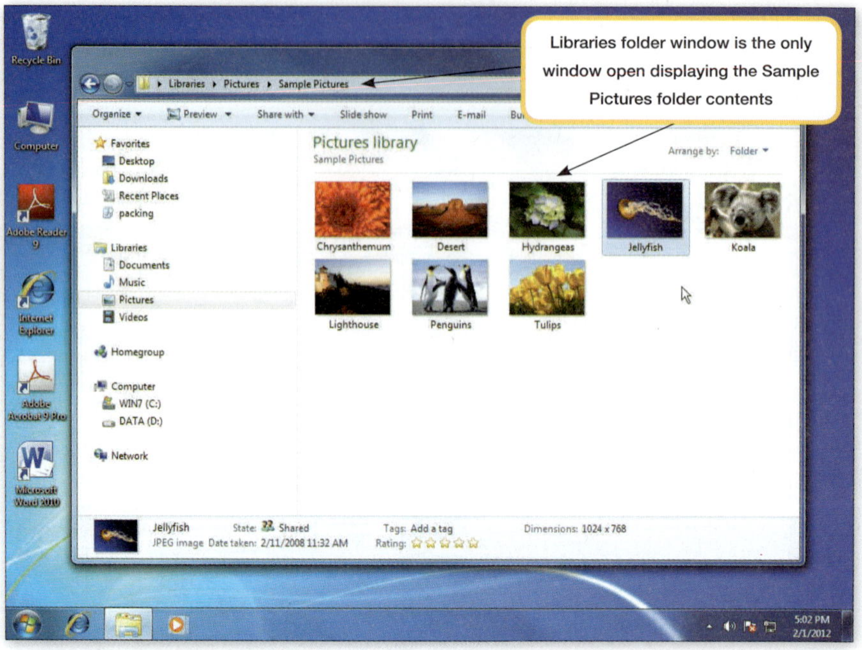

Figure 1.69

Windows Live Photo Gallery and Windows Photo Viewer are both closed and the Sample Pictures folder window is visible again.

6

- **Click Close to close the window.**

Shutting Down Windows 7

Additional Information

To avoid damaging files, always follow the procedure below to shut down Windows 7 before you turn off your computer.

It is always important to follow the correct procedures for shutting down your computer to ensure that all data is saved and all files are closed. You can shut down Windows 7 in one of two ways. When you want to stop working and turn off your computer, use the Shut Down command in the Start menu. If, on the other hand, you share a computer and someone else will use it next, use the Log Off command to end your session but leave the computer running at full power for the next user.

1

- **Click Start and point to the next to the Shut down button to access the Shut down menu options.**

Your screen should be similar to Figure 1.70

Additional Information

Depending upon the setup of your computer, the Sleep or Hibernate option may not appear.

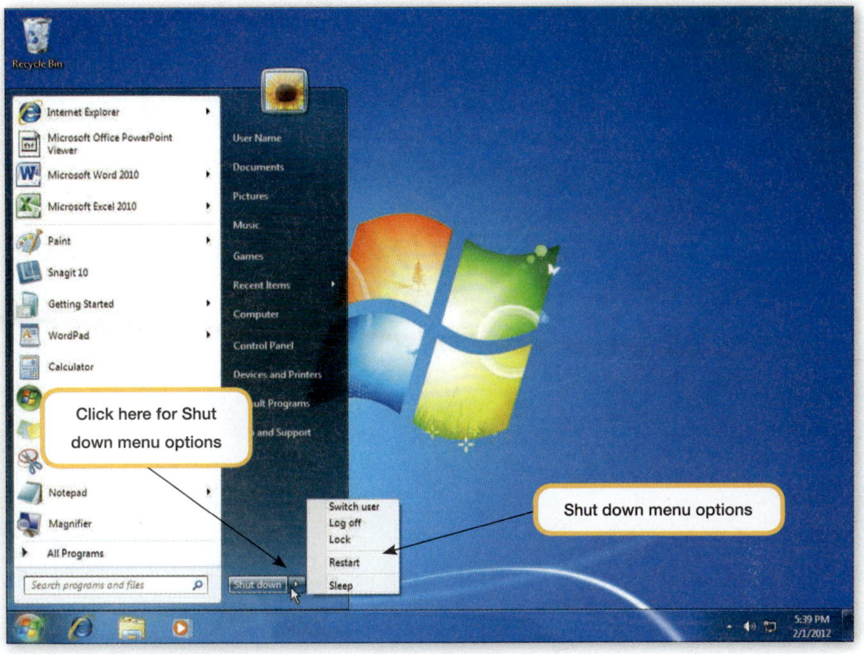

Figure 1.70

The following table describes each of the Shut down menu options.

Option	Effect
Switch User	Allows another user to log on and use the computer while your programs and files remain open. You can easily resume work by logging in again and everything is just as you left it. Because Windows does not automatically save files that are open before switching users, if the other user shuts down the computer, any unsaved changes you have made to files will be lost. Be sure to save any open files before switching users.
Log Off	Closes your programs and files and ends your Windows session but does not turn the computer off. Another user can then log on without the need to restart the computer.
Lock	Locks the computer without turning it off. Once locked, your computer cannot be used until you unlock it with your password.
Restart	Saves any settings you have changed in Windows 7, writes anything stored in memory to the hard disk, and restarts Windows. This is called a **warm start**. A warm start does not perform a memory check, but it does initialize the equipment for use. This feature is commonly used when a program stops running and the system freezes up on you or after installing a program or program update.
Sleep	Saves open documents and programs to memory and puts computer in low-power state in order to maintain your work in memory. Depending on your computer setup, the work session can be quickly resumed by pressing the power button or any key on the computer, by clicking a mouse button or by opening the lid on a mobile PC. Sleep is the default power setting.
Hibernate	Saves open documents and programs to hard disk and turns off the computer. Depending on your computer setup, the work session can be quickly resumed by pressing the power button or any key on the computer, by clicking a mouse button or by opening the lid on a mobile PC. Because hibernation turns the computer off, it uses the least amount of power of all the power-saving states.
Shut Down	Saves any settings you have changed in Windows 7 and turns the computer off. You must save your work and exit each program before you shut down the computer. You restart the computer using the computer's power button. Then, you must restart the programs and open the files you want to use. Use shut down only when you need to install or repair hardware, add memory, or do not plan to use the computer for several days.

2

- **Click on a Shut down menu option, or simply click on the Shut down button to turn off your computer.**

WARNING Always log off or shut down the computer using the above procedures. Do not turn off the computer by pressing the power button, as it is possible that data may be lost.

Lab 1 CONCEPT SUMMARY

Windows 7 Basic Skills

Operating System (WN1.5)

An operating system is a collection of programs that helps the computer manage its resources and that acts as the interface between the user and the computer.

Desktop (WN1.10)

The desktop is the opening screen for Windows 7 and is the place where you begin your work using the computer.

Menu (WN1.13)

A menu is one of many methods used to tell a program what you want it to do. When opened, a menu displays a list of commands.

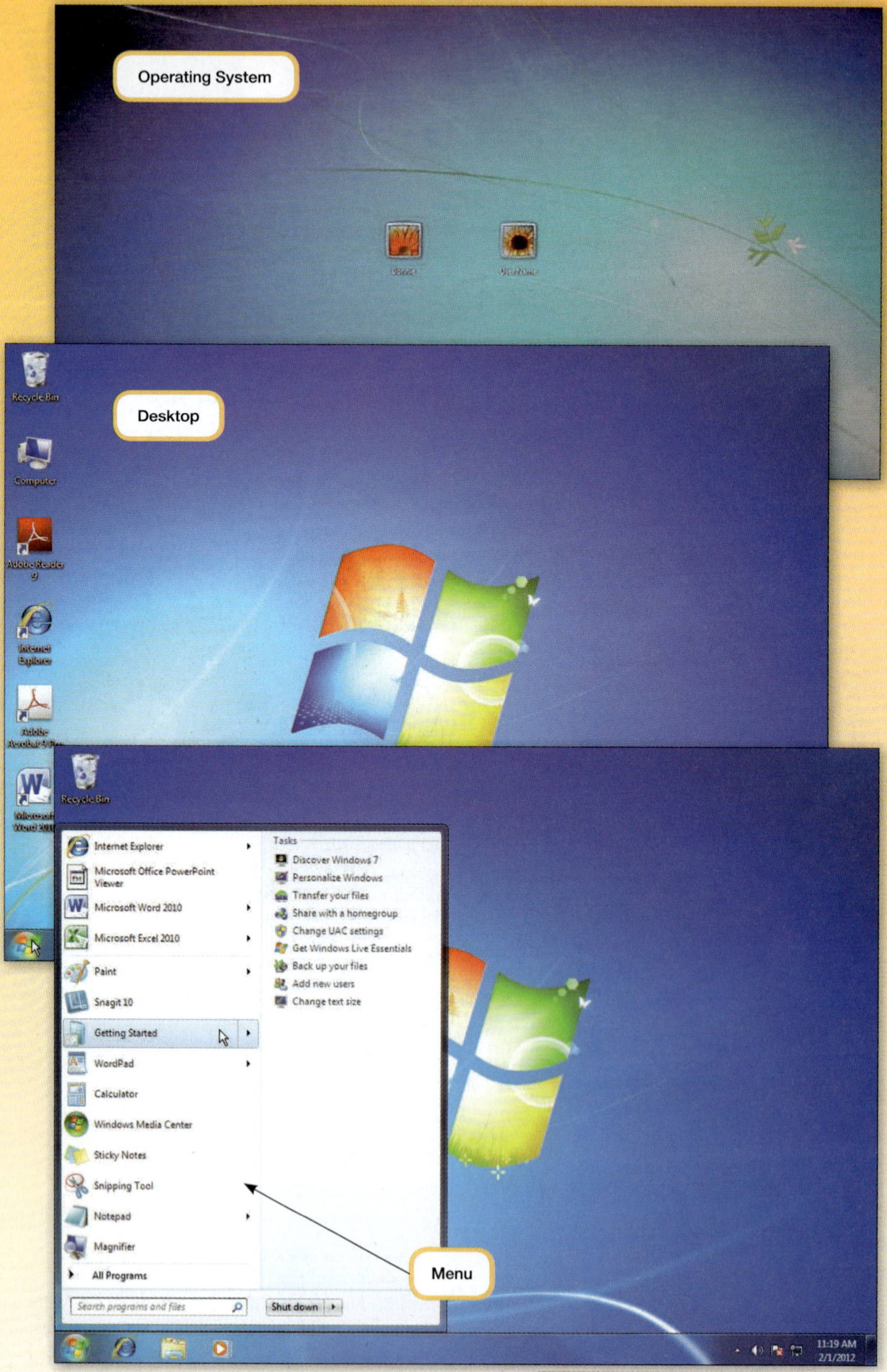

Window (WN1.16)

A window is a rectangular section of the screen that is used to display information and other programs.

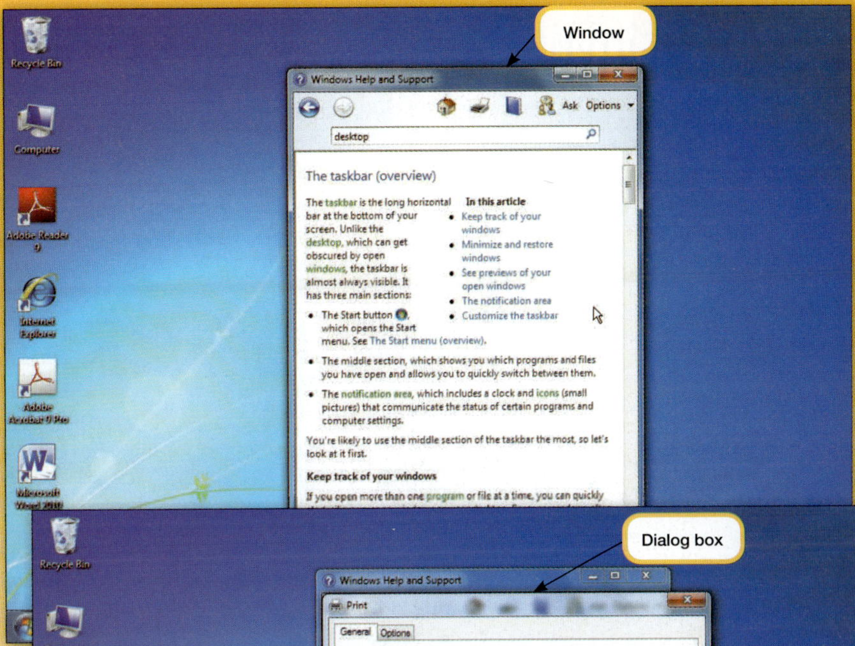

Dialog Box (WN1.33)

A dialog box is a window that is displayed whenever the program requires additional information from you in order to complete a task.

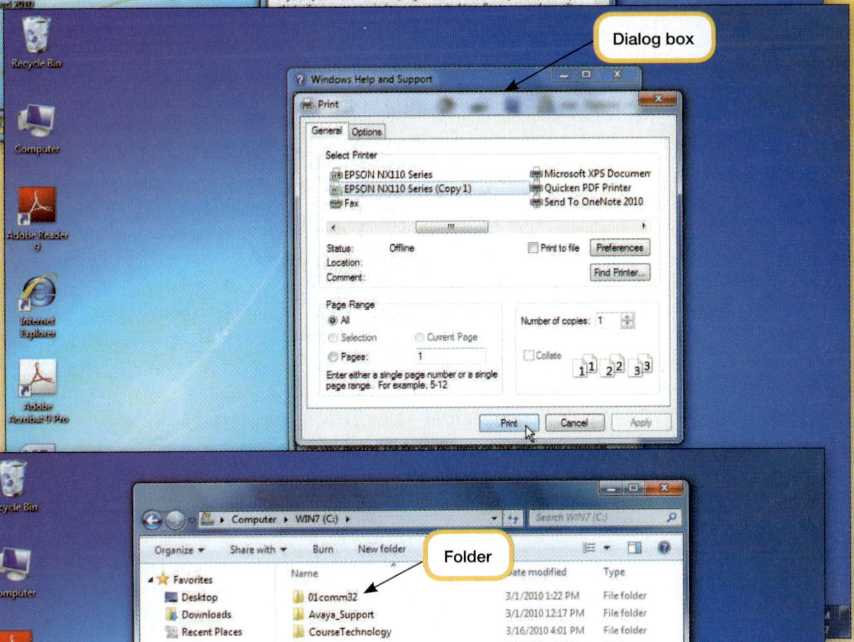

Folders and Libraries (WN1.50)

Folders and libraries are used to manage and organize the files on your computer.

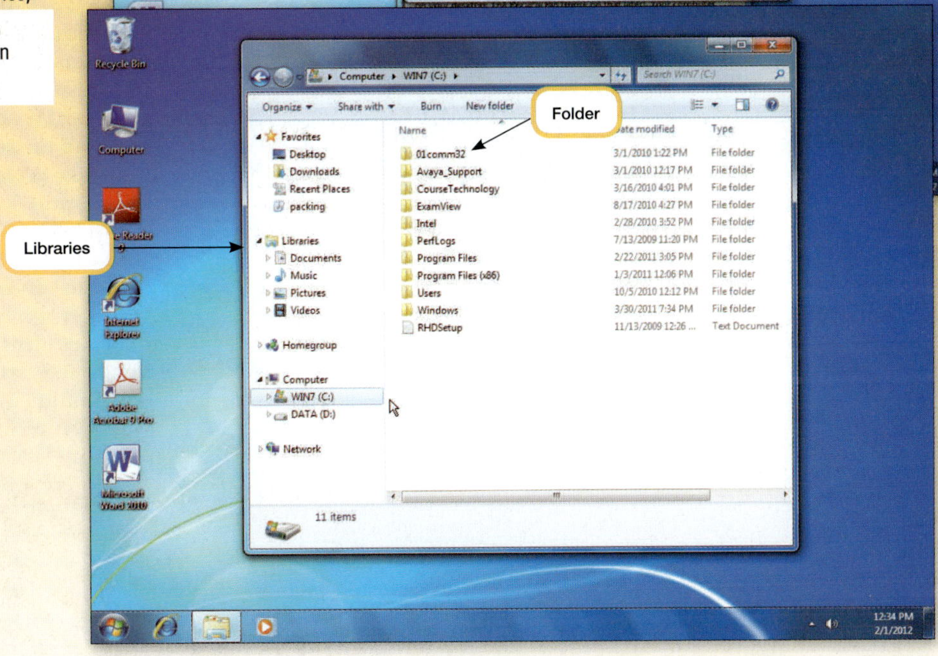

LAB REVIEW Lab 1 Windows 7 Basic Skills

KEY TERMS

active window WN1.38
Aero WN1.5
Aero Peek WN1.22
application software WN1.4
associated file WN1.59
button WN1.11
cable WN1.7
capacity WN1.54
cascade WN1.39
cascading menu WN1.13
click WN1.8
cold start WN1.6
data file WN1.49
desktop WN1.10
desktop gadget WN1.10
details pane WN1.52
dialog box WN1.33
disk size WN1.54
double-click WN1.8
drag WN1.8
file WN1.5, WN1.49
file list WN1.51
folder WN1.50
graphical user interface (GUI) WN1.5
home page WN1.28
horizontal scroll bar WN1.23
hyperlink WN1.25
icon WN1.10
insertion point WN1.9
left button WN1.7
library WN1.50
location WN1.50
maximize WN1.17
menu WN1.13
menu bar WN1.16
minimize WN1.17
mouse WN1.7
mouse pointer WN1.7
multitasking WN1.37
navigation pane WN1.52
object WN1.10
operating system WN1.5
optical mouse WN1.7
page WN1.25
pane WN1.13
path WN1.55
pin WN1.11
pinned items list WN1.13
point WN1.8
preview pane WN1.52
program WN1.5
program file WN1.49
properties WN1.10
restore WN1.17
Ribbon WN1.69
right button WN1.7
ScreenTip WN1.11
scroll arrow WN1.22
scroll bar WN1.22
scroll box WN1.22
search terms WN1.4
secondary folder WN1.50
selection cursor WN1.13
Shake WN1.46
shortcut menu WN1.41
Snap WN1.46
subfolder WN1.50
submenu WN1.13
tag WN1.69
taskbar WN1.11
taskbar button WN1.11
text box WN1.9
thumbnail WN1.23
tile WN1.41
title bar WN1.16
toolbar WN1.16
Undo WN1.42
user account WN1.6
Vertical Scroll bar WN1.23
warm start WN1.71
wheeled mouse WN1.7
window WN1.16

COMMAND SUMMARY

Command	Shortcut	Action
Start		Opens Start menu
Start Menu		
Documents		Opens the Documents folder
Computer		Opens the Computer folder
Help and Support	⊞ + F1	Opens Windows Help and Support
Folder Window		
Close	Alt + F4	Closes active window
Organize ▾/Layout		Turns on/off display of Details, Preview, and Navigation panes
Views		Cycles through Details, Tiles, Large Icons, and List views
Views/Extra Large Icons		Displays extra large icons of graphic files
Views/Large Icons		Displays large icons of graphic files
Views/Medium Icons		Displays medium icons of graphic files
Views/Small Icons		Displays small icons of graphic files
Views/List		Displays objects in a list
Views/Details		Displays all folder and file details
Views/Tiles		Displays objects with medium icons and file names
Content / Large Icons		
Slide show		Displays pictures in folder as a full-screen timed slide show
Help and Support		
Back	Alt + ←	Displays previously viewed Help topic
Forward	Alt + →	Displays next-viewed Help topic after using Back
Home		Displays Help home page
Print		Prints displayed Help topic
Browse Help		Displays Help table of contents list
Ask		Accesses other sources of Help
Options ▾		Changes Help settings

LAB EXERCISES

SCREEN IDENTIFICATION

1. In the following Windows 7 screen, several items are identified by letters. Enter the correct term for each item in the space provided.

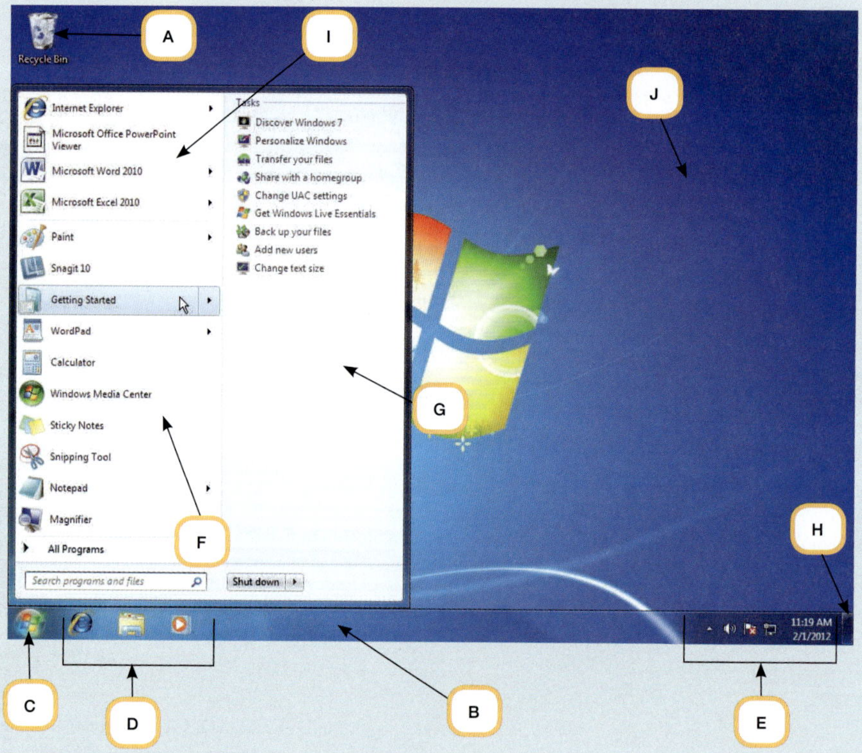

A. ____________________
B. ____________________
C. ____________________
D. ____________________
E. ____________________
F. ____________________
G. ____________________
H. ____________________
I. ____________________
J. ____________________

2. In the following folder window, several items are identified by letters. Enter the correct term for each item in the space provided.

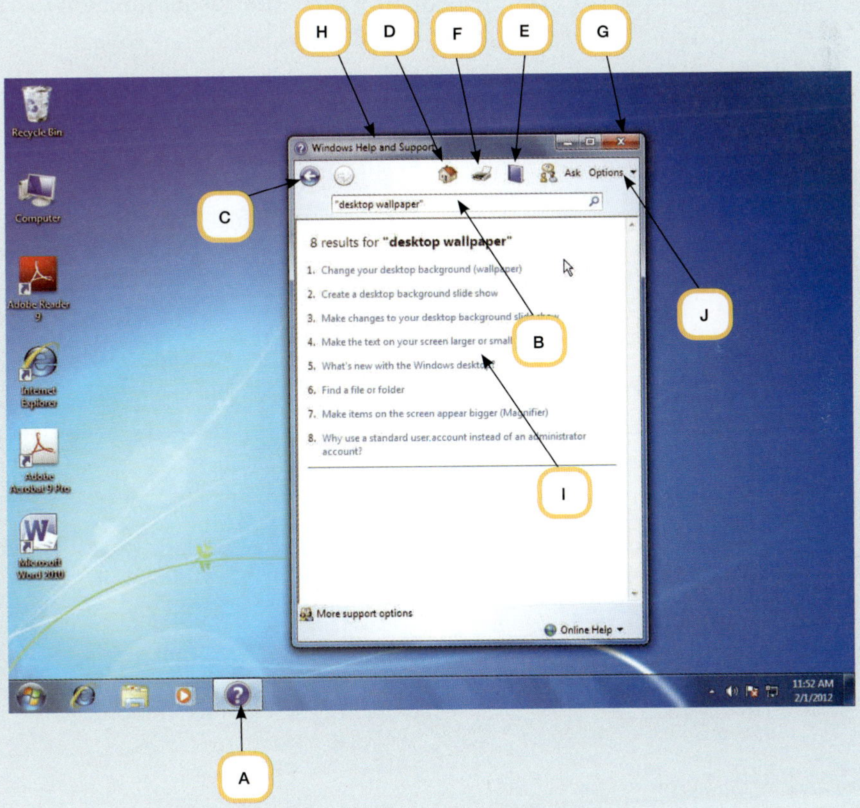

A. ____________________
B. ____________________
C. ____________________
D. ____________________
E. ____________________
F. ____________________
G. ____________________
H. ____________________
I. ____________________
J. ____________________

LAB EXERCISES

MATCHING

Match the letter to the correct item in the numbered list.

1. 
2. scroll bar
3. 
4. 
5. dialog box
6. 
7. 
8. 
9. window
10. 

_____ a. restores a maximized window
_____ b. a mouse pointer
_____ c. opens the Start menu
_____ d. used to provide information to complete a command
_____ e. displays Help home page
_____ f. minimizes a window
_____ g. used to bring additional information into view in a window
_____ h. rectangular section on the screen that is used to display information and other programs
_____ i. used to change the appearance of the folder list
_____ j. closes a window

MULTIPLE CHOICE

Circle the correct response to the questions below.

1. A collection of programs that helps the computer manage its resources and acts as an interface between the user and the computer is called a(n) ____________________.
   a. application
   b. operating system
   c. program
   d. software
2. The ____________________ is the opening screen for Windows 7.
   a. window
   b. pane
   c. desktop
   d. monitor
3. ____________________ provide ways for the user to interact with a program.
   a. Menus
   b. Dialog boxes
   c. Icons
   d. all the above
4. Related groups of folders can be housed together in _____.
   a. libraries
   b. programs
   c. organizations
   d. files

5. When a program requires more information to complete a task, a ________________ may be displayed.
   a. menu
   b. command button
   c. dialog box
   d. control panel
6. The feature that allows you to quickly minimize multiple windows on your desktop is called ________________.
   a. Snap
   b. Aero peek
   c. Shake
   d. Preview
7. To organize the information on a computer, related files are stored in ________________.
   a. folders
   b. directories
   c. objects
   d. none of the above
8. To make a window its largest size, the ________________ button is used.
   a. 
   b. 
   c. 
   d. 
9. Displaying open windows with all the title bars showing is called ________________.
   a. cascading
   b. tiling horizontally
   c. tiling vertically
   d. arranging
10. ________________ are settings and attributes associated with an object on the screen.
   a. Properties
   b. Positions
   c. Assets
   d. Possessions

LAB EXERCISES

TRUE/FALSE

Circle the correct answer to the following questions.

1.	The desktop is the opening screen for Windows 7.	**True**	**False**
2.	Small pictures, called items, represent the objects on the Windows desktop.	**True**	**False**
3.	The menu bar displayed across the bottom of the screen is used to interact with a program.	**True**	**False**
4.	A window is a rectangular section on the screen that is used to display information and other programs.	**True**	**False**
5.	A scroll bar is used to move more information in a window.	**True**	**False**
6.	The information a computer uses is stored electronically as a variety of different folders on a disk.	**True**	**False**
7.	A maximized window cannot be custom sized.	**True**	**False**
8.	Windows arranged in the stacked format are arranged vertically across the window space.	**True**	**False**
9.	The Lock feature prevents other users from accessing the computer.	**True**	**False**
10.	The function that allows you to preview the content of a window by pointing to the taskbar icon is called Aero peek.	**True**	**False**

FILL-IN

Complete the following statements by filling in the blanks with the correct terms.

1. ____________________ are groups of related folders that allow better organization of your files and folders.
2. The ____________________ program controls computer system resources and coordinates the flow of data to input and output devices.
3. When you turn the computer on to start Windows 7, you have performed a(n) ____________________.
4. Each object consists of settings and attributes called ____________________ that are unique to the object.
5. Storing related files in ____________________ keeps the disk organized and makes it much easier to locate files.
6. The ____________________ is displayed in the Address bar.
7. A(n) ____________________ provides a connection to information at another location.
8. A(n) ____________________ scroll box indicates that only a small amount of the total available information is displayed in the window.
9. The three window arrangements are ____________________, ____________________, and ____________________.
10. The capability to run several different programs at the same time is called ____________________.

LAB EXERCISES

Hands-On Exercises

RATING SYSTEM

★	Easy
★★	Moderate
★★★	Difficult

STEP-BY-STEP

REINFORCING YOUR KNOWLEDGE ★

1. Windows Help and Support includes links to Windows 7 getting started video clips, which introduce and explain many of the basic Windows 7 features. This problem will use the videos to reinforce many of the features presented in this lab.

    a. In the Windows Help and Support window, click on the How to get started with your computer link.

    b. Click the Click to open Getting Started. This will open another window on your desktop.

    c. Under the main heading, double-click Go online to find out what's new in Windows 7.

    d. Select and watch the video clips to help you answer these questions:

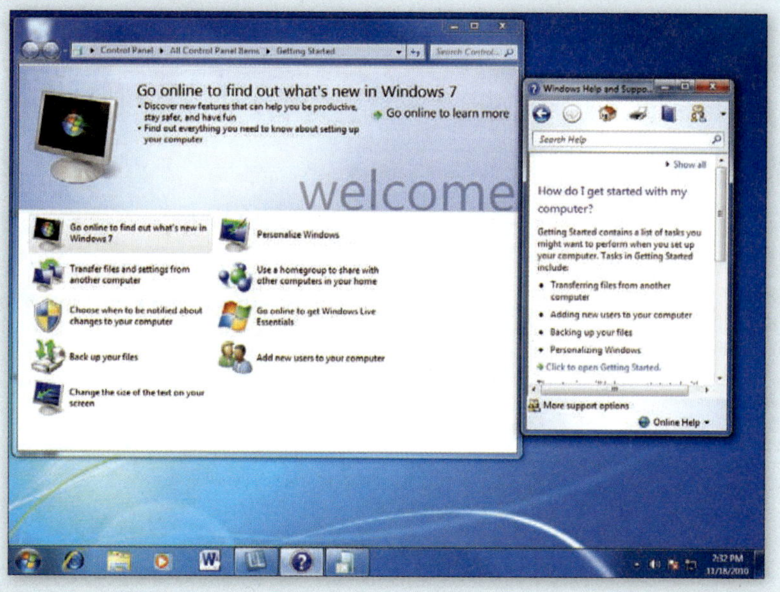

1) Name 3 special Windows 7 features.
2) What are two ways to include programs on the taskbar for easy access?
3) Give an example of a desktop gadget.
4) How are desktop gadgets useful?
5) Where can you find jumpllists?
6) When a program is open, what is displayed on the taskbar?
7) How can you use the taskbar to organize programs you use frequently?
8) What button do you click to make open windows "disappear?"
9) Give 2 reasons "snap" is helpful.
10) How can you easily find your recently accessed files?

    e. When you are finished, close all windows.

ARRANGING AND SIZING WINDOWS ★

2. As you learned in the lab, windows can be both sized and moved. This is an important skill to develop because many times windows will cover other information you want to see or may be an inappropriate size when they are opened. To develop this skill, you will open, move, and size several windows while learning about Aero Peek.

   a. Open the Computer window. Open Windows Help and Support. Restore both windows if necessary.
   b. Enter the word **preview** in the Help search box. Display the topic "Preview an open window on the desktop using Aero Peek." Scroll the Help topic and follow the directions on how to preview open files using Aero Peek.
   c. Move the Help window to the lower-right corner of the desktop.
   d. Move the Computer window to the upper-left corner of the desktop.
   e. Size the Help window until it covers the lower-right quarter of the desktop.
   f. Size the Computer window until it covers the upper-left quarter of the desktop.
   g. Maximize the Help window. Another way to make a window active is to click on the taskbar icon of the window. Using this method, make the Computer window active. Then use it to make the Windows Help and Support window active again.
   h. Cascade the open windows. Undo the cascade.
   i. Click Show desktop on the lower-right corner of the taskbar to display the desktop. Right-click on the taskbar to display the taskbar shortcut menu to display all open windows.
   j. Return the Computer and Help windows to their approximate original size and location.
   k. Close all open windows.

LAB EXERCISES

LEARN MORE ABOUT: SNAP, SHAKE, AND JUMP LISTS ★★

3. Windows Help and Support includes articles and tutorials on a variety of topics. You will learn more about some new features of Windows 7.

   a. Start Windows Help and Support. Scroll down on the Help home page to "What's new in Windows 7."

   b. Click on the link, which will take you to the Microsoft Web site where you can explore some of the new features and answer the following questions.

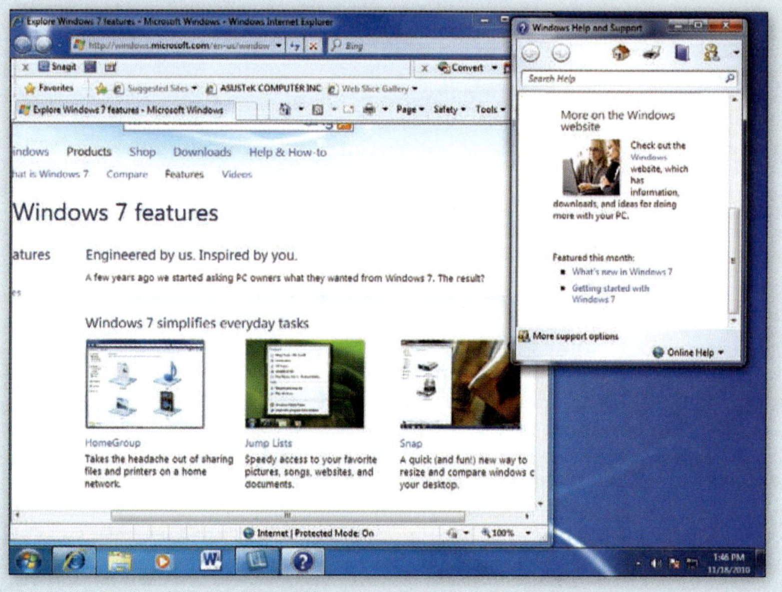

      1) What is the Snap feature? Why is this helpful? Be sure to try it with two open windows on your desktop.

      2) Search for the Shake feature. Open three windows on your desktop (the Help and Support window is one; you can also use Computer and Internet Explorer windows). Follow the instructions for Shake in Help.

      3) What are Jump lists? How can you "pin" frequently used files to your Jump list?

   c. Close all open windows.

PERSONALIZING YOUR PC ★★

4. In this problem, you will use Windows Help and Support to learn more about personalizing your computer.
   a. Start Windows Help and Support. Type **personalize your pc** in the search box.
   b. Choose the Personalizing your computer, topic and then answer the following questions.

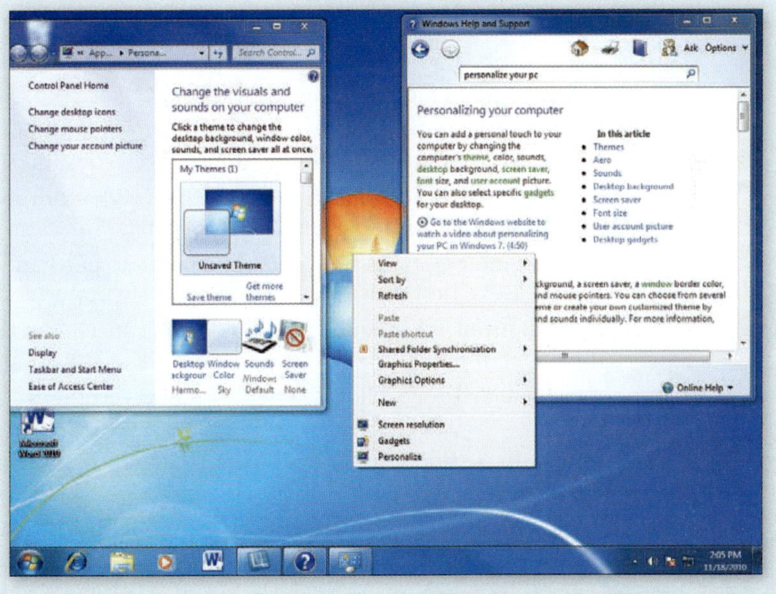

   1) What are ways you can customize your desktop?
   2) What are screen resolution settings?
   3) How do you change your user account picture?

   Next, you will use Windows Help and Support to locate information about using screen savers to personalize your desktop.

   c. Under the Screen Saver heading, click on the Change your screen saver link.
   d. After reading the information on this topic, click the link to Change a screen saver, then the link Click to open Screen Saver Settings.
   e. Open the Screen Saver drop-down list and select the Mystify screen saver. Click Preview to see it full screen and then press Esc to return to the dialog box. Preview other screen savers.
   f. When you are done, click Cancel to close the dialog box without making any changes.

   Next, you will use Windows Help and Support to locate information about customizing your keyboard settings to personalize your computer.

   g. Enter the word **keyboard** in the search box. Choose the Change keyboard settings topic.
   h. After reading the information on this topic, click on the link To change the delay before keyboard characters repeat.

LAB EXERCISES

i. Click on the link Click to open Keyboard Properties.

j. In the Keyboard Properties dialog box, adjust the Repeat delay and Repeat rate settings. Test out the new settings in the test area to see the effects of your changes. Change the cursor blinking rate. Click Cancel to cancel any changes you made and close the dialog box.

Next you will use the Help search box to locate more information about using and customizing the mouse.

k. Enter the word **mouse** in the search box. Choose the Change mouse settings topic from the list.

l. Display all the information on this topic. After reading the information on this topic, choose any one of the Click to open the Mouse Properties links.

m. Look through all the tabs in the dialog box. What are some of the mouse property settings and why would you want to change these settings?

n. In the Pointer Options tab, adjust the pointer speed and turn on the Display Pointer Trails option. Move the mouse to see the results of your selections.

o. In the Buttons tab, change the double-click speed and then try out your changes by double-clicking in the test area.

p. When you are done, click Cancel to cancel the changes you have made and close the dialog box.

Next you will use the Help search box to locate more information about using and customizing the desktop.

q. Enter the word **desktop** in the search box. Choose the Change your desktop background (wallpaper topic).

r. After reading the information on this topic, select Click to open Desktop Background.

s. From the Background list box, select several background pictures to see how they would look on your screen.

t. When you are done, click Cancel to cancel the changes you have made and close the dialog box.

u. Close Windows Help and Support.

CUSTOMIZING THE TASKBAR ★★

5. The taskbar can be customized in many ways. In this problem, you will learn about other features of the taskbar.

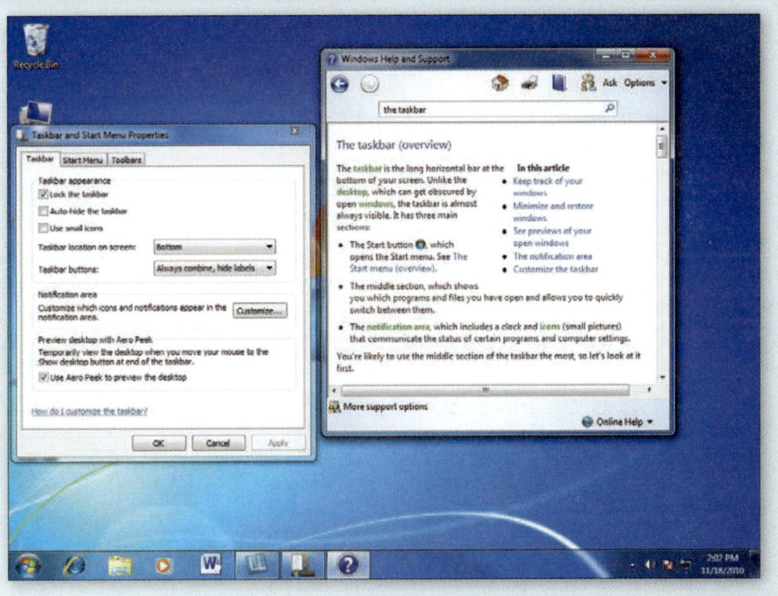

a. Use Windows Help and Support to find information about sizing the taskbar, setting the date and time, using Auto-hide, displaying toolbars in the taskbar, and moving it. Next, follow the steps below to try out several of these features.

b. Click on the time in the taskbar. Try changing the date and time properties. Click Cancel to close the dialog box without making any changes.

c. Choose Properties from the taskbar shortcut menu. Describe the five options in this dialog box. Clear the Lock the taskbar option. Turn on the Auto-hide the taskbar option. Click Cancel. Close the dialog box. What happened to the taskbar? To redisplay the taskbar, move the mouse pointer to the bottom of the window.

d. Drag the top border of the taskbar up to increase the size of the taskbar to two rows. What happened to the arrangement of items on the taskbar?

e. The taskbar can be moved along any border of the desktop. Move it to each border and describe what happens to the desktop and the taskbar. Return the taskbar to the bottom of the screen.

f. Resize the taskbar to a single row at the bottom of the screen. Reset the taskbar properties to lock it and turn off the Auto-hide feature.

g. Close the Windows Help and Support window.

LAB EXERCISES

ON YOUR OWN

WHAT ELSE IS NEW IN WINDOWS 7? ★

1. Read several articles about Windows 7. Then use Windows Help and Support to find out about more new features in Windows 7. Identify and describe three more new features of the program, compatibility, and ease of use.

PASSWORD PROTECTION ★★

2. Windows 7 has several built-in security features. One is the use of passwords for user accounts. Read about this topic in Windows Help and Support. Handwrite a brief paper about how to create a strong password and how to protect them.

ACCESSIBILITY RESOURCES ★★

3. Windows 7 includes many special features to enhance accessibility for people with special needs. Use Windows Help and Support to find out about these features. Describe the four programs that are included in Windows 7 to enhance accessibility. Get more information about the Magnifier program and try out this feature on your system. When you are finished, exit the Magnifier.

UPGRADING TO WINDOWS 7 ★★★

4. If you were the operations manager of a large company and had to decide whether to upgrade to Windows 7, what factors would you need to take into consideration? For example, what are the minimum hardware requirements to use Windows 7 effectively and will the current hardware and software at your company need to be upgraded? At what cost? With what benefits?

PLAYING MUSIC ★★★

5. You can play many types of audio files using accessories provided with Windows 7. The Media Player accessory is used to play audio and video files from the Internet, play your CDs or DVDs, or listen to Internet radio stations. You also can easily play music stored on your computer. You must have a sound card to use these features. If your system does not include speakers, check with your instructor about using a headset to listen to the sound. Use Help to locate information about the Media Player. Run the Media Player Tour to learn about this feature. Start the Media Player application. Open the Media Library and play the sample audio file by Aaron Goldberg. Select a Skin of your choice and use it to play the same audio file. Return to Full Mode when you are done. Close the Media Player. Using Help as a guide, search for information about playing music stored on your computer. Use the Favorite link to the Music folder. Select and play several of the sample music files in the Music folder.

File Management Lab 2

Objectives

After completing this lab, you will know how to:

1. Use the Documents Library.
2. Create folders.
3. Rename and delete folders and files.
4. Copy and move files.
5. Filter, group, and arrange files.
6. Use drag and drop.
7. Modify file properties.
8. Select multiple files.
9. Find files.
10. Use the Recycle Bin.
11. Open, edit, print, and save a Notepad document.

CASE STUDY

Adventure Travel Tours

As advertising coordinator, you create many different types of files that are used for different purposes to promote the Adventure Travel Tours company. You often find that it takes you a considerable amount of time to locate a file. Consequently, you decide you need to organize the files on your computer. Organizational skills are very important skills in any profession. When you are disorganized, it takes much longer to complete tasks accurately. In this lab, you will learn to use Windows Explorer to organize the folders and files on your disk. You will learn how to create folders and copy and move files into folders to make it easy to quickly locate files. Additionally, you will learn about many other file management features and shortcuts that will improve your efficiency.

Frequently while working, you want to quickly jot down ideas or reminders. A simple application program that is included with Windows 7, Notepad, can be used to create basic text documents quickly. You will use Notepad to create a simple list of items to include in a packing list for a Colorado River kayaking adventure. The features you will use to edit and print this document are features that are common to all applications that run under Windows. Learning about many of these features now will make it easier for you to learn to use new applications in the future.

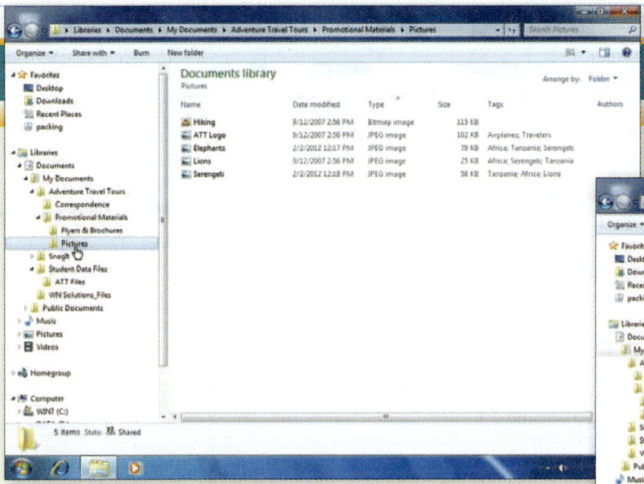

Storing related files in separate folders keeps the information in your computer organized.

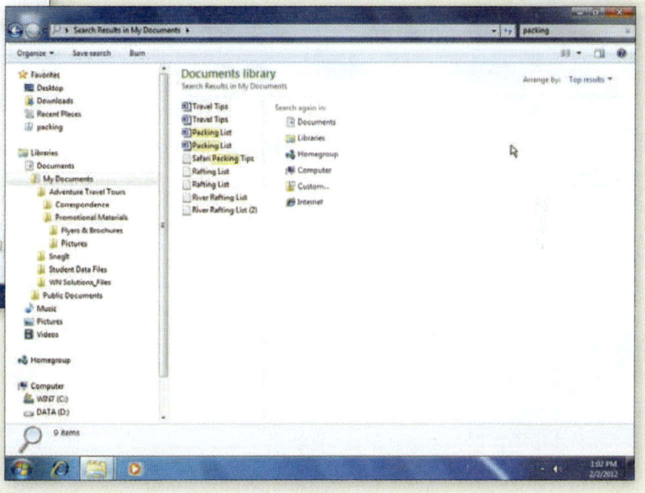

Locating files is quick and easy using the Search box.

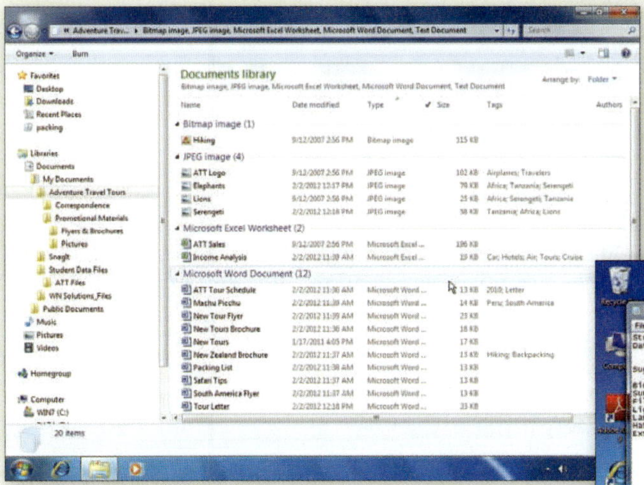

Filtering, grouping, and arranging files helps organize files.

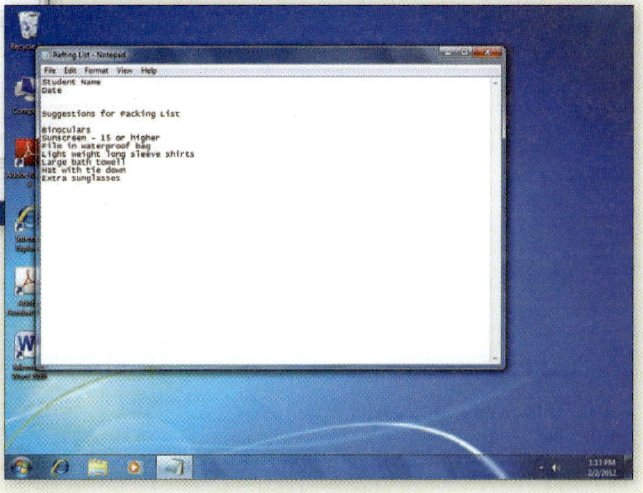

Notepad can be used to quickly create simple text documents.

Concept Overview

The following concepts will be introduced in this lab:

1. **Hierarchy** The graphic representation of the organization of folders on a disk is called a hierarchy.
2. **File and Folder Names** When a file or folder is created, it must be assigned a file name that identifies its contents. File and folder names should be unique and easy to recognize.
3. **Copy and Move** All Windows applications include features that allow you to copy and move selected information from one location to another.
4. **Filter, Group, and Arrange** To help you find files that share something in common, you can filter, group, and arrange files.
5. **Drag and Drop** Common to all Windows applications is the ability to copy or move selections using the drag-and-drop feature.
6. **Search** The search feature provides a quick method to find files, folders, programs and e-mail messages stored on your computer.
7. **Editing** One of the advantages of using a computer is that you can easily change or edit your documents.
8. **Saving Files** When you save a document you are working on, a permanent copy of your onscreen document is electronically stored as a file on a disk or other storage device.

Managing Files Using Folders and Libraries

As the advertising coordinator for Adventure Travel Tours, you create many different types of documents to promote the different products offered by the company. As you create more files, it is taking you longer to locate the file you want to use because they are not organized. You decide to create folders to help organize the files.

1

- **If necessary, turn on the computer.**
- **Log on to Windows.**
- **Click Start and choose Documents.**

Additional Information

You also can use /All Programs/ Accessories/ Windows Explorer to open the Libraries location.

- **Maximize the window.**
- **If necessary, change the icon view to Tiles.**

Having Trouble?

Your window will display different folders and files than those in Figure 2.1.

Your screen should be similar to Figure 2.1

Additional Information

Pointing to a file will display a Screen Tip showing some of the properties of that file.

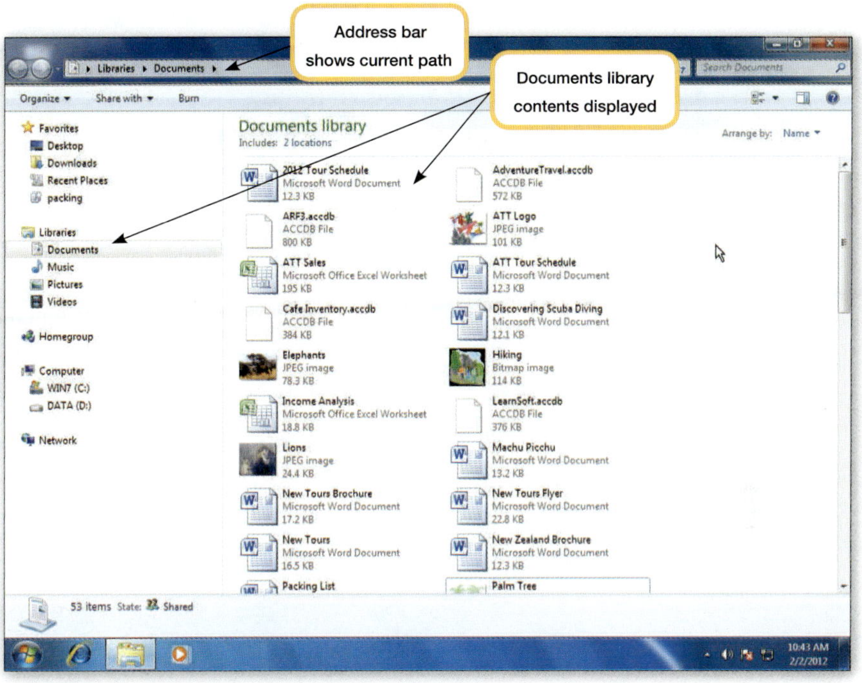

Figure 2.1

The Documents library is the current location and the address bar displays the path as links. The files and folders accessed by the Documents library are displayed in the file list.

When looking at the contents of your computer in Lab 1, you used many different navigation features to change locations to display the files and folders on your computer. These features included using links in the Address bar, clicking on displayed folders in the file list, and using the Navigation pane to display the contents of the selected location. You also used the button or the Address bar to return to a previous location and move to the next-higher-level folder. Using these methods to navigate is convenient if you want to work on files in a single location or in folders available in the Documents library but is not very efficient when you need to move between locations to work with files that are in locations that are not visible in the folder window.

USING THE DOCUMENTS LIBRARY

As briefly introduced in Lab 1, another way to view disk contents is to use the Documents library. Because libraries display folders and files from various locations, they provide quick access to these items. You also learned that the Documents library displays files contained in the My Documents and Public Documents folders. To see these locations, you expanded the Documents library in the Navigation pane by clicking the ▷ next to Documents. Another way to expand an item in the Navigation pane is to double-click on the item's name.

1

- **Double-click on the Documents library in the Navigation pane.**
- **Move the mouse pointer to point to My Documents in the navigation pane.**

Your screen should be similar to Figure 2.2

Having Trouble?

The expand and collapse symbols gradually fade when you move your mouse off the navigation pane.

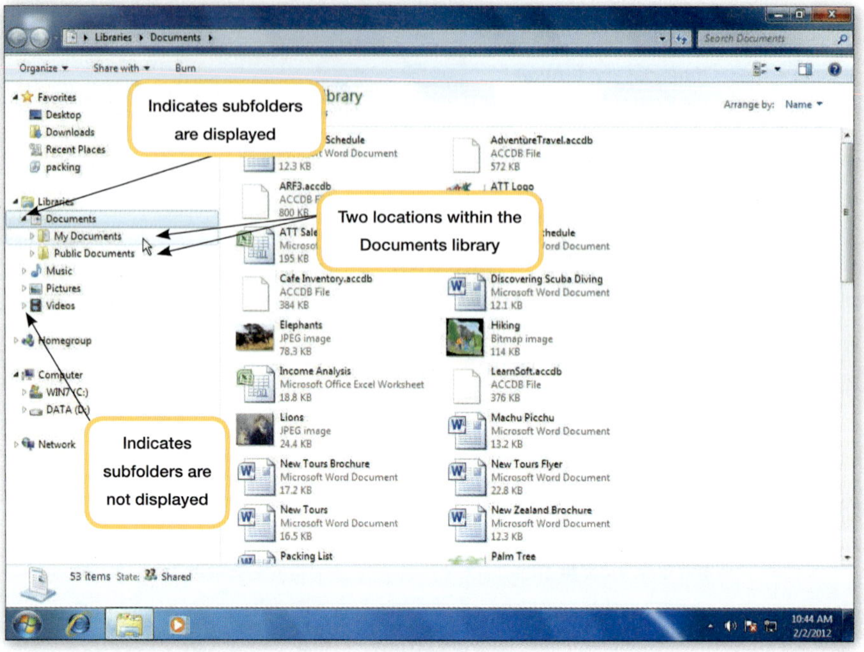

Figure 2.2

Now, in the Navigation pane, you can see the two folder locations accessed by the Documents library. The primary purpose of the navigation pane is to help you find, navigate through, and organize the folders and files on a disk. Because the Documents library is the current location, it is highlighted in the navigation pane. Notice the ◢ and ▷ symbols that appear before many of the items in the navigation pane. The ▷ (expand symbol) indicates the item contains additional items or folders that are not currently displayed in the list.

In addition, when the Computer area of the Navigation pane is expanded, the folder list is displayed. The **folder list**, also called the **folder tree**, displays the contents of the hard drive locations as a hierarchy.

Additional Information

You can adjust the size of the panes by dragging the bar that separates them.

Concept 1 Hierarchy

The graphic representation of the organization of drives and folders on your computer is called a **hierarchy.** The top-level folder of a storage location is the **main folder,** also called the **root folder.** On the hard disk of most computers, the main folder is represented by the C: drive. On a CD disk, the main folder is generally represented by the drive icon. The main folder always appears at the top of the hierarchy. Folders created in the main folder appear indented below the main folder. Subfolders appear indented below other folders. Because of the branching nature of the hierarchy, it is sometimes also called a **tree.**

You will next display the contents of the hard drive on your computer.

2

- **If necessary, scroll the navigation pane to see the Computer item.**
- **If necessary, expand Computer in the Navigation pane to display the drive locations.**
- **Double-click (C:) (or the appropriate drive for your system) in the navigation pane.**
- **If necessary, scroll the Navigation pane to see the entire folder list.**

Your screen should be similar to Figure 2.3

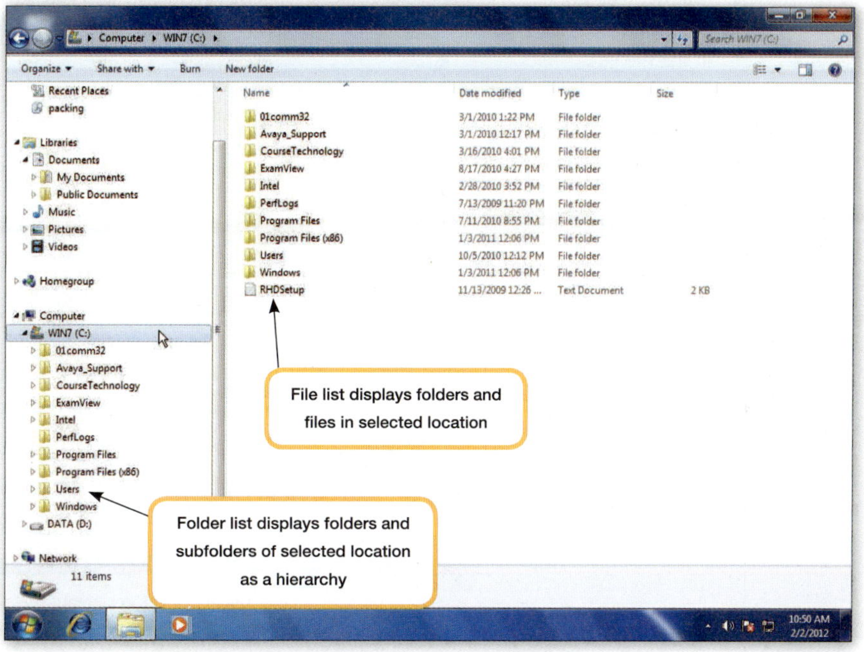

Figure 2.3

Using the Navigation pane, you quickly located the Computer section and expanded it to display the folder list of the selected hard drive. The folder list displays the folders and subfolders at that location. The file list displays both the folders and the files at this hard drive location.

Next, you will view the contents of the Program Files folder. This folder is used to store the files used to run most of the applications on your computer. Notice the same folders that are visible in the Navigation pane also are displayed in the file list. You also can display the subfolders in the Program Files folder by double-clicking on the folder name in the file list.

Additional Information
Your screen will reflect the folders and files on your computer's hard drive.

Additional Information
Pointing to a file or folder name that is too long to fully display in the navigation pane will display the complete name in a ScreenTip. You also can drag the right edge of the Navigation pane to change the width of the pane to display more or less information.

3

- **Double-click the Program Files folder in the file list.**

Having Trouble?

On some folders, Windows 7 may not initially display the folder contents and an advisory message appears indicating that you should not need to modify the files in this folder.

- **If necessary, click Show the contents of this folder to continue.**

Your screen should be similar to Figure 2.4

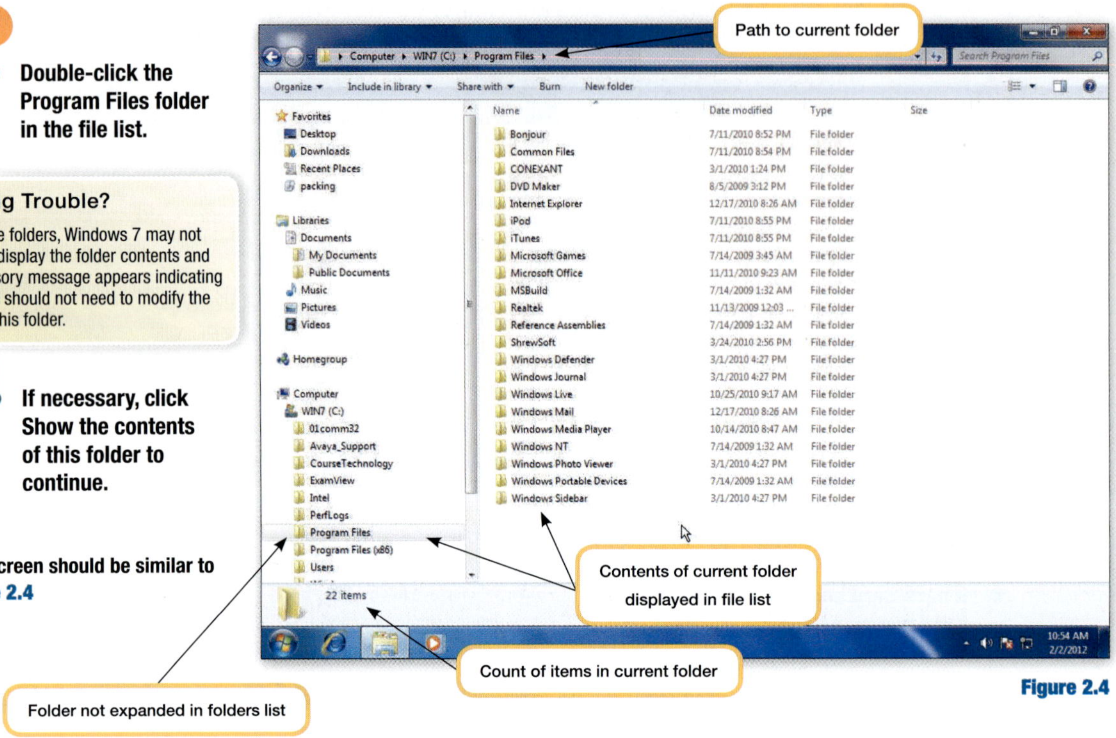

Figure 2.4

The folder name is highlighted in the folders list, indicating that it is the **current folder** or the folder that will be affected by your next actions. The Address bar displays the path as links to the selected location. The Details pane displays a count of the number of items in the folder and also may indicate the number of hidden files. Hidden files are files that Windows does not display by default to protect them from accidentally being altered. The folders list, however, did not expand and does not display the subfolders in the Program Files folder. Similarly, when you use the expand indicators in the Navigation pane to display subfolders, the file list does not display the information at that location. This is because using this method does not make the location the current location. You will expand the Users folder in the folders list to see how this works.

4

- **If necessary, scroll the folders list to display the Users folder.**
- **Click ▷ next to Users.**

Your screen should be similar to Figure 2.5

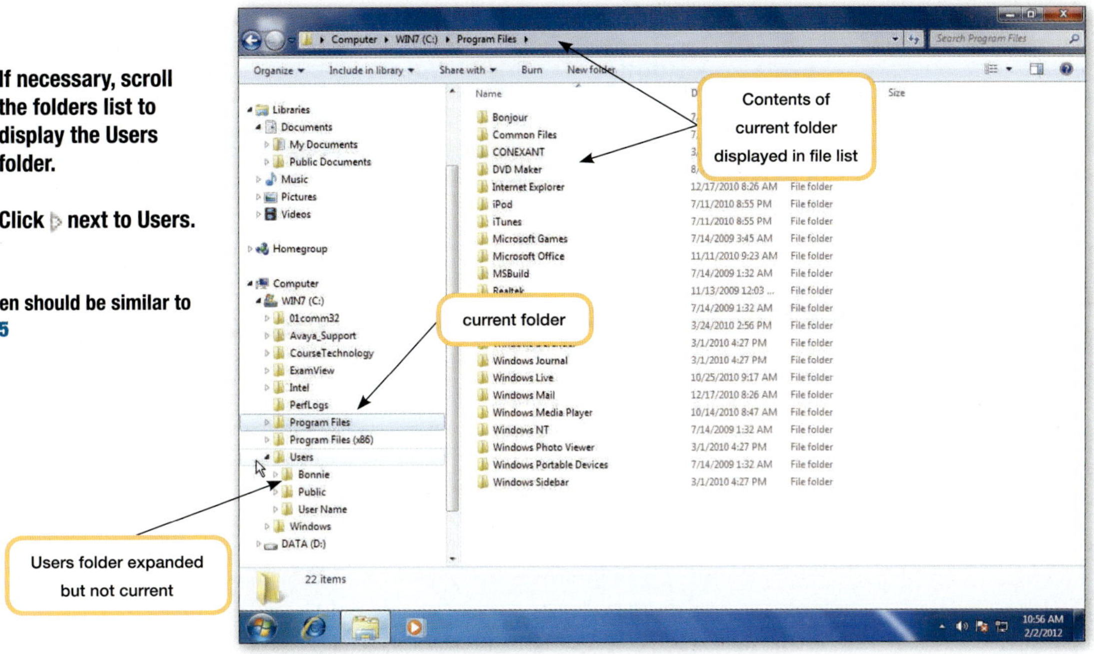

Figure 2.5

Although the Users folder is expanded in the folders list, the file list still displays the contents of the Program Files folder. This is because the Users folder is not the current folder. Clicking on the folder name makes the folder current.

5

- **Click Users.**

Your screen should be similar to Figure 2.6

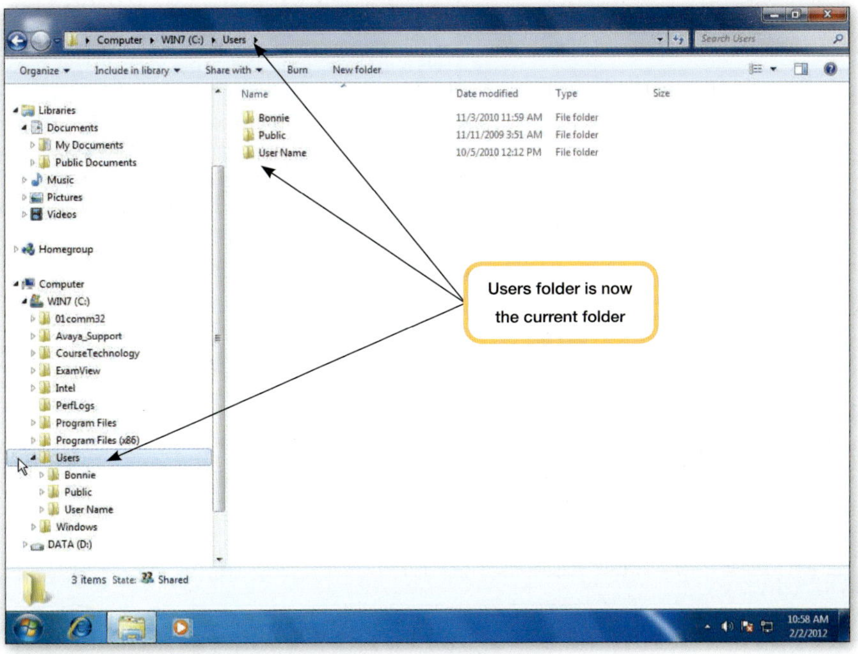

Figure 2.6

The contents of the Users folder are displayed in the file list.

At any time, you can hide or collapse the expanded list of items in the folders list by clicking the ◢ and ▷ symbols without affecting what is displayed in the file list.

6

- **Click ◢ to the left of Users.**

Your screen should be similar to Figure 2.7

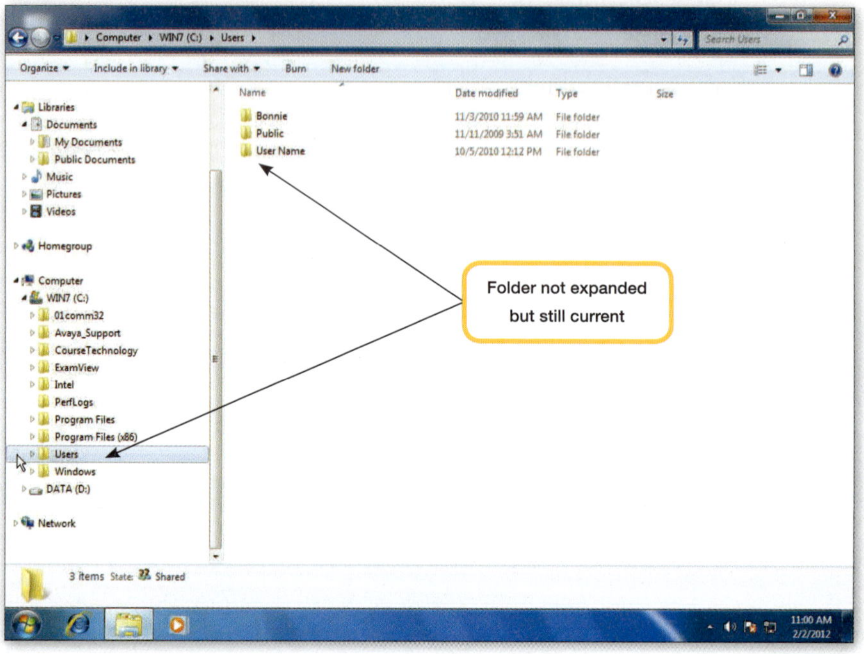

Figure 2.7

The Users folder is no longer expanded in the folders list. However, the file list continues to display the contents because it is still the current folder.

Using the Navigation pane and the folders list makes it easier to navigate through the contents of your computer and is especially helpful when you need to use files located in folders in different storage locations on your system. This is because you can easily see the entire drive and folder structure and can quickly go to a specific location without having to move sequentially up or down along a path from one folder to another.

USING THE ADDRESS BAR

The Address bar, as you learned in Lab 1, provides several methods for navigating to a particular folder on your computer. The first method, which you have already used, is to click on a link displayed in the address bar to move to it. A second method is to type the name of the folder or the path to the folder to which you want to move. Another method is to click on one of the arrows ▸ to the right of the link in the Address bar and select a location from the list that appears. The list displays the names of all subfolders in the selected location. You'll use both methods next.

Additional Information

When typing a path, the drive location is specified first, followed by a colon. A backslash is used to separate each folder (such as C:\Users\Public).

1

- **With the Users folder still current, click on the ▸ to the right of (C:) in the Address bar.**

Additional Information

The menu lists all folders located on your C drive.

- **Choose Windows, or, if this folder is not available, any folder from the menu.**

Your screen should be similar to Figure 2.8

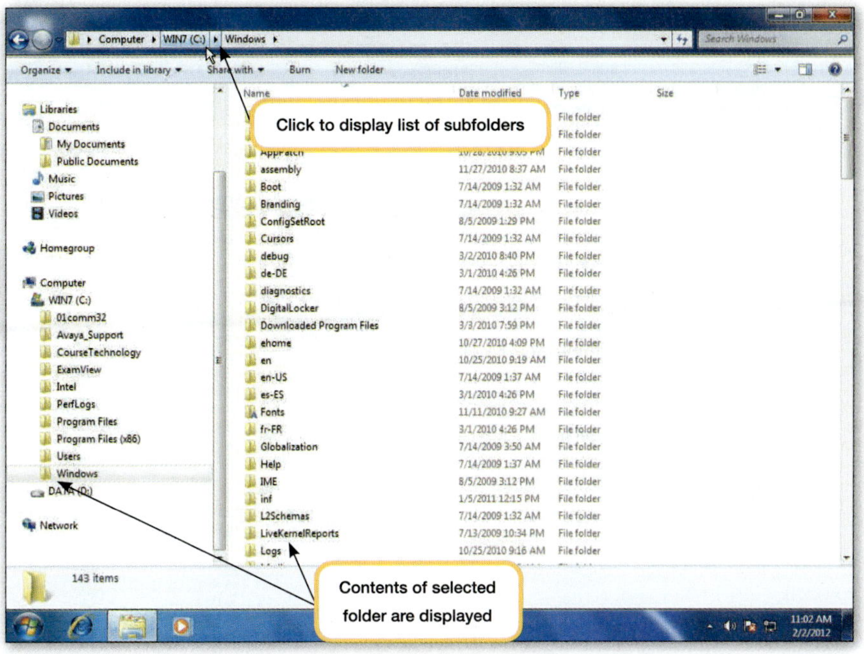

Figure 2.8

The contents of the selected folder are now displayed in the file list. Next, you will type a location directly into the Address bar.

2

- **Click on the ▸ on the left side of the address bar.**

Additional Information

The path to the current location is highlighted, indicating it is selected, and will be replaced by the new text you type.

- **Type computer and press ←Enter.**

Your screen should be similar to Figure 2.9

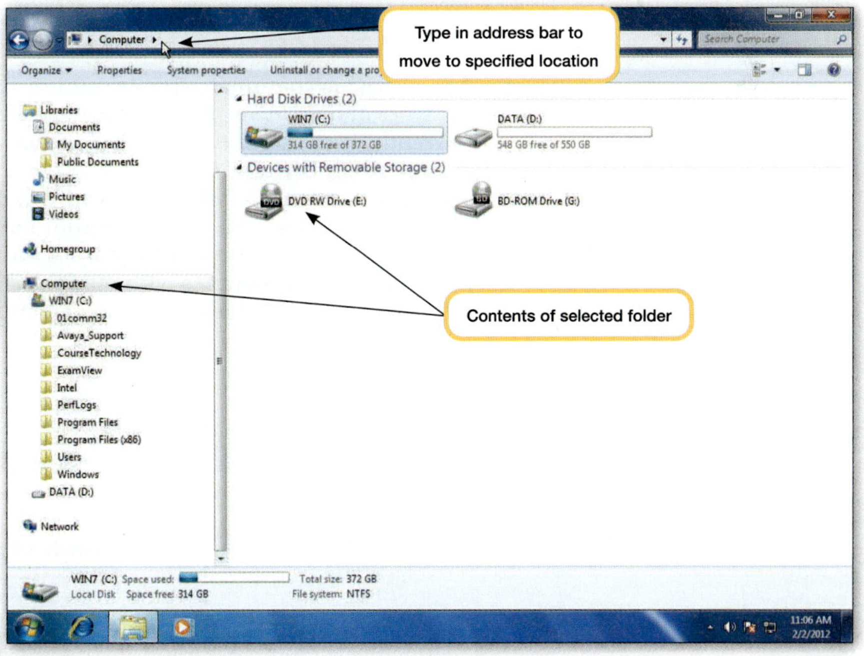

Figure 2.9

Additional Information

You also can type a word or phrase to search for information or a Web address (URL) in the Address bar. This opens Internet Explorer and displays a list of located search results or the Web page at the URL you specified.

The contents of the Computer folder are displayed. This method is easy to use if you want to quickly access common locations such as Documents, Computer, or Pictures. For most other locations, you'll need to type in the complete folder name or path (such as C:\\Users).

Additional Information

The Refresh button at the end of the Address bar will update the display of information in the current folder.

Finally, you can quickly return to a previously viewed location by selecting the path from a list of locations. The button at the end of the Address bar displays a list of previously used links by the Address bar. If you moved to locations using the Navigation pane, these locations will not be displayed.

3

- **Click at the end of the Address bar.**
- **Choose C:\Windows**

Your screen should be similar to Figure 2.10

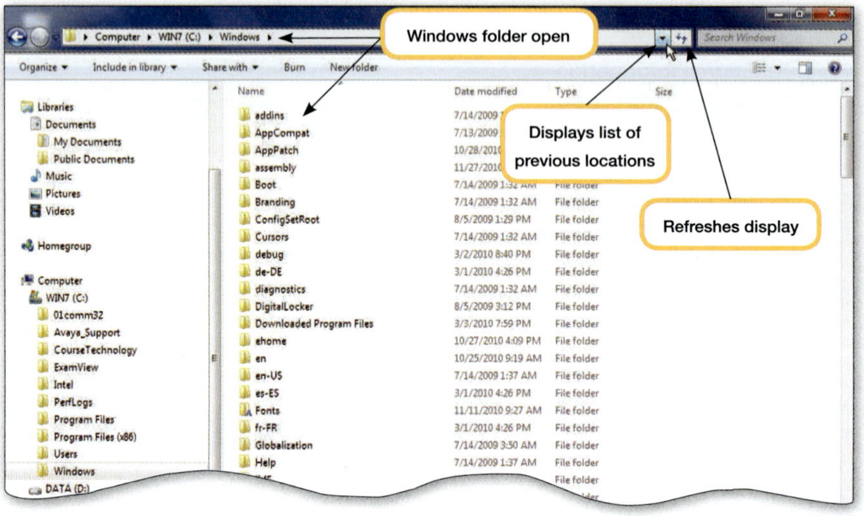

Figure 2.10

The Windows folder is open and displayed in the file list.

CREATING FOLDERS

As advertising coordinator for Adventure Travel Tours, you create many different types of documents to promote the different tours offered by the company. Currently, your files are in a single location that has become very crowded and disorganized. Because of this, it is often difficult to find the file you want to use. To help organize your files, you will create folders to hold the different categories of files. For example, promotional documents such as flyers and brochures you develop for Adventure Travel Tours will be stored in a subfolder named Flyers & Brochures within a folder named Promotional Materials. The folder and subfolder hierarchy you will create is shown here.

Additional Information

This text uses the My Documents folder as the location where students will save their work. If necessary, substitute the location where you save your work in place of this location throughout this lab.

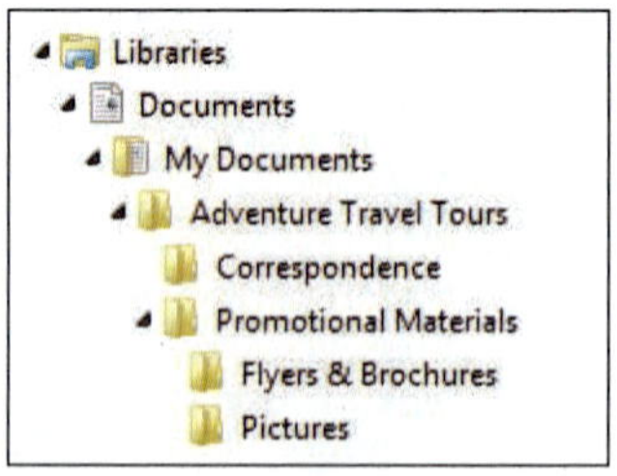

To indicate where you want the folder created, the drive or folder in which you want it created must be current first. However, if you create a folder in a library, the folder is created automatically in that library's default save location, which, for the Documents library, is the My Documents folder. You will create your new folder in the My Documents folder within the Documents library (or use your own storage media as directed by your instructor).

1

- Click ◢ next to the ◢ WIN7 (C:) to collapse the hard drive folders list.
- Using the navigation pane, make the My Documents folder (or the location where you will store your work) current.
- If necessary, change the view to Tiles.
- Click New folder on the toolbar.

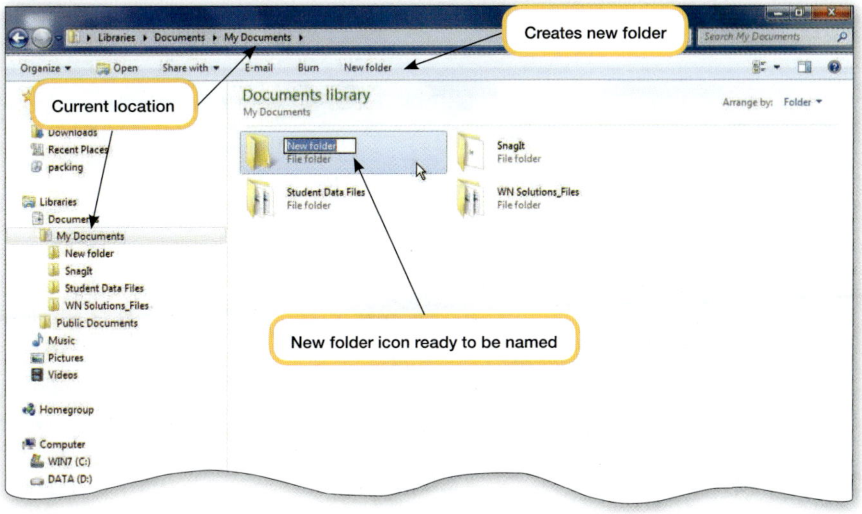

Figure 2.11

Your screen should be similar to Figure 2.11

A New folder icon is displayed in the file list. The temporary folder name is highlighted and the cursor is displayed at the end of the folder name. This indicates that Windows 7 is waiting for you to replace the default name with a descriptive name for the folder you are creating.

Concept 2 File and Folder Names

When a folder or file is created, it must be assigned a **file name** that identifies its contents. The name you assign a file must be unique for the folder it is in. For example, if you give a new file the same name as an existing file in the same folder, the contents of the original file will be replaced by the contents of the new file. Folder names also must be unique.

In addition to a file name, a **file name extension** may be added. A file name extension is up to four characters and is separated from the file name by a period. Generally, a file name extension is used to identify the type of file. This information establishes the file association that Windows uses to identify the proper program to use to open the file. Most application programs automatically add the identifying file name extension to any files created using the program. For instance, a file created using Microsoft Word 2010 has a file name extension of "docx." A folder extension is not generally used and is never supplied by the operating system.

The parts of a file name are shown below.

Safari Itinerary.docx

File name   File name extension

Windows 7 and programs that are designed to operate under Windows 7 allow you to use long folder and file names of up to 215 characters, including spaces. They can contain the letters A to Z, the numbers 0 to 9, and any of the following special characters: underscore (_), caret (^), dollar sign ($), tilde (~), exclamation point (!), number sign (#), percent sign (%), ampersand (&), hyphen (-), braces ({ }), parentheses [()], "at" sign (@), apostrophe ('), and the grave accent (`). Spaces are allowed in file names, but the following characters are not allowed: \ / : * ? > <l. The same character restrictions apply to file name extensions.

You need to replace the default folder name with a name that is descriptive of the folder contents.

2

- **With the text "New folder" highlighted, type Adventure Travel Tours.**

Having Trouble?

If you make a typing error, use the Backspace key to delete the characters to the left of the cursor and retype the entry correctly.

- **Press ←Enter.**

Having Trouble?

If your new folder did not automatically move to the correct alphabetical location click Refresh.

Your screen should be similar to Figure 2.12

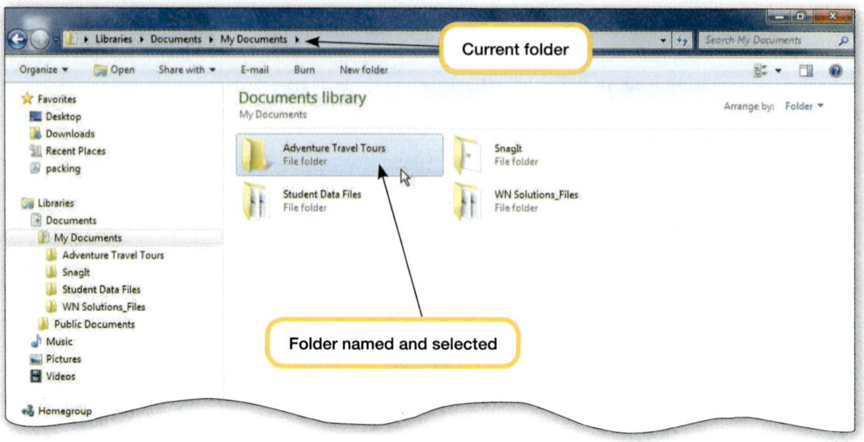

Figure 2.12

The folder name appears exactly as you typed it (including case). The cursor is no longer displayed, but the folder is still selected. It automatically moved to the correct alphabetical order by name.

Next, you want to create two folders under the Adventure Travel Tours folder, one to hold files for promotional materials such as flyers and another for correspondence such as letters and memos. Although the Adventure Travel Tours folder is selected in the file list, the location My Documents is still current, as you can see from the Address bar. When creating subfolders, you must first make the folder under which they are to appear the current folder.

3

- **Double-click the Adventure Travel Tours folder icon in the file list.**
- **Create a new folder named Promotional Materials.**
- **Create another new folder named Correspondence.**

Your screen should be similar to Figure 2.13

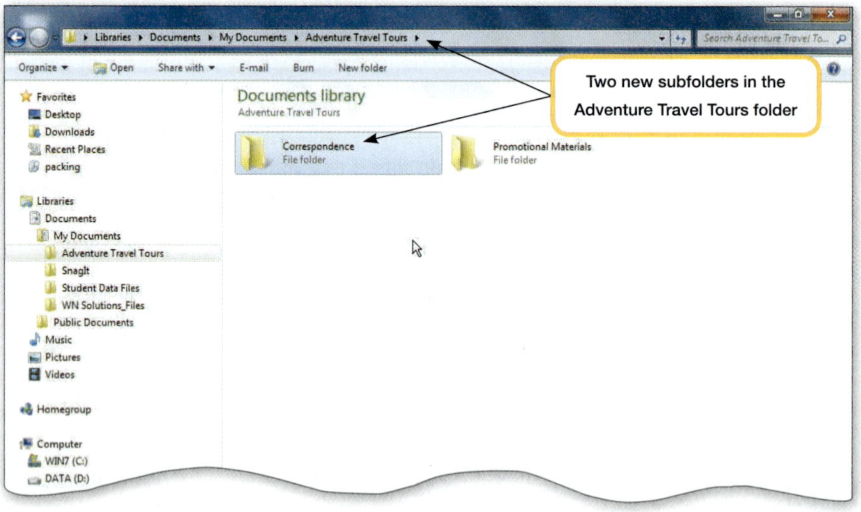

Figure 2.13

Another Method

You also can create a new folder using the file list shortcut menu. Just right-click anywhere in the white space of the file list and select NEW, then choose Folder from the menu.

Because you create many different types of promotional materials such as flyers, brochures, advertisements, and catalogs, you want to further subdivide your files in the Promotional Materials folder by the type of material. You also use pictures in these materials, which you want to include in a separate subfolder. You will create subfolders under the Promotional Materials folder for flyers, brochures, and pictures.

You will create the three new subfolders and then expand the My Documents folder in the Navigation pane to confirm the location where the folders were created.

4

- **Make the Promotional Materials folder current.**
- **Create a new folder named Flyers.**
- **Create a second new folder named Brochures and a third named Pictures.**
- **In the Navigation pane, expand the Documents library, the My Documents folder, the Adventure Travel Tours folder, and then the Promotional Materials folder.**

Your screen should be similar to Figure 2.14

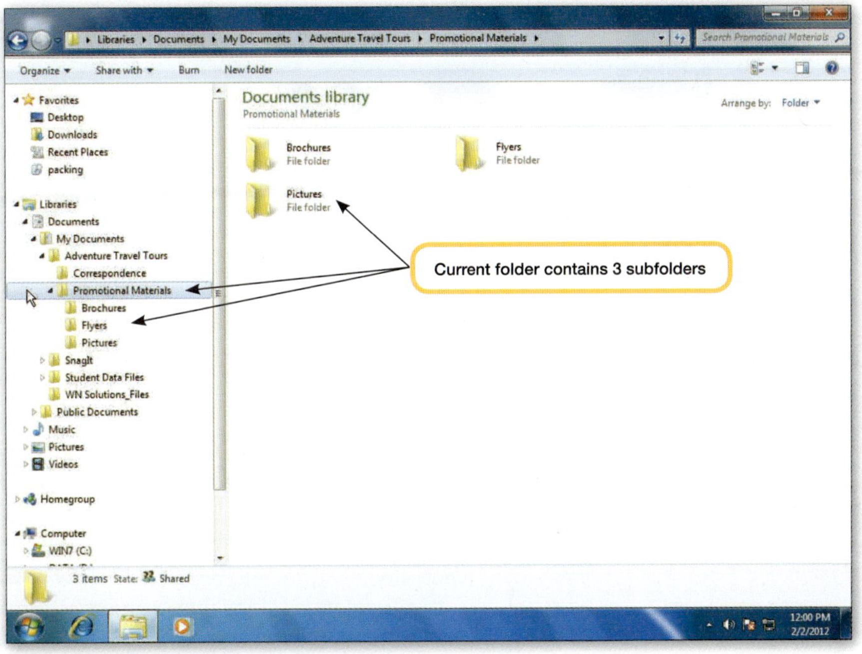

Figure 2.14

The Adventure Travel Tours folder was correctly created in the default My Documents folder. The Navigation pane shows the hierarchy of folders within the Adventure Travel Tours folder.

RENAMING FOLDERS

As you think about your folder organization, you decide to combine flyers and brochures into one folder. You will rename the folder first to reflect this change so that it is more descriptive of the information it contains.

1

- **Click on the Brochures folder icon slowly twice.**

Your screen should be similar to Figure 2.15

Another Method

You may also right-click on the selected folder and choose Rename from the file shortcut menu options.

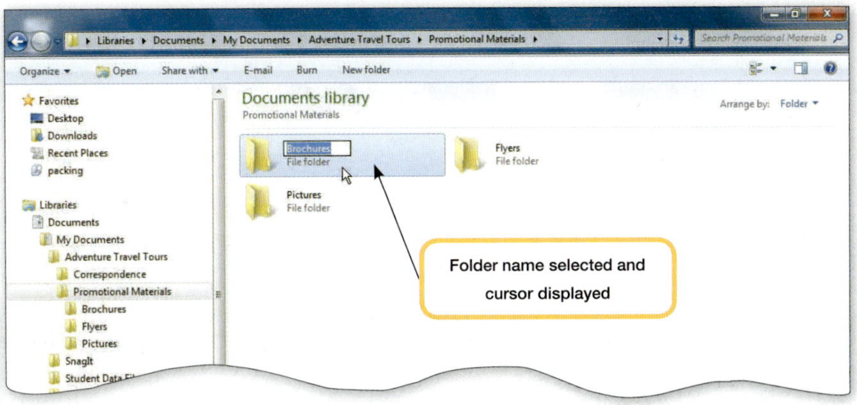

Figure 2.15

The folder name appears highlighted and with an insertion point, just as a new folder name appears. You will move the insertion point to the beginning of the file name and add the text "Flyers &" to the folder name.

2

- **Press** Home.
- **Type Flyers &.**
- **Press** Spacebar.
- **Press** ←Enter.

Your screen should be similar to Figure 2.16

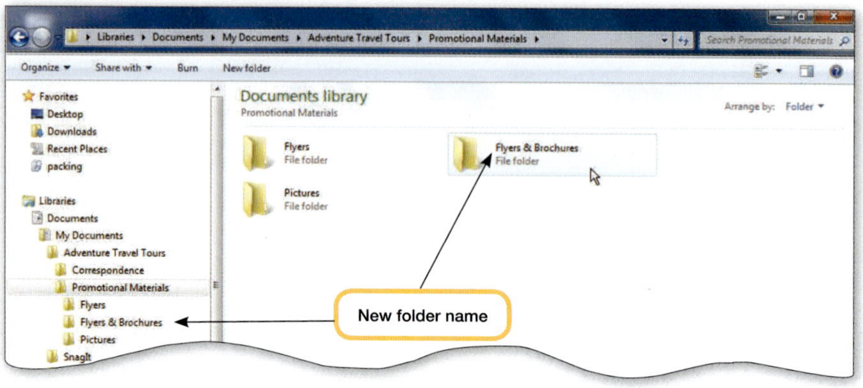

Figure 2.16

The folder name changes to its new name, Flyers & Brochures.

DELETING FOLDERS

Next, since you no longer need the folder you created for flyers, you will delete it. If you delete a folder that contains subfolders and files, all the files and subfolders contained within that folder also will be removed.

1

- **Select the Flyers folder icon.**
- **Press** Delete.

Another Method

The menu equivalent is Organize ▾ /Delete or Delete on the icon's shortcut menu.

Your screen should be similar to Figure 2.17

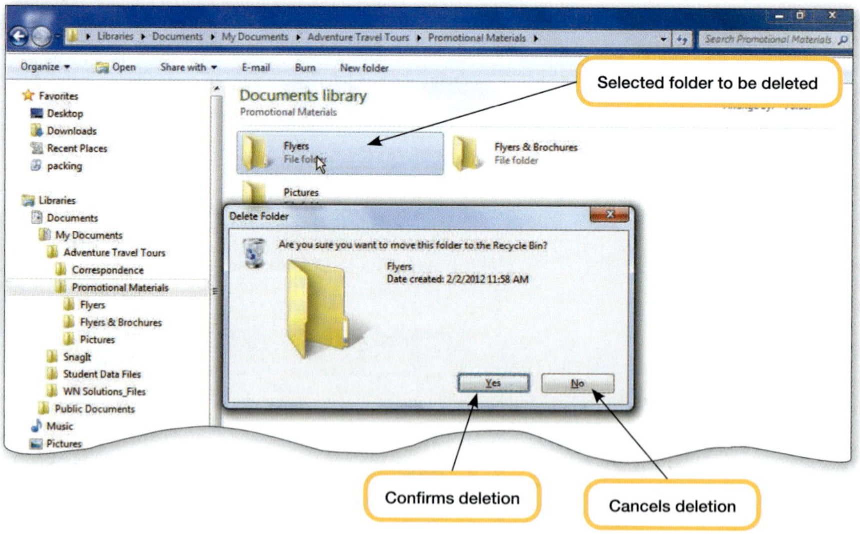

Figure 2.17

Additional Information

You will learn more about the Recycle Bin later in the lab.

The Delete Folder message box asks you to confirm that you want to delete the folder and its contents. This is especially important when deleting items from any external storage media because they are permanently deleted. Files and folders that are deleted from the hard disk are not permanently deleted but are placed in the Recycle Bin, where they are held until they are permanently deleted from that location. If you changed your mind, choosing No would cancel the procedure. You will confirm the deletion.

2

- Click Yes.

Your screen should be similar to Figure 2.18

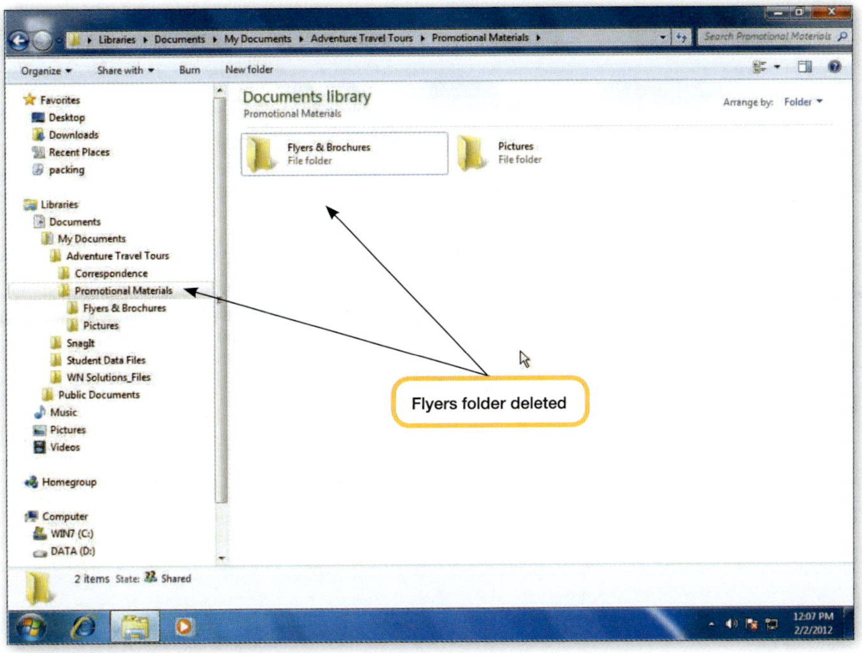

Figure 2.18

The Flyers folder is removed.

Working with Files

NOTE If you need to download the data files to complete the lab, see Appendix A for procedures on how to download and extract files from the McGraw-Hill Web site.

Now that you have created folders, they can be used to store files. The files you want to place in these folders may be located in a folder on your hard disk or on a network drive. First, you need to make current the folder containing the data files you will use in the lab.

NOTE In this section, you will be using data files that are located on your local hard drive in the Student Data Files\ATT Files subfolder. If your school uses a different folder name, or your computer is on a network and the data files are in a folder in another location, your instructor will provide additional instructions.

1

Locate the Student Data Files folder and make the ATT Files subfolder current.

Your screen should be similar to Figure 2.19

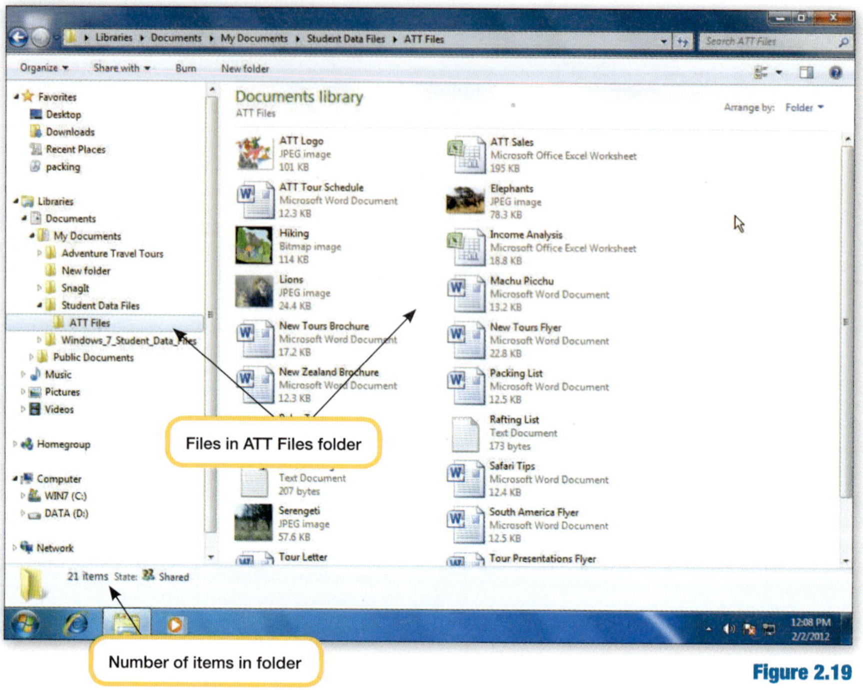

Figure 2.19

This folder contains 20 files that need to be placed in different folders. One of the major purposes of using folders is to help you manage files on your computer. This commonly involves copying and moving files to other locations, either on the same disk or drive location or to another.

Concept 3 Copy and Move

All Windows applications include features that allow you to **copy** and **move** selected items from one location to another. When an item is copied, the item remains in the original location and a duplicate is created in the new location. When an item is moved, it is deleted from the original location and a duplicate is created in the new location. You can copy and move entire folders, including all the files and subfolders contained in them, and entire files. Content contained in files also can be selected and copied or moved to another file. (You will learn about copying between files in Lab 3).

You can move and copy items using several different procedures. The basic procedure uses the Cut, Copy, and Paste commands located on the Organize ▾ menu in a folder window. These commands also are available in most Windows application programs. The item to be copied or moved must first be selected by highlighting it. The location that contains the information you want to cut or copy is called the **source.** Then, choose Copy to create a copy of the selection or Cut to move a selection. In both cases, a duplicate of the selection is copied to a temporary storage area in memory called the **Clipboard.** The Clipboard holds one block of copied information at a time. If you copy another item, it replaces the old contents in the Clipboard. Next, you select the location, called the **destination,** where you want the copy of the information that is stored in the Clipboard to appear. Finally, you use the Paste command to actually insert the item in the new location. Because an item that is stored in the Clipboard remains there until it is replaced by a new copied item, it can be pasted multiple times.

COPYING USING THE MENU

Now that you have organized the location where you want to store these files into folders, you will copy the files needed to complete this lab (and others your instructor may be using) to this location. First, you will copy all of the data files to the Adventure Travel Tours folder you just created.

To specify the files you want to copy, you first need to select them. You have already selected individual files and folders simply by clicking on the folder or file icon. Many times, however, you will want to select multiple files at the same time. How you select items depends on whether the items are in a consecutive group (adjacent to each other) or are nonconsecutive. The following table explains how to select multiple items.

To select	Procedure
Consecutive items	Click the first item in the group, hold down ⇧Shift, and click the last item.
	Drag the mouse pointer to create a selection around the outside of all items you want to include.
Nonconsecutive items	Hold down Ctrl while clicking on each item you want to select.
All items in a folder	Click Organize ▾ and choose Select All or use the keyboard shortcut Ctrl + A.

You also can use a combination of these methods. For example, after selecting a group, you can remove items from or add items to a group selection by holding down Ctrl while clicking on the files to add to or delete from the selection.

NOTE The text assumes My Documents\Adventure Travel Tours as the location where students will save their work.

You will select and copy all the files in the folder.

1

- **Click on the first file in the folder, then, while holding down ⇧Shift, click on the last file in the folder.**
- **Click Organize ▾ and choose Copy.**
- **In the navigation pane, click on the Adventure Travel Tours folder you created to specify the destination.**
- **Click Organize ▾ and choose Paste.**

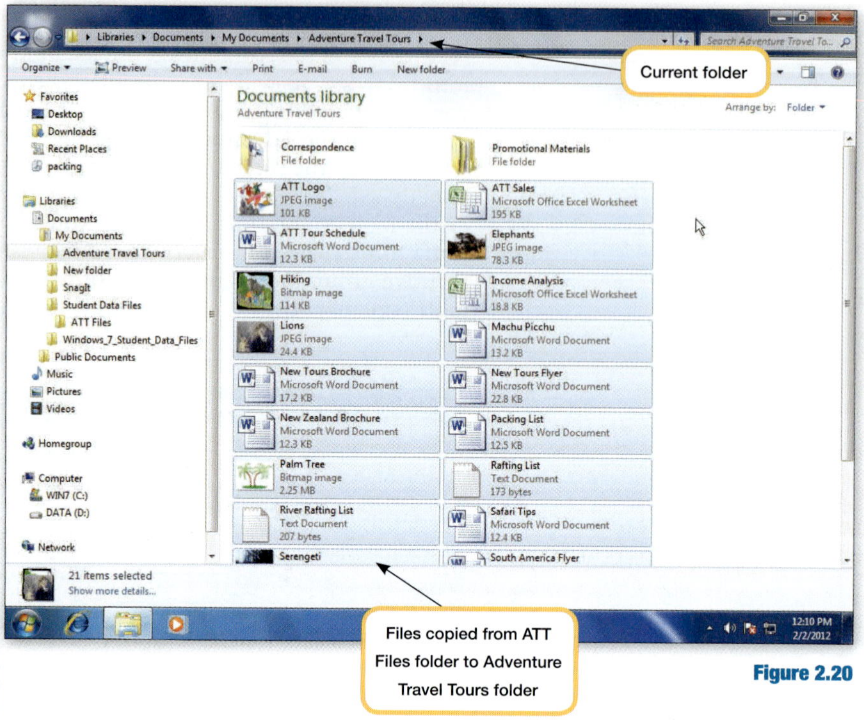

Figure 2.20

Another Method

You also could use the keyboard shortcuts to copy, Ctrl + C, and to paste, Ctrl + V.

Your screen should be similar to Figure 2.20

The files are copied to the Adventure Travel Tours folder and the file list displays icons of the copied files. The same files are still also in the ATT Files subfolder in the Student Data Files folder.

ADDING FILE PROPERTIES

Before you move the files to their specific folder locations, you may want to include additional file property documentation with several files. Many file properties such as the type of file and the dates it was created or modified are automatically added to a file by the application in which it was created. Others such as the author name and tags can be added by the user to add further identification to the file. These properties can be added within the application program or by entering the information in the Details pane of the folder window.

Additional Information

The properties that are available vary by file type. Properties cannot be added to some file types such as .RTF and .TXT files.

Because your view is still Tiles, the file list headings are not visible. You will change to Details view and display the Authors and Tags information in the file list so you can see this information for each file without having to select the file and look at its properties in the Details pane.

1

- **Click Views and select Details to change to Details view.**
- **Right-click anywhere on the file list column headings bar.**
- **Choose Authors from the shortcut menu.**
- **If necessary, display the Tags property column next.**
- **If necessary, adjust the size of the columns by dragging the column borders.**

Additional Information

The mouse pointer appears as ↔ when dragging to size a column.

Having Trouble?

The information in your Details pane may be displayed in a different order then shown here.

- **Select the Elephants file.**

Your screen should be similar to Figure 2.21

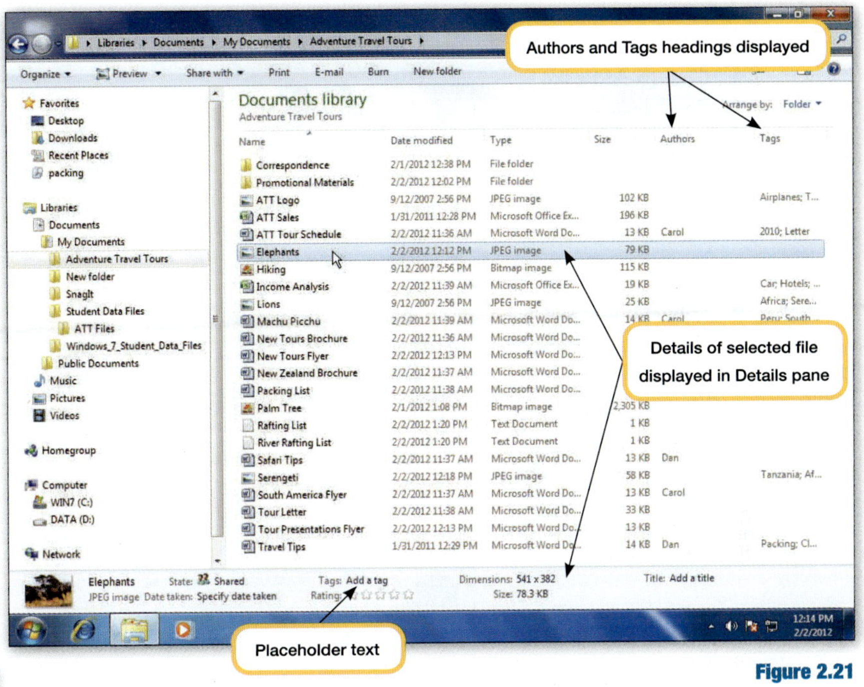

Figure 2.21

Now the Tags and Authors property information for all of the files is displayed. The Details pane displays the information for the selected file, Elephants.

You will add tags and author information to the Elephants file first. The Tags area in the Details pane displays "Add a tag" when the file does not include a tag. This text is a **placeholder** whose purpose is to provide directions. The placeholder is automatically removed as you enter the information.

2

- **Click on Add a tag in the Details pane.**

Additional Information

The Add a tag placeholder text will be replaced by the text you enter.

- **Type Africa and then click Save.**

Additional Information

As you type, a pop-up list of previously used tags that begin with the characters you type appears. You can click in the box next to an item in the list to complete the entry rather than type it in.

Your screen should be similar to Figure 2.22

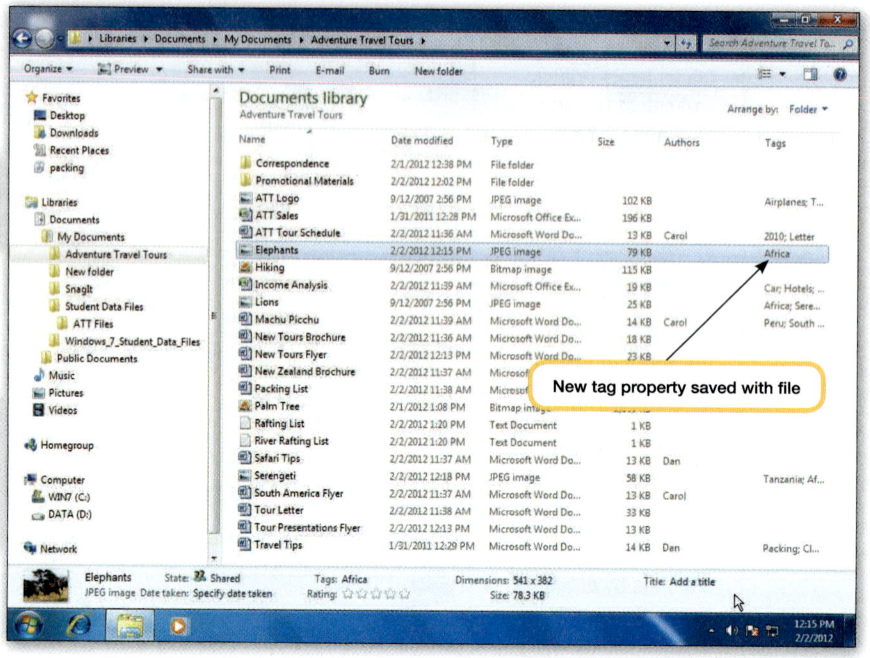

Figure 2.22

Additional Information

You will learn about searching for files shortly.

Additional Information

Some file types do not allow you to modify all properties, such as tags, author, or title.

The tag is saved with the file and displayed both in the Details area and in the Tags column of the file list. You decide to add two more tags to this file. Defining multiple tags makes the file easier to locate when you search for files using tags as the identifier. Multiple tags are separated by semicolons (;).

3

- **Click following the word Africa in the Tags box of the Details pane.**
- **Type Tanzania.**

Additional Information

If you choose a tag from the pop-up list, you do not need to press ⇥ to begin the next entry.

- **Press ⇥ to begin a third tag.**
- **Type Serengeti.**
- **Click Save.**

Another Method

You also can press ←Enter to save the changes.

Your screen should be similar to Figure 2.23

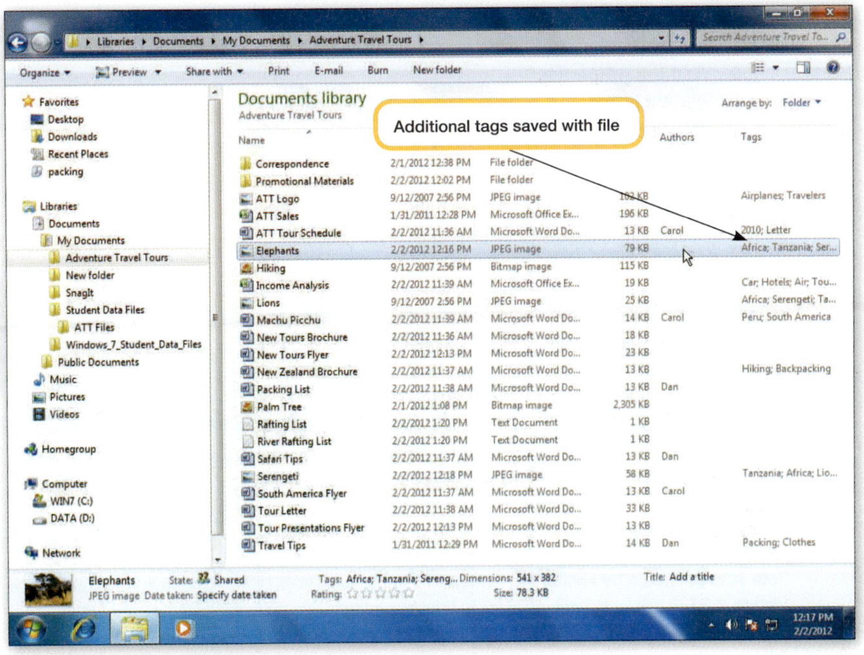

Figure 2.23

The new tags are saved with the file. The property information that is added to a file also can be easily modified or removed using the Details pane. To delete an existing property, select it and press Delete. To edit an existing property, select it and then click on it again to display the cursor. Edit the entry as you want it to appear. Remember to save the changes when you are done editing the properties.

4

- **Add the properties shown in the following table to the specified files:**

File	Tags	Author
Serengeti	Tanzania; Africa; Lions	
Tour Letter		Your Name
Tour Presentations Flyer		Your Name

- **In all files that display Student Name as Author, replace it with your name.**

Your screen should be similar to Figure 2.24

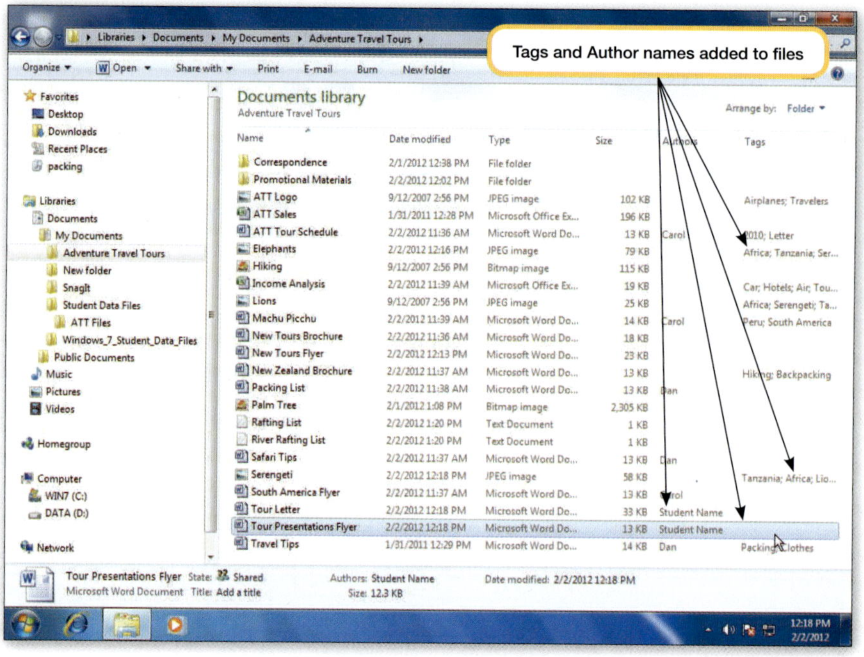

Figure 2.24

FILTERING, GROUPING, AND ARRANGING

To help organize files, you can filter, group, and arrange files.

Concept 4 Filter, Group, and Arrange

To help you find files that share something in common, you can filter, group, and arrange files. When you **filter** the contents of a folder, only those files that meet certain criteria are displayed. For example, you could filter the list to display only files of a specified type or author. When you **group** the contents of a folder, all the files are reorganized by a common file property into groups. For example, the files could be grouped by type or author. When you choose to **arrange** your files, Windows presents your files in a completely different way. The criteria for arranging will vary according to what type of files you may be working with. For example, you can arrange your pictures by month or your song files by artist. Or you may arrange your files by type. Windows will stack your files accordingly.

First, you will filter the file list to display only those files with a picture file type.

1

- **Point to the Type heading and click ▾ to open the menu.**
- **Click the box to the left of the Bitmap image and JPEG file types.**

Your screen should be similar to Figure 2.25

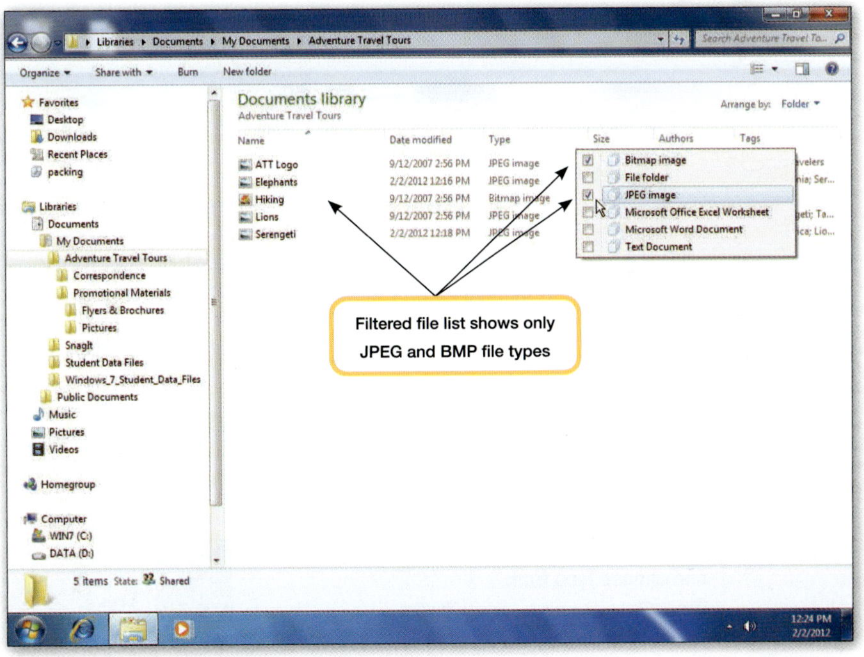

Figure 2.25

Now, only files with the selected file type appear in the file list. The other files are simply hidden; they have not been deleted.

Next, you will select all the file types, except File folder, and change the file list to display them in groups.

2

- **Select all the file types except File folder.**
- **Right-click on an empty space in the file list.**
- **Select Group by and choose Type from the shortcut menu.**

Your screen should be similar to Figure 2.26

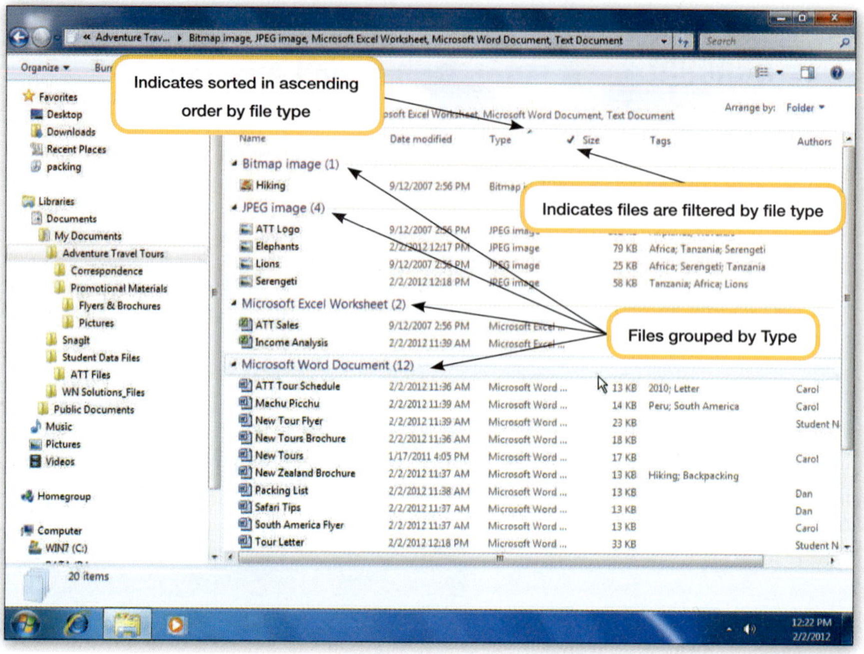

Figure 2.26

The files are still filtered (File folders are not displayed) and are arranged in ascending alphabetical order within groups according to the file type. Grouping the files creates visual breaks to more easily identify and locate files. You can group files without filtering first and all files and folders in the current location are grouped according to the selected heading.

Finally, you can arrange the files.

3

- **Click** Arrange by: Folder ▾ **in the library pane and choose Type from the menu.**

Another Method

You can also access the Arrange By options from the file list shortcut menu.

Your screen should be similar to Figure 2.27

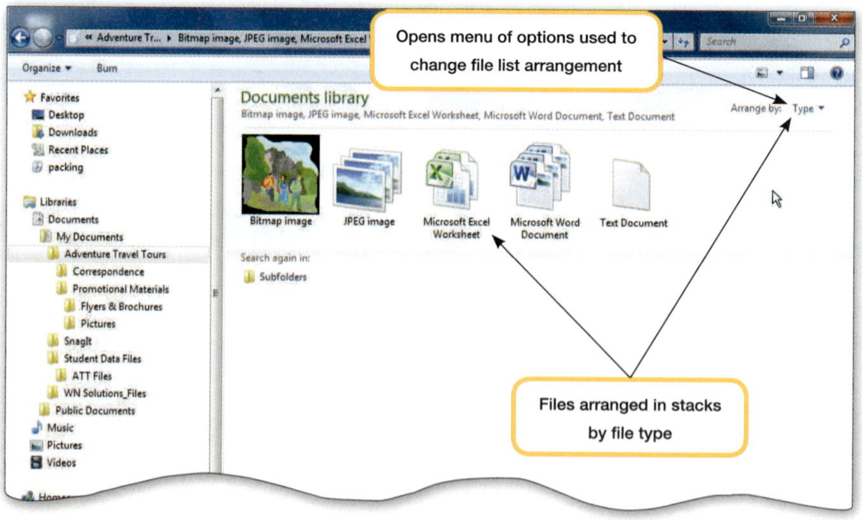

Figure 2.27

Having Trouble?

The Arrange by commands are only available when working in a library. If your current location is not a library, choose None from the Group by submenu, display folders again, and skip to the next section.

Now, all the files that appeared in the groups are hidden in a stack behind icons that are named according to the file type. To see the files, you need to open the stack of files by double-clicking on it.

4

- **Double-click the JPEG Image icon.**

Your screen should be similar to Figure 2.28

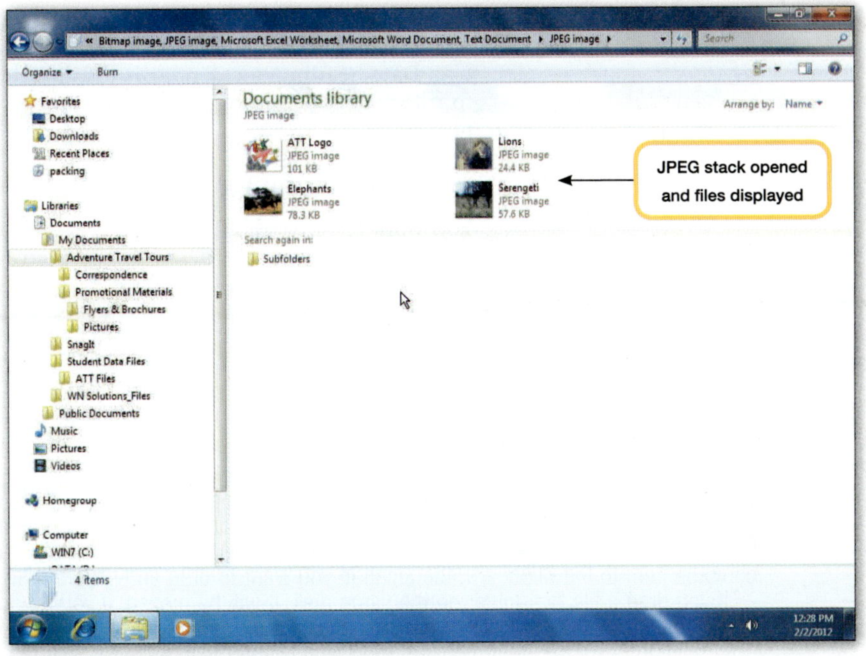

Figure 2.28

The files in the stack are displayed. Now that you know how to use these features, you will use them to organize the files that you want to move into the separate folders.

You will now clear the changes to the folder arrangement, which will remove the grouping and Type filter. The Type column will remain in sorted order.

5

- **Click Back to return to the stacks.**
- **Display the file list shortcut menu and choose Clear changes from the Arrange by submenu.**
- **If necessary, change to Details view.**

Your screen should be similar to Figure 2.29

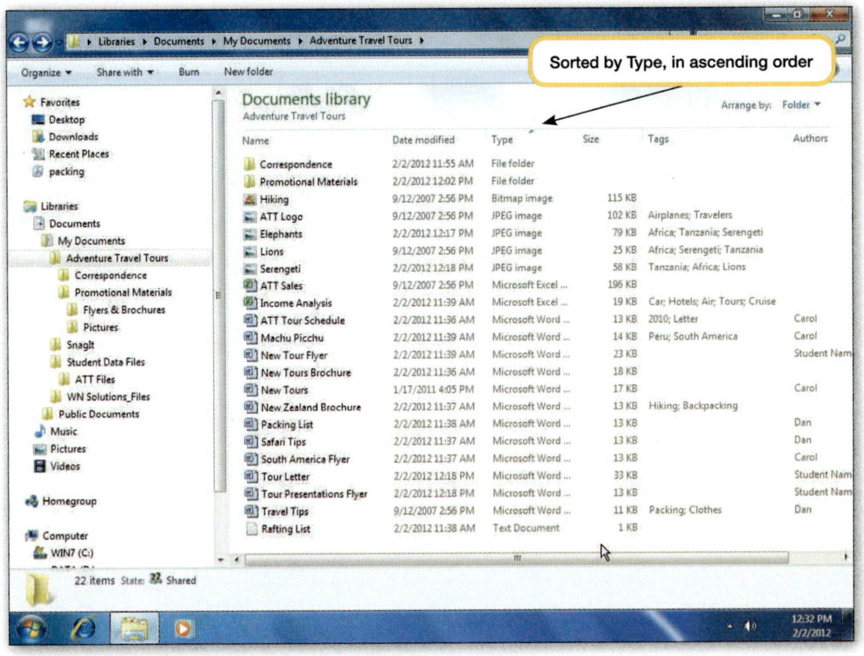

Figure 2.29

Grouping, arranging, and filtering are available in all headings in Details view. The filtering features vary with the heading type. For example, when filtering by a Date heading, a calendar is displayed from which you can select the date to filter on. The Arrange by commands are available only when working in a library.

USING DRAG AND DROP

You want to move the files into the appropriate folders you created. First, you will move the picture files into the Pictures folder. Another way to copy or move a file is to use the drag-and-drop feature.

Concept 5 Drag and Drop

Common to all Windows applications is the ability to copy or move selections using the **drag-and-drop** feature. After selecting the item to be copied or moved, pointing to it and dragging the mouse moves or copies the selection to the new location specified when you release the mouse button. Because drag and drop does not copy the item to the Clipboard, the location you want to drag and drop to must be visible in the window.

If you drag a file to a folder on the same disk, it will be moved. If you drag a file to a folder on another disk, it will be copied. You can hold down ⇧Shift while dragging to always move a file or Ctrl to copy a file. If you drag holding down the right mouse button, a shortcut menu appears with options to either copy or move the selection.

You will move the five picture files into the Pictures subfolder in the Promotional Materials folder using drag and drop.

1

- **If necessary, expand the Promotional Materials folder in the navigation pane.**
- **Filter the file list to display only the picture file types.**
- **Select all five files.**
- **With the mouse pointer on the selected file icons, drag the selection to the Pictures subfolder in the navigation pane and release the mouse button when the mouse pointer displays Move to Pictures.**

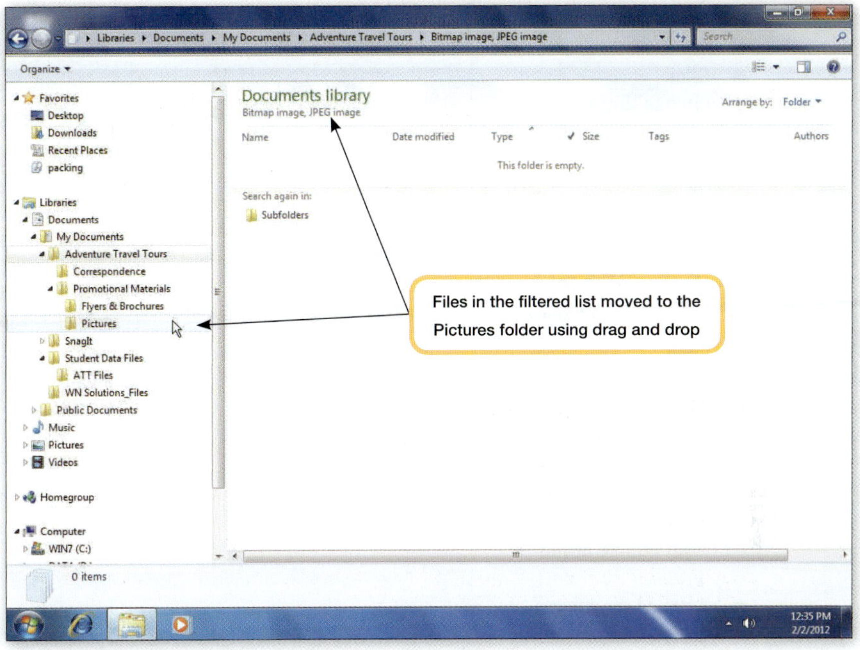

Figure 2.30

Additional Information

The mouse pointer appears as [pointer icon] when pointing to an area where the file cannot be copied or moved.

Another Method

You also can move a file using the Cut and Paste commands on the Organize ▾ or shortcut menus.

Your screen should be similar to Figure 2.30

The move is complete and the file icons for the five picture files are no longer displayed in the current folder. Another way to copy or move files is to drag the selection using the right mouse button. Using the right-drag method gives you the option of choosing to move or copy the selection from a shortcut menu that is displayed when you release the mouse button. Although it requires an additional step, it prevents accidentally moving files. If you do accidentally move files rather than copy them, you can always undo your last action. Undo reverses the last performed action.

You will undo the move you just did and then repeat the move using the right-drag method. When you undo the last action, the move will be reversed and the five files will be removed from the Pictures folder and placed back in the Adventure Travel Tours folder.

2

- **Click Organize and choose Undo.**

Additional Information

The keyboard shortcut is Ctrl + Z.

- **If necessary, click [refresh] to refresh your view.**
- **Select the five picture files again and drag the selection to the Pictures folder while holding down the right mouse button.**
- **Release the mouse button and choose Move Here from the shortcut menu.**
- **Make the Pictures folder current.**

Your screen should be similar to Figure 2.31

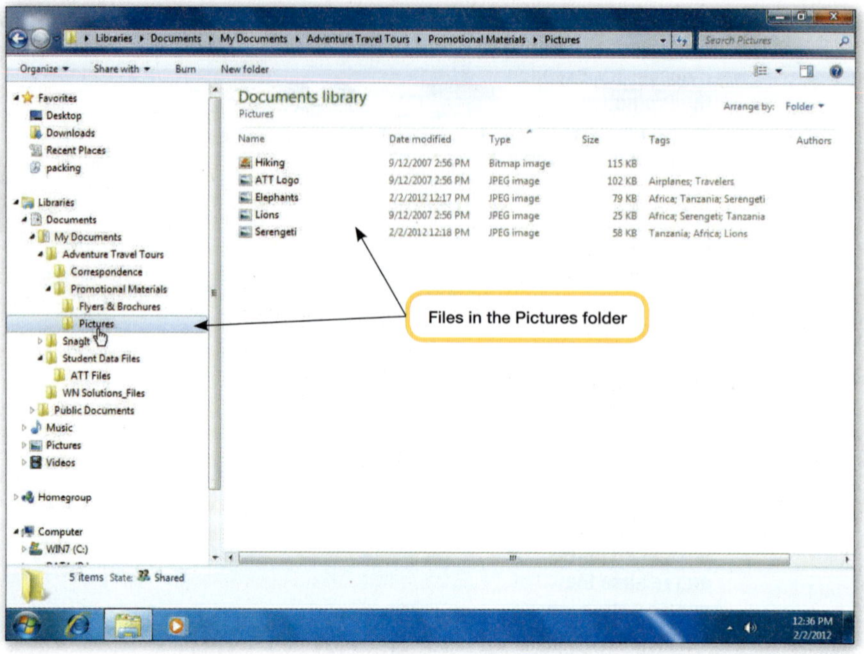

Figure 2.31

The five picture files you moved are now in the Pictures folder.

SELECTING NONADJACENT FILES

Now you want to move the remaining files into the appropriate folders. You will begin with moving files into the Flyers & Brochures folder. Several of the files are easy to identify because the file name includes the word brochure or flyer.

Unfortunately, these files are not next to each other in the file list. Rather than moving the files individually, you can select several files to move at the same time by holding down Ctrl and clicking on each file name.

1

- **Make the Adventure Travel Tours folder current.**

Additional Information

The filter is automatically cleared and all the files are displayed when you return to a folder after making another folder current.

- **Select the New Tours Flyer file.**
- **Hold down Ctrl while clicking on the following files: New Tours Brochure, New Zealand Brochure, South America Flyer, and Tour Presentations Flyer.**
- **Release Ctrl when all five files are selected.**
- **Point to any selected file and drag to move the selected files to the Flyers & Brochures subfolder under the Promotional Materials folder.**
- **To verify that the files were moved, make the Flyers & Brochures folder current.**

Your screen should be similar to Figure 2.32

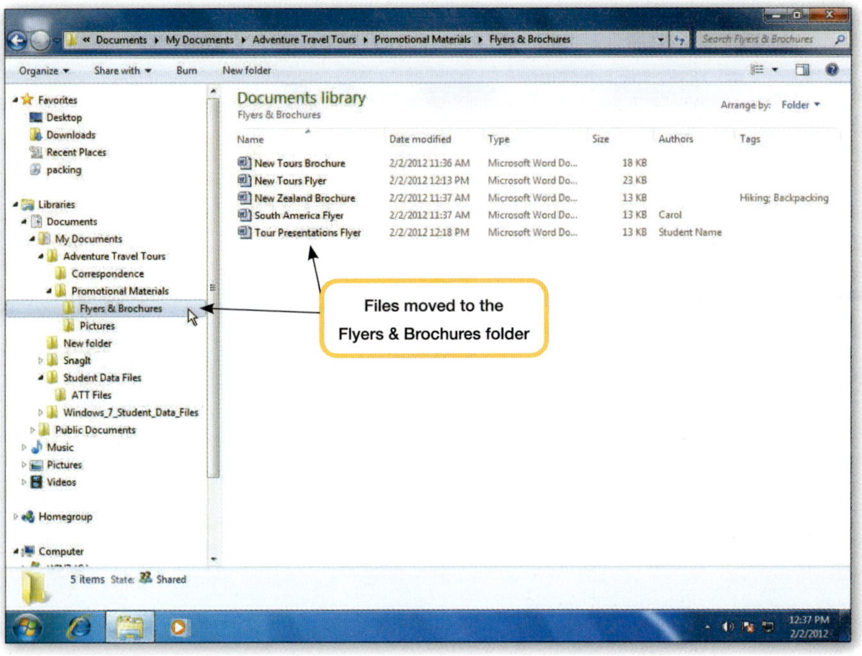

Figure 2.32

The five nonadjacent file icons for the files you selected and moved are displayed in the file list of the Flyers & Brochures folder window.

Next, you want to move files into the Correspondence folder.

2

- **Make the Adventure Travel Tours folder current.**

Additional Information

Remember, you can click to quickly return to a previous location.

- **Select the following three files: ATT Tour Schedule, Tour Letter, and New Tours.**
- **Move the selected files to the Correspondence folder.**
- **Make the Correspondence folder current.**

Your screen should be similar to Figure 2.33

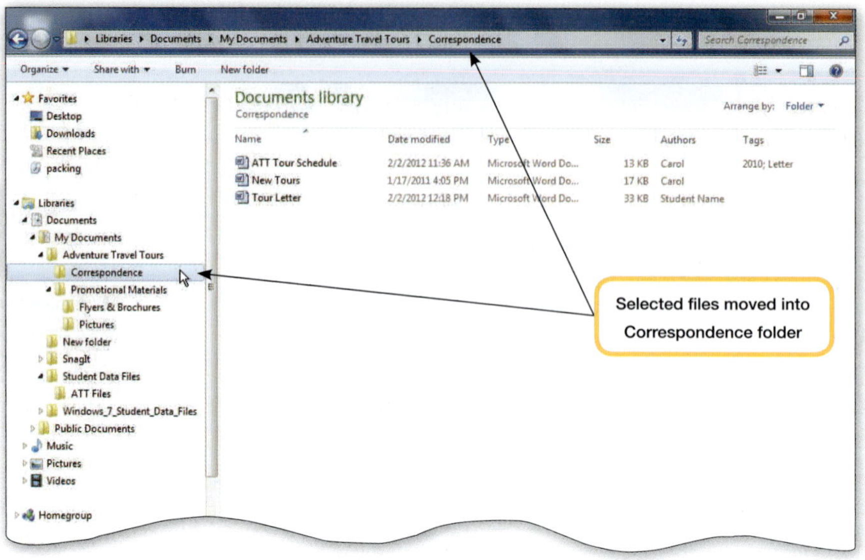

Figure 2.33

The files you selected have been moved into the Correspondence folder. You will now look at the files remaining in the Adventure Travel Tours folder and sort them by Name.

3

- **Make the Adventure Travel Tours folder current.**
- **Change the file list display order to ascending by Name.**

Your screen should be similar to Figure 2.34

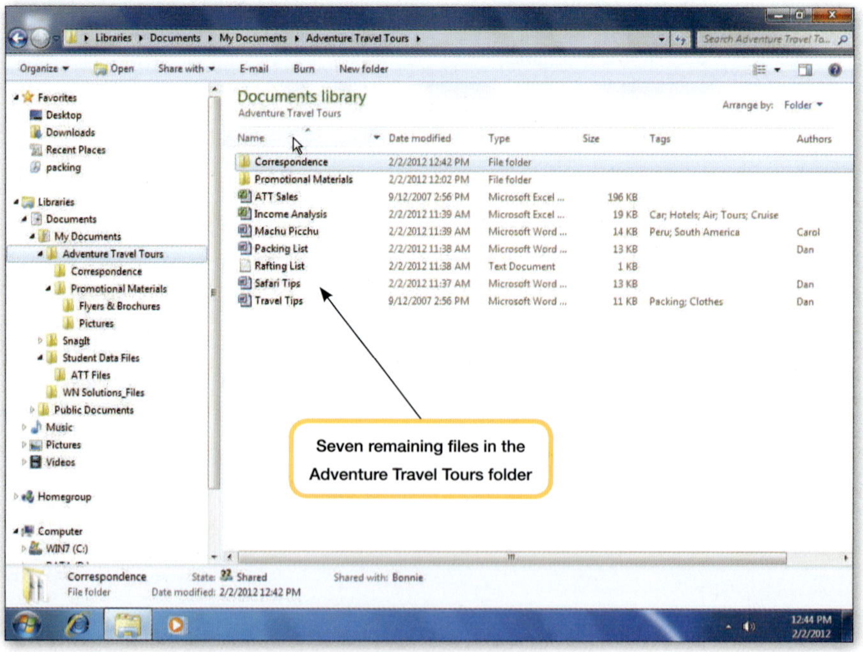

Figure 2.34

You decide to leave the remaining files in the current folder for now.

RENAMING AND DELETING FILES

Like folders, you want the names of files to be descriptive of their contents. The Adventure Travel Tours Tour Schedule file actually contains the proposed schedule for the year 2012, so you decide to rename this file 2012 Tour Schedule.

1

- **Make the Correspondence folder current.**
- **Click on the ATT Tour Schedule file name slowly twice.**

Having Trouble?

If you click on the file name too quickly, you will open the program in which it was created. If this happens, click [X] in the window title bar to close the program and try again.

Additional Information

You also can use Organize /Rename or Rename on the shortcut menu.

- **Press Home.**
- **Press Delete three times.**
- **Type 2012.**
- **Press ←Enter.**

Your screen should be similar to Figure 2.35

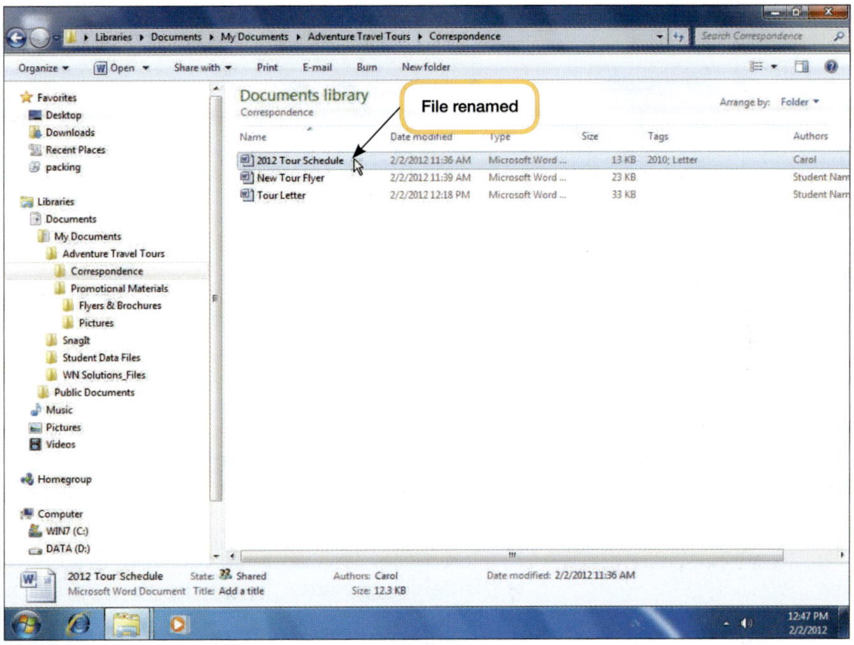

Figure 2.35

The file name has been changed to its new name, 2012 Tour Schedule.

Likewise, just as with folders, you can easily delete files you no longer need. You will delete the Machu Picchu file since the information it contains has been incorporated into another document.

2

- **Make the Adventure Travel Tours folder current.**
- **Select the Machu Picchu file icon.**
- **Press Delete.**
- **Click Yes to confirm the deletion.**

Additional Information

The menu equivalent is Organize ▾ /Delete.

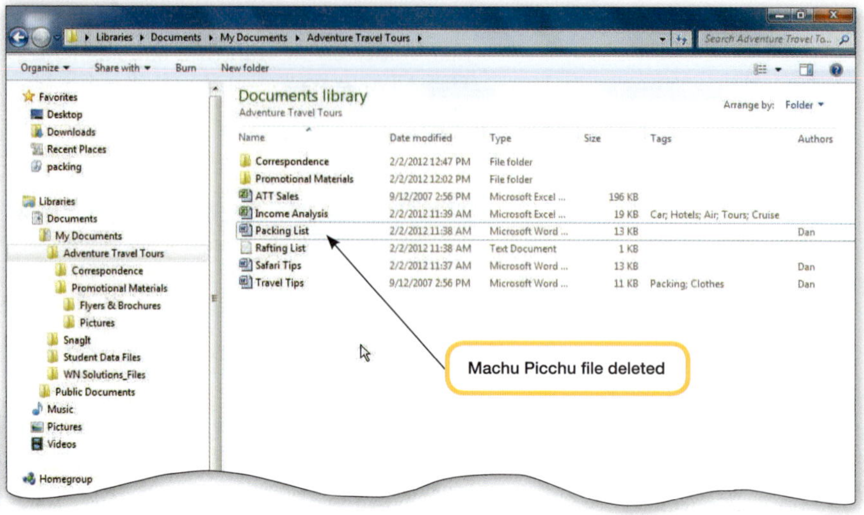

Figure 2.36

Your screen should be similar to Figure 2.36

The file is removed from the folder and is no longer displayed in the file list.

USING THE RECYCLE BIN

When a folder or file is deleted from the hard disk, it is moved to the Recycle Bin, a special folder used to store deleted items until they are permanently removed. This protects you from accidentally deleting files or folders that you might want later. When the Recycle Bin contains files, the icon appears full ; otherwise it appears empty . You will open the Recycle Bin to see the items you deleted.

1

- **Choose (click) Desktop under Favorites in the Navigation pane.**
- **Double-click Recycle Bin in the file list.**

Another Method

You also can double-click  on the desktop to open the recycle bin.

Having Trouble?

Your Recycle Bin may display many additional items that have been deleted on your computer.

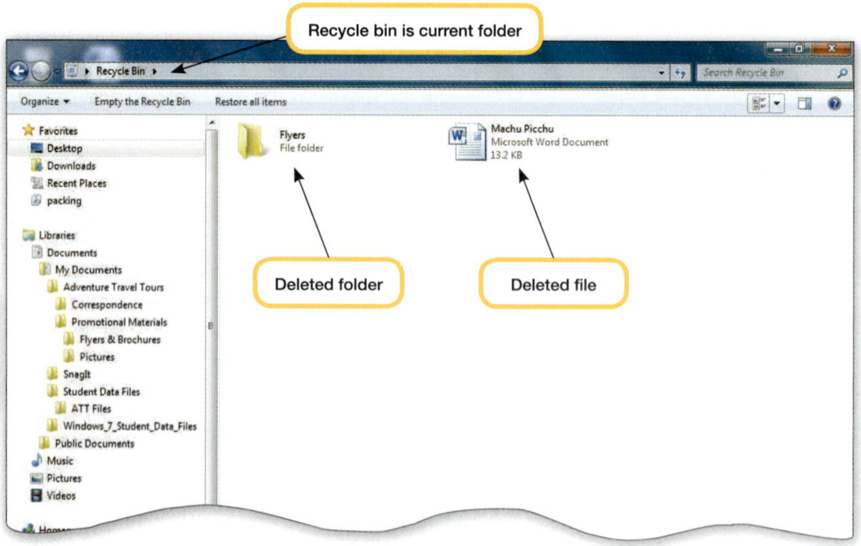

Figure 2.37

Your screen should be similar to Figure 2.37

The Recycle Bin folder is current and displays icons for all deleted files and folders in alphabetical order in the file list. The folder you deleted earlier and the file you just deleted are listed in the file list. You recover files you may need from the Recycle Bin and restore them by using the [Restore this item] or [Restore all items] buttons in the toolbar. When restored, the file is automatically returned to its original location. You can permanently remove all or selected files from the Recycle Bin. To remove all files, click the [Empty the Recycle Bin] button in the toolbar.

You will permanently remove the Machu Picchu file.

2

- **Select the Machu Picchu file icon.**

Having Trouble?

You may need to scroll the file list to see this file.

- **Press [Delete].**
- **Click [Yes] to confirm the deletion.**

Your screen should be similar to Figure 2.38

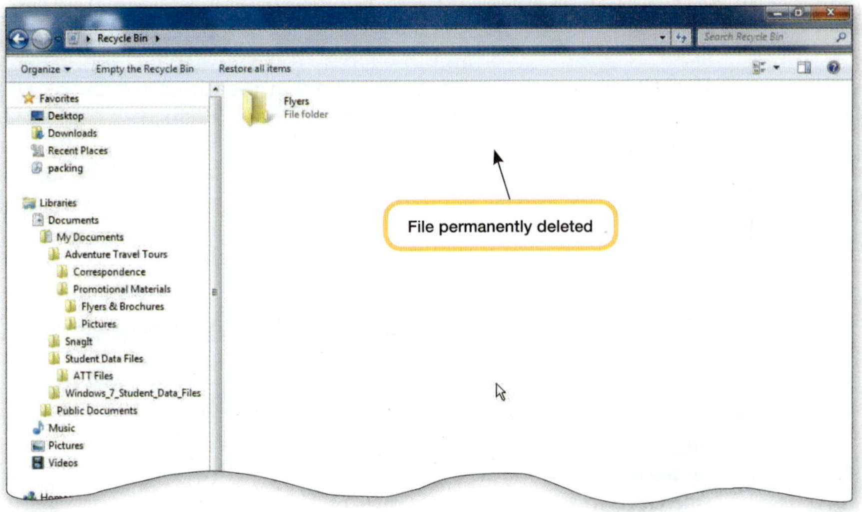

Figure 2.38

The number of items the Recycle Bin can hold is determined by the storage size (in megabytes) of the bin. You can adjust the size and other settings of the Recycle Bin by right-clicking its icon on the desktop and choosing Properties. It is a good idea to occasionally empty the Recycle bin to reclaim all of the hard disk space being used by unwanted files.

FINDING FILES

As you add more and more files to your hard disk, you may have trouble remembering what folder you stored a file in or what you named it. Windows 7 includes a search feature that helps you locate files or folders anywhere on your computer.

Concept 6 Search

The **search** feature provides a quick method to find files, folders, programs and e-mail messages stored on your computer. Search looks for matching text in file names, properties, and file content to the text you type in the search box and displays only those items that match your search text. Searching is very fast because it uses an **index** to keep track of the files on the computer. The index stores information about files, including the name and properties. Rather than searching through the entire hard disk for a file name or property, it searches the index. By default, the most common files on your computer and the files in libraries are indexed automatically. Program and system files are not indexed because you rarely need to search for those files. When it searches nonindexed locations, it searches file names only.

Windows 7 includes two basic methods that you can use to search. The first is to use the search box at the top of each folder or library to perform a fast search of the current folder and all its subfolders. In a library, the search includes all folders and subfolders in the library. The search box will reflect the name of the current location. The second method is to use the search box in the Start menu. This method finds items stored anywhere on your computer and allows you to perform more comprehensive searches.

When you know where to start looking for a file, it is easiest to make the location current and use the folder search box. You will use this method to find a file that Carol, a travel agent, created to help clients prepare for a trip. She gave you this file in case you wanted to make it available to other agents and to clients. You know that it will be somewhere on the C drive but do not recall exactly what location. You do recall, however, that the file content had to do with packing for a trip.

Before you begin a search, it's important to remember to select the location that you'd like to search. When searching, you can enter words that you think may be in the file name, file content, or properties such as tags or author names. The more precise the information you provide, the closer the matches that are found. You decide to search using the word "packing."

1

- **Make the My Documents folder (or the location where you created your folders) current.**
- **Click in the search box.**

Additional Information

The keyboard shortcut is Ctrl + E.

- **Type pa in the search box.**

Additional Information

You can enter the search terms in any case letters, as the search feature is not case sensitive by default.

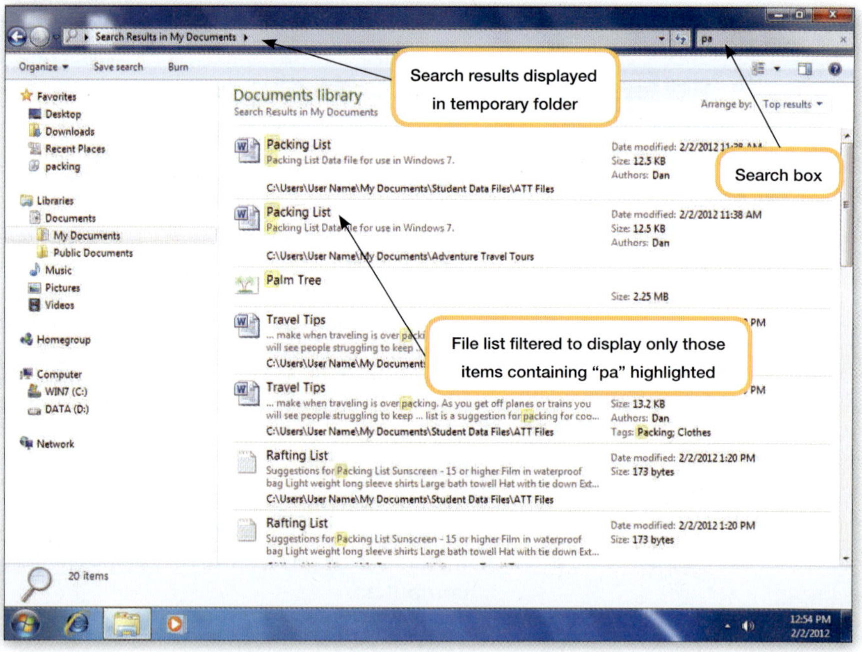

Figure 2.39

Your screen should be similar to Figure 2.39

Having Trouble?

Your search results may include additional files if your My Documents folder includes other files meeting the search criteria.

If your view does not match what's displayed, click Arrange by: Top results and choose Clear changes.

As you type in the search box, the file list instantly filters the current view to display only those items that contain the letter you type. Many files were located containing the letter "p." When you typed the next letter, "a," the search was narrowed to locate only those files containing "pa." The results of the search are displayed in a temporary Search Results folder. The default view for this type of folder is Content view, which displays the file name and some of the content from the file. The matching letters used in the search box are highlighted in yellow.

You will continue typing to narrow the search even more.

2

- **Continue by typing cki in the search box.**

Your screen should be similar to Figure 2.40

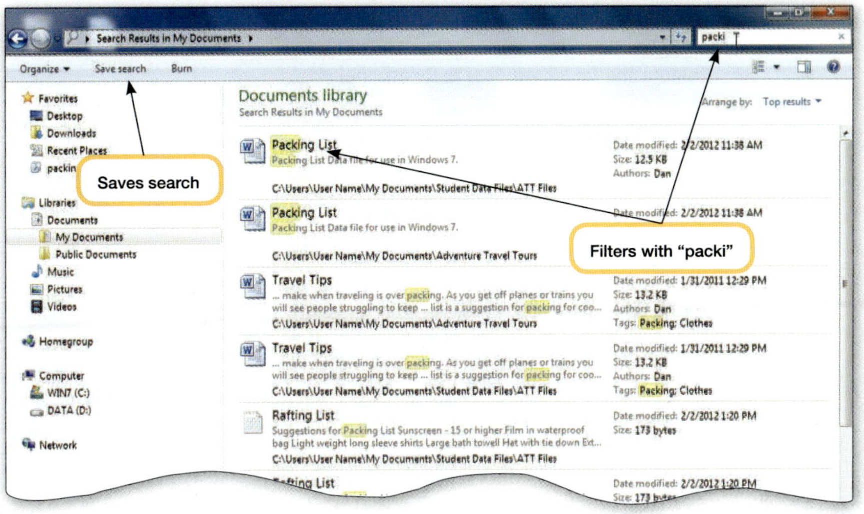

Figure 2.40

Additional Information

Click ✕ in the Search box to close a search.

Now you see the file you are looking for, Packing List. The other files that appear in the filtered results include files that have the search term in a tag or file content. If you plan to perform the same search frequently, it is helpful to save your search results so that you do not need to set up the search again. You will use this feature next.

3

- **Click Save search in the toolbar.**
- **Click at the end of the name in the File name text box and complete the proposed file name by typing ng.**
- **Click Save in the Save As dialog box.**

Having Trouble?

If this saved search already exists, click Yes to replace it.

Your screen should be similar to Figure 2.41

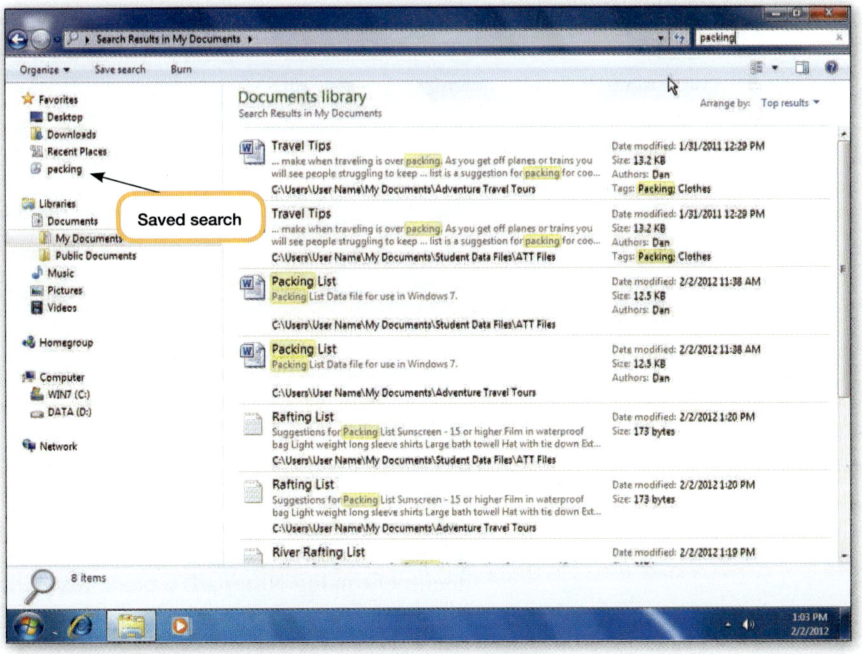

Figure 2.41

The search you just saved is listed under Favorites in the Navigation pane. Now, when you select this saved search, a rapid search will be performed and only the most current files that match the original search will be displayed in a temporary folder window.

4

- **Restore the folder window to its original size.**
- **Close the folder window.**

The program is closed and the icon is removed from the taskbar.

Running Applications

The primary activity for which a computer is used is to run application programs to accomplish various tasks such as creating a letter or a picture. In addition to the programs that run as part of Windows 7 such as Computer, Windows 7 includes many other application software programs that are designed to help you with your work, or amuse you while passing time. Several of these applications are described in the following table.

Application	Used To
Microsoft Internet Explorer	Explore the World Wide Web.
Windows Live Movie Maker	Transfer analog or digital audio and video to the computer for editing and playing.
Windows Live Photo Gallery	Download photos from a digital camera and then organize, edit, view, and share them.
Windows Media Player	Create and listen to CDs, watch DVDs, listen to radio.
Games	Play electronic versions of some familiar games.
WordPad	Create text documents with complex formatting.
Notepad	Create simple text documents.
Paint	Create simple line drawings and display and edit scanned photos.
Calculator	Perform basic arithmetic tasks.
Task Scheduler	Run scheduled computer tasks automatically.

You will use Notepad to create a simple text document.

STARTING NOTEPAD

Recently you went on the Adventure Travel Tours Colorado river rafting trip and you used Notepad to jot down several items to include in the suggested packing list for this trip. Since creating this document, you have thought of another item to include in the list. You will view, modify, and print this document using Notepad, a basic text-editing program that is included with Windows 7.

1

- **Click Start and choose All Programs/ Accessories/Notepad.**
- **If necessary, size the Notepad window to the approximate size as in Figure 2.42.**

Your screen should be similar to Figure 2.42

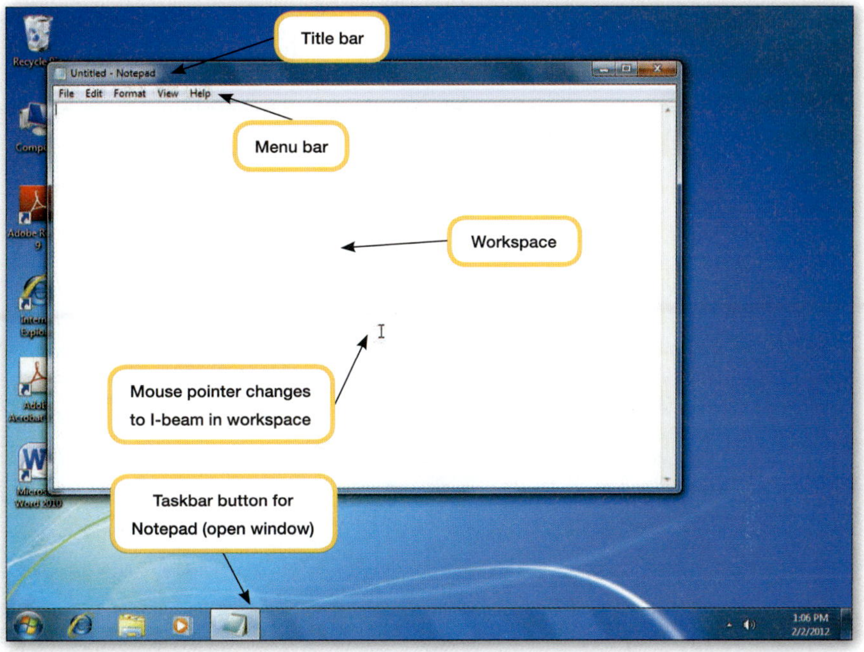

Figure 2.42

The Notepad application program is opened in its own window. The Notepad window includes a title bar and menu bar of five menu items. Clicking on a menu item opens a drop-down menu of commands from which you can choose. The large blank area below the menu is the **workspace** where your work is displayed.

OPENING A FILE

When Notepad first opens, a blank workspace is ready for you to begin typing to create a new document. Alternatively, as you will do in this case, you can open and then modify an existing document.

1

- **Click File in the menu bar and click Open to choose it.**

Additional Information

The keyboard shortcut is Ctrl + O.

Your screen should be similar to Figure 2.43

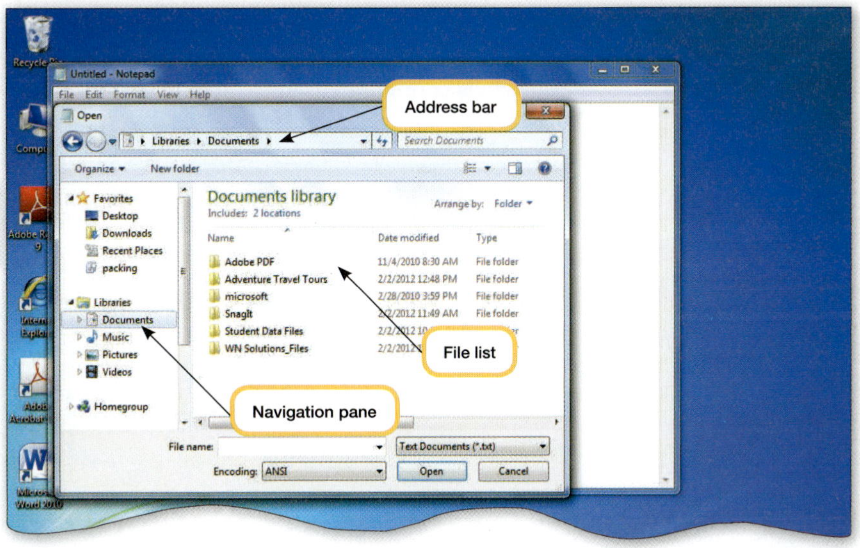

Figure 2.43

The Open dialog box is used to specify the location and name of the file you want to open. This dialog box is common to all applications running under Windows 7 and is similar to a folder window in that it includes an address bar, Navigation pane, and file list. Notice the Documents library is the current location.

Just like in a folder window, you can locate a file by selecting from the Navigation pane or by using the Address bar. You will now use the Navigation pane to locate the document you need to open.

2

- **Expand the Documents library and My Documents folder (or the location containing your work) and make the Adventure Travel Tours folder current.**

Your screen should be similar to Figure 2.44

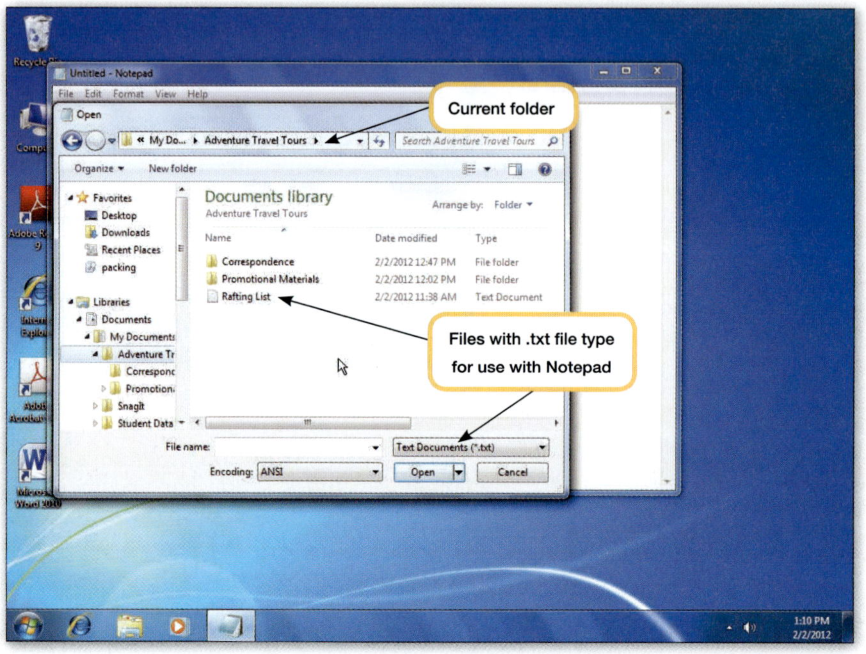

Figure 2.44

Now the file list box displays the names of all folders and text files in your Adventure Travel Tours folder. Only text files with a file extension of .txt are displayed because the Files of Type list box shows that the currently selected type is Text Documents. This type of file can include text characters only and is commonly used to quickly jot down notes.

3

- **Select the Rafting List file.**
- **Click Open.**

Another Method

You also could double-click on the file name to open it.

Your screen should be similar to Figure 2.45

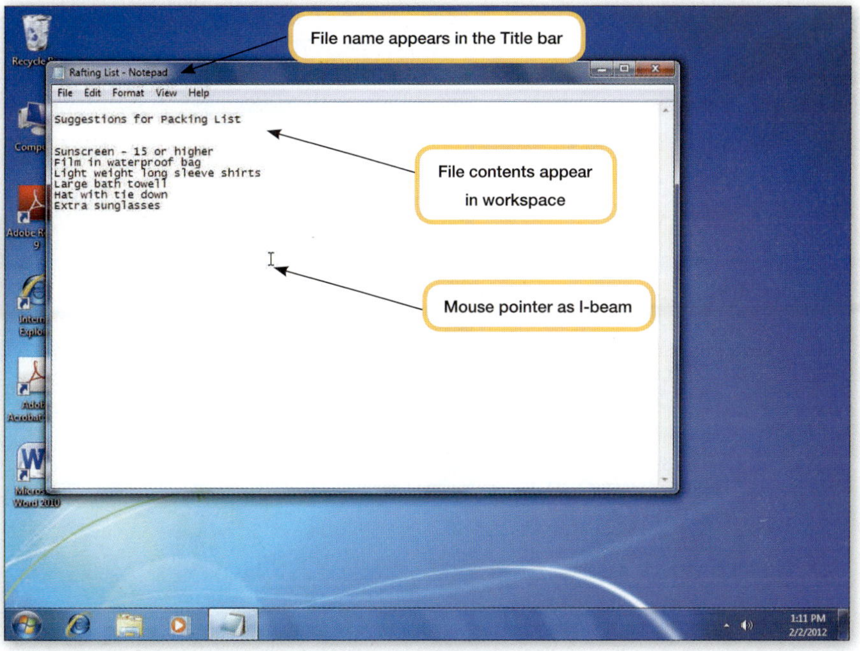

Figure 2.45

The file is loaded and displayed in the workspace and the file name is displayed in the title bar. The cursor in the upper-left corner of the document shows where the next character will appear when you begin to type. When the mouse pointer is positioned in the workspace, it appears as an I-beam, just as it does in a text box of a dialog box, and is used to position the cursor in the document.

EDITING A DOCUMENT

You want to add an item to the list and include your name and the current date at the top of the document. To make these changes, you will edit the document.

Concept 7 Editing

One of the advantages of using a computer is that you can easily change or **edit** your documents. While typing, you may make typing errors, or you might want to change what you have typed. The changes you make can be as simple as correcting spelling or adding or removing some text or as complicated as rearranging the content and redesigning the layout of the document.

To add the item to the top of the list, you must first move the cursor to that location. You can use the directional keys or the mouse to move the cursor within the text. To move the cursor with the mouse, position the I-beam at the location in the text where you want the cursor to be and click the left mouse button. The directional arrow keys also can be used to move the cursor one space in the direction indicated by the arrow.

As you are typing, do not be concerned if you make mistakes, as they can be easily removed and corrected. The two most common means to remove text are to use the Backspace key to delete unwanted characters to the left of the cursor or the Delete key to remove the character to the right. Then you can retype the text correctly.

1

- Press ↓ three times.
- Type **Binoculars**.
- Click on the top (blank) line of the document.
- Type **your name**.
- Press ←Enter.
- Type the current date.
- Press ←Enter twice.

Your screen should be similar to Figure 2.46

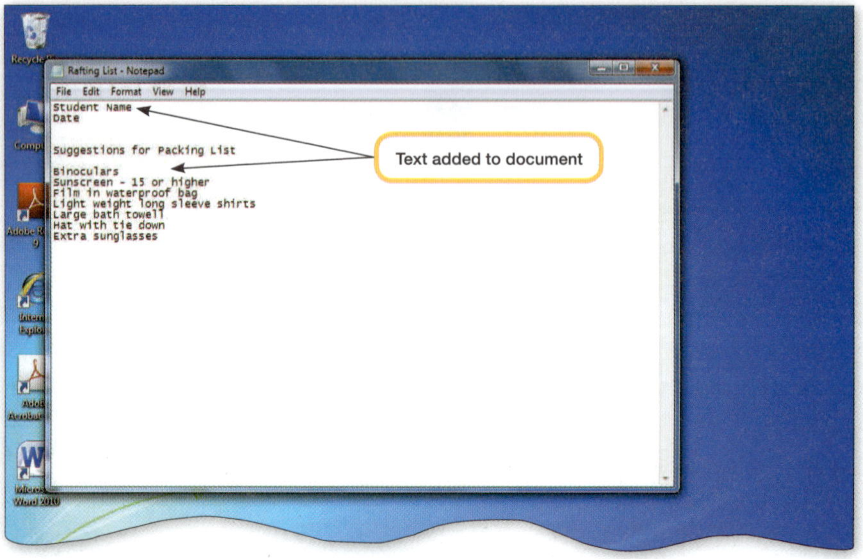

Figure 2.46

Pressing ←Enter ends a line and moves the cursor to the beginning of the next line. When the cursor is at the beginning of a line and ←Enter is pressed, a blank line is created.

PRINTING A DOCUMENT

Next, you want to print a copy of the document.

1

- If necessary, turn on the printer and make any necessary adjustment to prepare the printer to print.
- Click File and choose Print.

Additional Information

The keyboard shortcut to print is Ctrl + P.

Your screen should be similar to Figure 2.47

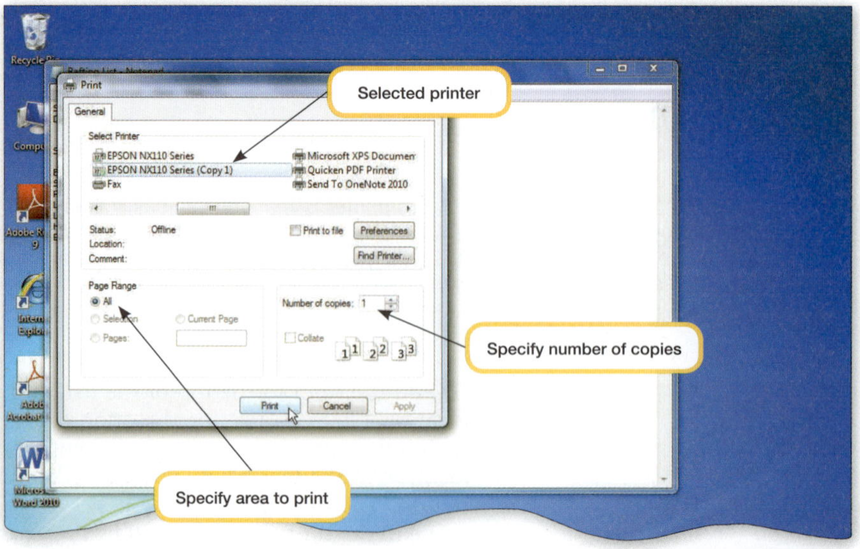

Figure 2.47

Notice the Print dialog box includes the same features as the Print dialog box that appeared when you printed a Help topic. This is part of the common user interface that makes learning and using different applications much easier.

2

- **If necessary, select the printer from the Select Printer box as specified by your instructor.**
- **Click Print.**

The printer indicator icon is displayed in the taskbar while printing is in progress. If you double-click on the indicator, the Printer dialog box is displayed so you can see the printer status and settings and cancel a print job if needed.

SAVING A FILE

Now you will save the document with the changes you made to it.

Concept 8 Saving Files

When you **save** a document you are working on, a permanent copy of your onscreen document is electronically stored as a file on a disk or other storage device. While working on a document, the changes you make are stored temporarily in the computer's memory. Not until you save the document as a file on a disk are you safe from losing your work due to a power failure or other mishap.

Two commands found on the File menu of all Windows programs can be used to save a file: Save and Save As. The Save command saves a document using the same path and file name as the existing disk file, by replacing the contents of the file with the changes you made. The Save As command allows you to select a different path and/or provide a different file name. This command lets you save both an original version of a document and a revised document as two separate files.

When you save a file for the first time, either command can be used. Although many programs create automatic backup files if your work is accidentally interrupted, it is still a good idea to save your work frequently as the backup features are not always foolproof.

Additional Information

The Save command keyboard shortcut is Ctrl + S.

You want to save the document with a more descriptive file name. Whenever you save a file for the first time or use the Save As command, the Save As dialog box is displayed so you can specify where you want the file saved and the file name. Like the Open and Print dialog boxes, the Save As dialog box is common to all programs running under Windows 7.

1

- **Choose File/Save As.**
- **Click at the beginning of the file name in the File Name text box.**
- **Type River before the existing file name and press Spacebar.**

Your screen should be similar to Figure 2.48

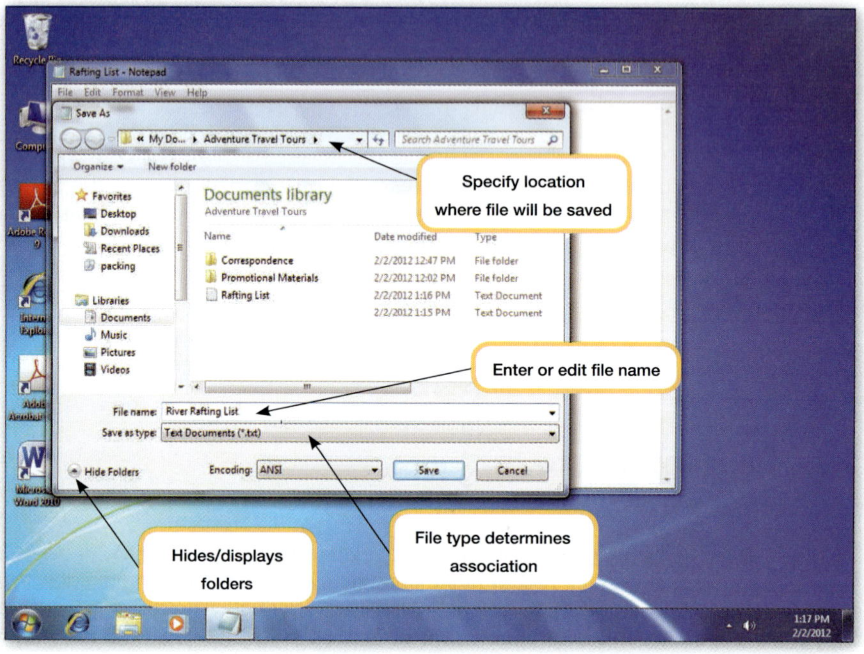

Figure 2.48

Additional Information

Your computer may associate the file with another word processor or with Notepad.

The Save As Type drop-down list box displays the name of the application that will be associated with the saved file. You can change the association by selecting another file type from the drop-down list or by including a specific file extension when naming the file to override the selection. The file extension is used by Windows to determine the application program to load when a document is opened. In this case, Notepad will automatically add a .txt extension to the file name, establishing the file type as a plain text format file.

The location to save the file is the same as the location where the file was opened. Since this is where you want to save the revised file, you do not need to make any changes to the location.

2

- **Click Save.**

Your screen should be similar to Figure 2.49

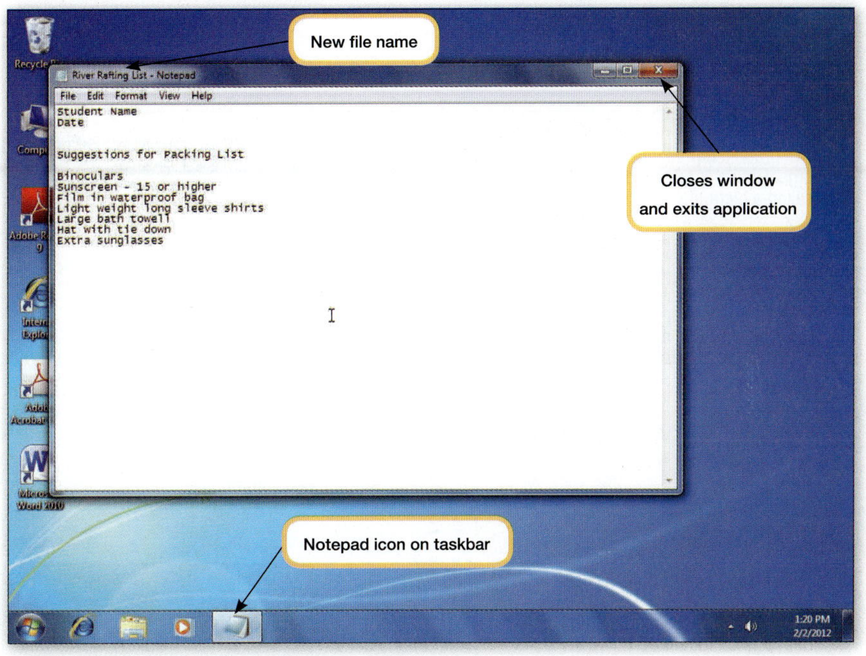

Figure 2.49

The document is saved using the specified file name. The new file name now appears in the title bar.

3

- **Click [X] to close the Notepad window.**
- **Log off or shut down Windows 7 as appropriate.**

LAB 2 CONCEPT SUMMARY

File Management

Hierarchy (WN2.6)

The graphic representation of the organization of folders on a disk is called a hierarchy.

File and Folder Names (WN2.13)

When a file or folder is created, it must be assigned a file name that identifies its contents.

Copy and Move (WN2.18)

All Windows applications include features that allow you to copy and move selected information from one location to another.

Filter, Group, and Arrange (WN2.25)

To help you find files that share something in common, you can filter, group, and arrange files.

Drag and Drop (WN2.28)

Common to all Windows applications is the ability to copy or move selections using the drag-and-drop feature.

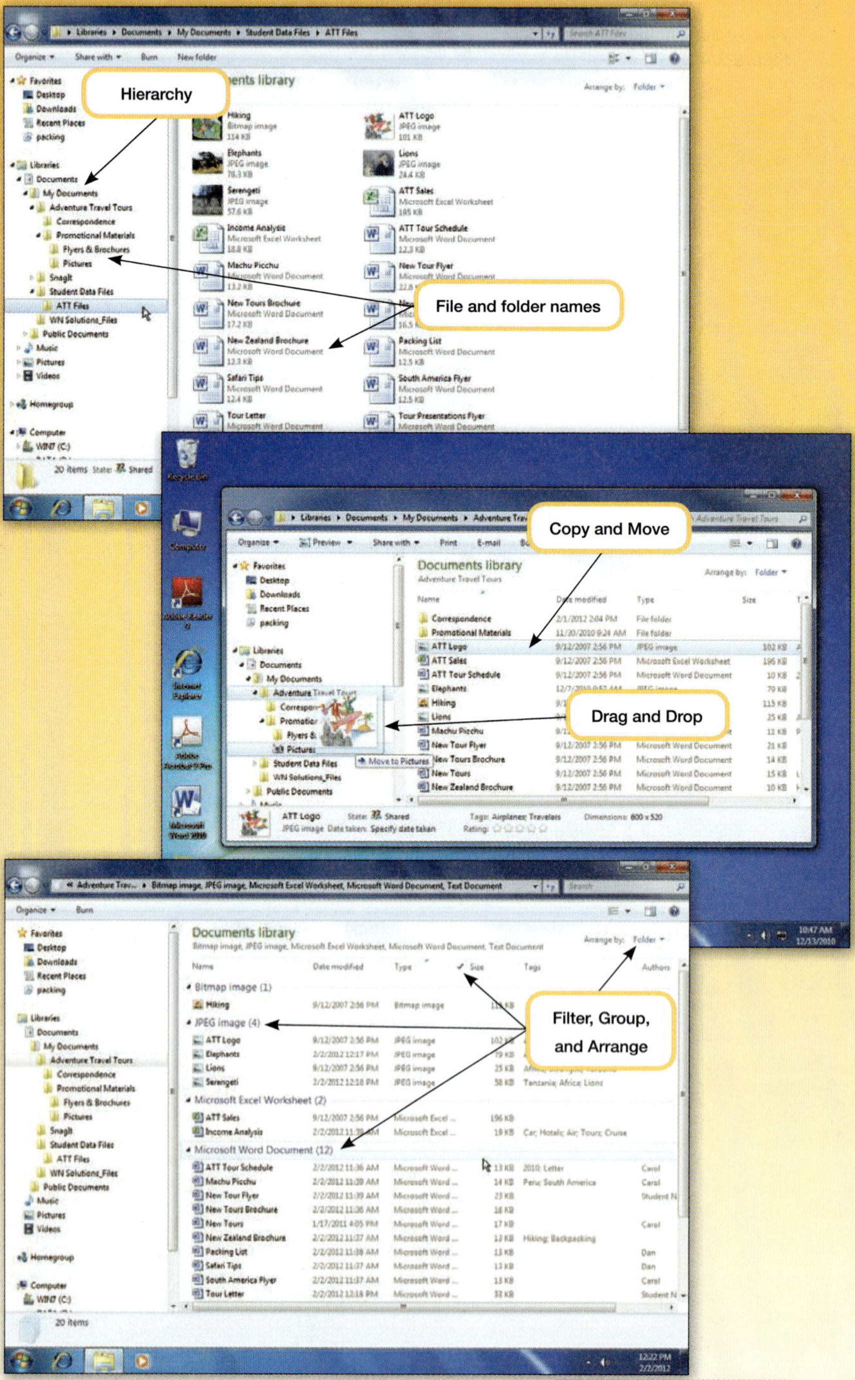

Search (WN2.35)

The search feature provides a quick method to find files, folders, programs and e-mail messages stored on your computer.

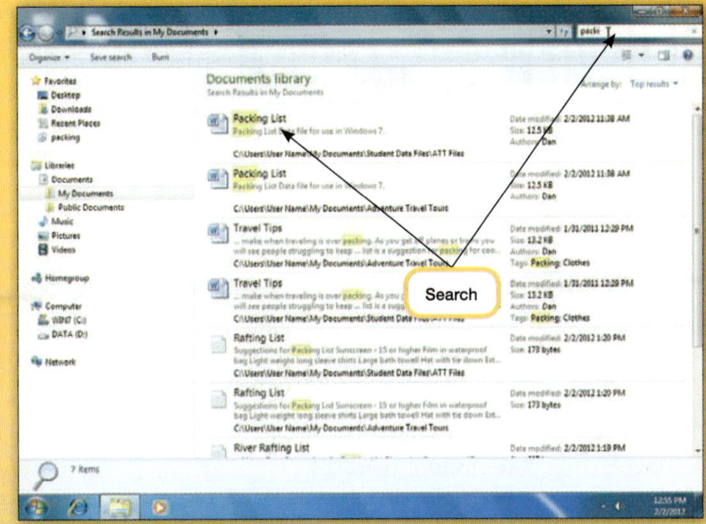

Editing (WN2.41)

One of the advantages of using a computer is that you can easily change or edit your documents.

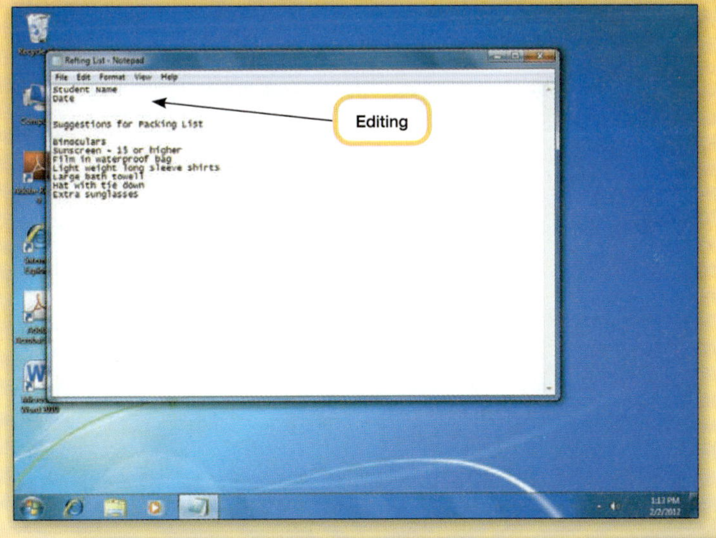

Saving Files (WN2.43)

When you save a document you are working on, a permanent copy of your onscreen document is electronically stored as a file on a disk.

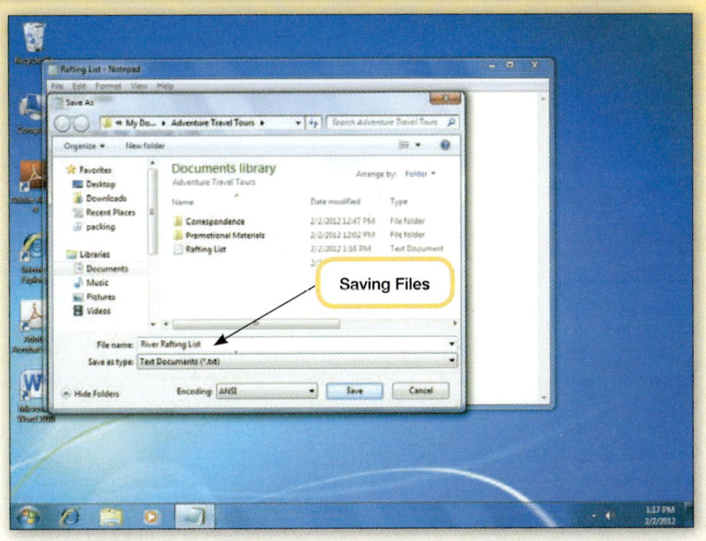

LAB REVIEW Lab 2 File Management

KEY TERMS

arrange WN2.25
Clipboard WN2.18
copy WN2.18
current folder WN2.8
destination WN2.18
drag and drop WN2.28
edit WN2.41
file name WN2.13
file name extension WN2.13
filter WN2.25
folder list WN2.6
folder tree WN2.6
group WN2.25
hierarchy WN2.6
index WN2.35
main folder WN2.6
move WN2.18
placeholder WN2.21
root folder WN2.6
save WN2.43
search WN2.35
source WN2.18
tree WN2.6
workspace WN2.39

COMMAND SUMMARY

Command	Shortcut	Action
Folder window		
Start/Search	Search programs and files	Locates files and folders on disks
Organize/New Folder		Creates a new folder
Organize/Delete		Sends selected item to Recycle Bin
Organize/Rename		Changes name of selected item
Organize/Undo	Ctrl + Z	Undoes the last command or action
Organize/Cut	Ctrl + X	Removes selected object and places it in Clipboard
Organize/Copy	Ctrl + C	Copies selected object to Clipboard
Organize/Paste	Ctrl + V	Pastes object from Clipboard to new location
Organize/Select All	Ctrl + A	Selects all items in active window
Heading/Sort		Sorts icons by selected heading
Notepad		
Start/Programs/ Accessories/Notepad		Starts Notepad application program
File/Open	Ctrl + O	Opens an existing file
File/Save	Ctrl + S	Saves a file with same name
File/Save As		Saves a file with a new name
File/Print	Ctrl + P	Prints document
File/Exit	X	Closes an application
Recycle Bin		
Empty the Recycle Bin		Empties Recycle Bin of all files
Organize/Delete	Delete	Deletes selected item from Recycle Bin
Restore all items		Returns items to their original locations.

LAB EXERCISES

SCREEN IDENTIFICATION

1. Use the figure below to identify each action and match it with its result.

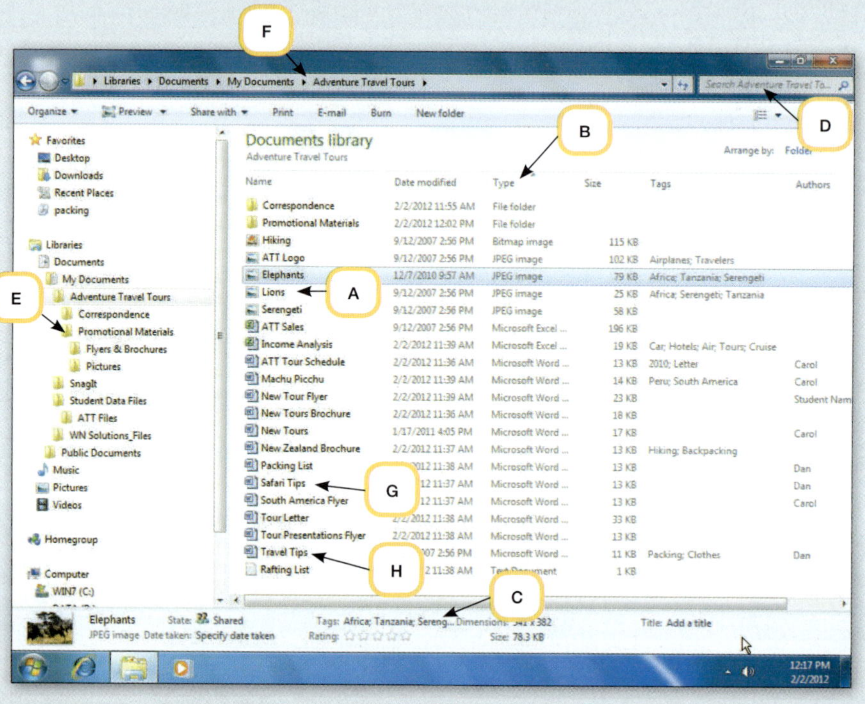

Action	Result
1. right-click A	____ a. starts a search
2. click B	____ b. displays list of folders
3. click C	____ c. adds a tag
4. type in D	____ d. opens the file
5. click E	____ e. renames file
6. click F	____ f. sorts files by file type
7. double-click G	____ g. opens the Promotional Materials folder
8. click H twice slowly	____ h. opens a file shortcut menu

MATCHING

Match the following with the correct definition or function.

1. .txt
2. source
3. 
4. Clipboard
5. hierarchy
6. Notepad
7. 
8. 
9. right-click heading
10. destination

____ a. indicates the folder is expanded
____ b. indicates icon is a shortcut
____ c. temporary storage area
____ d. plain text word processing program
____ e. the location you copy or move from
____ f. represents a Word file type
____ g. graphical representation of the organization of folders on a disk
____ h. a file name extension
____ i. the location you copy or move to
____ j. choose file headings to display

MULTIPLE CHOICE

Circle the correct response to the questions below.

1. _____ appear indented below other folders in the Navigation pane.
   a. Tree folders
   b. Subfolders
   c. Current folders
   d. Selected folders
2. The graphic representation of the organization of folders on a disk is called a _____.
   a. hierarchy
   b. tree
   c. file system
   d. both a and b
3. The Address bar displays the _____ to your current location.
   a. map
   b. path
   c. directions
   d. trail
4. The location where you want the copy of the information to appear is called the _____.
   a. source
   b. destination
   c. Clipboard
   d. storage location

LAB EXERCISES

5. A temporary storage area in memory is called the _____.
   a. source
   b. destination
   c. Clipboard
   d. storage location
6. Making changes to a document is called _____.
   a. copying
   b. moving
   c. saving
   d. editing
7. The large blank area called the _____ is where your work is displayed in Notepad.
   a. work site
   b. workspace
   c. active space
   d. form
8. When a file or folder is created, it must be assigned a(n) _____ that identifies its contents.
   a. symbol
   b. icon
   c. file name
   d. drive
9. The selected folder is the _____ folder, or the folder that will be affected by the next action you perform.
   a. current
   b. source
   c. destination
   d. active
10. The location on a disk that contains the information you want to cut or copy is called the _____.
    a. source
    b. destination
    c. Clipboard
    d. storage location

TRUE/FALSE

Circle the correct answer to the following questions.

1. The graphic representation of the organization of folders on a disk is called a tree.	**True**	**False**
2. Subfolders are also called primary folders.	**True**	**False**
3. Holding down Shift while dragging a file always copies it to the new location.	**True**	**False**
4. If you give a new file the same name as an existing file in the same folder, the contents of the original file will be replaced by the contents of the new file.	**True**	**False**
5. Windows 7 and programs that are designed to operate under Windows 7 allow you to use long folder and file names of up to 255 characters.	**True**	**False**

6. When a file is copied using the Copy menu command, a duplicate of the selection is copied to a temporary storage area in memory called the Clipboard.	**True**	**False**
7. Search is very fast because it looks for matching text to your search term in file names only.	**True**	**False**
8. Spaces are not allowed in file names.	**True**	**False**
9. Arrange by is a command associated with libraries, whose criteria can change depending on the type of library.	**True**	**False**
10. When a folder, file, or shortcut is deleted from the hard disk, it is moved to the Recycle Bin.	**True**	**False**

FILL-IN

Complete the following statements by filling in the blanks with the correct terms.

1. A(n) ____________________ or tree is a graphic representation of the organization of folders on a disk.
2. Copying a selection creates a ____________________.
3. When used in the folder window, ____________________ displays column headings and allows additional information to be added to file properties.
4. A(n) ____________________ is used to identify the contents of a file.
5. A temporary storage area called the ____________________ holds cut or copied information.
6. To cancel the last action or command, use the ____________________ command.
7. The Address bar displays the ____________________ to your current location.
8. Clicking a(n) ____________________ icon opens the associated program or file.
9. All Windows applications include features that allow you to ____________________, ____________________, and ____________________ selections.
10. Saving a document stores a(n) ____________________ copy of what you see on your screen in a file.

LAB EXERCISES

Hands-On Exercises

RATING SYSTEM

★	Easy
★★	Moderate
★★★	Difficult

STEP-BY-STEP

USING WINDOWS 7 GAMES ★

1. Windows 7 includes some additional application programs designed for your enjoyment. In this problem, you will learn how to play Spider Solitaire.

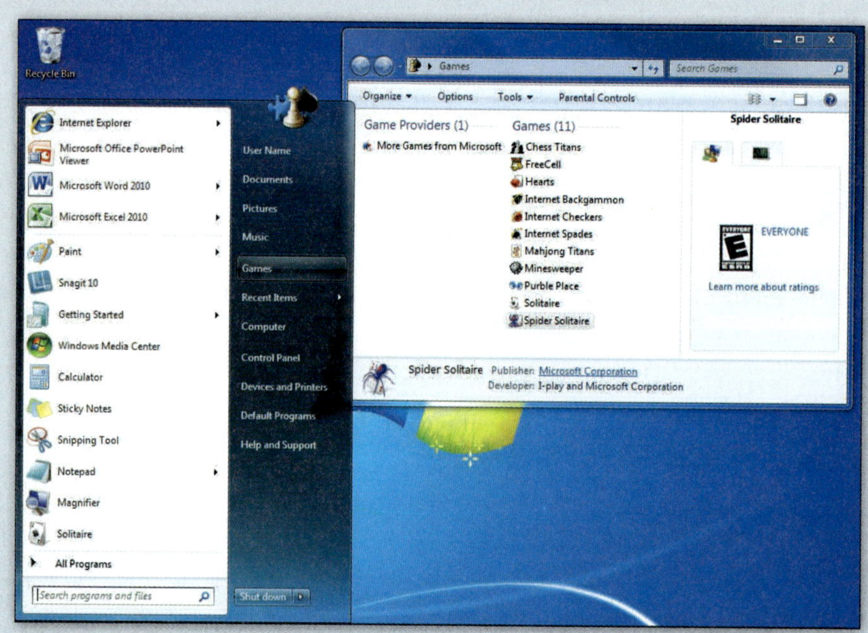

a. Open the Start Menu and choose Games.
b. Double-click Spider Solitaire.
c. If you have never played before, use Help on the menu bar to learn the rules.
d. Start with the "easy" level and work your way up.
e. Close the window(s) when finished.

ADVENTURE TRAVEL TOURS ★★

2. After creating folders and moving files into these folders, you still have several files under the main Adventure Travel Tours folder. You want to create another folder for these files and move them to the new folder. Your completed folder hierarchy will be similar to that shown here.

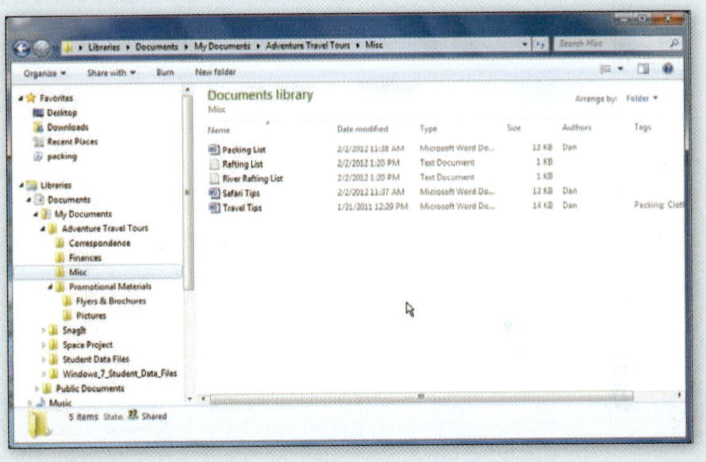

a. Create a new folder under the Documents\Adventure Travel Tours folder named **Finances.**

b. Filter the files in the Adventure Travel Tours folder to display only Excel Worksheet files.

c. Move these files to the Finances folder.

d. Create another folder under the Adventure Travel Tours folder named **Misc** for documents that do not have any particular category.

e. Search the Adventure Travel Tours folder to locate all files that contain List and move all located files to the Misc folder.

f. Search the Adventure Travel Tours folder to locate all files containing the word Tips. Move any located files that are not already in subfolders into the Misc folder.

g. In Notepad, open the file wn02_Safari Tips from the Student Data Files\Windows 7 location. Add the following to the document:

- Change the title to **Safari Packing Tips.**
- Enter **Essentials** to the middle blank line above the first group of items.
- Enter **Clothing** to the middle blank line above the second group of items.
- Enter **Accessories and Toiletries** to the middle blank line above the third group of items.
- Enter **More Essentials** to the middle blank line above the last group of items.

h. Add your name and the date at the end of the document.

i. Save the document as Safari Packing Tips to the Misc subfolder in the Documents\Adventure Travel Tours folder.

LAB EXERCISES

ORGANIZING FILES FOR A GROUP PROJECT ★★

3. You are working on a group project for a science class. Your group has decided to write a paper on the topic of space exploration. Each member of the group has been assigned a topic to research and write. You are responsible for coordinating the project. To make the project easier to manage, you decide to create folders for the different project topics to organize the documents as you receive them from the members of the group.

   a. Create a new folder in your solution file location to store the files for this project and name it **Space Project.**

   b. Copy the files wn02_Space Exploration Pre-1900, wn02_Space Exploration 1900–1950, wn02_Space Exploration 1960-Present, wn02_Moon, wn02_Shuttle, and wn02_Exploration Expenses from the Student Data Files\Windows 7 folder (or the location specified by your instructor) to the Space Project folder.

   c. Create three subfolders in the Space Project folder for the different sections of the project. Name the subfolders **History, Expenses,** and **Pictures.**

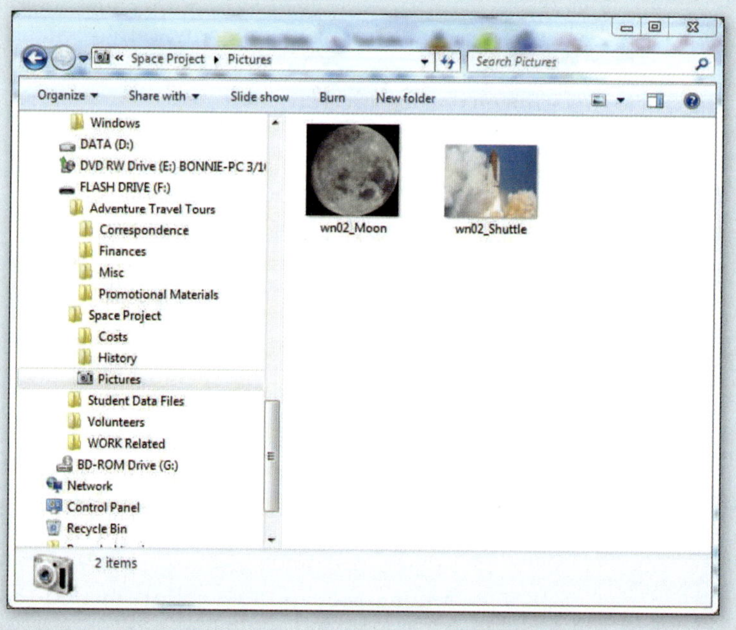

   d. Move the files wn02_Space Exploration Pre-1900, wn02_Space Exploration 1900–1950, and wn02_Space Exploration 1960-Present to the History folder.

   e. Move the files wn02_Moon and wn02_Shuttle to the Pictures folder.

   f. Copy the file wn02_Exploration Expenses to the Expenses folder.

   g. Delete wn02_Exploration Expenses from the main folder.

   h. Rename the Expenses folder **Costs.**

   i. Confirm that all the files have been moved or copied to the correct folders.

   j. Close the window.

ORGANIZING VOLUNTEER AND DONOR RECORDS ★★

4. You work for the Animal Rescue Foundation and are in charge of organizing the volunteers and donations. The volunteers are divided into two categories: Animal Angels, who work at the Foundation to care for the animals, and Foster Angels, who temporarily adopt animals until a permanent home can be found. Donations also come in from two main sources: individuals and businesses. You have several files already pertaining to these areas. You want to make it easier to locate the files and decide to create folders to help organize the information.

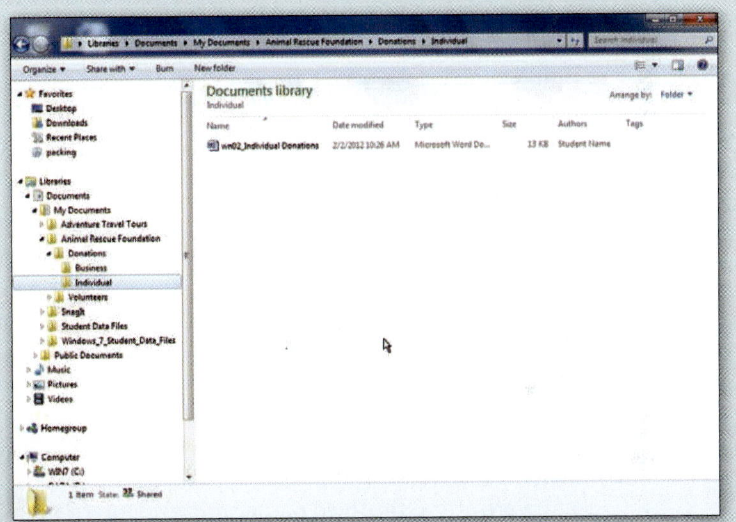

   a. Create a new folder in your solution file location named **Animal Rescue Foundation.** Create two new folders in the Animal Rescue Foundation folder and name them **Donations** and **Volunteers.** Under the Volunteers folder, create two subfolders: **Animal Angels** and **Foster Angels.** Under the Donations folder, create two subfolders: **Individual** and **Business.**

   b. Copy the files wn02_Foster Volunteers, wn02_Animal Angels Volunteers, wn02_Business Donations, and wn02_Individual Donations from the Student Data Files\Windows 7 folder (or the folder location specified by your instructor) to the Animal Rescue Foundation folder.

   c. Copy the wn02_Foster Volunteers file to the Foster Angels subfolder. Rename the file Foster Volunteers.

   d. Delete the wn02_Foster Volunteers file from the main folder.

   e. Copy the wn02_Animal Angels Volunteers file to the Animal Angels subfolder. Rename the file Animal Angels Volunteers.

   f. Delete the wn02_Animal Angels Volunteers file from the main folder.

   g. Move the two files wn02_Business Donations and wn02_Individual Donations from the main folder to the Donations folder. Rename the wn02_Individual Donations file Individual Donations 2012 and the wn02_Business Donations file Business Donations 2012. Move these files into the appropriate subfolders.

   h. Confirm that all the files have been copied or moved to the folders.

   i. Close the window.

LAB EXERCISES

EDITING A DOCUMENT ★★

5. You have been working on a brief report about why it is important today to have good, basic computer skills. Although the report includes several paragraphs, you still need to add topic headings. You will open, edit, and save this document.

   a. Start Notepad and open the wn02_Computer Competency document from the Student Data Files/Windows 7 location (or the location specified by your instructor).

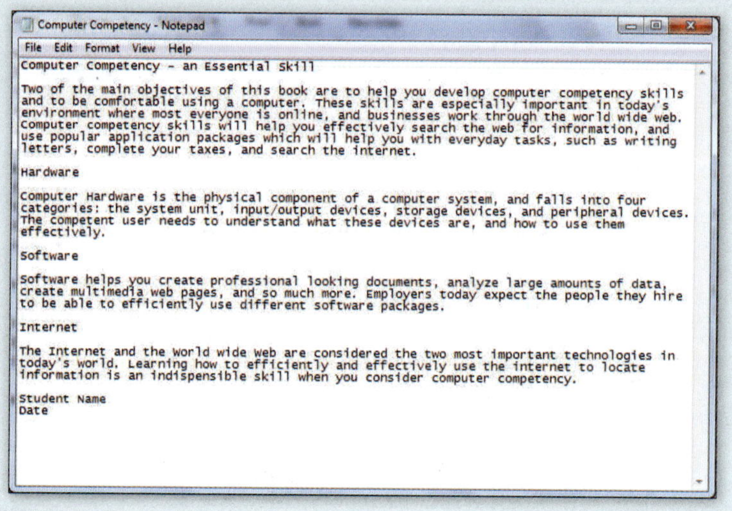

   b. Choose Format/Word Wrap to wrap the text to the window size.

   c. At the top of the document, add the title **Computer Competency–an Essential Skill.** Enter two blank lines below the title.

   d. Change the word "tool" in the last paragraph to "skill."

   e. Enter the headings **Hardware** above the second paragraph, **Software** above the third paragraph, and **Internet** above the fourth paragraph. Include blank lines above and below each heading.

   f. Enter your name and the current date below the last paragraph.

   g. Save the document using the file name Computer Competency to your solution file location.

   h. Print the document.

ON YOUR OWN

SEARCHING YOUR COMPUTER ★★

1. The Search command on the Start menu can be used to locate files on your computer. Use Search to locate all the files on your local hard drive (C:) that contain the word "window" in the name. How many were found? Refine the search to locate "Windows 7." How many were located? Finally, locate all picture files containing the text "leaves." How many files did you find? When you are done, close the Search window.

   Create a document using Notepad containing the answers to the above questions. Include your name and the current date in the document. Save the document as Search Results to your solution file location. Print the document.

ORGANIZING A GROUP PROJECT ★★

2. You are working on a group project with 12 other students. You have been allocated space on a server for the files you will create and share. As project manager, you want to organize the files to make access by all participants easy and quick. Use Notepad to describe the folder structure you plan to use that would allocate a private folder for each student and additional folders for the accounting, research, and cost management projects the students will be working on. Include your name and date in the document. Save your completed document as Project Folder Structure to your solution file location. Print the document.

LEARNING ABOUT HARD DISK CONSTRUCTION ★★

3. While using the Computer window, you looked at the files stored on the hard disk of your computer. Using your text and the library as a resource, learn about the construction of the hard disk and explain how a hard disk stores data. Use Notepad to create a short document about your findings. Include your name and the date in the document. Save the file as Hard Disk to your solution file location. Print the document.

WORKING WITH FILES ★★

4. The Briefcase and Sync Center are tools that allow you to easily transfer files between computers on a network location. Use Help to learn more about these tools. Then use Notepad to write a brief report explaining both tools. Be sure to include answers to the following questions:

   a. What is the purpose of Briefcase? Sync Center?

   b. What is synchronization? How do you synchronize files between the Briefcase and the main computer?

   c. What are the steps for using Briefcase?

   d. When you are copying files from your main computer into Briefcase, the two computers must be connected by what means?

   e. When is it best to use the Sync Center? When is it best to use Briefcase?

   f. What happens when you reconnect to the network after using offline files?

   Include your name and the date in the document. Save the file as Briefcase and Sync Center to your solution file location. Print the document.

LAB EXERCISES

ENCRYPTING FILES ★★★

5. One method to make your data secure is to encrypt the files. Use Help to learn more about data encryption. Then use Notepad to write a brief report explaining this feature. Be sure to include answers to the following:

   a. What is the purpose of encryption?

   b. How do you encrypt and decrypt a file?

   c. What is the system Windows 7 uses to encrypt files?

   d. Discuss the advantages to encrypting a folder.

   Include your name and the date in the document. Save the file as File Encryption to your solution file location. Print the document.

Appendix A

Downloading Files and Extracting a Zip File

The data files supplied with the Windows 7 and the Microsoft Office 2010 texts are available online at the McGraw-Hill O'Leary Series Web site. Your instructor may ask you to access the data files by downloading them from this Web site to your data file storage location. If this is the case, follow the instructions provided here to download the files and extract the zip file. Your computer must have a connection to the Internet to access these files.

DOWNLOADING FILES

Downloading a file means to copy a file from one computer to another using a network or Internet connection. When you download a file from the Internet, the file is copied from the computer where the Web site is stored over your Internet connection to the location you specify on your computer. Many files that you download are provided as zip files. A zip file is a single file that contains files (and folders) that are compressed. Compressed files are smaller in size, making them faster to download and reducing the amount of space they use on your disk. Additionally, because they can contain many files and folders, it makes the process of transferring files to other computers faster.

The student data files on the McGraw-Hill Web site are contained in zip files. To access the data files on the Web site, you will start the browser program on your system. Then you will enter the address of the Web site location where the data files are located.

1

- **Start your browser program.**
- **Maximize the window.**
- **Type www.mhhe.com/oleary in the Address box.**
- **Press ←Enter.**
- **Click on any Office 2010 text icon.**
- **Maximize the window.**

Your screen should be similar to Figure A-1

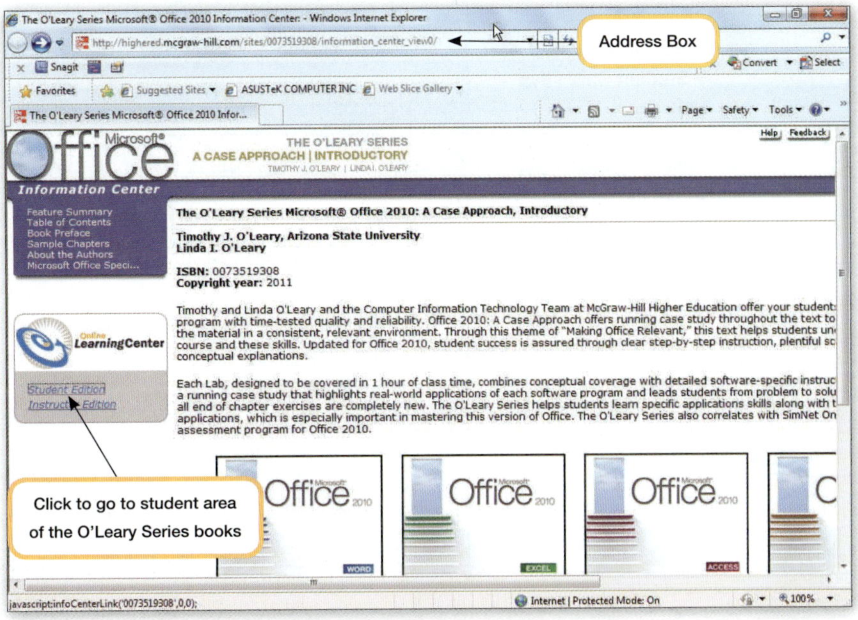

Figure A-1

The O'Leary Series Web site for the Microsoft Office 2010 text is open in your browser window. You want to download the Windows 7 data files from the Student Edition area of the Online Learning Center for this text.

2

- **Click Student Edition in the Online Learning Center section of the window.**
- **Click [Choose one... ▾] to open the menu of texts.**
- **Choose Windows 7.**
- **Click Student Data Files.**

Your screen should be similar to Figure A-2

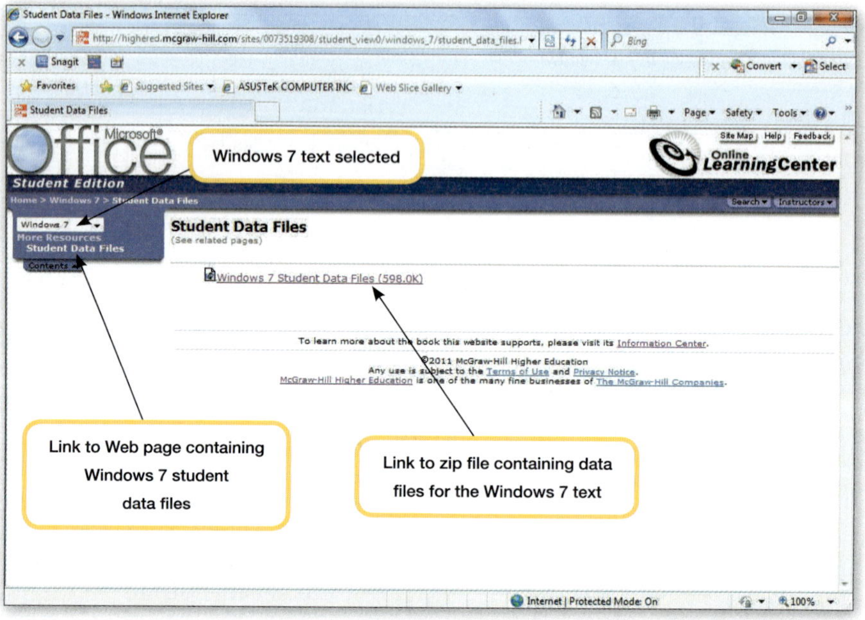

Figure A-2

The Student Data Files page of the Online Learning Center displays a link to the data files used in the selected text. You want to download and save the Windows 7 Student Data Files to your data file location on your computer.

3

- **Click the Windows 7 Student Data Files link.**
- **Click [Save] in the dialog box.**

Your screen should be similar to Figure A-3

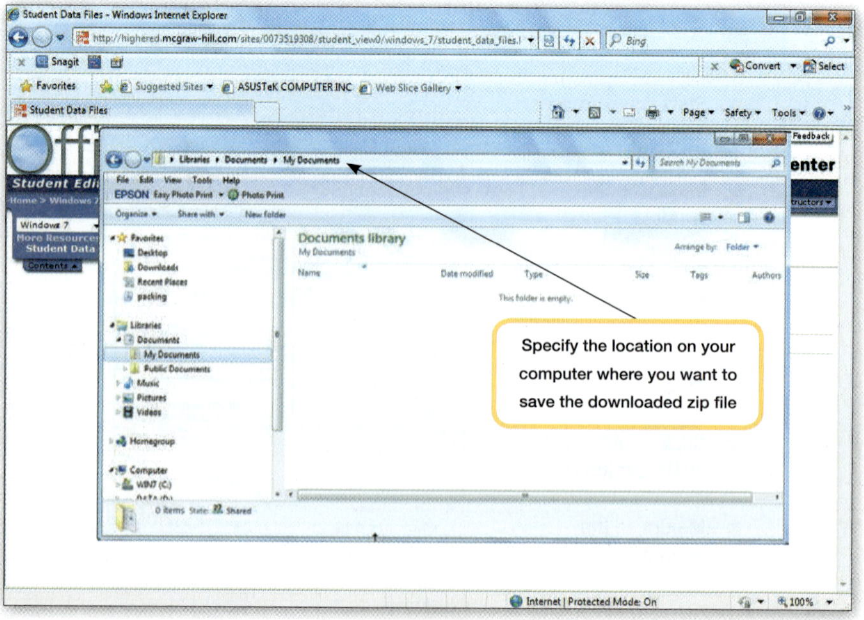

Figure A-3

Next, you need to specify where you want the file saved on your computer.

4

- **Specify the My Documents folder (or the location your instructor recommends as the location to save the zip file).**
- **Click Save.**
- **Click Open Folder in the Download Complete dialog box.**

Having Trouble?

Open the folder location where the zip file was saved.

Your screen should be similar to Figure A-4

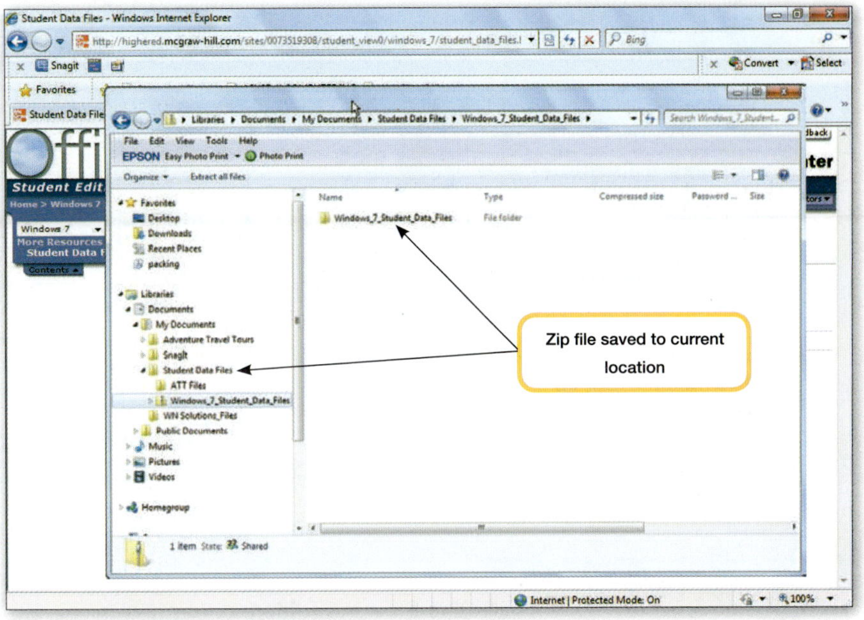

Figure A-4

The folder location where you saved the downloaded folder is open in a folder window.

EXTRACTING ZIPPED FILES

Most zip files are self-extracting files. This means that you do not need the software application to unzip the file. Simply clicking on the file begins the extraction process. By default, the extracted files are saved in the current location.

1

- **Right-click on the Windows_7_Student_Data_Files icon.**
- **Click** Extract All... **from the shortcut menu.**

Your screen should be similar to Figure A-5

Additional Information

Using this method allows you to specify the location of the extracted files, or to modify the folder name.

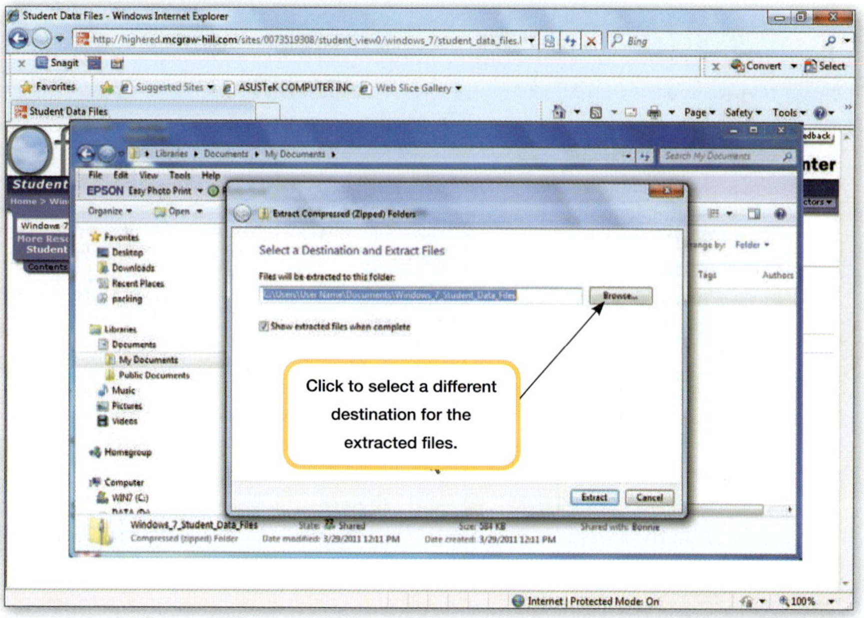

Figure A-5

Additional Information

The default destination location is the current location.

The files and folders contained in the zip file are listed in the window. Next, you need to specify the destination location on your computer where you want the extracted files stored.

2

- **If necessary, click** Browse... **to change the destination location for the extracted files and click** OK**.**
- **Click** Extract**.**

Your screen should be similar to Figure A-6

Additional Information

If there is a folder in the zip file, then only the folder is displayed. You will need to open the folder to see those files also.

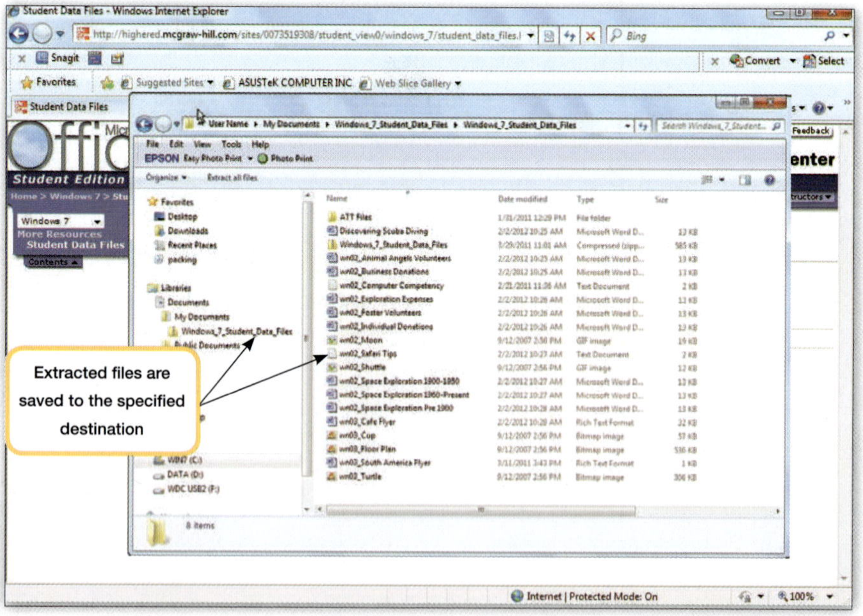

Figure A-6

The files contained in the zipped file have been copied to a folder that has the same name as the zipped file. This folder is not compressed and the files are ready for you to use.

3

- **Close all open folder windows and exit the browser application.**

WINDOWS 7 COMMAND SUMMARY

COMMAND	SHORTCUT	ACTION
Start		Opens Start menu
Quick Access Toolbar		
Save	Ctrl + S	Saves document using same file name
Undo	Ctrl + Z	Restores last editing change
Redo	Ctrl + Y	Restores last Undo or repeats last command
Start Menu		
Documents		Opens the Documents folder
Computer		Opens the Computer folder
Help and Support	⊞ + F1	Opens Windows Help and Support
Search programs and files		Locates files and folders on disks
Shut down		Turns the computer off, or gives other shut-down options (switch user, sleep, lock, restart, hibernate)
Folder Window		
Organize /Cut	Ctrl + X	Removes selected object and places it in Clipboard
Organize /Copy	Ctrl + C	Copies selected object to Clipboard
Organize /Paste	Ctrl + V	Pastes object from Clipboard to new location
Organize /Undo	Ctrl + Z	Undoes the last command or action
Organize /Select All	Ctrl + A	Selects all items in active window
Organize /Layout		Turns on/off display of Search, Details, Preview, and Navigation panes
Organize /Delete		Sends selected item to Recycle Bin
Organize /Rename		Changes name of selected item

WINDOWS 7 COMMAND SUMMARY

COMMAND	SHORTCUT	ACTION
Slide show		Displays pictures in folder as a full-screen timed slide show
Organize ▾ /New Folder		Creates a new folder
X	Alt + F4	Closes active window
▾ Views		Cycles through Details, Tiles, Large Icons, Content, and List views
Extra Large Icons		Displays extra large icons of graphic files
Large Icons		Displays large icons of graphic files
Medium Icons		Displays medium icons of graphic files
Small Icons		Displays small icons of graphic files
List		Displays objects in a list
Details		Displays all folder and file details
Tiles		Displays objects with medium icons and file names
Content		Displays small icon with file name, date modified, and file size
Help and Support		
Back	Alt + ←	Displays previously viewed Help topic
Forward	Alt + →	Displays next-viewed Help topic after using
Home		Displays Help home page
Print		Prints displayed Help topic
Browse		Displays Help table of contents list

WINDOWS 7 COMMAND SUMMARY

COMMAND	SHORTCUT	ACTION
Ask		Accesses other sources of Help
Options ▾		Provides options to change text size, find text on a page and changes Help settings
Recycle Bin		
Organize ▾/Delete	Delete	Deletes selected item from Recycle Bin
Empty the Recycle Bin		Empties Recycle Bin of all files
Restore all items		Returns items to their original location
Notepad		
Start/All Programs/ Accessories/Notepad		Starts Notepad application program
File/Open	Ctrl + **O**	Opens an existing file
File/Save	Ctrl + **S**	Saves a file with the same name
File/Save As		Saves a file with a new name
File/Print	Ctrl + **P**	Prints document
File/Exit	X	Closes an application
WordPad Menu		
New	Ctrl + **N**	Opens a blank (new) document
Open	Ctrl + **O**	Opens existing document file
Save	Ctrl + **S**	Saves document using same file name
Save as	F12	Saves document using a new file name, file type, and/or location

WINDOWS 7 COMMAND SUMMARY

COMMAND	SHORTCUT	ACTION
Print	Ctrl + P	Prints document
Print / Print preview		Displays document as it will appear when printed
Exit	Alt + F4	Exit WordPad application
Home tab		
Clipboard Group		
Paste	Ctrl + V	Pastes items from Clipboard
/ Paste special	Alt + Ctrl + V	Used to imbed a graphic or paste a link
Copy	Ctrl + C	Copies selection to Clipboard
Font Group		
Calibri Font family		Changes typeface
11 Font Size		Changes text size
B Bold	Ctrl + B	Adds/removes bold effect
I Italic	Ctrl + I	Adds/removes italic effect
U Underline	Ctrl + U	Underlines selected text with single line
A Text Color		Changes text to selected color
Paragraph Group		
Center		Centers text between margins
View Tab		
Settings Group		
Word wrap		Provides wrapping options to change how text appears on screen

WINDOWS 7 COMMAND SUMMARY

COMMAND	SHORTCUT	ACTION
Paint Menu		
New	Ctrl + N	Opens a blank (new) document
Open	Ctrl + O	Opens existing document file
Save	Ctrl + S	Saves document using same file name
Save as	F12	Saves document using a new file name, file type, and/or location
Print	Ctrl + P	Prints document
Print preview		Displays document as it will appear when printed
Exit	Alt + F4	Exits Paint application
Home tab		
Clipboard Group		
Copy	Ctrl + C	Copies selection to Clipboard
Image Group		
Select		Lists menu of image selection shapes and options
Select / Select all		Selects entire graphic
Rotate		Rotates or flips the picture or selection

WINDOWS 7 COMMAND SUMMARY

COMMAND	SHORTCUT	ACTION
Tools Group		
Fill with color		Automatically fills an area of the graphic with selected color
Eraser		Erases part of the picture and replaces it with selected background color (Color 2)
Text		Adds a text box to graphic
Brushes		Provides options for different types of brush effects
/Brush		Creates a solid line effect
/Airbrush		Creates an airbrush effect
Shapes group		
Oval		Creates an oval shape
Fill		Provides options for different mediums for the shape fill
Size		Selects line width for selected drawing tool
Colors Group		
Color 1		Changes foreground to selected color
Color 2		Changes background to selected color
Color palette		Provides current color options
Edit colors		Creates custom colors

WINDOWS 7 COMMAND SUMMARY

COMMAND	SHORTCUT	ACTION
Text Tools Tab		
Font Group		
Calibri Font family		Changes typeface
11 Font Size		Changes text size
B Bold	Ctrl + B	Adds/removes bold effect
I Italic	Ctrl + I	Adds/removes italic effect
U Underline	Ctrl + U	Underlines selected text with single line
Background Group		
Transparent		Allows color behind text box to show through
Colors Group		
Color 1		Choose for text color
Color 2		Choose for background color of text area
Colors /Color palette		Provides current color options
Edit colors		Creates custom colors